WATERLOO PUBLIC LIBRARY
W9-BSX-636

St. Peter and a deacon, from the Homily of St. Gregory.
(© Gianni Dagli Ortis/CORBIS)

NEW CATHOLIC ENCYCLOPEDIA

NEW CATHOLIC ENCYCLOPEDIA

SECOND EDITION

11
Pau–Red

Detroit • New York • San Diego • San Francisco • Cleveland • New Haven, Conn. • Waterville, Maine • London • Munich

in association with
THE CATHOLIC UNIVERSITY OF AMERICA • WASHINGTON, D.C.

The New Catholic Encyclopedia, Second Edition

Project Editors
Thomas Carson, Joann Cerrito

Editorial
Erin Bealmear, Jim Craddock, Stephen Cusack, Miranda Ferrara, Kristin Hart, Melissa Hill, Margaret Mazurkiewicz, Carol Schwartz, Christine Tomassini, Michael J. Tyrkus

Permissions
Edna Hedblad, Shalice Shah-Caldwell

Imaging and Multimedia
Randy Bassett, Dean Dauphinais, Robert Duncan, Leitha Etheridge-Sims, Mary K. Grimes, Lezlie Light, Dan Newell, David G. Oblender, Christine O'Bryan, Luke Rademacher, Pamela Reed

Product Design
Michelle DiMercurio

Data Capture
Civie Green

Manufacturing
Rhonda Williams

Indexing
Victoria Agee, Victoria Baker, Francine Cronshaw, Lynne Maday, Do Mi Stauber, Amy Suchowski

For more information, contact
The Gale Group, Inc.
27500 Drake Rd.
Farmington Hills, MI 48331-3535
Or you can visit our Internet site at
http://www.gale.com

LIBRARY OF CONGRESS CATALOGING-IN-PUBLICATION DATA

New Catholic encyclopedia.—2nd ed.
p. cm.
Includes bibliographical references and indexes.
ISBN 0-7876-4004-2
1. Catholic Church—Encyclopedias. I. Catholic University of America.
BX841 .N44 2002
282' .03—dc21
2002000924

ISBN: 0-7876-4004-2 (set)
0-7876-4005-0 (v. 1)
0-7876-4006-9 (v. 2)
0-7876-4007-7 (v. 3)
0-7876-4008-5 (v. 4)
0-7876-4009-3 (v. 5)
0-7876-4010-7 (v. 6)
0-7876-4011-5 (v. 7)
0-7876-4012-3 (v. 8)
0-7876-4013-1 (v. 9)
0-7876-4014-x (v. 10)
0-7876-4015-8 (v. 11)
0-7876-4016-6 (v. 12)
0-7876-4017-4 (v. 13)
0-7876-4018-2 (v. 14)
0-7876-4019-0 (v. 15)

Printed in the United States of America
10 9 8 7 6 5 4 3 2 1

For The Catholic University of America Press

Foreword

This revised edition of the *New Catholic Encyclopedia* represents a third generation in the evolution of the text that traces its lineage back to the *Catholic Encyclopedia* published from 1907 to 1912. In 1967, sixty years after the first volume of the original set appeared, The Catholic University of America and the McGraw-Hill Book Company joined together in organizing a small army of editors and scholars to produce the *New Catholic Encyclopedia.* Although planning for the *NCE* had begun before the Second Vatican Council and most of the 17,000 entries were written before Council ended, Vatican II enhanced the encyclopedia's value and importance. The research and the scholarship that went into the articles witnessed to the continuity and richness of the Catholic Tradition given fresh expression by Council. In order to keep the *NCE* current, supplementary volumes were published in 1972, 1978, 1988, and 1995. Now, at the beginning of the third millennium, The Catholic University of America is proud to join with The Gale Group in presenting a new edition of the *New Catholic Encyclopedia.* It updates and incorporates the many articles from the 1967 edition and its supplements that have stood the test of time and adds hundreds of new entries.

As the president of The Catholic University of America, I cannot but be pleased at the reception the *NCE* has received. It has come to be recognized as an authoritative reference work in the field of religious studies and is praised for its comprehensive coverage of the Church's history and institutions. Although Canon Law no longer requires encyclopedias and reference works of this kind to receive an *imprimatur* before publication, I am confident that this new edition, like the original, reports accurate information about Catholic beliefs and practices. The editorial staff and their consultants were careful to present official Church teachings in a straightforward manner, and in areas where there are legitimate disputes over fact and differences in interpretation of events, they made every effort to insure a fair and balanced presentation of the issues.

The way for this revised edition was prepared by the publication, in 2000, of a Jubilee volume of the *NCE,* heralding the beginning of the new millennium. In my foreword to that volume I quoted Pope John Paul II's encyclical on Faith and Human Reason in which he wrote that history is "the arena where we see what God does for humanity." The *New Catholic Encyclopedia* describes that arena. It reports events, people, and ideas—"the things we know best and can verify most easily, the things of our everyday life, apart from which we cannot understand ourselves" (*Fides et ratio,* 12).

Finally, I want to express appreciation on my own behalf and on the behalf of the readers of these volumes to everyone who helped make this revision a reality. We are all indebted to The Gale Group and the staff of The Catholic University of America Press for their dedication and the alacrity with which they produced it.

Very Reverend David M. O'Connell, C.M., J.C.D.
President
The Catholic University of America

Preface to the Revised Edition

When first published in 1967 the *New Catholic Encyclopedia* was greeted with enthusiasm by librarians, researchers, and general readers interested in Catholicism. In the United States the *NCE* has been recognized as the standard reference work on matters of special interest to Catholics. In an effort to keep the encyclopedia current, supplementary volumes were published in 1972, 1978, 1988, and 1995. However, it became increasingly apparent that further supplements would not be adequate to this task. The publishers subsequently decided to undertake a thorough revision of the *NCE,* beginning with the publication of a Jubilee volume at the start of the new millennium.

Like the biblical scribe who brings from his storeroom of knowledge both the new and the old, this revised edition of the *New Catholic Encyclopedia* incorporates material from the 15-volume original edition and the supplement volumes. Entries that have withstood the test of time have been edited, and some have been amended to include the latest information and research. Hundreds of new entries have been added. For all practical purposes, it is an entirely new edition intended to serve as a comprehensive and authoritative work of reference reporting on the movements and interests that have shaped Christianity in general and Catholicism in particular over two millennia.

SCOPE

The title reflects its outlook and breadth. It is the *New Catholic Encyclopedia,* not merely a new encyclopedia of Catholicism. In addition to providing information on the doctrine, organization, and history of Christianity over the centuries, it includes information about persons, institutions, cultural phenomena, religions, philosophies, and social movements that have affected the Catholic Church from within and without. Accordingly, the *NCE* attends to the history and particular traditions of the Eastern Churches and the Churches of the Protestant Reformation, and other ecclesial communities. Christianity cannot be understood without exploring its roots in ancient Israel and Judaism, nor can the history of the medieval and modern Church be understood apart from its relationship with Islam. Interfaith dialogue requires an appreciation of Buddhism and other world religions, as well as some knowledge of the history of religion in general.

On the assumption that most readers and researchers who use the *NCE* are individuals interested in Catholicism in general and the Church in North America in particular, its editorial content gives priority to the Western Church, while not neglecting the churches in the East; to Roman Catholicism, acknowledging much common history with Protestantism; and to Catholicism in the United States, recognizing that it represents only a small part of the universal Church.

Scripture, Theology, Patrology, Liturgy. The many and varied articles dealing with Sacred Scripture and specific books of the Bible reflect contemporary biblical scholarship and its concerns. The *NCE* highlights official church teachings as expressed by the Church's magisterium. It reports developments in theology, explains issues and introduces ecclesiastical writers from the early Church Fathers to present-day theologians whose works exercise major influence on the development of Christian thought. The *NCE* traces the evolution of the Church's worship with special emphasis on rites and rituals consequent to the liturgical reforms and renewal initiated by the Second Vatican Council.

Church History. From its inception Christianity has been shaped by historical circumstances and itself has become a historical force. The *NCE* presents the Church's history from a number of points of view against the background of general political and cultural history. The revised edition reports in some detail the Church's missionary activity as it grew from a small community in Jerusalem to the worldwide phenomenon it is today. Some entries, such as those dealing with the Middle Ages, the Reformation, and the Enlightenment, focus on major time-periods and movements that cut across geographical boundaries. Other articles describe the history and structure of the Church in specific areas, countries, and regions. There are separate entries for many dioceses and monasteries which by reason of antiquity, size, or influence are of special importance in ecclesiastical history, as there are for religious orders and congregations. The *NCE* rounds out its comprehensive history of the Church with articles on religious movements and biographies of individuals.

Canon and Civil Law. The Church inherited and has safeguarded the precious legacy of ancient Rome, described by Virgil, "to rule people under law, [and] to establish the way of peace." The *NCE* deals with issues of ecclesiastical jurisprudence and outlines the development of legislation governing communal practices and individual obligations, taking care to incorporate and reference the 1983 *Code of Canon Law* throughout and, where appropriate, the *Code of Canons for the Eastern Churches.* It deals with issues of Church-State relations and with civil law as it impacts on the Church and Church's teaching regarding human rights and freedoms.

Philosophy. The Catholic tradition from its earliest years has investigated the relationship between faith and reason. The *NCE* considers at some length the many and varied schools of ancient, medieval, and modern philosophy with emphasis, when appropriate, on their relationship to theological positions. It pays particular attention to the scholastic tradition, particularly Thomism, which is prominent in Catholic intellectual history. Articles on many major and lesser philosophers contribute to a comprehensive survey of philosophy from pre-Christian times to the present.

Biography and Hagiography. The *NCE,* making an exception for the reigning pope, leaves to other reference works biographical information about living persons. This revised edition presents biographical sketches of hundreds of men and women, Christian and non-Christian, saints and sinners, because of their significance for the Church. They include: Old and New Testament figures; the Fathers of the Church and ecclesiastical writers; pagan and Christian emperors; medieval and modern kings; heads of state and other political figures; heretics and champions of orthodoxy; major and minor figures in the Reformation and Counter Reformation; popes, bishops, and priests; founders and members of religious orders and congregations; lay men and lay women; scholars, authors, composers, and artists. The *NCE* includes biographies of most saints whose feasts were once celebrated or are currently celebrated by the universal church. The revised edition relies on Butler's *Lives of the Saints* and similar reference works to give accounts of many saints, but the *NCE* also provides biographical information about recently canonized and beatified individuals who are, for one reason or another, of special interest to the English-speaking world.

Social Sciences. Social sciences came into their own in the twentieth century. Many articles in the *NCE* rely on data drawn from anthropology, economics, psychology and sociology for a better understanding of religious structures and behaviors. Papal encyclicals and pastoral letters of episcopal conferences are the source of principles and norms for Christian attitudes and practice in the field of social action and legislation. The *NCE* draws attention to the Church's organized activities in pursuit of peace and justice, social welfare and human rights. The growth of the role of the laity in the work of the Church also receives thorough coverage.

ARRANGEMENT OF ENTRIES

The articles in the *NCE* are arranged alphabetically by the first substantive word using the word-by-word method of alphabetization; thus "New Zealand" precedes "Newman, John Henry," and "Old Testament Literature" precedes "Oldcastle, Sir John." Monarchs, patriarchs, popes, and others who share a Christian name and are differentiated by a title and numerical designation are alphabetized by their title and then arranged numerically. Thus, entries for Byzantine emperors Leo I through IV precede those for popes of the same name, while "Henry VIII, King of England" precedes "Henry IV, King of France."

Maps, Charts, and Illustrations. The *New Catholic Encyclopedia* contains nearly 3,000 illustrations, including photographs, maps, and tables. Entries focusing on the Church in specific countries contain a map of the country as well as easy-to-read tables giving statistical data and, where helpful, lists of archdioceses and dioceses. Entries on the Church in U.S. states also contain tables listing archdioceses and dioceses where appropriate. The numerous photographs appearing in the *New Catholic Encyclopedia* help to illustrate the history of the Church, its role in modern societies, and the many magnificent works of art it has inspired.

SPECIAL FEATURES

Subject Overview Articles. For the convenience and guidance of the reader, the *New Catholic Encyclopedia* contains several brief articles outlining the scope of major fields: "Theology, Articles on," "Liturgy, Articles on," "Jesus Christ, Articles on," etc.

Cross-References. The cross-reference system in the *NCE* serves to direct the reader to related material in other articles. The appearance of a name or term in small capital letters in text indicates that there is an article of that title elsewhere in the encyclopedia. In some cases, the name of the related article has been inserted at the appropriate point as a *see* reference: (*see* THOMAS AQUINAS, ST.). When a further aspect of the subject is treated under another title, a *see also* reference is placed at the end of the article. In addition to this extensive cross-reference system, the comprehensive index in volume 15 will greatly increase the reader's ability to access the wealth of information contained in the encyclopedia.

Abbreviations List. Following common practice, books and versions of the Bible as well as other standard works by selected authors have been abbreviated throughout the text. A guide to these abbreviations follows this preface.

The Editors

Abbreviations

The system of abbreviations used for the works of Plato, Aristotle, St. Augustine, and St. Thomas Aquinas is as follows: Plato is cited by book and Stephanus number only, e.g., Phaedo 79B; Rep. 480A. Aristotle is cited by book and Bekker number only, e.g., Anal. post. 72b 8–12; Anim. 430a 18. St. Augustine is cited as in the Thesaurus Linguae Latinae, e.g., C. acad. 3.20.45; Conf. 13.38.53, with capitalization of the first word of the title. St. Thomas is cited as in scholarly journals, but using Arabic numerals. In addition, the following abbreviations have been used throughout the encyclopedia for biblical books and versions of the Bible.

Books

Acts	Acts of the Apostles
Am	Amos
Bar	Baruch
1–2 Chr	1 and 2 Chronicles (1 and 2 Paralipomenon in Septuagint and Vulgate)
Col	Colossians
1–2 Cor	1 and 2 Corinthians
Dn	Daniel
Dt	Deuteronomy
Eccl	Ecclesiastes
Eph	Ephesians
Est	Esther
Ex	Exodus
Ez	Ezekiel
Ezr	Ezra (Esdras B in Septuagint; 1 Esdras in Vulgate)
Gal	Galatians
Gn	Genesis
Hb	Habakkuk
Heb	Hebrews
Hg	Haggai
Hos	Hosea
Is	Isaiah
Jas	James
Jb	Job
Jdt	Judith
Jer	Jeremiah
Jgs	Judges
Jl	Joel
Jn	John
1–3 Jn	1, 2, and 3 John
Jon	Jonah
Jos	Joshua
Jude	Jude
1–2 Kgs	1 and 2 Kings (3 and 4 Kings in Septuagint and Vulgate)
Lam	Lamentations
Lk	Luke
Lv	Leviticus
Mal	Malachi (Malachias in Vulgate)
1–2 Mc	1 and 2 Maccabees
Mi	Micah
Mk	Mark
Mt	Matthew
Na	Nahum
Neh	Nehemiah (2 Esdras in Septuagint and Vulgate)
Nm	Numbers
Ob	Obadiah
Phil	Philippians
Phlm	Philemon
Prv	Proverbs
Ps	Psalms
1–2 Pt	1 and 2 Peter
Rom	Romans
Ru	Ruth
Rv	Revelation (Apocalypse in Vulgate)
Sg	Song of Songs
Sir	Sirach (Wisdom of Ben Sira; Ecclesiasticus in Septuagint and Vulgate)
1–2 Sm	1 and 2 Samuel (1 and 2 Kings in Septuagint and Vulgate)
Tb	Tobit
1–2 Thes	1 and 2 Thessalonians
Ti	Titus
1–2 Tm	1 and 2 Timothy
Wis	Wisdom
Zec	Zechariah
Zep	Zephaniah

Versions

Apoc	Apocrypha
ARV	American Standard Revised Version
ARVm	American Standard Revised Version, margin
AT	American Translation
AV	Authorized Version (King James)
CCD	Confraternity of Christian Doctrine
DV	Douay-Challoner Version

ERV	English Revised Version
ERVm	English Revised Version, margin
EV	English Version(s) of the Bible
JB	Jerusalem Bible
LXX	Septuagint
MT	Masoretic Text
NAB	New American Bible
NEB	New English Bible
NIV	New International Version
NJB	New Jerusalem Bible
NRSV	New Revised Standard Version
NT	New Testament
OT	Old Testament
RSV	Revised Standard Version
RV	Revised Version
RVm	Revised Version, margin
Syr	Syriac
Vulg	Vulgate

P

PAUCAPALEA

Author of early glosses and a *Summa on the Decretum* of GRATIAN. His work was written before 1148 when it is referred to in the *Summa Rolandi*, which is of that date. We know practically nothing about him, the dates of his birth and death, his place of origin, etc. It seems certain that he taught at Bologna, where it is possible he had been a student of Gratian. He was responsible for some of the earliest *paleae*, or additions, to the *Decretum* of Gratian; the division of parts I and III into *distinctiones* appears also to be his work. He gives evidence of a good knowledge of Roman law and is a canonist of some competence. His *Summa* is also characterized by the many *historiae* or exegesis of passages of Scripture already noted in the *Decretum*. His work is frequently referred to by canonists after his time. For example, the author of the *Summa Parisiensis* mentions him by name about 20 times and seems to have had his work constantly before him. From time immemorial Paucapalea has been called ''the first decretist.'' More recently that title has been challenged seriously and perhaps successfully. He now appears to have made use of one or two earlier works on the *Decretum* that have lately come to the attention of scholars.

Bibliography: *Die Summa des Paucapalea über das Decretum Gratiani*, ed. J. F. SCHULTE (Giessen 1890). A. VETULANI, ''Le Décret de Gratien et les premiers décrétistes . . . ,'' *Studia Gratiana* 7 (1959) 273–353; ''Nouvelles vues sur le Décret de Gratien,'' *La Potogne au Xe Congrès international des sciences historiques à Rome* (Warsaw 1955) 83–105. G. FRANSEN, ''La date du Décret de Gratien,'' *Revue d'histoire ecclésiastique* 51 (1956) 521–531. S. KUTTNER, *Repertorium der Kanonistik* (Rome 1937). F. MAASSEN, ''Paucapalea: ein Beitrag zur Literargeschichte des canonischen Rechts im Mittelalter,'' *Sitzungberichte der Akademie der Wissenschaften in Wein* 31 (1859) 449–516. A. MOCCI, ''Documenti inediti sui canonista Paucapalea,'' *Atti della Reale accademia delle scienze di Torino* 40 (1905) 316–326.

[T. P. MCLAUGHLIN]

PAUL, APOSTLE, ST.

In his apostolate to the Hellenistic world St. Paul traveled extensively from Jerusalem to Rome, preaching, teaching, and founding churches in the name of Christ. His principal message was that both Jew and Gentile, through faith and acceptance of the gospel, could enter into redemptive solidarity with the risen Christ. In the labors and perils of his ministry Paul drew strength from his personal life in Christ, the urgency of his gospel, and an indomitable will. During Paul's lifetime, and chiefly through his ministry, the hesitant and uncertain group of Jesus' disciples made its decisive break with Judaism and turned its energies to the worldwide mission of converting all men to Christ. The Church entered fully into the Gentile world. Paul's conversion was not merely a call to personal sanctification; it was both a germinal source to aid Paul in the maturation of his gospel and an apocalyptic command to carry that gospel to the ends of the earth before the imminent return of Christ. Characteristic of Paul's preaching was his emphasis on the risen Christ as the center of a new existence radically transformed by the death and Resurrection of Christ—a reality Paul experienced through his transformation ''into Christ.''

This article is divided into three main sections treating, in order, of St. Paul's life, personality, and theology.

LIFE

After treating of the sources on which any account of the life and teachings of St. Paul must be based, a summary will be given here, first of the chronology of his life, and then of his youth, his role as a persecutor of the Church, his conversion, his apostolic activity, his imprisonments, and his last years and death.

Literary Sources. St. Luke's Acts of the Apostles (7.58; 8.3; 9.1–30; 11.25–30; 12.25; 13.1–28.31) and the Epistles of St. Paul are the only reliable accounts of Paul's life. The 20th century saw extensive debates about whether all 14 Pauline Epistles except the Epistle to the HEBREWS (held by most exegetes to be the work of a dis-

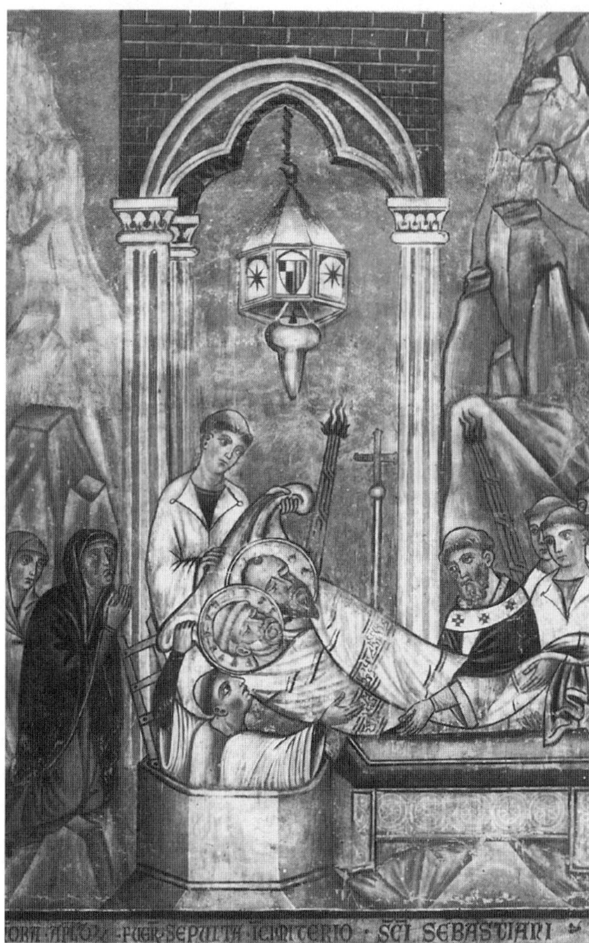

The burial of SS. Peter and Paul, 11th century fresco in the church of San Piero, in Grado, near Pisa, Italy.

ciple of Paul) should be attributed to Paul. The prevailing scholarly conclusion is that only Romans, First and Second Corinthians, Galatians, and (with some exceptions), First Thessalonians, Philippians, Colossians, and Philemon are authentic. Second Thessalonians, Ephesians, First and Second Timothy, and Titus are recognized as Pauline in the sense that they contain Pauline elements, and are perhaps the work of a Pauline school. (For the apocryphal *Acti Pauli,* see *The Catholic Encyclopedia* [New York 1907–22] 11:567.)

Paul's Epistles were both letters (substitutes for conversation) and epistles (formal literary compositions), occasioned by the needs and conflicts of the early Christian communities. As such they became normative in Church development. These sources outline the occasions and become the very manifestation of Paul's gospel (i.e., Jesus revealed through the life of Paul).

The relation between Acts and the Epistles is as interesting as it is complex. Most modern scholars agree that Acts is best read for historical purposes in the light of the Epistles, not conversely. The Epistles give many historical details and personal insights into the providential growth and transformation of Paul. Much of this information is not in Acts. (For difficulties in the Acts-Epistles relationship, see Munck, 78–86.) Yet, the multiple purposes of the ACTS OF THE APOSTLES can cross-fertilize the Epistles. Information on the last years and deaths of the Apostles come only from early tradition.

Chronology. The proconsulship of Junius Annaeus Gallio in Achaia dates very probably between the spring of A.D. 52 and the spring of A.D. 53 (see Acts 18.12–17). The assumption by Festus of the procuratorship in Judea occurred in A.D. 59 or 60 (see Acts 25.1). Paul was arrested in Jerusalem around Pentecost of A.D. 58 and taken to Rome between the fall of A.D. 60 and the spring of A.D. 61. The specific dates in the following narrative of Paul's life are based on these assumptions (see A. Wikenhauser, *New Testament Introduction* 360–361).

Youth. Paul was born, probably, a few years after the birth of Jesus, into a double world symbolized by his double name: Saul-Paul. Under Jewish parents of the tribe of Benjamin (Rom 11.1; Phil 3.5), Saul became a ''Hebrew of the Hebrews'' (Phil 3.5), conscientiously instructed in strict Pharisaic tenets and intensely loyal to religious traditions. At the age of five he would have learned the principal contents of the law (cf. Dt 5–6). At six he would have attended the ''Vineyard,'' a kindergarten attached to the synagogue. Studying the Scriptures until the age of ten, he would be introduced to the oral law and its multiple prescriptions (the MISHNAH). But Paul was also a Roman citizen born in Tarsus of Cilicia, a bustling maritime center of Hellenistic culture (Gal 1.14; 2.15; Acts 22.3; 25.12), so that in his boyhood he also absorbed a certain amount of Greek culture. His Epistles manifest youthful interest in wrestling, military drills, parades, and games.

At the age of 15 Saul went to the temple college in Jerusalem under the venerated GAMALIEL to learn the subtleties of rabbinic teaching with its mass of legal interpretations (HALAKAH) and folklore literature (HAGGADAH).

It was an obligation of the PHARISEE and the duty of an ordained rabbi to marry. But 1 Cor 7.7 seems to indicate that Paul never did. One unmarried rabbi justified himself thus: ''What shall I do? My soul cleaves to the Torah. Let others keep the world going.'' As a Christian, Paul looked upon his celibacy as a mystical betrothal to Christ and the Church.

Since a trade was needed by rabbis, who were not allowed to make money in giving instructions on the Law,

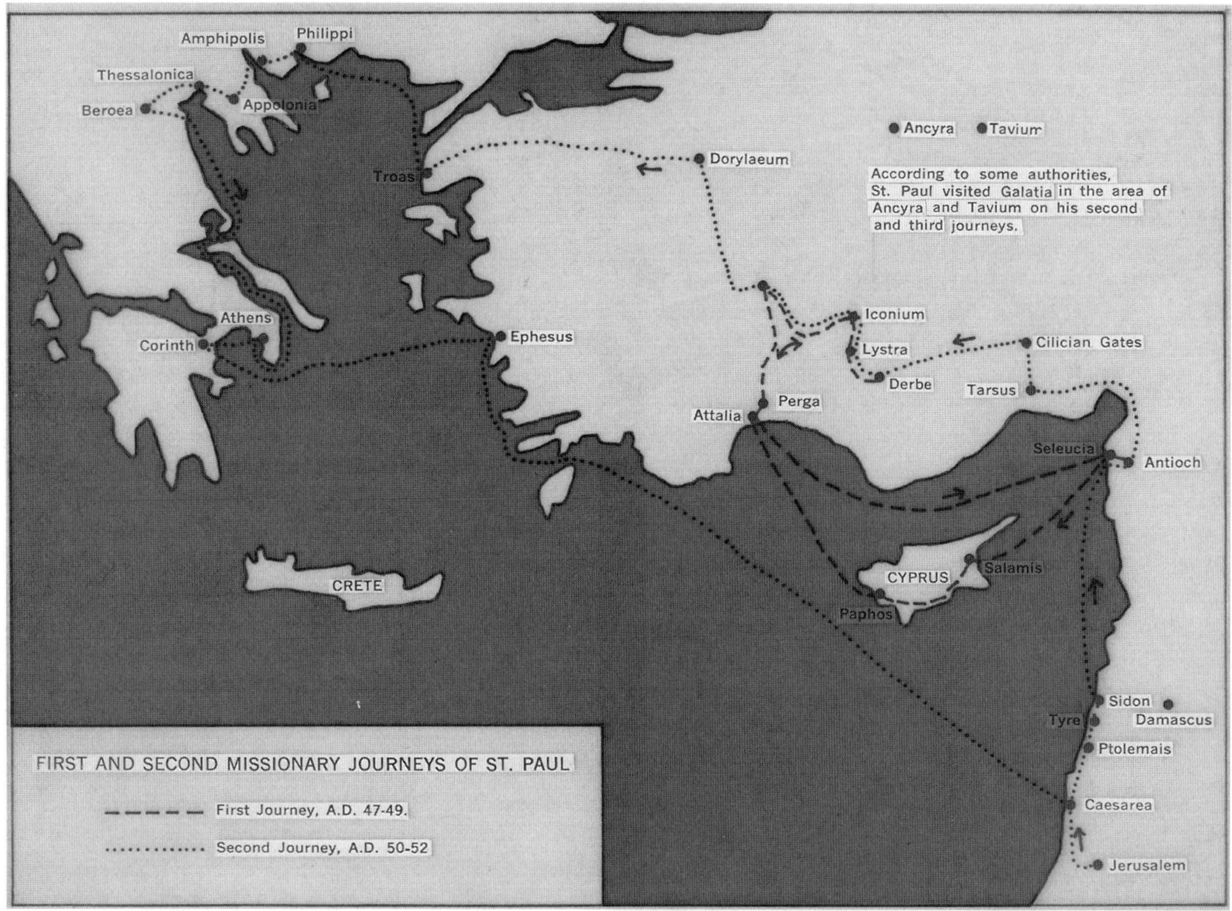

The first two journeys of St. Paul. The first journey began in Antioch; the second, in Jerusalem.

Saul learned the trade of ''maker of tent cloth'' (Acts 18.3).

Persecutor of the Early Church. About A.D. 34, in Jerusalem, Stephen, full of grace and power, was preaching the risen Christ (Acts 7); eventually, he was stoned to death. Paul, the Scribe witness, ''approved of his death'' (Acts 7.60). Stephen had prayed, ''Lord, do not lay this sin against them.'' Later Augustine said, ''If Stephen had not prayed thus, the Church would not have had Paul'' [*see* STEPHEN (PROTOMARTYR), ST.].

Stephen's death signaled one of the bloodiest persecutions against the infant Church. Zealous for the traditions of his fathers (Gal 1.14), Paul became grand inquisitor for the persecution, since he clearly saw Christianity as mortal enemy to Jewish legalistic tradition (Gal 1.13–23; 1 Cor 15.9). That the Mosaic Law was now supplanted by a new Christian dispensation seemed an outrageous blasphemy. Given spies, temple soldiers, and legal authority, ''Saul was harassing the church; entering house after house; and dragging out men and women, he committed them to prison'' (Acts 8.3).

Conversion. In the midst of his hostile activity against the emerging Church, Paul was unexpectedly converted to Christ. The most remarkable note of Paul's conversion was its suddenness. It was hardly expected that the zealous Pharisee, Saul, as he set out from Jerusalem armed with letters to harass the young Christian community of Damascus, would enter that city a convert and disciple of Jesus. Yet, on the outskirts of the city Paul, favored by grace with a miraculous and objective vision of Christ, heard the words, ''Saul, Saul, why dost thou persecute me?'' (Acts 9.4). ''Who art thou, Lord?'' was almost a rhetorical question; he already knew the answer that he would hear: ''I am Jesus whom thou art persecuting.'' One of Paul's most characteristic teachings, the doctrine of the MYSTICAL BODY OF CHRIST, finds its genesis here. A light from without blazed forth within him, ''the light of the knowledge of the glory of God on the face of Christ'' (2 Cor 4.6). Already a slave of Christ, Paul inquired, ''Lord, what wilt thou have me do?'' (Acts 9.6). He now realized that it was a matter, ''not of him who wills nor of him who runs, but of God showing

St. Paul. (Archive Photos)

The high altar of the Basilica of St. Paul-Outside-the-Walls, Rome, over the traditional site of the grave of the Apostle. (Alinari-Art Reference/Art Resource, NY)

mercy'' (Rom 9.16). The Lord simply directed Paul to Ananias, and Ananias baptized him.

Although there is no direct evidence for it, it is possible that Paul, haunted by the fear of sin and subconsciously but deeply impressed by the holy deaths of men such as Stephen (Acts 7.55–60; 26.10–11), may thereby have been prepared for his liberating encounter with Christ. But Paul himself regarded his conversion as an ἔκτρωμα, ''untimely birth'' (1 Cor 15.8). Suddenly he was freed from the uncanny power of the Law that had held him in psychological bondage. His was an utterly unexpected birth into the power of Him who was dead and risen.

The blindness that followed this event and remained for several days was probably the natural result of his psychological collapse. Possibly, Luke ''baptizes'' the ancient notion that blindness befalls the man who gazes on the divine. While all three accounts of Paul's conversion (Acts 9.3–9; 22.6–11; 26.13–18) agree in substance, they differ in detail because of the literary forms and differences of polemic, purpose, and author in each case [see D. Stanley, *Catholic Biblical Quarterly* 15 (1953) 315–338].

Apostolic Activity. St. Paul's apostolic ministry, as far as it is known from the NT, can be conveniently divided into four main periods: (1) early years, A.D. 34 to 47; (2) first missionary journey, A.D. 47 to 49; (3) second missionary journey, A.D. 50 to 52; (4) third missionary journey, A.D. 53 to 58.

Early Years in the Apostolate. No psychology of religion can fully explain the profound reconstruction of Paul's religious world whereby another Person took possession of him in an experience of mystic death to the old and resurrection to the new. At first there must have been a clearing away of the debris of his old world, while the new life in Christ was being built up within him. Yet nothing worthwhile, cosmopolitan polish, intellectual acuity, or vitality, was lost. For many years the process of conversion continued. An inner change, both intellectual and emotional, was wrought in him because of Christ, whose new life he now lived: ''I count everything loss because of the excelling knowledge of Jesus Christ, my Lord, for whose sake I have suffered the loss of all things'' (Phil 3.8).

In Gal 1.17 Paul says that immediately after his Baptism he retired into Arabia, i.e., the semidesert Nabataean country southeast of Damascus, and there spent three years, while his ''knowledge of the mystery of Christ'' (Eph 3.4) grew deeper. At the end of this period he returned to Damascus, where he preached ''that Jesus is the Son of God'' (Acts 9.20). But when the Jews of Damascus made a plot to kill him, he escaped from the city by being lowered over its walls in a large basket—an incident of which he later boasted as evidence of his human weakness (2 Cor 11.32–33).

From Damascus Paul went to Jerusalem, where BARNABAS introduced him to Peter and the other Apostles (Acts 9.25–29; Gal 1.18–19). After two weeks spent in preaching to the HELLENISTS of Jerusalem, however, another Jewish plot compelled him to leave the city. This time he retired to his native Tarsus (Gal 1.21; Acts 9.26–30), where the process of his transformation continued. These years seem to have been for Paul a time of training, while he waited for a new command from the Lord. Through reflection and prayer he was developing and maturing his gospel. His total involvement in the dead and risen Christ absorbed him to a point where his own personality found wholeness in the reality of Christ risen in him. Thus it was at this time that he had the famous ecstatic vision of which he later wrote in 2 Cor 12.1–7.

The earliest spread of Christianity was less through intentional missionary journeys than through the storm of persecution that scattered the first believers. Some went to Antioch, the capital of Syria, which was destined soon to become more important than Jerusalem as the center of the Church in the East. About the year 44 Barnabas was sent by the Apostles at Jerusalem to act as their representative in the Christian community at Antioch. When he saw the constant growth of believers in this city, he went to Tarsus, found Paul, and brought him back with him to Antioch to help him there in the ministry. In this community of predominantly Gentile Christians, Barnabas and Paul were blessed with great success (Acts 11.25–26). A few years later this community commissioned the two to bring the ''famine collection'' to Jerusalem for the relief of the brethren there (Acts 11.27–30; perhaps also in Gal 2.1–10).

First Missionary Journey. After their return from Jerusalem, Barnabas and Paul, with John Mark (*see* MARK, EVANGELIST, ST.), Barnabas's nephew, acting as their assistant, were commissioned by the Antioch community, under the inspiration of the Holy Spirit, to preach the gospel beyond the confines of Syria. Thus Paul began his first missionary journey (A.D. 47–49: Acts 13.1–14.27). The missionaries sailed first to the island of Cyprus, Barnabas's homeland (Acts 4.36). There the proconsul Sergius Paulus, who resided at Paphos, was converted to Christianity. From this point on in Acts, the Apostle is no longer mentioned by his Hebrew name Saul; apparently he now preferred to be known by his Greco-Roman name Paul, either in honor of his first important convert, Sergius Paulus, or more likely, to indicate by his ''Gentile'' name that his apostolate was now primarily to the Gentiles (Gal 2.7–9: Rom 15.16). Now, also, the leadership passed from Barnabas to Paul; the phrase in Acts is no longer ''Barnabas and Saul,'' but ''Paul and Barnabas.''

From Cyprus the three missionaries journeyed onward into the southern part of central Asia Minor, where at Perga, because of some disagreement, John Mark turned back. Paul and Barnabas evangelized the southern region of the Roman province of GALATIA, including the key cities of ANTIOCH in Pisidia, Iconium, Lystra, and Derbe. At Lystra Paul was stoned and left half dead (see also 2 Tm 3.11), perhaps then receiving the wounds whose scars he called the στίγματα, ''tattoo'' or ''brand marks,'' that marked him as the slave of the Lord Jesus (Gal 6.17). In spite of Jewish hostility, the missionaries were so successful that on the return journey they appointed PRESBYTERS and organized the Christian communities as they passed through the same cities.

The rapid spread of Christianity among the Gentiles brought on a crisis in the Church. A strong Judaistic movement in Jerusalem demanded that Gentile Christians should be circumcised and made to observe the Mosaic Law. Paul clearly saw the practical consequences of this. If the movement prevailed, Christianity would be turned into a merely Jewish sect that Gentiles would be loath to enter, or it would be split into a Judeo-Christian Church and a Gentile-Christian Church. But what was much more fundamental, Paul saw in the position of the Judaizers a repudiation of the very basis of Christianity—that man is saved by faith in Jesus Christ and not by the observance of any law, even though after initial salvation man is not without the law of Christ (Gal 6.2).

When the Judaistic demands were forced on the Christian community at Antioch, Paul and Barnabas were sent to Jerusalem to request a settlement of the dispute. The resultant meeting of these envoys from Antioch with the Apostles and presbyters in Jerusalem is commonly known as the Council of JERUSALEM.

According to some exegetes, Paul wrote his Epistle to the GALATIANS shortly before he left Antioch, or even on his way to Jerusalem, to attend this meeting. These scholars argue that in this epistle, which is primarily concerned with this dispute, there is not the slightest reference to any decision having been given on it at Jerusalem and that the dispute between Peter and Paul at Antioch mentioned in Gal 2.11–14 would hardly be possible after the Council of Jerusalem. Yet, because of the great similarity between Galatians (especially 3.1–4.31) and Romans (especially 4.1–25), which was written *c.* A.D. 57, most exegetes hold that Galatians could not have been written before A.D. 54.

In any case, the Council of Jerusalem (A.D. 49 or 50) decided that no burden should be laid on the Gentile converts except abstinence from meat offered to idols (for Paul's authentic interpretation of this see 1 Cor 10.25–30; Rom 14.14–23), from immorality, and from blood and meat containing blood. In spite of the decree, the hostility and agitation of the Judaizers continued to hound Paul throughout the rest of his life.

Second Missionary Journey. Shortly after the Council of Jerusalem Paul began his second missionary journey (A.D. 50–52: Acts 15.36–18.22). Barnabas wanted to bring his nephew Mark along, but Paul refused. Thus, the original mission team was dissolved. Barnabas and Mark journeyed again to Cyprus, while Paul took with him SILAS, valuable as a Roman citizen and a member of the mother church in Jerusalem. Paul revisited the Christian communities of (south) Galatia and at Lystra chose TIMOTHY (whom he circumcised for acceptance by the Jews) to be his constant companion and secretary. From here they traveled westward into Phrygia and northward along the western border of Galatia. They would have continued further north into Bithynia had they not been prevented by the Holy Spirit. Turning westward, then, through Mysia, they came to Troas on the coast, where Luke joined them (*see* LUKE, EVANGELIST, ST.). In obedience to a vision, Paul crossed the sea to Macedonia. Europe, grown sick of paganism, was calling him. Paul established vigorous Christian communities at Philippi, Thessalonica, and Beroea in spite of Judaistic hatred, which brought scourging and imprisonment at Philippi and persecution elsewhere.

Paul came to Athens by chance. Awaiting the arrival there of Timothy and Silas, he defended monotheism in a scholarly discourse before the Stoic and Epicurean philosophers on the AREOPAGUS; but results were small when he announced the risen Christ as judge of the whole world. Resolved henceforth to depend entirely on Christ and His power, not on polemic ability, he founded a large community at Corinth (1 Cor 1–2), where he worked for a year and a half (from about the beginning of A.D. 50 to the summer of A.D. 51). Here he was assisted by PRISCA (PRISCILLA) AND AQUILA (Rom 16.3; 2 Tm 4.19), a Jewish married couple expelled from Rome under edict of Emperor Claudius. Soon after his arrival at Corinth Paul wrote the First and Second Epistles to the THESSALONIANS.

Third Missionary Journey. Not long after Paul's return to Antioch, a third missionary journey (A.D. 53–58) led him back to the Christian communities of Galatia and Phrygia (Acts 18.23). At EPHESUS he worked for three years (Acts 19.1–40; 20.31), successfully building up the Mystical Body. Here he wrote the First Epistle to the CORINTHIANS and, according to the more common opinion, Galatians. Finally, led by Demetrius, the silversmiths, whose income from their images of Diana (Artemis) decreased with Paul's preaching, instigated a riot that forced him to leave Ephesus [*see* DIANA (ARTEMIS) OF THE EPHESIANS]. He revisited Macedonia (where he wrote his Second Epistle to the Corinthians) and Corinth, a hotbed of problems, in which Paul became dramatically involved (2 Cor 1–7; 10–13). Here he wrote his Epistle to the ROMANS in preparation for his proposed visit to Rome (Acts 19.21).

In the spring of A.D. 58 he returned to Philippi, where he celebrated the Passover. At Miletus he bade farewell to the presbyters of Ephesus. Despite numerous warnings at CAESAREA in Palestine (e.g., the prophetic symbolic actions of AGABUS: Acts 21.10–11) and his own sinister forebodings (Rom 15.31; Acts 20.22; 21.13), Paul delivered the collection for the poor of Jerusalem (Rom 15.25–29).

Imprisonments. In 2 Corinthians, written in A.D. 57, Paul says that he was ''in prisons frequently'' (2 Cor 11.23). Although direct evidence is lacking, it seems probable that one of these imprisonments was at Ephesus during his third missionary journey (see 1 Cor 15.32); and it is possible that the so-called CAPTIVITY EPISTLES were written at the time of this imprisonment. However, there is certain knowledge only of his imprisonments at Jerusalem, Caesarea, and Rome.

At Jerusalem and Caesarea. Advised by James, Paul accompanied and paid the expenses of four men who were completing their vows as NAZIRITES in Jerusalem. Here the Judaizers from the province of Asia stirred up a riot, accusing him of bringing a Gentile Christian (Trophimus) into the inner court of the temple. The Roman soldiers took him, as a Roman citizen, into protective custody. As Jewish hostility mounted, Lysias, the Roman commander at Jerusalem, had Paul taken to Caesarea, where the governor resided. Here Paul was kept in confinement for two years (A.D. 58–60) by the governor Marcus Antonius FELIX. But Porcius FESTUS, successor of Felix, became inclined to accede to the wishes of the Sanhedrin that Paul should be returned to Jerusalem for trial. Knowing that Sanhedrin justice would mean death, Paul exercised his right as a Roman citizen: he appealed to Caesar.

At Rome. To Rome, therefore, Paul was sent, and on the voyage he suffered shipwreck at Malta (Acts 27). For another two years he was ''imprisoned'' in ''house custody'' (*custodia libera*), allowed to rent his own dwelling, to receive visitors, and to preach the Gospel to them.

Last Years. With Paul's two-year imprisonment in Rome the Book of Acts comes to an end. A tradition of the early Church presupposes that Paul was set free. According to Clement of Rome (Pope CLEMENT I) Paul journeyed ''to the end of the West'' (*1 Clem* 5.5–7), i.e., Spain. The MURATORIAN CANON (lines 38–39) and the apocryphal Acts of Peter (1 and 3) repeat the same tradition.

The PASTORAL EPISTLES, if authentic, indicate that Paul revisited his missionary territory in the east, leaving TITUS and Timothy in Crete and Ephesus, respectively, with full authority to combat error and organize the Church there (Ti 1.5; 1 Tm 1.3). Whether the Spanish or eastern journey came first is uncertain. Once more, however, Paul was arrested and imprisoned in Rome, this time more strictly, and finally his desire ''to depart and be with Christ'' (Phil 1.23) was fulfilled by martyrdom in the reign of Nero (A.D. 67 according to Eusebius; A.D. 64 according to Clement of Rome and Tertullian). According to ancient, reliable tradition, Paul was beheaded at a place called *Ad Aquas Salvias* on the Ostian Road (*Via Ostiensis*), a short distance southwest of Rome, and buried along the same road, but somewhat nearer the city, in an area shown by archeological excavations to have been a pagan cemetery of the 1st and 2d centuries. The Basilica of St. Paul-Outside-the-Walls, erected over the Apostle's tomb by Constantine the Great, was enlarged and restored several times, most recently after a disastrous fire in the 19th century.

PERSONALITY

St. Paul's personality will be considered here from the viewpoint both of his character and physical condition and of his qualities as a writer.

Character and Physical Condition. Paul's natural temperament and character indicate, above all, a profoundly inspired religious spirit. As a Jew, he was led by his dedication to the Law zealously to persecute the Church. As a Christian, he adhered to Christ by heroically giving himself to all men. Paul was also a powerful dialectician, as shown by the march of his ideas in Romans, with the native temper of a debater. His dialectic method is clear but could lead to misunderstanding through exaggeration (e.g., in condemning the Law or in taking a dim view of human nature). Yet he possessed exquisite sensibility and an overall charm revealing his capacity for weakness, fear, and discouragement (e.g., 1 Cor 2.3; 2 Cor 1.8). His letters, especially Second Corinthians and Galatians, reflect depths of emotional response—the fears, hopes, affection, indignation by which his soul was torn and tossed. This lively play of emotion, expressed by look and gesture (e.g., Acts 13.9; 14.12–14; 20.34; 23.1–6; 26.1; see also Gal 3.1; Phil 3.18), was firmly controlled by judgment; he ascribed his effectiveness to the Spirit of Christ possessing him (2 Cor 13.3–4; Col 1.29; 1 Thes 1.5, etc.).

However, the qualities of Paul's character are best perceived as he functions in his ministry. Paul was a man of vision who developed the profound reality of the cosmic Christ, dead and alive, into an original system of thought called Pauline theology. Paul's mind was ''essentially intuitive'' (P. van Imschoot), grasping religious truths by direct contemplation rather than by intellectual reasoning. Paul was a mystic who penetrated deeply the inner reality of all things in Christ. His profound experience of seeing all ''in Christ'' sustained him through 30 years of extraordinary hardship and safeguarded him from the intemperances of the fanatic. Paul was an ascetic who steeled himself (1 Cor 9.27; 2 Cor 6.5), in spite of a nervous temperament, to endure all things for Christ. His will, aflame with love, dominated all circumstances and surmounted all difficulties. Paul was a pastor who manifested the tenderness of his Master in solicitude deep and total: ''Who is made to stumble and I am not inflamed?'' (2 Cor 11.29). Warmhearted, natural affection for others was joined to his all-consuming love for Christ. Paul was an organizer who combined born leadership with courage and critical tact. He was able to resist the authority of Barnabas (Acts 15.37–40) as well as to confront publicly the authority of Peter (Gal 2.11–14). With leaders selected by careful judgment, Paul solidly established community after community in ample evidence of his power to organize. Timothy and Titus, two powerful bishops, became extensions of his dynamic personality. All of these qualities combined to make Paul a missionary whose overwhelming desire was to bring Christ to all men. To this purpose he tirelessly spent himself.

Paul's personality reflects and yet transcends its many sources: Pharisaic upbringing firmly rooted in his religious heritage; Greek formation with its love of freedom; rabbinic training with its dialectic; mystic experiences; and the Christian catechesis. It was his personal encounter with the Lord that transformed these various potentials into a unified revelation of God's Son. This absorption in Christ, in whom all things have their meaning (Col 1.15–20), made Paul tolerant of everything beautiful, simple, honorable, and true (Phil 4.8).

Physically, Paul has been traditionally stylized as short, bald, with thick beard and prominent nose, with eyebrows meeting and legs somewhat bowed, but, on the whole, a distinguished man of dignified bearing. This description, found in the apocryphal *Acts of Paul,* derives from the legend of Paul and Thecla and is unflattering enough to be authentic (cf. 2 Cor 10.10; 12.6). His reference to a certain affliction that he calls a ''thorn in the flesh'' (2 Cor 12.7) refers more likely to the persecution he suffered, especially from the Judaizers, than to any physical ailment.

Paul as a Writer. If, as both Horace and Quintillian maintain, true eloquence is the fruit of feeling and strong conviction, not of literary artifice, Paul is sublimely eloquent. Although his style abounds in anacolutha, ellipses, and similar stylistic liberties, Paul is an artist who often and unconsciously creates great literature (e.g., Rom 8.28–39; 2 Cor 6.1–10; 11.21–29). Burning with zeal to shout out the ''good news,'' Paul may forget grammatical sequence, but he always delivers his message with force (e.g., Phil 3.1–14), frequently in the style of the Greek diatribe (Rom 3.1–20). Inflamed with love for Christ and all men in Him, Paul's letters betray indifference to none, least of all to his fellow Jews who rejected Jesus Christ.

Paul writes in a compressed style. His pet phrase, ''in Christ'' (used about 50 times), is a gospel in itself. A thousand ideas clamor for expression. Unified in an ever-changing mosaic of Christ, they are permeated with compelling conviction. Frequently, this pressure of crowding thoughts is forced into tight summaries. Paul is not a stylist with the studied eloquence of his time. His interest is not in words of wisdom but in the wisdom of the Word (1 Cor 1.17–2.5). In an effort to describe the indescribable impact of union with Christ, Paul impressed his creative personality on the Greek he used, giving new meaning to some words, at times even coining words or new combinations [for further discussion, see B. McGrath, *Catholic Biblical Quarterly* 14 (1952) 219–26].

Paul should be interpreted, not only against the background of his Greek world, but also, and primarily, in the context of OT thought processes. Paul thought and spoke cultured Greek, but his literary background was almost exclusively the OT and other Jewish writings. He used Greek words with their Septuagint (LXX) meaning, his thought patterns following Jewish tradition. For example, the body-soul-spirit relation is not Greek but Hebrew; the body (σῶμα, Heb. *bāśār,* ''flesh''), soul (ψυκή, Heb. *nepeš*), and spirit (πνεῦμα, Heb. *rûaḥ*) are, accordingly, three phases of an indivisible unity.

Paul, as a ''Christian rabbi'' (J. Bonsirven), saw Scripture alive only in Christ, who is the revolutionary fulfillment of God's plan and power. Christ is the lifegiving spirit of the letter of the OT (2 Cor 3.6, 17). Yet in Paul's use of the Scriptures—quotations (some 80), allusions, and reminiscences abound—Paul can be understood only in light of the Palestinian exegetical tradition that concerned itself more with applied adaptation and messianism of texts than with the literal sense. Thus, frequently in rabbinic fashion, Paul transcends not only historical accounts (e.g., Gal 4.21–31) but also the Prophets (Rom 1.17; 2.24) and the Psalms (Rom 10.8; Acts 13.33) in his determination to proclaim only Christ. Even though Paul is steeped in rabbinic interpretations of Hebrew Scripture, it is the LXX he uses; the Hebrew text, where it differs from the LXX, is quoted only five times.

THEOLOGY

The religious teaching of the Apostle of the Gentiles will be considered here, first in the sources from which he derived it, then as he presented it in his ''gospel,'' and finally in the important role that it played in the Church.

Sources. The teachings of St. Paul are primarily based on those of the OT, with certain of the OT doctrines as interpreted by the Pharisaic rabbis of his time. What is typically Christian in his teachings he owes partly to the teachings of Jesus as interpreted by the early Church and partly to the revelations that he received directly from God in his mystical experiences.

Jewish Pharisaic Beliefs. The doctrines of providence and the divine ordering of the world, reward and punishment beyond the grave, the resurrection of the dead, the Decalogue, charity toward God and men, belief in angels and demons—these were all a part of the spiritual patrimony Paul inherited as a Jew and a Pharisee. From the Bible Paul acquired the deep sense of God and the sense of sin—the religious attitude that was the treasure of Judaism.

There are striking similarities between Paul and the members of the QUMRAN COMMUNITY—expressions (e.g., ''earthen vessels,'' ''a share in the heritage of the sons''), ideas (e.g., mystery, revelation, knowledge, distinction between light and darkness, the theology of the spirit), and names (e.g., Belial and Satan disguised as an angel of light: see 2 Cor 6.14–18). Yet this similarity in terms and concepts derives mostly from the use of the OT Scriptures common to both Paul and the Qumranites.

Teachings of Jesus and Belief of the Early Church. The 19th-century rationalists saw radical differences between Jesus and Paul. Now, however, it is agreed that these apparent differences are complementary, one to the other, and not opposed. Paul is now seen in full accord with the teachings of Jesus, explicitly in 1 Cor 7.10 (cf. Mt 5.32); 1 Cor 9.14 (cf. Lk 10.7); 1 Cor 11.23–25 (cf. Mt 26.26–29; Lk 22.15–19); cf. also 1 Thes 4.8 with Lk 10.6; Gal 4.17 with Lk 11.52; 1 Cor 4.12–13 and Rom 12.14 with Lk 6.27; 1 Cor 5.4 with Mt 18.20; 1 Cor 13.3 with Lk 12.33; 2 Cor 10.1 with Mt 11.29; Rom 2.1 and 14.13 with Mt 7.1; Rom 14.14 with Mt 15.11; Rom 16.19 with Mt 10.16. The Gospel stress on love (ἀγάπη) is Paul's "way" (1 Cor 13.1–13). The traditions (παραδόσεις) of the early Church are reflected by Paul in 1 Cor 11.23 and 15.3. He gives details of Christ's earthly life (1 Cor 11.23; 15.3–7; 2 Cor 5.21; 8.9; Gal 4.4–5; Phil 2.5–11; Rom 1.3; 8.3; 1 Thes 2.15), His authority (1 Cor 7.10, 12, 25; 1 Thes 4.2–8, 15; 1 Cor 15.24; Acts 20.35), and His teaching (1 Cor 11.25; 9.14; 7.10). Paul determined to transmit the sacred deposit of revelation intact and free from error (Eph 4.14–15; Col 2.7–8; 1 Tm 2.5–7; 6.20; 2 Tm 1.14).

Revelations of Paul. In essence, Paul received everything from "the face of Christ Jesus" at his inaugural vision. Other revelations (or sacred traditions) deepened the Damascus experience or offered guidance to Paul's ministry (Gal 1.11–16; 2 Cor 12.1–4; Eph 3.3–10; see also Acts 18.9–10).

Paul's Gospel. To Paul, the GOSPEL (principally a Pauline term) is God's saving activity as constantly revealed and manifested in Christ's death and Resurrection. Death and Resurrection in Christ are the two powers, the only two powers, of man's new existence; they are the founts of salvation. A total, irrevocable commitment to Christ as Redeemer is man's necessary response to this saving act of God.

Paul's gospel (Rom 2.16; 16.25; 2 Tm 2.8; 2 Cor 4.3; 1 Thes 1.5; 2 Thes 2.14) refers to his personal experience of involvement in Christ's death and Resurrection. In his inaugural vision Paul came into transforming contact with Christ. Yet deeper growth into Christ came through the circumstances of his life.

Christocentric. Paul's interpretation of human existence is Christocentric, all men finding their *raison d'être* in Christ. The Apostle sees Christ's death and Resurrection as God's activity not so much for us as to us, as shown by the word "constitute" in Rom 5.19. By Baptism, Christians are fully and totally incorporated into Christ, into His death and Resurrection (Rom 6.4–6). Through these two transforming powers, Christians encounter Christ in the experiences of all reality, which has been created in, by, and for Him. In this sense, Paul declares that "To live is Christ" (Phil 1.21).

The Death-and-Resurrection Power of Christ. The patristic notion that the union of the Word with human flesh enriches our nature is not Paul's (or the Gospels'). Christ's earthly existence was "according to the flesh" (Rom 1.3). Though sinless, the flesh (i.e., human nature) that the Son of God took on Himself was the flesh of sin (Rom 8.3), and without His death and Resurrection it would be neither powerful nor glorious (Phil 2.7–11). The Father's plan of salvation had Christ enter into solidarity with man, even appearing as man-to-be-redeemed (Heb 5.7–9). Although, ontologically, Christ was always the Son of God, He Himself became "justified in the spirit" (1 Tm 3.16), a "life-giving spirit" (1 Cor 15.45), and was "constituted" (ὁρισθέντος), soteriologically, Son of God in power only with the climax of the Resurrection (Rom 1.3–4; see also Acts 13.33; Heb 1.5).

Death-and-Resurrection, seen as a single mystery, offers complementary facets: death to sinful flesh and entry into divine life. Paradoxically, Christ entered into glory through His Passion—He found life in death itself. His emptying of Himself (Phil 2.7) was a movement toward glory, corresponding to the ambivalent Johannine "hour" in which Christ was "lifted up" on the cross in glory.

The phrase "Christ dead and alive" (F. Durrwell) is significant. "Christ dead" refers to that power present in the risen Christ but grounded in a lifelong dying to "this world" (in its ethical, unredeemed sense) and climaxed by His final redemptive death, in which the baptized die to sin and are buried with Christ in death to this world (Rom 6.3–4; Col 2.20; 2 Tm 2.11). Our sharing in this death stems from a unifying solidarity in Christ, the second Adam. In one death all have died (2 Cor 5.14), not by way of substitution, but by way of mystic identification.

"Christ alive" refers to His life-giving presence in the new creation of eschatological existence, brought about by His Resurrection, in which the baptized are initiated and already share His glorious victory (Rom 6.4–5; see also 4.25).

Christians' Union with the Dead-and-Risen Christ. In Baptism we thus share in the death-to-sin and the becoming-alive-to-God in Christ's death-and-Resurrection. The Eucharist nourishes (1 Cor 10.16) this same reality and joins us in deeper union with Christ and all men (1 Cor 10.16–17). Paul's expression "the body and blood of the Lord" (1 Cor 11.27) shows that he identifies Christ's Eucharistic body with His risen body, for "the Lord" is Paul's name for the risen Christ.

This sense of sharing (κοινωνία) gives the Pauline ethic its distinctive form. No schism (1 Cor 1.10–13), no self-conceit (Gal 5.26), but a spirit of gentleness (Gal 6.1) must prevail among members of the same body. Toward this ideal Paul constantly admonishes, exhorts, warns, and encourages.

The significance of the Resurrection overpowered Paul at his conversion. But the significance of Christ's death became clear amid the birth pangs of his apostolate. Persecution, humiliation, and weakness became raw material for further transformation. Crucified together spiritually with Christ, he no longer lives, but Christ lives in him (Gal 2.20; see also 6.14). In union with Christ's death he would celebrate the perpetual passover (1 Cor 5.7–8) from death to life in Him. The life-giving law of the apostolate was to extend the death-and-Resurrection of Christ.

Paul thus speaks of a present sharing in Christ's Resurrection (Eph 2.4–8). Our whole self, body-soul-spirit, is being formed in the image of the risen Christ. The divine, unseen glory is already bestowed (in part) on our body. Our bodies are Christ's, and to use them for sin, especially sins of the flesh, is tantamount to sacrilege (1 Cor 6.12–20). The PAROUSIA does not effect—it manifests—the glorified risen state already possessed by Christians (Col 3.1–4; cf. the "spiritual body" of 1 Cor 15.44).

Mystical Body of Christ. In the Captivity Epistles, Paul concentrates on the Mystery of Christ risen and acting in His Church as the unifying force of the universe. As one body, Jew and Gentile alike are the object of God's mercy, subject to Him as head (Eph 1.22; Col 1.18), who rules through the "mighty power" of His Resurrection. In His body, sacrificed and glorified, Christ has slain all enmity (Eph 2.14). The entire universe is infused by the divinity and drawn into unity through the redeeming Christ. Thus is all created reality redeemed by God, who through Christ is at the beginning and end of all this work of the new creation (Col 1.15–20).

Although the key to Paul's theology, whether moral or dogmatic, is Christ's death-and-Resurrection, the function of the Holy Spirit is identified with that of the risen Christ (e.g., 2 Cor 3.17; 1 Cor 15.45). St. Ambrose calls Christ the body of the Holy Spirit. The Father pours out the Spirit to us through the risen Christ so that the raising of Christ and our participation in His new life are a single actuality. Paul refers to the activity of the Spirit as a "renewal" (ἀνακαίνωσις: Ti 3.5), a Greek word used in the NT to connote something utterly new, a surprising and transforming force. In Christ's death-and-Resurrection the Church, as God's community, is rebuilt on the cornerstone rejected by His own people (Rom 9.33).

Freedom from the Mosaic Law. In proclaiming Christ, dead and alive, as the only power of salvation, Paul encountered two chief doctrinal obstacles: the "wisdom" of the Gentile, and the "Law" of the Jew. The Gentiles proposed reason as a saving power. In 1 Cor 1.17–4.20 Paul magnificently praises the wisdom of God in Christ crucified. Salvation does not rest on the wisdom of men but on the power of God in Christ (1 Cor 2.5). Hence, the gospel is essentially a divine force, not a form of human reasoning.

The Judaizers posed the Law, both moral and ceremonial, as a cause of salvation. Paul saw that the Christian, by God's magnanimity, fully and personally receives Christ, dead and risen, who alone becomes the principle of saving life. The Law leaves man without hope. It has no power in itself to save; rather it condemns. Being itself holy (Rom 7.12) and spiritual (Rom 7.14), it reveals man in his sinful state. Thus, it works wrath (Rom 4.15), makes sin abound (Rom 5.20), is the power of sin (1 Cor 15.56), brings knowledge of sin (Rom 3.20; 7.7), and is a curse (Gal 3.13). These aspects of the Law died in Christ (Rom 7.4; Gal 2.19) and in Paul through Baptism. With Christ the Law was nailed to the cross and died (Col 4.14). The Law is for the unjust, not the just (1 Tm 1.9). It serves as a negative, protective pedagogue (Gal 3.24) to those not fully in the faith (Gal 3.25), or as an expression of true faith informed by charity for those wholly committed to Christ (Gal 5.6).

Such independence from the Law (Rom 3.21–28) is demanded by the gratuity of Redemption. Man, in original sin, is radically unable to save himself; history and Scripture attest universal sin (Rom 3.1–18). At best, his egocentric autonomy inclines him to turn all his law-keeping into a self-redemptive effort (Rom 10.3; Phil 3.4–9). Only through that faith that is total commitment to Christ can man accept salvation (*see* JUSTIFICATION).

Providential Role. The life-and-death struggle in the early Church between the Law and Christian freedom is difficult to overestimate. Had the early Christian community succumbed to the Judaizer's insistence upon the Law as a means of salvation, there would be no Christianity today. Providentially, Paul arose as the man preeminently qualified to transplant Christianity, without destroying any of its roots, from the ancient earth of Israel to fertile, Gentile soil.

Paul's life, however, reveals an even more profound role. All great movements are initiated and sustained by ideas. But Paul's is not mere intellectual genius; his is a vision of God's saving activity joined and compenetrated into man's entire human existence. For Paul, a man of many worlds, Christianity is no isolation. Jew, Greek, Roman, workman, intellectual, evangelist—through unbelievable hardships and great joys—all brought Paul, the many-faceted personality, to drink deeply of the death-and-Resurrection ''mystery of Christ'' (Eph 3.4; Col 4.3).

Historically, Paul's influence on Christianity is unsurpassed. His impact is ''the first after the One''—of the first in the One. Paul is ever real and contemporary. In his inspired letters, he continuously proclaims the eruption of Christ into man's life by which he is radically remade: ''If then any man is in Christ, he is a new creature. The former things have passed away; behold, they are made new'' (2 Cor 5.17). Paul himself stands as a model of self-renewal and of Church-renewal: ''Be imitators of me as I am of Christ'' (1 Cor 11.1).

Dynamically, Paul reveals the unifying force and life-giving principle of all created reality: Christ, who identified with the Church, is the now present ''mystery of God'' (Col 2.2). By his personal witness to Christ's death-and-Resurrection, Paul, Apostle to the Gentiles, has become the revealed archetype both of Christian theology and of the ecumenical Church.

Iconography. St. Paul has been portrayed very frequently in Christian art (sculptures, mosaics, paintings) since the 4th century, either alone or more often together with St. Peter. One of the oldest-known representations of him is on the beautiful sarcophagus of Junius Bassus (middle of the 4th century), in the crypt of St. Peter's, Rome. Here he is shown as being led away by a sword-bearing executioner. The scene of Paul's martyrdom is the predominant theme in early art, and his specific symbol since the 13th century has been the sword by which he was put to death. Later art, however, also shows various other scenes from his life, especially his conversion on the way to Damascus. Even scenes from the apocryphal Acts of Paul and Thecla are reproduced in art. At times various scenes are combined in so-called cycles, e.g., the ten scenes from his life in the mosaics at Monreale, Sicily, and the five scenes in tapestry from designs by Raphael for the Sistine Chapel, now in the Vatican Museum. Another celebrated masterpiece is Michelangelo's fresco of Paul's conversion, in the Pauline Chapel of the Vatican.

Bibliography: M. DIBELIUS and W. KÜMMEL, *Paul,* tr. F. CLARK (Philadelphia 1953). W. M. RAMSAY, *St. Paul the Traveller and the Roman Citizen* (3d ed. Grand Rapids 1949). J. MUNCK, *Paul and the Salvation of Mankind,* tr. F. CLARKE (Richmond 1960). E. HAENCHEN, *Die Apostelgeschichte* (12th ed. Göttingen 1959). F. PRAT, *Theology of St. Paul,* tr. J. L. STODDARD from 10th Fr. ed., 2 v. (Westminster, Md. 1958). L. CERFAUX, *Christ in the Theology of St. Paul,* tr. G. WEBB and A. WALKER (New York 1959). D. M. STANLEY, *Christ's Resurrection in Pauline Soteriology* (Rome 1961) with extensive bibliog. F. X. DURRWELL, *The Resurrection: A Biblical Study,* tr. R. SHEED (New York 1960). A. BRUNOT, *Saint Paul and His Message,* tr. R. MATTHEWS (New York 1959). F. AMIOT, *The Key Concepts of St. Paul,* tr. J. DINGLE (New York 1962). Paul and the Law. S. LYONNET, ''St. Paul: Liberty and Law,'' *The Bridge* 4 (1962) 229–251. J. KNOX, *The Ethic of Jesus in the Teaching of the Church* (New York 1961). Paul's Conversion. D. M. STANLEY, ''Paul's Conversion in Acts: Why the Three Accounts?'' *Catholic Biblical Quarterly* 15 (1953) 315–338. W. PROKULSKI, ''The Conversion of St. Paul,'' *ibid.* 19 (1957) 453–473. N. A. DAHL, *Studies in Paul* (Minneapolis 1977). *Anchor Bible Dictionary* 5 (New York 1992) 186–201. J. MURPHY-O'CONNOR, *Paul: A Critical Life* (Oxford 1996). J. D. G. DUNN, *The Theology of Paul the Apostle* (Grand Rapids, Mich. 1998).

[F. SCHROEDER/EDS.]

PAUL, MISSIONARY JOURNEYS

Of all the great wayfarers of antiquity, the journeys of Paul of Tarsus (*see* PAUL, APOSTLE, ST.) are among the best documented. His travels by land and sea in the Roman dominated eastern regions of the Mediterranean during the relatively peaceful era of the Pax Romana are most reliably reconstructed by placing primary reliance upon those epistles judged authentically his (Rom, 1–2 Cor, Gal, Phil, 1 Thess, Phlm). The traditions about Paul's movement in the deutero-Pauline letters function as secondary sources and must be critically evaluated for possible supplementary data. The massive material about Paul in the Acts of the Apostles functions as a secondary source, one most difficult to assess, since its author, Luke, clearly knew much about Paul. Luke implies that he had at times traveled with Paul (see the so-called we-passages in Acts 16:10–17; 20:5–15; 21:1–18; 27:1–28:16), yet he often gives (or appears to omit) information that does not correlate with Paul's letters.

Paul has long been described (and mapped) as having made three missionary journeys, followed by a fourth as a prisoner, nevertheless indomitably still preaching, when taken under custody to Rome. The superimposition of the three-journey structure upon Paul's life and travels, derived by interpreters of Acts, wherein it is merely implicit in 13:1–14:28; 15:36–18:22 and 18:23–21:14, can be used as a convenient aid for readers of the NT to organize their own understanding of the biblical text (see Brown, 431). This should be recognized as an artificial device that affects how Paul is seen. For example, the division into journeys, in which the demarcation between the second and the third (18:22–23) is not very clear, suggests that Paul's point of initial departure and final return was consistently Antioch, thus that the Antiochene church was his home base. Yet it is uncertain that Paul considered himself so integrally linked to that church, especially after his controversy with Peter there (Gal 2:11–14).

If the conventional three-journey structure has its drawbacks in sketching Paul the missionary traveler, its helpfulness and ongoing widespread use as a framework for his post-Damascus Road years should be balanced with the apostle's own description of what he was doing. Paul's imagery divides his life into two periods rather than a sequence of journeys. In Gal 1 he speaks of a time denoted as ''my earlier life in Judaism'' (1:14), which he says ended ''when God . . . was pleased to reveal his Son to me . . .'' (1:16). In Phil 3 he describes what he was doing after that revelation as ''straining forward to what lies ahead'' (3.13), ''press[ing] on toward the goal for the prize of the heavenly call of God in Jesus Christ'' (3:14), his goal being ''to know Christ and the power of his resurrection and the sharing of his sufferings'' (3:10) so that he Paul, too, might ''attain the resurrection of the dead'' (3:11). The resurrection of the righteous dead by God was a belief that Paul as a Pharisee must have held. Resurrection, however, had become for him, once ''Christ Jesus had made [Paul] his own'' (3:12), attainable not by a righteousness based on the Mosaic law, but by ''a righteousness . . . that comes through faith in Christ,'' (3:9). As he announced that faith far and wide, Paul unabashedly set forth that he was ''not ashamed of the gospel . . . the power of God for salvation to everyone who has faith, to the Jew first and also to the Greek'' (Rom 1:16).

In Paul's Philippian imagery of pressing on and straining toward completion, expressed as well in Gal 2:2 where he describes his evangelizing work as ''running,'' which he hoped was not ''in vain,'' he sees himself as one always moving urgently ahead, yet not without the great effort of struggling on many levels. It is possible that this language of progressing toward a goal was among Paul's most frequently used and best remembered metaphors for himself since the deutero-Pauline writer of 2 Tim 4:7 represents him as saying near the close of his life: ''I have fought the good fight, I have finished the race.'' This picture which emerges of Paul the runner, ever contending to stay on course and struggling even against great odds, is not incompatible with a supposed journey structure. Yet Paul's own imagery more vividly conveys a sense of relentless effort in evangelization, even when sidetracked by opposition, his own sickness, disputes with other co-religionists and co-workers, and imprisonment.

Various chronologies compete in dating the events in Paul's life (see Roetzel, 178–183). In spite of the widespread disagreement about timing, the sequence of activity in Paul's cursus vitae is generally similar, a major exception being the question of whether the Jerusalem conference (*see* JERUSALEM, COUNCIL OF) preceded or followed the travels described in Acts 15:35–18:22, the ''second journey.'' A traditional chronology and sequence is relied upon here (see e.g. Brown, 428–429; Fitzmyer, 1330–1337; cf. Murphy-O'Connor, 1–31).

After Damascus (Gal 1:16). Following his Damascus Road experience (*c.* 36 A.D.) and probably a brief period in Damascus itself, Paul went to Arabia, i.e. Nabatea (Gal 1:17). There he apparently preached on behalf of the risen Jesus, not only to other Jews living there but to Nabateans as well (see Hengel/Schwemer, Paul, 106–113), and in doing so stirred up opposition from the Nabatean king, Aretas IV. Paul returned to Damascus, remaining there for three years (Gal 1:18) until he was forced to escape when Aretas, into whose jurisdiction Damascus had passed under the Emperor Caligula (37–41), tried to arrest him. Paul proceeded to Jerusalem (*c.* 39), where he stayed with Cephas (*see* PETER, APOSTLE, ST.) for fifteen days and says he met no other apostle except James, the brother of the Lord (Gal 1:18–19). Paul's perspective is that he was unknown by sight to the churches of Judea at this time (Gal 1:22) (whether he intends ''Judea'' to include Jerusalem is not evident). Acts 9:26–30, however, offers a picture of Paul briefly preaching in Jerusalem and encountering problems that led members of the church to escort him to Caesarea Maritima, where they sent him off to his home city of Tarsus in Cilicia. Paul partially confirms the latter element of the Acts narrative in his statement that following this time in Jerusalem he ''went into the regions of Syria and Cilicia . . . proclaiming the faith'' (Gal 1:21–22). This period, (see Hengel/Schwemer, passim) during which Paul's activities are not known, has generally been dated from *c.* 40–44.

In the absence of further information from Paul himself concerning the next five years (*c.* 44–49), Acts 11:25–26 supplies this scenario: Barnabas went to Tarsus and recruited Paul to minister in the church at Antioch, where he did so for a year (*c.* 44–45), a year which was followed by or included a visit with Barnabas to Jerusalem to deliver famine relief (11:27–30). This Jerusalem visit, which Acts places about five years after Paul's prior one, is hard to reconcile with Paul's statement in Gal 2:1 that his second trip to Jerusalem in his Christian period was fourteen years after the first, i.e. after his return to Jerusalem following the Damascus Road event.

Proclaiming the Gospel among the Gentiles (Gal 2:2): Paul's ''First'' Journey. Acts 13:1–3 states that as a result of prayer and fasting in the church at Antioch, the prophets and teachers there determined that the Holy Spirit had set apart and called BARNABAS and Paul to do certain work. The Antiochene believers therefore ''laid their hands on them'' (13:3) and sent them off. John Mark (*see* MARK, EVANGELIST, ST.), the cousin of Barnabas, went with them. Because Barnabas's name is mentioned before Paul's throughout the Acts narrative up to this point, Barnabas is assumed to have been the senior partner (Daniels, 610).

Barnabas, Paul, and John Mark sailed from the seaport of Seleucia (16 miles west of Antioch) to Salamis in Cyprus, and thence went to the extreme west of the island to the capital city of Paphos. There they contended with a villainous magician, Elymas, and after temporarily blinding him, converted the Roman proconsul, Sergius Paulus. In Acts more prominence is from this point on accorded to Paul. In 13:13 the group of missionaries is denoted as ''Paul and his companions'' and Paul is then named before Barnabas several times (13:43, 46, 50). The crowds are also said to have recognized Paul as ''the chief speaker'' (14:12).

From Paphos the three sailed to Perga in Pamphylia, where John Mark left to return to Jerusalem (13:13). Acts does not specify John Mark's reasons but does imply that Paul considered this a desertion (15:38). He and Barnabas then continued on to Pisidian Antioch, Iconium, Lystra, and Derbe. Because of the opposition they encountered in the synagogues, both said, ''We are now turning to the Gentiles'' (13:46). From Derbe they retraced their steps through Lystra, Iconium, Pisidian Antioch, and Perga, setting sail from Attalia for the journey back to Syrian Antioch.

This course has come to be called the ''first journey'' (13:4–14:28) and widely dated *c.* 46–49. While Paul's undisputed letters give no information about such a journey, he mentions in 2 Cor 11:25 that he was once stoned, which accords with the report that this happened to him in Lystra (Acts 14:19). Further correlation is found in Gal 2:2, where Paul indicates that he had preached to the Gentiles before the Jerusalem meeting (*c.* 49), confirming that the debate over the integration of the Gentiles into the Jesus movement was an issue from his earliest evangelizing period.

Paul in Jerusalem (Gal 2:2). In the Acts narrative, Paul and Barnabas are said to have returned to Antioch only to encounter ''no small dissension and debate''(15:2) with certain individuals, presumably PHARISEES (15:5), Judaizing believers who had come there from Judea. The controversy concerned the conversion of Gentiles and the Mosaic requirement of circumcision. Paul, Barnabas, and others were appointed to go to Jerusalem to discuss this with the apostles and elders (15:2). The resulting meeting, which has come to be called the Council of Jerusalem and dated *c.* 49, is recounted in Acts 15:6–29. Scholarship has widely, though by no means unanimously, judged Paul's account in Gal 2:1–10 to be of the same event, for both narratives include the involvement of Paul, James the brother of the Lord, and Peter, and both involve a group opposed to Paul and holding that the converted Gentiles should be circumcised.

In Paul's perception the meeting resulted with recognition from the leaders, the ''acknowledged pillars'' (Gal 2:9), that Paul ''had been entrusted with the gospel for the uncircumcised'' (2:7), i.e. those who once they became Christian would remain uncircumcised, and that even his Gentile companion and apparent co-worker in evangelization, Titus, was not compelled to be circumcised (2:3). Acts 15 correlates with the decision for non-imposition of circumcision upon the Gentiles but describes a letter sent from Jerusalem to Antioch stipulating that believers of Gentile origin in Syria and Cilicia were to observe certain food laws. Paul himself expresses no knowledge of this letter and certainly promotes no stipulations concerning food eaten by believers in his later ministry (see e.g. 1 Cor 8).

The accounts of the Jerusalem conference in both Gal and Acts agree that upon its close Paul and Barnabas returned to Antioch. What is strikingly missing from Acts, yet very prominent in Paul's narrative in Gal 2:12–14, is that shortly after the conference Paul had a major public conflict in Antioch with Peter and with Barnabas, who sided with Peter. At issue, at least from Paul's perspective, which is the only one available to us, was Peter's inconsistency in sometimes eating with Gentile believers and at other times, notably when members of the Jerusalem circumcision party were present, eating only with the Jewish Christians. While it is difficult to reconstruct all the dynamics Paul saw at work in this event, it is widely thought that he must have lost the battle about food laws at Antioch since, from that time on, Antioch's role as the base of his missionary operations receded (Brown, 432).

En Route to Illyricum (Rom 15:19): The ''Second'' and ''Third'' Journeys. The missionary activity of Paul described in Acts 15:40–21:15, covering the years of *c.* 50–58, is commonly divided in to the ''Second'' (15:40–18:22) and ''Third'' Journeys (18:23– 21:15). Paul himself subsumes his activities of these years into a general description covering all of his evangelizing. He envisioned an arc extending from Judea north and west around the Mediterranean, reaching to the Dalmatian coast on the northeastern shores of the Adriatic Sea. Paul alludes to this in writing to the churches of Rome (*c.* 58), which he had not yet visited. He comments that up to that time in his life ''from Jerusalem all the way around to Illyricum I have finished preaching the gospel of Christ'' (Rom 15:19). This could have been meant literally, or it may have been Paul's way of saying that he had evangelized from East to West, since neither the epistles nor Acts indicate that he had actually made it to Illyricum by 58. Either way, Paul perceived that he had covered a vast amount of territory, and both his own letters and Acts 15:40–21:15 support extensive traveling in the years after the Jerusalem conference and his conflict with Peter at Antioch.

While Paul does not tell of his next move after the confrontation over table fellowship with Peter (and Barnabas), Acts 15:36–39 says that after the Jerusalem conference he invited Barnabas to make a return journey to the people they had earlier converted. In agreeing, Barnabas suggested enlisting John Mark again, but Paul refused to take someone who had not been dependable. Thus, he and Barnabas parted company. The tenor of this information from Acts 15:36–39 is corroborated by Paul's remark in Gal 2:13 about Barnabas's apparent hypocrisy at the table fellowship, namely, that it was during their return to Antioch after the council of Jerusalem that Paul and Barnabas had serious disagreements that precluded their continuing ministry together. Acts 15:41 says that Paul chose SILAS, whom he called Silvanus (1 Thes 1:1; 2 Cor 1:19), to travel with him. The two went through Syria and Cilicia to the churches of southeastern Asia Minor that Paul and Barnabas had previously established. In Lystra Paul converted Timothy, who then joined him and Silas as they went north ''through the region of Phrygia and Galatia'' (Acts 16:6), probably meaning the area northwest of Iconium. Acts 16:6–7 makes the enigmatic statements that they had been ''forbidden by the Holy Spirit to speak the word in Asia'' and that when they attempted to go into Bithynia ''the Spirit of Jesus did not allow them'' so that instead they went to the coast at Troas. A choice to make haste, or a divine restriction they felt imposed upon them, or some other reason to not missionize in certain areas they traversed may be reflected in Paul's later comment to the Galatians: ''You know that it was [only?] because of a physical infirmity that I first announced the gospel to you'' (Gal 4:13).

From Troas, via the island of Samothrace, Paul and his co-workers crossed over to Macedonia. Reaching the port of Neapolis, they went into the nearby city of Philippi, and thence, following the Egnatian Way (Via Egnatia), to Amphipolis, Apollonia, and Thessalonica. If Paul had continued west along this major Roman route as far as the Adriatic coast at Dyrrhachium, he would have been just south of the border of Illyricum. Nothing in his own letters nor in Acts, however, suggests this extended journey west either at this point nor later in his travels (see below) when he retraced his Egnatian route, although this would have been Paul's obvious route to Illyricum. The Acts' traditions instead indicate that Paul departed from the Egnatian Way at Thessalonica and went southwest to Beroea. Then, leaving Silas and Timothy behind, Paul went to the coast and shipped out to Athens. After preaching there with little success, he went on to Corinth, where Silas and Timothy eventually joined him. The tradition in Acts 18:12–17 that in Corinth Paul was brought before Gallio, the Roman proconsul of Achaia, has become the pivotal point in determining Pauline chronology since Gallio's proconsulship can be dated to a relatively narrow period, i.e. *c.* June through October of 51. The 18 months Paul is said to have stayed in Corinth (Acts 18:11) are therefore generally assessed as falling with the years 51–52.

Because Paul wrote to the Thessalonians (1 Thess) during his months in Corinth and would later write to the Philippians (Phil) and the Corinthians (1–2 Cor), a large legacy of his own literary evidence exists to illuminate this period and to compare it with the narrative of the same time in Acts 16:11–18:17. Within the limitations of this brief overview, it is important to point out that these were the travels in which Paul met and, in some cases converted, various important church leaders and some of his prominent co-workers, such as Lydia in Philippi (Acts 16:14–15; 40), Prisca and Aquila in Corinth (Acts 18:1–4), and probably at this time as well, Phoebe, who lived in the Corinthian port of Cenchreae (Rom 16:1–3) (see F. Gillman, passim).

Paul had worked at his trade of tent-making along with PRISCA AND AQUILA (a practice of self-support he followed throughout his missionary years). When he decided to leave Corinth in 52 to return to Syria, Prisca and Aquila left as well. They accompanied him as far as EPHESUS. Paul sailed on to Caesarea Maritima, while Prisca and Aquila stayed in Ephesus (Acts 18:19), where they led a church (1 Cor 16:19). It was during their Ephesian tenure that the eloquent, but theologically misinformed Apollos of Alexandria visited that city and preached. Prisca and Aquila corrected Apollos and became his references when he moved on to Corinth to address the Christians there (Acts 18:26–28). His presence in Corinth would eventually lead to factions in the church, a problem over the years for Paul (1 Cor 1:12).

Acts 18:22 says that after Paul's arrival in Caesarea he went to Jerusalem to greet the church and then proceeded on to Antioch. Because Acts 18:23 says he spent ''some time'' in Antioch (between 53–54), and because that city had earlier been his base of operations, this Antiochene ''break'' has become the conventional separation between the second and third journeys. But seeing an end to one trip and the beginning of another here is merely an interpretative perspective. In any case, Paul moved on, once more visiting GALATIA (confirmed by Gal 4:13 which implies that Paul made at least two visits there) and Phrygia, and then settling for a long period (*c.* 54–57) in Ephesus (see 1 Cor 16:8–9 and compare with Acts 19:1–20:1).

Much of Paul's known correspondence derives from this Ephesian period. It is widely held that he wrote GA-

LATIANS (*c.* 54) rather early in his stay. Much of Pauline scholarship would also place the writing of PHILIPPIANS and PHILEMON from this city as well. If that judgment is accurate, since both letters were written when Paul was imprisoned, the suspicion that 1 Cor 15:32 and 2 Cor 11: 23–26 allude to an Ephesian period of incarceration for Paul would be validated. Paul's extensive correspondence with the CORINTHIANS, with whom he was involved in multiple serious disagreements, also began in Ephesus, from which he certainly wrote 1 Corinthians (*c.* 57; cf. 1 Cor 16:8) and probably the so-called ''former'' (1 Cor 5:9) and ''tearful'' letters (2 Cor 2:4). Paul may also have made a brief visit under painful circumstances to the Corinthians in this period (2 Cor 2:1).

Acts 19:8–10 situates Paul's preaching in Ephesus first in a synagogue, where he spoke out boldly for three months (19:8). In the face of opposition within the congregation, Paul moved to the hall of Tyrannus where he ''argued daily'' for some two years (18:9). Acts also says that Paul converted former disciples of John the Baptist in Ephesus where he came into conflict with itinerant Jewish exorcists (the seven sons Sceva) and caused a riot among the silversmiths who made shrines of Artemis, the great mother goddess of the Ephesians [*see* DIANA (ARTEMIS) OF THE EPHESIANS]. Sometime after Pentecost (see 1 Cor 16:8), in the late springtime of 57, Paul departed for Troas to catch a ship to Macedonia, having sent his companions Timothy and Erastus on ahead. After meeting up with Titus in Macedonia (in Philippi? see 2 Cor 2:12–13), who informed Paul a reconciliation had been effected between him and the Corinthians, Paul wrote 2 Corinthians (at least in part; some judge this letter to be a composite). Paul then proceeded to Corinth, where he stayed for three months (Acts 20:2–3), i.e. late 57 into 58.

During this Corinthian period Paul envisioned himself on the verge of a major transition. He wrote to the ROMANS in 58, indicating that having proclaimed the good news of Christ from Jerusalem to Illyricum, he saw ''no further place for [himself] . . . in these regions'' (Rom 15:23) and thus he would proceed to Spain. He planned to visit the Roman Christians on the way, although he would first make a trip to Jerusalem to deliver a collection he had been taking up for the believers there (Rom 15:24–26). Acts says that when he was about to set sail to the east, however, he heard of a plot against him and therefore retraced his steps through Macedonia, sailing from Philippi to Troas, and then to Miletus, where he gave a farewell address to the elders of the church of Ephesus (Acts 20:18–38). From Miletus, Paul sailed to Cos, Rhodes, Patara, Tyre, Ptolemais, finally arriving at Caesarea, where he stayed with the evangelist Philip and his four prophesying daughters. The Acts traditions imply a foreboding of imprisonment and death during Paul's return trip from Miletus to Caesarea. This may reflect the knowledge of the author of Acts in retrospect, yet accords with Paul's statement in Rom 15:30–31, where he asks for prayers concerning his visit to Judea that he might be ''rescued from the unbelievers in Judea'' (Brown, 435).

The Road to Rome (Rom 15:23). When Paul sensed in 58 that his work in the east-northeast quadrant of the Mediterranean was over, he was correct, although the ensuing years, *c.* 58–64, played out differently than he planned. This period is chronicled only by Acts 21:15–28:31, unless Philippians and Philemon were not written during the Ephesian imprisonment but come from Paul's detentions in Caesarea (58–60) or in Rome (61–63). Of the plans Paul was making in 58, he did manage to reach Rome and to ''reap some harvest'' (Rom 1:13) among the Christians there, albeit in shackles. But his intention to evangelize in Spain after turning over his collection in Jerusalem were thwarted by his arrest and subsequent imprisonment at Caesarea (*c.* 58–60).

The story of Paul's transferal to Rome, due to his ''appeal to the emperor'' (Acts 25:12), offers one of the most detailed narratives of an ancient maritime journey. Following storms, shipwreck, and a winter marooned on Malta, Paul, under the guard of a centurion named Julius, disembarked at Puteoli, near the Roman naval base at Misenum. He was escorted into Rome, where he lived as a prisoner, but was able to continue his Christian proclamation. Acts ends abruptly, and puzzlingly, in 28:30–31 with the statement that Paul lived thus for two years (*c.* 61–63), implying in the judgment of many that he was released after that. If that is indeed what happened, it remains uncertain whether Paul went on further missionizing travels, either to Spain or elsewhere in the Mediterranean. CLEMENT of Rome (*c.* 95) observed that Paul had preached in ''the furthest limits of the West'' (1 Cor 5:7), although what Clement meant by this is not clear. As for information about Paul's death, history has relied upon information from Eusebius (*Ecclesiastical History* 2.25) that Paul was beheaded in Rome during the Neronian persecution. If there is any historical data underlying the tradition that Paul's death and burial took place on the Ostian Way (Via Ostiensis), near the basilica of St. Paul-Outside-the-Walls, then the very last leg of Paul's decades of dedicated missionary travel was on that busy, major Roman road going to and from Rome's seaport of Ostia. From the Damascus Road to the Ostian Way, the race to the finish had been completed by an indefatigable sprinter.

Bibliography: H. D. BETZ, ''Paul,'' *ABD* V, 186–201. R. E. BROWN, *An Introduction to the New Testament* (New York 1997) 422–442. J. B. DANIELS, ''Barnabas,'' *ABD* I, 610–611. J. A. FITZMYER, ''Paul,'' *NJBC*, 1329–1337. F. M. GILLMAN, *Women Who Knew Paul* (Collegeville 1992). J. L. GILLMAN, ''Silas,'' *ABD* VI,

22–23; idem, ''Timothy,'' *ABD* VI, 558–560. M. HENGEL and A. M. SCHWEMER, *Paul between Damascus and Antioch* (Louisville 1997). J. MURPHY-O'CONNOR, *Paul: A Critical Life* (New York 1996). C. ROETZEL, *Paul: The Man and the Myth* (Minneapolis 1999).

[F. M. GILLMAN]

PAUL, SS.

Paul the Hermit, third-century native of the lower Thebaid in Egypt. During the persecution of Decius (250) Paul fled to the desert and lived as a hermit. Though he intended to return to the world after the persecution ceased, he so enjoyed his life of solitude and contemplation that he remained there until his death, near the year 341. Legend said that Christ fed him daily with bread carried in the beak of a raven. St. Paul is usually considered the first hermit.

Feast: Jan. 15.

Paul the Simple, fourth-century hermit, was an elderly laborer who became a disciple of St. ANTHONY in the Thebaid Desert when he discovered that his wife had committed adultery. Though Anthony was reluctant to receive Paul as a hermit because of Paul's advanced age, he put him to severe test, but Paul proved his great humility and obedience. Finally Anthony accepted Paul as a hermit and revered him as a powerful servant of God. St. Paul died in the desert about 339.

Feast: March 7.

Paul I of Constantinople, bishop, elected probably in 336; d. 350. Most of his episcopal career was spent combating ARIANISM. After a series of exiles and returns to his see, Paul was finally banished to Cappadocia during the reign of CONSTANTIUS II (337–361) and there he was strangled to death.

Feast: June 7.

Of *St. Paul and St. John* history records only their names and their Christian martyrdom. Relics, supposedly theirs, were found in a house on the Coelian Hill that was converted into a Christian church in the fourth century. Their cult was widely spread by a spurious *passio* telling of their gallant military service under Constantine I (306–337) and their martyrdom under JULIAN THE APOSTATE (361–363).

Feast: June 26.

Bibliography: St. Paul the Hermit. H. WADDELL, tr., *The Desert Fathers* (New York 1936) 35–53. A. BUTLER, *The Lives of the Saints*, rev. ed. H. THURSTON and D. ATTWATER, 4v. (New York 1956) 1:91–93. St. Paul the Simple. A. BUTLER, *The Lives of the Saints*, rev. ed. H. THURSTON and D. ATTWATER, 4v. (New York 1956) 1:513–514. St. Paul of Constantinople. *Acta Sanctorum* June 2:13–24. A. BUTLER, *The Lives of the Saints*, rev. ed. H. THURSTON and D. ATTWATER, 4v. (New York 1956) 2:492–493. St. Paul and St. John. *Acta Sanctorum* June 7:138–142. A. BUTLER, *The Lives of the Saints*, rev. ed. H. THURSTON and D. ATTWATER, 4v. (New York 1956) 2:645–646.

[E. DAY]

PAUL II, PATRIARCH OF CONSTANTINOPLE

Reigned Oct. 1, 641, to Dec. 27, 653. Elevated at the accession of the Byzantine emperor Constans II, who succeeded HERACLIUS, and just prior to the pontificate of Pope Theodore I, Paul became patriarch at a time when MONOPHYSITISM was fragmenting the Byzantine Church. At first he declared his adherence to the orthodox Christology, then (646–647) accepted the compromise position of MONOTHELITISM put forward by his predecessors, Patriarchs SERGIUS and PYRRHUS. In 648 he backed with his authority the decree of Constans, known as the *TYPOS*, which simply forbade all further discussion of the Christological question. Then in 649, along with Sergius and Pyrrhus, he was excommunicated and anathematized by the Lateran Synod called by Pope MARTIN I. This action, coupled with the fact that Martin's elevation had taken place without imperial sanction, resulted in the Emperor's seizing the pope and exiling him to the Chersonesus in 653, the year of Paul's death. Imperial attempts to solve the Monophysite controversy, either by compromise or enforced silence, lost their urgency by the end of Paul's tenure; by that time Arab conquests had overrun the most strongly Monophysitic provinces of the Byzantine Empire. The Monothelite compromise was abjured by the Byzantine Church itself at the sixth ecumenical council, CONSTANTINOPLE III (680–681), which declared Paul, among others, heretical.

Bibliography: V. GRUMEL, *Les regestes des actes du patriarcat de Constantinople* (Kadikoi-Bucharest 1932–47) 1.1:120–121. Letter to Theodore, J. D. MANSI, *Sacrorum conciliorum nova et amplissima collectio* (Graz 1960) 10:1020–26. C. J. VON HEFELE *Histoire des conciles d'après les documents originaux,* tr. and continued by H. LECLERQ (Paris 1907–38) 3:398–400, 426–432. H. PARGOIRE, *L'eglise byzantine* (Paris 1905) under ''Monothéletisme.'' *Histoire de l'église depuis les origines jusqu'à nos jours*, ed. A. FLICHE and V. MARTIN (Paris 1935) 5:165–168. F. X. SEPPELT, *Geschichte der Päpste von den Anfängen bis zur Mitte des 20. Jh.* (Munich 1954–59) 2:59–63, 65ff. G. OSTROGORSKY, *History of the Byzantine State* (Oxford 1956, New Brunswick NJ 1957) 92, 97. H. G. BECK, *Kirche und theologische Literatur im byzantinischen Reich* (Munich 1959) 55, 432–433.

[D. A. MILLER]

PAUL IV, PATRIARCH OF CONSTANTINOPLE, ST.

Patriarchate, 780–84; b. Cyprus, 724; d. Florus Monastery, Aug. 31, 784. Sometimes designated in the sources as Paul the Younger of Salamis, Paul of Cyprus, etc., Paul IV is known to have been selected for that office by Emperor Leo IV in 780 on the condition that he take an oath to pursue the imperial policy of iconoclasm. Nothing is known of Paul's background or education; but while he accepted the emperor's condition for the patriarchal nomination, he does not seem to have been a fanatic iconoclast. He used the emperor's favor, however, to extend the territorial and governmental authority of the patriarchate apparently without interfering with papal prerogatives. With the accession to power of the Empress Irene as regent (780) the religious policy of the empire was changed, and Paul, after signifying his repudiation of ICONOCLASM, submitted his resignation from his office and retired to the monastery of Florus. On his deathbed he received clerical emissaries from the empress, gave them a solemn retraction of his errors, and pronounced an anathema against iconoclasm. He was criticized severely by Byzantine historians; but the empress succeeded in obtaining his canonization from the pope, in order that, as she requested, he might serve the cause of the veneration of images better by his death than by his life.

Feast: Aug. 28.

Bibliography: *Acta Sanctorum* Aug. 4:96. J.D. MANSI, *Sacrorum Conciliorum nova et amplissima collectio*, 31 v. (Florence-Venice 1757–98); reprinted and continued by L. PETIT and J.B. MARTIN 53 v. in 60 (Paris 1889–1927; repr. Graz 1960–) 12:951–1154. G. OSTROGORSKY, *History of the Byzantine State*, tr. J. HUSSEY from 2d German ed. (Oxford 1956); American ed. by P. CHARANIS (New Brunswick, N.J. 1957) 102–106.

[F. CHIOVARO]

PAUL I, POPE, ST.

Pontificate: May 29, 757 to June 28, 767. A member of an important noble family in Rome, Paul's career prior to his election as pope was spent in the service of the papal curia. During the pontificate of his brother, Pope STEPHEN II (III) (752–757), he served as a key papal adviser at a crucial moment that witnessed an interrelated sequence of events that revolutionized the political map of Italy and the position of the papacy in the Christian world. Included among those events were the precipitate decline of the power of the eastern Roman Empire in political and religious life of Italy, and the end of papal subordination to and dependence on the emperor in Constantinople. It also saw the formation of a papal alliance with the Franks, and the military intervention of the Franks in Italy, which prevented LOMBARD domination the peninsula, as well as the creation of the Papal States as a sovereign entity ruled by the pope. Those massive changes created a wide range of uncertainties that would dominate Paul I's pontificate, as the concerned parties struggled to adjust to the change and to seek advantage from the new conditions.

Although his election to the papacy was briefly challenged by another candidate, Paul I began his career as pope from a position of strength bequeathed by his predecessor. He was firmly linked to a strong ally, the Frankish king PEPIN III (751–768). Pepin was indebted to the papacy for the approval granted him in 751 by Pope Zacharias (741–752) to replace the MEROVINGIAN dynasty with his own family, the CAROLINGIANS, as rulers of the kingdom of the Franks. Then in 752 the new Frankish king had entered into a pact with Pope Stephen II, which among other things promised Frankish protection for the papacy, a restoration of territories that belonged to the pope, and papal sanctification of Pepin and his heirs as legitimate rulers of the Frankish kingdom. In two military campaigns in 755 and 756 against the Lombards Pepin III had demonstrated that he was prepared to protect an independent pope ruling the "special people" (*peculiarem populum*) of St. Peter inhabiting the Republic of St. Peter. The territory ruled over by the new pope had been substantially expanded as a result of the Donation of Pepin bestowed on the papacy as a consequence of the Frankish victory over the Lombards. The Lombard kingdom, defeated by the Franks shortly before Paul's accession, was ruled by a king, Desiderius (757–774), who owed his crown to papal support and who was well aware of the military impotence of the Lombards in the face of the Frankish threat. The position of the eastern Roman emperor in Italy had been fatally weakened by widespread opposition to ICONOCLASM and by the territorial losses resulting from Pepin III's concessions to the papacy after the Frankish victory over the Lombards in 755 and 756. From the beginning of his pontificate Paul I demonstrated his intention of keeping or even improving that position.

Immediately upon his election Paul I wrote to Pepin III in terms that indicated his dependence on the Frankish king for protection of the Papal States and for restoration of other territories claimed by the papacy. His understanding of the Donation of Pepin and promises made by the Lombard king prompted Paul I to envisage the extension of the Papal States over a large part of Italy. Throughout his pontificate Paul I never ceased conveying that message to Pepin III; so insistent were his claims that some historians have concluded that territorial acquisition was his only concern as pope. The Frankish king remained steadfast in his alliance, although not always acting in accord with the pope's demands.

From Paul I's perspective, the chief obstacle to gaining the territories he claimed was the Lombard king, Desiderius, who had made promises to surrender territories to the papacy in return for the support of Pope Stephen II in securing his election to the Lombard throne. Having become king, Desiderius showed little inclination to abide by his promises or to accede to papal demands. He was determined to continue a policy initiated by earlier Lombard kings aimed at establishing a united Lombard kingdom as the dominant political force in Italy, a goal that threatened the independence of the papacy and the Papal States. During the early years of Paul I's pontificate, extending from 757 to 762, the demands of the king resulted in a series of confrontations. Aside from spurning papal demands for territory, Desiderius on occasion threatened to use force to keep Paul from aiding those who resisted Lombard overlordship, especially the dukes of Spoleto and Benevento. Paul in turn pleaded with Pepin to force Desiderius' compliance to papal demands. His appeals were couched in terms that sought to convince the Frankish king the Republic of St. Peter was in dire danger. Although Pepin did mediate between Paul I and Desiderius, he was unwilling to commit himself to new military campaigns in Italy. Aside from problems in his own realm, the Frankish king was never persuaded that the Lombards offered as serious a threat to the papacy or the Papal States. Fully aware of Frankish military power, Desiderius was too astute a political leader to mount a threat on the papacy so serious that Pepin would feel compelled to repeat his earlier military attacks on the Lombard kingdom. Gradually, Paul I came to realize that he could not depend on the Frankish military to gain all the territory he claimed. During the last years of his pontificate, his territorial demands were greatly reduced. He was content to negotiate with Desiderius only minor adjustments of his boundaries of the Papal State and to avoid a major confrontation. Therefore although the boundaries of the Papal States were slightly enlarged, the pope and the Lombard king tacitly agreed to accept a state of equilibrium that constituted part of the newly emerging power structure in Italy.

Paul I was also always mindful of the eastern emperor, CONSTANTINE V Copronymos (741–775). The pope's concerns were both political and religious. Despite his weak political and military position in Italy and serious problems in the East, Constantine V nurtured hope of reestablishing an imperial political presence in Italy. Although on occasion Paul I sent alarmist reports to Pepin about impending invasions of Italy from Constantinople, Constantine V simply lacked the military resources to undertake such ventures. As a consequence, he sought to weaken the papacy by diplomatic means, but none of his ventures succeeded. During Paul I's pontificate it became clear that the eastern emperor was no longer a major factor in the Italian power structure.

Of greater concern to Paul I was the relentless effort of Constantine V to promote his iconoclastic policy. As had been the case with his predecessors, Paul I condemned iconoclasm as heretical and made every effort to defeat it. To offset Constantine V's efforts to propagate iconoclasm, Paul I offered refuge to large numbers of monks who fled the eastern Roman Empire to escape persecution for opposing iconoclasm and granted them freedom to worship according to their own liturgy and in their own language. He appealed by letter and by embassy to the emperor to abandon his heretical position. Some evidence suggests he may have been involved in an effort to persuade the eastern patriarchs to speak out against iconoclasm. He was especially concerned about the emperor's attempt to exploit reservations held by some in the Frankish church about the use of icons, but Paul was able to retain the loyalty of Pepin III and the Frankish Church to Rome's position on iconoclasm. Although Paul I was not successful in persuading Constantine V to abandon his policy on icons, his efforts restricted the spread of iconoclasm and fortified the papal position as the guardian of orthodoxy.

The surviving record provides little information about Paul's activities beyond his campaign to enlarge the Papal States and to defeat the heretical eastern emperor. There are hints indicating that he encouraged and advised those who were engaged in reforming the Frankish church, thereby strengthening the bonds linking the papacy and the Franks. He maintained contacts with the English hierarchy and with the newly established ecclesiastical structure put in place by Boniface in Bavaria and Germany. His biographer reported that some of his subordinates in the papal curia were tyrannical, suggesting that he introduced measures to strengthen papal administration in the Papal States. Perhaps his administrative actions were necessitated by the major enlargement of the papal territory that occurred under his predecessor, Stephen II, but they also helped to create the opposition to his regime that surfaced in the disputed election of his successor, Pope STEPHEN III (768–772). Paul was credited with initiating and supporting efforts to rebuild and redecorate churches in Rome. He also removed many relics from the catacombs and installed them in various churches in Rome. Perhaps these activities were a tangible response to iconoclasm. All these bits of evidence indicate his awareness of his role as a spiritual leader whose influence was spreading throughout western Europe. But the fact remains that Paul I's chief accomplishment was his successful effort to clarify the boundaries of the Papal States, to stabilize the administration of his realm, and to establish the pope as the political sovereign of that new political entity during a period of uncertainty following the changes that had occurred while he was a key adviser to his brother and predecessor, Pope Stephen II.

Feast: June 28.

See Also: CAROLINGIAN REFORM.

Bibliography: *Le Liber Pontificalis*, ed. L. DUCHESNE, 3 v., 2nd ed. (Paris 1955–1957) 1:463–467, English trans. in *The Lives of the Eighth-Century Popes (Liber Pontificalis). The Ancient Biographies of Nine Popes from AD 715 to AD 817*, trans. with intro. by R. DAVIS, Translated Texts for Historians 13 (Liverpool 1992) 77–84. *Regesta Pontificum Romanorum ab condita ecclesia ad annum post Christum MCXCVIII*, ed. P. JAFFÉ, 2 v., 2nd ed. (Leipzig 1885–1888) 1:277–283. P. CONTE, *Regesto delle lettere dei papi del secolo VIII: saggi* (Milan 1984) 97–117, 222–229. *Codex Carolinus*, Epp. 12–43, ed. W. GUNDLACH, *Monumenta Germaniae Historica, Epistolae: Epistolae Merowingici et Karolini aevi,* v. 1 (Berlin 1892; reprinted, 1994) 507–558. *Concilia aevi karolini,* Part 1, ed. A. WERMINGHOFF, *Monumenta Germaniae Historica, Concilia,* v. 2/1 (Hannover and Leipzig 1906; reprinted, 1997) 64–71.

[R. E. SULLIVAN]

PAUL II, POPE

Pontificate: Aug. 30, 1464 to July 26, 1471; b. Pietro Barbo in Venice, Feb. 23, 1417. Having spent his youth in Florence, he became archdeacon of Bologna and then bishop of Cervia and Vicenza before being created cardinal at the age of 23 by his uncle, Pope EUGENE IV. A man of considerable fortune, he had great influence in the Curia under Popes NICHOLAS V and CALLISTUS III and in 1456 became governor general of Campania and the maritime regions.

The CAPITULATIONS drawn up by the cardinals on the eve of the election of the successor to Pope PIUS II stated that the new pope, once elected, was to fix the number of cardinals at 24, reform the Curia, open a general council within the third year of his pontificate, and resume the war against the Turks. Paul was elected on the first ballot, but steadfastly refused to publish a bull confirming the provisions of the election pact. Supremely jealous of his authority, he ruled as an ostentatious monarch, imposing on the papal court a style in the mode of the first Italian Renaissance. Yet he himself was not a humanist in the full sense of the word; e.g., in 1468 he dissolved the Roman Academy founded by Pomponius Laetus, whose paganizing attitude struck the Pope as dangerous. (Paul's biography by Bartolomeo Platina, a member of the Academy, is understandably prejudiced.) On the other hand, Paul surrounded himself with scholars and encouraged the founding of Italy's first printing shop at SUBIACO (1465). His taste for pomp and luxury was expressed in the famous Palace of St. Mark, today the Palazzo Venezia, which he began in Rome as early as 1455 and made his principal residence from 1466 on.

Paul's pontificate was dominated by the intensification of the war against the OTTOMAN TURKS. Immediately, in 1464, Paul collected the funds necessary to renew the struggle, and in 1466 he gave his support to the Albanian chieftain Scanderbeg. To the profit of the Holy See he strengthened its alum monopoly by prohibiting any trading in alum with the Turks, but he could not prevent the fortress of Negropont (Euboea) from falling (July 1470). He was distracted from the struggle only when he felt it his duty to intervene in Bohemia in opposition to King George Poděbrad and the HUSSITE church. At the Pope's instigation, Matthias Corvinus, King of Hungary, declared war on Poděbrad (March 31, 1468), whom Paul had already declared deposed. Corvinus received the crown of Bohemia from the pope in March 1469. Poděbrad, meantime, had obtained the support of King Louis XI of France, and together they demanded the convocation of a general council of the Church and initiated a process against Paul's former favorite, Cardinal Jean Balue. To mollify Louis XI, who had earlier consented to the abolition of the PRAGMATIC SANCTION of Bourges (1461) despite the Parlement, Paul officially gave him and his successors the title ''Most Christian King.'' Paul also devoted himself to the extirpation of the heretical FRATICELLI, initiating a process against them in 1466 and prosecuting their adherents in Germany. By his bull of Aug. 19, 1470, Paul decreed that in the future HOLY YEARS would be held every 25 years (beginning 1475). In the spring of 1471 he actually contemplated the convocation of a council in Ferrara. He tried for a reconciliation with the BYZANTINE CHURCH and was negotiating an alliance with the Iranian Prince Uzom-Hassan against the Turks when he died suddenly. His famous Renaissance tomb in the Vatican is the work of Mino of Fiesole and Giovanni Dalmato.

Bibliography: Pius II, . . . *Commentarii* . . . (Frankfort 1614). M. CANENSIUS, *Pauli II. Pontificis Maximi vita* . . . (Rome 1740). B. DE P. SACCHI, *Platinae hystoria de vitis pontificum,* 2 pts. (Paris 1505). P. MÜNTZ, *Les Arts à la cour des papes . . . Paul II* (Rome 1884). L. PASTOR, *The History of the Popes from the Close of the Middle Ages* (London-St. Louis 1938–61) 4:3–194, 475–504. R. WEISS, *Un umanista veneziano: papa Paola II* (Rome 1958). A. BOCK, *Die ''Sala Regia'' im Vatikan als Beispiel der Selbstdarstellung des Papsttums in der zweiten Hälft des 16. Jahrhunderts,* (Hildesheim 1997). D. S. CHAMBERS, ed., *War, Culture, and Society in Renaissance Venice* (London 1993). A.J. DUNSTON, ''Pope Paul and the Humanists,'' *The Journal of Religious History* (Sydney 1973), 287–306. A. ESCH, ''Deutsche, Frühdrucker in Rom in den Registern Papst Paul II.:'' *Miscellanea Domenico Maeffei dicata. Historia. Ius. Studium* (1995), 439–47. G. L. GEIGER, *Filippino Lippi's*

Carafa Chapel: Renaissance Art in Rome (Kirksville, Missouri 1986). P. LA BELLA, ''Considerazioni sulla cultura a Roma durante il pontificato di Paolo II (1464–1471),'' *Studi Romano* 44 (1996) 10–20. A. MEYUHAS GINIO, ''Rêves de croisade les Sarracins dans la Castille du Xve siécle'' *Revue de l'Histoire et de Religions* (Paris 1995) 145–74. M.D.C. MORALES MUÑIZ, *Alfonso de Ávila, rey de Castilla,* (Ávilla 1988). R. J. PALERMINO, ''The Roman Academy, the Catacombs and the Conspiracy of 1468,'' *Archivum Historiae Pontificiae* 18 (Rome 1980) 117–55. J. RAINER, ''Die zweite Romfahrt Kaiser Friedrichs III,'' *Geschichte und ihre Quellen. Festschrift für Friedrich Hausmann zum 70. Geburtstag* (1987), 183–90. B. RESTANI, ''La scomunica come arma politica. Sigismondo Pandolfo Malatesta, Ludovicio II Gonzaga e la Santa Sede,'' *Studi Romagnoli* (Faenza 1996), 486–515. F.J. WORSTBROCK, *Krieg und Frieden am Horizont des Renaissancehumanismus,* (Weinheim 1986). G. ZANDER, ''La possible ricomposizione del monumento sepolcrale di Paolo II,'' *Atti della Pontifica Academia Romana di Archeologia. Rendiconti* (Rome 1982–1984), 175–243. J. N. D. KELLY, *Oxford Dictionary of Popes* (New York 1986) 251.

[M. FRANÇOIS]

Pope Paul II, marble bust by the 15th-century Venetian Bartolomeo Bellano, in the Palazzo Venezia, Rome. (Alinari–Art Reference/Art Resource, NY.)

PAUL III, POPE

Pontificate: Oct. 13, 1534, to Nov.10, 1549; b. Alessandro Farnese, Canino, February 29, 1468. He was a member of the distinguished Farnese family whose lands around the Bolsena Lake made them a powerful force in Italian history from the twelfth century. Alessandro was educated at Rome under Pomponius Laetus and later in Florence in the Medici house, where he was friendly with Giovanni de' Medici (later Leo X). Farnese's rise to prominence in the Church proved swift. He was created a cardinal by Alexander VI in 1493, partially because of the Pope's association with his sister, Guilia. Contemporaries dubbed him ''Cardinal Petticoat.'' In time he served under four other pontiffs, Julius II, Leo X, Adrian VI, and Clement VII, until he became dean of the Sacred College. Alessandro's career was marked by living habits that reflected his position as a Renaissance cleric. He fathered four bastards, Pierluigi, Paolo, Ranuccio, and Constanza. Of these Pierluigi became Duke of Parma, Piacenza, and Castro, married Girolama Orsini, and was murdered in 1547. Ranuccio died in 1509, and Constanza married Boso II of the house of Sforza. After his elevation he raised to the cardinalate two of his grandsons, Alessandro Farnese and Ascanio Sforza. His scandalous life, coupled with his NEPOTISM, provoked many complaints from both Catholics and the newly formed Protestant groups. Alessandro was ordained in 1519 and from that time his moral life improved. However, he remained a son of the Renaissance, very much addicted to worldly pleasures. He loved the hunt and the brilliant pomp of ceremonies, and he was a devoted patron of the arts. He began the FARNESE palace; and he commissioned Michelangelo to construct St. Peter's Basilica and ordered him to paint the Last Judgment and the ceiling of the Sistine Chapel. Paul censured Michelangelo for the nudity of the figures in the painting, and for this the artist depicted the Pontiff among the damned with an ass's ear and a serpent round his body. Paul supported also the construction of the Sala Regia in the Vatican and the interior decoration of the papal apartment in Castel Sant' Angelo. For these commissions he was severely criticized because the tone of the frescoes and of other decorations was considered pagan in its genre. He selected Giulio Mazzoni to begin the Palazzo Spada. Paul III's tomb in St. Peter's, the work of Michelangelo's student, Giacomo della Porta, is considered one of the basilica's finest monuments.

Reform of the Church. Despite his preoccupation with the cultural trends of the Renaissance, Paul was able to lead the Church into an important period of reform. Modern historians have called him ''the first reform pope,'' and the first Pope of the Counter-Reformation, and there is little doubt that he did create the atmosphere and the machinery that produced reform. At the time of his elevation, he was 67 and had twice before, in 1521 and 1523, almost been elected. Although the opposition of the Colonna and Medici families had previously prevented it, on October 13, 1534, he was unanimously

Pope Paul III.

elected. This man of violent temper, intelligence, and skilled diplomacy directed his varied talents to the problem of reform.

The pontificate of Paul III proved stormy, but had its major accomplishments. In 1538 he placed England under the interdict and excommunicated HENRY VIII. In that same year he was able to persuade Francis I of France and the Emperor Charles V of Germany to sign the Truce of Nice. He urged the Catholic princes of Germany to take up arms against the Lutheran SCHMALKALDIC LEAGUE, in addition to persuading the French King to adopt a policy of severity toward the Huguenots. In the midst of these upheavals he labored for reform and an ecumenical council.

In the early months of his reign he ordered the cardinals to adopt a more modest way of life. He recognized that unless the Roman clergy were first reformed he could accomplish nothing for the rest of Christendom. One of the distinctive features of Paul's program was the appointment to the Consistory of new cardinals who were committed to a program of ecclesiastical reform. Among these were John FISHER; Reginald POLE; Giovanni Pietro Carafa, cofounder of the Theatines and later PAUL IV; Marcello Cervini, who became MARCELLUS II; and such outstanding humanists as Girolamo Aleandro and the layman Gasparo CONTARINI.

By the bull *Sublimis Deus,* Paul appointed a commission to examine the conditions of the Church and to suggest reform. Pole, Contarini, Carafa, and others composed the commission, and their report, published in January 1538, became the basis of much of the work of the Council of Trent. Paul also recognized the Society of Jesus in 1540 and the Ursulines in 1544, encouraged the Barnabites and Theatines, and suggested the foundation of the Somaschi. In 1542 a reformed Inquisition was created in Rome to fight ''against all those who had departed from or who attacked the Catholic faith and to unmask such persons as were suspected of heresy.'' The Index followed, and in the next year enacted penalties for those who sold any condemned books. Paul made important strides toward reform, but his problems were compounded by difficulties in seeing his reforms carried out. Opposition came from the religious and, above all, from the secular rulers of the European world.

Imperial and French Opposition. The problems that the Pope faced seemed insurmountable. What should be included on the agenda of an ecumenical council? Should the Protestants be invited and, if so, should they be allowed to participate in the debates and discussions? Where should a council be held? Would it be better to accomplish reform simply by papal edict rather than run the risk of a resurgent conciliarism? Despite these obstacles, Paul announced that a council would convene at Mantua in May 1537. Unfortunately, the refusals of the French King and the German Emperor to allow their clergy to attend forced the Pope to postpone it. A similar opposition prevented its convocation for May 1, 1538. Francis I was playing a double game: he assured his Lutheran friends of the Schmalkaldic League that all was well, while he sought to frustrate any papal reforms for fear they would impair his control over the French Church. Charles V, who was also king of Spain, was a champion of reform for Spain, but he was opposed to it in the Holy Roman Empire. He regarded Lutheranism as a purely German problem and sought to resolve the logical differences himself.

The Council of Trent. On November 19, 1544, the bull *Laetare Jerusalem* announced that a council would meet at Trent on March 15, 1545. After eight years of frustration, Cardinal del Monte was able to celebrate the Mass of the Holy Ghost in the cathedral of Trent with four cardinals, four archbishops, 21 bishops, five generals of orders, and 50 theologians and canonists present. Despite the success in convoking the Council, Paul faced serious obstacles. The Germans insisted upon disciplinary reforms first so as not to alienate the Lutherans. The French, aided by national antagonisms, were suspected of Calvinistic leanings. The Spanish, who adopted a haughty attitude, felt that they were the sole defenders of the faith. Nonetheless, Paul had selected his papal legates wisely. These were men committed to reform and they included Giovanni del Monte; Marcello Crescenzi; Ercole Gonzaga; Giovanni Morone; Marcello Cervini; the Jesuits Claude Le Jay, Diego Laynez, and Alfonso Salméron; the Augustinian, Girolamo Seripando; and others.

In these first years of Trent important matters were settled. These included the role of the Holy Scriptures as a rule of faith, justification, the Sacraments, and the doctrine of original sin. Disciplinary reform of the bishops was also adopted. However, in May 1547, a plague struck Trent; and although Paul transferred the Council to Bologna in February 1548, Charles V refused to permit the German and Spanish bishops to attend. Paul was forced to suspend the Council on September 17, 1549. He died November 10, at the age of 82.

The judgment of history has been favorable to Paul III. Despite a wayward life in his younger years, a tendency to support the Renaissance in an extravagant manner, and a weakness for his family, he remains best described as follows: ''The supreme merit of Paul III is that he listened to this manifold voice, the voice of Christian conscience, and that he did its bidding according to his means.''

Bibliography: B. SACCHI et al., *Historia . . . de vitis Pontificum romanorum . . . ad Paulum V* (Cologne 1611). P. S. PALLAVICINO, *Istoria del concilio di Trento,* 3 v. (Rome 1656–57). L. PASTOR, *The History of the Popes from the Close of the Middle Ages,* (London–St. Louis 1938–61) v.11–12. P. ACCAME, *L'elezione del papa Paolo III* (Finalborgo, Italy 1907). W. H. EDWARDS, *Paul III. oder die geistliche Gegenreformation* (Leipzig 1933). W. FRIEDENSBURG, *Kaiser Karl V und Papst Paul III* (Leipzig 1932). L. DOREZ, *La Cour du Pape Paul III,* 2 v. (Paris 1932). C. CAPASSO, *Paolo III, 1534–1549,* 2 v. (Messina 1923–24); *La politica di papa Paolo III e l'Italia* (Camerino, Italy 1901). H. JEDIN, *History of the Council of Trent,* tr. E. GRAF,. P. JANELLE, *The Catholic Reformation* (Milwaukee 1949). H. DANIEL-ROPS, *The Catholic Reformation,* tr. J. WARRINGTON (History of the Church 5; New York 1963). L. MARCHAL, *Dictionnaire de théologie catholique,* ed. A. VACANT et al., 15 v. (Paris 1903–50; Tables générales 1951–) 12.1:9–20. R. BIRELEY, *The Refashioning of Catholicism: A Reassessment of the Counter-Reformation* (Washington D.C. 1999). *Epistolae ad Principes. Leo X–Pius IV (1513–1565)* ed, L. NANNI (Vatican City 1993). C. ROBERTSON, *''Il Gran Cardinale.'' Alessandro Farnese, Parton of the Arts* (New Haven 1993). P. PRODI and W. REINHARD, eds. *Il concilo di Trento e il moderno* (Bologna 1996). B. H. MCCLUNG, *Italian Cardinals, Reform and the Church as Property, 1492–1563* (Berkeley 1985).

[C. L. HOHL, JR.]

Pope Paul IV, statue by Pirro Ligorio on the Pope's tomb in the church of S. Maria sopra Minerva, Rome. (Alinari–Art Reference/Art Resource, NY.)

PAUL IV, POPE

Pontificate: May 23, 1555, to Aug. 18, 1559; b. Gian Pietro Carafa, Sant'Angelo a Scala (Avellino), Italy, June 28, 1476. His family were of the counts of Maddaloni, a branch of the noble CARAFA (Caraffa) family of Naples. Much of his education he obtained at Rome in the household of his uncle, the brilliant Cardinal Oliviero Carafa. The exceptional quality of this instruction is apparent from the fact that Erasmus corresponded with him as a young man, praising his knowledge of the three academic languages and once inviting his assistance in translating into Latin the Hebrew and Greek Scriptures. Cardinal Jacopo SADOLETO, the famed humanist, knew him as a fellow student in Cardinal Carafa's home and bears witness to his sanctity and learning. During this formative period he served blamelessly in the corrupt court of Alexander VI as a *cameriere pontificio.*

The Theatines. As bishop, Carafa gave an edifying example for those times by living and working zealously in his Diocese of Chiete in Abruzzi (*c.* 1506–13). To this activity he added valuable experience abroad as a papal envoy and observer. He was in England as legate of Leo X to Henry VIII for collecting Peter's Pence (1513–14); then he visited Flanders (1515–17) and Spain (1517–20).

In 1524 Clement VII allowed him to resign his bishopric so that he and Gaetano da Thiene of Vicenza could fulfill their desire of founding a congregation of clerks regular dedicated to restoring the apostolic way of life. From Carafa's former Diocese of Chiete (Lat., *Teate*) they acquired the nickname of ''Teatini.'' In 1527 the sack of Rome by the imperial forces put an end to the first Roman house of the THEATINES. Fleeing to Venice, they established another house, where Carafa remained until Paul III called him to Rome to make him a cardinal, December 22, 1536. In his 19 years as cardinal he was consistently anti-Spanish and anti-imperial. He aligned himself with the reform group in the Curia. In 1550 Julius III named him one of the six inquisitors of the Holy Office.

Reform Pope. At the death of Marcellus II (1555), Cardinal Alessandro Farnese turned all his influence in favor of Carafa, then dean of the Sacred College, and soon obtained the necessary votes for the 79-year-old Neapolitan. Carafa chose the name Paul out of respect for his earlier Farnese benefactor, Paul III.

Elected as a reformer, he lost some of his initial momentum and prestige by declaring an ill-considered war against the Spaniards, then in possession of a large part of Italy. He was in no sense a Julius II, however much he desired to drive the foreigner from the sacred soil. Moreover, to entrust the conduct of the war to his intriguing, self-aggrandizing nephew Carlo was an irremediable error. The Carafa family was defeated by the Duke of Alva, who was viceroy of Naples; the war ended with the generous peace of Cave, Sept.12, 1557. After 1557 the aged Pope devoted himself entirely to the reform of the Church. Opposing conciliar methods, he did not resume the Council of Trent. Instead, he relied on the establishment of a commission to which he named good and learned cardinals, chiefly men whom he had elevated. He fought an uncompromising war against simony and eventually struck a decisive blow at nepotism by exiling his own nephews. He also insisted that bishops reside in their sees and not spend their time in Rome and elsewhere, and ordered the arrest of vagrant monks in Rome.

Unpopular Reign. His zeal for the Inquisition was common knowledge and the terror it provoked earned him great unpopularity. Even during his war with Spain he attended its sessions. The number and types of cases exceeded by far those of his predecessors. Virtuous men, such as Cardinal Giovanni MORONE, were called before it on frivolous charges. Moreover, a new and more rigorous *Index Librorum Prohibitorum* was enacted and enforced. He forced the Jews to wear a distinctive badge and in 1555 established the ghetto in Rome.

Despite his vigilance against heresy, Protestantism made bold advances throughout northern Europe, often abetted by political considerations. Furthermore, Paul's policies toward the great powers of Europe were usually shortsighted and often arbitrary and not adapted to the political realities of the sixteenth century.

When the Pope died, the Romans rioted, tore down his statues and opened the prisons of the Inquisition, displaying their relief that his severe, unpopular rule was over. Although the positive side of his reign was long obscured by the memory of the excesses of the Inquisition, it was an era of important reforms as well.

A good likeness of the Pontiff, almost the only one extant, is the statue on his tomb, which Pius V had built in 1566 in the Carafa chapel of S. Maria sopra Minerva, Rome. Although idealized, it seems to have caught the spirit of the elderly, stern, fiery, and erratic Neapolitan aristocrat.

Bibliography: L. PASTOR, *The History of the Popes from the Close of the Middle Ages,* (London–St. Louis 1938–61) 14:56–424; 15:381–429. G. M. MONTI, *Ricerche su papa Paolo IV Carafa* (Benevento 1925); *Studi sulla riforma cattolica . . .* (Trani, Italy 1941). P. PASCHINI, *S. Gaetano Thiene, Gian Pietro Carafa e le origini dei chierici regolari teatini* (Rome 1926). G. SCHWAIGER, *Lexikon für Theologie und Kirche,* ed. J. HOFER and K. RAHNER, 10 v. (2d, new ed. Freiburg 1957–65) 8:200–202. C. V. DONATA, *Paolo IV e il Processo Carafa* (Milan 1993). T. TORRIANI, *Una tragedia nel cinquecento. Paolo IV e i suoi Nepoti* (Rome 1951). M. FIRPO, *Inquisizione romana e Controriforma* (Milan 1992). *Epistolae ad Principles. Leo X–Pius IV (1513–1565)* ed. L. NANNI (Vatican City 1993). E. G. GLEASON, ''Who was the First Counter-Reformation Pope?'' *The Catholic Historical Review* 81 (April 1995) 173–184. A. AUBERT, *Paolo IV Carafa nel giudizio della eta Contrariforma.* (Città di Castello 1990).

[H. H. DAVIS]

PAUL V, POPE

Pontificate: May 16, 1605, to Jan. 23, 1621; b. Camillo Borghese, Rome, Italy, Sept. 17, 1552. Camillo's family was Sienese and traced a distant relationship to St. Catherine of Siena. His ecclesiastical career began with studies in jurisprudence at Padua and Perugia. He was appointed extraordinary envoy to Philip II of Spain in 1593 and created cardinal in 1596 and vicar of Rome in 1603. In the conclave of 1605, although the youngest cardinal, he became a compromise choice. His esteem for law made him an unbending adversary in controversy, but did not prevent him from the indulgence of nepotism. To his nephew, Scipione Cafarrelli Borghese, he gave the cardinalate (1605), a large number of benefices and the Secretariate of State.

As pope, Paul took great interest in the city of Rome. His name is perpetuated there through the chapel in the Basilica of Santa Maria Maggiore, where his body was

Monument of Pope Paul V, sculpture by Silla da Viggi-, in the basilica of Santa Maria Maggiore, Rome. (Alinari–Art Reference/Art Resource, NY.)

buried after temporary interment in St. Peter's, and through the Villa Borghese built outside the ancient walls by his nephew, Cardinal Scipione Cafarelli Borghese. His plans for the renewal of Rome resulted in the lengthening of the nave of St. Peter's, the erection of the façcade (designed by Maderno), additions to the Vatican Palace, the restoration of two aqueducts and the erection of many fountains, including those at the Ponte Sisto, the Castel Sant' Angelo, and St. Peter's Square. He established a grain storehouse for the poor (1606) and to aid the farmers of the Papal States, he established a credit agency on October 19, 1611.

Paul, during his pontificate, was confronted by three grave international religious problems. First, a resurgence of religious hostility between Catholics and Protestants in Germany led, in 1618, to the start of the THIRTY YEARS' WAR. He helped to subsidize the Catholic League. Then James I of England demanded from his subjects a new oath that denounced the papal claim to depose a ruler. Paul condemned this oath on September 22, 1606, and again in the following year. Finally, when the Republic of Venice climaxed a policy of increased usurpation of the rights of the Church by subjecting a bishop and an abbot to trial in the secular courts, Cardinal Alessandro Ludovisi, the future GREGORY XV, was sent to Venice to negotiate a settlement. An interdict was laid on the city and excommunication inflicted on the Doge and his senators from April 17, 1606, until April 21, 1607. The Theatines, Capuchins, and Jesuits were expelled, but the rest of the clergy disregarded the papal sanctions and supported the government. The schism was ended through the mediation of Henry IV of France.

During the pontificate of Paul V, the Copernican system was proposed again by Galileo GALILEI of Pisa. Chiefly because of the precipitate fashion in which the scientist questioned Biblical exegesis, the heliocentric theories received negative judgment by the Congregation of the Index, March 5, 1616.

Among the achievements of Paul's reign were the publication of the *Rituale Romanum* on June 20, 1614; the permission for the use of literary Chinese in the liturgy of the Chinese missions (later suspended after the creation of the Sacred Congregation de Propaganda Fide); and the ban of September 5, 1607, upon further discussion of disputed topics related to grace. He followed with interest the growth of the Church in Latin America, particularly the Jesuit REDUCTIONS OF PARAGUAY. He gave many volumes to the Vatican Library and, being a scholar, he directed the religious orders to teach their members Latin, Greek, Hebrew, and Arabic in the universities. He also provided an archive to preserve the documents of the Holy See. Paul promoted the cult of saints, canonizing Charles Borromeo and Frances of Rome in a double ceremony on November 1, 1610. He beatified Ignatius of Loyola and Francis Xavier in company with the genial Philip Neri and the mystic Teresa of Avila. On February 24, 1612, he approved the Congregation of the Oratory founded by Philip Neri, and on May 10, 1613, the similar French Oratory of Pierre de Berulle. With his encouragement the Benedictine Congregation of St. Maurus was formed in 1618, and the first Visitation convent was organized by St. Francis de Sales and St. Jane Frances de Chantal. Paul also commissioned St. VINCENT DE PAUL in 1610 to represent the Pope at the court of King Henry IV of France.

Bibliography: P. PASCHINI and V. MONACHINO, *I Papi nella storia,* 2 v. (Rome 1961) 2:682–687. L. PASTOR, *The History of the Popes from the Close of the Middle Ages,* (London–St. Louis 1938–61) v. 25 and 26. L. MARSCHAL, *Dictionnaire de théologie catholique,* ed. A. VACANT et al., 15 v. (Paris 1903–50; Tables générales 1951–) 12.1:23–27, full bibliog. F. X. SEPPELT, *Geschichte der Päpste von den Anfängen bis zur Mitte des 20 Jh.,* (Leipzig 1931–41) 5:248–268. I. BEGAZZI, *Memoriale di Pierto di Vincenzo Strozzi* (Florence 1986). R. WOLFGANG, *Papstfinanz und Nepotismus unter Paul V* (Stuttgart 1974). P. SARPI, *Considerazioni sopra le censure di Paolo V* (Turin 1977). R. FELDHAY, *Galileo and the Church* (New York 1995). S.F. OSTROW, *Art and Spirituality in Counter-Reformation Rome* (New York 1996).

[T. F. CASEY]

PAUL VI, POPE

Pontificate, June 21, 1963, to Aug. 6, 1978; b. Giovanni Battista Montini, at Concesio, Lombardy, Italy, Sept. 26, 1897; d. Castel Gandolfo, Italy.

Early Career

Born in Concesio, at the country home of the Montini family five miles from Brescia, Giovanni Battista was the second of three children. His brothers were Lodovico and Francesco. The family atmosphere was deeply religious with great interest in literary and political issues. His father, Giorgio (1860–1943), was a lawyer, landowner, editor of the daily newspaper, *Il Cittadino di Brescia*, and member of the Italian Chamber of Deputies (1919–26). His mother, Giuditta Alghisi (1874–1943), instilled a love of music, art, and languages in her sons that lasted throughout their lives. She was president of Women's Catholic Action in Brescia.

The young Montini was devout and intelligent, but plagued by medical problems that he never fully overcame. Educated in the Jesuit primary and secondary school, Cesare Arici Istitute (1903–14), he also attended the state school, Liceo Arnaldo da Brescia, where he received the license (1916). The Oratorians at the Church

Pope Paul VI.

of Santa Maria della Pace in Brescia were a major influence in his youth. He was especially close to the Oratorian priest, Giulio Bevilacqua, who broadened his cultural and intellectual interests. When he began studying for the priesthood, he attended lectures at Brescia's diocesan seminary, but studied and lived at home. Following his ordination at the age of 22 on May 29, 1920, he was sent to Rome to do graduate study in literature at the Sapienza University and philosophy and canon law at the Gregorian University. In 1922, he was selected to attend the Pontifical Academy of Noble Ecclesiastics, the school for training Vatican diplomats.

Secretariat of State. Montini began his thirty years of service in the Vatican Secretariat of State in October 1924 as an *addetto* (attaché); six months later he was promoted to the rank of *minutante* (secretary). During those years, he was also active as a chaplain to the Catholic students at the University of Rome. In 1925, he was appointed spiritual moderator to the Federation of Italian Catholic University Students (Federazione Universitaria Cattolica Italiana known as FUCI) which faced the growing threat of the anti-clerical Fascist movement among university students. He and Igino Righetti, President of FUCI, founded Studium, a small publishing company, and *La Sapienza*, a weekly newspaper. Montini published three books that were collections of his conferences. He also translated two French books into Italian: *Three Reformers* by Jacques Maritain (1928) and *Personal Religion* by Léonce de Grandmaison (1934).

In addition to his work in the Secretariat of State, in 1931 Montini began teaching a course on the history of papal diplomacy at the Academy of Noble Ecclesiastics. In December 1937, he was named *sostituto* (undersecretary or surrogate) for ordinary church affairs serving Cardinal Eugenio Pacelli, the secretary of state. When Pacelli became Pope PIUS XII in 1939, Montini continued in the same post with the new secretary of state, Cardinal Luigi Maglione. When the latter died in 1944, Pius XII did not

Cardinals Karol Wojtyła (l) (later Pope John Paul II) and Stefan Wyszynski arriving from Poland for the funeral of Pope Paul VI, Rome, 1978. (AP/Wide World Photos)

appoint a secretary of state, and Montini worked directly with the Pope in charge of internal affairs of the Holy See. Msgr. Domenico Tardini handled external affairs. During World War II, Montini had many duties: to deal with the relief efforts of the Holy See, to oversee the tracing of prisoners of war, to protect political prisoners, especially Jews, and to assist displaced persons throughout Europe. After the war, he helped organize the Holy Year in 1950 and the Marian Year in 1954. In 1952, Pius XII asked both Montini and Tardini to accept the cardinalate, but they both declined the honor. In a gesture of appreciation for their work, the Pope gave both of them the title of Prosecretary of State.

Archbishop of Milan. Unexpectedly, Pius XII appointed Montini the Archbishop of Milan (Nov. 1, 1954)—a decision that may have been prompted by some internal conflicts within the CURIA. He departed Rome with some anxiety, but he was determined to face the pastoral challenges in Milan with its three and a half million people, 1,000 churches, and 2,500 priests. He rebuilt churches that had been bombed during the war and revitalized the social apostolate in this highly industrialized city that had been inundated by immigrants from the poorer areas of Italy. One of his goals was to win back the working class from Communist influences. Calling himself, ''the archbishop of the workers,'' he visited workers throughout the archdiocese and preached the social mission of the Gospel. Devoted to the disadvantaged, he was a frequent visitor to hospitals, orphanages, homes for the aged, and prisons. Using his excellent organizational skills, he planned an intense mission for three weeks in November of 1957. Priests, bishops, and hundreds of laypersons, delivered some 7,000 talks in parishes, cinemas, factories, and city streets to encourage lapsed Catholics to return to the Church. In his eight and a half years in Milan, he wrote eight pastoral letters to the faithful in the archdiocese, and each Holy Thursday he wrote a pastoral letter to his priests.

Cardinal. It had been expected that Pius XII would name Montini a cardinal soon after his appointment to Milan, but it did not happen, and the Pope died in 1958. At the papal election, Montini's name appeared on several of the ballots, thus becoming the first non-cardinal in centuries to receive votes in an election. The conclave chose Cardinal Angelo Roncalli, Patriarch of Venice, who became JOHN XXIII on Oct. 28, 1958. In his first consistory (Dec. 15, 1958), he created 23 new cardinals. The name of Archbishop Montini led the list of names that included his former fellow-worker in the secretariat of state, Msgr. Tardini. When John XXIII announced his intention to convene the Second VATICAN COUNCIL on January 25, 1959, he appointed Montini to both the Central Preparatory Commission and the Technical-Organizational Commission. Between 1959 and 1962, Montini delivered several important lectures on the nature of the forthcoming Council and devoted a 1962 pastoral letter to the faithful of Milan on that subject. He enthusiastically welcomed the Council, which he perceived to be a *kairos*, an exceptional opportunity for the Church to respond to the grace of God.

Although he was convinced that that Council would benefit the Church, he realized that it would not create a Church without imperfections. During the first session, he wrote weekly articles from Rome on the Council for *L'Italia*, the Catholic daily newspaper in Milan. He spoke twice at the first session: once on the schema on the liturgy (Oct. 22, 1962) and a second time on the schema on the Church (Dec. 5, 1962) in which he supported the views of Cardinal Léon-Joseph SUENENS on COLLEGIALITY.

Pontificate

At the death of John XXIII (June 3, 1963), Montini was favored as his successor by those who felt that he would continue the *aggiornamento* of Pope John. Not all the electors were of the same mind, however. It took six ballots on June 21 before he gained the two-thirds of the votes necessary for election. Elected at the age of 65, he appeared as a slim and austere figure who, at the time of his election, was 5 feet 10 inches tall and weighed 154 pounds. Taking the name Paul, he was determined that, like Paul the Apostle, his pontificate would spread the Gospel to the entire world. In his first message as Pope, the day after his election, he set forth his agenda: to continue Vatican II, to revise Canon Law, to work for peace and justice at all levels, and to seek Christian unity. Paul VI was crowned on June 30, 1963, giving his address in nine languages. He later sold his tiara to Cardinal Francis Spellman of New York and gave the money to the poor. Subsequently, he used the miter customarily worn by bishops.

Vatican II. As he had promised, Paul VI convened the second session of the Council, September 29, 1963. In his opening address he spoke of the purposes of the Council: to seek a fuller definition of the Church using proper images and to have a deeper understanding of the episcopate; to renew the Catholic Church; to restore the unity of all Christians and to ask forgiveness for the faults of the Catholic Church; and to initiate a positive dialogue with contemporary society that conveys the truth of the Gospel.

Paul VI was well equipped to deal with the Council because of long administrative experience in the secretariat of state and in Milan. He knew the Curia thoroughly. Their actions may not have always pleased him, but they rarely surprised him. He was actively involved in the three sessions of the Council over which he presided. He decided that the Council would not discuss birth control, since the Pontifical Study Commission on Family, Population,and Birth Problems that was established by John XXIII in 1963 had not completed its work. Some of the Fathers wanted the Council to discuss clerical celibacy, but the Pope did not agree. He explained his reasons in a letter (Oct. 10, 1965) to the Council: ''It is not opportune to debate publicly this topic. Our intention is not only to preserve this ancient law, but to strengthen its observance.'' His hope during the Council was that the final documents would be supported by the entire body and not just a slight majority. He was reluctant to stop debate on critical issues. At the end of the third session, for example, Cardinal Tisserant, speaking for the Council Presidency, announced that the preliminary vote on the hotly debated issue of religious liberty would be postponed to the next session. In response to that decision, some 1,000 Council Fathers signed a petition that was brought to the Pope requesting ''urgently, very urgently, most urgently'' that the schema be voted on in that session. Paul VI did not change the ruling of Tisserant.

As a member of the Council as well as its head, he suggested amendments to several of the documents: ecumenism, missionary activity, revelation, Eastern Catholic Churches, and religious liberty. Yet not all of his interventions were accepted. His suggestion that the Constitution on the Church (*Lumen gentium*) state that the Bishop of Rome is responsible to the Lord alone was not approved by the Theological Commission. Nor was another request, made in the first session before he was pope, that the Council declare ''Mary Mother of the Church,'' accepted. Nonetheless Paul VI used this title of Mary in his allocution closing the third session in November 1964. He invited a certain number of laymen, lay and religious women, and priests to attend the Council as auditors. Forty Orthodox and Protestant observers were present in the first session of the Council. With the support of Paul VI, their number grew to 100 by the end of the Council.

Implementation. Vatican II ended Dec. 8, 1965, and the Pope proceeded to implement its 16 documents. He soon discovered that it was a daunting task as he faced unrealistic expectations of the Council, curial opposition, and a crisis in culture in the 1960s that questioned the very existence of authority and tradition. One of the first tasks of Paul VI was the reform of the Curia, a move which many older prelates resented. The apostolic letter *Ecclesiae sanctae* (Aug. 6, 1966) decreed that bishops are to submit their resignations to the Pope no later than their seventy-fifth birthday. The apostolic constitution *Regimini ecclesiae universae* (August 15, 1967) urged greater consultation and cooperation among the curial offices and set a five-year term for heads and members of Roman congregations which may be extended by the Pope. Finally, the *motu proprio Ingravescentem aetatem* (Nov. 21, 1970) ruled that cardinals in charge of departments in the Roman Curia are to submit their resignation at the completion of their seventy-fifth year, and that on completion of eighty years of age cardinals cease to be members of the departments of the Roman Curia and lose the right to elect the Pope and to enter the conclave. Several cardinals, Eugène Tisserant and Alfredo Ottaviani among them, were bitterly opposed to this ruling. In addition, the Pope internationalized and expanded the College of Cardinals by adding new members from the Third World. In all he created 144 cardinals. The number of cardinals eligble to vote in papal elections was set at 120 (Apostolic constitution *Romano Pontifici Eligendo*, October 1, 1975).

The Pope established three permanent offices to carry out the major directives of the Council: the SECRETARIAT FOR NON-CHRISTIANS, the SECRETARIAT FOR NON-BELIEVERS, and the Secretariat for Promoting Christian Unity. A day before the end of the Council, he issued a decree reforming the Holy Office which was to be called the Congregation of the Doctrine of the Faith (*Motu proprio Integrae servandae*, Dec. 7, 1965) and abolished the four-century old Index of Forbidden Books. The Pope also decided to continue the Commission for the Revision of Canon Law, which John XXIII had established in 1959, but appointed its first members only in March 1963. John Paul II finally approved the revised Code of Canon Law in 1983.

Collegiality—the cooperation between the Pope and the bishops—was an important part of the postconciliar efforts of Paul VI. For him, the episcopate was not in opposition to the Pope, ''but working with him and under him for the common good and supreme end of the Church itself.'' In 1966, the Pope in *Ecclesiae sanctae* mandated that each nation or territory establish a permanent conference of bishops, if one did not already exist. The Synod of Bishops is another important organ of collegiality that was formally established by Paul VI on Sept. 15, 1965, by the motu proprio *Apostolica sollicitudo.* The purpose of this consultative body is to foster a close relationship between the Pope and the bishops and to facilitate agreement on essential points of doctrine and policy. The five synods he convoked were all held in Rome and dealt with the following issues: 1967—the relationship between the primacy and the episcopacy; 1969—dangers to the faith, revision of canon law, seminaries, mixed marriages, and liturgy; 1971—the ministerial priesthood and justice in the world; 1974—evangelization (*see* *EVANGELII NUNTIANDI*); and 1977—catechetics.

Liturgical rites were extensively revised after the Council. The Pope approved the use of the vernacular in the liturgy and new translations of liturgical texts. After a long process, approval was given for a new Order of the Mass and a revised breviary. By the apostolic letter *Sacrum diaconatus ordinem* (June 19,1967), Paul VI authorized the restoration of the permanent diaconate in the Latin rite that allowed married men to be ordained to that office. The apostolic letter *Ministeria quaedam* (August 15, 1972) decreed that laymen could be installed in the ministries of lector and acolyte. Laws of fasting and abstinence were modified; the Eucharist fast was reduced to one hour before reception.

Archbishop Marcel LEFEBVRE, a leader in the traditionalist movement, who vehemently opposed most of these liturgical changes, founded the Society of St. Pius X, which attracted a large number of followers. Efforts by Rome at reconciliation failed. In June 1976, Paul VI withdrew canonical approval of the Society of St. Pius X and prohibited Archbishop Lefebvre from exercising his priestly powers. When Lefebvre ordained four bishops in 1988 without Roman approval, he and the four bishops he ordained were automatically excommunicated.

International Travel. Like the Apostle Paul, Paul VI was an itinerant preacher of the Gospel. He was the first Pope to travel outside of Italy since Napoleon took Pius VII into captivity in 1809. He was also the first reigning Pope to travel by air, as well as the first to visit the United States, India, Africa, and the Holy Land. During his pontificate he travelled some 70,000 miles. He had planned to join the celebration of the 1,000th anniversary of Christianity in Poland in 1966, but the Polish government did not allow it.

In all Paul VI made nine pastoral pilgrimages. 1) In January 1964, in Jerusalem he embraced and exchanged the kiss of peace with Athenagoras, the Ecumenical Patriarch of Constantinople, and together they recited the Lord's Prayer. 2) In December 1964, he stopped in Lebanon on his way to Bombay, India for the International Eucharistic Congress. 3) In a moving address in French to the General Assembly of the United Nations in 1965, he said that the Church is ''an expert in humanity,'' and he pleaded for world peace: ''No more war. War never again.'' He concluded his one day visit to New York by celebrating Mass at Yankee Stadium before 90,000. 4) The occasion for his visit to Portugal in 1967 was the fiftieth anniversary of the appearances of Our Lady at Fatima. 5) In July 1967, meeting with Patriarch Athenagoras in Istanbul, Paul VI said that Rome and Constantinople regard each other as sister Churches. 6) The occasion of his visit to Colombia, August 1968, was the Eucharistic Congress at Bogotá and the meeting of the Latin American Bishops' Conference (CELAM) at Medellín. 7) In Geneva, Switzerland, June 1969, the Pope attended ceremonies celebrating the 50th anniversary of the International Labor Organization. He also visited the headquarters of the World Council of Churches and introduced himself with the words: ''We are here among you. Our name is Peter.'' 8) Uganda July 1969. In Kampala he prayed at the shrine of the 22 Ugandan martyrs that he had canonized in 1964. He encouraged the African bishops to develop a genuine African Christianity. 9) Far East, November 1970. This ten-day visit was his longest. He stopped at Tehran, Karachi, Manila, Samoa, Australia, Jakarta, and Sri Lanka. At the Manila airport, he narrowly escaped an assasination attempt by a knife-wielding Bolivian painter. The Pope forgave him on the spot.

Ecumenism. Paul VI had an unswerving commitment to the unity of all Christians, but he was realistic about the difficulty his own office posed. In an address to the Secretariat for Promoting Christian Unity (April 29,1967), he said: ''The Pope, as we well know, is undoubtedly the greatest obstacle in the path of ecumenism.'' His relationship with Athenagoras, the Ecumenical Patriarch of Constantinople, is legendary. They met three times. At their first meeting during the Pope's trip to the Holy Land in January of 1964, they exchanged gifts of special significance, and later in September of 1964, Paul VI returned the head of St. Andrew the Apostle, the brother of Simon Peter, to the Orthodox Church in Patras, Greece. This relic, taken by the Crusaders, had been in the possession of the Vatican since 1462. Before the Council Mass on December 7, 1965, a joint statement from the Pope and the Patriarch was read, lifting the mutual anathemas that were made by representatives of the two Churches in Constantinople in 1054. In his visit to Turkey in July 1967, Paul visited Athenagoras a second time in Istanbul. The Pope spoke of ''the dialogue of charity'' between the two Churches, and the Patriarch welcomed the Pope as ''the very holy successor of Peter who has Paul's name and his conduct as a messenger of charity, union, and love.'' A third meeting took place in Oct. 1967, when Athenagoras visited the Pope in Vatican City. It was the first time a reigning Ecumenical Patriarch had ever been to Rome. Athenagoras called the Pope the ''Bishop of Rome, bearer of apostolic grace,'' and described the See of Rome as ''the first in honor and order in the living body of the Christian Churches scattered throughout the world.''

The Pope also received visits from two Anglican Archbishops of Canterbury: Michael Ramsey and Donald Cognan. He gave a warm fraternal embrace to Archbishop Ramsey when they met in March 1966 and said to him: ''By your coming here you rebuild a bridge which for centuries has lain fallen between the Church of Rome and Canterbury.'' The Pope gave his own episcopal ring to the Archbishop who in turn gave the Pope a pectoral cross. This meeting led to the establishment of the ANGLICAN-ROMAN CATHOLIC INTERNATIONAL COMMISSION (ARCIC). In 1966, the Pope had a lengthy conversation with the Reformed theologian Karl BARTH. In 1973, he met with the Buddhist Patriarch and with the Dalai Lama. Paul VI's deep desire for Christian unity is reflected in his will published shortly after his death: ''The work of drawing closer to our separated brethren should continue with great understanding, with great patience, and with great love, but without deviating from the true Catholic understanding.''

Diplomatic Relations. Paul VI's willingness to negotiate with countries behind the Iron Curtain was his most controversial diplomatic initiative. This policy of *Ostpolitik* continued the ''opening to the left'' of John XXIII. The Pope condemned atheistic materialism and all violations against social justice, but he felt that accommodation was more productive than confrontation in improving relations between the Church and Communist countries. Cardinals József Mindszenty of Hungary and Josef Slipyj from Ukraine, both of whom had been imprisoned by the Communists, severely criticized the Vatican's negotiations with the East. Yet the policy of détente produced some favorable results and led to the restoration of the hierarchy and greater freedom for Church activities. Hungary and Czechoslovakia, for example, made significant concessions that allowed the Church greater freedom. The Pope met with several Communist leaders: President Nikolai Podgorny and Foreign Minister Andrei Gromyko of the Soviet Union, Premier Nicolas Ceausescu of Romania, Marshall Tito of Yugoslavia, and other high-ranking officials from Poland, Hungary, and Bulgaria. Many Western leaders also visited the Pope, including Presidents Kennedy, Johnson, Nixon, and Ford. Paul VI established diplomatic relations with more than 40 countries. In 1964, the Holy See established an office of permanent observer at the United Nations.

Writings and Other Activities. Paul VI wrote seven encyclicals. 1) *Ecclesiam Suam* (August 6, 1964) anticipated some of the themes that were to appear in *Lumen Gentium* of Vatican II. The Pope urged the Church to have a greater awareness of itself, to undertake necessary reforms, and to establish a dialogue with the world. 2) *Mense maio* (April 29, 1965) called for Christians to pray for the success of the Council and for world peace. 3) *Mysterium fidei* (Sept. 3, 1965) presented thhe traditional teaching of th Church on the mystery of the Holy Eucharist. 4) *Christi matri* (Sept. 15, 1966) appealed for prayers for peace and explained the value of devotion to the rosary. 5) *Populorum progressio* (March 26, 1967) discussed the development of peoples. It warned that the disparity between nations jeopardizes peace and that wealthier nations should help poorer ones. All nations have the duty to promote human solidarity. ''Development.'' he said ''is another name for peace.'' 6) *Sacerdotalis caelibatus* (June 24, 1967) reaffirmed the role of celibacy for clerics in the Latin Church. He described priestly celibacy as ''a heavy and sweet burden'' and a ''total gift'' of the priest to God and to the Church. 7) *HUMANAE VITAE* (July 25, 1968) condemned abortion, sterilization, and artificial birth control. It taught that ''each and every marriage act must remain open to the transmission of life'' (No. 11). This last encyclical created a crisis in the Church, especially in the Western world. Some had expected change in the traditional teaching, especially since the majority of the papal commission on birth control recommended some modification. Others argued that Paul VI did not follow the principle of collegiality, since he failed to consult adequately with the episcopal conferences. Large numbers of Catholics ignored the teaching of the encyclical and many priests resigned over it. On the tenth anniversary of *Humanae vitae* in 1978, Paul VI referred to it as ''a painful document of our pontificate,'' but he remained convinced that its teaching was correct.

Two of the most significant documents written by Paul VI were not encyclicals. The apostolic letter *Octagesima adveniens* (May 14, 1971), issued on the 80th anniversary of the encyclical *Rerum novarum* (1891) of Leo XIII, recognized that the world faced new social challenges and that Christians, relying on their faith, have a personal responsibility to promote justice in their particular situations. The apostolic exhortation *EVANGELII NUNTIANDI* (Dec. 8, 1975) taught that the proclamation of the Gospel, evangelization, is linked to social justice and must oppose all forms of cultural, political, or economic domination. In other addresses, Paul VI emphasized the essential unity of the human race and pleaded for peace in Vietnam, Northern Ireland, and the Middle East. He condemned all forms of oppression, but opposed violence or terrorism as acceptable ways to promote justice. In January 1967, he established the Pontifical Commission for Justice and Peace, and in 1968 he instituted the World Day of Peace to be observed annually on January 1. With good reason, he called himself an ''apostle of peace.''

The pope named St. TERESA OF AVILA and St. CATHERINE OF SIENA as Doctors of the Church in 1970, the first women to be so honored. He canonized 84 saints including the 22 Ugandan martyrs, the 40 martyrs of England and Wales, and two Americans: Elizabeth Ann Bayley Seton and John Nepomucene Neumann. Throughout his pontificate he created 144 cardinals with a great number coming from the Third World. He had appointed 100 of the 111 cardinals who were eligible to vote for his successor. Paul VI held more than 700 general audiences.

Assessment

The last ten years of his pontificate (1968–78) were difficult for Paul VI. He was more withdrawn and troubled by the negative reaction to *Humanae vitae*, the polarity between conservatives and liberals, the massive departure from priestly and religious life, and the lack of vocations. The Pope told Jean Guitton that Archbishop Lefebvre, who defiantly opposed the reform of the liturrgy, was ''the greatest cross of my pontificate.'' Rumors that Paul VI would resign on his 70th birthday or later on his 80th were unfounded. In fact, he remained quite active during that decade in writing, travelling, and caring for his flock. His increasing lament over international terrorism and the ''renaissance of barbarism'' touched him personally when his close friend, Aldo Moro, former premier of Italy, was kidnapped and murdered by the Red Brigades in May 1978.

Debilitating arthritis and acute cystitis weakened him in the summer of 1978. On August 6, he died of a heart attack at Castel Gandolfo. The Pope requested a simple funeral: ''I would like to be in real earth with a humble sign indicating the place and inviting Christian mercy. No monument for me.'' He was buried in a simple wooden coffin in the crypt of St. Peter's. His cause for beatification was introduced on May 11, 1993.

Some observers have compared Paul VI to Hamlet—vacilating, weak, and indecisive. Certainly by nature he was cautious and circumspect. His 30 years experience in the Curia taught him to favor an orderly administrative process and to avoid rash decisions. His style was to move slowly, to examine all aspects of an issue before taking action. Paul VI was aware that some saw him as timid and apprehensive. Toward the end of his pontificate in 1975, when he was 78 years old, the Pope reflected on his life. He noted: ''What is my state of mind? Am I Hamlet or Don Quixote? On the left? On the right? I do not feel I have been properly understood. My feelings are '*Superabundo gaudio*.' I am filled with comfort, overcome with joy, throughout every affliction.''

Paul VI was a man of the Church devoted to God's people. Labels do not easily apply to him. As he noted: ''A Pope must be neither a reactionary nor a progressive. He must be a Pope—that's all.'' He tried to be even-handed and not vindictive or petty. Although he felt criticism deeply and was given to occasional moments of isolation and self-doubt, he never personally condemned those who disagreed with him. He showed extradordinary patience in dealing with those who dissented from *Humanae Vitae*, with priests who left the active ministry and sought laicization, with problems in the Dutch Church, and with theologians such as Hans Küng and Ivan Illich. The only condemnation he made was his suspension of Archbishop Lefebvre whose continued defiance of Vatican directives left the Pope no other choice.

Paul VI's two greatest achievements were the continuance of Vatican II and its implementation. In both instances, he showed by his remarkable resolve and decisiveness that he was far removed from the attitude of Hamlet. In his decision to continue Vatican II, he manifested his acceptance of the Council and its importance in the life of the Church. His active engagement in the conciliar proceedings and interventions at difficult moments enabled the Council to complete its work successfully. The implementation of the Council, which occupied the remaining years of his pontificate, was often a continuing and painful struggle for the Pope. Yet in the turmoil of the postconcilar period, he avoided schism within the Roman Catholic Church. Through skillful oversight, he was able to affirm the value of the world without diminishing the uniquenss of the Church; to encourage collegiality and still preserve papal prerogatives; to reform the Curia without losing its support; to support ecumenism without sacrificing Catholic identity; and to revise the liturgy without jettisoning its traditional richness. In a word, the Pope accomplished his greatest challenge: to balance tradition and reform without compromising either.

Bibliography: P. ARATÓ and P. VIAN, *Paulus PP. VI, 1963–1978. Elenchus Bibliographicus* (Brescia 1981). *Insegnamenti di Paolo VI, 1963–1978*, 16 v. (Vatican City 1965–1979). *The Teachings of Pope Paul VI 1968–1975*, 9 v. (Vatican City 1968–1975). The Istituto Paolo VI in Brescia regularly publishes: *Quaderni, Notiziario*, and reports of conferences. J. G. CLANCY, *Apostle for Our Time: Pope Paul VI* (New York 1963). J. GUITTON, *The Pope Speaks: Dialogues of Paul VI with Jean Guitton* (New York, 1968). P. HEBBLETHWAITE, *Paul VI: The First Modern Pope* (New York 1993). *Paul VI et la modernité dans l'Église: Actes du colloque organisé par l'École française de Rome* (Rome and Brescia 1984). N. VIAN, ed. *Anni e opere di Paolo VI* (Rome 1978).

[P. GRANFIELD]

PAUL OF BURGOS

Spanish bishop, exegete, apologist; b. Burgos *c.* 1351; d. Burgos, Aug. 29, 1435. Since he was born of a wealthy Jewish family (and first known as Solomon ha-Levi), he began his career as a learned rabbi. The study of Sacred Scripture and philosophy, particularly the *Summa theologiae* of St. Thomas, led him to the Christian faith. He was baptized in 1390, when he took the name of Paul of St. Mary, and, not long after, following the death of his wife, he was ordained a priest. In 1405, he became bishop of Cartagena, and in 1415 bishop of Burgos. The next year he was appointed lord chancellor of Castile. His principal works are his *Additiones* (1429–31) to the *Postilla* of Nicholas of Lyra on all the Sacred Scriptures, and his *Dialogus . . . contra perfidiam Judaeorum,* finished in 1434, and printed several times (Mantua 1475; Mainz 1478; Paris 1507, etc.). The 1591 Burgos edition of the latter work contains a biographical sketch of Paul by C. Sanctotisius. Paul surpassed Nicholas of Lyra in his knowledge of Hebrew, but not in exegetical skill.

Bibliography: M. KAYSERLING, *The Jewish Encyclopedia,* ed. J. SINGER, 13 v. (New York 1901–06) 9:562–563. H. HURTER, *Nomenclator literarius theologiae catholicae,* 5 v. in 6 (3d ed. Innsbruck 1903–1913) 2:812–814.

[L. F. HARTMAN]

PAUL OF CANOPUS

Egyptian monk, patriarch of Alexandria from 536 to 539. Nothing is known of Paul's background or education. He was one of the monks sent to Constantinople in 536 to complain to JUSTINIAN I about the Origenistic disturbances in Egypt. While there he made the acquaintance of the Roman deacon and future pope, PELAGIUS I, who recommended him to the emperor to succeed Theodosius, the deposed Monophysite patriarch of Alexandria. Paul was consecrated at Constantinople in the presence of Pelagius by the patriarch MENNAS toward the end of 536 or early in 537 and was sent to Egypt with orders to pacify the religious situation. He had to use military assistance to take possession of his patriarchal see, and he conducted himself with such violence against Monophysite groups that he worsened the situation. He was accused of having demanded the torture and death of the deacon Psoïs, suspected of intrigue against the patriarch. This execution caused a great stir (Liberatus, 23; Procopius, *Hist. arcana,* 150–152); and in its wake, the city magistrate Arsenius and the augustal prefect Rhodon were executed. Paul fled to Gaza, where at the instance of Justinian, a synod was held in 539 by the patriarchs Ephrem of Antioch, Peter of Jerusalem, and Hypatius of Ephesus and the imperial official Eusebius, in the presence of the deacon Pelagius. Paul was deposed and exiled, and another monk, Zoïlus, was nominated patriarch of Alexandria.

Bibliography: J. MASPERO, *Histoire des patriarches d'Alexandrie* (Paris 1923) 129ff. A. FLICHE and V. MARTIN, eds., *Histoire de l'église depuis les origines jusqu'à nos jours* (Paris 1935–) 4;455. L. DUCHESNE, *L'Église au VI*[e] *siècle* (Paris 1925) 103–105; 169–170.

[P. ROCHE]

PAUL OF SAMOSATA

Heretical bishop of Antioch (260–268); b. Samosata on the Euphrates. He had acquired wealth and influence under Odenatus II, King of Palmyra, after the Persian defeat of the Roman Emperor VALERIAN (260). Under Queen Zenobia, Paul succeeded Demetrianus as bishop of Antioch, while retaining his secular position. In 264, as a result of widespread criticism of his conduct and doctrine, Bps. FIRMILIAN of Caesarea and Helenus held a synod of local bishops in Antioch to consider those accusations that referred to his financial interests and misconduct as well as to his encouragement of East Syrian usages, such as the *VIRGINES SUBINTRODUCTAE* and the chanting of psalms by alternating choirs of virgins and men. He was also accused of banning hymns in honor of Christ since ''he considered Him but an ordinary man'' (Eusebius, *Hist. eccl.* 7.27.2). Paul was judged in two further synods at Antioch, and was deposed in 268. Credit for his final condemnation is given to the priest Malchion, who had been head of a school of rhetoric at Antioch (Jerome, *De vir. ill.* 71).

Paul of Samosata's doctrine is known only from records of the debate with Malchion preserved in the works of HILARY OF POITIERS (*De synodis* 81.86); St. Basil (*Ep.* 52); the *De sectis* (3.3); JUSTINIAN I; and in the account given by Eusebius (*Hist. eccl.* 7.27), who says that the council that condemned Paul sent an encyclical letter to Pope DIONYSIUS and Bp. Maximus of Alexandria for distribution in all the provinces. A *Letter to Hymnaeus* supposedly sent by six bishops to Paul before the Council of 268 seems apocryphal, as are the *Orations to Sabinus.*

The Council that condemned Paul is said to have repudiated the term *HOMOOUSIOS,* or consubstantial, which is the orthodox term explaining the equality of Godhead in Christ and the Father, because Paul used it in a modalist sense. He is accused of having ''given the name of Father to God Who created all things, that of Son to Him Who was purely Man, and that of the Spirit to the grace which resided in the Apostles'' (*De sectis* 3.3) and of having considered Jesus to be greater than Moses, but not to be God. His doctrine thus recognized a Trinity merely of names, for he taught MONARCHIANISM; in the area of CHRISTOLOGY he is considered one of the founders of ADOPTIONISM.

Bibliography: G. BARDY, *Paul de Samosate* (*Spicilegium sacrum Lovaniense* 4; 1923); *Dictionnaire de théologie catholique,* ed. A. VACANT et al. (Paris 1903–50) 12.1:46–51. J. QUASTEN, *Patrology* (Westminster MD 1950) 2:140–142. H. J. LAWLOR, ''Sayings of Paul of Samosata,'' *Journal of Theological Studies* 19 (1917–18) 20–45, 115–120. F. LOOFS, *Paulus von Samosata* (Leipzig 1924). H. DE RIEDMATTEN, *Les actes du procès de Paul de Samosate* (Fribourg 1952). R. M. GRANT, *Vigilae christianae* 3 (1949) 225–229.

[P. LEBEAU]

PAUL OF THE CROSS, ST.

Mystic, missionary, spiritual director, and founder of the PASSIONISTS; b. Ovada, Italy, January 3, 1694; d. Rome, Italy, October 18, 1775. His parents, Luke Danei and Ann Marie Massari, although members of nobility, were neither wealthy nor privileged. Even though the town hall at Castellazzo had been at an earlier date the family manor, Luke Danei, a cloth merchant, was in constant financial distress. Paul Francis, the second of 16 children, had to discontinue his education at a boarding school in Genoa, and once pawned his possessions to relieve his father's embarrassment. Deprived of a formal education, he completed his studies through his own initiative and industry. His correspondence manifests a thorough study of Sacred Writ (especially the New Testament), a mastery of his native Italian, and a competency in Latin. A leader by nature, strong willed but gentle, Paul easily won the confidence of his contemporaries. Long before his own vocation was definite, he was instrumental in determining the vocations of many of his companions by his counsel and example. Simultaneously with compassion for others whose spiritual and physical poverty he keenly felt, there existed in his soul an equally strong attraction toward contemplation, solitude, and penance. The resultant tension was not resolved until he established a new order of penitential missionaries, combining a vigorous apostolate with exact monasticism.

The Vocation. In 1713 Paul was stirred by a parish sermon to serve God. Two years later he enlisted in the army of the Venetian Republic, desiring to die for his faith in the Turkish Wars. In prayer he recognized his destiny would be otherwise, and he returned to Castellazzo, where in 1720 he had what he called the ''great vision,'' beholding himself in God clothed in the habit that was to become the distinctive garb of his congregation. Under the direction of Arborio di Gattinara, bishop of Alessandria, he spent 40 days in prayer and penance and composed his rule. Although it took Paul of the Cross only five days to write it, the years before its approval were long and trouble-laden. Twenty-one years elapsed before BENEDICT XIV in 1741 approved the Passionist rule and institute and admitted Paul's first followers to religious profession. In the meantime Paul had been ordained together with his saintly brother, John Baptist (1727), and had begun one of the most illustrious missionary careers of the 18th century.

From his first mission at Grazi's Ferry in 1730 to his last at the age of 75 in the Basilica of Santa Maria in Trastevere, Rome, he exemplified the primary apostolate of his congregation, the *ministerium verbi.* For him the parochial mission was a confrontation of the Christian with Christ in the paradox of the cross that evoked a commitment to concrucifixion in the continuing passion of Christ and its redemptive work in the daily lives of his hearers. To achieve this he developed a participated mission method that involved the laity in an active role in processions, street preaching, vigils, penitential works and sacrifices, hymns, prayers, and at times in the sermon itself. Its success accounts for the solid growth of the order in its first period.

Role as Organizer. Besides carrying on a strenuous missionary apostolate, Paul governed his rapidly expanding congregation. Before his death he had made 12 foundations, established two provinces, and presided over six general chapters in addition to founding a second order, the strictly enclosed Passionist Nuns. He also found time for the difficult and delicate task of directing souls. One-fourth of his extant letters (not more than 3,000 have come down out of a conservative estimate of more than 10,000) are concerned with spiritual direction; many of them are small treatises on ascetical and mystical theology.

Mystic of the Cross. The impressive external works of Paul of the Cross, as founder, preacher, missionary, and spiritual director, were crowned by remarkable mystical experience. Above all else Paul is the mystic of the cross. Nothing was more contemporary to him than the Passion of Christ. To keep not its memory but its actuality effective in present society was the purpose of his life. Three periods are discernible in his mystical progress: 12 years of extraordinary visions and graces mingled with trials (1713–25); followed by 45 years of interior desolation, vicarious reparation, and intense sufferings (1725–70); and finally, the last years dominated by astonishing mystical phenomena, consolations, and extraordinary favors. Paul's importance to ascetical and mystical theology is studied in the works of R. Garrigou-Lagrange, J. de Guibert, M. Villet, Jules Lebreton, C. Brovetto, and others. Paul of the Cross was canonized by PIUS IX on June 29, 1867.

St. Paul of the Cross, after a painting from life, 1733, by Domenico Porta, original at motherhouse of the Passionists at Rome.

Feast: Oct. 19 (formerly April 28).

Bibliography: *Lettere di S. Paolo della Croce,* ed. A. DELLA MADRE DEL BUON PASTORE, 4 v. (Rome 1924); ''Diary of St. Paul of the Cross,'' *Cross and Crown* 6, 127–146; *Lettere a laici ed ecclesiastici,* ed. C. CHIARI (Rome 1974); *Words from the Heart: A Selection from the Personal Letters of Saint Paul of the Cross,* tr. E. BURKE, ed. R. MERCURIO and S. ROUSE (Dublin 1976); *La muerte mistica,* ed. and tr. A. M. ARTOLA (Bilbào 1986). B. DE SAN PABLO, *La espiritualidad de la Pasión en el magisterio de S. Pablo de la Cruz* (Madrid 1961). E. ZOFFOLI, *S. Paolo della Croce* (Rome 1963–). C. ALMERAS, *St. Paul of the Cross,* tr. A. BOUCHARD (New York 1960). FATHER EDMUND, *Hunter of Souls* (Westminster, Md. 1947). M. BIALAS, *Das Leiden Christi beim hl. Paul vom Kreuz* (Aschaffenburg 1978) tr. as *The Mysticism of the Passion in St. Paul of the Cross* (San Francisco 1990). J. MEAD, ed., *St. Paul of the Cross: A Source/Workbook for Paulacrucian Studies* (New Rochelle, N.Y. 1983). B. KELLEY, *Listen to His Love* (Union City, N.J. 1985); *Spiritual Direction According to St. Paul of the Cross* (Staten Island, N.Y. 1993). A. CALABRESE, *Maestro e mistico* (Rome

1993). A. LIPPI, *Mistico ed evangelizzatore* (Cinisello Balsamo, Milan 1993).

[C. J. YUHAUS]

PAUL THE DEACON

Carolingian historian of the Lombards, poet, grammarian; b. *c.* 730; d. Monte Cassino, 799(?). Paul was apparently of noble Lombard family, the son of Warnefrid and Theodolinda. As a youth he was sent to the court of King Rachis at Pavia, where he received an excellent education under Flavianus. He knew some Greek and Hebrew. While associated with the Lombard Princess Adelperga, beautiful daughter of King Desiderius, he composed (*c.* 770) in her honor a poem, a chronology of world history in which the acrostic *Adelperga pia* appears. She induced him to join the court of her husband, Duke Arichis of Benevento, an important ally of the Lombards in southern Italy. Paul remained there until the conquest of the LOMBARDS by CHARLEMAGNE (773–774), when he entered MONTE CASSINO. It seems unlikely that he was ever a monk at St. Peter's in Civate near Milan, as some have thought. Paul's brother, involved in a revolt (776) of Duke Hrodgaud of Friuli against Charlemagne, was imprisoned, and his property was confiscated. In 782 Paul addressed a plea in elegaic verses to Charlemagne, asking the king to release his brother, whose family was suffering from want. Charlemagne, attracted by the obvious scholarship of the monk, ordered Paul to come to Aachen, and there for several years Paul was an honored member of the court circle, which included ALCUIN, THEODULF OF ORLÉANS, PETER OF PISA, and PAULINUS OF AQUILEIA (*see* CAROLINGIAN RENAISSANCE). Although there is no record of his brother's release, it is practically certain.

Paul added the free Italian spirit (F. J. E. Raby) to the court circle as well as a knowledge of Vergil, Ovid, Lucan, FORTUNATUS, ARATOR, and many others. He was primarily a grammarian in the palace school, and he undertook an abridgment of Festus's *De verborum significatione,* important for a knowledge of archaic Latin and for miscellaneous bits of information about Roman religion and law. He wrote many poems, occasional verses, epitaphs, and letters to Peter of Pisa and Charlemagne. Two poems on St. Benedict were written in 774 when he first went to Monte Cassino. Two other of his poems rank among the best examples of Carolingian poetry: the one written for his brother's release and a description of Lake Como in epanaleptic lines. At Charlemagne's order, he compiled a homiliary (*Patrologia Latina,* 217 v. [Paris 1878–90] 95:1159–66) using the sermons of Ambrose, Augustine, Jerome, and others. He wrote a life of St. Gregory the Great and, at Bishop Angilramnus's request, compiled a history of the bishops of Metz. He did not write the commentary on the Benedictine Rule long attributed to him. Three hymns are said to be his: *Fratres, alacri pectori* (*Analecta hymnica* [Leipzig 1886–1922] 50:118–120) in honor of St. Benedict, one in honor of the Assumption (*Analecta hymnica* 50:123–125), and *UT QUEANT LAXIS*. The last is famous for its use by GUIDO OF AREZZO in determining the syllable names of the diatonic scale and is one of the best Carolingian hymns. Today Paul's authorship is seriously questioned or denied.

It is as a historian, however, that Paul is chiefly remembered. About 770 he edited Eutropius's *Breviarium ab urbe condita,* an abridgment of Roman history (753 B.C. to A.D. 364), which he extended by adding passages from Jerome and Orosius. His greatest work is the incomplete *Historia Langobardorum,* in six books. It covers the history of the Lombards from their legendary beginnings to the death of King Liutpard in 744, and is based on two earlier lost sketches of Lombard history, the chronicle of Secundus and *Origo gentis Langobardorum,* and works of other historians, such as GREGORY OF TOURS, GREGORY I THE GREAT (*Dialogues*), BEDE, and ISIDORE OF SEVILLE. Paul also used his own experience and observation, oral tradition, folk legends, and omens. The style is simple and unadorned, vivid in descriptive passages and dramatic in others. The work is weakest in chronology, sometimes erring by vagueness, for example, Paul's use of *circa haec tempora,* at other times by being from 30 to 40 years off the mark. It is a very important work because it preserved the memory of the Lombards, who were doomed to disappear as a political entity. It is unfortunate that Paul did not complete it at least to the fall of the Lombards in 774.

Bibliography: *Die Gedichte des Paulus Diaconus,* ed. K. NEFF (Munich 1908); *Sexti Pompei Festi de verborum significatu . . . Pauli epitome,* ed. W. M. LINDSAY (Leipzig 1913); *Historia Romana,* ed. A. CRIVELLUCI in *Fonti per la storia d'Italia* 51 (Rome 1914); *Monumenta Germaniae Historica: Scriptores rerum Langobardicarum* (Berlin 1926—) 45–187; *Monumenta Germaniae Historica: Gesta epp. Mett.* (*ibid.*) 2:260–270. M. MANITIUS, *Geschichte der lateinischen Literatur des Mittelalters,* 3 v. (Munich 1911–31) 1:257–272. W. WATTENBACH, *Deutschlands Geschichtsquellen im Mittelalter. Vorzeit und Karolinger,* ed. W. LEVISON and H. LÖWE, 4 v. (Weimar 1952–63) 1:212–224. F. A. WRIGHT and T. A. SINCLAIR, *A History of Later Latin Literature* (New York 1931) 149–157. F. J. E. RABY, *A History of Christian-Latin Poetry from the Beginnings to the Close of the Middle Ages* (2d ed. Oxford 1953) 162–167; *A History of Secular Latin Poetry in the Middle Ages,* 2 v. (2d ed. Oxford 1957) 1:197–199. M. L. W. LAISTNER, *Thought and Letters in Western Europe,* A.D. *500 to 900* (2d ed. New York 1957) 219–222, 279–280. E. OMLIN, ''Guido von Arezzo und der Johannes-Hymnus, *Ut queant laxis,*'' *J. B. Hilber: Festgabe* (Altdorf 1951) 46–54. A. KOLLAUTZ, *Lexikon für Theologie und Kirche,* 10 v. (Freiburg 1957–65) 8:230–231. L. J. ENGELS, *Observations sur le vocabulaire de Paul Diacre* (Nijmegen 1961). J. SZÖVÉRFFY, *Die*

Annalen der lateinischen Hymnendichtung. Ein Handbuch, 2 v. (Berlin 1965–65) 1:186–189. K. GAMBER, ''Il sacramentario di Paolo Diacono: La redazione del Gelasiano s. VIII in Paria,'' *Rivista di storia della Chiesa iri Italia* 16 (1962): 412–438.

[C. M. AHERNE]

PAULA, ST.

Widow, ascetic; b. Rome, Italy, May 5, 347; d. Bethlehem, Palestine, Jan. 26, 404. She was born into a rich patrician and Christian family. At age 15 she married Toxotius, and they had five children: (St.) Eustochium, (St.) Blesilla, Paulina (the wife of the Senator (St.) PAMMACHIUS), Rufina, and Toxotius. A widow at age 31, Paula consecrated her household to an ascetical way of life together with similar groups of noble Roman women on the Aventine and Coelian hills in Rome. St. JEROME was their spiritual director. With Eustochium, she followed Jerome to the Orient in 385, visited Palestine and the monks of Nitria under his guidance, and in 386 settled in Bethlehem, where she used her wealth to construct a convent for nuns, a monastery for monks, and a guest house for pilgrims. There she devoted her life to works of charity and penance and to the study of the Scriptures, which Jerome says she knew by heart. Jerome wrote her eulogy (*Epist.* 108). Her granddaughter Paula, the daughter of her son Toxotius and Laeta Caecina, cared for Jerome in his old age.

Feast: Jan. 26.

Bibliography: *Acta Sanctorum* Jan. 3:326–337. F. LAGRANCE, *Histoire de sainte Paule* (8th ed. Paris 1931). G. DEL TON, *S. Paolo romana* (Milan 1950); F. L. CROSS, *The Oxford Dictionary of the Christian Church* (London 1957) 1035. F. X. MURPHY, ed., *A Monument to Saint Jerome* (New York 1952). D. GORCE, ed. and tr., *Vie de sainte Mélanie* (*Sources Chrétiennes* 90; 1962).

[F. X. MURPHY]

PAULICIANS

An Armenian dualist sect that apparently arose in the 7th century in reaction against hierarchical church organization. The name is first mentioned in the works of the Armenian Catholicos JOHN OF OTZUN and at the Synod of Dwin (719), but its origin is obscure. It comes from Paul; but it is not clear whether this is Paul, the son of the legendary Manichaean woman Kallinike—who sent her sons John and Paul to Armenia to spread the heresy and who is falsely identified with the followers of the 3rd-century heretic PAUL OF SAMOSATA—or St. PAUL, whom they held in high honor.

The Paulicians distinguished between the good God, the creator of souls and ruler of heaven, and the evil God, the ruler of the material universe. They rejected the Old Testament and parts of the New Testament, Baptism, the Eucharist, marriage, hierarchy, and cult, especially of the cross and pictures. They denied the reality of Christ's body and His Redemption and considered His teaching His most important work. The organization consisted of ''apostles'' and ''prophets'' who established the sect diversely, taking the names of disciples of St. Paul.

The first Paulician community was founded at Kibossa, near Colonia in Armenia, by Constantine of Mananali during the reign of the Emperor Constans II (641–668). Apostles who followed were Symeon or Titus, the Armenian Paul, his son Gegnesius or Timothy, Joseph or Epaphroditus, Zachary, Baanes, and Sergius or Tychicus. They founded congregations in Armenia and Pontus and gave them names of Pauline churches. A reformation within the sect itself resulted in division of the party into Sergites (the reformed sect) and Baanites (the old sect). Through his new schism Sergius strengthened the Paulicians, spreading the sect and concurrently fighting the Baanites.

Persecutions during the first half of the 9th century drove the Paulicians into alliance with the Saracen emir of Melitene, who joined them in their fight against the Byzantine emperor. Under the former Byzantine officer Karbeas (d. 863), and Chrysocheir (d. 872), they oppressed the whole of Anatolia until 872, when Tephrik, their headquarters, and other fortifications were destroyed.

The heretics continued to live throughout the empire, and groups that had been deported to Thrace founded a new military headquarters at Philippopolis from whence they terrorized their neighbors throughout the 9th and 10th centuries. The Emperor ALEXIUS I COMNENUS put an end to the heresy when in residence at Philippopolis. Yet traces of it were left: in Bulgaria the BOGOMIL sect, which spread to the West in the form of Manichaean heresies, lasted through the Middle Ages; and in Armenia there were derivative sects.

Bibliography: R. JANIN, *Dictionnaire de théologie catholique*, ed. A. VACANT et al. (Paris 1903–50) 12.1:56–62. H. G. J. BECK, *Lexikon für Theologie und Kirche*, ed. J. HOFER and K. RAHNER (Freiburg 1957–65) 8:205–206. F. L. CROSS, *The Oxford Dictionary of the Christian Church* (London 1957) 1035.

[E. D. CARTER]

PAULINE FATHERS AND BROTHERS

Popular name of the Society of St. Paul for the Apostolate of Communications (SSP, Official Catholic Directory #1020); founded, 1914, Alba, Italy, by Rev. James

Alberione as a religious congregation of priests and brothers engaged in the apostolate of bringing Christ to the world through the mass media and the internet. In the U.S., the society operates a publishing house (Alba House), in addition to St. Paul Publications. The generalate is in Rome.

[J. DUNN/EDS.]

PAULINE PRIVILEGE

The term used to express the right to dissolve the marriage bond, contracted between two unbaptized persons, after the baptism of one of the spouses and the refusal of the other spouse to cohabit peacefully. The term is based on the supposition that St. Paul grants this privilege in 1 Cor 7.12–15, but it is rather a privilege granted by the Church through a broader interpretation of the Pauline text than this in itself allows. Paul teaches here that the Christian convert from paganism should not use baptism as a pretext for divorcing an unbelieving spouse (μὴ ἀφιέτω); ''but if the unbeliever departs, let him depart (χωριζέσθω).'' The latter Greek verb refers merely to the desertion of the marital bed. When the Apostle adds in 1 Cor 7.15 that ''a brother or sister [i.e., a Christian man or woman] is not under bondage in such cases,'' he means that the convert need not oppose the desertion of the unbelieving spouse. But he nowhere expressly states that the marriage bond is dissolved by such desertion or that the convert is free to contract another marriage. However, since the 4th century the majority of Catholic commentators have interpreted 1 Cor 7.15 to mean that the marriage bond between two unbaptized persons is dissolvable when the unbaptized spouse refuses peaceful cohabitation with the baptized spouse, and that it is actually dissolved when the baptized spouse contracts a sacramental marriage.

See Also: MARRIAGE, LEGISLATION (CANON LAW).

Bibliography: P. DULAU, ''The Pauline Privilege: Is it Promulgated in the First Epistle to the Corinthians?'' *The Catholic Bible Quarterly* 13 (1951) 146–152.

[R. KUGELMAN]

PAULINUS OF AQUILEIA, ST.

Patriarch and theologian; b. Friuli, Italy, *c.* 750; d. January 11, 802. Widely renowned in northern Italy for his learning, Paulinus was called by CHARLEMAGNE (*c.* 776) to his court school, where he formed a lasting friendship with ALCUIN. By 787 he had written *Liber exhortationis* (*Patrologia Latina* 99:197–282) and *Paulinus Magister in tres epistulas Pauli ad hebraeos* (still in MS). In 787 Charlemagne appointed him patriarch of AQUILEIA, where he governed wisely and firmly. Remaining in contact with the Frankish court, he kept abreast of theological discussions on Spanish ADOPTIONISM and the insertion of the FILIOQUE in the Creed. Paulinus attended the synod of Aix-la-Chapelle in 789; the convocation of Regensburg, which condemned the adoptionism of Felix of Urgel (d. 818) in 792; and the synod of Frankfurt in 794, at which he drafted the *Libellus Sacrosyllabus* (*Patrologia Latina* 99:151–166), a condemnation of adoptionist errors. He convoked and presided over the provincial synod of Cividale in 796 or 797, which prescribed the addition of the filioque to the Creed and condemned Spanish adoptionism. He advised this assembly that the best answer to adoptionism was the Constantinopolitan Creed and insisted that his clergy memorize the text of it that he distributed to the synod, which is approximately that in use in the West today. At the bidding of Charlemagne, he wrote *Contra Felicem Urgellitanum libri tres* (*Patrologia Latina* 99:343–468). He sat at the Synod of Aix-la-Chapelle in 801, which procured a guarantee for free episcopal elections. In view of his theological writings, hymns, poems, and letters, and his zeal for the conversion of the AVARS, Paulinus deserved to be called *lux Ausoniae patriae.*

Feast: Jan. 28 (formerly Feb. 9 and Jan. 11).

Bibliography: *Patrologia Latina* 99:1–684. *Monumenta Germania Poetae* 1:123–148. *Monumenta Germania Epistolae* 4:516–527. C. GIANNONI, *Paulinus II, Patriarch von Aquileia* (Vienna 1896). G. ELLERO, *S. Paolino d'Aquil* (Cividale 1901). *Geschichte der lateinischen Literatur des Mittelalters* 1:368–370. J. REVIRON, *Dictionnaire de théologie catholique* 12.1:62–67. P. PASCHINI, *San Paolino patriarca e la Chiesa aquilei[e]se alla fine del secolo VIII* (Udine 1977). *Paulinus Aquileiensis Contra Felicem*, ed. CETEDOC (Turnhout 1990).

[J. M. O'DONNELL]

PAULINUS OF NOLA, ST.

Meropius Pontius Paulinus, bishop of Nola from 409 to 431, and man of letters; b. Bordeaux, France, *c.* 353; d. Nola, Campania, Italy, 431. He came of a rich and powerful family with extensive property in Aquitaine, Gallia Narbonensis, Nola, and probably also in Spain. Paulinus was placed under the special patronage of St. FELIX OF NOLA at an early age (*Carmen* 21. 348–350). He studied under Decimus Magnus Ausonius at Bordeaux and later corresponded with him in verse letters. At the age of 30, he had been consul (probably *consul suffectus*) and governor of Campania (*c.* 379) and had married Therasia, a wealthy Spanish woman of distinguished family.

Baptized at Bordeaux in 389, he settled near Barcelona, where his only child, a son Celsus, died eight days after birth. Soon both he and his wife adopted an ascetic mode of life and began distributing their goods to the poor. At Christmas in 395, despite his objections, he was ordained a priest, and in the following year he and his wife went to Nola, where he devoted himself to promoting the cult of St. Felix. About 409 Paulinus succeeded Paulus as bishop of Nola. Paulinus built or restored a number of churches dedicated to the cult of St. Felix and may well have been the first to use the bell in church. Of his episcopal administration little is known.

Paulinus wrote in both prose and verse. In prose, some 50 letters are extant, addressed to SULPICIUS SEVERUS, Bp. (St.) Delphinus of Bordeaux (instrumental in Paulinus's conversion, d. 404), AUGUSTINE, RUFINUS OF AQUILEIA, and others. Of them Goldschmidt said, ''His loquacity . . . spoils his lucidity,'' and ''not one of his contemporaries interlards his writings with so many Biblical quotations.''

Of his 35 poems, the most interesting are a series of *carmina natalicia* commemorating each year, from 395 to 407, the feast day of St. Felix on January 14. In these Paulinus shows considerable narrative skill. In one passage (*Carmen* 16.82) he describes how Felix escaped his persecutors when he slipped through a hole in an old wall and a spider promptly spun a web over the opening. In such passages there is a good sense of liveliness and verve.

Feast: June 22.

Bibliography: P. G. WALSH, tr., *Letters of St. Paulinus of Nola*, 2 v. (Westminster, Md. 1966–67); *The Poems of St. Paulinus of Nola* (New York 1975). W. VON HARTEL, ed. (*Corpus scriptorum ecclesiasticorum latinorum* 29, 30; 1894). B. ALTANER, *Patrology*, tr. H. GRAEF from 5th German ed. (New York 1960), 482–483. R. HELM, *Paulys Realenzyklopädie der klassischen Altertumswissenschaft*, ed. G. WISSOWA et al. 18.4 (1949) 2331–51. R. C. GOLDSCHMIDT, ed., *Paulinus' Churches at Nola* (Amsterdam 1940). P. FABRE, *Essai sur la chronologie de l'oeuvre de Saint Paulin de Nole* (Paris 1948); *Saint Paulin de Nole de l'amitié chrétienne* (Paris 1949). R. P. H. GREEN, *The Poetry of Paulinus of Nola* (Brussels 1971). J. T. LIENHARD, *Paulinus of Nola and Early Western Monasticism* (Cologne 1977), with annotated bibliography. K. KOHLWES, *Christliche Dichtung und stilistische Form bei Paulinus von Nola* (Bonn 1979). G. LUONGO, *Lo specchio dell'agiografo: S. Felice nei carmi XV e XVI di Paolino di Nola* (Naples 1992). F. CEPARANO and D. RUOCCO, eds., *I gigli di Nola* (Naples 1994). D. E. TROUT, *Paulinus of Nola: Life, Letters, and Poems* (Berkeley, Calif. 1999). C. CONYBEARE, *Paulinus Noster: Self and Symbols in the Letters of Paulinus of Nola* (New York 2000). R. COURCELLE, *Revue des études latines* 25 (1947) 250–280, and St. Jerome. F. MURPHY, *Revue des études augustiniennes* 2 (1956) 79–91, and Rufinus.

[M. P. CUNNINGHAM]

PAULINUS OF VENICE

Franciscan bishop, diplomat, and historian; b. Venice, *c.* 1274; d. Pozzuoli, late June 1344. He was *custos* of Venice (1304) and inquisitor in the March of Treviso (1305–07). He served from 1321 to 1326, as chaplain, apostolic penitentiary, and inquisitor under Pope JOHN XXII at Avignon. As inquisitor he was examiner of the famous *Liber secretorum fidelium crucis* by Marino Sanudo (d. *c.* 1343). Paulinus's diplomatic services were used by both the republic of Venice and the Holy See. Venice sent him as an intermediary to Robert of Naples in 1315–16 and again in 1321 when Robert was in Provence. Paulinus became a friend of this king and later, as bishop, his adviser. In 1322 John XXII sent Paulinus to Venice to persuade the republic to cease hostilities against Rimini, and then to Ferrara, which was in rebellion against the Holy See. In 1324 he was named bishop of Pozzuoli, but did not take possession of his see until 1326 because of his diplomatic activity. As a historian Paulinus developed the *Historiarum epitome* into the *Satyrica gestarum rerum regum atque regnorum* . . . , a world history from the creation to Emperor Henry VII (1308–13). This work, written between 1316 and 1322, has little historical value. It has wrongly been attributed to a certain Jordan. The *Chronologia magna,* a world history, is unimportant except for sections pertaining to the FRANCISCANS that have been published separately. His most significant work is the *Provinciale ordinis fratrum minorum,* a catalogue of Franciscan provinces, custodies, and convents. The best critical edition is by P. C. Eubel [Quaracchi 1892; an appendix in *Bullarium franciscanum,* 5 (1898) 579–602]. Between 1313 and 1315 Paulinus composed *De regimine rectoris* in the Venetian dialect. Its three parts treat of government of self, of the family, and of the republic. It has been edited by A. Mussafia, *Trattato de regimine rectoris di fra Paolino Minorita* (Vienna and Florence 1868).

Bibliography: K. EUBEL, ''Handschriftliches zur Chronik des sogen. Jordanus,'' *Historisches Jahrbuch der Görres-Gesellschaft* 14 (1893) 603–608. G. GOLUBOVICH, *Biblioteca bio-bibliografica della Terra Santa e dell'Oriente francescano,* 5 v. (Quaracchi-Florence 1906–23) v.2. J. H. SBARALEA *Supplementum et Castigatio ad scriptores trium ordinum S. Francisci a Waddingo* (Rome 1936) 2:307–308. A. GHINATO, *Fr. Paolino da Venezia* . . . (Rome 1951). L. SPÄTLING, *Lexikon für Theologie und Kirche* 2 8:210–211.

[J. J. SMITH]

PAULINUS OF YORK, ST.

Benedictine (?) monk, missionary to Northumbria, first bishop of York; d. Rochester, England, Oct. 10, 644. Probably while a monk of St. Andrew's monastery,

Paulist Press headquarters, Glen Rock, New Jersey.

Rome, he and others were sent by Pope GREGORY I THE GREAT in 601 to assist AUGUSTINE OF CANTERBURY in England. Nothing certain is known of his activities before his Northumbrian mission but possibly he worked among the East Angles. Consecrated bishop by Abp. JUSTUS OF CANTERBURY on July 21, 625, he went north as chaplain to ETHELBURGA, the Christian bride of King EDWIN OF NORTHUMBRIA. Once Edwin was converted two years later, Paulinus established his seat at YORK and then traveled extensively throughout the north, preaching and baptizing. This work was cut short by the death of his patron Edwin in the battle of Hatfield (632), and Paulinus, who withdrew to Kent, was given the vacant See of ROCHESTER. In 634 he received the PALLIUM from Pope HONORIUS I, but since he had already deserted York, a see for which the pope had intended metropolitan rank, it remains disputed whether Paulinus should be counted its first archbishop. He was buried at Rochester.

Feast: Oct. 10.

Bibliography: BEDE, *Ecclesiastical History* 2.9–20; 3.14. A. W. HADDAN and W. STUBBS, eds., *Councils and Ecclesiastical Documents Relating to Great Britain and Ireland,* 3 v. in 4 (Oxford 1869–78) 3:75–88. W. BRIGHT, *Chapters of Early English Church History* (3d ed. Oxford 1897). F. M. STENTON, *Anglo-Saxon England* (2d ed. Oxford 1947) 113–116.

[R. D. WARE]

PAULISTS

The Society of Missionary Priests of St. Paul the Apostle (CSP, Official Catholic Directory #1030), popularly known as the Paulist Fathers or the Paulists, is a canonically approved clerical society of apostolic life. Members are men, priests or those preparing for ordination to the priesthood, committed by promise to the apostolic mission of the community and to an evangelical life in common in support of that mission and for their own ongoing conversion as disciples. The mission of the Paulists to North America is focused on sharing Catholic faith and life with those outside of or not active in the Catholic community and engaging in a Catholic witness to and dialogue with modern society.

Origin. The Paulists were founded in New York City in 1858 by Reverend Isaac Thomas HECKER, in association with Augustine F. HEWITT, George DESHON, Francis BAKER, and, shortly thereafter, Clarence WALWORTH. All were priest converts to Catholicism in the antebellum period of social reform and religious revival in the United States. These men were drawn to the Catholic Church in the process of their own religious quests. They had then joined the REDEMPTORISTS at a time when that congregation in the United States was generally regarded as a German group dedicated to the care of German immigrants.

Hecker and his companions believed that their mission work would prosper and American vocations would increase if the congregation established an American house and addressed itself to the wider American public. Father Hecker went to Rome to plead the cause of such a new foundation before the Redemptorist major general. Misunderstanding and conflict over his intentions and his right to make the journey led to Hecker's expulsion from the Redemptorists. He appealed to the Holy See and, with the support of Cardinal Alessandro Barnabo, secured a decision from Pius IX granting the release of Hecker and his confreres from their Redemptorist vows, with the suggestion that they form a new American missionary community. Hecker himself became convinced that a new religious community was needed to help supply the wants of the Church in the United States and to carry the message of Catholicism to Americans and their society. He and his companions drew up a Programme of Rule that was approved by Archbishop John Hughes of New York. On July 10, 1858, the Paulists were founded, the first religious community of men begun in the United States. In place of vows of religion, they took solemn promises (which they regarded as binding as vows), committing themselves to the evangelical counsels and life in community. Stressing the personal guidance of the Holy Spirit, apostolic flexibility, and individual initiative, Hecker believed that in all their apostolic works the Paulists should be faithful to their distinctive mission, the conversion of America.

Early Development. In 1868, a general chapter greatly expanded and enlarged the Programme of Rule, which then became the official constitutions. Revised by succeeding chapters, these constitutions were submitted in 1925 and received final approval from the Holy See in 1940. They provided for regular General Chapters and a governing structure consisting of a Superior General with four Consultors. Father Hecker was elected as the first Superior General, holding office until his death in 1888. Father Hewitt succeeded him as Superior General, and then Father Deshon.

With the founding of the Paulists in 1858, the motherhouse of the community was established in New York City. This was also the site for the Paulist studentate until the opening of The CATHOLIC UNIVERSITY OF AMERICA in Washington, D.C., when the Paulists became the first religious community to establish a house on campus (1889). In 1914, they opened St. Paul's College, adjoining the campus. A separate novitiate was begun in 1923.

In conjunction with their motherhouse, the Paulists were entrusted with the establishment and pastoral care of St. Paul the Apostle Parish in New York. Parish missions across the United States and Canada, aimed not only at reviving the active practice of the faith by Catholics but also drawing others to the Catholic faith, were a central work of the community's apostolate. Hecker started the *Catholic World* in 1865 to bring the best of Catholic theological and literary work to the attention of educated American Catholics in order to better equip them for their role in the Catholic mission in America. In 1866, he began the Catholic Publication Society, the forerunner of the Paulist Press (1916), especially noted for widespread dissemination of pamphlets and other works of an educational and apologetic nature, aimed both at Catholics and other inquirers. The Apostolic Mission House (1902) was established in Washington, D.C., to provide training for diocesan clergy in missions to Catholics and non-Catholics. A parish and base for parish missions was taken on in San Francisco (1894).

Catholic and American. Father Hecker had brought to the foundation of the Paulists a deep appreciation for positive values in the spirit and institutions of the United States, along with a trenchant critique of the deficiencies of American society, defects which he believed could only be remedied by Christ's truth and grace embodied in Catholicism. The tension inherent in being both Catholic and American was intensified by the condemnation of AMERICANISM (1898), based in part on European interpretations of Hecker and related controversies in both Europe and America. The Paulists (along with Cardinal Gibbons and others) were strong in affirmation of their Catholic loyalty and denied that the condemned tendencies were theirs or present in the Catholic Church in the United States.

The next decades saw an expanded commitment of the Paulists to the institutions of North American Catholicism, establishing or taking charge of urban parishes (in Chicago, Portland, Toronto, Los Angeles, and other major cities), rural missions (especially in Tennessee) and the emerging ministry of the Newman apostolate at state and private colleges (at the University of California at Berkeley, the University of Texas at Austin, and University of California at Los Angeles, among the early Newman Clubs and Centers). The mission of promoting Catholic organizational unity and the Church's role and voice in American life was evident in the work of Monsignor John J. Burke, CSP, who was instrumental in the establishment of the National Catholic War Council during World War I and its successor organization, the National Catholic Welfare Conference. In 1922, the Paulists were entrusted with the pastoral care of Santa Susanna, the American parish in Rome.

St. Paul the Apostle Church, New York City.

Missionary Outreach. Through the middle decades of the twentieth century, the Paulist Fathers continued to develop ways of evangelizing beyond the Catholic community. Beginning in 1937, trailer missions went on the road throughout rural areas of the South and the Midwest. Catholic Information Centers were established in New York, Boston, Grand Rapids, Toronto, and additional sites, while most other Paulist parishes and Newman Centers offered regular classes for inquirers interested in Catholicism. The Paulist Radio Station WLWL broadcast from 1928 to 1935 and initial forays into television were begun in the 1950s. The community took on additional parishes and Newman Centers, most in predominantly non-Catholic areas, in the 1940s and 1950s, a trend that continued into the 1970s.

Post-Vatican II Developments. Following the call of the Second Vatican Council for the renewal of religious life, the Paulist Fathers Renewal Chapter (1967–68) produced an experimental constitution for the

Society which, after successive modifications, received approval from Rome in 1989. Quadrennial General Assemblies continued the traditional role of the general chapter. A President and General Council, elected by all members in final profession, constituted the community's governing body. The President is assisted by two of these Consultors on a full-time Presidential Board, meeting regularly with the other Consultors as a General Council.

Revend Thomas F. Stransky, CSP, was elected the first President of the Society (1970). He had served under Cardinal Augustin Bea, SJ, in the Secretariat for Christian Unity in Rome and brought with him an expertise in both missiology and ecumenism, areas central to the postconciliar mission of the Paulists. The new community Constitution committed the Paulists to the work of Christian unity and interreligious dialogue, along with the continued mission of invitation and welcome of individuals into the Catholic Church. The social justice dimension of evangelization was also clearly acknowledged. In light of the needs evident after Vatican II, the Paulists took a special interest in outreach to and reconciliation with Catholics who had been alienated from the Church. Parish missions were redeveloped, first to serve the needs of renewal immediately after the Council and then to promote evangelization and reconciliation outreach by parish communities. Information centers provided leadership in a number of dioceses in the transition from the traditional convert apostolate to the process of implementing the Rite of Christian Initiation of Adults. Reverend Alvin A. Illig, CSP, emerged as a North American leader in responding to the call for new Catholic evangelization efforts made by Paul VI in *EVANGELIUM NUNTIANDI* (1975). Father Illig founded the Paulist National Catholic Evangelization Association in 1977. The Paulist General Assembly of 1986 recommitted the Society to the threefold mission directions of evangelization, reconciliation, and ecumenism, emphasizing collaboration with the laity in these mission areas. The Paulists established a coordinating Office for Ecumenical and Interreligious Dialogue in 1999.

The Paulist Press undertook a wide variety of new publishing ventures in and after the 1960s. Parish renewal programs, biblical studies and spirituality series with an ecumenical appeal, works promoting Jewish-Christian and interreligious dialogue, and basic Catholic adult education materials constituted a major portion of the publications of the Paulist Press during these decades. Other Paulist media ministries spanned the spectrum of radio, television, video, film, and the internet. Paulist Productions (1968) brought a Catholic dimension to the television and movie industry. Paulist Communications (1970), later Paulist Media Works, produced and disseminated Catholic radio programs and assisted Catholic communities and institutions in their media efforts. This has evolved into helping religious organizations communicate through the internet. The Paulist Young Adults Ministry (2000), an attempt to reach a population segment often with tangential relations to the church, focused on internet communications as a key component of its wider outreach.

The postconciliar Paulist Constitution affirmed life in community, in established community houses, as central to Paulist life. Diverse efforts to renew the Paulist life of communal prayer and mutual support in discipleship and ongoing conversion were given further impetus by the Community Direction Statement of the 1994 Paulist General Assembly. Paulist Associates involved individuals and groups (largely of lay men and women) appropriating and living the charism of Fr. Hecker and the Paulists in their own contexts of family, work, and society. The Paulist Associates program was authorized by the 1998 General Assembly and implemented in the following year. Efforts by members of the Paulist Fathers and their Associates to return to the sources of the Paulist charism were significantly aided by the publication of *The Paulist Vocation* (2000), a new and greatly expanded edition of selected writings of Father Hecker.

Bibliography: J. MCSORLEY, *Isaac Hecker and His Friends* (New York 1952). V. F. HOLDEN, *The Yankee Paul: Isaac Thomas Hecker* (Milwaukee 1958). J. FARINA, *An American Experience of God: The Spirituality of Isaac Hecker* (New York 1981). D. J. O'BRIEN, *Isaac Hecker: An American Catholic* (New York 1992). *The Paulist Vocation*, revised and expanded (New York 2000).

[R. J. O'DONNELL]

PAULUS, NIKOLAUS

Church historian; b. Krautergersheim (Alsace), Dec. 6, 1853; d. Munich, Jan. 29, 1930. After theological studies in Strasbourg, he was ordained Aug. 4, 1878, and served as a curate until 1883. Because of sickness he had to withdraw from parochial work and settled near Munich, where he led the quiet life of a scholar until his death. He earned a doctorate in theology in 1896 at the University of Munich.

Paulus was first brought into contact with the Reformation period and the religious culture of the Middle Ages by his studies in the history of his Alsatian homeland. It was J. JANSSEN's work on the history of the German people that led him to devote all his efforts to a study of the Reformation period, especially of Luther's Catholic literary opponents until then neglected by scholars. In about 50 publications he saved a great number of these theologians from oblivion. With a genuine love for truth he sought to do justice to Luther's reputation, but he also helped to undo the legends about him: *Luthers Lebensende* (Frankfurt 1898); *Johann Tetzel, der Ablassprediger* (Mainz 1899); *Hexenwahn und Hexenprozess im 16. Jh.* (Frankfurt 1910); *Protestantismus und Toleranz im 16. Jh.* (Frankfurt 1911). His chief work, however, is *Geschichte des Ablasses im Mittelalter* (3 v. Paderborn 1922–23). Because of his search for the whole truth and his faithfulness to the facts, he prepared the way toward a new Catholic outlook on the Reformation.

Bibliography: L. PFLEGER, *Historisches Jahrbuch der Görres-Gesellschaft* 50 (1930) 205–226; *Nikolaus Paulus, ein Priester- und Gelehrtenleben, 1853–1930* (Kevelaer 1931). R. BÄUMER, *Lexikon für Theologie und Kirche*, ed. J. HOFER and K. RAHNER (Freiburg 1957–65) 8:235.

[E. ISERLOH]

PAULUS ALBARUS

Writer, polemicist and central figure in the ''voluntary martyr movement'' of mid-ninth century CORDOBA; b. probably between 800 and 815; d. probably in Cordoba, late 862 or early 863.

All that is known of Paulus Albarus has to be gleaned from his own writings and those of his close friend and confidant, the martyr EULOGIUS. The spelling of his cognomen is Albarus rather than the customary Alvarus. He was probably born in or around Cordoba. Nothing is known of his parents beyond the fact that his father made a donation to a monastery. Nor is it known if Paulus Albarus had brothers and sisters. He belonged to a well-to-do, land-owning family of uncertain prominence in Cordoban life. The honorific titles (Aurelius Flavius) that Paulus Alvarus and his friend, John of Seville, applied to each other in their letters are suggestive of those used by the Visigothic kings of Spain but may simply reflect friendly respect between equals. Other respectful terms (''illustrissimus'' or ''serenissimus'') were used in letters to Albar who only used such language in his correspondence with Romanus, a doctor and former high official in the Christian community (epistle 9).

Albarus's ancestry is uncertain. While debating with Bodo, a convert to Judaism, Albarus seems to indicate his own Jewish background (''I am a Hebrew both by faith and race.'' ep. 18.). This may be a metaphorical claim that Christians represented the fulfilment of God's covenant with Israel. As Albarus, who certainly attended a monastic school, reported that he did not know the Hebrew language, he is unlikely to have converted directly from Judaism. His claim to Gothic descent (ep. 20) is also very plausible.

As a boy, Albar was educated at the monastery of Abbot Speraindeo. There he met Eulogius, with whom he forged a life-long friendship based on their shared love of learning. Albar recalled with great affection his debates with Eulogius over points of Holy Scripture, which were continued by letter, in verse form, although as adults they wisely chose to destroy such juvenilia. The literary output of Albar is enriched with quotations from Holy Scripture, patristic writers, especially St. JEROME, and Spanish authors, especially St. ISIDORE. He was also familiar with non-Christian Latin authors. In some cases, it is clear that Albar's knowledge was derived at second-hand from St. Isidore. On his return from a journey to northern Spain in 848, Eulogius brought back books unknown in Cordoba, which introduced Albar to other Christian and pagan writers. Both Speraindeo and Eulogius showed respect for Albar's scholarship by submitting their own writings to him for criticism.

Unlike Eulogius, Albar was a married layman. In the preface to his *Vita Eulogii,* Albar contrasts the priestly status of Eulogius with his own. Greetings in John of Seville's letters to ''the adornment of your household'' and ''the beauty of your household'' are, undoubtedly, references to Albar's wife (and, possibly, daughters). Even less certainly, the death of ''trium ancillarum vestrum,'' which drew sympathetic comment from John of Seville, may refer to servants rather than daughters.

Between 840 and 860, Albar was the outstanding figure in Latin literary culture in Cordoba. Apart from an indication that he had practiced law, Albar does not appear to have held any civil or ecclesiastical post. This may have permitted him the leisure to pursue his intellectual interests and develop impressive skills in Latin composition, which included the writing of verse. It also suggests that he was a man of independent financial means.

The start of Albar's known literary activity is his correspondence with Bodo-Eleazar. There are seven letters (four by Albar and three, badly conserved, by Bodo-Eleazar), with one clearly dated to 840. In 838, Bodo, a deacon, left the German imperial court to go on a pilgrimage to Rome. On his way there, for unknown reasons, Bodo converted to Judaism, married a Jewish woman and changed his name to Eleazar. He travelled on to Cordoba where he began to urge the Muslim authorities to persecute Christians and is last heard of in 847. It is noteworthy that Albar, a layman, should try to win back Bodo-Eleazar for Christianity and prove that Christ was the true Messiah. Albar's correspondence becomes increasingly abusive in response to what he regarded as Bodo-Eleazar's provocation. The letters show the state of Christian-Jewish polemic and the bitter tone of medieval disputes between the faiths.

An undated pair of letters to Abbot Speraindeo, Albar's former teacher, probably belongs to the period before 853. Albar described the errors into which some had fallen and asked Speraindeo to write a treatise refuting them (ep.7).

A group of six undated letters make up Albar's correspondence with his friend John of Seville, another educated layman with literary tastes (ep.1–6). Albar's use of citations from Virgil's *Aeneid* and St. Augustine's *City of God,* works only known in Cordoba after Eulogius's return from northern Spain in 848, suggests that the letters should be dated between 848 and 851, when the Muslim persecution began.

Albarus and Eulogius were central figures in the voluntary martyr movement that convulsed Cordoba in the mid-ninth century. A disparate group of Christians challenged Muslim authorities in Cordoba by the public denunciation of Muḥammad or by the breaking of Islamic law, actions that carried the death penalty. Between 851 and 859, 49 Christians are reported to have been executed by the Muslim authorities. Their actions also caused a split in the Christian community between those who supported open resistance and those who wished to avoid a confrontation with the ruling power. In 859, the execution of Eulogius, who is the principal source for these events, seems to mark an end to the martyr movement.

Neither Albar nor Eulogius originated the martyr movement although each gave it his full support. They shared a concern at the rising rate of conversion to Islam and at the increasing adoption of Arabic culture among the Christian community. Their solution was a self-conscious attempt to revive Latin letters, looking back to a Visigothic past and drawing especially on Isidoran writings, as an emblem of Christian identity for a community under threat. While Eulogius's writings dealt esentially with the passions of the Cordoban martyrs, Albar's defended them against their Christian detractors and made a direct attack on Islam.

Little is known of Albar during the decade of the persecutions. He seems to have had a direct acquaintance with few of the martyrs. While he championed their actions, Albar does not appear to have incited them. In his only recorded conversation with a would-be martyr, Albar's cautionary words are heard and then rejected by Aurelius (*Memoriale Sanctorum II,* 10). Neither Albar nor Eulogius presented himself as a voluntary martyr. Although Eulogius was to be martyred in 859, Albar's writings, in line with his advice to Aurelius, show no self-reproach for not sharing his friend's martyrdom. In 854, Albar produced the *Indiculus Luminosus,* his most ambitious work. It followed two lines: attacking Christian critics of the martyrs and arguing that Muḥammad fulfilled some of the prophecies of ANTICHRIST. Albar promised a second book which would gather the judgements of the DOCTORS OF THE CHURCH to support his view. This has not survived or, more probably, was not written.

Albar corresponded with Eulogius, giving moral support during his time of imprisonment in 851. Eulogius, in turn, sent Albar two works, the *Memoriale Sanctorum* and the *Documentum Martyriale,* for approval. Soon after Eulogius's execution in 859, Albar wrote the *Vita Eulogii.* It celebrated his friend's life and death, treating him as a saint. He also composed poetry in honour of Eulogius.

From the evidence of epistles 9 to 13 of his collected letters, Albar's final years seem to have been dogged by poverty and sickness. Around 861 he fell dangerously ill and received the sacrament of penance. On recovering, he was obliged to do public penance and abstain from the Eucharist. In his letters to Bishop Saul of Cordoba, Albar made typically forceful requests to be allowed to take Holy Communion. There may be undertones of an earlier confrontation over the martyrs but Bishop Saul refused Albar's demands (epp. 11–13). At this time, Albar wrote his *Confessio*, which was not a personal confession but a short treatise on penance. This outstanding figure of the Cordoban Church slipped into an obscure death by 862 or early 863.

In 961, Bishop Reccemund wrote a calendar, dedicated to Caliph al-Hakam (961–976), in which he listed the liturgical feasts that had been celebrated at Cordoba in the previous century. For November 7, it names the feast of Albar (*In ipso est festum Albari in Cordubam*).

Bibliography: Writings by Paulus Albarus. Collection of 20 letters between Albar and five other known men: Bodo/Eleazar (7), John of Seville (6), Bishop Saul (3), Abbot Speraindeo (2), Romanus the doctor (1) and a letter without identification; *Indiculus Luminosus*; *Vita Eulogii*; *Confessio*; 11 poems, following in style and content late Visigothic models, representing virtually all of the surviving material from Christian Cordoban writing of his day. Modest in quality, they were the fruit of Eulogius's attempt to revive Latin letters. Sources. J. GIL, *Corpus Scriptorum Muzarabicorum,* v. 1 (Madrid 1973). E. P. COLBERT, *The Martyrs of Cordoba* (Washington, DC 1962). R. COLLINS, *Early Medieval Spain; Unity in Diversity, 400–1000* (London 1995). C. M. SAGE, *Paul Albar of Cordoba* (Washington, DC 1943). K. B. WOLF, *Christian Martyrs in Spain* (Cambridge 1988).

[J. WREGLESWORTH]

PAULUS DE LIAZARIIS

Canonist; b. probably at Bologna, toward the end of the 13th century; d. Bologna, Feb. 8, 1356. He studied at the University of Bologna, numbering among his teachers JOANNES ANDREAE, and received his doctorate in both civil and canon law. Married three times (last in 1349), he had three children. He taught at the University of Bologna until 1321 when, in violation of the university statutes, he went to teach at Siena. In 1325 he left Siena to teach at Perugia, but by 1333 he was again teaching at Bologna. He headed a legation to Benedict XII at Avignon in 1338. His most famous work was the *Lectura super Clementinas,* written probably at Perugia and completed before 1330. It is often cited by later writers. He wrote also *Casus summarii* or *Epitome Clementinarum.*

Bibliography: J. F. VON SCHULTE, *Die Geschichte der Quellen und der Literatur des kanonischen Rechts* (Graz 1956) 2:246–247. G. ERMINI, *Storia della Università di Perugia* (Bologna 1947) 138–139. S. KUTTNER, ''The *Apostillae* of Johannes Andreae on the Clementines,'' in *Études d'histoire du droit canonique dédiées à Gabriel LeBras,* 2 v. (Paris 1965).

[C. M. ROSEN]

PAULUS EUERGETINOS

Eleventh-century Byzantine monk and ascetical writer; d. Constantinople, April 16, 1054. Paulus is known as the founder of the monastery of Euergetis near Constantinople (1048) and for the collection of ascetical writings (*Paterikon*) that he prepared for his monks known as his *Synagoge.* It consists of 50 chapters divided into four books, so ordered as to provide an ascetical education in godliness for the members of the monastery. The collected texts include selections from almost all the ascetical literature of the early Church from the vita of St. Anthony by Athanasius to the dialogues of St. Gregory I. It makes no pretense at original considerations but is a reelaboration. Its principal sources are a *Gerontikon* that is identical with the so-called *Alphabeticon Coteliers* and a collection of *anonyma.* These sources account for seven-eighths of the *Synagoge.* A *Horologion* also contains a homily on the Mother of God attributed to Paulus.

Bibliography: H. G. BECK, *Kirche und theologische Literatur im byzantinischen Reich* (Munich 1959) 587. S. VAILHÉ, *Échos d'Orient* 7 (1904) 268–276. *Bibliotheca hagiographica Graeca,* ed. F. HALKIN (Brussels 1957) 3:1450s–50z. W. BOUSSET, *Apophthegmata,* ed. T. HERMANN and G. KRÜGER (Tübingen 1923) 15–18.

[F. CHIOVARO]

PAVILLON, NICOLAS

Jansenistic reform bishop of Alet in Languedoc; b. Paris, Nov. 17, 1597; d. Alet, Dec. 8, 1677. For five years he was a coworker with St. VINCENT DE PAUL, who recommended him to Richelieu for the See of Alet in 1637. His asceticism attracted him to the Jansenists of Port-Royal, whom he openly favored after Vincent's death. He was one of four bishops who, contrary to the order of Alexander VII, refused to sign the formula of 1653 condemning five propositions that summed up the doctrine of JANSEN. The bishops urged the distinction that the Church is infallible in matters of right, but not in matters of fact. Pavillon signed the compromise formula of Clement IX in 1668, although he clearly indicated verbally his distinction between right and fact. His insistence on episcopal prerogatives appears also in his refusal, together with Bishop CAULET, to sign the declaration of Louis XIV on the Droit de Régale in 1673. Pavillon's main theological treatises favor Jansenism. His Jansenistic *Rituel d'Alet* (1667) was condemned by Clement IX but was used in Alet and other dioceses. There is no edition of his complete works. Manuscripts are scattered in French libraries. The *Oeuvres* of ARNAULD (v.36, 37) contain documents relating to Pavillon.

Bibliography: E. DEJEAN, *Un prélat indépendant au XVII e siècle* (Paris 1909). J. CARREYRE, *Dictionnaire de théologie catholique,* ed. A. VACANT et al. (Paris 1903–50) 12:77–79. P. BROUTIN, *La réforme pastorale en France au XVII e siècle* (Paris 1956). H. WEBER, *Lexikon für Theologie und Kirche*, ed. J. HOFER and K. RAHNER (Freiburg 1957–65) 8:237.

[J. J. SMITH]

PAX CHRISTI INTERNATIONAL

Pax Christi International, an international Catholic organization for promotion of world peace, was formed in March 1945 by a French Catholic laywoman, Madame Dortel-Claudot, and Bishop Pierre Theas of Montaubon. Its original objective was to promote reconciliation between the French and Germans, initially, through an apostolate of prayer. It soon expanded its vision to peace among all nations. The organization received encouragement in 1947 from Pope Pius XII. By 1950 it had grown into an international federation of European groups with its headquarters in Fribourg, Switzerland, and later moved to Paris. Cardinal Maurice Feltin, Archbishop of Paris, was its first international president. Its objective was ''the unity and pacification of the world through the promotion of international order based on the natural law and on the justice and charity of Christ.'' Pax Christi was a significant inspiration for Vatican II's teaching of the right to conscientious objection and of its condemnation of nuclear war. It has promoted a wider understanding of the social teaching of popes John XXIII, Paul VI, and John Paul II whereby peace, grounded in justice and directed by charity, must be further based on a just economic development of poorer nations. In 1965 its headquarters moved to the Netherlands under the presidency of Cardinal Alfrink, and in 1978 to Belgium under the secretariat of Etienne de Jhonge. Pax Christi has been active in peacemaking in Northern Ireland, Poland, South Africa, East Timor, and the Middle East. In 1983 it received the UNESCO Peace Prize, and in 1987, the UN Peace Messenger Award. In the midst of the Vietnam War, Pax Christi USA was established in 1972 as an affiliate of Pax Christi. In a development of Pax Christi's original broader mission, Pax Christi USA promotes a gospel-inspired non-violence: ''Pax Christi USA commits itself to peace education and, with the help of its bishop members, promotes the gospel imperative of peacemaking as a priority in the Catholic church in the United States.'' Two American bishops were its first moderators, Carroll T. Dozier (d. 1985) of Memphis and Thomas J. Gumbleton of Detroit. By 2000, membership in Pax Christi USA had grown to more than 11,500 members, including more than 120 bishops.

[D. P. SHERIDAN]

PAYNE, PETER

Wyclifite, Hussite; b. Hough-on-the-Hill, near Grantham, England, *c.* 1380; d. Prague, 1455. He was the son of a French father and an English mother and graduated from Oxford by 1406. There he had become converted to Wyclif's heresies through the efforts of a few remaining LOLLARDS. Not being a man to keep his beliefs to himself, Payne wrote letters to John HUS and the Bohemian reformers in 1406, praising the character and orthodoxy of John WYCLIF, and managed to attach the university's seal to them. The ensuing furor prompted Abp. Thomas ARUNDEL to investigate orthodoxy in the university. The university resisted Arundel's invasion of its privileges but had no desire to protect heresy. A university committee examined Payne but found him free of heresy. He then became principal of St. Edmund's College (1411–13). He was soon engaged in controversy with the mendicants. Faced with an oath of orthodoxy in 1413, he fled England for the more congenial atmosphere of Prague (1415). There, for 40 years, he played a very prominent part in the religio-political disputes that wracked Bohemia. Payne drifted more and more to the extreme reformist position of the TABORITES, whom he represented at the Council of BASEL. After rejecting the settlement proposed at Basel, he became rector of the HUSSITE monastery of Emaus in Prague and a supporter of John of Rokycana.

Bibliography: T. GASCOIGNE, *Loci e libro veritatum* (Oxford 1881). K. B. MCFARLANE, *John Wycliffe and the Beginnings of English Nonconformity* (New York 1953). A. B. EMDEN, *A Biographical Register of the University of Oxford to A.D. 1500* (Oxford 1957–59) 3:1441–43.

[J. E. HEALEY]

PÁZMÁNY, PÉTER

Cardinal, archbishop of Esztergom, often called Hungary's second apostle because of his leadership of the COUNTER REFORMATION; b. Nagyvárad, Oct. 4, 1570; d. Pozsony (now Bratislava, Slovakia), March 19, 1637. He was born of a noble Protestant family, but his Catholic stepmother and the first Hungarian Jesuit, István SZÁNTÓ, brought him into the Catholic Church when he was 13. At the age of 17 he entered the Society of Jesus (JESUITS) at Kolozsvár (Transylvania) and he was an outstanding student at the universities of Cracow, Vienna, and Rome. He taught philosophy and theology at the University of Graz, Austria (1597–1607), and then at the request of Hungary's primate, Cardinal Francis Forgách, he returned to his homeland. As the primate's counselor, he became the chief promoter of Catholic restoration. Pázmány wrote about 40 books in both Latin and Hungarian, of which *As Isteni Igazságra Vezérlő Kaulauz* (1613, ''A Guide to the Divine Truth,'' since 1637 known as *Hodoegus*) is the most important; all his works are apologetic and polemical. His translation of Kempis's *IMITATION OF CHRIST* and his sermons, characterized by a matchless vigor of speech, led 30 noble families and whole communities to the Church. His masterly prose style set a standard unmatched for three centuries. In 1616, after Cardinal Forgách's death, King Matthias, with the approval of Pope Paul V, appointed Pázmány archbishop of Esztergom, and in 1629 Urban VIII made him a cardinal. He founded the Pazmaneum in Vienna (1623), for the education of the clergy, and the University of Nagyszombathely (1635), now the University of Budapest. In his political views, despite severe criticism, Pázmány was faithful to the Hapsburg kings, seeing them as the defenders of Christianity against the Turks.

Bibliography: *Opera omnia: Series latina,* 6 v. (Budapest 1894–1904); *Ungarische Serie,* 7 v. (Budapest 1894–1905); *Epistolae collectae,* 2 v. (Budapest 1910–11). J. KORNIS, *Le Cardinal Pázmány, 1570–1637* (Paris 1937). S. SÍK, *Pázmány* (Budapest 1939). N. ÖRY, *Doctrina Petri Cardinalis Pázmány de notis ecclesiae* (Chieri 1952).

[O. J. EGRES]

PAZZI

Merchant and banking family of FLORENCE, for which there are records from the late 12th century. Members of the family held offices in the government; its bank with several branches was second only to the MEDICI bank. Brunelleschi designed the new palace and built the handsome chapel (both still standing) for *Andrea* and his eldest son, *Jacopo. Piero,* another son, was one of the learned men in the city. Their nephew *Guglielmo* married

Bianca, sister of Lorenzo de' Medici. The Pazzi were part of the unsuccessful 1478 conspiracy led by Girolamo Riario, nephew of Pope Sixtus IV, against the Pazzi family rivals, the Medici. Giuliano de' Medici was killed, but Lorenzo survived. Disgrace, executions, and confiscation of properties followed for the Pazzi family. Early in the 16th century, however, the Pazzi began to serve in the government again. In later generations two members brought renown. Mary Magdalene de' PAZZI, a Carmelite nun, was canonized in 1669. Giangirolamo Pazzi (1681–1743) was a member of several academies, a translator, and the founder of the *Società Colombaria.*

Bibliography: P. LITTA, et al., *Famiglie celebri italiane,* 14 v. (Milan 1819–1923) v.11. L. PASTOR, *The History of the Popes from the Close of the Middle Ages* (London-St. Louis 1938–61) 4:300–312, 512–515. *Acta Sanctorum* May 6:175–348. VESPASIANO DA BISTICCI, *Vite di uomini illustri del secolo XV,* ed. P. D'ANCONA and E. AESCHLIMANN (Milan 1951). F. MORANDINI, "Il conflitto fra Lorenzo . . . Sisto IV," *Archivio-storico italiano* 107 (1950) 113–154. A. POLIZIANO, *Della congiura dei Pazzi* (Padua 1958).

[M. L. SHAY]

PAZZI, MARIA MADDALENA DE', ST.

Carmelite mystic; b. Florence, Italy, Apr. 2, 1566; d. there, May 25, 1607. She was born of a noble family, the daughter of Camillo de' Pazzi and Maria di Lorenzo Buondelmonti, and was given the name Catherine at her Baptism. Precociously pious, she learned to meditate at the age of nine from the family confessor, the Jesuit Andrea Rossi. She was less than ten years old when she made her first Communion, one month after which she made a vow of virginity. She attended school, first as a day student (1574–78) and then as a boarder (1580–81), at the monastery of S. Giovanni dei Cavalieri, where, with the help of the sisters and the nearby Jesuits, she completed the solid spiritual formation begun in the family and revealed her desire to become a nun.

The CARMELITE convent in Florence, S. Maria degli Angeli (founded in 1474), attracted her because of its privilege of daily Holy Communion. In August of 1582 she sought admission and spent the customary ten-day probationary period in the convent. On December 1 she was received as a postulant, taking the name Maria Maddalena (Mary Magdalene), and the following Jan. 30, 1583, she entered the novitiate. A year later she became critically ill, and in spite of the best medical treatment she seemed at the point of death. On Trinity Sunday, May 27, 1584, her superiors allowed her to make her profession *in articulo* in a private ceremony on a cot in the chapel. It marked the beginning of extraordinary ecstatic experiences whose number, intensity, and variety were to gain her the title of the Ecstatic Saint.

Immediately after the profession, she fell into an ecstasy that lasted about two hours and was repeated after Holy Communion on the following 40 mornings. These ecstasies were rich experiences of union with God and marvelous insights into divine truths. Visions and locutions, as well as the symbolic mystical graces, such as the exchange of hearts or the invisible stigmata, abounded within them. Similar transports but without the insensibility of ecstasy, "excesses of love," in which she talked and moved about, likewise began to occur. As a safeguard against deception and to preserve the revelations, the convent confessor, Agostino Campi, directed her to dictate her experiences to sister secretaries, who would also write down what they observed. This is the origin of the works of Mary Magdalene de' Pazzi. Over the next six years, five large volumes were filled. The books were properly attested by witnesses and approved by ecclesiastical authorities and theologians. They are preserved in the archives of the convent now called the convent of S. Maria Maddalena de' Pazzi in Florence.

Book 1, called *The Forty Days,* covers the first period from May 27 to July 26, 1584, and includes intermittent ecstasies until August 15. Book 2, *The Colloquies,* records experiences between Christmas of 1584 and the following July 4, 1585. However, Pentecost week, June 8 to 16, 1585, is recorded separately in Book 3, *Revelations and Intelligences.* This week was a preparation for a severe, five-year trial that began on Trinity Sunday. Book 4, *The Probation,* records this trial, which lasted until 1590. After this time ecstasies were less frequent. The majority occurred in the two-year period (1584–86). The final volume, Book 5, *The Renovation of the Church,* recounts only one ecstasy but includes 12 letters concerning reform and renewal that were dictated in July and August of 1586 and were directed to important personages in the Church (and apparently never delivered to them).

One other literary work remains, the so-called *Admonitions* (manuscript title: *Ammaestramenti, avvisii, e ricordi della Madre Beata Maria Maddelena,* Arch. Monast., Pal IV, N. 57 and 65; pub. as *Avvertimenti et avvisi . . . ,* 1669). This is a collection of her sayings and owes its existence to the pedagogical roles she fulfilled in the convent. Beginning in 1589 she was either assistant novice mistress or instructor of the young; in 1598 she became novice mistress, and in 1604, subprioress. Although her vocation was a contemplative one of love and suffering for the Church, her own capable novice mistress and prioress throughout her convent life, Mother Evangelista del Giocondo, saw to it that Mary Magdalene de' Pazzi collaborated in the formation of the young. Her disciples showed their appreciation by collecting the lessons they learned and preserving them as a last testament. She died at the age of 41, was beatified by URBAN IV, on May

8, 1626, and canonized by CLEMENT IX, on April 28, 1669.

Mary Magdalene de' Pazzi has been a popular saint, especially in her native Italy. Two contemporary biographies, those of V. Puccini and V. Cepari, SJ, and the publication of her writings (however uncritical and truncated the published editions to date have been) have given rise to an abundant devotional literature concerned with her. But until the mid-twentieth century there were only a few scientific studies of her life or her spiritual doctrine. The publication in the 1960s of the original texts of her works should lead to better studies of her life and work. The style of the writings is a hindrance: it is baroque, pedantic, excessively allegorical, and repetitious. But this poor vehicle conveys a rich doctrinal spirituality that is Trinitarian, Christological, and especially Eucharistic. Her teaching is preeminently liturgical and ecclesial.

Feast: May 25 (formerly May 29).

Bibliography: *Tutte le opere di Santa Maria Maddalena de' Pazzi dai manoscritti originali,* ed. F. NARDONI (Florence 1960–1966). F. BAERTIUS and C. JANNINGUS, *Acta Sanctorum* May 6 (1866): 175–348. ERMANNO DEL SSMO. SACRAMENTO, ''I manoscritti originali di S. Maria Maddalena de' Pazzi,'' *Ephemerides Carmeliticae* 7 (1956): 323–400. M. MINIMA, *Seraph among Angels: The Life of St. Mary Magdalene de' Pazzi,* ed. and tr. G. N. PAUSBACK (Chicago 1958). S. THOR-SALVIAT, *Secrets of a Seraph: The Spiritual Doctrine of St. Mary Magdalene de' Pazzi*, ed. and tr. G. W. PAUSBACK (Downers Grove, Ill. 1961). *Portrait of a Seraph; a Pictorial Life of Saint Mary Magdalen de' Pazzi*, tr. G. N. PAUSBACK (Fatima, Portugal 1965). B. SECONDIN, *Santa Maria Maddalena de' Pazzi: esperienza e dottrina* (Rome 1974). A. MAGGI, *Uttering the Word: The Mystical Performances of Maria Maddalena de' Pazzi* (Albany, N.Y. 1998).

[E. E. LARKIN]

PEACE

A state of untroubled tranquility between persons (social) or within an individual's own self (personal). Social peace is dealt with under other headings; this article is concerned only with peace in the personal sense. So understood, it is the tranquil composure of soul that an individual experiences in the absence of a strong conflict of urge or desire between different elements of his own being.

The positive basis of such peace, theologically speaking, is the virtue of CHARITY. In one who has charity the functionings of all the appetites are united in a constant effort of love toward the ultimate point of focus that is God, the Supreme GOOD. This causes a unity of desire within the individual and eliminates the strife or contention that exists when there is contrariety of desire. Peace postulates order or harmony of conation, whereas conflict is always devisive. One cannot have internal peace if he is torn within himself between good and evil desires; such conflicts make personal peace impossible.

Personal peace, since it is based upon or is an effect of charity, can be had only by one who is in the state of sanctifying grace. In other words, there can be no true internal peace except when the appetite is directed to a true good, for an evil object or action, though it may have the appearance of good and thus be able to satisfy the appetite in some respects, nevertheless has many defects, which cause the appetite to remain restless and disturbed. Moreover, even a total dedication to evil could not produce a true peace in a wicked man because evil, unlike good, is not a unifying principle. The completely evil man, if such were possible, would remain a victim of conflict between his evil desires. Thus the peace of the wicked is not true peace, but at most a counterfeit of it (cf. Thomas Aquinas, *Summa Theologiae* 2a2ae, 29.2 ad 3).

Although the highest and most genuine personal peace is the consequence of a perfect unity of desires made cohesive by charity and thus directed, at least implicitly, to the Supreme Good, a lesser degree of peace is possible when the intellect and will control and curb the irrational impulses that spring spontaneously from the sense appetite and that would issue in sin if indulged. The occurrence of such impulses indicates a measure of division within a man, but not on the rational or moral level.

Although charity causes peace in the individual by uniting all his desires in the love of God above all else, it also brings about the peace of the individual in relation to other men, insofar as in loving his neighbor as himself, he wishes in some manner at least to fulfill his neighbor's will as though it were his own (*Summa Theologiae* 2a2ae, 29.3). The will of his neighbor thus becomes part of the unity of a man's own desires.

Although peace is directly the work of the essential unitive force of charity, indirectly it is also ''the work of justice'' (Is 32.17), insofar as justice removes obstacles to peace, for example, the possible conflict of wills concerning the rights that should be conceded to another.

True peace can be either perfect or imperfect. Perfect peace is achieved in the eternal beatitude, which will unite all of a man's desires by giving them permanent rest in one object. Only imperfect peace is possible in this life; for although a person may habitually have his will united to God in love and thus enjoy basic peace within himself, still his will is free and he may fall from grace. Moreover, there are many other things and situations, both within man and external to him, that can disrupt his essential peace and make it imperfect, e.g., the constant threat that his senses and emotions may escape the control of his will or the opposition to virtue of wicked men with which he has to contend (*Summa Theologiae* 2a2ae, 29.2 ad 4).

Peace is implicitly listed among the beatitudes enunciated by Christ: ''Blessed are the peacemakers, for they shall be called the children of God'' (Mr 5.9). It is also one of the fruits of the Holy Spirit (Gal 5.23).

Bibliography: T. AQUINAS, *Summa Theologiae* 1a2ae, 69.3; 2a2ae, 29, 37, 38, 39; *C. gent.* 3.34. E. SCHICK and A. AUER, *Lexikon für Theologie und Kirche,* ed. J. HOFER and K. RAHNER, 10 v. (2d, new ed. Freiburg 1957–65) 4: 361–363. B. H. MERKELBACH, *Summa theologiae moralis* (Paris 1949) 1:920, 954. W. R. FARRELL, *Companion to the Summa,* 4 v. (New York 1932–42) 3:104–106, 118–121.

[P. C. CURRAN]

PEACE (IN THE BIBLE)

The Hebrew word for peace, *šālôm,* translated in the Septuagint most often by the Greek word, *eirēnē,* has a wide semantic range including the notions of totality or completeness, success, fulfillment, wholeness, harmony, security and well being.

Peace in the OT. The most comprehensive description of shalom is a cosmic order ordained by God through creation (Gn 1) and established with God's people in the covenant (Ex 20–23). In this cosmic order each part finds its meaning and function as it conforms to God's purpose. Shalom describes the ''realm where chaos is not allowed to enter'' (Hanson, 347), chaos being understood as sickness, war, social strife, or the violation of the covenant.

Peace can result from military victory (Jgs 8:9), or from diplomacy (Est 9:30; 10:3). The phrase ''to ask the peace'' (2 Kgs 9:11, 19; cf. Dt 20:10), often serving as more than a common greeting, signals the process of initiating negotiation, whereas ''go in peace'' (Jgs 18:6; 1 Sm 20:13; 2 Sm 15:9) functioning as more than a farewell, appears to be used predominantly ''as the *conclusio* of successful negotiations'' (Wiseman, 323).

As the Hebrew Scriptures frequently attest, peace in its fullness is possible because Yahweh is its source and the giver of peace to others (Lv 26:6; Ps 29:11; 122.8; Is 26:12; Ez 34:25; Zec 8:12). In the well-known Aaronic blessing, ''The Lord look upon you kindly and give you peace'' (Nm 6:20), peace is associated with God's presence. There is no peace for the wicked (Is 48:22), but the one who keeps God's law has great peace (Ps 119:165). Frequently peace and righteousness are linked together (Ps 72:7; 85:10; Is 9:7; 48:18). Those who proclaimed peace when injustice and greed prevailed were berated by the prophets (Jer 6:14; 8:11; Est 13:16). In the ''covenant of shalom'' (Nm 25:12; Is 54:10; Ez 34:25; 37:26), peace is experienced as the result of living in fidelity to the covenantal stipulations. During the period of the monarchy, Israel's kings hastened the return of chaos as they abandoned trust in Yahweh, relying instead on the strength of their armies. Peace comes to the nation that trusts in God (Is 26:3).

After the collapse of the Southern Kingdom, at the time of the Exile, the restoration of Shalom was announced. The era of shalom would encompass the whole world with its center in Zion (Is 60–61). The coming of the day of salvation is linked with the Prince of Peace (Is 9:6–7), who is God's anointed (Is 61:1). Peace became the mark of the awaited Messianic kingdom and is announced along with salvation by its heralds (Is 52:7).

New Testament. The term *eirēnē* occurs in all the NT writings except 1 John, appearing most often in Luke-Acts, Romans, and Ephesians. Occasionally, *eirēnē* is used in its classical sense to designate a condition of law and order or the absence of war, as experienced, e.g., during the *Pax Romana* (Mt 10:34 par; Lk 11:21; 14:32; Acts 12:20; 24:2; Rv 6:4). Usually, however, the term is used to refer to the experience of salvation that comes from God or the harmonious relationships between persons.

In Luke-Acts Jesus is proclaimed as the one who brings ''peace on earth,'' understood as salvation for (not from) the world (2:14), and who guides others ''into the way of peace'' (1:79). In fact, peace is used as term for salvation (7:50; 8:48). It is a peace that Jerusalem (the ''city of peace'') unfortunately has failed to understand (19:45) because it failed to recognize its ''king'' of peace.

The disciples are instructed to have peace among themselves, i.e., to form a community of peace (Mk 9:50) and to seek reconciliation among themselves before worship when the communal peace has been disturbed (Mt 5:23–26; 18:15–20). They are sent on mission to bring peace, but only the person receptive to God's salvation receives it; those who are non-receptive come under God's judgement (Mt 10:13 pa.; cf. Acts 10:36). Those who decide against Jesus can expect not peace but the sword (Mt 10:34–36 par).

In John's Gospel, the ''world'' is portrayed as a hostile place neither able to give, nor easily receptive to the peace that already exists between Jesus and his disciples (Jn 14:27; 16:33). Accompanying the gift of the Spirit is the risen Jesus' gift of peace (Jn 20:19, 21, 26), a gift that drives out fear.

In the Pauline letters, the reconciling love of God in Christ (Rom 5:6–11) has bestowed justification upon believers, resulting in ''peace with God'' (Rom 5:1; *see* Col

1:20; Eph 2:11–22). Those who live according to the Spirit know peace (Rom 8:6). Peace is a fruit of the Spirit (Gal 5:22), the hallmark of the gospel (Eph 6:15), and, along with righteousness and joy, the essence of God's kingdom (Rom 14:17). For this reason Paul urges his readers to be ''at peace'' not only with other believers (Rom 14:19; 1 Cor 7:15; 2 Cor 13:11), but with everyone (Rom 12:18). Similarly, in the other letters believers are called to cultivate peace (Jas 3:18; cf. Mt 5:9) among themselves, with outsiders (Heb 12:14), and even with their enemies (1 Pt 3:10–12, quoting Ps 34:12–16).

God is a God of peace (1 Cor 14:33; cf. Rom 15:33; 16:20; 1 Thes 5:23) who will keep our hearts in Christ Jesus (Phil 4:7); Christ is himself the peace between us (Eph 2:14).

Bibliography: H. BECK and C. BROWN, ''Peace,'' *Dictionary of New Testament Theology* 2 (1976) 776–783. J. I. DURHAM, ''Šālôm and the Presence of God,'' J. I. DURHAM and J. R. PORTER, eds., *Proclamation and Presence. Old Testament Essays in Honour of Gwynne Henton Davies* (Richmond 1970) 272–293. J. FOLK, ''Salvation as Shalom,'' *Dialog* 26 (1987) 104–110. V. P. FURNISH, ''War and Peace in the New Testament,'' *Interpretation* 38 (1984) 363–379. P. D. HANSON, ''War and Peace in the Hebrew Bible,'' *Interpretation* 38 (1984) 341–362. V. HASLER, ''eirēnē, ēs, hē eirēnē Frieden,'' *Exegetisches Wörterbuch zum Neuen Testament,* v. 1 (1980) cols. 957–964. D. J. WISEMAN, '''Is it Peace?' Covenant and Diplomacy,'' *Vetus Testmentum* 32 (1982) 311–326.

[J. L. GILLMAN]

PEACE OF GOD

A movement, largely of ecclesiastical inspiration, to arrest anarchy by means of censures and pacts of peace; it originated in Aquitaine toward the end of the 10th century and had spread to most parts of Europe by the middle of the 12th century.

By the time the Capetian dynasty took over in France (*c.* 987), the Carolingian organization had been in a shambles for over a century, particularly in the center and south: property was a prey of robber barons; private wars were common; the judicial system was next to powerless. Consequently, local churches were moved to take measures to protect property, lay as well as ecclesiastical. An early example comes from a council of the archbishop of Bordeaux and his suffragans (Poitiers, Périgueux, Saintes, Angoulême) at Charroux (Poitiers) in 989, where excommunications were pronounced against violators of churches, aggressors of unarmed clerics, and despoilers of the livestock of the poor (J. D. Mansi, *Sacrorum Conciliorum nova et amplissima collectio* [Paris 1889–1927] 19:90). At Le Puy in the following year, the local bishop imposed a ''peace pact'' on all his subjects; and a council called by Count William V of Aquitaine at Poitiers (1000–14) had as its theme ''A delicious name indeed is that of peace'' (J. D. Mansi, *Sacrorum Conciliorum nova et amplissima collectio* [Paris 1889–1927] 19:267). Later, with the consent of King Henry I of France, a Council of Peace was established by the bishops of Aquitaine at Bourges in 1031 (J. D. Mansi, *Sacrorum Conciliorum nova et amplissima collectio* [Paris 1889–1927] 19:507); its success allowed the Limousin bishops meeting at Limoges in 1033 to hope, as they formulated a stirring anathema against warlords, that the peace then prevailing in Aquitaine ''would soon be achieved among the Limousins'' (J. D. Mansi, *Sacrorum Conciliorum nova et amplissima collectio* [Paris 1889–1927] 19:529–530). Writing in 1046, Rodulphus Glaber, a Burgundian historian, described how the example of Aquitaine had inspired all France to hold councils ''for remaking peace'' at which those present cried out with hands uplifted, ''Peace! Peace! Peace!'' as ''a sign of a perpetual pact between them and God'' (*Historiarum libri quinque,* ed. M. Prou [Paris 1886] 103–105). In the principalities of Normandy and Flanders in the north, secular power was sufficiently strong to dominate the movement; thus Baldwin IV of Flanders organized a great collective oath of peace in 1030, while in Normandy the rulers commissioned the bishops to use excommunication and, if necessary, to call on the secular arm, against violators of peace pledges (Council of Lillebonne, 1080; J. D. Mansi, *Sacrorum Conciliorum nova et amplissima collectio* [Paris 1889–1927] 19:555).

Outside of France. In Italy, despite overtures by some French prelates to Italian bishops in 1040 and 1041, the peace was not introduced until Pope URBAN II and the Norman barons proclaimed it in 1089 in southern Italy. During the quarrels between Pope GREGORY VII and the Emperor HENRY IV, the bishops and nobles took the initiative in Lorraine and Germany, but the emperor assumed charge of the peace on his return from Italy in 1077. Spain lagged behind until *c.* 1124, while the peace was never more than a name in England, since an Anglo-Saxon regime in which the power of the lords never wholly impaired the freedom of others passed directly in 1066 to a vigorous, well-organized monarchy. In general the movement had a qualified success, relying greatly upon EXCOMMUNICATION and on the feudal homage due rulers, nobles, and bishops (*see* FEUDALISM). Sometimes the pledges of local lords were substantiated by hostages, and barons often undertook to bring to heel any of their ranks who should break the collective oath. On occasion the movement got out of hand, as in the reckless and ill-fated Militia of Berry, founded in 1038 by Aimon, bishop of Bourges, or in the popular ''Peacemaker'' groups founded in Le Puy in 1082.

Truce of God. Allied to the peace of God, but distinct from it, was a "Truce of God," during which hostilities would be suspended. First mooted, perhaps, at the Council of Toulouges (Roussillon) in the diocese of Elne in 1027, where certain "days of rest" from fighting, notably Sundays, were proclaimed (J. D. Mansi, *Sacrorum Conciliorum nova et amplissima collectio* [Paris 1889–1927] 19:483–484), this excellent idea was later overused to the point of extinction; by 1139 (Third LATERAN COUNCIL; *Conciliorum oecumenicorum decreta* [Bologna-Freiburg 1962] 169) it covered a weekly lull from sunset on Wednesday until sunrise on Monday, as well as the whole of Advent, the octaves of Christmas and Epiphany, and the period from Quinquagesima (from Septuagesima by 1179; *Conciliorum oecumenicorum decreta* [Bologna-Freiburg 1962] 198) to the Octave of Easter.

Bibliography: L. HUBERTI, *Studien zur Rechtsgeschichte der Gottesfrieden und Landfrieden* (Ansbach 1892). F. V. DUVAL, *De la Paix de Dieu à la Paix de Fer* (Paris 1923). Y. BONGERT, *Recherches sur les cours laïques du Xe au XIIIe siècle* (Paris 1949). B. TÖPFER, *Volk und Kirche zur Zeit der beginnenden Gottesfriedensbewegung in Frankreich* (Berlin 1957). M. BLOCH, *Feudal Society,* tr. L. A. MANYON (Chicago, Ill. 1961). K. BOSL, *Lexikon für Theologie und Kirche,* ed. J. HOFER and K. RAHNER (Freiburg 1957–65) 4:1106–07. D. KENNELLY, "Medieval Towns and the Peace of God," *Medievalia et humanistica* 15 (1963) 35–53. A. HOFFMANN, *Gottesfriede und Treuga Dei* (Stuttgart 1964).

[L. E. BOYLE]

PEACE OFFERING (IN THE BIBLE)

Also known as a communion offering, of which the main characteristic was that the victim was shared between God, the priest, and the person offering the sacrifice. The Hebrew terms for this kind of offering, *zebaḥ, zebaḥ šᵉlāmîm* or *šᵉlāmîm*, were almost interchangeable. *Zebaḥ* described the sacrifice by its outward ritual, a slaughtering, or immolation; *šᵉlāmîm* by the intention of the offerer, with opinions varying according to the derivation of *šelem* from *šālôm*, peace, or *šillam*, complete or make good (vows). Three types of peace offerings include sacrifices of praise, VOTIVE OFFERINGS, and the free-will offering. The distinctions between the three were not very precise, and the time allowed for consuming the portions varied (Lv 7.15–18). The principal ritual is described in Leviticus ch. 3 and corresponds to that for HOLOCAUST. The victims were also the same as those for holocaust, though birds were not allowed; they could have been male or female, and minor blemishes were tolerated in a victim offered as a voluntary sacrifice (Lv 22.23). Yahweh's portion was burned on the altar. It comprised all the fatty parts, since fat, like blood, was considered a life-giving part (Lv 3.16–17; 7.22–24). The breast (wave offering) and the right leg (raised offering) were assigned to the priest. The remainder of the animal belonged to the person who offered the sacrifice. He ate it with his family and any guests, all of whom had to be in a state of ritual purity.

Bibliography: R. DE VAUX, *Ancient Israel, Its Life and Institutions*, tr. J. MCHUGH (New York 1961) 417–418, 427–428. *Encyclopedic Dictionary of the Bible*, tr. and adap. by L. HARTMAN (New York 1963) 1784–85.

[J. B. FREUND]

PEARL, THE

A Middle English alliterative poem. The *Pearl-Gawain* MS, written in the last quarter of the 14th century, contains four alliterative poems, *Patience, Purity* (or *Cleanness*), *The Pearl,* and *Sir Gawain and the Green Knight.* This MS (in the Cotton Collection, British Museum) is the only extant version. All the poems are written in the same scribe's hand, but there is no agreement among scholars about common authorship. All the poems are excellent examples of 14th-century alliterative verse, but *Patience,* which relates the story of Jona, and *Purity,* which contrasts the virtue of Christ and the Blessed Virgin to the wickedness of all pagan gods and goddesses, are completely overshadowed by *Pearl* and *Gawain;* in the latter two poems Middle English alliterative poetry reaches its highest eminence.

Pearl, in 101 interlinked 12-line stanzas, is cast in the form of an elegy. The speaker, sorrowing over the loss of his not quite two-year-old daughter, falls asleep in his garden and is granted a vision of her. She instructs him about the joys of heaven, tells him not to weep for her since she is in the company of the virgins who dance before the throne of God, and finally shows him a vision of the Heavenly Jerusalem, with its golden buildings and towers of precious stones, as it is described in Revelation. The glories of the narrator's vision are matched by the ornate and intricate verse. Each stanza contains only two rhyming sounds, and each is bound to its fellows by the device of beginning each stanza with a line containing a key word, and closing the stanza with a line including the same word, so that one word runs through each of the sections as a unifying principle.

Pearl is now widely interpreted as an ALLEGORY, though critics are not agreed as to its significance. Allegorical readings generally suggest that the poem is concerned with the loss of grace or with a dark period in the narrator's spiritual life. Whatever the ultimate interpretation, the poem is obviously a powerful argument for submitting to God's will in adversity.

Sir Gawain and the Green Knight relates in 2,530 lines the story of Gawain's exchange of blows with the

Two book pages from the "Pearl-Gawain" manuscript, on left, painting of the Dreamer speaking to his lost Pearl, who is standing on the battlements of the New Jerusalem. The river represents the great gulf between this life and the next, English, c.1350–1400.

preternatural Green Knight, who survives a beheading by Gawain and demands the right to a return match one year later. Gawain's search for the Green Knight the next year ends in a castle at Christmas. The lord of the castle keeps Gawain there for three days, during which it is agreed that the lord will exchange the trophies of three days' hunting for whatever Gawain receives on those days. On two days Gawain receives kisses from the lady of the castle, who tries to seduce him, and he keeps his bargain with the host. On the third day he receives from the lady a magic girdle that is supposed to ward off all harm. This he does not give to the host but wears to his meeting with the Green Knight. The Green Knight, who only nicks Gawain's neck, reveals himself to be the lord of the castle and announces that all was done at the command of Morgan le Fay, to test the Round Table and to frighten Queen Guinevere. The poem is written in stanzas consisting of a varying number of alliterative lines, ending in one two-stressed line followed by a four-stressed quatrain (a device known as the bob-and-wheel).

Interpretations of *Gawain* vary greatly. Among them, the poem has been regarded as a straightforward romance, as an allegory, and as a repository of English and Celtic myths. All critics agree, however, that it is one of the greatest of Middle English poems, and it is universally praised for the intricacy of its structure, controlled diction, sure characterization, balanced composition, and general high poetic achievement. Recent interpretations have increasingly stressed the religious aspects of the poem, and it may well be that Gawain represents the Christian in the world—virtuous, following his duty as he sees it, but occasionally fallible and in need of testing and correction.

Bibliography: *Patience,* ed. I. GOLLANCZ (2d ed. London 1924). *Purity,* ed. R. J. MENNER (New Haven, Conn. 1921); under the name *Cleanness,* ed. I. GOLLANCZ and M. DAY, 2 v. (London 1921–33). *Pearl,* ed. E. V. GORDON (Oxford 1953); ed. and tr. M. V. HILLMANN (Convent Station, N.J. 1961), valuable introd, and notes. *Sir Gawain and the Green Knight,* ed. J. R. R. TOLKIEN and E. V. GORDON (London 1925); ed. I. GOLLANCZ et al. (Eary English Text Society, orig. ser. 210; 1940); ed. J. KREUZER and tr. J. ROSENBERG

(New York 1959), with excellent introd. G. L. KITTREDGE, *A Study of Sir Gawain and the Green Knight* (Cambridge, Mass. 1916). M. BORROFF, *Sir Gawain and the Green Knight: A Stylistic and Metrical Study* (New Haven, Conn. 1962). M. W. BLOOMFIELD, ''Sir Gawain and the Green Knight: An Appraisal,'' *Publications of the Modern Language Association* 76 (1961) 7–19, invaluable summary of previous scholarship. SR. MADELEVA, *Pearl: A Study in Spiritual Dryness* (New York 1925), the first fully allegorical study. D. W. ROBERTSON, ''The Heresy of The Pearl: The Pearl as Symbol,'' *Modern Language Notes* 25 (1950) 152–161. J. SPEIRS, *Medieval English Poetry: Non-Chaucerian Tradition* (London 1957). D. EVERETT, *Essays on Middle English Literature,* ed. P. KEAN (Oxford 1955).

[N. D. HINTON]

PEASANTS' WAR (1524–25)

The Peasants' War was a rebellion by the poor agrarian classes against their overlords, which began in 1524 at Stühlingen and spread to most of the areas of southern and southeastern Germany, including Austria, the Tyrol, Alsace, and the provinces of the lower Rhine. Eventually, the rebellion touched off calls for reform in some South German cities as well, with the urban poor adding their calls for reform to those of the rural peasantry. The causes for unrest were many, including: economic pressures stemming from the commercial revolution; the increasingly burdensome demands of the landed classes; the growing sense of release from traditional social discipline resulting from the events and popular preaching of the early Reformation; the reception of Roman law, which lowered the social position of the German peasants and urban proletariat in relation to the authority of the Holy Roman Empire's princes, magistrates, and nobles; and the tradition of militant peasant action which had produced a number of peasant revolts during the previous half century, including the disturbances at Niklashausen in 1476, the uprisings of the *Bundschuh* of 1502, of Armer Konrad in 1514, and of Styria and Carinthia in 1515. Nineteenth-century historians once stressed that the Peasants' War resulted from a tragic misinterpretation of the doctrine of Christian freedom, as expressed most vigorously by Martin LUTHER in his *On Christian Liberty* of 1520. Scholarship since the 1970s has stressed multiple and complex causes for the event and has often styled the Peasants' War as an early social revolution that eventually came to challenge aristocratic institutions and privileges and the hierarchical nature of the social structure.

Peasant demands were codified in the Twelve Articles of Memmingen, widely circulated in 1525, which included: the right of congregational election of pastors, modification of tithe payments, abolition of serfdom, discontinuance of land enclosure, elimination of traditional feudal dues, and reform in administration of justice. The relationship between the German Protestant REFORMATION and the Peasants' War, while not immediate, was perceived at the time to be very real. In his ''An Exhortation to Peace in Response to the Twelve Articles of the Swabian Peasants'' of 1525, Luther initially counseled Germany's peasants against the use of force and the empire's nobles to conciliate with their subjects. As the conflict escalated to include Thuringia, and as the the peasants of Swabia and Franconia were won over to the doctrines of Thomas Münzer, Luther reacted decisively against the movement. In ''Against the Murderous and Robbing Horde of the Peasantry'' (1525), he issued a violent attack on them, advising the princes to make every effort to crush the rebellion. PHILIP OF HESSE, the Elector John of Saxony, and the Dukes Henry and George of Saxony met and defeated Münzer's force at Frankenhausen on May 15, 1525, slaughtering more than 5,000 peasants and capturing and executing their leaders, including Münzer. Anton of Lorraine annihilated the rebel bands in Alsace, while George Truchsess, with the Electors of Palatine and Trier, destroyed those under Metzler at Konigshofen.

Bibliography: P. BLICKLE, *The Revolution of 1525,* trans. T. BRADY, JR., and H. C. E. MIDELFORT (Baltimore 1981). G. FRANZ, *Der deutsche Bauernkrieg* (Darmstadt 1956); *Die Religion in Geschichte und Gegenwart*[3], 7 v. (Tübingen 1957–65) 1:927–930. F. ZOEPFL, *Lexikon für Theologie und Kirche*[2], ed. J. HOFER and K. RAHNER, 10 v. (Freiburg 1957–65); suppl., *Das Zweite Vatikanische Konzil: Dokumente und Kommentare,* ed. H. S. BRECHTER et al., pt. 1 (1966) 2:58–59. B. GEBHARDT, *Handbuch der deutschen Geschichte,* ed. H. GRUNDMANN, 4 v. (Stuttgart 1954–60) v. 2. J. BÜHLER, *Deutsche Geschichte* (Berlin 1954) v. 3.

[P. L. HUGHES]

PECIA

A ''piece'' or section of a manuscript used in university bookstores of the 13th and 14th centuries. The newly established universities created a great demand for books. The bookstores carried official copies, or exemplars, whose accuracy was vouched for by university professors; these were rented out in small sections, or *peciae,* usually of four leaves, to students to have copied. If the next *pecia* was in use, the student rented the following one, and his scribe left space for the one not available. In the MSS so produced the telltale indications are: (1) the abbreviation *p, pe,* or *pec* (for *pecia*), in the margins where *peciae* began or ended; often these were numbered serially; (2) change of hand or ink at the beginnings of *peciae;* (3) space left between *peciae* when a scribe, being forced to skip, wrote smaller than necessary; (4) crowding at the end of a *pecia* when not enough room was left.

The changes wrought by the new system, though considerable, arose naturally out of earlier practices. Previously when a book had to be copied quickly, the quires were divided among several scribes. Now a smaller unit, the 8-page *pecia,* was substituted for the 16-page quire; thus greater speed was made possible. The number of scribes must have increased considerably. Monks no longer sufficed for the task, and professional scribes largely supplanted them in the transcription of schoolbooks. The sudden demand (four universities were founded in Italy between 1222 and 1231) caused the multiplication of inaccurate copies and brought about university control of official copies, the heart of the new system. The net result was cheaper textbooks (for the prices were fixed), more rapidly produced, with the text guaranteed by the bookseller (called stationer). On a small scale this was an industrial revolution. The new system began about 1225. By 1264 it was so well established that the statutes of the University of Padua could declare that without exemplars a university could not exist.

J. Destrez's epoch-making book and his posthumous article brought the *pecia* into prominence. He examined more than 15,000 MSS of approximately 300 authors and found 82 exemplars. He confined himself to authors represented in the university curricula, chiefly in the fields of theology, law (civil and Canon), and medicine, to which he added Aristotle. The liberal arts he covered incompletely and scantily; hence it is not possible to say to what extent the system was employed for them. It seems, however, that few arts books were produced under it. When such are found, they deserve particular attention.

Destrez devoted his investigations largely to the Universities of Paris, Bologna, Oxford, and Naples. He noted the distinguishing characteristics of each in script, abbreviation, etc. The paleography of the MSS involved and their textual criticism are greatly affected by practices connected with the *pecia.* Naturally, exemplars are preferred to copies in the editing of texts.

Bibliography: J. DESTREZ, *La Pecia dans les manuscrits universitaires du XIIIe e du XIVe siècle* (Paris 1935). J. DESTREZ and M. D. CHENU, ''Exemplaria universitaires des XIIIe e XIVe siécles,'' *Scriptorium* 7 (1953) 68–80. G. FINK-ERRERA, ''Jean Destrez et son oeuvre,'' *ibid.* 11 (1957) 264–280. K. CHRIST, ''Petia,'' *Zentralblatt für Bibliothekswesen* 55 (1938) 1–44.

[B. L. ULLMAN]

PECOCK, REGINALD

Bishop, English philospher of religion; b. Wales, probably Saint David's diocese, between 1392 and 1395; d. Thorney Abbey, 1460 or 1461. He entered Oxford in 1409, took a B.A. in 1413, and in 1414 was elected to a fellowship at Oriel College. By 1424 he was bachelor of theology; by 1444, a doctor of theology. He was ordained in the Diocese of Lincoln (1420 or 1421). On July 19, 1431, he became rector of St. Michael in Riola and master of Whitington College, London, a body of five secular chaplains, two clerks, and four choristers, in the patronage of the Mercers Company. While there, he carried out part of his design to win back the LOLLARDS to the orthodox faith through philosphical argument in English and in Latin in the form of expository works outlined in his *Afore Crier.* The key work of the series was the *Book,* or *Rule of Crysten Religioun:* soon after this came the *Donet,* then the *Just Apprising of the Holy Scriptures.* These and other works, circulated among his friends before they had received final shape, got him into trouble with conservative theologians, who detected in his ''cleer witt'' the elements of heresy, particularly when in his *New English Creed* he propounded a doctrine of belief that could not be reconciled with the classic understanding of the symbol, or creed. Meanwhile at the insistence of his Lancastrian friends he received promotion to the bishopric of SAINT ASAPH (1444) and then to CHICHESTER (1450). But as a member of a court group of bishops, he became unpopular with the working clergy; and as one who was not prepared to attribute infallibility to the FATHERS OF THE CHURCH and one who held that bishops were not bound by their office to preach, he incurred the enmity of the powerful and passionate chancellor of Oxford, Thomas Gascoigne. In 1456 his enemies charged him with trying to disturb the faith of England. He was put on trial at the request of the council (October 1457) by a specialist tribunal, convicted before a great council, and forced (December 1457) to repudiate his errors. He was not deprived, having made his peace with Rome, but his enemies continued to pursue him, this time for offenses against the Great Statute of PRAEMUNIRE, and a new inquiry into his books was commissioned (September 1458). Pecock resigned (1458), but he was not allowed to go free. He was confined to the monastery of THORNEY, limited in his reading to the Sciptures and service books, and not allowed to write.

Bibliography: V. H. GREENE, *Bishop Reginald Pecock* (Cambridge, Eng. 1945). T. KELLY, *Reginald Pecock* (Manchester U. diss. 1950). E. F. JACOB, ''Reynold Pecock, Bishop of Chichester,'' *Proceedings of the British Academy* 37 (1951) 121–53. Emden 3:1447–49. E. H. EMERSON, ''Reginald Pecock: Christian Rationalist,'' *Speculum* 31 (1956) 235–242.

[E. F. JACOB]

PECTORIUS, EPITAPH OF

An inscription found (1830) in seven fragments in an ancient Christian cemetery near Autun, France, and published by Cardinal PITRA. He and G. de Rossi ascribed it to the beginning of the 2d century; E. Le Blant and J. Wilpert attributed it to the end of the 3d century. Both dates are too early; the form and style of its letters indicate as the period of its origin sometime between 350 and 400. The phraseology, however, resembles the inscription of ABERCIUS (end of the 2d century) and clearly reflects the discipline of the SECRET. It is quite possible that the first part of the epitaph is a quotation from an older poem.

The inscription consists of three distichs and five hexameters; and the first five verses are bound together by the acrostic ΙΧΘΥΣ, a word that appears five times in the text. The content falls into two parts. The first (verses 1 to 7) is addressed to the reader and is of doctrinal character. Baptism is called "the immortal fountain of divine waters"; the Eucharist, "the honeysweet food of the Redeemer of the saints"; Christ, "the light of the dead." The second part (verses 8 to 11) is personal. Here Pectorius prays for his mother and asks his deceased parents and brothers to remember him "in the peace of the Fish." The words "holding the Fish in your hands" recall the ancient Communion rite in which the Eucharist was placed in the hands of the recipient.

Bibliography: J. QUASTEN, ed. *Monumenta eucharista et liturgica vetustissima* (Bonn 1935–37) 24–27, text, and Lat. tr. QUASTEN, *Patrology* (Westminster MD 1950) 1:173–175, with bibliog. F. J. DÖLGER, ΙΧΘΥΣ?, v.1 (Rome 1910) 12–15, 177–183; *ibid.,* v.2 (Münster 1922) 507–515. M. GUARDUCCI, *Rendiconti della Pontificia Accademia di Archeologia* 23–24 (1947–49) 243–252.

[J. QUASTEN]

PEERS, EDGAR ALLISON

Hispanic scholar and authority on Spanish mysticism; b. Leighton Buzzard, Bedfordshire, England, May 7, 1891; d. Liverpool, Dec. 21, 1952. He was educated at Dartford Grammar School and Christ's College, Cambridge. After a distinguished university career, he taught modern languages. In 1920 he was appointed to the Gilmour Chair of Spanish in Liverpool University, a post he held until his death.

Professor Peers made an important contribution to Spanish studies, in both teaching and research. He organized vacation courses in London and Liverpool and eventually in Spain. He founded the Institute of Hispanic Studies and its *Bulletin* and was for some time educational director of the Hispanic Council. He was a brilliant but also a patient teacher who took a personal interest in his pupils. He published a definitive annotated translation of the works of SS. TERESA OF AVILA and JOHN OF THE CROSS, based on the critical text of P. Silverio de S. Teresa and on discussions with the latter and Dom Edmund Gourdon, Prior of Miraflores charterhouse (Burgos). Peers (himself an Anglican) produced numerous other works on Spanish mysticism. He wrote ably on the Spanish Civil War, and under the name of Bruce Truscot produced several books calling attention to the potentialities of the modern "red-brick" universities.

Edgar Allison Peers.

Bibliography: E. A. PEERS, *Studies of the Spanish Mystics,* 3 v. (London 1927–60). Translations. *Complete Works of St. John of the Cross,* 3 v. (London 1934–35; rev. ed. London 1953). *Complete Works of St. Teresa,* 3 v. (London 1946); *Letters of St. Teresa* (Westminster, MD 1950). BERNARDINO OF LAREDO, *Ascent of Mount Sion* (London 1952). *Bulletin of Hispanic Studies* 30 (1953) 1–20, memorial number with bibliog.

[K. POND]

PEGIS, ANTON CHARLES

Philosopher, educator, editor; b. Milwaukee, Wisconsin, Aug. 24, 1905; d. Toronto, Canada, May 13, 1978. He received a B.A. in 1928 and an M.A in 1929 from Marquette University. In 1929 Pegis entered the Institute of Mediaeval Studies in Toronto, where he studied under Etienne Gilson and Gerald Phelan, and in 1931 received the Ph.D. in philosophy from the University of Toronto. He lectured at Marquette from 1931 to 1937 and at Fordham University from 1937 until 1944, when he returned to the Pontifical Institute of Mediaeval Studies in Toronto as professor of the history of philosophy. He also taught as professor in the graduate department of philosophy at the University of Toronto.

Pegis served as president of the Pontifical Institute from 1946 to 1952 and subsequently became editorial director of the Catholic textbook division of Doubleday and Company in New York. He remained a fellow of the institute, returning to Toronto to teach full time from 1961 until his retirement in 1974. In his last years he supervised the new Graduate Center of Thomistic Studies at the University of St. Thomas, Houston, Texas, and lectured there on the philosophies of St. Thomas, Husserl, and Heidegger. Pegis was elected president of the American Catholic Philosophical Association in 1946 and in 1975 received its Aquinas Medal.

Pegis readily accepted the notion of Christian philosophy proposed by Pope Leo XIII in *AETERNI PATRIS.* He defended the rationality of philosophy and thought that Christian revelation, far from destroying that rationality, strengthened and deepened it. Though Pegis's research and writing in the history of philosophy and his own philosophical reflections touched upon many topics, his focus was the Augustinian themes of God and the soul.

To Pegis, the philosophy of St. Thomas appeared as the finest example of Christian philosophy. He saw Thomism as first and foremost a theology, one that employed philosophy as its handmaiden. The modern Thomist, he insisted, accepts the task of creating an autonomous philosophy true to the principles of Aquinas in a dialogue with contemporary philosophers and scientists that is open to the light of Christian revelation.

See Also: THOMISM.

Bibliography: *Essays in Honour of Anton Charles Pegis,* ed. J. R. O'DONNELL (Toronto 1974) 9–16. A. C. PEGIS, *St. Thomas and the Problem of the Soul in the 13th Century* (Toronto 1934); *St. Thomas and the Greeks* (Milwaukee 1939); *Basic Writings of St. Thomas Aquinas,* tr., 2 v. (New York 1945); *Introduction to St. Thomas Aquinas,* tr. (New York 1948); *The Wisdom of Catholicism,* ed. (New York 1949); *St. Thomas Aquinas: On the Truth of the Catholic Faith, Book One: God,* tr. (Garden City, NY 1955); *A Gilson Reader,* ed. (Garden City, NY 1957); *Christian Philosophy and Intellectual Freedom* (Milwaukee 1960); *At the Origins of the Thomistic Notion of Man* (New York 1963); *The Middle Ages and Philosophy* (Chicago 1963); *St. Thomas and Philosophy* (Milwaukee 1964).

[A. A. MAURER]

PÉGUES, THOMAS

Thomistic theologian; b. Marcillac, France, Aug. 2, 1866; d. Dax, April 28, 1936. He entered the Dominican order in 1888 and was ordained in 1892. He taught theology at Toulouse (1892) and Rome (1909). He became regent of studies for the Toulouse (1921) and Roman provinces (1928–35). Pégues' principal works are *Jésus-Christ dans l'évangile* (Paris 1899), *Initiation thomiste* (Toulouse 1921), *Aperçus de philosophie thomiste et de propédeutique* (Paris 1927), and *Commentaire français littéral de la Somme Théologique de Saint Thomas d'Aquin,* 21 v. (Toulouse-Paris 1907–32). In his monumental commentary he carefully followed the text of the *Summa theologiae* and explained St. Thomas's meaning by citing almost exclusively from his other works to show continuity and consistency of doctrine. Among his many articles the most noteworthy historically is ''L'hérésie du renouvellement'' against MODERNISM. It appeared in the *Revue Thomiste* (1907) two months before the promulgation of the encyclical *Pascendi* by Pius X (d. 1914).

Bibliography: R. GARRIGOU-LAGRANGE, *Revue thomiste* 41 (1936) 441–445. *Memoire domenicane* 53 (1936) 193–197.

[W. D. HUGHES]

PÉGUY, CHARLES PIERRE

French poet and essayist; b. Orléans, Aug. 7, 1873; d. Battle of the Marne, Sept. 5, 1914. He was of a peasant family and was raised by his mother, his father having died when Charles was a year old. He was educated at the lycée in Orléans, the lycée La Kanel, and, after military service, the École Normale (1894). He became a bookseller and later director of *La revue de la quinzaine,* in whose pages he showed himself to be a socialist, but opposed to the ''Socialists,'' and an intellectual opposed to the ''Intellectual party.'' In 1900 he founded *Cahiers de la quinzaine,* which introduced many young writers—and much of his own work—to the public. *Jeanne d' Arc* (1897; in the form of a medieval mystery play, 1910) strikes the note of exalted patriotism that was to mark all his work. This is evident also in *Notre patrie* (1905) and *Notre jeunesse*, his vigorous defense of Alfred Dreyfus. *Clio* (1909) sets forth a theological concept of history, and *L'argent* exalts French culture. His later *Mystéres* and *Tapisseries* give witness to his ''conversion'' and reveal a new poetic inspiration. He had early come under the influence of BERGSON, to whom he paid homage in *Note sur M. Bergson* (1914). He deliberately lived a poor life and, though devoutly Catholic, was somewhat unique in his manifestations of his faith.

Restless and full of pent-up violence, Péguy recalls BLOY and BERNANOS. The evil of the time, he conceived, rested in a disembodied intellectualism that belonged to a world of fantasy. Liberty is not derived from a philosophy or a political regime, but from daily struggle at the price of rigid discipline and constant effort. Love of liberty demands the help of the mystic. In some epochs of history the mystic controls human actions and, sustaining their impetus, gives them a direction consistent with honor; in other periods the mystic is consumed by politics—liberty of mind and heart are replaced by an unfeeling, rigid dogmatism. Persons on the scene, Péguy thought, are incapable of illuminating true history, which is what man knows ''by the Gospels of these fishermen, boatsmen, and tax-collectors who actually encountered Christ.'' The people alone are able to bear witness, for they alone are ''charged with the memory that preserves the essential against the alterations of time.'' The *Cahiers* foretold the ''city harmonious'' in which the theoreticians would give way to people of enthusiasm and faith.

Above all else, Péguy mistrusted the atheism of a progress that masqueraded under the aegis of science, as in RENAN and Jean Jaures. His goal was to foster a salvation that would join the spiritual with the temporal, intellectual, and vocational. In *Jeanne d'Arc* he proclaims the Christian dogmas of the reality of the Incarnation and Redemption. In some of his poems he portrays God speaking almost in the accents of a French peasant, in an effort to make real His loving providence. At one and the same time a chronicler of the Middle Ages and an illuminator and prodigious producer of words and ideas, Péguy created a language suitable for the poetic presentation of the irresistible march of Christianity since the paradise of Adam. This is the theme of *Eve* (1913).

Bibliography: *Oeuvres complétes,* 15 v. (Paris 1917–34); *Oeuvres poétiques complétes,* introd. F. PORCHÉ (Paris 1962). *Cahiers de la quinzaine,* ed. C. P. PÉGUY, 229 v. (Paris 1900–14). J. ROUSSEL, *Péguy* (Paris 1963). A. ROUSSEAUX, *Le prophète Péguy,* 2 v. (Paris 1942–46). R. ROLLAND, *Péguy,* 2 v. (Paris 1945). H. DANIEL-ROPS, *Péguy* (rev. ed. Paris 1935). A. SUARÈS, *Péguy* (Paris 1915). D. O'DONNELL, *Maria Cross: Imaginative Patterns in a Group of Catholic Writers* (New York 1952), C. MOELLER, *Littérature du XX e siècle et christianisme,* 4 v. (Tournai 1953–60).

[G. MOURGUE]

PEIRCE, CHARLES SANDERS

American philosopher, pioneer in symbolic logic, originator of one version of pragmatism, outstanding neorealist; b. Cambridge, Mass., Sept. 10, 1839; d. Milford, Pa., April 19, 1914.

Life and Work. A close associate of Chauncey Wright, John Fiske, Josiah ROYCE, and William JAMES, Peirce studied at Harvard University and lectured there briefly in philosophy in 1864. Besides another brief teaching stint at Johns Hopkins University (1879–84), he worked as a physicist for the U.S. Coast Survey. Peirce

Charles Sanders Peirce.

was known for his broader philosophical speculations by only a few contemporaries familiar with his articles, lectures, reviews, and correspondence. He wrote no single definitive philosophical work that clearly establishes the unity of his thought. The first presentation of a unified portion of his work appeared in M. R. Cohen's edition titled *Chance, Love and Logic* (New York 1923), containing the first Peirce bibliography. Between 1931 and 1953 appeared the first eight volumes of the *Collected Papers of Charles Sanders Peirce* (Cambridge, Mass.). Because of the lack of any certain order in Peirce's treatment of essential aspects of his philosophy, the extensive indexes in the *Collected Papers* are indispensable for the study of Peirce. (In references to Peirce, the general practice is to indicate the volume and paragraph number of this edition, e.g., 5.432.)

Teaching. Under the influence of his father, Benjamin Peirce, a Harvard University professor, Peirce became a complete mathematician. He made extensive and original contributions to the then-growing symbolic logic. I. KANT was his first philosophical mentor, although he grew critical of Kant as he studied British EMPIRICISM, ARISTOTLE, and scholastic sources, especially

Duns Scotus. He sums up his position thus: ''I should call myself an Aristotelian of the scholastic wing, approaching Scotism, but going further in the direction of scholastic realism'' (5.77).

Although this statement is arguable, Peirce tried to establish a complete system by relating all his conclusions to his three categories: firstness, secondness, and thirdness. He claimed that these are not only the categories of all experience as revealed in phenomenology, but that they are also the essential categories of thought, of sign relations, and of reality itself. Independent of, and perhaps prior to, E. HUSSERL, Peirce determined the role of phenomenology (or phaneroscopy, as he called it) and worked out its details along lines remarkably similar to those of Husserl. This he related to a theory of meaning that embraced his metaphysical realism, asserting that things have meaning insofar as they embody triadic relations. It was in this sense that he maintained; ''General principles are really operative in nature. This is the doctrine of scholastic realism'' (5.101).

His teaching that general principles are signs operating in nature is essential to an understanding of his doctrine of pragmatism, which he called pragmaticism to distinguish it from William James's version. James, he contended, borrowed the idea of pragmatism from him and badly misinterpreted it. Peirce modified his conception of pragmatism several times, finally concluding that it is a method of determining the meaning of signs, completely in accord with his version of scholastic realism.

Moreover, Peirce incorporated into his system a thorough evolutionism, in which respect he compared with H. BERGSON and A. N. WHITEHEAD. Chance and law, he maintained, were two sides of evolution. The theory that chance is an objective reality operating in the universe he called tychism. The operation of law he called synechism, explaining it thus: ''Synechism is founded on the notion that the coalescence, the becoming continuous, the becoming governed by laws, the becoming instinct with general ideas, are phases of one and the same process of the growth of reasonableness'' (5.4). Metaphysics, taken as ontology and cosmology, is fundamentally concerned with this evolution of law as reality, which is the heart of his category of thirdness.

It is strongly debated as to whether Peirce was indeed a realist or an objective idealist. The complexity of his thought and its wide range make it unwise to offer any certain critique this early in the development of Peircean studies. He is generally considered to be far superior to his contemporary American philosophers and particularly relevant to the statement of present scholastic philosophy.

Bibliography: W. P. HAAS, *The Conception of Law and the Unity of Peirce's Philosophy* (Fribourg 1964). J. BOLER, *Charles Peirce and Scholastic Realism* (Seattle 1963). M. G. MURPHEY, *The Development of Peirce's Philosophy* (Cambridge, Mass. 1961).

[W. P. HAAS]

PELAGIA, SS.

The name of six saints listed in the Roman MARTYROLOGY (1961 ed.); three are significant.

Pelagia of Antioch, d. 311? As a girl of 15, Pelagia of Antioch is said to have thrown herself from the rooftop to protect her virginity when soldiers came to arrest her during a persecution of DIOCLETIAN. St. JOHN CHRYSOSTOM praised this martyr's action in a homily preached probably in the church erected over her tomb (*Patrologia Graeca* 50:579–584). Her name is included in the canon of the Milanese Mass.

Feast: June 9.

Pelagia of Jerusalem, also known as Pelagia the Penitent, d. *c.* 457. According to a probable eyewitness writing under the pseudonym James the Deacon, Pelagia lived a dissolute life as an actress and dancer. Converted by the preaching of St. Nonnus (d. *c.* 458), an Egyptian bishop living at Antioch, Pelagia, disguised as a man, lived a life of penance in the Garden of Olives. Although a cult to St. Pelagia already existed in 530, the *Vita* by James the Deacon is the contamination of a sermon of St. John Chrysostom on an anonymous Syrian penitent (*Hom. 67 in Mt.; Patrologia Graeca* 58:636–637), mixed with the life of Pelagia of Antioch and the theme of the virgin monk. Her story is similar to that of several other saints, including Margaret, Marina, Euphrosyne, and Theodora.

Feast: Oct. 8.

Pelagia of Tarsus, d. 302? This Pelagia is said to have become a Christian after breaking her engagement with the son of Diocletian. When her fiancé then committed suicide, Diocletian summoned her and found her so beautiful that he proposed marriage, then ordered her burned to death when she declined.

Feast: May 4.

H. Usener tried to demonstrate that these three saints are the Christian sublimation of a Venus theme since Pelagia connotes ''from the sea.'' But his theory is untenable.

Bibliography: *Acta sanctorum* May 1:458–463, June 2:153–162, Oct.4:248–268. H. USENER, ed., *Legenden der heiligen Pelagia* (Bonn 1879). H. DELEHAYE, *The Legends of the Saints,* tr. D. ATTWATER (New York 1962). A. BENETTI, *S. Margherita dei Lessini e le pievi della Postumia* (Verona 1976). P. PETITMENGIN, *Péla-*

gie la pénitente: métamorphoses d'une légende, 2 v. (Paris 1981–84). *Die mittelniederdeutsche Margaretenlegende*, ed. K. O. SEIDEL and G. DREXEL (Berlin 1994).

[R. K. POETZEL]

PELAGIUS I, POPE

Pontificate: April 16, 556 to March 4, 561. Pelagius inherited a daunting situation—much of his own making—from his predecessor Vigilius (537–555), and his pontificate was consumed with it. Pelagius was by birth a Roman, son of a civic official named John. He was a deacon under AGAPETUS (535–36) and dealt with diplomatic matters, joining that pope on an embassy to Constantinople to convince the emperor JUSTINIAN I (527–565) to depose the Monophysite patriarch of Constantinople, Anthimus. He replaced Vigilius as the papal representative in the imperial city when Vigilius returned to Rome to succeed the deposed Silverius (536–537) as pope. Since Vigilius had concurred with the imperial deposition of the pope, Pelagius found himself rumored to have worked against SILVERIUS, but that accusation is unproven. He was a success in Constantinople, becoming a confidante of Justinian, whom he convinced to denounce officially the teachings of the long deceased Alexandrian theologian Origen (*c.* 185–*c.* 253).

But friendship with the emperor did not deter him from his duties. He was in Rome in 544 when Justinian, to pacify the Monophysites in Egypt, condemned some writings of three Chalcedonian theologians, the famous THREE CHAPTERS. Pelagius promptly requested the theological opinion of the North African Ferrandus of Carthage (d. 546), who opposed the condemnation of three theologians who had died in the peace of the Church. The emperor assumed that Vigilius would agree with the imperial line, but when he balked at the Three Chapters ploy, Justinian's agents kidnapped him in 545. He would never return to Rome. The Romans rejected any imperial appointees as head of the local church, and so Pelagius assumed that role as vicar of Vigilius. When the Goths besieged the city in 547, the vicar used much of his personal wealth to alleviate the sufferings of the people, and after the Goths had captured Rome, he bargained with their king Totila and avoided a massacre. Quite taken by Pelagius, Totila sent him as ambassador to Justinian to try to win a peace in Italy, but the negotiations failed.

In 551 he went again to Constantinople and met with Vigilius who, after six years of captivity, was ready to acquiesce to the emperor's demands. Pelagius stiffened the pope's resolve but only temporarily. When Vigilius capitulated, Pelagius split from him. Justinian had Pelagius imprisoned in a monastery, and from there he wrote a scathing attack on Vigilius. After the pope had attended and approved the fifth ecumenical council, CONSTANTINOPLE II (553), Justinian allowed him to return to Rome. He never made it, dying in Sicily on June 7, 555. The crucial point in Pelagius' life had arrived.

In the absence of both pope and vicar, a priest named Mareas had governed the Roman church and looked to be the next pope. But Justinian wanted Pelagius, a former friend who, even in his most stringent writings against the condemnation of the Three Chapters, had not censured the emperor. Pelagius accepted the offer. Scholars debate whether he saw the opportunity for the papacy and could not resist it or whether he accepted Constantinople II and the condemnation of the Three Chapters as a fact of ecclesiastical life and was reconciled to the emperor. Most likely both motives played a role. When Mareas died in August of 555, the way was open for Pelagius' election in September of that year. But the pope-elect could not become pope because, in the laconic words of the *Liber Pontificalis,* "there was not a bishop to ordain him." Seven months later, on April 16, 556, two bishops and a priest agreed to do the job, but neither of the bishops were from Ostia, Portus, or Albinum, whose bishop traditionally ordained the pope.

Most Western bishops considered Pelagius an opportunist who had sold out for the papal office, and these included the bishops of suburcarian Italy, the regions around Rome. The new pope had to restore his authority. His imperial patron was eager to help. When the African bishops raised objections to Pelagius, Byzantine troops forced them to recognize him. But this tactic could not work everywhere. The pope sent an embassy to the king of FRANKS, Childebert I, to assure him of his orthodoxy, a dangerous precedent since the popes usually represented orthodoxy and could demand that other bishops assure him of theirs. When the Gallic bishops were slow to acquiesce, Pelagius urged Childebert to force them into agreement. The bishops of northeastern Italy refused communion with the pope, who urged them to come to Rome to judge his orthodoxy for themselves—a remarkable offer. But these bishops remained recalcitrant, so Pelagius asked the Byzantine *exarch* (ruler of foreign territory) in Ravenna to use troops against them, but the *exarch* refused. Pelagius was, however, successful in winning over the suburcarian Italian bishops, who accepted not only him as pope but also the authenticity of Constantinople II and the condemnation of the Three Chapters.

Aside from the schism (which lasted in Italy into the next century), Pelagius enjoyed much success. Relations with Byzantium were generally good, and the Goths ceased to menace Rome. The war against the barbarians as well as the decade-long absence of Vigilius from the city had depleted the ranks of the Roman clergy, whose numbers and moral quality Pelagius considerably augmented. The war had also ruined papal finances, and the pope brought in the first lay papal finance minister, a banker named Anastasius. Pelagius was a scholar, a patron of monasticism, and translator into Latin of some sayings of prominent Eastern monks. Few popes have led so full a life or worked against such formidable odds.

Bibliography: L. DUCHESNE, ''Vigile et Pélage,'' *Revue des questions historiques* 36: 369–440; 37 (1885) 579–593. *L'Église au VIe siècle* (Paris 1925) 225–238. R. DEVREESSE, ed. and tr., *Pelagii diaconi ecclesiae romanae In defensione trium capitulorum* (*Studi e Testi* 57; 1932); *Dictionnaire de théologie catholique,* ed. A. VACANT et al., 15 v. (Paris 1903–50) 12.1:660–669. P.M. GASSÓ and C. M. BATLLE, eds., *Pelagii I papae epistulae quae supersunt* (Monserrat 1956). L. ABRAMOWSKI, *Vigiliae christianae* 10: 160–193. E. STEIN, *Histoire du Bas-Empire,* tr. J. R. PALANQUE, 2 v. in 3 (Paris 1949–59) v. 2. B. ALTANER, *Patrology,* tr. H. GRAEF from 5th German ed. (New York 1960) 555–556. R. ENO, *The Early Papacy* (Wilmington, Del. 1990) 134–139. E. FERGUSON ed., *Encyclopedia of Early Christianity* (New York 1997) 2:890. H. JEDIN, *History of the Church* (New York 1980) 2:445–446, 628–629. J. N. D. KELLY, *Oxford Dictionary of Popes* (New York 1986) 62–64. J. RICHARDS, *Popes and Papacy in the Early Middle Ages* (London 1979) 143–162.

[J. F. KELLY]

PELAGIUS II, POPE

Pontificate: Nov. 26, 579, to Feb. 7, 590. Because the Lombards were besieging Rome and the situation at the time was critical, a new pope was elected and consecrated as the successor of BENEDICT I without waiting for imperial confirmation. The deacon (later Pope) Gregory was dispatched to Constantinople to explain the omission and beg for military help. Pelagius II, born a Goth (son of Unigild), was the second pope of Germanic extraction. The emperor could spare few troops, hard pressed as he was by the Persians, but he advised the pope to bribe the Lombard dukes and to obtain the help of the Frankish King. The pope's appeal to the Frankish bishop of Auxerre (580) was without success, but it is an anticipation, by some 200 years, of a move that was ultimately to alter the course of history profoundly. The Byzantine exarch of Ravenna finally managed in 585 to secure from the Lombards a truce that lasted until 589.

The interval was used by the pope to end the Aquileian schism. The deacon Gregory was brought back from Constantinople to assist in the negotiations. Unfortunately the patriarch of Aquileia-Grado and the bishops of Venetia and Istria were unyielding in their refusal to restore communion with Rome. The pope asked Smaragdus, Byzantine exarch in Italy, to use force against the recalcitrant bishops, but the exarch was powerless to bring about the desired reconciliation, in spite of the pressure he brought to bear.

The pontificate of Pelagius II saw the beginnings of the controversy between Rome and Constantinople over the title of ''ecumenical patriarch,'' regularly used by the patriarchs of Constantinople since the fifth century. Pelagius II refused to accept the use of that title by Patriarch John IV the Faster and also the acts of a council held at Constantinople, which John had confirmed.

In spite of the perilous political situation, Pelagius II provided a number of important adornments to Rome. It was probably he who began to raise the presbyterium of St. Peter's so that the high altar would be directly over the shrine of St. Peter while a covered passageway would lead to a small chapel directly behind the shrine for daily Masses. The earliest Lateran monastery of San Pancrazio dates perhaps from this reign, though it is uncertain whether the Benedictine monks from Montecassino, fleeing from the destruction of the famous abbey by the Lombards in 577, were received there as a body. The pope's personal residence nearby, which he converted into a hospital, may have given rise to the present Ospedale di San Giovanni. Recent excavations seem to show that he was responsible for adding a second adjoining basilica to San Lorenzo fuori le Mura, where his portrait in mosaic appears on the triumphal arch. Pelagius II perished in a plague that followed an unusually severe flooding of the city by the Tiber in early 590. He was buried in the portico of St. Peter's.

Bibliography: *Clavis Patrum latinorum,* ed. E. DEKKERS 1705–07, 6 genuine letters. *Patrologia latina,* ed. J. P. MIGNE (Paris 1878–90) 72:703–60. *Liber pontificalis,* ed. L. DUCHESNE (Paris 1886–1958) 1:309–311; 3:92–93. H. LECLERQ, *Dictionnaire d'archéologie chrétienne et de liturgie* (Paris 1907–53) 13.1:1222–24. G. B. LADNER, *Die Papstbildnisse* (Vatican City 1941–). P. VIELLIARD, *Recherches sur les origines de la Rome chrétienne* (Mâcon 1941; repr. Rome 1959) 142. G. FERRARI, *Early Roman Monasteries* (Rome 1957). J. TOYNBEE and J. B. WARD PERKINS, *The Shrine of St. Peter* (New York 1956). R. U. MONTINI, *Le tombe dei papi* (Rome 1957) 112. G. SCHWAIGER, *Lexikon für Theologie und Kirche,* ed. J. HOFER and K. RAHNER (Freiburg 1957–65) 8:250. R. ENO, *Rise of the Papacy* (Wilmington, DE 1990) 139–142. E. FERGUSON, ed., *Encyclopedia of Early Christianity* (New York 1997), 2:890–891. H. JEDIN, *History of the Church* (New York 1980) 2:629. J. N. D. KELLY, *Oxford Dictionary of Popes* (New York 1986) 65. J. RICHARDS, *Popes and Papacy the Early Middle Ages* (London 1979) 166–168.

[J. CHAPIN]

PELAGIUS AND PELAGIANISM

A fifth-century heresy, Pelagianism was concerned with grace and freedom of the will; it is named after Pelagius, its principal author.

PELAGIUS

Born probably in Britain *c.* 354, Pelagius arrived in Rome *c.* 380, and although not a priest became a highly regarded spiritual director for both clergy and laity. His followers were few but influential, and their rigorous asceticism was a reproach to the spiritual sloth of many of their fellow Catholics. Before the capture of Rome by Alaric (410), Pelagius left for Africa with Coelestius, a close friend and collaborator. The latter remained there in the hope of becoming a priest, while Pelagius proceeded to Palestine, which became his home until 418, after which date he disappears from history.

Pelagius had received a solid training in the classics and achieved a fairly good knowledge of the Bible and the works of the Greek and Latin theologians. Many of his writings were formerly attributed to AUGUSTINE, JEROME, and other orthodox scholars. Some of his works, such as *De fide Trinitatis,* have disappeared. Three have been preserved: *Expositiones XIII Epistularum Pauli* (completed by 405); *Epistola an Demetriadem* (414), and *Libellus fidei* (addressed to Pope INNOCENT I in 417). There remain only fragments of some letters as well as of his *De natura* (414), *De libero arbitrio* (416), and *Liber testimoniorum,* a methodical collection of texts from Sacred Scripture. C. Caspari and G. de Plinval regarded him as the author of other anonymous or pseudonymous letters and treatises.

Pelagian Theological System. The doctrine of Pelagius, which can be reconstructed from his authentic writings, rests on freedom of the will and divine grace. According to him the human will is completely free and is equally ready to do either good or evil. This freedom would be destroyed if the will were inclined to evil because of another's sin or had to be strengthened by another's help. Divine grace is for him something external, as the free will itself, or the precepts of the Old and the New Testaments. Its purpose is merely to facilitate what the will can do by itself, and it is always given in proportion to one's merits.

These two basic principles led to the following conclusions: Adam's sin was purely personal; therefore it would be unjust for God to punish the human race for his transgression. Death is not a punishment of sin, but a necessity of human nature. Since all are born without sin, infant baptism is useless, and infants who die without the Sacrament go immediately to heaven. The Redemption does not give new life to the human race; Christ merely helps by His good example. Prayer for the conversion of others is futile since it cannot help them in saving their souls.

Pelagianism, therefore, denied the supernatural order, explained away the mystery of predestination, and made God only a spectator in the drama of human salvation.

Opposition to Pelagianism. These doctrines created no stir in Rome because Pelagius seems to have taught them only to a carefully selected audience, but soon after his departure from the city they were proclaimed openly in many parts of the Christian world. This was due mainly to the untiring propaganda of Coelestius. The first opposition was raised in 411 when Aurelius, Bishop of Carthage, summoned Coelestius to a local council. He was there ordered to retract his statements rejecting original sin and infant baptism. On his refusal, he was excommunicated and forced to leave the country.

Augustine. Augustine was not present at this council but, as he claims in his *Retractationes* (1.9.6), he was the enemy of Pelagianism long before it appeared. In 412 he wrote *De peccatorum meritis* and *De spiritu et littera.* In them, as in all his later anti-Pelagian writings, he emphasizes the weakness of man's will as a result of original sin and man's continuous need of God's help in order to be saved; and insists that grace is something personal, intrinsic, and above all a gratuitous gift of God, for if it were not gratuitous it would no longer be grace.

Orosius. While Coelestius was under excommunication, Pelagius was being honored and consulted by the clergy and laity of Palestine, and even DEMETRIAS in Rome sought his advice before dedicating herself to a life of virginity. In 414 Augustine sent a young and intelligent Spanish priest named OROSIUS to alert Jerome in Bethlehem and the hierarchy of the Holy Land to the dangers of the new heresy.

Orosius and Pelagius appeared before a meeting of bishops at Jerusalem on July 28, 415, where Orosius charged Pelagius with heresy. As Orosius did not know Greek, he was hindered in his presentation of the evidence, and Pelagius, who had become fluent in this language, easily refuted him by his equivocal statements. Bishop John of Jerusalem decided to refer the matter to the Holy See, urged both men to remain silent, and hinted that Orosius himself was not above suspicion. The latter professed his orthodoxy in his *Liber apologeticus* and also insisted that Pelagius should be condemned.

Jerome. In this same year Jerome wrote two treatises against the Pelagians: one is in a letter to Ctesiphon and the other is called *Dialogus adversus Pelagianos.* In both he weakened the force of his arguments by the use of vituperation and violent personal allusions. Jerome also exaggerated when he addressed Pelagius: ''You boast a justice in men which is perfect and equal to that of God Himself'' (*Epistolae* 133). Pelagius never went that far, for he carefully reminded his followers that they were inferior to God. His mistake, as Augustine repeatedly pointed out, was in teaching that man could acquire even a relative degree of justice by his own unaided efforts.

Synod of Diospolis. Eulogius, Metropolitan of Caesarea, did not wait for Rome's reply to the hierarchy of Palestine. Urged on by two exiled bishops of Gaul, Heros and Lazarus, he summoned Pelagius before a council of 14 bishops at Diospolis (ancient Lydda) on Dec. 20, 415. Since no accuser appeared, Pelagius was questioned about the doctrines attributed to him. When the incriminating passages were read he either denied that he had ever taught them or else offered an orthodox explanation. The bishops therefore exonerated him from the charge of heresy. Augustine later wrote a detailed account of this council, *De gestis Pelagii,* in 417, and showed that Pelagius had been forced to disavow Coelestius in some points of doctrine and to anathematize one of his essential principles: that grace is given according to man's merits.

The African Bishops. When the hierarchy of Africa first heard of this council they believed that it had given its approval to Pelagianism. Therefore, in 416 sixty-seven bishops from the province of Africa assembled at Carthage and fifty-eight from the province of Numidia at Milevis. Both councils sent letters to Pope Innocent I in which they pointed out the errors of the Pelagians concerning freedom of the will, the futility of prayer, and infant baptism, and implored him to condemn its two principal leaders. On Jan. 27, 417, the Pope wrote three letters in reply. In them he approved of what the African bishops had written and excommunicated Pelagius and Coelestius.

Commenting on this exchange of letters Augustine declared: "The reports of two councils concerning this case [Pelagianism] were sent to the Apostolic See. From there replies have come; the case is closed" (*Serm.* 131). This was later popularized as "Rome has spoken, the case is closed." Pelagius at once forwarded a profession of faith, *Libellus fidei,* to Rome, and Coelestius went there in person to vindicate himself.

Roman Phase. When Innocent died on March 12, 417, the matter was brought to the attention of ZOSIMUS, his successor.

Pope Zosimus. The new Pope was satisfied with the orthodoxy of Pelagius after reading his profession of faith and restored him to unity with the Church. He was also lenient with Coelestius, but warned him not to teach in public. Through his correspondence with the hierarchy of Africa, however, he became aware of the real danger of the doctrines that Pelagius and Coelestius had concealed by their ambiguous language. He was also disillusioned by the disobedience of Coelestius, who challenged his opponents to debates that often ended in riots. With the Pontiff's approval, therefore, the Emperor HONORIUS expelled the Pelagian leaders from Rome on April 30, 418.

The following day, 214 African bishops assembled for the Sixteenth Council of Carthage. They condemned nine specific errors of Pelagius on original sin and its transmission (c. 1–3), the nature and necessity of grace (c. 4–6), and human impeccability (c. 7–9). In the summer of this year Zosimus issued the so-called *Epistola tractoria* in which he gave a brief history of Pelagianism, pointed out its falsehoods, ratified the acts of the Council of Carthage, and renewed his predecessor's excommunication of Pelagius and Coelestius. All the bishops of the Church were ordered to sign this letter.

A council at Antioch summoned by the Patriarch Theodotus accepted the letter of the Pope and Pelagius was expelled from Palestine; he disappeared from history leaving only conjectures about his subsequent fate. Coelestius refused to accept the verdict of the Holy See, escaping punishment because of his protectors.

Julian of Eclanum. The leader of the Pelagians after 418 was JULIAN, Bishop of Eclanum. He and 17 other bishops of Italy would not sign the *epistola tractoria* and demanded that a general council should be summoned to reopen the case. All were excommunicated, deposed, and exiled, and Julian began a literary war with Augustine in defense of the condemned heresy. He was more radical than Pelagius or Coelestius and was quoted as saying: "The freedom of the will is that by which man is freed from God" (*Contra Iulianum, opus imperfectum, Patrologia Latina*, ed. J. P. Migne [Paris 1878–90] 45:1102), but his principal argument is that original sin, as approved at Carthage and Rome, was a revival of MANICHAEISM.

Augustine refuted Julian in four major works: *De nuptiis et concupiscentia* (419–420), *Contra duas epistolas Pelagianorum* (420), *Contra Iulianum* (421), and his final work, begun in 429 and not finished at the time of his death (430), *Contra Iulianum opus imperfectum.*

SEMI-PELAGIANISM

In his last years Augustine had to refute the teachings of the monastic leaders, such as John CASSIAN, who repudiated Pelagianism but taught that man was capable of making an initial act of faith without the aid of divine grace. They also objected to Augustine's theory of predestination

Against these Semi-Pelagians (*see* SEMI-PELAGIANISM), as they were later called, Augustine wrote *De gratia et libero arbitrio* and *De correptione et gratia* in 427, and *De predestinatione sanctorum* and *De dono per-*

severantiae in 428 or 429. Despite the cogency of his arguments, the struggle against Semi-Pelagianism did not end until the Second Council of Orange (529).

Some of the bishops who had resisted the order of Pope Zosimus eventually made their submission. The rest were forced into exile in the East where they were befriended by THEODORE OF MOPSUESTIA. In 428 or 429 Julian of Eclanum and three other bishops arrived in Constantinople, where they met Coelestius and were received by NESTORIUS who had just become bishop there (April 428).

The Council of Ephesus. In 431 the general council, which Julian had demanded in 418, met at EPHESUS. It condemned not only Nestorianism, but Pelagianism as well (c. 1 and 4), and in the synodal letter of July 22 the bishops ratified the deposition of the ''impious Pelagians.'' This council gave the deathblow to Pelagianism, for East and West were now united against it, and it ceased to exist as an organized movement.

Later History. There is no further mention of Coelestius after 431, and Julian, disgraced and discredited, died *c.* 455. Some traces of the heresy persisted, however, as is clear from a letter of Pope GELASIUS I to the bishops of Picenum on Nov. 1, 493. Either before or during his pontificate, Gelasius also wrote the *Dicta adversus pelagianam haeresim.* No papal pronouncements against Pelagianism were necessary in the sixth century.

The Pelagian heresy led Catholic theologians to make a profound study of original sin and the Redemption of Christ, but its principal result was a vindication of the supernatural character of Christianity, and the unqualified assertion that grace is a gratuitous and undeserved gift of God. The Church of Africa was the uncompromising foe of Pelagianism from the beginning, and its most illustrious member, Augustine, has been called ''the Doctor of Grace'' because his teachings on this dogma have been adopted in great part by the Catholic Church.

Bibliography: R. HEDDE and É. AMANN, *Dictionnaire de théologie catholique*, ed. A. VACANT et al., (Paris 1903—50) 12.1:675–715. AUGUSTINE, *Gest. Pelag.*, ed. C. F. URBA and J. ZYCHA (*Corpus scriptorum ecclesiasticorum latinorum* [Vienna 1866–] 42; 1902); *C. Pelag.*, ed. C. F. URBA, and J. ZYCHA (*Corpus scriptorum ecclesiasticorum latinorum* 60; 1913). PELAGIUS, *Expositions of the Thirteen Epistles of St. Paul,* ed. A. SOUTER, 3 v. (Texts and Studies 9.1–9.3; Cambridge, Eng. 1922–31). C. CASPARI, *Briefe, Abhandlungen, Predigten* (Oslo 1890). G. DE PLINVAL, *Pélage: Ses écrits, sa vie et sa réforme* (Lausanne 1943). J. FERGUSON, *Pelagius: A Historical and Theological Study* (Cambridge, Eng. 1956). J. TIXERONT, *A Handbook of Patrology* (St. Louis 1930). E. PORTALIÉ, *A Guide to the Thought of St. Augustine* (Chicago 1960). T. DE BRUYN, *Pelagius's Commentary on St Paul's Epistle to the Romans: Translated with Introduction and Notes* (Oxford; New York 1993). B.R. REES, *Pelagius: Life and Letters* (Rochester, N.Y. 1998); *Pelagius, a Reluctant Heretic* (Woodbridge 1988). J. FERGUSON, *Pelagius: A Historical and Theological Study* (New York 1978). R. F. EVANS, *Four Letters of Pelagius* (New York1968); *Pelagius; Inquiries and Reappraisals* (New York 1968). C. C. BURNETT, *God's Self-revelation in the Theology of Pelagius* (diss.; Catholic University of America 1998).

[S. J. MCKENNA]

PELCZAR, JÓZEF SEBASTIAN, BL.

Bishop, founder of the Servants of the Most Sacred Heart of Jesus; b. Jan. 17, 1842, Korczyna, Poland; d. March 28, 1924, Przemyśi, Poland. Józef Pelczar founded the Servants of the Most Sacred Heart of Jesus (1894), which came to the United States in 1959. He was consecrated titular bishop of Meletopolis (Feb. 20, 1899) prior to assuming the see of Przemyśi, Poland (Jan. 13, 1901), which he guided through the horrors of World War I. He is remembered for his selfless heroism following the invasion of Russia (March 1915), as well as for opening medical centers to care for the wounded and victims of epidemics. At Pelczar's beatification in Rzeszów, Poland, June 2, 1991, Pope John Paul II remembered the bishop as ''the man who did the will of the Father.''

Bibliography: *L'Osservatore Romano*, 23 (1991).

[K. I. RABENSTEIN]

PELICAN

In the Christian tradition, the pelican is identified as a symbol of Christ the Redeemer. The long beak of the white pelican is furnished with a sack which serves as a container for the small fish that it feeds its young. In the process of feeding them, the bird presses the sack against its neck in such a way that it seems to open its breast with its bill. The reddish tinge of its breast plumage and the redness of the tip of its beak fostered the folkloristic notion that it actually drew blood from its own breast. The *Physiologus* found the action of the pelican, so interpreted, as a particularly apt symbol of Christ the Redeemer:

> The little pelicans strike their parents, and the parents, striking back, kill them. But on the third day the mother pelican strikes and opens her side and pours blood over her dead young. In this way they are revivified and made well. So our Lord Jesus Christ says also through the prophet Isaiah: ''I have brought up children and exalted them, but they have despised me'' (Is 1:2). We struck God by serving the creature rather than the Creator. Therefore he deigned to ascend the cross, and, when his side was pierced, blood and water gushed forth unto our salvation and eternal life.

Under the influence primarily of the *Physiologus*, the pelican as a symbol of Christ the Redeemer, a symbol al-

St. Maria Euphrasia Pelletier.

ready familiar to St. Augustine (Enarr. In Psalm. 101:7), has a wide usage in Christian literature. As important and typical examples of medieval use, it will suffice to mention the allusion in the hymn *Adoro te devote* and that in Dante's *Paradiso* (25:113). In Christian art it is employed from the late Middle Ages, but especially in the Renaissance and in the baroque period. From the late Middle Ages the pelican is employed also as a symbol of the Eucharist. In art, particularly in baroque art, the pelican is found frequently as an ornament on altars, pyxes, chalices, and tabernacle doors.

[M. R. P. MCGUIRE/EDS.]

PELLETIER, MARIA EUPHRASIA, ST.

Foundress; B. Noirmoutier (Vendée), France, July 31, 1796; d. Angers, France, April 24, 1868. Rose Virginie Pelletier was sent for schooling to Tours where she joined (1814) the Religious of Our Lady of Charity of the Refuge and took the name Maria of St. Euphrasia. In 1825 she became superior of this autonomous community engaged in caring for women in need of moral reform. The house, which had been struggling to reestablish itself after suppression during the FRENCH REVOLUTION, flourished under her capable leadership.

In 1829 Mother Euphrasia established a house in Angers and became its superior in 1831. She received papal approval (1835) to centralize the administration of several independent convents under one superior general. The Sisters of Our Lady of Charity of the GOOD SHEPHERD, as they came to be known, grew rapidly. During the lifetime of the foundress, who acted as superior general, 110 foundations were started, including several in the U.S. For penitent women, Mother Euphrasia founded the Sisters Magdalens as a cloistered group of religious women dedicated to reparation. In 1950 they became affiliated as a branch of the Good Shepherd Sisters, and in 1964 they were renamed Contemplatives of the Cross. Mother Euphrasia was beatified on April 30, 1933 and canonized on May 2, 1940.

Feast: April 24.

Bibliography: *Conferences and Instructions* (Westminster, Md. 1943). SISTERS OF THE GOOD SHEPHERD, *In Truth, I Am Their Foundress (SME): Selections from and concerning St. M. Euphrasia Pelletier Compiled from Our Contemplative Communities* (s.l. 1978). *Lettres*, 8 v. (Angers 1995–1996). G. BERNOVILLE, *Saint Mary Euphrasia Pelletier: Foundress of the Good Shepherd Sisters* (Westminster, Md, 1959). J. T. MCVEIGH, *Rose Virginie Pelletier: The Woman and Her Legacy* (Lanham 1997).

[M. ANDREOLI]

PELLICANUS, KONRAD (KÜRSCHNER)

Pioneer Christian Hebraist; b. Ruffach, Alsace, January 1478; d. Zurich, April 6, 1556. He entered the Franciscan monastery in Ruffach (1493) and was later transferred to their monastery in Tübingen for his theological studies (1496). After his ordination (1501) he taught Scripture in the Franciscan monasteries of Basel (1502–07) and Ruffach (1508–11) and was then made local superior in Pforzheim, Ruffach, and Basel. While in Basel (1519–26), he became acquainted with the writings of M. LUTHER. When he was deposed from his office as superior because of his Protestant tendencies, he accepted the professorship of Scripture at the University of Basel (1523). In February 1526, when he accepted U. ZWINGLI's invitation to teach Scripture in Zurich, he definitively left the Catholic Church in favor of the Reformation.

Having taken a special interest, even as a seminarian, in the study of Hebrew, Pellicanus was the first Christian to publish a Hebrew grammar [*De modo legendi et intelligendi Hebraeum* (Strassburg 1504)]. He was highly regarded as the outstanding Hebraist of his day; thus he had a great influence on contemporary Scripture scholars and was an important collaborator on the German translations of the Bible made at Zurich. Besides other works, he wrote also the *Commentaria Bibliorum* (7 v. Zurich 1532–37) and in 1544 an autobiography [*Chronicon,* ed. B. Riggenbach (Basel 1877)] that is important for the study of the history of the Reformation.

Bibliography: O. VASELLA, *Lexicon für Theologie und Kirche*, ed. J. HOFER and K. RAHNER (Freiburg 1957–65) 8:254–255. H. R. GUGGISBERG, *Die Religion in Geschichte und Gegenwart* (Tübingen 1957–65) 5:208.

[L. F. HARTMAN]

PEMBROKE, PRIORY OF

Also known as Monkton, former Benedictine monastery in Pembroke, Saint Davids diocese, Wales. It was founded in 1098 as a cell to St. Martin's Abbey, Séez, Normandy, by Arnulf Montgomery, Lord of Pembroke, and was further endowed by later earls of Pembroke. Richard II, because of the French war, seized it into his hands (1378). Henry IV restored it (1399), but it was evidently again seized, since Henry VI granted it (1441) to Humphrey, Duke of Gloucester, who in turn granted it to the Abbey of SAINT ALBANS (1443). Under Saint Albans, Pembroke had a prior and probably three or four monks. Henry VIII dissolved it (1539). Dugdale describes the priory church, prior's mansion, dove house, and two chapels. The church, dedicated to St. Nicholas, and mother of two other Pembroke churches, continues in (Anglican) ecclesiastical use.

Bibliography: W. DUGDALE, *Monasticon Anglicanum* (London 1655–73); best ed. by J. CALEY et al., 6 v. (1817–30) 2:243–244; 4:320–323; 6.2:999. *Calendar of Documents Preserved in France,* ed. J. H. ROUND (London 1899–) v. 1. J. E. LLOYD, *A History of Wales from the Earliest Times to the Edwardian Conquest,* 2 v. (3d ed. New York 1939) v. 2. D. KNOWLES and R. N. HADCOCK, *Medieval Religious Houses: England and Wales* (New York 1953).

[R. W. HAYS]

PEÑA MONTENEGRO, ALONSO DE LA

Bishop of Quito; b. Villa de Padrón, Spain, April 29, 1596; d. Quito, May 12, 1687. In 1611 he entered the University of Santiago de Compostela, where he received the degrees of bachelor and licentiate in arts and philosophy. He continued his studies into theology, earning the doctorate in 1621. Two years later he won the position of teaching canon at the Colegiata de Iria and at the same time held a professorship at the University of Compostela. He had acquired these high ecclesiastical positions without becoming a priest, but in February of 1639, he was ordained and went to Salamanca to compete for a fellowship in the old Colegio de San Bartolomé. There he became a friend of Gaspar Bracamonte y Guzmán, later president of the Council of the Indies. In January of 1653 Peña Montenegro was appointed bishop of Quito and set out for the diocese with a large library and a retinue of 18 servants. He was consecrated in Bogotá by Abp. Cristóbal de Torres in April 1654, and took over his diocese September 23. After making his pastoral visitation, he wrote *Itinerario para párrocos de Indias* to instruct his clergy in parochial administration. He fostered vocations to the priesthood, restored the cathedral, founded the Carmelite monastery of Talacunga, helped in the establishment of the Dominican Colegio de San Fernando, served as interim president of the *Audiencia,* and promoted culture generally in the area.

[J. M. VARGAS]

PEÑALVER Y CÁRDENAS, LUIS IGNACIO

Bishop; b. Havana, Cuba, April 13, 1749; d. Havana, July 17, 1810. He studied in Havana at St. Ignatius College until 1768, when a decree of King Charles III of Spain closed this and other Jesuit institutions. He moved to the University of Havana and earned a doctorate in theology (1781). After Peñalver's ordination in 1772, Bp. Santiago José de Echevarria Felguezua placed him in charge of contributions and legacies made to the Diocese of Santiago de Cuba. In 1773 Peñalver became vicar-general and ecclesiastical judge. He also held the post of administrator of the diocese for two years. He assisted in founding a public library; organized an asylum for the poor, the Casa de Beneficencia; and inaugurated a program to promote better relations between the upper classes and the common people of Cuba. He spent much of his fortune in relief work for victims of a hurricane that swept Cuba in 1792.

When Pius VI created the Diocese of Louisiana and the Floridas in 1793, he appointed Peñalver the first bishop. He arrived in New Orleans July 17, 1795, and found the religious life of the people at a very low ebb. There were approximately 11,000 Catholics in New Orleans and its environs, but hardly more than a fourth of them ever attended Mass. Accompanied by his secretary, Rev. Ysidro Quintero, and the pastor of St. Louis Cathedral, Rev. Antonio de Sedella, Peñalver made a visitation (1796) of the 14 parishes and, in lieu of a synod, which he did not consider feasible, he issued detailed letters of instructions. These had the force of synodal regulations and helped stem some deeply rooted abuses. After six years, he could claim only qualified success for his efforts in Louisiana. On Nov. 3, 1801, he departed for Guatemala City, Guatemala, to whose archbishopric he had been promoted. After five years there, he retired to Havana.

[H. C. BEZOU]

PENANCE, PRACTICES OF

Concrete expressions of the penitential spirit involving either ascetical deeds or the sacrifice of legitimate pleasure for a spiritual purpose have been characteristic of the Christian Church since its foundation. The source of the penitential ideal is the life of Jesus Christ. For example, He praised the ideal of virginity, which renounces the great good of marital love, the better to love God, and the bestowal of one's earthly goods on the poor, the more easily to seek heavenly goods (cf. Mt 19.12, 16–22). And He emphasized His teaching by embracing these penitential practices in His own life.

The teaching and practice of Jesus were continued by His disciples. St. Paul noted that freedom from marriage gives a virgin opportunity to think about the things of the Lord, that she might be holy in body and spirit (1 Cor 7.25–35). St. John spoke of a special closeness to Christ that is a prerogative of the virgins in the Kingdom of Heaven (Rev 14.1–5). The faithful at Jerusalem gave up the ownership of their goods for the support of the community (Acts 2.44; 4.32); St. Paul presented his self-inflicted chastisement as an example for all Christians (1 Cor 9.27); the four daughters of Philip the Deacon dedicated themselves to a life of virginity (Acts 21.9); it was recorded of St. James the Less by Hegesippus, who lived in mid-second century, that James denied himself meat and wine and the use of razor and bath.

The Fathers of the Church praised such works of penance and reflected its practice in their own times. It is clear that the motives behind the various penitential practices were uniform: principally, a desire to answer the Lord's invitation to imitate Him in carrying a cross (Lk 9.23); reparation for sin, personal or otherwise (*see* REPARATION); and the mastery of all their human inclinations (1 Cor 9.27).

During the first centuries the penitential ideal was expressed in the lives of the chosen few, the virgins and ascetics, but also in the program of fasting that came into use throughout the Church, with varying local observances. There are signs that, very early, Friday was kept as a day of fast, in memory of the Lord's suffering and death on that day. In pre-Nicaean times there was a period devoted to pre-Paschal fast, roughly parallel to present-day Lent, with local variances in length and rigor. In some places it lasted only a few days, with one meal taken late in the day; in other places it was longer but less rigorous. The sackcloth (*see* HAIR SHIRT) spoken of by Christ (Mt 11.21) was always the garb of the penitent. In both East and West there were grades among these penitents, depending on the severity of their penances: for example, the ''weepers,'' who accompanied their pleas for prayers with tears, and the ''prostrati,'' who begged prayers while lying on the ground. Kneeling during religious services began as a penitential practice and at one time was not permitted on feast days. Manual labor, once the badge of slavery, was given a penitential aspect by the monks of the desert and later was adopted by religious rules. The monasteries, in due course, became schools of penance each with its own penitential pattern.

The detail of penitential practice differs in intensity from one culture to another; in extreme times there were many extremes, but they were generally short-lived. The rigors of the Egyptian hermits and the Irish monks, for example, passed quickly, but the reality of penance remains. Every age, even the present one, witnesses the attraction of the Christian to follow the Master by taking up a cross of some kind.

Bibliography: M. VILLER and M. OLPHE-GAILLARD, *Dictionnaire de spiritualité ascétique et mystique. Doctrine et histoire*, ed. M. VILLER et al. (Paris 1932–) 1:959–977. J. DE GUIBERT, *ibid.* 1:977–990. S. SOLERO, A. MERCARTI, and A. PELZER, *Dizionario ecclesiastico*, 3 v. (Turin 1954–58) 3:143. L. GOUGAUD, *Devotional and Ascetic Practices in the Middle Ages,* tr. G. C. BATEMAN (London 1927). H. THURSTON, *Lent and Holy Week* (London 1904).

[P. F. MULHERN/EDS.]

PENANCE, SACRAMENT OF

The sacrament of penance is the sacrament through which Christians ''obtain pardon from the mercy of God for offenses committed against him, and are, at the same time, reconciled with the Church which they have wounded by their sins and which by charity, by example, and by prayer labors for their conversion'' (LG 11). Conversion (*metanoia*) and reconciliation were central to the mission of Jesus and remain the foundation of disciples' life in Christ. Those preparing for baptism and Eucharist learn to be part of a converting and reconciling community. Those already baptized who sin return to the path of conversion and to Eucharist in this second sacrament of conversion. Though the understanding and practice of the sacrament have changed over the centuries, the essential elements (*substantia*) have remained constant: calling sinners to conversion and supporting those who respond (''binding''); reconciling the repentant who have undergone conversion (''loosing'').

Terminology. The earliest name for this sacrament was *paenitentia secunda*, from the Latin translation of the

Emperor Henry IV begging Matilda, Countess of Tuscany, before Hugo Abbot of Cluny at her castle, Canossa, Italy, manuscript illumination. (©Archivo Iconografico, S.A./CORBIS)

Pilgrims at a public square at Fatima do penance by walking around a designated path on their knees, Portugal. (©Tony Arruza/CORBIS)

Greek *metanoia* (conversion, repentance): baptism was the first conversion and penance the second. In the early Middle Ages ''confession'' became the usual term because of its ritual prominence and this usage has continued into our time. The twentieth century saw the return of ''penance'' to common use, and Vatican Council II and its new ritual stressed reconciliation. Theologically, this is a sacrament of both conversion (penance) and reconciliation, with the two mutually required: conversion leads to reconciliation with God and Church, and reconciliation requires conversion.

Origins. The sacrament is broadly based in the ministry of Jesus who preached repentance and conversion to the reign of God. Forgiveness of sins was prominent in his ministry (Mk 2:3–12), and the early Church believed it was authorized to continue his ministry (Mt 16:l9, 18:18; Jn 20:22–23). Baptism was the most striking expression of this authority, but sinners in the community also had to be dealt with. The ministry of binding and loosing included both the authority to exclude serious sinners from the community and its Eucharist and the authority to restore to the community of salvation those who underwent conversion (1 Cor 5:5; 2 Cor 2:11). Some communities were reluctant to forgive certain sinners (1 Jn 5:14–17; Heb 6:4–8; 10:26–31; 12:16–17), but generally conversion was the only prerequisite to welcoming them back.

Ancient Penance. *The Shepherd of Hermas* (c. 140) contains the earliest evidence of a second penance entrusted by Christ to the Shepherd. It was limited, like baptism, to once only but was open to all sinners. Other early authors—Clement of Rome (d. c. 96), Ignatius of Antioch (d. c. 110), Polycarp (d. c. 156), and 2 Clement (c. 150)—witness to this sense of clemency but say little about procedures. As pastor, the bishop was responsible for this ministry.

Everyday sinners repented and generally found support and reconciliation in the Eucharist. Practice varied on which sins required ecclesial ministry. The practice of penance took several forms, including fasting, almsgiving, wearing sackcloth and ashes, prayer and works of charity. Tertullian's description of *exomologesis* (confession, in the sense of celebrating God's greatness) in the *De Paenitentia* gives us some detail on the making of penitents in a liturgy confessing God's mercy. Sackcloth symbolizing the goats separated from Christ's flock, ashes symbolizing exclusion from the paradise of the Church, penitential practices (kneeling, prayer, fasting, works of charity), and community prayer for penitents were major ritual actions marking a person's entrance into the communal process of conversion called the order of penitents.

Cyprian of Carthage (d. 258), in the mid-third century, speaks of the laying on of hands in exorcism at the entry into penance and again at its completion, this time granting peace with the Church through communion with the Holy Spirit. These show how he understood the operational dynamics of conversion and reconciliation and also the liturgical orientation of the penitential works that characterized the time of penance: they expressed in practice the repentance manifested to the Church in becoming a penitent; at the same time they, together with the community's prayer and example, moved that repentance toward maturity.

Controversy over how to maintain the Church's holiness and opposition to reconciling some sinners helped shape Western development. The East, largely unaffected by this rigorism, kept more of a gospel leniency that gave priority to healing the community by healing sinners.

The elitist ecclesiology of third-century Montanists and Novatianists challenged the bishop's authority to forgive certain sins; e.g., Tertullian in *De paenitentia* held out hope of pardon to all sinners through *exomologesis* (liturgical conversion) but as a Montanist in *De pudicitia* denied the bishop's power to forgive those guilty of certain unpardonable sins. Such puritans, as they were termed at Nicaea, called the guilty to conversion but refused reconciliation. Cyprian of Carthage went against this when he authorized penance and reconciliation for the dying and, expecting another persecution, for all sinners, even those who had earlier apostacized. Rome followed a similar policy.

Nicaea upheld the Church's authority over all sinners, calling for the Eucharist to be given to the dying, even those who could not enter penance. This exceptional adaptation of procedures suggests that forgiveness was understood as due to divine mercy, not the penitent's efforts. Pacian (d. before 392) and Ambrose (d. 397) both upheld the Church's full authority as expression of divine mercy.

Communal disciplinary and liturgical structures developed to highlight the Church's authority over sin. Those who had begun to repent spoke privately with the bishop or his delegate. They entered the order of penitents in a public liturgical rite. The order of penitents provided community ministry parallel to the catechumenate. Fasting, prayer, and works of charity symbolized turning from self-centeredness to God and neighbor. The process of conversion often took years and frequently required celibacy and withdrawal from public life.

We know little of the liturgy reconciling penitents until after the resolution of the PENITENTIAL CONTROVERSIES and the emergence of canonical penance. The liturgy then became increasingly dramatic, perhaps to compensate for an abbreviated and less committed conversion, but certainly to highlight the Church's authority to reconcile all repentant sinners. In the fifth century the ritual of reconciliation took place after the dismissal of catechumens, at the time when penitents normally ''came under the hand'' to receive the community's exorcism-blessing and prayer. Penitents expressed their sorrow, their prayer became the community's, the bishop was asked to reconcile them, he prayed to voice the penitent's prayer now become the prayer of the Church, and he imposed hands to show that the penitents from freed from sin and restored to the Eucharist.

Penitents reached the completion (*absolutio*) of their conversion in a public liturgy just before Easter. Ritual dynamics expressed that both conversion and forgiveness were in and through penitents' relationship to the community of salvation: they were reconciled to God by being reconciled to the Church. However, the refusal to allow more than one such reconciliation (a parallel with baptism) signaled a failure to reflect in practice the doctrine of the Church's full authority.

Canonical regulation of the order of penitents in the fourth and fifth centuries also failed to take adequate account of the changing socio-cultural situation of the Church where sin was no longer the experience of a return to pagan ways. Coercive penalties were often inconsistent from one region to another; their severity discouraged many people from undertaking the ecclesial conversion that was increasingly experienced as punitive. Not surprisingly, there was a rise in deathbed penance, as many sought to avoid or mitigate the harshness of doing penance and the public stigma of being branded a public penitent. Voluntarily joining the ranks of the *conversi* was much like religious profession for the pious—Francis later founded three orders of penance—but those forced to undergo the canonical discipline were often penalized for life.

A priest listens to a woman's confession in an open confessional, Puerto Rico. (©Corbis)

The demise of the catechumenate meant that the developing season of Lent took on a penitential rather than baptismal spirit. In the fifth and sixth centuries others began to join the penitents and by the tenth century all were expected to. Lent thus became a communal form of penance.

In many places, particularly the East and Gaul, repentant sinners undertook conversion on their own or with the assistance of a spiritual advisor but without the official and liturgical support of the Church. The East, however, provided prayers for forgiveness in the Hours and Liturgy that maintained a communal orientation to penance.

Medieval Penance. Doing penance privately without official ecclesial and liturgical support increased in the early Middle Ages. In the West Celtic monks extended to the laity the ministry of soul-friend. Spiritual advisors, usually nonordained monks or nuns, gave counsel on how best to compensate for sin (a perspective of Anglo-Saxon and Celtic culture also evident in Anselm's theory of redemption). Advisors adapted the celtic penal system with tarriff and commutation in evaluating the penance that needed to be carried out for sin. This took the form of penitentials, lists of sins and appropriate remedies or penalties which generally functioned as tariffs imposed on sins.

The depth of the penitent's contrition was, however, taken into account. Unlike canonical penance, there was no public stigma, penalties were often mitigated by commutations and redemptions (later, indulgences), and, most importantly, penance could be done repeatedly for any sin at any time to reassure the anxious. All that was needed was contrition (sincere repentance), detailed confession, and the performance of assigned penances.

''Confession'' grew in importance. This was no longer the praise of a merciful God calling the sinner to conversion (*exomologesis*) but the detailed admission of sinfulness to the advisor for the purpose of receiving an appropriate ''penance.'' After this was done, the individual could return to eucharistic communion. If what was later called ''absolution'' existed—and this is doubtful—it was given by lay as well as ordained advisors who heard confession.

After unsuccessful efforts to revive canonical penance during the ninth-century Carolingian reformation, the official structures were adapted in a fashion that accepted private confession and penance for grave sins not publicly known. With the growing popularity of the Celtic practice of confession, a private liturgy of penance began to develop. At first this was simply confession (in the sense of admitting one's sins to receive the benefit of the confessor's advice and assignment of penance), but in the tenth century reconciliation (absolution) was added immediately after the confession. The private ritual contained many elements from the canonical liturgy but lost the public, communal process that liturgy engendered and the consequent sense of identity for both community and penitents. Priests were to serve as confessors and, after penance, to give an official declaration of completion, the absolution, as an exercise of the power of the keys. The penitent's active participation was largely limited to responding to the priest's questions regarding sin, listening to the Latin prayers, affirming faith and confidence in response to the priest's questions, and receiving the declaration of forgiveness (absolution). Confession and absolution were the ritual foci. It was the failure of penitents to return for absolution after doing their penance led to absolution being joined to confession in the tenth century.

Medieval theologians debated how penance fit into the new category of sacrament and how the penitent's acts (contrition, confession, and satisfaction as phases of personal conversion) and the priest's absolution related to one another in effecting forgiveness. These debates developed out of the private individual experience of repentance and the lack of a clear sense of reconciliation to the Church that had been expressed in the ancient liturgy.

Influenced by the spirit of Celtic culture that had shaped private penance, some theologians emphasized the penitent's efforts to make satisfaction. However, the displacement of confession-penance by confession-absolution meant that penance (satisfaction) diminished in importance and became more lenient. This led many twelfth-century theologians to emphasize contrition, interior penance or repentance manifested in confession, as the source of pardon (e.g., Abelard). Others (e.g., the Victorines) emphasized the power of the keys removing guilt. Bonaventure saw confession and absolution disposing a person to contrition, with that the cause of forgiveness, and there were other attempts at synthesis.

Aquinas achieved a balance between the personal and ecclesiastical factors by regarding the penitent's acts as the matter of the sacrament and the priest's absolution as the form. The two act as a single cause, with the penitent's acts sacramental signs and the absolution dominant. Grace is the formal, efficient, and final cause of both contrition and forgiveness; contrition and forgiveness are the material cause of grace and dispose the person to receive it; absolution serves as the instrumental cause. Attrition (incipient contrition) is the remote disposition for grace. In the sacramental ritual attrition matures into contrition and becomes the proximate disposition for grace. There is thus a single means of postbaptismal justification, in the sacrament or outside it: contrition as the expression of faith and love in response to grace.

Later scholastics exploited ambiguities in Thomas' explanation to relate the subjective and objective elements in a more extrinsic manner. Duns Scotus distinguished sharply between attrition and contrition (on the basis of motive, whether self-love or the love of God above all things) and gave prominence to the absolution by seeing only attrition as needed in the sacrament but ''perfect'' contrition required outside it.

In addition to private confession, the Middle Ages made use of other forms of penance: solemn penance (the rarely used remnant of ancient canonical penance's liturgy), the Lenten season, pilgrimage, and general (public) absolutions in the liturgy. Lay confession continued to be used into the fourteenth century, especially when a priest was not available, and was often considered sacramental or quasi-sacramental, although Scotus' view of absolution as the essence of the sacrament eventually led to it not being regarded as sacramental.

Modern Penance. Lateran IV (1215) began the transition from medieval to modern penance by requiring each Christian of the age of reason to make an annual confession to his or her priest for the sake of receiving absolution. Confessors were encouraged to interrogate penitents, a sign that penitents' understanding of sin and penance was shallow. Yet, in the face of Albigensianism, confession became a sign of loyalty to the Church and the obligatory means of forgiveness. Most lay people, submitted reluctantly to the priest's judgment. Most commentators saw this compulsory confession as binding only those conscious of mortal sin, a view given tacit approval by TRENT and incorporated into the 1983 Code of Canon Law.

The official requirement of confession and absolution began a shift from medieval understanding and practice. Confession became the ordinary means to gain forgiveness of serious postbaptismal sin. For some this was onerous discipline; for others, consoling grace.

LUTHER's understanding of justification by grace through faith led him to regard penance as the gospel promise of grace encouraging the sinner to confident trust in divine forgiveness. He criticized requiring integral (full) confession of all mortal sins. By limiting the power of the keys to proclaiming the gospel of forgiveness he rejected priestly absolution as a juridical act.

Trent's response (Session 14, 1551) was to insist on penance's institution by Christ for the forgiveness of postbaptismal sin. It solemnly reaffirmed integral confession of mortal sins to the priest and his absolution as a judgment reconciling the sinner with God. Both were declared to be *iure divino*, but at the time the term's meaning varied from a custom in line with the divine will to something essential by God's will.

The importance of the penitent's confession and the priest's absolution grew in response to Reformation criticism. The 1614 *Rituale Romanum* removed or diminished liturgical elements, including prayer, to show the centrality of integral confession and juridical absolution. As a consequence, few penitents experienced confession as ecclesial worship.

The Counter-Reformation continued the medieval association of confession and communion, and as communion became more frequent, so did confession. The introduction of the confessional, intended to prevent accusations of sollicitation, strengthened the sense of privacy and isolation. When Pius X's *Quam singulari* (1910) lowered the age of first communion, penance, rather than confirmation, became the ritual transition between baptism and Eucharist, and the age of this first confession became a matter of controversy following Vatican Council II. Throughout the era of the Counter-Reformation, highlighting confession as a sign of Catholic loyalty made its ritual performance the *only* ordinary means of postbaptismal justification. Devotional confession (the confession of venial sins or of already- forgiven mortal sins) became a common practice.

Vatican Council II. The ancient theme of experiencing reconciliation with God through reconciliation with the Church in the context of community worship (Xiberta, K. Rahner) was restored to prominence as a result of nineteenth- and twentieth-century historical study. Theologians consequently shifted focus from contrition (interior penance) to reconciliation with the Church in speaking of how God's action enters sacramentally within human experience (the *res et sacramentum*, to use the scholastic term).

Vatican Council II emphasized conversion as both personal and ecclesial and called for a reform to express the sacrament's social and ecclesial character (*Sacrosanctum concilium* 72). It stressed that the penitent sinner is reconciled at the same time with God and Church (*Lumen gentium* 11; *Presbyterorum ordinis* 5). Theological consensus on the priority of reconciliation with the Church was matched pastorally by grassroots development of communal celebrations of the sacrament.

The 1973 *Rite of Penance* provides three sacramental forms (for reconciling an individual, for reconciling several penitents with individual confession and absolution, for reconciling several penitents with general confession and absolution) and nonsacramental penitential celebrations to support conversion. The Introduction reflects theological consensus of the mid-twentieth century. Conversion to God is a personal process in community and the traditional acts of the penitent are restated in this context. Reconciliation is fundamental to the Church's character and responsibility, with bishops and priests exercising the ministry of this sacrament. Reconciliation with the Church is sacrament of reconciliation with God. For the first time in an official ritual social dimensions of sin and reconciliation and the sacrament's orientation to justice are noted.

Rite I, i.e., the rite for reconciling an individual penitent has also been enhanced liturgically with prayer, scripture, and fuller participation. It too is described as the liturgy by which the Church renews itself (RP 11). A pleasant room rather than a dark booth is the appropriate place for this liturgy, although penitents may choose to use a grille to maintain anonymity. Overall, practice has changed little, and focus is still more on confession and absolution than shared prayer.

Rite II situates individual confession and absolution in a new, communal context. Individual confession and absolution follow an initial communal celebration (including a Liturgy of the Word with homily and examination of conscience), ending with a proclamation of praise and prayer of thanksgiving. The difficulty of finding enough confessors to celebrate Rite II properly often means a truncated celebration still focusing on individual confession and absolution and eliminating communal praise and thanksgiving. However, when carried out in full, the communal context of Rite II is able to aid in the formation of one's conscience and a deepened sense of sin, conversion, and reconciliation that is both personal and communal.

Rite III provides a fully communal celebration for reconciling the repentant. The communal celebrations consist of introductory rites (song and prayer), celebration of the Word (including homily and examination of conscience), the rite of reconciliation, and a concluding rite. The rite of reconciliation begins with a general or communal confession, including the Lord's Prayer. Provision is made for a general or communal absolution and a proclamation of praise. The use of Rite III is governed by the provisions of canon 961 of the 1983 Code of Canon Law, which restricts its use to the following situations: (i) where danger of death is imminent and there is insufficient time for the hearing of individual confessions (c. 961 §1, 1), and (ii) there is grave necessity, i.e., when in view of the number of penitents, there are not enough confessors available for individual confessions within a suitable period of time in such a way that the penitents are forced to be deprived for a long while of sacramental grace or holy communion through no fault of their own (c. 961 §1, 2). The competent person to judge whether such conditions exist is the diocesan bishop (c. 961 §2).

The post-Tridentine increase in frequency of confession slowed and began to reverse in the second quarter of the twentieth century. A changed sense of sin, dissent from Church moral teaching (especially on artificial contraception), and the experience of reconciliation in other contexts (especially Eucharist, with more frequent communion) have been major factors in what amounts to a return to the medieval standard of frequency.

Bibliography: B. POSCHMAN, *Penance and the Anointing of the Sick* (London 1963). K. RAHNER, ''Forgotten Truths Concerning the Sacrament of Penance,'' *Theological Investigations* 2 (1963) 135–174. K. DOOLEY, ''From Penance to Confession: The Celtic Contribution,'' *Bijdragen* 43 (1982) 390–411. K. DOOLEY, ''Development of the Practice of Devotional Confession,'' *Quaestiones Liturgiques* (1983) 89–117. J. DALLEN, *The Reconciling Community* (Collegeville, MN 1986); J. FAVAZZA, *The Order of Penitents* (Collegeville, MN 1988); K. OSBORNE, *Reconciliation and Justification* (New York/Mahwah, NJ, 1990). INTERNATIONAL THEOLOGICAL COMMISSION, ''Penance and Reconciliation'' (1982); JOHN PAUL II, ''On Reconciliation and Penance in the Mission of the Church Today'' (1984).

[J. DALLEN]

PENITENTIAL CONTROVERSY

The problem regarding the practice of sacramental penance in the early Church. No unequivocal evidence exists for the formal method whereby sins were submitted to the priest and absolution given to the penitent during the first four centuries, although the practice of Penance and the forgiveness of sins is an essential fact of Christian belief from the beginning of the Church. During the second and third centuries, controversy broke out in various local churches as to whether formal absolution for sins committed after Baptism could be obtained more than once, and likewise regarding the possibility of the Church's granting pardon for certain grave sins—adultery, homicide, and idolatry—committed after Baptism. Finally, the readmittance to Communion in the Church of those who had committed acts of apostasy during persecution, particularly the LAPSI, or fallen, and the LIBELLATICI , or those who obtained certificates without sacrificing, was disputed. This difficulty also involved the intercessionary powers of the martyrs and confessors of the faith.

Postapostolic Documents. Although the DIDACHE and the so-called *Second Epistle* of CLEMENT I indicate that penance for the forgiveness of sins was a common Christian belief, neither of these documents specifies the technical machinery of effecting pardon other than through reconciliation with the leaders of the Church. In the *Shepherd of HERMAS*, there is evidence of a dispute regarding the number of times pardon can be extended to postbaptismal sinners, and the writer indicates the possibility of a time of pardon that has been variously interpreted by modern authors to mean a period of jubilee, although this season is identified with the building of a tower that represents the Church under an eschatological or chiliastic perspective. Hence the time of pardon could be coextensive with the perdurance of the Church. Hermas also spoke of one penance, μετάνοια μία (Mand. 4.1.8, 3.6); but this could mean one type rather than the usual significance of a single opportunity.

Tertullian and Cyprian. It is with TERTULLIAN (d. after 220) that the polemic concerning the possibility of only one absolution for postbaptismal sins comes clearly into focus (*De pudicitia*). He spoke of *duabus plancis* in the sense of Baptism and one other chance for safety given to those who relapsed into grave sins after the total forgiveness in Baptism (*De paenit.* 12.9). In his Montanist period (after 196), he likewise challenged a bishop, whom he ironically termed the supreme pontiff, for having declared that the irremissible sins of adultery, murder, and idolatry (*De pud.* 9.20; 21.14; 19.25; *Adv. Marc.* 4.9) can be forgiven by the Church. He termed these sins *exitiosa* and said their forgiveness is reserved to God (*De pud.* 19.6). The supreme pontiff to whom Tertullian referred was probably Agrippinus, Bishop of Carthage (218–22), and not the bishop of Rome. St. Cyprian of Carthage, half a century later, commented on Tertullian's opinion regarding unforgivable sins and said it did not represent the true teaching of the Church (*Epistle* 55); and Augustine in the 5th century also made reference to it as an error (*De libro Act. Apost.; Patrologia Latina*, ed. J. P. Migne, 217 v., indexes 4 v. (Paris 1878–90) 34:994).

Hippolytus and Novatian. Contemporary with Tertullian, however, a dispute had broken out in the Roman Church between Pope CALLISTUS (217–22)and the antipope, later reconciled martyr, HIPPOLYTUS. The latter in his *Philosophumena* (9.2) accused the Pope of laxity in his dealing leniently with Christians who had been guilty of grave sins. It is not certain whether there was an immediate connection between the Roman and Carthaginian disputes. However, both at Carthage and at Rome, during the Decian persecution (249–51), Pope CORNELIUS (251–53) and Cyprian were faced with the difficulty of dealing with the *lapsi.* Cyprian tried to curb the presumption of certain confessors who had suffered for the faith and were granting bills of pardon to the fallen without due penance and at the same time he had to assert the priestly power of forgiving sins even for apostates (*De lapsis* 16; *Epist.* 61.3). In Rome Novatian had dealt with the problem during the vacancy of the apostolic see before the election of Cornelius. In two letters to Cyprian (*Epist.* 30, 36), Novatian described the Roman doctrine of the possibility of forgiving sins of apostasy during persecution; but he cautioned that for the time being, this should be done only in case of imminent death. After the election of Cornelius (March 251), however, Novatian reversed his stand and claimed that apostates should be excommunicated forever. He went into schism (*see* NOVATIAN AND NOVATIANISM) when his position was rejected. He was condemned by a Roman synod of 60 bishops (Eusebius, *Hist. eccl.* 6.43.2).

Origen and Clement. In the Oriental Church, Origen (*De orat.*) and Clement of Alexandria (*Quis dives; Stromata* 2.12.55; 7.16.102) testify to the Church's teaching that postbaptismal sins of all gravity are forgiven in the Church through the use of God's power, but insist upon the necessity of long and vigorous penance. The third-century document called the *Didascalia Apostolorum* condemns those who deny that God grants pardon for sins through reconciliation by the Church's bishops and priests.

In the 12th and 13th centuries, when this matter was disputed at length, it was generally agreed that there are three kinds of penance: solemn, public, and private. The first, for those guilty of capital sins that hurt the Church, required a special ceremony of absolution and could be given only once since it meant retirement from worldly affairs including cohabitation in marriage (Peter Lombard, *Sent.* 4.14.3); the second was the penance performed publicly by ecclesiastical acts of prayer, fasting, almsgiving; the third was that made *cotidie coram sacerdote*—daily before the priest (Alain de Lille, *Lib. poenit.; Patrologia Latina* 210:297).

See Also: PENANCE, SACRAMENT OF.

Bibliography: A. MICHEL, *Dictionnaire de théologie catholique*, ed. A. VACANT et al., 15 v. (Paris 1903–50) 12.1:749–1127. A. D'ALÈS, *L'Édit de Calliste* (Paris 1914). B. POSCHMANN, *Paenitentia secunda: Die kirchliche Busse in ältesten Christentum bis Cyprian und Origenes* (Bonn 1940). H. KOCH, *Cyprianische Untersuchungen* (Bonn 1926). P. BATIFFOL, *Études d'histoire et de théologie positive: Première série.* (7th ed. Paris 1926). P. GALTIER, *L'Élise et la rémission des péchés* (Paris 1932); *Aux origines du sacrement de pénitence* (Rome 1951). E. F. LATKO, *Origen's Concept of Penance* (Quebec 1949). K. RAHNER, *Recherches de science religieuse* 37 (1950) 47–97; 252–86, 422–56. *Zeitschrift für katholische Theologie* 72 (1950) 257–81. J. T. MACNEILL, *The Celtic Penitentials and Their Influence* (Paris 1923). R. C. MORTIMER, *The Origins of Private Penance in the Western Church* (Oxford 1939).

[F. X. MURPHY/EDS]

PENITENTIAL PSALMS

A group of seven Psalms especially suitable for the use of penitents and considered, at least since the 6th century (e.g., by Cassiodorus), as forming a class by themselves. They are Psalms 6, 32, 38, 51, 102, 130, and 143. The number seven was interpreted allegorically by Cassiodorus to indicate seven means for obtaining forgiveness: baptism, martyrdom, alms, forgiving spirit, conversion of a sinner, love, and penance. By order of Innocent III they were to be prayed in Lent, and under Pius X they became part of the Friday ferial office of Lent. Although no longer officially mandated, they are still widely used in the liturgy, especially Psalm 130, the *De Profundis* (Out of the depths I cry to you, O Lord), and Psalm 51, the *Miserere* (Have mercy on me, O Lord). Although they are the classic Christian prayers of repentance for sin, they are not always directly concerned with this (particularly Psalms 6, 102, and 143). All of them, however, can be classified as laments (on this form, *see* PSALMS, BOOK OF).

"Hearing a confession," woodcut in an edition of "Eruditorum poenintentiale," printed at Paris by Antoine Caillaut, c. 1488–1490, Latin inscription above and below (Rosenwald Incu. X.E7).

Bibliography: E. HERTZSCH, *Die Religion in Geschichte und Gegenwart,* 7 v. (3d ed. Tübingen 1957–65) 1:153–39. B. FISCHER, *Lexikon für Theologie und Kirche,* ed. J. HOFER and K. RAHNER, 10 v. (2d, new ed. Freiburg 1957–65) 2:822–823.

[R. E. MURPHY/EDS.]

PENITENTIALS

Manuals for confessors, setting forth allotments of penance for specified sins. They originated in the Celtic Church (Wales?), became established in Ireland in the 6th century, and were introduced to the Franks and the Anglo-Saxons along with the Irish mission. Such manuals became necessary when private confession and penance, originally a monastic practice, began to replace the public confession and canonical penance of the early Church. This pastoral practice was inaugurated, it seems, by St. CAESARIUS OF ARLES; it was fully developed in Wales and Ireland by the middle of the 6th century. Its principal features were: (1) Penances were graded according to the status of the sinner as well as to the nature of the sin. (2) The penance was enjoined by a private confessor (normally a priest) of the penitent's choice. (3) Most penances were of limited duration, which made it possible to receive the Sacrament of Penance repeatedly. (4) Long penances were often performed in monasteries; i.e., the penitent temporarily joined a monastic community. (5) Long penances could be converted into more austere ones of shorter duration. (6) Ordinary penances consisted mainly in periods of fasting (often on bread and water) and the recitation of Psalms; alms could be substituted for fasting in case of sickness or for other reasons. Some commutations (*arrea*), however, were reminiscent of the more austere forms of Irish asceticism.

Welsh and Irish Penitentials. The private character of the "Celtic" penance and the absence of diocesan organization and episcopal jurisdiction in these countries explain why the penitentials were not decreed by synods but were the work of individuals, often of abbots of great monasteries. These authors fixed penances in accordance with Sacred Scripture, canonical and monastic tradition, and their own spiritual judgment; an element of secular law was the admission of *wergeld.* The penitentials had no other authority than their compilers' reputation for sanctity and holy wisdom.

The penitential ascribed to Gildas fixes penances for monks only. The penitentials of Vinnian (Finnian of Clonard, d. 549?) and of St. Columbanus (after 591?), who draws largely on Vinnian, have specific penances for clerics and laymen. Both penitentials are of rather loose composition. The most comprehensive of Irish penitentials, that of Cummean (probably Cummaine Fota, "the Long," d. 662) and the Old Irish penitential (of the Culdees of Tallaght near Dublin, 8th century), are based on Cassian's ogdoad of deadly sins. Both Vinnian and Cummean emphasize the remedial aspect of penance beside and above its vindictive aspect, that is the "healing" of the soul besides atonement for offending God. For example, Cummean (following Gildas) allows a long-term penitent to receive the Eucharist after 18 months "lest his soul perish utterly through lacking so long the celestial medicine." Much consideration is given to sinful thoughts and their expiation—another monastic element. The "medicine of souls" that the penitentials offered had doubtless a salutary influence also on social life: it curbed blood feuds and brawls, condemned sexual perversion and the practice of causing abortion by magic potions; it insisted on a minimum of hygiene by enacting some of the Old Testament dietary laws, etc. It had to compromise with the firmly rooted pagan custom of keening: the penance for keening decreased according to the higher rank of the dead person.

Later Penitentials. Columbanus brought the Irish penitential system to the Continent, where it soon became established. The Anglo-Saxons received it through the Irish from Iona who convened Northumbria. Even after the synod of Whitby (664) it was not abandoned. The penitential texts that go under the names of Theodore of Canterbury (d.*c.* 690), Bede, and Egbert (8th century) are still in the Irish tradition.

The two largest and best known Frankish penitentials of the 8th century, the *Excarpsus Cummeani* (Pseudo-Cummean) and the penitential of *Codex Bigotianus* (Paris, Bibl. nat. lat. 3182, 10th century), draw, *inter alia,* on both Cummean and Theodore. As a counterpart, one began to collect the penitential canons also in the native conciliar collections. Such compilations as the Saint Gall *Tripartitum,* or the *Capitula iudiciorum,* put, side by side, the *iudicia canonica* (and *iudicia Columbani*), the *iudicia Theodori,* and the *iudicia Cummeani.* The Carolingian reformers criticized the penitentials for their lack of canonical authority, the discrepancies of specific penances found between one penitential and another, and the abuses to which the option of substituting alms for fasting had led in course of time. New penitentials were composed from such canonical sources as the *HADRIANA COLLECTIO* and the *HISPANA COLLECTIO*, e.g., the *Collectio Dacheriana*, which was combined with a ''Roman'' penitential (actually a *tripartitum*) by Halitgar of Cambrai (817–831), but only as far as the latter would agree with Roman discipline. The penitential of Hrabanus Maurus is strictly canonical; it is based almost entirely on the *Hadriana* and *Hispana.*

A late descendant of the Franco-insular penitential tradition is the ''Corrector,'' b. 19 of the *Decretum* of BURCHARD OF WORMS in the beginning of the 11th century. It contains questions to be asked by the confessor, with the appropriate penance for each sin confessed. Later penitentials, beginning with that of Alan of Lille, are general guides for confessors and not ''tariff books,'' that is, books simply listing specific penances appropriate to certain sins.

Bibliography: C. VOGEL, *La Discipline pénitentielle en Gaule des origines à la fin du* VII*e siècle* (Paris 1952). F. W. H. WASSERSCHLEBEN, *Die Bussordnungen der abendländischen Kirche* (Halle 1851), texts and introd. H. J. SCHMITZ, *Die Bussbücher und die Bussdisciplin der Kirche* (Mainz 1883); *Die Bussbücher und das Kanonische Bussverfahren* (Düsseldorf 1898), historical, with ed. and analysis of many texts. J. F. KENNEY, *The Sources for the Early History of Ireland*, v. 1: Ecclesiastical (New York 1929) 235–246, survey with bibliog. P. FOURNIER and G. LEBRAS, *Histoire des collections canoniques en occident depuis les fausses décrétals jusqu'au Décret de Gratien* (Paris 1931–32) v.1, *passim.* G. LE BRAS, *Dictionnaire de théologie catholique,* ed. A. VACANT et al. (Paris 1903–50) 12.1: 1160–79. T. P. OAKLEY, ''Celtic Penance: Its Sources, Affiliation and Influence,'' *The Irish Ecclesiastical Record* 52 (1938) 147–164, 581–601. J. T. MCNEILL and H. M. GAMER, *Medieval Handbooks of Penance* (New York 1938), introd., Eng. tr., notes, bibliog., list of penitential MSS. *Le Pénitentiel de St. Columban,* ed. J. LAPORTE (Tournai 1958). C. VOGEL, *Lexicon für Theologie und Kirche*, ed. J. HOFER and K. RAHNER (Freiburg 1957–65) 2:802–805. L. BIELER, ed., *The Irish Penitentials,* app., D. A. BINCHY (Scriptores Latini Hiberniae, Dublin 1963), introd., critical eds., Eng. tr., notes, indexes.

[L. BIELER]

PENITENTIARY, APOSTOLIC

One of the three tribunals of the Holy See (along with the Roman Rota and the Supreme Tribunal of the Apostolic Signatura), which have the task of upholding moral conduct and safeguarding justice in the comportment of both individuals and of the diverse offices of the Apostolic See. The Roman Pontiff is the supreme judge for the entire Catholic world; he tries cases either personally or through the ordinary tribunals of the Apostolic See or through judges delegated by himself (*Codex iuris canonici c.*1442).

History. The early history of the Apostolic Penitentiary is marked by a gradual development of the penitential discipline of the Church of Rome particularly as applied to the pilgrims who came to Rome to honor the memory of the early Christian martyrs, to obtain forgiveness of their sins, in many cases to be freed from censures reserved to the Roman Pontiff, or to obtain graces and dispensations reserved to him. According to documents of 1200, a certain Cardinal Giovanni ''de S. Paolo'' heard confessions for the pope. Quite probably he was assisted by other confessors placed under his authority. In the time of Pope HONORIUS III (1216–1227), the cardinal who exercised that office was known as ''Penitentiary,'' ''General Penitentiary,'' then ''the Highest Penitentiary,'' or as he is known today, ''Major Penitentiary.'' He had collaborators among whom were some ''friars'' later called ''Minor Penitentiaries.''

Under Pope BONIFACE VIII (1294–1303) there were ten or more minor penitentiaries, almost all of whom were members of the Mendicant Orders. In the colleges of the minor penitentiaries functioning in three of the major basilicas there were also Franciscans, later known as Conventual Franciscans. PIUS V (1566–1572) introduced a radical reform of the three colleges of penitentiaries, and because of the widespread suppression of the Conventuals, misinformed (*malus informatus*) as Pope SIXTUS V (1585–1590) would later write (see Gatti, 176), he dismissed them from the office of confessor (penitentiary) in the Lateran Basilica and appointed the Friars

Minor of the Observance in their stead while at the same time appointing the Jesuits as confessors for St. Peter's Basilica. When CLEMENT XIV (1769–1774) reluctantly suppressed the Society of Jesus he appointed the Conventual Franciscans to the college of the penitentiaries in the Basilica of St. Peter. The Friars Minor of the Observance (today known simply as ''Friars Minor'') continue their service in the Lateran Basilica. The Dominicans are confessors at the Basilica of St. Mary Major, and since 1933 the Benedictines offer their services as confessors in the Basilica of St. Paul outside the walls. The minor penitentiaries, despite their name and the fact that they depend upon the Apostolic Penitentiary for their nomination, authority, and specific government, are not strictly speaking members of the Apostolic Penitentiary.

The Council of Vienna (1311–1312) decreed that the authority of the cardinal major penitentiary continue even during the interregnum (*sede vacante*) of the papacy. BENEDICT XII (1334–1342) with the bull *In agro domini* gave precise norms for the working and organization of the penitentiary, creating the office of ''canonist'' to assist the cardinal penitentiary in all juridical questions. In the course of time the competence of the cardinal major penitentiary extended beyond matters of conscience (the internal forum) to those concerning the external forum (public affairs and the government of the Church). PIUS IV (1559–1565) tried to reduce the exorbitant jurisdiction of the cardinal penitentiary, but it was PIUS V (1566–1572) who, after revoking all the faculties of the major penitentiary, went on to suppress the Apostolic Penitentiary entirely so as to radically reform it, reducing the cardinal penitentiary's authority in the external forum to a minimum and creating the office of ''theologian'' (which by privilege is reserved to the Jesuits). BENEDICT XIV and St. PIUS X enacted further modifications, while BENEDICT XV, in 1917, transferred to the Apostolic Penitentiary all matters concerning the granting and use of indulgences that St. Pius X had reserved to the Holy Office.

The most recent reorganization of the norms of this tribunal was undertaken by PIUS XI in the constitution *Quae divinitus* (March 25, 1935), which presents the fundamental structure and norms that govern the penitentiary. These norms were reconfirmed by JOHN PAUL II in his apostolic constitution on the ROMAN CURIA, *PASTOR BONUS* (1988).

Structure. Since Pius V and Benedict XIV, except for an occasional difference of nomenclature, the Apostolic Penitentiary is structured as follows: the Cardinal Major Penitentiary, the Regent, the Theologian, the Canonist and three Councilors, and three minor officials.

The *cardinal major penitentiary* assumes in his person all the faculties of the penitentiary. He is assisted by the regent and three minor officials. In the exercise of his authority, he acts collegially both in the Congress (which is the union of his ordinary collaborators for day-to-day solutions and decisions), and in the Signature (the collegial body made up solely of the prelates). He is not subject to the Congress; in other words, he may act contrary to the mind of his collaborators, but not without them; neither is he subject to the Signature. In the latter case, however, should he take a different stand, the fact must be noted in the protocol.

The *regent* has a position corresponding to that of the prelate secretary in the congregations of the Curia. He presides at the Congress—unless the cardinal himself presides—and directs the ordinary work of the office with ordinary or delegated powers according to the prescribed norms.

The *theologian*, the *canonist*, and the *three councilors* are prelates who together with the regent form the Signature. The cardinal must seek their advice in cases of special difficulty or importance. The prelates may offer their assistance either as individuals or as a group in which they express their opinion by majority vote according to the rules prescribed for the Roman Curia. Matters exceeding the competence of the cardinal penitentiary are brought to the attention of the pope in the semi-annual audience which the cardinal has with him.

The *minor officials* are the *aiutante di studio*, the archivist, and the *adetto di segretaria*, who assist in carrying out the ordinary business of the Apostolic Penitentiary.

Competence. The Apostolic Penitentiary has two major areas of competency: matters of the internal forum and indulgences. The apostolic constitution *Pastor bonus* (nos. 117–120) asserts that this tribunal has jurisdiction over all that concerns the internal forum, sacramental and non-sacramental, and whatever refers to the concession and use of indulgences, with due regard for the right of the Congregation of the Faith to examine questions that touch dogmatic doctrine in reference to indulgences. To the internal forum (typically ecclesial as opposed to civil) pertain what takes place in the intimacy of conscience and has immediate relation to God, and also occult (hidden) actions as long as they remain such.

The Apostolic Penitentiary grants absolution from sins and censures reserved to the Holy See. The reservation of sins as such has been done away with in the 1983 Code of the Latin rite but has been retained in the *Code of the Canons of the Oriental Churches*, which has reserved to the apostolic See (concretely the Apostolic Penitentiary) the absolution of the sin of direct violation of the sacramental seal and that of the absolution of one's accomplice in a sin against chastity (c.728 '1,1° and 2° *Codex Canonum Ecclesiarium Orientalium*, cc. respectively 1388 and 1378 of the *Codex iuris canonici*). The Apostolic Penitentiary also grants dispensations from private vows (public vows belong to the external forum) and oaths; dispensations from irregularities and matrimonial impediments whenever these are actually occult, even though public by nature; the commutation of vows and other obligations; the validation of religious professions and of marriage; and the condonation of obligations to the Church and third parties. It may be approached even by members of the Oriental rites for the solution of practical cases of conscience.

In the vast array of matters within the competence of the Apostolic Penitentiary, it has the authority to resolve concrete, individual cases, whereas the solution of problems under the aspect of universality belongs to the Congregation for the Doctrine of the Faith. The solutions of the Apostolic Penitentiary are authoritatively binding—preceptive or freeing from an obligation, according to the nature of the case—only for the concrete circumstances which are submitted for examination. It is clear, however, that the doctrinal and disciplinary direction furnished with the solution can prudently be applied by analogy on a broader scale.

Procedure. The modus operandi of the Apostolic Penitentiary may be illustrated in the case of a priest who attempts marriage, even though civilly only, and thereby incurs an irregularity, reserved to the Holy See only in public cases (c.1047, '3 *Codex iuris canonici*), and an automatic suspension (c.1394, '1 *Codex iuris canonici*). If the penitent priest wants to exercise the priestly ministry, he must obtain a dispensation from the irregularity by recourse to competent authority. The censure of suspension, of its nature public, though not reserved, will be lifted by the same authority, competent to dispense from the irregularity.

Under the 1983 Code, there is no automatic excommunication consequent upon the crime of attempted marriage by priests. Since the censure of suspension does not of itself prohibit the reception of sacraments, priests who have attempted marriage and, though contrite, cannot separate from the woman they are living with may seek and obtain absolution and be admitted to the reception of the sacraments like lay persons provided their situation is occult, that they are truly penitent, namely that they promise to live chastely with their companion in a brother-sister relationship, repair as far as possible whatever scandal was given, and seek to regularize their situation as soon as possible, and this because the obligation of celibacy which is reserved to the Roman Pontiff alone (cf. c. 291) remains.

Cases submitted to the Apostolic Penitentiary are resolved as far as possible within 24 hours of their receipt. This is in obedience to the disposition given already by Benedict XIV and confirmed by Pius XI. The reason for this rule and for the effort of the penitentiary to abide by it is very clear: *Salus animarum suprema lex* (''the salvation of souls is the supreme law''). This salvation does not admit procrastination. Should a case present special difficulties so that a reply cannot be given immediately, the penitentiary acknowledges the receipt of the case at least with an interlocutory reply. In connection with the exigency of the principle enunciated above, the Church has provided in c. 1357 (cf. c. 1048, by analogy, regarding the exercise of orders by one who is irregular) the means whereby the state of grace can be regained by sacramental absolution even before recourse is made. In giving an interlocutory reply, the penitentiary always reminds confessors of the faculties granted to them by this canon and of the opportuneness to grant absolution to the penitent.

The rescripts (written responses) of the penitentiary are not stereotype formularies but specific answers drawn up to respond to concrete and specific cases in order not to give the impression of impersonal bureaucracy. In conformity with the norms governing the Roman Curia modern languages are used in so far as possible, even though preference is still given to Latin when writing an answer to a confessor.

Although the replies of the penitentiary never contain personal information like the name and surname of the addressee of the provision or opinion, the rule is that the rescripts and replies are to be destroyed as soon as possible as a maximum safeguard of the sacramental seal or of the secret of conscience. However, if the decisions of the penitentiary have relevance for the external forum (e.g., permission to receive the sacraments that might be a motive or cause of scandal should the person not be able to adduce proof in the external form of the now regularized position), permission is given to keep the rescript so that, if necessary, it can be produced as evidence. All responses are sent in a double-sealed envelope, the first of which carries the protocol number by which the case can be identified in future correspondence should the need arise.

Recourse to the Apostolic Penitentiary. As in general regarding all the organizations of the Holy See, all the faithful have the right to have recourse to the penitentiary either directly or through someone else. The nature of the matters involved and experience indicate that recourse should be made anonymously, through the services of the confessor if the matter has to do with sin or through a spiritual director if it is a matter of the internal nonsacramental forum. The recourse should be made in a clear and succinct fashion, presenting elements regarding the theological and canonical connotations, serious circumstances impinging on the common good as well as the state of mind and psychology of the petitioner. The request is to be addressed to the cardinal major penitentiary or the Apostolic Penitentiary, Città del Vaticano.

External Forum. Finally, the Apostolic Penitentiary is entrusted with whatever concerns the granting and use of indulgences, with due regard to the competence of the Congregation for the Doctrine of the Faith in whatever has to do with the dogmatic aspect of indulgences (see *Pastor bonus*, no. 120; *Indulgentiarum doctrina* [January 1, 1967], AAS 59 [1967]: 5–24), a revision of the doctrine of indulgences).

Bibliography: JOHN PAUL II, *Pastor bonus* (June 28, 1988). *Enchiridion Indulgentiarum, Normae et Concessiones*, 4th ed. (Vatican City 1999). *Catechismus Catholicae Ecclesiae* (Vatican City 1987), nos. 1471–1498. F. M. CAPPELLO, *De Curia Romana*, 2 v. (Rome 1911–1912). L. CHIAPETTA, *Il Codice di Diritto Canonico*, 2 v. (Napoli 1988). L. DE MAGISTRIS and U. M. TODESCHNI, ''La Penitenzieria Apostolica'' in *La Curia Romana nella Cost. Ap. Pastor Bonus* (Vatican City 1990), 419–428. N. DEL RE, *La Curia Romana: Lineamenta storico-giuridici* (Roma 1970), 272–274. I. GATTI, ''Da 50 anni i Frati Minori Conventuali nello Stato della Città del Vaticano (1948–1998)'' in *Commentarium Ordinis Minorum Conventualium* 95 (1998):165–193. E. GOELLER, *Die Päpstliche Pönitentierie von Ihrem Ursprung bis zu Ihrer Umgestaltung unter Pius V*, 2 v. (Roma 1907–1911). C. H. HASKINS, ''The Sources for the History of the Papal Penitentiary,'' *The American Journal of Theology* 9 (1905): 421–450. L. ICHONET, *La sacrée Pénitentierie Apostolique: Etude de droit et d'histoire* (Lyon 1908). L. LARRAONA and S. GOYENECHE, *De SS.Congregationum, Tribunalium et Officiorum constitutione et interna ordinatione post const.* Sapienti consilio, in *Romana Curia a B. Pio X* ''Sapienti consilio'' *reformata* (1951), 123–129. V. PETRA, *De sacra Paenitentiaria Apostolica* (Roma 1712). F. ROBERTI, ''De Curia Romana ante Pianam reformationem'' *Appollinaris* 25 (1952): 13–34. F. TAMBURINI, ''Per la storia dei Cardinali Penitenzieri Maggiori,'' *Rivista di Storia della Chiesa in Italia* 36 (1982): 332–380.

[B. HEISER/D. KOS]

PENN, WILLIAM

Quaker statesman and colonizer; b. London, England, Oct. 14, 1644; d. Ruscombe, Berkshire, England, July 30, 1718. He was the son of Adm. Sir William Penn and received an education suited to good social position. About 1667 he became a Quaker; he was subsequently imprisoned a number of times for nonconformity and he became a leading spokesman for general religious toleration. As a friend of King James II, Penn was suspected of being a Jesuit and was regarded with suspicion under succeeding Protestant monarchs. In 1681, in payment of a debt due his father from the Crown, he received from Charles II a grant of land in America. As sole proprietor of PENNSYLVANIA, Penn developed the province into a ''holy experiment'' of his ideals of religious and political freedom, with the support of many Quakers and others who settled there. He framed a liberal government for the colonists and made just peace treaties with the native peoples. Unfortunately, he had political and financial difficulties at home and spent only two two-year periods in Pennsylvania. He wrote numerous religious and political tracts and preached extensively until a stroke of apoplexy in 1712 disabled him mentally.

Bibliography: Of Penn's writings (see list in Peare), most fully collected in 1726, only a few are now reprinted. A well-chosen anthology is *The Witness of William Penn,* ed. F. B. TOLLES and E. G. ALDERFER (New York 1957), bibliog. 203–205. Biographies include M. R. BRAILSFORD, *The Making of William Penn* (New York 1930). W. I. HULL, *William Penn* (New York 1937). W. W. COMFORT, *William Penn* (Philadelphia 1944). C. O. PEARE, *William Penn* (Philadelphia 1957), bibliog.

[H. J. CADBURY]

PENNINGS, BERNARD HENRY

Missionary; b. Gemert, Holland, June 9, 1861; d. De Pere, WI, March 17, 1955. He joined Berne Abbey in Heeswijk, Holland, in 1879 and was ordained on June 19, 1886. He volunteered for the American mission undertaken by the abbey in 1893 in response to a request from Bp. Sebastian G. Messmer of Green Bay, WI. Messmer wanted assistance in combating the work of Joseph Rene Vilatte, ''Archbishop of the Old Catholic Church in America,'' who was proselytizing among the Belgian immigrants in northeastern Wisconsin. In September 1898 Pennings became prior of the first permanent foundation of the Premonstratensian Order in North America, established at West De Pere, WI. In 1925 Pius XI raised the De Pere house to the status of an abbey, and Pennings was blessed as abbot on May 27. At the time of his death, his community conducted five high schools and St. Norbert College, West De Pere; operated one television and two radio stations; and served parishes in eight dioceses. Papal honors conferred on Pennings were: the *cappa magna* and *purple pileolus* (1934), the purple biretta (1936), and the title of knight commander of the Order of the Holy Sepulchre (1951). In 1951 the Belgian government named him a knight of the Order of the Crown in recognition of his work among Belgian immigrants.

[R. J. CORNELL]

PENN'S CHARTER OF LIBERTIES

The Charter of Liberties was drawn up by the PENNSYLVANIA Legislature and approved by William PENN, proprietor of the colony. It was the culmination of enlightened progress toward securing personal freedoms against a capricious proprietor and crown, and served as the constitution of Pennsylvania from 1701 to 1776. Its most notable features were the establishment of a popular assembly with the right to initiate legislation and the affording of persons accused of crimes the right to counsel. It was not until 1836 that English law gave the defendant an absolute right to counsel in all cases.

Background. The charter that King Charles II gave to William Penn in 1681 made him the absolute proprietor of the area in America where Penn was to establish a colony. The crown did, however, reserve to itself certain rights, including that of approving or disallowing acts passed by the General Assembly. Penn's first plan of government, the Fundamental Constitutions of Pennsylvania, granted freedom of conscience and provided for an Assembly with privileges like those of the House of Commons. Some of Penn's ideas failed to please prospective land buyers, and he modified them somewhat.

A new Frame of Government, issued in 1682, gave freemen the right to elect members to both the Council and the Assembly—a departure from the usual practice of having the upper house or council appointed. But the Assembly could not initiate legislation. Another Frame of Government, reducing the size of the Council and the Assembly, was issued in 1683 while Penn was in Pennsylvania. After Penn returned to England to defend his rights, his deputy governor, William Markham, issued a new Frame of Governement in 1696. The Assembly approved this, but Penn never gave his consent, and the law could not be considered as binding. When he returned to Pennsylvania in 1700, Penn advised the colonists to change the Frame of Government, if it did not suit them. The Council studied the Frames of Government of 1683 and 1696, took what was best in each and presented the results to Penn for his approval. On Oct. 28, 1701, Penn gave his consent. The required six-sevenths of both houses voted to replace the Frame of Government of 1683 with the new Charter of Liberties, and on Nov. 8, 1701, it became the constitution of Pennsylvania.

Provisions. In this charter Penn granted and confirmed to ''all the Freemen, Planters and Adventurers, and other Inhabitants of this Province and Territories, these following Liberties, Franchises and Privileges,'' to be kept and enjoyed by them forever. Liberty of conscience was guaranteed to all who acknowledged one almighty God, the creator, ruler, and upholder of the world. Those who professed to believe in Christ were eligible for service in any legislative or executive capacity, providing they solemnly promised allegiance to the king, fidelity to the proprietor and governor, and took the attests established by law.

Bernard Henry Pennings, founder of St. Norbert's Abbey.

Each October freemen of the colony were to choose four persons from each county for the Assembly that would meet in Philadelphia two weeks later. The Assembly had the power to choose a speaker, appoint committees, prepare bills, decide on adjournment, impeach criminals, and redress grievances. It also had ''all other Power and Privileges of an Assembly, according to the Rights of the free-born Subjects of England, and as is usual in any of the King's Plantations in America.'' If a county refused to choose representatives, or if those chosen refused to serve, the rest of the properly chosen delegates meeting together had the full power of the Assembly, providing that two-thirds of the whole body was present.

The freemen also nominated two men for sheriff and two for coroner. The governor then chose one man for each office, and those men selected served three years. In the case of death or default, the governor filled the vacancies until the end of the term. If the freemen failed to choose candidates for these posts, the incumbents remained in office until a new election was held. Justices of the counties nominated three persons for the position of clerk of the peace, and the governor appointed one of these to serve during his good behavior.

Other parts of the charter dealt with the recording and preservation of laws; the giving to criminals the privileges of counsel and of calling witnesses; the safeguarding of a citizen's property from actions by the governor and Council, except in the ordinary course of justice; the preventing of the forfeiture of property in the event of suicide or death by accident; and the licensing of taverns and public houses.

The charter could not be amended in whole or in part except by the consent of the governor and six-sevenths of the Assembly. The one exception to this was the article on liberty of conscience, which was so basic to the true intent of the charter that it must be kept forever without alteration. Penn promised on behalf of himself and his heirs to do nothing that would impair the liberties expressed in the charter.

Bibliography: R. L. PERRY, ed. *Sources of Our Liberties* (Chicago, Ill. 1959). E. B. BRONNER, *William Penn's Holy Experiment: The Founding of Pennsylvania, 1681–1701* (New York 1962). C. O. PEARE, *William Penn: A Biography* (Philadelphia, Pa. 1957). W. I. HULL, *William Penn: A Topical Biography* (New York 1937).

[H. D. LANGLEY]

PENNSYLVANIA, CATHOLIC CHURCH IN

The second of the original 13 states to ratify the U.S. constitution (Dec. 12, 1787), Pennsylvania is bordered by the Delaware River that separates it from New Jersey on the east, Delaware, and Maryland on the south, West Virginia on the southwest, Ohio on the west, by about 40 miles of Lake Erie shore at the northwest corner, and New York on the north. More than 80 percent of the population lives in metropolitan areas. Philadelphia is the largest city, followed in size by Pittsburgh, Erie, and Allentown. Harrisburg is the capital.

The eight dioceses in Pennsylvania comprise the ecclesiastical Province of Philadelphia, anchored in the eastern end of the state by the metropolitan see of PHILADELPHIA, and in the west by PITTSBURG. These two oldest dioceses in Pennsylvania also have the largest population of Catholics in the state, both by numbers and by percentage—Philadelphia with approximately 1,400,000, faithful and Pittsburgh with 750,000, each about 38 percent of total residents. Though both dioceses are centered in large metropolitan areas they have very different characters; it has often been said that the Midwest begins in western Pennsylvania, while Philadelphia has an atmosphere of established catholicity that it shares with other East Coast sees such as New York and Boston. In the middle of the state the diocese of Harrisburg, centered in the rural agricultural counties of the Susquehanna valley, comprises the lowest percentage of Catholics in the state,

Archdiocese/Diocese	Year Created
Archdiocese of Philadelphia	1875
Diocese of Allentown	1961
Diocese of Altoona-Johnstown	1957
Diocese of Erie	1853
Diocese of Greensburg	1951
Diocese of Harrisburg	1868
Diocese of Pittsburgh	1843
Diocese of Scranton	1868

with 238,000 faithful out of a total population of 1,940,000 (12 percent). The other dioceses are Allentown, Altoona-Johnstown, Erie, Greensburg, and Scranton. In 2001 there were about 3.5 million Catholics throughout the state, about 30 percent of the total population of almost 2 million.

Colonial Times. William PENN embarked on a unique experiment in religious liberty in his colony of Pennsylvania. As Sally Schwartz has observed: ''Other colonies experienced migration of German and Scotch-Irish peoples to their frontiers, but conceded at best only the privilege of toleration to newcomers, not the right of freedom of conscience. Only in Pennsylvania was there no 'establishment' to dispense or withhold favors.'' (*''A Mixed Multitude'': The Struggle for Toleration in Colonial Pennsylvania*, 292). Catholics benefitted more than most from this freedom of conscience. Though barred by the provisions of the Test Oath (1693–1775) from office-holding and the exercise of the franchise, Catholics enjoyed greater opportunities for worship and the practice of their faith in Penn's colony than in any of the 13 colonies.

That said, when, in 1708, news of Catholic activity in the province first reached the ears of Governor Logan, he complained to Penn of the ''scandal of the Mass.'' The Proprietor responded by warning Logan to be on the watch for an anti-Catholic backlash. None ensued, and indeed Jesuit missionaries regularly traveled north into Pennsylvania from their farm at Bohemia Manor on Maryland's eastern shore. Sources indicate that the priests were routine visitors at the Wilcox farm in Ivy Mills near Chester, and were certainly celebrating the Eucharist there by 1720. In 1729 Fr. Joseph Greaton was living in Philadelphia, celebrating the Mass in private homes, and the year 1732 saw his purchase of a plot of land off Walnut St., where by 1734 he had erected a small chapel and residence, frequented by a small congregation of about 40 persons (mostly German). St. Joseph's was the first place of public Catholic worship in the colonies since the chapel at St. Mary's City in Maryland was demolished in 1704.

St. Vincent College and Archabbey, first permanent Benedictine foundation in U.S., Latrobe, Pennsylvania.

In 1741 two German Jesuits arrived to care for the sizable number of Catholics who were migrating to southeastern and south-central Pennsylvania. William Wappeler found about 300 Catholics in Lancaster, and soon established three mission stations at Conewago (where a chapel serving Catholics from nearby Maryland had already been founded in 1730), Codorus Creek (near York, where a chapel would be built in 1750) and Lancaster itself (Wappeler would purchase land there in 1742 for a church that would come to be known as ''old St. Mary's''). Theodore Schneider, a former university professor from Heidelberg, was the other missionary who disembarked in 1741; he traveled to Berks county and set up his headquarters on a farm which Greaton had purchased at Goshenhoppen (present-day Bally, named in honor of a famous 19th century pastor). From there he and his successors were able to attend to congregations in Reading (where a ''meetinghouse'' existed by 1753), Lebanon, Pottsville (which boasted a wood church in 1827), Bethlehem, Easton (the mother church of the Lehigh Valley was erected there in 1836), Sunbury and Williamsport.

A census of Catholics in Pennsylvania in 1757 enumerated 1,365 communicants, of whom 948 were Germans and 416 Irish. About 40 percent of the Catholic population was centered in Philadelphia, Chester and Bucks counties. The increasing number of Catholics in the city of Philadelphia required the erection of a new church; St. Mary's was completed in 1763, its congregation made up mostly of Irish. The city was well served by priests such as Ferdinand FARMER, SJ, who cared for the poor and needy of the city as well as immersing himself in its intellectual life, serving as a Trustee of the fledgling University of Pennsylvania. A zealous pastor, who found time to make missionary journeys throughout Pennsylvania and New Jersey, he was mourned at his death in 1786 as a ''father of his people and friend of civilized humanity.''

Western Pennsylvania, unlike the east, traces its Catholic roots to France. Fr. Joseph Bonnecamps, SJ, accompanying a military expedition, offered Mass in what would become Westmoreland county in 1749, while the first site of public Catholic worship in the area was at the Chapel of the Assumption of the Blessed Virgin Mary of the Beautiful River, located in Fort Duquesne, at the confluence of the Allegheny and Monogehela rivers (Pittsburgh). The chapel, which functioned till its destruction four years later by British forces, was served by Fr. Denis Baron, and his extant baptismal register serves as an eloquent testimony to his pastoral labors.

Just as England's victory in western Pennsylvania brought an end to Fr. Baron's work, so the French and Indian War saw heightened anti-Catholic tensions in the eastern half of the state. News of General Braddock's defeat in 1755 touched off mob violence in Philadelphia, and St. Joseph's church was only saved from destruction by the intervention of a group of Quakers. In that same year in Goshenhoppen, a Corpus Christi procession was mistaken by neighbors for a military drill, and the Berks County Justices wrote to Gov. Morris in alarm. Yet Catholics retained their liberties throughout this period, and by the time of the War for Independence many of them supported the colonials, though Clifton's Regiment, a company of 180 men from St. Mary's church, did fight on behalf of the British. St. Mary's, though, could also boast of a number of prominent patriots, including Stephen Moylan (1734–1811, a merchant and aide-de-camp to Washington), Thomas Fitzsimmons (1741–1811; a financial backer of the colonial cause and Congressional delegate), and Commodore John Barry (1745–1803, honored as the ''father of the American Navy''). The church of St. Mary's itself would play a role in the birth of the new nation, serving as the setting for a number of liturgical celebrations attended by members of Congress and foreign dignitaries, including a Te Deum on July 4, 1779, and a service of Thanksgiving for the victory at Yorktown on Nov. 4, 1781.

A Diocese and Turmoil in Philadelphia. The new state Constitution granted all the rights of citizens to Catholics in Pennsylvania, and as the eighteenth century waned their numbers continued to increase. John CARROLL, the newly appointed Bishop of Baltimore, estimated in 1790 that there were 7,000 Catholics in Pennsylvania, 2,000 of these living Philadelphia and its environs. Finding clergy to care for such numbers was certainly a challenge (an outstanding young immigrant priest, Lorenz Grässel, died during the great Yellow Fever epidemic of 1793, soon after being named as Carroll's coadjutor). New churches were also needed, especially in Philadelphia. In 1789, the German Religious Society of Roman Catholics, under the guidance of Fathers John and Peter Heilbron, built Holy Trinity church. This premier ''national'' church would be but the first of many to seek autonomy in its choice of pastors and internal governance (leading to years of ecclesial strife). St. Augustine's church was begun in 1796 by newly arrived Irish Augustinians, and would soon, thanks to the generosity of its subscribers (including George Washington), rank as city's largest church.

The young nation's rapidly expanding Catholic population moved Bishop Carroll to request a division of his diocese. Among the four sees formed from Baltimore would be Philadelphia, which comprised at its establishment not only the states of Pennsylvania and Delaware, but also western and southern New Jersey. An Irish Franciscan, Michael Egan (who had labored at St. Mary's since 1803), was named the first Bishop of Philadelphia on April 8, 1808 — Carroll's only choice for that office. Though a fine preacher and a conscientious pastor, Egan was not possessed of a strong constitution, and his peaceable and pious nature was not equal to the conflicts that developed with the trustees of St. Mary's (which had become the new Cathedral). The contentious nature of the two Harolds, the Dominican William, and his uncle James, priests of the Cathedral, only exacerbated conflicts Egan had with the trustees over financial matters and personnel. Upon Egan's death in July of 1814, ecclesiastical affairs in Philadelphia had reached an impasse.

Following Egan's demise the see was vacant for six years. The War of 1812 and its aftermath hampered communications, and French and Irish factions in the United States and on the Continent feuded over the appointment. Both Louis de Barth (the administrator of the see, resident in Conewago), and Ambrose Maréchal (future archbishop of Baltimore) refused the nomination; finally Henry CONWELL, an Irishman from Armagh, arrived in the city in November of 1820, having received the appointment the previous year (Rome had given him his choice of Madras or Philadelphia).

Conwell was not a happy choice. He was 73 by the time he arrived in Philadelphia, and was an obstinate, vain man, lacking the oratorical skills so prized by the city's Catholics, and the talent for leadership so needed by the diocese. The bishop's lack of skill in the pulpit only added to the prestige of William Hogan, a flamboyant but troubled young priest, who soon could boast a following among St. Mary's congregants. The bishop sought to regulate Hogan's wayward lifestyle, while the priest denounced Conwell from the pulpit. The parish was soon divided—many of the trustees sided with Hogan—and both men were sued in court. A bloody riot even broke out on April 9, 1822. Rome was moved by the struggle to weigh in on the proper role of church trustees, and following the letter *Non sine magno* of Pius VII in August of 1822, Hogan's influence waned.

Troubles would flare up again in 1826, after the bishop agreed to a pact with the trustees of St. Mary's regulating pastoral appointments. Three of the lay leaders claimed that the deal gave them the authority to veto episcopal appointments. William Harold, now serving as Conwell's Vicar General, denounced the bishop's actions, whereupon the latter removed him from his post, only to see his cause taken up by the trustees. Rome criticized the terms of the pact, and Conwell was summoned to Rome. Suffering from the onset of senility, he fled from Rome after giving a report of his actions, and headed back to Philadelphia. In response to this bizarre turn of events, and prompted by the pleas of the American bishops, Rome appointed Francis Patrick KENRICK as Conwell's coadjutor, and entrusted the administration of the diocese to his care. He was consecrated in Bardstown, KY on June 6, 1830, and arrived in Philadelphia on July 7.

Kenrick, both a scholar and administrator, possessing gracious manners and steely determination, acted quickly to bring order to the diocese, which was, lamented his friend John Hughes (future bishop of New York) ''in a deplorable state.'' He placed St. Mary's under interdict until such time as the trustees renounced the right of naming pastors (which they soon did), and brought in Hughes to supervise the construction of a new church, St. John the Evangelist, which would have no trustees. Though hampered by the hostile and deluded meddling of Bp. Conwell (who besides criticizing Kenrick to all who would listen, on one occasion even threw his coadjutor's possessions out of the residence they shared), Kenrick was able to make great strides in the diocese. A synod was held in 1832 (whose pastoral provisions were soon copied by many U.S. bishops), a seminary begun, and a newspaper, the *Catholic Herald*, was founded. Heroic charitable assistance was offered during the cholera epidemic of the same year, most notably by the SISTERS OF CHARITY. Parishes were established to meet the needs of the thousands of immigrants streaming into the diocese, which numbered 100,000 souls by 1832, yet possessed only 38 priests. So great was the pastoral burden that already in 1835 Kenrick petitioned to have a new diocese erected in Pittsburgh. Though Rome put off a decision for eight years, finally on Aug. 11, 1843 the Diocese of Pittsburgh was established, comprising 21,000 square miles of territory and 45,000 Catholics. Michael O'Connor, formerly rector of St. Charles Seminary in Philadelphia, was named the first bishop.

Growth in Western Pennsylvania. During the time that the Church in Philadelphia was in turmoil, the rest of the state could boast of a growing number of Catholics. A band of the faithful from Goshenhoppen had migrated to Westmoreland county, and in 1789 Fr. Theodore Brouwers had joined them to provide for their pastoral needs. A 300-acre farm, Sportsman's Hall, near present-day Latrobe, was purchased by Brouwers and willed before his death in 1790 to whoever would succeed him in the care of the region's Catholics. The sad escapades of a rogue fortune-hunting priest would cloud much of the following decade, but finally Fr. Peter Heilbron (who had earlier served at Holy Trinity in Philadelphia) arrived to take up residence at the hall (a small cabin), and minister to the Catholics living throughout western Pennsylvania.

Demetrius GALLITZIN, who joined Heilbron, became known as the Apostle of the Alleghenies. The son of a Russian count and a German princess, Gallitzin completed his seminary studies in Baltimore and was sent by Bishop Carroll to care for Catholics living in the region of Magurie's Settlement (now known as Loretto), where he founded a church and school. From there he traveled for miles on horseback (and sleigh in old age) seeking out Catholics and ministering to their spiritual needs.

When Bishop O'Connor arrived in Pittsburgh, he found St. Patrick's Church, which had been built in 1811 by the city's first pastor, William O'Brien. His successor, Charles Maguire, had begun Pittsburgh's second Catholic church, St. Paul's, in 1820, which upon completion was the largest in the country. It was an obvious and impressive choice for O'Connor's cathedral church. The diocese was, however, in dire need of clergy and religious; while the bishop was in Europe for his consecration, he sought assistance in Ireland. He acquired eight seminarians from Maynooth, and the newly established Sisters of Mercy promised their support, and sent seven members to western Pennsylvania where they opened St. Xavier's Academy in 1844 and Mercy Hospital in 1846 (displacing the Sisters of Charity who had operated similar institutions in the city since 1835). The community would increase rapidly from this humble beginning, establishing foundations in Philadelphia, Erie and Scranton.

Attracted by the plight of German immigrants in the United States, the Bavarian Benedictine Boniface WIMMER and a band of companions arrived in the diocese in 1846 from the Abbey of St. Michael in Metten. Though their plans called for them to settle at Carrolltown, not far from Loretto, they found the land unsuited for farming, and Bishop O'Connor was able to entice them to Latrobe with the promise of the Sportsman's Hall property. There they founded St. Vincent's Priory (later Archabbey), the first Benedictine monastery in the country, and soon were staffing parishes and missions throughout western Pennsylvania, as well as an academy, college, and seminary.

Though he feuded with the headstrong abbot over the free education of his seminarians and the monk's brewery, O'Connor knew what a blessing the community was to his young diocese. Soon he was able to welcome another religious family, the Passionists, who sent a pioneer group of three priests and a brother to establish a foundation in Birmingham (the city's south side) in 1852.

The Rise of Nativism. All was not peaceful in Pittsburgh, though. The waves of Catholic immigrants flooding into the country in the 1840s had aroused the fear and suspicion of earlier immigrant groups. These Nativists sought to counteract the influence of the "Catholic menace" through political action and violent intimidation (*see* NATIVISM). The Protestant Association of Pittsburgh, for example, planned in 1850 to set fire to Mercy Hospital, which was saved only by the bishop's vigilance in ordering the facility to be guarded day and night. That same year, though, saw O'Connor arrested by the Nativist mayor of the city, who was ironically governing the city from his prison cell.

Tribulations far more deadly had occurred in Philadelphia, where Nativists were roused to action by the resistance Catholics offered to their children's use of the King James Bible in public schools, and their exposure to anti-Catholic materials in the schools' curriculum. Exacerbated by urban unemployment and ethnic strife, riots broke out in the Kensington section of the city in May 1844, during which two Catholic churches were burned (including St. Augustine's and its extensive library). Two months later, following reports that St. Philip Neri Church was being used to stockpile arms, a pitched battle ensued between a Nativtist mob and the state militia which had been ordered to guard the church. The violence claimed 20 lives and saw over 100 people injured before order was restored.

Given the challenges that immigrants faced in this climate of hostility, a number of proposals were made to found rural "colonies," where Catholics could live and work unmolested by their effects of prejudice. One such community was established in northwestern Pennsylvania, in Elk County. A settlement was established on 35,000 acres of land by German families from Philadelphia and Baltimore, who arrived on Dec. 8, 1842, and named their village St. Mary's. Though the first harsh winters tested the determination of the colonizers, and the Redemptorists who had initially backed the project turned it over to the Benedictines from St. Vincent's; in time the community flourished, developing mills and other small industries.

Despite the hostile climate for Catholic immigrants, the number of faithful in the diocese of Philadelphia continued to increase. The pastoral care of his flock was always Bishop Kenrick's first priority, and the arrival of new communities of religious women enabled the diocese to continue its ministry. The Sisters of St. Joseph were established in the city in 1847, and soon were running St. Joseph's Hospital (the first Catholic hospital in Philadelphia, established in 1849), a boy's orphanage, an asylum for widows, and a private academy. They were joined in their service to the Church by the School Sisters of Notre Dame (1848), the Good Shepherd Sisters (1849), and the Visitation nuns (1850). The Augustinians had recovered from the loss of their church during the Nativist troubles to embark on a college, Villanova, founded in 1842, and the Jesuits, not to be outdone, opened St. Joseph's College in 1851. The bishop, concerned not only with the spiritual but also economic welfare of his people, founded a diocesan bank in 1848. Finally, before his departure in 1851 to become archbishop of Baltimore, he had the satisfaction of purchasing land at 18th and Race streets, on which would one day be built a magnificent cathedral, modeled on the church of San Carlo al Corso in Rome. The diocese he left behind numbered some 170,000 Catholics, 101 priests, and 92 churches.

Philadelphia's Saintly Bishop. Upon his arrival in Baltimore, Kenrick found himself impressed by a quiet, humble Redemptorist then in residence in the city. He made a habit of making his confession to this priest, and when the time came for him to submit the name of his successor in Philadelphia to Rome, Fr. John NEUMANN's name was second on the list drawn up by the suffragans of the Baltimore province (only his "foreignness" — Neumann was from Bohemia — prevented him from officially occupying the first place, and Kenrick made it clear he was his personal choice). Neumann himself was horrified, but obediently submitted to the divine will, and was consecrated on March 28, 1852. He chose as his motto: "Passion of Christ, Strengthen Me."

Neumann had come to the United States in 1836 as a seminarian, and was ordained for the Diocese of New York. After a few years of pastoral work, he entered the Redemptorist community, and after professing his vows (the first in the country to do so), labored energetically in Baltimore and in St. Philomena's parish in Pittsburgh. He brought with him to Philadelphia a uniquely personal approach, spending much of his time in pastoral visitation; by September he had visited half the parishes in the diocese. The bishop referred to the promotion of Catholic parochial schools as his key project. Only a year after the establishment of a diocesan Board of Education in 1852, the number of children in diocesan parish schools had risen from 500 to 5000. To help in the evangelization of his ever-increasing flock, Neumann founded parishes, established the first diocesan-wide FORTY HOURS DEVO-

TION in the United States (1853), assisted in the foundation of a religious community of women, the Sisters of the Third Order of St. Francis (1855), and welcomed a second community, the Sisters, Servants of the Immaculate Heart of Mary, to the diocese in 1858.

Neumann was a man of paradox, beloved for his piety and devotion, yet criticized by some within and without his diocese for his foreignness and discomfort with Philadelphia ''society.'' As the diocese grew (in 1855 it already numbered 145 churches, the largest in the United States), Neumann proposed its division at the Eighth Provincial Council of Baltimore, suggesting that Pottsville be named the cathedral city of the new territory, and volunteering himself as the bishop of this more rural see. Some prelates, including O'Connor of Pittsburgh, urged Rome to accept Neumann's offer, but in 1857 it was decided that the diocese would remain as it was, but that Neumann would be given a coadjutor. James Frederic Wood, a financial genius possessed of a more urbane character, was the choice, and set himself at once to the task of straightening out the diocesan books. In this he was successful, yet his role as diocesan administrator remained nebulous while Neumann lived, even as the latter continued to long for a poorer, less cosmopolitan see. His strength sapped by pastoral labors, the saintly bishop of Philadelphia collapsed on the street on Jan. 5, 1860. He was beatified in 1863, and canonized in 1977.

New Dioceses for Pennsylvania. Bishop Wood finally came into his own as Bishop of Philadelphia, yet even as he came out of the shadow of his godly predecessor, he earned the nickname ''the Shadow,'' by remaining a quiet, reserved man. As an administrator, though, he guided the diocese with a vigorous and steady hand. The long anticipated Cathedral of Saints Peter and Paul, whose construction had been a long-standing burden to diocesan finances, was dedicated on Nov. 20, 1864, even as the bishop announced plans for a new seminary building in the suburbs at Overbrook (''Wood's Folly''). As the number of Catholic faithful continued to increase, Wood was forced to return to a subject dear to the heart of Bp. Neumann; namely, the division of the diocese. Acting on the recommendations of the Second Plenary Council of BALTIMORE (1866), and Wood's own proposals made to Pius IX while on a visit to Rome in 1867, the Holy See announced a major revision of diocesan boundaries, erecting three new sees on March 3, 1868. The Diocese of Wilmington was created, removing the state of Delaware from the jurisdiction of the bishop of Philadelphia (southern New Jersey had previously been reassigned to Newark in 1853). Bishop William O'Hara was given charge of the Diocese of Scranton, which was formed from ten counties in northeastern Pennsylvania. Catholic roots here stretched back not only to the pastoral work of Fr. Jeremiah Flynn, who as recently as 1825 had cared for Catholics throughout the whole region, but also to a settlement in Bradford County aptly named ''French Azilum,'' whose fifty dwellings and chapel awaited the arrival in 1793 of a band of royalist exiles to have been led by Queen Marie Antoinette herself. The Diocese of Harrisburg was created from 18 counties in the state's central section, where Jeremiah F. Shanahan was named bishop. Bishop Wood was relieved by this redistribution of his pastoral responsibilities, and no doubt honored when he became Archbishop of Philadelphia — the diocese having been raised to the dignity of a metropolitan see in March of 1875. Sadly, the last decade of his life would be plagued by increasing bouts of illness and paralysis, which lasted till his death on June 20, 1883.

By the time the Province of Philadelphia was created, it included not only the dioceses mentioned above, but also Erie, which had been created by Pope Pius IX on April 29, 1853 from 13 northwestern Pennsylvania counties soon after the recommendation of the Fifth Provincial of Baltimore (1852). Its first bishop was none other than Michael O'Connor, who was transferred by his request from Pittsburgh, but returned there seven months later following outspoken and vehement pleas from his former clergy and faithful. Erie's second bishop was the Maine convert Josue Moody Young, who was followed by Tobias Mullen. During the latter's tenure of three decades (1868–1899) the Catholic population of the diocese increased four-fold, and the number of parishes tripled.

Bishop O'Connor's return to Pittsburgh, though, was not to be long-lived. For many years the former seminary professor had struggled with a call to the Society of Jesus. Though counseled by the pope against following this aspiration at the time of his consecration as bishop, O'Connor decided to pursue his dream in 1860, resigning as bishop of Pittsburgh. He was followed by another seminary instructor from St. Charles in Philadelphia, the Spanish Vincentian Michael DOMENEC. His task as bishop was made perplexing, though, by financial difficulties, conflicts with numerous religious in his diocese, a restive clergy, and the financial intriguing of Fr. John Hickey, the rector of St. Paul's cathedral. Partly in aid of lessening the discord he was facing, Domenec recommended in 1875 that the diocese of Pittsburgh be divided, and proposed his own name for the newly created see. Accordingly, in January of 1876 Rome created the Diocese of Allegheny City (only a stone's throw across the Allegheny river from the city of Pittsburgh), appointed Domenec its bishop, and named John Tuigg (formerly pastor of St. John's church in Altoona) as his successor. Tuigg was shocked as he slowly discovered not only the level of indebtedness of many diocesan parishes, but also the reality that diocesan boundaries had been redrawn in such a way that the bulk of the financial (as well as other) problems were located in his, and not Domenec's, see. Following a local audit of diocesan records, the bishop requested the intervention of the Holy See. Bishop Domenec was called to Rome, and, unable to adequately respond to the evidence presented by Tuigg's representatives, was asked to submit his resignation as Bishop of Allegheny City. The dioceses were subsequently reunited by Rome, while Bishop Domenec, his health weakened by his ordeal, died in January of 1878 in his native Spain while enroute to America.

The see of Pittsburgh, thus reunited, saw its population continually increase as thousands of immigrants flocked to western Pennsylvania. Bishop Phelan first requested the division of the diocese in a meeting with Absp. Ryan of Philadelphia in 1899, and when a petition of the province's bishops met with no response from Rome, they repeated their entreaty in February of 1901. This latter petition met with a favorable response and eight counties were united to form the see of Altoona. Eugene A. Garvey (a Scranton priest) was chosen as the diocese's first bishop. Over half a century later the see city would be twinned with its neighbor to the west to become the diocese of Altoona-Johnstown.

The Challenges of an "Immigrant Church." The face of the Catholic Church in Pennsylvania continued to be altered by the tens of thousands of immigrants who arrived in its dioceses throughout the second half of the nineteenth century, drawn by promises of employment in the state's burgeoning coal mines, steel mills, oil rigs, and garment factories. Many of these new arrivals hailed from central and eastern Europe, and longed for an experience of the Church similar to that in their native lands. Pennsylvania's bishops responded by creating ethnic or national parishes, some (e.g., Scranton's St. Joseph's Slovak Church or Pittsburgh's St. Nicholas Croatian) were the first of their kind in the nation. Religious communities also sprang up to care for particular ethnic communities, such as Daughters of St. Cyril and Methodius in 1909.

A unique challenge was presented by the appearance in Pennsylvania of Eastern Rite Greek Catholics, almost half a million of whom had arrived in the United States by the beginning of the First World War. As early as 1884, a group of Ukrainians had settled in the town of Shenandoah, and had requested a pastor from the archbishop of Lviv. A priest, Fr. Ivan Volansky, arrived to care for the community, celebrating the first liturgy on December 19 of that same year. Other parishes were established in Freeland (1886) and Hazelton (1887). As occurred elsewhere in America when Greek and Latin rite Catholics came into contact, however, Volansky encountered opposition because of his marital status (he had a wife) and unfamiliar ways. Within five years, at the urging of the American hierarchy, he was recalled to the Ukraine.

In 1890, at the request of many U.S. bishops, Rome restricted Eastern rite clergy in the United States to celibates or widowers, and placed them under the jurisdiction of Latin rite bishops. A bishop for the Greek Catholics, Soter Ortynsky, was not appointed until 1907, and it would not be until 1914, in the decree *Cum episcopo,* that Rome would grant him full ordinary jurisdiction and independence from local bishops. Ortynsky based his exarchy (diocese) in Philadelphia. Following his death in 1916, and responding to tensions between Greek Catholics from Galicia (Ukrainians) and Greek Catholics from Hungary/Trans-Carpathia (Rusyns), Rome appointed two administrators, one for each nationality. On May 20, 1924, a bishop for each group would be named by the Holy See, Constantine Bohachevsky for the Ukrainians, and Basil Takach for the Rusyns. Both were consecrated in Rome in June, Bohachevsky becoming the bishop of Philadelphia (with pastoral charge of all Ukrainians in America), and Takach bishop of Pittsburgh (with pastoral charge of all Byzantine rite Catholics from Transcarpathia, Slovakia, Hungary and Yugoslavia). In 1958 Philadelphia was raised to an archeparchy (with Stamford, CT as a suffragan), while Pittsburgh became a metropolitan see in 1963 (with the addition of Passaic, NJ).

Many Greek Catholics joined the Orthodox church during the decades of their contentious relationship with the Latin rite hierarchy. Similar struggles occurred between the bishops and other ethnic groups, who aggressively, and at times stubbornly, advanced their demands. These cases often resulted in misunderstanding, enmity or worse, as in the case of Polish National Church. In 1897 a group of Polish Catholics in Scranton had completed construction of Sacred Heart Church, and asked Bp. O'Hara for control of the property. When he refused, as required by church law, the congregation of 250 families, led by their priest Fr. Francis Hodur, built a new church and refused to hand over the title to the property. O'Hara threatened sanctions, and the assembly was ultimately excommunicated, their appeals to Rome having been rejected. Hodur and many of his flock remained adamant, though, ultimately joining with similarly disaffected Polish Catholics from other dioceses to form a synod and electing Hodur as bishop of the Polish National Catholic Church, which would distinguish itself from the Roman church by its use of Polish in the liturgy, a married clergy, and lay control church property.

The growth of secret societies, often formed to protect the rights of unskilled laborers working in Pennsylvania's heavy industries, presented another challenge to the Church. Terence Powderly, a Catholic from Scranton, was the charismatic leader (1879–93) of the Knights of Labor, America's first national union. Unlike the Molly Maguires, miners who used violence in their struggle against the mine owners and operators, Powderly sought arbitration through peaceful means, and worked to conform the rituals and practices of the Knights to Catholic teaching. Working tirelessly in close consultation with Bp. O'Hara, Abp. Ryan, and others in the hierarchy, Powderly managed to receive the approval of the Catholic church for his organization in 1887, though sadly by then its decline had already begun.

Prominent Pennsylvania Catholics. Catholics in Pennsylvania were known not only as laborers in heavy industry, however. Priests such as the historian Peter Guilday (1884-1947) and Herman Heuser (1851-1932), editor of the *American Ecclesiastical Review*, were acclaimed in academic circles, while Maurice Francis Egan (1852–1924) and Agnes Repplier (1855–1950) were popular literary figures. In the field of medicine, Catholics could point with pride to such physicians as John M. Keating (1852–1893), a respected pediatrician, the surgeon Ernest Leplace (1861–1924), and Lawrence F. Flick (1856–1938) a leader in the fight against tuberculosis. Nicola A. Montani (1880–1948), the choirmaster of St. John the Evangelist Church in Philadelphia, was known to Catholics across the country for his work in restoring Gregorian chant to the liturgy, and his authoritative St. Gregory Hymnal (1920). Charles G. Fenwick (1880–1973), an expert in International Law, was a dedicated activist in the Peace Movement of the 1920s and 1930s.

The Church in Pennsylvania benefitted as well from the material success that had rewarded the labors of a number of her members. Nicholas and Genevieve Garvan Brady gave large sums of money to Catholic causes, and built an impressive novitiate for the Maryland province of the Society of Jesus at Wernersville. Charles Michael Schawb, who rose from being an engineer at Andrew Carnegie's Braddock works to become the president of US Steel, donated lavishly to Church-related institutions, including the Franciscan College of Loretto. Other Pennsylvania Catholic millionaires included Martin Maloney and John J. Sullivan, all of whom used their wealth to support the Church, and who were honored in turn with various awards and papal knighthoods.

One outstanding heiress who desired no earthly honors was Katherine DREXEL (1858–1955). Born into a wealthy banking family, which moved in the upper echelons of Philadelphia society, Katherine nonetheless was taught from her youth the importance of sharing the family's wealth with those in need (every week she joined her mother and sisters in distributing food and clothes to the poor who came to their house). As a young woman, Katherine sought to respond to the call of the Third Plenary Council of Baltimore to aid missions to America's African-Americans and Native Americans, but was taken aback somewhat when Pope Leo XIII suggested she found her own congregation of missionary religious. That, however, is precisely what she did, and after a novitiate with the Sisters of Mercy in Pittsburgh, she established the Sisters of the Blessed Sacrament for Indians and Colored People in 1891. Traveling across the country with her sisters, she used her substantial fortune (12 million dollars by the time of her death) to build churches and schools, and even a college (Xavier University in New Orleans). St. Katherine Drexel was beatified in 1988, and canonized in 2000.

The generosity of the Catholic laity made possible the founding of numerous colleges across the state, most notably those for women, run by ever-expanding orders of religious sisters, including: Marywood (1915) and College Misericordia (1924) in Scranton diocese; Villa Maria (1925) and Mercyhurst (1926) in Erie; Seton Hill (1918) and Mount Mercy [Carlow] (1929) in Pittsburgh; and Immaculata (1920), Rosemont (1921) and Chestnut Hill (1924) in the Archdiocese of Philadelphia.

The Twentieth Century. Philadelphia was fortunate to have a steady hand guiding it for much of the first half of the twentieth century. Dennis DOUGHTERY, ''God's Bricklayer,'' would serve as archbishop from 1918 to 1951, working with zeal and determination to found 112 parishes, 145 schools, four colleges and 12 hospitals, while personally ordaining over 2,000 priests to serve the needs of his ever-growing archdiocese. A formal and demanding administrator, Doughtery was named the state's first member of the college of cardinals in 1921.

Erie also was blessed with an ordinary of considerable longevity in John Mark Gannon, who served the diocese as bishop from 1920 to 1966. Known for his vigorous work in founding parishes, schools and even a college, Gannon was honored with the personal title of archbishop in 1953.

Pittsburgh also had a long-lived bishop in Hugh Boyle, whose tenure lasted from 1921 to 1950. As the city continued to grow, so did the diocese, which soon ranked as the eighth largest in the country. Most of this growth was the result of Pittsburgh's booming steel industry, which did not always receive praise from the Church for its labor practices. In fact, Pittsburgh priests and members of the Catholic Radical Alliance such as George Barry O'Toole, Carl Hensler and Charles Owen Rice were vocal critics of management and enthusiastic supporters of organized labor. The message of the Alliance helped to form Catholics such as Philip Murray, Patrick Fagan and John Kane, who all would become prominent union organizers in the steel and mining industry.

The diocese's postwar population growth soon provided an argument for a further division, and in May of 1951 four of Pittsburgh's eastern counties were united to form the Diocese of Greensburg. The first bishop was Hugh L. Lamb of the Archdiocese of Philadelphia, which itself was facing a rapidly expanding population. In 1961 Bp. Joseph McShea, who was serving as the administrator in the wake of the death of Cardinal O'Hara (1952–60), recommended to Rome that a new diocese be erected in either Bethlehem or Allentown. He was pleased by Rome's announcement on February 15 that a new Diocese of Allentown was to be created, but surprised by the news that he would be going there as the first bishop. The same momentous day saw the appointment of John KROL as the new archbishop of Philadelphia. Krol would serve as an undersecretary at the Second Vatican Council, as well as a member of the Central Coordinating Committee. The newly appointed bishop of Pittsburgh, John J. WRIGHT, would also distinguish himself as a member of the council's preparatory commission and worked to draft the celebrated chapter on the laity in the Constitution on the Church (*Lumen gentium*). Wright would subsequently be named a cardinal and Prefect of the Congregation of the Clergy in Rome. Krol too was named a cardinal in 1967, and remained in Philadelphia to guide the post-Vatican II church with a firmness and authority till his retirement in 1988, when he was succeeded by Anthony Bevilacqua, the bishop of Pittsburgh.

A number of Catholic dioceses in Pennsylvania faced the challenge of shrinking numbers of clergy as the century drew to a close, and many looked to the reorganization of their parishes as a means not only of ensuring a more effective distribution of priests, but also of revitalizing the faith. Pittsburgh, under the guidance of Bp. Donald Wuerl, took the lead in this initiative.

Serving as a helpful resource to the Church in Pennsylvania in the years following the Second Vatican Council was the Pennsylvania Catholic Conference. Formed in 1960 (as the Pennsylvania Catholic Welfare Committee) with constitutional lawyer William Bentley Ball as general counsel and executive director, the Conference was established to, in its own words "give witness to spiritual values in public affairs and . . . provide an agency for corporate Catholic service to the statewide community." It formulates policy positions, speaks on behalf of the Church before state government, and works to educate the public about Catholic teaching on morality, education, and human and civil rights. Most notable, perhaps, was the conference's advocacy on behalf of the Pennsylvania Abortion Control Act of 1989, which led to the U.S. Supreme Court's decision in *Planned Parenthood v. Casey*. After the Act went into effect in 1994, the number of abortions statewide fell 14 percent. The conference was also an outspoken champion of civil rights and seasonal farm workers rights, educational services for nonpublic school students, and the right of nonprofit charitable organizations to tax-exempt status. Figures provided by the conference placed the Catholic population at the beginning of the 21st century at approximately 3.5 million, or 29.7 percent of all Pennsylvanians. The dioceses of Philadelphia and Pittsburgh had the highest concentration of Catholics, at 38 percent, Harrisburg the lowest, at 12 percent.

Bibliography: Penn. Hist. and Museum Com., *Bibliography of Pennsylvania,* comp. N. B. WILKINSON, ed. S. K. STEVENS and D. H. KANT (2d ed. Harrisburg 1957). W. F. DUNAWAY, *A History of Pennsylvania* (2d ed. Englewood Cliffs, N.J. 1948). J. F. CONNELLY, *The History of the Archdiocese of Philadelphia* (Philadelphia 1976). L. G. FINK, *Old Jesuit Trails in Penn's Forest* (New York 1936). F. A. GLENN, *Shepherds of the Faith, 1843–1993: A Brief History of the Bishops of the Catholic Diocese of Pittsburgh* (Pittsburgh 1993). J. P. GALLAGHER, *A Century of History: The Diocese of Scranton, 1868–1968* (Scranton 1968).

[J. C. LINCK]

PENTATEUCHAL STUDIES

This survey of Pentateuchal scholarship comprises two parts. The first part examines the course of critical Pentateuchal scholarship from its beginnings down to 1965, while the second part extends the survey to the following decades.

Part I: Origins until 1965

The first five books of the Bible (Genesis, Exodus, Leviticus, Numbers, and Deuteronomy) are traditionally ascribed to Moses. The word Pentateuch, from the Greek πεντάτευχος, meaning the "five-scroll" work, was applied to these five books by the Jews of Alexandria at least from the beginning of the Christian Era. More commonly among the Jews, as already in the OT (2 Chr 23.18; Neh 8.1–2), these books were known as the Torah (Heb. *tôrâ*) or Law (of Moses). The Jewish title aptly designates much of the content; almost half of the material is legal in form. But the narrative portions give the theological meaning to the whole. It describes the religious history of mankind in very general terms from creation to Abraham (Gn 1–11), then in greater detail the patriarchal story (Gn 12–50) and the events surrounding the Exodus from Egypt and the wandering in the desert (Exodus through Deuteronomy). It is in the context of these latter events, in particular of the Sinai revelation, that the legal portion is conceived as an emergent of history. The Law, including all the religious, ethical, civil, and rubrical legislation in Israel, expressed Yahweh's will for His chosen people and accordingly was always related to the covenant of Sinai regardless of its actual date of formulation. Israel's concept of history had determined her concept of law. This article discusses the history of the origin and development of the Pentateuch as determined by Biblical scholarship. The following general outline will be followed: history of early scholarly opinion up to and including the Wellhausen documentary hypothesis; the four documents or traditions of the Pentateuch as determined by the classical documentary hypothesis; reactions to and refinement of the documentary hypothesis; summary and modern trends; Catholic opinion; Moses and the Pentateuch. (*See* GENESIS, BOOK OF; EXODUS, BOOK OF; LEVITICUS, BOOK OF; NUMBERS, BOOK OF; DEUTERONOMY, BOOK OF.)

Early Scholarly Opinion. Jewish and the earliest Christian tradition agreed in ascribing the Pentateuch as a whole to MOSES. As we shall see later in detail, this was in accord with a concept of authorship different from that of the modern Western world. By the time a more strict concept of the author's inviolability had been developed, in the Christian Era, the attribution to Moses was already traditional.

Richard Simon and Jean Astruc. In 1678 an Oratorian priest, Richard SIMON, published a critical work on the text, versions, and commentaries of the OT. On its appearance he was assailed by Catholics and Protestants alike, and his works were put on the Index. Despite this, he is called, and rightly so, the father of Biblical criticism, because of his pioneer work. It was 75 years later (1753) that another Catholic author, Jean ASTRUC, a French physician, published a literary analysis of Genesis in which he suggested the presence of two sources. By separating those sections using the name YAHWEH for God from those using ELOHIM he was able to reconstruct two fairly coherent stories. This was the beginning of the documentary hypothesis.

Early History of Documentary Hypothesis. Catholic reaction to Astruc's work was again not favorable. As a result, further development of the theory was undertaken mainly by German Protestant scholars. J. Eichhorn (1780) is generally credited with having systematized the investigation by drawing up certain principles of Biblical criticism and so assuring its development as a proper science. Moreover, he carried the analysis made by Astruc through to Leviticus and so made the problem of the origin of the Pentateuch an acute one for Biblical scholarship of the early 19th century. K. Ilgen (1798), Eichhorn's successor at the University of Jena, probed further into the Elohim sections and discovered two distinct sources there. Thus three documents had now become at least tentatively detached.

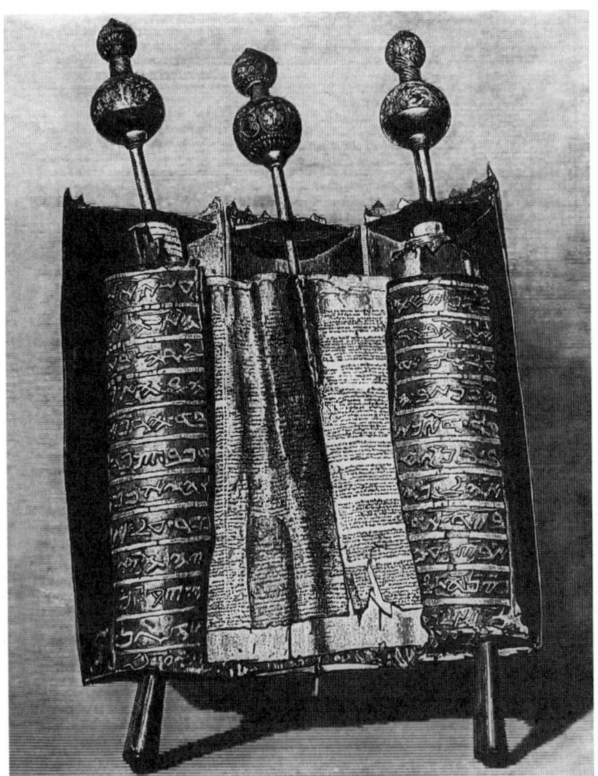

A paper scroll from the Pentateuch, written to Aaron's son, Eleazaar. (© Christel Gerstenberg/CORBIS)

The documentary hypothesis received its first major setback in the early part of the 19th century when a new theory, the fragment hypothesis, was championed. The seemingly complex tradition history of the material provided the basis for the theory. A. GEDDES (1792), an English Catholic priest, ascribed most of the material to the Solomonic era and considered it a conflation of a number of disparate documents. J. Vater (1802) further dissected the material and set the terminal date for its composition in the exilic period. W. M. L. De Wette (1805) concentrated on historical criticism and came to a similar conclusion, showing that much of the legislation could not have been made in the earlier period. But his outstanding contribution was the connection of Deuteronomy with the ''book of the Law'' found in the temple at the time of the reform of Josiah (2 Kgs 22.3–20; De Wette considered this ''finding'' a pious fraud on the part of the reformers); this had special interest for the next phase in the development of this hypothesis.

Further Development of Documentary Hypothesis. A partial return to this earlier theory was witnessed by G. H. A. Ewald's (1831) acceptance of a First Elohist (the modern "Priestly Code," abbreviated P; *see* PRIESTLY WRITERS, PENTATEUCHAL), a YAHWIST (abbreviated J after its German form), a redactor of these two, and De Wette's Deuteronomy (abbreviated D; *see* DEUTERONOMISTS). Though Ewald later changed to a supplement hypothesis, positing an Elohistic (the modern P) *Grundschrift* to which passages from other sources were added, his work prepared the way for the further development of the documentary hypothesis. This perfecting of the theory was heralded by H. Hupfeld (1853), who showed clearly the existence in Genesis of two Elohistic (the modern P and ELOHIST, abbreviated E) and the one Yahwistic (J) sources. Like his predecessors, Hupfeld considered P as basic and the oldest of all. Then E. Riehm (1854) proposed De Wette's Deuteronomy as the fourth distinct source in the Pentateuch. Thus the three sources in Genesis, first distinguished by Ilgen and then more clearly by Hupfeld, were proposed, together with Deuteronomy, as accounting for all the material for the Pentateuch. The task of substantiating this theory, revising some details, and filling in others remained.

The major revision was the reversing of the relative chronology of the sources. What had been considered the earliest of the Elohistic documents was, mainly through the work of E. G. E. Reuss (1833) and H. Graf (1866), considered to be postexilic in composition, at least with regard to its legislative sections. The latter scholar then followed W. Kosters (1868) in extending this conclusion to the narrative section of P. Thus, what once had been considered the oldest document of the Pentateuch was recognized as the youngest. The acceptance of this by the scholarly and influential A. Kuenen (1870) assured its acceptance by many others. The relative chronology as still held today had become more or less fixed.

Work of Julius Wellhausen. The great work of synthesizing all these conclusions and presenting them in a convincing way to the scholarly world was performed by J. WELLHAUSEN. The year 1876 marked the appearance of the first of his articles, which were later put in book form. This became the basis for almost all liberal critical work on the Pentateuch after that time. While he showed more clearly than any before him that the Yahwist was the oldest and the Priestly Code the youngest of the documents, he also provided an absolute dating for each, assigning the Yahwist to the 9th, the Elohist to the 8th, Deuteronomy to the 7th, and the Priestly source to the 5th centuries B.C. The determination was made on the basis of religious, social, and legal concepts supposedly found in the documents themselves.

Wellhausen made brilliant and full use of the science of literary criticism as developed at that time, a fact that helped in the wide diffusion of the documentary hypothesis as proposed by him. His writings, however, were partially vitiated by certain historical and philosophical preconceptions. He was completely skeptical about the ability to reconstruct any part of Israel's history that predated the beginnings of the monarchy. While some historical facts underlie the accounts of the Exodus, wandering, and conquest, they cannot be reconstructed, he argued, into any kind of organic story. And anything before that is, of course, pure legend or myth.

The lack of sufficient documentation for the history of the surrounding nations made it difficult also for Wellhausen, and others, to place Israel's history within its proper context. Hence they could more readily apply to OT literature criteria based on an evolutionary concept of religion. All the forms of religious belief, from animism to monotheism, were found to be expressed, and their expressions were dated in accord with the developing science of comparative religion. This science, as practiced by the majority at that time, left no room for the possibility of divine intervention and hence precluded any development of religion within Israel different than that among the pagan peoples.

Wellhausen's aprioristic reconstruction of Israel's religious history cast a shadow over the brilliance of his insights and presentation and was chiefly responsible for the reaction he met on the part of the more conservative scholars of his day, a reaction that has since been justified. The documentary hypothesis itself, however, in its determination of the four sources with their "constants" has retained the allegiance of the great part of the scholarly world, with the modifications to be noted.

Classical Four-Documentary Hypothesis. The characteristics of the documents or traditions, along with the principal passages attributed to them, determined by the process described above and as reflecting the generally accepted position, will be briefly presented.

Yahwist (J). This document was first recognized by its use, from the very beginning of its history, of the name "Yahweh" for God, although the name was revealed only in the time of Moses (Ex 3.15). The narrative is colorful and interesting; the painting of scenes and the delineation of characters are superb. The dialogues especially are presented with consummate skill and artistry (e.g., Gn 24). It is through the stories that J presents its religious convictions, which are quite profound and which reveal deep psychological insights into the human condition. The origin of evil, man's propensity to sin, the relationship between civilization and morality, the relevance of the apparently least significant events to the divine plan, and the grand sweep of that plan are all subjected to J's analysis. The underlying conviction is that God has intervened in Israel's history and manifested His loving concern for this people. In presenting this God, J makes bold use of anthropomorphisms, which easily distinguish it from E and P. God forms man, breathes into his nostrils, plants a garden, talks to man, walks in the garden, makes garments (Gn 2–3), is pleased (Gn 4.4), regrets, and is grieved (Gn 6.6), etc. Wellhausen and others placed the composition of J in the kingdom of Judah in the latter part of the 9th century B.C. There were to be later refinements of this, but the southern provenance during the monarchical period would continue to be maintained. Following are the principal passages attributed to J: Gn 2.4b–4.26; 6.1–8.22 (mixed with P); 9.18–27; 10.1–32 (mixed with P); 11.1–9; 12.1–13.19; 15.1–16.16; 18.1–19.38; 21.1–21 (mixed with P); 24.1–67; 25.1–26.35 (mixed with P); 27.1–45; 28.10–32.22 (mixed with E); 32.23–33.20; 34.1–31 (mixed with E); 37.1–36 (mixed with E); 38.1–39.23; 41.1–43.34 (mixed with E); 44.1–34; 45.1–48.22 (mixed with E and P); 49.1–33; 50.1–26 (mixed with E and P); Ex 1–2 (mixed with E and P); 3–5 (mixed with E); 7–11 (mixed with E and P); 14 (mixed with P); 32–34 (mixed with E); Nm 10.29–11.34 (mixed with E); 13.17b–16.35 (mixed with E and P); 20.1–24.25 (mixed with E and P); 32.1–42 (mixed with E and P). There is no universal agreement on all the attributions, and at times the conflation with other sources is such as to preclude a precise analysis.

Elohist (*E*). This document's careful use of the name ''Elohim'' for God in the pre-Sinai material is already an indication of its more exact theology. While the style is not as colorful as J's, it is more consciously didactic. E can be recognized by a preference for ''Horeb'' to ''Sinai,'' for ''Amorrites'' to ''Canaanites,'' etc. Its interest in the covenant is reflected in an emphasis on the obligations flowing from it (e.g., Gn 35.2). Similarly its morality is stricter than that of J (cf. Gn 20 with J's 26.6–11). Prophetic influence has probably colored E's description of Moses as charged with a prophetic office (Ex 3), and has determined its anachronistic identification of Abraham as a prophet (Gn 20.7). Finally, it avoids the bolder anthropomorphisms of J and presents God as speaking to man in dreams, from clouds or in the midst of fire, or through the medium of an angel. While the early critics debated the relative date of E and J, they all agreed in placing the composition of E in the northern kingdom, and the majority concurred on the time as the middle of the 8th century B.C. E was conflated with J, to J's advantage, in Juda some time after the fall of the northern kingdom. Following are the principal passages attributed to E: Gn 20.1–18; 21.22–22.24; 40.1–23; Ex 17–18; 20 (mixed with P); 21–24. See also the many passages conflated with J.

Deuteronomist (*D*). Early in the 19th century De Wette had already pointed out the special character of the book of Deuteronomy and argued that it had been composed as the basis of a reform program during the reign of Josiah. Riehm (1854) confirmed its special character. All critics accepted their principal conclusions. Within the Pentateuch D is confined, for the most part, to the book of Deuteronomy, whence its name, and is easily distinguished by its marked literary style. In vocabulary it makes frequent use of expressions such as ''choose,'' ''the good land,'' ''with all your heart and with all your soul,'' ''make his name to dwell,'' ''a mighty hand and outstretched arm,'' etc. These and its manner of presenting its material in the form of Mosaic addresses that are strongly hortatory and moving readily characterize it as a separate document. Its theology, too, is marked, stressing the law as a loving response to the God who chose Israel out of love and who made His name to dwell in the one Temple of Jerusalem where pure worship can alone be offered. While the critics did not endorse De Wette's thesis that Deuteronomy was composed and then put in the Temple to be ''found,'' they did agree that it was a document of the 7th century B.C. that bore some relation to Josiah's reform. As will be seen, later scholars recognized D in other books of the OT. As already stated, within the Pentateuch D is confined to the book of Deuteronomy except for a few brief passages in Exodus (Ex 12.24–27; 13.3–6; 15.26).

Priestly Document (*P*). The identification of P was relatively easy once E had been separated from it and recognized as a separate document. P's vocabulary tends to the abstract. Stereotyped expressions abound. The style is pedantic and redundant. P makes much use of genealogies, gives minute descriptions especially of ritual matters, and delights in chronological precision. Its presentation of history is liturgical in character, which accounts for the systematic and precise way in which the events are said to occur. As might be expected, God is presented in P less anthropomorphically than in any of the other documents. God ''appears,'' although it is not always indicated how, and speaks to man. The conversation is usually one-sided; man's attitude is one of respectful listening (Gn 17). P is responsible for most of the legal collections in their canonical form, and this interest is reflected in the whole composition. The critics agreed on a postexilic date for the document and that it was the work of priests attempting to restore liturgical worship in Jerusalem. Following are the principal passages attributed to P: Gn 1.1–2.4a; 5; 17; 23; 27.46–28.9; Ex 6; 16; 25–31; 35–40; the whole of Leviticus; Nm 1.1–10.28; 13.1–17a; 17–19; 25–31; 33–36. See also the passages conflated with J and E. Toward the end of the 7th century B.C., D had been joined to the conflated JE. The addition of P at some time in the 5th century B.C. would have completed the work, and the Pentateuch would have existed in its canonical form.

Reactions to the Documentary Hypothesis. In the succeeding years the Wellhausen hypothesis was subjected to many attacks that resulted in extensive revisions. While the outer shell of the theory, represented by the fourfold siglum of JEDP, has held up well and still claims the majority of supporters, the inner construction has been radically changed. The change was brought about by work in three major directions. The first and second of these were a more intense application of the principles of literary criticism and of a form-critical analysis. It is not always easy to distinguish the two, since the latter was a natural development of the former. Scholarly research led to the recognition that much of the material of the "documents" that had been the object of the classical literary criticism had developed from originally independent units. The attempt to recognize these units and trace their development through their varying "life situations" (*Sitze im Leben*) until they reached the final stage represented in the canonical books was an approach initiated principally by H. GUNKEL (1910) in his commentary on Genesis. The approach was called form criticism (*see* FORM CRITICISM, BIBLICAL). Thus, single stories or legal units were examined to see what could have given rise to them in early history. They would then be studied in relation to the complex cycle of stories or code of laws of which they became a part. Since the form critics agree that the fixing of these cycles or codes had already taken place to some extent within the period of oral tradition, this would throw considerable light on the role of the authors of the classical "documents" or "sources." These, whether individuals or schools, would not have been authors in the modern sense of the word. Rather would they be editors of already developed material, but with no little freedom to rearrange, conflate, revise, and, in general, cause the material to reflect their theology. It is clear that such an approach demands a much more extensive knowledge of history, in particular of the social, political, and religious institutions, and of situations that would have occasioned the origin or influenced the shaping of the unit in question. Such a knowledge was not possible in the 19th century and only in the 20th century was it becoming such that the form-critical approach could be used with some degree of confidence.

Literary Criticism. As indicated, there was first a more intense literary analysis that showed that the four documents were much more complex than generally suspected. Thus J was seen to reveal several strata in some of its stories. In the face of this, several scholars have posited a fifth source, called L (*Laienschrift* or Lay Document) by O. Eissfeldt, K (Kenite Document) by J. Morgenstern and S (South, or Seir Document) by R. Pfeiffer. These proposals, though differing in detail from one another, indicated that the documents in the Pentateuch had developed over a long period of time. This was strengthened by A. Welch's tracing of D to an earlier and northern origin, by G. von Rad's division of P into two strands, and by many other attempts along the same lines.

At times, the results of literary criticism took on absurd proportions that did much to discredit the science in the eyes of those who were suspicious of its conclusions from the outset. Thus B. Baentsch (1900) divided Leviticus into seven distinct P sources and worked with primary and secondary redactors of secondary documents, etc. A mere listing of his sigla indicated the extreme complexity of his analysis. On the other hand, there were a few who thought that the number of independent documents should be reduced. P. Volz, followed in part by W. Rudolph (1933), denied the independent existence of E and P, at least in Genesis. S. Mowinckel (1930) similarly expressed doubts about E, describing it rather as the product of several centuries of oral tradition. Later (1963) he dated J, which for him is equivalent to what others consider JE, to the 8th century B.C. but considered historiography to have begun in Israel with the Solomon saga, to which was later added a David story that included events dealing with Saul and Samuel.

These revisions, based principally on literary analysis, have not all been accepted. But they have influenced greatly the conception of the development of the sources within Israel. It is fairly commonly agreed that behind J and E there does stand some common source (e.g., M. Noth's *Grundschrift*) that would account for the many parallels in the two documents. Many, too, are more confident of being able to identify, at least partially, an older stratum (such as Eissfeldt's L) in J that would go back to the 10th or 9th century B.C. and a later stratum that shows the influence of the prophetic movement. In general it would be agreed that historiography began in Juda in the 10th or 9th century B.C. with J or one of its strata, that it continued in both kingdoms with succeeding editions of both J and E, and that the two were conflated in Juda after 721 B.C.

As for D, indication has already been made of the proposal that the development of its theology and of the resulting legal code in Deuteronomy took place over a long period of time, deriving its motivating force from the emphases of the Prophets, especially from Hosea in the North and Jeremiah in the South. More significant has been the identification of the vocabulary, style, and theology of the book of Deuteronomy with certain editorial passages in the historical books from Joshua to 2 Kings. It was concluded that these books form a long history based on material that had been passed on down over the years in both literary and oral form and had been given its definitive shape by the addition of editorial reflections and revisions in the appropriate places. Since these reflections and revisions echo the spirit of the Book of Deuteronomy, the entire history was called by M. Noth (1943) the ''Deuteronomistic History'' and the fifth book of the Pentateuch was considered its introduction. While this D history was probably not written at any one time, its final form must have been given in the exilic period, since it records the Babylonian Exile and seemingly looks forward to some kind of restoration (2 Kgs 25.27–30). Later in the postexilic period, perhaps around the time of Ezra, the historical books were detached from the introductory Deuteronomy, which was now attached to the first four books to form the Pentateuch. This now isolated corpus, with its emphasis on legal content, thus became the Torah, or Law, for later Judaism.

The development of P is similarly complex. All accept the final formulation of P in the postexilic period but admit also that it contains much older material. This is true especially of the legal sections that formed distinct codes in an earlier period. The Holiness Code (or H = Lv 17–26) was early recognized by A. Klostermann (1877) as forming a distinct unity that would later have been incorporated into the Priestly Code. The date of H has been placed as early as the period of the Judges (E. Robertson) and as late as the end of the kingdom of Judah (H. Cazelles, Von Rad). All would agree that it underwent a long development in accord with the same historical processes that helped to shape the other documents, that the Priestly Code of which it was made a part had similarly been developing over the centuries, and that the final redaction of the entire P did not take place until the postexilic period. (*See* HOLINESS, LAW OF.)

Form Criticism. Out of all this work there has come in recent years a more fruitful attempt to apply the principles of form criticism to the Pentateuchal material. Von Rad (1938), for example, isolated what he regarded as the ancient creeds of Israel (e.g., Dt 26.5–9; Jos 24.2–13) and considered them, or some form of them, to be the most primitive expression of SALVATION HISTORY (*HEILSGESCHICHTE*). The *Sitz im Leben* for the creed would have been a cultic celebration at the ancient shrine of Galgal (Gilgal). A separate tradition preserved the account of the Sinai covenant and its resulting covenant code; the covenant festival celebrated at SHECHEM would have been the original *Sitz im Leben* for this tradition. With this as his basis, Von Rad then gradually builds up to the profoundly constitutive work of J and to the gradual development of the Pentateuch along the classical lines.

Analyzing in greater detail the tradition history of the material, Noth (1948), who had already detached the great Deuteronomistic history (1943), attempted to identify and trace the basic themes of the Tetrateuchal history (the first four books of the Pentateuch). He found five of these themes, each of which he attempted to trace to its ultimate origin and then through its later development. While the extreme complexity of the task precluded a final solution to the whole problem, and while many of Noth's reconstructions were influenced by a regard for an underlying historical character more skeptical than generally held by scholars, he provided many insights that later scholars gratefully used in their own reconstructions. In both Von Rad's and Noth's studies we can detect a clear appreciation of the constitutive value of the classical documents or traditions, at least to the extent that they are seen to provide a basic theology to the heterogeneous material of which they are composed. This represents a reaction to the fragmentation of documents resulting from an overly critical literary analysis.

Besides the richer insights into the constitutive traditions, form criticism has already provided much deeper understanding of the individual elements of the traditions. Thus, working on a distinction proposed by A. Jirku (1927) and A. Jepsen (1927) between the type of laws proper to Israel and those common to the ancient Near East, A. Alt (1934) distinguished the former as apodictic and the latter as casuistic (*see* LAW, ANCIENT NEAR-EASTERN). G. Mendenhall (1954) and others then proceeded to show the close relationship between the Covenant Code (Ex 21–23), the oldest body of laws in the Pentateuch and the center of the attention of the other scholars, and the Hittite treaties, in which the concept of overlord-vassal relationship is presented in the same form as in the ancient Israelite Code. All this helped to give a more profound appreciation of the covenant itself and of its role in Israel's life.

In appraising the work of the form critics it can be said that they have confirmed the antiquity of much of the material of the Pentateuch, thrown greater light on the developing theologies within Israel and shown the need for much further study before any hypothesis can be accepted with all its details. The excesses in this field have not vitiated the value of the approach.

Uppsala School. A third approach that had its influence on Pentateuchal criticism was that of the so-called Uppsala School. Scandinavian scholars, such as Mowinckel (1930), J. Pedersen (1931), H. Nyberg (1935), and I. Engnell (1945), contributed in varying ways to the prestige of this school. In general there was a great stress put on the predominance and fidelity of oral tradition in ancient history and a consequent disregard for any supposed written documents in the early period. Even after the material had been consigned to writing (and Engnell would more readily accept an early written form for some of the legal matter), oral tradition was considered to have had its influence on the written documents. Such an approach would clearly be detrimental to the documentary hypothesis. In fact, Engnell, one of the most enthusiastic supporters of the approach, rejected the four classical documents and replaced them with a P Work, a symbol standing for the heterogeneous material in the Tetrateuch (Genesis through Numbers), and a D Work, Noth's Deuteronomic history. In both cases the emphasis is not on fixed literary traditions that can be precisely marked off as J, E, P, or D, but on a long history of oral tradition that was finally edited in the postexilic period in two principal works.

The vehemence with which these proposals were made, including occasional violent attacks on scholars of an opposite view, did not hasten their acceptance. Today most scholars would agree that the Uppsala School has not paid sufficient attention to the importance of writing, and consequently of written documents, in the early period of Israel's history. On the other hand, the emphasis on oral tradition and especially on its fidelity in transmission was a welcome stress, since it contributed to a healthier respect for the antiquity of much of the material of the Pentateuch. The school has also shown a reluctance to accept variant readings of the Masoretic Text, a reluctance that has frequently been justified on the basis of further studies.

Summary and Mid-20th Century. What has been stated above already affords some idea of the present situation with regard to the origin of the Pentateuch. Almost all would agree to the extreme complexity of the picture. Israel's Torah represented both a literary and a religious heritage that was kept ever alive by its adaptation to the constantly changing historical scene. The adaptation necessitated the addition of new material and the revision of the old. Today the emphasis is being placed on the successive stages of this adaptation and the development of the theological concepts. When the attempt is marked by sound methodological principles, the results are positive and valuable.

Throughout the long and occasionally heated history of the documentary hypothesis the question of historicity was constantly being raised. As we have seen, in the earlier stages of the theory's history grave doubts were cast on much of the historical character of the Pentateuch, in particular on the Genesis narratives. This situation has changed, owing in great part to the results of archeological work. The ruins themselves and, above all, the literature of other ancient peoples have provided an authentic background against which the Pentateuchal narratives can be seen. The patriarchal stories, for example, have been convincingly shown, in a series of articles by R. de Vaux (1946–49), to reflect the first half of the 2nd millennium B.C. This does not mean that these contain history in the modern sense; not even the later stories of the Exodus, wandering, and conquest do that. But it does mean that they contain a sufficient historical basis to support the weight of the credal interpretation that is their principal object. Once the concern for that historical basis can be satisfied, at least to the extent that is possible, greater emphasis can be correctly placed on the theological development.

Pentateuchal criticism in the future, then, will most probably concentrate on three general aspects of this theological development. The first aspect is that of the individual units and their meaning before their introduction to a particular cycle of tradition. The second is that of the principal cycles of tradition, such as the Yahwist, Elohist, and others. Some of the richest theological meaning was given to the material at this stage, and for that reason this aspect will continue to be studied for further insights. The third is that of the canonical Pentateuch. At times this is neglected by the scholars in their interest in the earlier stages. But it is in this aspect that the Pentateuch was made a part of the Christian Scriptures and that it has influenced the greater part of Christian history. It is likely that the canonical Pentateuch will be the object of the most intensive work in the future.

Catholic Opinion. Despite the fact that Catholics were among the first to cast doubts on the literary unity of the Pentateuch, the history of Pentateuchal criticism has been marked chiefly by Catholic opposition to its results. The opposition was to a great extent justified by the failure of the critics to distinguish properly between literary and historical criticism. The conclusions of the former were bound to have an undue influence on the latter. Also, the rationalistic philosophy of the 19th century vitiated much of the work of the liberal scholars and made all their conclusions suspect to the more conservative Christians. Toward the end of the 19th century a few Catholic scholars, notably, M. J. LAGRANGE, made an attempt to extract what was scientifically valid in the work of the critics. Lagrange, for example, accepted the distinction of the four sources, admitting that D and especially P represented, for the most part, post-Mosaic development. This Catholic beginning in literary criticism was again hampered by the flowering of the Modernist crisis early in the present century. MODERNISM accepted the most radical of the conclusions of the literary critics, including the evolutionary concept of Israel's religion. Catholic scholarship was placed once again on the defensive, and Pentateuchal criticism, as exercised by Catholics, was practically brought to a standstill. In a four-part decree, issued June 27, 1906, the PONTIFICAL

BIBLICAL COMMISSION stated that, although the use of sources and of secretaries by Moses could be admitted along with the introduction of some post-Mosaic modifications, the arguments of the critics were not at all convincing. Despite the guarded wording of the decree, it had a strong negative influence on Catholic scholarship in the area for many years.

Between the two world wars some attempts were made by Catholic scholars to adopt the most certain of the conclusions of the literary critics and combine them with the theory of substantial Mosaic authenticity. In non-Catholic circles, where scholarship had already done much to correct some of the exaggerations of the Wellhausen school and had forged ahead in new areas, these attempts were little noted. But they played their part in paving the way for the encyclical *DIVINO AFFLANTE SPIRITU* in 1943, which opened the door to Catholic scholarship in all areas of Biblical study. This remarkable document must be read in the light of all the controversy that preceded; only then will its vigorous championing of scientific investigation in all fields be fully appreciated. The Pentateuchal question is not brought up *ex professo* in this encyclical. Rather, Pius XII is dealing with the general principles that must underlie all Biblical work. But these principles are such that their application would necessarily involve a broader interpretation of the Pentateuch.

This conclusion is confirmed by a letter, sent on Jan. 16, 1948, by the secretary of the Pontifical Biblical Commission to Cardinal Suhard of Paris. It was in response to a query regarding the liberty of Catholic scholars to investigate the two problems of Pentateuchal sources and the historicity of the first 11 chapters of Genesis. The secretary first states that, in the light of the encyclical of Pius XII, the earlier decree of the Commission can be interpreted as not opposing "further and truly scientific examination of these problems." For this reason the Commission did not wish to promulgate a new decree at the time. Going into more detail, it has this to say about the origin of the Pentateuch: "There is no one today who doubts the existence of these sources or refuses to admit a progressive development of the Mosaic Laws due to social and religious conditions of later times. . . . Therefore, we invite Catholic scholars to study these problems, without prepossession, in the light of sound criticism and of the findings of other sciences connected with the subject matter." Attention should be called here to the complete objectivity of scholarly approach urged by the Commission in this letter. It is in marked contrast to the historically conditioned defensive attitude of the earlier decree.

The incentive given to Catholic scholars by the encyclical of Pius XII and again by the letter to Cardinal Suhard produced its fruits. The most recent studies in Pentateuchal criticism by Catholic scholars will, as a result, show few differences from those of respected non-Catholic scholars, and most of the differences would not be on the confessional level. Among the modern Catholic studies that reflect this new attitude mention can be made particularly of the commentaries on Genesis where the acceptance of the classical sources (more commonly called "traditions" by Catholics to indicate their long historical development) is presumed. J. CHAINE (1948), H. Junker (1949), De Vaux (1951), A. Clamer (1953) and B. Vawter (1956) are among those who accept them or develop their own reconstruction of the complex problem.

Moses and the Pentateuch. With regard to Mosaic authenticity a more subtle approach, but one more in keeping with the primitive concepts of authorship, is taken. Lagrange had long ago (1897) remarked that the modern concept of the inviolability of the author, with its repugnance to successive and extensive redactions of material over a long period of time, is a development of the Christian Era. It was not shared by the ancient Near East or by Israel. For them authorship was seemingly determined more by the one who provided the initial and pervading spirit of the work than by the one who oversaw its final redaction. This is evidenced, for example, in the tradition of the Davidic authorship of the Psalms and, in a much more remarkable way, in the completely pseudonymous attribution of Ecclesiastes and Canticle of Canticles to Solomon. Moses' historical role in the events of the Exodus, of Sinai and of the wandering, a role which must be accepted if only to explain the unity that is found in the Pentateuchal traditions, provided the basis for the literary role, which flowed from it and was conditioned by it. Because Moses, therefore, is at the heart of the Pentateuchal history and theology, Israel had no hesitation in attributing the entire literary work to him.

See Also: BOOK OF THE COVENANT; COMMANDMENTS, TEN; COVENANT (IN THE BIBLE); LAW, MOSAIC; PATRIARCHS, BIBLICAL; PRIMEVAL AGE IN THE BIBLE; SINAI, MOUNT.

Bibliography: J. COPPENS, *The Old Testament and the Critics,* tr. E. A. RYAN and E. W. TRIBBE (Paterson 1942). R. H. PFEIFFER, *Introduction to the Old Testament* (rev. ed. New York 1948). C. R. NORTH, "Pentateuchal Criticism," *The Old Testament and Modern Study,* ed. H. H. ROWLEY (Oxford 1951). H. F. HAHN, *Old Testament in Modern Research* (Philadelphia 1954). H. J. KRAUS, *Geschichte der historiach-kritischen Erforschung des Alten Testaments* (Neukirchen 1956). F. ROBERTI and A. TRICOT, *Guide to the Bible,* tr. E. P. ARBEZ and M. P. MCGUIRE, 2 v. (Tournai–New York 1951–55; v. 1 rev. and enl. 1960) 1:157–282. D. N. FREEDMAN, *The Interpreters' Dictionary of the Bible,* 4 v., ed. G. A. BUTTRICK (Nashville 1962) 3:711–727. J. BRIGHT, "Modern Study of Old Testament Literature," *The Bible and the Ancient Near East,* ed.

G. E. WRIGHT (Garden City, N.Y. 1961). H. CAZELLES, *Dictionnaire de la Bible,* supp. ed. L. PIROT et al. (Paris 1928) 7:687–767. A. SUELZER, *The Pentateuch: A Study in Salvation History* (New York 1964).

[E. H. MALY/C. T. BEGG]

Part II: From 1965 to the Present

The older scholarship on Pentateuchal studies up to 1965 was overwhelmingly diachronic in focus, i.e., it was concerned to get behind the present complex of books Genesis through Deuteronomy to the earlier materials underlying it. In this enterprise, the formative stage which received particular attention was that of the ''documents'' or ''sources'' held to extend over one or more of our existing Pentateuchal books. Such sources, it was believed, could be reconstructed on the basis of indications offered by the present Pentateuch, e.g., duplications of content, terminological variations, differences of anthropology, theology, and presupposed background, etc.

More specifically, for the books Genesis-Numbers (the ''Tetrateuch''), scholars reckoned with three long-established sources, namely, the Yahwist (J), dated *c.* 950 B.C., the Elohist (E) of *c.* 800–750 B.C., and the Priestly (P) deriving from the Exilic/post-Exilic period. A fourth source, the Deuteronomic, from *c.* 700–650 B.C., was seen as comprising an earlier form of the Book of Deuteronomy and as having stronger links with the following books (Joshua-Kings) (cf. M. Noth's 1943 theory of the ''Deuteronomic History''). In the decade beginning 1964, scholars like H. W. Wolff, W. Brueggemann, and P. E. Eliis strove to identify a distinctive ''kerygma'' for the various sources, reflective of the particular moment in Israel's history from which they emanated.

Given the above, this article explains the evolution of Pentateuchal studies over the last quarter of this century by first surveying diachronically-oriented scholarship of the most recent period and then touching upon the newer synchronic approaches where the focus is not on hypothetical earlier forms of the Pentateuch, but rather on the complex (and/or its component parts) in its actual existent shape.

Diachronic Approaches. Especially since about 1976, the ''three-source model'' for the origin of the Pentateuch/Tetrateuch (the special case of the ''Deuteronomic source'' will be left largely out of account here), as cited above, has become the object of intense controversy within diachronic Pentateuchal scholarship itself. It seems possible to divide participants in the controversy into three main groups: those who uphold the one-time independent existence of all three of the traditional sources, authors denying that any of the three sources (as traditionally understood) ever existed separately, and scholars ready to accept one or two but not all three of the classical sources. Each of these positions will now be considered in turn.

Maintenance of the Three Source Theory. In view of the controversy currently surrounding the theory of sources, it is important to note, at the outset, that the theory has not lacked weighty advocates throughout the period under discussion. Among these may be mentioned: W. Resenhöfft (1974), P. Weimar (1977, 1985), E. Otto (1977), H. Seebass (1977, 1978, 1983), R. Smend (1978), H. Vorländer (1978), R. E. Clements (1979), E. Zenger (1980, 1982), R. E. Friedman (1981, 1987), W. H. Schmidt (1982, 1984), L. Schmidt (1983, 1986), L. Ruppert (1985) and F. Kohata (1986). All these authors attempt, both negatively and positively, to counter the arguments against the existence of the various sources advanced by scholars of other persuasions. At the same time, the group under consideration is markedly heterogeneous in many respects.

The scholar who most clearly goes his own way with regard to the others is Resenhöfft. For him, each of the three sources extends into the Book of Kings. In addition, Resenhöfft takes source division further than any previous critic; e.g., he partitions the ''P chapter'' Genesis 17 among his three sources. By contrast, the other scholars listed tend to minimalize the content at least of J and E, ascribing much material earlier authors attributed to one or other of these documents rather to later redactors, R^{JE}, R^{D} and R^{P} (this tendency is especially marked in the works of Zenger and Weimar).

Authors in this group also diverge regarding the date and extent of the three sources. Friedman, e.g., assigns P to the reign of Hezekiah as compared with the traditional Exilic/post-Exilic dating advocated by the others. Vorländer, for his part, dates both J and E to the Exilic period. Similarly, Friedman finds J's conclusion in Nm 25.5, whereas Weimar, after earlier identifying Nm 14.9 as the last extant text of the source, has more recently proposed that J's final occurrence is in Ex 14.30. Again, Smend is unsure whether the compilation of J took place already in Solomon's time or only towards the end of the royal period. Thus even among contemporary ''documentarians'' significant differences do exist.

Rejection of the Three Sources. There are recent diachronic scholars who deny that J, E, and P ever existed as independent, free-standing documents. Positively, these authors espouse what in the history of scholarship has been called a ''supplementary hypothesis.'' In this conception, the Pentateuch originated, not via a combination of originally separate sources, but by the repeated reworkings/expansion of a ''foundational document'' (or documents). Advocates of this approach claim for it the advantage of being a more "economical" account of the Pentateuch's formation in which one no longer has to reckon with a combiner of J and E (R^{JE}), etc.

Differentiations are also in order within this group. The variety existing within the contemporary supplementary hypothesis is perhaps best illustrated by a summary presentation of the more specific conceptions of several of its leading representatives.

1) S. Tengström (1976, 1982) traces the Pentateuch (Hexateuch) back to a very early (11th century B.C.) "foundational narrative" comprising material now found in Genesis 11.27–Joshua 24, which related how the confederation of the 12 tribes came into possession of its land. This document is not to be identified with either J or E; it contains material normally assigned to both of these sources. Subsequently, the basic narrative underwent reworkings by assorted Deuteronomistic and Priestly redactors.

2) The views of J. Vermeylen (1981, 1986) are much more reminiscent of the standard documentary hypothesis. Vermeylen recognizes distinctive bodies of Yahwistic, Elohistic, and Priestly material present throughout the Tetrateuch and assigns these a content and a date largely along traditional source critical lines. For him, however, the Pentateuch came into existence by a process in which a Solomonic Yahwistic stratum (itself incorporating discrete materials from the reign of David) was reworked first by an Elohistic and then by a whole series of Deuteronomistic and Priestly redactors.

3) J. van Seters (1975) advocates the thesis of a late (Exilic, post-Deuteronomistic) Yahwistic history extending from Genesis to Joshua 24. This work took up existing "pre-Yahwistic" and Elohistic material and was itself subject to a Priestly redaction. H. H. Schmid (1976, 1981) and N. E. Wagner (1977) put forward similar views.

4) R. Rendtorff (1977, 1983) and his pupil E. Blum (1984) maintain, at opposite extremes from Tengström, that a continuous narrative extending from creation to the death of Moses came into existence only quite late, thanks to Deuteronomistic and Priestly redactors working in the Exilic and post-Exilic periods. Up until that time the various thematic blocks recognizable in the present Pentateuch, i.e., the primeval and ancestral histories, the complexes concerning Exodus, Sinai, and the desert wanderings, had circulated and developed independently. Thus for them one cannot speak of any continuous Yahwistic and Elohistic strands. A somewhat comparable conception is advocated by C. Houtman (1980). He holds that the books Genesis, Exodus-Numbers, and Deuteronomy each had a distinctive pre-history before finally being assembled by a Deuteronomistic redactor into a complex encompassing Genesis through Kings (the "Hennateuch").

5) The contemporary tendency to discard the classical documents reaches its culmination in the work of R. N. Whybray (1987). After an extended critique of the presuppositions and criteria operative in the identification of both "sources" and longer redactional strata in the Pentateuch, Whybray advances an "alternative approach" regarding the origin of the Pentateuch. Briefly his suggestion is that the Pentateuch be seen as the work of a single author writing in the sixth century B.C. who had available to him, as far as narrative material is concerned, little more than scattered items of tradition which he arranged and embellished with considerable creativity in a way reminiscent of his near-contemporary, the Greek historian Herodotus. For Whybray, this author should not be identified with any particular theological or literary current, that is to say, the Deuteronomistic or the Priestly; like Herodotus he would deliberately have varied his mode of presentation over the course of his work.

Compromise Positions. There remain a large group of diachronically minded scholars whose views on the formation of the Pentateuch (Tetrateuch) fall somewhere between those of the "documentarians" and the "supplementists." C. Westermann (1981) and A. H. J. Gunneweg (1985), for example, admit both a J and a P source (as well as the traditional dates for these), while viewing the Elohistic material as intended from the start as a supplement to J. Conversely, F. M. Cross (1973) accepts distinct J and E sources, even though he denies that "P" ever existed independently.

Three other recent authors to be mentioned here can be categorized basically as "supplementarists" except as regards the P material. H.-C. Schmitt (1980, 1985) suggests that "proto-Yahwistic" materials going back to the Solomonic period were, during the Exile, worked over by an Elohistic redactor whose composition was, in turn, supplemented by a post-Exilic "late-Yahwist" (cf. van Seters). P, however, did originate as a distinct document.

M. Rose (1981) also thinks in terms of a late Yahwistic body of material which utilized pre-existing "Elohistic" matter. More specifically, Rose holds that J was written in dependence on the Deuteronomistic history and was intended to stand together with it as its corrective introduction. For him too P constitutes a formerly freestanding document. E. Cortese (1983, 1986), unlike Schmitt and Rose, admits the existence of a continuous early J stratum (cf. Vermeylen). Subsequently, this underwent a large-scale supplementation by a Yahwistic redactor to whom Cortese likewise attributes the material normally ascribed to E. Corresponding to these early and late J strands are Cortese's source P which was reworked by a later Priestly redactor. Finally, under this heading may also be mentioned O. Kaiser (1984) who while advocating Exilic/post-Exilic dates for all three bodies of material J, E, and P, leaves it undecided whether these sigla are to be understood as representing ''sources'' or redactional strands.

Synchronic Approaches. As in Biblical studies in general Pentateuchal scholarship of the last two decades has witnessed a spectacular emergence of synchronic approaches in which the text in its currently extant form becomes the center of interest. Negatively, this development reflects the frustration felt by many faced with the hypothetical and conflicting character of diachronic scholarship's results. More positively, it bespeaks the impact on contemporary Biblical studies from the side of such disciplines as ''Orientalistics,'' literary theory, and theology. Against this background, mention may be made of several representative synchronic approaches to the Pentateuch all of which concentrate on unifying features within the material which cut across the sources or redactional strands distinguished by the diachronists.

C. J. Labuschagne (1982, 1986) and C. Schedl (1986) discover recurring numerical patterns throughout, e.g., the divine speeches of the Pentateuch. G. Larsson (1983, 1985) finds a self-consistent chronological/calandrical system undergirding the complex. R. P. Knierim (1985) identifies an overall genre for the present Pentateuch, i.e., a ''biography of Moses.''

On a more theological level, A. J. H. Clines (1978) ascertains an overarching theme, i.e., the (partial) fulfillment of God's promises governing both the Pentateuch's movement and its ending with Moses dying outside the land. Similarly, B. S. Childs (1979) attempts to uncover the ''canonical function'' of the Pentateuch in its ''canonical shape'' for those faith communities which recognize it as their authoritative Scripture.

Finally to be noted are the increasing number of studies which examine a particular segment of the Pentateuch from a synchronic perspective, e.g., G. J. Wenham (1977) on the flood narrative, B. W. Anderson (1978) on the primeval history, J. L. Ska (1986) on Exodus 14 and R. W. L. Moverley (1984) on Exodus 32–34.

All of the above authors explicitly acknowledge that the extant Pentateuch and/or its components have a prehistory which is a legitimate object of study. Indeed, e.g., Childs affirms his acceptance of J and E as distinct sources and of P as partly a source and partly a redactional stratum, while Labuschagne notes that his findings lend support to the supposition of an extensive Deuteronomistic redaction in the Tetrateuch. At the same time, their investigations do, inevitably, serve to shift attention to the remarkable degree of unity (literary, thematic, etc.) which resulted when the Pentateuch was given its present form.

Some scholars would go further, however, claiming that synchronic approaches vitiate the whole notion of the heterogeneity of the materials underlying our Pentateuch. Y. Radday, et al. (1982) claim, for example, on the basis of computer study of word frequency and linguistic patterns in Genesis, that there are no grounds for distinguishing between J and E, just as the linguistic differences between the P and non-P material are explainable in terms of the peculiar subject matter of the former. In a similar vein, I. M. Kikawada and A. Quinn (1985) appeal to the Ancient Near Eastern parallels and to stylistic considerations in upholding the unity of authorship for the primeval history in Genesis 1–11.

Reflections and Prospects. The foregoing account makes clear that contemporary Pentateuchal studies are characterized by diversity and fluidity. This state of affairs, while confusing, does have a positive side. It forces scholars continuously to rethink and refine their positions in view of other ways of explaining the data which are being put forward.

With regard to diachronic approaches to Pentateuchal study, it seems that the long-standing documentary hypothesis will not and should not be abandoned too readily. Respondents to Rendtorff point out the connections existing between the different blocks of material already at the pre-Deuternomistic and pre-P levels: they cite, by way of example, how the account of Abram's ''Egyptian interlude'' in Gn 12.10–20 foreshadows developments in the Joseph and Exodus narratives. In addition, the analogy of Chronicles in relation to the Deuteronomistic history (or the Gospels of Matthew and Luke in Mark) would suggest that when, in Biblical times, the need was felt for a ''revised version'' of events that need was met by the production of a new, free-standing document, rather than simply by a corrective reworking of an existing one. Or to put the point differently: the P material's peculiar slant on the Patriarchs' activities emerges far more effectively when that material is taken for and by itself, whereas it is largely neutralized when read in conjunction with the non-P matter, i.e., a ''P-redaction'' seems like a self-defeating procedure.

The above remarks notwithstanding, it must likewise be recognized that the material of the Pentateuch (Tetrateuch) allows itself to be partitioned among the three sources only to a quite limited degree. This point is widely recognized even by present-day documentarians whose reconstructed sources tend to contain far less material than those of their predecessors (see above). Thus also these authors acknowledge the presence of much redactional material in the Pentateuch—a fact relativizing the opposition between the documentary and supplementary approaches. Future Pentateuchal study needs to investigate more intensively the various redactions the complex has undergone in terms of, e.g., their relations to the sources, dating, and contextual thrusts. Thereby, diachronic scholarship's excessive preoccupation with the stage of the sources will, it may be hoped, receive a needed corrective.

The various synchronistic approaches to the Pentateuch outlined above are long overdue. They hold out the promise for furthering appreciation that the Pentateuch as a finished product makes sense. On the other hand, however, they should not be allowed to become what the Pentateuchal documentary hypothesis was for so long, i.e., the only scholarly "respectable" way of looking at the data. As most synchronists themselves recognize, diachronic investigation of the Pentateuch remains perfectly legitimate. Moreover, it should be kept in mind that the synchronic approaches are not without their own problems of hidden presuppositions, subjectivism, arbitrariness, and defective conceptualization [see, e.g., the critiques of the methods of Labuschagne and Radday by P. R. Davies and D. M. Gunn (1984) and S. L. Portnoy and D. L. Petersen (1984), respectively].

Bibliography: P. E. ELLIS, *The Yahwist. The Bible's First Theologian* (Collegeville 1968). F. M. CROSS, *Canaanite Myth and Hebrew Epic* (Cambridge, Mass. 1973). W. RESENHÖFFT, *Die Genesis im Worlaut ihrer drei Quellenschriften* (Bern 1974). J. VAN SETERS, *Abraham in History and Tradition* (New Haven 1975). S. TENGSTRÖM, *Die Hexateucherzählung* (Lund 1976). *Die Toledotformel und die literarische Struktur der priesterlichen Erweiterungsschicht im Pentateuch* (Lund 1982). H. H. SCHMID, *Der sogenannte Jahwist* (Zurich 1976). "Auf der Suche nach neuen Perspektiven für die Pentateuchforschung," *Congress Volume Vienna 1980*, J. A EMERTON, ed. (Leiden 1981) 375–394. G. J. WENHAM, "The Coherence of the Flood Narrative," *Vetus Testamentum* 28 (1977) 336–348. H. SEEBASS, "Zur geistigen Welt des sog. Jahwisten." *Biblische Notizen* 4 (1977) 39–47; *Geschichtliche Zeit und theonome Tradition in der Josephserzählung* (Gütersloh 1978); "Num xi, xii und die Hypothese des Jahwisten," *Vetus Testamentum* 28 (1978) 214–223; "Gerhörten Verheissungen zum ältesten Bestand der Vätererzählungen?" *Biblica* 64 (1983) 189–210. N. E. WAGNER, "A Response to Professor Rolf Rendtorff," *Journal for the Study of the Old Testament* 3 (1977) 20–27. E. OTTO, "Stehen wir vor einem Umbruch in der Pentateuchkritik?" *Verkündigung und Forschung* 22 (1977) 82–97. P. WEIMAR, *Untersuchungen zur Redaktionsgeschichte des Pentateuch* (Berlin-New York 1977); *Die Meerwundererzählung* (Wiesbaden 1985). R. RENDTORFF, *Das überlieferungsgeschichtliche Problem des Pentateuch* (Berlin-New York 1977); *The Old Testament: An Introduction*, tr. J. BOWDEN (Philadelphia 1983). R. SMEND, *Die Entstehung des Alten Testaments* (Stuttgart 1978). B. W. ANDERSEN, "From Analysis to Synthesis: the Interpretation of Genesis 1–11," *Journal of Biblical Literature* 97 (1978) 23–39. H. VORLÄNDER, *Die Entstehungszeit des jehowistischen Geschichtswerkes* (Bern 1978). D. A. J. CLINES, *The Theme of the Pentateuch* (Sheffield 1978). R. E. CLEMENTS, "Pentateuchal Problems," *Tradition and Interpretation*, G. W. ANDERSON, ed. (Oxford 1979) 96–124. B. S. CHILDS, *Introduction to the Old Testament as Scripture* (Philadelphia 1979). C. HOUTMAN, *Inleiding in de Pentateuch* (Kampen 1980). H.-C. SCHMITT, *Die Nichtpriesterliche Josephsgeschichte* (Berlin-New York 1980); "Die Hintergründe der 'neuesten Pentateuchkritik' und der literarische Befund der Josefgeschichte Gen 37–50," *Zeitschrift für die alttestamentliche Wissenschaft* 97 (1985) 161–178. E. ZENGER, "Wo steht die Pentateuchforschung heute?" *Biblische Zeitschrift* 24 (1980) 101–116; "Auf der Suche nach einem Weg aus der Pentateuchkrise," *Theologische Revue* 78 (1982) 353–362; *Israel am Sinai. Analysen und Interpretationen zu Exodus 17–34* (Altenberge 1982). C. WESTERMANN, *Genesis 12–36* (Neukirchen-Vluyn 1981). J. VERMEYLEN, "La formation du Pentateuque à la lumière de l'exégèse historico-critique," *Revue théologique de Louvain* 12 (1981); *Le Dieu de la Promesse et le Dieu de l'Alliance* (Paris 1986). M. ROSE, *Deuteronomist und Jahwist* (Zurich 1981). R. E. FRIEDMAN, *The Exile and Biblical Narrative* (Chico, Calif. 1981); *Who Wrote the Bible?* (New York 1987). W. BRUEGGEMANN and H. W. WOLFF, *The Vitality of the Old Testament Traditions* (2nd ed. Atlanta 1982). Y. RADDAY, et al., "Genesis, Wellhausen and the Computer," *Zeitschrift für die alttestamentliche Wissenschaft* 94 (1982) 467–481. C. J. LABUSCHAGNE, "Divine Speech Formulas in the Pentateuch," *Vetus Testamentum* 32 (1982) 268–281; "Neue Wege und Perspketiven in der Pentateuchforschung," *Vetus Testamentum* 36 (1986) 146–162. W. H. SCHMIDT, "A Theologian of the Solomonic Era? A Plea for the Yahwist," *Studies in the Period of David and Solomon*, T. ISHIDA, ed. (Tokyo 1982) 55–73; *Old Testament Introduction*, tr. M. J. O'CONNELL (New York 1984). E. CORTESE, "Il Pentateucho oggi: la teoria documentaria in crisi?" *Scuola cattolica* III (1983) 79–88; *Da Mose a Esdra. I libri storici dell' Antico Israele* (Bologna 1985). L. SCHMIDT, "Pentateuch," *Altes Testament* (Neukirchen-Vluyn 1983) 88–101; *Literarische Studien zur Josephsgeschichte* (Berlin-New York 1986). A. H. J. GUNNEWEG, "Anmerkungen und Anfragen zur neueren Pentateuchforschung," *Theologische Rundschau* 48 (1983) 227–253; 50 (1985) 107–131. G. LARSSON, "The Chronology of the Pentateuch: A Comparison of the MT and LXX," *Journal of Biblical Literature* 102 (1983) 401–409; "The Documentary Hypothesis and the Chronological Structure of the OT," *Zeitschrift für die alttestamentliche Wissenschaft* 97 (1985) 316–333. P. R. DAVIES and D. M. GUNN, "Pentateuchal Patterns. An Examination of C. J. Labuschagne's Theory," *Vetus Testamentum* 34 (1984) 399–406. S. L. PORTNOY and D. L. PETERSEN, "Genesis, Wellhausen and the Computer: A Response," *Zeitschrift für die alttestamentliche Wissenschaft* 96 (1984) 421–425. O. KAISER, *Einleitung in das Alte Testament* (5th ed. Gütersloh 1984). E. BLUM, *Die Komposition der Vätergeschichte* (Neukirchen-Vluyn 1984). R. W. L. MOBERLY, *At the Mountain of God. Story and Theology in Exodus 32–34* (Sheffield 1984). I. M. KIKAWADA and A. QUINN, *Before Abraham Was: The Unity of Genesis 1–11* (Nashville 1985). D. A. KNIGHT, "The Pentateuch," *The Hebrew Bible and Its Modern Interpreters*, D. A. KNIGHT and G. M. TUCKER, eds. (Philadelphia/Chico, Calif. 1985) 262–296. R. P. KNIERIM, "The Composition of the Pentateuch," *SBL 1985 Seminar Papers*, ed. K. H. RICHARDS, (Atlanta 1985) 395–415. L. RUPPERT, "Pentateuchdiskussion und Joseferzählung," *Biblische Zeitschrift* 29 (1985) 31–48. C. SCHEDL, *Zur Theologie des Alten Testaments* (Freiburg 1986). E. E. CARPENTER, "Recent Pentateuchal Studies," *Asbury Theological Journal* 41 (1986) 19–36. J. L. SKA, *Le Passage de la Mer. Etude de la construction, du style et de la symbolique d'Ex 14,1–31* (Rome 1986). F. KOHATA, *Jahwist und Priesterschrift in Exodus 3–14* (Berlin-

Basket of fruit gathered for the Jewish feast of Shavuot, or Pentecost. (©Hanan Isachar/CORBIS)

New York 1986). D. J. MCCARTHY, ''Twenty-Five Years of Pentateuchal Study,'' *The Biblical Heritage*, J. J. COLLINS and J. D. CROSSAN, eds. (Wilmington 1986) 34–57. R. N. WHYBRAY, *The Making of the Pentateuch* (Sheffield 1987).

[C. T. BEGG]

PENTECOST

The second great annual pilgrim feast of ancient Israel was the Harvest Feast or *qāṣîr* (Ex 23.16) celebrated at the completion of the wheat harvest in Palestine. It was called also the Feast of Weeks and later, the ''fiftieth day'' or Pentecost, and was primarily an agricultural festival. The celebration of this feast to commemorate the giving of the Covenant at Sinai began only in late Old Testament times.

Origin and Terminology. The custom of presenting the first fruits of the harvest to a god is an ancient one among agricultural peoples. The Hebrews borrowed from the Canaanites, in whose land they settled, a feast of thanksgiving at the end of the harvest of cereal grains, offering to Yahweh the first fruits, two loaves made from the new flour. Originally the date of the feast must have varied according to the condition of the crops (Ex 23.16; 34.22). When the commemoration of the Passover was joined to the Feast of the Unleavened Bread (*maṣṣôt*) in the Priestly Code, the date for the ''feast of the first fruits'' (*bikkûrîm*) was set seven weeks after the *maṣṣôt,* hence the name ''feast of Weeks'' (Ex 34.22; Nm 28. 26; Dt 16.10).

Since the time that elapsed between the offering of the first fruits of the barley harvest (on the day after the Sabbath of the *maṣṣôt*) and the day after the 7th Sabbath was a period of 50 days, the feast was called πεντηκοστή or ''fiftieth day'' or Pentecost by the later Greek-speaking Jews (2 Mc 12.31–32; Tb 2.1 in Septuagint).

Nature and Rites. Pentecost was a joyful feast, a ''thanksgiving day'' celebrating the first real harvest of the year. At the Feast of the UNLEAVENED BREAD, the loaves were presented without yeast; on Pentecost the use of leaven was ritually prescribed (Lv 23.17), signifying a sacrifice of the ordinary food of the Palestinian peasant and marking the close of the harvesting of cereal grains. The earliest liturgical calendars used in Israel (in the Elohistic Code of the Covenant, Ex 23.14–17 and in the Yahwistic Code, Ex 34.18–23) call the feast of the grain harvest a *ḥag,* or pilgrimage, the *ḥag* of the *šābu'ōt* (weeks). At first the feast would have been kept at the local shrines on a date determined by local crop conditions but with the growing centralization of cult under the monarchy, the celebration became the occasion for a true pilgrimage to the central shrine chosen by Yahweh (Dt 16.11).

The ritual found in the Priestly Code (Lv 23.15–22 and its commentary in Nm 28.26–31) prescribes the offering or ''waving'' of the newly baked wheat loaves, the sacrifice of seven yearling male lambs, two young bullocks, and one ram (one bullock and two rams in the earlier Lv 23.18) as a holocaust or burnt offering (*'ôlâ*), cereal offerings of flour and oil (*minḥâ*) and libations of wine and of blood from the slain animals. A he-goat was slain as a sin offering (*ḥattā't*), according to Leviticus 23.19, and two other yearling male lambs were offered for a thanksgiving sacrifice (*zebaḥ šᵉlāmîm*). The liturgy would normally include also processions, hymns and psalms of praise and thanksgiving, and the offering of gifts. In return the blessing of Yahweh would be bestowed on the pilgrims through the benediction pronounced by the priest.

Date of Pentecost. There was fixed, in Lv 23.11, 15–16, a period of 50 days from ''the day after the Sabbath'' of the *maṣṣôt,* counting seven weeks to ''the day after the seventh week'' on which the Pentecostal feast was to be observed. Later, the Pharisees identified the Sabbath of the Feast of Unleavened Bread with the feast-day itself on the 15th of the 1st month (Nisan) and, computing the 50-day period from the 16th, they celebrated Pentecost of the 6th day of the 3d month. The Boethuseans (a sect of the SADDUCEES), interpreting the Sabbath as the ordinary Sabbath that fell during the week of the *maṣṣôt* between the 15th and 21st day of Nisan, kept Pentecost on the Sunday following the 7th Sabbath. The calendar of the Book of Jubilees numbered the 50 days from the Sabbath after the whole Passover festival, i.e., beginning with the 26th day of Nisan. Consequently, Pentecost always fell on Sunday, the 15th day of the 3d month.

Commemoration of the Giving of the Law. The tendency of Israel to found its cult in its history affected the Feast of Pentecost comparatively late. According to Exodus 19.1 the Hebrews arrived at Sinai in the 3d month after leaving Egypt. When the feasts of the Passover and of Unleavened Bread were combined and fixed in the middle of the 1st month, the following seven-week period until Pentecost would approximate the time between the Exodus and the arrival at Sinai. A feast celebrated by Asa in the 3rd month of the 15th year of his reign to renew the Covenant may have been the Pentecostal feast (2 Chr 15.10–12) but the first unequivocal testimony to the commemoration of the giving of the Law at Pentecost is in the late noncanonical Book of Jubilees. The QUMRAN COMMUNITY, which followed this calendar, celebrated Pentecost as the chief feast of the entire liturgy because of this association with the Covenant. The calendar found in Ez 45.18–25, however, does not mention the feast and the more orthodox Jews after the Exile seem to have considered it a secondary feast. Not until the 2d century A.D. was its connection with the Covenant generally admitted by the rabbis.

Christian Pentecost. The events of the first Christian Pentecost are recounted in Acts of the Apostles 2.1–41. The text is structured as follows: (1) Introductory notice on the gathering together of the Christian community; description of charismatic phenomena: a roar like that of a mighty wind fills the house, and tongues like tongues of flame rest on everyone present. They are filled with the HOLY SPIRIT and begin to ''speak in foreign tongues'' (verses 1–4). (2) Following an introductory notice on the ''devout Jews from every nation under heaven'' staying in Jerusalem, there is described the gathering of a crowd, drawn by the sound of the community's charismatic prayer. Foreign visitors hear God praised in their own native tongues and ask, ''What does this men?'' Some, however, dismiss the phenomenon with ''They are full of new wine'' (5–13). (3) The discourse of Peter, which has three parts. Part one (14–21) explains the phenomenon of the community's prayer: not wine, but the outpouring of the Holy Spirit as promised in the Prophets. Part two (22–36) gives the explanation of how it is that

A detail of a retable by J. Cascalls depicting the Apostles at Pentecost. (©Ramon Manent/CORBIS)

the Spirit has come. And this explanation is the KERYGMA: the recounting of Jesus' ministry and Passion, the proclamation of His Resurrection and messianic enthronement at the right hand of the Father: ''*He* has poured forth this Spirit which you see and hear.'' And all this is in fulfillment of the prophecies of old. Part three (38–40) is spoken in answer to the crowd's bewildered query, ''Brethren, what shall we do?'' The answer is, ''Repent and be baptized every one of you in the name of Jesus Christ for the forgiveness of your sins; and you will receive the gift of the Holy Spirit'' (14–40). (4) A concluding notice narrates, ''Now they who received his word were baptized, and there were added that day about three thousand souls'' (41).

The Meaning of Pentecost. The eschatological expectations of the Old Testament and Judaism are supposed by the meaning of Pentecost. According to ancient rabbinical teaching, all the pious and upright in the age of the Patriarchs had been initiated through the Spirit of Yahweh into the whole range of God's mysteries. But from the time of Israel's adoration of the golden calf, God had restricted this gift to a chosen circle of Prophets and high priests.

Still later, with the death of the last of the chosen Prophets, the Spirit was altogether denied Israel; God spoke to His people exclusively through ''the heavenly voice'' and through omens. Only with the coming of the Messiah and the outbreak of eschatological SALVATION would the Spirit reappear. At that privileged moment Israel would be purified of its sins and again become ''a people of prophets'' (cf. Nm 11.29; Is 59.21; Jl 3.1–5).

In this context it becomes clear why the prophetic figures of John the Baptist and of Jesus had wakened expectations of imminent salvation. But above all the meaning of the Pentecostal event is illuminated. For, at Pentecost salvation is realized in the messianic blessings of ''the forgiveness of your sins'' (Acts 2.38; cf. 5.31; 10.43; 13.38; 26.18; see also 3.19; 22.16) and ''the gift of the Holy Spirit'' (Acts 2.38; cf. 1.5; 2.4, 17–18, 33; 4.31; 5.32; 8.15–19; etc.).

These are truly messianic blessings, accorded a community messianic not simply by aspiration but in the full consciousness of an already accomplished messianic event: the enthronement of Jesus at the right hand of God. Jesus made ''Lord and Christ'' (Acts of the Apostles 2.36) is the final explanation of the Pentecostal gifts (cf. verse 33), and these gifts, in turn, are the consummation of His ministry, death, and RESURRECTION.

Pentecost, then, is a salvific and messianic event, but it is also and par excellence an ecclesial event: (1) In the forgiveness of sins and the outpouring of the Spirit Israel is supremely blessed by its Savior. But these gifts are offered it only on condition of entry into the community of the saved (verses 38–40). For it is precisely this community of believers in Christ that is now revealed as the object and organ of salvation. (2) By the outpouring of the Spirit the messianic community is equipped to accomplish its salvific purpose. The immediate effect of the Spirit's advent is the joyous proclamation of the *magnalia Dei* in ecstatic prayer (Acts 2.11; cf. 4.31; 8.17–18; 10.45–46) and in kerygmatic discourse (Acts 2.14–40; cf. 4.8; 5.32). That is, the inner life of the community is created anew, and with Peter's summons to salvation its apostolic mission is launched. (3) With the gifts of Pentecost the Scriptures find fulfillment: the promise of Israel's purification and renewal in the Spirit (Is 32.15–20; 44.3; 59.21; Ez 11.19; 36.25–27; 39.29; Jl 3.1–5), the image of eschatological Sion drawing the whole world to salvation (Is 2.2–4; Jer 3.17; Zec 2.14–15), the prophecy of the messianic remnant [see F. Dreyfus, ''La Doctrine du reste d'Israël chez le prophète Isaïe,'' *Revue des sciences philosophiques et théologiques* 39 (1955) 361–68; cf. ''the saved'' of Septuagint Is 37.31; 45.20 with Acts 2.21, 47]. (4) Finally, it is the Spirit given on Pentecost that guarantees the growth of the new ἐκκλησία (Acts 2.41; cf. 9.31).

Details of the Account. It is probable on the basis of parallels (Acts 1.14; 2.42–47; 4.31–32) that the gathering together described in verse 1 refers to the entire community, not merely to the Twelve, and consequently that the ''tongues like flames'' rested on each of the 120 (cf. Acts 1.15), all of whom were inspired to pray ''in foreign tongues.''

The explanation of the phrase in verse 4 λαλεῖν ἑτέραις γλώσσαις, ''to speak in foreign tongues,'' is disputed. Elsewhere in Acts of the Apostles (10.46; 19.6) λαλεῖν γλώσσαις, ''to speak in tongues,'' refers to glossolalia, the ''language'' of ecstatic prayer, intelligible only to those to whom the Spirit has given the gift of interpretation. It is likely that this was the original sense of verse 4 (cf. the taunt in verse 13, ''They are full of new wine''). But at some stage in the tradition, perhaps at the stage of final redaction, the ''tongues'' motif was connected, by insertion of the word ἑτέραις, ''foreign,'' in verse 4, with another and quite distinct theme: salvation made known to all the peoples of the earth (verses 6–11). In connection with ''tongues'' this theme recalls, perhaps consciously and intentionally, both the confusion of tongues that according to Genesis chapter 11 divided mankind into distinct and hostile peoples, and the rabbinic legend of the preaching of the Law of Sinai to the nations. On the supposition that these allusions are consciously intended, the Pentecostal event is presented as the restoration of mankind's unity, the reverse of Babel, and as a new Sinai in which the law of the Spirit takes the place of the Mosaic Law. (Pentecost even prior to the Christian era was celebrated as a covenant renewal in commemoration of Sinai.)

The literary background of the list of the nations (verses 9–11) is with some probability to be located in ancient astrological-geographical catalogues [S. Weinstock, ''The Geographical Catalogue in Acts 2, 9–11,'' *Journal of Roman Studies* 38 (1948) 43–46], but the theological point of the list is to accent the universalism of salvation in Christ. It is furthermore likely that the list was originally intended, in Luke's source, to evoke the Isaian theme (Is 2.2–4; 11.10–12; 25.6–8, 10; 42.6; etc.) of the eschatological pilgrimage to Sion, center of the world and source of salvation in the last days [A. Causse, ''Le Pèlerinage à Jérusalem à la première Pentecôte,'' *Revue d'histoire et de philosophie religieuses* 20 (1940) 120–41]. This corresponds to the primitive Christian conception of the coming of the nations into salvation as a centripetal movement of all the world to ''the holy mountain,'' a conception founded on certain images used by Jesus Himself [e.g., Mt 8.11–12; see J. Jeremias, *Jesus' Promise to the Nations,* tr. S. H. Hooke (Naperville, Ill. 1958)].

The Pentecostal discourse is of interest on several counts: (1) As elsewhere (e.g., Acts 3.12–16), the proclamation of salvation through the paschal mysteries of Jesus and in particular through His glorification is made to serve an immediate, *ad hoc* purpose—in this case, to explain the pneumatic phenomena of Pentecost. But the proclamation transcends this purpose. Its ultimate intent is to win Israel over to repentance, belief, and aggregation to the eschatological community (verses 37–41). (2) The speech is argumentative, its central argument being that messianic prophecy is fulfilled in and through Jesus and Him alone. The scriptural loci, here taken from the Psalms, are interpreted as prophetic testimony to His glorification. (The accent on glorification is characteristic. In the schematized discourses of Acts explicit scriptural citations bearing on the Person of Christ are in every instance concerned with His Resurrection and exaltation in glory.) It is noteworthy that the community, in the person of PETER, regards itself not merely as ''measured and judged'' by the Scriptures, but more profoundly, as their charismatically guaranteed interpreter (cf. QUMRAN COMMUNITY). (3) The Christology of the discourse draws on three motifs: the Davidic Christ (verses 25–31, 33–36), the LORD (verse 21, 36), and the Name (verses 21, 38). The archaic character of certain aspects of this Christology and the lack of interest in the Crucifixion as itself a salvific mystery indicate the text's relative antiquity.

Lucan Theology. In the specifically Lucan perspective, Pentecost inaugurates a new era in SALVATION HISTORY, defined at its temporal extremes respectively by Jesus' already accomplished enthronement as Lord and His still future coming as judge. Concern over an imminent PAROUSIA gives way to concentration on the Church's inner life and apostolic mission. As the Lucan Gospel is conceived in terms of movement from Galilee to Jerusalem, so the dynamic of the early Church's life and growth as portrayed in Acts is conceived in terms of movement from Jerusalem to Rome. It is the glorified Christ who governs this movement through the Spirit bestowed on Pentecost.

See Also: MISSIONS, DIVINE; SOUL OF THE CHURCH.

Bibliography: W. F. ALBRIGHT, *Archaeology and the Religion of Israel* (Baltimore 1953). R. DUSSAUD, *Les Origines cananéennes du sacrifice israélite* (Paris 1921). A. S. HERBERT, *Worship in Ancient Israel* (Richmond 1959). A. ARENS and N. ADLER, *Lexikon für Theologie und Kirche*, ed. J. HOFER and K. RAHNER, 10 v. (2d, new ed. Freiburg 1957–65) 8:421–23. H. HAAG, ed., *Bibel-Lexikon* (Einsiedeln 1951–) 1:1324–27. J. A. BRINKMAN, ''The Literary Background of the *Catalogue of the Nations* (Acts 2,9–11),'' *The Catholic Biblical Quarterly* 25 (1963) 418–27. D. M. STANLEY, ''The Conception of Salvation in Primitive Christian Preaching,'' *The Catholic Biblical Quarterly* 18 (1956) 231–54.

[B. F. MEYER/J. L. RONAN]

PENTECOST, ICONOGRAPHY OF

The PENTECOST, or Sending of the Holy Spirit, was the last stage in the glorification of Christ, although He

Pentecost, painting by El Greco. (©Francis G. Mayer/CORBIS)

was not present. It occurred directly after the Ascension. In early Christian iconography of Pentecost, the 12 Apostles are grouped in a circle around the Virgin Mary (6th century, Gospel Book of Rabbula; Biblioteca Laurenziana, Florence), who appears in the scene probably as a symbol of the Church. Above their heads the Holy Spirit is represented in the form of a dove, from which golden rays of light emanate or tongues of fire dart upon them. The hands of the Apostles are shown making a variety of gestures following the linguistic miracle that has enabled them to go forth and spread the gospel to the four corners of the world.

Although not nearly so common as those with the Virgin, there occur representations of Pentecost with the Apostles alone (11th century, Gradual of Reichenau; Bibliothèque Nationale, Paris). The fire of the Holy Spirit is shown also as a flaming wheel with the Apostles grouped around it (11th century, Book of Pericopes; Munich Library). On occasion, instead of the dove, the hand of God is represented with rays of light coming from the extended fingers. Representations of the 12 Apostles alone, with Peter and Paul at either side of the throne of Christ, a doorway of a church, or an archway with the nations in it, depict the foundation of the Church.

In the typological art of the late Middle Ages (e.g., the *Speculum humanae salvationis*), the TOWER OF BABEL is shown alongside the miracle of Pentecost. The parallel is based on an early literary and pictorial tradition alluded to in homilies and sacramentary texts of the Feast of Pentecost, in both East and West. The Tower of Babel represented, according to interpretation, a confusion of tongues and the dispersion of the peoples of Earth; at Pentecost, on the contrary, there was a gift of tongues and a regathering through the power of the gospel.

The representation of the "Throne, Gospel Book, and Dove," called the Etimasia, became an accepted symbol and an important part of Pentecost representations. The Etimasia has been taken to mean the gospel preached by Christ and confirmed by the Holy Spirit; or a Trinitarian symbol in which the "Throne" stands for the Father, the "Gospel Book" for the Son, and the "Dove" for the Holy Spirit. The Russian Orthodox connect the symbol with the seat of the Last Judgment and the "preparation of the Throne" (*Hetoimasia tou Thronou*) of Christ's Second Coming.

The Etimasia is in the center of the Pentecost dome mosaic of St. Mark's, Venice. There is a similar mosaic in the dome of St. Luke in Phocis, Greece. In the Pentecost frescoes of the Cappadocian rock churches the Etimasia comes at the top of the picture; this arrangement has been copied into many illuminated manuscripts.

Frequently, below the group of the Apostles are depicted representatives of the 16 nations (mentioned in the Acts as present in Jerusalem at the time of the descent of the Holy Spirit) who marveled on hearing the Apostles speaking their native tongues. In the dome mosaics in Venice and Phocis, the nations appear between the windows of the drum supporting the dome. In Venice, each nation is represented by a pair of figures, male and female. In later miniatures, to avoid the difficulty of representing 16 nations, an old man symbolizing "Time," with rolls of the Gospel in his arms, is placed in a central arched doorway. The central doorway occurs in many Pentecost miniatures. In the Syrian miniatures of the Orthodox Convent, St. Mark's, Jerusalem, the doorway is interpreted as the door of the Cenacle through which Christ passed when He appeared to the Apostles, who testify to His Resurrection. The figure of the Virgin also may occur in the central doorway.

In the Anglo-Saxon MS of the famous Winchester School, the Apostles are seated in two groups but without either the Throne or the Virgin Mary in the center. From the same period, the Gospel Book of St. Paul's Outside-the-Walls, Rome, shows the Virgin in the center of the design. The Gospel Book from Cologne (now in Brussels, dating from 1250) goes so far as to place St. Peter in the center. In England, however, in the 13th-century St. Alban's Psalter, the Virgin Mary maintains the central position.

In later centuries Pentecost has been represented by the 12 Apostles surrounding Our Lady. The subject was frequently represented in the 16th and 17th centuries: Titian (S. Maria della Salute, Venice); Tintoretto (Victoria and Albert Museum, London); El Greco (Prado, Madrid); Zurbarán (Cadiz Museum). The 16 nations are not often referred to, nor are the 120 persons present in the Cenacle given much attention.

Bibliography: G. DE JERPHANION, *Les Églises rupestres de Cappadoce,* 5 v. (Paris 1925–42) 1:297–376. A. M. GRABAR, *La Schéma iconographique de la Pentecôte* (Prague 1923). A. FABRE, "L'Iconographie de la Pentecôte et le Portail de Vézelay," *Gazette des beaux-arts* (1923). S. SEELIGER, *Die Ikonographie des Pfingstwunders* (Munich 1956). L. RÉAU, *Iconographie de l'art chrétien,* 6 v. (Paris 1955–59) 2.2:591–596.

[J. U. MORRIS]

PENTECOSTAL CHURCHES

The Pentecostal churches originated out of the Holiness movement, especially in the wave REVIVALISM that swept through the U.S. during the early decades of the 20th century. They are characterized by a distinctive emphasis on sanctification that includes a conversion process in which an adult makes a decision or has a conversion experience; a cleansing from sin, or justification; a baptism of the Holy Spirit as an instantaneous spiritual transformation separate from and following justification; and, as a specific characteristic, a renewal of the gifts of Pentecost (Acts 2.1–4) consequent to baptism, especially the climactic charismata of glossalalia and faith healing. Many adherents of the Pentecostal movement are found in bodies that do not include the Pentecostal name, such as Elim Missionary Assemblies, International Church of the FOURSQUARE GOSPEL, and the largest of the Pentecostal bodies, the ASSEMBLIES OF GOD.

World interest in the Pentecostal movement stems from the sensational accounts of a prayer meeting held in Los Angeles, Calif., on April 9, 1906, at which an African-American boy began to speak in tongues. Although some Pentecostal churches predate this event, 1906 is regarded as the birth year of the Pentecostal movement. Another source of development has been secession and merger. The Pentecostal Assemblies of the World, orga-

Morning Star Pentecostal Church, Petersburg, Virginia. (©TimWright/CORBIS)

nized in 1914 as an interracial body, split in 1924 when the white members withdrew and formed the Pentecostal Church, Inc., which in turn merged with the Pentecostal Assemblies of Jesus Christ in 1945 to form the United Pentecostal Church with its distinctive anti-Trinitarian formulation of doctrine. Other Pentecostal churches that are the result of mergers are the Assemblies of God, the Pentecostal Holiness Church, International Pentecostal Assemblies, and the Pentecostal Fire-Baptized Holiness Church.

The Bible is the sole doctrinal authority, interpreted from a fundamentalist position. In addition, the Scriptures are looked upon as furnishing rules of order and discipline for all conditions of the life of man. Some of the Pentecostal churches accept the Lord's Supper, but allow a free interpretation of its significance. Many practice foot washing as part of the divine ordinances. Faith healing is common.

Good works, as part of the ''spirit-filled life'' and as a preparation for the coming of the Lord, are urged on all Pentecostalists. They include visiting the sick, strengthening the weak, encouraging the fainthearted, and pointing out the way of salvation. The Pentecostal ethos prescribes a strict abstinence from worldly pleasures, obedience to civil laws, the support of the church through tithes, and a complete cleansing of heart and soul from all remaining sin. In addition members are constrained from participating in war, destroying property, or injuring human life.

Worship is informal rather than ritualistic or liturgical, and freedom is encouraged. A large degree of emotionalism often permeates the devotional life of Pentecostalists. Favorite themes of preaching include atonement through the blood of Jesus, spiritual baptism, and the second coming.

Government is generally along the lines of congregational polity, although in some instances the organization of the church includes district conferences, annual conferences, and a general conference, all somewhat similar to those of the Methodist system. Missionary work is vigorously carried on at home and in many foreign countries under the guidance of local or denominational missionary boards.

Bibliography: D. GEE, *The Pentecostal Movement* (London 1941). S. H. FRODSHAM, *With Signs Following* (rev. ed. Springfield, Mo. 1946). R. M. RIGGS, *The Spirit Himself* (Springfield, Mo. 1949). S. DURASOFF, *The Bright Wind of the Spirit* (Englewood Cliffs, N.J. 1972). W.J. HOLLENWEGER, *The Pentecostals* (Minneapolis 1972). V. SYNAN, *The Holiness-Pentecostal Movement in the United States* (Grand Rapids, Mich. 1971). W.W. MENZIES, *Anointed to Serve* (Springfield, Mo. 1971). F.S. MEAD, S.S. HILL and C.D. ATWOOD, eds., *Handbook of Denominations in the United States*, 11th ed (Nashville 2001).

[R. MATZERATH]

PENTECOSTALISM

Pentecostalism began as a modern religious movement in 1900 at the Bethel Healing Home in Topeka, Kansas. Its fusion with revivalist forms of piety produced the Holiness Movement and a bewildering number of Protestant Pentecostal churches. More recently Protestant Pentecostalism has manifested growing ecumenical interest and openness. Neo-Pentecostalism is an interdenominational movement involving Christians from almost every existing church communion, including Roman Catholics. One must then distinguish denominational Protestant Pentecostalism from Neo-Pentecostalism.

Protestant Pentecostalism. Protestant Pentecostal piety is Biblical piety. It looks to Scripture as divinely inspired and infallible, and regards the Word of God as superior to reason and conscience, though not contrary to either. Protestant Pentecostals tend to regard every word of Scripture as divinely inspired; and their fundamentalistic tendencies incline them to be suspicious of "modern theology" and "liberal exegesis," which they believe often ignores or distorts the literal sense of Scripture. Such devotion to the inspired Biblical word endows the Pentecostal use of Scripture, in both personal and shared prayer, with ultimate authority and ritual significance. Protestant Pentecostals are more inclined to celebrate God's Word as a personal grace than to reflect on it with academic scholarship.

As a group Protestant Pentecostals hold to orthodox trinitarian theology, although a small group of Unitarian Pentecostals reject the Trinity as scripturally unfounded. As a group, Protestant Pentecostals affirm the two natures of Christ, the virgin birth, and the redemptive atonement effected by the blood of Jesus.

Protestant Pentecostal piety is preoccupied with personal religious conversion. It insists that Jesus has already fulfilled the divine conditions for spiritual regeneration and that the experience of conversion and Spirit baptism are therefore available to all. In the act of conversion, one turns away from sin and receives salvation in Christ. The Spirit baptized are, however, said to receive a "second blessing," subsequent to the grace of conversion. Most Protestant Pentecostals equate Spirit baptism with the reception of the gift of tongues, although some see tongues only as the inauguration of Spirit baptism. This belief is largely grounded in the more fundamental belief that the experience of Spirit baptism described in Acts 2 is normative for all Christians. The theological dissociation of conversion from the reception of the Spirit and the equation of the latter with the gift of tongues are both commonly rejected by theologians of other communions.

Some Protestant Pentecostals distinguish a third stage in the conversion process, that of sanctification. "Third-stage" Pentecostals are, however, divided over the question of the instantaneous or gradual character of sanctification.

Protestant Pentecostals believe that all the Pauline gifts are available to believers today, including tongues, prophecy, healing, and miracles. They practice faith healing and claim both physical cures and the psychic "healing of memories." In their approach to healing there is the tendency to affirm that no sickness, depression, and poverty can be sent by God and that these sufferings are often demonic in origin.

Protestant Pentecostals as a group recognize only two sacraments: baptism and the Lord's Supper. They regard baptism as an external sign of an inner grace that has already been given. Many reject infant baptism, but a significant minority practice it. The Lord's Supper is looked upon as a memorial meal symbolizing the atoning sacrifice of Jesus and expressing the personal faith of the worshiping community. Some Protestant Pentecostals also practice foot washing in obedience to Jesus' command in Jn 13.14, but they are divided as to its obligatory character.

As a group Protestant Pentecostals are ethically conservative. They believe in the Sabbath rest, and some practice tithing. Some are religious pacifists and reject military service. Most are opposed to smoking and alcoholic beverages. Some reject the consumption of pork and ban musical instruments, movies, slang, jesting, swimming, fairs, theaters, make-up, hairwaving, loud clothes, short skirts, etc. These rigoristic tendencies are both a protest against moral laxity and an ascetical bulwark against backsliding.

Protestant Pentecostal piety often has a chiliastic character. It tends to affirm the immanence of the second coming of Jesus. Its other-worldly caste leads it to minimize the importance of political involvement and social reform. Classical Protestant Pentecostalism tends to be suspicious of ecumenicism.

Neo-Pentecostalism. The fusion of Protestant Pentecostal piety with the religious traditions of other mainline churches has given rise to Neo-Pentecostalism. Neo-Pentecostals reflect the doctrinal pluralism of the different communions to which they belong. As a group they are ecumenical in bent, although they derive much of their popular forms of piety from the Protestant Pentecostal tradition.

Whatever their church affiliation, Neo-Pentecostals gather regularly for spontaneous shared prayer. These gatherings are either denominational or ecumenical in tone. In their prayer they are concerned to ''focus on the Lord.'' This phrase usually implies that the presence of the Lord will become manifest in the activities of the praying community: in the reading of Scripture, in praying and singing in tongues, in prophecy and the interpretation of messages in tongues, in personal witness to graces received, in spontaneous and rote prayers, in hymns, and in healings.

The fusion of Pentecostal forms of piety with that of the more traditional, institutional churches can produce pastoral concern and even apprehension among the hierarchy and ''non-Pentecostal'' membership. Neo-Pentecostals are most often criticized for the ''elitist'' and ''fundamentalistic'' tone of their rhetoric and for their lack of active involvement in social reform.

Catholic Neo-Pentecostalism began as a movement in 1966 at Dusquesne University. It spread throughout the United States and Canada and has taken hold in South America and in Europe. On Nov. 14, 1969, the American bishops gave a cautious and tentative approval to the movement and encouraged prudent priests to provide sacramental and pastoral ministry to charismatic Catholics. Since then it has won a growing acceptance from the hierarchy. In 1973 a meeting of the international leadership of the movement was held in Rome.

Among Catholics, the Neo-Pentecostal movement tends to be referred to as the ''Catholic charismatic renewal.'' Catholic charismatics as a whole manifest strong devotion to the institutional, sacramental Church and welcome priestly leadership. Most attend Mass in their parishes and are concerned to be accepted by their fellow Catholics. They tend to regard the charismatic renewal as Church renewal and believe that the renewal of charismatic piety was prepared providentially by Vatican Council II, which refocused attention on the Holy Spirit and his gifts.

The Neo-Pentecostal movement is forcing a theological reevaluation within the Catholic community of the gifts and their place in a sacramental, hierarchical tradition. And it is providing many Christians of different communions with a meaningful shared prayer experience.

See Also: PENTECOSTAL CHURCHES.

Bibliography: F. D. BRUNNER, *A Theology of the Holy Spirit* (London 1971). J. DUNN, *Baptism in the Holy Spirit* (Naperville, Ill. 1970). W. HOLNWEGER, *The Pentecostals: The Charismatic Movement in the Churches* (Minneapolis 1972). E. O'CONNOR, CSC, *The Pentecostal Movement in the Catholic Church* (South Bend 1971). D. L. GELPI, SJ, *Pentecostalism: A Theological Viewpoint* (New York 1971).

[D. L. GELPI]

PEOPLE OF GOD

Essentially, a segment of the human race, freely selected and set apart by God, the recipient of special divine blessings. Thus God chose ABRAHAM and ISAAC, Patriarchs, promising them the land of Canaan. In return, God made certain demands on His chosen ones, entering into a formal pact, or covenant, with them. [*See* COVENANT (IN THE BIBLE).] After narrowing down the line of Isaac to the Patriarch JACOB's descendants (the Israelites), God established the Mosaic covenant with this ethnic group. The elements of both nationality and religious fidelity, then, formed the basis of the Old Testament people of God.

The purification of this chosen nation entailed further selection. Only a remnant of Israel survived the Assyrian and Babylonian captivities. Later, in the second century before Christ, the Syrian persecution took its toll. Second Isaiah, in fact, describes the remnant under the figure of the Servant of Yahweh, whom New Testament writers—especially St. Mark—were to identify with Jesus Christ.

Christ's choice of the TWELVE Apostles inaugurated the New Covenant envisaged in Jer 31.31–34, and His death on Calvary sealed it in His blood. After His Resurrection the new people of God manifested a striking similarity to the synagogue. Like the *qāhāl* of old, it was convoked by the proclamation of the word of God, to which was added the breaking of bread (cf. Nehemiah ch. 8; Acts 2.42). Nationality no longer served as a basis for the selection of members. Indeed, a distinctive feature of the New Covenant was the admission of gentiles into the Christian community without discrimination. The people of God, however, did not come together by a spontaneous coalescence, but by apostolic activity as outlined in Christ's discourse (Mt ch. 10). The Apostles and their successors are the connecting links referred to in Eph 2.20.

In developing the theology of the new chosen people, St. Paul sees them as constituting a living organism that he designates as the Body of Christ. Following the lead of such exegetes as P. Benoit and L. Cerfaux, more and more theologians are adopting a position of physical realism in treating the union between Christ and His members. According to *MYSTICI CORPORIS*, the terms Church and MYSTICAL BODY are coextensive. The term people of God does not represent a different reality, but rather the same. This New Testament counterpart of Israel will continue to expand until, in Pauline terminology, the pleroma, or fullness, of Christ has been attained.

Mid-twentieth-century exegesis also led to a new emphasis on the use of the term people of God in dogmatic treatises on the Church. In its dogmatic constitution on the Church, Vatican Council II gave it preference over the term Mystical Body. Chapter 2 of the constitution is entitled *De populo Dei.* Transcending both Old and New Testaments, ''people of God'' lends itself better to a synthetic approach to the Church. It takes its origin from the raw material from which the community of the redeemed is constructed: those diverse races that have been amalgamated into a single religious unit through the Holy Spirit. The term Mystical Body, on the other hand, suggests the end product: the organism with its charisms and functions sustained by the sacramental bond.

The generic designation of the Church by the term ''People of God'' suggested also a way in which one could speak of various levels or degrees of''membership,'' not all of which require full sacramental communion. The council documents envisage Catholics as''incorporate,'' non-Catholic Christians as ''linked'' or ''joined,'' and non-Christians as ''related'' to the Church (*Lumen gentium* 14–16; *Unitaris redintegratio* 3). Within the full communion of the Church, the People of God have responded to this title by the assumption of new roles, notably in the Eucharistic celebration: permanent deacons, readers, commentators, and lay ministers of Communion. Team ministries have become commonplace, often including persons of both sexes. Catholic education and communications have witnessed an increase in lay leadership. Lay spirituality, although developing along its own proper lines, has been freed of the ''double standard'' of perfection which relegated it to a lower level of holiness than that demanded of priests and religious.

Even if Christ and His people are identified in a truly ontological sense, there remains a principle of opposition preventing any pantheistic fusion of divinity and humanity. Creating a wholesome polarity, this ambivalent relationship between Head and members is perhaps best subsumed under the Church's title Spouse of Christ. He is one with His people insofar as they have become apostolic instruments of SALVATION to others; He is other than they to the degree in which they themselves are still in the process of salvation. This consideration brings out clearly the eschatological character of the people of God: only at the end of time will Jesus become totally one with His Spouse, the people of God, the Church.

See Also: CHURCH, ARTICLES ON; KINGDOM OF GOD.

Bibliography: H. STRATHMANN, G. KITTEL, *Theologisches Wörterbuch zum Neuen Testament* (Stuttgart 1935–) 4:29–57. G. BERTRAM, *ibid.* 2:362–366. J. SCHARBERT, ''Volk (Gottes),'' in J. B. BAUER, ed., *Bibeltheologisches Wörterbuch,* 2 v. (2d ed. Graz 1962) 2:1147–58. P. GRELOT in *Vocabulaire de théologie biblique, ed.* X. LÉON-DUFOUR (Paris 1962) 815–826. J. HAMER, *L'Église est une communion* (Paris 1962) ch. 2. A. VONIER, *The People of God* (London 1937). R. SCHNACKENBURG, *God's Rule and Kingdom,* tr. J. MURRAY (New York 1963). A. DULLES, *Models of the Church* (New York 1974).

[M. K. HOPKINS/EDS.]

PEPIN III, KING OF THE FRANKS

First king of the Carolingian dynasty; Mayor of the Palace, 741–751; King, 751–768; b. 714 or 715; d. St-Denis, Sept. 24, 768.

The second son of CHARLES MARTEL by Chrotrude, his first wife, Pepin was educated at the monastery of St-Denis, near Paris. In 737 he was sent to the court of the Lombard king Liutprand (712–744) in Italy. There, Pepin had his hair cut in the Lombard style, was adopted as a son by Liutprand, and returned home, loaded with gifts. The significance of this is unclear. Since Liutprand already had a named successor, his treatment of Pepin did not affect the Lombard throne. In Francia, the Merovingian king Theuderic IV (721–737) had died and not been replaced, so there is a possibility that Charles Martel was cultivating royal connections with the eventual aim of placing his own son on the throne. The most likely explanation is that Charles was using his younger son to confirm an alliance with the Lombards, who were to give assistance against Muslim invaders in 739.

Towards the end of his life, Charles Martel divided Frankish territory between his two sons by Chrotrude. CARLOMAN, the elder, received Austrasia, Alamannia, and Thuringia; while Pepin acquired Neustria, Burgundy, and Provence. At the request of Swanachild, his second wife, Charles also made territorial provision for their son, Grifo, although the details are not now known. On Charles Martel's death in 741, the succession was disturbed, as it had been during his rise, with crises at the heart of the dynasty and rebellions by dukes of the peripheral regions.

Pepin and Carloman acted promptly to assert themselves over other family members. Their sister, Chiltrude, fled to Bavaria and married its duke, Odilo. The two mayors of the palace then moved against their half-brother, Grifo. He was captured at Laon in late 741 or early 742 and imprisoned; his mother was placed in the royal convent at Chelles. Another possible rival, Theudoald, a half-brother of Charles Martel, was killed in unknown circumstances (741).

Pepin and Carloman Establish Their Power. Having secured Francia, Pepin and Carloman campaigned, separately and together, against their enemies on the frontiers of Francia until 746. Like their father, they were able to muster enough supporters and resources to subdue widely dispersed opponents in Alamannia, Aquitaine, Bavaria, and Saxony. The Alamans were punished especially hard by Carloman, whose victory at Canstatt (near Stuttgart) in 746 was followed by mass executions. In the southwest, the Aquitanians were a test for Pepin until 768.

After an interregnum of six years, the brothers reestablished a member of the Merovingian family, the traditional ruling dynasty, on the throne of Francia. In his final years as mayor of the palace, Charles Martel had governed without a Merovingian king. His sons extricated a member of the dynasty from a monastery and raised him up as King Childeric III (743–751). Such a restoration might have disarmed opponents by restoring a veneer of legitimacy to the status of the Carolingians, the descendants of Charles Martel. It points to the political vulnerability of the brothers. There is also a possibility, from limited charter evidence, that Carloman may have been the driving force behind Childeric's elevation, suggesting a difference between the brothers as Pepin, alone, was to depose their Merovingian figurehead in 751.

The brothers exerted real power under their Merovingian figurehead until 746 when Carloman chose to retire to monastic life. This was surprising, but there were precedents in Anglo-Saxon kings laying down office and making a pilgrimage to Rome. According to later historiographical tradition, Carloman, having entrusted his son Drogo and his territory to Pepin's care, left for Italy in 747, where he entered the monastery at Monte Cassino and became a monk. Pepin's takeover of Austrasia was resisted by Drogo until his capture and imprisonment in 753.

In the fluid circumstances surrounding Carloman's abdication, another family member challenged Pepin. Grifo, his half-brother, escaped or was released from captivity in 747. He fled first to the Saxons, then to Bavaria. On the death of Duke Odilo, Grifo was able to exploit a claim to power through his sister and succeed him. Pepin

Pepin III. (Archive Photos)

defeated the Bavarians in 749, installing his young nephew, Tassilo III, as duke. Grifo was treated generously, being ceded rule over 12 counties at Le Mans in Neustria, but remained irreconcilable to Pepin. He fled to Aquitaine and the protection of Duke Waiofar (744–768), whose family had long resisted Carolingian authority. In 753, after Pepin had demanded his return, Grifo was cornered and killed by Frankish forces while en route for Italy.

Pepin Becomes King. Against this background of continuing unrest within his family and on the peripheral areas of Francia, Pepin took the profoundly significant step of deposing his Merovingian ruler and installing himself as the legitimate king of a new dynasty. In 751, he was elected king of the Franks, anointed, and raised to the throne at Soissons, while King Childeric III was tonsured and returned to a monastery. The sources describing these events are too late in date, too vague, and too partisan in defense of the Carolingians for a clear understanding of Pepin's actions and intentions. The earliest account (the *Continuator of the Chronicle of Fredegar*) reports that Pepin's emissaries went to Rome

Pepin III, 12th-century relief in parish church at Petersburg, near Fulda, Germany.

to seek approval for his proposed elevation to the throne. Having obtained this, Pepin was ". . .chosen as king by all the Franks, consecrated by the bishops and received the homage of the great men." In later versions of the mission and its results, unreliable details were added or altered, Pope Zacharias (741–752) becomes Pope Stephen II (III) (752–757), papal approval becomes a papal command, and St. BONIFACE alone is made responsible for anointing Pepin as king. Anointment with consecrated oil was a new element in Frankish ritual practice, which became increasingly important, and, with its biblical connotations, demonstrated the special status of the new king and his line.

To justify the change of dynasty, Pepin needed the seal of divine authority which would come from papal approval. In the eighth century the papacy was under constant threat from Lombard kings, especially Liutprand (712–744) and Aistulf (749–756). Its traditional guardian, the Byzantine empire, was unable to give protection because it was distracted by warfare against Arabs and Avars. Relations with Constantinople were also soured by Rome's opposition to its religious policy of iconoclasm and to Byzantine moves to increase taxation in Italy. In its quest for support, the papacy seems to have approached the Aquitainians (c.721) and Bavarians (743) and, as late as 752, appealed for Byzantine aid.

By the mid-8th century, the Franks were attractive as allies. There was a long tradition of Franco-papal relations, furthered by the work of Anglo-Saxon missionaries, especially Boniface, and reformist church councils who increased contact between the Franks and Rome. Papal overtures in 739 to Charles Martel for an alliance failed, as Lombard support against Muslims was evidently held to be more to Frankish advantage. In 751 Pope Zacharias's need for an ally against Lombard encroachment coincided with Pepin's need for a higher authority to sanction his deposition of the Merovingians. Curiously, there is no mention of these events in the *Liber pontificalis,* with its contemporary 8th-century lives of the popes. The promotion of Pepin was ultimately made possible by the power, prestige, and wealth that had been accumulated by his family over the past two generations. He was elevated to the throne by the Franks and anointed by their bishops in events that were endorsed, rather than commanded, by the papacy.

Further Lombard aggression in Italy tightened Franco-papal ties and produced more tangible results for the papacy. The Byzantine empire was unable to halt the advance of King Aistulf, who, by 752, had overrun the exarchate of Ravenna and now threatened the duchy of Rome. Early in 753, Pope STEPHEN II (III) (752–757) sent an appeal to Pepin, who dispatched a diplomatic mission to investigate the situation. After the failure of a mediated settlement with Aistulf at Pavia, Pope Stephen crossed the Alps to Ponthion, where he was greeted by Pepin in an elaborate piece of public theatre. In response to the request for aid, Pepin promised the restitution of papal territories, including the Byzantine exarchate of Ravenna. Despite some reluctance shown by the annual assembly of the Franks in 754, Pepin sent an unsuccessful embassy to Aistulf, demanding the return of occupied lands. Aistulf's shrewd response was to call Pepin's brother, Carloman, out of his monastic retirement and send him to Francia in the hope of blocking aid for the papacy. Pepin's reaction is unknown. Carloman failed in his mission, being promptly relegated to a Frankish monastery where he died, apparently of natural causes, in 755.

At St. Denis in July of 754, Pope Stephen anointed Pepin as king (again), along with his wife, Bertrada, and their sons, Charles (Charlemagne) and Carloman. Once more, the Carolingians had been legitimized as the true rulers of the Frankish kingdom. Pepin and his sons were awarded the title "Patrician of the Romans", probably indicating some form of protectorate over Rome. The ceremonies deepened the ties between the papacy and the Carolingians. Future kings of the Franks were to be chosen only from Pepin's family, while the Franks would defend papal interests, with prayers being offered in the Roman liturgy for the CAROLINGIAN DYNASTY.

In 755 and 756, Pepin carried out two successful campaigns of limited scale against the Lombards. Aistulf was eventually forced to surrender the disputed regions. An optimistic appeal by Byzantine ambassadors for the return of former imperial lands (the exarchate of Ravenna) was rejected by Pepin, who bestowed on the papacy the lands that had been surrendered by the Lombards. Despite appeals by Pope PAUL I (757–767) for help against the threats of the Lombard king, DESIDERIUS (757–774), Pepin carried out no further campaigns in Italy during the rest of his reign. He was anxious to avoid a possible Byzantine-Lombard alliance while facing persistent problems with Aquitaine, especially, and Saxony. The Frankish involvement with the papacy and the Lombard kingdom was to have important consequences in the reign of Pepin's son, CHARLEMAGNE.

Pepin's Significance. The traditional view of Pepin as king is that he was a reformer and defender of ecclesiastical interests whose work was developed by Charlemagne. During the seventh century, powerful local families had taken control of bishoprics with their resources, extending their authority over independent churches and monasteries. Control over ecclesiastical appointments enabled noble families to exploit the church's resources. Charles Martel was singled out, unfairly, in the mid-9th century, for secularization of church property. Modern research recognizes Pepin's patronage of reform, but now emphasizes his determined use of the church to attain political objectives.

The stern criticisms of the Frankish church's education, discipline, and organization made by Boniface (675–754), the great Anglo-Saxon missionary, may well have been distorted by his personal experiences in the mission field from the time of Charles Martel. Through church councils, Carloman (Concilium Germanicum, 742 or 743; Les Estinnes, 744) and Pepin (Soissons, 744) attempted to address the problems. Carloman, especially, was a patron of Boniface. On Carloman's retirement in 747, Boniface no longer seems to have been involved at the heart of Frankish church life. Under Pepin, CHRODEGANG OF METZ became the most prominent bishop in the Frankish kingdom. He revived the church councils (Ver, 755; Verberie, 756; Compiègne, 757; Attigny, 760–762; Gentilly; 767) which seem to have lapsed after Carloman's withdrawal from public life, and continued Boniface's reform program. Above all, he aligned the Frankish church with Roman liturgical practice.

Pepin's encouragement of reform within the church did not exclude his right to exploit its wealth for economic or political reasons. He systematically weakened the great families with aristocratic bishops by taking away their land and substituting royal rather than aristocratic rule over monasteries. After Boniface's death (754), Pepin turned his foundation at Fulda and others in its circle into a royal monastery. In recently converted or newly conquered areas, monasteries under royal control were a cornerstone of Frankish and, especially, Carolingian power. As a result, Pepin's reforming zeal was to his own advantage, as well as those of the church and the kingdom. The combination of royal influence over the church, the drive for reform and contact with the papacy was to be important under Pepin's successors.

Following the bloodless coup d'état of 751, there is an essential continuity between Pepin's activities as mayor of the palace and those as king. He continued to campaign to assert control over the kingdom's peripheral regions, such as in Saxony (753, 758). Here, effective Frankish conquest was checked militarily by the decentralized nature of Saxon society and culturally by the stubborn resistance of the region's inhabitants to Christian missionaries. Aquitaine, especially, resisted Carolingian rule and preoccupied Pepin throughout his reign. In the disturbed period after the death of Charles Martel, Pepin and Carloman had campaigned there in 742 to curb Duke Hunoald, the son of Eudo. Grifo, Pepin's irrepressible half-brother, took up residence at the court of Hunoald's son, Duke Waiofar, until 753. To end Aquitaine's independence, Pepin needed to win over the loyalty of the nobles and to establish control over the church. With one exception there were annual campaigns in Aquitaine between 759 and 768. This pressure brought about the murder of Waiofar by his own followers, which signaled the effective end of the war and Aquitanian independence.

During his final campaign in Aquitaine, Pepin fell ill and returned north to the royal monastery of St. Denis, where, *c.* 754, he had begun the construction of a new church. He died there on Sept. 24, 768, and was buried, like his father, in the ancient pantheon of the Merovingian kings. Shortly before his death, Pepin divided the Frankish kingdom between his two sons, Charles (768–814) and Carloman (768–771), who had been designated as heirs and anointed by Pope Stephen in 754. Relations between the brothers were uneasy until the death of Carloman in 771, but there was no succession crisis for the Carolingian dynasty.

Bibliography: P. FOURACRE, "Frankish Gaul to 814" in *New Cambridge Medieval History*, v. 2 (Cambridge 1995). R. MCKIT-

St. Jean-Gabriel Perboyre.

TERICK, *The Frankish Kingdom under the Carolingians* (London and New York 1983). T. F. X. NOBLE, *The Republic of St. Peter: The Birth of the Papal Republic* (Philadelphia 1984). M. ROUCHE, *L'Aquitaine des Wisigoths aux Arabes* (Paris 1979). J. M. WALLACE-HADRILL, *The Frankish Church* (Oxford 1985). I. N. WOOD, *The Merovingian Kingdoms* (London and New York 1994).

[J. WREGLESWORTH]

PERBOYRE, JEAN-GABRIEL, ST.

Martyr, priest of the Congregation of the Mission of Saint Vincent de Paul; b. Le Puech (Lot), Mongesty (diocese of Cahors), France, Jan. 6, 1802; d. Wuchangfu (near Hu-pei), CHINA, Sept. 11, 1840.

The eldest of eight children (five of whom became Vincentians) of the farmers, Pierre and Marie Rigal Perboyre, Jean-Gabriel attended minor seminary with his brother Louis at Montauban, founded by their uncle Jacques Perboyre, a Vincentian who had survived the French Revolution. In 1818 Jean-Gabriel became the first French Vincentian seminarian since the revolution. He studied theology in Paris, then accepted an appointment as professor at Montdidier College (1823), and was ordained in 1826.

After working as a teacher, spiritual director, and in other capacities in various Vincentian seminaries and training centers in France, he went to east central China (1835) to replace his brother, Fr. Louis, who had died en route. In the missions of Hunan and Hu-pei Provinces, he acquired a familiarity with the Chinese language and dedicated himself especially to instructing abandoned children. When persecution broke out, he was arrested (Sept. 16, 1839) at Cha-yüan-kou for entering China illegally to spread Christianity. Imprisoned at Wuchangfu, he was interrogated many times by mandarins and by the viceroy and tortured in a vain effort to make him reveal the hiding places of other priests. After eight months' imprisonment he was strangled to death Chinese-style (on a cross) on Ou-tch'ang (Red Mountain), and was buried in the nearby cemetery in Wuchangfu close to the remains of his confrere and fellow martyr, Bl. François Clet.

He was beatified Nov. 10, 1889, the first of the Chinese martyrs to receive the honors of the altar. On June 2, 1996, Pope John Paul II canonized Perboyre, the first saint of China, Patron of the VINCENTIAN missionaries.

Feast: Sept. 11 (since 1969).

Bibliography: *Life of the Bl. Servant of God, the Heroic Martyr, John Gabriel Perboyre . . .*, tr. C. FEILDING (New Orleans 1894). *L'Osservatore Romano,* English edition, no. 23 (1996): 1–2, 5, 12. J.L. BAUDOT and L.CHAUSSIN, *Vies des saints . . . avec l'historique des fêtes,* 9: 252–255. A. CHATELET, *Jean Gabriel Perboyre, Martyr* (Paris 1943). L. CHIEROTTI, *Il beato Gian Gabriele Perboyre: Lo strangolarono ad una croce* (Genoa 1995). A. SYLVESTRE, *Jean-Gabriel Perboyre: prêtre de la mission, martyr en Chine* (Moissac 1994).

[J. KRAHL]

PERCY, THOMAS, BL.

Seventh Earl of Northumberland, martyr; b. 1528; beheaded at York, England, Aug. 22, 1572. Thomas and his younger brother, sons of Sir Thomas Percy and Eleanor Harbottal, were brought up by Sir Thomas Tempest of Tong Hall, Yorkshire, after the execution of their father at Tyburn (1537) for his part in the PILGRIMAGE OF GRACE of 1536. The brothers were restored in blood by the crown in 1549. Thomas's loyal adherence to the Catholic faith brought him favorable notice from Queen Mary, who made him governor of Prudhoe Castle. Knighted and created Baron Percy, he was, in consideration of ''his noble descent, constancy, and virtue, and value in arms,'' made earl of Northumberland (1557). Shortly afterward he was nominated a member of the Council of the North and high marshal of the army in the north and was appointed captain of Berwick, lord-warden-general of the East and Middle Marches toward Scotland.

On the accession of Elizabeth I, however, the earl resigned his office. Despite Lord Burghley's suspicions,

Percy was made a knight of the Garter in 1563. At Mary Queen of Scots' flight into England, Northumberland insisted the custody of Mary should by right be his as the chief magnate of the north. When admitted to an interview with Mary at Carlisle, he expressed sympathy with her misfortunes. This angered the London government, and the Earl was ordered to withdraw from Carlisle and Mary was placed under the guardianship of Sir Francis Knollys.

Resentful at this treatment, desirous of religious freedom and for liberty for Mary Stuart, Percy joined the northern rebellion (1569). At the imprisonment of the Duke of Norfolk in the Tower, Northumberland and the Earl of Westmorland were summoned to court at London. Knowing this meant imprisonment and probable death, the Earl of Westmorland agreed with the fiery desires of the gentry for a rising. Northumberland accidentally stumbled into this nascent rising as he sought safer refuge from the queen's agents in his Yorkshire house and was finally convinced to throw in his lot with the rebels. It was another Pilgrimage of Grace. Under the banner of the five wounds of Christ crucified, the forces, led by Northumberland, took Durham, where Mass was said in the cathedral for the last time, Nov. 14, 1569. Four days later they were at Ripon. But the earls were no generals, nor had they any plans. By December 16, the royal forces were upon them, forcing the earls to flee to Scotland. Percy led a hunted life there, while his wife Anne, daughter of Henry Somerset, second earl of Worcester, did her best to raise ransom for him from her own exile in Antwerp, but without success. He was finally handed over to Elizabeth in August 1572 by the regent of Scotland, the earl of Mar, for £ 2000. He was taken to York and offered his life if he took the oath of supremacy and abandoned Catholicism. He refused and was beheaded. His last words were a renewed declaration of his faith as a Catholic and in family: "I am a Percy in life and in death." Pope Leo XIII beatified him in 1886.

Feast: Aug. 26 (Dioceses of Hexham, Leeds, and Middlesborough).

See Also: ENGLAND, SCOTLAND, AND WALES, MARTYRS OF.

Bibliography: P. HUGHES, *The Reformation in England* (New York 1963). C. READ, *Mr. Secretary Cecil and Queen Elizabeth* (New York 1955). C. SHARP, ed., *Memorials of the Rebellion of 1569* (London 1841). E. B. DE FONBLANQUE, *Annals of the House of Percy*, 2 v. (London 1887) v.2. J. H. POLLEN, *English Catholics in the Reign of Queen Elizabeth* (New York 1920). *Calendar of State Papers, Domestic* (1569–70), ed. M. A. E. GREEN, 7 v. (London 1856–72).

[J. D. HANLON]

Walker Percy. (©Jerry Bauer)

PERCY, WALKER

Novelist, essayist; b. Birmingham, Alabama, May 28, 1916; d. Covington, Louisiana, May 10, 1990. After the suicide of his father, LeRoy Pratt, in 1929 and the death of his mother, Martha Susan Phinizy, in an automobile accident in 1932, Percy and his two younger brothers were adopted by their father's cousin, William Alexander Percy, the lawyer-planter-poet of Greenville, Mississippi. Percy always respected "Uncle Will" for his noble ideals and romantic appreciation of the arts, but he ultimately rejected the mournful stoicism to which his relative gave classic expression in his memoirs, *Lanterns on the Levee* (1941).

Percy turned away from such a melancholy heritage by pursuing a secular faith in science. He majored in chemistry at the University of North Carolina at Chapel Hill and graduated from Columbia University's College of Physicians and Surgeons in 1941. Then Percy faced what he called "the cataclysm." He contracted tuberculosis while interning at Bellevue Hospital in 1942 and confronted a spiritual crisis. During a two-year rest cure at Trudeau Sanatorium (which formed the basis of an early, unpublished novel, "The Gramercy Winner"), Percy read his way to better health. He learned from the work of Tolstoy, Dostoyevsky, Kafka, and Mann, but found the most salutary understanding of his own dilemma through discovering the religious philosophy of Soren KIERKEGAARD. He discovered that science could speak about humanity in the abstract, yet it could say nothing about what it meant to live and die as Walker Percy. In seeking to appreciate that mystery, Percy discontinued his career in medicine, married Mary Bernice Townsend in 1946, converted to Catholicism in 1947, and began writing fiction as well as scholarly articles about language and Southern culture.

Although Percy published a collection of his essays on semiotics (*The Message in the Bottle*, 1975) and a parody of self-help books for an age near semiotic catastrophe (*Lost in the Cosmos*, 1983), he made his most distinctive contribution in his novels about quests to understand the perplexing signs of the spiritual life. Percy's fictional Southerners live out their faith through sharing in the same kind of despair, wandering, discovery, and return to daily work that marked the story of his own religious search. *The Moviegoer* (1961), for which he won the National Book Award, chronicles how Binx Bolling is drawn to stoicism, scientism, and aestheticism before accepting the Catholicism of his mother's family as a way of placing himself in the everyday world. As Percy shifted from such wryly understated comedy to the picaresque adventures of *The Last Gentleman* (1966) and the satiric science fiction of *Love in the Ruins* (1971), he portrayed religious faith as a scandalous alternative to lives and worlds that increasingly seemed on the verge of disaster.

The crisis of modern life exploded in a vitriolic tour de force, *Lancelot* (1977). While Percy's knight of the unholy grail tells of how he pursued the mystery of his wife's infidelity, he reveals his own more horrifying faithlessness as a vengeful champion of a morally-purified America. After such a bleak apocalypse, Percy wrote his most joyous novel, *The Second Coming* (1980), in which Will Barrett of *The Last Gentleman* discovers that his romance with Allie Huger may be the unexpected sign of God's presence in his life. Percy looked to the future with greater anxiety in *The Thanatos Syndrome* (1987). As Dr. Tom More of *Love in the Ruins* investigates a mysterious plague, he learns to oppose the scapegoating and social engineering that seek to undermine a semiotic understanding of humanity.

Percy repeatedly maintained that fiction must not preach, yet he viewed his Catholic faith as central to his artistic vision. The Judaeo-Christian understanding of humanity as fallen but engaged in a search deepened his conviction that the novel should focus on people in trouble in particular places, moments, and predicaments. Percy's fiction embodied this faith through its rootedness in the physical world, commitment to historical time, and exploration of spiritual wayfaring. Renouncing the fatalism of the Old South and the naive optimism of the New South, Percy's seekers may come to themselves and to others as they discover how they may finally come to God.

While Percy has been criticized for his moralizing, muddled plot details, and reductive portrayals of women, he is recognized as one of the pre-eminent novelists of the South. His writing combines philosophical depth, linguistic resourcefulness, wide-ranging comedy, clinical powers of observation, and trenchant social criticism as it explores the religious vision of a constant seeker. Percy's fiction contemplates not only the sadness and craziness of humanity's spiritual isolation but also the surprising possibility of overcoming that aloneness by living with others under God.

Bibliography: W. R. ALLEN, *Walker Percy: A Southern Wayfarer* (Jackson, MS 1986). R. H. BRINKMEYER, *Three Catholic Writers of the Modern South* (Jackson, MS 1985). G. M. CIUBA, *Walker Percy: Books of Revelations* (Athens, GA 1991). R. COLES, *Walker Percy: An American Search* (Boston 1978). J. E. HARDY, *The Fiction of Walker Percy* (Urbana, IL 1987). L. W. HOBSON, *Understanding Walker Percy* (Columbia, SC 1988). M. D. HOWLAND, *The Gift of the Other* (Pittsburgh 1990). L. A. LAWSON, *Following Percy* (Troy, NY 1988). M. LUSCHEI, *The Sovereign Wayfarer* (Baton Rouge 1972). P. L. POTEAT, *Walker Percy and the Old Modern Age* (Baton Rouge 1985). P. SAMWAY, ed., *Signposts in a Strange Land* (New York 1991). T. R. SPIVEY, *The Writer as Shaman* (Macon 1986). J. TAYLOR, *In Search of Self* (Cambridge, MA 1986). J. TOLSON, *Pilgrim in the Ruins* (New York 1992). R. C. WOOD, *The Comedy of Redemption* (Notre Dame 1988).

[G. M. CIUBA]

PEREIRA, TOMÁS

Missionary in CHINA; b. San Martinho do Valle, Province of Braga, Portugal, Nov. 1, 1645; d. Beijing, Dec. 24, 1708. He entered the Society of Jesus in Coimbra in 1663, left for the Indies in 1666, and in January 1673 arrived in Beijing. By his rare musical talents, he won the good favor of the Emperor Hsüan-Yeh and retained this esteem until his death. In 1689, he and Jean Gerbillon, SJ, assisted the Chinese delegates in the negotiations at Nerchinsk that led to the first peace treaty between the Chinese and the Russians. In recognition of the success of the two Jesuits in this mission, K'ang-Hsi in 1692 granted the first edict of toleration for Christianity. On this occasion Pereira spoke for all the missionaries and publicly thanked the emperor. Pereira became rector of the Jesuit College in Beijing and from June 1692 to June 1695, was vice provincial of the Chinese Vice-Province of the Society of Jesus. After his death, the emperor contributed toward a splendid funeral and composed an epitaph in his honor.

Bibliography: L. PFISTER, *Notices biographiques et bibliographiques* (Shanghai 1932) v.1. J. SEBES, *The Jesuits and the SinoRussian Treaty of Nerchinsk, 1689* (Rome 1961).

[E. HAGEMANN]

PEREIRA Y CASTELLÓN, SIMEÓN

Nicaraguan ''martyr bishop''; b. León, Nicaragua, July 2, 1863; d. there, Jan. 29, 1922. He was a member of a family of high social status, the son of Pedro Pereira and Dolores Castellón. In 1879 he entered the Society of Jesus and attended the Colegio de San Ignacio de Loyola in Matagalpa. When the Jesuits were exiled in 1881, he went with them to Ecuador, where he completed his studies at the University of Quito. He then taught for several years, first in Bogotá and then in Medellín. Ill health caused him to return to NICARAGUA in 1892. He was ordained in León and celebrated his first Mass on March 19, 1894. On the expulsion of the vicars general from Nicaragua, the vicariate was entrusted to him. He too was ordered into exile, but influential friends persuaded President José Simón Zelaya to cancel that decree, and Pereira remained in Nicaragua.

On July 25, 1896, he was consecrated auxiliary bishop of Nicaragua with the right of succession to Bp. Francisco Ulloa y Larios (1880–1902). As bishop he continued to be harassed by the political authorities to such an extent that he gained his epithet ''Martyr Bishop.'' When he wrote a strong pastoral letter against the anti-Catholic decrees of President Zelaya, he was first imprisoned in the barracks at Managua and then (Nov. 3, 1898) exiled to Costa Rica. He was again exiled in 1905 when clerical garb was forbidden in Nicaragua. This time he went to Rome and on the way preached in Spain, in Toledo and Zaragoza, and was acclaimed by the press as a representative of the American pulpit. He also lived in Mexico, Panama, Colombia, and Costa Rica before he was able to return in triumph to Nicaragua.

Bishop Pereira y Castellón reorganized the minor seminary in León and repaired and decorated the cathedral. With the permission of the Holy See he turned over the episcopal residence for the use of the Colegio de la Asunción. He founded a catechetical institute and, largely with his own funds, built an orphanage. He arranged to have Christian Brothers and Dominicans come into the diocese. He founded, and had printed on his own press, a diocesan newspaper. When the archdiocese was created in Nicaragua in 1912, he remained bishop of León, but the pope made him titular archbishop of Sísico. Benedict XV later gave him the titles of Roman Count and Attendant at the Pontifical Throne. In 1914 the national congress passed a resolution of public gratitude to Bishop Pereira and authorized the erection of a monument to him after his death.

Bibliography: A. AGUILAR, *Reseña histórica de la diócesis de Nicaragua* (León 1927).

[L. LAMADRID]

PÉREZ, ESTEBAN

Discalced Franciscan mission preacher in Peru; b. Olite, Navarre, Spain, 1854; d. Lima, Peru, 1934. Starting out from the Colegio de Ocopa and from the Descalzos of Lima, which gave them their name, Discalced missionaries constituted the most powerful force for the preservation and consolidation of Christian life in PERU and neighboring countries from the middle of the 19th century. The Catholic Church was in a critical state because of the continued shortage of priests, the spread of rationalism, secret societies, regalistic governments, antireligious laws, secular teaching, and sectarian propaganda. The evangelical action of the Discalced Fathers extended itself throughout Peru, embracing the aristocracy, the middle class, the clergy, religious communities, and reaching even to the Quechua and Aymará–speaking native population and the eastern jungle tribes. The missionaries, in well-trained groups of two, four, or six, traveled through the territory of more than a million square kilometers giving missions of one-and-a-half or two months in the principal cities, one month or 15 days in the smaller cities, and a proportional length of time in less-populated areas. To the clergy, the intellectuals, influential groups, students, and religious communities they gave courses of religious exercises. Esteban Pérez was a typical example of these missionaries. A vigorous man of convincing eloquence, great zeal, and untiring activity, he gave missions in Peru, Chile, Bolivia, Ecuador, and California. He encouraged social work and organized and gave new life to Lima's devotion to the Señor de los Milagros. In order to consolidate the mission gains, he wrote various works, among them the *Devocionario manual* (Lima 1960, 42 ed.), of which it has been said that ''it has converted more souls than it has letters.'' In 1932 he delivered the funeral oration for Leguìa, former president of Peru.

Bibliography: T. MORI, ''El padre Esteban Pérez,'' *Colección Descalzos* 6 (Lima 1944) 12–14.

[O. SAIZ]

PÉREZ, JUAN

Spanish Franciscan, patron of COLUMBUS; date and place of birth uncertain; d. c. 1515. He was once confused with Antonio de Marchena, another Franciscan patron of Columbus, but the two are distinct. Marchena in 1473 was probably guardian of San Esteban de los Olmos in Burgos, and in 1485 of La Rábida, where he gave Columbus shelter and approved his plans. Marchena also was versed in astronomy. He became custos of the Observant Franciscans of Andalusia in 1487; vicar provincial of Castile, 1499 to 1502; and guardian of Murcia, 1502 to 1505. As a youth, Pérez was employed in the office of accounts of Isabella I, and as a friar was for a time her confessor. He probably is the Juan Pérez de Segovia of the friary of Arrizafa in Córdoba, to whom Isabella gave aims in 1485. As guardian of La Rábida in 1491, he befriended Columbus, going to the court to commend him to Isabella and in his name, April 17, 1492, signing the agreement for the voyage of Columbus. He helped in the preparations for the voyage, especially by persuading Martin Yáñez Pinzon, the most eminent mariner of Palos, to take part in the venture. He heard the confessions of the crew and gave them his blessing for the voyage. He probably accompanied Columbus on his second voyage, on which Marchena did not go despite the wishes of the king and queen. The Franciscan Order contributed to the discovery of America with the learning of Marchena, the social and political patronage of Juan Pérez, and the understanding and charity of both.

Bibliography: A. ORTEGA, *La rábida,* 4 v. (Seville 1925–26) v.2. A. BALLESTEROS Y BERETTA, *Cristóbal Colón,* 2 v. (Barcelona 1945). A. YBOT LÉON, *La iglesia y los ectesiásticos españoles en la empresa de Indias* (Barcelona 1954—) v.1. A. URIBE, "Una *bula inédita de Paulo II . . . ,*" *Archivo Ibero-Americano,* 2d ser. 4 (1944) 464–472. J. MESEGUER FERNÁNDEZ, "Iñigo de Mendoza y Antonio de Marchena en an documento de 1502," *Hispania* 12 (1952) 401–411; Archivo Ibero-Americano, 2d ser. 19 (1959) 163–164, 167.

[J. M. FERNÁNDEZ]

PÉREZ DE RIVAS, ANDRÉS

Jesuit missionary, historian, and administrator; b. Córdoba, Spain, 1575; d. Mexico City, March 26, 1655. Little is known of his early years other than that he studied at the Jesuit school in his native city. He did not enter the Jesuit order until 1602, after he had been ordained a diocesan priest. Departing from custom in the order, Pérez de Rivas, while still a novice, was sent in 1602 to Mexico and completed his novitiate in Puebla. By the fall of 1604, he was at work in the San Felipe mission on the Río Sinaloa. By 1605 he had learned the native languages of the area and moved farther north to the Fuerte River region of Sinaloa, where with Jesuit companions he established several mission stations. Pérez de Rivas was next assigned to the Yaqui mission in Sonora. This whole missionary movement in the present Mexican states of Sinaloa and Sonora contributed greatly to extending the frontier up the mainland coast of the gulf and ultimately to Alta California. By the end of 1619 poor health forced the recall of Pérez de Rivas from the missions. Administrative positions in the order and historical writing occupied the rest of his life.

Of his works, *Historia de los triumphos de nuestra sante fee entre gentes los más barbaros y fieros del Nuevo Orbe* (Madrid 1645) is the most important. In 12 books, the author covers the Jesuit missionary endeavor in northern New Spain from 1591 to 1643. The first part of the work tells of the mission expansion from the Río Sinaloa up along the coast, over the rivers that fall into the Gulf of California, and up hundreds of miles into the Sonora Valley. The second part narrates the missionary development in the Sierra Madre Mountains of the west, and on the eastern plains in present Durango and Coahuila. The third part, consisting of only the 12th and last book of the work, treats of the early Florida mission. It is one of the finest accounts that exists concerning mission history and the gradual development of the colonial frontier. Under the title *Páginas para la historia de Sinaloa y Sonora; Triumphos de nuestra santa fee,* it was reedited in Mexico City in 1944. Pérez de Rivas's other published work of considerable importance is his *Corónica y historia religiosa de la provencio de la compañía de Jesús de Mexico en la Nueva España,* 2 v. (Mexico City 1896), which traces the history of the order from the coming of the first Jesuits to New Spain in 1572, to 1654. The published edition of the work omits numerous chapters, most of which are biographical. A short treatise on the life of Father Juan de Ledesma was printed in Mexico in 1636, and an answer to the Bishop of Puebla, Juan de PALAFOX, concerning some financial aspects of certain Jesuit schools in 1641. At least four other known works exist in manuscript form and deal with theological matters and different phases of the history of the order in New Spain.

Bibliography: P. M. DUNNE, *Andrés Pérez de Ribas: Pioneer Black Robe of the West Coast, Administrator, Historian* (New York 1951).

[N. F. MARTIN]

PÉREZ FLORIDO, PETRA DE SAN JOSÉ, BL.

Foundress of the Congregation of the Mothers of the Helpless and of St. Joseph of the Mountain; b. December 7, 1845, Málaga, Costa del Sol, Spain; d. August 16, 1906, Barcelona, Spain. From her youth Pérez desired the religious life. Full of compassion for the poor, she begged in the streets on their behalf despite her father's opposition. With the approbation of the bishop of Málaga, who also named the congregation, Petra and three companions formed (1880) the Mothers of the Helpless. Mother Petra labored (1895–1901) to build the royal sanctuary of Saint Joseph of the Mountain (Montaña Pelada), while guiding her growing religious communities. She was beatified by Pope John Paul II, October 16, 1994.

Feast: Aug. 16.

Bibliography: F. DE LA HOZ, *Desde el valle a la montaña* (Seville 1961). MOTHERS OF THE HELPLESS, *Sobre la 'piedra'* (Valencia 1972).

[K. I. RABENSTEIN]

PERFECTION, ONTOLOGICAL

Etymologically, perfect and perfection derive from the Latin *per facere or per-factum,* meaning made through or thoroughly; they imply a state of completion or totalization, as in that which is fulfilled or consummated. The perfect thing, then, suffers no lack or defect within the order of its perfectiveness. The concept is obviously a transcendental one, realizable on different levels of being (*see* TRANSCENDENTALS).

Kinds of Perfection. It is possible to discern at least two ontological significations of perfection, the first permitting a distinction between absolute and relative perfection, the second between substantial and accidental perfection.

Absolute vs. Relative. Absolute perfection, meaning that to which nothing whatsoever is lacking, embraces the total plenitude of being and is nowise compatible with defect. Such absolute perfection may be posited either as real, subsisting of itself outside the mind (thus identical with traditional concepts of GOD), or as ideal, having objective existence only within mind, as an IDEA.

By contrast something may be only relatively perfect, its perfection limited to a given order, inferior to the absolutely perfect, and bespeaking a greater or lesser removal from absolute perfection, with reference to which it is measured. The perfection of man, for instance, is at once greater than that of the irrational animal or the vegetable and less than that of intellectual substances, the angels of Christian tradition.

Substantial vs. Accidental. The second and wider sense of the word means that which lacks nothing due to its nature, possessing everything answering to its objective CONCEPT. Distinguishable here is substantial perfection, whereby a thing is constituted as an existent ESSENCE, and accidental perfection, bespeaking whatever completeness accrues to the thing in a consequential way. This latter in turn includes the indispensable properties and the common accidents added only contingently; operative perfection as well as entitative; and the final fulfillment of a thing, consisting in the attainment of its end or destiny.

Relationships. It is entirely accidental to perfection as such that it be realized as the term of a process; it is itself only completeness. The formality of perfection is ordinarily to be found, in the real order, resident in a being that is in other respects imperfect. The transcendentality of the concept lies in its conceptual proximity to BEING and the GOOD. A thing is perfect to the extent that it is; its actuality formally determines its perfectness. The PURE ACT of being is thus the sole instance of absolute perfection; to exist substantially is to have first perfection; to *be* in accidental ways is to achieve secondary perfection; to be actually in possession of the end is for any nature to reach the ultimate term of its relative perfection. The formal constitutive of perfection is this actuality. In turn, the actuality or perfection of a being, bespeaking its capacity to perfect another, gives rise to the relationship toward others of desirability. Goodness, or the good, is thus fundamentally (not formally) the perfection of a being.

A fuller understanding of the meaning and kinds of ontological perfection can be achieved by tracing the development of the notion in Greek, Thomistic, and modern thought.

Greek Thought. PARMENIDES, founder of the Eleatic school, reacting strongly against the doctrine of HERACLITUS that all things are in a state of constant change, developed a doctrine of being in opposition to the becoming of Heraclitus. For Parmenides, the very fact of knowledge determined his position: to think means postulating something that is; what is not cannot be thought. Becoming and change are illusory; there is only being, which is homogeneous and unchangeable—indeed there is only One Being without any inner differentiation; even the plurality of individual things is not real. Nothing can be added to being, so it is complete, i.e., perfect; thus it is immovable, eternal, continuous, and immune to evil. True enough, Parmenides regarded this Perfect Being as finite, but in the sense of determined and definite, as avoiding the imperfection of indetermination and indefiniteness. Melissus (fl. 440 B.C.), a disciple of Parmenides, reversed this and granted infinity to being. The evidence favors seeing Melissus's position as a monistic materialism; being is there seen as limited, at least in space, for outside of it there is the ''void.'' In short, the notion of perfection in this school is that of a totality that does not escape the restrictions of matter.

PLATO attempted to reconcile the many of Heraclitus and EMPEDOCLES with the one of Parmenides, deriving his insight from the teaching of PYTHAGORAS that all things exist by participating in the numbers. Things are thus multiple, composed and imperfect; yet at the same time each is what it is by participating in the Ideas that exist separately as simple, unchangeable, infinite, and perfect. All perfection is thus in the Ideas, which are said to be real and subsistent and are ranged hierarchically among themselves, the Idea of the Good being supreme. Without an explicit concept of efficient causality, Plato explained the sensible world as coming to be through the Ideas ''uniting'' themselves to matter.

This Platonic concept of perfection is basically an essentialism; the ideal order is not distinguished from the real, and there is a failure to recognize the all importance of existence. The Ideas are thus reified and the perfection they embody is that of pure essence without reference to actual existence. From this it follows that the distinction in perfection between an Idea and the varied instances of PARTICIPATION in it is merely one of degree in possessing a univocal essence.

ARISTOTLE rejected the Ideas of Plato, which he called poetic metaphors (*Meta.* 991a 21), as abstract universals enjoying existence only in the mind. Perfection lies only in the real order, where it is to be distinguished from a principle of imperfection. Imperfection is POTENCY capacity for being; perfection is ἐνέργεια, ACT, being itself. If ἐνέργεια means first of all a process whereby form is realized in matter, it comes to mean eventually the being or act so achieved. Potency and MATTER are infinite (τὸ ἄπειρον) and unknowable but in the traditional Greek sense of indefinite and undetermined—that outside of which there is always something. FORM and act, as the very opposite of this, mean that which is complete and whole (ὅλον), from which nothing is left out (Phys., 207a 1–10), that which is perfect (τέλειον). There is no unending process of development; each thing attains its maximum perfection when all the potentialities with which its NATURE is endowed are realized.

The transition from potency to act can be effected only by a being already actual. In the *Metaphysics* (1072a 25), Aristotle reasons to an Unmoved First Mover whose perfection is such as to account for all becoming, at least in the order of final causality. Whether the logical structure of his thought should have allowed this or not, Aristotle does appear to give real existence to this all perfect Nous (1072b 5, 25).

Thomistic Analysis. Perfection in the thought of St. THOMAS AQUINAS is developed along two distinct lines—the theological and the philosophical. While the latter order remains intrinsically free of any illumination from faith, still there are Christian presuppositions that extrinsically give direction to the philosophical endeavor. Nonetheless, St. Thomas's concept of perfection is basically an explication of that of Aristotle (see *In 5 meta.* 18), with a new shift of emphasis on the primacy of EXISTENCE over essence. ''To the extent that something is in act, to that degree it is perfect'' (*Summa theologiae* 1a, 5.1; 1a2ae, 3.2; *C. gent.* 1.39, 2.41, 3.22). And the supreme and ultimate act of all is existence, ''. . . the actuality of all acts . . . the perfection of all perfections'' (*De pot.* 7.2 ad 9). The primacy of the Ideas in Plato and of substance in Aristotle thus gives way in St. Thomas to the primacy of existence (*esse*). Potency, as the principle of mutability and determinability, is the source of imperfection; it limits the act that accrues to it (see POTENCY AND ACT). Thus essence, as potential to esse, limits the infiniteness of being and in so doing explains finiteness and plurality.

Divine Perfection. This composition, or potency-act relationship, between essence and existence establishes the caused nature of finite things and leads the mind by a natural dialectic to posit the real existence of Pure Act, Unreceived Being. This subsistent act of being suffers no limitation; it is thus the sole absolutely perfect being, i.e., God. The procedure is a negative one, denying of God any composition and thus any imperfection. The human mind is incapable of any quiddative knowledge of Perfect Being (ST 1a, 3.4 ad 2); it acknowledges Him in an analogical way only by an inference from the FINITE BEING it does know.

None of the perfections of being can be lacking to God (*ibid.* 4.2 ad 3); thus the perfections of all things preexist in Him, but as really identified with Himself and distinguishable only by the human mind in a conceptual way. Perfections of the created order derive causally from God and, because of their state of limitation by potency, are finite participations of infinite perfection. Some of them are pure perfections in their own order, the objective concept being one that excludes all imperfection, even though the perfection may be extrinsically conjoined with an imperfect subject. Others are intrinsically of such limited perfectness as to bespeak imperfection of themselves. Life and intelligence are examples of the first kind; rationality, sensibility, and the virtues of faith and hope belong to the latter category. In scholastic terminology the prior are designated as perfections *simpliciter simplex,* the latter as perfections *secundum quid.*

The subject possessing any given perfection may be said to have it either formally, i.e., according to its proper concept as expressed in the definition (e.g., rationality in man); or virtually, i.e., in a causal way only, lacking the perfection in actual fact but having the power to achieve the effect of such perfection (e.g., rationality in an angel); or eminently, i.e., in terms not of the proper form but of a higher form expressive nonetheless of whatever perfection is in the lower (e.g., rationality in God).

Supernatural Perfection. Approached theologically, however, in the light of Christian faith, the Perfect One is discerned not only to be eminently whatever there is of perfection in the natural order, created or even creatable, but to be of an entirely other order of perfection—the supernatural. The Subsistent Being in His inner trinitarian life is perfection in a transcendental sense that will not admit of manifestation in the universe of nature. Intellectual creatures, however, can in a totally gratuitous way be elevated to another universe, that of grace, wherein they are enabled to know and love God as He is in Himself.

Modern Views. R. DESCARTES, opening the era of modern philosophy, posited an absolutely perfect being, really existent and transcendent over the universe. His THEISM, however, is purely rationalistic, seeing an all perfect God in terms of function, i.e., as explaining the universe of things. The Infinite and Eternal is necessary to establish the universal laws for all things and to guarantee the validity of man's distinct and clear ideas. The direction of thought is a priori; the reality of the infinitely perfect Being is not demonstrated discursively; nor need it be acknowledged in faith, for this is the first intuitive truth from which all others derive. The human mind thus possesses a complete idea of the Perfect, which is no longer the incomprehensible *Ipsum Esse* of St. Thomas, but rather self-caused essence.

The RATIONALISM of B. SPINOZA is pantheistic in nature, beginning with a ''Being absolutely infinite and consummately perfect'' that is no other than the totality of nature. This is God as the cause of things, in an immanent rather than transcendent sense, however, and thus ultimately identified with all things. Spinoza marks a return to the doctrine of Parmenides; there is only one substance and all things are modes of it, ways in which it exists and operates. As infinite, substance produces its own existence.

G. W. LEIBNIZ continued the rationalist approach with the same apriority in gratuitously positing God as supreme perfection. The finite world derives from this pure essence, yet in such fashion that both belong to the same order. An underlying univocity of being means that God and creature differ only in degree of perfection. The will of the Perfect Being is limited by His essence and by the objects of His intelligence; God is even constrained morally to the creative act, since He can do only what is best. The way is thus open for the finite god of contemporary PANENTHEISM; ontological perfection is qualified.

I. KANT, influenced by empirical philosophy, reacted strongly against the apriority of the rationalists. All that can be known are the appearances of things, knowledge being what the senses furnish to certain structures of consciousness. The perfect being, then, while probably really existent, remains unknowable. The idea of God as the infinitely perfect Being has only logical validity; it enjoys only ideal existence. No analysis of that idea will reveal, a priori, the real existence of deity; nor may it be used to deduce the finite world. The supremely perfect is, then, for Kant, merely a form of thought.

G. W. F. HEGEL and the idealists (J. G. FICHTE, F. W. J. SCHELLING, and others) carried the IDEALISM of Kant to the point where every vestige of theism disappeared. Whereas Kant left God as unknowable in His transcendence, Hegel brought forth a metaphysics of the ABSOLUTE to replace the idea of God. The Absolute is spirit, ultimately pure thought, yet totally immanent within human consciousness. It develops as the process of finite things, moving through nature and history in self enrichment. The real world represents transient determinations of the impersonal Absolute. The perfection of the Absolute, however, is not total, for it is itself the internal developing principle of historical process. It seems not to enjoy consciousness apart from the conscious striving of finite minds, and thus to stand in need of human rational effort.

Critique of Modern Thought. These modern doctrines concerning the supremely perfect Being represent radical departures from the traditional teaching of St. Thomas and Aristotle. This latter, for example, is opposed to the rationalism and essentialism of Descartes and Leibniz. It argues that there is no basis in man's experience for innate ideas (see INNATISM). Rather, man's conscious knowing life originates from the real material world through sense activity. Even were there such, moreover, the existence of the idea in the mind could not of itself establish the real existence of the object; the most that one could conclude would be the notion of actuality, not the real exercise thereof. Also, both Descartes and Leibniz saw essence as ultimate perfection, reducing existence to another merely formal perfection.

Much the same can be said for the pantheism of Spinoza. The contingency of finite things reveals their caused nature, and the principle of causality, rightly understood, demands a real distinction of effect and cause. The Uncaused Necessary Being transcends the world of contingents; these latter cannot be mere modes of the necessary Substance.

In criticism of Kant's idealistic agnosticism, to say that one cannot know (but only believe, as a postulate of practical reason) whether a reality corresponds to one's idea of a totally Perfect Being is to limit human knowledge to the order of sensible appearances. This is to fail to acknowledge the evidence that the very being of things presents, namely, that existents are not only sensible but also intelligible. Also, the movement from CONTINGENCY to an Uncaused Necessary (and hence Perfect) Being is not a result merely of a synthesizing need on man's part; it lies in the very intelligibility of contingency as such. Nor does it follow, as Kant maintains, that the perfection of such a Being would then be relative, because His causal relation to the world is not in virtue of an action distinct from His very substance. The misunderstanding results from restricting ANALOGY to a mere symbolic function, from failing to see its ontological fundament with the implied underlying causal connectives.

In the dialectical monism of Hegelian idealism there is an unresolved ambivalence. Either Absolute Consciousness is sufficiently actual in itself, and then the world is mere illusion, or else the Absolute is realized only in conscious human striving, and then there is no Absolute Spirit or Pure Thought. Also, the reason for change is enrichment of the changing subject, and this bespeaks an underlying imperfection. Whatever perfection lies in pure process, then, cannot be absolute.

See Also: GOD; INFINITY OF GOD; BEAUTY.

Bibliography: THOMAS AQUINAS, *Summa theologiae* 1a, 4, Eng. *Existence and Nature of God,* ed. and tr. T. MCDERMOTT (*Summa Theologica* 2; New York 1964); *Commentary on the Metaphysics of Aristotle,* 2 v., tr. J. ROWAN (Chicago 1961). G. DI NAPOLI, *Enciclopedia filosofica,* 4 v. (Venice-Rome 1957) 3:1282–90. R. EISLER, *Wörterbuch der philosophischen Begriffe,* 3 v. (4th ed. Berlin 1927–30) 3:427–4:29. R. GARRIGOU-LAGRANGE, *God: His Existence and His Nature,* tr. B. ROSE, 2 v. (St. Louis 1934–36) v.2. É. H. GILSON, *God and Philosophy* (New Haven 1941). J. D. COLLINS, *God in Modern Philosophy* (Chicago 1959). C. HARTSHORNE and W. L. REESE, eds., *Philosophers Speak of God* (Chicago 1953).

[W. J. HILL]

PERFECTION, SPIRITUAL

The concept of perfection, as applied to Christian life, is scriptural in origin. Christ admonished His disciples: ''You therefore are to be perfect, even as your heavenly Father is perfect'' (Mt 5.48). The word translated into English as ''perfect'' is the Greek τέλειοι, which fundamentally implies the attainment of goal or end.

Notion. The term perfection as applied to human life in general, however, was used in antiquity even by the barbarians, who thought of it as fortitude, as is frequently evidenced in their legends. The idea that human perfection consists in fortitude has reappeared in recent times. Indeed, some have explained Christian perfection as the supreme act of fortitude, which is martyrdom. Others would have had the essence of perfection consist in penance and mortification. Quietism, on the contrary, rejecting all human efforts in the struggle for perfection, made it consist, rather, in a complete passivity that suppresses personal mortification as well as acts of charity toward one's neighbor. Some Greek philosophers explained perfection in terms of wisdom. Their error has been revived in modern theosophy, which makes perfection a consciousness of the divine in man. Something analogous to this is found in the doctrine of those who hold that the essence of Christian perfection consists in the contemplation that issues from the gift of wisdom.

In opposition to the above explanations, the majority of theologians have insisted upon charity as the formal element in true Christian perfection. In so doing, they are merely following the doctrine of the Scriptures which teach that ''God is love, and he who abides in love abides in God and God in him'' (Jn 4.16). St. Paul confirms this by his insistence upon charity as ''the bond of perfection'' (Gal 3.14). These words of St. Paul only summarize the teaching of Christ that the whole law depends on these two precepts of love: ''Thou shalt love the Lord thy God with thy whole heart, and with thy whole soul, and with thy whole strength, and with thy whole mind; and thy neighbor as thyself'' (Lk 10.27).

In order to understand this explanation more clearly it is necessary to understand the two senses in which the term can be used. St. Thomas Aquinas speaks of a first and second perfection. ''The first perfection is the form of the whole, the form which results from the whole, complete with all its parts. The second perfection is the end, which is either operation, as the end of the harpist is to play the harp; or something that is attained by operation, as the end of the builder is the house he makes by building'' (*Summa theologiae* 1a, 73.1). Applying this division of perfection to Christian life, one is said to possess first perfection, or is substantially perfect as a Christian, when he possesses sanctifying grace, through which he participates in the supernatural life of God. As the human soul constitutes a body truly human, and brings with it the powers necessary for human development, so sanctifying grace elevates the soul to supernatural life and brings with it all the infused theological and moral virtues and the gifts of the Holy Spirit.

Considered integrally or as the sum total of things necessary, second perfection will require all the virtues and gifts. But in the operation of which virtue does man attain his end, or union with God, while still on earth? Not in the operation of the moral virtues, since they are concerned rather with the means to the end than the end itself; nor can it be found in the operation of faith, which no longer exists in one who enjoys heavenly vision of

God; nor in hope, which also disappears in the possession of the Divine Good in glory. Charity alone remains as the source of effective union with God in this life. ''A thing is said to be perfect in so far as it attains its proper end, which is its ultimate perfection. Now it is charity that unites us to God, who is the last end of the human mind, since 'he who abides in charity abides in God, and God in him' (1 Jn 4.16). Therefore the perfection of the Christian life consists chiefly in charity'' (*Summa theologiae* 2a2ae, 184.1). Thus St. Thomas concluded: ''Primarily and essentially, the perfection of the Christian life consists in charity, principally as to the love of God, secondarily as to the love of neighbor, both of which are the matter of the chief commandments of the divine law'' (*ibid.* 2a2ae, 184.3).

Although everyone in a state of grace receives the virtue of charity, which gives him the capacity for supernatural friendship with God, the mere capacity for such friendship does not make him a perfect Christian in the proper meaning of second perfection. When charity is referred to as second perfection, which is perfection in the formal and proper sense, it is not the habit but the act of charity which is meant. Charity is a virtue, a power ordained by its nature to make the Christian capable of loving God as the supreme Good. But power is made perfect only in actual operation. For this reason the formal or second perfection of the Christian life consists in actual charity, not in the mere capacity for love. Nevertheless, in order to be perfect in charity in this life, one need not be engaged at all times in the actual exercise of the love of God; such uninterrupted love of God will be possible only in heaven. What is required for such perfection in this life is that all the other activities of Christian life should flow from the love of God.

It is precisely because man cannot always be actually loving God in this life that the other virtues have a role to play in Christian life here on earth. In this life the Christian, according to his state in life, must be concerned with actions and objects other than God. Nevertheless, he must preserve the state of grace and concern himself with other occupations in such a way that charity is not lost. The virtue of charity should rule over the acts of all the other virtues, for it is from charity that such acts receive their supernatural merit.

Degrees. While man can never exhaust God's capacity to be loved, for He is the Infinite Good, nor can the Christian always be actually loving God except in heaven, there are recognizable differences of degree of perfection that depend upon the extent of man's efforts to remove the obstacles to the love of God in this life. The first and lowest degree consists in the removal of all that is directly contrary to charity, i.e., the avoidance of mortal sin. A higher degree of perfection is achieved in the effort to remove whatever in man's affections might hinder him from tending wholly to God. St. Thomas summarized the traditional teaching concerning these degrees when he wrote: ''The various degrees of charity are distinguished according to the different pursuits to which the increase of charity brings man. For it is first incumbent on man to occupy himself chiefly with avoiding sin and resisting his concupiscences, which move him in opposition to charity. This concerns beginners, in whom charity has to be fed or fostered lest it be destroyed. In the second place, man's chief pursuit is to aim at progress in good, and this is the pursuit of the proficient, whose principal aim is to strengthen their charity by adding to it. Man's third pursuit is to aim chiefly at union with God and enjoyment of Him: this belongs to the perfect who 'desire to be dissolved and to be with Christ' (Phil 1.23)'' (*Summa theologiae* 2a2ae, 24.9). Even in this final degree of charity in this life, perfection is only relative, however, because, in a true sense, there is no limit to growth in the love of God in this life.

Perfection and the Counsels. Although some have held that the perfection of charity goes beyond the precept to love God with the whole heart, this opinion does not follow from the above explanation. Were this opinion true, the perfect love of God would go beyond the precept and require certain counsels of charity (Súrez, *De statu perfectionis,* 11.15, 16). The perfection of charity is not a matter of counsel, which the individual Christian is free to choose, but is commanded as the end to which all Christians must tend. As indicated above, the perfection of Christian life consists in the love of God and neighbor. But precisely in this love the whole of the law is summarized. The precept to love God is a command to love with the *whole* heart. Christ, by these words, explicitly excluded the placing of a limit beyond which one need not advance in love by reason of the commandment. Since the very perfection of Christian life terminates in being united to God as perfectly as possible—a union possible only through charity—the precept to love God is without limitation. ''Now the love of God and neighbor is not commanded according to a measure, so that what is in excess of the measure be a matter of counsel. This is evident from the very form of the commandment, pointing, as it does, to perfection—for instance, in the words: 'Thou shalt love the Lord thy God with thy whole heart'—since 'whole' and 'perfect' are synonymous. This is so because, according to the teaching of the Apostle, 'The end of the commandment is charity' (1 Tm 1.5). Now the end does not present itself to the will subject to a measure'' (*Summa theologiae* 2a2ae, 184.3).

Hence, with regard to the perfection of charity, one must distinguish what is essential and what is not. Perfection consists, primarily, in a program for all Christian life; namely, the observance of the commandments, which are directed to removing obstacles to charity. One attains the lowest degree of charity by doing nothing contrary to charity. Secondarily, however, it consists in the observance of certain counsels which remove the primary obstacles to the actual exercise of charity, even though these obstacles might not be directly contrary to charity. The counsels are good works, better than their omission, proposed to the faithful by our Lord, and commended by Him as useful for the attainment of the perfection of charity. In general, they are reducible to the three evangelical COUNSELS of poverty, chastity, and obedience. While without the counsels one cannot reach the higher degree of the perfection of charity, the counsels are free from precept and hence of obligation. Religious make the counsels an obligation by reason of vow.

One must note the distinction between Christian perfection and the *state* of perfection. Christian perfection is subjective and personal, a most intense habit of charity, hence a grade of perfection; the state of perfection is objective and external. A lay person who has supernatural charity and is keeping the commandments has personal perfection. One enters the state of perfection by binding himself solemnly to those things that pertain to Christian perfection.

Bibliography: J. AUMANN and D. L. GREENSTOCK, *The Meaning of Christian Perfection* (St. Louis 1956). R. GARRIGOU-LAGRANGE, *The Three Ages of the Interior Life,* tr. T. DOYLE, 2 v. (St. Louis 1947–48). J. DE GUIBERT, *The Theology of the Spiritual Life,* tr. P. BARRETT (New York 1953). A. A. TANQUEREY, *The Spiritual Life* (Westminster, Md. 1945). T. AQUINAS, *Summa theologiae* 2a2ae, 184. B. HÄRING, *The Law of Christ,* tr. E. G. KAISER, 3 v. (Westminster, Md. 1961–).

[R. MASTERSON]

PERGOLESI, GIOVANNI BATTISTA

Baroque composer of the Neapolitan school; b. Iesi (The Marches), Italy, Jan. 4, 1710; d. Pozzuoli (near Naples), March 17, 1736. Between 1720 and 1724 he attended the Conservatorio di Poveri di Gesù Cristo at Naples. His brief but successful career began in the summer of 1731 with the production of a *dramma sacro, La Conversione di San Guglielmo,* and thereafter his finest works were operas and sacred music. The popularity of his music caused many anonymous works to be attributed to him; thus the majority of extant compositions carrying his name are spurious. To the early Pergolesi period belong a Mass in D major, a *Dominus ad adjuvandum me,* and the psalms *Dixit Dominus* and *Confitebor,* probably commissioned by the city of Naples toward the end of 1732. In May 1734 he conducted his two-choir Mass in F major (commissioned by Duke Carafa Maddaloni and rewritten several times) in San Lorenzo in Lucina, Rome. In content and quality these works were far superior to the general music of that period. Long *al fresco*-like counterpoint or contrapuntal phrases alternate with concerto passages for solo and choir, solo ensembles, and arias, in which the unusual melodic talents of Pergolesi are effectively expressed.

Pergolesi's Masses consist only of *Kyrie* and *Gloria.* To the late Pergolesi period belong the psalm *Laudate pueri,* in which he finds a new form of expression in the exchange between solos and choir, and probably also the very popular *Stabat Mater* for two solo voices and strings and the *Salve Regina* in C minor for soprano and strings. All are outstanding examples of the sentimental style in Catholic sacred music. At the end of 1735 Pergolesi was forced by serious illness (probably bone tuberculosis) to retire.

Bibliography: *Opera omnia,* ed. F. CAFFARELLI, 5 v. (Rome 1939–42), performing edition. G. RADICIOTTI, *G. B. Pergolesi* (Rome 1910; 2d ed. Milan 1935). A. DELLA CORTE, *Pergolesi* (Turin 1936). W. KAHL, ''Pergolesi und sein Stabat Mater,'' *Kirchenmusikalisches Jahrbuch* 35 (1951) 84–97. H. HUCKE, *Die Musik in Geschichte und Gegenwart,* ed. F. BLUME (Kassel-Basel 1949–) 10:1048–64. P. H. LANG, *Music in Western Civilization* (New York 1941). P. M. YOUNG, *The Choral Tradition* (New York 1962). H. E. BECKWITH, ''Giovanni Battista Pergolesi and the Chamber Cantata'' (Ph.D. diss. University of Maryland, 1983). F. DEGRADA, ed., *Studi Pergolesiani: Prolusione el Convegna ''Lo stato attuale degli studi su Pergolesi e il suo tempo'' (Jesi, 18–19 novembre 1983)* 2 v. (Florence 1986). H. HUCKE and M. E. PAYMER, *The New Grove Dictionary of Music and Musicians* ed. S. SADIE (New York 1980) 14:394–400. D. E. MONSON, ''*Adriano in Siria,*'' *International Dictionary of Opera* 2 v., ed. C. S. LARUE (Detroit 1993); ''*La Serva Padrona,*'' *ibid.* M. E. PAYMER, ''The Instrumental Music Attributed to Giovanni Battista Pergolesi: A Study in Authenticity'' (Ph.D. diss. City University of New York, 1977). D. M. RANDEL, ed., *The Harvard Biographical Dictionary of Music* (Cambridge 1996). N. SLONIMSKY, ed. *Baker's Biographical Dictionary of Musicians* (8th ed. New York 1992).

[H. HUCKE]

PERICHORESIS, CHRISTOLOGICAL

The mutual indwelling of the divine and human natures in Jesus Christ. Trinitarian perichoresis (CIRCUMINCESSION) is the sacred indwelling of the three Persons in one sole God. The second is the compenetration of Divine Persons in one NATURE; the first, the compenetration of the human nature in Christ by the divine in the one Person of the LOGOS. Trinitarian perichoresis affirms the CONSUBSTANTIALITY of the Divine Persons against ARIANISM and the distinction of Persons against SABELLIANISM. Christological perichoresis proclaims (*a*) one sole PERSON in Christ against NESTORIANISM'S concept of two persons morally united and (*b*) two distinct natures against MONOPHYSITISM's confusion of the elements of Christ in one nature.

Only the Second Person possesses human nature, for only the WORD was made man and lived among men. Only He can say, ''This is my body.'' Both natures subsist mutually in each other without any modification of the Logos, but with, in predication, reciprocal interchange of attributes because of the oneness of Person. Thus the HYPOSTATIC UNION is the basis for the perichoresis that is reflected in this interchange or COMMUNICATION OF IDIOMS.

Incarnational perichoresis must be studied in its concrete existential richness, not merely in abstractive repetition of the great (and eternally true) Chalcedonian formula: two natures, one Person, unconfused, undivided, the difference of nature preserved in one SUBSISTENCE. The unifying power is from the Logos alone: the theologian must explain the concrete human subject, totally sanctified by the divine, existing with all the perfection of mind, will, and heart, profoundly conscious of itself, possessing tremendous initiative in the work of Redemption. Diverse from the Logos, it can be studied only as united to the Logos, only diversity explaining the unity, and unity giving insight into the diversity (Rahner).

Christ's human nature is God's presence among men. It is the divine plan that men are to find in Jesus Christ. Only in His human face can they see God, only in His word hear God, only in His GRACE become close to God. For this reason the Son of God took on visible human form. Even in His humanity He is the Son of God. Therefore Christ is God in a human way, and man in a divine way. As man He acts out His divine life in and according to His human existence. Everything He does as man is an act of God the SON, a divine act in a human form, His human love the human embodiment of the redeeming love of God, His humanity concretely intended by God as fulfillment of the promise of SALVATION. Because the human deeds are divine deeds, personal acts of the Son of God, divine acts in human form, they bring salvation, cause grace (Schillebeeckx).

In this light of the Incarnational perichoresis one studies the IMPECCABILITY OF CHRIST, for His humanity is substantially sanctified by uncreated holiness, His human nature and existence actuated by the divine Logos. In this light, also, the theologian studies the knotty problems of the one or two existences in Christ, of the human consciousness of the Savior and His ''psychological'' personality. Devoutly men commit themselves to Christ in whom alone they encounter God, for He is the primordial sacrament, the divine invitation and human response. In His Eucharistic presence both Trinitarian and Incarnational perichoresis promise the eternal encounter.

Giovanni Battista Pergolesi.

See Also: HYPOSTASIS; INCARNATION; JESUS CHRIST, III (SPECIAL QUESTIONS); PERSON, DIVINE; THEANDRIC ACTS OF CHRIST.

Bibliography: F. MALMBERG, *Über den Gottmensche (Quaestiones disputatae* 9; Basel 1960). E. H. SCHILLEBEECKX, *Christ: The Sacrament of the Encounter with God,* tr. P. BARRETT (New York 1963). K. RAHNER, *Theological Investigations,* v. 1, tr. C. ERNST (Baltimore 1961). I. SOLANO, *Sacrae theologiae summa* (Madrid 1962) 3:1.46. L. KÖSTERS, *The Believer's Christ,* tr. J. W. GRUNDNER (St. Louis 1939).

[E. G. KAISER]

PERICOPES

A Greek word meaning excerpt, pericope was used in early Christian times to designate any passage in Holy Scripture [Justin Martyr, *Dialogus cum Tryphone* 65.3 (*Patrologia Graeca*, ed. J. P. Migne, 6:625); Clement of Alexandria, *Stromata* 7.14 (*Patrologia Graeca* 9:517)]. Since the 16th century it has become a technical term for a Biblical passage read according to a determined order in the liturgy. This article treats the practice of reading Scripture in the liturgy, the meaning of terms used for such readings, the historical evolution of the Service of the Word, and a description of the various pericopal systems.

Biblical Reading in Liturgy

Sacred Scripture, which "is of the greatest importance in the celebration of the liturgy" (*Constitution on the Sacred Liturgy* 24), can be read in a more or less continuous fashion (*lectio continua*) or in passages that are chosen for their appropriateness for the liturgical day, season, or special objective. Prescinding from the mosaic type of lesson (found in certain liturgies, e.g., Gallican and Spanish), made up of verses from different Biblical books or chapters of the same book, and from the pericopes constructed out of Gospel-harmonies, generally the text is altered only by introductory and concluding formulas, by individual words that help establish the context, and occasionally by the omission of individual verses. The liturgical use of Scripture is a very weighty witness to the canon of the Bible.

The most important place for the reading of Scripture in all liturgies from the earliest days of the Church has been the Mass. "The liturgy of the Word and the Eucharist are so closely connected with each other that they form but one single act of worship" (*Constitution on the Sacred Liturgy* 56). The readings of the Service of the Word share the memorial character of the Mass and indeed specify it in the course of the year (*ibid.* 102–104, 109). The Liturgy of the Hours also has Biblical pericopes in Matins and brief passages called chapters or short readings in the other hours. Pericopes are provided for other sacramental rites, e.g., Baptism, Matrimony, and the Anointing of the Sick.

Meaning of Terms

When manuscripts of the Bible were used for the liturgical readings, the beginning and end of the passage to be read were indicated by means of signs (a cross) or words (e.g., *lege, finit*) and a liturgical title usually written in the margin (Klauser numbers 11 manuscripts from the 7th to 14th centuries with Roman marginal notes).

Capitulare. In time manuscripts with marginal notes were replaced by lists arranged according to the calendar and containing the necessary details for the Gospels (Klauser notes 429 such lists from the 8th to 15th centuries), less frequently for both Epistles and Gospels (Klauser has 179 for the same period), and very seldom for only the Epistles (Klauser has only seven; these and the following figures represent only Roman manuscripts). Such lists stand either at the front or at the end of manuscripts. The most frequent name for a Gospel list, at least since the 8th century, was *Capitulare* (also *Breviarius*) *Evangeliorum;* it was so called precisely because it gave the chapter (*capitulum*) and verse numbers for the selections to be read. Numerous names were used for the other lists.

Comes. Books containing the full text of the pericopes arranged according to the calendar began to appear, at the latest, in the 5th century. For the period from the 8th to the 17th centuries, Klauser numbers 397 providing only the Gospel text, 147 only the Epistles, and 113 both readings one behind the other. Ancient names for this type of book were many. Modern liturgical science distinguishes between Evangelary, Epistolary (often bound together with Evangelaries), and Full-Lectionary. An Epistolary, Full-Lectionary, or a list (even a Homiliary) was frequently called *Comes* (companion) or *Liber Comitis.* This is not to be confused with the Mozarabic name for the Full-Lectionary, *Liber Commicus* (*comma* meaning excerpt).

It is often said that Lectionaries appeared later than the marginal notes and the lists. However, both manuscript and literary witnesses to Lectionaries are almost older than those for the lists and marginal notes. Lectionaries were cheaper, more handy, and for areas using cento pericopes, indispensable. The *Admonitio Synodalis* (J. D. Mansi, *Sacrorum Conciliorum nova et amplissima collectio* 14:841), which stems probably from Caesarius of Arles (d. 542), required that every priest possess a plenary Missal, Lectionary, Antiphonary, and Homiliary. Musaeus of Marseilles (d. 461) and Claudianus Mamertus of Vienne (d. *c.* 474) are known to have compiled Lectionaries. See Gennadius, *De viris inlustribus* 80 (ed. E. C. Richardson, *Texte und Untersuchungen zur Geschichte der altchristlichen Literatur* 14.1:88); Sidonius Apollinaris, *Epist.* 4.11 (*Monumenta Germaniae Historica: Auctores antiquissimi* 8:63).

Christian Reading Service and Synagogal Worship. There is a formal parallelism between the Service of the Word, especially of the Roman Mass and synagogal worship: two readings separated by a psalm (sung responsorially in early times), intercessory prayers (to be reintroduced according to par. 53 of the *Constitution on the Sacred Liturgy*), explanation of Scripture, and a blessing. The NT itself already attests to the reading to the people of NT writings not only in those communities to which they were addressed (1 Thes 5.27; Ap 1.3, 11; 2.1, 8, 12, 18; 3.1, 7, 14; 22.18), but also in others (Col 4.16). First of all, all the texts of the NT were composed, transcribed, and preserved precisely for public reading.

Despite the absence of testimony, one must admit that the OT was read in the liturgy, whether from whole books, florilegia, or *testimonia.* In favor of this, one can adduce the knowledge of the OT presupposed in the NT (1 Thes, 2 Thes, Phil, Col, 2 Tm, and Ti are, however, without explicit Scripture citations; there is only one in 1 Tm, and three in Eph). But there is no proof that the OT was read according to the order of the synagogue, i.e., the entire Pentateuch continuously (in a cycle of one or three years, known since the 3d century A.D. as the Babylonian or older Palestinian usage) and, in a secondary position, only short selections from other books such as readings from the "Prophets." Moreover, not only Psalms, but also other spiritual songs were sung (Eph 5.19; Col 3.16; cf. Ap 5.9; 14.3). A continuous reading of the Pentateuch (consider Lv, Nm, and Dt) seems unthinkable in face of the Christian teaching on the Law, especially the teaching of Paul. The chief emphasis was precisely on the Prophets. New Testament quotations from and allusions to the prophetic books are twice as numerous as references to the Pentateuch. The ratio between the Pentateuch and the prophetic books in the Jewish sense is approximately one to four. The Psalter is either quoted or alluded to as often as the first four books of Moses together; the book of Daniel (never read in the synagogue) as often as Deuteronomy, but a little less frequently than Exodus; and Job (another book never read in the synagogue) not much less frequently than Numbers.

The *Apostolic Constitutions* (Syria, *c.* 380) testifies that: "After the reading of the Law and the Prophets, of our Epistles and the Acts, as well as the Gospels, the bishop greets the assembly" (8.5.11; F. X. Funk, ed., *Didascalia et constitutiones apostolorum* 1:477). From this statement authors usually conclude that there were four pericopes (some speak of five or three). In another obscure place, the Constitutions seem to require at least four (six or eight) readings from the OT before the two (or three) from the NT (2.27.5–7; *Didascalia et constitutiones apostolorum* 1:161).

The thesis that the ancient Church originally had two pericopes from the OT (as the synagogue) followed by two from the NT is usually based on the Apostolic Constitutions (8.5.11; *Didascalia et constitutiones apostolorum* 1:477). However, the pericope system found in the Constitutions is to be taken as typical only for the Syrian Church, which was ecumenical-minded toward the synagogue (Kunze, "Die Lesungen," 135–138). This is supported by the actual state of the Liturgies: only the East Syrian Liturgy has two readings from the OT alongside the two from the NT. The West Syrian Liturgy as a rule adds a pericope from the Sapiential books. Historically, many liturgical rites have one pericope from the OT before the two from the NT, namely, the Armenian, the Ambrosian (only in the high Mass; however, on some occasions the first lesson is also from the NT, on others there are only two readings, one of which may be from the OT), the Mozarabic (always three readings, but the first is not always from the OT nor the second always from the NT). There are no OT lessons in the Byzantine (two lessons), Coptic and Ethiopian (all four readings are from the NT, but often the first is hagiographical). The Roman Missal of 1570 had only two readings; the first is taken from the OT on Lenten ferias, on 110 saints' feasts (on many of which the same pericope is repeated), in 11 votive Masses, and in 30 Masses *pro aliquibus locis.* In the 1969 reform of the Roman Missal, a three-reading (one OT, one Epistle, one Gospel) framework was adopted.

The Georgian Lectionary from Jerusalem of the 5th through the 8th centuries [ed. M. Tarchnischvili, *Corpus scriptorum Christianorum orientalium* (Louvain 1959) 188–89, 204–05; cf. *idem, Muséon* 73 (1960) 261–96] supplies for the numerous simple feasts only two pericopes, both from the NT; three, or less frequently four, readings are provided for Sundays and greater feasts, and according to the character of the feast the first or the first two are often taken from the OT (rarely from the historical books, however). On the few days having more than four readings (as many as nine), the number of pericopes from the NT varies from two to seven; the number from the OT, from one to six. The Armenian-Palestinian Lectionary of the 5th century [ed. C. Conybeare, *Rituale Armenorum* (Oxford 1905) 518–27; A. Renoux, *Muséon* 75 (1961) 361–85; 76 (1962) 385–98] and the Syro-Palestinian Lectionary of the 9th century [ed. A. Smith-Lewis (London 1897; supplement London 1907)] usually have two pericopes from the NT. A preliminary reading on saints' feasts is taken from the OT for saints of the OT, otherwise from the NT or hagiographies.

In general scholars have claimed that originally the Byzantine Liturgy had three pericopes, the first of which was taken from the OT. The examples brought forward [Chrysostom, *Homil. in Acta* 19.5, 29.3 (*Patrologia Graeca* 60:156, 218); *Homil. in 2 Thes.* 3.4 (*Patrologia Graeca* 62:486); *Homil. in Hebr.* 8.4 (*Patrologia Graeca* 63:75); Maximus Confessor, *Mystag.* 23 (*Patrologia Graeca*91:700)], insofar as they deal with the Mass, as in Maximus, prove only that there were pericopes from the OT (only the first of two?). The three pericopes spoken of by Basil of Caesarea (Is, Acts, Mt: *Homil.* 13.1 *de bapt.; Patrologia Graeca* 31:425) belong to a catechetical service. The one place that unequivocally attests to three lessons in the Mass, with the first from the Prophets, is the biography of Bp. Theodore of Anastasiopolis in Galatia, who died in 613 (16; *Acta Sacntorum* 3:36).

Of the ancient liturgy of Milan, Ambrose has this to say: "First the Prophets are read, then the Apostle, and finally the Gospel" (*In ps.* 118.17.10; *Corpus scriptorum ecclesiasticorum latinorum* 152:382.17). The Milanese Sacramentary of Bergamo from the 9th century (ed. A. Paredi, Bergamo 1962) contains three pericopes (the first from the OT outside paschal time) for a few Sundays and feast days; otherwise there are only two, the first being from the OT only in Lent and on a few other days.

According to Augustine's homilies, three pericopes (the first from the OT) were read on a few major feast-days, otherwise only two were read [*Sermo* 13.4.4, 112.1.1, 165.1, 176.1.1, 180.1 (*Patrologia Latina*, ed. J. P. Migne, 38:197, 643, 841, 950, 972); the first was sometimes taken from the OT: *Sermo* 45.1, 48.1, 2, 289.3 (*Patrologia Latina* 38:262, 319, 1309)]. The genuine homilies of Maximus of Turin (*Corpus Christianorum. Series latina* 23) and Peter Chrysologus [A. Olivar, *Los sermones de S. Pedro Crisólogo* (Montserrat 1962)] show that both pericopes were taken from the NT.

For Gaul, the writings of Gregory of Tours [*Hist. Franc.* 4.1.6 (*Monumenta Germaniae Historica: Scriptores rerum Merovingicarum* 1.1:149–50); *Mirac. S. Martini* 1.5 (*Patrologia Latina* 71:918)] and Pseudo-Germain [*Exposit. ant. lit. gall.;* ed. J. Quasten (Münster 1934) 13; cf. *Patrologica Latina* 72:90] give evidence of a prophetic pericope from the OT before the two from the NT (cf. Caesarius of Arles, *Sermo* 73.2; *Corpus Chistianorum. Series latina* 103:307). Among the old Gallican Lectionaries, that of Weissenburg, from the 5th through the 6th centuries, contains nine Mass formularies with two pericopes and ten with three (in paschal time, even the first is from the NT). That of Luxeuil, from *c.* 700, has 39 formularies with three pericopes, and 13 for lesser feasts with two readings (from the NT). The Bobbio Missal from *c.* 700 has 12 formularies with three pericopes and 51 with two (only six times is the first pericope taken from the OT). The Lectionary of Schlettstadt contains only the pericopes from the OT.

It is almost universally believed that the ancient Roman Mass had three pericopes. A statement of Tertullian, often cited in support of this view, ''the Roman Church mixes (*miscet*) the Law and the Prophets with the evangelical and apostolic writings and thus nourishes the faith'' (*Lib. de praescr.* 36.5; *Corpus Christianorum. Series latina* 1:217), can be said equally of the Roman Missal, which as a rule has only two pericopes (the first sometimes from the OT). Seldom are three called for (the Wednesday of Embertides, of the 4th week of Lent, and of Holy Week and Good Friday).

In addition, Roman sources of the 7th through the 9th centuries have three pericopes for Christmas and some other days. But when the Comes of Würzburg provides four Epistles for other occasions, a choice is intended. This is proved by the practice observed in later Lectionaries: if they do not introduce new readings, they choose two of the four readings offered by the older books.

That the Roman Mass had as a rule only two pericopes, at least in the 6th century, is shown by a notice in the Liber pontificalis about Celestine I. He is supposed to have introduced the singing of Psalms, whereas before ''only the Epistle of blessed Paul and the Gospel were read at Mass'' (*Liber pontificalis*, ed. L. Duchesne, 1:88). In the homilies of Leo I and Gregory I there is not a trace of a three-pericope system.

One cannot invoke in favor of a three-pericope system the fact that the fragments of the 10th-century Missal of Zurich-Peterlingen-Lucerne (like some other Sacramentaries) occasionally have before the Secret three Orations, the first two of which were to be sung before the Epistles. In these fragments the first two Orations stand together before the first reading, and they are found also on days of lesser rank with only two pericopes; on the other hand, there are a few days with three pericopes that have only one Oration provided.

Lectio Continua. Arguments are often given in support of the thesis that originally the Bible was read in a continuous fashion at Mass. However, they do not hold up under examination. A dependence on the continuous reading of the synagogue is very improbable. As regards the formula *Sequentia sancti Evangelii,* it first appeared about the 9th century when there was certainly no continuous reading (Roman Ordinal 5.35; M. Andrieu, *Les 'Ordines Romani' du haut moyen-âge*, 2:216); in early manuscripts, in other rites such as the Milanese and Mozarabic, and in the Breviary, the word *Sequentia* is lacking. Besides, it means nothing more than ''The following passage is from the Gospel according to . . .'' Nor are the references in Justin (1 *Apol.* 67, J. Quasten, ed., *Monumenta eucharista et liturgica vetustissima* 19: ''as long as there is time''), Pseudo-Hippolytus, and Basil [cc. 37 and 97; W. Riedel, *Die Kirchenrechtsquellen des Patriarchats Alexandrien* (Leipzig 1900) 224, 273: the readings are to continue until all the faithful have assembled] necessarily to be understood as a continuous reading of the Bible.

Patristic homilies on whole books of the Bible, insofar as they were truly homilies preached at Mass and not at purely catechumenal services, offer a sound argument. Augustine preached his 35 homilies on Jn 1.1–12.50 in the year 413, but he may not have preached them at Mass. During this period, however, not only was there a long interruption from Monday of Holy Week until the 5th Saturday after Pentecost because of paschal time, but also Augustine suspended his series of Johannine homilies again and again on other days, even Sundays. Other evidence in Augustine of a continuous reading is rare and concerns almost always short passages. The same holds for Peter Chrysologus. On the other hand there is no evidence at all of such a continuous reading at Mass in the homilies of Ambrose, Maximus of Turin, Leo I, or Gregory I.

Although according to Augustine the reading of certain Biblical books was obligatory during paschal time [*In epist. Ioh. prolog; Sermo* 227.1; 231.1; 315.1; *In evang. Ioh.* 6.18 (*Patrologia Latina* 35:1977; 38:1100, 1104, 1426; *Corpus Christianorum. Series latina* 36:62.1)], he repeatedly alludes to the freedom used in choosing pericopes, often occasioned by rather banal circumstances [*Sermo* 93.1.1; 302.1; 362.1 (*Patrologia Latina* 38:573, 1385; 39:1611)]. Peter Chrysologus also mentions the fact that pastoral necessity frequently caused him to change the pericopes (*Sermo* 114, 120; *Patrologia Latina* 52:512, 529).

The continuous reading obtaining in some current liturgies is a late phenomenon influenced in part by the monastic lectio continua. That for ferias in the Byzantine Liturgy goes back only to the 9th century and is not always carried out strictly. The Epistles of the Roman Missal for the post-Pentecostal Sundays are selected according to the Biblical order; for 18 of these Sundays they hark back to the 41 pericopes in the Würzburg list that are arranged one after the other, following the order of the Pauline Epistles, but without any explicit liturgical determination. This same Würzburg list was the source of many different arrangements in later Lectionaries. The only time of the year in which the continuity of Epistle pericopes is almost complete in the Roman Missal (and Würzburg list) is the season after Epiphany (1st–4th Sundays, Rom 12.1–21, 13.8–10).

In conclusion, it is certain that at the very beginning there was a continuous reading of the NT, at least of the Pauline Epistles; it is equally certain the pericopes from the OT were not read according to strict synagogue order. Freedom to choose pericopes as well as whole books declined sharply as the temporal and sanctoral cycles were formed. A hard-and-fast system of continuous or semicontinuous readings was a secondary phenomenon.

Sundays After Pentecost. The greatest differences—prescinding from the sanctoral cycle—among the various witnesses to the Roman pericope system are found in the Sundays after Pentecost. The Würzburg Epistle list did not yet have fixed pericopes for these Sundays, and its Gospel list was incomplete. Other reasons for differences were the varying ways of designating the Sundays, either as grouped around principal sanctoral feasts (Peter and Paul, Lawrence, etc.) or as numbered after Pentecost, which changed date from year to year; the existence of an octave day for Pentecost in some sources; and variations in the date of the summer and fall Embertides and in the number of Advent Sundays (four or five).

Non-Roman Latin. Non-Roman Latin rites are too numerous to attempt here an adequate description of the evolution of their pericopal systems. Let it suffice to indicate the principal sources for each area.

Gaul. In his *Lectionnaire de Luxeuil* (Rome 1944), P. Salmon constructed pericope tables from 12 very diverse (and mostly fragmentary) sources from the 5th to the 8th centuries: Gamber 250, 255, 258, 260 c and d, 265, 266, 220, 240, 369 b; the notes in the Kilian-Gospel Book from Würzburg [P. Salmon, *Revue Bénédictine* 61 (1951) 38–53, 62 (1952) 294–96]; and the Freising manuscript of the Pauline Epistles (Clm 6229).

Northern Italy except Milan. Besides the above-mentioned Bobbio manuscripts (Gamber 220, 240), Cod. Vat. Regin, lat. 9 (Gamber 242) is important for the Epistles. Godu has published tables from the notes in the more or less related Cod. Rehd., Foroj., Clm 6224, and Ambros. C 39. The last four have also been described by Gamber [*Münchener theologische Zeitschrift* 13 (1962) 181–201] along with the notes from the Gospel Books, Cod. Vercell. A and Verona VII, the Evangelaries from Constance (Gamber 261) and Ambros. 28 (Gamber 543), and the Lindisfarne list (Gamber 405, 406).

Milan. The pericopes of the Ambrosian Missal (ed. *typica* 1902) are based on the Lectionary in the Sacramentary of Biasca of the 9th and 10th centuries (Gamber 515). The 9th-century Sacramentary of Bergamo (Gamber 505), except for later supplements, lacks the first reading; this reading is found in a 12th-century manuscript (Gamber 548). The Evangelary of Busto Arsizio (Gamber 541, 542) contains on older Gospel list. For pre-Carolingian pericopes in a few fragments of Sacramentaries, see Gamber 501, 502, 540.

Elsewhere in Italy. Sources for the Pauline pericopes are the list and notes in the NT of Bp. Victor of Capua (d. 554), Gamber 401; sources of importance for the Gospels are the lists of the Lindisfarne Gospel Book (Gamber 405, 406) and the notes in the Burchard Gospel Books (Roman admixture, Gamber 407). For Benevento and the rest of southern Italy, special pericopes have been preserved in a palimpsest of the 10th century (Gamber 434) and in some otherwise Roman sources of the 10th to the 12th centuries (Gamber 430–432, 440, 442, 455, 1411, 1412).

Spain. Beissel constructed an incomplete list of gospels from the *Missale Mixtum* of 1500 (*Patrologia Latina* 85:109–1036) and indicated parallels in the Silos Lectionary of the 11th century (Gamber 360). The latter was one of the sources (others in Gambar 362–365) of the *Liber Commicus Mozarabicus* (Madrid 1950–55), edited by J. Perez de Urbel and A. Gonzáles. A large fragment from the 9th century (Gamber 361) was published in 1956, with tables comparing it with the above-mentioned Lectionaries and the somewhat older notes in Biblical manuscripts of the 8th to the 10th centuries (Gamber 369).

Bibliography: A. G. MARTIMORT et al., *The Liturgy and the Word of God* (Collegeville 1959). O. CULLMANN, *Early Christian Worship,* tr. A. S. TODD and J. B. TORRANCE (Studies in Biblical Theology 10; Chicago 1953). K. DICK, ''Einleitungsund Schlussformeln in der Perikopenlesung der römischen Messe,'' *Archiv für Musikwissenschaft* 4.1 (1955) 73–80. H. JEDIN, ''Das Konzil von Trient und die Reform des römischen Messbuches,'' *Liturgisches Leben* 6 (1939) 30–660. K. GAMBER, *Codices liturgici latini antiquiores* (Spicilegium friburgense subsidia 1; Fribourg 1963). G. KUNZE, *Die gottesdienstliche Schriftlesung,* v.1, *Stand und Aufgabe der Perikopenforschung* (Göttingen 1947); ''Die Lesungen,'' *Leiturgia: Handbuch des evangelischen Gottesdienstes,* ed. K. F. MÜLLER and W. BLANKENBURG, (Kassel 1954–) 2:87–187. A. BAUMSTARK, *Comparative Liturgy,* rev. B. BOTTE, tr. F. L. CROSS (Westminster, Md. 1958) 111–29, 201–35. S. BEISSEL, *Entstehung der Perikopen des römischen Messbuches* (*Stimmen der Zeit* Ergänzungsband 24.96; 1907). P. GLAUE, *Die Vorlesung heiliger Schriften im Gottesdienste,* v.1, *Bis zur Entstehung der altkatholischen Kirche* (Berlin 1907). W. BAUER, *Der Wortgottesdienst der ältesten Christen* (Tübingen 1930). G. GODU, *Dictionnaire d'archéologie chrétienne et de liturgie,* ed. F. CABROL, H. LECLERCQ, and H. I. MARROU, 15 v. (Paris 1907–53) 5.1:245–344, 852–923. W. CASPARI, J. J. HERZOG and A. HAUCK, eds., *Realencyklopädie für protestantische Theologie,* 24 v. (3d ed. Leipzig 1896–1913) 15:131–59. K. DIENST, *Die Religion in Geschichte und Gegenwart,* 7 v. (3d ed. Tübingen 1957–65) 5:220–24. G. G. WILLIS, *St. Augustine's Lectionary* (London 1962). J. A. JUNGMANN, *Missarum sollemnia* (4th ed. Freiburg 1962) 1:501–83. E. C. RANKE, *Das kirchliche Pericopensystem aus den ältesten Urkunden der römischen Liturgie dargelegt und erläutert* (Berlin 1847). W. H. FRERE, *Studies in Early Roman Liturgy,* 3 v. (Oxford 1930–35) v.2, 3. T. KLAUSER, *Das römische Capitulare Evangeliorum* (Münster 1935). A. WILMART, ''Le Lectionnaire d'Alcuin,'' *Ephemerides theologicae Lovaninses* 51 (1937) 136–97. R. J. HESBERT, ''Les Séries d'évangiles des dimanches après la Pentecôte,'' *Maison-Dieu* 46 (1956) 35–39. A. CHAVASSE, ''Les Plus anciens types du lectionnaire et de l'antiphonaire romains de la messe,'' *Revue Bénédictine* 62 (1952) 3–94, cited in the text as Chavasse; ''La Formation de l'*Antiphonale Missarum,*'' *Bulletin du Comité des Études* 32 (1961) 29–41. T. MAERTENS, ''L'Avent,'' *Mélanges de science religieuse* 18 (1961) 47–110. E. STOMMEL, ''Messperikopen,'' *Trierer theologische Zeitschrift* 61 (1952) 205–13. H. SCHÜRMANN, ''Eine dreijährige Perikopenordnung für Sonn- und Festtage,'' *Liturgisches Jahrbuch* 2 (1952) 58–72. H. KAHLEFELD, ''Ordo lectionum,'' *ibid.* 13 (1963) 133–39. G. FRÉNAUD, ''Les Péricopes évangéliques et fériales,'' *ibid.* 4 (1954) 210–29. P. JOUNEL, ''Pour une réforme des lectures du missel,'' *Maison-Dieu* 66 (1961) 36–69. O. STEVENS, ''Gedanken zur Perikopenverteilung,'' *Liturgisches Jahrbuch* 13 (1963) 140–50. R. W. PFAFF, ed. *The Liturgical Books of Anglo-Saxon England* (Kalamazoo, Mich. 1995). L. LARSON-MILLER, *Medieval Liturgy: A Book of Essays* (New York 1997). E. PALAZZO, *A History of Liturgical Books from the Beginning to the Thirteenth Century* (Collegeville, Minn. 1998).

[E. J. LENGELING/EDS.]

PÉRIN, HENRI CHARLES XAVIER

Principal representative of Catholic social thought in 19th-century Belgium; b. Mons, Aug. 29, 1815; d. Ghlin, near Mons, April 4, 1905. An attorney, he was named to the faculty of law at Louvain in 1844 and the next year succeeded Charles de Coux as professor of political economy. He taught for 35 years, quitting in 1881 only when a warning issued by Leo XIII to placate Conflicting Catholics prejudiced his position. Accused of too strongly defending civic freedoms, Périn withdrew to his home at Ghlin and completed in the years that followed many of his major works. He was a vigorous critic of the 19th-century economic liberalism that held that the self-regulating mechanism of the market provided justice for all. He did not share, however, the confidence of other Catholic social critics in the role of the state as the provider of welfare. He supported free workingmen's associations as well as those of management. He was one of the organizers of the congresses of Malines of 1863, 1864, and 1867. His works include: *Les économistes, les socialistes, et le christianisme* (1849), *Le socialisme chrétien* (1879), and *Économie politique d'après ''Rerum Novarum,''* (1891).

Bibliography: P. MICHOTTE, *Études sur les théories economiques qui dominèrent en Belgique de 1830 à 1886* (Louvain 1904). R. KOTHEN, *La pensée et l'action sociales des catholiques 1789–1944* (Louvain 1945)

[E. T. GARGAN]

PERJURY

In a broad sense perjury is an unlawful oath, one lacking a condition required for a licit oath, viz, truth, prudence, or justice. In a strict sense, perjury is a false statement supported by an oath. Usually perjury refers only to declaratory OATHS, but in some European law systems the willful violation of a promissory oath is treated as perjury. Theologians in general say that if such an oath was sincere when uttered, a violation of the promise would be sinful—the gravity depending on the promise—but would not be perjury.

A lying, or perjured, oath is always a mortal sin because it involves contempt for God and disrespect for His attributes. The perjurer asks God to be a witness to a lie or supposes that God can be deceived. Perjury is one of the most serious offenses against the virtue of religion; it contains the malice of contempt for God. Hence only an imperfection in the act can excuse a perjurer from grave sin, for example, if he lacked sufficient reflection on, or full consent to, the oath or its falsity.

Imprudent or useless oaths usually are venial sins, similar to profane use of the holy names. But perjury in a strict sense is always a grave sin, as is shown in the condemnation of the contrary opinion: ''To call God to witness to a small lie is not a great irreverence because of which God would wish to or could condemn a man'' (H.

Denzinger, *Enchiridion symbolorum,* ed. A. Schönmetzer [32d ed. Freiburg 1963] 2124). Perjury in a wide sense, where required prudence is lacking, would not normally be a grave sin if it does not violate justice directly, because no serious irreverence is shown to God thereby. But such an oath could be gravely sinful because of scandal. If the virtue of justice is violated, perjury in the broad sense is considered a mortal sin *ex genere suo,* i.e., one that admits of light matter.

It is not lawful for a private person to seek or receive an oath from one who he is sure will commit perjury. With sufficient reason, however, one may seek and receive an oath without knowing whether the person swearing will do so truly or not.

Formal cooperation in an act of perjury is never lawful because it would make the cooperator share the guilt. Hence he who by command, counsel, promise, etc., induces another to swear falsely is guilty as the principal or as an accessory to the crime. Material cooperation is permissible if there is sufficient reason for it. For example, a public official may demand an oath required by law from one who he knows will swear falsely. In such a case, the public good demands that the oath be administered, even though for this person it is an occasion of perjury. The lawgiver, however, should not lightly multiply demands for sworn statements; otherwise the oath can become a mere formality that is thus deprived of probative value, and the temptation to perjury is thereby increased.

Bibliography: THOMAS AQUINAS, *Summa theologiae,* 2a2ae, 89. N. JUNG, *Dictionnaire de théologie catholique,* ed. A. VACANT et al., 15 v. (Paris 1903–50; Tables générales 1951–) 14.22:1939–55.

[M. HERRON]

PERNET, ÉTIENNE CLAUDE

Religious founder; b. Vellexon (Haute Saône), France, July 23, 1824; d. Paris, April 3, 1899. During his studies in the major seminary at Besançon scruples about his worthiness caused him to leave the institution (1848) contrary to the advice of his superiors. In 1850 he joined the recently founded ASSUMPTIONISTS, whose founder Emmanuel d' ALZON persuaded him to proceed to ordination (1858). Pernet taught at the Assumption college in Nîmes (1849–52, 1860–63). Together with Marie Fage, he founded the LITTLE SISTERS OF THE ASSUMPTION (1865). He also organized three societies of laymen and laywomen to collaborate with his congregation and to engage in charitable and other apostolic works. During the Franco-Prussian War he served as a military chaplain. The decree introducing his cause for beatification was issued in 1931 and the preparatory congregation concerning his virtues met in 1956.

Étienne Claude Pernet.

Bibliography: *Acta Apostolicae Sedis* (1931) 341–344.

[I. M. THIERRY]

PÉROTIN

The most gifted composer of the Notre Dame school, places and dates of birth and death unknown. Little is known of Pérotin's life; the assertion that he was court composer to the French kings has been challenged, and scholars set his death year as early as 1200 and as late as 1230: Called *optimus discantor* (most excellent composer of discant), he was probably the first composer to write in as many as four parts, and he developed the use of unifying devices such as imitation, exchanged voices (*Stimmtausch*), and melodic variation, which he inherited from earlier generations and which have been standard contrapuntal practice ever since. Like J. S. BACH and MOZART after him, he blended diverse national influences into well-organized, large-scale masterpieces that were the high points of his period.

A Pérotin organum consisted of a liturgical chant melody and text that formed the tenor of the polyphonic section but with its rhythm altered. In approximately the same vocal range he added one, two, or three voices, in one of six rhythmic patterns known as *modi.* Although these patterns were varied at irregular intervals by different devices, the variations never obscured the patterns. The added voices crossed and recrossed one another in clear-cut phrases that usually began and ended on perfect consonances, touching on unisons midway. But the particular color of 12th-century polyphony was conveyed by occasional sharp dissonances on the weak beats, and sometimes even on the strong beats. The syllabic parts of the tenor were extended beneath the added voices into very long notes, sometimes lasting 40 measures and sounding more like a series of drones at different levels than like a melody. This liturgical melody, however, was known to the hearers; an impression of two mental worlds could be conveyed. The melismatic sections of the chant tenor were also reshaped rhythmically into one of the *modi,* often a slower *modus* than that of the added voices; these sections were called *clausulae.* Typical unifying devices are the fragments of imitation in measures three and four and the varied repetition of whole phrases as in measures one and two, seven and eight. There is also a typical Pérotin coda on a prolonged tenor note, with the change to iambic rhythm and descending scale in the added parts.

Pérotin set also sacred and perhaps secular Latin verse in the *conductus* style. This had no liturgical tenor, and the voices, all in the same *modus,* were sometimes set syllabically throughout and sometimes with melismatic sections on a single syllable, called *caudae.* Pérotin's works have survived, along with others of his school, in four ''Notre Dame Manuscripts.'' The pitches in these MSS have been deciphered, but the rhythm problems have not been fully solved. LÉONIN's *Magnus liber organi,* which was partially rewritten by Pérotin, has not yet been found.

Bibliography: H. HUSMANN, *Die Drei- und vierstimmigen Notre-Dame-Organa* (Leipzig 1940) contains Pérotin music in modern notation; ''The Origin and Destination of the *Magnus liber organi,*'' tr. G. REANEY, *Musical Quarterly* 49 (1963) 311–330; ''The Enlargement of the *Magnus liber organi* and the Paris Churches, St. Germaine l'Auxerrois and Ste. Geneviève-du-Mont,'' tr. A. P. BRINER, *Journal of the American Musicological Society* 16 (1963) 176–203. H. TISCHLER, *The Motet in Thirteenth-Century France* (Doctoral diss. unpub. Yale U. 1942) 1:42–54, lists attributions in Middle Ages and in modern research; *The Earliest Motels, Corpus mensurabilis musicae,* ed. American Institute of Musicology, v.1– (Rome 1947–), v.30 (in press). *New Oxford History of Music,* ed. J. A. WESTRUP, 11 v. (New York 1957–). v.2. G. REESE, *Music in the Middle Ages* (New York 1940). A. WULF, ''Denken in Tönen und Strukturen: Komponieren im Kontext Pérotins,'' *Musik-Konzepte* 107 (2000), 53–100. I. D. BENT, ''Pérotin'' in *The New Grove Dictionary of Music and Musicians, vol. 14,* ed. S. SADIE (New York 1980) 540–543. D. M. RANDEL, ed., *The Harvard Biographical Dictionary of Music* (Cambridge 1996) 683–684. N. SLONIMSKY, ed. *Baker's Biographical Dictionary of Musicians, Eighth Edition* (New York 1992) 1391. J. STENZL, ''Perotinus und das *Ereignis* Notre Dame: Auswahlbibliographie,'' *Musik-Konzepte* 107 (2000), 101–105. H. TISCHLER, ''Pérotin and the Creation of the Motet,'' *Music Review* 44 (1983), 1–7.

[E. THURSTON]

PERPETUA AND FELICITY, SS.

Martyrs. The *Passio Perpetuae et Felicitatis* is one of the most ancient reliable histories of the martyrs and recounts the martyrdom of Perpetua, her slave Felicity, and companions in the arena of Carthage on March 7, 202. Perpetua and Felicity were commemorated in Rome in the fourth century on March 7, and their names were inserted in the list of saints in the canon of the Mass.

During the persecution of Septimius Severus, the catechumens Vibia Perpetua, a noblewoman of 22 and her infant; Felicity, a pregnant slave; Revocatus; Saturninus; Secundulus; and later their catechist Saturus were arrested. While under arrest, they were baptized, and Perpetua's father besought her to apostatize. Perpetua, removed to prison, had a vision of a ladder guarded by a dragon and strewn with arms that prohibited ascent, but she walked over the dragon and reached a beautiful place. Again her father besought her, and he repeated his appeal in the forum before the people. They were condemned to the wild beasts for the feast in honor of Caesar Geta. Perpetua had another vision that her small brother, Dinocrates, who had died of cancer, was in heaven following her prayers for him. A few days before the spectacle they were transferred to a camp prison, where Perpetua had her last vision. At first Felicity was not with them, since it was illegal to execute a pregnant woman; but three days before the spectacle, Felicity gave birth prematurely to a girl. After being flogged, they were led into the amphitheater and eventually beheaded. In the *Passio* four other martyrs are recorded: Jocundus, Saturninus, Artaxius, and Quintus, who had already suffered in the same persecution.

Part of the *Passio* (3–10) was written by Perpetua, and part (11–13) by Saturus; the introduction and conclusion, by an eyewitness, formerly thought to be TERTULLIAN. The Latin text is probably the original. The *Passio* is famous for its account of the visions and important for early Christian ideas on martyrdom. It was frequently quoted by St. AUGUSTINE. These martyrs were greatly venerated in Carthage, and a basilica was erected there over their tomb, which was identified in 1907.

Feast: March 7 (formerly 6).

Bibliography: C. VAN BEEK, ed., *Passio sanctarum Perpetuae et Felicitatis, Florilegium Patristicum,* ed. J. ZELLINGER et al, (Bonn 1904–) 43; 1938. S. MAITLAND, ed., *The Martyrdom of Perpetua* (Evesham 1996), incl. the sermons of St. Augustine. V. L.

KENNEDY, *The Saints of the Canon of the Mass* (Vatican City 1938). J. QUASTEN, *Patrology*, 3 v. (Westminster, Md. 1950–) 1:181–183. A. J. FRIDH, *Le problème de la Passion des saintes Perpétue et Félicité* (Göteborg 1968). R. PETRAGLIO, *Lingua latina e mentalità biblica nella Passio sanctae Perpetuae: analisi di caro, carnalis e corpus* (Brescia 1976). P. HABERMEHL, *Perpetua und der Ägypter, oder, Bilder des Bösen im frühen afrikanischen Christentum* (Berlin 1992). C. M. ROBECK, *Prophecy in Carthage: Perpetua, Tertullian, and Cyprian* (Cleveland, Ohio 1992). J. E. SALISBURY, *Perpetua's Passion: The Death and Memory of a Young Roman Woman* (New York 1997).

[E. HOADE]

PERPETUAL ADORATION, SISTERS SERVANTS OF THE HOLY SPIRIT OF

(S.Sp.S.deA.P., Official Catholic Directory #3540); a cloistered contemplative congregation founded in 1896 at Steyl, Netherlands, by Arnold JANSSEN, SVD, with the collaboration of German-born Mother Mary Tönnies (d. 1934). The rule received final papal approval in 1950. Besides adoration of the Blessed Sacrament and the chanting in choir of the Liturgy of the Hours, the sisters engage in manual and literary work. In 1915 the congregation went to the U.S. and took charge of the newly erected Chapel of Divine Love in Philadelphia. The generalate is in Bad Driburg, Germany. The U.S. headquarters is in Philadelphia, Pa.

Bibliography: A. FREITAG, *Tabernakelwacht und Weltmission* (2d ed. Steyl 1924).

[V. J. FECHER]

PERPETUAL ADORATION OF THE BLESSED SACRAMENT, NUNS OF THE

(AP, Official Catholic Directory #3190); a cloistered community of nuns with papal approbation, dedicated to an apostolate of contemplative prayer, primarily through the perpetual adoration of the Blessed Sacrament. The order was founded at Rome, Italy, on July 8, 1807, by Mother Mary Magdalene of the Incarnation (Catalina Sordini Movizzo, 1770–1824), a Franciscan sister from the convent on the island of Ischia in the bay of Naples. The nuns, who take solemn vows, are engaged in constant prayer, including the Divine Office, before the exposed Blessed Sacrament. In the U.S. they are located in El Paso, Texas (1925), and San Francisco, Calif. (1928). Worldwide, the congregation has houses in Spain, Mexico, Chile and Africa.

[J. H. MCNEELY]

PERPETUUS OF TOURS, ST.

Bishop; d. 491. Perpetuus, of a senatorial family, was bishop of TOURS for 30 years (461–491). He zealously restored discipline in his diocese, regulated fasts and vigils, and built churches, including the magnificent basilica of St. MARTIN OF TOURS described by GREGORY OF TOURS (*Hist. Franc.* 2; 10) and by the fifth–century poet–bishop, SIDONIUS APOLLINARIS (*Epist.* 4). St. Martin's body was transferred to the apse of this basilica, and Perpetuus himself was buried there. His presence at the provincial councils of Tours (461) and Vannes is attested to, but his epitaph and will were proved to be 17th–century forgeries of Jérôme VIGNIER.

Feast: April 8, Dec. 30.

Bibliography: *Acta Sanctorum* April 1:744–748. L. DUCHESNE, *Fastes épiscopaux de l'ancienne Gaul*, 3v. (2d ed. Paris 1907–15) 2:300–301. E. GRIFFE, *La Gaule chrétienne à l'époque romaine* (Paris 1947). H. LECLERCQ, *Dictionnaire d'archéologie chrétienne et de liturgie* ed. F. CABROL, H. LECLERCQ and H. I. MARROU (Paris 1907–53) 15, 2:2619–20. J. L. BAUDOT and L. CHAUSSIN, *Vies des saints et des bienheureux selon l'ordre du calendrier avec l'historique des fêtes*, (Paris 1935–56) 4:182–188. A. BUTLER, *The Lives of the Saints*. rev. ed. H. THURSTON and D. ATTWATER (New York 1956) 2:53. H. DELEHAYE, "Saint Martin et Sulpice Sévère," *Analecta Bollandiana* 38 (1920) 5–136.

[L. M. COFFEY]

PERRET, AUGUSTE

French architect important for original contributions to civic and ecclesiastic architecture; b. Brussels, 1874; d. Paris, 1954. His use of reinforced concrete (invented by the French engineers Hennébique and Coignet in the 1890s) for an apartment at Rue Franklin, Paris (1903), was the first such use of concrete in frame construction. This and subsequent structures liberated concrete from a basement-hidden material into a frankly expressed, monolithic constructional system that bears considerable influence on contemporary building. His church of Notre-Dame du RAINCY (1922–23) was the first to break with the accumulated styles of the past and to house a congregation on 20th-century terms. It is built of reinforced concrete with slender concrete nave columns supporting the roof; its side walls are independent, prefabricated concrete grills filled with colored glass, so that the interior is light and open. The altar is placed nearer to the congregation than in earlier churches. After the similar church of Sainte-Thérèse de Montmagny (Seine-et-Oise, 1925–26) his work became increasingly formalistic with even classic qualities. The rigid postwar rebuilding of Le Havre is punctuated by his last work, St. Joseph's Church (1952–55), a kind of "spiritual lighthouse" that towers some 350 feet above the city.

Bibliography: A. HENZE and T. FILTHAUT, *Contemporary Church Art,* ed. M. LAVANOUX, tr. C. HASTINGS (New York 1956) 21–23. J. PICHARD, *Modern Church Architecture,* tr. E. CALLMANN (New York 1962). B.CHAMPIGNEULLE, *Perret* (Paris 1959). G. E. KIDDER SMITH, *The New Architecture of Europe* (Cleveland 1961) 105–106; *The New Churches of Europe* (New York 1964).

[G. E. KIDDER SMITH]

PERRONE, GIOVANNI

Theologian; b. Chieri (Turin), March 11, 1794; d. Castelgandolfo, Aug. 28, 1876. He entered the Society of Jesus Dec. 14, 1815. A year later he began teaching dogmatic theology, a task he performed for the rest of his life, first at Orvieto for seven years (1817–24) and then at the Collegio Romano (1824–48), except for a short period when he was rector of the college at Ferrara (1830–34). Because of the revolutionary agitations of the Roman Republic in 1848, he went to England, where he taught theology at the Jesuit scholasticate at Benhart (Wales) from 1848 to 1851. He then returned to the chair of theology at the Collegio Romano where he was rector (1853–55) and prefect of studies until his death.

He played a principal role in the struggle against G. HERMES and in the preparation for the definition of the dogmas of papal infallibility and the Immaculate Conception, which he defended in his work, *De immaculato B. Marina conceptu* (Rome 1847, 10th ed. Milan 1852). He had an excellent grounding in patristics and positive theology; at the same time he possessed a clear, concise, and methodical style.

He was the author of many doctrinal and controversial works. His principal doctrinal works were: *Praelectiones theologiae dogmaticae* (9 v. Rome 1835–42), which had 34 editions up to 1888; *Praelectiones . . . in compendium redactae* (5 v. Rome 1845), which had 47 editions up to 1892; *De virtute religionis* (Paris 1866); *De Domini Nostri Jesu Christi divinitate adversus huius aetaris incredulos* (3 v. Turin 1870); *De matrimonio christiano* (3 v. Turin 1870); and *De romani pontificis infallibilitate* (Turin 1874). His controversial works include: *L'hermesianismo* (3 fasc., Rome 1838–39); *Il protestantesimo e la regola di Fede* (3 v. Rome 1853); and *Catechismo intorno al protestantesimo* (2d edition, Turin 1883).

Bibliography: C. SOMMERVOGEL et al., *Bibliothèque de la Compagnie de Jésus* (Brussels-Paris 1890–1932) 6:558–571. H. HURTER, *Nomenclator literarius theologiae catholicae* (Innsbruck 1903–13) 5.2:1496–98. C. BOYER, *Dictionnaire de théologie catholique,* ed. A. VACANT et al. (Paris 1903–50) 12.1:1255–56. W. KASPER, *Lexicon für Theologie und Kirche,* ed. J. HOFER and K. RAHNER (Freiburg 1957–65) 8:282.

[C. TESTORE]

PERSEVERANCE

Perseverance is a moral virtue that perfects the irascible appetite so that a person is reasonably inclined to continue in the practice of virtuous action in spite of difficulties arising from the protracted period during which the effort must continue. It is one thing to be called upon to perform a single virtuous act; it is quite another thing to be expected to continue to act in a virtuous manner for a long time. There is a kind of fatigue that overcomes the emotions when they must persist in a course of action and this fatigue inclines a person to abandon what he has undertaken.

In a broader sense, perseverance means the pursuit of some course of action or some undertaking until it is completed. Final perseverance is the continuance in the state of grace until death (*see* PERSEVERANCE, FINAL). Both the virtue of perseverance and final perseverance play important roles in the spiritual life, but they have completely different functions. Perseverance provides the fortitude of spirit that is necessary for the continued daily practice of virtue. It is the bulwark of all virtuous life. Virtue, by its very nature, demands a certain immobility and stability; all good habits demand a certain permanence. Without the virtue of perseverance, no virtue would be practiced for a prolonged period of time, and thus it would be impossible to attain the perfection of virtue demanded by the Christian life.

For the exercise of the virtue of perseverance man in his present state of fallen nature has a special need for actual graces. The Council of TRENT declared: ''If anyone should say that he who is justified can, without the special assistance of God, either persevere in the justice of God received or with that assistance cannot persevere, let him be anathema'' [H. Denzinger, *Enchiridion symbolorum,* ed. A. Schönmetzer (Freiburg 1963) 1572]. Thus the virtue of perseverance and the grace of perseverance cooperate in the ultimate work of salvation. The virtue gives man the ready disposition to continue in the life of virtue, but because of the ever-present possibility of sin—especially to a human nature wounded by original sin—man needs special actual graces to cause the virtue to be constantly operative.

The virtue of perseverance is opposed by the vices of inconstancy or cowardice and of pertinacity or stubbornness. There is a reasonable endurance of the tedium and fatigue involved in a life of virtue and the mean can be violated either by refusing to endure reasonably, or by continuing to act when it is no longer reasonable to do so. The Latin term for inconstancy (*mollities*) indicates a kind of softness or effeminacy of spirit. Hard, stubborn pertinacity lies at the other extreme. A person with this disposition will not abandon a course of action when he should. For example, such a man will attend a Confraternity meeting (for he has never missed one) while his wife is home sick and there is no one to care for the children.

The virtue of perseverance is extolled in Sacred Scripture. ''Take all that shall be brought upon thee and in thy sorrow endure'' (Sir 2.4). ''Be steadfast and immovable, always abounding in the work of the Lord, knowing that your labor is not in vain in the Lord'' (2 Cor 15.58). ''He who has persevered to the end will be saved'' (Mt 10.22).

Bibliography: F. L. B. CUNNINGHAM, ed., *The Christian Life* (Dubuque 1959). A. ROYO, *The Theology of Christian Perfection,* tr. and ed. J. AUMANN (Dubuque 1962). THOMAS AQUINAS, *Summa theologiae,* 2a2ae, 137–138. A. MICHEL, *Dictionnaire de théologie catholique,* ed. A. VACANT et al., 15 v. (Paris 1903–50) 12.1:1256–1304.

[R. DOHERTY]

PERSEVERANCE, FINAL

Living and dying in the grace of Christ is final perseverance. The simplicity of this description has a twofold merit. It bypasses, as exceptional cases, the situation of the baptized who never reaches the age of reason and the situation of the sinner who finds RECONCILIATION with God only at the hour of death. It stresses the two essentially related elements that constitute the grace of final perseverance. The first is a certain continuance in grace. This depends on God's special help. The second is the fact of death in the state of grace. This depends on God's special protection. St. Thomas combines these elements in defining final perseverance as ''the abiding in good to the end of life'' (St. Thomas, *Summa theologiae,* 1a2ae, 109.10). The Council of Trent speaks of ''the great gift of final perseverance'' [H. Denzinger, *Enchiridion symbolorum,* ed. A. Schönmetzer (32d ed. Freiburg 1963) 1566] and links it with the mystery of predestination:

> No one . . . so long as he lives in this mortal life, ought to be so presumptuous about the deep mystery of divine predestination as to decide with certainty that he is definitely among the number of the predestined, as though it were true that, because he is justified, either he cannot sin again, or, if he does sin, he should promise himself certain repentance. [H. Denzinger, *ibid.,* 1540; see, for tr. of this and subsequent passages, J. F. Clarkson et al., *The Church Teaches* (St. Louis 1955)]

It is important to distinguish between perseverance and final perseverance. Many receive grace who do not persevere in grace to the end of life (St. Thomas, *Summa theologiae,* 1a2ae, 109.10). It is likewise important to distinguish between the power to persevere in grace and actual perseverance. Every just man receives the grace of potential perseverance [H. Denzinger, *ibid.,* 1536]. It does not follow that every just man actually perseveres in grace until death. These distinctions become clear when the mystery of final perseverance is placed in its proper theological context. This is the task of this article. At the end, attention is given to the question, how does the just man obtain the all important grace of final perseverance?

Special help of God. Theologians commonly teach that the justified adult, who has made a fundamental option for God and is habitually disposed to the avoidance of serious sin, has the need of special help from God—if he is to persevere in justice. As early as the 5th century, it was the authentic teaching of the Church that ''no one, not even he who has been renewed by the grace of Baptism, has sufficient strength to overcome the snares of the devil and to vanquish the concupiscence of the flesh unless he obtains help from God each day to persevere in a good life'' [H. Denzinger, *ibid.,* 241]. The Council of Trent speaks of ''the special help of God'' in this regard (*ibid.* 1572). This canon is open to various interpretations [see A. Michel, *Dictionnaire de théologie catholique,* ed. A. Vacant et al., 15 v. (Paris 1903–50) 12.1:1283–86]. Sacred Scripture, by teaching that man's life is warfare (Eph 6.11–17) and by insisting on the need for prayer (Mt 6.13), makes men very much aware that sanctifying grace, while making them God's sons, does not remove the weaknesses of fallen nature. Special help from God is a moral necessity. While the Church has never defined this special help with any precision, theologians usually speak of it in terms of God's providential protection in the external order of a man's life (see St. Thomas Aquinas, *C. gent.* 3.155) and the actual graces that illuminate the intellect and give inspiration to the will. Whatever its nature, this special help is given to all the just. St. Paul writes, ''But the Lord is faithful, who will strengthen you and guard you from evil'' (2 Thes 3.3; cf. 1 Thes 5.23–24; Rom 8.31–33; 1 Cor 10.13). The Church also authoritatively expresses this teaching by quoting St. Augustine: ''God 'does not abandon' those who have been justified by his grace 'unless they abandon Him first''' [H. Denzinger, *ibid.,* 1537].

Death in the State of Grace. So much for the grace of potential perseverance, a great benefit from God. Theologians speak of an even greater benefit, the grace of final perseverance. This grace, inestimable because of the utter seriousness of man's hour of death, is the coinciding of the state of grace with the hour of death. It is the watchful protection of God, who so arranges—in the inscrutable mystery of His providential designs—the events of a man's life that the moment of death comes while he is persevering in the grace of Christ. Dying in the state of grace is no accident. It is God's most special gift, most special because it is distinct from all other graces and benefits, and most special because it is had only by those who are saved. One is face to face here with the mystery of God's grace and man's liberty. If a man dies in the grace of Christ, the thanks belong to God. If a man dies in serious sin, the fault is his own. Theologians disagree in their ultimate explanations of this mystery because of differing views on predestination and the mystery of efficacious GRACE. However, all Catholic theologians agree that final perseverance is a greater benefit from God than the grace of potential perseverance. The magisterium of the Church has never solemnly defined the matter. It is the common teaching of Catholic doctrine.

The Bible contains no explicit teaching on the grace of final perseverance. The doctrine, however, is an expression in theological categories of the biblical theme of divine election. The question developed in the consciousness of the Church at the time of the struggles with the Pelagians. As the theologian reflects on this doctrine at the present time, it is a theological conclusion that flows from the mystery of divine predestination and efficacious grace.

How does the just man obtain the grace of final perseverance? Does he MERIT this conjoining of grace and death? The answer is in the negative. The GOOD WORKS of a man in grace are gifts from God. They are also the good merits of the man himself. According to the Council of Trent, good works merit an ''increase of grace, life everlasting, and, provided that a man dies in the state of grace, the attainment of that life everlasting and an increase of glory'' [H. Denzinger, *ibid.,* 1582]. As this text illustrates, final perseverance is not an object of merit. Rather it is the condition for meriting the attainment of everlasting life. St. Thomas gives us the explanation [*Summa theologiae,* 1a2ae, 114.9]. The object of merit is the term of a good action, not the principle. Final perseverance depends on God's action that inclines the just man to good works until death. This motion from God is the principle of the good action. Thus, final perseverance cannot be merited. It is the very ground for meriting the attainment of eternal life. How, then, is the just man to persevere to the end, if such a grace is not the object of merit? The answer is prayer. The Scriptures give assurance that God infallibly hears the prayers that seek the true well-being of the just man (Mt 7.7; Mk 11.24; Lk 11.9). The theologians have discussed the conditions necessary for such infallible prayer [see St. Thomas, *Summa theologiae,* 2a2ae, 85 ad 2]. The grace of final perseverance is the supreme object of the just man's prayer. The just man will receive this grace—if he assiduously seeks it in true prayer.

See Also: DEATH (THEOLOGY OF); GRACE, ARTICLES ON; PREDESTINATION, ARTICLES ON.

Bibliography: A. MICHEL, *Dictionnaire de théologie catholique,* ed. A. VACANT et al., 15 v. (Paris 1903–50) 12.1:1256–1304. K. JÜSSEN, *Lexikon für Theologie und Kirche,* ed. J. HOFER and K. RAHNER, 10 v. (2d, new ed. Freiburg 1957–65); suppl., *Das Zweite Vatikanische Konzil: Dokumente und Kommentare,* ed. H. S. BRECHTER et al., pt. 1 (1966) 2:123–124. THOMAS AQUINAS, *Summa theologiae,* 1a2ae, 114.9. J. JAROSZEWICZ, *De dono perseverantiae finalis* (Kielce 1932). S. GONZÁLEZ, *Sacrae theologiae summa,* ed. Fathers of the Society of Jesus, Professors of the Theological Faculties in Spain, 4 v. (Madrid 1958–62); *Biblioteca de autores cristianos* (Madrid 1945–) 3.3:60–70. H. LANGE, *De gratia* (Freiburg 1929).

[J. J. CONNELLY]

PERSIA

Persia is the European name for the plateau land in the Near East extending from the lowlands of Mesopotamia to India. The native name has always been Iran, from Aryan. The name Persia is derived from the southwestern province of modern Fars, called Persis by the Greeks and Parsa by the ancient Persians. The political boundaries of Persia have changed throughout its long history, but at its peak, it encompassed not only the sovereign nation now known as Iran, but also the entire Iranian cultural area, including Afghanistan, Central Asia, and the Transcaucasus.

The Aryan invaders of the plateau probably came from the north in successive waves, beginning about the 16th century B.C. or earlier. Cuneiform inscriptions from this early period reveal Aryan personal names and Aryan deities. Although the Aryans or Indo-Iranians may have come into the Near East and into India both from over the Caucasus and through Central Asia, the expansion of the Iranians in the 9th century B.C. seems to have come mostly from the Caucasus. The Iranian tribes spread over the plateau and settled down in areas to some of which they gave their names. The two main tribes of the western section were the Mada or Medes and the Parsa or Persians. Others were the Asagarta or Sagartians in the central portion, and the Parthians, Bactrians, Sogdians, Khwarazmians, and others in eastern regions. From the Avesta and from the Old Persian inscriptions, one may surmise that the Iranian tribes were subdivided into clans and extended families. For example, Darius, son of Vishtaspa, belonged to the family of the Achaemenids, the clan of the Pasargadai, and the tribe of the Parsa. When the tribes settled down, the clans lost their importance, and tribal loyalties were tempered by a greater national or imperial allegiance.

The earliest Iranian state recorded in history was that of the MEDES. The frequent raids of the Assyrians probably brought the Medes together into a confederacy and then into a kingdom (*c.* 700 B.C.). At that time an invasion of Cimmerians and Scythians from the north disrupted the Median state. The Medes recovered and defeated the Assyrians, taking their place in creating an empire. The Medes in turn were overthrown (*c.* 549 B.C.) by the Persians under CYRUS II.

Achaemenid Dynasty. Cyrus II (559–530) took over the empire of the Medes and extended its frontiers. He captured Sardis (*c.* 547 B.C.) and took prisoner Croesus, king of Lydia, annexing his kingdom. The Greek cities of Ionia were absorbed later, one by one. In 539 Cyrus entered Babylon and brought an end to the kingdom of Nabu-na'id (Nabonidus). He further incorporated Syria and Palestine into his extensive empire. Evidence points to the tolerance of Cyrus in respect to subject peoples; his ending of the Jewish Exile in Babylon is well known from the Bible. Cyrus was killed while fighting against nomads in Central Asia.

Cambyses II (530–522), the son and successor of Cyrus II, conquered Egypt; but then a revolt broke out in Persis, and during his return journey Cambyses died, probably from an accident. According to the Behistun inscription of DARIUS I (522–486) and classical sources, the revolt in Persis was led by a Magian who claimed to be Bardiya (Greek Smerdis), Cambyses' brother who was supposed to have been secretly murdered by Cambyses before he left for Egypt. Some scholars discount Darius's story and claim that Bardiya was the true brother of Cambyses and that Darius overthrew him in 522. In any case, Darius was the real organizer of the Achaemenid empire.

Darius started building palaces at Persepolis; his capital, however, at least in winter, was at Susa, although Ecbatana and Babylon retained their past importance. Herodotus (8.98) tells of the various institutions of the Achaemenid empire, such as the postal service, the royal road from Susa to Sardis, the special agents of the king, and the bureaucracy. The lingua franca of the bureaucracy was apparently Aramaic, and inscriptions in this language have been found all over the area of the Achaemenid empire. It would seem that Darius also instigated a revision and codification of the laws in use in various parts of the empire. The Iranian word for law, *dāta,* was borrowed by Akkadian, Hebrew, and Aramaic, indicating the importance of law to the Achaemenid rulers. Darius also made a new division of satrapies or provinces of the empire, and Herodotus (3.89) lists 20. Darius further reorganized the system of taxes and tribute. The ruling Persians were exempted from paying taxes, since they supplied troops and officials. The royal guard was called "the Immortals" by Herodotus (7.83), but in time of war a vast army of various peoples from all over the empire could be assembled. Herodotus (7.61) gives a description of the various contingents of the army of Xerxes that invaded Greece.

The coinage of the Achaemenid empire was in gold, silver, and copper. The first, the daric, called στατήρ by the Greeks, shows the king kneeling with a bow and could have been minted only by the Achaemenid ruler. Silver and copper coins were struck by satraps and generals, while some autonomous cities, such as the Phoenician seaports, also struck their own coins. The striking of gold coins by a satrap was usually a sign of rebellion. The gold daric, probably so called after Darius, weighed 8.4 grams, and the silver shekel, Greek σίγλος, was 5.6 grams. The silver-to-gold ratio was $13\frac{1}{3}$ to 1. The imperial coinage, however, apparently did not have a wide circulation, for Greek silver coins have been found in various parts of the Achaemenid empire, from pre-Alexander hoards, which attest the importance of Greek commerce in the 4th century B.C.

The empire reached its largest extent under Darius, who invaded the Balkans and south Russia *c.* 510 B.C. He was unsuccessful in this campaign against the Scythians (Herodotus 4.83–92), but many lands north of Greece submitted to the Persians. The defeat of Darius at Marathon in 490 B.C. is well known, but only after the final defeat of the Persians in 478 B.C., in the time of Xerxes (486–465), was the Achaemenid empire put on the defensive. Egypt proved to be the most rebellious province of the empire and was lost and regained several times before Alexander's conquests. Persian gold and bribery proved more effectual than the army of Xerxes in Achaemenid relations with the Greeks.

The history of the empire after Xerxes, from the time of Artaxerxes I (465–424) on, is one of intrigues, assassinations, and dominance of the central government by the harem. That the empire was able to survive is a tribute to the fine organization of the state and bureaucracy by the early Achaemenids. One attempt to seize power is known through Xenophon's *Anabasis,* the story of 10,000 Greek mercenaries employed by Cyrus the Younger in his ill-fated attempt to overthrow his brother Artaxerxes II (404–359) in 401. Later, Egypt and several satrapies in Anatolia were able to gain and maintain their independence. It seemed as though the Achaemenid empire were falling apart. The accession of the capable monarch Artaxerxes III (359–338) was the beginning of a reconsolidation of the empire. Egypt was reconquered, and the rebel satraps were won back to allegiance. The murder of Artaxerxes, however, coincided with the conquest of Greece by Philip of Macedon. The last Achaemenid, Darius III Codommanus, had to face ALEXANDER THE GREAT and lost his empire at the battle of Gaugamela in 331 B.C.

The οἰκουμένη (world) of the Achaemenids made a great impression on later peoples, but the lack of a historical tradition in their homeland caused the Persians to forget the Achaemenids, although the memory of a Persian world empire did persist in legend in later times. The bureaucracy, using Aramaic, was maintained by Alexander and his successors of the Seleucid dynasty side by side with Greek. For the Persians, however, the period from the death of Alexander in 323 B.C. to the establishment of the Sasanian dynasty *c.* A.D. 225 was a dark age of warring princes.

Hellenism had an even greater influence in the Orient than Achaemenid culture had, and the Seleucid empire, as well as the Greco-Bactrian kingdom in the area of present Afghanistan, maintained Greek political dominance until the Parthians took over the Seleucid heritage in the west and the Kushans that of the Greco-Bactrians in the east of the Iranian Plateau. The founding of many cities by Greeks in the east, with the Greek πόλις (city-state) culture, provided important avenues of influence on the local populations. Undoubtedly the Greek colonists were influenced also by the Iranian peoples among whom they settled. The mother of Antiochus I, son and successor of Seleucus I, who was killed in 281 B.C., was an Iranian noblewoman. The mixture of Greeks and Iranians must have proceeded apace. Strabo in his geography (11.509) well characterized Seleucid rule in the east when he said that they were so occupied with wars (in the Mediterranean area) that they could not attend to their remote possessions.

A chronological list of the rulers of the Achaemenid Dynasty follows:

1. Achaemenes (Hakhamanish)
2. Teispes (Chishpish)
3. Cyrus I (Kurush)
4. Cambyses I (Kambujiya)
5. Cyrus II (559–530 B.C.)
6. Cambyses II (530–522)
7. Smerdis (Bardiya or Gaumata; 522)
8. Darius I (Darayavahush; 522–486)
9. Xerxes I (Khshayarsha; 486–465)
10. Artaxerxes I Longimanus (Artakhshassa; 465–424)
11. Xerxes II (424–423)
12. Darius II Nothus (423–404)
13. Artaxerxes II Mnenon (404–359)
14. Artaxerxes III Ochus (359–338)
15. Arses (Arsha) (338–336)
16. Darius III (336–330)

Arsacid Dynasty. The heirs of the Seleucids in Persia were the Parthians. Parthia was the Achaemenid satrapy covering most of the modern Province of Khurasan, but the rise of Parthia was caused probably by nomadic invaders from Central Asia, chief of whom was a tribe called the Parni by Strabo (11.508). The first ruler of the new state was Arsaces (Parthian Arshak), a name that became a generic term for later rulers. Most of the Parthian coins have only ''Arsaces'' on them, making identifications of various rulers very difficult. The Arsacid Dynasty was founded *c.* 250 B.C., but the expansion of the state was slow. The Seleucids regarded the Parthians as rebels against their authority similar to other rebels in the East. The Seleucid Antiochus III probably brought the Parthians back under Seleucid suzerainty between 209 and 189 B.C., when Antiochus was defeated by the Romans at the battle of Magnesia.

The real founder of the Parthian empire was Mithradates I, who became ruler *c.* 171 B.C. He had to fight against ANTIOCHUS IV EPIPHANES, who tried to restore Seleucid hegemony but died in 164. In 141 Mithradates entered Seleucia on the Tigris. The Seleucid King Demetrius II Nikator was defeated and captured by Mithradates in 139. In the reign of Phraates II (138–128), son and successor of Mithradates I, Antiochus VII tried to restore Seleucid rule in Mesopotamia and Persia. Although successful at first, he was subsequently defeated and slain by the Parthians. Phraates, however, lost his life in battle against nomadic invaders in eastern Iran. His uncle and successor Artabanus II (128–123) also was killed in the east, but Mithradates II (*c.* 123–87 B.C.), son of Artabanus, restored Arsacid power in the east, defeated the Armenians, and concluded the first treaty with Rome in 92. Even before the death of Mithradates II, however, the Parthian state suffered from revolts, and a period of disorders prevailed. King Tigranes of Armenia extended his boundaries, much at Parthian expense. It was not until Phraates III (69–57 B.C.) that Parthian unity was restored.

Although the early Parthian kings were known as Philhellenes and used Greek on their coins, their empire was variegated under many local feudal rulers and local influences. There were many vassal states and autonomous Greek cities in the Parthian domain. The most important of the latter was Seleucia on the Tigris.

The actual territory of imperial rule under the Parthians was not extensive, comprising mostly the lands on the plateau following the trade route described by Isidore of Charax in his *Parthian Stations.* In the east, the region of modern Kandahar in Afghanistan was probably under an independent Indo-Parthian state, although at times it may have submitted to Arsacid rule. In Mesopotamia there was a series of vassal states: OSRHOENE (Edessa), Gordyene, Adiabene, and in the south, Mesene, also called Characene. Ancient Elam was a kingdom called Elymais, and in Persis there were local rulers called *frataraka* (more likely than *fratadara*). Azerbaijan in the north, called Atropatene, also was a vassal state, and there may have been others.

The Parthians had their own era of time reckoning beginning from 247 B.C., but the Seleucid era, from 311 B.C., was widely used all over the Near East. Although remains from the early Parthians show an overwhelming influence of Hellenism in both art and objects of material culture, native features became more prominent with the passage of time. The first Christian century seems to have been the period of greatest change, when Parthian replaced Greek as the language of administration, and Parthian appeared together with a debased Greek in the coin legends. A token of the change was the seven-year revolt of Seleucia (A.D. 35–42) and the subsequent founding of a new though short-lived capital, Vologesia, by the Parthian king.

During the last two centuries of Parthian rule, the kingdom was on the defensive, against the Romans in the west and the Kushans in the east. The latter, invaders from Central Asia, established a kingdom in the area of present-day Afghanistan and northwest India in the 1st Christian century. Under the Kings Kanishka and Huvishka, whose dates are uncertain, the Kushans expanded, in the west probably at the expense of the Parthians, although there is no source material. The Kushan rulers were patrons of BUDDHISM and of the Buddhist art called Gandharan.

The wars with Rome began with the defeat and death of Crassus at Carrhae in 53 B.C. Mark Antony defeated the Parthians in 36 B.C. but suffered a setback in the following year. Under Augustus, peace was made between the two empires, and for a time pro-Roman rulers sat on the throne of Parthia. In the middle of the first Christian century a conflict over Armenia broke out, and a Roman army under Corbulo invaded Parthian domains. In A.D. 63 peace was restored, leaving Roman suzerainty over Armenia but with the presence of a Parthian royal family, the origin of the Arsacids of Armenia.

The later history of Parthia is filled with civil wars and rival claimants to the throne. The Romans took advantage of the internal struggles of the Parthians to invade Mesopotamia, under Trajan. He occupied Ctesiphon, the Parthian capital opposite Seleucia, in A.D. 115 and then sailed down the Tigris to the Persian Gulf. In 117, however, Trajan had to retreat, and after his death his successor Hadrian made peace and evacuated Parthian domains. The Parthians under Vologeses III (148–192) in turn invaded Syria in 161, provoking a Roman reaction. A Roman army again conquered Ctesiphon in 165, but an epidemic caused the Romans to retreat. Septimius Severus fought the Parthians, and in 198 he captured Ctesiphon but again could not hold it long. None of the Roman expeditions succeeded in taking the Arab-fortified city of Hatra in northern Mesopotamia, which always remained a threat to the Roman line of communications in Mesopotamia. As a result of internal strife and the Roman invasions, the Parthian state was greatly weakened. From *c.* 211 to the end of the kingdom (*c.* 227) there were two rival kings in Parthia, Vologeses V and Artabanus V, known from their coins. The invasion of Parthian territory in the north by Caracalla was matched by the rebellion of a vassal prince in Persis. By 226 Ardashir I, founder of the Sasanian empire, had overthrown both Parthian kings.

The rulers of the Arsacid Dynasty are listed below (most dates are approximate):

1. Arsaces I (247–? B.C.)
2. Tiridates (?–211)
3. Artabanus I (211–191)
4. Priapatius (191–176)
5. Phraates I (176–171)
6. Mithradates I (171–138)
7. Phraates II (138–128)
8. Artabanus II (128–123)
9. Mithradates II (123–87)
10. Gotarzes I (91-*c.* 80)
11. Orodes I (?–77)
12. Sinatrukes (80–69)
13. Phraates III (69–57)
14. Mithradates III (57–55)
15. Orodes II (57–37)
16. Phraates IV (38–2)
17. Tiridates II (30–25)
18. Phraataces (2 B.C.–A.D. 4)
19. Orodes III (4–7)
20. Vonones I (7–12)
21. Artabanus III (12–38)
22. Tiridates III (36)
23. Vardanes (39–47)
24. Gotarzes II (38–51)
25. Vonones II (51)
26. Vologeses I (51–80)
27. Artabanus IV (80–81)
28. Pakores (79–115)
29. Oroses (109–128)
30. Vologeses II (105–147)
31. Mithradates IV (128–147?)
32. Vologeses III (148–192)
33. Vologeses IV (191–207)
34. Vologeses V (207–227)
35. Artabanus V (213–224)
36. Artavasdes (226-*c.* 227)

Sasanian dynasty. The rise of Ardashir, son of Papak, descended from Sasan, parallels the story of

Cyrus, founder of the Achaemenid Dynasty. Papak established his capital at Istakhr, near Persepolis, and he and then Ardashir extended the frontiers of their principality. The conquest of Mesene by Ardashir brought him into conflict with his Parthian overlords. Much fighting was necessary before Ardashir was able to take the place of the Parthian ruler. His victory over Artabanus V is symbolically represented on a bas-relief at Naqsh-i Rustam, near Persepolis; another success, possibly over Artavasdes, son of Artabanus, is depicted on a rock carving near Firuzabad.

In the east, Ardashir wrested much territory from the Kushans and possibly secured Kushan submission to his overlordship. Unfortunately the chronology of the early Sasanian rulers is disputed, and dates of accession and other events may vary by as much as 3 years. Ardashir became "King of Kings," with more power than the Parthian monarch, who had ruled more as the chief of many feudal princes than as a king or emperor.

Shapur I, son and successor of Ardashir, seems to have been the Darius of his time. Shortly after becoming king he defeated the Romans in a battle in which the Emperor Gordian III (238–244) was killed. The new Emperor, Philip the Arab (244–249), sued for peace and paid a heavy tribute to the Persians. A decade later a dispute over Armenia led to an invasion of Roman territory by Shapur in 256 (or in 253 according to some scholars). Antioch, capital of the Roman East, was captured, as well as many cities in Syria and Cappadocia. In 259 the Roman Emperor Valerian (253–260) was defeated and captured by Shapur, who proclaimed this extraordinary event on several bas-reliefs and in a great trilingual (Greek, Parthian, and Middle Persian) inscription at Naqsh-i Rustam. Persian troops again ravaged Syria and Anatolia, but on the return trip to Ctesiphon, Odenathus, king of PALMYRA, defeated the Persian army and secured much booty. From 260 to 263 the troops of Palmyra dominated northern Mesopotamia. The Romans put an end to Palmyra, and in 283 the Emperor Carus captured Ctesiphon. Internal disorders and wars in the East reduced Persian resistance, but the Romans retreated. Sporadic warfare ended in 296 with a truce favorable to Rome, by which Armenia and parts of northern Mesopotamia remained under Roman rule.

The long rule of Shapur II (309–379) saw a renewal of the struggle with Rome. The conversion of the king of Armenia to Christianity *c.* 298 and of the Roman Emperor CONSTANTINE I two decades later brought religious factors into the struggle of the two powers. In 337, the year Constantine died, Shapur II laid siege to NISIBIS, but fighting was desultory until Julian the Apostate (361–363) invaded the Sasanian domain. He was killed near Ctesiphon, and his successor, Jovian (363–364), made peace by relinquishing Armenia and many Roman possessions in northern Mesopotamia, including the key fortress of Nisibis, to the Persians. One of the features of the reign of Shapur II was his persecution of the Christians living within the Sasanian empire. Persian policy in this matter varied, and under Yazdagird I (399–421) Christians were not molested, although at the end of his reign persecutions were resumed. Varahran (Bahram) V (421–439), known to popular tradition as Gor (the onager) because of his prowess in the hunt, lost a war to Rome in 422, and in the peace treaty he guaranteed freedom of worship to the Christians.

In the second half of the 5th century the Sasanian empire in the east was subjected to invasions of HUNS or Hephtalites from Central Asia. Peroz (459–484) lost his family and his life in fighting them. His son Kavad I (488–531) was restored to the throne in 499 with the aid of the Hephtalites, after a revolution had deposed him. These eastern successors of the Kushans usually proved more than a match for the Sasanian armies. It should be noted that NESTORIANISM became the dominant form of Christianity in Iran, especially after a synod in 483 favored Nestorianism in the Sasanian domains.

Kavad I (488–531) is noted for his espousal of the Mazdakites, a communist sect of Zoroastrianism (*see* ZOROASTER) that flourished at the beginning of his reign. Toward the close of Kavad's reign, however, his son together with the chiefs of the Zoroastrian faith instigated a massacre of the Mazdakites. Afterward the name Mazdakite vanished, but it reappeared again and again in Persia as the term for arch-heretics even in Islamic times.

Khusrau I (Khusro, Chosroes; 531–579), surnamed Anushirvan (immortal soul), reestablished orthodoxy and made peace with the Byzantine Emperor JUSTINIAN I (527–565) in 532. He instituted a new system of taxation, based probably on a post-Diocletian Roman model, with a fixed sum based on the land, rather than a variable amount based on yield. A reform of the bureaucracy was carried out, especially after the disruption caused by the Mazdakites. Later in Khusrau's reign, war against Justinian broke out again. Khusrau was able to capture Antioch, but the armistice of 561 left matters much the same as before the hostilities.

Following Khusrau's reign, the throne of Persia changed hands several times in a short period, and weak rulers and rebels hindered stability in the empire. The Hephtalites in the east were defeated by new invaders from Central Asia, the Turks, and after initial cooperation, hostilities between Persians and Turks followed. Under Khusrau II Parviz (591–628), the Sasanian empire reached a pinnacle, but after his time it suffered a rapid decline. In 602, after the assassination of the Emperor Maurice (582–602), Khusrau invaded the Byzantine Empire. Antioch was taken in 611, Jerusalem in 614; and shortly afterward Egypt was conquered, and Persian troops appeared before Constantinople. A brilliant counterstroke by the Emperor Heraclius (610–641) carried the war to the heart of the Sasanian empire. In 624 he invaded Azerbaijan and then Mesopotamia. Khusrau was assassinated, and the Sasanian empire fell into disorder. The Persians, by the terms of the peace treaty, evacuated all Byzantine territories. Thereafter one Sasanian ruler followed another in rapid succession, until Yazdagird III (632–651), the grandson of Khusrau, ascended the throne.

The rulers of the Sasanian Dynasty are listed as follows:

1. Papak King (208–222?)
2. Shapur King (*c.* 222)
3. Ardashir I King of Kings (222?–240)
4. Shapur I King of Kings (240–*c.* 272)
5. Hormizd I Ardashir (272–273)
6. Varahran (Bahram) I (273–276)
7. Varahran II (276–293)
8. Varahran III (293)
9. Nerseh (293–302)
10. Hormizd II (302–309)
11. Shapur II (309–379)
12. Ardashir II (379–383)
13. Shapur III (383–388)
14. Varahran IV (388–399)
15. Yazdagird I (399–421)
16. Varahran V (421–439)
17. Yazdagird II (439–457)
18. Hormizd III (457–459)
19. Peroz (459–484)
20. Valash (484–488)
21. Kavad I (488–531)
22. Zamasp (496–498)
23. Khusro I (531–579)
24. Hormizd IV (579–590)
25. Varahran Chobin (590–591)
26. Khusro II (591–628)
27. Kavad II (628)
28. Ardashir III (628–629)
29. Boran (629–630)
30. Hormizd V Khusro III (630–*c.* 632)
31. Yazdagird III (*c.* 632–651)

Persia under Islam. The rise of Islam in the Middle East brought a speedy end to the Sasanian empire. In the battles of Qadisiya in 637 and Nihavend in 641, the Persians were defeated, and Yazdagird fled from the Arabs eastward until he was killed (651) near the city of Merv in Central Asia.

The Arab conquest of Islam brought an end not only to the state but also to the official Zoroastrian church. Zoroastrians became fewer; eventually only a few thousand existed in the country, primarily in Yazd and Kirman. Others, however, fled to India, where their descendants, primarily in Bombay, the PARSEES, became a flourishing community.

The early history of Persia under Islam should be distinguished from the history of the Arabs in Persia. For several centuries, under the Umayyad and early 'ABBĀSID Caliphates, many conversions to Islam took place, but old Persian customs, such as the celebration of Noruz or new year's day, remained little changed. The writing of Persian in the cumbersome Pahlavi script became more and more restricted to Zoroastrian priests, while Arabic became the language of government and bureaucracy and also of literature and learning. There are indications, however, that spoken Persian was widely used in the eastern Islamic world, not only by natives but also by the Arabs as a lingua franca. Probably in the second half of the 9th century, Persian was written down in the Arabic alphabet. The resultant flowering of New Persian literature at the court of the independent dynasts in Bukhara, the Samanids, ushered in a new phase of Persian culture. The New Persian renaissance, as it has been called by some scholars, was based on an Islamic-Persian language and literature, a brilliant and successful fusion of ancient Iranian (not just Persian, but also Sogdian, Parthian, and Khwarazmian) elements with the Arab-Islamic culture from the Arabic-speaking Near East. Henceforth Islam was not bound to Arab or Bedouin mores and backgrounds but became universal, a manifold and variegated world culture. The Samanids ruled Central Asia and Khurasan from *c.* 875 to 999.

Boyid, Turkish, and Mongol Dynasties. The 10th century saw the rise also of petty principalities in western Persia, the most important of which was the Boyid Dynasty, which ruled western Persia and Mesopotamia, including the caliphal capital Baghdad, until 1055. Under the Boyids there was an interesting flowering of pro-Islamic motifs in art and other domains. For example, the ancient title *shah an-shah* (king of kings) reappears in the sources. The Boyids participated also in the New Persian renaissance, but rule passed from the hands of the Iranians to the Turks after the turn of the millennium.

The SELJUK Turks took Baghdad in 1055 and soon established a large empire extending from Central Asia to the Mediterranean Sea. The empire was organized along feudal lines, and the Persian language was generally the language of administration. The extent of Persian influence on the Turks is revealed by such books as the *Siyasat name* (book of state) by Nizam al-Mulk, the prime minister of the Seljuk Sultan Malikshah. The Turks were replaced by Mongols, who ruled over Persia from *c.* 1256 to 1335.

Turko-Mongol rule in Persia brought into the land many influences from Central Asia and even China. Pottery and miniature painting both reflected strong Far Eastern elements, and the administration and army also were greatly influenced. This can be seen in the many words and terms introduced into Persian from the Turkish and even Mongolian languages, e.g., *ordu* (army) and *tufangchi* (rifleman). Persian influence on the Turks, however, was much stronger than the reverse, and even OTTOMAN sultans composed poetry in Persian rather than Turkish.

After the Mongol Dynasty of the Il-Khans, Persia was ruled for a short period (*c.* 1380–1469) by TIMUR (Tamerlane) and his successors. These Central-Asian Turkish rulers, with their capitals of Samarqand or Herat, were great patrons of the arts and literature. Under them the regions of Central Asia and present Afghanistan experienced a flowering of culture, the architectural remains of which still embellish the cities mentioned above.

Safavid Dynasty. The modern history of Persia really begins with the rise of the SAFAVID dynasty in 1500. Although these rulers were also Turkish in origin, they espoused the SHI'ITE form of Islam and established a state church different from the SUNNI faith that prevailed elsewhere. The land again had a national solidarity closely resembling that of Sasanian and even Achaemenid times. The militant Shi'ite state soon came into conflict with its neighbors, and just as in the past, Persia had to fight on two fronts, the Ottoman Empire in the west and a new Özbek Turkish state in Central Asia, both Sunni. So the wars of the 16th and 17th centuries were religiously as well as politically motivated.

The greatest of the Safavid rulers was Shah 'Abbas I (1587–1629), who defeated both Ottoman Turks and Özbeks (or Uzbeks, a Turkic people of the region north of Afghanistan), but who is known chiefly for his building activity, especially in his new capital of Isfahan, where some of the masterpieces of Persian architecture are found. Shah 'Abbas also moved rebellious people from one part of his kingdom to another, a common practice as old as the Assyrian Empire. Some Kurds were moved from their homeland in western Persia to Khurasan, while Armenians were transferred from Julfa in Transcaucasia to a suburb of Isfahan that they called New Julfa. The Armenian church and other buildings of New Julfa are surviving masterpieces of Safavid architecture. Under Shah 'Abbas, Europeans began to arrive in Persia as merchants, missionaries, and even as mercenaries. The British East India Company established a base on the island of Hormuz in the Persian Gulf (*c.* 1622).

The later Safavids proved so weak that in 1722 a force of Sunni Afghans under a chief called Mahmud was able to take the Safavid capital of Isfahan. As a result of the ensuing disorders in Persia, foreign powers were able to annex parts of the land. In the north, PETER I (THE GREAT) OF RUSSIA took the Caspian Provinces of Gilan and Mazandaran (1723), as well as Baku and parts of Transcaucasia that had been under Persian rule. The Ottoman Turks invaded Azerbaijan, Kirmanshah, and Hamadan and in 1724 made a treaty with Russia that in effect divided northern Persia between them.

For the Safavid period of history there are fortunately many European travel accounts and a valuable chronicle of the Carmelites who were established at Isfahan. As a result of the disintegration of central authority following the Afghan occupation, however, many of the western Europeans established in the country left, so that there is less information about the 18th century than about the earlier periods.

The Safavids represented the high point of culture in modern Persian history. From the time of their rule come the finest rugs, miniatures, and architecture in the history of Persia. Such was the fame of Shah 'Abbas as a builder that even today the common folk believe most Islamic ruins in the country were edifices raised by the Safavid ruler. The elegance of the court of the grand sophy, as the ruler of Persia was called in Western sources, has been described by several European embassies. The importance of Safavid religious leaders, such as Mulla Muhammad Baqir al-Majlisi, in laying the present foundations of Shi'ite Islam must be emphasized. Philosophy also, which enjoyed little development in the Ottoman Empire, experienced a revival in Persia, especially in the Ishraqi (illuminist) school of Mulla Sadra of Shiraz and others.

The Afghan occupation did not last long, for a new conqueror rose in Khurasan, a Turk called Nadir from the Afshar tribe. In 1729 he took Isfahan from Mahmud's successor, Ashraf the Afghan, but Nadir was not crowned ruler until 1736, when he deposed 'Abbas III, the boy Safavid ruler. Nadir Shah made many military expeditions, enlarging Persia's frontiers. In 1739 he took and plundered Delhi, and in the following year he obtained the submission of the Özbeks in Turkistan, including Bukhara, Samarqand, and Khiva. In 1742 he conquered part of Daghistan and much of the Caucasus area. The empire built by Nadir Shah quickly fell apart, however, after his assassination in 1747.

The chronology of the rulers of the Safavid Dynasty is as follows:

1. Ismail I (1500–24)
2. Tahmasp I (1524–76)
3. Ismall II (1576–77)
4. Muhammad Khudabanda(1577–87)
5. 'Abbas I (1587–1629)
6. Sail I (1629–42)

7. 'Abbas II (1642–67)
8. Sulaiman (1667–94)
9. Husain (1694–1722)
10. Tahmasp II (1730–32)
11. 'Abbas III (1732–36)

Qajar Dynasty. From 1750 to 1779 Karim Khan Zand, with his capital at Shiraz, maintained unity and order in the country, but at his death troubles recurred, and only in 1794 did a eunuch Called Aga Muhammad reunite the country. This tyrant was assassinated in 1797, and his nephew Fath 'Ali Shah ascended the throne as the real founder of the Qajar Dynasty. During Fath 'Ali Shah's reign, the European powers brought Persia into the international politics and diplomacy of the Napoleonic period. British and French rivalry in Persia was replaced by British and Russian rivalry, after the final defeat of Napoleon. In 1813, after a disastrous war with Russia, Persia was obliged by the Treaty of Gulistan to cede her Transcaucasian possessions, save Armenia, to Russia. Another war ended in 1828 with the Treaty of Turkmanchai, whereby the boundary between Russia and Persia was set at the Aras River and Russia obtained extraterritorial rights in the domains of the shah.

The 19th-century history of Persia is largely the story of Russian and British diplomacy trying to obtain a favored position at the court of the shah. A new religious movement called BABISM was partially suppressed with the execution of its leader, the Bab, in 1850, but his successor, Baha Allah, changed the movement and founded the religion known as BAHA'ISM, which, with the flight from Persia of the leader and many of his followers, became an international faith. Baha'is, however, have continued to exist in Persia down to the present day.

The Persians captured Herat from the Afghans in 1856, but the British declared war on Persia and forced it to give up all Afghan territory in a treaty of 1857; the boundary between the two countries was not settled until 1872. Rivalry between the British and Russians was intensified with the Russian conquest of Central Asia in the second half of the 19th century. The growth of foreign influence usually took the form of loans to the shah, although more obvious indices of influence were the Persian Cossack brigade, trained and led by Russian officers, established in 1878, and the Imperial Bank of Persia opened by the British in 1889.

Nasir al-Din Shah was assassinated in 1896, a sign that the absolutism and tyranny of the Persian rulers would not last long. Not until December of 1905, however, did the revolution begin. The Persian revolution, from which dates the rise of contemporary Persia, began as a movement against the extension of foreign influences and as a protest against the corruption and tyranny of the prime minister of the shah. The revolutionary movement that began as a protest soon changed to a demand for a constitution and a representative assembly. After a great demonstration in the grounds of the British legation in July of 1906, the shah was constrained to agree to the convocation of an assembly (*majlis*) that met in the autumn of 1907 and drew up a constitution. Muzaffar al-Din Shah signed the order creating constitutional government in Persia shortly before his death on December 30 of the same year.

At the same time, the discovery of oil in the area heightened the interest of both the British and Russians in finally establishing hegemony. This conflict was temporarily resolved in 1907 with the Anglo-Russian Entente, which divided Persia into spheres of influence. During World War I, Persia was occupied by both Britain and Russia, but in 1921 the newly formed Soviet government renounced imperial claims to Persian lands.

The rulers of the Qajar Dynasty are as follows:

1. Aga Muhammad (1794–97)
2. Fath 'Ali Shah (1797–1835)
3. Muhammad Shah (1835–48)
4. Nasir al-Din Shah (1848–96)
5. Muzaffar al-Din Shah (1896–1906)
6. Muhammad 'Ali (1906–09)
7. Ahmad Shah (1909–25)

Pahlavi Dynasty. In 1921, a popular military officer named Reza Khan engineered a coup that established him as minister of war and later as prime minister. As Reza Khan's popularity eclipsed that of Ahmad Shah, the latter was forced into exile; in December of 1925, the *majlis* officially deposed the last of the Qajar rulers and elected Reza Khan hereditary shah.

Pro-Western in his approach, Reza Shah Pahavi enacted a number of reforms intended to modernize Persia, including the official renaming of the country as Iran in 1935. His son and successor, Muhammad Reza Shah Palevi (1941–79), continued with pro-Western, promodernization reforms, but nationalist and Islamic opposition grew steadily. In 1979 the shah was deposed in a violent revolution and Iran officially became an Islamic republic under the cleric Ayatollah Ruhollah Khomeini.

See Also: IRAN, THE CATHOLIC CHURCH IN

Bibliography: Pre-Islamic history of Persia. R. N. FRYE, *The Heritage of Persia* (Cleveland 1963), extensive bibliog. The rise of the Safavids. L. LOCKHART, *The Fall of the Safavī Dynasty and the Afghan Occupation of Persia* (Cambridge, Eng. 1958). P. M. SYKES, *A History of Persia,* 2 v. (3d ed. London 1951), gen. popular hist. G. BARDY, ''Les Églises de Perse et d'Arménie au Ve siècle,'' *Histoire de l'église depuis les origines jusqu'à nos jours,* ed. A. FLICHE and V. MARTIN (Paris 1935) 4:321–336, with bibliog. R. MAYER and W. DE VRIES, *Lexikon für Theologie und Kirche*, ed. J. HOFER and K. RAHNER (Freiburg 1957–65) 8:283–287, with bibliog.

[R. N. FRYE]

Bas-relief depicting winged monster, late 6th century B.C., Palace of Darius, Susa, Persia. (©Vanni Archive/CORBIS)

PERSIAN RELIGION, ANCIENT

Persian religion is defined here as the religion that prevailed in Persia from about the 6th century B.C. until the Muslim conquest in the 7th or 8th century A.D. and its subsequent replacement by Islam. It is now the faith of a very small minority in Persia and of the PARSEES settled in India since the 10th century A.D. It is often called Zoroastrianism, after the Greek form of the name of its traditional prophet or reformer Zoroaster, or Mazdaeism after the epithet of its supreme God AHURA MAZDA (Wise Lord), later Ohrmazd. The inadequacy of written documents and the lack of monuments explain the disagreement among specialists on even the most important points. To present a ''generally accepted view'' would be misleading. All that can be done is to describe sources and outline the most probable theories.

Sources. The main ancient source is the *AVESTA*, the sacred book of the Zoroastrians. It was discovered among the Parsees and deciphered by A. H. Anquetil-Duperron, who published a French translation (2 v. Paris 1771). The ancient form of Iranian, now known as Avestan, was soon seen to be akin to Sanskrit. Its interpretation was solidly established as a result of the progress of Indo-European philology in the 19th century. The *Avesta* is a series of books used mainly for liturgy. The *Yasna* is the text of the HAOMA sacrifice parallel to the Indian Soma. The rubrics are in middle Persian (i.e., Pahlavi) and, with greater detail, in Gujarati, an Indian language of the Bombay area. The oldest stratum, in an archaic dialect, are the *GĀTHĀS*, metrical poems attributed to ZOROASTER himself. The *Visprat* is a short addition to the *Yasna.* The *Vidēvdāt* (incorrectly *Vendidad*) comprises a miscellaneous collection of instructions regarding purifications after death and a penal code. Quite different in character is the collection of *Yashts,* some of them older than the *Yasna,* but some, late and awkward imitations; they are hymns to the gods presiding over each day of the month.

The *Khortak* (short) *Avesta* is a collection of prayers for the various hours of the day.

Other Avestan texts have survived only in Pahlavi commentaries; the *Dēnkart,* a Pahlavi encyclopedia compiled and partly composed in the 10th century A.D., summarizes the original books (*Nasks*) known in Sassanid times, most of which are now lost. The *Yasna* and *Vidēvdāt* were translated into and commented upon in Pahlavi. There is one ancient book dealing with eschatology, the *Zand i Vohuman Yasht,* preserved in a Pahlavi paraphrase, and portions of the *Nask* on the life of Zoroaster are embedded in a continuous narrative in book 7 of the *Dēnkart.*

Most of the extant Zoroastrian literature in Pahlavi dates from the 9th or 10th centuries. It is of great value because it is based on older tradition. The *Būndahishn* (Cosmology) gives an embryonic theology; the *Zātspram* contains the cosmological and eschatological myths; the *Artāg Vīrāf* describes a visit to heaven and hell; the *Mēnōk-i-Khrat* is a miscellaneous collection of ethical teachings; the *Shkand Gumānīk Vicār,* a philosophical refutation of Judaism, Christianity, Islam, and Manichaeism, betrays the influence of Greek philosophy and of Islamic theology.

The Gods. In the *Gāthās* the Yazatān (Worshipful Beings) form a group round Ahura Mazda, the one great God. They are Vohu Mann (the Good Spirit), Arta Vahishta (Best Righteousness, in a vast range of meanings), Khshathra Vairya (Desirable Rule),Āramaiti (Devotion, Obedience), the twins Haurvatāt (Integrity, Health), and Ameretāt (Immortality). G. Dumézil has shown that these are typically Iranian transformations of the earlier Indo-Iranian gods. Ahura Mazda, the supreme God, has taken the place of Varuna, while the other gods have been reduced to the status of his servants, Khshathra Vairya, for instance, taking the place of the warrior-god Indra.

The group was later called the AMESHA SPENTA, i.e., the Beneficent Immortals. Their rank is clearly less divine than that of the Adityas, their Indian parallels. The Amesha Spenta are patrons of the different spheres of creation: man, fire, metals, earth, plants, and waters. Some scholars have described them as aspects of the one God, though Mazdaean tradition clearly depicts them as His ''creatures.'' However, they are considered worthy of veneration, and the place they occupy in cult shows that they participate in the divine.

Zoroastrianism could thus be characterized as a qualified monotheism—with Ahura Mazda, as paramount God, alone described as creator—but with a certain vagueness about the status of the Amesha Spenta, probably because they come from beings who had a divine sta-

Ancient Persian fire altars, 5th century B.C., at Naksh-I-Rustem, Achaemenid Necropolis, near Persepolis, Iran. (The Catholic University of America)

tus before the *Gāthās.* Another indication of such a change is their vague and shifting character in the *Gāthās.* This makes it difficult to distinguish them without considering them in the light of their earlier history.

Other primeval entities in the *Gāthās* are the Beneficent and the Evil Spirits whose conflict is described chiefly in *Yasna* 30. It is not clear what their relation is to the Amesha Spenta or whether the Evil Spirit was created by Ahura Mazda. The description of their personalities and conflict may reflect not a fully worked out system of thought but a myth expressing ethical and ritual dualism, good and bad ways of worship as well as of action. The ethical aspect became dominant and colored the subsequent cosmology. *Yasna* 30 may have been the theological interpretation of the myth of the god Zurvan (Time). He gives birth to the twins Ormazd and Ahriman, who triumph for alternating periods in the world they have created until the Good is finally victorious and Evil destroyed. Evidence of this myth is hardly earlier than the Sassanid period, and it was always repudiated by orthodox Mazdaeans. Yet it was certainly more than a bookish phantasy (*see* MANICHAEISM), since later Muslim historians speak of it at length.

The *Gāthās* denounce those who do wrong to the Cow. Zoroaster is promised as its protector on earth, just as he is the helper on earth of the poor against violence and depredation. There is an obscure allusion to the slaying of the Bull, which is probably not so much a condemnation of animal sacrifice as of violence and orgiastic cults. The allusion may reflect, too, a remnant of Indo-Iranian reverence for the cow as providing milk and the necessities of life. Other helpers are Saoshyant (the Savior) and a chief Vishtāspa, who is the special protector of Zoroaster. Thanks to Vishtāspa, the cult will be maintained.

The eschatology of the *Gāthās* is fairly well worked out. Souls are tried at the Bridge, the world will be submitted to a fire of molten metal, the righteous will be saved and the wicked purified. The *Yasna Haptanhati* (*Yasna* of the Seven Chapters), which, judging by linguistic evidence, is slightly later than the *Gāthās,* stresses the importance of the fire cult, always paramount in Persian religion, and especially in the *Yasna* sacrifice. Many small fire shrines have been located by Muslim geographers and modern archeologists. Later parts of the *Yasna* name many other gods. There are hymns to Mithra, the god of contract (*Yasht* 10); to Ardvi Sura Anāhīta, the only important goddess, patroness of rivers and fecundity (*Yasht* 5); to Verethragna (later Vāhrām), the multiform god of strength, who gives his name to one of the most important fires (*Yasht* 14); to the FRAVASHIS, doubles of all men alive or to be born (*Yasht* 13, containing a long list of ancient heroes, a sketch of the mythical history of Iran). There is a similar passage in *Yasna* 9–11 in honor of the Haoma, the personified sacrificial plant offered with water and milk in the ceremony of the *Yasna.*

Zarathustra. Zarathustra (in Greek, Zoroaster) is given an important part in all these texts. Since the *Gāthās* do not mention the main gods of the *Yasna* and the *Yashts*, Zarathustra has been taken by most modern scholars to have been a reformer who repudiated the traditional Indo-Iranian gods and condemned the Haoma cult. According to the scholars mentioned, these two phases of worship were later reintroduced into the religion, which was still considered, however, to be that of Zarathustra. They have therefore sought to reconstruct the pre-Zoroastrian state of Persian religion from the data in the non-Gathic texts that are incompatible with the content of the *Gāthās.* Zarathustra thus appears as the prophet of a new reformed religion, approximating the role given to him in the *Dēnkart.* The problem is to explain how notions that are incompatible with the prophet's teaching were later reconciled with it. More recent research (e.g., that of M. Molé and R. C. Zaehner) suggests that the antagonism between the *Gāthās* and the later *Avesta* can be exaggerated and that in this case the argument *a silentio* is especially dangerous.

Zarathustra may have belonged to a priestly circle using an esoteric terminology. The date traditionally given to him is 258 years "before Alexander," i.e., probably 258 years before the sack of Persepolis in 330 B.C. Were the *Gāthās* written by him, or were they a liturgical text attributed to him as the priest par excellence (Molé)? His legend must have developed rapidly, since the Pahlavi resume of it is interspersed with literal translations from an Avestan text now lost. It presents the prophet's birth and childhood in a framework of miracles. Then come his Revelation as a dialogue with the Amesha Spenta, the wars waged by Vishtāspa on behalf of the new religion, and lastly the epochs of world history ending with Sōshyans.

In the Pahlavi works, *Bundahishn* and *Zātspram,* the cosmic dualism is fully worked out. Ahriman attempts to invade his rival's domain. Ohrmazd drives him out and, after an unsuccessful attempt at peace, creates the world as a bulwark against him. It is first created in spirit (*mēnōk*) and so remains 3,000 years. It then passes into actuality (*gētī*) and is mingled with the creatures of the Evil Principle. The fight lasts for 6,000 years with alternating triumphs and defeats, but the Good finally wins. *Mēnōk* and *gētī* are not opposed as spiritual and material. There is no trace of Platonic dualism, since all things have a *mēnōk* phase. This type of dualism is combined with another, that of the microcosm corresponding to the macrocosm, much as in the *Corpus Hippocraticum.* That the Iranian idea had priority over the Greek (A. Goetze) is no longer undisputed (J. Duchesne-Guillemin).

The Spread of Zoroastrianism and Its Problems. The geographical environment of the oldest parts of the *Avesta* is Eastern Iran. When did Zoroastrianism come to Western Asia? The oldest texts, the inscriptions of the Achaemenids, contain the name of the supreme God, written *Auramazda* (the Behistun inscription of Darius I, 486 B.C.), and he is mentioned with "other gods," e.g. with Anāhīta and Mithra by Artaxerxes II (404–358 B.C.). Zarathustra is never mentioned, but that is not decisive in itself, and it should be noted that the ethical attitude is not unlike that of the *Gāthās.* It is possible that the Persian kings reflect a royal rather than a priestly form of Zoroastrianism. An inscription of Xerxes (486–65 B.C.) proclaiming the destruction of "the lairs of the *DAĒVAS*" shows only that various cults were in opposition to one another. *Daēva* came to mean demon in Persian, but in India it is the name for a class of gods. The Persians may have worshiped exclusively the other class, the Ahuras, of whom Varuna, renamed Ahura Mazda, became predominant and tended towards a monotheistic status. In

India, there was no such antagonism between the classes of gods as in Persia, nor was there a tendency towards monotheism.

The earliest Greek author to speak of the Persian religion, Herodotus, describes the cult rendered to the elements and insists on the presence of the Magi, described as a Median tribe expert in ritual. These may have been responsible for much of the later development of Zoroastrianism as exemplified in the *Vidēvdāt,* which furnishes rules for the disposal of the dead (by exposure to carnivorous birds on the so-called ''Towers of Silence,'' still in use among the Parsees), against coming into contact with dead matter, and on the great ceremony of purification called *Bareshnūm;* it presents also a code of law covering injury and assault, and the sacredness of the dog and sins against it.

Dualistic Features and Their Influence. In the Pahlavi books dualism is hardened into a thoroughgoing opposition on the cosmic as well as moral plane. Personal eschatology describes how three days after the soul has left the body it has a vision of a maiden, beautiful or repulsive; this is the soul's *dāenā* (religion) and leads it to the Bridge, which expands or narrows, and to judgment by Mithra, Sraosha, and Rashnu. These judge it according to its merits, and weigh it. The soul is then awarded heaven or hell. Hell is ultimately purified by a river of molten metal. Creation is not absorbed into it, and creatures find the perfection they have lacked. The *gētī* world returns to the *mēnōk* state. Time is not cyclical, despite Plutarch's account, and there is no transmigration of souls as in Indian religion.

The later literature of Zoroastrianism contains philosophical vindications of the dualist position. Most Muslim treatises on apologetics refute Zoroastrianism and describe its heresies. Manichaeism used Zoroastrian patterns, though Manichaean theology is decidedly opposed to Zoroastrianism. To appraise the influence of Zoroastrianism on Judaism one would need a detailed knowledge of Zoroastrianism as it was when the two religions were in contact during the Exile. Its apparent polytheism would have repelled the Jews, but the overwhelming personality of Ahura Mazda may have reminded them of Yahweh. Zoroastrian eschatology seems to have stimulated the development of their own, but it is very unlikely that Khshatra gave rise to the idea of the Kingdom of God. Even if Iranian dualism is the source of the myth of the two spirits in the *Manual of Discipline* (*see* DEAD SEA SCROLLS) and in late Jewish pseudepigraphical writings, it has there been transformed so as to preserve the paramount sovereignty of God and to assign a subordinate role to the Devil.

See Also: ZOROASTER (ZARATHUSHTRA); PARSEES; MITHRAS AND MITHRAISM.

Bibliography: J. DARMESTETER, *Le Zend-Avesta* (2d ed. Paris 1960). E. W. WEST, *Pahlavi Texts I–V* (Sacred Books of the East 5, 18, 24, 37, 47; Oxford 1880–97). *Zand-Akāsīh, Iranian or Greater Budahishn,* ed. with Eng. tr. B. T. ANKLESARIA (Bombay 1956). *Shkand Gumānīk Vicār: La Solution décisive des doutes,* ed. with a Fr. tr. J. P. MENASCE (Collectanea Friburgensia 30; Fribourg 1945). E. BENEVENISTE, *The Persian Religion according to the Chief Greek Texts* (Paris 1929). J. BIDEZ and F. CUMONT, *Les Mages hellénisés* (Paris 1938). J. DUCHESNE-GUILLEMIN, *The Western Response to Zoroaster* (Oxford 1958); *La Religion de l'Iran ancien* (Paris 1962). E. PAX, *Lexikon für Theologie und Kirche*, ed. J. HOFER and K. RAHNER, 10 v. (2d, new ed. Freiburg 1957–65) 8:111–15. R. C. ZAEHNER, *The Dawn and Twilight of Zoroastrianism* (London 1961). M. MOLÉ, *Culte, mythe et cosmologie dans l'Iran ancien* (Paris 1963). F. KÖNIG, *Zarathustras Jenseitsvorstellung und das Alte Testament* (Vienna 1964).

[J. P. DE MENASCE]

PERSICO, IGNATIUS

Cardinal; b. Naples, Italy, Jan. 30, 1823; d. Rome, Italy, Dec. 7, 1895. He received his early training with the Jesuits, entered the Capuchin Order in 1839, and was ordained Jan. 24, 1846. He volunteered for the missions and departed the same year for the Vicariate of Patna, India. In 1849 he became secretary to Bp. Anastasius Hartmann, OFM Cap., vicar apostolic of Patna and administrator of Bombay. In 1850 he became the first editor of the Bombay *Catholic Examiner.* Later, as commissary of the vicars apostolic of India, he helped bring the threatening Goanese schism to an end and obtained limited government recognition of the Catholic missionaries in India. Persico was consecrated coadjutor to Hartmann at Bombay on June 4, 1854, and successively became visitator (1854), administrator (1855), and vicar apostolic (1856) of Agra. He resigned (1860) because of illness and returned to Italy. Upon recovery he offered his services in 1867 to the Diocese of Charleston, South Carolina. In 1869 he was present at the Tenth Provincial Council of Baltimore, where he was permitted to vote. While attending Vatican Council I, he was appointed the fourth bishop of Savannah, Georgia (March 20, 1870), but illness again forced him to resign in 1872. In 1874 Rome entrusted him with a secret mission to Canada. He also went to Malabar, India, in 1877 to settle the Syro-Chaldean schism and to prepare for the erection of the Indian hierarchy. In 1878 Persico was made consultor of the Propaganda Fide and the following year became bishop of the united dioceses of Aquino, Pontecorvo, and Sora, Italy. Illness forced his resignation (1886), and he was named titular archbishop of Damietta, Egypt. In 1887 he went as a papal envoy to Ireland. Upon his return he was named vicar of the Vatican Basilica and secretary of the Propaganda Fide. Leo XIII made Persico a cardinal priest and prefect of the Congregation of Indulgences and Relics on Jan. 16, 1893.

Bibliography: B. A. FINN, *Twenty-four American Cardinals* (Boston 1947). D. C. SHEARER, *Historical Records and Studies of the U.S. Catholic Historical Society of New York* 21 (1932) 54–137, with sources and bibliog.

[N. MILLER]

PERSON (IN PHILOSOPHY)

A term derived from the Latin *persona,* traceable to the Greek πρόσωπον, and originally used to denote the mask worn by an actor. From this it was applied to the role he assumed; and finally, to any character on the stage of life, i.e., to any individual. The term has taken on a special significance in SCHOLASTICISM, where it has figured importantly in theological discussions of the INCARNATION and the Holy TRINITY. This article is restricted to a consideration of the notion as used in scholastic philosophy and is divided into two sections: the first sketches the historical development of the concept and the second provides a metaphysical analysis. (For the psychological treatment and the use of the term in modern philosophy, *see* INDIVIDUALITY; PERSONALISM; PERSONALITY; and SELF, THE; for the theological discussion of the term, *see* PERSON [IN THEOLOGY]; PERSON, DIVINE.)

History. The main stages in the evolution of the concept are its early formulation by Boethius, its adaptation by St. Thomas Aquinas, and its various refinements by later scholastics.

Boethius. The classical definition is given by BOETHIUS in his *De persona et duabus naturis,* where he teaches that person is ''an individual substance of a rational nature'' (ch. 3; *Patrologia Latina,* ed. J. P. Migne, 271 v., indexes 4 v. [Paris 1878–90] 64:1345). Boethius uses the term ''SUBSTANCE'' in the definition primarily to exclude accidents: ''We see that accidents cannot constitute person.'' The term ''substance,'' as Boethius understood it, can be used in two senses, one referring to the concrete substance as existing in the individual and called first substance, the other referring to substance conceived abstractly as existing in the GENUS and the SPECIES and called second substance. It is disputed which sense of the term was here being used by Boethius. It seems probable that he prescinded from the technical significations of first substance and second substance, but used the qualifier ''individual'' to make his meaning equivalent to that of first substance. Individual, in turn, refers simply to what is undivided in itself; unlike the higher branches of the PORPHYRIAN TREE, namely, genus and species, it cannot be further subdivided. Boethius does not seem to attach any further signification to the term, but makes it a mere synonym for singular. The most important part of his definition is the expression ''of a rational nature.'' This serves to indicate that person is predicated only of intellectual beings. The generic term that includes all individual existing substances is supposit (*see* SUBSISTENCE); supposit may be applied equally to rational and irrational, to living and nonliving individuals. The sense of Boethius's definition is that a person is a particular type of supposit, namely, one with a rational nature.

Thomas Aquinas. The definition proposed by Boethius is not completely satisfactory as it stands, since the words taken literally can be applied to the rational soul of man and also to the human nature of Christ. St. THOMAS AQUINAS accepted it nonetheless, possibly because by his time it had become the traditional definition. The terms in which St. Thomas explained it, however, practically constitute a new definition. ''Individual substance'' becomes, for him, a substance that is complete, subsists by itself, and is separated from others (*Summa theologiae* 3a,16.12 ad 2). When the remainder of Boethius's definition is added to this, there are five notes that go to make up a person: (1) substance—this excludes accident; (2) complete—the person must have a complete nature, and thus that which is but part of a nature, either actually or aptitudinally, does not satisfy the definition; (3) subsistent by itself—the person exists in himself and for himself, being the ultimate possessor of his nature and all its acts, and therefore is the ultimate subject of predication of all his attributes; (4) separated from others—this excludes the universal notion of second substance, which can have no existence apart from the individual; and (5) of a rational nature—this excludes all supposits that lack rationality. To the person, therefore, there properly belongs a threefold incommunicability expressed in notes (2), (3), and (4). The human soul belongs to the nature as part of it, and is therefore not a person, even when existing separately (*see* SOUL, HUMAN). The human nature of Christ does not exist by itself alone, but in another, i.e., in the divine personality of the Word; thus it is not a person. Lastly, the divine essence, though subsisting by itself, is so communicated to the three Persons that it does not exist apart from Them; it is therefore not a person.

Later Scholastics. Further scholastic discussions of the notions of person have been largely disputes over the ultimate foundation of personality, i.e., to ascertain the precise determination of a nature that, if present, will make it subsistent and a person, and, if absent, will not.

According to John DUNS SCOTUS, as he is usually understood, the ultimate foundation of personality is a mere negation. An individual intellectual nature is a person if, in its nature, it is neither destined to be communicated, as is the human soul, nor actually communicated, as is the humanity of Christ. Were the hypostatic union to cease,

Christ's humanity would, ipso facto, without any further determination, become a person.

To Duns Scotus's position it is commonly objected that the person possesses the nature and all its attributes, and it is difficult to regard this possessor, as distinct from the objects possessed, as constituted only by a negative. Consequently, traditional Thomists, following Tommaso de Vio CAJETAN, hold that personality must be based on a positive determination, which they call the MODE of subsistence. It is the function of this mode to make the nature incommunicable, terminated in itself, and capable of receiving its own *esse,* or EXISTENCE. Without this mode the human nature of Christ subsists only by the uncreated *esse* of the Word.

F. SUÁREZ also insists that the ultimate foundation of personality cannot be a mere negation but must be a positive perfection. Since he holds that there is no real distinction between nature (or essence) and existence, he does not regard personality as something that prepares the nature to receive its own proper existence. In his view, personality is something added to a nature conceived as already existing. Subsistence can be added to a substance actually existing because, according to his teaching, existence itself is quasi potential. The sense in which personality or subsistence consists in incommunicability is that it excludes only communication to another as to the ultimate term of existence (*De incarn.* 11.3; *Disp. meta.* 34). Thus personality, for Suárez, is the final term or complement not of a substantial essence but of existence itself.

Other thinkers have attempted to define the formal constitutive of personality without employing Cajetan's mode or Suárez's conception of a positive determination. Some hold that a substance is a supposit, and an intelligent substance a person, from the mere fact of its being a whole, a *totum in se.* This totality, it is contended, is a positive note that adds no reality, just as the whole adds nothing to the parts that compose it. Those who reject this explanation do so because the concept of totality seems to reduce, according to their analysis, to the Scotistic concept of a mere negation. Still others consider personality to be ultimately constituted by the *esse,* the actual existence of an intelligent substance. That which subsists with its own *esse* is by that very fact incommunicable. This theory finds some support among the writings of the early Greek Fathers, but otherwise has not been regarded as completely satisfactory by philosophers and theologians.

Analysis. In the light of the foregoing, a more systematic analysis of the concept of person may be given, drawing mainly on the insights of St. Thomas and other scholastics but making their presentation more relevant to contemporary discussions among philosophers.

Ontological Foundation. The problem of the metaphysical definition of person is basically that of ascertaining what the notion of person adds to the more general concept of supposit, and, whatever this may be, of determining its ultimate ontological foundation. St. Thomas points out that person has a special dignity, that it represents what is most perfect in all of nature, and that its special excellence consists in having dominion over its own activity (*Summa theologiae* 1a, 29.1). Although in explaining this dignity he does not refer to the special mode of subsistence, there can be no doubt that for him the special excellence of the person derives from its entitative sufficiency for independent existence. The person is thus superior to the THING, which, although something in the order of substance, has a substantial form that is limited in its existential capabilities (*see* MATTER AND FORM). For example, the substantial form of a material thing, although itself a formal principle of substance, has no immediate aptitude to existence, because of its essential dependence on matter for both its becoming and its being. To this extent its ability to subsist is minimal, since the union of matter and form can be disrupted at any time under the influence of external physical agents. The human soul, on the other hand, although the substantial form of a body, by reason of its spirituality has a special aptitude for existence that it actually communicates to the body (*see* SPIRIT). Because of this, it has a more perfect type of subsistence than a material thing; at least on the part of the soul, existence is independent of any extrinsic causal influences. Thus the primary note that distinguishes human persons—and a fortiori ANGELS—from lower types of beings is the perfection of their spiritual forms, which confers on them a more perfect and enduring manner of existing.

The metaphysical basis of personality is thus traceable to a special mode of subsistence that is rooted in the spirituality of the form or substantial act of the intellectual substance. It is true, of course, that man's spiritual substantial form, or his soul, though complete in the order of substance, is not complete as a species and is thus not to be identified with the human person (*De anim.* 1; *De spir. creat.* 2, 2 ad 5, 2 ad 16). This notwithstanding, the proper perfection of man as a person derives from the subsistent character of his soul, because man exists and subsists only through the existence and subsistence of his spiritual soul. For this reason, the spirituality of man may be regarded as the metaphysical root of his personality; it is this characteristic that confers on him a more perfect type of subsistence than that found in other corporeal creatures.

Corollaries. As a consequence of this existential independence of material conditions, certain corollaries follow that relate to the person's activities and to his relationships to others.

The human person, precisely as spiritual, is free from the limitations of space and time that circumscribe irrational beings. Although he has a beginning in time, his subsequent duration in being is in a certain sense extratemporal; he cannot be considered merely as an integral part of the physical universe, completely subject to the laws of its history. Viewed from another aspect, he exhibits a type of IMMATERIALITY that is best seen in his rational or intellectual character. He is able to possess abstract and universal knowledge that transcends the data of sense (*see* INTELLECT). He has the capacity also of reflecting on his activities and even on himself; thus he is said to be endowed with CONSCIOUSNESS. Having dominion over his own activity, he also possesses FREE WILL. From this follows his moral character and all that this implies, e.g., the personal responsibility that is his for having dominion over his own activities.

Other properties of the human person are associated with the complex of relationships man may have with beings below him, with other finite persons, and with God. Because he transcends the rest of corporeal creation, the human person has a type of dominion over it and can use it for his own proper good. Since he stands in the relationship of EQUALITY to other humans, he may not derogate from their personal independence and liberty or deprive them of their rights. Even more, his community of nature with other humans provides the ontological basis for FRIENDSHIP and for LOVE. Similarly, man's personal character provides the foundation for all his social relationships, whereby he and others strive to attain the common good in civil SOCIETY. Finally, the person, precisely as rational or intellectual, is an image of his Creator and thus stands in special relationship to God. His autonomy and freedom are not absolute, but are limited by his dependence on God, i.e., on the divine will and on the eternal law. His ontological limitation as a finite person is the ultimate reason in the natural order why man should love God more than himself and should order his entire life toward God as his final end and ultimate completion.

See Also: MAN, 2, 3; SOUL-BODY RELATIONSHIP.

Bibliography: M. J. ADLER, ed., *The Great Ideas: A Syntopicon of Great Books of the Western World,* 2 v. (Chicago 1952); v. 2, 3 of *Great Books of the Western World* 2:1–41. R. EISLER, *Wörterbuch der philosophischen Begriffe,* 3 v. (4th ed. Berlin 1927–30) 2:393–401. L. W. GEDDES, *The Catholic Encyclopedia,* ed. C. G. HERBERMANN et al., 16 v. (New York 1907–14) 11:726–727. L. STEFANINI, *Enciclopedia filosofica,* 4 v. (Venice-Rome 1957) 3:1297–1304. C. DE KONINCK, *De la primauté du bien commun* (Quebec 1943). J. MARITAIN, *The Person and the Common Good,* tr. J. J. FITZGERALD (New York 1947). R. GUARDINI, *Welt und Person* (Würzburg 1940). M. DEANDREA, *Praelectiones metaphysica,* v. 2 (Rome 1957). J. B. METZ, *Christliche Anthropozentrik* (Munich 1962).

[L. W. GEDDES/W. A. WALLACE]

PERSON (IN THEOLOGY)

Christianity is love and its ''God is love'' (1 Jn 4.8, 16). Love manifests personality—a person loving and a person loved. Hence Christianity is an eminently personal religion and its God a very personal God. Three personalist mysteries summarize Christianity: (1) God, the absolute and infinite, unique and wholly ''other'' One, is three Persons; (2) Jesus Christ, the one mediator between God and man, is the Person of the WORD having both a divine and human nature; (3) there is a mystical personality of Christ, in which Christians enter into personal communion with God. All theology is ultimately a reflection on and seeking an understanding of these three personal realities. Because the developments of the concept of personality in Trinitarian and Christological theology are so intimately interconnected, these are here treated together. There follows a consideration of person in MYSTICAL BODY theology.

Person in Trinitarian-Christological Theology. Hebrew is without a term for our concept ''person.'' There are instances in the Old Testament when the word *pānîm* (face) practically corresponds to our understanding of person. The Greek word for face, πρόσωπον, likewise has the meaning of person (cf. 2 Cor 1.11). Postapostolic Christian teachers soon discovered that mere repetition of biblical phrases inadequately preserved the integrity of the Christian faith taking root in the Greco-Roman world. Because of the central place personality has in the mysteries of the Trinity and of Christ, there was need of a gradual clarification of the notion of person in Catholic theology. We shall trace this theological development of the notion of person in the mysteries of the Trinity and INCARNATION through four general stages.

Nicaean-Chalcedonian Formulation. The Trinitarian-Christological controversies of the 2d to the 5th centuries in the Greco-Roman world occasioned the first development in the notion of person. Christian Trinitarian monotheism had to be preserved while being incarnated in a new culture steeped in Neoplatonic philosophy and language. Whereas the starting point of Eastern writers was the distinction of Persons with an ever-present danger of SUBORDINATIONISM, the Western writers looked to the unity of the divine substance, with a dangerous tendency toward MODALISM. It was Tertullian's exact egalistic mind that gave precision to Western terminology at a very early date. *Persona* referred to that which is threefold in the Trinity and one in Christ; *natura* or *substantia,* later also *essentia,* designated that which is one in the Trinity and dual in Christ. In the East, however, four Greek words (πρόσωπον, φύσις, ὑπόστασις, οὐσία) signified our concept of person, the latter three words also designating nature. Moreover, πρόσωπον, taken in its etymological sense (face, mask, appearance), was capable of a modalistic meaning. The Nicaean-Chalcedonian formulas gave the first doctrinal clarification to the terms nature and person. NICAEA I (325) defined that the Son is of the Father's substance and ὁμοούσιος (consubstantial) with the Father, while Chalcedon (451) defined that Christ is one Person (πρόσωπον, or ὑπόστασις) with two natures (φύσεις, or οὐσίαι). These doctrinal formulas are both an end and a new beginning, for every propositional form of the divine mysteries is necessarily incomplete. Christianity's personalist message has to be constantly restated with ever-greater depths of understanding.

Relationship Pertains to Divine Personality. The mystery of the Trinity appears in the Bible in reference to distinct roles in the economy of salvation, but in the theology of the Greek Fathers as distinct Persons. The oneness of the divine substance is preserved by their doctrine of perichoresis, i.e., the coinherence of the Divine Persons in a dynamic compenetrating existence (*see* CIRCUMINCESSION). Though perichoresis contains an implicit mutual relationship between the Divine Persons, this aspect of Trinitarian theology reaches greater development in Western theology.

St. Augustine, faithful to the Western viewpoint, took the divine essence as the starting point of his investigation, but then had difficulty maintaining the distinction of Persons. He solved this difficulty when he saw that the term ''Person'' in the Trinity can only mean subsistent relation—a discovery that had a great impact on future Trinitarian theology. ''Substance comprehends unity, relation multiplies Trinity'' (Boethius). Starting with the unique divine nature in developing a doctrine of subsistent relations is admittedly not a New Testament approach to the Divine Persons. Nevertheless by returning to the biblical data now, it will be discovered that the description there of the Divine Persons can be taken in the sense of mutual relations. Moreover these mutual relations bring Western theology once more in contact with the dynamic Trinitarianism of Eastern theology. The mutual relations place in the Godhead eternal begetting, being begotten, and proceeding. The Divine Persons are now seen to reveal God in terms of His own inner life. Analogies are now easily discovered in man's spiritual, intellectual, and volitional life: Memory, Understanding, Will; Lover, Beloved, Their Love.

Ontological Precision of Person. Boethius, an Italian philosopher-statesman of the 6th century, defined person as an individual substance of a rational nature. This definition, explained by later theologians, especially St. Thomas, has become classic in theology. All recognize the term ''rational'' to mean any intellectual nature, not merely human, and the term ''substance'' to designate first substance, the subsistent subject or hypostasis. The precise clarification in this third stage is that the notion of SUBSISTENCE, existence in itself, and therefore INCOMMUNICABILITY, belongs to the notion of person. Person is the subsistent, incommunicable subject of an intellectual nature—theology now has a notion of person that accounts for the distinct roles of the Father, Son, and Holy Spirit in the biblical description of the economy of Redemption. This ontological notion of person, while far from adequate, offers a secure basis for theological consideration of the Trinitarian and Christological mysteries.

Relation of Person, Nature, Existence. Catholic dogma teaches that Christ is one Person (that of the Word) with two natures, divine and human. Consequently, human nature cannot of itself mean human person. Christ is a human but not a human person. Theology now had to come to a more precise understanding of personality or subsistence. Prescinding from particular modifications, the commentators on St. Thomas offer three principal explanations. (1) The Scotists see in subsistence a negative element—not being assumed. Christ is not a human person because His human nature is assumed by the Person of the Word. (2) Proper existence itself is subsistence in the view of Capreolus reaffirmed by Billot. Christ is without human personality because His human nature does not have a proportionate human existence but shares in the infinite act of existence of the Word. (3) For Cajetan subsistence is a substantial mode added to nature, terminating it in ultimate incommunicability, which makes nature immediately apt for existence. In Christ there is no such human substantial mode and hence no human personality.

That is where the matter lies today—one of free and divergent opinion. All three views are not without shortcomings. The nonassumption of the Scotistic view hardly seems an adequate explanation of so rich a reality as personality. The Capreolus-Billot view runs into serious metaphysical difficulties and seems to endanger the reality of Christ's human nature. Christ exists as God and exists as man; how can these existences be more one than His divinity and humanity are one? Even positing real existential unity of the person, there still seems a necessary parallel unity and distinction in essence and in existence. Cajetan's substantial mode seems to be a made-to-order explanation of the HYPOSTATIC UNION without much corroborating evidence from an examination of human personality as such.

Contemporary Psychological Notion of Person. The ontological categories that have prevailed in the theology of the Trinity and of Christ, fruitful as they have been, have not sounded the depths of the inexhaustible source—Scripture. New approaches are usually along three lines: (1) taking a more theological view of human personality, considering also what is known from the Trinitarian-Christological mysteries; (2) using the data of contemporary psychology in theologizing about the mysteries of the Trinity and Incarnation; and (3) complementing the ontological notion of person (a definition according to common notions of singularity, *Summa theologiae* 1a 29.1 ad 1) with existential aspects of personality (descriptions of singular uniqueness and dynamic vitality). In all of these the Catholic theologian is not questioning the ontological foundation of personality; hence no Günther-Rosmini identification of personality with self-consciousness.

Significant theological insights manifesting a new vitality in theology have resulted from these new perspectives. Human personality is seen as a center of relationships through self-consciousness (self-possession) and self-giving. A person is therefore someone complete in himself but also someone who is constituted by his relations. This is theologically significant, for we know that the relatedness of one Person to another in the Trinitarian mystery stands at the core of personality. This insight into personality gives new pertinency to RICHARD OF SAINT-VICTOR's trinitarian analogy—the Lover, the Loved, and the Love as Initial Gift. The New Testament definition ''God is love'' is understood no longer in an essentialistic sense of an absolute attribute of the divine nature, but in the strictly personalistic sense that God is Self-Giver, Responsive Self-Giver, and Mutual Gift.

It is impossible to overestimate the contribution made by the mystery of the Incarnation to our understanding of the human person. Christ's human consciousness and freedom reveal a Divine Person who is truly mediator in His humanity. The human person, radically in relationship to God, can then realize himself only in union with Christ. But this involves the human person in the mystery of Christ crucified and risen. In this life, the person finds it impossible to give himself without losing himself, so that the ultimate fulfillment of self-possession and self-giving is attained only after death and then not as a result of man's endeavors but of God's Self-giving. Made one with the Spirit, the human person is caught up in the Self-giving life of the Divine Persons.

Person in the Theology of the Mystical Body. The Old Testament presents a double theme on human personality: a gradual development of a sense of individual responsibility is intimately bound up with the collective—of the specially chosen PEOPLE OF GOD. There is a solidarity of the group and of the individual persons that constitutes a form of ''corporate personality.''

The full harmonization of the individual person and the corporate person is realized in Christ. Already St. Augustine speaks of Christ and Christians as constituting a certain oneness of personality (*una quaedam persona*). So basic is this oneness of all mankind in Christ that it can be said to be constitutive of the Christian viewpoint. As a consequence it is absolutely impossible for there to be any real opposition between the individual person and the community of persons.

A wonderful harmonization of personality and community is contained in the Church's theology of the Sacraments. Each Sacrament constitutes the Christian an ecclesial person in a particular way—either in state or in action. Through this being-a-person-in-society, the Christian comes into immediate contact with Christ inasmuch as that society is also the living organism, Body, of Christ, who is head. By the life that flows from that head to the members, the Christian becomes a more perfect person in Christ by opening himself in love and service to other persons: God and neighbor.

The consummation without absorption of human personality in the mystical personality of Christ is the elevation of the natural inviolability of the human person. Catholic theology has always taken its stand against any form of collectivism that reduces the human person to a means. The human person is an absolute value and therefore an end in regard to the entire material and spiritual universe, precisely because of its immediate ordination to God. The special dignity of the human person consists of an openness that enables him to relate himself consciously to God. Most perfectly and most eminently is this immediate communion with God realized by the hypostatic union in Christ. Dependent on and modeled after this hypostatic union is the mystical union of all Christians in the mystical personality of Christ. Here the Christian becomes as perfectly as possible a self-possessor, possessing self in Christ, and a responsive self-giver by the Spirit of Christ, joining him to Christ and in and through Christ to the Father.

''A person means that which is most perfect in nature'' (*Summa theologiae* 1a. 29.3). Catholic doctrine acknowledges the necessity of revelation for fallen man to know completely the more exalted natural truths. Where would this need of divine guidance be more acute than when man comes to search the meaning of himself at the deepest and central point of his being—personality. How deficient man finds his rational method whenever he comes to consider anything in its totality. Such is the person. The history of human thought certainly seems to confirm Cajetan's suspicion that man would never have even directed his attention to the subtleties of human personality had not the revealed mysteries of the Trinity and the Incarnation invited him to do so. If these mysteries have raised new problems in the understanding of personality, theology does not hesitate to seek in these same mysteries new insights into human personality. And from this better understanding of human personality, we can return to a fuller understanding of mystical personality and divine personality in Christ and in God.

See Also: ANALOGY, THEOLOGICAL USE OF; CONSUBSTANTIALITY; CREATED ACTUATION BY UNCREATED ACT; HOMOOUSIOS; HYPOSTASIS; INCORPORATION IN CHRIST; JESUS CHRIST, III (SPECIAL QUESTIONS); JESUS CHRIST, ARTICLES ON; LOVE; PERSON, DIVINE; PERSON (IN PHILOSOPHY); RELATIONS, TRINITARIAN; SUBSISTENCE (THEOLOGICAL ASPECT); TRINITY, HOLY; TRINITY, HOLY, ARTICLES ON.

Bibliography: A. MICHEL, *Dictionnaire de théologie catholique,* ed. A. VACANT et al., 15 v. (Paris 1903–50) 7.1:369–437. A. HALDER and A. GRILLMEIER, *Lexikon für Theologie und Kirche,* ed. J. HOFER and K. RAHNER, 10 v. (2d, new ed. Freiburg 1957–65) 8:287–292. A. GUGGENBERGER, *Handbuch theologischer Grundbegriffe,* ed. H. FRIES, 2 v. (Munich 1962–63) 2:295–306. I. M. DALMAU, *Sacrae theologiae summa,* ed. FATHERS OF THE SOCIETY OF JESUS, PROFESSORS OF THE THEOLOGICAL FACULTIES IN SPAIN, 4 v. (3d ed. Madrid 1958) 2.2. I. SOLANO, *ibid.* (4th ed. Madrid 1961) 3.1. J. MARITAIN, *Distinguish to Unite, or The Degrees of Knowledge,* tr. G. B. PHELAN (New York 1959), ''App. 4: On the Notion of Subsistence—Further Elucidations, 1954.'' K. RAHNER, *Theological Investigations,* v. 1 *God, Christ, Mary and Grace,* tr. C. ERNST (Baltimore 1961). H. DE LUBAC, *Catholicisme. Hier, aujourd'hui et demain,* ed. G. JACQUEMET, tr. L. C. SHEPPARD (New York 1950; 1958). B. COOKE, ''Theology of Person,'' *Spiritual Life* 7 (1961) 11–20. H. DIEPEN, ''La Critique du Baslesme selon saint Thomas d'Aquin,'' *Revue thomiste* 50 (1950) 82–118, 515–562. J. HAWKINS, ''On Nature and Person in Speculative Theology,'' *Downside Review* 80 (1962) 1–11. J. B. REICHMANN, ''St. Thomas, Capreolus, Cajetan and Created Person,'' *New Scholasticism* 33 (1959) 1–48, 202–230.

[M. J. DORENKEMPER]

PERSON, DIVINE

This article successively examines the scriptural foundation of the doctrine, the testimonies of early tradition, and finally the theological formulation.

Scripture. The Trinitarian mystery of God's inner life, remotely foreshadowed in the Old Testment (Prv 8.22; Sir 24.3–21 for the Word; Ez 3.12, 14; 36.26; Jl 3.1–5 for the Spirit), is unfolded in its totality, but gradually, by Christ Himself. Old Testment monotheism, deeply rooted in the Jewish mind (Dt 6.4–5; Mt 22.37) is the basis on which the new mystery is built and at the same time its main doctrinal obstacle. Yahweh's divinity needs no proof for a Jew. Paul, reared in the purest Jewish tradition (Phil 3.5), reserves the title ὁ θεός exclusively to GOD THE FATHER (Rom 15.5, 13, 33; 1 Cor 2.11; Col 1.3).

Jesus Christ is the only Son of God (Mk 1.11, where ἀγαπητός is the equivalent of only). Though rarely called God in the New Testment, Christ is endowed with strictly divine attributes: He is the spouse (Mt 9.15) and shepherd of the people (John, ch. 10), titles which were strictly divine in the Old Testment (Hos 2:16–25: spouse; Ezekiel ch. 34: shepherd). He forgives sin (Lk 5.20) on His own authority (Mk 2.7), perfects and completes the Law (Mt 5.17), is the supreme master of the Sabbath (Mt 12.8; Mk 3.1–6), and supreme judge of all men (Mt 25.31; Rom 2.16), who knows His Father as intimately as His Father knows Him (Mt 11.27). Christ is called directly God by Paul in Rom 9.5 if the Christological character of this doxology is admitted (*see* SON, GOD THE).

As for the distinct, divine personality of the HOLY SPIRIT, it is at the Last Supper that Jesus discloses it in full: He is the PARACLETE (John 14.16, 26), who hears (Jn 16.13), speaks (*ibid.*), announces (Jn 16.13–15), and teaches (Jn 14.26; 16.13). In Paul, the expressions ''to live in Christ'' and ''to live in the Spirit'' are practically synonymous: man is justified in Christ (Gal 2.17) and in the Spirit (1 Cor 6.11), sanctified in Christ (1 Cor 1.2) and in the Spirit (Rom 15.16), sealed in Christ (Eph 1.13) and in the Spirit (Eph 4.30). Both, Son and Spirit, preexistent in God, are sent by Him into the world (Gal 4.4–6; Rom 8.15–16).

Early Tradition. The doctrine is definitely shaped by NICAEA I (325, divinity of the Son) and CONSTANTINOPLE I (381, divinity of the Spirit). Simultaneously with the fixing of the doctrine itself, the thorny problem of terminology is thrashed out. After some initial hesitation (Tertullian, Novatian), the term *persona* is adopted in the West. This word translates the Hebrew *pānîm* (face), and originally designated a mask, then a theatrical role, and finally any concrete individual. The use of the word reflects Hebrew usage, easily recognizable in the literal Vulgate: ''facies mea praecedet te'' (Ex 33.14); ''in tempore vultus tui'' (Ps 20.10); ''ab increpatione vultus tui'' (Ps 79.17). In 2 Cor 1.11 the word *persona* has the meaning of an individual (see H. Lesètre, *Dictionnaire de la Bible,* ed. F. Vigouroux [Paris 1895–1912] 5.1:159–160). The word πρόσωπον (person) is applied to the Persons of the Trinity already by Hippolytus (*Cont. haer. Noet.* 7, 14; *Patrologia Graeca*, ed J. P. Migne [Paris 1857–66] 10:813, 822), but the definite formula ''three Persons, one substance'' is due to Tertullian (*Adv. Prax.* 11–13; *Patrologia Latina*, ed. J. P. Migne [Paris 1878–90] 2:166–170). After him, this terminology spreads throughout the West (Damasus, Hilary of Poitiers, Ambrose).

In the East there are similar uncertainties with regard to terminology: the HYPOSTASIS (ὑπόστασις) of Biblical origin (Heb 1.3) is now taken to mean a concrete individual with definite characteristics of his own, as opposed to a common substratum, or οὐσία, which can be shared by several individuals (see Basil, *Ep.* 236.6; *Patrologia Graeca* 32:884). Therefore in God οὐσία expresses what is common to all three, such as goodness and divinity; whereas ὑπόστασις signifies respectively paternity, FILIATION, and sanctifying power (Basil, *Ep.* 214.4; *Patrologia Graeca* 32:789). It is Gregory of Nazianzus who brings about final reconciliation between the conflicting terminologies of East and West (*Orat.* 42.16; *Patrologia Graeca* 36:475–478). Hereafter the Greek terms οὐσία and ὑπόστασις will be equivalent to the corresponding Latin *substantia* and *persona* (*Orat.* 21.35; *Patrologia Graeca* 35:1125). At the explicit request of Basil and Jerome, Pope Damasus authoritatively pronounces the validity of Basil's formula (Damasus, *Ep.* 2.1; *Patrologia Latina* 13:350). In 382 the East accepts the Latin formulation (Theodoret of Cyr, *Hist. eccles.* 5.9; *Patrologia Graeca* 82:1212–17), and, conversely, the West agrees to the Greek formula (Theodoret, *op. cit.* 5.3; 82:1202).

Theology. A Divine Person is essentially constituted by a SUBSISTENCE that is both individual and incommunicable. Divine personal PROPERTIES cannnot be shared among the three Persons. Yet, this concept of Divine Person, far from suggesting a nature that is closed up within itself, signifies rather an essential openness, an outward tendency relating each Person to the other two. In man, this social, outward bent is counterbalanced by and rooted in an unavoidable self-centeredness that is to be surpassed and perfected by an external acquisition. This social tendency in man fills up his own innate poverty. In the Trinity, on the contrary, each Person lacks this self-centeredness: a Divine Person is nothing else than an infinite, eternal, loving, centrifugal force, necessarily related to the other two centrifugal forces. In God that outward inclination has as its origin not poverty to be filled, but superabundance to be communicated. Each Person is nothing but a total self-gift to the other two, and this communication is so peculiar as to constitute a personal, distinct trait, a distinct Divine Person. A Divine Person is the supreme pattern of man's unselfish generosity.

See Also: TRINITY, HOLY, ARTICLES ON; PERSON (IN THEOLOGY); NATURE; INCOMMUNICABILITY; PATERNITY, DIVINE.

Bibliography: A. MICHEL, *Dictionnaire de théologie catholique*, ed. A. VACANT et al., (Paris 1903–50) 7.1:369–437. A. GRILLMEIER, *Lexikon für Theologie und Kirche*, ed. J. HOFER and K. RAHNER (Freiberg 1957–65) 8:290–292. A. MALET, *Personne et amour dans la théologie trinitaire de st. Thomas d'Aquin* (Paris 1956). F. PRAT, *The Theology of St. Paul,* tr. J. L. STODDARD, 2 v. (London 1926–27; repr. Westminster, Md. 1958). T. DE RÉGNON, *Études de théologie positive sur la Sainte Trinité,* 4 v. (Paris 1892–98).

[A. M. BERMEJO]

PERSONALISM

Although any philosophy that insists upon the reality of the person—human, angelic, or divine—may legitimately be classified as personalist, the name personalism more commonly designates a movement of some significance in 19th-century philosophy. This developed as a reaction to MATERIALISM, evolutionism, and IDEALISM, and has assumed various forms both in Europe and the U.S. It is usually theistic in orientation, and places great stress on personality as a supreme value and as a key notion that gives meaning to all of reality. This article treats briefly of currents in European philosophy that contributed to the origins of personalism.

During the 19th century there was considerable reaction to the crass materialism of the 18th century as propounded by thinkers such as C. A. Helvétius (1715–71) and P. H. D. HOLBACH; the reaction was accompanied by a growing and firm opposition on the part of many philosophers to the determinism and reductionism of some followers of Isaac Newton. Such personalists protested against reductionist systems that did not recognize a real distinction between man and the rest of nature. Again, whereas some of the followers of Charles DARWIN tended to integrate man into the rest of nature so completely that he ultimately lost his distinctive spiritual character, personalists stressed the value of man as a person, a moral self, with freedom, dignity, and responsibility. In stressing man's dignity some of these thinkers tended to denigrate material things and treat them as mere appearances or flux without any substantial character. Others, particularly among the Americans, thought that the common identification of both man and God as persons places a limitation on God, and thus they spoke of God as ''finite.''

Another formative factor in the development of personalism was a protest voiced against the absolutism inherent in the philosophy of G. W. F. HEGEL. In Hegelianism, humans allegedly are mere phenomenal beings who easily lose their identities in the collectivities of the family, the community, and the state. In opposition to such an absolutist tendency, personalists have frequently developed a form of idealism that allows the human self a kind of uniqueness and autonomy. In this vein the British personalist A. Seth Pringle-Pattison (1850–1931) wrote: "Each self is a unique existence, which is perfectly impervious . . . to other selves. . . . I have a centre of my own, a will of my own, which no one shares with me or can share—a centre which I maintain even in my dealings with God Himself."

Prominent European personalists such as C. B. Renouvier, Maurice BLONDEL, and E. Mounier (1905–50) have all embraced philosophies that continue to stress the distinctive worth of human striving. In 1932, Mounier founded the journal *Esprit,* and this has become a major source of materials for those wishing to trace the development of the European movement. Since the 1930s, such thinkers have been greatly concerned with the problems of modern man seeking to retain his freedom and authentic spiritual character in the face of a massive technology that is more dominated by material considerations than by spiritual values. Because of their strong stand for human freedom as against domination by the forces of a spiritually barren mass society, existentialists such as Gabriel Marcel, Jean Paul Sartre, and N. A. BERDÎAEV should be included as personalists (*see* EXISTENTIALISM). Also listed among the personalists are such distinguished Thomistic philosophers of freedom as Jacques MARITAIN, Yves SIMON, and Etienne GILSON (*see* THOMISM).

For the development of personalism in Catholic teaching, see PERSONALIST ETHICS.

Bibliography: G. MARCEL, *The Philosophy of Existence* (New York 1949). J. MARITAIN, *The Person and The Common Good,* tr. J. J. FITZGERALD (New York 1947).

[J. A. MANN/EDS.]

PERSONALIST ETHICS

The expression "personalist ethics" has a wide range of applications. The feature common to the diverse and, at times, contradictory positions of which it can be predicated is that all insist on defining value in terms of persons in community. For all advocates of personalist ethics the human person is central and foundational. Personalists note, first of all, that ethical questions arise only for persons, because only persons are capable of determining their lives by their own free choices. Only persons stand in need of moral norms to help them, prior to choice, discover which alternatives are morally good, i.e., truly fulfilling of human beings as persons, and which are morally bad, i.e., inimical to their fulfillment as persons. In addition, according to all forms of personalist ethics the norms for making true moral judgments and good moral choices are grounded in the being of human beings precisely insofar as they are persons.

Diverse forms of personalist ethics give widely different and frequently contradictory answers to such questions as the meaning of person, the source, scope, and universality of moral norms, the meaning of personal fulfillment, etc. Thus the expression "personalist ethics" can be and has been predicated of a wide spectrum of ethical thought, ranging from such disparate forms of existential personalism as those espoused by Martin BUBER, Jean Paul SATRE, Gabriel MARCEL and others, through the type of situation ethics championed by Joseph Fletcher, for whom persons are "front and center," and the varied types of phenomenological analyses of ethics found in such writers as Max Scheler and Dietrich von Hildebrand, to several types of personalist approaches advocated by contemporary Catholic theologians as diverse in their thinking as Louis Janssens and Karol Wojtyła (Pope JOHN PAUL II). This article will focus on the emergence of "personalist ethics" in current Catholic thought and on the form of personalist ethics developed by Karol Wojtyła.

Development of Catholic Personalism. The personalist movement had its beginnings in the 19th century thought of such figures as J. M. Seiler and J. B. Hirscher, but it was not until the 20th century, with the work of O. Schilling and Fritz Tillman in fundamental ethics and the efforts of Dietrich von HILDEBRAND, Herbert Doms and others in marital and sexual ethics that the "personalist" approach took root in Catholic ethical thought. Personalist writers were representative of Catholic thinkers who faulted the standard manuals of Catholic moral theology for their legalism and minimalism and insensitivity to the personalism central to the gospel. These authors stressed the gospel call to love as Jesus did and to live a new kind of life made possible by personal union with Christ and the community of his disciples gathered in the Church. This phase of Catholic personalism culminated prior to Vatican Council II in the work of Gérard Gilleman and Bernard Häring, with the former's *The Primacy of Charity in Moral Theology* and the latter's *The Law of Christ* standing as landmark works reflecting this early phase of Catholic personalism.

Vatican II gave impetus to this movement. It did so preeminently by the emphasis it placed, particularly in *Gaudium et spes* and *Dignitatis humanae* on the inherent worth of the human person, created in the image and likeness of God and called to be, with Jesus, a child of God and member of his family. *Gaudium et spes* insisted on the objectivity of moral norms, but taught that these "are drawn from the nature of the human person and human action" (n. 51).

Personalist Ethics of Karol Wojtyła. Among contemporary Catholic proponents of personalist ethics

Karol Wojtyła (Pope John Paul II) is by far the best known. His rich but complex thought in its ethical dimensions can best be understood initially by focusing on four key ideas: the centrality of free choice; the significance of the human body; the personalist norm for making good choices and the human person's call to love; and the mystery of Christ as the deepest revelation of what it means to be human.

Freedom at the Core of the Person. Wojtyła seeks to deepen the Boethian definition of the person as an ''individual substance of a rational nature'' by stressing, with St. Thomas, the fact that the person, as person, is not a mere individual instance of a rational nature, but subsists in that nature as a being in mastery of itself, with dominion over its own actions. It is for this reason that the person is truly incommunicable, *sui iuris.* Through his freely chosen acts the human person determines himself and gives to himself his identity as a moral being. The acting person constitutes himself as a person, as one utterly unique from others, by his freely chosen acts, which are not mere physical events—happenings—but rather constitutive elements of the being of the person. In short, we are the persons that we are because we make ourselves to be our unique selves by the actions that we freely choose.

The Significance of the Body. While stressing that it is through free, self-determining actions that we make ourselves to be the persons that we are, Wojtyła insists that ontologically all members of the human species, from conception onward, are persons. Rooted in the being of the human person is the natural capacity to make free choices, although, it is true, this capacity must be developed before it can be exercised. Yet for Wojtyła every living human body, consciously aware of itself or not, is a person. The human body is the expression or sign or indeed ''sacrament'' of the person, for the human body is an integral and constitutive dimension or aspect of the person. By stressing the bodily character of human personhood, Wojtyła separates himself from some purely phenomenalist types of personalism according to which only those members of the human species who are actually conscious of themselves as selves are persons.

Self-consciousness, self-cognition, and self-determination through free choice are indeed, for Wojtyła, the hallmarks of the person. Nonetheless he insists that our personhood is rooted in our being, and the being of the human person is inescapably bodily or corporeal. Thus the human body is the expression of the human person; the body participates in the dignity of the person. It is not some tool or instrument of the person. It is thus a good of the person, not merely a good for the person.

The ''Personalist'' Norm. Wojtyła holds that the basic normative principle that should inwardly shape our free choices and actions is the personalist norm. Negatively expressed, this norm states ''that the person is the kind of good which does not admit of use and cannot be treated as an object of use and as such the means to an end.'' Stated positively, this norm holds that ''the person is a good toward which the only proper and adequate attitude is love.''

Love, for Wojtyła, is at heart a gift freely given. It is rooted in the willingness of the acting person to give to other persons what is their due, to revere and respond fully to their awesome dignity as persons. To love another, moreover, we cannot be guided by blind choice. Rather we must be guided by the truth, and by the truth of persons. Our whole endeavor, then, must be to discover the goods that are truly perfective of human persons, the goods meant to flourish in them and contribute to their being fully themselves. Such goods include the good of life itself, of knowledge of the truth, of peace and harmony and fellowship with others and with God. The personalist norm requires that we will that persons flourish in these goods. It requires, above all, that we never make another person an object of enjoyment or use.

Thus, for Wojtyła, sensuality, or the natural and spontaneous response to the sexual values of another person, and affectivity, or the feeling of tenderness one experiences when in the presence of another person are not of themselves authentic human love. Rather, they are the raw materials of love and they must be integrated into a wholehearted response to the irreplaceable value of the person as such, as a good to be loved for its own sake. Thus bodily union through sexual coition is right and good only when it is an expression of the *communio personarum* brought about by the irrevocable gift of one person to another in marriage. If it is not the expression of this kind of personal communion, it is a lie.

The Mystery of Christ and the ''Human.'' Wojtyła's personalism is at its depths a Christian personalism, for he sees in the mystery of Christ's Incarnation, life, death, and Resurrection the ultimate disclosure of what it means to be human. Indeed, because of the reality of sin and of the concupiscence which entered into the human heart as a result of sin, Wojtyła holds that it is only in union with the redeeming Christ that human persons can fully be themselves and respond to the call of love that God has put into their hearts. Christ has revealed to us the depths of God's love for human persons and the glorious vocation to which human persons are called: to love, even as they have been and are loved by God in Christ, with a total, complete, disinterested gift of their very selves, of the persons they have made themselves to be by their self-determining choices, to other persons in love. In and through Christ, human persons can redeem suffering and conquer evil, including the evil of death. This can be accomplished by enduring evil in love for God and those irreplaceable and priceless bodily beings, human persons, whom God has created for their own sake.

See Also: PERSONALISM.

Bibliography: B. ASHLEY, *Theologies of the Body* (St. Louis 1984). J. C. FORD and G. KELLY, *Contemporary Moral Theology,* v. 1 *Questions in Fundamental Moral Theology* (Westminster, Md. 1963). B. HÄRING, *The Law of Christ,* 3 v. (Westminster, Md. 1960–); *Free and Faithful in Christ,* 3 v. (New York 1978–). L. JANSSENS, ''Norms and Priorities in a Love Ethic,'' *Louvain Studies* 6 (Spring 1977) 207–238. R. LAWLER, *The Christian Personalism of John Paul II* (Chicago 1982). A. SZOSTEK, ''Karol Wojtyła's View of the Human Person in the Light of the Experience of Morality,'' *Existential Personalism, American Catholic Philosophical Association. Proceedings of the Annual Meeting,* v. 60 (Baltimore 1986) 50–64. G. H. WILLIAMS, *The Mind of John Paul II* (New York 1981). K. WOJTYŁA, *Love and Responsibility* (New York 1981); *The Acting Person* (Boston 1979); *The Original Unity of Man and Woman* (Boston 1981); *Redemptor hominis* (papal encyclical; Wash., D.C. 1979). A. M. WOZNICKI, ''Revised Thomism: Existential Personalism Viewed from Phenomenological Perspectives,'' *Existential Personalism, American Catholic Philosophical Association. Proceedings of the Annual Meeting,* v. 60 (Baltimore 1986) 38–49; *Karol Wojtyła's Existential Personalism* (New Britain, Conn. 1980).

[W. E. MAY]

PERSONALITY

In philosophy and theology the term personality is relatively new, having been introduced by thinkers with longstanding psychological interests, such as W. JAMES, E. S. BRIGHTMAN and S. A. KIERKEGAARD. The older philosophical tradition preferred to center its discussion on the concept of PERSON, of which personality is a more abstract derivative. With St. THOMAS AQUINAS one may trace the origins of the formal definition of person to BOETHIUS, the earliest of the Christian Aristotelians in the West (*Summa theologiae* 1a, 29.1). The absence of any significant discussion of person or personality among the Greeks or Romans is itself meaningful. It reveals that this concept, which occupies so prominent a place in the 20th century, was of little interest to the ancients. It likewise is an indication that the concept of person was of minor concern in palco-pagan culture, just as the person has lost significance in the cult of the masses in the neopaganism of K. MARX.

In a sense, then, personality is a concept that belongs to Christian tradition, and only in an environment that maintains contact with its Christian origins does this concept achieve its full significance. This follows logically from the central Christian dogma of the Incarnation of the Word and the priceless gift of divine adoption that God conferred on man. Only a person can be adopted, and the entire economy of salvation is based on the relation of person to person. In view of this ultimate orientation, the human person is discussed in this section from three different points of view: the psychological, the philosophical, and the theological.

Psychological Aspect. The psychological dimension is man as he is known and as he knows himself. This is the empirical or existential personality, the aspect of man that has already been discussed. Psychological description of the person attempts to resolve a complex unit, MAN, into patterns of observable traits and inferred internal dynamics. The danger in this method is one of losing contact with the functioning whole in the preoccupation with traits and syndromes. Gestalt psychology, existential analysis, and clinical studies aim to avoid this pitfall and keep in focus the individual person in all his uniqueness and originality. Other studies of empirical or existential personality give rise to the variety of personality theories already noted. Most of these reflect the clinical methods and research interests of particular psychologists or schools of thought. They do not penetrate to the metaphysics of man or to the philosophy of the human person.

Philosophical Aspect. Without conflicting with empirical studies of personality, the philosophical aspect of the study of man is concerned with the metaphysical question, ''What does it mean to be a human being?'' and the ethical and juridical question, ''What rights and immunities accrue to man by reason of his being a person?''

Historical Genesis. Aristotle's balanced formula for man, animal rationale, was ''baptized'' by St. Thomas in the 13th century and remained current until the decline of SCHOLASTICISM. Even among the scholastics, however, there was a persistent tendency to upset this balance and to extol reason at the expense of man's animal or organic functions. Finally, R. DESCARTES (1596–1650), with only a sketchy background in 17th-century scholastic thought, introduced a complete divorce between mind and body through his doctrine of the two substances. In his psychophysical model of man, mind became the seat of exclusively spiritual functions, whereas organic activities were reduced to the domain of physics.

With the Cartesian disruption of man's psychosomatic unity and the exploitation of reason by later philosophers, the individuality and uniqueness of human personality were soon lost, particularly in the abstractions of Kantian transcendentalism. The age of the Enlightenment carried the angelism and excessive RATIONALISM of Descartes still further, until it reached its climax in

Hegel's dialectic of subject and object. Even the launching of the new science of psychology in the latter half of the 19th century did little to offset this development. In fact, experimental psychology in its early decades was entirely dominated by POSITIVISM and ASSOCIATIONISM, which stemmed ultimately from the philosophies of T. Hobbes and J. Locke.

With the beginning of the 20th century, however, a massive reaction to the rationalistic concept of man began to take shape. This reaction was due in great measure to Darwin's glimpse of an evolutionary pattern underlying all organic life and to Freud's sometimes crude but persistent probing of human emotion and unconscious drives.

Psychosomatic Unity. As a result, there has emerged a concept of man as a psychosomatic unit that gives full meaning to the Aristotelian-Thomistic definition without ignoring man's organic or animal nature. Pope Pius XII gave currency and authority to this concept when defining personality in his address to the Rome Congress of Applied Psychology shortly before he died: ''We define personality as the psychosomatic unity of man insofar as it is determined and governed by the soul.''

In medical contexts, the term psychosomatic refers to ailments in which physical symptoms are caused or influenced largely by emotional conflicts and psychic tensions. But the word itself, derived from the Greek ψυχή (soul or mind) and σῶμα (body), is admirably suited to signify any interaction between organic and mental components in man. Used in conjunction with unity, this term expresses the organic uniqueness of human beings among other forms of animal life, excludes interpretations that split human beings into two substances (body and mind), and signifies the incommunicable uniqueness of the individual person that is studied by empirical enquiry or clinical analysis.

All the important philosophical conclusions concerning humanity also follow from this psychosomatic unity. In particular, human sexuality and emotional life have their origin in this organic complex that functions also at the spiritual or psychic level (*see* SEX; EMOTION). They are not something foreign to humans, contracted by association with brute animals. At the same time, autonomy, the continuity of self-consciousness, and a sense of responsibility establish humanity's rights and immunities as a person.

While the philosophical or metaphysical concept of human personality goes beyond the conclusions of contemporary psychology and is the foundation of humanity's rights and immunities as a person, it in no way contradicts current scientific views of man. In fact, when contemporary clinical and existential psychologists insist upon the necessity of a unified and self-integrated personality as the *sine qua non* of normal functioning and of sound adjustment, they are very close to demanding a return to such a concept of humanity.

Theological Aspect. This organically integrated and spiritually sensitive being is likewise the subject of elevation to the supernatural plane by the action of the Holy Spirit, which is made connatural to man through the mediation of Christ. This constitutes the supernatural or theological aspect of personality. Supernatural man, the sublime concept of Christian humanism, stands out in sharp contrast to the cult of the superman of F. W. NIETZSCHE, A. Hitler, and the proponents of neopaganism. Entirely the creation of grace, supernatural man could not have come to be except through the Incarnation of the Word. This is the ''new man'' who is created in ''the justice and sanctity of truth'' and of whom St. Paul speaks so eloquently to his new converts of Galatia, ''My little children, with whom I am in labor again, until Christ is formed in you'' (Gal 4.19).

The unobtrusive transformation of nature by grace does no violence to the human personality because it begins with faith, the free assent of the mind to God's redeeming word. The first word spoken in a dialogue, faith is a person-to-person communion with Christ that reaches its climax only in the life after this. Thus the liturgy, the Sacraments, ascetical practices, and prayer take on the character of a personal encounter with the Transfigured Christ. Hence, even the possibility of redemption rests upon the fact of human personality.

The doctrinal epitome and guarantee of this teaching is found in the dogma of the Resurrection, which St. Paul places in the very center of the affirmation of Christian faith. This is a twofold dogma. It begins with the simple affirmation of the Creed that Christ suffered, died, was buried, and rose again. From this central doctrine a corollary follows: those who believe in Christ, whose lives are engrafted on His, the True Vine, who strive to conform their lives to His, will rise in glory with Him on the Last Day. This doctrine of the resurrection of the body, undreamed of in pagan philosophy, can be grasped by faith alone. Yet, what could be more fitting than that the psychosomatic unity so harshly disrupted by death be restored at the moment the human person enters into his glorified state? The organic complex preceded the soul in existence, called forth its unique creation, and, throughout the life span of the person, participated in every advance of the soul in virtue. Since the body has a real part in the preparation of the soul for beatitude, it is only fitting and proper that it be reunited to the soul to share in the life of glory.

Indeed, one may say that only in the light of the dogma of the Resurrection does the true dignity of the human personality stand fully revealed. Humans are surely rational animals, as they are social and emotional animals, but they are much more. Thay are spirit vitalizing matter, living under the laws of protoplasm, but destined to lead matter to a life in which only the laws of spirit hold sway. Such is the conclusion that the gospel accounts of Christ's appearance to His disciples after the Resurrection force upon us; it represents the complete transformation of the human personality in Christ.

Bibliography: T. J. GANNON, *Psychology: The Unity of Human Behavior* (Boston 1954). M. B. ARNOLD and J. A. GASSON, eds., *The Human Person* (New York 1954). A. WALTERS and K. O'HARA, *Persons and Personality* (New York 1953). J. E. ROYCE, *Man and His Nature: A Philosophical Psychology* (New York 1961). G. P. KLUBERTANZ, *The Philosophy of Human Nature* (New York 1953). T. V. MOORE, *The Driving Forces of Human Nature and Their Adjustment* (New York 1948). B. FROGET, *The Indwelling of the Holy Spirit in the Souls of the Just,* tr. S. A. RAEMERS (Westminster, Md. 1950). PIUS XII, ''Venus du monde'' (address, April 10, 1958) ''Applied Psychology,'' tr. P. J. OLIGNY, Pope Speaks 5 (1958) 7–20.

[T. J. GANNON]

PERSONS, ROBERT

Robert Persons.

English Jesuit; b. Nether Stowey, Somersetshire, June 24, 1546; d. Rome, Apr. 15, 1610. He was educated at Stogursey and Taunton and earned his degree at Oxford, becoming a fellow and later bursar of Balliol. In 1575 he left England to study medicine in Padua; but in Louvain, after a retreat under W. Good, SJ, he was probably reconciled to the Church. Having entered the Society of Jesus in 1575, he left Rome with (Bl.) Edmund Campion on April 18, 1580, for England. There he exercised considerable influence on Catholics by his pastoral work, as well as by his writing. In August of 1581, after Campion's arrest, he left England to consult Dr. William ALLEN, but he was forbidden to return by the Jesuit general, Claudius ACQUAVIVA, since he and Allen had been declared traitors by the government. He retired to Rouen to write. He made two journeys to win support for invasion plans to aid James VI, king of Scotland, and his captive mother, Mary, Queen of Scots: one to Philip II in Lisbon in May of 1582, the other to Gregory XIII in August of 1583. Both plans failed because Philip II, though urged by the pope, refused military aid. Such political activity must be viewed in the light of contemporary practice, when popes often employed Jesuits on political missions, for example, the missions of Antonio Possevino and Francisco Toledo. Nor was there any other person to send on a mission that demanded dispatch and secrecy.

Back from Rome, Persons worked closely with Allen, residing chiefly in Rouen and Saint-Omer, writing books and preparing priests for the English mission. In September of 1585 he journeyed to Rome with Allen to do his tertianship and to expose the intrigues of English councilors, who employed an agent, Solomon Aldred, to bribe leading personalities in the papal court to the jeopardy of the Catholic cause. In this the two Catholic leaders were successful. In Rome Persons took his final vows on May 9, 1587 and was instrumental in promoting Allen to the cardinalate.

After the failure of the Spanish Armada, Acquaviva sent Persons to Spain society business. Persons won high commendation for his work in Spain. He founded English seminaries at Valladolid and Seville and residences for English priests at San Lucar and Lisbon, and he brought about the foundation of a school for English Catholic boys at Saint-Omer in 1593.

Recalled to Rome in 1597 to settle the longstanding troubles in the English College, he succeeded in restoring peace and became rector of the college, a post he retained until his death. His plan for organizing the English Jesuits, proposed to Acquaviva while in Spain, was put into effect in 1598. They were to form a quasi province under a superior in Rome, to which post Persons was appointed, with prefects in Flanders and Spain and a superior in England. In the same year George BLACKWELL was appointed archpriest and superior of seminary priests in England. Persons had proposed a plan for two English bishops, one in Flanders, the other in England, explaining it to the cardinals concerned; but Rome decided that the time was not propitious for such appointments. In the resistance of a few priests to the new institution and their ensuing controversy with Blackwell, Persons supported the archpriest and strove vainly to reconcile both parties in the disputes (*see* ARCHPRIEST CONTROVERSY).

Of Persons' writings the most famous is *A Christian Directory,* published in 1582 under the title *The First Book of the Christian Exercise.* The book went through many editions and translations. The *Book of Succession* was not written by Persons alone, but was the joint production of several contributors. Among his controversial works, the most outstanding is his *Answer to the Fifth Part of Coke's Reports* (1606), with his reply to Coke's answer, *A Quiet and Sober Reckoning* (1609). His *Briefe Apologie* is remarkable for its rich documentation.

Bibliography: ''Memoirs,'' ed. J. H. POLLEN, *Publications of the Catholic Record Society* 2 (1906): 12–218; 4 (1907): 1–161; ''Letters and Memorials to 1588,'' ed. L. J. HICKS, *ibid.* 39 (1942). T. FITZHERBERT, ''Letters,'' ed. L. J. HICKS, *ibid.* 41 (1948). P. RENOLD, ed., ''The Wisbech Stirs,'' *ibid.* 51 (1958). L. J. HICKS ''Fr. Persons, S.J. and the Seminaries in Spain,'' *Month* 157 (1931): 193–204, 410–417, 497–506; 158 (1931): 26–35, 143–152; ''The Growth of a Myth: Fr. Robert Persons, S.J. and Leicesters Commonwealth,'' *Studies* 46 (1957): 91–105; ''The Embassy of Sir Anthony Standen in 1603,'' *Recusant History* 5 (1959–60): 91–127, 184–222; 6 (1961–62): 163–194; 7 (1963–64): 50–81. For further articles of L. Hicks see C. READ, ed., *Bibliography of British History: Tudor Period, 1485–1603* (23 ed. New York 1959). C. SOMMERVOGEL, *Bibliothèque de la Compagnie de Jésus,* 11 v. (Brussels-Paris 1890–1932) 6:292–316.

[L. HICKS]

PERU, THE CATHOLIC CHURCH IN

The Republic of Peru is bound on the northwest by ECUADOR, on the northeast by COLOMBIA, on the east by BRAZIL and BOLIVIA, on the south by CHILE and on the west by the South Pacific Ocean. Peru has three distinct regions. Its *costa* or coastal area, a narrow strip of desert that is fertile where irrigated by mountain streams, while the central region, the *sierra,* is formed by the Andes mountains that run north to south through the center of the country. Peru's vast jungle area, the *selva,* encompasses nearly two-thirds of the country and is sparsely populated by indigenous groups and Spanish-speaking settlers who live along the rivers that feed the Amazon basin. Natural resources include copper, silver, gold, petroleum, iron ore and phosphates, while agricultural produce consists of coffee, cotton, sugarcane, rice, wheat plantains and potatoes. Fishing is also an important industry in Peru, where fishmeal is one of its major exports, as is the cultivation and export of coca, which is processed into cocaine in neighboring countries. In 1999 the government curtailed production of coca by 24 percent as a way of curtailing the presence of the illegal drug trade in Peru.

Capital: Lima.
Size: 496,222 sq. miles.
Population: 27,012,900 in 2000.
Languages: Spanish, Quechua, Aymara.
Religions: 24,041,480 Catholics (89%), 1,971,850 Protestants (7.3%), 268,500 practice indigenous faiths (1%), 731,070 are without religious affiliation.

Peru was part of the Spanish viceroyalty of Lima until 1821, when José de San Martín proclaimed independence. Under a republican government, the region joined with Bolivia in the Peruvian-Bolivian Confederation from 1836 to 1839; from 1879 to 1884 it engaged in a bloody war with Chile. Under military rule from 1968 to 1980, Peru returned to democratic government and experienced stable economic growth in addition to making progress in combating both outbreaks of guerrilla violence and the activities of traffickers in illegal drugs. Almost half the population is ethnic Amerindian, with 37 percent mestizo and the remainder of European, Asian or African descent.

Early Christianization. In Peru, the seat of many cultures thousands of years old, there arose in the 14th century an Andean state, the empire of the Incas, which constituted a social and economic structure without equal, although lacking in individual liberty. In 1532 Spanish explorer Francisco Pizarro, at the head of a group of 200 conquistadores, put an end to that political organization by defeating Incan leader Atahualpa, and ten years later, Lima was created as a viceroyalty of Spain, its jurisdiction the entire southern continent, although it was effective only along the Pacific Coast. Catholicism was introduced by the regular clergy at the same pace as the conquest, and by 1550 Dominicans, Franciscans, Mercedarians, Augustinians and Jesuits were all active in Peru. The Incas continued to revolt against the Spanish conquest, leading full-scale rebellions as late as 1814, all without success.

Although the Church was aided in its work by Spain, there were several obstacles present in evangelizing a vast area housing three million inhabitants. Altering tribal customs and rituals, while not difficult with children, was extremely difficult with adults in whom such customs were deeply rooted. The number of unfamiliar Amerindian languages made communicating the scriptures difficult, for mastering one such language did not make the others spoken any easier to comprehend. In addition, the region suffered a shortage of clergy, which forced missionaries to gain the help of Spanish-speaking natives called *alguaciles* or *fiscales de doctrina.* These individuals helped the priest, leading repetitions of minor catechism, and tending the general management of the parish. After 1570 settlements of native converts were formed from which the *doctrinero* or rural priest operated. From these settlements the doctrineros, who served entire provinces, would also establish mission centers that they visited according to distance and necessity.

Besides their primary objective, the orders undertook to protect their converts and to disseminate culture. The DOMINICANS and JESUITS particularly worked in higher education, the Dominicans having opened 60 schools by 1548. The University of San Marcos in Lima was created in 1551. The Jesuits directed the Colegio de San Martín in Lima, San Bernardo in Cuzco, the University of St. Ignatius of Loyola in Cuzco, schools for the children of caciques in the Lima and Cuzco regions and schools in Juli. In addition, orders attended to evangelization, distributing the Peruvian territory among themselves. By the end of the 1500s the Dominicans had founded 22 convents, which attended to a total of 57 *doctrinas;* the Mercedarians had 13 convents with 47 *doctrinas;* the Franciscans, 22 with 28; the Augustinians, 13 with 28; and the Jesuits, in addition to residences in Lima, Arequipa and Cuzco, took charge of *doctrinas* in Huarochiri and Juli as well as of the native people living in Lima.

Despite the many challenges posed in Peru, the Jesuits and Franciscans went on to excel in Marañón and Ucayali and in the eastern region of present-day Bolivia. The Jesuits founded flourishing missions in the areas of the Morona, Santiago and Chinchipe Rivers; tragically, these missions would disintegrate when the Jesuits were expelled from South America after 1760. The Franciscans from the Colegio de Propaganda Fide de Santa Rosa de Ocopa (valley of the Mantaro) projected their evangelizing labor over the Pampa del Sacramento toward the Ucayali. At the beginning of the 19th century the Franciscans established themselves in the remote headwaters of the Yavarí, Yuruá and Purús Rivers. The bishopric of Maynas, erected in 1802, embraced the entire Amazon region and the tributary missions, in which neophytes were abundant.

In the 17th century new orders of men and women entered Peru, among them the Benedictines, the Hospitallers of St. John of God, the Minim Fathers, the Bethlemites and the Oratorians. In the 18th century the Camillians or Ministers of the Sick began their activities.

Archdioceses	Suffragans
Arequipa	Puno, Tacna y Moquegua
Ayachucho	Huancavélica
Cuzco	Abancay
Huancayo	Huánuco, Tarma
Lima	Callao, Carabayllo, Chosica, Huacho, Ica, Lurín
Piura	Chachapoyas, Chiclayo, Chulucanas
Trujillo	Cajamarca, Chimbote, Huarez

There are 11 prelatures, eight apostolic vicariates, and a military ordinariate in the country.

The two hospitaller orders of St. John of God and Our Lady of Bethlehem (the latter founded in America) expanded rapidly. The first took over the convalescent hospital in Lima; in Cuzco, Ayacucho and Huancavelica, they staffed previously established institutions. The Bethlemites took charge of hospitals in Lima, Cajamarca, Trujillo, Chachapoyas, Piura and Cuzco.

Development of the Hierarchy. While missionary work was carried out by the religious orders, the tasks of direction and coordination fell to the episcopate. The Church in Peru was first subject to Seville, but in 1529 the first see was erected in Túmbez. In 1537 Cuzco was created, its first bishop the Dominican Vicente de Valverde. Lima followed in 1541, and was raised to an archdiocese by Paul III in 1546. In 1559 Lima Archbishop LOAYSA founded the 12-room hospital of Santa Ana for Amerindians, which continued to operate for centuries on archdiocesan funds; later the hospital of San Bartolomé was opened for blacks, that of San Pedro for priests and that of Nuestra Señora de Atocha for orphans; and in Cuzco that of San Juan de Dios (1555) and that of Nuestra Señora de los Remedios for Amerindians. In addition the Church founded schools for children of all races, with instruction suited to their needs. During the third council (1582–83) the conversion of natives was of special concern. The knowledge of native languages was made obligatory, to aid priests in confession (up until the mid-16th century interpreters had been tolerated). In addition, a single catechism and *confesionario* in the Quechua and Aymara languages was adopted.

It was a general rule of the Church in Peru to elevate to the priesthood Creoles (whites born in Peru), and soon they outnumbered clerics from Europe. Mestizos (mixed white and Amerindian) were not excluded from religious

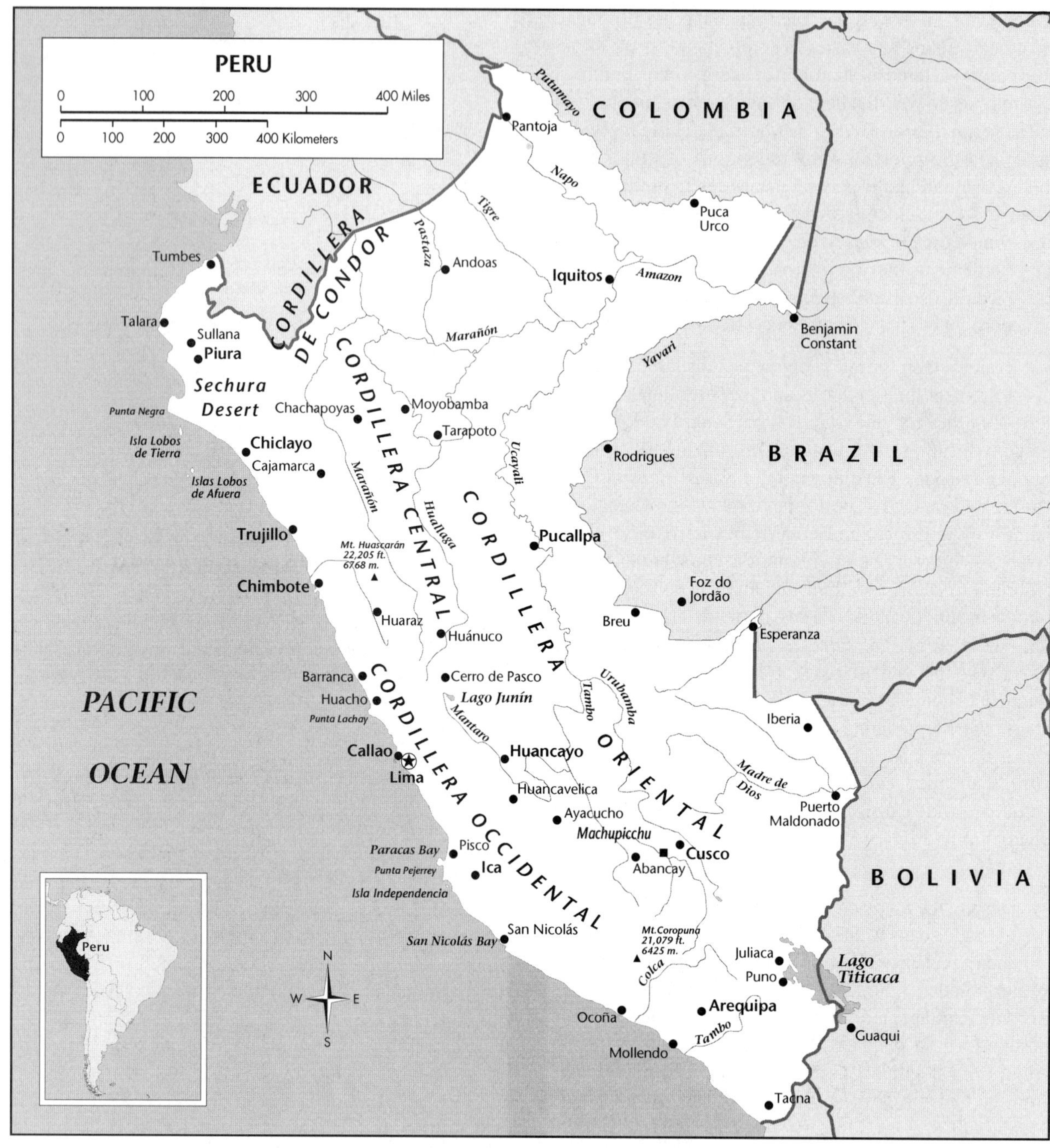

orders, and after 1588 their ordination was authorized if they had the qualities necessary for the priesthood. Since natives were new to the faith and, because of their lack of familiarity with Western culture, did not possess the formation necessary for a priest, it is understandable that the early councils closed the way to them. However, as Amerindian converts adapted to Christian customs and gained the necessary ability and skills, there was no reason to keep them from the altar. Among the first Amerindians admitted to orders were a Dominican lay brother, Francisco de San Antonio (1585–1635) and a Mercedarian lay brother. A 1769 decree of Charles III encouraged prelates to admit into the seminaries one-fourth Amerindians or Mestizos so that their compatriots would strengthen themselves in the faith. However, few made use of this privilege; native vocations appeared very slowly and increased only in modern times. At the end of the 17th century, a religious house was opened for native women: the Beaterio de Copacabana in Lima, under the direction of the Concepción Order.

View of Cuzco City and Cathedral, Peru. (©Brian Vikander/CORBIS)

Independence, Decline and Revival. As the stirrings of nationalism filtered throughout South America, the Creole clergy were sympathetic to the cause of independence, which the Spanish authorities, both civil and ecclesiastic, tried in vain to combat. Among the cathedral clergy, Peninsulars were more numerous because the king filled many of the offices, and the natives of Spain took advantage of this. Many pastoral letters like those of the bishop of Arequipa La Encina (1811 and 1815) and of the bishop of Cuzco Orihuela (1821), which introduced the apostolic brief of Pius VII (Jan. 30, 1816), tended to calm dissident citizens.

The Church could not remain indifferent to the struggle that divided her followers. Royalists and insurgents each attempted to win Church leaders to their side, realizing the Church's power and influence over its subjects. Royalists knew that the Church was obligated to preserve fidelity to the sovereign and would make use of the canonical resources within its reach to repress insurrection. Insurgents knew that many of the clergy, both religious and secular, were inclined by their birth toward separatism, and they took advantage of the indirect influence these priests could exert, even if they could not intervene actively.

In 1821 José de San Martín stormed Lima and proclaimed political independence. Three years later, following the Battle of Ayachucho, Spanish troops were withdrawn from the region. After almost three hundred years of Spanish rule, Peru was now a sovereign nation. Under the dictatorship of Simón Bolívar, Peru briefly entered the alliance of Gran Colombia, but this dissolved by 1830. A period of civil war was ended with the presidency of Ramón Castillo (1844–62), who ended slavery in Peru and nationalized education.

Political independence caused a temporary crisis of leadership within the Peruvian Church as Spanish-born bishops, who had taken an oath of loyalty to the Spanish crown, departed the country. From 1821 until 1835 there was no resident archbishop in Lima. Gradually, however, the crisis of episcopal leadership was solved as the Peruvian Congress, exercising the *patronato* in the name of the Republic, named bishops that Rome eventually recognized. A large number of highly trained and politically progressive priests helped the Church survive the immediate post-independence period and forge a working relationship with the new state. 33 served as members of the first Congress that made Catholicism the state religion.

Roman Catholic cathedral, Plaza de Armas in forefront, Lima, Peru. (AP/Wide World Photos)

The economic resources of the Church had permitted an untroubled existence up to the beginning of the 19th century. Its patrimony had slowly increased because the monarchs fulfilled conscientiously their duty of placing at the disposal of the Church the tithe-rents that had been conceded by the Holy See. To this had been added voluntary contributions of the faithful in the form of chaplaincies, legacies and other agencies and the contribution of tithes and first fruits. In the 1830s, as the government descended into civil war, the economic contribution of the Church, demanded alternately by each political faction, sped its impoverishment, since many properties and treasures were consumed in the struggle. Both factions seized what they could, confiscating the treasures of local churches and real estate tied to charitable foundations and works. The situation grew worse as the economy faltered later in the century, and laws were introduced regarding the suppression of convents; expropriation of their properties; suppression of tithes and first fruits (1856) and of ecclesiastical entailment (1856); redemption of encumbrances and chaplaincies (1864); administration of the properties of brotherhoods (1889); abolition of MORTMAIN (1903); and consolidation of usufruct (1911). In the law of 1856, the state provided that the public treasury give the bishops and clergy their income. The political change also negatively affected the orders: the superiors could not carry out canonical visits, the religious were divided among political parties and many left the cloisters to become secularized. Under a 1826 decree many convents were closed and towns were prohibited from having within them more than one house of the same order. The government, without consulting the Holy See or the ordinaries, took over the vacated places and mismanaged rural properties, except in the few cases in which these were converted into educational institutions.

The independence movement brought with it direct contact with the Holy See, of which the Peruvian Church had been deprived because of the PATRONATO REAL, although the orphaned state suffered for many years until the mechanism for the naming of prelates could be reestablished. The right of patronage began to be exercised by the heads of state when they assumed that they had subrogated the privilege given to the kings of Spain by the popes. The Holy See did not recognize this, and although it accepted the presentation of subjects for the bishoprics, this was not mentioned in the appointment bulls that were issued *motu proprio*. This irregular situation was normalized, in the absence of a suitable instrument (such as a concordat), through a bull signed by Pius IX in 1874, in which the chief of state's right to patronage and to the exercise of the inherent prerogatives under certain conditions was recognized *pro tempore*. The regulations and prerequisites indicated in the bull were complemented by the provisions of the constitution, which fixed Peruvian birth as a requisite for an archbishop or bishop. The congress was also given the right to create new sees or to suppress them at the initiative of the executive power. The president of the republic made the selection of pastors in the Peruvian Church with the counsel of his ministers, the legislative power being excluded from any participation. The president of the republic enjoyed the privilege of also making presentations for the dignitaries and canories of the cathedrals and of conceding or denying approval to pontifical rescripts, with the consent of congress.

Clergy Suffers a Reduction. While from the 16th to the 19th century Peru had attracted more than enough priests for its growing faithful, after 1800 a progressive reduction in the number of the clergy could be seen. While the clergy was still numerous enough to serve almost all the parishes by 1850, a shortage of seminarians was already evident and vacancies were difficult to fill. The causes were varied: the poverty of the Church forced the bishops to turn away some candidates who requested scholarships; civil strife drew into the services many youths who would not normally have taken up military life; the loss of Christian spirit in the home influenced the lack of vocations. In addition, some young men who might have become priests were attracted to new careers through the opening of technical institutes, normal schools and art and trade schools. New laws also contributed to the decline in the number of religious by raising the required age for the profession and placing other impediments in the way of entrance into the cloisters.

Although the clergy began to shrink, increasing communities of religious devoted themselves to charity, teaching and the general welfare of Peru. The Sisters of the Sacred Heart of Picpus dedicated themselves to teach-

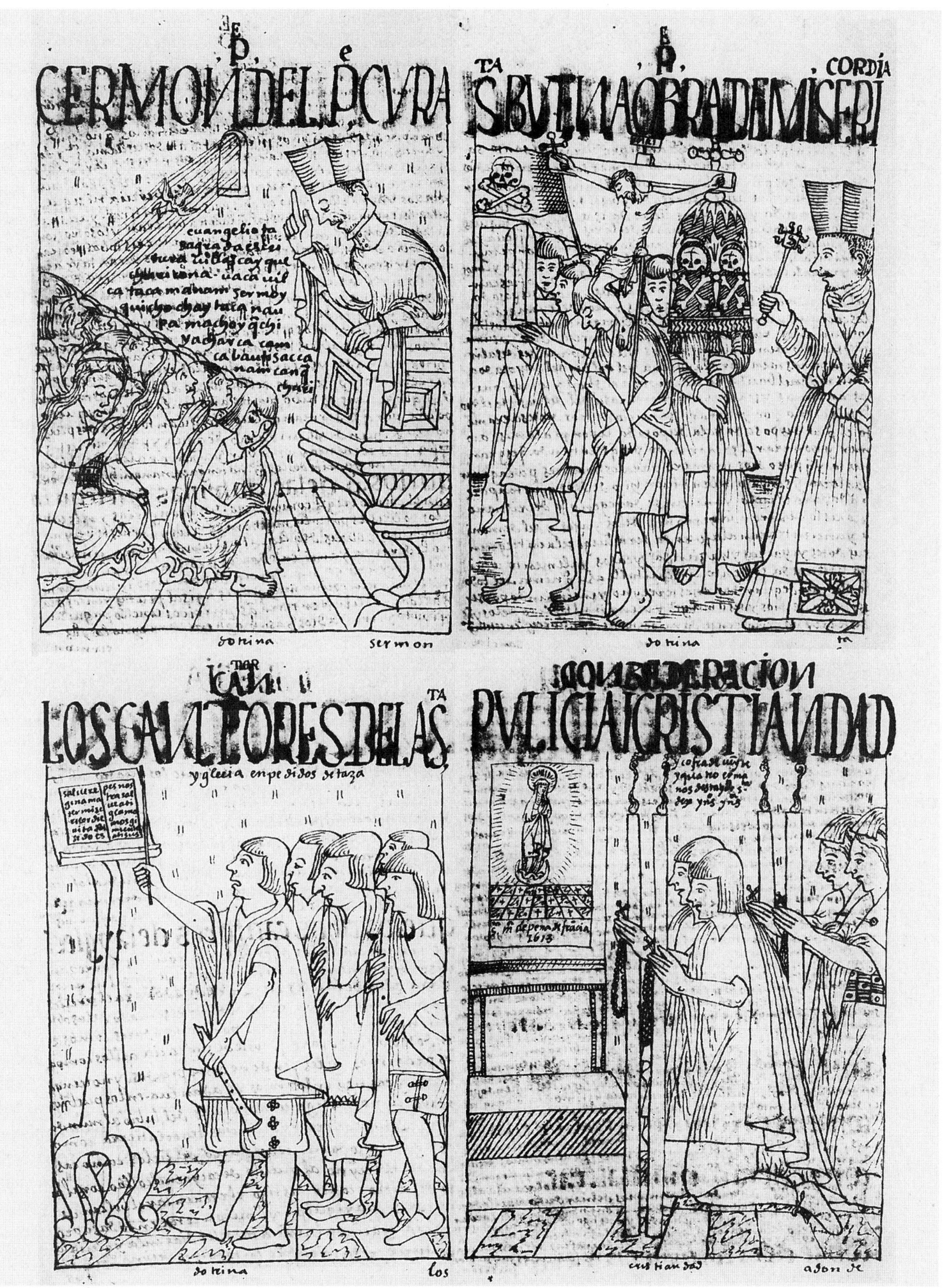

Church life in the missions of Peru during the early 17th century, four drawings from the manuscript of the ''Nueva coronica'' of Felipe Huaman Poma de Ayala, preserved in the Royal Library, Copenhagen.

Believers congregate to pay homage to Peru's most revered Catholic religious icon, the "Purple Christ" or "Lord of Miracles" (Senor de Los Milagros), Lima, Peru, Oct. 18, 2000. (©Reuters NewsMedia Inc./CORBIS)

ing, while the Sisters of Charity, Daughters of St. Vincent de Paul assumed the care of public hospitals in Lima and other cities. During the second half of the 19th century, new orders arrived to replace the old, many of which had seriously declined in numbers and some of which had disappeared completely. The Redemptorists dedicated themselves to the study of Quechua; the Jesuits returned; and the Salesians spread themselves through various parts of the country, taking charge of the education of needy children.

Contributions to Peruvian Culture. The influence of the Church in the development of Peruvian culture was significant throughout the colonial era and into the republic. Noted writers included Dominican Diego de Hojeda, author of the religious epic poem *La cristiada*, while mystical poetry was written by the Augustinian Fernando Valverde, the Jesuit Juan de Alloza and the Dominican Adriano de Alessio. Catholics contributed to the study of native languages: Domingo de Santo Tomás, Luis Gerónimo de ORÉ, GONZÁLEZ HOLGUÍN and Torres Rubio documented Quechua, while BERTONIO wrote on the Aymara language. Convent chroniclers reflected in their works not only internal history and events but also the daily life, customs and events of society. Among them were the Augustinians Antonio de la Calancha and Bernardo de Torres; the Franciscans Diego de CÓRDOVA Y SALINAS and Fernando Rodríguez Tena; and the Dominicans Reginaldo de LIZÁRRAGA and Juan de MELÉNDEZ. Theologians included the Jesuit Hernando de Avendaño, with his *Thesaurus indicus* (in six volumes) and the Augustinian Gaspar de VILLARROEL; in mysticism and asceticism were the Jesuit Diego Alvarez de Paz, Toribio RODRÍGUEZ DE MENDOZA, pedagogical reformer of the end of the 18th century and the bishop of Trujillo MARTÍNEZ COMPAÑÓN, who compiled invaluable manuscript and graphic material on the ethnology and life of his diocese (1779–90). The Catholic press, although limited, also had a considerable tradition, beginning with *El Bien Público*, which was published in 1865.

Despite the many contributions of Peru's Catholic population, by the 1850s the relationship between the government and the Church began to break down as certain members of the Peruvian oligarchy took up the causes of liberalism and POSITIVISM. Influenced by intellectual and political trends in Europe and North America, some were overtly anticlerical, accusing the Church of medievalism and questioning the patriotism of bishops because of their loyalty to Rome. Although a tiny percentage of the population, this Lima-based elite controlled national politics, often forcing the Church into a defensive position. The battle between political liberals and the Peruvian Church continued well into the 20th century.

As relations between Church and State became increasingly secular, religious fervor in Peru declined. Many priests abandoned their *doctrinas,* at times voluntarily, out of loyalty to political principles, at other times, forcibly, because of preference for the party out of power. Many sees remained without a bishop, and many resignations resulted from the republican government's favor of secularization. While liberal governments, to avoid wounding the religious sentiments of the people or alienating the good will of the clergy, showed themselves respectful, they were not inhibited from enacting their increasingly secular agendas. The dissemination of writings contrary to the Catholic faith was permitted, showing defections by many writers influenced by the rationalist philosophy of the Enlightenment. Among them were Manuel Lorenzo Vidaurre (1773–1841), who won renown with his ecclesiastical code; Benito Laso;

Francisco Javier Mariátegui, the grand master of Peruvian Masonry; and above all, the heretic Vigil.

As the century continued, non-Catholic Christian influences began to appear in Peru. The constitution of 1860, in force until 1920, restricted the influence of other faiths by stating that the public exercise of any cult besides the Catholic was not permitted. Until 1895 what little Protestant propaganda existed in the country passed almost unnoticed, partly because very few Protestants preached their doctrines in Peru. After 1900, however, Protestant evangelicals appeared with increasing frequently. Owing to the lack of Catholic priests and other social factors, Protestantism would successfully infiltrate many areas of Peru during the 20th century.

Bibliography: R. VARGAS UGARTE, *Historia de la iglesia en el Perú,* 5 v. (Lima 1953–62). R. LEVILLIER, *Organización de la iglesia y órdenes religiosas en el virreinato del Perú en et siglo XVI,* 2 v. (Madrid 1919). A. TIBESAR, *Franciscan Beginnings in Colonial Peru* (Washington 1953).

[G. LOHMANN VILLENA]

Francisco Pizarro. (Corbis)

The Modern Church

Toward the end of the 19th century an influx of missionaries from Europe and North America sparked a renaissance within the Church. Schools and hospitals were opened and rural parishes that had been abandoned due to the shortage of Peruvian priests were now staffed. Several universities were founded, among them the Pontificia Universidad Católica del Peru in 1917; the Universidad de San Martín de Porres, operated by the Dominicans; the Universidad de Santa María, in Arequipa, under the Marianists; and the Universidad del Pacífico, under the Jesuits. A second influx of missionaries after World War II, many from English-speaking countries, also helped the Church reestablish its presence in Peruvian society. In the 1950s a new generation of committed young Peruvian Catholics sowed the seeds of revival. Members of the Catholic Student Association (UNEC; an offshoot of Catholic Action), these students went on to assume prominent positions in both secular society and the Church in the 1960s and 1970s.

The Church after Vatican II. When the Second Vatican council opened in 1962, over 30 Peruvian bishops were present. Most returned to Peru committed to a new vision of the Church, especially the country's primate, Juan Landázuri Ricketts (1955–1990), who established new parishes in poor urban areas and invited foreign missionaries to work among the poor. In addition to staffing parishes, these new clergy also opened up cooperatives, schools and dispensaries to alleviate the poverty of Lima's new inhabitants, most of whom were newly arrived from the *sierra.* This scenario was repeated in other urban areas, and because of this new contact between the institutional Church and the poor, lay leaders who would have a profound impact on the direction of the Peruvian Church in subsequent years began to emerge. Large parishes gave birth to small Christian communities in which committed Catholics deepened their faith through prayer, study and social action. The energy and optimism of the 1960s was reflected in the Peruvian episcopal conference, which publicly advocated economic and political justice for all Peruvians, unheard-of themes from a Church once noted for its theological and political conservatism.

Despite the enthusiastic reception of Vatican II, some obstacles to liturgical reform were present in Peru, one of which was the region's great cultural and linguistic diversity. In the Andean areas, efforts to assimilate indigenous culture and language in rituals such as the eucharist progressed slowly because the number of priests who spoke fluent Quechua and Aymara was extremely small. In addition, the historic tension between the institutional Church, which in the minds of many symbolized European culture, and the indigenous society with its many languages, cosmic vision and ritual tradition, acted upon the growth of the faith. Meanwhile, liturgical reform got caught up in the more complex issues of ecclesiology and the limits of INCULTURATION.

Political Instability. In 1968 two events took place that affected both the Church and society: the Latin American Episcopal Conference held in Medellín, Colombia, and a military revolution. The purpose of the conference was to apply the teachings of Vatican II to the reality of Latin America. The Peruvian bishops were one of the most articulate groups at the conference, their insightful contributions due to the presence of Peruvian theologian Gustavo Gutiéeerz. The MEDELLÍN conference addressed the need for structural change in Latin American society. Condemning the growing gap between the rich and the poor as contrary to the Gospel, the bishops also recognized that the Church was sometimes more concerned with maintaining its social power than with proclaiming the gospel.

Peruvian bishops returned from Medelín better prepared to face the events that would confront them beginning in October when the military coup that ousted the country's civilian government unleashed what became known as the ''Peruvian Revolution.'' Intent on modernizing the country, the military government began to reform many facets of Peruvian society. Education was universalized and land was redistributed. The government opened up new universities and created agricultural cooperatives to help the impoverished rural population. The Church, while generally supporting these reforms and issuing pastoral letters focusing on the rights of workers and the question of land for Peru's indigenous peoples, maintained a certain distance from the government. In many respects, the Church was more visionary than the government itself, whose reforms began to bog down and generate opposition by the mid-1970s. Government leaders accused the Church of being too radical, and a period of tension ensued. In 1979 nearly all connections between the Church and the State were dissolved, although the constitution continued to recognize the special place of Catholicism in Peruvian society. When the military relinquished power and elections were held in 1980, tensions lessened.

Gustavo Gutiérrez and Liberation Theology. In 1971, following his contribution to the Medellín Conference, theologian Gustavo Gutiérrez published *A Theology of Liberation,* a work that gave a theological grounding to Christians involved in the transformation of Latin American society. This book became a classic text in a movement Gutiérrez helped name, LIBERATION THEOLOGY. In 1974 he founded the Bartolomé de las Casas Center in Lima to carry out theological and social scientific investigation of Peruvian society. Staffed by young Peruvians, many of whom were members of UNEC, the center exerted great influence on the Church throughout Latin America. In the Andes, where the Church had been dominant for decades, new life emerged. The five bishops of Peru's southern dioceses took up the cause of the country's Quechua- and Aymara-speaking peasants, and helped establish the Andean Pastoral Institute in Cuzco. Known in Spanish by the acronym IPA, this institute generated theological and social scientific studies about Peru's Andean peoples that led to new pastoral strategies and training programs for indigenous lay leaders, and sparked the eventual translation of the Bible into these languages. During the 1970s and 1980s the Church of the Sur Andino, comprising the five southern dioceses of Cusco, Sicuani, Ayavira, Puno and Juli, was considered one of the most dynamic sectors of the Peruvian Church.

Not all Catholics agreed with the theological and social trends engendered by liberation theology. For more traditional Catholics, many of whom came from the upper and middle classes, liberation theology and new forms of Christian community among the poor were sources of concern. More conservative bishops were likewise alarmed at what they perceived as an excessive concern with the social and economic issues on the part of progressive Catholics. While tensions continued to exist through the end of the century, destructive polarization in the Church was avoided, in part because no one in the Church, conservative or progressive, denied the need for the Church to address social issues.

A Rising Tide of Violence. In the late 1980s, as the Peruvian economy neared collapse, the resulting political instability created a climate of violence as Peruvians found themselves engulfed in poverty. A serious political menace surfaced in the form of *Sedero Luminoso*, or Shining Path, a group of ultra-violent Maoist guerillas that wreaked havoc in the late 1980s and early 1990s. Nearly 30,000 deaths resulted from the campaign of violence waged by both the Shining Path and extremist members of the Peruvian military, as the radicals assassinated Church leaders and religious due to a belief that articulate, socially involved Christians threatened its goal of becoming the sole voice of the poor. Through the efforts of both the Archbishop of Lima and the government, the Shining Path surrendered to the government in 1991, leaving in its wake a group of saints and martyrs whose deaths represented a tragedy but also a tribute to the Peruvian Church. Two years later *Sendero Luminoso* founder Abimael Guzmán was arrested and imprisoned, although terrorist acts by other Marxist guerrilla groups would continue into the 21st century.

Through the 1990s the Church continued its efforts on behalf of the poor by responding to the continuation of a government-led austerity program of drastic economic cutbacks. In addition to feeding and otherwise caring for the millions of Peruvians made destitute by the economic collapse, bishops noted that the private sector, not just the state, was responsible for reducing poverty. In 1996 a government program of forced sterilization of poor women drew strong Church condemnation as a violation of personal freedom, and the program was disbanded in 1998. A new coalition government, which took office after a contested election in 1999, expressed its intention to sustain Peru's economic stability into the 21st century and asked for the help of the Church in addressing social issues.

Into the 21st Century. By the year 2000 there were 1,400 parishes tended by 1,300 diocesan and 1,200 religious priests, with vocations on the increase. Other religious included approximately 2,050 brothers and 5,400 sisters, many of whom operated the 514 primary and 471 secondary schools operated by the Church throughout Peru. The Church, as a significant influence on Peru's development, continued to receive benefits from the government in the areas of tax-exemption and funding for education, and most public schools devoted a portion of time to Catholic study. A move by the government to scale back religious education under a restructured secondary program was a point of concern for Lima Archbishop Juan Luis Cipriani Thorne, who in 1999 called religious education ''not a privilege but . . . a right that belongs... to the Peruvian people.''

Despite the fact that under 20 percent of Peruvian Catholics regularly attended Mass by 2000, the country retained a fervent Marian cult and a special devotion to the Crucified Christ. The latter sanctuaries included the Señor de los Milagros in Lima, which dated back to the 17th century; the Señor de Luren in Ica; the Church of Huamán in Trujillo; and the Church of Los Temblores in Cuzco. The devotion to the Mother of God opened the way for pilgrimage centers as important as the sanctuary of Our Lady of Guadalupe in La Libertad, that of Cocharcas in Apurimac (Replica of Copacabana in Bolivia) and those of Chapi and Characato in Arequipa. Peru is the birthplace of the first South American-born saint, Rosa of Lima, a Dominican who was canonized in 1671.

Bibliography: J. HEMMING, *The Conquest of the Incas* (New York 1970). J. KLAIBER, *The Catholic Church in Peru: 1821–1985* (Washington DC 1992). J. C. MARIÁTEGUI, *Seven Interpretive Essays on Peruvian Reality* (Austin and London 1971).

[C. R. CADORETTE/EDS.]

PERUGINO (PIETRO VANNUCCI)

The leading Umbrian painter at the close of the fifteenth century, best known as Raphael's teacher; b. Città del Pieve, *c.* 1448; d. Fontignano, 1523. He is recorded as a pupil of the Umbrian artist Piero della Francesca and

Perugino. (Archive Photos)

of the Florentine Verrocchio and by 1472 was a member of the Florentine painters' guild. Of his most important commission, for frescoes and an altarpiece for the Sistine Chapel, all but the ''Delivery of the Keys'' (1481–82, Vatican) were destroyed. Here the balanced symmetry and lucid arrangement of figures in relation to architecture are clearly the legacy of Piero della Francesca. A mural of the ''Crucifixion'' within a triple arcade (1493–96; S. Maria Maddalena dei Pazzi, Florence) shows gentle figures placed in a serene, expansive landscape, which serves to unify the painting. Perugino was at the height of his powers from about 1495, executing the fresco cycle of the Sala del Cambio, Perugia, between 1496 and 1500. Raphael seems to have spent a year with Perugino from 1499, and the work of the two artists can be distinguished only with difficulty at that period. By 1506 Perugino's style was outdated, and he retired to Perugia. In his late paintings the figures with their tilted heads became repetitive and sentimental. The young Raphael is nevertheless indebted to him for his idealized types and classical serenity.

Bibliography: E. CAMESASCA, *Tutta la pittura del Perugino* (Milan 1959). R. WITTKOWER, ''Young Raphael,'' *Bulletin of the Dudley Peter Allen Memorial Art Museum of Oberlin College* 20 (1963) 150–168.

[M. M. SCHAEFER]

PESCH, CHRISTIAN

Jesuit theologian; b. Cologne-Mulheim, May 25, 1835; d. Valkenburg, Holland, April 26, 1925. He entered the Society of Jesus in 1869. After completing the course of studies, he was sent to Ditton Hall in England, where he taught dogmatic theology from 1884 to 1895, after which he taught for 17 years at Valkenburg. The influence of St. Thomas, Suárez, and De Lugo is apparent in both his doctrine and methodology. At the time when modernism was influencing the thinking of many German theologians, Pesch became a leading authority and proponent of orthodoxy and contributed notably to the eradication of modernism in Germany. The best-known of his works is the *Praelectiones dogmaticae* (9 v. Freiburg 1894–97). This work is still a popular textbook of dogmatic theology because of its clarity, precision, and order. The *Compendium theologiae dogmaticae* (4 v. Freiburg 1913–14), is a résumé of the one previously mentioned. Pesch's other well-known book is *De inspiratione Sacrae Scripturae* (Freiburg 1906).

Bibliography: H. WEISWEILER *Dictionnaire de théologie catholique,* ed. A. VACANT et al. (Paris 1903–50) 12.1:1305–06.

[G. V. KOHLS]

PESCH, TILMANN

Jesuit philosopher whose works constitute a major contribution to the textbook, or manual, tradition in the Thomistic revival of the late 19th century; b. Cologne, Feb. 1, 1836; d. Valkenburg, Holland, Oct. 18, 1899. He entered the Society on Oct. 15, 1852, and was ordained in 1866. From 1867 to 1869 he taught philosophy at Maria-Laach. After a lapse of seven years, during which he was exiled in Belgium and devoted himself to pastoral work and philosophical polemics in the vernacular, he taught philosophy at the Jesuit College at Blyenbeek, Holland, from 1876 to 1884. Thereafter he spent his life in writing and pastoral care. His textbooks constitute the following parts of a series called *Philosophia Lacensis,* all published in Freiburg im Breisgau: *Institutiones philosophiae naturalis* (2 v. 1880; 2d ed. 1.897), *Institutiones logicales* (3 v. 1888–90; 2d ed., 2 v. 1914–19), and *Institutiones psychologicae* (3 v. 1896–98). Inspired by *AETERNI PATRIS,* Pesch explicitly followed St. Thomas Aquinas and Albert the Great, while incorporating material from F. de TOLEDO, the Conimbricenses, F. SUÁREZ, S. MAURUS, and J. Kleutgen. His tract on Iogie includes Aristotelian logic (*Dialectica*), epistemology (*Critica*), and *quaestiones ontologicae*. Consequently the Cartesian and Kantian traditions, though rejected, condition the place and function of epistemology in his synthesis.

Bibliography: J. L. PERRIER, *The Revival of Scholastic Philosophy in the 19th Century* (New York 1909). *Stimmen aus Maria-Laach* 57 (1899) 461–475. H. HURTER, *Nomenclator literarius theologiae catholicae* (Innsbruck 1903–13) 5:1873–74.

[N. J. WELLS]

PESHITTA

(Syriac *pᵉšīṭtā*), the official Bible text of Syrian Christians. The name, in use since the 8th century, means "common" or "simple," in contradistinction to elaborate, which is applicable to versions such as the Syro-Hexaplar and the Harklean [*see* BIBLE (TEXTS), 2]. Although it was once believed to be the oldest version in the Syriac tongue, the Peshitta is no longer accorded this honor; yet it does have a venerable past, since it claims the heritage of the whole of Syrian Christianity despite the doctrinal separations that began in A.D. 431. One sign of its great antiquity is its limited New Testament canon, which did not include 2 Peter, 2 and 3 John, Jude, and the Revelation.

[A. VÖÖBUS]

PESSIMISM

The term pessimism, formed by analogy with the word OPTIMISM, appeared first in the writings of Coleridge in 1815. It signifies either a permanent attitude of mind and settled feeling, or a philosophical doctrine. The former manifests itself in man's tendency to see the world in its worst aspect and is exemplified in the lyrical pessimism of Byron, Leopardi, Musset, Baudelaire and Heine, which is basically a pathetic affirmation of evil in the world.

As a philosophical doctrine, pessimism asserts that, on the whole, the world is bad rather than good. This doctrine presents itself variously as (1) empirical pessimism, (2) metaphysical pessimism and (3) pessimisms confined to special areas of thought. According to empirical pessimism only the present terrestrial existence is bad. Metaphysical pessimism, on the other hand, declares that the world as such is essentially evil, that it would be better if it did not exist at all. In more restricted usages, pessimism becomes concerned with particular spheres of human activity that seem to be hopelessly unsuccessful. Thus, sociological pessimism despairs of ever finding a satisfactory solution to the social problem; ethical pessimism believes man radically incapable of moral improvement; eudaemonistic (hedohistic) pessimism affirms that the amount of evil in this world surpasses the happiness of even the happiest individuals; cultural pessimism emphatically denies the possibility of any real advancement in culture. Suggestive of such views are the writings of Jean Jacques ROUSSEAU, Renouvier, LESSING and TOLSTOI.

Pessimism and Religious Thought. While many great religions of the world are optimistic in promising their faithful final salvation and eternal happiness, they are pessimistic when considering man's present condition. They look upon this world as a vale of tears, and its pleasures as vanity and deception, from which the faithful should in great part abstain by the practice of heroic abnegation. Particularly restrictive is BUDDHISM with its famous ''Four Noble Truths on Suffering.'' Moreover, Buddhism teaches that only *arhats,* that is, perfect monks, can obtain salvation immediately after death. Christianity, when explaining the doctrine of future happiness, exhorts its disciples to become accustomed to live in hope, and to see in their present life a time of trial. But a man who loses Christian faith falls easy prey to pessimism. We see this clearly in atheistic EXISTENTIALISM and in some lyrical pessimism.

Some critics err in seeing a radical pessimism in the Books of Job and Ecclesiastes. The expressions of poignant distress that we find in these books are counterbalanced by other texts that are highly optimistic. Moreover, their authors sincerely believed in God, and whoever believes in God is implicitly satisfied with the world in which God has placed him. Certain Gnostics, in particular MARCION and his followers, pushed pessimism so far as to attribute the creation of the world to a demiurge, who is distinct from the supreme God. A number of Christian apologists have also placed undue emphasis on the evil, which causes men to suffer in this world. For example, ARNOBIUS THE ELDER calls man ''an unhappy and miserable being who deplores that he exists.''

Philosophical Pessimists. The most radical pessimist in antiquity was Hegesias, a Cyrenaic philosopher. Many of his pupils are said to have reduced his teaching to practice by committing suicide. For this he was called Πεισιθάνατος, that is, persuading to die. Stoic philosophy also contained much empirical pessimism, as did EPICUREANISM.

At first following a deistic optimism, VOLTAIRE wrote a poem two months after an earthquake in Lisbon, November 1755, in which he proclaimed a gloomy view of the world. Moreau de Maupertuis (1698–1759) taught that the evil in the world far surpasses the good. In the writings of David HUME, pessimism appears intrinsically connected with the thought expressed, which is particularly skeptical and radically phenomenalistic. Atheistic existentialism professes that man has been thrown into existence by an unknown Being without a reasonable goal and has been abandoned to his own forces, which are insufficient to procure for him even elementary happiness. Existence itself is said to be irrational, blind, fatal and absurd.

Schopenhauer's Philosophy. Since the pessimism of Arthur SCHOPENHAUER (1788–1860) and Eduard von HARTMANN (1842–1906) was erected into a system of philosophy, it merits more careful consideration. Immanuel KANT had taught that only representations of our mind—pure PHENOMENA—can be objects of our intelligence. Schopenhauer, on the other hand, held that things in themselves could also be known by man; in reality, they are nothing else but products of will. Man's will, being deprived of any knowledge, pushes ahead blindly and thus becomes an inexhaustible source of suffering. The present world is the worst of all possible worlds; if it were only a little worse, it would not exist. Pleasure is purely negative: ''want, depression, pain—these are positive.'' Again, ''suffering is the true destiny of life.'' Man's redemption or salvation can be obtained only by ''the negation of the wish to live,'' for then the world itself, ''which is the reflection of our will,'' will disappear.

Hartmann's Position. Eduard von Hartmann tried to correct the system of his master, Schopenhauer. On the irrational will he grafted the Absolute Idea of HEGEL, but he replaced Hegelian dialectic by an inductive-scientific method. In order to explain the finality existing in nature, Hartmann postulated a particular reality that is diffused in it. As the activity of this reality (digestion, growth and many psychic acts) does not betray any consciousness, he called it the Unconscious. When, in pursuit of its ends, the will encounters an opposition, consciousness appears and with it, pain. The sum total of pain far surpasses that of pleasure. ''The existence of this world is worse than its nonexistence.''

Critical Evaluation. The pessimism of many people can be explained almost entirely by psychological factors. Leopardi's pessimism is the crying out of his soul, so to speak, in rebellion against the natural deformity of his body and his continuous misfortunes. Schopenhauer suffered from chronic nervousness with paranoid tendencies. Not all pessimists, however, are to be considered insane. Some arrive at a pessimistic view of the world through imitation or by whim. Others profess it in theory, but practice optimism in their lives. Here can be mentioned, in particular, Hartmann and some modern existentialists.

Another condition that leads many people to pessimism is their lack of experience, which makes them unable to face life realistically. In this way they expose themselves to bitter disappointments, become irritated and rebel. This possibly explains why pessimism finds most of its followers among young people. Schopenbauer published his theory of pessimism when he was 31 years old; Hartmann when he was only 26.

The philosophical foundations of pessimism are certainly questionable. Schopenhauer's assertion that the present world is the worst possible one was rejected even by many pessimists themselves (for example, Hartmann). His doctrine about the purely negative nature of pleasure is refuted by consciousness and experimental introspection. Although Hartmann taught that evil surpasses good in the world even in "the happiest of individuals," he never proved it. Many individuals declare that they feel happy rather than unhappy. How could they be convinced of the contrary? Helen Keller, blind and deaf all her life, was an enthusiastic propagator of optimism.

The Darwinian "struggle for life" finds its proper corrective in the help that living creatures give one another. In order to understand the meaning of evil, one must take care not to mutilate this life. Moreover, pessimists consider only one fragment of human life, namely, terrestrial life; they reject a priori the immortality of the soul and its eternal destiny. Perhaps this explains why pessimism develops in men a sense of discouragement and leads many to suicide, which they see as the only logical conclusion to be drawn from pessimistic premises.

See Also: EVIL; SUFFERING; DEATH (THEOLOGY OF); DUALISM; IRRATIONALISM.

Bibliography: P. SIWEK, *The Philosophy of Evil* (New York 1950) 145–198. G. MORRA, *Enciclopedia filosofica,* 4 v. (Venice-Rome 1957) 3:1329–36. R. EISLER, *Wörterbuch der philosophischen Begriffe,* 3 v. (4th ed. Berlin 1927–30) 2:404–408.

[P. SIWEK]

PESTALOZZI, JOHANN HEINRICH

Swiss educator and social reformer; b. Zurich, Jan. 12, 1746; d. Brugg (Aargau), Feb. 17, 1827. He was born of a distinguished and strict Protestant family and was educated by his devoted mother after the early death of his father. He attended schools in his native town and ultimately the Collegium Carolinum, where such men as Johann Bodmer (1698–1783) and Johann Breitinger (1701–76) were his teachers. Influenced by physiocratic ideas, Pestalozzi attempted to organize a farm, Neuhof (near Brugg, Aargau), which he continued as a charity school after its financial ruin in 1773. When the same disaster struck his school, Pestalozzi was forced to support himself only by his writings. During the French Revolution, he sided with the Swiss Unitary State (centralized government) and was in charge of an almshouse in Stans (Nidwalden) in 1798, after the bloody suppression of the popular revolt. In 1799 he taught in Burgdorf (Berne), where he founded an educational establishment (1801), which he transferred to Münchenbuchsee (Berne) and to Yverdon (Neuchâtel) in 1805. Difficulties with his fellow teachers forced him to close this school in 1825. Returning to Neuhof, he wrote autobiographical accounts in which he explained his failure in terms of "lack of foresight and inability to govern," shortcomings that are in sharp contrast to his fervent love for and devotion to mankind. His ideas, however, had profound and lasting influence. In the contemplative review of his life, *Die Abendstunde eines Einsiedlers* (1780), he paints an ideal picture of a man who is at peace because he has worked for the development of men's inner powers through faith in God, a healthy family life, and an individual, vocational, and professional education adapted to the good of the community.

To Pestalozzi elementary education was the natural right of every child, who should be afforded the opportunity to develop his physical, moral, and intellectual powers. He was convinced that every child, if properly trained, could be prepared to earn a living while developing his intelligence and moral nature. Noting carefully the results of his educational experiments, Pestalozzi declared: "There unfolded itself gradually in my mind the idea of an ABC of observation to which I now attach great importance, and in the working out of which the whole scheme of a general method of instruction in all its scope appeared, though still obscure, before my eyes." He considered it an important principle of instruction to reduce all subject matter to its simplest elements and adapt observation of these elements to the level of the child's development. "The starting point of thought is sense-perception, the direct impression produced by the world on our internal and external senses," he said, adding, "These impressions give the child his first ideas and at the same time awaken the desire to express them, first by signs, then by words." Pestalozzi therefore stressed that sense-perception or observation was the foundation of instruction and that it should be joined with expression in language, for, he says, "We can only speak clearly and exactly of those things from which we have received clear and exact impressions." In keeping with these views, Pestalozzi used a great variety of objects upon which he expected the children to exercise their sensory powers in the process of learning: field trips in the study of geography; elements of computation taught by counting steps and objects about the room; and moral training to grow out of occurrences in the daily lives of the children. There was oral discussion based on observation of the object of the lesson, a separation of the essential from the accidental and eventually the formulation of a definition. The procedure was chiefly oral: textbooks were not used, the pupil was active throughout the process, and the teacher instructed orally. This required of the teacher careful organization, resulting from proper preparation of the materials for each lesson, and skill in the art of questioning.

Influenced by J. J. ROUSSEAU's *Social Contract* and *Emile*, Pestalozzi introduced a vocational course of instruction as the ideal way to better the condition of the poor. The Neuhof experiment (1774–80) was intended to further this idea. Here the boys studied farming, the girls were taught sewing and housekeeping, and both learned spinning and weaving in a good home environment. Later in Stanz, (1798–1825), as he himself related: "I tried to connect study with manual labor, the school with the workshop, and make one thing of them." Earlier he had corresponded with Philip Emmanuel von Fellenberg, Swiss educator and agriculturist, explaining his ideas relative to this. Fellenberg, a man of means, established an institute at Hofwyl that emphasized practical training in agriculture and industrial arts. Pestalozzi did not include history and literature in his program because they were not readily adaptable to object teaching and because of his prejudice against books, which may have been influenced by Rousseau's *Emile*.

To Pestalozzi the principal center for the education of children was a well-regulated home, the center of love and cooperation. This spirit should also permeate the atmosphere of the classroom, where a "thinking love" should become the basis of the relationship between teacher and pupil. The school, he maintained, should be the focal point of activity wherein the individuality of the child would be regarded as sacred and instruction would be in harmony with his nature and inborn powers. He believed strongly in the development of head, heart, and hand in surroundings resembling those of a good Christian home.

Fellenberg's application of Pestalozzian principles were used effectively in the rehabilitation of juvenile delinquents in Germany and England. The manual labor movement in American education stemmed from the same source as did, also, the changes brought about in reform schools, e.g., segregation of young offenders from hardened criminals, and the growth of the cottage plan that grouped juvenile delinquents in homelike situations. The spirit and methods of the Swiss reformer later became the foundation of the Prussian system of education whose leaders had studied under him at Burgdorf and Yverdon. The report of Victor Cousin, the French philosopher, on "The Study of Public Instruction in Germany, Particularly Prussia" (1831) influenced French education and its translation into English in 1834 was widely distributed in England and America. Visitors to European schools disseminated their views upon their return through various educational journals, e.g., Henry Barnard's *American Journal*, the *American Annals*, and Horace MANN's *Seventh Report*. Pestalozzian methods came to be emphasized in American teacher's institutes. Edward A. Sheldon (1823–97), Superintendent of Schools at Oswego, N.Y., introduced the methods into the schools of his district. A teachers training school developed from the in-service training given the teachers, and in 1865 gave rise to the Oswego state normal school whose influence spread throughout the state and the Middle West in what came to be known as the "Oswego Movement."

Johann Heinrich Pestalozzi. (Archive Photos)

Pestalozzi was essentially a reformer interested in the social regeneration of the poor, which he thought could best be effected through instruction. His ideas introduced changes ranging from an enlightened atmosphere in the classroom to an improved methodology that was based upon and in accord with the natural development of the child. His experiments and observations emphasized the need for prospective teachers to know how as well as what to teach. This factor, together with his advocacy of universal elementary education, added impetus to the establishment of an increasing number of teacher training institutes in the U.S. and abroad.

Pestalozzi was a religious man and considered religious and moral education a very important aim. However, influenced no doubt by Rousseau, he abandoned dogmatic Christianity, although believing in God, and adhered to a purely rationalistic interpretation of a natural religion. His educational ideals inspired two great German educators, J. F. Herbart and F. W. FRÖBEL, who developed further many of Pestalozzi's theories.

Bibliography: *Sämtliche Werke: Kritische Ausgabe* (Zurich 1927–). F. DELEKAT, *Johann Heinrich Pestalozzi* (2d ed. Leipzig 1928). T. LITT, *Der lebendige Pestalozzi* (2d ed. Heidelberg 1961). K. SILBER, *Pestalozzi: Der Mensch und sein Werk* (Heidelberg 1957), Eng. tr. (London 1960). H. HOFFMANN, *Die Religion im Leben und Denken Pestalozzis* (Bern 1944). W. BOYD, *The History of Western Education* (6th ed. London 1952). E. P. CUBBERLEY, *Readings in the History of Education* (Boston 1920). F. P. GRAVES, *Great Educators of Three Centuries* (New York 1912). P. J. MCCORMICK, *History of Education,* ed. F. P. CASSIDY (3d ed. Washington 1953). P. MONROE, *Founding of the American Public School System,* 2 v. (v.1, New York 1940; v.2 n.d. microfilm). G. O'CONNELL, *Naturalism in American Education* (Washington 1936). F. V. N. PAINTER, ed., *Great Pedagogical Essays* (New York 1905). G. COMPAYRÉ, *The History of Pedagogy,* tr. W. H. PAYNE (5th ed. London 1903). J. H. PESTALOZZI, *How Gertrude Teaches Her Children,* tr. L. E. HOLLAND and F. C. TURNER, ed. E. COOKE (Syracuse 1915); *Pestalozzi's Leonard and Gertrude,* tr. and ed. E. CHANNING (Boston 1897). R. H. QUICK, *Essays on Educational Reformers* (new ed. New York 1896). H. STETTBACHER, *Lexikon der Pädagogik,* ed. H. ROMBACH, 4 v. (3d. ed. Freiburg 1962) 2:373–374.

[J. B. KELLER/W. G. WIXTED]

PETAU, DENIS (PETAVIUS)

Jesuit theologian and patrologist; b. Orleans, France, Aug. 21, 1583; d. Paris, Dec. 11, 1652. He received his master of arts degree at 16, defending his dissertation in Greek instead of Latin, and at 19 began to teach philosophy in Bourges (1603–05). He studied theology at the Sorbonne, and under the guidance of Isaac Casaubon devoted himself to patristic studies. In 1605 he became a Jesuit and was ordained in 1610. From 1611 to 1621 he taught rhetoric at the Jesuit colleges in Reims and La Flèche, and from 1621 to 1644 he taught positive theology at the Collège de Clermont in Paris, where after his retirement from teaching, he served as librarian until his death. Philip IV of Spain and Pope Urban VIII both sought his competent and erudite services, but without success.

Works. Guided by Fronton de Duc at Clermont, Petau edited the works of the fourth-century bishop SYNESIUS (1612), the 16 orations of the fourth-century Greek rhetorician Themistius (1613), three orations of JULIAN THE APOSTATE (1614), the *Breviarium historicum* of NICEPHORUS I (1616), and the complete works of St. EPIPHANIUS OF CONSTANTIA (1622). Petau's *Doctrina temporum* (2 v., 1627) was a thorough revision of SCALIGER's standard work of world chronology; the abridged version, *Rationarium temporum* (1633), was used by Bossuet for his *Discours sur l'histoire universelle.* Petau also wrote works of humanist and apologetical interest, as well as polemics against the Jansenists and Calvinists. His correspondence with famous persons was published in 1652.

The fame of Petau rests on his contribution to positive theology in his *Dogmata theologia* (4 v. 1644–50), in which he follows the lead of M. CANO and J. MALDONATUS and traces the Church's doctrines to sources in Holy Scripture and tradition. Of ten books planned, five appeared: *De Deo, De Trinitate, De angelis, De mundi opificio,* and *De Incarnatione*—each accompanied by an exhaustive discussion of the history of the topic, opposing heresies, the Church's decisions, and allied problems. Jansenists and other enemies of the Jesuits at the University of Paris caused a poor reception for the first three volumes in 1644; but outside scholars recognized their worth and the fourth volume appeared in 1650.

Theology. In his *Prolegomena* to the work, Petau discusses the nature and scope of theology in a fundamental manner and ''leaves to others the frequently contentious and subtle theologizing of many scholastics.'' Recognizing that scholastic methods were useful in the clarification of positions and the refutation of heresy, he points out that some authors had trapped themselves in purely dialectical exercises or relied too much on the opinions of schools or champions. Petau's purpose was to make convenient for dogmaticians the evidence of the Scriptures and patristic theology as a basis for further study and development.

On two problems in particular, public penance and the indwelling of the Holy Spirit, Petau's contribution has been of considerable value. While editing the works of Synesius and of St. Epiphanius, he had already studied the history of penance in the early Church. In 1644 he published *De la Pénitence publique et de la préparation à la communion* to refute A. ARNAULD's Jansenistic propositions in the tract *De la fréquente Communion.* Citing the Fathers of the first three centuries and the Council of Nicaea, Petau argued that, while certain sins had been generally regarded as unabsolvable, the Church had never hesitated to grant absolution at the hour of death; and that in the first four centuries the practice of penance varied considerably from one period to another and from one church to another. In conclusion, he upheld the practice of frequent confession and Communion on the principle that the Church had power to regulate its discipline even in the matter of the Sacraments. While many of Petau's statements on the practice of penance in the early Church are open to question, he brought forth much new evidence on a historical problem that has not yet received a satisfactory solution.

In discussing the indwelling of the Holy Spirit in the soul (*De Trinitate* 8.4–7), Petau contended that theologians of his day stopped short of the true scriptural doctrine taught by the Greek Fathers. Granting that justification is caused by the presence of created grace in the soul, Petau maintained that, since both the Scriptures and the Fathers insist that sanctification is the work of the

Holy Spirit: (1) the other Persons are present in the soul only through being inseparable from the Holy Spirit; and (2) as the Holy Spirit is called the"sanctifying power" of the Father and the Son, His action in the soul requires a special title, and a special mode whereby the union of the soul with the divinity terminates in the Person of the Holy Spirit. Though completely different from the hypostatic union, which is singularly characteristic of the Incarnation, this union of the Holy Spirit with the soul is still substantial, "so that the very substance of the Holy Spirit is joined with us in some mysterious and unusual way." Petau's theory was rejected by most theologians but in a modified form found favor with L. THOMASSIN (*De Incarnatione,* 6.11) and J. B. FRANZELIN (*De Deo uno,* 341–342). More recently M. SCHEEBEN (*Die Mysterien des Christentums,* 30), T. de Régnon (*Études de théotogie positive sur la sainte trinité,* 4:524–526), and G. Waffelaert (*L'union de l'âme aimante avec Dieu*) have sought to render Pétau's theory acceptable by modifying his explanations.

Petau called the attention of theologians to the hesitations, misconceptions, and inexactitudes of many of the early Fathers with regard to the theology of the Trinity in the primitive Church, and was immediately accused of making "almost all the Fathers of the first three centuries deny the divinity of the Son of God" by the Jansenists, and the Anglican theologian G. Bull in his *Defensio fidel Nicaenae,* 1685. Actually Petau's work was of crucial significance in the appreciation of the development of doctrine through the centuries, as J. H. NEWMAN early came to realize. As a proponent of positive theology, Petau is one of the great theologians of all time.

See Also: PATRISTIC STUDIES.

Bibliography: Theological works pub. in editions of: *Opus de theologicis dogmatibus,* 6 v. (Antwerp 1700); as *Dogmata theologica,* 8 v. (Vivès ed. Paris 1865–67). P. GALTIER, *Dictionnaire de théologie catholique,* ed. A. VACANT et al. (Paris 1903–50)12.1:1313–37. A. MICHEL, *Dictionnaire de théologie catholique,* ed. A. VACANT et al. (Paris 1903–50) 15.2:1851–54. P. DE LETTER, "Sanctifying Grace and the Divine Indwelling," *Theological Studies* 14 (1953) 242–272. J. C. V. CHATELLAIN, *Le P. Denis Pétau d'Orléans* (Paris 1884). C. BAUMGARTNER, *Lexicon für Theologie und Kirche*, ed. J. HOFER and K. RAHNER (Freiburg 1957–65) 8:314. P. DI ROSA, "D. Petau e la chronologia," *Archivum historicum Societatis Jesu* 29 (1960) 3–54.

[F. X. MURPHY]

PETER, APOSTLE, ST.

This article will discuss Peter's name, his career as presented in the Gospels, position in the Apostolic Church, death and burial, and representations in early art.

Name. In all likelihood, Peter's original name was *šim'ôn* (transliterated Συμεών twice: Acts 15.14; 2 Pt 1.1). The form Simon (Σίμων), a genuinely Greek name, is used much more often, about 50 times. This could be simply a NT adaptation of the Hebrew name, but it is also quite possible that Peter, like many of his compatriots, used two names, one Hebrew and one Greek. However, it was by neither of these names that he came to be generally known. Jesus gave him a new name, the Aramaic word for rock, *kêpā'*. In the primitive Church, which was at first Aramaic-speaking, this form of his name would have been most common. Later it was transliterated into Greek as Κηφᾶς (Cephas), but this form turns up only nine times in the NT, once in John and eight times in the letters of Paul. In fact, only once does Paul refer to him in any other way; in Gal 2.7 he calls him Peter (Πέτρος). This is intended as a Greek translation of *kêpā'* and is used more than 150 times in the Gospels and Acts. It told the Greek-speaking Christians more about Peter's function than the noncommittal Cephas. Finally, there is the double name, Simon Peter, which occurs about 20 times, mostly in John.

Career as Seen in the Gospels. That Peter was accorded a special place among the Apostles appears from an examination of the Gospel material.

Early Background. Before his call to follow Jesus, Simon, son of Jonah (Mt 16.17) or of John (Jn 1.42;21.15–17), was a commercial fisherman. He and his brother ANDREW worked in partnership with another pair of brothers, JAMES and JOHN, the sons of Zebedee (Lk 5.10). The family home was in Bethsaida of Galilee (Jn 1.44), but by the time Jesus began His public ministry, Simon had married and moved to Capharnaum (*see* CAPERNAUM). His mother-in-law lived with him there, and on one occasion Jesus cured her of a fever (Mk 1.30–31). There is no direct mention of his wife or of any children, but 1 Cor 9.5 is commonly interpreted to mean that he took his wife about with him on his missionary travels.

The Synoptic and Johannine traditions do not agree on the circumstances of his initial call to discipleship. According to John, the first meeting took place at "Bethany beyond the Jordan," where Peter, Andrew, and John were listening to the preaching of John the Baptist, who called their attention to Jesus (1.28, 40–42), and on this occasion Andrew recognized Jesus as the Messiah, and Jesus gave Simon his name of Peter. According to the Synoptics (Mt 4.18–22; Mk 1.16–20; Lk 5.11), the call took place in Galilee; Matthew and Mark differ somewhat from Luke in point of detail. It is, of course, possible to reconcile the two traditions. Peter may well have had his first meeting with the Master in the valley of the Jordan, with the definitive call to discipleship coming only later, after the return to Galilee. After all, John was an eyewitness. On the other hand, there is reason to suspect that John's account is influenced more by theological than by strictly historical considerations. In this account it is Andrew who first recognizes Jesus as the Messiah, and this is immediately at the beginning of the public ministry. In the Synoptics, it is Peter who first attains to this knowledge, and then only after several months of association with Jesus. Furthermore, it is in connection with this later avowal of Jesus' messianic dignity by Simon that the Lord changes his name to Peter. But John often telescopes historically separate incidents in order to make his ''witness'' more impressive. Using a sort of concentric-circle method of composition, he tends, from the very beginning of his Gospel, to present the whole truth about Christ in each episode. A striking example of this tendency to anticipate occurs in the passage under discussion. Even before he records Simon's change of name to Peter (1.42), he writes: ''Now Andrew, the brother of Simon Peter, was one of the two.'' (1.40) (*see* JOHN, GOSPEL ACCORDING TO ST.).

In the Synoptics. Simon Peter figures prominently in the Gospels, especially in the Synoptics. His leadership is indicated in many ways. He is pictured as taking the initiative on several occasions and as acting quite consistently as the spokesman of the disciples. With surprising boldness, he asked Jesus to let him walk across the water to meet him (Mt 14.28). He usually spoke for the whole group of disciples, and their acknowledgement of his leadership is no less eloquent for its being tacit. In their name he asked for an explanation of the parable of the Alert Servants (Lk 12.41). When Jesus asked them their opinion of His identity, it was Peter who answered and proclaimed that He was the Messiah (Mt 16.16; Mk 8.29; Lk 9.20). Immediately after this he objected to Jesus' prediction of the Passion and was reprimanded for his trouble (Mt 16.22–23; Mk 8.32–33). On another occasion he reminded Jesus of the sacrifice they had made in answering His call and asked what sort of reward they could expect (Mt 19.27; Mk 10.28; Lk 18.28). Even in some instances where one Gospel attributes a question to the disciples as a group, another makes it clear that it was Peter who was the interlocutor (cf. Mk 7.17 with Mt 15.15; Mt 21.20 with Mk 11.21).

Whenever the Twelve are listed, it is always Peter who is mentioned first (Mt 10.2; Mk 3.16; Lk 6.14; Acts 1.13), and Matthew underscores his preeminence by starting his catalogue thus: ''first Simon, who is called Peter.'' Even within the circle of the favored three, Peter, James, and John, he is always named first. This privileged trio witnessed the raising of Jairus's daughter (Mk 5.37), the Transfiguration (Mk 9.1–7), and the Agony in the Garden (Mk 14.33). In many instances where a group of the Apostles is involved in an incident, only Peter is mentioned by name (Mk 1.36; 16.7; Lk 8.45; 9.32).

Quite often in the Gospel narrative, Peter is singled out for special attention. It was from his boat that Jesus addressed the crowd on the lake shore (Lk 5.3), and it was to Peter's house that Jesus went in Capharnaum (Mk 1.29). It was with Peter that Jesus discussed the paying of the Temple tax, and immediately afterward He sent Peter to catch the fish in whose mouth was found the coin that covered the payment for both of them (Mt 17.23–26). Peter was the first of the Apostles to make a public declaration of his faith in Jesus as the Christ, and was selected as the Rock (his name!) on which the Church would be built (Mt 16.16–19). This selection was confirmed at the Last Supper when Jesus assured him that He was praying for the staunchness of Peter's faith in order that he, in turn, might be a bulwark for his fellow Apostles (Lk 22.31–32). When Peter answered that he was prepared to follow Him to prison and to death, Jesus predicted that, for all his protestations of loyalty, he would deny Him publicly before dawn (Lk 22.33–34; Mt 26.33–35; Mk 14.29–31). The sorry fulfillment of this prediction is recorded in all the Gospels. But the Synoptics record also the fact that when he realized what he had done, Peter wept in repentance. Shortly before this, when Jesus' enemies were preparing to lead him from the garden, Peter, again displaying his characteristic impetuosity, cut off the right ear of a servant of the high priest (Mk 14.47; cf. Jn 18.10). That Jesus recognized the sincerity of Peter's sorrow and forgave him is attested by the fact that He favored him with a special appearance after the Resurrection (Lk 24.34; 1 Cor 15.5).

In John. Peter does not figure quite so prominently in John as in the Synoptics. But then, the Johannine tradition has theological centers of interest quite different from those of the Synoptic tradition. John's anticipation of the recognition of Jesus as the Messiah and of the change of Simon's name to Peter is mentioned above. After the Eucharistic discourse (Jn 6.22–68), when Jesus asked the Apostles if they also were minded to leave Him, Peter replied: ''Lord, to whom shall we go? Thou hast words of everlasting life, and we have come to believe and to know that thou art the Christ, the Son of God'' (Jn 6.69–70). At the Last Supper he protested when Jesus approached to wash his feet (Jn 13.6–10), and he motioned to John to ask Jesus the identity of the betrayer about whom He had been speaking (Jn 13.23–24). In concert with the Synoptics, John records the prediction of Peter's denial (Jn 13.38) and its fulfillment (Jn 18.17–18, 25–27). He alone identifies Peter as the disciple who cut off the ear of the high priest's servant (18.10). On the morning of the Resurrection, Mary Magdalene brought news of the empty tomb to Peter and John. Together they hurried to the spot, but it was Peter who entered first (Jn 20.1–10). Simon Peter's decision to return to his fishing is recorded in Jn 21.3. While he and his companions were at their work, Jesus appeared on the shore. After He had successfully guided them to a good catch, John realized who He was and immediately told Peter. The latter jumped overboard and waded ashore (Jn 21.4–8). And when Jesus asked for some fish for breakfast, Peter dashed out and dragged in the whole catch (21.10–11). After they had eaten, Jesus elicited from Peter a threefold profession of love and gave him the commission to feed His lambs and His sheep, thus confirming him in his primacy (21.15–17). He then foretold Peter's martyrdom (21.18–19).

Primacy. Because of its theological importance, Peter's confession in Mt 16.16–19 calls for special comment. All three Synoptics record his avowal of Jesus' messiahship, but Matthew alone includes his profession of faith in Jesus' divine sonship and the promise of primacy that follows. This passage presents several problems. First, is the matter peculiar to Matthew authentic, and if it is, why did Mark and Luke omit it? It used to be the fashion in certain circles to deny flatly the authenticity of the Matthean material. Now, however, there is general agreement that Mt 16.17–19 is part of the original Gospel according to St. Matthew. But there is still some question as to whether the promise was made on this specific historical occasion. The question is not an idle one. Mark and Luke both record the event that took place at Caesarea Philippi, but both give a shorter version of Peter's confession: ''Thou art the Christ'' (Mk 8.29); ''the Christ of God'' (Lk 9.20). And neither of them makes any mention of the change of Peter's name or of the promise of primacy at this point. Interestingly enough, even in Matthew's account, Our Lord brings the incident to a close with the charge ''to tell no one that he was the Christ'' (16.20).

The explanation may lie in Matthew's method of composition, which is obviously synthetic. He groups incidents and sermons topically rather than chronologically. The section in which this passage appears (13.54–19.1) is concerned with the structure of the Kingdom, and within this section Matthew has gathered several incidents that point up Peter's prominence: his walking on the water, his role in the drama of the Transfiguration, his finding of the coin for the Temple tax (for himself and Jesus) in the fish's mouth, and his inquiry about the forgiveness of offenses. It is quite possible that, following his method of logical grouping, he filled out the incident at Caesarea Philippi with another confession of Peter from the post-Resurrection period, the profession of faith that occasioned the bestowal of the primacy. In the Johannine tradition, this bestowal took place in a post-Resurrection context. Such a remarkable act of faith would seem more in place in this context. At any rate, whether or not it is in its proper historical setting in Mt ch. 16, the text is certainly authentic and retains its full force (*see* MATTHEW, GOSPEL ACCORDING TO ST.).

In the Early Church. After Christ's Ascension Peter is undisputed leader of the Church. He takes the initiative in the election of Matthias to the Apostolic college (Acts 1.15–26). At Pentecost he explains to the curious crowd the meaning of the strange phenomena that accompanied the descent of the Holy Spirit (2.14–40). His cure of the lame beggar is the first recorded miracle of an Apostle (3.1–11). He takes advantage of this occasion to preach Christ within the Temple precincts (3.12–26), and when the authorities arrest him and his companion, John, he fearlessly defends himself before the Sanhedrin (4.1–22). So great did his renown become that people brought their sick on stretchers and placed them on the ground in the hope that his shadow might fall upon them as he passed (5.15). And when all the Apostles were arrested, Peter again spoke in their defense (5.29–32). Once they were released on the advice of Gamaliel, they continued steadfastly to spread the Good News, in spite of the fact that they had been flogged as a warning (5.40–42). Peter vigorously condemned Ananias and Sapphira in the name of the Church (5.1–11). Leaving James in charge of the local community, he visited the churches in Samaria (8.14) and Galilee (9.31–32), Lydda (9.32), Sharon (9.35), and Joppa (9.36). In Lydda he cured the paralytic Aeneas, in Joppa he raised Tabitha from the dead. In Caesarea he received the centurion Cornelius into the Church (10.9–48).

This last incident illustrates the forthrightness and decisiveness of Peter's leadership. The question of the admission of Gentiles into the Church was far from being settled. In fact, it took a supernatural vision to form Peter's convictions on the matter, but, once convinced, he acted fearlessly. The reaction of the Jerusalem community was not favorable, but when Peter explained his action they acquiesced (11.1–18).

Not long after this, Herod Agrippa I arrested Peter, but he was miraculously released from prison; thereupon he departed, and went ''to another place'' (12.1–17), the identity of which is unknown. Antioch in Syria is a good possibility. At any rate, he was back in Jerusalem for the council called to discuss the still burning question of the admission of Gentiles into the Church. The matter had been somewhat clarified. It was no longer a question of whether or not they should be admitted, but rather of the terms on which they could be admitted—whether or not they needed to observe the Law. After a preliminary discussion among the Apostles, Peter settled the matter by citing the case of Cornelius (Acts 15) (*see* JERUSALEM, COUNCIL OF).

It is uncertain whether Paul's altercation with Peter at Antioch, as recounted in Gal 2.11–14, preceded or followed the council (*see* GALATIANS, EPISTLE TO THE). Peter was associating freely with the Gentile members of the Antioch church until some of the Judaizers came from Jerusalem. Apparently in an attempt to avoid trouble, he avoided the Gentiles while this group was in town. This created a nasty situation. The Gentiles were hurt and bewildered, and Paul, their champion, remonstrated with Peter for his disturbing inconsistency.

Death and Burial. It is quite certain that Peter spent his last years in Rome. The first of the two epistles ascribed to him was written from "Babylon," a code name for Rome. It is, however, impossible to say how long he stayed there. An old tradition that he spent 25 years in Rome is quite unacceptable. All that can be said with certainty is that he went to Rome and was martyred there. St. Clement of Rome wrote, about A.D. 95, in his *Epistle to the Corinthians* (5–6): "To these men [Peter and Paul], whose lives were holy, there is joined a great multitude of elect ones who, in the midst of numerous tortures inflicted for their zeal, gave amongst us a magnificent example." St. Ignatius of Antioch, in his *Epistle to the Romans* a few years later, says that it is not for him to give them orders as Peter and Paul did. In the first half of the 2d century Papias wrote that Mark's Gospel was a record of Peter's Roman preaching (Eusebius, *Hist. Eccl.* 3.39.15). From the second half of this century comes the testimony of Irenaeus, a man well acquainted with the universal Church of his day; he is quite explicit on the activity of Peter in Rome (*Adversus haereses* 3.3.3). By the late 2d and early 3d centuries, the tradition of Peter's Roman sojourn and martyrdom is solidly established. The martyrdom is usually dated 64 or 65 during the Neronian persecution. The tradition that he was crucified goes back to Tertullian (*De praescriptione* 36; *Scorpiacus* 15).

The earliest testimony to Peter's burial on Vatican Hill comes from the Roman priest Caius during the reign of Pope Zephryinus (199–217). The tradition has been constant since then, and recent archeological discoveries beneath the Basilica of St. Peter have confirmed it. For details see the article on the VATICAN.

Peter in Early Christian Iconography. The earliest known painting of Peter is in a house in Dura-Europos, a city in the Syrian desert not far from the Euphrates. One of the rooms of this house, which was built in 232–233, was used as a Christian chapel. The walls are covered with paintings, one of which depicts the miracle of the walking on the lake. Peter is on the point of sinking, and Jesus is stretching out his hand to him. The figure of Peter is very well preserved and portrays him as bearded and with a fine head of curly hair. In the mausoleum of the Valerii, discovered during the recent excavations beneath St. Peter's, there is a scratching of just the head of an old man, bald, with wrinkled brow and pointed beard. The accompanying Latin inscription has been translated as follows: "Peter, pray Christ Jesus for the holy Christian men buried near your body." Both the picture and the inscription have been dated about 280.

Peter is depicted also in the friezes decorating Christian sarcophagi. In the center of one such frieze, from the 4th century, Christ is pictured predicting Peter's denial, and Peter himself is shown being arrested and striking a rock to procure water for the baptism of his jailer. On another type of sarcophagus, of Asiatic columnar construction, he is pictured at the head of the Apostles, carrying a cross and receiving from Jesus the scroll of the New Law.

With the coming of peace under Constantine and the building of churches, portraits of the Apostles become more common. An interesting example of the differences in art traditions comes from the Basilica of San Lorenzo Fuori le Mura at Rome. The mosaics, which date from 578, show a definite Byzantine influence, and Peter is pictured at Christ's right. In the Roman tradition, from the 4th to the 13th century, he appears always at Christ's left. St. Peter is traditionally represented as carrying two keys, a symbolism based on "the keys of the kingdom of heaven" of Mt 16.19, their number probably determined by the "two swords" of Lk 22.38.

Feast: June 29 (Ss. Peter and Paul).

Bibliography: U. HOLZMEISTER, *Vita S. Petri Apostoli* (Paris 1936). O. CULLMANN, *Peter, Disciple, Apostle, Martyr: An Historical and Theological Study,* tr. F. V. FILSON (2d rev. ed. Philadelphia 1962). O. KARRER, *Peter and the Church: An Examination of Cullmann's Thesis,* tr. R. WALLS (New York 1963). J. LEBRETON and J. ZEILLER, *The History of the Primitive Church,* tr. E. C. MESSENGER, 4 bks. in 2 (reissue; New York 1951), pub. as *A History of the Early Church,* 4 v. (1962). J. FINEGAN, *Light from the Ancient Past* (2d ed. Princeton 1959) 297–304. J. DUPONT, "Pierre et Paul dans les Actes," *Revue biblique* 64 (1957) 35–47; "Pierre et Paul à Antioch et à Jérusalem," *Recherches de science religieuse* 45 (1957) 42–60, 225–239. D. STANLEY, "Études matthéennes: La confession de Pierre à Césarée," *Sciences Ecclésiastiques* 6 (1954) 51–61. R. E. BROWN, K. P. DONFRIED, and J. REUMANN, eds., *Peter in the New Testament* (Minneapolis 1973). R. PESCH, *Simon-Petrus* (Stuttgart 1980). T. V. SMITH, *Petrine Controversies in Early Christianity* (Tübingen 1985). *Anchor Bible Dictionary* 5 (New York 1992) 251–63.

[J. J. CASTELOT]

PETER, CARL JOSEPH

Priest, theologian, and teacher; b. Omaha, Nebraska, April 4, 1932; d. Washington, D.C., Aug. 20, 1991. Oldest of four children born to Carl J. and Anne Marie (Schinker) Peter. Gifted with a brilliant mind and eidetic memory, the younger Carl excelled at school. As a seminarian for the Archdiocese of Omaha, he studied philosophy and theology at the Pontifical Gregorian University in Rome where he was ordained a priest in 1957. After two years as assistant pastor at St. Patrick's Church and dean of studies at Archbishop Bergan Central Catholic High School (1958–60) in Fremont, Nebraska, Peter returned to Rome for doctoral studies. For the next four years he held the posts of assistant vice-rector and repetitor at the North American College, earning the S.T.D. at the Gregorian (1962) and the Ph.D. at the University of St. Thomas Aquinas (1964). His dissertations, both published in their entirety (1964), treated Aquinas' views on the beatific vision and the eviternity of rational souls.

In 1964 Peter was appointed assistant professor of dogmatic theology at the CATHOLIC UNIVERSITY OF AMERICA in Washington, D.C., where he spent his academic career. He chaired the Department of Theology (1975–77) and served for two terms as dean of the School of Religious Studies (1977–85). In 1990 he became the first occupant of the Founders (Caldwell-Drexel-Duval) Chair in Theology. He was also a visiting professor at St. John's University (Collegeville, Minnesota) during summer sessions (1970–91 *passim*) and a visiting lecturer at Princeton Theological Seminary (1974, 1976).

Peter's theological expertise was also widely esteemed outside the university. He was active in ecumenical dialogues, beginning as a member of the U.S. Bilateral Roman Catholic-Presbyterian and Reformed Churches Consultation (1967–72) and then as a prominent participant in the Roman Catholic-Lutheran Bilateral Ecumenical Consultation in the U.S. (1972 until his death). He served as a Roman Catholic observer (1969–70), as a member of the Interdemoninational Study Group on Intercommunion (1970–71), and as a commission member (1971–72) of the Department of Faith and Order in the National Council of Churches. He was elected president of the CATHOLIC THEOLOGICAL SOCIETY OF AMERICA (1971–72) and received the society's John Courtney Murray Award for Distinction in Theology (1975). He was a peritus to the American delegates to the International Synod of Bishops in 1971, 1983, and 1985. Pope John Paul II appointed him to two five-year terms (1980, 1985) as a member of the International Theological Commission. Beginning in 1986 he was also a theological advisor to the Committee on Doctrine of the National Conference of Catholic Bishops. Peter had a reputation for being open-minded regarding the positions of others and moderate—''centrist''—in positions he himself espoused.

His numerous publications were in the form of articles and reviews. At the time of his death from a sudden, massive heart attack, he was at work on a book about academic freedom in Catholic theology and the Catholic University of America. Forthright yet prudent, hard working, and deeply concerned about others, he was lavish in his generosity to the University in support of scholars and scholarship and to the needy.

Bibliography: For a bibliography of Peter's books and articles, see *Church and Theology: Essays in Memory of Carl J. Peter*, ed. P. C. PHAN (Washington D.C. 1995) 280–84. His personal writings and notes are preserved in the archives of the Catholic University of America, Washington, D.C.

[N. H. MINNICH]

PETER, EPISTLES OF

Since the two Epistles that bear St. Peter's name are quite different in many ways, they are treated separately here, according to the contents, authenticity, destination, time and place of composition, and theology of each.

1 Peter. After the writings of the Pauline corpus, this is probably the best-known and most important of the New Testament Epistles. It is written with rare unction. Among the catholic epistles, it has the greatest claim to have been written by the person whose name it bears, contemporary scholarship generally holds that it was written some time after the death of the Apostle Peter.

The author opens with a salutation (1.1–2) and blesses God, who has given rebirth, through the Resurrection of Christ, and an imperishable inheritance (1.3–5). He states that this is a source of joy even under trials (1.6–7) and that Jesus is now the object not of sight but of faith (1.8–9). Christian salvation was foreseen by the prophets (1.10–12); his readers must therefore be holy (1.13–17), being aware that they were ransomed by the blood of Christ (1.18–21). They are to love one another since they have been born anew of imperishable seed (1.22–25). They are newborn infants, living stones in God's building, a holy priesthood, God's own people (2.1–10). They must keep clear of fleshly passions, conduct themselves becomingly among the Gentiles, and be subject to human authority (2.11–17). Servants should be submissive; for all Christians must be willing to suffer, even unjustly, since Christ did so for them, dying on the cross that they might live (2.18–25). Wives and husbands are to practice the virtues appropriate to each (3.1–7). Mutual love is to prevail among all (3.8–12). They should be zealous for good, even if this involves suffering (3.13–17), since Christ, the righteous one, died for sinners and saves people, in Baptism, though His Resurrection (3.18–22). In conformity with Christ, who suffered in the flesh, they should live no longer by human passions, as formerly, and as the Gentiles now do (4.1–6). In view of the proximity of the end, they must practice all virtue (4.7–11). They are not to be surprised that they must suffer; rather, they should rejoice in sharing Christ's sufferings (4.12–19). The elders are to tend the flock with diligence, and the young are to be subject (5.1–5). All are to be humble and watchful; God will soon restore and strengthen them (5.6–11). The author concludes with a final greeting (5.12–14).

Authorship. The Petrine authorship of this letter—asserted in 1.1, confirmed by the reference to Babylon (a veiled reference to Rome; *see* BABYLON, CITY OF) and Mark (*see* MARK, EVANGELIST, ST.) in 5.13, and never challenged in antiquity—in modern times has been and remains the subject of considerable debate. Reasons for questioning authenticity include: (1) the excellent Greek style of the letter an ready familiarity with the Septuagint Bible, both of which would scarcely be possible for an unschooled Galilean fisherman (see Acts 4.13); (2) numerous similarities to Pauline theology and expression; (3) references to persecutions in the provinces (especially 4.12–17), which would be historically improbable until several decades after the death of Peter. In answer to these objections it is pointed out that: (1) In 5.12 Silvanus (SILAS) is mentioned as the one through whom the letter has been written. In accordance with ancient practice in writing letters, this prominent Christian (Acts 15.22) and companion of Paul's journeys (Acts 15.22–17.15; 1 Thes 1.1; 2 Cor 1.19) may be responsible for the literary qualities of the letter. (2) Much of the similarity to Pauline writings may be attributable to a tradition of Christian doctrinal and paraenetic formulas common to New Testament authors. Likewise the influence of Silvanus's extensive contact with Paul is pertinent. (3) The allusions to persecutions do not necessarily imply official governmental persecution of Christianity as such, particularly in view of the exhortation to submission to temporal authorities in 2.13–17.

While nothing in the letter is directly contrary to Petrine authorship, many tend to see it as a pseudonymous work of the 80s (Elliott, Brown). Nonetheless, the composition's use of fictional details is relatively sparse when compared with other samples of the pseudepigraphical genre (Brox). Although Brox is skeptical about the oft-repeated notion that this is a deliberate amalgam of Pauline themes and Petrine window dressing written in the interests of Church unity, he points out that further work is yet to be done.

The familiar thesis of Preisker (1951) that 1.1–4.11 constitutes a baptismal homily, followed in 4.12–5.14 by parenesis about persecution has been seriously called into question. Though a two sermon approach still has its defenders (Blevins), the style is more and more seen as consistent throughout the letter (Shimada), and 1.3–12 has been thought to establish the program of the whole letter (Kendall).

There is growing consensus that the letter is wholly parenetic, and it is a parenesis affected partly by liturgical language: the ''spiritual sacrifices'' of 2.5 refer both to the Eucharist and to the addressees' everday lives (Hill); the ''appeal'' to God for a clean conscience (3.21) is derived from the baptismal adjuration to leave the way of death by obeying God's commands (Tripp).

The author has adapted some imagery from Judaism, including ''convenantal'' language (Pryor). One Old Testament phrase, ''aliens and strangers'' (2.11) has been argued to be a technical term in addition, referring to resident aliens/migrant workers brought to Asia Minor to work in the fields or from rural areas to be house servants (Elliott). In this view, ''persecution for the name'' need not be linked to a major threat either from Nero or Domitian, but may refer to the ongoing hostility and suspicion accorded the resident aliens by their neighbors.

The injunctions to slaves and wives to obey the head of the household (2.13–3.12) have been seen as a needed apologia (3.15) to a culture deeply suspicious of the dire consequences for the Empire of adopting Eastern deities perceived as promoting egalitarianism (Balch). The thesis Presupposes as common currency the notion in Aristotle, among others, that the Household of the gods, of the state, and of the individual are interrelated. The Thesis seems supported by the fact that the ''code'' is surrounded by reference to the slander of pagans (2.12; 3.13–16). The thesis has been criticized for asserting, though not sufficiently proving, that there were Christian households in which this egalitarianism was functioning (Neyrey). Moreover, the codes may serve as much to provide internal cohesion as to provide the group a defense to outsiders (Elliott).

The codes have been seen as part of a late-stratum of material imposed on the Pauline and Petrine corpus (Munro) and have been called a corruption of the original ideal of ''equal discipleship'' (Schüssler-Fiorenza). The attitude of 1 Peter toward the codes is further complicated by the partial critiques of patriarchy which may exist in his presentation of them (Balch).

Interpretive Problems and Models. Suggestions for more accurate translations have focused on 1.2, ''because of the obedience and the sprinkling of the blood of Jesus Christ'' (Agnew); 3.2, ''chaste behavior with reverence (to your husbands)'' (Sylva); 4.15, ''let none of you suffer as a murderer, thief, sorcerer, or embezzler'' (Bauer).

Concerning the term ''spirits'' of 3.19, 4.6, since 2 Peter may have been aware of 1 Peter, 2 Peter may be helpful in understanding general problem passages in 1 Peter. On this theory, the spirits of 3.19 are seen to be evil because of the portrait in 2 Pt 2.4, 5; those who have died, but are ''alive in the spirit'' (4.6) are those who have died awaiting a new heaven and earth (2 Pt 3.9, 13) (Dalton).

2 Peter. This Epistle is a precious witness to the trials that were being inflicted on the Church by false teachers toward the end of the apostolic age.

The author opens with a salutation (1.1–2). He states that the divine goodness and promises, which include even a participation in the divine nature, should motivate Christians to the practice of all virtue, by which they may enter into the eternal kingdom (1.3–11). In view of his imminent death, the author wishes to leave this written memorial to the faith, based on his personal witness (e.g., of the Transfiguration) and on the prophetic testimony of the Scriptures (1.12–21). His readers are to beware of false teachers (2.1–3), whose punishment will correspond to that of the sinners of old (2.4–9); they give themselves over to every kind of evil, lead others astray, and revert to their original corruption (2.10–22). His readers must not be misled by those who scoff at the delay of the Lord's coming (3.1–10), Rather, their lives are to be lived in holy expectation, in accord with the genuine (not the twisted) teaching of the letters of Paul (3.11–18a). The author concludes with a doxology (3.18b).

Author and Genre. There is a general willingness to see the 2 Peter work as pseudepigraphical, and one commentator suggests that the letter comes from turn of the century Rome that also gave us 1, 2 Clement and Hermas (Bauckham). Whatever its geographical origins, the author is seen as having used Jude and straightened out its chronology (Neyrey). However, the reference to ''my first letter'' (3.1) is not a reference to Jude, but to 1 Peter (Johnson). The choice of a Petrine pseudonym is seen as a necessity in view of the Pauline canon being already known as closed (Farkasfalvy).

The parenetic nature of the letter is defended with the thesis that it displays appeals to memory (1.9; 1.12–15; 3.1–2, 5, 8), models (2.6), and maxims (1.5–7) typical of parenesis (Johnson).

There is a renewed appreciation of the fact that a denunciation of false prophets is appropriate to literature describing the End Time (Cavallin). This motif is often present in testamentary literature, and works with the author's prediction of his imminent dissolution (1.13, 14) to justify the description of the letter as a testament of sorts.

The appeal to the transfiguration is used by the author as a defense of the proclamation about the parousia (Neyrey). The author is not so concerned to defend the meaning of parousia as the second coming per se, since he feels free to use parousia for the ''presence'' of Jesus at the Transfiguration (Kee). But the author is concerned to answer those, Probably influenced by Epicurean notions, who think that death brings only Dissolution and not judgment. He attacks as false, the ''freedom'' which such a notion can offer (2.19), and insists on God's power to judge, both in the past and in the future (Neyrey). The letter, therefore, amounts to a Christian theodicy.

The letter shares with some gnostic texts the description of a deity who punishes throughout successive ages of world history; indeed, a study that traces the Petrine trajectory in relation to the Nag Hammadi library suggests that the letter is aimed at gnostics (Smith). But that position might be called into question in part because the letter was known in Justin's time, a generation before Irenaeus fought the gnostics (Thiede). More importantly, the anti-Epicurean polemic described by Neyrey does not need gnostics on the horizon to be coherent.

Recent suggestions about the translation of individual verses include a defense of the reading ''found'' at 3.10, a term often used absolutely in an eschatological context of both persons and things (Lenhard); and an interrogative reading of the same passage: ''shall the earth and everything in it be found?'' (Overstreet).

Bibliography: E. BEST, *I Peter* (1971; Grand Rapids 1982). E. G. SELWYN, *The First Epistle of Peter. The Greek Text With Introduction, Notes and Essays* (1947; 2nd ed. Grand Rapids 1981). L. GOPPELT, *Der Erste Petrubrief*, ed. F. HAHN (Gottingen 1978). D. KENDALL, ''The Literary and Theological Function of 1 Peter 1.3–12,'' C. H. TALBERT, ed., *Perspectives on First Peter* (Macon, Georgia 1986). W. MUNRO, *Authority in Paul and Peter. The Identification of a Pastoral Stratum in the Pauline Corpus and 1 Peter* (Cambridge 1983). J. CALLOUD and F. GENUYT, *La première épître de Pierre: Analyse semiotique* (Paris 1982). D. C. ARICHEA and E. A. NIDA, *A Translator's Handbook on the First Letter from Peter* (New York 1980). C. PERROT, ed., *Études sur la première lettre de Pierre* (Paris 1980). D. L. BALCH, *Let Wives Be Submissive: The Domestic Code in 1 Peter* (Chico, California 1981). J. NEYREY, ''Let Wives Be Submissive'' (review), *The Catholic Biblical Quarterly* 49 (1987) 690–91. R. E. BROWN and J. P. MEIER, *Antioch and Rome* (New York 1983). J. W. PRYOR, ''First Peter and the New Covenant,'' *Reformed Theological Review* 45 (1986) 1–4; (1986) 44–51. E. SCHÜSSLER-FIORENZA, ''Discipleship and Patriarchy: Early Christian Ethos and Christian Ethics in a Feminist Theological Perspective,'' *Annual of the Society of Christian Ethics Dallas, Texas* (1982) 131–72. D. HILL, ''To Offer Spiritual Sacrifices . . . (1 Peter 2.5): Liturgical Formulations and Christian Parenesis in 1 Peter,'' *Journal for the Study of the New Testament* 16 (1982) 45–63. D. SYLVA, ''Translating and Interpreting 1 Peter 3, 2,'' *Bible Translator* 34 (1983) 144–47. D. H. TRIPP, ''Eperotema (1 Peter 3.21). A Liturgist's Note,'' *Expository Times* 92 (1981) 267–70. W. J. DALTON, ''The Interpretation of 1 Pet 3, 19 and 4, 6; Light from 2 Peter,'' *Biblica* 60 (1979) 547–55. J. B. BAUER, ''Aut maleficus aut alieni speculator (1 Petr 4, 15),'' *Biblische Zeitschrift* 22 (1978) 109–15. N. BROX, ''Tendenz und Pseudepigraphie im ersten Petrusbrief,'' *Kairos* 20 (1978) 110–20. N. BROX, ''Der erste Petrusbrief in der literarischen Tradition des urchristentums,'' *ibid.* 20 (1978) 182–92. D. L. BALCH, ''Early Christian Criticism of Patriarchal Authority: 1 Peter 2.11–3.12,'' *Union Seminary Quarterly Review* 39 (1984) 161–73. J. L. BLEVINS, ''Introduction to 1 Peter,'' Rev 79 (1982) 401–13. F. H. AGNEW, ''1 Peter 1.2—An Alternative Translation,'' *The Catholic Biblical Quarterly* 45 (1983) 68–73. J. H. ELLIOT, *1 Peter* (AB 37B; New York 2000). P. J. ACHTEMEIER, *1 Peter* (Hermeneia; Minneapolis: Fortress 1996). T. SMITH, *Petrine Controversies in Early Christianity: Attitudes Toward Peter in Christian Writings of the First Two Centuries* (Tubingen 1985). R. E. BROWN, et al., eds., *Peter in the New Testament* (New York 1973). J. H. NEYREY, ''The Form and Background of the Polemic in 2 Peter,'' *Journal of Biblical Literature* 99 (1980) 407–31; ''The Apologetic Use of the Transfiguration in 2 Peter 1.16–21,'' *The Catholic Biblical Quarterly* 42 (1980) 504–19. R. L. OVERSTREET, ''A Study of 2 Peter 3.10–13,'' *Biblioteca Sacra* 137 (1980) 354–71. H. C. C. CAVALLIN, ''The False Teachers of 2 Pt as Pseudo-Prophets,'' *Novum Testamentum* 21 (1979) 263–70. H. LENHARD, ''Noch einmal zu 2 Petr 3.10 d,'' *Zeitschrift für die neutestamentliche Wissenschaft und die Kunde der älteren Kirche* 69 (1978) 136. F. W. DENKER, ''2 Peter 1: A Solemn Decree,'' *The Catholic Biblical Quarterly* 40 (1978) 64–82. D. FARKASFALVY, ''The Ecclesial Setting of Pseudepigraphy in Second Peter and Its Role in the Formation of the Canon,'' *Second Century* 5 (1985–86) 3–29. C. P. THIEDE, ''A Pagan Ready of 2 Peter: Cosmic Conflagration in 2 Peter 3 and the Octavius of Minucius Felix,'' *Journal for the Study of the New Testament* 26 (1986) 79–96. J. H. NEYREY, *2 Peter, Jude* (AB 37C; New York, 1993).

[T. W. LEAHY/M. KILEY]

PETER, SARAH WORTHINGTON KING

Lay leader and philanthropist; b. Chillicothe, Ohio, May 10, 1800; d. Cincinnati, Ohio, Feb. 6, 1877. Sarah was the daughter of Thomas and Eleanor Van Swearingen Worthington. Her father, descended from an ancient Lancashire (England) Catholic family, whose Virginia branch had become Episcopalians, was the first U.S. senator from Ohio and its sixth governor. Sarah attended private schools in Kentucky and Baltimore, Maryland. At 16 she married Gen. Edward King, son of U.S. Senator Rufus King, a former member of the Continental Congress and ambassador to England. In 1831 the Kings moved to Cincinnati where they became prominent in social life. Sarah took part in various charitable activities and worked for St. Paul's Episcopal parish until Edward's death in 1836. Three of their five children predeceased their father.

Sarah spent the next four years at Cambridge, Massachusetts, while her sons, Rufus and Thomas, attended Harvard University. Meanwhile, she continued her own studies, becoming fluent in German, French, and Italian. In 1844 she married William Peter, British consul at Philadelphia, Pennsylvania, and former Member of Parliament. At their home in Philadelphia, they received many of the most distinguished literary men and influential citizens of the country. Sarah founded the Philadelphia School of Design for Women, the first of its kind and a model for similar schools in other cities. She helped to establish a Quaker home for magdalens, and interested herself in a projected Episcopalian religious order for women.

When her husband died in 1853, Sarah returned to Cincinnati where she organized the Ladies Academy of Art, from which developed the Cincinnati Academy of Fine Arts and School of Design, later absorbed into the Cincinnati Art Museum. While collecting masterpieces in Europe she had been impressed by the liturgy of the Catholic Church and the social work of Catholic nuns. On March 25, 1855, she was received into the Church at Trinità dei Monti convent, Rome. With her own fortune and with funds collected from European nobility and royalty, she increased her charitable works. Through her instrumentality, the Sisters of Mercy, Sisters of the Poor of St. Francis, Sisters of the Good Shepherd, Little Sisters of the Poor, Religious of the Sacred Heart, and the Passionist Fathers were brought to Cincinnati. Thereafter, she gave them substantial assistance, frequently helping them to make foundations in other cities.

During the U.S. Civil War Sarah was a field nurse with the Franciscan sisters and worked in Cincinnati hospitals and war prisons, even nursing a soldier who had falsely accused her of spying. While living the life of a semireligious in an apartment of the mansion she had given to one of the sisterhoods, she pursued her civic and apostolic works until her death.

Bibliography: *Rufus King Papers,* Cincinnati Historical Society, Cincinnati. J. H. LAMOTT, *History of the Archdiocese of Cincinnati, 1821–1921* (New York 1921). A. S. MCALLISTER, *In Winter We Flourish: Life and Letters of Sarah Worthington King Peter, 1800–1877* (New York 1939). M. R. KING, *Memoirs of the Life of Mrs. Sarah Peter,* 2 v. (Cincinnati 1889).

[J. D. SAUTER]

PETER I (THE GREAT), EMPEROR OF RUSSIA

The greatest and most controversial of the Russian czars, chiefly responsible for the country's emergence as a great power; b. Moscow, May 30, 1672; d. St. Petersburg, Jan. 28, 1725. Peter, the son of Czar Alexis Mikhailovich and his second wife, Natalia Naryshkina, succeeded to the throne in 1682 as co-czar with his mentally disabled brother, Ivan V. Until Peter came of age, his sister Sophia ruled as regent while Peter lived a largely unsupervised life with his mother at Preobrazhensk, a village away from Moscow and the court. There he first sailed a boat and learned the rudiments of war in games with the local boyar and peasant boys. Sophia's plot to have herself proclaimed czarina brought Peter back to Moscow at 17. He deposed his sister, sent her to a monastery, and put the affairs of state largely into the hands of the Naryshkins, his maternal relatives. The palace guard (Streltsy) was so suspect that Peter built his personal forces around his boyhood regiments, the Preobrazhensky and Semenovsky, and put his trust in non-Russians, Gen. Patrick Gordon, a Scot, and the Swiss Col. Franz Lefort.

Window on the West. Russia's landlocked mass led Peter to attack and finally to overcome the Turkish controlled fortress of Azov. However, Turks still controlled the Black Sea. Therefore, Peter arranged a mission to the Christian West to seek allies against the Turks, but also to learn of western European culture and to hire specialists in various fields to work in Russia. He accompanied his own mission to the various courts, but only as a scarcely disguised Peter Mikhailov, private citizen. Peter's mission did not win allies, but in the shipyards of Holland and England Peter became a master shipbuilder. Even Vienna was not congenial, but there Peter began to think of exploiting the Catholic desire for reunion with the Orthodox, in the hope of a campaign in the Baltic regions against Sweden. Another revolt of the palace guard brought about their liquidation at the cost of more than 2,000 lives. With his position secure at home Peter embarked on his 21-year war with Charles XII of Sweden, a war that, at the Peace of Nystadt (1721), finally secured for Peter his ''window on the west'' at the east end of the Gulf of Finland. In relief and triumph the senate hailed Peter as Emperor and gave him the epithets Great and Father of His Country.

Program of Reform. Peter's reforms began with the boyars, in whom he had no confidence. The Boyars' Duma (council) was abolished, and in its place Peter created a specially selected senate, which was, after the czar, the highest organ of state and empowered to propose laws, supervise other state organs, and substitute for the absent ruler. A special procurator's office supervised administrative legality and the procurator-general controlled the senate itself. At first nine, then 12, collegia were established with various portfolios, such as foreign affairs and war. Internally, Russia was divided into eight administrative regions (*guberniya*) and subdivided into provinces. Each *guberniya* was ruled by a gubernator appointed by the senate and responsible to the senate. These administrative reforms made for better centralized government. Peter's reforms extended also to the Russian Orthodox Church. Both the Patriarch Joachim and his

Peter the Great.

successor Adrian opposed Peter and condemned his personal and public actions. Therefore, when Adrian died (1700), Peter abolished the office of patriarch, and replaced it with the Holy Synod, supreme in ecclesiastical affairs, although subordinated to the senate and to the procurator-general in all else.

Further reforms affected public education, economic and agricultural life, and especially the nation's cultural life. Although poorly educated himself, Peter saw the value of an intellectual life for the nation. He opened libraries, schools, and museums; he sent the sons of boyars to Western universities; he introduced a new and more simplified alphabet and writing style, encouraged printing, and even inaugurated the first Russian newspaper, *Vedomosti* (The Gazette). Never very tactful, he aroused great opposition when he abandoned the old church calendar (from the creation of the world) in favor of the Julian calendar (Old Style). His tax on beards, mustaches, and the old form of Russian dress was especially distasteful. He recognized and used talent where he found it; the Procurator-General Paul Yaguzhinsky was said to have been a swineherd as a boy; his Minister for Foreign Affairs, Peter Shafirov, had been a sales clerk; and ''Prince'' Alexander D. Menshikov, Peter's First Councilor, had sold meat pies in the Moscow streets. Gordon,

Lefort, and the Dutchman Carsten Brandt were his military advisers and friends.

Building of St. Petersburg. On an island in the Neva River, Peter built the Fortress of Peter and Paul (1703). With a few surrounding houses this fortress constituted the beginning of Peter's city. The larger city Peter called St. Petersburg and proclaimed it the new capital of Russia. History says it was constructed on the bones of the 40,000 peasants and serfs who died building Peter's dream. The swamps were filled, the forests were felled. While surveyors laid out the broad, straight *prospekts* and boulevards, foreign architects planned the great stone buildings and the numerous parks with their varied fountains. Nowhere, perhaps, is Peter's love of water better illustrated than in the planning and building of his summer palace, Peterhof, overlooking the Gulf of Finland—the estate is replete with fountains of all sorts for adornment, recreation, and irrigation.

Family Life. Peter endured only what family life he could not escape. As a boy he had witnessed family feuds and blood baths. He ended his first marriage with Eudokia Federovna Lopukhina by forcing her to enter a monastery. His son, Alexis, with whom Peter never troubled himself, was accused of plotting against the throne and on his father's orders was imprisoned and died under torture (1718) in the Peter and Paul Fortress. A commoner, Martha Skavronska, lived with Peter for several years before she embraced the Orthodox faith and took the name of Catherine. In 1712 Peter wed her officially, and she bore him 11 children, of whom only two, Anna and Elizabeth, survived. When Peter abolished the traditional succession of inheritance to the throne (1722), he made Catherine an empress and proclaimed her his successor. He died during the night of Jan. 27–28, 1725, as a result of an illness contracted while trying to save some soldiers caught in a storm at sea off Petersburg.

Czar Peter and Catholicism. Although the Roman Catholic Church could not be said to possess any great strength in Russia, it was ever interested in bringing back the Russian Orthodox to Christian unity and, in Peter's time, desirous of using the Russian land route to China. Peter tried to use this interest to his own advantage. During Sophia's regency, Leopold I of Austria had sent an embassy to Moscow to enlist aid against the Turks and to safeguard the precarious position of the few Catholics in Moscow. The two Jesuit priests in that mission discussed reunion with Boris Galitsyn, the regent's councilor. Nothing came of the mission or of the talks, but John Schmidt was allowed to remain in Moscow as chaplain to the Catholics. Later Albert de Boye joined him, and until 1689 two Jesuits served some 100 Catholic families in Moscow. General Gordon, a Catholic and a confidant of Peter, even helped them to open a small school. When a few boyar families became Catholics, Orthodox opposition increased. In 1689 Boris Galitsyn fell into disfavor and was exiled by Peter to Siberia. The Jesuits were also ordered to leave Moscow. A Dominican and later two secular priests also served for a while in Moscow. However, Peter was offended when he learned that the Jesuit Philippe AVRIL had mentioned his epilepsy in a book on the Catholic missions to Russia, and even the intercession of Gordon was unable to check the Emperor's growing hostility to Catholicism.

Two other Jesuits, John Milan and John Berula, and a Veronese missioner, Casagrande, accompanied another mission from Leopold I in 1698. Casagrande was allowed to attend to the spiritual needs of the Venetians in Voronezh; the two Jesuits remained in Moscow. There they reopened the school and even made some converts among the boyars. Since the Jesuits in their school were doing what Peter felt was needed, he did not hinder their work, despite the opposition of the Orthodox, even after the death of their protector, Gordon (1699). But when the friendship between Austria and Russia cooled, the Jesuits again were unwanted in Russia. When they departed in April 1719, they left behind some 2,000 Catholics, including some Russians, a bishop, three priests, and about 25 boyars. Rome replaced the Jesuits with Franciscans, Conventuals, and Capuchins, who, in turn, were expelled in 1724. Dominicans were planned for the Moscow mission, but after Peter's death they were never sent.

Peter was not a religious liberal. Although Catholics of the Latin rite were generally left in peace, such was not the case with the Eastern Catholics in the western regions of Russia. Although promised protection by Peter, they were constantly harassed by Russian troops. Some priests even died at the hands of the soldiers. Peter's tolerance for Catholics came from his desire for Vatican support against Charles XII of Sweden. He protested concern for reunion, but Pope Clement XI recognized his aims as political and refused to endorse the campaign against Sweden. After the battle at Poltava (1709), Peter had no further use for the Vatican and all talk of reunion ceased.

It was Peter the Great who catapulted Russia, for a time, into the mainstream of the West. This is recognized even by the Soviets, who claim that the spirit of Peter was that of a "first Bolshevik," despite the fact that it was Peter who was responsible for autocracy in Russia.

Bibliography: V. O. KLIUCHEVSKY, *Peter the Great,* tr. L. ARCHIBALD (New York 1961). M. JUST, *Rome and Russia* (Westminster, Md. 1954) 78–88. R. N. BAIN "Peter the Great and His Pupils, 1689–1730," *Cambridge Modern History* (London–New York 1902–12) 5:518–557. J. GLAZIK, *Lexikon für Theologie und Kirche,* ed. J. HOFER and K. RAHNER, 10 v. (2d, new ed. Freiburg 1957–65)

8:364–365. C. B. O'BRIEN *Russia under Two Tsars, 1682–1689* (Berkeley 1952). C. DE GRUNWALD, *Peter the Great,* tr. V. GERWIN (New York 1956). B. H. SUMNER, *Peter the Great and the Emergence of Russia* (New York 1951). R. WITTRAM, *Peter der Grosse: Der Eintritt Russlands in die Neuzeit* (Berlin 1954). R. T. MCNALLY, ''Chaadaev's Evaluation of Peter the Great,'' *Slavic Review* 23 (1964) 31–44. R. K. MASSIE, *Peter the Great, His Life and World* (New York 1980). E. J. PHILLIPS, *The Founding of the Russia Navy: Peter the Great and the Azov Fleet, 1688–1714* (Westport, Conn. 1995). A. G. CROSS, *Peter the Great through British Eyes: Perceptions and Representations of the Tsar since 1698* (Cambridge 2000). P. BUSHKOVITCH, *Peter the Great: The Struggle for Power, 1671–1725* (Cambridge 2001).

[W. C. JASKIEVICZ]

PETER ACOTANTO, BL.

Benedictine recluse; b. Venice, *c.* 1115; d. Venice, 1180 or 1187. Peter was educated in the BENEDICTINE monastery of San Giorgio in Venice as a result of a vow made by his noble parents when he was very ill. After marrying a girl from Crete, Peter went off on pilgrimage to the Holy Land, returning three years later. Finding that his wife had died, he entered San Giorgio a second time and later obtained permission to live near it as a recluse. His body is now in San Trovaso. CLEMENT VIII approved his cult.

Feast: Sept. 23, Aug. 15.

Bibliography: *Acta Sanctorum* Sept. 6:651–655. *Bibliotheca hagiographica latina antiquae et mediae aetatis* (Brussels 1898–1901) 6690–91. G. ZAPPERT, *Vita beati Petri Alcontati* (Vienna 1839). J. STADLER and F. J. HELM, *Vollständiges Heiligen-Lexikon,* v. 4 (Augsburg 1875) 843–844. A. M. ZIMMERMANN, *Kalendarium Benedictinum: Die Heiligen und Seligen des Benediktinerorderns und seiner Zweige* (Metten 1933–38) 3:93–94. A. MERCATI and A. PELZER, *Dizionario ecclesiastico* (Turin 1954–58) 204.

[M. CSÁKY]

PETER ARBUÉS, ST.

Augustinian canon, first inquisitor of the Spanish INQUISITION in Aragon; b. Epila, near Saragossa, Aragon, Spain, 1441; d. Saragossa, Sept. 17, 1485. After studies in philosophy at Huesca, he earned a doctorate in theology at the College of Albornoz in Bologna (1473). He became a canon regular of St. Augustine (1474) in Saragossa, where he helped revise the missal and wrote several works in MSS. He was made inquisitor in 1484 by Ferdinand V and preached vigorously against apostates. Although he was not responsible for a single sentence of death or torture, two arrests led to the attack on his life. He died after being stabbed at prayer in the cathedral at the instigation of MARRANOS and nobles who were threatened by the Inquisition. He was buried in the cathedral, beatified in 1664, and canonized on June 29, 1867.

Feast: Sept. 17.

Bibliography: *Acta Sanctorum* Sept. 5:728–754. G. COZZALUZI, *Della vita, miracoli e culto del martire S. Pietro de Arbues* (Rome 1867). F. DE LATASSA Y ORTÍN, *Bibliotecas antigua y nueva de escritores aragoneses,* ed. M. GOMEZ URIEL, 3 v. (Saragossa 1884–86). H. C. LEA, *A History of the Inquisition of Spain,* 4 v. (New York 1906–07) v. 1. A. ALCALÁ, *Los orígenes de la Inquisición en Aragón: S. Pedro Arbués, mártir de la autonomía aragonesa* (Epila, Aragon 1984).

[D. W. LOMAX]

PETER ARMENGOL, BL.

Martyr; b. Guardia de Prats, Spain, 1238?; d. April 27, 1304? Data for his vita derive from questionable documents ''discovered'' in the 17th century for the canonization of St. PETER NOLASCO. According to these sources, he was a descendant of the counts of Urgell, arrogant and vindictive, who left his fellow students to become a bandit leader with immunity from ordinary justice. In 1258 he repented and joined the MERCEDARIANS in Barcelona, probably as a knight. On his second trip to ransom captives, he remained in Moslem Algeria as a hostage for 18 Christians. He was hanged for his apostolic efforts, but the Blessed Virgin sustained him miraculously. Bearing the marks of his ordeal, he returned home and devoted himself to prayer and penance. His immemorial cult in Catalonia was confirmed in 1686.

Feast: April 27.

Bibliography: R. LECHAT, *Analecta Bollandiana* 39 (1921) 214. B. DE GAIFFIER, *ibid.,* 58 (1940) 88. D. MANSILLA, *Lexikon für Theologie und Kirche,* ed. J. HOFER and K. RAHNER, 10 v. (2d, new ed. Freiburg 1957–65) 8:349. *Acta Sanctorum* Sept. 1:317–335. F. BONET I ARMENGOL, *Pere Armengol i Cornet, penitenciarista català* (Barcelona 1994).

[E. P. COLBERT]

PETER AUREOLI

French Franciscan theologian and archbishop, known by the scholastic titles *Doctor facundus* and *Doctor ingeniosus;* b. near Gourdon, Aquitaine, *c.* 1280; d. Aix, Provence, January 1322. After entering the order he was sent to Paris, where he may have known Duns Scotus. By 1312 he was lector in Bologna, where he wrote *Tractatus de paupertate et usu paupere* (ed. Paris 1511) and an unfinished *Tractatus de principiis.* In 1314 he was lector in Toulouse and won fame for defending the doctrine of the IMMACULATE CONCEPTION. His *Tractatus de conceptione beatae Mariae Virginis* (ed. Quaracchi 1904) was completed on Dec. 20, 1314. Attacked for his views, he replied toward the beginning of 1315 with *Repercussorium editum contra adversarium innocentiae Matris Dei* (ed. Quaracchi 1904). At the general chapter of Naples in 1316, his name was submitted as a candidate for the Franciscan chair at Paris. The new minister general, MICHAEL OF CESENA, immediately assigned him to Paris to lecture on the *Sentences* (1316–18). Two versions of this important commentary exist. The first version (bk. 1, ed. E. M. Buytaert, 2 v. New York 1953–56) may have been written in 1317 or even before he arrived in Paris. The important definitive version was written in 1318–19 (2 v. Rome 1596–1605). Apparently Peter had some difficulty in obtaining license to incept as master, for on July 14, 1318, JOHN XXII ordered the chancellor to grant this license. A university list of *magistri actu regentes,* dated Nov. 13, 1318, carries the name of Peter as regent master in theology. As master he composed a highly respected *Compendium sensus litteralis totius sacrae scripturae* in 1319 (ed. Quaracchi 1896). He also determined one series of quodlibetal questions in 1320. Toward the end of 1320 he was elected provincial of the province of Aquitaine. On Feb. 27, 1321, John XXII named him archbishop of Aix-en-Provence, and the Pope consecrated him at Avignon on June 14, 1321.

Aureoli was an independent and highly original thinker, having a tendency to criticize doctrines that were generally received by his predecessors and contemporaries. His thought is highly speculative and subtle. In his works he frequently revels in disagreeing with the foremost masters of the immediate past, among them St. BONAVENTURE, St. THOMAS AQUINAS, DUNS SCOTUS, HENRY OF GHENT, and GODFREY OF FONTAINES. He is especially fond of ARISTOTLE and AVERROËS and not always aware of the dangers implicit in some of their positions.

For Aureoli the role of reason in theology is much more modest than it is for Aquinas. In the teaching of Aureoli the unity of the human composite, the immortality of the human soul, and even the fact of intellectual knowledge cannot in the final analysis be demonstrated by human reason. Contrary to many Franciscans of his day, he maintained that reason cannot establish with strictly demonstrative arguments the doctrines of creation and divine omnipotence. As opposed to Scotus, he maintained that intuitive knowledge does not require the presence of the existing thing.

Though often called a conceptualist and a forerunner of WILLIAM OF OCKHAM, Aureoli did not deny UNIVERSALS. For him, universals have a foundation insofar as several similar beings can be created by God.

Bibliography: J. BEUMER, ''Der Augustinismus in der theologischen Erkenntnislehre des Petrus Aureoli,'' *Franziskanische Studien* 36 (1954) 131–171. J. HALVERSON, *Peter Aureol on Predestination: A Challenge to Late Medieval Thought* (Leiden 1998). T. KOBUSCH, *Philosophen des Mittelalters: Eine Einfuhrung* (Darmstadt 2000). S. R. STRUER, *Die theologische Einleitungslehre des Petrus Aureoli: Auf Grund seines Scriptum super Primum Senteniarum und ihre theologiegeschichtliche Einordnung* (Werl/ Westf 1968).

[J. J. PRZEZDZIECKI]

PETER CANTOR

Theologian, glossarist; b. probably Reims, France; d. Longpont Abbey, Sept. 22, 1197. In 1171 he was canon and professor of theology at the cathedral school in Paris, and from 1184 held the office of cantor in the cathedral of Paris, whence his name. His reputation as an ecclesiastic and a theologian soon spread beyond Paris. The people and clergy of Tournai chose him in 1191 for their bishop, but his election was opposed by William of Champagne, archbishop of Reims, on grounds of irregularity. In 1196 he accepted the office of dean of the cathedral chapter of Reims. He died in the Cistercian abbey of Longpont. His works cover a wide range of subjects: dogmatic and moral theology, Sacred Scripture, canonical legislation, and monasticism. They are *Verbum Abbreviatum,* first published in 1693 and reproduced in Migne (*Patrologia Latina,* 205:21–554); *Summa de sacramentis et animae consiliis; Distinctiones Abel; De tropis theologicis;* and glosses on most of the books of the Old and the whole of the New Testament. With the exception of *Verbum Abbreviatum,* his works have remained unpublished.

Bibliography: *Chartularium universitatis Parisiensis,* ed. H. DENIFLE and E. CHATELAIN, 4 v. (Paris 1889–97) 1:46. M. GRABMANN, *Geschichte der scholastischen Methode,* 2 v. (Freiburg 1909–11) 2:478–485. F. S. GUTJAHR, *Petrus Cantor Parisiensis* (Graz 1899). N. IUNG, *Dictionnaire de théologie catholique,* ed. A. VACANT et al., 15 v. (Paris 1903–50; Tables générales 1951–) 12.2:1901–06.

[G. M. GRABKA]

PETER CHRYSOLOGUS, ST.

Archbishop and Doctor of the Church; b. Imola, Italy, *c.* 400; d. Imola?, Dec. 3, *c.* 450. The oldest vita by Agnellus of Ravenna *c.* 830 (*Patrologia latina* 106:553–566; *Patrologia latina* 52:13–28), confuses him with two other bishops of Ravenna named Peter (*Acta Sanctorum* Dec. Propyl. 560). The confusion arose because Peter was not distinguished as ''Chrysologus'' (of the golden word) until the seventh century. Ravenna, then the Western capital of the empire, became a metropolitan see following his installation (*c.* 431) as bishop. His relations with SIXTUS III and LEO I were close. When EUTYCHES, father of MONOPHYSITISM, was condemned at the synod of CONSTANTINOPLE in 448, he asked Peter in 449 to intervene in his favor. Peter replied, ''In the interest of peace and the faith we cannot judge in matters of the faith without the consent of the Roman bishop'' [see *Patrologia latina* 52:255; *ibid.* 54:743; and E. Schiltz, *Nouvelle revue théologique* 55 (1928) 265–276]. Besides the letter to Eutyches, Peter has left 183 *sermones* (ed. A. Olivar in *Corpus Christianorum*). The *Catalogus Felicianus* of Felix, archbishop of Ravenna (709–725), which contains 176 *sermones* (badly edited in *Patrologia latina* 52: 183–666), includes some apocryphal sermons [A. Olivar, *Revue Bénédictine* 59 (1949) 114–136] and lacks some authentic sermons [D. de Bruyne, *Journal of Theological Studies* 29 (1927) 362–368].

Most of the sermons offer biblical exegesis for reading in the liturgical Office; they are without theological depth or original speculation, but full of moral applications for daily life. They have considerable historical importance for the authentic picture they give of Christian life in Ravenna in the fifth century. The *Catalogus* contains also doctrinal homilies on the Incarnation and the mysteries of Christmas (140–160), and sermons for catechumens on the Apostles' Creed (56–62) and the Lord's Prayer (67–72). The sermons are brief (10–15 minutes) but sacrifice clarity for classical rhetoric. Despite his title ''Chrysologus,'' Peter was not as eloquent as AMBROSE or AUGUSTINE, or his Greek opposite JOHN CHRYSOSTOM.

Feast: July 30 (formerly Dec. 4).

Bibliography: J. H. BAXTER, ''The Homilies of St. Peter Chrysologus,'' *Journal of Theological Studies* 22 (1921) 250–258. C. JENKINS, ''Aspects of the Theology of St. Peter Chrysologus,'' *Church Quarterly Review* 103 (1927) 233–259. O. BARDENHEWER, *Geschichte der altkirchlichen Literatur* (Freiburg 1913–32) 4:606–610. R. H. MCGLYNN, *The Incarnation in the Sermons of St. Peter Chrysologus* (Mundelein, IL 1956). F. SOTTOCORNOLA, *L'anno liturgico nei sermoni di Pietro Crisologo: ricerca storico-critica sulla liturgia di Ravenna antica* (Cesena 1973). R. BENERICETTI, *Il Cristo nei sermoni di S. Pier Crisologo* (Cesena 1995).

[J. VAN PAASSEN]

PETER COMESTOR

Theologian and exegete; b. Troyes, *c.* 1100; d. Paris, *c.* 1180. He was dean of the cathedral of Troyes (1145–67?) and chancellor of the cathedral school in Paris (1164–68; 1178–80); he taught theology there (1164–68) and became a canon regular of Saint-Victor (1169). He wrote the *Historia scholastica* (*Patrologia Latina,* 198:1053–1644), a Bible history supplemented from the Fathers and profane historians (1169–73), *Sententiae de sacramentis* (ed. R. M. Martin, *Pierre le Mangeur, De sacramentis, Spicilegium sacrum Lovaniense,* 17, Appendix [Louvain 1937]), some 150 sermons (13 scattered in *Patrologia Latina,* 171:339–964), commentaries on the Gospels and on Peter Lombard's *Commentary on the Psalms,* and perhaps a commentary on the Lombard's *Sentences,* and on Romans 1 and 2 Corinthians. Unauthentic are commentaries on the other Pauline Epistles and the *Liber pancrisis* (compiled 1220–25). G. Raciti suggests his authorship of Pseudo-Augustine's *De spiritu et anima* (*Patrologia Latina,* 40: 779–832).

Bibliography: N. IUNG, *Dictionnaire de théologie catholique,* ed. A. VACANT et al., 15 v. (Paris 1903–50; Tables générales 1951–) 12.2:1918–22. R. M. MARTIN, ''Notes sur l'oeuvre littéraire de Pierre le Mangeur,'' *Recherches de théologie ancienne et médiévale* 3 (1931) 54–66. A. LANDGRAF, ''Recherches sur Pierre le Mangeur,'' *ibid.,* 292–306, 341–373. F. STEGMÜLLER, *Repertorium commentariorum in Sententias Petri Lombardi,* 2 v. (Würzburg 1947) 1:669–673. F. STEGMÜLLER, *Repertorium biblicum medii aevi,* 7 v. (Madrid 1949–61) 4:6543–92. B. SMALLEY, *The Study of the Bible in the Middle Ages* (2d ed. New York 1952). M. M. LEBRETON, ''Recherches sur les manuscrits contenant des sermons de Pierre le Mangeur,'' *Bulletin d'information de l'Institut de Recherches et d'Histoire des Textes,* 2 (1953) 25–44; 4 (1955) 35–36. O. LOTTIN, ''À propos de la date de deux florilèges concernant Anselmo de Laon,'' *Recherches de théologie ancienne et médiévale* 26 (1959) 307–314. G. RACITI, ''L'autore del *De spiritu et animo,*'' *Rivista di filosofia neoscolastica* 53 (1961) 385–401. L. HÖDL, *Lexikon für Theologie und Kirche,* ed. J. HOFER and K. RAHNER, 10 v. (2d, new ed. Freiburg 1957–65) 8:357–358.

[J. N. GARVIN]

PETER CRISCI OF FOLIGNO, BL.

Franciscan tertiary; d. Foligno, Italy, July 18, 1323. He lived for some time as a hermit at Pesaro, where he built the church of S. Maria di Montegranaro. He spent the latter part of his life in his home city of Foligno, where he was noted for his spirit of piety, poverty, penance, and good works. He is mentioned in the autobiography of ANGELA OF FOLIGNO under the name of Petrucius. He is buried in the cathedral church at Foligno, where he is still honored.

Feast: July 19.

Bibliography: *Acta Sanctorum* July 4: 663:668. M. FALOCI PULIGNANI in *Analecta Bollandiana* 8 (1889) 358–369. ANGELA DA FOLIGNO, *L'autobiografia. . . ,* ed. M. FALOCI-PULIGNANI and M. CASTIGLIONE HUMANI (Città di Castello 1932). J. L. BAUDOT and L. CHAUSSIN, *Vies des saints et des bienheureux selon l'ordre du calendrier avec l'historique des fêtes* (Paris 1935–36) 7:455–456. A. MERCATI and A. PELZER, *Dizionario ecclesiastico* (Turin

1954–58) 3:204. E. GRAU, *Lexikon für Theologie und Kirche* (Freiburg 1957–65) 8:362.

[K. NOLAN]

PETER DAMIAN, ST.

Benedictine cardinal (1057), Doctor of the Church; b. Ravenna, Italy, 1007; d. Faenza, Italy, Feb. 22–23, 1072. The traditional account of Damian's childhood, featuring abandonment by his parents, rearing by sacerdotal foster parents, and hardships bordering on starvation, stems from hagiographical embroidering by his biographer, JOHN OF LODI (*Patrologia Latina,* 144:113–146). His later career points to a sound primary education provided by his older brother at Ravenna and continued later at Parma, Modena, and Faenza. A brief but successful teaching career in Ravenna and ordination to the priesthood preceded his entry into the religious life at FONTE AVELLANA (1035). By 1043 he was elected prior of this congregation of hermits; as prior he reorganized their life by statutes combining the ideals of St. BENEDICT and St. ROMUALD. The result was an Eremitico-cenobitic amalgam, with stern but rational practices of asceticism, in which Damian claimed to carry out the mind of St. Benedict.

From this self-reforming base, Damian turned his attention to the reform interests of the Church at large, making contact with the German court of HENRY III and with the papal Curia. At first tentative in the reigns of GREGORY VI and CLEMENT II, his role matured during the pontificate of LEO IX. Two of his significant reform writings, the *Liber gratissimus*, defending the validity of orders conferred gratis by simonists, and the *Liber gomorrhianus*, attacking the moral decadence of the 11th-century clergy, date from this period. Unlike HUMBERT OF SILVA CANDIDA and GREGORY VII (Hildebrand), Damian viewed the reform movement as a joint project, conducted by both papacy and empire (*see* GREGORIAN REFORM).

As a churchman his services to reform stemmed primarily from his relation to the papal Curia. He was elevated to the cardinalate against his will by STEPHEN IX. Damian's active participation in the public life of the Church by synodal work, by diplomatic missions, and by his writings, which display an almost compulsive need to communicate, spanned nearly a quarter of the 11th century. His missions took him to Milan (1059–60) to settle the conflict between the archbishop and the PATARINES, soothing Milanese sensibilities while pointing up the Roman primacy. During the schism of antipope Honorius II (Cadalus of Parma), he strenuously defended the interests of ALEXANDER II, in whose cause he produced the *Disceptatio synodalis*, a fictitious debate between representatives of church and state, attempting to settle Alexander's disputed election. CLUNY was the beneficiary of his *Iter Gallicum* (*Monumenta Germaniae Historica: Scriptores*, 30.2:1034–46) in 1063 when, by on-the-spot arbitration, he upheld Abbot HUGH in his exemption dispute with Bp. Drogo of Mâcon.

During the last decade of his life he traveled to Mainz (1069), hoping to stabilize the marriage of young King HENRY IV and his wife, Bertha. In 1071, at the invitation of his friend Abbot Desiderius (*see* VICTOR III), he took part in the dedication of the basilica of St. Benedict at MONTE CASSINO. In 1072 he paid a last visit to his native Ravenna, working for better relations with the Roman See. On his return he died in the monastery of S. Maria in Faenza; his remains now rest in the cathedral. In 1828 his cult was approved when he was declared a Doctor of the Church.

Few medieval writers can compare with Damian in the number and range of his writings. His extant letters (*c.* 170), sermons (53), vitae (7), treatises, and minor works in prose and verse (epigrams, prayers, hymns, liturgical Offices) mark him as one of the great Latin stylists of the Middle Ages. The sources of his inspiration range from the Sacred Scriptures, allegorically interpreted, through the Latin and Greek Fathers (the latter in translation—Damian knew no Greek), the works of the Carolingian age, the Latin writings of antiquity, Roman law, and to a surprising degree, the pre-Gregorian collections of Canon Law. His favored canonical source was the *Decretum* of BURCHARD OF WORMS; he made no direct use of the FALSE DECRETALS of Pseudo-Isidore. The content of his theological and ascetical writing is distinguished by its practicality rather than by its theory. He preferred anecdote and example to the methodical presentation of principle. In contact with most of the problems of his day, he nevertheless showed a perplexing unconcern for the contemporary struggle between the Greek and Latin Churches (*see* EASTERN SCHISM). Affairs of church and state outside of Italy and the Empire—in England, Spain, and the Middle East—seem to have been beyond his horizon of interest. The ''dialectic'' of his career was that between the active and the contemplative life, which he resolved classically in his search for an ordered society in a world to which he always remained a stranger.

Feast: Sept. 21 (formerly 23).

Bibliography: Editions. *Patrologia Latina* 144, 145. Opusc. 4, 6, *Monumenta Germaniae Historica: Libelli de lite* 1:15–94. Opusc. 13, 36, 45, 58, ed. P. BREZZI and B. NARDI, *S. Pier Damiani: De divina omnipotentia, e altri opuscoli* (Florence 1943). *Vita Romualdi*, ed. G. TABACCO (Fonti per la storia d'Italia 94; Rome 1957). *Die Briefe des Petrus Damiani*, ed. K. REINDEL, 4 v. (Munich

1983–1993). Hymns, ed. G. M. DREVES and C. BLUME, *Analecta Hymnica* 11, 22, 48, 51. O. J. BLUM, *Traditio* 12 (1956) 87–148; tr. *Letters,* 5 v. (Washington, D.C. 1989–1998). Literature. *Acta Sanctorum* (Paris 1863—) 3:416–27. O. J. BLUM, *St. Peter Damian: His Teaching on the Spiritual Life* (Washington 1947). F. DRESSLER, *Petrus Damiani Leben und Werk* (Rome 1954). J. J. RYAN, *Saint Peter Damiani and His Canonical Sources* (Toronto 1956). P. MCNULTY, tr., *Selected Writings on the Spiritual Life* (New York 1960). J. LECLERCQ, *Saint Pierre Damien: Ermite et homme d'église* (Rome 1960). *Studi su san Pier Damiano in onore del Cardinale A. G. Cicognani* (Rome 1961). K. REINDEL, ''Studien zur Überlieferung der Werke des Petrus Damiani,'' *Deutsches Archiv für Erforschung des Mittelalters* 15 (1959) 23–102; 16 (1960) 73–154; 18 (1962) 317–417. J. SZÖVÉRFFY, *Die Annalen der lateinischen Hymnendichtun. Ein Handbuch* (Berlin 1964–65) 1:393–398. M. LOKRANTZ, *L'opera poetica di S. Pier Damiani* (Goteborg-Uppsala 1964). A. BENEDETTI, *Contemplazione e poesia in Pier Damiano* (Brescia 1975). A. CANTIN, *Les sciences séculières et la foi: les deux voies de la science au jugement de S. Pierre Damien* (Spoleto 1975). H. P. LAQUA, *Traditionen und Leitbilder bei dem Ravennater Reformer Petrus Damiani* (Munich 1976). L.-A. LASSUS, *Saint Pierre Damien, l'homme des déserts de Dieu* (Paris 1986). I. M. RESNICK, *Divine power and possibility in St. Peter Damian's De divina omnipotentia* (Leiden 1992). T. WÜNSCH, *Spiritalis intellegentia: zur allegorischen Bibelinterpretation des Petrus Damiani* (Regensburg 1992). M. GRANDJEAN, *La cs dans l'Eglise* (Paris 1994). S. FREUND, *Studien zur literarischen Wirksamkeit des Petrus Damiani* (Hannover 1995), includes German tr. of John of Lodi's 11th-century *Vita Petri Damiani.* G. FORNASARI, *Medioevo riformato del secolo XI: Pier Damiani e Gregorio VII* (Naples 1996).

[O. J. BLUM]

PETER DES ROCHES

Bishop of Winchester; b. Poitiers, France, late 12th century; d. Farnham, England, June 9, 1238. Peter was a royal knight and chamberlain of King RICHARD I and trusted counselor of King JOHN. When he was elected bishop of WINCHESTER in 1205, the election was disputed, but he was consecrated by Pope INNOCENT III in person on Sept. 25, 1205. Peter was among the king's most faithful adherents during the Interdict of 1208 to 1213 and the struggle leading to MAGNA CARTA in 1215, and he was justiciar from 1213 to 1215. His influence continued into the minority of Henry III, whom he crowned in 1216 and whose tutor he was for a while, but his power began to decline after 1219, and especially after 1223 when he came into competition with Hubert de Burgh (d. 1243). Dismissed from office in 1227, he went on crusade with Emperor FREDERICK II and returned to England in 1231. A reversal of fortune led to the eclipse of De Burgh and the supremacy of Peter's adherents in 1232 to 1234, but he again fell out of favor, this time through the hostility of Abp. EDMUND OF ABINGDON, and went into exile in 1235. He supported Pope GREGORY IX in his campaigns against the Romans and returned to England in 1236; after his death he was buried at Winchester.

Peter's work as bishop is reflected in the papal letters he received and in his synodal statutes, dating probably from 1224, implementing the canons of the Fourth LATERAN COUNCIL of 1215, which he did not attend, and of STEPHEN LANGTON's synod of Oxford in 1222. He was the founder of many churches and religious houses and a distinguished manager of his episcopal properties as is shown from the earliest pipe rolls of the bishopric of Winchester, which survive from his time and record an exceptional maturity of estate administration. A great and magnificent prelate, both hated and respected, at once bishop, statesman, warrior, and diplomat, Peter transcended the merely regional interests of the kingdom and was a European figure in Church and State alike.

Bibliography: W. E. RHODES, *The Dictionary of National Biography from the Earliest Times to 1900.* (London 1885–1900) 15:938–942. M. GIBBS and J. LANG, *Bishops and Reform, 1215–1272* (London 1934; repr. 1962). F. M. POWICKE, *King Henry III and the Lord Edward,* 2 v. (New York 1947); *The Thirteenth Century* (*Oxford History of England* 4; 2d ed. 1962); *Councils and Synods,* ed. F. M. POWICKE and C. R. CHENEY, 2 v. (Oxford 1964) 2:125–137. *Selected Letters of Pope Innocent III concerning England,* ed. C. R. CHENEY and W. H. SEMPLE (London 1953). *The Pipe Roll of the Bishopric of Winchester, 1210–1211,* ed. N. R. HOLT (Manchester, Eng. 1964).

[C. DUGGAN]

PETER GEREMIA, BL.

Preacher, theologian, and reformer; b. Palermo, Italy, Aug. 1, 1381; d. there, March 3, 1452. Born of distinguished parents, Peter took a doctorate in law at BOLOGNA where he joined the DOMINICANS *c.* 1401. His preaching won him the title of preacher general and the admiration of St. Vincent FERRER. In 1427 the master general, Bartholomew Texerius, sent him as visitator to Sicily (1427) where he encouraged the Dominican Observantines at the priory of St. Zita in Palermo, and developed the reform in other priories. Pope EUGENE IV invited him to the Council of FLORENCE (1439) and then appointed him apostolic visitator to Sicily where he was distinguished as a reformer. Five volumes of his *Sermones* have been published (Brescia 1502). His *Dictionary of Morals* and several theological works are unpublished. He is buried at St. Zita's, Palermo. PIUS VI confirmed his cult, May 12, 1784.

Feast: March 10.

Bibliography: J. QUÉTIF and J. ÉCHARD, *Scriptores Ordinis Praedicatorum* (Paris 1719–23) 1.2:810–811. I. TAURISANO, *Catalogus hagiographicus ordinis praedicatorum* (Rome 1918) 38. A. BUTLER, *The Lives of the Saints,* rev. ed. H. THURSTON and D. ATTWATER (New York 1956) 1:550–552. M. A. CONIGLIONE, *Pietro Geremia* (Catania 1952). A. WALZ, *Lexikon für Theologie und Kirche,* ed. J. HOFER and K. RAHNER (Freiberg 1957–65) 8:363.

[A. DABASH]

PETER GONZÁLEZ, ST.

Spanish Dominican, patron of sailors; b. Astorgá, Spain, before 1190; d. Túy, Spain, *c.* 1246. He is called also "St. (T)Elmo" through confusion with Erasmus (*see* ELMO, ST.), another patron of sailors. Peter was a worldly young noble of Palencia, educated by an uncle, Bp. Tello of Palencia; but he surrendered his canonry and prospects in order to enter the recently founded DOMINICANS. A great preacher, he became chaplain to King Ferdinand III of Castile and reformed the Castilian court. He advanced the Spanish crusades by his preaching and advice. At CÓRDOBA's surrender (1236), he won easier terms for the Muslims. Thereafter Peter evangelized along the coast and in Galicia. Because of his particular concern for sailors, he is pictured carrying a ship. He was buried in Túy cathedral, beatified in 1254, and canonized in 1741.

Feast: April 14.

Bibliography: "Legends b. Petri Gundisalvi," H. FLÓREZ et al., *España sagrada,* 54 v. (Madrid 1747–1957) 23:245–285. *Acta Sanctorum* April 2:385–396. A. BUTLER, *The Lives of the Saints,* rev. ed. H. THURSTON and D. ATTWATER, 4 v. (New York 1956) 2:94–95. P. ÁLVAREZ, *Santos, bienaventurados, venerables de la Orden de los Predicadores,* 4 v. (Vergara 1920–23) 1:121–177. A. DÁVILA, *San Telmo: notas sobre el desarrollo de su culto en las Antillas* (Santo Domingo 1983), with bibliography.

[R. I. BURNS]

PETER GROSSOLANO

12th-century theologian, bishop of Savona, then archbishop of Milan from 1101 to 1116; b. Greece or Sicily, *c.* 1050; d. Rome, Aug. 6, 1117. Nothing is known of Peter's career or of his election to the See of Savona, but upon the death of Anselm IV de Buis (Sept. 11, 1101) Peter became the archbishop of Milan. His election displeased the reform party in Milan, and they appealed to King Liutprand, through whose intervention Peter was forced to leave Milan (1103) and appeal to Pope Paschal II. In a Roman council held in 1105, Peter's position was upheld, and he was restored to his see. However, he was again deposed by the civil authorities and given Jordanus as a successor in 1112. He then embarked on a voyage to the Near East and, after a sojourn in Jerusalem, visited the court of ALEXIUS COMNENUS in Constantinople. Invited to attend a synod held in the Emperor's presence, he pronounced a discourse justifying the use of the filioque in the creed; this greatly upset his Greek hosts, and John Phurnes felt himself obliged to reply.

Grossolano's position was based on the thesis that to deny that the Holy Spirit proceeds from the Son is to lower the Son's glory and His equality with the Father. Grossolano's intervention was ill taken and caused a further renewal of polemic between Byzantium and Rome on the question of the procession of the Holy Spirit and the use of unleavened bread in the liturgy. A second discourse to the Greeks, attributed to Grossolano, repeated the same argument with considerable documentation and closed with an invitation to the emperor to bring about the reunion of the churches. Eustratis of Nicaea says Grossolano spoke frequently at the synod, but there is no further record of these interventions.

In 1116 both Peter and the intruded archbishop of Milan, Jordanus, appealed to the Council of the LATERAN for a settlement of their rival claims; and despite the support of the pope, the Council decided that Peter should return to his first see at Savona. Peter preferred to retire to the Monastery of St. Sabas in Rome, where he died a year later.

Bibliography: *Patrologia Latina* 162:1005–15. *Patrologia Graeca* 127:909–919. LANDULPHUS JUNIOR, *Historia Mediolanensis, Patrologa Latina* 173:1447–1546. V. GRUMEL, *Dictionnaire de théologie catholique* 12.2:1939; *Échos d'Orient* 22 (1933) 22–33. *Bibliotheca casinensis,* 5 v. (Monte Cassino 1873–94) 4:351–358, text. J. DRÄSEKE, *Byzantinische Zeitschrift* 5 (1896) 328–329, Eustratis.

[F. CHIOVARO]

PETER IGNEUS, BL.

Cardinal bishop of Albano; b. Florence, Italy, *c.* early 11th century; d. Jan. 8, 1089. He entered the VALLOMBROSAN Order in the lifetime of its founder, and he was given the name of "Igneus" because in 1068, by order of his abbot, he passed through fire unharmed to prove the guilt of Pietro di Pavia, bishop of FLORENCE, who was accused of SIMONY. He was prior at Passignano and abbot at Fucecchio, and he was made cardinal bishop of Albano, one of the SUBURBICARIAN dioceses of Rome, in 1074 by Pope GREGORY VII, who made frequent use of him as legate in Italy, France, and Germany. He showed great zeal for the reform of the clergy, and soon after his death he was venerated as a saint in Vallombrosa Abbey, where he was buried. His cult was not officially approved until 1673, and his name was then inserted in the Roman Martyrology.

Feast: Feb. 8.

Bibliography: *Acta Sanctorum* July 3 (1863) 297, 298, 330, 331. G. M. BROCCHI, *Vite de' santi e beati fiorentini,* v. 1 (Florence 1742) 143–158. A. SALVINI, *Vita di s. Pietro Igneo* (Alba 1928). A. M. ZIMMERMANN, *Kalendarium Benedictinum: Die Heiligen und Seligen des Benediktinerorderns und seiner Zweige,* 4 v. (Metten 1933–38) 1:185–187. J. L. BAUDOT and L. CHAUSSIN, *Vies des saints et des bienheureux selon l'ordre du calendrier avec l'historique des fêtes,* 12 v. (Paris 1935–56) 2: 185–186.

[S. OLIVERI]

PETER JOHN OLIVI

Franciscan philosopher and theologian; b. Sérignan, near Béziers (Hérault), 1248; d. Narbonne, March 14, 1298.

Life. He entered the order at the age of 12 in the monastery of Béziers and studied under Fra Raimondo Barravi, a Joachimite and proponent of the most rigorous evangelical poverty. After preliminary studies he was sent to Paris, where WILLIAM DE LA MARE, JOHN PECKHAM, and MATTHEW OF AQUASPARTA, all disciples of BONAVENTURE, were teaching. There he attended the lectures Bonaventure delivered on the seven gifts of the Holy Spirit in 1268 and on the Hexaëmeron in 1273.

After becoming a bachelor in theology, he declined further study, considering the title of doctor incompatible with the status of a humble Franciscan. He returned to Provence and devoted himself entirely to writing. With his brilliant and independent talent, and because of his zeal for the rigorous observance of the Franciscan Rule, especially the observance of evangelic poverty (*usus pauper*), he soon won the unreserved, almost fanatical, esteem and admiration of the zealous (called Spirituals), as well as the no less fanatical envy and enmity of those who interpreted the obligation of Franciscan poverty less strictly. This gave rise to a long series of accusations, defenses, and counter-accusations.

In 1279 Olivi was in Rome on a commission charged with drawing up the decretal *Exiit, qui seminar,* the most important interpretation of the Franciscan Rule. Olivi himself, by order of the minister general, wrote a treatise on Franciscan poverty. He also may have written the question *De indulgentia Portiunculae* (Quaracchi 1895) at this time. After accusations were leveled at him at the general chapter of Strasbourg (1282), a commission was appointed to examine his writings; it compiled a series of 34 propositions, declaring some false and others heretical. At the same time the commission prepared a letter with 22 articles, all beginning with the words ''we firmly believe,'' and all opposed to the propositions of Olivi. Since each of the seven members of the commission placed his seal on the letter, it was called the letter of the seven seals, *Littera septema sigillorum* [ed. G. Fussenegger, *Archivum Franciscanum historicum* 47 (1954) 45–53]. Olivi's writings were withdrawn from circulation, and he was summoned to Avignon, where, in the presence of the minister general, he was obliged to accept and sign the letter.

Olivi replied to 20 of the 34 accusations, leaving aside the philosophical questions, and devoting a separate, extensive declaration to his doctrine concerning the divine essence [D. Laberge, ''Fr. Petri Ioannis Olivi, O.F.M. tria scripta sui ipsius apologetica annorum 1283 et 1285,'' *Archivum Franciscanum historicum* 28 (1935) 115–155, 374–407, 595–608; 29 (1936) 98–141, 366–387]. Elsewhere he demonstrated that the propositions he held had already been defended by authors such as Thomas Aquinas and Bonaventure, and he protested that in all he had done he had been motivated solely by zeal for the faith and love for the Church. But his enemies gave him no peace; at the general chapter of Milan (1285) he was accused again of heading a rebellious and superstitious sect that was spreading errors and creating divisions within the order. The chapter accordingly directed the confiscation of his writings. He was summoned to appear before the general chapters at Montpellier (1287) and at Paris (1292) regarding his teachings on Franciscan poverty, but both times he escaped censure. After the chapter at Montpellier, Matthew of Aquasparta, the new minister general, invited him to be lector at the *studium* at Santa Croce in Florence; a few years later he was transferred to the *studium* at Montpellier. This was tantamount to a complete rehabilitation. He was in Narbonne (*c.* 1295) and spent the last few years of his life there. Soon after his death he was venerated as a saint.

Works. Olivi's works, according to UBERTINO OF CASALE, were 17 times larger in volume than the *Sententiae* of Peter Lombard [F. Ehrle, ''Zur Vorgeschichte des Concils von Vienne,'' *Archiv für Literatur- und Kirchengeschichte des Mittelalters* 2 (1886) 406]. D. Pacetti enumerates 64 writings and divides them into four groups: (1) philosophical and theological works, 1–15; (2) expositions or readings on the Scriptures, 16–42; (3) works dealing with evangelic perfection and Franciscan life, 43–52; and (4) ascetic and mystic works, 53–64. His most important philosophical and theological works are *Quaestiones ordinatae,* or *Summa super Sententias,* the second book of which was edited by B. Jansen [*Bibliotheca Franciscana scholastica medii aevi* (Quaracchi 192–226) 4–6]; *Commentarius in quatuor libros Sententiarum*; and *Quodlibeta* (Venice *c.* 1509). Concerning the Franciscan life and evangelic perfection the following works are of capital importance: *Expositio super regulam fratrum minorum* [ed. in *Speculum Minorum seu Firmamentum trium Ordinum* (Venice 1513) pars. 3, 106a–124c] and the *Quaestiones de perfectione evangelica.* Of the 12 short ascetic and mystical works, four have been published (*Spiritulis e Beghini in Provenza* 274–290).

Teachings. Olivi remained faithful on many points to the teachings of St. Bonaventure, although he abandoned the theories of seminal reasons and divine illumination. For him, St. Augustine is the greatest authority after the Scriptures. He was well acquainted with Aristotle, Averroës, and Avicenna but thought it absurd that the authority of pagan and Muslim philosophers be admitted without discussion, as if they were inspired writers. He himself did not attribute great importance to purely philosophical questions; in his view, philosophy must serve theology.

He conceived the soul as essentially dynamic and active. In the act of knowing, the intellect integrates or assimilates itself to the object. Hence there is no need for *species impressae,* either of sensibles or of intelligibles. The human soul is a spiritual substance composed of spiritual matter and of formal or constitutive parts that are the vegetative, sensitive, and intellective powers of the spiritual matter. The soul is the substantial form of the body, yet the intellective part does not unite with the body immediately, as form to its matter, but consubstantially. Olivi advanced this theory to safeguard the freedom of the will and the immortality of the soul. In the field of physics he was among those who explained the motions of bodies by the theory of IMPETUS.

Olivi's influence as a philosopher and theologian was not great, but his writings on evangelic perfection and his ascetic tracts were a source of inspiration for St. BERNARDINE OF SIENA as leader of the Observance, the most important reform movement within the Franciscan Order.

Bibliography: C. BERUBE, *De l'homme a Dieu: Selon Duns Scot, Henri de Gand et Olivi* (Roma 1983). D. BURR, *The Persecution of Peter Olivi* (Philadelphia 1976); *Olivi and Franciscan Poverty: The Origins of the Usus Pauper Controversy* (Philadelphia 1989). K. B. OSBORNE, ed., *A History of Franciscan Theology* (St. Bonaventure 1994). F.-X. PUTALLAZ, *Figures franciscaines: De Bonaventure a Duns Scot* (Paris 1997).

[G. GÁL]

PETER LOMBARD

Theologian; b. Lumellogno (Novara), *c.* 1095; d. Paris, Aug. 21 (22), 1160. After studies at Bologna, or possibly Vercelli, he went to France, according to St. Bernard [*Epist.* 410; *Patrologia Latina,* ed. J. P. Migne (Paris 1878–90), 182:618], about 1134 to visit the schools of Reims and Paris. He then decided, or was persuaded, to remain at Paris, where he finished a commentary on the Psalms before 1138 and a gloss on St. Paul from 1139 to 1141, and began his teaching career in the school of Notre Dame. By 1143 he was known as a "celebrated theologian" (*Metamorph. Goliae Episc.* 197), and while in minor orders, he became a canon of Notre Dame in 1144 to 1145. Meanwhile, he had begun the composition of his *Book of Sentences,* which attained final form *c.* 1157 to 1158. He took part in the Paris consistory of Eugene III, April 21, 1147, and again in the Council of Reims, March 21, 1148, both of which concerned errors attributed to GILBERT DE LA PORRÉE. By 1156 he was one of the archdeacons of Paris, and perhaps as such made a journey to Rome, likely with Bishop Theobald in late 1154. He was elected bishop of Paris in 1159 and consecrated about June 29; he died the following year.

Sermons and Exegetical Works. Some 30 sermons at least are acknowledged as Lombard's, many of them published among those of Hildebert of Lavardin [*Patrologia Latina* 171:339–964]. Most likely, however, the list is far from complete. An English disciple, Heribert of Bosham, later secretary of St. Thomas Becket, related that Peter himself told him he had begun his scriptural commentaries as private works designed to clarify the brevity and obscurity of the glosses of ANSELM OF LAON, and only later were they used in the schools. The text of Lombard reveals that he also used the glosses of Gilbert de la Porrée. Recognizing this mutual dependence, the scholastics named Anselm's work the *Glossa ordinaria;* Gilbert's, the *Glossatura media;* and Lombard's, the *Major* (or *Magna*) *Glossatura* [B. Smalley, *The Study of the Bible in the Middle Ages* (New York 1952) 64].

The commentary or gloss on the Psalter (*ibid.*) must have been written immediately after Lombard's arrival at Paris, for there is no influence evident of the anonymous *Summa Sententiarum* (*c.* 1137–38). Doctrinal development proves that it antedates the gloss on St. Paul, while extant manuscripts show the author did not apparently subject it to a later revision. In content, like all 12th-century glosses on the Psalms, it offers primarily a moral and spiritual exegesis, to render the Divine Office more intelligible and fruitful. Only occasionally does it touch on theological doctrine.

By contrast, the *Collectanea* (a title used only since the edition of 1535) on the Epistles of St. Paul (*ibid.*) presents many literary and doctrinal problems. Since the *Summa Sententiarum* is an important source, and since the commentary on Philippians is cited by Gerhoch of Reichersburg in 1142, the *Collectanea* was very likely composed between 1139 and 1141. Yet this must have been only a primitive redaction, as Heribert of Bosham indicates Lombard constantly revised it while using it in teaching. It is rather evident that Lombard began his course in theology with a commentary on the Apostle, then transferred much material from this and the gloss on the Psalter to a more systematic *summa,* the *Book of Sentences,* and continued to rework both the latter and the Pauline gloss. An early redaction of this gloss is found in the MS Vat. Lat. 695, which contains many questions that reappear in the *Sentences* but are not to be found in the printed text of the gloss. The latter represents rather the final redaction, but fails to distinguish between the body of the text and Lombard's later marginal additions. The gloss was later used as a standard text in the schools. It seems doubtful that Lombard wrote any of the other scriptural works attributed to him [F. Stegmüller, *Repertorium biblicum medii aevi,* 7 v. (Madrid 1949–61), 6625–36, 6639–53].

Book of Sentences. Partly in reaction to the extreme use of dialectic in theology, partly in keeping with the trend of medieval teaching after Peter ABELARD, the *Sentences* presents the whole of Christian doctrine in one brief volume on the basis of Scripture, the Fathers, and the Doctors, with speculation held in firm control. This work is divided into four books and chapters (the grouping of chapters into distinctions was introduced most likely by ALEXANDER OF HALES).

The work is largely a compilation from older and contemporary sources: Augustine, whose thought and spirit is evident throughout; Ambrose (and Ambrosiaster); Hilary; Julian of Toledo (on the Last Things); the older *Glossa ordinaria* (especially for the first part of book 2); Lombard's own glosses; Hugh of St. Victor; the *Summa Sententiarium;* and the *Decretum* of Gratian; as well as the canons of Ivo of Chartres. Yet such was Lombard's genius in organizing this material, in relating it to all the questions and controversies of the day without digressing into the merely curious or engaging in useless polemics, and in presenting a sound, brief, objective summary of doctrine, that the *Book of Sentences* was quickly recognized both for its contents and for its didactic qualities as the best of its kind. It influenced medieval thought also by its defects and omissions: little or nothing is said of the Church or the role of the Roman pontiff; while certain aspects of the Redemption and of the doctrine of grace in it leave much to be desired.

Long before Alexander of Hales introduced it in Paris (*c.* 1222) as the manual of his theological course, whence it passed into the curriculum of the university and eventually to other schools, the *Liber Sententiarum* had gained renown throughout Europe (as the number of early manuscripts attests) and had become the subject of numerous glosses and abbreviations (details in Landgraf, *Einführung* 96–102; *Introducción* 167–176). On the other hand, the work did not meet complete acceptance. Within Lombard's lifetime certain doctrines were attacked by Maurice de Sully and ROBERT OF MELUN. In particular, his apparent acceptance of so-called Christological nihilism (*Quod Christus secundum quod est homo non sit aliquid*) implicated him in the censures of Alexander III (1170, 1177). At the same time he was unmercifully and stupidly attacked for this and other teachings by Walter

Peter Lombard.

of St. Victor in his violent diatribe *Against the Four Labyrinths of France* (1177–78). At the end of the century, Lombard's Trinitarian doctrines were opposed by followers of Gilbert de la Porrée as well as by JOACHIM OF FIORE. This last polemic carried over to the Fourth Council of the Lateran (1215), which, instead of condemning the *Book of Sentences,* anathematized Joachim and in an extraordinary move acknowledged Lombard's orthodoxy (H. Denzinger, *Enchiridion symbolorum*, ed. A. Schönmetzer [32 ed. Freiburg 1963] 804).

Nonetheless, not every position of Lombard found adherents among the scholastics. The 13th and 14th centuries produced lists of ''articles in which the Master of the Sentences is not commonly held by all.'' The number grew with the years. Despite such mild disagreement, however, the *Sentences* continued to be used and commented on in all the schools of Western Christendom until well into the 17th century, though it was often replaced by St. Thomas after the work of CAJETAN (TOMMASO DE VIO).

Bibliography: J. DE GHELLINCK, *Dictionnaire de théologie catholique,* ed. A. VACANT et al., 15 v. (Paris 1903–50; Tables générales 1951–) 12.2:1941–2019; *Le Mouvement théologique du XIIe siècle* (2d ed. Bruges 1948); ''La Carrière de Pierre Lombard: Nouvelle précision chronologique,'' *Revue d'historie ecclésiastique* 30 (1934) 95–100. D. VAN DEN EYNDE, ''Essai chronologique sur

"St. Peter Martyr," fresco by Fra Angelico.

l'oeuvre de Pierre Lombard," *Miscellanea Lombardiana* (Novara 1957) 45–63. A. M. LANDGRAF, *Einführung in die Geschichte der theologischen Literatur der Frühscholastik* (Regensburg 1948), revised as *Introducción a la historia de la literatura teológica de la escolástica incipiente* (Barcelona 1956). P. DELHAYE, *Pierre Lombard: Sa vie, ses oeuvres, sa morale* (Paris 1961). N. ESPENBERGER, *Die Philosophie des Petrus Lombardus* (Beiträge zur Geschichte der Philosophie und Theologie des Mittelalters 3.5; Münster 1901). J. SCHNEIDER, *Die Lehre vom dreieinigen Gott in der Schule des Petrus Lombardus* (Munich 1961). J. SCHUPP, *Die Gnadenlehre des Petrus Lombardus* (Freiburg 1932). E. F. ROGERS, *Peter Lombard and the Sacramental System* (New York 1917). V. DOUCET, *Commentaires sur les Sentences* (Quaracchi-Florence 1954).

[I. C. BRADY]

PETER MARTYR, ST.

Preacher, miracle worker, first Dominican martyr; b. Verona, Italy, *c.* 1205; d. near Milan, Italy, April 6, 1252. Peter, born of heretical parents, embraced the Faith and *c.* 1221 entered the Dominican order. He preached in the important cities of central and north Italy, founding militant, pious confraternities of laity to counteract heretical influences. At Florence (1244–45) he aided the seven founders of the SERVITES. He was prior of Dominican houses at Asti (1240), Piacenza (1241), and Como (1251). In 1232, and again in 1251, he was named papal inquisitor (*see* INQUISITION). Because of his vigorous preaching and numerous converts, he aroused the hatred of the CATHARI. At Paschaltide, 1252, he was assassinated on the road between Como and Milan. INNOCENT IV canonized him the following year. St. Peter, patron of inquisitors, enjoyed a wide cult in the Middle Ages and was frequently depicted in art. His tomb is in the church of Santo Eustorgio, Milan.

Feast: April 20 (formerly 29).

Bibliography: *Acta Sanctorum* April 3:686–727. *Una vita per il credo, notizie biografiche storiche artistiche nel VII centenario del martirio di s. Pietro da Verona* (Seveso, Italy 1952). R. FRANCISCO, *S. Pietro da Verona* (Alba 1952). G. EDERLE, *San Pietro da Verona* (Verona 1952). E. LIBERTI, *Seveso deve qualcosa al sangue di un martire* (Milan 1968).

[J. F. HINNEBUSCH]

PETER MONOCULUS, BL.

Abbot of CLAIRVAUX; b. Burgundy, France; d. Foigny, France, Oct. 29, 1186. Peter, the son of a noble family, joined the Cistercian community in his early youth. In 1164 he was elected abbot of Valroy, where in a nearly fatal illness he lost an eye. He became abbot at Igny (1169), then at Clairvaux (1179). A worthy successor of St. BERNARD in his humility and love of poverty, he was held in the highest esteem by the popes and monarchs of his time. He died while on a tour of visitation at Foigny, but was buried at Clairvaux. Sixteen of Peter's letters have been edited (*Patrologia Latina* 201:1391–1404). Although never officially canonized, his cult is widespread among Cistercians.

Feast: Oct. 29.

Bibliography: Sources. *Acta Sanctorum* Oct. 8:53–90. *Patrologia Latina* (Paris 1878–90) 209:1007–36. P. L. PÉCHENARD, *Histoire de l'Abbaye d'Igny* (Reims 1883). S. LENSSEN, *Hagiologium cisterciense* (Tilburg 1948–49) 1:254–257. A. A. KING, *Cîteaux and Her Elder Daughters* (London 1954).

[L. J. LEKAI]

PETER NIGRI (SCHWARZ)

Dominican philosopher, theologian, and Hebraist; b. Kaaden, Bohemia, 1434; d. Eger, 1483. In 1481, at the request of King Matthias Corvinus, he became rector of the University of Budapest. Peter was a champion of THOMISM, defending it especially against the nominalists. His chief theological work is *Clypeus Thomistatum* (1481); he wrote also a commentary on the Psalms and possibly on the *Isagoge* of Porphyry and the *Categories* of Aristotle. Because of his acquaintance with Oriental languages, he may be considered the chief Hebraist of the late Middle Ages. He sought to convert the Jews through instruction and persuasion, and was active in religious concourses, delivering theological sermons. The rabbis, however, were usually reluctant to engage in disputation. Noteworthy was the seven-day session at Regensburg in 1474. The substance of this event was published as *Tractatus contra perfidos Judaeos de conditionibus veri Messiae, scilicet Christi vel uncti* (1475). In 1477 Peter expanded this work and published it in German as *Der Stern des Messiah.* The *Tractatus* is a rare incunabulum and possibly the first book printed in Hebrew characters. Peter published also a Hebrew primer or grammar, the first produced in Europe by a Christian.

Bibliography: R. BAUERREISS, *Lexikon für Theologie und Kirche,* ed. J. HOFER and K. RAHNER (Freiburg 1957–65) 8:372. B. WALDE, *Christliche Hebraisten Deutschlands am Ausgang des Mittelalters* (Münster 1916) 70–152; *Die deutsch Literatur des Mittelalters,* ed. W. STAMMLER and K. LANGOSCH (Berlin-Leipzig 1933–55) 4:130–134, 5:1045.

[J. F. HINNEBUSCH]

PETER NOLASCO, ST.

Founder of the Order of Our Lady of Ransom (MERCEDARIANS); b. probably Barcelona, Spain, perhaps Languedoc (Saint-Papoul or Masdes-Saintes-Puelles), France, *c.* 1182; d. Barcelona, Dec. 25?, *c.* 1249. Peter's vita is obscured by legends (e.g., that he crusaded against the ALBIGENSES, that he tutored King JAMES I OF ARAGON), but especially by a plethora of false documentation. Forgeries of the 17th century, promoting his canonization, furnish much of his traditional biography; genuine documents tell little about him. Involved controversies between Mercedarian and Dominican scholars add further confusion. Peter was born probably of merchant or improbably of knightly family. It is questionable whether simultaneous visions to Peter, RAYMOND OF PEÑAFORT, and King James of Aragon caused them to cofound the Mercedarians. More likely, perhaps, Peter was the procurator of Peñafort's lay confraternity for ransoming, which became an Order (1218 or 1223 or 1228 or better 1234). As master-general until 1249, Peter supposedly ransomed 400 Christians on one trip to Muslim Valencia and Granada, and a total of 890 during several ransom tours. King James fostered the Mercedarians, but much of his connection with Peter seems legendary. Perhaps Peter was on the Valencian crusade; he appears at Valencia in 1244. He was canonized 1628.

Feast: Jan. 28 (formerly Jan. 31).

Bibliography: P. N. PÉREZ, *San Pedro Nolasco, fundador de la orden de la Merced* (Barcelona 1915). E. VACAS GALINDO, *San Raimundo de Peñafort, fundador de la orden de la Merced: Estudio histórico-critico* (Rome 1919). F. D. GAZULLA GALVE, *La orden de Nuestra Señora de la Merced: Estudios históricocriticos, 1218–1317* (Barcelona, 1934). J. M. DELGADO VARELA, ''Sobre la canonización de San P. N.,'' *Estudios* [mercedarios] 12 (1956) 265–295. E. GOMEZ, ''San P. N. en la espiritualidad mercedaria,'' *ibid.* 329–355; and other studies in this journal. P. F. GARCÍA GUTIERREZ, *Iconografia mercedaria: Nolasco y su obra* (Madrid 1985). A. REMÓN, *Las fiestas solemnes de San Pedro Nolasco* (Madrid 1985), cult in Spain. A. PRONZATO, *Un mercante di libertà* (Turin 1986). L. O. PROAÑO, *Miscelánea histórica,* 2 v. (Ibarra, Ecuador 1986–1995).

[R. I. BURNS]

PETER OF AILLY (ALLIACO)

French scholastic theologian, cardinal; b. Compiègne, 1350; d. Avignon, Aug. 9, 1420.

Life. He began his study of philosophy in 1363 at the College of Navarre in Paris, where he became master in arts in 1368 and was influenced by the ideals of ROGER BACON. Beginning theological studies in 1372, he commented on the *Sentences* in 1375 (4th ed. Venice 1500), deeply influenced by the NOMINALISM of WILLIAM OF OCKHAM. As delegate of the ''French nation,'' he presented the university's obedience to CLEMENT VII in Avignon in the spring of 1379. Becoming master of theology and professor at the Sorbonne on April 11, 1381, he defended before the royal council the authority and right of a general council to end the WESTERN SCHISM. Appointed rector of the College of Navarre in 1384, he became extremely active in academic, ecclesiastical, and political affairs. When John of Montson attacked the doctrine of the IMMACULATE CONCEPTION in 1387 and appealed to the pope in the matter, Peter energetically defended the doctrine before Clement VII. His most illustrious pupil was Jean GERSON. On Oct. 7, 1389, Peter became university chancellor. In 1390 or 1391 he was appointed chaplain and confessor to Charles VI and (1391) archdeacon of Cambrai. The pope named him bishop of Laon, but the king, not wishing to release him, made him treasurer of Sainte-Chapelle and allowed him to retain his many lucrative benefices; he had as many as 14 benefices at one time. On April 2, 1395, BENEDICT XIII appointed him bishop of Le Puy; although consecrated, he never visited his see. He was made archbishop of Cambrai on June 5, 1397.

Although he was convinced that the schism could be repaired only by a general council, which he considered to be higher than a pope, he held a moderate position at the 1406 synod of Paris that considered withdrawing obedience from Benedict XIII, the antipope. He arrived too late at the Council of PISA to exert any influence. The an-

"Vision of Saint Peter Nolasco," painting by Francisco de Zurbaran. (©Francis G. Mayer/CORBIS)

tipope JOHN XXIII won his allegiance by creating him cardinal (Dec. 19, 1412) and administrator of Limoges and Orange and appointing him legate to Germany (March 18, 1413). At the Council of CONSTANCE (1414–18), which he himself had prepared, he adopted an opportunist attitude, changing views whenever it seemed useful to reach agreement. The legitimate pope, MARTIN V, elected at the council, appointed him legate at Avignon, where he died. His body was brought to Cambrai in 1422.

Works and Influence. His 175 writings [listed by P. Tschackert, *Peter von Ailli* (Gotha 1877) 348–366] cover practically the whole domain of human knowledge of concern to his contemporaries. Most of them, however, concern canon law and theories pertaining to the constitution of the Church. Among his more influential works, besides the commentary on the *Sentences,* are *Tractatus brevis de anima* (ed. Paris 1503), *Destructiones modorum significandi, Libellus sacramentalis* (ed. Louvain 1487), *Imago mundi* (ed. Louvain 1480; Paris 1930), *De materia concilii generalis tres partes, Tractatus super reformatione ecclesiae* [ed. in *Joannis Gersonis Opera omnia* (Antwerp 1706) 2:903–916], and *Tractatus et sermones* (ed. Brussels *c.* 1484).

Although facile and versatile, he was frequently contradictory in his teachings. In his scientific writings concerning nature he showed the influence of Roger Bacon. In philosophy and theology, however, his nominalism was tempered somewhat by THOMISM. He denied not only the infallibility of the pope but also that of the council, so that for him it is possible to appeal from one council to another. Concerning the EUCHARIST, he considered impanation as a possible alternative to TRANSUBSTANTIATION; in this he prepared the way for the doctrine of Martin LUTHER and other Reformers.

As a man of action, he was greatly concerned for the welfare of the Church. He strove harder than any of his contemporaries to restore unity to the Church, at whatever the cost. However, he was too much of an opportunist, strongly influenced by the needs of the moment; he disenchanted many friends because often they could not rely on him at crucial moments.

The influence of his writings was considerable, particularly on Gabriel BIEL, Jacques ALMAIN, John Major, DENIS THE CARTHUSIAN, and Martin Luther. Gallicanists considered him one of their foremost authorities.

Bibliography: A. CARDIN, *Enciclopedia filosofica,* 4 v. (Venice-Rome 1957) 1:113–114. F. STEGMÜLLER, *Repertorium biblicum medii aevi,* 7 v. (Madrid 1949–61) 1:306–309. L. SALEMBIER, *Dictionnaire d'histoire et de géographie ecclésiastiques,* ed. A. BAUDRILLART (Paris 1912–) 1:1154–1165; *Le Cardinal Pierre d'Ailly* (Tourcoing 1932); *Dictionnaire de théologie catholique,* 15 v. (Paris 1903–50) 1:642–654. J. P. MCGOWAN, *Pierre d'Ailly and the Council of Constance* (Washington 1936). L. R. LOOMIS, tr., *The Council of Constance,* ed. J. H. MUNDY and K. M. WOODY (New York 1961). B. MELLER *Studien zur Erkenntnislehre des Peter von Ailly* (Freiburger theologische Studien 67; Freiburg 1954).

[A. EMMEN]

PETER OF ALCÁNTARA, ST.

Friar Minor, ascetic, mystic, Franciscan reformer; b. Peter Garavita, in Alcántara, Estremadura, Spain, 1499; d. Arenas, Spain, Oct. 18, 1562. Peter, of noble parentage, entered the Franciscan order in the discalced vice province of Estremadura in 1515. Although not its founder, Peter is closely linked with the discalced reform, a controversial movement within Spanish Franciscanism. Because of his adherence to it, the movement spread from Spain to Portugal, Italy, Mexico, the East Indies, the Philippines, and Brazil, and his followers became known as Alcantarines. By his followers he was hailed as the restorer of the Franciscan Order and, as such, his statue was placed among the other founders of religious orders in the Vatican basilica. Peter is known for the severity of his mortifications, some of which are related in the autobiography of St. TERESA of Jesus, whom, in his last years, he advised and encouraged in her Carmelite reform. He wrote little. His justly famous *Tratado de la oración y meditación* was already popular in his lifetime, although its authenticity has not escaped challenge. It has gone through more than 175 editions and numerous translations. Peter died at Arenas, where his remains are still venerated in the shrine built at royal expense. He was beatified in 1622 and canonized in 1669. In 1826, by decree of the Sacred Congregation of Rites, he was made the patron saint of Brazil; in 1962 he was declared copatron of Estremadura.

Feast: Oct. 19.

Bibliography: "Estudios sobre San Pedro de Alcántara," *Archivo Ibero-Americano* 22 (Madrid 1962). PETER OF ALCANTARA, *Treatise on Prayer and Meditation,* tr. D. DEVAS (London 1926; repr. Westminster, Md. 1949). E. A. PEERS, *Studies of the Spanish Mystics,* v. 2 (London 1930). PETER OF ALCANTARA, *Vida y Escritores de San Pedro de Alcantaro,* ed. R. SANZ-VALDIVIESO (Madrid 1996). CONFERENCIA DE MINISTROS PROVINCALES, OFM., *Misticos Franciscanos Espanoles* (Madrid 1996), bibliography.

[J. B. WUEST]

PETER OF ALEXANDRIA, ST.

Bishop (300–311), martyr; d. Alexandria, Egypt, Nov. 25, 311. After serving as head of the catechetical school at Alexandria, Peter succeeded Theonas as bishop *c.* 300, and was "beheaded in the ninth year of the persecution" (EUSEBIUS, *Hist. eccl.* 7.32.31). This intrepid churchman reflected the milder school in his attitude toward the *LAPSI.* While Peter was in hiding during the persecution of DIOCLETIAN (303), Meletius, bishop of Lycopolis, assumed his episcopal rights. Meletius, whose view of the *lapsi* was more rigid, was declared excommunicate by a synod in 306, deposed, and banished to Palestine until 311; but the MELETIAN SCHISM of which he was the cause continued for several centuries after his death.

Peter's most important writing is the Paschal epistle; it contains 15 canons for the reconciliation of the lapsed (*c.* 306). Those who denied the faith under torture are assigned a 40-day fast for three years; those who lapsed without torture are assigned an additional year; those who obtained certificates of sacrifice are given a six-month penance; those who fell but later confessed are forgiven, but the clergy are not to be reinstated; those who sacrificed wealth and fled into exile are forgiven (*Patrologia Graeca* 18:468–508).

Peter's works exist mostly in Greek and Coptic fragments, and include treatises against ORIGEN AND ORIGENISM, *On the Godhead* (quoted at EPHESUS in 431), and a Letter on the Meletian schism. He was a courageous and enlightened churchman, and despite the tragic effects of the Meletian schism, his canons were a milestone in primitive Church discipline. The *Acts of the Martyrdom of St. Peter of Alexandria* (Latin, Greek, Syriac, and Coptic) is not authentic.

Feast: Nov. 26.

Bibliography: PETER OF ALEXANDRIA, *Patrologia Graeca* 18:449–522. J. QUASTEN, *Patrology* 2:113–118. B. ALTANER, *Patrology* 239–240. G. FRITZ, *Dictionnaire de théologie catholique* 12.2:1802–04. F. KETTLER, *Paulys Readenzyklopädie der klassichen Altertumswissenschaft* 12.2 (1938) 1281–88. T. Y. MALATY, *Pope Peter of Alexandria: The Deans of the School of Alexandria* (Jersey City, N.J. 1994). W. TELFER, "St. Peter of Alexandria and Arius," *Analecta Bollandiana* 67 (1949) 117–130; *Harvard Theological Review* 48 (1955) 227–237, and Meletius. M. RICHARD, *Mélanges de science religeuse* 3 (1946) 357–358, Christology. H. I.

BELL and W. E. CRUM, eds., *Jews and Christians in Egypt* (London 1924). É. AMANN, *Dictionnaire de théologie catholique* 10.1:531–536.

[H. MUSURILLO]

PETER OF ANAGNI, ST.

Bishop, crusader; b. Salerno, Italy, 1030 or 1035; d. there, Aug. 3, 1105. Peter entered a Benedictine monastery in Salerno. He later became a papal chaplain, and in 1062 ALEXANDER II created him bishop of Anagni. In 1071 Peter became the pope's representative to the Byzantine Emperor Michael VII Ducas. When Michael fell ill, Peter cured him and was lavishly rewarded. He returned to Anagni, where he commenced to rebuild the city's cathedral. Before the reconstruction was finished, Peter left Anagni to participate in the First CRUSADE as a member of the expedition led by Bohemund I. After the capture of Jerusalem, Peter returned to Italy and retired to Salerno. He was buried in the city's cathedral, and then translated to Anagni. By a decree of June 4, 1109, PASCHAL II authorized his feast day.

Feast: Aug. 3.

Bibliography: *Acta Sanctorum* Aug. 1:231–242. J. L. BAUDOT and L. CHAUSSIN, *Vies des saints et des bienheureux selon l'ordre du calendrier avec l'historique des fêtes* (Paris 1935–56) 8:59–60.

[J. A. BRUNDAGE]

PETER OF APAMEA

Sixth-century Monophysite bishop of Apamea in Syria (II). A disciple of the Monophysite theologian, Patriarch Severus of Antioch (512–518), Peter was installed in Apamea as metropolitan, but deposed in 518 by a synod under the bishop of Mariamne in Syria upon the accession of the Catholic emperor JUSTIN I. In 535 Peter accompanied Severus to Constantinople at the invitation of Empress THEODORA (1), but in the synod held there by Patriarch MENNAS the following year (May 2 to June 4, 536), he was condemned with his master. In a letter from JUSTINIAN I to the patriarch (June 10, 536), his name, together with those of Anthimus, the deposed patriarch of Constantinople, Severus of Antioch, and the monk Zooras, was anathematized. This condemnation passed into Justinian's *Codex juris* as *novella* 42. It enjoined the banishment of the four guilty men from Constantinople and all the major cities of the empire. Severus fled to the desert of Egypt, but nothing further is known of Peter.

See Also: MONOPHYSITISM.

Bibliography: J. D. MANSI, *Sacrorum Conciliorum nova et amplissima collection* (repr. Graz 1960) 8:578, 1068–82, 1093–1138. P. PEETERS, *Mélanges Henri Grégoire,* v. 2 (*Annuaire de l'Institute de philologie et d'histoire orientales et slaves,* 10; Brussels 1950) 5–51. A. GRILLMEIER and H. BACHT, *Das Konzil von Chalkedon: Geschichte und Gegenwart,* 3 v. (Würzburg 1951–54) v. 2. A. FLICHE and V. MARTIN, eds., *Histoire de l'église depuis les origines jusqu'à nos jours* (Paris 1935) 4:427, 452.

[P. ROCHE]

PETER OF AUVERGNE (ALVERNIA)

Secular master of Paris and later bishop of Clermont; b. Crocq, Auvergne, between 1240 and 1250; d. Clermont, Sept. 25, 1304. As a secular master of the arts, Peter taught philosophy at Paris for many years and wrote commentaries on all the Aristotelian books. He was still in the faculty of arts when Simon de Brie, the papal legate, appointed him rector of the university on March 7, 1275, in order to prevent an irreparable split between the followers of SIGER OF BRABANT and those of Alberic of Reims. Although an admirer and close associate of THOMAS AQUINAS, he could not attend Aquinas's lectures in the theology faculty and can be called his disciple only in a limited sense.

After the death of Aquinas he completed Aquinas's commentaries on the *Politics,* 3.7–end; *Meteora,* 2.1–end; and *De caelo et mundo;* 3.9–end. Before 1290 Peter enrolled in the faculty of theology and studied under HENRY OF GHENT and GODFREY OF FONTAINES. His commentary on the *Sentences* is no longer extant. Becoming master in theology in 1296, he taught as regent master until December 1301. His only theological writings extant, six *Quodlibeta,* stem from this period of regency.

Already a canon of Clermont before 1296, Peter obtained a canonry in Paris on June 18, 1296. On Jan. 21, 1302, he was named bishop of Clermont by BONIFACE VIII. After a visit to Rome that year, he returned to Paris, where he subscribed to the Parisian appeal to a council against Boniface VIII (June 1303).

Ptolemy of Lucca called Peter *fidelissimus* discipulus of Aquinas; and historians of THOMISM generally consider him an early representative of the Thomistic school in France. However, his fundamental orientation is Aristotelian and Averroist, with a certain dependence on Avicenna and Aquinas. This is particularly true of his *Quaestiones in metaphysicam* (10 qq., ed. A. Monahan). He interpreted Aristotle's concept of being as primarily a form, maintained that a being's *esse* differs only logically from its essence, and expounded the analogy of being solely in terms of attribution without reference to proper proportionality. For Peter, metaphysics is divided into general ontology and natural theology; ontology should be taught before all other sciences and theology should be taught last. His denial of a real distinction between essence and existence followed Henry of Ghent in literary structure, but his rejection of Henry's "intentional" distinction expressed the personal opinion of Godfrey of Fontaines. Similarly, Peter recognized only a logical distinction between the individual and its essence. In the *Quaestiones in metaphysicam* the principle of individuation is said to be a relation to a given efficient cause. In later writings, however, Peter followed Godfrey of Fontaines's view that form is the principle of individuation.

Bibliography: P. GLORIEUX, *Répertoire des maîtres en théologie de Paris au XIIIe siècle* (Paris 1933–34) 1:412–417. P. GLORIEUX, *La Littérature quodlibétique* (Kain 1925) 1:257–263. P. STELLA, *Enciclopedia filosofica* (Venice-Rome 1957) 3:1374. A. P. MONAHAN, "Peter of Auvergne's 'Quaestiones in Metaphysicam,'" *Nine Mediaeval Thinkers,* ed. J. R. O'DONNELL (Toronto 1955) 145–181; "The Subject of Metaphysics for P. of A.," *Mediaeval Studies* 16 (1954) 118–130. É. H. GILSON, *History of Christian Philosophy in the Middle Ages* (New York 1955) *passim.* F. J. ROENSCH, *Early Thomistic School* (Dubuque 1964).

[A. P. MONAHAN]

PETER OF BERGAMO

Dominican theologian and lexicographer; b. Bergamo, Italy, early 14th century; d. Piacenza, Oct. 15, 1482. He entered the order and was ordained at Bergamo in the Dominican province of upper Lombardy. His career was one of teaching theology, principally at the *studium generale* in Bologna. He was master of students in 1461, lecturer on the *Sentences* in 1466 and 1467, and regent of studies from 1471 to 1476. He had the highest reputation as a teacher and many revered him as a saint. Among his outstanding disciples were DOMINIC OF FLANDERS, Paul Soncinas (d. 1494), and Ambrose Alemannus. His greatest contribution to THOMISM consisted in an *Index universalis* to all the works of St. THOMAS AQUINAS, completed in 1475; a *Concordantia locorum doctoris angelici, quae sibi invicem adversari videntur* (ed. Bologna 1473) that harmonized apparently contradictory passages; and a table of biblical passages quoted by St. Thomas. These three works were collected under the general title of *Tabula aurea* and published in Bologna (1475) and again in the Piana edition of the complete works of Aquinas (Rome 1570; photocopy, Rome 1960).

Bibliography: J. QUÉTIF and J. ÉCHARD, *Scriptores Ordinis Praedicatorum* (New York 1959) 1.2:863–864. A. WALZ, *Lexikon für Theologie und Kirche,* ed. J. HOFER and K. RAHNER, 10 v. (2d, new ed. Freiburg 1957–65) 8:351. I. COLOSIO, "La *Tabula Aurea* di Pietro da Bergamo," *Divus Thomas* 64 (1961) 119–132.

[J. F. HINNEBUSCH]

PETER OF BRUYS

An itinerant priest in Daupiné and Languedoc; d. 1126 (according to Borst), or *c.* 1132–33 (according to Manselli). Documentation of Peter of Bruys' career and ideas is provided by PETER THE VENERABLE, who addressed his tract against the PETROBRUSIANS to the bishops of Embrun, Gap, and Die, as well as to the archbishop of Arles. Peter was also condemned as a subverter of the Church by ABELARD and TANCHELM of Flanders. For 20 years Peter spread his teaching in southern France, including Gascony, until he was seized and burned by the faithful at Saint–Gilles in Languedoc for desecration of the cross.

Peter's ideology is just one example of the variety of religious fermentation that occured in many parts of France during the first third of the 12th century, but whereas other itinerant preachers, such as Bl. Robert of Arbrissel, St. BERNARD OF TIRON, and VITALIS OF SAVIGNY, urged reform along apostolic lines within the ecclesiastical fabric, Peter moved from attacks on clerical delinquency and worldliness to bitter criticism of hierarchy and Sacraments, demonstrating the difference between legitimate, extraordinary preachers and a mere *gyrovagus.* He spurned as imposters regular and secular clergy alike. Accepting only the Gospels, Peter cast doubt on other portions of the Bible. He rejected infant Baptism and discounted the Mass and transubstantiation, affirming that each individual is to be saved by his own faith.

Peter disapproved of all ceremonies and outward forms, even the erection of churches. He held that one may pray as effectively in tavern or church, in market place or temple, and may commune with God before a stable as well as before an altar; that crosses are to be broken and burned because, as the instrument of the Passion, they are not worthy of veneration; and that sacrifices, prayers, alms, and good works of the living are not efficacious for the dead. Peter rejected art and ridiculed hymns, since what pleases God is the pious sentiments of the soul, not outbursts of the human voice or musical instruments. Upon Peter's death his followers were dispersed or joined the heretical monk, HENRY OF LAUSANNE.

Bibliography: Sources. PETER THE VENERABLE, *Epistola sive tractatus adversus Petrobrusianos haereticos, Patrologia Latina,* ed. J. P. MIGNE (Paris 1878–90) 189:719–850. P. ABELARD, *Introductio ad theologiam* 2:4, *Patrologia Latina* 178:1056. **Literature.** S. M. DEUTSCH, J. J. HERZOG and A. HAUCK, eds., *Realencyklopädie für protestantische Theologie* (Leipzig 1896–1913) 15:219–221. F. VERNET, *Dictionnaire de théologie catholique*, ed. A. VACANT et al. (Paris 1903–50) 2.1:1151–56. R. MANSELLI, *Studi sulle eresie del secolo xii* (Studi storici 5; Rome 1953) 25–43. E. VACANDARD, *Vie de Saint Bernard* (4th ed. Paris 1910). A. BORST, *Die Katharer* (Stuttgart 1953) 83–84.

[E. W. MCDONNELL]

PETER OF CASTELNAU, BL.

Legate, martyr; b. Château-Neuf, Montpellier, France; d. near Saint-Gilles, Belgium, Jan. 14, 1208. While Peter was archdeacon of Maguelonne (Montpellier), INNOCENT III made him papal legate to Languedoc to deal with the ALBIGENSES (1199). Peter gained the recantation of Raymond VI of Toulouse whose domains were rife with heresy. In 1202 Peter joined the CISTERCIANS at FONTFROIDE ABBEY. In 1207 Innocent III again made him legate to cope with Raymond, who had lapsed. With the support of the nobles of Provence and Languedoc, Peter issued a bull of excommunication and placed Raymond's domains under interdict, thus bringing him to submission. On January 15, a henchman of Raymond assassinated Peter. This led to the Albigensian Crusade led by Simon de Montfort l'Amaury. Peter is honored as a martyr in the Midi dioceses.

Feast: Jan. 15 (formerly March 5); Diocese of Nîmes, March 15.

Bibliography: *Acta Sanctorum* March 1:409–415. A. FLICHE and V. MARTIN, eds., *Histoire de l'église depuis les origines Jusqu'á nos jours.* (Paris 1935–) 10. S. LENSSEN, *Hagiologium cisterciense* (Tilburg 1948–49) 1. B. GRIESSER, ''Rainer v. Fossanova,'' *Cistercienser-Chronik* (1953) 151–167. K. SPAHR, *Lexikon für Theologie und Kirche*, ed. J. HOFER and K. RAHNER (Freiberg 1957–65) 8:354–355.

[M. A. MULHOLLAND]

PETER OF CELLE

Cluniac, abbot, bishop, Latin stylist, and spiritual writer; b. Champagne, *c.* 1115; d. Chartres, Feb. 20, 1183. Peter was abbot of Montier–la–Celle, near Troyes, from 1145 or 1150 to 1162, and then of Saint–Rémi, Reims, from 1162 to 1181, and bishop of Chartres from 1181 until his death. His Christocentric piety and ascetic ideals, expressed in a prolixity of Biblical allegorizing, and his administrative abilities, demonstrated early in his reform of Celle and in continuous assistance to diocese and papacy, made him the admired counselor, confidant, and correspondent of nearly all the great personalities of his time, to whom he addressed a flow of letters, sermons, and tracts (*Patrologia Latina*, ed. J. P. Migne [Paris 1878–90] 202: 397–1146).

Bibliography: J. DE GHELLINCK, *L'Essorde la littérature latine au XIIe siécle* (Brussels-Paris 1946) 1:100–101, 194, 225. J. LECLERCQ, *La Spiritualité de Pierre de Celle 1115–83* (Paris 1946); ''Nouvelles lettres de P. de C.,'' *Analecta monastica* v. 5 (St Anselm 43; 1958) 160–179, works, bibliog. P. GLORIEUX, ''Candidats à la pourpre en 1178,'' *Mélanges de science religieuse* 11 (1954) 5–30. JOHN OF SALISBURY, *Letters,* ed. and tr. W. J. MILLOR et al. (New York 1955–) 1:ix–1iii.

[P. EDWARDS]

PETER OF DIEBURG

Also known as Dieppurch; chronicler of the Hildesheim house of the Brethren of the Common Life; b. Dieburg, east of Darmstadt, Germany, *c.* 1420; d. Hildesheim, 1494. Dieburg is known chiefly as the author of the annals (1440–94) of the house of the BRETHREN OF THE COMMON LIFE in Hildesheim. These Latin annals, which are generally dependable, begin in 1440, the year the Brethren were founded at Hildesheim. They lived first in the Luremanshof in the Old Market, then purchased the Löchtenhof in 1443. Shortly before 1440, Dieburg had joined the Brethren in Herford; in 1440 he went to Hildesheim as a novice. He worked first as a kitchen helper, then as a copyist. After ordination, he became rector of the Hildesheim house in 1476 or 1477 and remained in office until his death, even though he tried to resign in 1491 because of his age. While rector, he maintained strict discipline, putting an end to the high-handed dealings of some of the Brethren.

A *domus scolarium,* or college, where students were boarded and educated by the Brethren, was founded during his rectorship. As in other houses of the Brethren, e.g., in Deventer and in Emmerich, the school aimed mainly—or even exclusively—at giving religious training to suitable young candidates for the community, or at least at inculcating a pious way of life in every student. Actual scholastic instruction was usually left to others. While Dieburg was in office, new houses of Brethren were founded from Lüchtenhof—one in Magdeburg (1482) and one in Berlicum in Friesland (1483), although the Friesland house perished in 1488. Dieburg was a pious, modest man who lived and acted entirely in the spirit of the DEVOTIO MODERNA.

Bibliography: *Annalen und Akten der Brüder des Gemeinsamen Lebens im Lüchtenhofe zu Hildesheim,* ed. R. DOEBNER (Hanover 1903). E. BARNIKOL, *Bruder Dieburgs deutsches Christentum* (Eisleben 1933). K. ALGERMISSEN, *Lexikon für Theologie und Kirche*, ed. J. HOFER and K. RAHNER (Freiberg 1957–65) 8:361.

[W. J. ALBERTS]

PETER OF IRELAND

Teacher of Aquinas; b. probably in Ireland, *c.* 1200; d. probably at Naples, after 1260. As a professor in Naples, he taught THOMAS AQUINAS natural philosophy, and probably logic (*c.* 1239–44). Peter's commentaries on PORPHYRY's *Isagoge* and on Aristotle's *De interpretatione* and *De longitudine et brevitate vitae* (*De morte et vita*) survive in manuscript and still await full study. A *determinatio magistralis* (or master's judgment) of a scholastic disputation in natural philosophy given by

Peter, probably at Naples in the presence of King Manfred (*c.* 1260), has been published (Baeumker). It shows that Peter was well versed in Aristotelian natural philosophy and was under the influence of Averroës. Peter's early career is still largely a matter of conjecture. He must have gone abroad for his studies, as Ireland had no university in the 13th century. His interest in Aristotelian natural philosophy might suggest Oxford; his logic and his methods of commentary have been thought to indicate Paris. His becoming a professor in the Norman kingdom of Naples strongly suggests that he was Anglo-Norman and not native Irish by race.

Bibliography: C. BAEUMKER, ''Petrus de Hibernia . . . und seine Disputation vor König Manfred,'' *Sitzungsberichte der Bayerischen Akademie der Wissenschaften zu München* (1920). M. GRABMANN, ''Magister Petrus von Hibernia . . . seine Disputation vor König Manfred und seine Aristoteleskommentare,'' *Mittelalterliches Geistesleben,* 3 v. (Munich 1926–56) 1:249–265. A. PELZER, ''Le Cours inédit d'Albert le Grand sur la Morale à Nicomaque . . .'' *Revue néo-scolastique de philosophie* 24 (1922) 333–361. M. B. CROWE, ''Peter of Ireland, Teacher of St. Thomas Aquinas,'' *Studies* 45 (1956) 443–456; ''Peter of Ireland's Approach to Metaphysics,'' *Miscellanea mediaevalia,* 2 (1963) 154–160. A. B. EMDEN, *A Biographical Register of the University of Oxford to A.D. 1500,* 3 v. (Oxford 1957–59) 3:xxx. A. PELZER, *Études d'histoire littéraire sur la scolastique médiévale* (Paris 1964) 272–335.

[M. B. CROWE]

PETER OF JERUSALEM

Patriarch from 524 to 552. Nothing is known of his origin or career until he succeeded John of Jerusalem in 524. The latter had held a synod in 516 that condemned both NESTORIUS and the Monophysites, EUTYCHES and SEVERUS OF ANTIOCH. Peter was of a similar theological orthodoxy. He accepted the appointment of Anthimus as patriarch of Constantinople in the fall of 535, for, as Zachary Rhetor said, ''he disliked to be quarrelsome or a heretic'' (*Hist. eccl.* 9.19); but he was reproached by Pope AGAPETUS I for so doing, and he accepted the rebuke (*ibid.*). Peter was represented by two monks, THEODORE ASCIDAS and Domitian, at the Constantinopolitan council (Aug. 6, 536) that confirmed the deposition of Anthimus by the pope, and condemned Severus of Antioch and Peter of Apamea. Peter called a synod of his own (Sept. 19) that accepted the Constantinopolitan decisions.

Troubled by the Origenistic monks in Palestine who were supported by Theodore Ascidas and Domitian, become bishops in Constantinople, Peter complained secretly against them. Called to Gaza in 539, he took part in the synod that deposed Paul of Alexandria and appointed ZOÏLUS as the new patriarch. Peter welcomed the Roman deacon and future pope, PELAGIUS (I), to Jerusalem and had his monks provide him with information that resulted in the condemnation of ORIGEN by JUSTINIAN I (543), but that in turn occasioned the emperor's edict against the THREE CHAPTERS (544). Peter refused to sign this document, and wrote to his monks in favor of THEODORE OF MOPSUESTIA; but he was called to Constantinople, forced to sign, and, at the insistence of Theodore Ascidas, accepted two Origenistic *syncelli* or counselors, who aided the Isochristic monks in their attempt to have Origen's doctrine accepted by the Palestinian monks. Peter's reign ended in great difficulties. He was succeeded by an Isochristic monk, Macarius, but the latter was quickly deposed and replaced by Eustachius in December 552 or early 553.

Bibliography: F. DIEKAMP, *Die origenistischen Streitigkeiten* (Münster 1898). *Histoire de l'église depuis les origines jusqu'à nos jours* 4:458–462. G. FRITZ, *Dictionnaire de théologie catholique* 11.2: 1574–80. L. DUCHESNE, *L' Église au VIe siècle* (Paris 1925) 169–176, 206–209.

[P. ROCHE]

PETER OF JULLY, BL.

Monk; b. England; d. June 23, 1136. Peter met STEPHEN HARDING in Burgundy, and together they made a pilgrimage to Rome, after which Stephen entered the Abbey of MOLESME. Peter, however, spent some time in solitude before he followed Stephen's example. At the request of Bl. HUMBELINE, sister of St. BERNARD OF CLAIRVAUX and prioress of Jully-les-Nonnais (Diocese Langres), the abbot of Molesme appointed Peter to be the chaplain of her convent, an office he held until his death. His cult was revived in the Diocese of Sens in 1884 after it had lapsed in the 16th century. He is sometimes referred to as ''saint.''

Feast: June 23.

Bibliography: *Acta Sanctorum* June 5:517–523. A. M. ZIMMERMANN, *Kalendarium Benedictinum: Die Heiligen und Seligen des Benediktinerorderns und seiner Zweige* (Metten 1933–38) 2:374–375, 377. J. L. BAUDOT and L. CHAUSSIN, *Vies des saints et des bienheureux selon l'ordre du calendrier avec l'historique des fêtes* (Paris 1935–56) 6:382–383. A. BUTLER, *The Lives of the Saints* (New York 1956) 2:622.

[V. GELLHAUS]

PETER OF LA PALU (PALUDANUS)

French Dominican theologian and patriarch of Jerusalem, known by the scholastic title *Doctor fructuosus;* b. Varambone (Ain), *c.* 1277; d. Paris, Jan. 31, 1342. The sixth son of Gerard of La Palu, lord knight of Varembone and allied territory, Peter entered the Dominican order at Lyons. After studying theology at Toulouse, he was sent to Paris to lecture on the *Sentences* (1309–10) as successor to DURANDUS of Saint Pourçain. He incepted in theology on June 13, 1314, and remained regent master until 1317. After the general chapter of Metz in 1313, he, together with HARVEY NEDELLEC and JOHN OF NAPLES, was appointed to a commission entrusted with examining the works of Durandus for errors. The first investigation resulted in a list of 91 errors that were sent to the 1314 chapter of London; a second investigation (1316–17), in which Peter examined bks. 2 and 3 of Durandus's commentary, resulted in a list of 235 errors. Beginning with his Advent quodlibet of 1314, Peter defended the rights of mendicant orders against the attacks of John of Pouilly (fl. 1301–21); this prolonged controversy culminated in a three-year trial at Avignon in which Peter showed his skill as a prosecutor. The trial ended with the condemnation of John of Pouilly on July 24, 1321. Simultaneously, Peter composed his *Commentaria in universa biblia.* Between April and June 1318, he was sent by the pope to make peace between Flanders and France in the ultimate hope of organizing a crusade. Having failed to secure the desired peace, he was twice charged with treachery by the king of France, but he was vindicated. At Avignon during the trial of John of Pouilly, Peter was also on a commission with six other theologians to examine the *Postilia* on the Apocalypse by PETER JOHN OLIVI; this commission censured 60 propositions. Between 1321 and 1329 he returned to Saint-Jacques in Paris, continued his commentary on Scripture, undertook various missions for the Church and crown, and wrote two important works on ecclesiology: *De causa immediata ecclesiasticae potestatis* (ed. Paris 1506) and *De potestate papae* (*c.* 1324).

In 1329 Peter became patriarch of Jerusalem. Commissioned by JOHN XXII and the King of France to inquire diplomatically whether the Sultan of Egypt would negotiate a return of the Holy Places to Christians, he accompanied William Durant, bishop of Mende, to Cyprus. Failing to reach agreement, he returned to Avignon and suggested a new crusade. Apathy and enmity among Christian princes rendered all attempts impossible. On Dec. 19, 1333, the king of France established a commission of 29 Paris masters to study the view of John XXII concerning the state of the blessed before the Last Judgment. Peter was one of the leading theologians; some scholars believe that he directed the entire discussion. In a letter to the king, the commission asserted that the pope neither held nor taught the view attributed to him, but only mentioned and examined it. In 1335 BENEDICT XII called Peter to Avignon to assist in drawing up the bull settling the controversy over the beatific vision. He was then successively administrator of the Diocese of Limisso in Cyprus (1335–36) and of Conserans in St. Lizier (1336). In 1338 he tried to dissuade the pope from changing the Dominican constitution in matters of poverty.

Peter was one of the most eager promoters of THOMISM in the early 14th century, but this apparently was not based on an extensive reading or profound comprehension of St. Thomas Aquinas. He was more successful as a polemicist and diplomat than as an original and speculative thinker. Although he had great prestige among his confreres, James of Lausanne compiled a list of teachings ''in which Peter departs from Thomas,'' and John CAPREOLUS frequently rejected Peter's views as unfaithful to St. Thomas.

Bibliography: F. STEGMÜLLER, *Repertorium commentariorum in Sententias Petri Lombardi* (Würzburg 1947) 1: 327–328. J. KOCH, ''Der Prozess gegen Magister Johannes de Polliaco und seine Vorgeschichte,'' *Recherches de théologie ancienne et médiévale* 5 (1933) 391–422. P. FOURNIER, *Histoire littéraire de la France* 37 (1938) 39–422. J. QUÉTIF and J. ÉCHARD, *Scriptores ordinis praedicatorum* (New York 1959) 1.2:603–609. W. ECKERT *Lexicon für Theologie und Kirche*, ed. J. HOFER and K. RAHNER (Freiburg 1957–65) 8:374–375. P. STELLA, *Enciclopedia filosofica* 3:1379–80. F. J. ROENSCH, *Early Thomistic School* (Dubuque 1964).

[J. A. WEISHEIPL]

PETER OF LUXEMBURG, BL.

Cardinal deacon; b. Ligny-en-Baurrois, Lorraine, July 20, 1369; d. Villeneuve-les-Avignon, July 2, 1387. He was the son of Guy of Luxemburg, count of Ligny. Despite his extreme youth, Peter was appointed to several ecclesiastical offices and finally, in 1384, was named bishop of Metz and cardinal by the antipope CLEMENT VII. Clement hoped to strengthen the AVIGNON papacy through Peter's well-founded reputation for extraordinary asceticism and charity and through his family attachments in Luxemburg. Weary of the controversies accompanying the WESTERN SCHISM, Peter renounced his bishopric in 1386 and, leaving Avignon, retired to a nearby Carthusian monastery, where he died, at age 18. He was beatified by the valid Pope CLEMENT VII on April 9, 1527; his relics are now in Saint-Didier, Avignon.

Feast: July 2 (formerly July 4).

Bibliography: *Acta Sanctorum* July 1:428–551. H. FRANÇOIS, *La Vie du B. Pierre de Luxembourg* (Nancy 1927). J. L. BAUDOT and L. CHAUSSIN, *Vies des saints et des bienheureux selon l'ordre du calendrier avec l'historique des fêtes* (Paris 1935–56) 7: 51–59. A. BUTLER, *The Lives of the Saints* (New York 1956) 3:9–10. J. CAMBELL, *Lexikon für Theologie und Kirche* (Freiburg 1957–65) 8:369.

[J. C. MOORE]

PETER OF MOGLIANO, BL.

Franciscan; b. Mogliano, in the March of Ancona, Italy, 1442; d. Camerino, Italy, July 25, 1490. Peter studied law at Perugia until 1464. Three years later, after hearing a sermon preached by the pious and zealous Franciscan observant, Dominic of Leonessa (d. 1497), at that time vicar-provincial of the Marches, Peter at once chose to enter the order. An exemplary and apostolic religious, he was assigned as companion to JAMES OF THE MARCHES. In 1472 the General Congregation of Aquila sent him to Crete as their representative. He was appointed three times (1477, 1483, and 1489) to be vicar-provincial in the Marches and once, in Rome (1474).

Peter was spiritual director to Bl. Baptista Varano (d. 1524) of the order of Poor Clares of Camerino, who left an account of his last days. On July 2, 1490, it was revealed to Peter that he was about to die. On July 4 as had been foretold, he was stricken with a raging fever. In spite of his suffering and the harassment of the devil, he retained a noble serenity throughout the ordeal and died advocating the observance of the rule.

Peter was at once venerated as a saint, and many miracles were attributed to him. In 1502 his relics and those of John of Parma were transported to the city of Camerino; later, following the suppression of the religious orders after 1860, they were transferred to the cathedral. His cult was confirmed in 1760.

Feast: July 30.

Bibliography: *Archivum Franciscanum historicum* 4 (1911) 329. *Le opere spirituali della beata Battista Varani,* ed. M. SANTONI (Camerino 1894) 61–101. L. OLIGER, *Lexikon für Theologie und Kirche,* ed. M. BUCHBERGER, 10 v. (Freiburg 1930–38) 8:169. J. L. BAUDOT and L. CHAUSSIN, *Vies des saints et des bienheueux selon l'ordre du calendrier avec l'historique des fêtes,* 12 v. (Paris 1935–56) 7:622. LÉON OF CLARY, *Lives of the Saints and Blessed of the Three Orders of Saint Francis,* 4 v. (Tauton, England 1885–87) 3:1–8. I. BRANDOZZI, *Il beato Pietro da Mogliano* (Rome 1968).

[J. CAMBELL]

PETER OF ONESTI

Founder and superior of an establishment of regular canons at the church of S. Maria in Portu on the isle of Isola adjoining Ravenna (known also as de Honestis); b. mid-11th century; d. Ravenna, 1118–19. At the request of Peter, Pope Paschal II confirmed his rule Dec. 21, 1116. Mercati denied the authenticity of Peter's letter and questioned the papal confirmation. He maintained that the rule was not composed by Peter, but was already in existence between 1025 and 1050. Whether it was Peter's or not, the rule adopted at S. Maria in Portu obtained a wide diffusion, and the church became regarded as the head of its own congregation with associated foundations in many Italian cities and in Germany. Writers of the 14th and 15th centuries frequently confused Peter of Onesti with St. PETER DAMIAN.

Bibliography: Text of the rule in E. AMORT, *Vetus disciplina canonicorum,* 2 v. (Venice 1747) 1:339 ff., and *Patrologia Latina,* ed. J. P. MIGNE, 271 v., indexes 4 v. (Paris 1878–90) 163:703–748. G. MERCATI'S criticisms in his ''Pietro Peccatore,'' *Studi e documenti di storia e diritto,* 16 (1895) 3–47, reprinted in *Opere minori,* v. 1, *Studi e Testi* 76 (1937) 170–201. P. F. KEHR, *Regesta Pontificum Romanorum. Italia Pontificia,* 8 v. (Berlin 1906–35) 5:96–97.

[F. COURTNEY]

PETER OF PISA

Deacon, grammarian, and poet at the court of Charlemagne; b. Lombardy, first half of the 8th century; d. Lombardy, sometime before 799. Peter probably learned grammar and rhetoric in Lombardy where he took part in public disputations. When ALCUIN was a youth on a trip to Rome, he heard Peter speak in Pavia in a disputation on the Jews. Later Peter came to CHARLEMAGNE's court, probably after the destruction of the Lombard kingdom (773–774). Already an old man, he was Charles' honored guest for several years and an integral part of his learned court circle (*see* CAROLINGIAN RENAISSANCE). Two other Lombards later joined this group, PAUL the Deacon and PAULINUS OF AQUILEIA. A close bond existed between Charles and Peter as well as between Peter and Paul, but Peter apparently was not much liked by either EINHARD or Alcuin. Peter seems to have been proud of Paul's intellectual superiority over the others, including himself. He instructed Charles in Latin grammar and probably read the Latin authors with him. Einhard mentions this fact (ch. 25) and describes Peter as elderly. It seems likely that both Peter and Paul brought manuscripts from Italy that kept Carolingian scribes busy for many years.

Charles used Peter's poetic talent when writing letters in verse to Paul; when Charles wrote to Peter, in turn, he pieced together verses from the works of the poets with Alcuin's help. One poem that Peter wrote in Charles's name can be dated 783; addressed to Paul, the letter asks him to remain in the Frankish kingdom to give instruction in Greek to clerics accompanying Hrotrude. Of this exchange of poems, at least one is lost. The surviving pieces contain riddles, admonitions to Christian charity, a vision, and the like.

Like Paul the Deacon, Peter was important as a grammarian. In a manner typical of the 8th century, he illustrated his teaching with writings of ancient pagan and

Christian authors. His grammar is preceded by a dedication preface in elegiac verse stating that the work was composed "by Peter for love of his lord" and praising Charles as conqueror of the Lombards, builder of churches, converter of heathen, and punisher of evildoers. Noa, Samson, Gideon, and David are held up to Charles as models. He prays that Christ may help Charles in the future; the Saxon wars were not yet completed. In his grammar, Peter borrowed from Donatus, Probus, Sergius, Augustine, Cominian, Priscian, and Vergil. This work, dealing chiefly with declensions and conjugations, treated pronouns, adverbs, participles, conjunctions, and prepositions very much as did the anonymous author of MS Bern 207, fol. 112a–127b. Peter's treatise appears in the same MS, and its editor, H. Hagen, believes both are reproductions of a common source. Reichenau MS 821 (B 6:403) is a 10th-century copy of the grammar, complete with its dedicatory poem to Charles. Peter promised additional treatises, but if he wrote them, they are no longer extant.

Bibliography: H. HAGEN, *Anecdota Helvetica* (Leipzig 1870) 159–171, partial ed. of Peter's grammatical works. PAUL THE DEACON, *Die Gedichte des Paulus Diaconus,* ed. K. NEFF (Munich 1908) 57–, critical ed. of poems of Peter of Pisa with those of Paul the Deacon. M. MANITIUS, *Geschichte der lateinischen Literatur des Mittelalters* (Munich 1911–31) 1:452–456. F. J. E. RABY, *A History of Christian-Latin Poetry from the Beginnings to the Close of the Middle Ages* (Oxford 1953) 150–279. M. L. W. LAISTNER, *Thought and Letters in Western Europe, A. D. 500 to 900* (New York 1957) 219–222, 279–280. F. J. E. RABY, *A History of Secular Latin Poetry in the Middle Ages* (Oxford 1957) 1:181182, 197–199.

[C. M. AHERNE]

PETER OF POITIERS

Theologian and chancellor of Paris; b. Poitiers (or in the Poitou) *c.* 1130; d. Paris, Sept. 3, 1205. Peter was in Paris and had begun his theological studies before 1159 if, as appears probable, he studied under Peter Lombard, whose election as bishop of Paris in 1159 ended his teaching career. Peter of Poitiers began his own career as a teacher of theology in 1167. In 1193 he was named chancellor of Paris. The chancellor was primarily an officer of the cathedral chapter, and he was charged with the direction of the higher schools within the jurisdiction of the bishop of Paris. This made him, in effect, chief officer of the university, and his chancellorship from 1193 to 1205 came during the transition of the cathedral schools into the university.

Peter of Poitiers was one of the late 12th-century theologians to whom is attributed the development of Paris into a great medieval center of theology. In this lies his importance. His first interest was in the dogmatic and moral questions to which the study of Scripture gave rise. His outstanding work is the *Sententiarum libri quinque,* a systematic and comprehensive exposition of these questions. In this work he draws heavily upon PETER LOMBARD, who was the father of the 12th-century *Sentence* books, but at the same time he is largely independent of the Lombard. Thus, at least half of the questions he discusses are not found in the *Sentences* of his master. Then, he was one of the most enthusiastic champions of the application of dialectics to theology. This gave reason a much greater role and changed the traditional theology, which was based entirely or almost entirely on authorities. This enthusiasm for dialectics followed in the wake of ABELARD and the introduction of the works of Aristotle into the West. In applying dialectics, and also grammar, to the solution of theological questions, Peter and his contemporaries initiated the scholastic method, which reached its greatest perfection in the *Summa theologiae* of St. Thomas in the 13th century. While Peter's *Sentences* follows the general systematic pattern of topics of the Lombard, he divided them into five books instead of four. Book one treats of the Trinity, book two of creation, book three of grace and the virtues, book four of Christology, and book five of the Sacraments and eschatology. Under the virtues he deals with a great many moral questions, thereby giving much more prominence to moral theology than did the Lombard. Among the technical terms that he was one of the first to use are *apere operato* and *apere operantis, spiratio,* and *synderesis.* Peter also devoted much time to the interpretation of Holy Writ according to the four senses or meanings of Scripture, which constituted medieval exegesis. These senses were the historical, allegorical, tropological, and anagogical. Peter was also interested in a third branch of the medieval theological curriculum, sacred history. One work on this subject, the *Compendium historiae in genealogia Christi,* certainly belongs to him, and the *Historia Actuum Apostolorum,* the last part of the famous *Historia Scholastica* of Peter Comestor and long attributed to this master, is most probably from the pen of Peter of Poitiers. On the other hand, he scrupulously avoided the subject of Canon Law, though he must have been well versed in law because he was appointed several times by the pope as judge-delegate in ecclesiastical disputes. To his teaching in the classroom, Peter added preaching from the pulpit. Fifty-nine sermons have been preserved and, from a study of their construction and diction, B. Hauréau placed him among the best preachers of the 12th century. Among the works that have been attributed to Peter but of which he certainly was not the author, the most important are the *Glossae super sententias,* which remains anonymous, and the *Allegoriae super vetus et novum testamentum,* which belongs to Richard of Saint Victor [*The New Scholasticism* 9 (1935) 209–225].

Bibliography: PETER OF POITIERS, *Sententiarum libri quinque,* ed. H. MATHOUD (Paris 1655), repr. in *Patrologia Latina,* ed. J. P. MIGNE, 217 v., indexes 4 v. (Paris 1878–90), 211:789–1280. *Sententiae Petri Pictaviensis,* ed. P. S. MOORE and M. DULONG (Publications in Medieval Studies 7, 11; Notre Dame, Ind. 1943, 1950), critical ed. of bks. 1–2. *Allegoriae super tabernaculum Moysi,* ed. P. S. MOORE and J. S. CORBETT *(ibid.* 3; 1938). P. S. MOORE, *The Works of Peter of Poitiers* (*ibid.* 1; 1936), with extensive bibliog. of unpub. and pub. sources and secondary works, both books and articles.

[P. S. MOORE]

PETER OF RUFFIA, BL.

Inquisitor, martyr; b. Ruffia, Piedmont, Italy, *c.* March 1320; d. Susa, Piedmont, Feb. 2, 1365. Born of the noble Cambiani family, he entered the DOMINICANS when he was 16 years old. A brilliant student of Scripture, theology, and law, he directed his learning against the heretical WALDENSES. Because of his knowledge of Piedmont and its people, INNOCENT VI named him inquisitor general there in 1351. Peter worked in the Diocese of Turin until mid-January of 1365, when he began a tour of the Alpine valleys near Switzerland. At the Franciscan friary in Susa he was assassinated by two heretics. He is buried in the church of St. Dominic, Turin. PIUS IX approved his cult on Dec. 4, 1856.

Feast: Nov. 7.

Bibliography: *Acta Sanctorum* Nov. 3:684–686. I. TAURISANO, *Catalogus hagiographicus ordinis praedicatorum* (Rome 1918) 1:29–30. A. BUTLER, *The Lives of the Saints* (New York 1956) 4:291–292.

[A. DABASH]

PETER OF TARENTAISE, ST.

Archbishop; b. near Vienne, Dauphiné, France, 1102; d. Bellevaux, Sept. 14, 1174. Peter (Pierre), who was of poor peasant stock, joined the Cistercian abbey of Bonnevaux. In 1132 he became the first abbot of Tamié in Savoy, and in 1141 was elected archbishop of Tarentaise. He reformed his diocese, effectively supported ALEXANDER III against Emperor FREDERICK I Barbarossa, and, for the same pope, undertook several successful diplomatic missions. For his charity and healing powers, Peter was venerated as a saint even in his lifetime. He was canonized by CELESTINE III, May 10, 1191.

Feast: May 8; May 10 (Cistercians).

Bibliography: *Acta Sanctorum* May 7:317–345. J. M. CHEVRAY, *La Vie de Saint Pierre II, archevêque de Tarentaise* (Baume-les-Dames 1841). G. MÜLLER, ''Der hl Petrus, Erzbischof von Tarentaise,'' *Cistercienser-Chronik* 3 (1891). S. LENSSEN, *Hagiologium cisterciense* (Tilburg 1948–49). *Les Saints de tous les jours,* ed. A. MAI (Paris 1957). H. RIGUET, *Printemps en chrétienté, l'aventure spirituelle de saint Pierre de Tarentaise* (Mercury, Savoie 1967).

[L. J. LEKAI]

PETER OF TIFERNO (CAPUCCI), BL.

Dominican preacher and wonder-worker; b. Città di Castello (Tiferno), Italy, 1390; d. Cortona, Italy, Oct. 21, 1445. After being clothed in the Dominican habit (1405) and professed at Tiferno (1406), he was sent to St. Dominic's Priory, Cortona, where he began his preaching career. Austere, prayerful, and mortified, he developed in his preaching the theme of death with extraordinary power, performing miracles to move men to penance. His relics were placed in the main altar at Cortona (1597) and then moved to the church of St. Liberius, Colorno (1786); they were finally returned to St. Dominic's at Cortona. PIUS VII confirmed his cult on May 11, 1816.

Feast: Oct. 21.

Bibliography: P. ÁLVAREZ, *Santos, bienaventurados, venerables de la Orden de los Predicadores,* 4 v. (Vergara 1920–23) 2:176–178. I. TAURISANO, *Catalogus hagiographicus ordinis praedicatorum* (Rome 1918) 37. J. L. BAUDOT and L. CHAUSSIN, *Vies des saints et des bienheureux selon l'ordre du calendrier avec l'historique des fêtes* (Paris 1935–56) 10:673–674.

[B. CAVANAUGH]

PETER OF TREVI, ST.

Italian preacher; b. Roccabotte, near Subiaco, Italy; d. Trevi, Italy, Aug. 30, 1052. From the usual medieval tale of prodigy and marvel the story of his life emerges, verified by contemporary accounts and later papal documents. He was born in what is now Roccabotte, about ten miles from Subiaco and 20 from Trevi, the pivotal towns of his apostolate. As a young man he was introduced to Gregory, bishop of Tibur, who educated him for his ministry and conferred his TONSURE. He died after two years as a bitterly persecuted itinerant preacher in the region around Trevi. INNOCENT III canonized him Oct. 1, 1215. Later popes honored Peter as a patron of Subiaco and the ''holy protector'' of Trevi, where his relics are preserved. His aid is invoked as protection against wolves by the inhabitants of the neighboring countryside.

Feast: Aug. 30.

Bibliography: *Acta Sanctorum* Aug. 6:634–647.

[N. M. RIEHLE]

PETER OF VAUX-DE-CERNAY

French chronicler; b. *c.* 1194; d. after 1218. He became a CISTERCIAN monk at VAUX-DE-CERNAY near Paris, where his uncle Guy was abbot. He accompanied Guy on the Fourth Crusade. From 1212 on he was with the royal army in the war against the ALBIGENSES, and he became the historian of that war. His account, titled *Hystoria Albigensis,* begins in 1203 and ends in 1218, shortly before its author's death, undoubtedly. In it Peter was especially interested in extolling the exploits of Simon de Montfort l'Amaury, chief of the expedition, whom he admired. Peter's *Hystoria* is the work of a fierce adversary of heresy; it is a passionate but well-composed work, full of details that are precise and objective when relating the excesses and weaknesses of the Crusaders.

Bibliography: *Hystoria Albigensis,* ed. P. GUÉBIN and E. LYON, 3 v. (Paris 1926–39). *Histoire littéraire de la France* 17:246–254. U. CHEVALIER, *Répertoire des sources historiques du moyen-âge. Biobibliographie* (Paris 1905–07) 2:3753. A. BORST, *Die Katharer* (Stuttgart 1953). A. MERCATI and A. PELZER, *Dizionario ecclesiastico* (Turin 1954–58) 3:215.

[É. BROUETTE]

PETER OF VIENNA

Theologian; b. France; d. in 1183. He studied under Gilbert of Poitiers (d. 1154), and before 1155 went to Austria, where he became known as Master Peter of Vienna. To defend Gilbert, his teacher, he soon turned against Gerhoch of Reichersberg (d. 1169) who had been attacking the ''novel'' doctrines of the French schools since 1141. He accused Gerhoch mainly of not distinguishing clearly between Christ's divine person and his human nature. Peter and his friend HUGH OF HONAU wrote to Hugh Etherian, asking him to provide them with translations of passages in which Greek Fathers teach a distinction between nature and person in God. In 1179, Hugh's answer was brought to the West. Little is known about Peter's official task or position in Austria. As Master Peter he signed a charter issued in 1158 by Bishop Conrad of Passau. In a later document (1161) he is called a member of ''the Order of Chaplains'' (*de ordine cappelanorum*). He taught in Vienna and may have written a compendium of theology (MS Zwettl 109).

Bibliography: PETER OF VIENNA, letter addressed to Otto of Freising (d. 1158), ed. H. WEISWEILER, *Scholastik,* 13 (1938) 231–246; letter addressed to Hugh Etherian, ed. A. DONDAINE, *Archives d'histoire doctrinale et littéraire du moyen-âge* 27 (1952) 131–132. H. FICHTENAU, *Mitteilungen des Instituts für österreichische Geschichtsforschung* 63 (1955) 283–297.

[N. HARING]

PETER ORSEOLO, ST.

Doge of Venice, Benedictine recluse; b. Venice, 928; d. Cuxa Abbey, Prades, France, Jan. 10, 987. Married at age 18, Orseolo (Urseolus) and his wife lived in continence after the birth of a son. In 948 he commanded the fleet in a war against pirates. After a revolution (976) during which Doge Peter IV Candiano was murdered, Orseolo was elected doge of Venice. He promoted peace, built hospitals, and cared for widows, orphans, and pilgrims. Using his own money he began the reconstruction of St. Mark's Cathedral and the doge's palace, both having been destroyed in the revolution.

At Mass one day, Peter heard, ''And he who does not carry his cross and follow Me cannot be my disciple'' (Lk 14:26), and he determined to join Marinus and ROMUALD, hermits living in the Po Delta. They refused to accept him, but shortly afterward he met Abbot Guarin of Cuxa, the great reformer of northern Catalonia and southern France, who took Orseolo and two other Venetians, John Gradenego and Morosone, as well as the two hermits, back to CUXA ABBEY on Sept. 1, 978. Orseolo was immediately a model religious, seeking the most menial tasks and undertaking severe penances.

As for Venice and her affairs, Peter contented himself with instructing his son, Otto, then doge, in the virtues of a Christian ruler. After Peter's death a cult sprang up; his body was translated in 1027; his cult was approved for Cuxa and Venice in 1731 and later for all Benedictines and CAMALDOLESE.

PETER DAMIAN (*Vita s. Romualdi, Patrologia Latina,* ed. J. P. Migne [Paris 1878–90] 144:959–963) claimed that Orseolo entered Cuxa in reparation for his share in the revolt and murder of his doge predecessor. Orseolo's chaplain, John the Deacon of Venice (*Chronicon Venetum, Monumenta Germaniae Historica* [Berlin 1826–] Section: Scriptores. 7:4), gave other reasons. And while it is likely that the Candiano family deliberately fostered the story given in Damian's account, it remains a fact that Orseolo's election was somewhat mysterious. The piety of certain chronicles may conceal the factional strife to which Orseolo owed his office. Furthermore, mild and tolerant, he probably encouraged local mischief and was happy to go to a monastery to fulfill an old vow. Peter called himself duke of Venice, Dalmatia, and Croatia, a title that reflected his ambition rather than an historical reality.

Feast: Jan. 10.

Bibliography: *Vita* (1027) by a monk of Cuxa, in J. MABILLON, *Acta sanctorum ordinis S. Benedicti* 5:851–860. *Bibliotheca hagiographica latina antiquae et mediae aetatis* (Brussels 1898–1901) 2:6784–86. H. TOLRA, *St. Pierre Orséolo* (Paris 1897).

B. SCHMID, *Studien und Mitteilungen aus dem Benediktiner- und Cistercienser-Orden* 22 (1901) 71–112; 251281. A. M. ZIMMERMANN, *Kalendarium Benedictinum: Die Heiligen und Seligen des Benediktinerorderns und seiner Zweige* (Metten 1933–38) 1:81–84. R. CESSI, *Enciclopedia Italiana di scienzi, littere ed arti* (Rome 1929–39) 25:603. G. F. VON PÖLNITZ, *Venedig* (Munich 1949) 78–84. A. BUTLER, *The Lives of the Saints*, rev. ed. H. THURSTON and D. ATTWATER (New York 1956) 1:64–65.

[C. M. AHERNE]

PETER PAPPACARBONE, ST.

Bishop, monastic reformer; b. Salerno, Italy, *c.* 1038; d. March 4, 1123. He was a hermit at LA CAVA and received his formative monastic training in the BENEDICTINE order at CLUNY under Abbot HUGH OF CLUNY. Peter was responsible for the reform of the monastery of Cilento in 1068; and although he accepted the bishopric of Policastro in 1070, he returned after a few years to La Cava, became coadjutor abbot in 1076, and succeeded Abbot LEO OF CAVA in 1079. Peter imposed the Cluniac customs at La Cava and secured from GREGORY VII the establishment of a congregation on the Cluniac model, thus beginning the monastic reform of central Italy. Under his rule, La Cava's domestic organization was improved, and many religious houses were placed under its jurisdiction. His cult was approved in 1893, and his relics were enshrined under the high altar at La Cava.

Feast: March 4.

Bibliography: *Vita,* L. A. MURATORI, *Rerum italicarum scriptores, 500–1500,* 25 v. in 28 (Milan 1723–51) 6.5:16–28. P. GUILLAUME, *Essai historique sur l'abbaye de Cava* (Naples 1877). P. LUGANO, *L'Italia benedettina* (Rome 1929) 164–179. P. SCHMITZ, *Histoire de l'ordre de saint-Benoît,* 7 v. (Maredsous, Bel. 1942–56) 1:185–187. K. HALLINGER, *Gorze-Kluny,* 2 v. (*Studia anselmiana* 22–25; 1950–51) A. BUTLER, *The Lives of the Saints,* rev. ed. H. THURSTON and D. ATTWATER, 4 v. (New York 1956) 1:481. A. M. ZIMMERMANN, *Kalendarium Benedictinum: Die Heiligen und Seligen des Benediktinerorderns und seiner Zweige,* 4 v. (Metten 1933–38) 1:28:2–284.

[B. D. HILL]

PETER PASCUAL, ST.

Bishop and martyr; b. Valencia, Spain, 1227; d. Granada, Spain, Dec. 6, 1300. He was of noble birth. He became a doctor of theology in Paris and a priest (*c.* 1250), taught in Barcelona and administered the Diocese of Toledo (1266–75) for its young Archbishop Sancho, son of James I of Aragon. He then traveled on foot, performing works of mercy. In Paris, he defended the Immaculate Conception, and in 1296 he was consecrated bishop of Jaén by BONIFACE VIII in Rome. He was captured by the Moors in 1298 and died in prison. His relics are in the cathedral of Baeza; his cult was approved in 1673. Peter wrote several religious works in Catalan and Castillan and a gloss on the Lord's Prayer against the teachings of Judaism and Islam.

Feast: Dec. 6.

Bibliography: *Opera,* ed. P. A. VALENZUELA, 4 v. (Rome 1906–08). F. FITA, ed., *Bulls of Boniface VIII, Boletín de la Real Academia de la Historia* 20 (1892) 32–61. *Analecta Bollandiana* 23 (1904) 507–508; 58 (1940) 88. D. MANSILLA, *Lexikon für Theologie und Kirche,* ed. J. HOFER and K. RAHNER, 10 v. (2d, new ed. Freiburg 1957–65) 8:375. *Homenajes de las entidades culturales de Valencia a San Pedro Pascual en el III centenario de su canonización* (Valencia 1973), anonymous author. F. COLOMBO, *Resumen de la vida del glorioso mártir San Pedro Pasqual de Valencia,* ed. J. B. MEREGA (Valencia 1979). W. METTMANN, *Die volkssprachliche apologetische Literatur auf der Iberischen Halbinsel im Mittelalter* (Opladen 1987).

[E. P. COLBERT]

PETER PETRONI, BL.

Carthusian; b. Siena, Italy, 1311; d. there, May 29, 1361. He demonstrated great piety as a youth and devoted himself to the care of the sick and lepers. At the age of 17 he joined the CARTHUSIANS at the charterhouse of Maggiani near Florence. The prior there wished to ordain him a priest, but Peter, feeling himself unworthy of this office, cut off the index finger of his left hand in order to disqualify himself for ordination. He is reputed to have warned BOCCACCIO to mend his ways. Peter was venerated by the faithful for his many virtues during his lifetime, and numerous miracles are reported to have occurred at his tomb in the charterhouse, where his relics were translated some 60 years after his death. He is honored as blessed, although he has never been officially beatified; his tomb was for a long time the object of local pilgrimages. His vita was written by JOHN COLOMBINI.

Feast: May 29.

Bibliography: *Acta Sanctorum* May 7:184–228. L. LE VASSEUR, *Ephemerides ordinis cartusiensis,* 2 v. (Montreuil 1890) 2:169–270. A. BUTLER, *The Lives of the Saints* (New York 1956) 2:421–422. J. L. BAUDOT and L. CHAUSSIN, *Vies des saints et des bienheureux selon l'ordre du calendrier avec l'historique des fêtes* (Paris 1935–56) 5:574.

[B. J. COMASKEY]

PETER RIGA

Canon of Notre Dame of Reims, later canon regular of Saint-Denis, student at Paris (1165), prolific writer of Latin verse; b. *c.* 1140; d. 1209. Riga's fame rests on the

Aurora, a metrical paraphrase of most of the books of the Bible with allegorical interpretations and moral applications, completed toward the end of the 12th century. It incorporates pieces appearing originally in the *Floridus aspectus,* compiled *c.* 1162 at the request of Samson, archbishop of Reims. Recapitulations in 23 sections summarize the content of each book. These are ingeniously composed: in the first poem the letter "a" does not occur in any word, in the second, no "b," etc. Three successive editions of the *Aurora,* the last revision containing more than 15,000 lines, attest to its popularity. Educators recommended it to their pupils (MS Dresd. 120 is glossed for schoolroom use); poets freely appropriated it (Chaucer, *Book of the Duchess;* Gower, *Vox clamantis;* Macé de la Charité, Old French verse Bible); clerics and religious used it for devotional reading. The first printed text of the poem appeared in *Aurora Petri Rigae Biblia Versificata,* ed. P. E. Beichner, 2 v. (Notre Dame, Ind. 1965).

Bibliography: M. MANITIUS, *Geschichte der lateinischen Literatur des Mittelalters* (Munich 1911–31) 3:820–831. K. YOUNG, "Chaucer and Peter Riga," *Speculum* 12 (1937) 299–303. P. E. BEICHNER, "The Old French Verse 'Bible' of Macé de la Charité, a Translation of the *Aurora,*" *ibid.* 22 (1947) 226–239; "The *Cursor Mundi* and P. R.," *ibid.* 24 (1949) 239–250; "Gower's Use of *Aurora* in *Vox Clamantis,*" *ibid.* 30 (1955) 582–595; "La Bible versifiée de Jehan Malkaraume et l'*Aurora,*" *Moyen-âge* 61 (1955) 63–78; "The Champagne Letter Writer and P. R.," *Recherches de théologie ancienne et médiévale* 30 (1963) 336–340.

[M. I. J. ROUSSEAU]

PETER THE DEACON OF MONTE CASSINO

Librarian and forger; b. Rome, probably 1107; d. after 1153. Peter went as a boy to MONTE CASSINO. He was a deacon by 1128 when Abbot Seniorectus exiled him as a sympathizer of the deposed Abbot Oderisius II. After his recall in 1130, he became *bibliothecarius* and supervised the compilation of the chartulary of the monastery, the *Registrum Petri Diaconi.* In 1137 he defended Monte Cassino's stand during the schism before the German Emperor LOTHAIR III at Lago Pesole (*see* PIERLEONI).

Peter is known only from his own numerous writings, many of which survive in the autograph codices *Casinenses* 361 and 257. Both MSS contain his autobiography. His handwriting is therefore known; it is "an uneven ordinary minuscule" (Willard), not the Beneventan calligraphy used in the *Registrum Petri Diaconi* and the *Registrum s. Placidi,* a corpus of hagiographical works pertaining mainly to St. Placidus, composed by him. Hence, as Meyvaert proved, Peter "wrote" neither these MSS nor the *marginalia* of MS Munich Clm 4623 of LEO MARSICANUS of Ostia's Chronicle of Monte Cassino and of codex *Casinensis* 413 (*Translatio s. Mennatis*).

Many of Peter's writings are careless excerpts from the works of others (e.g., the exegetical treatises in codex *Casinensis* 257) or outright forgeries. He may be one of the most prolific and brazen forgers in history, and studies in progress will show him to have been a pathological case. Some of these forgeries center around saints such as Placidus or MAURUS, St. Benedict's pupils, or Mark of Atina, an alleged disciple of St. Peter, and are buttressed by works of his invention ascribed to earlier authorities. The Atina papers, believed to be lost, were rediscovered in 1951 and will be edited by H. Bloch. Peter's historical works include the *Liber illustrium virorum archisterii Casinensis* and the *Ortus et vita iustorum cenobii Casinensis,* dictionaries of Monte Cassino's outstanding men and saints. His exact contribution to the *Chronica mon. Casinensis,* started by Leo of Ostia, continued by his own teacher Guido, and brought up to 1138 by Peter himself, remains to be determined.

Bibliography: E. CASPAR, *Petrus Diaconus und die Monte Cassineser Fälschungen* (Berlin 1909), fundamental. H. BLOCH, "The Schism of Anacletus II and the Glanfeuil Forgeries of P. the D.," *Traditio* 8 (1952) 159–264. P. MEYVAERT "The Autographs of P. the D.," *The Bulletin of the John Rylands Library* 38 (1955) 114–138; "The Exegetical Treatises of P. the D.," *Sacris Erudiri* 14 (1963) 130–148. P. MEYVAERT and P. DEVOS, "Autour de Léon d'Ostie et de sa *Translatio S. Clementis,*" *Analecta Bollandiana* 74 (1956) 211–223, with ref. to the earlier articles by W. Smidt and H. W. Klewitz on the *Chronica Casin.* A. MANCONE, "Il Registrum P. D," *Bullettino dell'Archivio paleografico Italiano* 2–3 (1956–57) pt. 2:99–126. H. WOLTER, *Lexikon für Theologie und Kirche,* ed. J. HOFER and K. RAHNER (Freiberg 1957–65) 8:360–361.

[H. BLOCH]

PETER THE DEACON OF ROME, BL.

Friend and fellow student of Pope GREGORY I; d. Rome, *c.* 605. He came to Gregory's monastery of St. Andrew's in Rome, traveled to Sicily in the interest of the pope (590–592), and as subdeacon of the Roman church (592–593) was charged with caring for its temporalities. Created cardinal deacon, he was Gregory's constant companion and appears in the *Dialogues* (4.57) as the pope's partner in discussing the problems of the day. Peter is cited as evidence for the appearance of the Holy Spirit in the form of a dove inspiring Gregory and for certain marvels occurring at the pope's death (*Bibliotheca hagiographica latina antiquae et mediae aetatis* 3640–41); but both accounts are late and legendary. He was at first buried in Rome near Gregory; later his remains were translated to Vercelli, and since 1480 they have rested in Salussola, in the Diocese of Biella, Italy.

Feast: March 12.

Bibliography: *Acta Sanctorum* Mar. 2:208–209. J. MABILLON, *Acta sanctorum ordinis S. Benedicti* (Paris 1668–1701)

1:484–485. A. M. ZIMMERMANN, *Kalendarium Benedictinum: Die Heiligen und Seligen des Benediktinerorderns und seiner Zweige* (Metten 1933–38) 1:323.

[O. J. BLUM]

PETER THE HERMIT

Crusade preacher; b. Diocese of Amiens, *c.* 1050; d. Neufmoûtier Monastery, July 8, 1115. Peter's early career is obscure. He was known as Peter the Little to his contemporaries, who described him as short and swarthy, with a long, bony face. The name Peter the Hermit derived from the hermit's cloak he usually wore. He went barefoot at all seasons, never bathed, and abstained from bread and meat, subsisting mainly on fish and wine. He was probably not present when Pope URBAN II proclaimed the First CRUSADE in November of 1095, but shortly thereafter Peter was preaching the crusade to enthusiastic audiences in northern France. By April of 1096, when his recruits left Cologne, Peter had collected a numerous army, which he led through Hungary and the Balkan provinces of Byzantium to Constantinople. In Asia Minor, most of Peter's forces were quickly annihilated by the Turks. Peter and the few survivors fled to Constantinople and joined the ranks of the major crusading armies in the spring of 1097. At Antioch in 1098 he deserted from the crusade but was brought back in disgrace. After the capture of Jerusalem in 1099, Peter returned to the West and became prior of the Canons Regular of St. Augustine at Neufmoûtier, near Huy, Belgium.

Feast: July 8.

Bibliography: ALBERT OF AACHEN, ''Historia Hierosolymitana,'' in *Recueil des historiens,* 16 v. (Paris 1841–1906) *Historiens occidentaux* 4:265–713. H. HAGENMEYER, *Peter der Eremite* (Leipzig 1879). A. WAAS, *Lexikon für Theologie und Kirche,* ed. J. HOFER and K. RAHNER, 10 v. (2d, new ed. Freiburg 1957–65) 8:333. J. FLORI, *Pierre l'ermite et la première croisade* (Paris 1999).

[J. A. BRUNDAGE]

PETER THE PAINTER

Latin poet, known also as Petrus Pictor; fl. *c.* 1100. All that is known of this remarkable figure is that he was a canon of the cathedral at Saint-Omer, where he probably received his education. By 1120 a number of his poems are already to be found in the *Liber floridus,* a compilation of LAMBERT OF SAINT-OMER. These works are typical of the *carmina,* or short poems, produced in the cathedral and monastic schools of the late 11th and early 12th centuries, and Peter is one of the better authors to practice this genre. Mention should be made of his eloquent *Contra simoniam,* a bitter attack against the Roman clergy in 70 rhyming hexameters, and his *De sacra Eucharistia,* which explores the nature and doctrine of the EUCHARIST in 688 verses. The *De vita Pilati* presents in 369 rhyming couplets the various legends concerning Pontius PILATE; the *Dominus vobiscum* is a 152-verse satire on clerical ignorance and materialism; and the *De illa quae . . . filium adamavit* is a drama in 246 leonine hexameters on a classical theme. Peter was also the author of the charming *De laude Flandriae,* written—judging from internal evidence—between 1100 and 1110; it is a poem of 43 hexameter lines with a variety of rhyme combinations, a eulogy in praise of his native Flanders. Seventeenth-century scholars often attributed much of this author's work to either PETER OF BLOIS or HILDEBERT OF LAVARDIN, but more recent research has assured Peter his rightful place in literary history.

Bibliography: Works. *Contra simoniam, Monumenta Germaniae Historica Libelli de lite,* (Berlin 1826–) 3:708–10; *Dominus vobiscum* in *Notices et extraits des manuscrits de la Bibliothèque nationale et autres bibliothèques* (Paris 1884) 31a:130–132; *De sacra Eucharistia, Patrologia Latina,* ed. J. P. MIGNE, 217 v., indexes 4 v. (Paris 1878–90) 207:1135–54; *De illa quae impudenter filium suum adamavit,* in B. HAURÉAU, ed., *Notices et extraits de quelques manuscrits latins de la Bibliothèque nationale,* 6 v. (Paris 1890–93) 5:220–226; *De laude Flandriae,* ed. W. WATTENBACH, *Neues Archiv der Gesellschaft für ältere deutsche Geschichtskunde* 18 (1893) 509–510. A. BOUTEMY, ''Quelques oeuvres inédites de Pierre le Peintre,'' *Latomus* 7 (1948) 51–69. Literature. *Histoire littéraire de la France* (repr. Paris 1865) 13:429–433. L. WILLEMS in *Biographie nationale de Belgique* 17:466–470. M. MANITUS, *Geschichte der lateinischen Literatur des Mittelalters,* 3 v. (Munich 1911–31) 3:877–883. É. AMANN, *Dictionnaire de théologie catholique,* ed. A. VACANT et al, 15 v. (Paris 1903–50; Tables générales 1951–) 12.2:2036–38. W. WATTENBACH, *Deutschlands Geschichtsquellen im Mittelalter. Deutsche Kaiserzeit,* ed. R. HOLTZMANN, v. 1.1–4 (3d ed. Tübingen 148; repr. of 2d ed. 1938–43) 1.4:710773. E. R. CURTIUS, *European Literature and the Latin Middle Ages,* tr. W. R. TRASK (New York 1953) 472. F. J. E. RABY, *A History of Secular Latin Poetry in the Middle Ages,* 2 v. (2d ed. Oxford 1957) 2:2630.

[B. J. COMASKEY]

PETER THE VENERABLE, BL.

Ninth abbot of Cluny (*see* CLUNY, ABBEY OF) and a significant personality in the monastic and literary renaissance of 12th-century Europe; b. Auvergne, *c.* 1092; d. Cluny, Dec. 25, 1156. Committed to Cluniac life as an oblate at an early age by his noble parents, Peter made his profession at Cluny under St. HUGH (1109). During the troubled administration of Pons de Melgeuil (1109–22) he was advanced to claustral prior at VÉZELAY, then to conventual prior at Domène, and finally swept by acclamation to the abbatial throne, Aug. 22,

1122, to rule the 300 to 400 monks at Cluny and the 2,000 dependent houses throughout western Europe. Although unable to check Cluny's decline beyond his lifetime, and eclipsed by St. BERNARD OF CLAIRVAUX in ecclesiastic as well as monastic spheres, Peter struck a note, remarkable in a polemic age, of peace and reasonableness in official and personal contacts and through the letters, tracts, and other writings by which he is known (*Patrologia Latina,* 189:15–1072). He was the last of the great "holy abbots,"—humane administrator, a controversialist, and an "occasional" theologian—and was much esteemed as a counselor. He won reconciliation for Peter ABELARD after the Council of Sens (1140), but his attempts to divert the crusading spirit from combat and conquest to dialogue and conversion went unheeded. He was called "venerable" in his lifetime by both St. Bernard and Frederick Barbarossa; his cult at Clermont was approved by Pius IX in 1862.

Feast: Dec. 29.

Bibliography: G. CONSTABLE and J. KRITZECK, eds, *Petrus Venerabilis, 1156–1956: Studies and Texts Commemorating the 8th Anniversary of His Death* (*Studia anselmiana,* 40; 1956), bibliog. of classic sources and continuing study. D. KNOWLES, *The Bulletin of the John Rylands Library* 39 (1956) 132–145. G. CONSTABLE, ed., *The Letters of Peter the Venerable* (Cambridge 1967). J. MARTIN and G. CONSTABLE, eds., *Peter the Venerable: Selected Letters* (Toronto 1974). *Pierre Abélard, Pierre le Vénérable,* proceedings of colloquium at Cluny Abbey, July 2–9, 1972 (Paris 1975). *Petrus Venerabilis, Adversus Iudaeos,* ed., Centre de Traitement Electronique des Documents (CETEDOC), Catholic University of Leuven (Turnhout 1985). J. L. BAUDOT and L. CHAUSSIN, *Vies des saints et des bienheureux selon l'ordre du calendrier avec l'historique des fêtes,* (Paris 1935–56) 12:674–678, bibliog. J. KRITZECK, *Peter the Venerable and Islam* (Princeton 1964). J. P. TORRELL and D. BOUTHILLIER, *Pierre le Vénérable, Abbé de Cluny* (Chambray 1988).

[P. EDWARDS]

PETER THOMAE

Franciscan scholastic (Petrus Thomae); b. probably in Compostella or nearby, *c.* 1280; d. *c.* 1340. Peter was lector at the Franciscan *studium generale* of Barcelona sometime after 1317 (more likely after 1322), and seems to have continued teaching until 1333. In that year he became apostolic penitentiary at Avignon. Nothing is known of him after 1336 although some older writers, confusing him with the Carmelite, St. Peter Thomas (d. 1366), Bishop of Patti in Sicily, claimed he ended his days as a bishop.

At least nine works of theology and philosophy are known to be from Peter Thomae. Of his *Sentences* only a reportation of the first book is extant. This is followed by his *De esse intelligibili,* nine questions on the ontological status of ideas both in creatures and in God, perhaps an answer to a work of like title by WILLIAM OF ALNWICK. The 15 (unpublished) questions on being (*De ente*) appear to be merely the first part of a work on the TRANSCENDENTALS in general; it defends Scotus's doctrine of BEING, ANALOGY, and univocity, and gives some attention to the attacks on RICHARD OF CONINGTON. Peter again reveals his debt to Duns Scotus in two works on formalities about the formal distinction and its applications. Both seem to have brought Peter considerable fame in the late Middle Ages. The *Quodlibet,* one of his later works, is incomplete in the only extant manuscript (ed. M. R. Hooper and E. M. Buytaert, St. Bonaventure, New York 1957). While Peter's last philosophical work was the *De unitate minori,* there is considerable evidence that he wrote a commentary on Aristotle's *Metaphysics* and perhaps on the *Physics.*

In the field of theology, Peter wrote the exegetic-moral work "On the Christian Rich Man," as well as the more important *Liber de originali Virginis innocentia.* This is the first extensive defense of the IMMACULATE CONCEPTION after those of Duns Scotus and PETER AUREOLI (both of which are primary sources for the theological reasoning); it contains the first earnest effort to find positive support for the doctrine in Sacred Scripture. Unfortunately, the work did not exert a real influence until 50 or more years after its appearance when it was used by Peter of Candia (later antipope ALEXANDER V), Andrew of Neufchâteau, John Vitalis, and John of Segovia.

In his own day, Peter Thomae was called "a great Scotist" and given the titles *Doctor strenuus, invincibilis, proficuus,* and *serenus.* He is viewed today as a faithful disciple of the Subtle Doctor, important for his clarifications of the Scotist synthesis (*see* SCOTISM).

Bibliography: É. BUYTAERT, "The Scholastic Writings of Petrus Thomae," in J. AUER and H. VOLK, eds., *Theologie in Geschichte und Gegenwart* (Munich 1957). G. G. BRIDGES, *Identity and Distinction in Petrus Thomae OFM* (St. Bonaventure, N.Y. 1959). A. MAIERU, "Logica e Teologia Trinitaria ne Commento Alle Sentenze Attributo a Petrus Tomae," in J. JOLIVET, Z. KALUZA, and A. DE LIBERA, eds., *Lectionum Varietates: Hommage à Paul Vignaux, 1904–1987* (Paris 1998), 177–198. I. BRADY, "The Later Years of Petrus Thomae," in *Studia Mediaaevalia et Mariologica* (Rome 1971), 249–257.

[I. C. BRADY]

PETER TO ROT, BL.

Martyr, married man, father, lay catechist; b. Rakunai, New Britain Island, northeast of Papua New Guinea, *c.* 1912; d. Vunaiara, Papua New Guinea, *c.* 1945.

As the son of the local chieftain, Angelo To Puia and his wife Maria la Tumul, Peter was baptized by the Missionaries of the Sacred Heart when his father invited his people to become Catholics. During his 40 years as chieftain, Angelo promoted the faith, but felt it was unwise for his son Peter—or any of the new Christians—to become priests or religious. He did allow Peter to study at Saint Paul's Mission School (1930–33) to become a catechist. After receiving his diploma, Peter taught effectively in Rakunai. He married (Nov. 11, 1936) another Catholic, Paula La Varpit, with whom he had three children (the last born shortly after Peter's death).

When the Japanese invaded (1942), the clergy and religious were imprisoned; however, Peter was allowed to continue his work. In the absence of priests, he led other laity in ministering to the extent permitted them: baptizing, witnessing marriages, visiting the sick with the presanctified Eucharist, conducting communion services, catechizing, and running charitable organizations. He even built a church from branches on the outskirts of the village to replace one destroyed by the Japanese.

Peter protested against the 1945 Japanese prohibition against Christian religious instruction and worship, as well as the imposition of polygamy. For this he was arrested (1945) and beaten repeatedly during his two-month incarceration in a cave. Finally he was killed for refusing to espouse polygamy. A fellow prisoner, Arap To Binabak, testified to Peter's martyrdom.

Pope John Paul II beatified him at Port Moresby, Papua New Guinea, on Jan. 17, 1995. In his address to the bishops of Papua New Guinea and the Solomon Islands during their *ad limina* visit (Nov. 30, 1998), John Paul II pointed to Peter To Rot as an example that young people "have a role and responsibility in the Church's life" that must be encouraged.

Feast: July 7.

Bibliography: *The Martyrs of Papua New Guinea: 333 Missionary Lives Lost during World War II*, ed. T. AERTS (Port Moresby 1994). *Acta Apostolicae Sedis* (1995): 166–68.

[K. I. RABENSTEIN]

PETERBOROUGH, ABBEY OF

Former BENEDICTINE monastery in the town of the same name, Northamptonshire, England. The original monastery, called Medehamstede, was founded *c.* 655 by King Peada of Mercia and by Saxulf, the first abbot. Destroyed by the NORMANS in 870, it was restored *c.* 970 by ETHELWOLD OF WINCHESTER. It proved to be an important Anglo-Saxon monastery, especially under Abbot Leofric, who died in the year of the Norman Conquest, 1066. Peterborough continued to be one of the wealthiest and most important abbeys in Anglo-Norman England. The year after Abbot Arnulf of Beauvais was made bishop of Rochester in 1115, the abbey church burned. It was rebuilt in Norman style (with later emendations) and consecrated by ROBERT GROSSETESTE in 1237. BENEDICT OF PETERBOROUGH, chronicler of BECKET and friend of King Richard I, the Lion-Heart, was abbot from 1177 to 1193. The Black Death reduced the number of monks there from 64 to 32. In 1534 the abbot and monks subscribed to the Act of Supremacy, and when King HENRY VIII created the new Anglican diocese of Peterborough, comprised of Northampton and Rutland, the last abbot, John Chambers, became the first Anglican bishop, while the abbey church became the cathedral in 1541. CATHERINE OF ARAGON is buried there, as was MARY STUART, Queen of Scots, until transferred to WESTMINSTER ABBEY in 1612.

Bibliography: Sources. *The Peterborough Chronicle,* ed. C. PLUMMER in *Two of the Saxon Chronicles Parallel,* 2 v. (Oxford 1892–99). *The Peterborough Chronicle, 1070–1154,* ed. C. CLARK (London 1958). *The Peterborough Chronicle,* tr. G. N. GARMONSWAY in *The Anglo-Saxon Chronicle* (New York 1953). W. T. MELLOWS, ed., *The Last Days of Peterborough Monastery* (Kettering 1947); *Peterborough Local Administration* (Kettering 1941). *Carte nativorum: A Peterborough Abbey Cartulary of the 14th Century,* ed. C. N. L. BROOKE and M. M. POSTAN (London 1960). Literature. W. DUGDALE, *Monasticon Anglicanum* (London 1655–73); best ed. by J. CALEY et al., 6 v. (1817–30) 1:344–404. J. BRITTON, *History and Antiquities of the Abbey and Cathedral Church of Peterborough* (London 1828). *The Victoria History of the County of Northampton,* ed. W. R. D. ADKINS et al. (Westminster, Eng. 1902–). L. H. COTTINEAU, *Répertoire topobibliographique des abbayes et prieurés,* 2 v. (Mâcon 1935–39) 2:2262–63. D. KNOWLES and R. N. HADCOCK, *Medieval Religious Houses: England and Wales* (New York 1953) 73, 299, 34.7. D. KNOWLES, *The Monastic Order in England, 943–1216* (2d ed. Cambridge, Eng. 1962). D. KNOWLES, *The Religious Orders in England,* 3 v. (Cambridge, Eng. 1948–60). F. L. CROSS, *The Oxford Dictionary of the Christian Church* (London 1957) 1057.

[M. J. HAMILTON]

PETER'S PENCE

Originally an Anglo-Saxon tax of obscure origin, paid to the Holy See and theoretically levied on every English hearth not specially exempted. It was probably distinct from money gifts made to Rome by the rulers of newly converted subkingdoms, such as that by King OFFA OF MERCIA. It seems, rather, to have originated under King ALFRED THE GREAT OF WESSEX, at least as early as 889, and to have been imposed throughout the English kingdom built up by him and his immediate successors. The practical difficulties of collecting such a tax under contemporary conditions were not inconsiderable, but payment was regular for some time, being annual under EDWARD THE CONFESSOR. If a later authority is to be believed, the proceeds were originally shared between the Roman See itself and the Schola Saxonum at Rome.

In the reign of King WILLIAM I the Conqueror the tax was in arrears: these payments were requested by Pope ALEXANDER II in a letter that also asserted a claim to feudal suzerainty over England, though it is not certain that the two claims were connected. William consented to pay the traditional Peter's Pence but rejected the claim to feudal suzerainty. Collection of the tax continued to be difficult, and in the course of the 12th century payment was commuted into an annual payment of 299 marks (£199 6s 8d) for which each diocese was assessed according to its means. Prosperity and population were then increasing, with the result that the bishops who levied Peter's Pence were making a profit from the transaction. Pope INNOCENT III protested vigorously but fruitlessly against this, and all attempts to increase the valuation proved quite unsuccessful.

In later times the sum involved was usually small, and payment of it was irregular. By the time of the Reformation, Peter's Pence was a very small item in the complex financial relationship of the English Church and the papacy. It was abolished by King HENRY VIII in 1534 (25 Henry VIII, *c.* 21) along with other payments.

It seems that during the Middle Ages not only was Peter's Pence (called also Rome-Scot, *heorðpaenning*, denarius, or *census s. Petri*) extended into Ireland and Wales, but the denarius-per-household was offered the Holy See by the northern nations whose religious background had known England's influence, e.g., Sweden, Norway, and Iceland. Other areas, such as Hungary, Istria, Dalmatia, and Poland, may also have paid a ''Peter's Pence'' distinct from their feudal tribute. As in England, Peter's Pence in these areas did not survive the Reformation.

The modern Peter's Pence collection originated under Pope Pius IX in the 1860s as a subsidy to compensate the papacy for the loss of revenue from the STATES OF THE CHURCH. Through the encyclical *Saepe venerabiles fratres* (1871), it was given official approval. Even after the Lateran Pacts, it remains a free offering of Catholic dioceses to the pope.

Bibliography: O. JENSEN, ''The *Denarius Sancti Petri* in England,'' *Transactions of the Royal Historical Society,* NS 15 (1901) 171–247. S. L. OLLARD et al., eds., *A Dictionary of English Church History* (Milwaukee 1912; 3d ed. New York 1948) 457–458. W. E. LUNT, *Financial Relations of the Papacy with England to 1327* (Cambridge, Mass. 1939) 3–84.

[M. J. HAMILTON]

PETERSHAUSEN, ABBEY OF

Former BENEDICTINE monastery on the Rhine River, near Constance, Germany (Latin, *Petridomus*). It was founded by Bp. GEBHARD II of Constance (983), who built the abbey church facing west in imitation of St. Peter's, Rome, and decorated it with magnificent frescoes and wood, silver and gold ornamentation. The bishop enshrined there the head of Pope Gregory I the Great, which he had brought from Rome (hence Gregory was first patron, Gebhard second). The original monks were from EINSIEDELN. The HIRSAU Reform was introduced by Bp. GEBHARD III. Under Abbot Theoderic (1086–1116), Petershausen monks went to Andelsbuch, MEHRERAU, KASTL, NERESHEIM, Wagenhausen, and Fischingen, at the request of those houses. After the fire of 1159 the Constance architect Wezilo (1162–80) built the new cruciform basilica. The first provincial chapter of the Mainz-Bamberg province of Benedictines was held there in 1417, with all Benedictines at the Council of CONSTANCE in attendance. The abbey was in a poor financial and domestic state in the mid-15th and early 16th century, but after 1519, under Abbot J. Merk, there was improvement. The Reformation in Constance forced the monks to leave their monastery from 1529 to 1549, and its buildings were a ''quarry'' for the bridge being built across the Rhine. In 1583, Pope Gregory XIII incorporated the Benedictine monastery of STEIN AM RHEIN and the Kingenzell provostry into the revived Petershausen. Abbot Wunibald Saur (1671–85), the ''second founder'' of the abbey, was a good administrator, and he undertook much building activity in the parishes dependent on the abbey and in the monastery itself. In 1769 Petershausen gained the status of an independent imperial abbey. It was suppressed in 1802, and its goods were assigned to the state of Baden. The church was demolished in 1832; its columned, Romanesque portal is preserved in the Landesmuseum, Karlsruhe. The abbey archives are in Karlsruhe Generallandesarchiv; the library is in Heidelberg University Library. The monastic buildings are presently a barracks.

Bibliography: *Life of Gebhard and the Petershausen Chronicle,* written *c.* 1156 by an unnamed monk, *Monumenta Germaniae Historica: Scriptores* (Berlin 1826–) 10:582–594. P. LINDNER, *Professbuch von Wessobrunn* (Kempten 1909). P. MOTZ, ''Die Neubauten der ehemaligen Benediktiner- und Reichsabtei Petershausen bei Konstanz im 18. Jahrhundert,'' *Schriften des Vereins für Geschichte des Bodensees* 79 (1961). J. N. HAUNTINGER, *Reise dutch Schwaben und Bayern im Jahre 1784* (Weissenhorn 1964), with illustrations and bibliography.

[G. SPAHR]

PETERSON, JOHN BERTRAM

Bishop, educator; b. Salem, Mass., July 15, 1871; d. Manchester, New Hampshire, March 15, 1944. Peterson studied at the Marist College in Van Buren, Maine, and at St. Anselm's College, Manchester, New Hampshire, before entering St. John's Seminary in Boston, Mass. He was ordained on Sept. 15, 1899 and spent two years studying church history at the Institut Catholique in Paris and at universities in Rome. Upon returning to St. John's Seminary, he became professor of church history, and two years later, professor of moral theology, a post he held for 20 years. While rector of St. John's (1911–26), he was named domestic prelate and held the archdiocesan posts of tribunal judge, defender of the bond, synodal examiner, moderator of ecclesiastical conferences, and consultor. In 1926 he was appointed pastor of St. Catherine of Genoa parish, Somerville, Massachusetts, and a year later was named titular bishop of Hippo and auxiliary to the archbishop of Boston. He was consecrated on Nov. 10, 1927. On the death of Bp. George A. Guertin, he was named to the See of Manchester and installed on July 14, 1932.

In New Hampshire, his influence was felt through his efforts to alleviate industrial problems. On the national scene, he was one of the founders (1904) of the National Catholic Educational Association and served as its president for five years. In 1930 President Herbert Hoover appointed him to a national commission that surveyed the U.S. educational system. He was vice chairman of the Administrative Council of the National Catholic Welfare Conference and episcopal chairman of its education department. He served as a trustee of both the Catholic University of America in Washington, D.C., and of the North American College in Rome. In 1934 he was named an assistant at the pontifical throne.

[J. J. MARKHAM]

PETIT, LOUIS

Archbishop and orientalist; b. Vuiz-laChiésaz (Haute-Savoie), France, Feb. 21, 1868; d. Menton (Alpes-Maritimes), France, Nov. 5, 1927. After joining the ASSUMPTIONISTS (1885) in Osma, Spain, where they had taken refuge from France, he made his perpetual profession at Livry near Paris (1887), studied at Rome, was ordained (1891), and then went to the East. From 1895, when he became superior of the scholasticate at Kadiköy (formerly Chalcedon), Turkey, he devoted himself to the religious past of Byzantium. In 1897 he founded the periodical *Échos d'Orient,* which he directed for the next decade, while contributing to other learned journals. As a member of the Russian Archeological Institute and the Greek literary Syllogue of Constantinople, he explored MOUNT ATHOS with Jules Pargoire in 1901 and 1905, and published his findings, together with M. Millet, in *Recueil des inscriptions chrétiennes de l'Athos* (1904). Together with other scholars, he edited *Les Chartes des monastères grecs* (5 v. 1903–11). In collaboration with Jean B. Martin, he was editor for the reprinting and continuation of MANSI, *Sacrorum Conciliorum collectio* (60 v., 1899–1927). Petit was responsible for 12 of the additional volumes, including five on Vatican Council I. He went to Rome in 1908 and acted as adviser to the Armenian Catholic bishops who met there in council (1911). When he became Latin archbishop of Athens and apostolic delegate to Greece (1912), he continued his scholarly labors and won recognition from even the most rigid Orthodox. He was instrumental in the foundation of the Pontifical Oriental Institute (1917) and of the Roman Congregation for the Oriental Church, for which he acted as consultor. In 1926 he resigned the archbishopric of Athens, and became titular archbishop of Corinth. His *Bibliographie des acolouthies grecques* appeared in 1926. Petit contributed to the *Dictionnaire de théologie catholique* numerous articles concerning Greek ecclesiastical writers and a long, highly regarded article on Armenia.

Bibliography: S. SALAVILLE, *Mgr. Louis Petit, Échos d'Orient* 15 (1912) 97–105; 27 (1938) 129–137. *Ibid.* 137–144, bibliog. of P.'s works. J. RODRIGO, "Necrologia," *Religion y Cultura* 1 (1928) 147–160. R. JANIN, *Dictionnaire de théologie catholique* 12.1:1345.

[J. DAOUST]

PETIT-DIDIER, MATTHIEU

Benedictine theologian; b. St. Nicholas-du-Port (Lorraine), Dec. 18, 1659; d. Senones (Lorraine), June 15, 1728. After his early studies with the Jesuits at Nancy, he entered the Abbey of St. Mihiel (1675), where he was appointed professor of theology and philosophy (1682). He was elected abbot of St. Leopold in Nancy (1705–08; 1711–15), and of Senones (1715). His *Traité théologique pour l'autorité et l'infaillibilité du pape* (Luxembourg 1724) was attacked by the Jansenists and suppressed by the parlements of Metz (June 8, 1724) and of Paris (July 1, 1724). After his appointment as titular bishop of Macra in 1725, he lived in Senones until his death. Other of his works are *Remarques sur la Bibliothèque ecclésiastique de M. Dupin* (Paris 1691–93); *Dissertation historique et théologique dans laquelle on examine quel a été le sentiment du Concile de Constance et des principaux théologiens qui y ont assisté, sur l'autorité du pape et sur son infaillibilité* (Luxembourg 1724); *Dissertationes historico-critico-chronologicae in Vetus Testa-*

mentum (Toul 1699); *Justification de la morale et de la discipline de Rome et de route l'Italie* (1727).

Bibliography: J. CARREYRE, *Dictionnaire de théologie catholique,* ed. A. VACANT et al., 15 v. (Paris 1903–50; Tables générales 1951—) 12:1346–48, bibliog. H. HURTER, *Nomenclator literarius theologiae catholicae,* 5 v. in 6 (3d ed. Innsbruck 1903–13) 4:1108–10. G. HEER, *Lexikon für Theologie und Kirche,* ed. J. HOFER and K. RAHNER, 10 v. (2d, new ed. Freiburg 1957–65) 8:323. O. L. KAPSNER, *A Benedictine Bibliography: An Author-Subject Union List,* 2 v. (2d ed. Collegeville, Minn. 1962) 1:444.

[N. R. SKVARLA]

PETITE ÉGLISE

The ''Little Church'' was a schism that arose in France and French-controlled territories in Belgium because of opposition to the CONCORDAT OF 1801 and the related Organic Articles. In accordance with article three of this concordat, Pius VII issued the brief *Tam multa* (Aug. 15, 1801) requiring the resignation of the entire hierarchy in French territories in order that new appointments could be made to all sees. Obedience to this unprecedented exercise of papal authority was particularly difficult for clerics imbued with GALLICANISM. In June 1802 Joseph Fouché, French Minister of Police, demanded that bishops and priests swear by oath their adhesion to the concordat and recognize the newly appointed bishops. In London (April 6, 1803) 36 bishops who had refused to resign their sees, joined by two others who had previously submitted, claimed that they alone retained jurisdiction over their dioceses. Eventually all of them submitted, but two of them delayed their submission for several years, during which they encouraged priests and laymen to follow their example. Many priests were the more ready to do so because they too were removed from office. Bishop de Coucy, formerly of La Rochelle, submitted in 1817 and was made archbishop of Reims. Bishop de Thémines, formerly of Blois, was the principal figure in the origin of the schism. His followers claimed that in virtue of extraordinary powers conferred on bishops during the French Revolution and never retracted, De Thémines retained a jurisdiction that had no territorial limitations. Eventually De Thémines severed relations with the Jansenistically inclined Petite Église of Lyons. Shortly before his death (1829) in exile in Brussels, he submitted to the pope and received the Last Rites. By 1850 the communities had lost all their priests. The schism declined in membership, but three groups still existed without priests. In 1955 the Petite Église of Lyons had about 400 members; the Petite Église in the Vendée region another 3,500; and the Stevenists, named after Canon Corneille Stevens (d. 1828), in Belgium approximately 400, concentrated around Leerbeeck and especially in the small village of Hal. Although these Petites Églises were independent of one another, they all maintained similar religious practices. Pius XII, as well as his predecessors, repeatedly sought reunion with these groups and eased the way to return by not requiring individuals to make a formal abjuration of schismatic beliefs.

Bibliography: C. LATREILLE, *L'Opposition religieuse au Concordat de 1792 à 1803* (Paris 1910); *Après le Concordat: L'Opposition de 1803 à nos jours* (Paris 1910); *La Petite Église de Lyon* (Lyons 1911). E. MANGENOT, *Dictionnaire de théologie catholique*, ed. A. VACANT et al., (Paris 1903–50) 1.2:1372–78. R. DE CHAUVIGNY, *La Résistance au Concordat de 1801* (Paris 1921). C. G. VAN RIEL, *Internationale kirchliche Zeitschrift* 28 (1938) 30–43, 65–77, 141–155. E. TORFS, *Le Stévenisme dans le sudouest du Brabant* (Enghien 1955). C. DE CLERCQ, *Dictionnaire de droit canonique*, ed. R. NAZ (Paris 1935–65) 6:1438–47.

[L. P. MAHONEY]

PETRARCH, FRANCESCO

Italian poet and humanist; b. Arezzo, July 20, 1304; d. Arquà, July 19, 1374. He was the son of one of the Florentine Whites who were banished with DANTE (*see* GUELFS AND GHIBELLINES). His father, a notary, frustrated in his hope that the coming of Emperor Henry VII would open the way for his return to Florence, moved (1312) to Avignon, the seat of the papacy, after Henry's failure. The town, however, was so overcrowded that the family had to find a home in Carpentras, about 15 miles from the court. There young Francesco attended grammar school under Convenevole da Prato; it was probably he who aroused in the youth a lifelong love for Latin eloquence. At the age of 12, Francesco was sent to the famous university at Montpellier to begin the study of civil law. He remained there four years and then with his brother, Gherardo, went to Bologna to continue his law studies, remaining there until his 21st year. How much progress he made in the legal studies to which his father had set him is not known, but it is clear that he was attracted by other interests: as early as Montpellier he had acquired some works of Latin literature, including the works of Cicero; his father had opposed this interest and even burned some of the books but finally allowed Francesco to have Vergil and the *Rhetorica ad Herennium,* falsely ascribed to Cicero. In 1325 he bought a copy of *De civitate Dei* of St. Augustine, the author who (with Cicero) was to dominate his thought.

At that time the association between classical studies and religious aspirations that became the central theme of his life was probably to some degree already established in his mind. He stated later that the harmonious beauty of the classic language was at first the chief attraction and that he was to discover, ''under the cortex,'' the fruit, the moral value, only some years later. But then the conviction that the classics could be the basic element of Christian perfection became firm and ineradicable in his mind. During those years in Bologna, literature, especially poetry, was his chief love, and that stay was above all decisive in his formation as a poet in the vernacular. He encountered the poetry of Guido Guinizelli (1230?–76) and Cino da Postoia (*c.* 1270–1337) and probably began to write poems in Italian. His father's death (1326) marked the end of young Petrarch's life of intimate literary friendships in a prosperous, cultured, and peaceful town. Upon his return to Avignon he abandoned any thought of a legal career and for some years spent his time in fashionable ease, writing verses, meeting people, and taking an excessive care of his own appearance in an effort to attract attention. In 1327 he met a young woman, Laura, who became his lifelong love. His affection was unreciprocated but endured as a dream-fantasy to be ceaselessly relived in poetry.

Abandonment of Neoplatonism. Realizing the need to order his life, Petrarch became a cleric and probably took minor orders in 1330. Perhaps he thus sought refuge from unhappy love; perhaps he thought that a dream-love was not incompatible with a clerical status. At any rate, he shared for a time the view of the poets of the *dolce stil nuovo* that beauty and love lead to perfection. At a certain point, however, he fully realized that love can be an estrangement from God and not a ladder to Heaven. With deep Christian awareness he refuted the neoplatonic, pagan theories of the dolcestinovist poets in his *Secretum* (1342), yet he was not able, at that time, to free himself from the passion that had so affected him. Finally, after Laura's death in the plague of 1348, he was reluctant to dismiss thoughts then tempered with a deep sense of remorse and repentance and a sincere longing for God's mercy. Laura had become the symbol of the fascination of the beauties of the world and at the same time a challenge God had given him to prove his soul.

Petrarch entered the service of Cardinal Giovanni Colonna, serving as a household chaplain until 1337 and later enjoying the cardinal's friendship and generous patronage. He traveled widely, searching for books in monastic libraries; in Liège, for instance, he found copies of two orations of Cicero. About 1333 Petrarch had become a friend of the Augustinian monk Dionigi da San Sepolcro, the man who probably most deeply influenced his life. Dionigi gave him a miniature copy of the *Confessions* of St. Augustine, which he carried about with him until his death. The Augustinian, a man of vast erudition and deep piety, probably encouraged Petrarch in his love for classical literature. Petrarch had discovered by himself, however, the sterility of late scholastic culture. In contrast to the syllogisms and the garrulous arguments of

Francesco Petrarch. (© Michael Nicholson/CORBIS)

scholastic dialecticians, the works of the ancients appeared to him to be full of concrete examples of humanity, virtue, and human dignity. The beauty and elegance of classical literature became for him synonymous with *humanitas*—moral value, illumination. A list made by the poet himself (1333) of *libri mei peculiares* shows clearly that the works of Cicero, Vergil, and Horace, together with those of St. Augustine and St. Jerome, were, to the complete exclusion of any scholastic book, his preferred reading.

Espousal of the Classics. The Christian world of Petrarch's epoch was in a state of degenerate turmoil: war, superstition, ignorance, violent outbreaks of extreme mysticism, heresy, despair, rebellion, and brutal materialism were rampant. The papacy itself was wholly absorbed in secular matters. To Petrarch this sad state of affairs was related to the disappearance of the classical heritage, the advent of Aristotelian scholasticism, the corruption of taste, the spread of atheistic naturalism, the forgetfulness of the great ancient examples of virtue, magnanimity, and human dignity. Against the culture of the "schools" and the prevailing Aristotelianism, the study of the great classical works appeared to him to be the only means to restore spiritual values in the world. These classical studies were to be called *litterae humanae,* a school for being humane, but certainly they did

15th-century Florentine manuscript illumination of "The Triumph of Death," from Petrarch's "Rime i Trionfi." (©Archivo Iconografico, S.A./CORBIS)

not imply any rejection of religious beliefs or attitudes; they rested on the assumption, and indeed on the explicit statements (clearest and most uncompromising in Petrarch himself), that the effort to perfect what is humanly most noble is acceptable to God and a way to perfection. It is known, however, that anti-Christian attitudes were to be found, in fact, only in those writers and scientists who did not accept or who rejected the culture of *litterae humanae,* men such as Leonardo da Vinci, Pulci, Pomponazzi, and MACHIAVELLI.

A good part of Petrarch's work could form a treatise or an anthology on the theme "Christianity and Culture," pointing out the indispensable connection between the two. If his familiarity with and appreciation of Cicero's work were so great that he inevitably felt resounding in his own conscience the warning that St. Jerome had once heard, "tu es ciceronianus," his answer was as assured and as sincere: he was and intended to remain a Christian; he was a Ciceronian in the sense that "Cicero himself would have been a Christian had he known Christ" (*De sui ipsius ignorantia*). With the same confidence and with an honesty that should forestall speculation about his personal failures, he proclaimed: "licet peccator, certe christianus sum" (*ibid.*).

Petrarch is too frequently thought of merely as the author of love sonnets and the founder of modern lyricism. He was both, but far more important, he was one of the authors who have exercised the deepest influence on the culture of the Christian world. As a matter of fact, there resulted from this renewed contact with the Ancients a new Christian attitude divorced from despair, anxiety, and dialectical subtleties, and based upon confidence in nature and in human forces. His work revealed the Christian vision that not only inspired most of the literature and art of the Renaissance but also led to the martyrdom of St. Thomas MORE, supported the action of St. IGNATIUS LOYOLA, opened the way to the recovery of the great teaching of St. Thomas, and resulted in the vast Catholic synthesis that the Council of TRENT was to codify. He was really a teacher to Christian Europe.

A New Christian Vision. Economic and political forces that gave birth to what has been called the *essor* of Europe were obviously independent of Petrarch and were at work long before him. Indeed, many elements of the civilization of the 15th and 16th centuries were unaffected by Petrarch's humanism or even ran counter to it. The world of politics with its violence and restless ambitions, the world of Cesare Borgia and of the other *condottieri,* for instance, were untouched by Petrarch's ideals of virtue and piety. It was, in brief, the world of the Counter-Renaissance. But the moral and religious ideas, together with the artistic and literary ideals of the epoch, had their source for the most part in the work of Petrarch. Probably in no other instance can a new epoch of the Christian world be traced so distinctly to the work of one man. Further, Petrarch's own spiritual career was most coherent. He has been described as a man continually in doubt, divided between his attachment to the old faith of the Middle Ages and to the new secularism of the Renaissance. The facts are quite different. On the one hand, Petrarch rejected the Middle Ages, judging them to be a period in which religion had been adulterated, especially in the preceding century, by dialecticism, Arab naturalism, heresy, and superstition—in a word, *immanitas.* On the other hand, Petrarch did not hide, either from himself or others, his own failures: his fondness for poetry, human beauty, and glory. He spoke at length of his ardors, of his vanity, of his real passion for Laura. His major Latin work, the *Secretum,* is a sincere, soul-searching, courageous, and public confession of his folly. But it is not simply an ascetic work. To St. Augustine, who, in the imaginary dialogues reported in the *Secretum,* urges him to think on death and the salvation of his soul and to renounce the vanities of the world, he confesses the weakness of his will but goes on to express his hope that even amidst the occupations and errors of the world one may find a way to God. Too often overlooked by critics, this humanistic conclusion contains the true meaning and value of the *Secretum;* it is the definitive expression of Petrarch's vision.

Petrarch wrote the *Secretum* about 1342, after his brother Gherardo had become a Carthusian monk, as a kind of justification of his decision not to follow his brother's steps. The opinion that it was written in a period of asceticism following a spiritual crisis does not correspond to the character of the work. Moreover, the letter in which the poet gave an allegorical description of the ascent of Mont Ventoux in France, made by Gherardo and himself in 1336, expresses the same thought.

Previously, in his early 30s, Petrarch had written many sonnets and *canzoni,* in which substantially he was still faithful to the manner of the stilnovist poets, writing verse as a manifestation of literary skill and praising the ennobling influence of his lady. But his deepening familiarity with the ancient poets, chiefly Propertius, soon turned him from the abstractions of the *dolce stil nuovo* and taught him to speak of his real experiences, of the aspects of nature, of a true woman. At the same time he realized how delusive were the neoplatonistic views about love as a ladder to perfection. The beauty of the world and of women, he recognized, was all too prone to divert one from God. He was not able to free himself from a passion that, despite the fact that it was not returned, had become extremely ardent. Yet he was willing to accept the test that was given him for his soul's sake. He lived this experience with the full awareness of its limits and its dangers, through moments of abandon and deep feelings of repentance, finding himself in a state of mundane ecstasy and then awakening to the sense of his failure and his misery, with "shame being the fruit of his raving." Petrarch's attitude, therefore, reflected a true Christian concept of love: something made of acceptance and penance, joy and sadness, entirely distant both from the fearful condemnations of medieval asceticism and from the pagan idealizations of the poets of the 13th century. His sonnets are full of expressions of pain caused by the unresponsiveness of Laura. But other poems that reveal his feeling of shame are filled with deep sorrow and fervent prayer to Christ to be delivered from his bondage.

It is this alternation of moments of weakness and moments of repentance, an essential characteristic of a Christian life, that is the substance of Petrarch's poetry. After the death of Laura in 1348, he continued to think of and to write poems about her. Some part of his soul was linked to the memory of his beloved, and he did not want or was not able to heal the wound that was for him a reminder of his weakness and of his need for God's help. He had begun to make collections of his poems in Italian. They were to him, then, only "fragments in the vernacular." After Laura's death, however, he began to regard them as fragments of his own soul and decided to divide them into *Rime in vita* and *Rime in morte* (for Laura, after her death). He finally assembled 366 of them to signify that all the days of his life were there gathered. He included among them poems about politics and other matters: *Il Canzoniere,* as the work was later called, was to be the testimony of his whole life. It begins with an introductory sonnet that summarizes the entire story and concludes with the *Canzone alla Vergine,* probably the most sublime poem ever dedicated to the Virgin Mary. It is on the whole his "confession," a revelation of his life that is pervaded with the final sense of misery, repentance, and hope.

Writing in Latin. Petrarch labored at this work to the last days of his life. From the beginning, however, Petrarch's creative work in Italian had been accompanied by, and had even given place for long periods to, an extraordinary amount of work in Latin. When he realized (*c.* 1337) the insidiousness of the courtly theories on love and had read *Le Roman de la Rose,* he wrote a *Triumphus Cupidinis* in Italian to show, in contrast with the French work, the slavery and the misery caused by love. Later he added other Triumphs: those of *Pudicitiae, Mortis, Famae, Temporis,* and *Aeternitatis.* He worked on these separate parts until his last years. But he was never completely satisfied with it, realizing that he had not succeeded in composing an organic, wholly inspired work.

Petrarch gathered a great number of letters in various collections: *Familiares* (24 books), *Seniles* (17 books), and *Sine nomine.* Two other collections were assembled posthumously: *Variae* and *Miscellaneae.* In 1337 Petrarch started a vast work, *De viris illustribus,* on which he labored intermittently until his last years. It was to be a collection of biographies, mainly of Roman heroes. By 1343, Petrarch had written 23; later he added other biographies, devoting extended treatment to Scipio and Caesar. Scipio was also chosen as the protagonist of the epic Latin poem *Africa,* the most ambitious of all of Petrarch's works. The inspiration came from the very core of the humanistic vision of the poet. Dealing with the war between Rome and Carthage, the pious Scipio and the dire Hannibal, *Africa* was to exalt the *humanitas* of Rome and its providential mission: the work was intended to evoke for Italy and the world the great pre-Christian values of the Roman world.

Petrarch began *Africa* in 1338–39, pinning his hopes for literary immortality on it. In 1341, thanks to the fame he had already achieved but not without solicitation on his part, he was given the laurel crown at the Roman Capitol. *Africa,* however, remained unfinished and Petrarch was not satisfied with what he did complete: he realized that he had not transfused the subject matter with a vivifying historical imagination. The poem reflected only a part of Petrarch's larger dream that Rome, the city, would be restored to its ancient glory and that the spirit of Roman civilization would renew the world. In this hope Petrarch supported the attempt of Cola di Rienzo to found a free Roman republic in 1347. He heard the news of the successful revolution with deep excitement, immediately wrote several letters in Cola's behalf and others to offer him his services. He was profoundly distressed at Cola's failure. Other political events won Petrarch's interest and intervention. Several passionate poems included in the *Canzon iere,* many poems in Latin (*Epistolae metricae),* and a great number of letters manifest his moral and religious concern with the problems of the time and his effort to mediate for peace. As it had for Dante, religion for Petrarch entailed concern for the political and moral condition of the world; yet there was nothing in Petrarch of the eschatological, prophetic element so characteristic of the author of the *Divina Commedia.* Yet this fact does not mean that Petrarch's faith was less profound.

One of Petrarch's last important works was *Invectiva de sui ipsius ignorantia* (1367), an answer to the charge made by four young Venetian Averroists that he was a ''good but uneducated man.'' He admitted his ignorance of science and natural philosophy but opposed to such knowledge his ceaseless search for the moral and religious wisdom necessary to the soul. The treatise typically exalted humanistic studies in opposition to science and natural philosophy and opposed Augustine and Cicero to Aristotle and Averroës. It was Petrarch's last and most vigorous battle against naturalism in defense of classical learning and Christian values, a superb example of what is called *littérature engagée.*

His Achievement. Yet Petrarch did not subordinate poetry to politics or ethics. The remarkable characteristic of his personality is that contrasting attitudes somehow found in him an extraordinary fusion and harmony. He had not only St. Augustine's sense of human misery and of the transience of life but also his deep consciousness of personal failure; together with these there were the clarity and reasonableness, the sense of human relationship of Cicero. He was perhaps as great a thinker, writer, and promoter of ideas as either ERASMUS or MONTAIGNE. More original than they, he was one of the most delicate and elegant poets of world literature. Petrarch gave to European poetry themes, movements, expressions, and above all, examples of classic style that were to be imitated for centuries in Spain, France, and England, as well as Italy.

From both the theoretical and the practical points of view, Petrarch's work also marked one of the most decisive evolutions in the history of aesthetics and taste. With it one passes from the aesthetic ideals of the Middle Ages, with their search for complication, artfulness, and subtlety, to the aspirations for simple elegance and naturalness. The Gothic yielded to classicism. Even for Dante, some few decades before, poetry was still ''something made with rhetoric and music''; beauty consisted in correspondence of sounds and was the result of *art,* technique, the use of rules. For Petrarch, beauty resided in measure, purity, and simplicity. *Art* gave way to imitation; Petrarch completely rejected the *artes,* the colors, the figures, alliterations, and metrical complexities that had been the characteristics of Gothic literature, and he exalted constant familiarity with the great authors, the assimilation of their taste, the imitation of their direct example. Poetry became the ''remembrance of experienced things.'' It was a very definite shift and one of which he was fully aware. From it also stemmed Petrarch's detachment front Dante, which has too often been explained by historians on the grounds of Petrarch's jealousy and weakness of character. His letters constantly return to the great theme of imitation. Classicism, the essence of the new artistic and literary civilization, had in Petrarch's *Canzoniere* and the theoretical statements of the *Epistolae* its clear, unmistakable foundation.

Other works of Petrarch were: *De otio religiosorum, De remediis utriusque fortunae, De vita solitaria, Invectivae, Rerum memorandarum libri,* and *Psalmi penitentiales.*

Bibliography: Editions. Latin works (Basel 1496); complete ed. J. HEROLD (Basel 1554); *Scritti inediti di F. P.,* ed. A. HORTIS (Trieste 1874); *Africa,* critical ed. N. FESTA (Edizione nazionale 1; Florence 1926); *Le familiari,* critical ed. V. ROSSI and U. BOSCO, 4 v. (*ibid.* 10–13; 1933–42); *Rerum memorandarum libri,* ed. G. BILLANOVICH (*ibid.* 14; 1945); *Epistolae e metricae,* v.2–3 of *Poemata minora,* ed. D. ROSSETTI, 3 v. (Milan 1829–34); *Bucolicum carmen,* ed. A. AVENA (Padua 1906); *Sine nomine,* critical ed. P. PIUR, *Petrarchas 'Buch ohne Namen' und die päpstliche Kurie* (Halle 1925); *De otio religioso,* ed. G. ROTONDI (*Studi e Testi* 195; 1958); *Invectivae,* ed. P. G. RICCI (Rome 1950); *Rime, Trionfi, e poesie latine,* ed. F. NERI et al. (Milan 1951); *Prose,* ed. G. MARTELLOTTI et al. (Milan 1955), includes *Secretum, De vita solitaria, Invectivae,* etc.; *The Sonnets, Triumphs and Other Poems,* ed. T. CAMPBELL (London 1859; repr. at various dates); *Some Love Songs,* ed. and tr. W. D. FOULKE (London 1915); *Sonnets,* tr. J. AUSLANDER (London 1931); *Secret,* tr. W. H. DRAPER (London 1911); *Sonnets and Songs,* tr. A. M. ASCOLI (Armi, pseud.) (New York 1946); *The Life of Solitude (De vita solitaria),* ed. and tr. J. ZEITLIN (Urbana, IL 1924); *On His Own Ignorance and That of Many Others (De sui ipsius et multorum ignorantia),* tr. H. NACHOD in *The Renaissance of Man,* ed. E. CASSIRER et al. (Chicago 1948); *The Triumphs,* tr. E. H. WILKINS (Chicago 1962); *Petrarch, the First Modern Scholar* *and Man of Letters: A Selection of His Correspondence with Boccaccio and Other Friends,* ed. and tr. J. H. ROBINSON and H. W. ROLFE, 2d ed. (New York 1914). Studies. *Studi petrarcheschi* (Bologna 1948–). A. SOLERTI, *Le vite di Dante, Petrarca e Boccaccio: Scritte fino al sec. XVI* (Milan 1904). R. SABBADINI, *Le scoperte dei codici latini e greci ne'secoli XIV e XV* (Florence 1905). P. DE NOLHAC, *Pétrarque et l'humanisme,* 2 v. (new ed. Paris 1907). A. FORESTI, *Aneddoti della vita di F. P.* (Brescia 1928). C. CALCATERRA, *Nella selva del Petrarca* (Bologna 1942). U. BOSCO, ''Il P. e l'umanesimo filologico,'' *Giornale Storico della Letteratura Italiana* 120 (1943) 65–119. G. BILLANOVICH, *Petrarca letterato,* v.1, *Lo scrittoio del P.* (Rome 1947). E. H. WILKINS, *The Making of the ''Canzoniere'' and Other Petrarchian Studies* (Rome 1951); *Studies in the Life and Works of Petrarch* (Cambridge, MA 1955); *The Life of Petrarch* (Chicago 1961). M. BISHOP, *Petrarch and His World* (Bloomington, Ind. 1963). G. TOFFANIN, *History of Humanism,* tr. E. GIANTURCO (New York 1954). É. H. GILSON, *History of Christian Philosophy in the Middle Ages* (New York 1955). G. MARTELLOTTI, ''Linee di sviluppo dell'umanesimo petrarchesco,'' *Studi petrarcheschi* 2 (1949) 51–81. P. O. KRISTELLER, *Renaissance Thought* (New York 1961). R. R. BOLGAR, *The Classical Heritage and Its Beneficiaries* (Cambridge, England 1954). F. DE SANCTIS, *Saggio critico sul P.,* new ed. B. CROCE (Naples 1907). H. HAUVETTE, *Les Poésies lyriques de P.* (Paris 1931). G. DE ROBERTIS, *Studi* (Florence 1944). U. BOSCO, *Francesco Petrarca* (2d ed. Bari 1961). R. MONTANO, *L'estetica del Rinascimento e del Barocco* (Naples 1962). J. VIANEY, *Le Pétrarquisme en France au XVIe siècle* (Montpellier 1909). H. K. HASSELKUSS, *Der Petrarkismus in der Sprache der englischen Sonnettdichter der Renaissance* (Barmen 1927). A. MEOZZI, *Il petrarchismo europeo* (secolo XVI) (Pisa 1934). C. CALCATERRA, ''P. e il petrarchismo,'' in *Problemi ed orientamenti critici di lingua e di letterstura italiana,* ed. A. MOMIGLIANO, 5 v. (Milan 1948–59) 3:167–273. L. BALDACCI, *Il petrarchismo italiano nel Cinquecento* (Milan 1957). J. G. FUCILLA, *Estudios sobre el petrarquisme en España* (Madrid 1960). C. TRINKAUS, *In Our Image and Likeness* (Chicago 1970). C. TRINKAUS, *The Poet as Philosopher* (New Haven 1979). R. WITT, *In the Footsteps of the Ancients* (Leiden 2000). M. O'ROURKE BOYLE, *Petrach's Genius* (Berkeley 1991).

[R. MONTANO]

PETRE

Family resident in Essex since 1539, with houses in Ingatestone and vicinity. Its members figured prominently in post-Reformation Catholic history; their wealth financed religious institutions; and their homes served as centers of Catholic life. They intermarried with many influential Catholic families; the title of Baron Petre of Writtle was granted in 1603.

Sir William, lawyer and civil servant; b. Tor Newton, Devonshire, 1505?; d. Ingatestone, Essex, Jan. 13, 1572. He was a pliable tool in carrying out the widely fluctuating policies of four sovereigns, and he also successfully established his own family fortunes. Sir William's sympathies probably remained Catholic, but were not put to the test; his son John, first Lord Petre, conformed at least externally.

Sir William Petre.

William, third son of William, second Lord Petre; b. Ingatestone, Essex, July 28, 1602; d. Stanford Rivers, Essex, 1677. He started the Petre line of Bellhouse. His father had financed the Jesuits in East Anglia, and he himself translated Pedro de Ribadeneira's *Flos Sanctorum* in 1669. Two daughters and six granddaughters became nuns and two grandsons were priests.

William, fourth Lord Petre, nephew of William Petre; b. Essex, 1627; d. London, Jan. 5, 1684. He suffered much with great constancy for his religion, both financially under the Commonwealth and by imprisonment at the time of the OATES PLOT (1678). Accused of having received from the Jesuit general a commission as ''lieutenant-general in the popish army,'' he was imprisoned in the Tower, where he died. A letter written by him to the King shortly before his death aroused public sympathy for the persecuted Catholics.

Sir Edward, SJ, confessor of James II; b. London, 1631; d. Watten, France, May 15, 1699. Cousin of the Petres of Ingatestone, Edward, of Cranham, England, entered the Jesuits in 1652. In England at the time of the Oates Plot (1678), Edward succeeded to his brother's title (1679) but was jailed in 1680 and 1683. Afterward, as Jesuit vice provincial, he was chosen by James II to be head of the chapel royal. The King, perhaps seeking to make amends for the Jesuits martyred in 1678 and, like most Catholics, overestimating his power to reverse the course of religious history, sought to have Petre made a cardinal; but Pope Innocent XI refused. When James nominated him privy councilor his enemies accused him of being bewitched by the Jesuits. Father Petre fled to the Continent in 1688.

Benjamin, bishop, vicar apostolic; b. Fithlers, Essex, Aug. 10, 1672; d. there, Dec. 22, 1758. Benjamin was educated and ordained at Douai. Largely because of his family wealth he was consecrated (1721), very unwillingly, coadjutor with right of succession to Bp. Bonaventure Giffard. After succeeding as vicar apostolic of the London district in 1734, he continually sought to resign, and at his insistence Richard CHALLONER was appointed coadjutor, whereupon Petre retired to his family estate.

Bibliography: *Essex Recusant* (Brentwood, Eng. 1959–) *passim.* F. G. EMMISON, *Tudor Secretary: Sir William Petre at Court and Home* (Cambridge, Mass. 1961). M. D. PETRE, *The 9th Lord Petre . . .* (London 1928). T. COOPER et al., *The Dictionary of National Biography from the Earliest Times to 1900*, 63 v. (London 1885–1900; repr. with corrections, 21 v., 1908–09, 1921–22, 1938) 15:976–983.

[D. SHANAHAN]

PETRE, MAUDE DOMINICA

Modernist, theological writer; b. Essex, Aug. 4, 1863; d. London, Dec. 16, 1942. Descended from a titled recusant family, Petre was the daughter of Arthur Petre (whose own father was the 13th Lord Petre) and Lady Catherine Howard, a convert to the Catholic faith. At age 22, Petre, with the encouragement of a Jesuit advisor, went to Rome to study scholastic thought under private tutelage. In 1890 she entered the Society of the Daughters of the Heart of Mary in London. She held several leadership positions in the community, but was refused permission to renew her vows in 1907 over a dispute concerning her book *Catholicism and Independence,* which had appeared the same year.

Petre befriended many of the major figures involved in the MODERNIST controversy: Friedrich von HÜGEL, Alfred LOISY, and most notably George TYRRELL. When Tyrrell became mortally ill shortly after his expulsion from the Society of Jesus, he moved to a cottage on Petre's property, and it was there that he died in 1909. A prolific writer of articles on literature and philosophy, Petre authored over a dozen books, including the *Autobiography and Life of George Tyrrell* (1912); *Modernism: Its Failure and Its Fruits* (1918); the autobiographical *My Way of Faith* (1937); *Von Hügel and Tyrrell: The Story of a Friendship* (1937); and *Alfred Loisy: His Religious Significance* (1944).The major female figure involved in Modernism, her approach to the movement at times mingled approval with a critical perspective.

Petre served as a nurse in France in World War I, and as a fire warden in London during the Blitz. She frequently spoke out on social and spiritual issues, and was a strong proponent of the League of Nations. She died at her home in London in 1942. A requiem funeral Mass was accorded her at her Kensington parish in the diocese of Westminster. She was buried, however, at Storrington in the diocese of Southward, and no priest was permitted to be in official attendance at the graveside services.

Bibliography: C. F. CREWS, *English Catholic Modernism: Maude Petre's Way of Faith* (Notre Dame 1984). E. LEONARD, *Unresting Transformation: The Theology and Spirituality of Maude Petre* (Lanham, Md. 1991)

[C. F. CREWS]

PETRI, OLAUS

Principal Swedish reformer under Gustavus Vasa; b. Örebro, Diocese of Strengnäs, Jan. 6, 1493; d. Stockholm, April 19, 1552. Petri received his preparatory education in Strngnäs's Carmelite school and his advanced education at Wittenberg (1516–18). Upon returning to Strengnäs in late 1518, he was ordained by and became secretary to Bp. Mattias Gregorii. Petri won to his cause Laurentius Andreae, Sweden's great church politician and chancellor of the king's privy council, who, in turn, converted King Gustavus Vasa to LUTHERANISM.

Olaus Petri was a gifted theologian, a great popular preacher, and an able writer. He was not a fighter like LUTHER, but more a man of peace and seriousness. He had a genius for absorbing materials from Luther or other reformers (for example, the *Ratschlag* of Osiander of 1524) and reworking them into literature adapted to his countrymen. While his work was not original, neither was it slavish translation. Petri published his doctrinal tract *An Useful Teaching* and had translated the New Testament into Swedish by 1526, but his greatest contribution was made in 1527 to 1528 when in the Lutheran-Catholic disputes he stressed that Sweden had strayed from the Christian church established by English missionaries, which he now aimed to restore. His writings covered the sacraments, marriage, monastic life, the primacy of God's Word and other fields. As a result of these efforts, the Diet of Västerås (1527) voted to break with Rome and introduce reforms. At the Council of Örebro (1529), Chancellor Andreae paved the way for a "Reformed Church" as proposed by Olaus and his younger brother Laurentius, then archbishop of Uppsala.

The period of 1529 to 1531 was productive of liturgical and homiletical writings for use in the emerging Lutheran Church: a *Manual of Service* (1529), *Hymn Book* (1530), *Catechism* (1530), and a Swedish form of *The Mass* (1531) modeled upon German forms in Wittenberg and elsewhere. The Petri brothers collaborated further in the translation of the Swedish Bible published in 1541. By the 1544 Diet of Västerås most of the Catholic usages had disappeared, and by 1552 Sweden was definitely Lutheran. Olaus engaged in a series of disputes with Gustavus Vasa over the position of the Church within the State. The Petri brothers also opposed any efforts at reconciliation with Rome during the early years of the Council of Trent. Gustavus honored Petri by placing him in charge of the *Ecclesia Stockholmensis*, supervising all churches in addition to his own church, St. Nicholas, where he had been pastor for more than 20 years.

Bibliography: O. PETRI, *Samlade skrifter,* ed. B. HESSELMAN, 4 v. (Uppsala 1914–18). C. J. I. BERGENDOFF, *Olavus Petri and the Ecclesiastical Transformation in Sweden* (New York 1928). W. GÖBBEL, *Die Religion in Geschichte und Gegenwart* (Tübingen 1957–65) 5:246. G. SCHWAIGER, *Lexikon für Theologie und Kirche,* ed. J. HOFER and K. RAHNER (Freiberg 1957–65) 8:326.

[E. G. SCHWIEBERT]

PETRILLI, SAVINA, BL.

Foundress of the Sisters of the Poor of Saint Catherine of Siena; b. Aug. 29, 1851, Siena, Italy; d. there April 18, 1923. At the age of ten, Savina was introduced to and inspired by the life of Saint CATHERINE OF SIENA and the saint's eucharistic devotion. Her family, the parish Children of Mary Sodality, and her pastor all nourished her spirituality and encouraged her generosity toward the poor. During an audience with Pope Pius IX (1869), she was told to follow Saint Catherine. In 1873, she requested permission from the archbishop of Siena to found a religious order. He instructed her to draw up the Rule. With three friends Savina founded (1874) a small group to care for the poor, beginning in a small apartment with an abandoned baby. Mother Savina continued working with the Sisters of the Poor of Saint Catherine of Siena, approved by the Holy See in 1875, until her death from cancer. The order spread to India, Italy, the Philippines, and Latin America. She was beatified by Pope John Paul II on April 24, 1988.

Feast: April 18.

Bibliography: *Acta Apostolicae Sedis* (1988): 583. *L'Osservatore Romano,* English edition, no. 16 (1988): 12.

[K. I. RABENSTEIN]

PETROBRUSIANS

The followers of PETER OF BRUYS, who were widely spread throughout southern France during the first half of the 12th century. Their views concerning hierarchy, Sacraments, and ecclesiastical observances were typical 12th-century protests that deteriorated into heresy. Peter of Bruys's contemporary, the monk HENRY OF LAUSANNE, spent most of his career in France, first in Le Mans, where his insistence on evangelical life spent in penance and poverty finally persuaded Bp. HILDEBERT OF LAVARDIN to expel him. In the south he accepted the teachings of Peter of Bruys, which, according to PETER THE VENERABLE, he modified and elaborated (*Patrologia Latina,* ed. J. P. Migne 189:723A). Although he did not at first hold the cross in horror as did Peter, he too developed an antisacerdotal and antisacramental aspect in his teaching. Henricians were accordingly identified with Petrobrusians. There is no evidence that they prepared the way for the WALDENSIANS. More probable is their indebtedness to the MANICHAEAN current (as Vacandard and Döllinger once suggested). Support for such a connection has been deduced from a passage in the *Exordium magnum Cisterciense* 17 (*Patrologia Latina,* ed. J. P. Migne 185:427C), where BERNARD OF CLAIRVAUX, on his way to refute the Henrician heresy, is described as setting out for Toulouse ''to confute the heresy of the Manichaeans.'' But this work was written *c.* 1210 in the full tide of ALBIGENSIAN influence, when no careful distinctions were drawn. Furthermore, in place of subscribing to thoroughgoing DUALISM, the Petrobrusians did not reject marriage, though they urged continence. They denied only infant Baptism. The Second LATERAN Council (1139) condemned some Petrobrusian ideas but not the movement itself. Canon 22 (H. Denzinger, *Enchiridion symolorum,* ed. A. Schönmetzer 718), reproducing word for word canon three of the Council of Toulouse (1119; *see* J. D. Mansi, *Sacrorum Conciliorum nova et amplissima collectio,* 21:226), dwells on the denial of the Eucharist and the rejection of infant Baptism and of the priesthood, but the repudiation of Matrimony attributed to them belongs probably to other sects.

Bibliography: R. MANSELLI, *Studi sulle eresie del secolo XII* (Studi storici 5; Rome 1953) 1–23. E. VACANDARD, ''Les Origines de l'hérésie albigeoise,'' *Revue des Questions Historiques* 55 (Paris 1894) 50–83; *Vie de Saint Bernard* (4th ed. Paris 1910). F. VERNET, *Dictionnaire de théologie catholique,* ed. A. VACANT, 15 v. (Paris 1903–50; Tables générales 1951–) 6.2:2178–83. J. J. I. VON DÖLLINGER, *Beltrāge zur Sektengeschlchte des Mittelalters,* 2 v. in 1 (Munich 1890) 1:75–97.

[E. W. MCDONNELL]

PETRONAX OF BRESCIA, ST.

Refounder and abbot of Monte Cassino; b. Brescia, Italy, *c.* 670; d. May 6, 750. Petronax went to the tomb of St. BENEDICT in 718 on the advice of Pope GREGORY

II. Among the ruins of MONTE CASSINO, destroyed in 581 by Lombards, he found a few solitaries with whom he remained. They elected him their superior, and their numbers grew. With the assistance of prominent nobles and three popes (among them Pope ZACHARY, who gave him [742] the autograph copy of the BENEDICTINE RULE), he succeeded in rebuilding Monte Cassino. In 729 St. WILLIBALD, an English monk who was afterward bishop of Eichstätt, arrived at Monte Cassino, where he remained for ten years as Petronax's disciple. Willibald's biographer (*Acta Sanctorum* July 7:509–510) credits him, rather than Petronax, with the restoration of genuine Benedictine observance, which he himself had experienced from his childhood in WALTHAM Abbey (Hampshire).

Feast: May 6.

Bibliography: H. LECLERQ, *Dictionnaire d'archéologie chrétienne et de liturgie,* ed. F. CABROL, H. LECLERCQ, and H. I. MARROU, 15 v. (Paris 1907–53) 11.2:2461–65. J. CHAPMAN, "La Restauration du Mont-Chassin par l'abbé Petronax," *Revue Bénédictine* 21 (1904) 74–80.

[C. MCGRATH]

PETRONILLA, ST.

Probably third century, authentic Roman martyr. Since no certain acts of her martyrdom exist, it is impossible to determine the date of her death and the persecution in which she perished. The opinion that she died of a natural death, as stated in the Roman MARTYROLOGY, stems from the apocryphal *Passion of Nereus and Achilleus.* Certain Gnostic writings quite probably led to the erroneous identification of the saint with the daughter of St. PETER THE APOSTLE. Petronilla's tomb, as marked in an *itineraria* of the seventh century, was located in the cemetery of St. Domitilla on the Via Ardeantina. A fresco of the fourth century depicts a holy woman entering heaven and bears the inscription "Petronilla martyr." During the pontificate of Pope SIRICIUS (384–399), a basilica was erected over the saint's tomb. Though G. B. de Rossi contested the allegation that Petronilla was a martyr, the opinion that she died for the faith has prevailed. In art Petronilla is represented as a little girl holding a palm and a book in her hand. She is a special patroness of France.

Feast: May 31.

Bibliography: A. BUTLER, *The Lives of the Saints,* rev. ed. H. THURSTON and D. ATTWATER, 4 v. (New York 1956) 2:434. R. DALL'ARA, *Petronilla e le altre: il mestolo dalla parte di lei* (Mantua 1998).

[E. DAY]

PETRUS COLLIVACCINUS (BENEVENTANUS)

Canonist and cardinal; b. Benevento, of the noble family of the Collis Vaccini; d. Rome, Sept. 21, 1219 or 1220. He studied and taught canon law in Bologna, probably with Lothar of Segni, later Pope Innocent III, in the school of HUGUCCIO. He may have followed Lothar to Rome, where he appeared as early as 1205 as Capellanus Domini Pupae. In 1210 he was called by the pope himself *subdiaconus et notarius noster.* He is recorded as cardinal deacon of S. Maria in Aquiro from March 15, 1212, to March 7, 1216, and as cardinal priest of S. Lorenzo in Damaso from April 13, 1216, to March 1217; before April 19, 1217, Pope Hanorius III named him cardinal bishop of Sabina. As confidant of two popes he took part in various missions, of which the most important was the legation of 1214 and 1215 for the Albigensian territory. Another of his achievements was the compilation of the *Compilatio III Antiqua.* This compilation was commissioned by Innocent III in 1210; it arranged the decretals of the first 12 years of the pontificate of Innocent III in five books and was the first such collection officially given to school and forum. He was probably the author of the *Summa Reginensis* on the *Decretum* of Gratian (*see* GRATIAN, DECRETUM OF).

Bibliography: F. HEYER, "Über Petrus Collivaccinus von Benevent," *Zeitschrift der Savigny-Stiftung für Rechtsgeschichte, Kanonistische Abteilung* 6 (1916) 395–405. S. KUTTNER, *Repertorium der kanonistik* (Rome 1937) 355; *Studi e Testi* (Rome 1900—) 71. S. KUTTNER, "Bernardus Compostellanus Antiquus," *Traditio* 1 (1943) 30.1, n. 54. A. M. STICKLER, "Decrefisti Bolognesi dimenticati," *Studia Gratiana* 3 (1955) 375–410. A. TEETAERT, *Dictionnaire de droit canonique,* ed. R. NAZ, 7 v. (Paris 1935–65) 3:1000–02.

[A. M. STICKLER]

PETRUS DE CRUCE

Composer and theorist, active in Paris at the close of the 13th century (also called Pierre de la Croix). In 1298 King PHILIP IV requested a musical Office for St. Louis from a Petrus de Cruce of Amiens, who was probably the composer-theorist. Two motets, *Au renouveler* and *Aucun one trouvé,* are identified as his work by the 14th-century theorist Jacques de Liège. Of the writings ascribed to Petrus, only some excerpts preserved by the theorists Robert de Handlo and John Hanboys and a *Tractatus de tonis* remain. Even though the conservative De Liège lauded him as a model of the 13th-century *ars antiqua,* Petrus was in fact a bold innovator. Going beyond the rhythmic novelties of FRANCO OF COLOGNE, he increased the number of semibreves subdividing the breve from two or three, to from four to nine, and separated such groups of semibreves from one another by means of a dot of division, the *punctus divisionis.* By introducing note values (minims) smaller than the officially recognized semibreve, Petrus accorded his music an unparalleled rhythmic freedom. His innovations were transformed by 14th-century composers and theorists into the *quatre prolations* of the *ars nova.*

Bibliography: PETRUS DE CRUCE, *Tractatus de tonis,* H. COUSSEMAKER, *Scriptorum de musica medii aevi nova series,* 4 v. (Paris 1864–76) 282–292. G. REESE, *Music in the Renaissance* (rev. ed. New York 1959). W. APEL, *The Notation of Polyphonic Music* (4th, rev. ed. Cambridge, Mass. 1949) 318–324, 338, 369. PETRUS DE CRUCE, ''Ambianensi Tractatus de tonis.'' in *Corpus scriptorum de musica, vol. 29,* D. HARBISON, ed. (Rome 1976) vi–xxv. D. M. RANDEL, ed., *The Harvard Biographical Dictionary of Music* (Cambridge 1996) 688. E. H. SANDERS, ''Petrus de Cruce'' in *The New Grove Dictionary of Music and Musicians, vol. 14,* ed. S. SADIE (New York 1980) 598–599.

[E. R. LERNER]

PETRUS DE DACIA

Dominican, Swedish author; b. probably Gotland Island, *c.* 1235; d. Visby, 1289. Of Petrus's early life nothing is known except that he entered the Dominican Order of the province of Dacia. Presumably he was educated in the Dominican monastery of Visby (founded 1228). In 1266 be was sent to the *studium generale* of the order in Cologne, and in 1269 he went to Paris, where he may have studied under THOMAS AQUINAS. Returning to Sweden in 1270, he became lector in the monastery of Skänninge; after a short time as prior of the Vüsterås monastery (1278–79), he was appointed lector in the monastery of Visby, becoming prior in 1284.

During his stay in Cologne, Petrus met the visionary virgin Christina of Stommeln, around whom had gathered a circle of followers. Petrus became one of her ardent admirers, and from Paris and later on from Sweden he carried on correspondence with her. Twice (1279, 1287) he journeyed to Stommeln to see her, and before his last visit he had written a Latin biography of her, the *Vita Christinae Stumbelensis,* which he brought with him, along with Christina's letters to him. The whole correspondence, as well as Petrus's biography of Christina, was copied in a manuscript (*Cod. Juliacensis*) that is now the chief source of knowledge of the *idylle monacale,* as E. RENAN named her. Petrus's writings reveal him as a master of elevated prose style, a scholar with profound theological insight and knowledge, and a sensitive and sometimes mystical mind.

Bibliography: H. SCHÜCK, *Vår Förste Författare* (Stockholm 1916). *Ny illustrerad svensk litteratur-historia,* ed. E. N. TIGERSTEDT, 5 v. (Stockholm 1955–58) 1:143–150; bibliog. 380.

[T. D. OLSEN]

PETTAZZONI, RAFFAELE

Historian of religions; b. Persiceto, Italy, Feb. 3, 1883; d. Rome, Dec. 8, 1959. He was professor of the history of religions at Bologna (1914–23) and then at Rome (1923–53). In his early career he was concerned primarily with the scientific study of religion in specified areas and periods, as in his *La religione nella Grecia antica fino ad Alessandro* (Bologna 1921; 2d ed. 1953). Subsequently he developed an original phenomenologico-historical comparative method, which he exemplified in his ethnographical study *La confessione dei peccati* (3 v. Bologna 1929–36) and in his *L'omniscienza di Dio* (Turin 1955; tr. H. J. Rose, *The All-Knowing God* [London 1956]). The last study was the culmination of investigations of the primitive ''high god,'' which he had begun some 30 years earlier. Special mention should be made, too, of his *Saggi di storia delle religioni e di mitologia* (Rome 1946; tr. H. J. Rose, *Essays on the History of Religions* [Leiden 1954]). He was the founder and director of the journals *Studi e Materiali di Storia delle Religioni* (1925–54) and *Numen* (1954–59), and he was cofounder (1950) and president (1950–59) of the Association Internationale pour l'Histoire des Religions.

Bibliography: C. M. EDSMAN, *Die Religion in Geschichte und Gegenwart,* 7 v. (3d ed. Tübingen 1957–65) 5:263–264. M. GANDINI, ''Nota bibliografica degli scritti di R. Pettazzoni,'' *Studi e materiali di storia delle religioni* 31 (1960) 3–21. A. BRELICH, ''Discorso di commemorazione,'' *ibid.* 191–202. V. VAN BULCK, *Gregorianum* 42 (1961) 797–800.

[G. SANDERS]

PEYTO (PETO), WILLIAM

English cardinal and Franciscan friar, a courageous figure at the time of the Reformation; b. Warwickshire, *c.* 1477; d. probably Greenwich, 1558. Presumably legitimate but of uncertain parentage, he was a relative of the Throckmorton family of Coughton, Warwickshire. He was educated at Oxford and Cambridge, and as a member of the Observant Franciscans (the Grey Friars), he acted as confessor to MARY TUDOR when she was a girl. On Easter Sunday, March 31, 1532, as head of the English province he preached a sermon before HENRY VIII condemning the proposed marriage to Anne Boleyn. The warden at Greenwich, Henry Elston, supported Peyto's statement some weeks later. In consequence, both priests were imprisoned, and on their release in 1533 they immediately fled to Antwerp. Peyto, attainted in 1539, spent 20 years on the Continent working with the COUNTER REFORMATION. In 1543 Paul III appointed him bishop of Salisbury, but he later resigned from this purely nominal position. After the accession of Mary, he returned to England and lived quietly in the restored friary at Greenwich. When Paul IV recalled Cardinal Reginald POLE from England, he appointed Peyto to succeed him as cardinal and legate (June 1557) despite the friar's plea that he was too old and otherwise unsuitable.

Bibliography: M. HAILE, *The Life of Reginald Pole* (New York 1910). D. KNOWLES, *The Religious Orders in England,* 3 v. (Cambridge, Eng. 1948–60) v. 3. L. PASTOR, *The History of the Popes from the Close of the Middle Ages,* 40 v. (London–St. Louis 1938–61) v. 14. J. GILLOW, *A Literary and Biographical History or Bibliographical Dictionary of the English Catholics from 1534 to the Present Time,* 5 v. (London-New York 1885–1902; repr. New York 1961) 5:300–303. J. GAIRDNER, *The Dictionary of National Biography from the Earliest Times to 1900,* 63 v. (London 1885–1900; repr. with corrections, 21 v., 1908–09, 1921–22, 1938; suppl. 1901–) 15:974–975.

[M. R. O'CONNELL]

PEYTON, PATRICK JOSEPH

The "Rosary Priest"; b. Carracastle, Attymass, County Mayo, Ireland, Jan. 9, 1909; d. San Pedro, California, June 3, 1992. One of nine children, Patrick Peyton grew up praying the rosary daily with his parents in their three-room cottage. In 1928 he emigrated to Scranton, Pennsylvania, where he worked as a janitor in St. Peter's Cathedral. Upon entering the Congregation of the Holy Cross, he studied at the University of Notre Dame. Diagnosed with incurable tuberculosis in 1939, he regained his health through faith and prayer and was ordained a priest on June 15, 1941. In January of 1942, Peyton decided that in gratitude for his recovery he would give the Blessed Mother ten million homes in which the Family Rosary would be prayed.

As the chaplain at Vincentian Institute High School (Albany, New York), Peyton preached the rosary at parishes throughout the eastern United States and Canada. In 1945, the Mutual Broadcasting Company permitted him to offer a radio program for Mother's Day that coincided with the national celebration of Victory in Europe Day. Two years later, he inaugurated the Family Theater (Hollywood, California), a national radio show featuring Loretta Young, Bing Crosby, and other stars of stage and screen. Airing weekly, it ran for 22 years. Peyton coined the slogan, "The family that prays together stays together." In the 1950s, Peyton sponsored several award-winning television programs. During 1956 and 1957 he produced 15 films on the life of Christ, each treating one mystery of the rosary. In 1973, he arranged the first satellite transmission to North America of the Christmas Midnight Mass at St. Peter's Basilica in Rome.

Peyton also established the Family Rosary Crusade (Albany, New York). Assisted by Holy Cross religious, he organized diocesan crusades, culminating in inspirational outdoor rallies. The first crusade was held in London, Ontario, in 1948. In 1952 Peyton assembled 75,000 people in New York City, 83,000 in London, England, and 150,000 in Melbourne, Australia. In 1960, he gathered 550,000 people in Santiago, Chile; in 1961, 500,000 in San Francisco; in 1962, one million people in Bogotá, Colombia; in 1964, two million in Sao Paolo, Brazil; and in 1985, two million in Manila, the Philippines. In all, Peyton spoke at rallies in more than 40 countries on 6 continents to approximately 27 million people. Peyton is buried at Stonehill College (North Easton, Massachusetts).

Bibliography: J.G. ARNOLD, *A Man of Faith* (Hollywood 1983). R.E. GRIBBLE, *The History and Devotion of the Rosary* (Huntington IN 1992). P. PETYON, *The Ear of God* (Garden City 1951); *Rosary Prayer Book* (Albany 1952); *All For Her: The Autobiography of Father Patrick Peyton* (Garden City 1967).

[R. KRIEG]

PFÄFERS, ABBEY OF

Former Benedictine abbey near the spa of Ragaz, St. Gall, Switzerland. It was founded *c.* 750 under the influence of St. PIRMIN and REICHENAU and became with CHUR and DISENTIS a spiritual center of Rhaetia. The free imperial abbey, under the protection of the Carolingian Lothair I by 840, came under the bishops of Constance (905), St. Gall (909), and Chur (920) before becoming independent (950). After an association with EINSIEDELN (*c.* 1000), Pfäfers was made exempt of the bishop of Basel (1116) during the investiture controversy, in which the abbey sided with the papacy. Territorially dependent on feudal lords in the 13th and 14th centuries, it came under the Swiss Confederation in 1482. Abbot Johann Jakob Russinger (1517–49) joined Zwingli but returned to Catholicism after the battle of Kappel (1531). Johann Heider (1586–1600) and Bonifaz Tschupp (1677–1706) headed revivals during which the baroque church was built (1694), but an economic and disciplinary decline led to suppression (1838). Since 1845 the abbey has been converted to use as a mental institution while the church serves a parish. From medieval times the abbey owned the spa Tamina-Ragaz.

Bibliography: H. WARTMANN, *Das Kloster Pfäfers* (St. Gallen 1883). M. GMÜR, *Urbare und Rödel des Klosters Pfäfers* (Bern

1910). L. H. COTTINEAU, *Répertoire topobibliographique des abbayes et prieurés*, 2 v. (Mâcon 1935–39) 2:2271–72. R. HENGGELER, "Der Untergang des Klosters Pfäfers," *Jahrbuch Heimatbund Sarganserland* 1 (1930) 25–238; *Professbuch der Benediktinerabteien Pfäfers, Rheinau und Fischingen* (Einsiedeln 1933). E. ROTHENHÄSLER, ed., *Die Kunstdenkmäler des Kantons St. Gallen*, v.1 (Basel 1951). F. PERRET, *Aus der Frühzeit der Abtei Pfäfers: Ein Kulturbild aus dem Ende des ersten Jahrtausends* (St. Gallen 1958). O. L. KAPSNER, *A Benedictine Bibliography: An Author-Subject Union List*, 2 v. (2d ed. Collegeville, Minn. 1962) 2:249. I. MÜLLER, *Lexikon für Theologie und Kirche*, ed. J. HOFER and K. RAHNER, 10 v. (2d, new ed. Freiburg 1957–65) 8:392–393.

[A. MAISSEN]

PFANNER, FRANZ

Trappist abbot, African missionary, religious founder; b. Langen, near Bregenz, Austria, Sept. 21, 1825; d. Emmaus, Natal, SOUTH AFRICA, May 24, 1909. After university studies in Innsbruck and Padua, Franz (whose baptismal name was Wendelin) studied for the priesthood (1846–50) and was ordained. He served in parish work at Haselstauden until 1859 when he became chaplain to the Sisters of Mercy in Zagreb. In 1863 he joined the TRAPPISTS at the priory of Mariawald, located in the Eifel region in the Diocese of Aachen. An attempt to expel him from the order (1867) because of a quarrel with the Trappist vicar-general was overruled by the Holy See. In 1869 Pfanner founded Mariastern in Bosnia and acted as its prior. In response to the appeal of Bp. James Ricards, Vicar Apostolic of the Eastern Districts of the Cape of Good Hope, before the Trappist general chapter (1879), Pfanner set out with 31 monks for South Africa, erected the priory of Dunbrody, and acted as its prior until 1882. Since this location was unsatisfactory, the community moved to Natal at the invitation of Bp. Charles Jolivet and began near Pinetown a priory called Mariannhill. In 1885 the priory became an abbey, with Pfanner as abbot. To further his missionary work among the Zulus he founded the MISSIONARY SISTERS OF THE PRECIOUS BLOOD and the MARIANNHILL MISSIONARIES. Under Pfanner's direction Mariannhill developed into the most important missionary center in South Africa, with 11 mission stations. Difficulties over the conflicting demands of the Trappist rule and evangelization led to Pfanner's suspension for a year as abbot (1892). Within that period he resigned and spent his remaining years laboring on the mission station at Emmaus, despite great suffering from arthritis.

Bibliography: B. HOFMANN, *The Founder of Mariannhill* (Dearborn, Mich. 1948), adapted from the Ger. B. HUSS, *Mariannhill: Half a Century of African Mission Life* (Detroit 1935). J. DAHM, *Mariannhill* (Mariannhill, Natal, S. Africa 1953). F. SCHIMLER, *Mariannhill: A Study in Bantu Life and Missionary Effort* (Mariannhill 1953); *Against the Stream* (Mariannhill 1949), W. BROWN, *The Catholic Church in South Africa from Its Origins to the Present Day* (New York 1960). A. WILMOT, *Life and Times of the Rt. Rev. James David Ricards* (Cape Town 1908).

[J. E. BRADY]

PFEFFERKORN, IGNAZ

Jesuit missionary; b. Mannheim, Germany, July 31, 1725; d. date unknown. He entered the Society of Jesus on Oct. 21, 1742. In 1754 he received permission to go to the New World as a missionary. Late that year he arrived in Cádiz, where he waited until Dec. 25, 1755, before sailing for New Spain. He arrived in Veracruz on March 19, 1756 and after a few months in Mexico City was sent to the missions of Sonora. In late 1756 he was assigned to the mission of Atí among the Pima natives. For reasons of health he was transferred to Cucurpe among the Eudebes; he worked there until the expulsion of the Jesuits from the Spanish dominions in 1767. A prolonged journey under guard brought him and his companions back to Cádiz on July 12, 1769. Pfefferkorn, with several other Sonoran missionaries, was held prisoner in Spain because their knowledge of Spain's outlying possessions was considered potentially dangerous. He returned to his homeland in 1777 and spent his last years writing *Bechreibung der Landschaft Sonora samt andern merkwerdigen Nachtrichten von den inneren Theilen NeuSpaniens und Reise aus Amerika bis in Deutschland* (2 v., Koln am Rheine, 1794–95). A projected third volume of this work was never published.

Bibliography: I. PFEFFEKORN, *Sonora: A Description of the Province,* tr. T. E. TREUTLEIN (Albuquerque 1949).

[F. B. WARREN]

PFEFFERKORN, JOHANNES

Controversial opponent of Jewish literature; b. Nuremburg, 1469; d. Cologne, 1524. A converted Jew, Pfefferkorn began a campaign to purge Germany of Jewish literature suspected of being subversive of Christianity. Supported by the Dominicans in Cologne, he secured a mandate from Emperor Maximilian I (1509) permitting the indiscriminate confiscation and destruction of Hebrew books. Protests, however, forced the emperor to seek opinions from theologians and private scholars, especially Johann REUCHLIN, humanist and renowned Hebraist. Reuchlin's courageous defense of many Hebrew writings prompted violent recriminations by Pfefferkorn, and a war of pamphlets ensued, Pfefferkorn and the original issue concerning questionable Jewish literature were dwarfed during the Reuchlin affair, which culminated in a widespread controversy between the conservative schoolmen of the universities and the humanists who defended the "new learning." As for Pfefferkorn, his reputation has since suffered considerably because of his fanaticism and the caricature of him in the popular writings of the humanists.

Bibliography: J. JANSSEN, *History, of the German People at the Close of the Middle Ages,* tr. M. A. MITCHELL and A. M. CHRISTIE, 17 v. (London 1896–1925) 3:48–52. F. ZOEPFL, *Lexikon für Theologie und Kirche,* ed. J. HOFER and K. RAHNER, 10 v. (2d, new ed. Freiburg 1957–65) 8:416. J. MACKINNON, *The Origins of the Reformation* (New York 1939). J. LORTZ, *Die Reformation in Deutschland,* 2 v. (Freiburg 1941).

[J. T. COVERT]

PFLUG, JULIUS VON

Theologian and bishop; b. Eyra, near Leipzig, 1499; d. Zeitz, Sept. 3, 1564. His father, Caesar, had an important role in the Leipzig disputation of 1519 as councillor to Duke George of Saxony. Pflug's education, begun at Leipzig and continued later in Italy at Padua and Bologna, imbued him with humanistic ideals of reform but gave him little formal training in theology. The noted humanist Peter Mosellanus was his master at Leipzig. Later the two corresponded frequently. More than 100 of Pflug's letters are extant [M. C. G. Müller, *Epistolae Petri Mosellani. . . ad Julium Pflugium* (Leipzig 1802)]. Because of his temperament and reputation as a moderate, he was often invited to negotiate a conciliatory statement of doctrine acceptable to Lutherans and Catholics. At Regensburg in 1541, Gropper, ECK, and Pflug, the Catholic conferees, met with MELANCHTHON, BUCER, and Pistorius. The resulting formula of twofold justification, examined later at the insistence of Seripando by the Council of Trent, was rejected. Though Gropper and Pflug wanted to save the conference with another formula, however vague, it broke up over the question of the Eucharist.

In 1548 Pflug drew up the document that was to become the basis of the Interim of Augsburg (*see* INTERIMS). Many alterations were introduced in the course of the discussions, but the main outlines of the original draft were not changed. The dogmatic content, stated in the mildest and most general terms, is nonetheless basically Catholic. When the Elector Maurice of Saxony demanded further concessions for the Protestants of his jurisdiction, Pflug and Melanchthon worked out the Leipzig Interim (1548). Although Lutheran in tone, it was a compromise in that some externals of Catholicism were allowed. Pflug presided over the Colloquy of Worms in 1557 and won high praise from his friend Peter CANISIUS for his patience and tact.

Pflug was the last Catholic bishop of Naumburg. The cathedral chapter elected him in January 1541, but a year passed before Pflug, assured of imperial support, accepted the appointment. Meanwhile the Elector John Frederick forced Nikolaus von AMSDORF, an avowed Lutheran, into the see. Only after Emperor CHARLES V defeated the Elector at Mühlberg in 1547 was Pflug established in his diocese. Pflug tried to win people back to Catholic practices but without notable success. Forced by the realities of the situation, he sought approbation for married priests and Communion under both species for the laity. In 1559 Pflug was named president of a council of German bishops, formed with the encouragement of Peter Canisius, to promote local reform. Pflug was residing at the collegiate church in Zeitz when he died. No successor was named; the Elector Augustus expropriated the See of Naumburg for himself.

Bibliography: L. CHRISTIANI, *Dictionnaire de théologie catholique,* ed. A. VACANT et al., 15 v. (Paris 1903–50; Tables générales 1951–) 12.1:1366–69. F. LAW, *Die Religion in Geschichte und Gegenwart,* 7 v. (3d ed. Tübingen 1957–65) 5:319. H. JEDIN, in *Lexikon für Theologie und Kirche,* ed. J. HOFER and K. RAHNER, 10 v. (2d new ed. Freiburg 1957–65) 8:429–430. W. OFFELE, *Ein Katechismus im Orient der Glaubenseinheit* (Essen 1963).

[B. L. MARTHALER]

PFORTA, ABBEY OF

(Schulpforta, *Porta*), Cistercian abbey in Thuringia, Germany, Diocese of Naumburg; founded 1132; secularized 1540. In 1127 Count Bruno of Pleissengau founded, near Schmölln, a convent for nuns. They were replaced in 1132 by Benedictine monks, who were followed by Cistercians invited from Walkenried, Brunswick, by Bishop Udo of Naumburg. In 1137 the Cistercians moved to Pforta, a more favorable location. Within a century Pforta founded three other abbeys: LEUBUS (1163), Altzelle (1170), and Dünamünde (1208). Through model farms and advanced agricultural methods, Pforta contributed to the economic growth of medieval Thuringia. Under the pressure of the Protestant Duke Henry of Saxony, the abbey was secularized in 1540 and made a secondary school. As such, "Schulpforta" achieved a reputation for scholarly excellence; it is still a school. The early church, in transitional style, was built (1137–50) after French models, but has been preserved as remodeled in 13th-century Gothic.

Bibliography: W. HIRSCHFELD, *Zisterzienserkloster Pforte* (Burg, Ger. 1934). R. BÄUMER, *Lexikon für Theologie und Kirche,* ed. J. HOFER and K. RAHNER, 10 v. (2d, new ed. Freiburg 1957–65) suppl., *Das Zweite Vatikanische Konzil: Dokumente und Kommentare,* ed. H. S. BRECHTER et al., pt. 1 (1966) 8:430.

[L. J. LEKAI]

PHANTASM

In its current acceptance, the term phantasm signifies a representation or apparition distinct from the ordinary reality of things and frequently subjective in character. In the latter case it is commonly attributed to the IMAGINATION. For Aristotle, φάντασμα means image (*Anim.* 432a 9), a representation similar to sensation (except that it is immaterial) and needed for the activity of the INTELLECT. Scholastics such as St. THOMAS AQUINAS define phantasm functionally as a likeness of a particular thing (*Summa theologiae* 1a, 84.7 ad 2). It is found at the level of the internal senses and constitutes an indispensable step in man's knowing process, where its principal role is to supply a representation of concrete reality from which the intellect extricates the essential meaning (*C. gent.* 2.77; *Comp. theol.* 1.83; *Summa theologiae* 1a, 84.7).

Explanation. Because the internal SENSES reach material reality only through the medium of the external senses, they generally (i.e., with the exception of the CENTRAL SENSE) need a representation of this reality to serve as the expression (*species expressa*) of their knowledge. When transmitting the integral object of their sensations to the internal senses, the external senses are unable to know the meaning or function of certain aspects of reality perceived by the COGITATIVE POWER (*In three de anim.* 3). Moreover, imagination and MEMORY store the impressions of the central sense and the cogitative power respectively (*Summa theologiae* 1a, 78.4), since the reality affecting all the senses changes continually. A representation of this reality as known by these three internal senses is thus required to complete their knowing activity. The need for the phantasm must therefore be admitted not only in the imagination, as many scholastics teach, but also in the cogitative power and memory, as St. Thomas expressly holds (*C. gent.* 2.73). Besides, since the *species expressa* is to represent the object as known, the latter two senses cannot elaborate their specific activity of knowing if they do not express this knowledge through a phantasm distinct from that of the imagination.

While phantasms, as expressed species, are representations of things other than themselves, they are realities of the organic order (*In lib. de memor.* 3), as are the cognitive powers that produce them. It is possible to detect their presence in particular areas of the brain by means of suitable techniques. Phantasms are subject to the physiological and psychological conditions of the internal senses and are liable to change with time (*C. gent.* 2.73); thus they can become weak and disappear.

Related Phenomena. While ILLUSION is primarily a sensory phenomenon of the external senses, to the extent that it implies a perceptual judgment concerning the data of SENSATION it also involves the internal senses. Imagination and memory can be active, particularly when there is interference of past experiences in the knowing process. The phantasms of these internal senses are joined to images directly brought on under the stimulus of actual sensations, and proportionately modify the whole as perceived and evaluated by the central sense and cogitative power. Such cases of illusion are limited because, in the wakened state, the imagination generally follows reason in preference to natural influences (*Summa theologiae* 2a2ae, 172.1 ad 3). However, because susceptible to the disturbing action of these influences, imagination is justly regarded as a source of error, and much more so than the external senses (*Summa theologiae* 2a2ae, 11.1 ad 3; *De ver.* 1.11). The typical illusion brought on by the imagination consists in presenting its phantasms to the consciousness of the subject with sufficient intensity to make it difficult to distinguish between things that are present and those that are merely representations of the imagination (*Summa theologiae* 1a, 17.2 ad 2).

Illusion consists principally in a distorted perception of a reality actually present to sensation. Hallucination, on the other hand, is produced by the interposition of an internal representation that is substituted, on the field of consciousness, for the perception of external reality. Its cause is the paroxysmal activity of the imagination's conserving and reproducing functions.

Following Aristotle, St. Thomas did not hesitate to attribute this hyperproduction of phantasms to biological factors—e.g., humoral circulation produces some phantasms (*Summa theologiae* 1a, 111.3)—or to the action of stupefacient substances (*De ver.* 13.1 ad 12). Devils also can bring on these apparitions (*De malo* 3.4).

The scholastic theory of phantasms is considerably elaborated with respect to dreams because of the related moral problems (*Summa theologiae* 2a2ae, 154.5), and even more so because of the paranormal states involved in visions and prophecies (*Summa theologiae* 2a2ae, 173.2, 3). A DREAM is essentially a product of phantasms appearing during sleep, while the senses are inhibited, so that the phantasms occupy almost exclusively what is left of the sleeper's consciousness. The causes of the production of these phantasms include everything that can act upon the imagination during sleep. St. Thomas draws up a systematic list (*Summa theologiae* 2a2ae, 95.6): first, internal causes, including those of a psychic nature (previous evening's preoccupation persisting during sleep), and those of a corporal nature (sleeper's organic disposition—whence Aquinas notes the usefulness of the study of dreams by doctors); and then external causes, including those of a physical nature (ambient temperature), and those of a spiritual nature (God, through the ministry of angels, or even the devil). As the central sense frees itself of hypnogenetic inhibitions, the subject begins to make a distinction between phantasms and the reality affecting the senses, although this distinction remains imperfect so long as the central sense is not completely awakened (*Summa theologiae* 1a, 84.8 ad 2).

See Also: SPECIES, INTENTIONAL; KNOWLEDGE, PROCESS OF.

Bibliography: F. GAETANI and M. L. FALORNI, *Enciclopedia filosofica* 2:264–268. R. EISLER, *Wörterbuch der philosophischen Begriffe*, 3 v. (4th ed. Berlin 1927–30)2:434, 424–433. R. E. BRENNAN, *Thomistic Psychology* (New York 1952). F. A. WALSH, ''Phantasm and Phantasy,'' *New Scholasticism* 9 (1935) 116–133. T. M. BARTOLOMEI, ''Le immagini,'' *Divus Thomas* (Piacenza) 58 (1955) 124–142.

[A. M. PERREAULT]

PHARISEES

The predominant sect or religious party among the Jews in the time of Christ. After outlining their history and principal teachings, this article considers the NT references to them.

History and Teachings. The Pharisees were those who had ''separated themselves'' (Heb. *p^e^rûšîm;* Aram. *p^e^rîšayyā* from which comes the Gr. φαρισαῖοι) from others on the basis of ritual purity through minute observance of the Law. It would seem that the sect arose during the Greek period, as a continuation and development of the HASIDAEANS. At the time of the Maccabees, they were strong enough to offer efficacious support to the HASMONAEANS; they came into conflict with this dynasty, however, during the reign of John Hyrcanus (135–10.5 B.C.). In NT times the Pharisees were in conflict with the priestly SADDUCEES; the latter were conservatives who rejected the oral tradition accepted by the Pharisees. Most Pharisees were lay, but some priests as well as many of the doctors of the Law or SCRIBES joined their number.

The teaching of the sect was based on oral tradition as well as on the written Law. The Pharisees held for such religious truths as the resurrection of the body and the existence of angels. Since these doctrines were not clearly taught in the Pentateuch (the only Scripture accepted by the Sadducees), the Pharisees founded their belief in them upon later writings and oral traditions. In the field of morals the Pharisees taught a rigorous observance of the SABBATH and insisted on legal purity and the payment of tithes. They offered various opinions on minute observance of these and other precepts, to such an extent that their opponents accused them of degenerating into rigorism and casuistry and focusing on sterile externalism destructive of a real religious spirit.

After the destruction of the Temple and the overthrow of the Jewish state, the Pharisees became practically the only influential group among the Jews. Through the uncertain centuries that followed, they held the Jewish people together. Later rabbinical schools looked back with admiration upon the Pharisees as the true upholders of Israel's Law and traditions. The rabbis of the TALMUD were their spiritual descendants.

In the New Testament. The fact that Jesus rejected much of the legalistic tradition of the Pharisees (Mk 7.1–23), sought to free people from its burden (Mt 11.28–30) and to interpret to them the profounder meaning of the Law (Mt 5.20–48), inveighed against externalislic pietism (Mt 6.1–18; 23.5–12, 23–31), and taught that redemption would come from Him (Mk 10.45) brought Him inevitably into conflict with the Pharisees. After His Ascension this conflict continued between the Christians and the Pharisees. While the debates between Jesus and the Pharisees recorded in the Gospels do recount historical events of His public ministry, their very preservation and the manner in which they are cast reflect the later struggle of the Church against the Pharisaic spirit both within and without.

The NT writers frequently mention the Pharisees, sometimes favorably, sometimes unfavorably. The Gospels narrate conflicts between the Pharisees and Jesus in Galilee (Mk 2.6–3.5; Lk 5.17–6.5; Mt 9.1–17; 12.1–45), in Jerusalem (Mk 11.27–12.40; Lk 20.1–47; Mt 21.23–22.46), and in several other less well-defined circumstances (Mt 15.1–20; Mk 7.1–23); and a strong condemnation of Pharisaism is found in Mt 23.1–36. Yet St. Luke relates incidents in which the Pharisees appear in a more favorable light (Lk 13.31; Acts 5.34; 23.6–9). It should be noted also that the Evangelists do not emphasize the activities of the Pharisees against Jesus in the Passion narratives. Only a few times are the Pharisees explicitly mentioned among those who brought about Jesus' death (Mt 27.62; Jn 18.3). The same reluctance to identify Pharisees as enemies is found in the Synoptic tradition about the predictions of the Passion (Mt 20.17–19; Mk 8.31; 10.33; Lk 9.22; 18.31).

In spite of, or because of, this ambivalent attitude toward the Pharisees as manifested in the Gospels, some modern critics consider the Evangelists biased and their testimony about the Pharisees untrustworthy. Other scholars attempt to vindicate the Evangelists in their apparent hostility to the sect.

In recent years exegetes have sought to rediscover the literary origins of the narratives, to analyze the religious background of a given pericope in the life of the early Church, and to stress the theological purposes that led an Evangelist to incorporate a narrative into his Gos-

"Pharisees Instructing a Man Not to Transport a Bed on the Sabbath," manuscript illumination by Cristoforo de Predis from the "Predis Codex." (©Archivo Iconografico, S.A./CORBIS)

pel. (*See* FORM CRITICISM, BIBLICAL.) It should be noted that many of the Gospel incidents mentioning the Pharisees are concerned with disputes between them and Jesus. It would seem that the narratives in which these incidents are recounted reached their present form during the heated Judaizing crisis in the early Church. The Judaizers insisted on the strict observance of the Mosaic Law by Gentile Christians as well as by those of Jewish origin. It was on the authority of the Lord that such a dispute had to be settled, and the early community recalled the occasions on which He had debated with the Pharisees concerning the observance of the Sabbath, circumcision, distinction of foods, legal purity, etc. As the orthodox Christians recalled these discussions and repeated them against the Judaizers (and to some extent against the Pharisees outside the Church), it is obvious that the Pharisees as a group would be depicted in a poor light. The Evangelists then used these ready-made narratives in their Gospels. Their intent was not to disparage the Pharisees as such, but rather to prevent Christian readers from failing into the evils of the Judaizers and the externalism of many Pharisees. Their motive was not a national or party bias but a deep concern for Christian believers.

The Evangelists mentioned the Pharisees with a theological intention in mind. Their chief purpose was to preserve for their Christian readers the authentic teaching of Jesus regarding the primacy of the spirit over the letter, of inner religion over sterile externalism.

Bibliography: L. FINKELSTEIN, *The Pharisees: The Sociological Background of Their Faith,* 2 v. (3d ed. rev. Philadelphia 1962). J.W. BOWKER, *Jesus and the Pharisees* (Cambridge 1973). J. NEUSNER, *Formative Judaism: Religious, Historical and Literary Studies: Third Series: Torah, Pharisees, and Rabbis* (Chico, Calif. 1983). S. MASON, *Flavius Josephus on the Pharisees: A Composition- Critical Study* (Leiden 1991). D. B. GOWLER, *Host, Guest, Enemy, and Friend: Portraits of the Pharisees in Luke and Acts* (New York 1991). G. STEMBERGER, *Jewish Contemporaries of Jesus: Pharisees, Sadducees, Essenes* (Minneapolis 1995). J. NEUS-

NER, *The Rabbinic Traditions about the Pharisees before 70* (Atlanta, Ga. 1999). A. J. SALDARINI, *Pharisees, Scribes, and Sadducees in Palestinian Society: A Sociological Approach,* new ed. (Grand Rapids, Mich. 2001). J. WELLHAUSEN, *The Pharisees and the Sadducees: An Examination of Internal Jewish History* (Macon, Ga. 2001).

[R. MERCURIO/EDS.]

PHELAN, DAVID SAMUEL

Priest, editor, author; b. Sydney, Nova Scotia, July 16, 1841; d. St. Louis, Mo., Sept. 21, 1915. As the son of Alexander and Margaret (Creedon) Phelan, he moved with his family to St. Louis, Mo., in 1853. On completion of his studies for the priesthood under the Vincentians at Cape Girardeau, Mo., he was ordained by Abp. Peter Richard Kenrick (May 30, 1863) and assigned as assistant at the cathedral in St. Louis. Within a few months he became pastor at Indian Creek, Mo., and shortly afterwards, at Edina, Mo. Here he purchased the machinery and type of two small, often anti-Catholic newspapers and began publication of the *Missouri Watchman.* In 1868 he was named pastor of Annunciation parish in St. Louis. In 1873, after serving at Pacific, Mo., he became pastor of Our Lady of Mount Carmel parish, St. Louis, a post he held until his death. Phelan organized parishes in Ferguson and Spanish Lake, Mo., and was involved in the establishment of a Carmel in New Orleans, La., by nuns from the St. Louis Carmel. Phelan was best known as a journalist. At Edina, where his newspaper attacked the test oath demanded by the Missouri constitution, he was arrested when he refused to take the oath. He was released without conviction. His newspaper, renamed the *Western Watchman,* in St. Louis, often indulged in controversy. Phelan frequently criticized the actions of the hierarchy, including his own superiors. He was outspoken, for instance, against Cahenslyism, attempts to recruit American volunteers for papal service against Garibaldi, the condemnation by some bishops of the Ancient Order of Hibernians, and the educational provisions of the Third Council of Baltimore. He was a great admirer of Abp. John Ireland, who supported him in several disputes. In addition to exposing the American Protective Association in St. Louis, Phelan usually favored Democratic foreign and domestic policies and reflected contemporary Irish-American antipathy to Britain. Besides his editorial contributions, he produced two volumes of sermons, *The Gospel Applied to Our Times* (1904) and *Christ the Preacher* (1905). He also compiled and translated from the French three works in ascetical theology.

Bibliography: J. E. ROTHENSTEINER, *History of the Archdiocese of Louis,* 2 v. (St. Louis 1928). M. C. SMITH, *Our Pastors in Calvary: Biographical Sketches of Parish Priests of St. Louis, 1854–1924* (St. Louis 1924).

[M. F. HASTING]

PHELAN, GERALD BERNARD

Philosopher, psychologist, medievalist; b. Halifax, Nova Scotia, Aug. 26, 1892; d. Toronto, Ontario, May 30, 1965. He was ordained a priest of the Archdiocese of Halifax Dec. 27, 1914. The next year he received an S.T.B. from The Catholic University of America; in 1918, an M.A. from St. Francis Xavier University, Nova Scotia; in 1924, a Ph.D. from the University of Louvain; and in 1925, an Agrégé en philosophie from the same institution. He was made a domestic prelate on Jan. 15, 1960. From 1914 to 1918 Phelan was engaged in parochial work in Nova Scotia and Bermuda. He lectured in philosophy at St. Mary's College, Halifax, from 1917 to 1922. In 1925 he was appointed professor of psychology at St. Michael's College, the University of Toronto, and from 1926 to 1946 he was professor of philosophy there. He served as librarian of the Institute of Mediaeval Studies, Toronto, from 1929 to 1931; as codirector with Étienne Gilson; and as president from 1937 to 1946. He was the founder and director of the Mediaeval Institute at the University of Notre Dame from 1946 to 1952 and head of the department of philosophy at Notre Dame during those years. From 1952 until his retirement in 1962 he was professor of philosophy at St. Michael's College, and from 1958 professor of philosophy in the Pontifical Institute. He served as president of the American Catholic Philosophical Association in 1931. He received the Cardinal Mercier medal in 1925 and the Cardinal Spellman-Aquinas medal in 1959.

He received his training in psychology under A. Michotte. He excelled in teaching the philosophy, especially the metaphysics, of St. Thomas Aquinas. A collection of his essays was published by the Pontifical Institute of Mediaeval Studies in 1966.

Bibliography: Works. *Feeling, Experience and Its Modalities* (Louvain 1925); *Jacques Maritain* (New York 1937); *St. Thomas and Analogy* (Milwaukee 1941); *Some Illustrations of St. Thomas's Development of the Wisdom of St. Augustine* (Chicago 1946); *On the Governance of Rulers* (Toronto 1935; New York 1939), tr. of THOMAS AQUINAS'S *De reg. princ.; The Wisdom of St. Anselm* (Latrobe, Pa. 1960).

[A. MAURER]

PHELAN, GERARD, MOTHER

Religious superior, educator; b. Kilkenny, Ireland, Jan. 17, 1872; d. Tarrytown, New York, March 22, 1960.

Baptized Anastasia Phelan, Mother Gerard was educated by the Sacred Heart of Mary Religious, Waterford and Lisburn, Ireland. She entered their congregation at Béziers, France, in 1893. After taking temporary vows, she attended Cambridge University and served as headmistress at Crosby, England before she was called to the United States in July of 1907. On December 8 of the same year, she and Mother M. Joseph BUTLER founded the first MARYMOUNT at Tarrytown, New York. After taking the M.A. and Ph.D. at The Catholic University of America in Washington, D.C., and Fordham University, New York, New York, she specialized in educational work. As Mother Butler's closest collaborator, she also filled successive offices—from conventual superior to superior general. Under her administration the Sacred Heart of Mary apostolate became global as foundations doubled in number and extended as far as Africa. In 1952, Fordham University, in conferring its honorary Litt.D., paid tribute to her extension of Mother Butler's work.

Bibliography: K. BURTON, *Mother Butler of Marymount* (New York 1944).

[F. S. BORAN]

Gerald Bernard Phelan.

PHENOMENA

Phenomena, or appearances, are attributes that make accessible to sensible perception the objects of the visible world. They are interpreted variously. According to PARMENIDES, they are the ''untrue.'' For Protagoras, they are subjective and relative; as the thing appears to a person, so it is for him (frag. 1). For ARISTOTLE, not every phenomenon is necessarily true (*Meta.* 1010b 1–29); however, when critically evaluated, phenomena make objective truth accessible and one should therefore study them (*Meta.* 986b 31). In the thinking of I. KANT, the phenomena are generally valid and objective, but only for man since he constitutes them. More specifically, perceptions are formed by space and time, ''which contain a priori the condition of the possibility of objects as appearances'' (*Critique of Pure Reason,* A 89); i.e., they are the pure intuitions that are contained a priori in sensible nature. The phenomena are then conceived by reason, through its a priori concepts and categories, as objects, while cognition remains limited to the thing–for–us, and never reaches the thing–in–itself (*ibid.* B 164). Likewise, we know ''our own subject only as appearance'' (*ibid.* B 156). As opposed to this view, E. HUSSERL returns ''to the things themselves''; these he understands as the contents of CONSCIOUSNESS that manifest themselves as the result of eidetic and phenomenological reduction and are comprehended by INTUITION or ideation (*see* PHENOMENOLOGY).

See Also: NOUMENA; KANTIANISM; PHENOMENALISM.

Bibliography: G. CAPRONE BRAGA, *Enciclopedia filosofica,* 4 v. (Venice–Rome 1957) 2:329–334. R. EISLER, *Wörterbuch der philosophischen Begriffe,* 3 v. (4th ed. Berlin 1927–30) 2:415–416.

[J. B. LOTZ]

PHENOMENALISM

Strictly taken, phenomenalism is a theory of knowledge attributing existence only to appearances or to sense data precisely as experienced. The commonsense thing, along with its philosophical counterpart, SUBSTANCE, is banished as an illicitly inferred and superfluous entity. ''Mr. Jones'' then becomes a shorthand term standing for a congeries of sense data, such as lowpitched sounds associated with a certain color, height, configuration, and so on. The statement ''Mr. Jones will be there,'' translated into phenomenalistic idiom, roughly reads: ''If you perform certain operations, you will receive such-and-such sensory impressions (summarily named Mr. Jones).'' The *esse est percipi* of G. BERKELEY was its first pure formulation: a thing is simply an aggregate of percepts, upheld by God. Shifting the phenomenal basis to the associative activity of the percipient, J. S. MILL defined matter as the permanent possibility of sensation. B. RUSSELL added logical sophistication by reducing a physical object to a logical construct or class of appearances. To avoid hypostatizing appearances, A. J. Ayer proposed linguistic techniques for replacing sentences about physical objects with sentences about sense data alone.

Broadly taken, phenomenalism admits extraphenomenal objects. I. KANT maintained that a thing-in-itself underlies the PHENOMENA. The ''Unconditioned'' of W. HAMILTON and the ''Unknowable'' of H. SPENCER, both quasinoumenal realities, betray a like spirit of Kantian compromise.

An empiricist bias restricting all immediate cognition to *sensibilia* bars phenomenalists from reaching noninferred substance, but the very formulas allegedly excluding substance admit the notion through the back door. SOLIPSISM aside, permanently possible sensations imply publicly permanent objects able to be sensed. Too, a class embraces appearances objectively similar, i.e., regularly emanating from one objective whole. Again, it is impossible to phenomenalize the self. Only an already unified subject can systemize data; a linguistic fiction cannot construct a linguistic fiction. Finally, while claiming to treat things as phenomena, phenomenalists in fact treat phenomena as things.

See Also: KNOWLEDGE; KNOWLEDGE, THEORIES OF; SENSE KNOWLEDGE.

Bibliography: G. CAPONE BRAGA, *Enciclopedia filosofica,* 4 v. (Venice–Rome 1957) 2:314–329. R. EISLER, *Wörterbuch der philosophischen Begriffe,* 3 v. (4th ed. Berlin 1927–30) 2:416–419.

[J. M. QUINN]

PHENOMENOLOGY

From the Greek φαινόμενον and λόγος, the setting forth or articulation of what shows itself. [For an etymological derivation and exposition of the term, *see* M. Heidegger, *Being and Time,* tr. J. Macquarrie and E. Robinson (New York 1962).] The word was first used in the 18th century by J. H. Lambert (1728–77), then by I. Kant; finally it became a fundamental notion in the celebrated work of G. W. F. HEGEL, *Phänomenologie des Geistes* (Würzburg 1807). In the 20th century the term was revived and given fresh meaning by E. HUSSERL, and it is from his work that contemporary usage derives its basic connotation.

Intentionality. Guided by the doctrine of the INTENTIONALITY of CONSCIOUSNESS, which he had acquired from his teacher F. BRENTANO, Husserl was led to repudiate and criticize his own earlier views on the nature of knowledge. In the *Logische Untersuchungen* (2 v. Halle 1900–01), he laid bare the logical inconsistency in PSYCHOLOGISM, the prevalent view that the laws of thought and the nature of thinking were attained by inductive generalization from the observation or INTROSPECTION of one's mental states. Thus, J. S. MILL held that the principle of CONTRADICTION was a generalization from the fact that belief and disbelief were two different ''mental states'' excluding one another. Husserl showed that such formulations not only could never attain the certainty and specific character of logical laws, but that they disastrously confused the act of thinking and the object of thought, so that *what* one thought was conceived as a content of the mind (and as subject to its laws) just as much as the thinking itself. In opposition to this, he argued that what presents itself to consciousness—what one judges, imagines, and remembers—is not an element or ingredient of the stream of conscious acts (judging, imagining, remembering, etc.) but transcends them in some way, as evidenced by the fact that one can return to the same thought indefinitely many times. To speak of consciousness as intentional is to refer to this essential characteristic of all conscious experiences, their intrinsic reference to an object that is not a real element of the experience. All consciousness is consciousness of something beyond it, something presented to it but not contained in it (i.e., the mind is not a container).

This doctrine of the intentional structure of consciousness is the cornerstone of phenomenology, but it is only the cornerstone. The influence and importance of phenomenology lie not in the recovery of this notion, but in its twofold analysis: one toward the ontological ground of this structure (and from this emerges contemporary EXISTENTIALISM) and the other toward the classification and clarification of the many different types of intentionality and intentional objects (perceptual, volitional, aesthetic, psychic, etc.).

Once the OBJECTIVITY of the objects of consciousness is secured, Husserl lays out the foundations of phenomenology as a ''prephilosophical'' descriptive protoscience, whose concern will be with the systematic delineation and classification of (not the stream of consciousness, but) the fundamental types of intentional objects and, correspondingly, the intentional acts of the subject presenting them. If this can be done, one will have at hand the fundamental data on which all systematic knowledge is founded.

Phenomenological Method. Such an effort, to be successful, requires that the phenomena be described as they really give themselves, free from any cultural, philosophical, or ontological bias: it requires an ascetic neutrality in one's attitude toward the phenomena of one's awareness. To achieve this neutrality is the purpose of the reductions that are sketched in bk. 1 of the *Ideen zu einer reinen Phänomenologie und phänomenologischen Philosophie* (Halle 1913); tr. W. B. Gibson, *Ideas: General Introduction to Pure Phenomenology* (New York 1931). There is, first, the philosophical *epoché,* or bracketing, the setting aside of all philosophical presuppositions about reality, the world, man, the distinctions of primary and secondary qualities, the exterior and interior worlds, etc. The eidetic reduction focuses one's attention on the essential structures of what appears, so that one is dealing not with an empirical description, nor with a description of subsistent Platonic Forms, but with the sense or meaning of what appears. The phenomenological reduction crowns this process by bracketing the reality of the phenomena (whether psychical or physical) that one spontaneously and implicitly accepts as existing. To do this is not to deny or ignore their reality, but rather to focus on precisely what in their appearance or mode of appearing gives them the index of real.

At this point, one is at the center of the labyrinth of phenomenological method and presumably prepared to proceed with an absolutely pure (i.e., unbiased) description of the structures of conscious experience: its temporality, the acts by which various intentional objects are constituted or rendered present, and the various types of objects themselves—perceptual, imagined, etc. Husserl goes further and seems to contend that the intentional acts and objects of consciousness exist absolutely, whereas physical objects exist only for consciousness, being nothing more than the system of their concordant appearances. Although the word is not used in the *Ideen,* it seems that IDEALISM is the direction of development here indicated. At least, this is the way in which many of Husserl's ''first generation'' of students read it and repudiated it, while accepting the phenomenological reduction (or the transcendental-phenomenological reduction, as it was later called) as a methodological device. To this first group belonged such eminent thinkers as Jean Hering, Alexander Koyré, and a notable group of later converts to Catholicism such as Dietrich von HILDEBRAND, Max SCHELER, and Edith Stein.

Meaning and Experience. Some other characteristic elements of Husserl's phenomenology developed in the *Ideen* and later works are the following. First is the distinction between empty and filled meaning-intentions, corresponding roughly to the distinction between ''I understand what you mean'' and ''I see that it is the case.'' The formulation of a hypothesis and its verification would exemplify this, but so also would the anticipation of how a melody now being heard will be resolved and

Doctor Dietrich von Hildebrand.

its actual heard resolution. The latter example is significant because the anticipation is not a hypothesis, nor is it conceptual, but it is part of the meaning of the unfinished melody in process.

Second is the affirmation that every object of awareness (perceptual, conceptual, etc.) is given in a horizon or field of other objects or meanings that contributes to its significance. Thus Husserl holds, as do the Gestaltists, that PERCEPTION is not of the individual object but of a figure on a ground of some kind. Moreover, Husserl extends the notion of horizon to the implicitly anticipated perceptions that one could have of the object before him if, e.g., he walked around it. He calls this the internal horizon of the object and insists that the not-yet-given-but-anticipated perceptions (the ''protentions'') are part of the meaning of the aspect of the object that is actually given to the perceiver. His view of perception, therefore, is not Humean in the sense that one is presented with naked sense data: there is a potential as well as an actual element in the objects of which man is perceptually aware. Moreover, the protentions are pre-predicative or pre-conceptual: they are not, as has been noted, hypotheses about what will come next. This reflects the phenomenological position that it is the appearing of the object that constitutes the phenomenon, not apparent objects about whose external status one has still to decide.

Third is the distinction between noesis and noema. Every conscious experience is, phenomenologically, extraordinarily complex. The fundamental composition is that of the intentional object, or noema, and the act of intending, or noesis: for example, that which one judges and the act of judging. Noesis and noema are correlative in the sense that every distinct kind of intentional object is rendered present to man's awareness by a distinct type of noetic act. Moreover, each intentional object is itself a synthetic unity of many distinct noematic aspects. Thus every noema, in addition to its fundamental sense or meaning, presents itself with the index of really existing, or being unreal (imagined, dreamt, etc.); with this or that aspect focused on by attention; with affective and volitional aspects (desirable, valued, sacred, etc.); and with a ''doxic'' character (possible, probable, problematic, doubtful, etc.). To each of these aspects of the full or complete noema corresponds a noetic element of consciousness (e.g., for the last series of doxic modalities: supposition, conjecture, question, and doubt).

Phenomenology and Idealism. In the later works of his middle period, Husserl's idealism grew more pronounced and more explicit. In the *Cartesian Meditations* (Paris 1931; tr. D. Cairns, The Hague 1960), phenomenology is described as a ''transcendental idealism,'' and every dimension of conscious experience is said to fit into the schema *''ego-cogito-cogitatum.''* Already in this work and increasingly in the 1930s, there are elements that resist subsumption into such idealism: the notions of history and the alter ego, of a time both constituted and constituting, of passive constitution and the genesis of meaning, and, perhaps most importantly, of the world as the passive pre-given ground of all intentional objects. Two posthumous works, *Erfahrung und Urteil* (ed. L. Landgrebe, Prague 1939) and the essays collected under the title of *Die Krisis der europäischen Wissenschaften und die transzendentale Phänomenologie* (v.6 of *Husserliana,* The Hague 1954), have a decidedly more realistic tone, and in their development of the notion of the *Lebenswelt,* or vital world of everyday life, served to lay out the frame of an ontological structure of consciousness as being-in-the-world.

It is as yet not possible to pass definitive judgment on the import of these late years for Husserl's own conception of phenomenology. What is clear is that it is primarily from the problems and orientation of this last period that the existential phenomenology of the 1940s and 1950s took its bearings. Among the themes of these writings, still only partially published, perhaps the most influential has been that of the *Lebenswelt.*

Lebenswelt. The *Lebenswelt* is the encompassing world of man's daily life, whose primordial structures tend to be lost sight of under a ''clothing of ideas,'' basically the ideas or attitudes of the physical sciences. For example, there is, according to Husserl, a primordial experience of spatiality that is neither Euclidean nor Riemannian nor Lobachevskian, i.e., not geometrical at all. It is structured around such basic poles as near and far, home ground and away, etc. Its central foundation is the earth, not in the sense of the circling globe of Copernicus, but as the ground upon which all motion takes place and which itself neither moves nor is stationary. All concrete, perceived motion requires a ground against which the motion is given. True, one can think about the motion of particles in mechanics without reference to this ground, but to do so is precisely to abstract from one's concrete experience and to leave behind part of its essential structure. The abstraction may indeed be truly revealing of a dimension of the real world, but insofar as it is taken to be the fundamental world-picture on the basis of which one must account for the perceived world, it represents an inversion of viewpoint rooted in a forgetfulness of its origins.

It is this forgetfulness of its concrete origins that underlies the contemporary crisis of the sciences of the West, in Husserl's view. To overcome this crisis, what is needed is a reduction that recovers (or rather uncovers) the primordial levels of the experience of living-in-the-world. Only then will one be able to secure the foundations of scientific knowledge by seeing how it arises out of, and hence is rooted in, the *Lebenswelt.* It was to the phenomenological exploration and description of the *Lebenswelt* that most of Husserl's work in the 1930s was addressed, and it is in large part around this theme that the later development of phenomenology has crystallized. A good example of this is the *Phenomenology of Perception,* by M. MERLEAU-PONTY (Paris 1945; tr. C. Smith, New York 1962), which provides descriptive accounts of the basic structures of living-in-the-world: perception, the body, things, space, time, other persons, etc.

Existential Phenomenology. In spite of the continuity of theme and approach, however, there are fundamental criticisms of Husserl's transcendental phenomenology in the writings of these more recent philosophers, so much so that it is appropriate to distinguish a second major phase of the phenomenological movement as a whole, a phase that has been called existential phenomenology. Three of these fundamental differences may be noted: the status of reduction and constitution, the role of pre-predicative intentionalities, and the significance of the body.

Reduction and Constitution. The transcendental *epoché* had as its goal the reduction of all objects of consciousness whatsoever to the status of *cogitata,* i.e., intentional-theoretic objects of the transcendental ego, the absolutely disengaged observer. The obverse of the reduction is the "constitution" of the mundane objects from which one began: once one has "unpacked" all the implicit and explicit intentionalities that make up the meaning of the objects he experiences, he is in a position to see and say how these objects are constituted for himself, namely, by the thus delineated intentional acts of the transcendental ego. For a transcendental idealistic phenomenology, then, reduction and constitution are coextensive and exhaustive: every possible nonego element of conscious experience can be reduced and produced. For the existential phenomenologists, however, the reduction does not reveal a disengaged transcendental ego for whom all else can be rendered objective, but discovers a world whose reality coconstitutes the ego rather than being constituted *for* the ego. It discovers a radical and irreducible involvement of consciousness with the world. It discovers, in sum, an ontological structure of participation: being-in-the-world. (Merleau-Ponty attributes this discovery to Husserl, in the form of the distinction between the intentionality of the acts of the ego and an operative intentionality that others have called "exsistence.")

Pre-predicative Intentionality. For existential phenomenology, then, there is a gap between reduction and constitution. The world as the encompassing ground of all constituted objects is itself pre-given, pre-objective, and unconstituted. The genesis or constitution of the "true and exact" world of objective science is still a problem consequent upon the reduction to the pre-objective world of the *Lebenswelt,* but the latter is only to be described, not constituted or constructed. The fundamental structures of the *Lebenswelt* underlie and thus escape from what Husserl in his idealist period considered to be the all-encompassing matrix of meaning: the *ego-cogito-cogitatum.* There are perceptions of meaning (e.g., of sexuality, of other persons, of the world) that are not *cogitationes* envisaging *cogitata.*

Intentionality remains, for the existential phenomenologists, the "defining" characteristic of awareness, although it is not primarily the intentionality of ego related to object through its thetic or explicit acts, but the irreducibly pre-reflective intentionality of an ontological situation. The critical operative element in this ontological structure, that which effects the in-the-world dimension of the being of consciousness, is its incarnation.

Significance of the Body. Perhaps no difference between classical modern philosophy and phenomenology is more striking and at the same time more significant than that of the status of the body. From R. DESCARTES on, the body has been an object for consciousness, bound to the ego in a unique way, no doubt, yet on the same footing with other objects in the world. This is still true for the early Husserl. For the existential phenomenologists, on the other hand, it is the lived body as a dimension of one's subjectivity that is the source of the (pre-reflective) intentionalities that structure the *Lebenswelt.*

Problems of Evaluation. The difficulty involved in making any final evaluation of Husserl's thought was mentioned, and it is perhaps clearer now why this is the case. It is simply not clear as yet (and may never be so) whether in his late years he abandoned the project of a transcendental idealism or whether the solidity of the *Lebenswelt* represented merely a temporary detour in the path of the transcendental reduction. In any case the phenomenological movement is beyond question the dominant philosophical current on the Continent. It seems to have laid to rest the epistemological problem of "inside" and "outside" worlds and to have at least blunted the conflict between science and philosophy by basing philosophy on the description of a pre-objective world of experience.

Causality. At the same time, a number of basic questions remain unanswered or answered unsatisfactorily. One of these is the relation of CAUSALITY to intentionality. The phenomenologists tend to deny any causal relation between nature and consciousness: the physical world acts on consciousness only by "offering it a meaning"; by at most, then, a kind of solicitation. Although they have addressed themselves to such objections as, e.g., an aspirin eliminating a headache, there is as yet no general consensus on how to state the relation between the "lived body" and the "object-body." Yet the latter is clearly involved in causal interactions with nature.

Eternal Truths. A second problem is that of eternal truths. There are, according to Merleau-Ponty, for example, no absolute certainties or eternal truths about anything other than the ontological structures of being-in-the-world; and since these are not objects of consciousness but dimensions of its subjectivity, there are no eternal truths about things in the world. However, it appears that this position commits the same fallacy as did that of D. Hume; namely, it purports to state an eternally true rejection of eternal truths. (*see* TRUTH.)

Metaphysics. A third problem, related to both the former, is the relation of phenomenology to METAPHYSICS. Merleau-Ponty and J. P. SARTRE, among others, have leveled lethal criticisms at the pretensions of modern RATIONALISM to pass from being-for-us to being-in-itself. The only meaning that being can have for man, according to them, is the meaning that it presents to him in his experience; in other words, it can have no consistent transphenomenal meaning. What is at issue here is the possibility of a metaphysics in general and of statements about a transcendent being in particular, but it seems that the challenge is to a metaphysics vitiated by a rationalistic univocity rather than to one recognizing that there is no common *res significata* that is realized imperfectly in the finite and perfectly in the infinite being. If one recognizes for certain terms, of which man grasps only a ''phenomenal'' meaning, that they are predicable of a transfinite being, without knowing precisely what they mean in Him, this seems to be sufficient both to establish the possibility of a metaphysics and to avoid this type of criticism.

Extent of Movement. In Germany, Husserl's former disciples have gone from describing the basic structures of *Dasein,* or human existence to focusing on the question of the meaning of being. The work of HEIDEGGER, in particular, has been an influential source for the transmission of the phenomenological problematic and method to theology, philosophy of religion, and psychology. Among Husserl's earlier students who did significant work in phenomenology, one may note the writings of Alexander Pfänder in logic and psychology, Adolf Reinach on essences and social philosophy, Moritz Geiger on aesthetics, Edith STEIN on psychology and social philosophy, as well as the relation between Thomism and phenomenology, Max SCHELER in ethics and religion, and Roman Ingarden in ontology and aesthetics.

In France, apart from the writings of former students such as Jean Hering in religion, Alexander Koyré in history of science, Gaston Berger, and Emmanuel Levinas, the major sources of phenomenological influence have been the works of Sartre, Merleau-Ponty, and Paul RICOEUR.

In the U.S., where phenomenological writings and interest in them have thus far been scant, the studies of Marvin Farber stood almost alone until the rise of Hitler brought a number of German phenomenologists to America. Men such as Alfred Schuetz, Felix Kaufmann, Fritz Kaufmann, Aron Gurwitsch, and Herbert Spiegelberg have had a definite influence on the growth of interest in phenomenology among American philosophers. The corresponding interest in existentialism and the increasing prominence of the phenomenological approach in theology, psychology, psychiatry, and the social sciences suggest that its present influence is likely to increase.

See Also: OBJECTIVITY; SUBJECTIVITY; CONSCIOUSNESS.

Bibliography: H. SPIEGELBERG, *The Phenomenological Movement,* 2 v. (The Hague 1960). The Husserl Archives at Louvain are publishing a series of studies on or influenced by phenomenology, *Phenomenologica* (The Hague; 1958–). Recent translations of Husserl include *The Phenomenology of Internal Time-Consciousness* (1904–10), ed. M. HEIDEGGER tr. J. CHURCHILL (Bloomington, Ind. 1964); *The Idea of Phenomenology* (from 1907), tr. W. ALSTON and G. NAKHNIKIAN (The Hague 1964). A yearbook was founded by Husserl, *Jahrbuch für Philosophie und phänomenologische Forschung* (Halle 1913–30); the American journal *Philosophy and Phenomenological Research* was founded by M. FARBER in 1940 as its continuation. In France the collection *Épiméthée* directed by J. HYPPOLITE has pub. several trs. of Husserl's works and studies of his thought, as well as original phenomenological studies. M. FARBER, *The Foundations of Phenomenology* (Cambridge, Mass. 1943). P. RICOEUR, *Philosophie de la volonté,* 2 v. in 3 (Paris 1950–60). M. MERLEAU-PONTY, *The Structure of Behavior,* tr. A. L. FISHER (Boston 1963).

[F. J. CROSSON]

PHILADELPHIA, ARCHDIOCESE OF

The Archdiocese of Philadelphia (*Philadelphiensis*) comprises the city and county of Philadelphia, and the counties of Bucks, Chester, Delaware, and Montgomery, an area of 2,182 square miles in the southeastern part of PENNSYLVANIA. In 2001, there were 1,430,161 Catholics, 39 percent of the general population of 3,707,238

Early History. William PENN's colony, founded in 1682, as a ''holy experiment'' by which ''all persons living in this Province shall in no way be molested or prejudiced in their religious persuasion or practice or in matter of faith or worship,'' became a refuge for persecuted Catholics.

First Catholics. There were Catholics in the Philadelphia area from the beginning of its colonization. In 1681 the first governor of what is now Pennsylvania, Anthony Brockholes, was a Catholic. Pehaps the first Catholic resident of ''Penn's Province'' was a servant of Daniel Pastorius, the founder of Germantown. One of the richest men of the time was J. Gray (alias John Tatham), a Catholic from London who had extensive holdings in New Jersey and in Bucks County. His residences were stopping places, where the Jesuits traveling between Maryland and New York celebrated Mass. The Jesuits visited the home also of the wealthy Frenchman Daniel Debuc (d. 1693). There is record of Mass being celebrated publicly in Philadelphia in 1707. Repeated complaints were made to London about this ''Popish Mass,'' but Penn's ''Great Law'' protected the religious freedom of the Catholics.

In 1720 Joseph Greaton, SJ (d. 1753), was given charge of the Catholics in Pennsylvania. He made his headquarters in Maryland but regularly traveled from Bohemia Manor to Concord, Chester County, Conewago, Lancaster, Philadelphia, and back. Greaton decided to reside permanently in Philadelphia, and in 1733 he purchased land and built the first Catholic church in

Student Library, St. Joseph's College, Philadelphia.

Philadelphia, St. Joseph's, which had about 40 parishoners. A year later the governor questioned the right of Catholics to have this public chapel, but he was overruled by the city council. In March 1741 Greaton received an assistant, Henry Neale, SJ (d. May 5, 1748), and the services of two priests from Germany to take care of the German Catholics in Pennsylvania. Father William Wappeler resided at Conewago; Father Theodore Schneider at Goshenhoppen (the present parish of Bally, near Reading). Both also ministered to the Germans in Philadelphia. Financial support for the Church in Pennsylvania was given by Sir John James of London, who set up a fund of £4,000, called the Sir John James Fund.

When Greaton retired to Bohemia Manor in 1749, English-born Robert Harding, SJ (1701–72), succeeded him. Eight years later Harding reported that in Pennsylvania there were 1,365 Catholics (from 12 years of age) who received the Sacraments; 378 of them were living in Philadelphia.

During the French and Indian War the loyalty of the Catholics was questioned and there was a move to keep all papists out of the Philadelphia militia, but without success. Harding purchased ground for another church and cemetery, and St. Mary's was opened in 1763, becoming the parish church of Philadelphia with Harding as pastor; St. Joseph's remained a chapel. The German Jesuit known in the colony as Father Ferdinand FARMER (d. 1786), came from Lancaster to assist Harding in Philadelphia, but he also continued ministering to the German Catholics in Pennsylvania, New Jersey, and New York. In 1772 Robert MOLYNEUX, SJ, succeeded Harding as pastor.

Revolutionary Era. During the Revolution, many of St. Mary's parishioners were leaders of the colonial forces. One exception occurred when General Howe withdrew from Philadelphia in the summer of 1778, taking with him a ''Roman Catholic Battalion'' of about 180 men with Col. Alfred Clifton of St. Mary's parish in charge. In general, however, the Catholics of Philadelphia fought bravely for the Revolution. After the French entered the war, St. Mary's Church became the outstanding Catholic church of the colonies. On Sept. 7, 1777, members of the Continental Congress were present there for the Requiem Mass of General du Coudray. They were present again on July 4, 1779, for the first public religious commemoration of the Declaration of Independence. On Nov. 4, 1781, the Congress met with General Washington at a Solemn Mass of Thanksgiving for victory over the

Barbelin Building, St. Joseph's College, Philadelphia.

British. On Feb. 22, 1800, the Congress met there for a memorial service for President Washington.

After the war, Molyneux built the first parish school in Philadelphia at St. Mary's in May 1782. The practice of pew rent was introduced to offset some of the cost. In October 1785 John CARROLL, then prefect apostolic, administered the Sacrament of Confirmation for the first time in Philadelphia. A year later when Farmer died, his funeral was attended by the members of the American Philosophical Society, the professors and trustees of the University of Pennsylvania, and a large number of non-Catholics. Molyneux retired and was succeeded by the Reverend Francis Beeston, SJ, who built the rectory for St. Joseph's. By 1790 there were reputed to be 2,000 Catholics in Philadelphia. Five years later Holy Trinity Church for German Catholics was completed, and Father John Heilbron was assigned as pastor. Carroll had reluctantly consented to the erection of this national parish, warning the parishioners against a feeling of separatism and denying them the right to name their own pastors. Meanwhile, a large number of destitute persons from the West Indies arrived in Philadelphia during the spring and summer of 1793, bringing the yellow fever mosquito with them. An epidemic ensued, causing about one-half of the inhabitants to flee Philadelphia, which became practically a quarantined city. All the priests of St. Mary's died from the fever, among them Father Lorenz Grässel, who had been chosen as coadjutor to Bishop Carroll, with residence in Philadelphia.

Early Trusteeism. In December 1793 the Reverend Leonard NEALE was appointed pastor of St. Mary's and coadjutor to Carroll. Because of trouble in Europe, the bulls did not arrive until 1800. The appointment in 1796 of Father John Goetz as Heilbron's assistant marked the beginning of TRUSTEEISM at Holy Trinity. Heilbron was forced to retire to St. Joseph's, where he conducted services for the loyal Germans. Although Goetz was suspended, he persisted in his opposition and was joined by Father William Elling, who came to Holy Trinity from Reading to teach in the school that the trustees were forming. At length, Carroll, in February 1797, was constrained to publicly excommunicate both Goetz and Elling. There was a falling out among the schismatics. Four months later, Goetz was forced to resign, and the trustees made Elling pastor. When the trustees tried to make common cause with another group of German schismatics in Baltimore, Carroll came to Philadelphia in 1798. A court case ensued during which the trustees argued that Carroll

Cathedral Basilica of Saints Peter and Paul, Philadelphia; during Mass for Holy Thursday. (AP/Wide World Photos)

was bishop of other nationalities, but not of the Germans. The case reached Rome and the Holy See backed Carroll against the trustees. But it was not until 1802 that Elling, the trustees, and the parishioners of Holy Trinity, which had been put under interdict, publicly recanted. Their abjuration was taken by Thomas Matthew Carr, OSA, the vicar-general.

Under Carr, the Irish Augustinians began another parish in 1796. But it was not until 1801 that St. Augustine's, ''the largest church in Philadelphia,'' was dedicated. President Washington, Commodore John Barry, and Stephen Girard were among the largest contributors. When the trustees of St. Mary's petitioned Carroll to send them a pastor capable of preserving the dignity of ''the leading church in the United States,'' he appointed Michael EGAN, OSF (d. 1814), who had been stationed at Lancaster, and gave him Father John Rossiter as assistant.

Diocese. On April 8, 1808, Egan was appointed bishop of the new Diocese of Philadelphia, which included the entire states of Pennsylvania and Delaware, and the western and southern part of the state of New Jersey, up to a line running west to east and slightly south of Barnegat Bay. St. Mary's was selected as the cathedral. Napoleonic difficulties in Europe prevented the bulls from arriving until 1810, so during the interval Egan remained at St. Mary's as Carroll's vicar-general.

Egan. At its beginning the Diocese of Philadelphia had 16 churches attended by 11 priests, who ministered to 30,000 Catholics. Unfortunately, the trustee problem at St. Mary's marred the new bishop's administration from the first. In 1808 Egan accepted William HAROLD, an Irish Dominican, as a priest of the diocese and in 1810 made him his vicar-general. The next year Father James Harold, an uncle of William Harold, was accepted into the diocese. Trouble, instigated by the Harolds, then developed between the bishop and the trustees of St.

Rosemont College, a Catholic women's college in Philadelphia. (©Kevin Fleming/CORBIS)

Mary's. Although the Harolds returned to Ireland and a schism was averted, the trustees of St. Mary's had acquired such ill fame that it was five years before a successor was named after Egan's death on July 22, 1814. John David, later Bishop of Bardstown, Ky.; Ambrose Maréchal, future Archbishop of Baltimore; and Louis De Barth, pastor of Conewago, all refused the Diocese of Philadelphia. During the interval De Barth was the administrator of the diocese. Finally Henry CONWELL (1748–1842), vicar-general of Armagh, Ireland, was nominated. Having been consecrated in London by Bishop Poynter on Sept. 24, 1820, he arrived in Philadelphia on November 25.

Conwell. The most urgent problem awaiting him was the case of William HOGAN, a priest from Albany, N.Y., whom the administrator had admitted into the diocese without proper credentials, and who preached a sermon against Conwell in the bishop's presence within a week after he took possession of the see. At length a schism began that is known as Hoganism. At Conwell's invitation, William Harold returned to Philadelphia in November 1821 and allied himself with Father Ryan (former rector of the College of Corpo Santo in Lisbon, Portugal) in defense of Conwell against Hogan and his followers. Defeated and disgraced, Hogan left Philadelphia in August 1824, but the trustees of St. Mary's continued to fight against their bishop. Finally, on Oct. 9, 1826, Conwell signed the notorious pact with the trustees giving them the right to veto his appointment of their pastors. This pact was rejected by the Congregation of the Propaganda and the rejection was approved by Pope Leo XII on May 6, 1827. Further trouble ensued when Harold, who had been appointed pastor of St. Mary's and vicar-general, was suspended by Conwell on April 3, 1827. There were appeals to Rome and to the U.S. government. Finally, the aged Conwell was summoned to Rome; Harold and Ryan were transferred from the diocese, and the Holy See named Francis Patrick KENRICK (1796–1863) coadjutor with right of succession. Conwell returned unexpectedly to the U.S. and gave many anxious moments to Kenrick and to the Holy See until his death in 1842 at the age of 94.

Kenrick. On June 6, 1830, Kenrick was consecrated in the Cathedral of St. Joseph at Bardstown, Ky. He arrived in Philadelphia that July 7, but it was not until August of 1831 that Pope Gregory XVI approved the brief that entrusted all ecclesiastical jurisdiction to Kenrick alone. The trustee problem at St. Mary's continued until

Kenrick closed the church and the cemetery on April 16, 1831. The greatest problem confronting him was the lack of priests, so in June 1832 he opened the diocesan seminary of St. Charles Borromeo, which obtained a state charter six years later. During the first three years of his administration, he doubled the number of the churches. St. John the Evangelist, built by Father (later Bishop) John Hughes before he was transferred to New York (1838), was dedicated April 8, 1832 (it became the cathedral in 1838). Next, St. John the Baptist, Manayunk, was dedicated with Father Thomas Gegan as first pastor; and on April 8, 1833, the cornerstone of St. Michael's in Kensington was laid, with Father Terence J. Donoghue as founding pastor. By 1832 the diocese numbered 100,000 Catholics, 38 priests, and 50 churches.

When the cholera epidemic devastated Philadelphia in 1832, the Sisters of Charity at St. Joseph's and St. John's Orphan Asylums gave heroic nursing service to the victims. Michael HURLEY, OSA (d. 1837), pastor of St. Augustine's, turned his school and convent into a hospital where 367 patients were treated. In the following year the city council passed a formal resolution of gratitude and gave a purse to the Sisters of Charity. Parochial expansion characterized these years; St. Francis Xavier parish was founded for the Fairmount district and St. Patrick's for the Schuylkill suburb (1839). The following year St. Philip Neri's parish was established in the Southwark district, with Father John P. Dunn as pastor. In 1842 the Redemptorist Fathers were given the new parish of St. Peter's which was built for the Germans in Kensington. In 1843 St. Paul's was founded in the Moyamensing section and St. Stephen's parish in Nicetown near a spot where the early missionaries had celebrated the first Masses in Philadelphia.

When the western portion of Pennsylvania became the Diocese of Pittsburgh (1843), Philadelphia was left with 58 churches, seven missions, 43 priests, and a Catholic population of 100,000. Despite the bitter NATIVISM of these years, which erupted in the 1844 riots in Philadelphia and the burning of two churches, Kenrick continued to direct the steady progress of his diocese. On Nov. 16, 1848, St. Anne's, founded in Port Richmond, was dedicated by Father Francis X. Gartland, later Bishop of Savannah, Ga. On Sept. 28, 1845, Bishop de la Hailandière of Vincennes, Ind., laid the cornerstone for St. Joachim's church in the Frankford district. On June 29, 1846, Bishop Kenrick issued a pastoral letter announcing his determination to build a cathedral. It was to be modeled after San Carlo al Corso in Rome with Napoleon Lebrun as its architect. Other foundations included the Church of the Assumption (1848) with Charles I. H. Carter, a convert and later vicar-general of the diocese, as pastor; St. Dominic's (1849) in the far north suburb of Holmesburg; the parish of St. James (1850) in West Philadelphia; and St. Malachy's church, the cornerstone of which was blessed on May 25, 1850. Before its completion Kenrick transferred to the Metropolitan See of Baltimore. The suburb of Germantown received its parish when St. Vincent de Paul's was founded on July 13, 1851, and placed under the care of the Vincentian Fathers, who conducted the seminary. The first pastor was Father Michael Domenec, later Bishop of Pittsburgh.

Kenrick also opened the first Catholic hospital in Philadelphia, St. Joseph's, staffed by the Sisters of St. Joseph, in June 1849. Educational facilities were expanded with the arrival in March 1846 of the Sacred Heart nuns to conduct a private school for girls, and of the Sisters of St. Joseph, who came the following year. In 1850 the Christian Brothers arrived to teach the boys in the Assumption parochial school. Two colleges for men were established also: Villanova (Augustinians) in 1842 and St. Joseph's (Jesuits) in 1851. When Kenrick left in 1851 to assume his new duties as archbishop of Baltimore, Philadelphia had 92 churches, eight chapels, 101 priests, 43 seminarians, two colleges, six academies for girls, seven charitable institutions, and 170,000 Catholics.

Neumann. John Nepomucene NEUMANN, the fourth bishop of Philadelphia, was consecrated on March 28, 1852. He had immigrated to the U.S. from Bohemia in 1836, was ordained for the Diocese of New York, June 25, 1836, and was the first Redemptorist to be professed in America (1842). During his episcopate, Neumann constantly pressed for parochial schools. He was unsuccessful in his relations with the trustees of Holy Trinity, but he undermined their influence when he established the parish of St. Alphonsus (1852) for German-speaking Catholics. In the same year he established St. Mary Magdalen de Pazzi Church, the first parish for Italian-speaking Catholics. He also introduced the FORTY HOURS DEVOTION in the diocese at St. Philip Neri's Church.

In 1853 the New Jersey section of the diocese was taken to form part of the Diocese of Newark, leaving Philadelphia with 121 churches, 32 missions, 119 priests, and 175,000 Catholics. On April 26, 1857, Neumann received as coadjutor with right of succession, James Frederick Wood, to whom was committed the work of completing the cathedral. He succeeded to the see upon Neumann's death on Jan. 5, 1860. The latter's cause was introduced in Rome in 1897 and on Oct. 13, 1963, Pope Paul VI beatified him. He was canonized by Pope Paul VI on June 19, 1977; his feast day is January 5.

Wood. The fifth bishop had been baptized a Unitarian but was received into the Catholic Church in 1838 and the next year was sent to Rome to study at the Propaganda College. He was ordained in Rome on March 25,

1844, and returned to Cincinnati, Ohio, where he served as curate at the cathedral and pastor of St. Patrick's Church until his consecration on April 26, 1857. His thorough knowledge of the financial world was one of the reasons for his appointment to Philadelphia. In the first year of his administration, Wood established the parishes of the Annunciation in South Philadelphia and All Saints, Bridesburg. His cathedral was nearing completion, but because of the Civil War, he did not have the happiness of singing the first Mass there until Nov. 20, 1864. On Dec. 8, 1865, he announced the purchase of 100 acres at Overbrook (called by some, ''Wood's Folly'') as the site for a seminary. By 1871 this seminary had 128 students.

During a visit to Rome in 1867, he petitioned the erection of two dioceses. On March 3, 1868, the new Dioceses of Harrisburg, Scranton, and Wilmington were founded, leaving Philadelphia with 93 churches; 67 missions; 157 priests; 42 parochial schools; 491 sisters; and a Catholic population of 200,000. Wood was prominent at the Second Plenary Council of Baltimore and attended also Vatican Council I (1869–70), but ill health forced an early return from Rome. He was unanimously appointed treasurer of the episcopal board of the new North American College in Rome. On Oct.15, 1873, he solemnly consecrated the diocese to the Sacred Heart of Jesus.

Archdiocese. In 1875 Philadelphia became the metropolitan see for the state of Pennsylvania with Wood as archbishop. Although in poor health, he went to Rome in 1877 for the golden jubilee of Pius IX's episcopate. On May 23,1880, he presided over the first provincial council of Philadelphia. When he died, he left 127 churches, 53 chapels, and 58 parochial schools.

Ryan. The see was vacant for one year until Rome appointed St. Louis's coadjutor, Bp. Patrick J. RYAN, second Archbishop of Philadelphia. Ryan, often referred to as the ''Bossuet of the American Church'' and perhaps the outstanding pulpit orator of his day, took formal possession of Philadelphia on Aug. 20, 1884. Under his care the archdiocese was provided with such charitable institutions as St. Joseph's Protectory for Girls, Norristown; St. Vincent's Home and Hospital, Philadelphia; St. Francis Vocational School, Eddington; and the Philadelphia Protectory for Boys, near Phoenixville. In 1890 Cahill High School for Boys (later called Roman Catholic High School), Philadelphia, was opened as the first free central Catholic high school in the U.S. In 1908 Ryan announced that a free central high school for girls (later called the John W. Hallahan Catholic Girls' High School) was opened, but he died before its completion in September 1912. A leading figure in the development of Philadelphia's Catholic school system was the diocesan superintendent of schools, Philip McDevitt, later Bishop of Harrisburg.

Ryan took paternal interest in the founding of the motherhouse of the Sisters of the Blessed Sacrament for Indians and Colored People, whose foundress, Mother Katherine DREXEL, dedicated her life and her fortune to the salvation of African Americans and Native Americans. At his death on Feb. 11, 1911, he was suceeded by Edmond Francis PRENDERGAST who had been consecrated auxiliary bishop to Ryan on Feb. 24, 1897.

Prendergast. The third archbishop directed the building of many new institutions: Misericordia Hospital, the Chapel of Divine Love, the Archbishop Ryan Memorial Institute for the Deaf, St. Edmond's Home for Crippled Children, the West Philadelphia Catholic High School for Boys, and the Archbishop Ryan Memorial Library at the seminary. He also renovated the cathedral. He died in Philadelphia on Feb. 26, 1918, and was succeeded by Bp. Dennis DOUGHERTY of Buffalo, N.Y., the first native son to be appointed the archbishop of Philadelphia.

Dougherty. The new archbishop was enthroned by Cardinal James Gibbons on July 10, 1918. During his 33-year administration 112 parishes, 145 parochial schools, 53 Catholic high schools, four Catholic colleges, 12 hospitals, and 11 homes for the aged were established. He consecrated 15 bishops and ordained over 2,000 priests. On March 7, 1921, Pope Benedict XV made him a cardinal priest. He died at his residence on the 61st anniversary of his ordination and was buried in the crypt of the Cathedral of SS. Peter and Paul. At that time the archdiocese had 1,896 priests (1,224 diocesan), 401 parishes, nine chapels, 62 missions, 6,825 sisters, seven colleges, 35 parochial and diocesan high schools, 21 private high schools, 330 parochial elementary schools, 20 private elementary schools, and 1,114,122 Catholics.

O'Hara. On Nov. 28, 1951, John F. O'HARA, former Bishop of Buffalo, was appointed the ninth ordinary of Philadelphia and was solemnly installed on Jan. 9, 1952. Although he was never in good health, O'Hara's episcopate in Philadelphia was most active and vigorous. Embarking on a bold and imaginative program to expand education facilities, he created 30 parishes, opened 55 new parish schools, and improved about 300 others. Fourteen new high schools were built, including Cardinal Dougherty High School with a capacity of 6,000 students. He was actively interested also in the education of the mentally retarded. He continued the unique system of financing Catholic education in the archdiocese, under which the pastors of the students, not the students, are responsible for their tuition. On Nov. 16, 1958, he was named cardinal priest by Pope John XXIII. Two years later on August 28, he died in his see city; his remains were interred in Sacred Heart Church at the University of Notre Dame, South Bend, Ind. After his death the archdiocese was further divided when the Diocese of Allentown was established Jan. 28, 1961, with Joseph McShea, former auxiliary bishop of Philadelphia and administrator of the archdiocese, as first bishop. The counties of Philadelphia, Bucks, Chester, Delaware and Montgomery were left to Philadelphia.

Krol. On Feb. 11,1961, John Joseph KROL (b. Oct. 26, 1910), former auxiliary bishop of Cleveland, was nominated archbishop of Philadelphia and installed on March 22. Born in Cleveland, Ohio, Krol was ordained on Feb. 20, 1937, and served as chancellor of the Cleveland diocese. He was appointed auxiliary bishop of Cleveland and vicar-general on July 11, 1953, and consecrated September 2.

In the wake of Vatican II, Philadelphia itself was caught up in the dramatic changes in church life, as well as the societal changes of America itself. If the city escaped some of the unrest which sprung from the Civil Rights Movement, it was in no small measure attributable to the success the newly created Archbishop's Commission on Human Relations, which helped bring the different factions together.

A first English-language Mass was celebrated Nov. 29, 1964; new rituals, increased roles for the laity and the reinstitution of the permanent diaconate came in time fashion, however introduction of Saturday evening Mass was delayed until 1983, when it was mandated for the entire American Church. Krol had opposed the change, but on some other issues he was quite open; for example, the Philadelphia archbishop was vocal in his support of disarmament and opposition to nuclear weapons. On June 26, 1967 he was created cardinal, along with another Philadelphian, Francis Brennan, dean of the Holy Roman Rota.

In 1976, the Bicentennial Year, Philadelphia hosted the 41st International Eucharistic Congress. Among the dignitaries who attended the Congress were MOTHER TERESA of Calcutta, Dorothy DAY, Archbishop Fulton J. SHEEN, Cesar CHAVEZ, Dom Heldar CAMARA and President of the United States Gerald Ford. Absent for reasons of health was Pope Paul VI, but almost unnoticed among the host of prelates attending was the future Pope JOHN PAUL II, Poland's Cardinal Karol Wojtyła, who had received his red hat with Krol and who had become a fast friend.

In 1977 Philadelphians traveled to Rome for the canonization of their fourth bishop, John Neumann, as America's first male saint. The cause had begun under Cardinal Dougherty, then languished until it was given new life by Krol, with beatification in 1963. Under his administration too, the cause for Mother Katharine Drexel was also begun and seen through the critical early stages.

After the death of Paul VI and the brief pontificate of John Paul I, Krol was able to participate in the 1978 election of Cardinal Wojtyła as John Paul II. The new pope visited Philadelphia as part of an American tour the following October, and his Mass on Logan Square facing the cathedral attracted more than a million people of all faiths. On Dec. 8, 1987, Cardinal Krol, then 77 and in poor health, announced his retirement.

Bevilacqua. On Feb. 11, 1988, Anthony J. Bevilacqua (born June 17, 1923), was installed as Archbishop of Philadelphia at the Cathedral Basilica of SS. Peter and Paul. Ordained a priest for the Brooklyn Diocese June 11, 1949 and possessing degrees in both canon and civil law, he was ordained as an auxiliary bishop for Brooklyn on July 24, 1980 and was named 10th Bishop of Pittsburgh on Oct. 7, 1983, before his appointment to the Archdiocese of Philadelphia.

As Archbishop of Philadelphia one of his first priorities was a reorganization of the archdiocesan administration to a system of regional vicariates overseeing the parishes and secretariats to administer the diocesan offices. This established a chain of command which freed the archbishop from much of the administrative detail, affording more time for pastoral care. An early pleasant duty for Bevilacqua was that of leading a pilgrimage to Rome for the Nov. 20, 1988 beatification of Mother Katharine Drexel (1858-1955), the Philadelphia born heiress who had renounced her wealth to found the Sisters of the BLESSED SACRAMENT, a congregation devoted to the evangelization and care of Native Americans and African-Americans.

A major challenge in Philadelphia — as elsewhere — were problems associated with shifts in Catholic population from the core city to the suburbs, and skyrocketing costs which were driving students away from the archdiocese's vaunted parochial school system. During Bevilacqua's administration, after exhaustive study some under-utilized churches would close or be twinned with another parish, as would schools. In certain cases the closed parishes were replaced by evangelization centers which would be charged with reintroducing the Church to the affected region. The archdiocesan high schools were a special problem; and in 1992 consultants recommended drastic reduction in the number of schools. Through aggressive fund-raising and elimination of restrictive territorial admission policies, most of the schools were saved; tuition increases were reduced to affordable levels and enrollment stabilized. Parishes also underwent self-studies, and were formed into clusters which enabled group cooperation and joint programs.

Bevilacqua, who was elevated to the College of Cardinals on June 28, 1991, fostered the spirituality of his archdiocese through a nine-year renewal leading up to the Jubilee Year 2000. As part of the renewal, a ''Bless Me'' hotline was inaugurated in 1997 on telephone and Internet, resulting in thousands of inquiries from people who wished to be reconciled with the Church or counseling by a priest. Ecumenism and interfaith relations were also encouraged during the Bevilacqua years with special outreach to Philadelphia's Jewish community. Seminary formation was also enhanced in 1991 through the addition of a separate ''Spirituality Year'' away from St. Charles Borromeo Seminary, Overbrook at Mary Immaculate Seminary in Northampton, Pa., which was acquired from the Vincentians for this purpose. A shortage of Spanish-speaking clergy was partly addressed in 1999 through the adoption of a parish in Arecibo, Puerto Rico where Philadelphia priests and seminarians could become accustomed to the special needs of Hispanic Catholics, and in that same year a Spanish-language radio program was launched by the archdiocese. With the Oct. 1, 2000 canonization of Mother Katharine Drexel, Philadelphia had the unusual distinction, at least at the time, of being the only diocese in the United States with two canonized saints. Her Feast day is March 3.

Bibliography: D. MAHONEY, *Historical Sketches of the Catholic Churches and Institutions of Philadelphia* (Philadelphia 1895). J. L. J. KIRLIN, *Catholicity in Philadelphia* (Philadelphia 1909). H. J. NOLAN, *The Most Reverend Francis Patrick Kenrick* (CUA *Studies of American Church History* 37; Washington 1948). G. E. O'DONNELL, *Saint Charles Seminary, Overbrook,* 2 v. (Philadelphia 1943–53). *American Catholic Historical Researches* (Overbrook, Pa. 1885–). Archives, Archdiocese of Philadelphia. T.J. DONAGHY, *Philadelphia's Finest: A History of Education in the Catholic Archdiocese, 1692–1970* (Philadelphia 1972). J.F. CONNELLY, *The History of the Archdiocese of Philadelphia* (Philadelphia 1976).

[J. F. CONNELLY/L. BALDWIN]

PHILEAS OF THMUIS, ST.

Martyr, first known bishop of THMUIS in the Nile Delta, Egypt; d. Feb. 4, 306. Phileas was a learned and distinguished native of Thmuis who held many civil offices before his conversion and consecration as bishop. Imprisoned during the Diocletian persecution, he joined with three other Egyptian bishops, Hesychius, Pachomius, and Theodorus, in addressing a protest to Meletius, bishop of Lycopolis. Meletius's adherents had invaded their dioceses as well as that of Alexandria, thus beginning the MELETIAN SCHISM. The *Acta* of Phileas's martyrdom and EUSEBIUS in his *Ecclesiastical History* (8.9.7–10, 12; 8.13.7) tell of Phileas's trial and beheading with Philoromus, an eminent Roman official. The *Acta* and a stirring letter of Phileas to his people of Thmuis, given by Eusebius, are regarded by most scholars as authentic.

Feast: Feb. 4 (Latin Church); Jan. 9 (Greek Church).

Bibliography: EUSEBIUS, *Patrologia Latina,* ed. J. P. MIGNE, 271 v., indexes 4 v. (Paris 1878–90) 23:687; *Ecclesiastical History (Die griechischen christlichen Schriftsteller der ersten drei Jahrhunderte* 9.1–3; 1903–09) 2:758–764, 772–773. R. KNOPF and G. KRUEGER, eds., *Ausgewählte Märtyrerakten* (Tübingen 1929) 111–116. *Patrologia Graeca,* ed. J. P. MIGNE, 161 v. (Paris 1857–66) 18:509–510, letter of bishops. H. LECLERCQ, *Dictionnaire d'archéologie chrétienne et de liturgie,* ed. F. CABROL, H. LECLERCQ, and H. I. MARROU, 15 v. (Paris 1907–53) 14.1:703–709. F. L. CROSS, *The Oxford Dictionary of the Christian Church* (London 1957) 1061. H. DELEHAYE, *Analecta Bollandiana* 40 (1922) 299–314. F. HALKIN, *ibid.* 81 (1963) 1–27. *Revue d'histoire ecclésiastique* 58 (1963) 136–139. M. SIMONETTI, *Studi agiografici* (Rome 1955) 109–132. *Apologie de Philéas, évêque de Thmouis,* ed. V. MARTIN (Cologny-Genève 1964).

[M. C. MCCARTHY]

PHILEMON, EPISTLE TO

This shortest of PAUL's letters has occasioned some interesting discussion in the history of interpretation. Though even Marcion had not challenged its authenticity, in the fourth century Jerome, Chrysostom, and Theodore of Mopsuestia had to defend it against detractors who claimed that it taught nothing of theological interest or ecclesiastical discipline and that it had not been written by Paul. Luther and Calvin expressed appreciation for it, and even F. C. Baur, who sought to reduce the Pauline corpus to Romans, Galatians, and the Corinthian correspondence, was impressed by its attractive form and Christian spirit. Paul's authorship of the letter is generally recognized today. As with Philippians, the other undisputed captivity epistle, the place of writing is unclear; Caesarea, Ephesus, and Rome have been proposed. Probable dates range from the mid-50s to early 60s.

The most thorough treatment of this epistle is a 1985 work by Norman Petersen. He maintains that if the letter is lacking in theological concerns, it is of great interest from a sociological perspective. He moves from examining the narrative world of the letter to the symbolic universe of the complete undisputed Pauline corpus (Rom, Gal, 1 & 2 Cor, Phil, Phlm, 1 Thes) in an effort to ascertain the sociological interactions among Paul, Philemon and his house church, and the wider Christian community.

Despite the fact that interpretations of Philemon often stress its private, domestic character, J. D. G. Dunn notes that Apphia, probably Philemon's wife, is addressed with the feminine singular form ''the sister,'' suggesting that a serious effort was being made to treat women as individuals and as Christians in their own right. Also, the designation of Archippus as ''fellow soldier'' probably indicates one who had carried out an independent commission in the service of the gospel. Finally, the church in Philemon's house is addressed, intimating that Philemon probably recognized the church's right to advise on internal matters, even though slaves probably constituted part of the house church.

While it is often argued that Onesimus simply ran away from Philemon, reputable scholars maintain that Onesimus had offended Philemon but did not feel completely in the wrong and left with the purpose of seeking Paul's intercession in mending matters. Dunn suggests that if this is true the dynamics of this three-way relationship cause the letter to be even more fascinating than Petersen suggests. It would mean that what Onesimus perceived as most likely to work in his favor was Philemon's character as a Christian who had not enforced his belief on his entire household; it might also suggest that Onesimus was already attracted to Christianity. Thus perhaps there is more of theological interest in this letter than is sometimes presumed.

Modern aversion to SLAVERY as an institution is probably not a fair standard against which to judge the acceptance of the institution in ancient times. The ethical question then was the *treatment* of slaves. Paul's ultimate appeal to Philemon clearly reflects the baptismal formula of Gal 3.28. Onesimus is now ''in Christ'' and the distinction between master and slave no longer exists within that relationship.

Bibliography: D. L. ALLEN, ''The Discourse Structure of Philemon: A Study in Text Linguistics,'' in *Scribes and Scriptures: New Testament Essays in Honor of J. Harold Greenlee*, ed. D. A. BLACK, (Winona Lake, Ind. 1992). 77–96. J. M. G. BARCLAY, ''Paul, Philemon and the Dilemma of Christian Slave-Ownership,'' *New Testament Studies* 37 (1991): 161–86. J. D. G. DUNN, *The Epistles to the Colossians and to Philemon* (New International Greek Testament Commentary; Grand Rapids, Mich.-Carlisle 1996). D. B. MARTIN, *Slavery as Salvation: The Metaphor of Slavery in Pauline Christianity* (New Haven, Conn. 1990). N. R. PETERSEN, *Rediscovering Paul: Philemon and the Sociology of Paul's Narrative World* (Philadelphia 1985).

[V. KOPERSKI]

PHILIBERT OF REBAIS, ST.

Abbot; b. Eauze, Gascony, France, *c.* 616–620; d. Abbey of Noirmoutier, France, Aug. 20, 685. He was the son of a noble family. His father, Philibald, became bishop of Aire. Philibert entered the household of King Dagobert I (d. 630), where he met OUEN OF ROUEN, and *c.* 636 he joined Ouen's BENEDICTINE foundation at Rebais. He succeeded AGIL as abbot, but left to study other monastic observances, visiting especially LUXEUIL and BOBBIO. In 654 he founded the monastery of JUMIÈGES and a convent for women at Pavilly. His criticism of Ebroin (d. 681), the mayor of the palace of Neustria, led to his imprisonment in Rouen. After his release he founded Noirmoutier, perhaps refounded Quinçay near Poitiers, and supervised Luçon. His kindness to neighboring families is particularly remembered. He died at Noirmoutier, but because of the unsettled times, the travels imposed on the monks with the relics of their saint spread his cult widely. In 875 his body was buried in the abbey church of St. Valerian at TOURNUS, where it remains.

Feast: Aug. 20.

Bibliography: *Monumenta Germaniae Historica: Scriptores rerum Merovingicarum* (Berlin 1826–) 5:568–606. R. POUPARDIN, *Monuments de l'histoire des abbayes de Saint-Philibert* (Paris 1905). J. L. BAUDOT and L. CHAUSSIN, *Vies des saints et des bienheureux selon l'ordre du calendrier avec l'historique des fêtes,* 12 v. (Paris 1935–56) 8:372–377, full bibliog. A. M. ZIMMERMANN, *Kalendarium Benedictinum: Die Heiligen und Seligen des Benediktinerorderns und seiner Zweige,* 4 v. (Metten 1933–38) 2:597, 600–601. *Bibliotheca hagiographica latina antiquae et mediae aetatis,* 2 v. (Brussels 1898–1901; suppl. 1911) 2:6805–10. L. JAUD, *Saint Filibert . . .* (Paris 1910). H. CURÉ, *St. Philibert le Thaumaturge* (Marseille 1936).

[V. I. J. FLINT]

PHILIP, ANTIPOPE

Pontificate: July 31, 768. Philip was chaplain of the monastery of St. Vito on the Esquiline in Rome; nothing else is known of his earlier life. In the confusion after the antipope Constantine II (767–68) had been taken captive, a Lombard priest named Waldipert attempted to install Philip as pope. Constantine had represented the interests of the military elite, and the former papal chancellor, Christophorus, had approached the Lombards to help depose Constantine. Waldipert, serving as a personal envoy of the Lombard king Desiderius (757–74), accompanied Christophorus' brother Sergius in an attack on Rome that ended Constantine's papacy. Upon entering Rome, Waldipert found Philip, managed to have him acclaimed pope by some citizens, and took him to the Lateran. When Christophorus heard of this, he appeared outside the city and swore he would not enter until Philip was removed. At this, one of Christophorus' partisans, a military official named Gratiosus (who would later become duke of Rome), forced Philip to return to his monastery. Then Christophorus entered the city and soon oversaw the election of Pope Stephen III (IV)(768–72). No harm appears to have come to Philip, and nothing more is known of him.

Bibliography: L. DUCHESNE, ed. *Liber Pontificalis* (Paris 1886–92; repr. 1955–57) 1.470–71. P. JAFFÉ, *Regesta pontificum Romanorum* (Leipzig 1885–88; repr. Graz 1956) 1.284. H. K. MANN,

The Lives of the Popes in the Early Middle Ages (London 1902–32) 1(2).367–74. T. F. X. NOBLE, *The Republic of St. Peter* (Philadelphia 1984). J. N. D. KELLY, *The Oxford Dictionary of Popes* (New York 1986) 94–95.

[P. M. SAVAGE]

PHILIP, APOSTLE, ST.

A native of Bethsaida (Jn 12.21) and one of Our Lord's first disciples (Jn 1.43–44). In the Synoptic Gospels he is mentioned only in the lists of the Apostles (Mt 10.3; Mk 3.18; Lk 6.14; see also Acts 1.13). In St. John's Gospel, however, he has a larger role: he was one of the first disciples called by Our Lord and was instrumental in introducing Nathaniel to Jesus (Jn 1.45–49); moreover, he is mentioned in connection with the miraculous feeding of the five thousand (6.5–7) and with Jesus' discourse at the LAST SUPPER (14.8–9). Certain friendly Gentiles singled out Philip as an intermediary in their desire to meet Jesus (Jn 12.20–23). Apart from these facts, nothing more is known about the Apostle. In the 2d century, Polycrates, Bishop of Antioch (Eusebius, *Hist. Eccl.* 3.31.3), and Clement of Alexandria (*Strom.* 3.6.16) identified him wrongly with PHILIP THE DEACON. Papias of Hierapolis (*c.* A.D. 140) may have been responsible for this idea (see Eusebius, *ibid.* 3.39.9). Epiphanius (*Heres.* 26.13) mentions a Gospel forged in the name of Philip that was used by the Egyptian Gnostics. In the *Pistis Sophia*, a remarkable Gnostic work of the 3d century, Philip is accorded a prominent place. The feast of the Apostle St. Philip, together with that of St. James the Less, was celebrated in the West on May 1 until 1955, when it was transferred to May 11; the Greeks celebrate it on May 14.

Bibliography: A. WIKENHAUSER, *Lexikon für Theologie und Kirche,* ed. J. HOFER and K. RAHNER (Freiburg 1957–65); suppl., *Das Zweite Vatikanische Konzil: Dokumente und Kommentare,* ed. H. S. BRECHTER et al. (1966) 8:465–466. H. KÖSTER, *Die Religion in Geschichte und Gegenwart,* 7 v. (3d ed. Tübingen 1957–65) 5:337–338. *Encyclopedic Dictionary of the Bible,* tr. and adap. by L. HARTMAN (New York 1963) from A. VAN DEN BORN, *Bijbels Woordenboek,* 1835–36. H. H. PLATZ, *The Interpreter's Dictionary of the Bible,* ed. G. A. BUTTRICK (Nashville 1962) 3:785.

[C. H. PICKAR]

PHILIP I, KING OF FRANCE

Reigned from 1060–1108; b. 1052. The son of Henry I (1031–1060) and Anne of Kiev, Philip was consecrated king at Reims in 1059 prior to his father's death. Owing to Philip's accession to the French throne at a young age, Baldwin V of Flanders, his father's brother-in-law, served as regent from 1060 until 1066. In 1072, Philip married Bertha of Frisia, the mother of Louis VI, but he later repudiated her because of his affection for Bertrada of Montfort, wife of Fulk IV of Anjou in 1092. In 1095 at the Council of Clermont, URBAN II excommunicated Philip over his marriage to Bertrada of Montfort, but support from French bishops, who were eager to limit papal interference in the French church, lessened the impact of the papal condemnation. Although most French bishops sided with Philip, the canonist Ivo of Chartres strongly voiced his opposition, which Philip ignored. Philip's antagonism toward the papacy continued throughout his reign. GREGORY VII's attempts to intervene in French episcopal elections, especially those that involved simony and lay investiture, met with stiff resistance from Philip. These issues reached a climax under Pope Urban II, who challenged the elections of the archbishop of Sens and the bishop of Orléans. In an age of religious reform, Philip's contemporaries often regarded him as no friend of ecclesiastical authority. Despite previous quarrels, Philip eventually came to terms with Pope Paschal II at the Council of Troyes (1107), where they reached an agreement over lay INVESTITURE. To enrich his own royal coffers, Philip plundered episcopal lands and religious houses. Yet, Philip provided for some monastic houses, especially those with Cluniac affiliations. In 1079, he reestablished his father's house of Saint-Martin-des-Champs as a Cluniac priory. He was buried at the abbey of Saint-Benoit-sur-Loire at Fleury.

Bibliography: SUGER, *The Deeds of Louis the Fat*, ed. and tr. R. C. CUSIMANO and J. MOORHEAD (Washington, DC 1992). R. FAWTIER, *The Capetian Kings of France*, tr. L. BUTLER and R. J. ADAM (New York 1960). E. HALLAM, *Capetian France, 987–1138* (London 1980). A. LUCHAIRE, *Les Premiers Capetians* (Paris 1901). A. FLICHE, *Le Règne de Philippe Ier, roi de France, 1060–1108* (Paris 1912).

[P. D. WATKINS]

PHILIP II AUGUSTUS, KING OF FRANCE

Reigned 1180 to July 14, 1223, seventh of the Capetian dynasty and the first to control most of France; b. Paris, Aug. 21, 1165; d. Mantes. As king he first overcame attempts by the houses of Champagne and Flanders to control his policies, and then in the late 1180s blunted the greater threat posed by HENRY II's Angevin Empire by inciting Henry's sons to rebellion. When the Angevin died in 1189, Philip's position was so secure that he willingly joined Richard I, the Lion Heart, in the Third CRUSADE.

Home again in 1191, Philip attacked Normandy soon after, hoping for gains during Richard's imprisonment in

Austria. Richard's release led to reverses for Philip, but victory ensued after JOHN's accession in 1199. Condemned by Philip for contumacy in 1202, John was easily driven from Normandy; the conquest of his other northern French lands quickly followed; and at Bouvines in 1214 Philip Augustus ensured his supremacy by defeating the forces of John, Otto IV, and Ferrand of Flanders.

Governmental reforms helped to consolidate these gains. Salaried bailiffs were appointed for local administration while the king's council became more competent and professional. The semifeudalized great offices of the crown were suppressed, bourgeois support was gained, and attempts to introduce legislation and taxation were made. Philip emphasized his royal position by refusing to do homage to anyone, and his conscious distinction between his powers as a private and a public person led to more modern concepts of political authority.

Philip's relations with the Church were mixed, and his religious policy was often dictated by political considerations. He left the Holy Land purely to add to his domains, and refused INNOCENT III's appeals to head the Albigensian Crusade (*see* ALBIGENSES). Only an interdict forced him to renounce his third wife in favor of his second; and while his 1213 plan to depose John had been drawn up at Innocent's request, it took threats of excommunication to stop his invasion after John submitted to the pope. Marital problems aside, his personal life showed religious devotion, and he both encouraged the building of Notre Dame and in 1200 granted clerical status to the students of the University of Paris.

Bibliography: L DELISLE, *Catalogue des actes de Philippe-Auguste* (Paris 1856). H. F. DELABORDE, *Recueil des actes de Philippe-Auguste* (Paris 1916). A. LUCHAIRE, *Les Premiers Capétiens,* in *Histoire de France,* ed. E. LAVISSE, 9 v. (Paris 1900–11) 3.1:83–284. A. CARTELLIERI, *Philippe II. August, König von Frankreich,* 4 v. (Leipzig 1899–1922). J. W. BALDWIN, *The Government of Philip Augustus: Foundation of French Royal Power in the Middle Ages,* (Berkeley and Los Angeles 1986). J. BRADBURY, *Philip Augustus: King of France, 1180-1223* (London and New York 1998). G. SIVERY, *Philippe Auguste* (Paris 1993). G. DUBY, *The Legend of Bouvines: War, Religion and Culture in the Middle Ages,* tr. C. TIHANY (Cambridge 1990).

[C. T. WOOD]

PHILIP IV, KING OF FRANCE

Reigned 1285 to 1314, called the Fair; b. Fontainebleau, 1268; d. Fontainebleau, Nov. 29, 1314. Philip brought the French monarchy to new heights of power, yet many of his contemporaries and some modern scholars assert that his ministers deserve all the credit (or blame) for his policies. It is true that his agents (Flotte, Nogaret, and Marigny) were forceful personages and that

Philip IV, King of France. (Archive Photos)

Philip himself always let them speak for him on formal occasions. But general policy remained the same for 29 years while ministers changed, and the records show that behind the scenes Philip worked with unflagging industry. Those who have studied the period most carefully suspect that he was responsible for the events of his reign.

The Reign and Its Problems. Philip was a devoted husband, a loyal friend, and a pious Christian. But his piety, without flaw in his private life, showed two peculiarities in public. First, he had no great respect for the leadership of the Roman CURIA. His father's death in the disastrous Crusade against Aragon, a death that left Philip at the age of 17 to cope with a hopeless war and a heavy debt, may have engendered his doubts about papal policies. Second, Philip, the heir of crusaders, the grandson of a saint, the ruler of the largest Catholic country in Europe, believed that the French monarch was as necessary for human welfare as the Roman See. Philip's duty to God and to his people was to strengthen the Kingdom of France, and anyone who interefered with this task, baron or emperor, bishop or pope, was to be swept aside.

He and his advisers had a fairly clear concept of sovereignty. Everyone who was ''in and of the kingdom'' owed obedience to the king. But what was the kingdom? There were bishops in the south who were virtually independent; there were lands on the border of the Empire that had both French and German connections; worst of all, the two great and wealthy fiefs of Guienne (held by England) and Flanders had almost escaped royal control.

Some of these problems were easily solved. Self-governing towns, many barons, even the great bishops of the Midi had to accept the oversight of royal officials. The French boundary was pushed east at the expense of the Holy Roman Empire; the city of Lyons was annexed. But England fought to retain Guienne, and Flanders fought to keep its autonomy. To gain English neutrality, Philip had to relinquish most of Guienne and marry his daughter to the Prince of Wales (thus creating the later English claim to the French throne). Even then, Philip could not win a complete victory over the Flemings; he acquired only the towns of Lille, Douai, and Bethune.

These wars, fought with paid soldiers, were very expensive. Philip was always short of money; his greatest innovations and his greatest mistakes were due to the fact that he was near bankruptcy during most of his reign. He imposed the first general taxes in French history; he inflated the currency; he expelled the Jews and confiscated their property; he abused judicial procedures to extort large fines from clergy, barons, and towns.

Relations with Boniface VIII. Both financial need and the desire for sovereign independence led to his quarrel with Pope BONIFACE VIII. Philip wanted to tax the clergy without securing papal consent; Boniface forbade this in the bull *CLERICIS LAICOS* (1296). Philip's ministers accused the clergy of disloyalty and harassed them so that they begged the pope to remove his prohibition. Boniface finally ruled that in an emergency for the defense of the realm the clergy could be taxed by the king.

The second stage of the quarrel came when Philip sought to condemn Bishop Bernard Saisset for treason. Boniface demanded the bishop's release; Philip's ministers charged that this was an attack on the authority of the king and the independence of France. A meeting of representatives of clergy, nobility, and *bourgeosie* was held at Paris in 1302, where Pierre Flotte denounced the pope. When the Flemings defeated the French and killed Flotte at Courtrai, there was a brief lull, but Guillaume de Nogaret was soon ordered to carry on the case. He accused the pope of simony, vice, and heresy, and persuaded most French communities, including cathedral chapters and monasteries, to appeal for a general council to depose Boniface. Nogaret went to Italy in 1303 to arrest the pope and succeeded in holding him prisoner at Anagni for a few days. A popular uprising freed the aged pontiff, but he died of the shock within a month.

The next pope, BENEDICT XI, did not live long enough to settle the affair. After his death, mysterious intrigues, still imperfectly known, resulted in the election in 1305 of the archbishop of Bordeaux as CLEMENT V. Clement, throughout his pontificate, acted as if he were under obligation to Philip. To end the scandal caused by continued attacks on Boniface's memory, he praised the king's pious zeal and absolved Nogaret and his aides. When Philip accused the Knights TEMPLAR of heresy, probably because he coveted the wealth that they had gained by operating as bankers, Clement suppressed the order even though its guilt was not proved. Worst of all, disorders in Italy gave Philip a chance to urge Clement to remain north of the Alps. The pope finally settled at AVIGNON, just across the Rhone from France. Thus began the ''Babylonian Captivity'' (*see* AVIGNON PAPACY).

Philip's determination to be a strong king in a united France made a lasting impression on the French government. All branches of the administration were professionalized, and the number of royal officials greatly increased. The high court of Parlement at Paris was strengthened and a much more efficient financial administration was created. France was already on the road to becoming a bureaucratic state, but Philip accelerated the process.

Nevertheless, whereas Philip's administrative structure survived, his unscrupulous methods tarnished the prestige of kingship. Revolts broke out after his death, and for the next century, the French monarchy rocked from crisis to crisis. Philip had very nearly exhausted the reservoir of goodwill that had been left by his grandfather. St. LOUIS IX. It took another saint, JOAN OF ARC, to replenish it.

Bibliography: R. FAWTIER, ed., *Camptes royaux, 1285–1314,* 3 v. (Paris 1953–58); *Registres du trésor des chartes* (Paris 1958). J. VIARD, ed., *Les Journaux du trésor de Philippe IV le Bel* (Paris 1940). A. A. BEUGNOT, ed., *Les Olim, ou registres dec arrêts,* 4 v. (Paris 1839–48); *Ordonnances des roys de France,* ed. E. J. DE LAURIÈRE et al. 23 v. and suppl. (Paris 1723–1847). *Recueil des historiens des Gaules et de la France* (Paris 1738) v.21–24, contains many important documents and chronicles of the reign. P. DUPUY, *Histoire du différend d'entre le pape Boniface VIII et Philippe le Bel* (Paris 1655). C. V. LANGLOIS, *Saint Louis, Philippe le Bel, les derniers Capétiens directs, 1226–1328,* v.3.2 of *Histoire de France,* ed. E. LAVISSE, 9 v. (Paris 1900–11). R. FAWTIER, *L'Europe occidentale de 1270 à 1380. 1 ptie. De 1270 à 328,* v.6.1 of *Histoire générale,* ed. G. GLOTZ (Paris 1933). G. A. L. DIGARD, *Philippe le Bel et le Saint-siège de 1258 à 1304,* 2 v. (Paris 1936). K. WENCK, *Philipp der Schöne v. Frankreich: Seine Persönlichkeit u. das Urteil der Zeitgenossen* (Marburg 1905). R. SCHOLZ, *Die Publizistik zur Zeit Philipps des Schönen und Bonifaz' VIII* (Stuttgart 1903). J. R. STRAYER and C. H. TAYLOR, *Studies in Early French Taxation* (Cambridge, Mass. 1939). J. R. STRAYER, ''Philip the Fair: A 'Constitutional' King.'' *American Historical Review* 62 (1956–57) 18–32. J. R. STRAYER, *The Reign of Philip the Fair* (Princeton 1980). D. POIREL, *Philippe le Bel* (Paris 1991).

[J. R. STRAYER]

PHILIP II, KING OF SPAIN

Reigned 1556 to 1598: b. Valladolid, May 21, 1527; d. the Escorial, Sept. 13, 1598. He was the son of Charles I of Spain (the Emperor CHARLES V) and Isabella of Portugal. He received his early education from Juan Martínez Siliceo, Bishop of Cartagena, an indulgent tutor, and Juan de Zúñiga, grand-commander of Castile, who provided a more systematic education, imparting piety and seriousness to his pupil as well as an extensive knowledge of history and an appreciation of scholarship, the arts, and politics.

His Empire. Philip's apprenticeship in government began in 1543 as regent in Spain during his father's absence in Germany. From 1549 Philip traveled in the Low Countries and Germany, and in 1554 played his first major role in the Emperor's foreign policy with his marriage to Mary Tudor, Queen of England, on which occasion his father gave him the Kingdom of Naples and the Duchy of Milan. When the Emperor decided to retire, he abdicated to Philip on Oct. 25, 1555, the sovereignty of the Low Countries; on Jan 16, 1556, Philip received the crown of Castile with Navarre and the Indies, the crown of Aragon-Catalonia with Sardinia, and the crown of Sicily. He was now the ruler of a world empire. But it was not the empire of Charles V. After the Peace of Cateau-Cambrésis with France in April 1559, Philip returned from the Low Countries to the Iberian Peninsula, where he remained for the rest of his reign. Financial difficulties forced him to settle in Spain, impose his authority, and withdraw from the widepread commitments of his father. In the process, the empire he ruled changed, not in size, but in character. Less ecumenical than that of Charles V, who had already lost Germany, it was also more solid, being firmly based in the Iberian Peninsula, and was essentially Castilian in character.

Philip II, King of Spain. (Archive Photos)

Domestic Tragedies. Philip II, whose accession was exceptionally free of complication, found it less easy to provide for his successor. He married Maria of Portugal in 1543; within two years she had died in bearing him the Infante Don Carlos. In 1554 he married MARY TUDOR, but the union was barren of children and, on Philip's side, of love. His marriage to Elizabeth of Valois in 1559 was also a diplomatic arrangement, but Philip grew to love his third wife and was desolate when she died in 1568, having borne him two surviving daughters. Her death was preceded by that on July 25, 1568, of Philip's problem son, Don Carlos, who had been mentally and physically abnormal. As a result of his deranged and dangerous meddling in affairs of state, Philip regarded him as permanently unfit to rule. He therefore confined him in January 1568, partly in his son's own interest but above all to prevent his succeeding to the throne, and perhaps with the intention of disinheriting him. His enemies accused the King of poisoning his son, a charge not proved by available evidence. In 1579 he married his fourth and last wife, Anne of Austria. Of the five children she bore him, only one survived, and he was to succeed his father as Philip III. These personal tragedies left their mark on Philip II, who behind the mask of sovereignty, was a sensitive man and devoted to his family.

Exercise of Power. In other ways, however, Philip was completely attuned to the exercise of power; he took the disaster of the ARMADA with the same equanimity as the triumph of Lepanto. He had a high sense of royal prerogative and with it a notion of personal duty that made him one of the most hard-working monarchs in history. He ruled his empire from his desk, dealing personally with all affairs of state. His distrust of subordinates was due to his anxiety to prevent the crown becoming a cipher in the hands of the aristocracy; his notorious slowness was not simply a defect of character but was imposed by circumstances, for he had to measure the distant repercussions of his acts, governing as he did an immense empire

"Philip II, King of Spain," portrait by Titian, 1551.

formed of constituent kingdoms separated by vast distances. His system of government was one of absolute monarchy; he was assisted, but never controlled, by his councils and secretaries. He completed the unification of the peninsula, annexing Portugal in 1580 and crushing a separatist revolt in Aragon in 1591. But he always respected the semi-autonomous status of the constituent kingdoms. In the administration of justice, he wrote that "in cases of doubt the verdict must always be given against me."

Concern for Religious Orthodoxy. Philip's religious beliefs were firmly based and carefully practiced. The affairs of the Church were his daily concern, and he was known to be a friend of religious reform, as St. Teresa of Jesus acknowledged when he assisted her Discalced Carmelite reform. His religious devotion, combined with a taste for literature, art, and science, gave birth to the greatest architectural monument of his reign, San Lorenzo de El Escorial, which was at once a monastery and a palace. Like other contemporary rulers, he was intolerant of religious dissent. One of his first actions when he returned to Spain in 1559 was to attend an *auto de fe,* one of a series that eliminated the faint traces of Protestantism in Spain; and in 1570 he ruthlessly suppressed a rebellion of *Moriscos* (convert Moors), in Granada, which the intemperance of the Spanish Inquisition itself had provoked. Philip even permitted the Inquisition to try the Archbishop of Toledo, Cardinal Carranza, whose orthodoxy it questioned and to keep him in prison for 17 years. Philip regarded these as essential measures of state to strengthen his power, the first because Protestantism itself was unapproachable, the second because Granada was a potential bridgehead for his Islamic enemies in the Mediterranean. His concern for orthodoxy was also seen in the support he gave Pope PIUS IV for reconvening the Council of TRENT in 1562 and for the Council's adoption of a specifically Catholic position.

Relations with Rome. However, on two issues (episcopal jurisdiction and the prerogatives of the crown, especially in ecclesiastical appointments), Philip II adopted a national point of view, and he published the decrees of Trent in his dominions only with the proviso that they would not encroach on the ecclesiastical rights of the Spanish crown. Philip supported the Spanish INQUISITION against Rome as well. Indeed, on ecclesiastical jurisdiction and on foreign policy Philip clashed with almost every pope with whom he dealt, which makes it impossible to regard him as "the secular arm of the Counter Reformation." After the victory of LEPANTO (1571), Philip withdrew from the papal-led Holy League and, in spite of the Pope's pressure, began a policy of disengagement from the Turks. In northern Europe, he was equally reserved about papal policy. He long repudiated aggressive Catholic plans against ELIZABETH I, for he had no wish to further the cause of MARY, QUEEN OF SCOTS, and thus of his enemy, France. When he finally decided to invade England, it was for a series of political and economic reasons rather than religious ones; his objective was to strike at the source of English harassment of Spain and its empire. Philip wanted the cooperation of the papacy for financial reasons and for moral support of his claim to dispose of the crown of England. But his alliance with SIXTUS V in 1587 was not a fruitful one. The Pope had little faith in the Armada and feared that a Spanish victory would overthrow the balance of power in Europe; for the same reason, he and his successors refused to support Philip II in his claim to the French throne in the last years of his reign. Philip II, on the other hand, believed that his own cause and that of the Church were identical.

Bibliography: J. LYNCH, *Spain Under the Hapsburgs* (Oxford 1964–) v.1. R. B. MERRIMAN, *Rise of the Spanish Empire in the Old World and in the New,* 4 v. (New York 1918–34) v.4. F. BRAUDEL, *La Méditerranée et le monde méditerranéen à l'époque de Philippe II* (Paris 1949). L. FERNÁNDEZ Y FERNÁNDEZ DE RETANA, *España en tiempo de Felipe II, 1566–1598,* 2 v. (*Historia de España,* gen.

ed. R. MENÉNDEZ PIDAL 19; Madrid 1958). J. H. ELLIOTT, *Imperial Spain, 1469–1716* (Toronto 1963). H. LAPEYRE, ''Autour de Philippe II,'' *Bulletin Hispanique* 59 (1957) 152–175. P. GALLAGHER and D. W. CRUICKSHANK, eds., *God's Obvious Design: Papers for the Spanish Armada Symposium, Sligo 1988* (London 1990). M. J. RODRIGUEZ-SALGADO and S. ADAMS, eds., *England, Spain and the Grand Armada 1585–1604: Essays from the Anglo-Spanish Conferences, London and Madrid 1988* (Edinburgh 1991). H. KAMEN, *Philip of Spain* (New Haven and London 1997). J. MARTÍNEZ MILLÁN, ed., *Felipe II, 1527-1598: Europa y las monarquía católica* (Spain 1998). E. MARTÍNEZ RUIZ, ed., *Madrid, Felipe II y las ciudades de la monarquía* (Madrid 2000).

[J. LYNCH]

PHILIP BENIZI, ST.

Fifth general of the Servite Order; b. Florence, Italy, Aug. 15, 1223; d. Todi, Umbria, Italy, Aug. 23, 1285. Born of the renowned Benizi and Frescobaldi families, Philip studied first in Paris and then in Padua, where he completed his course in medicine. After practicing medicine among the poor in Florence for a year, he entered the SERVITES (1254) as a lay brother and was sent to Monte Senario near Florence. While on a journey to Siena in 1258, his great ability and learning, hitherto hidden from his brethren, was accidentally discovered; he was immediately required to prepare for Holy Orders and was ordained to the priesthood the following year. On June 5, 1267, Philip was elected the fifth superior general. He proved to be a great administrator and zealous apostle. He preached and reputedly worked miracles throughout Europe; the order gained many members, e.g., Peregrine Laziosi and Andrew Dotti. In the GUELF-GHIBELLINE controversy he acted as peacemaker throughout Italy with great success. Aware that his death was approaching, Philip placed the order in the hands of Bl. Lotharingus Stufa in 1285 and retired to a poor Servite convent in Todi. He was buried in the Servite church there; many miracles followed. Pope LEO X approved his cult in 1516, and CLEMENT X canonized him in 1671.

Feast: Aug. 23.

Bibliography: P. SOULIER, *Life of Saint Philip Benizi* (New York 1886). P. SOULIER et al., eds., *Monumenta Servorum Sanctae Marine*, 20v. (Brussels 1897–1930) v. 2. L. PAZZAGLIA, *S. Filippo Benizi nella storia e nella leggenda* (Rome 1953). A. BUTLER, *The Lives of the Saints*. rev. ed. H. THURSTON and D. ATTWATER (New York 1956) 3:385–388. G. M. BESUTTI, *Saint Philippe Benizi*, tr. J. M. DESGRANDCHAMPS, ed. A. M. CIMICHELLA (Montreal 1985). L. DOMINICI, *Todi e S. Filippo Benizi: itinerario storico artistico* (Todi 1985).

[M. B. MORRIS]

PHILIP OF GRÈVE

Canon and master at Notre Dame, a native of *Gravia Parisiensis,* today the site of La Place de l'Hôtel-de-Ville, Paris; d. *c.* 1220–22. Since the 16th century most histories of medieval literature mistakenly identified him with his more famous contemporary PHILIP THE CHANCELLOR, theologian and chancellor of the University of Paris (1218–36) and outstanding poet of his time. Henri Meylan shattered this age-old identification (1927): manuscripts and obituaries prove that the two are not the same. Philip of Grève was a canon at Notre Dame, Paris (since 1182), and *magister* since 1104; he was teaching canon law there *c.* 1200. He died as dean of the cathedral chapter of Sens. He is not the author of the poetry formerly ascribed to him nor of any known writings. Philip the Chancellor was the poet, and he is always identified in the manuscripts as ''the Chancellor,'' never as Philip of Grève.

Bibliography: H. MEYLAN, *Les questions de Philippe le Chancelier* (Thèse de l'École Nationale des Chartres; Paris 1927). P. GLORIEUX, *Répertoire des maîtres en théologie de Paris au XIIIe siècle* (Paris 1933–34) 1:282–284; v. 17–18 of *Bibliothèque Thomiste* (Le Saulchoir 1921–). M. MANITIUS, *Geschichte der lateinischen Literatur des Mittelalters,* 3 v. (Munich 1911–31) 3:930. H. TISCHLER, ''New Historical Aspects of the Parisian Organa,'' *Speculum. A Journal of Mediaeval Studies* 25 (1950) 25. N. WICKI, *Lexikon für Theologie und Kirche,* ed. J. HOFER and K. RAHNER, 10 v. (2d, new ed. Freiburg 1957–65) 8:450.

[G. M. COOK]

PHILIP OF HARVENGT

Praemonstratensian abbot and ecclesiastical writer; b. Harvengt(?), near Mons (Belgium), early 12th century; d. Bonne-Espérance, April 11 (13?), 1183. He received a good classical education, probably at the cathedral school at Cambrai. He entered the monastery of Bonne-Espérance and in 1130 was made prior under the first abbot, Odo. Difficulties ensued with St. BERNARD OF CLAIRVAUX over an incident involving a monk from Bonne-Espérance who wished to join the house of Clairvaux. The conflict caused considerable notoriety, and opposition to Philip was aroused. In 1149 he was removed from his position by the general chapter of the order, and with seven other monks he was sent to another monastery. He was reinstated at Bonne-Espérance in 1151, and in 1158 he succeeded Odo as abbot. Under Philip's rule the abbey prospered, the collection of manuscripts continued, and intellectual activity among the monks flourished.

His writings reveal a vast knowledge of the ancient classics, the Bible, and the writings of the Church Fathers. He stands as a distinguished representative of prescholastic Augustinian philosophy. Many of his works were written for the education and inspiration of his own monks. Of these, the *De institutione clericorum* is a mirror of his views on monastic and clerical life. In his commentaries on Scripture, of which that on the Canticle is most important, he employed the allegorical explanations typical of his time. He wrote also a number of biographies, including those of St. Augustine and Odo of Rivreuille. In his theological teaching he failed to do complete justice to the human nature of Christ and its capacity to suffer, and, although he accepted the idea of the Assumption of the Blessed Mother, he denied the Immaculate Conception in the sense in which it was propounded at that time.

His works were edited at Douai in 1621 by Nicolas Chamart, Abbot of Bonne-Espérance, and were included in Migne (*Patrologia Latina* v.203). However, modern scholarship has ascertained that certain treatises in these editions have been falsely ascribed to Philip of Harvengt.

Bibliography: *Analecta Praemonstratensia* 14:37– and 189–; 15:129–166; 35:336-; 37:5–30, 177–231. M. FITZHUM, *Die Christologie der Praemonstratenser im 12. Jahrhundert* (Marienbad 1939) 62–129. F. PETIT, *La Spiritualité des Prémontrés aux XIe et XIIe siècles* (Paris 1947) 129–. A. ERENS, *Dictionnaire de théologie catholique* 12.1:1407–11.

[J. C. WILLKE]

PHILIP OF HESSE

Landgrave, confidant of Martin LUTHER, Philipp MELANCHTHON, and Ulrich ZWINGLI; b. Marburg, Hesse, Nov. 13, 1504; d. Kassel, Hesse, March 31, 1567. The son and successor of Landgrave William II, he married Christina of Saxony in 1523. He was called ''the Magnanimous'' because of his interest in political, church, and educational reform. He established a model government in Hesse before 1526 and founded the University of Marburg in 1527.

After his conversion to LUTHERANISM in 1525, his diplomatic and military activities greatly affected the process of the German reformation. Influenced by correspondence with Zwingli, Philip attempted to reconcile Zwingli and Luther at the abortive Disputation of Marburg in 1529. In the next year he publicly subscribed to the Confession of AUGSBURG. After his defeat of the peasant forces under Thomas Münzer at Frankenhausen in 1525, he was a recognized leader of the Protestant princes and was instrumental in the formation of the SCHMALKALDIC LEAGUE in 1531. His bigamous marriage with Margaret von der Saal in 1540 aroused strong controversy within the ranks of the reformers and alienated the support of certain of the princes. In the consequent weakening of the league, Philip was forced into signing the Treaty of Regensburg (1541). The War of the Schmalkald (1546–47) was disastrous to the landgrave. Defeated at Mülberg he was imprisoned until 1552; he displayed little interest in German affairs after his release.

Bibliography: W. HEINEMEYER, *Die Religion in Geschichte und Gegenwart,* 7 v. (3d ed. Tübingen 1957–65) 5:332–333. S. SKALWEIT, *Lexikon für Theologie und Kirche,* ed. J. HOFER and K. RAHNER, 10 v. (2d, new ed. Freiburg 1957–65) 8:452–453. K. SCHOTTENLOHER, *Bibliographie zur deutschen Geschichte im Zeitalter der Glaubensspaltung,* 1517–85, 6 v. (Leipzig 1933–40; repr. Stuttgart 1956–58, v. 7, 1962–) 6:450–451.

[P. L. HUGHES]

PHILIP OF THE BLESSED TRINITY (ESPRIT JULIEN)

Discalced Carmelite theologian and writer; b. Malaucene, (Vaucluse), July 19, 1603; d. Naples, Feb. 28, 1671. Philip took the Carmelite habit and was professed on Sept. 8, 1621. In 1629 he was sent to the Carmelite Missions; first to the mission of Ispahan, Syria, then to the mission of Malabar (now Kerala, India), where for 12 years he taught philosophy and theology. From 1634 to 1639 he was prior in Goa, where he received and professed Bl. Denis of the Nativity, the protomartyr of the DISCALCED Carmelites. He returned in 1659 to Europe, where he was appointed consultor of the Congregation of the Index; he was elected definitor general, and finally became general of the Discalced CARMELITES of the Italian Congregation (1665–68). Although reelected to the office (1668–71), he died on a visit to the convent of Naples before the completion of his term. Among his many works are the fruits of his years of teaching: *Summa Philosophica* (Lyons 1648); *Summa Theologiae Mysticae* (Lyons 1656); *Cursus Theologicus* (Lyons 1653–65); *Itinerarium Orientale* (Lyons 1649); *Tractatus de Immaculata Conceptione* (Lyons 1667).

Bibliography: MELCHIOR DE STE. MARIE, ''Pour une biographie du P. Philippe de la Trinitè,'' *Ephemerides Carmeliticae* 2 (1948) 343–403. H. KUMMET, *Die Gotteserfahrung in der ''Summae Theologiae Mysticae'' des Karmeliten Philippus a SS. Trinitate* (Würzburg 1938). B. HONINGS, ''La Contemplazione secondo Filippo della SS. Trinitè,'' *Ephemerides Carmeliticae* 13 (1962) 691–713. ANASTASE DE SAINT-PAUL, *Dictionnaire de théologie catholique*, ed. A. VACANT et al., (Paris 1903–50) 12.1: 1412–13.

[O. RODRIGUEZ]

PHILIP THE CHANCELLOR

Theologian and philosopher; b. Paris, between *c.* 1160 and 1185; d. Paris, Dec. 23, 1236. H. Meylan has shown that Philip is not the same as PHILIP OF GRÈVE, with whom he has been identified from the first edition of his *Distinctiones super psalterium* (ed. J. Bade, Paris 1523). Philip was a son of the archdeacon Philip of Paris. There is no record of his youth and education, but it is certain that he studied theology, and probably Canon Law, in Paris. He was first mentioned in a charter of 1211 as archdeacon of Noyon, an office he held until his death. In January 1217, however, he received from Honorius III the dispensation *pro defectu natalium* and permission to change to the Diocese of Paris. He is first mentioned as chancellor in the testament of Bp. Peter of Nemours (June 1218). The office of chancellor, although subordinate in the chapter, was important in Paris because of the statute of Innocent III (1215) giving to the chancellor limited jurisdiction over professors and students of the university.

The first half of Philip's tenure was disturbed by conflicts with the university. In 1219 he was summoned to the papal Curia for excommunicating masters and students, but was discharged in grace by Honorius III because his accusers did not appear. In the controversy over the appointment of WILLIAM OF AUVERGNE as bishop of Paris (1228), Philip supported Philip of Nemours, who had been elected by the chapter. In the university strike of 1229 to 1231, he sided with the university and the pope against the bishop and the regent, Blanche of Castile. In a sermon in Orléans he exhorted masters and scholars who had retired there to return to Paris. He readily submitted to the *Parens scientiarum* of Gregory IX, April 13, 1231, that ended the university strike.

Philip was a prominent preacher, often charged with special commissions. At the famous assembly of the masters of theology at Paris in 1235, he defended the permission of the benefice cumulation, which was probably a cause of the Dominicans' enmity. He remained friendly with the Franciscans and was buried in their church. The *Summa quaestionum theologicarum* (*Summa de bono*), Philip's chief work, dates from between 1230 and 1236 and probably was never finished. It is a systematic presentation of theology from the point of view of the good. Although the materials originate from the Augustinian tradition, most of the solutions it proposed were new, influenced by Aristotelian philosophy. He also wrote many sermons and approximately 20 theological *Quaestiones.*

Bibliography: É. GILSON, *History of Christian Philosophy in the Middle Ages* (New York 1955). *Chartularium universitatis Parisiensis*, ed. H. DENIFLE and E. CHATELAIN (Paris 1889–97) v.1. H. MEYLAN, *Les Questions de Philippe le Chancelier* (Paris 1927). P. GLORIEUX, *Répertoire des maîtres en théologie de Paris au XIIIe siècle* (Paris 1933–44) 1:282–284. A. M. LANDGRAF, *Einführung in die Geschichte der theologischen Literatur der Frühscholastik* (Regensburg 1948) 132–133. V. DOUCET, ''A travers le manuscrit 434 de Douai,'' *Antonianium* 27 (1952) 531–580. J. B. SCHNEYER, ''Philipp der Kanzler—ein hervorragender Prediger des Mittelalters,'' *Münchener theologische Zeitschrift* 8 (1957) 174–179. N. WICKI, ''Philipp der Kanzler und die Pariser Bischofswahl von 1227–1228,'' *Freiburger Zeitschrift für Philosophie und spekulative Theologie* 5 (1958) 318–326. J. B. SCHNEYER, *Die Sittenkritik in den Predigten Philipp des Kanzlers* (Münster 1963).

Philip of Hesse.

[N. WICKI]

PHILIP THE DEACON

One of the seven men chosen by the Apostles to perform certain administrative tasks for the poor in the early Christian community at Jerusalem (Acts 6.5–7). Because of his zeal in preaching the gospel he became known as Philip the Evangelist (Acts 21.8). According to Acts 8.4–5 Philip was among the Christians who were forced to leave Jerusalem after the martyrdom of Stephen. He preached the gospel with great success in Samaria (Acts 8.5–12), where Simon Magus became one of Philip's converts (Acts 8.13). On the road from Jerusalem to Gaza Philip instructed and baptized the Ethiopian minister of Queen Candace (Acts 8.26–39), and thereafter he apparently preached the gospel in every coastal city from Azotus (Ashdod) to CAESAREA in Palestine (Acts 8.40), where he became a permanent member of the early Christian community. Years later at the end of St. Paul's third missionary journey (A.D. 58), Philip acted as host to him and his party (Acts 21.8–9). In this same context mention is made of the fact that Philip had four virgin daughters endowed with the gift of prophecy; these, like Agabus and other Christian prophets, foretold the trials and difficulties that awaited Paul upon his return to Jerusalem. According to St. Basil (*Menol.* 1.69; *Patrologia Graeca* 67:103) Philip became bishop of Tralles. He is mentioned in the Roman Martyrology on June 6.

Bibliography: A. WIKENHAUSER, *Lexikon für Theologie und Kirche,* ed. J. HOFER and K. RAHNER (Freiburg 1957–65); suppl., *Das Zweite Vatikanische Konzil: Dokumente und Kommentare,* ed. H. S. BRECHTER et al. (1966) 8:464. G. STRECKER, *Die Religion in Geschichte und Gegenwart,* 7 v. (3d ed. Tübingen 1957–65) 5:338. *Encyclopedic Dictionary of the Bible,* tr. and adap. by L. HARTMAN (New York 1963) from A. VAN DEN BORN, *Bijbels Woordenboek,* 1835. H. H. PLATZ, *The Interpreter's Dictionary of the Bible,* ed. G. A. BUTTRICK (Nashville 1962) 3:785.

[C. H. PICKAR]

PHILIPPA MARERI, BL.

Poor Clare abbess; b. Petrella Salto, Cicoli, Abruzzi, Italy, 1200; d. Villa Casardita, Feb. 16, 1236. Philippa was the daughter of Philip, first lord of Mareri. She early became acquainted with the work of St. FRANCIS OF ASSISI. Not wishing to become involved in the quarrels between her brother Thomas and FREDERICK II, she refused all marriage proposals and withdrew with a few of her friends to a grotto near Mareri for a life of prayer and penance. Thomas reconciled himself to her decision and on Sept. 28, 1228, gave her a church in Villa Casardita, now known as Borgo San Pietro. She restored the building and built a convent that is the POOR CLARES' oldest convent in the kingdom of Sicily. On July 21, 1231, GREGORY IX took the house under his protection and integrated its community with the Poor Clares. The pious abbess recruited many young women of quality, was recognized for her humility, austerity, and charity, as well as for her organizational ability, and governed the monastery until her death. Her spiritual director, ROGER OF TODI, was present at her deathbed and delivered the eulogy at her burial. Philippa's reported apparitions and miracles gave rise to a local cult, and on June 27, 1247, INNOCENT IV granted an indulgence of 40 days annually on her feast day. In the 14th century a rhythmic office was composed in her honor (ed. Rome 1545, Naples 1668). In 1806 the cult was extended to the Franciscans and to the Dioceses of Rieti and Sulmona; new lessons in her honor were approved in 1838.

Feast: Feb. 16.

Bibliography: A. CHIAPPINI, "S. Filippa Mareri," *Miscellanea francescana* 22 (1922) 65–119. L. ZILIANI, *La baronessa santa* (Bergamo 1935). LÉON OF CLARY, *Lives of the Saints and Blessed of the Three Orders of Saint Francis,* 4 v. (Taunton, Eng. 1885–87) 1:257–260. *Vies des saintes et des bienheuruex* 2:365–367. G. FUSSENEGGER, *Lexikon für Theologie und Kirche* 2 8:457.

[J. CAMBELL]

PHILIPPIANS, EPISTLE TO THE

Place, Date, and Unity of Composition. Philippians has in the past generally been classified with the "CAPTIVITY EPISTLES," although the disputed status of Ephesians and Colossians leaves only Philippians and Philemon remaining in this category. The question of where Philippians was written continues to be debated. Four suggestions have been made as to provenance: Rome, Ephesus, Caesarea, and, more recently, Corinth. In the absence of compelling evidence, however, it seems best not to base one's exegesis of the epistle on the issue of where it was written.

Because of its association with what might have been Paul's final captivity, Philippians was long held to be one of Paul's later letters. However, even though Paul contemplates his death within the letter, he ends up expressing strong confidence that he will continue to live for the sake of the Christians in Philippi. In her detailed study of Rom 6:5, Florence Morgan Gillman has argued that the terminology there has been influenced by the *morph-* vocabulary in Phil 3. Additionally, there appear to be indications that the Letter to the Philippians was composed around the time of the Corinthian correspondence, most likely before 2 Corinthians. The first two chapters of 1 Corinthians, like Philippians, appear to share a background which contrasts a human view of wisdom with the Wisdom of God that 1 Cor 1:24 identifies as the crucified Christ. 2 Cor 8:1–5 appears to be a later reflection on the situation described in Philippians, and 2 Cor 8:9 seems to echo Phil 2:5–11.

Another point of debate regards the integrity of the letter. Particularly since the mid-20th century, it had become fashionable in discussion of this letter to propose that in fact Philippians is composed of parts of two or even three letters. Since 1981, however, the pendulum seems to be swinging in the other direction, initially stimulated by an article by David Cook that exposed the pseudo-scholarship of a number of exegetes who claimed to find early evidence for the "partition theory" in the 17th century writing of Stephanus LeMoyne. The fact that advocates of a partition theory are by no means in agreement as to where the supposed "obvious breaks" in the letter occur has led to the existence of at least 16 versions of this theory, as David Garland has pointed out. Wolfgang Schenk (1983) has attempted to "objectively" demonstrate the lack of integrity of the letter using the methodology of text linguistics, but in fact an appeal to linguistics cannot conclusively resolve the issue either way, as Jeffrey Reed has demonstrated. There is no manuscript evidence to indicate that the text ever existed in anything other than its canonical form. Also, as recent commentaries (*see* bibliography) have demonstrated, good sense can be made of the extant letter.

The Relationship between Paul and the Philippians. One item that has never been in dispute is the manifest affection between Paul and this community and the high regard in which its members were held by Paul, evidenced not only in this letter, but also in 2 Cor 8:1–5. The mutual participation in the gospel which extended to sharing of material resources is indicated by the frequency of *koinōnia* terminology (Phil 3:10). This was the only one of the churches Paul founded from which he accepted financial support for his own use ''from the beginning of the gospel'' (Phil 1:5, 4:15–16; cf. 2 Cor 11:9), contrary to his usual practice as illustrated in 1 Thes 2:9 and 1 Cor 9:1–15.

While in every one of his undisputed letters Paul at times uses the terms brother(s) or sister to indicate the addressees' equal status with him in the gospel, normally this is balanced by indications of his superior status as one who has a right to teach, as illustrated, for example in the use of *apostle* (Rom 1:1, 1 Cor 1:1, 2 Cor 1:1, Gal 1:1; cf. Phlm 1:14), *father* (1 Cor 4:15, 1 Thes 2:11; cf. 2 Cor 12:14), or *mother* (1 Thes 2:7; cf. Gal 4:19 and 1 Cor 3:1–1). Only in Philippians is there no explicit claim to superior status. At first glance this appears more remarkable insofar as modern scholars are increasingly inclined to agree with the observation of Chrysostom that it appeared to him the women mentioned in Phil 4:2 were the heads of the church at Philippi. In appealing to them to resolve their dispute, which may have been due to serious concerns regarding the threat of persecution, Paul is extremely courteous, although he takes the almost unprecedented step of naming persons involved in a dispute. This may indicate that Paul can rely on the strength of their relationship. In Galatians and 1 Corinthians, while he expresses disapproval in much stronger terms, the only person who is named as being party to an earnest disagreement is Peter (influenced by James; see Gal 2). The difference between his report of undisguised anger at Peter and the gentle courtesy extended to Euodia and Syntyche is understandable if Paul was expressing sensitivity to their serious situation which involved the threat of persecution.

Koinōnia in Suffering (Phil 3:10). The tendency to read Philippians as dealing with relatively minor problems in intra-community harmony has increasingly been replaced by a viewpoint which recognizes that most likely the letter was directed to a community in danger of persecution and even death for its belief in the gospel Paul preached. The initial impetus for this change of perspective was the 1930 commentary of Ernst Lohmeyer, which read the epistle against the background of the possible impending martyrdom of Paul (Phil 1:20–23) and also of the Philippian community (Phil 1:29–30). Such a reading makes better sense of Phil 2:5–11, which is preceded by an exhortation to have the same ''mind'' as Christ (or ''as you have in Christ''). Earlier objections to such an ''ethical'' interpretation of 2:5–11 were primarily based on the perceived incongruity between putting forth the model of Jesus' obedience even unto death as an incentive for the community to improve its internal relations. However if the disputes within the community are viewed not as petty squabbles, but rather as serious disagreements as to how to deal with the possibility of impending persecution, the exhortation to obedience in Phil 2, immediately following the example of the freely chosen obedience of Jesus unto death, makes better sense. Likewise, Paul's impassioned plea in Phil 3 to beware of the advocates of circumcision is more understandable if perhaps some in the community might have been considering the option that accepting this mark of Jewishness could be a means of avoiding Roman persecution. Philippi was a city in which abstaining from participation in Roman cult would have been noticeable, but Jews were exempt from such participation.

Reversal of Values. Phil 3:7–11 testifies to a profound reversal of values on Paul's part as the result of his encounter with the risen Christ. Not only his former privileged status in Judaism, but everything other than Christ is now accounted as worthless. The 15th century mystical writer Dionysius the Carthusian pointed out the similarity of this passage to Wis 7:7–9. It is in the Book of Wisdom that the notion of a righteous sufferer apparent in the Book of Isaiah becomes explicitly linked with the hope of resurrection for the just. In encouraging this community which, together with him, is ''knowing'' the koinōnia of Christ's sufferings, Paul holds out to them his own hope that he and they will likewise experience the power of Christ's resurrection (Phil 3:10), when the one who did not consider equality with God something to be used for his own advantage (Phil 2:6) ''will transform the body of our humiliation that it may be conformed to the body of his glory, by the power that also enables him to make all things subject to himself'' (Phil 3:20–21, NRSV).

Bibliography: D. A. BLACK, ''The Discourse Structure of Philippians: A Study in Text Linguistics,'' *Novum Testamentum* 37 (1995): 16–49. M. BOCKMUEHL, *The Epistle to the Philippians*, Black's New Testament Commentary 11 (London 1998). G. F. HAWTHORNE, *Philippians*, (Word Biblical Commentary 43; Waco, Texas 1983). V. KOPERSKI, ''Feminist Concerns and the Authorial Readers in Philippians,'' *Louvain Studies* 17 (1992): 269–292. V.

KOPERSKI, "Textlinguistics and the Integrity of Philippians: A Critique of Wolfgang Schenk's Arguments for a Compilation Hypothesis," *Ephemerides theologicae Lovanienses* 68 (1992): 331–367. V. KOPERSKI, *The Knowledge of Christ Jesus my Lord: The High Christology of Philippians 3:7–11,* Contributions to Biblical Exegesis and Theology 16, (Kampen, Netherlands 1996). P. T. O'BRIEN, *The Epistle to the Philippians: A Commentary on the Greek Text,* New International Greek Testament Commentary (Grand Rapids, Mich 1991). L. PORTEFAIX, *Sisters Rejoice: Paul's Letter to the Philippians and Luke-Acts as Received by First-Century Philippian Women,* Coniectanea Biblica, New Testament 20 (Stockholm 1988). J. T. REED, *A Discourse Analysis of Philippians: Method and Rhetoric in the Debate over Literary Integrity,* JSNTSuppl 136, (Sheffield 1997). W. SCHENK, *Die Philipperbriefe des Paulus* (Stuttgart 1984). M. SILVA, *Philippians,* Wycliffe Exegetical Commentary (Chicago 1988).

[V. KOPERSKI]

PHILIPPINE INDEPENDENT CHURCH

Also known as Iglesia Filipina Independiente (IFI), or more popularly as the Aglipayans, after its founding leader and first supreme bishop, Gregorio Aglipay. The IFI emerged out of the intense nationalism that accompanied the 1898 Philippine revolt against the Spanish and the resulting strong anti-Spanish and anti-friar sentiments directed against the PATRONATO REAL system that resulted in a church dominated by bishops and clerics appointed by the Spanish Crown. It is in communion with the U.S. Episcopal Church since 1961 and the Old Catholic Union of Utrecht since 1965. Its national office is located in Manila.

History. During the Philippine Revolution (1898), Gen. Emilio Aguinaldo and other Filipino leaders, wishing to overthrow both the political power of the Spaniards and the spiritual power of Spanish friar-bishops, persuaded Gregorio Aglipay (1860–1940) to head the Church in the Philippines by appointing him military vicar-general (Oct. 20, 1898). For his anti-Spanish rhetoric and anti-friar efforts, he was excommunicated by Abp. Nozaleda of Manila (April 29, 1899). Aglipay had been ordained (1889) and had labored in the Manila Archdiocese. He tried to obtain spiritual jurisdiction by persuading the imprisoned bishop of Nueva Segovia to appoint him ecclesiastical governor of that diocese. Supported by the Filipino clergy, Aglipay assembled the "synod" of Paniqui (October 1899). Forced to flee before the advance of the U.S. army of occupation, he led the Filipino resistance in Ilocos Norte but surrendered with other guerrilla leaders (April 1901).

In April of 1901 two priests representing the anti-Spanish nationalist movement went to Rome to request papal recognition of the actions of Aguinaldo and Aglipay, and the establishment of an indigenous hierarchy to replace the discredited Spanish patronato real bishops. Finding themselves rebuffed, the resolve of the Filipino nationalist clergy hardened. Isabelo de los Reyes, Sr. (1864–1938), newly returned from political imprisonment in Spain, proclaimed the establishment of the Philippine Independent Church (Iglesia Filipina Independiente or IFI) on Aug. 3, 1902. Aglipay was chosen supreme bishop and had himself "consecrated" bishop by 12 priests. About 36 Filipino secular priests joined him, some of them being similarly "consecrated." Consecration by priests was defended on the ground that the priesthood was the essential order, while the episcopacy was merely a title of rank.

Highly successful at first, the IFI could claim the loyalty of some one-quarter to one-third of the total Christian population of Philippines at the peak of its influence in 1904. The Aglipayans seized Catholic churches, rectories, and cemeteries. These were ordered restored to the Catholic Church by a Philippine Supreme Court decision (Nov. 24, 1906). Because no bishops joined the movement, the church lost the apostolic succession. It maintained a presbyteral transmission of the threefold ordained ministry until 1948, when the U.S. Episcopal Church consecrated three bishops with valid apostolic succession, who in turned transmitted the historic episcopate to other IFI bishops.

Teachings. The original doctrines of the IFI are contained in the epistles (1902–03) and the doctrinal books published after 1904. Their author, Isabelo de los Reyes, Sr., a Philippine senator and trade unionist, returned to the Catholic Church in 1936. Aglipay was unsuccessful in his attempt to be elected president of the Philippines in 1935. In 1940 the former Senator Santiago Fonacier succeeded him as supreme bishop.

From its early days, two principal factions co-existed uneasily within the IFI, one Unitarian and the other Trinitarian. This situation lasted until 1946, when a bitter feud erupted between these two factions. The Trinitarian faction had its bishops reconsecrated by U.S. Episcopalians in 1948 and sued the Unitarian faction for sole rights to the name and property of the original IFI. After prolonged litigation, in 1955 the Trinitarian faction, under Isabelo de los Reyes, Jr., as supreme bishop, was awarded by the Filipino Supreme Court the right to the name and possessions of the original IFI.

Bibliography: P. S. DE ACHÚTEGUI and M. A. BERNAD, *Religious Revolution in the Philippines: The Life and Church of Gregorio Aglipay, 1860–1960,* 2 v. (Manila 1960–66). I. R. RODRÍGUEZ, *Gregorio Aglipay y los origenes de la Iglesia Filipina Independiente (1898–1917),* 2 v. (Madrid 1960).

[P. S. DE ACHÚTEGUI/M. A. BERNAD/EDS.]

PHILIPPINES, THE CATHOLIC CHURCH IN

Capital: Manila.
Size: 115,651 sq. miles.
Population: 82,841,518.
Languages: Filipino (based on Tagalog) and English (both official); eight major dialects: Tagalog, Cebuano, Ilocan, Hiligaynon or Ilonggo, Bicol, Waray, Pampango, and Pangasinense.
Religions: Catholics 85% (this places the Philippines as the world's third largest local Church, after Brazil and Mexico). The population of southwestern Mindanao and Sulu is predominantly Muslim.

The Philippine archipelago consists of 7,107 islands stretching southward from the southern coast of China; the largest are Luzon in the north and Mindanao in the south. Central Philippines comprises several medium-sized islands known as the Visayan Islands. Stretching from the southwestern tip of Mindanao toward Borneo is a chain of small islands collectively known as the Sulu Archipelago.

There is evidence of human settlements in the islands as early as 20,000 B.C. First to arrive were the small black people called Negritos by the Spaniards. They were driven into the mountainous interior when brown-skinned Malays migrated to the islands. Today, one finds various hill tribes such as the Aetas and Ifugao of Luzon and the Mansakas, Mandayas, and Bukidnon of Mindanao, many of whom still practice their traditional religions. Malay Filipinos occupy the lowlands and constitute the majority of the population. The modern Republic of the Philippines is one of only two countries in Asia that have a predominantly Roman Catholic population (the other country being East Timor).

Arrival of Spaniards. In March 1521 Ferdinand Magellan arrived in search of spices and converts for Charles I (Emperor Charles V). It was his son Prince Philip, later King PHILIP II, whose name was bestowed on the islands by Villalobos in 1542. Lapulapu, a native chieftain of Cebu, resisted Magellan's claim of Spanish sovereignty and mortally wounded him. In 1565 Miguel Lopez de Legazpi established the first permanent Spanish settlement in Cebu. In 1571 Legazpi moved his headquarters to Manila, making it the capital of the colony. By the end of the century, most of the lowlands were under Spanish rule, except for some southern islands, which had been Muslim since the late 14th or early 15th century. When the Spaniards encountered the Muslims in the Philippines, their hostile attitudes based on Muslim-Christian encounters in Europe (the struggle for independence from Moorish rule in the Iberian Peninsula) colored their outlook and relations; these very negative attitudes were also transmitted to non-Muslim Filipinos.

Systematic Christianization. An organized program of evangelization of the Philippines was begun in 1565 by the AUGUSTINIANS who accompanied Legazpi's expedition. They were followed by FRANCISCANS (1578), JESUITS (1581), DOMINICANS (1587), and AUGUSTINIAN RECOLLECTS (1606) from both Spain and Mexico. Manila became a bishopric in 1579 and an archbishopric in 1595. The Spanish system of the *PATRONATO REAL* facilitated the implementation of the evangelization program. Under this arrangement, the Spanish crown gave financial support and protection to the Church in the Philippines while exercising a large measure of control over its activities. Missionaries traveled to the Philippines in the king's ships. While engaged in mission work, they were entitled to a stipend drawn from either the colonial government directly or from the right to tribute in certain territories *(encomiendas)* into which the country was initially divided. The *encomienda* system was gradually abandoned during the 17th century after widespread criticism of extortion and other abuses.

On the other hand, the appointment of missionaries to a parish or mission station was subject to the approval of the governor as vice-patron. In fact, it was Philip II himself who determined that each missionary group should have its own section of the country for evangelization purposes. Under this system the Church in turn exerted great influence on government policy. The early missionaries often sought to protect the natives from the abuses of the conquistadors and *encomenderos*; they had a vigorous leader in Fray Domingo de SALAZAR, OP, the first bishop of the Philippines. The synod that he summoned in 1582 clarified many difficult problems regarding the conquest, settlement, and administration of the country in accordance with Christian ideals and principles of justice.

The Philippine Church of the 16th century certainly took sides, and it was not with the rich and powerful nor with their fellow Spaniards, but with those who were oppressed and victims of injustice. Church historian J. N. Schumacher notes: ''Skeptics have often questioned the reality of the rapid conversion of 16th-century Filipinos. If one wishes the answer, it is to be found right here, that the Church as a whole took the side of the poor and the oppressed, whether the oppressors were Spaniards or Filipino *principales.*''

Mission Methods. The Spanish missionaries in the Philippines employed a variety of approaches to evangelization. The scattered clan villages were gathered together into larger communities (pueblos, *cabeceras*); often

Metropolitan Sees	Suffragans
Caceres	Daet, Legazpi, Masbate, Sorsogon, Virac, Libmanan (prel.)
Cagayan de Oro	Butuan, Malaybalay, Surigao, Tandag
Capiz	Kalibo, Romblon
Cebu	Dumaguete, Maasin, Tagbilaran, Talibon
Cotabato	Kidapawan, Marbel
Davao	Digos, Mati, Tagum
Jaro	Bacolod, Kabankalan, San Carlos, San Jose de Antique
Lingayen-Dagupan	Alaminos, Cabanatuan, San Fernando de la Union, San Jose, Urdaneta
Lipa	Boac, Gumaca, Lucena, Infanta (prel.)
Manila	Antipolo, Imus, Malolos, San Pablo
Nueva Segovia	Bangued, Laoag
Ozamis	Dipolog, Iligan, Pagadian, Marawi (prel.)
Palo	Borongan, Calbayog, Catarman, Naval
San Fernando	Balanga, Iba, Tarlac
Tuguegarao	Bayombong, Ilagan, Batanes and the Babuyan Islands (prel.)
Zamboanga	Ipil (prel.), Isabela (prel.)

Vicariates apostolic: Baguio, Bontoc-Lagawe, Calapan, Jolo, Palawan, San Jose in Mindoro, Tabuk, plus a military ordinariate.

this implied radical lifestyle changes and hence could only be accomplished with difficulty and very gradually. Instruction was given in native languages, as few Filipinos outside the Intramuros area of Manila were ever able to read, write, or speak Spanish with any proficiency. In most missions primary schools supplied the new Christian communities with catechists and local officials. Religion was made to permeate society by substituting splendid liturgical and paraliturgical observances (fiestas, processions, novenas) for the traditional rites and festivals; many pious associations of prayer and charity were formed and promoted.

Education and social services were almost exclusively the concern of the Church during the entire period of Spanish rule. By the end of the 16th century, Manila had three hospitals, one for Spaniards, another for natives, and a third for the Chinese. The first two were administered by Franciscans, the third by the Dominicans. In 1611, the Hospitallers of St. John of God established their hospital ministry in the Philippines. In 1595, the Jesuits opened a grammar school for Spanish boys that later developed into the University of San Ignacio and had attached to it the residential college of San José, founded in 1601 and today the San José Seminary. The year 1611 saw the beginnings of the Dominican University of Santo Tomás, which continues today as a vibrant educational center. In 1640 the Dominicans also took charge of the College of San Juan de Letrán, started about a decade earlier by a zealous layman for the education of orphans. Various religious communities of women established themselves in Manila in the 17th and 18th centuries; frequently, they undertook the education of girls. In 1684, Ignacia del Espírito Santo founded the first religious institute for local Filipino women, the Religious of the Virgin Mary (RVM).

The considerable funds required for the support of these schools, hospitals, and charitable works came from pious donations and legacies, called *obras pías*; they were often invested in the galleon trade or in large agricultural estates, the so-called friar lands. At the same time, the friar lands were leased to tenant cultivators for development and administration, an arrangement that led to frequent conflicts of interest and a deepening resentment of the Church as landlord. This background must be borne in mind for a balanced understanding of the anticlerical reaction that developed in the latter 19th century among a people deeply and sincerely Catholic.

Native Clergy. By the 18th century, Catholicism had taken permanent root in the Philippines as the religion of the people. However, it had one serious weakness: the retarded development of the native clergy. The unsatisfactory results of early experiments in Latin America had made the Spanish missionaries in the Philippines extremely cautious in admitting native candidates to the priesthood. Apparently, only in the late 17th century were native Filipinos ordained. A proposal of Gianbattista Sidotti, a member of Cardinal Charles de TOURNON's entourage, to erect a regional seminary in Manila for the whole of East Asia was sharply rejected by the Spanish Crown in1712. Bishops became increasingly eager for a diocesan clergy completely under their jurisdiction when conflicts over parish appointments continued—conflicts between the bishops and the religious orders on the one hand, and the bishops and the government on the other. Since very few secular priests came to the Philippines from Spain, this meant ordaining large numbers of natives. Archbishop Sancho de Santa Justa y Rufina of Manila (1767–1787) threatened to take away their parishes from the religious who refused to submit to episcopal visitation; he also ordained natives even when they lacked the necessary aptitude and training. The results proved disastrous, confirming the prevailing opinion that natives, even if admitted to the priesthood, were incapable of assuming its full responsibilities. Some improvement in formation and an increase in vocations occurred after the arrival of the VINCENTIANS (1862), who took charge of diocesan seminaries. Even so, the departure of a large proportion of Spanish clergy after the transfer of sovereignty from Spain to the United States (1898) left over 700 parishes vacant.

Religious Clergy. The privileges of the *Patronato Real* conferred by the Holy See on the Spanish crown were a mixed blessing; they promoted constructive collaboration between the Church and the colonial government, but also led to friction. The focus of difficulty was the religious parish priest and the extent to which he was subject to episcopal visitation and control. The conflict gave rise to series of crises that began as early as the administration of Bishop Salazar (1581-1594). In 1744 the Holy See ruled that religious parish priests were subject to the jurisdiction of the ordinary in all matters pertaining to their parish duties (*in officio officiando*) and to their religious superiors in their personal conduct. With the advent of the revolutionary era in Europe and the loss of Spain's American colonies, the terms of the problem in the Philippines changed. It became widely believed in official circles that the presence of the religious in the parishes was a political necessity, not so much because they were religious as because they were Spaniards and could be relied upon to keep the population loyal. This seems to have been the thinking behind the royal decree of 1862 transferring the Mindanao missions from the Augustian Recollects to the newly returned Jesuits (they had been expelled in 1768) and giving the former an equivalent number of parishes in Manila and Cavite, which were consequently taken away from the native clergy. The result was mounting disaffection among the native priests thus deprived or threatened with removal. Naturally, the Filipino priests assailed the government policy; among their active leaders and spokesmen were Fathers Gómez, Burgos, and Zamora, who were executed by the government for alleged complicity in a mutiny of native garrison troops in Cavite (1872).

Emerging Nationalism and Change in the Church. The deaths of these Filipino priests gave a powerful impetus to the emergence of Filipino nationalism by sensitizing Filipinos to injustices by the Spanish colonial government. The movement began as an initiative for colonial reforms led by Dr. José Rizal (1862–1896). After Rizal's arrest and execution for treason, it developed into a separatist movement. The ensuing revolution (1896–1898), which was markedly anti-friar, though usually not anticlerical or anti-Catholic, was cut short by the intervention of the United States, which demanded cession of the Philippines at the conclusion of the Spanish-American War.

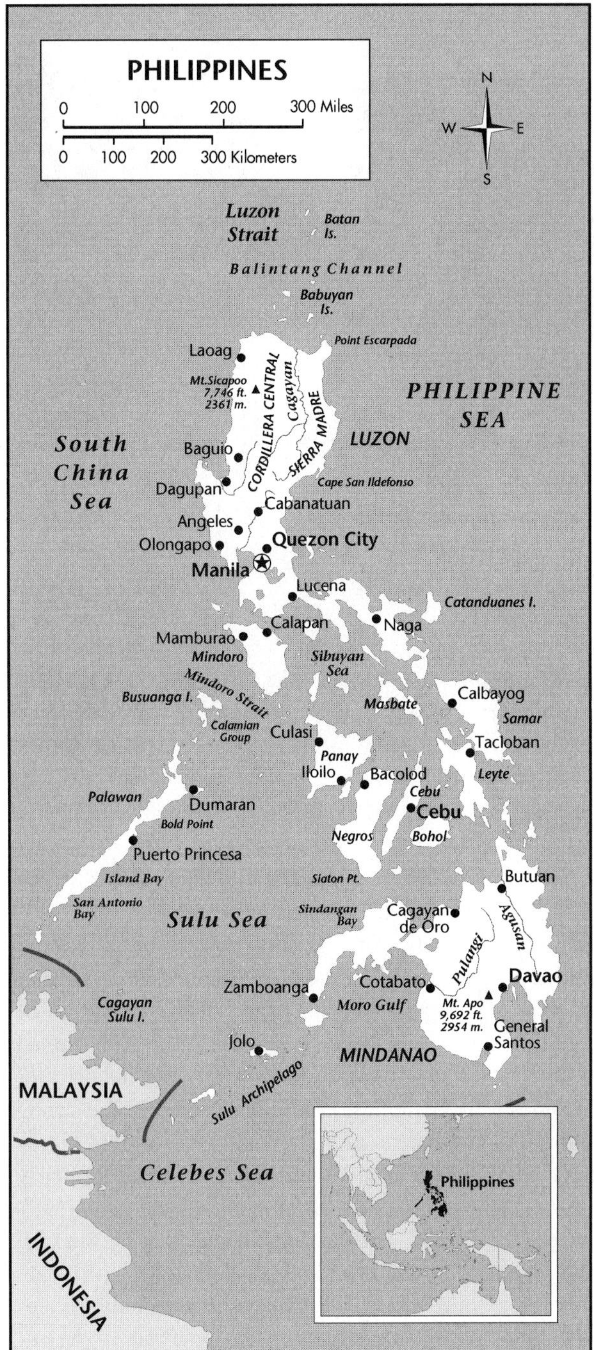

Ricardo Cardinal Vidal, Archbishop of Cebu. (Photo by James H. Kroeger)

The change of sovereignty ended the *Patronato* system. The U.S. policy of Church-State separation was extended to the Philippines, but interpreted in a manner much less favorable to the Church. Thus, a system of nonsectarian public education was established that failed to take into account that the overwhelming majority of Filipinos were Catholics. In addition, there was the strong influence of hundreds of American public-school teachers, most of whom were Protestants. They were popularly known as the Thomasites; a group of 540 arrived in 1901 aboard the U.S.S. Thomas and many others followed. The professed neutralism in religious matters of the state university, founded in 1911, was copied by other privately founded nonsectarian universities, resulting in the undermining of religious belief among the educated class.

One consequence of the revolutionary upheaval was the formation by Gregorio Aglipay, a Filipino secular priest, of a schismatic church along nationalist lines, the Philippine Independent Church or Iglesia Filipina Independiente (1902). Initially it drew a considerable following; however, it soon broke up into factions, some of which rapidly deserted Catholicism in doctrine as well as in discipline. The Supreme Court in 1907 also restored to the Catholic Church much of the property that had been taken over by the Aglipayans. The largest Trinitarian faction was received into full communion by the Protestant Episcopal Church of the United States, established in the Philippines since the beginning of the century.

Protestant denominations sent mission personnel to the Philippines almost as soon as the transfer of sovereignty was effected. In 1901 Presbyterian, Baptist, Methodist, and United Brethren groups, along with societies such as the Christian Missionary Alliance, the YMCA, and the American Bible Society, formed an Evangelical Union to coordinate their activities. A denomination of local origin with an evangelical orientation, the Iglesia ni Cristo, was founded in 1914.

The Church suffered disastrously during the years following 1898; in several respects it would be decades before a condition approximating normalcy would again be reached. From 1898 to 1900 there were almost no resident bishops; diocesan priests remained in very short supply and some had defected to the Aglipayans; seminaries were closed in 1898 and did not reopen until 1904. From 1898 to 1903 the total number of friars decreased over 75 percent from 1,013 to 246. In a word, the Church was in chaos. The true beginnings of the reorganization of the Church began with the persistent efforts of Monsignor Guidi through his negotiations with the U.S. government and the Filipino clergy. Pope LEO XIII, in his apostolic letter *Quae mari sinico* (1902) reorganized the hierarchy, created four new dioceses, and strongly recommended to the Philippine hierarchy the formation of a native clergy. The first official Provincial Council of Manila was convened in 1907 with the goals of reviving the faith of the Filipinos, restoring the local church, and inspiring in the clergy a spirit of apostolic zeal.

Meanwhile, the severe shortage of priests and religious was met in part by new, non-Spanish missionary congregations of women and men from Europe, Australia, and the United States. For example, male missionary societies that responded to the pressing needs in the 1905-41 period are: Irish REDEMPTORISTS (1905), MILL HILL MISSIONARIES (1906), Scheut-CICM (1907), Sacred Heart Missionaries and Divine Word Society (1908), De La Salle Brothers (1911), Oblates of Saint Joseph (1915), Maryknoll Missioners (1926), Columban Missioners (1929), Society of Saint Paul (1935), Quebec-PME Society (1937), and Oblates-OMI (1939). Many dedicated female religious came as missionaries to the Philippines, often working in partnership with the societies just mentioned.

By the mid-1920s, the situation was taking a turn for the better; some significant factors in the survival and resurgence of the Church were: the revitalization of Catholic education, growth of Filipino diocesan and religious vocations, a more educated laity, Church involvement in social questions and the labor movement, and the involvement of Catholics in national life. The celebration of the 33rd International Eucharistic Congress in Manila (1937) focused the attention of the Christian world on the Philippines and deeply inspired thousands of Filipino Catholics.

The Church from 1941 to 1965. Japanese forces invaded the Philippines in December of 1941. Allied forces under General MacArthur returned in 1944, but intense fighting continued until the Japanese surrender in August of 1945. Manuel Roxas became president of the second independent Republic of the Philippines on July 4, 1946. The war inflicted heavy damage; 257 priests and religious lost their lives. Priests, brothers, sisters, and dedicated Catholic women and men exhibited great faith and heroism during the war; many suffered imprisonment.

The origins of what is known today as the Catholic Bishops' Conference of the Philippines (CBCP) can be traced back to February 1945 when Apostolic Delegate William Piani, even as the war was still raging, appointed John Hurley, S.J. to take charge of relief work and created the Catholic Welfare Organization (CWO). As the very name indicates, the primary purpose of the CWO was to assist in alleviating the immediate suffering and destruction brought on by the war. On July 17, 1945, the bishops met in Manila for their first meeting after the Japanese Occupation; they requested that the CWO become the official organization of the Hierarchy of the Philippines. In subsequent years, the CWO continued to be largely engaged in relief services and the rehabilitation of Church institutions; it also became the vehicle through which the interests and values of the Church were protected and furthered.

The period from 1945 to 1965 was characterized by rapid recovery from the ravages of war, greatly expanded school system at upper levels, involvement of Catholics (laity, sisters, clergy) in social action, and growing Filipinization of Church structures and administration. The First Plenary Council of the Philippines (1953) focused on the ''preservation, enrichment, and propagation of Catholic life'' and offered Church resources ''to renew the social order.'' The Church became involved in CATHOLIC ACTION programs with farmers (FFF) and workers (FFW). Guidance from the hierarchy continued; from 1945 to 1965 the CWO issued 39 joint pastoral letters and statements on a variety of subjects relevant to Church and civil society. The Philippine bishops sponsored a Marian Congress in Manila (1954) and inaugurated the Pontificio Collegio-Seminario Filippino in Rome (1961). The period saw renewal programs introduced; the Christian Family Movement (CFM) came to the Philippines in the 1950s; the Cursillos de Cristianidad introduced in 1963

Philippine Roman Catholic church leader Jaime Cardinal Sin kisses the doors of the Manila Cathedral after closing them to symbolically end celebrations marking the 2000th birth of Jesus Christ, or the Jubilee year. (©AFP/CORBIS)

(and the evangelization seminars for various Church sectorial groups they inspired) ignited a renewed fervor of lay involvement in the Church.

In mid-1965, the nation observed a six-day renewal celebration of the quadricentennial of evangelization in the Philippines (1565–1965). The bishops established the Mission Society of the Philippines, signifying Filipino's commitment to spread the faith they had received to other lands. Two more events would prove to shape significantly the experience and mission of this local Church. The first was the election of Ferdinand Marcos as president of the Philippines; the second was the conclusion of the Second Vatican Council.

Authoritarian Rule and Revolt. The Philippine constitution, modeled on that of the United States, established a democratic form of government. Ferdinand E. Marcos, first elected president in 1965, declared martial law in 1972 and imposed a form of ''constitutional authoritarianism.'' The martial law period posed new, challenging questions for the Church and nation. Among the more pernicious effects of the two-decade Marcos era (1965–1986) were increased militarization, insurgency, the absence of juridical procedures, the destruction of

José Rizal.

democratic processes, economic decline, and pervasive fear. The end result, in the words of a Filipino social scientist, was to place the country ''on the trembling edge of a social volcano.'' This period proved a time of testing and growth for the Church. Prophetic stances were often met by military abuse, imprisonment and torture, and even deportation for foreign missionaries. The Church evolved a position of ''critical collaboration,'' cooperating with the regime on programs beneficial to the populace while criticizing government actions judged harmful.

An important 1977 pastoral letter, *The Bond of Love in Proclaiming the Good News,* addressed many social problems as well as the divisions within the Church created by various positions taken regarding martial law (e.g. the absence of a clear stance and the long-delayed response on the part of most members of the hierarchy; the infiltration of Church structures and institutions by left-leaning priests and religious). The pastoral letter sought to enunciate a clear, holistic vision to guide the Church's mission of integral evangelization.

President Marcos announced the lifting of martial law on Jan. 17, 1981. It was carefully timed—three days before the inauguration of President Ronald Regan, and one month before Pope JOHN PAUL II's visit to the Philippines. In view of the broad range of authoritarian controls that Marcos retained, the lifting of martial law was recognized by the Filipino people as purely cosmetic. The papal visit brought two clear messages to Filipinos: a need for dynamic faith in their lives and an emphasis on justice and peace. Specifically, John Paul II told the president and government leaders: ''Even in exceptional situations that may at times arise, one can never justify any violation of the fundamental dignity of the human person or of the basic rights that safeguard this dignity.''

The assassination of opposition leader Benigno Aquino on Aug. 21, 1983, ushered in a period of national mourning and a widespread clamor for justice and truth. In this highly charged atmosphere the Church's response was crucial. Jaime Cardinal Sin, Archbishop of Manila since 1974, cautioned Filipinos: ''If we allow his death to fan the flames of violence and division, then he will have died in vain.'' Events moved rapidly in the ensuing years. Filipino consciousness had been awakened; Philippine society had been galvanized. In 1986, Marcos attempted to forestall his overthrow by staging elections. Corazon Aquino, widow of the slain Benigno, won the popular vote, and when the national assembly nevertheless declared Marcos the winner, the Filipino people took to the streets in protest. The Church did not remain on the sidelines during this national crisis. In the volatile context that followed the elections, the Catholic bishops issued a statement declaring that fraud provides no moral legitimacy for any regime. If citizens agreed that the election had been stolen, they should oblige the regime to respect their will. However, resistance ''must always be according to the Gospel of Christ, that is, in a peaceful, non-violent way.''

An analysis of the story of the ''bloodless revolution'' of February 1986 and the roles played by church people and Cardinal Sin is instructive. The overthrow of the Marcos regime was ''a victory of moral values over the sheer physical force on which he had relied'' [J. Carroll]. It signaled people's determination not to shed Filipino blood. The revolution was a ''movement for active non-violence which was promoted by Church-related groups'' [*ibid.*]. In addition, ''the February Revolution was a political event, not a social revolution'' [*ibid.*]. Basic social issues of wealth and power that plagued the nation for generations remained. Many Filipinos still found themselves outside the mainstream of national social, political, and economic life.

The Aquino Presidency. Corazon Aquino, catapulted into office with little experience, served as Philippine president from 1986 to1992. Her main contribution was the reestablishment of a democratically functioning government. In May 1986, Aquino appointed a constitutional commission (including church people) and asked that a new document be produced within three months. This constitution was ratified overwhelmingly by a national referendum in 1987. Difficult issues facing Aquino included a bankrupt economy, the status of the U.S. military bases, continuing political insurgency (including militant Islamic separatists), natural disasters, a burgeoning population, foreign debt, agrarian reform—the list appeared endless. Yet she guided the Filipino people to free and fair elections in May 1992 and the orderly transfer of power to President Fidel Ramos (1992–1998), the first Protestant to become President of the Philippines.

The Marcos years further accentuated the mass poverty that had long been and continues to be the most tragic aspect of Filipino life. Fifteen years after he was overthrown, his ruinous legacy was still felt: 50 percent of Filipinos lived below the poverty line; servicing the domestic and foreign debt absorbed an average of 40 percent of the government budget; unemployment was at 11.8 percent and underemployment stood at 22 percent; 10 percent of the total population had to work abroad as migrant workers; graft and corruption remained prevalent—even endemic; environmental degradation remained unabated; and infant mortality rated among the highest in Asia. In stark contrast to the widespread immense poverty, there remained pockets of great luxury, brutally emphasizing the gross inequity of income distribution. In the political system, power, like wealth, remained concentrated in the hands of a few influential politicians, business and military people. There appeared to be a self-perpetuating social system and political culture. Politicians, for the most part, had not introduced truly transformative social programs into their platforms.

The Implementation of Vatican II. VATICAN COUNCIL II promoted a major ecclesiological paradigm shift, entailing changes in theologies, values, and orientations. Received by the local Church of the Philippines, it prompted the Filipino bishops to launch a New Evangelization; the social apostolate was among its emphases. Early efforts centered on the formation and support of unions and cooperatives for farmers, laborers, and fishermen. The bishops issued several pastoral letters on social action, justice and development. They sponsored a National Rural Development Congress in 1967, the slogan of which, ''The Church Goes to the Barrios,'' became axiomatic for the Church's commitment to development and social justice. The bishops established and funded the National Secretariat for Social Action, Justice, and Peace (NASSA) as their means of coordinating the social justice apostolate. In 1971, the influential Mindanao-Sulu Pastoral Conference (MSPC) was established. In the late 1960s and early 1970s, the Church's vision of human development as integral to evangelization expanded from a concern for social change to include the need for structural change. It became clear that efforts that had improved the conditions of the farming and working classes could not be sustained without corresponding political leverage. Church involvement in broader social, political, and economic questions became imperative.

Priests leading procession of new missioners during National Mission Congress. (Photo by James H. Kroeger)

Vatican II's ecclesiology took root in the Philippine Church, resulting in a mature, vibrant local Church. The presence of strong BASIC CHRISTIAN COMMUNITIES (BCCs) provided grass-roots structures for spiritual, catechetical, ministerial, and social growth. Important strengths developed within this Church: the inductive and experimental approach of theology; its inculturated social teaching; its spirituality of human development; its renewed ecclesiology/missiology; its concrete service to many Filipinos facing diverse dehumanizing social ills; its engagement in social issues in a non-partisan but active manner; its efforts to promote and practice nonviolent approaches to socio-political crises; its commitment to create structures of participation in Church and society. The Church also had its witnesses and martyrs: Bishop Benjamin de Jesus, OMI (Feb. 4, 1997), Father Rhoel Gallardo, CMF (May 3, 2000), and Father Benjamin Inocencio, OMI (Dec. 28, 2000).

Priest raising chalice during celebration of the first mass by Spanish missionaries in Philippines, painting. (Photo by Alfredo Juson; James H. Kroeger)

The Philippine bishops have continued, with moderate effectiveness, to use pastoral letters to communicate their holistic vision of the Church's evangelizing mission. The CBCP (Catholic Bishops Conference of the Philippines, canonically constituted in 1967) has issued more than 125 pastoral letters and statements in the period 1965 to 2000, two-thirds of which address social, political, and economic matters. Bishop Claver noted that they have generally proven to be quite accurate barometers of Philippine life. This effective tool of evangelization has promoted a basic Christian ''faith-realism'' and continually needs to be actualized within viable Christian communities.

The Church today retains moral authority and credibility in Philippine society; its witness to justice and solidarity with the poor, marginalized, and oppressed has established a reservoir of good will and credibility. Yet, as a living organism, she has clear limitations. There were unfortunate divisions in Church leadership, particularly in the mid-1970s; this resulted in missed pastoral opportunities and negative influences on the broader Church membership. Some bishops were hesitant to engage in human development programs and prophetic evangelization especially during the early years of martial law. Although indigenous clergy and religious continue to increase, that growth rate is below the percentage of population increase. There is also a glaring inequitable distribution of apostolic personnel within the country, with an over-concentration in urban areas.

Catechesis and Education. Given the large and rapidly expanding population of the Philippines, catechesis for Catholics remains a basic area of Church renewal. The catechetical ministry has shown considerable growth in vision, publications, institutes, and personnel. The Episcopal Commission on Catechesis and Catholic Education (ECCCE) has published several works and sponsored a variety of national workshops and congresses. Significant publications include *The Shape of Religious Education in the Philippines* (1979), *National Catechetical Directory for the Philippines* (1982-1985), *Filipino Family Growing in the Faith* (1983), *The Catechists' Basic Formation Program* (1992), *Catholic Faith Catechism* (1989-1993), *Catechism for Filipino Catholics* (1997) and its Tagalog translation *Katesismo para sa mga Pilipinong Katoliko* (2000). ECCCE publishes a quarterly catechetical review, *Docete,* which has raised interest in and the quality level of catechesis throughout the country.

Significant catechetical congresses were sponsored by ECCCE in the 1990s, beginning with the celebration of the National Catechetical Year (1990). Diocesan catechetical institutes were established in major cities (e.g. Bacolod, Cebu, Davao, Iloilo. Manila, Naga, Vigan, etc.). Other national centers which prepare women and men for their vocation as catechists (e.g. Mother of Life Center, Manila) continue their decades of service. The Philippine constitution affords opportunities for religious education in public schools; this critical area of the catechetical ministry is limited by inadequate numbers of adequately formed catechists.

The Philippine Church continues to operate hundreds of high schools and grade schools as well as over 300 colleges and universities. The Catholic Educational Association of the Philippines (CEAP), founded in 1941, continues to represent the interests of Catholic educational institutions and promote religious instruction. Similar activities are the focus of the Association of Catholic Universities of the Philippines (ACUP), established in 1973.

A unique and successful form of religious education and renewal has evolved in the Philippine Church with the holding of large national congresses, dedicated to particular themes. Delegates were expected to become trainer-facilitators upon their return home; audio and video tapes as well as printed materials of the congresses are made available. This approach proved particularly effective in the years connected with the Great Jubilee 2000. A partial list includes the following: Marian Year (1985), Eucharistic Year (1987), Bible Year (1989), Catechetical Year (1990), World Youth Day (1995), Eucharistic Congress (1997), two Holy Spirit Congresses (1998), Congress on God the Father (1999), Congress on the Trinity (2000), and the National Mission Congress (2000).

Catholic Bishops Conference of the Philippines (CBCP). The 50th anniversary celebrations of the CBCP in 1995 became an opportunity to review and assess the CBCP''re, structure, mission, and functions. The CBCP amended its constitution and bylaws; it established the new offices dedicated to media, legal matters, research, bioethics, women, and the cultural heritage of the Church. The CBCP now has 33 departments, commissions, and offices to address the many concerns of this local Church. In addition, the bishops relaunched the *CBCP Monitor* in a new format, initiated a weekly radio program, and established the CBCP Website [http://www.cbcp.net]. Responsive to the call for renewal in *Tertio Millennio Adveniente,* the CBCP issued a series of exhaustive and in-depth pastoral exhortations, designed to address vital aspects of Philippine life and Christianity: Philippine Politics (1997), Philippine Economy (1998), Philippine Culture (1999), and Philippine Spirituality (2000). The bishops concluded the series with their document on the Philippine Church's Mission in the New Millennium. The CBCP also sponsored the large National Mission Congress, which they saw as the ''fitting culminating activity'' of the Jubilee Year celebrations and the ''first step as a Local Church into the Third Millennium.''

Additional Ministries. Dialogue and peace-building with a variety of partners remain a continuous commitment of the Philippine Church. It strove to be an instrument of reconciliation during the Marcos years; along with the National Council of Churches in the Philippines, she made several overtures to various leftist and armed groups. In their 1990 pastoral letter, *Seek Peace, Pursue It,* the bishops laid out a ten-point path to peace. The Church also engages in interfaith dialogue with indigenous and Muslim peoples; the Silsilah movement and the pivotal Bishops-Ulama Forum have worked to foster Muslim-Christian harmony in Southern provinces. The annual Mindanao Week of Peace was begun in 1999.

Local Theologies. The Philippines has an impressive growing body of local theology emerging from local communities. Recurrent themes include evangelization, prayer, spirituality, peace-making and reconciliation, dialogue with peoples, cultures, and religious traditions. Several important theological, pastoral, catechetical, and mission journals are published. Prominent among Filipino theologians are C. Arévalo, T. Bacani, F. Claver, A. Co, D. Huang, A. Lagdameo, L. Legaspi, L. Mercado, J.-M. de Mesa, O. Quevedo, and L. Tagle.

Continuing Renewal and Commitment. A definite sign of a vibrant local Church is its mission outreach. In mid-2000 Catholic Filipino missionaries numbered 1,329 women and 206 men from 69 religious congregations serving in some 80 countries. The bishops established the Mission Society of the Philippines (1965). Maryknoll founded the Philippine Catholic Lay Mission (1977). Cardinal Sin established the San Lorenzo Mission Institute (1987), whose goal is serving the Chinese; its patron is San Lorenzo Ruiz, the first Filipino saint, canonized in 1987. Pedro Calungsod, beatified on March 5, 2000, inspired the successful National Mission Congress 2000.

A major Church milestone was achieved in the 1991 month-long Second Plenary Council of the Philippines (PCP-II). After three years of intense preparation, a total of 504 participants (including 165 lay faithful) gathered for a comprehensive review and renewal of Christian life. The Council challenged the local Church to be ''a Community of Disciples, a Church of the Poor, committed to the mission of renewed integral evangelization, toward building up of a new civilization of life and love in this land.'' A systematic implementation scheme was elaborated in the National Pastoral Plan, *In the State of Mission: Towards a Renewed Integral Evangelization,* approved by the bishops on July 11, 1993.

In January of 2001, delegates gathered for the National Pastoral Consultation on Church Renewal (NPCCR) and reflected on ''how far we as a Church have fulfilled the grand vision and mission proposed by PCP-II and the National Pastoral Plan.'' The evaluation was both sober and hopeful: ''The Church in the Philippines has, to our shame. . . remained unchanged in some respects. . .;we, as Church, have to confess some responsibility for many of the continuing ills of Philippine society. . . . We rejoice, however, in the perseverance and increase of many movements of renewal. . .; we hear anew God's call to renewal.'' NPCCR recommitted the Church to nine focused pastoral priorities for the first decade of the new millennium; they center on faith, formation, laity, the poor, the family, community-building, clergy renewal, youth, ecumenism-dialogue, and ad gentes mission.

Providentially, the NPCCR, as originally scheduled, took place during the week immediately following the People Power II events of Jan. 16–20, 2001 that removed Joseph Estrada from the Philippine presidency after only a little over two years of his six-year term; Gloria Macapagal-Arroyo became the fourteenth president and the second woman to hold the highest office in the land. There was muted euphoria; the Church had played a significant role; the event was described as "the gift of national and moral renewal which God empowered the Filipinos to receive." The tasks ahead were clear: democratic institutions needed strengthening; confidence in government awaited restoration; poverty demanded amelioration; the economy needed rebuilding. The Philippine Church's commitment to "renewed integral evangelization" took on new depths and urgency.

Bibliography: P.S. DE ACHUTEGUI, ed., *The "Miracle of the Philippine Revolution* (Manila 1986). C.G. ARÉVALO, "Filipino Theology," in K. MÜLLER, et al.,eds. *Dictionary of Mission* (Maryknoll 1997) 161-167, with extensive bibliography. T.C. BACANI, *Preparing Our Future: The Pope and the Filipino Youth* (Manila 1994). F.B. BAUTISTA, *Cardinal Sin and the Miracle of Asia* (Manila 1987). P. BERNIER and M.G. GABRIEL, eds., *Journeying with the Spirit: A Commentary on PCP-II* (Quezon City 1993). J.J. CARROLL, *Forgiving or Forgetting? Churches and the Transition to Democracy in the Philippines* (Manila 1999). Catholic Bishops Conference of the Philippines, *Acts and Decrees of the Second Plenary Council of the Philippines* (Manila 1992); *Catechism for Filipino Catholics* (Manila 1997); *In the State of Mission: Towards a Renewed Integral Evangelization* [National Pastoral Plan] (Manila 1993). F.X. CLARK, *Mission and the Philippines: Past, Present, Future,* 2d ed. (Pasay City 2000). F.F. CLAVER and P.C. QUITORIO, eds., *Anamnesis 1995* (Manila 1996). D. J. ELWOOD, *Toward a Theology of People Power* (Quezon City 1988). P. GIORDANO, *Awakening to Mission: The Philippine Catholic Church 1965–1981* (Quezon City 1988). H. M. GOMEZ,, *The Moro Rebellion and the Search for Peace: A Study on Christian-Muslim Relations in the Philippines* (Zamboanga City 2000). *Kasaysayan: The Story of the Filipino People I-X* (Hong Kong 1998). J.H. KROEGER, *The Philippine Church and Evangelization: 1965-1984* (Rome 1985), with extensive bibliography. J. H. KROEGER, ed., *Telling God's Story: National Mission Congress 2000* (Quezon City 2001). W. J. LAROUSSE, *A Local Church Living for Dialogue: Muslim-Christian Relations in Mindanao-Sulu (Philippines) 1965–2000* (Rome 2001), with extensive bibliography. P.C. QUITORIO, ed. *CBCP: On the Threshold of the Next Millennium* (Manila 1999); *Pastoral Letters: 1945–1995* (Manila 1996). J. N. SCHUMACHER, "Has the Philippine Church Been on the Side of the Poor?" *Life Forum* 16/3-4 (1984) 13-20; *Readings in Philippine Church History,* 2d ed. (Quezon City 1987). R. L. YOUNGBLOOD, *Marcos against the Church* (Ithaca, New York 1990).

[J. H. KROEGER]

PHILIPPISM

Named after Philipp MELANCHTHON, designated a Melanchthonian interpretation of Lutheranism, whose conciliatory tone was opposed by Gnesio (genuine) Lutherans (*see* GNESIOLUTHERANISM). The differences became open and often bitter controversies after Martin Luther's death (1546) and lasted more or less continuously until the end of the 17th century. The disputes were various and were named for content or for prominent spokesmen, e.g., the Adiaphoristic (indifferent), Majoristic (*see* MAJOR, GEORG), Synergistic (*see* SYNERGISM), Interimistic (*see* INTERIMS), Crypto-Calvinistic (*see* CRYPTO-CALVINISM), and Calixtine (*see* CALIXTUS, GEORG) controversies. Sometimes these have received separate treatment without proper emphasis on their common character of Philippism. The questions in dispute were not unimportant, e.g., the role of good works (Solafideism); the nature of Justification; efforts in the direction of ecumenism involving relations with Catholics (for a time some Philippists discarded even the Lutheran German hymns for Latin ritual) and with Calvinists (having mainly to do with the nature of the Real Presence in the Lord's Supper). Among Philippists, besides Georg Major, were Melanchthon's son-in-law Caspar Peucer (1525–1602), Justus Menius (1499–1558), Johann BUGENHAGEN and Nikolaus Crell (1550–1601).

Philippism had practically disappeared by the end of the 16th century—partly because of Melanchthon's inadequacies as a leader and his lack of realistic political sense; and also because certain Gnesiolutheran leaders, especially Matthias FLACIUS ILLYRICUS, were single-minded, as well as erudite and gifted with the power of poignant popular expression; and finally because of shifts in personnel of princely powers. Philippism received new strength in the era of Georg Calixtus. The Philippists helped preserve an irenic, ecumenical tradition in Protestantism.

Bibliography: O. RITSCHL, *Dogmengeschichte des Protestantismus,* 4 v. (Göttingen 1908–27) v. 2. H. W. GENSICHEN, *Damnamus: Die Verwerfung von Irrlehre bei Luther und im Luthertum des 16. Jahrhunderts* (Berlin 1955). V. VAJTA, ed., *Luther and Melanchthon in the History and Theology of the Reformation* (Philadelphia 1961).

[Q. BREEN]

PHILISTINES

The Philistines were a people from the area of the Aegean Sea who invaded the southern coast of Palestine and threatened the Israelites. This article, after discussing their origin and name, treats of their history, language, culture, and religion.

Origin and Name. In the latter half of the 2d millennium B.C., invading Indo-European tribes forced many people living on the islands and coast of the northeastern Mediterranean out of their original homeland. These displaced people attacked the HITTITES in Asia Minor and the cities of the North Syrian and Palestinian coast; they finally invaded Egypt in the reign of Ramses III, who defeated them in a land and naval battle fought on the coast (*c.* 1170 B.C.). When these so-called Peoples of the Sea were forced out of Egypt, one group, the Tsikal, settled in the coastal area of Palestine at the vicinity of Dor (South of Carmel). Another group that are called *prst* in

"Samson Captured by the Philistines," by Guercino. (©Geoffrey Clements/CORBIS)

the Egyptian records settled along the Palestinian coast south of Dor.

Their Egyptian designation, pronounced approximately *pulastu,* corresponds to the name *p^elištîm,* Philistines, by which they were known to the Israelites. The name Palestine is derived from it. In a short time the Philistines took over the area between Joppe and the Wadi Ghazzeh and formed a pentapolis, a group of "five cities," consisting of Gaza, Ashkelon, and Ashdod (later Azotus) on the coast and Gath and Ekron inland. The area was one of the richest tracts of land in Palestine. These independent cities were governed by *s^erānîm* (lords), who met in council and could overrule a decision made by an individual "lord" that did not advance the common good (1 Sm 29.1–7). Such ability for concerted action was an important factor in their successful expansion, particularly in the face of the disunited activity of the early Israelites.

History from the Beginnings to David. Early references in the Bible connect the Philistines with this region long before their arrival in the 12th century B.C. Abraham is spoken of as "residing a long time in the land of the Philistines" (Gn 21.34), and Abimelech is named as the king of the Philistines at the time of Abraham (Gn 21.32) and Isaac (Gn 26.1, 8, 18). These references are clearly anachronistic, although based perhaps on some Aegean colony in the Gerar area. The Philistines arrived shortly after the Israelite conquest of the hill country of Palestine and captured the sites of their pentapolis from the Canaanites. The Canaanite population remained as subjects. Apparently the Philistines were well-disciplined soldiers with a strong military tradition, who had a local monopoly on iron, which they used widely in their weapons. Inevitable conflict arose between Israel and the Philistines as the latter expanded into the nearby areas. The first tribe of Israel to feel the force of the Philistines was that of Dan. The elaborated story of the unsuccessful resistance of Samson, as they were pushed out of their holdings on the coastal plain to areas in the far North, is told in Judges ch. 13 to 16 and ch. 18. The Philistines were able to make definite advances also into the hill country of Judah. The Israelites suffered a major defeat *c.* 1050 B.C. near Aphek and Ebenezer, though they had brought the ark from Shiloh in the hope of stemming the advance of the Philistines by confronting them with the presence of Yahweh. Not only was the army of Israel defeated, but the ark was captured and held by the Philistines, who then spread out through the land (1 Sm 4.1–11). Even the town of Shiloh was captured and the tribal sanctuary destroyed. Although the Philistines did not gain control over all the land (parts of Galilee and the area east of the Jordan were still free), they constituted a grave problem to Israel. This menace was one of the chief reasons for the institution of the Israelite monarchy. The first king of Israel, Saul, had some initial success in stopping the advance of the Philistines (1 Sm 13.1–14.47), but later was decisively beaten and killed in the battle of Gilboa (1 Sm 31.1–10); the Philistines now recouped their recent losses and had Israel at their mercy.

After David, who had been a Philistine vassal in the latter days of Saul, was anointed king, the Philistines attacked his armies in the Valley of Rephaim (near Jerusalem); but David defeated them and drove them back to Gezer (2 Sm 5.17–25). Although the way in which it was effected is not entirely clear, the cities of the Philistine pentapolis were made vassals to King David (2 Sm 8.12), and with this subjugation the Philistine threat to Israel was ended. Subsequently, the Philistines and related peoples (the Cherethi and Pelethi) served as mercenaries in David's army (2 Sm 8.18). From this time on, the history of the Philistines is one of individual cities rather than of a unified people.

Philistia from Solomon to Roman Times. During the reign of Solomon, the Philistines continued as vassal states of Israel, but after his death and the consequent splitting of his kingdom, the Philistine cities, with the exception of Gath, which was controlled by Judah, existed independently and suffered from various encroachments on their territories. In about 815 B.C. the city of Gath was captured by Hazael, King of Damascus, when he invaded Judah (2 Kgs 12.18). Adad-Nirari III of Assyria (811–784 B.C.) forced tribute from the Philistines. Tiglath-Pileser III (745–728) captured both Gaza and Ashkelon in 734. Sargon II (721–705) attacked Gaza and installed his brother as governor of Ashdod. Sennacherib (705–682) also invaded the area and captured several cities, including Ashkelon.

With the fall of the Assyrian Empire, the Philistine cities were beleagured by Egypt. In his turn, NEBUCHADNEZZAR of Babylon (605–561) assaulted Ashkelon (604 B.C.) and deported its people and their rulers. During the Persian period the provincial organization centered on Ashdod. Gradually this area became almost completely Hellenized and its people allied themselves with the Syrians against the Jews in the Maccabean wars. Still later they became part of the Roman Empire. In the 2nd century of the Christian Era the southern part of the province of Syria was called ''Syria Palestina'' and thus the name Palestine became extended to the Holy Land generally.

Language, Culture, and Religion. There are no surviving documents written in the Philistine language, and practically nothing is known about it. Most likely the Philistines, soon after their arrival in Palestine, adopted the prevalent Canaanite dialect of the area. The word *s^e^rānîm* (Jos 13.3), used of the heads of the Philistine cities, is equated by many with Greek τύραννος, becoming English ''tyrant.'' This, however, is presumably the Greek borrowing from one of the indigenous languages of Asia Minor, and does little to advance our knowledge.

The absence of adequate archeological excavation of the cities of the Philistine pentapolis is another reason why our information on Philistine culture is limited. The most typical find from scattered sites is the well-known pottery called ''Philistine ware.'' This includes two-handled bowls and beer jugs with strainer spouts; it is generally buff in color and decorated with panels painted with black and reddish-purple designs, either geometric figures or sketches of swans preening themselves. It is almost identical with a type of Mycenaean pottery (stratum III C 1 b) discovered at Sinda and Enkomi in eastern Cyprus. From scenes at Medinet Habu in Egypt it is known that the Philistine soldiers wore plumed headdresses and kilt-like garments. They used a long, leaf-shaped sword that suggests a Danubian provenance.

Little more is known about Philistine religion. All their gods had Semitic names such as DAGON (Jgs 16.23), Ashtaroth (1 Sm 31.10), and Beelzebul (2 Kgs 1.1–16). The Philistines did not practice circumcision, which set them apart from the Israelites and the neighboring peoples who almost universally had this custom. Moreover, the Bible makes allusion to Philistine preoccupation with soothsaying (Is 2.6). At Gezer and Beth–Shan there are indications of burial customs in which the mouth of the corpse is closed with a gold mouth plate. This practice, perhaps reminiscent of the royal burials of Mycenae in the 16th century B.C., is known also from Phoenicia. At Beth-Shan and Tell Fara (in the south) coffins of pottery have been found that have lids with human features roughly modeled on them; this custom could be linked to the Egyptian sarcophagi. There is also evidence for the practice of cremation at Ashkelon, a custom accepted by the Philistines but entirely foreign to Israel. It seems most likely that the religion of the Philistines was a syncretistic one that assimilated notions and practices from the Canaanites, the Egyptians, and their original Aegean habitat.

Bibliography: R. A. S. MACALISTER, *The Philistines: Their History and Civilization* (London 1914), the most complete work in Eng. though now somewhat outdated. G. VON RAD, "Das Reich Israel und die Philister," *Palästinajahrbuch* (Berlin 1905–41) 29 (1936) 30–42. W. F. ALBRIGHT, *The Archaeology of Palestine* (rev. ed. Pelican Bks; Baltimore 1960) 112–117. J. GRAY, *Archeology and the Old Testament World* (New York 1962). G. A. WAINWRIGHT, "Some Early Philistine History," *Vetus Testamentum* (Leiden 1951–) 9 (1959) 73–84. O. EISSFIELDT, *Philister und Phonizier* (Leipzig 1936). K. M. KENYON, *Archeology in the Holy Land* (New York 1960), esp. ch. 9 which summarizes the archeological evidence gathered at Philistine sites.

[D. A. PANELLA]

PHILLIMORE, JOHN S.

Classical scholar; b. Boconnoc, Cornwall, Feb. 26, 1873; d. Sheffield, Hampshire, Nov. 16, 1926. At Westminster School and at Christ Church, Oxford, he won a succession of honors in classics. Christ Church appointed him a lecturer in 1895, and a tutor in 1898. The following year he succeeded Gilbert Murray in the chair of Greek at the University of Glasgow. Upon the retirement of G. G. Ramsay in 1906, he was transferred to the chair of humanity, a position that to him was most congenial. He produced critical editions of Propertius (1901; 2d ed. 1907) and Statius, *Silvae* (1905), and an excellent translation of Philostratus, *Apollonius of Tyana* (2 v. 1912). Throughout his life he published a large number of scholarly articles and learned notes in the *Classical Quarterly, Classical Review, Mnemosyne,* and similar journals. Phillimore was also a gifted poet, as is evidenced by his *Poems* (1902) and *Things New and Old* (1918), and a brilliant lecturer and writer on classical and literary themes in general who exercised a marked influence on Scottish intellectual life. Following his conversion to Catholicism in 1906, he became an occasional contributor to the *Dublin Review* and developed an interest in Christian Latin poetry. His last work was *The Hundred Best Latin Hymns* (London 1926).

Bibliography: S. N. MILLER, *The Dictionary of National Biography from the Earliest Times to 1900,* 63 v. (London 1885–1900; repr. with corrections, 21 v., 1908–09, 1921–22, 1938; suppl. 1901—) (1922–30) 675–677.

[M. R. P. MCGUIRE]

PHILLIP, ROBERT

Priest and court chaplain; b. in Scotland, probably in the 1580s; d. Paris, Jan. 4, 1647. Robert was a descendant of the family of Phillip of Sanquhar, but his early life remains almost wholly unknown. The first definite dates for him are those of his ordination as a seminary priest at the Scots College in Rome in 1612 and of his arrest in Edinburgh as a traitor on Sept. 14, 1613. The sentence of death was, however, commuted to exile, and he withdrew to France, where he joined the newly founded Oratory of Cardinal Bérulle. In 1628 he went to England as confessor to Queen Henrietta Maria, and as such he became identified with the interests of the court. His negotiations with Rome for papal financial aid at the time of the Long Parliament and a letter of his to the exiled Walter Montagu led to his denunciation by the parliamentary leaders as a spy and a pernicious influence on the Prince of Wales. Concern for Richelieu, whose name had been introduced into the proceedings, and eventually a direct intervention by Henrietta Maria terminated the inquiries, and Phillip was remanded to Somerset House. When the queen left England for the Hague in March of 1642, he accompanied her and resumed his role as her chaplain in Paris after 1644 until his death.

Bibliography: J. GILLOW, *A Literary and Biographical History or Bibliographical Dictionary of the English Catholics from 1534 to the Present Time,* 5 v. (London–New York 1885–1902; repr. New York 1961) 5:304–305. M. J. HAVRAN, *The Catholics in Caroline England* (Stanford 1962). G. ALBION, *Charles I and the Court of Rome* (London 1935).

[R. I. BRADLEY]

PHILLIPS, GEORGE

Legal historian, canonist; b. Königsberg, East Prussia, Jan. 6, 1804; d. Aigen, near Salzburg, Austria, Sept. 6, 1872. Phillips, whose father was English and whose mother was Scottish, studied law in Berlin and Munich, where he was greatly influenced by Friedrich von Savigny and Johann Eichhorn. Phillips taught history and law at the Universities of Berlin (1827–28), Munich (1834–47), Innsbruck (1850), and Vienna (1851–72). His friend Karl Jarcke influenced his conversion to Catholicism (1828). Together with Guido Görres he founded the *Historischpolitischen Blätter* (1838). He played a leading role in the revival of German Catholic life and scholarship, but his thought and politics became progressively more conservative. As a champion of ULTRAMONTANISM, he contributed greatly to popularizing in Germanic countries the doctrines of papal primacy and infallibility and to the utramontane victory at VATICAN COUNCIL I. Joseph de MAISTRE's views had much influence on Phillips, who

Philo Judaeus.

has been called a German de Maistre. Phillips's numerous writings, composed in clear, elegant German and replete with erudition, were widely read and at one time very influential. He ranks as one of the leading German canonists of the 19th century.

Bibliography: Works. *Versuch einer Darstellung des Angelsächsischen Rechts* (Göttingen 1825); *Deutsche Geschichte mit besonderer Rücksicht auf Religion, Recht und Verfassung,* 2 v. (Berlin 1832–34); *Deutsche Reichs und Rechtsgeschichte* (Munich 1845); *Die Diözesansynode* (Freiburg 1849); *Kirchenrecht,* 7 v. (Regensburg 1845–72); *Vermischte Schriften,* 3 v. (Vienna 1856–60). Literature. J. F. VON SCHULTE, *Allgemeine deutsche Biographie* 26:80–88. J. F. VON SCHULTE, *Die Geschichte der Quellen und der Literatur des kanonischen Rechts,* 3 v. in 4 pts. (Stuttgart 1875–80; repr. Graz 1956) 3.1:875–886. G. VON PÖLNITZ, ''George Phillips, ein Grossdeutscher Konservativer in der Paulskirche,'' *Historische Zeitschrift* 155.1 (1937) 51–97. J. FUCHS, *Magisterium, Ministerium, Regimen* (Bonn 1941). B. POEHLMANN, *Lexikon für Theologie und Kirche,* ed. J. HOFER and K. RAHNER, 10 v. (2d, new ed. Freiburg 1957–65) 8:468.

[S. J. TONSOR]

PHILO JUDAEUS

The greatest Jewish philosopher and theologian of the Greco-Roman period; b. Alexandria, Egypt, *c.* 13 B.C.; d. there, between A.D. 45 and 50. To distinguish him from other Philos of antiquity, he is known as Philo Judaeus (the Jew) or Philo of Alexandria. His family was wealthy and influential. Although attracted to a life of speculation and contemplation, he was forced into an active, political life for the sake of defending his coreligionists who were victims of anti-Semitic movements or discriminatory legislation. He fought to have their rights recognized and to strengthen them in the faith of their fathers. About A.D. 40 he was senior member of a delegation sent to Rome to have Emperor Caligula grant the Jews the right to live according to their own laws and to be dispensed from the obligation of taking part in the rites of emperor worship. These are about the only facts known concerning his life.

His Works and Their Nature. The principal writings of Philo, some of which are preserved only in part or in ancient translations, can be divided into four groups: (1) historical and apologetic: *In Flaccum, De legatione ad Gaium, De vita contemplativa* (hereafter *Contempl.*), *Apologia pro Iudaeis, De vita Mosis*; (2) philosophical: *De aeternitate mundi, Quod omnis probus liber sit* (hereafter *Prob.*), *De providentia, De Alexandro*; (3) expository on the Pentateuch: *De opificio mundi* (hereafter *Opif.*), *De Abrahamo* (hereafter *Abr.*), *De Josepho* (hereafter *Jos.*), *De decalogo, De specialibus legibus* (hereafter *Spec.*), *De virtutibus* (hereafter *Virt.*), *De praemiis et poenis*; (4) *Legum allegoriae* (hereafter *Leg.*), an allegorical commentary on Genesis—his most important work. Some of his other works are referred to in the course of this article.

As a commentator on the Scriptures, Philo limited himself almost entirely to the Books of Moses (according to the Septuagint translation); he seldom even cited the other books of the OT. For him the Prophets were but the ''disciples of Moses.''

Allegorical interpretation is characteristic of Philo's method. This manner of exposition seems to have been customary in the schools of that period, both among the Greeks, who used it to draw a moral lesson from the poets or to give meaning to the religious myths (the ''physical'' allegory of the Stoics), and among the rabbis. By means of his commentaries Philo seems to have wished to reduce the symbolic ''philosophy'' of Moses to formulas drawn from that syncretism of which Posidonius was the outstanding representative and which contained Platonic, Neo-Pythagorean, and Stoic themes. The extent and variety of Philo's vocabulary have led scholars to discover in him the most diverse influences: Greek (of various schools of philosophy), Jewish (of both Palestinian and Alexandrian Judaism), Egyptian, and Oriental (mystery religions). He can be regarded as a witness of the development of classical thought toward the different forms of later NEOPLATONISM, which are actually in germ in his works. He can also be considered another kind of witness—one showing the fermentation of Jewish thought at the very time when Christianity came into being. He, in turn, certainly had great influence on the early Fathers of the Church. Since lack of space here prevents even a summary exposition of the many studies that have been made on these different points of view, the rest of this article is limited to an endeavor to show in what the originality of Philonic thought consists.

His Education and Teaching on Education. Philo is a good representative of the intellectual training that a man of the cultured class received in Alexandria at the dawn of the Christian Era. In this cosmopolitan city, education was fostered and flourishing. Philo makes allusion to it when he speaks of the ἐγκύκλιος παιδεία. This "general education," or preliminary instruction, has a special meaning in his system, although several passages seem to refer to the historical reality of this institution. Philo calls it also μέση παιδεία (intermediate education) to indicate that it is a middle stage between unculture and perfect knowledge [*De congressu quaerendae eruditionis gratia* (hereafter *Congr.*) 22]. He lists the program of studies [*De agricultura* (hereafter *Agric.*) 18; *Congr.* 11, 15, 74; *De somniis* (hereafter *Somn.*) 1.205] as consisting, in an ascending order, of grammar, the study of the poets and historians, arithmetic and geometry, music, rhetoric, and dialectics. These serve as preparation for philosophy, which in turn has two phases: the lower one gives to the different individual sciences their principles and basic definitions (*Congr.* 146) and furnishes the moral principles for governing the passions in self-control, the ἐγκράτεια of the Stoics (*Congr.* 80); the upper one is concerned with the knowledge of God and leads to Wisdom [*De fuga et inventione* (hereafter *Fug.*) 141; *Congr.* 79]. The "profane" studies that Philo made extended from the course in grammar to instruction in the lower phase of philosophy. This school philosophy was nothing else than the syncretism then in fashion.

A good student, Philo retained much of his early education, and in his system he allotted to the common truths thus acquired the "intermediate" place that belonged to them. All this, however, was merely his intellectual equipment; it was not his own thought. To investigate the sources that he used is an interesting enough enterprise, but it is of little utility for understanding Philo himself. What belonged to him as his own lies in the upper phase of philosophy, his religious doctrine that directed the organization of all his knowledge and reflection. No doubt, on this level also he was subject to certain influences, some of them more purely Platonic, others of Jewish origin. His tendencies were not foreign to those that are dominant in sapiential literature (the idea of Wisdom). His purpose was the same as that expressed by Ben Sirach's grandson in his Prologue (Sir Prol.) to his Greek translation of the Book of Sirach: to instruct the Jews of the DIASPORA, who were in danger of losing the faith of their fathers and to render them fit to help "those outside" (καὶ τοῖς ἐκτος: Sir Prol. 4), i.e., the Gentiles.

Philo's display of profane learning does indeed too often mask the fidelity of his thought to the heritage of his faith; his skill in the use of allegory runs the risk of making one suspect that he is juggling the content of the Mosaic revelation; his rather simplistic moralism gives the impression of a banal spirituality and hides the originality of his mystical ideal. Learned investigations of his sources have made no small contribution in setting in bold relief the personal traits of his thought. The works of E. R. Goodenough and H. A. Wolfson, each in its own way, by showing the Alexandrian-Jewish and Palestinian-Jewish side of Philo, have brought light to bear on this question. In recent years detailed studies of Philonic ideas and images have been made directly in the texts themselves, so that now one recognizes more clearly that Philo was a genuine thinker who had a doctrine quite his own.

Active and Contemplative Life and Their Union. At the beginning of the third book of the Special Laws, Philo conjures up the time of his youth when he devoted himself to speculative philosophy: "I imagined myself raised in the air on high and ever carried away by divine inspiration. . . . Then I leaned over from the heights of the heavens and, as if looking down from a summit, I fixed the eyes of my soul and viewed the innumerable theories regarding the beings that are on earth. I was glad at heart to have fled, as far as possible, from the miseries of mortal life." But "discontent, the enemy of good," forces him to mix in political life. Although he suffers from it, he thanks God that he was not submerged in it and that he kept enough vision to understand the Holy Commentaries of Moses and make them known to the multitude who were ignorant of them.

Philo was drawn by nature to contemplation. In the *De vita contemplativa* he speaks with sympathy of the THERAPEUTAE, their way of life, and their manner of meditating on the Law as understood allegorically. Besides, the ideal of the ESSENES seems to have been his; of the three parts of philosophy, they neglected both logic, as being useless for the acquisition of virtue, and physics, as surpassing the possibilities of human nature (except when it treats of the existence of God and of creation); but they applied themselves to ethics in a study of the laws of their forefathers, inspired laws that human nature of itself could not attain to (*Prob.* 80). It is a matter, therefore, of revealed, religious morals. This is precisely the order of values that Philo respected: to meditate on God and His powers (creative, royal, and legislative) and to return to God both by a literal observance of the Law and by an effort to conform interiorly to the real values that are revealed there by means of symbols. Therefore, it is necessary to flee the corporeal for the incorporeal realities, the sensible for the intelligible world.

Philo, however, saw the insufficiency of this naïvely Platonic schema. Plato wanted the wise man to go down again into the cave; Philo wished to keep him there only for a certain time. He merely delayed his departure for the heights. As a young man, he could think that, in order to realize his ideal, he would have to retire to the desert, far from human affairs. Yet he did not neglect the course of studies established in his city; he saw in this a means by which he could attain to philosophy. ''As for me, when I began to be urged on by Philosophy's goads to desire knowledge, I frequented, while still young, one of her handmaids, Grammar, and all that I engendered from her . . . I offered to her mistress . . .'' (*Congr.* 74). He then passed in review all the branches of study. But the profit he drew from them he did not devote to the search for worldly interests; he turned it toward philosophical activity. This preparation was indispensable, since it is dangerous for a soul to cast itself too quickly into research of the purely intelligible.

Commenting on Gn 27.42–45, Philo imagines Rebecca speaking thus to Jacob: ''When you see a wicked man breaking out in invectives against virtue and making much fuss over things that should be held of no account, such as good fortune, glory, or pleasure, or when you hear him praising injustice as the means for winning such things . . . , do not turn forthwith in the opposite direction, toward renouncing wealth and pride and striving to lead a life of austerity in the desert, for thus you will only provoke your enemy and arm him as a still more dangerous foe against you'' (*Fug.* 25). It is necessary to know the world in order to fight against it and make it better: ''Truth would rightly censure those who, without looking into it, would abandon the business of political life'' (*Fug.* 33). ''Become acquainted with your body, know yourself and the parts of which you are composed, understand what each one is, the purpose for which it was created, how it acts according to its nature, and who He is who puts its wonderful mechanism in motion and who, Himself invisible, invisibly cares for His children—is this the spirit that it is in you or the Spirit of the universe? When you have examined yourself, study closely that which stands out as proper to Laban and his successful deeds, which vain opinion thinks are brilliant. . . . When, having become involved in a troubled, political life, you show that you have a strong character, sustained by a good education, I will take you back from down there'' (*Fug.* 46). There is, then, a relationship between practical life and education (*Leg.* 2.89).

The same idea is developed in his treatise *De ebrietate* (33–80). Philo well saw that education receives its definitive form from the political regime, from the social and moral state of the city that gives it. Thus it may be used for merely human ends; of itself it does not attain to perfection. But if God comes to its aid, it becomes an indispensable basis and means. Besides, he who rises directly to the vision of truth in itself can no longer speak to men in their language (cf. Moses and Aaron).

Thus, the originality of Philo consists in having discovered a middle term in education, wisdom, virtue, the soul, and life [*De plantatione* (hereafter *Plant.*) 94; *Leg.* 1:93; *Opif.* 154; *De mutatione nominum* (hereafter *Mut.*) 30; *Quod deterius potiori insidiari solet* (hereafter *Deter.*) 68]. Indeed, he found in Plato, in Aristotle, and in the development of the moral teaching of the Painted Porch school toward a new Stoicism examples of an opening on the material reality of human life that would soften the rigors of a pure spirituality or an absolute rationalism. For the philosophers, however, it was merely a matter of making concessions to ordinary human conditions; for Philo, since the creative act reaches all creatures in their most material and insignificant reality, it is from this lowest level of their being that they must return to God. In a sense, everything in them is good, for God devoted the same art and the same care in forming all of them [*Quis rerum divinarum heres* (hereafter *Her.*) 159].

Good and Evil. This being the case, all that is required for a being to be GOOD is that it return and be united with God. Philo writes: ''The perfect take their point of departure in the body, in sensation, in the different parts of their organism without which it is not possible to live (for these parts are useful to education applied to the life that accompanies the body), and they come to their end at the side of the wisdom of God. . . . Beginning with what is mortal, improvements are produced in the direction of what is incorruptible'' (*Her.* 315–316). ''It is good to bring to an end the combats of practical life before struggling for the contemplative life; this serves as a prelude to a more perfect combat'' (*Fug.* 36). The whole moral and religious system of Philo is swept by a fresh breeze of hope, improvement, and progress, which end in joy and goodness. But this presupposes effort and asceticism, for evil must be conquered. EVIL is out of place in creation inasmuch as it contrasts with the creative power that is all good. By this power God satisfies ontologically and physically the needs of all creatures; to none of them does He refuse anything that they can receive, since He loves to give. Evil is not in matter, the existing thing that, bereft of quality, form, and activity,

God has completed by giving it what it lacked. Nor is evil in sensation or even in the pleasure taken in it. Evil is pure disorder, a turning upside down of order. It comes from the fact that creatures, which should be subordinate to God, are taken for primary causes and last ends. Man's free will is responsible for this. In this sense the possibility of evil is enveloped in creation and in God who knew it beforehand. Having made in His LOGOS the intelligible plan of the universe, He wished to give to all the forms that the material world could receive at its various levels a definite place, so as not to leave any void in the projected ensemble. Minerals, which are ruled by their ἕξις (state of being), involuntarily follow their own laws; the same for vegetables, with their φύσις (natural instinct), and for irrational animals, with their ψυχή (animal life). All these are still in the domain of the involuntary. At the other extreme, pure intelligences are constantly attached to truth and intelligible goods. But man is an intermediate being, made of a mixture, and he must be so in order that there may not be a discontinuity in the universe [*De confusione linguarum* (hereafter *Confus.*) 176–179]. The reason for the disorder in man lies in his φιλαυτία (self-love), which is present both on the level of sensation, attaching itself then to sense pleasure, and on the level of intelligence when, unmindful of God, it thinks itself superior to everything else (*Spec.* 1.333–338). Another form of this evil is οἴησις (self-conceit, presumption). Besides these vices, which come from the ἐπιθυμίαι (sensual desires) that nothing can satiate, there is a false wisdom by which a man regards everything from his own viewpoint, the wisdom of the δοκησίσοφος (self-conceited sage), portrayed by Cain and Jethro. True wisdom is the fruit of the upper phase of philosophy, all turned entirely toward God. Evil results, therefore, from a voluntary choice of a center of life that is something other than God.

Thus, even though Philo makes no place for any sin of the angels (who are divine λόγοι, forming an army that cannot disobey), Adam's trespass brought into the world a permanent principle of subversion and corruption that has effects just as serious as those of original sin in Christianity. It entrains the dissolution of being. The Logos, transcendent intelligible unity of the world, enjoys, on the plane of immanence, the role of τόνος (cohesive force); it is a bond, a "glue" (*Her.* 188; *Fug.* 110–111; *Plant.* 8–10). It binds beings to their Creator even while making them distinct from Him. It is also called God's "angel" or archangel [*Her.* 205; *Somn.* 1.239; *Quod Deus immutabilis est* (hereafter *Deus*) 162; *Leg.* 3.177; *De Cherubim* (hereafter *Cher.*) 35]. Wrongdoing, however, withdraws man from this unifying action, for it detaches him from the creative plan and from God. Thus, he cannot save himself; he needs a savior. By himself he cannot attain to the light; he needs inspiration and revelation. In the order of creation man was penetrated with this light, which poured forth in him all the graces of the God of goodness. It is so no longer; θεός (God, name of the Creator) has become for him ὁ Κύριος (the Lord), who, while not abandoning him, rules him henceforth by another of His powers, the royal power that is legislative and punitive. This restores and saves what is good.

Ontology of Salvation. Being is not divided up between the creative power and the royal power; these two are united in the divine Logos, the firstborn, the elder brother of the world (*Cher.* 27). These powers manifest their duality and distinctness only in regard to man (*Fug.* 94–104). They are arranged in hierarchical order on the way of salvation. Man meets first the power of punishment, then that of mercy, and finally that of creative goodness. He finds them first in himself, within his conscience, and then in themselves. Having arrived at perfection, man is in relation to both the creative power and the royal power, since he is united to the Logos that embraces both (*Mut.* 19). To create the mixed nature of man in his intermediate condition, God made use of assistants: "Let us make man," it is written—in the plural; for the Father cannot be the cause of the evil that He knows must be born of His creature. He made man in His image, which is His Logos. Man, therefore, because of his complex nature, cannot escape from the royal power that sets him aright. But the perfect one, united to the Logos and unified by it against the disintegrating force of evil, recovers a state of innocence, as if he came forth, like the firstborn Logos, from God alone. This state of perfection is a result, not of nature, but of a grace of adoption that bestows on man, as on the Logos, the whole heritage of God. So it is explained in the *De mutatione nominum.* Thus, whereas Jacob, who had attained to virtue through effort and exercise, received the name of Israel but continued to be called Jacob also, since effort, even when sustained by God, does not guarantee an unchangeable result, Abraham, who by a pure gift of grace begot perfect virtue, joy (Isaac, who did not change his name, which means "he laughs"), was no longer called Abram. Therefore, the punitive power corrects the wicked; the creative power sustains man in progress. But the two powers in union, that is, the Logos, bring definitive salvation to the man who thus receives the lot of perfection.

Man's Need of God's Grace. It would be too much to say that in Philo there is a doctrine of the supernatural life in the Christian sense. Yet it is certain that beyond the mixed nature of man there is a transcendent nature, pure light, the light of the Logos in which the "friend of God" can participate by a gift of grace. The immanentism of the Stoics has no real value. The virtues defined by the Porch were taken up by Philo, but with this correction, that man by his own efforts cannot practice them consistently. The Stoic ideal (*see* STOICISM) can be realized only as a result of an absolute divine initiative. Inasmuch as man is mere man, he remains a mixed being, and his virtues are never perfectly pure. He must become a "man of God." True virtue is not a moral qualification of the soul; it is a sharing in the divine virtue and in the power that God has to create what is good. Man, in his intermediate condition, cannot truly do good; he is fortunate if he does not do evil. Intermediate education has value only if it is assumed by God, through His call and the ἀφορμή (start) that He gives to the soul.

Man's Cooperation. God, however, does not do it all; He demands an effort, and He urges one on through the Law. Philo used the image of athletic combat to express the fight against the body and its passions. This dualism of the intelligible and the sensible has meaning only in the intermediate phase of progress. Here the victory remains precarious, and it does not give access to a higher order of reality. The fight may even wear one out, and one should not become stubborn about it (*De migratione Abrahami* 26). Should one flee from it? A flight from the passions, when it is a human undertaking, suits those souls that love virtue without perfection (*Leg.* 2.90–91). There is another flight, one that is in answer to a divine call. In this case, the Logos "congeals" the passions, like the waters of the Red Sea, and he who looks to God can pass through them (*Leg.* 3.172). Having reached his goal, man, like the Logos that he shares in, does not retreat from the troubled world, but wages an all-out war against evil (*Leg.* 2.91). From God and His Logos comes the victory that consists not in resisting by such-and-such particular virtue such-and-such particular assault of evil, but in reestablishing the universal order thanks to the most generic virtue that begets, rules, and unifies all the others (*Leg.* 1.59).

Man's Need of Divine Revelation. What is true of virtue is true also of truth. Both are ontological realities in God before being human moral or intellectual values. Truth is the splendor of virtue (*Contempl.* 26; *Spec.* 1.209; *Virt.* 102; *Fug.* 139; *Somn.* 1.216–218; *Deus* 96; *Jos.* 68). Just as man, in the acquisition of virtue, cannot surpass the limits of his own efforts without divine aid, so also he cannot advance beyond the intermediate education without a revelation from God. True wisdom is connected with prophecy. Human language cannot express sublime realities unless God lets man hear an echo of them here below. The verb ὑπηχεῖν (to echo) is often used by Philo. It is to be compared with the noun ὑπόνοια (conjecture, hidden meaning) used in regard to symbolism and allegory. The allegorical method is connected with this concept of prophecy and with the idea of a sudden and gratuitous intervention of God. The prophet, who is a "seer," must have an interpreter who speaks for him (as Aaron spoke for Moses). The commentator on God's word goes in the opposite direction: starting with the words, he goes on to unveil the light.

Relation between the Sensible and the Intelligible. Having made use of the Stoic formulas to speak of the immanence of this world, Philo employs a Platonic vocabulary to express his religious thought. But it is still merely a matter of language. If Philo sets the intelligible in opposition to the sensible, he does not construe the former by means of a dialectic; God has created it in His Logos with all the relations that it implies. Plato made the sage descend again into the cave, to organize the demotic virtues there in the image of the dialectic virtue; in Philo's view, the perfect man, united to the Logos and armed with its power, contributes to the accomplishment of its work on earth, and he is then "pleasing in the eyes of God" (*Mut.* 39–40). He does good to men as God does good to His creatures. The relationship between the sensible and the intelligible becomes a personal relationship between man and God in the work of salvation. Even the break between human effort and divine grace has a Platonic aspect. In Plato's *Symposium* (210E), at the last stage of a man's ascent toward the beautiful in due order and succession (ἐφεξῆς), he has a sudden (ἐξαίφνης) revelation of Beauty in itself; Philo writes: "When God bestows on us the gift of the precepts of eternal wisdom, suddenly, without expecting it (ἐξαίφνης οὐ προσδοκήσαντες), we find the treasure of perfect happiness." He means the true gift of grace of a personal Being.

Conclusion. Despite these resemblances, Philo's profound thought remains just as foreign to the Platonic as to the Stoic system. Philo's God is the living God of the Bible. His God cannot be brought into comparison with the παντελῶς ὄν (absolute being) of Plato's *Sophist* (248E–249A) that lives and has life but is only a notion (τὸ ὄν, being—in the neuter). Philo's God is He who is (ὁ ὤν, the Being—in the masculine: *Somn.* 1.231; *Mos.* 1.75; *Opif.* 173; etc.). He is the cause of all life and the source of eternal life (*Fug.* 198). He is "faithful" because He is unchangeable, and all confidence must be placed in Him. Faith in God gives consolation and encouragement in life (*Abr.* 268). Here is a theology of faith, hope, and love that shows the man essentially engaged in the word of God (cf. *Cher.* 85; *Spec.* 1.310; *Fug.* 58). Between God and man there is a perpetual exchange of gifts from the One and acts of thanksgiving from the other, of which the Jewish cult is the symbol.

Philo thus does right by all the philosophical tendencies of his time: he puts each one in its place, using it where it can express a partial truth. But his religious thought is well above all this, and that is what he wished to show in thus justifying his basic faith in the preeminence of Moses, who infinitely surpasses all the other philosophers.

Bibliography: Editions. *Philonis Alexandrini Opera quae supersunt*, ed. L. COHN et al., 7 v. in 8 (Berlin 1962), with complete *index verborum; Philo*, tr. F. H. COLSON and G. H. WHITAKER, 10 v. (Loeb Classical Library; London-New York-Cambridge, Mass. 1929–62); *Philo: Supplement*, tr. R. MARCUS, 2 v. (Loeb Classical Library; London-New York-Cambridge, Mass. 1953), fragments preserved only in Armenian; *Oeuvres de Philon d'Alexandrie*, tr. R. ARNALDEZ et al. (Paris 1961–). Bibliographical studies. J. HAUSSLEITER, ''Nacharistotelische Philosophen 1931–1936,'' *Jahresbericht über die Fortschritte der klassischen Altertumswissenschaft* 281–282 (1943) 107–116. R. MARCUS, ''Recent Literature on Philo (1924–1934),'' *Jewish Studies in Memory of George A. Kohut*, ed. S. W. BARON and A. MARX (New York 1935). E. R. GOODENOUGH and H. I. GOODHART, *The Politics of Philo Judaeus, Practice and Theory* (New Haven 1938). L. H. FELDMAN, ''Scholarship on Philo and Josephus (1937–1959),'' *The Classical World* 54 (1960–61) 281–291; 55 (1961–62) 36–49, reprinted with some unauthorized changes by Yeshiva University, *Scholarship on Philo and Josephus, 1937–1962* (New York 1963). Literature. É. BRÉHIER, *Les Idées philosophiques et religieuses de Philon d'Alexandrie* (2d ed. Paris 1925; reprint 1950). E. R. GOODENOUGH, *By Light, Light: The Mystic Gospel of Hellenistic Judaism* (New Haven 1935); *An Introduction to Philo Judaeus* (2d ed. rev. New York 1963). H. A. WOLFSON, *Philo: Foundations of Religious Philosophy in Judaism, Christianity, and Islam*, 2 v. (Cambridge, Mass. 1947). J. DANIÉLOU, *Philon d'Alexandrie* (Paris 1958). C. MONDÉSERT and R. ARNALDEZ, ''Philon d'Alexandrie,'' *Dictionnaire de la Bible,*, suppl. v.7, ed. L. PIROT et al. (Paris 1928–).

[R. ARNALDEZ]

PHILO OF BYBLOS

Phoenician scholar who flourished *c.* A.D. 100. Philo of Byblos is the author of several works in Greek, of which fragments have been preserved in the citations of later Greek writers. Of these works, the most important is Τα, Φοίνικα, a history of Phoenicia, of which sections are transcribed in books 1 and 4 of EUSEBIUS OF CAESAREA's *Praeparatio evangelica.* These sections of the work recount the theogonic and cosmogonic myths of ancient Phoenicia, and picture the contemporary world state as derived from a dark and infinite chaos that gave birth to successive generations of divine beings. The first several of these generations include hypostatized natural forces, such as Desire, Death, Light, Fire, and Flame; these, however, are succeeded by the gods proper, successive generations of whom engage in a conflict whose outcome determines their permanent hierarchical relationship. Philo represented this history as the translation of a work written by Sanchuniaton, a native Phoenician of a remote age who gathered in written form the traditions of his country.

Despite evident editorial additions by Philo himself—notably his euhemeristic explanations of myths and his comparisons with Hellenistic religious concepts—the antiquity claimed by Philo for his material has been largely justified by comparison with ancient Near Eastern texts discovered in the 20th century. Thus, the names of several of the gods of Philo's pantheon, hitherto unattested elsewhere, are found in the Ugaritic texts of the 14th century B.C. (*see* UGARIT), and details of his myths recur in Hittite texts of the second millennium B.C. (*see* HITTITES). Therefore, while one must allow for the influence of Greek thought in Philo's history, the work in its essentials must be judged to be representative of ancient Phoenician religious thought. Those parts of it that have been preserved, therefore, offer a source of great importance for a knowledge of the Canaanite religious conceptions that surrounded Israel in the early period of its history. Fragments of two further works of Philo, *On Cities* and *On Forming a Library*, have been preserved by Stephen of Byzantium (5th century) and Serenus. Nothing remains of a composition *On the Reign of Hadrian* mentioned by Suidas (late 10th century).

Bibliography: L. B. PATON, *Encyclopedia of Religion and Ethics*, ed. J. HASTINGS (Edinburgh 1908–27) 9: 843–844. H. EISING, *Lexikon für Theologie und Kirche*, ed. J. HOFER and K. RAHNER (Freiberg 1957–65) 8:471. C. MÜLLER, ed., *Fragmenta historicorum graecorum*, 5 v. (Paris 1878–85) 3:560–576. W. F. ALBRIGHT, *Archeology and the Religion of Israel* (Baltimore 1946; 4th ed. 1956) 69–71. O. EISSFELDT, *Sanchunjaton von Berut und Ilumilku von Ugarit* (Halle 1952); *Taautos und Sanchunjaton* (Berlin 1952).

[R. I. CAPLICE]

PHILOLOGY

A term derived from the Greek φίλος ''lover'' and λόγος ''speech, word.'' In time this meaning of ''lover of the word, fond of literature or study'' came to be applied especially to lovers of the languages of Greece and Rome and then to include their whole culture.

In the early Alexandrian age, the philologists safeguarded the textual purity of the ancient Greek epic and dramatic writers and set up canons of criticism. Suetonius tells us that Crates brought philology from Greece to Rome in 169 B.C. Here philological study for a time concerned itself with older Latin writers, such as Plautus and Terence, whose texts were particularly liable to corruption at the hands of theatrical producers. This interest spread to other writers, such as Virgil; commentaries on him by Servius and Donatus are still extant. Christian writers, such as St. Jerome, were well acquainted with the general principles of textual criticism. Cassiodorus established a monastery where the principal work was the copying of religious and secular manuscripts. Even pagan authors were copied, and writers such as Isidore of Seville attempted a reconciliation of pagan and Christian thought. Irish monks preserved classical texts during the barbarian invasions and re-Christianized Europe afterward largely through their monastic centers of prayer, learning, and classical culture.

With the rise of scholastic philosophy in the 11th century, the texts of Aristotle attracted philologists. For well over a century before the fall of Constantinople, Greek scholars had been teaching in Italy. With the invention of printing and the spread of learning a great need arose for accurate texts of the classics. During the Reformation, both Catholic and Protestant scholars used the same Biblical and patristic texts to vindicate their stands. Later the Maurist Benedictines and the Jesuit Bollandists widened the scope of philology by using such auxiliary sciences as chronology, diplomatics, and palaeography. (*See* MABILLON, JEAN; BOLLANDISTS.)

Richard BENTLEY showed how literature and classical antiquity opened up new vistas in scholarship. After him Friedrich Wolf (1759–1824) attempted a new science of philology, naming it *Altertumswissenschaft.* He pleaded for an encyclopedic view of all antiquity, defining the 24 divisions of the field: metrics, grammar, history, geography, mythology, public and private law, religion, etc. This concept influenced the chief manuals of A. Boeckh (1785–1867), I. von Müller (1830–1917) for classical philology, L. Geiger (1856–1943) and E. Kuhn (1846–1920) for Indo-Iranian, J. Bühler (1837–98) for Sanskrit, H. Paul (1846–1921) for Germanic, and G. Gröber (1844–1911) for Romance. It underlies L. Traube's (1861–1907) concept of medieval Latin philology.

Bibliography: J. E. SANDYS, *History of Classical Scholarship* (New York 1958). C. H. HASKINS, *The Renaissance of the Twelfth Century* (Cambridge, Mass. 1927). U. VON WILAMOWITZ-MOELLENDORFF, *Geschichte der Philologie* (3d ed. Leipzig 1959).

[R. T. MEYER]

PHILOMENA, ST., THE LEGEND OF

In 1802 archeologists unearthed a tomb in the Catacomb of St. Priscilla. The remains appeared to belong to a young woman of the second or third century. Nearby were tiles painted in red: LUMENA PAXTE CUM FI, with images of a whip, arrows, anchors, a lily, and palm. They reconstructed this as PAX TECUM FIILUMENA, "Peace [be] with you, Filumena." The tiles were thought to have sealed the original tomb. The images were taken to be instruments of a martyr's suffering and emblems of her purity and heavenly victory.

Nothing was known of any historical Philomena. Eminent archeologists insisted that the tiles came from a nearby tomb. Despite these efforts to dampen the enthusiasm of those who declared these the bones of a martyr, within two decades there was a flourishing cult of Philomena, a detailed biography, and reports of many miracles. In 1961 the Congregation of Rites struck her feast from the Roman Calendar for lack of historical evidence of her existence, along with that of St. Christopher. The rise of Philomena's cult and her continuing veneration into the twenty-first century need to be read against the background of the duel between traditional religiosity and modern rationalism.

The cult of St. Philomena arose and spread in this environment. Religious orders including the newly reestablished Jesuits appreciated Philomena as model of Christian perseverance in a time not unlike the period of persecution by the ancient Roman empire. Bishops who visited Rome in the 19th century often brought home relics as this was a period when many catacombs were being excavated. In 1805, Father Francesco di Lucia of Mugnano del Cardenale petitioned for the relics. After being denied them, he was cured of a fever. He attributed his cure to Philomena. After much persistence he was granted the relics and enshrined them in his home town in 1832.

Reports of miracles during and after the relics were brought to the shrine advanced the cult. Sister Maria Louisa, Superior General of the Sisters of Sorrow of Mary (d. 1875), recorded visions of Philomena whose biography stressed chastity and resistence to persecution. In 1832 di Lucia recorded the biography, the story of the discovery of the relics, and many miracles, along with an essay on chastity. Eminent Catholics supported her cause including John Vianney, Madeleine Sophie Barat, Pierre-Julien Eymard, and Pauline Jaricot. In 1855 the Congregation of Rites established a feast day (Sept. 9), Mass, and Office for her.

Even when her feast was officially suppressed, her devotees continued to ask for and attribute cures to her intercession. Her omission from the calendar was not a prohibition of private devotion, but it does mean that the Congregation of Rites found insufficient evidence regarding her to mandate a place in the calendar or to allow the naming of official Catholic institutions for her.

Bibliography: F. DI LUCIA, *Relazione istorica della translazione del sacro corpo e miracoli di santa Filomena vergine e martire da Roma a Mugnano del Cardenale* (1834). A. BUTLER, *The Lives of the Saints,* rev. ed. H. THURSTON and D. ATTWATER, 4 v. (New York 1956) 3:299–301. *Acta Apostolicae Sedis* 53 (1961) 174. S. LA SALVIA, "L'inventione di un culto: S. Filomena de taumaturga a guerriera della fede," in *Culto de santi e classi sociali in età preindustriale* (1984).

[M. A. TILLEY]

PHILOSOPHY

Of Greek origin (φιλοσοφία), the term philosophy is a neologism attributed to PYTHAGORAS; it means literally ''love of wisdom,'' and represents philosophy as a high or supreme achievement of man and philosophers as aspirants to or proponents of WISDOM. In this relatively strict sense, philosophy implies both the process of questioning and the results of this interrogation as embodied in a personal or public enterprise of value to mankind. Such expressions as ''the philosophy of *X*''—when *X* can stand for art, advertising, government, and so forth—reveal that philosophy is taken to mean also an outlook on or a background to a given topic, subject, or enterprise. This broader meaning embraces academic philosophy as well as the philosophy of the man on the street; it makes philosophy equivalent to the sum total of basic views or principles accepted by a particular age or group.

Even this general meaning of the term, however, implies a distinction between philosophy and its proponents. Each philosopher has a personal conviction, and this even before he may make this public by means of verbal or written symbols. Yet one praises and esteems or deprecates and condemns not philosophers but what they proffer. Thus arises the basic question: What is philosophy? Any significant answer implies some ability to identify the content of philosophy as distinct from that of other branches of learning or to characterize the invariants in different forms of philosophizing. The difficulty of this task arises from the very nature of philosophy itself. Unlike other branches of knowledge, philosophical knowledge is both involutional (in the sense of growing more inward through reflection) and evolutional (in the sense of opening new domains for consideration). Accordingly, as a whole it is not static and closed; rather, it is dynamic and evolutionary. Each generation, and each philosopher for that matter, limits or enlarges its scope and colors or shades its meaning.

This dynamic and evolving character helps to account for the disagreement among philosophers themselves and for the phenomenon of philosophical schools or systems (*see* PLURALISM, PHILOSOPHICAL). Through such disagreement, however, as well as by genuine rapport, philosophers function as catalysts for the philosophical enterprise itself. Sometimes their efforts are misunderstood; this serves as the occasion for the rise of antiphilosophers, who attack philosophy from their own notions of what philosophy should be. They may underscore its failures in contrast with scientific success, deride its abstractness as opposed to the needs of daily life, or belittle its expressions as vacuous in comparison to religious vision. When the issues at stake have been settled, philosophy may have adopted a new position within culture or assisted in clarifying important issues for its very accusers. Thus man can be regarded as somehow trapped in a philosophical net; he can escape such confinement only by some point of view, but this itself will constitute his philosophy.

History. Granted that one may write the history of philosophy from a variety of points of view, there seem to be some common traits that the past life of philosophy reveals. In the first place, the philosophical enterprise seems to be a constant search for an integral and unified master plan as coextensive with, and explanatory of, the entire range of human experience. A second trait of philosophy derives from its constant renewal from the exigencies of practical life. Whether the problems be labeled as personal, social, political, or religious and whether they spring from technology or from other developments, man's everyday questions lead him to philosophical reflection. A third, and possibly more controversial, trait of philosophy is its zeal for TRUTH and for CERTITUDE in knowing. This is at once its most demanding and its most frustrating characteristic, one that seems to motivate all philosophers but that leaves many of them unsatisfied with their accomplishments. The philosophical task requires, moreover, that the philosopher express his insights in meaningful symbols. This relatedness to the LIBERAL ARTS is a fourth trait that seems to characterize most philosophical investigation.

Prior to Christianity. Considering philosophy in its broadest sense, one cannot name the first philosopher or delineate precisely philosophy's moment of nativity. Restricting consideration to academic philosophy, however, one may say that Western philosophy began with the Greeks partly as a result of their own genius and partly as an offshoot of Eastern thought. Compared, then, to the total age of the universe or of man, the life span of philosophy is short.

Western philosophy, which is of primary concern in this article, first began to take on a recognizable form or structure among the Greeks about the 6th century B.C. Its primitive trait can be designated as interest, or WONDER, over the changes taking place in the universe. The first philosophers, far from being presumptuous in their attempts to understand nature and being, spoke of themselves not as wise men but as lovers of wisdom. Philosophy, wisdom, knowledge, and truth—all were seen by them as synonymous and as valuable in themselves. They tended to identify philosophy with all true knowledge. Gradually, and especially in the eyes of the Ionians, it became a matter of privilege to have an orderly set of responses to questions concerning the nature and origin of both the universe and its contents, and especially of man himself. The ability to answer questions, then, came to be presupposed in the philosopher; the asking of the questions themselves, however, represented the first stage of the art of philosophizing.

Classical philosophy as a total outlook on the world and as somehow equivalent to knowledge in general developed largely with SOCRATES, PLATO, and ARISTOTLE. The latter two thinkers especially can be regarded as having broached the major issues with which Western philosophical thought has concerned itself to the 20th century, albeit in different ways. What does it mean for anything to be or to become? What are the origins, the conditions, and the final terms of being and becoming? Who is man and how is he related to being? What does it mean to know and to be known, and what are the conditions and requirements of knowing? In what ways are being and knowledge related? The major branches or areas of interest for philosophers also were marked out during this period: orderly thought was pursued in logic, then came mathematics and the philosophy of nature, after which personal and political activity was studied, and all was finally seen to culminate in metaphysical wisdom.

Again, already with Socrates and Plato, philosophy became self-conscious. Anything worthy of the name philosophy was expected to possess certain attributes: (1) it was to be universal, orderly, and systematic; (2) it was not to be transitory but necessary, even an eternal type of knowledge; and (3) it was not merely a response to questions by the ordinary man, but something attained by the very few. In brief, it was to be SCIENCE in the strict sense, and thus it came to be equated with all true and certain knowledge. To be a mathematician or a metaphysician, to be an astronomer or a musician was, in some participative sense at least, to be a philosopher. After about 400 years of growth, then, philosophy was considered as an open but all-embracing system, asking and answering questions about anything and everything, but answering them securely and definitively.

There were many attempts during this period, even by philosophers themselves, to challenge this concept of total and supreme wisdom. The SOPHISTS and the various proponents of SKEPTICISM introduced subsidiary currents that were to reappear in later centuries. But, by and large, the classical Greek thinkers had the greater influence. They set the course that philosophy was to follow, for the most part, in its subsequent history.

Philosophy and Christianity. It is somewhat surprising that philosophy survived the dramatic opposition of Christianity to its own world-view. Offering a set of new proposals, new terminology, and a complete way of life, Christianity claimed superiority over current and earlier forms of wisdom that were merely human. But philosophy was too well entrenched to succumb readily, and the need for a *rapprochement* soon became evident. True, in this first confrontation, there was the tendency of Christians to denigrate philosophy and of philosophers to ridicule or degrade Christianity. Both movements, however, survived and benefited from the encounter. Christianity opened new domains for philosophical consideration: the notion of a personal God and the possibility of knowing about His inner life; the idea of God as creator and as related to men and the world; the conception of a basic value of each man in God's sight. Christianity benefited likewise, especially in its aim to make all things Christian: it aspired to join the words of Christ with those of men to provide a unified outlook on the world. This task, however, was not accomplished with any *tour de force* for centuries. The first successful synthesis, in the 5th century, still perdures as the Augustinian-Platonic current of thought (*see* AUGUSTINIANISM). An alternate synthesis, Thomistic ARISTOTELIANISM, took form in the 13th century after assiduous preparation by such thinkers as ANSELM OF CANTERBURY, Arabian and Jewish philosophers, ABELARD, and countless other Christians and non-Christians (*see* THOMISM). A third proposal was the *via moderna* of the 14th and 15th centuries, originating with WILLIAM OF OCKHAM (*see* OCKHAMISM; NOMINALISM). Others may yet be in the offing, for the rapport between Christianity and rational thought is a perennial problem facing Christians, one that they may well solve differently in succeeding generations. (*See* PATRISTIC PHILOSOPHY; SCHOLASTICISM; CHRISTIAN PHILOSOPHY.)

Philosophy and the Sciences. The new sciences of the 17th century and later did not originate completely *de novo.* The currents of ancient philosophy reappearing in the Latin West in the 12th and succeeding centuries, along with countless other influences, conspired to make science possible. No one can fail to give credit, of course, to Galileo and his fellow pioneers. But the contributions of medieval philosophers also played an important role, particularly by way of synthesizing and transmitting the aggregate of human knowledge to the innovators.

The first and most immediate effect of the new sciences on philosophy was that of deliberate or implicit imitation. As the sciences grew and expanded, a retinue of philosophers, with F. BACON in the forefront, hoped to found a "new philosophy" that would be, in effect, a universal science. R. DESCARTES, B. SPINOZA, and G. W. LEIBNIZ were among those who sought to model the new philosophy on mathematics. British empiricists inclined more to the experimental sciences as a basis for their philosophizing. The many thinkers who conceptualized within the framework of KANTIANISM and HEGELIANISM, as well as LOGICAL POSITIVISM, endeavored to use both mathematics and the positive sciences as models for their philosophies. More recently, philosophers such as H.

BERGSON and W. JAMES saw philosophy and science as two complementary but radically distinct branches of learning.

Another effect of the new sciences on philosophy was the attempt to assimilate scientific findings into philosophy or even to erect philosophies exclusively on a scientific theory or viewpoint. Thus Darwin's theory of evolution, Einstein's theory of relativity, Brouwer's intuitionism, and Freud's libido have formed the basis for much philosophizing, to say nothing of the ''scientific philosophy'' of Hans Reichenbach and the Vienna Circle. Related to this development is the problem of philosophical methodology as contrasted with that of the sciences. Are the sciences themselves unified or distinguished by their methods; and, in any case, are their methods distinct from those of philosophy? [*See* METHODOLOGY (PHILOSOPHY)].

The increasing concern of science with problems earlier regarded as those of philosophy has forced philosophers to reconsider the various dimensions of the philosophical enterprise. The tendency of some to regard all knowledge as science and to leave the domain of spirit, *élan vital,* will, aesthetic experience, and life to philosophy occasionally has manifested itself. Others have seen the overlap of interest as an indication of the basic unity of science and philosophy as these seek satisfactory, if complementary, solutions to the same problems (*see* PHILOSOPHY AND SCIENCE).

Transitional and Contemporary Trends. Apart from the concern with science, philosophers in the 20th century have become increasingly aware of man and his problems. Even the new philosophers of despair are as much prophets of hope as they are of man's ill-fated condition. Before pretending to discuss the very being of all things, these thinkers philosophize about man and his experience in the everyday world. They designate man as historical, as consciousness, as body-self, as transcendence, and in general as a being-in-process toward a future; but they also see an ontological dimension in human modes of being and activity. They regard men as the responsible authors, with or without God, of their private and public philosophies and their effects. In their opinion science, concerned with specialized experience, builds an abstracted world of its own; but, through technology, science can help free man for his historical tasks. Religion and the arts are seen as closer to man's workaday world, adding to the meaning of life in the present and for the limitless future.

Definition. There is no definition of philosophy that is agreed upon uniformly by all philosophers. However, if the consideration is restricted to views of philosophy that are commonly accepted in the classical and scholastic tradition on the one hand, and in the modern tradition on the other, it becomes possible to mark out fairly broad areas of agreement.

Classical and Scholastic Tradition. Thinkers in the classical and scholastic tradition tend to regard philosophy as a HABIT of mind or a body of natural KNOWLEDGE that results from the use of special methods and that enables one to explain in a more or less profound way the sum of human experiences. It differs from common knowledge in that it is acquired and evolved systematically, although it must take its beginnings from ordinary experience. Insofar as it considers everything knowable and is not restricted to one or other species or kind of entity; it is more universal in its concern than are the special sciences; in a certain way it includes even them and their objects in its consideration.

A more detailed description of philosophy, as considered in this tradition, may be had by enumerating the questions and problems it commonly treats. Thus one of its areas of inquiry concerns the procedures to be used in the acquisition of knowledge; another concerns the world of nature and related topics such as motion, time, and space; yet another concerns life and its meaning, the nature of man, and his various cognitional and appetitive activities; another concerns morality, social and political life, the nature of law and other institutions that preserve the common good; still another concerns being, its attributes, its categories, and its principles.

Thinkers in the Aristotelian-Thomistic tradition, particularly, accent the certain and causal character of philosophical knowledge. Though not holding that every subject investigated by philosophers permits absolutely certain judgment, they regard truth and certitude as the goal of philosophy and insist on the availability to the human mind of at least some starting points on which philosophical reasoning can be solidly grounded. Philosophy, in their understanding, remains ever open to further extension and development, but it is not subject to change with regard to FIRST PRINCIPLES and other self-evident truths on which this development is based, except in the sense that these come to be more deeply comprehended and understood with the passage of time. Thus they define philosophy as all certain and evident knowledge, grasped either directly or through causal analysis and DEMONSTRATION, that man can attain through human reason alone, and this both in the speculative order and in the practical order, but in the latter only as this enables man to reach his ultimate end. Being concerned with all knowledge, philosophy is not merely one science but is an aggregate of several different sciences; since its unity is merely analogical, it cannot be defined strictly. Its certain and evident character separates it from conjecture and from mere personal OPINION, and also from divine FAITH which, though certain, is not evident to the human mind. Again, it is purely natural knowledge, and this separates it from sacred THEOLOGY, which makes use of knowledge that can be had only through the acceptance of divine revelation.

Modern Tradition. Attempts by modern philosophers to define philosophy can be explained in terms of the interrelationship between SUBJECT and OBJECT; for them, the confrontation of subject and object is what generates philosophical content. No philosopher in the modern era denies the function of subject in philosophizing. Materialists, empiricists, and phenomenalists may reduce the subject or his experience to brute matter or to sense imagery, and a monist or a subjective idealist may merge subject with object. But all seem to concur that philosophy is a reflection on the subject's experience; it is the response of the self to whatever appears to be nonself. In the early 20th century greater emphasis than theretofore was placed on the subject as central in all philosophizing. Though philosophy may be a true report or counterpart of extramental objects, like all knowledge it is regarded as indigenously personal; it is evoked from, surrounded by, and presented in symbols that spring from a field of CONSCIOUSNESS also manifesting the philosopher himself. From this point of view, philosophy is what a philosopher considers it to be. He himself is the final referent for its veridical meaning. Philosophers employ a wide variety of designations—such as science, wisdom, freedom, *Weltanschauung, Dasein,* and *Lebenswelt*—to denominate this personal aspect of the subject-for-philosophy.

But philosophy is generally conceded to be about something—whether this be termed object, being, idea, matter, principle, self, cause, thing, spirit, or will. The object of philosophy is regarded by some as that which comes to or is conveyed into the subject; others consider the object as that to which the subject reaches out, as that toward which he is tendential, or even as that which he finally attains. Object, as the counterpart of subject, is thus accorded different values by various philosophers. It is therefore evident that one can have philosophical content in the modern sense at its sober minimum in the solipsist subject or at its ecstatic maximum as concerned with a great plurality of objects. No matter which factors are highlighted, however, philosophy comes out to be a reflection on, and a derivative of, the fusion between subject and object. It is a content by way of personal reflection, and a content that is reflected also in the dialogue philosophers have, at least among themselves, about intersubjective relationships (*see* SUBJECTIVITY; OBJECTIVITY).

Scope. The following survey of the branches or domains of philosophy adopts the traditional classification of knowledge into speculative, with its three degrees or levels, and practical, with its realms of art, prudence, and moral science (*see* SCIENCES, CLASSIFICATION OF). It may be argued that this distinction is either indefensible or inapplicable to modern thought, but the fact remains that no newer classification is generally accepted. The problem here proposed, of course, presupposes an answer to the question: What kind of totality is philosophy? Some hold that it is an integral, organic unity: it studies being in general and in particular: it encompasses large issues and ferrets out minor details; but it is uniform in outlook, the sole differentiation within it arising from the variety of topics it considers. Others view philosophy as, say, primarily metaphysics or logic: other branches they regard as philosophical only by way of participation. Whatever position is maintained, however, contemporary philosophy can be understood without too much distortion as a historical development from the following branches of classical philosophy: logic; philosophy of nature and psychology; mathematics and its philosophy; metaphysics, including epistemology and natural theology; and the practical domains of art, ethics, and politics.

Logic. Traditional philosophy views LOGIC in one way as propaedeutic to higher learning. Logic teaches the modes of correct thinking in terms of the CONCEPT, the JUDGMENT, and REASONING. Throughout ancient and medieval times, logic was closely allied to other branches of learning, though there were some noteworthy attempts at liberating it from its affinity to psychology and to metaphysics. Bacon, Descartes, Leibniz, and Kant are key figures in the struggle to give logic an outlook and a domain of its own as distinct from metaphysics; G. Boole, G. Peano, G. Frege, B. RUSSELL, and E. HUSSERL, on the other hand, are prominent among those who strove to depsychologize logic. As a result of these influences, one may identify at least three aspects of logic. In its first aspect, which is more traditional, logic functions as a tool or instrument subserving other branches of learning. In its second aspect, logic becomes a discipline in its own right that is concerned with the forms of thought; this usage is best exemplified in logistics, or mathematical logic, or symbolic logic. PHENOMENOLOGY unveils a third aspect of logic. It proposes a methodology whereby answers can be sought to the question: What is involved in, or what is the very meaning of, concepts such as God, or velvet, or atom? (*See* LOGIC; LOGIC, HISTORY OF; LOGIC, SYMBOLIC.)

Philosophy of Nature and Psychology. The earliest philosophies of nature served as a background for the rise of the physical, biological, and psychological sciences. Plato's *Timaeus* and its many commentaries, together with Aristotle's physical treatises and their medieval and early modern commentaries, go far to explain why 17th-century scientists came to regard themselves as the new philosophers of nature. A series of epochal discoveries, however, altered this situation and gradually separated the philosophical from the scientific world-view. Evolutionary theory and such sciences as biology, paleontology, geology, and anthropology challenged the static conception of nature latent in some presentations of ancient thought. The discovery of analytical geometry, of the calculus, and of non-Euclidean geometries provided new instruments for investigating the world of change. Similarly, new concepts associated with quantum theory and the theories of relativity led to the questioning of all centuries-old world pictures. As a result, the very possibility of a philosophical outlook on the world independent of scientific knowledge was seriously challenged. Philosophy was confined to the roles of evaluating the proposals of science and of defending human values against the encroachments of technology. More recently, however, the philosophy of science has made its appearance, and one finds scientists returning more to philosophical conceptions of the world of nature. The traditional philosophy of nature likewise has strong support among those who aspire to harmonize its basic tenets with the changed outlook of science. (*See* PHILOSOPHY OF NATURE.)

A similar upheaval led to the divorce of philosophy from psychology and its branches. The nature, function, and ultimate disposition of man is an age-old question treated extensively in the Platonic and the Aristotelian traditions. For both, the study of man was primarily the study of psyche or soul, and the problem of the body-soul relationship was of paramount importance. With the rise of new sciences more directly concerned with man, however, various philosophies (dualistic, monistic, materialistic, etc.) were developed in attempts to answer the question: Who is man? Psychology and its attendant disciplines, separated in time from these philosophies, developed a closer affinity to the natural sciences.

Mathematics and Philosophy. No branch of learning has longer or closer contact with philosophy than mathematics. Except for extreme empiricists and materialists, philosophers have frequently regarded mathematical science as the exemplar of sophisticated thought, as the limit of certitude toward which other branches of learning converge. Early philosophers, regarding mathematics as the science of quantified being, conceded it a position intermediate between those of metaphysics and of the philosophy of nature. Modern thinkers, influenced by new discoveries in mathematics, have modified these views. But the closeness of mathematics to philosophy still is witnessed in current concerns over the foundations of mathematics and related topics in the philosophy of mathematics. (*See* MATHEMATICS, PHILOSOPHY OF.)

Metaphysics, Epistemology, and Natural Theology. No subject of learning in man's history has been the recipient of warmer accolades or more virulent gibes than metaphysics. For some, metaphysics is more divine than theology; for others, more diabolical than astrology. Nor is any other subject matter as much confounded with other subjects and forced to wear the masks now of a logic, now of a psychology or an anthropology, and so on. Traditionally, metaphysics is the science of being in general, as contrasted with other branches of learning whose proper concern is particular being. Metaphysics, then, functions as a wisdom to all the sciences and arts, including the art of life itself. After its hegemony in this latter regard was challenged by the Christian faith, metaphysics became an instrument for exploring Christian mysteries. Throughout the early Christian and medieval periods of thought, it thus retained its contact with other branches of learning. The new sciences, however, made sport of metaphysics along with the decadent science with which it was associated. All too often, metaphysicians reacted by continuing to expound their science in traditional form—neither receiving from, nor contributing anything to, the new sciences.

The outstanding success of these sciences, however, together with the rise of totally new philosophies, has served to awaken metaphysics from its slumber. Some scholars, appalled at the implications of the new sciences and their methods, raised the cry "back to metaphysics." The problem of the nature of human knowledge was reopened and led to the development of the branch of metaphysics called EPISTEMOLOGY—a discipline of key importance in modern philosophy. From the throes of these and other movements, a renewal of metaphysics is currently in progress. The new metaphysics sees man as intentional-toward-being, as consciousness, as freedom, as transcendence—as a questioner to whom being is both manifest and hidden. (*See* METAPHYSICS; METAPHYSICS, VALIDITY OF.)

Traditionally, metaphysics culminates in natural theology, with its proofs for God's existence and its study of His nature. This is another area of metaphysics that is undergoing renewal as the result of many factors, e.g., the problems associated with the theories of evolution and relativity, the question of man's function in this world as a being-toward-death and his ultimate disposition, and the renewed interest in Eastern philosophy. Thus the principal questions of theodicy are again being brought into focus: Can God be conceptualized in human categories and regarded as totally immanent to all being? Does He transcend all human categories? Is He at once immanent and transcendent? A greater merging of religious, philosophical, and scientific thought is in evidence; and channels are being opened by Christian philosophers that may lead to more agreement on the concepts of God in metaphysics and in revealed religion. (*See* THEOLOGY, NATURAL; EXISTENTIAL METAPHYSICS.)

Arts and Philosophy. The ordering of the arts among themselves and the function and meaning of art were discussed by Greek thinkers as well as by their medieval heirs. A much discussed question was whether or not BEAUTY is to be enumerated among the transcendental properties of being as such. The beauty of human works of art was seen to lie in their successful imitation of nature or in their exemplification of a truth of religious message. The introduction of Greek and Roman classics in the Renaissance gave great impetus to the arts, with the result that new theories of the nature of art were proposed by artists themselves and by philosophers. AESTHETICS generally has limited its analyses to the fine arts; its current tendency is to stress the creativity of the artist and the modes in which he symbolizes his cultural milieu [*See* ART (PHILOSOPHY); POETICS (ARISTOTELIAN); LIBERAL ARTS].

Ethics and Politics. In traditional thought, the intellect has always been viewed as directive of human action. As in art, so in moral science, reason serves as a counselor and guide affording practical principles for all of man's activity. Two main areas have consistently been recognized: ethics, relating to the sphere of individual man and his responsibility, and politics, concerned with man's social and political nature.

The traditional outlook on ethics has insisted that the GOOD is in things and that man's choice and conformity to this good affords him whatever happiness is available in this life. This doctrine, accepted for centuries, gave way in modern thought to Kant's ETHICAL FORMALISM. The notion of value, more recently, has opened up new directions for studying man's significance and his role in forming his future. (*See* ETHICS; ETHICS, HISTORY OF; VALUE, PHILOSOPHY OF.)

Among the Greeks, the social and political orders held primacy over the individual and his personal concerns. This effective subordination of ethics to social and political philosophy was only gradually challenged in the modern era by such writers as J. J. ROUSSEAU, T. HOBBES and the British empiricists. Contemporary discussions are concerned with the basic tenets of social and political philosophy and how these are to be differentiated from, and at the same time related to, the findings of the social and political sciences.

Philosophy and the Catholic Church. The historical relationship of the Catholic Church to philosophy is a patchwork of light and darkness. No one can deny, of course, the greatness of an AUGUSTINE or of a THOMAS AQUINAS. Lights of the philosophical world as well as of the Church, such thinkers are symbolic of the positive aspect of this relationship: the interest, concern, and support of philosophy by the Church. This general belief in reason and in philosophy is attested in various ways: (1) official pronouncements on the value of philosophy for Catholic and specifically for seminary education; (2) the traditional role of philosophy in the Church as subserving theological interests and needs; (3) discussions on the possibility of a Christian philosophy; (4) the notion of a *philosophia perennis* that continually reworks and reshapes a basic philosophical message in accord with Christian revelation. In the U.S., Catholics manifest their interest in philosophy by requiring it not only in seminaries but in collegiate education as well; by sponsoring philosophical journals; and by their membership and support of the American Catholic Philosophical Association and similar congresses and movements.

On the other hand, one cannot fail to acknowledge that leading authorities in the Church have often been unfriendly or openly inimical to certain philosophers and their teachings or that they favor some doctrines over others—often for insufficient or prejudicial reasons. Some of these episodes are intelligible within their historical context, whereas others are not. Occasional clashes between philosophers and Church authorities illustrate the perennial tension within the Church itself between FREEDOM and AUTHORITY. It is not to the purpose to recount here the long history of these episodes. It need only be pointed out—while admitting that tactical blunders have been made in the past—that the Church can no more be indifferent to philosophy than philosophers can be to each other's proposals. If one believes in an open society and in the freedom of knowledge, he can no more deprive the Church of its say than he can other interested parties and critics.

Teaching of Philosophy. If the nature of philosophy and of its branches is difficult to describe and if the relationship of philosophy to other branches of knowledge is quite complex, what can be said of the teaching of philosophy? It is evident, in the first place, that this question can be asked (and answered) only by those who have a definite view of human knowledge and its personal and cultural functions. Both the order and the method of teaching philosophy must be determined by one's personal outlook as well as by cultural and student needs. For those who grant philosophy a place in the curriculum, its content and method of teaching vary depending on what philosophy is considered to be, viz, either a form of wisdom that completes other types of knowledge, or an introduction to religious knowledge, or a personal outlook on the totality of experience, or a rigorous academic discipline, or a combination of any or all of these views. Probably the best teachers of philosophy are those of Socratic lineage who are both generalists and specialists, who awaken their students to reflection and also give them material on which to reflect, and who thus propound the simple truth that philosophy is not only a search for wisdom but is itself the wisdom that is sought.

Bibliography: M. J. ADLER, *The Conditions of Philosophy* (New York 1965). V. MATHIEU, *Enciclopedia filosofica* 2:397–411. A. M. MOSCHETTI, *ibid.* 412–415. G. RABEAU, *Dictionnaire de théologie catholique*, 12.2:1459–94. *Encyclopedia Française*, v. 19 (Paris 1957). H. ROMBACH, *Lexicon für Theologie und Kirche*, 472–478. L. OEING-HANHOFF, *ibid.* 8:471–472. G. PATZIG, *Die Religion in Geschichte und Gegenwart* (3d ed. Tübingen 1957–63) 5:349–356. S. RAMÍREZ, ''De ipsa philosophia in universum secundum doctrinam aristotelico-thomisticam,'' *La Ciencia Tomista* 27 (1922) 33–62, 325–364; 28 (1923) 5–35; 29 (1924) 25–29, 207–220; ''De propria indole philosophiae Sancti Thomae Aquinatis,'' *Xenia thomistica* 1 (Rome 1925) 53–64. L. B. GEIGER, *Philosophie et Spiritualité*, 2 v. (Paris 1963). J. MARITAIN, *An Essay on Christian Philosophy*, tr. E. FLANNERY (New York 1955); *On the Use of Philosophy* (New York 1965). A. M. MALINGREY, *Philosophia* (Paris 1961). E. W. HALL, *Philosophical Systems: A Categorical Analysis* (Chicago 1960). K. JASPERS, *The Perennial Scope of Philosophy*, tr. R. MANHEIM (New York 1949). M. MERLEAU-PONTY, *In Praise of Philosophy*, tr. J. WILD and J. M. EDIE (Evanston, Ill. 1963). J. ORTEGA Y GASSET, *What Is Philosophy?*, tr. M. ADAMS (New York 1961). J. A. PASSMORE, *A Hundred Years of Philosophy* (New York 1957). J. H. RANDALL, *The Career of Philosophy: From the Middle Ages to the Enlightenment* (New York 1962). W. DILTHEY, *The Essence of Philosophy*, tr. S. A. and W. T. EMERY (Chapel Hill, N.C. 1954). M. HEIDEGGER, *Being and Time*, tr. J. MACQUARRIE and E. ROBINSON (New York 1962). E. HUSSERL, *Ideas: General Introduction to Pure Phenomenology*, tr. W. R. BOYCE GIBSON (New York 1931; pa. 1962). J. P. SARTRE, *Being and Nothingness*, tr. H. E. BARNES (New York 1956). J. H. RANDALL, *The Career of Philosophy: From the Enlightenment to the 19th Century* (New York 1965).

[E. A. MAZIARZ]

PHILOSOPHY, HISTORY OF

The history of philosophy is a special branch of the general history of CULTURE whose object is the critical study of the formation and development of PHILOSOPHY and its associated concepts from their first appearance to the present. This article surveys some general notions associated with the history of philosophy and then summarizes its chronological development through the ancient, medieval, modern, and contemporary periods.

GENERAL NOTIONS

The history of philosophy is a composite concept; to attempt to define it one must first take account of the concepts of philosophy and history upon which it obviously depends.

Philosophy. In ancient times and during the Middle Ages, the term philosophy had a broad meaning identical

Aristotle.

with that of SCIENCE (*SCIENTIA*). In conformity with this classical notion, the history of philosophy would be the same as the history of scientific thought. Yet from I. Kant and 19th-century POSITIVISM onward, the sciences came to be separated from philosophy; they ceased to be regarded as a whole and were set in mutual contraposition as though they constituted two distinct fields of knowledge. This division was aggravated by the fact that there was hardly a modern philosopher who did not propose a distinct notion of philosophy, attributing to it various functions in conformity with what he deemed to be the basic principle of reality. This limitation and diversity in the concept of philosophy had its necessary repercussions in the concept of the history of philosophy. For purposes here it is convenient to adopt the classical notion of philosophy, regarding it as synonymous with science and attributing to the history of philosophy a material object broad enough to embrace the formation and development of all human sciences. This does not prevent this history, once provided with a breadth and diversity of materials, from being subdivided into a multitude of particular histories corresponding to the development of each of the branches into which science can be divided. (*see* SCIENCES, CLASSIFICATION OF; PHILOSOPHY AND SCIENCE.)

History. The term HISTORY can be taken in two ways, namely, as an ontological reality and as a science

Clement of Alexandria.

(the German distinction between *Historie* and *Geschichte*).

In the ontological sense, the problem about the essence of historical being, or historicity, is a partial aspect of the general problem concerning being. All real things have duration, but not all of them have a history. God, the absolute and immutable Being, has duration (eternity), but not history. However, all contingent and changeable beings, such as minerals, plants, and animals, have a history. Historicity is a property of man, not as regards his essence, which is immutable, but in reference to the accidental result of some of his actions. Historicity does not constitute the essence of man, as taught by W. DILTHEY and the historicist school, but consists in an accidental modality acquired by some individual or collective human actions achieved in time. Historical reality is the result of a past action that is not completely past, since some virtuality of it remains to continue actuating into the future.

History as a science consists of the critical study and explanation of historical facts considered in their chronological succession, through the investigation of their mutual relations, their antecedents and consequents, their connections and affinities, and their influences and reactions. This is done in search for a meaning and interpretation, so that these facts are presented in a total or partial view of the whole. History is a true science, although historical facts, which constitute its material object, are particular; this is possible since, once they have occurred, such facts acquire a type of absolute necessity (what has been done cannot not have been done). At times one can arrive at an absolute CERTITUDE in the knowledge of historical facts, and, at others, at a probability sufficient to establish certain and true knowledge, and therefore scientific knowledge.

Historicity of Philosophy. Philosophy is historical and has a history, since it is a product that men have elaborated by their intellectual activity in the course of time. Achieved philosophy (*in facto esse*) is a present and actual reality. It is the term at which the human intellect has arrived in the process of investigating the truth. Yet TRUTH is absolute, unchangeable, and timeless. From the moment wherein philosophy arrives at the possession of truth, scientific knowledge remains beyond change and temporality and therefore outside of history. Nevertheless, in the process of its becoming or formation, philosophy consists in the temporal process of its formation and in the stages that man's mind must follow until it arrives at the truth. In this second meaning, it is as though philosophy constitutes the object with which the history of philosophy is concerned. For this reason the attention of the historian of philosophy must be focused more upon vicissitudes that have been encountered in the formation of philosophy throughout a temporal development than upon philosophy itself.

Philosophy is a historical reality and has a history, but it is not identified with history. G. W. F. HEGEL converts history into philosophy, whereas Dilthey converts philosophy into history. However, philosophy, once accomplished, is one thing; quite distinctly other is the process throughout the centuries by which it has come to be what it is presently. Historicity is not an ontological property of philosophy in itself, but affects only the process of philosophy's formation and the vicissitudes of its development in the course of time. One can indicate the following as differences: (1) Pure philosophy is concerned with the truth, which is unchangeable and timeless. The history of philosophy is concerned with the formation or becoming of philosophy and the changeable and temporal process pursued by the human mind until it arrives at the knowledge of the truth. (2) Pure philosophy aims at unity, which is identical for all men and for all times; this unity is achieved when one attains the truth. The history of philosophy attains the unity of a science when it succeeds in establishing the truth of historical facts; yet it should reflect the diversity and dynamism of the process through which men have arrived at the unity of science in the possession of the truth. (3) Pure philosophy moves in a region of abstract, universal, and necessary concepts, of absolute truths, independent of time and space. The field of historical research comprises concrete, particular, free, contingent, and variable facts. (4) The philosopher himself studies the scientific problems corresponding to distinct parts of philosophy, and can prescind from the past as well as from the opinions of other thinkers. The historian studies facts as they have occurred in the past, and cannot prescind from the opinions and distinct solutions proposed by philosophers. (5) The philosopher studies the essences of things, which are immutable; the historian considers existences, which are contingent. (6) Pure philosophy seeks, not what men have said, but what the truth is. The history of philosophy seeks the truth of what men have said and done in their efforts to attain the possession of the truth.

Philosophical problems. The problems that philosophers attempt to solve are as numerous and varied as reality itself. They can be reduced to three great themes, corresponding to the three great orders of being: God, the world, and man; or, again, being, knowledge, and function. However, each of these great themes for investigation unfolds, in turn, into almost an infinite number of particular problems within each branch of science. These include (1) ontological problems concerning being in itself; (2) logical problems concerning the order and relationships among concepts; (3) mathematical problems concerning the nature of quantity and number; (4) physical or cosmological problems concerning the nature of changeable beings in the material world; (5) biological problems concerning the nature of living things; (6) anthropological problems concerning the nature of man; (7) psychological problems concerning the nature and functions of the human soul; (8) epistemological problems concerning the nature and value of human knowledge as representative of reality; (9) social problems concerning the relations of man with his fellow creatures; (10) political problems concerning the relations between citizens and civil authority; (11) juridical problems concerning law, justice, and right; (12) theological problems concerning the existence and nature of God; (13) moral problems concerning human actions as these are viewed in their order to an ultimate end or to the perfection of man; (14) religious problems concerning man's relations with God; and (15) aesthetic problems concerning beauty and art.

The consideration of philosophical problems in themselves corresponds to the various branches of philosophy. What pertains to the history of philosophy is the study of the answers that philosophers have offered in their attempts to solve them. The historian of philosophy should take account of the temporal preponderance of determinate themes of thought in various eras. Philosophical problems did not arise simultaneously, nor have all branches of science appeared at one time nor have they had an equal development. One of the distinctive characteristics of philosophical eras and currents is precisely the predominance of interest in some particular problem. For example, theological and moral problems were prevalent in Neoplatonism and medieval scholasticism; political themes, during the 17th century; physical and biological questions, during the 19th century; and human and social problems, during the 20th.

Marsilio Ficino, Italian philosopher and Platonist.

Philosophy and philosophies. Reality is one, and the problems it poses are the same at all times and for all men. Nor is there more than one truth, which consists in the adequation of human concepts with things as they are in themselves. Scientific knowledge should be an exact mental representation of reality. For this reason there should be only one philosophy and only one system that is representative of reality. In fact, however, not only is there no one system, but there are many distinct and even contradictory systems (*see* PLURALISM, PHILOSOPHICAL).

José Ortega y Gasset. (AP/Wide World Photos)

There are many causes for this diversity, both subjective and objective.

Among the subjective causes may be enumerated: (1) the basic limitation of man's knowing faculties with respect to their proper object, and much more so with respect to transcendent objects; (2) the nature of his intellect, which is rational and discursive; (3) the incapacity of his mind to have an intuitive perception of the essences of things; (4) the influence of environment and of historical, social, and political circumstances peculiar to each era; and (5) the influence of philosophers upon each other. Frequently, philosophy has not developed by making a direct investigation of reality itself, but has been elaborated by discourse on the books and opinions of philosophers. Various systems give rise to others, sometimes by way of reaction, sometimes as attempts at reconciliation or advancement.

Objective causes of philosophical pluralism include (1) the very nature of reality and the intrinsic difficulty of the problems it presents to the human mind, and (2) the difficulty of acquiring the means and instruments needed for their investigation. Many beings fall within the scope of the proper object of the human mind, but others, such as God, are beyond the direct reach of human means of perception, and man can know them only by ANALOGY. Even in the realm of the directly knowable, moreover, there are many questions that can be answered only with the help of costly and complicated instruments, and these were unavailable.

Nevertheless, there are also causes of philosophical unity, such as the nature of reality, which is one and the same and presents the same problems at all times to the minds of all men. There is, for example, the identity of human nature, which is essentially the same despite accidental differences. From the conjunction of the causes of unity with those of diversity there results a historical process that is not rectilinear but rather exhibits advances and backward movements, as well as fluctuations and oscillations. The final result, however, has been real and positive progress in most branches of philosophy.

Philosophical Systems. From the diversity of attitudes among philosophers in the presence of problems posed by reality, as well as from the multitude of their solutions, there arises a great variety of philosophical systems.

Being. As regards the basic problem of being, upon which all other problems depend, the following systems may be enumerated. REALISM holds that beings really exist and that man's faculties are able to know them. IDEALISM distrusts the veracity of the senses, breaks the contact with external reality, and imprisons itself within its own interiority, elaborating logical systems based upon combinations of mental concepts. According to MONISM, reality consists in one sole finite, spherical, compact, undifferentiated, and immovable being, or in one sole infinite being, of which all other beings are nothing more than emanations or modalities that do not alter its essential unity. According to PLURALISM, on the other hand, reality is constituted by a multitude of existent, individual, and distinct beings (ARISTOTELIANISM, THOMISM). MATERIALISM deems matter to be the sole reality. SPIRITUALISM holds that, in addition to sensible, bodily realities, there are spiritual realities that cannot be perceived by the senses. Essentialism limits itself to necessary and immutable essences, whereas EXISTENTIALISM focuses its attention upon existences or on concrete and particular existing things.

Truth. Positions concerning the problem of truth can be classified as positive or negative. The positive positions include realism, eclecticism, and dogmatism. According to realism, truth really exists. It is one, identical, absolute, and unchangeable, and all minds can attain it in a complete or partial way. ECLECTICISM holds that each philosophy succeeds in attaining only one part or some aspect of the truth; purged of their errors, these aspects can be coordinated into a single system. DOGMATISM locks itself within systems expressed in absolute formulas of pretended universal value. Among negative positions may be enumerated skepticism and relativism. SKEPTICISM, complete or partial, holds that the truth does not exist, or at least that it cannot be discovered by the human mind. According to RELATIVISM, there are no immutable essences. The truth is partial, relative, and changeable; it depends upon the way in which the subject perceives it, and it varies according to the circumstances of place and time.

Knowledge. As regards the problem of knowledge, there are the positions of SENSISM, EMPIRICISM, INTELLECTUALISM, etc. (*see* KNOWLEDGE, THEORIES OF).

God. Concerning the problem of God, the most important positions may be listed as atheism, theism, and pantheism. ATHEISM denies the existence of a personal God distinct from the world. THEISM can be divided into two positions. One holds that there is an eternal, infinite, and intelligent God, but that He is not a creator, nor does He exercise providence over the world; at the same time, there is an eternal and finite world (Aristotle). The other position is that there is an infinite, eternal, intelligent, and free God, Creator and Ruler of the world, and that there is a created, finite, and temporal world that is dependent upon God (St. THOMAS AQUINAS). PANTHEISM holds that there exists only one being, the universal principle of all things, and that the world is identical with this principle. Pantheism can be partial or total. According to partial pantheism, God is either the soul of the world, primary matter, or the existence of the world. Total pantheism can be distinguished into various forms: the static, introdynamic, emanationistic, and evolutionistic. The static form holds that there exists only one finite, spherical, undifferentiated, and immovable being (*see* PARMENIDES). The introdynamic form teaches that there is only one substance having infinite attributes and modes (B. SPINOZA). According to the emanationistic view, beings flow as descending emanations from the One (PLOTINUS). Evolutionistic forms teach that particular beings are the products of evolution from one sole principle, whether this be the Absolute (F. W. J. SCHELLING), the idea (Hegel), the will (A. SCHOPENHAUER), matter (K. MARX), life (H. BERGSON), or some similar principle.

Method. The history of philosophy must be preeminently history. It is a branch of the historical sciences, and its particular method is essentially that of historical investigation. A priori dialectical methods that make the history of philosophy a branch of logic (Hegel) or an exercise of pure reason are inadmissible. History is not concerned with possible, abstract, or universal essences, but with concrete facts and particular and real events. The historian's mission does not lie in imagining how matters should have occurred but in investigating and reporting how and why they did occur. The historical method embraces two functions, namely, the heuristic and the hermeneutical.

The heuristic function serves to investigate the facts and to reconstruct these as they happened. First, the historian of philosophy should reconstruct the authentic thought of philosophers by studying their writings, with the help of direct and indirect sources and auxiliary sciences. Second, he should state this thought faithfully, without alteration or falsification. He should classify thinkers and their systems in conformity with an order based upon reality itself. He should establish them in their coordinates of place and time, and take account of their relations of dependence to other philosophers and their thought.

The hermeneutical function is necessary since the statement of the facts should be completed by their explanation and interpretation. The historian should investigate not only the facts themselves but also the reasons for the facts, and explain one by the other without recourse to nonhistorical elements. Furthermore, he may rightfully pass judgment on the intrinsic value of the systems. However, he may not attribute a sapiential mission to history, as though it were a superphilosophy coordinating the divergencies of the systems and unifying their plurality. Even less acceptable are the Hegelian asides of Dilthey, who uses history to explain the relativity of systems, as a sort of reflection of spirit upon itself that includes the partial philosophies developed in the course of time.

Division. A priori divisions based upon determinate concepts of philosophies of history are inadmissible. Hegel adjusts the development of philosophy to the stages in the evolution of the Absolute Spirit. Influenced by the historical progressionism of CONDORCET and Turgot, A. COMTE establishes three stages, namely, the theological, the metaphysical, and the positive, but these have no basis in the reality of history. G. SANTAYANA indicates three great peaks in thought: naturalism, supernaturalism, and romanticism, which culminate in three great poets, namely, Lucretius, Dante, and Goethe.

The best division is one resulting from the reality of the facts. It can be made in conformity with various criteria. The first of these is chronology. Taking account of the temporal succession of the facts is basic and indispensable. In the history of philosophy, however, it is not enough merely to pursue the horizontal line of development in time. Thought has not followed one straight and ascending line of homogeneous progress; rather the many sources of diversity have dispersed the efforts of philosophers into different directions. From this there results a complicated process wherein some systems influence others, at times over many centuries and in quite distinct geographical localities. It is necessary to make the relation and connection among currents of thought evident. For example, Aristotelianism (4th century B.C.) and Neeplatonism (3rd century A.D.) had an influence on Persian Islam (10th century), and this, in turn, had an influence in Spain (12th century) and on SCHOLASTICISM (13th century). The currently accepted division of philosophy into ancient, medieval, modern, and contemporary is based upon Western history, but is defective since it does not coincide with the development of Oriental cultures, nor does it suit the effective development of philosophy itself.

The second criterion is geography. The development of philosophy can be manifested as it occurred in Greece, Rome, Italy, France, Germany, Spain, etc. Yet philosophy is supranational. Speaking of Greek, Roman, Italian, French, or German philosophy is less exact than saying that there are Greek, Roman, Italian, French, and German philosophers.

The third criterion is the enumeration of problems. To clarify philosophical problems, it is useful to group the systems and opinions of philosophers around some concrete problem, as, for example, some ontological, epistemological, or theological problem. Yet this procedure fails to offer a panoramic and articulate view of the whole development of philosophy. Associated with it are divisions according to schools and attitudes. Platonism, Aristotelianism, Neoplatonism, Thomism, Scotism, etc., can be presented, each one separately from the others; or, pursuing basic options, one can follow the lines of realism, empiricism, idealism, skepticism, etc.

Metahistory of philosophy. The history of philosophy, too, has its own history, which may be referred to as a metahistory of philosophy. The recognition of history as scientific knowledge is rather recent. Among the Greeks, the anecdotal had a predominance over the doctrinal. Aristotle, Plutarch, Diogenes Laertius, and Sextus Empiricus expounded the ''opinions'' of the various sects (doxography) without establishing a relation among them and without a perspective of integration within a universal process. These are documents of inestimable value, but they do not properly constitute histories of philosophy. During the Middle Ages, there was no intention of producing a history of philosophy. The scholastics expounded, criticized, and used the opinions of philosophers, but without trying to order and systematize them within a unified panorama. During the Renaissance, there appeared numerous monographic studies on the life and teaching of ancient philosophers, all based upon references in the Greek and Latin doxographies, but having the same deficiency of information and historical perspective. Something like this occurred during the 17th century in works dominated by the eclectic preoccupation of reconciling distinct philosophical ''sects.'' During the 18th century and the early part of the 19th, preoccupation with criticism was reflected in plans to apply it to the history of philosophy, and yet there was wanting a solid basis of information. The ENCYCLOPEDISTS contributed the concept of unity, continuity, and progress in the process of historical development. Despite his apriorism, Hegel took a very important step toward presenting philosophical systems as included within the framework of universal history, as stages in the dialectical development of the absolute spirit.

The greatest step, however, in the scientific study of history in all its branches started during the middle of the 19th century and was based upon a critical and objective investigation of facts and documents, upon attaining an ever greater freedom from fantasies and a priori interpretations. From this period date the great general histories of philosophy, completed with innumerable monographic studies on personages and schools. The result bas been a moving revelation of the process involved in the formation and development of philosophy, itself a magnificent conquest attained by the efforts of the human mind as these efforts have been multiplied over the span of centuries.

See Also: HISTORY, PHILOSOPHY OF; HISTORY, THEOLOGY OF.

Bibliography: F. C. COPLESTON, *History of Philosophy,* (Westminster, Md. 1946). F. UEBERWEG, *Grundriss der Geschichte der Philosophie,* ed. K. PRAECHTER et al., 5 v. (12th ed. Berlin 1923–28). N. PETRUZZELLIS, *Enciclopedia filosofica* 2:415–419; 4:982–993. G. FRAILE, *Historia de la filosofía* (*Biblioteca de autores cristianos* 160, 190; 1956–), esp. v.1. W. WINDELBAND, *History of Philosophy,* 2 v. (Torchbks; New York 1958). E. VON ASTER, *Geschichte der Philosophie* (11th ed. Stuttgart 1956), Fr. (Paris 1952).

[G. FRAILE]

ANCIENT PHILOSOPHY

By ancient philosophy is meant primarily ancient Western philosophy from its beginnings among the Greeks on the Ionian coast of Asia Minor to its last manifestation in Neoplatonism. At the same time, ancient philosophy rightly includes those forms of Chinese and Indian thought that contain elements of philosophical thinking under a moralistic or religious exterior.

Origins of philosophy. The desire to know, begotten by wonder at the marvels of nature, said Plato (*Theaet.* 155) and Aristotle (*Meta.* 980a 22), led men to philosophize. Not all human thought is by its very nature philosophical; but as men began to penetrate into the deeper nature of things and to seek by reason the most basic causes of what they knew by experience, they became philosophers. Thus philosophy, at least among the Greeks, stood in marked contrast to credulous acceptance of the theogonies and mythological cosmologies, the time-worn traditions of the race embodied in the poets Homer and Hesiod. These ancient teachers of Greece often spoke the truth, but they used the language of belief, not of proof (cf. Aristotle, *Meta.* 1000a 19). GREEK PHILOSOPHY emerged as a conscious reaction to such dogmatism, when men took experience, rather than tradition, as the starting point of their thought.

Only with the Greeks did ancient philosophy reach consciousness of its nature as a rational investigation of things. In contrast, the philosophical thought of the East remained hidden in religious beliefs or in the traditions of national culture. The ''Great Master'' of CHINESE PHILOSOPHY, K'ung or CONFUCIUS, was content to ''transmit and comment on the teachings of the ancients,'' without inventing anything new in his ethical reform. LAOZI, perhaps, was more metaphysical in his Way (DAOISM), yet even this was primarily a mystical-philosophical exposition of the principles that should govern one's moral life. Much more rational was the INDIAN PHILOSOPHY of the Brahmans, since the Upanishads formulate a speculative system that is essentially metaphysical. But it was elaborated by the priestly caste primarily as a wisdom of salvation, a quest for union with a higher being; and as such, endowed with the attributes of a religion. Like Brahmanism, of which it is a corruption, BUDDHISM proposed an anthropocentric philosophy of self-salvation. The Persian dualism of ZOROASTER was a mixture of religion, mythology, and reason in a non-philosophical form. One can well agree with Diogenes Laertius, an ancient collector of facts and fables on the philosophers: ''Thus it was from the Greeks that philosophy took its rise; its very name refuses to be translated into foreign speech'' (1:4).

Early Greek philosophy. If the Greek quest for philosophical wisdom showed a marked reaction to myth and uncritical tradition, it did not thereby represent a break with the general culture of the race. The Greek regard for the individual and his personal freedom and for the ideals of παιδεία, i.e., the shaping and educating of man to his true form, was constantly reflected in the philosophers. Of equal and even greater importance, perhaps, was the Greek feeling for the whole, an architectonic sense that looked for the bond that integrates individuals and events into a greater unity: the ἁρμονία, the ''golden chains'' (*Iliad* 8:18–26) that bind all things together. For Plato, the philosopher must be synoptic, since he is to see particulars together in one Idea; for Aristotle, even the study of man is to show how he is a part in relation to the whole (*Pol.* 1252a 24–1253a 38).

In different degrees this ideal pervaded Greek philosophy in all its history. In what is called the pre-Socratic period, for all their lisping thought (Aristotle, *Meta.* 993a 16), the early thinkers were searching for the one source; the φύσις or nature, whence come the scattered particulars of everyday experience. The first to do this were the ''physicists'' of Ionia, in the 7th and 6th centuries B.C., viz, Thales, Anaximander, and Anaximenes. Though each gave a different answer—Thales, water; Anaximander, the boundless or unlimited; and Anaximenes, air—all held to one principle, a φύσις, from which things evolve. More obscure, perhaps, was the thought of PYTHAGORAS and his followers, who studied the φύσις in terms of number. Yet this, too, was a search for the harmony and inner unity of the cosmos.

Two later thinkers, HERACLITUS and PARMENIDES, were inclined to brush this earlier thinking aside as failing to penetrate by reason (λόγος) behind the world of ceaseless change to discover that which truly is. Not the philosopher of pure becoming (despite the judgment of Plato and Aristotle), Heraclitus was primarily a teacher of moral wisdom who discerned behind the physical world and human life an all-abiding, all-ruling law or λόγος as the principle of unity amidst universal change and opposition. The physical world process interested Heraclitus chiefly as an illustration of this law, that men might learn from the order of the cosmos to order their own lives. In contrast, Parmenides was exclusively the physicist whose epic poem concentrated on the reality, the being (''that which is''), of the physical world, in opposition to current illusions on the nature of the universe. Reason alone, not sense knowledge or the traditions and ''opinions of mortals,'' must be man's instrument in penetrating nature. Though a physical philosopher, Parmenides had insight into the basic problem of philosophy, the problem of being: λόγος or reason proves the existent cannot be what one's senses reveal to him, something manifold and in motion; it is rather something whole and indivisible, motionless and perfect. Hence ZENO OF ELEA, his follower, sought to prove that ''there is no many.''

The last of the physicists, EMPEDOCLES, ANAXAGORAS, and DEMOCRITUS, turned from the search for the principle of the universe to study nature as found in ordinary things. To retain Parmenides's position that being alone is, and yet explain obvious motion and change, these thinkers, each in his own way, posited basic unchanging elements whose combination would give rise to the things of experience. Empedocles adopted four basic elements; Anaxagoras, an infinite number of principles; and Democritus and the school of Abdera, unchanging atoms (*see* ATOMISM; MATERIALISM).

Classical period. None of these early philosophers, save Anaxagoras and those of Abdera, lived on the mainland of Greece, much less in Athens. The scene shifted with the coming of the classical period of Greek philosophy, even as philosophy itself passed from concentration on the physical world to the truly metaphysical and universal thought of Plato and Aristotle. In this change the SOPHISTS provided the transition, since they focused attention on man and the city-state. Not philosophers but teachers, whose aim was to prepare men for public life and political activity in the new democracies, the Sophists revitalized παιδεία through a comprehensive cultural program, the beginnings of the liberal arts. Unfortunately, they often emphasized rhetoric and eloquence at the expense of truth. In reaction to their ideal of speaking well, SOCRATES professed a new σοφία, the wisdom of thinking well, a wisdom of the inner man who lived what he thought: the true philosopher. In this he set the pattern for Plato and Aristotle, who as true Socratics and lovers of wisdom sought to penetrate reality and human life to the fullest.

For PLATO, the philosopher is not primarily the metaphysician, though the doctrine of the Ideas is at the heart of his philosophy. He is rather the man liberated by right παιδεία from slavery to the senses, whose life is formed and guided by true knowledge of true being (which is found only in the Ideas). His life is his philosophy, since he has built within himself a city that he rules in peace. He alone is thus fit to rule others: the philosopher-king. To build this inner city, he must pursue true virtue and wisdom: his conduct must not be based on his own opinions but modeled on what is the transcendent "form" of virtue, the Idea of justice, temperance, and the other virtues. Thus does the "man within man," the rational part of the soul, achieve mastery over the less noble elements within him. True knowledge, man soon realizes, is not found in sense experience, since this sense world does not contain true being. Hence he strives for a knowledge derived from the stable and fixed being of things beyond transient phenomena: the world of Forms or Ideas, and comes at last to the best and highest of the Ideas, the Good itself. Philosophy is thus for Plato essentially the life of the spirit, "the culture of the soul," the guide of human life. Of its very nature, it does not give final answers even to the deepest questions, but spurs the philosopher ever upward to a more perfect vision of the absolute.

ARISTOTLE, "the Philosopher," as he has long been known, lacked the lyrical quality that pervades the doctrine of Plato, and was more scientific and coldly logical in the pursuit of knowledge. Yet as a true Socratic, he too did not separate philosophy and life, since philosophy and virtue are means to the well-being of the soul and steps to happiness. As the disciple of Plato, he was convinced that philosophical knowledge is not concerned with the particular sensible, but with the essence of things and their ultimate causes and principles. Against Plato, however, he refused to have recourse to a separate world of Ideas to answer the problem. Man does not start with things only to push them aside as empty of being and intelligibility. Since one says of things that they are, one should rather analyze the very being he attributes to them. This is the first step in a new science of being, which later came to be called metaphysics. But since even the form (εἶδος) of sensibles, which is the primary instance of being within them, is subject to potency and change, one must postulate the existence of suprasensible beings that are actual and imperishable, the heavenly bodies, and find beyond them one perfect principle whose very entity is perfect act. The god of Aristotle is thus an entity "which moves without being moved, being eternal, substance, and actuality," the final cause that produces motion by being desired (*Meta.* 1072a 25). But such a god, whose inner life is self-subsistent thought, has no knowledge of, or care for, the world, which he did not produce and does not govern. It is in terms of such a doctrine on being that Aristotle studies man and soul in his "On the Soul," a treatise that created many problems and spawned a host of commentaries. Since he is not sure that soul or mind survives the body, Aristotle's ethics and politics are earth-bound, pagan, and centered on the perfection of the individual within the city-state. Despite its limitations, however, the doctrine of Aristotle represents the peak of Greek thought. All succeeding philosophers, Greek, Arabian, Christian, and modern, stand in some debt to him (*see* ARISTOTELIANISM).

Post-Aristotelian developments. Greek philosophy after Aristotle reflected, and to some extent caused, a change in Greek political outlook. With the conquests of Alexander the Great, human thought burst the confining limits of the city-state to emphasize the world as a commonwealth and men as members of a world society.

The CYNICS, lesser followers of Socrates, had professed to be cosmopolitans, citizens of the world rather than of a particular city-state. Directly influenced by them, Zeno of Citium (the founder of STOICISM), Cleanthes, and later Chrysippus elaborated a physics whose monistic materialism made of the world a harmonious whole, a city of gods and men. The active principle of this universe, called god, fire, mind, fate, is above all law or λόγος. If such a doctrine recalls Heraclitus, the Stoics gave his teachings some new interpretations. The ethical ideal is a life in agreement with nature, that is, the inexorable law of nature and of the individual. The virtuous man thus conforms his will to the divine reason, in a passionless and calm detachment from all self-love and worldly interests. Even as it sought to answer ethical questions untouched by earlier philosophers, Stoicism attracted many by the nobility of its ideals. Less appealing because more individualistic, EPICUREANISM resembles Stoicism as an ethics based on a monistic physics. Pleasure, less in the hedonist sense of the CYRENAICS than in peace of mind and freedom from pain, formed the goal of EPICURUS. To rid men of fear of the gods and fear of death, he adopted a form of atomism in which the gods have nothing to do with the world or with men, wherein death brings dissolution of soul as well as of body. The SKEPTICISM that marked other Greek thinkers of this period was itself intended to be a step toward happiness.

Further witnesses to the spread of Hellenistic culture are to be found in the JEWISH PHILOSOPHY of PHILO JUDAEUS and in the smattering of philosophy that appeared in the Roman republic and empire. Jewish tradition was marked by a general distrust of reason and philosophy, so that Philo appears as an exception. Not properly a philosopher, he nonetheless sought to develop his religious belief by elements taken from Plato and the Stoics. After him there is little or no speculative thought among the Jews until AVICEBRON, whose *Fons vitae* was manifestly Neoplatonic in inspiration; and Moses MAIMONIDES, whose *Guide for the Perplexed,* written to solve apparent conflicts of faith and reason, is preeminently Aristotelian in spirit. Among the Romans, philosophy was hardly more than a reflection of Greek thought tempered and shaped by the Roman spirit. Stoicism as expounded by SENECA, EPICTETUS, and MARCUS AURELIUS had a special appeal for its rugged moral tone, as a help in forming the good citizen.

Neoplatonism. The last great philosophical movement of pagan antiquity was a revival of PLATONISM reaching its climax in what is now known as NEOPLATONISM. In many instances, the movement was marked by a deeply religious coloring as philosophy came to be used as a medium for union with the divine. Middle Platonism (in Plutarch, Celsus, and others) accented the transcendence of God, multiplied intermediaries between God and the world, contrasted to an extreme the dualism of matter and spirit, and laid great force on revelation, mysticism, and ecstasy. These characteristics carried over into the teachings of PLOTINUS, the first of the Neoplatonists. At the same time, Plotinus drew from Plato, Aristotle, and the Stoics to construct a synthesis that was the last stand of intellectual paganism against the growing appeal of Christianity. His map of the intelligible world, derived from an analysis of human knowledge, was designed to point the way to union with the One, the first principle of all. The school of Plotinus thrived in such disciples as PORPHYRY and PROCLUS; through them, if not through the works of Plotinus himself, it left its mark on patristic culture, in NEMESIUS OF EMESA, PSEUDO-DIONYSIUS, and St. AUGUSTINE. The direct descendants, however, of Plato, Aristotle, and Plotinus were the proponents of ARABIAN PHILOSOPHY.

Ancient philosophy came to a kind of official end in 529, when Justinian banished the philosophers from Athens and confiscated their schools. By that time, however, it had left its mark on Christian thinkers and had produced the new movement of Christian philosophy.

Bibliography: F. C. COPLESTON, *History of Philosophy,* v.1. (Westminster, Md. 1946). F. UEBERWEG, *Grundriss der Geschichte der Philosophie,* ed. K. PRAECHTER et al., 5 v. (12th ed. Berlin 1923–28). I. C. BRADY, *A History of Ancient Philosophy* (Milwaukee 1959). J. OWENS. *A History of Ancient Western Philosophy* (New York 1959), A. H. ARMSTRONG, *An Introduction to Ancient Philosophy* (3rd ed. London 1957). E. ZELLER, *Die Philosophie der Griechen . . . ,* 3 v. in 6 (5th–7th eds. Leipzig 1920–23), W. K. C. GUTHRIE, *A History of Greek Philosophy* (Cambridge, Eng. 1962) v.1.

MEDIEVAL PHILOSOPHY

Christianity is not a philosophy, but a revealed religion, a means of salvation. Yet because it answers many of the same questions asked by philosophy, dialogue and even conflict between these two forms of knowledge was almost inevitable from the beginning of the Christian Era—whether in the early centuries, the period of patristic culture, or later, in the Middle Ages, in what has come to be called scholasticism. Under medieval philosophy, then, we shall consider both periods, that of patristic philosophy and that of scholastic philosophy.

Patristic philosophy. The first dialogue between Christianity and philosophy, held by St. Paul in the Areopagus of Athens (Acts 17.17–34), was an apparent failure, as this new wisdom was ridiculed by the philosophers as foolishness (1 Cor 1.23), an old wives' tale. In succeeding centuries, many philosophers continued to regard Christianity as a specious doctrine of little or no value; some bluntly opposed or attacked it. On their part, many Christians refused to have anything to do with philosophy. For some, as Clement of Alexandria remarks, it was the invention of the devil for the ruin of man. For Tertullian, it was the source of error and heresy: what then has Athens to do with Jerusalem? Did not the blasphemous errors of GNOSTICISM arise from overconfidence in philosophy? Or again, it represented purely human wisdom incapable of teaching the truth; faith alone and the wisdom of Christ were sufficient for the Christian. Perhaps in many this attitude was but part of their wider opposition to secular learning or to anything that savored of the pagan life they had abandoned in accepting Christ.

Greek Fathers. On the other hand, those philosophers and rhetoricians who had been converted to Christianity were not inclined to abandon entirely the wisdom they had acquired by rational methods, but proposed to put it to use in the service of Christianity. An early instance of this new attitude is found in the Greek APOLOGISTS of the 2nd and 3rd centuries, who employed the techniques of rhetoric, law, and philosophy to defend their new-found faith. At the same time, they came to see, as did St. JUSTIN MARTYR and CLEMENT OF ALEXANDRIA, that whatever truth is found in the philosophers is but a fragmentary sharing in divine wisdom; while, in the providence of God, as Clement and EUSEBIUS OF CAESAREA held, Greek philosophy itself is intended to be a preparation for the gospel and a pedagogue to Christ. For Clement, it not only retained this role, as a "preparatory discipline" for those still to be converted; it also had actual value for Christianity itself, in defending the faith from assault and presenting it in such fashion as to win a hearing. Properly used, it perfected the Christian, helping him to understand what he believed and to grow in virtue, thus making him a true Gnostic, a learned and holy man.

Once secular learning had thus been brought into the service of Christ (however poorly Clement may have accomplished this in specific details), the way was open to a greater collaboration of philosophy and Christianity. Yet the approach of ORIGEN was not that of Clement, his master in the School of Alexandria. He was primarily a theologian, one of the most penetrating if daring minds in the history of the Church. He had no use for philosophy for its own sake; rather, he felt the need to know it and use it that he might meet the philosophers of his day on their own grounds and expound Christian dogma to them in their own terms and in relation to current philosophical problems. Often at fault because he went too far in many of his speculations, and the center of a long controversy after his death, Origen nonetheless paved the way for others, who followed his ideals in more orthodox form. Even his adversaries, such as St. METHODIUS OF OLYMPUS, an admirer of Plato, owed him more than they admitted (*see* ORIGEN AND ORIGENISM).

The Origenist controversy was prolonged perhaps because it was related to a deeper problem that faced Christian thought in the 4th century. As the Church gained her freedom and her belief and worship became the state religion, she confronted the problem of absorbing or being absorbed by the culture of HELLENISM: would the empire be Christianized or the Church Hellenized? More than one heresy, e.g., Arianism and Apollinarism, was closely connected with Greek philosophy; more than one churchman, as was said of SYNESIUS OF CYRENE, was more Platonist than Christian. Yet others, such as EPIPHANIUS OF CONSTANTIA, were deadly enemies of all classical culture and Greek philosophy.

A happy balance is to be found in three great thinkers of Cappadocia who share a common love and admiration for Origen: St. GREGORY OF NAZIANZUS, who gave attention to man's knowledge of God in a series of sermons admired by St. Augustine; St. BASIL, who synthesized the cosmological and scientific knowledge of his day, and in a famous letter to his nephews showed how Christians could profitably use the classics; and St. GREGORY OF NYSSA, the best philosopher of the three, who continued his brother Basil's work with a study on man, *De hominis opificio,* the first of its kind among Christian philosophers, and another on death and the Resurrection in manifest imitation of Plato's *Phaedo*. Gregory's influence is apparent in the "On the Nature of Man" of NEMESIUS OF EMESA. A century later (between 500 and 528) the works of the enigmatic PSEUDO-DIONYSIUS the Areopagite made their appearance in Syria, presenting a curious blending of Christian teaching and Neoplatonic thought. The unknown author apparently sought to convert the Neoplatonists and turn their philosophy into a Christian one. Instead, his writings, with the scholia of John of Scythopolis and MAXIMUS THE CONFESSOR, had greater influence among Christians of both East and West. The last of the Greek Fathers to enter the scene, St. JOHN DAMASCENE, summarized Greek patristic thought in his "On the True Faith" and made ample use of Dionysius's doctrines.

Latin Fathers. Among the Latin Fathers before Augustine, one can trace no set pattern. MINUCIUS FELIX composed his *Octavius* in imitation of Cicero, with some dependence on Seneca. TERTULLIAN relied on Soranus the Stoic to explain the nature of the soul and thus fell into materialism. MARIUS VICTORINUS remained a Neoplatonist even after his conversion, since he used that philosophy to help explain the Trinity. On the other hand, St. JEROME forbade Christians even to read the philosophers or poets [*Patrologia Latina* 22 (ed. 1859):385]. Yet without the help derived from the Neoplatonists, St. AUGUSTINE would hardly have achieved a concept of the spiritual, so deeply had he fallen into Manichaean materialism. When he came to the Church, it was not to abandon whatever good he had found in philosophy, but to vindicate its use for the Christian. Whatever truth the philosophers have discovered must be taken away from them by the Christian, to be used in the structure of Christian wisdom (*Doctr. christ.* 2:40:60). Philosophy thus became for Augustine a step in the structure of Christian knowledge—not an independent discipline, but a means of penetrating the truths of the faith. Philosophy was a part of his search for God: "What do I love when I love Thee?" (*Conf.* 10:6); and every branch of philosophy was made to contribute to that search (*Conf.* 10:6–7; *In psalm.* 41:6–8).

After Augustine, in the period marked by the migration of nations, there was little philosophical thought beyond that of Boethius and Cassiodorus. Preeminently the mediator between ancient culture and the Middle Ages, BOETHIUS left his mark on logic, the problem of UNIVERSALS, LIBERAL ARTS, and theology; while CASSIODORUS, author of a *De anima,* introduced learning and intellectual culture into monastic life. St. ISIDORE OF SEVILLE and St. BEDE deserve mention as encyclopedists. In addition, Bede marks a transition to the Middle Ages, since from his monastic tradition came those who would achieve a rebirth of learning in the Carolingian renaissance. (*See* PATRISTIC PHILOSOPHY.)

Scholastic philosophy. Patristic philosophy in almost every instance is the philosophy of men who were Christian in all their thinking, who did not cut philosophy off from faith or seek it for itself and in itself. This tradition was not abandoned in the revival of learning under Charlemagne. ALCUIN and his pupil RABANUS MAURUS continued the ideal of Augustine, making philosophy and secular knowledge the handmaids of faith. At the same time, the court of Charles the Bald witnessed a philosophical controversy on the nature of the soul carried on by RATRAMNUS OF CORBIE and HINCMAR OF REIMS, and was intrigued if not scandalized by the bold thinking and writing of JOHN SCOTUS ERIGENA. Possessed of some knowledge of Greek and widely read in Pseudo-Dionysius, Maximus, and Gregory of Nyssa, as well as in Ambrose and Augustine, John undertook a daring and powerful synthesis of philosophy and theology in his *De divisione naturae,* to show how the multiplicity of things proceeds from the oneness of God and is in turn brought back to Him. Even here, however, philosophy was a meditation on Holy Scripture and the faith, not the exercise of pure reason for its own sake.

Early Scholasticism. Only after Erigena, and partly under his influence, did Western thinkers make any real distinction between philosophy and revealed doctrine, to the extent that they began to cultivate logic or dialectics for its own sake. Called by John Scotus ''the mother of the arts'' and ''the science of disputing well,'' and yet regarded as the science of being (*Patrologia Latina* 122:869–870), dialectics attracted fresh interest in the 11th and 12th centuries and often intruded itself in areas where it had no place (*see* DIALECTICS IN THE MIDDLE AGES). Yet it is here that one finds the real beginnings of the movement known as SCHOLASTICISM, which reached its high point in the 13th century. Often indeed this early scholasticism, as in Peter ABELARD, thought it could answer such metaphysical questions as the nature of UNIVERSALS by the doctrine and method proper to logic, or explain the mysteries of the faith by pure dialectics. At the same time, the sound use of reasoning in LANFRANC of Bec and St. ANSELM OF CANTERBURY opened the way to a wholesome flowering of doctrine in the 12th century. From the school directed by Anselm's pupil, ANSELM OF LAON, came many theologians who by the middle of the century had done much to systematize theology in numerous *Summae* and *Sententiae,* often in imitation and rivalry of Peter Abelard's theological synthesis. The same tendency to summarize theology marked the work of the Parisian School of Saint-Victor, under Masters HUGH OF SAINT-VICTOR and RICHARD OF SAINT-VICTOR, who at the same time were much interested in philosophy and in mysticism. The most complete and most influential of such books of Sentences was that of Master PETER LOMBARD, composed at Paris about 1155 to 1158. Finally, though Paris was gradually becoming the intellectual center of the West, in the early part of the 12th century it was rivaled as a center of philosophy and surpassed as a seat of classical humanism by the School of Chartres. The last and greatest of the pre-university cathedral schools of Europe, under BERNARD OF CHARTRES, GILBERT DE LA PORRÉE, and others, it became known for its feeling for antiquity, its Platonism, and its growing interest in science. Its most perfect representative was perhaps JOHN OF SALISBURY, who at the same time mirrored the learning of Paris and was a witness to the growing importance of its schools.

High Scholasticism. Those schools, organized about 1200 as the guild or ''university of the masters and scholars of Paris,'' prepared the way for the flowering of scholasticism proper in the 13th century. Yet without the influx of new literature and ideas, through the translation of hitherto unknown works of Aristotle and of the Arabian and Jewish philosophers and scientists, the intellectual horizon of the West would never have been broadened beyond the narrow limits of earlier centuries. Nurtured in the Augustinian tradition of Christian wisdom, the schoolmen were suddenly faced with another wisdom that proposed itself to them as the complete embodiment of rational thought. Hesitant at first—sometimes victims of their own enthusiasm as they labored, as said ROBERT GROSSETESTE, to make Aristotle Catholic; sometimes content, with SIGER OF BRABANT, to ''recite'' the opinions of the philosophers whether or not they agreed with the faith—the scholastics came gradually to sift truth from error and to incorporate and integrate these newfound treasures into the body of Christian thought. In this, the lead was often taken by the teachers of the mendicant orders at the direction of the papacy: the DOMINICANS under St. ALBERT THE GREAT and St. THOMAS AQUINAS meeting the problem directly; the FRANCISCANS under St. BONAVENTURE inclining more perhaps to the older tradition, yet ready to accept the truth wherever found. It is the merit and glory of St. Thomas above all that he produced a new synthesis of Christian wisdom in which Aristotle and Arabians alike were brought into captivity to Christ. Not all were willing to accept his work; some bogged down in criticism and correctives; others, such as John DUNS SCOTUS, tried to build a new and stronger synthesis after a reexamination of the problems involved.

Late Scholasticism. With the 14th century, which brought so many religious and political changes and upheavals, scholastic thought became even more critical in character. Metaphysics and its integration into Christian theology no longer occupied the center of attention. Logic received a fresh emphasis and almost usurped the role of metaphysics, as WILLIAM OF OCKHAM initiated what came to be called the ''modern way'' of NOMINALISM. The beginnings of modern physics appeared at Oxford, always most receptive to science, and somewhat at Paris. Yet among the theologians, thought began to crystallize into schools: THOMISM, followers of GILES OF ROME, SCOTISM, and even nominalism. Paris became a city of conflict and confusion, as its intellectual life lost its vitality and degenerated into a mere commentary on the great syntheses of the 13th century.

Yet, while the failings and weaknesses of the scholastics are often much in evidence, they should not obscure the real and solid accomplishments of the movement itself and its effect on European culture. Paris and the many universities modeled upon it contributed to the transformation of Western education and the formation of an intellectual elite that was henceforth to dominate Western culture. From these schools, marked by rigorous use of the art of logical thinking, even more than from the Renaissance, Europe and the West derived the critical intelligence and restless spirit of scientific inquiry that sets Western culture off from the East, and even from other forms of Christian culture, and is the ultimate source of modern science. To label scholasticism a barren system, to call it ''one of the greatest plagues of the human mind'' (Diderot), is to fabricate a calumny that has no foundation in history.

See Also: AUGUSTINIANISM; OCKHAMISM; SCIENCE (IN THE MIDDLE AGES).

Bibliography: É. H. GILSON, *History of Christian Philosophy in the Middle Ages* (New York 1955). F. C. COPLESTON, *History of Philosophy,* v. 3–4 (Westminster, Md. 1953, 1958). F. UEBERWEG, *Grundriss der Geschichte der Philosophie,* ed. K. PRAECHTER et al., 5 v. (11th, 12th ed. Berlin 1923–28). P. DELHAYE, *Medieval Christian Philosophy,* tr. S. J. TESTER (New York 1960). A. A. MAURER, *Medieval Philosophy* (New York 1962). D. KNOWLES, *The Evolution of Medieval Thought* (Baltimore 1962).

[I. C. BRADY]

MODERN PHILOSOPHY

The time span of modern philosophy reaches from about 1400 to 1900, although there is no sharp division setting it off from either its medieval roots or its contemporary fruits. The whole development includes three main phases: the Renaissance transition (1400–1600), the classical modern methods and systematic explanations (1600–1800), and the 19th-century attempts at philosophical reconstruction. Each period makes a distinctive contribution to the process. The painful work of producing fresh ideas and attitudes begins in the Renaissance age, whose transitional character is marked by the intermingling of old and new elements and by the tentative nature of the philosophies. There follows a two-century spurt of great creativity in all parts of philosophy, with the emphasis placed upon new methodologies and systematic unifications of knowledge. Many deep divisions kept recurring, however, thus provoking the 19th century to search for broader bases of synthesis between evolving nature and historical man.

Modern philosophy does not grow in isolation from the other modern cultural factors. The national context is seen in the widespread use of vernacular languages, with a technical vocabulary being forged for philosophy in each linguistic area. Modern philosophy is unusually sensitive also to the methods, concepts, and problems evolved in the physical and biological sciences. Another mark of philosophical modernity is its dissociation from any particular theological framework, even though religious faith and its attendant questions continue to have a definite bearing on philosophical inquiries. Moreover, the modern growth in historical awareness leads to a special philosophical interest in genetic questions and human historicity.

Renaissance philosophy. Cardinal NICHOLAS OF CUSA embodied the early Renaissance disenchantment with the medieval systems, its epistemological uneasiness, and its special concern to rethink man's relations with God and the world. Although religious faith held firm his conviction in God's reality and creative power, he shifted the inquiry about God from a causal basis to a symbolical use of concepts similar to the mathematical way of dealing with infinite figures. Thus Nicholas heralded the appeal of modern philosophical methodology to the procedures in mathematics and physics, as well as the modern dialectical correlation between God and a world regarded as His expressive image and locus for constant social reforms.

A form of Christian humanism was developed by the Florentine humanists M. FICINO and PICO DELLA MIRANDOLA. They strongly defended man's freedom, personal immortality, and ordination to beatitude in God, against the attacks of the Aristotelians at Padua. P. POMPONAZZI and other Renaissance Aristotelians removed the Christian interpretation of Aristotle's view of man, nature, and the prime mover, thus hastening the separation of philosophy from theology. Their strongest work was done in the fields of logic and the philosophy of nature, where they influenced Galileo on method.

Renaissance Stoicism and SKEPTICISM arose from a continued dissatisfaction with all current accounts of human knowledge and conduct. J. LIPSIUS urged that Platonism was too cabalistic; that pure Aristotelianism ran counter to faith in a personal, free, transcendent God and beatitude; and that a sounder view was obtainable from Stoic logic, physics, and ethics. The really radical challenge came, however, from the reformulation of Greek skepticism by MONTAIGNE and P. CHARRON. They produced a crisis by regarding man's knowing powers as unreliable, by pointing out the large mixture of fantasy and wish in human speculations, and by pitting one philosophical school against another. Right down to P. BAYLE, the skeptical attitude remained strong, thus providing a spur for the great systematic thinkers in the 17th century.

Three other facets of the Renaissance mind are captured in the thought of N. MACHIAVELLI, G. BRUNO, and the philosophers of nature. Machiavelli placed brackets around the social precepts of Christianity and took the attitude of the inquiring scientist toward the realities of political life. His stark findings on the drive toward power and the political management of men pointed up the need for a relevant and yet morally disciplined political philosophy. Bruno's pantheism expressed a passionate desire to comprehend and unite oneself with total cosmic reality, but it was hampered by taking the substance-and-mode relationship as regulative for explaining the relation between God and the world. Although B. TELESIO and T. CAMPANELLA took a qualitative and quasi-magical approach to nature, they testified to the need to understand it better and to reorder social life in new ways.

The counterpoint to all these movements was the steady current of Renaissance SCHOLASTICISM, which continued to achieve new forms. This was the period of the great commentaries on St. Thomas Aquinas, the new developments in the law of nations and colonial moral problems, and eventually the shift to the teaching manual as the main instrument of tradition. (*See* RENAISSANCE PHILOSOPHY.)

Systematic philosophies. The impetus for the great 17th-century systems came largely from the effort of the mechanical philosophers and Descartes to counterbalance skepticism with a positive theory of nature and man. A modest role was played by F. BACON, even though he did not appreciate the primary lead of mathematics in the study of nature. He gave a new rhetoric to the age by codifying the criticism of scholastic philosophy of nature, by directing attention to the moving efficient causes, and by raising doubts about whether philosophy can say anything about God and the spiritual principle in man. But it was GALILEO himself who regarded nature as a divinely grounded system of mathematical intelligibilities and who bifurcated the primary qualities in nature and the secondary qualities in the perceiver. And although Sir Isaac NEWTON was less confident about the ontological import of mathematical rules, he worked out their explanatory functions with unsurpassed thoroughness.

But how does man fare in the mechanically ordered universe? Divergent responses were given to this leading question by T. HOBBES and R. DESCARTES. The Englishman's importance lay as much in his presuppositions as in his particular doctrines. For he developed the always attractive procedure of generalizing the dominant scientific outlook and, at least in principle, confining the philosophical analysis of man to what is attainable through this generalized method. Descartes agreed that man can fare very well indeed in the mechanically constituted universe, but only on condition that the mechanical conception of nature be integrated with an adequate theory of method, knowing, and being. By ''adequate,'' he meant one that can meet the skeptical challenge better than do either the older realism or the newer MECHANISM. Descartes sought to combine mechanism with a reflective metaphysics of the self and God in so firmly grounded and closely knit a system that skepticism would be eliminated and the Christian faith would be liberated from an outmoded philosophy of nature.

During the second half of the 17th century, the Cartesian school was plagued by the breakdown of the unity of man, by the recrudescence of skeptical doubts over the relation between evidential reality and clear and distinct ideas, and by the eventual substitution of the Newtonian for the Cartesian physics (*see* CARTESIANISM). The great rationalists—B. SPINOZA, N. MALEBRANCHE, and G. W. LEIBNIZ—found it necessary to begin all over again with fresh principles of metaphysical speculation adapted to life's moral ends. Spinoza laid stress on the purgative and reforming functions of the theory of method, which had to bring the finite human intelligence to the point of regarding man as a composite modal modification and dynamic expression of the unique and powerful divine substance. The other side of the modern debate between monistic naturalism and pluralistic theism was taken by Malebranche and Leibniz, who defended the reality of many finite substances and volitional centers as being related to the personal God. All three thinkers agreed, however, that man can attain to metaphysical principles of certitude, that the crux of systematic explanation lies in the theory of human unity, and that the entire speculative effort deeply affects the moral reordering of human life and the search for happiness.

Historians of philosophy rightly caution against making a rigid contrast between Continental RATIONALISM and British EMPIRICISM. The two groups share many problems and presuppositions, especially on the direct ordering of the mind to its ideas and mental states and on the basic use of the method of analysis. Each group strives in its own way to blend experience and reason, the scientific view of nature and the life of reflective mind. Still, some characteristic emphases distinguish them on how to achieve this blending of the components in human life. The empiricists are much less confident about metaphysical principles and the dependence of moral judgment upon a metaphysical account of the God-man relationship.

Another salutary warning from the historians is to respect J. LOCKE, G. BERKELEY, and D. HUME in their quite distinct intellectual configurations, rather than to blur them together in a close series. The important thing about Locke is that he tempered all claims made for the human understanding with a caution born from his training as a physician and his observation of the nonmathematical methods of R. Boyle and T. Sydenham. Berkeley's immaterialism combined a delicate sensitivity to the skeptical objections on man's knowledge of the world with a reflective personal grasp of the relations between God and participant minds. Hume cut out his own path between skepticism and Newtonian science by making the study of human nature and associative beliefs the central theme for theoretical and moral philosophy.

The minor philosophical movements in the 17th and 18th centuries constituted an influential cultural background for the main endeavors. Among the lesser British thinkers must be counted the CAMBRIDGE PLATONISTS with their rational theology, the Deists ranging from mild minimalists in religion to virulent opponents of revelation (*see* DEISM), and the SCOTTISH SCHOOL OF COMMON SENSE, which tried to break out of the skeptical impasse and the Humean restriction of knowledge to perceptual objects and associative beliefs. The French and German Enlightenment embraced a broad spectrum of positions, ranging from the minimal rational THEISM of Voltaire and Mendelssohn to the naturalistic ATHEISM of Holbach and Diderot, and on to Rousseau's plan for educating man through the moral sentiments (*see* ENLIGHTENMENT, PHILOSOPHY OF).

The great genius of I. KANT was to transcend these Enlightenment divisions and renew the main philosophical task of integrating experience and reason. Unconvinced by metaphysics in the dogmatic form proposed by C. WOLFF, Kant worked out a critical method for inspecting the structure of human judgments and the a priori principles involved in the several domains of human activity: Newtonian science of nature, moral rules, biological research, aesthetic appreciation, religious belief, and the taming of political power. Kant reserved knowledge in the strictest sense for man's scientific grasp of phenomenal objects and for a metaphysical reflection upon the structure and principles of the mind. But he looked upon man as the active unifier of knowledge with the other uses of the mind in areas of belief and reflective judgment. (*See* KANTIANISM.)

19th century. Kant's synthesis of freedom and nature was too precarious to last, since it rested upon a dualism of self and appearances that provoked the search for a closer kind of unity in human experience. Philosophical ROMANTICISM flourished in Germany upon the demand for a principle of synthesis drawn from the inner life of the self and an imaginative view of nature. The drive of men such as F. von BAADER and F. SCHLEGEL was to expand the scope of vital intuition and to give greater play to the wisdom of the imagination and the passions, as aids in mastering the sharp contrasts in life. On the theological side, F. D. E. SCHLEIERMACHER emphasized man's basic feeling of dependence upon a superior power as furnishing the very springs of religious belief.

The German idealists were then confronted with the need to join Kant's methodic control over concepts with the romantics' feel for the unity and divinity of life. J. G. FICHTE made the fruitful suggestion that all phases of reality and thought respond to a common pattern of positional thesis, counterpositional antithesis, and resolving synthesis, and that they do so respond because this threefold pattern is the graven law of the absolute ego and its activity. F. W. J. SCHELLING tested this hypothesis from two sides, starting first from nature in order to reach spirit, and then proceeding in reverse from spirit to nature. But it required the surpassing mind of G. W. F. HEGEL to work out the dialectical development of spirit in all modes of experience. He interpreted all oppositions as expressing the tragic life of spirit. The creative travail of spirit shapes the logical sphere, the domain of nature, and especially the human world of psychic life and morality, history and art, religion and philosophy, as the encompassing system of knowledge. (*see* IDEALISM.)

Hegel's awesome synthesis seemed to be suffocating, however, to S. A. KIERKEGAARD as a religious critic and to L. FEUERBACH and K. MARX as naturalistic critics. They all agreed upon the need to deflate the theory of absolute spirit by referring it back to the human exister and agent. Where a new parting of the ways occurred was over how best to describe the existence and agency of man. Kierkegaard located these perfections primarily in the free individual, taken in his search for happiness, his moral responsibility, and his religious faith in the transcendent personal God. The other aspect of the human situation was explored by Feuerbach and Marx, for whom man is not fully real except in his social relations with other men and the natural world. Marx and F. ENGELS laid special stress upon the activity of work, the historical law of class struggle, and the vision of a classless society—the main tenets of communism or dialectical and historical MATERIALISM.

Two varieties of POSITIVISM were advanced by A. COMTE and J. S. MILL. Comte aimed at joining the search for the unity of knowledge with the social aspirations aroused by the French Revolution. Hence his objective synthesis ordered all the positive sciences, whereas his subjective synthesis placed these sciences at the disposal of man's moral aims and the positivist religion. Mill was soberly critical of this latter phase, since he was prolonging the empiricist analysis of knowledge and the utilitarian calculus of social happiness. Hence he allied positivism with his logic of science and his defense of human liberty in the democratic society.

Throughout the century, there was a strong attraction toward the philosophy of life. Its early version was advanced by A. SCHOPENHAUER, who taught the universal presence of a relentless will to live. He sought surcease from this drive partly in aesthetic contemplation and partly in ascetic denial of self. After Darwin's work on evolution appeared, the philosophy of life became expressly evolutionary. Whether it should merely echo biology or become a general cosmology and new morality was a disturbing question for F. W. NIETZSCHE. Within his conception of the will to power and the eternal cycle of becoming, there was no room left for God and an absolute standard of truth and morality. A paradoxical split opened between this philosophy and the religious view of God as the source of all life and truth.

Minor currents during the first part of the century included TRADITIONALISM and ONTOLOGISM, which based certitude on social transmission and a concept of being. In the latter part, there was a revival of Kantianism and a spread of idealism beyond Germany (*see* NEO-KANTIANISM).

Bibliography: G. BOAS, *Dominant Themes of Modern Philosophy* (New York 1957). É. BRÉHIER, *La Philosophie moderne,* v.2 of *Histoire de la philosophie,* 2 v. (Paris 1926–32). A. R. CAPONIGRI, *Renaissance to the Romantic Age* (A History of Western Philosophy 3; Chicago 1963); J. D. COLLINS, *A History of Modern European Philosophy* (Milwaukee 1954). F. C. COPLESTON, *History of Philosophy* v.3–7 (Westminster, Md. 1953, 1958, 1959, 1963). B. A. G. FULLER, *A History of Modern Philosophy,* v.2 of *A History of Philosophy,* ed. S. M. MCMURRIN, 2 v. (3rd ed. New York 1955). É. GILSON and T. LANGAN, *Modern Philosophy: Descartes to Kant* (New York 1963); *Recent Philosophy: Hegel to the Present* (New York 1966). H. HØFFDING, *A History of Modern Philosophy,* tr. R. E. MEYER, 2 v. (New York 1950). R. KRONER, *Speculation and Revelation in Modern Philosophy* (Philadelphia 1961). J. H. RANDALL, *The Career of Philosophy: From the Middle Ages to the Enlightenment* (New York 1962); *From the Enlightenment to the Nineteenth Century* (New York 1965).

[J. D. COLLINS]

TWENTIETH CENTURY

There is a narrower and a broader meaning for the expression ''contemporary philosophy.'' In the narrower and highly fluid sense, it signifies those problems and positions that are at the center of interest and discussion in a specific situation at present. In a broader way, contemporary philosophy includes the major currents active in the 20th century and relevant for its continued inquiries. The latter is the working historical meaning, being comprehensive enough to include the significant prolongations of previous philosophies as well as the basically new approaches developed in the 20th century. There are some special difficulties in studying contemporary philosophy: the sifting process has not gone on long enough to distinguish clearly between the weight of argument and cultural influences; the perspective is not fully attained for setting off the major from the minor, but temporarily impressive, contributions; and not all the systematic consequences have been worked out sufficiently to measure a philosophy in the round. However, the main lines of 20th-century development can be charted and the most prominent landmarks indicated.

Life philosophies. The theme of life was prolonged in the direction of man's interior activities by H. BERGSON, and in the direction of cultural unities by W. DILTHEY. In order to countervail the positivistic reduction of life processes to physical laws, Bergson cited the difference between the physicalist meaning of time as discrete movements along a spatial line and the reflective human meaning of time as interior duration. This opened up a metaphysical view of evolution as a striving toward freedom, and of human social life as a tension between the closed system of morality and religion and the open attitude best exhibited by the Christian mystics. Thereafter, P. TEILHARD DE CHARDIN gave a theistic and personalistic interpretation of the evolutionary character of life. The surge of life is at once from God in a creative outpouring and toward God in function of man's ability to concentrate the streams of life in order to advance, in community form, to the divine spiritual goal of the entire universe.

What impressed Dilthey was that human life finds its expression not solely in the individual's spiritual striving but also in the various modes of cultural activity. In a given historical period, these cultural modes of artistic, scientific, religious, and political life unite in a pattern, sometimes called the tone or spirit or characteristic outlook of the age. Dilthey made two methodological findings: the cultural pattern in history discloses itself better to the procedure of sympathetic understanding than to either the positivist sort of physical-causal explanation or the Hegelian dialectic of absolute spirit; and the great differences between one cultural outlook and another can be studied in terms of a common set of humane categories. The method of sympathetic understanding and categorical analysis of the expressive cultural forms was applied to the areas of language, myth, and science by E. CASSIRER. And it was related to the individual existent's free interpretation of his destiny by J. ORTEGA Y GASSET. (*See* LIFE PHILOSOPHIES; HISTORY, PHILOSOPHY OF).

Idealism. During the first part of the century, idealism flourished in England, the U.S., and Italy. Among the British idealists, B. Bosanquet wrote persuasively about the ideal and absolute factor in art and the tension in practical life between absolute standards and particular situations. The most powerful mind was F. H. BRADLEY, who used the principle that the absolute is the totality of experience to argue for the ultimate internality of all relations, the constant breakdown of perceptual objects and empirical facts in the field of appearance, and the reality of the one undivided life of the absolute. Nevertheless, he denied any direct knowledge of the absolute reality as the union of all differences, and stressed the relative nature of the particular theoretical and practical standards that men do determine in experience.

In the U.S., J. ROYCE strove to accommodate evolutionary science and modern logic within idealism by exploring the dynamic, intentional relationship between an idea and its fulfilling meaning. He compared the bond between finite individuals and the absolute self to that between the living components in an interpreting system and the whole system or community of interpretation itself. On the moot question of preserving the reality of the human selves, Royce was criticized by such personal idealists as G. H. Howison and E. S. BRIGHTMAN (*see* PERSONALISM). Personal idealism emphasized the distinction between the personal God and finite persons, although it added that the divine nature itself contains both infinite and finite aspects to account for the presence of evil.

The leading Italian idealists were B. CROCE and G. GENTILE. Croce identified philosophy with history, because the former is a reflection upon the very process of spirit that internally constitutes the latter. He also revived the systematic claims of idealism by following the course of spirit through the theoretical realms of aesthetic and logical expression and the practical realms of economic and moral activity. Act was the key to reality for Gentile, who worked out a theory of actualism extending from logic to education.

Philosophy of the spirit. There was a loose association between several French and Italian thinkers who examined the life of the spirit apart from the Hegelian framework, in order to preserve unequivocally the integrity of the human person and his religious relation to the personal God. M. BLONDEL accepted from the philosophy of life a stress upon striving interior action, and from the idealists a respect for the interrelatedness of all domains of thought and reality. In his own synthesis, the philosophical inquiry remained open to the initiative of divine revelation. This inductive spiritual notion of Christian philosophy exerted an appeal upon M. F. Sciacca. But the renewed need to consider the fundamental philosophical issues in knowledge, metaphysics, and the growing theory of values was felt strongly by L. Lavelle and R. Le Senne. They exhibited the resources of the spiritualist position in penetrating downward into human experience at the levels of perception, ontological participation, and moral activity. (*See* SPIRIT)

American philosophy. American philosophy came of age with the impact of evolutionary thought, the interest it aroused in scientific method, and the questions left unanswered by the idealistic interpretation of evolution, science, and morality. C. S. PEIRCE emphasized the role of the idea of consequences in determining a particular scientific concept. He also examined the scientific attitude of unrestricted fallibilism, as well as the abductive method whereby the scientific mind develops fruitful new hypotheses. Against the antimetaphysical bias of positivism, he proposed a theory of the categories and a description of reality in terms of chance, continuity, and love. PRAGMATISM as a theory of meaning and truth was popularized by William JAMES. He argued that a pluralistic and melioristic universe, complete with a developing God, is not only more stimulating to man's moral fiber but also closer to the truth about being. The test of practice remained ambiguous in his hands, however, because of the difficulty of distinguishing between the satisfaction and the validation of ideas.

NATURALISM arose as a way of meeting this difficulty without returning to the idealistic absolute. The version proposed by G. SANTAYANA rested on the dictum that everything ideal has a real basis in the natural material world, and everything real has an ideal mode of fulfillment in the order of imagination. Santayana viewed the human spirit as a constant act of transition from matter to imagination and back again, and reduced religion to a refined filtering of aspirations by the play of imagination. Even so, the verdict of J. Dewey was that Santayana flirted so perilously with transcendence that he ended with a broken-backed dualism. Dewey's own naturalism aimed at being antidualistic in respect to the soul-body and God-world distinctions, and yet antireductionist in respect to the evolutionary levels of experience. He identified the knowable real with the totality of nature that can be investigated by the scientific method. This placed considerable weight upon the logic of scientific inquiry, which Dewey patterned after the biological relation of organism to environment and which he applied to man's artistic, social, and moral experience.

Since his main philosophical work was done in the U.S., A. N. WHITEHEAD belongs in American philosophy. He mounted a sustained attack upon the empiricist bifurcation of nature into causal factors and those that appear in the mind, as well as upon the empiricist disruption of causal relations in experience. His own philosophy of process and of organism was a speculative theory combining cosmological and metaphysical features. It revolved around the concrescence of "actual entities" and their dynamic togetherness in weaving "eternal objects" and achieving constant novelty. The systematic consequences of Whitehead's process philosophy were worked out for the various domains of experience in the metaphysical realism of P. Weiss.

Logical positivism. As originally propounded in the Vienna Circle consisting of M. Schlick, R. Carnap, and O. Neurath, LOGICAL POSITIVISM had the threefold task of analyzing the basic kinds of propositions that give knowledge, of determining a criterion of verification for these basic types, and of achieving the unification of the sciences. The first task resolved itself into a rigid distinction between the analytic, a priori propositions found in logic and mathematics and the synthetic or empirical propositions expressing sense data. The second step was to reduce all cognitive meaning to what can be verified through a formal test or a purely empirical test. And the third step was to use the language of physics as the basis of unification of the sciences, regarding every proposition that resisted such reduction as being metaphysical, in the pejorative sense of having neither formal nor empirical cognitive meaning.

Although this plan was simplicity itself, it ran into trouble when A. J. Ayer popularized it in England. The sharp contrast between the analytic and the empirical was attacked, the verification principle was weakened to several modes of verifiability in principle, and the physical language was discovered to contain unexpected contributions of mind. Both Ayer and H. Feigl moved on to broader conceptions of empiricism.

Analytical philosophy. The British school of analysis built upon the pioneer work of G. E. Moore and B. RUSSELL. What counted most in Moore's refutation of idealism was his method of moving from metaphysical justification to clarification of what is already known. His positive analysis of perceptual and moral problems took of piecemeal approach, fastened upon ordinary modes of discourse, and ferreted out the logical kinds of questions and reasons involved in commonsense talk. Russell's collaboration with Whitehead not only led to modern mathematical logic but also suggested ways of overcoming misleading expressions. His theory of types and descriptions led Russell to distinguish between the apparent and the real logical form of a proposition, to construct ideal languages out of known entities, and thus to devise a metaphysically neutral method of handling the traditional puzzles.

WITTGENSTEIN, the leading analyst, regarded philosophy as an activity of elucidation rather than as a theory. He proposed to dissolve rather than solve metaphysical theories about the world by showing that they arose from a misunderstanding of the structure and limits of language or from an attempt to express that which cannot be expressed in language but only shown by contrast with what is sayable. Eventually, Wittgenstein concentrated on the rules for particular language games and the particular meanings determined by such uses. J. Wisdom and the Cambridge school took a therapeutic approach to metaphysical conflicts, whereas G. Ryle and J. L. Austin at Oxford stressed plural usages, category mistakes, and good reasons.

Phenomenology. E. HUSSERL took the first step toward founding PHENOMENOLOGY with his critique of psychologism, or the attempt of J. S. Mill and C. Sigwart to reduce logical meanings to psychic occurrences and their conditions. He distinguished between the act of judging as a psychic phenomenon and the judgmental content or structure of meaning itself. After also criticizing naturalism and historicism for failing to distinguish between the context and the validity of thought, Husserl sought to make philosophy a rigorous science. He put brackets around the natural attitude of unquestioning acceptance of the world, developed descriptive and reductional techniques for examining the essential structure of things (acts and objects), and traced meanings back to the transcendental ego and its constitution of self and world.

M. SCHELER and M. MERLEAU-PONTY developed phenomenology in the moral-religious and the psychological spheres respectively. Scheler found a corrective for ETHICAL FORMALISM in the careful study of actual states of soul and attitudes. He used the theory of intentionality to examine the religious believer's ordination to God, as well as his self-realization through prayer and love of neighbor. His research was distracted, however, by an evolutionary pantheism in which God and man evolve together in life. Such speculations were foreign to Merleau-Ponty, who made phenomenology speak the language of perception again, in order to locate reality in the mutual relation between man and the world. He used the theme of the living body and man's relation to his life world as a means of regulating the sciences and of vindicating the act of human interpretation of visible reality.

Existentialism. The existentialists made their own return to the existent reality of man, partly to liberate him from being a modalized phase of the idealistic absolute, partly to recover the sense of freedom and moral decision, and partly to gain orientation for the study of being. But each of them made a distinctive development and came eventually to resist classification along with the others.

K. JASPERS and G. MARCEL maintained a threefold kinship. They were highly critical of the depersonalizing effect of technological civilization; they regarded the free human existent as being related to transcendence as well as to the world; and they recognized the limiting effect of life situations upon the project of reaching God. Marcel worked out a theory of recollection and participation in being whereby the human searcher is united to God, whereas Jaspers remained fundamentally ambiguous about this relationship. For J. P. SARTRE's part, both the social and the religious projects of man are unavoidable and yet doomed to frustration. Sartre based this conclusion on a sharply dualistic theory of matter and consciousness in man, reminiscent of the idealistic thesis and antithesis taken in isolation from any unifying principle. M. HEIDEGGER's route led him backward from things-that-are to being, from technology to the pre-Socratic grasp of nature, and from the long philosophical tradition to the act of thinking in which being can perhaps be enshrined. His analyses of being in the world, being along with others, and being related to instruments and to integral things, were clues to the metaphysics of being for which he sought. (*See* EXISTENTIALISM.)

Scholasticism. In the wake of the papal recommendations after Leo XIII's *Aeterni Parris,* there was a quickening of traditional Christian philosophies. The historical labors of M. GRABMANN and M. DE WULF restored knowledge of the medieval philosophies, a task carried on by É. GILSON, who also gave special place to St. Thomas Aquinas. J. MARITAIN's work was to bring THOMISM into living relation with modern problems in science, art, and society. The task of rethinking the scholastic heritage was continued in all areas of thought. (*See* SCHOLASTICISM, 3.)

Bibliography: J. L. BLAU, *Men and Movements in American Philosophy* (New York 1952). I. M. BOCHEŃSKI, *Contemporary European Philosophy,* tr. D. NICHOLL and K. ASCHENBRENNER (Berkeley 1956). J. D. COLLINS, *Three Paths in Philosophy* (Chicago 1962). F. C. COPLESTON, *Contemporary Philosophy* (Westminster, Md. 1956). A. DONDEYNE, *Contemporary European Thought and Christian Faith,* tr. E. MCMULLIN and J. BURNHEIM (Pittsburgh 1958). J. FERRATER MORA, *Philosophy Today* (New York 1960). A. W. LEVI, *Philosophy and the Modern World* (Bloomington, Ind. 1959). J. A. PASSMORE, *A Hundred Years of Philosophy* (New York 1957). *The Library of Living Philosophers,* ed. P. A. SCHILPP (Evanston, Ill. 1939), separate volumes on Broad, Buber, Carnap, Cassirer, Dewey, Einstein, Jaspers, Lewis, Moore, Radhakrishnan, Russell, Santayana, and Whitehead. V. E. SMITH, *Idea-Men of Today* (Milwaukee 1950). H. SPIEGELBERG, *The Phenomenological Movement: A Historical Introduction,* 2 v. (The Hague 1960). M. F. SCIACCA, *Philosophical Trends in the Contemporary World,* 2 v. (Notre Dame, Ind. 1964).

[J. D. COLLINS]

PHILOSOPHY AND SCIENCE

Prior to the 19th century, the philosophy of nature and natural science were one and the same discipline (*see* PHILOSOPHY OF NATURE). Their union dates back to Greek antiquity, when Aristotle considered as a single science what are now called the philosophy of nature, cosmology, chemistry, and biology. Such a unified view of philosophy and science survives in the title of Isaac Newton's masterwork *The Mathematical Principles of Natural Philosophy* (1687) and, more than a century later, in John Dalton's *A New System of Chemical Philosophy* (3 v., 1808, 1810, 1827). Contrasted to the "mathematical philosophy" fostered by Newton was another study, "experimental philosophy." These mathematical, chemical, and experimental philosophies, as they were then called, are today considered as science—a term that, with the foundation of the British Academy of Science in 1831, came into vogue to designate modern physics, chemistry, biology, and related disciplines.

Status before Kant. The separation of science and philosophy and the restriction of the term science—which Aristotle had used in a sense broad enough to include his philosophy of nature—must also be viewed against the background of modern philosophy (*see* PHILOSOPHY, HISTORY OF). Aristotle had applied the term physics to the single science of nature whose parts are listed above, and contrasted this with another science subsequently called METAPHYSICS. Aristotle's physical science was a project to explain material realities in terms of the four causes: MATTER, FORM, AGENT, and END. But the philosophers Francis BACON and René DESCARTES restricted the scope of physics. Bacon held that the concern with form and end belonged to metaphysics; Descartes, removing from physics the concern with FINAL CAUSALITY, conceived the world of nature as a machine and identified the physical with the mechanical. These developments, which had great influence, effectively destroyed the philosophy of nature as a physical science, leaving the material world to be studied only in the spirit of those subjects officially labeled science in the Anglo-American world of 1831.

Bacon and Descartes left metaphysics standing. But in a series of philosophies climaxed by that of Immanuel Kant, metaphysics itself was declared impossible. Science in the spirit of Newton and his successors was thus left as the only legitimate body of speculative knowledge concerning existing things. At this historical stage of the relations between philosophy and science, it could be said that science stood alone as a study of things, whereas philosophy, with respect to science, was purely critical and epistemological, warning students of nature against treading beyond knowledge like that in Newtonian physics.

Idealism and Positivism. In the wake of Kant's work, two new philosophical currents were put in motion. One was IDEALISM, which reached a climax with Georg HEGEL. Hegel constructed a philosophy of nature but in a sense quite different from its Aristotelian version. For Hegel, the idealist, nature was Spirit or Idea externalizing itself; these external manifestations could be studied by the philosophy of nature in three disciplines: (1) mechanics, which begins with a study of empty space; (2) physics, a study of things in their totality; and (3) organics, a study of the living world where Idea or Spirit, fractured in the externalizing process, is struggling in a more intense way to recover its unity. Hegel's notion of the estrangement (externalization) of a primitive reality from itself, and the subsequent struggle, in various stages, toward reunion, is important not only for understanding the Hegelian notion of nature and its sciences, but also for understanding the Marxist philosophy of science to be sketched below.

The other 19th-century view of science is called POSITIVISM and was begun by Auguste COMTE. He regarded his so-called positive philosophy as having concern not with the causes or origins of things but with "their invariable relations of succession and resemblance." This apparently descriptive, as opposed to explanatory, program for the study of nature leaves the material world entirely to the positive sciences. Herbert SPENCER, a later positivist, assigned to philosophy the role of synthesizing scientific results. But most positivists conceived the main burden of speculative philosophy as one of accounting for the apparent necessity and universality in the laws discovered by the sciences.

This project dates back to Kant, who had prepared its way by his ban on metaphysics and by his restriction of valid knowledge to PHENOMENA. Kant had argued that the phenomenal world could not give rise to the universality and necessity found in physical laws, and that such universality and necessity had therefore to come from a priori structures in the human mind. Comte's own preference was to view all history as following a law of three stages: a theological stage, wherein the world is explained by an appeal to supranatural deities; a metaphysical stage, wherein things are explained by abstract essences; and a positivistic stage, wherein reality is accounted for by sciences like that of Newton. Necessity is attributed to nature's laws, according to Comte, because even modern man has not yet outgrown the so-called metaphysical stage.

Charles Sanders Peirce. (Bettmann/CORBIS)

Other positivists proposed different theories. Ernst Mach regarded scientific laws as economies of thought that make it psychologically easier for man to study nature. Henri Poincaré held such laws to be mere conventions. Karl Pearson (d. 1936) considered scientific law a mental shorthand. For Hans Vaihinger (d. 1933) law was a fiction, but since one could proceed practically "as if" laws were real, he called his view "the philosophy of 'as if.'"

Other Philosophical Views. At the end of the 19th century and the beginning of the 20th, the relations between philosophy and science, as indeed the whole fabric of Western philosophy, were elaborated in a context of idealism or of positivism. Early in the 20th century, Anglo-American philosophy experienced a return to REALISM in one or other of its forms. For this and other reasons associated with the 20th-century revolution in physics, the relations between philosophy and science took new turns. Even 20th-century idealist and positivist philosophies of science became different from philosophies of the 19th century bearing similar labels. Generally speaking, six theories of the relations between philosophy and science can thus be identified; pragmatism, idealism, linguistic philosophy, existentialism, dialectical materialism, and realism of scholastic and nonscholastic varieties.

Pragmatism. PRAGMATISM owed its immediate origin to Charles Sanders PEIRCE, who held that ideas could be made clear only by looking to their ''effects.'' This is the so-called pragmatic test. But Peirce, a self-styled scholastic realist, rejected positivism in its account of scientific laws and held to the existence of ''particular characters,'' analogues to ''natures'' in the Aristotelian sense. Somewhat like Aristotle also, and again in contrast to positivism, he regarded man's first questions about nature as being ''the most general and abstract ones.'' Unlike the arrangement in positivism, this would put philosophy, not after science, but before it.

Other pragmatists like William JAMES and John Dewey did not have the intellectual interests of Peirce. They did not make distinctions of any importance between philosophy and science. But both James and Dewey insisted that experience extends beyond the phenomena of Kant or the sense data of British EMPIRICISM. According to this larger view, there is personal experience, religious experience, experience of values, etc. Such an enlargement of the Kantian and positivist notion of experience, while important in itself, prepared the way for philosophies of science like Whitehead's.

Idealism. Idealism, as a philosophy of science, was defended in the 20th century principally by Arthur Eddington and James Jeans. Eddington was led to his position by arguments that science consists of ''pointer readings'' recorded on instruments. The scale for such readings, which determines how much of the real will register on us, is selected by the mind. Hence the mental or idealistic component in science. What lies behind the pointer readings escapes science, Eddington alleges. He likened this basic reality to spirit and consciousness, stressing once more his preference for ''idealism.'' Jeans was led to a similar position by the predominance in modern science of the mathematical, which he identified with the mental.

Linguistic Philosophy. Linguistic philosophy must be subdivided into LOGICAL POSITIVISM and analytical philosophy. Both have common ancestors in Bertrand RUSSELL and Ludwig WITTGENSTEIN. Like earlier positivisms, logical positivism recognized as meaningful the various propositions occurring in a science; these are alleged to be either about sense data (in the British empiricist sense) or about what is reducible to sense data. It is the work of philosophy to clarify the meanings of such empirical statements. A second type of meaningful expression is the analytic statement, which is true by the very meaning of its symbols, e.g., *A* is *A*. In working with both types of statement, philosophy is reduced to logic, and science alone is left to study the real. Even among those who do not accept it completely, logical positivism has heightened interest among philosophers such as Ernest Nagel in searching for criteria by which scientific laws and theories are accepted.

Because of its concern with the propositions of the science, logical positivism has been referred to as a philosophy of artificial language. In contrast, another branch of linguistic philosophy, represented by Gilbert Ryle, P. F. Strawson, R. B. Braithwaite, and Stephen Toulmin, insisted on the importance of analyzing ordinary language. Such analytical philosophers, apart from their other commitments, argue that language can be meaningful without being merely analytic or empirical in the logical positivist sense. By recognizing ordinary language as a layer of first-level meanings that must be examined before the technical second-level terminology of science, analytical philosophers, while strictly concerned with language, acknowledge as genuine at least some of the questions raised by Aristotle in his philosophy of nature.

Existentialism and Phenomenology. EXISTENTIALISM as a philosophy of science can be seen best in the work of Karl JASPERS (b. 1883). For him there is an authentic primordial experience of subjectivity, existence, and transcendence. But science, while not itself such authentic experience, enlarges the field within which the act of transcendence can be accomplished. In form, though not in content, Jaspers's view here is reminiscent of the PHENOMENOLOGY of Edmund HUSSERL, who launched a program for the reduction of knowledge to primordial intuitions, e.g., of time and space, which condition man's interpretation of scientific results. Such a phenomenology was advanced also by Maurice MERLEAU-PONTY.

Dialectical Materialism. Though initiated in the 19th century, dialectical materialism reached its climax in the 20th century (*see* MATERIALISM, DIALECTICAL AND HISTORICAL). It has always claimed to remain close to science. Its theorists have insisted that philosophy precedes science and lays down such truths as the union of opposites in the essence of matter. Science, by such findings as the wave-particle duality in quantum theory, is regarded as confirming the earlier philosophical commitment.

Nonscholastic Realism. Finally, several 20th-century philosophers of science can be associated with realism, if merely for want of a better term to characterize their opposition to positivism and to idealism. Peirce, the pragmatist, belongs among these. Other realist philosophers include Emile Meyerson, Henri BERGSON, and Alfred North WHITEHEAD. Meyerson held that there was an ontology in all science, as shown by the scientist's commitment to the existence of abiding identities in a changing world. Bergson maintained that science as such presents a geometricized, hence static, view of a world in motion, and that motion can be grasped only by an intuition that lies beyond the techniques of science. Whitehead proposed that the scientist, in advance of his science, commits himself to "half truths" that the philosophers must examine. Using experience in the wide sense given it by James, Whitehead elaborated a philosophy of organism. He used science more to confirm and correct this philosophy than to establish it.

Scholastic Positions. With the revival of Thomistic philosophy in the wake of Leo XIII's encyclical *Aeterni Patris,* scholastics began to develop their own distinctive views on the relation between science and philosophy. One of the earliest and most active centers of this revival was the University of Louvain; its dominant figure was Cardinal Désiré MERCIER. As a follower of Aquinas, he subscribed to Thomistic metaphysics; he also accepted a philosophical physics that preceded metaphysics in the pedagogical order. With later generations at Louvain, however, the philosophy of nature, under the name of COSMOLOGY, gradually lost its originality and came to be considered more or less as an applied metaphysics. The most extreme presentation of this view is that of Ferdinand Van Steenberghen, for whom the sciences are subdivided into epistemology, which includes logic; positive science, which includes mathematics; and metaphysics, which includes cosmology, psychology, and even moral science.

Jacques MARITAIN (d. 1973) departed from the position just outlined by his recognition of a philosophy of nature distinct from metaphysics. The philosophy of nature is called by him ontological knowledge, in contrast to the modern sciences, which are called empiriological and are subdivided into empirioschematic and empiriometric. At the physical level of ABSTRACTION Maritain proposed a distinct type of natural science, called empirioschematic; such science, for him, uses so-called qualitative models, like the theory of evolution in biology, as explanatory tools. Empiriometric knowledge, on the other hand, is a mixed or intermediate science, described in principle by Aristotle, Saint Thomas Aquinas, and Cajetan, and roughly equivalent to today's mathematical physics. In such empiriometric knowledge the explanatory tools are quantitative, and the resulting science may be considered terminally physical.

Charles DE KONINCK of Laval University proposed a view denying that Maritain's so-called empiriological knowledge represented a distinct type of science. For De Koninck the modern sciences are dialectical in Aristotle's sense, whereas true or demonstrative natural science, again in Aristotle's sense, is found only in the general philosophy of nature and philosophical psychology (*see* DIALECTICS; DEMONSTRATION). The modern natural sciences are thus dialectical continuations of the philosophical study of nature, where demonstration can be achieved and science thus attained.

The Albertus Magnus Lyceum in the United States, taking its inspiration fro Anicetus Fernandez and William H. Kane, agreed with Maritain that mathematical physics is a science distinct from the philosophy of nature. The Lyceum position agreed with De Koninck's in recognizing that empirioschematic knowledge is not a distinct science but a continuation of the philosophy of nature. However, this continuation of the philosophy of nature is regarded as not only dialectical; some of it is said to be demonstrative also. To this extent it continued the philosophy of nature not merely in a dialectical but also in a scientific way.

See Also: SCIENCE (IN ANTIQUITY); SCIENCE (IN THE MIDDLE AGES); SCIENCE (IN THE RENAISSANCE); SCIENCES, CLASSIFICATION OF; PHILOSOPHY OF NATURE

Bibliography: V. E. SMITH, ed., *The Philosophy of Physics* (Jamaica, New York 1961). J. MARITAIN, *Distinguish to Unite, or the Degrees of Knowledge,* tr. G. B. PHELAN from 4th French ed. (New York 1959). C. DE KONINCK, "Les Sciences expérimentales sont-elles distinctes de la philosophie de la nature?," *Culture* 2 (1941) 465–76. J. A. WEISHEIPL, ed., *The Dignity of Science* (Washington 1961). P. H. VAN LAER, *Philosophy of Science,* 2 v. (Pittsburgh 1956–62). S. STRASSER, *Phenomenology and the Human Sciences* (Pittsburgh 1963). R. MCRAE, *The Problem of the Unity of the Sciences: Bacon to Kant* (Toronto 1961). B. K. MILMED, *Kant and Current Philosophical Issues* (New York 1961). A. J. AYER, ed., *Logical Positivism* (Glencoe, Illinois 1959). S. E. TOULMIN, *The Philosophy of Science* (New York 1953). K. JASPERS, *Way to Wisdom: An Introduction to Philosophy,* tr. R. MANHEIM (New Haven 1960). C. S. PEIRCE, *Philosophical Writings of Peirce,* ed. J. BUCHLER (New York 1955). R. M. PALTER, *Whitehead's Philosophy of Science* (Chicago 1960).

[V. E. SMITH]

PHILOSOPHY OF NATURE

The philosophy of nature, variously referred to as natural philosophy, COSMOLOGY, and the science of nature, is the discipline that treats of the world of nature or the physical universe in its most general aspects. Traditionally it considers such topics as the definition of matter, nature, motion, infinity, time, life, soul, and similar concepts, and speculates about the elements and component parts of the universe. In the present day, philosophers of nature are faced with two major problems. One is how to distinguish their discipline from metaphysics; the other is to preserve it from being displaced by modern sciences, such as physics, chemistry, biology, and psychology.

While recognizing alternative views of the philosophy of nature, this article devotes major attention to that first propounded by ARISTOTLE in his *Physics,* and subsequently clarified and enriched by Greek, Arab, and Latin commentators, especially St. ALBERT THE GREAT and St. THOMAS AQUINAS.

Scope of the Philosophy of Nature

Aristotle characterized his study of nature as being both scientific, in contrast to Plato's ''likely story,'' and natural, in contrast to being mathematical or metaphysical. The first claim he justified by delineating the subject of the science, its concern with causes and principles, and its scientific order of development. The second he showed by differentiating the natural from other scientific approaches, particularly the mathematical. This article follows his order in establishing these foundations and in proceeding from them to outline the scope of the entire discipline.

Subject of the Science. The claim that the philosophy of nature is scientific can be approached in several stages. First, the subjects considered in the philosophy of nature are said to be known in terms of a universal sensible matter (*see* SCIENCES, CLASSIFICATION OF). The corresponding universal knowledge is abstract, although not in the way in which mathematical knowledge is abstract. Mathematics, in its abstractions, leaves behind the sensible, physical world, while natural science does not. It merely abstracts the universal, or the type, from the individuals that impress themselves upon man's senses; in this respect, physical science stays within the sensible world, although considering only what is general within it. ABSTRACTION from individual to common sensible matter thus constitutes the special intellectual light under which the philosophy of nature views its subject.

Second, this subject itself may be defined in a general way as mobile being, where mobile means capable of being changed in any way. It is by their mobile character that things in the physical world first come to be understood. Water, copper, maple trees, cows, even men are initially known by their behavior, their weight, their combustibility or lack of it, their growth, or other such activities. Thus it is appropriate to characterize physical reality as mobile.

On the other hand, to consider the subject of the philosophy of nature to be ''being'' as mobile, one would have to presuppose a metaphysics. Until proof is given that there exists at least one immobile being—such as a Prime Mover or a spiritual human soul—reason, unaided by faith, can make no real distinction between being and the mobile. This is why, in the language of Cardinal CAJETAN, the philosopher of nature has to consider mobile being as an unsegregated whole (*totum incomplexum*). In the same vein, Cajetan urges that it would be inappropriate for the philosopher of nature to consider his subject matter to be corporeal reality. That every mobile being is a body has to be itself established in the philosophy of nature.

Scientific Character. These considerations raise the question whether there can be a scientific knowledge of a subject such as mobile being. If SCIENCE (*SCIENTIA*) is defined in Aristotle's sense, it is certain knowledge of things through their proper causes (*Anal. post.* 71b 8–12). To fulfill this definition, natural philosophy must initially seek the primary causes or FIRST PRINCIPLES of this subject. Such an objective governs the initial development of natural philosophy, as pursued in the Aristotelian tradition.

An orderly search for these principles is guided in that tradition by the methodological conviction that the mind's natural tendency is to go from the known to the unknown. This explains why, though God is the most universal cause of all reality, man's knowledge of nature, as reached by unaided reason, does not logically begin with Him or with any other metaphysical subject. The search for first principles must stay within the proper order of nature. This again explains why, for Aristotelian Thomists, the study of metaphysics is postponed until after that of the philosophy of nature. Another application is that within the level of physical knowledge, what is best known to man are physical things as grasped in a universal and vague mode; only from such considerations does the mind advance toward notions that are more particular and distinct.

Order of Invention. This way of stating the progress of the mind from the known to the unknown is based on the fact that man has an imperfect knowledge of a thing before such knowledge grows more complete. To know a thing imperfectly is to recognize its common features without being able to differentiate it from other things. A GENUS, which includes its SPECIES in a universal and indistinct manner, is more intelligible to man than a species itself. The mind is able to recognize an entity such as a circle or a man (vague knowledge) before it can give a scientific DEFINITION of either (distinct knowledge). As indicated by his speech, a child first tends to regard all women as ''mother'' and all men as ''father''; then, as his knowledge increases, he is able to put a differential (hence distinct) structure into such notions.

The movement of the mind from general aspects of things toward their more particular features is a progress from what is most intelligible to man toward what is most intelligible in itself. The more generic man's considerations, the more remote these are from the world of actual being, which is the source of objective intelligibility; again, the more specific these become, the closer man gets to actuality, even though this more actual entitative level is less intelligible for him. This is why, though modern science analyzes nature in a highly specific and detailed way, it is frequently uncertain and hypothetical in its conclusions. In very detailed areas of science, e.g., quantum theory, notions become so hazy that the physicist no longer knows what his mathematics represents and hence no longer knows what he is studying.

Order in Natural Science. The methodological approach just outlined has two important consequences, one concerning the order of the subjective parts of the science of nature, and the other concerning the level at which the mind should search for the first principles of physical things.

Subjective Parts. In the study of any type of mobile or material being, its most generic level should be examined first: this most generic level is mobile being without regard to its types, such as water, iron, maple tree, dog, or man. Such a procedure avoids repeating the analysis of mobile being in general whenever an analysis of a particular type of mobile being is begun. The subject of this basic study, entitled the *Physics* by Aristotle, is mobile being in general (*ens mobile simpliciter*). After this, the philosophy of nature considers the first and most common type of mobile being, bodies undergoing local motion; this formed the subject of Aristotle's *On the Heavens,* whose content may be best described as cosmology, the science of the universe at large. In the progress to the even more particular, the next study is that of qualitative change, exemplified in *On Generation and Corruption,* Aristotle's rudimentary work on chemistry. Finally come the biological works, beginning with a study such as that outlined in Aristotle's *On the Soul.*

This sequence of books is mentioned here not to defend the content of Aristotle's cosmology or chemistry, but only to illustrate a formal order for treating the various materials concerning natural things. This issue must be reopened in discussing the relation between philosophy and science. The contents of the *Physics* alone are often described today as the philosophy of nature; although this restriction is not quite accurate, it can be used until further precisions are made.

Principles of the Philosophy of Nature. The proper order of invention thus requires a search at the universal level of mobile being for those first principles which, when discovered, assure that the philosophy of nature is scientific in the sense of the *Posterior Analytics.* The result of this search leads to the recognition that in all motion there are three factors: (1) a subject or MATTER; (2) a new qualification of this subject, called FORM; and (3) the previous lack or PRIVATION of this form in the subject able to possess it (*see* MATTER AND FORM). Moreover—and now at a level only slightly less general than before—two kinds of change are recognized: on the one hand, SUBSTANTIAL CHANGE, e.g., the burning of wood, whose subject is called primary matter and whose form is called substantial form; on the other, accidental change, e.g., the splitting of wood, whose matter is called secondary matter and whose form is known as accidental form. Primary matter, substantial form, and the previous privation of such form are the three first principles of all mobile being. The recognition that such principles exist in the world of nature is the clear assurance that a science of the natural world is possible.

Nature and the Natural. Aristotle is furthermore at pains to distinguish the meaning of the term ''nature.'' If the philosophy of nature is a natural science, then he must show that the subject as well as the middle terms for demonstrating about that subject are both natural. He does this by first defining nature.

Art. NATURE has several opposite poles to which, in different contexts, it can be contrasted. First of all there is art [*See* ART (PHILOSOPHY)]. In all types of art, but especially in mechanical art, man obviously does something to the given world. He finds iron ready-made but shapes it into a fence. He obtains wool from sheep but sews it into a garment. He cuts wood from a forest but arranges it into a house. All such products of art can undergo changes as in the rusting of the fence, the tearing of the garment, and the burning or collapsing of the house. But second thought shows that the changes take place not because of the artistic form but because of the natural matter. The fence rusts because it is iron, the garment tears because it is wool, and the house burns or collapses because it is wooden. Thus, what is by nature has a principle of motion within itself; what is by art, to the extent that it is art, has its principle extrinsic to it and in human reason.

Chance. Another opposite to nature is CHANCE—an interference between two lines of natural causality not determined, by the nature of either, to interfere with one another. Such happens when, say, a cosmic ray strikes a gene and results in the production of abnormal offspring. ''Nature is the first principle of motion and of rest in that in which it is [by contrast to art] primarily and essentially and not accidentally [by contrast to chance]'' (St. Thomas, *In 2 phys. 1.5*). In a briefer but less rigorous wording, nature is an intrinsic principle of motion.

Mathematical Physics and the Physical. But though the phenomena of art and chance may aid in the defining of nature, the most important modern opposite of the natural or physical is the mathematical, especially the kind of mathematical knowledge called mathematical physics. In listing Aristotle's major works in natural science, no mention was made of mathematical physics. The reason is that this is not a natural or physical science in its internal structure, as Aristotle explains in Book 2 of his *Physics.* It does not have a strictly physical subject, like water or sheep, but a mixed subject, e.g., sensible lines in optics, where the physical or sensible is compounded with the quantified or mathematical. Moreover, it is only the mathematical component of the mixed subject that the mathematical physicist explains. Evidence for this can be found in the fact that the middle term in a mathematico-physical argument, hence the causal knowledge employed in such an argument, is mathematical (cf. 193b 23–194a 18).

Physical Subjects. The philosophy of nature, by contrast, is strictly physical or natural. It studies the mobile world as known through the principles of motion. Whereas the mathematical physicist may measure motion to determine its velocity or acceleration, the philosopher of nature tackles the more fundamental question of what motion is. In a similar fashion, the mathematical physicist measures time, but to define time is a problem in the philosophy of nature. Unlike mathematical physics, which has a mixed subject—materially physical and formally mathematical (St. Thomas, *In Boeth. de Trin.* 5.3 ad 6)—the subject of a genuine philosophy of nature is strictly physical or natural; it is the mobile as such.

Middle Terms. Unlike the mathematical physicist, whose mathematical reasons show only ''that'' something is so without giving the physical ''why'' (cf. *Summa Theologiae* 2a2ae, 9.2 ad 3), the philosopher of nature uses middle terms that are physical. These middle terms ultimately represent one or other of the four causes (*see* CAUSALITY). The determination that there are such causes in every mobile being is made in the latter part of Book 2 of the *Physics* (198a 14–200b 9). Therefore, in their middle terms as well as in their subjects, mathematical physics and the philosophy of nature are distinct sciences.

Physical Interpretation. Mathematical physics is said, in the language of St. Thomas, to be terminally physical (*In 2 phys.* 3.8), or, in the language of 20th-century philosophers of science, to require physical interpretation. This problem of terminating or interpreting mathematical physics means finding, if possible, a physical reason or model for the facts that mathematical physics knows in only their mathematical reasons. Such interpretation or termination, for Thomists, is external to mathematical physics; it is a function of the philosophy of nature, where the physical causes of material things are properly sought.

Unity of the Philosophy of Nature. Having established in Book 1 of the *Physics* that the philosophy of nature is a science and in Book 2 that it is a natural or physical science, Aristotle turns in Book 3 to a definition of MOTION, the fundamental property of mobile being; Book 3 looks, later on, at a possible intrinsic characteristic of motion, that of infinity. Having shown that motion is not infinite but finite and hence measurable, Aristotle turns in Book 4 to the extrinsic measures of motion, PLACE, the measure of mobile being, and TIME, the measure of motion. Motion is divided in Book 5 into its subjective parts and in Book 6 into its quantitative or integral parts. Books 7 and 8 are devoted to the Prime Mover and associated problems (*see* MOTION, FIRST CAUSE OF).

Relation to Metaphysics. In a work devoted to the consideration of the universal causes and principles of mobile being, it is relevant to raise the issue of the universal efficient cause of motion. This is the point where, if the proper order of invention is followed, the philosopher discovers that being need not be necessarily mobile and material. It is this so-called common being, i.e., being as common to both material and immaterial things, that becomes the subject of METAPHYSICS.

Relation to Modern Science. To the extent that physics and chemistry are mathematical, they are grouped by Aristotelian-Thomists with the mathematical physics described earlier; similarly, to the extent that biology invokes mathematics, as in the study of genetics, it is treated likewise. However, to that extent that modern sciences are not mathematical but physical—as in parts of chemistry, much of biology, and many notions of modern cosmology—these sciences are regarded as natural and physical. For those who subscribe to the Aristotelian-Thomistic view on the order of learning, i.e., that the mind moves from the universal level to the specific level in its understanding of nature, such sciences become parts of a single physical science that begins at the general level of what is now called the philosophy of nature and reaches to the more specific levels of modern science.

Disputed Questions. Yet these are disputed points even for Thomists. Many agree that the modern sciences in which mathematics predominates are affiliated with the ''mixed sciences'' of Aristotle and the medievals. But there is great controversy as to the place of the natural sciences in the Thomistic hierarchy of knowledge. Among those who maintain that there is a philosophy of nature distinct from metaphysics, one group envisions a continuation between the philosophy of nature and such sciences, while another maintains that these sciences are themselves, formally distinct from the philosophy of nature. While there is common agreement about where the philosophy of nature begins, there is no consensus about where it ends when compared to modern science. (*See* PHILOSOPHY AND SCIENCE.)

Psychology and the Philosophy of Nature. For Thomists who reject the view that the philosophy of nature is an applied metaphysics, PSYCHOLOGY is considered to be a part of the philosophy of nature. This is in accord with the analyses of St. Thomas in various of his commentaries on Aristotle's texts. What is called philosophical psychology is not about the soul only, as the etymology of psychology (from Gr. ψῦχή, meaning soul) might suggest. It is about the composite, with the soul or form being the principle of the science rather than the subject.

According to Aristotle's ordering, the study of mobile being in general becomes more and more specific until it extends to that type of mobile being that is animate. But the study of the living has no first principles of its own; the principles of living things are still the matter and form discovered in Book 1 of the *Physics*. In any living thing there is simply a special type of form, called a SOUL, producing a special kind of effect in primary matter, rendering the matter not only corporeal but animated in this or that specific way. The study of the animate world thus is a subjective part of the scientific knowledge developed in the more general philosophy of nature.

In the light of the foregoing, it is incorrect to think of the philosophy of nature and philosophical psychology as two coordinate branches, or integral parts, of the science of material things. This misconception is likely to occur when the philosophy of nature is considered in the spirit of Christian WOLFF and labeled cosmology. On the other hand, writers who reject the Wolffian usage often employ the expression philosophy of nature to designate the philosophical study not simply of the inorganic world but of what all mobile beings, lifeless and living, have in common. Such a study should be more accurately labeled the general philosophy of nature; in this understanding, it would be appropriate to regard philosophical psychology as a proper subjective part.

Method in the Philosophy of Nature

By contrast to mathematical physics, which abstracts from nature only those features that can assume quantitative form, the philosophy of nature methodologically takes the whole of EXPERIENCE into account. One of the reasons alleged by modern scholars for Aristotle's failure to construct a better mathematical physics was his over-empirical temper; this possibly prevented him from abstracting from the medium through which a body, say a falling body, actually moved. At any rate, the philosophy of nature is through and through an empirical science; its conclusions must be ''terminated'' as St. Thomas said, or tested, as we would say in a later age, in sense experience. Because it depends so much on experience, St. Thomas locates the philosophy of nature after mathematics and mathematical physics in the order of learning.

Mode of Discourse. In regard to other aspects of method, the philosophy of nature, always remaining close to experience, progresses from universal truths—such as those involving mobile being in general—to more particular truths. This progress is called by St. Thomas ''the method of concretion'' and is further described as ''the application of common principles to determinate [types of] mobile beings'' (*In lib. de sensu* 1.2). In this descending movement, the philosophy of nature is far from a deductive science of a mathematical or rationalistic type. It does not predict, except in the trivial sense that if *x* is a mobile being, *x* will have for its first principles primary matter, substantial form, and privation, etc. In progressing by the method of concretion, the philosopher of nature must discover, through experience rather than by deduction, what exists in the mobile world; the application of common principles discovered in earlier experience can then be offered in explanation of what later and more refined experience reveals.

Aquinas contrasts the methods of mathematics with the more discursive method of the philosophy of nature. In mathematics, the mind considers, for instance, the essence of an object such as a triangle; without reverting to experience, it deduces the properties, e.g., the sum of its interior angles. But in the philosophy of nature the mind does not study one thing such as a triangle; in response to experience, it goes from one thing, an effect, to another, e.g., the extrinsic causes. Thus the philosophy of nature proceeds discursively or *rationabiliter,* whereas mathematics is said to proceed ''in the mode of learning,'' or *disciplinabiliter* (*In Boeth. de Trin.* 6.1).

Use of Induction. As another aspect of its experiential character, the philosophy of nature establishes its principles by INDUCTION (*In 8 phys.* 3.4). Even in the *Physics*, abstract as it is in contrast to the study of later ''concretions,'' the method is predominantly an inductive examination of the world revealed through sense experience. Such inductions require a pre-inductive dialectic that is not part of the philosophical science of nature. It prepares for induction, and it is this post-dialectical induction that gives the philosophy of nature its experiential mood. There are far more inductions in the *Physics* and in *On the Soul* than there are causal demonstrations. Moreover, when such demonstrations are made, as in the case of the two definitions of motion or two definitions of the soul, the premises themselves are the fruits of induction. Most of the demonstrations are from effect to cause (*demonstratio quia*), not from cause to effect (*demonstratio propter quid*). Since the latter type of demonstration is known as DEDUCTION, and since such demonstrations are not especially characteristic of the philosophy of nature, it would be an error to regard the philosophy of nature as a deductive science. Its method of proceeding discursively (*rationabiliter*) actually involves something quite different.

Recent Views of Natural Philosophy

The Aristotelian view of the philosophy of nature was commonly accepted until the beginnings of the Renaissance. Then, as modern philosophy and modern science began long periods of development, natural philosophy suffered a steady decline under successive attacks from MECHANISM, EMPIRICISM, and POSITIVISM. The 19th and 20th centuries, however, have witnessed a renewal of interest in this discipline. While differing in many respects from the traditional expositions by scholastics, these new philosophies show some sympathy and accord with the basic theses that had earlier been developed.

Philosophies of Matter. Original philosophies of nature, for example, were developed by the idealistic and romantic philosophers of the 19th century (see G. Hennemann, *Naturphilosophie im 19. Jahrhundert,* Munich 1959). These are important in themselves as well as for their historical bearing. Out of the Hegelian movement came MARXISM, with a philosophy centering on the world of matter. This was given a more or less systematic form in the 20th century, not only by Lenin but by the more recent work of Soviet philosophers. Somewhat as in the strict Aristotelian scheme, Soviet philosophers hold to a general and philosophical study of matter with its opposing principles of thesis and antithesis. Since, among Soviet thinkers, there is only one matter and one view of it, scientific findings are said to verify and reflect the results of the prior and more general analysis by philosophers (*See* HEGELIANISM AND NEO-HEGELIANISM; MATERIALISM, DIALECTICAL AND HISTORICAL).

Notion of Nature. In the West, Aristotle's insistence that mathematical physics does not function as a fully natural science was matched by similar insights of thinkers like Charles S. PEIRCE, Alfred North WHITEHEAD, Henri BERGSON, Pierre TEILHARD DE CHARDIN, and, more remotely, such 20th-century naturalists as Samuel ALEXANDER, Roy Wood Sellars, and John DEWEY (*see* NATURALISM). All of these writers had some more or less explicit notion of nature—Peirce's ''particular character''; Whitehead's ''organism''; Bergson's ''*élan vital*''; and Teilhard's ''psychic.''

If their language seems too biological and even, as in the last case, psychological, it should be remembered that the term ''nature'' itself had biological connotations in both its Greek and Latin origins. Softer and analogical meanings can be given to the similar terms of modern philosophers; one need not take as univocal, in all their occurrences, words like ''organism,'' ''vital elan,'' and ''psychic.'' Even with these qualifications, however, much work remains before 20th-century philosophers of nature can be brought into harmony with each other, into agreement with the valid insights of past thinkers, and above all into accord with reality as experienced.

Duality and Directionality. Again, the 20th-century philosophers of nature named above attest more or less to a dualistic character of natural things like that explained through primary matter and its form. The naturalists even speak of ''levels'' of process and ''the emergence of novelty,'' both of which give evidence that in all natural things there is a substratum, differentiated in various ways by what has been called form. But the same thinkers are inclined to take ''levels'' and ''novelty'' as something given, rather than to try to explain the given, as do Aristotle, Whitehead, Bergson, Peirce, Teilhard, and the Soviet philosophers.

Finally, all of the 20th-century philosophers of nature named above, including the Soviet theorists and Western naturalists, see directionality in the cosmos. These insights are intimations of the causality of the END (*see* FINAL CAUSALITY; TELEOLOGY). Whitehead is explicit in regard to the causality of purpose and, contrary to Hume, insists on man's power to grasp EFFICIENT CAUSALITY. Thus, though in different terms and a different context, such a philosopher as Whitehead recognized all four of the physical causes in a more or less conscious way.

Since 19th-century efforts to construct a priori philosophies of nature, such as IDEALISM, or to deny the philosophy of nature, as with positivism, important 20th-century Western philosophers seem to have rediscovered the need for a realistic evaluation of nature, one that considers mobile being at a level more general than the specialized natural sciences and at a level more natural than mathematical physics.

See Also: PHILOSOPHY; MATHEMATICS, PHILOSOPHY OF.

Bibliography: T. DE VIO CAJETAN, *De subjecto naturalis philosophiae,* ed. C. DE KONINCK and E. GAUDRON (*Selecta Lavallensia*; Quebec 1939). JOHN OF ST. THOMAS, *Cursus philosophicus thomisticus,* ed. B. REISER, 3 v. (Turin 1930–37). V. E. SMITH, *The General Science of Nature* (Milwaukee 1958); ed. *The Philosophy of Physics* (Jamaica, NY 1961). W. H. KANE, "The Nature and Extent of Philosophy of Nature," *Thomist* 7 (1944) 204–232. J. MARITAIN, *Philosophy of Nature* (New York 1951). F. RENOIRTE, *Cosmology,* tr. J. F. COFFEY (New York 1950). C. DE KONINCK, "Introduction à l'étude de l'âme," *Laval Théologique et philosophique* 3 (1947) 9–65. A. FERNÁNDEZ-ALONSO, "Scientia et philosophia secundum S. Albertum Magnum," *Angelicum* 13 (1936) 24–59.

[V. E. SMITH]

PHILOSTORGIUS

Fourth-century Church historian; b. Borissus, Asia Minor, *c.* 368; d. probably Constantinople, 425 or 433. A layman well read and widely traveled, Philostorgius wrote a church history in 12 books known only through a summary and epitome in PHOTIUS (*Biblioth.* Codex 40), and fragments in Suidas, the *Martyrion* of Artemius by John of Rhodes (ninth century), a *Vita Constantini* (H. Optiz, *Cod. Ang. Gr.* 22), and the *Thesaurus orthodoxae fidei* by Nicetas Acominatus. Philostorgius presented his work as a continuation of the *Ecclesiastical History* of EUSEBIUS OF CAESAREA, and covered the period from 315 to 425. He was, however, obviously an Arian partisan and favored the cause of the neo-Arian heretic Eunomius of Cyzicus. While praising his style and diction, Photius maintained that Philostorgius was frequently inaccurate, particularly when he praised Eunomius, Aëtius of Antioch, and Eusebius of Nicomedia or condemned Acacius of Caesarea in Palestine and Basil of Cappadocia. His history is important for the citation of Arian sources that have not been preserved, for the evidence it offers of the attraction Arianism had for the cultured Greek mind, and for its thesis that the acceptance of the theology of ATHANASIUS OF ALEXANDRIA spelled the destruction of the Roman Empire. Philostorgius mentioned an *Encomium* on Eunomius and a *Refutation of Porphyry* of his own composition, which have not been preserved.

Bibliography: *Patrologia Graeca,* ed. J. P. MIGNE, 161 v. (Paris 1857–66) 65:459–624. J. BIDEZ, ed., *Philostorgius: Kirchengeschichte* (*Die griechischen christlichen Schriftsteller der ersten drei Jahrhunderte* 21; 1913) 1–150. H. OPITZ, *Byzantion* 9 (1934) 535–593. J. BIDEZ, *ibid.* 10 (1935) 403–442. H. HESELER, *ibid.,* 399–402. H. BECKBY, ed. and tr., *Anthologia Graeca,* v. 3 (Munich 1958) 120–121. H. RAHNER, *Lexikon für Theologie und Kirche,* ed. J. HOFER and K. RAHNER, 10 v. (2d, new ed. Freiburg 1957–65) 8:478. J. QUASTEN, *Patrology,* 4 v. (Westminster, Md. 1950–86) 3:530–532. P. BATIFFOL, *Quaestiones Philostorgianae* (Paris 1891). J. MARQUART, *Theologische Literaturzeitung* 38 (1913) 705–709. G. FRITZ, *Dictionnaire de théologie catholique,* ed. A. VACANT et al., 15 v. (Paris 1903–50; Tables générales 1951–) 12.2:1495–98. B. ALTANER, *Patrology,* tr. H. GRAEF from 5th German ed. (New York 1960) 274. G. GEUTZ, *Paulys Realenzyklopädie der klassischen Altertumswissenschaft,* ed. G. WISSOWA et al. 20.1 (1941) 119–122.

[F. X. MURPHY]

PHILOTHEUS COCCINUS, PATRIARCH OF CONSTANTINOPLE

Patriarchate from 1353 to 1354 and from 1364 to 1376; Byzantine theologian and Hesychast; b. Thessalonica, *c.* 1300; d. apparently Constantinople, 1379. Born of a Jewish mother in poor circumstances, Philotheus paid for his education by serving as cook to his preceptor, Thomas Magistros. He became a monk on Mt. Sinai, then entered the Grand Laura on MOUNT ATHOS, where he served as abbot and defended the Hesychastic doctrine of Gregory PALAMAS. Although he had been appointed bishop of Heraclea in Thrace, he spent most of his time in Constantinople and was not present for the sacking of his episcopal city by the Genoese in 1352. He was appointed patriarch of Constantinople by Emperor John VI Cantacuzenus (November 1353), but with the fall of the emperor, Philotheus was forced to resign and was imprisoned for treason. Eventually he was allowed to return to his former bishopric of Heraclea, and through the good graces of the high official Demetrius CYDONES was rehabilitated (1363) and reappointed patriarch the following year. He took a vigorous part in the political affairs of the empire, and he strongly opposed the efforts made by the restored emperor John V Palaeologus (1354–76) in favor of union with Rome. This gained him the enmity of Demetrius Cydones, particularly when Philotheus called a synod (1368) to condemn his brother Prochorus CYDONES.

Asserting the independent primacy of his patriarchate, Philotheus canonized Gregory Palamas in the synod of 1368 and declared him a doctor of the Church. Pursuing his ecclesiastical policy, he successfully won the allegiance of the Orthodox Serbs, Bulgarians, and Russians to the empire faced with the Turkish menace, and took repressive measures against Byzantine Catholics. In 1376 he resigned his position as patriarch because of age and ill health.

While still a monk on Mt. Athos, Philotheus seems to have written two tracts against Gregorius Akindynos (d. 1349) in favor of Taborite spirituality; and as bishop of Heraclea he wrote 14 *Kephalaia,* or chapters, against the heresies of Akindynos and the Calabrian monk Barlaam. At the suggestion of Emperor John Cantacuzenus (before 1354) he produced the most imposing of his polemical works, the 15 *Antirrhetica,* or diatribes, against the historian Nicephorus Gregoras, a severe opponent of Palamitism in Constantinople. This work appeared in separate sections: books 1 and 2 with an epilogue (book 3) were published first; then the succeeding 12 books were published. From this period there is also an unedited letter to the Barlaamite monk Petriotes on the Divinity (Paris MS Gr 1276).

Philotheus was the author of one of the weightiest Palamite documents, the *Hagiorite Tome,* written *c.* 1339 and used by Palamas in his own defense in 1441. With Nilus CABASILAS he prepared a second tome for the synod of 1351; and as patriarch he produced the *Synodal Tome* of 1368, in which Prochorus Cydones was condemned. He also edited a confession of faith for bishops, and the anathemas for the Synodicon (1352) for the celebration of Orthodox Sunday.

His hagiographical writings are numerous and seem to have been aimed primarily at preventing the anti-Palamite writings of Nicephorus Gregoras from affecting the liturgy. Philotheus wrote a life of St. Anysia of Thessalonica, the martyr Febronia, the monk Germanus, his predecessor Isidore, Onuphrius, and Sabas the Younger. He preached *Encomia* in favor of the 12 Apostles, St. Demetrius, the Three Hierarchs, All Saints, his spiritual father Nicodemus the Younger (d. 1321), the martyr Phocas, and sermons honoring St. John Chrysostom, Theodore Teron, and St. Thomas the Apostle. He wrote the life and the liturgical office of Gregory Palamas, whom he had canonized. His sermons on the Feast of the Transfiguration, on orthodoxy, on the *Koimesis,* and on the Holy Cross have been preserved. He was the author of two canons or liturgical hymns and an *Acoluthion* for the Fathers of Chalcedon. However the *Homiliary* formerly attributed to Philotheus was actually a re-elaboration of the *Patriarchal Homiliary,* whose author was Patriarch John IX Agapetus (1111–34); and the 40 ascetical chapters under his name in the *Philocalia* were the work of Philotheus of the Thorn Bush Monastery on Mt. Athos (twelfth century). The same is true of 21 chapters on the Lord's Prayer.

While still abbot of the Grand Laura on Mr. Athos, Philotheus had written a *Précis of Divine Liturgy* and an *Order of Service for the Diaconia.* He attacked the validity of the anathemas passed against the canonical *Hexabiblos* of George Harmenopoulus (d. 1383), and he is said to have written scholia for that work. Of his exegetical writings, three homilies on wisdom (Prv 9.1) are known and two on the woman of the Gospel cured of a curvature of the spine (Lk 13.10). He wrote a homily on Psalm 37 and apparently an explanation of the Psalms, as well as a tract on circumcision, three letters on the beatitudes, an address to Empress Helene (wife of John V), and a sermon and consolatory epistle to Heraclea on the occasion of its sacking by the Genoese. Two anti-Roman polemical pieces ascribed to him are not authentic: the *Kata Latinos* belongs to Nilus Cabasilas; and the *Diologue on Dogmatic Theology* belongs to Philotheus of Selymbria. Many of Philotheus's works are still unedited; but his writings in favor of Palamitism and his patriarchal acts asserting the primacy of his see had a lasting effect on the development of the Orthodox churches.

Bibliography: V. LAURENT, *Dictionnaire de théologie catholique,* 15 v. (Paris 1903–50) 12.2:1498–1509; *Revue des études byzantines* 10 (1952): 113–123. R. JANIN, *Lexikon für Theologie und Kirche,* 10 v. (Freiburg 1957–65) 8:478–479. H. G. BECK, *Kirche und theologische Literatur im byzantinischen Reich* (Munich 1959) 723–727. *Patrologia Graeca,* 161 v. (Paris 1857–66) 151:551–656, 693–1186; 152:1303–1460; 154:719–826. F. MIKLOSICH and J. MÜLLER, eds., *Acta et diplomata graeca medii aevi,* v. 1 (Vienna 1860) 325–350, 448–594. G. MERCATI, "Notizie di Procoro e Demetrio Cidone," *Studi e Testi* 56 (1931) 243–246. P. JOANNOU, ed., "Germanus the Athonite" *Analecta Bollandiana* (1952) 35–115. O. HALECKI, *Un Empereur de Byzance à Rome* (Warsaw 1930) 152–154, 235–242. F. DÖLGER, *Historisches Jahrbuch der Görres-Gesellschaft* 72 (1953) 205–221. E. HONIGMANN, *Byzantinische Zeitschrift* 47 (1954) 104–115.

[F. CHIOVARO]

PHILOXENUS OF MABBUGH

Syrian bishop and influential Monophysite theologian; b. Tahal, Persia, *c.* 450; d. Philippopolis, Thrace, Dec. 10, 523. After studying in Edessa and rejecting the current Nestorianism of that school, Philoxenus was selected bishop of Mabbugh (Hierapolis in Syria) by Peter the Fuller, patriarch of Antioch, in 485. An ardent opponent of the doctrine of the Council of CHALCEDON, and a friend of the Emperor Anastasius I, he was humiliated at the Synod of Sidon (511); but in the following year he succeeded in having many of his orthodox enemies deposed from neighboring sees and had SEVERUS OF ANTIOCH installed as patriarch (512–518). Exiled to Philippopolis by the orthodox Emperor JUSTIN I in 519, he continued his polemical and ascetic writings despite the rigors of captivity.

A classical author in Syrian literature, Philoxenus is honored as a saint and doctor by the Jacobite (Monophysite) Church. Among his 80 major exegetical, dogmatic, homiletic, and ascetical writings, 13 orations on Christian life, 5 tracts on the Incarnation and the Trinity, and a collection of letters have been edited. Although vehement, his MONOPHYSITISM is more verbal than actual. He adhered to the pre-Chalcedonian, Cyrillian terminology and preached a dynamic Christology, which he opposed to a suppositious dualism of Chalcedon. Inspired by the Alexandrian theological school, his thinking was creative and original.

Bibliography: *The Discourses of Philoxenus,* ed. and tr. E. A. W. BUDGE, 2 v. (London 1894). E. LEMOINE, ed. and tr., *Sources Chrétiennes* v. 44 (1956). R. LAVENANT, ed. and tr., *Patrologia orientalis* 30.5 (1963) 725–894. I. ORTIZ DE URBINA, *Patrologia syriaca* (Rome 1958) 147–150, complete bibliog. E. STEIN, *Histoire de Bas-Empire*. tr. J. R. PALANQUE (Paris 1949–59) 2:157–159, 171–173, 232. A. DE HALLEUX, *Philoxène de Mabboug, sa vie, ses écrits, sa théologie* (Louvain 1963). E. TISSERANT, *Dictionnaire de théologie catholique*, ed. A. VACANT et al. (Paris 1903–50) 12.2:1509–32.

[G. T. DENNIS]

PHOENICIANS

A Northwest Semitic people who inhabited Palestine and Western Syria. The name is commonly used to designate the Canaanites after 1200 B.C. For a history of the Phoenicians *see* CANAAN AND CANAANITES. The term Phoenician is clearly derived from Greek φοῖνιξ, which means purple (or crimson) as well as Phoenician. Though the etymology of the Greek word is uncertain, two possibilities can be considered: (1) if the primary meaning of φοῖνιξ (and its derivatives) is purple, then the land received the name Phoenicia because of its purple dye industry; but (2) if the primary meaning of φοῖνιξ is Phoenician, then the Greek word is used later in the sense of purple because the discovery and earliest use of a dye of this color was ascribed to the Phoenicians.

Bibliography: *Encyclopedic Dictionary of the Bible*, tr. and adap. by L. HARTMAN (New York 1963) 1846–49. H. HAAG, *Lexikon für Theologie und Kirche*, ed. J. HOFER and K. RAHNER (Freiburg 1957–65) 8:481–482. For additional bibliography *see* CANAAN AND CANAANITES.

[A. A. DI LELLA]

PHOENIX

The unique bird of Eastern legend, brilliant and beautiful, that lived for 500 years (longer in some accounts), and after dying rose again from its own ashes. It appears in Old Sanskrit poetry, Egyptian religious texts, and in Greek and Roman writers from Hesiod onward. Herodotus is the chief source for details. Christians especially used the myth for paradise and resurrection themes.

The compiler of the *PHYSIOLOGUS* (original Greek *c.* A.D. 200) provided the phoenix story as ALLEGORY for Jn 10.18: ''I have the power to lay down my life and take it up again,'' for ''the phoenix is the symbol of our Savior who came from heaven with both wings full of fragrant perfume, that is divine words.'' With time, commentaries acquired length and variety, and its attractive symbolism passed into frequent use in patristic and medieval Latin and vernacular literature.

A Phoenician fertility goddess found at the Island of Moyta, Sicily in 1971. (©David Lees/CORBIS)

Paintings, mosaics, sarcophagi, and pottery show the bird rising from its ashes. What had symbolized for Egyptians the sun's daily return and for Romans imperial APOTHEOSES became for Christians a symbol of resurrection, Christ's and their own.

Bibliography: G. TÜRK, W. H. ROSCHER, ed. *Ausführliches Lexikon der griechischen und römischen Mythologie* (Leipzig 1921) 3:3450–72. A. RUSCH, *Paulys Realenzyklopädie der klassischen Altertumswissenschaft*, ed. G. WISSOWA et al. 20.1 (1941) 414–423. H. LECLERCQ, *Dictionnaire d'archéologie chrétienne et de liturgie*. ed. F. CABROL, H. LECLERCQ and H. I. MARROU (Paris 1907–53) 14.1:682–692. M. C. FITZPATRICK, *Lactanti de ave phoenice: With Introduction, Text, Translation and Commentary* (Philadelphia 1933). M. F. MCDONALD, ''Phoenix redivivus,'' *Phoenix* 14 (Toronto 1960) 187–202, with emphasis on its place in Judeo-Christian tradition.

[M. F. MCDONALD]

PHOTIUS, PATRIARCH OF CONSTANTINOPLE

Patriarchate from Dec. 24, 858, to Sept. 25, 867, and from 878 to December 886; b. of a noble family in CONSTANTINOPLE, *c.* 810; d. in the monastery of Armeniakon, after 893.

Photius, Patriarch of Constantinople.

Early Career. His father, Sergius, and his mother, Irene, were exiled by the emperor THEOPHILUS because of their opposition to his iconoclastic policy. In the Byzantine SYNAXARY the confessor Sergius and his wife, Irene, are commemorated on May 13 (*Acta sanctorum,* Propylaeum Novembris, ed. H. Delehay [Brussels 1902] 682). Photius revealed in one of his letters that the whole family and his uncle, the former patriarch TARASIUS, were anathematized by one of the iconoclastic synods (*Patrologia Graeca,* ed. J. P. Migne, 161 v. [Paris 1857–66] 102:877). In letters to his brother Tarasius and to the Oriental patriarchs, Photius also praised the piety of his parents and their sufferings for the true faith (*Patrologia Graeca,* 102:972, 1020). Although the property of his parents is said to have been confiscated, Photius and his brothers Sergius and Tarasius, who were left in Constantinople, were able to obtain a good education. In a letter addressed to the Oriental patriarchs, Photius confessed that he was attracted in his youth by the monastic life but that he chose a secular career. Because of his learning, Theoctistus, the prime minister of the empress THEODORA, appointed Photius professor of philosophy at the University of Constantinople, which he had reorganized. Photius's brother Sergius married Irene, the sister of the empress, and Photius became director of the imperial chancery and a member of the senate.

Despite his new functions Photius continued with his disciples to study philosophical and theological literature. Around the middle of the century, he led an embassy to the Khalif Muttawakkil and was absent from Constantinople when Bardas, the brother of Theodora, in connivance with the young emperor MICHAEL III, terminated the regency of his sister after plotting the murder of prime minister Theoctistus and made himself regent. Bardas found support among liberals and intellectuals, but conservative circles favored Theodora, who had restored the cult of images in 843. The patriarch IGNATIUS, who had been appointed by Theodora, lost the favor of the new government because he sided with the conservatives and gave credit to slanderous stories about Bardas's private life, circulated by his opponents. When an attempt at the restoration of Theodora had failed, the empress and her daughters were obliged to take monastic vows. Ignatius refused to bless their monastic garb. He resigned his office on the advice of bishops who were anxious to prevent a conflict between the Church and the government and asked his adherents to select a new patriarch. In a local synod the bishops of both parties recommended to the emperor the layman Photius, avoiding the election of bishops from the rival parties. Photius was recognized as legitimate patriarch by all the bishops, even the five most faithful supporters of Ignatius, after he had given them certain guarantees concerning the position of Ignatius after his abdication. Because the new patriarch had to function during the feast of the Lord's Nativity, which was approaching, Photius obtained all the degrees of Holy Orders in a week. He was consecrated by Gregory Asbestos, leader of the liberals, and by two Ignatian bishops. This was a sort of compromise arranged at the synod. Gregory had been suspended by Ignatius and had appealed from Ignatius's judgment to Rome. As yet Rome had not decided about the justification of Ignatius's measure, and Gregory was rehabilitated by the synod.

First Patriarchate. About two months after Photius's ordination, the extreme followers of Ignatius, assembled in the church of St. Irene, refused obedience to the new patriarch and demanded the reestablishment of Ignatius. The reason for this action may have lain in differing interpretations of the nature of the guarantees given by Photius to the five leaders of the Ignatian party. Photius convoked a synod in the church of the Holy Apostles (859). The opposing party prevented their condemnation by provoking a riot (Zonaras, *Patrologia Graeca,* 137:1004–), which had a political background and which was suppressed with bloodshed by the imperial police. Photius protested against the cruelty of the police and threatened Bardas with his abdication. After peace had been established, the synod was reconvened in the church of the Blachernae palace. In order to deprive the opposition of any claim concerning the legitimacy of Ignatius's patriarchate, the synod declared, on the request of Bardas, that the whole patriarchate of Ignatius was illegitimate because he had not been elected by a synod, but had been simply appointed by Theodora. During the riots Ignatius and some of his followers were imprisoned. Ignatius was interned in various places, finally in a monastery on the island of Terebinthus. Bardas must, however, have convinced himself that Ignatius was not responsible for the riots, because he allowed him to stay (860) in the palace of Posis in Constantinople, which had been built by Ignatius's mother.

Because of these troubles, only in 860 was Photius able to send a letter to Pope NICHOLAS I regarding his enthronement. In this communication he announced that he had accepted his election unwillingly after Ignatius had abdicated. The emperor Michael III and Photius also asked the pope to send legates to a new council in Constantinople, which would once more condemn ICONOCLASM and confirm the decision made by Theodora in 843 concerning the reestablishment of the cult of images. In his answer to Photius, Nicholas objected to the elevation of a layman to the patriarchate and sent Bishop Radoald of Porto and Zacharias of Anagni to the council with orders to reexamine the religious situation in Constantinople, while reserving to himself the definite decision concerning the legitimacy of Photius's elevation. According to the Byzantine practice, the case of Ignatius had been definitively settled by a local synod. The government and Photius were, however, willing to let the legates reexamine the whole affair on condition that they would pronounce their verdict in the name of the pope during the council. The legates accepted this compromise, seeing in it the confirmation by the Byzantines of the supreme jurisdiction of the pope over the Church. After the interrogation of Ignatius in the synod of 861, the legates confirmed the decision of the local synod of 859, suspending Ignatius and declaring his patriarchate illegitimate. The acts of this synod are partly preserved in the collection of canon law by Cardinal Deusdedit. The declarations of the bishops and legates that the BYZANTINE CHURCH, when allowing the legates to reexamine the affair, had accepted the canons of SARDICA (343), showed their recognition of the right of the bishops to appeal to the pope as the supreme judge in the Church. Ignatius, although protesting against the initiative of the legates, seems to have accepted the verdict of the synod when he declared: *Romam non appellavi nec appello.* Nicholas, not satisfied with the course of events, asked for more documentary evidence to justify the decision of the synod. Photius, regarding the case of Ignatius as closed, remained silent.

In the meantime, several extremely partisan monks led by Abbot Theognostus succeeded in reaching Rome and giving the pope their own biased account of events in Constantinople. Theognostus even presented the pope with an appeal in Ignatius's name although he was not authorized by Ignatius to do so. The pope, resenting Photius's negative attitude to his request, gave credit to the account of Theognostus, who exaggerated the importance of the opposition to Photius. Disapproving the attitude of his legates at the synod of 861, Nicholas condemned and excommunicated Photius at a Roman synod of 863 and recognized Ignatius as the legitimate patriarch, announcing his decision to Photius and the emperor. The Byzantines disregarded this decision, and in 865 Michael III protested bitterly against this intervention of the pope in Byzantine ecclesiastical affairs in a letter that provoked a sharp reaction from the pope.

The situation took a turn for the worse because of a new conflict between Rome and Byzantium over BULGARIA. The Bulgarian ruler BORIS I (Michael) became discontented because Photius would send only missionaries to his country and refused to give him a patriarch or an archbishop. He therefore turned to the Franks and to Rome. Nicholas sent Boris a long pastoral letter and two bishops, Formosus and Paul. The latter succeeded in winning over Boris to the cause of the pope and of Western Christianity. The Latin missionaries, in rivalry with the Greeks, criticized certain customs of the Byzantine Church and seem to have introduced the *FILIOQUE* into the creed. The emperor Michael invited all the Eastern patriarchs to a synod (867) to deal with this encroachment of Rome into the Byzantine sphere of interest and to condemn the innovations introduced by the Latins into Bulgaria, especially the *filioque.* Nicholas was condemned, and the German emperor Louis II was asked to depose him. Alarmed by the hostile reaction that the conflict of interests in Bulgaria had provoked in Byzantium, the pope requested several Western theologians to refute the Byzantine critics of Latin customs. This was the atmosphere in which the first Latin polemical treatises against the Greeks (by Aeneas of Paris, RATRAMNUS OF CORBIE) were written. Nicholas died before learning about the fateful decisions of the Eastern synod of 867, and the situation was changed by a political revolution in Byzantium.

Deposition and Second Patriarchate. The emperor Basil I, whom Michael III had promoted to be coemperor, murdered first Bardas, the emperor's uncle and regent, and in September 867, also his benefactor Michael III. On becoming emperor, being anxious to win the support of the zealots, of conservative circles, and of Rome, he deposed Photius, reinstated Ignatius, and asked Pope ADRIAN II to send legates to Constantinople for a new council that should pacify the Byzantine Church. Adrian II condemned Photius and his synods (869) and sent the bishops Donatus and Stephen and the deacon Marinus to the council in Constantinople. The legates were instructed to demand from the fathers the acceptance of the decision of the Roman synod. This angered Basil I, who wanted a new examination of the controversy by the synod, reserving the final decision to himself. Only 110 bishops attended the council (869–70), called the Council of CONSTANTINOPLE IV (eighth ecumenical) by the Latins. Photius and his followers were suspended and excommunicated, but the great majority of the hierarchy and the clergy remained faithful to Photius. This circumstance hampered Ignatius in the administration of the patriarchate. He soon became involved in a sharp conflict with Pope JOHN VIII because he accepted the decision of the Eastern patriarchs made at the end of the council. At the request of Boris I, Bulgaria became a part of the patriarchate of Constantinople. Ignatius established a Greek hierarchy in Bulgaria and gave the new Church a certain degree of autonomy.

In the meantime Basil I revoked Photius's exile and entrusted him with the education of his sons. Ignatius was reconciled with Photius and asked Rome to send legates to a new council of union. Unfortunately, before the papal legates, Bishops Paul of Ancona and Eugenius of Ostia, had reached Constantinople, Ignatius was dead and Photius had been reinstated as patriarch. John VIII sent Cardinal Peter to Constantinople with instructions to recognize Photius as the legitimate patriarch after the latter expressed to the legates and the fathers his regret for his former behavior. Photius could not accept this condition because he had been elected by a synod after Ignatius had abdicated and could not be held responsible for the troubles provoked by the zealots. The synod was to put an end to the strife between the two parties and give satisfaction to Photius and his followers for their unjust treatment. For this reason the letters sent by the pope to Photius and to the council were changed, with the consent of the legates, who had become convinced that Rome had been wrongly informed about the true situation in Constantinople. All passages that did not correspond to the spirit of the union council were left out in the Greek version read to the fathers of the council (879–80). It should be stressed, however, that the main scriptural arguments by which the pope confirmed his own primacy in the Church were left in the Greek version, a circumstance that shows that Photius, although defending the autonomy of his Church, did not deny the PRIMACY OF THE POPE. The anti-Photian council of 869–70 was suppressed. Because of the canceling of this council by the union synod, the genuine Greek acts of this council are not preserved. We have only their Latin translation made by ANASTASIUS THE LIBRARIAN and an extract in Greek, preserved in the anti-Photianist collection. Consequently, the ORTHODOX CHURCH accepts only the first seven councils as ecumenical, calling the Photian synod of 879–80 a union synod.

John VIII protested against the changes made in his letters by the Greeks, but he accepted the decisions of the union synod and recognized the rehabilitation of Photius. This explains the fact that in the West before the end of the 11th century the council of 869–70 was not counted among the ecumenical councils (*see* COUNCILS, GENERAL). It was given an ecumenical character by the canonists of the GREGORIAN REFORM who, during the INVESTITURE STRUGGLE, exploited for their cause canon 22 of this council, forbidding laymen to appoint bishops. The union synod was forgotten, and only Cardinal Deusdedit and IVO OF CHARTRES made some quotations from its acts. So it happened that the Photian legend grew in the West, picturing the patriarch as the father of schism and the archenemy of papal primacy (*see* EASTERN SCHISM).

During his second patriarchate Photius endeavored to bring about a reconciliation with all his former enemies, especially with Marinus and Stylianus. He made concessions to Rome in Bulgaria, but Boris I refused to return to the Roman jurisdiction. According to a version of the *Synodicon Vetus* (MS Sinaiticus 482 [1117], fols. 357–365), Photius himself canonized Ignatius, whose feast (Oct. 23) is marked in the *Typikon,* which was revised under the second patriarchate of Photius. The emperor LEO VI induced Photius to abdicate, probably because of his hostility to Theodore Santabarenus, promoted by Photius to be metropolitan of Euchaita, and appointed his brother Stephen as patriarch. The belief that the successors of John VIII—Marinus I, Stephen V, and Formosus—had broken with Photius is a legendary invention. Photius died in communion with Rome. His feast (Feb. 6) is noted in several *Synaxaria* from the end of the 10th and 11th centuries and is celebrated by all Orthodox Churches.

Churchman and Humanist. Photius was one of the leading figures in the Byzantine intellectual renaissance of the 9th century, and his learning commanded the respect of his bitterest enemies. His scholarly reputation is established through his Μυριόβιβλον (*Bibliotheca*), giving criticisms of and extracts from 280 works that Photius had studied, many of which are not preserved today. The other of his main works, the 'Αμφιλόχια, contains answers to more than 300 questions of a theological and profane nature. His writing against the *filioque* (*Mystagogia Spiritus Sancti*) was exploited by anti-Latin polemicists from the 12th century on. His 200 extant letters and his *Homilies* are written in an elegant style. In his Διήρησις he attacked the doctrine of the PAULICIANS. He reorganized the patriarchal academy for the education of the clergy and brought philosophical and theological speculation back to the foundation established by Aristotle. He manifested interest in philology by composing a *Lexicon* and an *Etymologicum.* The writing against the Roman primacy (M. Gordillo, "Photius et primatus Romanus," *Orientalia Christiana periodica* 6 [1940] 6–39) cannot be ascribed to Photius because the legendary tradition that St. ANDREW the Apostle was the founder of the Byzantine bishopric, which this writing contains, had not yet been developed in the 9th century (F. Dvornik, *The Idea of Apostolicity in Byzantium and the Legend of the Apostle Andrew* [Cambridge 1958]). He initiated the revision of the *Typicon* of HAGIA SOPHIA and of a *Nomocanon.* Photius sent his disciple Constantine-CYRIL and his brother Methodius to the Khazars for religious discussion and with the emperor entrusted to them the mission to Moravia (*see* SLAVS). He also attempted to reunite the Armenian with the Orthodox Church (*see* ARMENIA).

Bibliography: Editions. *Patrologia Graeca,* ed. J. P. MIGNE, 161 v. (Paris 1857–66) 101–104. Φωτίου . . . λόγοι καὶ ὁμιλίαι, ed. S. ARISTARCHOS, 2 v. (Constantinople 1900). V. LAOURDAS, ed., *Homiliai* (Thessalonike 1959). C. MANGO, tr., *The Homilies of Photius* (Cambridge, Mass. 1958). Letters. V. LAOURDAS and L. WESTERINK, eds., *Epistulae et Amphilochia,* 6 v. (Leipzig 1983–88). A. PAPADOPOULOS-KERAMEUS, Φωτιακά (St. Petersburg 1897); in *Pravoslavnij Palestinskij Sbornik* 11 (St. Petersburg 1891) 179–213, letter to the Catholicos Zacharias. R. HENRY, ed. and tr. (French), *Bibliotheca,* 9 v. (Paris 1959–91). C. THEODORIDIS, ed., *Lexicon* (Berlin, New York 1983). *On the Mystagogy of the Holy Spirit,* tr. HOLY TRANSFIGURATION MONASTERY (New York 1983). Sources. *Etymologicon magnum,* ed. T. GAISFORD (Oxford 1848). The anti-Photianist collection in J. D. MANSI, *Sacrorum Conciliorum nova et amplissima collectio,* 31 v. (Florence, Venice 1757–98) 16:209–534. Synods, *ibid.* 536–549; 17:371–530; *Patrologia Latina,* ed. J. P. MIGNE, 271 v., indexes 4 v. (Paris 1878–90) 129:9–262. DEUSDEDIT, *Collectio canonum,* ed. V. WOLF VON GLANVELL (Paderborn 1905). IVO OF CHARTRES, *Decretum, Patrologia Latina,* ed. J. P. MIGNE, 271 v., indexes 4 v. (Paris 1878–90) 161:59–1022. G. HOFMANN, ed., *Photius et ecclesial Romana,* 2 v. (Rome 1932). J. DUFFY and J. PARKER, eds., *The Synodicon Vetus* (Washington, D.C. 1979). Literature. J. HERGENRÖTHER, *Photius, Patriarch von Konstantinopel,* 4 v. in 3 (Regensburg 1867–69). É. AMANN, *Dictionnaire de théologie catholique,* ed. A. VACANT et al., 15 v. (Paris 1903–50; Tables générales 1951–) 12.2:1536–604. K. ZIEGLER, *Paulys Realenzyklopädie der klassischen Altertumswissenschaft,* ed. G. WISSOWA et al. 20.1 (Stuttgart 1941) 667–737. A. P. KAZHDAN, *Oxford Dictionary of Byzantium* (1991) 1669–70. F. DVORNIK, *The Photian Schism* (Cambridge, Eng. 1948); *The Patriarch Photius in the Light of Recent Research* (Munich 1958); "Patriarch Photius, Scholar and Statesman," *Classical Folia* 13 (1959) 3–18; 14 (1960) 3–22. V. GRUMEL, "Y eut-il un second schisme de Photius?" *Revue des sciences philosophiques et théologiques* 22 (1933) 432–457; *Échos d'Orient* 29 (1930) 257–264, 33 (1934) 257–288, 34 (1935) 129–138, 35 (1936) 5–42, 37 (1938) 357–372, 39 (1940–42) 138–156; "Photius et l'addition du *Filioque* au symbole du Nicée-Constantinople," *Revue des études byzantines* 5 (1947) 218–234; *Les Regestes des actes du patriarcat de Constantinople* (2d ed. Paris 1971–91) v. 2. P. STÉPHANOU, "Les Débuts de la querelle photienne vus de Rome et de Byzance," *Orientalia Christiana periodica* 18 (1952) 270–280; "La Violation du compromis entre Photius et les ignatiens," *ibid.* 21 (1955) 291–307. H. G. BECK, *Kirche und theologische Literatur im byzantinischen Reich* (Munich 1959) 520–528. R. J. H. JENKINS, "A Note on Nicetas David Paphlago and the *Vita Ignatii,*" *Dumbarton Oaks Papers* 19 (1965) 241–247. H. AHRWEILER, "Sur la carrière de Photios avant son patriarchat," *Byzantinische Zeitschrift* 58 (1965) 348–361. R. S. HAUGH, *Photius and the Carolingians: The Trinitarian Controversy* (Belmont, Mass. 1975). P. LEMERLE, "Photios and Classicism," in *Byzantine Humanism: The First Phase,* tr. H. LINDSAY and A. MOFFATT (Canberra, Australia 1986) 205–235. C. MANGO, "The Liquidation of Iconoclasm and the Patriarch Photios," in *Iconoclasm,* ed. A. BRYER and J. HERRIN (Birmingham, Eng. 1977). J. A. MEIJER, *A Successful Council of Union: A Theological Analysis of the Photian Synod of 879–880* (Thessalonike 1975). G. MENESTRINA, ed., *Forzio: tra crisi ecclesiale e magistero letterario* (Brescia 2000). L. SIMEONOVA, *Diplomacy of the Letter and the Cross: Photios, Bulgaria and the Papacy, 860s–880s* (Amsterdam 1998). D. STRATOUDAKI WHITE, *Patriarch Photios of Constantinople: His Life, Scholarly Contributions, and Correspondence Together with a Translation of Fifty-Two of His Letters* (Brookline, Mass. 1981). W. TREADGOLD, *The Nature of the Bibliotheca of Photios* (Washington, D.C. 1980).

[F. DVORNIK]

PHYLACTERIES

Phylacteries are small boxes containing certain verses of Scripture worn by Jews at prayer. The term is derived from the Greek word φυλακτήριον (safeguard, amulet). The Jewish name for them is tefillin (Heb. *tᵉpillîn,* which probably represents an Aramaic word meaning "attachments" but which was popularly connected with the Hebrew word *tᵉpillâ,* "prayer"). A minor pseudo-Talmudic tractate also is called Tefillin; it discusses the laws regarding the preparation and wearing of phylacteries. Most of the material in this tractate has been taken from the TALMUD proper.

According to the prescriptions of the Talmud, phylacteries are two small leather boxes with leather straps attached; in each box is a piece of parchment on which are written four passages from the Scriptures: Ex 13.1–10 (the law, on the use of unleavened bread at the Passover in memory of the Exodus from Egypt); Ex 13.11–16 (the law on the first born in memory of the sparing of Israel's first born at the Exodus); Dt 6.4–9 (the *Shema Yisrael* or the Great Commandment of the love of God); Dt 11.13–21 (the promise of a bounteous harvest as a reward

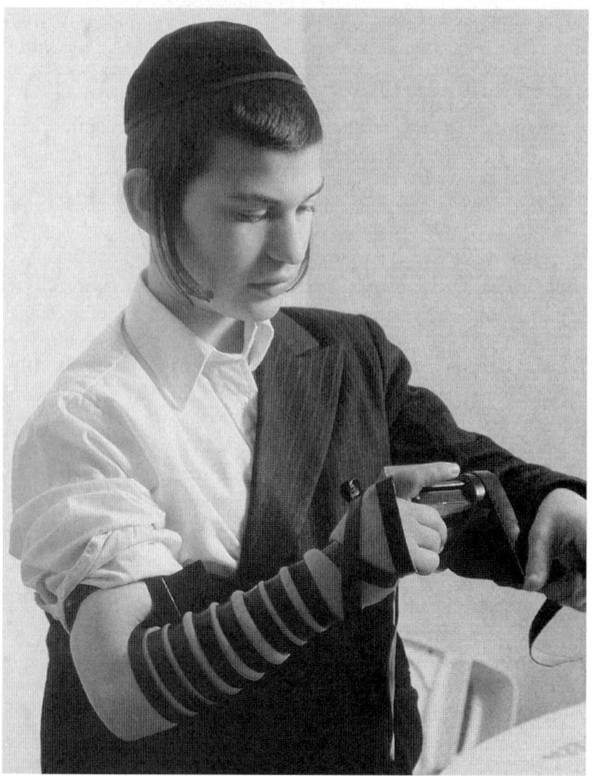

A Hasidic boy wears phylacteries for his morning prayers. (©Richard T. Nowitz/CORBIS)

for keeping the Law). Jewish men, when they say their morning prayers on weekdays (but not on Sabbaths or feasts), are to tie (literally ''lay'') one of the phylacteries on the forehead and one on the left arm. The custom of thus wearing phylacteries is still observed by Orthodox Jews, but not by Reform Jews.

The institution of the phylacteries is based on a literal interpretation of the injunctions in Ex 13.9 (''It shall be as a sign on your hand and as a reminder on your forehead'') and Dt 6.8, 11.18 (''Bind them at your wrist as a sign and let them be as a pendant on your forehead''); hence the choice of the four passages for the phylacteries. Originally, however, these injunctions were no doubt intended to be understood in a figurative sense, like the modern expression, ''Tie a string on your finger that you don't forget''; the Israelites were never to forget Yahweh's laws or His mighty deeds in rescuing them from bondage in Egypt. There is no evidence for the custom of wearing phylacteries before the last few pre-Christian centuries. But several phylacteries have been found at Qumran and further south in the Desert of Judah, e.g., at Murabba'āt, that come from about the time of Christ. The words of Jesus in Mt 23.5 show that the wearing of phylacteries was a common custom at His time; He did not condemn the custom as such, but only the hypocritical display of ''wide phylacteries.'' Among ignorant people phylacteries might have been regarded primarily as amulets; hence their name in Greek. It is possible that the wearing of phylacteries had certain affinities with the apotropaic practices of the ancient Near East; E. A. Speiser seeks to establish this connection by means of the words used to describe phylacteries in Dt 6.8, 11.18: *'ôt* (sign) and *ṭôṭāpōt* (pendants).

See Also: MEZUZAH.

Bibliography: *Encyclopedic Dictionary of the Bible,* tr. and adap. by L. HARTMAN (New York 1963), from A. VAN DEN BORN, *Bijbels Woordenboek,* 1853–54. J. H GREENSTONE et al., *The Jewish Encyclopedia,* ed. J. SINGER, 13 v. (New York 1901–06) 10:21–28. M. JOSEPH, *Universal Jewish Encyclopedia,* 10 v. (New York 1939–44) 8:522–523. J. SCHMID, *Lexikon für Theologie und Kirche*², ed. J. HOFER and K. RAHNER, 10 v. (Freiburg 1957–65) 4:554. E. A. SPEISER, ''TWTPT,'' *Jewish Quarterly Review* 48 (1957–58) 208–217. K. G. KUHN, *Phylakterien aus Höhle 4 von Qumran* (Heidelberg 1957).

[S. M. POLAN]

PHYSICAL LAWS, PHILOSOPHICAL ASPECTS

In considering physical laws, this article presents a historical survey of humanity's understanding of the nature and existence of these laws and a critique of various philosophical positions concerning them.

The conception that nature is regulated by physical laws in its properties and activities has received explicit formulation only in modern science, but it is rooted in notions that have been gradually formed through human experience. The animistic view of nature held by primitive peoples, through reflection and observation, have given place to a rational and philosophical concept of physical reality, and of natural events, as a regular concatenation of causes and effects. This rationalization of the concept of nature has been furthered by astronomical observations of the movements of the stars and by the development of technical arts—involving the construction of instruments and machines—that embody basic applications of mathematics. In these advances one can already detect a foreshadowing of physical laws in the modern sense.

Historical Survey. The mathematical conception of nature came into philosophy with PYTHAGORAS and the Pythagoreans, and with PLATO, who taught that God acts as the geometrician in the world. For ARISTOTLE, the existence of physical laws has a more solid basis in his conception of NATURE as the active principle of MOTION and rest in bodies. Moreover, Aristotle distinguishes events in the heavens from those on earth, the former being regulated by absolutely necessary laws admitting of no exception, the latter—while subject to determinate laws of nature and not merely to CHANCE—admitting of exception and thereby leaving room for chance events (*Phys.* 192b 20–23, 195b 31–198a 13).

After Aristotle, philosophy—and scholastic philosophy in particular—preserved and developed the Aristotelian concept of nature, while corroborating its philosophical analysis with the conception of the world proposed in the Bible. Sacred Scripture describes the universe as a work of the wisdom and omnipotence of God the Creator, by whom all things are disposed ''by measure and number and weight'' (Wis 11.20). According to St. THOMAS AQUINAS, ''since all things subject to divine province are ruled and measured . . . it is evident that all things partake the eternal law in some way, namely, inasmuch as, from its being impressed upon them, they have inclinations to their own acts and ends. . . . And this participation of the eternal law in the rational creature is called the natural law. . . . In the irrational creature, however, [the eternal law] is not shared in a rational way; so it cannot be called a law except by way of similitude'' (*Summa theologiae* 1a2ae, 91.2 and ad 3). All creatures, then, have from their Creator those determined natural inclinations to their own respective ends ''which we say are natural laws'' (*In Dion de div. nom.,* 10.1).

Thus, already in ancient and medieval thought, the lawfulness of physical nature is clearly stated, and the founders of modern science, especially GALILEO and Isaac Newton, were clearly conscious of the continuity of their thought with the foregoing philosophical tradition.

Ontological Value of Laws. Not only in Aristotelian and scholastic philosophy, therefore, but also for the founders of modern science, physical law has an ontological value. The regular and constant relation in the succession of physical phenomena, expressed by a mathematical function relating experimental variables in a determinate way, is, in its turn, and expression of an ontological necessity based upon the very nature of physical agents, which results from the directive will and divine wisdom of the Creator. Moreover, this conception, even when purified of its metaphysical and theological connotations, remained dominant in modern physical science until the 19th century. The classical POSITIVISM of A. Comte expressly acknowledged the realism of physical laws, which were deemed by him to be dogmatically universal facts, no less positively verifiable than singular facts [*Cours de philosophie positive* (Paris 1930) Lesson 1]. A similar realistic conception is defended by contemporary dialectical materialism, which, according to the teaching of K. MARX and F. ENGELS, holds that scientific knowledge is assimilated as a passive representation and faithful mirror of reality (*see* MATERIALISM, DIALECTICAL AND HISTORICAL).

Empiricism and Criticism. To this objective and rationalistic conception of physical laws is opposed EMPIRICISM, notably in the extreme form proposed by D. HUME. According to Hume, the necessity of phenomena expressed in physical law is something purely subjective, a mere psychological expectancy resulting from series of constant connections observed in the past (*Treatise of Human Nature,* 1.3.6). Wishing to save the necessity of physical laws thus compromised by Hume's skeptical empiricism, I. KANT had recourse to synthetic a priori judgments. For him, law is the application of a mental category to PHENOMENA, already ordered in representation through the subjective forms of space and time. In Kant's view, law is valid for the phenomenal world but cannot be acknowledged as valid for reality itself (*Critique of Pure Reason,* Analysis of Principles).

The motives prompting the criticisms by Hume and Kant coalesce, near the end of the 19th century, in the empiriocriticism of E. Mach. This resolves the world of perception into pure sensations and, therefore, the natural sciences into a mere analysis of sensation. For Mach, physical laws are not necessarily operative in reality, since this presupposes the inverifiable postulate of regularity in nature. They are merely a restriction that the subject imposes upon himself in anticipating future sensations, for the sake of economy and as a means of functional adaptation in the struggle for life (*Analyse der Empfindungen,* Jena 1900).

Conventionalism. Very close to this conception is the conventionalism of J. H. Poincaré, for whom general principles—both of mathematics and of physics—are free conventions or masked definitions, adopted as criteria of scientific convenience, i.e., for their simplicity and logical coherence (*La Science et l'hypothèse,* Paris 1902). Poincaré's conventionalism was inspired not so much by philosophical preconceptions as by the evolution of mathematics and physics during the 19th century, which had shown that many laws and principles, held to be necessary and eternal by classical science and by positivism, had to be revised and replaced by other principles and laws that were more in accord with experimental facts. From this is was easy to conclude that principles and physical laws are not absolutely imposed by experience and do not express objective relations or the causes of phenomena, but are posited by the scientist as apt conventions and as approximate and provisional expressions. Hence physical laws become mere algebraic relations connecting the numbers that result from experimental measurement; such relations can be approximated in an infinite number of ways by mathematical functions, from which the simplest relations are selected only for the sake of convenience and economy.

Neopositivism. The neopositivism of the *Wiener Kreis,* of Rudolf CARNAP and Otto Neurath, took up the teaching of Hume and Mach, eliminating its psychological elements and reducing empiricism to mere nominalism. For LOGICAL POSITIVISM the only meaningful propositions are ''protocol statements,'' which state an experimentally verifiable fact; physical laws, when enunciated as universals, cannot be verified. Rather, in their abstractness, they are not even complete propositions, but only propositional functions containing indeterminate variables in which determinate and concrete values can be substituted. Thus, for logical positivists, universal law is transformed into a protocol statement [J. Joergensen, *The Development of Logical Empiricism* (Chicago 1951) 30].

Critical Realism. The subjectivistic conception of physical laws is widely diffused in contemporary thought, being accepted even by neoscholastic philosophers such as J. MARITAIN and F. Renoirte, who deem it a legitimate purification of sciences from philosophical and metaphysical elements. Yet many scientists and philosophers defend the ontological value of physical laws by a kind of critical realism that steers a middle road between opposing extremes. Among these, the first to be cited are the founders of contemporary physics, namely, Max Planck and Albert EINSTEIN. Critical realism accords to empiricist and subjectivistic views the merit of having combated the exaggerated realism of a Platonic or mechanistic type that was dominant in classical physics. Thus it recognizes the essential activity of the mind in formulating scientific laws, which necessarily contain subjective, approximate, and provisory elements. At the same time, however, it admits the capacity of human thought to know material reality in itself and to penetrate into its essence through observed phenomena and by scientific reasoning.

Uniformity. The ontological value of physical laws can be justified by a critical theory of KNOWLEDGE in general, and then reinforced by a consideration of the practical value of science itself. If, in fact, physical laws lack all ontological value, the ability to predict phenomena from physical laws and the practical value of science in technical applications would be only casual and fortuitous coincidences, as even Poincaré noted in opposing the extremist interpretation given by E. Le Roy to his teaching [H. Poincaré, *La Valeur de la science* (Paris 1905) 220]. One must therefore admit that the constant and uniform regularity observed in experience, and stated in physical laws, has an ontological basis in the nature of physical agents. This nature is independent of human knowledge and is antecedent to action itself. Physical law thus objectively, *in actu primo,* as a causal antecedent of the activity regulated by it, even before being discovered and formulated by scientists, even before man appeared on the earth. The principles of UNIFORMITY in nature or of ontological determinism in physical agents offer, then, the ontological basis and rational explanation of physical laws.

Determinism. The ontological determinism of physical agents, or the principle of determinate causality, is a necessary presupposition for the formulation of physical laws and is also the ontological basis for scientific INDUCTION. As such, it cannot result from this type of induction, but must be seen as an application of the self-evident principle of SUFFICIENT REASON, according to which everything existing or happening has a reason for exiting or happening. If the physical agent, deprived of knowledge and choice, were not determined by its nature to one action rather than another, it would be indifferent to any action whatever and would therefore not act (St. Thomas, *C. gent.* 3.2). Even as regards physical determinism, however, contemporary physics has moderated the rigidity claimed by classical physics. This determinism is no longer absolute, but relative. Thus, from a metaphysical point of view, one can reject the illicit extrapolation of determinism from the physical world to the human will and, even more so, to the divine will. From a physical point of view, the discovery of statistical laws and of quantum indeterminism has shown the value of a conception of nature like that of Aristotle. While seeing determinism and necessity as arising from FORM, this recognizes the existence of indetermination and potentiality arising from MATTER and admits the existence of chance events as exceptions to natural law.

See Also: LAW; NATURAL LAW; INDETERMINISM; MECHANISM.

Bibliography: F. SELVAGGI, *Filosofia delle scienze* (Rome 1953). F. RENOIRTE, *Cosmology: Elements of a Critique of the Sciences and of Cosmology,* tr J. F. COFFEY (New York 1950). M. BUNGE, *Metascientific Queries* (Springfield, Ill. 1959). E. SIMARD, *La Nature et la portée de la méthode scientifique* (Quebec 1956). A. G. M. VAN MELSEN, *Science and Technology* (Pittsburgh 1961). R. B. LINDSAY and H. MARGENAU, *Foundations of Physics* (New York 1936). J. DE VRIES, ''Das Problem der Naturgesetzlichkeit bei Thomas von Aquin,'' *Scholastik* 10–24 (1949) 503–517.

[F. SELVAGGI]

PHYSIOLOGUS

Physiologus, composed in or near Egypt in the 2d century A.D., was the most widely known animal book during the Middle Ages. The author had before him unidentified descriptions of creatures known to classical literature (the phoenix, the sirens, the fox) and others deriving from accounts from India, Africa, and Asia Minor. To the short descriptions of physical traits of animals and mystic stones, he added Christian moralizations, illustrated by quotations from the Bible. The elements are fused with true artistry, and each chapter is something of a creative masterpiece.

In his critical edition of 1936, which replaces all earlier ones, F. Sbordone divided the Greek MSS into four versions. His *fontes* actually are parallels in the writings of the early Fathers and in a few cases borrowings, the sources proper being unknown. He adds the version of MSS AEIII, from which are derived the Armenian and all Latin translations. The fixed contents of this version are best presented alphabetically according to the 37 chapters of the Latin *versio B* correlated with the 49 of *versio Y* (names common to both are preceded by †, and those peculiar to *Y* are set in *italics*): †arbor peredixion; *arbor psycomora* (as "Amos" in *B*); †aquila; aspischeleon (*cetus*); asida, i.e., struthiocamelon; †autolops; caladrius (*charadrius*); caprea (*dorchon*); †castor; †cervus; †columbae; †elephas; †formica; fulica (*herodius*); †herinacius; †hyaena; hydrus (*niluus*); *hyrundo;* †ibis; ichneumon, as *echinemon;* lacerta (*saura eliace*); *lapis achatis;* lapis adamas (*lapis adamantinus* in two separate chapters); *lapis magnis;* lapis margarita [*l. sostoros* (i.e., "ostrea") *et margarita*]; *lapis senditicos,* i.e., "indicus"; lapides igniferi (*l. piroboli*); †leo; *mirmicoleon;* †mustela et aspis (plus a *vipera*); †nycticorax; †onager et simia (twice in *Y*); †panthera; †pelicanus; †perdix; †phoenix; *rana;* salamandra (*saura*); *serpens;* †serra; †sirenae et onocentauri; †turtur (plus a *cornicola*); unicornis (*monoceros*); upupa (*epops*); †vulpis; *vultur.*

The importance of the influence of India is evident in the mystic stones, the elephant, the mandrake, and the whale. The presence of any creature other than those listed proves later interpolation. Shorter versions include *versio L* (in 27 chapters, extant in some 15 MSS) and *De naturis duodecim animalium* (extant in over 70 MSS; *Patrologia Latina* 171:1217–24).

Versio B was in circulation by 386, when St. Ambrose quoted from it (*Hex.* 6.13:3), and was expanded in several steps, using St. Isidore of Seville and Solinus, until its final form as *De Bestiis et aliis rebus.* The four old French translations, by Philippe de Thaon, Pierre le Picard, Guillaume le Normand, and Richard de Fournival, make few innovations, except that the last develops a concept of love.

Even in the French, the original doctrines remain essentially unchanged. In stereotyped form, typical of the 2d century, a fluid demonology of fallen gods is described; and Satan is usually merely a symbol of death, wicked but not ugly; the association with the monkey relates to a moral idea. The work is violently antifeminist, and eternal damnation often results from mere imprudence: good intentions are of no avail, and a superhuman vigilance is required to frustrate the legions of Evil and their leader Satan. Both main Latin versions, rich in quotations from pre-Vulgate Bibles, add important variants for the *Afra* and the *Itala.* They also contain bold Hellenisms in addition to the names, and rare morphological and syntactical forms. Christianity took many symbols from *Physiologus,* the most important being the phoenix and the pelican; many animals represented in medieval stone and glass have no symbolic value, however, or are related to sermons and the works of HONORIUS OF AUTUN rather than to *Physiologus.*

Studies of *Physiologus* began with Ponce de León's edition (1587) of the Greek version attributed to St. Epiphanius of Constantia (*Patrologia Graeca* 43:517–534), but there was little further interest in the work until the beginning of the 19th century, when fragments began to be collected and translations made from Semitic languages: Angelo Mai (*Classici autores,* v. 7, Rome 1835), J. B. Pitra (*Spicilegium solesmense,* Paris 1855). The most useful single collection of Latin and French versions appears in C. Cahier's *Mélanges d'archéologie, d'histoire et de littérature,* 4 v. (Paris 1847–56). One major Greek version was edited by F. Lauchert, *Geschichte des Physiologus* (Strasbourg 1889).

Bibliography: *Physiologus,* Greek ed., F. SBORDONE (Milan 1936); *Versio B,* ed. F. CARMODY (Paris 1939); *Versio E,* M. R. JAMES, *The Bestiary* (London 1928); *Versio L* (in 27 chapters), G. HEIDER, *Archiv für Kunde österreichischer Geschichts-Quellen* 5 (1850); *Versio T* (in 12 chapters, attributed to Theobald), *Patrologia Latina,* ed. J. P. MIGNE, 217 v. (Paris 1878–90) 171:1217–23; Eng. tr. A. W. RENDELL (London 1928); *Versio Y,* F. CARMODY (Publications in Classical Philology 12.7; Berkeley 1941). K. AHRENS, *Zur Geschichte des sogenannlen Physiologus* (Plön 1885). E. DINKLER and V. SCHUBERT, *Die Religion in Geschichte und Gegenwart,* 7 v. (3d ed. Tübingen 1957–65) 5:364–365. B. E. PERRY, *Paulys Realenzyklopädie der klassischen Altertumswissenschaft,* ed. G. WISSOWA et al. (Stuttgart 1893) 20:1074–1129.

[F. CARMODY]

PIAGET, JEAN

Child psychologist; philosopher; b. Neuchatel, Switzerland Aug. 9, 1896; d. Geneva, 1980. Widely known as a psychologist of children's thinking, Piaget was a prolific researcher and writer with over 100 books and innumerable articles to his name. Piaget's chief aim was to transform philosophical epistemology into an interdisciplinary empirical science, involving notably psychology, biology, and the history of science. His typical methodology was to investigate the genesis of knowledge—in the individual, the species, society—hence the name ''genetic epistemology.''

Piaget limited his research to the most general structures of knowledge, what used to be called the universals or *a priori* categories, or more simply, the logical-mathematical framework that is assumed to structure all biological actions and human thinking. Piaget resolutely held to three basic assumptions: knowledge is an action, the relation of a subject acting on an object; the object is constructed (in evolution or individual development); this construction at all levels implies logical structures. Note that ''object'' in this context does not mean an external (objective) fact or event, untouched by ''subjective'' interactions, but almost the opposite: for Piaget subject (through active assimilation) and object (through passive accommodation) form a biological whole and reciprocally imply each other. With respect to human knowledge in particular, Piaget rejected the traditional dichotomies of heredity vs. environment, nativism vs. behaviorism, and idealism vs. empiricism, in favor of a *tertium quid*, namely, a radical constructivism.

Cognitive Development. In support of his thesis Piaget meticulously observed children first constructing sensorimotor know-how, shown in perception and movements in nearby space and time, which leads around age two to the transition from the undifferentiated object of action to the differentiated object of knowledge. The immediate consequence of object knowledge is the psychological representation of the desired object in symbol formation. Pretend play and gestures, mental image, and societal language are the major symbol types. Object knowledge ushers in a new stage of development in the form of ''pre-operations'' which between the ages six to eleven reach a partial closure with ''concrete operations,'' such as classification, seriation, number, and the subsequent full closure of ''formal operations,'' as shown in ordinary hypothetical and propositional reasoning.

Operations are the common and most general logical structures accessible to human consciousness, characterized logically by reversibility and universality, and psychologically by the subjective conviction of logical (as opposed to empirical) necessity. Development is here conceived as an active structuring and restructuring of general logical coordinations at sequentially more comprehensive stages. This developmental growth has repercussions on specific psychological acts, such as learning (in the strict sense of learning a particular skill or content), perception, imagery, memory, as well as moral and social conduct.

Stages are strictly defined in terms of the quality of logical understanding. Children are said not merely to know less but to know, and therefore to live in, a different reality than adults. Moreover, even though all healthy adults, regardless of external circumstances, can be assumed implicitly to share formal operations, the theory requires that this logical power is individually appropriated and applied. Any uniformity among people or across content areas is thereby excluded. In this manner Piaget's theory encompasses the tension between the freedom (and respect) for individual and cultural differences and the necessary constraints of logical implication and empirical confirmation. Only through the constructive interplay of these two conditions can knowledge attain a measure of—always relative—objectivity and certainty.

Knowledge and Freedom. For Piaget knowledge is not a ''point-at-able'' fact or merely information coded in the brain; it is alive and open-ended such that by its own motivation it cannot but lead to improvement and development. However, this growth is not an automatic internal program or a mere imitation from outside, but requires a serious personal commitment and contribution. Consequently in individual development genuinely new knowledge is constantly being constructed, just as throughout history social, artistic, and scientific achievements are the new products of human interactions.

In fact, the universal categories and their logical necessity are seen as the firm anchor against which true freedom of acting and thinking and moral autonomy can come to fruition. Human knowledge as relational translates into openness to other people's thinking, which must be restructured in one's own terms. In this sense operation is not something solitary and intrapsychic, but an interpersonal, social, and ultimately moral affair. For Piaget operation and cooperation, just as knowledge and development, are reciprocal notions: ''logic is the morality of thought just as morality is the logic of actions.'' Likewise, ''the logic of development is the development of logic.''

Piaget's theory can be appreciated as a reformulation of Kant's epistemology in a Darwinian and social-historical perspective. In contrast to other similar attempts, Piaget accepted the nature of Kant's a priori categories, but he rejected their temporal priority. Instead he offered an evolutionary description of their origin as an empirical answer to a heretofore purely philosophical question. ''Equilibration'' is Piaget's key concept through which he analyzes the developmental progress from instinctual know-how to the beginnings of a logic of action and ultimately to the necessary coordination of conscious logical operations.

On account of its unusual philosophical flavor Piaget's work is controversial and easily misunderstood.

Nevertheless, it has been widely applied wherever developmental considerations are relevant, including religious development and education. Three Piagetian notions seem particularly pertinent. First, his theory of symbol formation (Piaget 1946) is unique in being apparently the only scholarly attempt to go beyond the recognition of the specific power of symbols to an explanation of their psychological origin. Second, his study on children's moral judgment (Piaget 1932) stresses the important distinction between unilateral and reciprocal relations and how these affect the development of the moral person. Third, many facets of human life, particularly in interpersonal, artistic, and religious spheres, do not lend themselves to full operatory coordination. With Piaget (1926) the child's preoperatory conception of the world can be appreciated as something valuable in its own right and permanently affecting the deeper layers of a person's psychology.

Bibliography: J. C. BRINGUIER, *Conversations with Jean Piaget* (Chicago 1980). H. G. FURTH, *Knowledge as Desire: An Essay on Freud and Piaget* (New York 1987). H. E. GRUBER & J. J. VONECHE, eds., *The Essential Piaget* (New York 1977). J. PIAGET, *The Child's Conception of the World* (Totowa, N.J. 1969); *The Moral Development of the Child* (New York 1965); *Play, Dreams, Imitation in Childhood* (original title *Symbol Formation in the Child*) (New York 1951); *Insights and Illusions of Philosophy* (New York 1971). J. PIAGET and B. INHELDER, *The Psychology of the Child* (New York 1969).

[H. G. FURTH]

PIAMARTA, GIOVANNI BATTISTA, BL.

Diocesan priest, founder of the Congregation of the Holy Family of Nazareth and the Humble Servants of the Lord; b. Nov. 26, 1841, Brescia, Italy; d. April 25, 1913, Remedello, Italy.

Born into a poor but pious family headed by a barber and a seamstress, Piamarta received his education in local schools until he entered the seminary in 1860. Following ordination (1865) his ministry, first in rural parishes (Carzago Riviera and Bedizzole), then in Brescia, focused on working-class young people and their families.

With Msgr. Petro Capretti he founded (1886) the *Istituto Artigianelli* to provide working-class children with the moral foundation and professional skills needed in the newly industrialized society. He built housing and workshops for 100 boys, whom he served as a father and spiritual director.

With Fr. Bonsignori he established (1895) an agricultural research center on 140 hectares at Remedello to enhance the farming skills of peasants. Remedello gained an international reputation, and its structure was copied in many countries.

In 1902, he founded the Congregation of the Holy Family of Nazareth to perpetuate his work. A women's community, the Humble Servants of the Lord, was established, with the help of his mother and Elisa Baldo Foresti, to strengthen rural and urban families in the region through education. Piamarta gave precedence to the material and spiritual needs of others, while finding his own consolation in prayer.

He died peacefully surrounded by his brothers and Fr. Bonsignori. He was beatified by Pope John Paul II on Oct. 12, 1997 and is a patron of families and workers.

Feast: June 26.

Bibliography: *Acta Apostolicae Sedis* 20 (1997): 999. *L'Osservatore Romano,* English edition, no. 42 (1997): 1–2. *Lettere di P. Giovanni Piamarta e dei suoi corrispondenti,* ed. by A. FAPPANI (Brescia 1994). *Giovanni Piamarta e il suo tempo: atti del colloquio di studio: Brescia, 12 settembre 1987* (Brescia 1987).

[K. I. RABENSTEIN]

PIARISTS

The Order of the Poor Clerics Regular of the Mother of God of the Pious Schools (Sch.P.), popularly known as the Piarists, was established in 1597 by a Spanish diocesan priest, St. JOSEPH CALASANCTIUS (Calsanz) (1556–1648) in Rome. The founder wished to provide free education for youth, both rich and poor. All Piarists profess four religious vows, including a special vow to educate youth, especially the poor. The order, which dates its official foundation from March 25, 1617, has grown despite the numerous political persecutions it endured. In 1808, Napoleon destroyed the flourishing German-Swiss province; in 1832, the large and fruitful provinces in Lithuania and Poland were liquidated by Russia in the wake of the Polish revolution of the previous year. The Spanish Civil War (1936–1939) caused great destruction to the schools and the four provinces in Spain; 260 priests were killed. In the 1950s, foundations in Czechoslovakia, Hungary and Romania were abolished by communist governments.

Piarists are found in 33 countries in Europe; North, South, and Central America; Asia; and Africa. Established in 1975, the American province has its headquarters in Washington, D.C. Members of the American province serve in Washington, D.C.; Devon, Pennsylvania; Fort Lauderdale, Florida; Miami, Florida; Lackawanna, New York; Passaic, New Jersey; and Martin, Kentucky. Piarists also work in New York-Puerto Rico vice province and California vice province.

Alumni of the Piarists' schools include Pope Pius IX, who graduated from the Piarist school in Volterrs, Italy, and St. John Nepomucene Neumann, CssR, fourth bishop of Philadelphia and a graduate of the Piarist school in Straznice, Moravia. St. Anthony Maria Claret, founder of the Claretians, was also a student of the Piarists. Thaddeus Kosciusko, the American Revolutionary hero, Gregor Mendel, the father of modern genetics; the Spanish painter Francisco de Goya; Haydn; Mozart; Schubert: all had been educated by the Piarists. Prominent Piarists include Bishop Ladislaus Iranyi, the first bishop for Hungarians outside of Hungary, and Alfonso Mistrangelo, who became a cardinal in 1916 and was appointed archbishop of Florence. The Order has two saints among its members: St. Joseph Calasanctius and Pompilius Maria Pirotti (canonized, 1934), and several beati including Glycerius Landrinai, Peter Casani, and 13 Spanish martyrs of Spain.

Bibliography: J. C. BAU, *Biografía crítica de San José de Calasanz* (Madrid 1949). C. S. DURANT, *The Life of St. Joseph Calasanctius* (Los Angeles 1954).

[J. KERSHNER/D. POWERS]

PIBUSH, JOHN, BL.

Priest, martyr; b. Thirsk, North Riding, Yorkshire, England; d. hanged, drawn, and quartered at St Thomas's Waterings, Camberwell, Southwark, Feb. 18, 1601. John, probably the son of Thomas Pibush of Great Fencott and Jane Danby of Scotton, studied at Rheims (1580–87) before his ordination on March 14, 1587. He was confined to prison for most of his 12 years in the English mission. After his arrest at Morton-in-Marsh, Gloucestershire (1593), he was sent to London, then committed to the Gatehouse at Westminster for a year. After his trial at the Gloucester Assizes under 27 Eliz., c. 2, for being a priest, he was returned to Gloucester jail. He escaped for a day, but was recaptured at Matson. From Gloucester he was sent to the Marshalsea, London, and again tried in Westminster under the same statute, July 1, 1595. Although he was condemned for high treason, he was kept in prison at the Marshalsea and the Queen's Bench prison for more than five years. In the end he was permitted a single day to prepare for his death. He was beatified by Pius XI on Dec. 15, 1929.

Feast of the English Martyrs: May 4 (England).

See Also: ENGLAND, SCOTLAND, AND WALES, MARTYRS OF.

Bibliography: R. CHALLONER, *Memoirs of Missionary Priests,* ed. J. H. POLLEN (rev. ed. London 1924; repr. Farnborough 1969) I, 123. T. F. KNOX, *First and Second Diaries of English College, Douai* (London 1878) 169, 179, 198, 212, 214, 222. J. H. POLLEN, *Acts of English Martyrs* (London 1901) 333–6.

[K. I. RABENSTEIN]

PICARDS

A heretical group of semisecluded communities in Bohemia since the late 14th century. The name originated either as a Slavicized version of Beghards (*see* BEGUINES AND BEGHARDS), or from those supporters of the movement who immigrated to Bohemia from Picardy, France, due to the Inquisition in the early 1400s. Whether the Picards were originally heretical or merely unique in their communal way of life is questioned. The religious life of 14th- and 15th-century Bohemia was intricate, and the Picards can be understood only against that background.

Shortly after 1300, the Czech branch of the DEVOTIO MODERNA began to flourish under the bishop of Prague, John of Dražice. The Devotio had ties with the Netherlands, whence the Beghards, including Gerard GROOTE, who had studied at the Charles University in Prague, had spread through Europe. It is possible that this relationship between Bohemia and the Netherlands influenced the origin of the Picards. Furthermore, JOHN MILÍČ, a leading preacher in Prague, had insisted, as early as mid-14th century, on the usefulness of the semisecluded communities in which a brotherly life was practiced by Christian laymen. Although Milíč's own similar community in Prague, "New Jerusalem," remained orthodox, most of those outside the capital—including the Picards—eventually became contaminated with heresy. The fact that John ŽIŽKA, the military leader of the TABORITES, put to death a community of Picards in 1421 does not in itself prove that the Picards were or were not HUSSITES of some variety, as Žižka treated in like fashion anyone unwilling to submit to his leadership. Actually, the Picards were never orthodox Hussites, being more in sympathy with such radical Hussites as the Taborites and Adamites.

The Picards advocated a pseudorationalistic biblical criticism. They emphasized individual piety, and their mysticism, borrowed from the Beghards, became a pantheistic hedonism. Not unlike the WALDENSES in their criticism of the Church, they denied the priesthood, confession, the liturgy, and especially the role of the Holy Spirit in the Church. They denied the presence of Christ in the Eucharist and broke with orthodox Hussites, who were willing to compromise on the doctrine of transubstantiation. The Picards were still to be found in Bohemia and Moravia in the 19th century.

Bibliography: F. M. BARTOŠ, *Husitství a cizina* (Prague 1931). F. G. HEYMANN, *John Žižka and the Hussite Revolution* (Princeton 1955). R. KALIVODA, *Husitská ideologie* (Prague 1961). F. SEIBT, *Lexikon für Theologie und Kirche*, ed. J. HOFER and K. RAHNER (Freiburg 1957–65) 8:503–504.

[B. CHUDOBA]

PICCOLOMINI

A Sienese noble family, of Roman origin according to tradition and legend. Documentary evidence of its residence in SIENA goes back to 1098, when a *Martino* Piccolomini is mentioned. The family early engaged in commerce. By the 13th century it had several banks in Italy, France, and England, and eventually invested its wealth in land. Traditionally Guelf, the Piccolomini family played a significant role in Sienese political life. In 1458 they were granted the title of counts palatine by Emperor Frederick III. Besides PIUS II, his nephew, PIUS III, and Cardinal Jacopo AMMANATI DE' PICCOLOMINI, who had been adopted by Pius II, the family furnished many bishops of Siena and Pienza, and several cardinals. Other outstanding members of the family include the following.

Bl. Ambrogio, d. 1348, was one of the founders, and second superior, of the Olivetan BENEDICTINES.

Alessandro, humanist, theologian, and philosopher (b. Siena, June 13, 1508; d. Siena, March 12, 1578), was an author of sonnets and plays in his youth and later turned to philosophy and became professor of ethics in 1540. His works include translations of Ovid, Vergil, Aristotle's *Poetics* and *Rhetoric,* and several scientific and philosophical treatises. Made bishop of the nominal See of Patras in 1574, he was coadjutor of the archbishop of Siena during the last years of his life.

Francesco (b. Siena, 1582; d. Rome, 1651) was general of the JESUITS from 1649 until his death. *Celio,* d. 1681, was made cardinal in 1664, and archbishop of Siena from 1671 until his death.

Octavio, military commander during the Thirty Years' War (b. Pisa, 1600; d. Vienna, 1656), had joined the Spanish army in Italy and had become imperial cavalry commander and imperial field marshal in 1648, before he was made a prince by the Emperor in 1649. Several branches of the family still exist.

Bibliography: A. LISINI and A. LIBERATI, *Genealogia dei Piccolomini di Siena* (Siena 1900). A. BALDINI, *Enciclopedia Italiana di scienzi littere ed arti*, 36 v. (Rome 1929–39) 27:156–157. V. SPRETI, *Enciclopedia storico-nobiliare italiana,* 8 v. (Milan 1928–35) 5:325–337. F. V. CERRETA, *Alessandro Piccolomini* (Siena 1960).

[E. G. GLEASON]

The Piccolomini coat of arms, five crescents on the arms of a cross, shield flanked by two angels, above, two cherubs holding the papal tiara, relief in the Casa Piccolomini at Siena.

PICCOLOMINI, ALESSANDRO

Littérateur, philosopher, bishop; b. Siena, June 13, 1508; d. Siena, March 12, 1578. Piccolomini, a student of the classics in both Padua and Rome, also became a master of Petrarchan style. This author of more than 100 sonnets also composed several comedies, among them *Alessandro* and *Amor Constante.* He translated into Italian Ovid's *Metamorphoses,* Aristotle's *Poetics* and *Rhetoric,* and part of Vergil's *Aeneid.* His most famous work, *Raffaella o Dialogo della creanze aelle donne* (1540), written in the style of Aretino, was later repudiated by its author as too licentious. In the same year (1540), Piccolomini turned to philosophy, becoming a professor in Padua and later in Rome. He devoted himself principally to writing philosophic, scientific, and astronomical treatises. As a controversialist, Piccolomini attacked the Aristotelian theory concerning the extent of land mass on Earth; he also wrote in support of the Ptolemaic view of astronomy. Alessandro was converted from his youthful indiscretions, received Holy Orders, and in 1574 was appointed titular archbishop of Patras and coadjutor archbishop of Siena by Gregory XIII, whose interest in calendar reform Piccolomini shared.

Bibliography: A. POSCH, *Lexikon für Theologie und Kirche,* ed. J. HOFER and K. RAHNER, 10 v. (2d, new ed. Freiburg 1957–65) 8:492. *Il Cinquecento* (4th ed. Milan 1950).

[P. S. MCGARRY]

PICHLER, JOHANN AND WILHELM

Brothers distinguished in the field of catechetics and pastoral theology.

Johann, pastoral theologian; b. Grosskrut, Austria, March 22, 1860; d. Vienna, Oct. 22, 1927. Ordained in 1882, he was pastor in Maissau until 1903. He then went to Vienna, where he began his lifelong career in catechetics. With his brother, Wilhelm, he was the cofounder of the Viennese catechetical method and played a leading role in the Vienna Catechetical Union. At variance with the intellectualist catechetical method of the 19th century, he worked as a pioneer for the transformation of catechetical instruction of his day. His writings include *Kath. Volksschul-Katechesen* (Vienna 1905–07); *Katechesen für die Oberstufe . . . sowie für die Christenlehre* (Vienna 1911–14); with Wilhelm, *Lehrplan für den kath. Religionsunterricht an den Volks- u. Bürgerschulen Östr.s* (Vienna 1904).

Wilhelm, outstanding contributor to the field of catechetics; b. Grosskrut, May 11, 1862; d. Vienna, March 3, 1938. Ordained in 1887, he entered the field of catechetics in Vienna in 1903. There he quickly recognized the fruitlessness and formalism of the religious instruction of his time. He therefore exposed the deficiencies inherent in the current catechetical method and attempted to bring about a transformation in its form and methodology. He began by developing an entirely new curriculum in which Scripture, doctrine, and liturgy were united. In order to free catechetics from the methodological conflicts of his time, he called attention to its need of a strong Biblical foundation. In this he adhered closely to the thinking of Otto Wilmann, Augustin Gruber, and Johann Gustave Mey, contemporary workers in catechetical instruction and method. Pichler was strongly pastoral in his approach and saw pastoral concerns as basic to catechetics. His catechisms made him a pioneer for all Biblically grounded books of catechetical instruction. His writings include *Unser RU Seine Mängel u. deren Ursachen* (Vienna 1907); *Das Kath. Religionsbüchlein* (Vienna 1913); *Katechesen für die Unterstufe der Volksschule* (Vienna 1918–22); *Zur Methode des RU* (Vienna 1935); and *Hauptfragen des RU* (Vienna 1937).

On the practical level, he went far beyond the catechetical demands of his time, but failed to win complete understanding and sympathy for his work. Personal modesty and a shyness about making public his ideas were an obstacle to his success, and his co-workers remained few. Nevertheless, he had a marked influence on the application of religious instruction, especially to the lower grades. He also developed an interest in missionary catechetics and devoted the last years of his life to this area.

Bibliography: F. JACHYM, "Wilhelm Pichler: Sein Leben und Werk" in *Katechetische Besinnung* (Vienna 1951) 9–22. H. KREUTZWALD, *Zur Geschichte des biblischen Unterrichts* (Freiburg 1957). L. LENTER, *Katechetisches Wörterbuch* (Freiburg 1961) 623–624. A. HEUSER, in *Lexikon für Theologie und Kirche,* ed. J. HOFER and K. RAHNER, 10 v. (2d new ed. Freiburg 1957–65) 8:493.

[E. LEWIS]

PICHLER, VITUS

Canonist; b. Grossberghofen, Germany, May 24, 1670; d. Munich, Feb. 15, 1736. After ordination he entered the Society of Jesus on Sept. 28, 1696. He was professor of philosophy at Dillingen, and later of theology, controversial and scholastic. He taught canon law for 19 years at Dillingen and Ingolstadt, where he succeeded Franz SCHMALZGRUEBER. His first important literary work was *Examen polemicum super Augustana Confessione* (1708). His other controversial works were directed against the Reformers, such as *Lutheranismus constanter errans* (1709), *Una et vera fides* (1710), *Theologia polemica particularis* (1711), and *Cursus theologiae polemincae universae* (1713). It is said he was the first to make a clear distinction between fundamental theology and other divisions of the science. His important work on papal infallibility is *Papatus numquam errans in proponendis fidel articulis* (1709). He is better known as a canonist. His solutions to complex cases in jurisprudence kindled a wider interest in the study of canons and a better insight into the *Corpus iuris canonici.*

Bibliography: H. HURTER, *Nomenclator literarius theologiae catholicae,* 5 v. in 6 (3d ed. Innsbruck 1903–13) 4:1279–81. C. SOMMERVOGEL et al., *Bibliothèque de la Compagnie de Jésus,* 11 v. (Brussels-Paris 1890–1932; v. 12, suppl. 1960) 6:706–714. A. DE BACKER, *Bibliothèque des écrivains, S.J.,* 7 v. (Liège 1853–61).

[T. D. DOUGHERTY]

PICKERING, THOMAS, BL.

Benedictine lay brother and martyr; b. Westmorland(?), England, *c.* 1621; d. hanged, drawn, and quartered at Tyburn (London) May 9, 1679. Thomas was admitted to the Benedictines at St. Gregory's Abbey, Douai, in 1660. Upon returning to London (1665), he was procurator and steward of the community at the queen's chapel. Pickering, who was known to King Charles II, was allowed to stay in England after the expulsion of the Benedictines in 1675 because he was not a priest. He was unjustly implicated in the Titus Oates Plot in 1678. Although the queen upheld his innocence, the jury convicted and condemned him. The king made attempts to save Pickering while satisfying the public blood thirst by executing two others condemned for the conspiracy. However, after the House of Commons petitioned (April 26, 1679) for Pickering's execution, the king yielded and Pickering was martyred. Downside Abbey, Bath, preserves a relic. Pickering was beatified by Pius XI on Dec. 15, 1929.

Feast of the English Martyrs: May 4 (England).

See Also: ENGLAND, SCOTLAND, AND WALES, MARTYRS OF.

Bibliography: *Remarks on the tryal of Mr. Ireland, Mr. Pickering, and Mr. Grove* (London 1679). R. CHALLONER, *Memoirs of Missionary Priests,* ed. J. H. POLLEN (rev. ed. London 1924; repr. Farnborough 1969), II, 376. W. IRELAND, *The tryals of William Ireland, Thomas Pickering, and John Grove . . .* (London 1678). J. H. POLLEN, *Acts of English Martyrs* (London 1891).

[K. I. RABENSTEIN]

PICO DELLA MIRANDOLA

Surname of uncle and nephew Italian philosophers of the late fifteenth and early sixteenth centuries.

Giovanni. Count of Concordia; b. Mirandola, Feb. 24, 1463; d. Florence, Nov. 17, 1494. Giovanni Pico was the son of Gianfrancesco I and Giulia (Boiardo) Pico of the ruling family of Mirandola, a small independent duchy near Modena. At age 14 he went to Bologna to study canon law, and two years later he went to Florence, where he first made contact with M. FICINO and the Platonic Academy. At the University of Padua (1480–82) he began studying Aristotelian philosophy and also showed an interest in Hebrew and Arabic, becoming one of the first Europeans of the Renaissance to study these languages. In 1482 he returned to Florence, where he read Ficino's *Theologia Platonica,* studied Greek, and became fast friends with Angelo Poliziano. In 1485 Pico engaged in a famous controversy with Ermalao Barbaro on philosophical style, taking the position that philosophy must be judged by its truth value rather than by the literary style in which it is written. Later in the same year, he went to Paris to study scholastic philosophy and theology.

In 1486 Pico returned to Florence and made plans to hold a disputation in Rome in which he would defend against all challengers the truth of 900 selected theses in philosophy, theology, and science (Rome 1486). These theses, which include material from many sources, show the great breadth of learning of Pico at age 23. Before the disputation could take place, however, it was suspended by Pope INNOCENT VIII. Pico's *Apologia* (Naples 1487) only made matters worse, and his theses were condemned on Aug. 5, 1487, as containing heretical material. Pursued by a papal order for his arrest, Pico fled to France and was arrested there in January of 1488; he was released a short time later.

"Giovanni Pico della Mirandola," portrait by an unknown artist, in the Uffizi Gallery, Florence, Italy.

He returned to Florence, protected by the MEDICI family, and in 1489 composed his *Heptaplus* (Florence 1489), a commentary on the six days of creation dedicated to Lorenzo de'Medici. In 1492 he wrote *De Ente et Uno* (Bologna 1496), dedicated to Poliziano, the only completed portion of a projected longer work on the concord between Plato and Aristotle. In the same year Pico was absolved from the earlier charge of heresy by Pope ALEXANDER VI. In 1493 he finished *Disputationes contra Astrologiam* (Bologna 1496), the first of a proposed series of works to be written against the enemies of the Church.

Pico's works were published after his death by his nephew, Gianfrancesco II (*see below*), who prefaced them with a biography of his uncle (Bologna 1496) that Thomas More translated into English a few years later (London *c.* 1510). Although Pico's writings exhibit enormous erudition and extensive knowledge of source material, they are somewhat unsystematic and often inconsistent. Because of his early death, he was unable to finish many of his projected works, and, therefore, his philosophical system is incomplete. The extant works attempt to promote a universal accord of philosophical systems, a *pax philosophica;* their syncretic tendency to utilize what is best in all systems of thought is perhaps the most characteristic mark of Pico's thought.

His most famous single work, the *Oratio,* written as a preface to his proposed disputation, extols man's dignity. Man does not have a particular place or ability, as do the other animals, but he can raise himself to the level of the angels through his own efforts. Philosophy is of greatest assistance in the ascent toward the highest form of human life, the life of contemplation.

Pico was perhaps the first Christian of the Renaissance to study carefully the Jewish CABALA. His wide learning and originally of thought have attracted many thinkers to the study of his works.

Gianfrancesco II. Humanist thinker; b. Mirandola, 1469; d. there, Oct. 16, 1533. He was the author of numerous literary and philosophical works. The most important is *Examen vanitatis doctrinae gentium . . .* (Mirandola 1520), an extended attack on pagan philosophy in general and on Aristotle in particular, and a defense of Christian religion. He was the first Renaissance thinker to utilize the ancient skeptical writings of Sextus Empiricus (*see* SKEPTICISM).

See Also: RENAISSANCE PHILOSOPHY; PLATONISM.

Bibliography: Giovanni. Works. *Opera omnia* (Bologna 1496; Venice 1498, 1519, 1557; Strasbourg 1504; Reggio 1506; Paris 1517; Basel, 2 v. 1572–73, repr. 1601); modern edition, ed. E. GARIN (Florence 1942–); *Of Being and Unity,* tr. V. M. HAMM (Milwaukee 1943); "Oration on the Dignity of Man," tr. E. L. FORBES, in *The Renaissance Philosophy of Man,* ed. E. CASSIRER et al. (Chicago 1948) 223–254. Literature. E. CASSIRER, "Giovanni Pico della Mirandola: A Study in the History of Renaissance Ideas," *Journal of the History of Ideas* 3 (1942): 123–144, 319–346. A. DULLES, *Princeps Concordiae: Pico della Mirandola and the Scholastic Tradition* (Cambridge, Mass. 1941). E. GARIN, *Giovanni Pico della Mirandola: Vita e dottrina* (Florence 1937); *La cultura filosofica del Rinascimento italiano* (Florence 1961), Garin's volumes have fullest bibliog. P. KIBRE, *The Library of Pico della Mirandola* (New York 1936). E. MONNERJAHN, *Giovanni Pico della Mirandola: Ein Beitrag zur philosophischen Theologie des italienischen Humanismus* (Wiesbaden 1960). G. F. PICO DELLA MIRANDOLA, *Giovanni Pico della Mirandola: His Life by His Nephew,* tr. THOMAS MORE (London 1510), modern ed. J. M. RIGG (London 1890), and other short works tr. THOMAS MORE. Gianfrancesco II. *Opera omnis,* v. 2 of G. PICO DELLA MIRANDOLA, *Opera omnia,* 2 v. (Basel 1572–73; repr. 1601). E. GARIN, *La filosofia,* 2 v. (Milan 1947) 2:72–77. R. H. POPKIN, *The History of Scepticism from Erasmus to Descartes* (Assen 1960).

[C. B. SCHMITT]

PIDAL Y CHICO DE GUZMÁN, MARÍA MARAVILLAS DE JESÚS, BL.

Baptized María Christina Luisa Ildefonsa Patricia Josefa, also known as Mother Maravillas de Jesús, Discalced Carmelite; foundress of the Association of Saint Teresa; b. Madrid, Spain, Nov. 4, 1891; d. Dec. 11, 1974, in the Carmel of Aldehuela (Madrid). María Pidal was born while her father, Luis Pidal y Mon, the marquis of Pidal, was the Spanish ambassador to the Holy See. Her mother, Cristina Chico de Guzmán, was also a devout Catholic.

María did not enter religious life until she was nearly thirty. Drawn to the Carmelites after reading the works of saints JOHN OF THE CROSS and TERESA OF ÁVILA, she entered (1920) and was professed (1921) at the Escorial Carmel, Madrid.

In 1924, with three others, she founded the Carmel of Cerro de los Angeles at the geographical center of Spain, where she pronounced her solemn vows that same year. Because the carmel expanded so quickly, other communities, including one in Kottayam (1933), India, evolved from it.

During the Spanish Civil War (1936–39), the sisters lived in an apartment in Madrid, and their number continued to grow. In September 1937, they opened a carmel in the Batuecas near Salamanca. Following the war, Marí restored Cerro de los Angeles and continued to found other carmels (Mancera de Abajo, Duruelo, Cabrera, Arenas de San Pedro, San Calixto, Aravaca, Talavera de la Reina, La Aldehuela, and Montemar-Torremolinos) and restored that at El Escorial and Ávila. To bind these carmels together, Mother María obtained Vatican approval for the Association of Saint Teresa (1972).

A miracle attributed to her intercession was approved Dec. 18, 1997. Pope John Paul II beatified Mother Maravillas de Jesús on May 10, 1998.

Feast: Dec. 11 (Carmelites).

Bibliography: *Si tu le laisses faire: mère Maravillas de Jésus, Carmélite Déchaussée* (Montsûrs 1993), French tr. of *Si tú le dejas: vida de la Madre Maravillas de Jesus, Carmelita Descalza* (Madrid 1976). *Acta Apolstolicae Sedis,* no. 12 (1998) 599.

[K. I. RABENSTEIN]

PIE, LOUIS FRANÇOIS DÉSIRÉ

French cardinal, bishop of Poitiers; b. Pontgouin (Eure-et-Loir), Sept. 26, 1815; d. Angoulême, May 18, 1880. After studies at the seminary of Saint-Sulpice in Paris, he was ordained (1839), became curate at the cathedral of Chartres, and in 1844 vicar-general of the diocese. As bishop of Poitiers (1849–80) he constantly upheld the rights of the Church and the Holy See, notably during the invasions of the States of the Church after 1860. A discourse by him on this topic in his cathedral caused him to be haled before the Council of State. He defended the SYLLABUS OF ERRORS against DUPANLOUP and others. At VATICAN COUNCIL I Pie, who had been a strong promoter of ULTRAMONTANISM, was president of the commission on faith and took a leading role in the definition of papal infallibility. Naturalism, LIBERALISM, and other modern errors found in him a sturdy opponent. Politically he was a monarchist, a follower of the Bourbon claimant to the throne, Comte Henri de Chambord. A promoter of provincial councils, he was appointed by the bishops of the Bordeaux province to edit the statutes elaborated at diocesan synods. His episcopal ministry was marked by frequent pastoral visits, numerous discourses, the dedication of more than 120 churches, the introduction of many religious congregations into his diocese, the creation of a diocesan society of missionary priests called the Oblates of St. Hilary, the establishment of an institution of higher theological education entrusted to the Jesuits, and the development of various religious and charitable works.

Pie's numerous publications bear the stamp of his talent as writer and orator and of his scriptural, patristic, and theological knowledge, although he has been judged more facile than profound. His discourses of all types were collected in nine volumes, *Discours et instructions pastorales* (1858–79). The *Oeuvres de Mgr l'évêque de Poitiers* saw numerous editions between 1865 and 1894. In 1878 appeared volume 1 of *Oeuvres choisies,* comprising *Instructions synodales sur les principales erreurs du temps présent, suivies de l'Instruction synodale sur la première constitution dogmatique du concile du Vatican.* A two-volume selection of his sermons and instructions between 1839 and 1849 appeared in *Oeuvres sacerdotales* (1891–95). Many of his discourses, funeral eulogies, letters, and synodal instructions were printed separately. He also left in manuscript a large correspondence, numerous homilies, an *Essai sur le concile du Vatican,* and other longer works. In 1879 he became a cardinal.

Bibliography: L. BAUNARD, *Histoire du cardinal Pie,* 2 v. (Paris 1886). J. M. BESSE, *Le Cardinal Pie* (Paris 1903). E. CATTA, *La Doctrine politique et sociale du cardinal Pie* (Paris 1959). C. BUTLER, *The Vatican Council,* 2 v. (New York 1930), with photo. C. CONSTANTIN, *Dictionnaire de théologie catholique,* ed. A. VACANT et al., 15 v. (Paris 1903–50; Tables générales 1951–) 12.2:1740–43: R. AUBERT, in *Lexikon für Theologie und Kirche,* ed. J. HOFER and K. RAHNER, 10 v. (2d new ed. Freiburg 1957–65) 8:495.

[R. LIMOUZIN-LAMOTHE]

PIEDRA, ABBEY OF

Former Cistercian monastery in the Diocese of Tarazona, Saragossa province, Spain; founded in 1194 by Abbot Gaufrido de Rocaberti and 12 monks from Poblet, who occupied the *castrum de petra* and the surrounding land donated by Alfonso II of Aragon. Peter II in 1203, James I (1213–76), the lords of Albarracín and Molina, and bishops favored the abbey, which held many privileges and absolute jurisdiction over many places. The officials of the abbey, which depended on the Holy See, were elected by the community. Peter IV (1319–87) defended the monks from local outbursts and made them limit their prodigality to pilgrims. Martin de Vargas, the 15th-century Cistercian reformer, came from Piedra. Most of Piedra's art treasures were lost in the lootings that followed its suppression in 1835, when it was still a center of monasticism and spirituality. The buildings, which have been converted into a government tourist inn, contain architectural elements of Romanesque, Byzantine, Gothic, Renaissance, and churrigueresque styles. The setting, enriched by the famous cascades of the river Piedra, is remarkably beautiful.

Bibliography: J. PÉREZ DE URBEL, *Las grandes abadías benedictinas* (Madrid 1928) 227–236. *Enciclopedia universal ilustrada Europeo-Americana,* 70 v. (Barcelona 1908–30; suppl. 1934–) 44:724–731.

[J. PÉREZ DE URBEL]

PIERIUS, ST.

Fourth-century Alexandrian ecclesiastic and writer; d. apparently Rome, 312. A priest at Alexandria under Bp. Theonas (*c.* 281–300), Pierius was a noted exegete, preacher, and ascetic. He was a disciple of ORIGEN and successor of Theognostus as head of the School of Alexandria; he was the teacher of PAMPHILUS, and he suffered as a confessor in the Diocletian persecution, after which he settled in Rome. Philip Sidetes and JEROME speak of the elegance of his style and profundity of his teaching (*De vir. illus.* 76), and PHOTIUS mentions a collection of 12 λόγοι, or sermons, including a homily, *On Easter and the Prophet Osee,* and a treatise on St. Luke's Gospel (*Bibl. codex* 119). Philip Sidetes mentions a work, *On the Mother of God,* and a *Vita* of Pamphilus. Jerome was acquainted with his NT MSS in Caesarea. His close connection with Origen probably explains the loss of his works after the condemnation of Origenism.

Feast: Nov. 4.

Bibliography: *Patrologia Graeca,* ed. J. P. MIGNE, 161 v. (Paris 1857–66) 10:241–246. C. DE BOOR, *Texte und Untersuchungen zur Geschichte der altchristlichen Literatur* 5.2 (1888)

165–184. *Acta Sanctorum* Nov. 2.1:254–264. L. B. RADFORD, *Three Teachers of Alexandria* (Cambridge, Eng. 1908). J. QUASTEN, *Patrology,* 4 v. (Westminster, Md. 1950–86) 2.111–113. B. ALTANER, *Patrology,* tr. H. GRAEF from 5th German ed. (New York 1960) 239. G. FRITZ, *Dictionnaire de théologie catholique,* ed. A. VACANT et al., 15 v. (Paris 1903–50; Tables générales 1951–) 12.2:1744–1746.

[F. X. MURPHY]

PIERLEONI

Leading family of the Roman nobility in the 11th and 12th centuries, intimately and consistently associated with the papacy during the GREGORIAN REFORM. Its earliest known representative was the Roman Jew Baruch, whom the sources call Benedictus Christianus after his conversion (date unknown). He married a lady of the Roman aristocracy and died before Nov. 19, 1051. His son Leo, an important figure by 1051, supported Hildebrand in every way. Last mentioned in 1062, he was succeeded by his son Petrus Leonis, who gave the family its name. Their closeness to Hildebrand, a notice in the *Annales Pegavienses* [*Monumenta Germaniae Historica Scriptores* 16:238], and other circumstantial evidence gave rise to the highly controversial theory that GREGORY VI and GREGORY VII were related to them. URBAN II took refuge from the followers of the antipope CLEMENT III on the Tiber island, which was controlled by Petrus Leonis, and he died in Petrus Leonis's fortified house near the church of S. Nicola in Carcere (close to the theater of Marcellus). Petrus Leonis remained a faithful supporter of Urban's successors PASCHAL II, GELASIUS II, and CALLISTUS II. He died between 1124 and 1130, perhaps in 1128.

His son Petrus (called, like his father, Petrus Leonis) was for a time a student in Paris and a monk at Cluny and was raised by Paschal II not later than 1113 to the rank of cardinal deacon and by Callistus II in 1120 to that of cardinal priest. The growing influence of the Pierleoni aroused the enmity of the other leading Roman family, the FRANGIPANI. More important, under HONORIUS II, new forces opposed to the older cardinals of the reform began to rise in the Sacred College under the leadership of the chancellor, Aimeric of Santa Maria Nuova. Upon Honorius's death (Feb. 14, 1130), a committee of six cardinals dominated by Aimeric elected the cardinal deacon Gregory of Sant'Angelo pope (INNOCENT II). Later in the day the majority of cardinals (21) elected to the papacy Cardinal Pierleoni, who called himself Anacletus II. He prevailed for a time in Rome and most of Italy, but Innocent, with the powerful help of BERNARD OF CLAIRVAUX, was victorious. Upon the death of Anacletus in 1138 the schism came virtually to an end.

Anacletus's brothers remained prominent adherents of the papacy, except for Jordan, who in 1144 became the official leader of the rebellious populace of Rome after the restoration of the Roman Senate and received the title PATRICIUS. A nephew of Anacletus, Hugh was made bishop of Piacenza in 1154 and cardinal bishop of Tusculum in 1164 or 1165 (d. 1166). He was the uncle of another member of Alexander III's Sacred College, also named Hugh, cardinal deacon of Sant'Angelo (1173 to 1178), cardinal priest of San Clemente (1178 to 1182), and legate to England (1175 to 1176) and France (1176 to 1177).

Monuments of the family are found especially in Roman churches of the 16th and 17th centuries.

Bibliography: Main study still P. FEDELE, ''Le famiglie di Anacleto II e di Gelasio II,'' *Archivio della Società romana di storia patria* 27 (1904), 399–440. R. L. POOLE, ''Benedict IX and Gregory VI,'' *Proceedings of the British Academy* 8 (1917–18), 199–235, esp. 219–226. P. F. PALUMBO, *Lo Scisma del MCXXX* (Rome 1942), see index, 696. H. BLOCH, ''The Schism of Anacletus II and the Glanfeuil Forgeries of Peter the Deacon of Monte Cassino,'' *Traditio* 8 (1952), 159–264, esp. 159–182, with references to the earlier literature. F. J. SCHMALE, *Studien zum Schisma des Jahres 1130* (Cologne 1961), esp. 15–28, 66–82, weak. H. WOLTER, *Lexikon für Theologie und Kirche,* ed. J. HOFER and K. RAHNER, 10 v. (2d, new ed. Frieburg 1957–65) 8:496–497. P. E. SCHRAMM, ''Das Zeitalter Gregors VII,'' *Göttingische gelehrte Anzeigen* 207 (1953) 62–140, esp. 66–73, literature on the origin of Gregory VI and VII. V. FORCELLA, *Iscrizioni delle chiese e d'altri edificii di Roma,* 14 v. in 7 (Rome 1869–84). V. SPRETI, *Enciclopedia storico-nobiliare italiana,* 8 v. (Milan 1928–35), v. 5.

[H. BLOCH]

PIERS PLOWMAN

The full title of *Piers Plowman,* the master literary work of 14th-century England's alliterative revival in the West Midlands, is *The Vision of William concerning Piers the Plowman.* Common in the MSS and in early references are the Latin titles: *Visio Willelmi de Petro Plowman* and *Liber de Petro Plowman.* The poem survives in 49 MSS in three successive versions of unequal length, known as the A, B, and C texts; ten of the MSS are composed of parts from two of the texts. The A text (2,558 lines), written *c.* 1362 to 1373, is divided into a prologue, 11 *passus* (cantos) and a ''*Passus* XII'' of dubious character, written by a John But and printed as an appendix in recent editions. The B text (7,242 lines), written *c.* 1377, has a prologue and nine additional *passus* following the 11 of A, these earlier *passus* being altered in many respects. The C text (7,357 lines), written *c.* 1387 to 1398, is a revision of B, having no prologue and 23 *passus.* The first printed edition (B text) was by Robert Crowley in 1550.

Authorship and Organization. Although the famous controversy over the authorship is not completely resolved, *Piers Plowman* is now generally attributed to William Langland on the basis of two 15th-century notes in MSS and of internal evidence. He was possibly the illegitimate son of Eustace de Rokayle, was born at Cleobury Mortimer or Ledbury in Shropshire, and educated at the priory of Great Malvern in Worcestershire. All else about him seems speculation.

Each version of the poem follows the same basic organization of two large divisions, each containing several visions composed of one or more *passus.* The B text, the one most often read and translated today, includes the Vision concerning Piers the Plowman (Prologue-*Passus* VII), two dreams, and the Lives of Dowel (VIII–XIV), Dobet (XV–XVIII), and Dobest (XIX–XX), eight dreams, two of which are dreams within dreams.

The Visio and the Vita. In the *Visio,* Will, a persona for William the author and the will of every medieval man, recounts his dream of the various contemporary professions, of the "fair field full of folk," working out their fates between the Tower of Truth (eternal life) and the Castle of Care (eternal fire). A Lady (the Church), the first of many tutors to appear, explains the divine origin and destiny of men and their duties to God. There follows a series of dramatic scenes dealing with the proposed marriage of Lady Meed (reward) first to False, and then to Conscience. In the second dream, the folk repent their past sins and begin a pilgrimage in search of Truth. Piers now makes his first appearance, directing them first to plow their own half-acres, after which Truth sends a pardon to him and his true followers: "Et qui bona egerunt, ibunt in vitam eternam;/ Qui vero mala, in ignem eternum."

In the *Vita,* Will's quest for the three degrees of doing well (*bona egerunt*) moves mainly in his own mind; his search is a pilgrimage through the three grades of Christian perfection toward the ideal society. The pattern at the center of the poem, the lives of Dowel and Dobet, is progress through struggle. In the third vision, Will confronts his own faculties, such as Thought and Imagination, gradually learns the responsible use of man's distinguishing gifts, wit and will, and recognizes his sinfulness. In the fourth, under the tutelage of Conscience and Patience, he beholds Hawkin the Active Man's discovery of his stained coat (soul) and adopts an attitude of penance and poverty in preparation for the focusing of divine powers within his own soul, Anima. In the fifth vision, he then moves to the contemplation of the three theological virtues and the Trinity, and in the sixth, to a meditation on the Passion and its relation to his own salvation. It is in this last vision that Charity, who is also the Good Samaritan, takes on the flesh of Piers Plowman, who appears as Christ the Knight, come to joust at Jerusalem. In Dobest, Piers makes his third appearance as Christ's reeve, the Pope. The final two dreams present the testing of Will's love and poverty and of the 14th-century Church, which is attacked by Antichrist. Will recounts his own tribulations and the coming of old age; the poem concludes with his Conscience vowing that he will "walk as wide as the world lasts" in search of Piers the Plowman. Each *passus,* or "step," has made it clear that the pilgrimage is the poem's dominant motif, a fact that relates it to CHAUCER's *Canterbury Tales.*

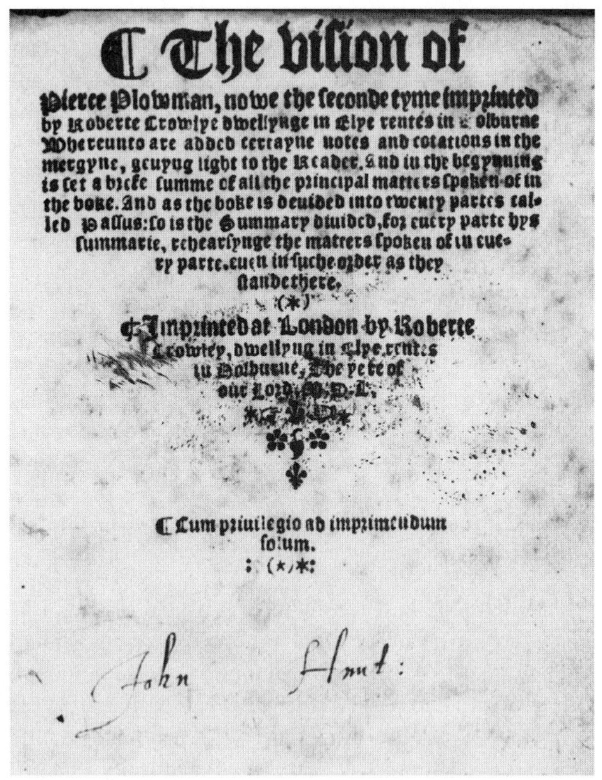
¶ The vision of Pierce Plowman, nowe the seconde tyme imprinted by Roberte Crowlye dwellynge in Elye rentes in Holburne Whereunto are added certayne notes and cotations in the mergyne, geuyng light to the Reader. And in the begynning is set a brefe summe of all the principal matters spoken of in the boke. And as the boke is deuided into twenty partes called Passus: so is the Summary diuided, for euery parte hys summarie, rehearsynge the matters spoken of in euery parte. euen in suche order as they standethere.

(*)

¶ Imprinted at London by Roberte Crowley, dwellyng in Elye rentes in Holburne, The yere of our Lord. M.D.L.

¶ Cum priuilegio ad imprimendum solum.

Title page from "Piers Plowman" written by William Langland. (Special Collections Library, University of Michigan.)

Relationship with Other Works. In form and technique *Piers Plowman* is related also to the works of other contemporaries. No other medieval poem presents such a mixture of genres. In keeping with the basic form of allegorical dream narrative, mental faculties (Reason), sins (Pride), virtues (Patience), institutions (Holy-church), and a great many other personifications, as well as divine persons (Holy Ghost), Biblical figures (Moses), and contemporary people (Friars) appear as characters, undergo a variety of transformations, and vanish unexpectedly. Parts of the personified action relate the poem to the morality plays, while mystery plays have clearly influenced other scenes (*see* DRAMA, MEDIEVAL).

The unifying action, a quest, connects it with the romance, and, inasmuch as the quest involves Will with a series of guides, it resembles the *consolatio* in which Boethius is tutored by Dame Philosophy. The character Will, uneducated but argumentative, is similar to the autobiographical *ingénu* of encyclopedic satire, and in the continual criticism of the actual in the light of the ideal, there are elements of complaint in the *de contemptu mundi* tradition. Other materials are derived from the sermon, the devotional, penitential, and ascetic handbooks, and the commentaries and glosses of the Bible. Langland "spoke Bible" and used at times both typology (*see* TYPOS) and the four allegorical levels of Scripture (singly or in combination) to shape a poem that, in its eschatological orientation and its scattered prophetic warnings, is apocalyptic. Some of the alliterative lines are macaronic and acrostic, and others contain repetition, riddles, puns, and word play of all kinds. All critics agree that *Piers Plowman* is one of the most puzzling poems in English literature.

Main Theme. If the author's aims and accomplishments are to be understood, the three versions should probably not be regarded as variants of the same poem, but as a cumulative work in which successive attempts are made to develop and clarify his main theme, the search for salvation. This is treated thematically as a pilgrimage, in keeping with the Augustinian definition of charity as the motion of the soul toward God, and is associated with plowing, the tending to the duties of one's own estate. The value of both depends on cooperation with the way of the cross, the pardon. These motifs of pilgrimage, plowing, and pardon are unified in penance, which is not only the ritual followed in the confession scenes for which the poem is well known, but a virtue related to poverty and patience. For the author, these three seem to define the life of perfection.

In depicting Will's search, Langland incorporates all the elements associated with the medieval spiritual life: the creed; the Ten Commandments; the seven deadly sins; the three theological virtues; the four cardinal virtues; the four daughters of God; the world, the flesh, and the devil; and the three types of chastity—in marriage, in widowhood, and in virginity. Key terms of medieval philosophical thought, such as Need, Fortune, and Kind (Nature), all receive systematic treatment as personifications, and the century's problems, such as the questioning of the value of learning and the rising emphasis on voluntarism, are given penetrating and balanced analysis. The poem, finally, is the most significant vernacular expression of English social thought in the Middle Ages; it makes explicit and detailed reference to the plagues, the Hundred Years' War, the Great Schism, and the wide variety of clerical and economic abuses; yet, grounded as it is in the actual religious practice, philosophical thought, and historical events of its time, it conveys, like no other English poem, the timelessness of Christian truth.

Scholarship Devoted to Piers. *Piers Plowman* has been fortunate in its editors and interpreters. The basic edition of all three texts is that of Skeat, but this is gradually being replaced by the new London edition, of which Kane's A text has already appeared. This edition, which was begun as a result of the famous authorship dispute between J. M. Manly, who argued that the composition of the three versions was the work of five men, and J. J. Jusserand and others, who argued for a single author, will probably not fully resolve the dispute for all, but Kane's book (1965) clearly indicates that the evidence points toward unity of authorship. Despite the speculations of A. Bright, little more is known about the author; the chief source for his biography is internal evidence, and most critics today agree that the events in the poem do not mirror his life in such close detail as has previously been argued. Chambers, Coghill, and Wells were among the poem's first great interpreters. Owst and Spearing have shown how much the poem has in common with the medieval sermon. Dunning's early study of the A text has left subsequent writers on all three versions in his debt, as has Donaldson's pioneering work on the C text. In more recent years, critical studies have focused on the B text and its Biblical, theological, devotional, and apocalyptic backgrounds; the best are those of Robertson and Huppé, Frank, Fowler, and Bloomfield. Interest in this important work is still very strong and further scholarship appears every year.

Bibliography: Editions. W. W. SKEAT, ed., *The Vision of William concerning Piers the Plowman in Three Parallel Texts, Together with Richard the Redeless,* 2 v. (London 1886). T. A. KNOTT and D. C. FOWLER, eds., *Piers the Plowman: A Critical Edition of the A-Version* (Baltimore 1952). G. KANE, ed., *Piers Plowman: The A Version* (London 1960). Translations. N. COGHILL, tr., *Visions from Piers Plowman* (New York 1949). J. F. GOODRIDGE, tr., *Langland: Piers the Ploughman* (Baltimore 1959). H. H. WELLS, tr., *The Vision of Piers Plowman* (New York 1935). Studies. A. H. BRIGHT, *New Light on 'Piers Plowman'* (London 1928). M. W. BLOOMFIELD, *Piers Plowman as a 14th-Century Apocalypse* (New Brunswick, N.J. 1962). R. W. CHAMBERS, *Man's Unconquerable Mind* (London 1939). C. H. DAWSON, *Medieval Religion and Other Essays* (New York 1934). E. T. DONALDSON, *Piers Plowman: The C-Text and Its Poet* (New Haven 1949). T. P. DUNNING, *Piers Plowman: An Interpretation of the A-Text* (New York 1937). W. ERZGRÄBER, *William Langlands 'Piers Plowman': Eine Interpretation des C-Textes* (Heidelberg 1957). R. W. FRANK, *Piers Plowman and the Scheme of Salvation* (New Haven 1957). D. C. FOWLER, *Piers, the Plowman: Literary Relations of the A and B Texts* (Seattle 1961). D. L. OWEN, *Piers Plowman: A Comparison with Some Earlier and Contemporary French Allegories* (London 1912). G. R. OWST, *Literature and Pulpit in Medieval England* (2d ed. New York 1961). D. W. ROBERTSON and B. F. HUPPÉ, *Piers Plowman and Scriptural Tradition* (Princeton 1951). A. C. SPEARING, *Criticism and Medieval Poetry* (New York 1964). E. M. TILLYARD, *The English Epic and Its Background* (New York 1954). H. C. WHITE, *Social Criticism in Popular*

Religious Literature of the 16th Century (New York 1944). G. KANE, *Piers Plowman: The Evidence for Authorship* (London 1965).

[G. L. O'GRADY]

PIERZ, FRANCIS XAVIER

Missionary; b. Kamnik, Carniola, Slovenia Nov. 20, 1785; d. Ljubljana, Carniola, Jan. 22, 1880. After study with the Franciscans in Kamnik and at the diocesan seminary in Ljubljana, Pierz was ordained on March 13, 1813 by Bp. Antonius Kautschitz. He spent the first 22 years of his priestly career in Yugoslavia as assistant at Kranjska Gora and Fuzine and as pastor at Pece and Podbrezje. His experiments in the development of fruit stock suitable for the region were recognized by the Carniolan Agricultural Society. In 1830 he published a text on the science of fruit growing, *Kranjski Vertnar* (The Carniolan Gardener), which remains a standard reference work in Slovenia. In 1834 Pierz went to the United States to work with his countryman Rev. Frederic Baraga, later the first bishop of Marquette, Michigan.

Baraga stimulated his interest in the evangelization of the Native Americans and persuaded him to volunteer for work among the Ottawas. From 1835 to 1871 Pierz labored among the natives of Michigan, Wisconsin, and Minnesota, achieving his most notable success with the Chippewas of Minnesota. He arrived there in 1852 and, from his headquarters at Crow Wing, traveled by foot and horseback to virtually every Chippewa village in the territory. As government policy restricted the Native Americans' domain, he worked to have their vacated lands settled by German and Sloveniane Catholics. Many Catholic communities in the Diocese of St. Cloud, Minnesota owe their origin to his efforts. He also brought the Benedictines to Minnesota from their foundation in Pennsylvania. In 1873, when he was 88 years old, he returned to his native land.

Bibliography: G. MCDONALD, ''Father Francis Pierz, Missionary,'' *Minnesota History* 10 (1929) 107–125. J. SELISKAR, *Acta et Dicta* 3 (1911) 66–90. W. P. FURLAN, *In Charity Unfeigned: The Life of Francis Xavier Pierz* (Paterson, N.J. 1952).

[W. P. FURLAN]

PIETÀ

An iconographic theme representing the Virgin (alone or with John and Mary Magdalen) grieving over the body of Christ on her knees. Late medieval religious spirit, preoccupied with pain and suffering, found its most pathetic expression in the Pietà, a devotional image of the compassion of Mary in the time between deposition and entombment.

''Pieta,'' wooden sculpture, on display at Mainfrankische Museum, in Marienberg Fortress, Wurzburg, Bavaria, Germany. (©Adam Woolfitt/CORBIS.)

Literary sources of the theme are Pseudo-Bonaventure's *Meditations,* St. Bridget's *Revelations,* and the sermons and poetry of the mystics, but its ultimate origin is a fusion of the Virgin's lamentation with either the entombment (Duccio, Maestà) or the deposition (Giotto, Arena Chapel) of Christ. The isolated, emotionally charged mother-son group in sculptural form is a specifically German achievement of *c.* 1300, most frequently and variously produced in Rhenish and Swabian centers.

The Pietà, is a synthesis of the Madonna enthroned with the slaughtered Innocents' mourning mothers. Three main types are distinguishable: Christ in a sitting position, His head and knees angularly bent—the earliest German manifestation; Christ in a horizontal position across the Virgin's lap (from the lamentation)—preferred in Italy; and Christ in a sloping position in an unbroken curve (from the deposition)—favored in France.

The small, sculptured Pietà in the Landeamuseum, Bonn, datable *c.* 1320, poignantly expresses human suffering and sorrow through the angularity of Christ's broken body and the Virgin's disproportionately large head. The great anonymous Pietà of Villeneuveles-Avignon, painted *c.* 1460, is moving in its noble constraint. With eyes cast down on Christ's rigid body, Mary prays, joined by John and the donor—her mute anguish intensified by the openly weeping Magdalen. Simple composition, subdued colors, and archaic gold-ground accentuate the concept of restraint. In 15th-century Italy the horizontal (entombment) type, with surrounding saints, prevailed (Crivelli, Tura, Perugino, Sellaio). In his earliest of four sculptured Pietàs (Rome, St. Peter's, 1498), Michelangelo replaced the horizontal form with a northern composite—creating through the monumental pyramid a transformation from agony to solemnity and heroic resignation. Although the theme continued intermittently (Carracci, Rubens, Guenther), not until the 20th century, e.g., Zadkine's small bronze Pietà (1952), has the original emotional impact been restored.

Bibliography: W. PINDER, *Die Pietà* (Leipzig 1922); ''Die dichterische Wurzel der Pietà,'' *Repertorium für Kuntswissenschaft* 42 (1919–20) 145–163. W. PASSARGE, *Das deutsche Vesperbild im Mittelalter* (Cologne 1924). R. HAMANN, ''Die Bonner Pietà,'' *Festschrift zum 60. Geburtstag von Paul Clemen* (Bonn 1926) 365–374. E. PANOFSKY, ''*Imago Pietatis:* Ein Beitrag zur Typengeschichte des Schmerzensmannes und der *Maria Mediatrix,*'' *Festschrift für Max J. Friedländer zum 60. Geburstage* (Leipzig 1927) 261–308. F. C. SCHNEIDER, *Die mittelalterlichen deutschen Typen und Vorformen des Vesperbildes* (Rendsburg 1931). É. MÂLE, *L'Art religieux de la fin du moyen âge en France* (5th ed. Paris 1949). W. KOERTE, ''Deutsche Vesperbilder in Italien,'' *Kunstgeschichtliches Jahrbuch der Bibliotheca Hertziana* 1 (1937) 1–138, W. H. FORSYTH, ''Medieval Statues of the Pietà in the Museum,'' *Bulletin of the New York Metropolitan Museum of Art* NS 11 (1952–53) 177–184.

[R. BERGMANN]

PIETISM

Broadly defined, pietism denotes a distinctive quality of religious life issuing in rigorous morality and personal piety. JANSENISM, PURITANISM, precisianism, and METHODISM share this quality. In a stricter sense, it refers to its expression within German Lutheranism, particularly by P. J. SPENER, A. H. FRANCKE, and N. L. von ZINZENDORF.

The spirit of Pietism, as set forth by Spener in his *Pia Desideria,* revealed the influence of Arndt's *Von wahren Christentum,* the writings of the English Puritans and the Reformed Christianity of Geneva. It called for a return to personal devotion and morality in response to the decay of German life following the Thirty Years' War and in reaction to the arid intellectualism of the Protestant scholasticism then dominating orthodox Lutheranism. It deemed Christianity more a matter of the heart than of the intellect; the mark of a Christian was more properly love of one's neighbor than right doctrines. Spener urged that a greater emphasis be given to devotional than to doctrinal and polemical studies in theological education, with a corresponding reformation of preaching. The errant and heathens were to be won by love and persuasion.

Pietism did not produce the sweeping reforms that Spener desired for the church. However, an improved moral climate was achieved and a greater emphasis given to the study of Scripture, along with a wider use of Scripture in preaching. Perhaps the greatest impact on church life occurred in Lutheran hymnody. Similarly the movement produced no immediate transformation of orthodox Lutheran theology, the two positions, indeed, differing not greatly in doctrines per se but rather in the emphasis given to doctrine. Nevertheless, Pietism revealed the weaknesses of Lutheran scholasticism and helped prepare the way for the theological resurgence of the 18th and 19th centuries.

The failures of Pietism were largely a result of its individualistic emphasis and a lack of organization. Spener never exercised the control over this movement that Wesley did over Methodism. Separatism was a constant threat in Pietism. Spener early founded the *collegia pietatis,* small devotional gatherings that he envisaged as a spiritual leaven *within* the church. Nevertheless, this drawing apart of a spiritual elite led to strained relations with the rest of Lutheranism. Some of Spener's more enthusiastic followers finally broke away from the Church but Spener (and Francke agreeing with him in this) being opposed to separatism broke with them and suppressed the *collegia.* Extremism plagued Pietism and detracted from its influence. Unlike Spener's, Francke's spiritual development had been traumatic and he regarded this as the norm for all true conversion, tending to impose this character upon the movement. Excessive and false religiosity both found frequent expression. In fact, Ritschl questioned Spener's classification as a Pietist because he confessed no such traumatic conversion. Extreme individualism in Biblical interpretation occasionally marred the Pietists' free study of Scripture, and subjective approaches to religion led to bizarre theological expressions, such as those of Zinzendorf. The deemphasis of doctrine inherent in Pietism also tended to weaken its impact. In reaffirming the necessary subjective aspect of faith, it tended to neglect the equally valid objective side. Consequently, the Halle school under Francke produced little scholarly research. In contrast, the less radical form of Pietism at Würtemburg under Bengel pursued scholarly research and continued as a significant force after the more extreme Pietism had disappeared.

A group of female Pietists at a Sunday afternoon gathering c. 1910. (©Hulton-Deutsch Collection/CORBIS)

The Pietist emphasis upon a quality of life rather than orthodoxy of belief tended to produce a softening of religious divisions and an improved relationship between the Lutheran and Reformed churches. Contact with like-minded Roman Catholics, initially inhibited by Spener's strong opposition to the papacy, developed late in the 18th century only to succumb to the ULTRAMONTANISM prevailing on the Roman side. The movement was, in this respect, a forerunner of religious freedom. Unlike the Puritans, the Pietists never became a political force. Nevertheless, they had considerable social impact, humanizing society and inspiring the growth of philanthropy. The Halle orphanage and schools under Francke were a precursor of the Innere Mission, the home mission, social service movement. Pietism fostered an upsurge of missionary effort. Inspired by Pietism, Frederick IV of Denmark commissioned two men from Halle for service in India. An active campaign was conducted to evangelize the Jews by establishing the Institutum Judaicum at Halle. The Moravians later gave a new impetus to the mission cause with their use of lay personnel. Pietism was influential also in the founding in England of the Society for Promoting Christian Knowledge, with its decidedly missionary purpose.

This movement was destined to be a factor in shaping the theologies of SCHLEIERMACHER and RITSCHL, and through the Moravians it promoted the rise of Methodism. Some cite a connection between Pietism and the rise of both rationalism and German nationalism. However, these latter movements in their developed expressions certainly did not reflect the spirit of Pietism.

Bibliography: A. RITSCHL, *Geschichte des Pietismus,* 3 v. (Bonn 1880–86). H. HEPPE, *Geschichte des Pietismus und der Mystik in der reformierten Kirche namentlich der Niederlande* (Leiden 1879). E. SACHSSE, *Ursprung und Wesen des Pietismus* (Wiesbaden 1884). H. SCHMID, *Die Geschichte des Pietismus* (Nördlingen 1863). M. STALLMANN, *Die Religion in Geschichte und Gegnwart,* 7 v. (3d ed. Tübingen 1957–65) 5:370–383. L. CRISTIANI, *Dictionnaire de théologie catholique,* ed. A. VACANT et al., 15 v. (Paris

1903–50) 12.2:2084–93. C. MIRBT, S. M. JACKSON, ed. *The New Schff-Herzog Encyclopedia of Religious Knowledge*, 13 v. (Grand Rapids, Mich. 1951–54) 9:53–67. J. T. MCNEILL, *Modern Christian Movements* (Philadelphia 1954).

[J. C. HOFFMAN]

PIETRANTONI, AGOSTINA LIVIA, ST.

Baptized Livia, nurse, a Sister of Charity of Saint Joan Antida Thouret (*Istituto delle Suore della Carità di Santa Giovanna Antida Thouret*); b. March 27, 1864 in Pozzaglia Sabina (between Rieti and Tivoli), Italy; d. Nov. 13, 1894, Rome.

Livia, the second of the eleven children of farmers, received little formal education. Responding to a call, Livia entered the Sisters of Charity at Rome in 1886. Sister Agostina became a nurse in the pediatric ward at Holy Spirit Hospital near the Vatican, where she cared for the critically ill. Later she was transferred to the tuberculosis ward, where she contracted the deadly disease but was miraculously cured.

Following a month of threatening notes, a former patient, Giuseppe Romanelli, stabbed Sister Agostina to death while attempting to rape her. As she died, she prayed for Romanelli's salvation and forgiveness. Agostina was beatified in 1972 and the miracle required for her canonization approved, April 6, 1998. She was canonized by Pope John Paul II, April 18, 1999.

Bibliography: *Acta Apostolicae Sedis* 65 (1973): 229–235. *L'Osservatore Romano,* Eng. ed. 47 (1972): 1–2. A. PRONZATO, *Una certa suor Agostina. Suora della carità di S. Giovanna Antida Thouret* (Turin 1971).

[K. I. RABENSTEIN]

PIETY, FAMILIAL

The virtue, akin to justice, that directs the interpersonal relationships of domestic society. It guides husbands and wives, parents and children, in their conduct toward each other. Whereas justice regulates the general relationships between individuals and between the individual and society, piety is concerned with the special relationships between the family and its members and between the members themselves. Without this thoughtful regulation of each person's activities, the frictions inevitable when people live very close to each other can make life unbearable and some form of escape attractive, whether this be divorce or simply leaving home.

Love. To understand the duties and rights of members of a family one should first reflect upon their basis, love, Christian love of one's neighbor. No neighbor is closer than husband to wife, parents to children. A self-seeking love that uses the object of love for the lover's own advantage cannot be a basis for union between members of a family. It can bring together only consumer and consumed. Even the love of friend for friend is insufficient as a basis for a family, for it lasts only so long as there are common interests—business, social, or emotional. When new interests supersede those on which the friendship was based, it ceases. If the family ceases there is a greater loss not only to its members but to society as a whole, for children need protection over a long period, and even after they are grown, the husband and wife still need the assistance each of the other, especially in sickness and old age. The only kind of love that can serve as a solid foundation for the family, exemplified by the Holy Family, is that which imitates the love whereby the Creator continually pours out His gifts upon His creatures.

Romantic love, which draws the man and woman together at the junction of their lives, does not endure forever, but rather settles down, in marriages that last, into that deeper, stronger current of married love that continually and actively promotes the well-being of the partner. It is, however, beset in the meantime by various dangers. Some of these arise from third parties. Thus, one parent may begin to think of ''my'' rather than ''our'' children, with the result that children come between the husband and wife. Again, husbands and wives may not detach themselves enough from their own parents in forming a new family. Such ''in-law trouble'' was foreseen long ago (Gn 2.24). Another danger is an attachment for an outsider, which, however ''platonic,'' gives to that person the husband's or wife's heart, leaving little love to the partner, or less if the attachment becomes adulterous. Assertions of man's natural tendency to promiscuity really deny his capacity for enduring love and contradict the evidence of the great majority of marriages, which do last.

Even if third parties are not a threat, a danger lurks in the human tendency to jealousy. This may be aroused by an imprudent action or a fault of the partner, or it may grow out from a mere suspicion on the part of an insecure person who is always fearing, yet seeking, a sign that love for himself, or herself, is waning.

Considerateness. Considerateness on the part of both husband and wife can do much to overcome these dangers. It implies, among other things, that they always try to control their tempers and to speak to each other in a normal tone. Considerateness also avoids sarcastic, belittling remarks, as well as nagging, ridicule, and undue silence. It bears no grudges. Considerateness implies a willingness to talk over difficulties. Many a marriage

Tapestry of Sister Agostina Livia Pietrantoni, hanging on St. Peter's Basilica. Agostina was a nurse in a Rome hospital stabbed to death by a crazed patient. (AP/Wide World)

ends because husband and wife can no longer communicate, can no longer talk with, but only at each other.

Considerateness implies also tolerance of the friends and relatives of the other partner. Partners cannot continue to spend excessive amounts of time with old friends from school or work. These must be replaced with new, mutual friends in their married circle. While the couple is developing shared interests, new social activities, and a fresh circle of friends, however, they should each be considerate of the other's feelings for the friends who are gradually slipping away.

Considerateness also involves respect of each for the privacy of the other, both with respect to mail and to professional secrets. It implies, too, that mealtimes will be calm, not sparring sessions, and that nightfall will bring an end to the day's problems so that each can relax and be ready to face those of the morrow. It includes care of one's personal appearance. After long association one may become careless and so offensive that cohabitation becomes distasteful. Certainly considerateness is required in love-making.

Duties of Husband and Wife. Love between members of the family should be orderly. The individuals involved are equal in regard to some things, such as their eternal destiny; however, in other things, such as government of the home, there must be subordination. The husband, in general, has the duty of taking the responsibility of head of the family, governing the home. The wife has a right to expect him to do this, not as a brute or as a weakling, but as a man who will do his best to protect his wife and children, support them, guide them, and handle wisely the family property and finances.

Improper management of finances can be avoided by the habit of openness and mutual management, for example, by the depositing of monthly salaries in a joint account. The handling of household expenses and the allotment of pocket money for husband, wife, and children should be agreed upon after careful discussion so that each person understands clearly the financial situation of the family. Without a family budget and careful regulation of charge accounts, there may be excessive spending, getting the family so deeply in debt that the wife is forced to go to work to help pay the bills. As a result the home is neglected and both husband and wife are continually so tired and nervous that they are no longer able to be considerate of each other. This frequently leads to separation.

The wife, in general, has a duty to respect her husband, unless by his conduct he forfeits his right to this. It is likewise her place to defer to him regarding the location and operation of the home and to care for it diligently. This, however, does not mean giving in to his every whim, or to demands that are contrary to her dignity as wife and mother. The degree and manner of the wife's subordination varies with persons, places, and the times. The wife may even have to take over the position of breadwinner, when the husband is incapacitated or cannot find employment. She may have to take over management of the family finances, if he is a spendthrift or simply a poor manager.

Finally, both husband and wife have a right to expect the help of the other, through prayer, example, and encouragement, to lead a virtuous life that will one day be rewarded in heaven. Marriage is intended to provide not only for the procreation and education of children, but also for mutual assistance by the spouses in the reaching of the goals of life, intermediate and ultimate.

Duties of Parents. The duties of parents and children are likewise mutual. The parents have a duty to love, educate, and provide for their children to the best of their ability, and children have a duty to love, respect, and obey their parents in all things lawful. In loving and taking an active interest in their children as they grow up parents should present a united front in dealing with them; one parent should not seek to win them as allies against the other. This united front is destroyed if the parents quarrel or speak ill of each other in the children's presence. Such quarreling infringes also upon the children's right to have a harmonious home in which to grow up.

Fairness in treatment of the children is another duty of parents. They cannot be partial to one and indifferent to the others, e.g., stepchildren. The whole family, however, parents and brothers and sisters, may well vie with each other to shower love upon one who is, for example, physically or mentally handicapped.

That is not true love which treats children as if they were mere extensions of the parents, instead of being individuals with their own responsibilities and eternal destiny. Thus, punishment administered to the children by the school or the court may reflect upon the training parents have given, but parents cannot complain of a violation of their rights when their children are held accountable for delinquency. Love needs to be moderate, not excessive; giving in on everything may hurt the child, either at the time, or later in life when he or she discovers that the rest of the world does not give in so easily.

Nagging the children, treating them harshly, and provoking them to anger by calling them vile names, all too often produces a rebellious attitude in children, which may result in their running away from home or their truancy from school to spite the parents, and, later, in more serious delinquency. On the other hand, regular rules of conduct and reasonable orders or suggestions regarding the running of the home, given after one has secured the children's attention, joined with moderate praise for good work done, develop an attitude of obedience to law as well as a sense of responsibility and of accomplishment.

The education of the children, if it is to be a progressive and harmonious development of all their faculties, has both spiritual and physical aspects. As to the former, the parents owe it to the children and to society to give them that religious and moral training without which they will not have those inner controls necessary for social living. Until these controls become second nature it may be necessary from time to time to correct the children, but physical punishment administered in anger, or in public, thus downgrading them in the eyes of their group, defeats its own purpose, as it draws the children's attention away from the reason for the punishment to its attendant circumstances. Disapproval of a child's conduct by a loved and loving parent is the best discipline, particularly when the reason for the disapproval is explained. When correcting conduct that is not acceptable, the parents do well always to remember that while they are correcting the fault they continue to love the child who has committed it.

When the children have questions the parents owe it to them to give honest and serious answers so far as they are able, and to direct them to sources from which they can obtain such further enlightenment as is necessary and proper. If this is not done, the child may be forced to get information, often inaccurate, elsewhere.

Besides giving good example as to the relative importance of spiritual and material things, of the law of God and the maxims of the world, parents should develop in their children sound judgment regarding companions, reading material, and entertainment, realizing that as the children grow older the parents will not always be available to advise them. They should also train their children to have respect for their own property and for that of others, lest later they become involved in vandalism.

The physical development of children requires protection of the life not only of the mother and fetus but also of infants too young and weak to care for themselves. It requires, further, and for some years, provision of food, clothing, and shelter in keeping with the economic condition of the family, at least to the extent that the law enforces contracts for such ''necessaries.'' Bodily development demands that the children have such exercise and engage in such labor as is suitable to their years, not being subjected to that overprotection that would leave them so poorly developed that they could not pass a physical test.

The parents have a duty to provide for the children's future, so far as they are able. This means seeing that they achieve a place in life suited to their temperament and aptitudes. They ought to be given an opportunity for such training, academic or in a trade, as will enable them later on to care for themselves in suitable fashion. Children will also need advice as to their choice of a state of life. Parents should not, however, interfere with the children's choices, except to the extent that their continued support is needed by the parents because of age or illness and requires the postponement of the pursuit of other objectives.

Duties of Children. Children, for their part, also have duties with regard to their parents, to each other, and to the society in which they live. They have a duty to love their parents in thought, word, and deed. There can be no question of hating, despising, or cursing parents, using harsh words to them, slandering them, or wishing them ill or dead. Striking them, provoking them to anger, mocking them, pretending not to recognize them if they are poor and shabbily dressed, or turning them out of the house, when they are not upsetting the family of the child with whom they may be living, is unconscionable. Further, children owe it to their parents not to sadden them greatly by consorting with evil companions, keeping unreasonably late hours, or neglecting their studies or training for a job. They have, also, a duty to help their parents when they are in need, whether spiritual or corporal.

OBEDIENCE is required of children, in all things licit, as long as they are at home and a part of the domestic society. When a parent gives a real command regarding a serious matter, the child is bound in conscience to obey. The matter is to be regarded as serious when disobedience would involve harm to the children, or to the family. Real commands, however, are not to be identified with what is intended only by way of counsel, or as an expression of preference. Similarly, obedience requires children who are not yet emancipated not to leave home unreasonably.

Obedience is also due, proportionately, to other persons who stand *in loco parentis,* i.e., guardians, older brothers and sisters who have taken over the responsibilities of their deceased parents, other relatives, and teachers.

Among themselves the children have mutual duties and rights to love, assistance, and protection in keeping with their developing abilities.

Bibliography: T. A. IORIO, *Theologia moralis,* 3 v. (5th ed. Naples 1960) v. 2. B. H. MERKELBACH, *Summa theologiae moralis,* 3 v. (8th ed. Paris 1949). D. JOHNSON, *Marriage Counseling* (Englewood Cliffs, N.J. 1961).

[T. O. MARTIN]

PIETY, GIFT OF

The gift of the Holy Spirit that perfects the acts of the infused virtues of religion and piety. By religion, one worships God as the Creator; the gift of piety moves the soul to venerate God as the Father of mankind. Thus the gift elevates the soul to approach God more perfectly than religion does. The infused virtue of piety prompts the soul to acts of respect for the members of one's own family. But the gift of piety raises this tendency to a higher plane, moving a person to acts of respect for those who belong to his spiritual family, all his fellow children of God. Three Beatitudes flow from the gift of piety: meekness, because it removes the obstacles to piety; justice, because piety perfects its work; mercy, because piety is exercised in its works. Goodness and benignity are piety's direct fruits, because it causes them; piety's indirect fruit is meekness, which removes impediments to acts of piety.

See Also: HOLY SPIRIT, GIFTS OF; RELIGION, VIRTUE OF.

Bibliography: B. FROGET, *The Indwelling of the Holy Spirit in the Souls of the Just,* tr. S. A. RAEMERS (Westminster, Md. 1950). A. ROYO, *The Theology of Christian Perfection,* ed. and tr. J. AUMANN (Dubuque, Iowa 1962) 447–454. R. CESSARIO, *Christian Faith and the Theological Life* (Washington, D.C. 1996). S. PINCKAERS, *The Sources of Christian Ethics,* tr. M. T. NOBLE (3d rev. ed.; Washington, D.C. 1995).

[P. F. MULHERN]

PIFFL, FRIEDRICH GUSTAV

Cardinal, archbishop of Vienna; b. Lanškroun (Landskron), Bohemia, Oct. 15, 1864; d. Vienna, April 21, 1932. The son of a bookbinder, he entered the CANONS REGULAR OF ST. AUGUSTINE at KLOSTERNEUBURG monastery (1883), was ordained (1888), and then took an active part in the parochial and educational work of the monastery before becoming its provost (1907). He became archbishop of Vienna (1913), apostolic administrator of Innsbruck (1922), and cardinal (1914). Charges of modernism were leveled against him by supporters of INTEGRALISM at that time, but they lacked foundation and had no effect. Thoroughly loyal to the monarchy and the emperor throughout World War I, as were the other bishops of AUSTRIA, Piffl urged Catholics to support the new Austrian Republic (Nov. 12, 1918). Known as the ''people's bishop'' because of his keen interest in the spiritual and material welfare of his flock, he played an important role in developing the Catholic response to the social problems of his day. Unpretentious and mild, he was the active leader of Austrian Catholics during two difficult decades.

Bibliography: A. M. KNOLL, *Kardinal Fr. G. Piffl und der österreichische Episkopat zu sozialen und kulturellen Fragen* (Vienna 1932). *Neue österreichische Biographie,* v. 9 (Vienna 1956) 175–187.

[W. B. SLOTTMAN]

PIGGE, ALBERT (PIGHIUS)

Theologian and humanist; b. Kampen, province of Overijssel, Netherlands, *c.* 1490; d. Utrecht, Dec. 29, 1542. Pigge studied at LOUVAIN where he became master of arts in 1509, but the date of his ordination is unknown. After a stay of several years in Paris, he went to Rome in 1522. Through his writings, as an adviser to papal nuncios, and by his participation in religious dialogues, he contributed much to the Catholic position in the 16th century.

Within the Church he belongs to the most caustic exponents of the papal system, which he especially defended in his principal work, *Hierarchiae ecclesiasticae assertio* (Cologne 1538). On the problem of JUSTIFICATION he supported the viewpoint of double JUSTICE, which was condemned at the Council of TRENT. His interpretation of papal infallibility went far beyond the then–current opinion and questioned even the possibility that a pope could be capable of HERESY. By his thorough study of the cases of LIBERIUS, ANASTASIUS II, HONORIUS I, and JOHN XXII, he attempted to prove that no pope had been a heretic. His views were accepted by many theologians, especially Robert BELLARMINE, and he was one of the more frequently quoted authors at the Council of Trent.

Pigge's critical examination of sources won him a recognized place in Church history. His theory that the acts of the councils of NICAEA II and CONSTANTINOPLE IV, which condemned Pope Honorius I, had been falsified was still current even in the 19th century. Several of his works, *De libero hominis arbitrio* (Cologne 1542) and the disputed passage on original sin in his *Controversiarum praecipuarum . . . explicatio* (Cologne 1541), were placed on the Lisbon INDEX of 1624.

Bibliography: Works. A. PIGGE, *Adversus novam Marci Beneventani astronomiam* (Paris 1522); *Apologia indicti a Paulo III . . . concilii* (Paris 1538); *Adversus furiosissimum libellum Henrici Angliae regis et senatus eius* in *Concilium Tridentinum. Diariorum, actorum, epistularum, tractatuum nova collectio,* ed. GÖRRES-GESELLSCHAFT (Freiburg 1901–38) 12:774–810. **Literature.** É. AMANN, *Dictionnaire de théologie catholique*, ed. A. VACANT et al., (Paris 1903–50) 12.2:2094–2104. H. JEDIN, *Studien über die Schriftstellertätigkeit Albert Pigges* (Münster 1931). L. PFEIFER, *Ursprung der katholischen Kirche und Zugehörigkeit zur Kirche nach Albert Pigge* (Würzburg 1938). J. FEINER, *Die Erbsündenlehre Albert Pigges* (Zurich 1940). R. BÄUMER, ''Die Wiederantdeckung der Honoriusfrage im Abendland,'' *Römische Quartalschrift für Christliche Altertumskunde und für Kirchengeschichte* 56 (1961) 200–214; ''Die Auseinandersetzungen über die römische Petrustradition in den ersten Jahrzehnten der Reformationszeit,'' *ibid.* 57 (1962) 20–57, esp. 51–56; *Lexikon für Theologie und Kirche*, ed. J. HOFER and K. RAHNER (Freiberg 1957–65) 8:502.

[R. BÄUMER]

PIGNATELLI, JOSEPH MARY, ST.

Spanish Jesuit who lived in exile in Italy after his expulsion from Spain (April 3, 1767) and the order's suppression (July 21, 1773) and who became a rallying point for his displaced brethren during the long period before the restoration (Aug. 17, 1814); b. Saragossa, Spain, Dec. 27, 1737; d. San Pantaleone, Rome, Italy, Nov. 11, 1811.

Early Years. Joseph's father, Don Antonio Pignatelli, was of the ducal house of Monteleone in Calabria; his mother, Marquesa Francisca Moncayo, was descended from the Spanish counts of Fuente. His mother died when Joseph was five and his father, four years later. Don Joaquín, the eldest of the eight children, assumed charge of Joseph and his younger brother Nicholás, another future Jesuit. For a time the boys live with a married sister, the countess of Acerra, and then, by special arrangement with the JESUITS at Saragossa, as the first resident students at their school; Father José Moreno was appointed their special instructor. Pignatelli, not yet 16, entered the Jesuit novitiate in Tarragona after securing the king's permission as was required of members of the nobility. During his studies at Calatyud (1756–59) and Saragossa (1760–63) he attained eminent success; but he contracted tuberculosis, which afflicted him with varying severity for the rest of his life. After ordination (1762) and the completion of his studies, he taught at Saragossa and served as chaplain of the prison. His merciful attention to those who awaited execution earned him the title ''Padre of the Condemned.'' Pignatelli and a companion would walk beside the sled to which the doomed man was lashed, holding a cloth sling under his head to keep it from pounding painfully on the cobbled street.

Edict of Expulsion. Pignatelli's unsuspected capacity for leadership was first tested in the Cloak and Sombrero Riots that flared in Saragossa and Madrid. His success in dissuading enraged Saragossans from arson and bloodshed was gratefully commended by Charles III, until his chief minister Pedro Pablo Aranda portrayed Pignatelli as the instigator of the rioting. This and similar distortions of Jesuit activities led to the edict of expulsion that was read to all Jesuits in Spain at dawn, April 3, 1767. Father Soldevilla, rector of Saragossa, judging himself unequal to the crisis, transferred his authority to Pignatelli, who, with his priest brother Nicolás, refused the offers of royal agents to return to their homes. The entire Jesuit province of Aragon converged on the port of Tarragona, where the provincial transferred his own extensive authority to Pignatelli, who in vain pleaded youthful inexperience. The assignment was to last ''as long as the emergency.'' In the flotilla of 13 ships, carrying 600 Jesuits to Civitavecchia, Italy, Pignatelli ferried from ship to ship to counsel and console the exiles.

At Civitavecchia, the Jesuits were refused entry because no authorization to disembark had been secured by the Madrid government. They then sought asylum in Corsica, first unsuccessfully at Bastia, where the ships waited offshore for 18 days because of an insurrection on land, then at Ajaccio, where a small Jesuit college, a Franciscan residence, and some vacant buildings lodged the exiles. From that time on Pignatelli's unfailing genius for providing food and shelter became a legend. Although his wealthy sister the countess of Acerra later aided with substantial sums, neither his family's generosity nor other sources of money known to his closest associates could fully account for the fact that funds were always sufficient.

After three weeks in Ajaccio the ships brought the refugees to San Bonifacio at the southern end of the island. There they remained until Corsica fell under French control 11 months later. The law that had banished the Jesuits from France in 1762 then drove them to the Ligurian Coast near Genoa, one of the few places in southwestern Europe where the Jesuits were not under Bourbon quarantine. When they disembarked Pignatelli learned that CLEMENT XIII, whose representatives had prevented their landing at Civitavecchia, would give them asylum at Ferrara 300 miles away. In that city Monsignor Francesco Pignatelli awaited them with hospitality that was typical of the family. As soon as Pignatelli had settled his exiles, by then doubled in number by Jesuits evicted from the missions of Mexico and Peru, he arranged class schedules and other academic projects before leaving for Rome to report to the general, Lorenzo RICCI.

Exile at Bologna. When CLEMENT XIV issued the brief of suppression in 1773, the Jesuits in Ferrara were disbanded and Pignatelli went to Bologna to live in enforced retirement. Forbidden to exercise the sacred ministry, he devoted his time to prayer, study, and collecting books and manuscripts on the history of the society; the library reached a total of 3,000 volumes. Many former Jesuits who gathered in Bologna were assisted by Pignatelli in finding employment and the means of subsistence. Upon hearing that the society had survived in Russia, he secured permission from PIUS VI to rejoin the order there.

However, he was prevented by a physical breakdown brought on by worry over his brother Nicolás, who indulged himself beyond his means and after a period of dissipation was sent to prison. When Nicolás was dying in Venice years later, Joseph overcame his resistance to grace and received him again into the order.

Eve of Restoration. The first effective step in restoring the Jesuits was taken in 1788 by Duke Ferdinand of Parma, who had been unable to take action earlier because of the opposition of his uncle Charles III of Spain. When Charles died, Ferdinand, with the encouragement of Pignatelli, secured the approval of Pius VI; of the Jesuit general in White Russia, Thaddeus Brzozowski (1749–1820); and of the new king, Charles IV of Spain, to establish a vice province in the Duchy of Parma to be attached to White Russia. In Parma on July 6, 1797, Pignatelli renewed his solemn profession and reentered the Society of Jesus. Duke Ferdinand was later poisoned, probably by enemies of the society, and died in Pignatelli's arms.

On Feb. 20, 1798, Pius VI was seized in Rome by French troops and hurried to Valence, France, where he succumbed to ill treatment. While he was being brought through Florence in chains Pignatelli eased his destitution with a substantial sum referred to by PIUS XI in the decree of beatification: "It gives me the opportunity as the eleventh Pope Pius to requite him in a measure for his memorable act of mercy to my predecessor in his distress, the sixth pontiff of my name."

Provincial of Italy. During this meeting Pius VI authorized Pignatelli to receive novices at Parma. As master of novices, Pignatelli directed their training with his characteristic gentleness. The novitiate was moved to Colorno, where, on May 7, 1803, he received word from the general in St. Petersburg that he was appointed provincial of Italy. Pignatelli, who had held great numbers of Jesuits together in northern Italy, as provincial of Italy sought to extend the society into the south. With authorization from PIUS VII, on Dec. 3, 1804, he presided at the restoration of the society in the Gesù in Naples, where 170 former members reentered the order. Despite crowded quarters this assemblage of aging Italian, French, German, Spanish, Portuguese, and American Jesuits resumed their work and prayer. The decree of Napoleon (March 30, 1806) proclaiming his brother Joseph, king of Naples, and the French seizure of the city, again dispersed the Jesuits and brought Pignatelli to Rome, where Pius VII turned over both the Gesù and the Roman College for Jesuit occupancy. Uneasy lest a too much publicized return to Rome incite hostility, Pignatelli purchased an abandoned house behind the Colosseum, named it San Pantaleone, and settled his Jesuits there, so that they escaped notice when Napoleon's forces swept through the city (1808) and carried Pius VII off to Savona and Fontainebleau. From Rome Pignatelli directed the reestablishment of the society in Sardinia (1807) and opened colleges at Rome, Orvieto, and Tivoli.

Last Days. The tuberculosis, which had flared intermittently throughout his life, now hastened the end. He offered his last Mass, Oct. 15, 1811, and received Communion each day thereafter until his death. In a final intimation of the future, Pignatelli, when dying, asked to be carried to the deathbed of Father Aloisi Panizzoni, his predecessor as provincial. He assured Panizzoni that he would not die, but despite his advanced age would succeed him as provincial, take a vital part in the restoration of the order, and live on into the term of his third successor in the provincialate. These events transpired as foretold, and Panizzoni, living into his 90s, was the recipient of the brief of restoration (Aug. 7, 1814). Pignatelli was beatified by Pope Pius XI in 1933 and canonized in 1954 by Pope Pius XII.

Feast: Nov. 28.

Bibliography: C. BECCARI, *Il B. Guiseppe Pignatelli* (Rome 1933). D. A. HANLY, *Blessed Joseph Pignatelli* (New York 1937). P. ZURBITU, *Blessed Joseph Pignatelli* (Bombay 1933). J. NONELL, *El ven. José M. Pignatelli y la Compañia de Jesús en su extinción y restablecimiento,* 3 v. (Manresa 1893–94). R. NASH, *Saint of the Displaced: St. Joseph Pignatelli* (Dublin 1955). L. PASTOR, *The History of the Popes from the Close of the Middle Ages* (London-St. Louis 1938–61) v.37. J. M. MARCH, *El restaurador de la Compañía de Jesús: Beato José Pignatelli y su tiempo,* 2 v. (Barcelona 1933–36; 2d ed. 1944). P. DELOOZ, "Canonizations récentes (21 Juin 1951–12 Juin 1960)," *Nouvelle revue théologique* 82 (Tournai-Louvain-Paris 1960) 723–72. M. BATTLORI, "José Pignatelli el hombre y el santo," *Razón y Fe* 149 (1954) 512–530. J. SCHAACK, "Saint José Pignatelli, S.J.," *Nouvelle revue théologique* 76 (Tournai-Louvain-Paris 1956) 673–688. *Acta Apostolicae Sedis* 46 (Rome 1954) 332–334, 357–358, 360–361, 374–375. H. WOLTER, *Lexikon für Theologie und Kirche,* ed. J. HOFER and K. RAHNER (Freiburg 1957–65); suppl., *Das Zweite Vatikanishe Konsil: Dokumente und Kommentare,* ed. H. S. BRECHTER et al. (1966) 8:503. C. TESTORE, *Il restauratore della Compagnia di Gesù in Italia: S. Giuseppe Pignatelli, S.J. (1737–1811)* (Rome 1954).

[R. F. COPELAND]

PIKE, WILLIAM, BL.

Lay martyr; b. in Dorset; hanged, drawn, and quartered Dec. 22, 1591 at Dorchester. He lived on the Moors, near Christchurch, Hampshire, and was an Anglican. On his way home from Dorchester one day, probably in 1586, he met Bl. Thomas Pilcher who convinced him of the truth of Catholicism. Thereafter he was reconciled to the Roman Church, and it was for this that he was arrested. At his trial he was asked to apostatize in order to save his life and that of his family, but refused, saying that it did not become a son of Mr. Pilcher to do so. Feast: Feb. 12. He was beatified by Pope John Paul II on Nov. 22, 1987 with George Haydock and Companions.

Feast of the English Martyrs: May 4 (England).

See Also: ENGLAND, SCOTLAND, AND WALES, MARTYRS OF.

Bibliography: R. CHALLONER, *Memoirs of Missionary Priests,* ed. J. H. POLLEN (rev. ed. London 1924). J. H. POLLEN, *Acts of English Martyrs* (London 1891).

[K. I. RABENSTEIN]

PILATE, PONTIUS

Roman procurator of Judea who condemned Jesus to be crucified. He was a Roman equestrian of the Samnite clan of the Pontii; hence his nomen Pontius. The meaning of his cognomen Pilatus is uncertain; his personal or first name is not known. In A.D. 26 the Roman Emperor TIBERIUS appointed him procurator of Judea, Samaria, and Idumea, subject to the legate (governor) of Syria. In 1961 a Latin inscription containing the words *Pontius Pilatus praefectus Judaeae* was discovered at CAESAREA IN PALESTINE [see *Journal of Biblical Literature* 811 (1962) 70–71].

Soon after his arrival in Palestine, Pilate offended the religious sensibilities of the Jews by having Roman troops carry into Jerusalem military standards bearing the emperor's image. The outraged Jews forced him to remove the images after five days (Josephus, *Bell. Jud.* 2.9.2–4; *Ant.* 18.3.1–2). When he hung votive shields inscribed with the emperor's name in Herod's palace in Jerusalem, Herod's four sons protested to Tiberius, who ordered the shields to be taken to a temple in Caesarea (Philo, *Leg. ad Gaium* 38). His other crimes against the inhabitants of Palestine included the financing of a Jerusalem aqueduct with money from the Temple treasury (Josephus, *Ant.* 18.3.2), the slaughtering of some Galileans who were subjects of HEROD ANTIPAS (Lk 13.1; 23.12), the minting of coins bearing pagan religious symbols, and, in A.D. 36, the attacking of armed Samaritans on Mt. Garizim. The Samaritans appealed to Vitellius, Legate of Syria, who ordered Pilate back to Rome to stand trial for cruelty and oppression. The Jewish attitude toward Pilate is further shown in a letter from Herod Agrippa I to Caligula, describing him as inflexible, merciless, and corrupt, and accusing him of executing men without proper trial (*Philo, Leg. ad Gaium,* 38). According to an uncertain tradition reported by Eusebius, Pilate killed himself on orders from Caligula in A.D. 30 (*Ecclesiastical History* 2.7; *Chronicles ad annum 39 AD*).

Philo and Josephus were very likely prejudiced, but Pilate's cruelty and injustice are exemplified also in the Gospel accounts of the TRIAL OF JESUS. All four Gospels describe Pilate's weak submission to the unjust accusations against Jesus and do not excuse Pilate in order to curry Roman favor. They portray him as superstitious, vacillating, and hostile to the Jews.

Justin (*Apol* 1.35.9; 1.48.3) and Tertullian (*Apol.* 5.2; 21.24) mention an official report sent by Pilate to Tiberius purporting to be about the life and death of Jesus. It is doubtful if a genuine report of such a nature ever existed. In any case, the so–called reports of Pilate to the Roman emperors that are contained in the apocrypha are certainly spurious. The chief apocrypha about Pilate are the *Acts of Pilate, Letter of Pilate to Claudius, Letter of Pilate to Tiberius, Anaphora Pilati,* and *Paradosis Pilati.* The legends in these works led the Abyssinian Copts to honor Pilate as a saint (feast, June 25). His wife, traditionally called Claudia Proc(u)la, is venerated as a saint by the Greeks (feast, Oct. 27).

Bibliography: *Encyclopedic Dictionary of the Bible* 1856–57, 1880. J. BLINZLER et al., *Lexikon für Theologie und Kirche*2 8:504–506. J. BLINZLER, *The Trial of Jesus,* tr. I. and F. MCHUGH (Westminster, MD 1959) 3–9, 177–184.

[F. J. BUCKLEY]

PILCHER, THOMAS, BL.

Priest, martyr; b. ca. 1557 at Battle, Sussex, England; hanged, drawn, and quartered March 21, 1587 at Tyburn or Dorchester. Pilcher earned his master's degree (1579) at Balliol College, Oxford, but resigned his fellowship in 1580. In November 1581, he began study in Rheims and was ordained priest at Laon in March 1583. That same year he went back to England to work in Hampshire and Dorset. In 1585, he was arrested and banished, but returned almost immediately to serve another two years before being apprehended in March 1587. Such was his zeal that during his two-week imprisonment at Dorchester, he converted 30 people to Catholicism. He was beatified by Pope John Paul II on Nov. 22, 1987 with George Haydock and Companions.

Feast of the English Martyrs: May 4 (England).

See Also: ENGLAND, SCOTLAND, AND WALES, MARTYRS OF.

Bibliography: R. CHALLONER, *Memoirs of Missionary Priests,* ed. J. H. POLLEN (rev. ed. London 1924). J. H. POLLEN, *Acts of English Martyrs* (London 1891).

[K. I. RABENSTEIN]

"Christ Before Pilate," from polyptych known as the "Liesborn Altarpiece," by Master of Cappenberg, c. 1525, National Gallery, London. (©National Gallery Collection/CORBIS)

PILGRIM HOLINESS CHURCH

A church in the Holiness tradition with a strong emphasis on the Wesleyan principles of sanctification of believers and evangelistic missionary work. In 1897 Martin Wells Knapp, a Methodist minister in Cincinnati, Ohio, organized the International Apostolic Holiness Union to restore the primitive spirit of John WESLEY on ''apostolic practices, methods, power and success.'' Twenty-five years later the International Holiness Church (derived from the Union) joined with the like-minded Pilgrim Church of California to become the Pilgrim Holiness Church. In 1968, the Wesleyan Methodist Church merged with the Pilgrim Holiness Church.

The church's stress on sanctification is based on Wesley's teaching that once a person is justified he may grow in holiness through his generous response to the Indwelling Spirit. This ''second blessing'' adds a sense of security that the sinner is now reconciled with God, and gives him an emotional experience that is unmistakable. In its accent on ''true Wesleyanism,'' the Pilgrim Holiness Church holds that sanctification is both possible and commendable; that man's sinfulness has not deprived him of the capacity for a willing cooperation with grace. The church also professes belief in millennialism, i.e., the belief in the early Second Coming of Christ (*see* PAROUSIA). The Pilgrim Holiness Church further believes that the Second Coming will precede this 1000-year period of the highest spiritual and material blessings on earth as a prelude to the end of the world.

Bibliography: F. S. MEAD, S. S. HILL and C. D. ATWOOD, eds., *Handbook of Denominations in the United States*, 11th ed (Nashville 2001).

[J. A. HARDON/EDS.]

PILGRIM OF PASSAU

Missionary bishop, of the noble Aribo family of Bavaria; d. Pssau, May 21, 991. The nephew of Abp. Frederick of Salzburg, he was educated in the monastic school of St. Pirmin, in NIEDERALTAICH; he became bishop of Passau in 971. When Henry the Wrangler, Duke of Bavaria, rebelled against OTTO II, Pilgrim remained steadfast on the side of the Emperor. As bishop he was gifted chiefly in the field of administration, as was shown in the reconstruction of churches and monasteries and in the restoration of Catholic life in great areas of his diocese, destroyed by Hungarian hordes. Pilgrim met the danger of fresh barbarian attacks by undertaking, on a grand scale, the task of converting the Hungarians to Christianity. The time was propitious, for the Germans on the west and the Byzantine Empire on the east had by then made it clear to the Hungarians that they had nothing to gain by warlike activities. The Hungarian leader, Geisa, married a Christian princess and was anxious to live in peace with his Christian neighbors. The transition from paganism was made easier by the presence in the area held by the Hungarians of two groups of Christians: a Slavonic element, a surviving remnant of the conquered population, and a Germanic group, a large number of prisoners of war brought home by the barbarians from their earlier successful expeditions. The missionaries sent by Pilgrim enabled these Christians once more to profess the Catholic faith. Not only did Pilgrim send considerable numbers of priests and monks to Hungary, but on occasion he took himself a place in their midst. He was thus in a position to send a personal account of the promising prospects to Rome. There were disappointments and setbacks, however, before the Hungarians, a generation later, were brought into the Christian fold by their own King STEPHEN.

Pilgrim's eagerness to establish dioceses in Hungary and to attach them to Passau as their metropolitan see led him to fabricate charters (the Forgeries of Lorch), showing that Passau, through its connection with Lorch, had an ancient right to archiepiscopal status. It is possible that he busied himself with the translation of old German sagas, especially with a Latin version of the *Niebelungenlied,* in which a ''Bishop Pilgerin'' is mentioned.

Bibliography: E. L. DÜMMLER, *Pilgrim von Passau und das Erzbisthum Lorch* (Leipzig 1854). A. HAUCK, *Kirchengeschichte Deutschlands* 3:163–180. I. ZIBERMAYR, *Noricum. Baiern und Oesterreich* (Horn 1956). R. BAUERREISS, *Kirchengeschichte Bayerns,* 2 v. (St. Ottilien 1949–55) 2:142–145. J. OSWALD, *Lexikon für Theologie und Kirche* 2 6:1142; 8:509.

[J. RYAN]

PILGRIMAGE OF GRACE

The name given to a series of uprisings in northern England in the reign of Henry VIII, but especially to the rebellion in Yorkshire in late 1536. The first outbreak, at Louth in Lincolnshire in early October 1536, quickly had most of that count in an uproar but collapsed within three weeks—though not before it had incited the southeast corner of the neighboring county of Yorkshire. Here a much more serious rebellion developed, led by Robert ASKE. By late October Aske had a large force behind him, carrying the banner of St. Cuthbert and badges of the Five Wounds of Our Lord. Had he marched southward he might have broken the king, HENRY VIII. But, insisting that he and his men were pilgrims seeking justice, not rebels, he halted at Doncaster to await a parley with Thomas Howard, Duke of NORFOLK. After six weeks of suspense, Pilgrim "councils" at York and Pontefract drew up a petition to the king that was presented to Norfolk on December 5. Norfolk made insincere promises and announced a dubious royal pardon, whereupon the Pilgrims, trusting Henry's goodness, disbanded. Two more rebellions broke out in January and February of 1537: one in Yorkshire, led by Sir Francis Bigod; the other in Cumberland. Both failed quickly.

These were sudden, popular, incoherent uprisings. Inevitably there was a wide variety of motives behind them. In particular, landlordism, heavy taxation, regionalism, and political conservatism all played a part. The Lincoln rebels, who recruited little help from either religious or gentry, made no mention of the pope and were even ready, some of them, to accept the Royal Supremacy, while the Yorkshire Pilgrims' articles included several purely secular demands. Bigod was a Protestant, driven to rebellion by motives far different from Aske's. The Cumberland peasants were stirred by oppression and hunger. But if these risings were not simply the protest of a Catholic north against the Reformation under Henry, they certainly had a large religious content. The Pilgrims' articles rejected explicitly the Royal Supremacy, called for a return to Rome (though not to papal fiscalism), and demanded that heresy in England be repressed and the Church's liberties restored. Above all, both the Lincolnshire and Yorkshire rebels opposed the suppression of the monasteries, then under way, and even asked that dissolved houses be restored. Had material and political motives not been added, the rebellion might have been smaller (and more coherent), but Aske claimed it would still have happened.

No other Tudor faced so large and courageous a domestic challenge as this. Henry bided his time, yielded nothing, and then wreaked terrible vengeance. Hundreds suffered death, including the admirable Aske, a number of religious (including several heads or former heads of houses), and some secular priests. The uprisings provided the excuse to suppress larger monasteries in the north, which had escaped the first act of dissolution.

Bibliography: M. H. and R. DOODS, *The Pilgrimage of Grace, 1536–1537, and the Exeter Conspiracy, 1538,* 2 v. (Cambridge, Eng. 1915), standard work. H. F. M. PRESCOTT, *The Man on a Donkey* (New York 1952), excellent historical novel about Aske. D. KNOWLES, *The Religious Orders in England,* 3 v. (Cambridge, Eng. 1948–60) v.3. A. G. DICKENS, *Lollards and Protestants in the Diocese of York, 1509–1558* (New York 1959), on Bigod.

[J. J. SCARISBRICK]

PILGRIMAGES

A pilgrimage may be described as a journey to a sacred shrine or sanctuary for a religious motive. Such journeys are a common religious phenomenon not restricted to any one people. This composite article examines pilgrimages in the Bible, in the early Christian period (to 600), in the Middle Ages (600 to 1500), and in modern times (1500 to mid-20th century).

1. IN THE BIBLE

Pilgrimages have a long history in the ancient Near East among Semitic peoples; they are as old as the sacred shrines uncovered by archeologists. To these various cultic centers the common man carried a part of the fruits of his land and livestock to offer it to the gods in homage and thanksgiving. The sanctuaries were places believed to be chosen by the gods as special abodes and manifested as such by peculiar natural phenomena (a height, a spring, a tree) or by a THEOPHANY, e.g., Jacob's dream (Gn 28.10–22).

Some of the Canaanite open-air shrines were merely converted to the use of the Yahwistic cult, e.g., SHECHEM, BETHEL, and Mamre. Because of Israel's tribal structure one shrine usually served as the central sanctuary, at least for partial confederations of the 12 tribes. The cultic center acted as politico-religious bond, an intertribal focus to which the federated clans periodically came on pilgrimage. At various times Gilgal, Shiloh, Mizpeh, and probably Gibeon served as such local centers. A description of a pilgrimage to a central shrine is found in the prescriptions for offering the first fruits of the grain harvest (Dt 26.1–10; cf. 1 Sm 1.3–7). Jerusalem became the focal point of religious gatherings after King David brought the ARK OF THE COVENANT there. Later, Jeroboam I, King of Israel, in order to have his own cultic centers in the Northern Kingdom, separated from Judah, established sanctuaries for Yahweh at Bethel and the city of Dan (1 Kgs 12.27–30).

Many other local sanctuaries attracted pilgrims during the time of the two kingdoms, as is clear from the preaching of the Prophets who condemned the evil influence of religious syncretism that these shrines fostered. These sanctuaries were destroyed by the centralizing reforms of Hezekiah (2 Kgs 18.4) and Josiah (2 Kgs 23.8–20), Kings of Judah, but flourished again after their deaths.

The custom of sacred pilgrimages was affirmed in ancient Israelite legislation concerning the religious FEASTS. The three *ḥag* (pilgrim) festivals, the Feast of PASSOVER, the Hebrew Feast of PENTECOST, and the Feast of BOOTHS (TABERNACLES), were times when the Israelites were commanded to appear before the Lord (Ex 23.14–17; Dt 16.16), a practice parallel to the Arabic *ḤAJJ*.

Israelite religious pilgrimages continued during and after the exile [Ps 41(42)]. Josephus (*Bell. Jud.* 6.9.3)

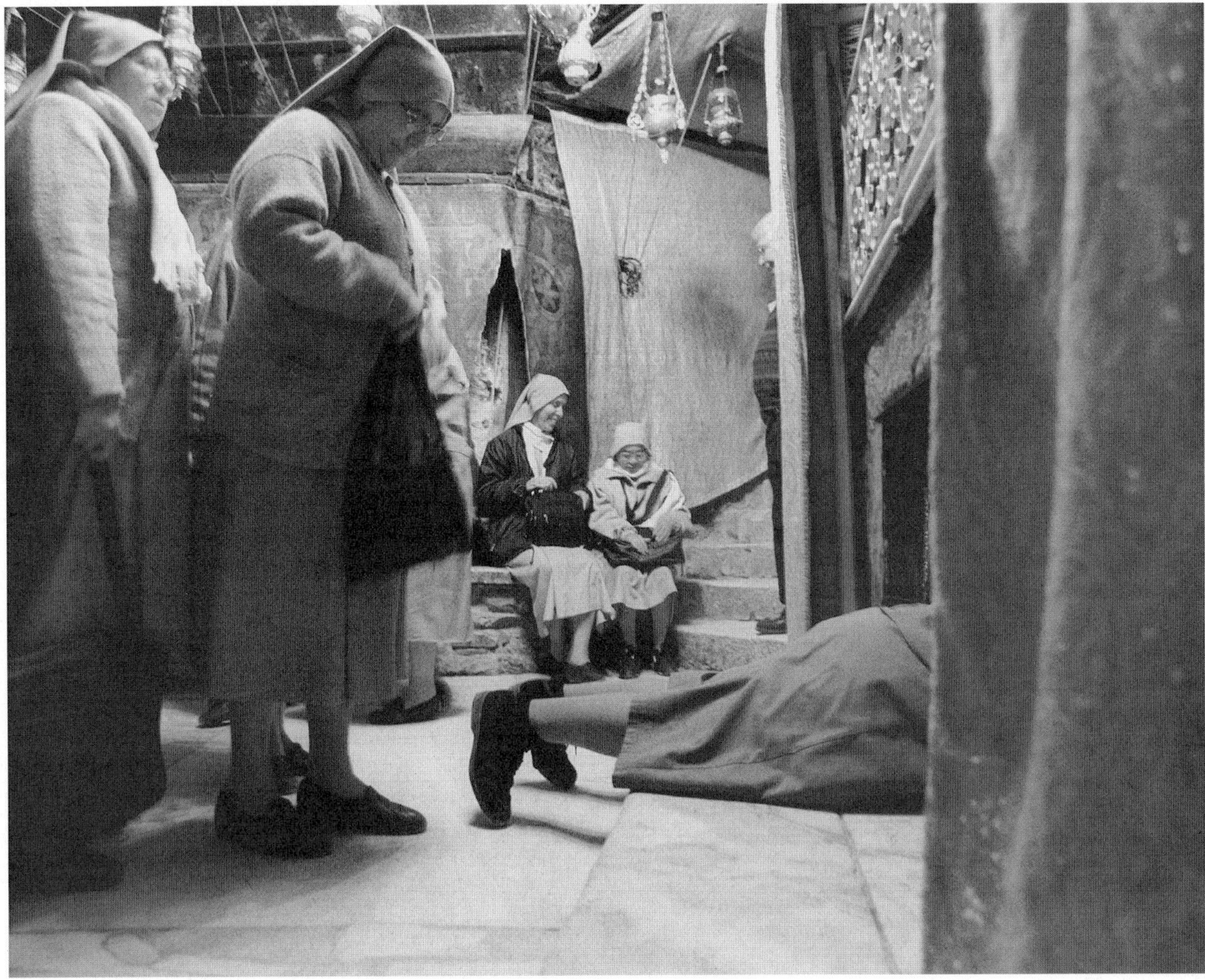

Catholic nuns on a pilgrimage from Italy, Church of the Nativity, Bethlehem, Israel. (AP/Wide World Photos)

speaks of the large gatherings at Jerusalem to celebrate the feasts of Yahweh. Evidence for them in the New Testament is found in Lk 2.41–42; In 2.13; 5.1; 7.2–10; 12.201; and Acts 2.1–11.

Bibliography: R. DE VAUX, *Ancient Israel, Its Life and Institutions*, tr. J.MCHUGH (New York 1961) 468–517. *Encyclopedic Dictionary of the Bible*, tr. and adap. by L. HARTMAN (New York 1963), from A. VAN DEN BORN, *Bijbels Woordenboek* 1858.

[S. M. POLAN]

2. EARLY CHRISTIAN

Journeys to holy places made by Christian men and women between the 1st and the 7th century. These voyages were undertaken to venerate places sanctified by the life of Christ; by the saints, especially the martyrs; or by miracles; and also to beg divine aid and to perform acts of penance or thanksgiving. After the Peace of the Church (313) and all through the 4th century, several events fostered the idea of making a pilgrimage: the honoring of the holy places in Palestine by CONSTANTINE I and his mother, HELENA; the publicity given the Holy Land by JEROME, and the monastic life he helped to foster there; the attention directed to the monastic life in Egypt by such works as ATHANASIUS's *Life of Anthony,* the anonymous *Historia monachorum in Aegypto,* and PALLADIUS's *Lausiac History;* and, in Rome, the work of Pope DAMASUS I in restoring the catacombs.

Pilgrimages will be treated here in three sections: (1) the Holy Land, the preferred place of pilgrimage; (2) the monasteries of Egypt and the tombs of Rome; and (3) shorter pilgrimages arising from local cults throughout the early Christian world. Despite difficulties of travel in ancient times, pilgrimages, especially to the Holy Land, were not unusual by the end of the 4th century, as the writings of the Fathers frequently attest.

The Holy Land. EUSEBIUS OF CAESAREA supplies information on a 2d-century pilgrimage of Bishop MELITO

Pope John Paul II greeting pilgrims during papal visit to Czestochowa, Poland, June 1, 1979. (Archive Photos)

OF SARDES (*c.* 160) to the land where the Scriptures were enacted (*Ecclesiatical History* 4.26.14) and on a 3d-century pilgrimage of Bishop Alexander of Cappadocia, who journeyed to Jerusalem (*c.* 216) in consequence of a vow and for the sake of information about the holy places (*ibid.* 6.11.2). Eusebius characterized Constantine and Helena as the most noble of pilgrims and described the great works they promoted in the Holy Land between 325 and 330. To Constantine he attributed the finding of the Holy SEPULCHER and the building of a great basilica on its site, and another on the site of Abraham's visit from the angels at Mamre, near Hebron; to Helena he attributed the building of magnificent basilicas on the sites of the Nativity, and of the Ascension from Mt. Olivet (*Vita Constantini* 3.25–40). Eusebius did not mention Helena's finding the true cross. However, by the end of the 4th century she was credited with this by AMBROSE, JOHN CHRYSOSTOM, Jerome, RUFINUS, the historian Socrates, and Aetheria.

Whether or not she found it, she and her son gave great impetus to the pilgrimage movement, as an increasing number of sources attests. A text of 333 details the stations of a pilgrimage from Bordeaux to Jerusalem and back via Rome to Milan (Geyer, 1–33). SOZOMEN notes that in 351, on the occasion of the appearance of a miraculous cross in the sky above Jerusalem, there were travelers from all parts of the world there for prayer and to visit the places of interest (*Ecclesiastical History* 4.5). By the end of the 4th century, references to pilgrimages can be found frequently in the FATHERS OF THE CHURCH, who especially valued them because they brought one to the land of the Sacred Scriptures. In a letter to a group of virgins who had returned from a pilgrimage to Jerusalem, Athanasius introduced a theme that was to become familiar: they can remain with Christ by a holy life, although they have left the scenes of His earthly life [ed. J. Lebon, *Muséon* 41 (1928) 170–203]. John Chrysostom spoke of the efficacy of pilgrimages in arousing devotion (*In Phil., Patrologia Graeca*, ed. J. P. Migne, 62:702–03).

Jerome has probably made himself the most famous of early Christian pilgrims to the Holy Land, not only as a resident there for over 30 years, but also as its most prolific writer and the greatest Scripture scholar of his age. He influenced the aristocratic Roman ladies PAULA, EUSTOCHIUM, and both MELANIA the Elder and the Younger to establish monasteries there. His own words show the impetus he was capable of giving to the pilgrimage movement, by pointing out the benefits to be derived from journeys to holy places:

> Just as one understands the Greek historians better when one has seen Athens, or the third book of Virgil when one has sailed to Troas or Sicily . . . so we also understand Scripture better when we have seen Judea with our own eyes, and discovered what still remains of . . . ancient towns . . . . That is why myself took care to travel through this land . . . . [Praef., *In lib. Paralip.*]

His friends Paula and Eustochium witness to the appeal of Christian pilgrimaging:

> Here one can see the most important people from everywhere . . . the best known in Gaul . . . . The Briton . . . comes . . . to seek a city which he knows . . . by what he has read of it in the Holy Scriptures. What shall we say of the Armenians, Persians, peoples of India and Ethiopia, from Egypt,. . . Pontus, Cappadocia, Coele-Syria, Mesopotamia and all the crowds from the East? . . . We shall be able to enter with you the cave of the Savior, weep at the Sepulchre, . . . kiss the wood of the cross, ascend . . . the Mount of Olives . . . . [Jerome, *Epist.* 46.]

Much more celebrated now than in her own time is the pilgrim nun Aetheria, famous for her account of the celebration of the liturgy in Jerusalem when she visited there (395) and for the extent of her travels, which included upper Syria as far as Edessa, the Sinaitic peninsula, and Egypt. Other noted Holy Land pilgrims also visited the DESERT FATHERS in Egypt; Rufinus and Melanie the Elder (371–372); Cassian (*c.* 385); Jerome (386); Palladius (388); the anonymous author of the *Historia monachorum* (394); Sylvania, sister-in-law of the Consul Rufinus (*c.* 396); and Postumianus, disciple of Sulpicius Severus (401–404). Some of the 5th-century abbots of

Lérins seem to have been Palestine pilgrims (*Acta Sanctorum* June 1:75–78; January 2:18–19). From the 5th or 6th century comes an enumeration of the sanctuaries of Jerusalem (Geyer, 151–155). The *De situ terrae sanctae* of Theodosius, an archdeacon from North Africa (*c.* 520–530; Geyer, 135–150), and an account of several pilgrims from Piacenza to Palestine (*c.* 560–570; Geyer, 157–218) are witnesses to the continued flow of pilgrims to Palestine through the 6th century.

One of the strongest witnesses to the popularity of early Christian pilgrimages and to sound teaching concerning them lies in the frequent warnings the Fathers uttered against their abuse: St. John Chrysostom (*Ad pop. Antioch hom.* 3, *Patrologia Graeca* 49:49), St. Jerome (*Epist.* 58), St. Augustine (*Epist.* 160), and especially St. Gregory of Nyssa (*Epist.* 2).

Pilgrimages to Egypt and Rome. In the 4th century, monasticism proved to be a link between Egypt and Palestine, the two famous places of early Christian pilgrimage. Athanasius's *Life of Anthony* not only fostered the monastic movement throughout the Mediterranean world but also drew pilgrims to seek counsel from the austere Desert Fathers. Those of Nitria, some 50 miles south of Alexandria, were fairly accessible, but as the author of the *Historia monachorum* relates, the journey to the THEBAID was arduous and dangerous. He had made it; so also did the intrepid Aetheria.

Although in the first six centuries Rome had not the same importance for pilgrimages as the Holy Land, the graffiti on the walls of the catacombs witness to a steady stream of pilgrims. The tombs of Peter and Paul were equally objects of pilgrimage, often made by visitors who had come to Rome on business. Polycarp of Smyrna visited Rome *c.* 150; both Abercius of Hierapolis in Phrygia (*c.* 216) and Origen seem to have made a sort of pilgrimage (*c.* 212), ''desiring to see the most ancient church of Rome'' (Eusebius, *Ecclesiastical History* 6.14). As in the case of the Holy Land, it was after the Peace of the Church that Roman pilgrimages increased. In the second half of the 4th century, Pope Damasus gave impetus to the movement by architectural restorations in the catacombs and by the inscriptions he had carved on the tombs. Jerome tells of his own visits to the catacombs when he was a youth studying in Rome and of the crowds of pilgrims: ''Where save at Rome do they crowd with such frequency to the churches and sepulchres of the martyrs?'' (*Comm. in Ezech.* 12.50; *Comm. in Epist. Galat.* 2). Ambrose (*Hymnus* 15) and Prudentius (*Peristephanon* 12) are among the many witnesses to the vast streams of pilgrims who flocked to Rome for the feast of Saints Peter and Paul on June 29.

This pilgrimage and others throughout the Christian world often gave rise to feasting and merrymaking, against which the clergy constantly had to preach. Prudentius in his *Peristephanon* is witness to a full flowering of the cult of the martyrs and the important role of pilgrimages in the century after the persecution of DIOCLETIAN and the Peace of the Church. He was especially moved by the great pilgrimages to Rome on the feast of the Passion of St. Hippolytus (*Peristephanon* 11). A dramatic feature of Roman PILGRIMAGES in the 4th century were those of Roman emperors to the tombs of the Apostles. The writings of John Chrysostom (*Patrologia Graeca* 61:582) and St. Augustine are among the witnesses to these events. In the words of St. Augustine: ''. . . the emperor comes to Rome: whither does he hasten? To the temple of the emperor, or to the memorial of the Fisherman?'' (*Patrologia Latina*, ed. J. P. Migne, 37:1830). In 450 Valentinian III came to Rome, according to Pope Leo the Great, ''to seek the Fisherman's intercession'' (*Patrologia Latina* 54:858). A steady stream of pilgrims to Rome seems to have continued unabated into the Middle Ages. At the opening of the 6th century, Pope Symmachus (498–514) built three hospices near the tombs of Saints Peter, Paul, and Lawrence. Later in the century, Gregory of Tours speaks of Roman pilgrimages from Gaul and describes an activity commonly connected with them, that of procuring relics for local shrines (*De gloria martyrum* 1.28).

Local Pilgrimages. Not far from Rome, at Imola and at Nola, pilgrimage cults in honor of the martyrs Cassian (Prudentius, *Peristephanon* 9) and Felix (Paulinus, *Carmina, Corpus scriptorum ecclesiasticorum latinorum* v.30) spread during the 4th century. By the end of that century, the cult of St. Felix was greatly extended by the devotion of the noted aristocrat and poet PAULINUS, who retired to the monastery he had built at Nola and celebrated in his poetry the throngs of pilgrims who came there, among them the noted Bishop NICETAS OF REMESIANA (*Carmen* 17). Important pilgrimage centers grew up in Gaul also. By the middle of the 4th century, a shrine had been established near the site of the martyrdom of St. Maurice and his THEBAN LEGION in Valais, Switzerland (d. probably *c.* 286). Pilgrims returning from Rome and, above all, pilgrims seeking cures came in such numbers that by the middle of the 5th century a large hostelry and infirmary had been built, and by the 6th, the still famous Abbey of SAINT-MAURICE d'Agaune. The late 4th century saw also the rise of Gaul's most extraordinary center of devotion and pilgrimage—the tomb of St. Martin at Tours. Gregory of Tours, who was one of Martin's most devoted episcopal successors, witnesses two centuries later to the unceasing stream of pilgrims to the tomb. They range from the Frankish King Chlotar (*c.* 560), making atonement for the murder of his son, to the simple youth Wulflaicus from Lombardy, who was so moved by the grace of him visit to Tours that he became an austere hermit near Yvois and converted many in the surrounding region (*Hist. Francorum* 8.15–16). In 5th-century Arles the throngs of pilgrims passing between the two shrines of St. Genesius on his feast were so great they broke the bridge over which they crossed (*Patrologia Latina* 50:1273–76).

Patristic literature bears witness that pilgrimages became an established part of Christian devotion, whether they involved traversing a city or more than half of the civilized world. The early Christian centuries gave the movement an impetus that took it wall into the Middle Ages.

Bibliography: P. GEYER, ed., *Itinera Hierosolymitana saeculi IV–VIII* (*Corpus scriptorum ecclesiasticorum latinorum* (Vienna 1866–) 39; 1898). *Library of the Palestine Pilgrims' Text Society,* 13 v. (London 1890–97). F. STUMMER, ed., *Monumenta historiam et geographiam Terrae Sanctae illustrantia* (*Florilegium Patristicum* 41; 1935). EUSEBIUS, *Ecclesiastical History,* and *Vita Constantini, Patrologia Graeca,* ed. J. P. MIGNE (Paris 1878–90) 20:45–1440. SOCRATES, *Ecclesiastial History,* and SOZOMEN, *Ecclesiastical History, Patrologia Graeca,* ed. J. P. MIGNE (Paris 1857–66) 67:29–1630. E. R. BARKER, *Rome of the Pilgrims and Martyrs* (London 1913). H. LECLERCQ, *Dictionnaire d'archéologie chrétienne et de liturgie,* ed. F. CABROL, H. LECLERCQ, and H. I. MARROU, 15 v. (Paris 1907–53) 14.1:65–176. G. BARDY, *Analecta Bollandiana* 67 (1949) 224–235, B. KÖTTING, *Peregrinatio religiosa* (Münster 1950). A. FLICHE and V. MARTIN, eds. *Histoire de l'église depuis les origines jusqu'à nos jours* (Paris 1935–) v.3, tr. E. MESSENGER (New York 1950) 504–512. J. M. THEURILLAT, *L'Abbaye de St-Maurice d'Agaune, des origines à la réforme canoniale, 515–830* (Sion, Switzerland 1954), F. VAN DER MEER and C. MOHRMANN, *Atlas of the Early Christian World,* ed. and tr. M. F. HEDLUND and H. H. ROWLEY (New York 1958). H. LHARKAMP, *Lexikon für Theologie und Kirche* ed. J. HOFER and K. RAHNER, 10 v. (2d, new ed. Freiburg 1957–65) 5:822–824.

[M. C. MCCARTHY]

3. MEDIEVAL AND MODERN

Pilgrimages in the sense of journeys to SHRINES or holy places for veneration, either to obtain favors through the intercession of the saints honored there or to render thanks for favors received, are a phenomenon common to all civilizations. In the Christian world they developed in all countries and in many fashions. As indicated above, the earliest documents of the pilgrimage as an institution link its origin with the veneration of places where Christ lived and of His tomb, the Holy SEPULCHER, in Jerusalem. But very soon pilgrimages began to be made also to the tombs of the earliest martyrs, ''witnesses'' of Christ. Well before the time of St. Augustine, who spoke very clearly on the point, it was held that complete remission of sins was obtained by going to the tomb of a martyr and meditating there.

Goals of Pilgrimages. If one excludes Jerusalem, the bodies of SS. Peter and Paul in Rome were the primary attraction for Christian pilgrims (*see* PILGRIMAGES, ROMAN). Later, alleged tombs of other martyrs came to be venerated, especially that of the Apostle JAMES (SON OF ZEBEDEE), once his supposed tomb was discovered in Galicia at *Campus stellae,* hence Compostela, in 830 (*see* SANTIAGO DE COMPOSTELA).

Soon pilgrimages acquired varied and diverse goals. The faithful began to venerate the tombs of nonmartyrs, e.g., those of the confessors MARTIN OF TOURS in Gaul (the most popular of all) and NICHOLAS OF MYRA, whose body was transported to Bari, Italy, in the 11th century, and much later those of SERGIUS OF RADONEZH in Russia and the saintly Jean VIANNEY in the Lyonnais, as well as the tombs of such penitents as Mary Magdalene in Sainte-Baume, Provence (*see* SAINT-MAXIMIN, ABBEY OF).

Pilgrimages were made also to places hallowed as the result of a reputed supernatural apparition. Thus it seems that from the 6th century many pilgrims went to Monte Gargano in Apulia, made famous by an apparition of the archangel Michael. After 710 pilgrims went for the same reason to MONT-SAINT-MICHEL on the borders of Normandy and Brittany.

There were also pilgrimages in honor of the Virgin Mary, Mother of God. Although they originated later than the early pilgrimages to the Holy Sepulcher or tombs of saints in general, certain Marian pilgrimages are obviously very old, dating back at least to the Frankish period so far as the West is concerned; e.g., Ambronay in Burgundy dates from the 7th century at least; EINSIEDELN in Switzerland goes back to 954; while Savona (near Genoa, Italy) claims to have received pilgrims as early as the age of Constantine.

Origins of Pilgrimage Shrines. Many pilgrim shrines owe their renown to origins so legendary that it is difficult to sift out the historical truth. More than one such shrine coincides with the site of a holy place that was previously a pagan shrine, e.g., at Fourvière (Lyons) a statue of Mercury was honored before that of the Virgin. Many new shrines have appeared even in modern times in the wake of revelations—quite often impossible to verify—made in dreams to simple folk. The sanctuary of St. Anne in Auray, France, was begun in the early 17th century by a simple Breton peasant, Yves Nicolazic, in obedience to repeated visions. In the following century it was a child who ''discovered'' the picture of the Virgin painted on a rock in Concepción, Chile. The miraculous icon of Tenos was found in the 19th century as a result of the dream of a Greek nun. Each of these events was the beginning of a new pilgrimage. Weeping statues, such as the ''Regina sanctorum omnium'' in the cathedral at Ancona during the French invasion in 1796 or the majolica madonna in a street in Syracuse, Italy, in 1953, have also resulted in pilgrimages.

Popular piety creates new sites of pilgrimage with disconcerting spontaneity, neither seeking nor tolerating, in many cases, counsels of prudence or warnings from the hierarchy. ''We have learned,'' wrote WILLIAM DE GRENEFIELD, the archbishop of York in 1313, ''that a statue of the Blessed Virgin newly installed in the parish church of Foston is stirring up many simple souls as if something divine were more apparent in this statue than in others.'' Every new instance of this sort raises the possibility that the unenlightened faithful will be victimized by illusions or fall into superstition.

In modern times Marian apparitions in rapid succession have generated immense new shrines and places of pilgrimage, whose renown has eclipsed that of the more ancient and traditional sites, e.g., Fatima has evidently eclipsed Compostela. But Marian pilgrimages are hardly all of modern origin. Well before LA SALETTE (apparition in 1846), LOURDES (1858), Pontmain (1871), or FATIMA (1917), waves of pilgrims had rushed to Laus in the Dauphiné Alps (17th century), to Garaison near Tarbes, France, to GUADALUPE in Mexico (16th century), and to Caravaggio in Lombardy (15th century). The ancient and venerable pilgrimage to Our Lady in Le Puy-en-Velay, southern France, likewise owes its origin to an apparition.

Chronology of Pilgrimages. It would be of interest to establish a chronology of Christian pilgrimages in an attempt to discover significant fluctuations throughout the centuries. No such chronological table has, in fact, ever been compiled. Were it to be, it would show the permanence of the pilgrimage phenomenon, which seems to live on despite the Reformation, the Wars of Religion, the Enlightenment, and despite the rationalism, materialism, and atheism of modern times. However, certain stages in the evolution of the pilgrimage are discernible.

Fourth-century documents testify that pilgrimages to Jerusalem had been going on without interruption since the Apostolic Age. EUSEBIUS OF CAESAREA stated that a bishop from Cappadocia had made a pilgrimage to Rome as early as 217. Constantine's work of pacification that made possible the rebuilding of Jerusalem, the finding of the Holy CROSS, and the erection of shrines, e.g., Holy SEPULCHER (326–336), in effect initiated the widespread popularity of pilgrimages that continued unabated throughout the Middle Ages, even though it was slowed down during the first centuries of the Moslem occupation. Rome, then Compostela, and later such sites as those of the relics of Mary Magdalene at Vézelay (succeeding Provence) and of Thomas BECKET in Canterbury (from 1171) all served to satisfy the piety of pilgrims who could not get to the holy places in Jerusalem. The Crusades began in 1095, and the fighting men considered themselves—and were consideredmdash;pilgrims, though there is scarcely any need to call attention to the extent to which the pilgrimage spirit had, in their case, been deflected from its original character. The influx of pilgrims at Canterbury (1220), Rome (1300), and Compostela was considerably augmented by the proclamation of the HOLY YEARS, which promised special spiritual favors to pilgrims.

The 16th century, understandably, was marked by a decline in pilgrimages in Europe, while the military advances of the OTTOMAN TURKS discouraged travelers to the Holy Land. Thus, when Ignatius Loyola went to Palestine in 1523, he found it deserted, and there were very few pilgrims in Jerusalem—at least from the West—down to the time of CHATEAUBRIAND. However, the newly Christianized areas in America were experiencing a rise and spread of pious pilgrimages in the 17th century, and Europe itself saw the road to Compostela become crowded once again after the THIRTY YEARS' WAR. The ''Holy House'' of Loreto, long after its singular appearance in central Italy at the end of the 13th century, attracted a growing number of pilgrims, and even a man so ''reasonable'' as Descartes traveled there in 1624 before he began publication.

After the great crisis of the French Revolution there was a renaissance of pilgrimage; and this despite the fact that many relics had been removed, many shrines burned or demolished since the religious crisis of the 16th century, either in the name of reform of the Church or as a result of the Enlightenment. Everything smacking of ''fanaticism'' was to be swept away. Yet, despite, or even because of, these excesses, western European Christians once again began to go on pilgrimage; other Christians, e.g., in Greece or Russia, had never ceased to do so. The movement turned instinctively toward the site of martyrdoms, including most recent ones; e.g., the people of Angers, France, would go on Sundays to the Field of the Martyrs where a number of nonjuring clergy had been executed during The Terror (1793–94). Pope Pius VII encouraged the resumption of the cult of Our Lady of Fourvière, whose statue had been burned by the Huguenots, and in 1836 Marseilles ''rediscovered'' the shrine of Notre-Dame de la Garde, which had been destroyed during the Revolution. In 1858 Pauline de Nicolay became a zealous sponsor of renewed Holy Land pilgrimages, which, like many others, were directed by the ASSUMPTIONISTS. Meanwhile the shrine at Lourdes had come into existence. Under the influence of Charles P. PÉGUY in the early 20th century a new movement was begun, designed to interest intellectual circles then sharply affected by scientism and positivism. The ''Chartres pilgrimages'' of Paris students, copied since then by various other universities, comprise one of the newest aspects of the modern pilgrimage spirit.

The Individual Pilgrim. It should be noted that from the time of the invasions by the barbarian nations a pilgrimage was often imposed as a penance on one who had confessed a particularly grave fault. Thus, in the 8th and 9th centuries and even later, murderers or other capital offenders were compelled to go on pilgrimages that often lasted years, wearing mean attire or even chains as a token of the incomplete remission of temporal punishment due to their sin. In certain regions, especially in the Low Countries, lay tribunals were allowed to sentence offenders to pilgrimages long after public penance had been abolished in the Church. However, the pilgrimage that has been important in the history of Christian piety and spiritual life is that undertaken by a free man as a spontaneous gesture in his quest for salvation.

Motives sending Christians on pilgrimages over land and sea may not always have been entirely pure: Sir John Mandeville, who set out for the Holy Land in 1322, was prompted as much by the desire to see the world, to have new and marvellous experiences, and to be accepted as an expert traveler as by a sincere desire for personal sanctification. And the same could certainly be said of many another pilgrim. But, just as John Chrysostom dreamed of being able to go to Rome simply "to see the chains and the prison" of the Apostle, many pilgrims in all ages expect nothing else from their journeys than the simple joy of being able to reach the holy place (*ad limina*), i.e., the tomb of a saint they were invoking, and there to saturate themselves with his *virtus,* to obtain full remission of their sins, to invoke the saint's power to cure their ills of soul or body, or to thank him for a cure already effected.

These two motives, entreaty and thanksgiving, seem constantly to alternate in pilgrimages. In both cases the object is frequently physical health, just as it was for those who sought out Christ during His earthly life. But many other graces and favors might also be solicited, e.g., liberation of a captive, victory over enemies, success in a temporal or spiritual undertaking. One of the first acts of King Richard I the Lion-Hearted after his release from the German prison following the Third Crusade was to visit the tomb of St. Edward the Confessor in WESTMINSTER ABBEY. During the national wars against the Turks in the 17th century, Prince Esterhazy and more than 10,000 faithful made the pilgrimage to Mariazell (Austria) to implore success in arms. Each of the great wars of the 20th century has seen a revival of pilgrimages to St. Leonard of Noblat, the popular patron of prisoners: 700 to 800 persons a day came to pray before his statue at Huyssinghem in Brabant (1914–18).

In the Middle Ages the pilgrim received a special liturgical blessing before setting out; he would have already put on a special dress reminiscent of a penitent, with a broad-brimmed hat, a wallet, or pouch, slung across his back, and a long iron-shod cane or "pilgrim's staff" in his hand. Before leaving, he would have been advised to put his affairs in good order, return any money unjustly acquired, make provisions for the support of his family in his absence, and give alms while retaining enough money to defray the expenses of his often long and costly journey. Furthermore, to claim the privileges to which the authentic pilgrim was entitled (for a pilgrim was protected by many conciliar decrees and was, in a certain sense, assimilated into the clergy), the pious traveler had, in fact, to get written authorization of his bishop (or abbot, if he were a monk). By the 12th and 13th centuries only the production of such testimonial letters (*testimoniales*) enabled him to escape being classified as an adventurer or pilgrimage profiteer. An ordinance of King Richard II of England in 1388 indicated that any pilgrim without such *testimoniales* risked arrest.

Today modern transportation has removed not only all danger for the majority of pilgrims but even, in most cases, any flavor of penance. But for centuries millions of Christian pilgrims suffered grim hardships, from both the length and the difficulties of their journeys. English pilgrims crossing to Compostela in the 14th century or Europeans going to the Holy Land in Venetian boats in the 15th were uncomfortable and in danger of shipwreck or capture by the infidels, harassed by poor sanitation and the extra fees often demanded by shipowners. The German Dominican Felix Fabri, who went from Ulm to Jerusalem in 1484, left a detailed account of such conditions.

For a long time pilgrims traveled on land by horse or mule. The Indians of Minas Gerâes still travel by mule over the Brazilian plateaus to Apparecida, a town whose name tells its story. Frequently, pilgrims traveled all or part of the way on foot. This is not unknown even today, e.g., Péguy's pilgrims and the Cologne pilgrims to SAINT-HUBERT in the Belgian Ardennes at the beginning of this century both went on foot. Many of the Portuguese peasants going to Fatima still travel on foot.

Very rare today, and constituting the exception even in the Middle Ages, were pilgrimages on which pilgrims went barefoot. King Louis IX walked five leagues barefoot on the road to Chartres; and Enea Silvio Piccolomini, the future Renaissance Pope PIUS II, walked barefoot through snow on pilgrimage to Our Lady of Whitekirk.

Pilgrim Roads. Popes and secular rulers early realized their duty to organize pilgrim roads and erect hostels and to ensure, as far as possible, the safety of the pilgrims. In Rome, for example, Pope SYMMACHUS concerned himself with pilgrim safety as early as the 6th century, and the famous Schola Saxonum was in existence in the 8th century (*see* HOLY SPIRIT, ORDER OF THE). In the 16th century the staggering influx of Holy Year pilgrims in the city of Rome prompted St. Philip NERI's work there. On the most dangerous parts of the journey refuges were built: Novalesa (on the road through the Mont-Cenis Pass) was encouraged by Emperor Louis the Pious (825); and Roncesvalles, a hostel for pilgrims to Compostela, was perhaps the most renowned of all such hospices and was showered with favors by the kings of Navarre. Certain orders were created expressly to aid pilgrims, such as the KNIGHTS OF ST. JAMES in Spain, the Knights TEMPLARS, and the KNIGHTS OF MALTA, who were initially intended to aid poor, unarmed, and sick pilgrims. The seal of the Templars bore the figure of a knight aiding a *pauper et peregrinus.* From the 13th century there appeared all over Christendom a great number of confraternities whose aim was to assist pilgrims. One of the most famous of these was that of Altopascio founded in Tuscany. Its influence in Paris is marked by its church of Saint-Jacques ''du HautPas,'' at the starting point of the Paris stage on the road to Compostela. A shrine-city like Lourdes today, or the hostels for pilgrims (in the widest sense of the word) founded in Chartres or Vézelay by PAX CHRISTI, are modern extensions of the efforts and the spirit of the medieval hospitallers.

Rarely does any pilgrim travel alone: he joins with companions for reasons of economy, security, or spiritual support. Thus, the pilgrimage as a mass phenomenon is of interest to the sociologist as well as to technical scientists, such as sanitation engineers and town planners.

Pilgrim Numbers. Sources tell of mob scenes at many medieval shrines, especially on certain dates (e.g., Holy Saturday at the Holy Sepulcher), with everyone wanting to be the first to reach the holy places; many were trampled in crowds carried away by misguided eagerness. The figures given by medieval sources seem astonishing; yet modern statistics tend to corroborate the huge numbers involved in pilgrimage statistics. Villani states that, during the first Holy Year in 1300, Rome had a steady 200,000 inhabitants above normal; 100,000 pilgrims are said to have congregated in Trier for the first solemn exhibition of the Holy Shroud in 1512. But then there were 300,000 pilgrims in Puy in 1853, close to 160,000 in Aachen in 1881, and at least 1,200,000 in Kiev in 1886 (the railroad had opened that year). Einsiedeln had 150,000 pilgrims a year at the beginning of the 20th century. Lourdes had 8,000,000 in 1958, the centenary year of the apparitions. The annual number of pilgrims in Lisieux (St. THÉRÈSE DE LISIEUX) still exceeds 1,000,000. In India a week-long exposition of the arm of St. Francis XAVIER in Goa attracted several million pilgrims who, incidentally, were not all Christians.

Pilgrim Ritual. The pilgrim usually brought an exvoto to the shrine, which he would leave there, e.g., a wax or metal reproduction of a limb that had been healed or a tablet telling of an accident that he had escaped. Different centuries and civilizations have seen pilgrims bring an infinite variety of such objects: *tammata* to Greek sanctuaries, silver orange trees with golden fruits to Tenos, wax ships to the shrine of St. GERALD OF BRAGA in the 13th century, silver ships recalling shipwrecks survived to Notre-Dame de la Garde in Marseilles in the 20th century, military medals and sabres to Notre-Dame des Victoires in Paris, crude and homely figurines of domestic animals for the little shrines in Carinthia, and innumerable marble plaques to Pontmain, to Sainte-Radegonde in Poitiers, and to Sainte Anne de Beaupré in Canada.

Usually the pilgrim offers gifts in money or in kind at the shrine. In fact, many shrine churches of the Middle Ages depended on offerings of oil and wax from their pilgrims for their illumination needs. Furthermore, a considerable number of old coins have been found in ST. PETER's, Rome; the Anglo-Saxon, 7th-century coins found there are one of the sources attesting to the early flow of English pilgrims to the tomb of Peter. In the 14th century gifts to the shrines of St. CUTHBERT OF LINDISFARNE and St. BEDE at DURHAM, England, were particularly abundant. In modern times CZĘSTOCHOWA in Poland was considered one of the richest shrines in the world. But even more modest shrine churches overflow with gifts; e.g., a little pilgrimage center in south Italy, Viggiano in Lucania, received sums amounting to 2,500,000 lire (or $4,000) in 1950, as well as some four pounds of gold.

The pilgrimage vow itself was discharged by prayer and penance at a shrine. The pilgrims generally prayed kneeling, and in consequence, e.g., the stone placed in front of the reliquary of Edward the Confessor in Westminster Abbey is now worn almost hollow. But penance was no less essential than prayer. Medieval pilgrims assumed a penitential posture as soon as they reached the *mons gaudii,* the height from which they first caught sight of their goal, and they retained this posture from that point on. Emperor Otto III thus approached the tomb of ADALBERT OF PRAGUE at Gniezno. One of the most constant penitential exercises was climbing a lofty staircase on hands and knees (Rocamadour; the *Scala sancta* in Rome; the shrine on Mt. Sinai; the oratory of St. Joseph in Montreal, Canada). Another penance was begging at the approaches to the shrine. Sometimes even more demanding penances were required of the pilgrim, such as those minutely codified for the pilgrim to the famous St. Patrick's PURGATORY.

A custom frequently observed at shrines, now as in the past, is the all-night vigil, in which a great number of pilgrims pass the entire night in the shrine itself or nearby in order to saturate themselves with the mysterious power of the saint. This is mentioned as early as the *Miracula* of St. HILARY OF POITIERS. In the 15th century Felix Fabri and his companions spent three nights in the church of the Holy Sepulcher. Even in the 20th century it used to be a frequent occurrence to see villagers camping out all night singing psalms and canticles during pilgrimages to Uzhgorod in the Ukraine, Russia, or to the Ostra Brama in Vilna, Lithuania. On Tenos, for the vigils of the Annunciation and the Assumption, the church is open for worshipers day and night.

Other pilgrim practices require the pilgrim to circle the tomb or pass under it if the architecture permits. This latter can often be observed in Breton ''pardons'' (pilgrimages). At some shrines the pilgrims circle the church itself, not unlike the practice in Mecca. Processions made over rocky ground at Fatima are considered especially penitential.

Receiving the Sacraments is one of the most appropriate acts for the pilgrim who has reached the goal of his pilgrimage, for he has journeyed all the way essentially to be freed from his sins. There are no pilgrim shrines without numerous confessionals; in Laus, hearing confessions is a steady and weighty duty of the chaplains. In Lourdes, during the peak pilgrimage period, pilgrims receive Communion for hours on end every day at the grotto. And it is a striking fact that even during the worst period of JANSENISM (1732) there were an average of 250 Communions a day at Notre-Dame de Hal in Belgium.

Bodily cures have always been sought by pilgrims, and in fact there is no shrine venerated by popular piety that has not at some point been the scene of cures. There is no way of verifying the cures reported—probably with exaggeration—in medieval sources. In modern times, however, a rigorous system of checking has been instituted, and the cures reported are all the more impressive. In many shrines the sick lie along the length of the processional route of the Blessed Sacrament or reliquaries of the saints, or they are immersed in the water of a miraculous spring. At the procession of Aug. 23, 1897, at Lourdes, when 350 miracles were recorded, there were 41 miraculous cures. At the 1891 Trier expositions 11 cures were officially reported. In England certain pilgrimages that were discontinued at the Reformation have been recently revived, and miraculous cures have been reported at the WALSINGHAM pilgrimage (revived in 1927).

Pilgrims' Return Home. Many pilgrims, especially in the past, could only regretfully bring themselves to leave the place where they had found peace of soul; in fact, some settled down at the holy site, especially Jerusalem, for months or even years, devoting themselves to works of mercy, to caring for the sick in the hospitals, etc. Even into the 20th century the faithful who went to the famous Solovetski Island shrine in the White Sea would often remain for some time in the service of the monks who were custodians of the shrine. Sources mention pilgrims who would express the wish that they might die there at the goal of their pilgrimage lest they fall again into sickness or sin. In exceptional cases this favor would be granted.

When pilgrims returned home, they always tried to take some tangible memento of their journey, some ''relic.'' Most had to be satisfied with a few drops of the oil used in the lamps burning before the tomb of the saint. This oil would be carried away in AMPULLAE, or phials, such as those preserved in the treasury of Monza in Lombardy. Or they would take minute fragments of the tomb itself, surreptitiously removed splinters of stone or a little of the dust scratched from the tombstone and carried away in a small bag. The ''dust of the Holy House'' at Loreto is still collected for pilgrims each year on Good Friday; rosaries with a lunula reliquary in their crosses containing ''earth of the catacombs'' are still sold just outside St. Peter's in Rome.

Many pilgrims in the Middle Ages were anxious to prove themselves bona fide returning pilgrims and to distinguish themselves from the swarms of pseudopilgrims, such as those Chaucer so mordantly denounces on the Canterbury roads. Their proof was the emblem (*signum*) they prominently displayed while returning home. The most renowned insignia were Holy Land palm branches broken off at Jericho (hence the term ''palmer'' to designate the pilgrim) and the St. James shell gathered on the beaches of Galicia when at Compostela. Insignia from Rome, which began to appear only about the 14th century, were more likely to be a Veil of Veronica with a reproduction of the Holy Face than an emblem picturing the heads of the two Apostles. The periodic exposition of Veronica's Veil in St. Peter's was enriched by popular indulgences. Other insignia included the picture of Thomas Becket on Canterbury phials, the Sinai torture wheel recalling the martyrdom of St. Catherine, the head of John the Baptist for Amiens, leaden statues of Our Lady of Walsingham, of Rocamadour, and other Marian sanctuaries, such as the statuettes that King Louis XI was fond of carrying.

Pilgrims generally wanted to repeat their pilgrimages. The case of Duke William V of Aquitaine (*c.* 1000) is famous: each year he went to Rome or else to Compostela. King Charles VII traveled to Puy five times, Louis XI went to Notre-Dame de Béhuard in Anjou 15 times,

King Henry III journeyed to Chartres 18 times. In 1843 a simple Austrian blacksmith made his 33d pilgrimage to Mariazell. There were perpetual pilgrims in the West during most of the Middle Ages and in Russia until modern times (called *peregrinantes* as opposed to *peregrini;* in Russia *startsy*). They went from shrine to shrine throughout most of their life, with no other aim than to proclaim Christ by their lonely wandering. St. Benedict Joseph LABRE was one of these "fools for Christ's sake," as late as the 18th century.

Reaction to Pilgrims. Both perpetual and ordinary pilgrims were often mocked, scoffed at, and sometimes insulted, as were those of La Salette in Grenoble (1872). Literary satire on pilgrims has been a constant phenomenon, from the *Roman de Renart* to attacks by Erasmus or Voltaire. Moralists, spiritual writers, and preachers have more than once deplored the abuses of pilgrimaging; one need only recall the remarks in the *Imitation of Christ* or Jerome's protest that the important thing was not to go to live in Jerusalem but to live a holy life, adding: "You can reach the court of Heaven just as well from Britain as from Jerusalem." And, though a pilgrimage well performed is an important means to salvation, he added, it is not a necessary means; it is hardly proper to neglect the duties of one's state in life to go wandering over pilgrimage roads, especially if one is a monk. More than once BERNARD OF CLAIRVAUX reminded his Cistercian confreres, "Your cell is Jerusalem." Yet despite these constant criticisms, despite the great popular credulity in relics and legends and the enormous number of pilgrims who were far from ideal, many great minds defended the principle of pilgrimaging. Sir Thomas More, for example, took pains to compose (1529) a treatise in defense of pilgrimages. "There was never a pilgrim," wrote CHATEAUBRIAND, "who did not come back to his village with one less prejudice and one more idea." Charles Eugène de FOUCAULD, for his part, maintained that the *haji* came back more tolerant, more just, and more pious than they had been before setting out for Mecca. These assessments are perhaps too optimistic. But this does not alter the fact that many Christian pilgrims have returned from their long journeys cured in body and at peace with God (*ad Deum conversi*).

Bibliography: J. J. JUSSERAND, *English Wayfaring Life in the Middle Ages* (4th ed. London 1892). J. SCHMITZ, *Sühnenwallfahrten im Mittelalter* (Bonn 1910). L. DE VALON, *Les Pèlerinages expiatoires et judiciaires de la Belgique à Roc-Amadour au moyen âge* (Marseilles 1935). W. J. MOORE, *The Saxon pilgrims to Rome and the Schola Saxonum* (Fribourg 1937). M. ROMANI, *Pellegrini e viaggiatori nell' economia di Roma dal XIV al XVII secolo* (Milan 1948). P. DEFFONTAINES, *Géographie et religions* (Paris 1948). L. VAZQUEZ DE PARGA et al., *Las Peregrinaciones a Santiago de Compostela,* 3 v. (Madrid 1948–49). C. BAUSSAN, *Lourdes et les pèlerinages de la Vierge* (Grenoble 1949). H. F. M. PRESCOTT, *Friar Felix at Large: A 15th Century Pilgrimage to the Holy Land* (New Haven 1950). B. KÖTTING, *Peregrinatio religiosa: Wallfahrten in der Antike und das Pilgerwesen in der alten Kirche* (Münster 1950). R. ROUSSEL, *Les Pèlerinages à travers les siècles* (Paris 1954), R. KRISS and H. KRISS-HEINRICH, *Peregrinatio Neohellenika: Wallfahrtswanderungen im heutigen Griechenland and in Unteritalien* (Vienna 1955). M. MARTINS, *Peregrinacões e livros de milagros na nosse idade media* (2d ed. Lisbon 1957). P. CABANNE, *Les Longs cheminements: Les Pèlerinages de tous les temps et de toutes les croyances* (Paris 1958). E. R. LABANDE, "Recherches sur les pèlerins dans l'Europe des XIe et XIIe siècles," *Cahiers de civilisation médiévale* 1 (1958) 159–169, 339–347. H. ENGELMANN, *Pèlerinages* (Paris 1959). A. M. BESNARD, *Le Pèlerinage chrétien* (Paris 1959). H. QUÉFFELEC, *La Bretagne des pardons* (Paris 1962). R. OURSEL, *Les Pèlerins du moyen âge: Les Hommes, les chemins, les sanctuaires* (Paris 1963).

[E. R. LABANDE]

Pilgrims gather in catacombs, Rome. (©Bettmann/CORBIS)

PILGRIMAGES, ROMAN

Devotional or penitential journeys to visit the center of Christendom, with its tombs of the Apostles Peter and Paul (*ad limina apostolorum*), its catacombs, and other famed sanctuaries and churches. Pilgrimages are a natural phenomenon in most ancient religions, and Rome itself in pagan times had sanctuaries that were the object of religious visits and celebrations by devotees from afar.

The first recorded Christian pilgrimage to Rome was made by ABERCIUS, Bishop of Hierapolis in Phrygia. On an epitaph written before 216, he left a record of his visit to Rome as the center of the Church, whose community was marked by the seal of Baptism (*sphragidion*). During the pontificate of Pope ZEPHYRINUS (198–217), ORIGEN visited Rome "to see the ancient Church of the Romans" (Eusebius, *Ecclesiastical History* 6.14.10). While the graves of the Apostles Peter and Paul were marked by monuments called *trophies* (*ibid.* 2.25.17) and were honored in the second century, there is no record of visits by specific strangers before the late third century, although *graffiti* inscriptions witness to the devotion of visitors at the tomb site beneath the main altar in St. Peter's and in the catacombs, particularly in the *triclia* of St. Sebastian's, which go back to the start of the cult of MARTYRS.

Peace of the Church. With the Peace of the Church (313) and the construction of the Constantinian basilica to St. Peter (*c.* 325–354); of the Sessorian basilica of the Holy Cross called "in Jerusalem," as well as of the Lateran basilica; of St. Paul's on the Via Ostiensis; of St. Lawrence; and of St. Agnes, new impetus was given to devotional visits to the Eternal City. Pope DAMASUS (366–384) provided for the proper care of the catacombs and decorated them with verse inscriptions that served as sign posts for pilgrims, from the fourth to the eighth century. The *DEPOSITIO MARTYRUM* preserved by the CHRONOGRAPHER OF 354 records the names of 52 martyrs whose feasts were commemorated annually by the Roman Church; almost a century later, the calendar of Pope BONIFACE I (d. 422) registers 300. St. JEROME has described the crowds of visitors to the catacombs and martyr churches in Rome (*c.* 365) that he witnessed as a youth (*Comm. in Gal.* 2; *Comm. in Ezech.* 45.5). In a hymn ascribed to St. Ambrose (d. 397), mention is made of three roads by which devotees arrived to celebrate the feasts of the martyrs: Via Aurelia for the Vatican; Via Ostiensis for St. Paul's; and the Via Appia for St. Sebastian's (*Hymn* 13.21–32). St. JOHN CHRYSOSTOM, writing in 387, spoke of the emperors, generals, and consuls who visited Rome to venerate the tomb of "a fisherman and of a tent maker" (*Cont. Jud. et gent.* 9), and deplored his own inability to visit the tomb of St. Paul (*Hom. in Rom.* 32.2–3).

Paulinus and Prudentius. While Rome was the scene of constant comings and goings by Church and imperial officials engaged in ecclesiastical and public affairs, there is no record of their pilgrim interests. At the end of the fourth century, PAULINUS OF NOLA informed St. AUGUSTINE of his annual visits to the shrine of the Apostles (*Epistolae* 17.1; 18.1; 20.2; 45.1) and mentioned visits to Rome in 400 and 403 by NICETAS OF REMESIANA (*ibid.* 29.14). Palladius, the monk, came from Palestine to Rome about the same time and mentioned a visit of the Galatian monk Philoromus (*Hist. Laus.* 45). During the fifth century, frequent visits were made by bishops, monks, and ecclesiastics, such as John Cassian, HILARY OF ARLES, and PROSPER OF AQUITAINE.

The Spanish poet PRUDENTIUS (348–405), in his *Peri Stephanon,* or verse in honor of the martyrs, spoke of the awe with which he beheld the places where the martyrs shed their blood and left innumerable relics (*Hymn.* 2.541–548; 11.1–2), and he described the catacombs and churches he visited, including the crypt of St. HIPPOLYTUS. There, for the saint's feast (Aug. 13), vast crowds assembled, having marched from the city in processions and been joined by men, women, and children, arriving on the roads from the Alban hills, Abruzzi, Etruria, Capua, and Nola (*Hymn.* 11.199–216).

Despite the sack of Rome by the barbarians in 410 and 452, GREGORY OF TOURS described pilgrimages made by St. BRICE (*Hist. Franc.* 2.1) and Bp. Aravatius of Tongres (*ibid.* 2.5); SIDONIUS APOLLINARIS was there in 456 and 467 (*Acta Sanctorum* Aug. 23: 603), and King Sigismund of Burgundy toward the end of the century. Sigismund had to write to Pope SYMMACHUS (498–514) for a further consignment of relics, having distributed all he himself obtained in Rome (*Monumenta Germaniae Historica* [Berlin 1826–]) division: Auctores antiquissimi, 6.2.59). Fulgentius of Ruspe (*c.* 500) described the custom of making regular rounds of pilgrim visits to the catacombs and churches, including St. Peter's, St. Paul's, St. Agnes', St. Lawrence's, St. Sebastian's, and SS. John and Paul's (*Vita* 13.27). CASSIODORUS (d. 583) spoke of the *universitas* of Christians who desired to visit the confessions or shrines in Rome (*Viv.* 11.2); and Gregory of Tours reported the return of his deacon (*c.* 590) from Rome with many relics (*Hist. Franc.* 10.1).

Roman Relics. Already in the early fifth century, so many pilgrims passed Spoleto on the Via Flaminia bound for Rome that Bishop Achilleus (402–418) thought it proper (on the inscription in his cathedral) to warn against possible superstition in the cult of relics; but later, another inscription in the same church informs pilgrims that the cathedral possessed a splinter of the true cross and a link of St. Peter's chain (De Rossi, *Inscript. Christ.* 2.8.114). Justinian I had written to Pope HORMISDAS (514–523) for *sanctuaria b. Petri et Pauli* or pieces of cloth that had touched the stone in the "second cataract" or level in the shaft that led down to tombs beneath the altar in St. Peter's and St. Paul's, as well as a piece of Peter's chain and, if possible, of the grill of St. Lawrence (Hormisdas, *Epist.* 77). In 595 the Bavarian Princess Theodelinda, as queen of the Lombards, asked Pope GREGORY I (590–604) for relics for the new church of St. John, which she had built at Monza, and received a consignment of ampules filled with oil that had been burning before the tombs of some 65 martyrs. Each ampule was marked with the location whence the oil was drawn (*Dictionnaire d'archéologie chrétienne et de liturgie*. ed. F. Cabrol, H. Leclercq and H. I. Marrou [Paris 1907–53] 1.2:1737–39). Contrary to Eastern practice, at Rome during this period bones were not distributed as relics, but openings were made above the tombs, and articles could be let down to touch the interior.

Schola Saxonum and Irish Pilgrims. The sixth and seventh centuries saw a great influx of monks and visitors from Byzantium, encouraged by the founding of a Greek monastery in Rome by anti-Monophysite monks. Likewise BEDE reported the visits of Danish and Anglo-Saxon princes and princesses who had put aside their diadems to visit the shrine of the Apostles, as well as visits of clerics and laity, men and women (*Ecclesiastical History* 5.7). BENEDICT BISCOP (628–689) made five journeys to Rome; Wilfrid of York (634–709) made two; and King Caedwalla of Wessex (d. *c.* 709) abdicated his throne, made a pilgrimage to Rome, was baptized in St. Peter's, and later was buried there (BEDE, *Ecclesiastical History* 5.7). MATTHEW PARIS credited King Ina of Wessex (689–726) with the foundation in Rome of the *schola Saxonum,* or pilgrim hostel, with the church of St. Mary, which burgeoned into an Anglo-Saxon colony and gave its name to the *borgo,* or neighborhood, in Trastevere, and was soon imitated by the hostels and churches of St. Savior for the Franks, St. Michael for the Frisians, and St. Justin for the Lombards (Matthew Paris, *Chron. Mai.,* ed. Luard, 1:331). Pope LEO III (d. 816) established a hospital for pilgrims in Rome, dedicated to St. Peregrinus of Auxerre.

From Ireland, so large an army of pilgrims followed Columbanus across the Continent on the road to Rome that in the vita of St. Gall, Gozbert remarked: ''Of late so many Scots [Irish] are pilgrims that it would appear that the habit of traveling is part of their nature.'' In the Irish lives of the saints, hardly a one does not mention *peregrinans pro Dei amore,* or *pro nomine Christi*—''on pilgrimage for the love of God'' or ''in the name of Christ''—thus the vitae of SS. Agilus, Kilian, and Fintan (J. Mabillon, *Acta sanctorum ordinis S. Benedicti* [Venice 1733–40] 2:324). St. Molua (d. *c.* 608), setting out on pilgrimage, said, ''Unless I see Rome, I will die soon.''

Pilgrim Guide Books. The ITINERARIA, based evidently on the Roman military maps and tax records, such as the Anonymous of Piacenza and the itinerarium of Einsiedeln, indicate that a number of private pilgrim guides existed for directing pilgrims on the Roman roads and conducting them to the various sites when they got there. A *notitia ecclesiarum urbis Romae* existed in the time of Pope HONORIUS I (625–638); it directed pilgrims from the church of SS. John and Paul on the Caelian Hill in a circle round the city from the Via Flaminia on the north, to the churches and cemeteries on the east and south, then west, and finished with a description of the wonders of St. Peter's. In the *De locis sanctis martyrum quae sunt foris civitatis Romae,* the pilgrim visits began with St. Peter's and made a round of the sanctuaries outside the city. The book was full of legends; it pointed out a kind of altar in St. Peter's constructed by Peter himself; on the road to Ostia was an *oratorium* on whose altar was a stone used in the stoning of St. Stephen; in the vestibule of St. Lawrence's, the rock used to drown St. Abundus was on exhibition; in St. Maria in Trastevere was a picture of the Blessed Virgin painted by herself; and the chains of St. Peter and St. Lawrence's grill, as well as other such relics, were carefully pointed out. In his *History of the English Kings,* William of Malmesbury (d. 1142) preserved a much older itinerary of Rome, which led the pilgrim out of 14 gates in the Aurelian Wall to visit all the cemeteries between the Porta Cornelia and the Porta Flaminia.

Dimissorial Letters. On the road to Rome, guest houses were constructed, and many monasteries, such as that at Rebais in northern France, were frequented by the Irish and offered free lodging overnight. Usually the pilgrims traveled in groups to ward off robbers; and they carried dimissorial letters supplied by the bishop with the acknowledgment of the civil authorities. In 514 CAESARIUS OF ARLES obtained the *Formulary* of Marculf (*Patrologia Latina,* ed. J. P. Migne [Paris 1878–90] 87:755) from Pope Symmachus granting the pilgrim safe-conduct and freedom from customs and other taxes. Pilgrims also made offerings to local churches or monasteries for prayers for their safe return; or made over their property to the bishop for safekeeping.

The custom of bishops, princes, and kings visiting the Eternal City continued during the eighth to early tenth century; they not only endowed St. Peter's and specific sanctuaries, but saw to the care for pilgrims on the routes to Rome and in Rome itself. They included Bp. CHRODEGANG OF METZ; Theodo, Prince of Bavaria; Bertrade, wife of Charlemagne; and Charlemagne himself, who visited Rome at least four times.

Penitential Pilgrimages and Abuses. In the nineth century, under Popes Nicholas I (858–867) and Stephen V (885–891), the custom of substituting pilgrimages for ecclesiastical penances and civil or criminal law penalties began; instead of excommunication, banishment, or exile for heresy, murder, arson, or breaking of the peace of God, the culprit was allowed to don pilgrim clothes and was supplied with a safe-conduct to a particular shrine. In the high Middle Ages, with the development of Canon Law, the ordinary penalty for striking a cleric was a pilgrimage to Rome, since the absolution of this crime was reserved to the pope. However, with the rise of the universities in the 12th and 13th centuries, this penalty had to be abolished since so many students were taking advantage of it.

Abuses and Complaints. As early as the fourth century, Gregory of Nyssa (*Epistolae* 2; 3) and Jerome (*Epistolae* 58.2–6) complained about the abuses committed by unruly monks and pilgrims in the Holy Land. Yet Jerome justified the veneration of images and the cult of the saints in his *Contra Vigilantium.* John Chrysostom (*Ad pop. Antioch.* 3.2.49) and Augustine (*Epistolae* 155.4.15; *Patrologia Latina* 33:672) reminded their parishioners that they were to honor God through the saints not by their feet, but in their hearts. The strongest voice raised against pilgrimage abuses connected with Rome was that of St. Boniface (*Monumenta Germaniae Historica* [Berlin 1826–] division: Epistolae, 3:354), who complained that despite synods and royal prohibitions, the majority of women making such trips to Rome lost their virtue. Claudius of Turin (*c.* 820) condemned images, relics, and pilgrimages and was answered by the Irish scholar Dungal and Jonas of Orléans, who in his *De cultu imaginum* (*Patrologia Latina* 106:305–388) followed the moderate doctrine of the *Libri Carolini.* Councils at Verneuil (755), Aquileia (796), and Châlons (813) forbade monks to go to Rome and cautioned against other abuses, and a poem in an eighth-century Irish manuscript admits, ''To go to Rome [*teicht do Roim*] means great labor and little profit; the king you seek can only be found there if you bring him within yourself'' [*see* R. Thurneysen, *Old Irish Reader,* tr. D. A. Binchyard O'Bergin (Dublin 1949) 41].

Erasmus. The author of the IMITATION OF CHRIST complained: ''Those who wander much are but little hallowed,'' and the 15th-century Dominican John Bromyard observed that many *peregrinamur a Domino:* pilgrimage away from God and toward the devil. The sharpest critic amid the voices raised against pilgrimages during the Reformation was ERASMUS, whose *Colloquies* [ed. E. Johnson (London 1878) 2.1–37] summed up the abuses as (1) neglect of home duties, (2) excessive credulity in relics and legends, (3) insistence on pilgrimages as if necessary for salvation, and (4) wantonness and evil conduct of pilgrims. However, he felt they were justified if entered on freely and with true piety.

Holy Years. Despite the break between the Roman and Eastern Churches, after 1054 relations, including pilgrimages to Rome, continued intermittently. The internal strife with which Rome was afflicted from the nineth to the 15th century had greatly lessened pilgrimages during that period; but the proclamation of the HOLY YEAR by Boniface VIII (Feb. 22, 1300), and the subsequent celebrations of jubilee years in 1350 under Clement VI, in 1390 under Urban VI, in 1400 under Boniface IX, and in 1423 under Martin V gave the movement new impetus. Paul II (1464–71) decreed the present system of 25-year intervals, which, with the exception of 1800 and 1850, has been followed to the present. Confraternities, such as that of the Holy Trinity established by St. Philip NERI in 1548 and those of the Gonfalone and the Holy Cross of St. Marcello, set up hostels and sanitary and hospital services and fed pilgrims down to modern times.

Secular and Religious Pilgrims. In the Renaissance period pilgrims' guide books, such as the *De mirabilibus civitatis Romae,* by N. Roselli (1314–62); the versified English *Stations of Rome;* and the *Itinerarium urbis Romae* (*c.* 1517), of the Franciscan Mariano da Firenze, provided pilgrims with information and direction in visiting the sites hallowed by the pagan, but more particularly by the Christian, heroes of Rome.

With the rise of the Renaissance, and more particularly during the Enlightenment period, the attention of the secular visitors to Rome, such as GOETHE on his *Wanderjahr,* was directed exclusively to pilgrimages to the ruins of ancient pagan Rome. This attitude has changed radically, and, with modern pilgrim movements arranged by the tourist industry, more emphasis is placed on the possibility of seeing the pope and visiting the shrines of the Apostles than on the relics of Rome's ancient glory.

Pope Boniface VIII had prescribed visits to the basilicas of St. Peter and St. Paul as requisite for the jubilee indulgence; Clement VI added St. John Lateran's; and Urban VI, St. Mary Major's. Visits to these four basilicas have become the custom for all true Roman pilgrimages.

Bibliography: H. LECLERCQ, *Dictionnaire d'archéologie chrétienne et de liturgie.* ed. F. CABROL, H. LECLERCQ and H. I. MARROU (Paris 1907–53) 14.1:40–65. J. HASENFUSS et al., *Lexikon für Theologie und Kirche*, ed. J. HOFER and K. RAHNER (Freiberg 1957–65) 10:941–946. B. KÖTTING, *Peregrinatio religiosa* (Münster 1950). E. R. BARKER, *Rome of the Pilgrims and Martyrs* (London 1913). G. SCHREIBER, ed., *Wallfahrt und Volkstum* (Düsseldorf 1934). G. BARDY, *Analecta Bollandiana* (Brussels 1882–) 67 (1949) 224–235. H. DELEHAYE, *Les Origines du culte des martyrs* (2d ed. Brussels 1933). D. GORCE, Les *Voyages, l'hospitalité . . . des IVe et Ve siècles* (Paris 1925). L. GOUGAUD, *Gaelic Pioneers of Christianity,* tr. V. COLLINS (Dublin 1923); *Revue d'histoire ecclésiastique* 9 (1908) 21–37, 255–277. W. KUBITSCHEK, *Paulys Realenzyklopädie der klassischen Altertumswissenschaft*, ed. G. WISSOWA et al. (Stuttgart 1893–) 9.2 (1916) 2308–65. K. MILLER, *Itineraria romana* (Stuttgart 1916). U. BERLIÈRE, *Revue Bénédictine* 7 (1890) 520–526, judicial pilgrimages. É. VAN CAUWENBERGH, *Les Pèlerinages expiatoires et judiciaires* (Louvain 1922). F. X. MURPHY, *American Ecclesiastical Review* 121 (1949) 164–180, Holy Year. G. B. PARKS, *The English Traveler to Italy* (Stanford, Calif. 1954–).

[F. X. MURPHY]

PIMENTA, SILVÉRIO GOMES

Brazilian archbishop; b. Congonhas do Campo, Minas Gerais, Jan. 12, 1840; d. Mariana, Aug. 30, 1922. One of the most outstanding ecclesiastical figures in Brazil at the beginning of the 20th century, Pimenta came from a very humble family. He made his first studies in his home town, and he began to work as a clerk in a commercial house to support the family when he was nine years old. His uncle and godfather, Manuel Alves Pimenta, aware of the great intelligence of the boy, asked the Vincentian Fathers of Congonhas to give him more education. Working to help his mother and studying at the same time in the most precarious circumstances, Pimenta nevertheless succeeded in excelling in Latin, French, and the humanities. In 1855 Antônio Ferreira Viçoso, Bishop of Mariana, knowing that Pimenta wanted to be a priest, took him under his protection and gave him a place in the seminary at the expense of the bishopric. On July 20, 1862, he was ordained. In 1871 Pimenta was chosen to teach Latin in the seminary, and he did this for 18 years, becoming a master in the language.

Pimenta's first writing was in defense of the Church, in 1872, in the famous Religious Question that had started in Rio between the Free Masons and Bp. Pedro Maria de Lacerda, former teacher of Pimenta in the seminary of Mariana. Pimenta worked as a journalist for four years. In 1875 he was named vicar capitular, in spite of some opposition because he was a person of color. In 1877, he was made vicar–general of the diocese of Mariana. In 1890, Father Pimenta was appointed titular bishop of Camaco and auxiliary bishop of D. Antônio Benevides of Mariana. Again there was criticism by those who did not wish to have a person of color as pastor.

He took over most of the administration of the diocese because the bishop was ill. Preoccupied with the shortage of clergy, he asked the Redemptorists and the Jesuits to come to his diocese. With the separation of Church and State in 1890, the bishops were free to rule over their territories, and D. Pimenta readily took advantage of it. On Dec. 3, 1896, he was named bishop of Mariana and was triumphantly received by his people.

His zeal was endless; he traveled dozens of miles on horseback to administer Confirmation and visit his priests in the vast diocese. Mariana became an archdiocese in 1906; and D. Pimenta, its first archbishop, having Goiás, Diamantina, and Pouso Alegre as suffragans. He established conferences for the clergy and founded an organization for fostering vocations. In 1920, he was elected a member of the Brazilian Academy of Letters, being the first clergyman to enter that house of poets and writers. Among other works, he wrote a biography of his predecessor Antônio Ferreira Viçoso.

Bibliography: J. SILVÉRIO DE SOUZA, *Vida de D. Silvério Gomes Pimenta* (São Paulo 1927).

[T. BEAL]

PINARD DE LA BOULLAYE, HENRI

Jesuit theologian, preacher, and author of numerous books and articles on philosophy, fundamental theology, apologetics, comparative religion, and Ignatian spirituality; b. Paris, Sept. 1, 1874; d. Lille, Feb. 9, 1958.

In 1893, a year after his graduation from the Jesuit College at Reims, he entered the Society of Jesus. Upon completion of his studies he was appointed professor of fundamental theology at the Jesuit theologate at Enghien. He held this post from 1910 to 1927. During this period he became interested in the study of comparative religion. He published the manual *De vera religione,* numerous theological works proper, and several studies on religious experience and the history of religions, contributing articles to *Dictionnaire de théologie catholique, Dictionnaire apologétique,* and *Recherches de sciences religieuses* on those subjects. In 1922 and 1925 the two volumes of his major work, *L'étude comparée des religions,* appeared. Throughout his life Pinard continued to revise and improve upon this book, producing several editions.

From 1927 to 1934 he taught the history of religions at the Gregorian University in Rome. He also preached a series of Lenten conferences at the Cathedral of Notre Dame in Paris from 1928 to 1937. Upon completion of these assignments he returned to Enghien, where he devoted himself entirely to his studies in comparative religion. He intended to produce a dictionary in this field, but his researches were interrupted by World War II, which made it impossible for him to complete his project. Frustrated in this pursuit he turned his energies to a study of the *Spiritual Exercises* of St. Ignatius and the spirituality of the society. Between 1940 and 1956 he produced several books and articles in this area.

All of Pinard's works were characterized by a great erudition. A man of rigorous logic and objectivity, he held sentiment, the irrational, and the subjective in suspicion. According to him, religion imposes itself on man first on a rational, deductive plane. For Pinard, God was concluded to before being seen, and religious experience was a complement or reward. His entire life was a total dedication to truth, seeking with all his energies to show that science and faith are not in conflict but ultimately proceed from the same source, the Giver of all truth.

Bibliography: V. VAN BULCK, *Annali Lateranensi* 24 (1960) 434–461. J. GOETZ, *Anthropos* 53 (1958) 1010–13. M. COLPO, *Archivum historicum Societas Jesu* 27 (1958) 481.

[E. J. MURAWSKI]

PINEDA, JUAN DE

Biblical scholar; b. Seville, 1558; d. there, Jan. 27, 1637. He became a Jesuit in 1572, taught philosophy at Granada for three years and at Seville for two years, and taught Scripture at Cordova, Seville (where he was also rector), and Madrid for 18 years. As a member of the staff of the Spanish INQUISITION, he edited, with P. Daza, the Spanish *Index librorum prohibitorum* (Madrid 1612–14; 2d ed. 1632). But his fame rests chiefly on his Biblical studies. Because of his wide knowledge of languages and history, his exegetical works had genuine scientific value for their time, though they are now outmoded. Chief among these are his commentaries on Job (2 v., Madrid 1597–1601), the Canticle of Canticles (Seville 1602), and Ecclesiastes (Seville 1619). Also very popular in its day was his *Salomon praevius* (Lyons 1609, Mainz 1613), a study of the reign of King Solomon.

Bibliography: C. SOMMERVOGEL et. al., *Bibliothèque de la Compagnie de Jésus* (Brussels-Paris 1890–1932) 6:796–801. H. HURTER, *Nomenclator literarius theologiae catholicae* (Innsbruck 1903–13) 3:770–772. A. ASTRAIN, *Historia de la Compañíá de Jesús,* 7 v. (Madrid 1902–25) 4:52–53, 234, 796.

[L. F. HARTMAN]

PINOT, NOËL, BL.

Martyr; b. Angers, France, Dec. 19, 1747; d. there, Feb. 21, 1794. After ordination (1771) he became a curate in Bousse (1771) and Corzé (1776), hospital chaplain in Angers (1781), and pastor of St. Aubin's Church in Louroux-Béconnais (1788). During the FRENCH REVOLUTION he refused to take the oath supporting the CIVIL CONSTITUTION of the Clergy and publicized from the pulpit his opposition to this legislation. As a result he was dismissed as pastor and ordered not to approach within eight leagues of his parish for two years. Disguised as a farmer he continued to perform priestly functions. When he persuaded the pastor and curates at Corzé to retract their oaths, he became an object of government search. When the army of the Vendée occupied Louroux-Béconnais, he celebrated Mass in his parish there (June 24, 1793), but he had to resume his disguise when the revolutionary army regained strategic territory. After being captured in the village of La Milanderie (Feb. 9, 1794), he was condemned to death as a "conspirator against the people," and guillotined, attired in priestly vestments. He was beatified Oct. 31, 1926.

Feast: Feb. 21.

Bibliography: F. TROCHU, *Le Bienheureux Noël Pinot* (Angers 1955). J. L. BAUDOT and L. CHAUSSIN, *Vies des saints et des bienhereux selon l'ordre du calendrier avec l'historique des fêtes,* ed. by the Benedictines of Paris, 12 v. (Paris 1935–56); v. 13, suppl. and table générale (1959) 2:445–448.

[M. LAWLOR]

PINY, ALEXANDER

Dominican theologian; b. Allos, Provence, Feb. 25, 1640; d. Paris, Jan. 20, 1709. He came from a middle-class family of noble lineage, and entered the Friars Preachers in his early youth. In 1676, after preaching and teaching philosophy and theology in Provence, he was named master in sacred theology and appointed professor of Sacred Scripture at the newly erected national Dominican studium in Paris, a post he retained for 16 years. Having already published two multivolume texts in Thomistic philosophy and theology, he brought out the first of many works in spiritual theology in 1680.

Piny represents the Thomistic viewpoint in the quietist controversy and resembles Fénelon and the semiquietists in his mode of expression, but his teaching was never unorthodox. He was influenced by St. Thomas and Tauler through Chadron, rather than by Molinos or Mme. Guyon. In 1685, before the condemnations of quietism, either on the advice of his superiors or through his own prudence, he stopped writing and devoted himself to the direction of souls.

Bibliography: *Anné Dominicaine* (Jan. 1912) 508–518. H. BRÉMOND, *Histoire littéraire du sentiment réligieux en France depuis la fin des guerres de religion jusqu'à nos jours* (Paris 1911–36) 8:78–178. M. M. GORCE, *Figures Dominicaines* (Juvisy, France 1935); *Dictionnaire de théologie catholique,* ed. A. VACANT et al. (Paris 1903–50)12:2119–24. J. QUÉTIF and J. ÉCHARD, *Scriptores Ordinis Praedicatorum* (New York 1959) 2.2:772–773.

[M. BEISSEL]

PIONA, ABBEY OF

Originally a Benedictine monastery in the Diocese of Como in Lombardy, northern Italy. It was founded by the CLUNIACS in the first half of the 12th century on a picturesque promontory at the point where the Adda empties into Lake Como and was dedicated to Our Lady and St. NICHOLAS OF MYRA. The solitude of the mountainous site and its distance from the main roads did not favor the numerical growth of the community, which always remained small and was governed, in accord with Cluniac usages, by a PRIOR rather than an ABBOT. It did, however, have numerous holdings on the banks of the lake and in the hinterland. In 1488, when the practice of COMMENDATION was introduced, the abbey was abandoned by the monks. In 1798 the commendation was itself suppressed and the property of the monastery was confiscated by the Cisalpine Republic. Partial restorations were undertaken in the late 19th and early 20th centuries. In 1937, the remaining buildings and grounds were given to the CISTERCIAN monks of the Casamari Congregation, who used it initially as a residence for the Abyssinian Community. It was abandoned by them shortly thereafter because of the rigors of the climate, and is now the home of Italian Cistercians. The monastery church is an excellent example of 12th-century Lombard Romanesque, while the cloister dates from the 13th century. Adjacent is a courtyard whose Cluniac style porticoes show strong local influences in design.

Bibliography: L. H. COTTINEAU, *Répertoire topo-bibliographique des abbayes et prieurés* (Mâcon 1935–39) 2:2286. A. K. PORTER, *Lombard Architecture*, 4 v. (New Haven 1915–17) 3:286–289. V. ADAMI, ''L'antica abbazia di Piona'' *Le Vie d'Italia* 32 (1926) 341–345. M. ZECCHINELLI, *Le tre Pievi* (Milan 1951) 197–210.

[I. DE PICCOLI]

The 13th-century cloister of the Abbey of Piona, Italy. (Alinari-Art Reference/Art Resource)

PIOUS DISCIPLES OF THE DIVINE MASTER

(PDDM, Official Catholic Directory #0980); a religious congregation of women with papal approval (1960), founded at Alba (Cuneo), Italy, in 1924 by Don Giacomo Alberione, the founder of eight congregations known collectively as the *Famiglia Paolina* or Pauline Family. Besides daily eucharistic adoration, the sisters perform domestic services in houses of the *Famiglia Paolina*; operate homes for sick or retired clergy; and engage in various forms of the liturgical ministries. The generalate is in Rome; the U.S. headquarters is in Staten Island, NY.

[M. F. MARCHEGIANI/EDS.]

PIOUS FUND

Originally associated with the Jesuit mission field of Lower California, the pious fund opened in 1697. The Spanish crown permitted the venture on condition that it should not be supported out of the royal treasury. As a result, throughout the 18th century various benefactors offered gifts of money and land for the new missions. These contributions were used as capital, the interest of which supported the apostolic undertaking. Eventually the Jesuits became administrators of the holdings, known as the Pious Fund of the Californias. Upon the expulsion of the Jesuits from Spanish dominions in 1767, the crown assumed management of the fund to support the Dominican missions in Lower California and those of the Franciscans in the new field of Upper California. After the Mexican Revolution, the fund was administered by the new government, which offered the income to support a bishop in California. In 1842, however, the Mexican government withdrew this offer, sold the fund's holdings, and placed the entire capital into the national treasury, acknowledging an annual indebtedness of six percent for religious purposes in California. After Upper California was annexed to the U.S., no payments were made until a protest was lodged before a joint commission by the bishops of the new state. In 1875 the umpire, Sir Edward Thornton, decided for the claimants and ordered back payments to be made. Mexico paid the past accrued interest, but gave nothing for the period following the decision. Protest was made again in 1902 before the Hague Tribunal, which ruled that Mexico should pay to the U.S., for the Church in California, both the delinquent interest on the fund and a perpetual annuity, in the future, of $43,050.99. Mexico paid this for a time but defaulted in

1913. In 1967, Mexico's Pious Fund debt was settled with a one-time payment of $719,546 to the archdioceses of San Francisco and Los Angeles.

Bibliography: J. A. BERGER, *The Franciscan Missions of California* (Garden City, N.Y. 1948). U.S. Senate, 57th Cong., 2d sess., *United States vs. Mexico. Report of Jackson H. Ralston, Agent of United States and of Counsel in the Matter of Pious Fund of the Californias before Permanent Court of Arbitration, The Hague, Sept. 15–Oct. 14, 1902* (Washington 1902).

[E. D. BURNETT/EDS.]

PIRHING, EHRENREICH

Canonist; b. Sigarthin, Bavaria, Apr. 12, 1606; d. Dillingen, Bavaria, Sept. 15, 1679. He entered the Society of Jesus and taught philosophy, moral theology, Scripture, and Canon Law at Ingolstadt. His classic work *Universum jus canonicum secundum titulos Decretalium distributum nova methodo explicatum* was written between 1674 and 1677 at Dillingen. An abridged edition of this massive work appeared in 1690 under the title *Facilius et succincta sacrorum canonum doctrina.* The Venice edition of 1693 was subsequently published under the title *Synopsis Pirhingana seu compendiaria S.S. canonum doctrina.* Pirhing's method in dealing with the *Corpus,* in contrast to the purely exegetical method in vogue of treating each title in sequence, was to choose the principal elements and coordinate them into a logical system.

Bibliography: R. NAZ, *Dictionnaire de droit canonique* (Paris 1935–65) 6:1504. J. F. VON SCHULTE, *Die Geschichte der Quellen und der Literatur des kanonischen Rechts* (Graz 1956) 3.1:143–144. A. VAN HOVE, *Commentarium Lovaniense in Codicem iuris canonici* (Mechlin 1928) 1:531, 537.

[B. R. PISKULA]

PIRKE AVOTH

One of the 63 tractates of the MISHNAH, placed at the end of Nezikin, the fourth order of the Mishnah. The Pirke Avoth (chapters of the Fathers), often cited as Avot, Avoth, or Aboth, is known also as the Ethics of the Fathers and *Capitula patrum.* It is a collection of ethical, moral, and philosophical maxims distilled from the flow of spiritual teachings of the rabbinic sages over a span of centuries. The Mishnah was compiled at the end of the second Christian century by Rabbi JUDAH HA-NASI with the collaboration of Rabbi Meïr, a student of Rabbi AKIBA BEN JOSEPH. Its six orders discussed religious, legal, domestic, agricultural, commercial, and physiological topics. The fourth order, Nezikin, dealt mainly with civil and criminal law and thus was appropriately followed by Avoth, which describes the desirable moral qualities of judges, wise men, and spiritual leaders.

The first chapter forms a chain of tradition reaching back to Moses and the Law received at Mt. Sinai, followed by the Prophets, through the generations to the men of the Great Synod, to Hillel and Shammai, and from them to the principal teachers of the Mishnah.

Chapter 2 begins with more of the wise sayings of Hillel, followed in verses 9 through 16 by quotations from the teachings of Rabbi JOHANAN BEN ZAKKAI and five of his disciples. When the Temple was destroyed in 70 A.D., the academy that Johanan founded at Jabneh became the cultural and spiritual center of Jewish learning and tradition. The closing verses in this second chapter are maxims quoted from Rabbi TARPHON.

Chapters 3 and 4 contain teachings of many sages, mostly of the Tannaic period. About 41 of them are cited by name.

Chapter 5 has a different format—the anonymous sayings have a numerical basis (10, 7, 4, 3), perhaps as a pedagogic aid to memory. For instance, Mishnah 19 uses the number 4: ''There are four types of those who sit before the sages: The sponge, the funnel, the strainer, and the sifter. The sponge soaks up everything; the funnel takes in at one end and lets out at the other. The strainer lets out the wine and retains the dregs; the sieve lets out the bran and retains the fine flour.'' This illustrates also the timelessness of the sayings of Avoth, for the wisdom of this truism is apparent to teachers and students of every generation. The only attributed authorship is toward the end of the chapter, where there is a reference to Ben Bag Bag and Ben He He.

Chapter 6 is a separate group of rabbinical sentences collected in a Baraita (addition to the Mishnah), called Kinyan Torah (Acquisition of the Law), added to the original five at a later date.

Raba, who died in 352 A.D., is quoted in *Baba Kama* 30a as advising: ''He who wants to become truly pious and virtuous, let him study and practice the teachings of Avoth.'' As early as the eighth century (according to the *Siddur* of Rabbi Amran Gaon) the Babylonian academies had inaugurated the custom of reading a chapter of Avoth on Saturday afternoons. This custom continues today. Throughout the summer months Avoth is studied in the synagogues on the Sabbath, after the afternoon service by the Ashkenazim and in the morning by the Sephardim. It has been translated into Latin, Italian, Spanish, German, English, and many other languages. With its central themes the love of God and man and the veneration of learning, Avoth has exerted widespread influence over many generations.

A midrashic expanded form of Avoth known as Avoth de-Rabbi Natan has been preserved in two variant versions.

Bibliography: H. GOLDIN, tr., *Pirke Abot: Ethics of the Fathers* (New York 1962). R. TRAVERS HERFORD, ed. and tr., *Pirke Aboth* (2d ed. New York 1930; pa. 1962). C. TAYLOR, *Sayings of the Jewish Fathers* (2d ed. Cambridge, Eng. 1897); *An Appendix to the Sayings . . .* (Cambridge, Eng. 1900). M. GUTTMANN, *Encyclopaedia Judaica: Das Judentum in Geschichte und Gegenwart* (Berlin 1928–34) 1:365–368. M. MEILZINER, *The Jewish Encyclopedia*, ed. J. SINGER (New York 1901–06) 1:81–82. J. KOHN, *Universal Jewish Encyclopedia* (New York 1939–44) 1:32–33.

[E. SUBAR]

PIRKHEIMER, CHARITAS

Learned abbess of the Nuremberg convent of St. Clara; b. Nuremberg, March 21, 1466; d. there, Aug. 19, 1532. Her family was prominent in the civic government of Nuremberg, and her brother, Willibald, won renown as a humanist. She entered the monastery of the Poor Clares and, in spite of her earnest remonstrances, was elected abbess Dec. 20, 1503. For 20 years her life was peaceful and studious. Under the guidance of her brother, she read Latin classics as well as the Fathers of the Church, of whom Jerome was her favorite. Through Willibald, she met many of the outstanding scholars of the day, and was in correspondence with Conrad Celtis, Georg Spalatin, Christopher Scheurl, Sixtus Tucher, Johann Cochlaeus, Albrecht Dürer, and Desiderius Erasmus. Charitas Pirkheimer remained unaffected by the great praise of these scholars, and her convent, though considered a center of culture, maintained its religious regularity. When Lutheranism reached Nuremberg, the peace and quiet of convent life ceased. Pirkheimer had written (1522) a letter to Luther's adversary, Hieronymus EMSER, in which she thanked him for his courage as the ''powerful defender of the Christian faith.'' The convent thus became a chief target of the governor of Nuremberg who from 1524 assigned to the convent Lutheran preachers to whom the nuns were obliged to listen. Until her death, despite the sufferings inflicted on her and her community, Pirkheimer defended her rights with courage and resourcefulness against the attacks of the town council, the abusive words of preachers, and the slanders of townspeople. The diary that she diligently kept during the stormy period of the Lutheran persecution came to light in 1852 in the archives of the convent of Bamberg. It adds much light to obscure points in the Reformation history of Nuremberg.

Bibliography: J. KIST, *Charitas Pirkheimer* (Bamberg 1948). *Caritas Pirkheimer: Quellensammlung* (Landshut 1961–). J. KIST, *Lexikon für Theologie und Kirche,* ed. J. HOFER and K. RAHNER, 10 v. (2d, new ed. Freiburg 1957–65) 8:516. G. PFEIFFER, *Die Religion in Geschichte und Gegenwart,* 7 v. (3d ed. Tübingen 1957–65) 5:385.

[M. DUFFEY]

PIRKHEIMER, WILLIBALD

A leading German humanist; b. Eichstatt, Dec. 5, 1470; d. Nuremberg, Dec. 22, 1530. The son of a distinguished lawyer, he studied jurisprudence, music, and classics at the Universities of Padua and Pavia (1489–95). In 1498, appointed one of the town councilors at Nuremberg, he became the center of the humanistic movement. He translated Greek classics into Latin and wrote a history of early Germany that won him the title of the German Xenophon. At the beginning of the Reformation, Pirkheimer sided with Martin Luther and attacked Johann Eck, Luther's opponent, in a bitter satire, *Eccius dedolatus.* He was included in the bull of excommunication of 1520, but he was absolved in 1521, after formally denouncing Luther's teaching. Later he attacked Protestantism with force when he learned of the persecutions to which his sister Charitas, abbess of the Poor Clares in Nuremberg since 1503, was subjected by Lutheran members of the city council. In that same convent his sister Clara and his two daughters, Katherina and Crescentia, were nuns.

Bibliography: *Opera,* ed. M. GOLDAST (Frankfurt a.M. 1610); *Briefwechsel,* ed. E. REICKE and A. REINMANN, 2 v. (Munich 1940–56). K. SCHOTTENLOHER, *Bibliographie zur deutschen Geschichte im Zeitalter der Glaubensspaltung,* 1517–85, 6 v. (Leipzig 1933–40; repr. Stuttgart 1956–58, v. 7, 1962–) 2:141–144; 5:219. H. LUTZ, *Lexikon für Theologie und Kirche,* ed. J. HOFER and K. RAHNER, 10 v. (2d, new ed. Freiburg 1957–65) 8:516–517. G. PFEIFFER, *Die Religion in Geschichte und Gegenwart,* 7 v. (3d ed. Tübingen 1957–65) 5:385.

[M. DUFFEY]

PIRMIN, ST.

Benedictine abbot, missionary bishop, founder of REICHENAU; d. Hornbach, *c.* 754. His ninth-century vita indicates he was a Visigoth from either Aquitaine or Spain. A Benedictine, Pirmin centered his missionary activity in the Upper Rhine region, and instead of being bishop of Meaux, as was earlier alleged, he was a CHORBISHOP, residing probably at some time in Medelsheim, a village near Hornbach. In order to evangelize the area of the Upper Rhine, Pirmin founded a number of monasteries in the area, notably Reichenau, *c.* 724, perhaps on a commission from CHARLES MARTEL. He founded there also Hornbach, Gengenbach, Schwarzach, and in Alsace, while in exile, MURBACH (726). He reformed Schuttern and Maursmünster. Although a contemporary of BONIFACE, he seems to have had little contact with him. Pirmin was buried in the monastery of Hornbach. His cult began in the early ninth century, and RABANUS MAURUS placed him in his martyrology for November 3 in the mid-ninth century.

Pirmin is almost certainly the author of the *Dicta Pirminii* or *Scarapsus* [G. Jecker, *Die Heimat des hl. P.* (Münster 1927) 34–73], a brief account of salvation history, as well as a commentary on the Apostles' Creed and a summary of Christian duties. The work is significant as an example of an eighth-century missionary's manual.

He is the patron of the Rhenish Palatinate, Alsace, and Innsbruck; he is invoked against rheumatism, rats, and snakes; the cities along the Inn River sought his intercession against the plague. In art he is portrayed as a monk and bishop holding a staff that is entwined with snakes.

Feast: Nov. 3.

Bibliography: *Acta Sanctorum* Nov. 2.1:2–56. *Monumenta Germaniae Historica: Scriptores* (Berlin 1826–) 15.1:17–35. A. ANGENENDT, *Monachi peregrini; Studien zu Pirmin und den monastischen Vorstellungen des frohen Mittelalters* (Munich 1972). U. ENGELMANN, ed., *Der heilige Pirmin und sein Missionsbüchlein* (Constance 1959); *Lexikon für Theologie und Kirche,* ed. J. HOFER and K. RAHNER (Freiburg 1957–65); suppl., *Das Zweite Vatikanishe Konsil: Dokumente und Kommentare,* ed. H. S. BRECHTER et al. (1966) 8:517–518.

[C. E. SHEEDY]

PIRROTTI, POMPILIUS, ST.

Baptized Domenico Pirrotti; b. Monteclavo, Naples, Italy, Sept. 29, 1710; d. Campo (Lecce), Italy, July 15, 1766. After a good rearing and early education he decided in 1727 to enter the Order of the Pious Schools (PIARISTS), and to dedicate his life to the apostolate of teaching. He took the name Pompilio (Pompilius) Maria of St. Nicholas, and after completing his studies taught in various schools of the order, particularly in the mountainous region of Abruzzi. His zeal for instructing and helping the poor was particularly manifest, and when he was appointed novice master in 1744 and sent to Naples his zeal only increased. He was among the first to propagate devotion to the SACRED HEART in Italy and to advocate daily Communion, which was most unusual at that time. His enthusiasm provoked suspicion and a campaign of slander that resulted in his exile by Charles III, king of Naples. The indignation of the people, however, forced Charles to revoke his decree. Pompilius was later sent to Manfredonia for two years and then to Campi, near Lecce, where he died. He was beatified in 1890 and canonized on March 19, 1934.

Feast: July 15.

Bibliography: F. GRILLO and G. TASCA, *Vita di San P. M. P.* (Novara 1934). F. LÁZARO MARTÍNEZ, *San Pompilio María Pirrotti: su persona, vocación, carácter y fisonomía espiritual* (Madrid 1976). S. LÓPEZ RUIZ, *S. Pompilio Maria Pirrotti, un escolapio místico y activo* (Salamanca 1984). L. PICANYOL, ed., *Lettere scelte di S. Pompilio* (Rome 1934). *Acta Apostolicae Sedis* 27 (1935) 223–234. A. BUTLER, *The Lives of the Saints*, rev. ed. H. THURSTON and D. ATTWATER, 4v. (New York 1956) 3:113.

[L. A. IRANYI]

PISA, COUNCIL OF

A council convened in 1409 by the concerted action of cardinals of both Avignon and Roman obediences in the hope of ending the WESTERN SCHISM, then of about 30 years' standing. It was first broached in June of 1408 at Livorno, when 13 Italian cardinals who had wearied of the procrastination of GREGORY XII joined forces with the estranged curia of Antipope BENEDICT XIII. The two rival popes were pressed to attend, but they stoutly resisted all overtures, each determining instead to hold a council of his own, Benedict at Perpignan, Gregory at an unspecified place, which was in fact to be Cividale. Some of the established areas of obedience decided to cling to their old loyalties. King Rupert of Germany, Hungary, Venice, and Rimini chose to follow Gregory, while Aragon, Castile, Scotland, and some parts of France rallied to Benedict's side. The moment was so critical, and the propaganda of the Pisan cardinals so persuasive, that the greater part of Western Christendom placed its faith in the gesture of the united cardinals. Opening at Pisa on March 25, 1409, the council was supported by four patriarchs, 200 bishops (102 in person), 287 abbots (180 by proxy), the generals of the mendicants and of most other orders, some 700 theologians and canonists, delegates from most of the Western states, and 13 of the greater universities.

Disappointed at the refusal of the contending popes to cooperate with it, the council gradually turned into what was, in effect, a legal process for a crime of schism which, because of its long duration, had passed into heresy. Thus, after evidence had been heard that the parties had been legally summoned and had failed to appear, the two popes were declared contumacious at the second session (March 27). A month later this sentence was extended to those cardinals who had remained faithful to them. A dissident element entered the assembly when envoys of King Rupert of Germany presented a pro-Gregorian memorial at the fourth session (April 15). However, they departed the council on April 21, without waiting to hear the promised reply. The central phase of the council began three days later (fifth session) with an indictment under 37 heads of those measures taken by the papal rivals to hinder union. The council, however, attempted at this crucial stage to be as legal and as unexceptionable as possible in its procedure: before going further, it had the amalgamation of the two cardinalatial colleges and the withdrawal of obedience from either pope declared "canonical and legitimate," on May 10, at the eighth session. Only then were witnesses examined (May 17–22) on the 37 charges, to which further articles were added later. Finally, at the 15th session (June 5) the two popes were formally deposed as schismatics and heretics. Three weeks later Peter of Candia, the Gregorian Cardinal of Milan, was elected as Pope ALEXANDER V. He presided over the remaining sessions, published some reform decrees and, promising to call a council for 1412, dissolved the assembly on Aug. 7, 1409.

Since the Council of Pisa was not convoked by papal authority, it is not recognized by the Church as ecumenical. At the time, however, it was warmly defended by many distinguished proponents of conciliar theory (*see* CONCILIARISM, HISTORY OF), e.g., by Jean GERSON, NICHOLAS OF CLAMANGES, and PETER OF AILLY. It had juridical support in the great exposition of the legal foundations of the conciliar doctrine written in 1408 by the Paduan canonist (later Cardinal) Francesco ZABARELLA. Because Benedict XIII and Gregory XII both refused to admit the sentence of deposition, the net result of the council was that the Church now found itself enmeshed with three popes. In fairness, however, it could be argued that members of the Council of Pisa meant well; it must be acknowledged that by complicating an already disastrous situation, they made imperative the solution adopted at the Council of CONSTANCE in 1415, when the three contending popes were persuaded to retire and Odo Colonna (one of the Pisan cardinals) was elected to the office in their stead as Pope MARTIN V.

For the Council of Pisa II (1511–12) *see* LATERAN COUNCIL V.

Bibliography: Sources. J. D. MANSI, *Sacrorum Conciliorum nova et amplissima collectio* (Florence-Venice 1757–98; reprint Graz 1960—) 26:1131–1256. C. J. VON HEFELE, *Histoire des conciles d'après les documents originaux* (Paris 1907–38) 7.1:1–69. "Acta Concilii Pisani," ed. J. VINCKE, *Römische Quartalschrift für christliche Altertumskunde und für Kirchengeschichte* 46 (1938) 81–331. J. VINCKE, *Briefe zum Pisanerkonzil* (Bonn 1940); *Schriftstücke zum Pisaner Konzil* (Bonn 1942). Literature. J. LENFANT, *Histoire du concile de Pise,* 2 v. (Amsterdam 1724). F. BLIEMETZRIEDER, *Das Generalkonzil im grossen abendländischen Schisma* (Paderborn 1904). E. F. JACOB, *Essays in the Conciliar Epoch* (2d ed. Manchester, Eng. 1953); "The Conciliar Movement in Recent Study," *John Rylands Library Bulletin* 41 (1958) 32–38. B. TIERNEY, *Foundations of the Conciliar Theory* (Cambridge, Eng. 1955). G. MOLLAT, *Dictionnaire de théologie catholique,* ed. A. VACANT et al. (Paris 1903–50) 12.2:2128–30. J. VINCKE, *Lexikon für Theologie und Kirche,* ed. J. HOFER and K. RAHNER (Freiburg 1957–65) 8:520–521.

[L. E. BOYLE]

PISANI, MARY ADEODATA, BL.

Benedictine nun. b., Naples, Italy Dec. 29, 1806; d. Mdina, Malta Feb. 25, 1855. She was baptized Maria (Marija in Maltese) Teresa on the day of her birth in the parish church of St. Mark at Pizzofalcone. Her father, Benedetto Pisani, was a Maltese baron, and her mother, Vincenza Carrano, a Neapolitan who, when Maria was still very young, separated from her husband because of his dissolute life. At first Marija lived with her paternal grandmother. After her grandmother's death she attended the Istituto di Madama Prota, a famous boarding school in Naples that catered to Neapolitan aristocracy, until she turned seventeen. Her father's involvement in politics resulted in his expulsion from Naples and deportation to Malta. Marija and her mother followed her father and settled in Rabat, in the vicinity of Mdina, the old capital city of Malta. Although her father continued to squander his life, Marija always showed him respect whenever she met him.

Marija chose a quiet and simple life. She attended church daily and helped the poor. Inspired by a sermon she decided to join the Benedictine Community of St. Peter's Convent at Mdina, taking the name Marija Adeodata. Her monastic life was exemplary and edifying. She held various official positions in her community. Her favorite duties were that of a porter so that she could be close to the poor and that of sacristan that allowed her to spend more time in the chapel. For four years (1847–51) she was novice mistress until she was elected abbess. Although ill health forced her to resign as abbess after two years in office (June 1853), she is credited with initiating changes to reflect more authentically the Benedictine way of life. Over the years she wrote her personal reflections on spiritual life and spiritual direction and composed prayers in both Maltese and Italian.

People revered sister Marija for her saintly life. The canonical process for her beatification, begun in 1892, culminated when Pope John Paul II visited Malta on May 9, 2001.

Feast: Feb. 25.

[E. MAGRO]

PISE, CHARLES CONSTANTINE

Educator, editor, historian; b. Annapolis, Md., Nov. 22, 1801; d. Brooklyn, N.Y., May 26, 1866. He was the son of Louis and Margaret (Gamble) Pise. After attending Georgetown College (later University), Washington, D.C., he joined the Society of Jesus and went to Rome as a scholastic. Shortly thereafter, he left the Jesuits to

Charles Constantine Pise.

prepare for the secular priesthood, probably at Mt. St. Mary's Emmitsburg, Md., although he may also have attended St. Mary's Seminary and College, Baltimore, Md. He taught at Mt. St. Mary's, where his students included two future archbishops of New York, John Hughes and John McCloskey. McCloskey later attributed his priestly vocation largely to the counsel Pise had given him at Emmitsburg. After his ordination March 19, 1825, Pise continued to teach at Emmitsburg and also for a time at the newly founded seminary in Cincinnati, Ohio. Between 1827 and 1832 he served at the cathedral in Baltimore and then at St. Patrick's in Washington, where he became friendly with Pres. John Tyler and Sen. Henry Clay and was elected Chaplain of the U.S. Senate (1832–33), the first Catholic priest to hold this position. At the invitation of Bp. John Dubois, Pise went to New York and served at St. Patrick's Cathedral and as pastor of St. Peter's parish. In 1850 he transferred to Brooklyn and was founder and pastor of St. Charles Borromeo Church until his death.

Pise achieved a national reputation as a preacher and polemicist; he delivered his noted panegyric on Charles Carroll of Carrollton at Georgetown a month after the death (1832) of the signer of the Declaration of Independence. In 1848, at the request of Bp. John Fitzpatrick, he lectured in Boston against the bigotry of the times. For a time he edited the *Metropolitan,* and he was coeditor with Rev. Felix Valera of the *Catholic Expositor* and with Rev. Joseph Schneller of the *Weekly Reporter and Catholic Diary.* Pise's works included a five-volume *History of the Catholic Church* (1827–30), *Christianity and the Church* (1850), *Aletheia* (1845), and a poem, "The American Flag," written to answer the Know-Nothing charge that a Catholic could not be a good American.

Bibliography: M. M. MELINE and E. F. MCSWEENEY, *The Story of the Mountain,* 2 v. (Emmitsburg, Md. 1911). J. GURN, *Charles Carroll of Carrollton* (New York 1932).

[W. K. DUNN]

PISTOIA

Town in Tuscany 20 miles northwest of FLORENCE; it is one of the most important in Italy for history and art. Of ancient origin, but with few ancient monuments, it resembles Florence with churches and palaces of the 12th and 13th centuries, a number of which, including the Romanesque cathedral of three naves, alternate black and white marble. Rich in all forms of art by many famous artists, the city has especially fostered music in the cathedral from the 14th century and in the theater from *c.* 1600. The Lombards, who influenced Pistoia's laws and customs, made it the seat of a gastaldo between dukes in Lucca and Florence. Bordering Byzantine Bologna and RAVENNA, Pistoia was important in the eighth century, but declined under the Franks, to revive in the tenth century. Its commune was very active (1100–1300), but from 1219 Pistoia was ruined in wars of Lucca and Florence and in internal struggles between GUELFS AND GHIBELLINES, Blacks and Whites, and Cancellieri and Panciatichi. The failure of its bankers in the 14th century left Pistoia in a bad state. Florence deprived it of autonomy in 1401. A synod under a Jansenist bishop made it noteworthy in 1786, and it took part in the Risorgimento. The Diocese of Pistoia, known from the fifth century, flourished with monasteries in the eighth century and came to possess 14 abbeys. Originally immediately subject to the Holy See, it has been suffragan to Florence since 1420; for some time Prato was united with Pistoia (1653–1954).

Bibliography: E. LUCCHESI, *I monaci benedettini vallombrosani nella diocese di Pistoia e Prato* (Florence 1941). P. PAOLINI, *Pistoia e il suo territorio* (Pistoia 1962).

[E. P. COLBERT]

PISTOIA, SYNOD OF

From Sept. 18 to Sept. 28, 1786, Pistoia was the site of a diocesan synod that had extraordinary significance in the history of JANSENISM. The Jansenist movement, which began at Louvain, followed a geographical trajectory that after PORT-ROYAL proceeded into Utrecht (*see* UTRECHT, SCHISM OF) and ended in Pistoia. The synod met in the church of the seminary and of the ecclesiastical academy, a church dedicated to Saint Leopold in honor of the Grand Duke Peter Leopold. The synod was held under the presidency of Scipione de' RICCI, Bishop of Pistoia-Prato, and the vice presidency of the grand ducal legate, Giuseppe Paribeni, with Pietro Tamburini, professor at the theological faculty of Pavia and theologian of Italian Jansenism, as promotor of the faith. Tamburini was assisted by Vincenzo Palmieri and other Jansenists and Jansenizing groups in Pistoia.

Preparation. The synod, convoked by a pastoral letter from Ricci (July 31, 1786), was preceded by a series of consultations with the Jansenists of Paris and leading spirits of the schismatic church of Utrecht and by publications and innovations condensed in the ''57 Points'' of ecclesiastical reform sent with the letter to all the pastors of the Pistoian diocese. The points were concerned with the renewal and updating or studies; the revision of the catechism and liturgical texts, including those of the Breviary, the Mass, and other sacred ceremonies; the economic reorganization of the clergy and a more just distribution of Church goods; and the purification of private and public piety of a devotionalism considered superstitious and contrary to the spirit and practice of the primitive Church. The points, showing a combative attitude toward the Roman Curia and the so-called papal monarchy, were accompanied by a list of books intended for distribution. Recurring among the authors' names were Saint-Cyran (DUVERGIER), P. QUESNEL, and Z. van ESPEN, while the titles of many other Jansenistic and Gallican works, together with others of an orthodox nature, were included.

Acts of the Synod. The synod held seven sessions and ten congregations, of which three were extraordinary and seven ordinary. Compelled by the at times violent insistence of the bishop, about 250 priests attended the synod: from the Diocese of Pistoia, ex officio, the parish priests, the parish chaplains, and the canons (called ''fathers of the council'') along with secular and regular priests who were expressly invited (called ''co-priests''). The development was rapid, even though the discussions dealt with almost the whole body of doctrine. From a neighboring residence Grand Duke Leopold himself kept watch, remaining aloof from ''the Romish meddlers'' and day by day receiving the result of each meeting ''with complete satisfaction,'' not, however, failing to intervene with secret letters to the recalcitrant. To obtain votes, violence and favors were resorted to. Amid the fear and the violence and unaware of the subtleties, equivocations, and ambiguities of wording, the pastors signed the synodic minutes, but their endorsement was only apparently unanimous, as became clear from their subsequent repudiations and retractions. The acts, published in their entirety in various languages, aroused the enthusiasm of not only the Italian Jansenists, but also and especially of foreign Jansenists. In a Latin codex of the Vatican Library one can read: ''a printer from Leghorn had earmarked 18,000 copies to be sent to Spain and France,'' and from Spain, Cardinal F. de Lorenzana and the nuncio made known that they could no longer prevent the reprinting of the acts in the Spanish language without a previous formal condemnation. Attending the synod were French, Austrian, German, Dutch, and Polish clerics and laymen. The bishops of the schismatic church of Utrecht, the archbishop of Salzburg (H. Colloredo), and French clerics such as Bellegarde, Maultrot, and Cleçment, by letters and the *Nouvelles ecclésiastiques,* the *Gazette universelle,* the *Gazette d'Europe,* and the *Gazette fran-*

Relief sculpture stands above the main doorway of the cathedral Santa Giovanni in the town of Pistoia, Tuscany, Italy. (©Hubert Stadler/CORBIS)

çaise, among the periodicals, extolled what in Tuscany was commonly referred to as the "Pistoian comedy."

Subsequent Events and Condemnation. As a sequel to the synod, as had been foreseen, there had to be a national council "at Florence to put an end to all the gossip the Roman court and its adherents would be able to start and the dealings they could attempt." The bishops, however, thwarted the project in the assembly held during April of 1787, in the Pitti Palace, in a hall called Novissimi. Fourteen bishops and three archbishops were present. In it arose a popular and ecclesiastical counter reform that had its epilogue in the bull *Auctorem fidei,* issued by Pius VI on Aug. 28, 1794.

The synod had affirmed, although in a form more prudent, the theories of C. O. JANSEN, A. ARNAULD, Quesnel, and Febronius (HONTHEIM), taking up again propositions that had already been condemned in the bulls *UNIGENITUS* and *In coena Domini,* the four articles of the Gallican clergy of 1682, the 43 presented by the Faculty of Louvain to Innocent XI in 1677, and the 16 presented by Cardinal L. Noailles to Benedict XIII in 1724, as Ricci himself was to confirm in a defensive letter sent to the Holy See and attested to in his *Memorie* (2:193–).

In the bull *Auctorem fidei,* which was drawn up by Cardinal H. Gerdil, seven of the 85 propositions taken from the synodic constitution (set forth under 14 titles according to the diverse subject matter) were condemned as heretical, and the others were proscribed under different censures, often according to the multiple meanings in which they could be presented (false, rash, scandalous, near-heresy, etc.). Also censured was the praise accorded the Gallican Articles in the decree on faith; the judgment pronounced against them by Innocent XI and Alexander VIII was renewed. The book of the acts of the synod was anathematized by name since it was not possible to single out each and every error (H. Denzinger, *Enchiridion symbolorum,* ed. A. Schönmetzer, 2600–2700).

Balanced View. It would be unjust, however, and ungenerous not to point out in the synodic reformist theme certain positive values, especially in regard to its pastoral and liturgical aspects. The letters of Bishop Ricci to the clergy and to the people, his personal letters, and the Memorie written toward the end of his life, admit of a calmer judgment than that which the historians of the 19th and early 20th centuries accorded them. It is true that there was a resentful anticurialism, heir to the spirit of P. SARPI and of SAVONAROLA; there was also a never-lulled anti-Molinism that turned the desire to purify the Church toward heterodox expressions formulated by the Jansenists and the Gallicans of the 17th and 18th centuries, and determined sympathies or antipathies in the various religious and theological schools. On the other hand, there is a correspondence and affinity between points discussed or decreed at Vatican Council II and some of the innovations attempted or desired by the Synod of Pistoia. Specifically, the synod gave great importance to the press, to the means of social communication. Ricci took an interest in the development of an enlightened culture. He saw to the translation of famous works. He founded reviews and other periodicals; he even had at his disposal various publishing houses. He reformed the program of studies in seminaries. There was a keen sense of the validity of the episcopal character (even if Ricci had the fault of episcopalism) united to a profound love of parish and parish priests (which, unfortunately, turned into parochialism). There was a constant attention to the theology of the faith drawn from the sources of the Bible and of tradition, for Ricci did make available the theological sources: biblical and patristic collections. There was an active concern to give new, expressive, and up-to-date form to the traditional catechesis. Versions of the catechisms that he patronized and diffused were numerous.

Finally, there were several positive elements of a liturgical nature. Here was revealed a certain appreciation of Protestant sensitiveness, at least in the theological conclusions. The Italian 18th century was stirred by a singular rebirth of liturgical studies, as seen in the works of Cardinal G. Bona and Cardinal P. Lambertini (later Benedict XIV). Even the historian Lodovico Muratori published, not without difficulties from the Holy Office, an excellent book, *Della regolata devozione dei cristiani* (1743). The polemical atmosphere of Jansenism brought about, however, an irritated and irritating psychological climate in which the essential values were confused with secondary elements, with the result that revisions and emendations were made of the Breviary, of the Missal, and the like that, instead of reforming, ended by deforming them. The history of the famous controversy on liturgical Communion, or *infra missam,* had as protagonists G. Nannaroni, a Dominican, and C. Traversari, a Servite; their conclusions, although attenuated, can be found in the acts of the synod and prove how correct insights and affirmations, in dispute and through dispute, become serious deviations from the authentic teaching of the Church.

But the Riccian experiment, intended to popularize the Latin language and make the people active participants in the celebration of the liturgy of the Word and the Eucharist, is not without significance. Perusing Ricci's circular letters, homilies, decrees, and books today [among them *Brevi preghiere ad uso delle parrocchie, con l'ordinario della messa ed altre divote orazioni* (Prato 1784); *La maniera di pregare e di assistere alla s. messa secondo l'intenzione delta Chiesa* (Pistoia 1785); *Della pronunzia del canone della messa* (Florence

1787)], together with a series of little works regarding the order of ceremonies and sacred rites, the translations of the liturgical texts, and an accurate historical and theological revision of the traditional exercises of Christian piety ''in which he avoided superstitious Pharisaism, and a licentious Sadduceism,'' one is enabled to understand some of the synodic reforms, despite their illegitimacy and intemperance.

The acts and decrees of the Synod of Pistoia, purified of episcopalist mania, all schismatic and misdirected zeal, and the passions of a reformist anticurialism, give some evidence of an ordered and legitimate progress of the reality of Christian piety and an improvement, not a rupture, in a tradition of the faith that continues to be ever-present and contemporary.

See Also: BAIUS AND BAIANISM; GALLICANISM

Bibliography: *Atti e decreti del concilio diocesano di Pistola del anno 1786,* ed. P. STELLA (Florence 1986). J. CARREYRE, *Dictionnaire de théologie catholique,* ed. A. VACANT et al., 15 v. (Paris 1903–50) 12.2:2116–99. A. BOLTON, *Church Reform in the 18th Century: The Synod of Pistoia 1786* (The Hague 1969). A. GERHARDS, ''Von der Synode in Pistoia zum 2ten Vatikanischen Konzil: zur Morphologie der Liturgiereform in 20ten Jahrhundert,'' *Liturgisches Jahrbuch* 36 (1986), 28–45. A. C. JEMOLO, *Il giansenismo in Italia prima delta rivoluzione* (Bari 1928). C. LAMIONI, ed., *Il sinodo di Pistoia del 1786* (Rome 1991). B. MATTEUCCI, *Scipione de' Ricci: Saggio storico-teologico sul giansenismo italiano* (Brescia 1941), bibliography 228–330. M. ROSA, *Giuridizionalismo e riforma religiosa nella politica ecclesiastica leopoldina. Rassegna storica toscana,* XI (1965). M. ROSA, ed., *Cattolicesimo e lumi nel settecento italiana* (Rome 1981). R. TANZNI, *Historia dell'assemblea degli arcivescovi e vescovi della Toscana tenuta in Firenze nel 1797* (Florence 1788). A. ZOBI, *Storia civile della Toscana dal 1717 al 1848,* 5 v. (Florence 1850–52).

[B. MATTEUCI/J. M. GRES-GAYER]

PITHOU, PIERRE

Canonist, in whose writings were initially codified the maxims of Gallicanism; b. Troyes, Nov. 1, 1539; d. Nogent-sur-Seine, Nov. 1, 1596. Pierre and his brother François, sons of a distinguished legal family, studied at Bourges and Valence under Cujas. Since his Calvinist background prevented admittance to the bar at Troyes, Pierre withdrew to the Protestant district of Sedan, where he codified the legal customs into law. He resided for a time at Basle and returned to France after the edict of pacification in 1570. Having escaped the Massacre of St. Bartholomew, he was converted to Catholicism in 1573. As an adherent of Henry IV, he published an anonymous letter in 1593 canonically defending the right of bishops to absolve Henry IV without papal consultation. In 1594 he codified the maxims of Gallicanism in the epic *Les Libertés de l'église gallicane* in 83 articles. Pithou's work formed the basis of the Four Articles of 1682. By decree of April 21, 1768, the Parlement of Daphiné gave legal enforcement to certain of Pithou's 83 articles. After resigning the post of procurator general of the Parlement of Paris he concentrated on juristic studies, editing, among other works, the *Capitularies of Charlemagne* and the *Corpus Iuris Canonici.*

Bibliography: R. NAZ, *Dictionnaire de droit canonique,* ed. R. NAZ, 7 v. (Paris 1935–65) 6:1506. L. DE ROSANBO, ''Pierre Pithou, biographie,'' *Revue du seizième siècle* 15 (1928) 279–305. J. CARREYRE, *Dictionnaire de théologie catholique,* ed. A. VACANT et al., 15 v. (Paris 1903–50; Tables générales 1951–) 12.2:235–38.

[B. R. PISKULA]

PITRA, JEAN BAPTISTE

Benedictine scholar and cardinal bishop; b. Champforgueil, France, Aug. 1, 1812; d. Rome, Feb. 9, 1889. After being ordained in 1836, he taught history and rhetoric at the seminary of Autun, where in 1839 he published a study of the third-century epitaph of PECTORIUS. In 1841 he joined the Benedictines at SOLESMES under Abbot P. GUÉRANGER. While prior of the new monastery of SAINT-GERMAIN-DES-PRÉS in Paris in 1843, he drew up the list of authors and their complete editions for MIGNE's Greek and Latin patrologies. From 1845 to 1850 he engaged in scholarly research while traveling in search of funds to restore Solesmes. His *Spicilegium Solesmense* (4 v. 1852–58; Graz 1963) contains texts discovered by him. He was called to Rome in 1858 to study the law of the Eastern Church, and during a profitable journey studying manuscripts in Austria and Russia (1859–60) he came to the conclusion that relations between the Greek and Roman churches had been close until the time of PHOTIUS. After he was made a cardinal in 1861, he published the *Juris ecclesiastici Graecorum historia et monumenta* (2 v. 1864–68). In 1863 he discovered the secret of Greek hymnography and published *Hymnographie de l'Église grecque* in 1867. After Vatican Council I, he returned to his publications in *Analecta sacra spicilegio Solesmensi parata* (8 v. 1876–83). In 1869 he was appointed Vatican librarian. He became bishop of Frascati in 1879 and bishop of Porto and St. Rufina in 1884. He made contributions to the history of ancient Christian literature that are still of value, but his works have not received the attention they deserve. He died alone at his work and poor, as he had lived; he left many notes that have not been studied.

Bibliography: F. CABROL, *Histoire du Cardinal Pitra* (Paris 1893). P. SÉJOURNÉ, *Dictionnaire de théologie catholique,* ed. A. VACANT et al., 15 v. (Paris 1903–50; Tables générales 1951–) 12.2:2238–45. U. ENGELMANN, *Lexikon für Theologie und Kirche,* ed. J. HOFER and K. RAHNER, 10 v. (2d, new ed. Freiburg 1957–65) 8:527. A. BATTANDIER, *Le Cardinal J.-B. Pitra* (Paris 1896).

[F. X. MURPHY]

PITTS, JOHN

Biographer; b. Alton, Hants, *c.* 1559 or 1560; d. Liverdun, Lorraine, Oct. 17, 1616. Pitts was nephew to Nicholas Sanders and a scholar of Winchester College (1571) and New College, Oxford (1578–79). He went abroad and entered the English College, Rome (1581), and was ordained (1588). Professor of rhetoric and Greek at the English College, Reims, Pitts earned further degrees at Pont-à-Mousson, Trier (1592), and Ingolstadt (1595). After two years as a canon at Verdun, he was for 12 years confessor and almoner to Antonia, Duchess of Cleves. Following her death, a former pupil, then bishop of Toul, appointed him dean of Liverdun.

Pitts published *Tractatus de legibus* (Trier 1592), *Tractatus de beatitudine* (Ingolstadt 1595), and *De peregrinatione libri septem* (Düsseldorf 1604); but his chief work is *Relationum historicarum de rebus Angliae,* of which only volume 1, *De Illustribus Angliae scriptoribus,* completed in 1613, was published (posthumously, Paris 1619, ed. William Bishop). Other sections, on the kings, bishops, and apostolic men of England, were left in MS at his death. Although he strove to replace John Bale's virulently anti-Catholic bibliography, and although he took pains to cite his authorities, Pitts, in exile, lacked opportunities for original research into the English medieval authors who occupy most of his volume, and he was seldom able to supersede or correct Bale's statements of fact by appealing to fresh sources. Concerning English Catholic writers who were his own contemporaries, however, he records valuable firsthand information.

Bibliography: J. PITTS, *De illustribus angliae scriptoribus* (Paris 1619) 816–817. J. GILLOW, *A Literary and Biographical History or Bibliographical Dictionary of the English Catholics from 1534 to the Present Time.* (London–New York 1885–1902) 5:318–319. T. F. KIRBY, *Winchester Scholars* (London 1888). *Publications of the Catholic Record Society* 37 (1940) 30. W. R. TRIMBLE, *The Catholic Laity in Elizabethan England 1558–1603* (Cambridge, Mass. 1964).

[D. M. ROGERS]

PITTSBURGH, DIOCESE OF

The diocese of Pittsburgh (*Pittsburgensis*), a suffragan of the Metropolitan See of PHILADELPHIA, comprises the six southwestern counties of Pennsylvania, an area of 4,092 square miles. The diocese, erected Aug. 8, 1843, originally included the entire western half of the state. It was reduced in 1852 when the Diocese of Erie was established, and in 1901 and 1951 with the erection of the dioceses of Altoona and Greensburg respectively. At the beginning of the 21st century, Catholics numbered about 40 percent of the total population. The Catholic Church in Pittsburgh is best known for the diversity of its ethnic communities and for the association of some of its well-known figures with the labor movement.

Early History. Catholicism was first brought to the area by the missionaries who accompanied the French expeditions of the early 18th century. The chapel of Fort Duquesne, built in 1754 and dedicated under the title of the Assumption of the Blessed Virgin, of the Beautiful River, was the first place of public worship within the territory. The chapel's register of baptisms and burials, still extant, records many Native American converts, as well as occasional Irish and German traders. When the French evacuated and burned Fort Duquesne in 1758, the British renamed the site Pittsburgh. For the next 40 years, there were no resident Catholic priests in the area.

In 1799 Rev. Theodore Brouwers purchased a tract of land called Sportsman's Hall in Westmoreland County not far from Greensburg and became the pastor for the whole of western Pennsylvania. Ten years later, in 1799, Rev. Peter Helbron arrived at the Sportsman's Hall parish, carrying out many years of arduous but fruitful labor there. In the same year, Rev. Demetrius A. GALLITZIN came to the McGuire Settlement, renamed it Loretto, and opened a mission and a school. The first resident pastor in the city of Pittsburgh was Rev. William F. X. O'Brien, who built Old St. Patrick's Church in 1808. In 1820, Rev. Charles B. MAGUIRE succeeded O'Brien. He built St. Paul's Church, which was the largest and most imposing church edifice in the United States at that time. His succcessor, John O'Reilly, completed St. Paul's, invited the Sisters of Charity into the diocese and established a Catholic school and an orphanage. Michael O'Connor became pastor of St. Paul's and vicar-general for western Pennsylvania in June 1841.

Diocese. *O'Connor.* Michael O'CONNOR was consecrated bishop of the new Diocese of Pittsburgh on Aug. 15, 1843. Within a year, he had opened St. Paul's parochial school, begun publishing the Pittsburgh Catholic (the oldest diocesan newspaper in the United States), opened a chapel for free Africans, and established a seminary. By 1852 the diocese had grown to such an extent that the Diocese of Erie was created, and O'Connor was transferred there to be its first bishop. Popular outcry in Pittsburgh against O'Connor's transfer was so great that in three months he was reassigned back to Pittsburgh. In 1860, he resigned to enter the Society of Jesus.

Domenec. Michael DOMENEC was consecrated Pittsburgh's second bishop on Dec. 9, 1860, beginning an episcopate that was marred by the Civil War unrest and the financial panic of the postwar era. Growth in the diocese and a financial crisis prompted Domenec to recommend dividing it. The See of Allegheny was created March 19, 1876, with its cathedral city just across the Allegheny River from Pittsburgh. (Allegheny was later annexed by Pittsburgh and is now known as the North Side.) Domenec became the first Bishop of Allegheny, and on the same day John Tuigg was consecrated third Bishop of Pittsburgh. The new arrangement took most of the wealthy parishes from the Diocese of Pittsburgh and left it with a crushing debt. Bitter resentment and recriminations ensued, and Domenec was summoned to Rome for an explanation. He resigned on July 27, 1877, and the See of Allegheny was reunited to the jurisdiction of the Diocese of Pittsburgh. It was suppressed July 11, 1889.

Tuigg. The third bishop of Pittsburgh, John Tuigg, successfully reorganized the reunited diocese, bringing it out of its financial difficulties. During his administration, the notorious railroad riots of 1877 resulted in the long struggle between labor and management that would frequently involve the Church on the side of labor. At his death on Dec. 7, 1889, his coadjutor, Richard Phelan, consecrated Aug. 2, 1885, succeeded to the see.

Phelan. During Richard Phelan's episcopate (1889–1904), tens of thousands of immigrant families from eastern and southern Europe came into western Pennsylvania to work in steel mills and coal mines. National or ethnic churches were established to serve those immigrants in their own languages, creating a diverse plurality of tongues, cultures and traditions that would characterize the diocese for a century. In the Homestead steel strike of 1892, priests emerged for the first time as labor leaders, since they were often the only ones who could translate the workers' languages. A miners' strike in 1894 had the same effect in the rural areas. To keep pace with the growth in population, the Diocese of Altoona was formed May 27, 1901.

Canevin. During the episcopacy of J. F. Regis Canevin (1904–21), the diocese experienced a threefold growth in population, and a corresponding expansion of facilities. Canevin sponsored the lay retreat movement, furnished spiritual care for blind and deaf children, and introduced the Confraternity of Christian Doctrine. The steel strike of 1919 again prompted some priests to take the side of the workers, among them. Rev. Hugh C. Boyle, who succeeded Canevin as bishop in 1921.

Boyle. Bishop Hugh C. Boyle (1921–50) oversaw the development of a flourishing parochial school system and many charitable institutions. In the Depression, the Catholic labor movement took a more definite shape, with Leo XIII's encyclical *RERUM NOVARUM* as its guide. Some prominent Pittsburgh ''labor priests'' were Rev. James R. Cox, who was the Jobless Party candidate for president of the United States; Rev. John Hugo, spiritual director to Dorothy DAY; and Msgr. Charles Owen Rice.

Dearden. The term of Bishop John F. DEARDEN (1950–59) was marked by significant expansion, but also by the first stirrings of the mass migration from city to suburbs. When Dearden was transferred to the Archdiocese of Detroit, he was succeeded by John J. WRIGHT, Bishop of Worcester, Mass., who was installed in Pittsburgh March 18, 1959.

Wright. A brilliant theologian with a talent for public relations, Wright (1959–69) made the bishop's office even more prominent in Pittsburgh public life. He was a pioneer in the ecumenical movement and in the expansion of the role of the laity, and his ideas on both topics were reflected in the diocese of Pittsburgh before they were enshrined in the documents of Vatican II. Wright was named a cardinal in March of 1969, and shortly afterward transferred to Rome as Prefect of the Congregation for the Clergy.

Leonard. Wright's successor, Bishop Vincent M. Leonard (1969–83), faced ecclesiastical, civil and economic upheavals during his episcopate with determined but charitable orthodoxy, and the diocese suffered less in those times than it might have suffered without his steady hand. In the early1980s, the steel industry collapsed suddenly, and more than 200,000 people left the Pittsburgh area to seek jobs elsewhere. Parishes in the industrial river valleys were devastated, and many of the ethnic parishes were among the hardest hit.

Bevilacqua. When Bishop Leonard retired in 1983, Anthony J. Bevilacqua was named to succeed him. During Bevilacqua's term (1983–87), an economic boom brought prosperity back to Pittsburgh, but the old industrial boroughs continued their decline. Bevilacqua reorganized the administration of the diocese and streamlined the parishes to bring finances under tighter control.

Wuerl. Upon Bevilacqua's appointment as Archbishop of Philadelphia in 1987, he was succeeded by Donald W. Wuerl, a native of Pittsburgh who had been Cardinal Wright's secretary in Rome. Recognizing the profound changes that migration to the suburbs and the collapse of the steel industry had wrought, Wuerl began an ambitious program of reorganization and revitalization. Many of the declining ethnic parishes were closed or combined into new territorial parishes, while ministries and services were established for new immigrant communities. Wuerl also reformed the diocesan school system, gaining it ac-

Idealized portrait of Pope Pius I in the Sistine Chapel.

creditation through the Middle States Association of Colleges and Schools, and creating foundations to give tuition assistance to poorer children.

Bibliography: A. A. LAMBING, *A History of the Catholic Church in the Diocese of Pittsburgh and Allegheny* (New York 1880). W. P. PURCELL, *Catholic Pittsburgh's One Hundred Years* (Chicago 1943). M. AQUILINA, *Building the Kingdom of God: An Illustrated History of the Diocese of Pittsburgh* (Pittsburgh 2002).

[C. BAILEY]

PIUS I, POPE, ST.

Pontificate: 142 or 146 to 157 or 161. According to Eusebius (*Chron.; Hist.* 4.11; 5.6, 24) Pius I reigned for fifteen years. Both Eusebius and Jerome placed his accession in the fifth year of Antoninus Pius (142). Although the Liberian and Felician catalogues make Pius the successor of Anicetus, he was his predecessor according to Irenaeus, Hegesippus, and Eusebius, who list him after Hyginus. (*See* POPES, LIST OF.) The fourth century LIBERIAN CATALOGUE reports that he was an Italian from Aquileia, the son of a Rufinus. Like the second-century MURATORIAN CANON, the catalogue records that he was the brother of HERMAS, author of the *Shepherd,* which was apparently written during Pius's episcopacy. Hermas's statement that he had been sold into slavery may suggest that the family was of plebeian origin. It also might explain why Hermas is a Greek name and Pius is a Latin one—slave owners were free to give slaves the names they (the owners) wished.

His attitude toward penance may be reflected in the theories exposed in the *Shepherd.* There is an indication that he excommunicated MARCION, the pupil of Cerdo, in 144, thus opposing a semi-Gnostic dualism and a stringent Paulinism that would deprive humans of their integrity as agents of their own salvation by making them helpless wards of an overpoweringly merciful Redeemer. The GNOSTICISM of VALENTINUS is said to have made great headway at this time. Along with the Gnostics came such famous scholars as HEGESIPPUS, JUSTIN MARTYR of Palestine, POLYCARP of Smyrna, and IRENAEUS of Lyons. These visitors testify to the existence of an influential episcopate in Rome as well as the city's growing significance as a major Christian intellectual center. ADO OF VIENNE was the first to include Pius in the martyrology. Modern excavations indicate that his supposed burial place next to Peter in the Vatican is without substantiation.

Feast: July 11.

Bibliography: J. QUASTEN, *Patrology* (Westminster, 1950–) 1:92–105, 268–272. É. AMANN, *Dictionnaire de théologie catholique*, ed. A. VACANT et al., (Paris 1903—50) 12.2:1612–13. G. SCHWAIGER, *Lexikon für Theologie und Kirche*, ed. J. HOFER and K. RAHNER (Freiberg 1957–65) 8:528. J. N. D. KELLY, *Oxford Dictonary of Popes* (New York 1986) 25–26. A. KIRKLAND, "The Literary History of the Shepherd of Hermas, Vision I to IV, Second Century." *A Journal of Early Christian Studies* (Abilene, TX 1992) 87–102.

[E. G. WELTIN]

PIUS II, POPE

Pontificate: Aug. 19, 1458, to Aug. 15, 1464; b. Enea Silvio Piccolomini, Corsignano, now Pienza, near Siena, Oct. 18, 1405; d. Ancona. The most distinguished representative of papal HUMANISM, he began his studies at the University of Siena (1423). In 1431 he accompanied Domenico CAPRANICA to the Council of BASEL, and under the direction of Niccolò ALBERGATI and others he began a brilliant diplomatic career. Rising rapidly in the council's service, he became secretary to Amadeus VIII of Savoy, who later became the antipope FELIX V. To his early poetical writings he added prose treatises in defense of CONCILIARISM. These, together with his unsurpassed oratorical ability, procured his coronation as poet laureate (July 27, 1442) by Emperor Frederick III. Sensing the growing futility of the council, he entered Frederick's service and left Basel in November 1442.

''The Pius II Book of Psalms'' manuscript with Gregorian chant annotations. The left page shows the Madonna and Child (initial ''O''), while the right shows St. John the Baptist baptizing Christ in the river, Orvieto Cathedral. (© David Lees/CORBIS)

His sojourn in Germany, although unhappy, was fruitful in literary activity, at times serious, at others frivolous, e.g., the celebrated *Historia de Eurialo et Lucretia.* Personal suffering and his conviction of the need for concerted action against the Turks instilled moral seriousness. He was reconciled with EUGENE IV in 1445 and in 1446 received Holy Orders. With NICHOLAS OF CUSA, he negotiated the reconciliation of Germany with the papacy (1447).

In 1447 NICHOLAS V named him bishop of Trieste, where he completed his *De viris claris* and *De Rebus Basileae gestis,* his final word on that subject. In 1450 he was translated to Siena. On Dec. 18, 1456, CALLISTUS III created him cardinal. His literary production continued. The important *Historia Frederici imperatoris* and other works date from this period.

Pontificate. Moved by the recent fall of CONSTANTINOPLE (1453), Pius placed a crusading counterattack in the first place of the papal agenda. In October 1458, following his election as pope, he summoned a congress of Christendom to meet the following June at Mantua to formulate plans for the crusade. Indifference, evasion, and insult awaited him there. The French denounced his recognition of Ferrante of Naples and diverted men and money already collected for the crusade to René of Anjou's invasion of Naples. To the levy of a crusade tax, the Germans replied with a personal attack on the pope, reminding him of the sins of his youth. Pius replied courageously to this opposition, and, immediately before the dissolution of the congress, issued the bull *Exsecrabilis* (Jan. 18, 1460; H. Denzinger, *Enchiridion symbolorum,* ed. A. Schönmetzer, 1375), which reaffirmed papal prerogatives by condemning appeals to ''future councils.''

Returning to Rome (October 1460), he brought order to the city and the states by courageous persistence and judicious nepotism. His love for Rome found expression in the bull (April 28, 1462) forbidding further destruction of ancient monuments. Pius never forgot his native soil. In 1461 he canonized CATHERINE OF SIENA and in 1462 made Corsignano an episcopal see. To the south, the struggle for Naples continued. Louis XI of France abrogated the PRAGMATIC SANCTION of Bourges (March 16, 1462), hoping to win papal support for the Angevin cause. Pius refused to abandon Ferrante, and thus sacrificed all possibility of French support for the crusade. Further, Louis replaced the sanction with a series of Gallican ordinances (1463–64).

The Crusade. Although his realistic appraisal of European attitudes had led Pius to attempt to convert the Sultan to Christianity by argument and exhortation (the famous *Epistola ad Mahumetem,* 1460–61), his crusading zeal remained strong. Undoubtedly his desire to avoid further distraction led him to lay aside the many proposals for Church reform submitted at his request. The final impulse to action was stimulated by appeals from Christians in the Levant, the scurrilous attacks on the papacy and himself made in Germany (see his moving reply, *In minoribus agentes,* April 26, 1463), and the actions of the heretical George Poděbrad of Bohemia. Angered by Pius's refusal to accept the Compacts of Basel, Poděbrad openly challenged papal direction of the crusade and the pope's traditional position as spiritual arbiter of Christendom. Encouraged by Cardinal BESSARION's success in persuading Venice and Hungary to join forces (Sept. 23, 1463), Pius declared his intention of leading the crusade in person and proclaimed the crusade on October 22. While there was some popular enthusiasm, his hopes for support from the princes proved illusory early in 1464. Nevertheless, having excommunicated Poděbrad (June 16), Pius assumed the cross and left Rome. He arrived at Ancona only to die there in the full knowledge that Christian Europe had proved indifferent to his appeals. His body was interred in the chapel of St. Andrew in Rome.

Appraisal. His heroic death did not receive appropriate recognition. Many humanists, feeling themselves neglected, vented their scorn on the dead pope. However, posterity has never ceased to value his writings. His *Commentaries,* a veritable autobiography and history of his reign, reflect his refreshingly ingenuous mind, his curiosity, delight in nature, and, above all, his firm grasp on abiding values. It is true that his reign witnessed the papacy's loss of control of the crusade as well as the final collapse of the moral unity of Christendom. Yet historians increasingly pay tribute to Pius's courage, self-control, judgment, and patient endurance. A sympathetic study of his life will carry one far toward a true appreciation of the grandeur and misery of the 15th-century Church.

Bibliography: Works. *Opera quae extant omnia,* ed. M. HOPPERUS (Basel 1551); *Orationes politicae et ecclesiasticae*, ed. J. D. MANSI, 3 v. (Lucca 1755–59); *Opera inedita,* ed. J. CUGNONI (Rome 1883); *Der Briefwechsel,* ed. R. WOLKAN, 4 v. (Fontes rerum Austriacarum 61–62, 67–68; Vienna 1909–18); *Lettera a Maometto II (Epistola ad Mahumetem)*, ed. G. TOFFANIN (Naples 1953); *Memoirs of a Renaissance Pope,* tr. F. A. GRAGG, ed. L. C. GABEL (New York 1959). Literature. L. PASTOR, *The History of the Popes From the Close of the Middle Ages* (London–St. Louis 1938–61) v.3. E. VANSTEENBERGHE, *Dictionnaire de théologie catholique,* ed. A. VACANT et al., 15 v. (Paris 1903–50; Tables générales 1951–) 12.2:1613–32. J. G. ROWE, "The Tragedy of Aeneas Sylvius Piccolomini (Pope Pius II)," *Church History* 30: 288–313. R. J. MITCHELL, *The Laurels and the Tiara: Pope Pius II, 1458–1464* (Garden City, N.Y. 1963). G. SCHWAIGER, *Lexikon für Theologie und Kirche,* ed. J. HOFER and K. RAHNER, 10 v. (2d, new ed. Freiburg 1957–65) 8:528–529.

[J. G. ROWE]

PIUS III, POPE

Pontificate: Sept. 22, 1503, to Oct. 18, 1503; b. Francesco Todeschini Piccolomini, Siena, *c.* 1440. His father was Nanno Todeschini; his mother, Laodinica Piccolomini, was a sister of PIUS II. Pius conferred upon him the use of the Piccolomini surname. Although his father had wealth, it was his uncle who fostered his studies in law at Perugia, where he received the doctorate. He was then made archbishop of Siena although only 20 years old and a deacon. In March 1460 he was created cardinal deacon of S. Eustachio. He served as papal legate under four pontiffs. His diplomatic service began in 1460 when Pius II sent him as legate to the Marches. Paul II made him legate in Germany. Having learned German, he defended the interests of the Church effectively both with the emperor and before the Imperial Diet at Regensburg (1471). Under Sixtus IV he remained in Rome, winning praise for his upright life, gentleness, and culture. Innocent VIII entrusted him with the task of restoring peace in Umbria, which was torn by factional strife. Alexander VI sent him as emissary to Charles VIII, but this mission was not successful.

The election of the reformist Cardinal Piccolomini as pope, following the death of Alexander VI, took place under unusual conditions. Cesare Borgia had gathered troops and amassed money in preparation for an attack on Tuscany. Though stricken by the same fever that had caused the death of his father, Alexander VI, Borgia still hoped to dominate the conclave, and his troops took possession of the Vatican. But the cardinals then assembled in the Church of the Minerva, where, defended by the Roman populace against troops under Michelotto Coreglia, they elected Cardinal Piccolomini. Eight days after his election Pius III was ordained by Cardinal Guiliano Della Rovere; he was consecrated on October 1 and crowned a week later. Pius III's brief pontificate marked the beginning of the collapse of Borgia power. After the election Borgia was permitted to reenter Rome, but without troops. While he was placed under protective guard in the Castel Sant' Angelo, local lords with Venetian help were moving into Rimini and Pesaro and other Borgia holdings. This shift in power affected the next conclave; for although Borgia hoped that the Spanish cardinals might prevent the election of Cardinal Guiliano Della Rovere, his weakened position led him to negotiate with Della Rovere and to assist in the latter's election as Julius II. Pius III is remembered in Siena for commissioning Pinturicchio to paint the frescoes in the cathedral library, which he founded.

Bibliography: L. PASTOR, *The History of the Popes from the Close of the Middle Ages* (London–St. Louis 1938–61) 6:191–207. E. PICCOLOMINI, "Il pontificato di Pio III . . . ," *Archivio-storico italiano* 32:102–138. J. SCHLECHT, *Pius III und die deutsche Nation* (Kempten, Ger. 1914). C. WIRZ, *Die Pontifikate Alexanders VI und Pius III* (Bern 1918). G. B. PICOTTI, *La Giovinezza di Leone X* (Milan 1928). G. VOIGT, *Enea Silvio de'Piccolomini, als Papst Pius der Zweite und sein Zeitalter,* 3 V. (Berlin 1856–63). J. A. F. THOMSON, *Popes and Princes, 1417–1517* (London 1980). R. BIRELEY, *The Refashioning of Catholicism, 1450–1700* (Washington D.C. 1999).

[D. R. CAMPBELL]

"Tomb of Pope Pius III," tomb effigy, located in the Grotto of the Vatican. (Alinari-Art Reference/Art Resource, NY)

PIUS IV, POPE

Pontificate: Dec. 25, 1559, to Dec. 9, 1565; b. Giovanni Angelo de' Medici, Milan, Italy, March 31, 1499. His family was of modest nobility and unrelated to the famous Medici of Florence. As the son of Bernardino de' Medici, who was deeply involved in the party strife of Milan, he experienced many changes of fortune. The family became so poor that he required free tuition, secured through the mediation of his father's friend, Girolamo Morone, in order to attend the college of Pavia. In 1525 he attained the doctorate in Canon and Civil Law at the University of Bologna. His oldest brother, Gian Giacomo, the *condottiere,* sent the youth to Rome for his personal safety in 1526. There he soon became a prothonotary. Later Giovanni left the Roman Curia to serve his brother again as secretary. His knowledge of the law and his native ability were eventually utilized by Paul III from the first year of his reign (1534), in the government of the States of the Church. He held the post of governor in several places, the last and most important being that of Parma, 1540.

His brother Gian Giacomo's marriage to an Orsini, the sister-in-law of Pierluigi Farnese, the pope's favorite son, greatly enhanced Giovanni's position at the court of Paul III, who even as cardinal had been his protector. He was made archbishop of Ragusa, Sicily, Dec. 14, 1545, only then receiving Holy Orders. He was appointed papal vice legate for Bologna, July 23, 1547; while in this office he hurried to Parma at the news of Pierluigi Farnese's assassination, and was largely responsible in saving that city for the Farnese. He served Paul III for 15 years before attaining the cardinalate in the pope's last consistory, held on April 8, 1549.

Cardinal Medici supported the Imperialist (Hapsburg) party and exerted much influence in the election of Julius III as pope; yet he managed to keep on good terms with the French. He was papal legate with the pope's army in the war around Parma, at the same time Gian Giacomo commanded the Imperial troops. He was altogether unsympathetic with PAUL IV's anti-Spanish policy, nor did he approve his often ill-advised zeal for Church reform. The Carafa pope made use of him principally as a consultant in legal matters. Happily Medici's health furnished a legitimate excuse for leaving Rome, June 13, 1558, for his Diocese of Foligno, awarded him in 1556 by a grateful emperor. From there he went to Florence to

Pope Pius IV. (©Archivo Iconografico, S.A./CORBIS)

consult with his patron, appropriately now the Medici duke, Cosimo I, who for dynastic reasons was interested in *Il Medichino* (''Little Medici'') as a future candidate for the papacy. Having continued then to his native Milan to settle the affairs of his brother, who had died, he remained there from Oct. 18, 1558, until the death of Paul IV on Aug. 18, 1559.

The conclave had lasted more than three months when Cardinal Medici was recognized as a candidate, being acceptable to both the French and Spanish governments. Christmas morning 1559 he was elected pope, assuming the name of Pius IV, saying that he wished to be *pius* in both name and deed. The Romans applauded the new pontiff for his tranquil manner and moderate disposition.

Papal Rule. In the light of his reputation for moderation Pius IV's treatment of the CARAFA, especially his permitting the brutal execution of Cardinal Carlo, who had worked hard for his election as pope, seems incongruous and remains an enigma. The theory, espoused even by Ludwig von Pastor, that he wished by such drastic means to show his opposition to the type of nepotism involving high political stakes, is hardly convincing. His relatives, the Hohenems (Altemps), the Serbelloni on his mother's side, and the Borromeo family descended on Rome soon after his election.

Two phenomena in Pius IV's pontificate tend to obscure for many readers his person and his just claim to fame. They are (1) nepotism (certainly much less objectionable than that of his predecessor), especially exemplified by the pope's high regard and affection for his cardinal secretary of state (and later saint), Charles Borromeo, son of his sister Margherita; and (2) the resumption and conclusion of the Council of Trent. However, with regard to the first matter, it must not be supposed that the pope with his good knowledge of law and wealth of experience in secular and ecclesiastical affairs ever relinquished the reins of Church government to his gifted young nephew. As to the second, even though not physically present at Trent, the pontiff made his influence felt through his legates, whom he chose with the greatest care to represent him and preside over the assembly, and to keep him informed promptly of their deliberations.

Conclusion of Trent. In fact, Pius IV's greatest accomplishment and enduring monument is the Council of Trent, which he caused to be resumed Jan. 18, 1562, after a ten-year suspension, and which, after many vicissitudes, he brought to a successful conclusion, Dec. 4, 1563. Although his own formation was not scientific and he had no real theological knowledge, he knew how to delegate technical matters to experts. After the council he was prudent in establishing a commission of cardinals, which later became a congregation, to interpret and enforce the council's decrees. Logical sequels to the council were the first Roman Catechism, designed to popularize the faith defined at Trent, and a new *Index Librorum Prohibitorum,* more practical and less rigid than that of Paul IV. Unlike his predecessor Pius IV did not attend sessions of the Inquisition, and he somewhat reduced its powers because he did not altogether approve of its strictness.

Although not a humanist, Pius IV appreciated scientific and literary merit, assisting many writers, and raising to the cardinalate a number of very learned men, e.g., Girolamo SERIPANDO, Stanislaus HOSIUS, and Guglielmo SIRLETO. He revived the Roman University, which was almost immediately staffed with a distinguished faculty. His zeal for building and urban public works knew no bounds. Allowed to bear the Medici coat of arms by the Medici duke of Florence, he patronized architects and artists, especially the titan MICHELANGELO. The drum of the dome and some other parts of St. Peter's, the Church of S. Maria degli Angeli within the Baths of Diocletian, and the Porta Pia in the Wall of Aurelian, named after the pope, are all examples of the collaboration of Pius IV and Michelangelo. The Borgo Pio, a section of the city between Castel Sant' Angelo and the Vatican, and the exquisite Villa Pia within the Vatican Gardens, also bear the name of him who completed them.

The pope's last days were disturbed by an abortive conspiracy directed against his life by Benedetto Accolti, a visionary of dubious antecedents, in a climate of public disgruntlement over the high taxes necessary to finance the Reform. The pontiff's recurring gout and its complications culminated in his death. Cardinal Borromeo arrived from Milan in time to assist his uncle in his last hours. Although first buried in St. Peter's, later (1583) in accordance with his testament, his remains were entombed, appropriately enough, in S. Maria degli Angeli. His simple but elegant monument, erected by his nephew Cardinal Altemps, is inconspicuous today behind the main altar in an area serving as the choir.

Bibliography: L. PASTOR, *The History of the Popes from the Close of the Middle Ages* (London–St. Louis 1938–61) v.15, 16, also Ital. ed., esp. v.17 (Rome 1963). G. CONSTANT, *Dictionnaire de théologie catholique,* ed. A. VACANT et al., 15 v. (Paris 1903–50; Tables générales 1951–) 12.2:1633–47. H. JEDIN, *Papal Legate at the Council of Trent: Cardinal Seripando,* tr. F. C. ECKHOFF (St. Louis 1947). G. SCHWAIGER, *Lexikon für Theologie und Kirche,* ed. J. HOFER and K. RAHNER, 10 v. (2d, new ed. Freiburg 1957–65) 8:530–531. M. A. MULLET, *The Catholic Reformation* (New York 1999). J. W. O'MALLEY, *Trent and All That* (Cambridge, Mass. 2000). A. TALLON, *La France et le Concile de Trent (1518–63)* (Rome 1997). *Epistolae ad Principles. Leo X–Pius IV (1513–1565)* ed. L. NANNI (Vatican City 1993). C. GUTIERREZ, *Trento, un problema (1552–1562).* (Madrid 1995). P. PRODI and W. REINHARD, eds. *Il concilo di Trento e il moderno.* (Bologna 1996).

[H. H. DAVIS]

PIUS V, POPE, ST.

Pontificate: Jan. 7, 1566, to May 1, 1572; b. Antonio Ghislieri, Bosco Marengo (Alessandria), Italy, Jan. 17, 1504. As a boy of a poor family he tended the flocks. At the age of 14 he entered the Dominican convent at Voghera, taking the name Michele in religion. He was professed a Dominican friar on May 18, 1521.

Early Career. After residence in Bologna for higher education, he was sent to Genoa, where he was ordained in 1528. For many years he was lecturer in philosophy and theology in the Dominican convent at Pavia as well as commissary of the Inquisition there. Twice prior of his convent, he was later elected definitor for Lombardy, second only to the provincial. In 1550 he was appointed to the difficult post of inquisitor at Como, which borders Switzerland, then a haven for heretics. His courage in opposing the bishop's vicar-general and the chapter, who challenged his methods, brought him to the attention of Cardinal Gian Pietro Carafa (later PAUL IV), a member of the Inquisition at Rome. The elder champion of orthodoxy recognized a kindred spirit in the other's purity of faith and firmness of position. Later Ghislieri twice acted as inquisitor at Bergamo.

Pope Pius V. (Archive Photos)

Appointed commissary general of the Roman Inquisition in 1551 by Julius III, he was confirmed in the same office when Paul IV ascended the papal throne. On Sept. 4, 1556, Michele was consecrated bishop of Sutri and Nepi, and appointed prefect of the palace of the Inquisition. On March 15, 1557, Paul IV created him cardinal and gave him the titular church of Santa Maria sopra Minerva. On Dec. 14, 1558, Cardinal Alessandrino, as Ghislieri was then called (from his native city), was named grand inquisitor of the Roman Church for life. Even the new grand inquisitor could not always please the choleric old pontiff, and toward the end of Paul's reign suffered papal rebukes. The zealous cardinal was soon out of favor with PIUS IV (1559–65), who was ever the moderate and diplomat, whether dealing with nations or persons. Cardinal Alessandrino thought of retiring to his bishopric of Mondovi in the Piedmont, to which he had been named in 1560, but serious illness prevented him.

In the nineteen-day conclave (Dec. 19, 1565, to Jan. 7, 1566) that followed the death of Pius IV, Cardinal Alessandrino, despite his reluctance to be pope, was the choice of the majority. Cardinal Charles BORROMEO's support had turned the balance in his favor; Borromeo overlooked the differences between his late uncle, Pius IV, and the person whom he regarded as best fitted to direct the Church's destinies.

Papal Reign. Pius V began his pontificate with the announced intention of carrying out the decrees of the Council of Trent. Ascetic in appearance and attitude, he introduced monastic austerity into the papal household, e.g., the solitary frugal meals of the pontiff that became the custom until mid-twentieth century. Although adamant against nepotism, he was prevailed on by cardinals of the Curia to raise his Dominican grandnephew, Michele Bonelli, to the cardinalate. Fra Michele, taking his uncle's former title of Cardinal Alessandrino, became, in effect, the papal secretary of state. The pope, however, still retained Girolamo Rusticucci, his private secretary of former days. He created him cardinal with the title of Santa Susanna, and at times entrusted him with matters of great importance, especially during the illness or absence of Cardinal Alessandrino.

The Romans were apprehensive about the new pope because of his long association with the Roman Inquisition, and vigilant struggle against heresy, fearing he might prove another Paul IV. The building of a new palace for the Inquisition—the first had been destroyed at the death of the hated Paul—reinforced their fears. Pius V, to be sure, made ample use of the dread tribunal in his pledge to root out heresy, but not with the caprice and lack of logic of Paul IV. Pius V, determined to preserve the unity and integrity of the Catholic faith in Italy, strengthened the Index Librorum Prohibitorum to which he gave new prestige by creating a new administrative congregation fashioned after those of the Inquisition and of the Tridentine Council.

Papal Reforms. Pius V proved energetic in his reforms of the Church, Curia, and the diocese of Rome. He insisted on the residence of bishops, threatening long-term absentees with deprivation of their revenues and jurisdiction. He also made a systematic review of the religious orders, exposing and correcting corruption. A few orders, such as the HUMILIATI, were abolished altogether. Seminaries were established; synods were held; and stated meetings of diocesan clergy, or larger groups, were emphasized. He was greatly assisted by Charles Borromeo in setting this example of conformity to the Tridentine decrees.

Pius V has an enduring monument in the liturgy and two published compendia thereof: the Roman Breviary (*Breviarium Romanum,* 1568), and the Roman Missal (*Missale Romanum,* 1570), whose title pages in all subsequent editions bear his name. These works supplanted, with very few permitted exceptions, the multiplicity of Breviaries and Missals, full of medieval accretions and often barbarous Latin, then in use. They advanced uniform recitation of the Divine Office and the Mass according to the restored (*restitutum*) earlier and purer tradition, and thus were useful instruments in Pius V's policy of centralizing Church control in Rome. The definitive Latin catechism for parish priests, decreed at Trent, and in large part prepared in the pontificate of Pius IV, was published. It was most appropriate for a Dominican pope to sponsor an edition, published in 1570 in 17 volumes, of the complete works of St. Thomas Aquinas, the theologian par excellence of the council, whom Pius V had declared a Doctor of the Church, April 11, 1567. A new edition of the Vulgate was projected, and the work assigned to distinguished scholars. In short, scientific criteria were being applied to most of the sacred sciences, e.g., liturgy, hagiography, and Canon Law.

International Relations. Pius V's policies toward the great powers of Europe proved unfortunate. His excommunication of Queen Elizabeth I (*Regnans in excelsis,* Feb. 25, 1570) had an effect contrary to the one he envisioned, and his support of the measures of the crafty Catherine de Médici against the Huguenots in France, as well as his dealing with the opportunist Emperor Maximilian II, were criticized. His statecraft always reflected the friar and theologian. Despite his shortcomings as a statesman from the secular viewpoint, his great popular renown, ironically enough, lies in the field of international politics, although his approach was heavily colored by religious mystique.

A primary goal of his pontificate had been to propagate the idea of a Holy League of the Christian powers in a crusade against the Ottoman Turks, who had so long threatened the bulwarks of Europe. It was his hope that the league would dispel a very real danger to Europe and Christianity, and unite Christian nations in the face of a common peril. After many months of rivalry and disagreement, Spain, Venice, Genoa, the Knights of Malta and the States of the Church joined forces in a great naval expedition. They met the Turkish fleet in the innermost part of the Gulf of Corinth (Lepanto), and inflicted a humiliating defeat, Oct. 7, 1571 (*see* LEPANTO, BATTLE OF). On that day, the Rosary Confraternity of Rome was meeting in the church of the Minerva, headquarters of the Dominican Order, to recite the rosary for the special intention of victory for Christian arms. When news of the victory reached Rome, it was attributed to the intercession of the Virgin invoked by their prayers. In the wake of Lepanto, the pope's prestige grew immensely, though he declined any credit for the success. In commemoration of the victory he established for the first Sunday in October the feast of Our Lady of Victory, which was changed by Gregory XIII to the feast of the Most Holy Rosary.

The pope did not long survive Lepanto, a fitting climax to his relatively short, but significant, pontificate. His death at the age of 68 caused considerable lamentation. On Jan. 9, 1588, Sixtus V had his remains transported from St. Peter's to St. Mary Major's, where they were committed to a splendid tomb, surmounted by a seated statue of the pontiff by Leonardo da Sarzana. He was beatified by Clement X, May 10, 1672, and canonized by Clement XI, May 22, 1712. Behind the image of stern lawgiver, of a new Moses, which he projected, lay kindness, and zeal for the well-being of the Church. Besides guarding it against heresy and the might of Islam, he encouraged its expansion through the missions, and was a patron of learning, especially the ecclesiastical sciences. He was not indifferent to the fine arts, considering them as ancillary to religion. Thus he left only a modest impression on the architecture of Rome.

Feast: May 5.

Bibliography: L. PASTOR, *The History of the Popes from the Close of the Middle Ages* (London-St. Louis 1938–61) v.17, with bibliog., and v.18. R. HEDDE and É. AMANN, *Dictionnaire de théologie catholique,* ed. A. VACANT et al., 15 v. (Paris 1903–50; Tables générales 1951–) 12.2:1647–53. A. FRANZEN, *Lexikon für Theologie und Kirche,* ed. J. HOFER and K. RAHNER, 10 v. (2d, new ed. Freiburg 1957–65) 8:531–532. H. H. DAVIS, "A Rosary Confraternity Charter of 1579 and the Cardinal of Santa Susanna," *American Catholic Historical Review* 48 (Washington 1962) 321–342. R. ANDERSON, *Saint Pius V* (Rockford, Ill. 1978). N. LEMAITRE, *Saint Pie V* (Paris 1994). A. SILLI, *San Pio V* (Rome 1997). F. A. P. FALLOUX, *Historie de Saint Pie V* (Paris 1844). M. FIRPO and D. MARCATTO, *Il processo inquisitoriale del Cardinale Giovanni Morone* 5 v. (Rome 1981–89).

[H. H. DAVIS]

PIUS VI, POPE

Pontificate: Feb. 15, 1775, to Aug. 29, 1799; b. Giovanni Angelo Braschi, Cesena, Italy, Dec. 25, 1717. His pontificate was the longest and most dramatic of the eighteenth century.

Prepapal Career. Gianangelo came of an ancient and noble, but far from wealthy, family of Cesena, in Emilia, North Italy. Following a youthful education in his home town, he studied law, became a *Doctor utriusque juris* (1735), and then entered the papal administrative service under the patronage of Cardinal Ruffo, legate to Ferrara. His aptitude for public affairs led to his rapid advancement under Benedict XIV. Under Clement XIII, he was named treasurer of the Apostolic Chamber, i.e., finance minister of the States of the Church. Only in 1758 did he become a priest. Clement XIV elevated him to the rank of cardinal in May 1771.

An amiable and rather ostentatious man gifted with excellent health and attractive presence, he had avoided the politico-religious debates that brought the Holy See into conflict with Catholic crowns concerning the sup-

Pope Pius VI. (Archive Photos)

pression of the JESUITS. Upon Clement XIV's death (Sept. 22, 1774), Braschi ranked high among the *papabili.* Adversaries and friends of the Society of Jesus counted equally on him, one group hoping to achieve the dissolution of the order decreed by the deceased pontiff; the other, to temper the application of the brief *Dominus ac Redemptor.* After a long conclave of 134 days, Cardinal Braschi emerged as successor to the throne of St. Peter. He received the tiara on February 21.

Decline of the Ancien Régime (1775–89). Between 1775 and 1789 Pius VI had to confront an almost universal hostility of governments and public opinion against the Holy See. Rulers maneuvered to wrench from the pope concessions designed to earn popular acclaim, or to increase their authority over the clergy in their domains. Under the influence of the ENLIGHTENMENT in France and England, incredulity infiltrated the educated classes, the upper ranks of society, and even the clergy. National churches, even when they preserved regularity and piety, displayed active defiance of the absolutism of the pope and the Roman CURIA. This "anti-curialism," bolstered by JANSENISM, aligned the bishops against the "pretensions of ULTRAMONTANISM."

A pope able to hold his own against these opposing forces, oblige lax clerics to reform, and impose respect for papal authority would have needed unparalleled genius and energy. Pius VI possessed neither quality. Sincerely intent on fulfilling his duties as administrator and defender of the Church's rights, he lacked firmness, and even clearsightedness, concentrating on secondary questions, personal considerations, and petty diplomatic quarrels.

Rome and the States of the Church. Although greater tasks demanded his attention, Pius VI became absorbed in the administration and defense of the STATES OF THE CHURCH. No doubt the ruinous condition and misery of that region clamored for remedies. Too much money, however, was spent on an unsuccessful attempt to drain the Pontine Marshes, and on lavish projects within Rome, e.g., the foundation of the Pio-Clementine Museum in the VATICAN, and the restoration of the Capitol. The Eternal City regained a rather artificial brilliance which attracted outsiders, but the pope did not enhance his prestige by his excessive nepotism, and his ostentatious entourage.

For years Pius VI persisted in demanding from his neighbor, the King of Naples, a feudal tribute of a white palfrey, symbolizing centuries-old papal suzerainty. Failing to obtain satisfaction, he kept dispatching protests to all the European courts until the outbreak of the French Revolution.

Catholic States. In his relations with Catholic kingdoms, Pius VI was able to attain some improvement. In Portugal the death of King Joseph I (1777) resulted in the disgrace of POMBAL, archenemy of religious orders and of the Holy See. The very devout Queen Maria I put an end to anticlerical violence. In Spain the situation improved during the final years of the reign of Charles III (1759–88). In France Louis XVI, ruler since 1774, was pious and personally well disposed. Both Madrid and Versailles, however, were prepared to take action against impiety only when the Holy See maintained great reserve in its interventions within their borders, and when it continued to effect the total destruction of the Jesuits.

Prussia and Russia. FREDERICK II, King of Prussia, and CATHERINE II, Empress of Russia, sovereigns who were not Catholics but maintained relations with the Holy See, constituted themselves protectors of the last small communities of Jesuits, whose educational talents they appreciated. Catherine II even authorized the Jesuits to establish a novitiate within her realm. Pius VI tried to have them apply the brief of Clement XIV suppressing the Society of Jesus, at the risk of displeasing two powerful rulers who controlled, since the Partition of Poland, the fate of large numbers of Catholics.

Febronianism. Germany was the source of the gravest fears during the 15 years preceding 1789. Anti-Roman tendencies there affected the leaders among the clergy. In 1763 ''Febronius'' issued against the authority of the Roman pontiff a veritable manifesto, repercussions of which were to be widespread. Pius VI succeeded in unmasking the author, HONTHEIM, coadjutor to the archbishop of Trier, and extracting from him a retraction, but FEBRONIANISM was not thereby checked in southern and western Germany. At the request of the Elector of Bavaria, Pius VI sought to establish (1786) a nunciature in Munich. This impelled the archbishops, who were also electors, to issue a public declaration, the Punctation of EMS, affirming that German Catholics depended only on their bishops, to the exclusion of any papal representative. Schism seemed imminent.

Josephinism. In the Austrian territories the situation during the same period was still more alarming. JOSEPH II, emperor since the death of MARIA THERESA (1780), had put into practice ideas inspired by the ENLIGHTENMENT and Febronianism, and constructed from them a system of ecclesiastical government known as JOSEPHINISM. He sought: (1) to submit the Church in Austria completely to the State; (2) to grant tolerance to all religious confessions; (3) to suppress houses of religious; (4) to oblige candidates for the secular priesthood to attend State colleges; (5) to abolish practices that he considered superstitious; and (6) to impose modifications in the liturgy and worship of the Church.

Pius VI was alarmed by the emperor's haste and uncompromising rigorousness. After his protests proved vain, the pope believed he could win over the ruler by an extraordinary move. Although no supreme pontiff had left Rome since 1533, he made a personal visit to Vienna, and resided there a month (March-April 1782). Joseph II received him courteously, visited him in return, but made no agreements. Joseph even persisted in carrying ahead his reforms, with so little regard for popular traditions that insurrections broke out in the more ultramontane provinces, notably in Brabant. At his death (1790) Belgium was aflame with revolt. Such was the determination of the population that this country was on the verge of obtaining concessions that Pius VI had been unable to gain from the emperor by persuasion.

Synod of Pistoia. The contagion of Josephinism reached Italy. In Tuscany Grand Duke Leopold I copied the reforms of his brother Joseph II. He found in Bishop Scipione de' RICCI a collaborator by conviction. The Synod of Pistoia (September 1786), an assembly of Tuscan priests with Ricci presiding, published decrees hostile to papal authority. As a result the Holy See beheld itself defied by anticurialists in ultramontane territory near Rome itself. This moved Pius VI to an unaccustomed outburst of energy. He roused the indignation of the faithful attached to orthodoxy, compelled Ricci to quit his See, and issued against his heretical theses the apostolic constitution *AUCTOREM FIDEI* (1794), a solemn condemnation of the aftereffects of Jansenism.

French Revolution (1789–99). The FRENCH REVOLUTION, far from ending the difficulties of the Holy See, posed more menacing perils.

Papal Attitude. Pius VI perceived events in France as signs of a rebellion against the social order ordained by God and of a conspiracy against the Church. He was convinced that the world faced a religious persecution. Doctrinally he condemned the principles formulated in the Declaration of the Rights of Man, while he supported the league against the Revolution.

Counterrevolutionary Actions. Pius's conduct up to the spring of 1791 seemed hesitant, either because he still counted on Louis XVI to preserve in France the constitution and Catholic traditions, or because he was uncertain about the will to resist on the part of the Gallican clergy. The enactment of the CIVIL CONSTITUTION OF THE CLERGY, the royal assent to it, and the firm opposition of the episcopal body induced him to act. In two briefs (*Quod aliquantum,* March 10, 1791, and *Caritas,* April 13, 1791) he condemned not only the ecclesiastical reforms decreed by the Assembly, but also the political principles on which they rested, represented by the pope as the negation of the fundamental truths of divine revelation. The uprising of the citizens of AVIGNON and of the Comtat Venaissin against his sovereignty served to render the Revolution detestable. Basically, however, his opposition arose from religious considerations. This explains his unwavering condemnatory attitude toward all the oaths of obedience required of the clergy by the revolutionary assemblies and his resolution to demand of all Catholics submission to the ''judgments of the Holy See on the affairs of France.''

Once diplomatic relations with France were broken with the recall of the nuncio Antonio Dugnani (May 31, 1791), Pius VI pressed for the formation of a counterrevolutionary crusade. His support of the First Coalition partially explains the enduring hate vowed against him by the Jacobins. The States of the Church, not yet menaced by the war, welcomed numerous *émigrés,* including aristocrats and priests who were victims of the deportation laws. Toward the priests particularly, Pius VI displayed extraordinary generosity. The Oeuvre pie de l'hospitalité française, confided by the pope to Monsignor Lorenzo Caleppi, enabled several thousand to live at the expense of the papal treasury.

French Antipapal Action. The invasion of Italy (1796) by Napoleon abruptly changed the situation by advancing the Revolution to the frontiers of the Papal States (*see* NAPOLEON I). The Directory intended to take vengeance on Pius VI, at least by exacting a ransom for Rome, and perhaps by destroying the papacy itself. For two years the prudence of General Bonaparte, who refused to be the destroyer of the Holy See, permitted papal diplomats to purchase a precarious peace at the cost of abandoning the LEGATIONS, or northern provinces of the States of the Church, at the armistice of Bologna (1796), and the Peace of Tolentino (1797).

Once Bonaparte left for Egypt, incidents inevitably occurred between Jacobins and zealous partisans of the Holy See. This furnished the pretext for a French punitive expedition against Rome. General Louis Berthier entered the city (Feb. 10, 1798), proclaimed the establishment of the Roman Republic, and drove out Pius VI and the Curia.

*Capture and Death.*The pope was placed in circumstances that made his spiritual government of the Church impossible. The French made him captive, and began (March 1799) forcing him from city to city toward France. The octogenarian pontiff was afflicted with a seizure depriving him of the use of his legs, yet he appeared a picture of courageous and serene resignation. Unexpected consolation came to him from the veneration accorded him by the French populace. He reached Valence, in southeastern France, on July 14, and was held prisoner there until his death, August 28. This marked the nadir of papal fortunes in modern times.

Bibliography: Sources. *Bullarium Romanum Continuatio,* ed. A. BARÈRI et al. (Rome 1835–57) v.5–10. A. MERCATI, *Raccolta di Concordati . . .* (Rome 1954) 1:493–560; [59]–[66]. Literature. J. GENDRY, *Pie VI, sa vie, son pontificat,* 2 v. (Paris 1906). G. BOURGIN, *Dictionnaire de théologie catholique,* ed. A. VACANT et al., 15 v. (Paris 1903–50; Tables générales 1951–) 12.2:1653–69. G. SORANZO, *Peregrinus Apostolicus: Lo spirito pubblico e il viaggio di Pio VI a Vienna* (Milan 1937). M. C. GOODWIN, *The Papal Conflict with Josephinism* (New York 1938). A. LATREILLE, *L'Église catholique et la révolution française,* 2 v. (Paris 1946–50) v.1. J. LEFLON, *La Crise révolutionnaire* 1789–1846 in A. FLICHE and V. MARTIN, eds., *Histoire de l'église depuis les origines jusqu'à nos jours* 20 (Paris 1949). L. PASTOR, *The History of the Popes from the Close of the Middle Ages* (London-St. Louis 1938–61) v.39–40. F. X. SEPPELT, *Geschichte der Päpste von den Anfängen bis zur Mitte des 20 Jh.,* (Leipzig 1931–41) v.5. P. PASCHINI and V. MOANCHINO, eds., *I Papi nella Storia,* 2 v. (Rome 1961) v.2. E. KOVACS, *Der Papst in Deutschland. Die Reise Pius VI in Jahr 1782* (Munich 1983). E. E. Y. HALES, *Revolution and Papacy, 1769–1816* (Notre Dame, Ind. 1966). J. MCMANNERS, *The French Revolution and the Church* (New York 1970). D. MENOZZI, ed. *La chiesa Italiana e la rivoluzione francese* (Bologna 1990). A. D. WRIGHT, *The Early Modern Papacy: From the Council of Trent to the French Revolution, 1564–1789* (London 2000).

[A. LATREILLE]

Pope Pius VII, portrait by Jacques Louis David, 1805.

PIUS VII, POPE

Pontificate: March 14, 1800, to Aug. 20, 1823; b. Barnaba Chiaramonti, Cesena (Emilia), Italy, Aug. 14, 1742.

PREPAPAL CAREER

He was from an old aristocratic family with a tradition of culture. Among his ancestors were the astronomer Scipione, famous for discussing with Galileo the nature of comets; jurists; and physicians of repute. His mother came from the Ghini family, closely connected with the Braschi, the family of Pius VI. Left a widow in 1750, she entered a convent of the Carmelites (1762) after rearing her five children. This background helps explain Chiaramonti's attraction toward positive sciences and his religious spirit. He exhibited also the characteristics of a native of the Romagna: independence, openness, vigor, vivaciousness. While studying under his first teachers, the Benedictines at Cesena, he often gave vent to his love for pranks.

Benedictine Monk. After entering the Benedictines (1756) he took the name Gregorio and pronounced his vows (1758) at the Abbey of Santa Maria del Monte of Cesena. During his studies at St. Justina's in Padua and later at St. Anselm's in Rome, which prepared professors of the Benedictine Congregation of Monte Cassino, Dom Gregorio was exposed to the influences of JANSENISM, and to a milieu receptive to modern sciences. At St. Anselm's, one of his teachers was the inventor of the seismograph, Andrea Bina, considered an excellent physicist. Italian Jansenism was then very influential, but less interested in doctrine than in reforms. From it Gregorio retained a desire to spiritualize the Church, and disengage it from temporal interests.

From 1766 to 1775 he was professor at the Abbey of St. John in PARMA, a city penetrated with French culture. There he acquainted himself with contemporary problems; witnessed Tillot's attempt to apply the principles of the Physiocrats; learned new bibliographical techniques after heeding the counsels of Paciaudi, organizer of the celebrated library in Parma; knew CONDILLAC, tutor of the young prince; and supported his method of introducing into psychology the principles of Isaac Newton.

Dom Gregorio's years as professor at St. Anselm's in Rome (1775–81) determined the orientation of his life. They coincided with the early years of the pontificate of Pius VI, a fellow native of Cesena and friend of the Chiaramonti family. The Abbey of St. Paul in Rome was experiencing domestic dissension. When the pope learned that the young professor was accused of supporting the young monks against the authority of the abbots, the pontiff named Dom Gregorio titular abbot, and in 1783 bishop of Tivoli.

Bishop of Tivoli and of Imola. In the small diocese of Tivoli Chiaramonti showed himself a model pastor, although he had to spend long months at the Quirinal familiarizing himself with what he termed "the great labyrinth of the Roman Court." Thanks to his influence he succeeded in defending his episcopal rights against the Holy Office.

Bishop Chiaramonti was transferred (1785) by Pius VI to the more important See of Imola, and raised to the cardinalate. At Imola the young cardinal displayed his abilities. Obliged to occupy himself with local civil administration since he was in the STATES OF THE CHURCH, he was able to ascertain the weakness of papal government. He was very energetic in repressing abuses, independent in his relations with the papal legate at Ferrara, and above all else careful of spiritual interests. His charity, firmness, broadmindedness, and tact were revealed especially during the FRENCH REVOLUTION. During the first French military invasion (1796), he intervened to prevent incidents between his flock and the invaders and opposed the uprising in Lugo. Under the regimes of the Cispadane Republic and the Cisalpine Republic, his attitude was very clear: to recognize the existing government, but to resist strongly whenever spiritual issues were at stake.

His Christmas homily (1797) admitted that democracy is not contrary to the Gospel, but recognized that it requires more than natural virtues, and cannot last if it disregards religion, which is ready to lend its support. On matters of principle he was inflexible, whether it was a question of taking an oath to support the Constitution of the Cisalpine Republic, or of the application of religious laws. His diplomatic skill and willingness to conciliate succeeded in conserving the essentials. When, for example, the Cisalpine Republic fell, he saved Imola, menaced by reprisals from General Hulin. Likewise he saved the Jacobin municipal government from being executed. He reproved the excesses of the anti-French reaction, preaching pardon and peace. So generous was the cardinal to French refugee priests in his diocese and to his own flock, suffering from a grave financial crisis and high food prices, that he had to borrow money to reach the conclave held in Venice after Pius VI's death (Aug. 29, 1799).

PONTIFICATE (1800–14)

During the fourteen-week conclave (Dec. 8, 1799, to March 14, 1800) Cardinal Chiaramonti voted with the more liberal group, the *politicanti.* The adroit intervention of Antonio Despuig, representative of Spain, and Ercole Consalvi, both future cardinals, broke the deadlock and settled the election.

From the beginning of his pontificate Pius VII left no doubt of his independence of Austria, which wanted to entice him to Vienna, and forbade him to traverse the Legations on his way to Rome. Forced to travel by sea to Pezzaro, he reached Rome, occupied by the Neapolitans, on July 3 and appointed CONSALVI as secretary of state.

Concordat with France. Overtures came a few days later from Napoleon for a concordat with France (*see* NAPOLEON I). Although taken unaware, the new pope proved decisive and revealed the spirit that was to animate his entire pontificate. Although he was pleased with the prospects of religious peace, he declared himself discontent that the First Consul should promise to safeguard the States of the Church provided the pope proved accommodating in religious matters. Effectively Pius VII was repudiating a confusion between the temporal and the spiritual, and making clear his intent to concentrate exclusively on the latter. He also discerned the difficulties involved in arranging an agreement, and still more in applying it. Yet he did not hesitate to accept the risks, for these delicate conversations could, he realized, reconcile the Church with the society that issued from the Revolution. Despite formidable obstacles; despite Bonaparte's brutalities; despite the opposition of Louis XVIII, the royalists, and the conservative *zelanti* group of cardinals, Pius VII succeeded in concluding the CONCORDAT OF 1801.

States of the Church. The reorganization of the States of the Church, whose richest provinces, the LEGATIONS, had been amputated, also posed problems. The pope relied heavily on his secretary of state. His solution was one of great moderation and adaptation. An amnesty, which exempted only the revolutionary leaders, prevented excess in the way of reaction. The question of alienated Church possessions was regulated by compromise. Lay persons, chosen from the nobility, entered the civil administration. The judicial system was simplified. Financial problems were faced by retiring the *monetaria erosa* to restore value to the coinage, and by improving the tax system. Chief among the innovations was the liberty accorded commerce. Efforts were made to improve agriculture, including a tendency to the partitioning of latifundia into tiny sections. Despite these measures the economy remained weak; nor were the reforms promoted by the opposition of the *zelanti* and the passivity of the bureaucracy.

Relations with Napoleon. The first part of the pontificate (1800–15), as indeed the whole history of Europe during these years, centered around the struggle against Napoleonic domination. The enterprises of Napoleon as first consul, then as emperor, imperiled the independence of the spiritual. Pius VII resisted this threat with increasing energy, conciliatory though he was in other respects. He protested against the Organic Articles, which reintroduced the GALLICANISM abolished in the Concordat. He also castigated the weaknesses of his legate CAPRARA for permitting the nomination of constitutional bishops to the new French sees. The government's doctrine on marriage met his further disapproval. Contrary to the *zelanti,* however, he resigned himself to the sometimes regrettable application of a Concordat that was on the whole very beneficial.

Italian Concordat. The Italian Concordat (1803) with the Italian Republic, eventually to become the Kingdom of Italy, disappointed the pope in other ways. Although it recognized Catholicism as the religion of the state and provided conditions more favorable to the Church than those in France, the Melzi d'Eril's decrees putting the accord into practice were inspired by JOSEPHINISM. Divorce was legalized with the introduction from France of the Civil Code.

Imperial Consecration. Despite the opposition of the cardinals, the Holy Father agreed to go to Paris for the consecration (Dec. 2, 1804) of Napoleon as emperor, although given only vague promises. Pius VII refused to demand the restoration of the Legations as a condition of his journey, in order to concentrate on matters spiritually advantageous. He agreed to modifications in the traditional ceremonial proposed to him beforehand by BER-

NIER, and consented to have Napoleon crown himself. He refused, however, to receive from the latter the constitutional oath, since the constitution contained clauses contrary to the Church's principles.

The pope's remonstrances to Napoleon to improve the religious situation in France were for the most part repulsed. From the constitutional bishops who had not retracted but remained obstinate the pope could obtain the submission of Bernier alone. Marriage legislation remained unchanged. Catholicism was not recognized as the state religion. Concessions were limited to assurance of a salary for 25,000 priests (*desservants*), the foundation of six metropolitan seminaries, the expulsion of married priests from teaching posts, and greater liberty to religious congregations dedicated to education and charity. To compensate for this, Pius VII made so deep an impression by his spirituality and won so much acclaim from the populace that his visit gained extraordinary prestige for the papacy.

Increasing Tension. Napoleon failed to gain acceptance from the pope of a concordat with Germany; but the pope was unable to prevent the secularization of ecclesiastical possessions in Germany. Pius VII distrusted DALBERG with good reason. He also feared that the emperor wished to extend to all Europe his religious system by introducing the spirit of the Revolution, as he had in Italy. Napoleon's coronation in Milan as king of Italy (1805) resulted in a new statute given to the clergy from abroad, one which Rome judged contrary to its rights. As this Napoleonic system extended to the Italian Peninsula and approached Rome, the danger mounted that the Holy See would become a vassal of France. After the papal conversations in Paris, the events at Milan caused an irremediable rupture in the entente between the priesthood and empire.

The agreements realized became more difficult to maintain for reasons at once strategic and economic. Napoleon found himself impelled to take possession of all Italy. This led him into a conflict of ever-increasing gravity with Pius VII, who wanted to maintain neutrality as head of the Church and to assure the spiritual independence guaranteed by his secular sovereignty. The occupation of Ancona (October 1805) provoked a strong papal protest. Napoleon replied after Austerlitz by demanding that the Holy Father expel from his States the agents of the Allies, and close his ports to their vessels. Pius VII categorically refused. The conquest of Naples and the occupation of the west coast completed the encirclement of Rome. The recall of FESCH, which provoked the resignation of Consalvi (June 17, 1806), heightened the tension. Napoleon went so far as to summon the pope to league with him against the heretical English and the infidels, and then to participate in the Continental Boycott.

Pius VII reacted by suspending the application of the Italian Concordat. After this the Holy See awaited the worst; but the emperor, who had crushed Austria and Prussia, waited until he was finished with Russia before regulating his accounts with "the old imbecile." After Tilsit he tried vainly to make the pope yield, but a negotiation carried on by Cardinal de Bayane failed. General Miollis invaded Rome (Feb. 2, 1808), and in 1809 annexed the Papal States to France. In return the supreme pontiff launched an excommunication against the instigators of this aggression, without explicitly designating Napoleon. The non-Roman cardinals were driven from Rome. Pius VII, who had opposed the arrest of Pacca, his Secretary of State, was seized, carried off from Rome (July 10, 1809), and deported to Savona, near Genoa.

Captivity of Pius VII. Deprived of his liberty and his counselors, the sovereign pontiff henceforth refused to exercise his papal authority. As a result he would not canonically appoint those nominated to bishoprics by the emperor. Numerous sees remained vacant, to the great embarrassment of the French government. An attempt was made to escape this predicament by compelling chapters to name vicars capitular the bishops chosen by the emperor; but the papal brief reproaching MAURY for accepting the See of Paris under these conditions was brought to France by reliable messengers and disseminated by Monsieur ÉMERY. A further effort to bend the Holy Father was made by a delegation of bishops sent to Savona from the National Council in 1811, but the pope did not weaken. The affair of the "black cardinals," those who refused to attend Napoleon's religious marriage (April 1810) with Marie Louise, as a religious one, marked the beginning of a police persecution that increased Catholic resistance.

Fontainebleau. Napoleon then (June 1812) transferred Pius VII to Fontainebleau, near Paris, to force his capitulation after the French victories in Russia. When the Russian campaign turned into a disaster, Napoleon hastened to finish with the pope. Under compulsion Pius VII appended his signature to a projected concordat, which was intended as a basis for future negotiations and to remain secret. But Napoleon published the document, the so-called CONCORDAT OF FONTAINEBLEAU, as if it were a final one. After the emperor's departure, Pius VII, exhausted, sick, and fearing his death, had drawn up in the form of a testament a text in which he annulled and abrogated the concessions granted in the project he had signed. This document, recently found in the private papers of PACCA, contradicts what Pacca says in his *Memorie.* He was not, nor were the cardinals who returned to Fontainebleau after their liberation, responsible for Pius VII's retraction. They only counseled the pope on how to inform the emperor of his decision. Pius VII wrote to

Napoleon in vigorous terms, but Napoleon kept the letter secret. Military reverses in France induced Napoleon to liberate his prisoner, who reentered Rome on May 24, 1814.

PONTIFICATE (1814–23)

Save for the crisis during the Hundred Days, which obliged the pope to retire to Genoa because of the impulsive act of Murat, who wanted to stir up all Italy, the second part of the pontificate (1814–23) proved less dramatic than the first. It was a period of attempted reorganization in the States of the Church, and restoration of the Church in various countries.

States of the Church. At the Congress of Vienna Cardinal Consalvi succeeded in obtaining the restitution to the Holy See of its temporal domain, with the exception of AVIGNON and the Comtat Venaissin, which the Most Christian King Louis XVIII intended to retain. Reorganization of the States of the Church posed grave problems. Two opposing tendencies clashed. Cardinal Pacca and the *zelanti* wanted to return to the conditions of the *ancien régime,* abolish French innovations, and severely punish collaborators in them. A second group, headed by Consalvi, now returned to the secretariate of state, judged excessive reaction unwise and adaptation to changed conditions necessary. "After a new deluge one cannot act as before," wrote Consalvi. He undoubtedly realized that a pope-king could not adopt a constitutional regime, since his temporal sovereignty was meant to assure his spiritual independence, which would no longer be guaranteed if his temporal authority were limited by assemblies capable of voting laws contrary to Church principles. Consalvi did not regard all French institutions as bad; indeed, he esteemed many of them as excellent. He also found it essential to take into account the marked change in mentality due to long French occupation, and the force of new ideas sprung from the Revolution. The cardinal sought, therefore, a compromise between past and present by a series of administrative, judicial, financial, and economic reforms. These provoked the opposition of conservatives without satisfying liberals, who organized in secret societies, with SANFEDISTS combating the CARBONARI and the followers of NEO-GUELFISM with their own methods.

A series of revolts (1816, 1817, 1820) resulted and was blamed on the secretary of state's weakness. Pius VII relied on Consalvi for administrative details and supported him more readily, since Metternich wanted the pope to supply military aid to crush the Neapolitan revolution, and unify the police and postal service of all Italian sovereigns in the battle against secret societies. Pius VII was as careful to safeguard his independence as under the Napoleonic regime and sharply refused.

Ecclesiastical Restoration. In Europe the Church everywhere, save in Austria, had been disorganized during the period of Revolution. A program of restoration had to take into account situations varying widely from country to country, and react against anti-Christian liberalism without becoming a party to the HOLY ALLIANCE. Pius VII braved both parties by restoring the JESUITS (1814). He had to conserve a sage equilibrium in dealing with governments in order to arrange agreements concluded at least by papal documents, if not by concordats.

Negotiations, carried on in a conciliatory spirit, succeeded in Piedmont, Naples, the Lombard-Venetian Kingdoms, the Principalities of Tuscany and Parma, Bavaria, Prussia, Baden, Württemberg, both Hesses, Saxony, and in Russia, concerning Poland. The way was prepared for future settlements with England and Switzerland. Only Spain, Portugal, and Austria remained aloof to this movement. In France the ultraroyalists sought to abolish the Concordat of 1801. Five years of negotiation and the defeat of two projects were required for a return to this Concordat.

In South America the revolt of the Spanish colonies was first reproved by Rome on the basis of information received solely from the Spanish court and the South American bishops (all appointed by the king of Spain). Better informed toward the end of his pontificate, Pius VII decided to send a papal mission to South America to investigate the situation and to prepare a reconciliation. The mission, under Muzi and Mastaï (the future Pius IX), took place after his death. North America left the pope with a freer hand, and offered much hope. Missions had suffered from the European crisis, and began to revive very slowly.

Conclusion. In eight years the aged and unwell pope could not solve all the problems of religious restoration of the Church and the reorganization of the States of the Church in a changing world. At least he labored constantly to discover a modus vivendi between the new society and the Church, which would preserve the Church's principles without violating those of the modern world. Pius VII's troubled pontificate was characterized by a desire for comprehension and conciliation without weakness and by an alternation of the most amiable suppleness with firmness to the point of inflexibility. For the monk become pope, detached from all temporal interests, what counted above all else was the spiritual, which he lived intensely. He was courageous, lucid, and although averse to administrative minutiae, able in critical moments to frame major decisions to orient the Church. He deserves to be called "the pope of the new age."

Bibliography: *Bullarium Romanum Continuatio,* ed. A. BARÈRI et al. (Rome 1835–57) v. 11–15. A. MERCATI, *Raccolta di*

Concordati (Rome 1954) 1:561–688. I. RINIERI, *La diplomazia pontificia nel secolo XIX,* 3 v. (Turin-Rome 1902–06). J. SCHMIDLIN, *Papstgeschichte der neuesten Zeit, 1800–1939* (Munich 1933–39) v.1. A. LATREILLE, *Napoléon et le Saint-Siège, 1803–1808* (Paris 1935); *L'Église catholique et la révolution française,* 2 v. (Paris 1946–50) v.2. G. BOURGIN, *Dictionnaire de théologie catholique,* ed. A. VACANT et al., 15 v. (Paris 1903–50; Tables générales 1951–) 12.2:1670–83. J. LEFLON, *La Crise révolutionnaire 1789–1846* (A. FLICHE and V. MARTIN, eds., *Histoire de l'église depuis les origines jusqu'à nos jours* 20; Paris 1949); *Pie VII* (Paris 1958–) v.1. (to 1800). A. FUGIER, *Napoléon et l'Italie* (Paris 1947). E. E. Y. HALES, *Revolution and Papacy 1769–1846* (New York 1960); *The Emperor and the Pope* (New York 1961). A. DANSETTE, *Religious History of Modern France,* tr. J. DINGLE, 2 v. (New York 1961) v.1. P. DE LETURIA, *Relaciones entre la Santa Sede e Hispanoamérica,* 3 v. (Analecta Gregoriana 101–103; Rome 1959–60) v.2, 3. P. PASCHINI and V. MONACHINO, eds., *I Papi nella Storia,* 2 v. (Rome 1961) v.2. L. PASZTOR, ''Per la storia del *Concordato* di Fontainebleau,'' *Chiesa e stato nell'ottocento: Miscellanea in onore di P. Pirri,* ed. R. AUBERT et al., 2 v. (Padua 1962) 2:592–603. M. O'DWYER, *The Papacy in the Age of Napoleon and the Restoration* (Lanham, MD 1985). R. ANDESON, *Papa Pio VII* (Rome 2000). M. CHAPPIA, *Pie VII et les Pays Bas* (Rome 1984). J. A. BRADY, *Rome and the Neapolitan Revolution of 1820–21* (New York 1976). H. H. WALSH, *The Concordat of 1801* (New York 1977). W. ROBERTS, ''Napoleon, the Concordate of 1801, and its Consequences,'' *Controversial Concordates: That Vatican's Relations with Napoleon, Mussolini and Hitler,* ed. F. J. COPPA (Washington D.C. 1999) 34–80. J. M. ROBINSON, *Cardinal Consalvi, 1757–1824* (New York 1987).

[J. LEFLON]

PIUS VIII, POPE

Pontificate: March 31, 1829, to Nov. 30, 1830; b. Francesco Saverio Castiglioni, at Cingoli (Ancona), Italy, Nov. 20, 1761. Educated first at Osimo, then at Bologna and Rome, he was ordained in 1785. A specialist in Canon Law, he served as vicar-general at Anagni and Cingoli until he was appointed bishop of Montalto (1800). His refusal to take an oath of allegiance to NAPOLEON I caused him to be imprisoned (1808). Pius VII, who held him in high esteem, made him a cardinal (1816), appointed him bishop of Frascati and summoned him to Rome as grand penitentiary (1821). In the conclave of 1823, which elected LEO XII, he was a leading candidate. During the five-week conclave in 1829 the pious and learned Castiglioni was a favorite of the moderates and emerged as Pius VIII, despite health problems.

Poor health plagued him during his brief pontificate and hindered his officiating at liturgical functions, but it did not prevent him from pursuing a vigorous policy that avoided the conservatism of his predecessor. In his first encyclical, *Traditi humilitati nostrae* (May 24, 1829), Pius VIII announced his intention to put into effect his authority, to combat religious indifferentism, to maintain marriage laws, to promote Christian education, and to oppose secret societies. The brief *Litteris altero* (March 25, 1830) renewed earlier papal condemnations of Freemasonry. In his government of the STATES OF THE CHURCH, Pius VIII was milder than Leo XII had been and sought to improve conditions economically and socially. In his relations with Prussia, he was faced with the problem of mixed marriage. After acquiring the Rhineland and Westphalia in 1815, Prussia sought to enforce in these Catholic regions its own legislation concerning mixed marriages. To conciliate Prussia, Pius VIII's brief of March 25, 1830, allowed priests to assist passively at these ceremonies when they were not accompanied by the guarantees usually demanded by the Church. This did not satisfy Prussia and the conflict became more tense during the following pontificate (*see* COLOGNE, MIXED MARRIAGE DISPUTE IN).

France was disturbed at this time by hierarchical opposition to Hugues Félicité de LAMENNAIS, who at this stage of his career favored ULTRAMONTANISM and attacked GALLICANISM. The pope did not give his approval to the program of Catholic liberalism advocated by Lamennais and his followers, but neither did he issue the condemnation sought by Archbishop De QUELEN of Paris and other legitimist French bishops.

When revolution erupted in Paris, July 1830, it soon became apparent that King Charles X lacked popular support. Because of the close union of throne and altar during the Restoration period (1815–30) the July Revolution assumed a decidedly anticlerical cast. When some legitimist bishops fled France, Pius VIII disapproved their conduct and refused them admission into the States of the Church. By September the pope expressed hopes that the July Monarchy under Louis Philippe would be firmly established and would maintain friendly relations with the Holy See. He called upon the French bishops and priests to rally to the support of the new regime and rejected the plan of Archbishop De Quelen to withhold the clergy's loyalty. Pius VIII insisted on applying the traditional title of Most Christian King to Louis Philippe, whose private life hardly warranted it. In this way the pope successfully detached the Church in France from any official tie with legitimism, insisted that this Church remain independent of any regime, and prepared it for the burst of spiritual activity that emerged during the next two decades.

Revolution in France was soon followed by revolution in the Netherlands, where a concordat between the Holy See and King William I had been signed in 1827. Pius VIII followed a conciliatory policy but William I had antagonized all segments in his southern provinces. Belgian Catholics united with Liberals in patriotic agitation and won independence for Belgium in 1830 after a successful revolt. Although Francesco Capaccini, the internuncio, and Cardinal Giuseppe ALBANI, the papal sec-

"Monument of Pope Pius VIII," sculptural group by the 19th-century Italian sculptor Pietro Tenerani, St. Peter's Basilica, Rome. (Alinari-Art Reference/Art Resource, NY)

retary of state, opposed the proceedings in Belgium, Pius VIII took no adverse action. However, he opposed liberal and national movements in Ireland and Poland.

In Latin America Pius VIII confronted problems caused by the movement toward independence from Spain.

The bishops of the U.S. held their first formal meeting, the First Provincial Council of BALTIMORE (October 1829). After the decrees had been submitted to the Congregation for the Propagation of the Faith, Pius VIII approved them granting the American bishops the faculties they had requested concerning baptisms.

Bibliography: R. BELVEDERI, in *I Papi nella storia,* ed. P. PASCHINI and V. MONACHINO, 2 v. (Rome 1961) 2:898–903. E. E. Y. HALES, *Revolution and Papacy, 1769–1846* (Garden City, N.Y. 1960). J. LEFLON, *La Crise révolutionnaire, 1789–1846* (A. FLICHE and V. MARTIN, eds., *Histoire de l'église depuis les origines jusqu'à nos jours* 20; Paris 1949). H. HAAG, *Les Origines du catholicisme libéral en Belgique, 1789–1839* (Louvain 1950). A. DANSETTE, *Religious History of Modern France,* tr. J. DINGLE, 2 v. (New York 1961) v.1. J. SCHMIDLIN, *Papstgeschichte der neuesten Zeit, 1800–1939* (Munich 1933–39) v.1. G. MOLLAT, *Dictionnaire de théologie catholique,* ed. A. VACANT et al., 15 v. (Paris 1903–50; Tables générales 1951–) 12:1683–86. P. DE LETURIA, ''Pio VIII y la independencia de Hispanoamérica,'' in *Miscellanea historiae pontificiae* 21 (1959) 387–400; repr. in *Relaciones entre la Santa Sede e Hispanoamérica,* 3 v. (Caracas 1959–60) v.2. O. FUSI-PECI. *La vita del papa Pio VIII* (Rome 1965). A. PENNACCHIONI, ed. *Il papa Pio VIII* (Cengoli 1994). J. D. HOLMES, *The Triumph of the Holy See* (London 1978).

[T. F. CASEY/EDS.]

PIUS IX, POPE, BL.

Pontificate, June 16, 1846, to Feb. 7, 1878; b. Giovanni Maria Mastai Ferretti, Senigallia (Ancona), Italy, May 13, 1792.

Prepapal Career. Born into a family of the lower nobility with moderate reform tendencies, the future pope studied (1802–09) in Volterra at the college run by the Piarists until he suffered an epileptic attack. His health restored, he studied theology at the Roman College, which was not yet fully reorganized after the French occupation, and was ordained (April 10, 1819). Initiated into Ignatian spirituality by the saintly Cardinal Carlo Odescalchi, for a short time he thought of joining the Jesuits. He spent his first priestly years at the Roman orphanage of Tata Giovanni. Then as auditor he accompanied (1823–25) Msgr. Giovanni Muzi, apostolic delegate to Chile and Peru, where his interest in the missions was roused. After returning to Italy, he refused to continue a diplomatic career and took charge of the Roman hospice of San Michele. As archbishop of Spoleto (1827–32) he confronted the revolutionary troubles of 1831 mildly yet firmly. Transferred to Imola (1832) and made cardinal (1840), he guided the diocese zealously until 1846 and was well regarded in liberal circles for his administrative qualities, good will, and avoidance of party spirit. It has been claimed by some that he was won over to the national and liberal program of GIOBERTI and Balbo by his friend Giuseppe Pasolini, but matters were not that clear-cut. Undoubtedly he disapproved the reactionary policies of GREGORY XVI and his secretary of state, Cardinal LAMBRUSCHINI, as well as their police regime in the STATES OF THE CHURCH. As early as 1845 he outlined administrative reforms (for the text, see A. Serafini, *Pio IX,* 1:1397–1406); but this program aimed to correct abuses rather than to modify structures. It did not envision political reforms or the introduction of a parliamentary regime, for lay participation in the government of the States of the Church seemed to him incompatible with the religious character of papal rule. Apparently he always regarded the program of NEO-GUELFISM as chimerical and believed that a pope, as spiritual head of the faithful throughout the world, should not act as president of a federated Italian state. Yet the highly emotional Mastai Ferretti sympathized with Italian national aspirations, nourished by the Romantic movement, to shake off the official and officious yoke of Austria that weighed on the various states of the peninsula.

After Gregory XVI's death, the mounting agitation of Italian patriots and liberals stirred a group of cardinals led by BERNETTI to support, in opposition to Lambruschini, favorite of the reactionary Austrophiles, a cardinal disposed to make some concessions to the spirit of the times and a native of the States of the Church, and thereby to appear more independent of foreign influences. Since they erroneously regarded Gizzi as too advanced in his ideas, they upheld Mastai Ferretti, who on the first ballot received 15 votes to Lambruschini's 17 and emerged as pope the next day (June 16, 1846). He took the name Pius IX in remembrance of Pius VII, who had aided him in his youth. Pius IX's pontificate was long, eventful, and significant.

Conservatism of Pius IX. The new pope was an enlightened conservative. Some regarded him as a liberal, and for a while his actions seemed to justify them, because he signed an amnesty decree (July 17); named as secretary of state Cardinal Gizzi; chose as counselor Msgr. Giovanni Corboli-Bussi (1813–50), a young prelate open to new ideas; showed favor to Father VENTURA DI RAULICA, an eloquent disciple of LAMENNAIS; and granted some ardently desired reforms, although this concession lacked a comprehensive plan. These limited gestures sufficed then to release mass enthusiasm. Heedless of the fact that the encyclical *Qui pluribus* (Nov. 9, 1846) renewed Gregory XVI's condemnations of liberalism's fundamental principles, many saw in Pius IX, as Ozanam did, ''the envoy sent by God to conclude the great business of the 19th century, the alliance of religion and liberty.'' All liberal Europe applauded the pope. For some months papal prestige attained its zenith, especially since Rome reached an agreement with the Ottoman Empire, which resulted in the reestablishment of the Latin Patriarchate of JERUSALEM (October 1847); Rome also signed a relatively favorable concordat with Russia after negotiating since 1845. Enthusiasm was highest in Italy, where all manifestations against the Hapsburg and other reactionary regimes were accompanied with the cry ''Viva Pio Nono!''

The myth of the liberal pope soon exploded. Despite concessions won by those who exploited Pius IX's yearning for popularity, it gradually became clear that the pope would refuse, in the name of the spiritual independence of the Holy See, to transform the States of the Church into a constitutional government and that he would never agree to participate actively in a war for Italian independence against Austria, because this would be incompatible with his role as common father of all the faithful, as he noted in his allocution of April 29, 1848. An economic depression and Pius IX's lack of political competence precipitated a crisis. After the assassination of the papal prime minister ROSSI by the radicals, the pope fled the uprising and took refuge in Gaeta in the kingdom of Naples (Nov. 24, 1848). Soon afterward Mazzini and his followers proclaimed the Roman Republic; but Pius IX, supported by European diplomacy and a French expeditionary force, reentered Rome (April 12, 1850). The papal regime, restored in an atmosphere of passionate resentment, justified Carboli-Bussi's designation of it as ''reactionary and maladroit.''

More important than the retrograde character of this political restoration was the changed mentality evident in Pius IX, whose preoccupation with religious reaction dominated and conditioned his ideas on political reaction. As often happened, he continued to allow his illusions to deceive him; and his entourage lost no opportunity to revive in his impressionable soul memories of the bloody Roman revolution. Apart from psychological considerations, the pope's theoretical conviction was reinforced, and so was his habitual distrust of principles whose dangerous results were becoming evident. Henceforth he was more firmly persuaded than ever that an intimate connection existed between the principles of the FRENCH REVOLUTION and the destruction of traditional values in the social, moral, and religious order. In this experience lay the seed of the entire Syllabus of Errors.

End of Temporal Power. The government of the States of the Church, directed by Cardinal ANTONELLI,

Pope Pius IX. (Archive Photos)

secretary of state (1848–76), put into effect administrative improvements too little noted by 19th-century historians; but the educated classes were exasperated by a regime that accorded no political liberty to its citizens. It was not difficult for Cavour to exploit this situation to hasten Italian unification. After the annexation of Romagna (March 1860) and of the Marches after the battle of Castelfidardo (September 1860), French military aid permitted the retention of Rome and its environs for another decade by the pope, who did not cease protesting and demanding the restitution ''pure and simple'' of the ''stolen'' provinces. To realists who tried to persuade him that sooner or later he must negotiate, Pius IX opposed a mystical confidence in divine providence, nourished by the conviction that the political convulsions in which he was implicated were only an episode in the great battle between God and Satan, in which Satan's defeat was inevitable. The conflict of liberal and anticlerical Italy against the papal temporal power seemed to the pope a war of religion, in which resistance to what he described more and more freely as ''the Revolution'' was no longer a question of the equilibrium of diplomatic or military forces, but a matter for prayer. Although he was merciless in his judgment of the concrete manner in which Italy realized its unification under the lead of anticlerical Piedmont, Pius IX was never disinterested in the national cause; and to the astonishment of many of his counselors, he had to restrain himself from manifesting publicly his union of mind with certain aspirations of the heroes of the RISORGIMENTO. Italian troops took advantage of the Franco-Prussian War, occupied Rome (Sept. 20, 1870), and ended the papal temporal power. Pius IX, who regarded himself less as a dethroned sovereign than as the custodian of a property for which he was responsible to all Catholics, refused to bow to the *fait accompli.* After refusing to accept the Law of GUARANTEES, proposed by Italy, he considered himself a prisoner in the Vatican.

Varied Activities. The ROMAN QUESTION and the bitter politicoreligious conflicts with Italy that resulted from the official world's incomprehension of the Holy See's preoccupations by no means absorbed all Pius IX's energies. The essential part of his pontificate was on another plane, i.e., the internal guidance of the Church. He concluded concordats with Russia (1847), Spain (1851), Austria (1855), and several Latin American states. Further, he promoted Catholic reinvigoration in Germany, where the KULTURKAMPF highlighted the new vitality of this Church, so weak only a half-century previously. He reestablished the hierarchy in England (1850) and in the Netherlands (1853), and erected 206 new dioceses and vicariates apostolic, notably in the U.S. and in British colonies. Under Vatican impulse missionary work expanded vigorously throughout the world.

Increased Centralization. Centralization of authority progressed continually and was one of the most striking phenomena of Pius IX's pontificate. It eliminated the remaining ecclesiastical particularism in various nations. This growth of Roman influence caused regrets among those who had known the advantages of pluralism; and it even aroused somewhat violent reactions in the Eastern Churches united with Rome, which did not acquiesce in the reduced autonomy of their bishops decreed in the bull *Reversurus* (1867). On the whole, this trend was beneficial in countries where the Church was weakened by the regalian traditions of the *ancien régime.* Diverse means were used after 1850 to accelerate this evolution, but the victory of ULTRAMONTANISM over the last centers of resistance by GALLICANISM or FEBRONIANISM has rightly been termed "the triumph of a man as much as that of a doctrine." In good part the explanation lies in the immense prestige, far surpassing that of any predecessors, that Pius IX enjoyed for more than a quarter-century among the Catholic masses and that manifested itself on the occasion of the pope's various anniversary jubilees: 50th as a priest (1869), 25th as pope (1871), 50th as bishop (1877). This prestige rested partly on the attractive personality of the pontiff, who multiplied personal contacts during innumerable private and group audiences, and partly on sympathy for his repeated misfortunes, such as the exile to Gaeta, the Piedmontese aggression, and the occupation of Rome, which led some to venerate him as a true martyr. In large segments of the Catholic world, above all in France, a true devotion to the pope resulted. This was a very important new phenomenon in Church history, which explains the facility with which the mass of the clergy and faithful rallied to the doctrine, obscured for centuries, of personal papal infallibility (*see* PAPACY).

The triumph of this movement toward closer and closer direction of the entire Church from Rome disquieted governments, which took it ill to see the local clergies freed from their control. The Kulturkampf in Germany, the rupture of the concordat in Austria, and numerous difficulties in Latin America are evidence of the vigorous reaction in some states, especially after 1870.

Shortcomings. Democratic opinion did not pardon Pius IX for his reversal of policy in 1848, and reproached him for the support supplied everywhere by the Church after 1848 to conservative parties, and especially for the repeated anathemas against modern liberties. Pius IX was maladroitly counseled by his advisers and failed to discriminate with the lucidity of LEO XIII between rationalist LIBERALISM and INDIFFERENTISM, and the legitimate elements in Catholic liberalism, combined as they sometimes were with imprudences. As a result the pope proved unable to adapt the Church to the profound political and social evolution that kept intensifying from midcentury. On the contrary, as he advanced in years he tended more and more to identify the Church's misfortunes with the forms of government inspired by liberal principles, without taking into account the danger of so insistently presenting political realities as associated with the triumph of an anti-Christian philosophy. At Pius IX's death the Catholic Church, though strengthened within, appeared isolated in a hostile world, the more so since he did not succeed in imparting on the scientific level the impulse needed to react efficaciously against the progress of RATIONALISM and POSITIVISM and to adapt certain traditional theological positions to contemporary intellectual movements, notably the progress of natural and historic sciences.

Doctrinal Accomplishments. Despite this grave lacuna, which caused Catholic teaching to lose precious time, Pius IX played an important doctrinal role. He issued warnings or condemnations against ONTOLOGISM and TRADITIONALISM; against the teachings of certain philosophers and theologians, notably Anton GÜNTHER and FROHSCHAMMER; and against the tendencies of the school of DÖLLINGER (*Tuas libenter,* Dec. 21, 1863). These measures favored the restoration of NEOSCHOLASTICISM. Pius IX also published numerous encyclicals and allocutions, which constitute a much more complete and systematic ensemble than Gregory XVI's, although they lack Leo XIII's originality. The pope also took frequent occasion to recall the principles that should guide the restoration of society, particularly in the encyclical *QUANTA CURA* and the accompanying SYLLABUS OF ERRORS, both of which were the objects of passionate discussions. In addition Pius IX solemnly defined the IMMACULATE CONCEPTION (Dec. 8, 1854), which promoted a flowering of Marian devotion. Above all he convoked VATICAN COUNCIL I (1869–70), important for its definition of papal primacy and infallibility, on which most contemporary attention concentrated, and also for its constitution *De fide catholica,* which was characteristic of Pius IX's positive contribution and marked a strong effort to eliminate the last traces of the naturalistic DEISM of the ENLIGHTENMENT and to refocus Catholic thought on the fundamental data of revelation.

Spiritual Achievements. This vast doctrinal effort had its counterpart in Pius IX's parallel effort to deepen the clergy's spiritual life and to stimulate the devotion of the faithful. The greatest of the many changes in the Church during his pontificate was the deepening spiritual quality of average Catholic life. Among the many factors contributing to this development, the pope's personal role was important, because he appeared to all as an exemplar of piety, and still more because he consecrated a good part of his efforts to activate and sometimes to hasten the evolution that followed the great revolutionary crisis. Precisely because he believed the success of this work permitted no concession to modern ideas, he always maintained an intransigent attitude, often without nuances.

Conclusion. Pius IX during his lifetime was exalted as a saint and criticized as a vain autocrat and unintelligent puppet maneuvered by obtuse reactionaries. A threefold disadvantage always impeded him. From his childhood malady he retained an excessive emotionalism, which explains his propensity to heed the most recent advice; yet when duty required, he could be unyielding in the face of difficulties. Second, like most Italian ecclesiastics of his generation, he had made only superficial studies, and he had scarcely an idea of modern scientific methods. As a result he did not always take into account the complexities of questions and the relativity of some theses. He was not, however, deficient in intellectual interests or in finesse; hence he grasped concrete situations with good sense when they were accurately presented. Unfortunately, his entourage constituted his third disadvantage; for if the men in his confidence were generally pious and zealous, they also tended to be quixotic or intransigent, theorists without practical viewpoints. Apart from these limitations Pius IX possessed numerous good qualities and merits. Notable were his touching simplicity, his great goodness, his serene courage in adversity, his lively practical intelligence, and his fervor that aroused the admiration of all who saw him at prayer and corresponded with his intimate sentiments. Still more remarkable were his pastoral virtues, his care to act always as a priest, and even under the torment of the Roman question to comport himself not as a sovereign defending his throne, but as a man of the Church cognizant of his responsibility before God for the defense of Christian values menaced by the rise of laicism, rationalism, and impiety. His admirers soon after his death introduced his cause for beatification. He was declared venerable in 1985, and was beatified by John Paul II, along with Pope John XXIII, on Sept. 3, 2000.

Bibliography: *Acta Pio IX. Pontificis Maximi. Pars prima acta exhibens quae ad Ecclesiam universam spectant (1846–1854).* (Rome 1855). *Atti del Sommo Pontefice Pio IX, Felicemente Regnante. Parte seconda che comprende I Motu-propii, chirografi editti, notificazioni, ec. Per lo stato pontificio,* 2 v. (Rome 1857). N. BLAKISTON, ed., *Extracts from the Dispatches of Odo Russel from Rome 1858–1870* (London 1962). C. BUTLER, *The Vatican Council: The Story Told from Inside in Bishop Ulathorne's Letters* (New York 1930). P. DALLE TORRE, *Pio IX e Vittorio Emanuele II. Dal loro carteggio privato* (Rome 1972); ''Cardinale Giacome Antonelli fra carte di archivio ed atti procesuali,'' *Pio Nono VIII* (1979). P. DE FRANCISCIS, ed., *Discorse del Sommo Pontefice Pio IX Pronuziati in Vaticano ai fedeli di Roma e dell'orbe dal principio della sua prgionia fino as presente* (Rome 1872). G. MAIOLO, ed., *Pio IX da Vescovo a pontice. Lettere al Card Luigi Amat, Agosto 1839–Luglio 1848* (Modena 1943). G. MARTINA, ed., *Pio IX e Leopoldo II* (Rome 1967). A. SERAFINI, *Pio Nono. Giovanni Maria Mastai Ferretti dalla giovinezzza alla morte nei suoi scritte e discorsi editi e inediti* (Vatican City 1958). *Servi Dei Pii posito super introducionem causae,* 2 v. (Rome 1954). R. AUBERT, *Le Pontificate de Pie IX* (Paris 1967). O. CHADWICK, *A History of the Popes, 1830–1914* (Oxford 1998). F. J. COPPA, *Pope Pius IX: Crusader in a Secular Age* (Boston 1979); *Cardinal Giacomo Antonelli and Papal Politics in European Affairs* (Albany 1990); ''The Modern Papacy Since 1789,'' *Longman History of the Papacy* (London 1998). A. FILIPUZZI, *Pio IX e la politica Austriaca in Italia dal 1815 and 1848* (Florence 1958). E. E. Y. HALES, *Pio Nono: A Study in European Politics and Religion in the Nineteenth Century* (Garden City, NY 1981). D. I. KERTZER, *The Kidnapping of Edgardo Montara* (New York 1998). G. MARTINA, *Pio IX (1846–1850)* (Rome 1986); *Pio IX (1867–1878)* (Rome 1990); *La Chiesa nell' età del liberalismo* (Brescia 1978). R. MORI, *Il tramonto del potere temporale* (Rome 1967). G. RADICE, *Pio IX e Antonio Rosmini* (Vatican City 1974).

[R. AUBERT]

PIUS X, POPE, ST.

Pontificate: Aug. 9, 1903 to Aug. 20, 1914; b. Giuseppe Melchiorre Sarto, at Riese (Treviso), Italy.

Early Life and Prepapal Career. Giuseppe Sarto was born on June 2, 1835 in the village of Riese in Vene-

Pope Pius X.

tia. He was the second of ten children of Giovanni Battista and Margherita (Sanson) Sarto. His family circumstances were humble. His father was a village messenger and postman, and his mother helped out as a seamstress. Especially from his mother, he received a deeply religious formation, and even as a child, he felt a strong call to the priesthood. After studies in his home village and Castelfranco, in 1850 at the age of 15 he entered the seminary of Padua. Ordained to the priesthood on Sept 18, 1858, he spent nine years as curate in Tombolo and eight years as a pastor in Salzano. These years of parish work helped to shape the future Pope with a pastoral sensitivity and a love for the common people. In 1875, he was called to Treviso to serve as the spiritual director of the major seminary and to work as the chancellor of the diocese. The Bishop of Treviso likewise made him a canon of the cathedral. As the spiritual director of the seminary, Msgr. Sarto was zealous and demanding but also warm and compassionate. He combined his work at the seminary with his duties as chancellor, and for a seven-month period, in 1879–1880, he served as the Vicar Capitular of the diocese following the death of the bishop.

In 1884, Msgr. Sarto was named the Bishop of Mantua, and, during his nine years there, he did much to revitalize the spiritual life of the diocese. He was especially devoted to catechetics, and the lessons he drew up formed the basis for what was to become *The Catechism of Pius X.* Likewise, he encouraged the laity in their pious associations, especially the Third Order of St. Francis to which he himself belonged. He was equally dedicated to fostering vocations to the priesthood. In 1885, he ordained only one priest, but by the end of his nine years as bishop of Mantua, he had ordained 175.

On June 12, 1893, Pope Leo XIII named Bishop Sarto of Mantua a Cardinal, and three days later, appointed him to be the next Patriarch of Venice. The Italian government delayed his entry into Venice, claiming that the state must approve such appointments. Eventually, the government relented, and Cardinal Sarto was permitted, on Nov. 24, 1894, to make his solemn entry into Venice as the Patriarch-Archbishop. In his new role, Cardinal Sarto continued to emphasize the need for sound catechesis, lay devotion and holy and well-educated priests. In a pastoral letter of May 1, 1895, he treated the subject of church music, and he underlined the importance of Gregorian chant. In August 1897, he presided over a Eucharistic Congress, and he encouraged the frequent reception of the sacrament.

Cardinal Sarto's time in Venice was marked by apostolic zeal, a spirit of poverty, concern for divine worship, directives in the field of Catholic action, and also for his professional, social and political interests. His pastoral letters of this period also afford a glimpse of his future work. Thus, a letter to the Mantuans (1887) reproved the principles and tendencies of what was later termed ''MODERNISM.'' His first pastoral to the Venetians underscored the need for obedience to the pope. As Cardinal Sarto noted, in matters concerning the Vicar of Christ, ''there should be no questions, no subtleties, no opposing of personal rights to his rights, but only obedience.'' His reforms as pope reflected, to a large extent, the needs and aspirations he had experienced and expressed as a pastor and bishop.

Papal Program. The conclave of 1903 (July31–August 4) elected him successor to Leo XIII, despite his entreaties. Cardinal MERRY DEL VAL, secretary of the conclave, became his secretary of state. His first encyclical, *E supremi Apostolatus* (October 4), together with his allocution to the sacred college (November 9), formulated the guiding principles of his pontificate: to battle against estrangement from God and against apostasy, which was becoming ever more ruinous to societies. To this end he would seek "to restore all things in Christ, in order that Christ may be all and in all." He desired to be merely the minister of the Most High; but this position he intended to fill completely. In no area of human activity, he promised, would he fail to affirm the authority of God, the rigorous obedience due His Church, and the limitless extent of the papal mission. Even political affairs, so far as they concern faith and morals, must not escape the need for universal "restoration"; as was reiterated in the encyclical *Jucunda sane* (March 12, 1904), commemorating the 13th centenary of Pope St. Gregory the Great. Pius X also resolved "to teach the Christian truth and law," and to defend them with circumspection against "the insidious maneuvers of a type of new science." He further aimed to promote social justice and charity, the sole guarantee of real order and peace among individuals and groups.

Modernism. Modernism provided the gravest concerns for Pius X in the realms of philosophy, theology and biblical exegesis. Since the time of the ENLIGHTENMENT, there had been various efforts to accommodate the Christian faith to newer philosophical and scientific movements. A certain tendency emerged that seemed to reduce revelation to subjective feelings and the aspirations of the human spirit moving towards transcendence. Modernism provided the gravest problems with which Pius X had to contend in the philosophical, theological, and exegetical realms. For some years this new trend had been infiltrating intellectual circles in Christian nations and gaining entrance into some periodicals in the U.S. As a result several works of unequal importance had been placed on the Index, including writings by LOISY, HOUTIN, LABERTHONNIÈRE, Fogazzaro, and others. The Pontiff revealed his attitude on several occasions, notably in the encyclical *Pieni l'animo* (July 28, 1906), and even more clearly, in the Consistory of April 17, 1907. Official condemnation came with the publication of *Lamentabili sane exitu* (July 3, 1907), a decree of the Holy Office approved by the Pope, which reprobrated 65 propositions containing in summary form the errors imputed to Modernism. The encyclical *Pascendi dominici gregis* (September 8) completed the repression of what it termed the "résumé of all the heresies." Pius X enacted in it a series of measures destined to protect the faith of the laity and, still more, of the clergy. The motu proprio *Praestantia* (Nov. 18, 1907) confirmed *LAMENTABILI* and *PASCENDI* under penalty of grave censures.

Despite these measures, supplemented by a number of excommunications, and several additions to the Index of Forbidden Books, resistance did not disappear. This led to the imposition of an oath against MODERNISM (September 1910) that created difficulties in Germany. To the end of his pontificate the Pope continued to denounce the Modernist peril and the "circuitous means" by which it maintained itself.

Excesses unfortunately accompanied the repression of Modernism. They were caused chiefly by the supporters of Integralism, particularly Monsignor Benigni and his SODALITIUM PIANUM (League of St. Pius V). As a result numbers of Catholics, savants among them, found themselves unjustly denounced. Ecclesiastical studies suffered a setback. Three papal letters encouraging the Sodalitium were published; but these did not mention all of its numerous secret activities. Never did the Pontiff accord it "formal and definitive approval."

Popular Action Groups. Unfavorable by nature to alliance with groups hostile or even foreign to Catholicism, Pius X desired Catholics to form a great union to effect a program of just and prudent social reforms. From the beginning of his pontificate he issued instructions of this tenor to the Italian Opera dei Congressi. His *motu proprio Fin dalla prima* (Dec. 18, 1903) tried to remove Italian popular action groups from the ardent political involvements in which Romolo MURRI and others were trying to engage them, contrary to the directives of the Holy See.

After dissolving the internally divided Opera dei Congressi, Pius X directed his attention to the followers of Christian Democracy led by Murri. In two encyclicals, *Il fermo proposito* (June 11, 1905) and *Pieni l'animo* (July 28, 1906), he affirmed the great social role (actually the role of prudent political preparation), which devolved on CATHOLIC ACTION, under the control of the heads of the Church. He also opposed the spirit of insubordination, shown by some ecclesiastics, which menaced young clerics. This insubordination had, in the Pope's mind, ties with Modernist errors. The Holy Office's condemnation (Feb. 13, 1908) of the journal of Abbé Naudet, *La Justice sociale,* and that of Abbé Dabry, *La Vie catholique,* manifested Roman disquietude concerning the activities of French Christian Democracy, which had oriented itself toward politics in the framework of the RALLIEMENT, as recommended by Leo XIII. The letter to the French episcopate *Notre charge* (Aug. 25, 1910) condemned the Sillon, directed by Marc SANGNIER, a man to whom the Pope was at first attracted. But the inter-confessional Sillon freed itself from ecclesiastical authority; adopted social, civic, and even religious theses in opposition at times to pontifical directives; "enfeoffed religion" to the party of democracy; and formed alliances that compromised the defense of the Church in a grave hour.

Distaste for inter-confessional groups appeared again in the encyclical *Singulari quadam* (Sept. 24, 1912), which authorized under certain conditions Protestant membership in some groups, but preferred in principle purely Catholic associations.

Internal Affairs of the Church. Pius X profoundly reformed the Church's interior life, while favoring its missionary expansion. Interest in public prayer and the splendor of divine worship inspired his motu proprio *Tra le sollecitudini* (Nov. 22, 1903), which supplied norms for sacred music, especially Gregorian chant. Breviary prayers were distributed anew, permitting the weekly recitation of the entire Psalter, by the apostolic constitution *Divino afflatu* (Nov. 1, 1911).

To modernize the vast body of ecclesiastical laws and bring them into agreement with one another, Pius X undertook the codification of the Code of Canon Law in the motu proprio *Arduum sane* (March 19, 1904). At his death the enormous labor was nearly completed.

The Church's central government was simplified, harmonized, and strengthened by the apostolic constitution *Sapienti consilio* (June 29, 1908). Among other provisions, it removed from the jurisdiction of the Congregation for the Propagation of the Faith the U.S., Canada, Newfoundland, England, Ireland, Holland, and Luxembourg.

Pius X commended the development of studies that conformed to the spirit of Christianity. Notable was his establishment (May 7, 1909) of the PONTIFICAL BIBLICAL INSTITUTE, destined to promote, despite some criticisms, the scientific knowledge of Sacred Scripture. The philosophy of St. Thomas Aquinas always found in the Pope a zealous champion. Pius X's dedication to Thomism was manifested in his, motu proprio, *Doctor Angelici,* of June 29, 1914. In this document, he ordered the ecclesiastical schools of Italy "to uphold religiously the first principles and major declarations of Thomas Aquinas" contained in the 24 metaphysical theses that he authorized for promulgation by the Congregation of Studies (cf. H. Denzinger, *Enchiridion symbolorum,* 32nd. ed., edited by A. Schönmetzer (Freiburg 1963) 3601-3624). However, after the death of Pius X, Pope Benedict XV qualified this mandate. In his March 19, 1917 letter, *Quod de fovenda,* to Wladimir Ledochowski, the Superior General of the Jesuits, Benedict XV explained that the 24 theses were to be understood as "secure directional norms" and there was no strict obligation "to accept all of the theses." To the Jesuits (some of whom were Suarezians instead of Thomists) this came as welcome news.

The importance of religious instruction and the catechism were emphasized in the encyclical *Acerbo nimis* (April 15, 1905). The greatness of the priesthood was extolled in the papal jubilee exhortation (Aug. 4, 1908). His devotion to the Blessed Virgin Mary appeared frequently, notably in the encyclical commemorating the 50th anniversary of the definition of the Immaculate Conception. As Pope of the Eucharist, he considerably advanced devotion to it, especially by the decree *Sacra Tridentina Synodus* (Dec. 20, 1905), recommending greater frequency of Communion. His decree *Quam singulari* (Aug. 8, 1910), concerning the reception of first COMMUNION by children, demolished the apprehensive resistance at first met.

Pius X canonized Alexander SAULI, Gerard MAJELLA, Joseph ORIOL, and Clement HOFBAUER. He also beatified numerous martyrs, and founders and foundresses of religious congregations.

Relations with Governments. The apostolic constitution *Commissum nobis* (Jan. 20, 1904) ended the veto power of Catholic governments resurrected by the Austrian Cardinal Puzyna at the 1903 conclave to defeat Cardinal Rampolla.

Pius X's pontificate coincided with the growth of ANTICLERICALISM in France, especially during the ministry of Émile Combes, which saw the prohibition of all teaching by religious congregations, and conflicts over episcopal nominations. It witnessed the rupture of diplomatic relations with the Holy See (July 30, 1904) subsequent to the note of Cardinal Merry del Val concerning the visit of President Loubet of France to the king of Italy, and also the summoning to Rome of the bishops of Dijon and Laval. A French law (Dec. 9, 1905) annulled unilaterally the CONCORDAT OF 1801, separated Church from State, and transferred the Church's goods to lay associations. Pius X condemned the legislation in the encyclical *Vehementer Nos* (Feb. 11, 1906). Despite the wish of the French bishops, who were concerned for the existence of their dioceses, the Pontiff opposed all projects for bettering the lay associations in the encyclical *Gravissimo officii munere* (Aug. 10, 1906). In his solicitude for the rights of God and the Church, he repeatedly displayed his hostility to the new legislation, which had been enacted in violent circumstances and which included expulsions and violations of the archives of the nunciature.

French Catholics were advised by the Holy See not to continue to identify the defense of their religion with union of Church and State. Pius X was remarkably indulgent toward the leader of the ACTION FRANÇAISE, Charles MAURRAS, when he left unpublished for a time the decree condemning several of Maurras' books.

In his relations with the government of Italy, Pius X upheld the temporal rights of the Holy See, while preparing the way little by little in diverse acts for the solution of the ROMAN QUESTION. He felt compelled to protest against the anticlerical violence of Ernesto Nathan, Mayor of Rome. Consideration for the country's general welfare dictated his encyclical *Il fermo proposito* (June 11, 1905), which allowed bishops in certain cases to remove the papal prohibition that kept the faithful from political elections.

One of the Pope's commemorative encyclicals, *Editae saepe* (May 26, 1910), dedicated to St. Charles Borromeo, roused some ill-feeling in Germany because one passage was interpreted as being severe toward the Reformation. Sympathy for the Poles won for the Pontiff the hostility of the Russian government. Similarly, the mission of Cardinal Vincenzo Vannutelli as legate to Ireland was viewed amiss in London. Catalan revolutionaries plunged the Spanish Church into mourning (1909); and the anticlerical government of Canalejas caused it extreme distress. The young republic of Portugal was reproved in the encyclical *Jamdudum in Lusitania* (May 24, 1911) for its law separating State from Church, which led to violent religious persecution.

Public opinion in the U.S. deplored the refusal of a papal audience (1910) to former Pres. Theodore Roosevelt, because he intended to speak in the Methodist church in Rome. On the other hand, Pius X praised the liberalism of the government of the U.S. He also approved (June 11, 1911) the Carnegie Endowment for International Peace. Frequently he praised and aided the fervor of North American Catholics.

Antireligious legislation in Ecuador merited papal disapproval (1905). Bolivia was reminded of certain ecclesiastical laws. The Holy See's prestige mounted with the arbitration of the pope's delegate, Monsignor Bavona, in the conflict involving Brazil, Bolivia, and Peru. The encyclical *Lacrimabili statu* (June 7, 1912) invited the Latin American bishops to do their utmost to improve the lot of the native peoples.

Conclusion. Pius X's grief at the outbreak of World War I appeared in his exhortation *Dum Europa fere* (Aug. 2, 1914). He died soon after (Aug. 20). Christendom recalled in manifold ways the sanctity of this pontiff of luminous faith and compassionate humility. The cardinals of the Roman Curia requested (Feb. 24, 1923) the introduction of his cause. After long investigations (1923–46), the approval of the required miracles, and the ritual formalities, Pius X was beatified (June 3, 1951) and canonized (May 29, 1954).

Devotion to Pius X was particularly strong in the U.S.A. from the 1930s through the 1950s. Edwin Vincent O'Hara, Bishop of Great Falls, Montana and later of Kansas City, Missouri, was especially committed to his cause. In part, this dedication was inspired by the growth of the Confraternity of Christian Doctrine (CCD) in America which had been mandated for every parish by Pius X's encyclical, *Acerbo Nimis,* of 1905. O'Hara led a popular movement that produced books, holy cards and prayer crusades to promote the cause for the Pius X's beatification and later canonization. Cardinal Cushing of Boston was also an enthusiastic promoter of the cause. During this period, Pius X was especially esteemed for his Eucharistic piety, humility, warmth and his love for children. In many respects, he was held up a ''people's Pope'' in a manner similar to that of John XXIII.

Since Vatican II, some scholars have become critical of Pius X for what they perceive as his overly harsh treatment of theologians accused of Modernism. The 1967 replacement of the Oath against Modernism with a simpler profession was welcomed as an end to an unfortunate era. On the other hand, many ''traditionalist'' Catholics, such as the followers of Archbishop Marcel Lefebvre, have associated themselves with Pope Pius X in his zeal against the Modernist heresy. This can be seen in the chosen name of the Society of St. Pius X, a group of priests who carry on Archbishop Lefebvre's resistance to many of the doctrines of Vatican II and the new Mass promulgated by Paul VI in 1969. Some Catholics resent this ''usurpation'' of the heritage of Pius X by a schismatic movement. They see no contradiction between the sanctity and Eucharistic piety of St. Pius X and the ''universal call to holiness'' promoted by Vatican II and the post-conciliar pontiffs. As for Pius X's resistance to Modernism, some Catholic theologians recently have become more sympathetic to the general spirit (if not every detail) of his opposition to this ''movement.''

Feast: Sept. 3.

Bibliography: M. C. CARLEN, *Dictionary of Papal Pronouncements: Leo XIII to Pius XII, 1878–1957* (New York 1958). PIUS X, *Acta,* 1903–08 (Rome 1905–14). Acta Apostolicae Sedis 1–6 (1909–14). V. A. YZERMANS, *All Things in Christ* (Westminster, Md. 1954), Eng. tr. of Pius X's papal documents. A. MARCHESAN *Papa Pio X nella sua vita e nella sua parola* (Einsiedeln 1904). R. MERRY DEL VAL *Memories of Pope Pius X* (Westminster, Md. 1951). É. AMANN, *Dictionnaire de théologie catholique 12.2:1716–40.* F. A. M. FORBES, *Life of Pius X* (London 1918). J. SCHMIDLIN, *Papstgeschichte der neuesten Zeit 1800–1939,* v.3 (Munich 1933–1939). R. AUBERT, ''Le Bienheureux Pie X,'' *Revue Nouvelle* 14 (1951) 386–399. G. DAL-GAL, *Pius X: The Life Story of the Beatus,* tr. and ed. T. F. MURRAY (Westminster, Md. 1954). C. LEDRÉ *Pie X* (Paris 1952); *Un Siècle sous la tiare* (Paris 1955). P. FERNESSOLE, *Pie X: Essai historique,* 2 v. (Paris 1952–53), Dansette. A. LATREILLE et al., *Histoire du catholicisme en France,* v.3 (Paris 1957–62). H. DANIEL-ROPS, *L'Église des révolutions: Un Combat pour Dieu,* Histoire de l'Église du Christ 6.2 (Paris 1963). Y. DE LA BRIÈRE, *Les Luttes presentes de l'Église,* v.1–2 (Paris 1913-). M. PERNOT, *La Politique de Pie X* (Paris 1910). J. RIVIÈRE *Le Modernisme dans L'Église* (Paris 1929). N. FONTAINE, *Saint-Siège: Action française et catholiques intégraux* (Paris 1928). V. MARTIN, *Les Cardinaux et la Curie* (Paris 1930); *Les Congregations romaines* (Paris 1930). M. RANCHETTI, *The Catholic Modernists* (London 1969). A. VIDLER, *A Variety of Catholic Modernists* (Cambridge 1970). L. KURTZ, *The Politics of Heresy: The Modernist Crisis in Roman Catholicism* (Berkeley and Los Angeles 1986). T. MCGOVERN, ''A Charter for Priestly Holiness,'' *Homiletic and*

Pope Pius XI. (Archive Photos)

Pastoral Review (March 1989) 13–19. R. MYERS, ''A Saint Speaks,'' *The Priest* (November 1993) 36–93. W. DIETHELM, *St. Pius X, The Farm Boy who Became Pope* (San Francisco 1994). *The Catechism of Pope Saint Pius X* (Kansas City nd). A. MAGGIOLINI, ''Magisterial Teaching on Experience in the Twentieth Century: From the Modernist Crisis to the Second Vatican Council,'' *Communio* (Summer 1996) 33:225–243. S. M. AVELLA and J. ZALAR, ''Sanctity in the Era of Catholic Action: The Case of St. Pius X,'' *U.S. Catholic Historian* (Autumn 1997) 15:57–80. G. SALE, ''Pio X, *'La Civiltà Cattolica'* e gli accordi Clerico-Moderati del 1904,'' *La Civiltà Cattolica*151 (1) (2000): 537–550.

[C. LEDRÉ/R. FASTIGGI]

PIUS XI, POPE

Pontificate: Feb. 6, 1922 to Feb. 10, 1939; b. Ambrogio Damiano Achille Ratti, at Desio, near Milan, May 31, 1857.

PREPAPAL CAREER

After ordination (1879) and studies at the Gregorian University, Rome (Ph.D., D.D., J.C.D.), he became (1882) a professor at the major seminary in Milan and was appointed to the staff of the Ambrosian Library, Milan (1888–1911, after 1907 director). During this period he became known especially for his work in paleography and published *Acta Ecclesiae Mediolanensis* (4 v. Milan 1890–99) and *Missale Duplex Ambrosianum* (Milan 1913). From 1911 to 1918 Ratti worked at the Vatican Library, first as proprefect under F. X. EHRLE, and after 1914 as prefect. In April 1918 Benedict XV entrusted Ratti with the difficult task of apostolic visitator to the young Polish Republic, which had just established diplomatic relations with the Holy See. Ratti was appointed nuncio to Poland in June 1919 and titular archbishop of Lepanto on Oct. 28, 1919. His mission, extending to the areas that had formerly been part of the Czarist Empire, acquainted him with the difficulties in reconstructing the State and Church in Poland and in the Baltic states of Lithuania, Latvia, and Estonia. He was also drawn into the rivalries and border disputes of these young states. Still more delicate was his task as papal delegate on the Inter-Allied Commissions for the plebiscite areas in Upper Silesia, where his sympathies were with Polish Catholicism. As national passions heightened, the nuncio's situation became so untenable that Benedict XV transferred him (June 13, 1921), making him archbishop of Milan and a cardinal. After the death of Benedict XV, Achille Ratti was elected pope on the fourteenth ballot on Feb. 6, 1922.

PONTIFICATE

Pius XI's 17-year pontificate was devoted to achieving the great task of peace and the reordering of the Church. After the collapse of the old systems in World War I, he strove for the *Pax Christiana* in a world that had not reestablished genuine peace. In the age of disappearing monarchies he referred the nations, war-weary and yet filled with unrest, to the kingdom of Christ. For him, the highest goal was the unification of humanity—a humanity seeking true peace and community—under the royal scepter of Christ.

Encyclicals. In his program of religious renewal, the Pope's encyclicals were of special significance. The first, *Ubi arcano* (Dec. 23, 1922), inaugurated CATHOLIC ACTION or ''the participation of the laity in the hierarchical apostolate'' for the purpose of restoring a society animated by Christian spirit and of permeating all manifestation of public life with the Catholic doctrines of faith and morals. Although the organization of Catholic Action in all countries was very close to the heart of Pius XI, it took on special importance for Italy, where it was linked up with existing organizations. The pope stressed repeatedly its nonpolitical, purely religious character. The encyclical on Christian education, *Divini illius magistri* (Dec. 31, 1929), lays the foundation for a genuinely Christian theory of education, opposes the modern state's monopoly of schools, and undertakes the demarcation and coordination of the education rights of the family, the Church, and the state. The marriage encyclical *CASTI CONNUBII* (Dec.

30, 1930) treats of the properties of marriage (children, mutual trust, holiness), warns against contemporary false solutions (marriage for a specified duration, trial marriage, marriage of comradeship, abortion, sterilization, infidelity, mixed marriage, divorce, birth control), and asks for respect for the divine commandments and esteem for the graces conferred by the Sacrament of Matrimony. Besides the primary purpose (children), the ''mutual and harmonious development of the partners'' is recognized as a ''primary reason for marriage'' (*Catechismus Romanus* 2:8, 13).

The encyclical on the Christian social order, *QUADRAGESIMO ANNO* (May 15, 1931)—forty years after LEO XIII's *RERUM NOVARUM*—is the second great social encyclical. Going beyond the demands of Leo XIII, it presses for social reform, and under this aspect develops the ideas of the principle of SUBSIDIARITY and of the ''corporate order.'' As a supplement to *Quadragesimo anno,* the encyclical *Nova impendet* (Oct. 2, 1931) treats of the world crises of financial distress, unemployment, and the international military arms race. The pope's concern over the growing distress after the 1929 world economic crisis found expression in the encyclical *Caritate Christi* (May 3, 1932). To offset the widespread misery in the world, the pope called for the Christian activity of love, prayer, penance, and devotion to the sacred heart of Jesus. In the face of growing dangers from the totalitarian systems of various states, Pius XI, in numerous addresses and writings, warned urgently against ideologies that alienated men from God, and he emphasized that the dignity of the individual, the sanctity of the family, and the order and security of society would be secured above all by religion and the apostolic work of the Church. These papal efforts culminated in *Non Abbiamo Bisogno* (July 5, 1931) against Italian Fascism, *Mit brennender Sorge* (March 14, 1937) against National Socialism, and *Divini Redemptoris* (March 19, 1937), a defense of human society and culture against atheistic communism. The encyclical *Ad Catholici Sacerdotii* (Dec. 20, 1935) was devoted to the priesthood of the Church.

Also directed to the goal of renewing and deepening religious- ecclesiastical life were the World Eucharistic Congresses; the Jubilee Years of 1925, 1929, and 1933; the encyclicals *QUAS PRIMAS* (Dec. 11, 1925), instituting the Feast of Christ the King, *Miserentissimus Redemptor* (May 8, 1928), *Caritate Christi* (May 3, 1932), and *Mens Nostra* (Dec. 20, 1929); and a decree concerning catechetical instruction of Jan. 1, 1935.

Beatifications and Canonizations. Among those beatified or canonized by Pius XI were St. THÉRÈSE OF LISIEUX, St. John VIANNEY, St. Robert BELLARMINE, St. John BOSCO, St. Peter CANISIUS, St. ALBERT THE GREAT, St. John EUDES, St. Madeleine Sophie BARAT, St. Marie Madeleine POSTEL, St. CONRAD OF PARZHAM, ST. BERNADETTE SOUBIROUS, St. Thomas MORE, St. John FISHER, St. Andrew BOBOLA, and others. Pius XI elevated to Doctors of the Church Peter Canisius, JOHN OF THE CROSS, Robert Bellarmine, and Albertus Magnus.

World Mission. In pursuit of the goals of Pope Benedict XV's *Maximum illud* (Nov. 30, 1919), Pius XI gave new direction to the Church's world mission by urging the renunciation of the prevailing Eurocentrism, by the planned training of a native clergy and the recognition of the intellectual-cultural individuality of the peoples to be evangelized, by the 1925 Missions Exhibit in the Vatican (thereafter housed in the Lateran as a missions and ethnological museum), and by the encyclical *Rerum Ecclesiae* (Feb. 28, 1926). Despite considerable opposition, the pope ordained the first six Chinese bishops in St. Peter's on Oct. 28, 1926, and the first Japanese as bishop of Nagasaki on Oct. 30, 1927. Additional episcopal ordinations of native priests from India, Southeast Asia, and China took place in 1933. At the beginning of Pius XI's pontificate there was no mission diocese under native direction; at the pope's death there were 40. In addition, the number of native priests in mission lands rose from 2,670 to more than 7,000, and about 200 apostolic vicariates and prefectures were established. The Catholic population in the mission countries increased from 9 million to 21 million. Moreover, the apostolic constitution *DEUS SCIENTIARUM DOMINUS* (May 24, 1931) officially included MISSIOLOGY among the subjects of theological study in colleges. A faculty of missiology was established at the Gregoriana and an institute in the same field at the Roman Propaganda College.

The Eastern Catholic Churches. The encyclical *Ecclesiam Dei* (Nov. 12, 1923) honored the memory of the martyr-archbishop Josaphat of Polozk. The abbot primate of the Benedictines was commissioned to promote the work of union by founding a special congregation. A novitiate of the Society of Jesus for the Greek-Slavic rite was established in Albertyn, Poland. The Oriental Institute founded by Benedict XV was promoted. Colleges for the training of priests of the Eastern rite Churches were founded or reorganized. The Ethiopian and Ruthenian Colleges in Rome were rebuilt. The encyclical *Rerum orientalium* (Sept. 8, 1928) called for greater understanding of the Eastern Churches, reviewing the past and planning for the future. In 1929 work was begun on the codification of Eastern Church law, under the direction of Cardinal Pietro Gasparri. In 1935 the Syrian rite Patriarch Tappouni was elevated to the cardinalate.

Non-Catholic Christendom. On the invitation of the learned Belgian primate and cardinal Désiré Mercier, conversations on the subject of union took place between Catholics and Anglicans at MALINES in the years 1921 to 1926, at first with the knowledge and toleration, later with the express approval, of the Holy See and the archbishop of Canterbury. However, the Holy See took a negative attitude toward the ecumenical movement of non-Catholic Christendom, which rapidly acquired strength especially through the support of the Protestant Archbishop Nathan SÖDERBLOM of Uppsala.

Art and Science. Having come from a scholarly background, Pius XI gave sustained support to art and science. Among other things he had a new building erected for the Gregoriana and combined with it the Bible Institute and the Institute for Oriental Studies. At the Gregoriana he established faculties for Church history and missiology. The apostolic constitution *Deus scientiarum Dominus* (May 24, 1931) produced a unified, improved arrangement of Church study on the college level. In 1925 the Pope established the Roman Institute for Christian Archaeology. He promoted the Vatican Library, published new editions, encouraged the establishment of Catholic universities (especially the University of the Sacred Heart in Milan), and interested himself in church music and church art.

Church Diplomacy. It was only in the pontificate of Pius XI that the catastrophic consequences of World War I became clear. In the states deranged by the aftereffects of war and revolution, the pope strove for Church consolidation. His pontificate was a new era of concordats. In part the preparatory work extended back into the time of Benedict XV. Aided by his two cardinal secretaries of state, Pietro Gaspatti (till 1930) and Eugenio Pacelli (1930–39), Pius XI concluded concordats with the following states: Latvia (Nov. 3, 1922), Bavaria (March 29, 1924), Poland (Feb.10, 1925), Rumania (May 10, 1927), Lithuania (Sept. 27, 1927), Italy (Feb. 11, 1929), Prussia (June 14, 1929), Baden (Oct. 12, 1932), Austria (June 5, 1933), Germany (July 20, 1933), and Yugoslavia (1935, not ratified). In addition he signed agreements with Czechoslovakia (1926, 1928), France and Portugal (1928), and Ecuador (1937). World War II and its consequences caused many of these treaties to lapse.

Roman Question. The most significant political event of the reign of Pius XI was the settlement of the ROMAN QUESTION, which had festered since 1870. This settlement meant reconciliation of the papacy with the Italian state, since 1922 under the dictatorial leadership of Benito Mussolini. After two and a half years of difficult negotiations the LATERAN PACTS were signed on Feb. 11, 1929. They comprised: (1) a treaty on the founding of the sovereign state of Vatican City (Stato della Città del Vaticano, 44 hectares in area) as a guarantee of the freedom and independence of the papacy in the governance of the Church; (2) a concordat of the Holy See with the Italian state whereby the Catholic religion was confirmed as the state religion in Italy, with freedom of pastoral work and of religious instruction in the schools and with state recognition of Christian marriage and religious orders and societies; (3) a financial agreement awarding the Holy See a lump-sum payment of 1,750,000,000 lire as compensation for damages sustained. For Italy this peaceful settlement meant the ideal conclusion of the RISORGIMENTO; for the Catholics, Rome was made secure as the center of the Catholic Church. After the fall of the monarchy (1946) the Lateran Pacts were incorporated into the new republican constitution of Italy.

Totalitarian States. In the aftermath of World War I and against the background of dictated peace treaties, powerful upheavals in economic life, and changes in social structure that affected all the Christian churches, there grew up in many parts of the world a completely new form of national life: the totalitarian state. Three principal forms developed: Russian Bolshevism of Marxist-Communist origin, Italian Fascism, and German National Socialism.

Between the Papacy and the Soviet Union there was no direct liaison whatever. In 1922 Pius XI made a vain effort, through diplomatic mediation, to achieve the cessation of Russian persecution of Christians. An attempt, through the Jesuit Michael d' HERBIGNY and the secret consecration of bishops, to strengthen the Catholic Church in Soviet Russia also miscarried. D'Herbigny was expelled, and the bishops were sent to penal camps. In the encyclical *Divini Redemptoris* (March 19, 1937) Pius XI issued a sharp condemnation of atheistic communism.

Mindful of the stable power of Catholicism, the Italian ''Duce'' Benito Mussolini sought to avoid conflict with the Church. In the Lateran Pacts of 1929 he made a satisfactory arrangement with the Holy See. In 1931 serious difficulties in the interpretation of the Italian concordat were compromised, though Catholic organizations were gravely damaged. The Vatican's relation to Fascist Italy worsened considerably in 1938, when National Socialist racial doctrine was introduced.

In 1933 it appeared that the way was being paved for a settlement with the National Socialist regime of Adolf Hitler. On the strength of his repeated and solemn assurances as Reich chancellor to make the two Christian churches ''the cornerstone of the work of national renewal,'' the German bishops believed that they had to modify their hitherto sharply negative attitude and that they could not withhold from the new state the cooperation of Catholics. On July 20, 1933, the Holy See concluded a concordat with the German Reich, the initiative for which had come from Hitler. Though the concordat was not the first international treaty concluded by Hitler's government (it was preceded by a trade agreement with the Soviet Union on May 5, and a treaty with England, France, and Italy on July 15) it enhanced Hitler's prestige in the eyes of foreign states. Combined with the German bishops' modification of their previous sharp condemnation of Hitler's movement (mentioned above) the concordat introduced an element of uncertainty into German Catholics' instinctive mistrust of the regime. In the atmosphere of increasing lawlessness and terror in Germany, the Holy See sought to bind the suspect new system to legal guarantees of Church rights. The German concordat was ''the attempt to save the Concordats with several states of the German Reich by means of territorial and substantive enlargements as Germany moved into a quite uncertain future'' (Pius XII on July 19, 1947). After its brief initial camouflage, National Socialism soon showed its atheistic face. Against the growing oppression suffered by the Catholic Church in Germany, between 1933 and 1936 Pius XI directed 34 notes of protest to the Reich government. Most of these went unanswered. These protests climaxed in the encyclical *Mit brennender Sorge* (Latin *Ardenti cura* [March 14, 1937], which was written by Cardinal Secretary of State Eugenio Pacelli with the help of Cardinal Michael von FAULHABER, Archbishop of Munich, and was read from all Catholic pulpits in Germany. The encyclical condemned with unusual sharpness the constant violations of law and the un-Christian teachings and practices of National Socialism. Taken together with the previous papal protests, the encyclical constituted a public demonstration of Hitler's duplicity the like of which was not attempted by any other sovereign power prior to the outbreak of World War II. From March 1937 on there began an intensified persecution of the Church in Germany, which was moderated somewhat only in World War II.

France. The relationship of the Holy See to France was substantially improved under Pius XI The encyclical *Maximam gravissimamque* (Jan. 18, 1924) confirmed a practical accommodation on the vexing issues consequent on the Law of Separation (1905). Aided by the resumption of Franco-Vatican relations in December 1921, Pius XI extended the efforts of Benedict XV to find a path of accommodation with the government of the French Third Republic. His primary objective was to encourage those elements in the French Church that wished to work constructively within the democratic framework. He opposed all extremist political statements and consistently appointed conciliatory candidates to the episcopacy and other key posts. The climax of this vigorous policy, properly termed the Second Ralliement, came with the condemnation of the nationalistic and monarchistic ACTION FRANÇAISE (letter to Archbishop and Cardinal Andrieu of Bordeaux, Sept. 5, 1926), which produced severe shock waves for parts of French Catholicism. The Pope, after long examination, excommunicated the adherents of this movement as atheistic and neopagan. The consequence was a release of the pent-up energies of French Catholics and the dawn of a new era in the French Church.

Other Countries. In Spain under the republican government (after 1931), anti-Catholic excesses occurred, including wild attacks on churches and monasteries. Against the harsh anti-Church separation of Church and State, decreed in 1931 on the French model, Pius XI raised a protest in the encyclical *Dilectissima nobis* (June 3, 1933). The civil war, begun in July 1936, led to frightful atrocities on both sides and the murder of many bishops, priests, members of religious orders, and Catholic laymen. In Portugal the situation of the Church visibly improved, and there was even a resumption of diplomatic relations with the Holy See. However, during the pontificate of Pius XI, Mexico witnessed a hard and bloody persecution of the Church there as President P. Calles (1924–28) executed the harsh anti-Church provisions of the Constitution of 1917. In the encyclical *Iniquis afflictisque* (Nov. 18, 1926), the pope described the ''Diocletian persecution'' of the Church in Mexico. In several addresses he repeated his complaints and protests and censured the ''conspiracy of silence'' in the world press toward the atrocities. After a temporary improvement, Pius XI again (1932, 1937) strongly protested the persecution in Mexico. Only after the 1930s did the situation of the Church gradually improve.

Jews and Anti-Semitism. Pius XI several times condemned anti-Semitism in the sharpest manner. In September 1938 Pius XI told a group of Belgian pilgrims: ''Anti-Semitism is inadmissable. Spiritually we are all Semites.'' Ten years previously, on March 25, 1928, the Holy Office, with papal approval, had issued a formal condemnation of anti-Semitism. In the summer of 1938, after the encyclical *Mit brennender Sorge,* Pius XI, wishing to expand that document's condemnation of racism, commissioned another encyclical which would condemn anti-Semitism. Drafted by the Jesuits John LaFarge, Gustav Gundlach, and Gustave Desbuquois, the text was not yet ready for publication at the death of Pius XI on Feb. 10, 1939. His successor, PIUS XII, felt that the rapidly deteriorating political situation in Europe required him to concentrate all his efforts toward preventing the outbreak of war. When these efforts failed, he incorporated portions of the draft in his first encyclical *SUMMI PONTIFICATUS* (Oct. 20, 1939).

Character. A man of simple, sober character and strong integrity, Pius XI was averse to all ostentation.

Quite conscious of the fragility of the peace in the interwar years, he made every effort to strengthen the will to peace, to encourage international organization, and to contain racism and excessive nationalism, which he saw as the major threats to peace. Despite the external misfortunes of his pontificate, Pius XI appears as one of the most significant and most able of the popes of modern times. He died shortly before the outbreak of World War II and was interred in the grotto under St. Peter's.

Bibliography: *Sixteen Encyclicals of His Holiness Pope Pius XI* (Washington 1938). *Acta Apostolicae Sedis* v. 14–31 (1922–39). *L'Osservatore Romano* (1922–39). M. NASALLI-ROCCA DI CORNELIANO, comp., *Concordatorum Pii XI P. M. concordatiae* (Rome 1951). *Pio XI nel trentesimo anno della morte 1939/69* (Milan 1969). G. BIANCHI et al., eds., *Il pontificato di Pio XI a cinquant'anni di distanza* (Milan 1991). M. AGOSTINO, *Le Pape Pie XI et l'Opinion (1922–1939)* (Rome 1991). *Achille Ratti, Pape Pie XI: Actes et documents du colloque organisé par l'École francaise de Rome. . . (Rome 15–18 mars 1989)* (Rome 1996). O. CAVALLIERE, *L'Archivio di Mons. Achille Ratti, Visitatore Apostolico e Nunzio a Varsavia (1918–1921)* (Vatican City 1990). S. WILK, ed., *Acta Nuntiaturae Polonae: Achille Ratti (1918–1921)* 6 v., (Rome 1995–2000). H. MÜLLER, *Katholische Kirche und Nationalsozialismus: Dokumente 1930–35* (Munich 1963). L. SCHÖPPE, *Konkordate seit 1800* (Frankfurt 1964). F. J.COPPA, ed., *Controversial Concordats* (Washington DC 1999). J. J. HUGHES, ''The Pope's 'Pact with Hitler': Betrayal or Self-Defense?'' *Journal of Church & State* 17/1 (1975) 63–80. L. SALVATORELLI, *Pio XI e la sua credità pontificale* (Turin 1939). C. A. BIGGINI, *Storia inedita della Conciliazione* (Rome 1942). G. DALLA TORRE, *Azione cattolica e fascismo: Il conflitto del 1931* (Rome 1945). J. NEUHÄSLER, *Kreuz und Hakenkreuz,* 2 v. (2d ed. Munich 1946). V. DEL GIUDICE, *La questione romona e i rapporti tra Stato e Chiesa fina alla Conciliazione* (Rome 1947). M. MACCARRONE, *Il nazionalsocialismo e la Santa Sede* (Rome 1947). G. DE ROSSI DELL'ARNO, *Pio XI e Mussolini* (Rome 1954). O. DIEHN, *Bibliographie zur Geschichte des Kirchenkampfes, 1933–1945* (Göttingen 1958). W. M. HARRIGAN, ''Nazi Germany and the Holy See, 1933–1936'' *American Catholic Historical Review* 47 (1961–62) 164–198. J. GUITTON, *L'Église et les laïcs de Newman à Paul VI* (Paris 1963). G. SCHWAIGER, *Papsttum und Päpste im 20. Jahrhundert* (Munich 1999) 193–270. J.GELMI, *Lexikon für Theologie und Kirche* (Freiburg 1995) 8:335–338. D. A. BINCHY, *Church and State in Fascist Italy* (New York 1941). D. ALBRECHT, *Der Notenwechsel zwischen dem Hl. Stuhl und dem Deutschen Reich, 1933–1937,* 2 v. (Mainz 1965–1969). G. PASSELECQ and B. SUCHECKY, *L'encyclique cachée de Pie XI* (Paris 1995). A. RAUSCHER, ed., *Wider den Rassismus. Entwurf einer nicht erschienenen Enzyklika* (1938). *Texte aus dem Nachlaß von Gustav Gundlach SJ* (Paderborn 2001). D. VENERUSO, *Il pontificato di Pio XI* in M. GRESCHAT and E.GUERRIERO, *Storia dei Papi* (Milan 1994) 758–794. K FUCHS, *Biographisch- bibliographisches Kirchenlexikon* 7 (1994) 680–682. A. FITZEK, ed., *Pius XI und Mussolini, Hitler, Stalin. Seine Weltrundchreiben gegen Faschismus, Nationalsozialsmus, Kommunismus* (Eichstätt 1987).

[G. SCHWAIGER/T. BRECHENMACHER/J. HUGHES]

PIUS XII, POPE

Pontificate: March 2, 1939, to Oct. 9, 1958; b. Eugenio Maria Giuseppe Giovanni Pacelli, Rome, March 2, 1876. He was the second of four children of Filippo Pacelli, a lawyer, and Virginia Graziosi.

PREPAPAL CAREER

He was educated in Rome, studying philosophy at the Gregorian University, and theology at Sant' Appollinare (today the Lateran University). After ordination (April 2, 1899), he studied Canon Law, and won a doctorate *in utroque jure* (1902). Entering the papal Secretariate of State (1901), he became (1904) the close collaborator of Pietro GASPARRI in the gigantic task of drawing up the Code of Canon Law. He was professor of ecclesiastical diplomacy (1909–14) at the Pontificia Accademia dei Nobili ecclesiastici. He became assistant secretary of state (1911), pro-secretary of state (1912), and secretary of the Congregation for Extraordinary Ecclesiastical Affairs (1914).

Nuncio. Consecrated titular archbishop of Sardes by Benedict XV (May 13, 1917), he was at the same time appointed nuncio to Bavaria, representing the Vatican in its peace efforts with Germany. He dealt with the German chancellors Von Bethmann-Hollweg and Michaelis and with Kaiser William II. Pius XII revealed in later years that the absence in the German reply of any assurance that the integrity and independence of Belgium would be reestablished were enough to frustrate papal mediation.

He became nuncio to Germany (June 22, 1920) and dean of the Berlin diplomatic corps. He signed the concordats with Bavaria (March 29, 1924) and Prussia (June 14, 1929).

Secretary of State. Created cardinal (Dec. 16, 1929), he replaced Cardinal Gasparri as secretary of state (Feb. 7, 1930), and concluded the concordat with Baden (Oct. 12, 1932). Cardinal Pacelli went as papal LEGATE to the Eucharistic Congress in Buenos Aires (October 1934), to the jubilee celebration in Lourdes (April 1935), to Lisieux to dedicate the basilica of St. Thérèse (July 1937), and to the Eucharistic Congress in Budapest (May 1938).

He traveled (October 1936) in an unofficial capacity to the United States, mainly to experience at first hand its Catholic life. Covering more than 9,000 miles by land and air, he visited 12 of the 16 ecclesiastical provinces, met 79 bishops, and observed Catholicism at work in education as well as in social and charitable endeavors. He was invited by President Roosevelt to dine at Hyde Park.

Concordat with Germany. Soon after the concordat (June 5, 1933) with Austria, whose chancellor was Dollfuss, another was concluded (July 20) with the German Republic. The Hitler regime had first proposed it at Easter; it was the German government that initiated the proceedings. Previously (March 24), the Center party and the Bavarian People's party, whom German Catholics rightly considered representatives of their interests, had approved the enabling act that gave Hitler unlimited powers. Also the German bishops had declared unequivocally (March 28) that Catholics could cooperate with the new state despite obviously irreconcilable differences between the Catholic Church and National Socialism. Cardinal Pacelli had in no way influenced either of these events; yet he had to take them into consideration. Since the new concordat agreed to all the demands of the Holy See, even to the continuation of Catholic schools and the earlier concordats with the German states, Rome would have put itself in the wrong and placed German Catholics in a dangerous situation by refusing to sign. At this time also German Catholics expected the Holy See to intercede in their behalf, because guarantees of their rights had become questionable since Hitler's accession to power (Jan. 30, 1933). The Holy See could fulfill these expectations only by negotiation and a treaty with Berlin. During the negotiations the dissolution of the Center party was not discussed. Cardinal Pacelli regretted very much this party's dissolution of itself (July 5, 1933) during the concordat negotiations, because, for good reason, he wanted to see it survive until the signing of the concordat.

Pope Pius XII.

Later negotiations between Pacelli and the Hitler government (1933–39) are contained in some 60 memoranda, written in Pacelli's own hand, which make clear his struggle to have the German government observe the concordat. The encyclical of PIUS XI, *Mit brennender Sorge* (March 14, 1937), climaxed this controversy.

PONTIFICATE

Cardinal Pacelli was elected pope March 2, 1939, and crowned March 12.

World War II. In the following months, until September 1, he sought to prevent war. The climax of these efforts was his diplomatic move (May 3) proposing that existing differences between Italy and France and between Germany and Poland be settled peacefully by a conference attended by these four powers and England. Many considered his proposal premature. Hitler thought it pointless. In August, with war imminent, the pope kept uninterrupted contact with both sides until the last moment, hoping to prevent the catastrophe. His appeal to the world (August 24) declared: ''Nothing is lost by peace; everything is lost by war.''

Pius XII relayed messages (November 1939–February 1940) between the German resistance movement and the Allies. The former wanted to know if the Allies would be ready for an armistice and peace negotiations in the event of a German general strike. Pius XII had at that time offered to leave nothing undone to end the war. As an important English official observed in 1944, he went as far as a pope could possibly have gone. In these communications it was presumed and understood that Poland would regain its former status, and that Austria would decide its own future, whether of independence or annexation to Germany.

Myron Taylor was named by President Roosevelt as his personal envoy to Pius XII (Dec. 25, 1939).

The meeting between Pius XII and Hitler's foreign minister, Joachim von Ribbentrop (March 10, 1940), could have no bearing on war or peace, since Ribbentrop refused any conversation on this topic.

The pope's efforts to keep Italy out of the conflict kept increasing from late 1939, and included personal meetings with King Victor Emmanuel III (Dec. 21 and 28, 1939) and correspondence with Mussolini. With Italy's entrance into the war (June 10, 1940) Pius XII intervened to save Rome. He wanted it declared an open city, recognized as such by the warring nations, and kept free of troops and commandos. This goal was realized in good part, although not perfectly, and only after the greatest difficulties. When Ernst von Weizsäcker was asked who saved Rome, he replied: ''Above all others it was the pope, who merely by staying in Rome forced the opposing armies to spare the city.'' Pius XII was determined not to leave Rome save under duress. Contrary to rumors, he did not leave Rome during the entire war.

Papal Mediation. The Allies declined to negotiate with Hitler under any circumstances. It was also inconceivable that Hitler would make any move to save the German people. This situation blocked the way to any kind of mediation. Of the two systems, National Socialism and Communist Bolshevism, Pius considered the latter more dangerous. But he never approved Hitler's war with Russia, nor did he consider it a crusade. He regretted very much the unconditional surrender terms promulgated at Casablanca (1943) because they could only lengthen hostilities. On the other hand, Berlin would not agree to let Rome intervene for the cessation or even lessening of aerial warfare because it hoped to develop a more lethal weapon than the enemy possessed. Italian Fascists were responsible for the bomb that fell on the Vatican (March 1, 1943).

Papal Charities. Assistance for needy individuals and countries was organized by the Pontificia Commissione Assistenza (PCA), which since 1952 has operated under the name Pontificia Opera di Assistenza (POA). Aid was extended without discrimination to all suffering persons during the war: prisoners of war, deportees, internees, refugees, the hungry and homeless, the politically and racially persecuted. Sums were also expended for the protection of buildings, especially churches and libraries. Papal kitchens during 1944 served 3,600,000 portions of soup monthly. Of the refugees who poured into Rome throughout the war, the PCA helped 52,000 to return to their homes. The pontifical information service received 9,891,497 inquiries about missing persons and in turn sent 11,293,511 inquiries of its own. Many of these appeals were handled under unusual circumstances.

Help to Jews. Jews received extensive aid. From the very start of his pontificate, Pius XII continued Pius XI's program of aid to Jews, especially to German Jews. Jewish refugees received financial aid, and Pius contributed his total private funds to them in cases of extraordinary urgency. After the German occupation of Rome (September 1943), the pope responded to Jewish pleas by offering them 15 kilos of gold in the event that they were unable to raise the 50 kilos demanded of them, but in this case his help proved unnecessary. Cloister regulations in religious houses were lifted to supply refuge to 4,447 Jews, exclusive of the large number in the Lateran and Vatican along with non-Jews. A special agency of the pontifical information service searched for Jews, especially in Germany, and handled 37,000 cases. Close cooperation existed between the pontifical St. Raphael Society and the Jewish Delasem to help Jews escape overseas. Pius XII's financial aid to Jews far exceeded $4 million. The Catholic Refugees Committee in the United States supplied the pope with plentiful financial means.

In his appeals for the humanizing of war and abolishing its brutalities and atrocities, Pius XII twice condemned unequivocally the exterminating of Jews, in his Christmas message (Dec. 24, 1942) and in his speech to the college of cardinals (June 2, 1943). One reason for a certain caution on the pope's part was the belief, which proved ill-founded, that a class of European Jews, for example those in Theresienstadt, would merely be restricted to their ghettos, but not exterminated. He did not want to endanger these people. All qualified judges, even those less favorably disposed to the pope, deny that any further formal papal move would have deterred Hitler from annihilating the Jews.

With the appearance of Rolf Hochhuth's play *The Deputy* in 1963 began the practice of distorting the actions of Pius XII with regard to the Nazis. A pope whose extraordinary efforts on behalf of Jews during the Nazi hegemony had hitherto been universally praised was now portrayed as the secret sharer of Nazi antisemitism if not an actual participant in the holocaust. Such libels were more than adequately addressed by Pincas Lepide in his magisterial *The Last Three Popes and the Jews* (1967). It was the careful calculation of this Jewish author that 860,000 Jews had been saved from certain death at the hands of the Nazis thanks to the efforts of Pius XII. No one has been able to refute the number given by Lapide—he thought the number could be as high as a million. Nevertheless, criticism of Pius grew—much of it fueled by popular books that distorted the historical record, but some prompted by a desire to give a responsible answer to the question whether the pope could (and should) have done more on behalf of the Jews.

Vatican Excavations. During and after the war Pius XII promoted the excavations under ST. PETER'S BASILICA. Msgr. Ludwig KAAS and the archeologists Bruno M. Apollonj Ghetti, Antonio Ferrua, SJ, Enrico Josi, and Engelbert Kirschbaum, SJ, were in charge. Their excavations resulted in discoveries important for Christian and secular archeology. Among other things they fixed with certainty the location of the original grave of the Apostle St. PETER (*see* VATICAN).

Pius XII as Teacher. In volume and scope the teachings of Pius XII surpassed those of any of his predecessors. His oral allocutions alone numbered nearly 1,000. He spoke 36 times to Catholics from the United States, and on five occasions asked help for hungry children from Catholic students of the United States. The fundamental theme of his principal speeches was the confrontation of contemporary civilization and culture with the Catholic outlook on life. He defended Catholic schools strongly. Topics common to the medical profession and Catholic moral theology received thorough treatment. Although disinclined to be hyperspiritual, he opposed the opinion that politics has nothing to do with religion. He held it a moral obligation, and a serious one under certain conditions, to exercise the right to vote.

Social Questions. In his numerous promulgations on social questions, Pius XII maintained the traditional Catholic social doctrine. He insisted that if the objectives of social reform and social policy are to be realized, then the social question must concentrate on preserving the dignity, freedom, and eternal value of the human person, and consequently on the proper functioning of the three indispensable divisions of social structure: the family, private property, and the state. The individual and the family take precedence over the state. The state cannot dispose of a guiltless individual's body and life, or sacrifice his moral or physical integrity in the interest of the common good, or compel him to act contrary to the dictates of his conscience. It is the purpose of society to serve the individual and not the contrary (*see* SOCIAL THOUGHT, PAPAL).

War and Peace. Pius XII gave a classic definition of the religious, psychological, and legal structure of a lasting peace, especially in his Christmas messages between 1939 and 1942. As a realist, he did not favor peace at any price. Presupposing these principles, he insisted on bilateral, controlled disarmament as the only effective means to prevent war. However, he maintained that as long as disarmament was not a reality, and any government could use an offensive war as a means of attaining an international political goal, then peaceful nations could not be denied the right to coordinate a system of defense, which, through its very existence and corresponding strength, might prevent enemy aggression (*see* WAR, MORALITY OF).

Government. Although Pius XII was legalistic by natural inclination and by training, he viewed governments and political systems with strict objectivity. His outward reserve toward the choice of the Italian people (May 5, 1946) between a monarchical or republican form of government was necessary, and in no way a ''Vatican revenge on the House of Savoy.'' The general principles that Pius XII supplied for the new order, during and after the war, excluded totalitarian systems. The democratic state, for its part, to be equal to its task, must make great demands on the moral responsibility of its people (Christmas message, 1944). He indicated to the Roman nobility (Jan. 14, 1952) that the age of privileged classes was past, and that they should place themselves at the service of the new state. The Prussian Concordat, which dealt with the rights of the Catholic Church in Prussia at the time of the Weimar republic, was the work of Pacelli as nuncio and the socialist minister President Otto Braun. The concordat with Spain (Aug. 27, 1953) permitted closer cooperation between the Church and State, and a stronger governmental influence in episcopal appointments than in the other concordats concluded since 1918; yet it did not mark a return to the PATRONATO REAL of the old Spanish monarchy. Pius XII was a man of the Church, who always strove to realize the Church's mission as well as possible under given circumstances.

Doctrinal Topics. The encyclical *HUMANI GENERIS* (Aug. 12, 1950) combated some recent theological trends. *MUNIFICENTISSIMUS DEUS* (Nov. 1, 1950) defined the ASSUMPTION OF MARY, while intentionally avoiding the question of the Blessed Mother's physical death. The encyclical *Ad caeli Reginam* (Oct. 11, 1954) dealt with the sublime dignity of Mary (*see* MARY, BLESSED VIRGIN, QUEENSHIP OF). Purposely he left the question of her MEDIATION and COREDEMPTION open to theological discussion. The encyclical *MYSTICI CORPORIS* appeared June 29, 1943.

On the subject of TOLERANCE, Pius XII stated (Dec. 6, 1953; Sept 7, 1955) that the Church, in its awareness of its divine mission to all men, practices tolerance toward other religious-ethical confessions mindful of the good faith of those living in invincible ignorance, and attentive to the common good of Church and state within individual nations, and also of the entire Church. On Sept. 7, 1955, he characterized as a product of the times the ''medieval concept'' that all temporal authority comes from God through the pope as Christ's representative.

In an address concerning man's nature and origin (*Richiamo di gioia,* Nov. 30, 1941), Pius XII insisted that the spiritual soul elevates man above all other living creatures, but that, on other questions regarding man's nature, nothing up to now has been positively ascertained. Concerning EVOLUTION, he declared in *Humani generis* that Catholic teaching holds the immediate creation of the soul by God and finds polygenism evidently irreconcilable with the testimony of Holy Scripture on original sin. The encyclical *DIVINO AFFLANTE SPIRITU* (Sept. 30, 1943) affirmed that the time, the character, and the literary style of the inspired writer can and should be considered by the Catholic exegete in establishing the literary meaning.

His important address to Italian midwives, *Vegliare con sollecitudine* (Oct. 29, 1951), supplemented the marriage encyclical of Pius XI, *Casti connubii.* On Sept. 29, 1949, the pope condemned any kind of artificial insemination. The natural performance of the marital act, he said, must remain an entirely personal function.

Pius condemned the concept of collective guilt (*Nessuno certamente,* Dec. 24, 1944; *L'ardua missione,* Feb. 20, 1946; Oct. 3, 1953).

The apostolic constitution *Sacramentum ordinis* (Nov. 30, 1947) dealt with the validity of ordinations of deacons, priests, and bishops, exclusive of the necessary matter and form. For theological inquiry, this was one of the most important decisions since the Council of TRENT (1545–63).

The *motu proprio In cotidianis precibus* (March 24, 1945) concerned the new translation of the Psalms by a commission of the PONTIFICAL BIBLICAL INSTITUTE, undertaken at the direction of Pius XII for use in the DIVINE OFFICE. The encyclical *MEDIATOR DEI* (Nov. 20, 1947) was of great importance for the LITURGICAL MOVEMENT. The encyclical *Musicae sacrae* (Dec. 25, 1955) summarized the norms for the lay participation in liturgical functions. Pius XII was willing to compromise with new musical trends and did not exclude instrumental music from liturgical ceremonies.

Disciplinary Matters. New regulations on the Eucharistic FAST appeared March 19, 1957.

The establishment of SECULAR INSTITUTES was treated in the apostolic constitution *Provida Mater Ecclesia* (Feb. 2, 1947) and in the motu proprio *Primo feliciter elapso* (March 12, 1948). In an allocution (Dec. 8, 1950) dealing with the relationship between religious and diocesan clergy, the Pontiff noted that Christ instituted one priesthood. The difference between the two forms of priestly life he attributed to the historical growth of the Church.

Pius XII terminated (Feb. 1, 1955) the long dispute concerning the KNIGHTS OF MALTA, and the reconciliation of their claim to sovereignty with their status of a religious order.

A decree of the Holy Office against communism appeared July 1, 1949. In the apostolic letter *Carissimis Russiae populis* (July 7, 1952) the pope distinguished between the communist-bolshevistic system and the Russian people.

Radio, television, and motion pictures were the subject of the encyclical *Miranda prorsus* (Sept. 8, 1957).

Pius XII called two consistories (Feb. 18, 1946; Jan. 12, 1953) to create 56 cardinals. The college numbered 57 at his death. He canonized 33 saints. Dioceses, excluding titular sees, increased from 1,696 in 1939 to 2,048 in 1958. Hierarchies were established in China (1946), Burma (1955), and several parts of Africa.

Conclusion. A man of genuine classical formation, extensive historical knowledge, level-headed realism, remarkable exactitude, and industry, Pius XII was highly esteemed in the ecclesiastical circles in which he had held office since 1900, as well as in the diplomatic and political world. He was well prepared to lead the Church through World War II and the postwar years, and did so with such wisdom that respect for the papacy reached an all-time high.

Bibliography: PIUS XII, *La personalità e la territorialità delle leggi specialmente nel diritto canonico* (Rome 1912); documents in *Acta Apostolicae Sedis* (1939–58); *Discorsi e radiomessaggi di Sua Santità Pio XII,* 20 v. (Vatican City 1939–58); *L'Osservatore Romano* (1939–58); *The Pope Speaks* 1–5 (1954–59); *Documents pontificaux de Pie XII, 1939–1958,* ed. S. DELACROIX and R. KOTHEN, 20 v. (Paris-St. Maurice, Switz. 1950–62); *Relations humaines et société contemporaine: Synthèse chrétienne; directives de S. S. Pie XII,* ed. A. F. UTZ and J. F. GRONER, tr. A. SAVIGNAT, 3 v. (Fribourg 1956–63); *Major Addresses of Pius XII,* ed. V. A. YZERMANS, 2 v. (St. Paul, Minn. 1961). M. C. CARLEN, *Guide to the Documents of Pius XII (1939–49)* (Westminster, Md. 1951); *Dictionary of Papal Pronouncements: Leo XIII to Pius XII (1878–1957)* (New York 1958). *Catholic Periodical Index* (1939–). P. CATTIN and H. T. CONUS, eds., *Sources de la vie spirituelle: Documents pontificaux,* 2 v. (2d ed. Fribourg 195861) v.2. C. C. CLUMP, ed., *The Social Teaching of Pope Pius XII* (Oxford 1956). I. GIORDANI, *Pio XII* (Turin 1961). D. TARDINI, *Pio XII* (Vatican City 1960). O. HALECKI and J. F. MURRAY, *Eugenio Pacelli: Pope of Peace* (New York 1951). *The Wartime Correspondence between President Roosevelt and Pope Pius XII,* introd. and notes by M. C. TAYLOR (New York 1947). R. COSTE, *Le Problème du droit de guerre dans la pensée de Pie XII* (Paris 1962). A. GIOVANNETTI, *Il Vaticano e la guerra, 1939–40* (Vatican City 1960). R. LEIBER, "Pius XII as I Knew Him," *Catholic Mind* 57 (1959) 292–304. R. C. POLLOCK, ed., *The Mind of Pius XII* (New York 1955). *Pio XII. Pont. Max. postridie kalendas martias, 1876–1956* (Vatican City 1956). J. S. CONWAY, "The Silence of Pope Pius XII," *Review of Politics* 27 (1965) 105–131. P. LAPIDE, *The Last Three Popes and the Jews* (London 1967). M. MARCHIONE, *Pope Pius XII Architect for Peace* (New York 2000). P. BLET, S.J., *Pius XII and the Second World War,* Eng. tr. (New York 1999). R. MCINERNY, *The Defamation of Pius XII* (South Bend, Indiana 2001).

[R. LEIBER/R. MCINERNY/EDS.]

PIUS X SCHOOL OF LITURGICAL MUSIC

The Pius X School of Liturgical Music was the first school founded to give Catholics in the United States the opportunity to share in the revival of church music urged by Pope St. Pius X. It was organized in 1916 at Manhattanville College of the Sacred Heart in New York City (now located at Purchase, New York). The school was founded as a partnership between Mother Georgia Stevens and Mrs. Justine B. Ward. The school was subsequently affiliated with the Pontifical Institute of Sacred Music in 1954. The school continued as a center of liturgical music until 1969, when a unilateral administrative decision combined the function of the School with that of the music department of Manhattanville College.

[J. FOX]

PLACE

An exclusively Aristotelian and scholastic notion, place serves a threefold purpose in their physical systems: (1) it is the condition of the possibility of local motion; (2) it is the external foundation for the category location (πoῦ, *ubi,* where), the internal foundation being quantity or structure; and, (3) as external reference of location, it constitutes the measure of the quantity of bodies. This article presents the historical development of the notion up to the high scholastic period, a systematic analysis following St. Thomas Aquinas, and an explanation of the modern rejection of the notion in favor of that of space.

Historical Development. Aristotle complains that he has inherited nothing about place from his predecessors (*Phys.* 208a 35). Nonetheless, there are two earlier traditions that he sets out to combat. The first proposes the concept of space (rather than place) as a basic constituent of the physical world—a concept expounded in Plato's *Timaeus,* where physical bodies are conceived of as parts of space limited by geometric surfaces (53B–55A). The second view, fostered by the atomists, also concentrates on space, designating it as a void contained within bodies and the condition of the possibility of their local motion. Against the background of these views Aristotle elaborates his own theory. Although he has a notion of space as a species of continuous quantity (*Cat.* 5a 7), which can be generalized into space as the summation of the dimensions of bodies (Jammer, 15), the notion is not developed and plays no part in his physical system. The emphasis is entirely on place.

Aristotle considers place primarily as a condition of the possibility of local motion, maintaining that the notion would never have come up except for the fact of local motion (*Phys.* 211a 12). His definition of place is ''the innermost motionless boundary of what contains'' (212a 20), or the unchanging surface of the surrounding physical environment in immediate contact with the contained body. It is a container, separable from the contained body, and neither larger nor smaller than it (210b 35). For Aristotle, all bodies in the universe are surrounded by other bodies, and are thus in place, but the universe as a whole is not in place (212b 22). This obviously implies the rejection of the void, or empty space, as upheld by the atomists. The ultimate reason for this rejection, however, is Aristotle's conception of natural places and natural local motion. ''Either nothing has a natural locomotion, or else there is no void'' (215a 12). For Aristotle the world is an interrelated system of concentric spheres, each in contact with that next to it. The natural place of heavy and inactive elements is at the center, that of more active elements farther and farther from the center in proportion to their activity or lightness. Voids or empty spaces would not allow for these interrelated activities, nor could a featureless void have a natural up and down.

It is sometimes maintained that Aristotle's basic notion of place can be accepted by one rejecting natural place. An argument for this is that Aristotle does not establish a close connection between the two in his treatment of place in the *Physics* (Solmsen, 127–129). Against this it can be argued that the apparent failure to make the connection is purposeful and methodological: Aristotle is there setting out general principles to be combined in his special treatment of natural local motion in the *De caelo.*

The history of the concept of place in late antiquity can be traced fairly clearly with the help of Simplicius, who has outlined much of it in his commentary on Aristotle's *Physics,* in a *Corollarium de loco* (Sambursky, 1–7). For the most part, the notions offered closely parallel one or other of the classical theories of Plato, Aristotle, or the atomists. The Epicurean LUCRETIUS expands the atomist notion of the void into infinite space; the Stoics accept Aristotle's plenum and make it the vehicle for the transmission of physical activity by giving it the qualities of a ''tension'' or field of force (Hesse, 76); the Neoplatonist PROCLUS identifies place or space with light; etc. In general, ''until the fourteenth century Aristotle's and Plato's conceptions were the prototypes, with only minor changes'' (Jammer, 21).

Analysis of the Concept of Place. In the Middle Ages, though there were some differences, the Aristotelian view is fairly represented by St. THOMAS AQUINAS. In general agreement with the other scholastics and with Aristotle, he defines place as the unchanging surface of the immediately surrounding body (bodies)—*terminus immobilis continentis primum* (*In 4 phys.* 6.16). Four properties follow from this definition. Place is a container, distinct from the thing contained. It is equal to the body contained and corresponds to it part to part. Every body surrounded by others is in place, and no physical body (except the universe as a whole) is without a place. Place implies natural place, a natural up and down both within a given place and in the universe as a whole.

There are two main divisions of place. The first distinguishes between common and proper place. Common place is the nearest immobile container or surrounding environment—immobile at least relatively to the body in question. Proper place is to be taken in strict accord with the definition—it is equal to the body in place, and its immobility is purely formal, as part of the whole system contained within an immobile common place (*In 4 phys.* 6.14–15).

The second division distinguishes natural from nonnatural place. The natural place of a body is its suitable physical environment—suitable for its proper activity in accord with its heaviness or lightness and for its consequent proper sense qualities. Nonnatural place is any other physical environment.

A necessary connection between place and natural place is demanded by the Aristotelian notion of natural motion or CHANGE. According to this notion, all nonnatural motion presupposes natural motion (*In 3 cael.* 5.2). The ultimate ground for this is the overall Aristotelian view of NATURE as an interrelated system, with quantity and such basically quantitative realities as natural local motion supplying the ground for qualitative changes, chemical reactions, etc. (cf. Jammer, 17–18).

Although Aristotle and some scholastics believed it did, this notion of natural place need not imply an absolute up and down. All that is required is a natural locus of operation within a given system such that the more massive and stabilizing elements, which are less active, are at the center, the unstable and highly active elements at the periphery. Neither does natural place imply an anthropomorphic conception of elements desiring their natural place as a known end; a directional tendency to a suitable functional environment suffices. The scholastic explanation of gravity follows as a direct consequence of this. Heavy bodies do not move themselves to their natural place by a sort of desire; their natural motion is simply a datum, given along with the nature of the body and in accord with it.

Modern Rejection of Place. The modern rejection of place belongs properly to the history of space. Some of the earliest rejections, however, should be mentioned, since they were proposed within a general Aristotelian framework. Aristotle had stated that the outermost of his celestial spheres was not in place, but that it did have a circular motion. His explanation of this (*Phys.* 212a 35–212b 10) did not satisfy all, and it was this problem of how a body without place could move locally that motivated most of the late medieval and Renaissance rejections of place in favor of space. Some, such as the natural philosophers of the Italian Renaissance, rejected the notion of place altogether, and postulated an infinite void in which the heavens could move. COPERNICUS chose the other alternative and made the heavens stationary.

None of these views alone, however, could have effected the total rejection of Aristotle, though they did contribute to the general disfavor toward him. The decisive grounds for rejecting place were three: the rise of the mathematical conception of nature, with its emphasis on a Euclidean notion of absolute space; the rejection of space dynamism and natural place, as represented in William GILBERT; and the revival of atomism, as represented by Pierre GASSENDI (Čapek, 7–31).

Since the Einsteinian revolution against Newtonian absolute space, a number of authors have remarked on the general resemblance between modern field theory and Aristotelian natural place, and some have spoken even of a return to Aristotle. Nevertheless, though the similarities are in some ways striking, the differences are important. Perhaps most important is the fact that, where natural place is a purely physical theory, Einstein's relativistic space is based on non-Euclidean geometry and other highly mathematical considerations (Čapek, 272–273).

In general, despite its rejection by classical physics, place can still be considered a valid concept. It is essential for modern Thomists who accept the natural, as opposed to the mechanistic, conception of MOTION. Again, the application of place is still the normal way for measuring the QUANTITY of a physical body, i.e., by surrounding the body with another body marked off in arbitrary units. And finally, especially in the context of relativity, it makes good sense to locate physical bodies relative to their nearest frame of reference (in a modified Aristotelian conception), rather than with respect to an absolute space.

See Also: CATEGORIES OF BEING; LOCATION (UBI); SITUATION (SITUS).

Bibliography: M. JAMMER, *Concepts of Space* (Cambridge, Mass. 1954). M. B. HESSE, *Forces and Fields: The Concept of Action at a Distance in the History of Physics* (New York 1962). ARISTOTLE, *Physics,* tr. and ed. W. D. ROSS (Oxford 1936). J. H. RANDALL, *Aristotle* (New York 1960). F. SOLMSEN, *Aristotle's System of the Physical World: A Comparison with His Predecessors* (Ithaca, N.Y. 1960). S. SAMBURSKY, *The Physical World of Late Antiquity* (London 1962). M. ČAPEK, *The Philosophical Impact of Contemporary Physics* (Princeton 1961). D. NYS, *Cosmology,* tr. S. A. RAEMERS, 2 v. (Milwaukee 1942) v. 2. F. SELVAGGI, *Cosmologia* (Rome 1959).

[P. R. DURBIN]

PLAGUES OF EGYPT

By the term plagues of Egypt is meant those prodigies that Yahweh inflicted upon the Egyptians as signs to them and to the Israelites that He alone was God and the Israelites were His chosen people, whom He would

Bible Illustration from Exodus Chapter 8, depicting frog plague on Egypt. (©Historical Pictures Archive/CORBIS)

bring out of Egypt with a mighty hand. The book of EXODUS (Ex 7.14–12.30) recounts ten plagues in all, occurring intermittently during a period of nine or ten months. The first nine of these prodigies and signs are founded upon natural phenomena characteristic either of Egypt, or of the Near East in general, but were miraculous in the manner in which they occurred. The last plague, the killing of the firstborn of the Egyptians, stands in a class by itself, both in its effect upon Pharaoh and the Egyptians and in its place in Israel's memory and liturgy.

Under divine inspiration, the final redactor of the PENTATEUCH has skillfully interwoven into a unified and dramatic account the mighty deeds with which Yahweh brought His people from the land of bondage, by selecting some of the traditional accounts of these divine acts as transmitted in Israel's memory and recorded by the YAHWIST, the ELOHIST, and the Pentateuchal PRIESTLY writers. The second plague would seem to be peculiar to the Yahwist and Priestly traditions; the third and sixth may come from the Priestly tradition alone, and the fourth and fifth from the Yahwist source. The rest of the plagues seem to belong to all three streams of tradition.

Conflict between Egypt and Yahweh. The divine drama opens when MOSES and AARON present themselves before Pharaoh to request that the Israelites be allowed to go into the desert to celebrate a feast to their God. ''Who is the Lord that I should heed his pleas to let Israel go?'' Pharaoh asks. ''I do not know the Lord; even if I did, I would not let Israel go'' (Ex 5.2). When Moses has recourse to the Lord, he is told ''Now you shall see what I will do to Pharaoh. Forced by my mighty hand, he will send them away. . . . You will know that I, the Lord, am your God when I free you from the labor of the Egyptians. . . . Yet I will make Pharaoh so obstinate that, despite the many signs and wonders that I will work in the land of Egypt, he will not listen to you. Therefore I will lay my hand on Egypt and by great acts of judgment I will bring the hosts of my people, the Israelites, out of the land of Egypt, so that the Egyptians may learn that I am the Lord, as I stretch out my hand against Egypt and lead the Israelites out of their midst'' (6.1–7; 7.3–5). The plagues are thus set in a religious context as divine signs that Yahweh is omnipotent Lord and the Israelites His chosen people with a special destiny in SALVATION HISTORY.

First Four Plagues. At the Lord's command, Moses and Aaron confront Pharaoh at the Nile. Moses tells him the water will be turned into blood, so that all the fish will die and the water will be unfit for use. Then Aaron strikes the water with his staff, the Nile turns into blood, the fish die, and the Egyptians must dig for drinking water. Here there is more than the usual reddening of the Nile at the flood season, for at that time the fish do not die and the water remains potable. Moreover, the effect is predicted beforehand, and follows upon a symbolic action evoking it as a divine sign, but Pharaoh ignores the event.

The second plague is one of frogs, with which Moses threatens Pharaoh seven days later if Pharaoh does not let Israel go. At the divine command transmitted through Moses, Aaron strikes the river with his staff and frogs infest Egypt in unprecedented numbers. This time Pharaoh summons Moses, asks him to pray the Lord to remove the frogs, and promises to let the people go. After Moses' prayer to the Lord, the frogs die, but Pharaoh becomes ''obdurate'' and will not let the people go.

The third and fourth plagues are similar to each other. In the third, at the Lord's command, Aaron strikes the dust of the earth, and a swarm of gnats comes upon men and beasts. Pharaoh remains obstinate. Again Moses and Aaron meet Pharaoh at the river. This time Moses announces a coming plague of flies, the fourth plague—with the added note, however, that an exception will be made in the land of Goshen, where the Hebrews live. Although flies are a normal part of Egyptian life, the Lord now sends them in thick swarms that exceed anything Egypt has known. Pharaoh is again ready to negotiate and promises to let the Israelites go. At Moses' prayer, the Lord removes the flies, but once more Pharaoh becomes obdurate.

Fifth, Sixth, and Seventh Plagues. The fifth plague strikes the livestock of the Egyptians with a severe pestilence, but that of the Israelites is spared. We are told that ''all of the livestock of the Egyptians died,'' but since some remained to be destroyed by hail, ''all'' may mean that every type of livestock was affected, or perhaps this is merely a case where the editor did not bother to harmonize one tradition with another. Pharaoh, however, remains obdurate.

As the sixth plague, Moses, at the Lord's command, scatters soot toward the sky in the presence of Pharaoh, and festering boils appear on the persons and beasts of the Egyptians, but the Israelites are spared. Pharaoh remains obstinate.

The seventh plague is a terrific hailstorm. Hail falls occasionally in Egypt, but the hailstorm the Lord now sends upon the Egyptians, as foretold by Moses, exceeds anything they have ever experienced, both in its intensity and in the lightning and thunder that accompany it. Beasts and servants left in the fields are killed, and the flax and barley crops are ruined. No hail falls in the land of Gesen, however. At this point, Pharaoh sends for Moses, confesses his fault, and begs him to pray the Lord to stop the hail. At Moses' prayer, the hail and thunder cease, but Pharaoh returns to his obstinacy.

Eighth, Ninth, and Tenth Plagues. The whole Middle East dreads the coming of locusts. At the Lord's command, Moses stretches his staff over the land of Egypt, and a strong east wind blows in swarms of locusts that destroy what has been left of the crops. Hastily summoned by a seemingly contrite Pharaoh, Moses begs God to remove the plague. At Moses' prayer, the Lord sends a strong west wind to blow the locusts into the Red Sea.

The ninth plague is a blinding sandstorm. When Pharaoh again becomes obdurate, the Lord sends a desert sandstorm, now called the *khamsin*, which comes when Moses stretches his hand toward the sky. Except for the land of Gesen, the whole of Egypt is plunged into thick darkness for three days. Pharaoh summons Moses and Aaron and tells them they may go, but to leave their herds in Egypt. When Moses insists their herds must accompany them, Pharaoh drives the two from his presence with threats.

Now the stage is set for the tenth and last plague, the killing of the firstborn of the Egyptians, which caused Pharaoh to send the Israelites away that very night. That a pestilence should strike every family in a given land is extraordinary, but that it should strike only the firstborn of every family and every beast puts the tenth plague in a class by itself. The poetic license to exaggerate should not be denied to the ancient storyteller even in the Bible, and the ones affected by the plague may have been in the vicinity of Gesen only, despite the statement of the text. The memory of this night, when the Lord spared the firstborn of the Israelites to kill those of the Egyptians, was liturgically perpetuated in the Israelite feast of the PASSOVER.

Special Problems. A true miracle is always a perceptible event, inexplicable by the normal course of nature, produced by God within a religious context as a sign of the supernatural. Judged by this definition, the plagues of Egypt can be seen to be true miracles, even though they do not in themselves transcend the powers of nature. As natural calamities they are of unprecedented intensity. Foretold by Moses as divine signs, they begin after symbolic gestures on the part of Aaron or Moses, and they cease abruptly when Moses asks the Lord to stop them.

The sacred writer sometimes says God hardened Pharaoh's heart, and again that Pharaoh hardened his own heart. How can this seeming contradiction be explained, for God cannot be the cause of moral evil? The answer will be found in the Semitic outlook that does not distinguish between direct and permissive causality. Other texts in Scripture throw light on the problem; for example, ''Why do you harden your hearts, as Egypt and Pharaoh hardened their hearts?'' (1 Kgs 6.6) indicates the personal responsibility involved. On the other hand, the place of this permitted obduracy in the divine plan is indicated in Ex 7.3–6; 9.16; Rom 9.17.

Bibliography: *Encyclopedic Dictionary of the Bible*, tr. and adap. by L. HARTMAN (New York 1963) 1861–62. G. STANO, EncCatt 9:1323–26. A. MALLON, *Les Hébreux en Égypte* (*Orientalia* 3; 1921) 138–147. R. E. MURPHY, *The Book of Exodus* (New York 1960) 16–21. M. NOTH, *Exodus,* tr. J. S. BOWDEN (Philadelphia1962) 62–102. J. H. NEWMAN, *Two Essays on Biblical and Ecclesiastical Miracles* (New York 1890) 3–94. J. C. CARTER, ''The Recognition of Miracles,'' *Theological Studies* 20 (1959) 175–197. R. LATOURELLE, ''Miracle et révélation,'' Greg 43 (1962) 492–509. F. TAYMANS, ''Le Miracle, signe du surnaturel,'' NouvRevTh 77 (1955) 225–245.

[M. J. REDLE]

PLANT LIFE (PHILOSOPHICAL ASPECTS)

The careful choice of paradigm, or typical cases, enables a broad distinction, at the descriptive level, of inorganic materials, plants, and animals. All three types of natural objects are alike in exhibiting an identifiably stable set of properties, so that it is appropriate, in each case, to speak of a natural mode of action. Beyond this general similarity, however, particular instances of each type exhibit marked dissimilarity.

Descriptive analysis. Plants differ markedly from inorganic systems in their tendency to carry on an active metabolic exchange of materials with the environment. Again, plants grow and mature and even enter resting phases of nearly total inactivity with respect to ordinary organic functions (respiration, metabolism). Plants may reproduce themselves either asexually (by budding or sporulation) or sexually (by pollination), producing one or more new individuals of the same organic type. Tendencies of this sort have no near analogues in inorganic systems. It should be noted, however, that these characteristics are dispositions and not continuously present properties or processes. Even as dispositions, they do not serve as necessary and sufficient conditions for the identification of all living things at the botanical level: sterile botanical forms may very well be referred to as living plants. Again, certain viruses reproduce only when allowed to infect a specific, nonimmune, bacterial host. Thus the question of the vitality of virus-like macromolecules may remain moot while a search is made of appropriate host organisms.

Animals exhibit vegetative activities usually considered philosophically indistinguishable from those found in plants, i.e., they metabolize, grow, pass through an orderly life cycle, and reproduce themselves. The distinction of plants and animals, within the context of the traditional scholastic philosophy of nature, is thought to rest upon the fact that animals possess powers of sensory cognition and appetition, while plants do not. Of course, plants do respond to a wide range of environmental stimuli with activities that are generally adaptive or beneficial to the continued survival of the organism or its species. On the other hand, a line may be drawn between organisms that exhibit definitely formed sense organs and coordinated neuromuscular systems and those that do not (or between those that exhibit plastic behavior patterns that become increasingly adaptive with repeated performance and those whose patterns are absolutely stereotyped or invariable in form). In other words, it seems more appropriate to attribute sensation to those organisms that seem to learn from EXPERIENCE or that spontaneously search out absent sources of food or other stimulation or that exhibit some analogue for affective experience, e.g., ''loyalty'' to a herd or to a master. One can speak of those higher animals that exhibit such behavior as knowing their environment or having feelings about it without appearing to indulge in metaphor, whereas the use of the terms know and feel with respect to plants is ordinarily regarded as metaphorical.

Evaluation. The descriptive distinctions drawn in the scholastic philosophy of nature between minerals and plants and between plants and animals are reasonable enough and, in fact, are quite compatible with ordinary ways of speaking and talking about these objects. What is contested by nonscholastics is the suitability of this same material as a base for an abstract theory of NATURE, requiring such explanatory principles as plant and animal souls and nutritive, sensitive, and appetitive faculties.

A number of contemporary points of view contest the distinctions in question as either inconsequential or injurious. The geneticist employs information gathered from the study of bacteria in the elaboration of a general theory of inheritance, hopefully applicable to all living things. The ecologist studies the interaction of all the elements of a given environment; a balanced population involves the commerce of all its organisms without specific regard for their botanical or zoological overtones. For the artist and the man of letters, the picture of nature as an unbroken, continuous chain may be a source of considerable inspiration. The alternative claim that nature is stratified into SPECIES and levels that are essentially distinct, while tenable, does not accord so simply with these points of view.

Once it is established that nature is essentially stratified, the traditional distinction between a substance and its powers (e.g., between a living thing and its powers of nutrition, growth, and reproduction) reflects the fact that one can adequately characterize a living thing only in terms of its dispositions or tendencies and that one may insist that a thing is living even when circumstances prevent the activation of these tendencies. It should be noted, however, that scholastic philosophers of science to date have not given biological problems the attention they deserve. With regard to plant life, for example, there is need for clarification of the grounds on which one may urge the view that nature is stratified rather than continuous and for adequate illustration of the point that these grounds can be made intelligible only through a system of substantial forms and powers.

See Also: SOUL; FACULTIES OF THE SOUL.

Bibliography: V. E. SMITH, ed., *The Philosophy of Biology* (St. John's Univ. Phil. Ser. 3; Jamaica, N.Y. 1962). A. O. LOVEJOY, *The Great Chain of Being* (Cambridge, Mass. 1936).

[A. E. MANIER]

PLANTIN, CHRISTOPHE

French bookbinder, printer-publisher; b. 1520?, near Tours, France; d. Antwerp, Belgium, July 1, 1589. He settled in Antwerp in 1549 as a bookbinder who turned to printing, achieving eminence in the late 16th century. Through employment of good type designers, such as Claude Garamond and Robert Granjon, his works reflected fine craftsmanship. His most famous publication was the eight-volume polyglot Bible (1569–73) in Aramaic, Greek, Hebrew, Latin, and Syriac, with text in parallel columns. The basic edition was 1,200 paper copies with an additional 13 on parchment for the patron, Philip II of Spain. In 1579, Plantin was designated by the Holy See and Philip as official printer of liturgical books for Spain and the Netherlands, a privilege held by his successors for two centuries. Between 1555 and 1589 he issued more than 1,600 works. His printer's mark, a hand from the clouds guiding a compass on earth, with the motto ''Labore et Constantia,'' symbolized his life's work. He was succeeded by his son-in-law, Jan Moretus (1543–1610). His original building with its typographical equipment has been preserved as the Plantin-Moretus Museum.

Bibliography: C. PLANTIN, *An Account of Calligraphy and Printing in the 16th Century from Dialogues Attributed to C. Plantin,* tr. R. NASH (Cambridge, MA 1940). T. L. DE VINNE, *The Plantin-Moretus Museum* (San Francisco 1929).

[E. P. WILLGING]

PLANUDES, MAXIMUS

Byzantine humanist and theologian. b. Nicomedia, *c.* 1260; d. Constantinople, *c.* 1310. Born of a family that migrated from Nicomedia to Constantinople after 1261, Planudes attempted a civil career, but because of religio-political difficulties entered a monastery (1283) and changed his name from Manuel to Maximus. He was appointed hegumen, or director, of the monastery of the Five Saints on Mt. Auxentius in Bithynia by the metropolitan of Chalcedon, but soon returned to Constantinople. Despite the opposition of the Patriarch Athanasius I, he founded a monastery for laymen and opened a school close to the Emperor's palace with access to the imperial library. Grammar, mathematics, and science, as well as Latin, were the main subjects taught. The success of this novel enterprise in Constantinople was guaranteed when the children of the imperial family were sent there.

Possessing an excellent knowledge of Latin, Planudes had consistently favored a *rapprochement* with the Roman Church, and he strove to defend the orthodoxy of the Western theology under the Palaeologi Emperors MICHAEL VIII and ANDRONICUS II; under pressure the latter forced him to reconsider his opinions. Planudes was sent on diplomatic mission to Venice in 1295; but since it proved a failure, he refused a similar assignment to Cilicia somewhat later.

Among his numerous writings was a defense of the Western doctrine on the procession of the Holy Spirit that has not been preserved. Later he wrote, evidently under the pressure from Andronicus II, a *De Spiritu Sancto adversus Latinos,* published first by Arcudius (Rome 1630), which, in manuscript played an important part in the 15th-century polemics between BESSARION, Gemistos PLETHON, and George METOCHITES. Of his correspondence, some 121 letters have been preserved, and they have importance for the history of his epoch. He translated St. Augustine's *De Trinitate* into Greek, as well as works of Cicero, Ovid, Boethius, and Caesar. He also wrote hagiographical tracts, including an encomium of SS. Peter and Paul and another of St. Diomedes, discourses, and poetry. He was a figure of importance in the debates surrounding JOHN XI BECCUS from 1282 to 1297.

Bibliography: V. LAURENT, in *Dictionnaire de théologie catholique,* ed. A. VACANT et al., 15 v. (Paris 1903–50; Tables générales 1951–) 12.2:2247–52. R. JANIN, in *Lexikon für Theologie und Kirche,* ed. J. HOFER and K. RAHNER, 10 v. (2d new ed. Freiburg 1957–65) 7:211–212. *Patrologica Grecia,* ed. J. P. MIGNE, 161 v. (Paris 1857–66) 147:1017–1130; 161:309–318. M. TREU, ed., *Epistulae* (Breslau 1890; repr. Amsterdam 1960). C. WENDEL, in *Paulys Realenzyklopädie der klassischen Alterumswissenschaft,* ed. G. WISSOWA et al. 20.2 (1950) 2202–53. S. KUGÉAS, *Byzantinische Zeitschrift* 18 (1909) 106–146. C. WENDEL, *ibid.,* 40 (1940) 406–445. H. G. BECK, *Kirche und theologische Literatur im byzantinischen Reich* (Munich 1959) 686–687. M. RACKL, *Miscellanea Francesco Ehrle* 1 [*Studi e Testi* 37; 1924] 1–38, Gr. tr. Augustine. S. VALORIANI, *Atti dello VIII º Congresso internazionale di Studi Bizantini,* v.1 (Rome 1953) 234. A. PERTUSI, *Mélanges H. Grégoire,* v.3 (*Annuaire de l'Institut de philologie et d'histoire orientales* 11; 1951) 301–322.

[F. CHIOVARO]

PLASDEN, POLYDORE, ST.

London martyr of 1591; b. probably London, 1563; d. there, Dec. 10, 1591. He is thought to have been the son of a humble craftsman. After studies at the English College formerly at Douai, then at Rheims, he was ordained in Rome in 1586. In the same year he signed the oath "to proceed to England for the salvation of souls," and in 1588 he did so. Little is known of his movements in the next few years, but possibly he labored in Sussex. In November of 1591, he was in London with Bl. Edmund GENNINGS and was in the house of Swithun WELLS when agents of the English government discovered them during the celebration of Mass. Plasden and Gennings, as Roman priests, were tried and sentenced for high treason; the others were condemned for aiding and abetting them. During his trial, Plasden defended his priestly calling. Later, on the scaffold, he protested his loyalty to Queen Elizabeth while remaining faithful to his religious convictions. Sir Walter Raleigh, who supervised the execution, ordered leniency, directing that he be hanged until dead before the process of dismembering began. Plasden was beatified in 1929 and canonized on Oct. 25, 1970, as one of the martyrs of ENGLAND, SCOTLAND, AND WALES.

Feast: Dec. 10; Oct. 25; May 4.

Bibliography: R. CHALLONER, *Memoirs of Missionary Priests,* ed. J. H. POLLEN (rev. ed. London 1924). J. GENNINGS, *Life and Death of Ven. Edmund Gennings* (London 1887). *Publications of the Catholic Record Society* 5:131–133, 204–208. J. H. POLLEN, *Acts of English Martyrs* (London 1891) 98–126.

[A. M. C. FORSTER]

PLATO

One of the greatest of Greek philosophers; he incalculably influenced the nature and orientation of subsequent thought. Plato was born in Athens (428 or 427 B.C.), of aristocratic parents, during the Peloponnesian War. Originally, he was called Aristocles, and only later was given the name Plato (πλάτων, meaning broad), a sobriquet for which various reasons have been offered: his wide forehead, his robust physique, the breadth of his knowledge. He was both athlete and poet, excelling in the Isthmian games at Corinth and composing dramatic and lyric verse. The most decisive influence in Plato's commitment to philosophy and in his intellectual formation was the life-and-death devotion of SOCRATES to truth.

Plato, bronze bust sculpture.

After the demise of Socrates in 399, Plato withdrew temporarily from the political tumult of Athens and found refuge with the philosopher Euclid at Megara. Between 390 and 388 he traveled extensively in Greece, Egypt, and Italy to acquaint himself with the principal schools of that time and to broaden his culture. About 387 he returned to Athens and founded his famous school, the Academy. Through this institution, Plato intended not only to promote philosophy and science but also to affect politics vicariously. His supervision of the Academy was interrupted on two occasions (367 and 361), when he journeyed to Sicily with the hope of making Dionysius II a philosopher-king and his city Syracuse an ideal state; both attempts, however, failed (*Epist.* 7). Henceforth, Plato remained at Athens, devoting all his powers of thought to philosophizing, teaching, and writing at the Academy, until his death at the age of 80. Already under way was the war that would bring Greece under the domination of Philip of Macedonia.

Works and Chronology. The authenticity of the writings in the Platonic corpus has been a matter of dispute since antiquity. The genuineness of four dialogues is still in question: *Hippias Maior, Menexenus, Alcibiades I,* and *Epinomis;* the first two are probably genuine, but the others are most likely spurious. Modern scholars generally agree that 24 dialogues and at least two epistles are definitely the work of Plato; they have also established the order of composition of these works. The chronology of Plato's writings represents the gradual evolution of his philosophy through four stages.

Initial Socratic Period (399–388). The dialogues of Plato's youthful philosophical life, before the foundation of the Academy, re-create and vindicate the spirit and mission of Socrates. In these dialogues of inquiry, there is a systematic pursuit of the one Form or Idea common to similar moral phenomena in order to arrive at the definition of a particular politicoethical virtue, e.g., courage. This group of writings is notably anti-Sophist in inspiration. In a manner characteristic of Socrates's confession of ignorance, most of these dialogues end without reaching any definite conclusion, thus emphasizing the need of seeking further enlightenment. This period includes the *Apology, Crito, Euthyphro, Laches, Ion, Protagoras, Charmides,* and *Lysis*—all distinctly ethical dialogues.

Transitional Period (387–380). As his intellectual and literary powers advanced, Plato found his way to a personal explanation of vexing contemporary problems. In addition to intensifying his polemics against the SOPHISTS, he undertook the building of the Socratic concept into a metaphysical theory of Forms. Whereas the earlier dialogues are limited in their scope to one facet of virtue, the works of this transitional and formational period manifest a broadening and deepening of Plato's speculation concerning the greater questions of wisdom and the good life. Here are found the *Gorgias, Meno, Euthydemus, Hippias Minor, Hippias Maior, Cratylus*, and *Menexenus*. These represent the inchoative constructive stage of the Platonic mind and the beginnings of a systematic philosophy.

Mature Period (380–361). At the height of his genius, Plato fully evolved his ontological theory of Forms and expressed the ramifications of this doctrine in epistemology, psychology, ethics, politics, and aesthetics. In dialogues of criticism and application, he subjected his speculative teachings to new facts and difficulties arising from other points of view. This period of maturity embraces the *Symposium, Phaedo, Republic*, and *Phaedrus*. Of all the dialogues, the *Republic,* Plato's teaching of the ideal state, appears as the full development of his constructive powers.

Final Period (361–348 or 347). In the last period of his activity, Plato's dramatic power declined, but his critical acumen advanced. A lifetime of reflective experience, the appearance of different problems, social and political changes—all these impressed on Plato the need for further investigation and for a reconsideration of his philosophy. With brilliant intellectual apperception, he critically elaborated his metaphysics and epistemology, modified his politicoethical concepts, made greater use of logic, and discovered new interest in the mystery of the cosmos. Written in the final period of his life were the *Theaetetus, Parmenides, Sophist, Statesman, Philebus, Timaeus, Critias, Laws,* and *Epistles 7* and *8*. The continual development of Plato's thought through these periods indicates that he never achieved a completely rounded-off system; it is an unfinished symphony of philosophy.

Platonic Method. The Platonic method, in general, consists in an intellectual and moral conversion from particular, concrete sense phenomena to universal, abstract Forms. Motivated by Eros, an inborn love of good, man can purge himself of bodily desires and rise to a knowledge of true being (*Phaedo* 65–68). This conversion is accomplished in three different, but complementary ways, according to the object under consideration. First, on the occasion of experienced sensible things, the mind can formulate a hypothesis and logically deduce from it true conclusions. The mathematician, for example, proceeds from a hypothesis such as a triangle to a knowledge of the essence of this object. Second, moral truths are treated by way of myth, the exposition of a concept or event in poetic imagery. The eschatological myths in the *Gorgias* (523–527), *Phaedo* (107–114), and *Republic* (613–621) present the soul as immortal, free within the limits set by necessity, and responsible, under God's government, throughout all its transmigrations. Third, the supreme means in the soul's ascent to the highest principles is dialectic, which ''by the light of reason only, and without any assistance of sense'' (*Rep.* 532A), advances ''from Forms, through Forms, and in Forms she ends'' (*Rep.* 511C). The dialectic method is masterfully dramatized by the give-and-take conversation of the dialogues, the major part often and very appropriately being taken by Plato's dynamic spokesman, Socrates.

Teachings. Plato's primary intuition is Form, the rest of his philosophy being a function of this central constant. With the influx of other insights, Plato critically explicated the implications of Form and developed what scholars generally recognize as a dynamic, dichotomous dualism, pervading four dominant aspects of reality—the epistemological, the metaphysical, the psychological, and the politicoethical.

Epistemological Dualism. In his famous Allegory of the Cave and Simile of the Line (*Rep.* 509E–511, 514–517), Plato distinguished between universal knowledge and particular opinion. Since sense perception, on the one hand, concerns only continually changing, relative, shadowy images, it admits at most fallible opinion. True scientific knowledge, on the other hand, is oriented toward the stable, absolute, and universal properties of cognition realizable only in intellection (*Crat.* 440B, C). In this clear distinction between sensation and understanding, Plato exposed the Protagorean error of confusing the former with genuine knowledge and refuted the RELATIVISM of the Sophists. Socrates's quest for truth, then, was defended and justified by Plato's epistemology.

Metaphysical Dualism. Corresponding to the two kinds of cognition, Plato also distinguished two radically different entities: the object of understanding is absolute reality; that of sense perception is relative phenomena. Universal concepts have an objective reference to transcendent Forms (*Phaedo* 102B)—unalterable, universal, intelligible realities. Since reality is rational only so far as it is unchanging, then immutable, suprasensible Forms alone, e.g., Justice itself, are fully real and fully intelligible (*Phaedo* 65C, D, 100C, E; *Symp.* 210B, D). In this realm of true reality, there is a hierarchy of beings culminating in the Form of Forms, the Good—the paramount principle of intelligibility, unity, and order. According to Aristotle (*Meta.* 987b 14–988a 15), Plato taught later a mathematical dualism in which the One is conceived as the supreme principle of limit and the indeterminate great-and-small as the cause of plurality. This doctrine of ultimate principles does not imply, however, that Plato ever dropped the theory of the Ideas. The identification of the One and the Good, confirmed both by Aristotle and Aristoxenus, must be accepted as well founded.

The lesser pole of Plato's ontological dualism is the empirical object of perception—relative phenomena. Because fluctuating phenomena are neither truly real nor fully knowable, the cosmologist cannot attain an exact and altogether self–consistent explanation of the physical world, but must be satisfied with a probable account (*Tim.* 29D). Yet the reality present in phenomena Plato discerned in terms of a rational order and uniformity, pointing to something fully real and implying its dominating presence. Sensible things are relatively real and intelligible only so far as they participate in absolutely real and intelligible Forms. For instance, a flower "can be beautiful only in so far as it partakes of absolute beauty" (*Phaedo* 100C). The unparticipating is the ultimate *raison d'être* of the participating. Participation or imitation, therefore, is the bridge by which Plato spanned the Parmenidean realm of being, unity, and permanence, and the Heraclitean realm of becoming and plurality.

Psychology. Between the realm of Forms and the purely sensible world there are mathematical objects, existing on an intermediate level (Aristotle, *Meta.* 987b 14–18). There is also Soul: the world-soul, celestial souls, and human souls. Souls share in both realms: in the ideal world insofar as they are immortal and closely related to the intelligible, and in the sensible world insofar as they are living and moving. The starting point in Plato's reasoning to the existence of a world-soul is the orderly motion and harmony in the empirical world. Since the motionless exemplary Forms by themselves cannot explain their exemplification in things, Plato found it necessary to posit the existence of a superlatively intelligent agent—the Demiurge. This preeminent intelligence is called God and Father of the world. As the Creator of Soul he must be ranked on the level of intelligible Being, which, in Plato's hierarchy, is placed directly under the One or the Good. The Divine Craftsman introduced harmony and symmetry into the primitive chaos of disorderly motion by fashioning the world according to the eternal exemplars (*Soph.* 265C–266C). Modeling the world after the Ideal Living Creature (*Tim.* 30B, C), the Demiurge formed the cosmic body by conferring geometrical patterns on the primary qualities in the indefinite space-receptacle—earth, water, air, fire—after having first formed the cosmic soul for its function of animating, ruling, and unifying the vast bodily sphere. Together with the world-soul, the Demiurge created the stars and planets with their souls, and next the souls of men. Then, at his request, the "created gods" (i.e., the star-souls) created bodies for the human souls.

Man is composed of soul and body, the former being akin to Forms and the latter to corporeal phenomena. The soul exercises two basic functions: as self-moving, it is the source of life; and as consciousness, it is the principle of intellectual and moral operations. From a fine analysis of the inner conflicting tendencies in man, Plato concluded to three diverse principles in the human soul: (1) the appetitive part, unruly and amenable to the siren of pleasure; (2) the spirited, noble and prompt to honor and courage; (3) the rational, the "god within man," able to contemplate Forms, and as charioteer, to check and direct the impulses of the instinctive and spirited steeds for the good of man (*Rep.* 436–441; *Phaedrus* 246–247). Thus the human soul is tripartite.

Nevertheless, Plato's dualism passes sharply and deeply through his notion of the human soul. The irrational parts, like the body, are mortal, whereas the rational principle is immortal. The immortality of the rational soul is maintained in four main arguments: (1) Opposites generate opposites; as the living die, so the dead return to life (*Phaedo* 70–72). (2) As self-moving, the soul necessarily lives and survives death (*Phaedrus* 245C, E). (3) The soul is akin to the Forms that it contemplates; it is simple and imperishable (*Phaedo* 79D, E). (4) The soul, living in virtue of its essential participation in the Form, Life, can never share in the contradictory Form, Death; a dead soul is an impossibility (*Phaedo* 95–106; *Rep.* 608–611). In the cognitional dualism between reason and Forms, Plato linked the knower and the knowable by his theory of anamnesis, or reminiscence. The repeated experience of changing, relative, particular, sensible images is the occasion of the soul's recalling the stable, absolute, universal, intelligible Forms it once contemplated in a preexisting state, but that have been forgotten since its ingression into the body. Knowledge is basically recollection (*Meno* 82, 86; *Phaedrus* 246, 248).

Politicoethical Dualism. The speculative dualism of Plato finds its practical application and extension in his contrast between ideal values and phenomenal values. Platonic ethics is objectively oriented toward ideal values, primarily the Form, Good, as its supreme ontological goal. The ethos of man's life is to care for his soul (*Apol.* 29; *Phaedo* 114D, E), gradually liberating it from the bonds of the body that, like Prometheus unbound, it may freely wing its way to an ever-clearer vision of the Good and True and Beautiful—man's foremost subjective happiness. The essential means by which man participates in formal values is virtue. Virtue is knowledge, and consequently, teachable (*Meno* 87B–89C); with knowledge of good, ''no man voluntarily pursues evil'' (*Prot.* 358C). The virtues are many in one, different expressions of wisdom in diverse fields of activity. Wisdom is the rational charioteer of the soul, courage the rein of the spirited steed, and temperance the rein of the appetitive steed, while justice is their proper functioning, right order, and cooperation for the good of the whole soul (*Rep.* 428–441). Plato admitted a phenomenal value to relative goods, e.g., innocent pleasure and moderate emotions. Hence, Plato's ethics is tensely dualistic, inasmuch as it attempts a delicate and harmonious balance between man's irrational attraction to relative goods and his rational proclivity to absolute Good.

Plato's political theory unfolds in the *Republic, Statesman,* and *Laws,* as inseparably related to his ethics. The disorders and injustices of actual empirical city-states can be rectified only by reforming and reorganizing them after the archetypal City-State. The organization of the ideal State parallels the threefold structure of the human soul: (1) The lowest class, the numerous workers who provide the economic necessities, are marked by a desire for things of the senses and so are in particular need of temperance. (2) Higher in hierarchy are the guardians—their membership including also qualified women—who valiantly defend the state against hostilities within and without, and faithfully enforce the decisions handed down by the rulers. The ideal State requires that all their property, wives, and children be possessed in common, lest these auxiliaries be impeded in their singular purpose of serving the common interest of the state. Rulers, however, must exercise strict eugenic supervision of marriages for the good of the social organism. (3) The political counterpart of human reason is the superior class of rulers, the elite in knowledge, bravery, and patriotism, who wisely govern in the light of ideal values. When each individual performs his due function, and the lower classes are properly subordinated to the prudent ruler, justice prevails. The unshakeable basis of the just state is absolute Justice.

The most important institution in the transmission of culture and the maintenance of virtue is education. The state has the primary authority to educate its citizenry, even under compulsion. Education has two branches: gymnastics for the body; art, science, philosophy, and religion for the soul. Since art is an imitation of an imitation of true reality, and a creation inspired by the Muses but originating also from irrational forces in the artist, it must be conscientiously superintended by the magistrates of the state. The ideal State is open only to beautiful art—the representation of the true and good and enjoyable. Love of artistic beauty can lead the soul to the vision of Beauty itself.

Various historical states more or less approximate the ideal State. Measuring up least to the Form is tyranny, the lawless rule of a strong man whose reason is a slave to brutish passion and whose subjects are his slaves. Closer to the ideal is democracy, government by the unqualified masses without fixed standards, devotees of freedom and equality to the point of anarchy; weak and inefficient, it is the worst of all lawful governments and the best of all lawless ones. More perfect is oligarchy, rule of the affluent few for their own profit. Superior to plutocracy, or government by the wealthy, is timocracy, government by a militaristic minority who, though prizing honor and valor, are wanting in rational purpose. The ideal State is philosophical, a true polity in which one or more philosopher-kings, enlightened by abiding norms of reason, are the real statesmen piloting the ship of state on the right course of civilization for the good of all classes.

Conclusion. Plato was among the noblest embodiments of the ideal philosopher and his *Dialogues* contain one of the finest philosophies ever envisioned by the human mind. His all-pervading dualism is tense with inner opposition and difficulties; yet the poles of his thought are unified in a grand Olympian synthesis under his fundamental Zeus-like insight—Form. His Academy survived from 387 B.C. to A.D. 529—an enviable longevity. Even more important, his philosophy has persisted for more than 2,300 years, profoundly influencing such luminaries as ARISTOTLE, St. AUGUSTINE, St. THOMAS AQUINAS, and Alfred North WHITEHEAD, and prodigiously advancing the life and thought of Western culture.

See Also: PLATONISM; NEOPLATONISM; CAMBRIDGE PLATONISTS.

Bibliography: Life. PLATO, *Epistles,* tr. and ed. G. R. MORROW (Indianapolis 1962), see *Seventh Epistle.* DIOGENES LAERTIUS, *Lives of Eminent Philosophers,* tr. R. D. HICKS 2 v. (Loeb Classical Library; London-New York-Cambridge, Mass. 1925) 1:3.2, 4–6, 45. Editions and commentaries. PLATO, *Platonis opera,* tr. and ed. J. BURNET, 5 v. (Oxford 1945–46); *Dialogues,* tr. and ed. B. JOWETT, 4 v. (4th ed. Oxford 1953); *The Republic,* tr. and ed. F. M. CORNFORD (Oxford 1942); *Plato's Theory of Knowledge: The Theaetetus and the Sophist, id.* (New York 1957); *Plato's Cosmology: The Timaeus, id.* (New York 1957); *Plato and Parmenides: Parmenides' Way of Truth and Plato's Parmenides, id.* (New York 1957); *Phaedrus,* tr. and ed. R. HACKFORTH (Cambridge, Eng. 1952); *Phaedo, id.* (Cambridge, Eng. 1955); *Statesman,* tr. and ed. J. B. SKEMP (New Haven 1952); *Philebus and Epinomis,* tr. A. E. TAYLOR ed. R. KLIBANSKY et al. (New York 1956). A. E. TAYLOR, *A Commentary on Plato's Timaeus* (Oxford 1928). For translations of Plato's works, see volumes of the *Loeb Classical Library.* General studies. L. STEFANINI and G. SANTINELLO, *Enciclopedia Filosofica* 3:1411–44 (Venice-Rome 1957). R. DEMOS, *The Philosophy of Plato* (New York 1939). G. C. FIELD, *The Philosophy of Plato* (New York 1949). P. SHOREY, *What Plato Said* (Chicago 1933; repr. 1957). A. E. TAYLOR, *Plato: The Man and His Work* (6th ed. London 1949; repr. 1955). W. JAEGER, *Paideia: The Ideals of Greek Culture* (New York 1945–) v. 2–3. C. J. DE VOGEL, ed., *Greek Philosophy,* 3 v. (Leiden 1950–59). J. OWENS, *A History of Ancient Western Philosophy* (New York 1959). F. C. COPLESTON, *History of Philosophy* (Westminster, Md. 1946–) 1:127–265. Bibliographies. G. A. DE BRIE, ed. *Bibliographia philosophica 1934–1945* (Brussels 1950–) 45–65. H. CHERNISS, "Plato 1950–1957," *Lustrum* 4 (1959) 5–308; 5 (1960) 321–648.

[P. J. ASPELL]

PLATONISM

A term with a variety of meanings in the history of philosophy. In its original imposition, it refers to the doctrines of PLATO himself, and by extension includes the teachings of others who developed characteristic Platonic themes such as (1) the teaching on forms or ideas, with its accompanying absolute REALISM, emphasis on mathematical intelligibility, and mistrust of sense knowledge; (2) the accent on recollection and use of a priori method; (3) the doctrines of a demiurge, PARTICIPATION, WORLD SOUL, and the relative nonbeing of MATTER; (4) the notion of the human SOUL as immaterial and endowed with various powers and virtues; and (5) the concept of the GOOD and its associated ethical idealism, theory of the state, and theory of education.

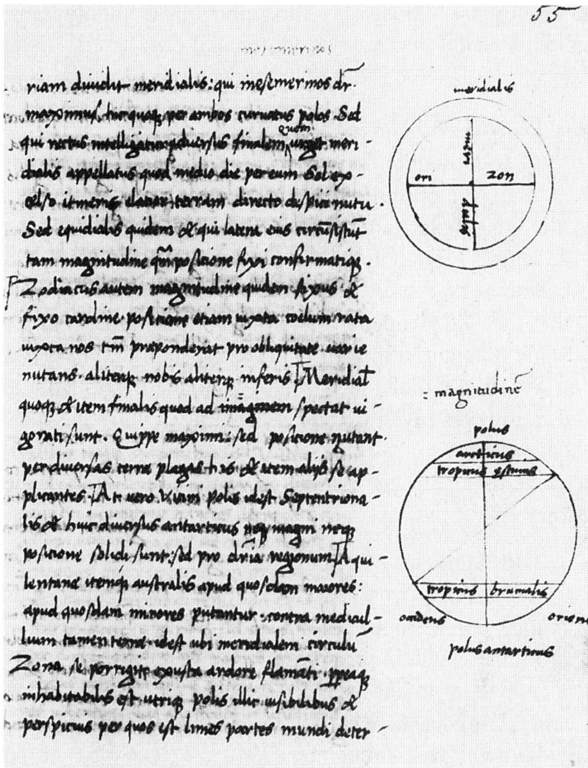

Manuscript page from Plato's "Timaeus," Latin translation of Greek, commentary by Calcidius, written in Italy, ca. 1500. Marginal diagrams depicting Platonic cosmology illustrate text. (MD Lat. 13, fol. 55, Charles Patterson Van Pelt Library, University of Pennsylvania).

In more specialized senses, Platonism refers first to the succession of philosophers of the Academy in Athens, and their associates, continuing—with some interruptions and possibly a loss of records—to the scholiarchate of Damascius, when an edict of the Emperor Justinian in 529 prohibited the teaching of philosophy in Athens. It is also used by some for Neoplatonism, although this is more commonly considered a separate philosophical movement closely related to Platonism. Among patristic, medieval, and modern scholars, the term is generally used to designate currents of thought of Platonic origin that flourished among the Greek and Latin Fathers, among medieval schoolmen, in the Platonic Academy of the Renaissance, or among the Cambridge Platonists. Not infrequently, Platonism has also influenced the elaboration of religious doctrines, and on this account is variously called Jewish, Islamic, or Christian.

This article is concerned mainly with the meaning of Platonism in the more specialized senses and is divided into two parts: the first treats of Plato's disciples and the schools they founded, under the title of Early and Middle Platonism; the second considers the use made of Platonic doctrines by Christian philosophers and theologians, under the title of Christian Platonism.

Early and Middle Platonism

Plato's thought continued to exert its influence after his death, particularly in the Academy he had founded. Although scholars are not unanimous on the status of the Academy's development, they usually speak of the Old Academy and the Middle and New Academies. Doctrinally, the Old Academy more or less maintained Plato's teachings intact, although it placed special emphasis on the Pythagorean elements that it contained. The Middle Academy was given over to SKEPTICISM, while the New Academy was more eclectic in its tendencies as it sought to develop a Platonic position in opposition to that of the Stoics (*see* STOICISM).

Old Academy. Speusippus (*c.* 407–339 B.C.), head of the Academy from 347 to 339 B.C., wrote numerous memoirs and dialogues of which only fragments remain. Favorinus related in the second book of his *Memorabilia* that Aristotle purchased Speusippus's writings for three talents (Diogenes Laertius, 4.5). His successor as head of the Academy was Xenocrates (396–314 B.C.), who served from 339 to 314 B.C. Xenocrates's writings were treasured in the Academy and presumed lost when the building was destroyed by fire in Sulla's siege and sack of Athens in 86 B.C. Polemon was then head of the Academy from 314 to 269 B.C.; he and Crantor were fellow pupils of Xenocrates.

A comparison between the teaching of these men and that of Plato is contained in the *Metaphysics* of ARISTOTLE (1028b 19–27). There the Stagirite says that Plato posited two kinds of substance—the forms and the mathematicals, and also a third kind, the substance of sensible bodies; that Speusippus posited several more kinds of substance, starting with the One, and assumed that there was a principle for each kind—one for numbers, one for configurations, and another for souls; and that other philosophers, presumably followers of Xenocrates, held that forms and numbers have the same nature, and that other things, e.g., lines and planes, and eventually the substance of the world and sensible bodies, are derived from these.

Middle and New Academies. Crates, pupil of Polemon, was head of the Academy in the 3d century B.C. One of his pupils was Bion; another was Arcesilaus, who was also a pupil of Crantor and the first to reject the traditional doctrine of Plato in favor of skepticism, being thereby named the founder of the Middle Academy by Diogenes Laertius (4.28). Lacydes was his successor (*c.* 242–216 B.C.), and, for Diogenes, founder of the New Academy (4.59).

Cicero has given a history of the chief persons in the New Academy (*Acad. prior.* 2.1–16). He starts his account with Arcesilaus, teacher of Lacydes, and says that Lacydes taught Evander, and Evander, Hegesinus. Carneades, "fourth in line from Arcesilaus," was then the pupil of Hegesinus, and served as head of the school for a long time, living to be 85 years old. Clitomachus succeeded him as head in 129 B.C. Then came Philo of Larissa (*c.* 140–*c.* 77 B.C.), and then Antiochus of Ascalon (*c.* 128–68 B.C.), both teachers of Cicero (*De nat. deor.* 1.6). Among the Roman Academicians, in addition to Cicero, should also be enumerated Atticus and Varro.

CICERO (106–43 B.C.) himself acknowledged that he was an Academic (*De nat. deor.* 1.11), and stated that sufficient reason for his allegiance had been given in the four books of his *Academics;* this survives in two editions, both incomplete, the first known as the *Lucullus,* and the second as the *Catulus,* after the leading interlocutor in each. Cicero also named the *ambulatio,* or place of exercise, in the lower level of his Tusculan villa near Rome the "Academia" (*Disp. tusc.* 2.9; 3.7). His *Tusculan Disputations, On the Nature of the Gods, Concerning the Last Object of Desire and Aversion, Laws,* and *Republic* are his important philosophical writings. At the end of the sixth book of the *Republic* (6.9–2.9) is a passage known as "Scipio's Dream," reminiscent of the story of Er at the end of Plato's *Republic* (614B–621D), upon which MACROBIUS commented at the end of the 4th century. Titus Pomponius Atticus (99–32 B.C.) was a fellow student and lifelong friend of Cicero; he edited the letters Cicero sent him, and these reflect his own philosophical opinions.

Marcus Terentius Varro (116–27 B.C.) also studied at Athens under Antiochus of Ascalon. A voluminous writer, he is reported as saying that up to the day he had entered upon his 12th hebdomad of years he had written 70 hebdomads of books, many of which were lost when his library was plundered at the time of his proscription. Among his books was one called *Images or Hebdomads,* fragments of which survive. His *Logistoricus,* a collection of philosophical and historical treatises, is lost.

Both Varro and Cicero were eclectic philosophers. Apart from his concern with the cult of the State, Varro was influenced by the number mysticism of NEOPYTHAGOREANISM and also by the teachings of the CYNICS. Cicero himself was hardly an original thinker, but his flair for expression enabled him to transmit a variety of Greek doctrines to Roman readers. His arguments against skepticism were not speculative but practical and based mainly on his personal intuition of moral consciousness. In his ethical teaching, he borrowed elements from the Stoics and from the Peripatetics, while in matters of religion he urged belief in divine providence and the immortality of the soul.

Middle Platonism. The Middle Platonists, as opposed to the earlier members of the Academies, were a group of writers of Greek who flourished from the beginning of the reign of Hadrian in A.D. 117 to the end of the reign of Marcus Aurelius Antoninus in 180. They continued the interest of the New Academy in eclecticism, while attempting to effect a fundamental synthesis between Platonism and Peripatetic thought, using Aristotelian logic to this end. Again, they were influenced by the mysticism of the Neo-Pythagoreans. In keeping with the practice of the times, they commented more than their predecessors on the Platonic *Dialogues,* and in so doing sought to develop an orthodox Platonist doctrine in opposition to the Peripatetics and the Stoics. The resulting tensions between orthodoxy and eclecticism left this intermediate stage of Platonism in a state of flux, from which a true synthesis was to be effected only with the emergence of Neoplatonism at the end of the middle period.

Plutarch of Chaeronea in Boeotia (*c.* A.D. 46–120) is the best known of the Middle Platonists, chiefly for his *Parallel Lives of the Greeks and the Romans.* His principal philosophical work is the *Moralia.* The 13th book contains Platonic questions, especially about the origin of the soul as expounded in the *Timaeus* and arguments against the Stoics. The 12th book includes a short treatise (945E–955C) dedicated to Favorinus (A.D. 80–150), from the city of Arelatum (Arles) on the Rhone River, who himself wrote on the tropes of Pyrrho.

Tiberius Claudius Herodes Atticus (A.D. 101–177), a student and protégé of Favorinus, also studied the doctrines of Plato with Calvisius Taurus of Tyre (2d century A.D.). The latter was scholiarch of the Academy in Athens during the rule of Hadrian and Antoninus Pius. His probable successor as scholiarch was Atticus, an Athenian philosopher, who is known to have written a commentary on the *Timaeus,* and another treatise quoted at length without title by Eusebius Pamphili of Caesarea (*c.* A.D. 260–399), both works surviving in fragments.

At Pergamum in the 2d century A.D. influence was exerted by a Platonist named Gaius (b. *c.* A.D. 75). In A.D. 144 Galen (*c.* 130–*c.* 200) attended the lectures of a "pupil of Gaius" at Pergamum, and in 151 or 152 went to Smyrna to make the acquaintance of the Platonist Albinus. The catalog in *Codex Parisinus Graecus 1962* mentions that Albinus edited the lectures of Gaius on the doctrines of Plato. All Gaius's writings have been lost, although some of his treatises were among those read in the school of Plotinus. Two writings of Albinus survive: a short prologue to the *Dialogues* of Plato, the introductory lecture of his course on Plato; and a much longer epitome of the doctrines of Plato, entitled *Didaskalikos* and usually published under the name of Alcinous. An unnamed Platonist, probably another pupil of Gaius, wrote a commentary on the *Theaetetus* that is extant (*Papyr. 9782*). Characteristic of the school of Gaius is esteem for the logic of Aristotle, in that this offered a respectable alternative to the tropes of Pyrrho.

Diogenes Laertius (3d century A.D.), it should be noted, has been thought an Epicurean because of his life of EPICURUS, which constitutes Book 10 of the *Lives and Opinions of Eminent Philosophers* and ends with 40 major maxims of Epicurus. However, Diogenes spoke approvingly of "an enthusiastic Platonist" (3.47), devoted Book 3 of the *Lives* to Plato, and in Book 4 wrote lives, many of high literary merit, of the important persons of the Academy from Speusippus to Clitomachus.

It is impossible to detect any systematic unity in the teachings of the Middle Platonists. Their attempts at synthesis, however, were incorporated into the movement that was later to be known as Neoplatonism, which had its proximate origin in Alexandria during the 3d century A.D. and its more remote beginnings at Apamea in Syria in the writings of the Stoic philosopher Poseidonius (*c.* 135–*c.* 51 B.C.) and the Neo-Pythagorean Numenius (2d century A.D.). For further details of this movement, *see* NEOPLATONISM.

Christian Platonism

Neoplatonism, in the view of one historian, "was the last breath, the last flower, of ancient pagan philosophy; but in the thought of St. Augustine it became the first page of Christian philosophy" (F. C. Copleston, *History of Philosophy* [Westminster, Md., 1946–75] 1:506). Apart from influences that are now recognized as Neoplatonist, however, Christian writers found much in the older Platonism that helped them in their understanding of Christian theology and much that helped them answer philosophical questions without compromising their theology. They found evidence for the unity of God, preexistence of the forms of things in the mind of God, creation of the world, providence, God the true and highest Good, memory as a way to know God, the virtuous life, and the spirituality and immortality of the human soul. Their main points of criticism, though not the only ones, are doctrines that they found to be irreconcilable with Christian theology.

Each period in history in which there occurs a movement identifiable as Christian Platonism is marked by a confrontation of Christian theologians with some newly available Platonic materials. As already noted, these periods were not restricted to reaction to the works of Plato;

in most cases they showed involvement with writings other than Plato's, especially those more recently classified as Neoplatonic. For purposes here, they may be divided roughly into periods corresponding to those of the Greek and Latin Fathers and the Middle Ages, and the special movements of the Platonic Academy, the Cambridge Platonists, and modern Platonism.

Greek and Latin Fathers. The Greek apologists during the reign of the Antonines were educated in the pagan schools of philosophy. They used their knowledge to point out to the emperors, themselves philosophers, that Christian doctrine was reconcilable with philosophy, and therefore not to be condemned, and also to furnish an answer to questions about God, life, and death, to which philosophers had found no satisfactory solution. ARISTIDES, a ''philosopher of Athens,'' wrote an apology to Hadrian (117–138), while JUSTIN MARTYR wrote one to Antoninus Pius (138–161) and another to Marcus Aurelius Antoninus (161–180) and his imperial partner, Lucius Verus (161–169). ATHENAGORAS, ''the Athenian, a philosopher and Christian,'' addressed his *Embassy for the Christians* to Marcus Aurelius Antoninus and his son, Lucius Aurelius Commodus (161–192). These apologies were written in Greek and are extant.

In Alexandria Christian scholars adapted Platonic thought to religious instruction and scriptural exegesis. Titus Flavius Clemens, or CLEMENT OF ALEXANDRIA, taught in the Christian catechetical school. He knew Greek philosophy and considered Plato to be the greatest of philosophers (*Paedagogus* 2.11). In his *Exhortation to the Greeks* he showed the acuteness, and yet the limitations, of the teachings of philosophers on the nature of God (6.59P–61P; cf. also *Miscellanies* 1.14). His pupil was ORIGEN, of whom EUSEBIUS quotes Porphyry as saying that he ''was most celebrated, and is still celebrated by the writings that he has left,'' and that ''he was always in company with Plato,'' but also read works of other philosophers (*Hist. eccl.* 6.19).

Somewhat more than a century later, after PLOTINUS and PORPHYRY, several of the Greek Fathers in Cappadocia continued the work of instruction in homilies. Thus GREGORY OF NYSSA wrote a dialogue *De anima et resurrectione,* modeled on Plato's *Phaedo,* in which Gregory's sister on her deathbed states the Christian doctrine of resurrection and of the restoration of the world (13). He said, after Plotinus, that the human mind is capable of direct experience of God, ''a divine and sober inebriation'' (*Beatitudes* 6; *In Canticum Canticorum* 10). About the same time, PALLADIUS (fl. 408) modeled his *Dialogue concerning the Life of Chrysostom* on Plato's *Phaedo;* and Methodius, the *Symposium* or *A Treatise on Chastity* on Plato's *Symposium.* Methodius wrote an answer, no longer extant, to Porphyry's attacks on the Christians. Under Porphyry's influence, NEMESIUS OF EMESA (fl. *c.* 400) wrote the *Nature of Man,* which was available in the Middle Ages in a Latin translation of Alfanus I, archbishop of Salerno 1058–85, under the title *Prennon Fisicon* (*Codex Abrincensis Bibl. Municipalis 221,* saec. XII).

In the Latin West, the predominant influences on Christian writers were Plato's *Timaeus* and Porphyry's *Isagoge* or introduction to Aristotle's logic. Cicero had translated the *Timaeus* in 45 or 44 B.C. after he had written the *Academics.* Four centuries later, CALCIDIUS translated the *Timaeus* anew, and wrote an elaborate commentary on it, dedicated to Ossius (*c.* 256–357 or 358), bishop of Cordoba. MARIUS VICTORINUS translated the *Isagoge* into Latin before 355, the year of his conversion to Christianity late in life, and also parts, if not all, of Plotinus's *Enneads.* AUGUSTINE OF HIPPO told the story of Victorinus's conversion as he had heard it from Simplicianus (*Conf.* 8.2–5).

The scene of the confrontation of the Latin Fathers with Platonism was in northern Italy: at Milan, where Augustine listened to Ambrose's homilies, and about 20 miles farther south at Pavia, where BOETHIUS was imprisoned. Ambrose later worked his homilies into treatises, some of which, notably the *Hexameron* and the *Funeral Orations,* indicate the use of Plotinus's ''On the Beautiful'' (*Enn.* 1.6). Augustine himself mentions in his *City of God* some books of Platonists he had read: Apuleius, *The God of Socrates* (8.14); Porphyry, *De philosophia ex oraculis haurienda* (19.23) and the letter to the Egyptian Anebo (10.11). In one chapter he lists those whom he means by the term ''Platonists'' (8.12): Plato, Speusippus, Xenocrates, Plotinus, Iamblichus, Porphyry, and Apuleius.

Anicius Manlius Severinus Boethius held high governmental positions under Theodoric the Ostrogoth (*c.* 454–526) but fell into disfavor. While imprisoned at Pavia, he wrote the *Consolation of Philosophy,* which includes autobiographical details. In his commentary on Aristotle's *On Interpretation* (comm. 3, proem.), he says that it is his intention to make available to his countrymen translations of all the works of Plato and Aristotle and a reconciliation of the seemingly different doctrines of the two. (*See* PATRISTIC PHILOSOPHY.)

Medieval Platonism. The Benedictine Abbey of SAINT-DENIS in the environs north of Paris, burial place of many kings of France, is the site of the next major development in Christian Platonism. Michael Bekkos, ''The Stammerer,'' emperor at Constantinople, sent a copy of the Greek writings of Dionysius the Areopagite (*Codex Parisiensis Bibl. Nat. grec. 437*) to Louis the Pious (778–840), son of Charlemagne and emperor in the

West, who received it at Compiègne in 827 and deposited it in the Abbey of Saint-Denis, where HILDUIN was abbot. Hilduin, on orders from Louis, translated the writings into Latin with the help of several collaborators (825–835). A few years later, in the reign of Charles the Bald, king of France from 840 to 877, JOHN SCOTUS ERIUGENA made, on the king's order, a new translation (*c.* 867) from the same manuscript. These writings consisted of four treatises: *On the Divine Names, On the Celestial Hierarchy, On the Ecclesiastical Hierarchy,* and *On Mystical Theology,* and ten letters, with an eleventh letter that Hilduin wrote and included. Their author, PSEUDO-DIONYSIUS, in effect presented summaries or quotations from PROCLUS (411–485): *Elements of Theology* (2.9–10), *Ten Doubts concerning Providence* (4.1–4), *On Providence and Fate* (4.15–17), *On the Subsistence of Evil* (4.18–35). He also showed the conformity of the doctrines to Sacred Scripture.

In the 12th century an interest in Platonism was maintained in the cathedral schools of CHARTRES, a town about 55 miles southwest of Paris. The chief Platonic document was the *Timaeus* in the partial translation of Calcidius (17A–53C), together with his commentary. JOHN OF SALISBURY was chronicler in his *Metalogicon.* The sequence of chancellors of the schools in the period was: BERNARD OF CHARTRES, GILBERT DE LA PORRÉE, and THIERRY OF CHARTRES. The first named was called by John of Salisbury ''the foremost Platonist of our time'' (*Metalogicon,* 4.35); he explained Porphyry (4.35), followed Plato in the doctrine of ideas (2.17), and tried to reconcile the teaching of Plato and Aristotle, ''a vain effort to reconcile in death ones who had disagreed in life'' (2.17).

WILLIAM OF CONCHES, ''most accomplished grammarian since Bernard of Chartres'' (*Metalogicon* 1.5), wrote a commentary on the *Timaeus,* of which fragments survive. He identified the ''soul of the world'' with the Holy Spirit. The *Timaeus* was read in the faculty of arts in Paris, along with explanations from his commentary, until 1255 or earlier, when it was superseded in the official curriculum by the works of Aristotle.

Several Latin translations of Plato and Proclus, from the Greek, were made in Sicily in the middle of the 12th century. Although they survive in a dozen manuscripts, they were known by few scholars before the Renaissance. Their production was a result of the enterprise of HENRICUS ARISTIPPUS, a Greek in the service of the king of Sicily. Henricus began a translation of Plato's *Phaedo* into Latin at the siege of Benevento in the spring of 1156 and completed it a short time later at Palermo; he also translated the *Meno* between 1154 and 1160. These are the only dialogues of Plato that name an Aristippus, and each has the name in the beginning of the dialogue (*Phaedo,* 59C; *Meno,* 70B).

Thus, toward the beginning of the 13th century a considerable collection of Platonic writings in Latin had been assembled. It included Calcidius's work on the *Timaeus;* works by Augustine, Boethius, Dionysius, al-KINDĪ, ALFARABI, and AVICENNA; Eriugena's *De divisione naturae,* the *LIBER DE CAUSIS*, and the *Fons Vitae* of AVICEBRON. The *Phaedo* and *Meno* of Plato and the *Elementatio physica* of Proclus had also been translated.

This material had been exploited by theologians at the Abbey of Saint-Denis, particularly by SUGER OF SAINT-DENIS; at the Abbey of Saint-Victor, by HUGH OF SAINT-VICTOR; at Cîteaux, where ALAN OF LILLE remonstrated with the Albigenses; and at Toledo in the original writings of DOMINIC GUNDISALVI. The wealth of material and its wide dispersion led to the use of it in a variety of ways. As a result, the Platonism of the 13th century was a many-sided jewel, with facets that were labeled Augustinian, Avicennian, Franciscan, Dionysian, Albertist, and mystical. (*See* AUGUSTINIANISM; SCHOLASTICISM.)

An important achievement toward the end of the century was the translation of Proclus from the Greek by WILLIAM OF MOERBEKE. The latter's translation of the *Elements of Theology* in 1268 was taken by St. THOMAS AQUINAS as the occasion for his commentary on the *Liber de Causis* and for a treatise *De substantius separatis.* Aquinas's commentary is practically also a commentary on the *Elements of Theology.* Before Thomas's death in 1274, William made a partial translation of Proclus's *Commentary on the Timaeus,* and in February of 1280 he completed at Corinth, where he was archbishop from 1278, the translation of the ''three little works'' that traditionally were together since the days of Dionysius: *Ten Doubts concerning Providence* (February 4), *On Providence and Fate and That which is in our Power, to Theodorus, the Mechanist* (February 14), and *On the Subsistence of Evil* (February 21). William also completed the translation of Proclus's commentary on the *Parmenides* just before his death at Corinth in 1285 or 1286 and before he could send a copy to his friend, Henry (Bate) of Mecheln, as he had promised. These translations were in harmony with the metaphysical disposition of St. ALBERT THE GREAT. Their influence was felt where his was greatest, among the German Dominicans.

Platonic Academy. In 1439 Gemistos PLETHON came from Mistra in Greece to Italy to attend the Council of Florence as a representative of the Eastern Orthodox Church. He met Cosimo de' Medici (1389–1464), leading citizen of Florence, who was so attracted by his enthusiasm for Plato's philosophy that he decided to have young Marsilio FICINO, native of Figline near Florence, trained by Plethon in philosophy and Greek with a view to translating Plato's complete works into Latin. Cosimo founded the Platonic Academy in 1459 in Florence and made Marsilio its first director.

Marsilio completed the translation of Plato, a translation of the *Enneads* of Plotinus, of Albinus's *Didaskalikos,* and of Proclus's *Elementatio physica, Elements of Theology, Hymns,* and part of the *Commentary on the First Alcibiades.* An original work of his, *Platonic Theology* (1482), was dedicated to Lorenzo de' Medici (1449–92).

Cardinal BESSARION was a pupil of Plethon and his defender *(In calumniatorem Platonis),* from charges made in George of Trebizond's (1396–1484) comparative study of Aristotle and Plato, that Plethon's philosophy was unchristian and that it was a new religion, neither Christian nor Muslim, but Platonic and heathen. Bessarion also defended Plethon in *De natura et arte* against Theodorus Gaza's (*c.* 1400–75) *De fato.*

Giovanni PICO DELLA MIRANDOLA proposed in 1486 his readiness to defend in a public disputation in Rome 900 theses; he based 55 of them on Proclus's *Platonic Theology.* Later he came to Florence and joined the Academy. He wrote *Of Being and Unity* (1492), part of a prospective treatise on the harmony of Plato and Aristotle.

In the early 16th century, a translation into Latin, perhaps the first, of the *Theology of Aristotle* was made from the Arabic by Francesco Rosi of Ravenna, putting it into Greek at Damascus, and Pier Niccolo Castellani, putting the Greek into Latin in Rome, where the Latin text was published in 1519. Fifty years later, Jacques Charpentier (1521–74) designated the earlier translation as bad, corrected it, and published the revision with notes in Paris in 1571. A translation by Geoffrey Lewis from the Arabic into English about 1959 was the occasion for Paul Henry's (1906–) establishing the work as that of al-Kindī, who excerpted it in large part from the *Enneads* of Plotinus.

Spiritus Martinus Cuneas made a Latin translation of Proclus's *Elementatio physica* (Paris 1542). Francesco Patrizzi translated the *Elementatio physica* and *Elements of Theology* into Latin (Ferrara 1583). Aemilius Portus (1550–1612) had his Latin translation of the *Platonic Theology* and the *Elements of Theology* published posthumously alongside the Greek text in Hamburg in 1618.

Giordano BRUNO and Jakob BÖHME were influenced by the writings of the Platonists; the former especially by Plotinus and Raymond LULL, the latter by Proclus and NICHOLAS OF CUSA.

Cambridge Platonists. In the 17th century, a group of Christian philosophers, most of them at the University of Cambridge, united in opposition to corpuscular physics and the mechanism of Thomas HOBBES as appropriate foundations for philosophy. They sought to reconcile science and religion in a Platonic framework and to establish ethics as law of nature. Their founder was Benjamin Whichcote (1609–83). The chief members were Ralph Cudworth (1617–88), Richard Cumberland (1631–1718), Joseph Glanvill (1636–80), Henry More (1614–87), and John Norris (1657–1711). *See* CAMBRIDGE PLATONISTS.

G. W. LEIBNIZ developed his philosophy in conscious opposition to the Cambridge Platonists, as he said in his *Discourse on Metaphysics* (10). He did not thereby accept a mechanist approach but simply pointed out that there was much more to Plato than the doctrines of world soul, subsistence of the ideas, and purification of the soul. He preferred Plato's teachings on virtue, justice, and the state; on the art of defining and classifying concepts; and on knowledge of the eternal verities and the innate principles of the mind.

Anthony Ashley Cooper, third earl of Shaftesbury (1671–1713), styled Lord Ashley from January of 1683, was sympathetic to the Cambridge Platonists. In 1698 he published the first edition of the *Sermons of Dr. Whichcote,* for which he wrote the preface; in *The Moralists: A Philosophical Rhapsody,* published in 1709, he spoke of Cudworth as ''that Pious and Learned man'' (2.3).

Jean Le Clerc (1657–1736), in his capacity as publisher, was in correspondence with Cudworth, Leibniz (whose philosophy he did not approve), Shaftesbury, and John LOCKE. He had great influence through his *Bibliothèque universelle et historique* (25 v. Amsterdam 1686–93), begun with J. C. de la Croze; *Bibliothèque choisie* (28 v. Amsterdam 1703–13); and *Bibliothèque ancienne et moderne* (29 v. Amsterdam 1714–26). In volumes 6 and 7 of *Bibliothèque choisie* he gave a sympathetic exposition of Cudworth's philosophy.

Modern Platonism. Unique among moderns is the philosophical position of Thomas Taylor, ''the Platonist'' (1758–1835). He abjured the Christianity of his day, openly avowed belief in the Greek gods, and wrote as a religious exercise hymns in their worship. He translated the complete works of Aristotle into English; and, with Floyer Sydenham (1710–87), the complete works of Plato. His chief interest was in the later Platonists, whose doctrine he approvingly designated, in their words, ''the Platonic theology.'' He translated much of Plotinus, Porphyry, Apuleius, Iamblichus, and Proclus.

The Platonism of the recent past is closely related to Platonic studies. Thus Victor COUSIN published unedited works of Proclus. G. F. Creuzer (1771–1858) edited Proclus and Plotinus. Clemens Baeumker edited Platonic writings of the Middle Ages. Constantin Ritter (1859–1936) edited Plato. Edward Caird (1835–1908) and F. M. Cornford (1874–1943) were interested in the evolution of theology in Greek philosophy. Charles Huit (1845–1914) and Ernst Hoffmann (1880–1952) took a scholarly interest in the history of Platonism.

Other names that must be mentioned are George Burges (1786–1864), George Grote (1794–1871), Benjamin Jowett (1817–93), Eduard Zeller (1814–1908), Walter Pater (1839–94), Charles Bigg (1840–1908), Thomas Whittaker (1856–1935), Stephen MacKenna (1872–1934), A. E. Taylor (1869–1945), William Temple (1881–1944), Émile Bréhier (1876–1952), Wincenty Lutoslawski (1863–1954), W. R. INGE, and C. S. LEWIS.

In the United States, a group of enthusiasts fostered Platonic studies in the Midwest as an antidote to the preoccupation with science and an alternative to Hegelianism. Their inspiration was Thomas Taylor, whose writings they carefully collected, but the spirit of their philosophy was consciously that of R. W. EMERSON and the Concord School. Leaders in the group were H. K. Jones (1818–1903) of Jacksonville, Ill., ''the Athens of the West,'' and T. M. Johnson (1851–1919) of Osceola, Mo. They associated with Thomas Davidson (1840–1900), Alexander Wilder (1823–1908), and K. S. Guthrie (1871–1940), translators of Platonic writings into English.

At the universities, Paul Shorey (1857–1934) and P. E. More (1864–1937) worked mostly with Plato; E. K. Rand (1871–1945), with Cicero and Boethius; C. S. PEIRCE, Josiah ROYCE, and A. N. WHITEHEAD with human values in a universe of science.

See Also: PLATO; NEOPLATONISM; SCHOLASTICISM; AUGUSTINIANISM.

Bibliography: F. UEBERWEG, *Grundriss der Geschichte der Philosophie* (Berlin 1932–28) 1:341–347, 513–556, 590–655 with bibliog. E. ZELLER, *Die Philosophie der Griechen,* 3 v. in 6 (5th–7th ed. Leipzig 1920–23). F. W. A. MULLACH, *Fragmenta philosophorum graecorum,* 3 v. (Paris 1881–83) 3:51–203. H. DÖRRIE, *Die Religion in Geschichte und Gegenwart* (Tübingin 1957–65) 5:411–415. F. W. BUSSELL, *The School of Plato: Its Origin, Development, and Revival Under the Roman Empire* (London 1896). R. E. WITT, *Albinus and the History of Middle Platonism* (Cambridge, Eng. 1937). P. MERLAN, *From Platonism to Neoplatonism* (2d ed. The Hague 1960). T. WHITTAKER, *The Neo-Platonists: A Study in the History of Hellenism* (2d ed. Cambridge, Eng. 1928). É. H. GILSON, *History of Christian Philosophy in the Middle Ages* (New York 1955) 11–128, 139–153, 250–294, 327–361, 431–471 with bibliog. R. ARNOU, *Dictionnaire de théologie catholique* (Paris 1903–50) 12.2: 2258–2392. J. HIRSCHBERGER, *Lexikon für Theologie und Kirche* (Freiburg 1957–65) 8:555–558. C. BIGG, *The Christian Platonists of Alexandria,* ed. F. E. BRIGHTMAN (rev. ed. Oxford 1913). M. P. GARVEY, *Saint Augustine: Christian or Neo-Platonist?* (Milwaukee, Wis. 1939). R. KLIBANSKY, *The Continuity of the Platonic Tradition During the Middle Ages* (London 1939). J. KOCH, *Platonismus im Mittelalter* (Kölner Universitätsreden 4; Krefeld 1948); ''Augustinischer und dionysischer Neuplatonismus und das Mittelalter,'' *Kant-Studien* 48 (1956–57) 117–133. E. HOFFMANN, *Platonismus und christliche Philosophie,* ed. H. G. GADAMER, et al. (Zurich 1961). R. J. HENLE, *Saint Thomas and Platonism* (The Hague 1956). M. GRABMANN, *Mittelalterliches Geistesleben,* 3 v. (Munich 1926–56). C. BAEUMKER, ''Der Platonismus im Mittelalter (1916),'' *Beiträge zur Geschichte der Philosophie und Theologie des Mittelalters* 25.1–2 (1927) 139–179; ''Mittelalterlicher und Renaissance Platonismus,'' *ibid.* 180–193. N. A. ROBB, *Neoplatonism of the Italian Renaissance* (London 1935). F. MASAI, *Pléthon et le platonisme de Mistra* (Paris 1956). P. O. KRISTELLER, *Renaissance Thought* (New York 1961). E. CASSIRER, *The Platonic Renaissance in England,* tr. J. P. PETTEGROVE (Edinburgh 1953). P. SHOREY, *Platonism: Ancient and Modern* (Berkeley, Calif. 1938). P. R. ANDERSON, *Platonism in the Midwest* (Philadelphia, Pa. 1963).

[J. O. RIEDL]

PLEASURE

A state of gratification, as opposed to pain or sorrow. The moralist usually associates this state with a situation of repose in a conative function and relates it to an object. Thus Aristotle considered pleasure to be a ''certain motion of the soul and a sensible establishing thereof all at once, in keeping with the nature of a thing'' (*Rhet.* 1369b33). Aquinas understood this to mean that pleasure is a passion of the soul, an actuation of the animal appetite arising from an apprehension of sense (*Summa theologiae* 1a2ae, 31.1). But pleasure may be taken more widely to include the satisfaction of the spiritual appetite, or will, arising from the contemplation of truth.

It follows from what has been said that for pleasure in the subjective sense four things are necessary: first, an appetite for the pleasant; second, something pleasant to satisfy the appetite; third, the union of the appetite and its object; and fourth, the perception of this union. Whenever these conditions are verified, there is pleasure.

Kinds of Pleasure. Pleasure is either sensible or intellectual. Sensible pleasure results from the gratification of some sense. Sensible pleasure has been called the feeling-aspect of a satisfying experience. Although it is neither feeling nor sensation but something attached to the experience, it means for the moralist the repose of the sense object in its proper object. Of these sensible pleasures the keenest one is that of the pleasure of touch; the highest and most intellectually useful is the pleasure of sight (*Summa theologiae* 1a2ae, 31.6).

Intellectual pleasure is spiritual, since it follows on the satisfaction of a spiritual nature and its appetite. This type of pleasure resides in the will and results from the possession of the truth. Special synonyms for it are joy, gladness, and delight.

Pleasure and Man's Final End. The view that pleasure is man's final end, and therefore, the right and proper motive of all human activity, has been held for centuries by various hedonistic schools of philosophy. These schools got their name from the Greek word for pleasure, ἡδονή. (*See* HEDONISM.) The fallacy latent in all forms of hedonism results from failure to distinguish pleasure as an end in itself and pleasure as the accompaniment of possession of a valued object which is the end. Pleasure, although subjective, depends partly upon the object that is ''pleasant'' as having a worth or goodness of its own. If pleasure is viewed as an end in itself, to which the object is made only a means, pleasure is ultimately found to be only a chimera.

It is nevertheless true that there is a sense in which pleasure is associated with the goal of life. There is no happiness without it. Pleasure accompanies and rewards all worthy achievement. It is the afterglow, the final repose of a will that has achieved its final end. But it is not itself the final end, the supreme good that is man's beatitude. ''What matters most'' Aquinas insisted, ''is the object that gives pleasure'' (*C. gent.* 2.26).

Moral Evaluation. While hedonists thought of pleasure as always good, that there is nothing right but pleasure, nothing wrong but pain, Stoics thought of it as always bad. For the hedonist pleasure was man's final end and therefore to be sought everywhere, always and at all costs; for the Stoic it was an animal gratification unworthy of a man. From the conclusions arrived at in the preceding paragraphs it appears that pleasure, viewed apart from its object, is neither good nor bad. Like all the passions of the soul it is in itself morally indifferent. The goodness or badness of pleasure depends primarily on its object. If a man takes pleasure in what is evil, e.g., bad thoughts, desires, or actions, his pleasure is evil. Not all pleasure is morally good because not everything pleasurable is morally good. The pleasurable, like the merely useful, is not necessarily honorable; to be honorable, one must sometimes forgo the pleasurable. On the other hand, there is always a pleasure attaching to the honorable, the virtuous good. The joy of a good conscience exceeds the pleasure of sense. The goodness or badness of a man's life can even be judged according to that in which he habitually finds his pleasure. For this reason Aquinas said ''the man is good and virtuous who takes pleasure in the works of virtue; and the man is evil who takes pleasure in evil works'' (*Summa theologiae* 1a2ae, 24.4).

It follows that pleasure must never be sought for its own sake and without reference to a reasonable and legitimate object. Only if the object be good will the pleasure be good. If, for any reason, the object cannot be legitimately desired, the pleasure must also be forgone. The pleasure of the act is the goal of the intemperate man (*Summa theologiae* 1a2ae, 13.3 ad 2). Intemperance means indulgence in pleasure without regard to reason. Innocent XI, therefore, censured these propositions: To eat and drink to satiety simply and solely for pleasure (*ob solam voluptatem*) is not a sin, provided that it is not injurious to health. The marriage act done solely for pleasure (*ob solam voluptatem*) is without any fault whatsoever, without even a venial defect [H. Denzinger, *Enchiridion symbolorum*, ed. A. Schönmetzer (32d ed. Freiburg 1963) 2108–09].

Apart from its obvious associations with morality, pleasure implicates the whole moral agent in ways that can be either valuable or devastating. Human experience provides ample evidence that individuals have a level of sense pleasure almost indispensable for well integrated life and for efficient work, and which is of no small significance as a protective shield against temptations due to the displacement of unsatisfied human drives.

Christianity has never enjoyed complete freedom from members unduly suspicious of human pleasure. This attitude finds no justification in its Judaic origins, but there have been recurrent revivals of it in Christian history. These appear to have stemmed in large part from various forms of dualism. Instances of this attitude in modern times are to be found in Puritanism and Jansenism, and among the immoderate devotees of supernaturalism.

See Also: EMOTION (MORAL ASPECT).

Bibliography: THOMAS AQUINAS, *Summa theologiae* 1a2ae, 2.6; 31–34. A. AUER, *Lexikon für Theologie und Kirche*, ed. J. HOFER and K. RAHNER, 10 v. (2d new ed. Freiburg1957–65) 4:361–364. H. ROST, *Die Fröhlichkeit in der Katholischen Kirche* (Westheim-Augsburg 1946).

[A. DOOLAN]

PLEGMUND OF CANTERBURY

Archbishop; b. Mercia, England; d. Aug. 2, 914. A hermit at Plegmundham (now Plemstall), in Cheshire, he became tutor and adviser to ALFRED THE GREAT and participated in the literary revival. Appointed archbishop of Canterbury in 890, he received the pallium in Rome from Pope FORMOSUS (891). Plegmund, the recognized leader against pagan influences, crowned Edward the Elder at Kingston (901), consecrated the New Minster at WINCHESTER (*c.* 903), and after a second journey to Rome (908) aided in the subdivision of the two West Saxon sees into five, consecrating seven bishops in one day (probably *c.* 909).

Feast: Aug. 2.

Bibliography: *Anglo-Saxon Chronicle,* tr. C. PLUMMER and J. EARLE, 2 v. (Oxford 1892–99; repr. New York 1952) 890, 891, 923, erroneous death-date. J. M. KEMBLE, ed., *Codex diplomaticus aevi saxonici,* 6 v. (London 1839–48). W. HUNT, *The Dictionary of National Biography from the Earliest Times to 1900,* 63 v. (London 1885–1900; repr. with corrections, 21 v., 1908–09, 1921–22, 1938; suppl. 1901–) 15:1306–07. E. BARBER, "St. Plegmund and His Connection with Cheshire," *Journal of the Architectural, Archaeological and Historical Society for the County and the City of Chester and North Wales,* NS 16 (1909) 54–69. C. COTTON, *The Saxon Cathedral at Canterbury and the Saxon Saints Buried Therein* (Manchester 1929).

[W. A. CHANEY]

PLESSINGTON, JOHN (WILLIAM), ST.

Priest, martyr; b. Dimples Hall, Lancashire, England, *c.* 1637; d. Chester, England, July 19, 1679. His family, always Catholic and royalist, maintained a chaplain in their house. Until the age of nine John was probably instructed by (Bl.) Thomas WHITAKER (later a martyr), who was chaplain at Dimples. Later John went to a Jesuit private school at Scarisbrick Hall, near Ormskirk, before crossing to St. Omer in Flanders to complete his education. Then he joined the English seminary at Valladolid, Spain, and was ordained at Segovia (March 1662). Leaving Spain in April 1663 he was sent as a missionary to Holywell in Flintshire, the shrine of St. Winefride, and a center of pilgrimage all through penal times. From his headquarters in Ye Crosse Keyes Inn he worked in Flintshire and the neighboring counties. It is uncertain when he left Holywell for Paddington Hall, the home of the Massey family, in the Wirral Peninsula, but he was certainly established there by 1670. For at least eight years Plessington was at Puddington, officially as tutor to the Massey children, in reality as a missionary. It was his firm stand against the marriage of a Catholic heiress to a Protestant that led to his betrayal and arrest at the time of the Titus Oates plot. The authorities were not able to involve him in the plot, but he was charged with being a priest. His popularity was so great that no witnesses could be found to charge him until three apostates came forward; one was the mentally deranged Margaret Plat; another he swore he had never seen before; the third was a valid witness. After condemnation for his priesthood he remained nine weeks a prisoner in an underground cell of Chester Castle. When visited by the undertaker sent to measure him for his coffin, he remarked to a friend that he was now giving an order for his last suit. He was executed at Chester on July 19, 1679. After a spirited speech the cart was drawn away, and he was heard to call out, "O Jesus, be to me a Jesus." His quartered body was returned to Puddington with instructions that it should be exposed on the four corners of the house. The Masseys flagrantly disobeyed this order and reverently buried the body in the neighboring churchyard of Burton. Although the burial was recorded in the Burton register, when the traditional grave was opened in 1962 no remains that could be certainly identified as the martyr's were discovered. Plessington was beatified by Pius XI on Dec. 15, 1929, and canonized by Paul VI on Oct. 25, 1970 as one of the Forty Martyrs of England and Wales.

Feast: June 20; Oct. 25 (Feast of the 40 Martyrs of England and Wales); May 4 (Feast of the English Martyrs in England).

See Also: ENGLAND, SCOTLAND, AND WALES, MARTYRS OF.

Bibliography: M. WAUGH, *Blessed John Plessington* (Pustalation Pamphlet; London 1961). R. CHALLONER, *Memoirs of Missionary Priests,* ed. J. H. POLLEN (rev. ed. London 1924). J. GILLOW, *A Literary and Biographical History or Bibliographical Dictionary of the English Catholics from 1534 to the Present Time* 5:322 (London-New York 1885–1902; repr. New York 1961). A. BUTLER, *The Lives of the Saints,* ed. H. THURSTON and D. ATTWATER (New York 1956) 2:599–600.

[G. FITZ HERBERT]

PLESSIS, JOSEPH OCTAVE

Eleventh bishop of Quebec, Canada; b. Montreal, March 3, 1763; d. Quebec, Dec. 4, 1825. He was the son of a blacksmith; his outstanding ability enabled him to complete his philosophical studies and to receive tonsure by the age of 17. While awaiting the required age for ordination, he taught in the Quebec seminary and was secretary to Bp. J. O. BRIAND. After ordination on March 11, 1786, he remained in Quebec, where he served on the bishop's council and at 29 became pastor of the cathedral. In 1797, when Bp. Pierre Denaut succeeded to the See of Quebec, he requested that Plessis be named his coadjutor. Because the bulls from Rome were delayed, the consecration did not take place until 1801; five years later he succeeded to the see. During his administration he energetically supported the rights of the church and of the French in Canada in opposition to the policies of Gov. James Craig and other Protestant high officials of Quebec. In recognition of his influence in ensuring the loyalty of French Canadians to the British cause in the War of 1812 with the United States, the English ministry expressly recognized his episcopacy and approved his appointments in 1815 and later named him an ex officio member of the legislative council (1817). His pastoral visits, accounts of which remain, finally convinced him that one bishop could not govern the 500 leagues of territory from Cape Breton to Red River. Thus in 1819 and 1820 he went to London and to Rome to urge a division of his diocese and succeeded in obtaining the creation of four suffragans as well as the status of archbishop for himself. However, in deference to the sensibilities of the English government, he did not assume the title, which was not used publicly by an incumbent of the see until 1844. His concern for education led him to establish many elementary schools, and he founded or encouraged the seminaries of Nicolet, St. Hyacinthe, and St. Roch, as well as the old Seminary of Quebec, where he resided and helped in the formation of future priests. He interested himself in school legislation and succeeded in neutralizing the Protestant-oriented system of *l'Institution Royale* (1801) and in having a parochial-based school system finally adopted in 1824. His *Journal de deux voyages apostoliques dans le Golfe Saint-Laurent et les provinces d'en bas, en 1811 et 1812* was published in 1865.

Bibliography: J. B. A. FERLAND, *Mgr. Joseph-Octave Plessis: Évêque de Québec* (Quebec 1878). H. TÊTU, *Les Évêques de Québec* (Quebec 1889). L. P. AUDET, *Le Système scolaire de la Province de Québec* (Quebec 1952–) v. 3, 4.

[H. PROVOST]

PLETHON, GEMISTOS

Late Byzantine philosopher and humanist; b. Constantinople, *c.* 1355 or 1360; d. Mistra, June 25, 1452. Apparently born George Gemistos, he was educated at Constantinople but as a youth spent considerable time at the Ottoman court in Brussa or Adrianople, where he studied occult arts and the teachings of Zarathustra (Zoroaster) with a Jewish savant named Eliseus. On the violent death of his mentor, Plethon, as he called himself, evidently in honor of Plato, moved to Mistra in the Peloponnesus, near Sparta, and opened a school of esoteric philosophy and religion. In 1413 he directed memoirs to Emperor Manuel concerning the affairs of the Peloponnesus and in 1414 another to the emperor's son Theodore, concerning the fortification of the Morean Isthmus, in which he proposed a complete reorganization of the civil and military society. In 1428 he was consulted by Emperor JOHN PALAEOLOGUS concerning the reunion of the Latin and Byzantine Churches and was brought to the Council of FLORENCE (1439) as one of the Greek theologians. He signed the decree of reunion, despite the fact that he later wrote an opposing treatise *On the Procession of the Holy Spirit.* While in Italy he presented the humanists with the tract *Difference between Aristotle and Plato.*

On his return to Mistra, Plethon published his chief work, *Nomōn Syngraphē,* in which he described a kind of political utopia. He proposed an idealized paganism built on elements of Neoplatonic philosophy: human felicity consists in the harmony between man's nature and the universe, of which man is only an element. Sin is but error; morality and religion can achieve only earthly, not heavenly, happiness; and in death, the soul returns to a spiritual, but not a supernatural, state and will exist in a sinless and happy condition.

Plethon's political philosophy was directed toward the complete reformation of life in the Peloponnesus, whose population he considered of pure Hellenic strain. In the reconstitution of society, he proposed three classes: the cultivators of the land, the merchants, and the imperial functionaries. The first two were to support the state with their products and money; the third, with military service. Among his many writings Plethon produced a treatise *On Virtues,* several tracts on the teachings of Zarathustra, a commentary on the *Analytics* of Aristotle, a tract on the Incarnation and on Latin theology, and orations for the death of the Princess Cleopas (1433) and the Empress Helen. His three books on the *Laws* contain a description of the liturgy of the new religion he desired to found. He was of original genius and had a strong influence on the Byzantine scholars who stimulated the Renaissance in Italy, but Plethon had no successors. His teachings were opposed by BESSARION, who had been one of his pupils in Mistra, and his *Laws* were publicly burned by George Scholarius after he became patriarch of Constantinople as GENNADIUS II.

Bibliography: *Patrologia Graeca,* ed. J. P. MIGNE, 161 v. (Paris 1857–66), 160:821–1020. S. P. LAMPROS, ed., v. 3–4 (Athens 1926–30). B. KOTTER, *Lexikon für Theologie und Kirche,* ed. J. HOFER and K. RAHNER, 10 v. (2d, new ed. Frieburg 1957–65) 8:561–562. E. STÉPHANOU, *Dictionnaire de théologie catholique,* ed. A. VACANT et al., 15 v. (Paris 1903–50; Tables générales 1951–), 12.2:2393–2404. *Échos d'Orient* 31 (1932) 207–217. F. MASAI, *Pléthon et le platonisme de Mistra* (Paris 1956); *Revue de l'Université de Bruxelles* 10 (1957–58) 392–412. H. DÖRRIE, *Die Religion in Geschichte und Gegenwart,* 7 v. (3d ed. Tübingen 1957–65), 2:1375–76. H. G. BECK, *Kirche und theologische Literatur im byzantinischen Reich* (Munich 1959), 754–755. M. V. ANASTOS, "Pletho's Calendar and Liturgy," *Dumbarton Oaks Papers,* 4 (1948) 183–303. J. P. MAMALAKES, *Georgios Gemistos Plethon* (Athens 1939), in Gr. D. J. GEANAKOPLOS, *Greek Scholars in Venice* (Cambridge, Mass. 1962) 35, 75, 85–86.

[F. CHIOVARO]

PLINY THE YOUNGER

Nephew and adopted son of Pliny the Elder, Roman orator, letter writer, and administrator; b. Comum (in north Italy), A.D. 61 or 62; d. before 114. After his adoption Pliny's name became C. Plinius Caecilius Secundus. As a member of the senatorial class he received the typical rhetorical education of the time and entered a career of public service. He served as *praefectus aerarii mili-*

taris under Domitian and was appointed *praefectus aerarii Saturni* by Nerva—both important financial posts. As consul suffectus in 100, he delivered the laudatory address that he developed subsequently into his elaborate and fulsome *Panegyricus.* He achieved a reputation as a prosecutor and defense counsel in political cases, but his forensic speeches are not extant. It is most probably owing to his special knowledge of Bithynia, exhibited when he defended two former governors of that province accused of maladministration, that Trajan sent him as an imperial legate to order the affairs of Bithynia. He served in this capacity from 111 to 113.

The nine books of letters Pliny wrote between 97 and 109 were originally intended for publication and lack the intimacy and sparkle of Cicero's *Letters to Atticus,* but they contain much personal information on both Pliny and his times. Book 10 of his *Letters* is different, however, because it is comprised of official correspondence between Pliny and Trajan respecting affairs in Bithynia—even those of minor import. It is only too evident that a provincial governor had very little scope for personal initiative—or at least did not deem it prudent to show any appreciable independence in action.

Letters 96 and 97 are of prime importance because they are about the policy to be adopted toward the Christiana. Pliny's letter (96) describes the Christian gatherings in some detail and makes the earliest non–Christian reference to the celebration of the Eucharist and Agape. Trajan's reply (letter 97) contains the first extant statement of imperial policy respecting Christians. Its inconsistency, as was pointed out later by TERTULLIAN, indicates that the Roman state was faced with a new and unique problem and was conscious of that fact.

Bibliography: R. G. C. LEVENS, *The Oxford Classical Dictionary.* ed. M. CARY et al. (Oxford 1949) 704–705. J. W. and A. M. DUFF, *A Literary History of Rome in the Silver Age . . .* (2d ed. London 1960) 425–443. M. SCHANZ, C. HOSIUS, and F. KRÜGER, *Geschichte der römischen Literatur* (Munich 1914–35) 2:656–673. M. SCHUSTER, *Paulys Realenzyklopädie der klassischen Altertumswissenschaft,* ed. G. WISSOWA et al. 21.1 (1931) 439–496. M. DURRY, *Pline le Jeune: Lettres X et panégyrique de Trajan* (Paris 1947). J. A. JUNGMANN, *The Mass of the Roman Rite,* tr. F. A. BRUNNER, 2 v. (New York 1951–55) 1:18.

[M. R. P. MCGUIRE]

PLOTINUS

Neoplatonic philosopher; b. probably in Upper Egypt, A.D. 205; d. Rome, 270. Plotinus's race is not known, but by education and cultural background he was thoroughly Greek, as the evidence of his own writings shows. He came to Alexandria to study philosophy in

Roman coin with portrait bust of Plotinus. (©Araldo de Luca/ CORBIS)

232, but could find no one to hold his interest until someone took him to hear Ammonius Saccas, a former Christian, with whom he remained 11 years. Fellow pupils of his were the two Origens, one a pagan Neoplatonist, and the other a future Christian theologian. Thus, Christianity was in some way associated with the very beginnings of NEOPLATONISM, but too little is known of Ammonius Saccas to ascertain how much his Christian upbringing may have influenced his teaching and, indirectly, the works of his more famous pupil, Plotinus. At any rate, Ammonius seems to have reconciled the teachings of PLATO and ARISTOTLE, perhaps after the manner of the Middle Platonists (*see* PLATONISM).

Character of Thought. In 243 Plotinus joined an expedition by the Emperor Gordian to the East, in the hope of making contact with Persian and Indian philosophers; but Gordian was murdered and Plotinus escaped to Antioch. He never made any contact with Eastern thought, and the balance of opinion among modern Neoplatonic scholars seems to find his entire system readily intelligible in terms of Greek philosophy, without postulating the introduction of Eastern elements. Plotinus came to Rome in 244 and taught philosophy until his death from a painful form of disease. From 254 onward he wrote, not a complete system, but tentative discussions of central points in his system, which have been rather arbitrarily arranged by his pupil PORPHYRY into six groups of nine treatises called *Enneads.*

The thought of Plotinus is a final synthesis of various elements of GREEK PHILOSOPHY. It expressly claims to follow the philosophy of Plato and merely to make explicit what was already implicit in his *Dialogues* and *Letters* (cf. 5.1.8), but it incorporates a great deal from Aristotle (especially through his great 2d-century commentator, Alexander of Aphrodisias), and from STOICISM, Neo-Pythagoreanism, and Middle Platonism. In fact, it may be regarded as the culmination of a movement toward the conflation of the various Greek schools of thought that began in the 1st century B.C., and gradually developed over the 1st and 2d centuries A.D. Hence Plotinus is not in the literal sense a Platonist, but in the wider sense of tradition, influence, and general viewpoint he most certainly is.

Teaching. For Plotinus the first substantial principle or hypostasis is the One or the Good. The double title reflects the influence of both Neo-Pythagoreanism and Middle Platonism, and ultimately of Plato himself, whose preoccupations were both ethical and mathematical. This first principle is also termed God and is beyond Being (following the *Republic* 509B).

Emanation. Next, by a process of necessary emanation, comes *nous* or intellect, also referred to as divine, in which the whole world of ideas or forms is contained. It is on this level that being, which always entails some multiplicity, and life appear. From intellect, in turn, comes soul, which at its highest level belongs to the world of intellect. The world-soul forms and rules the material universe, and at its lower level, where it acts as a principle of life and growth, receives the name of nature, which is almost a distinct fourth hypostasis. Each of these principles has proceeded from the previous, and then turned back in contemplation of it in order to be fully constituted, according to a law of abiding, procession, and reversion. But the last principle is too weak to produce anything further than the forms immanent in bodies, beneath which exists only formless matter.

Matter. This material visible world is therefore good, as emanating ultimately from the Good, but unformed matter is evil, in the ontological sense of lacking form, definition, or shape (1.8.3). Moral evil consists in the assimilation of the soul to matter, with all that this entails in terms of deficiency. Evil is simply the complete lack of good (1.8.5; 2.4.16). Some critics have taken matter in Plotinus to be a separate principle of evil that almost introduces a Manichaean dualism into his system, but a careful reading of the relevant texts does not seem to justify this conclusion (e.g., 4.8.6, 18–24).

Soul. Individual human souls are one with the universal soul, but with distinct identity, and descend by destiny into the body. Plotinus harmonizes the seemingly opposed views that the soul's entry into the body is somehow a fall, and yet at the same time for the benefit of the universe (4.8.5). But human souls are only expressions on the level of Soul of particular intellects within the sphere of intellect, and so man's highest and most real point never descends into union with the body. Each human soul has three levels—the transcendent intellect, the intermediate soul, and the lowest soul that immediately gives life to the body. Whether one's life is to be virtuous or not depends upon the decision of the intermediate soul, either to return in contemplation to the sphere of intellect, or to devote itself to the needs and cravings of the body.

Contemplation. The process of return to contemplation is much as Plato described it, the most suitable souls being those of the musician, the lover, and the philosopher. The first two still need to learn detachment from particular images of beauty, but the last can go straight on to the study of mathematics and then dialectic—the complete knowledge of the world of forms within the unity of intellect. One is led to this state of intellectual contemplation by the practice of the virtues—practical wisdom, courage, moderation, and justice. In their normal exercise these are civic virtues, but as specially directed toward detachment from the body they become higher virtues or purifications (1.2.3). The purified soul can rise still higher and be united to the One by the intellect, although only intermittently while it is still in this life (4.8.1). This union is beyond thought or expression in word; it is a unity of love in which the lover is no longer conscious of any distinction between him and the beloved. It is the simplicity of a single glance, and once attained all else seems worthless in comparison with it (6.7.34–36).

Influence. The philosophy of Plotinus immediately became dominant in the Greco-Roman world of the later Empire. Its terminology was used in the definitions of the Trinity at Constantinople in A.D. 381 with this difference: that for Plotinus procession entails inferiority, whereas the Christian Trinity is a procession of equals. St. AUGUSTINE found his inspiration in Plotinian thought, which led him out of the despair of MANICHAEISM and SKEPTICISM. Perhaps most important of all, the psychology of Plotinus became, via the medium of PROCLUS and PSEUDO-DIONYSIUS, the accepted framework of mystical theology, again with a difference. For Plotinus, the human soul at its highest level never descends into union with the body (a point upon which Proclus, following IAMBLICHUS, disagreed with him); thus it can by its own efforts return to the contemplative life of Intellect and even to union with the One, whereas, for the Christian mystic, the mind may be raised to the contemplation of God only by the freely bestowed grace or gift of union. However, the faculty of Nous was widely accepted as the nurtural vehicle of this grace by such authors as HUGH OF SAINT-VICTOR and RICHARD OF SAINT-VICTOR, St. BONAVENTURE, J. TAULER, and the Flemish and Spanish mystics.

See Also: NEOPLATONISM; EMANATIONISM; MONISM.

Bibliography: *Opera,* ed, P. HENRY and H. R. SCHWYZER, 2 v. (Paris 1951–59); *The Enneads,* tr. S. MACKENNA (3d ed. New York 1962); *The Enneads,* tr. A. H. ARMSTRONG (Loeb Classical Library; London-New York-Cambridge, Mass. 1912–). H. R. SCHWYZER, *Paulys Realenzyklopädie der klassischen Altertumswissenschaft,* ed. G. WISSOWA et al. (Stuttgart 1893–) 21:471–592. A. H. ARMSTRONG, *Plotinus* (London 1953); *The Architecture of the Intelligible Universe in the Philosophy of Plotinus* (Cambridge, Eng. 1940). É. BRÉHIER, *The Philosophy of Plotinus,* tr. J. THOMAS (Chicago 1958). M. P. DE GANDILLAC, *La Sagesse de Plotin* (Paris 1952). J. TROUILLARD, *La Procession Plotinienne* (Paris 1956); *La Purification Plotinienne* (Paris 1956). P. MERLAN, *From Platonism to Neoplatonism* (2d ed. The Hague 1960); *Monopsychism, Mysticism, Metaconsciousness* (The Hague 1963). E. R. DODDS et al., *Les Sources de Plotin* (Geneva 1960).

[W. H. O'NEILL]

PLOWDEN, CHARLES AND FRANCIS

Members of a distinguished Catholic family that contributed ten members to the Society of Jesus; lineal descendants of Edmund PLOWDEN.

Charles, rector of Stonyhurst College; b. Plowden Hall, Shropshire, Aug. 19, 1743; d. Jougne, France, June 13, 1821. Charles, the son of William and Frances Plowden, was educated at the Edgbaston Franciscan school. While registered at the College of ST. OMER under the alias of Simons, July 7, 1754, he entered the Jesuit novitiate at Watten (1759). After theological study at Liège and Bologna, Plowden was ordained at Rome, Sept. 30, 1770. When assigned to the English College at Bruges, he taught with John CARROLL, the future American bishop. Both were arrested and Plowden was imprisoned from September 1773 to May 1774, following the papal suppression of the Jesuits and the Austrian confiscation of Jesuit property in the imperial domains. Upon his release, Plowden joined a number of former Jesuits in conducting the Academy of Liège. He subsequently served as chaplain to the Smythe and Maxwell families, Jacobite exiles living on the Continent. In 1784, he became chaplain at Lulworth Castle, home of Thomas Weld, a prominent Dorset Catholic; there Plowden assisted and preached at the episcopal consecration of John Carroll (1790). Until Carroll's death (1815), the two maintained a correspondence that is of historical significance. Upon the provisional restoration of the Society of Jesus in 1803, Plowden became master of novices at Hodder Place. At its formal establishment by PIUS VII, he was named provincial and rector of Stonyhurst College (1817), which he and Weld had helped to found in 1794. It was while returning from the Jesuit General Chapter in Rome (1820) that Plowden died.

Francis, lawyer, historian, brother of Charles; b. Plowden Hall, Shropshire, June 28, 1749; d. Paris, Jan. 4, 1819. Francis had been educated at Edgbaston, St. Omer, and the Jesuit novitiate at Watten (1766), and was teaching at Bruges (1771–73) at the time of the Jesuit suppression. Since he was not yet ordained, he was released from his vows, and, returning to England, he entered the Middle Temple. When the Relief Act of 1791 relieved Catholics of legal disabilities, Francis expanded his law practice. His interest in research led to the publication of *Jura Anglorum* (1792), a commentary on English law, which brought him condemnation from his Jesuit brother Robert, but also an honorary degree from Oxford, a rare distinction for a Catholic. He abandoned his law practice to write extensively on Church-State relations. His *Historical Review of the State of Ireland* (1803), written at the request of the British government, was a harsh indictment of government policy and administration. A later volume, *Ireland since the Union* (1811), caused a libel suit in which Plowden was ordered to pay £5,000 to the government. The independent and forthright, if impractical, Plowden, refusing to pay the fine, fled to France, where he died in relative obscurity and poverty.

Bibliography: T. COOPER, *The Dictionary of National Biography from the Earliest Times to 1900,* 63 v. (London 1885–1900) 15 (1922) 1312–13, 1315–17. B. M. PLOWDEN, *Records of the Plowden Family* (privately printed 1884). B. N. WARD, *Dawn of the Catholic Revival in England,* 2 v. (New York 1909). J. GERARD, *Stonyhurst College* (Belfast 1894). C. SOMMERVOGEL et al., *Bibliothèque de la Compagnie de Jésus,* 11 v. (Brussels-Paris 1890–1932) 6:903–906. A. MELVILLE, *John Carroll of Baltimore* (New York 1955). J. GILLOW, *A Literary and Biographical History or Bibliographical Dictionary of the English Catholics from 1534 to the Preset Time,* 5 v. (London-New York 1885–1902) 5:322–323, 328–331.

[P. S. MCGARRY]

PLOWDEN, EDMUND

English recusant, jurist; b. Plowden Hall, Shropshire, 1518; d. London, Feb. 6, 1585. Plowden was educated at Cambridge for three years, but left to enter the Middle Temple in London (1538). He was a distinguished lawyer who additionally obtained a license in surgery from Oxford in 1552. Plowden was a member of the council of the Marches of Wales during the reign of Queen Mary I (1553), also serving in Parliament during those years. Upon succeeding to the Plowden estates in 1557, he devoted himself to his law practice, especially at the Middle Temple, where he served as treasurer (1561) and counsel of the court of the Duchy of Lancaster (1562).

Although a faithful Roman Catholic, he worshiped in the established church until Pius V issued the *Regnans in excelsis* (1570) excommunicating Queen Elizabeth I. During those years, Plowden appeared in litigations defending well-known Catholics, such as Bp. Edmund Bonner and Gabriel Goodman, dean of Westminster, when their religious authority was legally assailed. Along with Sir Thomas TRESHAM, Plowden was the leading Roman Catholic layman of his day. He suffered penalties for his religious convictions, and it is said that he sacrificed Elizabeth's offer of the Lord Chancellorship rather than renounce his Roman allegiance. His fame as a lawyer was very great. Both Sir Edward Coke and William Camden, the famous antiquarian, paid tribute to his learning and skill. Camden described him as ''second to no man of his profession.'' There seems to be little doubt that he was the ''foremost Catholic of cultural attainments of his day'' (Trimble 32).

Bibliography: T. COOPER, *The Dictionary of National Biography from the Earliest Times to 1900* (London 1885–1900) 15 (1922) 1314–15. W. R. TRIMBLE, *The Catholic Laity in Elizabethan England* (Cambridge, Mass. 1964). J. GILLOW, *A Literary and Biographical History or Bibliographical Dictionary of the English Catholics from 1534 to the Present Time* (London–New York 1885–1902) 5:325–327.

[P. S. MCGARRY]

PLUMMER, ALFRED

English theological and historical writer; b. Heworth, near Gateshead, England, Feb. 17, 1841; d. Bideford, England, April 17, 1926. From Lancing College he went to Exeter College, at the University of OXFORD, where he graduated in 1863. He was a fellow of Trinity College from 1865 to 1875 and tutor and dean there from 1867 to 1874. From 1874 to 1902 he was master of University College, Durham. He was admitted to the diaconate in 1866 by the bishop of Oxford, Dr. Samuel Wilberforce (d. 1873), but he never sought ordination to the priesthood.

He was a prolific writer, and his translations of DÖLLINGER's works introduced the latter to many English readers. His commentaries on the New Testament, noted especially for the section dealing with the Gospel of St. LUKE (Edinburgh 1906), and his introductions to the books of the Old Testament are scholarly and conservative. His devotion to ANGLICANISM appears in his historical writings: *Lectures on English Church History (1575–1649)* (1904), *The Church of England in the 18th Century* (1910), *The Churches in Britain before A.D. 1000* (1911). In 1887 he wrote *Handbook on the Church of the Early Fathers.*

Bibliography: *Who's Who* (London 1926) 2326. *London Times* (April 20, 1926) 18, obituary.

[T. C. CROWLEY]

PLUMMER, CHARLES

Scholar, fellow and chaplain of Corpus Christi College, Oxford, and deacon of the Church of England; b. Heworth, Durham County, England, Jan. 24, 1851; d. Sept. 8, 1927. The son of the Rev. Matthew Plummer, he won a scholarship to Corpus Christi in 1869 and was elected to a fellowship in 1873. While serving as college dean (1891–98) he edited Bede's *Historia ecclesiastica gentis Anglorum* (2 v. 1896) and later wrote the *Life and Times of Alfred the Great* (1902). Thenceforth he turned to Celtic studies and carried out John COLGAN'S design of publishing the lives of the Irish saints. The Latin lives edited in his *Vitae sanctorum Hiberniae* (2 v. 1910), as well as the vernacular lives in the *Bethada Náem nÉrenn* (2 v. 1922), are models of erudition. His *Miscellanea hagiographica Hibernica,* published by the Bollandists in the *Subsidia Hagiographica* (Brussels 1925), contains a valuable catalogue of hagiographical materials, and his British Academy lecture, *On the Colophons and Marginalia of Irish Scribes* (London 1926), is a classic. He is buried in Holywell Cemetery in Oxford.

Bibliography: P. GROSJEAN, *Revue Celtique,* 45 (1928) 431–435. Obituaries by P. S. ALLEN, F. M. STENTON, and R. I. BEST in *Proceedings of the British Academy* 15 (1929) 463–476.

[R. T. MEYER]

PLUMPE, JOSEPH CONRAD

Patristic scholar and editor; b. April 12, 1901, Cloverdale, Ohio; d. Dec. 8, 1957, Worthington, Ohio. He was the son of August H. and Mary (Gerding) Plumpe. He received his B.A. (1922) and M.A. (1924) from the Pontifical College Josephinum in Worthington, was ordained in 1928 at Toledo, Ohio, and studied at the University of Münster (Ph.D. 1932) and at the University of Berlin in Germany. He taught classical languages and German at the Josephinum (1932–41), and was professor of ecclesiastical Latin and New Testament Greek at the Catholic University of America (1954–57). His scholarly works include: *Wesen und Wirkung der auctoritas mai-*

orum bei Cicero (Münster 1935); a translation, *Life and Work of Prince Demetrius Augustine Gallitzin,* by Peter Henry Lemcke (London and New York 1940); and *Mater Ecclesia: An Inquiry into the Concept of the Church as Mother in Early Christianity* (Washington 1943). He was also joint founder-editor of the patristic series ''Ancient Christian Writers.''

[J. QUASTEN]

PLUNKET, OLIVER, ST.

Martyr, archbishop of Armagh, primate of Ireland; b. Loughcrew, near Oldcastle, County Meath, 1629; d. Tyburn, London, England, July 1, 1681. Oliver Plunket (Plunkett) was a member of a prominent Irish family that was related to the earls of Fingall and Roscommon. The young Oliver was educated by his kinsman Patrick Plunket, Benedictine abbot of St. Mary's, Dublin, later bishop of Ardagh and Meath. In 1647 Father Pier Francesco SCARAMPI, who had served as Innocent X's envoy to the Irish Catholic Confederacy (1643–45), returned to Rome accompanied by Oliver and four Irish seminarians. Plunket was enrolled in the Irish College, where he made an outstanding record. After his ordination in 1654, Oliver, instead of returning to Ireland, received permission to remain with the Fathers of Charity in Rome. He worked among the poor and also took degrees in canon and civil law at the Roman College. Plunket was appointed Roman representative of the Irish bishops and served as professor of theology and apologetics at the College of Propaganda until 1669. In that year Edmund O'REILLY, the exiled archbishop of Armagh, died in France, and Pope CLEMENT IX chose Plunket as the new archbishop.

Irish Mission. Plunket was consecrated in Ghent on Nov. 30, 1669. Clement also appointed bishops for the sees of Cashel, Tuam, Ossory, and Dublin. Plunket's cousin Peter TALBOT was named archbishop of Dublin. Plunket returned to Ireland by way of London. There he remained for several days as guest of Philip HOWARD, OP, almoner of Queen Catherine of Braganza, wife of Charles II. Plunket reached Ireland in the spring of 1670 after an absence of almost 25 years. Not only was Armagh a large and long-neglected ecclesiastical province, it was also a difficult area to administer. Fortunately, English Lord Lieutenant John Lord Berkeley of Stratton, whose wife was secretly a Catholic, was on friendly terms with Plunket and his priests; even a new school, conducted by the Jesuits, was opened in Drogheda. Berkeley's successor, Arthur Capel, earl of Essex (1672), was also considerate of Plunket's interests. Essex did not persecute Catholics, but he did stir up dissensions among the Catholic clergy over precedence and jurisdiction. Plunket and Talbot exchanged written arguments concerning Armagh's primacy over Dublin. Likewise, the FRANCISCANS and DOMINICANS engaged in rancorous disputes over parishes, foundations, and churches. The Franciscans, who had remained in Ireland during the persecutions of the 1650s and 1660s, were somewhat resentful of Dominican efforts to re-establish former Dominican foundations that they had abandoned when they had withdrawn from Ireland a few years before. The Franciscans had kept the faith alive, but their growth had been hasty and not carefully regulated. Plunket was fearful that the Irish province would become a dumping ground for undesirable friars. Plunket tried to restore peace by adjudicating the dispute between the Franciscans and Dominicans. The problems of begging and questing were as important as jurisdiction. Plunket resolved the conflict in favor of the Dominicans. He also tried to improve the character and discipline of the Franciscans by making formal recommendations to the Franciscan provincial chapter. The archbishop, a strict canonist, was anxious to eliminate irregularities and laxity. Shortly after Plunket began his efforts, the persecution of 1673 against Catholics changed the favorable attitudes of officials to hostile repression. Stemming in part from the passage of the Test Act of 1673, the persecution led to the closing down of religious houses, which dispersed friars, monks, and priests throughout the country. Plunket, along with Dr. John Brennan, later archbishop of Cashel, was forced to go into hiding.

Pastoral Work. Before the renewal of the persecution of 1673, Plunket had addressed himself to problems other than the squabbles and discipline of religious orders. One of his first actions was the summoning of the Synod of Clones (1670). Plunket set down rules for the education and ordination of priests. He also tried to raise money to overcome the dire poverty of the Church and its clergy. The primate warned his flock against cooperation with Tories, Irish outlaws who had turned to brigandage and robbery after the English had confiscated their property. Since the Tories were mostly Roman Catholic, Plunket was torn between sympathy for his coreligionists and his firm belief in law and order. The archbishop himself frequently went into their hiding places to plead with these outlaws to abandon their illegal activities. That Plunket knew that these criminals were often sentenced to exile in America far from the comforts and consolation of their religious faith did not make his task any easier. The English, however, held the clergy responsible for the rebellion and political activities of their parishioners. The persecution interrupted his work and forced Plunket to carry on his pastoral duties in disguise and secrecy.

Arrest, Trial, and Martyrdom. Plunket's letters to Rome described the hardships of these years (1673–79).

Priests were forced into hiding or exile. The Drogheda school was closed and the faculty driven out. Church services had to be conducted in secret. In 1677 James Butler, marquis, later duke of Ormond, replaced Essex as lord lieutenant. The suppression of convents and seminaries was ruthlessly enforced. Edicts of expulsion were widely circulated. Catholics were even forbidden to enter the city of Dublin or any other principal seaport (Nov. 20, 1678).

In the midst of these difficulties, the Titus OATES PLOT in England (1678) caused the English government to redouble its anti-Catholic efforts. Plunket, despite increased dangers, visited his aged relative Patrick Plunket, bishop of Ardagh and Meath, who was dying. The government had him arrested and imprisoned in Dublin Castle (Dec. 6, 1679). There he was denied all outside communication for six weeks. Finally, he was shown some consideration; he was able to attend Archbishop Peter Talbot, who had been jailed and who was close to death.

Plunket was accused of remaining in the kingdom despite the edict of expulsion and of conspiring to bring a French army into Ireland. These charges were based on statements given by several informers, among them some former friars and apostate priests who had suffered from Plunket's disciplinary measures. The grand jury hearing the case dismissed the charges because of the numerous contradictions in the witnesses' testimony. The government as well as the informers, aided and abetted by William Hetherington, an agent of Anthony Ashley Cooper, earl of Shaftesbury and one of the originators of the anti-Catholic campaign, drew up new charges. A trial was held at Dundalk in July of 1680. There Plunket was accused of fomenting a revolt that would lead to the murder of Protestants and the establishment of the "Romish religion." The government was fearful that it would not obtain a conviction in Ireland; thus, over Plunket's objections the trial was moved to London. The earl of Essex pleaded for him, but to no avail. Plunket was imprisoned in Newgate. At the Winter Assizes, a grand jury refused to find a true bill of indictment; but in June, after a trial in which Plunket was unable to present all of his witnesses, he was found guilty of high treason after the jury had deliberated for only 15 minutes. One of the prosecution's chief witnesses, Henry O'Neill (O'Neale), later confessed that he had perjured himself. A number of the other witnesses against the archbishop were later hanged as robbers. On July 1, 1681 (O.S.), the archbishop was brought to Tyburn, where he was hanged, drawn, and quartered.

Before his death, Plunket had written, "And being the first among the Irish, I will teach others, with the grace of God, by example, not to fear death" (Curtis, 172). For his courageous life and example, LEO XIII declared him venerable on Dec. 9, 1886, BENEDICT XV pronounced him blessed on May 23, 1920, and Paul VI canonized him on Oct. 12, 1975. His feast is celebrated in Ireland, Australia, New Zealand, and the Diocese of Clifton, England. His head is preserved in St. Peter's church, Drogheda, Ireland.

Feast: July 11.

Bibliography: E. CURTIS, *Blessed Oliver Plunkett* (Dublin 1963). A. CURTAYNE, *The Trial of Oliver Plunkett* (New York 1953). P. F. MORAN, *Memoirs of Most Rev. Oliver Plunket* (Dublin 1861). M. V. RONAN, *The Irish Martyrs of the Penal Laws* (London 1935). R. BAGWELL, *The Dictionary of National Biography from the Earliest Times to 1900,* 63 v. (London 1885–1900) 15:1328–1333. A. BUTLER, *The Lives of the Saints,* 4 v. (New York 1956) 3:73–77. E. CURTIS, *A History of Ireland* (6th ed. New York 1951). T. ÓFIAICH and D. FORRISTAL, *Oliver Plunkett: His Life and Letters* (Huntington, Ind. 1975). J. MCKEE, *A Martyr Bishop* (Houston, Tex. 1975). J. NOWAK, *Oliver Plunkett* (Hildesheim 1975). J. HANLY, *Oliver Plunkett* (Rome 1977). J. J. MEAGHER, *Saint Oliver Plunkett* (Dublin 1977).

[P. S. MCGARRY]

PLURALISM, PHILOSOPHICAL

The term pluralism has two uses in philosophy. In one it designates a philosophical position about the nature of reality and is opposed to MONISM. In the other it designates a phenomenon of philosophy itself, namely, that in history one does not find one philosophy but rather many philosophies. This raises a question of "metaphilosophy," that is, a question about philosophy: why are there many philosophies and not one? This article is concerned with the second use of pluralism and considers the problem it poses and various types of responses it elicits; a sketch of a solution along lines acceptable to Catholics is presented in conclusion.

The Problem of Philosophical Pluralism

A characteristic of philosophy as it is known in history is the multiplicity and diversity of philosophical systems. This is not merely a question of historical development, which obtains in all fields of human learning, nor is it a question either of the proliferation of divisions of philosophy as in the proliferation of the positive sciences, or of division within the sciences. Rather the historical situation is that philosophy exists not simply as philosophy, but as individual philosophies that are wholes or systems; these systems are in varying degrees different from and opposed to each other, and some tend to endure or to recur in the course of history.

Different Philosophies. To take the Greek period as an example, there are the classic philosophies of PLATO-

NISM, ARISTOTELIANISM, STOICISM, EPICUREANISM, SKEPTICISM, and NEOPLATONISM. Some of these systems are themselves repetitions in a more developed way of pre-Platonic philosophies (Stoicism of HERACLITUS, Epicureanism of DEMOCRITUS, skepticism of the SOPHISTS, etc.), and they are repeated again in the late medieval and Renaissance periods of European philosophy.

That they are designated as ''isms'' itself shows that they are not simply the thought of one man, but rather express a viewpoint and a doctrine that became a school and a tradition to which groups of philosophers adhere. They are in other words different philosophies. Moreover, they are not only different, but they are frequently explicitly and radically opposed to each other. Thus Aristotelianism is opposed to Platonism; Stoicism and Epicureanism are opposed to both and to each other; skepticism rejects all of them. In this feature of diversity and pluralism philosophy resembles religion and culture more than mathematics and the positive sciences. Thus, as there is a history of religions rather than religion, so there is a history of philosophical systems (see V. T. A. Ferm).

World Philosophy. The problem of philosophical pluralism can be situated within circles of narrowing dimensions. There is first the circle of the whole civilized world and the question of the comparison of Chinese, Indian, and Western philosophy. This question came into prominence after World War I with the increase of communication between all peoples (see C. A. Moore, S. Radhakrishnan). A difficulty with this comparison is the use of the term philosophy, how it is distinguished from religion and culture, and to what extent it is a Greek and therefore a Western phenomenon (*See* CHINESE PHILOSOPHY; INDIAN PHILOSOPHY).

Western Philosophy. Second, there is the circle of Western philosophy, which is traditionally divided into three periods: ancient, medieval, and modern. The ancient period is the time of the Greco-Roman philosophies mentioned above. The medieval period is the time of the religious philosophies: Jewish, Islamic, and Christian. Peculiar to the period was the problem of reconciling philosophy as developed by the Greeks (reason) with scripture (revelation, faith). Each religion had its polarity of Platonism and Aristotelianism (Jewish: Avicebron and Maimonides; Islamic: Avicenna and Averroës; Christian: Bonaventure add Thomas) (*see* JEWISH PHILOSOPHY; ARABIAN PHILOSOPHY; CHRISTIAN PHILOSOPHY).

The beginning of the modern period in philosophy witnessed the rebirth of the Hellenistic philosophies (Stoicism, Epicureanism, and skepticism) and of Platonism, the issuance of Averroism into rationalism (the rejection of a divine revelation and an effort to return to the pre-Christian Era), the division of Christianity into Greek Orthodoxy, Protestantism, and Roman Catholicism, and the continued development of new philosophies (Continental rationalism, British empiricism, Kantian criticism, German idealism, American pragmatism, Marxism, existentialism, analytical philosophy, etc.).

Catholic Philosophy. The third circle is that of Catholic philosophy and includes all the philosophies that have been developed in the Catholic community from its origins. There are in the main three families, or traditions, which are not, however, completely cut off from each other: the Greek Neoplatonic tradition (Pseudo-Dionysius, Erigena, Eckhart, Cusa); the Augustinian tradition (Anselm, Peter Lombard, Bonaventure); the Aristotelian-scholastic tradition (Boethius, Aquinas, Scotus, Ockham). This third circle has become especially significant in the third phase of the neoscholastic revival: for while the non-Thomistic scholastic schools have receded, nonscholastic philosophies have become increasingly important—philosophy of the spirit (M. Blondel, M. F. Sciacca), phenomenology (D. von Hildebrand), existentialism (G. Marcel), etc.

Scholastic Philosophy. The fourth circle is that of scholastic philosophy. Though three schools (THOMISM, SCOTISM, and NOMINALISM) eventually dominated the medieval scholastic period, historical study has concluded that SCHOLASTICISM was not a collection of two or three schools, but of many philosophical theologies: each master of theology was precisely a teacher and not a disciple. When nominalism moved in the direction of Protestant Christianity and modern rationalism, or scientism, its place in the scholastic circle was taken by SUAREZIANISM, which, however, intended to be a Thomism. The ''second scholasticism'' of the 16th century became largely a competition among these three schools. The first stages of the Leonine revival at the end of the 19th century brought back a repetition of this old competition, particularly between Thomists and Suarezians (R. Garrigou-Lagrange and P. Descoqs), but gradually the issue developed between Thomism and nonscholastic contemporary philosophies.

Thomism. The fifth circle is that of Thomism. The preferred status given to St. THOMAS AQUINAS within the Church led to a diversification within Thomism itself. Three categories can be designated: classical Thomism, which is the Thomism of the commentators and of the ''second scholasticism'' (Cajetan, Báñez, John of St. Thomas, J. Maritain); historical Thomism, which went behind the commentators and approached the 13th century from a historian's point of view (É. Gilson, C. Fabro); and developmental Thomism, which aimed to develop the thought of St. Thomas in relation with modern science (D. Mercier, American Dominicans, B. F. Lonergan) or with modern philosophy (J. Maréchal, K. Rahner).

Church Legislation. The issue of philosophical pluralism became particularly acute with the publication of the new Code of Canon Law for the Latin Church in 1918, which directed that theology and philosophy in seminaries must be taught *ad Angelici Doctoris rationem, doctrinam et principia* (1917 CIC c.1366.2). This raised two difficulties. One was the problem of determining what the ''doctrine'' of St. Thomas was, not to mention the method and principles, for there was controversy about this among the theologians and philosophers. Three schools of interpretation were discernible. One was literalist and restrictive and understood the doctrine of St. Thomas in the sense of the classical Dominican commentators. The second was broader and interpretative and understood the doctrine in the sense of an Aristotelian-scholastic *philosophia perennis* that fitted a Suarezian version of Thomism. The third maintained the Thomist position but reinterpreted it in the light of modern philosophy.

The other difficulty rose from the very idea of this sort of legislation in philosophy. It appeared to restrict Catholic philosophy to one particular historical system and to exclude or at most to tolerate all other philosophies past or present. First, this appeared to be the destruction of philosophy itself, for it seemed to close off the search for new philosophical understanding. Second, it seemed to put an impossible psychological burden upon philosophers who had elaborated a non-Thomist philosophy either by reason of having been formed in another Scholastic or Catholic tradition, or of having been converted to Catholicism as mature philosophers (e.g., Edith Stein, Von Hildebrand, Marcel), or of having come to philosophy with different problems and concerns than St. Thomas (e.g., contemporary science, evolution, history, socialism). Furthermore, the legislation tended to widen the gap between clerical and lay philosophy, since it applied directly and explicitly only to seminaries, though the encyclicals *Aeterni Patris* and *Humani generis* were directed to the Church at large. From these difficulties there arose the question of philosophical pluralism within the Church or within Thomism as intended by the Church.

Types of Responses

However, the problem of philosophical pluralism is broader than the question of philosophy in the Church. Catholicism adds another dimension and context to the problem because of the unity of faith and the completion of the deposit of faith in a definite time in the past. But the question arises also from the pluralism of Greek and modern philosophies. It is a question of ultimate truth and whether truth is one or many: and if one, in what way; and if many, in what way. There have been many responses to these questions. They can be summarized into the following five types.

Denial of Ultimate Truth. First, there are the various types of denial of a unified ultimate truth. The very phenomenon of the diversity and disagreement of philosophies was one of the arguments used by the Greek skeptics and by the skeptical tradition for rejecting absolute knowledge and speculative truth. Modern empiricism since D. Hume has denied the validity of metaphysical truth and granted meaning only to the empirically verifiable or to fruitful action (pragmatism). Though not adherents of the skeptical tradition, philosophers of the finite, such as N. HARTMANN, have rejected any overall system of thought and truth.

Unity of Ultimate Truth. At the opposite pole is the response asserting the absolute and univocal unity of ultimate truth and identifying this truth with a particular historical system or tradition in such a way that all other philosophies are measured by this system and are judged false or inadequate insofar as they differ from this system. Thus the true system is that of Plato, of Aristotle, of Thomas, of Kant, or of Hegel.

Philosophia Perennis. Next there is an intermediate response—that of the *philosophia perennis,* though this term itself has been used in different senses. According to this view philosophy is not a collection of different systems, but rather a continuous and gradual development by many philosophies and philosophers of an increasingly more adequate explanation of reality. Philosophy itself is continuous with nonphilosophical thought; there is a continuity between pre-Christian and Christian philosophy. The term seems to have been originated by A. Steuco in his *De perenni philosophia libri X* (Lyons 1540), but the idea harmonizes with the notion of the Catholic tradition since Justin and Origen. The general notion that there is truth in all systems and that they can be reduced to one synthesis was an ideal with G. W. LEIBNIZ. Both the notion and term are found in the documents of the neoscholastic revival along with the affirmation of Thomism. It was the position of the (German) Suarezian tradition, which, however, tended to limit the perennial philosophy to the Aristotelian tradition.

Parts of a Whole. Next there is the response that considers all particular philosophies even in their contradictions as parts of a whole or of an infinite unity. In one form of this position, the infinite can be expressed only in finite modes that are contradictory or opposite (Spinoza). In another, reality is dialectically structured so that opposition forms a stage in the process of the whole

(Hegel). This response is generally that of the pantheisms or monisms, whether Oriental or Western.

Different Expressions. Finally, there is the response judging that, though the many philosophies are apparently diverse and opposed, they are simply different expressions from different viewpoints and by different methods of one ultimate truth (R. P. McKeon, N. P. Stallknecht, and R. S. Brumbaugh). They can either be translated into each other if one studies the semantics involved or they simply point at the ineffable truth across the dialogue, as is stated in Plato's seventh letter.

Outline of a Solution

Only the general lines of a solution can be given here. It is necessary to note first of all that the solution itself does not escape the problem of pluralism, for any solution will involve a notion of philosophy and the notion of philosophy is itself involved in pluralism. The different philosophies conceive philosophy differently.

Personal Aspects. The reason for this is that philosophy is a reflexive science or WISDOM that includes its own subjective viewpoint in its philosophizing. This characteristic of philosophy is derived from the fact that philosophy aims at ultimate and universal understanding of reality. As a consequence of this aim philosophy must include itself in its investigation of the real, for the philosopher and his knowing are a part of the real. In other words, the philosopher must inquire not only into the world before him but also into himself and into his relation with the world. As a consequence of this, philosophy is intrinsically concerned with the question of the destiny of man as well as with the nature of the universe. That is why philosophy has always had two orientations, cosmological and scientific (Ionian), and humanistic and ethical (Italian). Both, if pressed to the ultimate as they must be, lead to the theological question and thus a third possible orientation is given, the theological. It is for this reason that philosophy shows some of the characteristics of religion as well as of science.

Because the reflexive character of philosophy so engages the subject in the work of philosophizing, personal choice and decision have a central role to play. For the philosopher determines his own fundamental orientation. That is, a man must ultimately determine his attitude toward the world, toward himself and his ultimate destiny. He may determine his attitude by default, that is, by not making any decision, by simply allowing himself to be carried along, or he may determine it by a series of minor decisions or by one major decision; but ultimately he must determine his basic freedom by a fundamental choice (cf. St. Thomas Aquinas, *Summa Theologiae* 1a2ae, 90.6).

Because the world and man himself are diversified and complex, many choices are possible to him. He may choose to rest in a polar opposite, in determinism rather than in freedom, in skepticism rather than in absolutism, etc.; or on a level of being, matter rather than spirit, nature rather than grace; or in a sphere of life, in art, political action, science, or business, etc.; or he may accept a contradiction between his way of life and his metaphysics. Thus according to J. G. FICHTE, the difference between idealism or materialism is determined by a choice—which, however, is conditioned by the kind of person the philosopher is—and William JAMES speaks in this connection of tough-minded and tender-minded men. The ultimate choice for a philosopher is whether he will open himself to the infinite and receive the word of the transcendent being (Blondel, K. Rahner), or whether he will close himself within the finite or the world of space and time. Thus ultimate philosophical truth depends upon the exercise of man's freedom.

Communal Aspects. This ultimate choice and orientation automatically makes a man a member of a community and a part of a tradition, the community and tradition of those who have made a like choice. This it is that makes for the fundamental diversity of philosophies in the world. Since the fundamental choice and orientation of the Catholic is the acceptance of the revelation of Yahweh and Jesus in the Church, he by that fact becomes a member of the community of the Church and a part of the tradition of the Church. His *philosophia perennis,* then, is determined by his membership in that community. But the community of the Church permits further determination and consequently there are communities within the community, specifications of the fundamental orientation. Typically these are the religious orders with distinctive spiritualities. Thus the diversity of philosophies in the Church frequently accompanies the diversity of spiritualities.

Philosophy therefore has both an objective, communal and traditional aspect, and a subjective, individual and creative aspect. It participates in the general conditions of all human knowing, which is developmental and dialogic, and hence social and historical. It never begins completely anew without antecedents, and consequently it shows continuity with its past. On the other hand, because it is seeking the ultimate and comprehensive, it must continually attempt to rethink the whole, to find a deeper integrating center or point of synthesis between itself and the world, the past and the future. Because philosophy is the work of finite thinkers in a complex and changing environment, it has many possible starting points. Because it is constantly striving to transcend its finite situation, it keeps trying new methods. Yet the philosopher works within a tradition, the larger tradition of the universal *philosophia perennis,* and the more specific tradition of his ultimate orientation.

Because of the personal element in philosophy, it is not possible to formulate the tradition once and for all. For philosophy is not a collection of single propositions that can readily be compared with other single propositions. Rather philosophy is a unity of viewpoints and totalities that are worked out in history not according to a straight, additive development, but by devious personal, social, and historical movements. Each philosopher is committed to remake the synthesis between the personal and traditional elements. He must recapitulate the tradition in himself, as did Aristotle, Plotinus, Aquinas, Suárez, Hegel, etc.

Catholics and Revelation. For the Catholic philosopher another possibility is given for determining the common elements and the tradition: revelation as developed in the Church. For revelation teaches ultimate truth. Besides drawing the fundamental distinction between the supernatural and the natural, it teaches truth directly or indirectly relevant to the natural investigations of man. These provide a center or outline for man's life and reflection. Like the universal tradition, the Catholic tradition is not formulated once and for all. It is gradually built up, by the work of many, over the centuries. This work of determining the Catholic tradition for philosophy must always be redone in the light of new knowledge and new problems.

The conclusion must be that philosophy cannot be only objective and communal; it must also be personal—not by moral obligation, as it were, but by the very nature of man and philosophy. Hence even within the Catholic community there will be different philosophies and schools. It is not possible to make one of these schools in its personal and individual elements the common philosophy of all, because these elements simply cannot be repeated by all. It is possible, however, to set one of the schools in its common and traditional elements as a norm for the developing tradition of the community. But this tradition will always be developed in personal and different philosophies.

Bibliography: J. D. COLLINS, *Three Paths in Philosophy* (Chicago 1962). V. T. A. FERM, ed., *A History of Philosophical Systems* (New York 1950). G. G. GRISEZ, ''Toward a Metaphilosophy,'' *American Catholic Philosopical Association. Proceedings of the Annual Meeting* 37 (1963) 47–70. H. GUTHRIE, *Introduction au problème de l'histoire de la philosophie* (Paris 1937). R. F. HARVANEK, ''Philosophical Pluralism and Catholic Orthodoxy,'' *Thought* 25 (1950) 21–52. B. J. F. LONERGAN, *Insight: A Study of Human Understanding* (New York 1957). G. A. MCCOOL, ''Philosophical Pluralism and an Evolving Thomism,'' *Continuum* 2 (1964) 3–16. R. P. MCKEON, *Freedom and History* (New York 1952); *Thought, Action, and Passion* (Chicago 1954). C. A. MOORE, ed., *Philosophy, East and West* (Princeton 1944). E. PRZYWARA, *Polarity,* tr. A. C. BOUQUET (London 1925). S. RADHAKRISHNAN, *Eastern Religions and Western Thought* (2d ed. New York 1940). N. P. STALLKNECHT and R. S. BRUMBAUGH, *The Compass of Philosophy: An Essay in Intellectual Orientation* (New York 1954).

[R. F. HARVANEK]

PLUS, RAOUL

Jesuit spiritual writer; b. Boulogne-sur-Mer, Jan. 22, 1882; d. Lille, Oct. 23, 1958. Plus entered the Society of Jesus at Saint-Acheul in 1899 and made his studies abroad because of the 1901 laws against religious orders in France. During his philosophical studies, his spiritual father was Germain Foch, SJ, who expounded the doctrine of incorporation into Christ that later became the core of Plus's spiritual writings. As a French army chaplain during World War I, he gave the soldiers talks that were to serve as the material for his first two books, *Dieu en nous* (Eng. tr., *God within Us,* New York, 1924), and *L'Idée reparatrice* (Eng. tr., *Ideal of Reparation,* New York, 1922). These were well received because of their style, as well as their doctrine, and were translated into other languages, as were many of his later works. For his wartime services Plus was decorated with the *croix de guerre.*

Between the wars Plus served as professor of religion and spiritual director at the Université Catholique at Lille, except during the years 1935 to 1939 when he taught at the Institut Catholique of Paris. This was the period of his greatest literary activity, from which eventually came more than 40 books and innumerable articles. In addition to his other work, he preached and gave retreats. After spending World War II at a retreat house, Plus returned to Lille as spiritual father for the Jesuit community and remained there until his death.

In his writings Plus popularized the principal chapters of the spiritual life, constantly reemphasizing the doctrine of the Mystical Body of Christ. A synthetic résumé of his teaching is found in his *Marie dans notre histoire divine* (Toulouse 1932; Eng. tr., *Mary in Our Soul-Life,* Cincinnati, 1940).

Bibliography: M. HOEHN, *Catholic Authors* (Newark 1948). J. JUAMBELZ, *Index Bibliographicus Societatis Jesus,* 4 v. (Rome 1938–53).

[F. J. BERGEN]

PLUSCARDEN PRIORY

Benedictine monastery near Elgin, Morayshire, Diocese of Aberdeen, Scotland. Founded and liberally en-

Pluscarden Priory. (© Hulton-Deutsch Collection/CORBIS)

dowed by Alexander II in 1230 for an austere community of VALLISCAULIAN monks from Burgundy, the monastery enjoyed the protection of popes and Scottish kings through the 13th century; and much of its present structure, finely restored, dates from this period. After the Scottish wars of independence, however, and particularly after being sacked and burned (1390), the monastery declined and was obliged to amalgamate with the Benedictine priory of Urquhart (1454). After the Reformation the priory with its lands passed into private hands. Purchased in 1897 by the Marquess of Bute, it was given by his son to PRINKNASH (Gloucester) with the hope that it would eventually become a daughterhouse. In 1948 a small band of monks reopened Pluscarden; they have restored much of the priory to its former use besides participating in the religious life of northeast Scotland.

Bibliography: F. J. H. SKENE, ed., *Liber Pluscardensis* (Edinburgh 1877–80). D. E. EASSON, *Medieval Religious Houses: Scotland* (London 1957) 55, 72. P. F. ANSON, *A Monastery in Moray: The Story of Pluscarden Priory, 1230–1948* (London 1959). O. L. KAPSNER, *A Benedictine Bibliography: An Author-Subject Union List,* 2 v. (2d ed. Collegeville, Minn. 1962): v. 1, author part; v. 2, subject part, 2:250.

[L. MACFARLANE]

PLYMOUTH BRETHREN

Also called the Christian Brethren. In 1827 groups of Christians in England and Ireland began to meet apart from the established churches to study the Bible, pray, and hold weekly communion services. John DARBY (1800–82), a former Church of Ireland clergyman, led the movement for many years. Members of these fellowships eventually were identified as Darbyites or Plymouth Brethren. The latter name came from the largest and most influential of these groups at Plymouth, England, but has no official acceptance. Beginning in 1838, Darby spent seven years in Switzerland; when he returned to England

and encountered opposition to his leadership, he started a rival body of Plymouth Brethren.

Most Plymouth Brethren congregations meet for worship in ''remembrance meetings,'' in private homes or rented halls, and include only 35 or 40 people. The Plymouth Brethren oppose seminary training, clerical titles, and ordination of ministers. Although they are devoted students of the Bible, they do not favor higher education. The various groupings of Plymouth Brethren have no national or international coordinating agencies. Local churches follow a congregational form of government. There are no official spokesmen or periodicals. The Brethren follow a fundamentalist theology based on the literal and verbal interpretation of the Bible. Their position is Calvinist, but they reject all creeds and confessions. The congregations hold a weekly communion service. In their preaching the Brethren emphasize the imminent Second Coming of Jesus Christ (*see* PAROUSIA).

Bibliography: F. S. MEAD, S. S. HILL and C. D. ATWOOD, eds., *Handbook of Denominations in the United States*, 11th ed (Nashville 2001)

[W. J. WHALEN/EDS.]

PNEUMATOMACHIANS

A 4th-century Christian sect that denied the divinity of the Holy Spirit; its devotees were known as Macedonians from the time of Pope DAMASUS I and had their center at the Hellespont. Relying solely on the Scriptures and repudiating metaphysical speculation, the Pneumatomachians denied that the Holy Spirit was God since the New Testament said nothing about His participation in the work of creation; they claimed He was not of the same essence as the Father and Son. As they denied the divinity of the Spirit, they received the name of opponents of the Spirit (*Pneumatomachoi*). The earliest information on this group was supplied by ATHANASIUS OF ALEXANDRIA in his *Ad. Serapion* (*Patrologia Graeca* 26:530). Ecclesiastical action against this group was taken in a synod at Alexandria (362) that declared a heretic whoever spoke of the Holy Spirit as a creature (*kstima*: *Patrologia Graeca* 26:800). The Cappadocian fathers opposed the theology of the Pneumatomachians and in a synod at Iconium (377) the heresy was condemned (*Patrologia Graeca* 39:93). In 379 Pope Damasus I, at a Roman synod, and the bishops of the Orient, in a synod at Antioch, likewise opposed this teaching. It was definitively anathematized at the Council of CONSTANTINOPLE I and condemned by a law of THEODOSIUS I (*Cod.* 16.5, 11–13). Despite the assertion of DIDYMUS THE BLIND (*c.* 380), Macedonius, the semi-Arian bishop of Constantinople (342–360), was not a founder of this sect.

Bibliography: J. QUASTEN, *Patrology* (Westminster, Md. 1950—) v. 3, index s.v. Pneumatomachoi. H. DÖRRIES, *De Spiritu Sancto* (Göttingen 1956). J. GRIBOMONT, *Dictionnaire de spiritualité ascétique et mystique. Doctrine et histoire*, ed. M. VILLER, et al. (Paris 1932—) 4:1257–72. G. BARDY, *Dictionnaire de théologie catholique*, ed. A. VACANT et al. (Paris 1903–50) 9.2:1464–74. T. SCHERMANN, *Die Gottheit des Heiligen Geistes nach den griechischen Vätern des 4, Jahrhunderts* (Freiburg 1901).

[F. HAUSER]

POBEDONOSTSEV, KONSTANTIN PETROVICH

Russian jurist, political philosopher; b. Moscow, Nov. 10, 1827; d. St. Petersburg, March 10, 1907. After studying law at St. Petersburg, he worked as a civil servant from 1846 until his death. He tutored Czar Alexander II's children in Russian law and history. He became a senator (1868), a member of the Council of State (1872), and lay head of the HOLY SYNOD (1880). The effect of his immense influence over Alexander III and Nicholas II was to make Russia's domestic policies reactionary and repressive, particularly in matters affecting religion, education, censorship, and religious and national minorities. Pobedonostsev was called the ''Grand Inquisitor.'' Until 1895, when his influence declined, he was feared as a symbol of the old regime by Russian liberals and radicals. He was a friend of Dostoevskiĭ and a good scholar fluent in several European languages. Yet his writings reflected his determination to destroy all Western influence in Russia. A collection of his essays, *Moskovskii sbornik* (1896), clearly manifested his hatred and fear of constitutional government, freedom of the press, religious liberty, trial by jury, and free education.

Bibliography: K. P. POBEDONOSTSEV, *Reflections of a Russian Statesman,* tr. R. C. LONG (London 1898). F. STEINMAN and E. HURWICZ, *K. P. Podjedonoszew, der Staatsmann der Reaktion unter Alexander III* (Königsberg 1933). R. F. BYRNES, ''P.'s Conception of the Good Society,'' *Review of Politics* 13 (1951) 169–190. K. ONASCH, *Die Religion in Geschichte und Gegenwart,* 7 v. (3d ed. Tübingen 1957–65) 5:423.

[R. F. BYRNES]

POETA SAXO

Medieval Latin poet; fl. last quarter of the 9th century. He was a monk of CORVEY in Westphalia, and is known only under the name of ''the Saxon Poet.'' About 888, early in the reign of the East Frankish king Arnulf (877–899), he composed a historical poem on Charlemagne in five books (2,683 lines). He titled books one to four *Annales de gestis Caroli Magni imperatoris*, and book 5 *De vita et obitu eiusdem.* The work exhibits no originality but is essentially an annalistic account of the reign of Charlemagne, based closely on the so–called *Annales Einharti,* Einhard's *Vita Caroli,* and similar earlier sources. While his poetic talent is of a low order, his prosody is relatively good. Books one to four are in hexameters, but he thought it would be more fitting to write his fifth book, on the last days of Charlemagne, in elegiac distichs.

Bibliography: P. VON WINTERFELD, *Monumenta Germaniae Historica: Poetae* 4.1:1–71. F. J. E. RABY, *A History of Secular Latin Poetry in the Middle Ages* (Oxford 1957) 1:260. M. MANITIUS, *Geschichte der lateinischen Literatur des Mittelalters* (Munich 1911–31) 1:583–584.

[M. R. P. MCGUIRE]

POETICS (ARISTOTELIAN)

The *Poetics,* in length, is one of Aristotle's slightest works, forming barely a hundredth part of the extant Aristotelian corpus. But short as it is, it ''is the most fundamental study we have of the art of drama'' (Fergusson, 2). Moreover, ''it is largely through the *Poetics* . . . that the main poetic 'kinds' are still distinguished, even in their names, through all the literature of Europe, as Tragedy, Comedy, Epic and Lyric'' (House, 14). Finally, there is widespread agreement that ''after twenty-two centuries it remains the most stimulating and helpful of all analytical works dealing with poetry'' (Cooper, 3). (*See* ARISTOTELIANISM.)

Content of the Work. A summary of the main parts of the work reveals an underlying logic of construction. The first five chapters constitute a general introduction to poetic art. The common genus is imitation; the various arts differ in terms of (1) the means of imitation (the medium in which the artist works), (2) the object of imitation (human action and passion), and (3) the manner of imitation (lyrical, narrative, and dramatic). The fourth chapter deals with the common origin of poetic art, with a brief history of tragedy, while the fifth chapter treats the origin of comedy and compares epic and tragedy.

Tragedy. Chapters 6 through 22 form the substance of the work and treat tragedy in considerable detail. After defining tragedy—''an imitation of an action that is serious, complete, having a certain magnitude, expressed in enriched language employing various kinds in different parts of the play, by means of action, not narration, through events arousing pity and fear which bring about the appropriate purgation of these emotions'' (1449b 24–28)—Aristotle lists the six elements of tragedy: plot, character, thought, diction, song, and spectacle. Diction and song relate to the means of imitation; spectacle or scenery pertains to the manner of imitation; and plot, character, and thought belong to the object of imitation. These are qualitative parts of a tragedy; the quantitative parts are acts or episodes of the play, and are discussed in chapter 12.

Plot. Plot occupies the chief attention, for it is ''the soul of tragedy,'' the metaphor by which Aristotle expresses plot as the life-giving principle that shapes human action into actual tragedy. He observes that eight conditions are realized in good plots: (1) an action is represented as complete in itself, that is, a whole with its appropriate beginning, middle, and end; (2) the plot has a fitting magnitude (''beauty is a matter of size and order'' 1450b 36); (3) it has unity, the parts being so ordered that if one of them is destroyed or removed or transposed the unity of the whole is lost; (4) it has dramatic possibility or plausibility, i.e., the plot deals with what *could* conceivably take place rather than what *actually* has happened; (5) it is not episodic, a series of events in which there is no inevitable or likely sequence of events, yet allows for the unexpected; (6) the plot contains something astonishing or marvelous, for in this way the tragic emotions of pity and fear are aroused; (7) it is complex, a course of events involving change, for example, from happiness to misery; a reversal, therefore, accompanied by discovery, a change from ignorance to knowledge; and (8) it contains some calamity, or painful action, in order to arouse sufficiently the emotions of pity and fear.

Character. Aristotle then proceeds to discuss (beginning with chapter 13) the sort of tragic character the poet chooses: a man who is good, but not eminently so, whose misfortune is brought about by a ''tragic flaw.'' The tragic emotions of pity and fear spring from the plot itself, not from the spectacle. The tragic character expresses moral qualities that are appropriate to him, and he should be consistent and coherent. After noting some practical rules that have guided the poet in his construction of a tragedy, Aristotle discusses the elements of thought and diction. The remainder of the *Poetics* (chapters 23–26) treats epic poetry, terminating in a comparative evaluation of epic and tragedy. Three key topics are here discussed briefly.

Imitation (Mimesis). Imitation is proposed by Aristotle as something common to all fine art, but its crucial role will be appreciated only if imitation is understood in a distinctive sense. It must first of all be distinguished from mere natural likeness or copying. A natural likeness is not an imitation at all; one egg may be like another egg, but it is not an imitation of it. The image of a man in the mirror is both a likeness and an imitation, for there is dependence of the image upon the original from which it proceeds. But this is mere duplication or reflection. In an artistic imitation, the image as expressed in some sense medium has a dependence upon some original referent in reality (such as a shape, color, sound, passion, or character), but there is also dependence upon man's creative conception and imagination. Aristotle's notion of imitation, therefore, does imply a creative vision on the part of the artist as well as something that relates in one way or another to the real. In the *Poetics,* Aristotle develops imitation chiefly in relation to the construction of plot that imitates "an action that is serious, complete, having a certain magnitude," (1450b 24) and so on. (*See* ART [PHILOSOPHY]; CREATIVE IMAGINATION.)

Hamartia. The translation of this as "tragic flaw" can be misleading if it is understood simply as moral fault. Rather, it is at once intellectual and moral, a flaw in the deliberation and judgment of prudence as inseparably bound up with some flaw in the ordering of man's appetite to good ends. It is a "mistake," therefore, but not one purely of the intellect, and is bound up with the elements of reversal and discovery in the development of the plot. The Greek word ἁμαρτία, as Aristotle uses it, means a failure or a mistake and is midway between ἀδίκημα (intentional wrong) and ἀτύχημα (a fault of ignorance). Hence when Aristotle speaks of the tragic character as one who is not wholly virtuous or one who suffers misfortune because of wickedness, we are led to understand that the tragic character, basically well-intentioned, is nonetheless brought to a downfall by mistaken judgment swayed by some moral defect in the impulse of desire.

Catharsis. The understanding of the cathartic effect in drama presupposes understanding the role pity and fear play in tragic representation. The two emotions are inseparably joined in good tragedy; one without the other becomes either mere sentimentality or sheer horror.

The first meaning of catharsis is medical, referring to some physical purgation in respect of the body. In an artistic context, Aristotle obviously extends this meaning. Just as a physical purgation eliminates a bodily disorder so as to achieve a better physiological state, so artistic catharsis is purgative and purifying in relation to the movement of human passion as the play is witnessed. We naturally have some emotional tension that is unresolved or is resolved somewhat unsatisfactorily. Good works of art, in arousing and resolving the emotions, bring us to the state of repose we need but often do not achieve in daily life; herein lies the great appeal of art, and not only tragedy. Elsewhere Aristotle speaks more explicitly of such catharsis in listening to music whereby persons can be restored as though they had found purgation and healing. "Those who are influenced by pity and fear, and every emotional nature, must have a like experience, and others insofar as each is susceptible to such emotions, and all are in a manner purged and their souls lightened and delighted" (*Politics,* 1342a 11–15).

Hence catharsis, as purgative and purifying, is basic to artistic enjoyment and appreciation. By artistic tension and release, the emotions receive an orderly subjection to reason as shaped by artistic form. Nevertheless, catharsis remains basically instrumental in art; it is ordered to the proper end of art—CONTEMPLATION and the ensuing delight we find in such contemplation.

Place in the Aristotelian Corpus. The usual order of Aristotle's works has the *Poetics,* preceded by the *Rhetoric,* at the very end, and some think that this may represent the ordering instituted at the Lyceum. The practical slant of the two works is one reason adduced for putting them at the end of the corpus.

Another tradition places the *Rhetoric* and the *Poetics* at the end of the *Organon* (the logical works). The *Organon* appears first because logic treats the common method for all knowledge. Within the *Organon,* the *Rhetoric* follows the *Topics* since, as Aristotle explains at the beginning of the *Rhetoric,* rhetoric is the counterpart of dialectic, the subject of the *Topics.* The *Poetics* follows the *Rhetoric,* first because of an affinity it has with rhetoric, and second because poetics, too, deals with a special type of argumentation.

The association of poetic art with argumentation is not acknowledged by all. The purpose of any argumentation, however, is to lead one to a new truth from previous knowledge, and poetic art has its own means of inducing assent to a truth. The poet does this by constructing a pleasing representation of what is true or plausible; for example, he composes metaphors and similes for the sake of presenting poetically imaginative meaning that conveys in its way a truth, or he constructs a plot so as to present a convincing similitude of the working out of human action. Thus Shakespeare induces us to accept the general judgment that jealousy can lead to a man's downfall; he does this by a particular representation of this in the person and action of Othello. Herein, lies the significance of the phrase "argument of the play" as often stated in a program. Such argumentation is properly found in the poetic arts, and in proportion as we speak of a poet's work of art as convincing, we acknowledge the existence of a poetic form of argumentation.

See Also: AESTHETICS; ARGUMENTATION; BEAUTY; RHETORIC.

Bibliography: S. BUTCHER, *Aristotle's Theory of Poetry and Fine Arts* (4th ed. London 1932). I. BYWATER, tr. *Aristotle on the Art of Poetry* (2d ed. London 1938). L. COOPER, *The Poetics of Aristotle* (rev. ed. Ithaca, N.Y. 1956). G. ELSE, *Aristotle's Poetics: The Argument* (Cambridge, Mass. 1957). F. FERGUSSON, ed. *Aristotle's*

Poetics, tr. S. BUTCHER (New York 1961). H. HOUSE, *Aristotle's Poetics: A Course of Eight Lectures* (rev. ed. London 1956).

[J. A. OESTERLE]

POGGIO BRACCIOLINI, GIOVANNI FRANCESCO

Humanist; b. Terranuova, near Arezzo, February 11, 1380; d. Florence, April 30, 1459. Early in his boyhood his impoverished family moved to Florence where Poggio was able to pay for instruction in Latin from Giovanni da Ravenna from fees earned in copying MSS. He probably learned Greek, of which he never had full mastery, on his own initiative. In 1404, at the age of 24, he entered the service of the apostolic chancery during the pontificate of Boniface IX, serving as a *scriptor;* he held that post as a layman under eight popes for almost 50 years. On June 8, 1453, he assumed the office of chancellor of the Republic of FLORENCE, and functioned in that capacity until shortly before his death. His proficiency in Latin epistolography, an accomplishment much admired in his time, exerted considerable influence on the development of the curial style of the papal chancery. Poggio's most enduring claim to distinction rests on his remarkable industry in ''recovering'' MSS of Latin authors in monastic libraries such as WEINGARTEN, REICHENAU, and SANKT GALLEN, where he found the complete text of Quintilian's *Institutio oratoria,* which he copied and forwarded to Leonardo Bruni.

As an author, Poggio is best known for his *Letters* and his most frequently translated *Liber facetiarum,* a collection of witty and generally indecent anecdotes filled with invective against clergy and religious. In imitation of Seneca he composed his *Historia disceptiva de avaritia, Historiae de varietate fortunae, In hypocritas et delatores,* and *De humanae conditionis miseria,* all of which show traces of a Christian STOICISM. The *Historia Florentiae,* modeled on Livy's history of Rome, is useful but labors under the defects of its annalistic approach. In his translations of Greek authors, such as Diodorus Siculus, Lucian, and Xenophon (*Cyropaedia*), Poggio's defective knowledge of Greek is all too evident; he was unable to render faithfully a Greek author's trend of thought. In controversies with Zeno of Feltre, Guarino, Ciriaco of Ancona, Filelfo, and Lorenzo Valla, to name but a few, he was frequently scurrilous and stirred up lifelong hatreds. Poggio's *Urbis Romae descriptio* and his interest in collecting Latin inscriptions give him a place of honor at the beginnings of classical archeology.

Bibliography: Editions. *Opera omnia,* ed. H. BEBELIUS (Basel 1538); *Epistolae,* ed. T. DE TONELLIS, 3 v. (Florence 1832–61). Literature. G. VOIGT, *Die Wiederbelebung des classischen Altertums,* ed. M. LEHNERDT, 2 v. (3d ed. Berlin 1893). L. PASTOR, *The History of the Popes from the Close of the Middle Ages,* 40 v. (London-St. Louis 1938–61) v.1, *passim.* J. E. SANDYS, *History of Classical Scholarship,* 3 v. (Cambridge, England) 2:25–34. E. WALSER, *Gesammelte Studien zur Geistesgeschichte der Renaissance* (Basel 1932). C. DA CAPODIMONTE, ''Poggio Bracciolini autore delle anonime *Vitae quorundam pontificum,*'' *Rivista di storia della Chiesa in Italia* 14 (1960) 27–47. M. SEIDLMAYER, *Die Religion in Geschichte und Gegenwart,* 7 v. (3d ed. Tübingen 1957–65) 5:424. F. ZOEPFEL, *Lexikon für Theologie und Kirche,* ed. J. HOFER and K. RAHNER, 10 v. (2d, new ed. Freiburg 1957–65) 8:577. H. BARON, *The Crisis of the Early Italian Renaissance,* 2 v. (Princeton 1955). M. E. COSENZA, *Biographical and Bibliographical Dictionary of the Italian Humanists and of the World of Classical Scholarship in Italy, 1300–1800,* 5 v. (2d, rev. and enl. ed. Boston 1962) 4:2858–59; 5:1445–46. P. BRACCIOLONI, *Lettere* (Florence 1984); *Poggio Bracciolini, 1380–1980* (Florence 1980). C. TRINKAUS, *In Our Image and Likeness* (Chicago 1970).

[H. DRESSLER]

POHL, ALFRED

Orientalist, author, and editor of scholarly publications on the ancient Near East; b. Köbernitz, Upper Silesia, Dec. 1, 1890; d. Rome, Oct. 23, 1961. He entered the Society of Jesus in 1912 and studied Assyriology under Bruno Meissner from 1924 to 1930. In 1930, he went to the Pontifical Biblical Institute in Rome as professor of Assyriology and of ancient Oriental history. In the next decade, he published several original editions of Babylonian and Sumerian economic texts: *Neubabylonische Rechtsurkunden aus den Berliner Staatlichen Museen,* 2 v. (Rome 1933–34), *Vorsargonische und sargonische Wirtschaftstexte* (Leipzig 1935), and *Rechts- und Verwaltungsurkunden der III. Dynastie von Ur* (Leipzig 1937). He became dean of the Oriental faculty of the institute in 1945.

Pohl was especially known for his long and successful career as an editor. Assuming charge of *Orientalia* in 1932, he built it into a periodical of international stature. As editor of *Analecta Orientalia,* he provided scholars with a series of basic grammars and historical studies on the ancient Near East, while his furthering of the *Materialien zum sumerischen Lexikon* (Rome 1937–) laid the groundwork for much-needed study on Sumerian lexicography. Scholars are further indebted to him for his founding and personal compilation of the indispensable *Keilschriftbibliographie* (1940—), the only comprehensive annual bibliography in Mesopotamian studies.

Bibliography: E. F. WEIDNER, *Archiv für Orientforschung* 20 (1963) 302–303. S. MOSCATI, *Orientalia* 31 (1962) 1–6.

[J. A. BRINKMAN]

POHLE, JOSEPH

Professor; b. Niederspay, Germany, March 19, 1852; d. Breslau, Germany, Feb. 21, 1922. After completing his studies at Trier, Germany, he attended the German College in Rome, as well as the Gregorianum. He received his Ph.D. in philosophy in 1874, his S.T.D. in 1879. He was ordained in 1878.

When prevented from accepting an official appointment in Germany by the restrictive laws of the Kulturkampf, he studied at Würzburg, Germany (1879–81), and was influenced by the noted botanist, Julius von Sachs. After teaching secondary school in Baar, Switzerland (1881–83), he became professor of theology and Scripture at St. Joseph's College, Leeds, England (1883–86). When episcopal seminaries were reopened in Germany by Bismarck's partial repeal of the Falk laws, Pohle became professor of philosophy (1886–89) at the seminary in Fulda. There, with Constantin Gutberlet, he served as cofounder and coeditor of the *Philosophisches Jahrbuch* of the Görres Society.

In 1889, at the request of Bp. John J. Keane, Pohle joined the faculty of the Catholic University of America in Washington, D.C., as professor of apologetics. In the United States his name came to be linked with the German-American party in the Cahensly dispute (*see* CAHENSLY, PETER PAUL). This may have prompted his acceptance of an offer to return to Germany in 1894 as professor of dogma at Münster. After transferring to Breslau in 1897, he continued to occupy himself with various scholarly pursuits until his death. Among his works were *Angelo Secchi* (1883), *Die Sternenwelten und ihre Bewohner* (1884), *Lehrbuch der Dogmatik* (1902–05), and *Soldatentod und Martyrertod* (1917). He collaborated on several other books and contributed to various learned journals. He also wrote 21 articles for the *Catholic Encyclopedia.*

Bibliography: P. H. AHERN, *The Catholic University of America, 1887–1896. The Rectorship of John J. Keane* (Washington 1949). J. GRUMMERSBACH, *Lexikon für Theologie und und Kirche,* ed. J. HOFER and K. RAHNER, 10 v. (2d, new ed. Freiburg 1957–65) 9:578. C. GUTBERLET, *Philosophisches Jahrbuch der Görres-Gesellschaft* 35 (1922) 181–184.

[J. F. WIPPEL]

POIDEBARD, ANTOINE

Archeologist, originator of aerial photography for archeological research; b. Lyons, France, Oct. 11, 1878; d. Beirut, Lebanon, Jan. 17, 1955. He entered the Society of Jesus at d'Aix on June 2, 1897; in 1904, with several confreres, he formed the nucleus of the Armenian mission entrusted to the Jesuits by Leo XIII. During this mission he studied Turkish and Armenian. From 1912 to 1914 he studied theology at Ore Place. During World War I he was a chaplain in the armed services and undertook several missions for the French government in the Near East. In 1924 he organized the services rendered to the Armenian refugees. He was commissioned a lieutenant-colonel of the reserve air force in 1925, and on Jan. 4, 1951, the air force medal was bestowed on him for outstanding services as a missionary explorer.

As a result of his aerial research, two works of considerable interest were published: *La Trace de Rome dans le désert de Syrie* (Paris 1934) and *Le Limes de Chalcis; organisation de la Steppe en Haute-Syrie romaine* (Paris 1945), a work done in collaboration with R. Mouterde as historian and epigraphist. This study marked a considerable advance in the knowledge of the history of Upper Syria. His observations concerning water supplies were used by the Syrian department of water services for supplying water to the nomad tribes. Poidebard's interest in aerial photography led to the discovery in the Mediterranean of an ancient seaport. The results were published in *Un Grand port disparu: Tyr; Recherches aériennes et sous-marines* (Paris 1939). In collaboration with J. Lauffray, he published *Sidon: aménagements antiques du Port de Saida; Études aériennes, au sol et sous-marines, 1946–1950* (Paris 1952). This new method of research inaugurated by Poidebard produced significant results. The use of aerial photography for archeological purposes is frequently employed today.

Bibliography: R. MOUTERDE, "A. Poidebard (1878–1955)," *Mélanges de l'Université St. Joseph* 31 (1954–55) 317–328.

[M. G. BULTEAU]

POIRTERS, ADRIAEN

Flemish Jesuit spiritual writer; b. Oisterwijk, The Netherlands, Nov. 2, 1605; d. Malines, July 4, 1674. Poirters attended the Jesuit secondary school at Bois-le-Duc and studied philosophy at the University of Douai before he entered the Society of Jesus on July 25, 1625. He was ordained in Louvain on March 20, 1638 and pronounced the four solemn vows at Roermond on Dec. 26, 1641. He was afterward active as a preacher and a confessor, mainly in Roermond and Malines. From 1640 on, he was remarkably productive as a popular writer. His main works are *Het Masker van de Wereldt afghetrocken* (1645, The Mask Torn from the World), *Het Duyfken in de Steen-Rotse* (1657, The Little Pigeon in the Rock), and *Den Spieghel van Philagie* (1671, The Mirror of Philagy), all of them reprinted as late as the 19th century.

These writings are in the current of the Counter Reformation, of which they represent the popular and pessimistic aspect; they aim at animating and deepening spiritual life among religious and laymen generally, and especially among women. In the course of his work Poirters mildly satirizes the contemporary love of splendor so eloquently illustrated in the paintings of Rubens, van Dyke, and Jordaens; he further resorts to somewhat sentimental and highly personal meditations on Christ's sufferings and death. In form, Poirters's works belong to emblematic literature, of which they represent the last phase: the inscriptions in verse and prose have come to be more important than the engravings. The verses are fluent and suggest the influence of the Dutch poets Cats and VONDEL. The pithy and colorful prose fragments have considerable literary value.

Bibliography: E. ROMBAUTS, *Leven en werken van pater Adrianus Poirters S.J. (1605–1674)* (Ghent 1930).

[E. ROMBAUTS]

POISSY, CONFERENCE OF

Held Sept. 9 to Oct. 18, 1561, the Conference of Poissy was summoned by the regent Queen Catherine de Médicis because France was on the brink of civil and religious war and she hoped for a theological compromise between Catholics and Huguenots. Several Catholic leaders, including the Queen and probably the cardinal of Lorraine, were content to seek a national settlement of religion without reference to Rome. The conference met in the refectory of the convent at Poissy near Paris. Of the Protestant deputies the chief was Theodore BEZA, from Geneva, later assisted by Peter Martyr Vermigli, from Zurich. The moderates hoped for formulas of compromise. But in an opening speech when Beza expounded the Calvinist doctrine of the Presence in the Eucharist, the Catholic prelates would hardly listen. A few days later it was evident that no agreement was possible. A legate, Cardinal Hippolyte d'Este, and shortly after, the Jesuit Diego LAÍNEZ, arrived and diminished the influence of those ready to compromise. The conference dwindled into a few private conversations among theologians. Its failure left Queen Catherine to walk a tightrope between the rival armies. Four months afterward the first of the French wars of religion broke out.

Bibliography: H. O. EVENNETT, *The Cardinal of Lorraine and the Council of Trent* (Cambridge, Eng. 1940). L. PASTOR, *The History of the Popes from the Close of the Middle Ages*, 40 v. (London-St. Louis 1931–61) 16:153–210.

[W. O. CHADWICK]

POKAGON, LEOPOLD AND SIMON

Father and son, Native American Catholics.

Leopold, a Native American chief; b. 1775?; d. July 8, 1841. Legend relates that Leopold was really a Chippewa, captured and adopted into the Pottawatomi; he married the daughter of the war chief and became a civil chief of the first rank. His name was really Pugegun, "the rib." His village was in Bertrand Township, Berrien County, Mich., about six miles from South Bend, Ind. The Pottawatomi had a fierce devotion to the teachings of the French Jesuits, who had attended the old St. Joseph Mission, Ind., as far back as 1690. These tribes on the St. Joseph River often made trips as far as Kaskaskia, Ill., and Quebec, Canada, to make their Easter duty. After Chief Leopold appealed for a priest for his tribe, Rev. Frederic Résé went to Leopold's village and baptized him, his wife, and about 30 others, registering them in the parish church of Bertrand, Mich. As a result of this eloquent appeal Rev. Stephen T. BADIN spent three years (1830–33) in Pokagon's village and won more than 350 converts. In September 1833 Leopold regretfully signed the treaty of cession of the Pottawatomi lands and four years later took up land in Cass County, near Dowagiac, Mich. There at Silver Creek he organized and built the first Catholic church; he was later buried under it.

Simon, b. 1830?; d. Jan. 28, 1899. One of Leopold's several children, Simon was regarded widely "as the best educated and most distinguished full-blooded Native American in America." He was educated at Notre Dame University, Ind., and Oberlin College, Ohio. He spent his entire life interpreting the Native Americans to the American public, the Congress, and several presidents and was successful in securing the annuities due the Pottawatomi. A noted public speaker, he made his most famous appearance at the World Columbian Exposition (1893) at Chicago, Ill. He wrote *Queen of the Woods,* a romance centering in events of his own life, as well as articles about Native American life, lore, and legend in magazines such as the *Forum, Harper's,* and *Review of Reviews.* He was buried in the Rush Lake (Mich.) church cemetery, with his two wives and four children. Pokagon State Park in Indiana is a memorial to the Pokagons.

Bibliography: C. B. BUECHNER, *The Pokagons* (Indianapolis 1933). J. H. SCHAUINGER, *Stephen T. Badin* (Milwaukee 1956).

[J. H. SCHAUINGER]

POLANCO FONTECHA, ANSELMO, BL.

Bishop of Teruel, Augustinian; martyr; b. Buenavista de Valdavia, Palencia, Spain, April 16, 1881; d. "Can Tretze" of Pont de Molins (near Gerona), Spain, Feb. 7, 1939.

Born to modest farmers, Anselmo Polanco was professed as an Augustinian friar at Valladolid (1896), studied at Santa María of La Vid Monastery, and was ordained in 1904. He began his priestly career teaching theology in the seminary, then served as prior until he was sent to the Philippines as provincial councilor. He returned to Valladolid upon his election as provincial superior (1932) of the Philippines Province, which entailed sending missionaries to various parts of the world. In that position he travelled to China, Colombia, Peru, and the United States.

Three years later he was named bishop of Teruel (Spain) and appointed apostolic administrator of Albarracín. Polanco remained in Teruel throughout the terrors of the Spanish civil war. In 1938, he was arrested and imprisoned by the Republican Army for refusing to remove his signature from a collective letter of the Spanish bishops denouncing the persecution of the Church. Shortly thereafter he was joined by his vicar general, Felipe RIPOLL. After thirteen months incarceration, the two were used as human shields as the soldiers disbanded at the end of the war. The bodies of both martyrs are enshrined in Bishop Polanco's cathedral.

During Bishop Polanco's beatification, Pope John Paul II observed: ''As a presentiment, [Polanco] said on the day he took possession of his diocese: 'I have come to give my life for my flock.' This is why, together with Felipe Ripoll, he chose to stay at the side of his flock in the midst of danger, and it was only by force that he was taken from them.'' John Paul II beatified Polanco, Oct. 1, 1995.

Feast: Feb. 7.

Bibliography: V. CÁRCEL ORTÍ, *Martires españoles del siglo XX* (Madrid 1995). J. PÉREZ DE URBEL, *Catholic Martyrs of the Spanish Civil War, 1936–1939*, tr. M. F. INGRAMS (Kansas City, Mo. 1993). *L'Osservatore Romano,* Eng. ed. 40 (1995): 1–3.

[K. I. RABENSTEIN]

POLAND, THE CATHOLIC CHURCH IN

Poland, the largest of the West Slavic States, has exercised a marked influence on the history of Eastern Europe. Under the Piast dynasty (960–1386), it was comprised of Great Poland (with its chief centers at Gniezno, Poznań, and Kruszwica), Little Poland (Cracovia), Mazovia, and Silesia. Under the Jagiellonian dynasty (1386–1572) Poland spread far to the east and became a great power. In the period of the Elective Monarchy (1572–1795) and of foreign rule (1795–1916) the Poles had a checkered history. Then, following the restoration of an independent Polish State (1919–39), came a new division of Polish territory in the wake of World War II and ultimately the formation of the Polish People's Republic (Polska Rzeczpospolita Ludowa), a Communist regime. Although Poland once had a mixed population of Poles, Germans, Lithuanians, Ukrainians, Russians, and White Russians, after World War II its inhabitants were overwhelmingly of Polish origin. The ecclesiastical history of Poland, which is the main concern of this section of the article, may be divided conveniently into five major periods. The main features in the history of the Church are presented systematically under each period.

The Middle Ages

The first traces of Christianity are found in the area of Cracovia during the second half of the ninth century and are connected with the missionary activity of Methodius, the Apostle of the Slavs, in Moravia. The spread of Christianity in Poland, however, really began under the Piast Prince Mieszko I (*c.* 960–992). In 965 he married the Czech princess Dobrava (Dabrówka) and was baptized the following year. In 968 a missionary bishopric was established for Poland, and Jordan, the first bishop, carried on his work from Poznań. To counteract the efforts of the German Church and of the first two Ottonian emperors to put the Polish bishopric under the jurisdiction of the archbishopric of Magdeburg, Mieszko placed his land in a kind of vassal status under the protection of the pope (990).

Establishment of the Polish Hierarchy. In the year 1000, the archbishopric of Gniezno was erected with Kolobrzeg, Wrocław, and Cracow as its suffragans. Pope SYLVESTER II, Emperor OTTO III, and Bolesław Chrobry, the son and successor of Mieszko (992–1025), all had an active part in this foundation. Chrobry continued his father's policy as a vigorous and successful promoter of Christianity in Poland, and a year before his death he received the royal crown from Rome. The boundaries of the archdiocese of Gniezno at first corresponded to those of the Piast realm. The archbishop was responsible for the care of souls in Great Poland. His suffragan bishops had the task of spreading and solidifying the Christian faith in the border areas: the bishop of Kolobrzeg, in Pomerania; the bishop of Cracow, in Little Poland and the adjacent territories acquired in the North and East; and the bishop of Wrocław, in Silesia. The establishment of the Polish hierarchy in the year 1000 was decisive for the incorporation of Poland into Western Christendom.

Growth in the 11th, 12th, and 13th Centuries. Among the missionaries at the end of tenth century and the beginning of the eleventh were the martyrs St. ADALBERT OF PRAGUE (d. 997), St. BENEDICT OF BENEVENTO,

John and companions (d. 1003), and BRUNO OF QUERFURT (d. 1009). The spread of the Church was threatened temporarily by a pagan reaction in 1046–47. In the eleventh and twelfth centuries Gniezno acquired new suffragans: Poznań, Włocławek, which replaced the shortlived bishopric of Kruschwitz, in Kujavia, Płock in Mazovia, Lebus on the Middle Oder, and later Wilna (Vilna), Lutsk, and Chełmno. Bishops, such as St. Stanislaus of Cracow (d. 1079), defended the rights of the Church against the encroachments of the state, and in the period of the division of inheritances among the Piasts, they maintained the consciousness of Polish unity. The metropolitans of Gniezno and other ecclesiastical princes emphasized the importance of the Polish language in the light of the threat of the German colonists whose immigration resulted in Polish decline in the western lands of the Piasts, especially in Silesia. The idea of Polish unity was kept alive also in the Polish kingship, and enjoyed the full support of the Church.

The monastic and cathedral schools, which were the vehicles for all education and culture, the cathedral chapters, the development of parish organizations, and the spread of the religious orders (BENEDICTINES, CISTERCIANS, PREMONSTRATENSIANS, FRANCISCANS, DOMINICANS, CARMELITES, AUGUSTINIANS, Hospitallers, and TEMPLARS) all contributed to the solid establishment and growth of Christianity. The Order of Knights, the Fratres Militiae Christi, or Knights of the Sword, founded by Duke Conrad of Mazovia in 1228, which because of its location was also called the Knights of Dobrin, passed in 1237 into the Order of the TEUTONIC KNIGHTS, which established a state of its own in Prussia. The interior growth of the Church in the age of the Piasts is evidenced by the number of saints and blesseds. Among them are: Bp. Wincenty Kadłubek of Cracow (d. 1223), author of the *Chronica de gestis (illustrium) principum ac regum Poloniae;* Bp. Jan Prandota of Cracow (1242–66), who represented in his person the ideal bishop of his time; the Dominicans, Czesław (d. 1222), who defended Wrocław during the great attack of the Mongols, and Hyacinth (Jaczko Odrowąź, d. 1257), who was active as a missionary in Prussia and South Russia; duchess Hedwig (Jadwiga, d. 1243), mother of duke Henry II of Silesia who fell in battle against the Mongols at Liegnitz; in 1241, a woman equally honored by Germans and Poles as a patroness of Christian charity; the Premonstratensian nun Bronisława (d. 1259); and the Poor Clares, Salomea (d. 1268), Kinga (d. 1292), and Jolanta (d. 1298).

Under the First Kings of the Jagiellonian Dynasty. In the middle of the fourteenth century Poland had again become a closely knit state. King Casimir III the Great (1333–70), the last famous Piast, extended its territory by the incorporation of the principalities of Halicz (Galicia) and Volhynia. To serve the spiritual needs of his Orthodox subjects, he brought about the restoration of the Galician metropolitanate, with Przemyśl, Chełmno, and Vladimir as its eparchies. Roman Catholic bishoprics arose also in these places. In 1367 he recognized the Armenian bishop of Lvov, so that three Christian confessions existed side by side in his realm. Shortly before 1364 he founded the *Studium generale* or University of Cracow. The marriage in 1386 of Casimir's granddaughter Hedwig (Jadwiga), the youngest daughter of King Louis of Hungary (1342–82) and Poland (1370–82) with the grandduke Jagiełło of Lithuania, who became King of Poland as Władysław II (1386–1434), inaugurated the union of Poland and Lithuania under the Jagiellonians. This union was more strongly established in the course of the fifteenth and sixteenth centuries and was sealed by the union of Lublin in 1569.

Capital: Warsaw.
Size: 120,756 sq. miles.
Population: 38,633,912.
Languages: Polish.
Religions: Roman Catholic 95%; Eastern Orthodox, Protestant, and other, 5%.

Władysław II, in 1387, founded the bishopric of Vilna, through which Roman Christianity was spread in Lithuania. This missionary work was aided very much by the establishment of the faculty of theology at the University of Cracow in 1397. Several Polish bishops and professors, among them the rector of the University of Cracow, Paul Vladimiri (Paweł Włodkowicz), were present at the Council of Constance. Paul in his tractate *De potestate papae et imperatoris respectu infidelium* condemned all conversion of pagans by force. Through this work he involved himself in the diplomatic battle between Poland and the Teutonic Order that took place after the military defeat of the German knights at Tannenberg (1410).

Under Casimir IV (1447–92) a thirteen-year war (1454–66) weakened the political independence of the Teutonic Order, and the bishopric of Ermland passed under the protection of the Polish king. The marriage of the king to Elizabeth of Hapsburg made possible the expansion of the power of the Jagiellonian house to Bohemia and Hungary. During Casimir's long reign the Orthodox population in Poland-Lithuania continued to enjoy toleration, but through the development of the Archbishopric of Lvov tensions arose between the Latin hierarchy and the Orthodox eparchs, and between those who went over to Catholicism and the majority of the population who were adherents of Orthodoxy. Bishop

Metropolitan Sees	Suffragans
Białystok	Drohiczyn, Łomża
Częstochowa	Radom, Sosnowiec
Gdánsk	Pelplin, Toruń
Gniezno	Włocławek
Katowice	Gliwice, Opole
Kraków	Bielsko-Żywiec, Kielce, Tarnów
Lublin	Sandomierz, Siedlce
Poznań	Kalisz
Szczecin-Kamien	Koszalin-Kołobrzeg, Zielona Góra-Gorzów
Warmia	Elbląg, Ełk
Warsaw	Łowicz, Płock, Warsaw-Prague
Wrocław	Legnica

Lódz is directly subject to the Holy See. The Latin-rite archdiocese of Przemysl has suffragans Rzeszów, and Zamość-Lubaczów. The Ukrainian-Byzantine rite has an archdiocese at Prezemysl-Warsaw with suffragan Wrocław-Gdánsk. A military ordinariate is also located in Poland.

Zbigniew Oleśnicki of Cracow (1423–55, cardinal from 1449) exercised, as an adviser for many years, a strong influence on the internal and foreign policies of the three first kings of the Jagiellonian dynasty. He suppressed the Hussite movement, which entered Poland from Bohemia, and his secretary Jan Długosz (1415–80) was the preceptor of the royal princes and the author of several historical works (among them *Historiae Polonicae libri XII*).

Spiritual Life in the Late Middle Ages. Polish bishops and professors who had participated in the reform councils spread HUMANISM in Poland-Lithuania, and in the second half of the fifteenth century the *Devotio Moderna* also made its influence felt. In the midst of the breakup of the rather circumscribed medieval outlook and of criticism against high ecclesiastics, benefices multiplied and churchmen devoted themselves more to political activities than to the care of souls. Yet, one should not overlook the contributions of outstanding pastors, especially the archbishops of Gniezno, such as Jakób Świnka (1283–1314) and Jarosław Bogorja Skotnicki (1342–74, d. 1376), or the first bishop of Vilna, the Franciscan Andrzej (d. 1398), or the holy and fruitful activity of provincial and diocesan synods. Besides the new monasteries erected by the orders already mentioned, foundations were made by HIERONYMITES, Bernardines, MINIMS, BRETHREN OF THE COMMON LIFE, and others.

Worthy of particular note also are the several distinguished saints and blesseds, among them Abp. Jakob Strepa of Halicz-Lvov (d. 1409); Jan Kanty (d. 1473), who was well known as a professor at the University of Cracow and as a friend and helper of needy students; the Bernardine Simon of Lipnica (d. 1482) a promoter of the veneration of the Holy Name of Jesus; the Jagiellonian prince Casimir (d. 1484), who was distinguished for his veneration of the Blessed Virgin Mary; the Bernardines Bl. Jan of Dukla (d. 1484), who despite his long blindness was famous as a preacher and confessor; and Władysław of Gielniów (d. 1505), who was active as a missionary in Lithuania and who as a writer of religious poems promoted the veneration of the Passion of Christ and devotion to the Mother of God.

The Jagiellonians defended the West against the Turks, who flooded southeastern Europe after their capture of Constantinople (1453), and in 1529 they penetrated as far as Vienna. Against them and the Orthodox Russians, Poland-Lithuania served as a bulwark of Christendom *(antemurale christianitatis, przedmurze chrześciańśtwa).*

Reformation to the Final Partitions

Numerous young nobles who had studied at foreign universities, for example, at Wittenberg, Geneva, and Strassburg, and the German burghers, who played a very important role in some cities, were favorably disposed to the ideas of LUTHER, CALVIN, and the other leading personalities of the Reformation. Following the secularization of the State of the Teutonic Order into a duchy (1525) and the conversion to Protestantism of the grandmaster Albrecht of Brandenburg-Ansbach, who became the first duke of Prussia (1525–68), Königsberg developed rapidly as a Protestant center from which the new teaching was channeled into Poland and Lithuania, where it was quickly absorbed.

Spread of the Reformation into Poland. The rapid spread of the Reformation is to be explained by the shortcomings of the higher clergy, by abuses in the lower clergy and numerous monastic establishments, and by the quarrels between the higher and lower nobility over the extent of ecclesiastical jurisdiction. Royal officials, men of learning, and politicians, such as Andrzej Frycz-Modrzewski (1503–72), and poets, such as Mikołaj Rej (1505–69) prepared the way for Protestantism in Poland. As early as 1520, King Sigismund I (1506–48) issued an edict against Luther's writings, but he did not succeed in halting the spread of Protestantism. After his death the

adherents of the Reformation put their hopes in Sigismund II Augustus (1548–72), who was in communication by letter with MELANCHTHON and Calvin. He did not abandon Catholicism, but the Protestant movement in Poland reached its zenith during his reign. At the imperial diet held at Piotrków in 1565, a constitution was drawn up and put into effect by which ecclesiastical courts were deprived of the jurisdiction they formerly enjoyed. The nobles could then establish PROTESTANTISM in their own properties and territories.

The Protestants in Poland at that time fell into three groups: the Lutherans, the Reformed, who were headed by Jan Łaski (1499–1560), and the BOHEMIAN BRETHREN. From 1555 they carried on negotiations among them with the object of establishing an independent Polish national church. At the convention held at Sandomierz in 1570 they reached agreement on the fundamental elements of belief. This *consensus Sandomirensis* has been called the first attempt at realizing the idea of Protestant universality. At any rate, it made it possible, following the death of Sigismund Augustus, for the dissenters to become politically united at the Warsaw Confederation of 1573. Temporarily, Stancarism, which stemmed from Francesco Stancaro (1501–74), and Socinianism, which took its name from Fausto Sozzini (Socinius, 1539–1604), played important roles. This anti-Trinitarian movement, whose adherents were also called Arians or Polish Brethren, was suppressed in 1658.

The Beginnings of the Counter Reformation. Sharp disputes among the various Protestant groups, Catholic reforms, and the Counter Reformation weakened the position of Protestantism, which had gained its chief support in the noble classes and in the higher levels among the burghers. Faced with the political threat to Poland-Lithuania of the Swedes in the north, of the advancing Russians in the east, and of Turkish attacks in the south, Polish political leaders and bishops emphasized the necessity of the abolishment of all ecclesiastical division and of return to the Catholic Church as a matter that

Stefan Cardinal Wyszyński, Primate of Poland 1948–81. (Archive Photos)

was absolutely vital to the national interest. Catholicism had already taken on new strength.

Numerous diocesan and provincial synods issued decrees against the abuses that had become widespread in the late Middle Ages, and they also came to grips with the Protestant religious views. The Archbishops Jan Łaski of Gniezno (1510–31) and Andrzej Krzycki (1535–37), who as bishop of Przemyśl (1523–27) had written against Luther, sought to check Protestantism. The polemical works of John Eck, Johannes Cochlaeus, and Georg Witzel (Wicelius) were disseminated throughout Poland. Stanislaus Hosius (1504–79) was especially zealous in defending the Church through his polemical and systematic writings (for example, his *Confessio catholicae fidei*) and his pastoral and ecclesiastico-political measures. As bishop of Chełmno from 1549, of Ermland from 1551, and as cardinal from 1561, he succeeded in bringing about a renewal of the life of the Church.

Work of Papal Nuncios and Jesuits. Polish Catholicism received essential help from Rome through admonitory papal briefs to the Polish kings and through the work of the nuncios, who by political means and visitations strove to put into effect the decrees of the Council of Trent. The nuncio Giovanni Francesco Commendone (1563–65) persuaded King Sigismund II Augustus to give the Jesuits the protection of the crown; the nuncio Alberto Bolognetti (1581–85) through his letters and sermons contributed to the return of many nobles to Catholicism; and the nuncio Germanico Malaspina (1593–97) made the preparations for the Union of Brest (1596), through which most of the Orthodox bishops of Poland-Lithuania were united with Rome. The Union of Brest was a great victory in the struggle for the unity of the Church. However, the national tensions between Poles and Ukrainians and the political altercations involving Poland-Lithuania, the Cossacks, and Russia hindered the development of the Union. The Basilian St. Josaphat Kuncevyč (1580–1623, archbishop of Płock from 1618) and the Jesuit St. Andrew BOBOLA (1592–1657) were murdered by fanatical Cossacks.

The nuncios were strongly supported by Cardinal HOSIUS and other members of the Polish episcopate. It will suffice to mention: Martin KROMER of Ermland (1579–89); Marcin Białobrzecki of Kamieniec (1577–86); Stanisław KARNKOWSKI of Włocławek (1567–81), and later archbishop of Gniezno (1581–1603), who as preacher, writer, and diplomat opposed Protestantism, and by synods, the erecting of seminaries, and patronage of the Jesuit order, hastened the re-Catholization of Poland; and Jan Dymitr Solikowski, archbishop of Lvov (1583–1603). In the religious strife of the age the Jesuits Melchior Grodziecki (1584–1619) and St. John SARKANDER (1576–1620) died as martyrs.

Success of the Counter Reformation in Poland. Sigismund III Vasa, king of Poland (1587–1632), and also king of Sweden (1594–1604), whom Rubens glorified as the ''Tamer of Heresy,'' completed the Counter Reformation in Poland-Lithuania. The JESUITS were its acknowledged champions. They were active as teachers and leaders in new educational institutions and as diplomats, preachers, missionaries, confessors, writers, and publicists. Typical representatives were Benedict Herbest (1530–93), Jakób Wujek (1540–97), Piotr Skarga (1536–1611), Maciej Kazimierz Sarbiewski (1595–1640), and Gaspar Druzbicki (1590–1662). The older orders, the Dominicans, Franciscans, Bernardines, Paulites, Augustinians, and Carmelites played an important role beside the Jesuits. The new orders or congregations as, for example, the Reformati (OFM Ref), PIARISTS, Capuchins, TRINITARIANS, VINCENTIANS, and others, spread rapidly. Orders and congregations of women engaged actively in education, in the care of the sick, and in other works of charity. Among the mystics of the age, the Carmelite Teresa Marchocka (1603–52) deserves mention.

When Swedes, Russians, and Turks poured into Polish territory, the Church gathered all her forces to drive

Solidarity demonstrators hold signs during the 1987 visit of Pope John Paul II to Poland. (©David & Peter Turnley/CORBIS)

out these enemies of her religion. The heroic defense of the Paulite monastery on the Jasna Góra at Częstochowa in 1655 was the occasion for raising this place of pilgrimage with its icon of the ''Black Mother of God'' to the status of a Polish national shrine. In 1666 King John II Casimir (1648–68) proclaimed Mary Queen of Poland *(regina Poloniae, królowa Korony Polskiej).* Pope ALEXANDER VII bestowed the title of *rex orthodoxus* on John and his successors. Marian devotion, which had struck deep roots in Poland in the Middle Ages, flourished anew. Catholicism was officially recognized as the religion of the state.

Political Decline and Repressive Religious Policy. In the period of the Elective Monarchy (1572–1795) Poland-Lithuania lost the position as a great power that it had attained under the Jagiellonians. Because King John III Sobieski (1674–1696) won victories against the Turks and played a major role in freeing Vienna from the Turkish siege in 1683, he received from Pope INNOCENT XII the title of *defensor fidei.* In the eighteenth century, Poland-Lithuania faced the catastrophe of partitions under the Saxon electors, Augustus II (1697–1733) and Augustus III (1733–63), who were forced upon it as kings by its neighbors.

The victory of the Counter Reformation led to measures that went beyond the solid establishment of Catholicism. Protestantism was suppressed, and in 1717 the erection of new Protestant churches was forbidden. Following an attack by the Protestant population on the Jesuit *Gymnasium* in Toruń in 1724, the burgomaster and nine other Protestants were executed. The United Catholics, or adherents of the Union, who even in the preceding century had to overcome external and internal difficulties, were now treated as Catholics of ''the second class;'' they were forced to accept certain forms and practices of the Roman Catholic State Church. The rights of the Orthodox were also curtailed. The kings of Prussia and the Russian czars took action to protect the Protestants and

Celebration of beatification of Karolina Kozka, Czestochowa, Poland. (©Peter Turnley/CORBIS)

Orthodox respectively under Polish rule. Catherine II (the Great) set her favorite Stanisław August Poniatowski (1764–95) upon the Polish throne. Through Gen. N. V. Repnin, her ambassador in Warsaw, she interfered in ecclesiastical affairs; e.g., in 1767 she had Bp. Kajetan Soltyk of Cracow (1759–88) and Bp. Jozef Andrzej Zaluski of Kiev (1759–74) arrested and deported to Russia. The patriotic Catholic opposition, under the leadership of Bp. Adam Stanisław Krasiński (1759–95, d. 1800), formed the Confederation of Bar. Jan Dołowicz, the Carmelite prior of Bar (d. 1801), even founded an ''Order of the Holy Cross'' to protect the faith, but after a four-year struggle the confederates were wiped out by the Russians.

The Partitions of Poland (1772–1815). In the first partition (1772) carried out by Russia, Austria, and Prussia, Poland lost about 30 percent of its territory and 35 percent of its inhabitants. In the attempts to stabilize conditions by reforms, several ecclesiastics took a prominent part. Among them should be mentioned as preacher, educational reformer, and statesman the famous Piarist Stanisław Konarski (1700–73), Abp. Michał Jerzy Poniatowski of Gniezno (1785–94), Bp. Adam Stanisław Naruszewicz of Lutsk (1790–96), the founder of modern Polish historiography, and Canon Hugo Kołłątej (1750–1812), who carried out important curricular reforms. They participated actively also in the formation of the Constitution of May 3, 1791, in which the Catholic religion was recognized as the official religion of the state, but in which also the free practice of religion was guaranteed for all dissenters.

The second partition of Poland by Russia and Prussia in 1793, and the third in 1795, by which the three neighboring Great Powers seized the rest of Poland, brought an abrupt end to the efforts at internal reform. The papal nuncio in Warsaw, Lorenzo Litta (1793–95), registered a solemn protest against the injustice done to Poland-Lithuania, but his protest died away unheard. Russia seized two-thirds, and Prussia and Austria the remaining third between them. The name of Poland vanished from the map. The Church was seriously weakened materially by the confiscations and secularization of her possessions. The grand-duchy of Warsaw, established by Napoleon, was abolished in 1813 and its territory divided between Prussia and Russia. The Congress of Vienna, which is rightly charged with the fourth partition of Poland, delivered the final blow in 1815: Russia received 82 percent, Austria 10 percent, and Prussia eight percent of the former Polish kingdom.

Foreign Domination, 1815–1918

The Poles did not meekly accept the loss of independent statehood, but held tenaciously to their national consciousness and to their language. As in earlier crises, the Catholic Church in this period also was a bond that united the Polish-speaking population at home and abroad. In the Congregation of the Resurrectionists, whose first members made their vows in Rome in 1842 *(Congregatio a Resurrectione Domini Nostri Jesu Christi;* in Polish, *Zmartwychstancy)*, belief in the Resurrection of Christ and the firm conviction that Poland would be restored were combined in a special way.

Polish Catholics under Russian Rule. In the parts of Poland annexed by Russia, the oppression of the Poles and of Catholicism, which was regarded as a foreign body, was especially severe. The Russian government conducted a continual campaign against the United, or adherents of the Union, in particular. Already under Catherine II eight million United were incorporated into the Orthodox Church by force. The eparchies, which had not been abolished earlier, comprising 1.5 million faithful and 1,500 parish churches, were placed under the control of the United-Greek College in St. Petersburg in 1829. Nicholas I (1825–55) granted the request of the Synod of Płock that the adherents of the Union should be reunited with the ''Old Orthodox Mother Church.'' Those who did not abandon the Union with Rome voluntarily were forced to do so. In 1875 the Diocese of Chełmno in Congress Poland (Russian Poland) was declared to be an Orthodox bishopric, and thus the Union was abolished in the whole territory under Russian rule. Small groups of faithful continued in secret to be loyal to the Union. The Edict of Toleration of April 17, 1905 permitted them to become Roman Catholics, but a return to their old United status was forbidden.

Dependent Status of the Roman Catholic Church. The Roman Catholic ecclesiastical administration was reduced to a condition of severe dependence under Russian rule. In Stanisław Sienstreńcewicz-Bohusz, whom she appointed to head her newly erected archbishopric of Mogilev (1782–1826), Catherine II found a willing helper. Alexander I (1801–25) established (1801) the Roman Catholic Ecclesiastical College in St. Petersburg in order to control the Church. In the grand-duchy of Warsaw, Polish Catholics had a short breathing spell. But in the period of the ''Kingdom of Poland,'' which from 1815 to 1830 was governed in personal union with Russia, it was soon evident that any cooperation with the Church was to be based purely on considerations of public policy. In order to break the influence of the bishop of Gniezno, who as primate of Poland possessed a measure of authority that extended beyond the boundaries of his own jurisdiction proper, Alexander I had Warsaw, which had been made a bishopric in the Prussian partition territory in 1798, raised to the status of an archbishopric in 1817. In the following year seven bishops were placed under its jurisdiction as suffragans.

Pope John Paul II kneeling at ''Death Wall,'' in former Auschwitz Concentration Camp, Auschwitz, Poland. (Archive Photos)

The expulsion of the Jesuits from Russia in 1820, the dissolution of the numerous monasteries, the possibility of divorce from a Catholic partner on the occasion of the other partner's conversion to the Orthodox faith, were all threatening portents. After the failure of the Polish revolution of 1830–31, they were followed by harsh measures against the Church. The government refused to give official approval to episcopal candidates (the archiepiscopal See of Warsaw, for example, was vacant from 1829 to 1836, and from 1838 to 1856); in 1832 it suppressed 200 monasteries; in 1834 it restricted freedom of movement on the part of the clergy; and in 1841 it confiscated the major portion of ecclesiastical property. In 1846 the priest Piotr Ściegienny, who advocated the freeing of the peasants and national revolt, was arrested in Kielce and condemned to hard labor in Siberia, from which he was not permitted to return before 1871. The convention of 1847 made between Nicholas I and Pope PIUS IX was never really implemented.

Statues of the Twelve Apostles rest atop the fence in front of Saints Peter and Paul Church in Cracow, Poland. (©Dave G. Houser/ CORBIS)

Tensions mounted under the government of Alexander II (1855–81), when the Poles rose in revolution against the Russian terror in 1863–1864, only to be suppressed with much bloodshed. Archbishop Zygmunt Szczęsny Feliński of Warsaw (1862–83, d. 1895), Bishops Adam Krasiński of Vilna (d. 1891), Wincenty Chościak-Popiel of Płock (archbishop of Warsaw 1883–1912), and Konstanty Lubieński of Sejny (1863–69), along with 400 clerics, were banished to Siberia. Almost all monasteries and Catholic societies were abolished, and processions outside churches and May devotions were forbidden. In 1866 the government repudiated the convention made with Rome in 1847. In 1869–1870 it ordered the use of the Russian language in divine worship and punished numerous bishops and clerics who opposed the new regulations with banishment to Siberia. No permission was given the bishops to attend VATICAN COUNCIL I.

Improvement after 1882. It was only after 1882, when Pope LEO XIII and Alexander III (1881–94) had worked out an agreement, that some alleviation of the oppressive conditions was introduced. The use of the Russian language in sermons and devotions was limited to communities with a Russian population. The use of Polish was permitted in Polish cities and Polish rural areas. In 1884 Leo XIII was able to fill the vacant sees. The Edict of Toleration of 1905 under Nicholas II (1894–1918) brought further alleviations, but restrictions were again imposed only two years later (1907). The government recognized and supported the MARIAVITES, whose leading personalities were excommunicated by Rome in 1906.

The Poles under Austria. In Galicia the situation for Polish Catholics was better. The government in Vienna was the only one of the three partition powers to give them assistance and support, although in the first half of

Rows of crosses in a field serve as a memorial to Polish Catholic victims at Treblinka, a Nazi concentration camp in operation during World War II. (©Ira Nowinski/CORBIS)

the nineteenth century the influence of the State Church of Josephinism was still active. The Concordat of 1855 and the autonomy granted to the Poles in 1867, with their own diet, were fruitful for the life of the Church. Education at all levels was conducted in Polish. The Academy of Cracow was founded in 1872. Cracow and Lvov with their universities and theological faculties were outstanding Catholic centers. From 1884 the Jesuits in Cracow published the monthly, *Przegląd Powszechny,* which became a vehicle for leading Catholics. Distinguished bishops were active as ecclesiastical statesmen, theological writers, and preachers. Special mention should be made of the Prince-Bishops of Cracow, Albin Dunajewski (1879–94) and Jan Kozielko Puzyna (1895–1911, cardinal from 1901), Abp. Józef Bilczewski of Lvov (Lemberg, 1900–23), and Bp. Józef Sebastian Pelczar of Przemyśl (d. 1924).

Between the Roman Catholic hierarchy and the United, who had acquired a separate archbishopric of Lvov in 1807, relations became strained, resulting essentially from the national opposition between Poles and Ukrainians. After long negotiations a formula of agreement was worked out at Rome in 1863, which dealt with disputed questions but did not clarify all points. The United, under the leadership of their metropolitans, especially Sylvester Sambrytovyč (1885–98, cardinal from 1895) and Andreas Count Szeptyckyj (1900–44), strove to gain political and ecclesiastical independence.

Polish Catholicism under German Rule. In the Prussian partition area the differences between the Protestant government and the Catholic, and especially the Polish-speaking, population became worse decade by decade, although the bull of Pope PIUS VII, *De salute animarum,* issued in 1821 had regulated anew ecclesiastical affairs in the eastern parts of Prussia. The bishopric of Posen (Poznań) was raised to an archbishopric and was united in a personal union with the archbishopric of Gnesen (Gniezno), which retained the greatly extended diocese of Kulm (Chełmno) as a suffragan. The dioceses of Ermland and Breslau (Wrocław), which meantime had been freed from their dependence on Riga and Gniezno respectively, were placed directly under the Holy See. Following the Polish revolution of 1830–1831, the Prussian Lord Lieutenant Eduard von Flottwell (1830–41) promoted German institutions and culture and Protestantism in order to restrict the influence of the Polish nobility and clergy. In 1839 the demands of the government on the question of mixed marriages led to the internment of

Reverend Jerzy Popiełuszko inside St. Stanisław Kostka Church, Warsaw, Poland. (©Ryszard Wesolowski/CORBIS)

Abp. Martin von Dunin of Gniezno (1831–42) in the fortress of Kolberg. His successor Leo Przyłuski (1845–65) in 1848 demanded the restoration of the national rights of the Poles.

The quarrel between the German government and the Poles reached its zenith in the period of the *Kulturkampf.* Through his policy Bismarck wished, among other things, to deprive the growing Polish nationalism of its spiritual leaders. Abp. Mieczysław Halka LEDÓCHOWSKI (1865–86) of Gniezno-Poznań (Gnesen-Posen), two auxiliary bishops, and numerous clergy were arrested, and their parishes left vacant. The pressure of the *Kulturkampf,* which slackened after some years, and other government measures, for example, the suppression of the Polish language in schools and in public life, did not have the success expected. Archbishop Julius Dinder (1886–90) tried in vain to bring about a settlement. After long negotiations, Abp. Florian Oksza-Stablewski (1891–1906) succeeded in obtaining permission for the use of Polish in religious instruction in the schools. An expropriation law was passed against Polish landed property in 1908, against which Cardinal Georg Kopp of Breslau protested in the Upper House of the German Parliament. This law enkindled a general outburst of anger that had repercussions beyond the borders of Germany. The tension remained, as was evidenced by the vacancy in the archiepiscopal See of Gniezno-Poznań during the years 1906 to 1914.

Along with the Polish bishops, who during the period of the domination of Poland by the partition powers defended the Catholic tradition, one must praise the old orders and new congregations for their splendid service in maintaining Catholicism and in spreading and deepening the knowledge of the Catholic religion. Mention should be made of the Jesuit writer and missionary Karol Antoniewicz (d. 1852), the Salesian August Czartoryski (d. 1893), the Carmelite Rafal KALINOWSKI (d. 1907), and the Redemptorist Bernard Lubienski (d. 1933). Several new Polish communities were founded in the second half of the nineteenth century. In 1855 Edmund BOJANOWSKI (d. 1871) founded the Little Servant Sisters of the Immaculate Conception, and Sofja Truszkowska founded the Felician Sisters (Felicjanki); in 1857 Jozefa Karska (d. 1860) and Marcelina DAROWSKA, the Sisters of the Immaculate Conception of Mary (Niepokalanki); in 1875 Franciszka SIEDLISKA (d. 1902), the Sisters of the Holy Family of Nazareth (Nazaretanki); in 1891–92 Brother Albert, ''the Polish Francis'' (Adam CHMIELOWSKI, d. 1916), the Albertines, including both men and women; in 1893 Bronislaw Markiewicz (d. 1912), the Sisters of St. Michael the Archangel (Michaelitki).

The Church in the Republic of Poland 1918–39

When the Polish Republic was created in November 1918, the bishops, who had cared for the faithful in the three partition areas, were faced with difficult problems of organization. In the rebuilding of Polish Catholicism, the leaders were the Archbishops Edmund Dalbor of Gniezno (1915–26) and Aleksander Kakowski of Warsaw (1913–38), who were made cardinals in 1919, and the nuncio Achille Ratti (1919–21), the later Pope PIUS XI. The Concordat of Feb. 10, 1925, and the bull *Vixdum Poloniae* of Pope Pius XI, issued October 28 of the same year, constituted the foundation for the new ecclesiastical order in Poland. Two new archbishoprics, Cracow and Vilna, were erected beside the existing archiepiscopal sees of Gniezno-Poznań (Gnesen-Posen), Warsaw, and Lvov, and four new dioceses were established: Częstochowa, Katowice, Lomza, and Pinsk. The new organization comprised five ecclesiastical provinces with a total of 15 suffragan sees.

The Polish census of 1936 indicated that Catholics comprised 75 percent of the population (Roman Catholics 63.8 percent, and adherents of the Union 11.2 percent), the Orthodox and Jews, 10 percent each, and Protestants, 3 percent. Catholicism, which was the acknowledged religion of the great majority of the Polish population, was respected even by religiously indifferent statesmen, as Józef Piłsudski (d. 1935) who as chief of state headed the Republic from 1918 to 1922 and guided it in the years 1926 to 1935 under several authoritarian governments. The generally harmonious relations between Church and State were seriously impaired by the new marriage legislation, the proposed penal code, and, above all, in the summer of 1938, by the expropriation and destruction of Orthodox churches in the Lublin area with governmental authority and support. The papal nuncio in Poland Filippo Cortesi (1936–47) and the Polish episcopate disassociated themselves definitely from this harsh action on the part of the government. Under the leadership of the bishops, at whose regularly held conferences the Primate Augustyn Hlond (1926–48) served as president, the Church, through an effective consolidation of its forces, exercised a strong influence on public life.

Flourishing Catholic Life. The number of bishops in the period from 1918 to 1938 rose from 23 to 51, and the number of diocesan and regular clergy increased by about 43, reaching a total of nearly 13,000. The religious orders enjoyed a marked growth in this same period. At the outbreak of World War II there were about 2,000 monastic foundations, 1,600 priests, 4,500 lay brothers, and 17,000 sisters. The numerous pilgrimages to the shrines of the Blessed Virgin at Częstochowa, Piekary, and Ostra Brama in Vilna and the increasing participation in the foreign missions and in religious congresses bore witness to a flourishing religious life. The Church intensified the care of souls by the multiplication of parishes, by the development of its social work in its organized charities and in its St. Vincent de Paul societies, by CATHOLIC ACTION, which furnished a more solid adult education program, and by the apostolate of the press. In 1939 there were more than 250 Catholic periodical publications, 38 of these being organs of the United Church. Every diocese had its own Sunday paper. The religious orders also exhibited marked zeal in the field of the Catholic press. The scholarly life of the Church, which had a solid foundation in obligatory religious education, was promoted through the theological faculties of Warsaw, Cracow, Lvov, and Vilna, by the Catholic University of Lublin, founded in 1918, and by the diocesan seminaries. This scholarly activity was reflected in a series of important theological journals.

The United Catholic Church of Poland was composed of the Armenian Bishopric of Lvov, which had 4,000 faithful, as well as the 3,500,000 members of the Greek-Catholic Church in East Galicia, and some parishes of the Eastern Slavic Church totaling about 25,000 faithful. They in common were opposed to the Polish government, which wished to restrict their separate status within the Church in favor of the Latin rite. The government hoped that Latinization would lead to the complete assimilation of the United faithful into the main stream of Polish life and culture.

The Church in Poland, 1939–65

Until the end of World War I, Polish Catholicism led a different kind of existence in the eastern provinces of Prussia, in the Russian Vistula area, and in Austrian Galicia, but within two decades an abrupt standardization was put into effect. The German-Soviet Pact and the German Polish campaign of September 1939 created a new political situation for the Church. The incorporation of the eastern Polish territory into the Soviet Union entailed the prohibition of religious propaganda, persecutions, and deportations of clergy and laity.

The Poles under the National Socialist Regime. The German National Socialist regime seized the territory of the ecclesiastical province of Gniezno-Poznań (Gnesen-Posen) and parts of the archbishoprics of Warsaw and Cracow, which it designated "the incorporated eastern territories," and established a general government that included the main parts of the ecclesiastical provinces of Warsaw and Cracow and the western border areas of the ecclesiastical provinces of Lvov and Vilna. Following the outbreak of the German-Soviet War, East Galicia, with the major portion of the ecclesiastical province of Lvov was added to the general government also. The harsh measures of the German authorities, the ideological outlook of Alfred Rosenberg, race theory, and Jewish persecutions threatened the Church, which was reduced to a slave status in the Warta District and was heavily oppressed in the general government.

In the Warta District members of the hierarchy were brutally beaten; the clergy was decimated; seminaries, numerous establishments of religious orders, and all Catholic schools and associations were abolished; ecclesiastical property was expropriated; sisters were driven from their convents; churches in large part were closed (in Poznań, for example, of thirty churches only two were left open for Polish-speaking Catholics and one for German-speaking faithful); wayside crosses and shrines were destroyed; Polish inscriptions on gravestones were effaced; and loyalty to religion was made extremely difficult. More than three million Polish Catholics were left outside the pale of the law and were at the mercy of the despotic whims of the National Socialists.

The Archbishop of Cracow, Adam SAPIEHA (1925–51, cardinal from 1946), served as spokesman for all the Polish bishops, making repeated representations to the administration of the general government in order to obtain alleviations in the treatment of priests under arrest and sent into exile, to provide for the recruitment and theological training of seminarians, and to maintain the charitable activities of the Church. Following the systematic elimination of the Church from public life, and especially after the liquidation of the Catholic press and of higher Catholic education, the spiritual activity of the Church under the general government was confined to divine worship, the care of souls, and religious instruction. The youth organizations and societies of men under the leadership of Catholic Action were forbidden, but in the underground they served in part as assistance organizations for persecuted clerics and Jews. The German occupation officials were bent on depriving the Church of her age-old function of being a protective shield for all that was characteristic in Polish life and culture. Their anti-ecclesiastical attack paralyzed Catholic life.

In all, 13 Polish bishops were exiled or arrested and put in concentration camps. Of these the following died: Auxiliary Bishop Leo Wetmanski of Płock on May 10, 1941, and Archbishop Antoni Nowowiejski of Plock on June 20, 1941, in Soldau (Działdowo); Auxiliary Bishop Michał Kozal of Włocławek on Jan. 26, 1943, in Dachau; and Auxiliary Bishop Wladyslaw Goral of Lublin at the beginning of 1945 in a hospital bunker in Berlin. There were 3,647 priests, 389 clerics, 341 brothers, and 1,117 sisters put in concentration camps, in which 1,996 priests, 113 clerics, and 238 sisters perished. On August 14, 1941, Maximilian KOLBE met his death in the concentration camp at Auschwitz. He offered his life in substitution for that of a father of a family who had been condemned to die. The diocesan clergy of the Polish Church, who at the beginning of World War II numbered 10,017, lost 25 percent (2,647). The National Socialist terror raged against leading Catholic laymen as well as against the clergy, and many laymen were also put to death.

Reorganization of the Polish Church. The collapse of the German East Front and the end of World War II introduced a new chapter in Polish history. The Polish Committee for National Liberation, the so-called Lublin Committee, in a manifesto of July 22, 1944 guaranteed, among other things, freedom of conscience and respect for the rights of the Catholic Church. Clergy and faithful devoted their efforts to healing the material and mental wounds caused by the occupation and the effects of the war. The Primate, Cardinal Augustyn HLOND—from 1946 also archbishop of Warsaw—undertook the rebuilding of ecclesiastical organization. He consecrated several bishops; restored the seminaries; made provisions for religious instruction, for the restoration of Catholic schools, and for the redevelopment of the ecclesiastical press; and revived the activity of the religious orders. Owing to the political territorial changes, modifications in the Polish ecclesiastical organization were necessary. In the East the largest part of the archdiocese of Vilna and Lemberg (Lvov) were lost. In the West, the new organization was fitted into the structure of the ecclesiastical province of East Germany. In the occupied German eastern territories, the so-called Polish West and North territories, five apostolic administrations were established in 1945 with their centers at Oppeln (Opole), Breslau (Wrocław), Allenstein (Olsztyn), Landsberg (Gorzów Wielkopolski), and Danzig (Gdańsk).

Difficulties of the Church under a Communist Government. On Sept. 12, 1945 the Polish government abrogated the Concordat of 1925. The nationalization of Catholic presses and the censorship of Catholic publications marked the beginning of restrictions on the freedom of the Church. They were followed (1948–50) by the censorship of all ecclesiastical publications, by the elimination of Catholic youth associations and broadcasts, by the dissolution of the Caritas Association, the nationalization of hospitals, and by the expropriation of the largest portion of ecclesiastical property. Primate Stefan WYSZYŃSKI (later cardinal) took over direction of the archdioceses of Gniezno and Warsaw after the death of Cardinal Hlond on Dec. 16, 1948. He made an agreement with the government on April 14, 1950, securing recognition of the bishops' dogmatic, liturgical, and catechetical demands, but the normalization of relations between Church and State, which they expected, did not take place.

Out of the latent battle between Church and State a more open conflict broke out in 1952. The government decree of Feb. 9, 1953, on the filling of ecclesiastical offices, subordinated episcopal jurisdiction to the supervision of the State. Bishop Czeslaw Mieczyslaw Kaczmarek of Kielce (1938–63) had already been arrested in 1951. In 1953 Cardinal Wyszyńiski, and, in 1954, Auxiliary Bishop Antoni Baraniak of Poznań (archbishop from 1957) were likewise deprived of their freedom. The absolute authority of the governmental office for ecclesiastical affairs; the dissolution of some major and minor seminaries, including seminaries of religious orders; the measures directed against the Catholic University of Lublin; the abolition of the Catholic faculties at the beginning of the winter semester of 1954; the prohibition of January 1955 against the imparting of religious instruction in the elementary schools; the arrest and imprisonment of priests; the frequent search of private domiciles by the police; and the expropriation of monasteries all endangered the independence of the Church. In addition to pressures from the outside, attempts were made to split the interior unity of Catholicism by means of the so-called "patriotic priests," who were pushed into key positions in the Church by the office of ecclesiastical affairs, and of "progressive Catholics" who organized themselves as the Pax-Movement and were supported by the government. These Catholics of leftist orientation developed the Pax Press and presented themselves as the true representatives of Polish Catholicism. The Church was pushed very much into the background in public life. The number of churches and chapels declined about 30 percent; the monasteries for men, 40 percent; and convents for women, about 45 percent. Because of the arrests, imprisonments, and banishments of priests, many parish posts could be filled in a temporary fashion only. On Dec. 8, 1955 concern for the unity of the Church in Poland moved Pope PIUS XII to address a letter to the Polish episcopate. He not only dealt with the persecution of the Church, but he emphasized, among other points, the danger of the ''Progressive Catholics.''

Church-State Relations 1956–57. In the fall of 1956, after the thaw that freed Poland from Stalinism, Władysław Gomułka took over the political leadership and the situation of the Church improved. Cardinal Wyszyński was freed and returned to Warsaw on Oct. 28, 1956. A commission made up of representatives of both Church and state was established to remove the existing tensions. The government decree of Feb. 9, 1953, was withdrawn. Imprisoned bishops and clergy were given their freedom, the vicars capitular who had been appointed in the Polish west and north territories by the office for religious affairs in 1951 were now selected from loyal supporters of the cardinal. Religious instruction was permitted as an elective subject in schools before and after the hours set for obligatory studies. The Catholic laity obtained influence in internal political affairs, the press, and journalism. In May of 1957 Gomułka declared that he saw the necessity of a coexistence between believers and nonbelievers, between the Church and socialism, and between the people's sovereignty and the hierarchy of the Church.

Polish Catholicism, 1956–1965. The Church utilized the alleviations that had been granted in 1956 to make itself heard. Through a carefully prepared and successfully conducted nine-year Novena (1957–66) the Church injected itself into the celebration of the millennium of Poland. The ideological reaction of communism was hesitant at first but soon became clearer. In the preparations for the Sejm (Parliament) elections of April 16, 1961, the watchword went out that Polish atheism must fight with the Catholic hierarchy, and that the domination of the souls of the whole nation was the issue at stake. On June 15, 1961, a law again abrogated the teaching of religion in the schools. The Church replied by constructing a thick network of catechetical support points that the ministry of education tried in vain to bring under its control. The State applied the screw of taxation against the Church; used the pretense of paper shortages against ecclesiastical papers and periodicals; attacked Cardinal Wyszyński and other bishops, charging them with demagoguery and fanaticism; and restricted the freedom of the Church in systematic fashion.

In 1965, the Church was seeking to overcome these threats through a concentration of her forces. Her interior development was evidenced by the sound training of numerous seminarians in the major seminaries (4,000 seminarians in 1965); by the further development of the Catholic University of Lublin and of the Catholic Academy in Bielany near Warsaw; by appropriate methods of pastoral care; by the zealous activity of numerous religious orders and congregations; by courageous argumentation against dialectic and practical materialism; by the publication of several theological journals of high standing, as, for example, the *Ateneum kapłańskie* (Włocławek), the *Collectanea theologica* (Warsaw), and the *Homo Dei* (Warsaw); by cooperation in the Ecumenical Movement; by close contact with Rome as the center of the Church; and by the implementation of the decrees and suggestions of VATICAN COUNCIL II. There was a flourishing religious life that was evidenced by zealous attendance at divine worship, the reception of the Sacraments, the intense devotion to the Blessed Virgin, and the restoration of old churches and erection of new ones. It was reflected also in the appearance of weekly Church papers like *Przewodnik Katolicky* (Poznań) and *Gość Niedzielny* (Katowice), in the sociocultural weekly *Tygodnik Powzechny* (Cracow), as well as in the monthly paper *Znak* (Cracow).

[B. STASIEWSKI]

The Church in Poland, 1965–2000

The Failure of the Five-Year Plan. The five-year plan introduced by the Władyslaw Gomułka regime ended in failure, further reducing living standards. It worsened shortages in consumer goods, stoked hidden inflation, and widened the gap between Poland and the West. The still-unsettled question of Poland's western borders on the Oder and Neisse Rivers continued to impede relations with West Germany (which did not recognize those frontiers) while heightening Polish dependence on the Soviet Union. In 1965 the Treaty of Friendship, Cooperation and Mutual Assistance between Poland and the Soviet Union was extended a further 20 years. Conflict with the Church grew over ecclesiastical preparations to mark the millennium of Christianity in Poland in 1966; the Polish government wanted to treat the occasion as merely the thousandth anniversary of the Polish State. The Polish episcopate addressed a letter to its German counterpart, ''forgiving and seeking forgiveness'' between Poles and Germans. This effort at mutual reconciliation resulted in Gomułka, now first secretary of the Polish United Workers' Party (PZPR), accusing Primate Wyszyński of interfering in the prerogatives of the State. Within the PZPR itself, dissidents succeeded for the first time in expanding civil rights, particularly in the area of culture.

In reaction to the conservatism of Gomułka and hard-line communists (''partisans''), a liberal dissident wing emerged within the PZPR, made up primarily of the party's intelligentsia, which enjoyed some support from youth and students. Gomułka and other hard-liners would seize upon events following the 1967 Arab-Israeli Six Day War and anti-Russian student protests in early 1968 following performances of Mickiewicz's play *Dziady* (''Forefathers' Eve'') to purge those ''revisionists'' in the name of ''anti-Zionism.'' This internecine party warfare, inspired from Moscow, resulted in the migration of about 10,000 Jews from Poland (not all of them party members) at the time.

The Gomułka regime lost further public credibility after the 1968 Soviet-led invasion of Czechoslovakia and the worsening economic situation in Poland. The ongoing failure of communist central planning only deepened Poland's dependence on the Soviet Union. Although the Gomułka regime sought to maintain control of the situation, it found itself increasingly isolated, distrusting even its closest collaborators; party and government purges continued.

Departing from its traditional anti-West German stance, however, the Polish government signed a treaty in December 1970 with Chancellor Willy Brandt's government, normalizing Polish–West German relations and recognizing Poland's postwar western borders. This resulted in the normalization of ecclesiastical government in those areas through the creation of dioceses and the appointment of ordinaries in lieu of apostolic administrators.

The economic crisis of 1968 to 1970 resulted, in part, in a weak supply of basic goods. Steep price increases announced just before Christmas 1970 spurred protests by workers in Gdańsk, Sopot, Gdynia, and Szczecin. The protests were put down bloodily, with 45 dead and about 1,200 wounded. In the wake of those protests, the Central Committee forced Gomułka and his coterie to resign. Edward Gierek became first secretary of the PZPR; Piotr Jarosiewicz replaced Józef Cyrankiewicz as premier. Gierek, who had begun his career as a communist activist in Belgium and France, gave the impression of a technocrat who promised to raise living standards and improve the economy, thereby buying a certain measure of social confidence (''Help us?'' ''We'll help!'' was a contemporary slogan). Gierek fostered the illusion of liberalization in the areas of culture (censorship became more elastic), social control (travel abroad became easier) and toward the Church. At the same time, persecution of the opposition in fact intensified; for example, a 1971 law provided for convictions in the absence of court decisions. These efforts went in tandem with slogans about patriotism and the building of socialism in close alliance with the USSR. One outcome of these campaigns was the approval by Parliament on Feb. 3, 1976, of constitutional changes previously adopted by the Seventh Congress of the PZPR that acknowledged the leading role of the party in the building of socialism and pledging Poland's indissoluble friendship with the USSR. Both the Church and dissident circles protested that decision, emphasizing that it conflicted with provisions of the 1975 Helsinki Final Act signed by Poland at the Conference on Security and Cooperation in Europe. Despite increased diplomatic contacts with the West, Polish dependence on the Soviets grew in the Gierek-Brezhnev era.

In the sphere of Church affairs, the government's authority grew as direct talks between the Polish government and the Vatican took place and efforts were made to repair relations with Cardinal Wyszyński. A new internal administrative division of the country into 49 voivodships occurred, although it served to intensify centralized party leadership while reducing the significance of the local party apparatus.

Economically, a boom in investments, overextension of western credit, and growth in consumerism in the period 1971 to 1975 were all passed off as evidence that Poland was growing closer to Western affluence. The lifestyle bought by over-indebtedness to Western credit eventually destabilized the economy by increasing the money supply even as the availability of real goods continued to decline. Starting in 1974, a new economic crisis (which, in socialist states also meant a new political crisis) began. Price increases announced by Premier Jarosiewicz on June 24, 1976 resulted in workers' protests in Radom, Ursus, and Plock. The militia suppressed the protests, resulting in about 1,000 arrests and 100 jailings.

Solidarność. The opposition acquired a new lease on life. On Sept. 23, 1976 the Committee for the Defense of Workers (KOR) was founded. The Church came out on the side of workers, providing shelter and succor for members of the opposition, irrespective of their religious convictions (or lack thereof). The government backed down from the price hikes, which simply hastened economic collapse. The majority of those convicted in the 1976 protests were pardoned in the amnesty of July 19, 1977, which still punished opposition activities with short-term punishments or punishment by time served.

Opposition labor organizing continued. On March 26, 1977 the Movement in Defense of Human and Civil

Rights (ROPCiO) was formed. In 1978 some free trade unions, the Self- Defense Committee of Farmers and the Trade Union of Farmers were all founded on local levels. Contacts were also formed with opposition movements in the other satellite countries. The Church, particularly through Primate Wyszyński, criticized the situation in Poland with the aim of fostering its improvement.

The election of Cardinal Karol Wojtyła as Pope JOHN PAUL II in 1978 and his first pilgrimage to Poland, June 2–10, 1979, emboldened society to take initiatives apart from party and government direction. Malaise in turn led to half-hearted prosecution of independent opposition organizations. The politico-economic crisis in the USSR was also slowly deepening.

One of the repercussions of this situation was the foundation in 1979 of a radical pro-independence organization led by Leszek Moczulski, the Confederation of Independent Poland (KPN). Independent trade unions also began asserting themselves more vigorously and the first strikes broke out in Lublin. Against this setting, the Eighth Congress of the PZPR in February 1980 resulted in nothing new. The only changes were at the level of personnel, e.g., Edward Babiuch replaced Jarosiewicz as premier.

Spring 1980 saw more shortages and price increases announced in July ushered in a wave of strikes in Lublin and Swidnik that spread on August 14 to the Gdańsk shipyards and all along the Polish seacoast. An Interfactory Strike Committee was formed in August in various production centers throughout the country. In contrast to 1970, this time the government did not use force. Instead, it negotiated with the strikers, under the proviso that permitting independent trade unions would not be allowed to undermine the leading role of the official government party nor seek changes to the Constitution. That process led the way to the formation in the Gdánsk shipyards of the independent trade union *Solidarność* (Solidarity) under Lech Wałęsa's leadership. Solidarity soon encompassed the whole country as regional trade unions were founded (the first in the Mazowsze region on Sept. 4, 1980). A National Committee for Understanding was set up in early September with Wałęsa as its head. The struggle to register Solidarity as an independent trade union went on until Nov. 10, 1980, when the Supreme Court confirmed the union's constitution.

Gierek was removed from office on Sept. 6, 1980 by the Sixth Plenum of the Central Committee of the PZPR. Stanisław Kania replaced him as first secretary. Kania advocated finding a political solution to the Polish crisis. But neither the party nor the government could constrain independent union organizing of diverse sectors of society: students, artists and scholars, farmers. Having begun with about 3.5 million members, Solidarity reached more than 9 million by the end of August 1981. The regime grew confused and fearful of a Soviet invasion. But the governing apparatchiks had no intention of giving up power and, under the leadership of General Wojciech Jaruzelski preparations for martial law began. Conflict between Solidarity and the government increased in 1981 as the regime took an increasingly hard line. Militia-initiated provocations (in Bydgoszcz, for example, Solidarity activists were beaten up in the local voivodship council's chamber) and efforts by the PZPR to limit Solidarity's local influence further fueled distrust and propelled events towards conflict. Ongoing Soviet pressure (e.g., the ''Letter of the Central Committee of the Communist Party of the Soviet Union to the Central Committee of the PZPR''), the radicalization of attitudes in the party and in Solidarity, and the May 1981 death of Primate Wyszyński, who had exercised a moderating influence, all brought confrontation closer.

The second half of 1981 saw an increase in mutual accusations between the party and Solidarity and a growing wave of strikes. During Solidarity's General Congress on Sept. 5, 1981, a ''Message to the Working People of Eastern Europe'' was adopted, expressing an interest in expanding the ideals of Solidarity to other satellite countries. Absent from the document were any traces of the postulates of socialist ideology or adherence to the doctrine of the party's ''leading role'' in society.

General Jaruzelski's assumption of the role of First Secretary of the PZPR in October 1981 signaled the beginning of a reckoning with Solidarity, which had already been suggested by the use of the army in quelling strikes. Solidarity sought to call a national strike. Its National Commission assembled on Dec. 11, 1981 in Gdańsk. On the night of December 12, martial law was declared in Poland and the majority of Solidarity activists interned. The Church, through the Primate's Committee for Assistance to Persons Deprived of Liberty, intervened in the name of human rights. Armed reserve militias (ZOMO) and army took over Solidarity-controlled factories. At the Wujek Mine in Silesia nine miners were killed. The regime transformed itself into the Military Council of National Salvation (WRON), with the Council for the Defense of the Nation acting as its shadow. The party nevertheless lost members, with about 700,000 quitting. Solidarity too lost members and went underground. Military commissars assumed control over the direction of all spheres of life, including the economy. Instead of the normalization that the WRON promised, however, chaos and acute shortages of basic goods afflicted the population.

The regime intended to liquidate Solidarity. The Trade Unions Act of Oct. 8, 1982 adopted by the Sejm sought to regulate the union without its consent. A Patriotic Front for the Rebirth of the Nation (PRON) was created, intended to facilitate the party's dialogue with society. That dialogue included gestures of reconciliation like the release of Wałęsa in November of 1982, the gradual freeing of other internees, and finally the suspension of martial law on Dec. 18, 1982. At the same time, more intense repression of the opposition meant losses for the underground Solidarity movement, now led by its Temporary Coordinating Commission (TKK) with offices in Brussels. Although Pope John Paul II's second pilgrimage in June 1983 and the formal lifting of martial law on July 22 were further conciliatory gestures on the regime's part, repression of the opposition continued. The Church paid for its public encouragement of Solidarity with the murder of several priests, including the Rev. Jerzy Popiełuszko. But even harsher punishments (the Criminal Code was updated on July 1, 1985, and there were 386 political prisoners by the end of 1986) could not staunch the hemorrhage of the regime's authority.

On Nov. 6, 1985 Jaruzelski further took over the Office of Chairman of the Council of State. The regime sought to reach some understanding with society by establishing a Consultative Council on December 6, 1986. Although limited participation in the Council by the opposition was permitted, it refused to take part.

Pope John Paul II's third pilgrimage to Poland, June 8–14, 1987, took place amid an atmosphere of the regime's weakening grip and the reappearance of active, though weakened, structures of Solidarity. On Oct. 25, 1987, the National Executive Commission of Solidarity was founded but, at the core of the union, permanent divisions in ideology and tactics had already occurred. In December 1987 regional structures of Solidarity reappeared publicly. Throughout 1987 and 1988, it was apparent that the government's economic program had failed. Following a wave of strikes General Kiszczak, the interior minister, met with Wałęsa on Aug. 31, 1988. On September 27, Mieczysław Rakowski became premier.

The End of the PZPR. The regime, while still displaying strength, called for roundtable dialogue with the opposition. The discussions took place from Feb. 6 to April 5, 1989. They guaranteed immunity to the departing regime. On April 7 the Sejm adopted a new electoral law and established a presidency and senate. The semifree elections of June 4, 1989 manifested social support for Solidarity and utterly discredited the regime. On July 19 General Jaruzelski was chosen by a majority of three votes in a joint session of Parliament to become president. On Aug. 24, 1989, Tadeusz Mazowiecki became premier. The PZPR formally ceased to exist in January 1990, although part of that grouping formed the Social Democracy of the Republic of Poland (SdRP) party, which included Aleksander Kwasniewski. Multiple other parties arose.

Solidarity, which had at first entered Parliament as the Citizens' Parliamentary Club (OKP) soon broke up into several political groupings of varying orientations. The "Centrist Understanding" (PC), formed in January 1991, eventually became a Christian-Democratic type party. Another faction that broke off in January 1991 later named itself the Democratic Union, taking the name Freedom Union in 1994.

Liberals and the left frequently found a coincidence of interests on various subjects, e.g., the exclusion of the Church from public life. *Gazeta Wyborcza,* at first the only independent daily newspaper independent of the communist regime, dominated public opinion. Public disorientation in political matters manifested itself in the 1990 presidential elections. The finalists were Wałęsa and Stanisław Tyminski, a candidate of indeterminate provenance who had outpolled Mazowiecki in the first round. Wałęsa won.

Jan Krzysztof Bielecki of the Liberal-Democratic Congress became premier. The electoral ordinance fostered Parliamentary fracturing (there were 29 parties) and made it difficult for the government to function. In 1991 Parliamentary elections eight parties and 29 smaller groups competed. The Democratic Union won 12.3 percent of the vote, followed by the Democratic Left Alliance (SLD), with the former communists assembled from various smaller groups also polling 12 percent. Solidarity won five percent. The government of Jan Olszewski (PC) lasted from December 1991 to June 4, 1992; Wałęsa's own ambivalence was decisive in Olszewski's fall, since that government had promised to undertake decommunization and lustration. The next government, from Waldemar Pawlak's leftist Polish Farmers' Front (PSL) lasted from June 5 to July 7, 1992. Hanna Suchocka's (UD) government endured until the end of May 1993.

The difficulties of successive governments were caused by the economic reforms of Finance Minister Leszek Balcerowicz, by the lack of a decisive break with the legacy of the communist regime, and by the contradictory interests among different parties and actors. A growing anticlericalism could also be felt, especially in the SLD, UW, the Union of Labor (UP) and parts of the PSL. One expression of this anticlericalism was the fight over the concordat between Poland and the Vatican, signed at the end of July 1993 but entering into force only in early 1998. In 1992 a new ecclesiastical reorganization of Poland took place, dividing the country into thirteen metropolitan and forty suffragan sees. Liberal circles, represented by journals like *Gazeta Wyborcza* and *Tygodnik Powszechny,* sought to divide Polish Catholicism into two camps: ''fundamentalist'' (i.e., those acknowledging traditional Catholic truths) and ''open'' (i.e., subordinating Catholicism to secularized ideology).

Political Division, Social Reform, and an Uncertain Future. On Nov. 17, 1992 Wałęsa signed the so-called ''Little Constitution'' that was to remain in force until adoption of a new fundamental law. A leftist alliance won the Nov. 19, 1993 parliamentary elections. Their victory was caused by divisions in the political landscape, discontent with the pain of economic reforms, and popular hopes fueled by the former Communists that they would spur economic growth. The SLD and PSL together won 45 percent of the vote. The decline of Wałęsa's and Solidarity's influence was the consequence of political conflicts, economic scandals, the communist past of various high-ranking officials, and the growing disparity between the generally poor (and growing poorer) public at large and the *nouveau riche* of the former communist *nomenklatura.*

In 1999 Poland became a member of NATO. Within the framework of preparing for accession to the European Union the government began economic reforms one consequence of which was the pauperization of villages and a rise in unemployment (caused by the sale of Polish factories that were then downsized or closed by their new owners). These reforms, in turn, generated opposition to the government, particularly among farmers. Reforms of the health service also struck hard at the poorest. Fractures within the governing coalition itself deepened while the left prepared for a populist campaign.

The lack of political stability in the decade after the fall of communism in Poland affected social morality, particularly in a growing crime rate and the continual legal sanctions. Sentimentality for the old Communist regime continued to be manifested in some social opinion.

Bibliography: N. DAVIES, *God's Playground: A History of Poland,* vol. 2, *1795 to the Present* (New York 1982). H. SLABEK, *Historia spoleczna Polski (1944–1970)* (A Social History of Poland: 1944–1970) (Warsaw 1988). J. HOLZER, *Solidarność* (Solidarity) (Warsaw 1990). T. MOLDAWA, *Ludzie władzy 1944–1991* (The People in the Government, 1944–1991) (Warsaw 1991). G. LONGWORTH, *The Making of Eastern Europe* (London 1991). I. PRIZEL and A. MICHTA, eds., *Polish Foreign Policy Reconsidered: The Challenges of Independence* (London 1995). W. ROSZKOWSKI, *Historia Polski, 1914–1991* (The History of Poland: 1914–1991) (Warsaw 1995). J. POPIELUSZKO, *The Way of My Cross: Masses at Warsaw* (Chicago 1986).

[Z. ZIELINSKI]

POLDING, JOHN BEDE

First bishop of Australia; b. Liverpool, England, Nov. 18, 1794; d. Sydney, Australia, March 16, 1877. Educated by the Benedictines, he joined the order (1811), was ordained (1819), and was assigned as a tutor at St. Gregory's College, Downside, England. In 1834 he was consecrated as first vicar apostolic of New Holland and Van Diemen's Land (Australia). He reached Sydney in 1835. After visiting Rome to request the establishment of an Australian hierarchy, he was named archbishop of Sydney and metropolitan of Australia in 1842. During a period when convict transportation was ending and immigration increasing, he consolidated the Church's position, making pastoral visitations through wild bush frontier country, establishing a Catholic education system, founding new dioceses and parishes, and bringing clergy from overseas. His original diocese was roughly the size of the U.S.; but when he died, there were 12 dioceses with 135 priests. His archdiocese of SYDNEY contained 82 churches, 53 schools, a Catholic hospital, and St. John's College within the University of Sydney.

Bibliography: P. F. MORAN, *History of the Catholic Church in Australasia* (Sydney 1897). H. N. BIRT, *Benedictine Pioneers in Australia,* 2 v. (London 1911). J. MCGOVERN, ''John Bede Polding,'' *Australasian Catholic Record* 11–16 (1934–39).

[J. G. MURTAGH]

POLE, MARGARET PLANTAGENET, BL.

Married woman, martyr; b. Castle Farley, near Bath, Aug. 14?, 1473; d. London, May 27, 1541. She was of the house of Plantagenet; the niece of Edward IV and Richard III; daughter of George, duke of Clarence; mother of Cardinal Reginald POLE. Margaret was three years old when her mother died (Dec. 22, 1476). A year later her father was arraigned on a charge of high treason and put to death in the Tower (Jan. 16, 1478). Margaret and her brother Edward, earl of Warwick, found their position insecure at the accession of Richard III (1483) since they were children of Richard's eldest brother. Edward, nearest male heir to Edward IV, was judicially murdered by Henry VII (1499). Margaret married Sir Richard Pole, son of Sir Geoffrey Pole, and was made countess of Salisbury (Oct. 14, 1513) by Henry VIII, partly to atone for her brother's murder. At the birth of Mary (1516), daughter of Henry VIII and Catherine of Aragon, Margaret carried the princess to her baptism at Greyfriars church in Greenwich and later, was also sponsor at her confirmation. As lady governess for Princess Mary, she gained the affection of the queen. Following Thomas Cranmer's pronouncement of Henry's divorce (1533), Margaret was separated from court, although she returned at the downfall of Anne Boleyn in 1536. In that year her son Reginald, soon to be a cardinal, wrote against the divorce and attacked the king's usurpation of the title of head of the Church in England. While Reginald's blunt outspokenness came from the relative safety of the Continent, it brought reprisals to Margaret and her family. Henry Pole, Lord Montague, a son of Margaret, was charged with treason and beheaded on Tower Hill. A cousin, Henry Courtney, marquis of Exeter, met a similar fate. A third son, Sir Geoffrey, under examination had incriminated his brothers and Exeter.

Parliament, in May 1539, passed an act of attainder against the executed men, Lady Margaret, and Reginald Pole. Thomas Cromwell produced a tunic of Margaret's bearing the five wounds of Christ, the banner of the PILGRIMAGE OF GRACE. Without trial, with no crime imputed to her, and upon this sole evidence, Margaret was thrown into the Tower. After two years, she was beheaded with only an hour's warning on the morning of May 27, 1541. Ludovico Beccadelli, Reginald Pole's first biographer, has recorded the words of the cardinal when the news of his mother's death was brought to him at Viterbo: ''Until now I thought that God had given me the greatest blessing of being son to one of the best and most honored ladies in England. . .but from now on He has wished to bestow an even greater blessing by making me the son of a martyr. . . .May God's will be done.'' Margaret was included in the decree of beatification of the English martyrs that was approved by Leo XIII on Dec. 29, 1886.

Feast: May 28.

See Also: ENGLAND, SCOTLAND, AND WALES, MARTYRS OF.

Bibliography: R. POLE, *Epistolae. . .et aliorum ad ipsum*, ed. A. M. QUIRINI, 5 v. (Brescia 1744–57). J. S. BREWER et al., eds., *Letters and Papers. . .of the Reign of Henry VIII*, 22 v. (London 1862–1932) v.3, 11, 13, 14. *Calendar of Letters. . .State Papers. . .between England and Spain*, ed. G. A. BERGENROTH et al., 13 v. (London 1862–1954). B. CAMM, ed., *Lives of the English Martyrs Declared Blessed by Pope Leo XIII in 1886 and 1895*, 2 v. (New York 1904–14) v.1; *The English Martyrs* (Cambridge, England 1929). J. GAIRDNER, *The Dictionary of National Biography From the Earliest Times to 1900* (London 1885–1900; repr. with corrections, 21 v., 1908–09, 1921–22, 1938; suppl. 1901–) 16:28–29. J. GILLOW, *A Literary and Biographical History or Bibliographical Dictionary of the English Catholics from 1934 to the Present Time* (London-NewYork 1885–1902; repr. New York 1961) 5:335–336. J. D. MACKIE, *The Earlier Tudors* (New York 1952).

[J. G. DWYER]

POLE, REGINALD

Cardinal, papal legate to the Council of Trent and to England under Queen Mary I, last Roman Catholic archbishop of Canterbury; b. Stourton Castle, Staffordshire, March 3, 1500; d. Nov. 17, 1558, Lambeth Palace, London, a few hours after the death of Mary Tudor. His simple monument is in Canterbury Cathedral near the tomb of Thomas Becket.

Patronage of Henry VIII. Pole's mother was Margaret of Salisbury, later beatified, daughter of George, duke of Clarence, and niece of King Edward IV. Sir Richard Pole, Reginald's father, was a cousin of Henry VII. Thus, Pole, of Tudor and Plantagenet descent, was cousin to King Henry VIII of England. He was tutored by William Latimer, a Greek scholar, was educated at the Carthusian monastery of Sheen and Magdalen College, Oxford, and continued his studies (1519–1527) in Rome, Padua, and Venice. Henry VIII paid for the early education of his kinsman, and Pole never forgot his debt of gratitude. Even in later years when bitter controversy marked their relationship, Pole wrote to him: ''May God be my witness that never has the love of a mother for her only son been greater than the love I have always had for you.''

On his return to England he refused to support the king's divorce proceedings against Catherine of Aragon, even though Henry offered him the sees of York and Winchester. In a stormy scene with Henry, Pole boldly defied the king. In 1532 he received permission to return to Italy. There an urgent appeal from Henry VIII sought Pole's opinion on the divorce. The result was Pole's *Pro ecclesiasticae unitatis defensione (De Unitate)* (1534–35), written for Henry VIII alone. It was a classic defense of the papacy and a strong statement of righteous indignation at Henry's moral and political transgressions. He begged Henry to repent and told him: ''I can conceive of no greater injury you could inflict upon the Church than to abolish the head of the Church from the face of the earth. . . . Nothing more ignominious could ever have been imagined than this pretentious title of supreme head of the Church in England.'' Henry, angered by this vigorous tone, reacted by having Pole's brother executed and then by imprisoning Pole's innocent and devout mother, Margaret of Salisbury, in the Tower, where she was later beheaded. In 1536 Pope Paul III created Pole cardinal. At the time of the PILGRIMAGE OF GRACE in England he was named legate, though when he reached Paris in April of 1537, the rising had been crushed, and Pole returned to Italy.

Leader of Reform. In July of 1536, Paul III had appointed Pole, with Cardinal Gian Pietro Caraffa (later Pope Paul IV) and three other prominent reform leaders to a special commission. The *Consilium de emendanda ecclesia* that resulted was a fearless statement on the existing abuses in the Church and contained the outline of the general reform program for the Council of Trent. In August of 1541, Pole was appointed governor of Viterbo and the Papal States in Italy, where tolerance and kindly sympathy marked his administration. Barely three weeks before the opening of the Council of Trent, on Feb. 22, 1145, Cardinals Giammaria Del Monte, Marcello Cervini, and Pole were empowered to preside. In the absence of one, the other two were to have full authority. At the Council of Trent Pole's dominating personality and his restrained and conciliatory approach impressed the delegates as he reminded them that they themselves were alone to blame for the evils burdening the flock of Christ. He exhorted them to acknowledge the spiritual wickedness existing in high places.

Following the death of Paul III on Nov. 10, 1549, and the political maneuvering at the conclave, Pole received a large number of votes but not the two-thirds necessary for election. The imperialist cardinals offered to elect Pole by acclamation and rendering homage (*per adorationem*), but Pole refused to cooperate with this devious strategy. After considerable haggling Cardinal Del Monte (Julius III) was elected with the aid of French cardinals who arrived too late to participate in the early voting.

Marian Restoration. In 1554 Pole was appointed papal legate to England. Mary Tudor, his cousin, was now queen. On Nov. 30, 1554, Pole absolved the English nation from schism and brought about the short-lived Catholic Restoration. He made every effort to restrain Mary from excessive retaliation against the Protestants, favoring instead a policy of moderation and reconciliation. He was ordained and consecrated archbishop of Canterbury (1556), and he introduced Tridentine discipline and reforms. Throughout Pole's time as archbishop he was hampered by the unfounded suspicions and criticisms of Paul IV, who distrusted him. Ill health also restricted his effectiveness.

Pole's Achievement. Pole's ideals represented a humanism tempered by personal sanctity, the cultivation of man's intellectual gifts, and unswerving defense of the apostolic succession to the papacy. His moral conduct was above reproach, and compared with the majority of his contemporaries he was conspicuously gentle, both in his opinions and in his language. His learning, generosity, and charity inspired warm friendships. If his total achievements appear minimal, his permanent contribution was in his firm stand on papal supremacy and his reasoned reform program for the Church Universal, which permeated the Council of Trent and later inspired Vatican Council II.

Reginald Cardinal Pole, after 1556 oil painting on panel, by an unknown artist.

Pope Paul VI in *Summi Dei Verbum* (1963) referred to Pole by recalling his decree to the London Synod of 1556. It was there that Pole first introduced the word *seminarium* (a seed-bed, seminary) for the proper training of candidates to the priesthood. He urged the bishops to imitate the example of St. Ignatius Loyola and his Roman College by founding adequate seminaries. This decree of Pole's became the model for the canon on the institution of seminaries that emanated from the Council of Trent in the *De Reformatione* decree approved on July 15, 1563.

Bibliography: R. POLE, *Epistolae . . . et aliorum ad ipsum*, ed. A. M. QUIRINI, 5 v. (Brescia 1744–57). Sources. J. S. BREWER et al., eds., *Letters and Papers of the Reign of Henry, VIII*, 22 v. (London 1862–1932). Literature. W. SCHENK, *Reginald Pole, Cardinal of England* (New York 1950). P. HUGHES, *Rome and the Counter-Reformation in England* (London 1942); *The Reformation in England,* 3 v. in 1 (5th, rev. ed. New York 1963). F. A. GASQUET, *Cardinal Pole and His Early Friends* (London 1927). M. HAILE, *The Life of Reginald Pole* (New York 1910). H. F. M. PRESCOTT, *Mary Tudor* (London 1952). H. JEDIN, *History of the Council of Trent,* 3 v. (Freiburg 1949–). J. GAIRDNER, *The Dictionary of National Biography from the Earliest Times to 1900,* 63 v. (London 1885–1900) 16:35–46. R. BIRON and J. BARENNES, *Un Prince anglais: Cardinal Légat au XVIe siècle, Reginald Pole* (Paris 1922). A. ZIMMERMANN, *Kardinal Pole: Sein Leben und seine Schriften* (New York 1893). G. B. PARKS, ''The First Italianate Englishmen,'' *Studies in the Renaissance* 8:197–216; ''The Parma Letters and the

Dangers to Cardinal Pole,'' *American Catholic Historical Review* 46 (1960) 299–317. E. G. BOLAND, ''An Appreciation of Cardinal Pole,'' *Unitas* 14 (1962) 120–126. T. STARKEYA, *A Dialogue between Reginald Pole and Thomas Lupset*, ed. K. M. BURTON (London 1948).

[J. G. DWYER]

POLIGNAC, MELCHIOR DE

Cardinal, diplomat, and apologist; b. Puy–en–Velay, Oct. 11, 1661; d. Paris, Nov. 20, 1742. Polignac studied at the Collège de Clermont and later at the Sorbonne, excelling in Cartesian philosophy. While at Rome in 1689, he refused to subscribe to the four Gallican Articles of 1682, thereby disavowing the schism (*see* ASSEMBLIES OF FRENCH CLERGY). In 1693 he was made ambassador to Poland by LOUIS XIV, and at the death of King John Sobieski (1696) he succeeded in having Prince François Louis de Conti chosen as candidate for the throne. When the Prince de Conti was displaced by Augustus II, Elector of Saxony, Polignac was recalled and confined to the Abbey of Bomport from 1698 to 1702. In 1704 he was elected to the French Academy to succeed Bossuet; two years later he was named auditor of the Rota and took up residence in Rome. He participated in the conferences of Gertruydenberg and in the Peace of Utrecht (1713). On March 8, 1712, he was created cardinal, and later became archbishop of Auch (1726).

Because he was involved in the conspiracy of A. Cellamare during the minority of Louis XV, he was confined to the Abbey of Auchin in Flanders. While in exile, he composed the famous poem *Anti-Lucretius sive de Deo et natura libri novem.* In this poem, containing nine books of 1,000 verses each, he refuted the ancient materialism of Lucretius and Epicurus, and that of his contemporary P. Bayle, and demonstrated the existence of God, the supernatural world, and the immortality of the soul.

Bibliography: *Anti-Lucretius sive de Deo et natura libri novem*, 2 v. in 1 (Paris 1247). J. CARREYRE, *Dictionnaire de théologie catholique,* eds., A. VACANT et al. (Paris 1903–50), 12.2:2416–18. P. PAUL, *Le Cardinal Melchior de Polignac* (Paris 1922).

[I. J. CALICCHIO]

POLISH NATIONAL CATHOLIC CHURCH

The Polish National Catholic Church was established on March 14, 1897 in Scranton, Pennsylvania. It came into existence as a result of the resentment of Polish Catholics to the lack of Polish-speaking clergy and disputes over legal, property, and other administrative issues. Its origins go back to the turn of the century when thousands of Poles arrived in the U.S. and, like most national groups, tended to settle among their own countrymen in Polish-speaking communities located in Massachusetts, Connecticut, New York, New Jersey, Pennsylvania, Ohio, Michigan, Illinois, and Wisconsin. The predominantly Irish and German hierarchy and clergy in these areas were unfamiliar with the ways of the Poles, who in turn wanted to have their own priests and to run their own parishes on a trustee basis, contrary to the decrees of the Councils of BALTIMORE. Conflict between the non-Polish clergy and some strongly nationalistic Poles led to small schisms and eventually to the formation of a separate and distinctly Polish National Catholic Church.

The first significant schism occurred in 1895, when Anton Koslowski, an assistant at St. Jadwiga's parish, Chicago, Ill., and a large group of parishioners clashed with the bishop over parochial administration. When Koslowski set up his own church, All Saints, he was excommunicated. After organizing several other parishes, he associated himself with the Old Catholic Church and received episcopal consecration (*see* OLD CATHOLICS). He then formed The Polish Old Catholic Church, which at the time of his death in 1907 had 23 parishes.

In Scranton, Pa., a similar and far more significant situation arose in 1897 in Sacred Heart parish. The parishioners, who had built the church, wanted to retain control of the property under lay trusteeship, but their bishop could not accept this arrangement and directed that the deed be turned over to the diocese. Under Rev. Francis Hodur, a group of 250 families built another church, St. Stanislaus, which the bishop refused to bless. When Hodur continued as rector after an unsuccessful appeal to Rome for support, he was subsequently excommunicated. Other dissatisfied Polish groups followed Hodur's example and in 1904 formed a synod, electing Hodur its bishop. His consecration by the Old Catholics was postponed until after the death of Koslowski; Hodur then united his church with the Chicago churches to form the Polish National Catholic Church (PNCC). This was externally distinguished from the Roman Catholic Church only by its use of Polish (later, English) in the liturgy and lay control of property and the appointment of pastors.

The sect grew quickly, from 16,000 in 1904 to 62,000 in 1926. It gained many adherents among Polish Catholics who felt at home in its parishes. By the 1950s and 1960s, membership had exceeded 280,000 members.

Hodur remained prime bishop of the church until his death in 1953; however, he did not hold complete authority. This is centered in the general Synod, which meets every four years. The function of the bishop primate is to preside at the Synods and consecrate bishops elected by it, to direct the church's sole seminary in Scranton, and to oversee the church's publications. Hodur himself rejected certain theological truths such as original sin and the existence of hell, but his opinions were not normative for his church. Over the years, decisions of the Synod accepted the teachings of the first four Ecumenical Councils as necessary, thereby deepening their separation from Roman Catholicism. The Synod also declared that there are seven Sacraments. The other five are identical with those of the Catholic Church. Synodal action likewise permitted a married clergy since 1921 and introduced new liturgical feasts expressive of Polish nationalism, such as the Commemoration of the Polish Fatherland. The PNCC catechism justifies its national character in these words: ''Christ called all men from all nations and races to serve God, each to contribute its particular spiritual and cultural gifts toward the building of the Kingdom of God on earth.''

Under the terms of an agreement made in 1946 between the PNCC and the EPISCOPAL CHURCH, U.S.A., each church admits members of the other to its sacraments; both remain independent and do not necessarily accept the other's doctrinal viewpoint, acknowledging only that the other holds essential Christian faith. However, this sacramental intercommunion was ended in 1978 over the issue of women's ordination in the Episcopal Church.

In 1921 the PNCC established a mission in Poland and in time set up 55 parishes for its 55,000 native Polish communicants. However, in 1951 the Communist regime suppressed all contact between the Polish and American branches. Since that date, a separate national church, the Polish Catholic Church, has been established in Poland.

Ecumenical endeavors have been especially encouraged by Hodur's successor, Leon Grochowski. The church holds membership in the NATIONAL COUNCIL OF THE CHURCHES OF CHRIST IN THE U.S.A. and the WORLD COUNCIL OF CHURCHES. It also maintains a close relationship with the Old Catholics of the Declaration of Utrecht.

Bibliography: T. ANDREWS, *The Polish National Catholic Church* (Society for Promoting Christian Knowledge; London 1953). C. J. WOZNIAK, *Hyphenated Catholicism: A Study of the Role of the Polish-American Model of Church, 1890–1908* (San Francisco 1998).

[T. HORGAN]

POLITICAL THEOLOGY

Political theology has two distinct meanings. Firstly, it is the implicit or explicit use of religious symbols to interpret, to justify, or to criticize political events, systems, or units. As implicit, it is almost coexistent with religion. As explicit, political theology is a distinct division of theology which, in middle Stoicism, was distinguished from mythic and natural theology. In the European Enlightenment and Catholic Restoration, it was contrasted with the notion of CIVIL RELIGION, and in the 1960s it was a theological response to existentialism that stressed the public significance of Christian ESCHATOLOGY. Secondly, in its other meaning, political theology stands for a foundational theology that analyzes the interrelation between political patterns and religious beliefs. Their mutual influence is studied to uncover the meaning, truth, and practice of religious symbols.

Historical Analysis. Although both meanings of political theology are quite clear, political theology has often been confused with political ethics or has often been identified either with traditionalism or with LIBERATION theology. A historical survey will underscore its distinctive meaning.

Antiquity. In middle Stoicism, political theology appears along with mythic and natural theology as parts of a tripartite division. This Hellenistic division became current in Roman theology when Pontifex Quintus Mucius Scaevola argued for the necessity of political theology as a defense of the Roman civil religion. This tripartite division is elaborated by Marcus Terentius Varro (116–27 B.C.) in his *Antiquities,* a major source of information about the tripartite division. Since it is no longer extant, it must be reconstructed from TERTULLIAN's *Ad nationes* and AUGUSTINE's *De Civitate Dei* and their discussions of political theology. In this tripartite division, each theology has a specific source, locus, and theme. Mythic theology consists of the poet's narration of divine stories and its locus is the theatre. Natural theology consists of the philosophical world views propounded by the philosophers in their schools. Political theology is attributed to priests and statesmen; its locus is the cities. Varro distinguishes between uncertain and certain gods, elucidates a natural theology, and gives an allegorical interpretation of Roman myths in order to salvage and defend the Roman political theology.

Both Tertullian and Augustine criticize political theology. For Tertullian, valid theology demands criteria of certitude, morality, and universality. Political theology lacks universality, for each city has its own religion. Augustine's criticisms are much more fundamental. Political theology rests upon a mythic theology. If the myths and fables are false, then the political theology is invalid. Likewise it is only as valid as its underlying metaphysical or natural theology. Augustine's analysis and critique contributes several insights. Political theology along with natural and mythic theology are viewed as three fundamentally distinct ways of speaking of God. They are distinct, but are radically intertwined. Moreover, Augustine challenges the adequacy of utilitarianism as a theological criterion of political theology. He argues against the immanence of the Roman natural theology and confronts political theology with his eschatological conception of the City of God.

Enlightenment and Restoration. Distinct evaluations of political theology appear in the ENLIGHTENMENT and Catholic Restoration. The tripartite division of theology is cited by such leading representatives of the Enlightenment as H. Grotius (1583–1645), E. Lord Herbert of Cherbury (1581–1648), P. Bayle (1647–1706), G. Vico (1668–1744) and M. Diderot (1713–1784). Just as they criticize positive religion and seek to replace it with a natural religion, so too do they criticize political theology. Rousseau introduces "civil religion" as a replacement for the confessional political theologies. It should become the basis of the social contract and should encourage citizens to love their civil duties and sacrifice themselves for them. Since the religious wars were seen as the consequences of confessional political theologies, a natural civil religion would avoid such strife. Nevertheless the notion of civil religion faces a dilemma since the particularity demanded by a civil religion is undercut by the universality of natural religion. Social utility and universal truth are often in conflict.

The Catholic Restoration, represented by Catholic nobility in exile, not only elaborated, but also defended, a political theology. J. Donoso Cortes (1809–53), Louis G. A. de Bonald (1754–1840), Joseph de Maistre (1773–1821), Carl Ludwig von Haller (1768–1854), and the early Félicité Lamennais (1782–1854) constitute this restoration and can all be classed under the heading of seeking to reconstitute society on the basis of religion. They perceived the interrelation between political ideas and religious ideas and asserted that changes in religious and philosophical world views led to changes in political patterns. Therefore, they saw the French Revolution as a result of the Enlightenment and criticized both. Against the Enlightenment they argued that no natural religion exists, but only positive religion. Only a positive religion, not a civil religion, could demonstrate its utility for the state. They developed an apologetic for the social necessity of positive religion, gave primacy to the social over the individual, and suggested political utility and common consent as social criteria of theological affirmations. Their political theology underscored the sinfulness of human nature, the need for strong authority, and the Lordship of God and Christ.

Current Usage. In Germany the term political theology was used in the 1960s by Johannes B. Metz to characterize a distinct theological approach and endeavor. It expressed a theological response to the secularization and privatization of religion in industrialized, technocratic societies. Against the individualism and subjectivism of EXISTENTIAL THEOLOGY and philosophy, political theology argued that existentialism failed to come to grips with the privatizing tendencies of modern society. In fact, it only reinforced and justified them. Political theology was therefore proposed primarily as a public theology or political hermeneutics that sought to draw out the public significance and practical import of religious symbols. It especially sought to retrieve the meaning of eschatology as a source of critique and amelioration in the sociopolitical order (*see* THEOLOGY OF HOPE).

Since political theology underscores the public significance of faith, it turned toward analyzing the questions of hermeneutics and the theory-practice relation. It sought to distinguish itself from previous Constantinian political theologies and to elaborate a post-Enlightenment conception of theology's relation to political practice. These issues moved political theology in the direction of fundamental theology.

Systematic Clarification. The historical survey indicates that, despite diverse uses, political theology primarily refers to the implicit or explicit use of religious symbols to legitimate or to criticize political reality. The contemporary use of political theology as response to the Marxist critique is an important shift, for whereas previously political theology justified and legitimated political systems, now it was ordered to their critique.

Although the Enlightenment distinguished between a confessional political theology and a natural civil religion, political theology generally refers to the reflective theological attempt to justify or defend civil or political religions. In its most recent usage, political theology was appropriated precisely as an explicit theological criticism of civil or political religions, even though some would see the civil religion itself as exercising a critical function within a country. This meaning of political theology distinguishes it quite clearly from political ethics and liberation theology.

Distinction from Political Ethics. Political ethics focuses on deontic judgments of moral obligation or on aretaic judgments of moral value and rightness; political theology analyzes how religious symbols either legitimate or criticize a political and social order. To the extent, however, that any symbolic vision leads to concrete action, it needs to be complemented by ethical reflection. On this point the advocates of political theology disagree; some demand that a specifically theological ethic as an integral part of the religious vision link theory and practice; others claim that the pluralism of modern society demands a more universal rational ethic.

Distinction from Liberation Theology. Political theology, moreover, differs from liberation theology as the general from the specific. Liberation theology is a specific political theology insofar as it is usually linked with a specific group (Blacks, women, minority groups, underprivileged nations). These appeal to their specific experiences; they then analyze their religious tradition in relation to their experience, and, drawing on their tradition, they propose a concrete vision and praxis of liberation. Since liberation theology is theoretically and practically concerned with the interrelation between religious symbols and political praxis, it is a political theology, but its methodic basis is formed by a specific experience as a starting-point and is ordered to particular political and social goals.

A Foundational Theology. In addition to its primary meaning, political theology has come to be understood as a FOUNDATIONAL THEOLOGY. As such its primary concern is not the practical application of religious symbols, but the analytical and reconstructive task of studying the pragmatics of religious symbols. It investigates their origin, development, and use in relation to the sociopolitical order. Political theology so understood seeks to come to terms with the sociology of religion and the sociology of knowledge insofar as these affect the foundations of faith and the basis of theology. It thereby extends the historical-critical method into a socio-critical method. Whereas the historical-critical method studies the historical context of diverse texts, political theology analyzes the social conditions and political effects of religious beliefs. Political theology would therefore come to grips with a Weberian analysis of the correlation between social status and religious beliefs, with a Durkheimian analysis of the correlation between religious and political patterns of organization, and with the Marxist analysis of the possible ideological function of religion. This foundational task would make systematic theology and theological ethics more explicitly self-reflective of their basis. Its method would not be simply hermeneutical or transcendental, but rather reconstructive, since it would take into account the history of the intertwinement of the religious and the socio-political.

Bibliography: G. BAUM, *Religion and Alientation* (New York 1975). W. R. COATES, *God in Public. Political Theology beyond Niebuhr* (Grand Rapids, Mich. 1974). H. FELD, et al., *Dogma und Politik* (Mainz 1973). A. FIERRO, *The Militant Gospel: An Analysis of Contemporary Political Theologies* (New York 1978). F. FIORENZA, ''Political Theology': An Historical Analysis,'' *Theology Digest* 25 (1977) 317–334; ''Political Theology as Foundational Theology,'' *Catholic Theological Society of America. Proceedings* 32 (1977) 142–177. R. D. JOHNS, *Man in the World. The Theology of Johannes Baptist Metz* (Missoula, Mont. 1976). A. KEE, ed., *A Reader in Political Theology* (Philadelphia 1974). J. B. METZ, *Theology of the World* tr. W. GLEN-DOEPEL (New York 1969); *Glaube in Geschichte und Gesellschaft* (Mainz 1977). H. PEUKERT, ed., *Diskussion zur 'politischen Theologie'* (Mainz 1969). C. SCHMITT, *Politische Theologie* (Berlin 1922). *Politische Theologie, II* (Berlin 1970). D. SÖLLE, *Political Theology* (Stuttgart 1976) excellent bibliog. S. WOLIN, *Politics and Vision* (Boston 1960). M. XHAUFFLAIRE, *La Théólogie politique* (Paris 1972). See also bibliog. for Liberation Theology.

[F. SCHÜSSLER FIORENZA]

POLLEN, JOHN HUNGERFORD

Historian and journalist; b. London, England, Sept. 22, 1858; d. Roehampton, April 8, 1925. He was the third of ten children born to John H. Pollen, professor of fine arts at the Catholic University in Dublin during Newman's brief rectorship, and Maria Margaret Laprimaudeye, daughter of the future Cardinal MANNING's curate at Lavington. After schooling in Münster, Westphalia, and later at the Oratory, Birmingham, Pollen entered the Society of Jesus in 1877. A year spent, between his philosophical and theological studies, in assisting Father John Morris, then vice-postulator of the cause of the English martyrs, determined the direction his own work was to take; after ordination (1891) he was appointed to the Jesuit House of Writers at Farm Street, London, where he led a life of single-minded devotion to the tasks of research, writing, and lecturing, mainly on the English martyrs and related matters. (*See* ENGLAND, SCOTLAND, AND WALES, MARTYRS OF.) He became vice-postulator of the cause, in succession to Father Morris, whose ''Life'' he wrote. He also edited and contributed to sundry volumes published by the Catholic Record Society, and contributed to the ''Lives of the English Martyrs,'' collaborating with Dom Bede Camm, OSB, in the first series, and with Canon E. H. Burton in the second.

For almost 40 years, although not formally attached to the staff of the Jesuit review, the *MONTH*, he regularly contributed articles that evidenced a first-class historical mind. These soon led to an invitation to speak before the Scottish Historical Society, which resulted in the publication of the documents contained in *Papal Negotiations with Mary, Queen of Scots* (1901) edited by Pollen with a long introductory study. He returned to the theme intermittently in the pages of the *Month* until 1922, when he published *Queen Mary and the Babington Plot.*

Pollen's most considerable work was *The English Catholics in the Reign of Queen Elizabeth: A Study of Their Politics, Civil Life, and Government, 1558–1580* (1920). It gave final shape to the conclusions he had reached in piecemeal studies published in the *Month* over the years, and was generally accepted as at once scholarly and authoritative. It has stood the test of time, as reference to such a work as Philip Hughes's *The Reformation in England* (5th ed. 1963) clearly indicates.

Bibliography: *Month* 145 (1925) 446–448.

[R. MOFFAT]

POLLIEN, FRANÇOIS DE SALES

Carthusian spiritual writer; b. Chèvenoz (Haute-Savoie), France, Aug. 1, 1853; d. Calabria, Italy, Feb. 12, 1936. He was ordained at Annecy in 1877, became a novice at La Grande Chartreuse in 1884, and took his vows the following year. He was coadjutor (i.e., guest master and spiritual adviser) in several charterhouses, became prior at Mougères in 1901, and at Pleterjé (now in Slovenia) in 1911. In 1914 he retired to St. Bruno's in Calabria.

Dom Pollien was accustomed to write as he meditated upon what he had been reading. The Scriptures and SS. Augustine, Thomas Aquinas, and Francis de Sales provided his favorite reading material, but he had the capacity to find inspiration for devout meditation even in juridical documents. His written meditations were sometimes given or lent to those who came to him for counsel, and in this way they began to circulate through Europe, often in more or less inaccurate copies. Several of his works were published, in some cases without his knowledge. He edited none of these writings himself. His *La Vie intérieure simplifyée* [he preferred *unifiée*] *et ramenée à son fondement,* edited by Joseph Tissot in 1894, became a spiritual classic that contributed greatly to the renewal of ascetical and mystical doctrine in the first quarter of the 20th century.

His voluminous *La Plante de Dieu* (cf. Is 61.3) is a sequel to *La Vie intérieure.* Whereas *La Vie* treats mainly the rational "creational" foundations of that life, *La Plante* is a powerful synthesis of the entire Christian life as far as mystical union, dealing with Christocentric aspects.

Bibliography: For a list of Pollien's works *see* F. DE SALES POLLIEN, *La pianta di Dio* (Florence 1949). P. BROUTIN, "Les 'Élévations monastiques' de Dom Pollien," *Revue d'ascétique et de mystique* 34 (1963) 196–221, with extensive extracts. D. MONDRONE, "Un solitario della vita e della penna, Don Francesco Pollien," *La civiltà cattolica* 104.4 (1953) 681–693, a critical study.

[B. DU MOUSTIER]

POLLO, SECONDO, BL.

Military chaplain, diocesan priest of Vercelli, martyr; b. January 2, 1908, Caresanablot (near Vercelli), Lombardy, Italy; d. December 26, 1941, on the plain of Dragali (near Montenegro), Yugoslavia.

Secondo Pollo completed the minor seminary at Montecrivello, then studied philosophy and theology at the Pontifical Lombard Seminary in Rome. Following his ordination he taught at his alma mater in Montecrivello, while ministering in various parishes, including Cigliano, Borgo d'Ale, Saluggia, Livorno Ferraris, and others. He was particularly gifted as a catechist, preacher, and spiritual director. Later he taught philosophy and theology at the archdiocesan major seminary, served as chaplain of the Italian Youth of Catholic Action (September 1936), and ministered to prisoners. Pollo enjoyed parochial ministry and administered a parish in Larizzate (1940–41) until he was drafted as a military chaplain.

He was assigned to the Val Chisone battalion of the Alpine regiment, which was sent to Montenegro. He died on the battlefront between Italian and Yugoslav forces as he comforted a wounded soldier. The mortal remains of this priest, who was declared venerable December 18, 1997, were translated to Vercelli's cathedral in 1968. Pope John Paul II beatified him, May 23, 1998, during a pastoral visit to northern Italy.

Bibliography: *L'Osservatore Romano,* English edition (26 May 1998): 2.

[K. I. RABENSTEIN]

POLTERGEIST

A term that signifies some type of force to which is attributed a set of spontaneous, puzzling, and troublesome occurrences. The term is derived from the German *Polter,* meaning noise, and *Geist,* meaning spirit. Paranormal occurrences reported in poltergeist cases are classified by parapsychologists as physical psi-phenomena. These take the form of noises, self-propelled stones, the popping of bottle caps, and the like. Apparently these occurrences are never dangerous to persons, but they are perturbing and frightening.

Poltergeist Phenomena. Series of poltergeist phenomena begin and end spontaneously. Such occurrences differ from the physical phenomena reported in séances. Raps, sounds, and "voices" that are part of a séance have a purpose: usually to confirm the power of the medium. Poltergeist phenomena occur for no obvious purpose and on no special occasion; they are completely unpredictable. For this reason, scientists have difficulty finding reliable methods of investigation. Frequently all that the trained specialist can do is report the occurrences and judge whether or not there is evidence of deception.

Poltergeist activities differ from cases of diabolic possession. In most reports of possession, a human person is possessed or obsessed. A poltergeist "force" remains aloof and operates through no human medium or instrument. Such phenomena differ also from reported cases of ''haunted houses.'' Poltergeist incidents are of relatively short duration and are of a mischievous nature; ''hauntings'' are reputed to be more permanent and threatening. Though the name suggests specters and goblins, poltergeist has become a technical term with no religious or occult connotations.

There have been reports of poltergeist phenomena throughout man's history and from every part of the world. Before man began to investigate such occurrences closely, there was a readiness to believe in the reality of occult phenomena and to attribute them to some ephemeral being. It is difficult to sift the legendary from the real; thus, most reports in history have to be discounted. Nonetheless, there are accounts of poltergeist phenomena that seem above suspicion of deception. Scientific proof does not rest on these alone.

Systematic Study. In England the Society for Psychical Research was founded in 1882 with the express purpose of studying all paranormal phenomena scientifically. Sir William Barrett and other cautious scientists have admitted that deception was not present in all of the many poltergeist cases investigated. Since its foundation the society has tried to study every report of poltergeist occurrence; reports of these investigations can be read in its *Proceedings.*

Meanwhile Charles Richet devoted himself to the study of poltergeists and other paranormal phenomena in France. His work attracted others: in 1919 the International Metapsychical Institute and in 1941 the French Association for Parapsychological Studies were formed. Both proposed to study psi-phenomena scientifically, although they did not bar practitioners of the occult from membership. In Belgium a similar committee was begun to research paranormal phenomena systematically; mediums and spiritists were there excluded.

In the U.S. the Society for Psychical Research was founded in 1884. Eminent scholars, such as Henry Sidgwick (1838–1900), William JAMES, and Josiah ROYCE, have been members. More than 500 poltergeist phenomena have been carefully investigated. None has been so thoroughly covered as the poltergeist reported at Seaford, N.Y., in 1958. J. G. Pratt, of Duke University, studied this occurrence while it was still active. While fraud was definitely ruled out, this one case did not provide sufficient material on which to base answers to all questions concerning poltergeists.

Explanation. The general conviction of those who have studied poltergeist phenomena is that there is definitely something in operation that cannot be explained by normal physical causes.

Examining the evidence compiled, one can detect some elements of uniformity. There seems to be one person, an ''agent,'' whose presence coincides with the occurrences. While this person is not the observed performer of poltergeist phenomena, his presence is apparently necessary. Also, such phenomena take place in homes in which there are children. The principal agent considered necessary is most often an adolescent; only rarely is he an adult.

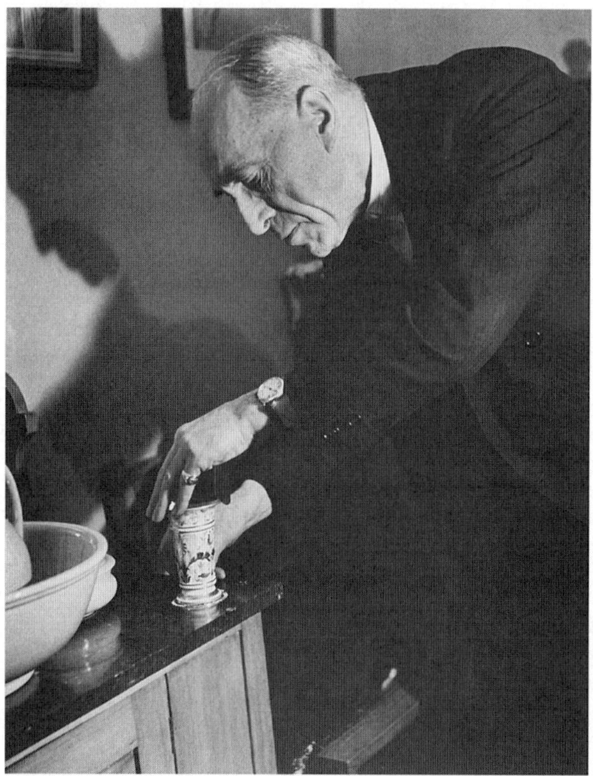

A man draws chalk rings around vases to see whether they will move during an investigation of paranormal activity inside the house. (© Hulton-Deutsch Collection/CORBIS)

Fraud has been discovered in some cases. Even young people can learn to perform magical tricks, and this could explain some of the reported phenomena. However, certain phenomena cannot be explained as sleight-of-hand. The presence of deception in some cases is not, in itself, reason to suppose that fraud is present in every case. Usually there is no evident motive for fraud. Nothing can be gained by the performance of complicated and difficult pranks, unless it is momentary notoriety. This seems an insufficient motive for all cases. Fraudulent cases would be stopped only by the decision of the deceiver. Yet in some cases the occurrences dramatically ceased after the recital of a religious prayer.

In those cases in which fraud cannot be proved, there is little on which to base a theory or explanation. The popular belief is that these occurrences, since they exhibit a certain intelligence, are the work of a ''playful ghost.''

There is no scientific foundation for such an explanation. A more technical hypothesis is proposed: poltergeist phenomena are merely psychokinetic phenomena set in motion by the subconscious mind of some uninhibited person in the household, e.g., the adolescent agent.

The reaction of the Catholic Church to poltergeists is one of caution. In her Ritual and manuals of theology, she advises her subjects to be very slow to attribute such phenomena to angelic or diabolic spirits. When it is clear that the occurrences are of a nonreligious nature, the Church does not interfere—particularly when the phenomena are under scientific investigation. It is only when some theory takes on religious implications that she speaks out. Indeed, she welcomes explanations providing natural or normal causes for occurrences once erroneously believed to be the work of God or the devil.

Bibliography: J. G. PRATT, *Parapsychology: An Insider's View of ESP* (New York 1964). R. OMEZ, *Psychical Phenomena,* tr. R. HAYNES (New York 1958). H. THURSTON, *Ghosts and Poltergeists,* ed. J. H. CREHAN (Chicago 1954).

[C. P. SVOBODA]

POLTON, THOMAS

Curialist, bishop; b. Mildenhall, Wiltshire, England, *c.* 1370; d. Basel, Aug. 23, 1433. A bachelor in laws of Oxford, he became commissary general in the Diocese of BATH AND WELLS. From 1394 he was a regular member of the Roman Curia, becoming an ABBREVIATOR of papal letters by 1401 and prothonotary apostolic by 1414. He was provided to the archdeaconry of Taunton in 1395 and later received other English benefices, some by PROVISION; in 1420 he held the deanery of York, a rectory, and three prebends. Royal pardons for accepting provisions indicate that Polton was useful as an agent for English interests. He returned to England as a papal envoy in 1413 and the next year was appointed King Henry V's proctor at the Curia. Polton was a prominent member of the English delegation at the Council of CONSTANCE. Afterward he resumed his curial duties under Pope MARTIN V, who provided him to the See of HEREFORD in 1420. Although the king recommended that he be promoted to the Diocese of London in 1421, John KEMP was chosen and Polton succeeded Kemp at Chichester. He was appointed a delegate for the English kingdom of France to the Council of Siena. He retired to England shortly before his translation to WORCESTER in 1426 (cf. *Cal. Patent Rolls* 1422–9, 283, and *Rotuli Parliamentorum* 3:296). He died while attending the Council of BASEL.

Bibliography: *The Register of Henry Chichele: Archbishop of Canterbury, 1414–1443,* ed. E. F. JACOB and H. C. JOHNSON, 4 v. (Oxford 1937–47) 2:485–495, 671. A. B. EMDEN, *A Biographical Register of the University of Oxford to A.D. 1500,* 3 v. (Oxford 1957–59) 3:1494–95.

[R. L. STOREY]

POLTZMACHER, JOHANN

Canonist. He first appears in 1436 as a *doctor juris regens* in Vienna, where he was dean of the faculty of law intermittently for six terms between 1436 and 1447. He fulfilled various political and diplomatic roles, such as legate to the Diet of Presburg and agent of Albert II. He produced one of the few canonical commentaries to emanate from the University of Vienna, *Lectura magistri Johannis Poltzmacher, ordinarii juris canonici in generali studio Viennisi, Pataviensis, pro annis 1439 et 1442 secundum Cardinalem et Panormitanum.* This work was based on the works of Zabarella and Panormitanus.

Bibliography: F. RUBOD, *Dictionnaire de droit canonique* 7:17.

[B. R. PISKULA]

POLYCARP, ST.

Bishop of Smyrna, 2d-century martyr. Polycarp, a disciple of St. John, probably the Apostle, was visited by IGNATIUS OF ANTIOCH in the course of Ignatius's journey to Rome for martyrdom (*c.* 116); and Ignatius wrote a letter to Polycarp from Troas, as well as a letter to the community at Smyrna. Some 40 years later Polycarp journeyed to Rome as representative of the churches in Asia Minor and dealt with Pope ANICETUS (155–166) on the QUARTODECIMAN question and the date for the celebration of Easter. During his stay in Rome he met many Valentinian heretics and came face to face with MARCION and his followers.

At the age of 86, on a ''great Sabbath,'' Polycarp was put to death in the Stadium at Smyrna, possibly on Feb. 22 or 23, 155 (*Mart. Poly.* 21), under the Proconsul Statius Quadratus. As EUSEBIUS OF CAESAREA (*Hist. Eccl.* 4.15.1) records his death in the reign of Marcus Aurelius (161–180), it is possible that the date should be between 161 and 169.

Information concerning Polycarp's life, though scanty in detail, is authentic. The acts of his martyrdom (*Martyrium Polycarpi*) are the earliest-preserved, fully reliable account of a Christian martyr's death; and Irenaeus (*Adv. Haert.* 3.3.4) and Eusebius (*Hist. Eccl.* 4.14.3–8; 5.20.4–8; 24.16–17) concur in the main facts. The *Vita* by Pionius (*c.* 400), however, is a legendary account of his life.

Polycarp's *Letter to the Philippians* is preserved in Greek (ch. 1–9.2) and wholly in an early, poor Latin translation. Eusebius recorded also ch. 9 and 13 (*Hist. Eccl.* 3.36.13–15), The letter was written in response to a request from the community at Philippi, who had also asked Polycarp to furnish them with a collection of the letters of Ignatius. It appears that in the MSS of the letter, ch. 13 is an interpolation that served originally as the covering note to the Ignatian letters (Harrison); while ch. 1–12 (and possibly 14) are a pastoral epistle that Irenaeus described as ''a vigorous letter . . . in which those seeking salvation can apprehend the nature of the faith and the teaching of the truth'' (*Adv. Haer.* 3.3.4).

Polycarp based his moral exhortation on the imitation of Christ in his patience (8.2; 9.1). He inculcated Christian virtue following the Gospels and St. Paul (2–3), citing liberally from these NT writings, and included all members of the community in his admonitions; bishop, priests, deacons, married couples, virgins, widows, young men, and orphans (4–6). Almsgiving was an essential practice (10.2), and the Christian was to pray for kings, powers, and rulers, for his enemies and persecutors (12.3–13).

Feast: Feb. 23

Bibliography: P. T. CAMELOT, ed. and tr., *Sources Chrétiennes* 10 (3d ed. 1958) 183–275. J. A. KLEIST, *Ancient Christian Writers* 6 (1948) 67–102, 184–204. P. N. HARRISON, *Polycarp's Two Epistles to the Philippians* (New York 1936). J. QUASTEN, *Patrology,* 4 v. (Westminster, Md. 1950–86) 1:76–82. P. MEINHOLD, *Paulys Realenzyklopädie der klassischen Altertumswissenschaft,* ed. G. WISSOWA et al. 21.2 (1952) 1662–93. H. I. MARROU, *Analecta Bollandiana* 71 (1953) 5–20. H. VON CAMPENHAUSEN, *Bearbeitungen . . . des Polykarpmartyriums* (*Sitzungsberichte der Akademie der Wissenschaften zu Heidelberg* 3; 1957). H. GRÉGOIRE et al., *Académie royale de Belgique: Bulletin de la classe des lettres,* 5th ser. 47 (1961) 72–83. L. W. BARNARD, *Church Quarterly Review* 163 (1962) 421–430. J. A. FISCHER, *Lexikon für Theologie und Kirche,* ed. J. HOFER and K. RAHNER, 10 v. (2d, new ed. Freiburg 1957–65) 8:597–598. F. W. WEIDMANN, *Polycarp & John: The Harris Fragments and Their Challenge to the Literary Traditions* (Notre Dame, Ind. 1999).

[F. X. MURPHY]

POLYCARPUS

A Canon Law collection, preserved in 14 manuscripts in two forms. The first (13 MSS) was written between approximately 1104 and 1106 by Cardinal Gregory, who lived during the pontificate of Pope Paschal II (1100–18). It is divided into eight books, subdivided into topics that are in turn subdivided into chapters; every topic has a summary preceding it and every chapter a title. The collection contains regulations on all areas of ecclesiastical life and was intended to serve the aims of the GREGORIAN REFORM. Its chief source is the collection of ANSELM OF LUCCA; other sources are numerous conciliar canons and papal decrees, passages from the letters of Gregory the Great, texts from the Fathers of the Church, etc. The collection, although not widely disseminated, exercised an influence on some later collections. The author of the second form (1 MS) is unknown, but he seems to have been close to the Roman Curia and to have been active about 1120. The number of books is the same as in the first form, but the number of topics has been increased. The new chapters are regularly taken from the same sources as the first form. The second form was less widely disseminated than the first.

Bibliography: H. HÜFFER, *Beiträge zur Geschichte der Quellen des Kirchenrechts und des Römischen Rechts im Mittelalter* (Münster 1862) 74–109. P. FOURNIER, ''Une Collection canonique italienne du commencement du XIIe siècle,'' *Annales de l'Université de Grenoble* 6 (1894) 400–409; ''Les Deux recensions de la collection canonique romaine dite le *Polycarpus*,'' *Mélanges d'archéologie et d'histoire de l'École Française de Rome* 37 (1918–19) 55–101. P. FOURNIER and G. LEBRAS, *Histoire des collections canoniques en occident depuis les fausses décrétales jusqu'au Décret de Gratien* (Paris 1931–32) 2:169–185. R. NAZ, *Dictionnaire de droit canonique*, ed. R. NAZ (Paris 1935–65) 7:18–20.

[G. MAY]

POLYGLOT BIBLES

Bibles containing the text in several languages, usually in parallel columns, for the purpose of comparison. The term ''polygot'' is taken from the Greek words, πολύ (many, several) and γλῶσσα (tongue, language). The derivative from better-known Latin words would be ''multilingual.'' Similarly formed words are ''triglot,'' ''hexaglot,'' ''heptaglot,'' used to designate Bibles in three, six, or seven languages, respectively.

Nature. Strictly speaking, the term polyglot is applied only to a Bible (1) that contains the whole biblical text of the Old and New Testament, according to the author's accepted canon; (2) that at least in its greater part is printed synoptically, i.e., in parallel columns, so that the reader has under his eyes the simultaneous reproduction of the same passage in all the different languages without turning a page—facing pages often being used for this purpose; (3) that contains the original language of each book and its oldest versions. Only a few polyglots fulfill these conditions adequately.

In a wider sense, the term is used when the original text and its ancient versions are reproduced only in part, or when modern translations are used, but hardly when the versions are not printed synoptically.

Purpose. The aim of a polyglot is to facilitate an immediate comparison between the different renderings for the purpose of establishing the genuine text and its interpretation. For various reasons, the era of such Bibles seems to be past, not because they have ceased to be very useful, but because the expenses and the herculean labor they demand are preferably spent on other kinds of equally useful and deeper scientific work, more readily condensed into smaller volumes.

Great Polyglots. The following points must be understood: (1) There is a considerable variety in the presentation of the various texts when dealing with the OT or the NT, or when dealing with the protocanonical or deuterocanonical books or passages. (2) Each polyglot uses its own manuscript sources, by which the individual text must be evaluated. Extensive studies have been published on this subject (*Dictionnaire de la Bible* 5:513–529). But sometimes the author of a later polyglot merely reproduces the text of an earlier one. (3) Of the major polyglots, only the fourth (Walton) was not published under Catholic auspices; the others were published with the approbation of the ecclesiastical authorities, which, in one case, was only reluctantly granted. (4) No single person is exclusively responsible for any of the major editions. Both the material and the scientific endeavors were shared and distributed among a number of men. Only the names of the most important are listed in the table. The patrons financed and favored and sometimes even initiated the enterprise.

The *Complutensis* was important for the fact that it was the first Catholic printing of the Hebrew, the Septuagint, and the NT Greek text. The *Antwerpiensis* was an improvement because of the larger number of languages and the magnificence of its printing. The *Parisiensis* was ill-fated from the beginning; it had no chance to compete with the *Londinensis,* which was and remains, as a whole, the best.

The most recent so-called polyglot is the *Biblia Polyglotta Matritensia,* published in Madrid by the Consejo Superior de Investigaciones Científicas and the Biblioteca de Autores Cristianos. In 1957 the *Prooemium* and the *Psalterium Visigothicum-Mozarabicum* were published. The *Psalterium S. Hieronymi ex hebraica veritate* appeared in 1962. The *Targum Palaestinense in Pentateuchum* has been announced. All these volumes are critical editions. The whole ambitious plan covers the entire field of the major polyglots, and so far it has been carried out in a very competent way by the foremost Spanish biblical scholars. However, it should not, strictly speaking, be called a polyglot, since each text is edited in a separate volume.

Bibliography: E. MANGENOT, *Dictionnaire de la Bible*, ed. F. VIROUROUX, 5 v. (Paris 1895–1912) 5:513–529. F. J. DELITZSCH, *Studien zur Entstehungsgeschichte der Polyglottenbibel des Kard. Ximenes,* 3 v. (Leipzig 1871, 1878, 1886). B. HALL, "Biblical Scholarship: Editions and Commentaries," *The Cambridge History of the Bible,* ed. S. GREENSLADE (Cambridge, Eng. 1963) 50–63. M. REVILLA RICO, *La políglota de Alcalá* (Madrid 1917). D. RAMOS FRECHILLA, "La políglota de Arias Montano," *Revista Española de Estudios Biblicos* 3 (1928) 27–54.

[X. G. ARCE]

POMBAL, SEBASTIÃO JOSÉ DE CARVALHO E MELLO

Portuguese prime minister; b. Soure, near Coimbra, Portugal, May 13, 1699; d. Pombal, May 8, 1782. The Marquis of Pombal, the title granted in 1770 by which Carvalho is generally known, was the son of Manuel de Carvalho, a cavalry captain and landowner. Pombal served in the army and was later a lawyer. In 1733 he secured a position at the Academy of History. It was at this time that he eloped with Dona Theresa Noronha, niece of Count Arcos, in a marriage opposed by the exclusive Portuguese aristocracy. In 1739, aided by Marc António de Azevedo Coutinho, an important relative, Pombal was sent as minister to London, where he tried to adjust Anglo-Portuguese differences over India, as well as problems arising from Portuguese neutrality during the War of the Austrian Succession. In 1744 he returned to Lisbon, but within a year was sent by King John V to act as Portuguese minister at Vienna and as mediator in a dispute between the King's niece, Empress MARIA THERESA, and Pope BENEDICT XIV. At Vienna he received news of his wife's death. Pombal, a childless widower, married the poor but noble Countess Leonor Ernestina Daun. Two children were born of the second marriage. His mediation successfully concluded, Pombal was recalled to Lisbon (1749), where his diplomatic experience and skill were to be employed by King Joseph I (1750–77), the successor of John V. Pombal, at first minister of foreign affairs and war, and later prime minister, dominated the Portuguese political scene for the entire reign of Joseph I.

Jesuit Controversy. Pombal was called upon to settle a dispute arising from the Colonial Boundary Treaty of 1750, which had settled rival Spanish-Portuguese claims in South America. Under the treaty seven of 30 Jesuit REDUCTIONS (missions) of Paraguay, where the Jesuits had attempted to set up a federation of Christian communities, were placed under Portuguese control. It was an area where 200 priests ruled 140,000 natives. The treaty of 1750 had called for Jesuit and native evacuation and emigration. The resulting resistance led to a series of revolts that lasted for three years. Pombal blamed the Jesuits for this turmoil and opposition. In 1755 Pombal issued an edict freeing the natives, denying civil authority to Jesuits and all priests, and establishing the Gran Pará

Trading Company to carry out all commercial transactions under civilian rule.

That year (Nov. 1, 1755) Lisbon was practically destroyed by a great earthquake and tidal waves. For three days the city was in chaos. Pombal efficiently organized the relief and rebuilding of the stricken city and reestablished law and order with remarkable skill and courage. The destruction of the city made a tremendous impact on all of Europe. A noted Jesuit preacher, Gabriel MALAGRIDA blamed the catastrophe on Pombal and his policies and described the earthquake as God's retribution, a work of divine wrath. Pombal attributed it to scientific causes and a royal edict condemned Malagrida's denunciation. The nobles, however, backed Malagrida against the ambitious and powerful minister.

Jesuit Expulsion. The Jesuit refusal to accept the boundary changes, their opposition to Pombal's scheme to reorganize colonial administration and trade, and their opposition and ill feeling toward him at Lisbon increased tension and led him into his campaign against them. In 1757 Joseph I ordered all Jesuit confessors to leave the court. In February of 1758 a Portuguese protest was filed at the Vatican, enumerating many charges against the Jesuits. Benedict XIV was prevailed upon to appoint Cardinal Saldanha, Patriarch of Lisbon, as Visitor and Reformer of the Society of Jesus. The Jesuits were forbidden by the patriarch to preach or hear confessions (June 1758). Their Portuguese superior was banished from Lisbon and the society stripped of all power and privileges.

A few months later, an effort to assassinate Joseph I (Sept. 3, 1758) gave Pombal another pretext for expelling the Jesuits. The assassination plot was organized by José de Mascarenhas, eighth Duke of Aveiro, and his brother-in-law, Francisco de Assis, third Marquis of Távora, whose wife was a fervent disciple of Malagrida. It was not until December that the plot and assassination attempt were publicly denounced. A decree called for the arrest of the principal conspirators, including Malagrida and 12 prominent Jesuits who were also accused of aiding the plot. In January of 1759 Aveiro and the Távora family were tried and condemned. The Jesuits were imprisoned and many accused nobles were racked, strangled, burned, or beheaded. Pending an appeal to Pope CLEMENT XIII, all Jesuit property in Portugal was to be sequestered. By this time all Jesuits, by order of Saldanha, were confined to their colleges and forbidden to communicate with anyone outside their walls. Pombal's policy was inspired in part by his hatred of the Jesuits and by his "rationalist" policy of establishing royal supremacy and independence in all ecclesiastical matters within Portugal and its colonies.

On Aug. 18, 1759, Clement XIII issued *Exponi nobis,* a brief granting the Portuguese government the right to put the accused priest conspirators on trial, but the decree did not authorize future trials. A month later Pombal issued a decree of expulsion (Sept. 3, 1759). The Jesuits were accused of crimes against God and King. Those Jesuits not solemnly professed who asked for release were permitted to leave the society. All others were removed without possessions and transported to the Papal States. Nearly 1,100 destitute and half-starved Jesuits were brought to Civitavecchia. Jesuits in Portuguese colonies were brought to Lisbon, where after imprisonment and interrogation they were deported to Rome. Pombal never put any imprisoned Jesuits on trial save Malagrida. Most of them were left in solitary confinement, where they died. The King's scruples probably prevented him from executing them. The unfortunate Malagrida, accused of heresy, blasphemy, and false prophecy, was condemned by the Inquisition and was executed by strangulation, and his body was burned (Sept. 21, 1761). At the time of their expulsion the Jesuits conducted 20 colleges and three seminaries in Portugal, 20 colleges in the islands of West Africa, 13 in Goa, ten in Malabar, and five in China.

Marquis de Pombal.

Religious and Political Aftermath of the Expulsion. Pombal continued his attack on the Church, ordering the papal nuncio to leave Lisbon and breaking diplomatic relations with Rome. Portuguese bishops were also compelled to exercise powers independent of Rome. In 1761 the former Jesuit schools were secularized, and free schools, as well as a College of Nobles for the children of the aristocracy, were established in their place. An abortive attempt at reconciliation with the papacy in 1767 was followed by further antireligious legislation limiting the amount of money that could be willed for Masses for the dead. Many convents were suppressed and those remaining forbidden to accept novices under 25 years of age. Bishops were appointed without papal approval. Pombal also inspired the publication of *Chronological Deductions,* a three-volume attack on the nefarious influence of the Jesuits on Portuguese history. Chief author of this masterpiece of vindictive indictment was José Seabra de Silva, later Pombal's secretary of state.

Pombal's expulsion of the Jesuits demonstrated the weakness of the society, and the governments of France, Spain, and Naples were quick to follow the Portuguese example. All the powers clamored for the suppression of the society. At first CLEMENT XIV resisted, but by degrees he modified his opposition. From 1769 to 1770 Pombal and the Pope negotiated an agreement in which Pombal's power over the Church was acknowledged. His brother Paul was given a cardinal's hat, although he died before it arrived at Lisbon. Pombal in return promised to restrain his campaign against the Jesuits. In June 1770 a nuncio returned to Lisbon. By 1773, however, Clement XIV had weakened so much that he issued *Dominus ac redemptor,* suppressing the Society of Jesus.

In 1756 Pombal had become minister of internal affairs and first minister. In this capacity he attempted to introduce many agricultural and commercial reforms. In his efforts to strengthen the depressed and faltering Portuguese economy, he established and encouraged printing, manufacturing, wine monopolies, and trading companies, and introduced and expanded widespread coffee, sugar, rice, cocoa, and indigo cultivation in Brazil. He reorganized the Portuguese army, rebuilt fortifications, and established a censorship board that, although it licensed or suppressed all books written or imported into Portugal, nevertheless encouraged the distribution of the works of Voltaire, Rousseau, and the Encyclopedists.

His Fall from Power. Pombal exercised almost absolute power over Portugal despite his advanced age. His ruthless methods included torture, bribery, espionage, and terror. He accumulated millions through gifts, pensions, properties and investments. His purchase of confiscated estates and the advantageous marriages of his children to grandees increased his family fortune. His power, however, also depended on the King's cooperation. By 1777 Joseph I was dying, and after Feb. 1, 1777, no edicts appeared under Pombal's name. Queen Maria I succeeded her father on his death (Feb. 24, 1777). Pombal, who had always taken the legal precaution of having the King countersign his edicts, was allowed to resign, but the Queen forbade him to reside within 20 leagues of the court. Pombal lived to see much of his work undone. Prisoners, including 60 surviving Jesuits, were freed; offenses were pardoned. The Távora verdict of 1759 was declared null and void (1780). The clergy persecuted by Pombal were restored. The Gran Pará Company was abolished (1778) and the Treason Tribunal dissolved (1777). Pombal himself was sued by a number of his victims, and despite his poor health he was accused of fraud and murder and stood trial. It ended with Pombal pleading for the mercy of the court (1780). In 1781 he was labeled an infamous criminal, but he was permitted to spend his declining years at his estate. The bishop of Coimbra, whom he had persecuted and imprisoned, consoled him at his death.

Bibliography: M. CHEKE, *Dictator of Portugal: A Life of the Marquiz of Pombal, 1699–1782* (London 1938). A. WELD, *The Suppression of the Society of Jesus in the Portuguese Dominions* (London 1877). T. D. KENDRICK, *The Lisbon Earthquake* (London 1956). E. G. JACOB, J. HÖFER and K. RAHNER *Lexicon für Theologie und Kirche,* 10 v. 8:600–601.

[P. S. MCGARRY]

POMBEIRO, ABBEY OF

Former Benedictine monastery of St. Vincent in Lugo province, Spain; founded in 964 by the widow of Sancho Ordoñez, Queen Goto of Galicia, who gave the surrounding land to Abbot Asterigo and his brothers. In 997 Bermudo II confirmed and increased the donation, but in the late 11th century Alfonso VI subjected the abbey to CLUNY, thus depriving it of its abbatial title and some of its prestige. This loss was real despite the statement of Alfonso VII in a donation of 1139 that the monks served the Almighty, under the governance of Cluny. Pombeiro survived the stormy end of the Middle Ages in Spain without event and in 1527 was attached to the nearby abbey of San Esteban de Rivas del Sil and incorporated into the Benedictine Congregation of Valladolid. The monastery disappeared with the dispersal of the monks in the suppression of religious orders (1834) but its church now serves the parish of the small town that grew up around it.

Bibliography: A. DE YEPES, *Crónica general de la Orden de San Benito,* ed. J. PEREZ DE URBEL, 3 v. (Madrid 1959) 2:347–350.

[J. PEREZ DE URBEL]

POMERIUS

Julianus, African ascetical writer; b. Mauretania, North Africa; d. Gaul, after A.D. 498. Nothing is known of the education or ecclesiastical career of Pomerius, who migrated to Gaul, opened a school of rhetoric in Arles, and was ordained to the priesthood. One of his pupils was CAESARIUS OF ARLES. Pomerius attained considerable fame in his lifetime, as is attested by letters addressed to him by several bishops. His treatise *De vita contemplativa* was famous in the Middle Ages, and owed its preservation to its ascription in most manuscripts to PROSPER OF AQUITAINE, perhaps because of its praise of St. AUGUSTINE. The Jesuit Jacques SIRMOND in the 17th century was the first to cast doubt on the ascription to Prosper; today no one seriously contests that Pomerius is the author of the work.

The *De vita contemplativa* describes the combined ideals of the contemplative and active life. The first two books are addressed to bishops and concern the manners and asceticism of priests, as a pastoral manual for clerics, and the third book is addressed to all Christians. Pomerius intended to set forth in the first book the contemplative life; in the second, the active life; and in the third, the vices and virtues of Christians. His distinction between the active and the contemplative life is founded on states of soul: that of the soul seeking perfection (the active life) and that of the soul possessing and enjoying it (the contemplative life). This conception is less exteriorized than the modern notion and seemingly more profound. The style is generally clear and smooth, more elegant than vigorous. Pomerius's knowledge of secular literature appears in his quotations from Terence, Cicero, and Vergil and in echoes from other authors.

From the middle of the 8th to the late 9th century the authority of the *De vita contemplativa* all but rivaled that of the leading Latin Fathers. BONIFACE quoted from it in 747, and several decades later it was mentioned by CHRODEGANG, Bishop of Metz. Copious quotations from it appear in the Church councils of the 9th century. Almost a 100 manuscripts of the work exist in codices of widely diverse provenence that date from the 8th to the 15th centuries.

Pomerius wrote three other works. Two of them, *De virginibus instituendis* and *De contemptu mundi,* have completely disappeared; but his eight books in dialogue form, *De anima et qualitate eius,* are known from summedes in Pseudo-Gennadius (*Vir. ill.* 99) and Isidore of Seville (*Vir. ill.* 25).

Bibliography: *Patrologia Latina,* ed. J. P. MIGNE, 217 v., indexes 4 v. (Paris 1878–90) 59:411–520. Trs. by J. G. PFISTER (Würzburg 1826), Ger., ascribed still to Prosper; J. B. BOUILLON (Paris 1576), Fr.; M. J. SUELZER, *Ancient Christion Writers* 4 (1947), Eng. O. BARDENHEWER, *Geschichte der altkirchlichen Literatur* (Frieburg 1913–32) 4:599–601. G. FRITZ, in *Dictionnaire de théologie catholique,* ed. A. VACANT et al., 15 v. (Paris 1903–50; Tables générales 1951–) 12.2:2537–43. F. DEGENHART, *Studien zu Julianus Pomerius* (Eichstätt 1905). A. C. PRENDERGAST, *The Latinity of the "De vita contemplativa" der altkirchlichen Literatur* (Catholic University of America, *Patristic Studies* 55; 1938). M. L. W. LAISTNER, *Miscellanea Giovanni Mercati,* 6 v. (Rome 1946); *Studi e Testi* 121–126] 2:344–358, influence. J. C. PLUMPE, *Vigiliae christianae* 1 (1947) 227–239.

[M. J. SUELZER]

POMMEREL, CELESTINE, MOTHER

Religious superior; b. Feillens, Burgundy, France, April 7, 1813; d. Carondelet, Mo., June 17, 1857. As the daughter of André and Louise (Pommiers) Pommerel, she was baptized Marie. Although educated by the Sisters of St. Charles in Mâcon, France, she entered the novitiate of another community, the Sisters of St. Joseph, in Lyons, France. As Sister Celestine she received the habit on May 18, 1831, and made her vows on Oct. 15, 1833. She then taught in the Diocese of Chamberry until the superior general, Mother St. John Fontbonne, selected her for the missions in St. Louis, Mo. Following a year's preparation in working with the deaf, Sister Celestine arrived in St. Louis on Sept. 4, 1837. After teaching for two years at Carondelet, near St. Louis, she became the first superior general of the Sisters of St. Joseph in the United States. By 1840 she had founded the novitiate of the Sisters of St. Joseph of Carondelet, opened the first U.S. school for the deaf, established seven elementary schools (one for black children), and formed an Native American mission. She also built three hospitals and established novitiates in Wheeling, W.Va.; Philadelphia, Pa.; Toronto, Canada; St. Paul, Minn.; and Buffalo, N.Y. At her death she left 149 sisters to continue her work.

Bibliography: M. L. SAVAGE, *The Congregation of St. Joseph of Carondelet* (2d ed. St. Louis 1927).

[ST. C. COYNE]

POMPALLIER, JEAN BAPTISTE FRANÇOIS

Missionary bishop in OCEANIA; b. Lyons, France, Dec. 11, 1801; d. Puteaux, near Paris, Dec. 21, 1871. Pompallier, who came from a family of silk manufacturers, was ordained in 1829. In 1836 he was appointed vicar apostolic of the newly created Vicariate Apostolic of Western Oceania, and he sailed from The Havre with the first group of MARIST FATHERS to evangelize the Pacific islands. On the way to NEW ZEALAND, his eventual destination, Bishop Pompallier left Pierre BATAILLON with one brother on Wallis Island and St. Peter CHANEL with another brother on nearby Futuna Island. Pompallier, accompanied by one priest and one brother, landed in New Zealand on Jan. 10, 1838.

Despite prolonged Protestant hostility, the vicar apostolic's success was remarkable. Two mission stations existed by January 1840, when British rule was established. In 1841 Pompallier reported about 1,000 Maoris baptized and another 45,000 under instruction. By 1844 there were 12 stations, 16 priests, 11 lay missionaries, 2,166 baptized Maoris, and about 1,400 European Catholics. The vicariate was divided in 1842 when the Vicariate Apostolic of Central Oceania was created, with Bataillon as its first vicar apostolic.

Pompallier visited Rome in 1846. His differences with Marist superiors induced the Holy See in 1848 to divide New Zealand into two dioceses. The Marists were transferred to Port Nicholson (later Wellington) in the south, with Philip Viard, SM, as bishop. Pompallier returned in 1850 with ten secular clerics to head the Diocese of Auckland. Retaining priests was a constant problem; despite fresh recruits, he had only ten in 1859. He returned from Europe in 1860, however, with 20 more. Maori wars during the 1860s and economic depression (1866–67) crippled missionary endeavors. When further support from Europe failed to materialize, Pompallier returned to France and resigned his see (1869). He had an impressive bearing, a winning personality, and a talent for attracting native peoples by his cordiality and respectful manner, but his forte was extension, not consolidation. He was one of the century's leading missionaries.

Bibliography: L. KEYS, *The Life and Times of Bishop Pompallier* (Christchurch, N.Z. 1957), with list of Pompallier's pub. works. *Fishers of Men,* ed. P. T. B. MCKEEFRY (Auckland 1938). J. J. WILSON, *The Church in New Zealand,* v. 1 (Dunedin 1910). J. S. C. DUMONT D'URVILLE, *The Voyage of the Astrolabe, 1840,* ed. O. WRIGHT (Wellington 1955). H. M. WRIGHT, *New Zealand, 1769–1840* (Cambridge, Mass. 1959).

[M. W. MULCAHY]

POMPONAZZI, PIETRO

Italian philosopher; b. Mantua, Sept. 16, 1462; d. Bologna, May 18, 1525. Pomponazzi, the son of a wealthy and noble family, studied at the University of Padua under the eminent Aristotelian, Nicolettus Vernias, and received a degree in medicine there in 1487. The next year he began teaching at the same university and continued to do so (except for a three-year interruption) until the university was closed in 1509. He then taught at Ferrara for one year and in 1511 went to the University of Bologna, where he taught until his death.

During his stay at Bologna, Pomponazzi published several philosophical works, the most important being *On the Immortality of the Soul* (Bologna 1516), which defended the position that the immortality of the soul cannot be demonstrated by reason but must be accepted on faith alone. This writing, though severely attacked, was never actually condemned by the Church. Soon afterward, Pomponazzi wrote two separate defenses: the *Apologia* (Bologna 1518), written against Gasparo CONTARINI, and the *Defensorium* (Bologna 1519), directed against Agostino NIFO. In 1520 he completed two other important works: *De fato, libero arbitrio, praedestinatione et providentia Dei* (Basel 1567) and *De incantationibus* (Basel 1556). At his death he left a number of unpublished works, the majority of which still remain in manuscript.

Pomponazzi has attracted attention in the 20th century for modern elements in his thought that anticipated attitudes common to 17th-century scientists. His *On the Immortality of the Soul* shows a favorable attitude toward reason and a reliance on sense experience that were uncommon in his day. The conclusions to which he came, combined with his professed orthodoxy and willingness to submit to the authority of the Church, led him to adopt what has been called the theory of DOUBLE TRUTH. Thus he held the immortality of the soul on the authority of the Church's teaching, but denied that this immortality could be demonstrated by reason unaided by faith.

See Also: ARISTOTELIANISM; RENAISSANCE PHILOSOPHY.

Bibliography: Works. *Tractatus acutissimi . . .* (Venice 1525); *Opera . . .*, ed. G. GRATAROLUS (Basel 1567); *Tractatus de immortalitate animae,* ed. G. MORRA (Bologna 1954), best bibliog. to 1954; *Libri quinque de fato . . .*, ed. R. LEMAY (Lugano 1957); "On the Immortality of the Soul," *The Renaissance Philosophy of Man,* ed. E. CASSIRER et al. (Chicago 1948) 280–381. P. O. KRISTELLER, "Two Unpublished 'Questions on the Soul' of Pietro Pomponazzi," *Medievalia et humanistica* 9 (1955) 76–101. Literature. A. H. DOUGLAS, *The Philosophy and Psychology of Pietro Pomponazzi,* ed. C. DOUGLAS and R. P. HARDIE (Cambridge, Eng. 1910). F. FIORENTINO, *Pietro Pomponazzi* (Florence 1868). C. CARBONARA, *Enciclopedia filosofica,* 4 v., (Venice-Rome 1957) 3:1507–11.

[C. B. SCHMITT]

POMPOSA, ABBEY OF

Former Benedictine abbey four miles from Codigoro in the Province of Ferrara and Diocese of Comacchio (Emilia), Italy. The remains of an inscription date the existence of the primitive church from the 7th century, but written records go back only to the 9th century. A letter of Pope John VIII (874) attests that the monastery came directly under the authority of the Holy See. Later it passed under the temporal jurisdiction of the archbishops of Ravenna, until Emperor Otto III made it a royal abbey. Its power increased with imperial and papal privileges and with donations from princes and private persons alike. From the 11th century on, Pomposa held large estates of cultivated land, as well as salt and fishing marshes. The abbot, as a prince of the Empire, exercised wide ecclesiastical and civil jurisdiction, and gave judgment according to the statutes of the abbey. It was a center of cultural activity as early as the 11th century; PETER DAMIAN wrote part of his works there, GUIDO OF AREZZO spent his youth at the abbey composing his musical system, and Emperor Otto II and the poets Dante and Tasso were its guests. In the 16th century increasingly bad climatic conditions and earthquakes obliged the monks to transfer to Ferrara, where the Duke of Este had offered land for a new monastery (San Benedetto). Pomposa itself continued to be used as a secular parish.

The numerous codices and manuscripts from the abbey's archives and library were dispersed when the abbey was suppressed during the Napoleonic period. The chief monuments remaining at Pomposa today are the basilica, the oldest building, with splendid mosaics and frescoes; the bell tower (11th century) in the Lombard style; and the Palazzo della Ragione, where the abbots administered justice. After the Napoleonic suppression it became private property and was turned into a farm. In the last few decades, however, considerable restoration has been undertaken.

Bibliography: P. FEDERICI, *Rerum Pomposianarum historia* (Rome 1781); v.2 in MS at Monte Cassino. G. MERCATI, ''Il catalogo della biblioteca di Pomposa,'' *Studi e documenti di storia e diritto* 16 (1896) 143–177. M. ROBERTI, *Pomposa* (Ferrara 1906). P. F. KEHR, *Regesta Pontificum Romanorum. Italia Pontificia,* 8 v. (Berlin 1906–35) 5:177–187. M. SALMI, *L'Abbazia di Pomposa* (Rome 1935).

[S. OLIVIERI]

View of the nave of the Abbey Church at Pomposa. Among the frescos are images depicting the Last Supper, and Lucifer Being Cast Out of Heaven, 12th century, Pomposa, Italy. (Alinari-Art Reference/Art Resource, NY)

PONCE, ALONSO

Franciscan chronicler; b. Castile, probably Ciudad Real, date unknown; place and date of death unknown. Ponce went to New Spain in 1584 as commissary general of his order. Between 1584 and 1592 he traveled 2,000 leagues, visiting the Franciscan provinces of Mexico, Guatemala, Honduras, San Salvador, Nicaragua, Costa Rica, and Granada. Some Franciscans denied Ponce's authority and he excommunicated them. Viceroy Villamanrique then ordered the exile of Ponce, who was obliged to embark ''under the staff of authority.'' Providentially the ship landed at Campeche, Mexico, and Ponce continued his visitation. The king confirmed him in his post and later summoned him to Spain. Fray Alonso de San Juan and Fray Antonio de Ciudad Real accompanied Ponce on his journeys and probably wrote the *Relación breve y verdadera de algunas cosas de los muchas que sucedieron at P. Fray Alonso Ponce en las provincias de Nueva España siendo comisario general de aquellas partes.* This famous and interesting work is a description of geography, hydrography, customs, clothing, climates, and crops. It is an unsurpassed work for the study of the first century of the Spanish colony and of many pro-Hispanic antiquities.

Bibliography: A. PONCE, *Viaje a Nueva España: Antología,* ed. A. HENESTROSA (Mexico City 1947). R. GUERRERO, *Índice clasificado de la Relación Breve . . . de Ponce* (Mexico City 1949).

[E. GÓMEZ TAGLE]

PONCE, MANUEL MARÍA

Popular Mexican composer, pianist, and teacher; b. Fresnillo (Zacatecas), Dec. 8, 1882; d. Mexico City, April

Manuel María Ponce. (©CORBIS)

24, 1948. At ten he was a choirboy; at 15, organist at San Diego church, Aguascalientes, where his brother was a priest. In 1906, after studying with Luigi Torchi in Bologna, he made his piano début in Berlin. In 1912 he was soloist at the première of his Piano Concerto, his first large work, in Mexico City. Gradually he turned less to European classics than to the Spanish-American melos for inspiration, and his ingratiating *canciones mexicanas* (including *Estrellita*) appeared in 1914. During another extended European residence (1925–32), his style matured contrapuntally and harmonically, and thereafter he made imaginative use of native materials. In 1941 he made a highly successful South American tour, during which his *Concierto del Sur* for guitar and orchestra (Andrés Segovia, soloist) had its first hearing. As a teacher Ponce introduced DEBUSSY and other moderns to Mexico City, and one of his first pupils was the distinguished composer Carlos Chávez.

Bibliography: M. M. PONCE, *Nuevos escritos musicales* (Mexico City 1948). R. M. STEVENSON, *Music in Mexico: A Historical Survey* (New York 1952). H. FERDINAND, *Die Musik in Geschichte und Gegenwart*, ed. F. BLUME (Kassel-Basel 1949–) 10:1437–38. O. MAYER-SERRA, *Música y músicos de Latinoamérica,* 2 v. (Mexico City 1947) 2:782–786. J. PENA, *Diccionario de la música Labor,* ed. H. ANGLÈS, 2 v. (Barcelona 1954) 2:1787–88. P. CASTELLANOS, rev. P. MELLO, *Manuel M. Ponce* (México City 1982). D. M. RANDEL, ed., *The Harvard Biographical Dictionary of Music* (Cambridge 1996) 700. N. SLONIMSKY, ed., *Baker's Biographical Dictionary of Musicians, Eighth Edition* (New York 1992) 1427. R. STEVENSON, ''Manuel (María) Ponce'' in *The New Grove Dictionary of Music and Musicians, vol. 15*, ed. S. SADIE (New York 1980) 74–75.

[R. STEVENSON]

PONTANUS ROMANUS, LUDOVICUS

Canonist; b. Spoleto, 1409; d. Basel, 1439. He was a student at Rome, assuming for this reason the surname Romanus. After pursuing his studies at Perugia and Bologna, he became a doctor in 1429. In 1431 he was nominated as an auditor of the Apostolic Camera. As a professor at Siena he compiled his famous *Singularia,* a series of legal questions, which he recorded daily in a notebook for future publication. By 1444, only five years after his death, they were widely known and circulated. He became a member of the Papal Curia in 1435 and was sent as an envoy to the Council of Basel to safeguard the interests of Alfonso V of Aragon. He was associated with PANORMITANUS at Basel. His premature death of plague brought to a close a decade of exceptional canonical studies. Besides the classic *Singularia*, he wrote commentaries on the *Corpus Iuris Civilis, Digestum vetus, Digestum novum*, and the *Codex.*

Bibliography: PIUS II, *De viris illustribus* (Bibliothek des Literarischen vereins in Stuttgart 1.3; Stuttgart 1842). C. LEFEBVRE, *Dictionnaire de droit canonique* 7:22–23. J. F. VON SCHULTE, *Die Geschichte der Quellen und der Literatur des kanonischen Rechts* 2:395.

[B. R. PISKULA]

PONTAS, JEAN

Moral theologian; b. Saint-Hilaire-du-Harcouet, Dec. 31, 1638; d. Paris, April 27, 1728. He studied at Rennes and Navarre and at the age of 25 was ordained. After receiving his doctorate in Canon Law, he became vicar of Sainte-Genevievedes-Ardents in 1666 and subpenitentiary at Paris in 1693. Although he wrote a number of works during his active career, his most important work was published during the long years of his retirement. The *Dictionnaire des cas de conscience* appeared first in two volumes (Paris 1715), but was followed by a supplement of three volumes in 1718. The entire work was reedited in 1724 and 1726, and several times edited after his death. Numerous editions were published in both French and Latin translation in the 18th century. Benedict XIV regarded Pontas as an eminent theologian.

Bibliography: J. CARREYRE, *Dictionnaire de théologie catholique* (Paris 1903–50) 12.2:2551–52, with bibliog. H. HURTER,

Nomenclator literarius theologiae catholicae (Innsbruck 1903–13) 4:1312–13.

[M. D. BARRY]

PONTIANUS, POPE, ST.

Pontificate: July 21, 230 to Sept. 28, 235. The *Liber pontificalis* states that Pontianus was from Rome and presided over that see for five years. Little is known of his pontficate, but the Roman church enjoyed peace under the tolerant emperor Severus Alexander (222–35). Alexander's successor, Maximus Thrax (235–238) exiled Pontianus to Sardinia with the theologian and antipope, HIPPOLYTUS. After maltreatment, he died in October of 235. His body and that of Hippolytus, with whom he had been reconciled, were returned to Rome for burial by Pope FABIAN in 236 or 237.

Pontianus may have been the first occupant of the new bishop's grotto in the Cemetery of Callistus. The *DEPOSITIO MARTYRUM* published by the CHRONOGRAPHER OF 354 lists him as the first Roman bishop-martyr, while his epitaph also lists him as a martyr; he is so celebrated. The date he resigned the episcopacy, Sept. 28, 235, although this designation is obviously an addition to the original inscription, is the oldest precise date in the history of popes. Under his direction a Roman synod reaffirmed the excommunication of ORIGEN pronounced by two Alexandrian councils in 231–232.

Feast: Nov. 19.

Bibliography: EUSEBIUS, 6:23, 29. L. KEOP, *Reallexikon für Antike und Christentum*, ed. T. KLAUSER (Stuttgart 1941 [1950]) 2:410–415. J. QUASTEN, *Patrology* (Westminster, MD 1950–) 2:235. J. SHOTWELL and L. LOOMIS, *The See of Peter* (New York 1927), 312–313. E. FERGUSON, *Encyclopedia of Early Christianity* (New York 1997), 2:935. J. N. D. KELLY, *Oxford Dictionary of Popes* (New York 1997) 16.

[E. G. WELTIN]

PONTIFF

This term, borrowed from the vocabulary of pagan religion at Rome, made its way early into Christian discourse. Lexicographers derive it, although with clear misgivings, from the Latin words *pons* (bridge) and *facere* (to make, build). If this derivation is accepted, it is easy to see how readily it applies to those who build a bridge to make a way for men to God. Nevertheless, in Roman religion it designated members of the council of priests forming the Pontifical College, which ranked as the highest priestly organization at Rome and was presided over by the *pontifex maximus.*

It is not clear when the term first made its appearance as a designation for Christian religious leaders, or whether Tertullian's ironic use of the designation *pontifex maximus* (in his *De pudicitia, c.* A.D. 220) for a Catholic bishop represents current terminology or not. In the Vulgate *pontifex* is used in Hebrews as a translation for the Greek ἀρχιερεύς (chief priest, high priest).

In present ecclesiastical usage the term "pontiff" (with its derivatives, "pontifical" and the verb "pontificate") is applied to bishops and especially to the pope. Although for the sake of clarity we still prefix supreme (sovereign) or Roman to the word pontiff in designating the pope, it is generally to him that there is reference when we speak of "the pontiff." The reference to all bishops is maintained in such expressions as "the Common of Confessor Pontiff" (in the Roman Missal and Breviary), "all holy pontiffs and confessors" (an invocation in the Litany of Saints). In the derived forms, too, the reference at times is clearly to all bishops: the Roman Pontifical is the liturgical book that contains the rites and formulas for liturgical acts performed by all bishops; and bishops (and certain other dignitaries) are said to pontificate when they celebrate the Eucharistic sacrifice and perform other liturgical acts with all the insignia of their office or dignity.

It is to be noted, however, that the English adjective pontifical has come more and more to designate that which is concerned with or belongs to the pope. Thus when institutes, colleges, universities, athenea, and societies are described as pontifical, the adjective indicates that the corporation in question has been directly established or approved by the pope or is immediately dependent upon him. In the Code of Canon Law (c.488.3) religious congregations that have received approbation from the Holy See are technically described as of "pontifical right"; others not yet so approved are said to be of "diocesan right." And when the expression "pontifical teaching" or "pontifical document" is employed, the reference is clearly to the Holy Father. The same exclusive reference is found in the cognate noun form pontificate (e.g., "in the pontificate of").

As a consequence of this restriction of meaning, the term that in earlier times looked to fullness of priestly and sacramental power (possessed by all bishops) is gradually becoming one that denotes the fullness of pastoral and teaching power and therefore applies (without addition of supreme or Roman) to the pope alone.

See Also: BISHOP (IN THE CHURCH); POPE.

Bibliography: M. BIERBAUM, *Lexikon für Theologie und Kirche*, ed. J. HOFER and K. RAHNER (Freiberg 1957–65) 8:613. G. J. LAING, *Encyclopedia of Religion and Ethics*, ed. J. HASTINGS (Edinburgh 1908–27) 10:325–335.

[S. E. DONLON]

PONTIFICAL, ROMAN

In Latin, *Pontificale Romanum*; one of the books of the Roman liturgy, it contains the rites for ordinations, consecrations, and all other liturgical rites and ceremonies reserved to bishops. The *Roman Pontifical* has its source in the early Roman Sacramentaries and Ordinals. Beginning with the 8th century, however, attempts were made to collect into one book the various rites proper to the bishop. *The Pontifical of Egbert,* archbishop of York (736–766), and the *Pontifical of Poitiers* (*c.* 800) are examples of this procedure. A more direct forerunner of the *Roman Pontifical* is seen in the *Romano-Germanic Pontifical* of the 10th century. Michel ANDRIEU gave this name to a compilation of 10th-century manuscripts containing episcopal rites and published part of it in the *Ordo L* in volume 5 of his *Ordines Romani du haut moyenâge* (Louvain 1962). Brought to Rome by the Ottos, it was adapted and later appeared in the 12th century as a papal pontifical. In the 13th century, the Roman Curia accepted an edition from Avignon.

In 1294 Bp. William DURANTI, the Elder of Mende, France, wrote a new edition for his diocese which, in less than a century, was used in nearly every European diocese. He transcribed some prayers of identical meaning, allowing bishops a choice, but this was discontinued in subsequent editions and repetitions became obligatory. Innocent VIII (d. 1492) charged Agostino Patrizi and John Burckard (d. 1506) with revising Duranti's book for the Roman Curia. This revision was approved on March 2, 1486, but it was not made obligatory. After several further revisions, by Alberto Castellani in 1520 and Pius V in 1561, Clement VIII in 1596 promulgated an official edition and forbade the use of any other pontifical in the Latin Church.

Until 1961 the pontifical remained unchanged. In that year a revision was prepared by a commission named by Pius XII (d. 1958). Promulgated by John XXIII (d. 1963) this was but a reform of Part II, in which some rites were reduced and placed into more logical order, and from which other repetitious, obsolete, or seldom-used ceremonies were eliminated. In its *Constitution on the Sacred Liturgy,* Vatican Council II ordered a revised edition of Parts I and III.

In the wake of Vatican II, the various liturgical rites of the pontifical were revised in stages, in keeping with the directives of Vatican Council II (*Sacrosanctum Concilium* 25, 71, 76, 80). Translations of these, prepared by the INTERNATIONAL COMMISSION ON ENGLISH IN THE LITURGY (ICEL), were first published separately. In 1978 the *Roman Pontifical*, Part I, appeared as a compilation of these rites. Except for two additions, the book corresponds in scope to the *Pontificale Romanum*, of Clement VIII, promulgated in 1596 in compliance with the decree of the Council of Trent on the matter (Session 25, Dec. 4, 1563: in *Conciliorum oecumenicorum decreta* 3d ed., p. 797).

The following are the contents of the 1978 *Roman Pontifical.* Part One contains rites for the celebration of the Sacraments of Christian Initiation, i.e., Baptism, Confirmation, and the Eucharist, along with the rites of admission to the catechumenate and reception of baptized Christians to full communion. At all of these rites the accompanying instructions recommend that the bishop preside (although priests may and often do so). Part Two is on the institution of lay ministers, specifically of readers and acolytes. Part Three contains the rites of ordination of deacons, presbyters, and bishops; also of admission to candidacy for diaconate and presbyterate and of commitment to celibacy (the latter as a part of diaconal ordination for unmarried men). Part Four comprises blessings for persons publicly dedicated to God: the rite of consecration to a life of virginity, the blessing of an abbot or abbess. In addition, the *Roman Pontifical* contains two other rites, belonging to Part II of the *Pontificale:* the Blessing of Holy Oils and Consecration of Chrism (English, 1972) and the rite for the dedication of a church and altar.

Bibliography: M. ANDRIEU, *Le Pontifical Romain au moyenâge* (Rome 1938–41). P. DE PUNIET, *Le Pontifical romain, histoire et commentaire,* 2 v. (Paris 1930–31). C. VOGEL and R. ELZE, eds., *Le Pontifical romanogermanique du Xe siècle,* 2 v. (*Studi e Testi* 226–227; 1963). G. CATALANI, *Pontificale romanum . . . commentariis illustratum,* 3 v. (1738–40; Paris 1850–52). N. K. RASMUSSEN, "Unité et diversité des pontificaux latins au VIIIe, IXe et Xe siècles," in *Liturgie de l'église particulière et liturgie de l'église universelle* (Rome 1976) 393–410. P. JOURNEL, "The Pontifical and the Ritual," in *The Church At Prayer Vol 3: The Sacraments,* A. MARTIMORT, gen. ed. (Collegeville, Minn. 1988) 1–10. M. KLÖCKENER, "Das Pontifikale: ein Liturgiebuch" *Archiv für Liturgiewissenschaft* 28:3 (1986) 396–415. E. PALAZZO, *A History of Liturgical Books from the beginning to the Thirteenth Century* (Collegeville, Minn. 1998).

[J. NABUCO/T. C. O'BRIEN/EDS.]

PONTIFICAL ACADEMIES

Pontifical academies are loose networks of scholars and representatives of various professions organized by the Holy See for the advancement of the arts, science, and culture. Each has its own by-laws and, in most cases, the members are appointed by the Roman pontiff. The *Annuario Pontificio* for the year 2000 lists the following pontifical academies: (1) the Pontifical Academy of Sciences; (2) the Pontifical Academy of Social Science; (3) the Pontifical Academy for Life; (4) the Pontifical Academy of St. Thomas Aquinas (formerly the Pontifical Academy of St. Thomas and Catholic Doctrine, founded in October, 1879); (5) the Pontifical Academy of Theology; (6) the Pontifical Academy of Our Lady Immaculate, founded in 1835; (7) the Pontifical International Marian Academy, founded in 1946; (8) the Distinguished Pontifical Academy of Arts and Letters of the Pantheon Virtuosi, founded in 1543; (9) the Pontifical Roman Academy of Archaeology, founded in 1810; and (10) the Pontifical Academy of the ''Cult of the Martyrs,'' founded in 1879. There have been other pontifical academies in the course of the centuries. Those listed here represent true pontifical academies. Additionally, institutions such as the Pontifical Ecclesiastical Academy, formerly known as the Academy of Noble Ecclesiastics, founded in 1701, enjoy the prerogatives of a pontifical academy, but are entrusted with special duties in service to the Church's diplomatic corps.

The most prominent pontifical academy is the Pontifical Academy of Science, the *senatus scientificus,* according to Pope Pius XI, dedicated to the mathematical, physical, and natural sciences. It attempts ''to pay honor to pure science, wherever it is found, and to assure its freedom and to promote its research, which constitute the indispensable basis for progress in science.'' At its full complement the membership stands at 80, a number established by Pope John Paul II in 1986. This academy is directly responsible to the Holy Father, who appoints the members, and its expenses are met through the Patrimony of the Holy See. Members, regardless of religious confession, are drawn from different countries, and they are appointed for life. By reason of their office, the directors of the Vatican Observatory and its Astrophysical Laboratory and the prefects of the Vatican Library and the Secret Archives of the Vatican are appointed ''Academicians *pro tempore.*''

The Pontifical Academy of Sciences has its roots in the Academy of the Lincei (*Academia Linceorum,* from its emblem, a lynx) which was founded in Rome in 1603 by Federico Cesi, Giovanni Heck, Francesco Stelluti, and Anastasio de Filiis, all contemporaries and sometime rivals of Galileo. In 1847 Pope Pius IX reestablished the Academy as the Pontifical Academy of the New Lincei. Pope Pius XI renewed and reconstituted the academy in 1936, and bestowed upon it its present name. The academy's activities range from a traditional interest in pure research to a concern with the ethical and environmental responsibility of the scientific community. The premises of the academy are in the Casina Pio IV, built in 1561, and it is there that members gather in plenary session.

The Pontifical Academy of Social Sciences was founded by Pope John Paul II on Jan. 1, 1994, with the *motu proprio* called *Socialum scientiarum.* Its statutes indicate that its objective to promote ''the study and progress of the social, economic, political and juridical sciences, and of thus offering the Church the elements which she can use in the study and development of her social doctrine.'' The academy is autonomous and at the same time, maintains a very close relationship with the Pontifical Council for Justice and Peace, with which it coordinates the planning of various initiatives. Its academicians are named by the pope and their number cannot be fewer than 20 nor more than 40. They are chosen because of their high level of competence without distinction to religious denomination. In its early years, the academy centered its plenary sessions and workshops on three themes: work and employment, in 1996, 1997, and 1999; democracy in 1996, 1998, and 2000; and social dimensions of globalization in 2000 and 2001. The headquarters of the academy are in the Casina Pio IV, in the Vatican Gardens. The Pontifical Academy for the Social Sciences has its own foundation to provide for its financial needs.

With the *motu proprio* titled *Vitae mysterium* of Feb. 11, 1994, John Paul II instituted the Pontifical Academy for Life. Its primary objective is to study problems of biomedicine and law, especially as they relate to the promotion and defense of life, in accord with Christian morality and the directives of the Church's magisterium. The Vitae Mysterium Foundation, instituted in October 1994, finances this academy which is linked to the Pontifical Council for Pastoral Assistance to Health Care Workers and various other dicasteries of the Roman Curia committed to the service of life. Seventy members are named by the pope and represent different branches of the biomedical sciences. The academy's activities focus on issues related to the HUMAN GENOME Project and specifically on the identity, localization, heterogeneity, and the mutability of those genes which constitute the hereditary patrimony of humanity. Further, because of the substantial unity of the body with the spirit—*corpore et anima unus: una summa*—the human genome has not only a biological significance, but is the bearer of an anthropological dignity, which has its foundation in the spiritual soul which pervades it and vivifies it (cf. Discourse of His Holiness John Paul II to Members of the Academy, Feb. 24, 1998).

The Pontifical Academy of St. Thomas took on renewed significance in view of Pope John Paul's encyclical *FIDES ET RATIO* (1999), in which the pontiff made a sustained plea for the value of the Angelic Doctor's work among moderns (see especially no. 57). Similarly, *Fides et Ratio* (nos. 92–99) would have the Pontifical Academy of Theology assist in the promotion of the sacred sciences, but always in dialogue with and in light of contemporary culture.

The Pontifical Academy of Our Lady Immaculate grew out of a small circle of students at the Gregorian University in Rome and became recognized by the Sacred Congregation for Studies, as it was then called, in 1847. One of its traditions has been presenting a ''floral homage'' before the statue of Mary Immaculate in the Piazza di Spagna on December 8. Pope John Paul II approved the new statutes for the academy in 1988 and 1995. Another Marian academy, the Pontifical International Marian Academy, founded by Carlo Balić, OFM, in 1946, promotes historical studies related to the Virgin Mary. In this connection (and largely through Balić's own scholarship), the academy has helped sponsor the herculean effort to develop a critical edition of the works of John Duns Scotus. It was also charged with the organization of various Marian congresses throughout the world. Raised to the status of a pontifical academy by Pope John XXIII in 1959 through the *motu proprio* called *Maiora in dies,* the academy enjoys a continued working relationship with the Friars Minor at the Antonianum in Rome.

Of the three remaining pontifical academies, the Academy of the Arts is the oldest, with a history stretching back to Pope Paul III in 1542. Its statutes were revised and approved by Pope John Paul II in 1995. The academy seeks to support sculptors, writers, architects, film makers, musicians, poets, and painters. The academy works cooperatively with the PONTIFICAL COUNCIL FOR CULTURE, and its virtuosi are nominated by the Holy Father. The Pontifical Academy of Roman Archaeology (formerly the Academy of Roman Antiquities) was founded in 1810, becoming a pontifical academy in 1829 under Pius VIII. It seeks to promote the study of archaeology and the history of ancient and medieval art. The Cardinal Secretary of State is its protector. Finally, the Pontifical Academy of the Cult of the Martyrs was founded as the Collegium Cultorum Martyrum in 1879 and collaborates with the Congregation for Divine Worship and the Discipline of Sacraments. Its work involves liturgical studies, archeology, and hagiography. Its statutes were revised and approved in 1995. The academy is historically based at the German College in Rome.

Bibliography: *Annuario Pontificio per l'Anno 2000* (Vatican City 2000), 1876–1893, 2018–2024. R. LADOUS, *Des Nobel au Vatican: La fondation de l'académie pontificale des sciences* (Paris 1994). MARINI-BETTELO and G. BATISTA, *Activity of the Pontifical Academy of Sciences, 1936–1986* (Vatican City 1987); *Historical Aspects of the Pontifical Academy of Sciences,* Oct. 28, 1986 (Vatican City 1986). ''Inter Munera Academiarum,'' *Acta Apostolicae Sedis* 91:9 (Sept. 1999): 849–853.

[P. J. HAYES]

PONTIFICAL BIBLICAL COMMISSION

In the history of the Pontifical Biblical Commission a sharp distinction must be made between its form and function before and after the Second Vatican Council.

Before Vatican II

The Pontifical Biblical Commission was created by Pope LEO XIII in 1902 through his Apostolic Letter *Vigilantiae* (*Enchiridium biblicum. Documenta ecclesiastica Sacram Scripturam spectantia* [Naples-Rome[2] 1954] 137–148). Its function was, according to this founding document, ''to strive and effect with all possible care that God's words will both be given, everywhere among us, that thorough study that our times demand and will be shielded not only from every breath of error but even from every rash opinion.''

The pre-Vatican II Commission consisted of a limited number of cardinals, named by the pope, the majority belonging to the Roman CURIA. To these members were joined as consultors Catholic biblical scholars from various tendencies and countries though most resided in Rome. The seat of the Commission was Rome. From 1938 until the post-Vatican reorganization the president of the Commission was Cardinal Tisserant. The last four secretaries were J. M. Vosté (1939–49); A. Miller (1949–58); A. Kleinhans (1958–62); and B. N. Wambacq from 1963 until the reorganization.

Activities. Between 1905 and 1953 a number of decrees or *Responsa* (''answers'') were issued. Some of those from the period 1905–1915 are well known for their negative impact, e.g., the *Responsa* on the narratives in the historical books (1905; EB 161), on the Mosaic authorship of the Pentateuch (1906; EB 181–184), on the authorship of the book of Isaiah (1908; EB 291–295), and on the historical character of the first three chapters of Genesis (1909; EB 336–343). Particular publications were judged to be inaccurate and their use in Catholic schools was forbidden.

The letter written by Commission's secretary to Cardinal Suhard of Paris (1948) struck a positive note. It allowed Catholic scholars considerable liberty ''concerning the time of the documents of the Pentateuch and concerning the literary genre of the first 11 chapters of Genesis'' (EB 577–581). The last intervention of the Commission occurred during the Council by way of the instruction *Sacra Mater Ecclesia* (1964; DS 3999) on the historical truth of the gospels. The open-mindedness of the document was praised, especially because of its distinction among the three stages of the gospel tradition: what Jesus of Nazareth actually did and said, what the disciples and apostles preached about what Jesus said and did, and what the evangelists wrote down from that preaching. Consequently, the gospels cannot be regarded as direct reports of the facts about and the words of Jesus. The content of this instruction has been integrated into the Dogmatic Constitution *Dei Verbum* of Vatican II (1964, paragraph 19).

Before its reorganization by Pope PAUL VI, the Pontifical Biblical Commission functioned as an organ of the magisterium. Twice, in 1907 and 1910, PIUS X emphasized that the decisions of the Commission require religious assent: ''All are bound in conscience to submit to the decisions of the Pontifical Commission pertaining to doctrine, whether already issued or to be issued in the future, in the same way as to the decrees of the Sacred Congregations approved by the Pontiff; nor can they avoid the stigma both of disobedience and temerity or be free from grave sin who by any spoken or written words impugn these decisions'' (1910, EB 341).

The rise of MODERNISM in the early years of the Commission explains, to a great extent, the defensive and apologetic character of many *Responsa* that caused serious conflicts of conscience for many Catholic scholars. Later letters and instructions manifested a more open approach, especially thanks to the encyclical *Divino afflante Spiritu* (1943; EB 538–569).

From 1904 until 1928 the Pontifical Biblical Commission alone had the power to grant Catholic academic doctoral degrees in Scripture.

After Vatican II

The Pontifical Biblical Commission was restructured by Paul VI through the promulgation of the apostolic brief *Sedula Cura* in 1971. The stated reasons for this action were both the prescription of Vatican II, ''that the rich treasures of the word of God be made more amply and plentifully accessible to the faithful,'' and the fact that ''progress of modern scholarship daily presents new questions in this discipline which are not easy to solve.''

The two most notable changes in the nature of the reformed Biblical Commission are its close linking with the Congregation for the Doctrine of the Faith and the constitution of its membership by biblical scholars and not, as formerly, by cardinals, who were assisted in their function by scholars merely as consultors.

The new regulation, which can be compared with the statutes of the International Theological Commission (created in 1969), is set forth in 15 points. (1) The chief function of the Commission remains that ''of rightly promoting biblical studies and of offering assistance to the magisterium of the Church in interpreting Scripture.'' (2) Its president is ''the Cardinal Prefect of the Sacred Congregation for the Doctrine of the Faith.'' (3) The membership is limited to 20 scholars ''from various schools and nations,'' considered to be ''outstanding for their learning, prudence and Catholic regard for the magisterium.'' (4) They are appointed by the pope on the recommendation of the cardinal president, ''after consultation with the episcopal conferences,'' for five years, a term that may be renewed. (5) The secretary is appointed by the pope for five years; he is also named a consultor of the Congregation for the Doctrine of the Faith. (6) A plenary meeting of the Commission is to be convoked annually. (7) Subcommissions may be set up to study particular problems, and can consult ''other experts, including non-Catholics.'' (8) Consultation of the membership by letter is made possible. (9) The pope or the president designate the questions to be studied. These may be proposed by the Congregation for the Doctrine of the Faith, by the Synod of Bishops, the episcopal conferences, the Biblical Commission itself, or by Catholic universities and biblical societies. (10) Conclusions reached in plenary session are to be submitted to the pope for use by the Congregation for the Doctrine of the Faith. (11) This latter body may ''publish with special mention of the Biblical Commission'' instructions or decrees ''which are the fruit of the scholarly investigation of the members.'' (12) Relations with ''institutions of biblical studies, both Catholic and non-Catholic,'' are to be cultivated by the Commission. (13) Before new norms concerning Scripture are issued within the Church, the Commission is to be consulted. (14) The Commission continues to confer academic degrees in biblical studies, but its members do not, as such, conduct the examinations leading to these degrees, as formerly. (15) Finally, secrecy ''in keeping with the character and importance'' of its business is to govern its transactions.

Paul VI appointed the 20 members of the postconciliar Commission in 1972. Bishop A.-L. Descamps, former rector of the Catholic University of Louvain, was named secretary in 1973. Although the international and collegial character of this postconciliar body is assured, it has been more than once noticed that in the first five terms (1972–2000) no woman scholar was a member of the Pontifical Biblical Commission.

The first plenary session of the Commission took place in 1974; its activities were devoted to reviewing the norms for examinations and degrees in biblical studies. The investigation of the second and the third sessions concerned the *Condicio mulieris in Sacra Scriptura* (1975) and *De munere mulieris in societate humana et in activitate religiosa ad mentem S. Scripturae* (1976). It became known that a majority of the Commission was of the opinion that Scripture is not enough to exclude women from priesthood. In 1977 the first group of the Commission met for the last time. They dealt with the use of Scripture in the writings on liberation theology. No publication of texts followed. There was no plenary session in 1978 (nor for that matter in 1984, 1990, 1996 and 2001).

The second group also had Bishop Descamps as its secretary. The theme of the 1979 plenary session was acculturation in Sacred Scripture itself. The majority of the discussion papers have been published in revised form in *Fede e cultura alla luce della Bibbia – Foi e culture à la lumière de la Bible* (1981). No common conclusions are offered. After the tragic death of Bishop Descamps in 1980, H. Cazelles replaced him as secretary. The four successive sessions (1980, 1981, 1982 and 1983) were devoted to recent questions concerning christology. The work of these sessions resulted in the publication of *Bible et christologie* (1984). The volume consists of two main parts: the official document of the Biblical Commission (in Latin and French, pp. 14–109) and nine contributions by individual members (all in French, pp. 113–287).

In 1984 H. Cazelles was named secretary of the Commission's third group as well. Four sessions (1985, 1986, 1987 and 1988) investigated the relation between local churches and the universality of the unique people of God. This examination led to the publication of the volume *Unité et diversité dans l'Eglise* (1989). The book contains the official French text of the Commission (pp. 9–28) and twenty contributions by individual members in different languages (pp. 31–311). The ecumenical importance of this publication is recognized. In the fifth session (1989) a new theme was approached: the interpretation of the Bible in the Church; this work was interrupted at the end of the five-year term.

In 1990 Prof. A. Vanhoye was appointed secretary of the fourth group. Within three sessions (1991, 1992 and 1993) the same theme, the interpretation of the Bible, was further studied and a joint document redacted. On Saturday, April 24, 1993, during a solemn audience at the Vatican, a double anniversary was celebrated: the encyclical *PROVIDENTISSIMUS DEUS* (Leo XIII, 1893; EB 81–134) and the encyclical *DIVINO AFFLANTE SPIRITU* (Pius XII, 1943; EB 538–569). This commemoration, however, did not take place with the issuing of a new encyclical. During that audience the Pontifical Biblical Commission submitted to Pope JOHN PAUL II its document *The Interpretation of the Bible in the Church.*

Why this new document? There have been, from different quarters, complaints about the scientific study of the Bible. Moreover, the historical-critical method is often attacked because of its so-called sterility; not seldom, it is said, doubt, if not unbelief, arises from its use. What about the new and seemingly more promising approaches? The Pontifical Biblical Commission was asked to reflect on this malaise. Could the Commission ''indicate the paths most appropriate for arriving at an interpretation of the Bible as faithful to its character both human and divine?''

The Commission presented its considerations in a lengthy document consisting of four main parts. First there is a discussion of the different methods and approaches: thirteen of them are analyzed and carefully evaluated (e.g., rhetorical analysis, narrative analysis, the sociological approach, the liberationist approach, the feminist approach). Then the document investigates the philosophical question of what ''hermeneutics'' actually involves and it deals with the question of the meaning or meanings of inspired Scripture (the literal, spiritual and fuller senses). In the third part the characteristics of a Catholic interpretation of the Bible are considered: what has exegesis done during the long tradition of the Church and how can the task of the exegete be defined today? The last part is concerned with the interpretation of Scripture in the life of the Church: how can the Bible be actualized? What kind of attention must be given to inculturation? Which are the different uses of the Bible, in liturgy, in individual or communal reading, in pastoral ministry and in ecumenism?

In his address during the 1993 audience Pope John Paul II praised the document for the spirit of openness in which it was conceived, for its balance and moderation, for its stress on the fact that the biblical Word is at work speaking universally, in time and space, to all humanity. The reactions from both scholars and religious leaders, not only Catholics, underline the importance of this document.

In the sessions of 1994 and 1995 a new theme of discussion was brought forward: what does the Bible say about the universalism of salvation through Christ? Because of lack of time no final document could be achieved. The individual contributions, which had been updated after discussion in the plenary sessions, were brought together and presented to the Theological Commission.

A. Vanhoye remained the secretary of the fifth group. In the sessions of 1997, 1998, 1999 and 2000 the Commission investigated the place of Israel in Scripture and a final document is now ready. The publication of *Le peuple juif et ses Saintes Ecritures dans la Bible chrétienne* is announced for 2002. Its three main parts are: I. ''Les Saintes Ecritures du peuple juif partie fondamentale de la Bible chrétienne''; II. ''Thèmes fondamentaux des Ecritures du peuple juif et leur réception dans la foi au Christ''; III. ''Les juifs dans le Nouveau Testament.''

Bibliography: The postconciliar Commission published the five following documents: 1. *Fede e cultura alla luce della Bibbia – Foi e culture à la lumière de la Bible. Atti della sessione plenaria 1979*, ed. J. D. BARTHÉLEMY (Turin 1981). 2. *Bible et christologie*, preface by H. CAZELLES (Paris 1984). 3. *Unité et diversité dans l'Eglise* (Città del Vaticano 1989). 4. *The Interpretation of the Bible in the Church. Address of His Holiness Pope John Paul II and Document of the P.B.C.* (Città del Vaticano 1993). 5. *Le peuple juif et ses Saintes Ecritures dans Bible chrétienne* (Città del Vaticano 2002). A. VANHOYE, ''Passé et présent de la Commission Biblique,'' *Gregorianum* 74 (1993) 261–275. J. A. FITZMYER, *Scripture and Christology: A Statement of the Biblical Commission with a Commentary* (New York/Mahwah 1986); *The Biblical Commission's Document ''The Interpretation of the Bible in the Church.'' Text and Commentary* (Subsida biblica 18; Rome 1995).

[J. LAMBRECHT]

PONTIFICAL COUNCIL FOR CULTURE

In 1982 Pope JOHN PAUL II created the Pontifical Council for Culture and with a sense of symbolism signed the letter on the feast of the Ascension. This new body was to serve at the crossroads between faith and lived realities, as an organization of encounter and of research; it was to deepen ''the relations of the Holy See with every manifestation of culture.'' Similar to other Vatican dicasteries involved with dialogue, this council was intended to communicate *ad extra*, and especially with those places where the meanings and values of humanity are being formed. Its very existence was to witness to the desire of the Church to collaborate with people of culture everywhere.

Three principal factors lay behind this papal initiative. At the Second Vatican Council, *Gaudium et spes* devoted a substantial chapter to the topic of culture, noting that the concept had widened from an older meaning of conscious development and creativity to include various ways of life in society. Second, the pastoral relevance of different cultural contexts came to the fore during the seventies, especially through the 1975 call of Pope Paul VI for an in-depth ''evangelization of cultures'' (*Evangelii nutiandi*). Third, Pope John Paul II had shown a personal interest in the whole field of culture and had often spoken of it as the key to what makes us human and as a crucial dimension for the very future of humanity, most notably visiting UNESCO on June 2, 1980.

In the letter of foundation the pope expressed his vision thus: ''The synthesis between culture and faith is not just a demand of culture but also of faith. A faith that does not become culture is a faith which has not been fully received, not thoroughly thought through, not faithfully lived out.'' Gradually the Pontifical Council entered into collaboration with international organizations and cultural institutions throughout the world. It organized many international conferences, such as a symposium on ''Christianity and Culture in Europe'' to prepare for the 1991 Synod of Bishops. It worked, in cooperation with other Vatican organizations, on a document on the presence of the Church in university culture. It is actively involved with Catholic Cultural Centers in many countries, seeking to be a channel of contact and communication between them.

In 1993 Pope John Paul II issued the *motu proprio* titled *Inde a Pontificatus,* which merged the previous pontifical councils for culture and for dialogue with nonbelievers under the title of Pontifical Council for Culture. With this refoundation the aims of the Council are further clarified. It has two sections: (1) faith and culture and (2) dialogue with cultures. Its aims are fourfold: to foster meeting places between the gospel and contemporary cultures; to help toward evangelizing cultures and inculturating the Gospel; to build up contacts with cultural institutions at the local level and to further intercultural dialogue; and to promote dialogue with unbelievers and reflection on this issue.

The council's publications include books arising from the various congresses organized over the years, and a quarterly review titled *Cultures and Faith.* Since its inception it has had only one president, Paul Cardinal Poupard.

[M. P. GALLAGHER]

PONTIFICAL COUNCIL FOR INTERRELIGIOUS DIALOGUE

The Pontifical Council for Interreligious Dialogue (PCID) is a dicastery of the Holy See responsible for relations with followers of other religions. The PCID promotes dialogue with other religions in accordance with the decrees of the Second Vatican Council, particularly *Nostra Aetate*. Founded at first as the Secretariat for Non-Christians during Pentecost 1964, it was raised to the dignity of a pontifical council in 1988 through the apostolic constitution *Pastor Bonus,* when it was renamed. In accordance with that constitution's regulation (§161), the PCID may at times, in the course of its work, consult with the Congregation for the Doctrine of the Faith, as well as the Congregations for the Eastern Churches and the Evangelization of Peoples. The PCID does not have responsibility for the promoting relations with Jews. That is the proper competence of the Commission for Religious Relations with Jews, an office of the Pontifical Council for the Promotion of Christian Unity.

The goals of the PCID are threefold: to promote mutual understanding, respect, and collaboration between

Catholics and the followers of others religious traditions; to encourage the study of religions; and to promote the formation of persons dedicated to dialogue. In aid of this task the PCID has produced several documents, ''The Attitude of the Catholic Church towards the Followers of Other Religious Traditions: Reflections on Dialogue and Mission'' (1984), ''Pastoral Attention to African Traditional Religions'' (1988), ''Dialogue and Proclamation'' (1991), ''Pastoral Attention to the Traditional Religions of Asia, America, and Oceania'' (1994), ''Journeying Together: The Catholic Church in Dialogue with the Religious Traditions of the World'' (1999), and an ''Interreligious Dialogue Directory.'' Other documents also serve as guides, particularly the papal encyclical letters *ECCLESIAM SUAM* (1964), *REDEMPTOR HOMINIS* (1979), and *REDEMPTORIS MISSIO* (1990).

The permanent staff in Rome includes staff members for Africa and Asia and a staff member for new religious movements. The PCID also has a special commission for religious relations with Muslims, instituted by Paul VI on Oct. 22, 1974. It engages in studies on different aspects of Christian-Muslim relations and has produced a document with special attention given to dialogue with Muslims.

The PCID usually publishes the acts of the dialogue meetings it organizes. A bulletin, called *Pro Dialogo*, is published regularly three times a year. Typically, the president of the PCID or his delegate sends greetings on the occasion of the major festivals of non-Christian religions. For example, widely published messages have been sent to Hindus around the world on the feast of Diwali, to Buddhists on the feast of Vesakh/Hanamatsuri, or to Muslims on the occasion of Ramadan.

Bibliography: F. ARINZE, *Church in Dialogue: Walking with Other Believers* (San Francisco 1990); *Meeting Other Believers* (Huntington, Ind. 1997). M. BORRMANS, ed., *Guidelines for Dialogue between Christians and Muslims by the Pontifical Council for Interreligious Dialogue,* tr. R. M. SPEIGHT (New York 1990). W. R. BORROWS, ed., *Redemption and Dialogue: Reading ''Redemptoris Missio'' and ''Dialogue and Proclamation''* (Maryknoll, N.Y. 1993). F. GIOIA, ed., *Interreligious Dialogue: The Official Teaching of the Catholic Church, 1963–1995* (Boston 1997). R. B. SHEARD, *Interreligious Dialogue in the Catholic Church since Vatican II: An Historical and Theological Study* (Lewiston, N.Y. 1987).

[P. J. HAYES]

PONTIFICAL COUNCILS

Pontifical councils operate on the fourth tier of the HOLY SEE's governing structure. They have within their competence special functions in connection to ecclesial life that the pope deems to be of primary importance. As such, they carry out their duties in an official capacity in the pope's name and by his authority (CIC, c. 360). At the end of the 20th century there were 11 pontifical councils, all of which fell under the regulations of *Pastor bonus,* the 1988 apostolic constitution of Pope JOHN PAUL II that reorganized the Roman CURIA. These include the Pontifical Council for the Laity, the Pontifical Council for the Promotion of Christian Unity, the Pontifical Council for the Family, the Pontifical Council for Justice and Peace, the Pontifical Council ''Cor Unum,'' the Pontifical Council for the Pastoral Care of Migrants and Itinerant People, the Pontifical Council for the Pastoral Assistance of Health-Care Workers, the Pontifical Council for the Interpretation of Legislative Texts, the Pontifical Council for Inter-religious Dialogue, the PONTIFICAL COUNCIL FOR CULTURE (which subsumed the Pontifical Council for Dialogue with Non-Believers in 1993), and the Pontifical Council for Social Communications.

Structures. All the pontifical councils are led by a cardinal or archbishop who takes title of the office of president (*Pastor bonus* I, a. 3, §§1). They are assisted typically by a secretary and undersecretary. Members are usually selected from the episcopate; consultors and professional staff are employed to assist in the work of each council. Lay participation is permitted on all councils, though clerics continue to dominate. Each dicastery may issue norms relative to its field of competence or may join with other curial bodies in issuing joint statements of mutual concern. The councils meet on a regular basis, sometimes in plenary assembly. Membership on each of the councils is by term appointment or at the pleasure of the Holy Father. Many of the pontifical councils are housed in offices located in the St. Callixtus complex in Rome's Trastevere neighborhood.

History and Aims. The history of pontifical councils varies, though they all sink their roots in the 20th century. Some, such as the Pontifical Council for the Laity and the Pontifical Council for the Promotion of Christian Unity, emerged directly from commissions established to participate in the Second VATICAN COUNCIL. Other dicasteries were shaped by Pope Paul's apostolic constitution *Regimini Ecclesiae universae* (Aug. 15, 1967) which established norms for the implementation of the conciliar decrees during an ''experimental period'' in which the local churches would seek ways to adapt to the new situation created by the Second Vatican Council. Pope John Paul II has established several pontifical councils either as entirely new entities (Health Care, Legislative Texts, Culture) or by raising already established secretariats or commissions to the dignity of a pontifical council (Christian Unity, Family, Justice and Peace, Migrants and Itinerant Peoples, Social Communications). What follows here is a brief history of each of the pontifical councils, together with a short description of their fundamental purposes.

Pontifical Council for the Laity. The Pontifical Council for the Laity seeks to engage the lay apostolate on all levels through sustained interaction with international lay groups, national laity councils, and institutions participating in CATHOLIC ACTION. It promotes the lay apostolate under the guidance of the relevant texts of the Second Vatican Council as well as the post-synodal apostolic exhortation *CHRISTIFIDELES LAICI* (1988). The council's history may be traced as far back as 1908 when Pope PIUS X issued the apostolic constitution *Sapienti consilio.* That text reformed the Roman Curia and was later made part of the universal law of the Church (1917), making the Sacred Congregation of the Council competent for ''the discipline of the secular clergy and of the Christian people.'' The importance of Catholic Action in the years preceding the Second Vatican Council provided the impetus for a more formal recognition of the lay apostolate in the council itself. The conciliar decree *Apostolicam actuositatem* proposed that a secretariat for the laity form part of the Roman Curia (AA 26), and this was formally constituted ''ad experimentum'' for five years by the *motu proprio Catholicam Christi ecclesiam* of Pope Paul VI (January 6, 1967). Pope Paul gave both recognition and definition to this secretariat. With *Regimini,* the ''Consilium de Laicis'' was given general and particular norms, the latter of which were altered with only minor changes in *Pastor bonus.* Nearly ten years after the creation of the ''Consilium de Laicis,'' Paul VI's *motu proprio Apostolatus peragendi* (Dec. 10, 1976) further solidified this dicastery by making it a pontifical council. The current council comprises sections pertaining to youth, Catholic international organizations, and (in conjunction with the Congregation for the Clergy) new ecclesial ministries within parishes and other contexts, as well as emerging associations of the lay faithful.

Pontifical Council for the Promotion of Christian Unity. In 1966, after the council had ended, Pope Paul VI confirmed the Secretariat for Promoting Christian Unity as a permanent dicastery of the Holy See. In *Pastor bonus* Pope John Paul II changed the secretariat into the Pontifical Council for Promoting Christian Unity (effective March 1, 1989). The council exercises a double role. First of all, it is entrusted with the promotion, within the Catholic Church, of an authentic ecumenical spirit according to the conciliar decree *Unitatis redintegratio.* It was for this purpose that an ecumenical directory was published in 1967–70 and a revised edition issued in 1993 as *Directory for the Application of Principles and Norms on Ecumenism.* The council also aims to develop dialogue and collaboration with other churches and world communions. Since its creation, it has established a cordial cooperation with the WORLD COUNCIL OF CHURCHES (WCC); 12 Catholic theologians have been members of the FAITH AND ORDER COMMISSION, the theological department of the WCC. The work of this dicastery is divided between an Eastern section, dealing with Orthodox churches of Byzantine tradition and the Oriental Orthodox Churches (Coptic, Syrian, Armenian, Ethiopian, and Malankara), as well as the Assyrian Church of the East; and a Western section, dealing with the different churches and ecclesial communities of the West and the World Council of Churches. This dicastery also maintains the Commission for Religious Relations with the Jews that Pope Paul VI established on Oct. 22, 1974. Although it is an autonomous unit, it is largely staffed by members of the pontifical council.

Pontifical Council for the Family. This dicastery was instituted by John Paul II with the *motu proprio Familia a Deo instituta* (May 9, 1981), replacing the Committee for the Family created by Paul VI in 1973. The committee had remained closely linked to the ''Consilium de Laicis'' and was governed by *Catholicam Christi Ecclesiam.* There are still links between the two pontifical councils, such as the presence of the two secretaries in each of the presidential committees. The council is responsible for the promotion of the pastoral ministry of and apostolate to the family, assisting in all dimensions of family life and encompassing such issues as responsible procreation, theology and catechesis of the family, marital and family spirituality, the rights of the family and the child, lay formation, and marriage preparation courses. Due to the influence that issues such as PORNOGRAPHY, PROSTITUTION, and drugs can have on the family, these topics also fall under the council's purview.

Pontifical Council for Justice and Peace. Pope Paul VI created the Pontifical Commission ''Iustitia et Pax'' in 1967 as an experiment (together with the Pontifical Council for the Laity) but made it a definitive dicastery of the Holy See with the *motu proprio Iustitiam et pacem* (1976). It became a pontifical council with *Pastor bonus.* The council's raison d'etre is to promote peace and justice in the world according to the gospel and the social doctrine of the Church. It is principally concerned with labor and human rights and frequently collaborates with other organizations, not necessarily affiliated with the Church, who share common goals.

Pontifical Council ''Cor Unum.'' The Pontifical Council ''Cor Unum'' was created by Paul VI who described it, in his *lettera autografa* (hand-written letter) *Amoris officio* (July 15, 1971), as a dicastery at the level of the universal Church ''for human and Christian promotion.'' The council is concerned with understanding the demands of solidarity and development and enacting them according to the principles of the gospel. The council promotes the catechesis of charity and stimulates the faithful to bear witness to it, coordinates initiatives of those Catholic institutions that help the less fortunate, helps promote a more just distribution of aid in times of disasters, and acts as a go-between with Catholic charitable and humanitarian organizations. Half of the council's members are bishops and representatives from developing countries, while the other half represent Catholic aid organizations. ''Cor Unum'' is also responsible for the Holy Father's charitable donations. From the World Council of Churches (Unit IV), the council receives information on aid programs for those countries that have been struck by natural calamities, ethnic conflicts, or civil wars. In 1984, Pope John Paul established the John Paul II Foundation for the Sahel, providing drought relief and and programs against desertification. In 1992, the Holy Father also founded the Populorum Progressio Foundation, which is at the service of indigenous, racially mixed, Afro-American, and campesinos of Latin America and the Caribbean.

Pontifical Council for the Pastoral Care of Migrants and Itinerant Peoples. Pope Pius XII drew attention in 1952 to a pressing pastoral need that had been fomenting throughout the aftermath of World War II, namely, the plight of the emigrant. The apostolic constitution *Exsul familia* (1952) established both the Superior Council for Emigration and the Work of the Apostleship of the Sea within the Consistorial Congregation, now known as the Congregation for Bishops. Six years later Pope Pius broadened the scope of the congregation's duties to include air travelers through an institution called ''Opera dell'Apostolatus Coeli o Aeris.'' In 1969, at the request of the Congregation for Bishops, Paul VI updated his predecessor's creations and the following year established a single entity with his *motu proprio Apostolicae caritatis* (March 19, 1970), calling it the Pontifical Commission for the Spiritual Care of Migrants and Travelers. This commission embraced all those pastoral ministries regarding human mobility: migrants, exiles, refugees, seafarers, air travel personnel and passengers, nomads, pilgrims, and tourists. To these were later added gypsies and ''circus people.'' With *Pastor bonus* the commission was raised to the dignity of a pontifical council.

Pontifical Council for Pastoral Assistance to Health-Care Workers. With the *motu proprio Dolentium hominum* (Feb. 11, 1985), John Paul II instituted the Pontifical Commission for the Pastoral Assistance to Health-Care Workers, which with *Pastor bonus* became a pontifical council. It stimulates and promotes the work of formation, study, and action carried out by the diverse international Catholic organizations in the health-care field. The council coordinates the activities of different dicasteries of the Roman Curia as they relate to the health care sector and its problems. It spreads, explains, and defends the teachings of the Church on health issues and favors its involvement in health-care practice. It also maintains contacts with the local Churches and especially with bishops' commissions related to health care.

Pontifical Council for the Interpretation of Legislative Texts. With his *motu proprio cum iuris canonici* (Sept. 15, 1917), Pope BENEDICT XV inaugurated a pontifical commission for the authentic interpretation of the Code of Canon Law, promulgated the previous May. At the time of the Second Vatican Council the commission became an instrument by which the council's legislation was prepared. In the post-conciliar era, the commission was responsible for delivering authentic interpretations of the conciliar texts as well as working toward a revised code of canons in light of the new legislation. That code was approved by Pope John Paul II in 1983. He later charged the commission with the task of interpreting the new code through his *motu proprio Recognito iuris canonici codice* (Jan. 2, 1984). *Pastor bonus* raised the commission to the dignity of a pontifical council, and placed it council in charge of all authentic interpretations of both singular and inter-dicastoral documents.

Pontifical Council for Culture. Dating back to the Second Vatican Council, this pontifical council's roots are grounded in *Gaudium et spes* 53–62. It did not emerge as a distinct entity until John Paul II founded it in 1982 (personal letter to the Cardinal Secretary of State, May 20, 1982). In his *motu proprio Inde a Pontificatus* (March 25, 1993), John Paul II merged the Pontifical Council for Dialogue with Non-Believers (founded in 1965 by Paul VI) with the Pontifical Council for Culture. The council's main tasks are to bring the gospel into diverse cultures and seek ways to enliven those in the sciences, letters, and arts through the Church's sustained interest in their work ''in the service of truth, goodness, and beauty.'' As such, this dicastery coordinates the activities of the pontifical academies and cooperates on a regular basis with the Pontifical Commission for the Cultural Heritage of the Church.

Pontifical Council for Social Communications. This dicastery has undergone a number of incarnations since the secretariat of state of Pope Pius XII first ordered that a Pontifical Commission for the Study and Ecclesiastical Evaluation of Films on Religious or Moral Subjects be established (Jan. 30, 1948, by letter, protocol no. 153.561). On Sept. 17, 1948, Pius XII approved the statutes of this new office and renamed it the Pontifical Commission for Educational and Religious Films, later to become the Pontifical Commission for Cinema, the statutes of which were approved Jan. 1, 1952. After consultation with bishops and Catholic film organizations, the name of the commission was once more changed, this time to the Pontifical Commission for the Cinema, Radio, and Television (Dec. 31, 1954). Pope John XXIII entrusted the commission with developing the Vatican Film Library. Pope John also added the responsibility of coordinating the communications media needed for the Second Vatican Council. Pope Paul VI transformed it into the Pontifical Commission for Social Communications (*motu proprio in fructibus multis,* April 2, 1964). It was responsible for dealing with the all the problems raised by cinema, radio, television, and the daily and periodical press in relation to the interests of the Catholic religion. With *Pastor bonus,* the commission became a pontifical council.

Bibliography: *Annuario Pontificio: 2000* (Rome: Libreria Editrice Vaticana, 2000). T. J. REESE, *Inside the Vatican: The Politics and Organization of the Catholic Church* (Cambridge: Harvard University Press, 1996). *Canon Law Digest,* vols. 5–8.

[P. HAYES]

PONTIFICAL INSTITUTE FOR FOREIGN MISSIONS

(PIME, Official Catholic Directory, #1050) an international society of secular priests exclusively dedicated to mission work, with a special emphasis on training local clergy and establishing local hierarchies. The society works under the umbrella of the Congregation for the EVANGELIZATION OF PEOPLES. Members of the society work in Africa, Asia and the Americas. The society is the result of a merger effected by Pius XI in 1926 of the Institute for Foreign Missions of Milan and the Pontifical Seminary of SS. Peter and Paul for Foreign Missions of Rome. The Milan branch, the larger of the two, is the second oldest foreign mission society in the Church. Under the direction of the hierarchy it was established in 1850 at the request of Pius IX by Angelo Ramazzotti, who later became patriarch of Venice, Italy. Pietro Avanzini (1832–74) founded the Roman branch in 1871, also at the request of Pius IX. Priests from this branch worked in the California missions at the beginning of the 20th century. One of its members, Giovanni Bonzano (1867–1927), was apostolic delegate to the U.S. from 1911 to 1922, after which he was raised to the cardinalate. The society officially came to the U.S. in 1948 when, on the advice of the Holy See, it decided to become international. Cardinal Edward MOONEY invited the fathers to establish their American headquarters in Detroit, MI. The generalate is in Rome.

[N. MAESTRINI/EDS.]

PONTIFICAL MISSION FOR PALESTINE

Founded by Pope Pius XII for the care of Palestinian refugees, presently the Holy See's relief and development agency for the entire Middle East. In the aftermath of the first Arab-Israeli wars, Pope Pius XII was concerned about the plight of more than one million Palestinians displaced or impoverished by the hostilities. He unified the Holy See's humanitarian and charitable assistance into one pontifical agency and appointed as its President the Secretary of the Catholic Near East Welfare Association.

On June 18, 1949, Eugene Cardinal Tisserant, Secretary of the Sacred Congregation for the Oriental Churches, announced the erection of the Pontifical Mission for Palestine and outlined its competence: ''. . .it has been decided to bring together under the Pontifical Mission, operating in the Holy Land, all those organizations and associations which are engaged in activities concerning the East, and which are scattered throughout many countries of Europe and other continents.''

Immediately a headquarters office was opened in Beirut, Lebanon and, following that, a local office in Jerusalem. Seven local emergency aid committees involving papal representatives, hierarchy, clergy, laity and charitable agencies were organized for Arab Palestine, Egypt, Gaza, Israel, Lebanon, Syria and Transjordan, and field staff were recruited.

In the years that followed, the Pontifical Mission not only distributed many tons of food, clothing, medical supplies, temporary shelters and cooking equipment to the newly dispossessed, but also constructed homes for those who had lost their own. An outstanding achievement of the Pontifical Mission was its encouragement and endowment of training and educational programs to enable the refugees to help themselves through newly acquired skills and trades and to accede to literacy and higher schooling.

With the Israeli occupation of the West Bank and Gaza in 1967, the Pontifical Mission moved from assisting displaced and refugee Palestinians to responding to the needs of an entire civilian population living under martial law. Besides supporting the humanitarian activities of the local churches, the Mission began to establish and subsidize social service institutions, including schools, libraries, hospitals and orphanages.

The new influx of Palestinian refugees into the Hashemite Kingdom of Jordan prompted the Mission to open an office in the capital city of Amman to provide the poor and the refugee—Jordanian and Palestinian—

with medical care, employment assistance and other social services. After the Gulf War in 1991, the Pontifical Mission also offered emergency assistance to Iraqi refugees seeking refuge in Jordan.

On the occasion of the twenty-fifth anniversary of the Pontifical Mission for Palestine in 1974, Pope Paul VI gave new impetus and new dimensions to its work:

> Our Mission for Palestine is thus about to be faced with a compelling task. In addition to continuing its assistance, without distinction of nationality or religion, to those who have suffered or are suffering in any way as a result of repeated conflicts which have devastated that region, the Mission will now have to expect, in the situation which is now evolving, to contribute to projects of aid, of rehabilitation and of development for the population of Palestine.

With the increase of civil strife in Lebanon in 1975, the beneficiaries of the Pontifical Mission there were no longer only Palestinian refugees, but Lebanese themselves too. After the cessation of hostilities in 1991, the Pontifical Mission launched—in addition to its substantial program of institutional support—a regional village rehabilitation and resettlement project.

The start of the Palestinian intifada, or uprising, in 1987 offered new challenges, as the Pontifical Mission aided grassroots organizations, providing medical assistance, agricultural aid, legal advocacy and other vital services.

Because of its modest administrative structure, its non-governmental nature and the confidence it enjoys among the local churches, the Pontifical Mission is able to act quickly, expeditiously and effectively to alleviate human suffering and aid human development. It concentrates especially on trying to meet those needs that are either too limited to be addressed by larger agencies or which fall outside of their funding guidelines.

The following have served as President of the Pontifical Mission for Palestine: Monsignor Thomas J. McMahon (1949–55); Monsignor Peter P. Tuohy (1955–60); Monsignor Joseph T. Ryan (1960–66); Monsignor John G. Nolan (1966–87); and Monsignor Robert L. Stern (1987–).

[M. J. L. LA CIVITA]

PONTIFICAL ROMAN UNIVERSITIES

This article is concerned with those institutions of higher learning in Rome that have been founded as universities by the pope or given university status by papal action. All such universities are subject to the governing structures set out in Pope John Paul II's apostolic constitution SAPIENTIA CHRISTIANA (1979) regulating ecclesiastical faculties and seminaries, together with the accompanying norms of the Sacred Congregation for Catholic Education, the Roman dicastery that has jurisdiction over them. The pontifical Roman universities provide service to the universal Church by lending their expertise to the Roman curia. While independent of one another, many of the universities share resources or are linked through agreements that have an impact on curriculum and formation of the student body. In 1991, several of the libraries of the major universities became part of the URBE (Roman Union of Ecclesiastical Libraries) network that allows students access to nearly four million volumes for specialized research.

The *Annuario Pontificio 2000* reported seventeen institutions comprising the ''Atenei Romani.'' Many of them contain specialized centers devoted to proscribed areas of study and many of these have degree-granting capabilities.

Pontificia Università Gregoriana. The Pontifical Gregorian University (PUG) is the largest of the pontifical Roman universities and is under the direction of the Society of Jesus. The prefect of the Sacred Congregation for Catholic Education is the chancellor, and the general of the Jesuit order is the vice-chancellor. Its faculties include theology, canon law, philosophy, church history, missiology, and social science. The PUG has three additional departments in spirituality, psychology, and religious studies. It also houses a school for the study of the Latin language. Finally, the PUG is home to the Pontifical Biblical Institute and the Pontifical Oriental Institute, both of which are discussed below.

The history of the PUG can be traced to St. IGNATIUS LOYOLA who, in 1551, founded the Collegium Romanum with St. Francis Borgia in what is today the Piazza d'Aracoeli. In 1555, a year before Ignatius died, the school was all but bankrupt, but in the next decade it prospered and grew. After the suppression of the Jesuit order in 1773, the Gregorian's faculty consisted mainly of alumni and secular clergy until the JESUITS were again assigned to staff the university by Pope Leo XII in 1824.

By a rescript of December 4, 1873, Pius IX granted the rector use of the title ''pontifical university.'' In 1876 the canon law faculty was added and in 1924, by his *motu proprio Latinarum litterarum,* Pius XI instituted the School of Latin Letters. His predecessor, Benedict XV, had the land for the present building set aside on the Piazza della Pilotta in 1919, although formal dedication ceremonies did not take place until 1930. By a letter of the Congregation for Catholic Education of May 20, 1958, the faculty of theology began the Institute of Spirituality. In 1970 and 1971, respectively, that same congregation established the Pontifical Institute ''Regina Mundi'' for research into societies of apostolic life and secular institutes and the Institute for Religious Studies. Also in 1971 the Institute of Psychology was established.

At the turn of the millenium, the library of the PUG contained some 1.2 million volumes, including those of the Biblicum and the PIO, for use by nearly 3,000 students and over 400 faculty. The PUG's publishing house prints books in the following series: *Analecta Gregoriana, Documenta Missionalia, Inculturation, Miscellanea Historiae Pontificiae*, and *Tesi Gregoriana*. Three periodicals are based at the Gregorian: *Gregorianum* (1920—), *Periodica de re Canonico* (1912—), and *Archivum Historiae Pontificiae* (1963—).

Pontifical Biblical Institute. The Pontifical Biblical Institute (PBI) is a university-level institution of the Holy See located on the Via della Pilotta. Its grand chancellor is the cardinal prefect for the Congregation for the Eastern Churches. Pope St. Pius X established it with the apostolic letter *Vinea electa* of May 7, 1909, in order to be ''a center of higher studies for Sacred Scripture in the city of Rome and of all related studies according to the spirit of the Catholic Church.'' From its foundation, the Institute was entrusted to the Society of Jesus, and Father L. Fonck served as organizer and first rector.

At the beginning the PBI prepared its students to take the examinations of the PONTIFICAL BIBLICAL COMMISSION. With the apostolic letter *Cum Biblia sacra* (August 15, 1916), Benedict XV authorized the institute to grant the academic degree of licence in the name of the Biblical Commission. The *motu proprio Quod maxime* (September 9, 1930) of Pius XI gave the institute academic independence from the Pontifical Biblical Commission and permitted it to grant the doctorate. With this same document, the PBI was officially associated with the Pontifical Gregorian University and the Pontifical Oriental Institute. These three institutions have the same vice-grand chancellor (the general of the Society of Jesus), but each has its own proper statutes. The grand chancellor of the institute is the prefect of the Congregation for Catholic Education. On August 7, 1932, the Faculty of Ancient Near-Eastern Studies (Oriental Faculty) was erected, with the same academic privileges accorded to the Faculty of Biblical Studies for the granting of the licentiate and doctoral degrees.

The purpose of the PBI is to cultivate and promote, by means of scholarly research, the biblical and relevant ancient near eastern disciplines, in order to obtain ''a more profound understanding and exposition of the meaning of Sacred Scripture'' (*Dei Verbum*, §12). Second, it is to offer to the students, by the teaching and the practice of these various disciplines, in particular the biblical languages, an adequate preparation both for scholarly research and for the teaching and spread of Sacred Scripture and of the disciplines connected with it. Third, it is to work toward ''a better understanding and explanation of the meaning of Sacred Scripture, so that through preparatory study the judgment of the Church may mature'' (*Dei Verbum*, §12) and that Sacred Scripture may have an ever more active role in the study of theology, in pastoral ministry, in ecumenical dialogue, in the sacred liturgy, and in the reading of the faithful. An indispensable means for the PBI to achieve this goal is a specialized library, presently at about 160,000 volumes with subscriptions to 600 periodicals. The PBI has its own publications, including the journal *Biblica,* as well as a branch in Jerusalem, which was begun in 1927 and staffed by the Society of Jesus. At 2000 the PBI had 375 students from approximately 60 nations.

Pontifical Oriental Institute. The Pontifical Oriental Institute (PIO) was founded by Benedict XV on October 15, 1917. Initially it was located in the Piazza Scossacavalli near the Ospizio dei Convertendi. It began academic life on December 2, 1918 under the rectorship of Alfredo Ildefonso Schuster, the abbot of St. Paul's Outside-the-Walls and future archbishop of Milan. In 1920 it obtained permission to grant academic degrees for studies of the eastern churches. In 1922, Pius XI entrusted the PIO to the Jesuit order and transferred it and the Pontifical Biblical Institute to the Piazza S. Maria Maggiore, though it was not until 1928 that the Gregorian ''consortium'' of the PIO, Biblicum, and university was formed. Pius XI, a former librarian of the Ambrosian library, generously supplied the library of the PIO with books pertaining to issues affecting the Eastern Churches. He continued to endow the school with leading faculty as well, largely through his exhortation *Rerum Orientalium* (1928) addressed to the world's bishops. By a decree of the Congregation for Catholic Education in 1971, the section of the Gregorian's canon law faculty pertaining to the Code of Canon Law for the Eastern Churches became its own faculty within the PIO. In 2000 the grand chancellor was the cardinal prefect of the Congregation for the Eastern Churches. Noted for studies of the Eastern Rites of the Church, the PIO has also been active as an ecumenical bridge between the Orthodox world and the Holy See. It houses a library of some 200,000 books and 2,500 periodicals. These served about 435 students in the year 2001, along with 52 faculty. The PIO publishes *Orientalia Cristiana Periodica.*

Pontificia Università Lateranense. The Pontifical Lateran University (PUL), under the chancellorship of the vicar of Rome, is organized into faculties and institutes. The four faculties are in theology, philosophy, civil law, and canon law. These last two faculties brought into being an institute that is the only one of its kind in the world, the Institutum Utriusque Iuris, for the study of both canon and civil law. It also contains the Pontifical Pastoral Institute, which has a special department for the social teaching of the Church. Formally recognized in May of 1996 by the Congregation for Catholic Education, this department can issue graduate degrees with a specialty in the Church's social doctrine. The PUL is home to the Religious Education Institute, Ecclesia Mater, which trains pastoral assistants and catechists. It was established by the Congregation for Catholic Education in 1973, and that same congregation formally approved its statutes on June 27, 1994, permitting it to grant the licentiate degree. One of the great achievements of the PUL is its publication of a 13-volume dictionary of saints, the *Bibliotheca Sanctorum* (ca. 1970), one of the most thorough reference works of its kind.

More than 30 institutes across the world are in some way linked to the Lateran, comprising a student body of over 6,000, from over 100 countries. One such institute is the Pontifical JOHN PAUL II INSTITUTE for Studies on Marriage and the Family. It was founded by John Paul II on October 7, 1982 with the apostolic constitution *Magnum Matrimonii Sacramentum*, according it the power to grant both the licentiate and doctorate with concentrations in marriage and the family. Although housed at the PUL, it is an autonomous body by statutes approved by the pope on November 21, 1992 and March 17, 1993. Its satellites have multiplied to include branches in Washington, D.C. (1988), Mexico City (1996), and Valencia, Spain (1994).

Three additional institutions are closely linked by statute with the PUL, the ''Alfonsiana,'' the ''Augustinianum,'' and the ''Claretianum.''

The Alphonsian Academy is a higher institute of moral theology founded in 1949 by the REDEMPTORISTS. On August 2, 1960, by a decree of the Sacred Congregation for Seminaries and Universities, the academy was elevated to full university status. Shortly after St. ALPHONSUS LIGUORI was proclaimed a doctor of the Church in 1871, the Redemptorists conceived the idea and began to make plans for the establishment of an institute dedicated to teaching and promoting the moral theology of St. Alphonsus. The Redemptorist General Chapter of 1894 approved a decree encouraging this. The first institute opened its doors in 1910 with six professors and 26 student priests. The faculty offered courses in dogmatic and moral theology, as well as canon law, philosophy, and Hebrew. The fledgling institute was forced to close its doors at the beginning of World War I. On February 9, 1949, Father Leonard Buijs, the Redemptorist superior general, founded the Alphonsian Academy as an internal institute of the Congregation. On March 25, 1957 the academy was formally recognized by the Vatican Congregation for Religious as a ''public internal institute'' entrusted to the Redemptorists, granting it the opportunity for extern students.

In 2001, the Alphonsian Academy was the academic home for over 287 post-graduate students, divided between the licentiate and doctoral programs. The students come from over 60 countries and all five continents. Twenty-eight professors, of whom 21 are Redemptorists, comprised the faculty. The Alphonsian Academy is responsible for publishing the journal *Studia Moralia* (1963—).

The Library of the College of St. Alphonsus was founded in 1855, when the Redemptorist Fathers opened their General House in Rome. Its modest beginning came from the legacy of Cardinal Clement Villecourt (d. 1867). By 1905, the library already contained 20,000 volumes and was considered among the best ecclesiastical libraries of Rome. In 2001 it housed almost 165,000 volumes in its collection, with its major strength continuing to be in the field of moral theology.

The Patristic Institute Augustinianum was founded in 1905 as an official organ for the general curia of the Augustinian order. It affiliated with the PUL in 1969. It is known for its distinguished publishing repertoire under the banner Analecta Augustiniana. By 1939 it had established itself as one of the leading houses for critical editions of patristic texts in philosophy and theology, as well as medieval AUGUSTINIANISM. In 1961, the periodical *Augustinianum* was begun by the Patristic Institute of the PUL, treating all aspects of Christian antiquity and the Church fathers.

The Theological Institute on the Religious Life ''Claretianum'' was affiliated with the PUL in 1972 and is in the care of the Sons of the Immaculate Heart of Mary (Claretian Fathers) on the Largo Lorenzo Mossa in Rome.

Pontificia Università Urbaniana. The Pontifical Urbanian University (PUU), the college of the Congregation for the EVANGELIZATION OF PEOPLES (Propoganda Fidei), is an international seminary with almost 90 affiliates worldwide, constituting a student body of about 11,000. Located on the Gianicolo Hill, its large complex is the center for 1,250 students in Rome, representing about 100 nations. It had 156 faculty in 2000. The grand chancellor is the cardinal prefect of the Congregation and the vice-chancellor is the secretary of that dicastery. The PUU is overseen by a rector magnificus. It is open to clerical, religious, and lay students. Its library contains some 300,000 volumes and is strong in mission studies.

The PUU offers the doctorate in theology, philosophy, missiology, and canon law. In addition to these faculties, the PUU is also home to an Institute for Missionary Catechesis, founded in 1970 by the Congregation for the Evangelization of Peoples. With the decree *Cum catechesis pars* of May 25, 1980, the Congregation for Catholic Education permitted this institute to issue baccalaureate degrees.

A number of joint programs emerged in the late 20th century. For instance, in 1986 the faculties of canon law and missiology began a joint venture. Similarly, by decree of the Congregation for Catholic Education, April 12, 1999, the faculty of missiology was given charge of the Higher Institute for Catechesis and Missionary Spirituality ''Redemptoris Missio'' in response to the John Paul II's encyclical letter of the same name.

Since 1949 there have been special sections devoted to languages, particularly those of Asian origin. In 1960, by university statute, the faculty of philosophy was placed in charge of administering the Higher Institute for the Study of Beliefs, Religion, and Culture. This institute, in turn, oversees two centers, one for the study of Chinese and the other, more generally, the Cardinal Newman Center, both of which were begun in 1975. John Henry Cardinal Newman was a student at the Urbaniana while preparing for ordination in 1847.

The PUU also boasts its own publishing organ, the Urbaniana University Press, founded on April 19, 1979. In addition to a book list, the press prints the theological journal *Euntes Docete.*

Pontificia Università di S. Tommaso d'Aquino in Urbe (Angelicum). The Pontifical University of St. Thomas in Rome, known as the Angelicum, is under the direction of the Order of Preachers (DOMINICANS). The master general of these friars is the grand chancellor. The Angelicum is the descendent of the medieval *studium* of the Dominican Order in Rome. Beginning in 1698, it had at its disposition the Biblioteca Casanatense. In 1906, Pope Pius X changed the title of the College of Saint Thomas to the Pontifical Angelicum College, and allowed for the recognition of its academic degrees. In 1908, Father Hyacinth Cormier, master of the Order of Preachers, erected the Pontifical International College ''Angelicum.'' Officials of the Italian government occupied the old building, constructed by Pius V, from 1873 to 1908, while the College of Saint Thomas operated on Via San Vitale. The government took control of the rich collection of manuscripts, palimpsests, and incunabula of the Biblioteca Casanatense. As part of a deal with Italian dictator Mussolini in 1931, a newer building was exchanged for the monastery's library. It has since grown to nearly a half million volumes.

In 1950 and 1955, respectively, the Institute of Spirituality and Social Sciences were added to the Angelicum. Founded in 1950 by Father Paul Philippe, OP (c. 1984), the Institute of Spirituality was approved by the Congregation for Seminaries and Educational Institutions on May 1, 1958. On March 7, 1963 (the feast of Saint Thomas), Pope John XXIII raised the school to the rank of a pontifical university through his *motu proprio Dominicianus ordo.* In the same year, a section of the theology faculty dedicated to ecumenism and patristics was erected in Bari, and in 1964, the Higher Institute of Religious Sciences Mater Ecclesiae, directed in particular to the laity, was annexed. In 1972, the Congregation for Catholic Education granted the Mater Ecclesiae power to issue graduate degrees. On Nov. 25, 1974, that same congregation allowed the Institute of Social Sciences to become a full-fledged university faculty.

Pope Paul VI visited the university in the spring of 1974 for the closing of the International Congress marking the 700th anniversary of the death of Saint Thomas. In his address, the pope emphasized the relevance of Thomism in the modern world, a position echoed by his successor, John Paul II, in his encyclical letter *Fides et ratio* (§§ 43–44). In 1983, the Institute of Saint Thomas was established to promote the study of the works of the Angelic Doctor. The school's periodical, *Angelicum,* continues this exploration of St. Thomas's thought.

Pontificia Università Salesiana. The Pontifical Salesian University is under the care of the Society of St. Don Bosco (Salesians). The head of the Salesian order is the grand chancellor. The school's rector, also a Salesian, oversees the faculties of theology, canon law, philosophy, education, and social communication. By his *motu proprio Magisterium vitae* of May 24, 1973, Paul VI elevated the Ateneo Salesiàno to university status and granted it the title ''pontifical.'' In 2001 the library of the Salesiana contained around 700,000 volumes and the largest number of serials in the URBE network, approximately 4,800 titles. These serve the needs of nearly 200 professors and over 1,600 students.

Among the oldest of the university's faculties is the education department, begun and shepherded by the Brazilian Salesian Carlos Leóncio da Silva, dean from 1940 to 1952. Paul VI made the Higher Institute for Pedagogy into a full-fledged faculty of education studies. The pope took the occasion to link the importance of the faculty with the charisma of Don Bosco. Education continues to be of prime interest to the university, as typified by the important collective work by this faculty, the three-volume *Enciclopedia delle Scienze dell'Educazione* and the *Dizionario di Scienze dell'educazione* (1997).

By a decree of the Congregation for Catholic Education, dated June 29, 1986, the Higher Institute for Religious Studies ''Magisterium Vitae'' was granted the power to award graduate degrees. On May 27, 1998, that same congregation elevated the Institute for the Study of Social Communications, created in 1988, to a permanent faculty.

The faculty of Christian letters and classics includes a Pontifical Higher Institute for Latin. Though recognized independently in the *Annuario Pontificio,* it is actually semi-autonomous. Its impetus was Pope John XXIII's apostolic constitution *Verum Sapientia* (art. 6) and made concrete by the action of Paul VI in his creation of the Pontificium Institutum Altioris Latinitatis through his *motu proprio Studia latinitatis* of Feb. 22, 1964. The institute's status was remanded to the Congregation for Catholic Education, which eventually wed it to the philosophy faculty of the Salesianum in 1971.

Pontificia Università della Santa Croce. The Pontifical University of the Holy Cross is under the care of the personal prelature of OPUS DEI. The grand chancellor of the university is the prelate of Opus Dei. The university is the realization of a desire of Blessed Josemaría ESCRIVÁ, the founder of Opus Dei, to promote a Roman educational institution at the service of the whole Church. Blessed Josemaría's successor, Monsignor Alvaro del PORTILLO, sought the approval of the Holy See for the project. This it granted by a decree of the Congregation for Catholic Education on Jan. 9, 1985, erecting the Centro Academico Romano della Santa Croce and linking it to the canon law faculty of the University of Navarra. Five years later to the day, this same congregation canonically erected the Ateneo Romano della Santa Croce, conferring upon it the right to grant academic degrees in theology and philosophy. On March 28, 1993 the canon law faculty was erected and on June 26, 1995 Pope John Paul II raised this institution to the status of a pontifical college. By a similar act of July 15, 1998, he bestowed on it the title pontifical university. At the turn of the millennium, the university had faculties of theology, canon law, philosophy, and the communications of social institutions, the latter of which was erected on Feb. 26, 1996, and given the power to grant licentiate and doctorate degrees. The Higher Institute of Religious Studies ''Apollinare'' has been subsumed within the theology department and has a faculty specializing in distance learning. It was established as a university entity on Sept. 17, 1986, but it was not until an act of the Congregation for Catholic Education on June 10, 1998 that it was enabled to grant graduate degrees in religious studies.

The faculty publishes *Annales Theologici, Ius Ecclesiae, Apollinare Studi,* and *Acta Philosophica.* The student body, which for the academic year 1999 and 2000 numbered nearly 1,300, was drawn from over 60 countries. Of these, 541 students were in the Apollinare. Aptly, the university campus is in the Palazzo di Sant'Apollinare. Both Pius XII and John XXIII were students in the Apollinare, from 1895 to 1903 and from 1901 to 1905, respectively. The library is housed in the via di Farnesi, near the Church of St. Girolamo della Carità, and possesses some 75,000 volumes.

Pontificia Ateneo di S. Anselmo. The College of Sant'Anselmo in Rome (Anselmianum) is an institute of theological studies operated by the Cassinese Congregation of the Order of Saint Benedict. Its grand chancellor is the Abbot Primate of the Benedictine confederation. Founded in the 17th century, it was granted the right to confer academic degrees by Leo XIII on Aug. 20, 1891. This was confirmed by Pope Piux X in his *motu proprio Praeclara inter opera* of June 24, 1914, in which he decreed ''that the College of Sant'Anselmo, like the other academies of Rome, should have the privilege of conferring all academic degrees in philosophy, sacred theology, and canon law upon both diocesan and religious seminarians.''

The Monastic Institute was erected as a division of the Faculty of Theology by decree of the Sacred Congregation for Seminaries and Universities on March 21, 1952. Among its faculty have been such noted scholars as K. Hallinger, B. Steidle, J. Leclercq, B. Studer, J. Gribomont, and A. de Vogüé. Since 1977 its program of teaching and research has concentrated on the preparation of students for the licentiate and doctorate in monastic studies. The institute also attempts to respond to the new demands of monasteries and of the Church by extending its interests to the study of Eastern monasticism, to ecumenical concerns, and to the emerging communities of Africa, Asia, and Latin America.

The Pontifical Liturgical Institute was erected by a decree of June 17, 1961 with its own statutes. By a decree of the Congregation for Catholic Education on Dec. 8, 1977, the Pontifical Liturgical Institute was incorporated into the Abbey of Santa Giustina in Padua and remains an affiliate of the campus in Rome. With a decree of Aug. 23, 1978, that same congregation raised the Pontifical Liturgical Institute to the level of a faculty with the authority to grant the license (SL.L.) and doctorate (SL.D.) in sacred liturgy. The general statutes of the Athenaeum and those of the faculties of philosophy, sacred theology, and sacred liturgy were approved by the Congregation for Catholic Education on April 21, 1987. Beginning in 1970, the theology faculty offered courses leading to the license and doctorate with specializations in sacramental theology. In the academic year 1997 and 1998, the faculty of philosophy began a new cycle leading to the license and doctorate with a specialization in philosophy and mysticism. A number of seminary programs in Italy are affiliated with the Anselmianum. In 2001 its library numbered approximately 100,000 volumes, serving about 400 faculty and students.

Pontificio Ateneo ''Antonianum.'' The Pontifical College ''Antonianum'' is under the care of the Friars Minor, with the minister general of these FRANCISCANS as grand chancellor. The vicar-general of the order is the vice-chancellor. The initial college, founded in 1887, was formally created the Collegium S. Antonii Patavini in Urbe by Leo XIII in 1890. In more recent times, the Antonianum has grown to include two off-site institutes, more notable of which is its house of biblical studies in Jerusalem. This Franciscan Biblicum's statutes were redrawn on Feb. 28, 1989 to reflect the changes brought on by the apostolic constitution *Sapientia Christiana.* Additionally, there is the Institute for Ecumenical Studies in Venice. The theology faculty allows its students to specialize in dogmatics, spirituality, evangelization, moral theology, church history, and Franciscan history. On site, the Franciscan Institute of Spirituality (coordinated with the Capuchin friars), the Higher School for the Study of Medieval and Franciscan History, and the Higher Institute for Religious Studies ''Redemptor Hominis,'' comprise additional institutes within the college. The Higher School for the Study of Medieval and Franciscan History is a member of the International Federation of Institutes for Medieval Studies (F.I.D.E.M.). The ''Redemptor Hominis,'' so named for John Paul II's first encyclical letter, was begun in 1982, but it was canonically erected by the Congregation for Catholic Education on July 31, 1986. It seeks to bring ''intelligence to the faith'' in the training of catechists and others in pastoral service. Lastly, the International Scotist Commission, producing critical editions of the works of John DUNS SCOTUS, is located at the Antonianum.

The library possesses nearly half a million volumes, with particular strengths in Franciscana. It boasts a large number of incunabula that are, as of the year 2001, at the disposal of about 460 students and 110 professors. The multi-lingual periodical *Antonianum* has been published quarterly since 1926, giving special attention to sacred scripture, theology (dogmatic, moral, and pastoral), history (of the Church, of theology, of spirituality), canon law, philosophy, the human sciences, and especially medieval and Franciscan studies.

Pontificio Ateneo ''Regina Apostolorum.'' Directed by the LEGIONARIES OF CHRIST, the Pontifical Athenaeum ''Regina Apostolorum'' was canonically erected by the Congregation for Catholic Education on Sept. 15, 1993, with a faculty of theology and philosophy. The superior general of the Legionaries is the grand chancellor and the Athenaeum is overseen by a ''retorre magnifico.'' On July 11, 1998, John Paul II granted it the title ''pontifical.'' It maintains an information center on the human sciences and a center for telecommunications. On April 23, 1999, the Congregation for Catholic Education erected the Higher Institute for Religious Studies ''Regina Apostolorum'' within the theology faculty and gave it the power to grant the graduate degree *Magisterium in Scientiis Religiosis.*

The Regina Apostolorum encourages certain pious devotions among its students and faculty, which at the turn of the millennium numbered 529 and 59, respectively. On the first Friday of each month, the Athenaeum community is invited to participate in adoration of the Blessed Sacrament which is solemnly exposed in the chapel. This adoration is offered for the special intentions of the Holy Father. Also, a plenary indulgence may be obtained (under the normal conditions) by visiting the Athenaeum Chapel on March 25 (Feast of the Annunciation), September 15 (Feast of the Virgin of Sorrows), December 12 (Feast of Our Lady of Guadalupe), December 25 (Feast of the Nativity of Our Lord), and on the Solemnity of the Sacred Heart.

Presently, the library of the Athenaeum contains more than 102,000 volumes and receives over 400 different publications. The library was enriched in 1993 by the acquisition of the De la Torre Villar Latin American collection consisting of over 13,000 volumes. The faculty publish a multilingual journal titled *Alpha and Omega.*

Pontificio Istituto di Musica Sacra. Located on the Via di Torre Rossa, the institute offers various music and liturgical disciplines—for instance, organography and Gregorian chant—with particular attention given to the practical, theoretical, and historical aspects expressed in the diverse cultures that comprise the Church. It trains musicians and forms teachers of sacred music for service around the world. The grand chancellor is the cardinal prefect of the Congregation for Catholic Education. It has an honorary president and a rector and a faculty of some 20 church musicians.

The institute offers the baccalaureate, the license, and the master's degree in a specialized field. Courses leading to the doctoral degree are also offered. The library is structured to cater to the needs of didactic liturgical activities, as well as for research within the institute. The reading room now occupies the spacious areas previously used by the Commission for the New Vulgate.

Pontificio Istituto di Archeologia Cristiana. The Pontifical Institute of Christian Archeology was created by the *motu proprio I primitivi cemeteri* of Pius XI on Dec. 11, 1925. Its grand chancellor is the cardinal prefect of the Congregation for Catholic Education. In the year 2000, it was the only institute of all the Atenei Romani that had a lay person as rector. Located on the Via Napoleone III, this institute has a fivefold mission. First, it is to gather and place at the researcher's disposal all those tools that will permit the scientific study of monuments and early Christian institutions (photographs, reproductions, books, journals, etc.). Second, it seeks to promote the scientific study of the ancient world generally and the antiquities of Christian Rome in particular. Third, the institute must develop new methodologies for the study of the Christian monuments of Rome, especially in their application to knowledge of the meanings of visible objects. These methodologies may be undertaken either in personal research questions, the exploration of the teaching of sacred archaeology or the institutions of the early Church, or conservation techniques. Fourth, the institute publishes the *Revista di Archeologia Cristiana* (1926—), together with important monographs on catacombs, monuments, inscriptions, pictures, and sculpture relative to early Christianity. Fifth, it acts as the center for the promotion of the International Congress of Christian Archeology, which meets occasionally in various cities.

Students in this institute enroll in a three-year course for the doctorate. A second course of studies, lasting one year, allows one to obtain a certificate.

Pontificia Facoltà Teologica "San Bonaventura" (Seraphicum). The Theological Faculty of St. Bonaventure is under the direction of the Friars Minor Conventual in Rome. Its patrons are St. ANTHONY OF PADUA (the Evangelical Doctor) and St. BONAVENTURE of Bagnoregio (the Seraphic Doctor), for whom the faculty is named. Erected on June 24, 1905 as the Collegio Serafico Internazionale di San Francesco, the faculty has its roots in the "studi generali" of the Franciscan order. It is thereby the oldest of all the Roman faculties, with its first impulse arising from Franciscan Minister General Elias of Assisi in 1236 and later Alexander of Hales, although it does not possess an unbroken tenure. After the suppression of religious orders in 1873 by the Italian government, it would be 37 years before the Franciscans could re-engage their work.

On July 15, 1561, through his apostolic letter *Ut ampliores et uberiores fructus,* Pius IV allowed the minister general of the Friars Minor Conventual to permit his faculty to grant the master's degree in the arts and theology. When Sixtus V formally inaugurated the faculty as a Roman college in 1587, he ennobled it with a cardinal protector. Sixtus V, himself a Conventual Franciscan, desired the college to concentrate on the thought of St. Bonaventure, later writing this into the college's statutes by the decree *Cum nuper* of April 13, 1590. In 1629, a number of Franciscan studia were granted the power to confer the doctorate, including the house in Rome. Extern students were allowed to enroll when the Congregation for Catholic Education approved the faculty's new statutes on March 14, 1973.

Among its distinguished alumni are Lorenzo Ganganelli, who would become Pope Clement XIV (d. 1774), and St. Maximillian Kolbe, who attended from 1912 to 1919. The present site of the Seraphicum is a short distance from the location of St. Paul's martyrdom. The building was formally inaugurated on January 4, 1964. The minister general of the Friars Minor Conventual is the grand chancellor. The faculty maintains a number of affiliations with other Franciscan institutes in Italy and abroad.

Pontificia Facoltà Teologica e Pontificio Instituto di Spiritualità "Teresianum." The Pontifical Faculty of Theology and the Pontifical Institute of Spirituality "Teresianum" are directed by the Discalced CARMELITES of Saints Teresa of Jesus and John of the Cross. The general of the Discalced Carmelite order is the grand chancellor. Through the efforts of the order's superior, William of St. Albert (1878–1947), and at the behest of previous general chapters, the college opened on November 14, 1926 for the theological and spiritual formation of postulants. In 1935 the faculty was authorized to grant licentiate and doctoral degrees in sacred theology. Two of the Carmelite fathers general, Siverio of St. Teresa (1878–1954) and his predecessor, Pier Thomas of the Virgin of Carmel (1896–1946), were able to construct the present campus in the Piazza San Pancrazio in 1954, with a solemn inauguration occurring in April of 1955.

In 1973 a revision of the Teresianum's statutes was approved by the Congregation for Catholic Education, permitting students to specialize either in theological anthropology, unique among the Atenei Romani, or spirituality, through the Institute of Spirituality. This institute, originally founded in 1957, was the hope of Father Gabriel of St. Mary Magdalene (d. 1953) and the Carmelite General Chapter of 1955. The Institute of Spirituality was canonically linked to the theology faculty on Sept. 8, 1964, by the Congregation for Seminaries and Universities. Thereafter it was empowered to grant the license and doctorate in sacred theology with a specialization in spiritual theology. For many years, the institute grew more autonomous from the rest of the Teresianum, both by virtue of its specialization and its statutory construction. Under the norms of the apostolic constitution *Sapientia Christiana,* the institute sought to re-establish its old links to the rest of the faculty, and on April 8, 1988, the Congregation for Catholic Education formally acknowledged the ''Pontificia Facoltà Teologica Teresianum e l'Istituto di Spiritualità.''

On April 28, 1987 the Congregation for Catholic Education incorporated the International Institute of Pastoral Theology Camillianum into the Teresianum. This is under the direction of the Camillians, who minister to the infirm. The same congregation aggregated to the Teresianum the Pontifical Faculty Studium de Notre Dame de Vie, with its center in Venasque, France, on Sept. 21, 1993, as well as the Theological Institute Leoniano di Anagni on June 21, 1995.

The Teresianum's library was started in 1735, when the headquarters of the Discalced Carmelites in the convent of Santa Maria della Scala was situated in the Palazzo Barberini. In 1896 it received a major gift when Cardinal Raffaele Monaco La Valletta bequeathed to it his library. Similarly, the two Carmelite cardinals, Gerolamo Maria Gotti (d. 1916) and Adeodato Giovanni Piazza (d. 1957), provided significant accessions from their personal collections. In 2001 the library possessed some 350,000 volumes, with important collections on Discalced Carmelite missions and spirituality.

Pontificia Facoltà Teologica ''Marianum.'' The Pontifical Faculty of Theology ''Marianum'' is an academic institution entrusted to the care of the Order of the Servants of Mary (the SERVITES). The prior general of the Servite order is the grand chancellor. On Jan. 1, 1971, with the decree of the Congregation for Catholic Education ''Theologicas Collegii S. Alexi Falconierii Scholas,'' the faculty received the title ''pontifical.'' It conferred all the rights granted to other pontifical universities and faculties, including permission to grant academic degrees with specializations in Mariology.

The faculty seeks to promote Christian theological reflection on the figure of the Virgin Mary through the six degree programs that it offers: a two-year certificate program in Marian theology; a three-year baccalaureate in theology; a two-year master's program in theology specializing in Marian theology; a doctoral program in theology specializing in Marian theology; a two-year certificate program in religious studies; and a two-year certificate program in the history and spirituality of the Order of the Servants of Mary. In 2000 it was home to 47 professors and 215 students, both clerical and lay.

Founded in 1950, the Marianum library is the successor of two previous Servite theological libraries in Rome, namely, the Henry of Ghent College library (1666–1870) and that of its successor school, Saint Alexis Falconieri International College library (1895–1950). In 1917 the Servants of Mary formalized a Marian section in the Saint Alexis library as part of an International Marian Center. As the library of the Marianum Pontifical Faculty of Theology, the Marian collection became its primary concern. By 2000 it numbered about 20,000 volumes and was one of the world's largest collections on the subject. In 1946 Pius XII placed about 3,000 volumes dealing with Marian subjects in the custody of the library. In 1956 Pius XII gave the library all of the documentation sent to the Holy See on the occasion of the Marian Year of 1954. In August of 1988, the Holy See's secretary of state gave the library the archive of the Consilium Primarium Anno Mariali, pertaining to the Marian Year of 1987 and 1988. Another section, while incomplete, nevertheless contains the largest amount of material on the Servite order in the world. In 2001, the library had a collection of about 105,000 books and close to 1,400 serials.

The faculty publishes the journal *Marianum,* founded in 1939 by Fr. Gabriele M. Roschini, O.S.M. as a multi-lingual periodical concentrating on Marian theology, especially from the Christological, ecclesiological, and ecumenical perspectives, and studies of the figure of Mary in doctrinal, historico-cultural, literary, and artistic aspects.

Pontificio Istituto di Studi Arabi e d'Islamistica. The Pontifical Institute of Arab and Islamic Studies began in Tunisia in 1926 and was canonically erected by the Congregation for Seminaries and Universities on March 19, 1960. It is directed by the Missionaries of Africa. The cardinal prefect of the Congregation for Catholic Education is the grand chancellor and the superior general of the Missionaries of Africa is the vice-chancellor. It was given the title ''Institut Pontifical d'Etudes Orientales'' and charged with developing pastoral sensitivities among clergy and laity to the Arabic language and letters, as well as the religion and institutions of Islam. In 1964 it was transferred to Rome, where later the Holy See renamed it the ''Pontificio Istituto di Studi Arabi.'' It is located on the Viale di Trastevere. The Congregation for Catholic Education, through decrees of May 18, 1965; May 19, 1966; and May 25, 1980, enabled the institute to confer the doctorate under the norms of its statutes.

Pontificia Facoltà di Scienze dell'Educazione ''Auxilium.'' The Pontifical Faculty of the Science of Education ''Auxilium'' was canonically erected by the Congregation for Catholic Education under the name of the ''Instituto delle Figlie di Maria Ausiliatrice'' on June 27, 1970. At the end of 1954, the original Instituto delle Figlie di Maria Ausiliatrice was founded in Torino as the International Institute of Pedagogy and Religious

Studies. It was reconstituted by the Congregation for Religious on July 13, 1956. On Jan. 31, 1966, through a decree of the Congregation for Seminaries and Universities, this institute was incorporated into the Higher Institute for Pedagogy at the Pontificio Ateneo Salesiano in Rome. It was made juridically and academically autonomous by statute in 1970. However, it has kept its links to the Salesianum insofar as the institute's grand chancellor is the major rector of the Society of Don Bosco, who is also the grand chancellor of the Salesianum. In 1978 the faculty occupied a site in Rome along the Via Cremolina. On July 25, 1986, the Auxilium was given power to confer the graduate degree of "Magisterium in Scientiis Religiosis" within the Higher Institute for Religious Studies. In 2000 there were 53 faculty members and 364 students enrolled. The library collection numbered about 50,000 volumes, with 663 periodicals.

Bibliography: Gregorian. *Annuaria Pontifica* (2000): 1833–1835, 2008. P. CARAMAN, *University of the Nations: The Story of the Gregorian University with Its Associated Institutes, the Biblical and Oriental, 1551–1962* (New York 1981). E. DES PLACES, "L'Institut Biblique de Rome," *La Nouvelle Revue des Deux Mondes* (October 1975). E. G. FARRUGIA, *The Pontifical Oriental Institute: The First Seventy-Five Years, 1917–1992* (Rome 1993). C. GALLAGHER, "Cenni storici sulla Facoltà di Dritto Canonico," *Periodica de Re Morali, Canonica, Liturgica* 66 (1977): 407–421. Lateran. *Annuaria Pontifica* (2000): 1835–1837, 2009. Urbaniana. *ibid.*, 1837, 2010. Angelicum. *ibid.*, 1838, 2010–2011. Salesianum. *ibid.*, 1838–1839, 2011. J. E. VECCHI, *Decreto di Pormulgazione degli Statuti dell'Università Pontificia Salesiana*, Prot. N. 01/2000, with accompanying "Statuti Generali" (Rome 2000). Santa Croce. *Annuaria Pont.* (2000): 1839, 2012. Anselmianum. *ibid.*, 1840, 2012–2013. G. J. BÉKÉS, ed., *Sant'Anselmo: Saggi storici e di attualità* (Rome 1988). P. ENGELBERT, *Geschichte des Benediktinerkollegs St. Anselm in Rom: von den Anfägen (1888) bis zur Gegenwart* (Rome 1988). Antonianum. *Annuaria Pontontifica* (2000): 1840–1841, 2013. *Pontificium Athenaeum Antonianum ab origine ad praesens* (Rome 1970). Regina Apotolorum. *Annuaria Pontontifica* (2000): 1841, 2013. Pontifical Higher Institute of Latin and Faculty of Christian Letters and Classics. *ibid.*, 1841, 2014. Pontifical Institute of Sacred Music. *ibid.*,1841–1842, 2014. Pontifical Institute of Christian Archeology. *ibid.*, 1842, 2014–2015. Seraphicum. *ibid.*, 31842, 2015. Teresianum. *ibid.*, 1842–1843, 2016. *Statuta Facultatis Theologicae Collegii Internationalis SS. Teresiae a Iesu et Ioannis a Cruce Ordinis Carmelitarum Discalceatorum Romae,* 1936. Marianum. *Annuaria Pontontifica* (2000): 1843, 2016. Pontifical Institute for Arab and Islamic Studies. *ibid.*, pp. 1843, 2017. Auxilium. *ibid.*, 1844, 2017.

[M. J. COSTELLOE/P. J. HAYES]

PONTIGNY, ABBEY OF

Second daughter abbey of CÎTEAUX (Lat., *Pontiniacum*), founded in 1114 in France in the former Diocese of Auxerre (the present Diocese of Sens). The first abbot, Hugh of Mâcon, entered Cîteaux with St. BERNARD and later became bishop of Auxerre (1136). The second abbot, Guichard, was archbishop of Lyons in 1165. William, archbishop of Bourges in 1199, had been a monk at Pontigny. Between 1160 and 1240, three archbishops from Canterbury in conflict with the English king found refuge at Pontigny: THOMAS BECKET (1164), STEPHEN LANGTON (1207), and EDMUND OF ABINGDON (1240); the last-named was buried at Pontigny and his grave became the object of pilgrimage. As a result of war, the abbey experienced serious financial difficulties. Conditions had begun to improve under the last abbot when the French Revolution broke out. The buildings were sold, the abbey church became a parish church, and the cult of St. Edmund was reestablished. The buildings were occupied for a time by the Fathers of the Society of Saint Edmond; later (1910–39) Paul Desjardins bought and restored the buildings for his *Union pour la verité,* a moral, areligious movement that inspired especially the *Nouvelle revue française*. Then, after having sheltered a Franco-American college, they became in 1952 the seat of a prelate *nullius* of the *Mission de France.*

Bibliography: "Historia Pontiniacensis monasterii," E. MARTÈNE and U. DURAND, *Thesaurus novus anecdotorum,* 5 v. (Paris 1717) 3:1221–66. C. É. CHAILLOU DES BARRES, *L'Abbaye de Pontigny* (Paris 1844). G. FONTAINE, *Pontigny, abbaye cistercienne* (Paris 1928). A. MOREAU, *Pontigny, de l'abbaye cistercienne au collége franco-américain* (Paris 1950). A. A. KING, *Cîteaux and Her Elder Daughters* (London 1954) 148–206.

[M. A. DIMIER]

PONTILLO, EGIDIO MARIA DI SAN GIUSEPPE, ST.

Baptized Francesco Antonio, also known as Giles Mary of St. Joseph, Franciscan lay brother; b. Nov. 16, 1729, near Taranto (Apulia), Italy; d. Feb. 7, 1812, Naples. He practiced his father's trade of rope making and supported the family with this skill after his father's death (1747). Before entering the Alcantarine Franciscans at Galatone, Lecce, Italy (1754) under the impetus of an extraordinary spiritual experience, he led a very devout life and participated zealously in the activities of the Sodality of Our Lady of the Rosary. From 1759 to 1812 Egidio lived at the friary of San Paolo a Chiara in Naples, where he labored as cook, porter, and alms gatherer (*quaestor*). His simplicity and serenity won him the affection of the Neapolitan sick and poor, among whom he propagated devotion to Mary and Joseph. He was beatified Feb. 5, 1888, and canonized by John Paul II at Rome, June 2, 1996.

Feast: Feb. 7.

Bibliography: P. COCO, *Cenni della vita del beato Egidio Maria di S. Giuseppe, taumaturgo di Taranto* (Taranto 1931). M.A.

HABIG, *The Franciscan Book of Saints* (Chicago 1959): 89–92. V. MUSARDO TALÒ, *S. Egidio Pontillo da Taranto: dalla marina tarantina a quella di Napoli* (Lecce, Italy 1996). *Acta ordinis minorum* (1888): 7:18–20.

[C. J. LYNCH]

PONTIUS OF BALMEY, BL.

Carthusian, bishop of Belley; d. Meyriat, France, Dec. 13, 1140. Of noble lineage, Pontius (Ponce) became a canon and schoolman at Lyons. In 1116, deeding his own property for the purpose, he founded the charterhouse of Meyriat, entered the CARTHUSIAN Order, and made his profession at the Abbey of La Grande-Chartreuse. Two years later Pontius was named prior at Meyriat, and in 1121 he was elected bishop of Belley. About 1134, however, he resigned from his see and returned to Meyriat to spend his last days in solitude. The theological works attributed to him by the anonymous author of a late 12th-century vita are lost.

Feast: Dec. 13.

Bibliography: *Bibliotheca hagiographica latina antiquae et mediae aetatis* (Brussels 1898–1901) 2:6895. L. LE VASSEUR, *Ephemerides ordinis Cartusiensis* 4 (1892) 492–496. É. BROUETTE, *Lexikon für Theologie und Kirche*, ed. J. HOFER and K. RAHNER (Freiberg 1957–65) 8:615.

[O. J. BLUM]

PONTIUS OF FAUCIGNY, BL.

Abbot; b. early 12th century; d. Abbey of Sixt, Savoy (now in Switzerland), Nov. 26, 1178. From a noble family of Savoy, Pontius (or Ponce) entered the Abbey of ABONDANCE near Chablais as a CANON regular of St. Augustine at about 20 years of age. He revised the constitutions of this foundation and was instrumental in the organization of a daughterhouse at Sixt, in Savoy, of which he was made the first abbot (1144). In 1154 he saw to the elevation of the Priory of Entremont to the status of an abbey. After about 26 years at Sixt, Pontius was elected in 1171 to succeed Burchard as abbot of Abondance. The following year he raised Grandval to the rank of an abbey. After a few years he resigned his office and returned to Sixt to die a simple monk. On Nov. 14, 1620, FRANCIS DE SALES, bishop of Geneva, who held the abbot in high esteem, opened his tomb and arranged for the translation of his relics to the abbey church. Pope LEO XIII confirmed his cult in 1896.

Feast: Nov. 26.

Bibliography: *Gallia Christiana* (Paris 1715–85; 1856–65) 16:500–501. *Acta Sanctae Sedis* (Rome 1865–1908) 29 (1896–97) 440–441. N. V. L. ALBERT, *Le Bx. Ponce de Faucigny* (Annecy 1904). A. BUTLER, *The Lives of the Saints*, rev. ed. H. THURSTON and D. ATTWATER (New York 1956) 4:426–427. J. L. BAUDOT and L. CHAUSSIN, *Vies des saints et des bienheureux selon l'ordre du calendrier avec l'historique des fêtes*, ed. by the Benedictines of Paris (Paris 1935–56) 11:881–882.

Cloister at Abbaye de Pontigny, France, 16th century. (© Bob Krist/CORBIS)

[B. J. COMASKEY]

POOR CHILD JESUS, SISTERS OF THE

(PCJ, Official Catholic Directory #3220); founded, 1844 at Aachen, Germany, by Mother Clara FEY for the care and education of children and young people. The constitutions were based on the Augustinian Rule and were approved definitively by Rome in 1888. Assisting in the foundation and early spread of the congregation were Bishop Laurent; André Fey, brother of the foundress; and Wilhelm Sartorius, her spiritual director and composer of the first rule. The congregation, expanded

Poor Clares, detail from "St. Clare Grieving Over the Body of St. Francis," by Giotto, Upper Church, Basilica of San Francesco, Assisi, Italy, 1300. (©Elio Ciol/CORBIS)

from the Rhineland throughout Germany, Austria, and Luxembourg. The sisters who were expelled from Germany during the KULTURKAMPF went to Holland, Belgium, France, and England. Upon their return, they reoccupied their former houses. During the 20th century new foundations were made in Italy, Spain, Latvia, Java, and the Americas. The sisters established their first American house at Parkersburg, West Virginia, in 1924. The generalate is at Simpelveld, Holland; the U.S. headquarters is in Columbus, Ohio.

Bibliography: I. WATTEROT, *The Life of Mother Clare Fey* (St. Louis 1923).

[J. SOLZBACHER/EDS.]

POOR CLARES

An order of contemplative nuns, originally called the Poor Ladies, founded at Assisi, Italy, in 1212. They comprised the Second Order of St. Francis and took their inspiration from him, under the leadership of St. CLARE OF ASSISI. At 18 years of age Clare received the habit from the hands of FRANCIS OF ASSISI in the Portiuncula (now incorporated into the basilica of St. Mary of the Angels in Assisi). After a sojourn with Benedictine nuns, Clare and her followers were established by Francis in the convent of San Damiano near Assisi, where she remained until her death in 1253. Her followers subsequently became known under various titles, among which the more prominent are: Poor Clares (PC), the Order of St. Clare (OSC), and Poor Clares of St. Colette (PCC).

See Also: FRANCISCANS, SECOND ORDER.

[H. F. ASCHMANN]

POOR HANDMAIDS OF JESUS CHRIST

(PHJC, Official Catholic Directory #3230); known also as the Ancilla Domini Sisters, a congregation of religious women founded in 1851 at Dernbach bei Montabaur, Germany, by Katharina KASPER (Mother Mary), with the sanction of Bp. Peter Joseph Blum of Limburg. When the foundress died in 1898, the congregation numbered 2,000 members and staffed 193 missions in Germany, Holland, England, and the U.S. The rules and constitutions of the Poor Handmaids, modeled on those of St. Vincent de Paul, received temporary papal approval in 1870 and were finally confirmed by Leo XIII.

In 1868, at the request of Bp. John Henry Luers of Fort Wayne, IN, the congregation made a foundation in his diocese at Hessen Cassel, where the sisters engaged in teaching and home nursing. Within a year they had established their motherhouse and a hospital (St. Joseph's) in Fort Wayne, with Sister M. Rose as first provincial. From it were founded St. Anne's and St. Elizabeth's in Chicago, IL; St. Mary Mercy, Gary, IN; St. Catherine's, East Chicago, IN; St. Mary's, East St. Louis, IL; and smaller institutions in Indiana, Wisconsin, and Minnesota. The congregation's Angel Guardian Orphanage in Chicago was opened in 1868 and early adopted the cottage system.

In the U.S., the congregation is involved in academic education at all levels, child care, healthcare, retirement homes, parish ministries, and retreats. The generalate is in Dernbach, Westerwald, Germany. Since 1922 the American motherhouse and novitiate has been located in Donaldson, IN.

Bibliography: G. T. MEAGHER, *With Attentive Ear and Courageous Heart: A Biography of Mother Mary Kasper* (Milwaukee 1957).

[M. H. BOLL/EDS.]

POOR SERVANTS OF THE MOTHER OF GOD

(SMG, Official Catholic Directory #3640); founded, 1869, in London by Frances Margaret TAYLOR, aided by Lady Georgiana Fullerton (1812–85). The congregation, which follows an adaptation of the rule of the JESUITS, received final papal approval in 1900. It engages in a variety of apostolic works. When the foundress died in 1900, there were 12 houses. The sisters came to the U.S. in 1947. In the U.S., the sisters are engaged in education, healthcare, pastoral ministries, retreats and spiritual direction. The motherhouse is in London, England; the U.S. headquarters is in High Point, NC.

Bibliography: F. C. DEVAS, *Mother Mary Magdalen of the Sacred Heart* (London 1927).

[M. GERALDINE/EDS.]

POOR SISTERS OF JESUS CRUCIFIED AND THE SORROWFUL MOTHER

A diocesan congregation (CJC; Official Catholic Directory 3240) founded in Pennsylvaniaby the Lithuanian Passionist priest, Rev. Alphonsus Maria Urbanavicius, C.P., for works of charity among newly arrived coal-mining families. The congregation is familiarly known as the ''Sisters of Jesus Crucified.'' The principal patrons of the community are theSorrowful Mother, St. Joseph, and St. Paul of the Cross. The congregation was begun in 1924 in the Diocese of Scranton, Pa., where its pioneer members received initial training under the guidance ofthe Sister Servants of the Immaculate Heart of Mary. The novitiate and motherhouse were established at Saint Mary's Villa, Elmhurst, Pa. With the gradual increase of members, the sisters began to teach the youth and nurse the aged in the states of Pennsylvania and Massachusetts,and later in Kansas, Connecticut, and New York. In 1945, in response to the invitation of Archbishop Richard J. Cushing, the motherhouse was transferred to the Archdiocese of Boston. The New headquarters and the novitiate were established at Our Lady of Sorrows Convent, Brockton, Mass. In the mid-1960s, the congregation reached its peak membership of over 100professed members. Even though the number of professed sisters has fallen, they still carry on the mission of the congregation: to extend the love and compassion of Jesus Crucified. The congregation conductshealthcare facilities, St. Mary's Villa Nursing Home and St. Mary's Villa Residence, in Elmhurst, Pa. In association with Covenant Health Systems, the Sisters of Jesus Crucified sponsor St. Joseph Manor Health Care, Inc. and Mater Dei Adult Day Care in Brockton, Mass.

[S. E. GLINECKIS]

POOR SISTERS OF NAZARETH

(PSN, Official Catholic Directory #3242); a religious congregation with papal approval (1899), set up in 1851 in London by Mother St. Basil (Victoire Larmenier, 1827–78) under the patronage of Cardinal WISEMAN. The sisters left France to begin work in England at the request of the cardinal, having for their purpose the care of the aged, together with the care and education of underprivileged infants and children. The first house in the U.S. opened in 1924. The motherhouse is in Hammersmith, London, England. The U.S. regional headquarters is in Los Angeles, CA.

[M. C. ROBERTSON/EDS.]

POOR SOULS

The term used to designate the souls of the just who are suffering in PURGATORY. The adjective ''poor'' has no sanction in the official language of the Church, probably being used to indicate that these souls cannot help themselves to escape the punishments that they must undergo for their sins.

See Also: DEAD, PRAYERS FOR THE.

[R. J. BASTIAN]

POPE

As a name, it is derived from the Latin *papa,* in turn derived from the Greek πάπας (πάππας), which in classical Greek was a child's word for father. *Papa* and πάπας appear in Christian literature from the beginning of the 3d century as a title used of bishops, suggesting their spiritual paternity. From the 3d to the 5th century the name was applied to all bishops, but in the 6th century it began to be reserved to the bishops of Rome. The first writer to do this with any consistency was Magnus Felix ENNODIUS (d. 521). The practice of restricting the title to the Roman bishops has been universal in the Western Church since the 8th century.

The office of the pope is described in the *Annuario pontificio* (official directory of the HOLY SEE) by the following titles: ''Bishop of Rome, Vicar of Jesus Christ, Successor of the Chief of the Apostles, Supreme Pontiff of the Universal Church, Patriarch of the West, Primate of Italy, Archbishop and Metropolitan of the Roman Province, Sovereign of the State of Vatican City.'' Of these titles, the basis of all the rest is the third, Successor of the Chief of the Apostles. VATICAN COUNCIL I defined that Christ constituted St. PETER chief of all the APOSTLES and visible head of the whole Church militant, granting him a PRIMACY not merely of honor but of true jurisdiction; that Christ established that Peter should have perpetual successors in this primacy; and that the Roman bishops are these successors (*Enchiridion symbolorum* 3055, 3058). The pope, then, being bishop of Rome and successor of Peter in his primacy, is the supreme PONTIFF of the universal Church. The term *pontifex*, used in classical Latin of the members of the college of high priests, began to be used of bishops late in the 4th century. The term supreme pontiff applied to the pope means that he is the first and chief bishop in the Church, and head of the episcopal college, having truly episcopal authority over all the faithful and all pastors, whether singly or all together (Vatican I, *Enchiridion symbolorum* 3060). As Christ, the good shepherd (Jn 10.11), before His Ascension appointed Peter pastor of all His flock (Jn 21.15–17), thus leaving him as His visible substitute or vicar on earth, endowed with the KEYS and the power of BINDING AND LOOSING (Mt 16.19), so also the pope, as successor to St. Peter, is the vicar of Christ for the spiritual government of the universal Church. The titles Patriarch of the West, Primate of Italy, and Archbishop of the Roman Province are based on the principle that the Roman see, being that of St. Peter, is the chief see of any jurisdictional area of the Church of which it is a part. The last of the titles in the *Annuario* is based on the Lateran Treaty, by which Vatican City is recognized by Italy as a sovereign state with the pope as its temporal ruler.

See Also: APOSTOLIC SEE; BISHOP (IN THE BIBLE); BISHOP (IN THE CHURCH); FATHER (RELIGIOUS TITLE); PAPACY; PATRIARCH; STATES OF THE CHURCH.

Bibliography: P. DE LABRIOLLE, ''Papa,'' *Archivum latinitatis medii aevi* 4 (1928) 65–75. H. LECLERCQ, *Dictionnaire d'archéologie chrétienne,* ed. F. CABROL, H. LECLERCQ, and H. I. MARROU (Paris 1907–53)13.1:1097–1111. M. MACCARRONE, *Vicarius Christi* (Rome 1952). M. J. WILKS, ''Papa est nomen jurisdictionis,'' *Journal of Theological Studies* 8 (1957) 71–91. P. MCCORD, *A Pope for All Christians?* (New York 1976). A BRANDENBURG and H. J. URBAN, eds. *Petrus und Papst* (Münster 1978). J. M. R. TILLARD, *The Bishop of Rome* (Wilmington, Del. 1983). J. N. D. KELLY, *The Oxford Dictionary of the Popes* (Oxford 1986).

[F. A. SULLIVAN]

POPE, ALEXANDER

Poet; b. London, May 21, 1688; d. Twickenham, May 30, 1744. His mother was a member of an old Catholic Yorkshire family and his father a devout convert to Catholicism. Pope's formal education was desultory and his life ill-starred in many ways: he belonged to a proscribed ''sect''; he was deformed and suffered ill health throughout his life; and he was hypersensitive. On the other hand, he had more than the usual allotment of courage, and he was unquestionably the most talented writer of his generation.

Early Work. His earliest published work, four graceful Vergilian *Pastorals* (1709), showed the poetic promise that was more than amply fulfilled in his *Essay on Criticism* (1711), which, if derivative, incorporating ideas from Aristotle, Horace, Vida, and Boileau, nevertheless possesses a sprightliness, a jauntiness of its own. Old truths are given a new relevance; each line, each couplet is marvelously felicitous. The first version of *The Rape of the Lock*, the most delightful of English mock-heroic poems, appeared in 1712. The occasion, a foolish quarrel between two prominent Catholic English families over a social indiscretion, the impulsive and playful snipping of a lock of hair from the head of Miss Arabella Fermor by Lord Petre, teased Pope into a jocular treatment designed to persuade the participants in the feud to make sense. The poem is, however, much more than an occasional piece; it was simultaneously lighthearted, amusing, good-humored, persuasive—and a profound study of the values men live by. Pope obviously found the poem a challenge and two years later published an expanded and far superior version.

The restless interest in technique exhibited by neoclassical poets has been largely unnoticed. Between the two versions of *The Rape of the Lock*, Pope tried another classical genre, the topographical poem. *Windsor Forest* (1713) is important on many counts. It not only suggests that Pope (and his contemporaries) could appreciate external nature, even before Wordsworth publicized the Lake District; it hints that the kind of moralized description of nature that James Thomson made popular in *The Seasons* (and that has accordingly been viewed as a kind of foreshadowing of English Romanticism) was not foreign to neoclassicism. Further, it shows Pope's deep concern with the urgent issues of his day, e.g., the Peace of Utrecht that brought a long war with France to an end and was looked upon as the dawn of a new age of peace and prosperity.

Translations. If neoclassical poets were very much aware of contemporary events, they were also excessively respectful toward the achievements of the past. Pope not only imitated the classical pastoral and eclogue (as in *Windsor Forest*), but he devoted many years of his creative life to translating Homer. Classical scholars even in his own day complained that he had done violence to the spirit of the original. He had. He meant to. Samuel Johnson, however, called Pope's *Iliad* (1715–20) ''a performance which no age or nation can pretend to equal.'' Johnson was much more perceptive than many of his contemporaries. He understood that Pope was not preparing a translation for schoolboys but rather a new poem for sophisticated readers.

This translation brought Pope a considerable fortune. He bought (not only for himself but for his mother, whom he idolized) a villa at Twickenham on the Thames, and amused himself with gardening and with the decorating of a fantastic grotto. He went on to translate the *Odyssey* (12 books, completed 1725), also a great financial success, and began work on an edition of Shakespeare's plays (completed 1725). His editorial principles in this labor are calculated to horrify a modern editor. But his determination to make Shakespeare available to his generation, to men brought up with the tastes (and prejudices) that he shared, makes his Shakespeare all of a piece with his Homer. The fact that his Homer has, to some extent, survived, while his Shakespeare is but a curiosity, is a kind of accident of history.

While Pope was still working on his translation of the *Iliad*, the first collected volume of his poetry appeared (1717), notable for its inclusion of two poems not hitherto published: *Verses to the Memory of an Unfortunate Lady* and *Eloisa to Abelard*. These two famous poems are often thought to represent a somewhat aberrant romantic strain in Pope; actually *Eloisa* is classical and Ovidian, and the *Verses* exhibit an awareness of the language and of the attitudinizing of classical tragedy. They remain interesting evidence of the many-sidedness of Pope's genius and of his interest in problems of form.

Satires. Pope's later work is chiefly satirical. His reworkings of the satires of Horace and Donne are notable, but perhaps the best known is the *Epistle to Dr. Arbuthnot* (1735), which became the Prologue to the *Satires* and which contains the famous sketches of Addison and Lord Hervey. The fundamental seriousness of the satires is also to be found in Pope's *Moral Essays* (1733), and the impetus behind the *Moral Essays* is the same impetus that gave the world the incomparable *Essay on Man* (1733–34). The profundity of this poem, its relationship to the permanent ethical problems that confront mankind, its dependence on traditional theology and philosophy, have only recently begun to be sensed. The ''sublime'' is one of the critical shibboleths of the 18th century. Pope's characteristic utterance was anti-sublime, but in the *Essay on Man* it mysteriously blended the cool common sense of the 18th century with an amazing awareness of the heights and depths of the mystery of the universe. He achieved the same kind of marvel in the *Dunciad* (1728–43). The conclusion of its fourth book is one of the most sublime and most frighteningly prophetic passages in English poetry.

Religious Background and Reputation. In spite of his family background, Pope's grasp of the fundamentals

Alexander Pope.

of his faith seems never to have been conspicuously firm. Not a few of his critics have accused him of paying lip service to Catholicism while actually professing the fashionable DEISM of his day. Doubtless Pope was somewhat affected by what seemed to be the enlightened and magnanimous principles of Deism, but careful readers have become increasingly convinced that these Deistic elements in his thought have been overly stressed. His lifelong adherence to Catholicism, even after the death of his beloved parents and even when the advantages of a change of allegiance were obvious and their practical benefits actively urged by influential friends, demonstrates that his religious profession was more than nominal.

The history of Pope's reputation is singularly complex: in his own time he was both extravagantly admired and hated for the cleverness and ruthlessness of his personal satires. To the 19th century in general, Pope's poetry seemed that of a bygone age; its power was not felt, and his genius not apprehended. And a myth grew in which Pope was represented as a venomous monster, twisted in body and mind. New perspectives have gradually developed, however, and Pope is now almost universally recognized as one of the outstanding geniuses in the English tradition. The alleged ''savageness'' of his attacks on the fools and dunces of his day is now seen to be a brave man's defense of himself against conscienceless enemies—and also an implicit profession of belief in a highly moral and nobly humane credo.

Bibliography: *Works*, ed. W. ELWIN and W. J. COURTHOPE, 10 v. (London 1871–89), rendered obsolete by *The Twickenham Edition of the Poems*, ed. J. BUTT, 6 v. in 7 (New Haven 1951–61). G. W. SHERBURN, *Early Career of Alexander Pope* (Oxford 1934), a model of careful biography. B. DOBREE, *Alexander Pope* (New York 1951), a good short study of his life. R. H. GRIFFITH, *Alexander Pope: A Bibliography*, 2 pts. (Austin 1922–27), an indispensable starting point. F. W. BATESON, ed. *The Cambridge Bibliographies of English Literature*, 5 v. (Cambridge, Eng. 1940–57) 2:294–305; 5:411–413.

[G. CRONIN]

POPE, HUGH

Scripture scholar and preacher; b. Kenilworth, Warwickshire, England, Aug. 5, 1869; d. Edinburgh, Nov. 22, 1946. Educated at the Oratory School under Cardinal NEWMAN, Henry Vincent Pope became a Dominican and received the name of Hugh in 1891. After his ordination at Hawkesyard, Staffordshire, in 1896, he became a lector of theology in 1898, and later professor of Scripture at Hawkesyard until his appointment to the same post in the Collegio Angelico at Rome in 1909. In that year he gained the doctorate of Scripture from the Pontifical Biblical Commission, and in 1911 the master's degree in theology. Returning home, he held, from 1914 to 1920, the priorship of Woodchester, where he began a course of open-air lectures on Christian doctrine that helped to develop the future nationwide Catholic Evidence Guild. From 1920 to 1932 he was in control as regent of Dominican studies in England, and afterward held in succession the priorship of Hawkesyard (1935–41) and the office of vicar of St. Albert's in Edinburgh, where he died. He was a preacher always in demand and a writer of an immense output, principally scriptural works, of which the chief are *The Date of Deuteronomy; Catholic Aids to the Bible,* 5 v.; *The Layman's New Testament; The Church and the Bible;* and *The Life and Times of Saint Augustine of Hippo.*

Bibliography: K. MULVEY, *Hugh Pope of the Order of Preachers* (London 1954). W. GUMBLEY, *Obituary Notices of the English Dominicans from 1555 to 1952* (London 1955).

[W. GUMBLEY]

POPES, ELECTION OF

Any consideration of the election of the pope is founded upon the teaching of the Church concerning succession to the papacy, the history of papal elections, and the present legislation governing such elections.

Catholics accept on divine and Catholic faith that the Holy Father is the successor of Peter. He attains the primacy of Peter by succeeding to the See that Peter established. But the method of selection, who selects, and how the Holy See is vacated are matters of ecclesiastical law and not divine decree. The pope has the freedom and the right not only to make, but also to abrogate, derogate, or alter a law concerning papal elections. Therefore the code of rules that is in effect is at the disposal of the pope. He could alter it, and he could even appoint a successor since there is nothing here that is determined by faith.

The ways in which the papacy may be vacated also admit of diversity. Physical death is the usual manner of vacating the see of Peter, but irremedial loss of reason (mental death) and resignation are legitimate means. The pope, however, since he has supreme power, can never be deposed.

History. Until the 4th century the method of election of the bishop of Rome did not differ considerably from that used in other bishoprics. The neighboring bishops, the Roman clergy, and the laity of Rome each participated in the election. Since the role of these various classes of electors was somewhat unclear and the office was one of extreme importance, the procedure was open to abuse. Consequently, with the advent of the Christian Roman emperors (4th century) the imperial influence was brought to bear on papal elections.

From the 4th to the 11th century the influence of temporal rulers in papal elections reached its zenith. Not only the Roman emperors but also, in their turn, the Ostrogoth kings of Italy and the Carolingian emperors attempted to control the selection of the Roman pontiff. This civil intervention ranged from the approval of elected candidates to the actual nomination of candidates (with tremendous pressure exerted on the electors to secure their acceptance), and even to the extreme of forcible deposition and imposition. It was at this time that, in an attempt to avoid the inevitable disputes that accompanied papal elections, two popes—Felix IV (526–530) and Boniface II (530–532)—proceeded to the rather striking innovation of naming their own successors. Their right to do so, however, was not generally accepted by the electors and, as a result, the attempts were for the most part ineffectual.

The history of papal elections from the 11th to the 16th century is characterized by the gradual development of the conclave as we know it today. The first important step in the attempt to reform papal elections was taken by Pope Nicholas II on April 13, 1059, at the Council of Rome. The decree, which he published, declared that the papal electors were henceforth to be only the higher clergy of Rome (i.e., the cardinals) with the rest of the clergy and the laity permitted merely to give approbation to the election. The emperor was likewise to be informed of the results of the election and allowed to confirm the choice that had already been made, although it was made clear that this was only a concession granted to him by the Holy See. Provisions were made also for holding the election outside the city of Rome if conditions warranted. (*See* PAPAL ELECTION DECREE [1059].)

At the Lateran Council of 1179 Pope Alexander III, in the apostolic constitution *Licet de vitanda discordia,* further stipulated that all cardinals were to be considered equal, and that a two-thirds majority of the votes was necessary for a valid election. With the passage of time it became apparent that the college of cardinals was on occasion prone to delay its selection of a pope and, as a result, to inflict upon the Church the harmful effects of a long interregnum. To remedy this situation, Gregory X, by means of his bull *Ubi periculum* (1274), instituted the conclave system of strict seclusion in order to secure a more rapid papal succession. Further modifications were added in 1562 by Pope Pius IV who issued regulations regarding the method of voting in the conclave through his bull *In eligendis.*

The method of election established by the end of the 16th century has remained for the most part intact, with various modifications and codifications of existing regulations effected by several pontiffs as the need arose. In 1882 Pope Leo XIII published his constitution *Praedecessores nostri,* which contained a number of modifications of electional procedure. Pius X, through his bull *Commissum nobis* (Jan. 20, 1904), effectively removed any remnants of secular influence, and on Dec. 25, 1904, he issued the constitution *Vacante Sede Apostolica* that was for the most part simply a codification of prior legislation. The current rules governing elections are those established by Paul VI (apostolic constitution *Romano pontifici eligendo* [1975]) and revised by John Paul II (apostolic constitution *Universi dominici gregis* [1996]).

Procedure. *Preparation for the Conclave.* It is the duty of the dean of the sacred college of cardinals to notify all the cardinals of the vacancy of the Holy See and to call them to the election of the new pontiff. These in turn are bound in virtue of holy obedience to respond to this summons and to proceed immediately to the place designated for the election, unless they are detained by a legitimate obstacle that is recognized as such by the sacred college of cardinals. After 18 days at most have elapsed since the vacancy of the Holy See, as many cardinals as are present enter the conclave and proceed to the business of the election. If a cardinal should arrive after the conclave has begun, but before a pope has been elected, he is admitted. In such a case, however, the newcomer must take up his duties at whatever stage of progress the conclave has reached at the time of his arrival.

The cardinals will be lodged in the *Domus Sanctae Marthae,* a new accommodation that will certainly do away with the strictures to shorten the length of the conclave as conceived by Pope Bl. Gregory X in his constitution *Ubi periculun* (1274). The cardinals will have to be transported to the traditional voting place: the Sistine Chapel. The chapel itself is to be carefully checked, by "trustworthy individuals of proven technical ability, in order to ensure that no audiovisual equipment has been secretly installed for recording and transmission to the outside" (*Universi dominici gregis* 51).

At the appointed time, after the dean of the sacred college has celebrated a Mass in honor of the Holy Spirit, the cardinals hear an oration warning them of the sacredness of their duties, and on the same day they begin the conclave. After a brief entrance ceremony all outsiders are excluded, the cardinals repeat their oath, and all others who have not yet taken the oath, now swear to abide by all the rules and prescriptions of the conclave. At this point the conclave is closed within and without, and its closure is duly certified.

The Conclave. On the morning following the sealing of the conclave, all the cardinals present gather in the appointed chapel for the celebration of Mass, the reception of Communion, and the recitation of the hymn *Veni, Creator Spiritus.* After this, they proceed immediately to the matter of the election.

The mode of the election is by secret, paper ballot. For a valid election the candidate must receive two-thirds of the votes of the cardinals; if the number of the cardinals present cannot be divided into three equal parts, another vote is required for the validity of his election.

Election by ballot is divided into three stages: preparatory steps, the actual casting of ballots, and subsequent tallying and recording of the votes. In the preparatory stage two or three ballots of a set form are distributed to each cardinal. Then, three tellers for the election are chosen from among the cardinals by lot, as well as three to bring the ballots of the sick, and three to review the results of the election. After all the officials are chosen, the cardinals write the name of the candidate they favor on the ballot. They alter the style of their penmanship to help prevent recognition, and they write only one name on the ballot. When finished, they fold the ballot once lengthwise.

In the actual casting of the ballots, each cardinal in turn approaches the altar according to the order of precedence. He carries the folded ballot between the first two fingers of his right hand. He kneels for a short prayer, and on rising he testifies in a clear voice that as Christ the Lord will be his Judge, he is choosing whom he judges according to God should be chosen. Then he places his ballot on the provided paten, and with the paten he places it into a chalice. He bows to the altar and returns to his place. After all the ballots have been cast, the first teller covers the chalice with the paten and shakes it a few times to mix the ballots. If the number of ballots corresponds to the number of cardinals, the election process continues; if not, all the ballots are burned and the vote must be taken up again. When all have been counted, the three tellers read each ballot successively, and the third one reads aloud the name appearing on each ballot. All the cardinals can keep a record of the voting. The last teller strings all the ballots together and puts the ensemble into an empty chalice or on a table to one side.

The tallying and recording of the votes is performed officially by the tellers, even if the outcome of the balloting is already obvious. They count all the votes any candidate has received. Not until one receives at least the necessary two-thirds of the votes, is a pope canonically and validly elected. The three official cardinal reviewers chosen at the beginning then verify the whole procedure by a careful examination. Then the tellers burn the ballots, whether a pope has been elected or not. If, when no one was elected, there is to be a second balloting immediately following, the ballots of both are burned together. There are to be two such sessions in the morning and two in the afternoon every day until a pope is elected.

When a pope has been canonically elected, the dean of the cardinals, in the name of the whole college, asks him if he accepts his election as pope. When he answers in the affirmative within the time set by the majority vote of the cardinals, he is duly elected and true pope having full and absolute jurisdiction over the whole Church. Once the pope-elect accepts his election, the conclave is at its end as far as any canonical effects are concerned.

Previously, at a time designated by the pope, the eldest cardinal deacon would crown the new pope with the triple tiara of the papacy. This has been replaced with the ''solemn ceremony of the inauguration of the Pontificate'' (*Universi dominici gregis* 92), the praxis introduced by John Paul I in 1978.

Current Legislation. The apostolic constitution *Romano pontifici eligendo* of Pope Paul VI (Oct. 1, 1975; *Acta Apostolicae Sedis* 67 [1975] 609–645) introduced numerous changes in the legislation regarding papal elections, while retaining many traditional elements.

Electors, Cardinals Only. In addresses given on March 5, 1973, and March 24, 1973, Paul VI announced his intention of consulting interested persons to see whether Oriental patriarchs who were not cardinals, as well as the members of the Council of the General Secretariat of the Synod of Bishops should participate in papal elections. The results of the consultation were not conclusive and, hence, only those persons who have been named cardinals of the Church were to be electors (*Romano pontifici eligendo* 33).

Number and Age of Electors. The number of electors is limited now to 120. While formerly the number of cardinals was fixed at 70, each cardinal could bring two or three assistants to the conclave. Currently, only in exceptional cases may an infirmarian accompany an elector, thus reducing the overall number of participants (*ibid.* 33, 45). Following upon the prescriptions of the *motu proprio Ingravescentem aetatem* of Nov. 21, 1970, only those cardinals who have not completed their 80th year of age are eligible to vote in papal elections (*ibid.* 33).

The Conclave. The conclave is not required for validity (*ibid.* 41), but is to be understood as a carefully determined place, a kind of sacred retreat, where the cardinal electors choose the supreme pontiff and where they remain day and night until the election is complete (*ibid.* 42). New norms regarding the observance of secrecy provide for an examination of the premises to determine whether listening devices or other such instruments have been introduced into the quarters (*ibid.* 55, 61). These precautions, as well as the other norms, have two purposes: to ensure a free election and to provide for a rapid carrying out of the business to be transacted.

Episcopal Character. If the newly elected pope is a bishop, he is immediately bishop of Rome and head of the episcopal college. He possesses and can exercise full and supreme power over the universal Church. If, however, the elected person does not possess the episcopal character, he is to be immediately ordained a bishop. This change is in line with Vatican Council II's teaching on the unity that is to exist between the power of orders and the power of jurisdiction (*Lumen gentium* 22).

Period of Prayer. If no person is elected after three days of voting, a day is to be allowed to pass without voting (*Romano pontifici eligendo* 76). The electors are to pray and may converse freely among themselves. Two other such days are foreseen if the ballots are not conclusive. After this point, forms of compromise may be adopted.

Pastoral Dimensions. The cardinals are strongly exhorted not to be guided by likes or dislikes in electing the pope, but to vote for the person whom they judge most fit to rule the universal Church (*ibid.* 85). Likewise, the entire Church is to be united in a special way with those who are electing a supreme pontiff: the election is to be considered the action of the entire Church, and, thus, prayers are to be offered in every city and in other places as well for the successful outcome of the election (*ibid.* 85).

Other Simplifications. Matters of lesser importance include changes in the various excommunications to be levied against those who do not observe secrecy (*ibid.* 46, 58) and prescriptions regarding photographs to be taken of the deceased pontiff (*ibid.* 30). An ecumenical council or a synod of bishops that may have been in progress at the death of a pope is automatically suspended pending authorization by the newly elected pontiff to proceed (*ibid.* 34).

Universi dominici gregis maintains all the essential elements of *Romano Pontifici eligendo:* the powers of the College of Cardinals during the vacancy of the Apostolic See are limited and well defined; the cardinals of age remain the sole electors of the pontiff; the election is to take place in the secrecy, under pain of excommunication, of the conclave; and two-thirds of the votes are required for election unless there is a prolonged deadlock. The introduction identifies the reason for the new document as ''the awareness of the Church's changed situation . . . and the need to take into consideration the general revision of Canon Law.'' But at the same time it has been careful ''in formulating the new discipline, not to depart in substance from the wise and venerable tradition already established.''

The most significant changes introduced by the constitution concern the rules for electing the pope. The previous legislation had established that if there was a deadlock after 33 ballots and periods of prayer, exhortation, and consultation, the cardinals could *unanimously* agree to change the required two-thirds of the votes for a valid election to election by an absolute majority or else a vote in which there are only two candidates, namely, the two who received the most votes in the immediately preceding balloting. *Universi dominici gregis* changed the required unanimity to an absolute majority; it also specified that if the cardinals agreed to hold a vote between the two previous leading vote-getters, only an absolute majority is required for election (no. 75). This last point had not been clearly specified before. The constitution also abolished two of the three methods of election: by acclamation and by compromise (in case of deadlock, allowed the cardinals to delegate their votes to a small committee of their own). Secret, paper ballot is now the only valid way to elect the Roman pontiff (no. 62). In a further, slight modification, the constitution requires two-thirds of the votes for a canonical election. Both Paul VI and Pius XII had required that one vote would be added to the traditional two-thirds established by Alexander III in his constitution *Licet de vitanda* in 1179. The reason behind the extra vote was to guarantee that the elected had obtained the traditional percentage even if he had voted for himself. The only instance in which the plus one vote will be required is if the total number of cardinals voting is not divisible by three (no. 62).

Universi dominici gregis maintains the limitation of the total number of electors to 120 and the prohibition of the cardinals who are 80 years of age from participating in the conclave, though it moves the date at which the age limit is enforced from the beginning of the conclave to the death of the previous pontiff (no. 33). The over-80 cardinals are asked, ''by virtue of the singular bond with the Apostolic See which the Cardinalate represents,'' to lead the prayers of the faithful in Rome and elsewhere asking for divine assistance for the cardinal electors (no. 85). The only reason a cardinal elector can be excluded from voting is if he refuses to enter the conclave or abandons it with no valid cause and without the permission of the majority of the participating cardinals (no. 40).

Bibliography: C. JOURNET, *The Apostolic Hierarchy,* 427–433, 479–482, v. 1 of *The Church of the Word Incarnate,* tr. A. H. C. DOWNES (London, New York 1955–); *The Primacy of Peter from the Protestant and from the Catholic Point of View,* tr. J. CHAPIN (Westminster, Md. 1954). G. C. VAN NOORT, *Christ's Church,* 274, v. 2 of *Dogmatic Theology,* tr. J. J. CASTELOT and W. R. MURPHY, 3 v. (Westminster, Md. 1957). K. BIHLMEYER and H. TÜCHLE, *Kirchengeschichte,* 3 v. (17th ed. Paderborn 1962), *Church History,* v. 1 *Christian Antiquity,* tr. V. MILLS (Westminster, Md. 1958). P. HUGHES, *A History of the Church* (New York, v. 1–2, rev. 1949; v. 3, rev. 1947) v. 2.

[A. SWIFT/F. G. MORRISEY/S. MIRANDA]

POPES, LIST OF

This list of popes is taken from *Annuario Pontificio* for 2001, and it reflects the results of the most recent historical research. For the first two centuries of the Christian era the dates of the pontificates are not secure, and until the middle of the eleventh century there often remain doubts as to the precise day and month. The *Annuario* has formatted this list so that ''two or three dates at the beginning of the pontificate indicate the election, ordination and coronation from which pontiffs were accustomed to calculate their pontificates.'' The last date reflects the pope's death, deposition, or resignation. When dates of consecutive pontiffs overlap, it is often because the validity of a papal election was disputed, and it is difficult to determine the party that has the legitimate claim, ''which, existing *de facto,* assures the legitimate and unbroken continuation of the successors of St. Peter (A.P., p. 12*).'' The names in square brackets are those of antipopes.

The liturgical books and hagiography of the Church consider as martyrs all popes before Sylvester I

(314–335) and as saints those from Sylvester I to Felix IV (526–530) inclusive. There are two exceptions, Liberius (352–366) and Anastasius II (496–498).

Throughout the almost 2,000 year history of the papacy, anomalies have arisen in regard to the sequential numbers given to popes who have had or chose certain names. Antipope Felix (355–366) was erroneously confused with St Felix, a Roman martyr and was given a place in the list of Roman pontiffs as Felix II. Thus the next two legitimate popes who were named "Felix" have been called Felix III (483–492) and Felix IV (526–530), instead of Felix II and Felix III. An antipope of the fifteenth century took the name Felix V (1439–1449).

A Roman priest named Stephen was chosen pope after the death of Zacharias (741–752), but he lived for only four days after his election and died before his consecration, which according to the canon law of the time was the true the beginning of a pontificate. A pope is now considered to be pope from the time of his election, so Stephen should today be counted as a legitimate pope, and this unusual circumstance has added to confusion to the numbering system. To make the matter more complex, the man who followed him to throne of St. Peter was also called Stephen. He now is given the name and number Stephen II (III) by the *Annuario Pontificio.* The same accommodation is made for all other popes named Stephen.

The most dramatic skewering of papal numbers concerns the name "John." The pontificate of John XIV (983–984) was erroneously attributed to two men with the same name. In addition, Antipope John XVI (997–998) has had his pontificate counted in the numbering system of legitimate popes. When Romanus of Tusculum, was elected pope in 1024, he took the number XVIII, his rightful number, but he was designated in documents recorded a little later as John XX. Since by the thirteenth century this corrupted numbering had been everywhere accepted, the next Pope John, Peter of Spain, took the name John XXI on his accession in 1276. Subsequently, Romanus of Tusculum's number was changed to John XIX (1024–1032), but since Peter of Spain remained John XXI (1276–1277), there is no Pope John XX listed in the *Annuario Pontificio.* All this explains what the *Annuario* calls the "the strange nomenclature" that can be found in the Basilica of St. Paul's Outside the Walls in Rome, where portraits of all the popes line the walls. Captions read "John XVI or XVII," "John XVII or XVIII," "John XVIII or XIX or XX," etc.

Simon of Brie became Martin IV (1281–1285) upon his election by placing Marinus I (882–884) and Marinus II (942–446) as well as Martin I (649–655) among the Martins. Oddo of Colonna took the name Martin V in 1417. An antipope, Ottaviano of Monticello called himself Victor IV (1159–1164) instead of Victor V. He did so, the *Annuario* speculates, because a previous antipope Victor IV (1138) reigned only two months before spontaneously submitting to Innocent II. Thus he was not counted when Ottaviano of Monticello assumed the name of Victor. Both are listed in *Annuario Pontificio* as Antipope Victor IV. Antipope Benedict X seems to have been included in the numbering of the legitimate popes named Benedict. Finally Alexander VI (1492–1503) should have become Alexander V, a name that had been assumed in 1409 by an antipope created by the Council of Pisa during the Great Schism.

In this edition of *New Catholic Encyclopedia* there is a separate article on every pope and antipope, which contains the important biographical and historical material relating to each individual.

St. Peter, . . . 64 or 67
St. Linus, 68–79
St. Anacletus (Cletus), 80–92
St. Clement I, 92–99 (or 68–76
St. Evaristus, 99 or 96–108
St. Alexander I, 108 or 109–116 or 119
St. Sixtus I, 117 or 119–126 or 128
St. Telesphorus, 127 or 128–137 or 138
St. Hyginus, 138–142 or 149
St. Pius I, 142 or 146–157 or 161
St. Anicetus, 150 or 157–153 or 168
St. Soter, 162 or 168–170 or 177
St. Eleutherius, 171 or 177–185 or 193
St. Victor I, 186 or 189–197 or 201
St. Zephyrinus, 198–217 or 218
St. Callistus I, 218–222
[St. Hippolytus, 217–235]
St. Urban I, 222–230
St. Pontianus, July 21, 230–September 28, 235
St. Anterus, November 21, 235–January 3, 236
St. Fabian, 236–January 20, 250
St. Cornelius, March 6 or 13, 251–June 253
[Novatian, 251]
St. Lucius I, June or July, 253–March 5, 254
St. Stephen I, March 12, 254–August 2, 257
St. Sixtus II, August 30, 257–August 6, 258
St. Dionysius, July 22, 259–December 26, 268
St. Felix I, January 5, 269–December 30, 274
St. Eutychian, January 4, 275–December 7, 283
St. Gaius (Caius), December 17, 283–April 22, 296
St. Marcellinus, June 30, 296–October 25, 304
St. Marcellus I, 306–January 16, 309 (His pontificate could have started in 307 or 308 and ended in 308 or 310)
St. Eusebius, April 18, 309–August 17, 309 (His pontificate could have ended in 308 or 310)
St. Miltiades, July 2, 311–January 10, 314
St. Silvester I, January 31, 314–December 31, 335

St. Mark, January 18, 336–October 7, 336
St. Julius I, February 6, 337–April 12, 352
Liberius, May 17, 352–September 24, 366
[Felix II, 355–November 22, 365]
St. Damasus I, October 1, 366–December 11, 384
[Ursinus, September 24, 366–367]
St. Siricius, December 15, 22, or 29, 384–November 26, 399
St. Anastasius I, November 27, 399–December 19, 401
St. Innocent I, December 22, 401–March 12, 417
St. Zosimus, March 18, 417–December 26, 418
St. Boniface I, December 28, December 29, 418–September 4, 422
[Eulalius, December 27, December 29, 418–April 3, 419]
St. Celestine I, September 10, 422–July 27, 432
St. Sixtus III, July 31, 432–August 19, 440
St. Leo I (The Great), September 29, 440–November 10, 461
St. Hilary, November 19, 461–February 29, 468
St. Simplicius, March 3, 468–March 10, 483
St. Felix III (II), March 13, 483–February 25 or March 1, 492
St. Gelasius I, March 1, 492–November 21, 496
Anastasius II, November 24, 496–November 19, 498
St. Symmachus, November 22, 498–July 19, 514
[Lawrence, November 22, 498–499, 502–506]
St. Hormisdas, July 20, 514–August 6, 523
St. John I, August 13, 523–May 18, 526
St. Felix IV (III), July 12, 526–September 20 or 22, 530
Boniface II, September 20 or 22, 530–October 17, 532
[Dioscorus, September 20 or 22, 530–October 14, 530 (Possibly a legitimate pope. See his biography.)]
John II, December 31, 532, January 2, 533–May 8, 535
St. Agapitus I, May 13, 535–April 22, 536
St. Silverius, June 8, 536–537
Vigilius, March 29, 537–June 7, 555
Pelagius I, April 16, 556–March 4, 561
John III, July 17, 561–July 13, 574
Benedict I, June 2, 575–July 30, 579
Pelagius II, November 26, 579–February 7, 590
St. Gregory I (The Great), September 3, 590–March 12, 604
Sabinian, March, September 13, 604–February 22, 606
Boniface III, February 19, 607–November 10, 607
St. Boniface IV, August 25, 608–May 8, 615
St. Deusdedit I (Adeodatus I), October 19, 615–November 8, 618
Boniface V, December 23, 619–October 23, 625
Honorius I, October 27, 625–October 12, 638
Severinus, October 638, May 28, 640–August 2, 640
John IV, August, December 24, 640–October 12, 642
Theodore I, October 12, November 24, 642–May 14, 649
St. Martin I, July 5, 649–September 16, 655
St. Eugene I, August 10, 654–June 2, 657
St. Vitalian, July 30, 657–January 27, 672
Adeodatus II (Deusdedit II), April 11, 672–June 16, 676
Donus, November 2, 676–April 11, 678
St. Agatho, June 27, 678–January 10, 681
St. Leo II, January 681, August 17, 682–July 3, 683
St. Benedict II, June 26, 684–May 8, 685
John V, July 23, 685–August 2, 686
Conon, October 23, 686–September 21, 687
[Theodore, 687]
[Paschal, 687]
St. Sergius I, December 15, 687–September 7, 701
John VI, October 30, 701–January 11, 705
John VII, March 1, 705–October 18, 707
Sisinnius, January 15, 708–February 4, 708
Constantine, March 25, 708–April 9, 715
St. Gregory II, May 19, 715–February 11, 731
St. Gregory III, March 18, 731–November 28 741
St. Zachary, December 3, 741–March 15, 752
Stephen II (III), March 26, 752–April 26, 757
St. Paul I, April, May 29, 757–June 28, 767
[Constantine, June 28, July 5, 767–July 30 768]
[Philip, July 31, 768]
Stephen III (IV), August 1, August 7, 768–January 24, 772
Adrian I, February 1, February 9, 772–December 25, 795
St. Leo III, December 26, December 27, 795–June 12, 816
Stephen IV (V), June 22, 816–January 24, 817
St. Paschal I, January 25, 817–February–May 824
Eugene II, February-May 824–August 827
Valentine, August 827–September 827
Gregory IV, September 827, March 29, 828–January 25, 844
[John, January 25, 844]
Sergius II, January 25, 844–January 27, 847
St. Leo IV, January, April 10, 847–July 17, 855
Benedict III, July, September 29, 855–April 17, 858
[Anastasius (The Librarian), September 21–24 855]
St. Nicholas I (The Great), April 24, 858–November 13, 867
Adrian II, December 14, 867–November or December 872
John VIII, December 14, 872–December 16, 882
Marinus I, December 882–May 15, 884
St. Adrian III, May 17, 884–August or September 885
Stephen V (VI), September 885–September 14, 891

Formosus, October 6, 891–April 4, 896
Boniface VI, April 11, 896–April 26, 896
Stephen VI (VII), May or June 896–July or August 897
Romanus, July or August 897–November 897
Theodore II, December 897–December 897 or January 898
John IX, December 897 or January 898–January–May 900
Benedict IV, January–May 900–July 903
Leo V, July 903–September 903
[Christopher, September 903–January 904]
Sergius III, January 29, 904–April 14, 911
Anastasius III, June or September 911–June or August or October 913
Lando, July or November 913–March 914
John X, March or April 914–May or June 928
Leo VI, May or June 928–December 928 or January 929
Stephen VII (VIII), January 929–February 931
John XI, March 931–January 936
Leo VII, January 936–July 13, 939
Stephen VIII (IX), July 14, 939–October 942
Marinus II, October 30, November, 942–May 946
Agapetus II, May 10, 946–December 955
John XII, December 16, 955–May 14, 964
Leo VIII, December 4, December 6, 963–March 965
Benedict V, May 964–July 4, 964 or 965
John XIII, October 1, 965–November 6, 972
Benedict VI, December 972, January 19, 973–July 974
[Boniface VII, June–July 974; then August 984–July 20, 985]
Benedict VII, October 974–July 10, 983
John XIV, November or December 983–August 20, 984
John XV, August 985–March 996
Gregory V, May 3, 996–February or March 999
[John XVI, February or March 997–May 998]
Silvester II, April 2, 999–May 12, 1003
John XVII, May 16, 1003–November 6, 1003
John XVIII, December 25, 1003–June or July 1009
Sergius IV, July 31, 1009–May 12, 1012
Benedict VIII, May 18, 1012–April 9, 1024
[Gregory, May–December 1012]
John XIX, April 19,1024–1032
Benedict IX, August or September 1032–September 1044
Silvester III, January 13 or 20, 1045–March 1045
Benedict IX (for second time), March 10, 1045–May 1, 1045
Gregory VI, May 1, 1045–December 20, 1046
Clement II, December 24, 1046–October 9, 1047
Benedict IX (for the third time), October 1047–July 1048
Damasus II, July 17, 1048–August 9, 1048
St. Leo IX, February 2, February 12, 1049–April 19, 1054
Victor II, April 13, 1055–July 28, 1057
Stephen IX (X), August 2, August 3, 1057–March 29, 1058
[Benedict X, April 5, 1058–January 1059]
Nicholas II, December 1058, January 24, 1059–July 27, 1061
Alexander II, September 30, October 1, 1061–April 21, 1073
[Honorius II, October 28, 1061–May 31, 1064]
St. Gregory VII, April 22, June 30, 1073–May 25, 1085
[Clement III, June 25, 1080, March 24, 1084–September 8, 1100]
Bl. Victor III, May 24, 1086, May 9 1087–September 16, 1087
Bl. Urban II, March 12, 1088–July 29, 1099
Paschal II, August 13, August 14, 1099–January 21, 1118
[Theodoric, 1100]
[Albert, 1101]
[Silvester IV, November 18, 1105–April 12 or 13, 1111]
Gelasius II, January 24, March 10, 1118–January 28, 1119
[Gregory VIII, March 10, 1118–April 22, 1121
Callistus II, February 2, February 9, 1119–December 13 or 14, 1124
Honorius II, December 15, December 21, 1124–February 13 or 14, 1130
[Celestine II, December 1124]
Innocent II, February 14, February 23, 1130–September 24, 1143
[Anacletus II, February 14, February 23, 1130–January 25, 1138]
[Victor IV, March 1138–May 29, 1138]
Celestine II, September 26, October 3, 1143–March 8, 1144
Lucius II, March 12, 1144–February 15, 1145
Bl. Eugene III, February 15, February 18, 1145–July 8, 1153
Anastasius IV, July 12, 1153–December 3, 1154
Adrian IV, December 4, December 5, 1154–September 1, 1159
Alexander III, September 7, September 20, 1159–August 30, 1181
[Victor IV, September 7, October 4 1159–April 20, 1164]
[Paschal III, April 22, April 26, 1164–September 20, 1168]
[Callistus III, September 1168–August 29, 1178]
[Innocent III, September 29, 1179–January 1180]
Lucius III, September 1, September 6, 1181–November 25, 1185
Urban III, November 25, December 1, 1185–October 20, 1187
Gregory VIII, October 21, October 25, 1187–December 17, 1187
Clement III, December 19, December 20,

1187–March 1191
Celestine III, April 10, April 14, 1191–January 8, 1198
Innocent III, January 8, February 22, 1198–July 16, 1216
Honorius III, July 18, July 24, 1216–March 18, 1227
Gregory IX, March 19, March 21, 1227–August 22, 1241
Celestine IV, October 25, October 28, 1241–November 10, 1241
Innocent IV, June 25, June 28, 1243–December 7, 1254
Alexander IV, December 12, December 20, 1254–May 25, 1261
Urban IV, August 29, September 4, 1261–October 2, 1264
Clement IV, February 5, February 22, 1265–November 29, 1268
Bl. Gregory X, September 1, 1271, March 27, 1272–January 10, 1276
Bl. Innocent V, January 21, February 22, 1276,–June 22, 1276
Adrian V, July 11, 1276–August 18, 1276
John XXI, September 16, September 20, 1276–May 20, 1277
Nicholas III, November 25, December 26, 1277–August 22, 1280
Martin IV, February 22, March 23, 1281–March 29, 1285
Honorius IV, April 2, May 20, 1285–April 3, 1287
Nicholas IV, February 22, 1288–April 4, 1292
St. Celestine V, July 5, August 29, 1294–December 13, 1294
Boniface VIII, December 24, 1294, January 23, 1295–October 11, 1303
Bl. Benedict XI, October 22, October 27, 1303–July 7, 1304
Clement V, June 5, November 14, 1305–April 20, 1314
John XXII, August 7, September 5, 1316–December 4, 1334
[Nicholas V, May 12, May 22, 1328–August 25, 1330
Benedict XII, December 20, 1334, January 8, 1335–April 25, 1342
Clement VI, May 7, May 19, 1342–December 6, 1352
Innocent VI, December 18, December 30, 1352–September 12, 1362
Bl. Urban V, September 28, November 6, 1362–December 19, 1370
Gregory XI, December 30, 1370, January 3, 1371–March 26, 1378
Urban VI, April 8, April 18, 1378–October 15, 1389
Boniface IX, November 2, November 9, 1389–October 1, 1404
Innocent VII, October 17, November 11, 1404–November 6, 1406
Gregory XII, November 30, December 19, 1406–July 4, 1415
[Clement VII, September 20, October 31, 1378–September 16, 1394]
[Benedict XIII, September 28, October 11, 1394–November 29, 1422 or May 23, 1423]
[Alexander V, June 26, July 7, 1409–May 3, 1410]
[John XXIII, May 17, May 25, 1410–May 29, 1415]
Martin V, November 11, November 21, 1417–February 20, 1431
Eugene IV, March 3, March 11, 1431–February 23, 1447
[Felix V, November 5, 1439, July 24, 1440–April 7, 1449]
Nicholas V, March 6, March 19, 1447–March 24, 1455
Callistus III, April 8, April 20, 1455–August 6, 1458
Pius II, August 19, September 3, 1458–August 14, 1464
Paul II, August 30, September 16, 1464–July 26, 1471
Sixtus IV, August 1, August 9, August 25, 1471–August 12, 1484
Innocent VIII, August 29, September 12, 1484–July 25, 1492
Alexander VI, August 11, August 26, 1492–August 18, 1503
Pius III, September 22, October 1 (consecrated), October 8, 1503–October 18, 1503
Julius II, November 1, November 26, 1503–February 21, 1513
Leo X, March 11, March 19, 1513–December 1, 1521
Adrian VI, January 9, August 31, 1522–September 14, 1523
Clement VII, November 19, November 26, 1523–September 25, 1534
Paul III, October 13, November 3, 1534–November 10, 1549
Julius III, February 7, February 22, 1550–March 23, 1555
Marcellus II, April 9, April 10, 1555–May 1, 1555
Paul IV, May 23, May 26, 1555–August 18, 1559
Pius IV, December 26, 1559, January 6, 1560–December 9, 1565
St. Pius V, January 7, January 17, 1566–May 1, 1572
Gregory XIII, May 13, May 25, 1572–April 10, 1585
Sixtus V, April 24, May 1, 1585–August 27, 1590
Urban VII, September 15, 1590–September 27, 1590
Gregory XIV, December 5, December 8, 1590–October 16, 1591
Innocent IX, October 29, November 3, 1591–De-

cember 30, 1591
Clement VIII, January 30, February 9, 1592–March 3, 1605
Leo XI, April 1, April 10, 1605–April 27, 1605
Paul V, May 16, May 29, 1605–January 28, 1621
Gregory XV, February 9, February 14, 1621–July 8, 1623
Urban VIII, August 6, September 29, 1623–July 29, 1644
Innocent X, September 15, October 4, 1644–January 7, 1655
Alexander VII, April 7, April 18, 1655–May 22, 1667
Clement IX, June 20, June 26, 1667–December 9, 1669
Clement X, April 29, May 11, 1670–July 22, 1676
Bl. Innocent XI, September 21, October 4, 1676–August 12, 1689
Alexander VIII, October 6, October 16, 1689–February 1, 1691
Innocent XII, July 12, July 15, 1691–September 27, 1700
Clement XI, November 23, November 30, December 8, 1700–March 19, 1721
Innocent XIII, May 8, May 18, 1721–March 7, 1724
Benedict XIII, May 29, June 4, 1724–February 21, 1730
Clement XII, July 12, July 16, 1730–February 6, 1740
Benedict XIV, August 17, August 22, 1740–May 3, 1758
Clement XIII, July 6, July 16, 1758–February 2, 1769
Clement XIV, May 19, May 28, June 4, 1769–September 22, 1774
Pius VI, February 15, February 22, 1775–August 29, 1799
Pius VII, March 14, March 21, 1800–August 20, 1823
Leo XII, September 28, October 5, 1823–February 10, 1829
Pius VIII, March 31, April 5, 1829–November 30, 1830
Gregory XVI, February 2, February 6, 1831–June 1, 1846
Pius IX, June 16, June 21, 1846–February 7, 1878
Leo XIII, February 20, March 3, 1878–July 20, 1903
St. Pius X, August 4, August 9, 1903–August 20, 1914
Benedict XV, September 3, September 6, 1914–January 22, 1922
Pius XI, February 6, February 12, 1922–February 10, 1939
Pius XII, March 2, March 12, 1939–October 9, 1958
John XXIII, October 28, November 4, 1958–June 3, 1963
Paul VI, June 21, June 30, 1963–August 6, 1978
John Paul I, August 26, September 3, 1978–September 28, 1978
John Paul II, October 16, October 22, 1978–

See Also: ANTIPOPE; PAPACY; POPE; POPES, ELECTION OF; POPES, NAMES OF.

Bibliography: A. MERCATI, ''The New List of the Popes,'' *Mediaeval Studies* 9 (1947) 71–80. H. LECLERCQ, *Dictionnaire d'archéologie chrétienne et de liturgie*, ed. F. CABROL, H. LECLERCQ, and H. I. MARROU (Paris 1907–53) 13.1:1111–1345. *Liber pontificalis*, ed. L. DUCHESNE (Paris 1886–92). G. B. LADNER, *Die Papstbildnisse des Altertums und des Mittelalters* 1 (Vatican City 1941). F. X. SEPPELT, *Geschichte der Päpste von den Anfängen bis zur Mitte des 20. Jh.* (Munich 1954–59). E. CASPAR, *Geschichte de Papsttums von den Anfängen bis zur Höhe der Weltherrschaft,* 2 v. (Tübingen 1930–33). L. PASTOR, *The History of the Popes from the Close of the Middle Ages,* 40 v. (London-St. Louis 1938–61). Much of the information in this article is taken from the notes that accompany the list of popes in the *Annuario Pontificio* (2001) 7*–20*.

[T. E. CARSON]

POPES, NAMES OF

It is an old custom, but not a regulation, that upon election every pope assumes a new name. The new name is practically always one already used by a predecessor. The last pope to assume an ''original'' name was Lando (913–914). The 144 popes from then until 1978 used only 32 names. Those of Clement, John, Benedict, Gregory, Innocent, and Pius have each been adopted more than ten times. In 1978 Albino Luciani combined the names of his two immediate predecessors, becoming Pope John Paul I.

Origins of the Change of Name. This custom originated shortly before 1000. Examples from earlier times of John II (533–535), previously Mercurius, and John XII (955–964), previously Octavianus, both pagan names, probably can be explained by their double names. In the first clear case of a change of name, Peter, bishop of Pavia, when elected to the papacy (983), exchanged his baptismal name for that of John (XIV). He did so doubtless out of reverence for the first pope, St. Peter: *quia Petrus antea extiterat* (Epitaph). Boniface VII and John XV, his immediate successors, kept their former names. Then followed the first transalpine pontiffs, Bruno of Carinthia (996) and Gerbert of Aurillac (999). The precedent of the change of name by John XIV encouraged them to change their ''barbarous'' sounding names to the genuinely Roman ones: Gregory (V) and Sylvester (II). After John XVII and John XVIII, another Peter, bishop of Albano, ascended the throne of Peter (1009) and called himself Sergius (IV). Since that time the practice of changing one's name has persisted to this day, except for two Renaissance pontiffs, Adrian VI and Marcellus II, who retained their baptismal names.

Motives. If at first pagan origin, or ''barbarous'' sound, or reverence for St. Peter induced several popes to drop their former names, people later interpreted this alteration as a determination to place the individual completely in the service of the new office. Moreover, the examples of the holy Apostles Peter and Paul were cited (e.g., Bernard of Clairvaux, *Ep.* 238, c. 1; Peter Lombard, *Collect. in Ep. ad Rom.*, c. 1). Persons changed their names upon entering religious orders, a custom that established itself in the 6th century. In the choice of the new papal name various, often complicated, motives are involved, such as veneration for a predecessor of the same name, accidental influence of date and locale, and familiarity with the works and ideas of earlier popes. A special attitude is noticeable during the century beginning with Clement II (1046–47), when all the popes wanted to circumvent the ''dark'' age of the papacy and reverted to the names of popes of the first centuries. As a result 13 of the 18 popes were the ''second'' of their name. With Eugene III (1145–53) began a long line of popes with the ordinal ''III.'' Only after 1276 were several names, such as John, taken once more from the period 867 to 1046.

The Ordinal Number The oldest example of an ordinal number added to a pope's name is most probably that of Gregory III (731–741). Two centuries older is the custom of calling the second of two popes with the same name *junior,* and the third, if there were three, *secundus junior.* Appending the actual ordinal number became common only in the 10th century. Since Leo IX (1049–54) the ordinal number has been on the lead seal. The ordinal number, however, is omitted even today in the declaration of the papal name (*intitulatio*) at the beginning of every papal document sealed with lead, and in the solemn papal signature: *Ego N. Catholicae Ecclesiae episcopus.*

Bibliography: A. KNÖPFLER, ''Die Namensänderung der Päpste,'' *Compte rendu du IVe Congrès scientifique international des catholiques,* 10 v. in 4 (Fribourg 1898) 3:158–167. R. L. POOLE, ''The Names and Numbers of Medieval Popes,'' *English Historical Review* 32 (1917) 465–478. P. RABIKAUSKAS, ''Papstname und Ordnungszahl,'' *Römische Quartalschrift für christliche Altertumskunde und für Kirchengeschichte* 51 (1956) 1–15. F. KRÖMER, ''Über die Anfänge und Beweggründe der Papstnamenänderungen im Mittelalter,'' *ibid.* 148–188 with bibliog.

[P. RABIKAUSKAS]

POPPE, EDWARD JOHANNES MARIA, BL.

Diocesan priest of Ghent; b. Dec. 18, 1890, Temse, East Flanders, Belgium; d. June 10, 1924 in Moerzeke, Belgium.

Edward Poppe, a baker's son, entered the diocesan seminary in May 1909. His first assignment following ordination (1916) was the working-class Sainte Colette's parish in Ghent, where he exhibited a special love for children, the poor, and the dying. Poppe's concern regarding the secularization of society led him to emphasize catechesis and the formation of Eucharistic associations.

He was appointed rector of a religious community in rural Moerzeke (1918) because of poor health. Although he was often too ill to get out of bed (1918–22), he used his time well for prayer, study, and writing about contemporary problems: ten short works, 284 articles, and thousands of letters.

He adopted the ''Little Way'' of Saint THÉRÈSE DE LISIEUX after a pilgrimage to her tomb in 1920 and began an intense campaign for re-evangelization centered around the Eucharist. Although he continued to concentrate on the religious instruction of young people, he also formed an association of priests, mobilized the laity, and invigorated social action in Flanders. He had a profound effect on a generation of Belgian priests when he was sent (October 1922) to Leopoldsburg as spiritual director to military chaplains.

He died two years later at age 34. On July 3, 1998, a miracle attributed to Poppe's intercession was approved, leading to his beatification by John Paul II, Oct. 3, 1999.

Bibliography: O. G. JACOBS, *Edward J. M. Poppe,* 5th ed. (Averbode 1965). M. LEKEUX, *La dure montée* (Bruges 1964). F. VAN DE VELDE, *De wereld van Edward Poppe* (Antwerpen 1983); *Edward Poppe en de Vlaamse beweging* (Veurne 1994). *Acta Apostolicae Sedis,* no. 19 (1999): 965.

[K. I. RABENSTEIN]

POPPER, KARL

Philosopher of science, political theorist, b. Vienna, July 28, 1902; d. London, Sept. 17, 1994. The son of a leading Jewish lawyer who had converted to Protestantism, Popper studied science, philosophy, and music at the University of Vienna, earning in 1928 a doctorate for a thesis on methodological issues in the psychology of discovery. He qualified in 1929 as a schoolteacher in mathematics and physics, a career he followed until his departure from Austria. Popper's masterpiece, *Logik der Forschung* (*The Logic of Scientific Discovery*) was published in 1934. In opposition to the doctrines of the Vienna Circle, it elaborated a radically new approach to the methodological problems of natural science and also articulated thorough-going objectivist interpretations of probability and quantum mechanics. For many years anxious for the safety of democracy in central Europe, and for their own safety in a totalitarian state, Popper and his wife eventually left Austria in 1937 for New Zealand, where he had been offered a lectureship at Canterbury University College. There he wrote *The Open Society and Its Enemies*, a rousing defense of democracy and of rationality, published in 1945.

Shortly after the end of the World War II, Popper returned to Europe to take up a readership at the London School of Economics. He was a frequent visitor to the United States and continental Europe beginning in 1950, the year he gave the William James Lectures at Harvard. That year Popper remained in London as professor of logic and scientific method, a post he held until his retirement in 1969. He was knighted in 1965, and made a Companion of Honour in 1982. He published scores of papers and several books on an extraordinary range of subjects: ancient Greek philosophy, the formalization of logic, the axiomatics and interpretation of probability, quantum mechanics, thermodynamics, indeterminism, evolutionary biology, logical problems in both natural and social science, political theory, the theory of knowledge, the body-mind problem, and more.

Philosophy. Central to Popper's philosophy is the Socratic maxim that there is no easy road to understanding the world we live in, and that any wisdom we have resides in acknowledging our lack of knowledge. This is not skepticism, since he insists that the irremediable unsureness of our ideas need not prevent some of them from being preferable to others and, perhaps, true. The achievement of *Logik der Forschung* was to show that scientific knowledge, usually thought to be the best founded of all our knowledge, consists not of laws established by the traditional empiricist methods of observation, experiment, and induction, but of a network of hazardous speculations whose pretensions to truth we probe constantly by empirical tests. Inductive inference, says Popper, has no role to play in science: hypotheses are not inferred, but invented; and the only inferences needed are the deductive ones used to derive testable predictions from them. More generally, according to Popper, rational argument has been universally misconstrued as a form of justification or proof, and not seen to be simply a method for uncovering mistakes. His methodological view of rationality, *critical rationalism*, restores some sense after more than 2,000 years of unsuccessful responses to skeptical and mystical assaults on man's claims to rational knowledge.

For Popper the methodological question, "How can we detect, and eliminate, mistakes?" replaces the unanswerable epistemological question "How do we know?" Likewise a question of social engineering, "How can we set up institutions that stop our rulers from doing too much damage?" replaces the authoritarian question, "Who should rule us?" that has dominated political philosophy since Plato. There is no authority that we may not challenge, in either intellectual or political affairs; though we may hope for the best, for enlightening thoughts and enlightened rulers, we should also prepare for the worst. Democracies are special not for the way in which they appoint good leaders, for they seldom do, but for the way they are able to dismiss bad ones without bloodshed.

Popper is widely recognized as one of the most important philosophers of science and as a social and political thinker of courage and imagination, but the impact of his revolutionary epistemological ideas on most traditional philosophical problems has been oddly underrated by the philosophical profession. His influence on the general public, and on those who value a philosophy that is both rational and humane, has been profound.

Bibliography: Principal works. *Logik der Forschung* (Vienna 1934), trans. as *The Logic of Scientific Discovery* (New York 1959); *The Open Society & Its Enemies* (Princeton 1950, 1966); *The Poverty of Historicism* (New York 1977); *Conjectures & Refutations* (New York 1968); *Objective Knowledge* (New York 1972, 1979); *Unended Quest* (La Salle, Ill. 1976, 1984); *The Self & Its Brain* [with J. C. ECCLES] (Heidleberg 1977); *The Postscript (Realism & the Aim of Science, The Open Universe, Quantum Theory & the Schism in Physics)* (Totowa, N.J. 1982, 1983). D. W. MILLER, ed., *Popper Selections* (Princeton, N.J. 1985). Studies. P. A. SCHILPP, ed., *The Philosophy of Karl Popper* (La Salle, Ill. 1974). B. MAGEE, *Philosophy & the Real World: An Introduction to Karl Popper* (La Salle, Ill. 1985) [previously published as *Popper* (New York, 1973)]. H. KEUTH, *Die Philosophie Karl Poppers* (Tübingen 2000).

[D. W. MILLER]

POPPO OF STAVELOT, ST.

Abbot and monastic reformer; b. Deinze, Belgium, 978; d. Marchienne-au-Pont, Belgium, Jan. 25, 1048. After a career in the army and pilgrimages to the Holy Land (1000) and to Rome (1005), Poppo renounced the world and entered the BENEDICTINE Order at the Abbey of Saint-Thierry near Reims in 1008. There he met Richard (d. 1046), abbot of VERDUN-SUR-MEUSE, who had him transferred to his own monastery as prior, to help in the reformation of several abbeys in Flanders. Poppo's work drew the attention of Emperor HENRY II, who had him transferred to the abbatial see of Stavelot-Malmédy in 1020. From there he proceeded to reform a network of abbeys in Lorraine and Flanders. Poppo showed his gratitude to the emperors by negotiating alliances between the Empire and France, and he is regarded as an example of the imperial abbot of that day. He was buried at Stavelot, where his relics were elevated in 1624.

Feast: Jan. 25.

Bibliography: *Monumenta Germaniae Historica: Scriptores* (Berlin 1826–) 9:293–316. J. HALKIN and C. ROLAND, *Recueil des chartes de . . . Stavelot-Malmédy* (Brussels 1909) 1:206–227. W. LEGRAND, ''Notes sur la culte de Saint Poppon, abbé de Stavelot,'' *Chronique archéologique du pays de Liège* (1943) 1–18, 25–44. E. DE MOREAV, *Histoire de l'église en Belgique* (2d ed. Brussels 1945–) 2:169–177. A. CASSIMAN, *Sint Poppo, de grootste burger van Deinze,* 978–1048 (Tielt 1949). H. GLAESENER, ''Saint Poppon, abbé de Stavelot-Malmedy,'' *Revue Bénédictine* 60 (Maredsous 1950) 163–179. A. M. ZIMMERMANN, *Kalendarium Benedictinum: Die Heiligen und Seligen des Benediktinerorderns und seiner Zwiege,* 4. (Metten 1933–38) 1:125–128. T. SCHIEFFER, *Lexikon für Theologie und Kirche,* ed. J. HOFER and K. RAHNER (Freiburg 1957–65); suppl., *Das Zweite Vatikanishe Konsil: Dokumente und Kommentare,* ed. H. S. BRECHTER et al. (1966) 8:617–618.

[D. S. BUCZEK]

POPULAR PIETY, HISPANIC, IN THE UNITED STATES

Hispanic popular piety in the U.S. encompasses a wide range of practices, rituals, meanings, and functions. It is highly affective, accessible to all, and often filled with color, pageantry, vivid religious imagery, lively participation, a fervent spirit of embodied prayer, and confident assurance in the tangible presence of Jesus, Mary, and the saints. Practitioners of Hispanic popular piety enact their faith expressions both individually and collectively, as well as both outside official Catholic rites and during sacramental liturgies. Although they consist primarily of lay-controlled practices, Catholic clergy have fostered particular faith expressions that evoked significant lay participation among their Latino co-religionists. The primary promoters and teachers of Hispanic popular piety are Latina mothers, grandmothers, aunts, godmothers, and other women, who for centuries have transmitted communal faith, identity, and values to the next generation through their leadership in celebrating familial and collective religious traditions.

Hispanic popular piety has been continuously extant within the continental U.S. since 1565, when Spanish Catholic subjects established the first permanent European settlement at St. Augustine, Florida. The Hispanic penchant for Marian devotion expressed in activities like constructing Marian shrines, for example, was evident in Florida as early as 1620, when Catholics at St. Augustine built the first Marian shrine in the United States. In 1973, Cubans in Miami dedicated a shrine to their national patroness, *Nuestra Señora de la Caridad del Cobre* (Our Lady of Charity).

In the latter half of the 20th century, the numbers and influence of Hispanics in the U.S. have increased dramatically. An influx of newcomers from such diverse locales as Puerto Rico, Cuba, the Dominican Republic, El Salvador, Guatemala, Nicaragua, Colombia, Peru, Ecuador, and Argentina, along with ongoing Mexican immigration, added to the ranks of an established Hispanic population comprised primarily of Mexican-descent Catholics. These arrivals from Latin America and the Caribbean bring their treasured expressions of faith with them. The faith expressions of Hispanic popular piety differ from group to group. While Mexicans are the principal Hispanic group that celebrates *las POSADAS* during the nine days before Christmas, for example, Puerto Ricans enact the *parranda*, in which devotees take images of the magi from house to house collecting *aguinaldo*, offerings used for a communal fiesta at the end of the Christmas season. Many national groups favor a particular Marian image such as *Nuestra Señora de la Altagracia* (Dominican Republic), *Nuestra Señora de Lujan* (Argentina), *Nuestra Señora del Carmen* (Colombia), and *Nuestra Señora de Guadalupe* (Mexico), the patroness of the Americas. Some national groups also exhibit strong devotion to particular saints or images of Jesus, like the Puerto Rican devotion to their patron San Juan, Guatemalan faith in *El Cristo Negro de Esquipulas* (the Black Christ), Peruvian veneration of Santa Rosa de Lima and *Nuestro Señor de los Milagros* (Our Lord of Miracles), and El Salvadoran dedication to Oscar ROMERO, the slain archbishop of San Salvador who is popularly acclaimed as a martyr and saint.

Some Hispanic faith expressions are common among several and even to all Latino groups. Although San Martín de Porres is a Peruvian saint, many Hispanics revere him for his life of charity and his perseverance in the face of the racist treatment he endured as a mulatto. Mexicans and some Central Americans retain the tradition of the *quinceañera*, which celebrates the maturing to adulthood of a young woman, usually in the context of the Eucharist around the time of her fifteenth birthday. Hispanics of various backgrounds also exhibit profound dedication to *el niño Jesús* (the child Jesus), the Sacred Heart of Jesus, and the Blessed Sacrament. Pilgrimages, processions, holy cards, crucifixes, saints medals, and other sacred images abound, as do the reception of ashes on Ash Wednesday and palms on Palm Sunday, the lighting of candles, and the keeping of *mandas* or *promesas* (offering promises in exchange for the granting of a petition).

Many Hispanics construct home altars, use *agua bendita* (holy water) to bless themselves and their children, place a strong emphasis on *padrinos* (godfathers) and *madrinas* (godmothers) in baptism and other sacraments, bless graves and hold novenas for loved ones who have died, offer special prayers for their beloved deceased on ALL SOULS DAY (known in some communities as *el Día de los Muertos*, the Day of the Dead), and ask priests to bless their homes, cars, and other possessions. One of the most widespread traditions among all Latino groups is the extensive devotion to the crucified Jesus and his suffering mother on Good Friday. In Hispanic communities this devotion encompasses rituals and devotions like a public reenactment of Jesus' way of the cross and crucifixion, the *siete palabras* or proclamation and preaching on the seven last words of Christ, the *servicio del santo entierro* (entombment service) for Jesus, and the *pésame* (condolence) offered to the Virgin on Good Friday evening.

Pastoral ministers respond in diverse ways to Hispanic popular piety; their responses are frequently shaped by the particular faith expression that they address in a given pastoral situation. Some pastoral ministers discourage or even condemn certain practices of Hispanic popular piety as inimical to Catholic faith and the Catholic tradition. Others try to incorporate traditions like Marian devotion into parish life and even into sacramental celebrations, often attempting to engage these traditions as a means to augment participation in parish and sacramental life. Still other pastoral ministers engage faith expressions like the Way of the Cross as a means to prophetically denounce the ongoing suffering of Jesus in today's suffering peoples and challenge devotees to live gospel and church teachings on social justice. In some instances, of course, pastoral ministers ignore or are unaware of home-based celebrations and faith expressions, making more visible or even accentuating tensions and separation between church officials and Catholic liturgy, on the one hand, and Hispanic devotees and religious traditions, on the other. Often missing in these various pastoral responses to Hispanic popular piety is an attempt to probe the complex and multi-layered meanings of Latino popular Catholicism from the practitioners' perspective. Pastoral responses to Hispanic popular piety are greatly enhanced by careful studies of these meanings, which collectively embody the worldview that underlies Hispanic faith expressions.

Recent studies highlight the rich meaning and underlying religious worldview in Hispanic popular piety. These studies provide critical insights about the theological significance of Hispanic faith expressions, as well as the pastoral opportunity and challenge to serve their practitioners in the life of local faith communities. Virgilio Elizondo contends that Mexican-American rituals and devotions reinforce identity and a sense of belonging, help a suffering people endure their pain and struggles, and enable this people to celebrate hope and new life. Ana María Díaz-Stevens states that many Puerto Rican migrants to the mainland brought the complex constellation of religious practices from their *jíbaro* (peasant or mountain dweller) roots. This constellation of practices illuminates God's action in daily life, enacts rites of passage, expresses devotees' desire for harmonious relations with nature, and reminds them of the need for mediators, both among the heavenly saints and the *hacendados* (major landowners) who so influenced their lives in their homeland. Roberto Goizueta proposes a theology of accompaniment rooted in the powerful network of relationships that popular faith expressions mediate between Jesus, Mary, the saints, and their Hispanic devotees. Orlando Espín has also proffered some analysis of the worldview that underlies expressions of Hispanic popular Catholicism. Espín posits that Latinos project many features of their familial relationships onto the sacred realm of the Trinity and the saints and that their popular Catholicism enables them to interpret and endure their personal and collective suffering. He also outlines basic tenets of the Latino popular worldview such as the constant intervention of the divine in human life, the belief that human existence always encompasses the conflict between good and evil, and the assumption that the only way people can change their state in life is through divine sanction granted after persistent prayer or fulfilling a series of challenges or tests.

Bibliography: A. M. DÍAZ-STEVENS, *Oxcart Catholicism on Fifth Avenue: The Impact of Puerto Rican Migration upon the Archdiocese of New York* (Notre Dame, Ind. 1993). V. ELIZONDO, *Galilean Journey: The Mexican-American Promise* (Maryknoll, N.Y. 1983). O. ESPÍN, *The Faith of the People: Theological Reflections on Popular Catholicism.* (Maryknoll, N.Y. 1997). E. FERNÁNDEZ, *La Cosecha: Harvesting Contemporary United States Hispanic Theology (1968–98)* (Collegeville, Minn. 2000). R. S. GOIZUETA, *Caminemos con Jesús: Toward a Hispanic/Latino Theology of Accompaniment* (Maryknoll, N.Y. 1995). T. MATOVINA and G.E. POYO, eds. *¡Presente! U.S. Latino Catholics from Colonial Origins to the Present* (Maryknoll, N.Y. 2000). J. RODRIGUEZ, *Our Lady of Guadalupe: Faith and Empowerment among Mexican American Women* (Austin, Tex. 1994). T. A. TWEED, *Our Lady of the Exile: Diasporic Religion at a Cuban Catholic Shrine in Miami* (Oxford 1997).

[T. MATOVINA]

POPULAR PIETY, POLISH

Polish-style Catholicism is an intimate network of popular religious practices, closely bonding home, church, and community. Since the Baptism of Prince Mieszko I in 966, the Gospel has rooted itself and gradually Christianized seasonal, life cycle, and national events, through blessings, family religious ritual, devotional prayer, and pilgrimages.

Blessings and devotional prayer celebrate the liturgical calendar as well as the religious nature of the seasons. This is particularly true of the Lent/Easter cycle. The ''Bitter'' Lamentations or *Gorzkie Żale* are congregationally sung reflections on the personal and cosmic dimensions of Jesus's passion. Their melodies, along with other Lenten hymns, inspire an intensely personal, yet communal, meditation on the Lord's suffering. This reflection culminates in the Holy Saturday prayer vigil at the Lord's Sepulchre. On this day, faithful pray at a Garden Tomb constructed in a special side chapel. This devotional dimension of the Paschal Triduum arose out of tenth-century reflection on the psalms and antiphons of the Liturgy of the Hours commemorating Christ's burial and repose.

The entire cycle reaches full completion in the early morning ''Sunrise'' procession on Easter Sunday: the glorious antithesis of Lenten lament. Parishioners gather at the now empty Garden Tomb to chant morning prayer and celebrate Christ's Resurrection in a jubilant outdoor eucharistic procession, ending with a solemn celebration of the Mass of Easter. Eucharistic devotion, stands at the heart of Polish piety, especially evident during city-wide processions on the Solemnity of Corpus Christi, parish feast days, and monthly Sacred Heart Devotions. This originally BAROQUE response to the Protestant Reformation solidified Catholicism among the general populous, during an era when official government policies promoted a national climate of religious pluralism.

Lenten and Easter practices give evidence to a mutually enriching relationship between the parish and home life. Children ask their parents for forgiveness in preparation for celebration of the sacrament of penance, as adults seek sacramental reconciliation during parish Lenten retreats. Throughout these 40 days, individuals fast and abstain from rich foods ascetically identifying with Christ's temptation in the desert. The fast is broken at the Eucharist of Easter morn. The celebration at the Lord's Table extends into the home through a domestic liturgy beginning with the characteristic egg-sharing ritual. The Holy Saturday rite of priestly blessing, with eighth-century Western Catholic roots, reveals the Resurrection symbolism of the holy day meal: round cross-breads and wine—the Eucharist, the ''butter'' lamb and smoked meats—the victorious Lamb of God; horseradish—the bitterness of crucifixion; pussy-willow branches and greens—the new life of Easter. Exquisite batik-style, dyed Easter eggs radiate with floral patterns dating to the tenth century. The colorful shells of the eggs suggest Jesus's miraculous tomb, while their yolks represent the Easter sunrise. Parishes, also, share blessed foods with the poor and the homeless.

On Christmas Eve families celebrate the holiest night of the year with a Vigil Supper, called *Wigilia.* This domestic liturgy begins only after the youngest child sights the first star of Christmas Eve, recalling the Wise Men in the Gospel. The head of the household initiates a bread-breaking ritual around a festive table set with a thin layer of pure hay and a white tablecloth—reminiscent of Bethlehem's manger. The leader extends wishes while the gathered share a fine, wheaten wafer or opłatek. This holy day exchange of wishes and bread breaking expresses the intimacy of familial love and reconciliation, as all present ''forgive and forget'' all wrongdoing. A meatless meal follows, gathering together the bounty of the entire year. The festival continues with an exchange of gifts and the singing of carols, the latter of which finds full expression at the parish Midnight/ Shepherd's Mass.

Other domestic liturgies include the Epiphany house blessing and the lighting of the ''thunder'' candle, blessed on February 2, as a prayer during storms or times of family crises. The liturgical feasts of the spring and summer months are occasions to bless palm bouquets, wreaths, wildflowers, herbs, seeds, and grain—symbols of the Pole's mystical solidarity with creation, a profound reverence for the environment, and divine solicitude. Senior tradition bearers lead family ritual with simple elements, blessed by the parish priest, expressive of the close relationship between the family and the parish, a hallmark of Polish popular piety.

Participation in parish and domestic celebrations forms an individual's faith, as well as community identity. Prior to beginning formal religious education, the mother teaches her children the content and value of personal prayer. This attitude matured in the nineteenth century when Poland ceased to exist as a political entity. During this time a ''domestic stronghold'' outlook developed where prayer, religious ritual, and the passing on of community values centered in the family home. Early immigrants to the United States were ''home-schooled'' in this very manner, and many of these attitudes remain operative to this very day. Family tradition bearers continue to creatively adapt agrarian customs to the more urban environment of the United States.

Milestones along the various phases of the human birth-life-death cycle emphasize annual name days (the feast of one's patron saint) over birthdays, patronal feast-days, anniversaries and commemorations of the deceased. National resistance to two centuries of totalitarianism and the tragedy of two World Wars demonstrate that suffering has been a part of recent Polish history. ALL SOULS' DAY, therefore, is a national holiday of homecoming. People return to the resting places of deceased family members to pray, light vigil candles, arrange flowers, and celebrate Mass. During the evenings prior to All Souls, cemeteries across the country blaze with thousands of candles. In the United States, similar practices emerge during Memorial Day celebrations.

Pilgrimages to religious shrines frequently celebrate national festivals, as the Polish word *święto* denotes both the holy day and holiday. Among these are famous, week-long, on-foot pilgrimages to Marian shrines, above all, to the Shrine of Our Lady of Częstochowa. Pope John Paul II best expressed the mysticism of this national "Upper Room" or spiritual capital in stating that Poles are accustomed to come here "to listen to the nation's heart beat in the heart of its Mother." Similar pilgrimages are held each August to the Salvatorian Fathers' Shrine southeast of Chicago and to the Shrine of the North American Martyrs in Midland, Ontario, Canada.

Bibliography: J. KŁOCZOWSKI, ed., *Uniwersalizm i swoistość kultury polskiej,* v. 1–2 (Lublin 1990). C. M. KRYSA, *A Polish Christmas Eve: Traditions and Recipes, Decorations and Song* (Lewiston, New York 2000); *Domesticae Ecclesiae Liturgia. The Easter Meal in Polish Tradition: A Cultural, Textual, and Pastoral Analysis* (Rome 2001). J. J. PAROT, *Polish Catholics in Chicago 1850–1920: A Religious History* (DeKalb 1981).

[C. M. KRYSA]

POPULATION

The systematic study of population has assumed growing importance in recent decades consequent to the maturing of demography as a scientific discipline and the increasingly evident implications of population trends for individuals, society, and the Church. Within the Church cognizance has been taken of population questions by the papacy under Pius XI, Pius XII, John XXIII, and Paul VI. A number of participating fathers of Vatican Council II expressed themselves as concerned about practical and ethical aspects of population growth. This concern is reflected in portions of the *Constitution on the Church in the Modern World.* Nevertheless, a full doctrinal appraisal of questions relating to population was not forthcoming during the council sessions but was referred for further study.

Inasmuch as the Church, by divine mission, is concerned with the salvation and spiritual well-being of the individual persons who compose human populations, it necessarily gives attention to their numbers, location, age-sex composition, and social characteristics, as well as to the impact of population trends and movement upon personal and societal behavior. It is not incorrect to say that the Church officially was interested in certain practical aspects of demographic analysis well before the science of demography as such developed. The Council of Trent (1545–63) made a great step forward in insisting that births, deaths, marriages, etc., be recorded in the respective parishes. The Code of Canon Law promulgated in 1917 is quite explicit about the obligation of keeping accurate records on the parish and diocesan levels (canon 470). On the international level, each year the *Annuario Pontificio* (Vatican Polyglot Press) publishes summary ecclesiastical statistics for the many dioceses and other circumscriptions of the world.

Doctrinal and Moral Aspects

Man is under moral obligation to use both the resources of the material universe and his own powers and abilities in a manner befitting a rational being. Moreover, rights of the individual, whether directly from the nature of man or by acquisition, have corresponding duties, including that to respect the rights of others and the legitimate claims of society. These broad principles apply in various areas of human activity and extend to the use of the procreative faculty.

The interrelation of population and the means of subsistence can occasion misunderstandings on both the dogmatic and the moral levels. Continuing analysis of this relation by competent scholars, without compromise of traditional doctrine, is called for in view of recent population trends, as well as of the mounting complexity of modern society and the valid findings of science. In his address to participants in the World Population Conference in Rome (Sept. 8, 1954), Pius XII indicated the timeliness of such study, also emphasizing the importance of maintaining doctrinal integrity.

Some Misconceptions. In the past, a misconceived belief held that Divine Providence would always see that human beings brought into the world are adequately provided for. If they are not, it was argued, the deficiency is traceable largely to social injustice, inefficient distribution systems, or both. This line of thought was pursued by some 18th-century French authors and by various advocates of social reform. Analogously, English critics of Malthus charged him on occasion with ignoring or minimizing the role of Providence. The truth is that Divine Providence always presupposes in rational beings the exercise of human providence and of prudence in using the goods of this world. Institutional change, then, is no substitute for needed personal reform or individual responsibility, as Pius XI pointed out in the encyclical letter *QUADRAGESIMO ANNO* (1931). History testifies to the many natural disasters that overtake even prudent men, and the Apocalypse suggests distress to come. It would, therefore, be improper to overlook the necessity of personal responsibility in entering marriage and using the same, or to exclude the implications thereof in economic life and for society.

Another incorrect interpretation concerns the relation of population to subsistence viewed in the light of the finality of creation. Some have proposed that since man is the one who consciously gives glory to God, it is incumbent upon individuals who marry to reproduce to the maximum extent possible or at least close to it. It is argued that in this way more individuals will come into existence and give glory to the Creator. As sometimes expressed, this position is doctrinally ambiguous. It seemingly implies, however, that the world should be populated as quickly as biologically possible, even though the process becomes disorderly and hardship results. If the position implies that no regard need be had for the welfare and education of children or for the family as a social institution, it is in contradiction of traditional Catholic teaching, which links procreation and education as the primary end of marriage (1917 *Codex iuris canonici* c.1013.1). Procreation without concern for the prospects of education (upbringing in the full sense), as well as willful neglect in actual upbringing of offspring, is not adequately rational and hence involves some moral defect.

If the argument set forth does not go quite that far but nevertheless suggests that only the welfare and education (upbringing) of the individual family need be taken into account, then it falls short of proper social responsibility. It would, in a sense, make of the family a fully autonomous social entity, which it is not. On the one hand, the family is composed of individuals with a personal destiny, and on the other, the society must look to the common good of all.

Another extreme of misunderstanding revolves around the idea that society has special claims upon individual members to the extent that they must subordinate their personal interests and welfare to the transcending interests of the body social. Pushed to the limit, this readily becomes a totalitarian position. Population policies based thereon can become grossly immoral, as became clear before and during World War II, when various minorities were systematically liquidated in the name of social policy.

Even in its more moderate form this position seemingly implies that society's claims have a priority that ordinarily supersedes those of its members. For example, some mercantilists of the pre-Malthusian era urged marriage and reproduction as social goals and social goods, going so far as to penalize celibates and bachelors. Such an approach involves infringement of personal freedom in the interests of social policy. As a general principle, individuals have a right not to marry should they so choose.

If, on the other hand, the position set forth merely means that man is by nature social and therefore should behave with the needs and legitimate claims of society in mind, it is in conformity with the traditional teaching of the Church and the conclusions of the perennial philosophy. It should not be overlooked, however, that society exists to enable individuals the better to fulfill their destiny to life. Society is not an absolute end in itself.

Necessity of Economic Development. The development of natural resources and of the local and regional economies whereby the material needs of men are met is not a convenience or luxury but a true necessity as population trends continue upward. If expansion of output in goods and services is insufficient to cover the requirements of the human numbers added annually, levels of living inevitably will decline. Where improved levels of living are sought—as is especially fitting in the less developed regions with low income and unsatisfactory conditions of health, nutrition, and education—the respective economies must expand at a rate significantly above that of population. Among other things, this means that those in positions of leadership or decision making have a responsibility to foster and facilitate such development. This responsibility, however, is shared by all to some degree, especially the more educated, in line with established principles and legal and distributive justice. Necessary economic growth and social improvement do not come to pass simply by good intentions or by attempting to implement schemes of redistribution of property or income. Economic progress is impossible without appropriate motivation, pride of achievement, acquisition of skills, and the kind and amount of investment calculated to raise output and job opportunities.

Furthermore, educational institutions, both public and nonpublic, have special responsibility to society to foster and facilitate the needed training and skills, according to their capacity and type of educational programming. In the developing regions especially, an adequate supply of individuals with the appropriate skills and motivation must be forthcoming if progress is to be genuine. It is noteworthy that for many decades, and even centuries, pioneering work in education on all levels has been done by Christian mission groups. With population growing at recent rates, the need for such educational effort is greater than heretofore.

Resource development and economic expansion cannot resolve all problems associated with the population-subsistence relation. As indicated in the demographic analysis of world and regional trends, populations have been increasing at rates unprecedented in history. These trends are likely to continue so long as the recent patterns of marriage and reproduction prevail. This increases the likelihood that in some instances, at least, famines, epidemics, and even wars will be instrumental in bringing births and deaths more nearly into balance.

Since, if long continued, such population growth eventually will exhaust space and meanwhile outstrip capacities for food production, the reduction of birth rates has been deemed necessary by a number of informed demographers and economists. Others point out that even if science and technology can multiply many times over the possibilities of food production, there still remains a problem in achieving economic expansion while populations multiply at such rapid rates. The reduction of birth rates that has been suggested involves ramifications for normative values as regards sex and marriage. Accordingly, a review of the authoritative teaching of the Church on sexuality, marriage, and reproduction is given here in summary form.

Applications of Sexual Morality. As a rational animal possessed of free will, man in his human acts is necessarily subject to moral law as ordained by the Creator. He therefore is obliged to use his capacities in accordance with properly ordered reason and his human nature. In the case of sexuality and the implementation of the reproductive capacity, this means acting both reasonably and responsibly, and not merely in line with passion or instinct.

It is the perennial teaching of the Church that concupiscence, in this case sex urge, is not fully subject to reason. Although God originally gave man the gift of bodily integrity, voluntary control over sexual appetite was not restored to mankind after the fall of Adam and Eve. Accordingly, in the present order of grace (that is, of man fallen but redeemed), it is not uncommon to experience conflict between moral duty and sexual passion. Hence it is the obligation of man to avoid deliberate actions that are prohibited and to develop self-control to the greatest extent possible.

Cultivation of the virtue of chastity is incumbent on the married and the single, each according to their state. In both the unmarried and the married there normally is recurring tension between reason and impulse, between instinctual response and moral norms. In view of man's composite nature of body and spirit this is not surprising. The difficulty of such spiritual development presupposes that one will avail himself of supernatural grace in attaining chastity. For believing and practicing Christians the acquisition of such grace is facilitated through the Sacraments, particularly those of penance and the Eucharist. The Church has always taught that habitual resolution of problems associated with sexuality cannot adequately be achieved apart from these supernatural aids. This teaching is stated in the Catechism of the Council of Trent (Roman Catechism, 1572), more especially the parts on sex in marriage (part 3, ch. 7). Recent popes, in addresses and statements, repeatedly have made the same point.

Traditional teaching, through the ordinary magisterium of the Church, and more explicitly in the Council of Trent (session 5, decree on original sin), has been that concupiscence in itself is not a sin. Sexual passion and impulse become sinful only when, and to the extent that, man deliberately arouses or indulges sex contrary to moral law. Thus the true Christian position is at variance with views on the integral sinfulness of sexual urges, as proposed over the centuries by MANICHAEISM, illuminati of various types, and some reformers of the 16th century and after. The doctrinal errors indicated by Trent with regard to original sin, concupiscence, grace, and the sacramental system should not be revived or repeated.

Periodic Continence. As for use of sex by the married, the Church has not taught, nor does it teach, that intercourse is permissible only when conception is possible and intended. It permits the marriage of those beyond reproductive age and does not prohibit natural intercourse to a couple unintentionally infertile. Whereas the Code of Canon Law notes appropriately that antecedent and perpetual impotence ''invalidates marriage by the law of nature itself'' (c.1068.1), it then clearly states that of itself ''sterility neither invalidates marriage nor renders it illicit'' (c.1068.3). Among humans conjugal society manifestly is more than an ad hoc mating procedure for reproducing the species. At very least, appropriate human upbringing of offspring is implied. Accordingly, canon law indicates that ''mutual aid and the allaying of concupiscence'' constitute a secondary end of marriage (c. 1013.1). The same is the underlying assumption of the discussion in the Roman Catechism of the reasons why people marry (part 2, ch. 8). Additional light was thrown on the subject by Pius XI in *CASTI CONNUBII* (22–25), the monumental encyclical on chaste wedlock (1930).

The use of marriage for its secondary ends has at times been misconstrued, so as allegedly to justify direct intervention in the reproductive process. Ignoring for the moment the question of abortion, feticide, or other intervention after conception has occurred, it is noteworthy that the Roman Catechism expressly rejects the direct prevention of conception. On the other hand, the authentic position of the Church always has been that regulation of offspring may licitly be accomplished by abstinence from intercourse. The implications of this position were not fully recognized until the basic facts about the female cycle were established scientifically in the 1840s. It then became evident that during much of the cycle conception is objectively impossible whatever the intentions of the spouses, and that it would be possible to avoid conception by confining marriage relations to the infertile days.

The question as to whether marriage might licitly be used on both the fertile and infertile days was substantially answered by traditional teaching and practice, including canonical acceptance of the validity of marriages among the overaged and sterile. The question as to whether marriage relations might licitly be restricted to days known or thought to be infertile was up for discussion. Queried at an early date about the matter by the bishop of Amiens, the Sacred Penitentiary replied (March 2, 1853) that "those mentioned in the petition should not be disturbed, so long as they do nothing to prevent conception."

Although some Catholics have questioned the legitimacy of periodic continence, the majority of moral theologians have taught that the practice is in itself lawful. Inasmuch as there is no specific obligation to have marital relations with any given frequency, periodic abstinence is then justifiable for a reasonable cause. This was pointed out by Pius XII in his address to the Italian midwives (Oct. 29, 1951): "Serious reasons, such as those often found in medical, eugenic, economic and social 'indications,' can exempt for a long time, perhaps even for the whole duration of the marriage, from this positive duty. From this it follows that the observance of the nonfertile periods can be morally licit, and under the conditions mentioned it is really so" (*Vegliari con sollecitudine, Acta Apostolicae Sedis* 43 [1951] 846).

Abortion. Direct intervention in the development of human life has always been reprobated by the teaching Church. Once conception has occurred, special malice attaches to any intervention that not only stops the reproductive process but also destroys the product of conception at whatever stage of development. Over the years the essential immorality of ABORTION, or feticide, as a means of controlling number of offspring, or of avoiding them altogether, has been stressed repeatedly. For example, on March 4, 1679, the Holy Office condemned the notion that the unborn fetus may be killed to escape personal or social complications. In the *Casti connubii* Pius XI referred to direct abortion as a "very grave crime" and repudiated the idea that it can be justified by "medical and therapeutic indications" or eugenic reasons. The same standard was applied by Pius XII in his address to the midwives and in other statements and addresses.

Sterilization. Direct sterilization, that is, the deliberate rendering sterile of the reproductive organs or processes, in order to avoid conception, is intrinsically immoral. This is the perennial teaching of the Church. The question is not a new one, as evidenced by discussions in centuries past as to when and under what circumstances surgical castration is permissible. In the period between World War I and World War II, however, the morality of sterilization became specially relevant, in view of various legislative enactments compelling sterilization for eugenic or social reasons. In *Casti connubii* (68–71) reference is made to eugenic sterilization, and the practice is rejected as immoral. Specific reference was made to laws enacted by the Nazis and other totalitarians in statements of Pius XI in 1933 and 1935. In 1936 the Holy Office was quite specific in discussing the enactments and in condemning the underlying assumptions.

In a specially noteworthy decree of Feb. 24, 1940, the Holy Office stated that "direct sterilization of man or woman, either perpetual or temporary," is illicit and "is forbidden by the law of nature." Pius XII was cognizant of the proposed condemnation and ordered its publication. The implications are far-reaching, since by that time experiments were under way with temporary (reversible) sterilization by biochemical as well as surgical means. Subsequently, in a series of addresses to professional groups, Pius XII clarified particular points as to what is and is not permissible in suppressing functions that relate to reproduction. It is clear that direct suppression of either ovulation or spermatogenesis, in order to avoid conception, cannot be approved morally.

Contraception. Artificial CONTRACEPTION, which is to be distinguished from both sterilization and destruction of the product of conception, is immoral. This is the perennial teaching of the Church, and problems of excess fertility do not and cannot render it permissible. Perhaps the best-known condemnation of the practice is that by Pius XI in *Casti connubii* (55): "No reason, however grave, can be put forward by which anything intrinsically against nature may become conformable to nature and morally good. Since, therefore, the conjugal act is destined primarily by nature for the begetting of children, those who in exercising it deliberately frustrate its natural power and purpose sin against nature and commit a deed which is shameful and intrinsically vicious." The teaching of the Church in this matter has not changed, as was indicated several times during 1964 and 1965 by Paul VI, amid ill-advised demands by some for change.

The Church is not unaware of the fact that many persons outside her membership do not perceive, at least clearly, the grave immorality of artificial contraception. She does not condemn their good faith or perhaps confusion of thought in the matter. But she rightly insists, and will continue to insist, that those calling themselves Catholics recognize her teaching authority in this regard.

The population trends of recent years make it clear that both research and instruction are needed on a continuing basis, in order to render periodic abstinence increasingly effective. Moreover, the doctrinal and pastoral aspects of the practice of periodic continence merit continuing attention. The values of chaste celibacy must not be minimized, and the prudent delay of marriage is quite properly to be encouraged for those who realize that the conjugal relationship does not resolve all the moral problems associated with sexuality.

Bibliography: Council of Trent, Session 6, *On Justification* (1547); Session 24, *On Matrimony* (1563). *The Catechism of the Council of Trent* (The Roman Catechism), tr. J. A. MCHUGH and C. A. CALLAN (New York 1923), esp. pt. 2, ch. 7, 8. Vatican Council I, Session 2, *Profession of Faith* (1870); Session 3, *Dogmatic Constitution on the Catholic Faith* (1870); Session 4, *Dogmatic Constitution I on the Church of Christ* (1870). Vatican Council II, Session 4, *Constitution on the Church in the Modern World* (1965). PIUS XI, ''Casti connubii'' (Encyclical, Dec. 31, 1930) *Acta Apostolicae Sedis* 22 (1930) 539–592. PIUS XII, ''Sacra virginitas'' (Encyclical, March 25, 1954) *Acta Apostolicae Sedis* 46 (1954) 161–191; ''Vegliare con sollecitudine'' (Address, Oct. 29, 1951) *Acta Apostolicae Sedis* 43 (1951) 835–854, to Ital. midwives; ''Nell'ordine della'' (Address, Nov. 26, 1951) *Acta Apostolicae Sedis* 43 (1951) 855–860, to the National Congress of the Family Front; ''Et maintenant'' (Address, Sept. 8, 1954), Eng. *The Pope Speaks* 1 (Oct. 1954) 625; *Catholic Mind* 53 (April 1955) 256, to participants in the World Population Conference. JOHN XXIII, Mat Magis; PacTerr. *Conciliorum oecumenicorum decreta* (Bologna-Freiburg 1962).

[W. J. GIBBONS]

POPULORUM PROGRESSIO

Encyclical letter, ''On the Development of Peoples,'' promulgated by Pope PAUL VI on the feast of Easter, March 26, 1967. The pope's intention is to encourage ''the development of those peoples who are striving to escape from hunger, misery, endemic disease, and ignorance; of those who are looking for a wider share in the benefits of civilization and a more active improvement of their human qualities; of those who are aiming purposefully at their complete fulfillment'' (no. 1).

The encyclical is divided into three principal parts. In the first part, ''On Man's Complete Development,'' the pope reflects on human development under three headings. First, in ''Data of the Problem'' (nos. 6–11), he isolates the problem that impedes human development: ''Freedom from misery, the greater assurance of finding subsistence, health, and fixed employment; an increased share of responsibility without oppression of any kind and in security from situations that do violence to their dignity as human beings; better education—in brief, to seek to do more, know more, and have more: that is what people aspire to now when a greater number of them are condemned to live in conditions that make this lawful desire illusory'' (no. 6). Next, in ''The Church and Development'' (nos. 12–21), he presents a Christian vision of development: ''Development cannot be limited to economic growth. In order to be authentic, it must be complete: integral, that is, it has to promote the good of every man and of the whole man'' (no. 14). Based on this vision, in the final subsection, ''Action to Be Undertaken,'' the pope recommends actions to enhance human development (nos. 22–42).

In part 2, ''The Development of the Human Race in a Spirit of SOLIDARITY,'' Pope Paul establishes as a point of departure that ''there can be no progress towards the complete development of humanity without the simultaneous development of *all* people in the spirit of solidarity'' (no. 43). He proposes specific mechanisms for achieving universal solidarity under three headings. In ''Aid for the Weak'' (nos. 45–53), he contends that human development requires ''building a world where every person, no matter what his or her race, religion or nationality, can live a fully human life, freed from servitude imposed by other people or by natural forces over which he or she has not sufficient control; a world where freedom is not an empty word and where Lazarus can sit down at the same table with the rich person.'' Ultimately, the achievement of this goal demands ''generosity . . . sacrifice . . . and unceasing effort on the part of the rich'' (no. 47). In ''Equity in Trade'' (nos. 56-65), the pope contends that ''efforts to assist developing nations . . . would be illusory if their benefits were . . . partially nullified as a consequence of the trade relations between rich and poor nations'' (no. 56). Thus, for international trade to be ''human and moral, social justice requires that it restore to the participants a certain quality of opportunity.'' To reach this long-range objective, ''we must begin now to create true equality in discussion and negotiations'' (no. 61). Additional factors that militate against universal solidarity include ''nationalism'' (no. 62) and ''racism'' (no. 63). Finally, in ''Universal Charity'' (nos. 66–75), the pope claims that the ''illness'' of the world ''consists less in the unproductive monopolization of resources by a small number of individuals than in the lack of brotherhood and sisterhood among individuals and peoples'' (no. 66). In view of this void, he emphasizes ''the duty of welcoming others—a duty springing from human solidarity and Christian charity—which is incumbent both on the families and cultural organizations of host countries.'' Conviviality of this sort offers protection from ''loneliness, the feeling of abandonment and distress, which undermine all moral resistance.'' In the end, ''hospitality should aim to provide . . . the warm atmosphere of a fraternal welcome, with the example of wholesome living, an esteem for genuine and effective Christian charity, an esteem for spiritual values'' (no. 67).

In part 3, ''A Final Appeal,'' the pope entreats all persons to assume responsibility for the cause of human development through universal solidarity. He prevails first upon Christian laypersons ''to take up as their own proper task the renewal of the temporal order.'' Their specific charge is, ''without waiting for orders and directives, to take initiative freely and to infuse a Christian spirit into the mentality, customs, laws, and structures of the community in which they live'' (no. 81). Next, he encourages ''all Christians . . . to expand their common cooperative effort in order to help humanity vanquish selfishness, pride, and rivalries, to overcome ambitions and injustices, to open up to all the road to a more human life, where each person will be loved and helped as a brother or sister, as his neighbor'' (no. 82). The pope also calls upon members of non-Christian religions to ''work with all their hearts and their intelligence . . . that all the children of humanity may lead a life worthy of the children of God'' (no. 82). Finally, to ''all people of good will who believe that the way to peace lies in the area of development''—particularly to ''delegates to international organizations, government officials, members of the press, and educators''—the pope acknowledges, ''all of you, each in your own way, are the builders of a new world'' (no. 83).

In his concluding remarks Pope Paul VI speculates that ''if the world is in trouble because of a lack of *thinking*,'' resolution will come from ''people of reflection and learning'' who are called to ''open the paths which lead to mutual assistance among peoples, to a deepening of human knowledge, to an enlargement of heart, to a more fraternal way of living within a truly universal human society'' (no. 85).

[K. GODFREY]

PORMORT, THOMAS, BL.

Priest, martyr; *alias* Whitgift, Price, Meres; b. *c.* 1560 at Little Limber, Lincolnshire, England; d. Feb. 20, 1592, hanged, drawn, and quartered in St. Paul's churchyard, London. He was probably related to the Pormort family of Great Grimsby and was the godson of Protestant Archbishop Whitgift. He studied at Cambridge for a short time, then at Rheims (1581–82), and Rome (1582–87). After his ordination, he entered the household of Bishop Owen Lewis of Cassano (March 1587) and served as prefect of studies in the Swiss College at Milan for a time before starting off for England. Upon reaching Brussels around Nov. 29, 1590, he used the name Whitgift to obtain a job as manservant to Mrs. Geoffrey Pole, traveling with her via Antwerp to England, where he was arrested in London on July 25, 1591. He managed to escape but was arrested again and convicted on high treason for having ''persuaded to popery'' a haberdasher named John Burrows. Archbishop Whitgift endeavored to delay the execution in order to persuade his godson to conform but without success. He was beatified by Pope John Paul II on Nov. 22, 1987 with George Haydock and Companions.

Feast of the English Martyrs: May 4 (England).

See Also: ENGLAND, SCOTLAND, AND WALES, MARTYRS OF.

Bibliography: Harleian Society Publications, LII (London, 1904), 790. R. CHALLONER, *Memoirs of Missionary Priests,* ed. J. H. POLLEN (rev. ed. London 1924), I, no. 95. J. H. POLLEN, *English Martyrs* (London 1908), 187–90, 208–2, 208–10, 292; *Acts of the English Martyrs* (London 1891), 118–20.

[K. I. RABENSTEIN]

PORNOGRAPHY

The term *pornography,* derived from the Greek *porne* (prostitute) and *graphein* (to write), came into common use in English in the 19th century to describe life, manners, and activities of prostitutes and their patrons. In present usage, the term is a generic label for a wide range of books, magazines, films, videos, broadcasts, Internet communications, taped phone messages, and live public performances intended to be sexually arousing. A further and relational characteristic of pornography is the removal of ''real or simulated sex acts from the intimacy of the partners in order to display them deliberately to third parties'' (*Catechism of the Catholic Church* 2354), a voyeuristic condition on which is based major moral objections to the material. In both popular speech and in the legal and cultural battles over this issue, a distinction is sometimes made between ''soft core'' and ''hard core'' pornography. The former denotes erotic representations conveyed suggestively, the participants displaying a degree of mutuality in the intimacies they share; the latter connects the sexual acts with violence, hatred, pain, and degradation, the principals relating to one another in purely instrumental ways. The word ''obscenity,'' often used interchangeably with ''pornography,'' is more usefully identified with a range of offensive conduct that extends beyond the sexual. Thus a rally of the Ku Klux Klan or an act of spousal abuse could be called obscene though free of any sexual content. On these definitions and their linguistic refinements hangs a complex history of legal and moral wranglings that has only increased in intensity over time.

Examples of pornography are found throughout human history and in many cultures, although attitudes toward it varied widely. Examples include the salacious songs associated with the fertility rites of Dionysus in ancient Greece and erotic paintings found on the walls of Pompeiian ruins. The craft, both visual and verbal, of these productions does not entirely remove them from invidious classification, their clear purpose being to celebrate the pleasures of the flesh exclusive of other human values. Other alleged pornographic practices have historically served the purpose of satirizing the pretensions and hypocrisies of individuals and institutions. Thus a medieval poet such as Boccaccio as well as an 18th-century graphic artist such as Hogarth employed the bawdy to skewer the self-righteous, the erotic subject matter dissolving in cathartic laughter. For this reason, societies with strong centralized governments and/or a state supported religion have used anti-pornography laws to prosecute political humorists as threats to civic order.

The invention of printing and subsequent advances in photography, motion pictures, and the electronic media have made possible the mass production of pornography in ever-increasing amounts. Thus a behavior confined to a primarily literate and privileged elite became in the 20th century a mass phenomenon, one that has come to permeate popular culture. It is this phenomenon that is the primary focus of this article, a summary of efforts by the Church, private interest groups, civil governments, and academics to deal with the issue.

Church. The Catholic Church, which affirms the dignity and sovereignty of all humans, individual and collective, and opposes all influences that threaten these values, entered most forcefully into the regulation of offensive print materials during the Counter-Reformation. The first general decree of prior censorship was promulgated by the Lateran Council of 1515; a half-century later, the Council of Trent (1562) issued the INDEX OF PROHIBITED BOOKS, which shaped Church policy well into the 20th century. The Index, a checklist of specific titles, established normative guidelines to regulate censorship, among which was one that forbade the publication, selling, reading, and possession of obscene works. Revisions over time and under different pontificates changed the titles but the norms remained intact.

As a consequence of the Second Vatican Council, the duties of monitoring the Index were transferred in 1965 to the Congregation for the Doctrine of the Faith. That body a year later issued a statement declaring the Index to have ''no ecclesial force,'' but reserved to itself as well as diocesan ordinaries and episcopal conferences the right to condemn writings for the protection of the faithful. These norms and the procedures for enforcing them have been codified in canon law. However, the explicit condemnation (*ex professo*) of obscene publications in the 1917 Code has virtually disappeared in the 1983 Code, which confines its concerns to works that carry or should carry the marks of Church orthodoxy in matters of faith and morals.

In the U. S. especially, the actions of the Church in defense of morality have been directed both internally and externally: individual bishops as well as national conferences have organized the faithful for their own moral protection, for example through such agencies as the Legion of Decency, which regularly published lists of unacceptable movies. Also, sometimes alone, often with the collaboration of other faith communions, Catholics have formed pressure groups to support censorship of the media, to oppose or limit the spread of ''adult'' venues such as bookstores and massage parlors, in direct actions such as boycotts and protest marches. Joining in these actions as well as promoting the enactment of prohibitory laws through at least the 1960s, Catholics mounted the most active opposition to pornography of any church or civic body. The effectiveness of that opposition—both in accurately targeting the offensive material and in limiting its spread—was not, however, always consistent. Norms as well as judgments of specific works of popular entertainment were often simplistic, their articulation paternalistic and condescending. At present the voice of the American Church has grown more nuanced in discussing the morality of popular entertainment, reflecting the increased educational level of the laity. But its counter-cultural position is perhaps more pronounced than ever.

U.S. Courts. European states, more concerned with sedition and subversive ideas than aberrant sexual behavior, exercised control over printed works in the name of established religious and state powers. In Catholic countries sexually explicit materials were not generally condemned except when they were blasphemous, undermined religious doctrine, or subjected clergy and nuns to ridicule. Colonial America, influenced by the Puritan ethos, also linked obscenity with disrespect toward civic and religious authority. Nathaniel Hawthorne's short story ''The Maypole at Merrymount,'' based on the short-lived 17th-century experiment in collective hedonism led by Thomas Morton, illustrates this connection: the civil authorities of Massachusetts Bay jailed and then deported the free-living colonists as a threat to orthodoxy. In 1711 the same government enacted a statute prohibiting the ''composing, writing, printing, or publishing of any filthy, obscene, or profane story, pamphlets, libel or mock sermon, in imitation of preaching or any other part of divine worship.''

The history of protective legislation and court actions in the American Republic is long and complex, characterized by a constant back and forth movement in a dynamic generated by the opposing values of individual freedom and community solidarity. States and local governments enacted obscenity statutes; and courts measured these norms against the materials actually proscribed. But in the course of time, the norms themselves came under constitutional scrutiny, resulting in an erratic if evolving judicial center.

Reviewing U. S. court cases over a period of 150 years, one can discover a limited understanding of this evolution. An early precedent turned on the distinction between authorial intent and actual content. Thus, although a work was recognized to have been written to secure a social value, the presence of scatological elements (whatever their purpose) rendered the work legally offensive. In a celebrated 1934 case before the Supreme Court, this principle was overturned: James Joyce's celebrated novel *Ulysses*, formerly banned because of obscene content, was found by reason of the artistic integrity of the whole work to be unobjectionable. This calculus pitting artistic merit against offensive content continues to be a source of judicial dispute, serious art by its very symbolic nature being resistant to easy reductions.

A second area of contention concerns the question of harm, and the obligations of the state to protect individual victims as well as the community. Restricting the distribution of pornography on this basis is regularly opposed by appeal to the First Amendment to the U. S. Constitution, the ''free speech'' clause. As this fundamental issue works itself out in case after case, more points of conflict are exposed. The Court in 1957 (*Roth v. U. S.*) found that publications ''utterly without redeeming social value'' deserved no protection. But this near absolute ''utterly'' condition caused considerable trouble for the bench, leading to minimal regulation for several years. The Burger Court stiffened the code in 1973 with two decisions: *Miller v. California* found that ''public portrayal of hardcore sexual conduct'' is far removed from the free exchange of ideas the Constitution is designed to protect; it went on to invoke ''contemporary community standards'' as the benchmark for specific judgments. In a related action decided on the same day in 1973, the Court in *Paris Adult Theater v. Slaton* defined an ''environmental'' principle for ruling against a chain of adult moviehouses, arguing that their presence alone was a threat to the quality of life of a neighborhood and could therefore be restricted by zoning laws.

The vigor of this prosecutorial offense—at one point demanding not just proscription of targeted materials but monetary damages to the victims—gradually weakened, again from a difficulty in identifying key conditions: e.g. ''taken as a whole,'' ''violates community standards,'' and ''inherent harm.''

This long history, linguistic and legal, ecclesiastical and civil, brings us in this new century to a point of impasse. The opposing camps, libertarian and communitarian, are themselves deeply divided. And their professional supporters, lawyers, social scientists, and moral theologians, multiply the points of contention. A third force, amoral at its center, is economic; the explosion of pornography as a market phenomenon—in 1996 there were 665 million pornographic video rentals, 150 titles were added each week, and this does not include electronic transmissions to millions of subscribers—has generated enormous profits in the industry shifted the balance of power between providers and society so radically that only the state can restore a measure of parity. And this does not take into account the role of organized crime, a steady and malignant presence.

At this writing, a new contest over the rights of the pornographer has reached the doors of the Supreme Court. However this matter is decided, the case illustrates many of the complexities of this long history as well a new element. Child pornography has long been one of the secure areas in the battle to protect community values. This is because the production process itself—the use of underage boys and girls to make the product—independent of the content or the merchandising, exploits and violates children. No area of this industry has so consistently drawn the enmity of the law and the courts, from village to nation, as child pornography. Congress has enacted Child Protection laws (1988) and the Supreme Court has upheld them (1994, *U. S. v. Knox*).

Recently, however, producers have moved to create and distribute *virtual* depictions of child sex, the images electronically produced, and hope thereby to avoid prosecution based on harm to the child ''actors.'' In moving through the appeals courts, the legal adversaries have also reenacted the debate over violence to women allegedly inherent in pornography; viz. does the consumption of pornography, child or adult, lead to anti-social behavior by devaluing women and children, portraying them as willing victims of sexual assaults, and thereby legitimizing violence? Does such material victimize the consumer by weakening their moral judgment, their capacity for mature relationships, alienating them from society, closing them off in addictive fantasies? Or, as libertarians argue, does such experience provide an ''innocent'' release of sexually aberrant impulses that otherwise might be spent in criminal acts? And does their repression too conveniently serve to cover a more pernicious attack on uncomfortable ideas?

However these things work themselves out in the future, if they work themselves out, what seems most certain is that pornography is one of a number of crucial lifestyle behaviors that have intensified a spreading culture war in the United States. Political parties, religious bodies, age groups, and even geographical regions have become polarized over these issues. Anyone who wants to track the direction of the United States at this millennial divide must attend to this unsavory issue.

Bibliography: J. A. CORIDEN, T. J. GREEN, and D. E. HEINTSCHEL, eds., *Code of Canon Law: A Text and Commentary* (New York 1985). J. BISHUPIC and E. WITT, "Freedom of Ideas," *Congressional Quarterly's Guide to the U. S. Supreme Court* 1 (1997). M. J. MCMANUS, *Final Report of the Attorney General's Commission on Pornography* (1987).

[P. MESSBARGER]

PORPHYRIAN TREE

A porphyrian tree is a diagrammatic representation of the relationship of GENUS, SPECIES, and individual in the category of SUBSTANCE. Based on a passage of the *Isagoge* of PORPHYRY, it became common in logic texts of the Middle Ages and was called the *scala predicamentalis* (κλῖμαξ). In its usual form, the predicamental line of the supreme genus, substance, is subdivided into its subjective parts by the specific differences given in the left-hand column. These divide the genus and constitute the species. In treating rational animal as a genus, Porphyry followed the Stoics, who posited the existence of another kind of rational being, eternal in time, with a body of a tenuous airlike matter. This type of division could be pursued in any of the CATEGORIES OF BEING.

See Also: PREDICABLES.

[W. BAUMGAERTNER]

PORPHYRY

Neoplatonic philosopher greatly influencing the development of philosophical and theological thought at the close of antiquity; b. Tyre, 234; d. Rome?, after 301. At Athens, in 254, he became a pupil and constant friend of the Platonist Longinus Cassius. In 263 he went to Rome to join the school of PLOTINUS, whose teaching led him astray from the outset. Yet he was not slow in becoming one of the most important members of this school. Five years later, possibly as a result of his intellectual labors, he fell victim to neurasthenia and contemplated suicide. Under advice from Plotinus, who discerned his difficulty, he went to Marsala (Lilybaeum) in Sicily. After Plotinus's death (270), he returned to Rome, became head of the school, and married Marcella, the widow of a philosopher.

Porphyry wrote an immense opus, comprising almost 70 treatises; only fragments of this work remain. It is not quite correct to hold, as many do, that Porphyry was content merely with popularizing Plotinus's teaching. Besides the edition of the *Enneads,* the only Plotinian thought in Porphyry's writings is that in the *Sententiae ad intellegibilia ducentes,* whose title J. Bidez has rendered "Treasury of thoughts for a soul wishing to arrive at the intelligible" (*Vie* 106). Here Porphyry reproduces complete sentences from Plotinus but often adds his own reflections. One can detect that, while seeking to systematize Plotinus, Porphyry distorts his thought, notably as regards the distinction of virtues into political, purificatory, contemplative, and paradigmatic (*Sent.* 32). Although he proposed to make a résumé of Plotinus (*Enn.* 1.2), Porphyry actually presented a quite different teaching. Yet this distinction among the virtues prevailed throughout the Middle Ages.

Generally, Porphyry seems not to have understood Plotinus perfectly, notably as regards the latter's teaching concerning the transcendency of the One in relation to the intelligible world. He seems instead to have remained partially faithful to the traditional Platonism of Longinus. When Plotinus violently criticized the Aristotelian teaching in the *Categories,* Porphyry wrote a commentary on this treatise and actually refuted Plotinus's objections. His *Isagoge,* a sort of introduction to Aristotle's *Organon,* systematizes the teaching on the PREDICABLES. By asking whether GENUS and SPECIES are realities subsistent in themselves or mere conceptions of the mind, Porphyry proposed the problem of UNIVERSALS to the Middle Ages. Moreover, he commented upon many dialogues of Plato, especially the *Timaeus* (traces of this commentary are found in CALCIDIUS, MACROBIUS, and PROCLUS) and the *Parmenides* (14 pages of this have been recently identified in a palimpsest at Turin). Porphyry identifies the first One, corresponding to the first hypostasis in the *Parmenides,* with the act of being, and the second One, corresponding to the second hypostasis with the subject receiving being. This distinction, found also in MARIUS VICTORINUS, was used by BOETHIUS in his *De hebdomadibus* and was eventually formulated in the Middle Ages as the difference between EXISTENCE (*esse*) and what exists (*quod est*).

Porphyry was much preoccupied throughout his life with moral and religious questions concerning the salvation of the soul and spiritual cult. Bidez maintains that his thought on this subject underwent an evolution. Before his encounter with Plotinus, he had written a work titled "Philosophy Drawn from the Oracles," a collection of oracles gleaned from various centers of cult. Here Porphyry professes a strong belief in the most uncouth superstitions and practices of paganism. He attacks Christianity, while admitting that Christ could have been a superior man. After meeting Plotinus, however, he discovered that the true salvation of the soul could come only from mystical union with the divinity. In his *De regressu animae,* of which fragments have been conserved by AUGUSTINE (*Civ.* 10), he claims nonetheless that the religious practices advised by the Chaldaic Oracles could afford salvation for the inferior part of the soul (*see* NEOPLATONISM). In his letter to the Egyptian priest Anebo, he enumerates a whole series of doubts and criticisms concerning the public cult given to the gods. These criticisms can be seen in his *De abstinentia:* bloody sacrifices cannot honor the gods; they can, at best, appease the evil demons. The philosopher, as a priest of the supreme God, refrains from these practices. As Bidez notes (*Vie* 101), the religious teaching of Porphyry recognizes three levels: the lowest is the public cult rendered by the cities—this protects the masses from evil demons; above this, the mystery rites purify man's imagination and turn it to the visible gods; and at the summit, the contemplation of the wise provides the only cult that is worthy of the supreme God.

In Sicily, after 268, Porphyry wrote his 15 books against the Christians, which deal with numerous points of chronological or philological detail and attack especially the veracity of the Gospel narratives. Despite his desire for objectivity, Porphyry makes many errors in details and quite simply represents the prejudices of the Greek mind against Christianity. Yet this great adversary of Christianity has exercised a great influence on Christian thought. To formulate the Trinitarian dogma, Marius Victorinus and SYNESIUS OF CYRENE (in his *Hymns*) employ the schemata Porphyry had used to translate into Platonic terms the data furnished by the Chaldaic Oracles. The Oracles placed, at the summit of all, a triad formed by the Father, His Power, and His Intellect. Porphyry identified the Father with the first One and the triad Father-Power-Intellect with the triad being-life-thought. Thus he compromised the transcendence of the Plotinian One. In similar fashion, Victorinus and Synesius identified the Father with the One and the Being, and made the Son and the Holy Spirit correspond to the Power and the Intellect (otherwise known as Life and Thought) to form a triad with the Father. St. AMBROSE and St. Augustine also seem to have been strongly influenced by the metaphysical and moral doctrine of Porphyry.

Porphyry's works are still poorly known; important fragments may yet be found in Arabian translations.

See Also: PORPHYRIAN TREE

Bibliography: PORPHYRY, *Lettera ad Anebo,* ed. A. R. SODANO (Naples 1958). F. C. COPLESTON, *History of Philosophy* (Westminster MD 1950) v.1. F. UEBERWEG, *Grundriss der Geschichte der Philosophie* (Berlin 1923–28) v.1–2. R. BEUTLER, G. WISSOWA, et al., eds., *Paulys Realenzyklopädie der klassischen Altertumswissenschaft* (Stuttgart 1953) 22.1; 273–313. J. BIDEZ, *Vie de Porphyre* (Leipzig 1913). H. DÖRRIE, *Porphyrios' "Symmikta Zetemata"* (Munich 1959). P. HADOT, "Fragments d'un commentaire de Porphyre sur le *Parménide,*" *Revue des études grecques* 74 (1961) 410–438. F. ALTHEIM and R. STIEHL, *Porphyrios und Empedokles* (Tübingen 1954). R. STIEHL, "New Fragments of Greek Philosophers: II. Porphyry in Arabic and Syriac Translation," *East and West* 13 (Rome 1962) 3–15. W. THEILER, *Die chaldäischen Orakel und die Hymnen des Synesios* (Halle 1942). J. J. O'MEARA, *Porphyry's Philosophy from Oracles in Augustine* (Paris 1959), but see review of this by P. HADOT, "Citations de Porphyre chez Augustin," *Revue des études augustiniennes* 6 (1960) 205–244.

[P. HADOT]

PORPHYRY OF GAZA, ST.

Fifth-century ascetic and bishop; b. Thessalonica, *c.* 347; d. Gaza, Feb. 26, 420. A generally authoritative but chronologically unreliable biography by Mark the Deacon records that Porphyry lived ten years as a monk in Egypt and Palestine, then sold his property in Thessalonica and distributed the money among the monasteries of Egypt and the poor of Jerusalem. Ordained in 392, he had in his charge the relics of the Holy Cross until in 395 he became bishop of Gaza, a hotbed of paganism. His success in making converts brought persecution on the small Christian community. He appealed to Emperor Arcadius, who closed the pagan temples, but they were soon reopened and the persecution resumed. Empress Eudoxia helped Porphyry obtain a new rescript. This time troops destroyed the temples. On the site of the largest, the Marneion, Porphyry built a basilica called Eudoxiana after the empress, who had donated plans and funds. Porphyry tirelessly instructed his people and made many converts despite continued pagan opposition.

Feast: Feb. 26.

Bibliography: P. PEETERS, tr., "La Vie Géorgienne de saint Porphyre de Gaza," *Analecta Bollandiana* 59 (1941) 65–216, Lat. tr. H. GRÉGOIRE and M. A. KUGENER, eds. and trs., *Marc le Diacre: Vie de Porphyre* (Paris 1930), review by F. HALKIN, *Analecta Bollandiana* 49 (1931) 155–160. C. BAUR, *John Chrysostom and His Time,* tr. M. GONZAGA, 2 v. (Westminster, Md. 1960–61). H. ENGBERDING, *Lexikon für Theologie und Kirche*, ed. J. HOFER and K. RAHNER, 10 v. (2d, new ed. Freiburg 1957–65); suppl., *Das Zweite Vatikanische Konzil: Dokumente und Kommentare*, ed. H. S. BRECHTER et al., pt. 1 (1966) 8:619–620.

[P. W. HARKINS]

PORPORA, NICOLA ANTONIO

Baroque opera and church composer of the Neapolitan school; b. Naples, Aug. 17, 1686; d. Naples, March 3, 1768. He began his music studies in Naples at ten and staged the first of his 44 operas there in 1708. After an interval (1711–25) as *Kapellmeister* to Landgrave Philip of Hesse-Darmstadt, he was invited in 1733 to direct the Opera of the Nobility set up in London to rival HANDEL's company. The venture failed, and he left after three years. A renowned teacher, he gave lessons in Dresden (1747) and in Vienna (1751), where Franz Joseph HAYDN was his student and protégé. Intermittently he held also teaching posts at conservatories in Venice and in Naples, where he lived after 1758. Besides his operas and some 11 oratorios, he composed many Masses and motets, most of them in the operatic style of the day. In both operatic and sacred forms his melodies reveal an elegance of line not usually found in the music of his contemporaries.

Bibliography: F. WALKER, ''A Chronology of the Life and Works of Nicola Porpora,'' *Italian Studies* 6 (1951). A. MONDOLFI, *Die Musik in Geschichte und Gegenwart*, ed. F. BLUME (Kassel-Basel 1949–) 10:1453–58. W. M. HIENZ, JR., ''The Choral Psalms of Nicola Porpora'' (D.M.A. diss. University of Illinois, 1980). D. E. MONSON, ''Nicola Antonio Porpora'' in *International Dictionary of Opera* 2 vols., ed. C. S. LARUE (Detroit 1993) 1036–1039. D. M. RANDEL, ed., *The Harvard Biographical Dictionary of Music* (Cambridge 1996) 702–703. M. F. ROBINSON, ''Nicola (Antonio) Porpora'' in *The New Grove Dictionary of Music and Musicians*, vol. 15 ed. S. SADIE (New York 1980) 123–127. N. SLONIMSKY, ed., *Baker's Biographical Dictionary of Musicians*, Eighth Edition (New York 1992) 1431. E. L. SUTTON, ''The Solo Vocal Works of Nicola Porpora: An Annotated Thematic Catalogue'' (Ph.D. diss. University of Minnesota, 1974).

[W. C. HOLMES]

PORRAS Y AYLLÓN, RAFAELA MARÍA, ST.

Known in religion as María of the Sacred Heart, foundress of the HANDMAIDS OF THE SACRED HEART OF JESUS; b. Pedro Abad (Córdoba), Spain, March 1, 1850; d. Rome, Jan. 6, 1925. She was the youngest of 13 children of well-to-do, pious parents, Ildefonso (d. 1854) and Rafaela (Ayllón y Castillo) Porras (d. 1869). She and her sister Dolores, four years her senior, became the first Spanish novices of the Society of MARY REPARATRIX (1875). When action by the bishop of Córdoba compelled the congregation to transfer to Seville, Rafaela followed the advice of her spiritual director, José Ortiz Urruela, and remained with her sister in Córdoba. Out of this situation the Sisters of Reparation of the Sacred Heart developed as a new congregation. Rafaela established the first community in Andújar, moving it to Madrid in 1877. With the assistance of Father Cotanilla, SJ, Rafaela wrote a rule that was approved by the archbishop of Toledo. Rafaela and Dolores, who became Maria of Pilar, pronounced their vows June 8, 1877. The institute devoted itself to perpetual adoration, teaching, and catechizing in order to make reparation for the outrages against the Blessed Sacrament. In 1886, when the congregation received approval from the Holy See, it changed its name to the present one. Rafaela became the first superior general. Mother Pilar, who had charge of the temporalities, caused domestic tensions by her poor administration; yet in 1893 she succeeded her sister as superior general. Rafaela continued to dwell humbly in the convent in Rome without any position of authority. She remained there as mistress of novices after Mother Pilar was removed as superior general (1903). Rafaela was beatified May 18, 1952 and canonized Jan. 23, 1977.

Feast: Jan. 6.

Bibliography: N. BIRCH, *Saint Raphaela Mary Porras* (London 1977). M. J. CABIZA, *La Beata Raffaela Maria del Sacro Cuore* (Rome 1952). W. LAWSON, *Bl. Rafaela Maria Porras* (Dublin 1963). E. ROIG Y PASTUAL, *La fundadora de las Esclavas del Sagrado Corazón* (Rome 1952). I. YÁÑEZ, *Cimientos para un edificio: Santa Rafaela Maria del Sagrado Corazón* (Madrid 1979). *Vies des saintes et des bienheuruex* 13:237241. PIUS XII, *Acta Apostolicae Sedis* 44 (1952) 456–460.

[I. BASTARRIKA]

PORRES, MARTIN DE, ST.

Peruvian Dominican; b. Lima, Dec. 9, 1579; d. there, Nov. 4, 1639; canonized May 6, 1962. His baptismal record states, ''Martin, son of an unknown father,'' but eight years after Martin's birth John de Porres, a noble Spanish gentleman and knight of the Order of Alcantara, acknowledged him as his son and provided for his education. The illegitimate son of a Spanish grandee and of Anna Velasquez, a free black woman, might have grown into an embittered boy and a violent man, for the Spanish were still the proud conquerors of his country. Instead, even as a child, Martin gave his heart and whatever few possessions he had to the poor and the despised. At 12 he apprenticed himself to a *cirujano,* who in those days was a barber, pharmacist, doctor, and surgeon. After a few years of medical apostolate among the poor, he applied to the Dominicans of the monastery of the Most Holy Rosary, asking to be admitted as a lay helper, since in his humility he did not even aspire to the rank of lay brother. He was accepted, but after nine years his superiors and the entire community were so impressed by his life of prayer, penance, humility, and charity that they asked him to make full profession as a religious. The remaining years of his monastic life after religious profession were spent exactly as the preceding ones. The extraordinary was ordinary in Martin de Porres's life: visions, ecstasies, terrifying penances, bilocation, infused theological knowledge, miraculous cures, and astonishing control over animals. He was judged to be a saint because of his perfect obedience, profound humility, and unbounded love of all God's creatures. This half-Spanish, half-black Peruvian loved all people without regard to race, color, or station, and he served Christ in all people without measuring the cost. In long nights spent in prayer and penance, he slaked his thirst for God, and in long days spent in unremitting nursing of the sick, caring for the poor, and laboring for his monastery, he slaked his thirst for the souls of humankind. Martin's sanctity was so clearly recognized by his own brethren that the religious of his monastery took him as their spiritual director, yet his humility was so great that he called himself only "a poor slave" or a "mulatto dog." His contemporaries called him "father of charity, father of the poor." Today he would be called a far-seeing social worker as well, and a champion of the rights of those denied full freedom because of their race or color.

Bibliography: G. CAVALLINI, *St. Martin de Porres: Apostle of Charity,* tr. C. C. HOLLAND (St. Louis 1963).

[C. C. HOLLAND]

PORT-ROYAL

Port-Royal was a Cistercian abbey of nuns situated in the Chevreuse Valley about nine miles from Versailles, and within the Diocese of Paris until 1802, famous for its role in the history of JANSENISM. It was established in 1204 by Mathilde de Garlande, wife of Matthieu de Marly. By the end of the 16th century the spirit of the abbey had deteriorated; 12 nuns lived there in mediocrity, without any well-defined rule or enclosure. In keeping with a practice current at that time, on July 5, 1602, the community received a 10-year-old girl as their abbess, Jacqueline Marie Angélique Arnauld, who later became Mère Angélique (1591–1661). She was the daughter of a Parisian lawyer, but owed this elevation to her maternal grandfather, a friend of Henry IV. At first the abbey was managed by the ARNAULD FAMILY, which partly restored its material prosperity.

The Reform of Mère Angélique. About March 25, 1608, the young abbess was converted. She resolved to reform her monastery and to reestablish the Cistercian rule in its full vigor. She overcame resistance from her nuns and, on Sept. 25, 1609, in the course of the famous *Journée du Guichet,* she broke the opposition of her own family by refusing to let them enter the cloister. Her renown as a reformer spread, and, with the help of Capuchin, Jesuit, and Feuillant confessors, Port-Royal became a center of spiritual life. In 1618 Mère Angélique received the mission to reform the abbey of Maubuisson, near Pontoise. She made the acquaintance of St. FRANCIS DE SALES, who was then at Paris and who became her director. He made a visit to Port-Royal in July 1619. After his death in 1622, she accepted Sebastian Zamet, Bishop of Langres, as her director. The unhealthy climate of the valley of Port-Royal decimated the nuns. On the advice of Zamet and the Jesuit Étienne BINET, she transferred her abbey to Paris and, in 1626, closed Port-Royal-des-Champs and installed her community in a house in the Faubourg Saint-Jacques, soon put under the immediate jurisdiction of the archbishop of Paris. In 1633, she left Port-Royal-de-Paris to establish, under Zamet's authority, a new order, called Institut du Saint-Sacrement. The new foundation was strongly attacked and its orthodoxy questioned with regard to a writing of Mère Agnès (1593–1671), a sister of Mère Angélique; the work, which was entitled *Chapelet secret du Saint-Sacrement,* was deferred to the Sorbonne.

St. Rafaela María Porras y Ayllón.

Direction by Abbé Saint-Cyran. Upon Zamet's entreaties, the *Chapelet* was defended by a theologian then enjoying a well-established reputation among the devout, Jean DUVERGIER DE HAURANNE, Abbé de Saint-Cyran (1581–1643). This was the occasion for Mère Angélique,

The Refectory of the Abbey of Port Royal. (© Archivo Iconografico, S.A./CORBIS)

who had known him superficially since 1621, to discover him as a spiritual director. She invited him to Port-Royal, where the nuns enthusiastically accepted his teaching and spread his rigoristic ideas about penance and the Eucharist, which occasioned public controversies. In August 1637, a nephew of Mère Angélique, the young and brilliant lawyer Antoine Lemaître, was converted and decided to live in seclusion and penance, without becoming a priest or religious. Saint-Cyran agreed to take him under his direction, but he was highly criticized for doing so.

The Solitaries of Port-Royal. Lemaître became the first of the Solitaries or gentlemen (*Les Messieurs*) of Port-Royal. Others joined him, including two of his brothers, the grammarian Claude Lancelot, and the priest Antoine Singlin, who was to play an important role as confessor at Port-Royal. Forty other men joined them later. However, Saint-Cyran openly criticized Cardinal RICHELIEU's policies regarding the welfare of Catholicism. To get rid of him, Richelieu had him arrested and imprisoned at Vincennes, May 14, 1638. In prison, Saint-Cyran continued his role as director by way of letters. The Solitaries and other witnesses were interrogated, but Richelieu could not discover any charge against Saint-Cyran, who was freed on Feb. 6, 1643, shortly after the cardinal's death. He died the following October 11, exhausted by his detention. In August 1643, one of the theologians of the group, Antoine Arnauld (1612–94) published a treatise *De la fréquente Communion,* a vigorous defense of Saint-Cyran's ideas. The AUGUSTINUS, a posthumous work of Saint-Cyran's friend Jansenius, had been previously published in 1640. Although Saint-Cyran had some reservations about this work, he had commanded his disciples to defend it. Furthermore, from 1646 onward, the Solitaries organized *Les Petites-lÉcoles* where many of them taught. Despite difficulties with the royal power, *Les Petites-Écoles* continued until 1660 and reared about 100 children, Jean Racine being among them. At that time Port-Royal enjoyed a great reputation and the number of nuns quickly mounted. The foundation of the Institut du Saint-Sacrement, which had not succeeded, was united with Port-Royal, and on Dec. 24, 1647, the nuns received the white habit with a scarlet cross on the scapular, and dedicated themselves to perpetual adoration. Their constitutions were redacted by Mère Agnés. In 1648, as the nuns became too numerous for the Parisian monastery, a group of them returned to occupy Port-Royal-des–Champs.

Jansenist Controversies. In France, the Jansenist controversies began in 1649 with the question of the five propositions. Seconded by the Solitaries, and especially by the theologian and moralist Pierre NICOLE, Arnauld defended Jansenius energetically. Since the court had taken a clear stand against Jansenism, the position of Port-Royal became perilous, especially from 1655, when Arnauld brought the debate to the public at large by his *Lettre à une personne de condition.* At one time the nuns feared they would be dispersed. But the *Lettres provinciales* of Blaise Pascal and, on March 24, 1656, the miracle of the Holy-Thorn, the instantaneous cure of a niece of Pascal who was boarding at the monastery, restored opinion in favor of Port-Royal and led to a period of calm. Persecution began again in 1661, when Louis XIV sought to force the nuns and *Les Messieurs* to sign a formulary condemning the five propositions and attesting that they were in the *Augustinus.* Though none of the nuns had read the book, they agreed to sign if certain restrictive clauses were added. After three years of waiting and negotiating, Hardouin de Péréfixe, archbishop of Paris, took rigorous steps in August 1664 and transferred 12 of the nuns to other convents. In July 1665, the 12 nuns who had signed were left at Port-Royal-de–Paris, now raised to the status of an independent abbey, and the nuns who refused to do so were interned at Port-Royal-des-Champs under police supervision and were deprived of the sacraments, while *Les Messieurs* hid through fear of imprisonment. Upon the initiative of Pope Clement IX, a compromise was reached in 1669 and the monastery at Port-Royal-des-Champs regained its freedom and remained separate from the abbey in Paris. This period of tranquillity, called ''Peace of the Church,'' was an exceptionally brilliant one for Port-Royal. The Duchess de Longueville, cousin of the king, protected it, and famous friendships surrounded it, including that of Madame de Sévigné. The group became distinguished by some outstanding publications, such as Pascal's *Pensées* and Saint-Cyran's *Considérations* (1670), as well as Lemaître de Sacy's translation of the Bible (1672).

Decline and Suppression. Upon the order of Louis XIV, who was irritated at finding resistance to his absolutism at Port-Royal, the new archbishop of Paris, Harlay de Champvallon, renewed persecution in 1679 by forbidding the monastery to receive novices and thereby condemned it to progressive extinction. Arnauld and other Jansenists went to foreign countries. However, the last years of the declining monastery were peaceful until 1706, when the nuns refused to sign the bull *Vineam Domini* against Jansenism. After troublesome chicanery, Louis XIV, urged by Madame de Maintenon, personally intervened and, on Oct. 29, 1709, the 22 old nuns still living in the house were deported to separate monasteries by the police. Two years later Louis XIV had the buildings destroyed, and the corpses in the cemetery exhumed and amassed in a common grave at nearby Saint-Lambert. The place became a center of Jansenist pilgrimages. Repurchased after the French Revolution by a lawyer named Louis Silvy, the ruins of Port-Royal are now the property of a private association that has had a small museum erected there. Another museum belonging to the estate is at the Granges de Port-Royal, in the house where *Les Messieurs* lived.

Bibliography: C. A. SAINTE-BEUVE, *Port-Royal,* ed. M. LEROY, 3 v. (Paris 1952–55). C. GAZIER, *Histoire du monastère de Port-Royal* (Paris 1929). A. GAZIER, *Histoire générale du mouvement janséniste . . .*, 2 v. (Paris 1922). A. MALVAULT, *Répertoire alphabétique des personnes et des choses de Port-Royal* (Paris 1902). M. SCHMIDT, *Die Religion in Geschichte und Gegenwart* [3] 5:465. L. COGNET, *La Réforme de Port-Royal* (Paris 1950); *Le Jansénisme* (Paris 1961). M. ESCHOLIER, *Port-Royal. The Drama of the Jansenists* (New York 1968). F. E. WEAVER, *The Evolution of the Reform of Port-Royal: From the Rule of Cîteaux to Jansenism* (Paris 1978). F. DELFOGE, *Les petites Écoles de Port-Royal* (Paris 1985). W. R. NEWTON, *Sociologie de la communauté de Port-Royal* (Paris 1999).

[L. COGNET/J. M. GRES-GAYER]

PORTER

Also known as doorkeeper, or ostiary. Historically, the first of the minor orders or steps that led to the priesthood. In the early Church the principal function of the porter was to guard the doors of the church and to exclude those who were not authorized to enter. The porter was also given the duties of ringing the bells to announce the divine services and of assisting the preacher.

This order, instituted by the Church, was not considered a sacrament by many theologians. In the rite of ordination the candidate was first instructed by the ordaining prelate in the duties of his office. The essential action in this rite was the presentation of keys to the candidate along with the words recited by the ordaining prelate as found in the Pontifical. The ceremony also included the opening and shutting of the doors of the church and the ringing of the church bell by the candidate.

By the apostolic letter *Ministeria quaedam* dated Aug. 15, 1972, Pope Paul VI suppressed, among other things, the minor order of the porter.

Bibliography: P. DE PUNIET, *The Roman Pontifical: A History and Commentary,* tr. M. V. HARCOURT (New York 1932) 122–140. M. ANDRIEU, ''Les Ordres mineurs dans l'ancien rite romain,'' *Revue des sciences religieuses* 5 (1925) 232–274. W. CROCE, ''Die niederen Weihen und ihre hierarchische Wertung,'' *Zeitschrift für katholische Theologie* 70 (1948) 257–314.

[T. J. RILEY/EDS.]

PORTER, FRANCIS

Irish Franciscan controversialist and historian; b. Kingstown, near Navan, County Meath, 1632; d. St. Isidore's College, Rome, April 7, 1702. It is not known where he received his early education. On Oct. 10, 1654, on the eve of his solemn profession in the FRANCISCAN order, he made a renunciation of his possessions, thus indicating that he had entered the order a year before. He studied for the priesthood, probably at St. Isidore's College, Rome. After ordination he became professor of philosophy and theology at that college, where he resided until his death. He did valuable work on some of the Roman Congregations and acted as one of the procurators at Rome for the Belgian anti-Jansenists (1680–84). His *Securis evangelica* (Rome 1674) is a fine piece of controversial writing, but it depends to a great extent on Bossuet's *Exposition de la foi.* His *Compendium annalium ecclesiasticorum regni Hiberniae* (Rome 1690) gives a brief account of the ancient kings and laws of Ireland and of its conversion to Christianity, but most of the material is derived from other Irish historians. He acted at Rome as procurator of the Franciscan province of Ireland (*c.* 1680). On Oct. 6, 1690, he was appointed theologian and historian to the exiled King James II, and on Dec. 19, 1695, he was commended for promoting the affairs of that monarch.

Bibliography: G. CLEARY, *Father Luke Wadding and St. Isidore's College Rome* (Rome 1925) 121–123. B. JENNINGS, ''Francis and Patrick Porter of Kingstowne, Meath,'' *Franciscan College Annual* (Multyfarnham 1951) 11–17. L. CEYSSENS, ''Romeinsche brieven uit de Ierse episode van het Belgisch antijansenisme 1680–1684,'' *Bulletin de l'Institut historique belge de Rome* 23 (1944–46) 73–121; ''François Porter, Franciscain Irlandais à Rome (1632–1702),'' *Miscellanea Melchor de Pobladura* 1 (Rome 1964) 387–419. A. TEETAERT, *Dictionnaire de théologie catholique,* ed. A. VACANT et al., 15 v. (Paris 1903–50; Tables générales 1951–) 12.2:2598.

[C. GIBLIN]

PORTIER, MICHAEL

Bishop; b. Montbrison, France, Sept. 7, 1795; d. Mobile, Ala., May 14, 1859. As a seminarian at Lyons, France, he volunteered for service in Louisiana when Bp. Louis Dubourg appealed for helpers in 1817. Upon arriving at Baltimore, Md., in September, he received the diaconate and proceeded to New Orleans, La., as a catechist. After being ordained in St. Louis, Mo., Sept. 29, 1818, he returned to New Orleans where he served as priest and educator. He was named to the new Vicariate Apostolic of Alabama and the Floridas in 1825, and was consecrated by Bp. Joseph ROSATI, CM, at St. Louis, Nov. 5, 1826. His vicariate had some 6,000 Catholics centered at Mobile, Ala.; and Pensacola and St. Augustine, Fla.; it was totally without clergy. In June 1828, he went to seek laborers and funds in Europe. Jean Mathias Pierre LORAS and others offered to join him, and the Society for the Propagation of the Faith at Lyons promised liberal assistance. While Portier was in Rome (May 1829), Pius VIII established the Diocese of MOBILE. Lack of clergy remained a chronic problem for Portier, who seldom had more than a dozen diocesan priests at his disposal. Nevertheless, Spring Hill College, Mobile, the oldest institution of its kind in Alabama, was founded in 1830, and conditions improved after 1847 when the Society of Jesus undertook to run the college. In the same year the Brothers of the Sacred Heart opened an orphanage and school for boys, while as early as 1832 four Visitandines arrived from Georgetown, Washington, D.C., to begin an academy for girls. The Sisters of Charity from Emmitsburg, Md., entered the diocese in 1841, and in spite of nativist opposition during the 1850s expanded their work to include education, two hospitals, and a girls' orphan asylum. Under Portier, Catholicism in Florida enjoyed a marked growth at Pensacola, and churches were built at Apalachicola, Tallahassee, Jacksonville, and Isle Key West. In Alabama he opened new parishes and missions in the vicinity of Mobile, and supplied pastors for Montgomery and Tuscaloosa. In 1850 at Mobile he consecrated the Cathedral of the Immaculate Conception.

Bibliography: M. T. A. CARROLL, *A Catholic History of Alabama and the Floridas* (New York 1908). R. H. CLARKE, *Lives of the Deceased Bishops of the Catholic Church in the U.S.,* 4 v. (New York 1887–89) v.1.

[O. H. LIPSCOMB]

PORTILLO, ALVARO DEL

Bishop, prelate of personal prelature; b. Madrid, March 11, 1914; d. Rome, March 23, 1994. Alvaro del Portillo held doctorates in civil engineering, history, and canon law. In 1935 he joined OPUS DEI, a predominantly lay organization founded by Josemaria ESCRIVÁ for the spiritual, ascetical, and doctrinal formation of persons in the world. As a close associate and collaborator of Escrivá, del Portillo remained with him during much of the Spanish civil war (1936–39).

After the civil war, del Portillo worked with Escrivá to rebuild Opus Dei in Spain and foster its spread elsewhere. As a layman, he traveled to Rome in 1943 on the founder's behalf in order to introduce the new organization to Pope Pius XII and curial officials and to prepare for the establishment there of its international headquarters. On June 25, 1944, del Portillo became one of the first three members of Opus Dei to be ordained as a priest.

Del Portillo was secretary general of Opus Dei from 1940 to 1947 and again from 1956 to 1975. From 1947 to 1950 he was counselor (regional director) of Opus Dei in Italy, and from 1947 to 1956 also served as its procurator general. He was first rector of the Roman College of the Holy Cross, a position he held from 1948 to 1953. He often accompanied Escrivá on trips to prepare for or consolidate the apostolic work of Opus Dei in Europe and, between 1970 and 1975, in Latin America.

In the preparatory phase for the Second Vatican Council, del Portillo was president of the preparatory commission for the laity and was among the first 100 *periti* to be named. During Vatican II he served as secretary for the Commission on Clerical Discipline and the Commission of the Christian People.

Beginning in the 1950s, successive popes—Pius XII, John XXIII, Paul VI, and John Paul II—named del Portillo a consultor to various dicasteries and other bodies of the Holy See. Among these were the Congregation for Religious, the Commission for the Revision of the Code of Canon Law, the Congregation for the Doctrine of the Faith, the Congregation for the Clergy.

Personal Prelature. Following Escrivá's death in Rome on June 26, 1975, a general congress of Opus Dei on Sept. 15, 1975 unanimously elected del Portillo to head the association of the faithful as its founder's first successor.

During the next 19 years, Opus Dei grew from approximately 60,000 members to approximately 77,000 while beginning apostolic activities in 21 new countries in Latin America, Africa, Europe, Oceania, and Asia. In the United States, where it was introduced in 1949, the number of cities with centers of Opus Dei rose from eight to seventeen, and apostolic activities were begun in several other places.

Another major initiative of Opus Dei during these years was the establishment in 1984 of the Roman Atheneum of the Holy Cross, with faculties in theology, canon law, and philosophy.

By the Apostolic Constitution *Ut sit* (Nov. 28, 1982) Pope John Paul II created the Prelature of the Holy Cross and Opus Dei, the first personal prelature of the Church, and named del Portillo its first prelate. Pope John Paul II ordained del Portillo titular bishop of Vita on Jan. 6,1991. Finally, in 1992, a cherished goal of del Portillo's was realized when, on May 17th, Pope John Paul II beatified Escrivá.

In 1994, del Portillo suffered a heart attack and died in the early morning of March 23.

Bibliography: P. BERGLAR, *Opus Dei: Life and Work of Its Founder Josemaria Escrivá* (Princeton 1994). D. LE TOURNEAU, *What Is Opus Dei?* (Dublin 1987). A. DEL PORTILLO, *Faithful and Laity in the Church* (Shannon, Ireland 1972); *On Priesthood* (New Rochelle NY 1974); *Meeting the Press: Two More Interviews on Opus Dei* (New Rochelle NY 1984); *Intervista sul Fondatore dell'Opus Dei, a Cura di Cesare Cavalleri* (Milan 1992).

[R. SHAW]

PORTIUNCULA

A rural chapel on the plain below Assisi, Italy, called also St. Mary of the Angels, favorite church and headquarters of St. Francis of Assisi. E. d'Alençon (1904) and L. Canonici (1963) have demonstrated that an alleged foundation of the chapel by Syrian monks in the 4th century and restoration by St. Benedict in the 6th were invented by S. Vitale in 1645. It was probably built in the 10th or 11th century; its site is first mentioned in a document of 1045, and the chapel itself about 1150. The chapel was originally known as St. Mary of the Angels because of local reports of angelic visitations, but it was called St. Mary of the Portiuncula in the mid-13th century; later both names were used. Its proper ecclesiastical title is uncertain: it may be the Assumption, or it may be the Annunciation (as is suggested by the polyptych behind the altar painted in 1393). The church belonged to the Abbey of San Benedetto on Mount Subasio, but it was abandoned late in the 12th century, until the young Francis repaired it in 1207. There he received his vocation and founded his first order (1208), acquiring the Portiuncula from the Benedictines (1210) and having it consecrated (1215?). There he vested St. Clare (1212), held general chapters, and died in an adjacent cell (1226). The church and friary, at first subject to the basilica of San Francesco, passed to the Observant Franciscans in 1415. A triple-naved basilica (papal since 1909) of St. Mary of the Angels was erected over the chapel and death cell (1569–78), and was later rebuilt after an earthquake (1836–40); a marble façade and portico were added in the 20th century (1926–30). Since about 1270 the Portiuncula has been one of the major Marian shrines of Europe, owing to the fame of the ''Pardon of Assisi'' or the Portiuncula Indulgence, a plenary INDULGENCE, without offerings, gainable by pilgrims yearly on August 2, which

Honorius III is reported to have spontaneously granted to Francis in 1216 at Perugia, upon hearing of a private revelation received by the saint. The prolonged controversies regarding its historicity and subsequent extensions have been documented by R. Huber. Its validity has not been questioned since the first extant papal briefs affirming it under Boniface VIII (1294–1303). In 1622 it was extended to all visitors to Franciscan churches; Benedict XV on April 16, 1921, made it a daily *toties quoties* indulgence, under the usual conditions [see *Enchiridion Indulgentiarum* (Rome 1952) n.698].

Modern scholars have questioned the granting of the indulgence in 1216 because: (1) it is not mentioned in early Franciscan biographies, chronicles, or official acts, or in a sermon by an archbishop of Pisa in Assisi in 1261 listing indulgences gainable at the basilica of San Francesco; (2) in 1215 the Fourth Lateran Council ordered that indulgences granted for consecrations of churches be restricted to 40 days; (3) Honorius III in 1222 conceded to the Basilica of St. Mary Major in Rome only a partial one of one year and 40 days; (4) plenary indulgences could then be gained only by participants in or material supporters of the various Crusades; (5) documents attesting the Portiuncula Indulgence date only from 1277 and are contradictory in details; and (6) two basic compilations by the Catalan Andrea Batlle (or Bajuli; *c.* 1315), edited by A. Fierens (1910) and J. Cambell (1963), and by Fra Francesco di Bartolo della Rossa of Assisi (*c.* 1334), edited by P. Sabatier (1900), include improbable visions, miracles, and legendary materials. (New biographical data on Francesco di Bartolo were published by A. Fortini in 1959.)

Historians who accept the granting of the indulgence in 1216 reply that the first compilation of evidence made by Bp. Theobald of Assisi about 1310 contained critically acceptable attestations by Friar Benedict of Arezzo (d. 1282) and Giacomo Coppoli (fl. 1276), a prominent Perugian friend of Bl. Giles of Assisi. They stated that they had heard it narrated by Brother Leo of Assisi (d. 1278), St. Francis's confessor, or by Brother Masseo, who accompanied the saint to Perugia in 1216. Benedict of Arezzo and a companion testified in 1277 that they frequently heard Masseo describe the granting; their testimony, incidentally, implies that Masseo was then dead and so did not die in 1280 as traditionally reported. In 1311 Bl. John of La Verna testified that numerous friars had informed him they had also received the account from the eyewitness Masseo. Fra Francesco Venimbeni of Fabriano (d. 1322) wrote in his minor *Chronica* [cf. partial ed. by G. Pagnani in *Archivum Franciscanum historicum* 52 (1959) 153–177] that he went to Assisi in 1268 to gain the indulgence and heard Leo tell about it. A treatise defending it by Peter John Olivi (d. 1291) indicates that it was accepted and disputed *c.* 1279. The spiritual writer Ubertino da Casale declared that he gained the indulgence in 1284. The testimony of such witnesses establishes the fact of the granting in 1216, in the judgment of P. Sabatier, M. Faloci Pulignani, L. Oliger, M. Bihl, G. Abate, and R. Huber. However, they question or reject a number of additional incidents narrated in the two late compilations.

One of several points still requiring clarification is whether St. Francis in 1216 publicly announced the indulgence at the Portiuncula in the presence of seven bishops; for, once proclaimed, how could it have been, in effect, ignored for 50 years? The late accounts stress that the Curia urged Honorius to retract it and induced him to restrict it to one day a year. That, owing to this potent official opposition, the saint voluntarily allowed it to lapse soon after receiving it is suggested by his reported advice to Leo to keep it a secret until near the end of Leo's life. A few writers have seen a discreetly cryptic allusion to the indulgence in a friar's vision, recorded by both Thomas of Celano in 1245 and St. Bonaventure in 1261, of a countless throng of men kneeling before the Portiuncula, imploring and obtaining God's mercy.

Bibliography: P. SABATIER, ed., *Fratris Francisci Bartholi de Assisio Tractatus de Indulgentia S. Mariae de Portiuncula* (Paris 1900). R. M. HUBER, *The Portiuncula Indulgence from Honorius III to Pius XI* (New York 1938). M. BIHL, ''Bibliographia,'' *Archivum Franciscanum historicum* 33 (1940) 199–210. G. FUSSENEGGER, *Lexikon für Theologie und Kirche,* ed. J. HOFER and K. RAHNER, 10 v. (2d, new ed. Freiburg 1957–65) 8:625–626. R. BROWN, comp. and tr., *Our Lady and St. Francis* (Chicago 1954). A. FORTINI, *Nova vita di San Francesco,* 4 v. in 5 (Assisi 1959). L. CANONICI, *La Porziuncola e gli inizi dell'Ordine Francescano* (Assisi 1963). J. CAMBELL, ''Glanes Franciscaines: La Première compilation de Barcelone,'' *Archivo Ibero Americano* 23 (1963) 77–78, 86–88, 439–448. O. ENGLEBERT, *St. Francis of Assisi: A Biography,* tr. E. M. COOPER, 2d augm. ed. by I. BRADY and R. BROWN (Chicago 1966).

[R. BROWN]

PORTLAND, ARCHDIOCESE OF

The metropolitan see of Portland (*Portlandensis*) erected as a vicariate apostolic Dec. 1, 1843; created Archdiocese of Oregon City July 24, 1846; name changed to Archdiocese of Portland in Oregon Sept. 26, 1928. It comprises 29,717 square miles in western Oregon, from the Cascade Mountains to the Pacific Ocean between California and the Columbia River, with a total population in 2001 of 2,869,750, including 297,841 Catholics. The metropolitan province of Portland includes the dioceses of Baker, Boise in Idaho, and Great Falls-Billings and Helena in Montana

Early History. During the period that the Oregon Country was jointly occupied by Great Britain and the

U.S. (1818–46), it was the home of native peoples, explorers and fur traders. Gradually the Hudson's Bay Company, under the guidance of Dr. John McLoughlin at Fort Vancouver, dominated the territory. French Canadians, mostly Catholics, and fur trappers settled in the Willamette Valley near St. Paul around 1830, and in 1834 they sent a letter to Bishop Joseph PROVENCHER of Red River, Canada, begging for priests. The bishop arranged to bring the Columbia area into his vicariate, and eventually responded to the settlers' requests. In anticipation of the arrival of priests, the French Canadians built a log church on French Prairie in 1836, the first Catholic church in Oregon.

The archbishop of Quebec selected Francis Norbert BLANCHET (Sept. 3, 1795–June 18, 1883) to be vicar general of the Columbia Mission on April 17, 1838. On May 3, 1838, Father Blanchet left Montreal for Red River, where Father Modeste Demers joined him; and the two missionaries reached Fort Vancouver on Nov. 24, 1838. Soon after their arrival Blanchet visited the log church on French Prairie, celebrating the first Mass in what became the state of Oregon and dedicated the chapel to St. Paul the Apostle (Jan. 6, 1839).

Peter DE SMET, SJ, working in the Rocky Mountains, learned of the priests in the northwest, and in 1842 he came to Fort Vancouver and St. Paul Mission to discuss the future of the mission with Blanchet and Demers. On their own initiative, the three men laid out a plan for the development of the church in the Oregon Country. De Smet left for Europe to secure personnel; Demers went to New Caledonia (now British Columbia) to expand the missions to native tribes; while Blanchet continued to serve the existing missions, writing to church authorities urging support for the plan.

In August of 1844, De Smet returned to Oregon with a party of five Jesuits and six Sisters of Notre Dame de Namur. Meanwhile, Blanchet's letters influenced the decision to elevate the Columbia Mission to a vicariate on Dec. 1, 1843. When the news reached Oregon on Nov. 22, 1844, Francis Blanchet reluctantly accepted the nomination as bishop of the Vicariate of Philadelphia (later changed to Drasa). Blanchet journeyed to Montreal, where he was consecrated bishop on July 25, 1845, and from there he sailed for Europe to gather personnel and financial support. Assisted by Vatican insiders, Blanchet convinced the Holy See to establish the ecclesiastical Province of Oregon City in the Oregon Country; it would have two suffragan bishops, a bishop of Walla Walla, and a bishop of Vancouver Island. On June 18, 1846, the U.S. Senate ratified the treaty bringing Oregon into the Union. On July 24, 1846, Oregon City became the second archdiocese in the United States.

Blanchet's triumphal return to St. Paul on Aug. 26, 1847, with a group of 21, including eight priests and seven more sisters, inspired a flurry of ecclesiastical activity. In December of 1848, Archbishop Blanchet officially moved to Oregon City, the seat of his see. Following the Whitman Massacre in 1848, during which the Cayuse tribe killed 14 people at the Protestant mission and for which Catholics were blamed, a time of widespread anti-Catholicism ensued. Along with the debts from building and departure of much of the male population to the California Gold Rush, the archdiocese struggled to avoid bankruptcy. The desperate archbishop made a successful two-year trip to South America to raise funds.

The Oregon Donation Land Law of 1850 drew population to the territory. Although few of the newcomers were Catholics, the church slowly recovered, and new parishes were established. Oregon City, however, failed to develop, and in 1862 Blancehet transferred his episcopal residence to Portland. In 1851 the Reverend James Croke had established the parish of the Immaculate Conception and the church he built became the procathedral. Twelve Sisters of the Holy Names came from Quebec to revive Catholic education in Oregon in 1859. They soon had schools throughout the state and by 1871 had a novitiate in Portland. Catholic lay societies began to grow, particularly in Portland. With the assistance of the St. Vincent de Paul Society, the Sisters of Providence opened St. Vincent's Hospital in Portland in 1875.

While Blanchet was in Rome attending the first Vatican Council (1868–1870), a Portland group established a newspaper, *The Catholic Sentinel*, still in existence. Blanchet used the paper to battle inequities in Grant's Peace Policy, which turned supervision of native reservations over to religious groups, most often Protestant ones.

Establishment of the Vicariate of Idaho in 1868 reduced the size of the archdiocese, but the resignation of its bishop in 1876 forced Blanchet to take over its administration once again. The aging Blanchet tried for some time to resign. Charles John SEGHERS, Bishop of Vancouver Island, became his coadjutor in 1878, arriving in Portland in July of 1879. Blanchet retired in 1880 and died June 18, 1883.

Bishop Seghers (Dec. 26, 1837–Nov. 28, 1886) left Vancouver Island reluctantly. While waiting for acceptance of Blanchet's retirement, Seghers toured the archdiocese, visiting places no priest had ever been before. A consummate missionary, Seghers paid special attention to the native peoples. During the Seghers administration the Benedictines came to Oregon and established an abbey at Mount Angel, while Benedictine Sisters took up educational work. The archdiocese was consolidated within the state boundaries when vicars apostolic were named for Idaho and Montana. While at a meeting in Rome, Seghers resigned from Portland to return as bishop to the Diocese of Vancouver Island. He was killed by a crazed assistant on Nov. 28, 1886, while on a missionary trip to Alaska.

A man of firsts, William Hickley GROSS, bishop of Savannah, became third archbishop of Oregon City on Feb. 1, 1885. Among other attainments, he was the first American-born archbishop of Oregon City, as well as the first American-born bishop in the west and first member of a religious congregation, the Redemptorists, to become an archbishop in Oregon. One of his first acts was the dedication of the second Cathedral of the Immaculate Conception in Portland, begun in 1878. By 1894 this building was replaced by a temporary cathedral elsewhere, as the area around the second cathedral became commercial.

Gross attracted many new religious communities to the state; and not content with importing nuns, he created his own congregation, now known as the Sisters of St. Mary of Oregon. During this period the church grew rapidly, with new parishes and a dramatically expanded parochial school system. With Gross' encouragement and support, the Benedictines founded Mount Angel College (1887) and a seminary (1889) at their abbey. Social work advanced with the arrival of several congregations of Sisters who opened institutions to serve various needy groups. Eastern Oregon parishes also grew during this period, with more parishes, schools and a Catholic hospital in Baker City.

Archbishop Gross died suddenly in Baltimore on Nov. 14, 1898, and was buried there. Again the Diocese of Vancouver Island provided an archbishop when Bishop Alexander Christie (May 28, 1848–April 6, 1925) became fourth archbishop of Oregon City in February of 1899. The archdiocese was deeply in debt, but the population was growing and more varied than before. In 1903 the archdiocese shrank to its current size, with the establishment of the Diocese of Baker City in the eastern part of the state.

Later Archbishops. Archbishop Christie purchased a former Methodist college in Portland in 1901 to found a school, originally named Columbia University. In 1902 Holy Cross priests and Brothers took over the institution, which became the University of Portland.

Anti-Catholicism, led by the Ku Klux Klan, played an important role in Oregon affairs in Christie's time. In 1922 the state legislature passed the Oregon School Bill intended to force all children up to the age of 16 to attend public schools. Designed to close parochial schools, it lead to the famous OREGON SCHOOL CASE. The Sisters of the Holy Names challenged the law and won. The State in turn appealed to the U.S. Supreme Court, which declared the law unconstitutional in 1925. Christie organized the Catholic Truth Society, which joined the Knights of Columbus in fighting for Catholics' rights. Visits from the chapel cars sponsored by the Catholic Church Extension Society beginning in 1909 led many towns to build churches. Archbishop Christie proposed a new edifice to replace the building that had served as a temporary cathedral but just as his dream for a new cathedral was about to be realized, he died on April 6, 1925.

His replacement was a former teacher and college president from Iowa, Edward Daniel Howard (Nov. 5, 1877–Jan. 2, 1983), destined to serve for over 42 years, from 1924 to 1966. He immediately moved to officially transfer the archdiocese from Oregon City to Portland, which was effected in 1928. With the archdiocese near bankruptcy, Howard consolidated financing and set up a chancery office. The Catholic Truth Society (today the Oregon Catholic Press) began publishing weekly missals that were distributed all over the country. Social work was coordinated under Catholic Charities, as was education under the superintendent of education. The archbishop supported Catholic Action and was deeply involved in social welfare problems, for which he received numerous awards; and he encouraged apostolates for racial minorities. One of his special projects was development of a diocesan-supported Central Catholic High School in Portland, to encourage candidates for the priesthood. Archbishop Howard was the oldest archbishop from the United States at Vatican II. He implemented changes and allowed innovations, starting a Priests' Senate and encouraging ecumenical programs. In 1966 he resigned at the age of 89, and died at the age of 105 years.

Robert Joseph Dwyer (Aug. 1, 1908–March 24, 1876), bishop of Reno, succeeded Howard. Having been a newspaper editor, he continued to write erudite, articulate columns for the *Catholic Sentinel.* While church programs and activities increased in the post Vatican II era, the loss of priests and nuns contributed to school closures. Conflicts over Vatican II changes caused turmoil. Dwyer set up a business manager for the archdiocese, and established a formal budget and accounting practices. He created a vicariate for the Spanish speaking and encouraged inner city social work. The Maronite rite came to the state; the permanent diaconate was reinstituted; Newman centers at colleges and universities expanded. Failing health forced Dwyer's resignation in 1974.

The first native northwesterner to become archbishop of Portland was Cornelius Michael Power (Dec. 18, 1913–May 22, 1997). Former bishop of Yakima, he was appointed as seventh archbishop of Portland on Jan. 22, 1974. Continuing the work of Archbishop Dwyer, he organized the archdiocese using a business model. Rome appointed two auxiliary bishops, Paul Waldschmidt, C.S.C., and Kenneth Steiner to assist him, and he divided the archdiocese into area vicariates, also establishing a Southeast Asian vicariate, and welcomed the Byzantine Rite to the area. Power retired in 1986.

Installed as eighth archbishop of Portland on Sept. 22, 1986, William Joseph Levada (June 15, 1936—), supported lay ministry, ecumenism, and social programs. He reorganized Catholic Charities and carried on a successful campaign to provide a retirement home for priests. Catholic school enrollment began to grow again. In 1993 the archdiocese formed a political action committee which carried on a vigorous but ultimately unsuccessful campaign against the Oregon Assisted Suicide bill. Levada left in 1995 to become archbishop of San Francisco.

For only the second time, a member of a religious community became archbishop of Portland when Francis George, OMI (Jan. 16, 1937—), who had been bishop of Yakima, came to Portland in 1996. His was the shortest administration of any Portland archbishop, not quite one year, before he was named archbishop of Chicago in 1997. The Most Reverend John Vlazney (Feb. 22, 1937—), bishop of Winona, was appointed Oct. 28, 1997 to succeed him.

Bibliography: L. M. LYONS, *Francis Norbert Blanchet and the Founding of the Oregon Missions, 1838–1848* (Catholic University of America *Studies in American Church History* 31; 1940). E. V. O'HARA, *Pioneer Catholic History of Oregon* (4th ed. Paterson 1939). P. BRANDT and L. PEREYRA, *Adapting in Eden* W. P. SCHOENBERG, *A History of the Catholic Church in the Pacific Northwest 1743–1983* (Washington 1987). J. R. LAIDLAW, *The Catholic Church in Oregon and the Work of Its Archbishops* (Smithtown, NY 1977).

[P. BRANDT]

PORTLAND, DIOCESE OF (MAINE)

The Diocese of Portland (*Portlandensis*) comprising the entire state of Maine is a suffragan of the metropolitan see of Boston. At the time it was established by Pope Pius IX (July 29, 1853), it included Maine and New Hampshire, formerly parts of the Diocese of Boston. After Henry B. Coskery (1808–72), Vicar General of Baltimore, refused, Rome appointed David William BACON (1815–74), a priest of the Diocese of New York, as Portland's first bishop (Jan. 23, 1855).

During Bacon's tenure, the diocese expanded to include the Madawaska territory which the United States had acquired under the Webster-Ashburton Treaty of 1842 but which had remained under the administration of Canadian bishops until the First Vatican Council. As a participant at Vatican I Bacon joined 18 other American bishops in stating, before its pronouncement as a dogma, that it was inopportune to proclaim the doctrine of papal infallibility. An energetic builder of churches and schools as well as an effective speaker, Bacon set the foundations of his new diocese firmly in place before his untimely death at the age of 59.

Bacon's successor, James Augustine HEALY (1830–1900), the first black American Catholic bishop, was named Feb. 12, 1875. He led the diocese for the next quarter-century during which time New Hampshire was separated from the Diocese of Portland with the creation of the Diocese of Manchester in 1884. The influx of a large French-speaking population from Quebec had helped to expand the Catholic population in cities like Biddeford, Lewiston, and Waterville so that it became necessary to provide even more schools and parishes for an ethnic group that constituted the majority of the state's Catholic population, almost 100,000 at the time of the bishop's death. Healey's work had been enhanced by the charitable and educational works of the Sisters of Mercy among the Irish and French as well as among the Native Americans on the reservations.

William Henry O'CONNELL (1859–1944), a native of Lowell, Massachusetts succeeded Healy, February 8. O'Connell remained in office until he was named Boston's coadjutor on Feb. 21, 1906. While his tenure in Portland was short, it was distinguished by his attempts to improve relations with peoples of different faiths and of different ethnic backgrounds within the state. By encouraging Catholics to become part of the social mainstream, O'Connell brought prestige to the church just as he did when he was appointed, Aug. 31, 1905, papal envoy to the Emperor of Japan in the wake of the Russo-Japanese War.

When O'Connell moved on Boston in 1906, Louis Sebastian Walsh (1858–1924), a native of Salem, Massachusetts, was named bishop of Portland. While Walsh provided national parishes for immigrants from Italy and Poland, his emphasis on education, including the founding in 1917 of what became Cheverus High School, and his advocacy of public funds to support the Catholic school system proved very controversial in an era when his coreligionists were defending their right to send their children to parochial schools.

The next two bishops were natives of Waterbury, Connecticut. On May 25, 1925, Rome named John Gregory Murray (1877–1936), who had been auxiliary Bishop of Hartford, to succeed Walsh. His facility in languages helped him to strengthen the faith among the state's immigrant groups. However, the financial stress induced by the worldwide Depression towards the end of his tenure severely handicapped the subsequent development of his diocese. After Murray was appointed Archbishop of St. Paul, Minnesota, Oct. 29, 1931, Joseph Edward McCarthy (1876–1955) became the bishop of Portland, on May 13, 1932. A heavy diocesan debt severely limited McCarthy in what he able to do by way of developing the parishes, schools, and other services of his geographically extensive jurisdiction. To his credit, McCarthy was able to lighten that burden and to become for his flock a good shepherd who was regarded with deep respect to his last days.

Portland's next bishop, Daniel Joseph Feeney (1984–1969) took office Sept. 8, 1955. As a native son who for ten years had served as auxiliary bishop and coadjutor to Bishop McCarthy, he was well prepared for the tasks that lay ahead. Once he effectively freed the diocese of its financial constraints, Feeney was able to undertake the construction of a number of new schools and churches. Feeney, who had attended the Second Vatican Council, moved forward to implement conciliar reforms even when the changes were controversial.

Peter Leo Gerety (b. 1912), who succeeded McCarthy on Sept. 15, 1969, served the diocese of Portland until March, 25, 1974 when he was appointed to the archiepiscopal see of Newark. Although Gerety's tenure in Portland was of short duration, it was distinguished for his innovations in revamping the Church's social services so that it reflected more comprehensively the teachings of the Second Vatican Council.

When Gerety moved on to Newark, Edward Cornelius O'Leary (b. 1920), who had served as Auxiliary Bishop of Portland since 1971, became the ordinary on Oct. 22, 1974, Bishop O'Leary resigned on Sept. 27, 1988, but in the 14 years he served as Portland's bishop, he brought the leadership of the church closer to the people. This was reflected, for example, in the appointment of Armadee Wilfrid Proulx (1932–1993), a Franco-American, as auxiliary bishop. Franco-Americans constitute the largest ethnic group among Maine's Roman Catholics.

With O'Leary's resignation on Dec. 21, 1988, Rome appointed the former abbot of St Anselm's Abbey and auxiliary bishop of Manchester, N.H., Joseph John Gerry O.S.B., (b. 1928), as the Tenth Bishop of Portland. Gerry brought with him his monastic love of the Holy Scriptures which emerged in his homilies, but at the administrative level Gerry had to face the consolidation of parishes and schools because of the shortage of priests, religious and laity necessary to staff them. With Bishop Michael Richard Cote as his auxiliary, Gerry's task of leading a flock of over 200,000 Roman Catholics is made easier by presence in the diocese of men religious like the Dominicans, Franciscans, Jesuits, and Brothers of Christian Instruction, women religious like the Sisters of Mercy, Sisters of St. Joseph, the Ursulines, and a host of others to help the diocese in its charitable, educational, and pastoral ministries.

Bibliography: J. P. ALLEN, *Catholics in Maine* (1970). W. L. LUCEY, *The Catholic Church in Maine* (1957). Newspaper Catalog, Portland Room, Portland Public Library.

[V.A. LAPOMARDA]

PORTUGAL, THE CATHOLIC CHURCH IN

The Portuguese Republic is located on the Atlantic coast of the Iberian Peninsula of Europe, and is bordered on the north and east by Spain. Mountains and the Douro, Mondego and Tagus Rivers divide the country into east-west regions. The south has a Mediterranean climate while the central and north have an Atlantic climate. Portugal, including the Azores and Madeira islands, possesses natural resources that include cork, tungsten, iron ore, uranium and marble. Among its agricultural products are grains, potatoes, olives, grapes, livestock, poultry and diary products. Earthquakes occur frequently in the Azores.

The region was visited by Celts from the 6th to the 2d century B.C., Romans *c.* 137 B.C., and Suevi in the 5th century, was invaded by the Moors between the 8th and 13th centuries, and received Jewish and African immigrants between the 15th and 18th centuries. In Roman times the area of modern Portugal covered most of the province of Lusitania and part of Galicia. Barbarian Suevi held the north from 411 to 585, and in the 10th and 11th centuries the county of Porto gradually spread south to include all Portuguese territory freed from the Moors in 1095. Since 1139 Portugal has been independent except for a period under Spanish rule (1580–1640). In 1910 the country adopted a republican form of government, and from 1932 to 1968 it was dominated by António de Oliveira Salazar (1889–1970) who ruled as a virtual dictator. A coup in April of 1974 brought constitutional democracy to the country following initial revolutionary instability. Subsequently, all the Portuguese overseas territories became independent, the last, Macau, returning to China in 1999. The liberation movement in the overseas provinces, especially in Angola, had far-reaching demographic and economic consequences because it caused many of Portuguese descent to seek refuge in Portugal. Portugal became a member of the European Union in 1986.

The following essay is in three parts. Part one covers the early church through 1495; part two covers the Church from 1495 to 1900; the third covers the Church through the 20th century.

Capital: Lisbon.
Size: 35,672 sq. miles.
Population: 10,048,230 in 2000.
Languages: Portuguese.
Religions: 9,445,335 Catholics (94%), 200,975 Protestants (2%), 25,000 Muslims (.2%), 376,920 practice other faiths or are without religious affiliation.

Ecclesiastical History to 1495

There were Christians in Portugal probably shortly after Apostolic times. The accounts of the early 4th-century martyrs Verissimus, Maxima and Julia in Lisbon and Victor in Braga are of later date. Bishops Liberius of Mérida, Vincent of Ossonoba and Quintianus of Évora attended the Council of ELVIRA *c.* 304; and Potamius of Lisbon (357) was an important adversary of Arianism. The 4th century was more noteworthy, however, for the lengthy controversy over Pelagianism, which exhibited the attraction of novel doctrines and rigorous asceticism in Galicia and Lusitania, as well as the strong reaction of local Christians against heresy. The monk Baquiarius and two priests of Braga named Avitus distinguished themselves in this controversy. By 400 Braga (Bishop Paternus) joined Ossonoba, Évora and Lisbon as a known Portuguese bishopric (metropolitanate of Galicia).

Barbarian Suevi, Vandals and Alans invaded and occupied the west of the peninsula in 411. While the Vandals and Alans moved on to Africa, the Suevi formed an independent kingdom (411–585) and revived paganism and Priscillianism before King Rechiarius (d. 457) became Catholic; but in 465 they adopted Arianism. Paul OROSIUS had to flee Braga, and in 460 HYDATIUS of Chaves was imprisoned. Religious decline was halted by St. MARTIN OF BRAGA, who *c.* 550 converted the Suevi king to Catholicism and organized the first rural parishes. JOHN OF BICLARO, a native of Scalabis (Santarém) and Apringius of Beja lived in this period, when Braga was extending its influence south at the expense of MÉRIDA. Christian prosperity under the Suevi was threatened by the Arian Visigoths conquest of 585, but continued after the conversion to Catholicism of Visigoth King Reccared in 587. With the establishment of the religious center of Spain in Toledo, Galicia became less prominent in the Christian world, but its bishops and those of Lusitania always attended the councils of TOLEDO. Only in 650, however, did Mérida regain the sees made suffragan to Braga in the previous century. St. FRUCTUOSUS OF BRAGA (d. 665) is famous for his pastoral and monastic activity under Visigothic rule.

Like Spain, Portugal experienced an Arab invasion from 711 to 713. Christians remaining under Muslim rule continued for the most part to practice their religion, yet little is known of the conditions of their life. Many bishops fled to the north, and used the titles of their sees in exile. Reconquest expeditions of the 9th and 10th centuries restored the Sees of Porto, Coimbra, Lamego and Viseu, but until the definite reconquests by the Castilians Ferdinand I (1055–64) and Alfonso VI (1093) life remained precarious. Although Braga was restored in 1070, the bishop of Coimbra administered Lamego and Viseu until the 12th century and Lugo retained the metropolitan rights it obtained during the exile of the bishop of Braga. The success of SANTIAGO DE COMPOSTELA as a pilgrimage center led its bishop to also claim metropolitan rights. Braga's rights to the pallium were thus not restored until 1101.

Saints FROILÁN (d. 905), ATTILANUS (d. 916) and Rosendus (d. 977) restored monasteries and reorganized Christian life throughout Galicia. Those cities abandoned in the face of warfare were slowly restored, especially the important economic and political center of Porto, although they continued as traditional ecclesiastical centers. Of more importance, especially north of the Douro, were the monasteries, strong points in the repopulation of the country and in close dependence on the rural nobility. In the 10th century were founded Guimarães, Cete, Vairão, Lorvão, Arouca, Paço de Sousa and Santo Tirso; in the 11th century, Pedroso, Pendorada, Rio Tinto, Vilar de Frades, POMBEIRO, Bostelo and others.

The French Influence: 1080–1185. Christian life changed course *c.* 1080 and became more vigorous after contact with French monks and knights and with pilgrims returning to the peninsula from abroad. Whereas previously the ideal had been to restore Visigothic tradition and institutions, now many influences from beyond the Pyrenees were incorporated with the support of Bishop Cresconius of Coimbra (d. 1098). Dioceses adopted the Roman liturgy and the organization of archdeaconries; monasteries adopted the Benedictine rule and the customs of CLUNY. In 1095 the county of Porto was granted to Henry of Burgundy, son-in-law of Alfonso VI of Castile. The See of Braga was occupied by St. GERALD (d. 1108), a monk of MOISSAC; the See of Coimbra by Maurice Burdin, from LIMOGES; and the See of Porto by Hugh, probably also a Frenchman. Cluny had three priories: Rates, S. Justa of Coimbra and Vimieiro. The GREGORIAN REFORM came into effect; simony, lay patronage, marriages of kinship and other abuses were suppressed.

Ecclesiastical Provinces	Suffragans
Braga	Aveiro, Bragança-Miranda, Coimbra, Lamego, Oporto, Viana do Castelo, Vila Real, Viseu
Lisbon	Angra (Azores), Funchal (Madeira), Guarda, Leiria, Fátima, Portalegre-Castelo Branco, Santarém, Setúbal
Évora	Beja, Faro

Lisbon was made a patriarchate of the Latin Church in 1716.

Before 1150, however, exempt monasteries were extremely rare.

When Alfonso I became king of Portugal in 1139, the prelates supported Portuguese independence from Castile, which was confirmed with the acknowledging of vassalage to the Holy See in 1143. Lisbon was reconquered in 1147 with the help of a Crusader fleet of English, Frisians and Germans, and the see was bestowed on an English crusader. In his domestic policy too, Alfonso relied on close collaboration with the clergy: restoring the Sees of Lisbon, Lamego, Viseu (1147) and Évora (1165), granting charters of immunity to almost all monasteries of any importance, strongly supporting the canonical reform (1131) of Telus and St. THEOTONIUS in SANTA CRUZ of Coimbra, introducing Cistercians in ALCOBAÇA with generous grants (1153), supporting the foundation of a military order in Évora (1164) and making concessions to the Templars in THOMAR (1160). With such royal backing, Cistercians and Augustinians spread widely, Cistercians in Tarouca, Lafões, Salzedas, Sever, Fiães and Aguiar; and Augustinians in Grijó, Moreira, S. Simão da Junqueira, Vilela, Roriz, Cárquere, Refojos de Lima and S. Vincente of Lisbon. The most powerful bishops were those of Braga and Porto, holding exempt lands from 1112 and 1120. The richest Benedictine monasteries had scriptoria to copy manuscripts (almost all lost), but most devoted themselves to a well-organized life of rural work. The MILITARY ORDERS, rich in lands, assured the defense and repopulation of central and south Portugal.

Tension between Church and Throne. The prosperity and influence of the Church in Portugal provoked stronger and stronger reactions from the civil authority, beginning with Sancho I (1185–1211), whose conflicts with Bishops Martin Rodrigues of Porto in 1208 and Peter Soares of Coimbra in 1210 were sporadic and personal. Alfonso II (1211–23) made the conflict a legal one, promulgating laws against the MORTMAIN of ecclesiastical goods and ordering inquiries as to whether or not clerical property had been acquired by usurpation. Jurists at court, such as Gonçalo Mendes and Mestre Vicente, followed the spirit of Roman law and supported royal claims. The failure of Sancho II (1223–45) to suppress disorders led to his deposition by Innocent IV after the Council of LYONS, at the request of the Portuguese bishops. The throne passed to his brother, Alfonso III (1245–70), count of Bologna, who, seeking to increase royal power, ordered new inquiries into ecclesiastical holdings in 1258 and maintained the struggle against the clergy until his death. The tension ended only under Denis (1279–1325), who established a concordat with the clergy in 1282.

Power struggles between the clergy and the crown were not a symptom of crisis; on the contrary, the secular clergy was growing in prestige and number, and gained official recognition of the privileges that gave them their own courts, military exemption, special jurisdiction with regard to wills and tax exemption. Only the first of these privileges was contested with frequency during this time. The new mendicant orders, Franciscans and Dominicans, favored by the royal family and the people, served as mediators in Church-State disputes. The military orders kept their powerful organizations, but after the reconquest of Portugal was completed in 1249, the king regarded them as a standing army to defend the country, and they turned to the cultivation of their extensive farm lands.

The 1282 concordat of Denis with the clergy began for the Church a period of peace and submission to the State. In 1361 King Peter I (1357–67) required that papal bulls be published only with royal approval. During the WESTERN SCHISM King Ferdinand I (1367–83) decided first to support the Roman claimant Urban VI (1378–89), then to observe neutrality (1379), then to follow Clement VII (1380) and finally to recognize Urban again (1381). The bishops were also undecided; some sees had two prelates, one named by Rome and one by Avignon. The Church's political decline showed itself in other ways, and by 1345 the immunity of the powerful bishop of Porto was suppressed. Benedictine, Cistercian and Augustinian monasteries, at odds with the ruling nobility and unable to keep pace with the urbanization of society, suffered in revenue and discipline. Dominicans and Franciscans multiplied, but were divided into conventuals and observants. The military orders organized their possessions into grants, which were distributed to their knights. Many instances of witchcraft and superstition occurred. Bishop ALVARO PELAYO OF SILVES (d. 1352) vehemently denounced the religious deterioration. Despite the decline, King Denis, on the initiative of several abbots and priors, founded in 1290 the University of Lisbon, which

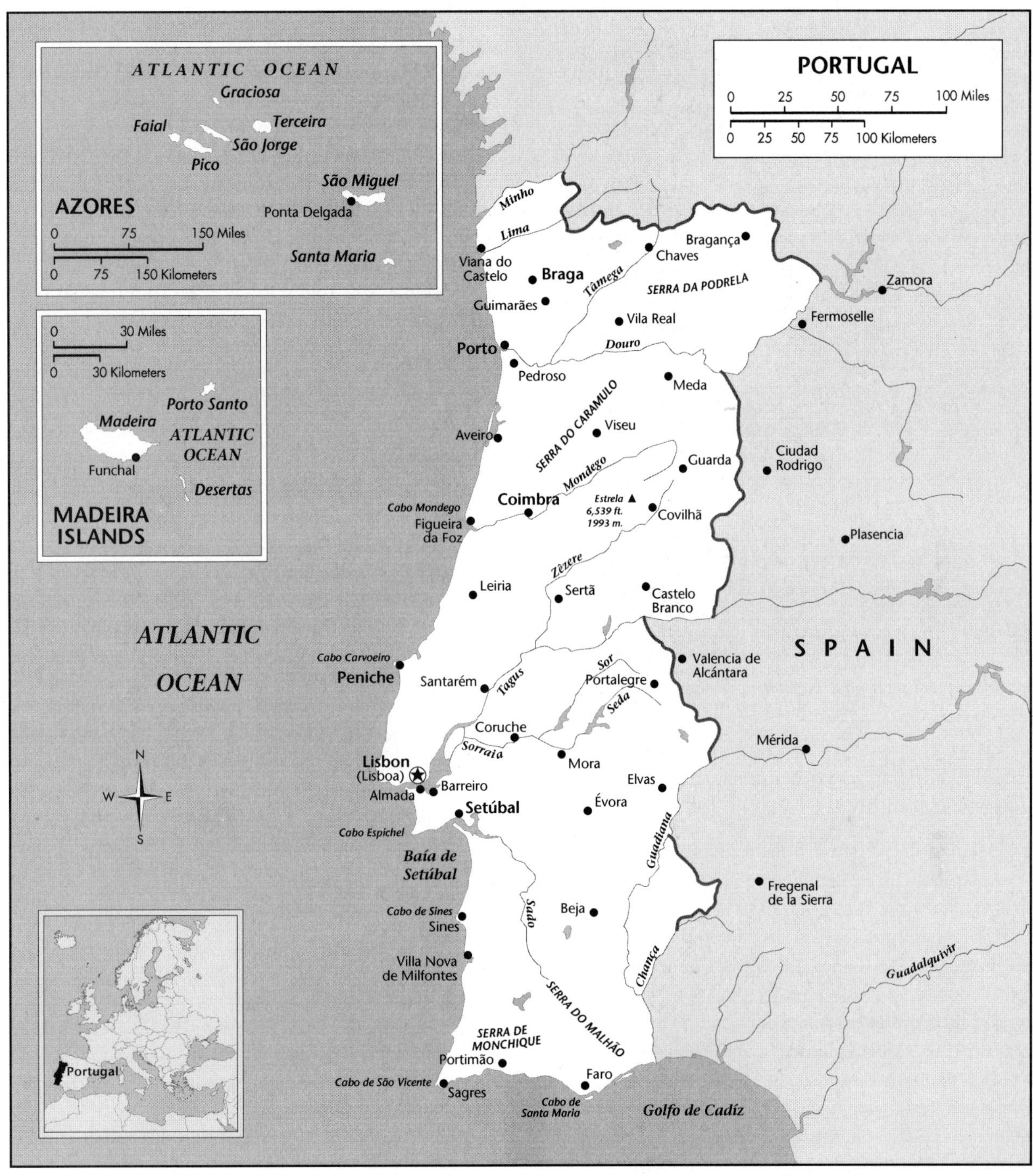

moved to COIMBRA in 1308. The military ORDER OF CHRIST was created in 1319 and endowed with the possessions of the Templars.

From Decline to Revivial: 1385–1495. The Aviz dynasty (1385–1580) in the person of John I (1385–1433) gained the throne of Portugal as the national hero Nuno Álvares Pereira defeated the Castilian attempt at succession in the battle of Aljubarrota (1385). The ensuing political renaissance was accompanied by a religious resurgence and conflicts between king and clergy arose in 1426, 1436 and 1455. Alfonso V (1438–81) again required royal approval of papal bulls, but King John II's repeal of the order in 1487 showed the strength of the revived Church, a strength that derived from the new spirit characteristic of the expansion overseas after the 1415 conquest of Ceuta. The expeditions sent along the coast of Africa by Prince Henry the Navigator almost always

Statue of St. Teresa behind the altar in Lamego Cathedral, Lamego, Portugal. (©Tony Arruza/CORBIS)

carried Franciscan and Augustinian missionaries who evangelized the natives.

Many events figured in the religious renaissance. A new metropolitan see was created in Lisbon in 1393 with Évora, Lamego, Guarda and Silves as suffragans. Portuguese sees incorporated territory hitherto subject to Spanish bishops. The Order of Christ assumed spiritual jurisdiction for overseas territories in 1456. The Holy See created the Portuguese nunciature and in 1460 gave the king the title ''Most Faithful.'' John Álvares and Gomes Anes of Florença reformed the Benedictines in Paço de Sousa and the Augustinians in Santa Cruz. Hieronymites entered Portugal in 1389; Carmelites, Augustinians and Hermits of Serra de Ossa prospered; and houses of strict observance appeared among Dominicans (1399) and Franciscans (1443). The order of Canons of St. John the Evangelist for charitable work was founded in 1420. Saints flourished: Gonçalo de Lagos (d. 1422), Nuno Álvares Pereira (d. 1431), the Infante Blessed FERDINAND (d. 1443), Princess Blessed JOAN (d. 1490) and Beatrice da Silva (d. 1490) foundress of the Conceptionists. However, by 1450 decline began to spread rapidly, especially in the old monastic orders and the secular clergy, among whom there were several unworthy bishops. The changes in society caused by overseas discoveries were becoming evident.

Ecclesiastical History since 1495

In 1415 Portugal began the conquest of MOROCCO and the exploration and colonization of the west coast of Africa: the Madeira Islands (1418–20), the Azores (*c.* 1430), the CONGO (1482), and the Cape of Good Hope (1487). In approximately 1497 Vasco da Gama reached India by an all-sea route, and in 1500 Pedro Álvares Cabral reached Brazil. Because of the 1494 Peace of Tordesillas with Spain, Portugal's empire extended from Brazil to the East Indies. A maritime empire was organized with centers in Ormuz, Goa and Singapore that evolved into a royal monopoly of the spice trade. In 1551 the king became grand master of the Order of Christ, which had ecclesiastical jurisdiction of the overseas possessions.

Missionary work was done by several orders. Missions to the Congo began in 1490–91 and had success under the native King Alfonso, whose son Henry was consecrated bishop in 1518; but after Alfonso's death (1543) the activity declined as Portugal directed her efforts to the East. The mission to Mozambique in 1560 had quick and spectacular success but failed almost as quickly and spectacularly, probably due to the opposition of Islam. The mission to Angola in 1560 failed, but another in 1578 succeeded, and in 1596 a bishopric was established at Massangano. An elaborately prepared mission to Christian Ethiopia (1545–56) came to nothing. The weakness of Portuguese missions was that the personnel were too few and far between to deal with continental areas and only a peripheral effort on the coasts could be made. The greatest success came in BRAZIL, where Jesuits expanded rapidly south from Bahia after 1549, and with only 63 missionaries, covered the coast by 1600. Missionaries exercised considerable civil authority in organizing the nomadic natives of Brazil, but their efforts were hindered by the disrupting practice of slavery pursued by Portuguese colonists. Missionary activity in the Portuguese empire declined after 1600; and in the 18th century, when the religious orders were expelled from Portugal, it dwindled further.

The Decline of the State: 1495–1580. The strong reign of Manuel I (1495–1521) was followed by a period of political decline that culminated in 1580 when Spain ended Portuguese independence. The Church then reformed herself for a new period of splendor. Sometimes brutal steps were taken to purify the faith, one of which was the expulsion of thousands of Jews and Muslims in 1496, an action that was motivated by Manuel's desire to marry a Spanish princess (deporting the Jews was a condition of marriage imposed by King Ferdinand and

Bom Jesus Church, Braga, Portugal. (©Tony Arruza/CORBIS)

Queen Isabella, who had done the same in Spain four years earlier). Rather than lose a valuable segment of society, Manuel forced many Jews to convert to Christianity, the threat of prison, torture or death at the stake serving as an inducement to many. Other steps to purify the faith included the initiation of the INQUISITION in 1536 by John III (1521–57) and its extension overseas. The Scot George Buchanan, who taught at Coimbra (1547–50), was imprisoned by the Inquisition (1550–52) and Damião de Goes, brought to trial for contact with Luther and Melanchthon, was abjured (1572). The Inquisition served mostly to increase royal authority.

More effective in raising the religious level were the Jesuits, established in 1540; the appointment of zealous bishops such as Jerónimo Osório of Silves (d. 1580), Baltasar Limpo of Porto and Braga (d. 1558) and Bartolomeu dos Mártires of Braga (d. 1590); the provincial synods of Lisbon, Braga and Évora (1566–67) to enforce the Council of TRENT; the creation of new dioceses in Leiria, Miranda, Portalegre and Elvas, and the new metropolitanate in Évora; the 18 new dioceses established outside the country, including Funchal (1514), which at first embraced all overseas possessions; the reorganization of the University of Lisbon and the creation of that of Évora in 1559; the building of seminaries in Lisbon and Braga; and the gradual suppression of commendatory abbots in Benedictine, Cistercian and Augustinian monasteries. Such measures as these reinvigorated spiritual and intellectual life. The monastic orders were reformed through the influence of the Hieronymites, Augustinians, Arrábidos and Jesuits. There were saints, such as St. JOHN OF GOD (d. 1550) and the overseas martyrs. In recognition of the missionary endeavor, the Holy See in 1514 granted the king of Portugal the padroado over the metropolitanate and all overseas possessions, a right of patronage that lasted in India until 1950.

The Intellectual Age: The 17th-18th Century Church. After King Sebastian (1557–78) was slain in an attempt to conquer Morocco, the aged and feeble Henry II (1578–80) was unable to prevent the annexation of Portugal by PHILIP II OF SPAIN. John IV (1640–56) restored Portuguese independence, which continued under the Bragança dynasty from 1640 to 1853. This dynasty was characterized by a period of religious stability characterized by a constant defense against heretics and an isolation that slowly drained the practice of the faith of vigor and originality. Several orders entered the country—Hospitallers in 1606, Capuchins in 1647, Theatines in 1650, Discalced Augustinians in 1663 and Apostolic Missionaries in 1679—but their influence was limited, and most attention was devoted to speculative theology, Canon Law, history and to sacred oratory. More serious was the refusal of the Holy See, on the request of Spain, to name bishops to Portuguese dioceses between 1640–70. One bishop served in Portugal and its overseas possessions from 1658 to 1668, and none in 1669. This attitude of Rome promoted a tendency to regalism. Only Oratorians (1659) were important, because of their educational work; their college in Lisbon (1750) became famous for studies in natural science and philosophy.

King John V (1706–50), titled ''Most Faithful'' by the Holy See in 1748, began a policy of regalism with Church support. In return for aiding Pope Clement XI against the Turks he received extraordinary powers for the archbishop of Lisbon (made a patriarch in 1716). While also presenting the pope with lavish gifts and constructing impressive monasteries at Mafra and Vila do Conde, John broke relations with Rome from 1728–31 and in 1728 made royal approval of papal acts necessary in Portugal.

John's successor, Joseph I (1750–77), influenced by the ENLIGHTENMENT and by his minister the Marques de POMBAL, pushed regalism further. He expelled the Jesuits from Portugal and its vast colonial holdings, closed the University of Évora (1759), severed relations with Rome (1760–69), promulgated decrees against the Oratorians, turned the Inquisition into a royal tribunal, suppressed several Augustinian monasteries, secularized education (1772), favored the spread of GALLICANISM and JANSENISM, and interfered in a number of religious congregations on the pretext of investigating the Jacobeu and Sigilista fanatical movements. Inevitably Christian life declined. The religious orders that entered Portugal—Camillians, Vincentians, Minims and Ursulines—were unable to turn the tide, and the traditionalist movement that followed the fall of Pombal had no lasting results.

The invasion by the French from 1807–11 ended the spread of revolutionary ideas in Portugal. The monarchy fled to Brazil from 1807 to 1820 until that region gained independence in 1822. Meanwhile, the revolution of 1820 in Portugal installed a liberal regime and suppressed clerical privileges, which the traditionalist and absolutist government of Michael I (1828–34) did not restore. In the struggle between liberals and absolutists the clergy were divided. In 1834 liberalism suppressed male religious orders and closed women's novitiates, expelled the papal nuncio and regarded as invalid the nominations of bishops by Michael I. Relations with Rome were restored in 1841, but property that had been confiscated was not restored to the Church. Gradually religious returned, but their presence was barely tolerated in an atmosphere wherein the Church was without prestige or social influence. Instead, it was subjected to constant attacks by the intelligentsia, ridiculed in the press and restricted in its activity by some public officials (*see* ANTICLERICALISM). The number of dioceses in Portugal was reduced in 1881, and apostolic life was evidenced only by the foundation of the National Center in 1874 and the Academic Center of Christian Democracy (CADC) in 1903; by the holding of several congresses; and by the beginning of a Catholic daily newspaper, *A Palavra,* in 1872.

Bibliography: Sources. C. ERDMANN, *Papsturkunden in Portugal* (Berlin 1927); *Das Papsttum und Portugal im ersten Jahrhundert der portugiesischen Geschichte* (Berlin 1928). J. DOS SANTOS ABRANCHES, *Summa do bullario portuguez* (Coimbra 1895). L. A. REBELO DA SILVA et al., *Corpo diplomático portuguez: Relações com a curia romana,* 16 v. (Lisbon 1862–1958). A. DA SILVA RÊGO, *Documentação para a história das missões do padroado português do Oriente,* 12 v. (Lisbon 1947–58). A. GARCIA RIBEIRO DE VASCONCELOS, *Nota chronologico-bibliographica das constituições diocesanas impressas* (Coimbra 1911). General works. F. DE ALMEIDA, *História da Igreja em Portugal,* 4 v. (Coimbra 1910–22); *História de Portugal,* 6 v. (Coimbra 1922–29). *História de Portugal,* ed. D. PERES, 8 v. (Barcelos 1928–37). R. KONETZKE, *Geschichte des spanischen und portugiesischen Volkes* (Leipzig 1939). H. LIVERMORE, *A History of Portugal* (London 1947). M. A. DE OLIVEIRA, *História eclesiástica de Portugal* (3d ed. Lisbon 1958); *As paróquias rurais portuguesas: Sua origem e formação* (Lisbon 1950); *Lenda e história: Estudos hagiográficos* (Lisbon 1964). B. J. WENZEL, *Portugal und der Heilige Stuhl* (Lisbon 1958). A. BRÁSIO, *Monumenta missionaria africana,* 12 v. (Lisbon 1952–64). L. M. JORDÃO, *Bullarium Patronatus Portugalliae regum in ecclesiis Africae, Asiae atque Oceaniae bullas,* 5 v. (Lisbon 1868–79). Early period. P. DAVID, *Études historiques sur la Galice et le Portugal du VI*[e] *au XII*[e] *siècle* (Lisbon 1947). M. MARTINS, *Correntes da filosofia religiosa em Braga dos s. iv a vii* (Porto 1950); *Estudos de literatura medieval* (Braga 1956). B. X. DA COSTA COUTINHO, *Acção do papado na fundação e independência de Portugal* (2d ed. Porto 1940). E. A. O'MALLEY, *Tello and Theotonio: The 12th-Century Founders of the Monastery of Santa Cruz in Coimbra* (Washington 1954). A. E. REUTER, *Königtum und Episkopat in Portugal im 13. Jahrhundert* (Berlin 1928). A. DOMINGUES DE SOUSA COSTA, ''Mestre Silvestre e Mestre Vicente, juristas da contenda entre D. Afonso II e suas irmãs,'' *Itinerarium,* 8 (1962) 87–136; 9 (1963) 249–311; 11 (1965) 54–97. J. C. BAPTISTA, ''Portugal e o cisma do ocidente,'' *Lusitania sacra,* 1 (1956) 65–203. A. DE J. DA COSTA, *O bispo D. Pedro e a organização da diocese de Braga,* 2 v. (Coimbra 1959).

[J. MATTOSO]

The Modern Church

Following the assassination of King Charles I in 1890, the republican revolution of 1910 expelled the papal nuncio, confiscated seminaries and episcopal residences, dispersed religious, forbade processions and the wearing of clerical garb, appointed lay committees to regulate church services, and tried, imprisoned and exiled priests and bishops. However, instead of destroying Christian life, it generated a reaction. The episcopacy united. New associations appeared, such as the Catholic Union (1913). In Coimbra an elite group of Catholic intellectuals formed, among them António de Oliveira Salazar, then a professor of economics at the University of Coimbra. In 1917 a military coup installed Sidonio Pais, who restored relations with the Holy See in 1918 and ended the harassment of the Church. The military coup of 1926 that brought Salazar to power six years later stabilized politics and finances and inaugurated a period of cooperation with the Church, during which the State gave special protection to missionary congregations. The concordat confirmed this cooperation with the Holy See in 1940, that among other things, permitted the government to veto the appointment of bishops nominated by the Church, upheld the denial of divorce in cases of Catholic marriage, provided that morality be taught in schools and gave the Church responsibility for religious education in public schools.

Salazar and the New State. While the ''New State'' introduced in 1933 by Prime Minister Salazar represented a welcome reaction against the anti-clericalism of the Republic of 1910–26, there remained some dissatisfaction among a minority of Catholics with the social and political shortcomings of the regime. The Portuguese hierarchy, led until 1971 by Manuel Gonçalves Cardinal Cerejeira, a student friend of Salazar, generally shared the government's vision of an orderly and stable regime well disposed toward the Church, whose social principles it claimed to follow, with overseas territories constitutionally incorporated into the state in 1951. Cerejeira naturally defended the Church's interests but usually accepted the regime's version of events. Opposed to totalitarianism, a category from which he excluded the ''New State,'' he warned his flock against collaboration with communists.

One episcopal exception to the general harmony was António Ferreira Gomes, bishop of Oporto, who in 1958 sent Salazar a letter, which became public knowledge, in which he advocated political pluralism and criticized the regime's social and labor policies. A year later, after Catholic activists in Lisbon had been arrested for conspiring to overthrow the regime, the bishop was refused entry when returning from Rome, being allowed back only in 1969 by Marcello Caetano, who succeeded Salazar as premier (1968–74). Other critics included Sebastião Soares de Resende, bishop of Beira in Mozambique, who clashed with the secular authorities over publication of his defense of human rights in that territory in 1965, and Manuel Vieira Pinto, bishop of Nampula (Mozambique), who was removed from his diocese in 1974 by Caetano's administration for criticism of colonial policies and opposing the expulsion of priests denouncing atrocities committed by Portuguese forces.

Church-state relations were also troubled by Pope Paul VI's visit to the Bombay Eucharistic Congress in 1964. Portugal's foreign minister called it a gratuitous insult, for by visiting India the pope was seen as condoning that country's forcible incorporation of Portugal's Indian territories (chiefly Goa) in 1961. The censorship of the visit in the Portuguese media led to the removal from state radio of António Ribeiro for opposing the government's line. The state then objected to Ribeiro's appointment to the see of Beira in 1967, the only known instance of a state veto under the terms of the Concordat of 1940. Ribeiro succeeded Cerejeira as patriarch of Lisbon in 1971 and was named a cardinal by Paul VI in 1973.

Effects of Vatican II. Forty-nine Portuguese bishops attended the Second Vatican Council in 1962–65. In the short term, the Council resulted in Mass in Portuguese, and the bishops formally acknowledged the Council's decrees, decisions and declarations. The majority of the Portuguese clergy and laity, however, were unenthusiastic about change, and debate was confined to members of the clergy and the (generally urban) lay elite. Differences of opinion on implementation of conciliar recommendations often overlapped with the widening divisions of opinion in Catholic circles from 1958 regarding the authoritarian practices of the ''New State'' regime and the colonial wars of 1961–74. Although the majority of the laity, like the older bishops and clergy, generally remained conservative in attitude, the application of Vatican II's recommendations made gradual but steady progress after the revolutionary disorientation of the mid-1970s.

The influence of Vatican II eventually found its way into a number of state-funded organizations. One success was the foundation of the Portuguese Catholic University in 1967 on the basis of the Faculty of Philosophy in Braga. It achieved juridical recognition in 1971 and by 1988 had 6,000 students in Faculties of Theology, Philosophy and Human Sciences in Lisbon, Braga, Oporto and Viseu. Prominent charitable institutions include diocesan *Caritas Portuguesa* and the *Santas Casas da Misericórdia.* Over 380 of these traditional welfare institutions, running hospitals, hospices, orphanages, homes for the elderly and disabled, and canteens, often with state support, were reorganized in 1976 into the Union of Portuguese Misericórdias. The Lisbon Misericórdia, under the Franciscan Vítor Melícias, funded by the state, was responsible for most welfare services in the capital. The Union of Private Institutions of Social Solidarity that oversaw social centers, youth clubs and crèches were also state supported.

A Radicalized Clergy. By 1974 Portugal contained a minority of activist clergy and lay persons among such groups as Portuguese Catholic Action, Catholic Workers' Youth, Catholic Workers' League, and in the male and female Catholic University Youth, caught up in campus protests. Battles for independence in Portugal's many colonies waged, sparking differences of opinion regarding many aspects of government and society. The relaxation of authoritarianism during Caetano's regime highlighted the increased diversity of Catholic opinion. In the elections of 1969 prominent Catholic laymen ran as candidates for the state's National Union as independents, as monarchists and in alliance with communists. After a military coup and the granting of independence to all of Portugal's African colonies in 1975, the minority of progressive Catholics channeled their energies into leftist parties, notably the Portuguese Democratic Movement (PSD) and Socialist Left Movement. Free Assemblies of Christians and radicalized priests called for the resignation of some or all of their ''collaborationist'' bishops. The bishops responded by exhorting Catholics to aid in building a pluralist system based on the Christian conception of democracy. Marxism was condemned, as was extreme capitalist individualism, but moderate socialism was specifically deemed within the parameters of political acceptability.

Constitutional Democracy Forms. As Portugal struggled through several years of political unrest, the revision of the concordat of 1940 was agreed by negotiation with the Holy See. The 1971 Law on Religious Freedom granted the Church favored status through tax exemptions and control over the naming of chaplains. Divorce was legalized for Catholic spouses. In 1975 the episcopacy expressed its growing concern over the nationalization of charitable institutions and the occupations of Catholic educational establishments and highlighted the need for freedom of education.

Following the election of President Antonio Eanes in 1976, a new constitution was promulgated that specified freedom of religion and freedom of education. A 1979 law ensured parity of treatment for Catholic schools. The bishops continued to condemn Communism and pure economic liberalism. The PSD, which governed either in coalition or alone from 1980, upheld ''Religion and Morality'' classes in the school curriculum, supported the Catholic University, subsidized the building of Braganza cathedral, allowed the clergy tax exemptions and awarded a television channel to a church consortium. The most serious clash between church and state occurred over abortion. A draft law for its decriminalization proposed in 1982 was denounced as immoral by the episcopacy. Despite Catholic street demonstrations, a law permitting certain abortions in cases of rape, when the mother's health was endangered or when the fetus was deformed, was passed in 1984. Legislation to legalize abortion was reintroduced in 1997 but was defeated by a single vote.

During the last decades of the 20th century Portuguese bishops voiced continuing concern over abortion, Catholic schooling, family life and values, housing, health care, the renewal of the Church, the role of the laity, the Church's cultural and historical patrimony, the problems of immigrants and the unemployed, corruption and social degradation, immorality, environmental conservation, the campaign against AIDS and such international issues as human rights in the former Portuguese colony of East Timor, China and elsewhere. Throughout the 1990s Manuel da Silva Martins, bishop of Setúbal, was a leading critic of social injustice and poverty.

A major obstacle to the fulfillment of the Church's mission continued to be a shortage of clergy. While the north and the Atlantic islands were relatively well provided with priests, numbers were lacking in the south. Vocations, never plentiful in Portugal, fell off dramatically in the 1960s and 1970s. By the early 1990s two-thirds of the clergy were over 56 and nearly a quarter over 70 years of age.

Despite the shortage felt among the clergy, popular religiosity continued to be impressively seen in the continuing pilgrimages of hundreds of thousands of Portuguese to FÁTIMA on May 13, the date of the first apparition of the Virgin before three children in 1917. Crediting the lady with saving his life during an assassination attempt on her feast day, Pope John Paul II paid three visits to Fátima. During the first, in 1982, he was assailed by the Spanish priest Juan Fernández Krohn, but visits in 1991 and 2000 were peaceful. Popular religiosity also survived in other pilgrimages, in traditional festivals such as those of St. Antony in Lisbon and St. John in Oporto and Braga, in veneration of local saints and village festivals and in romarias (often noisy outings to destinations of religious significance).

Into the 21st Century. By 2000 there were 4,359 parishes tended by 3,273 diocesan and 976 religious priests. Other religious included approximately 345 brothers and 7,000 sisters, many of whom attended to the operation of Portugal's primary and secondary Catholic schools. By 2000 the socialist government was attempting to diminish the privileged status of the Church through a bill that would fund religious education through the voluntary allocation of money from taxpayers rather than through a state payment. Discussion was also underway regarding renegotiation of the Concordat of 1940 with the Vatican.

Issues of continued concern to the Church into the next millennium included the migration from countryside to city, the changing role of women in society and the increased influence of the mass media on culture. In addition, the increased prosperity and the quest for upward social mobility continued to exacerbate materialism, individualism and hedonism, which Church leaders saw as corrosive to traditional and family values.

Bibliography: A. DA SILVA RÊGO, *O padroado português do oriente* (Lisbon 1940); *História das missões do padroado português do oriente* (Lisbon 1949–). E. G. JACOB, *Das portugiesische Kolonialreich* (Leipzig 1940). *Portugal 1140–1640: Festschrift,* ed. F. SCHALK, (Cologne 1940). J. S. DA SILVA DIAS, *Correntes do sentimento religioso em Portugal (s. xvi a xviii),* v.1 (Coimbra 1960). J. DE CASTRO, *Portugal no Concílio de Trento,* 6 v. (Lisbon 1944–46). J. L. D'AZEVEDO, *História dos cristãos novos portugueses* (Lisbon 1921). A. BAIÃO, *Episódios dramáticos da inquisição portuguesa,* 3 v. (2d ed. Lisbon 1936–53). E. BRASÃO, *D. João V e a Santa Sé* (Coimbra 1937). A. PEREIRA DA SILVA, *A questão do sigilismo em Portugal no s. xviii* (Braga 1964). J. HENRIQUES MOUTA, *Alexandre Lobo: Antítese de Alves Martins?* (Braga 1946). S. CORBIN, *Essai sur la musique religieuse portugaise au moyen âge, 1100–1385* (Paris 1952). J. CARDOSO and A. CAETANO DE SOUSA, *Agiologio lusitano,* 4 v. (Lisbon 1652–1744). F. DE CASTRO PIRES DE LIMA, *A Virgem e Portugal* (Porto 1963). F. DA SILVA CORREIA, *Origens e formação das misericórdias portuguesas* (Lisbon 1944). F. RODRIGUES, *História da Companhia de Jesus na assistência de Portugal,* 4 v. in 7 (Porto 1931–50). M. M. WERMERS, *A Ordem carmelita e o carmo em Portugal* (Lisbon 1963). M. ESPÍRITO SANTO, *A Religião Popular Portuguesa* (Lisbon nd). JUNTA DIOCESANA DE ACÇÃO CATÓLICA DE LISBOA, *A Acção Católica do Presente e do Futuro* (Lisbon 1985). M. DE A. TRINDADE, *Memórias de um Bispo* (2d ed. Coimbra 1994). *Católicos e Política de Humberto Delgado a Marcello Caetano,* ed. J. DA F. ALVES, (2d ed. Lisbon 1969). J. G. FREIRE, *Resistência Católica ao Salazarismo-Marcelismo* (Oporto 1976). M. DIAS, *Igreja: Que Opção?* (Oporto 1980). L. DE FRANÇA, *Comportamento Religioso da População Portuguesa* (Lisbon 1981). *História de Portugal,* ed. J. MATTOSO, 8 (Lisbon 1993). M. DAS NEVES, *Cardeal Cerejeira: o Homem e a Obra* (Lisbon 1988). CERP, *Perguntas á Nossa Igreja: Igreja e Política do 25 de Abril ao 25 de Novembro* (Lisbon 1976). *Textos Cristãos, 25 Abril-Novembro 25,* ed. J. FORTUNATO, (Lisbon 1977). *Os Bispos e a Revolução de Abril,* ed. H. B. RUAS, (Lisbon 1976). *Bulletin des études portugaises,* 22 (1959–60) 30–102. *Revue d'histoire ecclésiastique,* 48 (1953) 683–718, 49 (1954), 51 (1956), 53 (1958). *Análise Social,* 29 (1994) 287–317, 383. *Journal of Church and State,* 18 (1976) 463–490. *Revue Française de Science Politique,* 23 (1973) 473–513. *Studia monastica,* 1 (1959) 189–201. *Lusitania sacra* (Lisbon 1956–). *Portugiesische Forschungen* (Münster 1960–). *Dictionnaire de théologie catholique,* ed. A. VACANT et al., 15 v. (Paris 1903–50) 12.2:2612–34. *Espasa,* 46:670–746. *Portugal Hoje* (Lisbon 1995) 71–92. *Theologica,* 1 (1954) 67–85, 211–240.

[R. A. H. ROBINSON/EDS.]

POSADA Y GARDÜNO, MANUEL

Thirty-second archbishop of Mexico; b. San Felipe del Obraje, Mexico, Sept. 27, 1780; d. April 30, 1846. In 1818 he was appointed curate of the Sagrario in Puebla, later becoming vicar-general and diocesan administrator. In Mexico City in 1824 as senator from Puebla, he was named curate of the Sagrario and later doctoral canon there. When FONTE was forced to resign the See of Mexico, Pope Gregory XVI proclaimed Posada archbishop in December 1839, and he was consecrated in Mexico City on May 31, 1840. Posada actively defended the rights and privileges of the clergy. In 1823 he vigorously rejected an attempt by the military governor of Puebla to silence him, and in the following year he successfully stood as a candidate for the senate. Because of his staunch clericalism, Posada was forced to spend a year in exile in the United States by the liberal and anticlerical Gómez Farías government in 1833 and 1834. His reign as archbishop proved somewhat anticlimactic. His participation and influence in Mexican politics were minimal and even in ecclesiastical matters he accomplished little of significance. He established Forty Hours devotions, introduced some modest reforms in the seminaries, and secularized a few mission churches.

Bibliography: E. VALVERDE TÉLLEZ, *Bio-bibliografía eclesiástica mexicana (1821–1943),* 3 v. (Mexico City 1949). J. TRINIDAD BASURTO, *El arzobispado de México* (Mexico City 1901).

[K. M. SCHMITT]

POSADAS

A manifestation of popular piety in Mexican and Mexican-American communities in the U.S., celebrated between December 16 and Christmas Eve, Las Posadas comprise a festive procession whereby participants go from home to home singing carols, reenacting the journey of Mary and Joseph in search for lodging (*posada*). Participants play the various roles of Joseph and Mary, innkeepers, choir, and onlookers. At the first two homes, the participants are rejected, but at the third home, they enter and the fiesta of welcome begins. At the final house, the choir sings the same song of petition, but this time the innkeepers welcome them singing an additional verse of welcome. Each evening ends in a celebration, the final night usually a large fiesta hosted at the local parish church. The celebration generally consists of prayers and singing with refreshments of hot chocolate and sweet bread (*pan dulce*) for everyone. Blindedfolded children also attempt to hit a suspended, paper maché piñata, usually in the form of a star or animal and filled with candies that are released when the piñata breaks.

One tradition attributes the origins of Las Posadas to Spaniard Brother Pedro de San José Bentacur, a Third-Order Franciscan who settled in Guatemala. Historically, Spanish missionaries used Las Posadas as a catechetical device for explaining the Christmas story to the indigenous people. Among Mexican-American communities, the celebration of Las Posadas reminds immigrant families of their own journeys and experiences of rejection and welcome.

Bibliography: M. ARIAS, M. R. FRANCIS, and A. J. PÉREZ-RODRIGUEZ, *La Navidad Hispana at Home and at Church* (Chicago 2000). S. BRANDES, ''The Posadas in Tzinzuntzan: Structure and Sentiment in a Mexican Christmas Festival,'' *American Folklore* 96 (1983) 259–280. A. PÉREZ, *Popular Catholicism: A Hispanic Perspective* (Washington, D.C. 1988). S. VERTI, *El libro clasico de la Navidad en Mexico: costumbres y tradiciones de nuestro pueblo* (Mexico 1998). *Faith Expressions of Hispanics in the Southwest*, rev. ed. (San Antonio 1990).

[T. TORRES]

POSITIVISM

A name given to a doctrine taught in the 19th century by A. COMTE or to any one of a set of general philosophical views, of which Comte's is but one exemplar, that tend to limit human knowledge to what can be established by the methods of ''science.'' For the most important 20th-century version of positivism, *see* LOGICAL POSITIVISM; few contemporary philosophers, however, call themselves ''positivists'': they prefer the name ''logical empiricists,'' mainly in order to suggest their opposition to the narrow verificationism of the Vienna Circle. In what follows, consideration is given to the background of Comte's doctrine; then those elements of Comte's doctrine that continue to have importance are discussed, some later developments are reviewed, and finally a brief evaluation is made.

Historical Background. The history of positivistic views extends over the 3½ centuries of the modern period, in which the progressive expansion of modern science has taken place. What struck many thinkers, perhaps most notably I. KANT, was the contrast between the status of science and that of philosophy: progress in the former, stagnation and deadlock in the latter. A necessary condition of growth in established knowledge appeared to them to be the application of the techniques of science to the still backward areas of human thought; and philosophy itself was increasingly considered to be no longer the handmaid of theology, but rather the handmaid of science. Resistance from the ''metaphysicians'' who, the positivists said, claimed to have information about what lies beyond EXPERIENCE, aroused a progressively strong antimetaphysical reaction, a scornful and dogmatic reaction that reached its full strength in the late 19th and early 20th centuries. Anti-metaphysical bias tends to be the most striking property separating those in the positivist tradition from others who give full credit to the achievements of science.

Forerunners. It is impossible to do justice in a few words to the forerunners of 19th-century positivism, for given the fact that positivism can be seen as a variety of EMPIRICISM (which, as opposed to RATIONALISM or its variant, IDEALISM, emphasizes the role of experience and minimizes the role of reason), any of those who contributed to the development of empiricism can be considered as having contributed to the development of positivism. And if one speaks, rather vaguely, of ''positivistically inclined thinkers'' or of positivism as a ''temper of mind,'' one might range all the way from the SOPHISTS of the Greek Enlightenment through the *philosophes* of 18th-century France to the American pragmatists of the early 20th century—and even include, along the way, men such as DUNS SCOTUS, who is called a ''moral positivist'' because of his teaching that a thing is good (or bad) simply because God wills it to be good (or bad). Nevertheless it seems fairly clear that full-blown positivism had its day in the 19th century when *the* distinctive intellectual influence in the modern world, the natural sciences, had reached the high tide of their domination of the philosophical world.

As contributing to the development of 19th-century positivism, one might first mention Francis BACON, the ''trumpeter'' of the new sciences detached from philosophy in the 16th and 17th centuries. Bacon characterized past philosophy as mere childish prattling and expressed his utter confidence in the brilliant future of the natural sciences and of humanity under their guidance. (In his *New Atlantis* he gives a vivid picture of a mankind served and guided no longer by traditional aristocracies but by the new aristocracy of science.) Another important precursor of Comte in the field of social and legal philosophy was Thomas HOBBES, whose opposition to traditional ''natural-law'' positions clearly puts him in the ranks of the major forerunners of self-conscious positivists.

Major Influences. Certainly, however, the two major influences on Comte and other early positivists are those of D. HUME and Kant. The very notion of science as the study of the invariable relations of coexistence and succession observed to hold between elements of experience, the notion of scientific knowledge as relative and tentative, the notion of unknown and unknowable NOUMENA, the notion of metaphysics as a surrogate of science that offers a total (but false because characterized by a sort of mathematical necessity) explanation of the universe, the suggestion that perhaps the methods of science might be adapted to the solution of philosophical problems—all these themes had Humean or Kantian sources.

The most immediate and direct influences on Comte were those of J. d' Alembert, J. L. Lagrange (who first stated the principles of mechanics without any reference to ultimate cause or hidden forces, merely describing the laws by which phenomena were connected), CONDORCET, Turgot, and, most important of all, SAINT-SIMON, whom Comte served as secretary.

Comte's Doctrines. The most influential doctrines of Comte were three: the ''Law of Three States,'' the hierarchy of sciences, and his notion of sociology and the social sciences.

Three States. According to Comte, the structure of the human mind is such that all thought has followed a law of progress, the Law of Three States. There is first a primitive stage in which explanations of puzzling phenomena are theological, changes being attributed to the will of the gods, conceived of as very powerful human beings. The intermediate stage is that in which metaphysical explanations predominate, when forces or powers having abstract names take the place of superhuman agents. The third and final stage is that in which not explanation but pure description of phenomena takes the place of discarded powers or agents. Thus, for example, gravitation was first explained theologically as effected by divine beings attracting or repelling one another from their seats in the stars or planets; later, gravitation was explained anthropomorphically as a force or a power assumed to cause the movement of bodies; and only in the positive stage was a mathematical equation given that describes ''how'' but not ''why'' movement occurs. The positive method is well summarized by J. S. MILL: ''We have no knowledge of anything but phenomena; and our knowledge of phenomena is relative, not absolute. We know not the essence nor the real mode of production of any fact, but only its relations of other facts in the way of succession and similitude. These relations are constant, i.e., always the same in the same circumstances. The constant resemblances which link phenomena together, and the constant sequences which unite them as antecedent and consequent, are termed their laws. All phenomena without exception are governed by invariable laws, with which no volitions, either natural or supernatural, interfere. The essential nature of phenomena and their ultimate causes, whether efficient or final, are unknown and inscrutable to us'' (*A System of Logic,* bk. 2). One might note that there was a general consensus in the 19th century, shared, as Émile Meyerson (an important critic of positivist anti-ontologism) has shown, even by G. W. F. HEGEL, that empirical science must be purely descriptive, confined to establishing the regularities of observed phenomena; Hegel did not, of course, like Comte, deny value to explanation, for his idealistic philosophy of nature provided the grounds of all explanation.

Hierarchy of Sciences. A second key Comtean doctrine was his conception of the ''positive hierarchy'' of the sciences. The fundamental sciences were said to fall into a logical order (one depends on another for certain of its principles), a single linear order of decreasing generality and increasing complexity; and this is also the historical order in which they developed: mathematics, physics, chemistry, biology—and finally, with Comte's own work, sociology. Psychology, that ''last transformation of theology,'' was denied a special role in his hierarchy because Comte denied the possibility of knowledge through INTROSPECTION (it is impossible to observe one's own mental processes without at the same time destroying them). In the positive stage one will limit himself to a consideration of the organic conditions on which various psychic functions depend: as A. Bain put it, ''psychologus nemo nisi physiologicus.'' The *International Encyclopedia of Unified Science* (Chicago 1938–) is a contemporary answer to Comte's demand for a coherent synthesis of all science.

Sociology. The third important area of Comte's significance and influence is that of the social sciences or of sociology. Comte thought of himself as first and foremost a social reformer. He believed that satisfactory social organization could be achieved only after the spiritual foundation—the reorganization of all knowledge along ''positive'' lines—had been laid: institutions rest on morals, morals on beliefs; and once a stable and unified body of beliefs is available, social beatitude is possible. Of course, implied in Comte's notion of the hierarchy of science is the basing of social science on physical science, thus making it possible to treat social phenomena in purely physical, nonanthropomorphic language. A leading idea of positivist sociology was first given expression by Condorcet when he wrote that to an observer from another planet, physical and social phenomena would appear in the same light, ''a stranger to our race, he would study human society as we study those of the beavers and bees.''

Though an archenemy of anthropomorphism and the ''empathetic fallacy,'' Comte nevertheless thought of sociology as the study of the evolution of mankind as a sort of collective organism (''the whole of the object is here certainly much better known and more immediately accessible than the constituent parts''), conceiving of humanity as a ''social being,'' a kind of superperson. Comte and his followers thus committed what A. N. Whitehead has named ''the fallacy of misplaced concreteness.'' Such notions are quite consistent with the historicist orientation of 19th-century Continental social thought, an orientation best known today in the works of K. MARX and F. ENGELS.

The positivist view of society as organismic—humanity alone is real and the individual only an abstraction—clearly has the effect of suppressing or obliterating the freedom of the individual subject to it and of sanctioning a ''scientific'' despotism; J. S. Mill described the resulting system as ''liberticide'' and as ''the completest system of spiritual and temporal despotism which ever yet emanated from the human brain, unless possibly that of Ignatius Loyola.'' (Like his early mentor, Saint-Simon, Comte also founded a ''religion'' of veneration and cult of ''the Great Being: Humanity,'' well-described by T. H. Huxley in his epigram ''Catholicism without Christianity.'')

It is especially in treating social phenomena that Comte's practical bent most clearly shines through: ''I have a supreme aversion to scientific labors whose utility, direct or remote, I do not see.'' For him as for so many of the 19th-century positivists, science is the handmaid of humanity (though few went quite so far as Comte in considering sidereal astronomy—by contrast with the study of the solar system, in which man lives—a ''grave scientific aberration'' serving only to satisfy vain curiosity). For Comte and many later positivists, knowing is for the sake of foreseeing and then controlling: *voir pour prévoir, prévoir pour prévenir, prévenir pour pouvoir.*

Later Developments. Comte's influence on the later history of positivism was achieved in great part through his influence on Mill and a few other leading English thinkers. (The sixth book of Mill's *Logic,* which deals with the methodology of the moral sciences, is little more than an exposition of Comtean doctrine.) The writings and translations of George Lewes, Harriet Martineau, and George Eliot were important in making Comte known in Germany, where L. FEUERBACH became known as the founder of German positivism. Herbert SPENCER, though severely critical of Comte, attempted a not dissimilar task in attempting to formulate a law of progress and the development of a unified ''synthetic'' philosophy of science.

In sociology, Émile DURKHEIM was Comte's principal disciple and, though divesting sociology of Comte's religious and politically reactionary elements, continued to emphasize the group mind as the point of reference for all human knowledge. In legal philosophy, positivism confines itself to positive law (laws actually valid at a certain time in a certain place) and strongly opposes any ''higher'' law. The *Allgemeine Rechtslehre* in Germany, analytical jurisprudence in England, H. Kelsen's ''pure theory of law'' (which leaves no place for an ideal of justice), and American ''legal realism,'' though poles apart in some respects, are united in their common aversion to metaphysical theories in general and natural-law theories in particular, and so are generally known as types of legal positivism. (Legal positivism today is, however, under something of a cloud because of the ease with which a form of positivism facilitated Hitler's subversion of German law.) *See* POSITIVISM IN JURISPRUDENCE.

An important contribution to the development of contemporary philosophy was made by the left-wing positivists, the late 19th- and early 20th-century scientist-philosophers G. R. Kirchhoff (1824–87), E. Mach, W. K. Clifford (1845–79), and K. Pearson (1857–1936), all of whom had a phobia of the invisible and intangible and the thrust of whose thought led, not to an acceptance of the ''law of three states'' but to the discarding of all statements that cannot be reduced to perceptual data. The right-wing idealist, quasi-Kantian branch of positivism flowered but briefly in the writings of F. A. Lange (1828–75) and Hans Vaihinger (1852–1933), who believed that metaphysics is arrant nonsense considered as anything but poetry, though as poetry it may have a certain beauty.

Evaluation. It is clear, as H. Feigl has remarked, that the issues that divided G. BERKELEY and Locke, Hume and Kant, Mach and H. von Helmholtz, phenomenalists, neorealists and critical realists, cannot be solved by positivistic fiat. Second, the positivist, like all other antimetaphysicians (with the possible exception of the early Greek skeptics) is, as F. H. BRADLEY has remarked, a ''brother metaphysician with a rival theory of first principles.'' The assumption is made that there are facts, each distinct from every other, that man can observe and then correlate; but when an attempt is made to say what ''facts'' are, various positivists give as widely differing answers (Bacon's ''simple natures,'' Hume's ''impressions,'' Comte's ''special or general facts'') as do self-confessed metaphysicians. Third, though positivism may well have served as a useful reminder against the dangers of a priori speculation and formed a useful counterbalance to the yeasty absolutisms of idealist metaphysics, its attempt to show, for example, that FINAL CAUSALITY has no valid use or meaning because it has no place in mechanics or in an intellectual system based on mechanics is an unwarranted limitation on the range of human experience. Finally, even in their chosen field of scientific METHODOLOGY, the 19th-century positivists misconceived the role of hypothesis as a function of science (taking the relation between hypothesis and confirming evidence to be purely logical or analytic) and found no place for what science has no way of directly testing. This led them to condemn as meaningless many propositions later accepted as scientific truth, such as propositions about the chemical structure of the stars.

Perhaps one might accept the analogy of R. W. Sellars as a benign expression of the general impact of early positivism; this, he suggests, "might be compared to the action of a firm of scientific accountants going over the books of that ancient firm called philosophy. It has been a healthy thing for philosophy; and it may be that the accountants have also learned something."

See Also: SCIENTISM; METAPHYSICS, VALIDITY OF.

Bibliography: J. A. PASSMORE, *A Hundred Years of Philosophy* (New York 1957). B. MAGNINO, *Storia del positivismo* (Rome 1955). G. MILHAUD, *Le Positivisme et le progrès de l'esprit* (Paris 1902). F. A. VON HAYEK, *The Counter-Revolution of Science: Studies on the Abuse of Reason* (Glencoe, IL 1952). H. G. GOUHIER, *La Jeunesse d'Auguste Comte et al formation du positivisme,* 3 v. (Paris 1933–41). H. DE LUBAC, *The Drama of Atheist Humanism,* tr. E. M. RILEY (New York 1949), pt. 2. R. L. HAWKINS, *Positivism in the United States, 1853–1861* (Cambridge, MA 1938). R. HOFSTADTER, *Social Darwinism in American Thought* (rev. ed. New York 1959). H. FEIGL, "The Power of Positivistic Thinking," *Proc. and Addresses of the American Philosophical Assoc. 1962–63,* 36 (Yellow Springs, OH 1963) 21–41. R. W. SELLARS, "Positivism in Contemporary Philosophic Thought," *American Sociological Review* 4 (1939) 26–55. H. B. ACTON, "Comte's Positivism and the Science of Society," *Philosophy* 26 (1951) 291–310.

[R. L. CUNNINGHAM]

POSITIVISM IN JURISPRUDENCE

The term "jurisprudence" refers here to exercise of private and public decision-making functions involved in administration of the system of law of a particular political society, performance of functions related to making these decisions, scholarly critiques of these actions, and the knowledge and skill out of which these actions proceed. This is the classical notion of jurisprudence. The same term refers also to scholarly studies that principally concern the general nature of law, legal institutions, and legal processes in the application of law. Jurisprudence in both instances is a knowledge of law. In the first sense it is a working knowledge of a particular system of law. In the second sense it is a theoretical knowledge of law.

Scholars engaged in jurisprudence in the second sense are generally known in Anglo-American legal circles as jurisprudents. The position of positivist jurisprudents, whatever else it may include, may be described as minimally involving the assertion that in defining the nature of law of a political society the proper object is to separate the law as it is from the law as it ought to be, or to separate law from morality. Since in Western thinking positivism in the broad sense is much more extensive than the position of separating law from morality, it would be well to characterize the latter as "legal positivism." Some current discussions have attempted to distinguish legal positivism from a study called analytical jurisprudence. The latter has been asserted to be a neutralistic study of the meanings and usages of terms belonging to law and the relations of these terms to each other and to nonlegal language. The two concepts and studies that they are asserted to represent may be distinguished; however, the leading positivist jurisprudents, in elaborating their positions, either have not attempted or have not succeeded in the attempt to separate their analytical jurisprudence from their legal positivism.

Finally, although positivism in jurisprudence originated as a theory about the nature of law obtaining in political societies generally, and indeed is even called by its principal Continental exponent a "pure" theory of law, it is far from being a neutral theory free of practical implications for those engaged in jurisprudence in the primary sense. It is in fact inseparable from and probably is better described as a general theory concerning the proper interpretation of law of political societies. Positivism in jurisprudence was unquestionably intended by its proponents to have, and in fact has had, a profound impact on the practical jurisprudence of modern political societies. The jurisprudent, as H. Kelsen has put it, approaches the study of law as a law teacher, a law student, or a lawyer who seeks to determine what the law is. He does not concern himself with the specific meaning of particular legal rules of a given political society, but with a general theory of legal interpretation applicable to the legal system of any political society.

Principal Interpretations. Positivist jurisprudents have focused principally upon two problems of legal interpretation: the identification of law and the general method of expounding the meaning of what has been identified as law.

Identification of Law. In attempting to identify law, positivists have proceeded from at least two different vantage points. One of these is represented by the work of John Austin, the English jurisprudent, and the other by the work of Hans Kelsen, his Continental counterpart. Austin, a utilitarian, doubted whether even judges could engage in rational discourse concerning problems of justice presented in the administration of positive law, and whether they could agree on guidelines to be used or results to be reached in decisions resolving these problems. He expressed some hope for future generations in this respect as mankind progressed in knowledge of moral principles. Nevertheless, he developed his theory of law in light of his judgment that for the foreseeable future it would be impossible to obtain certain desirable goals of political society and at the same time admit into a working concept of positive law a working concept of justice. If one was to promote through a working concept of law the goals of societal stability, certainty in identification and elaboration of law, and ready obedience to law, one must necessarily exclude from that concept the uncertainty and imperfection inherent in human judgment about problems of justice.

Kelsen reached the same result because of his denial of the possibility of rational judgments about justice. He viewed a judgment about justice as a judgment of value always determined by emotional factors, subjective in character, and valid only for the judging subject. For this reason, jurisprudence as a scientific discipline whose aim is cognition of law must exclude from the domain of positive law the problem of the justice of law. Although it is certainly desirable, from this point of view, that the law of political societies will, when created, be considered generally to be just, administration of law is not a quest for justice but for cognition of legal norms.

Thus, for Austin and Kelsen, although for different reasons, the identification of law became a total separation of law from the morally just. They identified as law a working concept that might or might not in fact coincide with true moral justice (Austin) or with a subjective and merely emotional view of what is moral justice (Kelsen). As positivist jurisprudents are fond of saying, ''Laws, however morally iniquitous, would still be laws.'' In his effort to separate law from morality Austin sought to treat as law only those rules he could comprehend within the concept of a command. For Austin, a command involved the power to inflict an evil upon the person directed to do something if he failed to comply. All that could not be fitted within this mold was rejected as not being law. Similarly, Kelsen sought to embrace all law by the concept of a social order based upon directives to officials to apply coercive measures to persons engaging in specified conduct when these directives were issued in accordance with a basic norm.

H. L. A. Hart, in the mid-20th century, rejected the command theory of law as ''threadbare'' and the directives-to-officials theory as a dogmatic suppression of other aspects of law. To secure a more adequate separation of law from morality, Hart proposed both an ultimate ''secondary rule of recognition'' whose function is to provide merely procedural criteria by which may be determined the validity of ''primary rules of conduct'' in the legal system and certain less ultimate secondary rules that govern both the application and modification of the primary rules.

Expounding the Meaning of Law. In constructing a theory for expounding the meaning of such law, positivist jurisprudents have excluded the concept of justice from the theory either totally or in large part. Kelsen, for example, employed the concept of an ''objective meaning'' of law, essential to the very possibility of a science of law. This concept implied techniques for determining the meaning of legal rules that focus primarily upon the words through which they are expressed. On the other hand, in order to preserve the unity and meaningfulness of an entire legal system, he incorporated a number of principles of interpretation designed for resolving logical contradictions in that system. For example, in order to deal with rules that in the light of their ''objective meanings'' contradicted previously formulated rules, he included within his general theory the principle *lex posterior derogat priori.*

Austin was far more definitive in elaborating a general theory relative to expounding the meaning of legal rules, particularly when statutory in form. His most characteristic statement concerning statutes is that ''the law is one thing, the reason [for the law] another. . . .'' This bears a marked resemblance to his position that the existence of a law is one thing, whereas its merit or demerit is another. The expressions of statutory law, according to Austin, are to be viewed as having an objective meaning to be drawn from the provisions themselves and not from other indicia of meaning. Only if these provisions are ambiguous may the *ratio legis* and the history of the statute be considered. A fortiori, the judge must disregard considerations of justice that might move him to assign a meaning at variance with the objective meaning of the law. Moreover, Austin conceived of statutory law as precluding a judge from administering it except through the vehicle of the precise rules through which it was expressed, although he perceived an underlying principle that would logically indicate the propriety of other applications than the one expressed in the statute. Otherwise, the judge might engage in spurious interpretation, a process Austin condemned as subjecting administration of statutory law to the arbitrary disposition of tribunals. Although Austin recognized that traditional law was frequently administered in new ways by judges resorting to principles underlying specific rules for deciding cases, he strongly favored each political society's rejecting this form of law in favor of a statutory code of law wherever possible. He believed his general theory of interpretation as applied to statutory law would make possible a much greater measure of certainty in law administration. However, he and his followers conceded the necessity of judges making new law both in the traditional and statutory areas. But while deeming this necessity an ungovernable area of discretion except through precise legislation, they have not explored or elaborated an interpretative theory to provide for it.

Criticism. Four central criticisms of legal positivism have been made. They are objections to the positivistic interpretation given to legal process, identification of law, and law administration, and a warning that certain societal harms may arise from positivistic assumptions.

Legal Process. The first criticism asserts that the theory, in whatever form it has been stated, fails to reflect the reality of legal process, whether in identifying law or in elaborating and applying its meaning. In turning their attention away from the content of law by their mode of theorizing, legal positivists have necessarily had to turn away from the legal process by which that content is developed and modified in the course of time. This process throughout its extent is affected in fact by considerations of justice, conceptions of the purpose of law and political society, and a consensus concerning the modes and techniques of authority. The disregard for legal process by legal positivists indicates that their view is not realistic, however pure or analytical it may be. In prescinding to a greater or lesser extent from the content and processes of law, this theory deforms its object and, consequently, prevents its proponents and users from attaining the principal objective of the theory, which is the cognition of law that serves as part of a developing legal system.

Identification of Law. A second criticism of legal positivism is that its proponents misconceive what the problem of identifying or defining law really involves. In elaborating this criticism, L. L. Fuller has remarked that law is a social institution and that what is identified as law must be something with characteristics enabling it to serve the function of that particular social institution and, above all, to promote the objective of fidelity to law that legal positivists now generally concede is a prime objective of their theory. Inevitably, however, there are some characteristics about what legal positivists recognize or define as law that preclude the latter from adequately serving the function of law as an institution or of promoting fidelity to it. These objectives must be worked or planned for in the defining of law. A theory for defining positive law that prescinds from a consideration of these objectives is a faulty theory since it does not comprehend the necessary elements of the particular definitional problem.

Law Administration. A third criticism of legal positivism focuses upon the failure of its proponents to come to grips with undeniable difficulties of law administration. Their theory does not hide these; it may even highlight them. Currently, legal positivists are talking about the intersection or overlapping, especially in certain problem areas, between positive law and justice. Some of the major problem areas confronting them are the following: the assigning of meaning to laws where, according to any description of the task, law is being made; the field of procedural justice in the administration of law, which exacts objectivity and impartiality; the defining of the content of a legal system; the issuance of official decisions concerning the application of ''law'' to a transaction in light of its grossly immoral quality. By and large, legal positivists now recognize these problems, but only by way of acknowledging them as evidence of the inappropriateness of a total separation between law and morality in defining a working concept of law. They do not consider that their ''minor'' concessions of certain intersections weaken in any substantial way their effort to keep law separate from morality. Neither do they seek to resolve these problems but defer to other disciplines for their solution. The problems are, however, problems that those engaged in jurisprudence in the primary sense have to meet and solve. Critics of legal positivism insist that its proponents must also face them.

Societal Harms. The fourth criticism of legal positivism is that in proffering a working point of view regarding identification and elaboration of law, it may be responsible for certain societal harms. One of these is the failure of modern jurisprudents to discuss the prudential aspects of problems of justice involved in the operation of a legal system. Instead of making uncertainty or inability to attain science about questions of justice a reason for putting these questions beyond the pale of the legal discipline, jurists should make them the occasion of effort to understand as much as possible about the process of justice. To do so involves no necessary commitment to eternal verities about the minimal content of positive law, nor does it preclude affirmation of them. To the extent that it achieves acceptance, legal positivism defeats that inquiry into justice which ought to be one of its contributions to improvement of administration of law. Moreover, legal positivism can contribute to the dangerous tendency of men, including members of the legal profession, to accept as respectable law whatever has been officially recognized or proffered as such. One need not refer merely to the example of the legal profession in Germany, which, by its adherence to legal positivism, aided the Nazi drive for establishment of a dictatorship. One may see in the United States, positive harms resulting from practical effect being given in law administration to the views of legal positivism. Consider, for example, two decisions of the United States Supreme Court: *Korematsu v. United States,* 323 U.S. 214 (1944), and *Application of Yamashita,* 327 U.S. 1 (1946). These decisions were the product of the viewpoint of legal positivism. The doctrine provided a convenient principle for crediting as law what had been administratively formulated as the legal basis for placing a person in a concentration camp without regard to his innocence or guilt, in the first case, and as the basis for depriving a person of his life irrespective of any knowledgeable commission of wrong, in the second case. Legal positivism has also long provided in the Anglo-American legal systems the basis for an attempt to justify literalism and extreme devotion to precedent. To the extent that this has prevented the administration of law from proceeding in accordance with its purpose, the result has been to frustrate the realization of justice, and to some extent, the operation of the democratic principle. Legal positivism is possibly waning in significance as a doctrine of jurisprudence, but its practical legacy is still very much present in the practical administration of law.

Bibliography: J. AUSTIN, *Lectures on Jurisprudence,* ed. R. CAMPBELL, 2 v. (5th ed. London 1885). H. KELSEN, *General Theory of Law and State* (Cambridge, Mass. 1945). H. L. A. HART, *The Concept of Law* (Oxford 1961). L. L. FULLER, *The Law in Quest of Itself* (Chicago 1940); *The Morality of Law* (New Haven 1964). E. BODENHEIMER, *Jurisprudence: The Philosophy and Method of the Law* (Cambridge, Mass. 1962). S. I. SHUMAN, *Legal Positivism: Its Scope and Limitations* (Detroit 1963).

[J. P. WITHERSPOON]

POSSENTI, GABRIEL, ST.

Commonly known as St. Gabriel of Our Lady of Sorrows, Passionist seminarian; b. Assisi, Italy, March 1, 838; d. Isola del Gran Sasso (Teramo), Italy, Feb. 27 1862. Francesco (his baptismal name) was the 11th of 13 children of Sante and Agnese (Frisciotti) Possenti. His father was governor of Assisi and later assessor of Spoleto. Until 1856 Francesco studied at the Jesuit college in Spoleto, where he was known for meticulousness in dress, fondness for dancing and the theater, and an inclination to vanity. After twice failing to fulfill promises to enter religion made during grave illness, he experienced, while watching a religious procession honoring the miraculous icon of Spoleto, a strong urge to follow his vocation. Despite his father's objections he joined the PASSIONISTS at Morrovalle (1856) and took as his name in religion Gabriel of Our Lady of Sorrows. During the next six years he was a model seminarian, exact in his observance of his religious rule and noted for his spirit of prayer and penance. His spiritual director singled out devotion to the Blessed Virgin Mary as his preeminent characteristic and the source of his spirituality. He received minor orders in 1861 but died before advancing to major orders. He was beatified May 31, 1908, and canonized May 13, 1920. He has been declared patron of the Abruzzi region and copatron of Italian Catholic youth.

Feast: Feb. 27.

Bibliography: E. BURKE, *Happy Was My Youth* (Westminster, Md. 1962). G. POAGE, *Son of the Passion* (Milwaukee 1962; Boston 1977). V. FUENTE RODRÍGUEZ, *San Gabriel de la Dolorosa, pasionista* (Madrid 1973). F. D'ANASTASIO, *San Gabriele dell'Addolorata* (San Gabriele 1995). G. CINGOLANI, *Gabriel of Our Lady of Sorrows*, tr. S. B. ZAK (New York 1997); *Saint Gabriel Possenti, Passionist: A Young Man in Love*, tr. S. B. ZAK (New York 1997).

[E. BURKE]

POSSESSOR IN GOOD, BAD, OR DUBIOUS FAITH

A possessor is a person who exercises actual control over a thing in such a way that he can dispose of it at will, regardless of whether he enjoys rightful ownership of it. An owner, on the contrary, is a person who has full right to dispose of a thing, with or without the corresponding exercise of that right. Ownership thus indicates a condition of right, whereas possession is merely a condition of fact, which may, nevertheless, be protected by law and be productive of juridical effects.

This article will treat the possessor's rights and obligations in relation to the owner, whether they concern the property itself, the income derived from it, or the expenditures incurred during the period of possession. Since these rights and obligations vary according to whether the possessor is in good, bad, or doubtful faith, each kind of possession requires separate consideration.

In Good Faith. A possessor in good faith is one who sincerely believes that property in his possession belongs to himself when in fact it belongs to another. Thus he is unaware that he is violating another's rights. His obligations and rights are as follows.

In Relation to the Property Itself. (1) As soon as he becomes aware that the property belongs to another, he is obliged in justice to restore it to its lawful owner, if it still exists. (2) He is absolved from further obligation in justice if the property has perished and he is no richer for having had it in his possession. The same is true if he has given it away, although in this case, if it can be done conveniently, charity requires either that he admonish the present possessor to restore the property to the owner, or that he bring the matter to the owner's attention so that the latter may recover his own property. (3) He acquires true ownership of the property in question if he fulfills all the requirements for lawful prescription.

In Regard to the Products. (1) Since a thing fructifies to its owner, the possessor in good faith must restore to the owner the products of his property, whether they be natural products, such as animal offspring, or civil products, such as rent from his house. However, the possessor is not obliged to restore industrial products, or the fruits of his own labor, such as profits realized from a business. (2) Modern codes of civil law frequently allow the possessor to retain all products, whether natural, civil, or industrial, which he acquired during his period of good faith. The prescriptions of civil law may be safely followed in conscience.

In Regard to Expenditures. The possessor in good faith is entitled to compensation for all necessary and useful expenses incurred in the maintenance or improvement of the property. No compensation is due him, however, for superfluous expenses, that is, for those that have not benefited the owner, or which the latter would not have reasonably authorized.

In Bad Faith. A possessor in bad faith is one who culpably takes or keeps a thing that he knows to be the property of another. In general, he is bound to repair all foreseen damage caused to the lawful owner. Therefore: (1) He must restore the property itself, if it still exists, or its equivalent, if it has perished or passed into the hands of a third party. (2) He must compensate the owner for all ensuing loss, so that the owner receives as much as he would have had if he had not been unjustly deprived of his goods. This obligation, of course, presupposes that the unjust possessor foresaw the losses at least indistinctly. (3) Like the possessor in good faith, he must restore all natural and civil products, but may retain the fruits of his own labor, and is entitled to compensation for necessary and useful expenses. (4) Unlike the possessor in good faith, he may never acquire ownership of the property by prescription.

In Doubtful Faith. A possessor is said to be in doubtful faith if he has serious reasons for questioning the lawfulness of his possession. Since his obligations differ according to whether the doubt was present at the beginning of his possession or arose only during its course, both alternatives must be considered separately. In either case, however, he must undertake a reasonable investigation in proportion to the seriousness of his doubt and the value of the property in question.

When Doubt Is Subsequent to Possession. (1) If such a doubt persists after a diligent inquiry, the possessor may keep the property, since in this case the presumption is in his favor. (2) If, on the contrary, he discovers that the property belongs to someone else, he has the same obligation to make restitution as the possessor in good faith. (3) If he culpably neglects to settle the doubt, he becomes a possessor in bad faith.

When Possession Begins with Doubt. (1) If the disputed property had been taken away from another who possessed it in good faith, it must be restored to the former possessor since here the presumption supports his claim. (2) If, on the other hand, the property had been acquired by legal title, for example by purchase or donation, from a possessor in good faith, after fruitless attempts to dispel the doubt, the present holder may retain the disputed object. (3) If the property was acquired from a person in doubtful faith, or from one whose good faith was reasonably suspect (because, for example, he was known to have stolen in the past), and this doubt persists after the inquiry, the possessor must, according to the degree of his doubt, make restitution to the probable owner, or to the poor, if the owner is completely unknown.

Bibliography: D. M. PRÜMMER, *Manuale theologiae moralis,* ed. E. M. MÜNCH, 3 v. (12th ed. Freiburg-Barcelona 1955) 2:207–222. H. NOLDIN, *Summa theologiae moralis,* rev. A. SCHMITT and G. HEINZEL, 3 v. (Innsbruck 1961–62); 2:437–452. H. DAVIS, *Moral and Pastoral Theology,* rev. and enl. ed. by L. W. GEDDES (New York 1958) 2:317–325. F. ROBERTI et al., *Dictionary of Moral Theology,* ed. P. PALAZZINI et al., tr. H. J. YANNONE et al. from 2d Ital. ed. (Westminster, Md. 1962) 92.6–935. S. WOYWOD, ''Possessory Actions or Remedies,'' *Homiletic and Pastoral Review* 31 (1931) 957–965.

[J. J. MCDONALD]

POSSEVINO, ANTONIO

Missionary, linguist, educator, and papal diplomat; b. Mantua, 1534; d. Ferrara, Feb. 26, 1611. As a vigorous opponent of the Protestant Reformation, Possevino entered the Society of Jesus in 1559, and one year later was sent to Savoy to preach against the Waldenses. From 1562 to 1572 he preached in France with great success. In 1573 Everard Mercurian, the new Jesuit General, named Possevino as his private secretary

In 1577 Gregory XIII appointed Possevino as his personal representative to John III of Sweden because John had expressed a desire to become Catholic. Possevino arrived in Stockholm in December of 1577 with power to negotiate the matter. In May 1578 John III, without reservations, made his *obedentia* and was absolved from schism. The king insisted that the conversion of Sweden would be facilitated if the pope would make certain concessions: Mass in the vernacular, communion under both species, and marriage of the clergy. Possevino personally asked Gregory for these during the summer of 1578, but the pope refused. The legate's return to Stockholm in 1579 was anticlimactic, and John III, fearing the loss of his crown, lapsed from the Catholic faith. Possevino left Stockholm in August 1580.

Gregory next appointed Possevino as legate to Russia. Czar Ivan IV (the Terrible), having been decisively defeated by Stephen BÁTHORY, King of Poland, appealed to the pope for mediation and suggested the possibility of the reunion of the Russian Church. Possevino left Rome in March of 1581 with broad instructions to negotiate these points. He entered Russia in August, and after protracted discussions was able to secure a desired armistice. Once the armistice was signed, Ivan grew cool to the reunion proposals, and in May of 1582, the ambassador left for Rome with his mission only half accomplished.

In October Possevino was accredited as nuncio to Poland, with additional instructions to continue working for reconciliation with Russia, however, Ivan's death in 1584 terminated all official contact between Russia and the papacy. Possevino remained in the North for three additional years, preaching, writing, and founding schools. Although the Pope wished him to remain in Poland as his resident legate, the Jesuit General, Claudius ACQUAVIVA, insisted on his recall in 1587.

From 1587 to 1591 Possevino taught theology at the University of Padua where the most famous of his pupils was St. Francis de Sales. In 1595 he was instrumental in obtaining full papal absolution for Henry of Navarre. Possevino's writings include: *Moscovia* (Vilna 1586), an important early authority on Russian history; *Apparatus sacer ad Scripturam Veteris et Novi Test* (Venice 1603–06), an analysis of more than 8,000 books treating of Sacred Scripture; and the *Biblioteca selecta* (Rome 1593), which deals with the method of study, teaching, and practical use of various sciences.

Bibliography: L. KARTTUNEN, *Antonio Possevino: Un diplomate pontifical au XVIe siècle* (Lausanne 1908). H. BRIANDET, *Le Saint Siège et la Suède durant la seconde moitié du XIVe siècle,* 2 v. (Paris 1907–13). C. SOMMERVOGEL et al., *Bibliothèque de la Compagnie de Jésus* (Brussels-Paris 1890–1932) 6:1061–93. H. WOLTER, *Lexikon für Theologie und Kirche*, ed. J. HOFER and K. RAHNER (Freiberg 1957–65) 8:640. G. MARON, *Die Religion in Geschichte und Gegenwart* (Tübingen 1957–65) 5:476–477.

[J. W. ROONEY]

POSSIBILITY

A term taking its root meaning from the Latin *posse* (to be able, to have the power to) and thus closely associated with the term "POTENCY." When the notion of potency, or capacity, is referred exclusively to the order of BEING, it becomes possibility, i.e., the absolute potentiality, or capacity, to be. This article surveys the historical development of the concept from the Greeks to the present and concludes with a Thomistic explanation of how possibility is related to the divine omnipotence.

Early Origins. The concept of possibility, like many philosophical notions, had its beginning with the Greeks, and in particular with PARMENIDES (Fragments 2–3) and PLATO. Plato held the natures of things to be eternally subsistent Forms existing apart from the things of which they are Forms (*Phaedo* 100D–102B; *Phaedrus* 247C; *Parm.* 132D). Natures, or essences, have their truth and being in and of themselves. For Plato, therefore, there is a dichotomy between being and existence. True being is Form, whereas existence is a reflection of the world of true being in sensory changing matter, the world of opinion rather than of true knowledge (*Rep.* 509D–511E). In Plato's metaphysics, which may be referred to as a metaphysics of essence, the possible has a being of its own in the world of Forms.

For Aristotle, on the other hand, the ontological possible—which he identified with power and matter—is always located in the world of things. It is already a being, although potential to further actuality (*Phys.* 187a 12–192h 3, 200b 12–201b 15; *Metaphysics* 1045b 27–1052a 12). The possible thus denotes the state of that which is able to be or can be, and as such is contrasted with the impossible, that which is not able to be or cannot be. It is defined in relation to the actual, which itself is identified simply by pointing to examples, such as a bird flying or a man walking.

The possible has several analogical meanings for Aristotle. It may denote (1) that which is actively possible, as the sculptor's active possibility of carving a statue; 2) that which is passively possible, as the marble's passive possibility of being made into a statue; (3) that which is possible in the sense of being able, not only to be done, but to be done well, actively or passively, as one may speak of an able sculptor; and (4) that which is possible in the sense of being powerful and able to resist change, in contrast to that which is weak and unable to withstand transmutation from opposing forces. All of these meanings are reducible to the first, the possible as implied in active potency. Thus the actualization of passive potency is dependent on activity deriving from active potency. Similarly, to be able to act well depends on being able to act, but not conversely. And again, the possible understood as ability to resist change clearly requires an active source that is able to be resisted.

Medieval Thought. The transition from the notion of ontological possibility contained in Aristotle to that of logical possibility is traceable historically to the Christian doctrine of CREATION. In the context of Judeo-Christian revelation, "to be" no longer meant to be a thing, or a kind of being, but simply to exist. Thus the Aristotelian notion of potency, which was drawn from the operational order of substance and accident and from the essential order of matter and form, was extended to the existential order of ESSENCE AND EXISTENCE. As a consequence, essence came to be viewed as potency in the order of being, or potency to exist simply, which is actualized by the act of existence. This application was consistent with Aristotle's understanding, for potency in his view is always the power of a being, i.e., the potentiality of something already existent for further change or for realizing its actuality by the reception of other forms.

With the Neoplatonic interpretation placed on Aristotle by Arab philosopher Avicenna, however, a new element was introduced. As Avicenna conceived it, essence, if it is to receive existence, must possess a being of its own in its proper state as essence. Under his influence, the Platonic Forms, i.e, the essences of things existing apart from the things of which they are the essence, came to serve as the philosophical model for the conception of essence as that which *is* of itself, but then *exists* by its act of existence. HENRY OF GHENT, GILES OF ROME, and John DUNS SCOTUS (and later F. SUÁREZ) all seem to have accepted this notion of the possible essence as the logical possible (*possibile logicum,* as Duns Scotus termed it), distinguishing it from the Aristotelian ontological possible. A further development was the application of the Aristotelian ontological perspective to the existential order as the real possible (*possibile reale,* again in the terminology of Duns Scotus, *Opus Oxon.* 1.43.1.3, 6).

Christian thinkers generally have agreed that essences derive their truth or intrinsic possibility from God. But within this consensus they have disagreed as to the precise attribute of God that provides the ultimate foundation of possibility, the possible essence.

St. THOMAS AQUINAS and Thomists generally have taught that the formal and immediate foundation of essences is the divine intellect. The remote and ultimate foundation of the possibility of things is the divine essence. The essences of all things are reflections of the divine ideas, or exemplars, which in turn are the divine essence perceived as imitable in this mode or that by the divine intellect. Essences are knowable inasmuch as they are involved in being, and the origin of all beings is the divine essence.

WILLIAM OF OCKHAM and the nominalists, on the other hand, have taught that God's power is the ultimate foundation of possibility, or essences. The ability of God to make something explains why it is intrinsically possible. Likewise, something is intrinsically impossible simply because God cannot make it. Thus the ultimate explanation of the possibility of things lies not within things themselves but within the Being responsible for making them. The omnipotence of God is the ultimate foundation for essences.

Modern Philosophers. With the advent of modern philosophy, further developments were associated with attempts to discover the ultimate foundation of possibility. According to René DESCARTES, possibility derives from the divine will, not from the divine omnipotence or the divine essence. In fact, in a much-quoted illustration, Descartes claims that a triangle has three angles equal to two right angles not only because of its components, but because ultimately this is the way God has willed it. If God had willed it otherwise, then it would have been otherwise. Thus the absurd and the impossible would be possible if God willed them to be so.

In the view of G. W. von LEIBNIZ, possibility can be explained antecedent to and without actuality. The foundation of the analytic proposition or statement is possibility, or the autonomy of an order of the possibles. For Leibniz the present world is only one of an infinite number of possible worlds. Synthetic propositions are true of the actually existent world. But some statements are true of all possible worlds as well, and these are called analytic propositions. They are necessary or eternal truths such as are to be found in mathematics and in logic. Leibniz, though differing from Plato and St. Thomas, like them reduces possibility to conceivability. A statement is possible if its contradictory is inconceivable, i.e., if no contradiction follows from the assumption of its existence. The necessity of logic, the necessary analytic statement, thus depends on an order of possible being that is independent of and antecedent to existence.

For Christian WOLFF, the necessity of the possibles is identified with the necessity of the divine essence. Wolff taught that essences are dependent on God not in respect to their intelligible or ideal constituents, but only as regards their existence. The absolute necessity of the possibles is in the order of ideal essences; their existence depends on the necessary existence of God. Consequently, Wolff defined metaphysics as the science of essences, or of the possibles, a definition that has had a long history and is still influential in scholasticism. Essence, in his view, is the intelligible content from which is drawn the meaning of the thing, namely, what makes it to be the kind of thing it is, and this apart from its existence.

For Immanuel Kant, as for modern IDEALISM, essences, or the intrinsic possibilities of things, arise from the human intellect and from the conditions of knowledge. Possibility is thus defined as agreement with the formal conditions of experience, although as such it is definable only under the conditions that make sensible experience possible (*Critique of Pure Reason,* B266, A220). Kant does not concede possible being a being of its own apart from the actual world of sensation. Such an attribution, in his view, would be a result of the transcendental illusion. Contrary to Leibniz, he holds that possibility cannot be defined independently of the actual world of sensible intuition.

For E. HUSSERL, on the other hand, the possible, along with the probable, the questionable, and the doubtful, are ontic modalities. As ontic, these modalities can change without any type of (subjective) thought, i.e., without concepts or judgments playing any part in the change. Possibility, for him, is objective in a Cartesian rather than in a Kantian sense.

Contemporary Logicians. In the usage of contemporary logicians, logical possibility has greater extension than physical possibility. The criterion of logical possibility is the compatibility of a statement with the laws of logic. Since the laws of logic are reducible to the principles of CONTRADICTION and IDENTITY, this is a return to the position of Leibniz, to an abstract order of essences that *are* in themselves apart from existence. Bertrand RUSSELL, for example, conceives of number in this way, as does Alonzo Church. Numbers are not abstracted from concrete sense data; they simply *are,* like Platonic Forms. Similarly, an argument is sound only if it is not possible for its premises to be true and its conclusion false. Every conceivable situation in which the premises would be true would make the conclusion true.

According to Nelson Goodman, counterfactual conditionals explain possibility in the logical order. The empiricist or nominalist position is also behind the identification of meaning and evidence as circular. W. V. O. Quine's rejection of possibility by reducing it to the role of a modal operator offers a good illustration of how a thorough-going empiricism would eliminate possibility. In Quine's view, the object-directed pattern of man's thinking confuses defective nouns with propositions. Yet there is a metaphysical foundation of his criticism of possibility, which seems to be directed more against the idealistic possible, with a being all its own, than against the possible of scholastic philosophy.

Contemporary Scholastics. Interest in the problems posed by possibility has also been manifested by É. Gilson and other scholastic proponents of EXISTENTIAL METAPHYSICS, who claim St. Thomas as the source of their doctrine. They point to such texts of St. Thomas as ''That which entirely is not, is infinitely distant from act; it is not in potency in any way at all'' (*C. gent.* 1.43). In their view, instead of discussing possible being in terms of a second intention such as possibility or in terms of schematic metaphysical notions such as potency and act, it should be discussed in terms of the more immediate metaphysical principles of essence and existence. Formulated in this way, a possible is an essence without existence. Possible being is thus a relic of the Platonic essence, and as such contradicts an existentialism that finds in existence the source of all perfection, including that of essence. The possible essence, in this view, is simply an intentional being existing only in the mind by a mental divorce from existence (*esse*). The being (*esse*) of a quiddity is a kind of being of reason (*quoddam esse rationis—In I sent.* 19.5.1 ad 7). Between being (*esse*) and intentional being (*esse intentionale*) there is no alternative except the nonexistent world of Platonic Ideas and Avicennian essences.

For Leibniz and N. HARTMANN, existence is dependent on essence; this is why all that can be is. But this is a reversal of the values of being, according to the existentialist interpretation. Existence is primary and only that which is, is. Whatever can be is dependent on that which is, and what it is. Thus pure possibility can occupy a place in reality, play a role in the real, only if the essence possesses some mode of existence. Of course, man can know things that do not exist. But when he knows essences that are nonexistent, this is in virtue of a secondary act of the mind, a REFLECTION on human knowledge itself. In this case the intellect knows essences apart from their existence, but such essences themselves exist by the act of existence of the human knower. They exist in a precise mode of being, the mode of INTENTIONALITY. Possible essences exist as concepts, as accidental being, with the kind of existence proper to accidents. The unicorn, the gold mountain, the elder brother of the eldest brother are all brought into existence by an act of reflection on prior knowledge that is restructured and reconstructed in the mind of the knower. Those who would attribute to such possibles an extramental existence in their own right fall under the very criticism Thomas Aquinas made of the Platonic Forms (*In lib. de causis* 2). They consider things as they exist under the conditions of thought as if they were existing under the conditions of reality. In St. Thomas's moderate realism, the existence that grounds and supports the possible essence is the act of existence of the knowing subject, whether this be human or divine.

See Also: ESSENCE AND EXISTENCE; EXISTENCE; POTENCY AND ACT

Bibliography: A. FAUST, *Der Möglichkeitsgedanke,* 2 v. (Heidelberg 1931–32). A. C. PEGIS, *St. Thomas and the Greeks* (Milwaukee 1939). G. SMITH, ''Avicenna and the Possibles,'' *New Scholasticism* 17 (1943) 340–357. É. H. GILSON, *Being and Some Philosophers* (2d ed. Toronto 1952). A. FOREST, *La Structure metaphysique du concret selon S. Thomas d'Aquin* (2d ed. Paris 1956) 133–165. N. J. WELLS, ''Capreolus on Essence and Existence,'' *Modern Schoolman* 38 (1960–61) 1–24. W. N. CLARKE, ''What Is Really Real?,'' *Progress in Philosophy: Philosophical Studies in Honor of Rev. Doctor Charles A. Hart,* ed. J. A. MCWILLIAMS (Milwaukee 1955) 61–90. J. I. CONWAY, ''The Reality of the Possibles,'' *New Scholasticism* 33 (1959) 139–161, 331–353. E. W. MORTON, ''The Nature of the Possible According to St. Thomas Aquinas,'' *American Catholic Philosophical Association. Proceedings of the Annual Meeting* 32 (1958) 184–189. W. E. CARLO, ''The Role of Essence in Existential Metaphysics: A Reappraisal,'' *International Philosophical Quarterly* 2 (1962) 557–590. J. OWENS, *All Elemen-*

tary Christian Metaphysics (Milwaukee 1963) 30–37. L. SWEENEY, *A Metaphysics of Authentic Existentialism* (Englewood Cliffs, N.J. 1965). P. WEISS, *Modes of Being* (Carbondale, Ill. 1958).

[W. E. CARLO]

Possibility and Divine Omnipotence The possibility conceived of as already present in the nature of things and able to be actualized in the ordinary course of events, called natural possibility, is situated under a further, all-embracing possibility that includes and transcends the former, called by scholastic theologians absolute, or logical, possibility. The possible is this absolute, or logical, possibility. The possible in this absolute sense is the domain of the divine OMNIPOTENCE, an active potency infinite in extent. Unlike the case of created active and passive potency, in which the possibility of the former is circumscribed by the limitations of the latter, the divine active potency, identical with the divine nature and the divine actuality, is wholly unlimited and produces from nothing, according to the motion of the divine will and the dictates of the divine wisdom, the totality of all other being, including all natural potency or possibility, whether active or passive.

Strictly speaking, nothing is impossible to this divine potency, since that which is logically impossible by a repugnance of terms has, by virtue of its intrinsic contradiction, the status of nothingness. It is impossible in itself rather than to God. Things impossible to nature, on the other hand, such as the raising of the dead, the giving of sight to the blind, are so solely because of the determination of the limits of nature by the Author of nature. They are not impossible to the divine potency, which is infinite, but rather are connatural to it. Although past events cannot be reversed, as the discovery of America cannot now be made not to have happened, nevertheless this does not denote any limitation of the divine power. The occurrence of every event, past, present, or future, signifies instead a definitive realization, permissive in the case of sin, of the divine plan, to which, in the decree of the divine wisdom, no amendment of a more desirable nature can exist or be possible.

Divine activity in the production and conservation of things is not qualified by the necessary and the contingent, the possible and the actual, as these are present in things. Rather God, in producing being, also determines the mode of being, what will be and what cannot be, and, in what is to be, whether it will exist as that which cannot not be or as that which may or may not be. Those possible things that by nature do not occur with necessity but may or may not be, though proceeding according to the infallible sequence of divine providence and coming into being when so ordained, yet do so according to their nature, i.e., as contingent rather than as necessary. Hence the possible and the impossible, the necessary and the contingent in natural things should be considered as they are present in secondary, or natural, causes, since, barring divine intervention, that is the way their occurrence takes place.

The limitless potency inherent in the divine omnipotence, because man does not know positively the extent of that omnipotence, is discerned by man in a negative way as being everything that is not intrinsically contradictory. (An intrinsic contradiction is one in which two terms contradict each other as, for example, in the combination ''square circle.'') Hence the possibility that what it implies is called logical as well as absolute. A gold mountain would be considered possible in this sense, even should there be in the present nature of things no natural potency allowing for an accumulation of gold in one place sufficient for the amount to be qualified as a mountain. The concept of gold simply has nothing repugnant in it that would exclude its being present in a quantity equivalent to a mountain. A centaur, however, conceived as a creature half man and half horse, would not be considered possible even in the logical, or absolute, sense, since here one term by its very nature negates or excludes the other. The rationality proper to man could not be combined with the irrationality proper to a horse. The same internal contradiction makes it impossible for a man simultaneously to sit and not sit or, at a given moment in the past, to have been seated and not to have been seated (which latter would occur if an event in the past were able to be made not to have taken place). The all-embracing type of the possible, found in the divine omnipotence, grasped negatively by man as whatever is not internally contradictory, may be stated in the logical sense as ''that which, supposing it to exist, nothing (absolutely) impossible follows,'' or ''that whose contradictory is not necessarily true.''

See Also: CONTINGENCY; NECESSITY

Bibliography: THOMAS AQUINAS, *Summa theologiae* 1a, 25; *In 3 phys. 2; In 5 meta. 14; In 6 meta. 3; In 9 meta. 1–7; De pot. 1.* L. SCHUTZ, *Thomas-Lexikon* 606–608. V. MATHIEW, *Enciclopedia filosofica,* 4 v. (Venice-Rome 1957) 3:1545–58. W. KERN, *Lexikon für Theologie und Kirche,* ed. J. HOFER and K. RAHNER, 10 v. (2d, new ed. Freiburg 1957–65) 8:640–642. R. EISLER, *Wörterbuch der philosophischen Begriffe,* 3 v. (4th ed. Berlin 1927–30) 2:162–168.

[P. CONWAY]

POSSIDIUS, ST.

Fifth-century African bishop, biographer of St. Augustine; d. after 437. One of the first of Augustine's disciples at Hippo (*c.* 391), Possidius became bishop of Calama in Numidia *c.* 397. He took part in the 8th Council of Carthage, Aug. 25, 403 (Mansi, *Sacrorum Concili-*

orum nova et amplissima collectio 3:790); the 11th, in 407 (*ibid.* 806); and the 15th, June 14, 410 (*ibid.* 810). He served as spokesman for the Catholic bishops in their great discussion with the Donatists, held at Carthage in May and June 411 (Mansi 4:8). He participated in the Council of Milevis (416) against Pelagianism (*ibid.* 335; Augustine, *Epist.,* 137, 176), and was at the Council of Carthage in 419 (Mansi 4:433) (*see* PELAGIUS AND PELAGIANISM).

On a pastoral visitation in 404 Possidius was attacked by the Donatists (*Vita Aug.* 12; Augustine, *Epist.,* 105.4), and in 408 he retired before the fanaticism of the pagans of Calama. He was sent to Italy as ambassador to the imperial authority and visited PAULINUS OF NOLA (Augustine, *Epist.,* 95.1), but returned to Africa in 410. When the Vandals invaded Calama (428), Possidius took refuge at Hippo and assisted Augustine on his deathbed (*Vita Aug.* 28–29, 31). Forced to return to Calama in 435, he was expelled with other African bishops by the Vandals under Geiseric in 437 (Prosper of Aquitaine, *Chron.; Monumenta Germanica Auctores Antiquissimi* 9:475) and disappears from history.

His principal work, the biography of St. Augustine, composed between 432 and 437, delineates Augustine's career as a monk, priest, and bishop. A modest work, it avoids the overlaudatory style usual to that age. Its account of Augustine's activities is trustworthy for the most part; the *Indiculus* (list of Augustine's writings) is invaluable, though not complete or without error.

Feast: May 16 or 17.

Bibliography: *Patrologia Latina* 32.1:33–66. *Acta sanctorum* Aug. 6:427–440. M. PELLEGRINO, *Revue des études augustiniennes* 2 (1956) 195–229; ed., *Vita* (Alba 1955). A. WILMART, ed., in *Miscellanea Agostiniana,* 2 v. (Rome 1930–31) 2:149–233, ed. of *Indiculus.* W. ENSSLIN, *Paulys Realencyclopädie der klassichen Altertumswissenschaft* 22.1 (1953) 860–861. B. ALTANER, *Patrology* 488, 513. H. T. WEISKOTTEN, ed. and tr., *Vita* (Princeton 1919), critical ed. and Eng. tr. E. ELM, ''Die *Vita Augustini* des Possidius: 'The Work of a Plain Man and an Untrained Writer?' Wandlungen in der Beurteilung eines hagiographischen Textes,'' *Augustinianum* 37 (1997) 229–240.

[R. K. POETZEL]

POSTEL, MARIE MADELEINE, ST.

Foundress of the Sisters of the CHRISTIAN SCHOOLS OF MERCY; b. La Bretonne, Normandy, France, Nov. 28, 1756; d. Saint-Sauveur-le-Vicomte, Normandy, July 16, 1846. Postel was born in comfortable circumstances and was given the baptismal name of Julie. After attending school at Barfleur and at the Abbey of Valognes, she opened a school in La Bretonne for poor children (1774). During the French Revolution she continued to teach religion to them and to befriend nonjuring priests. Desirous of founding a religious congregation dedicated to the education of girls, she went to Cherbourg in 1805 and gathered around her three women who began leading the religious life. The four pronounced the vows of religion in 1807, and Julie took the name Madeleine. She composed a rule for her institute, but this was replaced in 1837 by the one written by St. John Baptist de LA SALLE for the CHRISTIAN BROTHERS. Sister Marie Madeleine, as superior general, moved her community to Tamerville in 1816, and it remained there until 1832. She then established its headquarters in the abandoned Abbey of Saint-Sauveur-le-Vicomte, which has since been the location of the congregation's motherhouse. During her remaining 14 years of life she restored the abbey church and supervised the growth of her institute, which in 1846 had 150 members and 37 convents. Sister Marie Madeleine was noted for her fortitude amid many trials. As an educator she improved the unimaginative curriculum then provided for poor girls by introducing sewing and embroidery and by supplementing Guizot's *Charte* with subjects such as poetry and singing. She was beatified in 1908 and canonized in 1925.

Feast: July 16.

Bibliography: G. GRENTE, *Ste. Marie-Madeleine Postel,* tr. K. HENVEY (New York 1928). SISTER CALISTA, *Love Endureth All Things: Life of St. Marie Madeleine Postel* (pa. Cork 1953).

[W. J. BATTERSBY]

POSTGATE, NICHOLAS, BL.

Priest, martyr; *alias* Watson, Whitmore; b. ca. 1596–97 atKirkdaleHouse, Egton (Eyton) Bridge, Yorkshire; hanged, drawn, and quartered Aug. 7,1679at York under Charles II. He studied at Douai (1621–1628), where he wasordained priest in 1628. On June 29, 1630, he began his fruitful, 49-yearapostolate in Yorkshire. He was apprehended by the exciseman Reeves at the house of MatthewLyth of Sleights, Little Beck (near Whitby), and was condemned for hispriesthood.Following his execution, his remains were given to his friends and interred.One of hishands was sent to Douai College and his portable altar-stone to Dodding Green,Westmoreland. He was beatified by Pope John Paul II on Nov. 22, 1987 withGeorge Haydock and Companions.

Feast of the English Martyrs: May 4 (England).

See Also: ENGLAND, SCOTLAND, AND WALES, MARTYRS OF.

Bibliography: R. CHALLONER, *Memoirs of Missionary Priests,* ed. J. H.POLLEN (rev. ed. London 1924), II, no. 204.E. HAM-

ILTON, *The Priest of the Moors: Reflections on Nicholas Postgate* (London 1980).J. H. POLLEN, *Acts of English Martyrs* (London 1891).D. QUINLAN, *The Father Postgate Story* (Whitby, Yorks. 1967).

[K. I. RABENSTEIN]

POSTULATE

A postulate is an assumption advanced with the claim that it be taken for granted as axiomatic. In reference to further investigation it is a statement so assumed as to require no proof of its validity. In the development of THEORY, it corresponds to the first principles of philosophy. Practically, a postulate is roughly the same as a hypothesis except that the postulate is considered to be the idea content of the assumption and the hypothesis the logical statement of the postulate. In scientific theory postulates are generally either laws or principles that are considered as established, e.g., Newton's laws of motion, or convenient concepts that can neither be proved nor disproved, e.g., the principle of the conservation of energy.

See Also: AXIOMATIC SYSTEM.

[L. A. FOLEY]

St. Marie Madeleine Postel.

POTENCY

Potency, a technical term used principally in philosophy and theology, is the capacity or aptitude in a being to receive some perfection or perform some action. Always a relative term, it means capacity ''for'' something, e.g., potency to receive energy, to grow, to learn mathematics, to become wise, virtuous. The correlate of potency is ACT, which expresses the fully present realization or completion of potency. (*See* POTENCY AND ACT.)

Origins with Aristotle. The general theory of act and potency, with its terminology, originated with ARISTOTLE and became the central doctrine of his philosophy (*Phys.* 187a 12–192b 3; *Meta.* 1045b 27–1052a 12). For him, potency was necessary to explain CHANGE, that is, the transition from one mode of being to another, or the coming-to-be of some new being or mode of being. Change, he argued, requires not only a state of being at its end different from that at the beginning, but also some underlying element or subject that remains throughout the process, thereby forming a bond of continuity between the two terms. This underlying element cannot be identified with either of its changing states or modes of being, since it is now without one, now without the other. It must have the capacity or potency to be now in one state, now in another, so that while in possession of one mode of being it still remains in potency to all other possible states. Thus water that is now actually cold is at the same time potentially hot; an acorn is in potency or has the potency to become an oak tree, and so on.

Every BEING that is capable of change must therefore be composed of two distinct but mutually interrelated principles called act and potency, the second of which is in act with respect to its present state of perfection and in potency with respect to all other acts within its range of change. In a nonessential or accidental change the potency corresponds to the whole SUBSTANCE or ESSENCE of the being, which is thus in potency to its various possible accidental states or modes (*see* ACCIDENT). In a substantial or essential change the potency corresponds to ultimate or primary matter, which is in potency to diverse substantial forms (*see* MATTER AND FORM).

Thus did Aristotle answer the question that had baffled early Greek philosophers, viz, how is change possible, since new being cannot arise out of pure nothingness, nor, it seems, out of already actualized existing being? His answer was that the new being appearing in change arises out of a relative or partial nonbeing, i.e., out of a preexisting potency that is ''not yet'' the new being, but has the positive aptitude to become it.

Thomistic Development. Aristotle applied the notion of potency only to the order of change or process.

Where no change is possible, according to him, there is no potency but only act. St. THOMAS AQUINAS, however, applied this doctrine more widely to explain the intrinsic reason for limited or FINITE BEING (*De pot.* 1.1–2; *C. gent.* 1.16,18; 2.52–54). He saw potency not merely as a positive aptitude for some attribute, but also as a capacity limiting the amount of perfection a being can possess or receive. Since different limiting capacities can determine different degrees or modes of possessing a common perfection, such as life, knowledge, or power, the notion of limiting potency also explained, for him, how perfection could be multiplied or shared by many different beings, each according to its own potency or receptive capacity (*see* PARTICIPATION).

Thus St. Thomas explains all degrees of being as different combinations of potency and act. God alone has no potency, either as limiting capacity or as aptitude for change. All beings below Him have at least the composition of the act of EXISTENCE with the limiting potency of essence, which makes them exist at this particular level, as this particular being. All beings except God have also the act-potency composition of accident and substance, allowing them an individual history of development and change. All material beings, moreover, are composed of substantial form and primary matter.

The notion of LIMITATION was already implicit in Aristotle's theory of potency as receptive capacity, but was never made explicit by him. The reason undoubtedly was that for Aristotle, as for practically all Greeks of the classical period, the finite was identified with the finished, the intelligible, the perfect, i.e., with FORM or act, and the infinite with the unfinished, the unintelligible, the imperfect, i.e., with MATTER as pure indeterminate potency. Hence in this perspective the role of limit was associated with act rather than with potency. St. Thomas, on the other hand, synthesized Aristotelian doctrine with the Neoplatonic participation theory developed during the first centuries of the Christian era. According to the latter, any participated perfection has its source in an unlimited plenitude; each subject participating in this perfection shares in it according to its own finite capacity (*see* NEOPLATONISM; EMANATIONISM). St. Thomas identified the infinite source with act and the limiting capacity with potency. Thus the two great currents of Greek metaphysics are synthesized in a basic Thomistic doctrine: ''No act is found limited except by a potency'' (*Comp. theol.* 1.18); ''Every act inhering in another is terminated by that in which it inheres. Hence, an act that exists in nothing is terminated by nothing'' (*C. gent.* 1.43).

Other scholastic thinkers, like DUNS SCOTUS and SUÁREZ, stay closer to Aristotle and incorporate less Neoplatonic doctrine than did St. Thomas. They do not hold or do not stress the role of potency as a necessary limiting principle for finite being, and explain the limitation of act merely by the extrinsic efficient cause or agent that makes the being such as it is.

Meaning and Kinds. The term potency, as understood by St. Thomas, means simply a real capacity for some act. It includes both the positive note of aptitude for act and the negative note of capacity limited to receive only so much act and no more. This potency may, but does not necessarily or always, imply aptitude for change. Because of its essentially relative character potency must be defined in relation to its proportionate act, and hence neither its existence nor its nature can be known except through its fulfillment in actuality.

Active Potency. Potency as aptitude or capacity for act is divided into two main types, active and passive. Active potency is the inner power of an agent to perform some action, though it may not be actually so doing, e.g., the power of an artist to paint a picture, of a bird to fly, or of God to create beings. Since active potency does not of itself imply imperfection, it can be found in both God and creatures. In creatures, however, which now act and now do not, it implies some inner change from inactivity to activity, usually stimulated by an outside agent. When divisions into act and potency are compared, active potency belongs more properly with act than potency; the latter, unless further specified, usually means passive potency. Hence, to avoid confusion in terminology, active potency is more safely referred to as active power.

Passive Potency. Passive potency is the capacity to receive or be enriched with some new perfection not previously possessed, e.g., to acquire new knowledge, to receive heat energy, and so on. This potency alone plays the role of limiting capacity already explained. No passive potency possesses in its own right the perfection or act that it receives; if so, it would itself be the act in question and not a potency for it. Therefore passive potency can be activated only through the action of a cause or causes already possessing, at least in some equivalent way, the perfection that is actualized in the recipient potency. This priority of act over potency is used by Aristotle, St. Thomas, and other scholastic philosophers as a key notion to demonstrate the existence of God as First Unmoved Mover, the PURE ACT required as ultimate cause of change (*see* MOTION, FIRST CAUSE OF; GOD, PROOFS FOR THE EXISTENCE OF).

Pure Potency. The only pure passive potency in the universe, according to Aristotle and St. Thomas, is primary matter. This doctrine has often been grossly misinterpreted to mean that pure potency is a distinct material thing existing on its own, like an atom. Since this potency is of itself pure indetermination, it can exist only as co-principle in a composite of act and potency that is itself structured or ''informed'' matter. Hence it can never be isolated or observed by laboratory analysis, and can be grasped only by philosophical analysis as a necessary condition for the properties of beings that can be observed. All complete real beings in the universe, therefore, are either Pure Act or varying combinations of act and potency. Apart from primary matter, all levels and kinds of passive potency are a blend of passive and active potency. Thus, whenever a new perfection is received by any being, this involves some aspect of passivity, or reception, and some aspect of activity, or assimilation of the new perfection into the being of the recipient.

Obediential Potency. Theologians also speak of a special passive potency in creatures as obediential potency. Unlike a natural potency, this does not flow directly from the nature of a thing, but is rather the basic openness or docility of the creature to elevation by God toward some level of perfection beyond its normal fixed status in the hierarchy of being. The principal instances of this type of potency actually given in the present historical order (endless others may be hidden in God's providence for the future) are: (1) the aptitude of rational creatures to be raised to the life of GRACE and the BEATIFIC VISION as adopted sons of God; (2) the aptitude of human nature to be assumed into a special HYPOSTATIC UNION with one of the Persons of the Blessed Trinity, as happened in the human nature of Christ in the INCARNATION, and (3) the aptitude of material things to be made efficacious instruments or channels of divine grace in the Sacraments. [*See* SACRAMENTS (THEOLOGY OF).]

Potency in Modern Philosophy. With the RENAISSANCE, the theory of act and potency fell into disrepute along with other Aristotelian and scholastic doctrines (*see* RENAISSANCE PHILOSOPHY). One of the reasons was that decadent SCHOLASTICISM often substituted this general metaphysical theory for proper scientific explanations relevant to particular areas of experience. To explain the phenomenon of sleep, for example, by postulating a dormitive potency might be quite correct, but this explanation is so general as to be scientifically sterile. Nor was the theory of potency and act ever intended for such purposes.

Most modern philosophers outside the scholastic tradition have attacked the notion of potency. The notable exception is LEIBNIZ (1646–1716), who attempted to restore it to use in his theory of the MONAD. A principal reason for this attack is that potency is knowable only through its fulfilling act and is not a complete entity that is discoverable by sense observation or scientific experimentation. Act and potency is the general model of a metaphysical composition of incomplete coprinciples within a complete being; when this notion was lost, the idea of real potency was distorted into that of a physical entity hidden somewhere inside a being, which, if real, should be able to be uncovered by a sufficiently probing scientific analysis. When nothing such was found, as of course it could not be, the notion itself was rejected as medieval superstition. The ''clear and distinct ideas'' of Cartesian RATIONALISM, the radical EMPIRICISM of the English tradition culminating in HUME, the conception of nature found in MECHANISM—all had no place for the authentic conception of potency.

Modern philosophies of change, such as that of BERGSON, make continuous process or succession of states the very essence of reality. Since, for them, no underlying immobile substances exist, they either deny the reality of potency as distinct from act or consider it a mere mental projection of the present into the past.

With the breakdown of mechanistic pictures of the universe in 20th-century science, and the recent return of metaphysics to respectability among philosophers outside the scholastic tradition, the notion of real potentiality is being restored as indispensable for an adequate analysis of reality. This is true not only among philosophers, but even among scientists, most notable of whom is Werner Heisenberg. Indeed it is difficult to see how one can explain any process of organic growth, or the range of unpredictable possibilities of action found in nature from man to subatomic particles, without the help of some such notion.

See Also: POSSIBILITY; POTENCY AND ACT; MATTER AND FORM; ESSENCE AND EXISTENCE.

Bibliography: A. POMPEI, *Enciclopedia filosofica,* 4 v. (Venice-Rome 1957) 3:1562–64. V. MATHIEU, *ibid.* 3:1545–58. A. MANSION, *Introduction à la physique aristotélicienne* (2d ed. rev. & enl. Louvain 1946). J. STALLMACH, *Dynamis und Energeia* (Monographien zur philosophischen Forschung 21; Meisenheim 1959). C. GIACON, *Atto e potenza* (Brescia 1949). R. GARRIGOU-LAGRANGE, *Reality: A Synthesis of Thomistic Thought,* tr. P. CUMMINS (St. Louis 1950). V. E. SMITH, *The General Science of Nature* (Milwaukee 1958). W. N. CLARKE, ''The Limitation of Act by Potency,'' *The New Scholasticism* 26 (1952) 167–194. J. WILD, *Introduction to Realistic Philosophy* (New York 1948). W. HEISENBERG, *Physics and Philosophy* (New York 1958). G. A. DE LAGUNA, ''Existence and Potentiality,'' *Philosophical Review* 60 (1951) 155–176. E. B. MOORE, ''Positivism and Potentiality,'' *Journal of Philosophy* 48 (1951) 472–479.

[W. N. CLARKE]

POTENCY AND ACT

Separate studies on POTENCY and ACT are demanded if one is to gain a knowledge of their significance and the range of their application. But these leave something to be desired. Since they isolate the notions from one another, they offer a static picture with only suspicion of the dynamic quality of potency and act. To supply this quality, one must seek a situation in which the two notions are involved in intimate relationship. This is found in the context of BEING that does not exceed the limits of the predicamental order (*see* CATEGORIES OF BEING). For it is of this being that potency and act are principles (*see* PRINCIPLE).

In such a context potency and act reveal themselves for what they are entitatively. They are simply principles, not things. Both are essentially incomplete, since neither is able to claim more than an imperfect participation in the form of being, Furthermore, they are naturally corroborative. Potency is the indetermined and perfectible element that looks to act as its determinate and perfecting complement. Because of their imperfect grasp on the form of being, the two necessarily require mutual assistance to exercise their role as principles of an existent. (For an exception, however, *see* SOUL, HUMAN, 4.)

Origin with Aristotle. It is Aristotle who must be credited with the discovery of the notions of potency and act. Initially it was his concern with the problem of CHANGE that provided the occasion for the discovery (*Phys.* 184a 9–192b 5). Prior to his time change was conceived as limited to the order of accidents; all the early naturalists steadfastly denied that it ever penetrated to the level of SUBSTANCE. Moreover, for them it was more a case of unveiling what was actual but hidden than of discovering the nature of change itself (see Saint Thomas Aquinas, *In 1 phys.* 9.2–3). With Aristotle's discovery of the notion of potency and his projection of that notion to the substantial order in the concept of primary matter, the whole picture was altered (*see* MATTER AND FORM). A true science of change was initiated. But important as this is, it is far from being the only application of the notions of potency and act in Aristotelian philosophy.

The further one ventures into the corpus of Aristotle's natural studies, the more evidence one encounters of the significance of these principles. These are, one learns, the basis of the theses that constitute the heart of his philosophy of nature and his psychology, such as, for example, the definition of MOTION (*Phys.* 201a 10) and that of the SOUL (*Anim.* 412a 6–28). But it is in his *Metaphysics* (1017a 35–b 9; 1045b 28–2052a 12) that Aristotle explicitly extends their horizons by bringing potency and act into the focus of being itself. Here he gives them a distinctively metaphysical aspect and lays the groundwork for the special use to which medieval philosophers would put them in their teachings concerning essence and existence.

Thomistic Development. With the ascendancy of ARISTOTELIANISM among the schoolmen, the doctrine of potency and act assumed great prominence in scholastic philosophy. But while all made it a major feature of their respective systems, none equaled Saint THOMAS AQUINAS in his fidelity to Aristotle's concepts or in the role he granted them in his philosophy. Whereas other outstanding figures, such as Duns Scotus and F. Suárez, adulterated the Aristotelian notions of potency and act, Saint Thomas preserved them in their original purity and made them the cornerstone of his philosophy of being. Special topics that deserve mention in that philosophy are the real distinction between the concepts, their relative priority, the limitation of act by potency, and the distinction between essence and existence.

Real Distinction. There are instances in which the actual separation of act and potency prove beyond doubt the reality of their distinction. It must be admitted, however, that such instances are too few and are verified in too limited a context (that of the soul's operative powers) to constitute a premise warranting a universal conclusion. It is for this reason that Thomists look in a new direction for a compelling proof, namely, to the conceptual order.

While aware that not every conceptual distinction is an actual reflection of the ontological order (e.g., the distinction between the concepts of GENUS and difference is a case in point), Thomists argue that the extensive distance between the concepts of potency and act is a proof of their real distinction. The concepts of potency and act far exceed the distance that separates concepts that are virtually distinct by a virtual major distinction, as is the situation with regard to the concepts of genus and difference (*see* DISTINCTION, KINDS OF). The latter share a commonness despite their distinction. Both signify the totum: the genus indeterminately, the difference determinately. Neither signifies a wholly new form but rather the same form, the sole variation arising from the mode of signifying. Consequently, their distinction, while having roots in the reality they represent, does not pass over from the conceptual to the ontological order. The case of the concepts of potency and act is altogether different. The concept of each stands diametrically opposed to that of the other, and there exists no ground on which this opposition can be resolved. The concept of potency formally signifies capacity or the absence of perfection, whereas that of act signifies perfection. Thus potency formally negates the very substance of act. Granting the correctness of each concept, it necessarily follows that the one and the other signify notions that defy identification, and this not only conceptually but also ontologically.

Relative Priority. In the order of knowledge, act naturally is prior to potency. Because potency signifies possibility and the measure of the knowableness of an entity depends on its actuality (*In 1 phys.* 1.7), potency can be known only through the act that is its fulfillment (*In 9 meta.* 7.1846).

In the ontological order, in which potency and act are constituent principles, potency is in most cases anterior to act. This follows because potency is generally the subject of act and therefore must be prior to it in time or solely in nature, or both in time and in nature. If one considers the matter absolutely, however—i.e., without reference to the circumstances associated with potency and act as constituent principles of being and attending solely to their respective natures—one must acknowledge the priority of act over potency. The reason for this is that the only source that can effect a transfer from potency to act is a being that is already in act (*see* MOTION, FIRST CAUSE OF).

Limitation of Act by Potency. The multiplication of act affords sufficient proof of the compatibility of the notions of limitation and of act. But the source of the compatibility is not quite obvious. Can the two notions be immediately joined or must they be mediated? Saint Thomas's answer is constant: the two notions can be associated only through the medium of potency.

Three alternatives suggest themselves as explanations for the limitation of act: act itself, potency, and the efficient cause. The first and third alternatives must be excluded. Were act self-limiting, it would negate itself, for it would be forced to assume a contradictory character, i.e., that of presenting itself as the principle of a perfection and of its negation. Similarly, appeal cannot be made to the efficient cause. It is not within the competence of this cause, be it infinite or finite, to resolve a natural incompatibility such as exists between the notions of act and self-limited act. There remains, then, potency as the final possibility, and here Thomists find the principle of act's limitation. The explanation follows from the nature of potency itself. Potency is self-limiting; it is a capacity for a definite act. Possessed of this inherent limitation, it naturally imposes limitation upon the act it receives; whatever is received must be received according to the measure, or limiting capacity, of the recipient (*see* PARTICIPATION).

Essence and Existence. The notions of potency and act provide maximum service within Thomism for solving the problem of the relationship between essence and existence. Other arguments can be given as a basis for maintaining the real distinction between essence and existence, but the doctrine of potency and act here assumes the greatest cogency. In particular, the Thomistic analysis of the nature of act and of its principle of limitation furnishes the middle term through which the real distinction between essence and existence is demonstrated (*see* ESSENCE AND EXISTENCE).

Later Scholasticism. One finds in the philosophy of the schoolmen a strong echo of Aristotle's evaluation of the importance of potency and act. Every major system of metaphysics elaborated within the scholastic tradition, whether of Thomist, Scotist, or Suarezian persuasion, places major emphasis on these notions. But while Aristotle's influence is far from negligible, it would be erroneous to see the thought of the scholastic tradition as a mere copy of that of the Stagirite. For one thing, a new use was made of potency and act by the scholastics; for another, though it is debatable whether this was a development, the Aristotelian notions came to be greatly modified.

The Thomistic application of the notions of potency and act to the problem of essence and existence, for example, was a wholly new venture. Though Aristotle himself did employ potency and act in his study of being, he did not consider the question of essence and existence in the context of the actual existent, nor did he apply the doctrine of potency and act to its general resolution. This was left to the scholastics, especially those of the Thomist school (*see* THOMISM).

Notable but regrettable changes in the structure of potency and act were much in evidence in both the Scotist and Suarezian systems. John Duns Scotus expanded the structure by attempting to introduce an intermediate between potency and act, viz, the notion of virtual act. F. SUÁREZ, in his turn, conceived of potency as an *actus imperfectus,* thereby restricting, rather than expanding, the traditional structure. These changes were significant. With the introduction of virtual act Scotus felt compelled to challenge the universality of the distinction between the moved and the mover (*Opus oxon.* 2.25.1.12), and consequently the metaphysical character of Saint Thomas's *prima via.* Suárez's interpretation of potency as an *actus imperfectus* had similar repercussions. Because of it he was forced to deny the basic opposition between potency and act in the systems of both Aristotle and Saint Thomas. Furthermore, he had to reject the principle "whatever is moved is moved by another" as not having metaphysical validity (*see* SCOTISM; SUAREZIANISM).

Modern Thought. So long as modern thought followed the pathways of IDEALISM or EMPIRICISM in any of their variations, the doctrine of potency and act could not hope for any type of recognition. The philosophical neglect of these principles varied in direct proportion to the rejection of REALISM, whether this was its complete repudiation, as in idealism, or merely its limitation to the sensibly perceived, as in empiricism.

In contemporary philosophy, however, a new interest in realism has begun to emerge. Rejecting idealism's attempt to impose its own image on the world of things, existentialists have become absorbed with the anguish of existence. Their concern with EXISTENCE, although presently fettered with the chains of IRRATIONALISM, could ultimately open the way for a renewed interest in potency and act (*see* EXISTENTIALISM).

See Also: POTENCY; ACT; ESSENCE AND EXISTENCE; MATTER AND FORM

Bibliography: J. M. RAMIREZ, *De ordine, Placita Quaedam Thomistica* (Salamanca 1963). G. M. MANSER, *Das Wesen des Thomismus* (3d ed. Fribourg 1949). A. FOREST, *La Structure metaphysique du concret selon S. Thomas d'Aquin* (Paris 1956). P. DESCOQS, *Essai critique sur l'hylémorphisme* (Paris 1924).

[J. C. TAYLOR]

POTTER, MARY

Foundress of the LITTLE COMPANY OF MARY; b. London, England, Nov. 22, 1847; d. Rome, Italy, April 9, 1913. She was the daughter of William Norwood and Mary Anne (Martin) Potter. Her mother, an Anglican, was received into the Catholic Church in 1845, and her five children were raised as Catholics. Mary was educated in a small private Catholic boarding school. She showed no inclination toward the religious life until her early twenties when, convinced that God was calling her to a life dedicated to the sick and the dying, she broke her engagement to be married. Given permission to influence others in devotion to the dying and to bring together in community life women with similar interests, she founded the Little Company of Mary at Hyson Green, England (1877). Several of her writings have been published. Her cause for beatification has been introduced in Rome (*Decretum super scripta,* July 25, 1952, and Nov. 25, 1956).

Bibliography: P. DOUGHERTY, *Mother Mary Potter* (London 1963).

[M. K. COUCH]

POTTHAST, AUGUST

Important German historian and editor of canonical sources; b. Houster, Aug. 13, 1824; d. Leobschutz, Feb. 13, 1898. After his studies in theology, philosophy, and history at the University of Halle, he was commissioned as a teacher in 1855. He was appointed custodian of the royal library in Berlin in 1868, and from 1874 to 1894 he was librarian of the legislative assembly of Germany. He was a fellow worker on the *Monumenta Germaniae Historia.* His most important works are the *Regista pontificum Romanorum inde a post Christum natum MCXCVII ad annum MCCCIV* (Berlin 1874–75) and the *Biblioteca historica medii aevi. . .* (Berlin 1862, 2d ed. 1896). This latter work is still considered an indispensable work for the history of the Middle Ages. It lists the original sources, with information on the chief collections, editions, and translations. In 1965 the first volume of an enirely recast edition of the *Biblioteca* was issued: *Repertorium Fontium Historiae Medii Aevi primum ab Augusto Potthast digestum, nunc cura collegii historicorum e pluribus nationibus emendatum et auctum, I: Series Collectionum* (Rome 1962), published by Istituto Storico Italiano per il Medio Evo.

Bibliography: H. OTT, *Lexikon für Theologie und Kirche,* ed. J. HOFER and K. RAHNER, 10 v. (2d, new ed. Freiburg 1957–65) 8:649. A. VAN HOVE, *Commentarium Lovaniense in Codicem iuris canonici 1,* v. 1–5 (Mechlin 1928–); v. 1, Prolegomena (2d ed. 1945) 1:363, 612.

[J. M. BUCKLEY]

POUGET, FRANÇOIS AIMÉ

Oratorian, author of a controversial catechism; b. Montpellier, France, Aug. 28, 1666; d. Paris, April 4, 1723. After his ordination, he obtained his doctorate at the Sorbonne in 1692. He was then attached to the church of Saint-Roch, Paris. While there, he reconciled La Fontaine to the Church. In 1696 or 1697, Pouget joined the Oratorians and returned to Montpellier, where he became rector of the diocesan seminary. Later, he served for a time as parish priest in the Diocese of Saint-Malo. His last years he spent in Paris. During this time, he was a member of Abp. Louis Antoine de NOAILLES' liturgical commission for the archdiocese, and also gave conferences in the seminary of Saint-Magloire.

Pouget's fame is due completely to one of his works, popularly known as the Montpellier Catechism, but to which he gave a long, rambling title in order, as he himself put it, ''to soften a little the name catechism, which most people falsely think to be written for children.'' Like many another catechism, it was a work on the Christian life and was written for adults. The first part explained the principles of religion, its beginnings and its growth from the creation to the end of the world, and the achievement of eternal life. The second part showed the way a person must live on earth in order to reach the kingdom of heaven. In the third part, he considered the means given men by which they can live rightly.

This work, published in a large and a small edition, the latter for the use of children, had immediate and widespread popular success. It went through 30 editions in French alone, from the first publication, in 1702, to 1710. Each edition, with corrections and annotations by the author, was an improvement over its predecessor. Very quickly, translations appeared in English and in most of the European languages.

The French versions were placed on the Index of Forbidden Books, Jan. 21, 1721, and the English version was similarly condemned, Jan. 15, 1725. Both original and translations were condemned as containing Jansenist doctrine. In his last years, Pouget, who was then almost blind, translated the catechism into Latin. He revised the original, adding citations from Scripture, definitions of the Church, and statements from the Fathers, but because of his blindness he had to depend on others. When the Latin version was published in 1725, it was so filled with inaccuracies that it immediately fell under the ban of local Church authorities.

Pouget's work had the misfortune to appear under the patronage of Archbishop de Noailles of Paris, always inclined to favor Jansenist doctrine, and Bishop Colbert of Montpellier, a militant Jansenist. The defenders of Pouget's orthodoxy sometimes charge that his condemnations were largely the result of politics. He himself once noted that the desire to vindicate one's own school of thought often dictated loyalties in the Jansenist controversy. However, even those who attempted to vindicate the catechism and its author had to note that the condemned editions contained expressions that were distinctively Jansenist in connotation.

The history of the numerous French editions and of Pouget's own Latin translation has been called bizarre, and it is so complicated as to be practically incomprehensible. Numerous French editions continued to be printed, each one the object of much discussion and controversy. A Polish version was issued in Warsaw in 1791. Finally, in 1836, a French version was adopted in the Diocese of St. Pierre, Martinique, apparently without objection. The final Latin version, published in Venice in 1764, had been purged of many, but not all the original faults.

Pouget wrote little else of note. In 1712, he published *Instructions sur les devoirs des chevaliers de Malte* (1712), a work of which he was editor, not author. Another work by him, *Instruction chrétienne sur la prière,* was published in Paris in 1728.

Bibliography: A. MOLIEN, *Dictionnaire de théologie catholique,* ed. A. VACANT et al., 15 v. (Paris 1903–50; Tables générales 1951–), 12.2:2664–68. E. MANGENOT, *Dictionnaire de théologie catholique,* ed. A. VACANT et al., 15 v. (Paris 1903–50; Tables générales 1951–), 2.2:1895–1968. CANON HÉZARD, *Histoire du catechisme depuis la naissance de l'Église jusqu'à nos jours* (Paris 1900).

[P. MULHERN]

POUGHKEEPSIE PLAN

A compromise educational plan initiated in New York State in 1873 in an attempt to avoid Church State conflict while maintaining the cooperation of both. It was similar in purpose to the plans from 1831 to 1852 in Lowell, Mass., and 1891 in Faribault and Stillwater, Minn. (*see* FARIBAULT PLAN; LOWELL PLAN).

On June 11, 1873, Rev. Patrick F. McSweeny, pastor of St. Peter's church, Poughkeepsie, with the approval of Abp. (later Cardinal) John McCluskey of the Archdiocese of New York, proposed a compromise arrangement with the public board of education on behalf of his parish school for boys on Mill Street and for girls on Clover Street. The board of education approved the plan on July 16 and signed the document on August 21, with Egbert Q. Eldridge acting for the Poughkeepsie board of education. Henceforth the schools were known as School 11 (which enrolled 413 pupils in the first year of the new arrangement) and School 12 (322 pupils).

This plan called for the school board to pay St. Peter's Church $1 per year for each of the school buildings and their furniture, each of the buildings constituting thenceforth a public school. The board was to care for the repair and insurance of the buildings, which were to be under the board's control during school hours, but at other times to revert to the owners. During school hours, the board's authority was to be as complete as in other public schools: teachers were to be selected, employed, paid, and subject to dismissal by the board; non-Catholics as well as Catholic pupils were to be admissible by board regulation and subject to the board's rules during school hours; and the schools were to be subject to visitation by members of the board. Either the board or the owners could terminate the lease at the end of any scholastic year by giving 30 days' notice. No religious exercises were to be held or religious instruction given during school hours, and no child was compelled to attend religious exercises given after school hours and during lunch hour except by parental wish. The Catholic teachers, including some nuns, were retained, and it was tacitly understood that Catholics would continue to be hired for these schools, provided they were equally competent with other teachers under the board's supervision.

The plan for the most part seemed satisfactory: an 1875 inspection by Wolcott Calkins, a Presbyterian minister and bitter foe of Catholicism, went well; Abp. John IRELAND lauded it in 1890; in 1898 it was praised by Orlando D. M. Baker, president of the board of education of Poughkeepsie, and by Charles W. ELIOT, president of Harvard. But there was some dissatisfaction: in 1887 Andrew S. Draper, state superintendent of public instruction, declared it illegal to employ as a public school teacher anyone wearing "an unusual garb worn exclusively by members of one religious sect"; in 1889 Bp. Bernard J. McQuaid of Rochester voiced disapproval for "many Catholics"; in 1890, Rev. James Nilan, McSweeny's successor, complained of some "harsh and witless" Catholic criticism. From 1891 the plan became involved in the heated debate aroused by Rev. Thomas Bouquillon, professor of moral theology at The Catholic University of America, whose pamphlet, *Education: To Whom Does It Belong?*, granted a wider right to the state in education than had been traditional among American Catholics (*see* BOUQUILLON CONTROVERSY). State Superintendent Charles R. Skinner in 1896 opposed the plan as "unwise as a matter of school policy, and a violation of the letter and spirit of the Constitution" and on Dec. 23, 1898, ordered its discontinuance. Church authorities immediately complied; Nilan reopened School No. 11 as a parochial school on Jan. 3, 1899, and leased School No. 12 to the city until 1902. Similar plans in other localities of the state (e.g., Lima, Corning, West Bridge, Niagara, Watervliet, and Ogdensburg) were also affected by Skinner's ruling. On April 17, 1906, the court of appeals of New York State, in the Lima case of *O'Connor v. Hendrick,* affirmed the decision, citing art. 9, sec. four of the New York State constitution, which prohibited the appropriation of public funds for schools wholly or partly under sectarian auspices.

Bibliography: E. M. CONNORS, *Church-State Relationships in Education in the State of New York* (Washington 1951).

[H. A. BUETOW]

POULAIN, AUGUSTIN

Jesuit mystical theologian and writer; b. Cherbourg, Dec. 15, 1836; d. Paris, July 19, 1919. Poulain entered the Society of Jesus in 1858 and after completing his studies, taught mathematics at Metz and Angers, directed the schools there, and was for five years director of the artists' guild in Paris. His publication of *Des Grâces d'oraison* (Paris 1901) surprised his associates, no one of whom seemed to have known that he was interested in, or capable of writing in, the field of mystical theology. The book won immediate success, going through nine editions during the author's lifetime, and was translated into several foreign languages. Poulain, though not a strong theologian and apparently without any direct experience of the purely mystical states that he described, succeeded in writing a clear didactic treatise on a delicate and difficult subject. By doing so he contributed to the revival of interest in mystical theology, which had been largely neglected since the 17th century. The clear distinction that Poulain maintained between the ascetical and mystical states aroused considerable controversy.

Bibliography: A. POULAIN, *The Graces of Interior Prayer,* tr. L. L. YORKE SMITH, ed. J. V. BAINVEL (St. Louis 1950). A. RAYEZ, *Lexikon für Theologie und Kirche,* ed. J. HOFER and K. RAHNER, 10 v. (2d, new ed. Freiburg 1957–65) 8:650.

[M. J. BARRY]

POULENC, FRANCIS

Contemporary composer noted for his religious works; b. Paris, Jan. 7, 1899; d. there, Jan. 30, 1963. Poulenc was one of the creative musicians who formed the *Groupe des Six* under the leadership of Erik Satie and Jean Cocteau (the other five were Darius Milhaud, Arthur Honegger, Germaine Tailleferre, Louis Durey, and Georges Auric). Strongly opposed to the refinement and elegance of DEBUSSY and Ravel, "Les Six" wished to be thought *barbares,* but Poulenc for one was much more than that. While his style revealed influences of SCHUBERT, FAURE, Satie, and Moussorgsky, his clarity, spontaneity, and irresistible melodic gift were his own. He composed some of the finest French art songs of the 20th century, as well as attractive instrumental works, such as the sparkling Organ Concerto (appreciated more in the U.S. than in France), and the operas *Les Dialogues des Carmélites,* based on the Bernanos-Bruckberger scenario for Gertrud von Le Fort's *Song at the Scaffold* (U.S. *première,* San Francisco Opera, 1957; also on NBC-TV), and *La Voix Humaine* (1960). His particular glory, however, is his choral writing, which ranges from *Petites Voix* for small girls to the demanding Mass (1937) for unaccompanied mixed chorus, in the spirit of the *motu proprio* on sacred music. In all his sacred choral works, which include a setting of the Prayers of St. Francis, the *Litanies à la Vierge Noire de Rocamadour* (1936), *Salve Regina* (1941), and *Stabat Mater* (1951), Poulenc gives free expression to a naturally religious temperament without falling into the banality of much religious music. The *Gloria,* commissioned by the Koussevitsky Foundation and first heard in Boston on Jan. 20, 1961, is not a Mass setting but, like the Vivaldi *Gloria,* a cantatalike work in several movements. Abounding in simplicity, humility, and joy, as well as in mystical sonorities, it places its composer among the masters of religious music. The *Sept Répons des Ténèbres,* commissioned by the New York Philharmonic for its opening season in Lincoln Center and first performed in April 1963, three months after Poulenc's death, takes its place with the classic TENEBRAE settings in "an enticement of sound that is an act of faith in itself," in the words of one commentator.

Bibliography: F. POULENC, *Entretiens avec Claude Rostand* (Paris 1954). H. HELL, *Francis Poulenc: Musicien français* (Paris 1958), Eng. tr. E. LOCKSPEISER (New York 1959); "La Musique religieuse de F. P.," *La Revue musicale* 212 (1952) 53–58; *Die Musik* *in Geschichte und Gegenwart*, ed. F. BLUME (Kassel-Basel 1949–) 10:526–529. C. ROSTAND, *La Musique Française contemporaine* (Paris 1952). R. H. MYERS, *Grove's Dictionary of Music and Musicians*, ed. E. BLOM 9 v. (5th ed. London 1954) 6:898–901. E. LOCKSPEISER, ''The Wit and the Heart,'' *High Fidelity* 8 (July 1958) 35–37. I. KOLODIN, ''The Merit of P.,'' *Saturday Review* 46 (Feb. 23, 1963) 49–50, 66. V. RASŠÍN, ''Les Six and Jean Cocteau,'' *Music and Letters* 37 (1957) 164–169. P. M. YOUNG, *The Choral Tradition* (New York 1962). P. BLAY, ''Francis Poulenc: *Le Concert champêtre*,'' *Analyse Musicale* 21 (1990) 37–44. R. BRANDT, ''Die religiöse musik von Francis Poulenc eine werkübersicht,'' *Kirchenmusikalisches Jahrbuch* 73 (1989) 97–117. K. W. DANIEL, ''*Dialogues des Carmélites*'' in *International Dictionary of Opera*, ed. C. S. LARUE (Detroit 1993) 340–341; ''*La Voix Humaine, ibid.* C. KIMBALL, ''Reach Out and Touch Someone: Poulenc's One-Act Phone Call,'' *The Opera Journal* 22/2 (1989) 2–12. W. LANDOWSKA, ''Thoughts On Modern Music: Francis Poulenc,'' in *Landowska On Music* ed. and trans. D. RESTOUT (New York 1964) 347. W. MELLERS, *Francis Poulenc* (Oxford 1993). C. B. SCHMIDT, *The Music of Francis Poulenc (1899–1963), a Catalogue* (Oxford 1995).

[C. A. PELOQUIN]

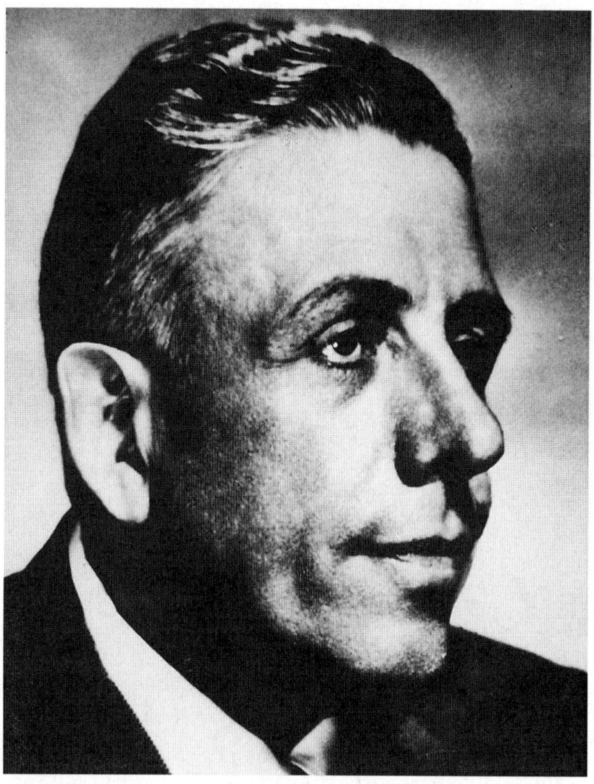

Francis Poulenc. (Archive Photos)

POULLART DES PLACES, CLAUDE FRANÇOIS

Founder of the Seminary and the Congregation of the Holy Ghost; b. Rennes, Brittany, France, Feb. 26, 1679; d. Paris, Oct. 2, 1709. He was educated at various Jesuit schools. Intellectually gifted, well-born and rich, Poullart des Places gave up his original plan to become a priest and studied law at Nantes and Paris. After obtaining his licentiate in law (1700), however, he made a serious retreat and decided to study for the priesthood at the Jesuit College of St. Louis-le-Grand, Paris. His attention was soon drawn to the many needy ecclesiastical students roaming the streets of Paris for food and lodgings, because the Tridentine type of seminary was still largely unknown in France. His charities to these students led him almost imperceptibly to the foundation of the Seminary of the Holy Ghost (May 27, 1703), in which he took care of their spiritual and material welfare, and provided for their solid training in ecclesiastical sciences. To secure the continuation of this work, the youthful founder associated carefully selected students with his work, thereby laying the foundation of the Congregation of the Holy Ghost. He was ordained in 1707, and died less than two years later.

Bibliography: C. F. POULLART DES PLACES, *Spiritual Writings*, ed. H. J. KOREN (Pittsburgh 1959). H. J. KOREN, *The Spiritans: A History of the Congregation of the Holy Ghost* (Pittsburgh 1958). J. MICHEL, *Claude-François Poullart des Places* (Paris 1962). J. RATH, *Lexikon für Theologie und Kirche*, ed. J. HOFER and K. RAHNER, 10 v. (2d, new ed. Freiburg 1957–65) 8:650.

[H. J. KOREN]

POUNDE, THOMAS

Jesuit lay affiliate and confessor; b. Belmont, near Winchester, England, May 29, 1539; d. Belmont, March 5, 1615. Thomas was the elder son of William Pounde, wealthy country gentleman, and Anne Wriothesley, sister of Thomas, Earl of Southampton. Until *c.* 1562 he was educated at Winchester, then at Lincoln's Inn, London. Thomas, admitted to Elizabeth's court and appointed esquire of the body, outwardly remained a Protestant until, following a humiliation at court (*c.* 1569–70), he retired to Belmont and was reconciled to the Church. Four years of spiritual preparation followed: two as a hermit, two with Thomas Stephens. In 1574 while preparing to leave for Rome, he was arrested in London. According to Pounde's own reckoning, over the succeeding 30 years there followed 15 imprisonments of varying lengths and in numerous prisons. During this time he was also fined £4,000 for recusancy. He was admitted to the Jesuits in 1579 by a letter from General Everard Mercurian that was smuggled to his prison cell in the Tower of London. His brief treatise ''The Six Reasons'' (1580), an attack on the *scriptura sola* position, was circulated in manuscript among English Catholics. In 1604 following James I's accession, he was released and retired to the seclusion of his Belmont home until his death. His lengthy imprisonment may well be the longest for any English Catholic layman of the period.

Bibliography: H. FOLEY, ed., *Records of the English Province of the Society of Jesus,* 7 v. (London 1877–83) 3.2:567–657, includes numerous documents in full. J. GILLOW, *A Literary and Biographical History or Bibliographical Dictionary of the English Catholics from 1534 to the Present Time* (London–New York 1885–1902) 5:354. *Publications of the Catholic Record Society* v. 22; 39; 51. W. R. TRIMBLE, *The Catholic Laity in Elizabethan England 1558–1603* (Cambridge, Mass. 1964).

[H. S. REINMUTH, JR.]

POURRAT, PIERRE

Theologian; b. Millery (Rhône), France, Feb. 7, 1871; d. Lyons, March 12, 1957. He was one of six children of thoroughly Christian parents, farmers in modest circumstances, and at an early age felt called to the priesthood. He did his minor seminary work in Lyons, studied philosophy at Alix, and, after three years of theology at St. Irénée in Lyons, completed his course at Saint-Sulpice in Paris, where he was ordained Dec. 19, 1896. Most of his teaching work was in dogma at the major seminary in Lyons, where from 1908 to 1926 he was rector and also a vicar-general of the archdiocese. In 1926 he was named superior of the Solitude, the quasi novitiate of Saint-Sulpice at Issy-les-Moulineaux. He held this post until 1945, when for reasons of health he returned to Lyons, where he spent an active retirement at the university seminary. His first major work, *Théologie sacramentaire,* published in 1907 (tr. *Theology of the Sacraments* [4th ed. St. Louis 1930]), grew in part out of the need he felt to refute the modernism of the day. From 1917 to 1928 he labored on the four volumes of his pioneering work *La Spiritualité chrétienne* (tr. *Christian Spirituality,* 4 v. [Westminster, Md. 1953–55]), a concise and critically sound history of spirituality from biblical to modern times.

[J. P. MCCORMICK]

POUSSEPIN, MARIE, BL.

Foundress of Dominican Sisters of the Presentation; b. Oct. 14, 1653 near Chartres in the village of Dourdan, France; d. in Sainville, France, Jan. 24, 1744.

Marie's well-to-do middle class parents, Claude and Julienne Fourrier, were hosiers and actively engaged in the local parish and in the Confraternity of Charity dedicated to works of mercy. When her mother died in 1675, Marie assumed responsibility for looking after her younger brother and rescued the family business from bankruptcy by expanding into the manufacture of woolen stockings and introducing the latest advances in looms. She also revolutionized the work place by abolishing the customary apprenticeship fee. In addition Marie was generous to the young employees, rewarding them with bonuses and offering them opportunities for advancement.

Sometime after 1690 she joined the Third Order of St. Dominic, and in 1696 she moved to Sainville, where she gathered a community of women to serve in the local parish, educating girls and ministering to the sick and poor of the area. Marie placed her sisters under the protection of Mary in the mystery of her Presentation in the Temple. They took simple vows, living according to the rule of the Third Order of St. Dominic, and they dedicated themselves to apostolic work at a time when most women religious lived a cloistered life.

When Marie died at the age of 90, the community had established 20 houses in northern France. Her tombstone bears the simple inscription: ''She saw what was good in the eyes of God and accomplished it.'' Pope John Paul II beatified her Nov. 24, 1994.

Feast: Oct. 14 (the anniversary of her baptism).

Bibliography: B. PRÉTESEILLE, *Marie Poussepin,* translated from the French by M. C. VAILLOT (Private printing). *L'Osservatore Romano,* English edition (Nov. 23, 1994).

[M. W. LAPOINTE]

POVEDA CASTROVERDE, PEDRO, BL.

Priest, martyr, scholar, founder of the Teresian Institute, and Carmelite tertiary; b. Linares, Spain, Dec. 3, 1874; d. Madrid, Spain, July 28, 1936. Although Pedro desired to become a priest, his family experienced financial difficulties, and he lacked the means to continue his studies at the diocesan seminary at Jaen. Fortunately he was offered a scholarship by the bishop of Guadix to attend his seminary in southern Spain. Following his ordination in 1897, Father Poveda taught in that seminary. In 1900, he earned his licentiate in theology at Seville, then worked in Guadix and Madrid. In 1906, he was appointed canon of the Basilica of Covadonga in Asturias. He returned to his first seminary at Jaen to again teach theology.

Throughout his adult life, Poveda's primary apostolate was education. He built an elementary school and started workshops for the cave-dwellers of Guadix. In 1911, he founded Saint Teresa of Avila Academy as a residence for students that became the basis for the Teresian Institute, an organization dedicated to the formation of teachers. It received diocesan and civil approval in Jaen, then Vatican approbation in 1924. Additionally, Poveda initiated pedagogical centers, opened the first university residence for women in Madrid (1914), and served as the spiritual director of Los Operarios Catechetical Center. He also continued to take an active role in teacher formation. He published articles and pamphlets and founded several periodicals to advance pedagogy in Spain.

After moving back to Madrid (1921), Poveda was appointed chaplain to the Royal Palace and sat on the Central Board Against Illiteracy. He continued to guide the growth of the Teresian Institute as it spread to Chile and Italy (1934) until he was killed at the beginning of the Spanish Civil War. He was beatified on Oct. 10, 1993 by Pope John Paul II.

Feast: July 28.

Bibliography: *La Radicalidad de una utopia: Pedro Poveda desde América* (Buenos Aires, Argentina 1993). P. ALASTRUÉ, *Inquietud y conquista* (Madrid 1976). D. GÓMEZ MOLLEDA, *La escuela, problema social: en el centenario de Poveda* (Madrid 1974); *Pedro Poveda et son temps* (Paris 1974); *Pedro Poveda, hombre interior* (Madrid 1971). D. MONDRONE, *Un prete scomodo,* 2d. ed. (Milan 1969). A. SERRANO DE HARO, *Una figura del pensamiento español: Don Pedro Poveda Castroverde* (Madrid 1974).

[K. I. RABENSTEIN]

A tenant farm family in a migrant camp, 1935, Maryville, California. (© Bettmann/CORBIS)

POVERTY

The Church's long history with poverty and the poor originated with Jesus' preferential treatment of the marginalized in society. Poverty became glorified as Jesus' regard for the poor was identified with the renunciation of personal property, a state considered to be a divinely intended way of life. The glorification of poverty also emanated from the works of the Eastern Fathers of the Church and the Eastern monastic traditions. A different view of the Christian life highlighted the role of charity, which requires both a donor and a recipient. In such a view, the role of the poor beneficiary is foreordained. The ''Life of Saint Eligius'' explains that God made the poor in order to give the rich an opportunity for redemption. While they were clearly the objects of the Church's concern, the poor were encouraged to accept their lot with humility.

After the glorification of poverty peaked with the rise of the MENDICANT ORDERS in the 12th and 13th centuries, a combination of human and natural upheavals significantly increased the number of those relying on charity. By the 14th century, poverty was linked with social disintegration and was regarded much more dimly. At the same time, the efficiency with which charitable institutions handled poverty came into question. In the 16th century the Catholic Church was challenged for its role in glorifying and thus spreading the social problem of poverty, even though throughout the Middle Ages Church policy clearly made the distinction between those who were poor due to an inability to work and the condemned state of vagrancy. In an effort at renewal, the Council of Trent called for an even greater charitable role for the Church as well as an attempt to reorganize the charitable systems for greater effectiveness. The Church struggled through the following centuries to maintain its relationship with the poor against the advancing claims of modernity that strove to place social responsibility completely in secular hands. Throughout the 16th and 17th centuries Rome, like most large urban areas, followed a policy of segregating the poor, particularly those able but unwilling to work. During the 18th and 19th centuries much attention was given to understanding the causes and the likely outcome of poverty. While some still contended that poverty is inevitable, advocates of socialism linked it to the after-effects of the labor-market economy. Others blamed it on laziness or addiction. In the 20th century an increasing number of theorists began to look to societal structures that limited the economic and general development of people.

The contemporary relationship between the Church and poverty should begin with the definition of terms. In the case of poverty difficulties arise. Extensive research has not produced a commonly agreed upon definition. Following on this point is the fact that the line at which one is poor also lacks clear distinction. The level of means generally considered adequate for existence in one population may fall well below tolerable conditions in another. Poverty and its definable boundaries have been linked to income-level relative to a percentage of national productivity. Poverty has been connected with dietary requirements, and it has been associated with the availability of the adequate necessities for survival. No one form of measurement has proven universally adaptable. Another concern with poverty research is that much of it is performed to support various social policies, not all of which are intended to alleviate the suffering of the poor. Social scientists have even gone so far as studying the utility value of the poor for the non-poor; the presence of poor people willing to perform undesirable tasks for very low wages frees the wealthy for other, more rewarding, endeavors.

Defining poverty as a lack of something sets it up as a conflict issue, a cause of strife and upheaval. It requires the transfer of whatever is lacking from those who have to those who do not. Theorists who insist that the economy need not be considered a zero-growth system challenge this view. Noting that the beginning of the modern era found the majority of the world's population poor by most standards, these thinkers suggest that more attention should be given to those who advanced from poor to non-poor and the path they followed. While many people benefitted in this way, certain demographic sectors of nearly every nation have not. Children, women, minorities, and the elderly continue to lag behind in sharing the benefits of growing economies. Changing trends in the societal value of children has affected both the children and their mothers. When children are not viewed as assets, neither is the maternal labor directed toward caring for them. This female labor-value stigma carries into the workplace where women, regardless of parental status, have been chronically paid lower wages for the same work as men. Equally vulnerable minority sectors of society have faced similar labor-value perceptions that are only overcome against great resistance. When a culture sets its value standards relative to economic productivity, the elderly are also drawn into the web of poverty, often in spite of their former contribution to the overall growth of the economy.

Most recent Church statements and positions on poverty set their foundation on the groundbreaking 1891 encyclical of Pope LEO XIII entitled *RERUM NOVARUM*. Leo attempted to counteract socialist efforts to usurp personal freedom. The socialist system called for the transfer of responsibility for human productivity to the state in the name of protecting the working poor. Leo was also interested in reversing the recurrent view that the poor endangered society. The focal point of this issue was the right to possess private property. Leo advocated a more equal distribution of goods that is voluntary yet encouraged and expected, while he maintained a strong position on the rights of individuals to hold private property. *Rerum novarum* set the tone for future Church statements that refuse to accept poverty as the inevitable condition of a portion of society. Forty years later, Pope PIUS XI reaffirmed *Rerum novarum* with the release of *QUADRAGESIMO ANNO*. The Great Depression had wiped away any lingering notion that poverty was a localized concern or that it was the lot of the lazy and weak. Pius advocated the use of capital to expand employment opportunities, and he called for a just wage that would allow for the eventual accumulation of wealth by the average working person. Pius was also a pioneering supporter of profit sharing.

Recent popes have promoted various economic activities in the hope of advancing the development of all people. Noting the unequal social and economic development in different parts of the world, Pope JOHN XXIII insisted, in his 1961 encyclical *MATER ET MAGISTRA*, that wealthy nations should assist under-developed nations in achieving similar levels of growth with a hoped-for ensuing equitable distribution. The encyclical also supports social insurance systems to reduce class imbalances. John related the security provided by such social insurance programs to appropriate human development in his later encyclical, *PACEM IN TERRIS*. From this point poverty is clearly considered a limitation to human development, and its effects are expanded to include cultural deprivation. Language emphasizing the development and advancement of the human person is prevalent in the Second Vatican Council's *Gaudium et spes*. Calling for an end to ''*excessive* economic and social differences,'' the council was concerned with structures that limit human freedom. The council supported the right to private property, but emphasized that this must be held along with the conviction that the goods of the earth are ultimately intended for the COMMON GOOD of all. Recognizing that the solution to poverty was not yet at hand, Pope PAUL VI, in *POPULORUM PROGRESSIO*, called upon people of intellectual capacity and social status to continue seeking answers to the problem of poverty. He appealed for the collaboration of governmental and non-governmental organizations to influence economic and trade initiatives that would positively affect the international poverty gap. The encyclical *SOLLICITUDO REI SOCIALIS*, released by Pope JOHN PAUL II in 1987, draws attention to certain governmental programs, arms-related in particular, that channel money away from opportunities to advance more just development. Concerned with equally dangerous threats to human development and to the human soul, John Paul challenges radical consumerism by noting the tension between ''being'' and ''having.'' Some have so little that their ability to be is impoverished, and some have so much that their ability to be is also impoverished.

With the demise of communism in the former Soviet Union and Eastern Europe, consumerism took center stage as a magnet to the poor and non-poor alike. John Paul recognized this situation when he recalled the 100-year anniversary of *Rerum novarum* in his 1991 encyclical *CENTESIMUS ANNUS.* While following the growth model of the non-poor allowed many of the previously-poor to share in some of the benefits of economic prosperity, a noticeable rise in the quality of life has been absent. Asserting that consumption does not directly equate to increased satisfaction, John Paul claimed that every economic decision must be made as a moral decision considering the enhancement of human integrity, the improved quality of life for those directly and indirectly affected by the decision, and the ecological ramifications. Based on these precedents, future efforts of the Church to confront poverty will be directed toward the overall advancement of the human person through a continuous struggle to justly embrace the many gifts God has bestowed for that purpose.

Bibliography: D. CHEAL, *New Poverty: Families in Postmodern Society* (Westport, Conn. 1996). R. G. CLOUSE, ed., *Wealth and Poverty: Four Christian Views of Economics* (Downers Grove, Ill. 1984). M. ESTOR, ''Women's Work is Never at an End: Paid and Unpaid Labor,'' in *Women, Work, and Poverty*, Concilium 194, ed. E. SCHÜSSLER FIORENZA and A. CARR, 3–9 (Edinburgh 1987). B. GEREMEK, *Poverty: A History*, tr. A. KOLAKOWSKA (Oxford 1994). E. ØYEN, S. M. MILLER, and S. A. SAMAD, eds., *Poverty, a Global Review: Handbook on International Poverty Research* (Oslo 1996). J. V. SCHALL, *Religion, Wealth and Poverty* (Vancouver 1990).

[D. MCCARTHY]

POVERTY, RELIGIOUS

The majority of people in the world today live in material POVERTY or destitution. Worse still is their inability to shape their own futures, with the result that they often experience a sense of fatalism and a loss of hope. Men and women throughout the world have paid a high price for the present affluence of many in our Western technological society. Part of the price has been extracted from the poor nations whose fields, forests, and factories have been exploited so that commodities may be produced for the rich in the world. Part too has been paid by the poor who in fact live and work within the wealthy countries but without sharing equitably in the profits. A great part has been paid by affluent people themselves, for they have purchased prosperity at the expense of a staggering impoverishment of their own humanity.

CONVERSION and change must begin in the hearts and life-style of the consumers. Not only must the poor be delivered from their poverty; modern men and women, and especially Christians, must allow themselves to be liberated from the oppression that comes from an acquisitive, consumerist mentality. The social and economic conditions of millions of poor people in the world are issuing a call from God to the wealthy and comfortable to be freed from the economic and political assumptions about affluence and power which shackle their own freedom as well as that of the destitute. There is no ultimate liberation of the poor from their destitution except through the deliverance of the wealthy from their blindness and greed. The Christian response to the situation must involve generous service to the destitute in terms of the caring love outlined in the twenty-fifth chapter of Saint Matthew's Gospel. It involves a willingness to share with others, rooted in gratitude to God who is the ultimate source of all good gifts. It implies an acknowledgment that goods are to be owned personally only if they are held in trust for the service of those in need.

The Christian response also involves just decision-making which realizes that efficacious charity must be rooted in justice. The enemy of justice today is often not malice or lack of good well but rather blindness and lack of vision. Poverty today requires that Christians reflect on their actual positions in society as persons and communities so that contemplation might free them from their blindness by revealing the truth of the situation and then call them to make radical decisions.

Finally there must be the response of witness through life-style, following the example of Christ's simplicity and detachment. This has always been the Church's clearest proclamation of the nature of ownership and of its essentially communal character. It also has revealed the reverence that human beings must have for created things which are more truly God's gifts than human achievements. At a time when many people are uninterested in or insensitive to theoretical teaching, they are keenly alert to detect what difference Christianity makes in the lives of those who profess it. Furthermore, many people in the world in fact yearn to be liberated from the sophisticated, domineering, and alienating consumer mentality which characterizes our technological culture. To that yearning, the life of Christians who espouse simplicity and a commitment to responsible stewardship can be a significant response.

Poverty in the Bible. In the Bible there is a development in the understanding of poverty, which is described both as that unavoidable distress which opens a person to God and as the humble, loving abandonment of one's own rights. Hence it is not simply an economic or social condition but also an interior disposition.

Initially the Old Testament writers usually represented wealth as a blessing, whereas poverty was a misfortune to be borne, often as a manifestation of divine retribution. The sapiential writers recognized that there were virtuous poor people, but experience taught them that destitution was often the result of laziness or disorder.

The prophets defended the poor who were often the victims of injustice. They denounced violence and robbery, fraud in trading, abuse of power, and enslavement of the lowly. The prophets echoed the Mosaic law which prescribed charitable attitudes and social measures to lessen the sufferings of the needy, for God had identified with the unfortunate people on the margins and shown compassion toward the poor. The prophets also proclaimed a Messiah who would defend the rights of the poor and destitute.

Even before the Exile the prophets had helped the Israelites to realize that the rich are apt to harden their hearts to the distress of others, to enclose themselves in self-righteousness, and to exploit the underprivileged. But in light of the humiliating experience of servitude in Babylon and the many disappointments after their return from exile, the Israelites were helped by the prophets and other sacred writers to understand poverty as a religious value, more or less synonymous with humility and piety. They came to see it as a virtue which enables people to find refuge in God and to await God's coming with trust.

The religious meaning of poverty was clarified with the incarnation of the divine Logos whose life of self-sacrifice and self-denial revealed God as one who always lives for giving. The incarnation was both a sacrament of God's love for us and an example for us to follow. In his inaugural discourse Jesus taught that the poor were the privileged heirs of the Kingdom he proclaimed. As the Messiah of the poor, he lived a life of simplicity and invited the weary and the burdened to come to him as their meek and humble savior. He sharply criticized the idolatries of power, pleasure, and possessions not by violently attacking them but by identifying himself with the materially or morally indigent, by sharing his life with all who came to him, and by inviting his followers to trust his Father who knows their needs. He promised salvation to all those who trusted him in time of hunger, but the food he promised was the Kingdom. He proclaimed that with him and in him the KINGDOM OF GOD had arrived, and that with the coming of the Kingdom men and women are placed in a situation in which they must make radical decisions about their lives. Jesus clearly affirmed that with the advent of the Kingdom human riches have become a danger and an obstacle to the acceptance of God's reign in human hearts, to such an extent that it is easier for a person to pass through the eye of a needle than for a rich person to enter the Kingdom of God.

The New Testament does not teach that possessions are immoral in themselves or that the absence of possessions constitutes a moral value. What it does say is that riches and the accumulation of possessions constitute a grave danger for people in that once they have become preoccupied with the cares of this world they tend to become blind to the presence of God's Kingdom, deaf to the cries of the poor, and unresponsive to the call to live according to the gospel. The person attached to riches does not have that spirit of freedom which is necessary for a whole-hearted acceptance of God's reign in human life. Hence Jesus requires that his disciples share their possessions with the poor and be prepared to become poor themselves. He did not commend poverty out of contempt for wealth or for purely ascetical reasons but because it helps men and women acknowledge their ultimate dependence and enables them to be open to the needs of others. In his teaching on discipleship Jesus requires that those who voluntarily decide to become poor for the Kingdom must give their riches to the poor who are brothers and sisters in the Kingdom. When faith in the Kingdom is lived out in the form of voluntary poverty, this faith must be expressed by the unity in love of all those who are united in the Body of Christ. Hence those who have faith do not defend their material goods as though they were the bastion of their own self-defense against others; rather they give others a share in their goods because they can look upon others in a spirit of trust and can love them as members of the Body of Christ. Hence the acknowledgment that all people have a right to the riches of God's creation is an intrinsic element in Christian poverty. Holding property in common is an expression of the community of all people in Christ.

The early Christian community had a clear understanding of the spirit of Jesus' teaching on poverty. They knew that a literal application of his teaching was neither essential nor always possible. They knew that Jesus himself did not live in destitution nor was he usually threatened by hunger. He was able to obtain support from his wealthy friends when he needed it. His lavish generosity at Cana and his sharing in the feast in Matthew's house suggest a spirit of MAGNANIMITY far distant from any puritanical condemnation of the enjoyment of good things. Yet he was radically free and detached in his use of goods because of his primary commitment to his mission. Likewise, Paul had a budget for his missionary and charitable work, but he often preached the gospel without any recompense and sometimes lived in want and distress. The early Christians shared what they had with each other and with those in need. Service rendered to the poor was an expression of their love for Christ, who being rich became poor for our sake, so that he might enrich us by his poverty.

Poverty and the Christian Tradition. The birth of MONASTICISM in about 270 in Egypt, Palestine, and Syria was partly an attempt to reassert the call to poverty. Antony heard the gospel call to the rich young man and then sold all that he had and entered the desert. The DESERT FATHERS and mothers realized that poverty in the material sense can never be permanently total, for men and women must eat, have shelter, and be clothed. Hence the first monastic men and women of the desert worked and received money with which they provided for their basic needs. While Antony was still alive, Pachomius established communities of monks who modeled themselves on the early Christians, with all things held in common and supported by their own work done under obedience.

In his *Dialogues* Saint Gregory says that Saint BENEDICT left all his possessions with the desire of pleasing God alone. It is within Benedict's Rule that we find the nucleus of the medieval monastic tradition on poverty. Benedict never uses the word ''poor'' or the abstract noun ''poverty'' when speaking of his monks. He directs that his disciples should have no other goal than to seek God. They are to give away all they possess; hence they are to be protected from all personal attachment. After profession the monk is unable to possess anything of his own; he shares everything with the community. Moderation is characteristic of the rule, yet Saint Benedict is adamant that possessions must be renounced. The monastery may possess goods, but the abbot is not to be oversolicitous for material possessions. The produce of the monastery is to be sold a little cheaper than it is sold by others in the world so that in all things God may be glorified. Saint Benedict was conscious that the monastery must share its goods with the poor, the sick, and the stranger. He feared avarice in his monks but prescribed that they should receive what they needed from the resources of the monastery. Throughout history the basic Benedictine attitude toward material goods has been that of stewardship. This tradition is in keeping with the second chapter of Genesis in which God places man in the garden of Eden not as a master but as a steward. In this regard Benedictines have something to say to men and women in the modern world. By establishing the right order of relationships between people and nature, among men and women themselves, and between men and women and God, Saint Benedict established the primacy of persons over things, and at the same time he saw the importance of respect for material things and an ordered and humane environment in helping his monks develop as persons whose whole life is directed to the glorification of God. However, there is the serious problem that a commitment to simplicity of life, celibacy, and obedience, when allied with hard work, can in the course of time make for corporate wealth simply because monks have limited needs and no families to consume the fruit of their labors. This is precisely what happened throughout the Middle Ages, for the principal dissolvent of monastic fervor was the possessiveness of both individuals and communities, including abbots. The urgent question was raised: Who would stand for God against Mammon?

The answer came from Saint FRANCIS OF ASSISI. He consciously and explicitly reacted against the monastic rules and constitutions in regard to their teaching on poverty. Akin to Antony and Macarius rather than Cassian and Benedict, he took the words of Christ literally and lived them. His was a direct and absolute imitation of Jesus, not as Jesus lived in Galilee or at Bethany, but as he died on the cross, with even his clothes appropriated by others. Francis stood not only for a literal interpretation of the poverty of Jesus but also for a sense of freedom which he could only describe by a romantic name, Lady Poverty. He felt that the most sordid enemy of this freedom was money, which he saw as a token of possession and security against the future. However, the early history of the Friars Minor gives sad evidence of the perpetual problem of embodying a spirit, a difficulty which was made visible in the case of Franciscan poverty because human beings, as embodied spirits, cannot fully divest themselves of the material world by taking a vow or joining a community. It was Saint BONAVENTURE who found a mean between the commands of Francis and the conditions of human life by establishing principles close to those in the Rule of Benedict. A serious dispute over the interpretation of Franciscan poverty resulted in a theological controversy of great bitterness which was finally ended by Pope John XXII, who insisted that even Christ and his apostles had a true right to own property; he handed back to the Franciscans the ownership of property of which they had been deprived.

The early Franciscans stood apart from the other orders of friars both in their interpretation of poverty as the center of their religious lives and in the various controversies which this brought upon them. The Dominicans, though standing for an austere life and accepting a mendicant status, interpreted poverty in line with the teaching of Saint THOMAS AQUINAS, who emphasized that the essence of the virtue of poverty was interior detachment. The use or even the ownership of goods was not illicit for Christians or even for religious communities, provided they observed the prescriptions of canon law in financial matters.

A review of the whole of monastic and medieval spirituality suggests that poverty is not the best word to describe a spiritual ideal. It was not the word used by patristic or monastic spiritual writers; nevertheless it found its way into the vow patterns of religious institutes from the late Middle Ages until the present time. The 1983 Code of Canon Law describes the vow of poverty in canon 600 which reminds those who take the vow that they are meant to imitate Christ and commit themselves to a life that is poor in fact as well as in spirit. They are obliged to work in accord with the nature and ends of the institute to which they belong and to live in dependence on the institute. This is not the poverty of destitution experienced by countless people who are deprived of the basic necessities of life and which Christ and the Church strive to eliminate. Unlike the vow of chastity, which is absolute, that of poverty admits of a wide variety of expressions in accord with the nature, spirit, and purpose of each institute. Hence the effects and obligations of a vow of poverty may differ widely from one religious institute to another. The various apostolates undertaken by religious and their institutes witness to the dignity of human work and the life of service to which religious are called. In addition to the traditional apostolates of education, social services, and health care, work in other areas is frequently undertaken by members of religious institutes to alleviate hunger, ignorance, sickness, unemployment, and the deprivation of basic human freedoms. Often from their own resources they provide for those in such circumstances.

At the heart of all religious life are values that directly oppose blindness, materialism, greed, and the structures that dehumanize persons and communities. These values are above all poverty of spirit, simplicity of life, sharing and giving, self-denial prompted by love, freedom of heart, gratitude, care for persons, and the kind of sound judgment with regard to created things that proceeds from exposure to God in prayer. Material privation is never an end in itself, and it is in no sense a part of religious poverty to assess everything economically by materialistic standards or to override aesthetic or other values for the sake of cheapness or squalor. Such a mentality narrows the human spirit and even creates those very evils accompanying destitution, which all Christians have the duty to eliminate from the earth. A life of simplicity, stewardship, and sharing of goods can surely help to counteract those forces that lie at the roots of world poverty today.

Bibliography: P. R. RÉGAMEY, *Poverty: An Essential Element in Christian Life* (New York 1950). M. D. LAMBERT, *Franciscan Poverty: The Doctrine of the Absolute Poverty of Christ and the Apostles in the Franciscan Order 1210–1323* (London 1961). K. RAHNER, "Poverty," *Sponsa Regis 33* (1962) 311–17, 348–57; 34 (1962) 15–24, 49–57. A. MCCORMACK, ed., *Christian Responsibility and World Poverty: A Symposium* (Westminster, Md. 1963). Y. CONGAR, *Power and Poverty in the Church* (Baltimore 1964). A. GEORGE et al., *Gospel Poverty: Essays in Biblical Theology* (Chicago 1977). D. REES et al., *Consider Your Call: A Theology of Monastic Life Today* (London 1978). M. GUINAN, *Gospel Poverty: Witness to the Risen Christ* (New York 1981). S. SCHNEIDERS, *New Wine-Skins: Re-Imagining Religious Life Today* (Mahwah, N.J. 1986). P. J. PHILIBERT, ed., *Living in the Meantime: Concerning the Transformation of Religious Life* (New York 1994). Y. SUGAWARA, *Religious Poverty from Vatican Council II to 1994 Synod of Bishops* (Rome 1997). C. BLOMBERG, *Neither Poverty nor Riches: A Biblical Theology of Material Possessions* (Grand Rapids, Mich. 1999).

[R. K. SEASOLTZ]

POVERTY CONTROVERSY

A term denoting a series of disputes over the nature and practice of poverty. Beside the mendicant controversy (1252–72) between the professors at the University of Paris and the friars over the issue of poverty and the sacred ministry (poverty controversy in the less strict sense), two further instances can be distinguished:

(1) First there was the practical controversy among Franciscans regarding the extent of the obligation of poverty under their vow. Whereas generally the community sought certain mitigations of the rule and adaptation to other orders, the FRANCISCAN SPIRITUALS, influenced by Joachimite doctrines (*see* JOACHIM OF FIORE), rejected papal interpretations of the rule and declared the life and the last will of the founder to be binding and poverty to be the summit of perfection. NICHOLAS III (*Exiit qui seminar,* 1279) and CLEMENT V (*Exivi de paradise,* 1312) were unable to achieve unity in the matter. Thereupon JOHN XXII (*Quorundam exigit,* 1317) censured the Spirituals, had four of them burned as heretics, and ordered other recalcitrants, later called FRATICELLI, to be prosecuted by the INQUISITION.

(2) There was further theoretical controversy between DOMINICANS and FRANCISCANS over poverty and its relation to evangelical perfection. In 1321 the Dominican John of Belna rejected the opinion that Christ and the Apostles had possessed nothing, either in common or individually, and that the highest perfection consisted in extreme poverty. Against John of Belna, the Franciscans appealed to the pope. But since John XXII tended toward the Dominican opinion, the general chapter of Perugia 1322 solemnly proclaimed that Nicholas III in *Exiit* had defined the doctrine concerning the poverty of Christ and the Apostles as an article of faith, a teaching that was now doubted by the pope. Angered by the chapter's action, John (*Ad conditorem canonum,* 1322) rejected the papal title to Franciscan property and forbade the friars to elect a procurator in the future. He then declared (*Cum inter*

nonnullos, 1323) that the opinion on the poverty of Christ was heretical. The general of the order, MICHAEL OF CESENA, together with Bonagratia and WILLIAM OF OCKHAM, joined the excommunicated Emperor Louis IV the Bavarian, who also, in the appeal of Sachsenhausen (1324), had rejected the papal decision as heretical. Cesena's successor, Geraldus Odonis, however, personally and in the name of the order, submitted to the pope, and apparently all the Michaelists were reconciled with the Church before their death. As a result of these disputes, devotion to the ideals of the order suffered a severe temporary decline.

Bibliography: K. EUBEL, *Bullarium Franciscarum,* ed. K. EUBEL (Rome 1898–1904) 5. H. DENIFLE and F. EHRLE, eds., *Archiv für Literarur- und Kirchengeschichte des Mittelalters* (Freiburg 1885–1900) v.–4, *passim.* H. HOLZAPFEL, *The History of the Franciscan Order,* tr. A. TIBESAR and G. BRINKMANN (Teutopolis, Ill. 1948) 32–53. K. BALTHASAR, *Geschichte des Armutsstreites im Franziskanerorden* (Munich 1911). B. GRATIEN, *Histoire de la fondation et de l'évolution de l'Ordre des Frères Mineurs au XIIIe siècle* (Paris 1928) 200–509. E. MÜLLER, *Das Konzil von Vienne* (Münster 1934). F. DE SESSEVALLE, *Histoire générale de l'Ordre de s. François,* 2 v. (Paris 1935–37) 1:75–143. O. ENGLEBERT, *St. Francis of Assisi: A Biography,* tr. I. BRADY and R. BROWN (Chicago 1966). G. GAL and D. FLOOD, eds., *Nicolaus Minorita: Chronica* (St. Bonaventure, N.Y. 1996).

[S. CLASEN]

POVERTY MOVEMENT

A trend among various classes and groups in the Middle Ages, identified by their adherence to the ideal of radical evangelical poverty. A more profound understanding of the religious life, as it had been awakened by the GREGORIAN REFORM (HUMBERT OF SILVA CANDIDA, PATARINES, GREGORY VII), inspired a striving for personal sanctification. The Crusades, in bringing the monasticism of the East into contact with the West, presented a concrete picture of the poverty that Christ and the Apostles encountered in their pastoral life (Lk 9.1–6), leading to a more vigorous reading of Holy Scripture and to an imitation by "Christ's poor"; of the *vita apostolica* which contrasted sharply with the monastic poverty of Cluny. Even after dualistic doctrines, under the influence of the BOGOMILS, were gradually accepted, the controversy still centered around the religious life and the Church, and as a result, the poverty movement often stood in opposition to the Church and was suppressed.

Problem for the Church. Until the 11th century, ecclesiastical discipline recognized religious life exclusively as the life of a religious order and distinguished between an order of the priesthood, whose function was the administration of the Sacraments and preaching, and an order of religious vocation, which consisted in striving for personal sanctification. Since, however, the poverty movement, as promoted by preachers and justified by reference to Mark 16.15, belonged to neither of these two "orders"; it was rejected as spurious religiosity and was referred to as *religio simulata* and as heresy without any indication at least in the beginning of any specific heretical teachings. In contrast to earlier sects, the movement had no definite founder. While its members might be called *rustici, idiotae, illitterati,* or *textores*, only the distinction between them and scholars *(docti, litterati, sapientes, clerici)* was underscored and nothing was said about their social origin, for members were recruited from amongst the nobles and the commoners, and might be clerics, monks, nuns, or laity who followed the profession of weavers only to earn a living in the manner of Saint Paul (Acts 18.9). Furthermore, the Church was scandalized because women belonged to the poverty movement, by virtue of 1 Cor 9.5. The membership were accused of sexual excesses, even though they were called *boni homines* by the people and no wrongdoings could be proved against them.

The Church's Position. The stand taken by bishops and popes was both inconsistent and vague, and there were no unified standards by which heresy could be judged. Heretics were recognized by ORDEAL or else bishops and popes hesitated inconclusively until the suspected "heretics" generally became victims of lynch justice. BERNARD OF CLAIRVAUX (*Patrologia Latina*, ed. J. P. Migne, 183:1101–02) was the first to call for the continuance of the traditional procedure for determination of heresy: to protect their good name and to allow them to fulfill their vows; to require men and women of the poverty movement to be placed in separate monastic communities; and to consider those who refused to comply to be guilty of heresy. Bernard's view soon became the official policy of the Church and, since at the time there were no definite canonical norms for determining heresy, only the heretics of southern France were punished by the Third LATERAN COUNCIL in 1179. However, when the WALDENSES and HUMILIATI, themselves enemies of the CATHARI, asked the council, because of their difficulties with the bishops, for permission to live the life of wandering mendicants, the pope and the council reverted to their former position and, without even examining their writings for orthodoxy, practically forbade them to preach. Finally, a fundamental norm was agreed upon by LUCIUS III and FREDERICK I BARBAROSSA at Verona in 1184: unauthorized preaching, disbelief in the Sacraments, and the express declaration of a bishop were to be accepted as evidence of heresy, and the suppression of such became the duty of the bishops. INNOCENT III was the first to use these new powers to the Church's advantage and permitted members of the movement to adopt apostolic poverty and to preach as long as they recognized the hierarchy and the Sacraments of the Church. It was thus possible for him to receive back into the Church the Humiliati (1210) and individual groups of Waldenses, and above all the Poor Catholics of Durandus of Huesca (1208) and the Society of Bernard Prim (1210). Although the Fourth Lateran Council condemned the use of ordeals for determining heresy, it established, as a criterion, a confession of faith (*Firmiter credimus Conciliorum oecumenicorum decreta* 206) and called for Church reform, but it also issued penal laws against recalcitrant heretics and made it compulsory for new orders to adopt already existing rules (*Ne nimia Conciliorum oecumenicorum decreta* 218), i.e., it attempted to force upon the pope the former position of the Church.

Relation to the Church. The development of this phenomenon is discernible in three distinct categories: (1) various heretical sects; (2) the older orders; (3) the new orders.

Heretical Groups. These also may be categorized as three types: the dualists, the spiritualists, and the antihierarchical group. (1) The dualists appeared among the heretical Cathari (ALBIGENSES), who taught either strict (Church of Dragovitsa) or moderate (Old Bulgarian) dualism. Since the movement's teaching on dualism was not completely formulated until 1270, its emphasis on the relationship to the world took precedence; poverty was considered the means to renunciation of the world. Furthermore, the Luciferians, who shared this dualism, demanded extreme renunciation and the rejection of marriage. (2) The spiritualists were individuals whose Catharist ideas were bound to those of JOACHIM OF FIORE: poverty was practiced as a protest against the possessions of the Church. The Franciscan Gerard of Borgo S. Donnino put forth the opinion in the *Introductorius in evangelium aeternum* (1254) that the promised spiritual Church, as realized in the Franciscan Order, would replace the established Church of the priests; in this regard, he was followed more or less by the FRANCISCAN SPIRITUALS and the FRATICELLI. The AMALRICIANS, who interpreted the pantheistic teachings of AMALRIC OF BÈNE as ''rules of life,'' and combined them with Joachimite ideas, also rejected the sacramental Church. In about 1250 their teachings were continued by the BROTHERS AND SISTERS OF THE FREE SPIRIT, who spread in the region of the Swabian Ries and along the Rhine (Cologne, Strasbourg, Basel). In this group were also the APOSTOLICI, founded by Segarelli of Parma (burned 1300) and his successor Fra DOLCINO (burned 1307), who were originally similar to the Franciscans, but after 1285 were prosecuted by the Church for having denounced it as the ''whore of Babylon''; (3) To the antihierarchical group belonged the unreconciled Waldenses and the rebellious Stedingers, who, following the Waldensian tenets, rejected the tithe and fought with the archbishop of Bremen; they were crushed after FREDERICK II placed them under the ban of the empire in 1253 and after a crusade was preached against them.

The Older Orders. (1) All Catholic wandering preachers, both men and women, cooperated with the work of the Church and, as Bernard of Clairvaux had proposed, fostered their ideal of poverty in separate monasteries (e.g., ROBERT OF ARBRISSEL at FONTÉVRAULT, NORBERT OF XANTEN at PRÉMONTRÉ, VITALIS OF SAVIGNY, and BERNARD OF TIRON). The exception was HENRY OF LAUSANNE, who consequently broke with the Church and was imprisoned in 1134. (2) Apostolic poverty led to the establishment of the Order of GRANDMONT, founded by STEPHAN OF MURET, whose members followed the BENEDICTINE RULE and were popularly called the *boni homines*. Poverty as an ideal prompted the founding also of the CISTERCIANS by ROBERT OF MOLESMES and Bernard of Clairvaux, who in his controversy with CLUNY (*Patrologia Latina* 182:895–918) proposed his interpretation of Benedictine poverty: the Cistercian nuns were chiefly women of the movement. (3) To the lay poverty movement were affiliated various HOSPITALLERS, male and female, among them the lay society of Saint Anthony, approved by Urban II in 1095 for the staffing of a hospital at Saint-Didier de la Mothe. Originally living without vows and unified by their interest in nursing, they eventually professed the Rule of Saint AUGUSTINE (1218) as prescribed by the Fourth LATERAN COUNCIL. The same development accounted for the Bridge-building brotherhood of BÉNÉZET of Avignon (117–99), approved by Clement III in 1189 as a pious lay society with the purpose of building bridges. In the category of the lay poverty movement belonged also the BEGUINES, who, as a society of women living by their own handiwork, were organized into communities by JACQUES DE VITRY with the approval of Honorius III; under the direction of MARY OF OIGNIES, they accepted mendicant poverty; their male counterparts were the Beghards. Since the Beguines were technically neither religious nor seculars, they were often accused of heresy, and in 1274 the Second Council of LYONS attempted to suppress them; they generally then became associated with the various Third Orders in the Church.

New Orders. (1) FRANCISCANS (Friars Minor, Poor Clares, Brothers and Sisters of Penance). Innocent III had previously approved only those dissenters who had sought reconciliation, but by his oral approbation of the rule of the Friars Minor (1209 or 1210), he established the first new order to emerge from the movement. For FRANCIS OF ASSISI poverty was the bride of Christ whom he personified as Lady Poverty. Contrary to the Fourth

Lateran Council's ban on new orders, Innocent III granted CLARE OF ASSISI the *privilegium paupertatis*, and Honorius III gave written approval to the rule of the Friars Minor in 1223, while Cardinal Hugolino (GREGORY IX) vitalized the Third Order of Saint Francis in 1221. (2) DOMINICANS. By preaching against heresy, DOMINIC came to found his order and adopted mendicant poverty as a prerequisite for a successful preaching crusade. After the Fourth Lateran Council had prohibited the founding of new orders, he chose, as a former canon, the Rule of Saint Augustine, to which he added special constitutions. (3) The CARMELITES, a previously existing order, adopted mendicant poverty in 1245 and, after changes in the rule (1247), founded also a third order. (4) The Hermits of Saint Augustine (AUGUSTINIANS), who also later founded a third order, came into existence when Innocent IV (1243) united various groups of hermits living in Tuscany, to which Alexander IV (1256) added all other hermits who professed the Rule of Saint Augustine, creating the fourth mendicant order. In the poverty controversy at the University of PARIS (1252–72), the antimendicant party wished the Church to return to its traditional position on poverty as held in the days before Innocent III. A similar attempt at the Council of Lyons (1274) was averted by the Franciscan Cardinal BONAVENTURE.

Modern Poverty Movements. Various poverty movements continue to persist in the poverty-based religious orders that have retained their identity and spirit. Additional claimants to this tradition may be added. Not motivated as heavily by the pursuit of spiritual perfection in the imitation of Christ, more modern movements have used poverty as a basis for transformative action in the world. Exemplifying the spirit of poverty in action are members of the Catholic Worker Movement, founded by Dorothy DAY and Peter MAURIN, and the practitioners of liberation theology. The Catholic Worker Movement formed in an effort to raise the dignity of the working poor and the underemployed in urban settings, as well as to bring attention to the plight of these sufferers. Liberation theology, based on the preferential option for the poor, seeks to highlight and reconstitute social and political structures that create conditions of injustice, predominantly in so-called third-world countries, for the most vulnerable, the poor. A tenet held by many liberation theologians is that one must be amongst the poor in order to stand with and for the poor.

The worker-priest movement in France involved ordained clergy and associated laypersons locating themselves completely within the social conditions of their industrially impoverished, urban, working parishioners. Poverty, as it is integrated with an active presence in the world, not only frees the practitioner to concentrate on the mission; it also makes a visible entreaty for the right of the most vulnerable to participate in the world. The Little Bothers and the Little Sisters of Jesus introduced this latter effort into their way of life, on the inspiration of Charles De FOUCAULD. These movements employed the ''sign-value of poverty'' to pre-evangelize the poor. The mere presence of those willing to embrace the lot of the poor in the name of Jesus opens a channel for the Good News to reach and transform the lives of the most marginalized in society. In a world economy increasingly dependent on consumerism, it should not be surprising to see the increasing use of the ''sign-value of poverty'' as a counter-balance to a possession-centered lifestyle.

Bibliography: J. B. PIERRON, *Die katholischen Armen* (Freiburg 1911). M. C. SLOTEMAKER DE BRUINE, *Het ideaal der navolging van Christus ten tijde van Bernard van Clairvaux* (Wageningen 1926). H. GRUNDMANN, *Religiöse Bewegungen im Mittelalter* (2d ed. Hildesheim 1961). L. SPÄTLING, *De apostolicis, pseudoapostolicis, apostolinis* (Munich 1947). A. MENS, *Oorsprong en betekenis van de Nederlandse Begijne en Begardenbeweging* (Louvain 1947). A. BORST, *Die Katharer* (Stuttgart 1953). E. W. MCDONNELL, *The Beguines and Beghards in Medieval Culture* (New Brunswick, N.J. 1954). S. CLASEN, *Die Armut als Beruf: Franz von Assisi* (*Miscellanea mediaevalia* 3; Berlin 1965). P. F. MULHERN, *Dedicated Poverty* (Staten Island, N.Y. 1973).

[S. CLASEN/D. MCCARTHY]

POWEL, PHILIP, BL.

Benedictine priest and martyr; *alias* Morgan, Prosser; b. Trallong, Breconshire, Feb. 2, 1594; d. hanged, drawn, and quartered at Tyburn (London), June 30, 1646. After completing grammar school at Abergavenny, Powel, son of Roger and Catherine Powel, became a law student at the Temple, London. There he fell under the influence of David Baker, who later became the Benedictine Augustine Baker. Philip joined the Benedictines (1614) at St. Gregory's and was ordained in Douai (1618). In 1622 he returned to the English mission where he labored for 20 years in Somersetshire and Devonshire. During the Civil War he was chaplain to the Catholic soldiers in General Goring's army in Cornwall. When the force was disbanded, he set sail for Wales, but the ship was captured, Feb. 22, 1646. Powel was recognized as a priest, arrested, taken to London, and imprisoned at St. Catherine's in Southwark. Following torture, he suffered from pleurisy. He was tried at Westminster Hall, June 9, convicted, and condemned. His mortal remains were buried in the old churchyard at Moorfields and some of his relics are preserved at Downside Abbey, Bath. He was beatified by Pius XI on Dec. 15, 1929.

Feast of the English Martyrs: May 4 (England).

See Also: ENGLAND, SCOTLAND, AND WALES, MARTYRS OF.

Bibliography: *Relation du martyre de Philippe Powel, autrement dit le Père Morgan, Religieux Bénédictin* (Paris 1647). R. CHALLONER, *Memoirs of Missionary Priests,* ed. J. H. POLLEN (rev. ed. London 1924; repr. Farnborough 1969), II, 297. J. H. POLLEN, *Acts of English Martyrs* (London 1891).

[K. I. RABENSTEIN]

POWELL, EDWARD, BL.

Theologian, priest, and martyr; b. Wales, *c.* 1478; d. hanged, drawn, and quartered at Smithfield (London), July 30, 1540. Powell, a fellow of Oriel College, Oxford (1495), earned his master's and doctorate in theology (1506) at Oxon. He was sometime rector of Bleadon, Somerset, and held a number of prebends.

King Henry VIII, who regarded Powell highly, ordered the priest to publish a reply to Martin LUTHER. This took the form of a dialogue in three books entitled *Propugnaculum summi Sacerdotii Evangelici, ac septem Sacramentorum, aeditum per virum eruditum, sacrarum literarum professorem Edoardum Poelum adversus Maratinum Lutherum fratrem famosum et Wiclifistan insignem* (London 1523), which won praise from the University of Oxford.

Powell was among those theologians selected to defend the legality of the marriage of Catherine of Aragon in the royal divorce proceedings. In connection with this, he wrote the *Tractatus de non dissolvendo Henrici Regis cum Catherina matrimonio* (London). Powell debated Hugh Latimer, then fell into further disfavor by denouncing Henry's marriage to Anne Boleyn.

He was discharged from the proctorship of Salisbury in January 1534. Upon refusing to take the Oath of Succession (November 1534), he was attainted for high treason along with Bishop John Fisher of Rochester, deprived of his benefices, and imprisoned in the Tower of London. Following a six-year confinement, he was executed together with BB. Thomas ABELL and Richard FETHERSTON. They were beatified by Pope Leo XIII on Dec. 29, 1886.

Feast of the English Martyrs: May 4 (England); July 30 (Wales).

See Also: ENGLAND, SCOTLAND, AND WALES, MARTYRS OF.

Bibliography: R. CHALLONER, *Memoirs of Missionary Priests,* ed. J. H. POLLEN (rev. ed. London 1924; repr. Farnborough 1969). J. H. POLLEN, *Acts of English Martyrs* (London 1891).

[K. I. RABENSTEIN]

POWER, EDMUND

Biblical scholar; b. Herbertstown, County Limerick, Ireland, March 2, 1878; d. Dublin, Ireland, Aug. 3, 1953. After his early education with the Christian Brothers in Limerick, he studied philosophy at Thurles and Maynooth (1893–96) and entered the Society of Jesus (Oct. 1, 1896). After his novitiate, he studied classical languages at the Royal University, Dublin, and Oriental languages at the University of St. Joseph, Beirut, where he received the doctorate (1906). He then completed his studies in philosophy at Valkenburg, Netherlands (1907–09), and in theology at Hastings, England (1909–13). After his ordination, he was appointed professor of Arabic and Syriac at the PONTIFICAL BIBLICAL INSTITUTE. During his long residence there (1914–38), in certain years he also taught biblical geography and archeology. From 1938 to 1953 he was professor of Sacred Scripture at Milltown Park, Dublin. He contributed many articles on biblical topics to *Biblica* (of which he was the editor 1926–31), *Verbum Domini, Catholic Commentary on Holy Scripture,* and *Dictionnaire de la Bible, Supplément,* v. 1–3.

Bibliography: E. VOGT and P. NOBER, *Biblica* 35 (1954) 122–126, with complete list of his writings.

[J. MCPOLIN]

POWER, EMILY, MOTHER

Educator; b. County Waterford, Ireland, Jan. 12, 1844; d. Sinsinawa, Wis., Oct. 16, 1909. The Power family came to the U.S. in 1851, settling in St. Louis, Mo. When the father died, his widow took the family to a farm near Sinsinawa. At the age of 13, Ellen Power entered an academy at Benton, Wis., established by the Rev. Samuel Mazzuchelli, OP, founder of the Sinsinawa Dominicans. At the age of 17 she was received into the community of the Dominican sisters in Benton and given the name of Sister Mary Emily. In 1867 she was chosen head of the community. With the aid of a wealthy Catholic, William Ryan, she moved the group, both sisters and students, from Benton back to Sinsinawa. On this base she built an organization that in 1961 staffed educational institutions in 20 states, Europe, and South America. Her educational apostolate included the elementary, secondary, and college levels. Rosary College, River Forest, Ill., and its branch in Fribourg, Switzerland; Edgewood College of the Sacred Heart, Madison, Wis.; and Pius XII Graduate School of Fine Arts, Florence, Italy, were all part of Mother Emily's plan. St. Clara of Sinsinawa was one of the first Catholic secondary schools to establish affiliation with a state university, and the curriculum of Corpus

Christi School, New York City, has been a model for many elementary schools. Mother Emily was one of the first superiors to send sisters to secular institutions and to the Catholic University of America, Washington, D.C. She was aware of the problems of poverty and sympathetic with workers, and was associated also with social movements. She directed aid for the miners of Spring Valley, Minn., for the locked-out workers of the Anaconda in Montana, and for the strikers of the Chicago stockyards. She anteceded Leo XIII in teaching the need for understanding between capital and labor; when the pope's pronouncement came, she put it into action as an educational factor of essential importance.

Bibliography: M. E. MCCARTY, *The Sinsinawa Dominicans: Outlines of Twentieth Century Development, 1901–1949* (Sinsinawa, Wis. 1952).

[M. SYNON]

POWER, JOHN

Missionary; b. Rosscarberry, County Cork, Ireland, June 19, 1792; d. New York City, April 14, 1849. He studied at St. Patrick's College, Maynooth, was ordained in 1814, and after serving as a curate at Youghal, taught in the diocesan college of Cloyne. In 1819 he immigrated to New York City, where he became a curate and then pastor at St. Peter's Church. As one of the most prominent Catholics in New York, he was named vicar-general and administrator of the diocese (1823–49); he attended the First and Second Provincial Councils of Baltimore, and accompanied Bp. John Dubois on a visitation of the entire diocese (1828). Power was keenly interested in the Catholic Orphan Asylum, and he encouraged the founding of the *Truth Teller*, New York's first Catholic newspaper. He distinguished himself by his zeal during the yellow fever epidemics of 1819 and 1822, and the cholera epidemic of 1832. Like all New York priests of the time, Power was an itinerant missionary and on occasion ministered to the Catholics of Brooklyn, N.Y.; Jersey City and New Brunswick, N.J., where he said the first Mass; and Connecticut. His tenure at St. Peter's was beset by TRUSTEEISM and financial difficulties that were climaxed by bankruptcy in 1844, when the church was auctioned to satisfy the creditors.

Power was an excellent linguist, with a good command of Latin, Greek, French, Spanish, Italian, and Gaelic. An able exponent of Catholic doctrine, he successfully answered the attacks of Calvinist ministers William Brownlee and John Breckenridge. His publications include several books of devotion, a translation of part of the Royaumont Bible, and a catechetical history of the Old Testament. His remains were interred in old St. Patrick's Cathedral, New York City.

Mother Emily Power.

Bibliography: J. T. SMITH, *The Catholic Church in New York* 2 v. (New York 1906) v. 1. L. R. RYAN, *Old St. Peter's, . . . New York 1785–1935*. (*U.S. Catholic Historical Society* 15; New York 1935). M. A. CORRIGAN, *Historical Records and Studies of the U.S. Catholic Historical Society of New York* 2 (1900) 42–43.

[F. D. COHALAN]

POWER, LIONEL

Church composer and singer; b. England, *c.* 1375; d. Canterbury, June 5, 1445. He ranks next to DUNSTABLE in importance among early 15th-century English composers, by reason of the artistic quality and quantity (about 50) of his works, all church music. Neither Power nor Dunstable was a member of the chapel royal, but Dunstable's membership in the Duke of Bedford's private chapel suggests that Power too may have accompanied the Duke into France. Most of his music is found in Continental MSS, although the Old Hall MS also provides examples of his early and later styles. Some of his liturgical music could have been written for Christ

Church Priory, Canterbury, for he was received there as a lay oblate as early as 1423. His early works were strongly influenced by the angular and often recondite features of the late *ars nova,* and two of his Mass sections exhibit many of the complexities of proportional notation. His later music, especially the 15 motets in honor of the Blessed Virgin Mary, assumes the flowing and consonant style developed and perfected by Dunstable.

Bibliography: M. F. BUKOFZER, ''English Church Music of the Fifteenth Century,'' *New Oxford History of Music*, ed. J. A. WESTRUP, 11 v. (New York 1957–) 3:172–176. F. L. HARRISON, *Music in Medieval Britain* (New York 1958). W. B. SQUIRE and A. HUGHES, *Grove's Dictionary of Music and Musicians*, ed. E. BLOM 9 v. (5th ed. London 1954) 6:903. *Baker's Biographical Dictionary of Musicians*, ed. N. SLONIMSKY (5th, rev. ed. New York 1958) 1274. M. BENT, ''Leonel Power'' in *The New Grove Dictionary of Music and Musicians*, vol. 15, ed. S. SADIE (New York 1980) 174–179. R. D. BOWERS, ''Some Observations on the Life and Career of Lionel Power'' in *Proceedings of the Royal Musical Association* (1975/1976), 103–127. D. M. RANDEL, ed., *The Harvard Biographical Dictionary of Music* (Cambridge 1996) 707. N. SLONIMSKY, ed., *Baker's Biographical Dictionary of Musicians*, eighth edition (New York 1992) 1439. B. G. SMITH, ''John Dunstable and Leonel Power: A Stylistic Comparison'' (Ph.D. diss. University of Sheffield, 1993).

[D. STEVENS]

POWERS, JESSICA

Religious name: Sister Miriam of the Holy Spirit; American poet and Carmelite nun; b. Cat Tail Valley, Wisconsin, Feb. 7, 1905; d. Pewaukee, Wisconsin, Aug. 18, 1988. Jessica Powers grew up in a small farming community near Mauston, Wisconsin. The grandchild of pioneers, she counted the Scottish poet Robert Burns among her ancestors. Catholicism, nature (especially winter), and death are major themes in her lyric poetry. Her formal education ended after one semester at Marquette University's School of Journalism (1922–23). For the next few years she worked in Chicago in a secretarial pool while nurturing her inner work of poetry. Her poems regularly appeared in newspapers, journals, and anthologies. However, when symptoms of tuberculosis appeared, she returned to Cat Tail Valley.

After her mother's sudden death in 1925, Powers gave up her dream of living and writing in New York in order to help her brothers with the farm. It was during the ''farm years'' she first read the poetry of JOHN OF THE CROSS, to whom she has been compared. Her brothers eventually married, and in 1937 she felt free to go to New York, where she was active in the Catholic Poetry Society. There she met Clifford Laube, a *New York Times* editor. Laube had his own publishing company, Monastine Press (after SS. Monica and Augustine) in the basement of his home. In 1939 he published her first volume of poems, *The Lantern Burns.*

As her poetic work was becoming recognized, Powers abruptly left New York in 1941 to enter the new Mother of God Carmelite monastery in Wisconsin. She lived there for the remaining 47 years of her life, exploring the secrets of the soul in prayer and poetry. Her largest collection, the *Selected Poetry of Jessica Powers,* was published posthumously in 1989. Her papers are in the Marquette University archives.

Bibliography: M. KAPPES, *Track of the Mystic: Carmelite Influence on the American Poet Jessica Powers* (Kansas City 1994). D. R. LECKEY, *Winter Music: A Life of Jessica Powers—Poet, Nun, Woman of the 20th Century* (Kansas City 1992). R. MORNEAU, *Mantras From A Poet* (Kansas City 1991). J. POWERS, *Mountain Sparrow* (Reno Carmel 1972) illustrated by Sr. Marie Celeste, OCD; *Journey to Bethlehem* (Pewaukee Carmel 1980); *The House at Rest* (Pewaukee Carmel 1984); *Selected Poetry of Jessica Powers* (Kansas City 1989; includes bibliography of secondary sources).

[D. R. LECKEY]

POYNTER, WILLIAM

English vicar apostolic; b. Petersfield, Hampshire, England, May 20, 1762; d. London, Nov. 26, 1827. Sent to the English College at Douai, France, by Bp. Richard Challoner, he was ordained (1786) and remained as prefect of studies at the college. Imprisoned during the French Revolution, he returned to England as vice president of the new College of St. Edmund, Old Hall Green (1795), becoming its president in 1801. In 1803 he was consecrated coadjutor to Bp. John Douglass of the London District. He succeeded to the vicariate at Douglass's death (1812), but retained the presidency of St. Edmund's until 1813. During his episcopate, Poynter opposed the rough controversial methods of Bp. John MILNER and won the support of leading Catholic laymen who had been dissatisfied with the position of the bishops on the Relief Act of 1791. Poynter also served after 1816 as the spokesman for English bishops seeking compensation for property lost during the French Revolution.

Bibliography: T. COOPER, *The Dictionary of National Biography from the Earliest Times to 1900,* 63 v. (London 1885–1900; repr. with corrections, 21 v., 1908–09, 1921–22, 1938; suppl. 1901–) 16:276–277. J. GILLOW, *A Literary and Biographical History or Bibliographical Dictionary of the English Catholics from 1534 to the Present Time,* 5 v. (London-New York 1885–1902; repr. New York 1961) 5:358–361. B. N. WARD, *Dawn of the Catholic Revival in England, 1781–1803,* 2 v. (New York 1909); *Eve of Catholic Emancipation,* 3 v. (London 1911–12); *The History of St. Edmund's College, Old Hall* (London 1893).

[D. MILBURN]

PRADO, JOHN OF, BL.

Restorer of the Morocco mission, martyr; b. Morgovejo, Spain, 1563; d. Marrakech, Morocco, May 24, 1631. John entered S. Gabriel Province, whence, as superior, in 1620 he established the new S. Diego province of Andalucia and became its provincial. With good prospects of reopening the Moroccan mission, in 1630 he was named its prefect apostolic. John left Cadiz with Father Matías de S. Francisco and Brother Ginés de Ocaña, and at Mazagan secured letters and safe-conducts of the Spanish governor to Sultan Muley Abd el-Malik. Upon reaching Marrakech, he learned that the benevolent sultan was dead and had been replaced by his brother, Muley el-Walid, who in the audience of April 3, 1631, rejected the credentials of the friars and threw them into prison, asking that the Spanish governor and garrison evacuate Mazagan in exchange for their release. Later the sultan violently attacked the Christian faith, while Father John with the eloquence of a saint moved the apostates among the Christian captives to repent. Summoned before the furious sultan on May 24, Father John asked him to renounce Muḥammad and to worship Christ. Instead, the sultan stabbed him to death. The martyr was beatified by BENEDICT XIII on May 14, 1728, and was chosen patron of the Morocco mission.

Feast: May 24.

Bibliography: FRANCISCO DE SAN JVAN DE EL PVERTO, *Mission historical de Marrvecos* (Sevilla 1708). J. LÓPEZ, *Memoria sobre la misión franciscana de Marruecos* (Tangier 1924). H. KOEHLE, *L'Église chrétienne du Maroc et la mission franciscaine 1221–1790* (Paris 1934).

[A. S. ROSSO]

PRADT, EL ABATE DE

William Poynter, after a painting by Ramsay.

French prelate, diplomat, and publicist who supported NAPOLEON I and promoted Spanish-American independence and other causes by his pen; b. Chateau de Pradt, Allanche, Auvergne, April 23, 1759; d. Paris, March 18, 1837. Born the second son of a large noble family, Dominique Georges Frédéric de Riom de Prolhiac de Pradt was ordained in 1784, and took a doctorate in theology at the Sorbonne (1785). His uncle Cardinal de Larochefoucauld made him canon and vicar at Rouen. He represented that diocese in the Estates General (1789). Initially hostile to revolutionary ideas, especially the CIVIL CONSTITUTION OF THE CLERGY, he emigrated in 1792. In 1798 he published the first of his 70 volumes, *L'antidote du congrés de Rastadt ou Plan d'un nouvel équilibre en Europe,* which revealed the influence of Montesquieu, Raynal, and the Encyclopedists but was still antirevolutionary. After 18 Brumaire, however, his relative General Duroc introduced De Pradt to NAPOLEON Bonaparte. He became the first consul's chaplain, bishop of Poitiers (1805), and archbishop of Mechlin (1808), although the last post was never confirmed by papal bull. De Pradt negotiated with the Spanish Bourbons at Bayonne (1808) and served ineptly as ambassador to the Grand Duchy of Warsaw (1812). Estranged thereafter from the emperor, De Pradt helped his friend Talleyrand engineer the Restoration (1814).

After 1815 De Pradt turned to prolific and facile writing on international politics and Church-State relations. In his books, which were widely read in the New World as well as in Europe, he developed liberal themes begun earlier in *Les trois âges des colonies* (1802). Most influential was his *Des colonies et de la révolution actuelle de l'Amérique* (1817), which brought him heavy criticism from the Ultra press and the admiration of such Spanish Americans as Rivadavia, Bolívar, and Servando Teresa de MIER. In *Les quatre concordats* (1818) De Pradt, a Gallican, bitterly denounced the political motivations of the papacy in withholding the bulls that destroyed his ambitions at Mechlin. Although not a systematic thinker, he proposed as a solution the clear separation of Church and State. This and other works on clerical problems attracted liberal attention in the infant Spanish-American republics. He wrote steadily until 1837; he died reconciled to the Church.

Bibliography: M. AGUIRRE ELORRIAGA, *El Abate de Pradt en la emancipación hispanoamericana, 1800–1830* (2d ed. Buenos Aires 1946).

[H. M. HAMILL, JR.]

PRAEMUNIRE, STATUTE OF

A statute of 1353 that forbade—on pain of outlawry, confiscation of goods, and imprisonment at the king's pleasure—all appeals to authorities outside England in cases cognizable before the royal courts. Ever since the 12th century, both secular and ecclesiastical judges in England had claimed jurisdiction over cases involving advowsons; and although the Statute of Praemunire did not specifically mention the papal Curia, its purpose was to prevent appeals to Rome in cases concerning English benefices. It was thus closely related to the preceding Statute of PROVISORS. Subsequent statutes of 1365 and 1393 explicitly forbade appeals to Rome, but none of these 14th-century acts was regularly enforced. They became of great importance in the 16th century when HENRY VIII invoked the medieval legislation, first to bring about the downfall of Thomas WOLSEY in 1529, and then to coerce the whole English clergy in 1531. Subsequent legislation extended the penalties of Praemunire to a wide variety of offenses, mostly political ones. The last such statute was the Royal Marriages Act of 1772.

Bibliography: Sources. H. GEE and W. J. HARDY, *Documents Illustrative of English Church History* (New York 1896) 103–104 (1353 statute), 122–125 (1393 statute). Literature. J. T. ELLIS, *Anti-Papal Legislation in Medieval England, 1066–1377* (Washington 1930). E. B. GRAVES, "The Legal Significance of the Statute of Praemunire of 1353," *Anniversary Essays in Mediaeval History, by Students of Charles Homer Haskins* (Boston 1929) 57–80.

[B. TIERNEY]

PRAEPOSITINUS OF CREMONA

Theologian; b. Cremona, 1130–35; d. Paris, Feb. 25, 1210. He was a student of MAURICE OF SULLY, ACHARD OF SAINT-VICTOR, and PETER COMESTOR. Before 1194 he taught at Paris and lived among the Cathari in Lombardy or Mainz; he was master of the episcopal school of Mainz (1194–1203), was used by the Holy See as judge-delegate, and was chancellor at the University of Paris (1206–09). His authentic writings include a *Summa theologica* (1190–94); the lost *Distinctiones Praepositini,* which was the source of the *Collecta ex distinctionibus Praepositini; Summa super psalterium* (before 1196–98); and the *Summa de officiis* (1196–98), which was used almost completely in Durandus of Mende's *Rationale divinorum officiorum.* Unauthentic are the Porretanian *Quaestiones Praepositini* (1170–80), *Summa contra haereticos* (*c.* 1200), and the *Summa de poenitentia iniungenda* (after 1202).

Bibliography: G. LACOMBE, *La Vie et les oeuvres de Prévostin* (*Bibliothèque Thomiste* 11; 1927); *Dictionnaire de théologie catholique* 13.1:162–169. C. OTTAVIANO, *Rivista de filosofica neoscholastica* 20 (1928) 366–371. O. LOTTIN, "Le Traité sur le péché originel des *Questiones Prepositini,*" *Recherches de théologie ancienne et médievale* 6 (1934) 416–422; *Psychologie et morale aux XIIe et XIIIe siècles,* 6 v. in 8 (Louvain 1942–60) v. 6. A. FRIES, *Urgerechtigkeit, Fall und Erbsünde nach Präpositin von Cremona and Wilhelm von Auxerre* (Freiburg 1940). D. VAN DEN EYNDE, "Précisions chronologiques sur quelques oeuvres théologiques du XIIe siècle," *Antonianum* 26 (1951) 239–241. A. M. LANDGRAF, *Introducción a la historia de la literatura teológica de la escolástica incipiente* (Barcelona 1956). J. CORBETT and J. N. GARVIN, eds., *Summa contra haereticos* (Notre Dame, Ind. 1958). L. HÖDL, *Die Geschichte der scholastischen Literatur und der Theologie der Schlüsselgewalt,* v.1 (*Beiträge zur Geschichte der Philosophie und Theologie des Mittelalters* 38.4; 1960) 273–289.

[J. N. GARVIN]

PRAEPOSITUS (JOANNES DE SAN GEORGIO)

Lay canonist; b. Bologna, Italy; d. Bologna, *c.* 1378. He completed his studies in law and became professor of Canon Law at Bologna in 1320. He left that position in 1347 and in 1352 became professor of Canon Law at Padua, where he remained until 1361. He married the daughter of another important canonist of this period, Joannes Andrea, and there was considerable communication between these canonists in their work. He was a member of a group of 14th–century commentators upon the *Decretum* of Gratian and upon papal decretals. His most important works were a commentary on the Clementine constitutions (*Reportationes super clementinis*) and a collection of commentaries on various juridic problems (*Quaestiones*). His *Reportationes* can be considered a supplement to Joannes Andrea's apparatus on the Clementine constitutions.

Bibliography: J. F. VON SCHULTE, *Die Geschichte der Quellen und der Literatur des kanonischen Rechts* 2:253. A. VAN HOVE, *Commentarium Lovaniense in Codicem iuris canonici 1* 1:490 501.

[J. M. BUCKLEY]

PRAETEXTATUS OF ROUEN, ST.

Archbishop; d. Rouen, France, April 14 or Feb. 25, 586. Raised to the episcopacy (*c.* 544), Praetextatus (or Prix) assisted at the synods of Tours (567) and Paris (556–73). His interference in affairs of state, justifiable or not, earned him the personal hatred of Chilperic and Fredegund and involved him in the political intrigue of his day. At a synod held in Paris (577), he was accused by Chilperic of treasonable activities, deposed, and placed in confinement on an island in the neighborhood of Coutances. GREGORY OF TOURS was the only bishop at the synod who spoke in his defense. After Chilperic's death (584), Praetextatus was recalled and honorably reinstated, despite the vigorous opposition of Fredegund. In 585 he assisted at the synod of Mâcon. The following year, at the instigation of Fredegund, he was murdered in his cathedral.

Feast: Feb. 24.

Bibliography: GREGORY OF TOURS, *Historia Francorum,* 5:18; 7:16; 8:20, 31, 41; 9:20, 39. *Monumenta Germaniae Historica: Scriptores rerum Merovingicarum* (Berlin 1826–) 1.1:216–217, 337, 387, 397, 407, 440, Eng. tr. O. M. DALTON, 2 v. (Oxford 1927). *Monumenta Germaniae Historica: Concilia* (Berlin 1826–) 1:135, 145, 151, 172, 174. E. VACANDARD, *Vie de Saint Ouen* (Paris 1902) 96–97. L. DUCHESNE, *Fastes épiscopaux de l'ancienne Gaule,* 3 v. (2d ed. Paris 1970–15) 2:206. C. J. VON HEFELE, *Histoire des conciles d'après les documents originaux,* tr. and continued by H. LECLERCQ, 10 v. in 19 (Paris 1907–38) 3.1:33–34. J. L. BAUDOT and L. CHAUSSIN, *Vies des saints et des bienheureux selon l'ordre du calendrier avec l'historique des fêtes,* 12 v. (Paris 1935–56); v. 13, suppl. and table générale (1959) 2:507–511. H. LECLERCQ, *Dictionnaire d'archéologie chrétienne et de liturgie,* ed. F. CABROL, H. LECLERCQ, and H. I. MARROU, 15 v. (Paris 1907–53) 15.1:120–121.

[G. M. COOK]

PRAETORIUM

The Greek word πραιτώριον was taken over directly from the Latin *praetorium,* which originally signified the headquarters of the commanding officer (the *praetor*) in Roman military encampments. In its military usage, the word came to be used also of the council of war held in the commanding officer's headquarters and of the bodyguard of the emperor (the Praetorian Guard) or of a Roman governor, whether his title was that of praetor or not. Finally, its meaning was extended in a local sense, as well, to designate the governor's official residence in a Roman province or administrative district.

In the Gospels. The praetorium is mentioned in the accounts of the Passion (*see* PASSION OF CHRIST, I) as the place where Jesus was mocked by the Roman soldiers (Mt 27.27; Mk 15.16) and interrogated by Pontius PILATE (Jn 18.28, 33; 19.9). Immediately in front of this praetorium at Jerusalem, or in an outer part of it, in a place called Lithostrotos in Greek and Gabbatha in Aramaic, the tribunal or curule chair of Pilate was apparently located, at least on this occasion, and there final sentence was passed on Jesus (Jn 19.13). Because of the diversity of the Gospel accounts, it is a matter of debate among Biblical scholars whether the scourging of Jesus also took place inside the praetorium, or outside of it, and whether it took place before or after the sentence of condemnation was pronounced. Further, whether the praetorium itself and the place called Lithostrotos or Gabbatha are also to be located at the Antonia fortress situated at the northwest corner of the TEMPLE area in the lower city, or at HEROD THE GREAT's palace in the western or upper part of the city, is likewise a subject on which scholars are fairly evenly divided. In favor of the Antonia as the place of Pilate's residence during the Passion is the argument that it would have been more likely for Pilate to choose as his headquarters this site close by the Temple area, where rebellious outbreaks often originated, in order to be on hand in case of trouble during the large gathering of the people for the feast of the Passover. Furthermore, recent excavations at the site of the Antonia have uncovered an extensive pavement of large stone blocks, dating from the time of Christ, that its discoverers have identified with the Lithostrotos of John's account. Since Lithostrotos (λιθόστρωτος) means ''paved with stones'' (cf. Septuagint of Est 1.6, Sg 3.10, 2 Chr 7.3) and is most probably used substantively in John 19.13 to denote a proper name, the name would appear to fit the place well. In addition, if, as seems probable, the name Gabbatha (*gabbātā',* called ''Hebrew'' in John 19.13, but really Aramaic) is connected with the root *gb'* (to be high), this name too would be appropriate for the same site, since the Antonia was situated on high ground overlooking the entire temple area. Against this view, however, is the fact that Philo (*Legatio ad Caium* 38) and Josephus (*De bello Judaico* 2.3.1–4; 2.9.4; 2.14.8) seem to indicate Herod's palace in the western sector of the city as the ordinary residence or praetorium of the Roman governors when they were present in Jerusalem. So the basic difficulty of identifying the Antonia as the praetorium of the Passion hinges on whether or not the term praetorium itself was used so loosely that it was applied indiscriminately to any place where the governor might have taken up residence, no matter how temporary that residence might have been. Also, Herod's palace was situated at a higher point in the city than the Antonia. It is possible, too, since knowledge of the ancient localities in Jerusalem, along with their names, is by no means complete, that there may have been another pavement made of large stones standing before this western palace that would be more in accord with the Gospel narrative than the one discovered at the

Ancient pavement discovered under the convent of the Sisters of Sion and the Franciscan Monastery of the Flagellation at the Ecce Homo Arch in Jerusalem. It formed part of the courtyard of the Antonia Fortress and may have been the praetorium where Pilate condemned Jesus. Cuts on the pavement were made for playing Roman games.

site of the Antonia, which appears to have been an inner courtyard rather than an outside plaza.

In Acts and Philipians. In Acts of the Apostles 23.35 mention is made of ''the praetorium of Herod,'' i.e., the palace that Herod the Great built for himself at Caesarea. In accord with the frequent practice of Roman governors in taking over the palace of the former ruler as their official residence or praetorium, this palace of Herod at Caesarea became the normal headquarters of the Roman procurators of Judea (cf. Josephus, *De bello Judaico* 2.14.8). There St. Paul was imprisoned under the procurator Felix. The meaning of praetorium in Philippians 1.13, where Paul writes that his imprisonment is known ''throughout the praetorium'' to be for the sake of Christ, depends largely on whether Paul is thought to have been writing from Rome, Caesarea, Ephesus, or elsewhere. Since a personal, rather than a local, interpretation of the phrase appears to be called for by the context in which it occurs, it is probable that, if Paul was writing from Rome, he was referring to the members of the Roman Praetorian Guard who, through periodic changes of the guard on Paul, would all have come to know his case. If, however, Paul was writing from Caesarea, Ephesus, or elsewhere, the word could be applied to the members of the Roman governor's guard, or possibly even to other members of the governor's court or household. However, if a local sense for the term is preferred, the praetorium could indicate the governor's palace at Caesarea, Ephesus, or elsewhere. But a similar local interpretation could not be supported under the hypothesis of a Roman origin of this letter, since the palace of the emperor in Rome is never called a praetorium, even though his palace outside of Rome is sometimes so named.

Bibliography: M. E. BOISMARD, *Lexikon für Theologie und Kirche*, ed. J. HOFER and K. RAHNER, 10 v. (2d, new ed. Freiburg

1957–65); suppl., *Das Zweite Vatikanische Konzil: Dokumente und Kommentare*, ed. H. S. BRECHTER et al., pt. 1 (1966) 4:477–478. *Encyclopedic Dictionary of the Bible*, tr. and adap. by L. HARTMAN (New York 1963), from A. VAN DEN BORN, *Bijbels Woordenboek* 1888–92. C. KOPP, *The Holy Places of the Gospels,* tr. R. WALLS (New York 1963) 365–373. E. A. CERNY, ''Lithostrotos,'' *The Catholic Biblical Quarterly* 4 (1942) 159–160. L. H. VICENT, ''L'Antonia et le Prétoire,'' *Revue biblique* 42 (1933) 83–113; ''Antour du Prétoire,'' *ibid.* 46 (1937) 563–570; ''Le Lithostrotos évangelique,'' *ibid.* 59 (1952) 513–530; ''L'Antonia, palais primitif d'Hérode,'' *ibid.* 61 (1954) 87–107. P. BENOIT, ''Prétoire, Lithostroton et Gabbatha'' *ibid.* 59 (1952) 531–550.

[W. K. LEAHY]

PRAETORIUS, MICHAEL

Church composer and theorist, authority on baroque organ; b. Kreuzberg (Thuringia), Germany, Feb. 15, 1571; d. Wolfenbüttel, Feb. 15, 1621. His full name was Michael Hieronymus Schultheiss, of which surname Praetorius is the Latin form. He was the son of a Protestant minister, and was at one time prior of Ringelheim Abbey (in Protestant possession 1570–1643), but resigned to devote himself to music. From 1612 until his death he was *Kapellmeister* in Wolfenbüttel. Praetorius published many oversized collections of his church music, much of it based on German chorale tunes, developed in the new Italian *concertato* style. Among these collections are the *Musae Sioniae* (1,244 settings in 16 v.; 1605–10); *Musarum Sioniarum* (1607); *Eulogodia Sionia* (60 motets ''for the conclusion of worship''; 1611); *Hymnodia Sionia* (1611); and *Kleine und Grosse Litanie* (1613). His great theoretical work is the *Syntagma Musicum.* Of its published volumes the first is a (Latin) treatise on ancient church music (1615); the second, with its illustrated appendix, is a primary reference on baroque instruments, particularly the organ [1620; tr. from German by H. Blumenfeld (St. Louis 1949)]; the third, a treatise on contemporary secular music.

Bibliography: M. PRAETORIUS, *Gesamtausgabe der musikalischen Werke,* ed. F. BLUME et al., 21 v. in 22 (Wolfenbüttel 1928–60). F. BLUME, *Michael Praetorius Creuzbergensis* (Wolfenbüttel 1929). A. FORCHERT, *Die Musik in Geschichte und Gegenwart,* ed. F. BLUME (Kassel-Basel 1949–) 10:1560–72. M. F. BUKOFZER, *Music in the Baroque Era* (New York 1947). W. BLANKENBURG, ''Michael Praetorius'' in *The New Grove Dictionary of Music and Musicians, vol. 15,* ed. S. SADIE (New York 1980) 188–192. S. HEAVENS and E. SEGERMAN, ''Praetorius' Brass Instruments and *Cammerthon,*'' *Fellowship of Makers and Researchers of Historical Instruments Bulletins* 78 (1995) 54–59. G. LYNDON-JONES, ''Praetorius' Keyless Curtals,'' *Fellowship of Makers and Researchers of Historical Instruments Bulletins* 74 (1994) 26–29. E. SEGERMAN, ''On Praetorius and English Viol Pitches,'' *Chelys* 17 (1988) 24–27; ''On Praetorius and the sizes of Renaissance bowed instruments,'' *Fellowship of Makers and Researchers of Historical Instruments Bulletins* 89 (1997) 40–52;

Michael Praetorius. (Archive Photos)

''Praetorius's *Cammerthon* Pitch Standard,'' *The Galpin Society Journal* 50 (1997) 81–108.

[W. C. HOLMES]

PRAGMATIC SANCTION

A fundamental law of the state regulating important affairs of Church or State, e.g., the Pragmatic Sanction of 1713 that determined the successor to the throne after the death of Emperor Charles VI. In France the term was used to designate the regulations of the general councils that, after lengthy legal advice, were enforced by the king. Royal sanctions of this type occurred in 1407 and 1418, but more famous and consequential than these was the Pragmatic Sanction of Bourges (1438).

Antecedents of Bourges. After the suspension of EUGENE IV by the Council of BASEL (Jan. 24, 1438), France, like the empire, sought to remain neutral in its relations with both the pope and the council. At a meeting convened at Bourges (May 1, 1438) King Charles VIII took the opportunity to discuss with the French clergy their attitude toward the threatened schism. After regaining most of the royal domain, thanks to JOAN OF ARC, Charles was able to consult with representatives from nearly all parts of France. When agents from the pope and from Basel had vigorously presented their opposing points of view, the assembly decided that the king should strive to restore harmony by sending envoys to both parties, by requesting them to end the controversy, and by allowing the council's reform decrees to be tested by a commission in France. The 23 decrees of Basel were accepted with partial modifications, and the changes were to be approved by the Council of Basel. The decisions became immediately effective with the king's endorsement on July 7. Six days later the Pragmatic Sanction was registered by the parlement. The council, however, did not give its approval until Oct. 17, 1439.

Content. Among the approved decrees were *Frequens* and *Sacrosancta,* which legislated respectively regarding the regular convening of councils and the supremacy of a council over the pope. Other decrees regarding elections, the granting of benefices, papal jurisdiction, and ANNATES sharply limited the rights of the pope. Still others affected the celebration of the liturgy and choir chant or were directed against current abuses in the Church, against concubinage and immorality, and also against excessive use of EXCOMMUNICATION, INTERDICT, and reservation. Nevertheless, the Pragmatic Sanction, with more concern than the council, wished to spare the person of Eugene IV and not deprive him of all his resources.

Conflict. The Pragmatic Sanction was a thorn in the side of the popes, not so much because it painfully restricted their income and limited their rights, but especially because, by its recognition of Basel's supremacy, it had furthered the demands and threats of CONCILIARISM. Thus the papacy's struggle against this legislation was quite understandable. However, the concordat negotiations, begun in 1442, produced no results. Cardinal G. d' ESTOUTEVILLE, as the legate of Nicholas II, demanded in vain that the Assembly of the Clergy of 1452 abolish its restrictions, offering a concordat instead.

Moreover, pragmatic decrees were often used by the king as a means of bargaining against concessions of the pope in French and Italian affairs, and in this period a spurious Pragmatic Sanction, signed supposedly by St. LOUIS IX in 1269, made its appearance. In the hope of gaining papal support in the struggle over Naples, Louis XI, much to the chagrin of the clergy and the parlement, abolished the Pragmatic Sanction in 1461. Since he did not achieve the desired objective, however, in 1463 he again issued a long list of decrees ''as a protection against Roman encroachments and for the reestablishment of ancient Gallican liberties.'' Both Julius II and Leo X condemned the Pragmatic Sanction as a work of the schism, but as late as 1510, an assembly of French bishops expressed the desire that it be observed. The bull of Leo X was read at the 11th session of the Fifth LATERAN COUNCIL (1516). But the popes paid a heavy price for the replacement of the Pragmatic Sanction by the French concordat of 1516. The Pragmatic Sanction lived on in the form of GALLICANISM, since it was generally held by the French clergy that only those articles had been abolished that were explicitly corrected or retracted in the concordat. Thus, some articles survived until the French Revolution. However, the maxim that ''the absolute and infinite authority of the pope has no place in France'' became a fundamental principle of Gallicanism.

Bibliography: C. J. VON HEFELE, *Histoire des conciles d'après les documents originaux* (Paris 1907–38) 7.2:1053–61. N. VALOIS, *Histoire de la Pragmatique Sanction de Bourges sous Charles VII* (Paris 1906). V. MARTIN, *Les Origines du gallicanisme,* 2 v. (Paris 1939) v. 2. L. BUISSON, *Potestas und caritas: Die päpstliche Gewalt im Spätmittelalter* (Cologne 1958). R. NAZ, *Dictionnaire de droit canonique* (Paris 1935–65) 7:108–113. P. DE VOOGHT, *Lexikon für Theologie und Kirche,* ed. J. HOFER and K. RAHNER (Freiburg 1957–65) 8:680.

[H. TÜCHLE]

PRAT, FERDINAND

Jesuit exegete; b. La Frétarie (Aveyron), France, Feb. 10, 1857; d. Toulouse, Aug. 4, 1938. After his ordination in 1886 and his studies in Oriental languages at Beirut and Paris and in exegesis under R. Cornely in Rome and J. Knabenbauer in England, he taught Scripture at various times in France, Belgium, and Lebanon. In Rome from 1902 to 1907 as one of the first consultors to the PONTIFICAL BIBLICAL COMMISSION, he influenced the earliest decisions on ''implicit citations'' and the historicity of the Bible and helped in the planning of the proposed Pontifical Biblical Institute. For his service as chaplain during World War I, he was awarded the *Croix de la Légion d'honneur.* Attached intermittently to the editorial staff of *Études,* he published many more than 100 articles in that and other journals. His books include *Origène: le théologien et l'exégète* (1907), *Saint Paul* (1922), *Jésus-Christ, sa Vie, sa Doctrine, son Oeuvre* (1933), and his most lasting work, *La Théologie de saint Paul* (2 v., 1908, 1912).

Bibliography: J. CALÈS, *Un Maître de l'exégèse contemporaine* (Paris 1942).

[J. R. KEATING]

PRAT Y PRAT, MERCEDES, BL.

Known in religion as María Mercedes; martyr of the Society of St. Teresa of Jesus; b. Mar. 6, 1880, Barcelona, Spain; d. July 24, 1936, Barcelona.

Mercedes' Christian parents, Juan and Teresa, died while she was still a child. She combined her special talents as a painter, needleworker, and catechist to evangelize other girls. In 1904, she entered the novitiate of the Society of Saint Teresa of Jesus at Tortosa, where she pronounced her initial vows (1907) and served as a dedicated teacher. From 1920, she was assigned to the motherhouse at Barcelona, from which the community was forced to flee (July 19, 1936) at the beginning of the Spanish Civil War. Stopped by militiamen, Mercedes was arrested on July 23 upon identifying herself as a religious. She was shot at dawn on July 24 on the road to Rabasada. Although mortally wounded she survived for some hours in extreme pain. Her cries attracted the attention of the passing militiamen, who shot her again.

At her beatification (April 29, 1990) Pope John Paul II said: "Her great love for God and neighbor brought her to engage in the apostolic work of catechesis. . . . Her love for her neighbor showed itself above all in her act of pardoning those who shot her."

Feast: July 24 (Carmelites).

Bibliography: V. CÁRCEL ORTÍ, *Martires españoles del siglo XX* (Madrid 1995). J. PÉREZ DE URBEL, *Catholic Martyrs of the Spanish Civil War*, tr. M. F. INGRAMS (Kansas City, Mo. 1993). *Acta Apostolicae Sedis* (1990): 578.

[K. I. RABENSTEIN]

PRATENSIS, FELIX

Editor of the first printed edition of the Hebrew Bible; b. Prato, Tuscany, toward the end of the 15th century; d. Venice, Dec. 5, 1558. Felix was born a Jew, the son of a rabbi, and was well versed in Hebrew. In 1506 he was baptized and entered the order of the Hermits of St. Augustine. He taught Hebrew to the famous printer Daniel BOMBERG of Venice. Bomberg in turn printed the edition of the Hebrew Bible prepared by Pratensis in 1518. This edition contained marginal notes of the rabbis and a Latin dedication to Pope Leo X. Another feature of this edition was the indication, in Hebrew letters, of the Christian division of the Bible into chapters. Felix's work influenced Jacob ben Chayyim in the preparation of his edition of the Hebrew Bible that was printed by Bomberg at Venice in 1525–26. This work became the principal edition of the Hebrew Bible until 1929, when it was supplanted by the third edition of Kittel's *Biblica Hebraica.* See C. D. Ginsburg, *Introduction to the Masoretic-Critical Edition of the Hebrew Bible* (London 1897) 925–974. Felix's writings and sermons were instrumental in attracting many Jewish converts.

Bibliography: D. A. PERINI, *Bibliographia augustiniana* 3 (1935) 100–102. W. HÜMPFNER, *Lexikon für Theologie und Kirche,* ed. J. HOFER and K. RAHNER, 10 v. (2d, new ed. Freiburg 1957–65) 4:70.

[S. M. POLAN]

PRATULIN, MARTYRS OF, BB.

Also known as Wincenty Lewoniuk and Companions or the Martyrs of Podlasie, martyrs; d. Jan. 24, 1874, Pratulin, Poland; beatified by John Paul II, Oct. 6, 1996.

The background for the martyrdom was the the Union of Brest (1595–96) that marked the reunion of Polish Orthodox to the Church of Rome. It retained the Byzantine-Ukranian Rite, while permitting their priests to marry. When Poland fell under Russian domination, "Uniate" Catholics were systematically persecuted by the Czarist regime. Bishops and priests who refused conversion to the Orthodox Church were deported to Siberia or detained in Siedlce or Biała Podlasie (now eastern Poland). By 1874, only the Byzantine Catholic Eparchy of Chelm remained.

When the Russian Kutanin, district prefect of Pratulin village, wanted to nominate an Orthodox priest to replace the pastor of Pratulin, the parishioners objected. Kutanin brought Colonel Stein and his Cossack troops into the town to make the transfer by force. The unarmed parishioners surrounded the church to defend it and refused to disperse despite promises of favors and then threats. Thirteen Byzantine Catholics, led by Wincenty Lewoniuk, were martyred when the soldiers shot them to death for their fidelity to the Catholic Church. Another 180 survived their wounds. The martyrs were buried without ceremony. The decree of martyrdom for the 13 killed was pronounced on June 25, 1996. Those beatified were

Andrzejuk, Jan (John), married, b. 1848, Derło; cantor in the church.

Bojko, Konstanty (Constantine), married, subsistence farmer, b. Sept. 25, 1826, Derło.

Bojko, Łukasz (Luke), unmarried farmer from the village of Legi; b. 1852, Zaczopki. Łukasz, the son of Dymitra Bojko and Anastazji Wojda, spread the news of the arrival of the Cossacks to encourage others to defend the church in Pratulin and rang the church bells throughout the attack. He was shot in front of the church doors.

Franczuk, Ignacy (Ignatius), married layman, b. 1824, Derło (age 50). Ignacy, son of Daniel and Akacja Franczuk, had seven children by his wife, Helena.

Hawryluk, Maksym (Maximilian), married farmer in Derło, b. May 22, 1840, Rolnik. Maksym and his wife, Dominika, had three children. He died at home of a wound in his stomach.

Hryciuk, Anicet, unmarried layman, b. 1855, Zaczopki. Anicet, the only son of Józef and Julianna Hryciuk, was shot in the head.

Łukaszuk, Konstanty (Constantine), married farmer, b. *c.* 1829, Zaczopki. Konstanty, husband of Irene and father of seven children, was pierced with a bayonet in the cemetery.

Karmasz, Daniel, married, layman; b. 1826, Odznaczał. He was the uneducated farmer from Legi who encouraged others to defend the church against the Cossacks and was shot holding the Cross in his hand.

Kiryluk, Filip (Philip), married farmer, b. 1830, Zaczopki. Shot.

Lewoniuk, Wincenty (Vincent), married layman; b. 1849, Krzyczewie. Vincent, husband of Marianna, was persecuted for supporting the Union of Brest. During the defense of Pratulin's church, he was shot to death.

Osypiuk, Bartołomiej (Bartholomew), married farmer; b. 1844, Bohukały. Son of Wasyla Osypiuk and Marty Kondraciuk; had two children of his own. He guarded the church, was wounded, and died at home praying for the pardon of his attackers.

Wasyluk, Onufry (Humphrey), married layman, village administrator; b. 1853, Zaczopki. Onufry's parents paid 800 rubles to the Russians to keep their son out of the army. He was shot in the head during the defense of the church.

Wawryszuk, Michał, layman, b. 1853, Derło. Michał had only recently been married in Olszyna before his martyrdom.

At their beatification Pope John Paul II declared: ''The martyrs of Pratulin defended not only the parish church in front of which they were killed, but the Church that Christ entrusted to the Apostle Peter, the Church which they felt a part of, like living stones.''

Feast: Jan. 24

Bibliography: K. DEBSKI, *Bohaterstwo unitów podlaskich* Warsaw 1993). J. HAWRYLUK, *Z dziejów Cerkwi Prawoslawnej na Podlasiu w X-XVII wieku* (Bielsk Podlaski 1993). T. KRAWCZAK, *Zanim wrócila Polska* (Warsaw 1994). R. SOSZYNSKI, *400-lecie Unii Brzeskiej, 1596–1996* (Warsaw 1996). *Acta Apostolicae Sedis* (1996): 999.

[K. I. RABENSTEIN]

PRAXIS

A transliteration of the Greek word, *praxis* is a noun of action that implies doing, acting, and practice. According to Aristotle there are three ways of knowing that he designates as *theoria, praxis,* and *poiesis,* roughly corresponding to three kinds of living that we might call the contemplative (philosophical) life, the practical (public) life, and the productive (creative) life. In the Aristotelian framework, praxis is directed to the right ordering of human behavior in the sociopolitical world. The term appears in medieval Latin (Albertus Magnus, *Meta.* 5.5.2; and John Duns Scotus, *Ord.,* prologus, 5.6), but it is only in the 19th century with G. W. F. Hegel and Karl Marx that the technical concept of praxis returns to the center of the philosophical debate and begins to influence theology.

The term has become commonplace and, according to many, the issue of praxis is *the* key question in contemporary theology. In spite of widespread use, however, it is not always clear what authors intend when they use the term ''praxis.'' The reason for this lack of clarity is that a plurality of philosophical backgrounds has been brought to bear on the theological usage of this term: ARISTOTLE, MARX, the FRANKFURT SCHOOL of Critical Theory, Paolo Freire, and Habermas. The purpose of this article is to shed some light on the different theological usages of this term and to indicate briefly the challenge they pose for the future of theology.

Liberation Theology. By far the most common use of the term ''praxis'' is to be found in Latin American LIBERATION THEOLOGY. In this regard it should be remembered that what is truly significant about liberation theology is not so much its content as its method. Within the method of liberation theology praxis plays a central role.

According to G. Gutierrez, theology is ''a critical reflection on Christian praxis in the light of the word.'' As such, theology is ''a second step'' coming after the praxis of involvement with the liberation of those who are oppressed in the world. The point of departure, therefore, for liberation theology is the existence of a prior commitment to the cause of the poor in the world today. The source of this commitment is humanity's intuitive awareness that there is something intrinsically wrong with ''the myth of things as they are.'' There is an instinctive consciousness abroad that the existence of so much poverty in the world is contrary to the fundamental solidarity of the human race; and that the dangerous divisions throughout the globe go against the grain of creation and human nature. Liberation theology reflects critically on this underlying commitment to liberation, seeking to make it more complete, and highlighting its connection with the gospel of Christ. In particular, liberation theology shows how liberation is an important step on the way to the gift of SALVATION.

A number of points should be noted here concerning the use of the word "praxis" in liberation theology. First of all, praxis is about that particular human activity that is directed toward the transformation of the conditions and causes of poverty. Further, this activity, once initiated, is guided and governed by a process of critical interaction with the gospel of Christ. Thirdly, the relationship between action and reflection, between theory and practice, is dialectical in liberation theology. Lastly, the experience of actually changing structures in the world is regarded as an important source of new knowledge that enables liberation to talk about the existence of an "epistemological break" within its praxis method. In brief, the praxis of liberation theology is intuitive and reflective, transformative, dialectical, and epistemologically significant.

While it is true that the importance of praxis in liberation theology has been the subject of much discussion, by and large it has won overall acceptance by the theological community. One example of this discussion can be found in the 1984 *Instruction on Certain Aspects of the "Theology of Liberation"* issued by the Congregation for the Doctrine of the Faith, which has both negative and positive comments to make about the place of praxis in theology. In that document the association of praxis with "the class struggle" and its identification with "partisan praxis" is seriously called into question (8.25). While this particular understanding of praxis may belong to some isolated instances of liberation theology, it can hardly be said to represent the mainstream of liberation theologies.

The praxis of liberation theology is not intended to promote the class struggle as an end in itself nor is it solely a partisan praxis. Instead the praxis of liberation theology is ultimately inspired by a radical commitment to justice for all animated by the great commandment of love and its gospel imperatives. Having criticized that form of praxis which promotes the class struggle, the 1984 *Instruction* went on to make two positive observations on praxis. It pointed out that a "healthy theological method no doubt will always take the praxis of the Church into account and will find there one of its foundations" (8.3). Further, the 1984 *Instruction* suggests "it is necessary to affirm that one becomes more aware of certain aspects of faith by starting with praxis, if by that one means pastoral praxis and social work which keeps its evangelical inspiration" (11.13).

Primacy of Method. The philosophical background to the primacy of praxis within liberation theology is, loosely speaking, Marx and Freire. This does not mean that liberation theology takes its primary inspiration from Marx or indeed that it identifies with his basic philosophy. Rather, liberation theology is only partially influenced by Marx. One area of this partial influence is Marx's Eleventh Thesis on Feuerbach: "Philosophers have only interpreted the world; the point is to change it." Equally, liberation theology is partially influenced by Freire who brings out the importance of reflective action for the conscientization of people to the possibility of determining their own destiny, of changing the given structures of oppression within society, and of moving beyond an understanding of knowledge as merely the transfer of information.

A similar emphasis on the place of praxis can be found in the POLITICAL THEOLOGY of Johann B. Metz. According to Metz, contemporary theology is undergoing a transition from a transcendentalist-idealist paradigm to (RAHNER and LONERGAN) a postidealist paradigm. Within this new postmodern situation the primary focus of attention is given to the dialectical relationship that can and should exist between theory and practice within Christianity. What is ultimately important for Metz is a practical discipleship of Christ. Within this paradigm shift, Metz acknowledges the power and influence of liberation theology on the rest of theology.

Likewise, much of FEMINIST THEOLOGY today shares with liberation theology a similar emphasis on the centrality of praxis. Feminist theology operates out of a prior commitment to the liberation of women from the constraints of patriarchy. The experience of women, like the experience of the poor in liberation theology, is a crucial category within the construction of feminist theology. The methodology of feminist theology is very close to the methodology of liberation theology—both emphasize praxis as the basic point of departure for the interpretation of the gospel.

What is common to liberation theology, political theology, and feminist theology is the presence of a strong emphasis on the primacy of praxis in the method of theology. This unified focus on praxis is inspired by a common reaction against a purely theoretical, essentialist, and universalist understanding of Christian faith. In particular, there is an emerging consensus within these three theologies that something is intrinsically wrong with the way society is structured and that the world as we experience it today is amenable to a radical process of making, unmaking, and remaking. The key to bringing about change in the world from the way it is to the way it might be is this new focus on the primacy of praxis within theory.

This does not mean that these three theologies naively think that there is ready to hand some social and political blueprint for the resolution of the problems facing humanity today. This charge, often made against these theologies, misreads the meaning of the primacy of praxis within theory. Instead, these theologies consistently emphasize the importance of social and cultural analysis of the circumstances surrounding the existing praxis as well as the need for a critical reflection on this praxis in the light of faith before any movement toward a new and liberating praxis can be effected.

Hermeneutical Theology. Alongside these developments there has also been the rung to HERMENEUTICS within European and North American theology. First World theology has witnessed a recovery of theology as a complex exercise embracing understanding, interpretation, and application—not as separate and independent activities but as internally related moments. Hermeneutical theology is not simply about putting forward new, theoretical interpretations of Christianity derived from interplay between the text and the interpreter, or human experience and the Christian tradition. Instead, hermeneutical theology also includes a critical reference to the praxis of the faith and as such intends to influence that praxis. To this extent hermeneutical theology also claims to embrace a turn to praxis within the process of interpretation.

The philosophical impulses behind this recovery of hermeneutics within theology are manifold. They include in a particular way the influences of Martin HEIDEGGER and GADAMER. For Heidegger the act of human understanding is not simply about the discovery of knowledge pure and simple; rather, human understanding is a self-involving existential act that affects the individual's mode of being and becoming in the world. In a similar but by no means identical way, the human act of understanding for Gadamer (who was influenced by Aristotle), involves practical reason in its application to particular social and political issues.

These philosophical influences can be found in the pioneering hermeneutical theology of David Tracy and Claude Geffré. Both of these theologians and others bring together hermeneutics and praxis in their understanding of the task of theology. Both claim that a Christian interpretation of text must also include reference to the contemporary praxis of the faith. As Tracy puts it, ''without some *applicatio,* there is no real hermeneutical *intelligentia* or *explicatio.* In that sense the contemporary hermeneutical concern with praxis is entirely correct'' (*Plurality,* 101). Going a step further, Geffré claims that Christian praxis is ''both a place of production of the meaning of Christianity and the place of the verification of that message'' (*The Risk,* 19).

Hermeneutics and Liberation. At this stage it should be quite clear that the word ''praxis'' is prominent in all the above forms of theology and that the language of praxis is by no means alien or unacceptable to the language of the magisterium of the Church as expressed through the teaching of the Congregation for the Doctrine of the Faith. What is not quite so clear is the particular meaning and direction of this common usage of the word ''praxis'' in First World and Third World theologies. This ambiguity derives ultimately from a difference of political ideology and social location concerning the context within which these theologies take place.

For one thing, the point of departure of hermeneutical theology and liberation theology seems to be quite distinct. Hermeneutical theology is primarily concerned with the interpretation of the text and the effect that this can have on the consciousness of the interpreter. This kind of praxis might be called individual noetic praxis. Liberation theology on the other hand is primarily concerned with the praxis taking place on the ground and the effect this has on the historical lives of people. This latter type of praxis can be described strictly speaking as social praxis. To this extent the impression is given that hermeneutical theology sets out to provide ''a theory for practice'' while liberation theology operates out of ''a theory of praxis'' i.e., the recognition of praxis as an important source of human understanding. Thus hermeneutical theology accords primacy to theory whereas liberation theology gives primacy to praxis insofar as theory follows praxis and reflects upon praxis. In other words, hermeneutical theology tends to relate theory to praxis via the principle of application. Within application to the relationship of theory to praxis, however unintentionally, tends to be extrinsic. On the other hand liberation theology sees that relationship between praxis and theory as one in which these two dimensions are constitutive of each other. According to the principle of constitution, the relationship between theory and praxis is intrinsic.

A second difference between hermeneutical theology and liberation theology concerns the particular pre-understanding out of which each operates. The pre-understanding of hermeneutical theology appears by and large to belong to that of the liberal human autonomy. On the other hand, the pre-understanding of liberation theology goes beyond liberalism to focus on the individual as bound to the community, highlighting the importance of social responsibility and structural change. Consequently, while hermeneutical theology calls for the fusion of horizons between text and interpreter and the transformation of the understanding of the interpreter, liberation theology demands a transformation of structures as a matter of justice.

Lying behind these two different emphases in hermeneutical theology and liberation theology is the presence of two distinct perceptions of society: a functionalist versus a dialectical understanding of society. By and large, hermeneutical theology sees society in functional and organic terms. Within the functionalist approach to society the principal emphasis is placed on maintaining order and harmony; changes are effected from within the given structures of society. On the other hand, according to liberation theology, society is seen as conflictual and dialectical. Within this dialectical understanding of society attention is placed on the importance of struggling against the social contradictions and injustices of the world; changes require a transformation of given structures; what is needed is a new recipe for the structuring of society and not simply an alteration of the ingredients.

A third difference between hermeneutical theology and liberation theology concerns the complex area of human understanding. For hermeneutical theology the risk of interpretation vis-à-vis the text is the source of human understanding generating new theory, whereas in liberation theology the risk of interpretation vis-à-vis praxis is the source of human understanding, generating new praxis. In both instances theory, however explicit or implicit, plays an important role. In hermeneutical theology theory animates new theory, initially inchoate and subsequently explicit, animates new praxis.

It would be a serious misrepresentation of both hermeneutical theology and liberation theology to reduce their differences simply to that of the former being concerned with the purely theoretical and the latter being concerned with the purely practical. This, not uncommon, misrepresentation is based on the illusion that there is such a thing as pure, nonhistorical theory and pure transhistorical praxis. The theoretical self-understanding of hermeneutical theology is colored by personal experience and social location. Likewise, the self-understanding of the praxis of liberation theology is influenced by some form of background interpretation and understanding, no matter how implicit or explicit this may be. Given this view of things it would be a great mistake to polarize the contributions of hermeneutical theology and liberation theology.

Hermeneutics and Praxis in Dialogue. Instead, the challenge facing theology today is to allow the developments of hermeneutical theology and liberation theology to critically complement each other. There is no reason why the interplay between text and interpretation cannot be brought to bear more explicitly on the interpretation of the contemporary praxis of faith. The dialogue between the present and the past in hermeneutics must begin to include explicit reference to the contemporary praxis of faith. Equally there is no reason why the contemporary praxis of faith cannot be allowed to interrupt constructively the conversation between the text and the interpreter. Is not this exactly what the praxis of the poor and the praxis of women has done with extraordinary result in liberation theology and feminist theology? If this interaction between hermeneutics and praxis could begin to take place, then the way might be opened for tackling one of the most intractable problems facing Christianity today, namely the existence of so much theory without praxis and of so much praxis without theory.

A second area within this conversation between hermeneutics and praxis that might be addressed concerns the mediation of the universal and the particular. Critical attention to the particular questions of praxis discloses the hazardous and ambiguous character of universalist Christian answers. In so many instances, especially relating to questions of justice, universal answers simply are not available or do not work on the basis of the application simply of theory to praxis. An explicit recognition of this limitation of the universal message of Christianity was made by Pope Paul VI in his Apostolic letter, *Octegesima adveniens,* where he points out: ''In the face of such widely varying situations it is difficult for us to utter a unified message and to put forward a solution which has universal validity. Such is not our ambition, nor is it our mission'' (a. 4). Similar recognition of the limitations of universal Christian claims was made by the Congregation for the Doctrine of the Faith in its 1986 *Instruction on Christian Freedom and Liberation* (*see* a. 2 and a. 72). Once this is admitted then it becomes clear, as the 1986 *Instruction* points out, that the teaching of the Church and the gospel message is far from being a closed system but is rather open to new questions that continually arise requiring the contributions of all charisms, experiences, and skills (1.72). An acknowledgment of this situation challenges theology to look in places other than texts and traditions for new light on the particularity of questions relating to justice. One such place must surely be praxis of liberation and its ability to shape new theory in and through the fragile experience of transforming structures.

A third area of mutual concern to hermeneutics and praxis is the whole concept of Christian TRUTH. Both hermeneutics and praxis are agreed on the need to go beyond a classical understanding of truth as some kind of correspondence or conformity between the mind and reality. Christian truth is more than an *adequatio intellectus et rei.* In this regard liberation theology is quick to point toward the contradictions and distortions that exist within social and political reality. For liberation theology truth is to be found not by conforming to the distorted social structures of reality but by engaging in the praxis of transforming these structures. According to liberation theology the individual as knower must be complemented by the individual and the community as agent of a transformative praxis. It is this focus on the importance of ''knowing by doing'' that prompts liberation theology to talk about an epistemological break.

This epistemological break, however, must be tempered by the call of hermeneutical theology to dialogue with the existing tradition. In making a case for dialogue with the past, hermeneutical theology warns against reifying the tradition, setting it up as something that simply exists in an nonhistorical vacuum. Tradition must always be interpreted in the context of the interpreter's historicity. The dynamics of dialogue with tradition in hermeneutical theology and the praxis of a solidarity with and for the poor in liberation theology provide complementary approaches to the question of truth. The truth that Christian theology seeks is something that is both revealed and concealed, both historically given within the tradition and eschatologically promised in the future.

A final area in which hermeneutics and praxis might enrich each other concerns the dialectical relationship that exists between praxis and theory. Accepting that there is a dialectical relationship between praxis and theory, and that praxis has an important epistemological contribution to make to theory, the question arises: what particular norms and criteria should guide this dialectical relationship must be guided by the basic principles of hermeneutics and praxis as outlined above, namely that of a dialogue between the particular praxis of Christian faith and horizons of contemporary understanding as retrieved from within the Christian tradition (theory) as well as the existence of a fundamental solidarity with and for those who are the weakest members of society.

These principles of hermeneutics and praxis in turn must continually be informed by explicit reference to the life, death, and Resurrection of Jesus. In the life of Jesus there is a dialectical relationship between praxis and theory, between words and deeds, between action and reflection. The vision of Jesus that dialectically embraces a radical praxis is contained in His parables about the coming Reign of God, in His teaching on the Beatitudes and the great commandment of love, and in the story about the final judgment scene in Matthew 25. Equally the praxis of Jesus that dialectically inspired this vision is illustrated in terms of healings, exorcisms, forgiveness, table fellowship and the presence of love in action unto the end. As *Dei Verbum* points out, ''Jesus perfected revelation by fulfilling it through His whole work of making Himself present and manifesting himself: through His words and deeds. His signs and wonders, but especially through His death and glorious Resurrection form the dead and final sending of the Spirit of truth. Moreover, He confirmed with the divine testimony what revelation proclaimed: that God is with us to free us from the darkness of sin and death, and to raise us up to eternal life'' (a. 4). In the end a Christian theology of hermeneutics and praxis must be guided and controlled by the vision and praxis of Jesus and the ongoing presence of His Spirit among us today.

Bibliography: M. LAMB, *Solidarity with Victims* (New York 1982). D. LANE, *Foundations for a Social Theology: Praxis, Process and Salvation* (New York 1984). C. BOFF, *Theology and Praxis: Epistemological Foundations* (New York 1987); *Theology and Praxis* (New York 1987) 57. G. GUTIERREZ, *A Theology of Liberation* (New York 1975) 13; ''Liberation Praxis and Christian Faith,'' *The Power of the Poor in History* (New York 1983). N. LOBKOWICZ, *Theory and Practice: History of a Concept from Aristotle to Marx* (Notre Dame, Ind. 1967). J. SOBRINO, *The True Church and the Poor* (New York 1984). J. B. METZ, ''Political Theology: A New Paradigm of Theology,'' *Civil Religion and Political Theology,* ed. L. S. ROUNDER (Indiana 1986). D. TRACY, *The Analogical Imagination* (New York 1981); *Plurality and Ambiguity* (New York 1987). C. GEFFRÉ, *The Risk of Interpretation* (New York 1987). W. JEANROD, ''Hermeneutics and Christian *Praxis,* Literature and Theology,'' v. 2 (1988).

[D. A. LANE]

PRAYER

Prayer, a universal phenomenon of religion, has passed through a long history in the development of mankind.

PRIMITIVE PRAYER

Primitive prayer is a rather complex phenomenon. It is treated here under its more significant aspects.

Definition. In its primal and elemental form it may be defined as an act of cult by which man enters into communion with a higher, superhuman, supersensuous being, somehow conceived as personal and experienced as real and present, upon whose power he feels himself dependent. In the world of primitive man there exist a great number of living things and inanimate objects that impress him as mysterious, charged with a preternatural dynamic energy producing effects beyond the ordinary limits of natural processes. In approaching them he treats them with reverential awe, but he does not pray to them. Because they are impersonal, there is no way of his coming into personal relations with them. In order to have prayer, more is required than just the presence of some supernatural, superhuman power. This power must be borne by a personal being capable of governing it by an act of will.

The objects of primitive man's prayer, therefore, are always personal supersensuous beings who possess superhuman power and make him feel this power. Moreover, because of the anthropomorphic conception primitive man has of them, they acquire the features of

A young boy watches adults as they perform the noon prayer at a mosque in Bandar Seri, Begawan, Brunei. (©Michael S. Yamashita/ CORBIS)

a human person. Hence, his way of dealing with them quite naturally takes the forms of the relations of human social life. Since speech, gesture, and countenance are the means of communication with his fellow man, it is by these means, also, that primitive man explains to the higher being he invokes all that moves his soul. His prayer is a communication between an "I" and a "thou," whether it is verbal or remains unspoken, whether it finds no outward expression at all or is expressed by gestures only, whether it is offered by an individual or performed collectively by a group, whether it is a free spontaneous creation of the moment or a fixed, stereotyped prayer formula.

Primitive Prayer and Magic Formula. Though primitive prayer and magic formula contain some common elements, such as the belief in the transcendent and a certain awe toward the beings or forces invoked, they differ in one essential point. While in prayer man tries by persuasion to move a higher being to gratify his wishes, the reciter of a magic formula attempts to constrain that being or to force the effect to his own ends by the very words of his formula, to which he ascribes an unfailing, immanent power. In the first instance the answer to man's invocation lies within the will of the higher being, in the second the binding of the higher being effected by the formula is considered to be absolute, automatically producing the result desired. In many ritual acts, it is true, the two attitudes exist side by side and often blend one into the other so completely that it is difficult, if not impossible, to decide which of the two attitudes is present or dominant. It is also true that of the two attitudes the one taken by the reciter of a magic formula is cruder. But this does not warrant the conclusion that the magic formula is older than prayer and that the latter grew out of the former. No factual evidence for the priority of the magic formula is adducible.

Motives and Content. The prayer of primitive man arises from concrete environmental needs in which the vital interests, either of the individual or the community, are at stake, and it is directed toward definite, material objectives. Longing for delivery from his predicament, primitive man turns to higher, mightier beings. To make them yield to his desires, he uses every means of persuasion: praise, flattery, allurement, manifestation of gratitude, complaint, self-commendation, apology, self-accusation, lament. If all these verbal artifices are of no avail, he does not shrink from reproaching or reprimanding the mightier beings, or even resorting to insults and threats.

To the various motives urging primitive man to pray correspond certain types of prayer. The commonest type is the petitionary prayer, which, in accordance with primitive man's childlike selfishness, is concerned almost exclusively with his own material well-being. Reflecting the conception of prayer as a give-and-take relationship between man and the higher being invoked, prayers of this type are often strengthened by vows or by sacrifices. Some primitive prayers contain, in place of a petition in the strict sense, an emotional complaint, man either simply pouring out his need and misery before a divinity, or quarreling with the deity, indignantly questioning its power, and even reprimanding and insulting it, because his previous prayers have remained unanswered. The same naïveté manifests itself in primitive man's prayers of cursing and vengeance, in his passionate appeals to higher beings for the destruction of enemies and evildoers. On the other hand, primitive man is not devoid of social feelings. The intercessory prayer for living and dead members, either of the family or the tribal community, has a surprisingly prominent place in primitive devotion. The same is true concerning the prayer of thanksgiving. Though many primitive peoples possess no special word for "thanks," they actually give thanks either by an offering or by simply acknowledging the bestowal of a gift by a benevolent deity.

Form, Prayer Formula, Sacred Language. Primitive prayer has a very simple form, consisting of two parts, the address and the prayer itself. The first word uttered in the invocation is usually the proper name of the divine being. In this way the attention of the deity, who may be either at some distance or not listening, is called to the presence of the worshipper. Sometimes a loud cry or a long, drawn-out whistle precedes the deity's name, or some such word as "Hear!" is added to it. Ordinarily, the worshipper is not satisfied with simply mentioning the name of the deity. He feels it necessary to add one or more epithets to pay tribute to the deity from whom he hopes to obtain a favorable hearing. Often he also ceremoniously apologizes, begging for only a moment's attention. This does not prevent him, however, from becoming verbose in the prayer proper, whose main theme he likes to repeat over and over with now slight and now more elaborate variations.

Primitive man appeals to higher beings not only in moments of distress. He brings to them also his permanent needs, concerns, and wishes. Thus, besides the extraordinary occasions of prayer, there are regular, customary ones suggested by such phenomena as sunrise and sunset, the changes of the phases of the moon, and the alternations of the seasons. Because of the frequent recurrence of these occasions and their connection with ritual acts, the prayer loses its originally flexible, elastic outline, tends to become more rigid in the arrangement of thoughts and their wording, and finally hardens into fixed formulas whose words are chosen with the utmost care to obviate any displeasure on the part of the divinities invoked. Deities whose power is especially feared are generally referred to by affectionate and flattering names that emphasize their beneficent character and veil the darker side of their nature with conciliatory euphemism. As a result, there arises a particular prayer language, marked by great solemnity, wholly ritual in character, and regarded as sacred.

PRAYER IN THE GREAT ANCIENT RELIGIONS

In the ancient Chinese, Vedic, Babylonian, Egyptian, Homeric and old Roman religions, prayer in general retains the peculiar qualities of primitive prayer. It is essentially eudaemonistic, that is, directed toward the attainment of material blessings. The feeling for ethical values is seldom powerful enough to serve as a motive of prayer. The prayer of the Chinese religion is characterized by ceremonial stiffness, that of the Roman religion by legal formalism. In the Vedic-Brahmanic religion prayer is the business of the priestly caste. In possession of a comprehensive collection of prayer formulas, the priests alone know "the right art of prayer."

On the other hand, of the numerous Egyptian and Greek prayer hymns that have been preserved, many not only show a high degree of artistic perfection, but they also contain a lofty conception of the Deity and promote the tendency toward monotheism. The vitality and personal character of the Greek religion keep prayer from stiffening into a ritualistic formula and enable it to rise to ever higher moral purity. Prayer finds its most sublime expression in the petition of Socrates for "inward beauty." By excluding eudaemonism from piety and purifying the conception of the divine from all anthropomorphic features, Greek philosophy creates a new ethico-religious ideal of prayer. It is the product of rational and ethical criticism. Its content is threefold: petition for moral blessings, perfect surrender to the eternal decrees of fate, adoration and praise of divine greatness.

In Mystic Religions of Redemption. The mystic religions of redemption arrive at a spiritualization of the prayer by another route. Mystical prayer tends to pass from prayer in words, either uttered aloud or inwardly framed, to wordless prayer, to meditative absorption in the spiritual or metaphysical. It may be called a state of prayer rather than an act of prayer. In the various ramifications of Indian mysticism the prayer is largely replaced by silent contemplation that, gradually perfected by the means of the Yoga exercises (correct sitting posture, control of the process of breathing, withdrawal of the senses from the external world, calm and concentration), aims at the liberation of the soul from the mechanism of the forces of life and its final absorption in the Absolute (*see* YOGA). In the Neoplatonic religion of redemption, the most sublime manifestation of Hellenistic mysticism, contemplative prayer leads the mystic, in an ascent of the soul in successive steps, from the transitory world to a union with the One, the imperishable foundation of all existence.

In the Prophetic Religions. In the Pentateuch and in the Gāthas of the Avesta, which reflect the prophetic experiences of Moses and Zarathustra (Gr. Zoroaster), respectively, prayer appears as the spontaneous, personal communion with the Godhead, in which the harassing emotions of fear and doubt are first overcome by the feelings of hope and trust, and finally replaced by the blissful certainty of being cared for by the infinite goodness of an all-wise, omnipotent God.

The same spirit of prayer is alive in the Psalms of the Old Testament, which often begin with a troubled question and a moving lament, and then shift to heartfelt outpouring of trust, joy, praise, and thanksgiving; it is present also in the entreaties of the prophets who intercede with Yahweh for faithless, wayward Israel. With the Babylonian captivity and the end of the old sacrificial cult there arises a purely spiritual congregational worship in which the psalter becomes the prayer book of the exiled Jewish community. The religious vitality of the Jewish people, strengthened by a succession of highly gifted mystics, has protected Jewish prayer from petrification.

The development in the Iranian religion is different. With later Zoroastrianism hardening into a constricted, legalist religion, spontaneous devotional intercourse gives way to regular recitation of ethical prayer formulas, a practice considered as the performance of a duty imposed by divine law and a meritorious work.

A similar development takes place in Islamic prayer. While the prayer life of Muḥammad and his disciples is, in its spontaneity, akin to that of the Old Testament prophets, and the devotional piety in the Ṣûfistic mysticism of Islam shows personal warmth and fervor, the daily obligatory prayers and the liturgical prayers recited on Fridays and holidays in the mosque become ritually fixed in wording and gesture.

See Also: PRAYER (IN THE BIBLE); PRAYER (THEOLOGY OF).

Bibliography: E. N. FALLAIZE et al., J. HASTINGS, ed. *Encyclopedia of Religion and Ethics,* 13 v. (Edinburgh 1908–27) 10:154–205. B. THUM et al., *Lexikon für Theologie und Kirche,* ed. J. HOFER and K. RAHNER, 10 v. (2d, new ed. Freiburg 1957–65) 4:537–540, prayer in the general history of man and in the OT. F. HEILER et al., *Die Religion in Geschichte und Gegenwart,* 7 v. (3d ed. Tübingen 1957–65) 2:1209–18, prayer in the general history of man, in the OT, and in Judaism. F. HEILER, *Prayer,* tr. and ed. S. MCCOMB and J. E. PARK (New York 1958). T. OHM, *Die Gebetsgebärden der Völker und das Christentum* (Leiden 1948). G. VAN DER LEEUW, *Religion in Essence and Manifestation: A Study in Phenomonology,* tr. J. E. TURNER (London 1938) 422–429 (par. 62), 519–526 (par. 78.2). E. CONZO, *Buddhist Meditation* (London 1956). J. B. PRITCHARD, *Ancient Near Eastern Texts Relating to the Old Testament* (2d, rev. ed. Princeton 1955) (Egyptian) 365–381; (Akkadian) 383–392; (Hittite) 393–401. H. SCHMIDT, *Veteres philosophi quomodo iudicaverint de precibus* (Giessen 1907). G. APPEL, *De Romanorum precationibus* (*ibid.* 7.2; Giessen 1909).

[R. ARBESMANN]

PRAYER (IN THE BIBLE)

There is no one definition of prayer that will completely cover all references to it in the Bible. Prayer is often described in terms of intercourse and spiritual communion with God, with or without the mediation of priests or heavenly beings; it is usually, but not necessarily, vocal. By it the petitioner's will and activities are identified with God, effecting an intimate personal contact and relationship with Him.

In the Old Testament. The most common Hebrew verb meaning to pray or intercede is *hitpallēl;* from it is derived the noun *t^epillâ* (prayer), which is often used in the Psalm titles. Several other Hebrew terms also are used in the sense of praying, e.g., *qārā'* (to call), *hitḥannēn* (to seek favor), *ṣā'aq* (to cry aloud), and *šāpak nepeš* (to pour out one's soul).

Prayer as expressed in the Old Testament was founded upon the realization of the Israelites that Yahweh was present in their midst and acting in their behalf; His personal presence invited their response [Ps 17(18).7; 139(140).7–10; 1 Kgs 8.23–58]. The response on their part was the fruit of abiding confidence (*see* FAITH, 1) that God would hear and answer their prayer, because He had revealed His covenanted love [*see* LOVE (IN THE BIBLE)] for them and was powerful to help them. Later, as they came to realize Yahweh's constant active intervention in their behalf, they saw Him as creator and sustainer of the universe, and this idea, too, was frequently expressed in prayer [e.g., Ps 103 (104)].

The prayer of the Israelite was always deeply rooted in confidence in Yahweh's response [Ps 24(25).1–4; 27(28).6–7; 45(46); 90(91)]; a confidence so firm that accompanying expressions of thanksgiving appeared even in anticipation of the reception of favors they had petitioned [Ps 13(14); 22(23); 26(27); etc.]. Yet on occasion a certain anxiety about prayers' not being answered introduced a note of pleading, challenging, and even wrestling with Yahweh, as in Jeremiah and Job.

Spiritual blessings and, more frequently, temporal prosperity were the objects of Israelite prayer [Ps 16(17); 32(33); 53(54); 87(88)]. They petitioned life in the full sense: good health, long life, prosperity, rich progeny, the happiness of seeing fellow Israelites flourish, and the joy of participating in the worship of Yahweh [Ps 38(39); 41(42); 83 (84); 125 (126); Tb 8.10; 1 Sm 1.10–11]. Spiritual values of the highest order came to be embraced in their petitions. They desired to share in the praise of Yahweh and pleaded for the preservation of true religion, associated always, however, with the idea of triumphant vindication of Yahweh's own nation and the punishment of its enemies [Jgs 13.6–9; Ps 3; 10(11); Jer 17.14–18]. Their prayer involved intercession for others: for the king, for the country in which they were exiled, for their brethren in the faith, and in the latest period of their history, for those who had departed this life (1 Mc 12.11; 2 Mc 12.44).

Three types of prayer are evident: petition, thanksgiving, and those of a penitential character. Those of petition stated not only what was desired, but also frequently the reasons for the request (e.g., Jgs 16.28). Occasionally such prayers were lengthened by the adding of a summary of favors previously granted and often became so verbose in expressing the praise of Yahweh for earlier favors that they developed into a review of Israelite history [2 Chr 20.6–12; 1 Kgs 3.6–9; Ps 102(103)]. Penitential prayers, requesting forgiveness of sin and remission of punishment following a simple confession of guilt, were sometimes joined to a plea for deliverance from threatening danger and a promise of amendment (Jgs 10.10, 15; 1 Sm 12.10; Est 9.6–15; Dn 9.4–19). Prayers of thanksgiving for blessings received usually included an admission of man's unworthiness to receive divine favors [2 Sm 7.19–29; Ps 12(13).6; 21(22).26].

Some fixed formulas of prayer for certain occasions are found in the Old Testament. The priestly blessing (Nm 6.24) and the words said in offering the first fruits (Dt 26.3, 5–10) and tithes (Dt 26.13–15) are examples of early liturgical prayer formulas. Later, certain passages from Scripture were used as fixed types of prayer, e.g., the confession of faith known as the Shema (Dt 6.4–9; 11.13–21; Nm 15.37–41) and the Hallel [Ps 112(113)–117(118)].

Prayer was not limited to the place of public worship, however, but was offered anywhere; it accompanied sacrifice [Ps 21(22).26; 53(54).8; 115(116B).8; Jn 2.10] and the making of vows [1 Sm 1.11; Ps 64 (65)]. A quiet room in the home with a window facing Jerusalem was a favorite place for family prayer (Tb 3.11; Dn 6.11; 1 Kgs 8.38; 2 Chr 6.34). Prayer was often communal (Jl 2.15–17; Jdt 4.7–9; Jgs 10.10;20.26–28). The Book of Psalms constitutes the inexhaustible source of relevant expressions for communication with God for all ages, places, persons, and conditions of earthly existence.

In the New Testament. The ordinary Greek terms used in the New Testament in regard to praying are προσεύχομαι (to pray) and προσευχή (prayer); several synonyms for praying, such as αἰτέω (to ask) and ἐντυγχάνω (to intercede), are used occasionally.

The Gospels often describe Christ in prayer (Lk 3.21; 5.16; 9.29; 10.21; 11.1; 22.32); He prayed, publicly as well as privately, before important acts and decisions (Lk 3.31; Mt 14.23; Heb 5.7). However, in virtue of His special relationship with the Father, He is presented as living in continuous prayer (Jn 1.51; 4.34; 8.29; 11.41). He taught His disciples to pray, giving them the sublime form expressed in the LORD'S PRAYER; yet, as is evident from its two variant recorded forms (Mt 6.9–13; Lk 11.2–4), He did not teach strict adherence to the formula, but to its spirit, ''In this manner you shall pray. . . .''

The new relationship by which Christians come to the Father through Christ, that of adoptive sonship, forms the basis of prayer in the New Testament. A joyful awareness of this relationship evokes a deepened childlike loving confidence and tender intimacy whereby Christians come to pray to God with ''unutterable sighs'' of the Spirit (Rom 8.15, 26; Gal 4.6). The requisites for prayer are explicitly set forth: unshakable confidence born of faith (Mt 11.24; Lk 17.5; Jas 1.5); perseverance with urgent insistence (Mt 7.7–1; 15.21; Lk 11.1–13; 18.1–8; Eph 6.18; 1 Thes 5.17); absolute inner sincerity, as opposed to the hypocritical externalism of the Pharisee (Mt 6.5–8); humility; and the loving fulfillment of God's commandments. Where prayer fulfills these conditions, its efficacy is unlimited (Mk 11.24). Particular efficacy is ascribed to communal prayer of the Christian community (Mt 18.10; 1 Tm 2.1–2).

The Acts and Epistles show that the prayers of the early Christians were dominated by interests of the kingdom of God and spiritual values (Acts 4.29; 16.25; Rom 15.30; 2 Cor 2.11; Eph 6.19). Objects of prayerful intercession included not only fellow Christians, but all men, especially those in authority (1 Tm 2.1) and even enemies and persecutors (Mt 6.44; Lk 6.28).

Usually in the New Testament, all prayer, private as well as public liturgical prayer, is addressed to God the Father through Christ. Yet, occasionally, prayer is directed to Christ as Lord (Jn 14.14; Acts 7.59; Rom 10.12; 1 Cor 1.2; 2 Cor 12.8; 1 Tm 1.12). The various doxologies and hymns of adoration and praise form a veritable treasure house of prayer formulas (Rom 9.5; 11.36; 2 Cor 11.31; 16.27; 1 Pt 4.11; etc.).

Bibliography: *Encyclopedic Dictionary of the Bible*, tr. and adap. by L. HARTMAN (New York 1963), from A. VAN DEN BORN, *Bijbels Woordenboek* 1892–1901. W. HILLMANN, *Lexikon für Theologie und Kirche*, ed. J. HOFER and K. RAHNER, 10 v. (2d, new ed. Freiburg 1957–65) 4:537–42. C. WESTERMANN and O. BAUERNFEIND, *Die Religion in Geschichte und Gegenwart*, 7 v. (3d ed. Tübingen 1957–65) 2:1213–21. D. R. AP-THOMAS, "Notes on Some Terms Relating to Prayer," *Vetus Testamentum* 6 (1956) 225–41. L. BOUYER, "Les Psaumes, prière du peuple de Dieu," *La Bible et l'évangile* (Paris 1951) 227–44. J. DE FRAINE, *Praying with the Bible*, tr. J. W. SAUL (New York 1964).

[M. R. E. MASTERMAN]

PRAYER (THEOLOGY OF)

Prayer in its general notion and its differences of kind is here presented in the light of revelation, according to the teachings of the Church and Catholic theology.

PRAYER IN GENERAL

Prayer (Greek, εὐχή, προσευχή; Latin, *preces,* but most frequently since the 2d century, *oratio,* meaning petition, request, pleading) is, in the strict sense, the filial expression of one's desires for self and others to the heavenly Father from whom come all good things, natural or supernatural. In a wider sense, it is the ascent of the mind to God; and in the widest sense, it is speaking with God. These three definitions are found in every age of the Christian Era.

History of the Christian concept. We are not concerned here with the notion of prayer in non-Christian religions (*see* PRAYER). For the idea of prayer as it is found in the Bible, *see* PRAYER (IN THE BIBLE).

Patristic Age. Prayer in the strict sense is a petition to God. St. Basil says prayer is "an appeal for good things made to God by devout people" (*Patrologia Graeca* 31:244). According to St. Augustine prayer is a petition (*Patrologia Latina* 38:409–414). St. John Damascene says, "To pray is to ask becoming things of God" (*Patrologia Graeca* 94:1089). The most perfect example of the Christian prayer of petition is the Our Father.

Prayer in a broad sense is "raising the mind to God" (St. John Damascene, *ibid.;* Evagrius of Pontus, PG 79:1173). In its broadest sense prayer is "speaking with God" [St. Gregory of Nyssa (*ibid.* 44:1124); St. Augustine, *Serm. 130 de temp.* (*Patrologia Latina* 39:1886); St. Jerome (*Corpus scriptorum ecclesiasticorum latinorum* 54:178)] or as St. John Climacus says, "Prayer considered in its essence, is a conversation and union between God and man" (*Patrologia Graeca* 88:1129).

Scholastic Age. In the scholastic period, the definitions of the Fathers and early Church writers were analyzed and retained. St. Thomas, quoting Augustine and John Damascene, defines prayer (*oratio*) as petition and considers it in this sense in 17 articles of the *Summa* (*Summa theologiae* 2a2ae, 83.1–17; 3a, 21.1; *In 4 Sent.,* 15.4.1.1). He also attests to the wider definitions, citing St. John Damascene (*Summa theologiae* 2a2ae, 83.1 ad 2) and St. John Chrysostom (*ibid.* 2a2ae, 83.2 ad 3). F. Suárez holds with St. Thomas that prayer in the strict sense is a petition to God and says that this is also the mind of St. Bonaventure, Richard of Middleton, OFM, and others (*De oratione,* 1.1.8).

Modern Age. With the decline of scholasticism, the notion of prayer was less and less restricted to petition, so that in the 16th and 17th centuries prayer frequently included meditation and the various degrees of contemplation. Consequently, while spiritual writers in the 20th century accept the patristic definitions of prayer and recognize that in the strict sense it is a petition, some show preference for the wide definition, "speaking with God." This wide sense has the advantage of including all the forms of prayer while at the same time it emphasizes that prayer is not a monologue but a dialogue in which man responds to God, who has first spoken through His word and especially through the Word made Flesh [A. Fonck, *Dictionnaire de théologie catholique* 13.1:175; J. de Guibert, *Revue d'ascétique et de mystique* (1930) 227].

Those who prefer the definition "the ascent of the mind to God" generally add the motive, or the end, since the elevation of the mind alone is insufficient for prayer. In study, for example, one thinks of God without praying. The "elevation of the mind," therefore, is further qualified as both an affective and a noetic act, as is done in the following typical modern definition: "Praying means raising our hearts to God to praise Him and thank Him or ask something of Him."

Value of prayer. There have always been some who find prayer worthless: the skeptics who say that God already knows one's needs, the Deists who say that contact with Him is impossible since He is not interested in the world, others who find petition an expression of selfishness, and those who find petition an unreasonable attempt on man's part to bend God's will to his own.

Against these errors Catholicism teaches that since God knows everything, prayer is not an attempt to inform Him of man's needs, but rather an act of acknowledgment of one's insufficiency and dependence on God. Furthermore, prayer is not selfishness since one seeks the object of prayer with humble submission to God's will and in obedience to His command (Lk 11.9–13). Finally, man cannot attain salvation without graces from God, and many of these according to divine providence are granted only in answer to prayer (*Summa theologiae* 2a2ae, 83.2). Prayer, therefore, is not useless or selfish but a postulate of man's filial relationship with God. It is an obedient and loving response of a child to his Father.

More specifically, prayer has four special values in relation to man; namely, satisfactory, meritorious, impetratory, and psychologico-moral. In common with every good work (e.g., giving alms), prayer has satisfactory and meritorious value; that is, when man is in the state of grace, his prayer can obtain satisfaction for temporal punishment due to sin and can merit for him an increase of grace. The impetratory value, distinct from the meritorious value, is proper to prayer. Something merited is given in justice. Something obtained by impetration is given because of the generosity of the donor, who is in no way obliged to grant the gift. For example, the increase of grace merited by the prayer of the just man is bestowed in justice, since God has promised it to him. On the other hand, the gift of final perseverance, in no way promised as a reward for prayer or good actions, cannot be merited but is given in answer to prayer solely through the mercy of God. Likewise, the sinner cannot merit sanctifying grace in strict justice through prayer, but his prayer moves God to show mercy (*ibid.* 2a2ae, 83.16). The psychologico-moral value of prayer is a particular spiritual refreshment (*ibid.* 83.13): prayer furnishes the intellect with religious knowledge; produces in the will sentiments of admiration, respect, fear, joy, and desire for God; and makes the virtues of faith, hope, and charity more vital and dynamic in a person's life.

In view of all these effects, it is not surprising that the habitual practice of prayer is sanctifying. Spiritual writers emphasize its role in effecting detachment from creatures with hatred for sin and imperfections, progressive union with God, and gradual transformation into Christ.

Ends of prayer. Prayer in the broad sense may be directed, as is sacrifice, to one or several of four ends: adoration, thanksgiving, propitiation, and petition. Other classifications of ends—praise, love, abandonment to God's will—may ultimately be reduced to this classical division. Praise, for example, which is the expression of joy in adoration, is a specification of adoration. The four ends are proximate objectives of prayer, namely, acknowledgment of God's excellence and man's absolute dependence, gratitude for benefits received, sorrow for sins, and petition for fitting things. These ends are intimately connected so that often they form parts or elements of the one prayer of petition. In every petition there is at least virtually adoration, thanksgiving, and sorrow. This is clearly seen in the Our Father, essentially a prayer of petition, in which one finds adoration (''hallowed be Thy name'') and sorrow (''forgive us our trespasses''). Thanksgiving for favors received is only implicitly expressed. While the prayer of the wayfarer is especially one of petition and sorrow, in heaven after the general judgment, when all petitions will have been fulfilled, the prayer of the blessed will be essentially one of adoration and thanksgiving.

Efficacy of prayer. To the prayer of petition alone Our Lord has added the promise of infallible efficacy. ''Amen, amen, I say to you, if you ask the Father anything in my name, he will give it to you. Hitherto you have not asked in my name. Ask, and you shall receive, that your joy may be full'' (Jn 16.24; Mt 7.7, 21–22). Theologians agree that this promise is infallibly fulfilled not only for the just man but even for the sinner, provided that a person prays for himself with the proper dispositions listed below and directs the prayers to an object that will be advantageous to his eternal salvation (*Summa theologiae* 2a2ae, 83.14; 83.15 ad 2). Prayer for another is not always infallibly heard because resistance to the grace of God on the part of others is not under the control of the one who prays. Finally, prayers for souls in purgatory, certainly effectual in general, may not be heard for a particular soul, for one does not know what conditions God requires for prayer to be efficacious for a particular suffering soul.

Necessity and obligation of prayer. While the Sacraments and meritorious works are also means of obtaining God's grace, nevertheless, in the ordinary providence of God, for an adult, prayer of petition is a necessary means of salvation (*ibid.* 3a,39.5; Suárez, *De oratione* 1.28; A. Liguori, 2:428–430, citing St. Augustine and other theologians). St. Augustine, writing against the Pelagians, who denied the necessity of both grace and prayer, says ''that God gives us a few things even when we do not pray, such as the beginning of faith, but that He has provided the rest, including final perseverance, only for those who pray'' (*Patrologia latina* 45:1017). According to theologians, one can reduce to three the divine graces that cannot be merited but can be obtained only by prayer of petition: internal efficacious graces, the gift of final perseverance, and external efficacious graces [P. de Letter, ''Merit and Prayer in the Life of Grace,'' *Thomist* 19 (1956) 472].

Because prayer is a necessary means of salvation, Christ has imposed upon man a precept to pray (Suárez, *De oratione* 1.28.4). ''And he also told them a parable that they must always pray and not lose heart'' (Lk 18.1). ''Ask, and it shall be given to you; seek, and you shall find; knock, and it shall be opened to you'' (Mt 7.7, 26.41; Col 4.2; Eph 6.17–18; 1 Thes 5.17; see Persons Who Pray, *infra,* for the time when the precept obliges).

Qualities of prayer. To be efficacious, prayer must be adorned with special qualities. It should be devout, attentive, full of confidence, and persevering.

Devotion. The will should be turned to God, humble and submissive, ready to do the things that concern His service (*Summa theologiae* 2a2ae, 83.1). True devotion should not be confused with spiritual and sensible consolation, which may be present or absent in true prayer, because even in the state of aridity the will can be determined to serve God promptly. The more devout one is, the closer his friendship with God and the more likely the prayer will be heard (*ibid.* 114.6). Nevertheless, the sinner, although lacking devotion, is obliged to pray, and Christ often invited sinners to pray (Lk 18.13–14). ''Oh, what a sweet consolation for a poor sinner, to know that his sins are no hindrance to his obtaining every grace he asks for, since Jesus Christ has promised that whatever we ask of God, through His merits, He will grant it all!'' (A. Liguori, 2:441).

Attention. Some attention is required in every prayer. In mental prayer, internal attention is necessary, that is, the application of one's intellectual faculties to the consideration of truths and the eliciting of affections. In the recitation of a vocal prayer, the minimum requirement is the intention of praying and external attention, that is, the avoidance of any act incompatible with the correct pronunciation of the words (e.g., writing or talking to another). Internal attention to the meaning of the prayer, while praiseworthy, is not necessary. Consequently, the recitation of prayers (e.g., the Divine Office in Latin) that one may not understand has satisfactory, meritorious, and impetratory value, and, if one's thoughts are devoutly centered, may not be wanting in spiritual refreshment. Perfect attention in vocal prayer consists in turning the mind to God in loving adoration and union. The devout Christian will always try to have his mind and heart centered on God and the meaning of prayer (1 Cor 14.14–15). Involuntary distractions that come and go during prayer do not destroy its value.

Full of Confidence in God. One should pray in the name of Jesus, that is, full of confidence in His redemptive love and in the power of His merits to obtain from the Father what one asks. Thus in many official prayers of the Church addressed to the Father, the petition ends with the words ''Through Christ our Lord.'' To approach God with little or no hope is to offend Him (Jas 1.6).

Perseverance. One should never cease to ask in prayer. ''And he told them a parable—that they must always pray and not lose heart'' (Lk 18.1–7; 11.5–13; 21.36). Short, frequent, devout prayers are preferable to long, tedious ones, which tend to discourage lasting prayer.

Psychology of prayer. When man speaks to God to ask something, the intellect and the will, the supernatural virtues, and the emotions all play a part. In prayer the whole man with his natural and supernatural faculties goes forth to meet God. Other factors that influence prayer are the following: imagination and memory, the conscious and the unconscious, temperament, education, mental health, the cultural ambient, and other circumstances recognized in applied psychology. [G. Frei, ''Gebet, psychologisch,'' *Lexikon für Theologie und Kirche* (Freiburg 1957–65) 4:550–551].

Prayer in its strict sense is an act of the intellect. The intellectual act here is not merely speculative, an act of simple apprehension, judgment, or reasoning, but practical, i.e., causative: man asks God to do something (*Summa theologiae* 2a2ae, 83.1). St. Thomas taught this doctrine against certain voluntarists such as Hugh of Saint-Victor (*Patrologia Latina* 176:474) and St. Bonaventure (*In 3 sent,* 17.1.1; ad 3), who considered prayer an affective motion of the will. As St. Bonaventure pointed out, the prayer of petition is not the desire of the heart, but the interpreter and expression of that desire (*Summa theologiae* 2a2ae, 83.1 ad 1). Both intellect and will are operative, it is true, but prayer is formally of the intellect because the will's role is to move the intellect to make the petition.

Besides the intellect and will there are other faculties, and these are supernatural, that function in Christian prayer. Prayer, while it involves the exercise of the theological virtues, is actually an act of the moral virtue of religion. The theological virtues are rather dispositions for prayer. They enable man to enter into divine intimacy with God. The virtues of faith and hope, for example, give man the proper and befitting disposition of belief and trust in the goodness of God, his Father, as he stands before Him pleading for his needs. The habit of charity, too, should be present, although the sinner who is without habitual grace and the habit of charity can and should pray with the help of actual grace. Perfect prayer, however, the prayer of the loving child, is the one that is directed by charity. Prayer should be an expression of one's friendship with God, just as it is an expression of one's faith and hope.

But to elicit an act of prayer is proper to the virtue of religion. Religion gives God the honor that His divine nature deserves. Every prayer is an act of homage in which man bows before God, recognizing that all good things come from Him. Prayer, then, is an act of the virtue of religion and after devotion the principal act of this virtue. Without prayer religion would be merely external, like a body without a soul.

The moral virtues, some more than others, are, like the theological virtues, dispositions for prayer. Humility, obedience, penance, and fortitude, for example, are virtues that provide the qualities of prayer mentioned in the preceding section: humility, submission, contrition, and perseverance. While prayer depends upon the infused virtues, the emphasis here is to show that the virtues depend on prayer for their increase and subsequent influence on man's moral conduct. The Church prays, ''Almighty, everlasting God, grant us increase of faith, hope, and charity'' (Collect for the 13th Sunday after Pentecost).

The intellect and will elevated and perfected by the virtues are thus the efficient cause of prayer. But in their complex activity at prayer, as at other things, these higher faculties are sometimes influenced for good or evil by the emotions, which can be useful or harmful to the spiritual life of man. In prayer, controlled or reasonable emotions can stimulate and help one to pray more intensely. Joy can excite one to fervent adoration and petition. On the other hand, uncontrolled emotions (e.g., violent anger and fear) can disturb the attention of the intellect and make prayer difficult or almost impossible. In general the emotions, controlled by reason and faith, should be made to aid prayer.

Persons who pray. Only intellectual beings can pray. In their order of excellence they may be listed as follows: Christ as man, the Virgin Mary, the angels, the blessed, the souls in purgatory, and wayfarers. The devils and damned souls cannot pray for they are turned irrevocably away from God.

Although our concern here is primarily with the wayfarer, it is important to observe that the object of prayer will vary according to the state of the one who prays. For example, Christ in His human nature adores the Father and renders eternal thanks to Him in heaven. He also intercedes for mankind. The Virgin Mary prayed on earth and prays now in heaven, where she intercedes for mankind, obtaining by her suppliant omnipotence the graces that man needs for salvation. The angels can pray for an increase in their accidental glory and for the salvation of mankind. The blessed can petition for the glorification of their body on the day of final judgment, for accidental glory of honor and cult, and for all the needs of men on earth. The souls in purgatory can pray for themselves, although they are not able to satisfy or merit a condonation of their punishment. St. Thomas thought that the souls in purgatory do not know the needs of the faithful and consequently cannot help them (*Summa theologiae* 2a2ae, 83.4 ad 3), but some theologians hold as a pious opinion that the souls in purgatory do intercede for the faithful (Suárez, *De oratione* 2.8.25–28). In spite of this opinion, in liturgical prayers the Church never prays to the poor souls but always prays for them.

As for the wayfarer, whether he be in grace or in sin, he should in the first place pray for himself. Second, charity urges him to pray for his neighbor, ''Pray for one another that you may be saved'' (Jas 5.16). In particular, prayer should be made for the Holy Father, bishops, priests, religious, members of the Church, catechumens, the suffering, enemies, the souls in purgatory, rulers of states, and for all outside the Church that there may be one flock and one shepherd. No one except the damned should ever be excluded from prayer, for charity must extend to all. In the mind of the Church, prayer's social value is immeasurable. ''This is truly a tremendous mystery upon which we can never meditate enough: that the salvation of many souls depends upon the prayers and voluntary mortifications offered for that intention by the members of the Mystical Body of Jesus Christ, and upon the cooperation which pastors and faithful and especially parents must afford to our Divine Saviour'' [Pius XII *MysCorp* 27–28]. Obviously, one does not pray for the blessed in heaven, except in the sense of praying that their name be held in higher esteem and their virtues be more widely imitated.

Those to whom prayer is addressed. Man prays to the one, triune God: the Father, the Son, and the Holy Spirit. One may direct his prayer to all three Persons or to one of them. Liturgical prayers usually address the Eternal Father through His only-begotten Son. But on some occasions, even during the Holy Sacrifice of the Mass, prayers are immediately directed to Christ, for the Man Jesus Christ is truly God (*ibid.* 81). The first known prayer addressed to Christ is that of St. Stephen, ''Lord Jesus, receive my spirit . . . Lord, do not lay this sin against them'' (Acts 7.60). One prays to the Blessed Virgin, to the angels and saints in heaven, but only in the sense that they may intercede before God for us. To God one prays, ''Have mercy on us''; to the saints ''Pray for us,'' as the litanies exemplify.

Objects of prayer. For what does one pray? One asks for all desirable goods and in the order that Christ has given us in the Our Father. One asks absolutely for God's glory, the coming of His kingdom, the fulfillment of His will by men and for salvation and the graces necessary and useful for it. ''All our prayers should be directed to the acquisition of grace and glory'' (*Summa theologiae* 2a2ae, 83.4). One asks for temporal goods conditionally, that is, if they are expedient for salvation. No one would expect from God anything that would be injurious. Consequently God does not grant every request for good health, gainful employment, and other worldly goods that He foresees may be spiritually harmful. Nevertheless, prayers for temporal goods are heard by God, and some spiritual good (e.g., merit and spiritual refreshment) can be obtained.

Circumstances of prayer. Although one can pray for fitting things at any time, in any place, and in any posture, there are certain principles that govern the order of prayer.

Time. When must one pray? It is difficult to determine precisely when this obligation binds. Nevertheless, it can safely be said that one is bound to pray many times a year. Some say that to omit prayer for one month or at least for two months could be a mortal sin [J. Aertnys and C. A. Damen, *Theologia moralis* (Turin 1958) 1.414]. "We must certainly pray in temptations that cannot, without prayer, be overcome; also when other precepts (e.g., the precept of confession) require prayer, and on occasions (such as war, famine, pestilence) when divine help is necessary. Lastly, we must pray at the hour of death if we are not in the grace of God, for then most of all it behooves us to be friends of God" [H. Davis, *Moral and Pastoral Theology* (London 1941) 2.7]. Catholics who pray at Mass on Sundays and feast days surely fulfill the divine precept to pray often. Although there is no precept to say morning and evening prayers or table prayers, these are laudable Christian customs and should not be neglected. The good Christian will pray many times each day.

Place. Certain places, such as a church or one's private room, lend themselves to recollection and are more conducive to prayer. But if one wishes to learn to pray always, one must become accustomed to speak to God in short prayers while walking, riding, sitting, or working. In a word, one can pray wherever one may happen to be.

Posture. The general rule is to assume a posture that helps one to pray better and with less hindrance. One may kneel, sit, stand, walk, or lie down. Exterior reverence, being an outward sign of interior sentiment, should regulate the circumstances of prayer, but in such a way as not to cause discomfort, admiration, or embarrassment to others. One's interior devotion or state of health will often indicate external behavior; for example, the sick will be forced to pray while lying down and fervent souls may be moved, as early Christians were, to stand erect with hands extended, imitating Christ on the cross.

MENTAL PRAYER

In general, prayer is mental when the internal acts of intellect and will are not expressed externally in words or gestures. In modern usage the term is not restricted to an internal petition but embraces every interior act of faith, hope, charity, every thought of God with the object of serving Him and of fostering charity and the other virtues, every movement of praise, thanksgiving, penance, petition, adoration, and love.

Kinds of mental prayer. As an exercise in the spiritual life, mental prayer may be either formal or diffused (virtual). It is diffused when internal acts are intermingled with other occupations, as in the practice of aspirations while cooking or sewing. It is formal when a definite space of time is devoted to making these internal acts to the exclusion of all other occupations.

Necessity of formal mental prayer. There are some simple souls with little education who cannot regularly practice formal mental prayer and nevertheless by the devout practice of vocal prayer and asceticism come to a high state of perfection. For this reason it cannot be said that formal mental prayer is necessary for all who strive for Christian perfection. Neverthless, it is a normal means of Christian perfection, and usually it cannot be neglected without spiritual loss (De Guibert, *The Theology of the Spiritual Life,* 210). Its daily practice is strongly recommended to the clergy and religious in Canon Law (1917 *Codex iuris canonici* cc.125.2, 595.1n2) and by numerous popes. Pius XII, writing to the clergy in *Menti Nostrae* [*Acta Apostolicae Sedis* 42 (1950) 657] says there is no substitute for it; and John XXIII in the first Roman Synod made the daily practice of prayerful meditation a law for clerics living in Rome because "this is very necessary to foster piety in souls" [*Prima Romana Synodus* (Rome 1960) 28]. St. Thomas says that meditation is necessary for devotion (*Summa theologiae* 2a2ae, 82.3).

Division of formal mental prayer. Since the 17th century, it has been common among spiritual writers to distinguish three degrees of formal mental prayer: (1) discursive, (2) affective, and (3) contemplative. The latter is subdivided into acquired contemplation (also called active contemplation or the prayer of simplicity) and infused contemplation (passive contemplation or mystical prayer). Here emphasis will be placed on the basic form of mental prayer, namely, discursive prayer or meditation. (For the other degrees, and infused contemplation, *see* CONTEMPLATION.)

Discursive prayer or meditation is most strongly recommended for beginners in the spiritual life, although it remains most useful even for the advanced (H. U. von Balthasar, *Prayer* 211). It is composed of reasoning, analyses of concepts, and comparisons, as well as affections, resolutions, and communion with God and the saints. Its characteristic element is the predominance of reasoning and consideration. It has always been practiced by God-fearing people in some form or other, as is evident in the Scriptures [Ps 38(39).4; 62(63),7; 76(77).13; 1:18(119); Eph 6.18; Col 4.2; 1 Tm 4.15; 1 Cor 14.15]. In the course of time, systematic methods of this type of prayer were constructed. Here only the principal ones and their value will be considered. All modern methods, as we shall see, are essentially the same, and one or another is used more or less regularly by seminarians, priests, religious, and devout lay people at set periods of the day. But history shows that this was not always so.

The early Christian Fathers and monks had daily periods of holy reading (*lectio divina*), during which they often meditated and prayed. The Rule of St. Benedict provided for about four hours of reading every day and recommended that the monks frequently give themselves to prayer.

Methods of Mental Prayer. It is only in the Middle Ages that the foundations of methodical prayer were prepared. Guigo II, a Carthusian, in his small masterpiece *Scala claustralium* (*c.* 1145) tells how monks prayed in the 12th century. He presents four steps of man's ''spiritual exercise'': reading, meditation, prayer, and contemplation. Reading is the application of the mind to the Holy Scriptures, meditation the careful consideration of the truths, prayer the heart beseeching God (petition), and contemplation the soul resting in God. These parts of prayer are intimately linked: the first are of little use without the others, and the last are rarely attained without the first. Through these four steps man ascends to union with God. St. Bernard made a remarkable contribution to the technique of mental prayer by teaching souls to center their meditations on the mysteries of Christ and by outlining a formula for meditation. Later, in the 14th and 15th centuries, under the influence of St. Bonaventure, who suggested how to apply the faculties in meditation and prayer (*De triplici via* 1.19), the Franciscans popularized meditation on the life of Christ [*Meditations on the Life of Christ, St. Bonaventure* (Princeton 1961)].

However, it was only in the 15th century with the DEVOTIO MODERNA that the first full-scale systematic methods of meditation were developed. In 1483 John Wessel Gansfort composed his *Scala meditatoria* and presented a method of 23 steps. This set the pattern for future methods, but with time they were simplified. In 1500, Ximenes Garcia Cisneros, abbot of Montserrat, produced such a simplified method, with subjects for each day of the week. St. Ignatius, who visited Montserrat after his conversion, was probably familiar with it. In the 16th century, many methods were developed among the new apostolic congregations—the Jesuits, Oratorians, Minims, and Theatines—all of them seeking a practical prayer for their active life. The most influential treatise in this development of methodical prayer was the *SPIRITUAL EXERCISES* of Ignatius Loyola. In the same century, another important method, often underestimated, was that of Louis of Granada, which was later simplified by Peter of Alcántara; this highly effective method was recommended by Teresa of Avila and influenced the method used among Carmelites and other religious orders [Gabriel of St. Mary Magdalen, *La mistica Teresiana* (Fiesole 1935) 52; K. Healy, *Methods of prayer in the Directory of the Carmelite reform of Touraine* (Rome 1956) 108–120]. In the following centuries Francis de Sales (2.2–7) and Alphonsus de Liguori evolved their own methods but with dependence on Ignatius and Louis of Granada. Finally came the method of Father Olier, later developed and known as the Sulpician method, which is highly affective and Christocentric. These methods, still in use, are helpful for progress in the spiritual life. But since the Holy Spirit is the principal guide in prayer, methods should be subordinated to His divine action.

Every method has three essential parts: the preparation, the body of prayer, and the conclusion. Although commonly considered in relation to discursive prayer, these three parts can be found also in affective prayer and the prayer of simplicity. We consider them here especially in relation to discursive prayer. The preparation is remote and proximate. The former consists in one's accumulated religious experience; the latter includes reading the subject before the meditation, or at least at its beginning, placing oneself in the presence of God, and asking His help to meditate well. The subject matter varies with individual tastes and needs. The body of prayer consists in the profound consideration of the subject matter with consequent affections. The memory, imagination, and intellect serve to arouse the will to elicit affections. Consequently the actions of these faculties should cease, once the will is moved. Even in times of aridity, ample attention should be given to thoughts and affections but without violently attempting to arouse the will to devotion. A specific resolution, although beneficial in every meditation, is not necessary.

The conclusion, especially important in the Ignatian method, always consists of a colloquy with God, our Lady, or the saints. Attention should also be given to acts of adoration, thanksgiving, and petition. Francis de Sales and others suggest a spiritual ''nosegay,'' that is, taking some thought or affection from the meditation to ponder during the day. In this way meditation extends its influence over the whole day.

Such is the general plan of mental prayer in all the methods. The various ways of developing the body of the meditation give rise to the different methods of prayer. (1) In the method of the three faculties, the best known of the many methods proposed by Ignatius (*Spiritual Exercises,* 1st week), the memory and intellect play an important part. The use of these faculties is important for beginners who stand in need of profound thought before conviction and affections are reached. (2) In the method of contemplation (*ibid.,* 2d week), the intellect with the aid of the imagination contemplates or considers a mystery in the life of Christ, for example, the Christ Child in the manger, the bleeding Christ of the cross. The persons, the words, the actions, etc., that pertain to the particular mystery are then considered (who, what, why, when, by what means, etc.). Finally, a practical application is made to oneself. (3) In the method of the application of the senses (*ibid.*), one employs the five senses to move the will to affections.

Other beneficial methods that can be used in the body of the prayer, especially for those who have difficulty with the standard discursive methods, are meditative reading and mixed prayer. In the first one reads, then reflects, in order to move the will. Such a process is repeated during the period of prayer, as often as necessary (Teresa, *The Complete Works* 2.69). In mixed prayer (oral and mental) one employs a fixed formula (e.g., the Our Father) and repeats it slowly, stopping to reflect after each thought or petition, with the intention of eliciting affections (Ignatius, 4th week).

Affective Prayer. This kind of prayer stands between discursive and contemplative prayer. It received this name in the 16th century (Philippe, ''Mental Prayer in the Catholic Tradition,'' *Mental Prayer and Modern Life* 51). It is not discursive prayer because it has little or no reasoning and the affections predominate. It is not contemplative prayer because it has a multiplicity of affections (e.g., humility, sorrow, hope, love), whereas contemplation is characterized by its simplicity of affection. Although it is proper to those who have progressed in mental prayer, Teresa of Avila, who practiced it, recommended it even for beginners (*The Complete Works* 1.71). In fact she defines mental prayer in terms of affective prayer. ''And mental prayer, in my view, is nothing but friendly intercourse, and frequent solitary converse, with Him Who we know loves us'' (1.50). Carmelite and Franciscan spirituality lean heavily toward affective prayer, as did the original method of Father Olier (Lercaro, *Methods of Mental Prayer* 2–36). Some even consider the method of contemplation and the application of senses in the spiritual exercises of St. Ignatius as forms of affective prayer (Tanquerey, *The Spiritual Life* 989–995).

Those who practice affective prayer must at times return to discursive prayer to keep the mind occupied and the will motivated. For unless convictions are deeply rooted, there is danger of mere sentimentality with little effect on one's moral life, especially in those of an affectionate temperament. But should the Holy Spirit invite one to leave discursive prayer for affective prayer, it is important to recognize the opportune time. The signs for the transition are the following: considerations become fruitless, convictions are so deeply rooted that the will is easily moved, and the soul tends easily and gladly toward God.

Diffused mental prayer (virtual prayer). Besides formal mental prayer, the soul may engage in exercises of mental prayer that consist in short, frequent internal acts in the midst of daily occupations. The chief forms of this practice are the following: (1) the exercise of the presence of God, (2) prayer of aspirations, and (3) the renewal of the good intention. Acts of conformity with and abandonment to the will of God and short periods of recollection and retreat may also accompany these practices. This value of diffused prayer consists in prolonging the thoughts and affections of formal mental prayer and thus influencing and pervading man's conduct throughout the day. For this latter reason it is called virtual prayer. By this prayer one does ''the work of Martha with the spirit of Mary'' (J. M. Perrin, ''Making One's Life a Prayer,'' *Mental Prayer and Modern Life* 113). Thus, the conjunction of diffused prayer with other spiritual exercises enables one to fulfill to an eminent degree the admonition of Christ to pray always and not to lose heart (Lk 18.1; 1 Thes 5.17).

The Exercise of the Presence of God. This is a practice in which the soul thinks lovingly of God frequently throughout the day and often speaks to Him in aspirations, ejaculations, or colloquies without interrupting or neglecting one's daily duties. This is dealt with elsewhere (*see* PRESENCE OF GOD, PRACTICE OF).

Prayer of Aspirations. According to their role in the spiritual life aspirations are brief, fervent elevations of the heart to God. Sometimes they are called ejaculations because like arrows shot toward their target, they go quickly to the object of the affections. In this sense they are affective prayers proceeding from charity. Generally speaking, therefore, the greater the charity, the more perfect and frequent the aspirations. The faithful practice of discursive prayer is a normal disposition for the prayer of aspirations, which is often considered a distinct exercise of prayer. Some, however, prefer to make aspirations the predominant part of the exercise of the presence of God, in which the memory recalls God's presence, the intellect focuses its attention upon Him, and the will fervently turns toward Him in aspirations (F. Blosius, *Book of Spiritual Instruction,* ch. 4, 6; A. Liguori, *Complete Ascetical Works* 1.508; and *Carmelite Directory,* 439–480). Such a mode of presentation has many advantages, but one should remember that the exercise of the presence of God does not always terminate in aspirations, but sometimes in loving thoughts or even colloquies.

The Good Intention. There is not a single action of the day that cannot be directed to God's glory, subjected to His will, and offered for the good of the Church and the salvation of souls. It is usually done through the good intention made in the morning offering and renewed at intervals throughout the day. ''I offer to Thee, O my God, all my thoughts, words, acts, and sufferings of this day; grant that they may all tend to Thy glory and my salvation.'' To make the intention more pure, one should have removed not only every bad motive but every natural motive and strive to act from love (J. M. Perrin, ''Making One's Life a Prayer,'' *Mental Prayer and Modern Life* 114). To act from lesser supernatural motives, e.g., obedience, gratitude, renders the act less perfect but still meritorious. However, sometimes only a lesser supernatural motive will be effective, and it is better to use it. One may act with many motives, e.g., desire for happiness, fear of hell, but should try to place them all under the direction of ''Making One's Life a Prayer,'' *Mental Prayer and Modern Life* love [A. Rodriguez, *The Practice of Christian Perfection,* (Chicago 1929)]. The renewal of the good intention not only exercises influence on one's actions but prolongs prayer throughout the day. Alphonsus de Liguori considers it along with aspirations as part of the exercise of the presence of God (*Complete Ascetical Works* 1.510).

Purity of intention is aided by joining it with acts of conformity to God's will. To say often ''Thy will be done'' in union with the good intention helps one to act from a more pure love (*ibid.* 604). Pope John XXIII granted a plenary indulgence to be gained once each day under the usual conditions by the faithful who in the morning offer to God their labor of the whole day, whether intellectual or manual, using any formula of prayer, and a partial indulgence of 500 days as often as with contrite heart they offer the work at hand, using any formula of prayer [*Acta Apostolicae Sedis* 53 (1961) 827].

Vocal Prayer

From the point of view of expression, prayer is vocal when it is manifested externally in words or, sometimes, in gestures. An internal act of the mind is always presupposed. Vocal prayer may be an intimate and personal cry that springs spontaneously from the heart, but more often than not it is a recitation of a fixed formula, for example, the Our Father, psalms, hymns, and such repetitive prayers as litanies, the angelus, and the rosary. (For an excellent collection of prayers, see A. Hamman.)

Usefulness. In opposition to Quietists the Church has defended the usefulness of vocal prayer for every state of the spiritual life (H. Denzinger, *Enchiridion symbolorum* 2234). Everyone should at times pray vocally for the following reasons: first, to awaken thoughts and desires that may have been dormant, and thus, to stimulate devotion; second, to serve God with the body as well as the soul, for the whole man should serve God with all that he has from Him; third, to express the feelings of the soul that naturally find their outlet in the body; and last, to give good example to others (*Summa theologiae* 2a2ae, 83.12; 91.1).

Kinds. Vocal prayer may be private (either individual or common) or public, depending on whether one prays in his own name or officially in the name of society. Private prayer is individual when said alone, communal when recited in a group (e.g., the family rosary). Public prayer, called by St. Thomas ''common prayer'' (*ibid.* 2a2ae, 83.12), requires the following three conditions: use of an approved formula, recitation in the name of the society, which for the Christian is the Church, and legitimate delegation. Consequently, a priest or cleric in major orders who recites the Divine Office alone, offers public prayer because he not only uses the approved formulas but because as the Church's official delegate he prays in her name (H. Denzinger, *Enchiridion symbolorum* 3757).

Liturgical prayer. The public prayer of the Church is called liturgical prayer and is found in liturgical actions, namely, in the Mass, the Sacraments, the Divine Office, the sacramentals, and Benediction of the Blessed Sacrament [J. H. Miller, *Fundamentals of the Liturgy,* (Notre Dame, Ind. 1960) 27–28]. In all liturgical prayer it is Christ who prays in the first place, and His members pray only insofar as they pray through Him, with Him, and in Him. In the Mass, for example, Christ is the High Priest and Victim with whom the faithful spiritually associate themselves and along with the priest at the altar offer themselves with Him and through Him to the Eternal Father.

The relative excellence of liturgical prayer in comparison with private prayer, especially mental prayer, has often been discussed [L. Bouyer, *Liturgical Piety* (Notre Dame, Ind. 1955) 243–256]. The Church's teaching is quite clear: ''It is true that liturgical prayer, being the public prayer of the august Bride of Christ, is superior to private prayers; but this superiority does not mean that there is any conflict or incompatibility between them'' (Pius XII, *Mediator Dei*). Indeed, there exists the greatest harmony between private prayers and liturgical prayer, and both are necessary if Christ is to be formed in man. Consequently, private devotions (e.g., the Rosary or the Way of the Cross) may be considered as aids to the liturgical cult. Through them the Christian is prepared to offer the Sacrifice of the Mass with better dispositions, to receive the Sacraments with more fruit, and to participate in the sacred rites with greater fervor and recollection. ''But these devotions should be so drawn up that they harmonize with the liturgical seasons, accord with the sacred liturgy, are in some fashion derived from it, and lead the people to it, since, in fact, the liturgy by its very nature far surpasses any of them'' (Vatican Council II, *Constitution on the Sacred Liturgy* 13).

Bibliography: ALPHONSUS LIGUORI, *Complete Ascetical Works,* ed. E. GRIMM, 22 v. (New York 1886–97), excellent meditations esp. in v. 1 and 2; *The Carmelite Directory of the Spiritual Life* (Chicago, Ill. 1951). J. C. FENTON, *The Theology of Prayer* (Milwaukee 1939). FRANCIS DE SALES, *Introduction to the Devout Life,* ed. and tr. A. ROSS (Westminster, Md. 1948). R. GARRIGOULA-GRANGE, *The Three Ages of the Interior Life,* tr. M. T. DOYLE, 2 v. (St. Louis, Mo. 1947–48), esp. v. 1. J. DE GUIBERT, *The Theology of the Spiritual Life,* tr. P. BARRETT (New York 1953). A. HAMMAN, *Early Christian Prayers,* tr. W. MITCHELL (Chicago, Ill. 1961). F. HEILER, *Prayer,* tr. and ed. S. MCCOMB and J. E. PARK (New York 1958) [non-Catholic]. JOHN OF THE CROSS, *Complete Works,* tr. E. A. PEERS, 3 v. (Westminster, Md. 1963). V. LEHODEY, *The Ways of Mental Prayer* (Dublin 1949). G. LERCARO, *Methods of Mental Prayer,* tr. T. F. LINDSAY (Westminster, Md. 1957), contains bibliog. of books of meditations. MARIE-EUGÈNE DE L'ENFANT-JÉSUS, *I Want to See God,* tr. M. V. CLARE (Chicago, Ill. 1953). P. P. PARENTE, *The Ascetical Life* (St. Louis, Mo. 1951). P. PHILIPPE, "Mental Prayer in the Catholic Tradition," *Mental Prayer and Modern Life,* tr. F. C. LEHNER (New York 1950), partial translation of *L'Oraison* (Paris 1947). R. PLUS, *How to Pray Always,* tr. I. HERNAMAN (London 1942); *How to Pray Well* (Westminster, Md. 1948). A. POULAIN, *The Graces of Interior Prayer,* tr. L. SMITH (6th ed. St. Louis, Mo. 1950). F. SUÀREZ, *De oratione, devotiones et horis canonicis, Bk. 1,* in *Opera Omnia,* 28 v. (Vivès, Paris 1956–78) v. 14. A. TANQUEREY, *The Spiritual Life,* tr. H. BRANDERIS (Westminster, Md. 1945). TERESA OF ÀVILA, *The Complete Works,* ed. SILVERIO DE SONTA TERESA and E. A. PEERS, 3 v. (New York 1946). THOMAS AQUINAS, *Summa theologiae* 2a2ae, 83.1–17. H. U. VON BALTHASAR, *Prayer,* tr. A. V. LITTLEDALE (New York 1961).

[K. J. HEALY]

PRAYER, CENTERING

The prayer of centering is a process of turning inward to gather the faculties to a center in the depths of the self. The integration of body, mind, and spirit in a point of stillness releases deeper levels of consciousness and opens the self to more contemplative union with God, not as an object of meditation but as a presence within and the source of all being. In contemporary writing on Christian prayer the term "centering" reflects the influence of Eastern spirituality and depth psychology and suggests the action of a potter bringing clay into a spinning, unwobbling pivot on the wheel. Commonly used techniques to facilitate centering are rhythmical breathing, process meditation, the use of a mantra, mandala, or sacred symbol, and the repetition of the JESUS PRAYER.

Centering Prayer is a modern name drawn from the writings of Thomas MERTON (Fr. Louis, OCSO of Gethsemani Abbey) for the ancient method of meditation or prayer found in the writings of Saint John Cassian (d. 435) and once attributed to Abba Isaac (Second Conference). It comes from the same source as the Jesus Prayer, namely, the Fathers of the Desert, but represents the greater suppleness with which it was passed on in the West. The most notable representative of this prayer form in English spiritual writings is the anonymous author of *The CLOUD OF UNKNOWING.* The method as refined and popularly presented by the Cistercian monks of Saint Joseph Abbey in Spencer, Massachusetts may be summarized in this way:

1. Sit relaxed and quiet.
2. Be in faith and love to God who dwells in the center of your being.
3. Take up a love word and let it be gently present, supporting your being to God in faith-filled love.
4. Whenever you become aware of anything else, simply, gently return to the Lord with the use of your prayer word.
5. After 20 minutes of meditation let the Our Father (or some other prayer) pray itself quietly within you.

See Also: CONTEMPLATION; PRAYER.

Bibliography: B. GRIFFITHS, *Return to the Center* (Springfield, Ill. 1976) 16–39. W. JOHNSTON, *The Still Point* (New York 1970) 67–85; *Silent Music* (New York 1974) 55–67. I. PROGOFF, *The Well and the Cathedral* (New York 1971). M. C. RICHARDS, *Centering in Pottery, Poetry, and the Person* (Middletown, Conn. 1964) 9–56. T. MERTON, "The Inner Experience," *Cistercian Studies* 18 (1983) 3–15; 121–134; 201–216; 289–300; 19 (1984) 62–78; 139–150; 267–282; 336–345. M. B. PENNINGTON, *Centered Living* (New York 1986); *Centering Prayer* (New York 1980); *Challenges in Prayer* (Wilmington, Del. 1982).

[D. KENNEDY/M. B. PENNINGTON]

PRAYER BOOKS

Collections of prayers, hymns, meditations, etc., intended for private or community devotions; to be distinguished from collections containing the official texts used in liturgical services. Some prayer books contain both private prayers and liturgical texts, while others contain various prayers—often paraphrases of the liturgical text—for silent reading during liturgical services. So common were these latter collections over the past century that the Missal itself has been frequently referred to in common parlance as a prayer book. It is noteworthy here that even the *Missale Romanum* includes private prayers as preparation for and thanksgiving after Mass for *ad libitum* recitation by the priest.

There is no extant collection of private prayers from the early Christian era; in fact there is not even a mention or intimation of such a collection in apostolic and patristic documents. While it is true that the Scriptures, the works of the apostolic Fathers, the Martyrology, and early papyri and ostraca contain individual prayers of many types, yet there is no actual collection of private prayers from the ancient Church that can be classified as a prayer book in the contemporary sense of the term. The

NEHIRO-IRINIUI
AIAMIHE
MASSINAHIGAN,
SHATSHEGUTSH, MITINEKAPITSH,
ISKUAMISKUTSH, NETSHEKATSH,
MISHT', ASSINITSH, SHEKUTIMITSH,
EKUANATSH, ASHUABMUSHUANITSH,
PIAKUAGAMITSH,
Gaie miſſi miſſi nehiro-iriniui Aſtſhitſh
ka tatjits, ka kueiaſku aiamihatjits ka utſhi.

UABISTIGUIATSH.
Maſſinahitſcetuau, BROUN gaie GIRMOR.
1767.

Title page of Jean Baptiste de la Bosse's prayer book for the Montagnais, printed in Quebec, 1767.

short collections of prayers found in the *Didache,* Hippolytus, the *Apostolic Constitutions,* and the *Euchologium* of Serapion—to name but a few—must all be considered liturgical rather than private. The systematic destruction of Christian documents during the persecution of Diocletian can be blamed for the paucity of extant documents from the early Church period.

The obvious question engendered by this dearth of evidence is: Did the early, literate Christian use any particular book for his private devotions? Although the testimony is somewhat indirect, there is evidence in the popularity of the commentaries on the Psalms by Augustine and Cassiodorus, as well as from statements by Cassian (*De coenob. inst.* 2.5; *Patrologia Latina* 49:34) and Eusebius (*In psalm.; Patrologia Graeca,* ed. J. P. Migne 23:647), that the Book of Psalms sufficed both for private and public devotion. Indeed the popularity of the Psalter (the texts of the Psalms along with liturgical and private prayers) during the whole of the Middle Ages lends additional strength to this judgment. The Psalms were to become the basis of the later Divine Office; and the famous teacher of Charlemagne's court, Alcuin, was to write a work on the use of the Psalter for private devotion (*De psalmorum usu liber; Patrologia Latina,* ed. J. P. Migne 101:465–508). The large number of extant Psalters from both East and West also bespeaks the popularity of this type of collection for private and liturgical devotion. It is often the case, however, that surviving manuscripts were ''collectors' items'' from the beginning, and their lack of use no doubt contributed to their survival. The very fact of their desirability as collectors' items is indirect evidence for the existence of innumerable other, simply executed Psalters worn to destruction by their devout readers.

Examples of Surviving Semiliturgical Prayer Books. The earliest extant Psalters from the Church of the East come only from the 9th and 10th centuries, but their illustrations and text frequently show that they had been copied from models dating back to the early centuries of the Christian Church. These books from the East, on the basis of the sumptuousness of their production, are generally divided into two groups: aristocratic and monastic. The first group is representative of those deluxe editions that only the wealthy could afford; they were produced for the aristocracy of Constantinople and for the members of the imperial court of that city. The manuscripts are frequently characterized by the typical Byzantine gold ink and purple dye, and often betray in their illustrations the neoclassic style that developed after the period of iconoclasm. Representative of the aristocratic or ''aulic'' Psalter are the *Paris Psalter* (Bibliothèque Nationale) and the *Psalter of Basil II* (Biblioteca Marciana, Venice), both of which are outstanding for their rich and extensive illumination. The second group, much less ornate, was intended for more ascetical tastes and practical use; but even among the manuscripts of this group marginal illustrations are to be found, and these were to become quite common in the prayer books of the East during the 10th and 11th centuries. Typical of the monastic group are the *Theodore Psalter,* named after its illuminator, Theodore of Caesarea, and a profusely illustrated Psalter of the 11th century. The former is now in the British Museum; the latter is designated as ''Ms suppl. 14'' in the Walters Art Gallery collection in Baltimore. Psalters were continuously copied for private devotion in the East throughout the Middle Ages up to the time of the fall of Constantinople in the middle of the 15th century.

In the West the Psalter was to remain a popular book of devotion into the 15th century, even after the later Book of Hours overshadowed its popularity to some degree. Extant Psalters from the 9th to the 15th centuries are generally illuminated and many of them represent the finest artistry of the period. Among the better known

Psalters of the age, the *Utrecht Psalter,* produced by the school of Rheims in the 9th century, presents enigmas both to the art historian and the paleographer. Its lively, unadorned outline drawings are a shocking contrast to the elaborately colored and static illustrations found in the typical books of the time. And where one would expect the usual Caroline minuscule writing, this Psalter has instead a combination of *scriptura communis* (rustic capital) for the general text and uncial for the titles and *incipits.* Although logically plausible explanations have been offered for these peculiarities, the *Utrecht Psalter* still remains a strikingly unique work of the Caroline period. As is usual with Psalters of the Middle Ages, this manuscript contains, in addition to the texts of the Psalms themselves, the Pater Noster, Ave Maria, Gloria, Credo, and other formulas used both for private and liturgical exercises. Every Psalm in the work contains an illustration that either literally or figuratively explains the text. The *Utrecht Psalter* was brought to England toward the end of the 10th century, where it was used as a model for other illuminated Psalters in later centuries, and had some influence on manuscript illustration there. The work is now owned by the university library at Utrecht.

British Psalters. From Britain, where the Canterbury school produced the first artistic books of southern England, comes the *Canterbury Psalter* (British Museum), known also as the *St. Augustine Psalter;* it was written and illuminated around the middle of the 8th century, and consequently is one of the earliest such works extant today. Its elaborate illumination presents a mine of material for the art historian as well as for the historian of books and writing. From the later Winchester School of book production come two important Psalters: the *Arundel Psalter* (British Museum) of the late 11th or early 12th century, whose illuminations have been described as in the finest style of English art; and the *Winchester* or *St. Swithin's Psalter* (British Museum) produced in the St. Swithin's scriptorium in the middle of the 12th century. During the 12th, 13th, and 14th centuries England produced a large number of truly beautiful Psalters, many of which are proud showpieces in the libraries that own them today. The *Windmill Psalter, Tickhill Psalter,* and a legion of other masterpieces are adequately described in the standard histories of manuscript illumination mentioned in the bibliography, and frequently the better known Psalters have been published in facsimile with elaborate introductions. Suffice it here to mention only one more of these prayer books that appeared in the later period of the Psalter's popularity as a book of private devotion: the so-called *Queen Mary's Psalter.* Although executed in the first half of the 14th century, it carries the name of Mary Tudor to whom it was presented in 1553, after it had been confiscated by customs officials on its surreptitious way to the Continent. It is profusely illustrated with outline drawings filled in with transparent washes, and represents one of the finest works of the East Anglian school of illumination. The manuscript is now a proud possession of the British Museum.

The few Psalters mentioned above are only representative of the many extant manuscripts that indicate the devotional and artistic trends of their times. The use of the Psalter is, of course, of particular interest to us in that it formed the basis of both the Divine Office and its offspring, the Book of Hours, which appeared as the popular prayer book of the laity during the last few centuries of the medieval period.

Books of Private Prayers. Contemporary with the Psalters of the Carolingian period were the first extant collections of private prayers: books containing prayers composed by the early Church Fathers, along with the usual Pater, Ave, and some popular Psalms. Several of these prayer books have been edited and published from manuscripts in recent years; four of them, written between the years 800 and 850, were published by Dom A. Wilmart (*Precum Libelli IV aevi Karolini,* Rome 1940) and represent collections of private prayers that are typical not only of the Middle Ages, but of modern times as well. The first book of the group, entitled *Libellus Trecensis* by its editor, was written in the early 9th century at Tours; it contains prayers composed by Augustine, Jerome, Gregory, Ephraem, Isidore, and other early writers, and includes some Psalms and prayers to be recited at certain hours. The second work in Wilmart's edition is entitled *Libellus Parisinus,* probably written at Tours also, *c.* 820; it has a prayer of St. Martin along with various anonymous prayers and devotions for certain hours of the day. The *Libellus Coloniensis,* third of the group, was composed probably in Cologne in 805; its contents include prayers for various activities of the day, prayers before each of the penitential Psalms, a prayer of Ambrose, and various others, and anonymous prayers. The final work of the collection is a comparatively large book called *Magnus Libellus Turonensis,* written in 850 at Tours. In addition to the usual prayers before various daily activities, it includes the *Confessio S. Fulgentii,* the litany, prayers after the penitential Psalms, hymns for different hours, various prayers and hymns for different seasons and feasts, and the "Little Psalter" of Bede.

Other early prayer books that are of interest include the famous *Book of Cerne* (Cambridge University Library), written in Mercia in the early 9th century and extensively illuminated. It is a compilation from various sources showing both Roman and Irish influences in its prayers. The collection includes 74 prayers and hymns, the *Psalter of Aethelwold,* and the apocryphal *Descensus ad inferna;* the book begins with the Passion story as told by the evangelists. This medieval prayer book was edited and published by A. B. Kuypens (*The Book of Cerne,* Cambridge, England 1902). Another British work of interest among prayer collections is the anonymous Royal MS 2.A.XX of the British Museum. This manuscript contains gospel passages, hymns, canticles, and prayers of various saints; it is 52 leaves in length and had its origin in England during the 8th century.

Among medieval collections for private devotion the *Liber Manualis* of Dodana, written for her son Wilhelm in 841, is well known, although it might be considered more a handbook of Christian perfection than a collection of prayers (*Le Manual de Dhuoda,* ed. E. Bondurand, Paris 1887).

J. P. Migne's *Patrologia Latina* (101.1383–1416) contains a miscellaneous collection of prayers and devotions that dates from the last part of the 9th century. In its published form it is entitled *Libellus sacrarum precum* (ex MS floriacensi, *c.* 900), and its contents include prayers and hymns of Hilary, Ambrose, Augustine, Jerome, and other Fathers; the litany also is included.

Books of Hours. During the following centuries collections of private prayers continued to be compiled and copied, but one begins to notice in the later Middle Ages the growing popularity of the *Horae,* or Book of Hours. These devotional collections received the name of primer in England. The core of the Book of Hours was the Office of the Blessed Virgin Mary, a collection of Psalms, hymns, prayers, and readings arranged according to the canonical hours of the Divine Office. However, the extant *Horae* contain many other prayers and devotions, as will be seen later.

The fundamental work on the origin of this popular book of devotion is an article written by Edmund Bishop "On the Origin of the Prymer" in his *Liturgica Historica* (Oxford 1918, repr. 1962) 211–237. Since the work is readily available, it is sufficient to summarize Bishop's scholarly presentation: The origin of the Office of the Blessed Virgin can be traced to the extra devotions (*cursus*) added to the ordinary recitation of the daily Office in the monastery. Benedict of Aniane in the latter part of the 8th century is said to have introduced the recitation of 15 additional Psalms and other prayers before the singing of Matins (Ardo's life of Benedict, *Monumenta Germaniae Historica, Scriptores* 13) as well as the Office of the Dead as a further devotional supplement. Later in the 10th century, Vespers and Lauds of All Saints began to be added as a supplement to the regular Vespers and Lauds of the day in various monasteries; and in the latter half of this century the groundwork of the Little Office had been laid. For it was at this time that a *cursus* in honor of the Blessed Virgin was said, and more Psalms were added as extra devotions to the recitation of the regular Divine Office. In time these "extras" were incorporated into a special collection for lay use; Bishop believed that these "accretions" were adopted by the secular clergy from the monks, just as they had taken the practice of reciting the Office from monastic use. Finally, Bishop saw the adoption of the primer by the laity as growing out of a natural desire to imitate the clergy in their devotions. Bishop dates the beginning of the primer's popularity in England from the close of the 10th century as a result of a spread of devotion to the Blessed Virgin from this time until the Norman Conquest.

Distinction of Book of Hours from Psalter. From the 11th to the 13th century the Book of Hours and the Psalter are sometimes hard to distinguish, since some Psalters might contain the Little Office in addition to their ordinary contents. However, from the 13th century onward the two books went their separate ways. Certainly the vast number of Books of Hours extant from the last centuries of the Middle Ages and the beginning of modern times attests to the popularity of this collection of private devotions. Indeed, some of the most beautifully illuminated books of western Europe extant today are *Horae* meticulously produced for wealthy nobles and royalty in the 14th and especially the 15th centuries by accomplished lay artists of France, Italy, and the Low Countries. Although the contents of these collections might differ slightly among themselves, for the most part a Book of Hours would contain at least the following items: a liturgical calendar, gospel passages, the Office of the Blessed Virgin, the seven penitential Psalms, the 15 gradual Psalms, the litany, and the Office of the Dead.

Illumination of Books of Hours. Because of the nature of its contents the Book of Hours stirred the imagination of the medieval artist. The sequence of the hours of the Office represented events in the life of the Blessed Virgin and her Son; consequently one usually finds at least one illustration for each of the hours, as well as other pictures accompanying the liturgical calendar and the various other Psalms and devotions outside the text of the Office itself. A large number of the extant Books of Hours, particularly French, were produced by unknown artists in the service of noblemen; and so such books are described as originating in a certain atelier, or as being produced by the artist of such-and-such a work. The famous *Rohan Hours* (Bibliothèque Nationale), with its 11 full-page miniatures, is such an anonymous work, for its origin can be attributed only to the "Rohan atelier."

The first truly outstanding artist to illuminate a Book of Hours was the 14th-century painter Jean Pucelle, whose *Hours of Jeanne d'Evreux* (Metropolitan Museum) shows an early grasp of the art of perspective. Toward the end of that century the Limbourg brothers, who painted in the service of the Duke of Berry, produced the magnificent *Très Riches Heures* (Condé Museum, Chantilly). Their employer, Jean, Duke of Berry (d. 1416), brother of Charles V of France, has been called the ''prince of medieval bibliophiles''; the deluxe editions of his library represent the epitome of 14th- and early 15th-century French illumination. The *Belles Heures* illuminated for this nobleman, now in the Metropolitan Museum, is one of the most beautiful manuscripts of the late Middle Ages.

In the 15th century Jean Fouquet, an artist at Tours, produced, among other precious works of manuscript illumination, the *Hours of Étienne Chevalier.* His work shows an unusual independence of the Flemish school, although Italian influence is marked in his use of perspective and classical architecture for background. Among other well known *Horae,* brief mention might be made of the *Boucicaut Hours* (Jacquemart-André Museum, Paris), executed in the early 15th century for the Maréchal de Boucicaut and his wife. Instead of the usual ten to fifteen miniatures, this exquisite manuscript contains no less than 45 large pictures and shows a markedly improved grasp of artistic realism. From this time on, Books of Hours often contained 20 to 40 or more miniatures—their artists perhaps influenced by the ''Boucicaut master.'' The *Laval Hours* (Bibliothèque Nationale), indeed, contains 54 miniatures and many other illustrations; and in the profusion and richness of their illustrative material they are typical of the late 15th-century Books of Hours.

It is interesting to note that these beautiful manuscripts are more frequently studied for their artistic aspects than for their possible effect upon private devotion or personal piety. And it is highly probable that, in spite of their obviously devotional content, the purpose behind their original purchase lay in artistic acquisitiveness rather than piety. Certainly the almost spotless and perfect preservation of many such books betrays no extensive use on the part of their owners. However, it is encouraging, at least in the context of this article, to examine the small, anonymous, and comparatively unknown Books of Hours in the manuscript divisions of libraries—books that are dog-eared and often so worn from constant use that the lettering is extremely difficult to discern or completely worn off. These were the real prayer books of the period.

Printed Books. Since the French undoubtedly produced some of the most exquisite manuscript Books of Hours, they continued after the invention of printing to maintain this artistic excellence in their printed *Horae.* The Parisian printers and publishers chiefly associated with this work were Jean Dupré, Antoine Vérard, and Philippe Pigouchet, who frequently printed their *livres d'heures* on parchment and employed manuscript illuminators. These printed Books of Hours appeared from 1486 on into the 16th century. The first English *prymer* to be printed came, appropriately enough, from the press of the first English printer, William Caxton, at Westminster *c.* 1478. Other printed *Horae* followed in the next century, among which the *Horae eboracenses* (York Prymer) is well known. It was first printed in 1536 and reprinted as volume 132 of the publications of the Surtees Society (London 1920). This work presents the typical contents of the popular lay prayer book of the late Middle Ages: liturgical calendar, *formulae communes* (Pater Noster, Ave Maria, etc.), gospel passages on the birth of Christ, occasional prayers, Office of the Blessed Virgin, penitential Psalms, litany, *vigiliae mortuorum,* Psalms on the Passion of Christ, and various *suffragia.*

In this early age of the printing press the popularity of the *Horae* did not, however, exclude the printing of other prayer collections and books of devotion. Other pious compositions such as the *Hortulus Animae* (Strassburg 1498) and *Paradisus Animae* (Basel 1491) made their appearance, and frequently such collections would contain fantastic spiritual promises and indulgences; these latter were condemned by a bull of Pius V, dated March 11, 1571. It should be noted also that the first work to show the true culmination of the invention of Gutenberg was a Psalter printed in 1457 by the successors to his establishment, Johann Fust and Peter Schoeffer. During the period of the Counter Reformation many Catholic prayer books were published; these seem to have originated as a result of the activity of Peter Canisius, and often appear as manuals for the sodalities in honor of the Blessed Virgin.

In modern times every country has had its favorite prayer books, and accounts of these individual collections can be found in the various national Catholic encyclopedias. In English North America the first extant printed book was the 1640 metrical edition of the Psalms—again attesting to the popularity of the Psalter as a book of devotion. However, Challoner's *Garden of the Soul* (1740) became the first Catholic prayer book to be printed here.

Bibliography: For exhaustive bibliog. and source citations consult J. STADLHUBER, ''Das Stundengebet des Laien im christlichen Altertum,'' *Zeitschrift für katholische Theologie* 71 (1949) 129–183; ''Das Laienstundengebet vom Leiden Christi im seinem mittelalterlichen Fortleben,'' *ibid.* 72 (1950) 282–325. General literature. S. BEISSEL, ''Zur Geschichte der Gebetbücher,'' *Stimmen der Zeit* 77 (1909) 28–41, 169–185, 274–289, 397–411. G. DOMEL, *Entstehung des Gebetbuchs und seine Ausstattung* (Cologne 1921). T. SCHNITZLER, *Lexikon für Theologie und Kirche,* ed. J. HOFER and K. RAHNER, 10 v. (2d, new ed. Freiburg 1957–65); suppl., *Das*

John Eliot preaching to Native Americans in Massachusetts, drawing by J.A. Oertel, 1856.

ZweiteVatikanische Konzil: Dokumente und kommentare, ed. H. S. BRECHTER et al., pt. 1 (1966) 4:551–553. Illuminated Psalters and *Horae.* D. BLAND, *A History of Book Illustration* (Cleveland 1958) 33–83. D. DIRINGER, *The Illuminated Book* (New York 1958). Texts of prayers from the early Church and source citations. A. HAMMAN, *Early Christian Prayers,* tr. W. MITCHELL (Chicago 1961). Books of Hours and Psalters. H. LECLERCQ, *Dictionnaire d'archéologie chrétienneet de liturgie,* ed. F. CABROL, H. LECLERCQ and H. I. MARROU, 15 v. (Paris 1907–53) 9:1836–1906; 14:1950–67. V. LEROQUAIS, *Les Livres d'Heures manuscrits de la Bibliothèque Nationale,* 2 v. (Paris 1927; suppl. 1943). J. WRIGHT, *Early Prayer Books ofAmerica* (St. Paul 1896) 1–26. H. THURSTON, *The Catholic Encyclopedia,* ed. C. G. HERBERMANN, 16 v. (New York 1907–14; suppl. 1922) 12:350–354, 425–426. Individual prayer book citations are listed within the article itself.

[F. J. WITTY]

PREACHING, I (HISTORY OF)

The sermon by its nature is intended to be spoken and heard, and few sermons have been preserved exactly as they were preached. Those preserved in written form have generally been edited for publication. For the early Church no verbatim report of a sermon has survived. Even the accounts of the sermons of Christ recorded in the Gospels give us no more than extracts of the substance of His preaching.

Preaching of the Apostles. It may be assumed that the Apostles followed Christ's practice of speaking in the synagogues after the reading of the Sabbath pericope (Lk 4.14–22). Specific mention of such procedure is not infrequent (Acts 7.4–5; 9.20; 10.42; 1:3.16–41). While there is information about the Christians gathering for the ''breaking of the bread'' in apostolic times (Acts 2.42) and meeting for prayer, there is no surviving record of a sermon preached on such occasions. There are indeed records of seven discourses delivered by Peter (Acts 1.16–23; 2.14–37; 3.12.–26; 5.29–32; 10.34–44; 11.4–18; 15.7–11), and six by Paul (Acts 13.16–41; 14.15–18; 17.22–32; 20.17–36; 22.1–22; 26.2–23). With the exception of Peter's remarks in connection with the election of Matthias and the record of his unwillingness to impose the obligations of the Mosaic Law on Gentile converts, these addresses would be designated in later terminology as ''missionary sermons'' for prospective converts and may faithfully reproduce the preaching of these Apostles or may be an account of it as reported by a Christian writer near the end of the 1st century A.D. In either case this record yields little direct evidence for the history of the sermon preached in the Christian community. As sermons of traveling missionaries Peter's discourse delivered to the crowd after the healing of the

''Saint Giovanni Melchoir Bosco Preaching From His Balcony.'' (©Archivo Iconografico, S.A./CORBIS)

lame man (Acts 3.12–26) and Paul's address on the Areopagus (Acts 17.22–33) show some interesting parallels in their structure. Both begin with a formal greeting of the audience followed by a brief summary of the blessings God has conferred on mankind, a reference to guilt for offenses, a call to repentance, a reminder of the judgment to come, and finally a reference to Christ's Resurrection [cf. E. Norden, *Agnostos Theos,* 3–12 (Stuttgart 1912, repr. 1956)].

The preachers of the apostolic age were the Apostles and those appointed by them to be in charge of the Christian communities. It is difficult to judge how widespread was the charismatic speaking mentioned by Paul (1 Cor 12.1–11, 27–31; ch. 14; Eph 4.7–16). In any case, the phenomenon seems to have disappeared as the catechumenate developed.

Subapostolic and Early Patristic Age. IRENAEUS mentions the discourses that POLYCARP gave to the people in Smyrna (Eusebius, *Ecclesiatical History* 5.20.6), Irenaeus also spoke to the people, and his discourses were collected in a book still extant in Eusebius's day (*ibid.* 5.26). From this same era comes the earliest extant evidence showing the sermon as part of the liturgical service, JUSTIN MARTYR (*Apologia* 1.67) says that the Christians gathered on Sundays and that the memoirs of the Apostles, and writings of the Prophets were read. When the reader had finished, ''he who presides gives the admonition and invites us to imitate these noble men.'' Slightly later, TERTULLIAN makes two references to preaching in similar circumstances. In the *Apologeticum* (*Corpus scriptorum ecclesiasticorum latinorum*—CSEL— 69: 91–92) he relates, that the faithful met for prayer and the reading of the Scriptures; thereupon by admonitions they were strengthened in the practice of their teachings. In his *De anima* (*Corpus scriptorum ecclesiasticorum latinorum* 20:310) he specifically states that there were addresses (*allocutiones*) during divine services

"Christ Preaching" by Rembrandt van Rijn, c. 1635. (©Burstein Collection/CORBIS.)

(*inter dominica sollemnia*). This practice is clearly attested for the Church in northern Africa. Similar evidence for Asia Minor seems to be found in the homily on the Passion preached by MELITO, Bishop of Sardis in Lydia (J. Quasten, *Patrology,* 1.243). As an interesting item from the subapostolic age, the so-called *Second Epistle fo Clement to the Corinthians* (*c.* 150) deserves mention as the oldest extant Christian sermon. It is written in Greek and was read to the assembled Christian community. "Therefore, brothers and sisters, following the God of truth, I am reading you an exhortation to pay attention to that which is written, and that you may both save yourselves and him who is the reader among you" (*2 Clement* 19.1).

In sharp contrast to the unliterary style of *2 Clement* there is the sole surviving homily of CLEMENT OF ALEXANDRIA *Quis dives salvetur,* (Who is the rich man that is saved), on the text of Mk 10.17–31. This rather lengthy homily, if really preached, is possible early evidence of preaching by a priest, although scholars are not agreed on the priesthood of Clement. In any case, instances of preaching by priests and laymen occur in the early part of the 3d century.

During the pontificate of Zephyrinus (199–217), ORIGEN, Clement's successor at the catechetical school in ALEXANDRIA, came to Rome (Jerome, *De viris illustribus* 54) and was present in a church when HIPPOLYTUS preached a sermon in Greek, On the Praise of the Lord Our Savior (*ibid.* 61). This sermon has been lost; it is significant, however, that a priest (Hippolytus had not yet become bishop and antipope) preached in Rome some time before 215. After a brief stay in Rome, Origen returned to Alexandria and remained there until 215, when he left for Palestine, where he was eventually ordained a priest, to the displeasure of Demetrius, Bishop of Alexandria (*ibid.* 54). EUSEBIUS makes the following report on Origen's activity in Palestine:

> And although he had not yet received the presbyterate, the bishops there requested him to discourse and expound the divine Scriptures publicly in the church. That this is so is clear from what Alexander, the bishop of Jerusalem, and Theoctistus, the bishop of Caesarea, write with reference to Demetrius. They make their defense somewhat as follows: And he added to his letter that such a thing had never been heard of, nor taken place hither, that laymen should preach in the presence of bishops; though I do not know how he comes to say what is evidently not true. For instance, where there are found persons suited to help the brethren, they are also invited to preach to the people by the holy bishops, as, for example, in Laranda Euelpis by Neon, and in Iconium Paulinus by Celsus, and in Synnada Theodore by Atticus, our blessed brother bishops. And it is likely that this thing happens in other places also without our knowing it. [Bede, *Ecclesiatical History* 6.19]

All the places mentioned were important cities in Asia Minor: Iconium and Laranda in Lycaonia, Synnada in Phrygia. The statement of the bishops then indicates that laymen preached in this region (at least by Eusebius's time) even though such practice may have been unheard of in Egypt, if Demetrius's judgment was not clouded by his prejudice. Origen's preaching followed this structure; exordium, practical application of a chosen scriptural text in the allegorical interpretation, exhortation, and finally a doxology. There was no striving for rhetorical adornment. As a result of long preparation he had an extraordinary facility in speaking and, in his later years, permitted shorthand-writers to take down the discourses he delivered in public (*ibid.* 6.36).

Shortly after Origen's death a new manner of preaching appeared at least briefly in Antioch. Apart from his doctrinal errors, Paul of Samosata, Bishop of Antioch (*c.* 260–268), aroused disgust with his pulpit antics. Only a few fragments of his discourses are extant, so one can judge only from reports. Eusebius takes Paul to task for "the quackery in church assemblies that he devises, courting popularity and posing for appearance sake . . . with the tribunal and lofty throne that he prepared for himself not befitting a disciple of Christ. . . . He smites his hand on his thigh and stamps the tribunal with his feet; and those who do not applaud or wave their handkerchiefs, as in a theater, or shout out and jump up in the same way as do the men and wretched women who are his partisans—these he rebukes and insults. . . . He brags about himself as though he were not a bishop but a sophist and a charlatan" (*ibid.* 7.30).

The meager evidence extant for preaching in Latin down to the 4th century centers around the Church of north Africa. Tertullian's references to preaching have already been mentioned. That he himself may have preached can be inferred only indirectly from Lactantius when the latter states that Tertullian was not a persuasive speaker (*Divinae institutiones* 5.1, CSEL 19: 402). Cyprian's sermons, admired and praised by Lactantius (*ibid.*) as being diligently prepared for the faithful, are lost. One sermon in Latin, perhaps from Africa and preached *c.* 300, is preserved. It is the discourse *Adversus aleatores,* or *De aleatoribas* (CSEL 3.3.92–104), which inveighs against dice players as persons who have denied the faith.

With the end of the great persecutions and the peace that came to the Church with the accession of Constantine, a new era for preaching began. The preachers themselves, educated in the best schools of the day at Athens, Antioch, and Alexandria and trained by such outstanding masters of rhetoric as Himerius and Libanius, brought to the office of preaching a wealth of learning and an amazing familiarity with Sacred Scripture. As the Church penetrated the more educated strata of society, an audience was at hand that could relish the accomplishments of the preachers.

Greek Preaching. The great Cappadocians GREGORY OF NAZIANZUS, BASIL the Great, and JOHN CHRYSOSTOM dominate Greek preaching during the 4th century. Of these preachers, Gregory of Nazianzus is distinguished as both poet and orator. His fame in preaching rests on his proficiency in the panegyric (a form already Christianized by Gregory Thaumaturgus in his eulogy of Origen delivered in 238), the liturgical sermon, and the funeral oration. In this genre Gregory Christianized the pagan *epitaphios logos.* Of his four extant funeral orations, the one delivered at the death of St. Basil is the masterpiece of Christian Greek funeral speeches. The discourses of Gregory were greatly admired and were soon studied as models; marginal annotations (*scholia*), the earliest dating from the early 6th century, clearly show this. Rufinus translated nine of Gregory's discourses into Latin, *c.* 399.

Basil the Great made significant contributions to the exegetical homily by enhancing it with the embellishments of Greek rhetoric. This artistic effect is seen at its best in the homilies on the six days of creation preached during Lent while he was still a priest. AMBROSE, well versed in Greek, used these homilies freely for his *Hexaemeron.* A Latin translation of the homilies made by Eustathius the African appeared as early as 440.

GREGORY OF NYSSA, the younger brother of Basil and a teacher of rhetoric before he became a bishop, merits at least passing mention for his funeral orations, even though they fall short of the excellence of those preached by Gregory of Nazianzus.

John Chrysostom, who was renowned as a preacher both in Antioch and Constantinople, has left a larger legacy of discourses than any other orator of the golden age of Greek preaching. His oratorical skill is evident in the homily (exegetical, dogmatic, and polemical), the catecheses for those about to receive Baptism, the moral discourse, the liturgical sermon, the panegyric, and the occasional discourse. The best known of his sermons are probably the 21 homilies *On the Statues,* preached in Antioch in 387 and generally considered the finest examples of his eloquence, and the two homilies on the fall of Eutropius, delivered in Constantinople in January 399. The pleasing effect of the rhetorical adornment of his sermons frequently elicited spontaneous applause from his audience (Migne, *Patrologia Graeca,* 60:226).

Amphilochius of Iconium, who delighted in presenting scriptural personages engaged in dialogue in his sermons, and Asterius of Amasea, whose sermon on St. Euphemia bears early witness to the veneration of sacred images, are overshadowed by their contemporaries, Basil and Chrysostom.

The golden age of Greek preaching had its last moments of splendor in the early years of the 5th century. As the catechumenate fell into desuetude, the catecheses gradually disappeared. On the basis of extant evidence, however, the homily and sermon on special topics remained in use as can be seen in the works of Flavian of Antioch, SEVERIAN OF GABALA, Antiochus of Ptolemais, NILUS OF ANCYRA, THEODORET OF CYR, Basil of Seleucia, DIADOCHUS OF PHOTICE, GENNADIUS of Constantinople, John the Faster, JOHN DAMASCENE, and THEODORE THE STUDITE.

The sermon for special feast days, the panegyric of martyrs and other saints, and the funeral oration received special attention. In particular, sermons on the Blessed Virgin (Theotokos) became very frequent as CYRIL OF ALEXANDRIA, Hesychius and Chrysippus of Jerusalem, Theodore of Ancyra, Proclus of Constantinople, Abraham of Ephesus, John of Thessalonica, SOPHRONIUS of Jerusalem, GERMANUS of Constantinople, ANDREW OF CRETE, and TARASIUS of Constantinople clearly show. Significant for the history of Greek preaching is Canon 19 of the Trullan Synod (692), which directed bishops to instruct both clergy and laity daily, and especially on Sundays (Mansi 11:951). The synod bade the bishops in their treating of scriptural topics not to depart from, but to follow, the fathers, ''the luminaries and teachers,'' rather than to compose their own sermons. This synodal enactment explains at least in part the proliferation of collections of homilies especially for use on Sundays during the following centuries. Of all the forms of preaching, the panegyric was the most cultivated after the golden age of preaching had passed. In the long list of panegyrists the emperors themselves find a place. Leo VI the Wise and Constantine Porphyrogennetus are notable examples.

Latin Preaching. The surviving evidence that Latin sermons were preached in Gaul, Spain, and Italy becomes increasingly specific as investigation focuses on the 4th century. Hilary of Poitiers is, in Jerome's opinion, ''the Rhone of Latin eloquence'' (Migne, *Patrologia Latina,* 26:355A) even though the same critic does not admire Hilary's involved periodic sentences ''adorned with the flowers of Greece'' (*Epistola* 58.10). Victricius of Rouen is remembered for his sermon *De Laude Sanctorum* (Migne, *Patrologia Latina,* 20: 443–458). Gregory of Elvira is known especially for his homilies on the Canticle of Canticles; he is the earliest known preacher in the West to apply the bridal imagery of this book to Christ and the Church. The first preacher in Latin whose sermons survive in an appreciable number is ZENO OF VERONA. His 16 longer sermons show their author's skill in the use of anaphora, alliteration, and cursus. But Ambrose of Milan was the first real Latin rival of the great preachers in Greek. His sermons were a delight to the trained rhetorician (Augustine, *Confessor* 5.13). Ambrose as preacher has a twofold claim to distinction. He has great proficiency in the exegetical homily and is a pioneer and master in the Christian Latin funeral oration. In the first category he is indebted to Philo of Alexandria, Origen, and, as already noted, Basil. In the second, he is vastly more independent of pagan models than his Greek contemporaries and gives to the funeral oration a much more Christian tone.

Latin preaching in the 5th century was dominated by AUGUSTINE, whose preaching career began with his ordination to the priesthood in 391. Valerius, Bishop of Hippo, entrusted him with the office of preaching, although in many places it was not the practice for priests to preach in the presence of bishops (Jerome, *Epistola* 52.7). For more than 30 years, both as priest and as bishop, Augustine preached frequently and at times twice a day. He addressed his audience in the exegetical homily, in special sermons emphasizing the chief mysteries of salvation or commemorating saints' feast days, or in discourses on various moral topics. The style of these sermons ranges from the highly rhetorical to the almost colloquial, adapted to the capacity of those who lacked formal training. More important for the history of preaching is the fourth book of Augustine's *De doctrina christiana,* in which he gives guidelines for preaching based on his own personal experience.

JEROME preached exegetical homilies to his monastic community in Bethlehem. As in the case of Augustine, the text of the sermons we possess is the stenographic report taken down by secretaries (*notarii*) in the audience, Peter Chrysologus, Archbishop of Ravenna, and Maximus, Bishop of Turin, both popular and effective preachers, are overshadowed by Pope St. LEO I. His carefully prepared sermons, with their neatly balanced clauses and close attention to cursus, rival Augustine's in artistry. The topics of Leo's sermons are chosen chiefly from the liturgical cycle. From the doctrinal point of view, however, three sermons preached on the anniversary of his election to the papacy merit special attention. In these sermons Leo is the first pope to state specifically that the Roman pontiff is the heir to the petrine powers (Migne, *Patrologia Latina,* 54:144A, 147A, 155A). To the list of renowned preachers of this century must be added the names of Hilary of Arles and Gaudentius of Brescia.

6th to 9th Centuries. The year 529 has special significance for the history of preaching in the Latin Church. In that year the second council of Vaison met. The second canon approved at this council granted priests the right to preach: ''for the edification of all the churches and the benefit of all the people not only in the cities but also in the rural areas. If, because of illness, the priest is unable to preach let the homilies of the holy fathers be read by the deacons'' (*Monumenta Germaniae Concilia* 1:56; G. Morin, *S. Caesarii opera omnia* 2.86). Juridically this canon marked the end of the bishops' monopoly on the right to preach in the Latin Church (Hefele-Leclercq, *Histoire des Conciles* 2.2:1112). As already mentioned priests did *de facto* preach in the Latin Church, but it was not customary (cf. Jerome, *loco citato*).

It is worthy of note that CAESARIUS OF ARLES presided at this council. He was a very important bishop in 6th-century Gaul and a most zealous preacher. His *Vita* (G. Morin, *opere citato* 296–345) states that he preached every Sunday and on all feast days as long as his health permitted; if illness prevented him from preaching he had the deacons read the homilies of Ambrose. Augustine, and those of his own composition, which he also readily gave to those who asked for them. Frequently too, when people gathered in the church at the time of Lauds or Vespers, he had homilies read to them so that no one could plead ignorance of his religious duties. Even more, Caesarius sent sermons to churches in Italy, in Spain, and in distant places so that through preaching, the faithful would be incited to the pursuit of good works.

St. GREGORY I was the author of 40 homilies composed *c.* 590 and 591, of which 20 were read to the people by a secretary in the Pope's presence, and the rest preached by Gregory himself. These homilies, considered models of eloquence, were widely read in the Middle Ages. Extant also are 22 longer sermons explaining portions of Ezechiel. Even more important for the history of preaching is Gregory's *Liber regulae pastoralis,* the third section of which gives practical directives for preaching. This work enjoyed wide popularity and was translated into Greek during the Pope's lifetime. Other noteworthy preachers of this century were Avitus, Bishop of Vienne; Fulgence, Bishop of Ruspe; and the opponent of Faustus of Riez, Martin of Braga, author of the famous sermon *De correctione rusticorum* (used later especially by Eligius of Noyon and Pirmin of Reichenau).

The meager extant evidence on preaching in the 7th century makes it practically impossible to determine to what extent the legislation authorizing priests to preach was implemented. Apart from some general remarks about the eloquence of certain well-known bishops of this century, and sermons either incorrectly or doubtfully attributed to them, we know with certainty of a sermon of Ildefonsus of Toledo and a collection of homilies known as *Homiliae Toletanae,* which owes its origin either to Ildefonsus or Julian of Toledo.

Early in the 8th century Bede was ordained to the priesthood. His homilies, based on the Gospel pericopes for feast days and preached to the monks of his abbey, are indebted in great measure to the sermons of Jerome and Gregory the Great. The collection of patristic homilies made by Paul the Deacon and intended primarily for use in the monastic office in choir indirectly served the needs of the clergy in their office of preaching. A deplorable state of preaching, at least in the Frankish kingdom, is indicated in the *Admonitio generalis* (*Monumenta Germaniae Capitularia* 1:52–62) of March 789. The bishops were admonished to find out whether the priests themselves understood the Our Father and preached it to the people. They were also to see that priests preached according to the Scriptures and that they did not fabricate teachings of their own. To implement these directives, the *Admonitio* gave a summary of essential sermon material. Theodulf of Orleans in 797 presented an equally gloomy picture of preaching. He exhorted his priests to instruct the people. He who was versed in the Scriptures should preach scriptural sermons; he who was not should at least preach to the people that ''they turn away from evil and do good: seek after peace and pursue it. The eyes of the Lord are upon the just: and his ears unto their prayers'' (Migne, *Patrologia Latina,* 105:200A; Mansi, *Sacrorum Conciliorum nova et amplissima collectio,* 13:1001).

Preaching in the 9th century received invaluable aid from the collections of homilies and sermons made by Alcuin, Rabanus Maurus, and Haymo of Auxerre. Great as these contributions were, the progress of preaching was far more vitally affected by the third Council of Tours and the second Council of Reims, both of which met in 813. Canon 17 of the Council of Tours decreed that each bishop should have homilies containing the necessary admonitions for the instruction of his people. He was directed moreover to translate these homilies into the early Romance language or German so that ''all could more easily understand what is being said'' (Mansi 14:85). Canon 15 of the Council of Reims similarly instructed the bishops to preach the sermons and homilies of the holy Fathers in the vernacular ''so that all may understand'' (Mansi 14:78). Some 30 years later the first Council of Mainz (847) repeated the legislation of canon 17 of the Council of Tours (Mansi 14:903).

Medieval Preaching. After the legislation regarding the use of the vernacular in sermons, the Crusades, the flowering of scholasticism, and the founding of the mendicant orders were the most significant factors that influenced preaching in the Latin Church. From the 10th to the early 13th century important preachers were active. A selective list of the most outstanding must mention the following at least in passing: AELFRIC GRAMMATICUS, FULBERT OF CHARTRES, PETER DAMIAN, BERNARD OF CLAIRVAUX, ANSELM OF CANTERBURY, HONORIUS OF AUTUN, IVO OF CHARTRES, ROBERT OF ARBRISSEL, GUIBERT OF NOGENT, RUPERT OF DEUTZ, HUGH OF SAINT VICTOR, AELRED OF RIEVAULX, PETER COMESTOR, MAURICE OF SULLY, FULK OF NEUILLY, ALAN OF LILLE, and Adam Scotus. The sermon texts of medieval preachers have come down to us in Latin. This is not conclusive evidence, however, that the sermons were delivered in Latin. It is known that Bernard of Clairvaux preached to the lay brothers in the vernacular. Jacques de Vitry clearly states that sermons for clerics were in Latin while those for the laity were in the vernacular. The Latin text, moreover, was intended primarily for the preacher's own use in preparation, as can be concluded from the complaint of Adam of Perseigne that sermons, when translated into the vernacular, were like wine poured from one container into another; some of the color, taste, and bouquet of the original was always lost in the process (C. Langlois, *Revue des deux Mondes* 115:173–175).

The Scholastic Preacher. Toward the end of the 12th century the scholastic method of teaching had an effect on preaching. The logic and dialectic of the schools was applied to the sermon topic. The preacher announced his theme according to the method of propounding questions and defending conclusions in the schools of theology. He then proceeded to definition, division, subdivision, and distinction, citing numerous passages from Scripture and the Fathers and adding arguments from reason to prove his point. The tactful preacher generally left, as his parting impression, an outline of future bliss and glory ''to which may He lead us who lives and reigns forever. Amen.'' These scholastic sermons were delivered before faculty and students at such university cities as Paris, Oxford, and Cambridge by William of Auvergne, Odo of Chateauroux, Stephen Langton, and Robert Grosseteste. With the founding of the mendicant orders, the Dominicans and Franciscans became famous for such sermons delivered by Hugh of Saint-Cher, Thomas Aquinas, Peter of Tarantasia, John of Rupella, Bonaventure, Guibert of Tournai, and Matthew of Aquasparta.

The Popular Sermon. Popular preaching at the end of the 12th century was generally at low ebb. Conditions were such that few among the parish clergy, according to the Fourth Lateran Council in 1215, had the least proficiency in letters (*Concilliorum Oecumenicorum Decreta,* 226). To meet this deficiency, unauthorized preachers and laymen came forward, among whom were the HUMILIATI and WALDENSES. But their lack of training for preaching eventually involved them in doctrinal errors. As a consequence Alexander III forbade the Humiliati and Waldenses to preach, and Lucius III finally excommunicated them for failing to obey the prohibition.

The founding of the Dominicans and Franciscans provided a more effective remedy for the situation. Some of the friars distinguished themselves in the more academic type of preaching mentioned above, but great numbers of them gave themselves to apostolic preaching among the people. They preached in the vernacular upon concrete themes, and applied their message in a practical way to daily life. Homely expressions and examples as well as the Scriptures and the lives of the saints were freely used. The timeliness of this type of preaching can be judged from the Council of Vienne (Hefele-Leclercq, *Histoire des conciles d'après les documents originaux-opere citato* 6.2:674–678), which empowered the Dominicans and Franciscans with the apostolic authority to preach freely and ordered prelates and parish clergy to receive the friars kindly and cooperate with them. Distinguished preachers among them were David of Augsburg, Berthold of Regensburg, Raymund LULL, Bartholomew of Vicenza, Guido of Évreux, James of Lausanne, and Peregrine of Breslau.

A special form of the popular sermon was the sermon in verse, or rhymed sermon (*sermo rimatus*), which enjoyed special popularity in England. The Franciscan John of Grimston achieved fame in this type of preaching, which Peter of Limoges criticized as a deadly snare to seduce the ear rather than to convert the soul.

The beginnings of the mystical sermon can already be discerned in some of the preaching of Bernard of Clairvaux and Bonaventure, but the genre was developed later by Meister ECKHART, Johannes TAULER, HENRY SUSO, NICHOLAS OF STRASSBURG, JOHN OF STERNGASSE, Henry of Nordlingen, and Jean GERSON.

Literature. As the various types of sermons were developing, a wealth of sermon literature was produced. Technical treatises, the *artes praedicandi,* offered direction for the preparation and delivery of the sermon. Frequently, however, some of these *artes* were really ''sermon encyclopedias'' as, e.g., the work of Humbert of Romans. Among the best known medieval sources for sermon material were the *Exempla* of JACQUES DE VITRY and the *Legenda aurea* of JAMES OF VORAGINE. Sturdy competitors were the *Liber exemplorum* and the *Speculum laicorum,* written by two anonymous Franciscans, and the impressive *Summa predicantium* of the Dominican John of BROMYARD.

Preaching in the Open. Another development in the history of preaching in the Middle Ages must yet be noted. The sermon did not have to be delivered in the church during the celebration of Mass. In 1312 the Council of Vienne granted the Dominicans and Franciscans permission for street preaching (*in plateis communibus*) and ordered prelates, of whatever preeminence, and parish priests not to look askance at this procedure (*Conciliorum Oecumenicorum Decreta,* 342, 344). This decree did not introduce a novelty (Berthold of Regensburg had already preached in this manner), but gave formal legality to something already in existence.

14th and 15th Centuries. Preaching, which in the 13th and 14th centuries had attained an uncommon splendor, had, in the subsequent centuries, varying fortunes in different regions. Generalizations about its effectiveness are particularly hazardous. When the enthusiasm for the sermon was over and the preacher gone, fickle audiences, which ''like snails in fright had drawn in their horns . . . shot them out again as soon as the danger was over. Cards, dice, false hair, rouge-pots, and other tribulations even to chess boards'' might well be burned in Florence when Bernardine of Siena had finished his sermon, but the more calculating Englishman was not likely to be moved in similar fashion (G. Owst, *Preaching in Medieval England,* 190). At all events, the 14th century produced works noteworthy in the history of preaching. The most outstanding is the *Postilla litteralis* of Nicholas of Lyra. This treatise, of which 700 copies were made within one century, differentiated clearly between the literal and mystical meaning of Scripture and profoundly influenced subsequent preaching. Its impact on Luther, while perhaps oversimplified, was neatly expressed in the dictum: ''Si Lyra non lyrasset Lutherus non saltasset'' (Had Lyra not played the tunes, Luther would not have danced). Collections of sermons for Sundays and the feast days of saints were written by John of S. Geminiano, Francis of Meyronnes, and HENRY OF FRIEMAR; homilies on the Lord's Prayer, the Hail Mary, the Apostles' Creed, and sermons on the Blessed Virgin, by HENRY HEINBUCHE OF LANGENSTEIN. ROBERT HOLCOT produced the popular compendium of sermon material: *Lectiones super sapientiam Salomonis,* and Conrad of Waldhausen inveighed against the vices of his times and indulged in hackneyed invectives against the mendicants charging them with laxity and avarice.

In the 15th century there was a notable increase in the publication of collections of sermons. The most popular was that of Johannes of Werden (d. 1437) published under the forthright title *Dormi secure* (Sleep without Anxiety). The numerous editions of this work (almost 90 within 100 years) are an indication of its popularity and may also be a significant commentary on the condition of preaching at this time. Slightly less popular was the work of an unknown author, *Parati sermones,* which furnished several sermons for every Sunday and the feast days of certain saints. There were 17 editions of this sermon aid. The largest and most unusual collection of sermons was the *Hortulus reginae,* composed by Meffreth, a priest (*c.* 1447). This work supplied at least three sermons for every Sunday and for the feast days of certain saints. The sermons were long and, in addition to scriptural references, contained quotations—some quite lengthy—from Aristotle, Pliny, Horace, Ovid, Terence, Martial, Juvenal, Lucretius, the distichs of Cato, Sedulius, and Boethius. By 1500 there had already been ten editions of the *Hortulus,* and many more followed in the 16th and 17th centuries. Other well-known sermon collections of the period were those of Johann NIDER, Johann Herolt, and Anthony Rampegalus. Another noteworthy development of the century was the Lenten sermon, frequently mentioned in records of this period.

The mission sermon also attained eminence through such renowned preachers as VINCENT FERRER, BERNARDINE OF SIENA, JOHN CAPISTRAN, and JAMES OF THE MARCHES.

A selective list of important preachers of the period must include such names as: John of Retz, NICHOLAS OF DINKELSBÜHL, NICHOLAS OF CUSA, Leonard of Udine, Gabriel Barletta, Anthony of Vercelli, Pelbart of Temesvar, BERNARDINE OF FELTRE, Roberto CARACCIOLO, and Gabriel BIEL. The most widely known preacher of this century was undoubtedly Girolamo SAVONAROLA.

As the evidence shows, there was no dearth of preaching in the years immediately preceding the Reformation. There were, in fact, ecclesiastical benefices that obliged the incumbent to preach. The proliferation of ''sermon encyclopedias'' also made it possible for the laymen to read sermons, if they were neglected in church. On the other hand, that the quality of the sermons must have left much to be desired is deducible from the *Circa modum praedicandi* of the 11th session of the Fifth Lateran Council, dated December 19, 1516. This document deplores the fact that preachers were often more concerned with a display of their own talents than with the needs of the audience. The meaning of the Scriptures was distorted in sermons; preaching was often long-winded; the Gospel was not being preached, but fictitious miracles, false prophecies, and idle tales found their way into the sermon. Some even went so far as to proclaim the arrival of anti-Christ and the imminence of the Last Judgment. Bishops and prelates in positions of authority were being openly denounced (see *Conciliorum Oecumenicorum Decreta,* 610–614). It is difficult to determine how widespread these abuses were. The list of shortcomings does, however, contain many charges that the reformers themselves were soon to make.

The Reformation. With the Reformation, a new emphasis was placed on preaching. The sermon became the focal point of the revised divine worship. The duly called minister based his sermon on the literal meaning of Scripture. In the new theology, the sermon was the living voice of the gospel, and Christ spoke in the preacher's words. The new doctrines on justification and the role of Scripture as the sole rule of faith were proclaimed in the sermon.

This renewed emphasis on preaching was reflected also in the Council of Trent. The *Decretum super lectione et praedicatione, (ibid.* 645) declared that it was the duty of bishops, archbishops, primates, and other prelates to preach the holy Gospel of Jesus Christ. Pastors were to preach, either themselves or through suitable priests, at least on all Sundays and solemn feast days. Similar emphasis was placed on preaching at the 24th session in *De Reformatione,* where special sermons during Advent and Lent were recommended (*ibid.* 739). Among the early opponents of the new teachings were Thomas MURNER, Johann ECK, Wendelin Fabri, Johann Hoffmeister, and especially Peter CANISIUS.

In addition to determining responsibility for preaching, the Council of Trent took further steps to secure trained men for preaching by decreeing that seminaries be established to train priests (*ibid.* 726–729). This legislation was enacted to eliminate the recurrence of the plight deplored in the Fifth Lateran Council.

Charles BORROMEO was untiring in efforts to implement the decrees of Trent. He was personally a zealous preacher, as were JOHN OF AVILA and LOUIS OF GRANADA. Of the impressive number of preachers whose sermons were delivered entirely, or at least in great part, during the 17th century only the following can be mentioned: JOSEPH OF LEONESSA, LAWRENCE OF BRINDISI, Robert BELLARMINE, Procopius of Templin, and Paolo SEGNERI.

17th to 19th Centuries. The last half of the 17th and the beginning of the 18th century witnessed a brilliance of pulpit oratory rare in the annals of preaching. The era was dominated by Jacques BOSSUET, Louis BOURDALOUE, Valenten-Esprit Fléchier, François FÉNELON, and Jean Baptiste MASSILON. Two other preachers of the same era cannot go unmentioned: the inimitable ABRAHAM OF SANCTA CLARA and the great mission preacher, LEONARD OF PORT MAURICE. The conferences of Henri LACORDAIRE drew crowds to the cathedral of Notre Dame in Paris. Gustave RAVIGNAN and Joseph Felix also achieved fame for conferences in the same venerable cathedral. Sacred eloquence continued at a high standard in the preaching of Louis PIE, Bishop of Poitiers, often called the Hilary of the 19th century, and Étienne de Boulogne. Among English-speaking preachers, the three well-known English cardinals, WISEMAN, MANNING, and NEWMAN, hold places of distinction.

In large part because of the writings and example of the English cardinals there was new interest in the forms and frequency of preaching. In the United States the number of books and periodicals that addressed the technical aspects of preaching and the composition of sermons, as well as collections of sermons multiplied. In the United States the sermon was a regular feature of the Sunday Mass. Religious congregations, and some dioceses, organized bands of traveling preachers who conducted parish missions in which the sermon was a main feature. Lenten sermons and sermons during weekly holy hours and novenas were a regular part of parish life. Street preaching, often apologetic in purpose, and radio sermons were popular up to the advent of television. After World War II preached retreats for the laity became popular in midcentury, but it was the Second Vatican Council that brought new vitality to the preaching ministry by the emphasis that it gave in the various documents to theology of the word.

Bibliography: R. CRUEL, *Geschichte der deutschen Predigt im Mittelalter* (Detmold 1879). C. SCHIAN, J. J. HERZOG and A. HAUCK, eds., *Realencyklopädie für protestantische Theologie,* 24 v. (3rd ed. Leipzig 1896–1913) 15:623–747; 24:333–346. H. JORDAN, *Geschichte der altchristlichen Literatur* (Leipzig 1911) 184–211. G. R. OWST, *Preaching in Medieval England* (Cambridge, England 1926); *Literature and Pulpit in Medieval England* (2d ed. New York 1961). A. ZAWART, *The History of Franciscan Preaching and of Franciscan Preachers 1209–1927* (*Franciscan Studies* 7; New York 1928). H. CAPLAN, *Mediaeval Artes praedicandi: A Hand-List* (Ithaca, N.Y. 1934); *Mediaeval Artes praedicandi: Supplementary Handlist* (Ithaca, N.Y. 1936). H. CAPLAN and H. H. KING, "Pulpit Eloquence: A List of Doctrinal and Historical Studies in English," *Speech Monographs* 22 (Special issue 1955) 1–159; "Pulpit Eloquence: A List of Doctrinal and Historical Studies in German," *ibid.* 23 (Special issue 1956) 1–106. P. MANDONNET, *St. Dominic and His Work,* tr. M. B. LARKIN (St. Louis 1944) 120–155. Y. T. BRILIOTH, *Landmarks in the History of Preaching* (London 1950). B. REICKE, "Synopsis of Early Christian Preaching," *The*

Root of the Vine, ed. A. J. FRIDRICHSEN (New York 1953) 128–160. E. C. DARGAN, *A History of Preaching,* 2 v. in 1 (Grand Rapids 1954). M. H. VICAIRE, *Saint Dominique de Caleruega* (Paris 1955) 113–189. H. THYEN, *Der Stil der jüdischhellenistischen Homilie* (Göttingen 1955). A. NIEBERGALL, *Die Religion in Geschichte und Gegenwart,* 7 v. (3d ed. Tübingen 1957–65) 5:516–530. J. B. SCHNEYER, *Lexikon für Theologie und Kirche,* ed. J. HOFER and K. RAHNER, 10 v. (2d, new ed. Freiburg 1957–65) 8:705–713.

[H. DRESSLER/EDS.]

The Documents of Vatican II. The first document of the Council, the *Constitution on the Sacred Liturgy,* that deals with preaching relates it to three fundamental aspects of the mystery of Christ and the Church: (1) it reaffirms the primacy of the work of preaching in the mission of Jesus and his followers (*Sacrosanctum Concilium* 6); (2) it reaffirms also the necessity of preaching as the unique instrument of faith and conversion (ibid. 9), thus providing the basis for that intense ''evangelical'' preaching which is a notable feature of the ministry of the Word in the postconciliar world; (3) it designates the privileged place for preaching within the liturgical celebration itself, that is, in the HOMILY, by means of which ''the mysteries of the faith and the guiding principles of the Christian life are expounded'' (ibid. 52). Specific guidelines for liturgical preaching include the regrounding of the Homily in the scriptural Readings and its restored status as the natural climax of the Liturgy of the Word.

The various instructions and decrees implementing liturgical reform after the Council made it clear that the Homily is an integral part not only of the Eucharist but of the other Sacraments as well; and the new rituals for each of the Sacraments reflect this conception and this concern. Baptism, even when celebrated outside of Mass, has its own Liturgy of the Word and its own Homily; the same procedure is indicated for the rite of Penance when it is celebrated for more than one penitent and for the rite of Matrimony when celebrated outside of Mass; even the rite of Anointing of the Sick calls for a brief explanation of the scriptural texts when circumstances permit. The Homily following sacred Readings is now an integral part of the entire sacramental ritual, so that liturgical reform may be said to be governed everywhere by the necessary union of Word and Sacrament— *contactus fidei, contactus sacramenti* (cf. *Summa Theologiae* 3a. 48.6 ad 2)—in order to bring about a true interiorization of the sacramental encounter with Christ.

The documents of Vatican II are very rich also in their sensitivity to the ecclesial character of the preaching act and to the widespread sharing of the prophetic ministry throughout the Church. As in the *Decree on the Church's Missionary Activity* (*Ad gentes* 3) so in the Constitution on the Church the task of the Church is seen as always centered on the act of proclaiming the Gospel (*Lumen gentium* 17). This same Constitution, as well as other conciliar documents, clearly identifies those who are called upon to exercise this central ministry of preaching. First, bishops are said to ''receive from the Lord . . . the mission to teach all nations and to preach the Gospel to every creature'' (ibid. 24). More particularly they are to ''preach to the people commited to them the faith to be believed and put into practice'' (ibid. 25). According to the *Decree on the Pastoral Office of Bishops*, their prophetic mission is shared by pastors who are ''cooperators of the bishop'' in preaching and catechetical instruction (*Christus Dominus* 30), as well as by priests and lay people. ''By the power of the sacrament of Orders . . . they (priests) are consecrated to preach the Gospel . . . and to announce the divine Word to all'' (ibid. 28). According to an emphasis characteristic of the documents of Vatican II the laity also are designated as ''witnesses'' of the faith and ''powerful proclaimers of a faith in things to be hoped for'' (ibid. 35). The role of the laity as preachers is also affirmed in the *Decree on the Apostolate of the Laity* (*Apostolicam actuositatem*) wherein lay people are said to share in ''the prophetic office of the Church,'' not only ''by their efforts to permeate and perfect the secular order of things with the spirit of the Gospel'' but also by their more direct efforts ''to bring the news of the Gospel and the ways of holiness to mankind'' (*Apostolicam actuositatem* 2). The final document of Vatican II, the *Pastoral Constitution on the Church in the Modern World* underlines the same prophetic mission of the laity, a mission not only ''to penetrate the world with a Christian spirit'' but also ''to be witnesses to Christ in all things in the midst of human society'' (*Gaudium et spes* 43).

Along with the rehabilitation of the Homily, the phenomenon of lay preaching is one of the most distinctive developments in the prophetic mission of the Church after Vatican II. In practice this phenomenon covers a whole range of paraliturgical preaching, much of it very informal and spontaneous. Such ''preaching'' is usually based upon Scripture and can take the form of ''teaching'' or ''sharing'' or ''witnessing,'' the last-named having to do with the confession of personal experiences that have challenged or restored or deepened a person's faith. It is evident that the term ''preaching'' as it includes communications such as these takes on a very broad signification. It ceases to be restricted to public proclamation of the mysteries deriving from episcopal mandate and associated with clerical ministry. Preaching becomes, rather, any public communication of faith by any believer under a right and an impulse deriving from the baptismal character itself and, even more urgently, from Confirmation. Moreover, the rightful and fruitful exercise of such a ministry should be looked upon as normal in the Church, granted a right understanding of the dynamism of Baptism and Confirmation and a right understanding of the act of preaching as a charism or grace-of-words given by the Spirit in the Church for the building up of the Church in faith and love.

The Apostolic Exhortation on Evangelization. A second major source for renewed emphasis on the theology of preaching is the apostolic exhortation *On Evangelization in the Modern World*, issued by Pope Paul VI and inspired by the Third General Assembly of the Synod of Bishops (1974). In this document the term ''evangelization'' has both a specific and a general meaning: specifically, it refers to the initial proclamation of the Word of God or the Good News aimed at CONVERSION (Paul VI EvangNunt 10); in other contexts it refers to any exercise of the ministry of the Word. The specific meaning of evangelization, however, and the stress upon that meaning in the document reflect a growing awareness that Christian ministry is exercised today in an increasingly non-Christian and non-religious environment, so that preaching must be first defined as the call to conversion. Under this aspect preaching in the Catholic sector tends to link with the evangelical character of those forms of Protestant preaching which focus almost entirely upon the call to conversion and spiritual rebirth.

While the apostolic exhortation reflects this specific need and this specific mode of preaching, the entire document provides, in addition, a vital and eloquent restatement of the chief elements in a theology of preaching.

(1) The character of the preaching act is Christological after the example of the preaching of Jesus, the first evangelizer, and as the historical extension of his preaching (ibid. 7).

(2) An ecclesial character marks the act of preaching. The exhortation insists that evangelization or the proclamation of the Good News ''constitutes the essential mission of the Church. . . which exists in order to evangelize'' (ibid. 14). Preaching is never ''an individual or isolated act; it is one that is deeply ecclesial'' (ibid. 60).

(3) The preaching act is charismatic in so far as the Holy Spirit is its principal agent and the new humanity generated by the Spirit its very goal and purpose (ibid. 75). In an authentic theology of preaching it is the Spirit who moves both the preacher to preach efficaciously and the hearer to respond with a living faith.

(4) The content is revealed or God-given, a content which, however diversely expressed (the Love of the Father, the Good News, Salvation, Jesus himself) touches principally on ''a transcendent and eschatological salvation'' (ibid. 27), though secondarily and consequently on human liberation here and now from temporal evils (ibid. 31–38).

(5) Preaching is ministry, a ministry pertaining to the whole Church and to each of its parts. It pertains, first, to the ordained ministry of pope (ibid. 67), bishops and priests (ibid. 68); and to religious according to the silent witness of example or the overt witness of proclamation (ibid. 69). The document stresses also the ministry of the laity (ibid. 70), in virtue both of their presence in the midst of temporal affairs and of their direct service to the ecclesial community (ibid. 73). In this sense the apostolic exhortation supports the distinctive stress in the documents of Vatican II on the role of the laity in proclaiming the Good News and extending the Kingdom of Christ.

(6) Preaching as a ministry calls for such special virtues and qualities as the witness of a holy life (ibid. 76), the spirit of unity and amity among believers (ibid. 77), great reverence for truth (ibid. 78), authentic love for those to whom the Gospel is proclaimed (ibid. 79), and that spiritual fervor which makes the preaching of the Good News a matter of urgent personal necessity (ibid. 80).

(7) Finally, preaching is an act of discernment and accommodation, an act in which the specific character, needs, and life-situation of the hearers affect the mode of proclamation (ibid. 51–57; 62–63), though without prejudice to the universality of the preaching mandate (ibid. 49), or the claims of the universal Church (ibid. 64), or the unimpaired content of revealed truth expressed by the magisterium (ibid. 65).

In conclusion, it may be said that while the documents of Vatican II and the apostolic exhortation on evangelization clearly and persuasively restate a traditional theology of preaching—its source, its purpose, its content, its agency, both divine and human—these same documents give special emphasis and provide special insight into three distinct areas or concerns in the contemporary regime of preaching: (1) the importance of conversional preaching, or the initial moment in the proclamation of the Gospel; (2) the restoration or renewal of liturgical (homiletic) preaching, not only during the celebration of the Eucharist but as an integral part of the entire sacramental system; (3) the phenomenon of lay preaching grounded in the baptismal character of the believer and as the expression of the distinctive role of the laity in communicating the Gospel in the modern world.

Bibliography: E. ECHLIN, *Priest as Preacher* (Cork 1973). W. SKUDLAREK, *The Word in Worship: Preaching in a Liturgical Context*. (Nashville, 1981). G. S. SLOYAN, *Worshipful Preaching*. (Philadelphia, 1984). J. HOFINGER, *Evangelization and Catechesis* (New York 1976).

[T. D. ROVER]

PREACHING, II (HOMILETIC THEORY)

The theory of preaching in the Church has had a long development and several names In the Middle Ages it was called ''the art of preaching.'' In the 16th and 17th centuries it became ''ecclesiastical rhetoric'' and ''sacred eloquence.'' Since the end of the 17th century it has most commonly been called ''homiletics.'' This article traces the main outlines of its development in the contributions of Catholic authors in patristic, medieval, and modern times.

Patristic Times (until c. 600). Christian preaching appeared in the 1st century as a force unique in its origin, content, aim, and spirit. It had originated in a divine mandate (Mt 28.19–20), contained a divinely revealed message, aimed at the radical conversion of its hearers, and breathed a spirit of earnestness and power.

Apostolic Contrast. The Apostles and their successors found their models of Christian preaching in the instruction and example of Christ our Lord (e.g., Mt 10.16; 13.52), and of the Old Testament prophets. They continued the synagogue custom of explaining the Scriptures at divine services (Lk 4.16–20; Acts 42) in a type of free, familiar, artless discourse that came to be called a HOMILY, from the Greek word for familiar conversation (ὁμιλία); cf, 1 Cor 15.33; Lk 24.14; Acts 24.26). In writing to the Corinthians St. Paul disclaimed any reliance on ''sublimity of words or of wisdom,'' (1 Cor 2.1, 4; 2 Cor 10.10; 11.6), an apparent reference to the art of eloquence that played a dominant role in the Hellenic environment of the time.

Implicit in Paul's disclaimer is the abiding challenge of inculturation, and more specifically of maintaining the supernatural character and divine efficacy of the act of preaching while utilizing effectively principles of general rhetoric. In the four centuries preceding the Christian era the solid foundations of an authentic art of persuasion had been laid in Greek and Roman treatises. The challenge for the Church was how to perfect the natural eloquence of the preacher without succumbing to the superficiality and ostentation that characterized recurring periods of rhetorical decadence.

Classical Rhetoric. A classical rhetoric had been established by close observation of constant elements in the persuasive process. For the soundness of its basic doctrines it has sometimes been called ''the perennial rhetoric,'' by analogy with the *philosophia perennis* that developed beside it. It was ideally conceived by Plato (*Gorgias, Phaedrus*), philosophically analyzed by Aristotle (*Rhetoric*), studied in its practical applications by Cicero in seven separate works on the subject, and construed as a complete system of education by Quintilian. It was in the composite a body of doctrine divided into five tracts: invention, arrangement, style, memory, and delivery. Its aim was to give persuasive impact to the cause of truth and justice. In the early Christian centuries, however, this functional rhetoric had been overlaid by the contrived art of the so-called Second Sophistic, a decadent period marked by a recrudescence of the spirit of self-display and an obsession with stylistic ornament against which Plato had striven much earlier.

As Christianity won more converts from among the educated classes, the unsuitability of sophistic as a vehicle for the word of God became an acute dilemma as the values of Christianity and Hellenism clashed. To pagan listeners with a developed taste for sophistic discourse and a lofty disdain toward the uncultured masses who had embraced the Gospel, the plain-spoken artlessness of Christian preaching had little appeal. Yet to earnest believers, whatever their tastes before conversion, it now seemed desecration to embroider the simple directness of the Gospel with sophistic conceits. Scattered passages containing reflections on this dilemma are found in the works of Tertullian, St. Cyprian, Arnobius, Lactantius, St. Jerome, St. Clement of Alexandria, and Origen (see Labriolle, 1–28). The rigoristic view was that the principles of eloquence developed by pagan rhetors could be of no practical use to the preacher sent by God. The moderate view that gradually won out was that the really valid principles constant in the persuasive process should be taken into the service of Christian preaching, while the superficial mannerisms that entrusted and embarrassed them should be discarded.

The 3d Century. ORIGEN (d. 153) made a lasting impression on homiletics. His views, revealed only in passing, stressed a side to effective preaching that had to be developed by the preacher's own efforts (*Patrologia Graeca*, ed. J. P. Migne, 14:1215–16). He held that true preaching must combine instruction and persuasion, just as true fire gives both light and warmth (*Patrologia Graeca* 12:392). His chief influence, however, lay in his far-reaching principle of interpreting Scripture in the Alexandrian tradition of a fourfold exegesis. Each passage was explained in a literal, moral, and mystical sense, the mystical being subdivided into allegorical and anagogical. The belief that single verses and even single words of Scripture contained meanings hidden deep beneath the literal sense filled his homilies with allegory. The term homily itself took on the technical meaning of an explanation of a Scriptural passage, and the verse-by-verse explanation that this exegetical method required has become known as the ''first form'' of homily, or the ''lower homily,'' or the versicular homily.

The Golden Age of Patristic Eloquence. From the Peace of Constantine (313) to the Council of Chalcedon (451) there was progress toward a theory of Christian preaching and a solution of its basic conflict with sophistic. Large congregations in spacious basilicas, public celebration of Christian feasts, violent controversy on doctrinal issues, and prominent bishops who had spent their youth in the study of public speaking made for vigorous eloquence. Besides the versicular homily there now appeared funeral discourses and panegyrics on the martyrs and theological orations that established the thematic sermon as another form of Christian preaching, differing from the homily chiefly in that it set out to explain a certain doctrine or a certain event rather than a scriptural passage. The great Fathers of this age, influenced on the one hand by their early training and continued friendship with leading sophists, and on the other by their profound reverence for the word of God, gave their attention to the question of the relation of Christian preaching to general rhetoric. St. BASIL (d. 379), who had earlier followed the career of his renowned rhetorician father and sent students to the sophist Libanius (see Basil's *Letters* 335–360), made an indirect contribution in his treatise *To the Youths* by endorsing the principle that the genuine values of pagan literary achievement should be preserved. His brother, St. GREGORY OF NYSSA (d. 394), personally exemplified the Christian confronted with sophistic standards he could neither honor nor escape. St. GREGORY OF NAZIANZUS (d. 389) left more numerous obiter dicta on the problem. For him, the greatest ''wisdom'' (σοφία, cf. 1 Cor 1.22; 2.2–8) was to despise ''wisdom'' that consisted only in word play and false antitheses (*Patrologia Graeca* 35:935). He attacked the theatrical preachers who destroyed the simple eloquence of the Christian message (*Patrologia Graeca* 36:237). Yet he esteemed true eloquence as a most precious possession (*Patrologia Graeca* 35:635), a pearl of great price (*Patrologia Graeca* 35:727) that he had acquired by great efforts in his youth (*Patrologia Graeca* 35:762).

The great influence on preaching among the Greek Fathers was exercised by St. JOHN CHRYSOSTOM (d. 407). Following the preference of the Antiochian school for the literal rather than the allegorical sense of Scripture, he did much to develop the second or mixed form of homily, in which a Scriptural passage was first explained verse by verse and then its central thought was treated as a unified theme as in the thematic sermon. Although for this versicular-thematic homily he left no connected theory, he did devote the fourth and fifth books of his treatise *On the Priesthood* to the ministry of preaching. Because they lacked the apostolic power of miracles, he argued, later Christian preachers needed the power of eloquence, to acquire which they had to expend great effort, since not nature but training made a speaker. This was all the more essential because of ''the great passion for eloquence that has taken hold of the minds of Christians'' (*op. cit.* 5.8). But while these books dealt with the attitude of the preacher toward his office and the dangers surrounding it, they did not constitute a homiletic theory properly so called.

St. Augustine. The first technical theory of preaching was provided in 427 by St. AUGUSTINE (d. 430), in the fourth book of his treatise *On Christian Instruction (De doctrina christiana).* By devoting the first three books, which had been written much earlier (*c.* 397), to methods of interpreting Scripture, and the fourth to techniques of proximate preparation and delivery, he anticipated a modern distinction between material and formal homiletics. His major contribution, however, was to establish once for all time the principle that the Christian must press into the service of the Gospel all the perennially valid principles of general rhetoric. Clearly rejecting sophistic, he reached back to the works of Cicero for his rhetorical doctrine, adapting to Christian preaching the triple Ciceronian aims of teaching, pleasing, and persuading (*docere, delectare, movere*), and the corresponding concepts of instructive, affective, and persuasive styles. In a thorough discussion of the whole foundation of the theory of preaching he showed the way for very many subsequent treatises, so much so that what Aristotle, Cicero, and Quintilian were to the establishment of the perennial rhetoric, this work of St. Augustine was to homiletics. Another of Augustine's works that contained much advice for preachers is his *The First Catechetical Instruction* (*De catechizandis rudibus*) in which he provides practical suggestions on how to engage an audience and maintain their attention as well as contents for an introductory sermon for individuals inquiring about the faith.

Bibliography: C. S. BALDWIN, *Ancient Rhetoric and Poetic* (New York 1924; repr. Gloucester, Massachusetts 1959); *Medieval Rhetoric and Poetic (to 1400)* (New York 1928). P. C. DE LABRIOLLE, *History and Literature of Christianity,* tr. H. WILSON (New York 1924). J. QUASTEN, *Patrology,* 3 v. (Westminster, Maryland 1950–). CATHOLIC UNIVERSITY OF AMERICA, *Patristic Studies* 1, 2, 5, 23, 38, 42, 79.

[J. M. CONNORS/EDS.]

Medieval Times (c. 600–c. 1500). In the early Middle Ages (600–1100), there was a sharp decline in preaching. In the making of Europe after the fall of the Roman Empire, clergy were ordained with only the most essential preparation, books were scarce, the ministry of the word was closely reserved as the bishops' prerogative, and the ideal of monastic stability during these Benedictine centuries made traveling preachers exceptions to the rule. Those who did preach depended almost entirely upon the early Fathers for both doctrine and expression, being content merely to repeat or paraphrase some patristic homily on the scriptural lesson of the day, for which the more fortunate had at hand homiliaries such as the widely used collection edited for Charlemagne by Paul the Deacon. These conservative customs were reflected in the lack of any substantial developments in homiletic theory from the 5th to the 12th century. St. GREGORY THE GREAT (d. 604) did give detailed instructions in his *Pastoral Rule* on themes for different types of listeners, and in his *Homilies* and *Dialogues* set a precedent for the use of illustrations or *exempla* in preaching. CASSIODORUS (d. *c.* 575), St. Isidore of Seville (d. 636), St. Bede (d. 735), and ALCUIN (d. 804) did write concise summaries of general rhetoric. RABANUS MAURUS (d. 856) summarized St. Augustine's tract and St. Gregory's *Rule* in his treatise on the training of the clergy (*De clericorum institutione; Patrologia Latina*, ed. J. P. Migne, 107:297–420). But of any original technical treatise on preaching after St. Augustine's in 427 there is no trace for 700 years.

The late Middle Ages (1100–1500), by contrast, was a highly creative period in the history of homiletic theory. Seeds sown in the 12th century flowered in the 13th, but ran to seed again during the 14th and 15th centuries. Passages in St. BERNARD (d. 1153) give evidence of the 12th-century transition. On the one hand his sermons reveal a low opinion of rhetoric and a reluctance to allow monks to preach outside the cloister; on the other hand, they exhibit a unity of theme and an orderly progression and originality of conception that anticipate the flowering of medieval homiletics. His contemporary, the Benedictine Abbot GUIBERT OF NOGENT (d. 1124), also sowed new seed by his tract on how a sermon should be prepared (*Quo ordine sermo fieri debeat; Patrologia Latina* 156:21–32). While not a technical treatise, this little work has seminal suggestions about the fourfold interpretation of Scripture, the importance of moral application, the knowledge of the human heart to be gained by observing one's own inner life, the necessity of lively delivery, and the usefulness of examples from history and of allegories from observation of gems, birds, and beasts. More technical than this is the treatise published a little later by the Cistercian scholar ALAN OF LILLE (d. *c.* 1203). Its 48 chapters (*Summa Magistri Alani doctoris universalis de arte praedicatoria; Patrologia Latina* 210:111–198) are mostly illustrative sketches of how to develop sermons on certain virtues and vices (ch. 2–37) and different states of life (ch. 40–48). Only the first chapter, after repudiating all puerilities in preaching such as the rhyming sermon then popular, presents the technical theory. The recommended technique is to begin with a text from the Gospels, Psalms, Pauline Epistles, or Books of Solomon, since these afford many moral themes, for which confirmatory texts can be sought in other parts of the Bible. Then the preacher must get the good will of his listeners by his humility and his explanation of the usefulness of what he is about to say, promising to be brief and to the point. Then he must develop his text, bringing in other authorities to confirm the proposition, sometimes even quoting the classics, as St. Paul sometimes did. He must also employ pathos to soften hearts and draw tears. Toward the end he may clinch the lesson by using *exempla,* since teaching by stories is popular (*familiaris*). These suggestions foreshadowed the elements of the numerous treatises that in the following century were to establish a characteristic technique for the late medieval sermon.

The 13th Century. In the 13th century the Fourth Lateran Council's decree on preaching (X. *De praedicatorbius instituendis*) gave authoritative impetus the renewal of preaching already well underway. The rapid growth of the mendicant Orders, notably the Franciscans and Dominicans, the rise of the universities and scholasticism, and the determination to meet on their own ground the heretics who were spreading their doctrines by preaching, all conspired to produce a vast homiletic renewal. In contrast to earlier monastic stability, thousands of mendicant friars became itinerant preachers, while professors took turns in the university pulpits and required trial sermons of candidates for degrees. Many technical treatises appeared, gradually developing a fairly standardized theory. Authors of widely used treatises in the 13th century were WILLIAM OF AUVERGNE (d. 1249), the Franciscans John of La Rochelle (d. 1245) and John of Wales (d. *c.* 1300), and the obscure Richard of Thetford (13th century), whose tract inculcated the conventional eight modes of developing a theme, resembling the ''commonplaces'' or topoi (τόποι) of classical rhetoric. The fifth Dominican master general, HUMBERT OF ROMANS (d. 1277), published two books (*c.* 1240) on the training of preachers in a single volume *De eruditione praedicatorum,* which was used extensively by both Dominicans and Franciscans (Zawart, 374). The first book contains reflections on the preacher's office and conduct (translated in 1951 as *Treatise on Preaching,* ed. W. M. Conlon), and the second contains sermon models for all types of listeners and all occasions.

The 14th Century. In the 14th century, prominent authors were Robert of Basevorn (fl. 1322?), the Dominicans Jacques de Fusignano at Paris (early 14th century) and Thomas Waleys at Oxford (d. *c.* 1349), and the Augustinian Thomas of Todi (fl. 1380). Still later works were the Franciscan manual written by Christian Borgsleben after 1464 for student friars at the University of Erfurt, and the chapters on preaching included by the Dominican St. ANTONINUS of Florence (d. 1459) in part three of his *Summa theologiae moralis.*

Compilations of Sermon Material. Besides the the many technical treatises on preaching—the ARS PRAEDICANDI—as the genre was called, the medieval preacher had many promptuaries of sermon material indexed under such headings as the virtues and vices. His lapidaries and bestiaries afforded him abundant illustrations of sermon themes by way of analogy with the properties of gems and characteristics of animals. His collections of *exempla* or pious stories, which he liked to employ especially toward the end of a popular sermon, enabled him to preach on any theme with only short notice. In imitation of the 2nd century Alexandrian bestiary *Physiologus* and of the early Lives of the Fathers ascribed to St. Jerome's disciple PALLADIUS, and of the *Dialogues* of St. Gregory the Great, which was their counterpart in the West, many medieval authors edited such collections. Outstanding were the compilations of the Cistercian Abbot CAESARIUS OF HEISTERBACH (d. *c.* 1240), whose *Homiliae* and *Dialogus miraculorum* followed the methods of St. Gregory and of the Augustinian Cardinal JACQUES DE VITRY (d. 1240), whose published sermons contained as many as three and four *exempla* each. Major Dominican compilers were Étienne of Bourbon (d. 1261), William Peraldus (d. *c.* 1207), the above-mentioned Humbert of Romans (d. 1277), and much later Johannes Herolt (d. early 15th century). In England a *Summa praedicantium* was compiled by the Oxford-Cambridge Dominican and adversary of Wyclif, John Bromyard (d. 1390), running to nearly 1,000 folio pages containing some 1,200 *exempla* under 189 alphabetical headings, with a prologue and a little treatise on preaching under the heading *"Praedicator."* The Franciscan John of Kilkenny is credited with a 13th-century collection (Zawart, 366). A number of his confreres compiled a *Liber exemplorum Fratrum Minorum* somewhat later, and still another anonymous Franciscan edited the *Speculum laicorum* (*c.* 1285).

Technique. The technique of the late medieval sermon described in the standard treatises was the product of the scholastic spirit. It emphasized strict unity and sought to evolve the whole sermon systematically from a carefully chosen Scripture text that stated the theme. After the text came the pro-theme, which led to the invocation for divine help for preacher and listeners. The theme was then restated and divided, usually into three parts, which were then subdivided and developed according to conventional modes of amplification. Theme, protheme, invocation, division, declaration of parts, and development proceeded in a logical unfolding that was seen by the systematic scholastic mind as the homiletic equivalent of PORPHYRY's tree. In fact the medieval *artes praedicandi* often contained diagrams illustrating the sermon process by the organic structure of a tree, with its root (the theme) developing into the trunk (pro-theme), which then divided into the major limbs (three parts), these then subdividing into branches bearing leaves and fruit. In the declining Middle Ages, while the popular sermon to the uneducated laity, especially in the hands of preachers such as the Franciscan Berthold of Regensburg (d. 1272), could for the most part escape it, there lay in the formalism of the scholastic sermon a tendency to an obsession with style and excessive subtlety.

Bibliography: P. ARENDT, *Die Predigten des Konstanzer Konzils* (Freiburg 1933). C. S. BALDWIN, *Medieval Rhetoric and Poetic (to 1400)* (New York 1928). T. M. CHARLAND, *Artes praedicandi* (Ottawa 1936). M. M. DAVY, ed., *Les Sermons universitaires parisiens 1230–1231* (Paris 1931). A. LECOY DE LA MARCHE, *La Chaire française au moyen âge* (2d ed. Paris 1886). G. R. OWST, *Preaching in Medieval England* (Cambridge, England 1926); *Literature and Pulpit in Medieval England* (2d ed. New York 1961). J. T. WELTER, *L'Exemplum dans la littérature religieuse et didactique du moyen âge* (Paris 1927). A. ZAWART, *The History of Franciscan Preaching and of Franciscan Preachers 1209–1927* (New York 1927). M. MCC. GATCH, *Preaching and Theology in Anglo-Saxon England: Aelfric and Wulfstan* (Toronto 1977). D. L. D'AVRAY, *The Preaching of the Friars* (Oxford 1985).

[J. M. CONNORS]

Modern Times (from *c.* 1500). From the time that Poggio, on his way to the Council of Constance (1414), recovered the complete Quintilian in a tower of the Abbey of St. Gall and Gherardo Landriani in 1425 came upon Cicero's rhetorical treatises in the Duomo at Lodi, it was predictable that the Renaissance enthusiasm for classical rhetoric would influence the theory of preaching. Actually, the *Manuale curatorum* by Ulrich Surgant in 1503 was about the last well-known homiletic treatise in the medieval scholastic mold. The next year the renowned humanist Johann REUCHLIN published a brochure of concise notes on preaching as *Liber congestorum de arte praedicandi* in 1504. In less than 24 pages, he summarized the typical features of the perennial rhetoric: the five basic tracts on invention, arrangement, style, memory, and delivery; the *topoi* or commonplaces as tools of invention; the classic arrangement of exordium, narration, division, confirmation, confutation, and peroration; the stylistic modes divided into figures of thought and figures of words; orderly arrangement and frequent meditation as aids to memory; and treatment of delivery in sections on voice and on action. In several places he explicitly mentioned Cicero and Quintilian, revealing himself as the first of dozens of 16th-century authors who took timbers from the Greek and Roman treatises for the framework of their homiletic theory. The trend became more firmly established in 1535 with the publication of *Ecclesiastes sive de ratione concionandi* by ERASMUS. This very long and loosely organized treatise, begun at the urging of St. John FISHER (d. 1535) and published in the year of his martyrdom, shows the effects of Erasmus's personal hardships during its composition, but firmly advances St. Augustine's principle of adopting the perennial rhetoric as the framework for homiletic theory.

With these precedents, the way lay open for the many authors who saw a demand for homiletic manuals implied in the decrees of the Council of Trent on frequent preaching and on the establishment of seminaries with homiletic training in the curriculum. St. Charles BORROMEO worked these decrees out in fuller detail in his First Provincial Synod of Milan in 1565, and in 1575 published his instructions on preaching as *Instructiones praedicationis verbi Dei,* which went everywhere as part of the *Acta ecclesiae mediolanensis* [ed. Achille Ratti (1890) 2:1207–48], the bishops' handbook at many local councils after Trent. These decrees of Trent and Milan and the CATECHISM OF THE COUNCIL OF TRENT came to form the core of a Tridentine tradition in conciliar legislation on preaching for the next four centuries. To fill the great need for manuals thus created, leading ecclesiastics took up their pens. In 1562 the Franciscan Lucas Baglioni published *L'Arte del predicare.* An Augustinian preacher at the Spanish court, Lorenzo de Villavicente, put out in 1565 a work *De formandis sacris concionibus seu de interpretatione scripturarum populari,* reproducing the title and substance of a renowned earlier work by the Protestant writer Andreas Hyperius. Technical treatises also appeared by the famous Franciscan preachers Cornelius MUSSO (d. 1574) and Francesco PANIGAROLA (d. 1594), who have a controversial place in history as originators of the baroque *concetti.* In 1570 Alphonsus Garsias Matamoro, professor of rhetoric at the then thriving University of ALCALÁ, published *De tribus dicendi generibus sive de recta informandi styli ratione* and *De methodo concionandi juxta rhetoricae artis praescriptum.* Antonius Lanquier, a Carmelite, published in 1578 his *Synopsis ad faciendam piam concionem orthodoxis,* and in 1595 appeared the *Divinus orator vel de rhetorica divina* by Ludovico Carbone. To the Capuchin LAWRENCE OF BRINDISI (d. 1619) is attributed a long unpublished treatise for young preachers, *Tractatus de modo concionandi, quo instruuntur novi concionatores.*

The most successful authors, however, were Augustinus Valerius, Didacus Stella, and Louis of Granada, whose works so complemented each other that they were sometimes published together in subsequent editions. Valerius (d. 1606), Bishop of Verona, writing so closely under the observation of St. Charles Borromeo that he called him the true author of the treatise, based his three books on ecclesiastical rhetoric, *De rhetorica ecclesiastica sive modo concionandi libri tres* (1574), squarely upon Aristotle's Rhetoric. DIEGO OF ESTELLA, a Franciscan exegete (d. 1578), derived his theory more from the preacher's role as interpreter of the Scriptures in his *De ratione concionandi, sive rhetorica ecclesiastica* of 1576. Most widely used of all, and recommended even by Bellarmine and Bérulle, was the *Ecclesiasticae rhetoricae sive de ratione concionandi libri sex* published in 1576 by LOUIS OF GRANADA (d. 1588). This outstanding Dominican, praised by the Jesuit Rapin as the very model of a preacher, stressed in the preface to his work the importance of style and delivery as well as invention, and relied for his principles heavily on Quintilian.

The Jesuits. This movement to employ classical rhetoric as the framework of homiletic theory received strong and enduring support from the Jesuits. A zeal for preaching was evident from the beginning in the writings of the early Jesuit generals. St. IGNATIUS OF LOYOLA promulgated the 24 rules for preachers, and other directives. Diego LAÍNEZ wrote a long unedited treatise of advice for preachers, *Monita pro iis qui concionandi munus suscipiunt.* St. Francis BORGIA published a short but much-reprinted tract *De ratione concionandi,* and Claudius ACQUAVIVA (1581–1615) included an instruction for preachers in his *Instructiones ad provinciales et superiores societatis* in 1613. St. Robert BELLARMINE (d. 1621) also gave a half-dozen pages of instructions, *De ratione formandae concionis* (*Opera oratoria postuma, I; S. I. selecti scriptores* Rome 1942); and even in the foreign missions St. Francis XAVIER (d. 1552) wrote letters including extensive advice on preaching. More to the point concerning the perennial rhetoric, Gerónimo Nadal (d. 1580) gave detailed instructions on Jesuit homiletic training in his *De ministerio verbi Dei* (*Monumenta historica Societatis Jesu, Epistolae Nadal* 4.653–670), in which he explicitly called for a theory of preaching utilizing the best of Aristotle, Cicero, and Quintilian (p. 657). Execution of this clear policy was aided by the ardent classicism of the RATIO STUDIORUM, which took as its own objective Quintilian's ideal of "the good man skilled in speaking," and for more than two centuries trained Jesuit students on such compendia of classical rhetoric as the *De arte rhetorica* (1560) of Cyprian Soarez, SJ. The homiletic treatises of dozens of Jesuit authors in the 17th and 18th centuries reflected this background (see C. Sommervogel et al., *Bibliothèque de la Compagnie de Jésus*).

France. In the 17th century the initiative in homiletic theory passed to France, where the reform of preaching was a particular manifestation of the general Catholic revival. Influential beyond all proportion to its brevity was the *Letter to André Frémiot* on preaching written in 1604 by St. FRANCIS DE SALES (d. 1622). His effect on St. VINCENT DE PAUL (d. 1660) helped to shape "The Little Method," which the latter employed in his efforts to reform French preaching through the Tuesday Conference for the diocesan clergy and his own Congregation of the

Mission and his retreats for ordinands. He employed it everywhere also in the work of the internal missions, which he originated in 1617. As a spirit, The Little Method was a rejection of the sophistic taste that had once more revived in the form of the exaggerated classicism of the Renaissance. As a technique, it was a way of constructing a moral sermon on a sequence of motives, nature, and means pertaining to some virtue or vice, employing the most stirring stylistic modes or figures of speech and short texts and examples. Among others, J. J. Oiler, L. TRONSON, and even BOSSUET learned The Little Method from St. Vincent, and Tronson as tutor and Bossuet as colleague undoubtedly communicated at least its spirit to FÉNELON. Its influence is evident also in the tract on *The Apostolic Preacher* by St. John EUDES (d. 1680). Meanwhile, the *Orator christianus* (1612) by the Jesuit Charles Regius (d. 1612) had been made a standard manual for the Society by Acquaviva's instruction in 1613. A French Jesuit, formerly chaplain to Louis XIII, Nicholas Caussin (d. 1651) published the unwieldy and disorganized *Eloquentiae sacrae et humanae parallela* in 1619. Much shorter and clearer was the theory by which another Jesuit, Paolo SEGNERI (d. 1694), did much to combat the Sophistic taste of the early baroque period in Italy. In 1670 the Capuchin Amadeus Bajocensis (Amadée of Bayeux) published a huge work on homiletic theory based on St. Paul, *Paulus Ecclesiastes seu eloquentia christiana, qua orator evangelicus ad ideam Pauli efformatur.* René RAPIN, SJ, wrote *Reflections upon Eloquence,* (1671) and the Oratorian Bernard LAMY put out his *L'Art de parler* with a section on preaching in 1675.

Reaction to the Baroque. In the 18th century the plea for a return to apostolic simplicity and earnestness was characteristic of the major treatises. In France, Blaise Gisbert, SJ, produced his *Christian Eloquence in Theory and Practice* (1702), a volume of 23 chapters and 435 pages in its English translation, making an eloquent statement of the highest homiletic ideals, profusely illustrated from the works of St. John Chrysostom. In 1710 Jean Gaichiès published his less valuable but well-known *Maximes sur le ministère de la chaire.* A high point in the history of French homiletics was the work of Fénelon (d. 1715). In his *Letter to the Academy* of 1714 he called for scholars to construct an ideal rhetorical treatise by drawing from the best of the Greek and Roman classics, and for a comparable treatise on preaching based on the principles of St. Augustine. In 1717 his *Dialogues on Eloquence* were published posthumously. Much admired and quoted, they define eloquence as the art of persuading men to truth and goodness, demand full understanding of listeners' obligations and motives, list the aims of preaching as to prove, to portray, and to strike, prescribe careful preparation but extempore delivery, reject formal divisions and the artificial conceits dear to the baroque taste, insist on full knowledge of both Holy Scripture and human nature, advocate that pastors be chosen for ability to preach, propose a return to the patristic homily and a style of preaching that, because it did not make heroic demands in preparation, enabled the preacher to speak as often as his listeners desired. Fénelon is the zenith of the golden age of French homiletic theory, of which later treatises like Cardinal Jean Siffrein Maury's *Principle of Eloquence* in 1782 are but the sunset before the nightfall of the French Revolution in 1789.

Spain. In the 18th century, meanwhile, the campaign against baroque sophistic was cleverly waged by the Jesuit Jose Francisco de Isla (d. 1781), whose lampooning *History of the Famous Preacher Friar Gerund of Campazas* (Spanish 1758) became a classic of Spanish satire rivaling *Don Quixote.* This novel, which Benedict XIV stayed up all night to read and then highly praised, stirred up such opposition as to land on the Index until 1900, but it succeeded in overcoming the current bad taste by making ''Gerundianism'' a term of ridicule. Almost at the same time, in Italy St. Alphonsus Liguori (d. 1787), founder of the Redemptorists, circulated among bishops and religious superiors in 1761 his *Letter to a Religious on Apostolic Preaching.* It was one long appeal for simplicity and practicality, and repeatedly recommended the ideals expressed by Lodovico Antonio MURATORI in his *Dei pregi dell' eloquenza popolare* of 1750. In addition, St. Alphonsus wrote technically on homiletic theory in part three of his *Selva* (1760). For the Passionists, founded in Italy at the same time for the same work of internal missions, St. Vincenzo Strambi (d. 1824) dictated notes in 1789 that were later published as *A Guide to Sacred Eloquence.* This work, strongly classical in orientation, bears such intrinsic resemblance to St. Alphonsus's treatise as to indicate either dependence upon it or the sharing of a common source. Contemporary were the works of the two Capuchins, Gaetano da Bergamo, *L'uomo apostolico ixtruito nella sua vocazione al pulpito* (1729), and Andrea da Faenza, *Lettera didascalica sopra la maniera di ben comporre la predica* (n.d.).

Germany. In 18th-century Germany the ENLIGHTENMENT was followed by the appearance of the first Catholic homiletic works in German. Rudolf Graser, OSB, published *Vollständige Lehrart zu predigen* in 1766 and *Praktische Beredsamkeit der chr. Kanzel* in 1769. Ignaz Wurz, SJ, produced in 1770 his *Anleitung zur geistlichen Beredsamkeit,* many times republished. Another Jesuit, Joseph Anton Weissenbach, began in 1775 his nine-volume work on patristic eloquence, *De eloquentia patrum libri xiii,* which was abridged in Rome as *Ratio utendi scriptis sanctorum patrum ad conciones sacras*

(1825), only to have the abridgement translated back into German in 1844 by M. A. Nickel and J. Kehrein. It is a statement of homiletic theory filled out with abundant illustrations from the Fathers. The reorganization of theological studies by the Benedictine Abbot Franz Stephan RAUTENSTRAUCH (d. 1785) and the subsequent decree of Empress Maria Theresa that vernacular lectures on pastoral theology be held in all theological faculties of her empire created a demand for more manuals and established the German custom of writing large handbooks of pastoral theology comprising treatises on homiletics, catechetics, and liturgy. The appearance in 1788 of the lectures on pastoral theology, *Vorlesungen aus der Pastoraltheologie,* by the renowned Johann Michael SAILER set a new standard, in a time when even some theological manuals were tinged with rationalism, for sound theology and exact knowledge of Scripture, to which Sailer added, in treating homiletics, a sure grasp of technique. The homiletic part of the manual gave that constant attention to the connections between doctrinal themes, moral themes, and Scriptural Selections that became typical of German homiletics. Sailer's students followed his lead, especially Aegidius Jais and Ignaz Schüch, OSB, the homiletic part of whose phenomenally successful *Handbuch der Pastoraltheologie* was translated by Lubberman in 1894 as *The Priest in the Pulpit.* Less valuable than the untranslated parts of Schüch's manual that account for its many German editions, the translated treatise on homiletics has had little acclaim in English.

The 19th Century. In the 19th century the early decades of upheaval were followed by the restoration of the French seminary system and the supplementing of its traditional supervised refectory practice-preaching by extensive systematic courses in homiletic theory. Manuals appeared, such as those of J. X. Vètu (1840), L. H. M. Bellefroid (n.d., 2d ed. 1847), Mullois (1853–1863), and, at Mechlin in Belgium, Van Hemel (1855), whose work presented a plan for consecutive homiletic training throughout the seminarian's philosophical and theological courses. Most successful among the new French manuals, however, was the *Traité de la prédication* by the Sulpician André J. M. Hamon in 1844. In 1853 an anonymous abridgement of it was published by the Vincentian Joseph Lament in his *De la prédication,* and in 1866 Thomas J. Potter of All Hallows, the Dublin seminary for English-speaking countries, paraphrased its first part in his *Sacred Eloquence,* and in 1869 its second part in his *The Pastor and His People.* In this way the same basic theory of Hamon became standard for seminaries directed or influenced by the Sulpicians and Vincentians and emigrating Irish clergy, who together in the 19th century established prototype diocesan seminaries in English-speaking countries. Other technical treatises, not intended as textbooks, based mainly on Fénelon's *Dialogues,* were *The Art of Extempore Speaking* by L. Bautain (1856) and *The Ministry of Preaching* by the great DUPANLOUP (1866, tr. 1890). In 1851 the Jesuit Cyprien Nadal assembled an encyclopedia of homiletic theory for a Migne six-volume series, *Dictionnaire d'éloquence sacrée: Novyelle encyclopédie théologique.* Georges Longhaye, SJ, published his popular *La prédication, grands maîtres et grandes lois* in 1888.

The restoration of the Jesuits in 1814 and their assignment to the theological faculty at Innsbruck in 1856 were influential events in the development of German homiletic theory in the 19th century. In Rome in 1847 the German Jesuit Joseph Kleutgen published his *Ars dicendi,* which in the revised *Ratio Studiorum* achieved the place so long held by Soarez. Kleutgen tried to assimilate the aesthetic and belletristic tendencies of rhetoricians like Hugh Blair (*Lectures on Rhetoric and Belles Lettres,* 1783) without submerging the character of the perennial rhetoric as essentially a theory of public speaking in an omnibus treatise on all forms of prose and verse composition. Like Blair, however, and like other prominent Jesuit theorists (C. Coppens, F. P. Donnelly) he organized his treatise in such a way as to imply that homiletics is only a species of general rhetoric, or that the theory of preaching is little more than the theory of public speaking for priests. The same inclination to make general rhetoric the foundation rather than merely the framework of homiletic theory was visible in the *Grundzüge der Beredsamkeit* published in 1859 by Nikolaus Schleiniger, SJ, (tr. 1909 as *The Principles of Eloquence*). Schleiniger did, however, produce another specifically homiletic treatise on the ministry of preaching in *Das kirchliche Predigtamt* in 1861, in 1864 a manual on *Die Bildung des jungen Predigers* for training of young preachers, and in 1865 his sermon models in *Muster und Quellen des Predigers.* At Innsbruck, Josef JUNGMANN, SJ (d. 1885), after an earlier study on aesthetics, wrote his monumental *Theorie der geistlichen Beredsamkeit* (2 v. 1877–78), building his theory around his ''two supreme laws'' of popularity and practicality. In 1883 the popular spiritual writer Alban Stolz was author of a posthumously published work on how to preach the Gospel to the poor, *Homiletik als Anweisung den Armen das Evangelium zu predigen.* In 1888 the renowned apologist Franz HETTINGER published his maxims on preaching and preachers, *Aphorismen über Predigt und Prediger.*

While France and Germany in the 19th century enjoyed this abundance, and Italy had at least Guglielmo Audisio's *Lezioni di sacra eloquenza* (3 v. Turin 1839–58), the English-speaking countries had only the modest beginnings of a Catholic homiletic literature. After three centuries of Catholic disabilities, during which a vernacular tradition of Catholic pulpit eloquence had been utterly impossible, the Catholic Emancipation of 1829 and the rapid growth of the seminary system called forth the first efforts. Fénelon, Gisbert, Isla, Bautain, Mullois, and Maury had been translated, as also St. Alphonsus and St. Vincenzo Strambi, but the only original works in English by Catholic authors were Newman's essay on "University Preaching" (*c.* 1855), published as part of the *Idea of a University,* and in 1881 a poorly done *Sacred Eloquence* by Thomas MacNamara, CM. An English adaptation of the fourth part of Kleutgen was made by Charles Coppens, SJ, in his *Art of Oratorical Composition* in 1885. The standard theory of preaching in English-speaking countries in the 19th century, remained that expounded by Thomas J. Potter in his trilogy on *Sacred Eloquence, The Pastor and His People,* and *The Spoken Word.* Sharing its theory with Hamon and Lamant in a uniform Sulpician-Vincentian-Hibernian tradition of seminary training, drawing also from Bautain, Bellefroid, Van Hemel, and Newman.

Having no serious rival among Catholic authors in English, Potter's is the representative work of the late 19th and early 20th century. Briefly, he teaches that the general aim of preaching is to move to action, so that every proper sermon is persuasive, issuing in a practical resolution. A discourse that does not prove a proposition and issue in definite action cannot be called a sermon. Intermediate aims are St. Augustine's "to teach, to please, to move." The set sermon is a formal oration with sublime concepts and elevated style for special occasions; the familiar instruction, with simple ideas and colloquial style, is typically employed at Sunday Mass. The set sermon follows the classic Ciceronian plan; the familiar instruction may take the form of the various types of homily or of The Little Method. Unity in a sermon is essential, and may best be tested by reducing the sermon to a syllogism. Psychological steps in sermon preparation are to meditate the theme, to conceive the central idea that will unify the discourse, to write at a time when mind and heart are enlightened and warmed by the subject, and to revise and polish the hasty first draft. Extempore preaching is the ideal, although beginners must write and memorize. Delivery cannot be taught in a book, but coaching must produce vocal variety and effective action. For the rest, Potter's theory is not in the familiar mold of classically oriented treatises, except for the Ciceronian arrangement of the set sermon and the threefold intermediate aims. The *topoi* or "commonplaces" are not developed, but only listed and defined. Figures of speech are disposed of in a single paragraph. Types of style correspond vaguely to the set sermon and familiar instruction, with no vestige of St. Augustine's three styles. There is no effort to discuss the role of homiletics as a part of pastoral theology, or to treat in depth the question of sermon content.

The 20th Century. In the 20th century many historical studies and a few manuals appeared in French. At the behest of his superiors, Jacques M. MONSABRÉ, OP, published in 1900 his *Avant, pendant, après la prédication* as an official Dominican handbook. In 1923 Raoul Plus, SJ, published *Prédication 'reelle' et 'irreale': Notes pratiques pour le ministère paroissial.* Antonin G. Sertillanges, OP, put out *L'Orateur chrétien* in 1931. In German, Albert Meyenberg produced his huge *Homiletische und katechetische Studien* in 1903, which after great success was translated in 1912 as *Homiletic and Catechetic Studies.* Meyenberg borrowed his formal theory from Jungmann, but in the bewildering organizaton of his book, which must have become popular in German more for its liturgical than its homiletic content, Jungmann's thought is done little justice. Jacob Herr wrote *Praktischer Kursus der Homiletik* in 1913, the Capuchin Dionys Habersbrunner produced *Ein Weg zur Kanzel* in 1933, and Peter Adamer published *Predigtkunde* in 1937. The most vigorous activity in homiletic theory in the early part of the century, however, has been the movement carried on in Germany by Bishop Von Keppler and his associates, Adolf Donders and Franz Stingeder. A major aim in Von Keppler's campaign from the time of his articles in the *Tübinger Quartalschrift* in 1892, until death overtook him while he was preparing for a homiletic convention in 1926, was to restore the homily to a place of honor side by side with the thematic sermon, which had too long monopolized the pulpit. He also insisted that homiletics is independent of general rhetoric in its origin, content, and aim. It is not derived from rhetoric any more than Catholic theology is derived from scholastic philosophy, but it can make a similar use of the concepts and principles of the perennial rhetoric as tools of investigation and forms of expression for the content it derives from divine revelation. It is the difference between a foundation and a framework. Von Keppler's papers at the Ravensburg convention of 1910 were translated in 1927 as *Homiletic Thoughts and Counsels,* but they are not as representative of his theory as are his periodical articles and his "Homiletik" and "Predigt" in Wetzer-Welte, *Kirchenlexicon.* His *Predigt und Heilige Schrift* was published after his death in 1926. In 1910 Stingeder wrote a critique of contemporary homiletics as *Wo steht unsere heutige Predigt?* In 1920 he contributed a history of the use of Scripture in preaching, *Geschichte der Schriftpredigt,* to the nine volumes of homiletic studies edited from 1919 to 1931 by A. Donders and Thaddeus Soiron, OFM. Soiron was the most prominent of the Paderborn Franciscans who showed prolific zeal in homiletic publications; he edited from 1918 to 1935 a scientific homiletic journal called *Kirche und Kanzel.*

English-speaking Countries. In English-speaking countries, meanwhile, the turn of the century brought forth the first generation of Catholic authors of original homiletic treatises. Some of the theory was published incidentally as parts of books on other subjects. Rapid expansion of the seminary system after the Third Plenary Council of Baltimore (1884) and the growth of an indigenous English-speaking clergy prompted many works on the duties of the priesthood, which often contained chapters on preaching. At a time when the elocutionary movement led by the followers of François Delsarte had brought it into disrepute, it is not surprising that writers on preaching took a negative view of rhetoric.

Cardinal MANNING in 1883 devoted chapter 14 of *The Eternal Priesthood* to the importance of remote rather than proximate preparation for preaching, and to a plea for simple, earnest, extempore discourse. Cardinal GIBBONS wrote in the same vein in 1896 in *The Ambassador of Christ.* Bishop Hedley in *Lex Levitarum* in 1905 argued that "it would be a waste of time to enter too deeply on the study of rhetoric as an art" (p. 110). Arthur Barry O'Neill, CSC, in chapter 11 of his *Priestly Practice* in 1914, felt the need to refute the idea that "rhetorical" is a synonym for "artificial." The extempore method advocated by Manning was greatly furthered by J. Ward's biography of *William Pardow of the Company of Jesus* in 1915, and by C. C. MARTINDALE's *The Life of Monsignor Robert Hugh Benson* in 1916.

Of the treatises dealing *ex professo* with the technical theory of preaching before 1936, Bernard Feeney's *Manual of Sacred Rhetoric* in 1901, Win. B. O'Dowd's *Preaching* in 1919, and Charles H. Schultz's *Sacred Eloquence* in 1926 were general homiletic manuals, dealing, that is, with all aspects of sermon composition and delivery. Works consisting almost entirely of the proposal of a sermon formula and its explanation were George S. Hitchcock's *Sermon Composition* in 1908, which describes a sermon arrangement akin to the "Ignatian Method" in discursive meditation, and the Passionist Mark Moeslein's *Mechanism of Discourses* in 1915, which draws from St. Vincenzo Strambi. Presentations of a professedly simplified approach to the theory of preaching were Thomas Flynn's *Preaching Made Easy* in 1923, and Aloysius Roche's *Practical Hints on Preaching* in 1933. John A. McClorey, SJ, published *The Making of a Pulpit Orator* in 1934. In 1936 John K. Sharp published *Our Preaching,* followed in 1937 by his *Next Sunday's Sermon.*

The most prolific publishers of periodical articles on homiletic theory in the United States were the *American Ecclesiastical Review* (*AER*) since 1889 and the *Homiletic and Pastoral Review* (*HPR*). The outstanding contributor and most representative author of homiletic theory in English-speaking countries in his era was Monsignor Hugh T. Henry (d. 1946) of the Catholic University of America, who republished the best of his hundreds of articles from the *AER* and *HPR* in his *Hints to Preachers* in 1924, *Papers on Preaching* in 1925, and *Preaching* in 1941. Other books and brochures whose chapters first appeared as articles in the *AER* were the Jesuit Francis P. Donnelly's *The Art of Interesting* in 1920, Edmond D. Benard's *The Appeal to the Emotions in Preaching* in 1944, and the Passionist Luke Missett's *The Pews Talk Back* in 1946.

Earlier, in 1942 a layman, O'Brien Atkinson, skilled in modern advertising and street preaching, published *How to Make Us Want Your Sermon,* in which he challenged many concepts traditional in standard writers such as Potter, Henry, and Sharp. Also in 1942 appeared the Carmelite Albert Dolan's brochure of *Homiletic Hints.* In 1943 Thomas A. Carney built *A Primer of Homiletics* around St. Vincent's Little Method. In 1950 William R. Duffey's *Preaching Well* appeared as a substantial paraphrase of Bellefroid. Thomas V. Liske published his *Effective Preaching* in 1951 (rev. 1960). Ferdinand Valentine, OP, put out *The Art of Preaching* in 1952. *Unless They Be Sent* by Augustine Rock, OP, in 1953, was a theological study of the nature of preaching, based especially upon St. Thomas and St. Albert the Great. Like *The Canon Law on Sermon Preaching* by the Paulist James McVann in 1940, and *The Canonical Obligation of Preaching in Parish Churches* by Joseph L. Allgeier in 1949, it was done as a doctoral dissertation. Sylvester MacNutt, OP, published *Gauging Sermon Effectiveness* in 1960 as a method and checklist for judging sermon composition.

New Development. In retrospect, the year 1936 can be seen as the beginning of a new period in the development of Catholic homiletic theory. In that year Josef Andreas Jungmann, SJ, (not to be confused with the 19th century Jesuit who also taught in Innsbruck) published *Die Frohbotschaft und unsere Glaubensverkündigung,* and the fifth pastoral convention at Vienna raised the question of determining more clearly the theological nature of the ministry of preaching. Numerous studies began to appear concerning the content of preaching, and about "the whole Christ" as the core of the Christian message. The pastoral revival, of which the Catholic LITURGICAL MOVEMENT and the KERYGMA concept in catechetics were a part, had spread to homiletics and given to the German homiletic movement the theological dimension so eagerly sought earlier by Von Keppler.

Jungmann's call for a return to kerygmatic preaching as well as his subsequent *Missa Solemnia*, a history of the Roman Mass, exercised direct and indirect influence at Second Vatican Council, especially on *Lumen gentium*, the Constitution on the Sacred Liturgy. The Constitution did not attempt to formulate a homiletic theory but it contributed greatly to the building up of a theological tract ''on preaching'' that could stand beside the traditional tracts on the Sacraments and on the Church (see Alszeghy-Flick). It clarified the nature and aim of the preaching ministry and became the basis for the pastoral guidelines incorporated into Book III, ''The Teaching Office of the Church,'' in the 1983 Code of Canon Law.

Bibliography: Z. ALSZEGHY and M. FLICK, ''Il problema teologica della predicazione,'' *Gregorianum* 40 (1959) 671–744. H. CAPLAN and H. H. KING, ''Latin Tractates on Preaching: A Book-List,'' *Harvard Theological Review* 42 (July 1949) 185–206; ''Italian Treatises on Preaching: A Book-List,'' *Speech Monographs* 16 (1949) 243–252; ''Spanish Treatises on Preaching: A Book-List,'' *ibid.* 17 (1950) 161–170; ''Dutch Treatises on Preaching: A List of Books and Articles,'' *ibid.* 21 (1954) 235–247; ''Pulpit Eloquence: A List of Doctrinal and Historical Studies in English,'' *ibid.* 22 (Special Issue 1955) 1–159; ''Pulpit Eloquence: A List of Doctrinal and Historical Studies in German,'' *ibid.* 23 (Special Issue 1956) 1–106; ''French Tractates on Preaching: A Book-List,'' *Quarterly Journal of Speech* 36 (1950) 296–325. W. TOOHEY and W. D. THOMPSON, eds., *Recent Homiletical Thought: A Bibliography, 1935–65* (Nashville 1967). J. O'MALLEY *Praise and Blame in Renaissance Rome: Rhetoric, Doctrine, and Reform in the Sacred Orators of the Papal Court, ca. 1450–1521* (Durham, North Carolina 1979). J. O'MALLEY, ''Erasmus and the History of Sacred Rhetoric: The Ecclesiastes of 1535,'' in *Erasmus of Rotterdam Society Yearbook* 5 (1985) 1–29. J. M. MCMANAMON, ''Innovation in Early Humanistic Rhetoric: The Oratory of Pier Paolo Vergerio (the Elder),'' *Rinascimento*, NS 22 (1982) 3–32. E. ACHTEMEYER and M. AYCOCK, *Bibliography on Preaching, 1975–1985* (Richmond, Virginia 1986).

[J. M. CONNORS]

PREACHING, III (THEOLOGY OF)

In its broadest usage, the English term ''preaching'' comprises the multiple ministries of the word—evangelization, the liturgical homily, catechetical instruction, exhortation, mystagogy, et al.,—through which the Christian community announces and expounds the Gospel. The theology of preaching begins with the premise that the proclamation of the good news of salvation—the announcement that ''the reign of God is at hand''—constituted the focus of the life and ministry of Jesus and remains central to the life and mission of the Church.

Apostolic Proclamation. As preacher of the reign of God, Jesus stood within the prophetic tradition of announcing the saving power of God active in human history by calling to memory God's fidelity in the past, evoking trust in God's presence here and now, and rousing hope in God's promise to create a new future. Anointed by the power of the Spirit, Jesus proclaimed and embodied the presence and power of God at work in human life and throughout creation. The ''signs of the kingdom'' evident in Jesus's ministry confirmed the message of the saving rule of God which the prophets promised and which Jesus declared was ''at hand''–a ''year of favor'' when the poor would hear glad tidings, the brokenhearted be healed, captives set free, and prisoners released (Is 61, Lk 4). In his words, especially his characteristic mode of speaking in parables, as well as in his liberating deeds and relationships, Jesus reinterpreted the living tradition of Jewish faith he inherited, announcing the unlimited compassion and forgiveness of God. The Gospels of Matthew and John further portray Jesus as Wisdom (*Hokmah/Sophia*) the prophetic street preacher from the book of Proverbs who proclaims God's ways at the city gate, reaches out her hand to the needy, clings to truth, decides for justice, orders all things rightly, and invites her children to an abundant feast. Just as Sophia fashioned others into ''friends of God and prophets,'' Jesus gathered a band of disciples whom he sent to continue his preaching mission in the power of the Spirit ''even to the ends of the world'' (Lk 9:1–6; 10:1–12; Mt 28:12). Mounting resistance to Jesus's announcement of the reign of God culminated in his execution as a political rebel and false prophet. Historical-critical biblical scholars argue that the bold preaching of the disciples in the face of their devastation at the time of the death of Jesus gives testimony to the truth of the claim which formed the core of the apostolic kerygma (proclamation): Jesus who was crucified has been raised from the dead, and all who repent and believe in him will be saved (cf. 1 Cor 15:3–8; Acts 2:22b–24, 3:12b–26, 10:34–43).

The resurrection narratives testify to the necessity of the conversion of the preacher for effective proclamation of the good news of salvation. The New Testament records specifically the post-Easter commissioning of Mary Magdalene (Jn 20:17), the Twelve and their companions (Mt 28: 16–20, Mk 16:14–20, Jn 20: 19–23), and Paul (Gal 1:11–17). The Pentecost narrative in the ACTS OF THE APOSTLES further highlights the role of the Spirit in both the proclamation and the hearing of the word of God in diverse voices and cultures.

In the tradition of Jesus and the Hebrew prophets, the apostolic preachers announced the *dabar YHWH*—the word of God—as creative, dynamic, and saving event that brings about what it promises. Thus the Acts of the Apostles describes the success of the Church's ministry in a specific area with the summary statement: ''The word of God continued to spread'' (Acts 6:7). As the Hebrew roots of the word ''*dabar*'' indicate, to proclaim

God's word is to announce God's activity in history in such a way that renders salvation history present and operative in the present moment. Although distinctions based on purpose and style can be drawn between various modes of preaching such as *KERYGMA* (direct proclamation of Jesus as Lord and the good news of the reign of God), *didache/didaskalia* (teaching, catechesis, or doctrinal instruction), and the homily (liturgical preaching), all preaching from the standpoint of theology draws its power and effectiveness from the saving power of God. As a salvific event, the word of God effects what it signifies as promised throughout the scriptures: ''So shall my word be that goes forth from my mouth: it shall not return to me void, but shall do my will, achieving the end for which I sent it'' (Is 55:11); ''Indeed God's word is living and effective, sharper than any two-edged sword. It penetrates and divides soul and spirit, joints and marrow; it judges the reflections and thought of the heart'' (Heb 4:12).

Preaching and Teaching. The apostolic proclamation of God's fidelity throughout history focuses on the Word made flesh—the good news of what God had done in the life, death, and resurrection of Jesus. The proclamation of the Gospel identified by Paul as ''the power of God for salvation'' was a call to conversion (METANOIA)—radical turning towards God and away from sin. Claiming a vocation he identified with a ''compulsion to preach,'' (1 Cor 9:16), Paul stressed that the power of preaching is ''the power of God'' (Rom 1:16, 1 Cor 1:18), active in spite of human weakness (1 Cor 1:25), its persuasive source found not in wise argumentation, but only in ''the convincing power of the Spirit'' (1 Cor 2:4). Paul likewise insisted on the centrality of the cross in the Christian proclamation of God's wisdom: ''The message of the cross is complete absurdity to those who are headed for ruin, but to us who are experiencing salvation, it is the power of God'' (1 Cor 1:18; cf. 1 Cor 2: 1–5).

Endowed with the Spirit's charisms of ''wisdom in discourse'' (*logos sophias*) and prophecy (1 Cor 12:8–10), prophets, teachers, and apostles embraced their mission to proclaim the good news of God's salvation in Jesus Christ through diverse ministries of the word in the early Christian communities and house churches. The *First Apology* of JUSTIN MARTYR in the mid-2nd century gives evidence of liturgical preaching (the homily) as an integral part of the Christian eucharist. The closely related ministries of preaching and teaching shared the common intent of drawing both initial and more experienced hearers of the word into embracing the Christian life of discipleship. Concern for the authenticity of the tradition led to a growing emphasis on the ministry of bishops as the official preachers and teachers of the Gospel and overseers of the ministries of the word, although gifted and educated lay preachers such as ORIGEN, head of the catechetical school at ALEXANDRIA, were invited by bishops to preach even in the liturgical assembly.

By the 4th century, preaching had become predominantly doctrinal, catechetical, and mystagogical formation in faith. Convinced that God's word was revealed pre-eminently in Jesus Christ, preachers searched for the ''spiritual sense'' of the scriptures (seeking a Christological interpretation, for example, of the Hebrew scriptures) and pointed to the sacraments as continuations of God's saving work. AUGUSTINE articulated an early sacramental theology of preaching by identifying a sacrament as a ''visible word'' (*verbum visibile*) and preaching as an audible sacrament (*sacramentum audibile*). Although he outlined principles of rhetoric for Christian preaching in Book IV of *On Christian Doctrine*, Augustine viewed preaching as a share in Christian wisdom that goes beyond rhetorical skill. The preacher's interpretation of a biblical text was to highlight how the signs of the Trinity are to be found throughout creation and history. The ultimate hermeneutical key for the interpretation of any scripture passage, as delineated in *On Christian Doctrine*, is to be found in love of God and love of neighbor. Augustine maintained that when the preacher announces the word of God, it is in fact ''Christ who teaches; his pulpit is in heaven . . . and his school is his [mystical] body'' (*Sermo de disciplina christiana*, ML 40, col. 678).

Medieval understandings of preaching were grounded in the sacramental and incarnational conviction that in the divine economy all of creation, and every word of scripture, speaks of Christ (BONAVENTURE). The goal of preaching was to draw out the spiritual senses of scripture so as to ''offer instruction in matters of faith and behavior'' (ALAN OF LILLE, *The Art of Preaching*, ch. 1). THOMAS AQUINAS emphasized that the ''grace of speech'' was needed for one to speak in a way that not only instructs the intellect, but also moves the affections of the hearers so that they might love what is signified and want to fulfill what the word urges (*Summa Theologiae* II–II, q. 177,a. 1, reply). To emphasize that preaching communicates the word of God and not merely human words, Aquinas used scholastic terminology to identify God as the ''principal cause'' of preaching and the preacher as ''instrumental cause.'' CONVERSION requires not only the outer word of the preacher, but also the inner word of grace that is the effect of the anointing of the Holy Spirit (*Summa Theologiae* II–II, q. 1, a. 4, ad 4; q. 6, a. 1; q. 2, a. 9, ad 3).

Ministry of the Word. In the sixteenth century, Protestant Reformers Martin LUTHER and John CALVIN developed rich theologies of the word, but these were not developed in the post-Tridentine Roman Catholic tradition that continued to emphasize the Church's ministry of teaching and instruction. Post-Reformation disputes about the efficacy of preaching (preaching brings about faith, but cannot effect sanctifying grace), and the relationship between sacraments and preaching (preaching is not an eighth sacrament) dominated Catholic theologies of preaching well into the 20th century. In 1936 Joseph JUNGMANN charged that preaching had become ''the vulgarization of theological tracts'' rather than the announcement of good news. The kerygmatic renewal in catechetics which Jungmann promoted and the liturgical movement provided resources and impetus for a similar renewal in preaching.

Along with the developments in critical biblical scholarship and the ''return to the sources'' (resourcement) in theology, the impact of the liturgical and catechetical movements on the Church's understanding of preaching are evident throughout the documents of Vatican II. One of the central purposes of the Council as expressed by John XXIII in his opening address, was for the Church to make itself ''better fitted for proclaiming the Gospel to the people of the twentieth century'' (*Acta Apostolicae Sedis* 54 [1969] 792). Of particular note in the conciliar documents are the claims that ''The Church has always venerated the divine scriptures just as she venerates the body of the Lord'' (DV 21); that preaching is crucial to the mission of the Church (LG 17; AG 3); that preaching is the Church's chief means of evangelization (AG 6) and that preaching is necessary as a call to faith and conversion (SC 9). At various points the documents identify preaching as central to the ministries of bishop (LG 25; CD 12) and priest (PO 4; LG 28). At the same time the documents speak of all baptized members as sharing in the prophetic office of the Church (LG 12; AA 2,3; GS 43).

In a major liturgical reform, the Constitution on the Sacred Liturgy restored the ancient liturgical homily, by means of which ''the mysteries of the faith and the guiding principles of the Christian life are expounded,'' as ''part of the liturgy itself'' (SC 52, 35) and climax of the Liturgy of the Word. Likewise, the Decree on the Life and Ministry of Priests reestablishes the centrality of the preached word to the sacramental celebration since ''faith is born of the word and nourished by it.'' The homily, according to that document and numerous liturgical sources, is to be drawn from scriptural and liturgical texts of the day, and to ''apply the perennial truth of the Gospel to the concrete circumstances of life'' (PO 4; see also SC 10, 35, 51–52; General Instruction on the Roman Missal, n. 41; and second edition of the General Instruction on the Lectionary for Mass, n. 24).

Ten years after the close of the Council, Paul VI's apostolic exhortation ''On Evangelization in the Modern World'' (1975), used the term ''evangelization'' to refer both to the initial proclamation of the word of God as a call to conversion and to any exercise of the ministry of the word. The exhortation reaffirmed that preaching is an ecclesial act and that proclamation of the good news of the reign of God ''constitutes the essential mission of the Church'' (EvangNunt, 14). The document also accents the pneumatological dimension of a theology of preaching with the reminder that the Holy Spirit is the principal agent in preaching and that the new humanity generated by the Spirit is the goal of all preaching (ibid., 75). The Spirit is the authentic source of both the proclamation and the hearing of the word that moves the hearers to initial and ongoing conversion. The Spirit forms ministers of the word—both ordained and lay—so that the preacher's words can be supported by the witness of a holy life, the spirit of unity and friendship among believers, a reverence for truth, an authentic love of those to whom the Gospel is proclaimed, and the spiritual fervor that gives preaching its character of urgency (ibid., 76–80). The apostolic exhortation recalls the universality of the preaching mandate of the Church, but also recognizes that preaching requires careful pastoral discernment which takes account of the specific character, needs, and life-situation of the hearers of the word.

Ministry of the Word. Following on the kerygmatic renewal earlier in the century, Catholic theologians discovered rich resources for a theology of preaching in biblical theologies of the word as well as in ecumenical dialogue with Reformation traditions that have emphasized the saving power of the proclaimed word. Theologians such as Otto Semmelroth, Yves CONGAR, Edward Schillebeeckx, Michael Schmaus, Domenico Grasso, and Charles Davis all contributed to a renewed theology of preaching grounded in a sacramental theology of revelation. Semmelroth, for example, stressed that the Liturgy of the Word and the Liturgy of the Eucharist constitute an integral representation of the saving event of Jesus's total life of self-surrender from the time of the incarnation through his saving death on the cross. Word and Sacrament together make present the fullness of the paschal mystery embodied in Jesus Christ who is both God's saving Word of grace as offer (*Wort*) and the Spirit-empowered answer (*Antwort*) of self-offering obedient love. The incarnation constitutes ''God's own sermon'' to humankind; the goal of all preaching is to invite the gathered community into deeper participation in the paschal mystery (*The Preaching Word*, 1962).

Karl RAHNER's lament that Catholic theology lacked an adequate theology of the word was attenuated by his own groundbreaking insights into the word as sacrament and sacraments as the ''highest words'' of the Church's self-expression. Rahner's development of Augustine's insight that the proclaimed word is an ''audible sacrament'' provided an important theological foundation for contemporary Catholic theologies of preaching. While he did not develop an explicit theology of preaching, Rahner identified the proclaimed word as a sacrament in which grace (God's self-communication) is embodied in the explicitness of word. Thus the role of the preacher is to name the depth dimension of the mystery of human existence as God's self-offer and thus draw the hearers of the word into a deeper relationship with God. The Church is called to be the abiding sacramental presence in the world of the primal sacramental word of definitive grace—Jesus Christ. Preaching and the sacraments function as the self-expression of the Church, naming, proclaiming, and celebrating the deepest truth at the heart of reality—God's self-offer in love. According to Rahner, all the words of the Church, preeminently the words of liturgical preaching, are oriented toward the celebration of the sacraments. The eucharist functions as the ''highest word of the Church'' in which the Church locates its deepest identity in the proclamation of the death and resurrection of Jesus Christ.

William J. HILL also recognized the centrality of the apostolic kerygma, but Hill stressed that effective preaching involves the ''kerygmatic reinterpretation'' of texts and events from the tradition. That retrieval is possible, however, only from the perspective of the contemporary milieu. According to Hill, the task of the preacher is to render salvation history present and operative in the contemporary world in a way that moves the community to surrender to the unconditional claims of God. New questions and experiences—both those of the preacher and those of the community—elicit previously unrecognized dimensions of the biblical text and produce a genuinely new word. Remarking that effective preaching requires both the conversion of the preacher and serious theological reflection, Hill drew on the resources of Bernard LONERGAN to describe preaching as a moment in the theological process. The preacher's task is to discern the meaning God intends and the human response required today based on the normative expression of God's word located in the New Testament as proclaimed in the community of faith. The word of God—or as Hill states, ''God's meaning'' becomes incarnate in the words and deeds of the preacher. The word inaugurates the process of conversion in both preacher and community. In the process of mediating God's meaning to today's world both the preacher and the community are newly constituted. Through the process of discerning and announcing God's meaning, the preacher is constituted as a herald of the message of Christ and the community is constituted as ''the place where the word takes root.''

Edward Schillebeeckx's early writings on revelation and theology reflect a sacramental theology of revelation and the word very similar to that of Karl Rahner. In his later writings on revelation in his Christological trilogy (notably *Christ: The Experience of Jesus as Lord*, 1980), Schillebeeckx moved beyond the distinction between revelation-in-reality and revelation-in-word with the claims that all experience has a narrative structure and that revelation occurs within, but cannot be identified with, human experience. Christianity began with the first disciples' experience of salvation in and through Jesus and continues as a living story of discipleship. To announce salvation, Schillebeeckx emphasizes, is not only to proclaim a memory of God's fidelity in the past as recorded in the scriptures and handed on in the living Christian tradition, but also to preach the good news of how God's Spirit continues to work in the world today and promises a future even in the most desperate of situations. The goal of preaching and of every ministry of the word is to interpret the human story and the story of creation in light of the story of Jesus in such a way that people can find hope to believe that God is at work in the world in spite of all the evidence to the contrary. That kind of proclamation remains credible only if Christian communities give evidence of that hope by ''writing a fifth gospel'' with their lives.

Recent theologies of liturgical preaching stress the Spirit's activity in the community of the baptized and the claim of the Second Vatican Council's Constitution on the Sacred Liturgy that the presence of Christ is located in the gathered assembly and the word proclaimed as well as in the sacramental elements and the minister. That approach characterizes the implicit theology of preaching in *Fulfilled in Your Hearing: The Homily in the Sunday Assembly*, issued by the National Conference of Catholic Bishops' Committee on Priestly Life and Ministry in 1982. The document begins with the liturgical assembly and stresses that the purpose of the homily is ''to enable the gathered congregation to celebrate the liturgy with faith'' (20). Shifting the focus of preaching from the application of biblical texts to life, *Fulfilled in Your Hearing* suggests that ''the goal of the liturgical preacher is not to interpret a text of the bible . . . as much as to draw on the texts of the Bible as they are presented in the lectionary to interpret people's lives'' (20).

As the word of God is proclaimed around the globe in multiple and diverse communities of faith, and the Church responds to John Paul II's call for a ''new EVANGELIZATION'' that includes the ''evangelization of cultures,'' the Gospel's call to conversion takes on new meaning. The call to preach requires that preachers first listen to the word of God not only in the scriptures and liturgy, but also in the unique cultural contexts and life situations of the communities in which they preach. The word of God has been entrusted to the entire community of faith. Thus one of the roles of pastors and preachers is to encourage members of the community to share their own insights into the word of God as revealed in their daily lives. Likewise, the call to embody the word of God extends beyond sacramental praxis. As the 1971 Synod of Bishops' statement proclaimed, "action on behalf of justice is a constitutive part of the preaching of the Gospel" (*Justice in the World*, Washington: USCC, 1972, p. 34). The call to repent and believe the good news is a call that needs to be heard and embraced by the Church and its preachers—especially those from dominant groups and cultures—if it is to be proclaimed authentically beyond the boundaries of the Church.

Bibliography: Z. ALSZEGHY and M. FLICK, "Il problema teologica della predicazione," *Gregorianum* 40 (Rome 1959) 671–744. C. DAVIS, "The Theology of Preaching," *Clergy Review* 45 (London 1960) 524–547. R. T. HANLEY, *The Theology of Preaching in Modern Papal Teaching: St. Pius X-John XXIII* (Washington 1964). P. HITZ, *To Preach the Gospel,* tr. R. SHEED (New York 1963). J. A. JUNGMANN, *The Good News Yesterday and Today,* ed. and tr. W. HUESMAN (New York 1962). J. MURPHY-O'CONNOR, *Paul on Preaching* (New York 1964). O. SEMMELROTH, *The Preaching Word: On The Theology of Proclamation,* tr. J. J. HUGHES (New York 1965). K. RAHNER et al., *The Word: Readings in Theology* (New York 1964). D. GRASSO, *Proclaiming God's Message* (Notre Dame, IN 1965). BISHOPS' COMMITTEE ON PRIESTLY LIFE AND MINISTRY, National Conference of Catholic Bishops, *Fulfilled in Your Hearing: The Homily in the Sunday Assembly* (Washington, DC 1982). W. J. BURGHARDT, *Preaching the Art and the Craft* (New York 1987). W. J. HILL, *Search for the Absent God* (New York 1992). M. C. HILKERT, *Naming Grace: Preaching and the Sacramental Imagination* (New York 1997). P. JANOWIAK, *The Holy Preaching: The Sacramentality of the Word in the Liturgical Assembly* (Collegeville, MN 2000). W. SKUDLAREK, *The Word in Worship: Preaching in a Liturgical Context* (Nashville 1981).

[M. C. HILKERT]

PREACHING, IV (CANON LAW OF)

The *1983 Code of* CANON LAW treats the topic of preaching in Book III, "The Teaching Office of the Church." In that Book, preaching is treated as one facet of Title I, "The Ministry of the Divine Word." The other facet of Ministry of the Divine Word is catechetical instruction. However, there are references to preaching in other canons of Book III and in other sections of the Code, all indicating that the activity of preaching has several forms and various levels of relationship to the teaching authority of the Church. The most fundamental level of preaching is entrusted to the whole Church; that is, every member of the Christian faithful, by reason of baptism. A second level of preaching pertains to the ordained; bishop, priest or deacon, by reason of ordination. A third level of preaching is that undertaken by laity at the specific invitation of the ordained.

Preaching Entrusted to All the Baptized. The Code, reflecting the teaching of Vatican II, acknowledges the responsibility of all the baptized to preach the Gospel through the witness of their lives. This obligation, explicit throughout Chapter II of *Lumen gentium,* is implied in canon 204 which states that all who are baptized share "in their own way" in the priestly, prophetic and royal functions of Christ, and are called to exercise the mission of the Church "in accord with the condition proper to each." Canon 204 has its roots in *Lumen gentium.* This implication of the baptismal obligation to preach is repeated in canons 208, on the equality of all the baptized in dignity and action as they carry out the mission of the Church, and 211 on the right and obligation of all the Christian faithful to evangelize.

The obligation of all the baptized to preach the Gospel message is stated explicitly in canon 747, the opening canon of Book III, and again in canon 759. This most fundamental form of preaching is proper to all Christians and requires no permission or authorization from the hierarchy.

Preaching Entrusted to the Ordained. For the ordained—bishops, priests and deacons—preaching can take on a number of forms and purposes. For instance, the preaching done by bishops can be directly related to their role as teachers of the faith, while the preaching done by priests or deacons is not seen as an action of magisterial teachers. For all the ordained, preaching can take on a catechetical or liturgical character, depending on the context within which it is done.

Some norms on preaching are applicable to all the ordained. First, all the ordained are reminded in canon 762 that their principal duty is to proclaim the Gospel. Thus, preaching must be held in great esteem. This emphasis is placed on preaching because of the value of the Word of God for the community of believers as the cause of their gathering and their source of ongoing strength. As the canon states, "the people of God are first brought together by the word of the living God." The canon concludes with the statement, taken from the *Presbyterorum ordinis* 4, that the people rightly have the expectation to hear this word of God from the ordained.

Canon 768 provides guidance for the content of preaching, first in general and then more particularly. In general, preaching is intended to proclaim to the Faithful what must be done and believed "for the glory of God and the salvation of humanity." More specifically, preaching is to present magisterial doctrine on the "the dignity and freedom of the human person, the unity and stability of family and its duties, the obligations which people have from being joined together in society, and the ordering of temporal affairs according to the plan established by God.'' This canon is derived from *Christus Dominus* 12, on the preaching responsibilities of bishops, and from *Gaudium et spes* 40–42, which describes the vital relationship between the Church and the world and between faith and life. Together these sources provide a rich theological foundation for understanding preaching as the ministry which aims to make the Word of God active in the hearer.

The canon that follows (canon 769), builds on this goal of preaching to relate faith and life, by stipulating that Christian doctrine, that which is preached, is to be accommodated to its hearers and adapted to the needs of the times. This same theme is emphasized again in canon 770 which directs bishops and pastors to arrange for other forms of preaching in their respective dioceses of parishes, namely spiritual exercises or missions which meet the needs of their people. Then canon 771 widens the circle of concern by obliging all ''pastors of souls,'' that is, bishops and priests, to have concern that the word of God reaches both those who do not present themselves for ordinary pastoral care and those in the territory who are not believers in Christ.

Also applicable to all the ordained is canon 767 on the HOMILY. The homily, described by the canon as preeminent among all forms of preaching and an integral part of the liturgy, ''is reserved to the priest or deacon.'' The homily, according to the canon, is rooted in Scripture and is an explanation of ''the mysteries of faith and the norms of Christian life.'' Homilies are required at all Sunday celebrations and holy days of obligation when a congregation is present, unless a ''grave cause'' indicates otherwise (canon 767 § 2). Homilies are recommended at all other masses when people are present, especially during Advent and Lent (canon 767 § 3). Responsibility for seeing that these directives are observed falls to the pastor or rector of a church (canon 767 § 4).

Norms Specific to Bishops. The 1983 Code contains norms on preaching which apply only to bishops. They, in virtue of their role in the Church, have a right (*ius*) to preach everywhere in the world, ''including churches and oratories of religious houses of pontifical rite.'' In his own diocese an individual bishop may prevent another bishop from preaching, but this must be done explicitly and for a particular instance (canon 763).

Further, bishops are directed to preach frequently in person and propose in their preaching the truths of the faith and how those truths of the faith and how those truths are to inform Christian living. Lastly, bishops are obliged to oversee the proper implementation of the law concerning all aspects of the Ministry of the Word, especially homilies (canon 386 § 1).

Norms Specific to Priests. While bishops have a *right* to preach everywhere in the world, priests are given, in the law, the faculty to preach everywhere in the world. This faculty to preach may be restricted by the appropriate authority with respect to the person or with respect to certain territory (see canon 764). The exception to this world-wide faculty is that permission from the appropriate religious superior is required for a priest to preach to members of a religious institute in the institute's own church or oratory (canon 765).

Priests who are pastors of parishes are specially charged with the obligation of preaching to their people on the sacrament of marriage so that ''the matrimonial state is preserved in a Christian spirit and advances in perfection'' (canon 1063, 1°).

Norms Specific to Deacons. Deacons, similarly to priests, are given, by the law itself, the faculty to preach everywhere in the world. Deacons are subject to the same restrictions and permissions stipulated for priests in canons 764 and 765.

Preaching Entrusted to Laity. The 1917 Code was quite specific in stating that laity, even religious, were not permitted to preach in churches (1917 Code, canon 1342). The documents of Vatican II, specifically the Constitution on the Sacred Liturgy, n. 35, directed that in areas of the world where priests were not available, bishops should appoint deacons or lay persons to conduct ''Bible services.'' This directive was implemented by the instruction *Inter oecumenici* (issued September 26, 1964) which indicated that such Bible services could be presided over by deacons or laity, but only a presiding deacon, with proper permission, could preach. Both these documents are the indicated sources for canon 766 of the 1983 Code which states that lay persons are permitted to preach in churches or oratories ''if necessity requires it, in certain circumstances or it seems advantageous in particular cases.'' The canon also stipulates that in every country, lay preaching is regulated by norms issued by the conference of bishops, ''without prejudice to canon 767 § 1.'' That is, the homily is reserved to the priest or deacon.

Much of the discussion and development concerning lay preaching has revolved, not around canon 766 itself, which states the acceptability of lay preaching, but around canon 767 which excludes laity from preaching homilies. An early difficulty arose from a lack of consistency in the wording of canon 767 itself. The first paragraph of the canon refers to the homily at ''liturgy,'' while subsequent paragraphs refer to the homily at ''Mass.'' For any interpretation of the canon, the latter wording indicates the exclusion of laity from preaching at Eucharistic celebrations, while the former wording calls for wider application to all liturgical celebrations. A number of official documents issued subsequent to the 1983 Code indicate that the canon applies only to preaching at Mass. For instance, the Directory for Sunday Celebrations in the Absence of a Priest (issued May 21, 1988) and the interdicastery instruction ''Some Questions Regarding Collaboration of the Nonordained Faithful in Priests' Sacred Ministry'' (issued August 14, 1997) refer to laity preaching in at non-Eucharistic services. However, even these documents have not been entirely consistent, since the latter refers to laity giving ''homilies'' at non-Eucharistic liturgies, which seems to contradict the wording and intent of canon 767 to restrict homilies to the ordained.

A second area of difficulty over the relationship of canons 766 and 767 came in the early years of the implementation of the 1983 Code. Because the restriction of the homily to the priest or deacon stated in canon 767 was considered to be a disciplinary norm, diocesan bishops felt free to dispense from the norm, according to the common understanding of their dispensing power, thereby allowing laity to preach. An authentic interpretation of the law was issued on May 26, 1987 [see *AAS* 79 (1987) 1249] which stated that such dispensations were not permitted to bishops.

This authentic interpretation and continued effort to implement canon 766 has given rise to further discussion on the nature of the homily and the meaning of its restriction to the ordained. It leaves open the question whether the homily is to be defined by its content (an explanation of the Scripture which has been proclaimed), or by its placement in the celebration. For instance, were an ordained person to preach during a Eucharistic celebration on a topic other than the Scripture which has been proclaimed, would that be a homily? If the ordained person preaches before the Gospel rather than after, or at some other point in the celebration and explains the Scriptures which have been proclaimed, is that a homily? Likewise, if a lay person preaches after the Gospel, but does not speak on the Scripture which has been proclaimed, or speaks at some other time in the celebration but does comment on the Scripture readings, is that an acceptable implementation of canon 766?

There are many differences of opinion on these questions, and consequently many differing opinions on how and when canon 766 can be implemented. Clearly, lay persons are excluded from giving homilies, but there is not universal agreement on what constitutes the homily. Consequently, the forms of preaching available to laity according to canon 766 such as reflections, commentary, personal witness or testimony, are clouded by the ambiguity.

Acknowledging that there is the restriction concerning the homily, canon 766 states the broad principle that preaching by laity, when advantageous to the community in question, is appropriate. There is no mention that lay preaching is conditioned upon a lack of priests. However, laity who undertake this formalized preaching are invited to it by an appropriate ecclesiastical authority. The canon does not designate where decisions about necessity or advantage to the community are made, or by whom. Neither is the level of authority who invites the lay person to preach identified in the canon. However, such determinations may be stated in any norms established by a particular episcopal conference for its own territory. Examples of norms established by various conferences indicate that some conferences have restricted lay preaching by its placement in the liturgy. Others do not mention placement, but require special preparation for lay preachers and/or permission from the local ordinary before preaching is undertaken. (Examples in the *Canon Law Digest*, volume 11.) In the absence of any national norms or diocesan norms, decisions about lay preaching are made at the local level and in conformity with universal law.

Bibliography: J. BEAL, et al., eds., *New Commentary on the Code of Canon Law* (Mahwah/New York 2000). L. ROBITAILLE, ''An Examination of Various Forms of Preaching,'' *Canon Law Society Proceedings* 58 (1996) 308–325. J. PROVOST, ''Brought Together by the Word of the Living God,'' *Studia Canonica* 23 (1989) 345–371. P. STEVENS, ''La Prédication dans le Code de Droit Canonique: Quelques remarques critiques,'' *Revue de Droit Canonique* 48 (1998) 81–96.

[E. A. RINERE]

PREACHING, MEDIEVAL ENGLISH

Medieval English sermon literature (*c.* 1000–1500) was founded on the beginnings of English Christianity; the importance attached to the preaching function produced a pulpit literature important to the development of the English language and established literary traditions recognizable centuries after the close of the Middle Ages.

Early Collections. Among the earliest surviving collections of sermons in English is the Blickling Homilies, 19 sermons recorded *c.* 970 and named by scholars after an early home of the MS. In these sermons, the homilist is concerned more with exhorting his audience than with expounding doctrine. The sermons of AELFRIC GRAMMATICUS (d. 1020), a monk of Cerne Abbas and later abbot of Eynsham is perhaps the most important of the Anglo-Saxon sermon writers. He prepared a large body of sermons for delivery to the laity. Two homiletic collections have survived: *Sermones Catholicae* and *Lives of the Saints*. The first consists of two series of 40 sermons each, intended for use throughout the liturgical year. The second, describe saints "whom monks honor." Many of his sermons had a catechetical purpose. Their contents, following an English paraphrase of the gospel pericope, were adapted from the writings of the Latin church fathers. If Aelfric's sermons were intended for instruction in doctrinal matters, those of his contemporary, WULFSTAN, are calculated to stir their hearers to repentance.

From the earliest times, the sermon following the Gospel of the Mass could be replaced by the reading in the vernacular of a homily of one of the Fathers. Although little evidence survives from the 11th and 12th centuries, it is likely that the sermons of this time, however infrequent, were in English. *See*, for instance, Goulburn and Symonds, *Life, Letters, and Sermons of Bishop Herbert de Losinga* [of Norwich] (Oxford 1878), the Homilies of the Vercelli Book (*c.* 1100), and the sermons of MS Bodley 343 (*c.* 1175). Examples could be multiplied, although one should note that the existence in MSS of vernacular sermons does not demonstrate that they were preached in English. They may have been reproduced to edify or to serve as models for clergy not proficient in Latin. ROBERT GROSSETESTE, however, shortly after he became bishop of Lincoln in 1235, issued constitutions requiring the clergy of his diocese to teach their parishioners, in English, the Decalogue, the seven deadly sins, the seven Sacraments, and the Creed. His example apparently inspired others: in 1281 JOHN PECKHAM, Archbishop of Canterbury, for instance, issued the Constitutions of Lambeth, commanding every pastor, personally or by deputy, to explain to the people four times a year in their own tongue the 14 articles of faith, the ten Commandments, the two precepts of the Gospels, the seven works of mercy, the seven deadly sins, the seven cardinal virtues, and the seven Sacraments.

Whereas "the edicts of the Lateran Council in 1215 imply that the office of preaching was generally at that time either badly performed or totally neglected" (see A. Lecoy de la Marche, 30–31, in bibliography; the author is describing conditions in France, but the state of preaching in England was similar). However, the advent of the friars to England transformed that situation. "It seems clear that church-going increased in the later Middle Ages, and it is reasonable to attribute the growth of this situation. Sermons were no longer delivered infrequently, or even as seldom as four times a year." The importance medieval England attached to preaching is attested by the great number of manuals and books of models that survive. More than 80 MSS of 30-odd *artes praedicandi* (arts of preaching) have been discovered in English libraries, 12 of them from the 13th century. A number of the identifiable authors were Dominicans and Franciscans, and it is clear that the friars were responsible in large measure for the flowering of the preaching art that was such a force in England for 300 years after their coming.

The friars were not the only ones who preached in the vernacular. There is ample evidence of preaching in English by clergy of all kinds from the 13th century onward, and for those who needed them, there were abundant models, manuals, and collections of sermons and *exempla.* The sermon books were often in Latin, but there was no lack of them in English. Indeed, it is often difficult to determine whether a collection or cycle of sermons was intended for pulpit delivery or to serve as models. Instances are the Northern Homily Cycle, written in short couplets, presumably of single authorship; or the sermons of British Museum MS Royal 18 B. xxiii, which include a famous sermon preached by Thomas Wimbledon at Paul's Cross in 1388–89; and three sermons from John Myrc's *Festial;* besides 51 others. Some were apparently for pulpit use and others seemingly served as models.

Later Manuals. Among the interesting manuals besides the *Festial* are *Instructions for Parish Priests,* also by Myrc, largely a translation from the Latin of William de Pagula's *Oculus Sacerdotis; Jacob's Well* (early 15th century), developing in 95 sermons an elaborate allegory in which man is likened to a well that must be cleaned and protected from pollution entering through the five senses; the Lollard translation of the *Speculum Christiani,* prepared, doubtless, for the many unlearned Lollard preachers (*see* LOLLARDS). Two centuries earlier, *c.* 1200, Orm, or Ormin, a canon regular of the Order of St. Augustine, wrote the *Ormulum.* He states that he planned to present in English the Gospels in the Mass book for the year, with interpretations and applications, so that simple men might understand Church doctrines. He never completed his project, but his achievement is monumental; it is valuable today for linguistic study more than as sermon literature, but surely it was used as a sermon manual.

There are many other collections. Some are translations from Latin or French, and the authors of many of the individual sermons are identifiable. The Lambeth Homilies (MS Lambeth 487, *c.* 1200) include material from Aelfric, and the five Kentish sermons of MS Laud 471 (late 13th century) survive along with their French originals by Maurice de Sully. There is a large body of Wyclifite sermons; however, it is difficult to separate the writings of Wyclif from those of his followers. Most of the two volumes of sermons are probably his, but they are brief, and perhaps were meant as sermon notes for poor priests. G. R. Owst's great studies, *Preaching in Medieval England* and *Literature and Pulpit in Medieval England,* identify a large number of medieval preachers by name and affiliation.

Structure and Matter of the Sermons. The manuals are specific on the structure of the sermon, although not all sermons followed the directions set forth. First came the text or *thema,* taken from the Lesson, the Epistle, or the Gospel of the day, except on feast days, when any Bible text could be used. Next followed the *prothema* or *antethema,* an apology, which could be made elaborate; and a prayer (sometimes a prayer alone); sometimes the *prothema* was replaced by a ''prelocution'' that cited authority for proof of the *thema,* followed by a statement of the divisions of the sermon, and a prayer. Next came a restatement of the text, or *thema,* and the ''process,'' a statement of the divisions in which the text was to be treated. In the 13th century, at least, there were two types of division: *infra,* when the sermon was addressed to clerks; *extra,* when addressed to the people. Each division of the ''process'' was a ''principal,'' and each subdivision of the ''principal'' was a ''part,'' or *socius.* The amplification of the ''parts'' could be highly complicated. Traditionally, the rhetorical modes were the historical or literal, the allegorical or personified, the tropological or moralized, and the anagogical or mystical. The development often included citations of authority, parallels from natural history, and analogies from the Bible or saints' lives. Caplan lists 20 forms of amplification (''Classical Rhetoric . . . ,'' 88; see also his ''The Four Senses of Christian Interpretation . . . ,'' 282–290, and Bowers, *Publications of the Modern Language Association* 65 (1950) 590–600).

The mode and tone of the sermon varied with the audience, the occasion, and the talent of the preacher. Although the subject might be the same, the discourse would be different if the preacher addressed a popular audience at the crossroads than when his audience was a congregation of clerks, or when he preached before the king.

Sermons could be very short or very long. The prose ''Lithir lok'' in Trinity College, Cambridge MS 43 (a Dominican MS, printed by Carleton Brown, *Bulletin of the Modern Humanities Research Association,* 2.5, September 1926) is about 400 words; the verse sermon on the Lord's Prayer from Cambridge University Library MS Dd XI. 89 [printed by Frank A. Patterson in *Journal of English and Germanic Philology* 15 (1916) 406–419] is 592 short lines in couplets; whereas the ''Per Proprium Sanguinem'' of Austin Friar John Gregory (printed by Pfander, *The Popular Sermon of the Medieval Friar in England,* 54–64) runs to more than 5,000 words.

Sermons are frequently in pedestrian verse, intended apparently to be mnemonic rather than artistic; often a popular sermon would begin with a few lines from a popular song (St. Francis himself once used a secular couplet as a sermon text). Friar Nicholas Phillipp (15th century) interlards his prose sermons with rhymes and short poems; and Carleton Brown believed that the Franciscan Herebert's (d. 1333) translations of Latin hymns ''were designed primarily for pulpit use'' [*English Religious Lyrics of the Fourteenth Century* (Oxford 1924) xiv].

The subject matter of the sermons was also varied: interpretation of the Scriptures, the Creed, the Pater Noster, and the Decalogue was of first importance; exposition of the vices and virtues; reproofs for wrongdoing and commendation of uprightness; setting forth the rewards of right conduct and the punishment of evil—these made up the substance of the sermons.

When the Dominicans and Franciscans reached England in 1221 and 1224, they immediately addressed themselves to the neglected common man, and he responded with an enthusiasm of which there is abundant record. This concern for the common man led the preachers to learn his idiom, his hopes and fears and frustrations. They developed a new kind of vernacular sermon that was instrumental in bringing about the upsurge in church attendance from the 13th century onward.

Influence on Secular Literature. It is impossible to assess this influence adequately. To begin with, the popular preacher must have been a force during the later 11th and the 12th century, as he demonstrably was during the 13th, in the preservation of English as a worthy medium of expression; and he clearly was a major instrument during the 13th century in the fusion of the diverse elements that became the language of Wyclif and Chaucer. He dealt with the commonplace realistically and in picturesque, forceful language, and it cannot be doubted that the realism and vigor of the literature of the 14th and later centuries owes much to his style.

The association of the Church and early drama is a commonplace of literary history; and from pulpit treatment of life and death came the plots of morality plays and a tradition that is still recognizable in the speech on the Seven Ages of Man of Jacques in *As You Like It.* (*See* DRAMA, MEDIEVAL) The allegoric characters of Evil found in Langland are familiar in the homily books; the abstractions of Good and Evil in *Pilgrim's Progress* have their prototypes in the personified vices and virtues of medieval sermons and religious poems; the symbolic castles that dot the landscapes of 14th- and 15th-century literature—Langland's Tower of Truth, ''Maudelyn'' Castle in the Digby play, the *Castle of Perseverance,* and many more—were first homiletic symbol and metaphor. Chaucer's and all other attacks on corruption both within and without the Church have their counterparts in the *Summa Predicantium* of the great Dominican John BROMYARD.

Indeed, the whole body of the literature of satire and complaint reflects directly what Owst (*Literature and Pulpit,* 213) calls ". . . at once the profoundest and most abiding influence of the English pulpit." To cite but one of many available examples, the great collection of homiletic tales, the *GESTA ROMANORUM,* is a storehouse drawn on by Chaucer, Gower, Lydgate, and Hoccleve; it supplied Elizabethan dramatists with the plots of some of their best-known plays. Wherever one turns in examining the growth of secular literature in England, from the most sedate to the most ribald, one finds it firmly rooted in popular pulpit oratory and in homiletic writings.

See Also: PREACHING, I (HISTORY OF).

Bibliography: J. E. WELLS, *A Manual of Writings in Middle English, 1050–1400* (New Haven 1916; 9 suppls. 1919–52). G. R. OWST, *Literature and Pulpit in Medieval England* (2d ed. New York 1961); *Preaching in Medieval England* (Cambridge, Eng. 1926). R. H. BOWERS, "A Middle English Treatise on Hermeneutics: Harley MS 2276 32v–35v," *Publications of the Modern Language Association* 65 (1950) 590–600. H. CAPLAN, *Mediaeval Artes praedicandi* (Ithaca, N.Y. 1934); *Supplementary Handlist* (Ithaca, N.Y. 1936); "Classical Rhetoric and the Medieval Theory of Preaching," *Classical Philology* 28 (1933) 73–96; "The Four Senses of Scriptural Interpretation and the Medieval Theory of Preaching," *Speculum* 4 (1929) 282–290; "Rhetorical Invention in Some Mediaeval Tractates on Preaching," *ibid.* 2 (1927) 284–295. B. JARRETT, *The English Dominicans,* rev. and abr. W. GRUMBLEY (2d ed. London 1938). H. G. PFANDER, *The Popular Sermon of the Medieval Friar in England* (New York 1937). A. G. LITTLE, *Studies in English Franciscan History* (Manchester 1917); *The Grey Friars in Oxford* (Oxford 1892). A. LECOY DE LA MARCHE, *La Chaire française au moyen âge* (2d ed. Paris 1886). M. MCC. GATCH, *Preaching and Theology in Anglo-Saxon England: Aelfric and Wulfstan,* (Toronto 1977). D. L. D'AVRAY, *The Preaching of the Friars.* (Oxford 1985).

[J. E. CARVER/EDS.]

PREAMBLES OF FAITH

Classically, those conclusions taken from the natural and philosophic sciences that are of use in demonstrating the validity of the Catholic faith or of the apologetic that is designed to defend it. In the pyramidal structure of the 19th-century scientificohistorical apologetic, the *praeambula fidei* were presumed to have been previously demonstrated from first principles in the study of the several sciences that are related to apologetics, so that only relevant conclusions needed to be considered in the defense of faith. Thus, the objective validity of the human power to know, the existence and absolute nature of objective truth, the existence and spirituality of the soul, the freedom of the will, the existence of a personal God and His principal attributes, the ethical necessity for man to worship God, etc., were all included among the preambles of faith without which, it was felt, a scientific apologetic could not be constructed. These propositions were presumed to have been conclusions validly drawn in the sciences of epistemology, theodicy, psychology, and ethics. Any philosophic or scientific theory that impugned one or more of these fundamental propositions was to be rejected, while any theory that supported them was to be favored.

In more recent apologetic thought there is a departure, to some degree, from the closely reasoned and what many consider to be the almost rationalistic method of the 19th-century defense of the reasonableness of faith. The pioneer work of J. H. NEWMAN (*A Grammar of Assent*) raised the question regarding the reasonableness of the faith of the multitude of Catholic believers who are unable to grasp the reasoning involved in the apologetic employed to demonstrate its reasonableness. His conclusion was that it is by the convergence of evidence and the congeniality of orthodox beliefs among themselves that one comes to a reasonable basis for belief, rather than by the syllogistic method employed in scientific apologetics. Within the structure of his thought, the metaphysical question raised is how could there be such a convergence of evidence if the point toward which all the evidences gravitated were not the truth. This approach widens considerably the traditional definition of *praeambula fidei* to include not only the propositions previously noted, but a number of evidences that are personalistic in character and may be recognized only vaguely by the ordinary Christian. Newman's approach left room for the investigations of depth psychology and a consideration of the influential but not fully conscious convictions of the individual that form the context of his entire reasoning capacity.

In the 1960s the a priori conditions of faith were sought in the historical dimension of human existence experienced as transcendental openness to the absolute mystery of being and thus predisposing man to accept the revelation of God-man as the concrete historical and social realization as well as the historical, objective expression of his existential openness (*see* Bouillard, RAHNER, Darlap). As a consequence Rahner takes for a starting point of the way to faith man as the potential believer who, thanks to the abiding presence of the eschatological Christ-event in the world, is already in possession of what he is to believe, e.g., God's self-communication in Jesus Christ. Preambles of faith are therefore an implicit faith as an abiding feature of man's existence oriented to explicit faith as to its objective and conscious self-expression in the society of believers.

Since man discovers more and more the unlimited varieties of his own historical tradition, and thus a common philosophical ground for all believers and unbelievers is found extremely difficult, in the 1970s the preambles of faith were sought rather in the empirical fact of the already existing believing community. This conception of the preamble of faith does not assume any philosophical notion of human existence or religion in general by determining a priori which philosophy or religion should be the most adequate for man. It takes the community of believers as God-given, Christ-sign-event as puzzling datum strong enough to raise in man questions concerning God's personal presence in Jesus Christ.

Preambles of faith will be defined according to the concept of the apologetics they are designed to support. In an apologetic designed to arrive at the necessity of belief (credendity), they appear in strictly demonstrable, propositional form, whereas in the more recent Biblical and personalistic approaches to apologetics that strive to show no more than the reasonableness (credibility) and desirability of belief, they assume a less rigid and wider aspect that is more a way of life than the foundation for a syllogistic analysis.

See Also: APOLOGETICS; FAITH.

Bibliography: G. MUSCHALEK, *Lexikon für Theologie und Kirche*, ed. J. HOFER and K. RAHNER (Freiberg 1957–65) 8:653–657. K. RAHNER and H. VORGRIMLER, *Kleines theologisches Wörterbuch* (Freiburg 1961) 296–297. M. NICOLAU, *Sacrae theologiae summa*, ed. Fathers of the Society of Jesus, Professors of the Theological Faculties in Spain (Madrid 1962) 1.1:44–45. M. C. D'ARCY, *The Nature of Belief* (New York 1931; rev. ed. 1958). A. DULLES, *Apologetics and the Biblical Christ* (Westminster, Md. 1963). J. H. NEWMAN, *An Essay in Aid of a Grammar of Assent* (London 1870). J. ALFARO, ''Preambles of Faith,'' *Sacramentum Mundi. An Encyclopedia of Theology*, ed. K. RAHNER, C. ERNST, et al., 6v. (New York 1968–70) 2:324–326 H. BOUILLARD, *The Logic of Faith* (New York 1967). A. DARLAP, ''Theologie der Heilgeschichte,'' *Mysterium Salutis* 1 (Einsiedeln 1965) 1–156. T. HORVATH, *Faith Under Scrutiny* (Notre Dame 1975). B. J. F. LONERGAN, *Insight, A Study of Human Understanding* (London 1957). K. RAHNER, ''A Way to Faith,'' *Sacramentum Mundi. An Encyclopedia of Theology*, ed. K. RAHNER, C. ERNST, et al., 6v. (New York 1968–70) 2:310–317.

[J. P. WHALEN/T. HORVATH]

PRECA, GEORGE, BL.

Dun Ġorġ (in English, Father George) Preca; founder of a religious order, b. Feb. 12, 1880 in Valletta, the capital of Malta; d. July 26, 1962, in Santa Verera. The seventh of nine children born Vincenzo Preca, a businessman, and Natalina Ceravolo, a teacher, he was baptized Ġorġ on February 17. After completing his studies at the Lyceum, Dun Ġorġ studied philosophy and theology at the University of Malta. He attend the Seminary of the Archdiocese of Malta in Floriana, and was ordained to the priesthood Dec. 22, 1906.

Even before his priestly ordination Dun Ġorġ was inspired to devote his life to the catechetical ministry. He gathered a group of young men and instructed them in the teachings of the Church. His goal was that these educated and formed men devote their lives to the ministry of catechesis. In 1910 he founded a female branch. All members dedicate themselves to catechize the young for an hour every day and thereafter meet among themselves for personal continuing formation. They embrace a simple evangelical lifestyle and lead prayerful lives by saying short prayers at regular intervals during the day. He called the group *Societas Papidum et Papidissarum* (''Society of the Sons and Daughters of the Pope''). The locals nicknamed his association the Museum because of the rundown building where the members held their meetings. The members in turn adopted the epithet and created out of it an acronym in Latin: *Magister Utinam Sequatur Evangelium Universus Mundus* (''Divine Teacher, may the whole world would follow the Gospel'').

The innovative idea of the laity catechizing raised suspicions among the Church authorities. In 1909 the bishop ordered Dun Ġorġ to close down all the centers he had so far opened, but the parish priests rallied behind Dun Ġorġ and the ban was soon lifted. A few years later destructive articles about the Society appeared in the local press. As a response Dun Ġorġ required that the members take a vow of meekness. After further investigations by the Church, the bishop canonically established Dun Ġorġ's group as the Society of Christian Doctrine on Apr. 12, 1932, and in time the Society established branches in Australia, England, Albania, Sudan, Kenya, and Peru. Dun Ġorġ wanted his members to study, pray and proclaim God's word in their own native tongues. He translated parts of the Bible into Maltese and wrote a good number of books on systematic and moral theology as well as on spirituality, mainly for the continuing formation of the members of his society. He had a great devotion to the mystery of the incarnation and instructed his members to wear a badge with the words *Verbum Dei caro factum est* (''The Word of God became flesh''). Dun Ġorġ was a zealous apostle of the word of God, a faithful minister of catechesis. He was a priest of great humility, goodness, meekness and generosity. Dun Ġorġ died July 26, 1962 and was buried in the Church of Our Lady of the Miraculous Medal adjacent to the Society's motherhouse at Blata l-Bajda. He was one of three Maltese beatified by Pope John Paul II on his visit to Malta May 9, 2001.

Feast: May 9.

[E. MAGRO]

PRECEPT

A precept is a command by a legitimate authority that binds in conscience. Since this is also true of law, canonical usage has restricted the scope and meaning of the word precept. All laws are precepts but, conversely, not all precepts are laws. A further precision, then, is necessary. A precept is commonly understood as a command, by a qualified superior, given to an individual person, either temporarily or permanently, or to a community temporarily. The source of the authority imposing the precept may be either jurisdictional or nonjurisdictional power. The former is public power to govern a perfect society; the latter is either domestic power, by which qualified heads of private societies (e.g., conjugal or parental) exercise their respective authority over certain persons, or dominative power, by which properly constituted superiors of imperfect societies govern their subjects, e.g., parishes, some religious institutes.

With regard to the scope of the precept itself, to create a true obligation in those on whom it is imposed, it must be objectively just, possible, and morally good and useful; and finally, it must be made known to those whom it proposes to bind. On the part of the superior, it requires the requisite juridical relationship, by way of either jurisdiction, domestic power, or dominative power, by which the superior may impose the precept; and this relationship must be actual in order for the precept to be obligating, at least at the time of the issuance of the precept. A distinctive characteristic of precepts given to individual persons in virtue of nonjurisdictional power is that its prescriptions are personal and binding everywhere, and not only in a specific locality (unless this had been otherwise indicated by the superior or by the nature of the precept itself).

Precepts are usually temporary expedients and normally cease with the cessation of authority of the individual imposing the precept, through either death, resignation, transfer, or loss of official status. The precept is imposed by the superior and not by the law itself, and means of enforcement are limited to disciplinary measures such as paternal exhortation and the extrajudicial imposition of penances. A precept given to a community likewise is obligatory for the members of the group as individuals, in accordance with the above. On the other hand, precepts imposed on individuals in virtue of jurisdictional power are both personal and temporary, but lose their binding force with the cessation of the preceptor's juridical power, unless the precept had been imposed with the formality of a legal document or before two qualified witnesses. If this latter measure was taken, the precept could be enforced judicially, i.e., by an ecclesiastical trial. If the precept is given to a community, it seems that the common good requires its duration, even after the cessation of the official authority of its author. However, when for any reason the precept ceases to bind because of the superior's loss of office, the effects of it that have already been executed retain their force and remain unchanged, although the precept itself and its future effects lose their capacity to bind. Thus, a religious transferred to another in virtue of a precept must remain there although his superior who issued the precept has since lost his office.

The precept is akin to law in many ways: its imposition gives rise to moral obligation as is the case with law; its object must be morally good, possible, and reasonable; the excusing causes that obtain with regard to law, i.e., impotence, ignorance, revocation, etc., are the same. There are, however, some notable qualifications that distinguish precept from law: the law has as its object the common good, while the precept may be issued for the good of the individual himself or any other person, including the superior. Law requires legislative power, while dominative or domestic power (e.g., paternal or domestic) suffices for a precept. A precept can be imposed on a community that would not be capable of receiving a law. A law by its nature implies a relative stability and perpetuity, whereas a precept is usually ineffective after the authority of the superior ceases. Generally, laws are territorial, while the precept, unless otherwise stipulated, is personal.

Bibliography: J. ABBO and J. HANNAN, *The Sacred Canons,* 2 v. (St. Louis 1960) v. 1. M. CONTE A CORONATA, *Institutiones iuris canonici: De sacramentis,* 3 v. (Turin-Rome 1949–57) v.1. U. BESTE, *Introductio in codicem* (Naples 1961). E. F. REGATILLO, *Institutiones iuris canonici,* 2 v. (Santander 1961) v. 1. F. X. WERNZ and P.VIDAL, *Ius canonicum,* 7 v. in 8 (Rome) v. 1 (1952). M. ZALBA, *Theologiae moralis summa,* 3 v. [*Biblioteca de autores cristianos* (Madrid 1945) 93, 106, 117; 2d ed. 1957] v. 1.

[P. BALKAN]

PRECEPTS, CANONICAL

A canonical precept is an injunction given to a person or group of persons imposing an obligation to do something or to refrain from doing something [*Codex iuris canonici* cc. 35, 49; *Codex canonum ecclesiarium orientalium,* c. 1510]. A precept has binding force upon those to whom it is given, which distinguishes it from a counsel.

Precepts differ from law in many ways. Precepts are commands or orders given to individual persons, whereas law primarily affects territory and affects persons indirectly. Law is established to preserve and promote the common good; precepts are issued for the individual good. Laws bind within territorial limits; precepts bind the individual everywhere. Law by nature is relatively perpetual; precepts are relatively temporary in nature.

Penal precepts are primarily preventive measures to avert serious transgressions of the law [*Codex iuris*

Woodcut "Christ on the Cross with Three Angels," by Albrecht Dürer, ca. 1523-25, depicting angels catching Christ's precious blood in chalices, Eucharistic and Liturgical aspects, Northern Renaissance style.

canonici c. 1321 §1; *Codex canonum ecclesiarium orientalium,* c. 1414 §1]. There is a supposition of previous violation of the law that will be the occasion of further transgressions, or that may easily result in grave scandal. One who would issue a penal precept must employ a certain reserve. This is in keeping with the law's preference that penalties be employed as a last resort.

The canonical usage concerning penal precepts is that the offender is first admonished privately. If this fails to produce the desired effect, a public admonition follows, along with private or public correction. When these are likewise without deterrent effect, the precept is issued. This precept indicates what the party in question is to do or to avoid, along with a statement of the penalties that may be incurred if the precept is not obeyed.

Bibliography: G. MICHIELS, *De delictis et poenis,* 3 v. (Paris 1961). T. J. GREEN in J. A. CORIDEN et al., *The Code of Canon Law: A Text and Commentary* (New York 1985) 901. M. R. MOODIE, SJ in J. P. BEAL et al., *New Commentary on the Code of Canon Law* (New York 2000) 101, 109–110. T. J. GREEN in J. P. BEAL et al., *New Commentary on the Code of Canon Law* (New York 2000) 1540–1541.

[D. M. BURKE/EDS]

PRECIOUS BLOOD, I (IN THE BIBLE)

The term Precious Blood is traditionally used of the blood of Christ in keeping with the words of 1 Pt 1.18–19: "You were redeemed . . . with the precious blood of Christ," i.e., the blood that was the price of our Redemption.

The New Testament writers are anxious that Christians should see the excellence of Jesus' sacrifice. It surpasses the bloody sacrifices of the Old Law because blood is no longer merely a sign or symbol of the flow of life between God and man. The blood of Jesus is divine blood and bears the life of God in itself. It is the cause of the divine life that it brings to those in whose favor it works.

While the New Testament writers stress the preeminence of the sacrifice of Jesus, at the same time they develop a theology of the Precious Blood according to the sacrificial theology of the Old Testament. The Apostles' teaching enters three areas: the salvific death and RESURRECTION OF CHRIST, the Eucharistic liturgy, and the heavenly liturgy.

John recalls how blood and water flowed from the heart of the Savior (Jn 19.34; 1 Jn 5.6–8), assuring us that the Spirit of God, whom the water symbolizes, flows to us through the sacrifice of Jesus' blood. Peter, in a passage of great power, proclaims our Redemption through the Precious Blood (1 Pt 1.18–19). Paul assigns our Redemption (Eph 1.7) and justification (Rom 5.9) to the saving blood. Through it we are brought near to God (Eph 2.13). It has given us peace (Col 1.20) and "has been put forward" (i.e., displayed publicly) as a propitiation for our sins (Rom 3.25). The "great price" with which we have been bought (1 Cor 6.20; 7.22) is the blood of Christ (Acts 20.28). All the rich theology here is easily understood by referring to the theology of blood in the Old Testament.

The bloody sacrifice of Jesus is reenacted sacramentally in the Eucharist. When Jesus instituted the Eucharist and declared, "This is my blood of the new covenant" (Mk 14.24), He was resuming the words of Moses (Ex 24.8) by which the Sinai covenant had been inaugurated. Jesus' blood is the blood of the covenant because it effectively sets up a bond of friendship with those upon whom it is sprinkled. The Church repeats the Eucharistic action according to Christ's command, and the bread and wine become the body and blood of Jesus. The sacrificial blood of each Mass renews the covenant of Calvary. It effects a real union with God because the body and blood of Jesus are given to the redeemed as their food and drink. This banquet is the pledge of eternal glory for body and soul (Jn 6.54–58). In the resurrection of the body the total life-bearing efficacy of the Precious Blood is realized. Paul reminds us that the blood of the Eucharist joins us to one another as well as to Christ. The "sharing of the blood of Christ" (1 Cor 10.16; 1 Jn 1.7) makes Christians one.

In heaven the blood of Jesus remains the eternal bond joining the redeemed to the throne of the Father. Through it the saints have been victorious (Rv 7.14; see also 1.6), and they continuously proclaim the glory of the blood of the Lamb (Rv 5.9–13). The picture that Hebrews presents of Jesus entering the heavenly sanctuary with His own blood (Heb 9.11–14; 10.19–22) shows how acceptable the sacrifice of Jesus was. By His eternal priesthood He offers the sacrifice of His blood in glory (Heb 7.24–25). The tableau of the festive assembly of those in heaven and on earth gathered around the ''sprinkling of blood'' brings together the earthly and the heavenly liturgy in a tribute to the blood of Jesus (Heb 12.22–24).

Bibliography: *Encyclopedic Dictionary of the Bible*, tr. and adap. by L. HARTMAN (New York 1963) 258. A. VÖGTLE, *Lexikon für Theologie und Kirche*, ed. J. HOFER and K. RAHNER (Freiberg 1957–65) 2:539–541. W. NAUCK, *Die Religion in Geschichte und Gegenwart* (Tübingen 1957–65) 1:1329–30. J. BEHM, G. KITTEL, *Theologisches Wörterbuch zum Neuen Testament* (Stuttgart 1935–) 1:171–176. G. KITTEL, ''Aὂμα,'' *Theological Dictionary of the N.T.* (Grand Rapids 1964–). L. MORRIS, ''The Biblical Use of the Term *Blood*,'' *Journal of Theological Studies,* new series 3 (1952) 216–227. D. E. H. WHITELEY, ''St. Paul's Thought on the Atonement,'' *ibid.* 8 (1957) 240–255. R. T. SIEBENECK, ''The Precious Blood and St. John,'' *Proceedings of the 1st Precious Blood Study Week* (Carthagena, Ohio 1959) 65–92; ''The Precious Blood and St. Peter,'' *Proceedings of the 2d Precious Blood Study Week* (Carthagena 1962) 36–56. E. F. SIEGMAN, ''The Blood of Christ in St. Paul's Soteriology,'' *ibid.* 11–35; ''The Blood of the Covenant,'' *American Ecclesiastical Review* 136 (1957) 167–174. C. SPICQ, *L'Èpître aux Hébreux*, 2 v. (*Étude biblique* 1952–53).

[R. T. SIEBENECK]

PRECIOUS BLOOD, II (THEOLOGY OF)

The theology of the Precious Blood deals with the mystery of Redemption through the Blood of Christ in all its phases: the real shedding on Calvary as summation of the whole earthly redemptive work of Jesus, the mystic shedding in the central action of the sacramental Church and focal point of the life of GRACE, and the final consummation in the celestial liturgy and the eternal priesthood. It is the special function of this theology to explain the mystery in relation to the devotion to the Precious Blood. In both the basic concern is the whole work of Redemption: *totum opus redemptionis.*

This work is divine redemptive action on the part of the triune God offering mercy to man, wrought through Christ, the priest-mediator between fallen mankind and God. It is accomplished through the INCARNATION of the LOGOS, the Second Person in the Holy TRINITY, all His acts (called objective Redemption) bringing grace (and glory) to man (called subjective Redemption).

Who and Why. The mystery of Redemption by Blood properly involves the mystery of the *why* (motive) and the *who* (Person) of the Incarnation. Was the Incarnation eternally decreed because of the Redemption through the Blood? All agree that in this present sinful order it was. But some theologians (Thomist) maintain that had there been no sin, there would have been no Incarnation at all; others (Scotist), that there would have been an Incarnation without pain or Blood. Still other writers reject this ancient dispute as purely hypothetic and in no way dealing with the present world. The dispute, they say, assumes an order of priority in the divine decree. They hold that God, by one simple decree (with no interior order of priority), determined to create this universe in which sin would be permitted (not caused) by God and the sinful creature redeemed. A world redeemed, they contend, gives greater glory to God than a sinless world not in need of Redemption. In this view the Blood of Redemption is central in the universe, the source of grace to ADAM in his innocence and to the angels (F. Malmberg).

As to the who in the Incarnation, faith teaches that only the Second Person became man, though St. Thomas holds that either God the Father or Holy Spirit could have become incarnate, giving striking arguments *ex decentia* for the Incarnation of the Logos. But, it is being asked, is there not a more profound cogency to his argument? Perhaps the very order of origins in the Trinity makes it impossible that the Father eternally unborn be born in time; perhaps only the Son born from eternity in the Godhead could be born in time. This bold linking of the *oikonomia* (God's work outside the Trinity) with the *theologia* (the Trinity itself) would relate the work of Redemption to the very heart of the inner life of God.

Whether one accepts or rejects these insights (they are not presented as certain at all), there is a special significance (which no one denies) in the Second Person's being the image of the Father and His becoming man, having the created IMAGE OF GOD, patterned on the Logos in whom all things were made.

> Indeed this very relation of the two images . . . is the more basic reason why in the Incarnation the one image could be and should be hypostatically united with the other. For the Incarnation is . . . the penetration of the inner image of God into the external image, manifesting and communicating in and through it the entire inner glory externally. . . . And conversely, this external image of God is drawn to the internal. Thus the external image of God, which is man, is perfected and crowned through the inner image of God. [M. Scheeben, *Dogmatik* 3.147 (No. 356)]

The image is the Word, the Logos, eternally uttered in the bosom of the Godhead and uttered in time in the

''The Blood of the Redeemer,'' tempera painting on wood panel by Giovanni Bellini. (©National Gallery Collection; By kind permission of the Trustees of the National Gallery, London/CORBIS)

Incarnation. Through Mary mankind responded and accepted its mediator. Now He who spoke to man as the Word of the Father turns to God with Mary and a united mankind, offering homage of obedience and love to an offended majesty in the one sign and symbol that is the supreme act of submission, the loving acceptance of death in the shedding of Blood. It was MERIT, satisfaction, Redemption, efficacy, and sacrifice: it was death because the giving of one's life for friends is the most exalted act of love. It was death because Christ chose to share human existence and experience, a kind of life that is marked by death. In human existence all one's life acts receive their final impress and definitive integration in death (A. Grillmeier).

Calvary and the Church. Calvary was death, but it was bloody death, the death unto life. The climax of Good Friday, the culmination of Christ's merit, satisfaction, sacrifice was the glorious RESURRECTION OF CHRIST. Through the Resurrection-Ascension Christ has become the life-giving Spirit bestowing the Christ-life, the God-life of grace on man. Now man redeemed, purchased by Blood, is God's possession, no longer slave given to death: death has erased death and given immortality.

This divine life is given to men under the veil of SIGN, as all Christ's actions in the flesh are sacramental, grace-producing. He is the Sacrament of God, visible sign of SALVATION. And the Church that flowed from His riven side in the symbol of blood and water is His sacrament, for it is the sign of all His grace. In union with it men are one with Him, men's prayers mingling with those of the Church and His. In the Eucharistic prayer there is communion and communication with God through Him. All partake, the priest through official sacral order and indelible sign of priesthood, the laity through the sacerdotal signs of Baptism and Confirmation that link every member of the Church with Christ, the Priest. Though all the Sacraments are in the order of worship, these three are Sacraments of perpetual priesthood, deriving their meaning from the High Priest who forms the Church in its supreme duty of offering worship to the Father through Him and thereby sanctifying men. The bond is sealed in the Blood of covenant-love, between the Church, between High Priest and ministers, between ordained priest and members of the Society of Worship: the bond is the bond of Calvary's Blood.

Heaven. Awaiting the Second Coming of its Lord, the Church celebrates the memorials of His Passion and death under the sacramental veils. When He removes the veil, the Church will celebrate with Him the celestial liturgy. It seems preferable to follow the theologians (e.g., J. Alfaro) who place the resurrected Christ, resplendent in His Wounds, in the very center of the blessed congregation who adore the Lamb that was slain. This glorified humanity (as subjective disposing cause, not as a medium) prepares the blessed for the vision of God. Thus the redemptive action continues forever in eternal fruition, the work of the everlasting priesthood. The term itself, consecrated in theology, would have little meaning were the priesthood to end on the day of final judgment, and the wounds in glory to be merely a memory.

In explaining the devotion to the Precious Blood, theology goes far beyond the adoration of the blessed Humanity infinitely adorable in all its parts. It must embrace the *totum opus redemptionis.* The shedding of Blood is sign and symbol of that total work. Progress in this study parallels the progress in CHRISTOLOGY, MARIOLOGY, ECCLESIOLOGY, and the LITURGICAL MOVEMENT inaugurated by St. Pius X, attaining its climax in the liturgical constitution of Vatican II. As never before, because of the progress of theology, one today understands better Christ in His history (Scripture-tradition), in His MYSTICAL BODY, in His glory—and all this in the light of the Redemption through His Blood. The decisions of the Church through John XXIII, Pope of the Precious Blood (*Inde a primis*, a new Litany of the Most Precious Blood, the addition of ''Blessed be His Most Precious Blood'' to the Divine Praises) were official recognition of the importance of the devotion and its proper theology.

Bibliography: JOHN XXIII, ''Inde a primis'' (Apostolic Letter, June 30, 1960) *Acta Apostolicae Sedis* (Rome 1909–) 52 (1960) 545–550. R. HAUBST, *Lexikon für Theologie und Kirche,* ed. J. HOFER and K. RAHNER, 10 v. (2d, new ed. Freiburg 1957–65) 2:544–545. A. GRILLMEIER, *ibid.* 1156–66; 3:1024–30. *Precious Blood Study Week, Proceedings of the First and Second* (Carthagena, OH 1957, 1960). F. MALMBERG, *Über den Gottmenschen* (Basel 1960). K. RAHNER, *On the Theology of Death*, tr. C. H. HENKEY (Quaestiones disputatae 2; New York 1961). O. SEMMELROTH, *Die Kirche als Ursakrament* (Frankfurt 1952). J. ALFARO, ''Cristo Glorioso, Revelador del Padre,'' *Gregorianum* 39 (1958) 222–270. E. G. KAISER, ''Theology of the Precious Blood,'' *American Ecclesiastical Review* 145 (Washington 1961) 190–201.

[E. G. KAISER/EDS.]

PRECIOUS BLOOD, III (DEVOTION TO)

Devotion to the Blood of Christ is the Christian's response of love and gratitude to Jesus who offered His Blood for man in atoning sacrifice. Christ Himself spoke of it as the Blood of the new covenant shed for many unto the forgiveness of sins (Mt 26.28). With it He purchased the Church (Acts 20.28). It is precious (1 Pt 1.19). By it we are justified (Rom. 5.9), cleansed (Heb 9.14; 1 Jn 1.7), washed from sin (Rv 7.14, 22.14), and redeemed for God (Rv 5.9). Jesus called it ''my blood'' (Mk 14.24) and invited His followers to drink it that they might have everlasting life (Mt 26.28; Jn 6.54–57).

The Fathers re-echo these statements of Scripture in both the East (*see* Pollack) and the West (*see* Rohling) and not infrequently add some devotional sentiment in their commentaries and sermons, especially when speaking of the REDEMPTION or the Eucharist. Of the Fathers, St. John Chrysostom is the most eloquent. The liturgical devotion has its deepest roots in the celebration of Christ's triumph at Easter and in the offering of the Eucharistic Sacrifice together with the reception of the Holy Eucharist under the species of both bread and wine.

The devotion became more explicit as the minds of the faithful gradually emphasized the sufferings of Christ preceding the triumph of His Resurrection. Relics of the Precious Blood (not hypostatically united) were venerated at Mantua as early as 553, at Weingarten since 1090, and at Bruges since 1158. The many (supposed) relics that the crusaders returning from the Holy Land brought back to Europe tended to focus the attention of the faithful on the humanity of Christ, particularly on His sufferings and bloodsheddings.

While artists produced graphic representations of the effectiveness of the Precious Blood, medieval theologians and mystics, such as St. Albert the Great, St. Bonaventure, St. Mechtilde, St. Gertrude, and St. Catherine of Siena, found in the Blood the inspiration for the most profound mystical love. There is evidence of confraternities honoring it in Spain in the 17th century. Benedict XIV approved a Mass and Office in its honor in 1747.

The greatest epoch in the history of the special devotion began early in the 19th century, which witnessed the remarkable missionary activity of St. Gaspar del BUFALO in the Papal States and the founding of the Society of the PRECIOUS BLOOD (CPPS, 1815), the establishment of the Archconfraternity of the Precious Blood in Rome (1815), and the founding of several sisterhoods. The feast (previously celebrated only in the Society and in certain localities in Lent), at the suggestion of Don Merlini, third moderator of the Society of the Precious Blood, was extended (1849) by Pius IX to the whole Church, to be celebrated on the first Sunday of July. In 1917 the date of the feast was changed to July 1. The 1969 reforms of the liturgical calendar combined the Feast of the Precious Blood with the Feast of the Body of Christ (Corpus Christi), under the title "Solemnity of the Body and Blood of Christ" (CORPUS ET SANGUINIS CHRISTI).

The devotion also received official papal approval from John XXIII in 1960. He not only approved the Litany of the Precious Blood for private and public recitation throughout the world and ordered the ejaculation "Blessed be His Most Precious Blood" inserted in the Divine Praises, but even wrote an apostolic letter, *Inde a primis,* to the bishops of the world (June 30, 1960), urging them to foster the devotion to the Precious Blood.

Bibliography: JOHN XXIII, "Inde a primis," (Apostolic Letter, June 30, 1960) *Acta Apostolicae Sedis* 52 (1960) 545–550. *Precious Blood Study Week, Proceedings of the First and Second* (Carthagena, Ohio 1957 and 1960). F. W. FABER, *The Precious Blood* (new ed. Philadelphia 1959). J. H. ROHLING, *The Blood of Christ in Christian Latin Literature Before the Year 1000* (Washington 1932). A. J. POLLACK, *The Blood of Christ in Christian Greek Literature till the Year 444* (Carthagena, Ohio 1956). G. LEFEBVRE, *Redemption through the Blood of Jesus,* tr. E. A. MAZIARZ (Westminster, Md. 1960). C. GRIESSNER, *Das kostbare Blut Christi, Gedanken und Gebete* (Mindelheim 1957). R. MYERS, *Jesus Is Here: Devotions to the Sacred Heart and Precious Blood* (Huntington, Ind. 1986).

[J. H. ROHLING/EDS.]

PRECIOUS BLOOD, MISSIONARIES OF THE

A male Society of Apostolic Life, the Missionaries of the Precious Blood (C.PP.S.) were founded by St. Gaspar del BUFALO (b. Jan. 6, 1786, Rome, Italy) in 1815 in the Papal States. The purpose of the institute was the renewal of the clergy and laity through the preaching of popular missions and retreats. Gaspar had been inspired to a devotion to the Precious Blood by Canon Francesco Albertini, who had established an Archconfraternity of the Precious Blood in the church of St. Nicola in Carcere in Rome in 1808.

Early Years in Italy. As a result of his refusal to swear allegiance to Napoleon I when he gained control of the Papal States, Gaspar was imprisoned and exiled. It was at that time he originated the idea of establishing a society to perpetuate devotion to the Precious Blood. He found the society of missionary priests at Giano in Umbria on Aug. 15, 1815. According to his conception, the society was to include priests and brothers, and was to be dedicated to the task of giving parish missions and to fostering devotion to the Precious Blood. The members were not obligated by religious vows but by a bond of charity. They were to adhere to a common life and to be an example to the diocesan clergy. Their garb was the ordinary Roman cassock and cincture, with the distinguishing feature of a large crucifix and gold chain.

Pius VII had encouraged the establishment of the institute, and assigned the missionaries the task of converting the brigands in the southern parts of the Papal States. In this work the missionaries were quite successful. Despite various objections to the institute, Gaspar was able to establish it by the time of his death in 1837, when it numbered around 200 members. The rule for the missionaries was approved in 1841.

The turmoil involved in the unification of Italy hampered development of the institute in the 1860s and 1870s. That members were bound to the institute only by the bond of charity made it also unstable, as members could enter and leave as they wished. The limited nature of its work missions, novenas, and retreats also tended to restrict its usefulness to the larger Church. It often lacked the leadership needed for the times. Nevertheless, several of its members were selected as bishops of Italian dioceses, and notable among the moderators general were Biagio Valentini (1837–47), Ven. Giovanni MERLINI (1847–73), and Enrico Rizzoli (1873–90). Several communities of nuns were founded, and subsequently spread throughout Europe and America.

Development in North America. The acceptance of a Swiss priest, Francis BRUNNER, into the institute marked the beginning of a new era. As the first non-Italian member, he was sent to establish a foundation in Switzerland at Castle Loewenberg in Canton Graubünden. The turmoil in Central Europe at the time prevented establishing permanent foundations until one was begun at Trois Epis in Alsace. In 1843, Brunner set out with a small group of priests and seminarians for the diocese of Cincinnati, which at that time encompassed the entire state of Ohio, to answer an appeal of Bp. John Purcell for help in ministering to German immigrants. Brunner established himself in northern Ohio at Peru, near Norwalk. From there, some ten houses were established, principally in Seneca, Putnam, and Mercer Counties. Ties were relinquished with German-speaking Europe, except for a house in Schellenberg, Liechtenstein, which served as a place of entry for candidates for the American missions.

In the last four decades of the nineteenth century, the missionaries spread beyond the confines of Ohio, moving as far west as Missouri. An ill-fated plan to open a vicariate in northern California failed in the 1870s. In the 1880s a mission school for Native Americans was taken over from the diocese of Fort Wayne in Indiana; St. Joseph's College was founded there in Rensselaer, Indiana, in 1889.

The twentieth century saw the missionaries expanding as far west as California, and into Florida and Texas in the south. In 1946 a revised rule was approved by the Congregation for Religious for the entire institute. The burgeoning numbers in the American Province led to the division of the U.S. into three provinces, Cincinnati, Kansas City, and Pacific, in 1965. Meantime, the Italian Province had sent priests to minister among Italian immigrants in the U.S. and Canada. This foundation became the Atlantic Province in 1987, with headquarters in Canada. Among the notable members of the CPPS in America have been Bp. Joseph DWENGER, one of the major architects of the Catholic parochial school system, and pioneering biblical exegete Edward Siegman.

Worldwide Developments. Other foundations grew out of the institute in Italy as well. A foundation in Cáceres in Spain in 1898 led to the formation of the Iberian Province, embracing Spain and Portugal, in 1987. A province embracing the German-speaking countries began in 1922. Work in Latin America began in Brazil in 1929, followed by Chile in 1947, Peru in 1962, and Guatemala in 1982. A foundation began in Poland in 1982. Work in Africa began in Tanzania in 1966, and in Asia in India in 1988. Since then, the Missionaries of the Precious Blood are found in 18 countries around the world.

Charism, Mission, and Spirituality. Gaspar founded a missionary society dedicated to the renewal of the Church through preaching and retreats. This defined the work in Italy, and has always been part of the work in other parts of the institute. The revised 1969 Constitution defined the work of the institute as renewal of the Church through the ministry of the Word. As the institute has spread throughout the world, it has seen its work of renewal as meeting the needs of local churches in their moment of need: be that ministry to immigrant groups, setting up schools, building up the diocesan church where structures were not yet in place, to meeting the needs of special groups. Helping the Church in need, especially through the ministry of the Word, has become its hallmark. At its inception, devotion to the PRECIOUS BLOOD was the central spiritual focus of the institute. In the ensuing decades after Vatican II, its spirituality has expanded to encompass themes of covenant, cross, chalice, community-building, working with the suffering, the centrality of the Eucharist, and the ministry of personal and social reconciliation.

Bibliography: A. J. POLLACK, *Historical Sketches of the C.PP.S.* (Carthagena, Ohio 1984). R. J. SCHREITER, *In Water and in Blood* (New York 1988). V. SARDI, *Herald of the Precious Blood: Gaspar del Bufalo,* adapt. E. G. KAISER (Carthagena, Ohio 1954).

[R. J. SCHREITER]

PRECIOUS BLOOD SISTERS

Under this title are included several congregations of religious women who owe their origin, directly or indirectly, to the influence of St. Gaspare del BUFALO.

Adorers of the Blood of Christ. (ASC, Official Catholic Directory, #0100); founded, 1834 in Acuto, Diocese of Anagni, Italy, by Bl. Maria De MATTIAS, according to the plan of St. Gaspare del Bufalo and under the direction of Giovanni MERLINI. Dedicated principally to the education of the poor, the sisters opened 65 schools in central Italy before the death of the foundress in Rome (1866).

On Oct. 17, 1860, a group of Precious Blood Sisters, who had been established originally at Steinerberg, Switzerland, in 1845, and who later moved, because of government hostility, to Gurtweil, Baden, Germany, formally joined the Italian foundation. Ten years after this amalgamation the Gurtweil sisters opened a school in the U.S. at Piopolis in southern Illinois, when the KULTURKAMPF threatened them in Baden. While the majority of the sisters who went to America between 1870 and 1873 became an independent congregation (Sisters of the Most Precious Blood of O'Fallon, MO), the few sisters remaining at Piopolis under the direction of Mother Clementine Zerr, the novice mistress, continued under the Italian affiliation. When Mother Clementine was approved as superior of the U.S. foundation by the superior general, she transferred headquarters to Ruma, IL, in 1876. Subsequently, the sisters extended their work through Illinois, Missouri, and the Great Plains states, with a second central house and novitiate in Wichita, KS. The small band of German sisters who remained in Europe found a permanent home in 1879 in Banja Luka, Bosnia, whence new foundations were later made in Germany, Austria, Switzerland, and Poland. Sixteen sisters, brought from Banja Luka to the U.S. in 1906 by Mother Pauline Schneeberger, formed the nucleus of a third U.S. province with its central house in Columbia, PA.

In 1855 Pius IX granted initial approbation to the congregation; final papal approval of the constitutions was given in 1897. The spiritual ideal of the congregation is centered in the mystery of Redemption through the Blood of Christ, which the sisters worship in particular through daily eucharistic adoration. Their active apostolate consists primarily of work in schools and hospitals. The generalate is in Rome. There are three U.S. provinces: Ruma (1876), Wichita (1929) and Columbia (1925).

[A. MYERSCOUGH/EDS.]

Sisters of the Most Precious Blood. (CPPS, Official Catholic Directory #3270); a congregation with papal approbation whose motherhouse is in O'Fallon, MO. The community was founded originally in 1845 at Steinerberg, Switzerland, by Rev. Karl Rolfus and Magdalena Weber (Mother Teresa) to honor the Precious Blood in convents of perpetual adoration. In 1848 the Swiss government forced the young community into exile, and a new settlement was made at Ottmarsheim in the Alsace region of France. Some eight years later, at the invitation of Rev. Herman Kessler, 18 sisters went to Gurtweil, in Baden, Germany, to establish a school and open a home for delinquent girls. The combined responsibilities of perpetual adoration and the active apostolate of teaching posed serious problems. The conflict was resolved in 1860 when the sisters of Gurtweil separated from those of Ottmarsheim and became affiliated with the Sisters Adorers of the Most Precious Blood, a congregation dedicated to the active apostolate.

Difficulties with the government in Baden, which sought to establish nondenominational schools, led the sisters to answer a call for teachers from Rev. Blasius Winterhalter of St. John's, IL (later Belle Prairie, now Piopolis), in the Diocese of Alton (now Belleville). On Feb. 2, 1870, nine sisters set sail for America; others followed in the next few years. The majority of these sisters soon separated themselves from the European congregation and became known as the Sisters of the Most Precious Blood of O'Fallon, MO. This was accomplished in 1874 with the assistance of Abp. Peter Kenrick of St. Louis, MO, and his vicar-general, Henry Muehlsiepen. Mother Augusta Volk was the first superior general of the new community to which the Holy See granted final approval in 1938.

The congregation is engaged in academic education, catechetics, pastoral ministries, social outreach, care of elderly, parish ministries, and foreign missions.

[M. P. THAMAN/EDS.]

Sisters of the Precious Blood. (CPPS, Official Catholic Directory, #3260); a congregation with papal approbation whose motherhouse is in Dayton, OH. The community originated in 1834 at Castle Loewenberg in the Diocese of Chur, Switzerland. Mother Maria Anna Brunner, the foundress, was then an elderly widow and the mother of six children. In the previous year, during a pilgrimage to Rome for the Holy Year of 1833, she came in contact with the Society of the Precious Blood, whose founder was (St.) Gaspare del Bufalo. Inspired by his example, she determined to devote her remaining years to the adoration of the Precious Blood and to the spreading of this devotion. After returning to Castle Loewenberg, she soon attracted a sufficient number of associates to keep up nocturnal adoration before the Blessed Sacrament. By the time of her death in 1836 the nucleus of the future congregation was formed and its main features indicated. Her eldest son, Father Francis de Sales BRUNNER, guided the early years of the community and eventually transferred it to the U.S.

In 1844 three of the sisters went to Peru in northern Ohio. About six months later a permanent foundation was made at New Riegel, OH, where there now stands a convent adapted for the use of a cloistered group that was later formed within the congregation. The motherhouse in the U.S. was transferred from New Riegel to Maria Stein, OH, in 1846, and then to Dayton in 1923. The U.S. community was granted final approval by the Holy See in 1946.

In accord with the primary purpose of the foundress, daily eucharistic adoration is maintained in the community's principal houses. In fulfillment of Mother Brunner's secondary aim, the sisters from the beginning engaged in academic education and catechetics. Gradually their apostolate broadened to include care for the sick and the aged, healthcare, retreats and spiritual direction, social outreach to immigrants and homeless, and pastoral ministries.

Bibliography: *Not with Silver or Gold: A History of the Sisters of the Congregation of the Precious Blood, 1834–1944* (Dayton 1945).

[M. O. GUTMAN]

PRECIOUS STONES

From prehistoric times precious stones have been employed universally as personal ornaments and amulets and as elements of adornment in religious and profane art and architecture in general. Men of past ages prized many precious stones because they believed that they possessed magical properties and gave special protection and strength to their owners. An accurate classification of precious stones before the rise of modern chemistry at the end of the 18th century is impossible. Many of the stones mentioned as precious in ancient and medieval writers were not precious in the strict sense but merely resembled genuine diamonds, rubies, emeralds, etc.

Employment in Judaism and Early Christianity. There is frequent mention of precious stones in the Bible, the jeweled breastplate of the high priest, for example, being described in detail [*see* PRECIOUS STONES (IN THE BIBLE)]. In the Greco-Roman civilization, in which Christianity appeared and developed, the demand for precious stones was intense, and the amount of jewelry displayed or worn by possessors approached the fantastic. Pagan moralists attacked such ostentation in adornment as morally wrong, but their censures were not effective. The early Christian writers and Fathers of the Church did not condemn the use of precious stones as such, but warned repeatedly against the evil of luxury so often associated with them and, above all, against belief in their magical properties. Thus, Clement of Alexandria denounced luxury in dress and adornments, mentioning the excessive fondness for gold ornaments and precious stones. He ad-

A gold chalice studded with 500 diamonds and red and blue enamels. It was used by Pope Pius IX during the Mass for the Proclamation of Dogma of the Immaculate Conception on December 8th, 1854. Made in Rome by Peter Paul Spagna, it is part of the Treasury of the Sacresty of the Sistine Chapel. (©David Lees/CORBIS)

mitted, however, that women married to wayward husbands might need adornment to make themselves more attractive to such men, and he recognized the necessity of signet rings or seals for protecting property. But pagan devices on seals, especially those of a licentious and magical character, were strictly forbidden. The Christian should use a dove, a fish, a ship, an anchor, or a fisherman (see Clement, *Paedagogus* 2.12:118–129 and, esp. 3.11:57–60). All these symbols have important Christian meanings, and the references to them in literary texts are confirmed by the large number of seals and engraved precious stones brought to light by archeology (see ''Gemmes,'' *Dictionnaire d'archéologie chrétienne et de liturgie*, ed. F. Carroll, H. Leclerq, and H. I. Marrou, 15 v. (Paris 1907–53), esp. 816-). Luxury in jewelry was a persistent evil, however, and all the Christian writers of

East and West found it necessary to attack it again and again in the strongest terms.

Alleged Magical Properties of Gems. Diamonds were said to give protection against poison and evil powers; agate and sapphire, against despair and envy; emeralds and amethysts, against spells, hail, and locusts; serpentine, against snake bites. The sardonyx was a good luck stone. The beryl gave knowledge of the future and promoted marital harmony. The ruby furnished strength and was a charm against poison and evil spirits. Blood jasper stopped bleeding, and limonite aided pregnancy. Numerous other stones were regarded as efficacious in similar ways (see Pliny, *Hist. Nat.* bk. 37, and Apuleius, *Apol.* 31). For many centuries, precious stones in powdered form have been used as medicines. Symbols or formulas inscribed on gems gave them an important role in astrology and other kinds of magic. The employment of month-stones or birthstones, however, is largely modern. As is evident from medieval lapidaries, above all from the classic *De lapidibus* of Marbod of Rennes (1035–1123), with its description of 60 stones, belief in the marvelous powers of precious stones was widespread in the Middle Ages. It is still far from dead in the East—or even in the West.

Bibliography: W. M. F. PETRIE, J. HASTINGS, ed., *Encyclopedia of Religion and Ethics* 13 v. (Edinburgh 1908–27) 10:224–225. J. H. EMMINGHAUS, *Lexikon für Theologie und Kirche*, ed. J. HOFER and K. RAHNER, 10 v. (2d new ed. Freiburg 1957–65) 4:659. H. LECLERCQ, *Dictionnaire d'archéologie chrétienne et de liturgie* (Paris 1907–53) 6.1: 794–864, with copious illustrations and bibliog. A. HERMANN, ''Edelsteine,'' *Reallexikon für Antike Christentum* ed. T. KLAUSER [Stuttgart 1941 (1950-)] 4:505–550, with bibliog. O. ROSSBACH, *Paulys Realenzyklopädie der klassischen Altertumswissenschaft*, ed. G. WISSOWA et al. (Stuttgart 1910) 7.1:1052–1115. P. SCHMIDT, *Edelsteine* (Bonn 1948). A. FURTWÄNGLER, *Die antiken Gemmen,* 3 v. (Leipzig 1900; repr. 1963), of fundamental importance. J. EVANS, *The Magical Jewels of the Middle Ages* (Oxford 1923). L. THORNDIKE, *A History of Magic and Experimental Science*, 8 v. (New York 1923–58) 1:775–782. S. THOMPSON, *Motif-Index of Folk- Literature*, 6 v. (rev. and enl. ed. Bloomington, Ind. 1955–58), see index under ''Jewels'' and the names of the respective precious stones.

[M. R. P. MCGUIRE]

PRECIOUS STONES (IN THE BIBLE)

Humankind has always and everywhere been fond of using precious stones as personal ornaments. Whether a small stone was considered precious or not depended partly on its relative rarity and partly on custom or taste in any given culture. In the ancient Near East precious or semiprecious stones were commonly worn as necklaces. Gems were also cut and engraved in the form of seals (Sir 38.27) and scarabs. Since such valuable possessions were often buried with their owners, precious stones are frequently found in ancient tombs.

In Palestinian archeology it is generally only in the tombs of wealthy people that jewelry, consisting of precious metal and gems, is found. Hardly any precious stones are native to Palestine, so those that are found in Palestinian archeological sites must have been imported, mostly from south Arabia (Gn 2.12; 1 Kgs 10.2, 10–11; Ez 27.22), with the Edomites often acting as middlemen in the traffic (Ez 27.16). Actually, precious stones are mentioned rather rarely in the Bible. The longest list of gems is that given in connection with the description of the ''breastpiece of decision'' worn by the Israelite high priest (Ex 28.17–19; 39.10–12). This breastpiece consisted of a square of richly woven cloth on which were mounted 12 precious stones, in four rows of three stones each. On each stone the name of one of the 12 tribes of Israel was engraved. The meaning of most of the Hebrew words for these gems is obscure.

Nine of these gems are mentioned in the gloss that is added to the phrase addressed to the ''Paradise man'' in Ez 28.13: ''Every precious stone was your covering.'' This gloss is apparently connected with Ex 28.17–19, since these nine gems are the same, although in somewhat different order, as the stones in the first, second, and fourth rows of the high priest's breastpiece.

The Hebrew names of other gems mentioned in the Old Testament, together with terms used for them in the Confraternity Old Testament are: *p^e^nînîm,* coral (Prv 3.15; 8.11; Lam 4.7; etc.); *rā'môt,* coral (Jb 28.18); *kadkōd,* ruby (Is 54.12; Ez 27.16); *'eqdāḥ* carbuncle (Is 54.12); *šāmîr,* diamond (Jer 17.1; Ez 3.9: Zec 7.12). In the New Testament pearls (μαργαρῖται) are mentioned in Mt. 7.6; 13.45–46; 1 Tm 2.9; Rv 17.4; 18.16; 21.21.

In Rv 21.19–20 there is a list of 12 precious stones ''adorning the foundations of the walls of the city'' of the heavenly Jerusalem. The exact meaning of most of the Greeks names of these gems is uncertain.

Bibliography: *Encyclopedic Dictionary of the Bible*, tr. and adap. by L. HARTMAN (New York 1963) 1906–07. K. GALLING, *Biblisches Reallexicon* (Tübingen 1937) 139–140. F. NÖTSCHER, *Biblische Altertumskunde* (Bonn 1940) 233.

[L. F. HARTMAN]

PREDEFINITION

An absolute divine decree that a man shall perform a good act, infallibly effective before man's consent is given. Because such decrees are implied in scriptural teaching that every good act is the work of God, the gift of God, that His providence infallibly rules human action, Catholic theologians unanimously affirm these decrees for all good acts, but differ in explaining them. Some hold formal predefinition: God first absolutely decrees that a man shall perform good acts and consequently decrees efficacious graces to obtain them. So say they who reject God's middle knowledge (SCIENTIA MEDIA), affirming that the efficacy of grace comes from its intrinsic nature; and also say some who affirm middle knowledge, deriving the efficacy of grace partly from it—some of these affirm God would seek endlessly by middle knowledge to obtain effective grace, so determined is He to have these good acts.

Strict Molinists hold virtual predefinition: God simply intends to give man this grace to which, by middle knowledge, He sees man would consent, thereby intending the resulting good act; but He would give the same grace if He foresaw man's dissent, because He had no prior absolute intent to have a good act, but only if obtainable with this grace. This difference of Catholic opinion is due to differences about the condition under which God intends to save all men, and the source of grace's efficacy.

See Also: BÁÑEZ AND BAÑEZIANISM; FREE WILL AND GRACE; GRACE, EFFICACIOUS; GRACE, SUFFICIENT; MOLINISM; PERSEVERANCE, FINAL; PREDETERMINATION; WILL OF GOD.

Bibliography: C. WILLIAMS, *Lexikon für Theologie und Kirche*, ed. J. HOFER and K. RAHNER (Freiburg 1957–65) 8:659–660. J. M. DALMAU, *Sacrae theologiae summa*, ed. Fathers of the Society of Jesus, Professors of the Theological Faculties in Spain (Madrid 1962) v. 2. B. BERAZA, *De gratia Christi* (Bilbao 1929).

[F. L. SHEERIN]

PREDESTINATION (IN CATHOLIC THEOLOGY)

Predestination is the plan eternally conceived by God whereby He conducts rational creatures to their supernatural end, that is, to eternal life. Of necessity this plan is very complex. It must be concerned, first of all, with the SUPERNATURAL ORDER: its end, which is eternal life; its means, the complexus that we term supernatural GRACE (sanctifying and actual, efficacious and sufficient grace, the infused VIRTUES, and the gifts of the HOLY SPIRIT). Predestination also closely involves the divine foreknowledge of future free acts, the exercise of the FREE WILL of man, and divine predilection.

This article will consist basically of three parts: (1) an exposition of the nature of predestination and the concepts with which it is necessarily concerned; (2) a presentation of Catholic teaching concerning this great mystery (here emphasis will be on the historical development); and (3) a survey of the chief theological systems formulated by the great theologians of the Church in their attempts to delineate and clarify this revealed truth.

Predestination and related concepts. In its most general sense, predestination is a decree of God, an inner decision of the divine wisdom and will, whereby God resolves and determines what He Himself will bring to pass. According to St. Paul, it is the counsel of the divine will whereby God works all things (Eph 1.11), or, according to St. AUGUSTINE, it is that whereby He disposes within Himself what He intends to accomplish (*Persev.* 17.41; *Patrologia Latina* 45:1018). In this general sense, divine predestination has a bearing on all the works of God. Everything that He does and effects is predestined by Him through an eternal decree before it is carried out in time.

More precisely, however, predestination signifies the ordination of God by which certain men are led efficaciously to the attainment of SALVATION. On the part of God, this divine ordination involves two actions. There is, first, an act of the divine intellect, by which God infallibly foreknows which men are to be saved and the precise means whereby they will attain this salvation. Second, it includes an act of the WILL OF GOD by means of which He decrees to save these men in the very fashion that He Himself has planned.

For this reason, St. Augustine has defined predestination as ''the foreknowledge and preparation of those gifts of God whereby they who are liberated are most certainly liberated'' (*Persev.* 14.35; *Patrologia Latina* 45:1014). According to Augustine, the object of predestination is salvation, the freeing from servitude of SIN, and all the benefits through which salvation is attained, i.e., efficacious graces, including the gift of final PERSEVERANCE. The infallible connection between these benefits, that is, the means and the freeing from servitude, has its ultimate foundation in God Himself. The subject of predestination is all men who are in fact saved. Predestination, therefore, formally exists in God. It is an act of God in His divine ETERNITY. In the definition above, the ''fore'' in foreknowledge and the ''pre'' in preparation express the independence of the activity of God in this process rather than the ETERNITY OF GOD.

Although the definition of Augustine is classic, that of St. THOMAS AQUINAS is, perhaps, more exact. According to the Angelic Doctor, ''predestination is a plan existing in the divine mind for the ordering of some persons to eternal salvation'' (*Summa theologiae* 1a, 23.2). The object of predestination for St. Thomas, then, is the supernatural end to be attained by a rational creature and the infallible ordination of means to that end.

It is evident that the subject of predestination can only be an intellectual creature. It is also clear that predestination exists formally in God alone, that is, in the divine mind.

Viewed, therefore, in its totality predestination includes on the part of God the following: (1) the prevision of the end; (2) a determined grade or degree of glory; and (3) the ordination of the means. These three factors are concerned with acts of the divine intellect. In addition, there are the following, which are concerned with the divine will: (1) the first calling of the elect to JUSTIFICATION; (2) the decree to confer efficacious graces; and (3) the decree to confer the gift of final perseverance.

Although the act of the divine will is most simple, it nevertheless does not attain its created objectives in the same way. Hence, predestination has been considered by the theologians in concepts of varying comprehensiveness:

(1) Predestination viewed in its totality. This is predestination insofar as it is concerned with the complete series of graces by which man is saved. Predestination in this sense considers the entire process from beginning to end, from the first calling of a soul to the way of salvation to the conferral of final glory.

(2) Predestination partially viewed. This is predestination considered in only one aspect of the entire series of effects. It is derived from the division of the entire process of predestination into its logical, component parts. Thus, one may consider predestination to FAITH alone, predestination to justification alone, or even predestination to glory alone.

According to the teaching of the Church and of Sacred Scripture itself, predestination viewed in its totality is, in the fullest sense of the word, gratuitous; it is not merited, on the part of man; it is independent of all that is purely human or outside of God. The proper gratuitousness of predestination consists in this, that there is absolutely no reason or foundation on the part of any man why it should pertain to him to have the total series of effects that constitute predestination viewed in its totality, that is, from its initial step of first calling to the ultimate conferral of glory.

Despite the fact that the will of God cannot be moved by any created will, the question has, nevertheless, arisen whether the existence of this entire series of created effects, that constitutes total predestination, may not have some basis or foundation in the individual man who is saved?

The only answer that can be given to this question is that the ultimate and definitive reason for the salvation of any man is not to be found in man himself but rather in the mercy of God. However, this basic fact, fundamental though it may be, need not exclude, as the proximate reason for salvation, the meritorious acts of man himself.

Also, basic to any discussion of the theology of predestination is the distinction between the gratuitousness of the supernatural order, the destining of all mankind to a supernatural end, and the gratuitousness of predestination. One is not the other. The universal fact of the gratuitousness of man's supernatural destiny consists in the truth that God, by His mere liberality, gives to every member of the human race the possibility of salvation. It is, therefore, a gratuitousness in the order of merely sufficient graces. The gratuitousness of predestination adds this to the above, namely, that the ultimate reason for the actuation of this possibility of salvation is to be found in God Himself. It is a gratuitousness in the order of efficacious graces. This is what is called the principle of divine predilection. It is a special predilection of God toward those who are eventually saved. God is so disposed to these men not because of any good in them that attracts His love; He acts in this way simply because He so wills. In itself divine predilection is at the very core of the mystery of predestination.

Catholic teaching. The presentation of the nature of predestination according to Catholic teaching will become more clear and meaningful as it is viewed in its historical setting.

The mystery of predestination stands in the middle of two extremes, each of which either completely abandons one or the other of its two organically connected elements, or, at any rate, puts such excessive emphasis on one that the other is neglected. Either the independence and self-activity of man is overly stressed to the exclusion of God's initiation and guidance of man's preliminary steps and continued progress (Pelagianism and Semi-Pelagianism), or the divine initiative and guidance is represented as inexorably driving and hurrying man along in such a way that his own free movement and advance are obscured or completely denied (predestinationism).

Prior to the time of St. Augustine the Fathers of the Church were not preoccupied with the problem of predestination. It was the bishop of Hippo who first treated the mystery exhaustively, with the theological decisiveness so characteristic of him.

From 418 until 531, there took place in the Western Church many grave controversies concerned with explaining the ultimate foundation for the salvation of those who are saved (the elect) as well as ascertaining the reason for the condemnation of those who are in fact not saved (the reprobate). This theological ferment centered around the Pelagian and Semi-Pelagian controversies.

Pelagianism. This heresy (*see* PELAGIUS AND PELAGIANISM) denied the necessity of supernatural grace and consequently did not admit of predestination in the true sense of the word. It maintained that man, by the mere use of his free will and by his other natural powers, is able to believe and act in a salutary manner without the assistance of supernatural grace and thus obtain eternal beatitude. According to this doctrine, some species of predestination could be admitted. It would be nothing more, however, than the foreknowledge of God through which He foresees which men will attain salvation through their own efforts. Consequently God, through His divine prevision, chooses as the blessed those whom He has foreseen would be saved solely through their own powers.

Semi-Pelagianism. On the other hand, Semi-Pelagianism attempted to mitigate the extreme position of Pelagianism. It affirmed that without the assistance of divine grace fallen man is unable, by his natural powers, either to be justified or to posit acts that would be meritorious of eternal life. But above all else, the universal salvific will of God must be maintained. It was felt that this salvific will would really be denied, unless it was unequivocally affirmed that the ultimate foundation for the salvation of the saved and the condemnation of the reprobate is to be found in the good use or abuse of human freedom. If God truly and sincerely desires all men to be saved, He must, on His part, will the salvation of all with a complete equality and indifference. He must show no favoritism or special preference regarding the salvation of one man over that of another. If this were not the case, then the salvation of one man and the DAMNATION of another would be directly due to God's action alone. This would destroy any semblance of a universal salvific will and would be unjust.

Semi-Pelagianism claimed, therefore, that Augustine's basic principle, of the gratuitous predilection and preelection of God being the ultimate reason for the salvation of the elect, is irreconcilable with the dogma of the universal salvific will. The ultimate foundation for salvation must be found in man, not in God. Man, though he is fallen, is able through his own natural powers to desire and ask for salvation. He is able to believe and thus posit the first step in the process of salvation, which is faith. God then comes and confers the rest, i.e., justification, meritorious acts, and glory. Despite the disparity between man's meager natural efforts and the conferral of the supernatural gifts by God, it is, nevertheless, this unaided free use of his will directed toward God that is the ultimate reason why one man rather than another attains justification and salvation. In addition, Semi-Pelagianism rejected the doctrine that final perseverance is a gratuitous gift of God, the conferral of which depends solely on the divine largesse. This position would be untenable in view of God's necessary impartiality toward all men. God is not a respecter of persons.

Doctrine of St. Augustine. Against all of this St. Augustine and his followers denied emphatically that any man is predestined for salvation because God foresaw that he would attain this state through his own efforts. The contrary is true. Men lead holy lives and perform meritorious acts because they have been preelected by God. They were so chosen precisely that they might be justified by the grace of God, posit meritorious acts, persevere, and consequently be saved. That is, God did not choose these men from eternal salvation because they were already holy, but rather, for reasons known only to Himself, He chose them while yet unworthy in order that He Himself might make them holy and thus worthy of eternal glory (*Praed. sanct.* 17.34; *Patrologia Latina* 44:985).

According to Augustine, the decrees of the divine will are infallible regarding predestination not because God foreknows that man will give his consent; they are infallible because He is omnipotent and accomplishes what He wills (*Corrept.* 14.43; *Patrologia Latina* 44:942).

After the death of St. Augustine (430), a variety of pamphlets and treatises were written; some distorted the teaching of Augustine; others were frankly critical of it as being too extreme. Among the critics (Semi-Pelagians) were John CASSIAN, St. VINCENT OF LERINS, FAUSTUS OF RIEZ, and GENNADIUS OF MARSEILLES. Those who defended Augustine were PROSPER OF AQUITAINE, FULGENTIUS OF RUSPE, and St. CAESARIUS OF ARLES.

True to the teaching of the master, Prosper wrote: "We must most sincerely believe and profess that God wills all men to be saved. For this indeed, is the mind of the Apostle (1 Tm 2.4), who most urgently commands what is a most devout custom in all Churches, that suppliant prayers be offered to God for all men. That many of these perish is the fault of those who perish; that many are saved is the gift of Him who saves" (*Liber Responsionum* 2, *Patrologia Latina* 51:179; cf. Fulgentius, *Epist.* 17, *Patrologia Latina* 65:451–493; St. Caesarius, *Dictionnaire de théologie catholique* 2.2:2178).

The Semi-Pelagian controversy can be considered to have been terminated through the intervention of Pope BONIFACE II (530–532), when he approved as Catholic doctrine the teaching of the Second Council of ORANGE (529) concerning "the beginning of faith" (*initium fidei*): "by the sin of the first man, the free will of man was so inclined and attenuated that subsequently no one was able either to love God as he should, or to believe in God, or to accomplish what is good because of God, unless the grace of divine mercy first comes to him . . . in every good work, it is not we who first initiate it and only afterwards are assisted by the mercy of God, but it is He Himself, who, without any prior merit or good on our part, inspires us to faith and to love of Himself'' (H. Denzinger, *Enchiridion symbolorum* 396–397; *see* FAITH, BEGINNING OF).

Papal approval (Denzinger 398–399) equivalent to a dogmatic definition was given to the doctrine of Orange II; the Church afterward thus accepted the doctrine approved by Boniface II and already contained in the *Indiculus Caelestini* (Denzinger 238–249).

Although neither Orange II nor Boniface II expressly taught the gratuitousness of predestination itself, nevertheless, they did teach, as being of faith, the gratuitousness of an efficacious calling to faith; they taught that the ultimate source of man's faith, justification, and subsequent salvation is the gratuitous gift of God. It may be stated, therefore, that the gratuitousness of predestination viewed in its totality is contained at least virtually and perhaps formally implicitly in the above pronouncements of the magisterium.

Other Errors. Pelagianism and SEMI-PELAGIANISM, which deprived God of His rightful role in the total process of predestination, were followed by a variety of doctrines that went to the opposite extreme. These predestinationist teachings attacked the universality of God's salvific will. On the occasion of these errors, the doctrine of the Church was reaffirmed with still greater precision and clarity as the need required.

Substantially, predestinationism teaches that God does not sincerely will the salvation of all men. On the contrary, God wills absolutely the salvation of only some men; the rest He absolutely and unconditionally wills to condemn. In fact, the latter were created for the express purpose of being condemned to eternal punishment. Toward them God has never had a salvific intent. This pernicious doctrine was first taught by a priest of Gaul, Lucidus by name. It was condemned at the Council of Arles in 475 and again at Orange II (Denzinger 330–342, 397).

In the 9th century, the monk GOTTSCHALK OF ORBAIS renewed the same error. This was condemned in the Council of Quercy in 853 (Denzinger 621–624) and again by a synod of Valence in 855 (Denzinger 625–633). The latter was extremely important, because it explicitly posited a distinction between the foreknowledge of God and predestination itself.

The 16th century witnessed another form of the same heresy, as it was taught by CALVIN (1509–64). His position may be summarized as follows: (1) From all eternity, God chooses a certain portion of mankind to be saved; the others He positively and antecedently wills to condemn. (2) God not only wills the damnation of the latter, but also directly wills moral evil or sin itself in the same way that He wills moral goodness. (3) Predestination, therefore, is nothing more than the eternal decree of God by which He has decided upon the fate of each man. Some are preelected to eternal life, and others positively are preordained to eternal damnation.

In the 17th century, the followers of Calvin split into two groups. One group, the SUPRALAPSARIANS, maintained that God from all eternity, antecedently to the prevision of original sin, did not desire the salvation of all mankind, but rather predestined a portion of them to glory, while the rest He condemned absolutely to eternal punishment. A second group, the INFRALAPSARIANS, varied the above doctrine to the extent that this uneven decree of God came only after His prevision of the FALL OF MAN, not before.

Lastly, Cornelius Jansen of Louvain (d. 1638) agreed with the infralapsarians to the extent that he taught it is Semi-Pelagian to hold that Christ died for all mankind.

Teaching of the Church. Throughout the years, on the occasion of these pernicious doctrines, the Church condemned these aberrations from revealed truth. In addition, the Church reaffirmed with greater precision and clarity the revealed doctrine of the sincere universal salvific will of God.

The following are some of the declarations that are pertinent:

1. God predestines no one to evil (Denz 1567).

2. He wills, on the contrary, the salvation of all men (Denz 623).

3. Christ did not die solely for the predestined or the faithful (Denz 2005, 2304, 2430).

4. There is a grace that is truly sufficient and that is a true gift of God (Denz 2306).

5. The grace of conversion is offered to sinners (Denz 1542).

6. They only are deprived of it who, failing in their duty, refuse it; this is something which God permits but of which He is by no means the cause (Denz 1556, 1567, 2866).

To sum up, one must say that the Church affirms particularly three truths against Pelagianism and Semi-Pelagianism: (1) The cause of predestination to grace or justification is not the divine foreknowledge of naturally good works that are performed by men, neither is the cause preliminary to any act of the NATURAL ORDER that prepares man for salvation. This efficacious calling is due solely to God. It is initiated by Him because of His divine largesse. (2) Predestination to glory is not a result of foreseen supernatural MERITS that would continue to be effective apart from the special gift of final perseverance. (3) Predestination, viewed in its totality, that is, the entire series of graces from beginning to end, is gratuitous, and hence previous to the foreseen merits of man. In a word, that some are saved is the gift of Him who saves (Denz 623).

Against the various forms of predestinationism the Church teaches that: (1) God sincerely wills the salvation of all men and thus makes the fulfillment of His precepts possible for all. (2) There is neither predestination to evil as a final end nor predestination to any evil deed in particular. (3) Christ died for all men without exception. (4) Nevertheless, God has decreed from all eternity to inflict eternal punishment for the sin of final impenitence, which He has foreseen for all eternity. He is by no means the cause of the impenitence, but merely permits it.

In the words of St. Prosper, ''That many . . . perish is the fault of those who perish; that many are saved is the gift of Him who saves.''

Theological systems. The fundamental point at issue in this difficult problem is the necessity of reconciling predestination, viewed as a species of predilection for a select group, with God's will to save all mankind. Sacred Scripture emphatically declares that God wills all men to be saved (1 Tm 2.4), and yet God's sacred word asserts with equal force that in fact all are not predestined, but that those ''whom He has predestined, them He has also called; and . . . also justified; . . . and glorified (Rom 8.30). Hence the difficulty.

Is it human effort that makes God's help efficacious, or is it rather the intrinsic efficacy of God's help that prompts human effort? And if grace is of itself efficacious, how is it that God mercifully grants it to the elect and justly refuses it to the rest of men? Moreover, predestination is not concerned merely with two groups of souls, the saved and the unsaved, but it is especially concerned with individuals. The question is: why has God placed in the number of the elect this particular person and not that other? Why has He chosen James rather than John and not vice versa? This unequal distribution of such exceedingly important gifts to individuals who are equal both by nature and by reason of ORIGINAL SIN is seemingly unjust on the part of an all-loving God.

Such is the inherent difficulty of the problem or rather the obscurity of the mystery with which the theologians of the Church have grappled. They have attempted to formulate answers that would be within the framework of revealed doctrine and the magisterial pronouncements of the Church.

Different points of departure, a variety of diverse opinions concerning many basic theological problems (divine CONCURRENCE, divine foreknowledge of future free acts, human freedom and supernatural grace), led to serious theological controversy and to a plethora of theological systems.

Among the outstanding efforts on the part of the greatest minds in the Church are the following.

St. Thomas Aquinas. The Angelic Doctor defined predestination as ''a plan existing in the divine mind for the ordering of some persons to eternal salvation'' (*Summa theologiae* 1a, 23.2). It is, therefore, the plan conceived in the divine mind whereby a selected group of rational creatures is so governed by God that they will infallibly obtain eternal beatitude. Consequently, predestination is formally in the divine intellect, although it presupposes the act of the will (*De ver.* 6.1). Predestination is a single process which encompasses at one and the same time all the graces by which each person is led to his final end, as well as the conferral itself of glory (*ibid.* 6.1). The conferral of grace is the effect of predestination, insofar as it is the means that leads a creature to the attainment of his end. The granting of glory is also the effect of predestination, insofar as it is the end for the attainment of which efficacious grace was given to these select souls.

Logically, predestination may be distinguished into three operations: dilection, election, and formal predestination. Dilection is the absolute decree of the divine will whereby God wills eternal life, that is, a determined measure of eternal HAPPINESS for a select group of men. Election is the same act of the will, insofar as through it God chooses a certain group of men to be saved rather than others whom He could have chosen. Formal predestination is the plan existing in the divine intellect according to which God accomplishes the salvation of those whom He has chosen. These three divine operations are so united that logically dilection is prior to election, and election is prior to formal predestination (*Summa theologiae* 1a, 23.4; *In 1 Sent.* 41.1). According to Aquinas, the foreknowledge of merits is neither the cause nor the reason for predestination; meritorious acts are rather the effects of predestination (*Summa theologiae* 1a, 23.5).

Luis de Molina, SJ. The founder of MOLINISM, and along with him Francisco de TOLEDO, Gabriel VÁZQUEZ, and St. FRANCIS DE SALES, agreed substantially with St. Thomas concerning the nature of predestination. He agreed that it is the divine plan that is formally in the divine intellect, although conjoined with the will. Predestination is one. It concerns all the means from first calling to the attainment of beatitude itself (*Concordia* 23.1.1, 2) and is entirely gratuitous. Therefore, predestination is not granted because of the divine foreknowledge of the free will of the creature, as if God predestined some because He foresaw the good use of their free will and reprobated the rest because of His foreknowledge of the abuse of their free will.

MOLINA taught that there exists in God a knowledge of all possible beings, as well as a knowledge of all possible orders of things. As a result, God knows all possible free acts of all possible men in all possible world orders. Presupposing this knowledge on the part of God, He, for His own reasons, freely chooses one order of things and wills its fulfillment. Thus, He chooses, those men to be saved whom in this world order He has foreseen would make good use of the graces that would be granted to them in these particular circumstances, men whom He has foreseen would persevere and ultimately merit eternal felicity. There is absolutely no causal influence, on the part of rational creatures, that influences God to choose this particular world order over other possible world orders. As a matter of fact, the very men whom God has foreseen will attain the blessings of eternal life in this present world order He also has foreseen in another equally possible world order as the group constituting those who would die unrepentant and thus be condemned. For this reason, it must be firmly held that election and predestination itself is entirely gratuitous.

The absolute decree of God to choose this world order is directly concerned with His foreknowledge of graces, which for some will be efficacious and for others merely sufficient. In knowingly choosing this world order in which a select group of men will receive graces which will prove to be efficacious, God is exercising toward these men a special predilection that He does not exercise toward others. The choice of this world order, in a sense, can be said to be the basic reason why the men thus benefited are saved.

The explanation of Molina is founded on his opinion concerning the manner by which God knows future free acts. He maintains that this knowledge is in God independently of any decree of the will of God that would physically predetermine the will of man to one course of action, PREDETERMINATION, he holds, would destroy human freedom. He concludes, therefore, that each individual freely determines himself to cooperate with grace or not. Molina, therefore, believes that the conferral of glory can be decreed absolutely by God only after He has foreseen absolutely the cooperation with grace and hence the meritorious acts of man. The reason for this is that the decree of election and predilection is concerned only with the graces to be conferred. Accordingly, in Molina's system there exists neither antecedent positive REPROBATION nor antecedent negative reprobation. Consequently, after the prevision, as absolute futures, of the merits of the first group and the demerits of the second group, God absolutely wills to give glory to the first and eternal punishment to the second.

Domingo Báñez. In opposition to Molina the Spanish Dominican theologian held that predestination to glory, viewed in itself, is decreed before the provision of any merits whatsoever (*ante praevisa merita*). The very first action of God concerning the chosen group of men (the elect) is their election to glory, and, conversely, His very first action concerning the rest of men is their exclusion from glory or from an efficacious election to glory. This predestination of certain souls to glory before the prevision of their merits is, of course, not a result of any merit on the part of man, but is entirely gratuitous. God wills this by reason of His absolute dominion over all creatures and through His inscrutable counsel. This is the first decree of God in the order of intention.

God in His divine wisdom has decreed to confer glory to the elect as the reward of merit. Therefore, after the decree of predestination to glory, God absolutely decrees the meritorious acts that are to be posited freely by each of the elect. Following this second decree, God absolutely decrees to give for each meritorious act graces that are intrinsically efficacious, graces that will infallibly predetermine man's will to a meritorious act. To those who were not elected, the negatively reprobated, God, subsequently to the decree excluding them from glory or from an efficacious election to glory, decrees not to give them efficacious graces, but graces that are merely sufficient. He premoves them to the matter of sin and permits malice. Having posited these decrees, God knows infallibly that they will freely sin and perish unrepentant.

For the elect the execution of this divine plan is accomplished in the inverse order of its intention: (1) the granting of graces that are intrinsically efficacious; (2) the positing of meritorious acts, and death in the state of grace; (3) the conferral of glory because of merit. Conversely, for the reprobate, the nonelected, the execution of the divine plan is in a similar fashion. There is (1) the granting of merely sufficient graces; (2) permission to sin and the subsequent death of the unrepentant sinner; and (3) the positive reprobation of the sinner, subsequent to the prevision of his death in an unrepentant state. (*See* BÁÑEZ and BAÑEZIANISM.)

Congruists. The Jesuits St. Robert BELLARMINE and Francisco SUÁREZ presented a doctrine called CONGRUISM. In agreement with Báñez, congruism stated that there existed in God a predestination to glory for chosen souls, a predestination that is prior to the provision of any absolute merits on the part of the elect. By His middle knowledge (*SCIENTIA MEDIA*), God foresees as FUTUR-

IBLES the merits and demerits of all men. God's prevision of this, however, is not a factor that moves Him to choose this world order over any other. It is necessary, however, to posit this knowledge on the part of God in order to explain how He acts wisely and intelligently in His election of one group of men rather than another.

The first decree of God in the absolute order is the will to predestine a select group of men to glory before the provision of any absolute merits on their part. The reason for this decree of God is not a result of the provision of any goodness on the part of these chosen souls, but rather is a result entirely of the predestination and mercy of God. The choice is completely gratuitous. Following the will to select these chosen ones, God decrees to confer on them graces that through middle knowledge He foresees will be efficacious, that is, graces that are infallibly connected with SALUTARY ACTS. This decree of the divine will concerning efficacious graces and merits is necessary, and God has decreed to give glory to those whom He has chosen.

Conversely, God absolutely decrees to exclude the nonelect from an efficacious election to glory. It is important to note that He wills this exclusion antecedently to and in fact independently of the provision of any demerits on the part of the reprobate. He is able to do this because of His absolute dominion over all creatures and because of His inscrutable counsel. This is termed negative antecedent reprobation. As a consequence of this decree to exclude them from an efficacious election, He wills to exclude them from the order of efficacious graces. He confers upon them graces that are not congruous, graces that through middle knowledge He has foreseen will be merely sufficient. As for Báñez, so for Bellarmine, the order of execution of the divine plan is inverse to the order of intention.

Conclusion. Such were the answers given by the great theologians of the Church to the almost insurmountable problems involved in the doctrine of predestination. In matters of this type, theology may avert the evident contradiction, but it is not within its province to demonstrate philosophically the intrinsic possibility of mysteries. *See* MYSTERY (IN THEOLOGY). Just as the reality of the mysteries of the Trinity, Incarnation, and predestination remain obscure in this life, so does their intrinsic possibility (Denz 3015–20).

In this very difficult question of predestination, one must always bear in mind that he knows God merely by ANALOGY, through concepts that are completely unequal to the task of representing Him exactly as He is in Himself. For God unites in His essence various aspects that appear inharmonious to man for the simple reason that man's cognition is potential and imperfect.

Following the example of Christ, it is possible practically to consider the question under the light that shines forth in His preaching. The inspired description of the salvific will of God in the Gospels presents Christ weeping over Jerusalem and contains those heartrending words, ''Jerusalem, Jerusalem! thou who killest the prophets and stonest those who are sent to thee! How often would I have gathered thy children, as a hen gathers her young under her wings, but thou wouldst not!'' (Mt 23.37). The sincere unambiguous salvific will of God appears, indeed, forcefully in the Gospels; recall the widow seeking the lost drachma, the father and his prodigal son, and the Good Shepherd leaving the 99 sheep in the desert in order to find the one that is lost (Lk 15.1–32). Only Christ, who is one with the Father, can narrate what attitude of mind the Father has toward men, and from the above examples it is evident that it is one of infinite love and mercy.

See Also: FREE WILL AND GRACE; FREE WILL AND PROVIDENCE; GRACE, EFFICACIOUS; GRACE, SUFFICIENT; OMNISCIENCE; PREDESTINATION (IN NON-CATHOLIC THEOLOGY).

Bibliography: A. LEMONNYER et al., *Dictionnaire de théologie catholique*, 12.2:2809–3022. R. SCHNACKENBURG et al., *Lexicon für Theologie und Kirche,* 8:661–672. A. D'ALÈS, *Dictionnaire apologétique de la foi catholique* 4:195–270. X. M. LE BACHELET, *Prédestination et grâce efficace: Controverses dans la Compagnie de Jésus au temps d'Aquaviva,* 2 v. (Louvain 1931). V. BOUBLÍK, *La Predestinazione: S. Paolo e S. Agostino* (Rome 1961). J. FARRELLY, *Predestination, Grace, and Free Will* (Westminster, Md. 1964). M. FRANCESCONI, *La dottrina del Damasceno sulla predestinazione* (Rome 1945). R. GARRIGOU-LAGRANGE, *Predestination,* tr. B. ROSE (St. Louis 1939). M. J. SCHEEBEN, *The Mysteries of Christianity,* tr. C. VOLLERT (St. Louis 1946). E. ELORDUY, ''La predestinación en Suárez,'' *Archivo teológico granadino* 10 (1953) 5–150. T. FAHY, ''Romans 8.29,'' *The Irish Theological Quarterly* 23 (1956) 410–412. A. MCDONNELL, ''Those Whom He Has Chosen,'' *Dominicans* 48 (1963) 109–119. J. RABENECK, ''Grundzüge der Prädestinationslehre Molinas,'' *Scholastik* 31 (1956) 351–369. J. D. SHERIDAN, ''Predestination Up to Date,'' *Irish Monthly* 70 (1942) 227–231. S. TROMP, ''Tractatus S. Roberti Bellarmini iuvenis de predestinatione,'' *Gregorianum* 14 (1933) 248–268; ''Progressus doctrinalis in tractatibus S. Roberti Bellarmini de predestinatione,'' *ibid.* 315–355. H. J. VALLA, ''Metodología para una catequesis de la predestinación,'' *Didascalia* 15 (1961) 385–393. R. VELASCO, ''Providencia y predestinación: Estudio positivo de una cuestión disputada en la escuela tomista,'' *Revista española de teología* 21 (1961) 125–151, 249–287.

[A. G. PALLADINO]

PREDESTINATION (IN NON-CATHOLIC THEOLOGY)

At the very beginning of this article it should be clearly stated that actually there is no single doctrine concerning predestination that would be acceptable to all branches of Protestantism. Therefore, it would be inaccurate and ill-advised to present this article as being the Protestant theology of predestination. All that one can do is treat historic Protestantism as it has faced the problem of predestination, i.e., trace the theories of election and REPROBATION that can be found in the main currents of Protestantism as it has flowed through the history of the past 400 years. The approach, therefore, will be historical: the beliefs of some of the chief personalities will be delineated, the interrelation of their diverse opinions will be shown as far as possible, and, in conclusion, the doctrine of perhaps the most eminent of modern Protestant theologians, Karl Barth, will be set forth.

Martin Luther. The two men who played key roles in the early history of Protestantism, Martin LUTHER (1483–1546) and John Calvin, were both deeply influenced by the theological thinking of the centuries previous to those in which they lived. St. Augustine, as understood by them, was a great influence. So were Gottschalk of Orbais in the 9th century and, more proximately, John Wyclif in the 14th.

Luther, in his earlier years at least, maintained as extreme a doctrine of predestination as Calvin himself was later to profess. This is important to note since, by and large, modern LUTHERANISM rejects the extreme approach to predestination that was so emphatically taught by its founder. There are some who claim that in his later years Luther mitigated his doctrine of predestinarianism to a less rigid form of predestination. Actually, however, it seems that although there is a difference in the technical terminology utilized by Luther in the first and later form of his theology, nevertheless the later form does not constitute a radical departure from his earlier conception.

When Luther first began to grapple with the problem of predestination, about 1509 or 1510, he accepted the solution that was common among the schoolmen, that predestination is in some way to be explained by God's foreknowledge of man's conduct. But upon more assiduous study of the Bible and St. Augustine, Luther gradually underwent a complete reversal of opinion and finally professed the doctrine of predestinarianism, which he claimed to be the true teaching of the Bible as well as of St. Augustine.

The most complete sources concerning Luther's teaching on predestination are his commentary on the Epistle to the Romans and his work *De servo arbitrio* (The Will Enslaved), the latter being written in answer to Erasmus's attack on his doctrine, *De libero arbitrio* (Free Will). Essentially, the doctrine contained in these works may be summarized as follows.

There exists on the part of God an irrevocable election of some souls to eternal beatitude and positive rejection of the rest, who go to eternal perdition. As proof, Luther gives Paul's references to the scriptural stories of God's election and rejection in the three cases of Isaac and Ishmael, of Jacob and Esau, and of David and Saul.

According to Luther, all objections to predestination, as he understands it, come from human reason and not from the wisdom of God. The objections follow: 1. Man has been given a free will by which he can earn either merit or demerit. (Luther replies that man's will in itself has not the least ability to secure justification, because the will itself is totally corrupt, totally unable to choose anything but sin. Indeed, the will is not free but captive.) 2. Predestination, as held by Luther, is inconsistent with the teaching of Sacred Scripture, which states (1 Tm 2.4) that "God our Savior . . . wishes all men to be saved." (Luther's reply is that all such statements are realized properly in the elect. One must make a distinction between "the apparent will" and "the hidden will" of God. It is interesting to note that in his translation of 1 Timothy Luther renders the above as "God wills that all be assisted.") 3. If men sin of necessity, then they are unjustly condemned. (Luther replies that men are sinners of necessity and so are under condemnation, but no one is a sinner by external coercion or against his will. Man's will has been so corrupted by original sin that it interiorly always chooses evil and of itself is incapable of doing otherwise.) 4. God's hardening of the will of man makes God the cause of man's sin and condemnation. [Luther answers that what God wills cannot be unjust. For what right has the clay to criticize the Potter? God's law exists that the elect may obey it (for this divine grace is conferred) and that the reprobate may be caught in it (for this divine grace is withheld). Thus there is displayed both God's wrath and His mercy.]

Luther's presentation of this extreme position caused a violent reaction on the part of his humanist friends as well as of others. He was roundly criticized; most important of all, Erasmus broke with him and in two treatises bitterly attacked his former friend.

For the person who is tormented by the question as to whether or not he is among the elect, Luther's advice is to turn away from such thoughts and instead look to Christ. If one believes in Christ, then he may be assured that he is called; and if called, he may be sure that he is predestined to eternal salvation. Despite the efforts of certain followers of synergistic tendencies to maintain that Luther mitigated his earlier opinions concerning predestination (*see* SYNERGISM), it is fairly evident from many sections in his "Table Talk" of later years that Luther never retracted the rigid doctrine outlined above.

Huldrych Zwingli. The Swiss reformer (1484–1531) was a contemporary of Luther and according to many was profoundly influenced by him, though he himself was unwilling to admit it. Although ZWINGLI was much more under the influence of humanism than either Luther or Calvin, some scholars still believe that predestinarianism was the determinative principle in his theology. Zwingli taught a thoroughgoing determinism, declaring that all evil, as well as all good, is due to the causality of God. This generalization includes the fall of Adam. Faith is the fruit and present pledge of election so that he who has faith already knows that he is elected. Zwingli believed in the twofold character of predestination. Election is given to those who are to be saved, positive reprobation and rejection to those who are lost.

Philipp Melanchthon. At first an adherent of Luther's rigid predestination and the denial of free will in man, Philipp MELANCHTHON (1479–1560), perhaps because of humanistic tendencies, gradually changed his opinion. The AUGSBURG CONFESSION, in the formation of which he played the leading role, manifests a deliberate avoidance of the question of predestination. The Formula of Concord (*see* CONCORD, FORMULA AND BOOK OF) became the accepted Lutheran doctrine in the 17th century. This document states that predestination is the will of God that all who believe are saved. It states that foreknowledge deals with both the good and the evil, but that predestination deals with salvation. However, the promise of salvation is made to all men and not to just a few. Those whom God foresees will believe, He eternally elects. If certain men are not elected, the fault is their own. Thus it came to pass that the vast majority of Lutherans eventually held a position directly opposed to that of their founder.

John Calvin. A second-generation reformer, John CALVIN (1509–64) absorbed many of his ideas from the writings of Luther and Zwingli. In his *Institutes of the Christian Religion* (3.21.5, 7) Calvin teaches:

> We call predestination God's eternal decree, by which he determined with himself what he willed to become of each man. . . . eternal life is foreordained for some, eternal damnation for others. Therefore, as any man has been created to one or the other of these ends, we speak of him as predestined to life or death. . . . We assert that, with respect to the elect, this plan was founded upon his freely given mercy, without regard to human worth; but by his just and irreprehensible but incomprehensible judgment he has barred the door of life to those whom he has given over to damnation. Now among the elect we regard the call as a testimony of election. Then we hold justification another sign of its manifestation, until they come into the glory in which the fulfillment of that election lies. But as the Lord seals his elect by call and justification, so, by shutting off the reprobate from knowledge of his name or from the sanctification of his Spirit, he, as it were, reveals by these marks what sort of judgment awaits them.

It is evident from the above that the first and absolute intention of God at creation was that certain men should be saved and the rest condemned to eternal damnation. This will of God is incapable of being frustrated. It imposes on secondary causes, even man himself, a direct internal necessity. Freedom of the creature consists in mere immunity from extrinsic coaction. Only the elect are justified; grace cannot be lost. The rest of men God precludes from the possibility of life, since He refuses them grace, without which they are internally incapable of positing a morally good act. In fact, God actually wills that they sin and die in the state of aversion from Him. This, however, is truly sinful and blameworthy on the part of man, because he is free from external coaction. (*See* CALVINISM.)

Jacobus Arminius. A theologian of the Reformed Church and professor at the University of Leiden, Netherlands, ARMINIUS (1560–1609) and his followers protested against Calvin's doctrine of unconditional election and irresistible grace. They maintained that for God to elect some men to salvation and to deny the privilege to the rest would be unjust on the part of God, and injustice is impossible with Him. The truth is that God knows in advance that a man will sin by free choice, but He does not will nor does he predestine him to do so. Man's freedom must be in contrast to all compulsion, necessity, and spontaneity. Freedom exists only when there is the power of alternate choice. Man does face alternate choices and therefore is actually free. For Arminius grace is not irresistible. (*See* ARMINIANISM.)

In the face of this mitigated doctrine and the controversy that it engendered in the Reformed Church, the Synod of Dolt (1618–19) was convened. The Arminians were subsequently condemned and excluded from their pastorates; rigid Calvinism was strongly reiterated. There were, however, two groups among the members of the synod. One group, the SUPRALAPSARIANS, maintained that prior to any knowledge of original sin, and in fact independently of it, God eternally wills some men to be saved and positively reprobates the rest. The second group, the INFRALAPSARIANS, maintained that God's positive decree to predestine the elect to glory and to reprobate the rest came only after His prevision of the fall of man. The influence of Arminian theology was extremely important, because it was widely diffused when adopted by John Wesley and Methodism, as well as by related movements in the 18th century. The theological influence of Melanchthon, Arminius, and Wesley provided a basis for the fact that the united stand that the original reformers had taken regarding the doctrine of predestination of free will steadily lost ground. As a result, today most of Protestantism takes a synergistic position that in many ways is similar to that held by the Catholic Church in opposition to the reformers.

Karl Barth. No new development of importance occurred until that of the present day, when NEO-ORTHODOXY has produced a departure in an entirely new direction from historic reformed doctrine. This position is best exemplified in the theology of an outstanding Protestant theologian of the 20th century, Karl BARTH.

Election in Christ. For Barth predestination is essentially connected with Christology. The root of every error that has crept into the doctrine of predestination lies in the blindness of its classic exponents to the fact that the ground of the electing will of God is identical with the reality of Jesus Christ. The divine election of grace means that God in the eternal counsel of His will has chosen for Himself fellowship with man, and for man fellowship with Himself—thus a double choice and predestination. This double choice is revealed in Jesus Christ and takes effect in Him on the stage of time. Christ is both the electing God and the elected Man. As the eternal Son of the Father, He is very God. His will is one with God's will. There is no other will of God for man but what is expressed, realized, and fulfilled in Him. And Christ is also the elected Man. In Him, through Him, and for Him, man's humanity is laid hold of and gathered into the life of God. Jesus Christ is true man. In the light of Christ one can no longer speak of God purely in Himself or of man purely in himself. One can only speak of God and man united in that communion wherein God meets man in pure sovereign grace and man meets God in faith and obedience.

God not only chooses but He also rejects. He chooses to be man's God, and He chooses not to be not man's God. This negative decision is just as truly a decision as the positive. The man to whom God binds Himself is fallen man, who as such lies under divine rejection. But the election of grace, eternal in the counsels of God, is not nullified by man's sin and fall. In Christ, God takes upon Himself the sentence of rejection and bears it in man's stead. In Christ, God Himself enters into the dark shadow of man's rejection and dissipates it. There is, therefore, because of Jesus Christ no positive decision of God to reject man, but only the gracious decision to accept him. There are not, therefore, two spheres, one of election and the other of rejection, standing independently over against each other.

Old and New Israel. According to Scripture, the first reference about divine election is not to man in general but to a chosen community, named Israel in the Old Testament and the Church in the NT. It must be emphasized, however, that it is the individual man who is the object of divine election and not the community as such. Both Israel and the Church exist to serve the electing purpose of God, which is for the individual man. In their life and history they mirror and reflect the great divine events of election and rejection that took place in Him, and so bear witness to Him, mediate Him to the world. The peculiar function of Israel in this regard is to mirror and illustrate the sinful actuality of all mankind and the divine rejection that became event in the Crucifixion of the Son of God, and so of the world that passes away in Him. The peculiar function of the Church is to mirror the new humanity in Christ, to bear witness of the divine election that was manifested in His Resurrection, and so the new coming world of God. Israel and the Church are one and the same community with two historical magnitudes. The one community of God in its departing form as Israel serves to set forth the divine judgment and in its coming form as the Church serves to set forth the divine mercy.

It is necessary to recognize that election is no mere dead, stationary decree fixing in advance all that should follow after. The election of grace is a living, moving thing. It is the action of the living, electing God upon the acts and decisions of men. Predestination as such is salvation history and as such is the secret of all history.

Individual Man. It has been noted that it is not the community as such that is the real object of divine election, but individual man, the single man in his simple humanness, as he exists in relation to the various forms of collectivity with which he is related. What does this individuality mean from the standpoint of divine election? This individual man is a sinful individuality that strives continually to isolate itself from God and make itself its own God. As such, man stands under the rejection of God and must cease to be in order that the true individual, the elect man, may appear. This is attained by a judgment borne by Christ in His death on man's behalf in order that man may receive the promise of his true manhood in Christ's Resurrection.

The election of the individual man is in reality, therefore, a derivation from the election of Jesus Christ. As his life becomes a hearing and receiving of the promise that is his in the election of Jesus Christ, the election becomes the transcendent mystery of his own existence. The elect man allows himself to be loved by God in that he sets aside all claims of his own to that love and permits a love that he has not in any way earned or deserved to determine his life. He allows God's love to overflow to him and finds in that love his one sure ground of hope, his joy and blessedness. However, man is not simply the object of God's love and blessedness; he is also the subject of them. He does not just passively receive; he actively shares. This love and blessedness must pass beyond himself in the direction of the world, which God in His election of grace has chosen for His own. The elect man must be a witness of God's election to others. He must become a further stage along which God's election of grace takes effect in the world. This he does in the very living of his life as an elected man.

Rejection is but the reverse side of election, but nonetheless real. The rejected man, in the crisis into which God's election of grace places him, sets himself in opposition thereto. God is for him, but he is against God. The rejected man exists as the object of God's not willing; that is to say, his existence is determined by the fact that God will not have him as he is. He exists as rejected insofar as he attempts to live in withdrawal from that positive will of God that claims him for divine grace. His life is a life without meaning and substance, without future. It is such a life because it is determined as such by the will of God, which, in electing him for grace, condemns him as one who strives to live in independence of grace.

It is important to note that since God's love is universal, Barth rejects the idea of the predestination of only a certain number of men; instead he would leave the number of the elect indeterminate. However, he would not make this open number of the elect equal to the number of all men. This would limit God's freedom.

Some critics maintain that, since Barth states that all men are elect in Christ, the basic difference between believers and unbelievers is only that the unbeliever does not yet know that he is elected. Moreover, since Jesus took upon Himself the rejection of all men, no man therefore is rejected by God. His critics maintain that because of this basic doctrine, it is difficult to see how Barth can escape from the charge of universalism, the doctrine that holds that all men are *de facto* eventually saved. It seems that this part of Barth's exposition is as yet a bit uncertain. Despite this limitation, Barth's teaching on election and rejection, with its Christocentrism, has had a remarkable appeal to all forms of Protestantism.

See Also: PREDESTINATION (IN CATHOLIC THEOLOGY.

Bibliography: R. GARRIGOU-LAGRANGE, *Dictionnaire de théologie catholique,* ed. A. VACANT, 15 v. (Paris 1903–50) 12.2:2959–63. J. AUER, *Lexikon für Theologie und Kirche,* ed. J. HOFER and K. RAHNER, 10 v. (2d, new ed. Freiburg 1957–65); suppl., *Das ZweiteVatikanische Konzil: Dokumente und kommentare,* ed. H. S. BRECHTER et al., pt. 1 (1966) 8:660; H. FRIES, ed., *Handbuch theologischer Grundbegriffe,* 2 v. (Munich 1962–63) 2:334–339. J. MOLTMANN, *Lexikon für Theologie und Kirche,* ed. J. HOFER and K. RAHNER, 10 v. (2d, new ed. Freiburg 1957–65); suppl., *Das ZweiteVatikanische Konzil: Dokumente und kommentare,* ed. H. S. BRECHTER et al., pt. 1 (1966) 8:670–672. C. H. RATSCHOW et al., *Die Religion in Geschichte und Gegenwart,* 7 v. (3d ed. Tübingen 1957–65) 5: 479–489. A. S. MARTIN, J. HASTINGS, ed., *Encyclopedia of Religion & Ethics,* 13 v. (Edinburgh 1908–27) 10:225–235. M. LUTHER, *The Bondage of the Will,* tr. J. I. PARKER and O. R. JOHNSTON (London 1957); *Commentary on the Epistle to the Romans,* tr. J. T. MUELLER (Grand Rapids 1954). J. CALVIN, *Commentaries on the Catholic Epistles,* tr. J. HAROUTUNIAN and L. P. SMITH (Philadelphia 1958); *Institutes of the Christian Religion,* ed. J. T. MCNEILL, tr. F. L. BATTLES, 2 v. (Philadelphia 1960). K. BARTH, *Church Dogmatics,* tr. G. T. THOMSON et al. (New York 1955–) v.2. H. BOUILLARD, *Karl Barth,* 2 v. in 3 (Paris 1957) v.2. H. E. BRUNNER, *Dogmatics,* tr. O. WYNN et al., 3 v. (Philadelphia 1950–62) v.2. C. BERKOUWER, *Divine Election* (Grand Rapids 1948). H. BUIS, *The Doctrine of Eternal Punishment* (Philadelphia 1957); *Historic Protestantism and Predestination* (Philadelphia 1958). R. BULTMANN, "Grace and Freedom," in *Essays: Philosophical and Theological,* tr. J. C. G. GREIG (New York 1955). F. W. CAMFIELD, ed., *Reformation Old and New* (London 1947). W. M. HORTON, *Christian Theology, an Ecumenical Approach* (rev. and enl. ed. New York 1958). J. JUCZ, *Predestination: A Theology of Election* (London 1958). P. MAURY, *Predestination and Other Papers,* tr. E. HUDSON (Richmond 1960). H. ROWLEY, *The Biblical Doctrine of Election* (London 1950).

[A. G. PALLADINO]

PREDETERMINATION

Historically, a term connoting the controversies of the *CONGREGATIO DE AUXILIIS* (1598–1607), and which the Thomists came to accept as a term expressing the intrinsic efficacy of actual GRACE. The nature of this efficacy was described as a physical predetermination or as a help that predetermines physically (*Historiae Congregationum de Auxiliis,* 2:171B; 4:515C). Such expressions were more frequent than the expression "physical PREMOTION." Doctrinally the term raises the problem of the relationship between divine causality and the free human act and requires careful precision.

Divine Causality as Predetermination. The causality of God as intelligent first cause may be described as predetermination. The priority of this causality, so that it is a "pre-" determination, is its eternity. Identical with the divine being, the divine causality does not evolve but exists all at once. Thus it is prior to all the temporal effects to which it extends, including the voluntary actions of man.

This same causality is a determination because God is an intelligent cause. This determination can be taken as equivalent to the plan of divine PROVIDENCE, which extends to every created reality, all the way to singular beings and the events of their individual development and thus to the concrete acts of FREE WILL. Because this plan is divine, it is infallible; there can be no conjecture, no waiting or uncertainty about God's knowledge. God's eternity is itself a reason for this infallibility. In His knowing plan the actual events of all created history, including the voluntary acts of every man, are present before the simple, unevolving gaze of the divine mind. But this infallibility also presupposes that God's plan, His intelligent causality, is effective and not a mere theoretical apprehension of possible worlds. The source of that effectiveness is the decree of the divine will—the divine choice that certain beings and certain events, including the actions of men, should in fact exist. Thus, although the actual presence of all history in God's plan is explained by His eternity, that His knowledge be knowledge of the actually existent presupposes the sure source of all actuality, the efficacy of His own will. The infallibility of God's plan cannot be based on secondary causes; these are defectible, contingent and impedible. Thus because it is a knowledge of all events (including the act of free will) in their subordination to the efficacious decrees of His will, God's plan, His determination, is infallibly certain.

All of this, however, is rejected in MOLINISM. The Molinist *SCIENTIA MEDIA* is a knowledge anterior to any decree of the divine will. Its certainty lies in its being an eternal comprehension of all the free acts to which the human will might determine itself with the aid of a merely simultaneous concurrence (*Concordia,* 14.13.52). The bases for this certitude are variously assigned, but the point of opposition to St. Thomas Aquinas's teaching is that the *scientia media* is an infallible knowledge of the existent anterior to the decrees of God's will (see *Summa theologiae* 1a, 14.5, 8, 13). The divine plan actually operative, for the Molinists, is a *scientia libera.* As eternal, this could be called predetermination, but the term is not apt because the decrees underlying it follow upon the perception in the *scientia media* of the autonomous determination of the free creature.

Physical Premotion as Predetermination. The eternal and infallible efficacy of divine causality is the basis for referring to physical premotion as predetermination. Physical premotion properly designates the effect of God's causality in every created agent, an effect by which the agent actually is conjoined to its own action. As such, physical premotion may well be described as predetermined. This serves to emphasize its nature as an effect of God's causality, belonging to His government, the execution of the divine plan in time. Because premotion is from God, it bears the marks of its origin, corresponding to the infallible efficacy by which God as first cause determines all actual existents. Thus premotion is not indifferent; it is not an indefinite energy variously determinable by created agents, but is itself predetermined and causative according to the universally extensive causality of God, which reaches to the singular existent, even to the free act.

Again, premotion may be designated as predetermining. This simply emphasizes its being a causal influence by which the created agent causes in subordination to God, the first cause. As such, it is prior to the actual effect, the action itself, by a causal antecedence. Precisely as a divinely causal influence, it is determining and not indeterminate. This is again to say that it extends to each concrete act to be exercised.

Thus understood, premotion is contrasted with the merely simultaneous concurrence espoused by Molinists. Such concurrence is proposed as a divine help conferred on the action of free will, and not on the faculty itself; thus both the divine help and the will-act become coordinated causes of free choice. The divine help, in this explanation, is in itself indeterminate; by its own choice, the human will concretizes and diversifies the divine help so that it becomes effective of a particular act.

But what is left unexplained is the will's passage to actual choice from a prior state of potency. In the final analysis, premotion is invoked simply because of this suspension of the will faculty. The divine help must be truly causal because the human will is dependent; the divine help cannot be indifferent and determinable, simply because it is primarily causative; the human will is so subordinated to divine help that without such help it could not exercise its choice at all. Thus the will could not determine the divine help to this or that choice; rather it is the divine help that is itself determined, namely, the help the will needs precisely to exercise this concrete act of choice, to pass from potentiality to actual choice. It was, in fact, because a merely simultaneous concurrence is an indifferent divine help that would make the divine plan uncertain, fallible, determinable that *scientia media* had to be invented. The Thomist position, as opposed to the Molinist, rests the certainty of God's plan on the efficacy of His decrees, to which physical premotion as predetermination corresponds.

Predetermination and Freedom of Choice. No attempt to see the compatibility of God's primacy as cause with the freedom of the will's choices can rid itself of obscurity. But certain strands of the problem can be separated. Physical premotion as it relates to its source, divine causality, is predetermined; the infallibility of the divine plan and its efficacy require this. As it relates to the free choices of the will, premotion is predetermining, in the sense of being causal with regard to each particular free choice. This causality takes place in the movement by which the will passes from potentiality to the actual exercise of its act. But freedom itself exists in the actual exercise of choice. This means that both as to what is chosen and as to the choosing itself the will has dominance; not only is it not coerced, but its basic orientation toward man's fulfillment is not fully evoked. The object and act of willing do not necessitate the will. As it wills, the will fully achieves its choice both of object and of action. From the point of view of conjoining the will to actual choice, then, physical premotion no more takes away freedom than does the will faculty itself in actually choosing its own act.

Yet the ultimate problem remains: predetermination implies the incompatibility of a physical premotion conferred and the will not placing the corresponding act. The nonpositing of this choice is incompatible with the infallibility and efficacy of the divine causality itself. The Molinist position escapes this problem by leaving the divine assistance indifferent and by relying on the *scientia media.* St. THOMAS AQUINAS faces this natural mystery by pointing to the unique effectiveness of God's causality that reaches each effect according to the connatural mode of being and acting that is proper to the secondary cause (*Summa theologiae* 1a, 19.6; 22.4 ad 1, ad 2, ad 3; *C. gent.* 3.148; *De ver.* 24.1 ad 3). Thus, for him, physical premotion is not predetermining in the sense of necessarily coercing the will. All the dynamism that leads up to the point of free choice takes place connaturally. The apprehension of this choice as desirable has gone on because of its conformity with the abiding dispositions of the will. The choice itself is made when, with the indispensable help of premotion, the will actually causes its own act. That the premotion, while retaining its own infallibility, does not coerce the will, rests upon God's acting on the will according to its proper nature, dispositions and mode of acting. The will is moved to make the free choice, so to exercise its freedom.

See Also: PREMOTION, PHYSICAL; BÁÑEZ AND BAÑEZIANISM; MOLINISM; CAUSALITY, DIVINE.

Bibliography: J. H. SERRY, *Historiae Congregationum de Auxiliis* (5 v., 2d ed. Venice 1740) 2:171B; 4:515C. L. MOLINA, *Concordia,* 14.13.52.

[T. C. O'BRIEN]

PREDICABLES

The predicables (Gr. κατηγορούμενα) are the relations involved in saying something is one of many; they express the five basic ways in which one thing ''can be said'' of many as of a subject by way of formal predication. Such predication manifests a formal perfection of the subject; an otherwise unexpressed determination and is opposed to mere predicates of identity. The five predicables were enumerated in the third century by PORPHYRY in his *Introduction* (*Isagoge*) to the *Categories* of ARISTOTLE. They are the classic *quinque voces:* genus, species, difference, property and accident. The notions were examined at great length in medieval logic (*see* LOGIC, HISTORY OF).

Purpose. The predicables are used in the dividing of being into the ten supreme genera (Gr. κατηγορίαι, categories), which are divided and subdivided by specific differences that ultimately constitute the lowest species, the term of the process (*see* CATEGORIES OF BEING). Since the categories are drawn up in order to help in classifying and defining natural objects, it is obvious that the predicables also share this purpose. In a DEFINITION, several concepts, generic and differential, are ordered in such a way as to express distinctly the determinate kind of being of an object, thus setting it off sharply from other objects. Through the verbal formula that stands for these concepts, the mind knows a limited class of things with a peculiar identity. Thus it selects predicates that will set off a given class by its proper determinations. In the definitions sought, the whatness or QUIDDITY (*quod quid erat esse*) is known and expressed as the starting point of scientific knowledge.

Of the words used in formulating a definition, not all are equally effective. For example, an essential predicate will manifest the quiddity better than an accidental one. The several relations of these words to the subject being defined are called predicables. By an exhaustive division one discovers that there are five of these. Such words are predicable of a subject because they are first related to the subject, as a universal would look to its inferiors. Predicability presupposes that what is said of many is in some way in the many. Since predicability follows on universality as a necessary attribute, the relations of predicability correspond to the five relations of logical universality, wherein the mind recognizes the ways in which a nature, abstracted from singulars, may be found in them as in its inferiors (*see* UNIVERSALS).

Number and Definitions. The five predicables are attained in the following way: When something is said of a subject it can either (1) belong to the nature or essence of the subject and express its quiddity, or (2) belong to the subject in some other way beyond its essence, that is, as accidental to it. In the former case it will manifest either the whole NATURE or ESSENCE of the subject, or part of that nature. The predicable designating the whole nature is called SPECIES. The part of the essence that the subject has in common with other classes of things resembling it is called GENUS, or including class. The part that distinguishes the subject from all other classes is called the difference. In the latter case the predicate may indicate something outside the essence but necessarily following on it, the PROPERTY; or may indicate something contingently associated with the subject, the predicable ACCIDENT.

In the *Isagoge* the definitions follow in this order. Genus is the said universal of many differing in species, in answer to the question ''What is it?'' (''animal,'' of man and brute). Species is the universal said in answer to ''What is it?'' of many that differ only in number (''man,'' of Plato and Socrates). Difference is predicated as the qualitative part of the essence (*in quale quid*) of those differing in number or also in kind (''rational,'' of man; ''sensitive,'' of animal). Property is a universal said of a species as belonging only, necessarily and always to that species and its individuals (''able to speak,'' of man). Accident is a universal said of a species as belonging contingently to that species and its individuals (''white,'' of man).

The order in which the predicables are given reflects a proportionate share in the notion of universality. This is found more formally in essential predicates than in those that are outside the essence of the subject. And of the essential predicates, the generic are more universal than the specific, so that genus and species are given first as substantial predicates, then difference as a qualitative predicate, followed by property and accident as yet more distant from the essence of the subjects.

Predicates vs. Predicables. The predicables are distinct from the classes of predicates listed by Aristotle in the *Topics* (101b 11–103b 19). In this treatise on DIALECTICS, he sets out to classify problems concerning which arguments take place. Since dialectical reasoning inquires simply whether the predicate does or does not inhere in the subject in a given way (*quia est*), these problems can be reduced to four relations that the predicate of a proposition may have to its subject. The division is made on the basis of essentiality of predicate to subject, and of convertibility of predicate and subject. There are four possible combinations: (1) definition (Gr. ὅρος)—essential and convertible; (2) property—nonessential but convertible; (3) genus and generic difference—essential but not convertible; and (4) accident—nonessential and nonconvertible. Species is not listed separately because species is the subject of inquiry and not a predicate. Specific differences are tested in the same way as definition and may be reduced to it as a problem. Moreover, the question of specific difference is more proper to the specific science treating of the subject than to dialectics.

The division into classes of predicates is made so that the dialectician may discover the common means (*loci*) for testing each kind of predicate. The predicables, on the other hand, follow on the several relations of one to many, of one nature in many inferiors that are immediately contained under the superior or universal. These inferiors may be singulars or other universals. Thus species and difference constitute distinct relations of universality to inferiors, but not classes of predicates or problems for the dialectician. Individuals enter as terms of the relation of universality, but not as subjects of dialectical propositions.

See Also: PORPHYRIAN TREE; PREDICATION; INTENTIONALITY; LOGIC.

Bibliography: ''Isagoge et in Categorias commentarium,'' *Commentaria in Aristotelem Graeca,* 23, ed. A. BUSSE, (Berlin 1882–1909) 4.1. ARISTOTLE, *Organon,* tr. O. F. OWEN, 2 v. (London 1899–1900). H. B. VEATCH, *Intentional Logic* (New Haven 1952). P. COFFEY, *Science of Logic,* 2 v. (New York 1912; reprint 1938). I. M. BOCHEŃSKI, *History of Formal Logic,* tr. I. THOMAS (Notre Dame, Ind. 1961). BOETHIUS, *In Isagogen Porphyrii commenta,* ed. S. BRANDT (Vienna 1906). ALBERT THE GREAT, *Liber de Praedicabilibus,* v.1 of *Opera Omnia,* ed. A. BORGNET, 38 v. (Paris 1890–99). T. DE VIO CAJETAN, *Scripta philosophica: Commentaria in Porphyrii Isagogen,* ed. I. M. MAREGA (Rome 1934). JOHN OF ST. THOMAS, *Cursus Philosophicus,* ed. B. REISER, 3 v. (new ed. Turin 1930–37). JOHN XXI, *Petri Hispani Summulae logicales,* ed. I. M. BOCHEŃSKI (Turin 1947).

[W. BAUMGAERTNER]

PREDICATION

A predicate is a term affirmed or denied of a subject in a categorical or a simple modal PROPOSITION. Subject and predicate compose a sort of matter, which the copula, asserting agreement or variance between them, forms into the proposition. An individual TERM can be a predicate only if the subject also is individual. Other terms, whether concrete or abstract, positive or negative, are not so restricted. Since to be without an attribute is a kind of attribute, no distinction is made here between positive and negative terms.

Predication is the assertion that an attribute (signified by the predicate) does or does not characterize something (signified by the subject). There are thus two kinds of predication: affirmative, asserting such characterization; and negative, denying it. Consideration of the objective status of what the terms signify discloses that both affirmative and negative predication can be of two sorts, identical and disparate. Predication is identical when the attribute the predicate signifies does in fact characterize every referent of the subject; it is disparate when this attribute does not characterize any, or fails to characterize some, referent of the subject. Both of these can be either formal or material. The identical is formal when the predicate is the genus, difference, or property of the subject. Formal disparity results from incompatibility between what the predicate signifies and an attribute the subject signifies. When the subject neither entails nor excludes the predicate, the identity or disparity actually present is material.

Traditional LOGIC teaches that an affirmative proposition is true if and only if its predication is identical, and that a necessary proposition is true if and only if such identical predication is formal. The TRUTH and FALSITY of negative propositions are not determined by identity or disparity of predication.

See Also: PREDICABLES.

[J. J. DOYLE]

PREFACE

In current usage, the term ''Preface'' refers to that prayer of praise and thanksgiving addressed to God the Father located between the introductory dialogue (a.k.a. the *Sursum Corda*) and the SANCTUS.

Term. The word *praefatio,* used to designate in a general manner that part of the Mass to which it is applied in the present Missal, is found with certitude for the first time in the Hadrian edition of the Gregorian Sacramentary. While some have claimed the word should be understood as an introduction to the Canon, many liturgical scholars (spearheaded by J. A. Jungmann) think that the pre-Carolingian Roman liturgy employed the term in that sense used in ancient Roman religion. The ''before'' (*prae-*) would then have reference to place, designating the position assumed by the priest when speaking the words. Hence, *praefatio* would refer either to a formula or prayer uttered solemnly to God ''before'' or at the head of a gathered assembly, or to such an utterance proffered ''before'' or in the presence of God (possibly, some propose, a translation of the Greek *prophētia*). Thus the word is more properly applied not only to the section of the Mass to which it is restricted in the Missal today, but to the entire solemn Eucharistic Prayer or Anaphora. This solution brings out better the theological significance of the term, especially in the light of recent theology of the Church as the ''People of God'' and the *Qahal Yahweh.* Moreover, certain aspects in the historical evolution of our present Mass formulary seem to lend support to this hypothesis.

Historical Considerations. Whatever may be the original sense of the term, historical study leaves little doubt that today's Preface was initially an integral part of the Eucharistic Prayer (*eucharistia, actio*) or Great Prayer (*oratio, prex*), or *Canon Actionis* in some manuscripts. Several ancient Sacramentaries, in fact, place titles such as *Incipit canon actionis* before the dialogue that introduces the present Preface.

The solemnity of the Preface is heightened by an admonition to dispose oneself for the holy activity to follow (''Lift up your hearts''), and by the people's assurance that they are so prepared (''We lift them up to the Lord''). With the next phrase, which culminates the dialogue between celebrant and people, the specific purpose of the gathering is solemnly set forth in an expression that probably has its origin in a Biblical, Jewish context. ''Let us give thanks to the Lord our God'' may well be borrowed from the traditional Jewish form of thanksgiving at meals; ''Let us give thanks to Adonai our God,'' from the BERAKHOT. In these blessings God the Father is thanked and praised for His glory manifested in the history of the Chosen People, past, present, and future.

This link with the Jewish service, which seems borne out even more explicitly in the body of the Preface itself, aids in the understanding of the ''eucharistic'' aspect of what takes place. It is not thanksgiving in an abstract sense, nor in a narrow, isolated sense, but it primarily designates a response on the part of the present ecclesial community to the activity of God in the whole of salvation history. To the celebrant's solemn invitation to engage in actions of gratefulness, the people respond *Dignum et iustum est* (literally, ''It is right and just''), a formula possibly taken from Hellenism by which the citizenry ratified an election or an important decision. Thus the assembly or *ekklesia* acclaims its union with the celebrant with respect to the rest of the eucharistic prayer.

At this point dialogue ends, and the celebrant directs the Eucharistic prayer-action to God the Father in the name of all. In earliest times this whole prayer-action appears to have been uttered in a loud voice in a kind of speech-song. Moreover, the formula was by no means set in its details, and the celebrant was allowed to indulge in a degree of improvisation. Rather quickly, however, because of its nature, the latter portion of the prayer, including the words of institution, tended to become almost invariable, thus starting the historical process that would eventually lead to distinction between the various parts. In the earlier part of the prayer, in which God is praise-thanked for the whole mystery of salvation, the practice arose in the West for the celebrant, in his improvisation, to stress some particular aspect of the total mystery that the specific feast or circumstances brought into special focus. These elaborations tended to proliferate in number, style, and length, thus increasing the distinction between this first portion and the unvarying, brief, and sober ending. Thus the Leonine Sacramentary (late 6th century) has 267 examples of what we today call ''Prefaces,'' although even these seem to be only models or patterns to be imitated rather than definitive formulas. Through the centuries the number of variations fluctuated. The Tridentine Roman Missal (1570) contained 15 Prefaces, and certain dioceses and religious congregations had additional prefaces.

Other developments also tended to obscure the unity of the great Eucharistic Prayer. The SANCTUS chant was interpolated (probably about the 4th century) and seems to have introduced a split in the inner continuity of the prayer, especially when, about the 12th century, a new attitude of piety brought about the silent recitation of the words following the Sanctus. The cleavage was further heightened when, in the manuscripts, the initial ''T'' of the *Te igitur* prayer began to be stylized and finally became the full-page illustration of the crucifix that we find in today's Missals.

The oldest formula of the complete Eucharistic Prayer that we now possess, found in the *Apostolic Tradition*, traditionally attributed to Hippolytus, manifests much more explicitly the spirit of praise-thanksgiving for the wonders God has worked in history, with emphasis on the Christological aspects: through Christ we can offer fitting thanks because of the wondrous works the Father has performed in and through Him.

> We offer thanks to you, O God, through your beloved child, Jesus Christ, whom in the last days you have sent us as savior and redeemer and messenger of your will . . . whom you sent from heaven . . . who, fulfilling your will, . . . stretched out his hands when he suffered to free from suffering those who believe in you . . . [who] taking bread, making eucharist [i.e., giving thanks], said: Receive, eat: this is my body . . . Being mindful, therefore, of his death and resurrection we offer thee . . . [*Apostolic Tradition,* 4].

One can see in Hippolytus's prayer and its Christ-centered concern a specifically Christian adaptation of the ancient Jewish blessing prayer (*berakah*) of praise-thanksgiving to the New Covenant ANAMNESIS (memorial) of Christ's death and Resurrection. Historical studies suggest that the earliest anaphoras or Eucharistic Prayers were structured after the Jewish *Berakah* (or after-dinner thanksgiving) of the time of Christ, which was composed of a threefold, interconnected theme: (1) a statement of praise and adoration addressed to God as the creator and provider of food; (2) a solemn declaration of thanks to God for his redeeming actions in sacred history; and (3) a prayer of petition, asking God to continue to bestow his mercy and care on the people of Israel. The Jewish prayer had itself been an anamnesis of God's providence, His mercies and wonders worked for the Chosen People of the Old Covenant; it concluded with a petition for the coming of the Messiah. The basic structure of the berakah, certainly, is paralleled in certain New Testament prayers, e.g., ''Blessed be the God and Father of our Lord Jesus Christ, the Father of mercies and the God of all comfort, who comforts us . . .'' (2 Cor 1.3; cf. 1 Pt 1.3). Some scholars would argue that the eucharistic prayer appears to be a Christianization of that berakah, or thanksgiving.

It appears that two types of Eucharistic Prayer developed, one within a basically Eastern tradition which retained the tripartite form of the original, the other, more Western tradition, which assumed a bipartite pattern in which the first two parts of the original Jewish rite (praise and thanksgiving) coalesced into the initial ''thanksgiving'' that came to be known as the *Praefatio,* and which tended both to be variable according to the occasion and the feast and to appear somewhat isolated from the later supplication by reason of the *Sanctus* acclamation.

Developments since Vatican II. The ''General Instruction of the Roman Missal,'' first issued in 1969, indicates the official ecclesiastical acceptance of the assertion of the liturgical historians that the Preface, with its opening dialogue, is an integral part of the Eucharistic Prayer:

> The eucharistic prayer, a prayer of thanksgiving and sanctification, is the center and high point of the entire celebration. In an introductory dialogue the priest invites the people to lift their hearts to God in prayer and thanks: he unites them with himself in the prayer he addresses in their name to the Father through Jesus Christ. The meaning of the prayer is that the whole congregation joins Christ in acknowledging the works of God and in offering the sacrifice (*General Instruction of the Roman Missal* 54).
>
> The chief elements of the eucharistic prayer are these: a) *Thanksgiving* (expressed especially in the preface): in the name of the entire people of God, the priest praises the Father and gives him thanks for the work of salvation or for some special aspect of it in keeping with the day, feast, or season. b) *Acclamation:* united with the angels, the congregation sings or recites the *Sanctus.* This acclamation forms part of the eucharistic prayer, and all the people join with the priest in the singing or reciting it . . . (ibid. 55).

In its ''Index of Prefaces'' of the SACRAMENTARY there are 84 listed for various seasons, feasts, and occasions; most are provided with subtitles which rather clearly summarize the doctrinal or theological contents. Moreover, the impression is given that the further composition of other Prefaces suited to particular circumstances may be the rule rather than the exception.

The season cycle of the liturgical year has been quite liberally enriched by additional formulas which strive to bring out with increasing subtlety the thematic evolution of both the Christmas cycle and the Easter cycle. Thus, for example, the Advent-Christmas-Epiphany season now has seven Prefaces; the Lent-Passion-Easter-Ascension-Pentecost cycle has 21. For Sundays in ordinary time there is a variety of eight Prefaces, while six are for weekdays.

The sanctoral cycle is similarly enriched. The feasts and mysteries of the Lord account for 13 new formulas, while there are 16 for the feasts of the saints. Certain other celebrations have also been provided with their own Prefaces, e.g., marriage, religious profession, Order of Christian Funerals, such civic observances as Independence Day and Thanksgiving.

Bibliography: B. BOTTE, *L'Ordinaire de la messe* (Études liturgiques 2; Paris 1953). J. A. JUNGMANN, *The Mass of the Roman Rite,* tr. F. A. BRUNNER (rev. ed. New York 1959) 371–378. D'SOUBIGOU. *A Commentary on the Prefaces and the Eucharistic Prayers of the Roman Missal* tr. J. OTTO (Collegeville. Minn. 1971). C. GIRAUDO, *La struttura letteraria della preghiera eucaristica: saggio sulla genesi letteraria di una forma: toda veterotestamentaria, beraka giudaica, anafora cristiana* (Rome 1981). K. GAMBER, *Beracha: Eucharistiegebet und Eucharistiefeier in der Urkirche* (Regensburg 1986). A. BOULEY, *From Freedom to Formula : The Evolution of the Eucharistic Prayer from Oral Improvisation* (Washington, D.C. 1981). E. MAZZA, *The Eucharistic Prayers of the Roman Rite* (New York 1986). E. MAZZA, *The Origins of the Eucharistic Prayer* (Collegeville, Minn. 1995). P. F. BRADSHAW, *Essays on Early Eastern Eucharistic Prayers* (Collegeville, Minn. 1997). E. MAZZA, *The Celebration of the Eucharist : The Origin of the Rite and the Development of Its Interpretation* (Collegeville, Minn. 1999). B. D. STUHLMAN, *A Good and Joyful thing: The Evolution of the Eucharistic Prayer* (New York 2000).

[D. GRABNER/EDS.]

PRELATE

From the Latin, *praeferre,* to put before, is a general term for an ecclesiastical dignitary who has jurisdiction in the external forum, whether he is a secular or religious cleric (1917 *Codex iuris canonici* c.110). True prelates are those who, either in their own right or as a member of a college, are vested with some power to assist the pope in the governing of the Church. These include the following: (1) prelates *a flocculis* (i.e., those with specific offices, and who wear distinctive garb); (2) assessors and secretaries of the Roman Congregations; (3) the *Maestro di Camera,* the secretary of the Apostolic Signatura, the dean of the Roman Rota, and the substitute secretary of state; (4) four colleges of prelates—prelate auditors of the Roman Rota, clerics of the Apostolic Camera, prelates of the Apostolic Signatura, prelates *referendarii* of the Apostolic Signatura; (5) metropolitans; (6) bishops and all those listed as ordinaries in 1917 CIC c.198; (7) vicars-general; (8) superiors and provincial superiors of the institutes of exempt clerical religious.

Patriarchs, primates, metropolitans, archbishops, and bishops are classified as major prelates. Minor or subordinate prelates are those who have quasi-episcopal jurisdiction. The Code of Canon Law, when treating of minor prelates, speaks only of abbots *nullius* and prelates *nullius.* However, superiors in clerical exempt institutes as well as certain members of the household of the pope also are classified as minor prelates.

The title prelate is also granted by the Holy See to some clerics as an honorary distinction without jurisdiction. They do not enjoy any special office because of the prelacy but are entitled to the honorific rights of prelates.

Bibliography: J. ABBO and J. HANNAN, *The Sacred Canons* (St. Louis 1960). J. NABUCO, *Ius pontificalium: Introductio in caeremoniale episcoporum* (Tournai 1956).

[R. J. MURPHY]

PRÉMARE, JOSEPH HENRI DE

Missionary and sinologist; b. Cherbourg, July 17, 1666; d. Macau, Sept. 17, 1736. He was admitted into the Society of Jesus on Sept. 17, 1683, and departed for the mission to Middle China in 1698, where he labored principally in the province of Guangxi. Prémare was confined with his fellow missionaries to Canton after Emperor Yongtching forbade further Christian proselytizing. Another imperial edict exiled him to Macau. In his banishment he studied the language and literature of China, and his success in appreciating their subtlety and beauty is shown in his major work, *Notitia linguae sinicae* (Malacca 1831; Eng. tr. J. G. Bridgman, Canton 1847). Here he explains the rules for the use of the Chinese vulgar (*siao shue*) and literary (*wen tchang*) language. He also translated several pieces of Chinese poetry, including the Chinese tragedy *L'orphelin de la maison de Tschao* (1731). The Jesuit Joachim BOUVET proposed a theory of figurism, holding that Chinese characters suggest allusion to Christian mysteries. Prémare defended it in *Vestiges choisis des principaux dogmes de la religion chrétienne, extraits des anciens livres chinois* (Paris 1878). J. B. du Halde has published some of Prémare's letters in *Lettres édifiantes et curieuses* (Paris 1711) and *Description de la Chine et de la Tartarie chinoise* (Paris 1735; Eng. tr. E. Cave, 2 v. London 1738–41). Others are to be found in the Bibliothèque Nationale, Paris.

Bibliography: L. PFISTER, *Notices biographiques et bibliographiques sur les Jésuites de l'ancienne mission de Chine 1552–1773,* 2 v. (Shanghai 1932–34). C. SOMMERVOGEL et al., *Bibliothèque de la Compagnie de Jésus,* 11 v. (Brussels-Paris 1890–1932; v. 12, suppl. 1960) 6:1196–1201. M. EDER, *Lexikon für Theologie und Kirche,* ed. J. HOFER and K. RAHNER, 10 v. (2d, new ed. Freiburg 1957–65) 8:721.

[J. S. SCHWARZ]

PREMONSTRATENSIAN RITE

The liturgical usages proper to the Premonstratensian Order. They are not properly a rite.

History. Liturgical reform was integral to the reform of religious life in all medieval communities from Cluny to the mendicants. Thus, the particular forms of expression for consecrated life from the eleventh to the thirteenth centuries—the eremetical (CARTHUSIANS), the monastic (CISTERCIANS), the canonical (PREMONSTRATENSIANS) and the mendicants (especially DOMINICANS and CARMELITES)—legislated and enforced liturgical reform as strictly as the other aspects of their ritualized life. Liturgical uniformity was seen as necessary to the success of reform in these orders. Contrary to the prevailing opinion held throughout the twentieth century, liturgical uniformity among the Premonstratensians was not as strictly enforced as it was among the Cistercians. The early growth of the Premonstratensians was as much due to already existing canonical and collegiate chapters accepting the *ordo vivendi praemonstratensis* as it was to new foundations. These existing communities already were united by usages proper to the non-monastic liturgy of canons. They could not be expected to jettison their liturgical libraries immediately upon accepting the Premonstratensian way of life.

In the course of the second half of the twelfth century, the long and increasingly centralizing administration of HUGH OF FOSSE, successor to the founder St. NORBERT and first abbot of Premontre, the influence of Cistercian government and liturgy on the Premonstratensians and papal encouragement towards uniformity all contributed to greater, but never complete, liturgical uniformity throughout the order.

The oldest *Ordinarius* or basic description of the order's liturgy dates from the last quarter of the 12th century. In the Middle Ages it was a strong factor in maintaining continuity and solidarity throughout the order and served as a principal source for the spiritual formation of its members.

The liturgical books of the order were revised in the 15th and 16th centuries. In the wake of the Tridentine reform of the liturgy, all orders having a liturgical tradition of less than two hundred years were obliged to follow the revised Roman rite. In 1574 and 1578, during the administration of Abbot General Jean Despruets, the *processionale, breviarium,* and *missale* of the order were reprinted on the basis of authentic medieval manuscripts. In the same period, however, it became more and more the tendency to imitate the new Roman rite. The general chapter of 1618 voted to maintain the order's liturgy, but did adapt more Roman elements (*breviarium* of 1621, *missale* of 1622 and *Liber Ordinarius* of 1628). This hybrid liturgy was further adapted in 1739 and remained in force until the end of the 19th century.

In response to the liturgical renewal initiated by SOLESMES and PIUS X, the order decided to review and reintegrate elements of its medieval liturgy. A chant commission was established in 1904 and new liturgical books published: a graduale in 1910, a revised calendar in 1924, a *breviarium* in 1930, a *processionale* in 1932, and an *antiphonarium* in 1934. Throughout this period, the general chapters debated the value of an integral reintegration of medieval usage against one adapted to 20th–century life, especially in the many parishes served by Premonstratensians. The more adapted reintegration marks the *Liber Ordinarius* published in 1949.

The General Chapter of 1976 decided to retain its right to proper usages, but in conformity with the principles of liturgical renewal set forth by the Second Vatican Council. A revised calendar was approved in 1977 and a *Thesaurus Liturgiae Praemonstratensis* for the celebration of Mass and the Liturgy of the Hours appeared in 1988. In practice, almost all communities follow the Roman liturgy according to the order's calendar.

Description. The order's liturgical tradition places heavy emphasis on the celebration of the paschal mystery. In the pre-Vatican II usages, the expulsion of penitents and their reconciliation on Holy Thursday were solemnly celebrated. The Easter octave was celebrated with the greatest solemnity. Post-baptismal Easter Vespers was celebrated each day of the octave. The Order had an eighth "O antiphon," *O Virgo virginum*. The medieval Christmas sequence, *Laetabundus*, was retained. The rites of the *Ordo Romanus Antiquus* (*c.* 950) were retained in the celebrations of Candlemas, Ash Wednesday, Holy Week, and the Rogation Days. Some elements in the rites for the dying and burial went back to the Carolingian period. The older Mass rite was a canonical adaptation of the Carolingian version of the *Ordo Romanus primus* (Andrieu's *Ordo Romanus 5*) and was an important witness to the Romano-Germanic tradition of the Western liturgy. The order retained a proper chant dialect that was largely retrieved through the work of the chant commission established in 1904.

The most important change in the order's liturgy since Vatican II has had to do with its spirit. The hallmark of Premonstratensian liturgical prayer has shifted from that of *splendor cultus* to ecclesial prayer *in medio populi*. Throughout the twentieth century many Premonstratensian abbeys in Western Europe, especially Berne in the Netherlands and Tongerloo and Averbode in Belgium, were centers of liturgical renewal.

Bibliography: A. D. CIFERNI, *The Post-Vatican II Discussion of the So-Called Premonstratensian Rite: A Question of Liturgical*

St. Norbert Abbey, De Pere, Wisconsin.

Pluriformity, Ph.D. dissertation (Notre Dame 1978). P. LEFEVRE, *La Liturgie de Premontre* (Louvain 1957). A. A. KING, *Liturgies of the Religious Orders* (Milwaukee 1955). B. LUYKX, ''Essai sur les sources de l'Ordo Missae premontre,'' *Analecta Praemonstratensia* 23 (1947) 35–89. L.C. VAN DYCK and HERMAN JANSSENS, *Woordenlijst betreffende de Orde van Premontre* (Averbode 2000) 35.

[A. D. CIFERNI]

PREMONSTRATENSIANS

An order called also Norbertines, Canons Regular of Prémontré, and (in England) White Canons, the Premonstratensians (O. Praem.) were founded by St. NORBERT OF XANTEN at Prémontré, France, in 1120. This religious community was intended by its founder to blend the contemplative with the active religious life; it was one of the canonical orders of the 12th century that provided a link between the strictly contemplative life of the preceding period and the life of the MENDICANT ORDERS of the 13th century.

Foundation and Growth. At the outset Norbert's associates, attracted to him by his preaching and exemplary life, did not deem it necessary to form a new order or adopt a special rule; they considered the counsels and example of their director sufficient for their spiritual needs. When Norbert convinced them of the need for a definite rule of life, the Rule of ST. AUGUSTINE was a natural choice. Many of the members of the original Prémontré community were canons, and some reformed houses of canons had already adopted Augustine's rule. The canons of Prémontré then assumed the white habit customarily worn by the canons regular of that day. The first community, numbering about 40, made their profession of vows on Christmas 1121.

Following the example of other communities of canons, Norbert did not contemplate a centralized order. However, Bl. HUGH OF FOSSE, Norbert's successor at Prémontré and the first abbot of the original foundation, perfected the organization of the new religious institute with the adoption of practices and rules that were for the most part Cistercian in origin. Hugh persuaded the other Premonstratensian abbots of the need for some kind of federation of their otherwise autonomous houses.

With the help of papal bulls, culminating in that of Alexander III in 1177, the Order grew into a well-defined organization with an abbot general (the abbot of Prémontré), an annual general chapter of the heads of the various houses, the system of filiation of houses, and a method of visitation, all adopted largely from the system at CÎTEAUX with accommodations according to the peculiar needs of canons. The houses of Saxony, the chief of which was Magdeburg, resisted this attempt at centralization by appealing to the views and policies of Norbert. Traditionally, the Magdeburg-oriented houses also emphasized the active apostolate more than did the western European abbeys, where Cistercian influence was more pronounced.

In the 12th century the order spread rapidly over practically all of Europe and, with the Crusades, even to Palestine, where three Premonstratensian foundations had been made by 1145. The famous Abbey of FLOREFFE (Belgium) was founded as early as 1122, and St. Martin of Laon (France) became a Norbertine house when the church there was accepted by the Order in 1124. In the same year the Abbey of St. Michael was established in Antwerp, largely as the result of the successful preaching of Norbert's canons against the heresy of TANCHELM, who denied the Real Presence. It is because of his victory over this heresy that Norbert is often portrayed with a monstrance in his hands and with a figure representing Tanchelm under his feet.

Many of the abbeys that were founded during Norbert's time or shortly thereafter have either survived the turmoil of the centuries or have been refounded and still flourish today. In Belgium, the abbeys of Averbode, Tongerlo, Grimbergen, Park, and Postel are among the great Premonstratensian houses of the 20th century. Berne abbey in the Netherlands is the oldest continuously existing abbey in that country. It was founded as a house of Premonstratensian canons in 1134, the year that Norbert died. Henry Zdik, Bishop of Olmutz (d. 1150) was responsible for the erection of the great Abbey of Mount Sion at STRAHOV, Prague, in 1140. This abbey, along with several other Premonstratensian houses in the Czech Republic, Slovakia, and Hungary, were suppressed by the Communist government in 1950. Since the fall of Communism in those countries, these abbeys have been reopened and religious life has been restored.

By the middle of the 13th century, according to a conservative estimate, there were at least 500 abbeys or priories located in France, Belgium, Germany, Austria, Switzerland, Hungary, Spain, Greece, Palestine, Poland, Portugal, the British Isles, and the Scandinavian countries. Many of these were founded as double monasteries by colonies from established houses; others were existing communities, especially of canons regular, which were incorporated into the order. Foundations and donations were received from bishops and nobles who were interested in Church reform. In 1122, for example, St. Godfrey, Count of Cappenberg (1097–1127) ceded his vast properties to the order and received the habit himself. In 1139 Ven. Louis of Arnstein founded a magnificent monastery in his feudal palace. Some bishops invited Premonstratensians to take the place of their cathedral canons. At Laon and Magdeburg secular canons were replaced by canons of Prémontré. In some instances, as in the case of St. Alexis (Rome) and of St. James (Mainz), communities of monks were replaced by these reformed canons.

During this period of great fervor and growth, the Premonstratensians were particularly noted for their *xenodochia* (hospices), where the poor and the sick were assisted and pilgrims housed and fed. In this work the canons had the assistance of Premonstratensian nuns, whose communities were attached to most of the abbeys in the early period. While Norbert himself always remained an active preacher, the foundations that he made before Magdeburg were essentially contemplative and frequently located in isolated places. The original statutes provided that the Premonstratensians were not to serve parish churches except those attached to the abbeys. The numerous requests from ordinaries and the need for priests in churches located in the vicinity of Norbertine foundations led to a relaxation of this regulation concerning parochial ministry. In 1188 Clement III formally approved parish administration by the Premonstratensian canons. The abbeys soon became training centers for clerics, secular as well as regular, and eventually schools of humanities were established.

The Order's first century and a half witnessed not only great expansion, but also a rich harvest in spiritual and intellectual life. Among the saintly figures, in addition to those previously mentioned, were: Bl. Ricvera of Clastre, who aided Norbert in organizing the nuns of the order; St. GILBERT, who in 1150 founded the monastery of Neuffontaines (France) and became its first abbot; Bl. Hroznata, martyr (d. 1217), a member of the Bohemian nobility who gave himself and his possessions to the order, thus founding the Abbey of Teplá (Czech Republic); St. Evermode (d. 1178), a companion of Norbert who became provost of Magdeburg and later bishop of Ratzeburg; and St. Herman Joseph, canon of Steinfeld, (d. *c.* 1241), one of the earliest promoters of devotion to the Sacred Heart, who later became the patron of youth in his native section of Germany. Noteworthy among those who made important contributions to the intellectual tradition of the Premonstratensians were Gervase of Chichester (fl. 1170), Adam Scotus (Dryburgh), and PHILIP OF HARVENGT. Gervase was one of the more notable abbots general in the order's long history. During his lifetime he acquired a reputation for zeal and learning, and in 1215 he was called to Rome by Innocent III to assist at the Fourth Lateran Council. Gervase was eventually named bishop of Sées (Normandy) in 1220. Through the influence of such learned men, the Order of Prémontré contributed significantly to the medieval renaissance.

Decline and Recovery. By the late 13th century the first symptoms of decline in religious fervor appeared in the order. The wealth of some of the houses and the practice of *peculium* (funds for private use) were factors in this deterioration, and no doubt the increasing pastoral activity beyond the walls of the monasteries cooled the claustral spirit. The large land holdings of many abbeys led to the abuses of commendatory abbots, many of whom had no interest in the material or spiritual welfare of the communities whose properties they administered. Then, too, on some occasions plagues depopulated entire communities.

During the Reformation every Norbertine foundation in England was lost as well as the houses in Ireland and Scotland. A similar fate befell abbeys in northern Germany, Frisia, Hungary, and the Scandinavian countries. In the 16th century, as the Catholic reform spread throughout Spain, France, and the rest of Catholic Europe, the Premonstratensian Order also experienced a revival. The Norbertine Nicolas PSEAUME, Bishop of Verdun, was one of the influential figures of the Council of Trent. Especially noteworthy within the order was the reform of Lorraine, fostered by Servais de Lairuels (1560–1631), which spread through the monasteries of Lorraine and France. Eventually, by pontifical decree, the Congregation of Ancient Observance of Prémontré was withdrawn from the jurisdiction of the general chapter and authorized to govern itself by a separate chapter at which the abbot general or his personal delegate always presided. In 1630 new statutes based on decrees of the Council of Trent were adopted for houses of the common observance. So fruitful were these reforms that the 17th century might well be called the renaissance of the Order. Not only was there a rebirth of religious fervor in existing Premonstratensian houses, but some monasteries that had gone out of existence were reestablished, especially in Hungary. This was the period also when houses of study were established near the great European universities in order to provide for the higher education of the canons. The ancient privileges pertaining to the apostolate, previously granted by earlier pontiffs, were reconfirmed by Pope Benedict XIV in 1750.

The French Revolution and its aftermath, as well as the monarchical reforms in Austria, almost completely demolished the order. After 1791 not a single abbey remained of the 94 that had existed in France. The invasion of Belgium and the Rhenish lands by the revolutionary armies brought destruction or suppression. Some years previously, Joseph II of Austria sequestered Premonstratensian abbeys when the canons refused to conform to his decrees regulating the training and activities of religious within his realm. By 1820 the only Premonstratensian houses remaining in all Christendom were those in Spain, and a small number that had survived in Austria-Hungary. The Spanish monasteries were suppressed after the revolution there of 1833.

Modern Development. Revival in the 19th century was extremely slow. In the 1830s, after the separation of Belgium from Holland and the granting of religious freedom in the former colony, the surviving Premonstratensians reconstituted the houses of Averbode, Grimbergen, Park, Postel, and TONGERLOO. In France, the Abbey of FRIGOLET was founded in 1858, and the Abbey of Mondaye was restored in 1859 by canons from Grimbergen. Similarly, in 1857 there was a reestablishment of common life at Heeswijk, Holland, of Berne Abbey, which was the house destined to undertake the first permanent foundation in North America. General growth, however, was hampered by the lack of unity.

After the Abbey of Prémontré was suppressed in 1790, Jean-Baptiste L'Ecuy, the last abbot, was unable to function as abbot general until his death in 1834. After 1834 there was no abbot-general until a general chapter was convened in 1869 and Jerome Zeidler, the abbot of Strahov, was elected. He died before his confirmation by the Holy See. In 1883 a general chapter, convened in Vienna, again selected the abbot of Strahov, Sigismund Stary. To facilitate the handling of business before the Holy See, it was decided to have the procurator general reside in Rome. The election of Gummarus Crets of Averbode as abbot general in 1922 was evidence of the success of the revival in the Low Countries, where the abbeys are the largest in the order and have been most active in the missionary field and the liturgical apostolate. In 1937 the procurator general, Hubert A. Noots, a canon of Tongerloo Abbey, was elected to succeed Crets as abbot general. He separated the generalate from the administration of a particular abbey by taking up his residence in Rome.

In 2001 the order consisted of six circaries (provinces) organized along language lines. Within these six circaries there were thirty-six independent houses or canonries located on six continents in twenty-three countries. In addition to these houses there were several houses of sisters, under the jurisdiction of local bishops. There were also missions and dependent priories in various countries around the world.

The first permanent Premonstratensian foundation in North America resulted from an invitation in 1893 from the Bishop of Green Bay, Wis., Sebastian G. Messmer. He asked the canons of Berne Abbey to send missionaries to his diocese to combat the heresy of Joseph René Villatte among the Belgian settlers in northeastern Wisconsin. Bernard Henry Pennings was chosen to lead the first missionary group of three; the small community was later augmented by eight other religious. By February of 1898 the heresy was a dead issue, and Pennings turned his attention to the establishment of a Norbertine foundation in De Pere, Wis. Eventually, there were four independent Norbertine houses in the United States: St. Norbert Abbey (De Pere, Wis.), Daylesford Abbey (Paoli, Pa.), Immaculate Conception Priory (Claymont, Del.), and St. Michael's Abbey (Orange, Cal.).

Government, Spirit, and Apostolate. Supreme authority rests with the general chapter composed of the abbots and delegates from each autonomous Premonstratensian house. The general chapter regularly convenes every six years, and in the intervening period the enforcement of the will of the chapter is entrusted to the abbot general, who is elected for life, and his council (Definitory). The abbot general is represented in each circary by a vicar general. In a non-centralized order such as the Premonstratensian, the individual abbots enjoy considerable autonomous power in the administration of the spiritual and temporal affairs of their own houses. While the order had already received many papal privileges in the 12th century, it was in 1409 that Alexander V formally granted exemption from episcopal jurisdiction.

The Premonstratensian order is composed of priests, clerics, lay brothers, canonesses and lay sisters. The canonesses live a cloistered life. In the 19th and 20th centuries communities of third-order sisters were established in some countries of Europe to do work that did not involve a strictly cloistered life. While the order has for many centuries had lay third-order members, more recently there has been a move toward accepting oblate members and associate members who are more closely involved with the life and work of the order.

Norbertine life is intensely liturgical, with a strong paschal character most evident in the celebration of post-baptismal Easter Vespers and its proper chants in Eastertide. The so-called *Premonstratensian Rite* rooted in the medieval liturgical practice of Franco-Rhenish collegiate churches has largely been replaced since Vatican II with the renewed Roman Rite according to the calendar proper to the order. The order's earlier commitment to *splendor cultus* in the canonical tradition has been superseded by a commitment to ecclesial prayer *in medio populi*.

The Norbertine apostolate has varied throughout its history. Norbert at first envisioned preaching as the chief ministry of his disciples, but a diversification set in even in his lifetime, since it became customary for the order to assume work arising from the needs of the area in which the houses were located. The Norbertines of Belgium and France emphasize missionary activity and specialized apostolates, such as retreats, teaching, and the liturgical apostolate. In Austria and Germany the traditional parochial ministry prevails. Many members of the restored Hungarian, Czech, and Slovak houses are engaged in parochial ministry. In the U.S. the Premonstratensians until the mid-1970s were mostly active in the field of education, as well as in parochial ministry. Since then there has been a shift to view the abbeys as spiritual and liturgical centers. While teaching is still part of the work of some abbeys, activity in others has centered on retreats, spiritual direction and opportunities for prayer.

Bibliography: F. PETIT, *The Order of Canons Regular of Prémontré*, tr. and rev. B. T. MACKIN (De Pere, Wis. 1961). H. M. COLVIN, *The White Canons in England* (Oxford 1951). F. PETIT, *La Spiritualité des Prémontrés aux XIIe et XIIe siècles* (Paris 1947). N. BACKMUND, *Geschichte des Prämonstratenserordens* (Grafenau 1986). N. BACKMUND, *Monasticon Praemonstratense*, 3 v. (Straubing 1949–56). B. ARDURA, *Prémontré: Histoire et Spiritualité* (Publications de l'Université de Saint-Etienne 1995). D.-M. DAUZET, *La voie canoniale dans l'Église aujourd'hui* (Namur 1994).

[R. J CORNELL/T. J. ANTRY]

PRÉMONTRÉ, MONASTERY OF

From the Latin *praemonstratum* (the place shown forth), cradle of the Order of Canons Regular of Premontre or PREMONSTRATENSIANS (Norbertines), near Coucy, Aisne, former diocese of Laon, now Soissons. The land was given by Bishop Bartholomew of Laon to NORBERT OF XANTEN, who founded the monastery there (1120–21). The foundation was originally a double cloister. In 1128, Norbert was succeeded by HUGH OF FOSSE, an able organizer, and the order grew. The abbots of Prémontré became generals of the order, and annual general chapters were held there. The abbey was ruled by zealous abbots, but on three occasions free elections were interfered with, when Cardinals Francis of Pisa, D'Este (1535–71), and Richelieu (1636–42), were named commendatory abbots. The survival of this crisis and the reform of the order was attributed to Abbot Jean Despruets, freely elected in 1572. The abbey added several large buildings in the 17th and 18th centuries. It had 80 canons when it was suppressed in the French Revolution (1790). The large medieval church and Gothic chapterhouse were demolished, and subsequent attempts (1843, 1856) to rebuild the monastery failed. The bishop of Soissons sold the property, and it became an asylum of the Department of Aisne. The three 18th-century buildings surrounding the court of honor (the *praelatura*, the provisor's offices and the residence for older confreres) have been preserved as historic monuments while serving as offices for the asylum. The ruins of the first abbey church of St. John the Baptist built by St. Norbert have been incorporated into a wall of the property.

Bibliography: C. L. HUGO, *S. Ordinis Praemonstratensis annales*, 2 v. (Nancy 1734–36) 1:2–58. *Gallia Christiana*, v.1–13 (Paris 1715–85) 9:642–662. C. TAIÉE, *Prémontré*, 2 v. (Laon 1872–73). L. H. COTTINEAU, *Répertoire topobibliographique des abbayes et prieurés*, 2 v. (Mâcon 1935–39) 2:2359–61. B. RAVARY, *Prémontré dans la tourmente révolutionnaire* (Paris 1955). N. BACKMUND, *Monasticon Praemonstratense*, 3 v. (Straubling 1949–56) 2:521–530. P. BONNET, *Les Constructions de l'Ordre de Premontre en France aux XVIIe et XVIIIe siecles. Bibliotheque de la Societe Francaise d'Archeologie* 15 (Paris 1983). M. PLOUVIER, *L'Abbaye de Premontre aux XVIIe et XVIIIe Siecles. Histoire d'une Reconstruciton. Bibliotheca Analectorum Praemonstratensium* 16 (Louvain 1985).

[A. D. CIFERNI]

PREMOTION, PHYSICAL

A translation of the Latin *praemotio physica,* an expression that is itself contrived, connotative of controversy, and pleonastic. Historically it is tied to the Thomist side in the controversies of the *CONGREGATIO DE AUXILIIS* (1598–1607); yet it was in fact thrust upon Thomists as part of the case to be defended [see J. H. Serry, *Historiae Congregationum de Auxiliis* (5 v., 2d ed. Venice 1740) 2:171 B; 4:515 C].

Historical Background. The expression ''physical premotion'' certainly had arisen in theological circles at Salamanca earlier than the *Congregatio.* It is found, for example, in a work of Juan Vicente (Asturicensis) completed in 1589 and entitled *De origine gratiae* (MSS in Archivum Generale OP, Rome, XIV-366, fol. 816r–817v). In his rejection of the notion, as in the usage of the *De Auxiliis,* the formula used ordinarily is *praedeterminatio physica* (*see* PREDETERMINATION).

The reality underlying both expressions is a special divine causal influence upon all created causes, including man in his voluntary acts. The explication of the expressions is closely bound to the theological contexts in which they were disputed, viz, PREDESTINATION and FREE WILL, the efficacy of divine GRACE and human freedom, and divine CAUSALITY and the act of SIN. Yet the causal influence designated by physical premotion can also be subjected to a philosophical analysis in terms of the creature's dependence on God.

St. THOMAS AQUINAS proves that God is the cause of all causes' causing in three ways: as ultimate end, the source of all finality; as source and conserver of the operative, forms by which agent causes are constituted; and as applying or moving these operative powers to actual exercise (*Summa theologiae* 1a, 105.5). Physical premotion refers only to the last. In St. Thomas's terminology, the simple term motion would suffice; his followers accepted the redundancy of the complex term as expressing the meaning of *motus.* The causal influence is ''motion'' because it is transitory and also because it affects the agent's power to act. It is called ''pre-'' motion, or a previous motion, to indicate its causal priority with regard to the actual operation of the created agent. It is called ''physical'' with a view of the human will, to emphasize that the will faculty is interiorly affected by it.

By its redundancy the term opposes the Molinist conception of God's causality on the free act. Luis de MOLINA professed his incomprehension of St. Thomas's statement concerning the application of the created agent to its act [*Concordia* 14.13.26 (Paris 1876) 152]. He taught instead a divine causal influence only on the free act itself, and this coordinated with the will's causality of its own act. The two causalities are simultaneous, hence ''simultaneous concurrence,'' as opposed to premotion (*see* CONCURRENCE, DIVINE). For Molina, the only causal influence antecedent to the will-act is moral, that is, through the object of choice. The Molinists, throughout the *De Auxiliis* and subsequently, were at pains to interpret physical premotion as a kind of natural impulse, taking physical to mean natural and thus as necessitating the will. The Thomists, on the other hand, insisted on the insufficiency of the *SCIENTIA MEDIA*, the cornerstone of the Molinist position, to defend the infallibility of God's knowledge and of His causality; in their analysis, a motion that is merely moral and simultaneous concurrence are what make the *scientia media* indispensable to MOLINISM.

Premotion as Motion. Physical premotion is neither God's causality itself nor the causality of the created AGENT. God's causality is identical with Himself, with the operations of His intelligence and will with regard to creatures, and for this reason it is called His power (ST 1a, 25.1 ad 4). But this causality does not pass outside of God as does a transient action, for, if it did, God would be perfected by the developing process. The divine causality is itself immanent what does ''pass outside of God'' are the effects of His causality. Physical premotion is one of these—an acknowledgment resting upon God's being the first cause of all the acts of creatures as their first mover.

In receiving its own grade of being from God, every agent has a certain type of action that is proportionate or connatural to itself. But no created agent is identical with the exercise of its own activity. This is experientially plain from the transitoriness of actions and the perdurance of the agent with its operative form or power. The fact is seen also as an intelligible necessity: identity between agent and action presupposes identity between ESSENCE AND EXISTENCE. Thus only God is identical with His own action; only He is first mover. Every other being, thus every other agent, is composed of POTENCY AND ACT on the level of substantial existence, and again on the level of accidental existence, where action properly belongs. There is necessarily, then, a real distinction between an agent with an operative form and the actual exercise of its operation. Thus every agent is dependent on God as first mover, the source by which its potentiality to operation is actualized. Whether or not other movers are involved, God's causality always is. Other movers function only insofar as they themselves are reduced from potency to act; they are moved movers. The unique effect attributable to the divine causality is thus the created agent's overcoming its potentiality. It is this that is indicated in the term premotion (see Thomas Aquinas, *In two sent.* 37.2.2; *De pot.* 3.7 ad 7; *C. gent.* 3.67, 66, 89; *Summa theologiae* 1a2ae, 109.1; *In lib. de caus.* 1).

In English the term motion is active. Its active sense can be used to connote the reference of this effect to its source, God's causality as first mover, and also to indicate that God applies and moves the operative forms or powers to actual operation (ST 1a, 105.5). The same effect, however, might well be called MOTION in the sense of the Latin *motus,* according to which the action of the mover is motion in the subject moved (see Aristotle, *Phys.* 202a 13–22). This passive sense connotes the passivity of the created agent, viz, that it must receive the divine causal influence to undergo a transition from POTENCY to actual operation. Because it is not identical with its own operation, the created agent receives the divine effect that is premotion; it cannot communicate this to itself, for its passivity must be overcome by something extrinsic to itself. With the insight provided by this distinction one may avoid the error of seeing premotion as the anticipation of, or the substitute for, the creature's action. It is neither of these; rather it is the creature's passage to action. This action is the term of the premotion as this brings about the ultimate realization of the operative form, conjoining it to its actual operation. The action once begun, this formality of the creature's dependence on God ceases; the moment of action-motion ceases as the term is realized.

A merely simultaneous divine concurrence would have to be centered on the action itself, and thus would leave unexplained the agent's passage to activity. The real distinction between potency and act in regard to this activity is what causes St. Thomas to affirm: ''No matter how perfect any nature, corporeal or spiritual, may be, it cannot proceed to its action unless it be moved by God'' (ST 1a2ae, 109.1). And because this real distinction is found in the ontological structure of the creature, he further states that the autonomous power to move itself to act could not be conferred on any creature; this would be to transform it into the primary source of existence and act, to make it God (*De pot.* 3.7 ad 7).

Premotion as Prior. For St. Thomas to speak of motion is already to indicate a priority; this is what makes the term premotion itself redundant. But the priority in question must be properly understood. Actually it is a causal anteriority that permits a threefold distinction. It is verified first with reference to the action of the agent, the term of the premotion. Just as the agent itself, with its permanent operative form or power, is the cause of its own action, and thus its power is causally prior to the action, so the premotion by which the agent becomes ultimately active is causally anterior to the action. Certainly this premotion is not the temporal anticipation of the action itself.

The priority can be made more precise by reflecting on the one reality that is the agent's motion. There is a sense of priority here, but not a real priority, since the one reality cannot be prior to itself. Rather there is a conceptual priority: the connotation of origin in God's causality is prior to the connotation of the creature's passive passage to operation; the reference to God's giving is prior to the reference to the agent's receiving.

Finally, while the priority of premotion is emphasized to reject a merely simultaneous divine concurrence, it does not exclude simultaneous concurrence. God's causal influence on the agent continues during the exercise of the agent's action. For this action is a reality, and no reality perdures without God's continuing causality. But this causal influence is no longer a previous concurrence; the agent's own causal energies are actually engaged; the agent is simultaneously causing the action in subordination to the divine causality, which is thus designated simultaneous.

Premotion as Physical. This designation refers to the divine causal influence on the WILL. It does not mean that a corporeal or a compulsive necessitating impulse is exercised on the will. The connotation of the term physical is rather that, for the exercise of the will-act, man is dependent on God as first mover just as is every other created agent. The divine causal influence is received in, and exercised on, the faculty itself; the potency of the will to the exercise of its action is not overcome simply by the attraction of the object proposed by the intellect. This attraction is designated as a moral motion, in the sense that the object proposed functions as an END drawing the will and also determining the kind of act the will is to exercise. Such causality is necessary for the will to function, since the will is an APPETITE whose functioning is consequent upon knowledge; i.e., it is an elicited appetite. When, therefore, God influences the intellect to apprehend an object as good and desirable, the intellect's causality on the will-act is called a moral motion (ST 1a2ae, 9.1; 10.1–27). As has been said, it is the only antecedent causality upon the will faculty that is admitted by Molinists.

Efficient Causality. For St. Thomas, however, this moral premotion, though admittedly present, does not suffice to explain the will's activity. In his teaching, the object itself is not the efficient cause of the will's actual exercise; it remains a moral or final cause. Thus any causal influence on this level is insufficient to explain the effective exercise of activity (ST 1a, 82.2, 4; 1a2ae, 9.1; 10.2.). Because the will is in potency to actual operation, efficient (physical) causality must be exercised on the faculty itself.

In its natural choices, the will itself exercises such causality. It does so by accepting the object proposed by the judgment of reason, by following this as the last decisive practical decision to act. In so doing, it accepts not only some good to be chosen but its own act of willing, the choosing itself. The basis for this power to will or not to will is the same as the general dominion of the will over all objects of choice. The will is the faculty of human nature for its own good, its fulfillment. Every object proposed is a concrete good that contributes only to some degree to this fulfillment. Among the goods that can be chosen is the very act of choice itself. Thus the will has power over its own act, to will or not to will. When it exercises that power, it effectively causes its own act, it moves itself (ST 1a2ae, 9.3). But the exercise of this causality is the will's very act of choice. By choosing, by acting, the will causes its own act. At the point of choosing, however, the will is not identical with its choice; it is in potency to it. Like every other agent the will is subordinated to, and dependent on, God as first mover. It cannot exercise its own act; it thus cannot cause its own act, except insofar as it receives the divine causal influence, a premotion directed to the faculty itself. The influence of reason and the object proposed by the intellect do not effectively overcome the will's suspension from act. Thus the premotion required is physical.

In fact, the will is more plainly in need of divine assistance than is any other power precisely because no other mover can directly act on the will (ST 1a, 105.4; 106.2; 111.2; 1a2ae, 80.1; *De malo* 3.3; *De ver.* 22.9). With the help of God's premotion the will is reduced from potency to act; in acting, it chooses, and it chooses its own act. The premotion does not anticipate the will's act; it makes possible the act's exercise. Nor does it deprive the will of its own causality; rather, in bringing about the transition to act, it makes this causality effective. "The will, when beginning to make a new choice, is changed from its previous disposition in the sense that it was previously in potency to making a choice and then actually is making it. This change has its source in some mover, namely, in that the will moves itself to its act, and in that it is also moved by an exterior agent, namely, God. It is not moved by necessity" (*De malo* 6.1 ad 17).

Freedom. The last statement of this text is important in that it suggests the problem of FREEDOM and physical promotion. But the suggestion is somewhat misplaced in this context. The problem of freedom and the divine causality is more properly associated with premotion as this is also predetermination. Simply from the viewpoint of the will's need for physical premotion, there is no conflict with freedom. The will itself is truly the cause of its own act in choosing. Its acceptance of the decision of reason as final, and thus its causality of its own act, does not make this act necessary; it remains a choice. The object and the choice itself appeal to the will's thrust toward human fulfillment; they do not exhaust it, since they are concrete particular goods. When the will is actually engaged by its choice, its dominance over object and act is actualized. Thus the will, when choosing to act, is not acting under necessity but is exercising its freedom. Since, then, physical premotion does bring about the will's exercise of its own act, such promotion is not opposed to freedom. On the contrary, premotion brings this freedom to fruition in the act of choice that it causes the will to cause.

See Also: CAUSALITY, DIVINE; BÁÑEZ AND BAÑEZIANISM; MOLINISM.

Bibliography: Thomistic works. R. GARRIGOU-LAGRANGE, *God: His Existence and His Nature,* tr. B. ROSE, 2 v. (St. Louis 1934–36) v.2; *Dictionnaire de théologie catholique,* ed. A. VACANT, 15 v. (Paris 1903–50; Tables générales 1951–) 13.1:31–77. M. CANAL, "El Molinismo impugnado por Vitoria antes de nacer Molina," *Angelicum* 9 (1932) 447–481. T. C. O'BRIEN, "El enigma de francisco de Araújo," *Ciencia Tomista* 89 (1962) 221–226; 90 (1963) 3–79. V. D. CARRO, "La crítica histórica ante las controversias sobre la gracia en el siglo XVI," *ibid.* 87 (1960) 39–96; "Cayetano y la tradición teológica medieval en los problemas de la gracia," *ibid.* 54 (1936) 289–311; 55 (1936) 5–32, 260–285; 56 (1937) 231–242. B. DE HEREDIA, "El maestro Domingo Báñez," *ibid.* 47 (1933) 26–39, 162–179; "El Maestro Mancio del Corpus Christi," *ibid.* 51 (1935) 7–103. N. DEL PRADO, *De gratia et libero arbitrio,* 3 v. (Fribourg 1907) v.2–3. A. M. DUMMERMUTH, *S. Thomas et Doctrina Praemotionis Physicae* (Paris 1886); *Defensio doctrinae S. Thomae Aquinatis de praemotione physica* (Paris 1895). Molinist works. J. HELLIN, *Theologia naturalis* (Cursus philosophicus 5; *Biblioteca de autores cristianos* 60; 1960). V. FRINS, *Sancti Thomae Aquinatis O.P. doctrina de cooperatione Dei cum omni natura creata, praesertim libera* (Paris 1893). G. SCHNEEMAN, *Con-*

troversiarum de Divinae gratiae liberique arbitrii concordia initia et progressus (Freiburg 1881). L. DE MEYER, *Historiae controversiarum de divinae gratiae auxiliis I–II* (2d ed. Venice 1742). G. DE HENAO, *Litterarum Sacrarum, scientia media historice propugnata* (Lyons 1655; Salamanca 1665); *Scientia media theologice defensata* (Lyons 1674).

[T. C. O'BRIEN]

PRENDERGAST, EDMOND FRANCIS

Archbishop; b. Clonmel, County Tipperary, Ireland, May 3, 1843; d. Philadelphia, Pa., Feb. 27, 1918. Two brothers, Peter and Francis, were priests, and two of his sisters entered the religious life. One of his three priest uncles, Rev. Francis Carew of St. Rose of Lima's parish, Carbondale, Pa., arranged (1859) to have young Edmond begin his studies in the Philadelphia seminary for that diocese. He was ordained by Bp. James Wood on Nov. 17, 1865. After several assignments as curate and pastor, he became pastor of St. Malachy's, Philadelphia, and later was named vicar-general. On Feb. 24, 1897, he was consecrated auxiliary bishop of Philadelphia; he succeeded to the see and was enthroned as the third archbishop of Philadelphia on July 16, 1911.

Prendergast's 45 years as a parish priest in the archdiocese had given him a wide knowledge of personnel and parochial conditions. During his episcopate he increased the number of parishes from 297 to 327, provided parochial schools for 23,000 more children, erected the free West Catholic High School for boys, and opened the free Hallahan High School for girls. He doubled the capacity of the diocesan seminary by the additions of St. Edmond's Hall and the Archbishop Ryan Memorial Library, and he procured 13 religious communities for work in the archdiocese. He opened the Archbishop Ryan Memorial for the Training of Deaf Mutes, the Madonna House for Italian immigrants, a similar home for the Spanish-speaking immigrants, St. Francis Country Home for Convalescents, St. Edmond's Home for Crippled Children, a boarding home for working girls, and three new orphanages. He also relocated the Catholic Home for Destitute Children and St. Vincent's Home. He established the Catholic Home Bureau, sponsored the erection of the Misericordia Hospital, and provided a Catholic hospital for Allentown. At the cost of more than $250,000 he made the first major renovations of the cathedral. Under his direction the forerunner of the Newman Club was established at the University of Pennsylvania, Philadelphia.

Bibliography: *Installation and Investiture of Archbishop Prendergast* (Philadelphia 1912). Various references in *Records of the American Catholic Historical Society of Philadelphia* 1912–.

[H. J. NOLAN]

PRESBYTER

An official in the early Christian Church. This article treats of the use of this title, first as found in the Bible, then as employed in the early postapostolic Church.

In the Bible

After a consideration of the origin of the term, a brief description will be given of the nature of the office of the Christian presbyters as found in the New Testament.

Origin of the Term. The English word presbyter is derived, through the Latin, from the Greek word πρεσβύτερος, literally ''older'' (the comparative of πρεσβύτης, ''old man''), but often with no comparative force, ''elder.'' Although the English word priest is also derived from the same Greek term, in strict usage presbyter is not synonymous with priest.

The Septuagint sometimes uses the plural πρεσβύτεροι to translate the Hebrew word *z^eqēnîm* (Ex 19.7; Nm 11.16, 24; Ru 4.2; etc.), the Old Testament elders who had authority in the Israelite community. In the New Testament this Greek word is used for the Jewish elders, the members of one of the groups in the Sanhedrin (Mt 16.21; 21.23; 26.3; etc.). Apparently it was by analogy with this Jewish usage in Palestine that the first Christians employed this term for the officials of their own community. The Hellenistic use of the term, however, for officials of certain pagan associations may also have had some influence on New Testament usage. Greek-speaking Jews of the Diaspora do not seem to have employed the term for officials of their communities before the Christian era.

Christian Presbyters in the New Testament. According to New Testament usage Christian presbyters were dignified, mature officials of the Church (1 Pt 5.1, 5) who performed functions that would now be described as both episcopal and sacerdotal. The New Testament writers use the terms πρεσβύτερος and ἐπίσκοπος interchangeably (cf. Acts 20. 17 with v. 28; Tm 1.5 with v. 7; also the variant reading in 1 Pt 5.1–2: πρεσβυτέρους . . . ἐπισκοποῦντες). It was only in the postapostolic age that these terms took on the precise technical meanings of priest and bishop.

In an efficacious liturgical rite that included the IMPOSITION OF HANDS (Acts 14.23; 1 Tm 4.14; 5.22; 2 Tm 1.6), the candidate who satisfied the Church's moral and spiritual requirements (1 Tm 3.2–7; Ti 1.6–9) was raised to the presbyterate by Apostles, such as Paul and Barnabas (Acts 14.22), or by an episcopo-presbyter, such as Timothy (1 Tm 5.22) or Titus (Ti 1.5). The authority of the presbyter was not essentially dependent on a charismatic gift; it was mediated by ordination (2 Tm 1.6; see A. Farrer, 144–45). The sacerdotal aspect of his office was especially evident in the liturgical function he performed in the breaking of bread (see J. Colson, 42–43). The presbyter, by reason of his office, ruled and gave good example to his community (Acts 20.28; 1 Pt 5.1–3; Ti 1.5), corrected abuses (Ti 1.5), was vigilant against false teachers (Acts 20.31), anointed and prayed for the sick (Jas 5.14–15), presided at the celebration of the Eucharist (Acts 2.42; 1 Cor 10.16–21), and was an authoritative teacher and arbiter of doctrine, as seen especially in the Council of Jerusalem (Acts 15.2, 4, 6, 22, 23); if he was an episcopo-presbyter like Titus, he constituted and directed fellow presbyters (Ti 1.5–6).

See Also: BISHOP (IN THE BIBLE).

Bibliography: A. FARRER, ''Ministry in the New Testament,'' *The Apostolic Ministry*, ed. K. E. KIRK (London 1946) 115–82. C. SPICQ, *Les Epîtres pastorales de Saint Paul* (*Études Bibliques*; 1947) 84–97. A. EHRHARDT, ''Jewish and Christian Ordination,'' *The Journal of Ecclesiastical History* 5 (1954) 125–38. J. COLSON, *La Fonction diaconale aux origines de l'Église* (Bruges 1960) 41–49. E. SCHWEIZER, *Church Order in the New Testament*, tr. F. CLARK (Naperville, Ill. 1961).

[J. J. O'ROURKE]

In the Early Church

The term presbyter was used also to designate the ''companions of the disciples of the Savior'' who handed on the oral preaching of the Apostles (Papias of Hierapolis, quoted by Eusebius, *Ecclesiastical History* 3.39.4), as also bishops such as Papias himself and POLYCARP (Irenaeus, *Adversus haereses* 5.33.3). The precise meaning of the word or office it signified in the 1st and 2d centuries of the Church's existence has been the subject of considerable discussion.

From the End of the 1st to the Mid-2d Century. In CLEMENT I'S *First Epistle to the Corinthians, c.* A.D. 96, the term presbyter appears in the plural frequently. It has the meaning of ''older men'' to whom respect is due (1.3; 21.6), but also of priests who had been ''removed from the ministry *[λειτουργία]* which they performed blamelessly'' (44.5). Distinguishing clearly between the laity and the clergy, a reference is made to the malcontents ''disloyal to the presbyters'' (47.6); and they are cautioned to ''submit to the presbyters'' (57.1) and ''be at peace with the presbyters set over the flock of Christ'' (54.2). Describing the sources of authority in the Church, Clement says, ''The Apostles received the Gospel from the Lord Jesus Christ . . . the Christ sent from God'' and the Apostles ''appointed their earliest converts [ἀπαρχαί] . . . to be bishops and deacons of the future believers'' (42.1–43.1). He says the Apostles were given to understand by Christ ''that the office of bishop would give rise to strife'' (44.1); however, he calls those presbyters blessed ''who have before now completed life's journey, and taken their departure in mature age,'' for they have ''no fear of being dislodged from the place appointed to them'' (44.5).

The lack of consistency in referring to the ''bishops and deacons'' appointed by the Apostles, and the presbyters charged with the ministry of the community, to whom obedience was due, renders it difficult to form a precise idea of the organization of the Church under Clement. It has been suggested that the terms bishop and presbyter here are interchangeable, and likewise that the Church of Rome was governed by a group or college of presbyters. This latter interpretation seems to go against the tradition registered for the Church at Rome in Irenaeus, Eusebius, and the early lists of the popes. It is certainly contrary to the organization evident in the letters of IGNATIUS OF ANTIOCH (d. before 117), in which a hierarchy is described as of ''one bishop assisted by the presbytery and the deacons'' (*Ad Phil.* 4), and ''the bishop presides in the place of God while the presbyters function as the council of the Apostles'' (*Ad Magn.* 6.1). The presbyters are subject to the bishop (*Ad Ephes.* 4.1, 3; *Trall.* 12.2); and are delegated by the bishop for the functions of celebrating the Eucharist, baptizing, and holding an AGAPE (*Smyrn.* 8.1, 2).

Neither the DIDACHE nor the Shepherd of HERMAS employed the word presbyter. In the mid-2d century, Justin Martyr spoke of a president of the assembly and described his function in relation to religious cult and the life of the Christian society (*Apol.* 1.65), but did not use the word presbyter. However, Irenaeus of Lyons, before the turn of the same century, continued the post-apostolic usage and generally employed both bishop and presbyter indiscriminately, although he did distinguish at least once between bishops and priests in the Ignatian sense (*Adversus haereses* 3.3.3).

The evidence thus far available indicates that in the primitive Church the word presbyter was used generically to designate men invested with authority in the local Church, and that this authority was present through apostolic institution. Likewise, at the beginning of the 2d century there existed a monarchical type of episcopate to which the other grades, including that of the presbyter, were subordinate.

From Mid-2d to End of 3d Century. Beginning with the second half of the 2d century, the function of the presbyter in the ecclesiastical hierarchy is clear and in accord with the modern use of the word priest. While CLEMENT OF ALEXANDRIA did not speak of the hierarchy as such, he did distinguish the three grades of bishop, priest, and deacon (*Paed.* 3.11; *Strom.* 3.12; 6.13). ORIGEN did the same (*In Ezech.* 10.1; *In Ps.* 37, *Hom.* 2.6). Among the Latin Fathers, TERTULLIAN spoke in similar fashion of the priests and deacons, who came after the bishops (*De Bapt.* 17) and said that in the absence of the bishop, the priest presided over the assembly and distributed the Eucharist (*De corona* 3). Only after his defection to Montanism (after 196) did he agitate in favor of an ascendancy of the laity over the hierarchical priesthood (*De exhort. cast.* 7).

At the beginning of the 3d century, the Apostolic Tradition of Hippolytus described the organization of the Western Church in a precise fashion; and Cyprian of Carthage did the same. Cyprian described the priests as associated in the government of the diocese, which is the task of the bishop primarily; they formed his ordinary council (*Epist.* 14.4) and acted for him in cases of necessity in the administration of the Eucharist and Reconciliation (*De lapsis* 25; *Epist.* 18.1). In the East, the same hierarchical structure and function of the priest is described in the Didascalia, a document of the end of the 3d century (4.1; 9.3), and in the Apostolic Constitutions, which are a reworking of the Didascalia some time later (50.2, 27).

Bibliography: K. BIHLMEYER, ed., *Die Apostolischen Väter* (2d ed. Tübingen 1956–). J. A. KLEIST, ed. and tr., *The Epistles of St. Clement of Rome and St. Ignatius of Antioch* (*Ancient Christian Writers*, ed. J. QUASTEN et al Westminster, Md.-London 1946; *The Didache . . .* (*ibid.* 6; 1948). H. RAHNER, *Lexikon für Theologie und Kirche*, ed. J. HOFER and K. RAHNER, 10 v. (2d, new ed. Freiburg 1957–65) 8:725–26. G. BARDY, *La Théologie de l'église dès saint Clément de Rome à saint Irénée* (*Unam Sanctam* 13; Paris 1945) 40–41, 27–28, 109–11, 190–92. O. PERLER, in *L'Épiscopat et l'église universelle*, ed. Y. M. J. CONGAR and B. D. DUPUY (*ibid.* 34; 1962) 31–66. C. VOGEL, *ibid.* 591–636. J. COLSON, *ibid.* 135–69; *L'Évêque dans les communautés primitives* (Paris 1951) 18–21, 106–08, 117–22. W. JANNASCH, *Die Religion in Geschichte und Gegenwart*, 7 v. (3d ed. Tübingen 1957–65) 5:540–41. A. MICHEL, *Dictionnaire de théologie catholique*, ed. A. VACANT et al., 15 v. (Paris 1903–50) 11.2:1212–16, s.v. ''Ordre.''

[F. CHIOVARO]

PRESBYTERAL COUNCILS

The 1983 Code of Canon Law mandates the establishment of a presbyteral council in each diocese. According to the code, the presbyteral council ''is to aid the bishop in the governance of the diocese according to the norm of law, in order that the pastoral welfare of the portion of the people of God entrusted to him may be promoted as effectively as possible'' (c. 495n. 1).

The impetus for establishment of councils of this kind in Catholic dioceses throughout the world came from the Second Vatican Council intent on reforming diocesan consultative bodies, including the cathedral chapter. *Lumen gentium* (n. 28), *Christus Dominus* (n. 27) and *Presbyterorum ordinis* (n. 7) describe the theological relationship of presbyter to bishop as that of coworkers and friends. A circular letter of the Sacred Congregation of the Clergy (April 11, 1970) traces the development of presbyteral councils at Vatican II. In 1987, speaking in the United States, Pope John Paul II called ''the development of presbyteral councils committed to the solidarity of priests with one another and with their bishop in the mission of the Universal Church,'' a ''most encouraging sign.''

Role and function. The intention of the 1983 Code of Canon Law is clear: the more serious matters of diocesan governance require the collective wisdom of the presbyterate acting in concert with the bishop. Specifically, the presbyteral council must be consulted on such concerns as the advisability of a diocesan synod (c. 461 n.1), the establishment of parishes (c. 515 n.2), modification of parishes (c. 1222 n.2), offerings of the faithful on the occasion of parish services (c. 531), norms for parish pastoral councils (c. 536), and imposition of a diocesan tax (c. 1263).

The code determines the membership of the council. About half of the counselors are to be elected by the presbyterate (c. 497 n.1). The others are members by reason of their position in the diocese or by reason of being appointed by the bishop.

Canon law gives the resident bishop the right ''to determine the questions to be treated by [the presbyteral council] or to receive proposals from its members'' (c. 500 n.1). According to the code, the bishop of the diocese presides at council meetings, but in practice it is the custom in many places for the bishop to be a participant in the discussions while the meeting is chaired by an officer of the council. The content of council discussions and resolutions may be published. Each council is to draw up its own statutes (c. 496). The council ceases when there is no diocesan bishop (c. 501 n.2) or when the bishop determines the council needs restructuring. In either case, the new bishop or the bishop after dissolving the council has one year to establish the council anew.

College of consultors. The 1983 code calls also for a College of Consultors whose members are selected from among the members of the presbyteral council (c. 502 n.1). The consultors do not have a general mandate; their responsibilities are limited to those explicitly stated in canon law, namely, the election of the diocesan administrator when the see becomes vacant (c. 421 n.1); certain duties when the office of bishop is impeded or vacant (cc. 272, 413 n.2, 419, 422, 485, 501 n.2); and designated financial duties such as the hiring of the finance officer (c.

494), consent for acts of extraordinary administration (c. 1277), and consent for the alienation of certain ecclesiastical property (c. 1292 n.1).

The College of Consultors is to have between six and twelve members, serving for a five-year term. In some smaller dioceses the members of the Presbyteral Council are the same as those of the College of Consultors.

Bibliography: J. A. CORIDEN, et al., *The Code of Canon Law. A Text and Commentary* (New York 1985) 400–407, and *passim.* J. F. STAFFORD, ''Priests, Bishop and the Presbyteral Council,'' *Touchstone* 2:1 (Winter, 1986).

[R. P. HYNES]

PRESBYTERIAN CHURCHES IN THE UNITED STATES

Adherents of the Reformed (Calvinist) Church tradition implanted in Scotland under the name Presbyterian (Gr. *presbyteros,* the elder, an officer of the Jewish synagogue at Jerusalem before A.D. 70, then of the Christian congregations) and thereafter in other English-speaking countries and mission territories. The title denotes church government by elected representatives, in contrast with congregational government, and episcopacy, or government by bishops. Historically, Reformed Churches were Continental, and Presbyterian were British and North American.

Origin and Historical Development. Presbyterianism came to North America first as an interpretation of church order held by certain Puritan colonists in Massachusetts, against Increase and Cotton MATHER of Boston, who taught that church authority belonged solely to congregations. Solomon Stoddard (1643–1729) of Northampton, Mass., organized congregations in associations possessing authority to examine and ordain candidates for the ministry and determine disputes within or between congregations. Governing power in regional bodies, called presbyteries, is a distinctive mark of Presbyterianism; this usually includes the right to ordain, install, discipline, and remove ministers and governing (lay) elders of congregations; to establish discipline, refute error, remedy schism, and receive and determine appeals from congregations; to maintain a corporation for holding property; and to attend to the general spiritual welfare of the congregations in the membership of the presbytery. Although presbyteries are not sacerdotal in character, they may be compared with bishops, and they may be described as a form of corporate episcopacy.

American Calvinist churches were governed by elected elders in a number of colonies before 1700, but not until 1706 was a presbytery formed that survived, the Presbytery of Philadelphia, Pa. For a century Presbyterians lived on the seaboard and the Appalachian hinterland; after 1800 they moved west. Presbyterian church history in the U.S. is marked by major steps of reorganization, schism, and reunion.

First Presbyterian Church, Stamford, Connecticut. (©Francis G. Mayer/CORBIS)

Early Schism. The Presbytery of Philadelphia was composed of some clergy schooled in the Puritan piety of Old and New England and others formed in the controversies of the Church of Scotland. Scotland had just emerged from an epoch of bitter strife with the Church of England and had enforced strict Calvinist orthodoxy on its clergy as a defense against LATITUDINARIANISM. In 1729 the clergy of Philadelphia enacted an Adopting Act, declaring the WESTMINSTER CONFESSION of faith—composed by the Westminster Assembly of Puritan divines in England (1646), adopted by the General Assembly of the Church of Scotland (1647) and by the English Parliament (1648)—to be the confession of the new American church. Its ministers were required to subscribe to it. Dispute concerning the strictness or permissiveness of this measure was continuous until 1741, when rigorists of Scottish background expelled a core of Presbyterian clergy led by Gilbert Tennent of Freehold, N.J. Tennent's father was training ministers at a woodland academy at Neshaminy, Pa.; he was formed in the Puritan tradition of personal religion and had been a leader of the revival.

REVIVALISM is popularly associated with John and Charles WESLEY; in fact, the earliest outbreak of the GREAT AWAKENING occurred in New Jersey in Dutch Reformed and Presbyterian congregations about 1730. Gilbert Tennent and his associates protested against religious formalism, unspirituality, and materialism, and preached with a view to arousing consciences, renewing conviction, and strengthening Christian obedience. Their doctrine was orthodox, but they attacked their opponents as unconverted and unspiritual; they preached in parishes, training and ordaining ministers in the presbytery they controlled. The revival was immensely successful in winning volunteers for the ministry.

The schism of 1741, a consequence chiefly of revivalism, ended in 1758 with reunion of the Old Side (subscriptionist) and New Side (revivalist) Presbyterian churches. Tennent apologized for his excesses; yet the revival proved to be the vital force of the times. Led by Jonathan Dickinson of Elizabethtown, N.J., a friend of the revival, the New Side body had established the College of New Jersey (Princeton University) in 1746. Under a succession of able leaders, such as John WITHERSPOON, the college trained Presbyterian clergymen until the separate establishment in 1811 of Princeton Theological Seminary.

After the establishment of the new republic, the southern and westward movement of Presbyterianism called for new steps of organization. Although it originally consisted of a single presbytery, by 1758 Presbyterianism had nine, extending from the New York area to Virginia and west into the valleys of the Alleghenies. In 1788 the General Assembly of the Presbyterian Church in the U.S. was founded, uniting 16 presbyteries and four intermediate bodies or synods in a single national church extending from New York to Kentucky and the Carolinas. Ministers had increased from seven in 1706 to 177.

To assist the new settlements on the frontier, the Presbyterians formed a board (1816) authorized to organize, finance, and direct the mission to the west, reporting annually to the General Assembly. On a similar basis other agencies were established—theological seminaries, boards for education (1818), foreign mission (1831–37), academies and colleges, and a highly organized and effective system for promoting the interests of the Church.

Later Divisions. The second major division of American Presbyterianism (1810) was a consequence of the stresses of westward expansion and resulted in the founding of the Cumberland Presbyterian Church. A second wave of revival, first in Virginia (1790), then in Kentucky, had multiplied congregations greatly by 1810. Ministers were few in Kentucky, and the revival overtaxed the power of the College of New Jersey to supply the new congregations. Methodists and Baptists solved their problem by ordaining preachers with spiritual gifts, but little education, and assigning them to circuits, i.e, groups of congregations to be visited periodically. Presbyterians preferred a well-educated, settled ministry. Suspicious of the doctrinal reliability of untrained men, seaboard Presbyterians would not permit freer ordination; they were unable to supply clergy, and the Cumberland Presbytery revolted in 1810. The new church flourished, attaining a large membership by 1906, when the majority merged with the Presbyterian Church. Two continuing Cumberland Presbyterian churches remained, one white, the other predominantly African-American.

The third major division of Presbyterianism (1837) involved a complex range of issues: doctrinal controversy between rationalistic Calvinism (the Old School), fostered by such leaders as Charles HODGE of Princeton Seminary, and adherents of the New England Theology of Nathaniel TAYLOR and Samuel Hopkins (the New School); a trend toward denominationalism, specific for Presbyterians in the breakup of a plan of cooperation (the Plan of Union of 1801) with the CONGREGATIONALISTS that had united mission effort on the frontier while, according to its critics, introducing doctrinal error; an internal struggle for ecclesiastical power between the two parties; and the early stages of the sectional schism between North and South. The Old School party won the southern clergy by agreeing to exclude slavery from ecclesiastical discussion; the New School was generally abolitionist, more pragmatic than theological in orientation, and opposed to rigid discipline. After 20 years of friction (1818–37), the Old School captured control of the major action agencies established in the first quarter of the century, made its peace with southern Presbyterians, and expelled its critics.

Efforts at Reunion. The national sectional dispute did no further harm to this divided and realigned Presbyterianism until the Civil War broke out. Socially quiescent until President Abraham Lincoln called upon the nation to oppose the secession, the Old School then declared for national unity, and the Presbyterian Church of the Confederacy took shape immediately (1862). The small Southern branch of the New School that had existed since 1837 joined this body in 1864. After the Southern defeat, the Southern denomination became The Presbyterian Church in the U.S. By 1870 it had assembled certain independent Presbyterian groupings in Kentucky and Missouri.

American weariness with strife aided the movement of reunion in the North, however, and the schism of 1837 ended (1869–70) with the reunion of the northern Old and New School under the original name (1788), Presbyterian Church in the U.S.A. Insistence on doctrinal conformity was tacitly yielded by conservatives, but the organizational structure developed by the Old School before and during the schism became permanent. The trend toward denominational separatism yielded to concern for ecumenism and the Presbyterians entered into a variety of interdenominational groups: the World Presbyterian Alliance, formed in 1872; the Federal Council of Churches of Christ, formed in 1908 and absorbed into the NATIONAL COUNCIL OF THE CHURCHES OF CHRIST in the U.S.A. in 1950; and the WORLD COUNCIL OF CHURCHES (1948). Efforts for reunification of Presbyterianism were continued, with measurable success: Calvinist Methodist (Welsh) and some German groups were absorbed; in 1958, following failure of a plan for a three-way union that would have included the southern Presbyterians, the United Presbyterian Church of North America (1858–1958) merged with the Presbyterian Church in the U.S.A. (1788–1958) to form the United Presbyterian Church in the U.S.A.

The United Presbyterian Church of North America was formed in 1858 from two Scottish traditions of dissent from the Church of Scotland: the Covenanters of 1638 and the Seceders (official title: Associate Synod) of 1733. These Presbyterians originally imported Scottish disputes as the basis of their distinctness from one another, but these gradually lost their influence; in 1858 the United Presbyterian Church of North America was formed.

In 1982, the Southern and Northern churches were finally reunited, when the Presbyterian Church in the United States (PCUS) joined with the United Presbyterian Church of North America (UPCNA) to form the Presbyterian Church (U.S.A.). This healed the formal separation that began during the Civil War and lasted for 122 years. In 1988, the national headquarters of the united church was moved to Louisville, Ky., from the Southern Church's Atlanta headquarters and the Northern Church's New York offices.

Bibliography: J. CALVIN, *Institutes of the Christian Religion,* ed. J. T. MCNEILL, tr. F. L. BATTLES, 2 v. (Philadelphia 1960). P. MILLER, *The New England Mind: From Colony to Province* (Cambridge, Mass. 1953). *Minutes of the General Assembly of the United Presbyterian Church in the U.S.A.,* pub. annually Office of the General Assembly, Philadelphia. L. J. TRINTERUD, *The Forming of an American Tradition* (Philadelphia 1949). L. A. LOETSCHER, *The Broadening Church* (Philadelphia 1957). E. A. SMITH, *The Presbyterian Ministry in American Culture: A Study in Changing Concepts, 1700–1900* (Philadelphia 1962). L. VANDER VELDE, *The Presbyterian Churches and the Federal Union, 1861–1869* (Cambridge, Mass. 1932). W. W. SWEET, ed., *The Presbyterians, 1783–1840 (Religion on the American Frontier* 2; New York 1936). N. R. BURR, *A Critical Bibliography of Religion in America,* 1 v. in 2 (Religion in American Life 4; Princeton 1961). R. T. HANDY, "A Survey of Recent Literature: American Church History," *Church History* 27 (1958) 161–165. Periodicals. *The Journal of the Presbyterian Historical Society* (Philadelphia 1901–). *Church History* (Philadelphia 1932–). F. S. MEAD, S. S. HILL and C. D. ATWOOD, eds., *Handbook of Denominations in the United States,* 11th ed (Nashville 2001).

[E. A. SMITH/EDS.]

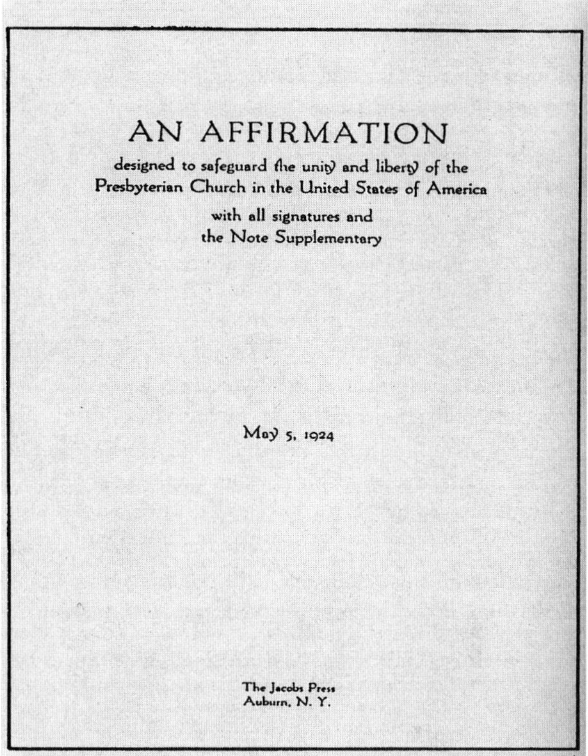
AN AFFIRMATION
designed to safeguard the unity and liberty of the
Presbyterian Church in the United States of America
with all signatures and
the Note Supplementary

May 5, 1924

The Jacobs Press
Auburn, N. Y.

Cover of the Auburn Affirmation, May 5, 1924.

PRESBYTERIANISM

One of the earliest, most influential, and enduring forms of Protestantism, essentially a system of ecclesiastical polity, namely, the government of the church by presbyters. In a larger sense, however, it connotes the theology, liturgy, and discipline that stem from John CALVIN and as such constitutes the general tradition in Protestantism called "Reformed." This entry surveys the origins, history and significant developments in the evolution of Presbyterianism in Europe.

The specific designation "presbyterian" derives from the Greek *presbuteros,* the "elder." The presbyter's function in the New Testament church provided a model for the Calvinist ideal of a reformed church that would be neither tyrannical nor anarchical. Calvin sought, by divine warrant, to avoid the two extremes of episcopal authoritarianism and congregational egalitarianism. The entire subsequent history of Presbyterianism can almost be summarized as the struggle to maintain and extend this scripturally based balance in church order.

By definition pre-Calvinist, Presbyterianism traces its origins to the OT, where the tradition of elders in Israel provided an obvious working pattern for the first Christian communities of the NT. The occasional references to elders (*presbuteroi*) and especially the apparent equivalence of that term with "overseers" (*episcopoi*) established a sufficient scriptural basis for the later Calvinist elaboration of an integral presbyterian polity. Nevertheless, the fact that neither Calvin nor the earliest Reformed churches stemming from him ever really insisted on the claims of presbyterianism to be the only polity with a scriptural sanction lessens the problem of the continuity of the presbyterian system through the centuries that extended from the apostolic age to the Reformation. Practically, then, Presbyterian history begins with Calvin.

Calvinist Origins. The Reformation in the Swiss cantons was already well under way when Calvin arrived in Geneva in 1536. Yet the intellectual eminence of his theology as evidenced in his *INSTITUTES* and the practical acumen of his organizational directives as seen in his *Ecclesiastical Ordinances* secured for him an ascendancy not only in Geneva but in Protestantism. Under his leadership Geneva became the "Protestant Rome," the model and training center of Reformed religion. Skillfully adapting biblical prescriptions to the circumstances of an autonomous, republican city-state, Calvin devised a system of church government that incorporated four basic features: (1) the autonomy of the church—independence from the state and competence to administer its own internal discipline; (2) the unity of the church—interdependence of the individual local congregations in a graded series of disciplinary courts, or judicatories; (3) the parity of ministers—corporate uniformity of clerical power substantiating the presbytery and its varied functions; and (4) the representation of the people—ratification by the laity of the clerical power and functions. All four features were thus mutually integrated and geared toward the ultimate realization of a church wholly incorporated in Christ.

The implementation of this Calvinist scheme was never complete, even in Geneva. Calvin had to accede to the demand of the secular magistrates that they share formally in the appointment of the elders—the lay members who were to complement the dual commission of the clerical ministers to preach the Word and administer the sacraments by their own dual commission to rule (i.e., legislate and enforce discipline) and care for the sick (and other temporalities). Moreover, a certain Genevan character remained impressed on all subsequent presbyterian polities: an aristocratic, homogeneous body, with a curious proclivity toward ERASTIANISM or sectarianism, or both. Not surprisingly, perhaps, an authentic Calvinist presbyterianism never succeeded in displacing the earlier and looser Zwinglianism as the dominant Protestant form in Switzerland.

Growth of Presbyterianism. In the other German-speaking lands Calvinism was likewise a late arrival; but within the lifetime of the founder it became a considerable force, particularly in the Palatinate. In 1563 the Heidelberg Catechism appeared and in 1566 the Second Helvetic Confession, two of the most influential documents in the Reformed tradition. A well-knit presbyterian system posed as much of a threat to the Lutheran territorial churches as to the Catholic Church, and this complicated the situation that eventually led to the THIRTY YEARS' WAR. In spite of the toleration finally secured for it at the Peace of WESTPHALIA—perhaps because of it—German Calvinism lapsed into a quiescence in which, after some 200 years, it was practically absorbed into the prevailing Lutheranism. Meanwhile in Eastern Europe the originally fast-growing Calvinism was effectively countered by a revitalized Catholicism under Hapsburg auspices. Of these German and eastern Reformed churches, the one that best survived the Catholic dominance of the 17th century, the "enlightened" laxity of the 18th, and the interconfessional confusion of the 19th has been that of Hungary, where a presbyterian Calvinism is still a vigorous minority.

Although Calvin's initial success lay in German-speaking Strassburg, while his initial plea to Francis I was a failure, his interest in his native France never flagged. Both Catholic and Protestant appreciated the centrality of this greatest kingdom in Christendom; and if the Catholics succeeded in maintaining possession of the crown and the majority of the nation, the Protestants, spearheaded from Geneva, proceeded with skill and momentum to build a powerfully based minority. The first Reformed, or Huguenot, congregation was established in 1555; by 1559 there were enough to justify the adoption of a Gallican Confession and the establishment of a national synod. This first presbyterian church on a nationwide scale was likewise the first to be organized according to a Calvin-inspired series of pyramided judicatories: the local congregations, or consistories (more commonly called sessions), forming regional colloquies (or presbyteries), which in turn were grouped into provincial synods (or simply synods), which finally reached a national unity in the National Synod (or General Assembly). The long politico-religious war that almost inevitably resulted from this organized rupture in French society ended (Edict of NANTES, 1598) practically where it began: a Catholic majority and a Protestant minority facing each other in an uneasy truce. Political absolutism (revocation of the Edict of Nantes, 1685) and cultural secularism (the Enlightenment) successively reduced the extent of that Protestant minority; but largely because of their tough presbyterian polity, the Huguenots retain a permanent position in France.

Already strongly affected by Lutheran and Anabaptist influences from Germany, the Netherlands quickly responded to the later and more organized impulses of Calvinism coming from France and the Palatinate. In 1566 a synod in Antwerp adopted the Belgic Confession, composed some years earlier by Guy de Brès, and published in Dutch in the Heidelberg Catechism. In the following years, while Spain pursued a policy of stern repression, refugees in Wesel and Emden organized the Dutch Reformed Church along the same lines as the Reformed Church of France. The declaration of independence of the United Provinces of the North introduced the ambiguous Church-State relationship that would remain a permanent feature of the new Dutch nation. Under the stress of the Spanish war the Calvinist religion assumed an increasingly ''established'' character, while the Estates-General assumed an increasingly ecclesiastical competence. This ambiguity was compounded by the Arminian controversy, which broke out in 1609 after the Spanish truce, and was finally resolved—in favor of rigid ''orthodox'' Calvinism—in 1619 by state intervention at the Synod of Dort. In spite of their numerical majority and political dominance, the Dutch Presbyterians underwent much the same vicissitudes in the subsequent centuries as did their coreligionists elsewhere on the Continent (*see* CONFESSIONS OF FAITH, PROTESTANT; REFORMED CHURCHES).

English, Scottish, and Irish Presbyterianism. While the militant ecclesiasticism called the Reformed religion was taking over the vanguard of Continental Protestantism, another wing of the movement was finding its greatest opportunity yet—and its greatest ultimate success—in the British Isles. England appeared precluded from direct Calvinist inroads by its formidably state-dominated and instinctively conservative Established Church. Scotland, on the other hand, presented a vacuum. Remote, feudal, and beset by a succession of royal minorities, the country was disunited and pressured by the alien, competing interests of England and France. In 1560, under the driving leadership of John KNOX, the Reformed Church of Scotland was officially inaugurated by the parliamentary approval of the First Scottish Confession and by the convocation of the first General Assembly of the Kirk, in which a Book of Discipline was adopted. The revised Genevan liturgy of the Book of Common Order completed the formulation of the Scottish Reformation in 1564, by which time the efforts of MARY STUART, the young widowed queen, to restore Catholicism had manifestly failed. Although Knox's Kirk was disposed to tolerate bishops as possibly useful superintendents, a rigid presbyterian reaction, claiming an exclusive scriptural sanction, was launched by Andrew MELVILLE in 1574 and codified in a Second Book of Discipline in 1581. Episcopacy thus became the classic point at issue between the churches of Scotland and England in the politico-religious crisis that became immediate in 1603 when both countries recognized the sovereignty of a common crown.

Despite the original harrying of radical Protestants under Henry VIII, both the momentum and the ambiguity of his schism indirectly favored the introduction of an integral Protestantism. The dominantly Lutheran and Zwinglian influence gradually yielded to the Calvinist in the course of Edward VI's reign, and this trend was confirmed by the sojourn of the Marian exiles principally in Frankfurt and Geneva. If on Mary's death it was clear that a schismatic Anglicanism would be politically reestablished, it was equally clear that this establishment would be strongly bent theologically toward Calvinism. This fact of a common theology, however, only intensified the quarrel over polity that the anonymous Admonition to Parliament brought to a head in 1572. Demanding a full-scale renovation of the liturgical and organizational fabric of the national church, and encouraged by the antiroyalist example of the Huguenots and the Scots, the ''Precisians,'' or ''PURITANS,'' as they were called, were repressed by Elizabeth I and her bishops as dangerous subversives. On their part the Puritans were not unanimously agreed regarding the right order in Church and State. The majority, led by Thomas CARTWRIGHT, advocated a formal presbyterian polity on a nationwide scale; only a minority as yet tended toward the Separatism (or Congregationalism) that would disestablish the church and dissolve it into independent local congregations.

The accession of the Stuarts signaled an ecclesiastical crisis in both kingdoms. In 1603 James I refused the millenary petition for certain Puritan reforms; in 1610 he reintroduced bishops into the Kirk. Against this alliance of high church Anglicanism and divine-right monarchy there coalesced an alliance of Puritans and parliament men, and under Charles I the inevitable crisis came. In 1638 the Scottish General Assembly abolished episcopacy and solemnly adopted the National League and Covenant. In 1641 the English Long Parliament began discussing a reformation of ''root and branch.'' In 1643 an Assembly of Divines of the dominant presbyterian party met in Westminster to formulate the new religious settlement for all three British kingdoms. The result of their four years of labor was the remarkable collection of documents that have been the standards of all English-speaking Presbyterians ever since: the WESTMINSTER CONFESSION, the Larger and Shorter Catechisms, the Directory of Public Worship, and the Form of Church Government. Ironically, the Westminster Standards were at the time successfully adopted only in Scotland, where they supplanted the earlier formularies of Knox. In England the brief Presbyterian triumph succumbed to the congregational Puritans, then called Independents, who abolished the monarchy and the state church. This revolutionary force could not survive Oliver CROMWELL, and the immediate reaction in 1660 meant not only the restoration of king and bishops but also the ''Great Ejectment'' of the presbyterian clergy. Thereafter, in spite of toleration secured by the Revolution of 1688 and the partial revival of Calvinist principles by the eventual Evangelical Movement, Presbyterianism as such retained but a small minority in England.

Outside England, in Wales and Scotland, where the LATITUDINARIANISM of the 18th century was less marked, the residual Calvinism of the early Reformation kept its vigor. In Wales this took the form of a revival, under the leadership of Howell HARRIS (1735), that anticipated and subsequently fused with John WESLEY's movement. Like Wesley, Harris had at first no intention of leaving the established Anglican Church. Only when his ''societies'' were proscribed did he ordain his own ministers and, in 1811, organize a regular presbyterian church. The Calvinist Methodist Church of Wales was structured like the Scottish, with which otherwise it has no connection: local societies (sessions) formed monthly meetings (presbyteries) and quarterly associations (synods) and finally a general assembly. In Scotland, meanwhile, the Kirk had been reestablished (1690); but the Patronage Act of 1712 introduced an Erastian irritant that provoked a series of secessions and partial reunions. The divisions, however, were jurisdictional, not doctrinal; and the basic presbyterian polity was never substantially modified in any of them.

Of almost equal significance with Scotland in the history of Presbyterianism was Ireland. From the first years of the 17th century a royal policy of promoting plantations in the conquered island gave rise to an immigration of Scottish presbyterians to Ulster. When the native Irish revolted in 1641, the Ulstermen, or ''Scotch-Irish,'' replied by forming a church of their own, a militant Presbyterianism modeled on the Kirk, and equally opposed to the Catholicism of the national majority and to the Anglicanism of the government. Although the victory of William of Orange over James II at the Boyne was a triumph for Ulster, nevertheless the Scotch-Irish felt neglected and discriminated against by the government at Whitehall. One reaction was the decidedly conservative trend of the two synods that later united in 1840 to form the General Assembly of the Presbyterian Church of Ireland; another was the emigration of many Ulstermen to America. Beginning even before 1688, they were laying the foundations of Presbyterianism in the future United States.

Seeing their church as a mean between the authoritarian and the anarchical, Presbyterians view it also as both an individual, autonomous entity and a constituent part of a larger whole. The first large-scale and lasting ecumenical achievement within Protestantism, the Alliance of the Reformed Churches throughout the World Holding the Presbyterian Order, established in 1875, represents 90 churches and nearly 50 million members. Through and beyond this world alliance, as well as participation in the World Council of Churches, Presbyterian Churches have committed themselves to the eventual realization of a Christian universality.

Bibliography: J. DALL, M. W. ARMSTRONG et al., eds., *The Presbyterian Enterprise* (Philadelphia 1956). C. M. DRURY, *Presbyterian Panorama* (Philadelphia 1952). UNITED PRESBYTERIAN CHURCH IN THE U.S.A., *Constitution . . . 1961–1962* (Philadelphia 1963). G. S. HENDRY, *The Westminster Confession for Today* (Richmond, Va. 1960). H. T. KERR, *A God-Centered Faith* (New York 1935). L. A. LOETSCHER, *A Brief History of the Presbyterians* (Philadelphia 1958); *The Broadening Church* (Philadelphia 1957). G. MACGREGOR, *Corpus Christi* (London 1958). J. A. MACKAY, *The Presbyterian Way of Life* (Englewood Cliffs, N.J. 1960). J. T. MCNEILL, *The History and Character of Calvinism* (New York 1954). H. H. MEETER, *Calvinism: An Interpretation of Its Basic Ideas* (Grand Rapids, Mich. 1939). N. SYKES, *Old Priest and New Presbyter* (Cambridge, Eng. 1956); *The English Religious Tradition* (London 1953). A. H. DRYSDALE, *History of the Presbyterians in England* (London 1889). J. VIÉNOT, *Histoire de la réforme française,* 2 v. (Paris 1926–34). E. O. JAMES, *A History of Christianity in England* (New York 1949). A. C. ZENOS, *Presbyterianism in America* (New York 1937).

[R. I. BRADLEY/EDS.]

PRESCRIPTION, THEOLOGICAL USE OF

Prescription is a legal term to express one way of acquiring property or extinguishing a debt. Natural law, as well as civil law, acknowledges that the public good requires that long possession of property or long failure by a creditor to claim a debt should be a title to property or a release from liability for debt. Moral theology accepts this position, stipulating that unless the civil law's ruling be effective in conscience, the public good would suffer harm. However, it imposes the conditions that the civil law's requirements be observed and that the beneficiary should throughout have good faith, which means that a person who knows that a property belongs to another or who culpably fails to pay a debt cannot by prescription acquire the property or be released from liability.

Tertullian (*De praescriptione haereticorum, c.* A.D. 200) transferred this juridical notion to theology, in order to prove that the teaching that the Church was its rightful possession from the time of the Apostles, from whom it received the teaching. Since his time this argument has been regularly used by theologians.

The nature of the argument is seen from its use. As in law, legitimate possession can be proved either by direct documentary evidence or by prescription, so too in theology Church teaching may similarly be proved. As in law, prescription is a legal title founded on long possession, so too in theology the long possession of a doctrine by the Church may give the Church a title to that teaching, i.e., be a proof that the teaching is an original possession of the Church.

The strict argument from tradition is that in which evidence is drawn from the records of tradition that a particular teaching has been faithfully transmitted from the Apostles to subsequent Christians. It is a difficult and long process, and sometimes impossible in that records going back right to the Apostles may be lacking. In these circumstances, the proof by prescription may be used. Since the early Church was extremely tenacious of tradition, novelty being strongly resisted, this argument gains in power. It may be propounded either as a purely historical argument or as a theological one. As a theological argument, the Church's infallibility is invoked to bring about, the conclusion that what the Church has long held to be revealed must be revealed—otherwise the Church would be in error. As a historical argument, the inherent improbability of a large number of people over a long period coinciding in the same error is invoked. In either case, the conclusion is the same: the undisturbed possession by the Church over a long period of some doctrine is a sure, though indirect, proof of its truth.

As an example, the belief in seven Sacraments may be cited. Although it was 1150 before the strict definition of a Sacrament was given, and that only in the West, nevertheless the Eastern Churches not in communion with Rome—the Orthodox who broke with the West in 1054 and the Nestorians and Monophysites who broke away in 431 and 451—all hold the belief in seven Sacraments and have done so over a long period. This fact alone proves the Church's prescriptive right to this teaching.

Bibliography: R. LAPRAT, *Dictionnaire de théologie catholique*, ed. A. VACANT et al., 15 v. (Paris 1903–50) 13.1:116–131. *Sacrae theologiae summa*, ed. FATHERS OF THE SOCIETY OF JESUS, THEOLOGICAL FACULTIES IN SPAIN, 4 v. *Bibliotheca auctores cristianos* (Madrid 1945—) 1:803–804. A. C. COTTER, *Theologia fundamentalis* (2d ed. Weston, Mass. 1947).

[B. FORSHAW]

PRESENCE OF GOD, PRACTICE OF

A spiritual exercise in which a person cultivates a habit of recalling the presence of God, with silent acts of love, without interrupting one's other occupations. Although, in a strict sense, placing oneself in the presence of God is an act of the intellect, one does this in order to raise the heart to Him in acts of adoration, love, contrition, etc. While a purely speculative exercise is not a prayer, the simple averting to God by an act of faith is a prayer, for it involves the will as well as the intellect.

The doctrinal basis for the practice is the presence of God in all things by His immensity, the divine indwelling, and the Eucharistic presence. Through His immensity, God is present in a threefold manner: by His power, inasmuch as all things are subject to His domain; by His presence, inasmuch as all things are bare and open to His eyes; by His essence, inasmuch as He is present to all things as the cause of their being (cf. Acts 17.28). God is present in the souls of the just through grace: "if anyone love me, he will keep my word, and my Father will love him, and we will come to him and make our abode with Him" (Jn 14.25). Also, in the Eucharist Jesus Christ is present, true God and true man.

One can respond to these modes of God's presence in different ways. By looking at, or considering, sensible creatures, as, for example, the sun, the stars, the flowers, one can raise his mind to God, who is present in these, and in all things, by His immensity. Or one may practice the "imaginative" presence by looking at a picture of Christ or by summoning up to the imagination an image of Christ as being present here and now. Further, one may practice the "intellectual" presence of God by thinking of Him with the aid of reason enlightened by faith, with little or no use of a particular image. Thus, one makes an act of faith in God's presence by His immensity or by the divine indwelling. Too, one can practice the "affective" presence of God, turning the will toward Him as present here, or one can make an act of "spiritual communion" by willing to receive Christ, who is present in the Eucharist.

Intellectual and affective acts of God's presence are inseparable. The former without the latter would be mere speculation, and the affective act is not possible without at least a fleeting thought of God. Thus, the exercise of the presence of God, like formal mental prayer, terminates in the act of the will. All types of practice of God's presence are useful in that they turn the mind to God. The affective, rather than the intellectual element should be fostered. If the affective element prevails, the will moves the mind easily to think of God, even when the mind is primarily occupied with some other subject.

The cultivation of this practice is recommended by the saints and other spiritual authorities. It helps one to acquire a firm will in the presence of temptation. It arouses a horror of sin, a strong desire to practice virtue, and a continual desire to serve and love God.

Bibliography: THOMAS AQUINAS, *Summa theologiae* 1, 8.3. PIUS XII, *Mystici Corporis* 79. TERESA OF AVILA, *Complete Works,* ed. SILVERIO DE SANTA TERESA and E. A. PEERS, 3 v. (New York 1946). *Mental Prayer and Modern Life,* tr. F. C. LEHNER (New York 1950).

[K. J. HEALY]

PRESENT, THE

In common usage taken in its secondary sense to mean an interval of time coextensive with this minute, this hour, or today. Purged of its crudities, the so-called specious present roughly corresponds to the minimal present immediately perceivable. The present as presented event is central in the making of the triadic continuum of past-present-future. In its primary sense, present signifies the punctiform now, distinguishing and linking past and future segments on the time-line. This existential present limits past and future; beyond it lies no part of the past, within it nothing of the future. As a divisor, the present must be indivisible. Were it a divisible common term, one of its parts would include something of the past, another something of the future. Without a divisor that cannot be divided, past and future would interfuse in an irrational mèlange. The existential present both divides and continues the parts of TIME. It is formally divisive because from the now, precisely as other, emanates actual otherness, the distinction of part from part in time. It is materially continuative, so far as the perduring identity of the now bears no essential reference to the plurality and diversity that are the properties of time.

See Also: INSTANT; ETERNITY.

[J. M. QUINN]

PRESENTATION, SISTERS OF MARY OF THE

(SMP, Official Catholic Directory #2450) A community with papal approbation (1959) whose motherhouse is in Broons, Côtes-du-Nord, France. The congregation was founded in 1828 by Rev. Joachim Fleury for the purpose of engaging in teaching, nursing, and other works of charity. The suppressions and confiscations carried out by the anticlerical government in France in 1902 caused the sisters to seek new foundations in other parts of Europe and in North America. They came to the U.S. in 1903 and established their novitiate in Spring Valley, Ill. The U.S. provincialate is in Valley City, ND. In the U.S., the sisters are engaged in academic education, catechetics, hospitals, homecare ministries, parish ministries, and social outreach.

[H. M. RICHARD]

PRESENTATION BROTHERS

The popular name for the Brothers of the Presentation of the Blessed Virgin Mary (FPM), a congregation of brothers whose principal ministry is the education of children and youth. In 1802 a mitigation in the Penal Laws, which had outlawed Catholic education in Ireland, permitted Edmund RICE, the founder, to open a school in Waterford for poor boys. He and a few companions began to lead a religious life according to the constitutions of the recently founded Sisters of the PRESENTATION OF MARY of Cork. In 1809 they took vows and were henceforth called Presentation Brothers. Schools were then opened in other cities. In 1821 Rice and a majority of the brothers voted to adopt the rule of the CHRISTIAN BROTHERS of St. John Baptist de LA SALLE. Thus originated the IRISH CHRISTIAN BROTHERS, whose first superior general was Rice. A few of the brothers, led by Brother Michael Augustine Riordan chose to remain with the original Cork community. Other brothers joined Riordan and continued to live according to the original Presentation rule. Each house was autonomous in regard to personnel and finances, and was subject to the local bishop. In 1889, however, the Holy See approved an amendment to the constitutions that allowed central government. Papal approbation was formally granted in 1899. Subsequently, the brothers expanded from Ireland into England, Canada, United States, the West Indies, Peru, and Ghana. The general motherhouse is at Mount St. Joseph, Cork, Ireland. In the U.S., the brothers have houses in Kissimmee, FL and Knoxville, TN.

[D. S. BURKE/EDS.]

PRESENTATION OF MARY

The only reliable and pertinent source concerning the presentation of Mary, mother of Jesus, in the Temple by her parents is the Mosaic Law; the apocrypha speak in detail of her birth and presentation, but with no definite historical basis.

Firstborn males were necessarily dedicated to God (Ex 13.12–16), and at the time of Jesus this was done by a ceremony in the Temple (Lk 2.22; *see* PURIFICATION OF

"Presentation of the Virgin in the Temple," oil on canvas painting by Titian, 1538.

MARY). Since the firstborn of humans and beasts were to be in general consecrated to God (Ex 13.1–2), there may have developed some pious custom of bringing firstborn girls to the Temple with the mother as she performed her duty of purification (Lv 12.5–8). When a woman gave birth to a daughter she was to spend 80 days in seclusion, after which she must present herself to the priest in the Temple with an offering of a yearling lamb as a thanksgiving holocaust and a pigeon or turtledove as a sin offering.

The apocrypha indicate that Mary was presented in the Temple as the result of a vow made by her parents rather than because of a law or universal custom. The Protoevangelium of James (7.1–2) has it that Joachim and Anna agreed to fulfill their vow only after Mary was three years old, lest the child be immature and long for her parents. She was then left in the Temple for permanent residence and applied herself more diligently than did the other virgins. According to the Gospel of Pseudo-Matthew (4), when Mary was three years of age her parents took her to stay in the Temple; at the gates she was so eager that she ran up the steps without ever looking back and never asked for her parents as would an ordinary child. It must be chiefly from the apocryphal accounts that there has arisen a special interest in Mary's presentation as a symbol of self-offering and dedication to the spiritual life. The feast was not finally extended to the universal Church until 1585, by Pope Sixtus V.

The presentation of Mary has been a favorite subject of Christian iconography from the Middle Ages on. Thus, for example, Giotto di Bondone, Domenico Ghirlandaio, Titian, and Tintoretto all painted their interpretations of the apocryphal material.

See Also: MARY, BLESSED VIRGIN, ARTICLES ON.

Bibliography: B. H. COWPER, ed. and tr., *The Apocryphal Gospels and Other Documents Relating to the History of Christ* (London 1897). M. R. JAMES, *The Apocryphal New Testament* (Oxford 1953). R. LAURENTIN, *Marie, l'Église et le sacerdoce,* 2 v. (Paris 1953). L. RÉAU, *Iconographie de l'art chrétien,* 6 v. (Paris 1955–59) 2.2:164–168.

[H. FRENCH]

PRESENTATION OF MARY, SISTERS OF THE

(PM, Official Catholic Directory, #3310); founded in France on Nov. 21, 1796, by Anne Marie Rivier. Despite the upheaval of the French Revolution, with its dispersal of religious orders and confiscation of property, by 1805, Madame Rivier, as she was called, had opened 20 schools throughout France in an effort to counteract the spiritual decline caused by the Revolution.

The congregation, which enjoys papal approbation, established its motherhouse in Bourg-Saint-Andeol, France, on the right bank of the Rhone. Houses of the Presentation of Mary were founded in France, England, Spain, Portugal, Italy, Switzerland, and the Madeira Islands. In 1853 the sisters went to Canada. From Canada, in 1873 they entered the U.S., where they maintained provincial houses at Manchester, NH, and at Methuen, MA. Besides teaching, the sisters are engaged in catechetics, healthcare, retreats and spiritual direction, care for the young and elderly, youth ministries, pastoral ministries and social outreach. The generalate is in Castel Gandolfo, Italy.

[M. LANDRY/EDS.]

PRESENTATION OF THE BLESSED VIRGIN MARY, SISTERS OF THE

A congregation (PBVM, Official Catholic Directory #3320 for the U.S. foundations, #3330 for the Irish foundations) of religious women begun in 1775 by Honoria (Nano) NAGLE, in Cork, Ireland. Because the Penal Laws banned the Catholic education of youth, Miss Nagle resolved to devote her life and fortune to the education of poor children. She began her noviceship with three companions in Douglas Street, Cork; on June 24, 1776, they received the habit of the newly established community to which Nano gave the title, Sisters of Charitable Instruction of the Sacred Heart of Jesus. One year later the novices pronounced their vows in the presence of Bp. John Butler of Cork, who appointed Nano, now Mother Mary of St. John of God, as superior of the community, which she directed for seven years.

During her years as superior Mother St. John examined the rules of three orders and, meanwhile, on Oct. 30, 1779, she accepted temporarily the rule drawn up by the curé of Saint Sulpice. Before she reached a final decision in this matter, Mother St. John died (1784) and was succeeded by Sister Angela Collins. Shortly afterward Bp. Francis Moylan and Rev. Lawrence Callanan of Cork drew up constitutions based on the Rule of St. Augustine; these were completed in 1793 and approved by Pius VI; final approbation was granted by Pius VII in 1805. The society was renamed Sisters of the Presentation of the Blessed Virgin Mary.

The special purpose of the congregation is to educate the young, and to minister to the sick, elderly, dispossessed and marginalized. Each motherhouse of the congregation is independent, but all are united in the observance of the same rule and traditions and in the recognition of the same foundress. The expansion of the Sisters of the Presentation included foundations in England, North America, Asia, Oceania and Africa. The first filiation from the motherhouse in Cork was established in the Kerry diocese, and the second in Dublin. In 1833 the first Presentation establishments were made in Newfoundland and England. Madras, India, received its first foundation in 1841. In 1875 the community was established in Australia, and by 1886, in Tasmania. Other foundations include Zimbabwe (1949); New Zealand (1950); and the Philippines (1960).

The first U.S. foundation was established in San Francisco in 1854. In the U.S., Presentation Sisters are engaged in education, youth ministries, campus ministries, parish ministries, healthcare, nursing, chaplaincies, care of the elderly and disabled, pastoral ministries, social outreach, retreats and spiritual direction. Since 1953 the U.S. Presentation houses have been amalgamated in the North American Conference of Presentation Sisters (Official Catholic Directory #3320). In addition to the U.S. foundations, a number of Irish foundations sent their members to the U.S. beginning in the 1950s to supplement the efforts of the U.S. foundations. In 1989, the Irish sisters established the U.S. Province of the Union of Sisters of the Presentation of the Blessed Virgin Mary (Official Catholic Directory #3330).

At the beginning of the 21st century, there were more than 1600 sisters in Australia, Papua New Guinea, Thailand, Africa, China, New Zealand, the Philippines, Latin America, India, Pakistan, North America, England, Ireland and Slovakia. In 1991, the Society of Australian Presentation Sisters, the Union of Sisters of the Presentation and the North American Conference of the Presentation Sisters established the International Presentation Association (IPA), with its headquarters in New York City, as a vehicle to promote international collaboration in joint projects and sharing of resources.

Bibliography: T. J. WALSH, *Nano Nagle and the Presentation Sisters* (Dublin 1959).

[M. R. O'CALLAGHAN/EDS.]

PRESTER JOHN

Legendary ruler of a Christian kingdom in the East. The name of Prester (priest) John appears first in 1145, in the chronicle of Otto of Freising, where John is described as a Christian king reigning "in the Far East, beyond Persia and Armenia," the vanquisher of the

Moslem kings of Iran. It was hoped he would come to the aid of the Holy Land. The victory alluded to here was actually that of the Khan of the Kara-Khitay over the Seljuk King of Persia (1141). But the name ''Prester John'' was certainly in use prior to 1141 and doubtless designated the Christian emperor of Ethiopia, whose existence was vaguely known in Palestine. After the victory of 1141, the Christian West tended to localize the kingdom of Prester John in the Indies. An apocryphal letter, widely disseminated from 1165 on, from this ruler to the Byzantine Emperor Manuel I Comnenus made Prester John the guardian of the tomb of the Apostle Thomas in Mylapore.

In the 13th century, John's name was interspersed throughout the West's information on the Mongol conquest. A text disseminated *c.* 1220 made Genghis Khan, under the name ''King David,'' the son of Prester John and a Christian as well. Later it was supposed by some that Genghis Khan had destroyed the kingdom of Prester John, a kingdom identified by some with that of one of the Christian peoples in Central Asia, the Kéraït, or the Naimans; and by others believed to be a kingdom located in India. The latter group further believed that the kingdom had escaped the Mongol conquest thanks to the miraculous intervention of the three royal Magi, or Wise Men, whose heir Prester John was reputed to be. Finally, John of Monte Corvino affirmed that Ongüt, king of the Turks, was the descendant of Prester John.

Another tradition, however, persisted in identifying Prester John with the emperor of Ethiopia; and when Western Christendom actually came into direct contact with this emperor in the 14th century, he seemed willing to seize the Muslim states from the rear in order to back up the Crusades and to aid in freeing the Holy Land. And so the name of Prester John survived until the 17th century.

Bibliography: E. CERULLI, *Lexicon für Theologie und Kirche*, ed. J. HOFER and K. RAHNER (Freiburg 1957–65) 5:1072. J. RICHARD, ''L'Extrême-Orient légendaire au moyen âge,'' *Annales d'Éthiopie* 2 (1957) 225–244.

[J. RICHARD]

PRESTON, THOMAS (ROGER WIDDRINGTON)

Theologian who defended James I in his quarrel with the pope; b. *c.* 1567, Shropshire(?), England; d. 1640, London. He was educated at Oxford and the English College, Rome, where he was ordained. He entered the Benedictines at Monte Cassino and was professed in 1592. He soon acquired the reputation of learning as a theologian and was chosen to be one of the first two Benedictine missionaries to England, arriving there in 1603. By 1605 he had become friendly with the Anglican Archbishop of Canterbury, Richard Bancroft, and later, with his two successors, George Abbot and William Laud. By arrangement with English authorities he was held in comfortable custody as a supposed prisoner of the faith; at the same time he produced learned justifications of the king's position in the oath of allegiance controversy. Most of these were published under the pseudonym of Roger Widdrington. Maintaining this disguise, he wrote more than 12 controversial works in both Latin and English. Several of these were censured by Roman authorities. He maintained his disguise until the end, having, according to Dr. Kellison, ''a conscience like an ostrich's stomach.''

Bibliography: W. K. L. WEBB, ''Thomas Preston O.S.B.,'' *Biographical Studies* 2.3 (1954) 216–268. D. KNOWLES, *The Religious Orders in England* (Cambridge, England 1948–60).

[T. H. CLANCY]

PRESTON, THOMAS SCOTT

Prothonotary apostolic, administrator; b. Hartford, Connecticut, July 23, 1824; d. New York City, Nov. 4, 1891. His parents, Zephaniah, an insurance agent, and Ann Canfield Preston, were of English ancestry. When Thomas graduated from Washington College (later Trinity), Hartford, in 1843, he gave the valedictory in Greek. He studied at the General Theological Seminary, New York City, but was refused ordination by the bishop of New York because of his pronounced Episcopal High Church views. He was ordained (Sept. 14, 1848) at Holy Innocents Church, West Point, by Bishop DeLancey of Western New York, and became a curate (November 1848) at St. Luke's Church, New York City, under Dr. John Murray Forbes. Preston, his brother William, and Forbes were received into the Catholic Church (Nov. 18, 1849) by Rev. James Roosevelt Bayley.

Preston studied at St. Joseph's Seminary, Fordham, New York, and was ordained on Nov. 16, 1850, by Bp. John McCloskey. After a brief curacy at Old St. Patrick's Cathedral, he became pastor of St. Mary's in Yonkers, New York, in July 1851. Successively secretary (1853), chancellor, and vicar-general (1853–91), he was named pastor of St. Ann's Church upon Forbes's return to the Anglican Church. Preston, a domestic prelate (1881) and a prothonotary apostolic (1888), was a notable administrator but was less successful in personal relations owing to the inflexible rectitude with which he applied the letter of the law to himself and to everyone else. He was deeply devoted to Abp. Michael Corrigan and regarded him as ''the finest ecclesiastic I have ever known.'' With Mother

Mary Veronica Starr, Preston founded the Sisters of the Divine Compassion. His published works include more than 12 volumes of sermons and conferences.

Bibliography: H. A. BRANN, *The Rt. Rev. Thomas Preston, Vicar General, 1824–91* (New York n.d.). M. TERESA, *The Fruits of His Compassion: The Life of Mother Mary Veronica* (New York 1962).

[F. D. COHALAN]

PRESUMPTION

The sin against the virtue of HOPE by apparent excess, the opposite extreme to the sin by real defect, which is despair. In presumption the excess is apparent rather than real, because it is impossible to hope too much, if by hope is meant aspiring to the good that God has promised and relying on the means that He has made available. Instead of hoping too much, one who presumes substitutes for the Christian virtue a distorted counterfeit that looks to a good or trusts in means other than those guaranteed by God's promise.

Like despair, presumption may be based upon a corruption of faith, in which case one presumes because he thinks perversely about the object or motive of hope. This is known as heretical presumption, which is a sin primarily and directly contrary to faith, rather than to hope. Such would be presumption based on the belief that God will not punish sin. In distinction to this, simple presumption, which is directly opposed to hope, supposes no false belief, but arises from a failure to make practical application to oneself of the truths known by faith.

There is a kind of presumption that is opposed to the moral virtue of MAGNANIMITY rather than to hope, as when one aspires to something humanly possible, but beyond the limits that a reasonable estimate of one's capacities should impose.

Theologians distinguish two kinds of the simple presumption opposed properly to hope. One kind is directly opposed to hope and essentially corruptive of the virtue (*praesumptio contra spem*); it either rejects hope's proper motive and looks for the attainment of eternal life by one's own unaided efforts, or it expects salvation by a gift of God that would be incompatible with the divine perfections (as when one expects salvation without repentance for sin). The other kind of presumption consists in trusting beyond the limits of hope (*praeter spem*), but in a way not essentially corruptive of the virtue, as when one looks rashly to God for what God could, but has not promised, to give; for example, extraordinary graces or an extended opportunity for repentance at the end of life.

Presumption directly contrary to hope is always a grave sin unless its malice is lessened by an imperfection of awareness or consent. As a sin directly opposed to a theological virtue, it is more serious, other things being equal, than a sin against a moral virtue. Because it involves a repudiation of God's plan for one's salvation, it is listed by some as a sin against the Holy Spirit. Nevertheless, it is not as grave as the sin of despair, because its affront to divine justice dishonors God less than that of despair to divine mercy, mercy being more characteristic of God than justice (St. Thomas Aquinas, *Summa theologiae* 2a2ae, 21.3).

Presumption of the kind called *praeter spem* may be seriously or venially sinful. Provided there is no serious want of submission to divine providence and no contempt of the ordinary means of salvation, it is not grievously sinful to hope for extraordinary graces or favors, although such hope is likely to be inspired by an inordinate vanity or egoism.

See Also: SIN AGAINST THE HOLY SPIRIT; TEMPTING GOD.

Bibliography: THOMAS AQUINAS, *Summa theologiae* 2a2ae, 21. B. H. MERKELBACH *Summa theologiae moralis* 3 v. (8th ed. Paris 1949) 1:833–837. E. VANSTEENBERGHE, *Dictionnaire de théologie catholique*, ed. A. VACANT et al., 15 v. (Paris 1903–50) 13.1:131–135.

[P. K. MEAGHER]

PRETERNATURAL

A concept used mainly for certain gifts of the state of ORIGINAL JUSTICE and for the theology of miracles.

Concept. Preternatural is a division of the SUPERNATURAL: generally it is defined, by contrast with the simply or absolutely supernatural, as the supernatural in a certain sense (*secundum quid*) or the relatively supernatural. (Some authors, however, identify preternatural with the modally supernatural as opposed to the substantially supernatural.) Whereas the simply or absolutely supernatural is a gift of God surpassing the powers and exigencies of every possible creature (e.g., the BEATIFIC VISION), the preternatural surpasses the powers and exigencies of only some particular nature (e.g., the immortality possible to Adam, which surpassed the powers and exigencies of human but not angelic nature). Thus the preternatural is supernatural only with respect to some particular nature. Further, unlike the simply supernatural, the preternatural does not elevate the creature to share the life of the Trinity but adds something that perfects this nature in its own order (thus Adam's gift of immortality would have perfected his human life by preserving it perpetually).

Word. Preternatural comes from Latin *praeter naturam,* a phrase used of miracles by, among others, Ambrose (*De Mysteriis* 9.51, 53), Peter Chrysologus (*Sermon* 156), Peter Lombard (2 *Sentences* 18.6), and Thomas Aquinas (*De potentia* 6.2 ad 3), who also applies it to a body's unnatural place and the separated soul's mode of knowing (*Summa theologiae* 1a, 89.1). John Damascene (in Burgundio's translation) speaks of a disordered moral life as *praeter naturam* (*De fide orthodoxa* 3.14). *Praeternaturalis* itself is used by Albert the Great of the heat of hectic fever (*Metaphysicorum* 2.11) and by Aquinas of a violent cause (*In 2 In libros de caelo et mundo expositio* 28.1; cf. *Contra gentiles* 1.19); in Albert it means *contra naturam,* in Aquinas it means that which is not in accord with nature. Cajetan, however, distinguishes *praeternaturalis* from *contra naturam* in describing the separated soul's mode of knowing (in *Summa theologiae* 1, 89.1 no. 13), and Suárez presents it as a mode of the supernatural when using it of miracles (*De gratia* 2.4.4; *De substantiis separatis, seu de angelorum natura* 2.29.2). Only in the 19th century does the word come into common use concerning certain gifts of original justice; in theology today this application tends to predominate.

Miracles. The notion of preternatural is strictly verified in those miracles where natural causes could produce the effect, but not in the mode employed by the divine power (e.g., a sudden cure): the mode of activity surpasses the power of the creature involved, but the creature is not elevated to a higher order of being. In this strict sense miracles *praeter naturam* form one class of miracles among others; some theologians, however, call all miracles preternatural to distinguish them from simply supernatural effects. By extension preternatural is applied to the extraordinary but not strictly miraculous effects of angelic or diabolic activity in lower beings; some, indeed, maintain this to be the proper use of the term in this area. (*See* MIRACLES (THEOLOGY OF).)

Gifts of Adam. Besides the simply supernatural gift of GRACE, Adam was given the gift of INTEGRITY and bodily immortality (on other gifts *see* ORIGINAL JUSTICE). The preternatural quality of these gifts other than grace is vital to Catholic teaching about the effects of ORIGINAL SIN: were they natural to man, their loss would entail an intrinsic corruption of human nature; since they were preternatural, their deprivation as punishment left man intrinsically whole and good. Although the Fathers and earlier theologians had with varying terminology taught the supernaturality of these gifts, M. Baius in the 16th century, and later the Jansenists, held that Adam's grace, integrity, and bodily immortality were natural as due to man by an exigency of his nature, that their loss brought evil to human nature intrinsically. (*See* BAIUS AND BAIANISM; JANSENISM.) The Church's rejection of this (H. Denzinger, *Enchiridion symbolorum*, ed. A. Schönmetzer [32d ed. Freiburg 1963] 1921, 1923–24, 1926, 1955, 1978, 2616–17) led to more detailed study of the supernaturality of Adam's prerogatives and to a clearer distinction of grace from the other gifts. The latter were now said to be supernatural *secundum quid* or *quoad modum* or *per accidens* and, later on, preternatural. While Biblical research and paleontology today lead theologians to reexamine the number and content of these gifts, they hold in common that those present in Adam were preternatural.

The concept of preternatural is also used in eschatology, where it is applied to the separated soul's mode of knowing and to the final perfecting of the entire created universe under the headship of Christ.

See Also: CONCUPISCENCE; ELEVATION OF MAN; GRACE, ARTICLES ON; MAN, 3; NATURAL ORDER; OBEDIENTIAL POTENCY; PURE NATURE, STATE OF; SUPERNATURAL ORDER.

Bibliography: A. MICHEL, *Dictionnaire de théologie catholique*, ed. A. VACANT et al., 15 v. (Paris 1903–50; Tables Générales 1951–) 14.2:2849–59. F. M. BERGOUNIOUX and P. HERMAND, *Catholicisme* 5:843–866. J. BRINKTRINE, *Die Lehre von der Schöpfung* (Paderborn 1956) 61–67. H. DE LUBAC, *Surnaturel: Études historiques* (Paris 1946) 354–402. M. FLICK and Z. ALSZEGHY, *Il Creatore: L'inizio della salvezza* (2d ed. Flourence 1961) 299–327, 411–439, 661–672. M. M. LABOURDETTE, *Le Péché originel et les origines de l'homme* (Paris 1953). "Die Erkenntnis des Übernatürlichen," in A.M. LANDGRAF, *Dogmengeschichte der Frühscholastik*, 4 v. (Regensburg 1952–56) 1.1:141–201. M. J. SCHEEBEN, *Handbuch der katholischen Dogmatik,* v.3–4 (3d ed. Freiburg 1961) 3:§§158, 161, 175–180, 183–184. M. SCHMAUS, *Katholische Dogmatik,* v.2.1 (6th ed. Munich 1962) 114–132. B. V. MILLER, "The Fall of Man and Original Sin," in *The Teaching of the Catholic Church,* ed. G. D. SMITH, 2 v. (New York 1949) 1:320–359. A. DENEFFE, "Geschichte des Wortes *supernaturalis,*" *Zeitschrift für katholische Theologie* 46 (1922) 337–360.

[W. H. PRINCIPE]

PREUSS, ARTHUR

Editor, lay theologian; b. St. Louis, Mo., March 22, 1871; d. there, Dec. 16, 1934. The son of Edward Preuss, convert and editor of the St. Louis *Amerika,* German Catholic daily, Preuss was educated at Canisius College, Buffalo, New York, and St. Francis College, Quincy, Illinois (M.A. 1890). After a year on the *Amerika* staff, he went to Chicago in 1892 as editor of *Der Weltbürger, Katholisches Sonntagsblatt,* and *Die Glocke.* On April 1, 1894, he began his own *Chicago Review.* He moved this to St. Louis in July 1895, where he again worked on the *Amerika* staff while continuing his own magazine, retitled the *Catholic Fortnightly Review* (1905–11) and the *Fortnightly Review* (1912–35). His magazine was important because of its independent and courageous opinions on such controversial questions as the FARIBAULT PLAN, Cahenslyism (*see* CAHENSLY, PETER PAUL), Americanization of the foreign-born, especially Germans, the MCGLYNN case, and most contemporary issues affecting the Church.

From 1896 to 1934, Preuss was literary editor for the B. Herder Book Co. of St. Louis, for which he translated three German theological texts, Joseph Pohle's often-printed 12-volume *Dogmatic Theology* (cited as Pohle-Preuss), Johannes Brunsmann's four-volume *Fundamental Theology* (1928–32), and Anthony Koch's 5-volume *Moral Theology* (3d ed. 1918). His own three books were: *The Fundamental Fallacy of Socialism* (1908), *A Study in American Freemasonry* (1908), and *A Dictionary of Secret and Other Societies* (1924). He also edited the one-volume translation of Hartmann Grisar's *Martin Luther* (1935) and the two-volume *Meditations for Religious* (1935) by Johannes Janssen. He served as literary adviser to the Society of the Divine Word Press at Techny, Illinois, and was a contributor to the Catholic papers the *Echo* of Buffalo, New York, and the *Wanderer* of St. Paul, Minnesota. He refused all of many honors offered except a doctorate from the University of Notre Dame.

[E. P. WILLGING]

PRICE, THOMAS FREDERICK

Cofounder of the Catholic Foreign Mission Society of America; b. Wilmington, N.C., Aug. 19, 1860; d. Hong Kong, China, Sept. 12, 1919. His parents, converts to Catholicism, were Alfred Lanier and Clarissa Bond; his father was editor of Wilmington's first daily newspaper, the *Daily Journal*. As a youth Price sometimes served the Masses of Bishop James Gibbons, vicar apostolic of North Carolina (and future archbishop of Baltimore), who resided in Wilmington's St. Thomas parish. After studies at St. Charles Seminary, Catonsville, Md. and St. Mary's Seminary, Baltimore, Price was ordained on June 20, 1886, becoming the first native diocesan priest of the vicariate of North Carolina. From 1887 to 1896 he was pastor of the vicariate's oldest parish at New Bern, traveling by horse and buggy to its over 17 dependent missions.

Toward a Wider Apostolate. Though widely scattered, Catholics were relatively few in North Carolina. Price concluded that more of the Church's efforts should be devoted to a wider apostolate. Influenced by the convert programs of the Paulist Fathers in the north, he secured authorization from the then vicar apostolic, Bishop Leo Haid, O.S.B., abbot of Belmont, to be released from his parish to engage in preaching to the mostly protestant general public. In 1896 he acquired land near Raleigh as a base for his work, naming it Nazareth. As he began his new preaching campaign, he launched *Truth* (1897), a monthly devoted to correcting misunderstandings about Catholicism. Edited entirely by Price, it was non-polemical in style and soon attracted a national readership. At Nazareth he established an orphanage, inviting the Sisters of Mercy, led by his sister, Sr. Catherine, to staff it. He also began seeking priests and seminarians who would join him as a community of missionary preachers. At Nazareth he built a center for this ''North Carolina Apostolate'' with a preparatory seminary for future apostles (1902). Although a few priests joined him and some candidates entered his training program, and while others, including some Northern seminarians, lent their services in summer months, the project did not succeed as he had hoped.

The Foreign Mission Challenge. In 1904 Price attended a meeting of the Catholic Missionary Union in Washington, D.C., an organization of leaders of the principal home missionary projects in the United States. Price presented a report on his methods. He also listened as the young director of the Society for the Propagation of the Faith from Boston, Fr. James A. WALSH, proposed that home mission interest and vocations might well be increased if the wider challenge of foreign missions were likewise promoted. Price was attracted to Walsh's vision. The foreign mission theme now appeared frequently in his editorials in *Truth*, and he followed Walsh's appeals in *The Field Afar*. During the next several years he began to feel that the future of his North Carolina project should be its becoming a national mission society for home and foreign missions. He also realized that Bishop Haid would not approve of his expanding the Nazareth project.

Cofounder of Maryknoll. In September of 1910 Price and Walsh met by chance while attending a Eucharistic Congress in Montreal. Price urged that they take steps together to establish the mission seminary they felt was needed by the U.S. Church. Walsh accepted the challenge. Price then conferred with Cardinal Gibbons and the apostolic delegate, Diomede Falconio, who were favorable to making the project a national one. Gibbons submitted the project to the U.S. archbishops, who approved it at their meeting on April 27, 1911, directing Walsh and Price to proceed to Rome to secure the authorization of the Congregation for the Propagation of the Faith (June 29). Upon their return, they established The Catholic Foreign Mission Society of America near Ossining, N.Y. on property they named Maryknoll. For the next seven years, Price traveled throughout the East and Midwest, promoting the new society and seminary, seeking vocations and raising funds. When he was at Maryknoll, he served as a spiritual director. During these years his personal spirituality became more mystical, marked by an intense devotion to Mary and to the Venerable Bernadette Subirous of Lourdes. The fact that the new society did not include missions in the United States was a disappointment to Price, and he continued to nourish the hope of eventually establishing such a society. In this effort he was not encouraged by Cardinal Gibbons. In 1918 Price accepted the charge of superior in the first group of four Maryknoll missionaries assigned to work in China. In 1919 he developed acute appendicitis and died at St. Paul's Hospital in Hong Kong. In 1936 his remains were returned to Maryknoll, N.Y., where they now rest beside those of Bishop James A. Walsh in the crypt of the society chapel.

See Also: MARYKNOLL FATHERS AND BROTHERS.

Bibliography: A. DRIES, *The Missionary Movement in American Catholic History* (Maryknoll, N.Y. 1998). J. C. MURRETT, *Tar Heel Apostle: Thomas Frederick Price, Cofounder of Maryknoll* (New York 1944). J. T. SEDDON, *When Saints Are Lovers: The Spirituality of Maryknoll Co-Founder Thomas F. Price* (Collegeville, Minn. 1997). R. E. SHERIDAN, ed., *Very Reverend Thomas Frederick Price, MM. Cofounder of Maryknoll: A Symposium, with Supplement 1981* (Maryknoll, N.Y. 1981). R. E. SHERIDAN, ed., *Collected Letters of Thomas Frederick Price, M.M.* (Maryknoll, N.Y. 1981).

[W. D. MCCARTHY]

''Pride,'' in kitchen, mid-19th century drawing by Louis Boilly. (©Historical Picture Archive/Corbis)

PRIDE

Pride is the inordinate desire to excel. Pride springs from a self-love that is exclusive of others. There is a self-love that is legitimate, necessary, and even virtuous; such a love embraces others and recognizes and rejoices in whatever excellence they may have. In this sense a man can be proud of certain talents or achievements that are his, while still recognizing their relative value in line with the talents and achievements of others. He has a place in the universe of which he can be justly proud, but it is alongside others and under God and God's visible authority.

When man isolates self from God and the rest of humanity and makes self absolute or central, either ignoring all others or using them solely toward the achievement of his own private ends, he has the vice of pride. It is in this sense that pride is traditionally regarded as one of the seven capital sins and the queen of vices. It is a capital sin because it is a source or foundation for other sins, especially such sins as presumptuousness, which inclines the proud man to attempt what is beyond his powers; inordinate ambition, which is the inclination to aim at an honor and dignity beyond one's deserts or to use sinful means in the pursuit of them; and vainglory, which is the inordinate effort to manifest one's own excellence, real or fictitious. At the root of all such sins there is an exaggerated love and concern for self that clouds one's knowledge and appreciation of the true self and the corresponding worth of others.

The malice of pride varies according to its degree or kind. There is, for instance, a pride that is satanic, that aims at withdrawing man from subjection to God and incites him to reject the commands of superiors. It breeds contempt for God and all authority and for every value and judgment that is not a man's very own. It is the father of all nihilistic thinking and acting. Such pride is, of course, most seriously sinful, and though rarely, if ever, starkly manifest, it nevertheless seems to be the undercurrent of much of present-day immorality. Wherever there is the tendency to debase and to level, to deny the relevance of God and of ethical values in the affairs of man, there is pride in its most grievous and satanic form.

Pride is less sinful when God and legitimate authority are not denied but simply disregarded at certain times. God's dominion, the authority in which it is manifest, and the worth of others are accepted, but still much is made of self unduly. For instance, a man may think he has gifts that in fact he has not, or he may unreasonably seek to be esteemed above others. Such cases of pride, though always harmful to a degree, are not generally seriously sinful, unless, of course, such pride causes grave injury to

Priest gives communion to a Jordanian Catholic at a large gathering to hear Pope John Paul II say Mass, Amman, Jordan. (AP/Wide World Photos)

another or is such that a man is prepared to commit serious sin because of it.

Bibliography: D. VON HILDEBRAND, *Christian Ethics* (New York 1953). J. LECLERCQ, *Christ and the Modern Conscience,* tr. R. MATTHEWS (New York 1962). B. HÄRING, *The Law of Christ: Moral Theology for Priests and Laity,* tr. E. G. KAISER (Westminster, Md. 1961–) v. 1.

[S. F. PARMISANO]

PRIESTHOOD IN CHRISTIAN TRADITION

Current interest in the use of the imagery and theme of priesthood in Catholic theology arises in great part from their use in the documents of the Second Vatican Council and in its aftermath. It is also affected by the ecumenical currents that found their focus in the Catholic Church after the Council. To relate the life and mission of the Church to Christ, the conciliar teaching distinguished the threefold mission or office of Jesus Christ as Priest, King, and Prophet. The Church, as a body and in each of its members according to their order, was then said to share in this threefold mission and office. To set this teaching within Christian tradition, an extensive investigation is needed into how images and definitions of priesthood have been used in the past, both in explaining Christ's salvific work and in explaining the life, mission, and ministry of the Church. While the immediate concern of this article is priesthood, it is apparent that its relation to kingship and even prophecy must be kept in mind.

Here it is only possible to offer a selective reading from a long tradition, and to some extent systematize a vast body of literature in which the terms are used in diverse ways. There is no uniform notion of priesthood or kingship at work, but at times the language is used symbolically and metaphorically and at times more conceptually, and contexts also change. A chronological approach is unavoidable in order to see how language and thought developed, but from the start four ways in which priestly and kingly images occur are noted: (a) to describe the salvific work of Christ; (b) to designate the Church, his Body; (c) to describe the share in the royal priesthood of the Church given through Baptism; and (d) to describe the share in it given through the laying-on of hands, or what came to be called the Sacrament of Order. New Testament texts, patristic literature, medieval writings, sixteenth-century controversies and their aftermath, and modern theology all need attention.

New Testament Texts

The New Testament provides the imagery and thematic of the priesthood of Christ and of the royal priesthood of the Church. The second however is not introduced as a deduction from the first, and they are to be considered separately.

The Priesthood of Christ. The texts which present the death of Christ as a SACRIFICE, or which attribute priesthood to him, belong in a larger context wherein other images and descriptions are used. There is a very varied soteriology in the works of the New Testament, and a proper placement of priesthood, kingship and sacrifice has to resist the temptation to reduce all understanding to such a thematic. It is asked rather what such imagery adds to the meaning of Christ's salvific suffering, death, and resurrection, as it is appropriated primarily from the Hebrew scriptures.

Several images used of Christ's work provide the context. Jesus is the new Paschal Lamb (e.g. 1 Cor 5:7). He is compared to Isaac (Jn 10:17; Rom 8:12). He is the victim offered in EXPIATION for sin (Mt 26:28; 1 Cor 15:3; Gal 1:4). Compared to the SUFFERING SERVANT of the songs of the Book of Isaiah, he is said to give himself in service for others (e.g. Jn 12:38). In such images, there is a ready appeal to a sacrificial background in explaining the death of Jesus as the culmination of his life and ministry, but the key to its understanding is the contrast made with the inefficacy of ritual action.

The *Letter to the HEBREWS* is the high-point of the appeal to notions of mediation, priesthood, and sacrifice, and it is this work which has exercised the primary influence in Christian literature in these areas of thought. The letter is written to encourage believers and disciples in communities that suffer and endure persecution. Its focus is on the mediation of a new covenant, according to the eternal plan of God, whose intention is to save humanity and all of creation from servitude to the devil and to subject them in obedience to his own will and rule. It is through Christ, the eternal Son made flesh, that this work is accomplished (1:1–4). Through his suffering in the flesh he showed perfect obedience to the Father and became for humankind the purification for sins (10:8–13). The comparison with God's covenant with Israel and with the levitical priesthood and its rituals is apparently prompted as a suitable way to convey the letter's message of salvation through Christ to its particular readership. Those addressed seem to have been nostalgic for the worship of the temple and steeped in a knowledge of the story of the covenant made with the people through Moses and sanctioned by sacrifice.

A priest waves an incense burner during Christmas Mass at a church in Kaysersberg. (©Owen Franken/CORBIS)

It is to demonstrate the dominance of the Son and his superiority over all creatures, his solidarity in the flesh with suffering humanity, and the perfect obedience which he learned through suffering, that the author introduces the themes of covenant, mediation, priesthood, kingship, and sacrifice. Heb 4:14–16 might be cited as a key text:

> Since therefore we have a great high priest who has passed through the heavens, Jesus the Son of God, let us hold fast to the faith we profess. Ours is not a high priest unable to sympathize with our weaknesses, but one who has been tested in every way as we are, only without sinning. Let us therefore boldly approach the throne of grace, in order that we may receive mercy and find grace to give us timely help.

Jesus Christ is a perfect high priest, who, being the SON OF GOD, has taken on our human weakness. He is declared so by divine oath from all eternity (5:5–10). He is the mediator of a new and more perfect covenant in which the forgiveness of sins shown to be impossible under the old covenant is brought about. His priesthood is unlike that of the old covenant, or that of Aaron, and is a priesthood according to the order of Melchizedek (chap. 7), for it has no human origin but only a divine one. The sacrifice of this mediator and high-priest is made once and for all, and his priesthood is now exercised in priestly intercession at the right hand of God in heaven (10:13).

There are five aspects of this priesthood, developed through chapters 5 to 10. First, Christ, Son of God, coming in the flesh in the fullness of time, is qualified to be a priest because he is declared so from eternity by divine oath and because he lived and suffered in perfect solidarity with those whom he is to save through his death. Second, this priesthood is perfect and unique, a priesthood according to the order of Melchizedek, not that of AARON. Third, through the offering of his death in perfect obedience to the will of the Father, this priest entered not an earthly sanctuary but a heavenly sanctuary and there continues to exercise his priesthood on behalf of sinners. Fourth, unlike the sacrifices of the earthly sanctuary, the offering of this priest achieves once and for all the forgiveness of sins, so that no further sacrifice is needed. Fifth, the notion of kingship is conjoined with that of priesthood, because through his sacrifice Christ has gained dominion over sin and the devil and has subjected all things in obedience to the rule of God (10:13).

Two acts constitute the exercise of this priesthood. The first is the death through obedience, the piercing through the veil of the flesh into the heavenly sanctuary. Second, there is what results from this, the eternal priestly intercession which Christ makes for his own at the right hand of the Father. For the writer of the letter, in his attention to the suffering of the faithful, this priesthood and its sacrifice is the foundation of the spiritual life of Christ's followers. It is to be confessed by them in faith and confidence (10:19–25). They are guaranteed the forgiveness of sin. They are given dominion over sin and the works of the flesh. They, too, through suffering can gain their salvation because of Christ's solidarity with them and of theirs with Christ.

Placed within the entire corpus of the New Testament, these notions of priesthood, sacrifice and kingship are not to be isolated as though they were the primary notions of teaching about salvation. They are used in conjunction with other images to give some understanding of what Christ achieved for a humankind that needed to be saved from sin and death, through his coming in the flesh, his ministry, his preaching, his suffering, even his rejection, and his death. It is the metaphorical transposition of these terms from a ritual and legal order to this work of Christ that carries weight and power. The contrast with what is sought and not achieved through ritual action and through the law is basic.

The Royal Priesthood of the Church. The idea of the Christian community as a royal priesthood may in fact predate the elaboration of the theme of Christ's priesthood, though in hindsight it has been understood in relation to this. The most commonly invoked text is I Peter 2:4–10.

While this text is often called upon in support of the priesthood of all baptized, or all believers, it is to be noted that it speaks of the people as a whole or as a unity. The aim of the letter is to encourage the followers of Christ in their suffering, especially in the suffering which comes from finding themselves aliens and disregarded. They can endure these sufferings through union with the redemptive suffering of Jesus Christ. According to the author, Christ leads them on the way of suffering. He can do so because he has released them from bondage through the ransom paid by the pouring out of his own precious blood. The letter compares Christ to the Passover lamb and makes of the death of Jesus a sacrifice of expiation (1:18–19).

Though they may sense themselves a people subjected to alien powers, his followers are in fact a chosen people, an elect people. They are built up as a household, or as a living temple, on the foundation who is Jesus Christ, who was himself rejected and spurned. Evoking the scene of the Covenant narrated in Exodus 19, the author calls the disciples whom he addresses a "royal priesthood." The term is taken from Exodus 19:5–6, which describes a scene of election and covenant. It is because they were a chosen people, a people with whom Yahweh makes covenant, that the Israelites were a royal priesthood, that is, a nation which has dominance over its enemies through God and which can engage in true worship, and indeed one in which all may be seen as kings and priests, unlike their Gentile neighbors. This is now applied to Christ's disciples. Chosen in Christ, redeemed by his blood, they are a royal priesthood, a people that has spiritual dominance and which can announce the good news of salvation to their neighbors. They are a people in which each and all are kings and priests, all anointed by the Spirit in the building up of the one household of God. It is the collective denomination which stands behind any application to individuals of the terms of chosen race, holy people, kingly priesthood.

Christ is said to be, in virtue of the RANSOM paid by his blood, the foundation of the people, this living temple of God's Spirit. If there is any reference in the letter to Christ himself as priest, it is oblique and is contained in the idea that the people offer spiritual sacrifices which are pleasing to God "through Jesus Christ" (2:5). The idea of Christ as king is more to the fore in the letter than that of Christ as priest, for it is his rule that now leads this new people as God's rule led the Israelites of old through the desert (cf. Is 43:20–21).

A comparable text is Revelations 1:6, which also draws on Exodus 19:5–6. There it is said that those saved in Jesus Christ are a kingdom (not kings) and priests (sic) for God, the Father of Jesus Christ. It is the rule of Christ which is here emphasized, for he is called the prince of the kings of the earth in virtue of being the firstborn of the dead. He is a faithful witness of God's love, who washed us from our sins with his own blood (v. 5). Being the people whom he thus acquired, the company of his disciples are a kingdom in which all are priests because all can give glory to God the Father. The same image of ruling as priests, because they are redeemed in the blood of Christ, is found in the chant of the elders before the throne in Revelations 5:9–10.

By way of postscript to New Testament usage, what has often been noted may be briefly recalled. Images of priesthood and sacrifice are never used to describe the role and function of the apostles or of the leaders of the community. This would contradict the sense in which these terms are used of the people, in their subjection to the way and the rule of Christ and in their reliance on him and on him alone for salvation, since it would suggest a dependence on ritual rather than on faith in Christ.

Summary. Those texts, especially Hebrews, which speak of Christ as priest and of his priestly work, do so by way of contrast with a ritual religion. Priestly and sacrificial imagery is allied with the imagery of a new rule and kingship. What is underlined is Christ's suffering, his solidarity with sinners and sufferers, and his obedience to the Father's will. Salvation given in this way is in sharp contrast with the search for salvation through obedience to the Law or through ritual sacrifice.

When the image of priesthood is used of Christ's followers, this is founded in the thought that Christ's people are a new kingdom, chosen by God and with whom he has made covenant. Living by faith in him and the power of his suffering, they have dominion in this world over their own selves, over sin, over all who oppose the rule of God, because they are redeemed by the blood of Christ. Where Christ is proposed as exemplar to the people in 1 Peter, it is in the endurance of his suffering. It is in suffering in witness to God's love and rule, that those who believe in him are one with him and can expect with him the resurrection from the dead, in which his and their dominion is perfected.

It is not possible to grasp the full import of this usage of priestly terms without noting the deliberate move away from any idea that God is to be served and glorified through dependence on ritual practice, as well as from the idea that priesthood belongs to only one portion of the people. It is not through cult and the observance of a law that we are saved but through the obedient dedication of Christ, his life and even his death, through his faithful witness. As a result of his death and resurrection, to live the life of the spirit is not to be dependent on cult or law. The people themselves are royal and priestly, a living temple. They can offer spiritual sacrifices in everything they do, their suffering is priestly and kingly, as they live in memory of the power of Christ's suffering and in faith in it. They have no need of further sacrifice and are free of the Law which subjects them because they are subject in spirit and have dominion over sin in virtue of the obedience and service of Jesus Christ. The symbolic and metaphorical quality of this language of priesthood, sacrifice, and kingship is what gives it its power.

Patristic Teaching

Early Christian Literature. In proclaiming salvation through the passion, death, and resurrection of Jesus Christ, writings of the apostolic and post-apostolic age develop the theme of sacrifice to some degree, especially in emphasizing the spiritual nature of Christian sacrifice, which is contrasted with the levitical cult. The imagery of Christ the Passover or Paschal Lamb is prominent in Paschal Homilies and in Irenaeus. Irenaeus acclaimed Christ to be mediator because in his flesh the conflict between good and evil, life and death is worked out and because in him there is a recapitulation of all creation, whereby all that was snatched from the Father is again surrendered to him in obedience (*Adversus Haereses* III, 18, 7. Irénée de Lyons. *Contre les hérésies*. Livre III. Ed. A. Rousseau et L. Doutreleau. Sources chrétiennes 211. Paris 1974). While the language of sacrifice is used, there are only occasional references to the priesthood of Christ, especially when authors draw on the Letter to the Hebrews, e.g. Ignatius of Antioch, *Letter to the Philadelphians* 4 (*Ignace d'Antioche—Polycarpe de Smyrne. Lettres—Martyre de Polycarpe*. Ed. T. Camelot, Sources chrétiennes 10. Paris 3e. ed., 1958).

On the other hand, in the life of the Church during this period, a distinction was made between clergy and laity which had an enormous effect on the way in which later centuries treated participation in the one priesthood of Christ. In this context, the canonical collection called the *Apostolic Tradition* associated priesthood with episcopacy. The bishop, it says, acts as priest in offering the gifts of the people, and in the teaching by which he brings them holiness of life (*La Tradition Apostolique de Saint Hippolyte. Essai de Reconstitution*. By Dom Bernard Botte O.S.B. Münster 1963. Pp. 7–11). By way of association, the presbytery of the Church is joined in this priesthood, since they extend hands with the bishop over the gifts in the prayer of thanksgiving.

In Letter 63 on the sacrament of the Eucharist (*Corpus scriptorum ecclesiasticorum latinorum 3*, 2.701–717), CYPRIAN of Carthage appealed to the figure of Melchizedek to typify the exercise and offering of Christ's own priesthood in this celebration. He then called the bishop a priest (*sacerdos*) because in his offering of the Eucharist for the people he acts *vice Christi* (Ep. 63. 14, loc. cit.). In some of his letters, he referred to presbyters as *consacerdotes*, people who in some way share in the priesthood of the bishop.

School of Alexandria. The themes of mediation, priesthood, and sacrifice were developed in the School of Alexandria, with mediation as the key term. This is found first in ORIGEN, and to some extent in CLEMENT, and later in ATHANASIUS and CYRIL. With these one may also associate the similar teaching of JOHN CHRYSOSTOM. The ideas of Philo influenced Origen and Clement. In the temple priesthood and in the figure of Melchizedek, Philo found images of the Divine Word. Remaining within a Jewish perspective, he spiritualized the act of sacrifice. He connected priesthood and Passover, and in his allegorical commentary on the vestments of the high priest he indicated the universal character of the new spiritual priesthood.

Origen attributed the work of mediation to the Logos or the Son. He located this mediation already within the Trinity in the procession of the Spirit (see his commentary on John's Gospel Bk. II.X.75, *Commentaire sur Saint Jean* 1–V, ed. Cécile Blanc. Sources chrétiennes 120. Paris 1966) and its manifestation in the world in the taking on of human nature. In line with this, he explained how Christ is High Priest, according to the Order of Melchizedek. Eternal Word, he never leaves the sanctuary of heaven, where he dwells in light inaccessible. There he offers himself as a gift to the Father. In the flesh, on earth, when he is able to sympathize with sinners and their weakness through his own experience, he offers himself for sins ''outside the camp'' (Homily XII on the Book of Leviticus, *Homélies sur le Lévitique*, texte latin, traduction et notes par Marcel Borret. Sources chrétiennes 287. Paris 1981). In his offering in the flesh he blotted out sins and the ''bond that was writ against us'' so that not even a trace is left. Thus Christ exercised both priesthood and kingship, winning dominion over principalities and powers, ''making a show of them openly'' when nailed to the Cross. The eternal and the earthly are not so much two stages of the one priesthood as two complementary offerings.

In several places, e.g. his commentary on John, Bk VI. 51), Origen relates the royal priesthood of the Church to the priesthood and kingship of Christ. The true Jerusalem, he says, is the Church, built of living stones, a royal priesthood in which spiritual sacrifices are offered. Martyrdom is the most perfect form of this spiritual worship, but it is exercised by all who live according to the Law of the Spirit. In the Eucharist, by drinking the blood of Christ the people are initiated into the mystery of the flesh and blood of the Word, who in his flesh rendered God propitious to sinners so that they might become one with him in his eternal offering (e.g. on Matthew 26:26–28, *Die griechischen christlichen Schriftsteller der ersten drie Jarhrhunderte, Origenes* 11, 196–200).

In Homily V on Leviticus, and in Homily XI on Numbers (*Homélies sur les Nombres*, introduction et traduction de André Méhat. Sources Chrétiennes 29. Paris 1951) Origen relates the ministry of the ordained to the priesthood of Christ. Christ is said to have ''eaten the sins of the people'' in his death. Bishops too must eat the sins of the people ''in a high place,'' which is that of perfect faith and charity, by teaching them sound doctrine and purifying their consciences. These priests are victims of the Word of God which they must teach. They propitiate the sins of the people by advising them, exhorting them, teaching them, and instructing them, and thus leading them to penance. Thus through their ministry Christ the High Priest sanctifies his people, making of them a royal priesthood, who offer spiritual sacrifices (On Numbers, Homily XXIV).

Thus it is that in Origen we see an early mention of the four aspects of priesthood. First and foremost, there is the priesthood of Christ, the Word made flesh, which is both heavenly and earthly. From this there arises the royal priesthood of the Church, which is the people saved and sanctified by his blood and his obedience to the Father, and with which it is particularly associated in the Eucharist. This priesthood is exercised by each and all of the faithful in offering spiritual sacrifices, in their daily lives and in the sacrament of the Eucharist. Finally, the ministers of the Church are configured to the priesthood of Christ by themselves eating the sins of the people, living in complete fidelity to the Word in order to sanctify the people by their teaching and spiritual guidance.

Athanasius and Cyril. In these writers, the theme of mediation is even more highly developed, but it is also more securely related to the mystery of incarnation than in Origen. Athanasius and Cyril relate Christ's role as Mediator to his genealogy from the tribe of Judah. Through this genealogy, priesthood and kingship are combined in the one person. Eusebius, it may be noted, in his *Ecclesiastical History* 5,3.13 (PG 22, 365,389) adds the title of Prophet, noting that in Christ the three Old Testament types of king, priest, and prophet are fulfilled.

The sense the Alexandrians give to Christ's priesthood, kingship, and sacrifice can be understood within the broader descriptions of his work of mediation. It is because Christ, the Word of God in his divine nature, took on human nature and human flesh that he is mediator between God and a fallen humanity. The imagery used of this is quite diverse, a typical example indeed of mixed metaphors. The core notion is that the Word took on human nature in the weakness of the state to which sin had reduced it in order to lift it up out of this state and bear it with him to the right hand of the Father. To do this he had to pass through death, death being portrayed as a conflict with death itself and with sinful flesh. He, holy and innocent, encountered sin and death on the earth, entered into conflict with them, and won a victory for all those for whom he chose to live, suffer, and die.

Athanasius and Cyril use various biblical metaphors to describe this mediation. Enlarging upon the language of painful but victorious conflict, they use the language of paying a debt, occasionally of paying a debt to the devil but most of all to death itself. The language of sacrifice, taken primarily from Paul in all the harshness of the victim's identification with sin, is also employed. They call the Mediator ''King'' because he was victorious over sin and death and now reigns over the faithful who have been redeemed and who dominate these enemies in their own flesh in the hope of being with Christ in eternity. Drawing especially on Hebrews, they call him Priest because he offered himself as sacrifice in the once and for all offering of his death and his entry into the heavenly sanctuary.

Commenting on Hebrews and on the Psalms, both Athanasius and Cyril contrast the priesthood of Aaron and the priesthood according to Melchizedek. They do this to show the distinctive character of the priesthood of Christ and the unique quality of his offering, through which cultic priesthood is not only replaced but surpassed. He is priest according to the order of Melchizedek because his priesthood had no origin in this world but comes from the eternity of the Word's communion with the Father. Being exercised once and for all in his transition through death to heaven, it is an eternal priesthood whose act of sacrifice need never be repeated but is forever efficacious.

The texts in both authors are numerous, but some specific examples may be mentioned. In his treatise *On the Incarnation* (*Patrologia Graeca* 25, 95ff.), Athanasius says that by the sacrifice of his own body Christ did two things: He put an end to the law of death which barred humanity's way to God, and he made a new beginning of life for those who obtained the hope of the resurrection (II.9). Christ settled humanity's account with death by paying the debt which was owing to it (IV.20). In IV.21 of this treatise, Athanasius elaborates quite dramatically on the struggle with death which Christ took on in his own mortal flesh for ''it was precisely in order to die that he had taken a body.''

In the Second *Oration Against the Arians* (*Patrologia Graeca* 26, 146ff.), Athanasius relates Christ's priesthood to the life of the Church. Having acted as High Priest in the sacrifice of his death, he became an eternal High Priest who entered through his death into the heavenly sanctuary. Now he acts as High Priest in the Church by sanctifying it through communion with his life-giving flesh, bringing believers near to God and offering to the Father those who in faith approach him.

A similar approach is found in Cyril, for example, in his *Commentary on Hebrews* (*Patrologia Graeca* 74, 967) where he says that our pontiff or *archiereus* subjected himself to the malediction of death, not that he might demand punishment from sinners, nor that he might subject those guilty of sin to judgment, but so that he might save them by faith, absolve their crimes, make them holy, and make them participants in his own nature. He joins the images of Priest and King together by relating them both to anointing. The Son of God was anointed for the apostolate in coming into the world, joining the created thing in union with himself and anointing humanity with his deity, making one out of the two. This is the basis for the power of his sacrifice and for the royal priesthood of the Church.

Athanasius briefly pursues this theme of the royal priesthood which derives to the Church from its Head by the anointing of the Spirit (Commentaries on Psalms 77 and 78: *Patrologia Graeca* 27). The members of the Church make spiritual offerings in union with its Head, who offers in the heavenly sanctuary. Not only has Christ entered into conflict with sin and death on our behalf, not only has he entered the heavenly sanctuary through his resurrection, but his flesh has become a life-giving flesh and the redeemed partake of his wonderful exchange. They are brought into communion with him in grace and so are his body, one with him in his communion with God in the Spirit.

In his Paschal Homelies XX to XXII, Cyril, drawing on Old Testament types, speaks at length of the self-offering of the faithful through the Lenten fast and Lenten exercises in preparation for the Pasch when Christ would unite them with himself in his glorified flesh, but he says little about priesthood. On the other hand, in *Homily* 142 on Luke 22, 17–22 (*Commentary on the Gospel According to Luke by St. Cyril of Alexandria*, trans. from the Syriac by Payne Smith. Oxford 1859, 664–669), he explains that the royal priesthood mentioned in 1 Peter 2 is exercised by drawing near to God with Christ through faith. The people are made holy through communion in the Word made flesh. They offer prayers of thanksgiving and praise, drawing near to the eucharistic table from which they receive life and blessing both spiritually and corporeally, ''for we receive in us the Word of God the Father, who for our sake became man, and who is life and life-giving.''

John Chrysostom. The work of John Chrysostom deserves special mention because he associates the priesthood of Christ and of his Body in a special way with the Eucharist. Though connected with the Churches of Antioch and Constantinople, John shares the Christology of the Alexandrians. He traces the priesthood of Christ to the Incarnation of the Word. There are two moments to its exercise: terrestrial and heavenly. The terrestrial culminates in the sacrifice of the Cross, where the testimony of the Word made flesh is sealed by the death of the testator. The heavenly exercise is located in the priestly intercession which continues for eternity. A special development of the theme is found in John's homilies on the Letter to the Hebrews, where he draws on other biblical texts that accentuate the KENOSIS of the Word in the flesh to elaborate on what Hebrews says of his suffering, his obedience to the Father and the prayer which he made for his sisters and brothers.

The Eucharist is the sacrament and representation of Christ's mysteries, as explained, for example, in *Homily* XIV on Hebrews 8, 1–2 (*Patrologia Graeca* 63, 329–336) and *Homily* VII on John (*Patrologia Graeca* 59, 61–66). Because of this, Chrysostom writes of the priestly character of the Bishop, since in the mysteries he represents Christ the High Priest. However, this share in Christ's priesthood is also connected with the bishop's teaching office and with his exercise of the power to bind and loose. As for the royal priesthood, this originates in Baptism, where John points to the anointings found in this rite. Christ, who is a descendant of the tribe of Judah and not Levi, is both king and priest (*Homily* XIII on Hebrews: *Patrologia Graeca* 63, 321–329). Through baptism, the faithful are made kings, priests and prophets (*Homily* IV on II Corinthians: *Patrologia Graeca* 61, 417–428). They are kings because they have been given victory over sin. They are priests because they immolate their bodies in offering a sacrifice to God. They are prophets because they are given a knowledge of what is to come. Their royal priesthood is founded in the communion with Christ, priest, and victim, given through the eating and drinking of his sacramental body and blood. By reason of this sacramental communion, the faithful are able to offer spiritual sacrifices by living a holy life and by offering prayers of thanksgiving to God. The hymns sung and the rites performed in the sacraments, whether this be the Eucharist or the act of binding and loosing in rites of penance, are done in concert with the heavenly choirs. Since this is a new and better covenant, Chrysostom waxes at some length on the promises which such priesthood hold forth.

When in *Homily* XVII, on Hebrews 9.24–26 (*Patrologia Graeca* 63, 345–352) Chrysostom elaborates on the death of Christ as his priestly and sacrificial offering, following the letter's own comparison with the ritual of *Yom Kippur*. He again points to the Eucharist as its remembrance. The sacrifice is not repeated, but what is performed is a remembrance of the sacrifice. Of this sacrifice those who have been initiated into the mysteries partake through communion but they must do so worthily, lest they face judgment for their sins.

Two aspects of the bishop's priesthood come together in the treatise *On the Priesthood*, which John wrote before his own ordination. In looking to the representative symbolism of the eucharistic mysteries, John likens the bishop to the High Priest ''standing over the sacrifice and praying,'' with the Lord sacrificed and lying before him (*On the Priesthood*, III. 4. *Patrologia Graeca* 48, 642). With more elaboration, however, he associates the priesthood of the ordained with the office of sanctifying through teaching the Word of God and with the office of purifying the people from their sins by leading them to do penance (Ibid. III, 5). Thus the episcopal priesthood in which the bishop is configured to Christ includes his sacramental ministry, his teaching ministry, and his office in leading the people to penance and the purification of their sins.

The Latin West

On developments in the Latin West during the patristic era, this survey is limited to the teaching of Saint AUGUSTINE of Hippo and to the influence of the notions of order and hierarchy on thought about the priesthood of the Church.

Augustine. In the western Church, it is the teaching of Augustine on priesthood which is the most important in the development of tradition. For Augustine, as for the Alexandrians, reference to the priesthood of Christ is to be found within his treatment of the mediation of Christ, or of Christ as mediator between God and a sinful humanity. Mediator is, as it were, the primary title given to Christ. His argument against Porphory and against sacrificial cult in *De Civitate Dei*, Book X (Corpus Christianorum, Series latina 47, 271–314) gave him ample occasion to enlarge on the theme of Christ's priesthood and sacrifice and on Christian sacrifice.

In X. 24 (Ibid., 297–298), Augustine relates the mediation of Christ to the notion of Principle or source of life and grace. The Principle is the Word and it is this Word who assumed human nature. The flesh of Christ purifies us and gives us life because it is the flesh of the Word. In the flesh he took on death, laid down his life in death, and so changed our nature to something better by the resurrection. In X. 29 (Ibid., 304–307), Augustine says that this Word, who is the Son, assumed humanity and thus gave humanity the hope of his love, bringing us near to God the Father, whereas we had been far off. Treating of the mediation of the Word made flesh, in Bk X. 20 (Ibid., 294) Augustine writes of him as Priest and sacrifice, a sacrifice to which all other sacrifices must give place. It is here that Augustine says that the Church has the Eucharist, which is the daily sign or sacrament of the one and unique sacrifice of Christ.

In relation to Christ's mediation in X.5 and 6 (Ibid., 276–279) Augustine discoursed on the sacrifice of Christians by way of contrast with pagan sacrifices and pagan mediators. True sacrifice is an attitude of soul before God and deeds done out of mercy. The visible sacrament of this invisible sacrifice is what makes clear that all are united with God as one holy fellowship (*una sancta societas*). The Eucharist is the sacrifice of Christians, for it is the sacrifice of the Body, head, and members. As a sign of the sacrifice of Christ's death, it includes in its offering both head and members because of the actions which the faithful perform as members of this head.

In the same work on the City of God we find a very clear statement about the royal priesthood of the Church. The priesthood, he says in XVII.5 (Corpus Christianorum, Series latina 48, 562–566), is "the people itself, of which Christ is the Priest who is the Mediator between God and men," and which the Apostle Peter calls "a holy people, a royal priesthood." Indeed, the people may also be called God's sacrifice, so that Paul says, "We being many are one bread, one body," adjuring them, "Present your bodies a living sacrifice." They are a priesthood and a sacrifice because they eat of the flesh of the Priest himself. Augustine here seems to mean eating by faith, but no doubt the saying also has eucharistic implications. The designation is collective, as it is in 1 Peter, though of course it has implications for the way in which each of the faithful partake in it (see also *Sermo* 272: *Patrologia Latina* 38, 1246–1248; *Sermo* 227: ed. Sources chrétiennes 116, 234–242; *Sermo* 7, ed. G. Morin, *Miscellanea Agostiniana* 1, 462–464).

There are a few places where Augustine relates the priesthood of Christ to his work in the Church in the present in a way that extends beyond the celebration of the Eucharist. In the commentary on Psalm 85:1 (*Patrologia Latina* 37, 1081) he says that Christ prays for us as our priest, prays in us as our head, and is prayed to by us as our God. Commenting on Psalm 44:17 (*Patrologia Latina* 36, 504) he makes a statement which was taken up by Isidore of Seville and had an influence in later medieval treatises. To keep the play on words, it is necessary to cite the Latin text: "Quomodo et sacerdos a sanctificando nos, ita et rex a regendo nos." This indicates that there is both a relation and a distinction between his work as priest and his work as king. From what has been said above, however, it seems clear that the claim to both titles comes from his offering sacrifice and ruling over sin and death by his death on the Cross and his entry into heaven.

In *De Civitate Dei* XX.10 (Corpus Christianorum, Series latina 48, 719–720), Augustine associates priesthood with resurrection from the dead. Christ's own resurrection is the ultimate anointing of his priesthood according to the order of Melchizedek. To this all believers are assimilated by the anointing with chrism and so live in the hope of the resurrection. In this chapter, Augustine makes a distinction between the special use of the title *sacerdos* when used of bishop and presybyters and the more general use when applied to all the faithful, but it is to emphasize the point that through the royal priesthood all share in the anointing of Christ as priest in his resurrection.

Hierarchy and Order. How the relation of the Church to Christ was seen, how clergy and laity were distinguished, was greatly influenced by the notion of *ordo/ order*. Roman bishops, and in particular Leo the Great (*see* LEO I, POPE, ST.), often speak of diverse orders in the Church and of the ranking of orders within the clergy. The ranking of laity, clergy, and bishop, however, for Leo is within the one royal priesthood and by the anointing of the Spirit, as he explains in commenting upon 1 Peter 2 in a sermon given on the anniversary of his episcopal ordination (*Tractatus in natale eiusdem*, IV. Corpus Christianorum, Series latina 138, 20–25). By the anointing with the Spirit at baptism, all are enabled to submit themselves to God in ruling their bodies and in consecrating themselves with a pure conscience through offering spiritual sacrifices. The grace of this anointing, however, flows out more fully over the bishop when he is ordained to his office, placing him in rank and dignity above all others so that the anointing may flow unsparingly from him over those whom he serves. What sets the bishop apart and fits him for his service is the more abundant outflow of the gift of the Spirit who consecrates all as priests within the one royal priesthood.

The strongest influence of the notions of order and hierarchy in the Latin west came through the translations of the writings of the Syrian monk, known to history as the PSEUDO-DIONYSIUS. Though he did not mention priesthood, he allied the idea of *hierarchy* or sacred power with that of rank to a vision of the cosmos and of Church order in particular. At the center of his mystical vision stands Christ, the Word of God manifesting the divine in the flesh. It is his role to draw humanity from this obscure and symbolic manifestation to a mystical contemplation of God, supreme light, and truth. The Christian must be drawn from attachment to the material world through a gradual process of purification, illumination, and perfective contemplation. Those closer to God in communion must lead those farther from this state to union with God along this threefold path.

In the work called *The Ecclesiastical Hierarchy* (English translation, *Pseudo-Dionysius. The Complete Works*, trans. Colm Luibheid. New York/Mahwah, 1987, 193–259), the bishop is called *hierarchés* or *hierarch*. This is a pagan word, meaning one who presides at sacred rites, or, indeed, high priest. The term *hierarchia* means sacred source or principle. It is defined in chapter three of the *Celestial Hierarchy* (Ibid., 143–192) as a ''sacred order, knowledge and activity'' which assimilates one to likeness with God and from which graces may flow to others. The bishop who is at the head of the ecclesiastical hierarchy is a font or source of the wisdom that brings others into communion with God. Presbyters, next in rank, are charged with the work of illuminating or teaching the divine mysteries as expressed in rites and symbols, while deacons are charged with the work of purification.

What this position says is that one does not lead others towards God unless one has entered into communion with him, at whatever degree of ordering one stands. This was given another twist in Latin theology when it resorted to legal and ontological categories to explain the hierarchy of bishop and presbyter, especially in the sacraments. Order was then applied more to official position and function than to the holiness of the minister. This accentuated the distinction in office and order between hierarchy or clergy and laity, and within hierarchy between the different ranks. The sharpening of the distinction between the holiness of the minister and his power was heightened toward the turn of the millennium as a result of disputes with those spiritual groups that questioned the validity of the sacramental celebrations of unworthy ministers.

Summary. During these early centuries, the images of priest and king are attached to a fundamental conception of Christ's mediation between God and humanity. The possibility of this mediation is rooted in the incarnation of the Word or Son and is effected through the combat with sin and death which he undertook in the flesh. The priestly character of this mediation is, on the one hand, by way of contrast with ritual acts of sacrifice. The comparison, on the other hand, with the process of priestly sacrifice shows that by his reason of his access through suffering into the heavenly sanctuary Christ continues to act as mediator in his heavenly intercession and through his active presence in the Church. The most central thought is that of suffering, conflict, and victory over sin and death. The use of the images and titles of king and priest comes mainly from scriptural commentary and is subordinate to the fundamental idea of the mediation of the Word, who reconciles God and humanity in his own person and in the work he was sent to do.

The imagery of sacrifice, priesthood, and kingship is used also of the Church. They are related more directly to the priesthood of Christ than is done in the New Testament itself, by way of showing that the Church, Christ's Body, exists and acts only by participation in the mystery of Christ himself. Initiated into the royal priesthood by baptism and Eucharist, the Church and its members are purified of sin through Christ's death, anointed with the anointing of Christ himself, and nourished by his life-giving body and blood. Sacramental participation makes possible daily spiritual sacrifices. Sacramental and spiritual participation in Christ's priesthood are one, neither making any sense except in relation to the other.

Within the royal priesthood of the Church, Christ's Body, there are various ministries and various manifestations of holiness, modes of participation in the one priesthood of Christ himself. Leadership and pastoral ministry in the name of Christ always stood out as special roles within the one royal priesthood. In particular, the more the word Priest was used of Christ in relation to the action of the liturgy, the more the term was transferred to bishops and presbyters who preside over it. It was, however, the growing, practical, and then theological distinction between clergy and laity, as well as use of the notions of hierarchy and order, that made for more sharply defined differentiations between the participation of the faithful and the participation of the ordained.

Liturgical Developments

Developments of language and thought that gave pride of place to the ordained in the use of sacerdotal terminology are linked with the liturgy. It was within the liturgy, or in relation to the liturgy, that the distinction between clergy and laity was given focus. On the one hand, this is nothing other than a practical distinction, prompted by the need to distribute charges and assure the financial arrangements necessitated by the call to ministry. The clergy are those who take their place at the altar, who also have other community responsibilities, and so must be by and large free of concern about their financial support. When TERTULLIAN (*De baptismo* 17.1: Corpus Christianorum latina I, 291) makes the distinction he refers to the fact that anyone can baptize, all being priests, but it is the *summus sacerdos*, the bishop, who retains the primary right to do this, and following him presbyters and deacons. This, he says, is a matter of peace and good order in the Church. Origen (*Homily on Josuah* 17.3: Sources Chrétiennes 71, 381) also has a practical approach but one heavy with symbolic meaning. It comes from the law of God that priests and levites are to be free of external preoccupations so as to dedicate themselves to the word of God, but then it is the part of the laity to assure their material needs. In *Letter* 1 (*Corpus scriptorum ecclesiasticorum latinorum* 3), Cyprian uses the same Old Testament typology to apply the distinction between clergy and laity to their different roles in the eucharistic sacrifice. As is known, this typology was pursued in the west in the papal decretals to underline the duty of the clergy to serve in the liturgy and to promote in tandem with this the call and obligation to clerical celibacy.

Distinctions in the relation of congregation and bishop to Christ were given meaning within the eucharistic action. The offering of the bread and wine was done by the priestly people, not necessarily in any ritual sense but in the sense that they provide them. The meaning of what the people offer in bread and wine comes from the fact that they are a free people, made free in the Spirit (Irenaeus), or Christ's priestly people (e.g. Augustine). Christ prays in them as they make an offering of their gifts and of themselves and in turn receive gifts in gratitude. However, liturgically in this offering the priest leads them in thanksgiving, that is, he offers on their behalf with thanksgiving for creation and for God's salvific work, and it is through his words that the sacramental sacrifice is perfected.

A distinction is made in Sermon 5. 7–8 of the mystagogical catechesis of Cyril of Jerusalem between the offerings of the people, the spiritual sacrifice of the prayer proclaimed, and the propitiatory sacrifice present on the altar when the spiritual sacrifice over the offerings has been completed (*Cyrille de Jérusalem: Catechèses Mystagogiques*, ed. A. Pièdagnel et P. Paris. Sources Chrétiennes 126. Paris). The idea that the offering of the gifts and the bread and wine sanctified by the prayer constitute a twofold sign of Christ's sacrifice appears, for example, in the anaphora of Basil of Caeserea (*Prex Eucharistica. Textus e variis liturgiis antiquioribus selecti*, ed. Anton Hängii et Irmgard Pahl. Fribourg), which distinguishes between *prosphora* or offering and *thusia* or sacrifice. The bread and wine laid on the table are an offering, a sign of the people's own self-offering and a sign of Christ's offering. In the course of the eucharistic prayer proclaimed by the bishop, with the people's assent, when the Word or the SPIRIT is invoked, or when Christ's supper words are proclaimed, as different authors variously explain the power of the prayer, the sacrament is perfected as the sacrament of Christ's sacrifice. Hence the blessed elements show forth the sacrifice of Christ the High Priest through which he entered the holy of holies, in which he is the one in whose humanity all are forgiven and made free, the Head of his body, which is one with him in this priestly offering and Passover. Though the priestly people make their offering through the sign of the bread and wine, their primary mode of participation in Christ's sacrifice and priesthood is through eating and drinking of his Body and Blood. It is in partaking of the sacramental sacrifice by eating and drinking of the body and blood of Christ that their royal priesthood is given its most fundamental sacramental and spiritual form.

Medieval Thought

The Order of Priesthood. In the work of ISIDORE OF SEVILLE in the Latin west, there is a formal treatment of orders and offices in the Church which had considerable influence on later writers. In commentaries on the books of the Pentateuch, Isidore associated both kingship and priesthood with anointing and pointed to the figure of Christ, who by his anointing with the Spirit became the true high priest and king. The Church shares as a body in this anointing by the Spirit and hence as the Body of Christ is a royal priesthood and a kingly people. Some share in it through baptism, others through ordination. In the Eucharist, the priestly people eats and drinks of the body and blood of Christ and is itself offered with Christ in the sacramental action.

Treating of the *ordo sacerdotalis* in the *Etymologiarum*, Liber VII.12 (*Patrologia Latina* 82, 291–292) and the *De Ecclesiasticis Officiis*, Liber II.5–7 (*Patrologia Latina* 83, 780–788) Isidore includes bishops and presbyters in this priesthood. The definition of *sacerdos* is ''to give the sacred or holy (*sacrum dare*).'' The word comes, he says, from *sanctificando* just as *rex* comes from *regendo*. He traced the *ordo sacerdotalis* back to the giving of the power of the keys to Peter (Matt 16:18). It is exercised in ruling and governing, in preaching and teaching, and in the consecration of the body and blood of the Lord. Within the priestly order, only the bishop bears the title of *Pontifex*, since he is the prince of priests by reason of his place in the apostolic succession.

After Isidore, ecclesiastical writers maintained this broad understanding of the nature and functions of the *ordo sacerdotalis* but focused increasingly on the priestly power exercised in the act of consecration in the Mass, drawing extensively on the Aaronic priesthood as type of the sacerdotal order in the Church. This meant that the consecration of the body and blood of Christ was also viewed as the act of eucharistic sacrifice. Authors made a distinction between the action of the priest in consecrating and that of the people in offering by distinguishing in sacrifice between *offerre* and *immolare*. In Christ's own death the consummation of the sacrifice is in his immolation. In the Mass this means it is found in the consecration when the bread and wine are changed into his body and blood and his immolation represented. All offer (themselves, bread and wine, even Christ) but only the ordained priest can consummate the sacrifice and represent the immolation of Christ's death [On this, see for example Amalar of Metz, *Liber Officialis* (ed. Hansenns II, 106–108), and Paschasius Radbertus (*Liber de corpore et sanguine Domini* (Corpus Christianorum, Series latina)].

An example of how this applied to liturgy may be found in an eleventh century writer, ODO OF CAMBRAI, in his work *Expositio in Canonem Missae* (*Patrologia Latina* 160:1053–1070), in which he explains the Canon of the Mass. Odo locates the sacrifice of praise, sung by all the people, in the *Sanctus* of the Mass, the consecration of the body and blood of Christ in his own words repeated by the priest, and the daily offering of this sacramental sacrifice by the whole Church (both present and absent) in the prayers of offering that follow the consecration when the body and blood of Christ are on the altar. The people are thus able to join their sacrifice of praise with the real sacrifice, which is that of Christ, now sacramentally represented in the Mass through the offering of his body and blood made really present through the words of Christ repeated by the priest.

Sacerdotium et Regnum. An important medieval influence on concepts of priesthood and the ordering of the Church came from the quarrel over *sacerdotium* and *imperium* or *regnum* that marked the relations of Pope and bishops with kings and emperors. With the emperor CHARLEMAGNE there emerged the idea and pursuit of a single *societas christiana* and a new vision of the divine commissioning of emperor and later of kings. The role of the Prince was to defend the Church and uphold a Christian society against its enemies. At times the claim was made that his task was to rule the Church when it came to the ordering of society. Liturgical books (e.g. *Ordines Romani* XLV, XLVI, XLVII, in Michel Andrieu, *Les Ordines Romani du haut moyen âge*, t. IV. Louvain 1965) of the time included rites for the consecration, and even the ordination, of emperors and kings, making of them a special order in the Church, distinct from both clergy and laity. The model was taken from the Old Testament, according to which kings, priests, and prophets were all anointed. The divine origin of temporal power, whether through natural law or by special ordinance, was confirmed by jurists, canonist, and even theologians. Though usually princely power was not related to Christ's kingship, at times the emperor or kings were called vicars of Christ in the exercise of their rule.

Around the cusp of the millennium, episcopal authorities found the encroachment on ecclesiastical affairs by princes impossible to concede and responded by an assertion of their supremacy over principalities in both religious and temporal matters, though without however claiming direct temporal rule for themselves. To limit trespass on affairs of the Church, strong popes like GREGORY VII and INNOCENT III thus found it necessary to claim some authority in temporal matters. Innocent was ready to admit that temporal rule came to lords of the realm from God, whatever be that process, but he asserted some control over the temporal in virtue of his spiritual authority. This came from the subordination of the temporal to the spiritual, so that temporal rulers needed to acknowledge papal superiority over the *regnum* in virtue of the higher order of *sacerdotium* (See the letter of Oct. 30, 1198, *Epistula ad Acerbum consulem Florentinum*: *Patrologia Latina* 216, 1186). Between the two luminaries set by God in the universe, the *pontificalis auctoritas* and the *regalis potestas*, the first to rule over souls and the second to rule over bodies, the greater dignity is that of the pontifical, so that from it, as the moon from the sun, the regal receives its dignity and splendour.

These attitudes were confirmed by THOMAS AQUINAS in his work on the rule of princes (*De Regimine Principum ad Regem Cypri*, ed. Joseph Mathis. Turin and Rome: Marietti, 1948). Kings, he taught, hold their authority from God, both by reason of the very nature of rule and by reason of the ordinances of divine providence. This power, however, is exercised in temporal things. He separated earthly rule clearly from the kingship of Christ since Christ's power has to do with the spiritual realm, the kingdom of God (chapter XIV). Christ is both king and priest, and from him there derives a royal priesthood (*regale sacerdotium*) in virtue of which all the faithful are kings and priests. The regimen of this kingdom is not given to earthly princes but to priests, especially to the High Priest, who is the successor of Peter and the vicar of Christ, the Roman Pontiff. Since this is the highest kingdom, the one that is the end of all earthly administration, earthly kings are subject to this high priest. This does not mean that the Pope, in virtue of his kingly priesthood as vicar of Christ, exercises temporal power as a matter of course. It only means that kings and rulers have to acknowledge his ultimate supremacy and that he may intervene in temporal affairs when this seems to be served by the spiritual end of the rule and priesthood which he holds from Christ. This reasoning placed the kingship of Christ clearly in the spiritual order but the theory of the subjection of the temporal to the spiritual provided popes and bishops a say in temporal affairs.

Scholastic Theology on Priesthood

All of these influences on the meaning of priesthood just outlined were present in the Church and in Christian thought about ministry and priesthood when the writers of the schools took on the challenge of offering a system of faith and doctrine. The Master, PETER LOMBARD, defined order and priesthood as a sacred power given through consecration and itself the power to consecrate the Body and Blood of Christ and this influenced those whose task it was to comment on his *Summa*.

A prior issue is the way in which authors deal with Christ's priesthood and mediation. Consideration is here confined to the primary authors of the period.

In THOMAS AQUINAS's *Summa Theologiae*, the question on Christ's mediation (III, Q. XXVI) comes several questions after that on priesthood. Attributing the role of mediator to the humanity of Christ, Thomas mentions two functions. The first is to give gifts and teaching to humans on behalf of God; the second is to offer satisfaction to God and to intercede for human beings on behalf of humanity (art. 2). There is no mention of priesthood or sacrifice here, though one recognizes that normally the act of intercession is listed as a priestly function.

On the priesthood of Christ, Thomas (*Summa Theologiae* III, Q. XXII) had said that what is proper to a priest is that he is the mediator between God and humankind. Being mediator involves three things: to give holy things (*sacra dans*), to offer the prayers of the people to God, and to satisfy for their sins. Where he says that Christ in his death is both priest and victim, quoting Augustine, *De Civitate Dei* X.5, he points to visible sacrifice as the sacrament of the invisible and adds that everything which is held out to God (*Deo exhibetur*) so as to bring the human spirit towards God may be called a sacrifice. Drawing parallels with levitical sacrifices, which according to Rom 4:25 and Hebrews 5:9 have been fulfilled in Christ, he says that the three purposes of sacrifice are to remit sins, to keep the human person in the state of grace, and to unite it with God. When it is said that Christ's priesthood is according to the Order of Melchizedek, this means that it is more excellent than any other priesthood and that it endures for ever in its end and purpose, which is to bring those for whom the sacrifice is made into union with God.

When Thomas treats of the sacrifice of Christ in *Summa Theologiae* III, Q. XLVIII, art. 3, he uses the definition of Augustine in *De Civitate Dei* X.6, namely that sacrifice is whatever good work brings us into holy fellowship (*sancta societas*) with God and then adds the note from this same book, X.20, that the perfection of Christ's sacrifice comes from the perfection of his charity or love. He also quotes Augustine from *In Tim* IV.14 to the effect that in every sacrifice we may distinguish the one to whom it is offered, the one by whom it is offered, what is offered, and those for whom it is offered. On this score, Christ's sacrifice is most perfect because he is one with the one to whom it is offered, he is the one who offers that which is offered, and one with those for whom it is offered.

There is no mention of the priesthood of Christ in Bonaventure's discussion of mediation in his *Breviloquium* IV and in the *Collationes in Hexameron* I, *reportatio* B, but he does take up the patristic themes of mediation with which the Fathers linked this priesthood. In the work on the *Hexameron* Bonaventure relates the mediation of Christ to the Cross. It is here, where he takes on sin for humanity's sake, that he is at the most distant point from the divine, but it is here also that the impotence of the crucified is united with the power of the Word. It is then in his ascension that Christ becomes the center, the mediating point, where the divine and a transformed humanity come together. Here and in the *Breviloquium* IV, 1 and 10, it is the image and function of Principle which stands out. In this, Bonaventure is in line with the thinking of Augustine. Christ as Word of God is principle of creation and principle of redemption.

At the same time, in his explanation of the Eucharist (VI.9) Bonaventure gave prominence to the sacrifice of immolation as an actual offering of the Church and of Christ in the Church. He says that in his suffering Christ offered to God a fully satisfactory obedience. The purpose of this offering is to make satisfaction for sin but it is also to inflame human hearts with the love of the Spirit and thus to unite them to God. It is this love which unites the Church to Christ as a body to its head (V.8). On the other hand, the concept of priesthood gets no treatment in his discussion of the sacrament of Order (VI.12), apart from the use of the title *sacerdos* in reference to the agent of the consecration of the bread and wine. It is of order and dignity that Bonaventure treats and in ordination he sees a sing of the giving of power (VI.12,5).

It is in his treatment of the sacraments, *Summa Theologiae* III, Q. 63, that Thomas deals with the participation of the Church in the priesthood of Christ, developing his thought around the notion of the sacramental character. Writers before him had spoken of the character as some share in Christ that undergirds the participation in grace, but it was his own insight to relate this to worship and to participation in Christ's priesthood. This participation is both passive and active. One shares passively in this priesthood by receiving of its fruits through the celebration of sacraments. Ministers share in it actively by serving as instruments in the instrumental action of Christ's priesthood through which the effects of his passion extend into the present. The power for passive participation is given through the sacramental character imprinted in baptism, which equips the baptized to take part in the public worship of the Church, which is his Body. The adjective *passive* does not signify that the people remain inactive in the liturgy, for indeed Thomas insists on the activity of their faith and on their part in the prayers and the rites. What it brings out is that Christ's grace is totally gratuitous, that not even faith merits or is any way causative of grace, for humans are always recipients in face of Christ's redemptive action.

If the character of the sacrament of order is said to give an active participation in Christ's priesthood this is strictly as instrumental cause, as the channel and expression of the sanctifying act whereby the passion of Christ is still operative in the present, as explained in Q. 48, art. 5. In Q. 83, art. 4, on the rites of the Mass, Thomas points to three actions of the ordained minister: to say the priestly prayer through which the offerings of the people are made acceptable to God, to consecrate the bread and the wine in the act which signifies Christ's immolation and which is itself a kind of immolation of these gifts since they are now changed, and to give communion to the people.

Aquinas did not get to the treatment of the sacrament of order in the writing of the *Summa Theologiae*. In other writings, he was so inclined to related order to priesthood and priesthood to the consecration of the Lord's body and blood, that he deemed the episcopacy not to be a sacrament but a higher order given to one who was already a priest in the order of presbyters. In the opusculum *De perfectione vitae spiritualis* he says that what the bishop possesses is a higher and a holy power which allows him to teach and to govern the Church, as well as to perform his own distinctive liturgical functions, such as consecrating, ordaining, and confirming, which go with this office and ministry. This is the power which Christ gave to the twelve apostles and which is passed on through apostolic succession. Though Thomas described this power as a jurisdiction, he retains enough of the vision of the Pseudo-Dionysius to look upon the episcopacy as a state of acquired perfection and to expect outstanding holiness from those who would exercise this power.

The Sixteenth Century

The Reformers. The Reformers of the sixteenth century were intent on applying Christ's titles of King and Priest to spiritual things and not to temporal, as they were intent to overcome the distinction between the baptized and ordained ministers associated with the doctrine of the sacramental character and priestly anointing.

Martin Luther. In his writings on the role of Christ in human salvation, as well as in what he says of the baptized, Martin LUTHER joins the function of king with that of priest. He elaborates on the sacrifice of Christ in several of his biblical commentaries in terms that often sound similar to those found in patristic writers, but with his own particular view of the imputation of Christ's righteousness to sinners and of justification by faith. In his incarnation, Christ took on the effects of Adam's sin, indeed took on his sin, in order to endure suffering and death on behalf of sinners and thus earn the right to have his righteousness imputed to them. It is by the death and the blood of Christ that the baptized are cleansed and sanctified. Taking on the form of a servant and offering himself in the flesh, Christ is the true Aaron, or fulfills the type of the Aaronic priesthood. None can share in this priesthood, because his sacrifice is unique and once and for all and does away with all sacrifices. His anointing as priest according to the order of Melchizedek is associated more readily with his present role in heaven and his present relation to the Church. By his anointing, like Melchizedek Christ is both king and priest and he enters into these offices through the sacrifice of his death.

While it is mentioned in several places in Luther's writings, a convenient and short presentation of his view of the priesthood and kingship that Christ now exercises and in which the faithful participate, is found in the 1520 treatise on *The Freedom of a Christian* (*Luthers Werke in Auswahl,* 31;333–377). He starts with the affirmation that under the Old Testament the birthright of the first-born male was that of priesthood and kingship, but that this is only a type of the priesthood and kingship of Christ, who is the first-born of the Father. Of his kingship, Luther says ''he reigns in heavenly and spiritual things'' that pertain to the righteousness by which God makes us righteous and rules over believers, protecting them against evil onslaughts. His priesthood is also exercised in spiritual things, not in outer ceremonies and is related by Luther to his heavenly prayer and intercession. In both cases, Christ exercises his kingship and priesthood through the living instruction of the Holy Spirit that guides those who believe in his word and receive his righteousness.

All faithful Christians have a share in this kingship and priesthood, because of the freedom they have been given through Christ and their faith in him. In virtue of a spiritual power, Christians are kings and lords of all things spiritual and cannot be harmed by evil, even though of course they are subject to suffering and the onslaught of the devil. As priests, Christians are able to appear before God and pray for others, as well as to teach one another spiritual things. In the *Babylonian Captivity* (*Luthers Werke in Auswahl* 36, 11–57), Luther elaborates on the many spiritual offerings which the baptized can make because of their life in Christ. These include prayer and alms-giving and the self-offering in which they cast themselves upon Christ. In later years Luther evolved his teaching on ministry, and while he recognized the need and Gospel mandate for ordained ministers of Word and Sacrament, he did not acknowledge any participation in Christ's kingship and priesthood other than that of baptism. To preach the Word and duly administer the sacraments, as ministers are called to do, is to exercise their baptismal priesthood.

Luther resolves the conflict between *regnum* and *sacerdotium* in his own unique way, for example, in the work *Secular Authority: To What Extent It Should Be Obeyed*, *Luthers Werke in Auswahl* 45, 81–129). He believes in Christendom, that is, that society should be organized and ruled to serve the kingdom of God and the mission of the Church. Secular authority is willed and ordained by God in the interests of the Gospel. Its role is to protect the followers of the kingdom and to punish the wicked. However, it is not said to be in any way a participation in Christ's kingly powers. Luther's fundamental principle is that through baptism all are of the royal priesthood, all are priests and kings without distinction. Within this priesthood or kingship, each must serve according to the position which he holds. Some are called to ministry, some to rule, others to do more ordinary tasks. It is by meeting these duties that one lives out the common priesthood or kingship that comes from Christ, through baptism and the Spirit.

John Calvin. While the division of the three offices of Christ was already developed to some extent by Erasmus, Osiander, and Bucer, in the sixteenth century it received its fullest and most lasting treatment from John CALVIN in the *Institutes of the Christian Religion*, Bk II, 15. For all three offices, Christ was anointed by the Father when he was sent into the world. The prophetic office was and is exercised through the proclamation of true doctrine. The royal office is the rule that he has over believers through his resurrection from the dead and his sitting at the right hand of God. To explain the priestly office, Calvin predicates it of Christ's role as Mediator and looks both to the sacrifice of his death and his heavenly intercession. Because of the adequacy of his satisfaction for sin, he is now our heavenly intercessor, and it is only through his prayers that we have access to the Father.

For Calvin, there is a sense in which the baptized participate in both roles of Christ's priesthood, that of offering and that of prayer: ''We are,'' he writes, ''defiled in ourselves, yet we are priests in him, offer ourselves and our all to God, and freely enter the heavenly sanctuary that the sacrifices of prayer and praise that we bring may be acceptable and sweet-smelling before God'' (II.15.6). In fact, to speak of another priesthood, as to speak of the Mass as an immolating of Christ, is ''detestable'' (ibid.).

With the special priesthood of the ordained in the Church, the Reformers have no truck. Among other things, both Luther and Calvin associate the claim to the chalice at the Lord's Supper with the baptismal priesthood (Luther, *The Blessed Sacrament of the Holy and True Body of Christ, and the Brotherhood*, *Luthers Werke in Auswahl* 35, 49–75; Calvin, *Institutes* Bk IV, 17. 44–47). Calvin eloquently appeals to the testimony of the Fathers in this regard, quoting what they say about the meaning of eating and drinking from the flesh and blood of Christ to which all are called without distinction. This reminds us of how early Christian writers saw participation together at the table of the Lord's Supper as the most fundamental exercise of the royal priesthood.

Council of Trent. It was not one of the tasks of the Council of TRENT to resolve questions of Christology and soteriology, which were not the issues in dispute. The Decree on Justification, chapters six and seven (H. Denzinger, *Enchiridion symbolorum,* 1526–1530), when speaking of the redemptive work of Christ used the categories of merit and satisfaction rather than those of priesthood and sacrifice, since these touched more closely on the dispute with Martin Luther. The Decree on the Sacrifice of the Mass (H. Denzinger, *Enchiridion symbolorum,* 1738–1750), whose separation from the Decree on the Sacrament was highly significant, explained that in the sacrifice of the Mass Christ is both priest and victim, the same priest and victim as offered on the Cross but now offered in an unbloody manner in this memorial representation, which he left to his Church. The immolation, deemed the essence of sacrifice as this had been spelled out in scholasticism, is located in the words of Christ at the Supper, repeated by the ordained priest who acts by the power of Christ. For the faithful, the best participation in this Mass, according to the conciliar decree, is to receive communion, but assistance at the priestly action, offering oneself in communion with Christ, is also a way to take part in the sacrifice and in its fruits.

The Decree on the Sacrament of Order (H. Denzinger, *Enchiridion symbolorum,* 1763–1778) affirmed the institution of the priesthood along with the institution of the eucharistic sacrifice at the Last Supper. In priestly ordination, the recipient is endowed with an indelible sacramental character, which distinguishes the ordained from the baptized. The Council did not resolve the debate about the sacramentality of the episcopacy but did affirm the superiority of bishops over presbyters, attributing to bishops the power to govern the Church, which they hold as successors of the apostles (H. Denzinger, *Enchiridion symbolorum,* 1767/8).

From Trent to the Twentieth Century

In the aftermath of the Council of Trent, marked particularly by the treatise *De Ecclesia* of Robert BELLARMINE, the royal priesthood of the baptized suffered an eclipse. The Church was viewed as a congregation of the faithful and a hierarchical society, the bishops being endowed with the powers of order and jurisdiction needed to govern the Church, Priesthood as such, and the Sacrament of Order, were practically identified with ordination to the presbyterate and with the celebration of the Eucharist. In his treatise, *De Christo Capite totius Ecclesiae* (*Opera Omnia*, Tomus Primus. Naples and Paris: Laureil, 1872), in chapter one Bellarmine treated Christ as Mediator, but without mentioning priesthood. He is mediator in four senses: he judges, he speaks to the people on behalf of God, he prays and makes supplication for others, and he makes satisfaction by shedding his blood for sin and offense, thus releasing sinners by his death. In the first three senses, others also can act as mediators, but it is in the fourth sense that Christ is the one mediator between God and humankind.

In the third book of the treatise, *De Romano Pontifice* (ibid.), in chapter XXI, Bellarmine connected mediation with priesthood in order to explain, against the attacks of the Reformers, how Christ acts in the actions of priests, especially in the Eucharist. Christ is a priest forever because he offered himself once and for all through his death in order to make satisfaction for sins. Contrary to what the Reformers said of Catholic doctrine, the Mass does not take from this offering, but it is the same priest now offering himself through the ministry of many priests in mystery. Bellarmine mentions the priesthood of Christ only in connection with ordained priesthood, and then the meaning which he gives to the offering of his death is that of making satisfaction for sins.

French School. To understand the theology that prevailed at the outset of the Second Vatican Council, one cannot pass over the influence on the ideal of priesthood of the French School of Spirituality, associated with Cardinal de BÉRULLE and Saint-Sulpice. Pierre de Bérulle's basic theological insight or intuition was what he saw as the intimate union between the ordained priest and Christ the mediator. Sacrifice, in communion with the sacrifice of Christ, is at the heart of this vision of the priesthood. This is not, however, understood in a narrow sacramental or liturgical sense, albeit the celebration of the Mass is at the core of the priest's ministry and of his life. Sacrifice is a gift of self and an act of mediation on behalf of others and must be operative in the entire ministry of the priest, in word and pastoral care as well as liturgy. The perfection of the priesthood in the order of mediation has to carry with it a perfection in the spiritual order, so that it constitutes a higher calling in the Church (see ''A Letter on the Priesthood,'' in *Bérulle and the French School: Selected Writings*, edited with an introduction by William H. Thompson, translated by Lowell M. Glendon. New York 1989, 183–185).

Monsieur OLIER consolidated Bérulle's ideal of priestly holiness by writing of the special union of the priest with Christ, priest, and victim. Olier's major influence on priestly life came through his conferences on the seven clerical orders, published posthumously as a treatise by Monsieur Tronson (*Traité des saints ordres, publié par M. Tronson selon les écrits et l'esprit de Jean-Jacques Olier*. Paris 1953). Priesthood is not purely a sacramental office but embraces the entire work of priests for the sanctification of the faithful. Sacrificing his Son as an act of divine sovereignty in restoring holiness to the world, God now unites the priest with himself, as well as with the victim, Jesus. The priest now shares with God the power to produce the Son, in the sacrament of the altar and in the lives of the faithful. He also shares the power to give or send the Spirit, for the sanctification of the Church. This calls for a profound holiness of life, which is nourished by the adoration of Christ in the Blessed Sacrament.

John EUDES (*The Priest: His Dignity and Obligations*, translated by William Leo Murphy. New York 1947) in turn wrote of priests as other Christs, ''walking among men,'' representing his authority and perfections. Eudes calls on the *Celestial Hierarchy* of the Pseudo-Dionysius to speak of them as visible gods, who take the place of God in this world. In godlikeness, the bishop is first in rank, the priest second, and the faithful third. Eudes did not neglect the priesthood of the baptized, since they too share in Christ's priesthood, but he ranked them lower than the ordained. He exhorts the faithful to respond to their calling by offering themselves with Jesus Christ as priests and as victim and to welcome Christ to dwell in them through sacramental communion.

Priesthood in Theology before the Second Vatican Council

Before the Second Vatican Council, there were two comprehensive studies of the priesthood of Christ and of the Church which amply cited texts from a long tradition and offered a theological synthesis. In *Das Priestertum Christi im Anschluss an den hl. Thomas von Aquin. Vom*

Mysterium des Mittlers in seinem Opfer und unserer Anteilnahme (Paderborn 1934), Emil J. Scheller offered a thomistic synthesis but within the boundaries of a long historical study. The nature of the priesthood is rooted in the incarnation of the Son of God and hence is an eternal priesthood. In his understanding of the Alexandrian and Augustinian traditions, Scheller identified mediation and priesthood without differentiation. In his view, for Thomas Aquinas the essence or constitutive form of Christ's priesthood is to reconcile, that is, to atone or make one God and sinful humanity. Scheller located the exercise of this priesthood in the sacrifice of Christ's death, which he called his immolation. Done once and for all on the Cross, this immolation continues to be sacramentally offered in the Eucharist.

For his part, in *Le sacerdoce dans le mystère du Christ* (Paris 1957) Joseph Lécuyer connected the priesthood of all the baptized and the priesthood of the ordained with the priesthood of Christ through an appeal to patristic writings. With priestly anointing, he associated kingly and prophetic, showing that for both Christ and the Church the three may not be separated. Amply quoting patristic texts, he offered a dynamic view of Christ's priesthood, tracing its origin and enactment through different stages. These are the incarnation, the anointing at the Jordan, the offering on the Cross, his consummation in the glorification of his resurrection and ascension, and finally his eternal priestly intercession. Jesus is the one true priest because he alone could offer the true sacrifice which reconciles humanity with God and penetrate with his immolated and glorified humanity into the heavenly sanctuary. The faithful are priests because through union with Christ and through the gifts of the Spirit, they participate sacramentally in his paschal mystery and can offer spiritual sacrifice in communion with Christ's sacrifice. Their anointing is prophetic and kingly as well as priestly. The ordained share in the threefold anointing of Christ, as did the apostles, that is, as ministers through whom the paschal mystery of Christ is enacted and participated in the Church. Lécuyer thus put the relation between ordained and baptized in the sacramental enactment of the paschal mystery. Ordained priesthood belongs first and foremost to bishops since it is they who are the successors of the apostles. Presbyters share in this priesthood through their communion with bishops. This reverses the medieval tendency to distinguish the two orders by identifying priesthood with presbyters and governing with bishops.

A third theological work of importance to thought on the priesthood was the historical concatenation of texts on the royal priesthood of the faithful by Paul Dabin, *Le sacerdoce royale des fidèles dans la tradition ancienne et moderne* (Paris 1950). While the author insists strongly on the distinction between the priesthood of the faithful and that of the ordained, and while the texts offered need study in context, the compilation made it clear that ecclesiology cannot be done without considering the royal priesthood of the baptized.

On a practical level, in the late nineteenth and early twentieth centuries, new perspectives on the relation of all the baptized to the priesthood of Christ and to his kingship began to emerge through their renewed way of taking part in the liturgy and through Catholic Action in the apostolate. While an official recognition of the priesthood of the faithful was already found in the encyclical letter of Pius XII, *MEDIATOR DEI* (H. Denzinger, *Enchiridion symbolorum,* 3851), the key work in giving this theological formulation may justly be said to be *Jalons pour une théologie du laicat* (Paris 1953) by Yves CONGAR. Congar evoked the words of Saint Augustine where he spoke of the *una sancta societas*, which is offered to God in the Eucharist, head and members. This communion in faith, service, and worship is the fundamental reality of the Church in which its members partake in different ways according to their order. By the baptismal character, all the faithful share in the priesthood and kingship of the Church and of Christ.

Priesthood is exercised in spiritual sacrifice and through an active participation in the liturgy, both intimately connected. Kingship, as well as prophecy, provide the ground for an active participation in the apostolate. Certainly, kingship (*Jalons*, 314–366) consists first and foremost, according to Congar, in dominion over the self and in submission to the will of God in all things. A Christian practices freedom of the Spirit in relation to temporal matters and thus in their exercise appears as an eschatological sign of the ultimate nature of Christ's kingship. However, it is also in virtue of this kingship that lay persons have some active role in the apostolate and in regulating the affairs of the life of the Church itself, something for which canon law should make provision.

The Second Vatican Council

Such writings amply prepared the way for consideration of the Church at the Second Vatican Council. In the course of the Council itself, one of the first issues which the bishops had to decide was whether the episcopacy is a sacrament or simply a governing and jurisdictional power added to the priesthood already received. Once it was decided to treat of it as a sacrament, it was clear that the ministry which flows from ordination could not be seen uniquely as sacramental or liturgical. Liturgical history, now better known through the critical edition of liturgical sources, made it clear that a person could be ordained to the episcopacy without receiving any previous order. It was also noted that bishops were ordained by the laying-on of hands to a ministry that comprised sacrament, teaching, and pastoral care.

The way found to allow for this ampler view of the episcopal office was to relate it directly to Christ's own mission and then to distinguish the threefold office of Christ as priest, prophet, and king, in each of which the bishops are said to share. This same distinction was used to explain the ordination and ministry of presbyters and deacons. It was likewise followed in presenting the relation of all the baptized to Christ and his Church. All the members of the Church, each in their own place, were thus said to participate in the priestly, royal, and prophetic anointing and office of Christ.

While the term ''royal priesthood'' was used by the Church or of the baptized in a comprehensive way (e.g., *Lumen gentium* 10), it is clear that in the documents of the Second Vatican Council priesthood is not the fundamental term by which to designate order and the role of the ordained. Mission, consecration, and anointing, as ways of participating in the reality of Church and of Christ's redemptive work, serve as more basic terms for both the baptized and the ordained. These terms provide the foundation for talking of a share in the anointing and mission of Christ as priest, prophet, and king.

The role or office of Christ as Priest is associated primarily with the Church's sacramental worship. In the composition of the conciliar texts, the comprehensive designation of the Church, the Body of Christ as ''royal priesthood'' gives way to a use of the separate terms of priesthood, prophecy, and kingship. Priesthood is usually predicated of liturgical participation, prophecy of a role in spreading or teaching the Gospel, and kingship of witness to the kingdom of God in the world and of the role of Church government. While these titles offered a useful way to face some of the emerging questions about episcopacy, laity, and the mission of the Church, the distinctions and the use of the titles are closer to the thought of John Calvin than to that of the patristic Church.

Though they have served good purpose in theology and in ecumenical dialogue, there are some problems about the use of these titles as a way of retrieving a scriptural and patristic tradition. Where it is said that the Church has been constituted as a royal priesthood by Christ the High Priest in LG 10, the scriptural texts cited are Revelations 1:6 and 5:9–10, and 1 Peter 2:4–10. However, in these texts the kingdom and the priesthood of the Church are said to flow from Christ as king and as witness, rather than as priest. This, as seen from the scriptures, is significant for the meaning of priesthood as a quality of the Church and of its members.

Differentiating priesthood from other offices, whether of Christ or of the Church, does not have a clear scriptural foundation. As already seen, in the early Church ''priest'' alone, or ''priest and king'' as a couplet, served as symbolic terms that presented and interpreted the entire work of Christ, often in this case being joined with ''sacrifice.'' In describing the redemptive work of Christ, his overcoming of sin and death, his reconciliation of humanity with God, these terms were used as metaphors to express the unique and distinct character of his atoning mission.

While the tendency has been to follow through with the Calvinistic and conciliar distinction, the theological elaboration of the insights contained in a larger view of the Church's mission and ministry would benefit from a careful study of scriptural and patristic tradition. The prevailing usage does not do full justice to the original use of the metaphor of priesthood and its relation to the overcoming of sin and death through the taking on of flesh, self-emptying, and suffering. Nor does it do justice to the image of royal priesthood. To list priesthood alongside other offices or to predicate it narrowly of sacrament and liturgy misses its comprehensive allusion to the whole life of the Body of Christ in its participation in Christ's mystery.

Conclusion

The overview of tradition has brought to light three ways of using the image or the idea of priesthood.

The first has its origin in scripture and patristic writings. Christ is called the priest or king of the new covenant, his death is called the sacrifice by which sin and death are blotted out and through which humanity is given access to God. This priesthood is from eternity because it springs from the Father's love and fidelity. It endures into eternity where Christ sits in his risen flesh at God's right hand. Priesthood, kingship, and sacrifice are terms used by the scriptures and by ecclesiastical writers to express the identification of the Son of God with weak humanity and the strength of the suffering through which he took on the powers that would undo humankind. Transformed in their own flesh by reason of the taking flesh of God's Son and their sacramental communion with him, those who are given access to God through Christ, the Church his body and his people, are a royal priesthood. In this, there is no difference of kind among his members and the only difference of degree is in the depth of communion with him, in the splendor of holiness that manifests and transmits God's love. It is this which readies for ministry and ordination to the service of others.

A second attribution of priesthood follows from this. The communion of Christ and his members in the one

Body is sacramentally celebrated through rituals of initiation and in the eating and drinking of his life-giving flesh and blood. Sacramental communion is the basic act of the royal priesthood and the offering of spiritual sacrifices flows from the sacramental gift. Within this context of sacramental representation, however, the role of the bishop took on its own representative character. His actions in the sacramental mystery represent the presence and the action of Christ and his teaching and pastoral ministry lead the faithful to this mystery. Hence there emerged a special attribution of priesthood, as well as of kingly power, to bishops, and thus to presbyters. However, this usage remains firmly grounded in the priority of the sacramental representation of Christ's life-giving sacrifice in the gift of his body and blood and so in the prior attribution of royal priesthood to the whole Church.

A third attribution of priesthood emerges later, particularly in the Latin West, and it is given to the ordained in virtue of their role and power to act as instruments of Christ in the sacraments and especially in the Eucharist. This attribution manifests a change of concern, language, and thought-structure wherein categories of being, power, order, and office prevail. The concept of Christ's own priesthood is affected, for it is closely related to his action in the sacraments and in the offering of the Eucharist. The combat with sin, suffering, and death, which is foremost in the Letter to the Hebrews, recedes in favor of the language of cult and satisfaction for sin. Instead of being used as metaphors to express the meaning of this combat and its efficacy, priesthood, sacrifice, and kingship are used as definable concepts in their own right.

In terms of the exercise of instrumental power, participation in Christ's priesthood was distinguished into passive and active, into being recipient and being instrument. Enough was retained of the scriptural and patristic imagery of priesthood, as in the French School of Spirituality, to see that being a priest must mean close identification with Christ in his suffering and his service of others. However, the concepts of office and power dominate. To be a bishop or a priest is a call to communion with Christ, priest, and victim, but it is fundamentally a communication of power. In contemporary documents and theological writing, rather than attributing a passive power to the priesthood of the baptized, they are said to have an active part in liturgy and in offering spiritual sacrifices in virtue of their baptism.

It is in regard to the third attribution of priesthood that the doctrine of the Second Vatican Council speaks of a difference not only in degree but in kind (LG 10). The meaning is clear, and a distinction of offices and roles in the Church is necessary for the sake of the ordering of community and of communion. The language of power is indeed tempered by the language of service, and it is often repeated that the mission of the ordained priesthood is to serve the priesthood of all the baptized. However, to speak of differentiation in priesthood through kind obscures the fundamental sacramental mystery of the royal priesthood of the Church as a sacramental and spiritual body. A preferable use of language may be to distinguish mission, ministry, and service. It would be more respectful of the first, fundamental and most original use of the language of priesthood which has to do with the power of Christ's suffering for sinful humanity and with the royal priesthood of his people, those who have been saved through this mystery.

Bibliography: K. BORNKAMM, *Christus—König und Priester. Das Amt Christ bei Luther im Verhältnis zur Vor- und Nachgeschichte* (Tübingen 1998). B. COOKE, *Ministry to Word and Sacraments* (Philadelphia 1976). P. DABIN, *Le sacerdoce royal des fidèles dans la traditionne ancienne et moderne* (Paris 1950). A. HOUSSIAU and J.-P. MONDET, *Le sacerdoce du Christ et de ses serviteurs selon les pères de l'église* (Louvain-La-Neuve 1990). T. HERMANS, *Origène, théologie sacrificielle du sacerdoce des chrétiens* (Paris 1996). J. LéCUYER, *Le sacerdoce dans le mystère du Christ* (Paris 1957). G. MATHON, ''Sacerdoce.'' *Catholicisme* 12, 245–260. M. MESSIER, ''Médiateur.'' *Catholicisme* 8, 1059–1084. K. B. OSBORNE, *Ministry. Lay Ministry in the Roman Catholic Church, Its History and Theology* (New York/Mahwah 1993). E. J. SCHELLER, *Das Priestertum Christi im Anschluss an den hl. Thomas von Aquin. Vom Mysterium des Mittlers in seinem Opfer und unserer Anteilnahme* (Paderborn 1934). R. SCHULTE, *Die Mess Als Opfer Der Kirche. Die Lehre frühmittelalterlicher Autoren über das eucharistiche Opfer* (Münster 1959). A. VANHOYE, *A. Prêtres anciens, prêtre nouveau selon le Nouveau Testament* (Paris 1980). G. WAINWRIGHT, *For Our Salvation. Two Approaches to the Work of Christ* (Grand Rapids, Mich. 1997).

[D. N. POWER]

PRIESTLY WRITERS, PENTATEUCHAL

Term applied to those responsible for one of the main traditions in Israel that was gradually edited to become the ''Priestly Code'' and conflated with the YAHWIST and ELOHIST traditions and with Deuteronomy to form the Pentateuch. The Priestly Code (abbreviated P) contains a story of creation, genealogies, a story of the flood, patriarchal narratives, an account of the Exodus and Covenant and a large number of laws. Because of its interest in laws and in the cult and because of the liturgical cast of its narratives, it is attributed to the priests of Judah. It is recognizable by its more didactic and redundant style, its numerical symbolism, chronological precision, and liturgical and legal emphases. P developed over a long period of time, many of its laws reflecting a primitive milieu. Probably in the postexilic period it incorporated the originally independent Holiness Code (or ''H,'' Leviticus ch. 17–26; *see* HOLINESS, LAW OF) and other material and, in the middle of the 5th century B.C. was conflated with the Yahwistic, Elohistic, and Deuteronomic traditions (J, E, D). P now provides the chronological and ethnological framework for the Pentateuch. (*see* PENTATEUCH for details and bibliography.)

[E. H. MALY]

PRIMACY OF THE POPE

The word primacy, which in general use means the state of being first, as in time, place, rank, etc., as applied to the pope means his state of being first of all the bishops, not only in rank or dignity, but in pastoral authority. The primacy of the pope, then, is that full, supreme, and universal authority over all the bishops and faithful of the Church which belongs by divine right to the bishop of Rome as the successor of St. PETER, who received such a primacy among the APOSTLES directly from Christ.

The doctrine of papal primacy, while always present in the deposit of revealed truth, was not always and in every part of the Church so clearly understood or explicitly professed as it has been in the Western Church since the time of Pope St. Leo the Great (d. 461). Lacking the space that would be needed to trace the history of this doctrine, this article will limit itself to presenting the three most authoritative statements that the Church has made on the nature of the papal primacy, namely, the decrees of the Council of FLORENCE and of the two Councils of the Vatican.

Council of Florence. The bull of union with the Greeks, *Laetentur caeli* (1439), contains the following solemn definition of papal primacy: ''We likewise define that the holy, apostolic see and the Roman pontiff hold the primacy over the whole world, and that the Roman pontiff himself is the successor of blessed Peter, prince of the Apostles, and that he is the true vicar of Christ, head of the whole Church and father and teacher of all Christians, and that to the same in blessed Peter was given the full power of feeding, ruling, and governing the whole Church, as is contained also in the acts of the ecumenical councils and the sacred canons'' (H. Denzinger, *Enchridion symbolorum* 1307). While this decree enjoyed only short-lived acceptance by the Greeks, it did mark a decisive victory in the West over conciliarism, the doctrine of the superiority of an ecumenical council over a pope.

Vatican Council I. In the canon concluding the third chapter of its dogmatic constitution *Pastor aeternus,* the first VATICAN COUNCIL solemnly defined that the Roman pontiff has not merely an office of inspection or direction, but the full and supreme power of jurisdiction over the whole Church, not only in matters that pertain to FAITH AND MORALS, but also in those that pertain to ecclesiastical discipline and government throughout the whole world; that furthermore he has not merely the greater share, but the whole plenitude of this supreme power, and that this power is ordinary and immediate, both over all the Churches as well as over all the pastors and faithful (Denzinger 3064). Other aspects of the doctrine of papal primacy contained in the decree, but not resumed in the canon, are the following. The end for which Christ instituted the primacy is to ensure the undivided unity of the episcopate, by which in turn the whole body of the faithful is maintained in UNITY OF FAITH and communion (Denzinger 3051). While the pope's power of jurisdiction over the whole Church is truly episcopal (3060), it does not conflict with the authority that the bishops have to rule their flocks as true pastors (3061). The pope has the right to communicate with the bishops of the whole world without interference from secular rulers (3062). He is the supreme judge to whom appeal can be made in all ecclesiastical cases; there is no higher authority in the Church to which appeal can be made over his judgment (3063).

In the Acts of the Council one finds an authoritative explanation of the terms episcopal, ordinary, and immediate, by which papal power is described in the decree. The intention of the council was to exclude the doctrines of such writers as J. von HONTHEIM, J. Eybel, and P. Tamburini, who had allowed the pope an authority outside of the Diocese of Rome only similar to that of a metropolitan archbishop with regard to the other dioceses of his province, that is, an authority of inspection rather than of true pastoral jurisdiction, limited to certain extraordinary cases of the neglect of their duties on the part of the local bishops. Against this, the council defined the pope's authority over the whole Church to be truly episcopal, meaning that he has the same kind of authority over the whole Church as each bishop has in his own diocese; to be ordinary, meaning that it belongs to the very nature of the papal office; and to be immediate, meaning that the pope can exercise his episcopal authority over the faithful of any diocese, without being required to use the bishop's mediation (J. D. Mansi, *Sacrorum Conciliorum nova et amplissima collectio* 52:1103D–06A).

On the other hand, as the official spokesman for the conciliar Commission on Faith explained, papal power is not unlimited or arbitrary. It is limited by the divinely given constitution of the Church, one of the basic elements of which is the episcopacy; hence the pope could neither in theory nor in practice deprive the bishops of their pastoral function or reduce them to the status of mere vicars of the pope [Mansi 52:715B–C; cf. Leo XIII, *Satis cognitum, Acta Sanctae Sedis* 28 (1895–96) 732].

St. Peter received his supreme power not for the destruction but for the building up of the Church, and in using it he was bound by the divine and natural law (Mansi 52:1105C–D; 1109A). Still, it must be admitted that there is no juridical appeal in the Church against a possible misuse of papal power. In the case of a publicly heretical or schismatic pope, most theologians hold that the other bishops collectively would have the authority to declare this man no longer pope, and to sanction the election of his successor. But against an abuse of papal power, the Church would have to resort to moral remedies: to persuasion and to prayer, relying on Christ's promises of divine aid (Mt 28.20).

Vatican Council II. In the third chapter of its *Dogmatic Constitution on the Church,* the second VATICAN COUNCIL, while affirming the collegial nature and authority of the episcopate, at the same time emphasizes the role of the pope as the divinely appointed head of the episcopal body or college. This college, it declares, has no authority except in union with its head, who has, in virtue of his office as vicar of Christ and pastor of the whole Church, the full, supreme, and universal authority over the Church, which he can always freely exercise. The college of bishops, always understood as united with the pope and never as separated from him, is likewise a subject of supreme and full power over the whole Church, but it cannot exercise this power without the consent of the Roman pontiff. It exercises this supreme power in a solemn manner in ecumenical councils, which it is the prerogative of the pope to convoke and to confirm; moreover, collegial authority can be exercised by the bishops dispersed throughout the world, provided that the head of the college summons them to a collegial action, or at least approves or freely receives their united action, so that it becomes a truly collegial act [22; *Acta Apostolicae Sedis* 57 (1965) 25–27].

From this it follows that there are two ways in which supreme authority can be exercised in the Church: either personally by the pope, or collegially by the whole episcopate, necessarily including the pope; there are not two separate supreme authorities that could ever come into conflict. The pope, as head of the body, remains free to decide whether a particular decision calls for collegial action or not. The other bishops, even collectively, have no authority to oblige the pope to choose the collegial rather than the personal exercise of supreme power in any given case. The fact that they can share in acts of universal jurisdiction does not give them such a right to do so as would conflict with the pope's liberty to exercise his supreme authority as he judges best [*Nota explicativa* 3–4; *Acta Apostolicae Sedis* 57 (1965) 74–75]. Hence there is no reason to see in the doctrine or practice of collegiality any conflict with the doctrine of papal primacy. To say that the pope, as head of the episcopal college, is in all his acts inseparably united with his fellow bishops, who by their membership in this body are made capable of sharing with him in the exercise of supreme authority, is in no sense to diminish that plenitude of authority which Vatican Council I defined the pope to have. The one visible head, to whom all the members are joined in love and obedience, is, by Christ's will, the manifest sign and the efficient cause of the unity of the episcopal body, by whose unity, under the guidance of the Holy Spirit, the whole Body of Christ is assured of its oneness.

See Also: APOSTOLIC SEE; APOSTOLIC SUCCESSION; AUTHORITY, ECCLESIASTICAL; BINDING AND LOOSING; BISHOP (IN THE BIBLE); BISHOP (IN THE CHURCH); CONCILIARISM (HISTORY OF); CONCILIARISM (THEOLOGICAL ASPECT); COUNCILS, GENERAL (ECUMENICAL), THEOLOGY OF; INFALLIBILITY; KEYS, POWER OF; PAPACY; UNITY OF THE CHURCH; CHURCH, ARTICLES ON.

Bibliography: G. GLEZ, *Dictionnaire de théologie catholique,* ed. A. VACANT et al. (Paris 1903–50) 13.1:247-344. U. BETTI, *La costituzione dommatica ''Pastor aeternus'' del concilio Vaticano I* (Rome 1961). G. DEJAIFVE, *Pape et évêques au premier concile du Vatican* (Bruges 1961). G. THILS, *Primauté pontificale et prérogatives épiscopales* (Louvain 1961). K. RAHNER and J. RATZINGER, *The Episcopate and the Primacy* (New York 1962). P.C. EMPIE and T.A. MURPHY, *Papal Primacy and the Universal Church* (Lutherans and Catholics in Dialogue 5; Minneapolis 1974). H.U. VON BALTHASAR, *The Office of Peter and the Structure of the Church* (San Francisco 1986). P. GRANFIELD, *The Limits of the Papacy* (New York 1987). R. B. ENO, *The Rise of the Papacy* (Wilmington, Del. 1990). K. SCHATZ, *Papal Primacy: From its Origins to the Present* (Collegeville 1996). M. BUCKLEY, *Papal Primacy and the Episcopate* (New York 1998). H. J. POTTMEYER, *Towards a Papacy in Communion* (New York 1998). J. R. QUINN, *The Reform of the Papacy* (New York 1999).

[F. A. SULLIVAN]

PRIMEVAL AGE IN THE BIBLE

The period of the origins of the world and of man as related in Genesis ch. 1–11. Although the Pentateuch as a whole is based upon four main sources, only two of these, the priestly (P) and the Yahwistic (J) sources, are represented in the first 11 chapters of Genesis (*see* PRIESTLY WRITERS, PENTATEUCHAL; YAHWIST). Moreover, the literary genre of these chapters is of such a peculiar nature that it must be studied in detail for a proper understanding of the narrative.

Ancient Traditions

The primeval age covers the period from the creation of the world to Abraham. It can be divided into three main parts: (1) the creation and the Fall: Gn 1.1–6.4; (2) the Flood: 6.5–9.17; (3) the Flood to Abraham: 9.18–11.32.

Structure and Contents. Although the J and P traditions are mixed in Genesis ch. 1–11, it is useful to list each tradition separately.

1. J tradition
   - *a.* 2.4b–3.24: creation of man and woman, paradise, temptation, and Fall
   - *b.* 4.1–26: Cain and Abel and genealogies
   - *c.* 6.1–8: increasing corruption of humanity
   - *d.* 7.1–8.22: Noah and the Flood (interwoven with P)
   - *e.* 9.18–27: sons of Noah; sin and curse of Canaan
   - *f.* 10.8–19, 24–30: peopling of Earth
   - *g.* 11.1–9: tower of Babel
2. P tradition
   - *a.* 1.1–2.4a: creation account
   - *b.* 5.1–32: genealogy from Adam to Noah
   - *c.* 6.9–22: Noah and the ark
   - *d.* 9.1–17: covenant with Noah
   - *e.* 10.1–7, 20–23, 31–32: descendants of Noah; Table of the Nations
   - *f.* 11.10–26: descendants of Sem

History and Nature of Traditions. The tradition called J (10th century B.C.) contributed the underlying structure and gave the theological bearing to Genesis ch.1–11. It assured continuity and provided perspective for patriarchal history, since the latter was based upon a history that went back to the world's origins. About the 5th century B.C., the tradition called P received its present form, having previously been fluid from the 10th to the 5th century. During these 500 years, both traditions, representing popular collections of oral and written material, some of which was very ancient, underwent a formative process of reshaping and rethinking. The men who formed J and P were not creators of traditions, but rather religious thinkers and interpreters of events that were significant in the life of ISRAEL. So too, when the final redactor integrated the traditions into the present Genesis account, he presented a highly evolved compendium of theological insights on Israel's experienced history.

An analysis of these isolated J and P sections discloses far-reaching agreements as well as marked differences. Common to both is the general content and the central theme of universal good and evil. The differences lie chiefly in details of the accounts. The creation accounts clearly show two distinct traditions. Even though P is later, it does not use J's earlier material. Substantial unity is evident; yet there are differences in style, vocabulary, and the method of representing God in His relations with men. Thus both J and P traditions must have been incorporated side by side in the final editing.

Such an arrangement, however, is not used throughout primeval history. The Flood story, ch. 7–8, is the best example of a composite account, or a combination of P and J sources. In this narrative, the editor, respecting his source material, did not alter either tradition, but skillfully intertwined the two as into an artistically woven tapestry. The intricate combination caused duplications (cf. 6.13–22 with 7.1–5), contradictions in regard to the number and kind of animals taken into the ark (cf. 6.19–20; 7.14–15 with 7.2–3), variations in the timetable of the Flood (cf. 7.24; 8.3–5, 13–14 with 7.4, 10, 12; 8.6, 10, 12), and separate sources of the Flood's water (rain in 7.4, 12; 8.3, but the fountains of the abyss and heaven's windows in 7.11; 8.2). The traditions, even when fused, were reverently left unaltered because they were sacred and untouchable history. Although the traditions were recounted side by side in writing and thus in all their glaring contrast, they could not be changed by whim, for the contrasts themselves had become parts of sacred history.

Literary Genre

Genesis ch. 1–11, along with the patriarchal history of ch. 12–50 (*see* GENESIS, BOOK OF) form a prologue to Israel's history that actually began with the experience of election and salvation in the exodus from Egypt. Both these introductory sections were added later and were composed in the light of Israel's experience. The first 11 chapters related Israel's particular history to that of the whole world. Through its constant experience of God's salvation, Israel had developed, over many centuries of theological reflection, a profound understanding of the human-divine relationship and of God's activity in history. Chapters 1–11 are the compendium of that reflection, written in a literary form that bound together a group of independent but meaningful narratives into a religious epic that reaches historical proportions.

Description of the Genre. The primeval age as described in this account is not prehistory in the modern sense of the word, for the aim of the biblical writers was not to present a scientific, biological, anthropological, or geological record of the past; nor were they capable of rendering such an account of either the universe or man's origins. This primeval history is not even history for its own sake; it has an altogether different purpose. It is, rather, interpreted history or faith—imbued perception and understanding of experienced history. It uses historical data as well as legendary or popular traditions and sagas to teach fundamental religious truths. The literary form chosen by the biblical author is not comparable to modern literary types, nor does it correspond to the classical categories and thus must not be judged according to their norms. The literary forms of Genesis ch. 1–11 are to be evaluated on the basis of how well they achieve their own authors' desired goal. The ancient historical form employed a simple, popular style proper to a recently civilized people who used concrete and graphic narratives vividly to impress religious truths of great importance.

Ethical monotheism is the essential, vital, and distinguishing mark of these early biblical accounts. The basic tenets of Israel's monotheism are expounded through the integration of vivid stories, which contained a theological message, into a drama for the purpose of expressing the doctrines presupposed in the plan of salvation, namely, creation by God at the beginning, the special intervention of God in the production of man and woman from whom all humanity is derived, an original state of moral integrity and happiness, sin of the first pair of humans, the Fall, and the hereditary trials and punishments for sin.

Through its experience of God and His mighty acts, through faith and reflection, as well as practical and speculative wrestling with the great problems of life, Israel arrived at the knowledge of these early events. The religious conviction of good and evil was reflected upon, universalized, and extended in a historical mode to the very beginning of God's creation. Cast into a loosely historical genre whose vagueness was inevitable because of the time span between the events and the date of the writing, the colorful pedagogic narrative was the vehicle most fitting for Israel to express and to teach its beliefs in the divine and human realities of its ethically monotheistic system.

Origin of the Genre. The external form of the biblical narratives of events before the time of Abraham was not something that had been invented by Israelite tradition; it was available from the traditions of other cultures. Biblical tradition was familiar with Mesopotamian stories; the Patriarchs, in fact, had come from this region. Among the many foreign etiologies, or origin stories, the most conspicuous sought to explain such insoluble mysteries as the origin of man and the universe, order, the diversity of peoples and language, the pain of childbirth, the attraction of the sexes, the necessity of labor, and the inevitability of death. Given the relationship in theme between the biblical and other ancient eastern narratives, the biblical authors were probably indebted to ancient models also in matters of arrangement, phraseology, and details. Of far greater moment was the intentional interpretation imparted by the authors of J and P to the independent stories, which resulted in the spiritual message that was conveyed through unifying the separate scenes into one drama of religious history. Through dominating religious themes, the etiologies were turned into a profound theology that was related to Israel's SALVATION HISTORY.

Contents and Themes. At the very outset, Israel manifested its polemic with polytheism by presenting the creation story in an ethicomonotheistic framework and by emphasizing that in the beginning all creation was good, since God had created it. The best known of various ancient creation myths was the Babylonian *ENUMA ELISH* (J. B. Pritchard, *Ancient Near Eastern Texts Relating to the Old Testament* [2d, rev. ed. Princeton 1955] 60–72). Purified of any suggestion of biological relationship or struggle between chaos and God, the P tradition simply affirmed that everything that is came from the effortless word of God. The J tradition colorfully affirmed the profound theological truth that the essential datum of man's life is his immediate, direct, and total dependence on God. Thus Israel declared its faith that its own history was inseparably related to the world's history and that Israel's role in the world had meaning only because Earth and all men were made and preserved by Israel's God. Israel's experience that God had created it as His people presupposed that He existed as the unique Master of all peoples (Ex 19.5). From the awareness of election, Israel developed its consciousness of God's creation of and concern for all mankind and the universe.

Creation and Fall. The stage had been set for a panoramic view of universal history with the creation stories that formed a basic structure for all reality. Written in what has been called a liturgical didactic hymn, the creation story of ch. 1 was part of Israel's all-including praise of God in which it depicted His original plan. God's goodness was shown in His establishing of man over all creation. But even more important was God's granting to man an intimate friendship and union with his Creator. The story of PARADISE with the TREE OF KNOWLEDGE and the TREE OF LIFE became a theological medium to express that God placed only one restriction upon man—that he acknowledge his character as creature by acknowledging his Creator. Otherwise man was free and autonomous. From this picture of what God intended life to have been, the rest of the creation account portrayed what life actually was, what man had become, and how he had arrived at his present sad state. God was good, and there was good in the world; but in Israel's experiences, evil, disorder, and man's unhappiness were obvious. How did evil originate? The condition of man surely was not the blessed state described in the paradise account. God's plan had somehow been thwarted. Israel explained evil's origin as the result of man's willful separation from God. The alienation from God was not willed directly by God, but was the result of man's rebellion. Couched in anthropomorphic symbolism, the dramatic scenes of the temptation by the SERPENT in Paradise, the fall of man, and its consequences, taught a theology of sin and punishment that explained the reason for man's dire situation. The determination of the specific character of the first sin was not the author's preoccupation; through disobedience man violated the one simple law of the creation COVENANT and thus denied his own status of dependency. The theme of condemnation following upon sin was commonplace throughout salvation history.

All was not lost, however. God, on His part, did not withdraw all the blessings of His creation pact; the human couple did not immediately die, but were condemned to a hard life that would end in death. Nevertheless, the battle against evil continued, indicating that man had not been completely conquered by the serpent. The PROTOEVANGELIUM had been proclaimed. God continued to have concern for man by clothing him (3.21) and by allowing him to use his function as the source of new human life (3.20; 4.1). Yet man could not himself undo sin's effects; only God could take away the curse.

As the narrative progressed, the effects of sin and evil became, however, more serious. Chapter 4 presupposes an already highly developed civilization (4.2), institutional worship (4.3), and widespread population (4.14). It does not relate, then, the fortunes of the first man's sons. Originally the tradition may have reflected the animosity between shepherds and farmers, but the story has been elevated from a tribal saga to a universal lesson by the biblical author. The bitter fruits of rebellion infected all the descendants of the first humans. Sin led to sin and gathered momentum; it had repercussions in every walk of life. The first sin resulted in a strained relationship between God and man that led to enmity between man and his brother. Murder, jealousy, bigamy, and revenge were added to the list of rebellion. In the story of Cain and Abel the author used the theme of freedom of divine choice or election, an undercurrent of all sacred history. Verse 6 summed up the author's purpose for inserting the story at this point. ''Sin is crouching at the door like a beast'' means that sin was loose in the world, but man could and must master its temptation. The entire story, however, ends on a note of hope by emphasizing God's mercy toward Cain. Throughout salvation history sin evoked God's punishment; but in punishing, God always tempered justice with mercy.

Genealogies. The schematic mnemonic device, adopted from oral transmission, that linked present men to their ancestors by name was a form common to the priestly tradition. Here in Genesis the lists are not historically genealogical trees, but serve to span immense time gaps. The biblical author, desirous of demonstrating the unity of the history of salvation and of building toward the climax of his epic, employed the genealogies of P and a few from J to achieve both ends. (*See* GENEALOGIES, BIBLICAL.) Neither P nor J traced the genealogies back to the first man merely for purposes of national history. Rather, they recognized that God transcended history and played the decisive role in it from the first man down to their generation. The Cainite list in J (4.17–26) was based on two combined streams of tradition that were not harmonized. To Cain's progeny (v. 17–24) was appended a parallel line of Seth (v. 25–26), which also contained Cainite names. The J tradition described the cultural progress of organized community life, new occupations, and new professions. But simultaneous with cultural progress, there was an apparent increase in sin, expressed in the increased brutality of the ''Song of the Sword'' (4.23–24).

The Sethite genealogy of P (5.1–33, continued in 11.10–26) was a continuation of Gn 2.4a. There were 10 Patriarchs before the Flood and 10 after, corresponding to Babylonian king lists. But the long lives are very moderate when compared to those in Babylonian lists. The symbolic significance of the numbers is not known, but with the diminishing life spans, the biblical author wished to teach that man was deteriorating morally, thus setting the stage for the FLOOD (*see* PATRIARCHS, BIBLICAL).

The Deluge. A warning of impending disaster is given in 6.1–4. This mysterious and isolated fragment is mythological in flavor and has been the source of many controversial opinions. Recently discovered Hittite texts containing translations of Hurrian myths with Mesopotamian elements, dating back to the 2d millennium B.C., relate a popular legend regarding the birth of Nephilim or giants (Nm 13.13) from the union between mortals and heavenly beings. (*See* SONS OF GOD.) The J author might have alluded to such a legend. Without making any judgment on its truth, he placed it in the context of the Flood for etiological reasons. The mixture of superhumans with men served as an example of the increasing human perversity that occasioned God's punishment. The 120 years of 6.5 was already a shortening of the life span because of increased depravity.

In the biblical traditions, the Flood was not described as a natural event. In J it is employed as a parable of God's mercy and justice. The essential difference between the Flood story in J and in other ancient versions of such a cataclysm lies in the religious interpretation of the disaster. The J tradition expanded legendary stories about what might originally have been a great Mesopotamian flood to universal proportions to emphasize that YAHWEH, in contrast to the mythological gods, was a moral God who did not act capriciously but with a righteous purpose. His judgment was tempered by the mercy shown to Noah and his family. Yahweh was a saving God, and from the small remnant, He would make a new beginning. A new covenant was made between God and man (9.1–17) in language that was almost the same as that of the creation covenant. Yahweh would never again destroy mankind by a flood; the regularities of nature and the rainbow (8.20–22) were signs of His faithfulness to the pact. The Flood thus marked the end of one epoch in the relationship between God and man and the opening of a new one.

From Noah to Abraham. The salvific mercy shown to Noah did not long hold in check man's inclination to evil (8.21). The story of the discovery of wine, Ham's sin, and the curse of Ham's son, Canaan, came from J and indicated its low esteem for the Hamites and CANAAN and the Canaanites (9.18–27). The J tradition concluded its epic by inserting the TOWER OF BABEL story. Since the diversity of nations was already contained in Yahwistic elements in ch. 10, which came mainly from P, the story of the confusion of languages must have been incorporated in order to inculcate a religious lesson. The actions of the men in this story implied that man's impulse to revolt was still deeply rooted in him. Mankind had made little progress in his relationship to God.

The narratives of paradise, Cain and Abel, the Flood, and the tower of Babel were progressive variations on one theme. Man was a creature who had rebelled by arrogantly defying his Creator. In each case the sin was punished by God. Man attempted to obtain control of creation by severing himself from God and by obtaining complete security by himself alone.

The Yahwist thus brought his primeval history to a close on a sad note. The human situation appeared irremediable; men were geographically dispersed, separated from their fellow men and alienated from God. Yet it was precisely toward this perplexing situation that the Yahwist had orientated his dramatic epic. From Adam to the tower of Babel, he portrayed man in his highest dignity and in his pitiful distress. Unable by his own strength to bring order into his disordered world, man had to wait patiently and trustingly for God to take the initiative in restoring him to the full measure of the inheritance he forfeited by sin.

Genesis ch. 1–11 ended in utter tragedy, but it described only a part of the whole plan of salvation; the story was not over. Beginning with the call of Abraham (ch. 12), God's redemptive activity was to initiate His salvation response to man's need.

Bibliography: *Encyclopedic Dictionary of the Bible,* tr. and adap. by L. HARTMAN (New York 1963), from A. VAN DEN BORN, *Bijbels Woordenboek* 19:20–26. G. VON RAD, *Genesis: A Commentary,* tr. J. H. MARKS (Philadelphia 1961). E. A. SPEISER, *Genesis* (Anchor Bible 1; Garden City, N.Y. 1964). H. RENCKENS, *Israel's Concept of the Beginning,* tr. C. NAPIER (New York 1964). J. CHAINE, *Le Livre de la Genèse* (Paris 1951). D. BONHOEFFER, *Creation and Fall,* tr. J. C. FLETCHER (pa. New York 1959). C. A. SIMPSON, *The Early Traditions of Israel* (Oxford 1948). C. HAURET, *Beginnings: Genesis and Modern Science,* tr. J. F. MCDONNELL (2d ed. Dubuque 1964). B. VAWTER, *A Path through Genesis* (New York 1956).

[L. STEINER]

PRÍMOLI, JUAN BAUTISTA

Jesuit missionary and architect; b. Milan, Italy, Oct. 10, 1673; d. Paraguayan Reduction of La Candelaria, Sept. 11, 1747. He entered the Society of Jesus in 1716 and went to Buenos Aires with another architect, Brother Andrés Blanqui. After completing their novitiate in 1719, they began their collaboration. Both were professional architects, and they acted also as builders, working well together. The contention that one worked as the architect, the other as the builder is not true. Together they were responsible for most of the constructions in La Plata during their lifetimes: the cathedrals of Córdoba and Buenos Aires; the churches of La Recoleta; Las Catalinas, San Francisco, and La Merced in Buenos Aires; the Monserrat School in Córdoba; and the Cabildo of Buenos Aires, as well as many churches in the Reductions and many private homes in Buenos Aires, Santa Fe, and Córdoba. They generally adhered to the prevailing style in the country, which had a charming simplicity of line and harmonious proportions. However, when circumstances demanded, they knew how to introduce innovations as in the church of San Francisco in Buenos Aires and the façade (now destroyed) of the cathedral of Buenos Aires.

Bibliography: G. FURLONG, *Arquitectos argentinos durante la dominación hispánica* (Buenos Aires 1946).

[G. FURLONG]

PRINCE-BISHOP

A medieval, ecclesiastical institution peculiar to the Holy Roman Empire—even beyond the boundaries of Germany proper—denoting certain bishops (and abbots) who possessed not only spiritual jurisdiction but also temporal authority. They were independent governors of specific civil territories under the exclusive sovereignty of the emperor, and, like the secular princes, they participated in the governing of the empire itself.

Origin and Development. The origins of this institution lie in the early Middle Ages when the Germanic tribes closely associated priesthood with authority either among kinsmen or within a tribe. They lie also in the advancement of the social position of bishops effected by Constantinian imperial Church law, even though the episcopal power of arbitration was unable to make headway in Germanic territories. Furthermore, during the period of the migration of the barbarian nations bishops became the protectors of their flocks, saw that their people were fed and their cities defended, and handled all negotiations with the enemies. In consequence, by Merovingian times they had become almost lords in their sees—a situation comparable to that of the popes in the STATES OF THE CHURCH. The MEROVINGIAN and the CAROLINGIAN rulers, who, with few exceptions, named all bishops throughout their kingdom, generally attracted these educated, usually noble, and, because of the Church's property, wealthy bishops into government service. The bishops were treated as secular nobles. CHARLEMAGNE entrusted all of them, as *membra imperii,* with the establishment of law and order. In return they were granted numerous civil privileges: tax exemption, legal immunity, and, eventually, such sovereignty rights as the privilege of market and mint. As early as 887 Emperor Charles III had granted the rank of count to the bishop of Langres, and in 927 Henry I did the same for the bishop of Toul.

The Ottonian System. This development reached its climax under Emperor OTTO I, who opposed the secular nobility within the empire by establishing a reliable aristocracy of churchmen who were extensively invested with imperial rights and property. The economic and military services that the bishops and abbots were to render the empire were precisely regulated, and with their help the German emperors ruled supreme. But difficulties arose when, because of the political influence of his prelates, the emperor felt he had the right to intervene in their appointment (*see* INVESTITURE STRUGGLE). The problem, however, was resolved in the compromise Concordat of Worms in 1122, after which the bitter investiture controversy subsided. Meanwhile the conceit of the hierarchy was severely shaken. During the Ottonian period they had considered themselves partners in the *regale sacerdotium,* living as they did in the security of an undivided secular and religious world (e.g., BRUNO OF COLOGNE, ULRIC OF AUGSBURG). But the investiture controversy had drawn them into a serious internal conflict, which each had to resolve differently, according to his own judgment and insight. Furthermore, the Concordat of Worms made them conscious of a certain independence and autonomy that they as churchmen possessed.

Religious Governors. The imperial reform of the 12th century connected princeship with a specific territory that was now within the feudal authority of the king. This was the origin of the first real ''imperial'' bishops and abbots. Through the letters of privilege of Emperor FREDERICK II (1220 and 1232), imperial bishops and abbots became completely sovereign within their territory: the *membra imperii* became *principes imperii* and were an integral part of the empire. The prince-bishops were elected by their cathedral chapters; they, in turn, through their superiors, the three ecclesiastical electors in the Rhineland (Mainz, COLOGNE, and TRIER), soon won great importance at the election of kings or emperors. On an even broader scale, the prince-bishop (e.g., Berthold of Henneberg, Archbishop of Mainz), concerned with the imperial reform that Emperor Maximilian I had initiated in his German lands, made common cause with the GRAVAMINA of the German nation against Rome. The character and level of religious devotion evidenced by prince-bishops varied greatly over time and from place to place. In the later Middle Ages and the early modern period anti-clerical polemic and peasant rebellions frequently singled out the prince-bishops for some of their harshest attacks. Following the Council of TRENT many of the prince-bishoprics remained noble dominated institutions that were resistant to reform efforts. In modern times the prince-bishops tended to become the chief supporters of the empire, great patrons of art and culture (e.g., SCHÖNBORN), and especially the exponents of the trend toward a German national church.

The territories controlled by prince-bishops were relatively small when compared with their political importance. Thus even the archbishop of Mainz, who from the 10th century was arch-chancellor of the empire, governed a territory that would be considered modest by modern standards. Besides the three Rhineland Archdioceses, Salzburg, AQUILEIA, Utrecht, LIÈGE, and Würzburg were among the larger prince-bishoprics of the Holy Roman Empire.

Secularization. The so-called reform of Emperor SIGISMUND had already broached the issue of secularization of ecclesiastical territories. Then, during the Reformation, the middle and northern German principalities were actually secularized; those of northwest Germany were preserved only through the military intervention of the house of Wittelsbach. Later FREDERICK II THE GREAT, as part of his anti-Hapsburg imperial policies, forced the dissolution of all prince-bishoprics in Germany. The 1803 enactment of the delegates of the empire (*Reichsdeputationshauptschluss*) under Napoleon abolished them entirely, with the exception of Abp. Karl Theodor von DALBERG, who remained for a few years more in Regensburg. A few dioceses in Austria still retained the title of prince-bishopric in the 20th century.

Not to be confused with the prince-bishops are those prelates of the very numerous (about 40) imperial monasteries, who did not hold lands through feudal tenure and who had a voice in the diet only insofar as they were associates of the bench of prelates, at whose invitation they could participate.

Bibliography: O. KÖHLER, *Das Bild dergeistlichen Fürsten in den Viten des 10., 11. und 12. Jahrhunderts* (Berlin 1935). T.

MAYER, *Fürsten und Staat* (Weimar 1950). F. HEER, *Die Tragödie des Heiligen Reiches* (Vienna 1952) 9–81. L. SANTIFALLER, *Zur Geschichte des ottonisch-salischen Reichskirchensystems* (Vienna 1954). H. E. FEINE, *Kirchliche Rechtsgeschichte,* v.1, *Die katholische Kirche* (Cologne 1964). E. KLINGELHÖFER, *Die Reichsgesetze von 1220, 1231–32 und 1235* (Weimar 1955). H. RAAB, *Die Concordata nationis Germanicae in der kanonistischen Diskussion des 17. bis 19. Jahrhunderts* (Wiesbaden 1956). H. SCHMIDINGER, *Patriarch und Landesherr* (Graz 1954). K. BOSL, ''Würzburg als Reichsbistum,'' *Festschrift für Theodor Mayer,* v. 1 (Lindau-Constance 1954). G. MAY, *Die deutschen Bischöfe angesichts der Glaubensspaltung des 16. Jahrhunderts* (Vienna 1983). K. HAUSBERGER, ed. *Carl von Dalberg* (Regensburg 1995) 161–181; *Lexikon für Theologie und Kirche*[2], ed. J. HOFER and K. RAHNER, 10 v. (Freiburg 1957–65); suppl., *Das Zweite Vatikanische Konzil: Dokumente und Kommentare,* ed. H. S. BRECHTER et al., pt. 1 (1966) 4:619–622.

[H. TÜCHLE]

PRINCIPLE

Something first in a certain ORDER, upon which anything else follows. An order of before and after is found in many things and in different ways. This article merely describes the scholastic notion of principle as applied to nature and to knowledge, and gives some distinctions that are commonly associated with it.

Principles in nature and knowledge. A succession of parts, one after another, is discernible in the material world, not only in the magnitudes of bodies but also in their MOTION and in TIME. The order of parts identifiable in local motion, itself most evident to man, enables him to understand the order in other changes. Hence he speaks of the principles of making or generating, which may be either intrinsic to the product or extrinsic to it. The foundation, or first part made in an edifice, is an intrinsic principle; likewise, the first part developed in organic generation, such as the heart or the brain, is such a principle. On the other hand, the mover or source of the motion is an extrinsic principle, as is the end or goal of the agent, insofar as the agent tends to a good beyond itself. The first principles in the order of nature are usually identified as matter, form, and privation (*see* PHILOSOPHY OF NATURE; MATTER AND FORM).

In the learning process, that which first becomes known and leads to further knowledge is called a principle. The basic truths prerequisite for all learning are named axioms; other propositions that are only relatively first and of particular application, whether true or merely probable, are called hypotheses or postulates. According to the natural realism of ARISTOTLE and St. THOMAS AQUINAS, axioms express reason's grasp of things as intelligible, with their necessary and universal reasons of being. According to Immanuel KANT, principles of thought merely express reason's understanding of necessary and universal relationships included in ordinary analytic judgments and, more especially, in judgments referred to as synthetic a priori. Kant doubted whether these principles are valid or true of things distinct from man's knowledge.

Furthermore, the rules and standards of art are called principles. In morals and politics, the rules of conduct and the standards of judgment are similarly referred to as principles, and this term is applied in law to the basic sources from which consequences flow. In each science and art, besides the first principles basic to the whole discipline, there are other principles proper to particular kinds of things included in the general subject. In arithmetic the basic principle is the unit, but each number is a principle of its own properties. Likewise, in geometry the point and the line are basic principles, but particular curves and figures serve as further principles. In physical science also, general principles hold for all natural things, and special principles for special kinds of things. In this way the principles of a science are about as numerous as its conclusions.

Common distinctions. A distinction is usually drawn between a principle and a cause. Every cause is also a principle, but some principles are not causes. Cause implies a certain influence on the being of the thing caused, and is defined as that upon which something follows of necessity and with dependence in being. But for a principle it is sufficient that it be first upon which something follows, whether or not it influences being in another. Moreover, a principle is not always something positive, as a point or part of a line, but may be something negative, as the darkness that precedes dawn, or something privative, as sickness that precedes health recovered.

From the examples given it is evident that the priority signified by a principle is often relative to a certain order under consideration and is not usually absolute or in every order. Only GOD is the absolutely first and strictly necessary principle (*see* UNIVERSE, ORDER OF). According to Catholic theology, there are certain principles even in the Holy TRINITY, as the Father is a principle with respect to the Son, and Father and Son are one common principle with respect to the Spirit.

What is a principle in one respect may be consequent in another respect. Some principles are first and prior in the nature of the case, that is, according to the order of being, whereas others are first only in regard to man's knowledge or consideration. Some principles are first in the order of theoretical knowledge, as the principle of CONTRADICTION or the principle of CAUSALITY, whereas others are first in the order of practical knowledge, as the

Two monks from Prinknash Abbey carry newly harvested wheat. The crop was grown on Abbey grounds. (©Hulton-Deutsch Collection/CORBIS)

principle of doing good and avoiding evil, and of preserving and perfecting the self (*see* SYNDERESIS).

See Also: CAUSALITY; ELEMENT; FIRST PRINCIPLES; AXIOMATIC SYSTEM; POSTULATE; LAW; THEORY.

Bibliography: M. J. ADLER, ed., *The Great Ideas: A Syntopicon of Great Books of the Western World* (Chicago, Ill. 1952) 2:420–436. V. E. SMITH, *General Science of Nature* (Milwaukee, Wisc. 1958). G. E. EKBERY, *First Principles of Understanding* (London 1949). A. FOSSATI, *Enciclopedia filosofica* 3:1615–16.

[W. H. KANE]

PRINKNASH ABBEY

Benedictine abbey outside Gloucester, southwest England. Anglican Benedictines under Aelred Carlyle (d. 1956) settled on Caldey Island (1906 and 1913); and, together with the nuns' Abbey of St. Bride, converted to Catholicism in 1913. They continued as Benedictines, but their conversion occasioned a decline in their material resources. CALDEY (now a Trappist abbey) was sold, and the Benedictines moved to Prinknash Park, given to them by Thomas Dyer-Edwardes (1928). Under Abbot Wilfrid Upson (1938–61) Prinknash flourished and founded priories at FARNBOROUGH and PLUSCARDEN (Scotland).

Bibliography: P. F. ANSON, *The Benedictines of Caldey* (London 1940); *The Call of the Cloister* (rev. ed. London 1964). O. L. KAPSNER, *A Benedictine Bibliography: An Author-Subject Union List*, 2 v. (2d ed. Collegeville, Minn. 1962) 2:250–251.

[J. STÉPHAN]

PRIOR

The official title of certain superiors in some religious communities. The Latin noun *prior* was used in the 6th century with a meaning close to that of the modern English ''superior''; with this meaning the word is used seven times in the *Rule of St. Benedict.* The contemporary meaning of prior came into use with the Cluniac reform and became common in England only after the Conquest. At this time the term appeared in reference to monastic officials who replaced and subsumed the *praepositi* and *decani* of the *Rule*—that is, those chosen by the abbot to share in the government of the community. From that time to the present, the Benedictines and the Cistercians have had three principal kinds of superior called prior. (1) The conventual prior is the elected superior of a conventual priory, an independent house that has not been elevated to the dignity of an abbey; with minor exceptions the conventual prior has the same power in his own house as the abbot does in his. According to the custom of the congregation, he is elected by his own monks for life or for a definite period. (2) The obedientiary or simple prior is the ruler of a dependent priory; he is appointed by the superior of the motherhouse and may be removed at the will of his superior. (3) The claustral prior is an official in an abbey and is appointed by the abbot; he shares as much of the rule of the monastery as is delegated to him by the abbot. To these three kinds of prior, found everywhere among the Benedictines, could be added the cathedral prior of medieval England, where the unique custom developed by which the bishop's chapter was constituted by an independent Benedictine priory. In some congregations of the 11th and 12th centuries, such as that of Cluny, in addition to the *prior claustralis,* there was a *prior major,* whose power extended to various dependencies of the monastery. In large medieval monasteries, second and third priors were sometimes appointed. The term prior passed over into the vocabulary of the later medieval institutions. The Premonstratensian canons preserved the full monastic vocabulary with respect to superiors. The Carthusians, Dominicans, Augustinian friars, Carmelites, and Servites preserved the use of the word prior to designate the superiors of their conventual priories; this usage was preserved, too, among some orders no longer existing, such as the Gilbertines and the military orders. Also, the word prior was used to refer to several new kinds of superior; thus the head of a group of priories is called a prior provincial among the Dominicans, Augustinians, Carmelites, and Servites; and the head of the order is called the prior general in the orders of the Augustinians, Carmelites, and Servites.

Bibliography: M. OTT, *The Catholic Encyclopedia,* ed. C. G. HERBERMANN et al., 16 v. (New York 1907–14; suppl. 1922) 12:427–428. D. KNOWLES, *The Monastic Order in England, 943–1216* (2d ed. Cambridge, England 1962). C. DU CANGE, *Glossarium ad scriptores mediae et infimae latinitatis,* ed. L. FAVRE, 10 v. (Niort 1883–88) 6:504–506.

[A. DONAHUE]

PRIOR MARRIAGE (IMPEDIMENT TO MARRIAGE)

Among the impediments to marriage, the Code of Canon Law lists that of prior marriage: ''One bound by the bond of a prior marriage, even if it was not consummated, invalidly attempts marriage'' (*Codex Iuris Canonicis c.* 1085 1). The Code of Canons of the Eastern Churches also states that one bound by the bond of a prior marriage invalidly attempts marriage (*Codex Canonum Ecclesiarium Orientalium c.* 802 §1).

The foundation of this impediment is not merely the law of the Church, but also the divine law. By both natural law and divine positive law, marriage possesses the property of unity. Therefore, any valid marriage precludes the possibility of entering another marriage by either consort unless the previous marriage has been dissolved. The Church teaches that the natural law itself forbids such a plurality of marriages, so that even the unbaptized cannot enter a valid marriage so long as the bond of a prior marriage exists.

The basis of this impediment is the property of unity that marriage enjoys and not the property of indissolubility. The prior marriage in question may be capable of dissolution for a cause other than the death of one of the spouses. Such would be the case in the use of the Pauline Privilege, whereby the marriage of two unbaptized persons is dissolved at the moment the marriage that favors the faith is contracted. Moreover, a marriage that has not been consummated may be dissolved by papal dispensation for a just cause (*Codex Iuris Canonicis c.* 1142; *Codex Canonum Ecclesiarium Orientatium c.* 862).

In the 12th century there was a dispute among two schools of canonists as to whether or not an unconsummated marriage was a perfect marriage. Some argued that a second marriage that was perfected by consummation would not be invalid because of the existence of the prior marriage. Pope Alexander III (1159–81) opposed such a theory, even though he probably held this opinion as a member of the School of Bologna before his accession to the Papacy. By the phrase ''even it was not consummated'' the code reaffirms the correct solution to this dispute.

''Even if the prior marriage should be invalid or dissolved for any reason whatsoever, it is not allowed to contract another marriage until it has been lawfully established that the former marriage was certainly invalid or dissolved'' (*Codex Iuris Canonicis c.* 1085 §2; *Codex Canonum Ecclesiarium Orientatium c.* 802 §2).

It is to be noted that the absence of a spouse for a long time is not in itself sufficient proof of death. If death cannot be proved from public documents, the diocesan bishop can issue a declaration of presumed death (*Codex Iuris Canonicis c.* 1707 §1; *Codex Canonum Ecclesiarium Orientatium c.* 1383 §1). The bishop must have moral certitude of the death of the spouse in order to issue the declaration (*Codex Iuris Canonicis c.* 1707 §2; *Codex Canonum Ecclesiarium Orientatium c.* 1383 §2). In uncertain and complicated cases, the Latin bishop must consult the Holy See (*Codex Iuris Canonicis c.* 1707 §3), while the Eastern bishop is to consult either his patriarch or the Apostolic See of Rome (*Codex Canonum Ecclesiarium Orientatium c.* 1383 §3).

Bibliography: J. ABBO and J. HANNAN, *The Sacred Canons* (St. Louis 1960) 2:1069. J. P. BEAL in J. P. BEAL et al., *New Commentary on the Code of Canon Law* (New York 2000) 1286–1288. P. J. JUGIS, *ibid.,* 1798–1799.

[J. F. DEDE/EDS.]

PRIORESS

The religious superior in certain houses of religious women. The word prioress is derived from the late medieval Latin word *priorissa,* which was certainly not in common use before the 11th century. This word was used to designate three kinds of superior: the claustral prioress, who assisted the abbess in government of the abbey; the prioress of a dependent house; and the prioress of an independent or conventual priory. The Benedictine prioresses of medieval England were often sophisticated aristocrats, as may be gathered from Chaucer's caricature, *The Prioress,* which was probably meant to represent the wealthy superior of an independent Benedictine house. The terminology has been preserved into modern times not only by the Benedictines and Cistercians, but also by the later medieval foundations that have survived: the Dominican nuns, the Poor Clares, the Carmelite nuns, the various congregations of the Canonesses Regular, and the Bridgettines.

Bibliography: E. E. POWER, *Medieval English Nunneries* (New York 1964).

[A. DONAHUE]

PRIORY

Any religious house governed by a prior or a prioress. The equivalent Latin word, *prioratus* (like the word *prior,* from which it is derived), did not come into common use until the 11th century. At this time there occurred a vast multiplication of religious houses, especially in France. Cluny was the principal, but by no means the only, house of this period that established many dependent houses. Some of these new houses, or priories, remained dependent on their motherhouse; others became independent, conventual priories; still others were advanced to abbatial status. In each case, the name priory was given because of the title of the superior, the prior or prioress. In England, besides the dependent and conventual priories of nuns and monks, there were also the cathedral priories attached to the cathedrals (*see* PRIOR). The term priory has been preserved not only by the Benedictines and Cistercians but also by many of the institutions of the later Middle Ages; thus today not only the monks but also the Premonstratensian Canons, the Dominicans, Carmelites, Carthusians, Augustinians, and Servites call some of their houses priories.

Bibliography: C. DU CANGE, *Glossarium ad scriptores mediae et infimae latinitatis,* ed. L. FAVRE, 10 v. (Niort 1883–88) 6:506. D. KNOWLES, *The Monastic Order in England, 943–1216* (2d ed. Cambridge, England 1962).

[A. DONAHUE]

PRISCA (PRICILLA) AND AQUILA

There are three references to Prisca (Priscilla) in the Pauline letters (1 Cor 16:19; Rom 16:2–5; 2 Tm 4:19) and another three in the Acts of the Apostles (Acts 18:2–3, 18, 26). In the Pauline letters she is called Prisca, whereas in Acts she is called Priscilla, which is the diminutive of Prisca. Among the individuals connected with Paul's evangelizing work, Priscilla and Aquila stand out because they are always mentioned together as a married couple. A Judeo-Christian couple, originally from Pontus in northern Asia Minor, they converted to Christianity most likely in Rome. Priscilla is usually named before her husband, which may imply that she had a stronger personality or that she was the more active of the two.

By examining the historical and social setting in which their mission took place, a more comprehensive view emerges of the couple's evangelizing activities. They moved from Rome to Corinth, as a result of the Emperor Claudius's edict, probably in 49 A.D., of expulsion against the Jews (Acts 18:1–2). In Corinth they met Paul. They hosted him in their home, offering him not only a place to stay but also employment in their tent-making workshop (Acts 18:2). When Paul left Corinth for Ephesus, the couple accompanied him (Acts 18:18). In Ephesus they hosted a community in their house and were actively involved in instructing Apollos ''more accurately'' about Jesus (Acts 18:26). The earliest reference to the couple is 1 Cor 16:19 when Paul, probably writing from their home in Ephesus, associates the couple in greeting the Corinthians. In the letter to the Romans (16:2–5) they head the long list of people greeted by Paul. Paul speaks highly of them and calls them ''my co-workers in Christ Jesus.'' The title ''co-worker'' is given by Paul to a limited number of people associated with his missionary work, and Prisca and Aquila are the only married couple given this title. As close friends of Paul, they even ''risked their own necks'' (Rom 16:3) for him; how or when is unknown. Since only Roman citizens would be sentenced to decapitation, one wonders whether this phrase hints to death by decapitation, thus revealing the social status of the couple as Roman citizens. Their willingness to face dangerous situations for a common cause strengthened the bond between Paul and the couple. Paul says then: ''To whom the Churches of the Gentiles give thanks.'' Though of Jewish origin (at least Aquila), the couple was supportive of Paul's mission to the Gentiles in Corinth and Ephesus.

The church that met in their home in Rome was probably a mixed assembly of Gentiles and Jews. Gentile Christians felt welcomed by Prisca and Aquila and were grateful to them. In 2 Tm 4:19 Paul, imprisoned in Rome, sends greetings to Aquila and Priscilla who are in Ephesus. If 2 Tm is an authentic letter of Paul, it provides additional information about Paul, Priscilla and Aquila, and if it is not written by Paul, it evidences how renowned Priscilla and Aquila were in the post Pauline era. Taking advantage of the sophisticated transportation system of the Roman Empire, Priscilla and Aquila traveled extensively and established themselves in some of the most bustling cities of the empire, like Rome, Corinth, and Ephesus. In these cities they opened their house to host other Christians. In early times of Christianity the house was the gathering place to celebrate their liturgy and to support one another. Of the four times (Phlm 2; Col 4:10; 1 Cor 16:19; Rom 16:4) in which the house churches are mentioned in the NT, two of them refer to Aquila and Priscilla's house in Ephesus (1 Cor 16:19) and Rome (Rom 16:4). The apocryphal Acts of Paul refers to Priscilla and Aquila when Paul enters their house in Ephesus. The Acts of Aquila mentions Clement and Niketas as the sons of this couple and describes the relationship of Aquila and Priscilla with Peter in Rome. Some archaeologists relate the church of St. Prisca in Rome to the site of the house of Prisca and Aquila on the Aventine.

Feast; Feb. 13 (Eastern Church), July 8 (Western Church).

Bibliography: M. BARBERO, *A First-century Couple, Priscilla and Aquila: Their House Churches and Missionary Activities,* (Ph.D. Dissertation. The Catholic University of America; Washington, DC, 2001); MURPHY-O'CONNOR "Prisca and Aquila: Traveling Tentmakers and Church Builders," *Bible Review* 8:6 (1992) 40–51.

[M. BARBERO]

PRISCA VERSIO

The *Prisca Versio* is a canonical collection from the fifth century. It is also called the *Itala Versio* and is dependent upon the *Atticus Versio.* It is different from the *HISPANA VERSIO* with which it should not be confused. The *Prisca* contains the canons of Nicaea and Sardica, with the same numbering, omits the Council of Laodicea, adds the Council of Chalcedon (whose canon 28 is attributed to the Council of Constantinople), and includes also some African canons. The *Prisca* was established at Rome. Its date is controversial. According to C. H. Turner, it was after Chalcedon; according to E. Schwarts, it was made under Pope Anastasius II (496–498) or Pope Symmachus (498–514). It is best preserved in the *Collectio Ingilrami* (also called the *Codex Chieti or Teatini*) of cod. Vat. Reg. 1997, and in the MS of Justel (Bodleian, Mus.100–102). According to W. M. Peitz, the *Prisca Versio* is the work of DIONYSIUS EXIGUUS.

Bibliography: G. VOELLUS and H. JUSTEL, eds. *Bibliotheca iuris canonici veteris,* 2 v. (Paris 1661) 1:277–320; reprint PL 56:747–816. E. SCHWARTZ, "Die Kanonessammlungen der alten Reichskirche," *Zeitschrift der Savigny-Stiftung für Rechtsgeschichte, Romanistische Abteilung* 25 (1936) 95–108. C. H. TURNER, "Chapters in the History of Latin MSS of Canons," *Journal of Theological Studies* 30 (1929) 337–347; 31 (1930) 9–20. F. MAASSEN, *Geschichte der Quellen und der Literatur des canonischen Rechts im Abendlande bis dem Ausgang des Mittelalters* (Graz 1956) 526–536. W. H. PEITZ, *Dionysius Exiguus-Studien,* ed. H. FOERSTER (Berlin 1960). C. J. VON HEFELE *Histoire des conciles d'après les documents originaux,* tr. and continued by H. LECLERQ (Paris 1907–38) 3.2:1149–1250. H. WURM, *Studien und Texte zur Dekretalensammlung des Dionysius Exiguus* (Bonn 1939).

[C. VOGEL]

PRISCILLA, ST.

Priscilla, also known as Prisca, was thought to be a Roman lady of the senatorial family of Acilii Glabriones. Her name is associated with the ancient cemetery on Via Solarea. She is not to be confused with the Prisca mentioned by St. Paul (Rom 16:3; 1 Cor 16:19) and in Acts 18:2, 18–26. In the 5th century there appeared in Rome a *titulus Priscae* on the Aventine, and this, as in like cases, became at the end of the 6th century *Sanctae Priscae.* However, in the Martyrology of St. Jerome for January 18, mention is made of a virgin Prisca or Priscilla; in one codex she is called a martyr and in later codices is connected with Rome. The 7th-century Itineraries know a Prisca martyr, buried in the cemetery of Priscilla and in the *Sacramentarium Gregorianum* there is the Mass of Bl. Priscilla martyr. The present Church of St. Priscilla on the Aventine stands over an ancient sanctuary of Mithras.

Bibliography: P. TESTINI, *Le catacombe e gli antichi cimiteri cristiani di Roma* (Bologna 1966), 50, 166. A. AMORE, *I martini di Roma* (Rome 1976), 66–67.

[E. HOADE/EDS.]

PRISCILLIAN

A highly educated Spanish nobleman after whom the ascetic movement of PRISCILLIANISM is named; b. Spain, *c.* 340; d. Trier, 386. After his conversion to Christianity Priscillian joined a lay community of ascetics, who became wandering preachers. After seeking to reform the clergy, they turned to a wider mission and encountered considerable success but also a fanatical reaction in Lusitania. Priscillian and his supporters, Bps. Instantius and Salvian, were denounced by Bp. Hyginus of Córdoba to their metropolitan, Bp. Hydacius of Mérida. The Council of Saragossa (380), at which only ten Spanish bishops were present, passed canons against the participation of women with men in religious gatherings; against lay doctors or teachers; and against Christians absenting themselves from church during Lent (c.1; 7.2). Canon five was probably directed at the rebellion of Priscillian, Instantius, and Salvian against their metropolitan. Despite this, Priscillian was elected bishop of Ávila. His opponents, Hydacius and Ithacius of Ossonoba, appealed against him to the secular authorities, alleging charges of Manichaeism and magic. Exiled from their province, Priscillian, Instantius, and Salvian traveled to Rome; Salvian died there, and the others journeyed to Milan. They failed to win the support of Pope DAMASUS or St. AMBROSE, but were reinstated by the civil authorities. Upon the successful revolt (383) of the usurper Maximus, however, their position was again jeopardized; and Instantius was deposed by a Council at Bordeaux (384–385). When Priscillian unwisely appealed to Maximus, he was condemned as a Manichaean, together with six supporters, and was executed at Trier.

Bibliography: *Works,* ed. G. SCHEPSS (*Corpus scriptorum ecclesiasticorum latinorum* 18; 1889), including *Pauli Apostoli epistolas: Canones,* rev. by an unknown Bp. Peregrinus, and *Tractatus* 9, possibly by Instantius. SULPICIUS SEVERUS, *Chronicon* 2.46–51 and *Dialogi* 2.11, ed. C. HALM (*Corpus scriptorum ecclesiasticorum latinorum* 1; 1866). *Patrologia Latina* 84:315–318, Council of Saragossa. E. BABUT, *Priscillien et le priscillianisme* (Paris (1909). J. M. RAMOS Y LOSCERTALES, *Prisciliano. Gesta rerum* (Salamanca 1952); *Clavis Patrum latinorum* ed. E. DEKKERS, 785–789. J. MARTIN, *Lexikon für Theologie und Kirche* [2] 8:768–769.

[J. N. HILLGARTH]

PRISCILLIANISM

Early Priscillianism was a mystical movement that originated in Spain during the late 4th century. It betrayed traces of that early Christian disdain for the institutions of the world that reminds one of DONATISM, and it became suspect because of its originally lay leadership and intense proselytism. Priscillianism created groups of devotees, especially among women, who withdrew from the regular church services to hold gatherings of their own. It made use also of apocryphal writings filled with a spirit hostile to marriage, wine, and meat, and it insisted on a theory of inspiration, based on the place given by the New Testament to prophecy in the early Church. Priscillianist asceticism seemed more coherent and logical than orthodox asceticism in that it directed its message intentionally to all the faithful and was not content with reaching merely a select minority.

The fragmentary and biased nature of the sources for the study of Priscillianism that is represented by the writings of adherents or of violent opponents makes it all but impossible to resolve the main problems concerned with this movement. Historians have not decided whether PRISCILLIAN himself was merely a leading ascetic and the founder of an ascetic movement or a heretic. It is important to distinguish rigorously between (1) the works ascribed to Priscillian himself or, alternatively, to his supporter, Bishop Instantius, (2) later Priscillianist writings, and (3) the references and quotations found in the works of adversaries of Priscillianism. The extreme asceticism recommended in authentically Priscillianist tracts can be paralleled in the practice of many contemporary Eastern ascetics, whose orthodoxy was never questioned.

The accusations of GNOSTICISM and MANICHAEISM leveled against early Priscillianism do not seem capable of proof; the condemnation of Priscillian himself and his execution at Trier were due mainly to political reasons and to the personal hatred indulged by Priscillian's opponents, Hydacius of Mérida, Ithacius of Ossonoba, and other worldly bishops. The execution was condemned not only by Priscillian's supporters, who saw him as a martyr, but by St. MARTIN OF TOURS, St. AMBROSE, and Pope SIRICIUS. The refusal of Pope DAMASUS and St. Ambrose to support Priscillian and his friends when they were first exiled in 381 seems to have been due to the fact that the Spaniards were canonically in the wrong, being in opposition to their metropolitan, Hydacius, and to the Council of Saragossa. Hydacius and Ithacius resigned or were deposed after the fall of their protector, the Emperor Maximus, in 388. But the stories they spread about Priscillianism were generally credited, and the Priscillianists themselves aroused legitimate suspicion among Catholics.

Having first dominated virtually all the province of Galicia, the movement deliberately aimed at obtaining the election of its leaders as bishops in Lusitania. Later it extended to southern France; and there was a Priscillianist bishop in Provence as late as 417 (Zosimus, *Epistolae.* 4.3). Almost inevitably, Priscillianism came into conflict with the not very strict Spanish bishops and later with the imperial authorities.

Priscillianism secured the support of some educated laymen, who produced apologetic works, now lost. After Priscillian's execution Galicia remained solidly Priscillianist until 400, when most Galician bishops were reconciled to the Church at the First Council of TOLEDO. Among them was Dictinius of Astorga, author of the *Libra,* which was denounced (*c.* 420) to St. AUGUSTINE because it justified lying to escape condemnation for heresy. After 400 Priscillianism survived in Galicia, where it was condemned by Orosius (*c.* 414), by Bp. Turibius of Astorga (*c.* 445), by Bp. Montanus of Toledo (*c.* 530), and by the First Council of Braga in 561. That council anathematized 17 errors, attributing them to Priscillianists. But Priscillianist works were produced after this date, and the errors denounced by opponents of later Priscillianism are a compound of SABELLIANISM, GNOSTICISM, and MANICHAEISM. The influence of Priscillianism can be noticed in the maintenance of the tradition of continence in clerical marriage already upheld at the Council of ELVIRA (*c.* 33); its effect on the text of the Bible should be noted also.

Bibliography: A. FRANZEN, *Lexikon für Theologie und Kirche*, ed. J. HOFER and K. RAHNER, 10 v. (2d, new ed. Freiburg 1957–65); suppl., *Das Zweite Vatikanische Konzil: Dokumente und Kommentare*, ed. H. S. BRECHTER et al., pt. 1 (1966) 8:769–771. A. D'ALÈS, *Priscillien et l'Espagne chrétienne* (Paris 1936). MARTIN OF BRAGA, *Opera omnia,* ed. C. W. BARLOW (New Haven 1950) 105–115, councils. OROSIUS, *Commonitorium de errore Priscillianistarum et Origenistarum,* ed. G. SCHEPSS (Corpus scriptorum ecclesiasticorum latinorum 18; Vienna 1889) 151–157. AUGUSTINE, *Ad Orosium contra Priscillianistas et Origenistas, Patrologia Latina,* ed. J. P. MIGNE, 217 v., indexes 4 v. (Paris 1878–90) 42:669–678; *Contra mendacium,* ed. J. ZYCHA (Corpus scriptorum

The beginning of the second tract of eleven tracts by Priscillian, Bishop of Avila, 6th-century MS (MS Mp. th. q. 3) in the collection of the Universitätsbibliothek, Würzburg, Germany.

ecclesiasticorum latinorum 41; Vienna 1900) 469–528; *Patrologia Latina*, ed. J. P. MIGNE, 217 v., indexes 4 v. (Paris 1878–90) v.33, letter 237. LEO I, *Patrologia Latina*, ed. J. P. MIGNE, 217 v., indexes 4 v. (Paris 1878–90) v.54, letter 15. TURIBIUS OF ASTORGA, *ibid.* 693–695. MONTANUS OF TOLEDO, *Patrologia Latina*, ed. J. P. MIGNE, 217 v., indexes 4 v. (Paris 1878–90) 65:51–58. JEROME, *De viris illustribus* 121–123, *Patrologia Latina*, ed. J. P. MIGNE, 217 v., indexes 4 v. (Paris 1878–90) v.23; *Patrologia Latina*, ed. J. P. MIGNE, 217 v., indexes 4 v. (Paris 1878–90) v.22, letters 75.3, 126.1, 133.3. *Clavis Patrum latinorum*, ed. E. DEKKERS (2d ed. Streenbrugge 1961) 785–797, 2302. MARTIN OF BRAGA, op. cit. 270–275. P. MONCEAUX, *Journal des Savants* NS 9 (1911) 70–75, 104–113. A. PUECH, ''Les Origines du priscilliansisme et l'orthodoxie de Priscillien,'' *Bulletin d'ancienne littérature et de l'archéologie chrétienne* 2 (1912) 81–95, 161–213. Z. GARCÍA VILLADA, *Historia eclesiástica de España,* 3 v. in 5 (Madrid 1929–36) 1.2:91–145, 357–361. J. A. DE ALDAMA PRUANO, *El símbolo Toledano I* (Analecta Gregoriana 7; Rome 1934). J. MADOZ, ''Arrianismo y Priscilianismo en Galicia,'' *Bracara Augusta* 8 (1957) 68–87. B. VOLLMANN, *Studien zum Priscillianismus Die Forschung, die Quellen, der fünfzehnte Brief Papst Leos des Grossen* (Kirchengeschichtliche Quellen und Studien 7, ed. H. S. BRECHTER; St. Ottilien, Ger. 1965).

[J. N. HILLGARTH]

PRITCHARD, HUMPHREY, BL.

Lay martyr; sometimes given as Humphrey ap Richard; b. in Wales; d. July 5, 1589, hanged at Oxford, England. While the pious Humphrey worked at St. Catherine's Wheel Inn, opposite the east end of St. Mary Magdalen's Church, Oxford, he covertly assisted refuge Catholics for 12 years. He was arrested and sent to Bridewell Prison, London, with BB. Richard YAXLEY, Thomas Belson, and George NICHOLS for assisting unlawful seminary priests. When told during his trial in Oxford that he did not know what it was to be a Catholic, he replied that he knew what he was to believe and that he would willingly die for so good a cause. He was beatified by Pope John Paul II on Nov. 22, 1987 with George Haydock and Companions.

Feast of the English Martyrs: May 4 (England).

See Also: ENGLAND, SCOTLAND, AND WALES, MARTYRS OF.

Bibliography: R. CHALLONER, *Memoirs of Missionary Priests*, ed. J. H. POLLEN (rev. ed. London 1924). J. H. POLLEN, *Acts of English Martyrs* (London 1891).

[K. I. RABENSTEIN]

PRIVATION (PHILOSOPHY)

Privation is the lack of a quality or form normally required by the nature of a thing. It is a type of contrariety, and is thus to be distinguished from simple negation, which is based on contradictory OPPOSITION. Privation (Gr. στέρησις) is opposed either to possession (Gr.ἕξις, Lat. *habitus*) or to form (εἶδος) as to its contrary.

Historical Development. ARISTOTLE claims, with justice, to have introduced the concept of privation into philosophy (*Phys.* 192a 3). His dialectic concerning the principles of CHANGE and the changeable shows that monistic cosmologists, such as Anaximenes, and pluralistic ones, such as Anaxagoras, invoked a sort of contrariety, but that all failed, as did PLATO, to distinguish between privation and the underlying substratum of change. St. THOMAS AQUINAS defines privation as neither an aptitude for form nor an inchoate form, nor some imperfect active principle, but the lack or contrary of form itself (*In 1 phys.* 13.4). For Aristotle and St. Thomas privation is an incidental (*per accidens*) principle of CHANGE.

A new note was added in the Renaissance philosophies of NICHOLAS OF CUSA and Giordano BRUNO. They made privation a third essential principle of change and the changeable, together with MATTER and FORM. For them, privation implies matter and form and reconciles their contrariety: their position thus anticipates in a way the Hegelian ''negation of the negation.'' Maurice BLONDEL, in his philosophy of action, perceived in privation the foundation of the inexorable process of human will and action, regarding it as the principle from which one should start when investigating the origins of will and of man's theandric destiny [*L'Action* (Paris 1893) 293, 368].

Privation is here considered from the Aristotelian-Thomistic viewpoint as a principle of change and of changeable being, with emphasis on its relationship to matter, its role in Aristotle's astronomical theory, its ontological status, and its causality.

Principle of Change. Although the concept of privation can be investigated through logical and linguistic analysis (cf. *Cat.* 12a 26–13a 36), its full richness is uncovered through the study of change. Here it is found that the coming-to-be of physical being requires three principles: an underlying subject or substrate that persists through the change; a determination of that subject, which is the term or end of the process; and a lack or absence of determination, which is its inception (*see* MATTER AND FORM). Both the substrate (matter) and its determination (form) are essential or *per se* principles of the coming-to-be; the third principle, privation, is incidental or *per accidens.* The term incidental or *per accidens,* sometimes associated with the contingent, has a special meaning in this context. Although privation is incidental, it is not contingent, for while it may be contingent that a subject have this particular form, or be deprived of it, it is still necessary that it be in one state or the other. Thus privation is a necessary principle of change. Incidental (*per accidens*) here has the meaning of ''through another'' (*per aliud*). It merely ''happens'' (*accidit*) that a subject lacks the form of which it is deprived, and therefore privation exists through this subject in an incidental or indirect way (*In 1 phys.* 13.3).

Relationship to Matter. The relation of privation to the subject can be understood only in terms of the pure potentiality of primary matter. Throughout the early chapters of bk. 1 of the *Physics,* Aristotle avoids the term matter (ὕλη), speaking rather of subject (ὑποκείμενον). Only in ch. 9 does he clarify his usage: ''For my definition of matter is just this—the primary substratum of each thing, from which it comes to be without qualification, and which persists in the result'' (192a 31). Until this point he has been concerned with change as it takes place in a determinate subject, e.g., in this gold or this man. Such a subject, while numerically one, must be twofold conceptually: it must contain an aspect that survives through change, a substratum, and an aspect that does not change, a privation (*Phys.* 190a 13–20).

Privation and Potentiality. Privation is intimately associated with matter, but can be distinguished from it in terms of matter's potentiality and natural appetite for form (*In 1 phys.* 15). Potency and act divide being and every genus of being, including that of substance. Potentiality is not a property of matter, but matter itself as ordered to substantial form. Privation bespeaks no such ordering. It is NONBEING by its very nature, while matter is nonbeing in a qualified sense, precisely as lacking determination to a certain form. Molten bronze in a crucible is nonbeing only as it is amorphous: it becomes a statue when poured into a mold. Again, although primary matter is, in St. Augustine's phrase, ''nearly nothing'' (*prope nihil—Conf.* 12.6), it is for St. Thomas ''nearly a thing'' (*prope rem—In 1 phys.* 15.4) because it is potency in the genus of substance. Privation, then, is not identified with the potentiality of matter.

Privation and Appetite. Aristotle describes matter as having a natural desire or appetite for form, as a woman desires a man, or the ugly the beautiful (192a 17–24). The simile is Plato's, but the application is quite different from his. Under the Platonic confusion of matter and privation, matter was conceived as desiring its contrary (form), and therefore its own destruction. For Aristotle, however, matter is ordered to form as to an end, and this ordination constitutes its natural appetite. Yet matter stands in different relationships to different forms: (1) It looks to forms it has not yet had with a sort of desire, for desire bespeaks a tendency to an absent good. In primary matter this natural desire is purely passive. (2) With regard to forms once possessed, but later passed away, matter may be said to have an inefficacious desire. The proportion between matter and form remains, but there is no potentiality in nature for the past, and no natural agent is capable of reintroducing the same numerical form. (3) As to the form actually possessed, the natural desire is quieted, but not satiated, for no natural form is infinite in act. Since matter possesses infinite potentiality, it has an inclination to all forms not possessed; this nonpossession is privation.

Principle of Changeable Being. A particular difficulty arises in connection with these distinctions. All scholastics agree that privation is a principle *per accidens* of change itself and of changeable being in coming-to-be. Several present-day manualists deny that privation is a principle of changeable being once it is constituted; for them, privation ceases with the coming of form. The position is understandable, but it is not that of Aristotle and St. Thomas. The latter states: ''But someone could object that privation does not happen to a subject when it is under a form; thus privation is not a *per accidens* principle of existing. Therefore it must be said that matter is never without privation because when it has one form it is with the privation of another form. . . . Thus the privation of the opposite form is the *per accidens* principle of existing'' (*In 1 phys.* 13.4, tr. Kocourek).

It should be noted, however, that the privation that is a principle of coming-to-be is not to be entirely identified with the privation that is a principle of being. The first is the contrary of the form that is the term of the process; the second is the lack of every form not now actually informing the matter, but that could inform it. In the second case, privation is the unfulfilled potentiality of matter.

Privation, then, is always associated (*per accidens*) with matter and changeable being, whether in coming-to-be or in being itself; it is a necessary principle of changeable being, furnishing the radical explanation of its changeability.

Aristotle's Astronomical Theory. Additional light is shed on privation by the use Aristotle makes of it in his astronomical theory. For him, privation is not found in heavenly bodies. Inadequate observational data and presuppositions now known to be untenable led him to assert a radical difference between sublunary and celestial bodies. The latter do not come to be, but are eternal and not subject to substantial, quantitative, or qualitative change. They are neither heavy nor light by nature, and hence have no natural MOTION, either upward or downward. Since the motion of terrestrial bodies, like all other kinds of change, is between contraries, the only type of motion possible to the heavenly bodies is rotation, which has no contrary.

Aristotle offered a reasoned explanation of these presuppositions in terms of HYLOMORPHISM. Since the heavenly bodies are eternal, they do not come to be, as do other bodies, in a subject and from a contrary. Nature has justly exempted them from the law of contraries. Thus there is no privation in their composition, and this can be learned from their rotational motion (*Cael.* 270a 12–22). St. Thomas examined this position in light of the teaching of previous commentators such as Simplicius, JOHN PHILOPONUS, and AVERROËS. In defending Aristotle's solution, he points out that heavenly bodies are indeed composed of matter and form, but their perfect forms so fulfill the potentiality of matter that no privation remains in them. Although matter is not act, in this case it has actuality completely; there remains only a certain privation of LOCATION (*In 1 cael.* 6.6). The entirety of this doctrine, of course, must be rejected.

Ontological Status. The problem of the ontological status of privation does not admit of easy solution. For some Thomists, privation has real existence. It is modally distinct from its subject, matter, and therefore is not merely a being of the mind (*see* MODE; DISTINCTION, KINDS OF).

Others hold that the nonbeing of form, or the lack of form, is found in the nature of things and not merely in the mind. However, the privation or nonbeing that is a principle of changeable being is conceived after the fashion of a positive entity. Precisely as nonbeing, it is not positive and can have no real existence. It is a being of the mind, existing only as an object of knowledge, but with a foundation in reality. The foundation in the extramental world is the unactualized potentiality of matter, the unfulfilled natural appetite always present in changeable being. Privation exists incidentally to changeable being because it is incidental (*per accidens*) to matter.

Is privation one or many? Since privation is the lack of form in an apt subject, there are as many privations as there are possible forms. Since the potentiality of primary matter for the reception of substantial forms is manifold, even when such matter is actually under a given form, privation must be multiplied according to the number of substantial forms.

Mode of Causality. Another problem is the mode of causality proper to privation. Although privation is an incidental principle of change, in that substantial change proceeds from the privation of form, it is difficult to see how causality can be attributed to nonbeing. It seems, then, that its mode of causality will be analogous to its mode of being. Just as privation exists through matter, as its unfulfilled potentiality, so too its causality is exercised in matter. The proper effect of privation is precisely the substantial mobility of changeable being. Privation is therefore in the order of formal causality, for it is the opposite of form, and its effect is produced in matter. *Eadem est ratio oppositorum:* opposites are to be defined by affirmation or negation of a common nature or note.

While the concept of privation is first considered in the PHILOSOPHY OF NATURE, its applicability is not limited to that science. The metaphysician makes extensive use of the concept in his treatment of evil and nonbeing.

See Also: EVIL.

Bibliography: V. E. SMITH, *The General Science of Nature* (Milwaukee 1958). J. GREDT, *Elementa Philosophiae Aristotelico-Thomisticae,* 2 v. (13th ed. Freiburg 1961), J. P. ANTON, *Aristotle's Theory of Contrariety* (New York 1957). G. M. SCIACCA, *Enciclopedia filosofica* (Venice-Rome 1957) 3:1620–21.

[W. B. MAHONEY]

PRIZEFIGHTING

A contest of punching between two men wearing padded gloves. No adequate definition applicable to boxing or even to its most important levels is possible without introducing many distinctions. This article is restricted to a moral analysis of a single type of prizefighting (professional), though amateur fighting at some levels possesses many of the characteristics of professional boxing and would share to some extent the same moral analysis.

The Catholic Church has made no official pronouncement on the morality of professional boxing. However, theologians applying traditional principles have found it increasingly difficult to defend the sport. In assessing its morality they have admitted its advantages: the opportunity it affords for the development of physical fitness, alertness, poise, confidence, sportsmanship, initiative, and desirable character traits. Furthermore the game has given countless underprivileged youngsters a chance to better themselves. It is generally accepted that the fatalities that occur are accidental to the sport and not central to the moral question. Three considerations have been basic in theological literature.

The Knockout. Many fighters aim for a knockout. Not a few theologians find it difficult to admit that the knockout is justifiable. Directly and violently to deprive oneself or another of the use of reason is morally reprehensible except for a sufficient reason because it is the rational faculties that distinguish man from brute. Sport, money, or fame do not qualify as sufficient reasons. If such violent deprivation of higher controls is reprehensible, then the intent to produce it is reprehensible. A sport in which this intent is integral must be condemned. The argumentation is not completely convincing. The knockout is understood in a limited sense (rendering unconscious). This is not a necessary sense of the word. It is realistically capable of meaning the incapacity to continue. Second, such deprivation of the use of reason, if it occurs, generally lasts only a few seconds. Independently of other factors (injury, injurious intent), it is doubtful that so brief a deprival would suffice to condemn the sport.

Intent of Injury. Professional boxing is the only sport in which the immediate object is to damage the opponent. In all other sports the immediate objective is something else, (e.g., to score a basket in basketball); injury and incapacity to continue are incidental. In boxing, however, injury of the passing or permanent variety is the object of direct intent. Intent of transient injury is clear. A puffed eye, a lacerated cheek, a bleeding nose are signals for an intensified attack on the vulnerable area. Intent of lasting damage is more difficult to show. Certainly few fighters would explicitly desire to maim permanently. However, it seems that every head-pommeling is likely to leave some portion of the brain tissue permanently affected. While such injury does not manifest itself clinically until later and while it need not imply malfunction of the brain, it is cumulative. Hence, though the fighter's only explicit intent is to win as decisively as possible, the means he chooses are directly injurious. Man does not possess the right to inflict damage on himself or another in this way. He is charged with the duty of a reasonable administration of his person. When he pounds another into helplessness, scars his face, jars his brain and exposes it to the danger of lasting damage, he has surpassed the bounds of reasonable stewardship of the human person. Hence, a sport in which such an intent is central is immoral.

Brutalizing Effect. Boxing as we know it today tends to foster the brutish tendencies in man by provoking him to take pleasure in the sufferings of another. The nearer the knockout, the more frenzied the howling of the crowd. The fighter is goaded by the crowd; his own intensified fury further stimulates them. Because the modern prizefight is too often the canonization of brute force and because man tends to grow in the image of that which he cheers, the sport is seen as one that fosters growth in the brutish responses.

In recent years there has been a growing consensus among theologians that the moral discussion must begin with the sport itself, not only with its circumstances. Theologians increasingly see the sport as involving a directly injurious intent and as unduly fostering the instinct of brutality. These conclusions are not necessarily true; nor are they factually true of all fights or fighters; but they are too generally true of the sport as a whole. Thus the

Rocky Marciano (left) and Joe Walcott. (AP/Wide World Photos)

overwhelming unfavorable, if still somewhat tentative, majority vote of the theologians who have discussed the moral question.

Bibliography: G. C. BERNARD, *The Morality of Prizefighting* (Washington, D.C. 1952). E. HILLMAN, "The Morality of Boxing," *Theological Studies* 12 (1951) 301–319. E. G. LAFORET, "Boxing: Medical and Moral Aspects," *Linacre Quarterly* 25 (1958) 56–67. G. PERICO, *Difendiamo la vita* (Milan 1960). A. BOSCHI, "Sports e Boxe: Per una guista valutazione morale," *Palestra de clero* 34 (1955) 769–786, 817–830, 865–881. L. L. MCREAVY, "The Morality of Boxing," *Clergy Review* 41 (1956) 413–416.

[R. A. MCCORMICK]

PRO JUÁREZ, MIGUEL AGUSTÍN, BL.

Mexican Jesuit martyr; b. Guadalupe, Jan. 13, 1891; d. Mexico City, Nov. 23, 1927. The son of Miguel Pro and Josefa Juárez, a well-to-do, socially prominent couple, as a child, Pro was noted for his open and sympathetic nature and his firm piety. He entered the Jesuit novitiate in El Llano, Michoacán in 1911 and devoted himself fervently to the religious life, believing "that God wanted him among His saints." Because of the religious persecutions under President Carranza, he studied in Los Gatos, Calif. (1914–1915). He was then sent to

Miguel Agustín Pro Juárez prepares for execution. (Catholic News Service)

Spain, where he stayed until 1924 except for the years (1919–22) during which he taught in Granada, Nicaragua, a task that proved very difficult because of his ill health. In 1924 he went to Enghien, Belgium, for special studies in sociology and was ordained there in 1925. He then became gravely ill. In 1926 he returned to Mexico City where public worship had ceased because of the persecutions of President Calles. Pro undertook so many religious duties that they would have exhausted even a well man. He was seized by the police on Nov. 13, 1927 and executed with his brother Humberto ten days later amid much public uproar. Officially, he had been accused of plotting against General Obregón, but his innocence was clearly proved. Father Pro was beatified by Pope John Paul II on Sept. 25, 1988.

Feast: Nov. 23.

Bibliography: A. DRAGON, *Vida intima del Padre Pro,* tr. R. MARTÍNEZ DEL CAMPO, 3d ed. (Mexico City 1961). R. MARTÍNEZ DEL CAMPO, *La prueba del Padre Pro y el proceso de su beatificación* (Mexico City 1952). F. ROYER, *Padre Pro* (New York 1954). J. CARDOSO, *Los mártires Mexicanos* (Mexico City 1953) 363–389. DAUGHTERS OF ST. PAUL, *God's Secret Agent* (Boston 1967). G. F. MULLER, *With Life and Laughter* (Notre Dame, Ind. 1969; rep. Boston 1996). R. RAMÍREZ T., *Miguel Agustín Pro* (Mexico 1976). L. BUTERA V., *Un martir alegre* (Mexico City 1987). J. M. GARCÍA DE ALBA, *Beatificación del P. Miguel Agustín Pro S.J.* (Guadalajara, Mexico 1988). A. BALL, *Blessed Miguel Pro: Twentieth-Century Mexican Martyr* (San Francisco 1996). J. ESCALADA, *Miguel Agustine Pro: Alter Christus* (Mexico 1999). J. N. TYLENDA, *Jesuit Saints and Martyrs* (Chicago 1984).

[R. TORRES]

PRO MUNDI VITA

Pro Mundi Vita (PMV), an international study and research center located in Brussels, served for almost 30 years as a clearing house for information about the challenges facing the Christian churches and, specifically, the pastoral response of the Roman Catholic Church to the Second Vatican Council. Shortly before Vatican II, a group of Western European and Brazilian bishops, major religious superiors, aid agencies, and scholars created a kind of clearing house named Pro Mundi Vita, motivated by concern over the lack of Church personnel in non-Western countries. Under the inspiration of a Dutchman, Montanus Versteeg, OFM, its center was located in Tilburg, the Netherlands. Following an international conference in Essen, Germany, in 1963, presided over by Bishop F. Hengsbach, the center moved to Brussels. Its first secretary general, Jan Kerkhofs, SJ, a professor at Louvain University, transformed the PMV foundation into an international study and information center, with an international team of multilingual scholars and an intercontinental board of directors.

The Center focused on the challenges facing the Roman Catholic Church, as well as the main Protestant Churches, and the pastoral responses inspired by Vatican II. PMV developed its activities in three directions. First, it published scientific studies (country profiles and major problem areas) that were sent free of charge to thousands of bishops, major superiors, and international Christian organizations. Second, a service for episcopal conferences and Church institutes in need of pastoral surveys and advice was established. Third, international meetings on a wide variety of topics were organized. The center published hundreds of bulletins and studies in English, Spanish, French, German, and Dutch that dealt with topics as varied as the Christian and Muslim, Hindu, and Buddhist dialogues; the Church in Russia, South Africa, and China; the family, pluralism, and polarization in the Church; and the evolution of vocations. It also published hundreds of dossiers in four series on Latin America (in Spanish), Africa (in English and French), Europe and North America (in English and French), and Asia (in English). PMV also published a worldwide information bulletin, Ministries and Communities, and a quarterly, CECC Newsletter, on China. The center had launched a group of China scholars called "Catholics in Europe

Concerned with China.'' Together with a China committee of the Church of England, PMV established the Ecumenical China Liaison Group. Often in cooperation with the Lutheran World Federation, PMV organized some forty international meetings on China alone. PMV coedited the review, Religion in the People's Republic of China: Documents.

PMV carried out surveys in Thailand, Nigeria, Ghana, Ethiopia, and Brazil. Particular attention was given to the role of women in the Church. The first ecumenical conference co-organized with the World Council of Churches, took place in Louvain in 1975, and many publications dealt with this topic: Women in Japan, Women in China, Women and the Priesthood, Cooperation of Women and Men in Church and Society. Among the main international conferences was a 1973 colloquium, New Forms of Ministry in Christian Communities, that in turn inspired the 1977 Hong Kong meeting of the FEDERATION OF ASIAN BISHOPS' CONFERENCES, cosponsored by PMV. In 1970 in Brussels, PMV coorganized the first world conference of the review Concilium. In 1978 PMV launched the European Values Study (EVS), surveying the evolution of values in the Western world. Later, the EVS became an independent foundation in Amsterdam and continues its surveys of all European countries, the United States, and Canada. After a period in the course of which PMV was transferred to Louvain, organizational and financial problems forced the center to close in 1991.

[J. KERKHOFS]

PROBABILIORISM

Probabiliorism is the moral system according to which, in a doubt of conscience concerning the morality of a certain course of conduct, one must follow the opinion for law unless the opinion for liberty is certainly more probable—which is equivalent to saying unless it is much more probable. If both opinions are about equally probable, the opinion for law must be followed. This system seems to have been commonly accepted in practice before Bartolomé de Medina, OP, in 1577 enunciated the fundamental principle of probabiliorism. It was revived, especially among Dominicans, through the approval of this system communicated by Alexander VII to the Dominican general chapter in 1656. One of the outstanding defenders of probabiliorism in the 18th century was C. Billuart, OP (1685–1757). St. Alphonsus was a probabiliorist in the early years of his priesthood, but later renounced this system because he thought that some of the decisions of its school were keeping the faithful away from the Sacraments. Few, if any, uphold this system today.

See Also: CONSCIENCE; MORALITY, SYSTEMS OF; DOUBT, MORAL; REFLEX PRINCIPLES.

Bibliography: D. M. PRÜMMER, *Manuale theologiae moralis,* ed. E. M. MÜNCH, 3 v. (10th ed. Barcelona 1945–46) 1:345–346. J. AERTNYS and C. A. DAMEN, *Theologia moralis,* 2 v. (16th ed. Turin 1950) 1:101–123. M. ZALBA, *Theologiae moralis compendium,* 2 v. (Madrid 1958) 1:676. C. R. BILLUART, *Summa Sancti Thomae,* 10 v. (new ed. Paris 1874–86) v.4 *diss.* 5.

[F. J. CONNELL]

PROBABILISM

Probabilism is the moral system according to which in a doubt of conscience about the morality of a particular course of conduct, a person may lawfully follow the opinion for liberty, provided it is truly probable, even though the opinion for law is definitely more probable. The defenders of this system apply their fundamental principle: ''A doubtful law does not bind'' (*Lex dubia non obligat*) to both divine and human laws, whether the doubt concerns the existence or the cessation of the law. However, they admit the exceptions to the use of reflex principles. Moreover, they require a person reasonably to seek direct certainty regarding the moral problem before seeking indirect certainty through the use of reflex principles. The outstanding exponents of this system emphasize that the opinion for liberty must be truly and solidly probable, for if it is only slightly probable it has no value against the opinion for law. Thus, probabilism is clearly distinguished from laxism. Jesuit theologians are the best known exponents of probabilism.

See Also: MORALITY, SYSTEMS OF; CONSCIENCE; REFLEX PRINCIPLES; DOUBT, MORAL; LAXISM.

Bibliography: D. M. PRÜMMER, *Manuale theologiae moralis,* ed. E. M. MÜNCH, 3 v. (10th ed. Barcelona 1945–46) 1:342. J. AERTNYS and C. A. DAMEN, *Theologia moralis,* 2 v. (16th ed. Turin 1950) 1:101. M. ZALBA, *Theologiae moralis compendium,* 2 v. (Madrid 1958) 1:679–703. J. M. HARTY, *The Catholic Encyclopedia,* ed. C. G. HERBERMANN et al., 16 v. (New York 1907–14; suppl. 1922) 12:441–446. T. DEMAN, *Dictionnaire de théologie catholique,* ed. A. VACANT et al., 15 v. (Paris 1903–50; Tables générales 1951–) 13.1:417–619.

[F. J. CONNELL]

PROBST, FERDINAND

Liturgist; b. Ehingen, Germany, March 28, 1816; d. Breslau, Dec. 26, 1899. After his ordination in 1840, he served as a curate in Ellwangen. The following year he was sent for higher studies to the University of Tübingen. In 1843 he was appointed pastor at Allgäu. In 1851 his doctorate in theology was conferred by the University of

Tübingen. He was called to teach pastoral theology at the University of Breslau in 1864; he became a canon in 1886, rector of the university in 1889, a domestic prelate in 1890, and dean of the cathedral chapter of Breslau in 1896. As the author of a prodigious number of books and articles, most of which deal with the liturgy, Probst gained a widespread reputation for scholarship. His studies were limited to the liturgy of the Church as it developed in the first few centuries. They manifested a facile acquaintance with patristic literature; but the author's conclusions were criticized in some quarters as being largely concoctions of his own imagination. Notable among Probst's works are his *Kirchliche Benedictionen und ihre Verwaltung* (Tübingen 1857), *Liturgie der drei ersten christlichen Jahrhunderte* (Tübingen 1870), *Sakramente und Sakramentalien in den drei ersten christlichen Jahrhunderten* (Tübingen 1872), *Geschichte der katholischen Katechese* (Breslau 1886), *Liturgie des 4. Jahrhunderts und deren Reform* (Münster 1893), and *Die abendländische Messe vom 5. bis zum 8. Jahrhundert* (Münster 1896).

Bibliography: H. LECLERCQ, *Dictionnaire d'archéologie chrétienne et de liturgie,* ed. F. CABROL, H. LECLERCQ, and H. I. MARROU, 15 v. (Paris 1907–53) 9.2:1731–32. H. HURTER, *Nomenclator literarius theologiae catholicae,* 5 v. in 6 (3d ed. Innsbruck 1903–13); v. 1 (4th ed. 1926) 5.2:2066–67. B. FISCHER, *Lexikon für Theologie und Kirche,* ed. J. HOFER and K. RAHNER, 10 v. (2d, new ed. Freiburg 1957–65) 8:780.

[C. R. MEYER]

PROCESS PHILOSOPHY

Broadly understood, process philosophy refers to any position that gives the central place to flux or BECOMING. HERACLITUS, HEGEL, SPENCER, BERGSON, PEIRCE, JAMES, S. ALEXANDER, C. Lloyd Morgan, Dewey, G. H. Mead, and TEILHARD DE CHARDIN have all been classified as philosophers of process. (The best survey of process philosophy in this sense is Nicholas Rescher's *Process Metaphysics.*) The term is used principally to refer to the philosophies of A. N. WHITEHEAD and C. HARTSHORNE, and this narrower usage has gained increasing currency since it was introduced by Bernard Loomer in 1946. In this philosophy events (actual occasions) are the primary actualities. Enduring substances are reconceived as series (societies) of these occasions, each repeating the society's common defining characteristic, which functions much like an Aristotelian substantial form. Each occasion is self-creative. In other philosophies causes are conceived as active agents producing passive effects. Whitehead reverses this, treating effects as actively producing themselves in appropriating their causes.

Whitehead. The model for such causation is perception, understood in a Kantian sense as the mind spontaneously organizing and unifying its sensations into a single, intelligible experience. Perception is then generalized by abstracting from it any necessary reference to consciousness. Prehension, the more general concept, means any (conscious or unconscious) taking account of another. An occasion is then the growing together or concrescence of its prehensions. The way B prehends A is the way A causally influences B. Thus physical causality and mental experiencing are unified to overcome Cartesian dualism.

Each occasion is an atomic unit of becoming. Physical (objective) time consists of these droplets of self-creation, each with its own temporal thickness. Each is a process of determination whereby an indeterminate multiplicity of causal factors is transformed into a determinate past. Past actualities are determinate and fixed, yet as objectified they function as causal factors for the occasions now prehending them. Whatever is objective (since determinate) is therefore past. This means that all present immediacy is subjective. Thus subjectivity is presentness, for the only present immediacy we can ever directly experience is our own subjectivity. Since only determinate elements can be prehended, even the objective components of our present experience must be considered past, for the events we directly experience must already have occurred in order to be experienced. This identification of subjectivity with temporal immediacy entails a pansubjectivity akin to PANPSYCHISM. Since every occasion concresces in the present, it must then enjoy its own subjective immediacy. Its present can only be expressed in subjective terms if distortion is to be avoided, since the present can never be objectively experienced.

However, we must not anthropomorphize subjectivity by endowing every occasion with the characteristics of human experience. Subjectivity is regularly confused with mentality and consciousness. If subjectivity is the general capacity to be influenced by actuality, mentality is the capacity to be influenced by possibility, especially by novel possibility. Consciousness is a more specialized contingent feature of some highly complex occasions displaying massive mental originality. Few occasions in the universe are conscious; many display noticeable degrees of mentality (novelty); all are equally subjective.

If each occasion actively produces itself, its "causes" need only be prehensible objects, which can include possibilities, values, and ideals in addition to past actualities. Since no occasion can integrate all the conflicting tendencies of its inherited past, each must have a "subjective aim" or ideal of what it should become. This aim functions as a principle of selection by which to appropriate the past. It both affects and is affected by the influence of the past, and this reciprocal interaction constitutes the occasion's freedom. Since it becomes the final form of the determinate outcome, the subjective aim is the dynamic, emergent counterpart of an essence or substantial form, but one particularized to each individual actuality.

The occasion's subjective aim cannot be derived from its own past taken collectively, since it must function as a means for selecting amidst this welter of incompatibilities. Nor can the ideal be derived from some single past actuality, since every occasion has a different past and needs a different principle of selection. Occasions may, and often do, have privileged past occasions to serve as their predecessors, but then the origins of these predecessors must be taken into account. Ultimately these individual ideals must be derived from an actuality that is not a temporal occasion, namely God. God's power is the worship he inspires through the ideals provided to each occasion. God creates by the way in which he persuades each creature to create itself.

Hartshorne. Hartshorne's conclusions are basically similar to Whitehead's, but his characteristic mode of argument differs. He sets up a series of polar opposites, and then asks which is the more inclusive, which can best account for its opposite. If neither can include the other, we have irreconcilable dualisms. Thus he argues for panpsychism on the grounds that mind can account for matter, but not matter for mind. Freedom can account for whatever causal determinism there is, while determinism can only account for freedom by explaining it away. Becoming (change) includes being as an abstract aspect of itself, while being cannot include change without thereby changing. God as the perfect being supremely worthy of worship is not to be conceived merely in terms of one set of these categories to the exclusion of their opposites, but as the eminent instantiation of both sets. Thus God's omniscience is abstractly absolute as utterly free from error and ignorance, but concretely relative to what in fact there is to know. In championing this logic of perfection, Hartshorne defends the ONTOLOGICAL ARGUMENT, but applies it only to God's abstract essence, not his concrete actuality. The abstract essence is eternal and necessary, but the concrete actuality is temporal, contingent upon the divine experience of an emerging world. God knows all there is to know, the actual as actual, the possible as possible, but future contingents cannot be known as determinate actuality.

Because of its clarity, cogency, and accessibility, Hartshorne's version of process philosophy has been enormously influential. A major divergence among process thinkers centers on whether Whitehead's concept of God as an everlasting concrescence is correct, or whether it must be revised as an ongoing series of divine occasions. Cobb has worked out this Hartshornean revision most extensively, while Christian and others favor the original concept. Ford also affirms an everlasting concrescence but has made other far-reaching modifications in order to insure God's effectiveness in the world.

New Developments. Whitehead's unfamiliar terms and conceptuality presented formidable difficulties to early readers of *Process and Reality*. Between 1958 and 1966 a new era in process studies was inaugurated by the publication of three excellent aids: Leclerc's introduction, Christian's commentary, and Sherburne's *Key*. The *Key* is a heavily abridged and rearranged version of *Process and Reality,* with notes and glossary, well designed to facilitate the reader's understanding of the system.

Besides its obvious relevance to PROCESS THEOLOGY, process philosophy has been applied to aesthetics, evolutionary theory, physics, biology, the analysis of religious language, biblical studies, literary criticism, political science, the theory of civilization, and the history of religions (particularly Buddhism). A Center for Process Studies has been established at the School of Theology in Claremont, California, which also publishes a scholarly quarterly, *Process Studies*.

Criticisms. Process philosophy has been criticized by proponents of alternative viewpoints on many different counts, but three persistent internal criticisms stand out as particularly worthy of notice. Many, including Hartshorne, have rejected Whitehead's theory of forms (eternal objects) as too Platonic, preferring a more temporalistic understanding of the emergence of possibilities. The eternal objects are not permanent forms, somehow always subsisting, for they are only intermittently temporally instantiated. On the other hand, they are uncreated and to that extent an exception to Whitehead's ontological principle, which grounds all reasons in actualities.

Others question whether a theory of persons as series of momentary selves does justice to our experience of continuous, persistent self-identity and the requirements of responsibility. But the theory can explain relative self-identity in terms of memory and anticipation, and questions whether absolute self-identity permits us to be radically constituted by our experience of others. As Hartshorne wryly observes, we cannot love our neighbors as ourselves if our relations to ourselves must be absolutely different from our relations to others. Nor does responsibility for past acts depend upon absolute self-identity. If officials can be held responsible for the actions of their predecessors, should not the same be true for momentary selves with respect to their predecessors?

Edward Pols, in the most thoroughgoing critique of Whitehead published to date, develops the objection also made by Paul Weiss that these actual occasions cannot do anything, that there are no real agents. This is true insofar as any action consists in the unity of intentional activity and causation, while in process theory this unity is split between two actualities: the first creates itself by its own intentional activity, and it only exerts causal influence as it is objectively appropriated by another. This simply means, however, that actions are inherently relational, necessarily involving the activity of the effect as well as the cause. Any theory vesting the action solely in one actuality as agent permits some causes to completely determine their effects, contrary to the postulate of universal creativity.

Bibliography: A. N. WHITEHEAD, *Process and Reality* (New York 1929); *Adventures of Ideas* (New York 1933); *Science and the Modern World* (New York 1925; repr. 1967). C. HARTSHORNE, *Creative Synthesis and Philosophic Method* (La Salle, Ill. 1970); *Whitehead's Philosophy: Selected Essays, 1935–1970* (Lincoln, Neb. 1972). I. LECLERC, *Whitehead's Metaphysics* (New York 1958). W. A. CHRISTIAN, *An Interpretation of Whitehead's Metaphysics* (New Haven, Conn. 1959). D. W. SHERBURNE, ed., *A Key to Whitehead's Process and Reality* (New York 1966). J. B. COBB, JR., *A Christian Natural Theology* (Philadelphia 1965); *Beyond Dialogue: Toward a Mutual Transformation of Christianity and Buddhism* (Philadelphia 1982). E. POLS, *Whitehead's Metaphysics: A Critical Examination of Process and Reality* (Carbondale, Ill. 1967). L. S. FORD, *Transforming Process Theism* (Albany, N.Y. 2000.) N. RESCHER, *Process Metaphysics: An Introduction to Process Philosophy* (Albany, N.Y. 1996). V. LOWE, *Alfred North Whitehead: The Man and His Work,* 2 v. (Baltimore, Md. 1985, 1990). T. E. HOSINSKI, *Stubborn Fact and Creative Advance: An Introduction to the Metaphysics of Alfred North Whitehead* (Lanham, Md. 1993).

[L. S. FORD]

PROCESS THEOLOGY

The core of process theology centers upon the understanding of God derived from the philosophies of A. N. WHITEHEAD and C. HARTSHORNE. In this philosophy God is not a casual adjunct introduced for reasons of religious apologetics, but is necessary for its overall coherence. At the same time this philosophy is thoroughly conversant with contemporary science, for it was originally conceived as an effort to do justice to the revolution in physics occasioned by Einstein's special theory of relativity. Whitehead, then an agnostic sharing Bertrand Russell's religious opinions, first came to appreciate that temporal presentness could not be adequately explained in terms of the purely objective categories of nature, and later concluded that the origins of subjectivity required an appeal to God.

Process theism is also significant for its challenge to classical theism, a challenge that may well further contemporary efforts at de-Hellenizing the Christian faith. Whitehead was particularly troubled by the problem of EVIL. If God wills or allows all that is, having the omnipotence to change whatever is, then He may be faulted for the evil that exists. Even if God permits our evil decisions for the sake of fostering human freedom, He could prevent or ameliorate their consequence. But need OMNIPOTENCE be understood in this fashion? It cannot mean the monopoly of all power, for then we would have no power, and power is essential for freedom. Hartshorne argues that perfect power means all the power appropriate to a divinely perfect being that is consistently conceivable with creaturely power. If God does not compete with creatures for power, his power must be persuasive, not coercive.

Whitehead's reinterpretation of causality leads to similar conclusions. Instead of causes producing their effects, the effects produce themselves out of their causes, guided by the lures received from God. Without the ordering possibilities of divine persuasion, finite occasions would simply be random combinations of their causal pasts, quickly degenerating into chaos. The occasion freely modifies and actualizes the divine aim. This is its self-creativity. It is free from the causal determinism of the past insofar as it selectively appropriates from that past according to the divine aim, but it is also free from divine determinism insofar as it allows that aim to be modified by the past it appropriates.

Now a plurality of free decisions, insofar as they are uncoordinated, will inevitably (though not necessarily) lead to conflict, which is the source of evil. Divine coordination prevents total chaos, but it can achieve total harmony only to the extent to which creaturely occasions freely actualize divine aims.

On this view freedom is ontologically basic. It is not as if God can create some creatures with freedom and some without, for any lacking freedom would be merely intentional objects of the divine imagination, having no separate reality. In place of the traditional dualism of an uncreated creator and creatures that cannot create, all actualities are self-creative. God's creative activity is exercised in guiding each creature in its self-creation.

Because each finite actuality requires a past to appropriate, there is an infinite chain of causal pasts. The world is seen as having no beginning. Hartshorne argues that the existence of the world, like God, is abstractly necessary, though the concrete character it assumes is contingent. For him the metaphysical principles (which entail, among other things, the necessary existence of some world or other) have no consistent alternative, and hence are determined by no one, not even God. For Whitehead, God's primordial envisagement determining all possibilities thereby also determines the metaphysical principles. He is not explicit on the point, but if the existence of God without a world is a valid metaphysical alternative, then God in determining the metaphysical principles would be in effect determining whether to create or not to create. But this is nontemporal decision, applicable to all times, including the infinite past.

Hartshorne and Others. Hartshorne's *The Divine Relativity* is sharply critical of the Thomistic claim that God in knowing creation is not really related to creatures. Generally, in knowing one's knowledge is affected and largely determined by the existence and character of what is known, and it would seem inconsistent to make an exception in God's case. That exception is made to protect God's IMMUTABILITY. Hartshorne argues that though God's formal attributes are abstractly necessary, their concrete content is contingent. God as the perfect being is necessarily all-loving, but what God loves is dependent upon whatever there is to love. Far from being absolute and immutable, God is supremely relative, sensitively responding to every change in the world. Our actions thus contribute to the enrichment of the divine experience, and find their ultimate meaning in being cherished by God forever.

Many have resisted this argument because it entails that God's experience is (partially) caused by the world. This objection derives its force from the traditional axiom that the cause is superior to its effect, which implies a hierarchy of causes culminating in God as first cause. If Whitehead's reinterpretation of causality is correct, however, the effect is superior as the creative, novel unification of its many causes. Thus God is supreme as the effect of the world as well as the ultimate source of all its final causes.

Schubert Ogden has forcefully developed Hartshorne's thesis that the meaningfulness of life can only be justified by its enrichment of the divine experience. John Cobb, in addition to writing some foundational studies, has explored some important ways in which process thought has enriched our understanding of, among other things, world religions, evolutionary biology, economics, ecology, and political theology. Bernard Loomer and Bernard Meland have examined the more empirical dimensions of Whitehead's thought, seeking to describe as sensitively as possible the impingement of divine activity upon human experience. Daniel Day Williams has attempted the first full-scale process theology centered on the interpretation of love. These theologians, together with Peter Hamilton, Norman Pittenger, David Pailin, and David Griffin, have been exploring the contours of a process Christology. Others have considered its implications for the doctrine of the Trinity.

Catholic Interest. Catholic interest in process theology has been increasing since Vatican II, as the static categories of the natural and supernatural have given way to more dynamic, biblical categories. Whitehead may well provide the philosophical foundations for TEILHARD DE CHARDIN's vision, even though there is a major conflict with respect to the nature of the future. Teilhard de Chardin, faithful to the biblical witness, looks forward to the final consummation of all things in God; while Whitehead, attuned to the unending advance of creative freedom, insists that there is no one perfection capable of embracing all other perfections within itself. God seeks the actualization of all perfections, each in due season.

Joseph Bracken, SJ has sought to interpret Catholic theology in process terms, especially with respect to the Trinity as three persons in interaction. There has been particular interest in correlating Whitehead with St. Thomas Aquinas, as evidenced by recent work by James W. Felt, SJ, and Stephen T. Franklin. Norris Clarke, SJ gives an excellent Catholic assessment of process theism in the book cited below.

God in Process Theism. For process theism, God is both abstract and concrete, necessary and contingent, unchanging and changing, independent and dependent upon the world. These contrasting predicates can be applied to the same individual, provided they apply to diverse aspects: God is abstract, necessary, unchanging with respect to metaphysical attributes, but concrete, contingent, and changing in the experience of the world. Insofar as God is held to be radically simple, excluding all but nominal distinctions, this logic is inapplicable. But Whitehead agrees with Duns Scotus in affirming formal distinctions. As the subjective unity of a multiplicity of prehensions, God experiences many distinct objective data, but these prehensions are not separable because of the indivisible unity, even simplicity, of their subject.

The use of formal distinctions grounded in prehensive unity obviates one need for analogy. Analogy would also be needed to speak about God if our experience were only sensory. Whitehead, however, defends our nonsensuous experience of divine purposing. In this he is reviving a version of Augustinian ILLUMINATION, yet in a context that takes full cognizance of the role of EFFICIENT CAUSALITY as developed in contemporary science. Nevertheless, the analogy of being plays a role in process thought: every instance of creativity is thoroughly analogous with every other, having with respect to creativity no univocal elements in common.

Because God is constantly being enriched by the experience of novel events in the world, many have assumed that the God of process theism must be finite. But God's contemplation of all pure possibilities is necessarily infinite, and God's actual experience of the past must also be infinite if the world has no beginning. The mathematical concept of the potential infinite (for any x, $x + 1$) applies to God more accurately than the notion of an actual infinite (which cannot be enriched). Although Whitehead holds all determinate being to be finite, God is by contrast infinitely becoming, constantly in process of determination.

Bibliography: E. H. COUSINS, ed., *Process Theology* (New York 1971). D. BROWN, R. E. JAMES, and G. REEVES, eds., *Process Philosophy and Christian Thought* (Indianapolis, Ind. 1971). C. HARTSHORNE, *The Divine Relativity* (New Haven, Conn. 1948). A. N. WHITEHEAD, *Religion in the Making* (New York 1926; repr. 1996). J. B. COBB, JR., *Christ in a Pluralistic Age* (Philadelphia 1975). J. B. COBB, JR., and C. BIRCH, *The Liberation of Life* (Cambridge 1981). S. M. OGDEN, *The Reality of God* (New York 1966). D. D. WILLIAMS, *The Spirit and Forms of Love* (New York 1968). B. E. MELAND, *The Realities of Faith* (New York 1962). P. HAMILTON, *The Living God and the Modern World* (London 1967). N. PITTENGER, *Process Thought and Christian Faith* (New York 1968). J. A. BRACKEN, *Society and Spirit: A Trinitarian Cosmology* (London and Toronto 1991). J. A. BRACKEN and M. H. SUCHOCKI, eds., *Trinity in Process: A Relational Theology of God* (New York 1997). W. N. CLARKE, *The Philosophical Approach to God: A Neo-Thomist Perspective* (Winston-Salem, N.C. 1979).

[L. S. FORD]

PROCESSIONS, RELIGIOUS

In the history of religion an important socio-religious ritual action or form of worship. It is found especially, but not exclusively, in the higher religions and is a worldwide custom. The procession was a marked feature of public religion, e.g., throughout the Near East and the Mediterranean world. Solemn processions were regularly held to honor a given divinity, as a part of the enthronement ceremony of a king, to celebrate the New Year and the harvest, to avert calamities, or to propitiate the god or gods when calamity had occurred. Statues or symbols of the gods were usually carried in religious processions and the ritual normally combined magical as well as religious elements. It is sufficient to mention the great religious processions connected with the enthronement of the Egyptian pharaoh, the elaborate processions of the Babylonians from the Sumerian Age to the end of the Chaldean Empire, the Athenian processions in honor of Athenae the patron goddess of Athens, and the long procession from Athens to Eleusis connected with the celebration of the Eleusinian mysteries. At Rome, procession was an essential feature of lustration ceremonies, and the Roman triumph was a solemn religious procession culminating in an act of thanksgiving to the Capitoline Jupiter for victory. The joyous pagan processions associated with bountiful harvests were usually accompanied or followed by much license, however religious their motivation. Hence, the frequent condemnation of such processions in the Old Testament and in the Fathers of the Church.

Group activity and movement spring so spontaneously from human religious psychology that the Church did not hesitate to adopt some of these rites from paganism, as in the substitution of the Rogation procession of April 25, for the Roman Robigalia, and to develop many more of her own. The Christian Church can never forget that its spiritual life has its roots in the Old Testament, when God accompanied His chosen people on their long pilgrimages out of Egypt and later back from exile. The Christian life is a continual "Passover" as we follow in the footsteps of Christ and His cross along the road leading to heaven. Processions, ordinarily led by the cross, are an expression of the fact that the Christian life is a constant movement toward God and that prayer is always a kind of "walking with God"; they are a public image of the Church in continual pilgrimage here on earth.

It is important to distinguish between strictly liturgical processions (e.g., the Palm Sunday procession), whose rite, chant and prayer are specified in liturgical books, and non-liturgical processions. There are two kinds of liturgical procession: (1) ordinary processions are those connected with certain feast days, such as the processions on CANDLEMAS, PALM SUNDAY, ROGATION DAYS, and CORPUS ET SANGUINIS CHRISTI. Extraordinary processions are those enjoined or permitted by the bishop for some special occasion, e.g., the solemn transfer of relics.

Some processions, such as those of the palms and of the EASTER VIGIL, relive a special event in the history of salvation. Others are called functional because they simply solemnize a necessary movement from one place to another, as, for example, funeral processions and the first entrance of a bishop into his see. Still others have as their purpose to bless and sanctify certain places, to provide public pilgrimages to sacred shrines, or to offer supplication to God for good weather or for help in time of war, famine, epidemic, etc.

The most popular processions are those that honor the Eucharist and the Blessed Virgin. Besides the Holy Thursday procession, the best known Eucharistic processions are those of Corpus Christi. At an early date processions in honor of Mary were introduced, especially in connection with her major feasts. The one with the longest history is that of the Assumption. The present-day May processions, while not strictly liturgical, are in accord with this tradition.

See Also: PILGRIMAGES.

Bibliography: F. LOUVEL, "Les Processions dans la Bible," *Maison-Dieu* 43 (1955) 5–28. J. PINELL, "La processione come componente dell'azione liturgica,'' in *Ricerche sulla religiosit. . . popolare* (Bologna 1979) 151–170. A. N. TERRIN, ''Il rito della processione: appunti per una interpretazione religiosa storico-comparata,'' in *Ricerche sulla religiosit . . . popolare* (Bologna 1979) 225–242. J. EVENOU, ''Processions, Pilgrimages, Popular Religion,'' in *The Sacraments*, ed. A. Martimort (Collegeville, Minn 1988) 241–262.

[B. I. MULLAHY/EDS.]

PROCESSIONS, TRINITARIAN

The MYSTERY of the one God revealed in history as Father, Son, and Spirit was from the very beginnings of Christianity never a mere mathematical or logical puzzle. Rather Christians experience this divine one-in-three or triune reality as a saving and gracious mystery, sharing its life with humans through creation, redemption, and sanctification. God is understood as a mystery of communion—communion among Father, Son, and Spirit, and communion between these three divine ''persons'' and each human person. Furthermore, this double communion is also experienced as the basis of and condition of possibility for the communion among humans themselves, in the Church and in the world at large. These three intrinsically interrelated communions—communion among the three divine persons, communion between the divine persons and each human person, and communion among all humans with and in the cosmos—constitute for Christians the goal and meaning of human history and the universe.

Pope John Paul II (center), flanked by cardinals and bishops, in procession to St. Peter's Basilica, St. Peter's Square, Vatican City, Italy, 1985, photograph by L. Mellace. (©Reuters/ Bettmann-CORBIS)

New Testament Roots. This faith in the one God as Father who communicates Himself to humans in His Son and by the power of His Spirit is already expressed in the New Testament, especially by means of triadic formulas that entail both distinction and equality among the three divine persons (e.g., Mt 28:19; 2 Cor 13:13; Eph 2:18; 3:14–17; 4:4–6; 5:18–20; Rom 8:14–17, etc.). Beside the Father, both Christ and the Spirit are referred to as ''Lord'' and divine attributes are predicated of Jesus and, to a lesser extent, of the Spirit. In His preexistence (Jn 1:1–18: Heb 1:1–3), conception (Mt 1:23; Lk 1: 32), baptism (Mk :11), transfiguration (Mk 9: 2–13), and Resurrection (Rom 1:4) Jesus is confessed to be the beloved Son of God in power. Similarly, though less explicitly, the Holy Spirit is depicted not only as a divine power but also as a divine ''person'' speaking though the mouths of the apostles (Acts 8:20), sending the disciples out on mission (Acts 13:4), leading the Church (Acts 20:28), and dwelling in Christians to give them life and to bear witness to their being a son or daughter of God (Rom 8:14–16; Gal 4:6). For this reason ''God,'' ''Lord,'' and ''Spirit'' can be used in parallelism to one another (1 Cor 12: 4–6; 2 Cor 3:17).

For the first Christians who were Jews, this faith in the triune God was bound to be baffling in light of their unqualified monotheism. As a result, there is already in the New Testament an attempt to justify this Trinitarian faith by clarifying the relationships among the Father, Son, and Spirit, even though there is no elaboration of a Trinitarian theology as such in the New Testament. Most prominent is the Fourth Gospel's teaching on the two ''sendings'' or ''processions,'' namely that of the Son from the Father (Jn 3:17, 34; 6:38; 20:21) and that of the Spirit from the Father and/through the Son (Jn 14:16–17, 26; 15:26). Of course, the focus in these Johannine texts is on the sendings and processions of the Son and the Spirit in the history of salvation (the *oikonomia*), on what is termed the ''economic Trinity,'' and not on their eternal origination in the Godhead (the *theologia*), within what will be termed the ''immanent Trinity.'' In later theologies of the Trinity, however, these texts will be invoked to explain the eternal relationships among the Father, Son, and Spirit within the Godhead itself, in other words, the divine ''processions.''

Underlying Theological Issues. The Christian understanding of God can be summarized in two statements.

First, in continuity with the faith of Israel, it is affirmed that there is only one God, and God is Yahweh, the Father. In light of later Latin theology, it is important to note that in the New Testament and in the pre-Nicene theology, ''the one God'' refers to the Father and not to the divine nature or substance that the three divine persons possess in common. Second, this one God the Father is confessed to have manifested himself in the End Time, that is, in the life-death-resurrection of Jesus and in the outpouring of the Spirit, as the Father of Jesus who is therefore the Son and as the Sender of the Spirit who therefore proceeds from Him. Hence, Jesus the Son and the Holy Spirit are divine and not created. The *one* God is therefore somehow a *Triad.* The theological challenge is how to maintain these two apparently contradictory statements together, in such a way that the one God does not become a monad, and a divine triad does not jeopardize the monotheistic faith, and to come up with a plausible explanation of how unity and trinity in God are not mutually contradictory.

Historically, three positions regarding the Triune God have been condemned as heretical. First, SUBORDINATIONISM, which holds that the Logos/Son and the Spirit are not divine but created. Arius, who taught that the Logos is not eternal but only a preeminent creature, was condemned by the Council of Nicaea (325), and the ''pneumatochoi'' or Macedonians, who held that the Spirit is a creature, were rejected by the Council of Constantinople (381). Second, MODALISM, which denies that Father, Son, and Spirit are distinct realities, and comes in two forms. Some, like Noetus, Praxeas, and Sabellius thought that ''Father,'' ''Son,'' and ''Spirit,'' are mere names for the various roles of the one Godhead in the economy (''Modalist Monarchians''), while others thought that Christ was a mere man indwelt or inspired in a special way by divine power (''Adoptionist'' or ''Dynamic Monarchians''). Third, Economic Trinitarianism, whose classic defender is Tertullian and which holds that God in His eternal being is a strict Monad, but becomes a Triad in His decision to create, when God's immanent Word (the *Logos endiathetos*) was uttered forth in creation and Incarnation (the *Logos prophorikos*) and when, in a similar fashion, God's inner Spirit was breathed forth into the world.

The first attempt at reconciling God's unity and trinity by way of processions was made by the Cappadocian Fathers who drew a distinction between that which is generic or common (*to koinon*) shared equally by all members of a class and that which is particular or individual (*to idion*) possessed by a particular member and no other. That which is common and answers the question of ''what'' is called nature (*ousia*), whereas that which is particular and answers the question of ''who'' is PERSON (*hypostasis*). Hence, *ousia* + *idioma* = *hypostasis.* Applying this distinction to God, the Cappadocians argue that what is common in God is the divine nature (*ousia*) and that this divine nature is particularized by the characteristics that constitute their persons (*hypostasis*). These characteristics (*idiomata*), which differentiate one divine person from another, are brought about by the ways in which the Son and the Spirit originate or proceed from the Father: The Father is unoriginated (*agennesia*), the Son is generated (*gennesia*), and the Spirit proceeds (*ekporeusis* or *ekpempsis*).

The Legacy of Augustine, Thomas Aquinas, and Scholastic Theology. The first comprehensive attempt at explaining the compossibility between unity and trinity in God was made by AUGUSTINE in his *De Trinitate.* Augustine chooses as the starting point of his Trinitarian theology the unity of the one divine substance or nature, which unfolds subsequently as it were into three persons, Father, Son, and Spirit. The bishop of Hippo effectively abandons the earlier tradition that the one God is first and foremost the Father, and that the unity and unicity of God resides in the Father. This is a momentous methodological change, with far-reaching implications for the way in which the relationships between each divine person and humans are understood. In fact, for Augustine, and through him, THOMAS AQUINAS and scholastic theology, since there is only one substance and since substance is the basis of action, all the divine attributes as well as the operations of God in the history of salvation (the *opera divina ad extra*) are to be predicated of God absolutely and not relatively of particular persons. Consequently, it is only by way of appropriation that these actions are attributed to a particular divine person on the basis of some affinity between these actions and the distinctive characteristics (*proprium*) of that person. An unintended but disastrous result of this approach is a separation between the Immanent Trinity (which is truly a Triad) and the Economic Trinity (which is not Trinitarian but fundamentally unitarian, namely, the divine substance).

Augustine devotes the second half of his *De Trinitate* to exploring the analogies of the Trinity in humans, since humans are created in the image and likeness of God. He first considers the triad involved in the phenomenon of human love—the Lover, the Loved, and the Love—but abandons it because it does not appear to him to adequately reflect the divine Triad's equality. He then investigates the rational processes of the human mind and finds them more satisfactory: the *mens* or *memoria,* the *intellectus,* and the *voluntas.* By *mens* or *memoria* Augustine means the person's self-consciousness. This self-consciousness is actualized in the act of knowing and the act of willing. There is then a three-in-one triad in human cognition: the mind, its knowledge of self, and its love of self. The mind, the originating source of the whole cognitive process, is analogized to the Father; the production of knowledge by the mind resulting in the knowledge of itself, i.e., the "conception" of the idea, is analogized to the generation of the Son/Word/Image by the Father; and the termination of the rational process in love is analogized to the procession of the Spirit from the Father and the Son, who, according to Augustine is the mutual love between the Father and the Son. These reflections serve as the foundation of the later theology of divine processions as elaborated by Thomas Aquinas and popularized by scholastic theology.

By "procession" is meant the origination or coming forth of one being from another. Derived from biblical texts such as Jn 15:26 ("the Spirit of truth, who proceeds [*ekporeuetai*] from the Father"), the term is used in theology to explain how the Son and the Spirit originate from the Father eternally in the Godhead. Thomas Aquinas's interpretation (*Summa Theologiae* I, q. 27) later popularized by scholastic theology, remains the best known. Thomas begins by positing a real distinction between the principle or source from which something proceeds, and the term or that which proceeds from the principle or source. Furthermore, he notes that there are two kinds of procession: the transient (*ad extra*), in which the term comes to exist outside the principle, e.g., the chair exists outside the carpenter, and the immanent (*ad intra*), in which the term remains within the principle, e.g., the idea or concept remains within the mind that conceives it.

The two eternal processions in the Godhead belong to the second kind. They are not produced in time by God the Father by way of efficient causality like creatures. Rather they are eternal "events" within the Godhead itself by which the Godhead is a triad, all three members of which are truly and equally divine. Taking a clue from Augustine, Thomas analogizes these two divine processions to the two activities of the human spirit, namely, knowing and loving. The first procession, that of the Son/Word, is termed by the Bible as "generation." In generation, there are three things: the vital act whereby something is given birth by another living thing, the specific resemblance between the generator and the generated, and the identity of nature between the two. These three things are found, analogously, in the generation of an idea by the mind, and the generation of God the Son from God the Father. The Father contemplates Himself eternally and generates in the divine mind a perfect idea or word or image of Himself, just as when a person conceives in the mind an idea that is identical in nature with the mind. Hence the Son can be said to be the Word, Wisdom, the Image of God.

Beside the procession of the Son by generation the Bible also speaks of the procession of the Spirit from the Father. This procession may be analogized to another act of the human spirit, namely, willing or loving. In the cognitional process of the human spirit, what is known is also often loved. The act of knowing is different from that of love, which proceeds from the will, and not the intellect. Analogously, God the Father loves the Son and vice versa, through the divine will. This mutual love between the Father and the Son is the Spirit. Whereas there is a specific term in the Bible to refer to the act whereby the Son proceeds from the Father, namely, generation, there is none to describe the procession of the Spirit. This procession ought not to be called "generation" but "spiration" or breathing-forth, an act of communication through love. Hence, the names of the Spirit are Gift and Love, and not Son.

In the Bible the Spirit is said not only to proceed from the Father (Jn 15:26) but also to have been sent by the Father *and* the Son (Jn 14:26; 15:26). In light of this, Latin theology (e.g., Augustine, Anselm of Canterbury, and Thomas) holds that the Spirit proceeds from the Father *and* the Son but as from one principle, even though the Creed of the Council of Constantinople professes only that the Spirit "proceeds from the Father." This so-called double procession of the Spirit constitutes a long-standing difference between the Latin and Orthodox Churches, a difference exacerbated by ecclesiastical and political rivalries.

Contemporary Theology. Despite the enormous authority of Augustine and Thomas Aquinas behind this "psychological theory" of the Trinity, many contemporary theologians have found it ultimately unsatisfactory. Though it clarifies in some way how faith in the one and trine God is not self-contradictory, the speculation on the divine processions by way of intellect and will is arid and unbiblical. As a result, some theologians have dropped it altogether and even suggest that no discourse on the Immanent Trinity is possible or useful. Others argue that the language of origination or procession implies hierarchy and subordination and negates the equality among the three divine persons.

The most serious critique, however, comes from Karl RAHNER and his many followers. For them, the psychological theory of the divine processions implicitly separates the divine nature from the divine persons, even though it explicitly affirms that the divine persons are identical with the divine nature. Because it is assumed that the starting point for the theology of the Trinity is the divine substance, and not the Father, God is said to act in the history of salvation through the divine substance, so that all the divine actions *ad extra* are to be attributed to the common substance and not to each of the divine persons. This is the teaching of the Fourth Lateran Council (1215), the Council of Florence (1442), and later scholastic theology: *opera divina ad extra communia sunt tribus personis tamquam uno principio* (divine actions outside of the Trinity are common to all three persons as one principle). It is only by way of appropriation that God's actions in history can be attributed to a particular divine person. As a consequence, there is a loss of the Economic Trinity in theology, and Christians, despite their professed faith in the Trinitarian God, are in fact ''monotheists'' or unitarians.

To retrieve the Economic Trinity Rahner affirms the principle that ''the 'economic' Trinity is the 'immanent' Trinity and the 'immanent' Trinity is the 'economic' Trinity.'' What Rahner intends with this formula is to assert that God acts in history not through the divine nature but through each divine person, each in a distinctive way, so that humans are related to each divine person relatively and distinctively, and not to the divine substance absolutely. In the concrete, ''God'' does not refer to the divine substance but to the Unoriginated and Originating Father who acts in history in two really distinctive (therefore not modalist) and ordered (therefore mutually conditioned) ways, in the Incarnation of the Logos under the aspects of origin, history, invitation, and knowledge, and in the grace of the Spirit under the aspects of future, transcendence, acceptance, and love. Consequently, the ways in which we experience God in history (the Economic Trinity) do tell us really and truly, though never exhaustively, about the ways in which the Father, the Son, and the Spirit are related to each other eternally (the Immanent Trinity). God's communication to us is indeed *self*-communication. This self-communication is therefore to be understood not by way of efficient causality by which God creates something distinct from Himself but by way of formal or more precisely quasi-formal causality by which the three divine persons indwell in humans, each in its distinctive way.

Consequently, speaking about the two temporal ways of God's self-communication by means of narrative and/or metaphysical language is already speaking about the two eternal ''processions'' from the Father. Trinitarian theology is not something one does *after* one has dealt with the ''one God'' (divine substance, its existence and its attributes). Rather it is the systematic and critical reflection on the two ways in which God the Father has acted in history by way of self-communication and on what these two ways reveal about who God is, that is, one and trine, or on how the Son and the Spirit ''proceed'' from the Father.

See Also: TRINITY, HOLY, ARTICLES ON.

Bibliography: K. RAHNER, *The Trinity,* tr. J. DONCEEL (New York 1974). T. MARSH, *The Triune God: A Biblical, Historical, and Theological Study* (Mystic, Conn. 1994). G. O'COLLINS, *The Tripersonal God: Understanding and Interpreting the Trinity* (New York 1999). C. LACUGNA, *God for Us: The Trinity & Christian Life* (San Francisco 1991). E. JOHNSON, *She Who Is* (New York 1993). D. COFFEY, *Deus Trinitas: The Doctrine of the Triune God* (New York 2000). P. C. PHAN, ''God in the World: A Trinitarian Triptych,'' in *New Catholic Encyclopedia, Jubilee Volume: The Wojtyła Years,* ed. B. L. MARTHALER (Washington, D.C. 2001) 33–42.

[P. C. PHAN]

PROCLUS

Also generally called Diadochus (successor) because he succeeded to the head of the Platonic Academy at Athens, a pagan Greek Neoplatonist who was hostile to the Catholic Church but who greatly influenced medieval and Renaissance Christian philosophy and theology; b. Byzantium, A.D. 410 or 412; d. Athens, April 17, 485. After his elementary education at Xanthus in Lycia, Proclus went to Alexandria, Egypt, where he studied rhetoric and Roman law, then mathematics and philosophy, the last under Olympiodorus the Peripatetic. Moving to Athens *c.* 430, he continued his study of philosophy in the Platonic Academy under Plutarch of Athens and, especially, under Syrianus. Shortly after the latter's death, Proclus assumed the leadership of the academy, which he held until his death.

Proclus wrote voluminously on literary, scientific, religious, and philosophical topics. The following are his most important writings still extant in whole or in part. On literature: commentary on Hesiod's *Works and Days.* On science: commentary on Euclid's *Elements*, on the introduction to Nicomachus' *Arithmetic*; *Sphaera,* on eclipses, elements of physics. On religion: several hymns, the hieratic art, on the Chaldean philosophy. In philosophy: commentaries on Plato's *Parmenides, Timaeus, First Alcibiades, Cratylus, Republic; Eighteen Arguments in Favor of the Eternity of the World Against the Christians; The Platonic Theology; Ten Doubts Concerning Providence; On Providence, Fate and Free Will; On the Existence of Evil; Elements of Theology.* Medieval and Renaissance authors were acquainted almost solely with the last four treatises and best of all with the fourth of these.

In *Elements of Theology* Proclus speaks of many items that may seem to be subsistent and autonomous: limit, infinity, being, eternity, wholeness, life, time. Eventually, though, all these merge with one or other of those hypostases that he clearly intends as somehow independent: the One, the intelligence, the soul, nature. Hence, his universe is made up of four levels, hierarchically arranged: the One (together with multiple ''ones'' or henads), the intelligence (and intelligences, both divine and merely intellectual), the soul (and souls, both supermundane and intramundane), nature and the sensible world. Proclus' view of this universe is a cosmogony, since at least two sorts of causality are operative in it, both of which are spontaneous and necessary. The one is a process of participation: participations come to be present in participants, which they complete and perfect as integral parts. The other is not: the participations themselves and their participants originate by emanating from the monads (e.g., the intelligence, the soul), which stand at the head of each level of reality and which ultimately arise from the One. Throughout the twofold causality two forces are constantly at work: a procession of everything downward from the One and a reversion of everything back to the One because of desire. Proclus' universe is also a monism since the effect is never totally distinct from the cause. Finally, in his *Weltanschauung* Proclus owes more to Plato, Iamblichus and Syrianus than to Plotinus; he leans heavily also upon the Orphic hymns and Chaldean oracles.

See Also: PLATONISM; SCHOLASTICISM, 1.

Bibliography: For a bibliog. of texts and trs. to 1945, see L. J. ROSÁN, *The Philosophy of Proclus* (New York 1949), 245–260. Texts. *Procli Diadochi Lycii Elementatio physica,* ed. H. BOESE (Berlin 1958); *Tria opuscula: De providentia, Libertate, Malo,* ed. H. BOESE (Berlin 1960); *Elements of Theology,* ed. E. R. DODDS (2d ed. Oxford 1963); *Commentarium in Parmenidem,* ed. R. KLIBANSKY and C. LABOWSKY in v. 3 of *Plato Latinus* (London 1953) 23–81; *La teologia platonica,* ed. E. TUROLLA (Bari 1957); *Commentary on the First Alcibiades of Plato,* ed. L. G. WESTERINK (Amsterdam 1954). C. VANSTEENKISTE, ed., ''Procli Elementatio theologica translata a Guilelmo de Moerbeke,'' *Tijdschrift voor philosophie* 13 (1951) 264–302, 491–531. Studies. L. SWEENEY, ''Origin of Participant and of Participated Perfections in Proclus' *Elements of Theology,*'' in *Wisdom in Depth* (Milwaukee 1966). J. TROUILLARD, ''La Causalité selon Proclus,'' *Revue des sciences religieuses* 37 (1958) 347–357; ''Âme et esprit selon Proclus,'' *Revue des études augustiniennes* 5 (1959) 1–12; ''La Monadologie de Proclus,'' *Revue philosophique de Louvain* 57 (1959) 309–320.

[L. SWEENEY]

PROCLUS, ST.

Theologian, bishop of Cyzicus, and archbishop of Constantinople *c.* 434–46; d. Constantinople, 446. Proclus was an admirer of JOHN CHRYSOSTOM. He served as episcopal secretary to, and was ordained a priest by, Bp. Atticus of Constantinople; he was selected by Sisinnius I as bishop of Cyzicus in 426, but because of popular opposition, he was not able to take possession of that see and remained in the capital. A renowned preacher, Proclus delivered a homily on the THEOTOKOS (*Hom.* 1) during the Christmas season of 428 in the presence of Archbishop NESTORIUS (428–431) that seems to have precipitated the Nestorian crisis, although Proclus did not play an important part in that controversy. At the instance of the Emperor THEODOSIUS II, he was selected archbishop of Constantinople (April 12, 434) to replace Maximianus, who had succeeded to the see after the deposition of Nestorius at the Council of EPHESUS (431).

In his sermons Proclus did not discuss contemporary events, but he attacked the beliefs and morals of the Jews in classical fashion. In 435 he received a request from the bishops of the Church in Armenia regarding the theology of THEODORE OF MOPSUESTIA whose works were being translated into their language, and whom they suspected of Nestorian teaching. In his famous answer, *Tomus ad Armenios de fide,* Proclus did not mention Theodore; he discussed the Church's teaching on the single hypostasis and the two natures in the incarnate Word, and intimated the errors that could be ascribed to Theodore. In 438 Proclus had the relics of the exiled John Chrysostom (d. 407) returned to Constantinople, and through his letters seems to have extended the authority of his see. He is also thought to have introduced the *Trisagion* (Holy God, Holy Almighty . . .) into the liturgy, but a fragment of a *De traditione divinae liturgiae* attributed to him is a 16th-century forgery.

Approximately 35 of Proclus' homilies about feasts of Christ and the saints have been preserved. Homily six has long been suspect because of an interpolation on virginity (ch. 2–7) and two acrostic dialogues (*see* ROMANUS MELODUS). The sermon itself, however, is contemporary and could be his. Recent research has restored to credit to him for a mystagogic homily on Baptism (27), a homily on Good Friday and the Trinity preserved in Arabic (30), and another on the credulity of St. Thomas (*Hom.* 33; *Patrologia Graeca*. ed J. P. Migne [Paris 1857–66] 59:681–688). Of the 17 letters preserved under his name, seven were written by him. The fourth letter contains the famous phrase *unum de Trinitate secundum carnem crucifixum* that became the center of the Theopaschite controversy in the following century.

Feast: Oct. 24.

Bibliography: *Patrologia Graeca* ed J. P. MIGNE (Paris 1857–66) 65:679–888. *Acta conciliorum oecumenicorum* (Berlin 1914–) I.1.1:103–107, Homily 1; IV.2:65–68, 187–195. J. QUASTEN, *Patrology* (Westminster, Maryland 1950–) 3:521–525. G. FRITZ, *Dictionnaire de théologie catholique*. ed. A. VACANT et al., (Paris 1903–50) 13.1:662–670. R. DEVREESSE, *Essai sur Théodore de Mopsueste* (*Studi e Testi* 141; 1948) 125–152; *Revue des sciences religieuses* 11 (1931) 543–565. J. A. DE ALDAMA, ''Investigaciones recientes sobre las homilías de San Proclo,'' *Estudios Eclesiásticos* 39 (1964) 239–244. V. INGLISIAN, *Oriens Christiana* 41 (1957) 35–50. F. J. LEROY, *Recherches sur l'Homilétique de Proclus de Constantinople* (Louvain 1963); *Orientalia Christiana peri-*

odica 23 (1962) 288–299; *Byzantion* 33 (1963) 357–384, Homily 6. *Quattro omelie copte*, ed. and tr. A. CAMPAGNANO, A. MARESCA, and T. ORLANDI (Milan 1977).

[F. J. LEROY]

PROCOPIUS OF CAESAREA

Byzantine historian; b. Caesarea, in Palestine, toward the end of the 5th century; d. after 562. Procopius was educated in Caesarea and in Gaza, where he studied rhetoric and law and went to Constantinople early in his life to practice law. There he became associated with BELISARIUS, the famous general of JUSTINIAN I, as his legal adviser and private secretary. He accompanied Belisarius during the first Persian war from 527 to 531; in Africa, during the war against the Vandals (533–34); and in Italy, against the Goths. He was still with Belisarius in 540, but whether he accompanied him in the second Persian war in 541 is uncertain. In 542 he was in Constantinople. He is known to have borne the title of *illustris* and then the title of *patricius.* Procopius, who was the prefect of Constantinople in 562, was most probably also this same historian.

Procopius was the author of three important historical works: the *History of the Wars* in eight books (*De bellis, libri VIII*); *Secret History* (*Historia arcana*); and *On Buildings* (*De aedificiis*). A detailed account of the Wars of Justinian, the *History of the Wars* is at the same time a general history of the reign of that Emperor. The first two books relate the history of the Persian wars: the next two, that of the campaign against the VANDALS; the next three, that of the war against the Goths. The last book is more general in nature and relates the history of the period 551 to 553. The first seven books were composed sometime between 545 and 550 and published in 550; the last, after 553. The *Secret History,* composed *c.* 550 but never published during the lifetime of the author, is a vicious libel upon the characters of Justinian and the Empress THEODORA, and upon Belisarius and his wife, Antonina. It is the principal source of what is known concerning the scandalous behavior of Theodora. The *Buildings,* composed probably between 558 and 560, is, on the other hand, an encomiastic account of the building activities of Justinian. Procopius modeled himself after Herodotus and Thucydides and is considered the most accomplished Greek historian since Polybius.

Bibliography: Best edition. *Opera omnia,* ed. J. HAURY, 3 v. in 4 (Bibliotheca scriptorum Graecorum et Romanorum Tuebneriana; Leipzig 1905–13), Eng. tr. H. B. DEWING, 7 v. (Loeb Classical Library; London 1914–40). Literature. J. B. BURY, *A History of the Later Roman Empire from the Death of Theodosius I to the Death of Justinian, A.D. 395–565,* 2 v. (2d ed. London 1923) 2:419–430. E. STEIN, *Histoire du Bas-Empire,* tr. J. R. PALANQUE (Paris 1949–59) 2:709–723. G. MORAVCSIK, *Byzantinoturcica,* 2 v. (2d ed. Berlin 1958) 1:489–500. M. E. COLONNA, *Gli storici bizantini dal sec. IV al sec. XV* (Naples 1956-).

[P. CHARANIS]

PROCOPIUS OF GAZA

Christian rhetorician and Biblical exegete; b. Gaza, *c.* 475; d. Gaza, *c.* 528. Procopius was the foremost member of the school of rhetoric that flourished in Gaza during the 5th and early 6th centuries; among his colleagues were Choricius, Aeneas, and his brother Zacharias. Here the programs and techniques of the Greek sophistic education were applied to Christian purposes. Among his nontheological works are a panegyric to the Emperor Anastasius I and a lost paraphrase of Homer. Modern scholarship rejects the Procopian authorship of several occasional pieces in rhythmic prose and assigns to Nicholas of Methone (12th century) the polemical treatise against the Neoplatonism of Proclus, an example of Byzantine pseudepigraphy. A collection of 163 elaborately rhetorical letters devoid of theological interest but supplying biographical data has survived. Further information about his life is contained in the funeral oration for Procopius by his pupil Choricius.

Procopius's major achievement was in the field of scriptural interpretation, specifically the compilation of *CATENAE* for a number of the books of the Old Testament. These *catenae,* or chains, of passages selected from earlier authors (e.g., PHILO, ORIGEN, BASIL the Great, Theodoretus, CYRIL OF ALEXANDRIA), are so arranged as to provide, along with the collector's personal exegesis, a continuous and comparative explanation of the Biblical text. Procopius composed two commentaries on the *Octateuch:* the shorter survives in a Latin translation with some Greek fragments, while the longer has been identified as essentially the *Catena Lipsiensis* assembled by Nicephorus Hieromonachus. Other genuine works by Procopius are the commentaries on historical books of the Old Testament, Isaiah, and Ecclesiastes (not yet edited). The Migne edition prints two commentaries on the Canticle of Canticles: one (*Patrologia Graeca* 87:1545–1754) is genuine, the other (*Patrologia Graeca* 87:175–580) is spurious. Scholars reject the authenticity of the commentary on Proverbs (*Patrologia Graeca* 87:1221–1544); however, some sections of a genuine work on this book have been discovered.

Bibliography: *Patrologia Graeca* 87:1–2842, works. R. HERCHER, ed., *Epistolographi Graeci* (Paris 1873) 533–598, letters. *Kirche und theologische Literatur im byzantinischen Reich* 414–416. W. ALY, *Paulys Realencyclopädie der klassischen Altertumswissenschaft* 23.1 (1957) 259–273. H. G. BECK, *Lexikon für*

Theologie und Kirche 2 8:787. R. DEVREESSE, *Dictionnaire de la Bible* suppl. ed., 1:1103–05.

[R. J. SCHORK]

PROFANITY

Profanity is the irreverent use of names, or irreverent reference to attributes or qualities of God or of holy persons or things held in esteem because of their relationship to God. Its essential relationship with the holy is gathered from the derivation of the word (from the Latin *pro* and *fanum*), according to which it indicates a quality of something outside the temple, i.e., unholy. Hence, if careless expressions have no connection with the holy, or if an original connection with the holy has been lost to sight in popular usage, they are not properly profane, but should rather be classified, if they are offensive to convention or good taste, as vulgar (*see* SPEECH, INDECENT AND VULGAR). Such, for example, would be expressions like ''oh hell,'' or ''damn it.''

However, even though profanity is properly thus connected with the holy, it is not to be confused with BLASPHEMY, understood as the utterance of contemptuous speech against God. Intent must be considered in distinguishing particular instances of blasphemy and profanity. If one wishes to dishonor God by his words, an expression that would in other circumstances be merely profane becomes blasphemous and gravely sinful. However, as it is generally understood, profanity involves no positive intent to show contempt for holy things. Rather, it does them less honor than is their due by careless, or too frequent, or inappropriate reference to them. There can be moral fault in this, but it is not serious enough to amount to mortal sin. Sometimes, indeed, there may be no sin at all, as when profane statements are simply ways by which the illiterate unthinkingly try to give emphasis to their statements, or when the expressions used have, through widespread social usage been more or less denatured and have lost their original sacred connotation. Profanity, however, always carries with it the danger of giving disedification or scandal, especially to the young.

Some use of profanity in literature can be fully justified, as when such language is put in the mouths of the characters for the purpose of indicating that such is the type of character being portrayed. However, an excessive use of this device might indicate a certain moral insensitivity or a penchant toward vulgarity or culpable irreverence.

Bibliography: H. NOLDIN, *Summa theologiae moralis,* rev. A. SCHMITT and G. HEINZEL, 3 v. (Innsbruck 1961–62) 2:178–181. H. DAVIS, *Moral and Pastoral Theology,* rev. and enl. ed. by L. W. GEDDES (New York 1958) v. 2.

[P. K. MEAGHER]

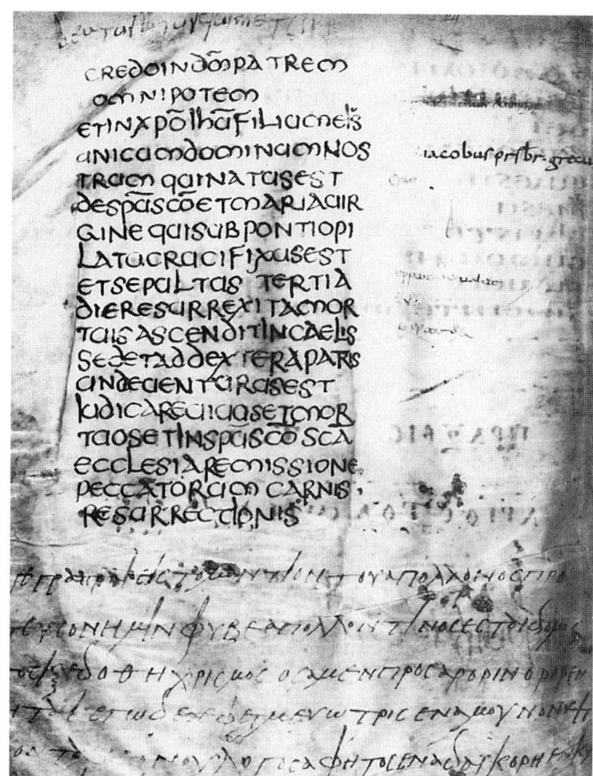

A Latin profession, or symbol, of faith inscribed in a manuscript of the 6th or 7th century.

PROFESSION OF FAITH

Faith is necessary for salvation. This means that there must be acts of FAITH (for those capable) that are at least internal (Mk 16.16; Heb 10.38; 1 Jn 3.23).

Theology. The Church teaches that a man must elicit acts of faith at least sometimes during life (H. Denzinger, *Enchiridion symbolorum* 2021). When such acts of faith are externalized in word or action they are called professions of faith. Certainly such professions are required of the Christian by divine precept. Christ Himself said explicitly, ''Therefore, everyone who acknowledges me before men, I also will acknowledge him before my Father in heaven. But whoever disowns me before men, I in turn will disown him before my Father in heaven'' (Mt 10.32–33). Such a precept is, moreover, in perfect conformity with man's nature. To avoid exterior profession would mean lack of conformity between actions and internal belief. Such conduct could not but weaken the belief of the Christian. Nor would it be in keeping with the social and visible nature of the Church to which he belongs.

Thus no one doubts the serious obligation to profess one's faith openly. But it is harder to determine the exact practice and extension of it. The precept would seem to be taken care of in the ordinary performance of duties prescribed under other laws; e.g., attendance at Sunday Mass involves profession of faith. So the real question is, when is a person obliged to profess his faith apart from the profession implicit in normal Christian duties? Theologians say that the obligation to profess one's faith in word and deed binds whenever the honor and glory of God or the salvation of one's neighbor demands it.

Denial of the faith is never justified under any conditions, not even the threat of torture and death. The above words of Christ do not allow fictitious or merely external denial whether by word or sign, even if the faith is upheld interiorly. Thus one may not simulate denial by externally venerating idols, for example, so as to escape danger or mockery.

While denial of faith is forbidden, temporary concealment can be justified for serious reasons (as long as it is not equivalent to denial). Eating meat in Muslim lands on days of abstinence can be licit (except where such partaking is imposed as a test of one's faith). One must confess one's faith in answer to legitimate questions by lawful authority, though evasive or equivocal answers may be given to private and unauthorized questioners—if good reason is had. Sometimes a convert is justified in delaying open profession of his faith, e.g., to prevent attacks on the Church, to avoid danger. But one is not allowed to continue formal practice of another religion. A person may not conceal his faith if such concealment imperils the faith of others, especially of those weak in their religion and looking to a leader. One is permitted to hide from or flee from persecution. Yet bishops and pastors may not forsake their people if there be reasonable hope of ministering to them (Jn 10.11–18). Flight can be justified by a long-range view of such care (Mt 10.23).

Formulas of Profession. Besides the normal outward expression of faith, the Church sometimes asks certain people to externalize their faith by means of determined formulas, called professions of faith. Such acts are considered acts of worship and are meant to edify others, or indicate the integrity of a bishop's or teacher's faith, or occasionally to unmask a deceiver.

The earliest profession of faith was, ''Christ is the Lord'' (cf. 1 Cor 12.3; Phil 2.11; Rom 10.9). This contained the whole Christian faith and from it the longer creeds developed. This original statement emphasized the point that Christians profess faith in the Person of Christ, or God in Christ, and not merely in a set of statements.

Soon the Trinitarian professions used in the rites of Christian initiation emerged (see the *Apostolic Tradition* of Hippolytus); before long the Apostles' Creed became the fixed profession of faith for Baptism in the West, as did the NICENE CREED in the East. By the 7th century candidates for orders, the bishopric, and even the papacy had to show their orthodoxy by professions of faith. Anyone suspect of heresy could clear his name in this way; thus Berengarius, accused of denying the substantial presence of Christ in the Eucharist, was asked to subscribe to a special profession of faith in 1079 (Denzinger 700).

At the time of the Protestant Reformation, Pius IV drew up the Tridentine Profession (Denzinger 1862–70). Public adherence to this soon became obligatory for all Catholics attaining degrees in theology or acquiring positions of authority in the Church. In 1877 Pius IX added certain details related to the Immaculate Conception and Vatican Council I. St. Pius X, in 1910, ordered that the profession be confirmed with an oath, and signed. In 1989 the Congregation for the Doctrine of the Faith issued a new formula of profession, the PROFESSION OF FAITH AND OATH OF FIDELITY.

[W. F. DEWAN/EDS.]

PROFESSION OF FAITH AND OATH OF FIDELITY

Canon 833 of the 1983 Code of Canon Law of the Latin Church requires a profession of faith, ''in accord with a formula approved by the Apostolic See,'' to be made by (1) everyone who has voting rights in an ecumenical or particular council, a synod of bishops, or a diocesan synod; (2) individuals named to the college of cardinals; (3) persons promoted to the episcopacy and those equivalent to a diocesan bishop; (4) diocesan administrators; (5) vicars general, episcopal vicars and vicars judicial; (6) pastors, rectors of seminary, professors of theology and philosophy in seminaries and those promoted to the diaconate; (7) rectors of Catholic universities and university teachers who teach disciplines dealing with faith and morals; and (8) superiors in clerical religious institutes and societies of apostolic life. At the end of February 1989, the Roman Congregation for the Doctrine of the Faith (CDF) issued a new formula of the profession in *L'Osservatore Romano* and at the same time introduced an oath of fidelity to be made by some, but not all, those listed in canon 833 ''on assuming an office to be exercised in the name of the Church.'' Both the profession of faith and the oath of fidelity were to become obligatory four days later, March 1, 1989.

Although the Latin texts printed in *L'Osservatore Romano* were accompanied by a ''note of presentation,'' the document as a whole had grave canonical defects. In addition to the inadequate interval before it was to go into effect, it lacked signatures and date. Neither did it explain the exceptional use of the newspaper for canonical promulgation, nor did it make mention of the requisite papal approval that is required for a significant innovation. Since 1917 the issuance of a such a general decree (i.e., a law) without papal delegation exceeds the power of the departments of the Roman Curia.

The question of the document's validity, however, became moot in the following October when the official *Acta Apostolicae Sedis* published a retroactive rescript dated September 19, and signed by the cardinal prefect of the CDF. The rescript stated that in an audience on July 1, 1988, Pope John Paul II had approved the action and ordered the decree promulgated. It also introduced a further norm: the approbation of vernacular versions of the two texts was reserved to the congregation.

Approved Formula. Canon 833 remained unchanged. The innovation lay in the new text itself. Prior to 1967 the approved formula of the profession of faith that was canonically required (and prefixed to the 1917 code) consisted of the creed of the councils of Nicaea and Constantinople, augmented by several paragraphs that summed up the teaching of the ecumenical councils of Trent and Vatican I. The additions to the fourth-century creed were removed in 1967 in the wake of Vatican II. Only a simple formula, with obvious references to the three modern ecumenical councils, was to be said at the end of the ancient creed:

> I firmly embrace and accept all and everything which has been either defined by the Church's solemn deliberations or affirmed and declared by its ordinary magisterium concerning the doctrine of faith and morals, according as they [the teachings] are proposed by it [the Church], especially those things dealing with the mystery of the Holy Church of Christ [Vatican II], its sacraments and the sacrifice of the Mass [Trent], and the primacy of the Roman pontiff [Vatican I].

The 1989 text replaced this 1967 formula with three new paragraphs. The oblique references to the modern councils were suppressed; more important, the suggestion of the diverse levels or modes of proposal of teachings was lost, although this had evidently been derived from the 1964 dogmatic constitution on the Church (*Lumen gentium* 24). The purpose of the new text, according to the note of presentation, was to update the profession of faith ''as regards style and content'' and to bring it ''more in line with the teaching of the Second Vatican Council and subsequent documents.'' The paragraph appended to the creed in the 1967 formula was modified ''in order to distinguish better the types of truths and the relative assent required.''

PROFESSION OF FAITH

(Formula for making the Profession of Faith in those cases where it is required by law)

I, N., with firm faith believe and profess everything that is contained in the symbol of faith, namely:

I believe .... [here follows the Nicene Creed].

With firm faith I also believe everything contained in God's word, written or handed down in tradition and proposed by the Church, whether by way of solemn judgment or through the ordinary and universal magisterium, as divinely revealed and calling for faith.

I also firmly accept and hold each and everything that is proposed definitively by the Church regarding teaching on faith and morals.

Moreover, I adhere with religious submission of will and intellect to the teachings which either the Roman Pontiff or the college of bishops enunciate when they exercise the authentic magisterium, even if they proclaim those teachings by an act that is not definitive.

Commentary and Explanation. (For the text, see accompanying box.) In the new formula the first paragraph simply mentions matters to be believed ''with firm faith,'' namely, matters taught ''as divinely revealed and calling for faith.'' The wording is derived from the teaching of Vatican I, and it corresponds roughly to the norm of canon 750.

The second paragraph requires the firm acceptance and holding of Church teachings that are ''definitively proposed.'' Nothing in the text suggests that this implicates an affirmation of divine and catholic faith. Theologians and canonists showed concern about the very nature of this ''acceptance,'' about the ambiguity of ''definitively proposed,'' about the distinction between truths of Christian faith infallibly defined and other teachings, about the possibility of future development or changes in such ''definitive'' teachings, and the like. When the text appeared, it was quickly noted that this dimension of Church teaching (unlike the first and third paragraphs) had not been touched upon in the canons of the code promulgated in 1983.

Finally, the third paragraph goes beyond matters of ''divine and catholic faith.'' It is an assertion of adherence to other teachings of the pope and the other bishops. Not unexpectedly this corresponds to the nondefinitive, noninfallible, nonirrevocable teaching similarly characterized by canon 752, namely, teachings enunciated by the Roman pontiff or the college of bishops ''when they exercise the authentic magisterium even if they do not intend to proclaim it with a definitive act.'' For this, the canon properly requires ''not the assent of faith [like the

OATH OF FIDELITY ON ASSUMING AN OFFICE TO BE EXERCISED IN THE NAME OF THE CHURCH

(Formula to be used by the faithful mentioned in canon 833, nos. 5–8)

I, N., in assuming the office of _____, promise that both in my words and in my conduct I shall always preserve communion with the Catholic Church.

I shall carry out with the greatest care and fidelity the duties incumbent on me toward both the universal Church and the particular Church in which, according to the provisions of the law, I have been called to exercise my service.

In fulfilling the charge entrusted to me in the name of the Church, I shall hold fast to the deposit of faith in its entirety, I shall faithfully hand it on and explain it, and I shall avoid any teachings opposed to that faith.

I shall follow and foster the common discipline of the whole Church and I shall observe all ecclesiastical laws, especially those which are contained in the Code of Canon Law.

In Christian obedience I shall unite myself with what is declared by the bishops as authentic doctors and teachers of the faith or established by them as those responsible for the governance of the Church; I shall also faithfully assist the diocesan bishops, in order that the apostolic activity exercised in the name and by mandate of the Church may be carried out in the communion of the same Church.

So help me God, and God's holy Gospels, on which I place my hand.

(Changes in paragraphs four and five of the formulary, for use by those faithful indicated in Codex Iuris Canonicis, canon 833, no. 8:)

I shall foster the common discipline of the Church, and I shall insist on the observance of all ecclesiastical laws, especially those which are contained in the Code of Canon Law.

In Christian obedience I shall unite myself with what is declared by the bishops as authentic doctors and teachers of the faith or established by them as those responsible for the governance of the Church; I shall also cooperate fully with the diocesan bishops, in order that, without prejudice to the character and purpose of my own institute, the apostolic activity exercised in the name and by mandate of the Church may be carried out in the communion of the same Church.

So help me God, and God's holy Gospels, on which I place my hand.

creed and other revealed truth embraced in the first appended paragraph] but a religious *obsequium* of intellect and will.''

The translation of *obsequium* is far from certain: it may mean anything from blind obedience or total submission to simple religious respect or docile reflection, even faithful, loyal dissent. The officially approved English text of the new profession of faith chooses ''submission.''

Oath of Fidelity. The 1989 Oath of Fidelity is distinct from the profession of faith, and different persons are canonically bound to take it ''on assuming an office to be exercised in the name of the Church.'' The text is a promissory oath; by definition it adds to a simple promise the invocation of the name of God and obliges the oath-taker by reason of the virtue of religion. A review of the text (see accompanying box) reveals that it is not, either strictly or conventionally, an ''oath of office,'' namely, an oath to fulfill the responsibilities of a given Church office. (Such oaths of office do exist in the Latin Church for certain officeholders, e.g., officers of tribunals required by canon 1254 to swear ''that they will fulfill their function properly and faithfully.'') The oath is rather a broad promise to preserve ecclesial communion and to maintain Church doctrine and discipline required of individuals on assuming of certain, but not all, ecclesiastical offices.

The note of presentation compares the new oath of fidelity to the oath of fidelity to the Apostolic See taken by bishops-elect (c.380), but the wording of the two oaths bear very little resemblance and have very different purposes. Even ''fidelity'' or faithfulness is not a common element: the new oath does not mention fidelity to the Roman See, and most of the promises seem concerned with the existing duties of all the Christian faithful, now to be confirmed by oath. Overall the text is a kind of pastiche of obligations, unexceptionable in themselves but without direct reference to the duties assumed by individuals appointed to Church offices.

Each of the five paragraphs deserves a word of explanation. (There are minor variants of the last two paragraphs for ''superiors in clerical religious institutes and societies of apostolic life.'')

Paragraph 1. The one taking the oath promises both in words and conduct always ''to preserve communion with the Catholic Church.'' This is partially based on canon 209, §1, and binds all the Christian faithful alike. The context demands only that this obligation be sworn to and seems to imply that officeholders have a greater obligation of communion than the rest of the faithful.

Paragraph 2. This section (alone) does have aspects of an oath of office, since one promises to carry out carefully and faithfully ''the duties incumbent on me toward the universal Church and the particular church in which . . . I have been called to exercise my service.'' The language, however, is derived from canon 209, §2, again a description of duties incumbent on all the Christian faithful. The ultimate source of the language is in *Lumen gen-*

tium 30 and the conciliar decree on the laity, *Apostolicam actuositatem* 10, although both passages refer to lay, nonordained members of the Church without reference to any Church office.

Paragraph 3. The paragraph begins, ''In fulfilling the charge entrusted to me in the name of the Church,'' a phrase that explicitly confirms the interpretation that the positions in question are true ecclesiastical offices to which appointments are made by Church authority, which acts officially ''in the name of the Church.''

The substance of the paragraph refers to doctrine; it is a promise to ''hold fast to the deposit of faith in its entirety,'' faithfully to ''hand it [the deposit of faith] on and explain it,'' and finally to ''avoid teachings opposed to that faith.'' The mention of handing on the faith appears to apply to those officials who exercise the ministry of the word through preaching, catechetical formation, and other means. More important, it is the DEPOSIT OF FAITH in the strict sense (as referred to in the profession of faith, both the credal text and the first added paragraph) that is at issue. The text is a digest of canon 750, concerning what must be believed with divine and catholic faith; the canon also requires the believer to avoid contrary doctrines and adds that revealed truth ''is manifested by the common adherence of the Christian faithful under the leadership of the sacred magisterium.''

Paragraph 4. As in the preceding paragraphs, it is the common duties of the faithful that are specified, with a mention of ''fostering'' as well as following ''the common discipline of the whole Church''—presumably the greater duty for Church officials. The second clause bears no relation to Church office: ''I shall observe all ecclesiastical laws, especially those which are contained in the Code of Canon Law [of the Latin Church, since the Eastern Catholics are not bound by the oath].'' The oath to observe all ecclesiastical laws involves one in the graver transgression of the virtue of religion when one does not observe the canon law.

Paragraph 5. The final paragraph of the promise is somewhat repetitive and has two parts. First there is a promise ''in Christian obedience'' to unite oneself with the bishops, both as teachers of the faith and as those responsible for Church governance. The reference is to both doctrine and Church order. It is clearly adapted from canon 212, §1, although in that context the duties are those of the Christian faithful in general rather than those of officeholders. Second, there is a promise faithfully ''to assist the diocesan bishops'' in carrying out apostolic activity. While this is surely both proper and desirable, the language is somewhat ambiguous in its reference to diocesan bishops; either the local bishop or diocesan bishops in general may be meant.

Such a commentary or critique of the text of the oath of fidelity reveals no responsibilities that are unacceptable, but it does raise the grave question of binding oneself so broadly with the invocation of the Name of God in support of the oath-taker's promise.

Persons Obliged to Take the Oath. The principal question asked by canonists and especially teaching theologians is, who are obliged to take the oath of fidelity? The document specifies many named in the latter part of canon 833 (numbers 5–8), but not all the officeholders listed in the second half of the canon are included. As the title of the oath indicates, it is to be taken by individuals ''on assuming an office to be exercised in the name of the Church.'' It is an important qualification for some of those enumerated in canon 833 do not hold Church office at all, much less one to be exercised in the name of or on behalf of the Church.

Perhaps the principal category of those simply unaffected by the new norm are teachers in colleges and universities ''who teach disciplines which deal with faith or morals.'' Such teachers do not receive an appointment to any ecclesiastical office, unless in some exceptional case. To take another example, the president (rector) of a Catholic university may or may not be appointed to a duly established Church office; if not, he or she is bound by canon 833, no. 7 to make the profession of faith, but not bound to take the oath of fidelity.

Bibliography: F. R. MCMANUS, ''Report on a Study of the Profession of Faith and Oath of Fidelity,'' *Proceedings (1991): Canon Law Society of America* (Washington 1992) 190–220; ''Preliminary Report of the CTS [College Theology Society] Committee on Profession of Faith/Oath of Fidelity,'' *Horizons* 17 (1990) 103–27; *Report of the Catholic Theological Society of America Committee on the Profession of Faith and the Oath of Fidelity* (1990). L. ÖRSY *The Profession of Faith and Oath of Fidelity: A Theological and Canonical Analysis* (Wilmington, Del. 1990). H. SCHMITZ '''Professio fidei' und 'Iusiurandum fidelitatis.' Glaubenbekennis und Treueid. Widerbelebung des Antimodernisteneides?,'' *Archiv für katholisches Kirchenrecht* 157 (1988) 353–429.

[F. R. MCMANUS]

PROFESSIONAL ETHICS

Within the broad field of applied ethics, professional ethics assesses the moral dimension of human activity in the classic occupations of law, medicine, ministry and by extension higher education, engineering, journalism, management and other occupations that aspire to professional status. Professional ethics is concerned with the standards and moral conduct that govern the profession and its members. More specifically, professional ethics examines issues, problems, and the social responsibility of the profession itself and individual practitioners in the light of philosophical and, in some contexts, religious principles among which are duty and obligation.

Occupations that by social consent enjoy professional status are generally characterized by the following criteria: technical training that implies generalized knowledge, detailed information and practical skills in a specific field; an institutionalized mode of validating or certifying mastery of this knowledge and the accompanying skills; and, an institutionalized means of insuring that they will be put to service in the public good. Associations made up of the professionals themselves set standards to secure the competence and integrity of members engaged in private practice and, in some fields such as medicine and law, structures to monitor their conduct. These same standards are in many cases reinforced by civil law through a process of examinations and licensing.

It is characteristic of professional ethics that, in addition to providing guidelines that govern the relationship of the professional with clients, as in the case of a doctor-patient relationship, they define norms that govern the professional's responsibility to colleagues and the public as a whole, as in the case of lawyers who are officers of the court and sworn to serve the cause of justice. This latter point is illustrated by the guidelines provided by the American Bar Association and the American Medical Association governing advertising. Lawyers and doctors may participate in programs that provide information and educate the public regarding services available in order that individuals be in a position to make informed choices regarding the selection of specialists who can address their needs. It is improper, however, for advertising to promote one lawyer or doctor at the expense of others.

Theoretical Issues and Specialized Questions. Professional ethics raise a number of theoretical and specialized questions that are not easily resolved. Among the theoretical issues is the extent to which the special norms and principles governing the professions override individual rights and other moral principles. Professional ethics is concerned with the obligations and responsibility that arise out of a particular kind of service performed for individuals or groups, and in that sense approximate obligations arising out of contractual agreements. In themselves the norms of professional ethics do not define the social or personal relationships of individuals towards one another.

Every code of professional ethics puts greater or lesser emphasis on the confidentiality that is intrinsic to every professional relationship. Counselors, accountants, clergy and other professionals are narrowly restricted in what they can discuss about their clients, and it goes without saying that they cannot reveal information that they have come to know through private conversation or examinations. The client's right to privacy must be safeguarded on the one hand, and the professional cannot use information for personal gain or aggrandizement. The right to confidentiality, however, is not absolute. Laws in many states require that doctors report gunshot wounds, and teachers, counselors, nurses, and others report evidence of child abuse.

Contribution of Catholic Ethics. Although philosophical and religious ethics hold much in common when analysis in each discipline is brought to bear on the dilemmas faced by and the virtues and character required of professionals, there is a specific meaning as well as a transcendent horizon or purpose that religious ethics generally, and Catholic ethics in particular, bring to the discussion.

The Roman Catholic understanding of professional ethics is based on a theology of work and vocation. In biblical and papal teaching, it is not just physical labor that is central to human identity, but work includes the notion of intellectual activity and service as well. The Church opposes every economic and political system that erodes the connection between human dignity and work. Catholic values, shared by other religious believers, see work as a calling from God, a sharing in divine creativity that is directed to the common good as well as the transcendent horizon, the Kingdom of God. The Second Vatican Council declared in *Gaudium et spes,*

> People are not deterred by the Christian message from building up the world, or impelled to neglect the welfare of their fellows. They are, rather, more stringently bound to do these very things (n. 34).

In LABOREM EXERCENS, Pope John Paul II stated, "Work serves to add to the heritage of the whole human family, of all the people living in the world" (par. 10).

"To profess" has clear resonance in the Catholic tradition. Members of religious orders and congregations profess their vows publicly. They affirm their membership in a community and proclaim their willingness to fulfill the mission of the group as set forth in the rules and constitutions. Similarly, Catholic social teaching reaffirms that the professional's primary obligation is to the public good in some form, with financial remuneration playing a distinctly subordinate role.

Crisis in Professional Ethics. In the 1980s the popular media reported a widespread collapse of ethical standards in general and in the professions in particular (*Time,* May 25, 1987). One reason for the crisis in professional ethics was said to be that professions had lost their heritage, one which is rooted in the Christian understanding of profession as commitment (Campbell 1982). This loss of heritage, however, is not an indictment of the professions so much as a statement that is descriptive of a cultural crisis presently facing Western civilization.

This loss of a cultural consensus has its roots in the profound changes wrought by technological innovation and scientific discovery in the middle of the 20th century: splitting the atom, developing the computer and telecommunications, and unlocking the genetic code. An emphasis on individualism, human freedom, and privacy (summed up as human rights) coupled with unprecedented economic power in a pluralistic/heterogeneous American society contribute to the loss of consensus that explains much of the present concern about professional ethics. The central question becomes "What is the social responsibility of the doctor, lawyer, minister, and by extension, educator, manager, engineer, accountant, journalist, social worker, and public policy maker?" It is a question that was not likely to be asked in a social context which assumed that certain standards and values were held in common. Professional behavior was virtually dictated by a consensus among the practitioners and popular expectations woven into the fabric of everyday life. (It must be acknowledged, however, that the consensus also resulted to some extent in a society in which women and minorities, whose roles were also sharply defined, found many of the professions closed to them.)

Although the moral complexity created by technological innovation and cultural pluralism is not of the individual's making, it is the responsibility of the individual professional—doctor, lawyer, scientist—to take a stance. Not everything that is medically and scientifically possible is permissible. To what extent does the technological imperative alone define the moral and legal context? The question is not one that individual professionals can be expected to resolve in principle even though, by default, they must resolve it in practice on a case-by-case basis. They face ethical dilemmas for which there is no precedent. Their responsibility to clients must be balanced against larger social issues as, for example, the right of an AIDS patient to anonymity and the need to safeguard the public from an infectious disease. Consequently, the requirements of social responsibility are central in any discussion of professional ethics.

The task facing the professions in the last decade of the 20th century is to discern ethical responsibility tentatively in an age of change while building a community in which the common good has primacy. The twin challenges of discerning personal moral behavior and the common good are no small matters. In Roman Catholic ethics this individual/social issue is clarified by the natural law tradition as well as by contemporary Catholic thinking which emphasizes historical consciousness and interprets the human person as responding to God's call in history and community.

To be designated a professional demands a commitment to the common good. Thus, to be a professional is to be called. It is to have a vocation, not just a career connoting upward mobility, success, and wealth. In the Catholic tradition, this call is from God and signifies that it is not only in our work (*in vocatione*) but through our work (*per vocationem*) that we carry out the task of continuing creativity and preparing for the Kingdom of God (Frankena 1976).

Bibliography: M. D. BAYLES, *Professional Ethics* (Belmont 1981). B. BAUMRIN and B. FREEDMAN, eds., *Moral Responsibility and the Professions* (New York 1983). J. N. BEHRMAN, *Essays on Ethics in Business and the Professions* (Englewood Cliffs 1987). R. N. BELLAH, et al., *Habits of the Heart: Individualism and Commitment in American Life* (Berkeley 1985). J. A. BOYAJIAN, ed., *Ethical Issues in the Practice of Ministry* (Minneapolis 1984). S. M. CAHN, *Saints and Scamps: Ethics in Academe* (Totowa 1986). P. CAMENISCH, *Grounding Professional Ethics in a Pluralistic Society* (New York 1983). D. M. CAMPBELL, *Doctors, Lawyers, Ministers: Christian Ethics in Professional Practice* (Nashville 1982). A. FLORES, ed., *Professional Ideals* (Belmont 1987). W. FRANKENA, "The Philosophy of Vocation," *Thought* (December 1976). A. H. GOLDMAN, *The Moral Foundations of Professional Ethics* (Totowa 1980). B. JENNINGS, et al., "The Public Duties of the Professions," *Hastings Center Report* (February 1987). M. S. LARSON, *The Rise of Professionalism: A Sociological Analysis* (Berkeley 1977). K. LEBACQZ, *Professional Ethics: Power and Paradox* (Nashville 1985). A. MACINTYRE, *After Virtue* (Notre Dame 1981). W. F. MAY, "Professional Ethics: Setting, Terrain, and Teacher," *Ethics Teaching in Higher Education*, eds. D. CALLAHAN and S. BOK (New York 1980). D. REECK, *Ethics for the Professions: A Christian Perspective* (Minneapolis 1982). T. L. SHAFFER *Faith and the Professions* (Albany, N.Y. 1987). N. O. HATCH, ed., *The Professions in American History* (Notre Dame, Ind. 1988).

[J. R. WILCOX]

PROKOPOVICH, FEOFAN

Russian Orthodox archbishop, theologian; b. Kiev, June 8, 1681; d. St. Petersburg, Sept. 9,1736. After studying theology in the Academy of Kiev he became a Catholic (1698) and joined the Basilian monks. During his graduate studies in Rome he was accepted as a member of the Society of Jesus. Instead of entering the order, however, he returned to Kiev and reverted to Orthodoxy. In 1704 he became a professor at the Kiev Academy and served as its rector (1711–16). Although Stefan accused him of Calvinism, he became bishop of Pskov (1720) and archbishop of Novgorod (1725). He was a close adviser of Emperor Peter I (the Great), who used him as his principal theorist on ecclesiastical policies. Prokopovich supported Peter's creation of the HOLY SYNOD (1721) and became its first vice president. The Holy Synod replaced the patriarchate as the governing body of the Russian Orthodox Church, which it subjected almost completely to state control. For his role in this change Prokopovich has been called the father of Russian CAESARO-PAPISM. He published numerous literary, philosophical, and theological works, mostly in Latin. Their influence lasted until 1836, when the reaction in favor of traditional Orthodox beliefs began. His work on ecclesiastical regulation, published in conjunction with the Czar in 1720, urged the Church's subjection to the State. In a treatise on the justice of the emperor's decision (1721), Prokopovich combined Western ideas on absolute power with Byzantine theocratic concepts. His views on the procession of the Holy Spirit, the cult of images, and the Blessed Virgin conformed to those of Orthodoxy, but his teachings on grace, free, will, justification, and ecclesiology showed strong Lutheran influences. The seminary that Prokopovich started in St. Petersburg, patterned on the Protestant one in Halle, became a center for spreading his ideas.

[J. PAPIN]

PROMISE, MORAL OBLIGATION OF A

A promise is an assurance one gives that he will do, give, or refrain from something to the advantage of another. A promise of some kind is involved in all contracts, but ordinarily when a moral theologian speaks of a simple promise he excludes from consideration mutual or onerous agreements and thinks only of unilateral, gratuitous commitments that an individual may make to the benefit of another.

A promise binds in virtue of commutative JUSTICE if it is contractual in the strictest sense of the term, for in that case the promisor intends to obligate himself seriously and the promisee accepts the assurance with that understanding. The deliberate violation of such a promise is therefore gravely sinful, provided that the matter with which it is concerned is not too trivial of its nature to be an object of serious injustice.

More commonly the promises of daily life bind only in FIDELITY. They involve no strict contract because there is no formal acceptance on the part of the promisee, and the promisor does not intend to put himself under grave moral obligation. The keeping of such promises, therefore, is not a matter of strict justice but is rather a form of truthfulness in which an individual makes his actions conform to his words. Fidelity is a most commendable quality of soul, but it is less urgently necessary to the social good than justice, and its violation under ordinary circumstances is not considered mortally sinful.

A promise, whether binding in justice or fidelity, ceases to oblige (1) if the promisee is willing that it should not be fulfilled, (2) if fulfillment becomes impossible, unlawful, useless, or harmful to the promisee, or (3) if it can be reasonably assumed that the promisor would not have bound himself had he foreseen some supervenient change of circumstance connected with the promise.

When what is promised is morally wrong, the promise is invalid and without binding force from the beginning.

Bibliography: B. H. MERKELBACH, *Summa theologiae maralis,* 3 v. (Paris 1949) 2:497–500. D. M. PRÜMMER, *Manuale theologiae moralis,* ed. E. M. MÜNCH, 3 v. Freiburg-Barcelona 1955) 2:226–229. H. NOLDIN, *Summa theologiae maralis,* rev. A. SCHMITT and G. HEINZEL, 3 v. (Innsbruck 1961–62) 2:481–482.

[P. K. MEAGHER]

PRÔNE

The Prône began in medieval times as a vernacular service in extra-liturgical settings that came later to be included in the Latin High Mass on Sundays and other feasts. In its more developed form the Prône included a translation or paraphrase of the Gospel reading, sometimes with an explanation, a catechetical instruction based on the creed, Lord's Prayer, or Commandments, bidding prayers, as well as notification of the banns of marriage and other announcements. The term also was used to refer to sermons, especially of an instructional type. The word itself is derived from the French *prône*, a grill separating the chancel from the rest of the church on which notices were posted.

In France the Prône became a common means of catechetical instruction as is evident in the following 17th century account:

> The Prône contains four parts: (1) Prayers for the Church, for princes, for the state, for public and special needs. (2) Instruction on how to serve God, explanation of the Pater, the Credo, the Sacraments, the Commandments, the Gospel. (3) Announcements of Church regulations, feasts and fasts, indulgences, processions, marriages, candidates for Holy Orders and all public acts of piety. (4) Promulgation of the commands of prelates, cases of excommunication, public sinners. . . . It is a public function that serves to carry out what the Fathers, the Councils, and the popes teach to the faithful, to instruct them in piety, to teach them the law of the Lord; the people, therefore, are obliged to assist at it and the parish priests to read it or have it read, as has been ordered by the capitularies of Charlemagne and since then by num-

berless councils, even by the first council of Orleans, as is reported by Ivo of Chartres: ''On Sundays and feast days, after the sermon preached during the solemn Mass, the pastor will, in accordance with the advice of the Apostle, have the people pray for all the different needs, to pray for the king, . . . for peace, for the sick of the parish, for the dead; and for each of these intentions each one will say privately the Lord's Prayer and the priest will say the appropriate orations.'' [M. F. Grancolas, *Les Anciennes liturgies* (Paris 1697) 1:525–526]

An edition of the Prône in French and in English, published in Quebec in 1874, after beginning with an instruction on avoiding servile works and attending Sunday Mass, adds a series of petitions:

> ''We offer Thee our prayers for Thy holy Church . . . for the peace and tranquility of this country . . . for widows and orphans. . . . We beseech thee to protect from all danger pregnant women, that their children may receive the holy Sacrament of Baptism . . . to preserve the just in a state of grace, to enlighten the mind and change the hearts of sinners . . . to unite in the bonds of charity all the inhabitants of this parish. And, in order that we may ask of Thee all that is necessary for us, we will offer to Thee the prayer which Jesus Christ Himself has taught us.''

The Lord's Prayer, the Hail Mary, the Apostles' Creed, the Ten Commandments, and the Precepts of the Church follow. Finally there is the Collect from the 22d Sunday after Pentecost (in Latin), the names of deceased, the *De Profundis,* and the prayer *Fidelium.*

In the United States a vestige of the Prône endured almost to the time of the Second Vatican Council. After the Epistle and Gospel of the day were read in Latin, the celebrant would then mount the pulpit or, where there was no pulpit, stand at the communion rail, make announcements, including the banns of matrimony, read an English translation of the Epistle and Gospel, and deliver a sermon that was often an exposition of the catechism (Creed, Commandments, sacraments, and prayer).

Bibliography: J. CARMODY, ''An American Use of the Prône,'' *Theological Studies* 19 (1958) 228–236. J. B MOLIN, ''Les Prières du prône en Italie,'' *Ephemerides liturgicae* 76 (1962) 39–42. G. OURY, ''Les Survivances de l'oratio fidelium au XIIe siècle,'' *Revue Grégorienne* 40 (1962) 142–148. T. MAERTENS, ''Pour un renouveau des prières du prône,'' *Paroisse et Liturgie* 43 (1960–61) 21–28, 89–98, 245–252. *Oxford Dictionary of the Christian Church,* s.v. ''Prone.'' E. GERMAIN, J. JONCHERAY in *Aux Origines du Catéchisme en France* (Relais-Desclée, 1989) 106–119; 229–246.

[J. M. CARMODY/EDS.]

PRONOUNCEMENTS, PAPAL AND CURIAL

The pronouncements of the Holy See, either directly from the pope, or through the various offices of the Roman Curia. Certain documents are used for teaching faith and morals; some for church governance, and others for disciplinary purposes.

Documents of the Pope. The *decretal letter* is one of the most solemn forms of papal proclamations. It is presently used for the canonization of saints and is generally presumed to invoke infallibility.

An *encyclical* is a pastoral letter written by the pope for the entire Church. Encyclicals are used to present the moral and social teachings of the Church, or to give counsel on points of doctrine which must be made more precise or which must be taught in view of specific circumstances.

The *APOSTOLIC CONSTITUTION* is the most solemn form of legal document issued by the pope in his own name; it is issued only in relation to very weighty matters. For instance, the *Code of Canon Law* for the Latin Church was promulgated as a constitution, *Sacrae disciplinae leges*, Jan. 25, 1983; the same for the *Code of Canons of the Eastern Churches*, Oct. 18, 1990. The *Catechism of the Catholic Church* was formally published through the constitution *Fidei depositum* (Oct. 11, 1992).

The apostolic letter *motu proprio* is the most common source of canonical legislation after the Code itself. It deals with matters that are significant, but would not merit a constitution. *Motu proprios* are legislative in nature and are directed to the Church at large. More recently, the pope has been using a more general form, simply entitled *Apostolic letter* to make proclamations. For instance, the letter *Ordinatio sacerdotalis* (May 22, 1994) addressed the issue of admission of women to priestly ordination: ''I declare that the church has no authority whatsoever to confer priestly ordination on women and that this judgment is to be definitively held by all the church's faithful.'' The preparations for the Jubilee Year 2000 were also announced in an apostolic letter, *Tertio millennio adveniente* (Nov. 10, 1994). The place this type of papal document will occupy in years to come is not yet totally clear. There is no doubt that it is considered to be a major papal document.

APOSTOLIC EXHORTATIONS are also a significant expression of the magisterium of the Church; although they are not legislative in nature, they are morally persuasive and quite influential because they are frequently the product of consensus.

Papal *allocutions* are the regular addresses given by the pope on the occasion of meetings with bishops, congresses, pilgrimages, and so forth. These express the ordinary papal magisterium; they are not legislative by nature. However, the repetition of a given theme in a number of allocutions gives particular insight into the personal thought of the pope on the matter. For instance, the annual addresses to the Roman Rota at the opening of the judicial year constitute a privileged opportunity for the pope to express his views of matters relating to the application of procedural law and the canons on marriage.

The Second Vatican Council recognized the diversity of texts and their particular significance when used by the pope to further his teaching. ''His mind and will . . . may be known chiefly either from the character of the documents, from his frequent repetition of the same doctrine, or from his manner of speaking'' (*LG* 25). Canon 754 addresses this in legislative terms: ''All Christ's faithful are obliged to observe the constitutions and decrees which lawful ecclesiastical authority issues for the purpose of proposing doctrine or of proscribing erroneous opinions; this holds particularly for those published by the Roman Pontiff or by the College of Bishops.''

Curial Documents. The *decree* is the highest form of document issued by a department of the Roman Curia. It is a law whose interpretation is governed by the canons on laws (see canon 29). The term *decree* is given many practical meanings: 1) where it is used in administrative matters, it is applied to designate the decisions of the Roman dicasteries (for instance, the approval of the Constitutions of a religious institute); 2) in legislative matters, the term is applied specifically to disciplinary laws (for instance, the undated decree of the Cong. for the Doctrine of the Faith prescribing an automatic excommunication for any person who abuses the sacrament of penance by using tape recorders and similar means of social communication — *AAS*, 80 (1988), p. 1367); 3) in judicial matters, the various procedural decisions taken by the judge (as, for instance, the decisions of the Supreme Tribunal of the Apostolic Signatura).

Instructions clarify the prescriptions of laws and determine an approach to be followed in implementing them (see canon 34).

Declarations are of three types: 1) the simple declaration, which must be interpreted in the light of existing legislation (such as the Declaration of the CDF relating to membership in Masonic organizations, Nov. 26, 1983); 2) authentic interpretations or declarations, which have the force of law and must be promulgated (such as those issued by the Pontifical Council for the Interpretation of Legislative Texts); 3) extensive declarations, which to a certain extent modify the law, by having it apply to instances not originally covered by the legislation.

Circular letters express the intentions and policies of the Roman Curia. When accompanied by rules, these letters explain the intention, spirit and purpose of these rules (for instance, the letter and norms governing dispensations from the obligations of priestly celibacy, Oct. 18, 1980, as revised slightly, June 6, 1997).

Directories, such as the 1993 *Directory for Ecumenism* (March 25, 1993) are given for the application of accepted principles and are seen as ''an instrument at the service of the whole Church . . . [whose] orientations and norms of universal application . . . provide consistency and coordination . . . with the discipline that binds Catholics together'' (No. 6). The importance of a directory lies in the fact that it provides the basic principles of pastoral theology, taken from the magisterium of the Church, by which pastoral action in the ministry can be more fittingly directed and governed.

Classification. Documents can be examined from a descriptive approach, according to form and the authorities who issued them. But they can also be classified according to their juridical value or weight. Some documents are magisterial (flowing from the *munus docendi*), while others are juridical (based on the *munus regendi*). Those that are juridical can be either laws in the proper sense of the term, or administrative documents for the whole community; they can bind only the executors of the law (such as texts addressed particularly to bishops), or even be non-binding (such as guidelines).

Bibliography: J. M. HUELS, ''A Theory of Juridical Documents Based on Canons 29–34,'' *Studia canonica* 32 (1998) 337–370. E. LABANDIERA, ''Clasificación de las normas escritas canónicas,'' *Ius canonicum* 29 (1989) 679–693. F. G. MORRISEY, *Papal and Curial Pronouncements: Their Canonical Significance in Light of the ''Code of Canon Law''* (Ottawa 1995). L. WÄCHTER, *Gesetz im kanonischem Recht: eine rechtssprachliche une systematisch-normative Untersuchung zu Grundproblemen der Erfassung des Gesetzes im katholischen Kirchenrecht*, Müchener theologische Studien, III, Kanonistische Abteilung, Bd. 43 (St. Otilien 1989).

[F. G. MORRISSEY]

PROOF

Proof is the means of ascertaining the truth of an alleged fact or proposition. It may consist in presenting empirical evidence, documents, or witnesses. More often it is taken to mean a reasoning process. Proof is inductive if it proceeds from the singular to the universal, or from the less to the more universal. It is deductive (syllogism) if it proceeds from the more to the less universal, or from one universal to another coextensive universal. From the viewpoint of truth-value, deductive proof is either demonstration, in which certitude is attained, or dialectics, in which probability is attained. Reasoning from hypothesis and analogy yields dialectical conclusions. Statistical proofs are a mode of induction. The ancients assigned proper modes of proof also to RHETORIC and POETICS.

See Also: ARGUMENTATION; DEMONSTRATION; DIALECTICS; INDUCTION.

[M. A. GLUTZ]

PROPAGANDA

The term applied to the content and the process of communication in which actual or alleged facts, arguments, and opinions are presented in such a way as to induce judgments and attitudes favoring the interest or point of view of those sponsoring the communication. In the United States, propaganda is associated with sinister activities, in that it is perceived as slanted and biased. It usually involves loaded or heavily weighted material to assure consent and agreement. The term came to be used by English and Continental writers in the late 18th and early 19th centuries, when some who were anticlerical and anti-Catholic identified this type of material with the publications of the Roman Congregation of the Propagation of the Faith (De Propaganda Fide). ''Propagating the faith'' was judged by these writers as ''sheer propaganda.'' However, the term lost its original connection with anti-Catholicism, and it is currently used to identify the vast body of political, partisan, and high-pressure mass communication designed to promote persons or causes in the modern world. Within modern communist movements, the term is associated with the agitation and indoctrination of the masses. Others associate the term with the highest degree of deception comparable to that of the Nazis' Ministry of Public Enlightenment and Propaganda. As a contemporary phenomenon, especially associated with wars and political strife, propaganda has been studied by social psychologists and political analysts in great depth. In moral society, propaganda falls under the same moral laws as do other forms of speech and communication.

Bibliography: M. ANGENOT, ''La propagande socialiste: elements de rhetorique et de pragmatique.'' *Texte-Revue de critique et de theorie litteraire* 8–9 (1989)159–97. P. BUITENHUIS, *The Great War of Words: British, American, and Canadian Propaganda and Fiction, 1914–1933* (Vancouver 1987). C.A. FLEMING, ''Understanding Propaganda from a General Semantics Perspective,'' *Etc: A Review of General Semantics* 52 (1995) 3–12. A.P. FOULKES, *Literature and Propaganda* (London 1983). R. FYNE, *The Hollywood Propaganda of World War II* (Metuchen, NJ 1994). S.C. SCHICK, ''Propaganda Analysis: The Search for an Appropriate Model,'' *Etc: A Review of General Semantics* 42 (1985) 63–71. X.-M. YANG, *The Rhetoric of Propaganda: A Tagmemic Analysis of Selected Documents of the Cultural Revolution in China* (New York 1994). J.W. YOUNG, *Totalitarian Language: Orwell's Newspeak and Its Nazi and Communist Antecedents* (Charlottesville 1991).

[A. S. FOLEY/EDS.]

PROPAGATION OF THE FAITH, CONGREGATION FOR THE

The Congregation for the Propagation of the Faith (*Congregationis de Propaganda Fide* or ''CPF'') was established to coordinate and spearhead the missionary activity of the Church. This entry deals with the history and activities of CPF from its founding to its reorganization by Pope Paul VI in 1967, when its name was changed to Congregation for the Evangelization of Peoples. For developments since 1967, see EVANGELIZATION OF PEOPLES, CONGREGATION FOR THE.

History. The idea of a special congregation in the Roman Curia to devote its attention to missionary matters appears to have originated with Raymond LULL, a Franciscan tertiary, who in the 13th century petitioned Celestine V and later Boniface VIII to establish such a congregation. Jean VENDVILLE revived the idea, proposing in 1567 that the pope institute a congregation for the conversion of the Greeks, another for alleviating the lot of Christian captives in Muslim lands, and one for the ''Christian apostolate.'' In 1568 at the urging of Francis Borgia, Pius V established two temporary commissions for the propagation of the faith, one in Protestant lands, the other in non-Christian lands. In 1573 Gregory XIII instituted a provisional congregation of three cardinals for the conversion of non-Christians. Clement VIII enlarged the importance of this commission of cardinals.

During Clement VIII's reign four things were being proposed: (1) a congregation of cardinals for the propagation of the faith, (2) an organization to procure financial support for the missions, (3) a publishing house to print Christian literature to be distributed among non-Christians, and (4) a seminary for the training of missionaries. Prominent among the promoters of these ideas were Cardinal Santori, the Capuchin Girolamo Narma, and the four Discalced Carmelites, Girolamo Graziano della Madre di Dio, Domenico di Gesu e Maria, Tommaso di Gesu, and Pietro della Madre di Dio. Clement VIII established a congregation of nine cardinals in 1599 for handling missionary affairs, and under this he placed the national seminaries founded by Gregory XIII.

This gradual evolution of a central missionary organization reached its climax and permanent institutional

The College of the Congregation for the Propagation of the Faith, building designed by Gian Lorenzo Bernini, 1935, Rome. (Alinari-Art Reference/Art Resource, NY)

character in the formal erection of CPF by Gregory XV on Jan. 6, 1622. It was confirmed by the bull *Inscrutabili Divinae* of June 22, 1622. The original congregation consisted of 13 cardinals, two prelates and one secretary. One of the prelates was John Baptist Vives, who presented his palace in the Piazza di Spagna to serve as its headquarters.

The two factors that necessitated a missionary congregation were the lack of unity and collaboration among the various religious orders charged with carrying out missionary work, and the excessive control that Spain and Portugal were then exercising over the administration of the missions under the terms of the right of patronage. (*See* PATRONATO REAL.) Pius V had earlier attempted to wrestle control of the Church's missionary activity from the Portuguese and Spanish Crowns, but was unsuccessful. The erection of the CPF was an important step in mission history, marking the transfer of authority over missionary activity from states to the Holy See. State control of this field had resulted in a hierarchical organization ill-suited to the needs of the missionaries. The frequent interference of colonial officials into the administration of missions, and the close identification between the colonial regimes and missionaries in the eyes of the indigenous people hindered the missionaries from winning over the hearts and minds of the local populace. Reform was urgently needed to institute reforms and to bring about more united and concerted missionary action.

The new congregation set to work at its first meeting on Jan. 14, 1622. The first order of the things was the momentous task of conducting a study of existing missions to identify areas of strengths and weaknesses. This task fell on Francesco Ingoli, a priest from Ravenna, who as secretary for the first 20 years, proved to be the driving force behind the early congregation. Through his painstaking efforts, the newly established CPF was able to accumulate a wealth of knowledge on missionary affairs that enabled it to draw up the fundamental principles destined to govern all future missionary activity. Some of the evils revealed by this study were: the insufficient number of missionaries, their ignorance of native languages and cultures, the mercenary preoccupation of some of them, the discord between missionary orders, the failure to train native clergy, and a lack of willingness to adapt to indigenous cultural values. Having learned the evils and the obstacles, CPF set out to improve missionary methods, to increase the supply of missionaries, and to foster the development of an indigenous clergy. It strove actively to centralize control of the missions, and to emphasize the spiritual character of mission work. Under CPF, the Catholic missions once again began to assume that supranational character that they had had during the Middle Ages. In its objectives one can see the lofty spiritual ideal with which it was concerned, yet it had to face a long and bitter struggle with the Spanish and Portuguese authorities before the necessary reforms could be carried out. Although CPF had been given exclusive jurisdiction over all missionary activity, including the mission territories and personnel, it was not immediately able to exercise its authority freely. It was opposed not only by the governments mentioned but also by religious orders jealously clinging to privileges and faculties granted in the past by the Holy See.

In order to promote unity and uniformity, the CPF assumed responsibility for granting all missionary faculties. Missionaries were obliged to report to it every year on the status, prospects, and resources of their missions. CPF also urged the generals of religious orders to found schools of languages and controversy for missionaries destined for the East. In 1627, under Urban VIII, a seminary of the CPF called the Collegium Urbanum was founded to train for the secular priesthood candidates from all nations. In order to circumvent the excessive authority claimed by Spain and Portugal under the right of patronage, CPF appointed the first three vicars apostolic for the Far East in 1659, at the same time furnishing them with wise and far-reaching directives relating to the preservation of indigenous values and the development of an indigenous clergy. In contrast to the colonizing policies of Spain and Portugal, which had unfortunate repercussions on mission methodology, CPF had insisted from the beginning on the preservation of cultural characteristics and social autonomy of the non-Western lands. Regrettably, however, CPF, while still young and relatively inexperienced, found itself embroiled in the bitter controversies about rites and jurisdiction. (*See* CHINESE RITES CONTROVERSY; PATRONATO REAL.)

In order to supply Christian books and literature for the mission world, CPF set up its own printing press in 1626. Much of this equipment, and books as well, were stolen during the Napoleonic invasion of Rome. Because of the revolutionary occupation of the city, CPF was closed between 1809 and 1814, but it was reestablished by Pius VII in 1817. In 1862 there was established within CPF a congregation for the Oriental Church. In Pius X's reorganization of CPF in 1908, the Oriental congregation was separated from CPF and given complete autonomy for Oriental affairs.

Administrative Competence. In the beginning, CPF's competence was very broad, embracing all matters related to missionary activity, the only limitation being that particularly serious affairs had to be referred to the pope. Its competence was exclusive for each and every mission region, and it included all persons and cases. The exclusive authority of CPF was guaranteed by the abrogation of all contrary legislation, including the privileges and indults that had been granted to different orders or congregations. Since it had the right to handle for its territories all matters that other Roman Congregations handled for European dioceses, it was commonly said of CPF *ceteras Congregationes habet in ventre.* It enjoyed not only administrative jurisdiction but also judicial, since it could judge cases, even in the first instance. It had legislative power also; in fact, its decrees had the force of apostolic constitutions and were to be observed inviolably by all persons. The conferral of this broad jurisdiction on CPF did not automatically assure its recognition and acceptance by all who were legally subject to it. For a long time CPF had much opposition to face.

These sweeping powers were modified by Pius X in his constitution *Sapienti Consilio* of 1908. This constitution abrogated CPF's competence in regard to extent of territory, matters of faith, matrimonial cases, the discipline of the sacred rites, and religious as missionaries, restricting it to mere regulatory authority over the various missions to ensure their proper administration. In reality, CPF had special faculties from the Roman pontiff, which dispensed it from ordinary canonical prescriptions under special circumstances prevailing in mission territories. It was vested with true legislative power, although it is restricted in its exercise. It was authorized to issue instructions in order to explain the practical application of laws or to suggest more efficacious means of the mission apostolate. These instructions did not have the force of law but were rather directive norms to be followed in general. More specifically, CPF was granted the power to erect mission territories, and divide them according to needs or opportunities. It had the power to name the ordinaries of these territories, and it regulated the proper administration of all mission regions, including local councils, seminaries and indigenous religious orders.

Territorial Competence. From its very beginning, CPF was entrusted with mission territories in those regions of Europe where Protestantism prevailed. It was only in 1908, according to the provision of *Sapienti Consilio,* that Great Britain, Holland, Luxembourg, southern Canada, and the U.S. were removed from its jurisdiction. The bulk of Central and South America were never under CPF because of difficulties with the Spanish and Portuguese crowns under the patronage system. Most of Africa and Asia, where the control of the Spanish and Portuguese colonial authorities were more tenuous, came to be subjected to CPF, except for those jurisdictions which had been ceded earlier to the Portuguese and Spanish crowns.

External Organization. The territory under CPF's jurisdiction was divided into dioceses, vicariates, and prefectures, ruled over respectively by bishops, vicars apostolic, and prefects apostolic. At one time there was a territorial organization known as the *missio sui juris,* which flourished particularly when Cardinal Van Rossum was prefect. Their number steadily diminished after his death in 1932. By the time of the 1967 reorganization into the Congregation for the EVANGELIZATION OF PEOPLES, only three remained. The general practice was to erect a new mission territory in the form of a prefecture, and elevate it to a vicariate after suitable growth, particularly in the number of local clergy.

The hierarchical organization, however, originated not as an indication of missionary development but in the endeavor to overcome the abuses, excesses, and failures of the right of patronage, so strongly defended by the Spanish and Portuguese crowns. Originally the Holy See appointed vicars apostolic for territories outside the effective control of the Portuguese authorities, but within already constituted dioceses. It was only later that vicariates and prefectures independent of dioceses were erected.

In the 19th century, the practice of CPF upon opening a new mission region was to entrust it to a particular religious order or mission society commissioned to develop the region, at the same time appointing as ecclesiastical superior a member of the same institute. This practice, formally known as ''*ius commissionis*,'' was abolished in 1966, and indigenous bishops took over the administration of these mission territories from superiors of religious orders.

Emphasis upon indigenous leadership received renewed impetus after World War I when Benedict XV assigned to CPF as its special task that of building up as soon as practicable an indigenous clergy and hierarchy, to whom the government of the Church in the mission territories should be turned over without delay. The fruits of this policy were quite remarkable; the first bishop of Asian origin was consecrated in 1923, and the first apostolic vicars of African origin were named in 1939. When Vatican Council II opened in 1962, there were a total of 90 Asian bishops and 58 African bishops present. The development of an indigenous episcopacy and the erection of the hierarchy in nearly all mission lands was a landmark development in the history of the Church's mission.

Bibliography: R. H. S. SONG, *The Sacred Congregation for the Propagation of the Faith* (Washington 1961). S. DELACROIX, ed., *Histoire universelle des missions catholiques,* 4 v. (Paris 1956–59) v.2. G. GOYAU, *Missions and Missionaries,* tr. F. M. DREVES (London 1932). L. PASTOR, *The History of the Popes from the Close of the Middle Ages* (London-St. Louis 1938–61) v.18; 19; 24; 27. T. TREDE, *Die Propaganda fide in Rom* (Berlin 1884). O. MEYER, *Die Propaganda, ihre Provinzen und ihre Recht,* 2 v. (Göttingen 1852). J. SCHMIDLIN, *Catholic Mission History,* tr. T. J. KENNEDY and W. H. ROBERTSON, ed. M. BRAUN (Techny, IL 1933); ''Die Gründung der Propagandakongregation (1622),'' *Zeitschrift für Missionswissenschaft und Religionswissenschaft* 12 (1921) 1–14. G. STANGHETTI, *Prassi della S. C. de Propaganda Fide* (Rome 1943). N. KOWALSKY, *Pontificio Collegio Urbano de Propaganda Fide* (Rome 1956). P. GUILDAY, ''The Sacred Congregation de Propaganda Fide, 1622–1922,'' *American Catholic Historical Review* 6 (1921) 478–494. M. CASTELUCCI, ''Il Risveglio dell'attività missionaria e le prime origini della S. C. de Propaganda Fide nella seconda metà del XVI secolo,'' *Le conferenze al Laterano, Marzo-Aprile 1923,* 117–254. J. METZLER, ed., *Sacrae Congregationis de Propaganda Fide memoria rerum: 350 Years in the Service of the Missions 1622–1972 3v.* (Freiburg 1971–75). J. A. GRIFFIN, ''The Sacred Congregation de Propaganda Fide: Its Foundation and Historical Antecedents,'' in *Christianity and Missions, 1450–1800* (Brookfield, VT 1997).

[R. HOFFMAN/EDS.]

PROPAGATION OF THE FAITH, SOCIETY FOR THE

The ''organ of the Holy See for collection everywhere of the alms of the faithful and their distribution among all Catholic Missions'' [''Romanorum Pontificum,'' *Acta Apostolicae Sedis* 14 (1922) 321]. It aids the Near East, Latin America, and the home missions of the United States, as well as those territories under the Congregation for the Evangelization of Peoples.

Origin. At 19, Pauline JARICOT (1799–1862) had her first intuition of the plan for the Propagation of the Faith. The French missionary establishment had been fatally hit by the revolution of 1789 and the three leading missionary institutes wiped out; only seven missionaries left France between 1793 and 1798. French organizations in Asia and Africa were cut off from the motherland for 25 years. Missionary societies lacked both vocations and monetary support. Aware of this situation and also of the fact that various organizations were trying to set up collecting agencies, Pauline Jaricot did not believe that particular and competing associations would advance the missions. She wished, rather, to establish a single collecting agency for all Catholic missions everywhere.

Three stages may be distinguished in the foundation of the Society for the Propagation of the Faith. The first, from 1818 to 1819, was Pauline Jaricot's implementation of a proposal by the directors of the Missions Étrangères for an association of prayer and good works for the missions—one, however, that culled but meager contributions. The second stage, from 1819 to 1822, was the organization of the association according to a plan she had conceived. Watching a family card game one evening, Pauline thought how easy it would be for each of her friends and relatives to find ten associates who would each donate a weekly sou to the missions. One among them would be chosen to receive the contributions of 10 groups of 10; another, 10 groups of 100, and so on. The future of the Society for the Propagation of the Faith, which was born that evening, appeared bright; however, only a few weeks later its very existence was threatened. Several Lyonese priests warned their parishioners against the society in their Sunday sermons, calling the association a schismatic enterprise dreamed up by an ambitious bigot, and they refused absolution to its associates. These attacks were triggered by the displeasure of the friends of certain missions in the United States who resented a general collecting association. Fortunately, through the efforts of influential laity and clergy, the society was saved and immediately afterward took a great step forward. The third stage was the universalization of the association and its subsequent reorganization. This began at a meeting on May 3, 1822, purportedly held to raise money for Bp. Louis William DUBOURG's missions in Lousiana and attended primarily by members of the *Congregation de la Vierge*, an organization dedicated to works of charity in post-Revolutionary France. They agreed to constitute themselves a provisionary council and adopted the collection method and name of the Society for the Propagation of the Faith. Pauline Jaricot was persuaded to bring her own collection groups into the generalized society, and for the next 30 years "left to whomever wished to assume it, the honor of having founded the Society for the Propagation of the Faith." However, in 1881, in a brief addressed to Julia Maurin, Pauline Jaricot's first biographer, Leo XIII designated her as the foundress.

History. The society spread with extraordinary rapidity on the national level. After Pius VII authorized it on March 15, 1823, what so far had been the concern of pious laity was enthusiastically promoted by bishops and clergy. By 1826 the society had become international; the first branch outside of France was established in Belgium in 1825, and two years later others followed in Germany, Italy, and Switzerland. By 1836 the society had spread over most of Europe. In 1839 local units extended to the land that was its first beneficiary, the United States, and in 1840 to South America.

In 1822, when the society sent its first donation to the United States, the Church there had only one archdiocese and eight dioceses, while Catholics numbered about 200,000. For the next ten years, the United States received 42 percent of the society's total allocations. In recognition of this, the First Provincial Council of Baltimore (1829) stated: "The bishops and clergy of the United States make it a duty never to offer the Sacrifice on our altars without thinking of the venerable Association of the Propagation of the Faith." In 1884 the Third Plenary Council of the United States bishops endorsed Cardinal James Gibbons' suggestion for a national organization of the Society for the Propagation of the Faith in the United States. No substantial work was done, however, until 1896, when at the proposal of Abp. Patrick Riordan of San Francisco, California, the metropolitans authorized the appointment of a national director and the American branch of the society was incorporated. The following year, 1897, Bp. Henry Granjon, a Sulpician missionary of Lyons, was appointed first national director, and headquarters were established at St. Mary's Seminary in Baltimore, Maryland.

Until 1922 the central council of Lyons and the central council of Paris decided on the distribution of the alms received, in accordance with the missionary demands brought to their attention. Displeased by the monopoly held by the French council over the distribution of monies collected in the entire Catholic world, the bishops of other countries, and especially the United States bishops, tried to bring about the transfer of the international center of the society to Rome. So did the heads of mission territories who complained that the central council did not understand their needs. Decided and prepared by Benedict XV, this transfer was realized by Pius XI in 1922 and carried through by a young prelate, Msgr. Angelo Roncalli (later Pope John XXIII), National Director for the Society for the Propagation of the Faith in Italy. Through his motu proprio *Romanorum Pontificum* of May 3, 1922, Pius XI established the society as a pontifical society to be governed by the Congregation of the Propagation of the Faith and directed by a general council selected among the clergy of the countries notably contributing to the collection. With its headquarters in Rome, the society received from the same Pontiff a new set of rules and regulations for its administration and coordination. Later Pius XI issued an important encyclical, *Rerum Ecclesiae*, which conferred upon the society in a certain way "Roman citizenship" and made it "all mission organizations . . . the principal one" [*Acta Apostolicae Sedis* 18 (1926) 65]. Through the same document it received "charge of all mission needs that exist at present, or that shall exist in the future."

Organization. The Pontifical Society for the Propagation of the Faith is administered by a supreme council chosen by the pontiff himself from among those nations that contribute to the work. Over this council presides the secretary general of the Congregation of the Evangelization of Peoples. The roster of officials administering the council, as well as the regulations for its conduct, have been laid down by *Romanorum Pontificum.* The two main functions of the council consist in augmenting its administrative sphere through the establishment of national and diocesan offices of the Society for the Propagation of the Faith and in centralizing the alms of the faithful in order to be in a position to effect a ''just division of the alms among . . . all the Catholic Missions'' (Pius XI, *Romanorum Pontificum, op. cit.* 321). Subject to the superior general council are the national and diocesan directors of the Society for the Propagation of the Faith. The national directors are directly responsible to the pope through the superior general council. Diocesan directors, named by the bishop in each diocese, assist their national director to whom they send the alms that have been donated to the society by the faithful in every parish throughout the world.

Distribution of alms collected through the society belongs strictly to the superior general council. Those in charge of the national and diocesan offices of the society are the trustees of the pope's mission money. Therefore it may not be disposed of by anyone except the superior general council without violating positive and natural rights. Accordingly, the same council found it necessary to declare that ''according to the motu proprio: *Romanorum Pontificum*, the right and duty of allocating to the Missions all offerings made to the Society belongs exclusively to the Superior Council'' (Plenary Session, Rome, April 26, 1938). It further asserted that ''all stringless offerings, even those made outside of Mission Sunday and membership ought to enter the General Fund to be placed at the distribution of the Superior Council'' (Dec. 15, 1951). This distribution is made at the annual international meeting in Rome.

Fides News Service. From its inception, the Society started a service of mission information — ''News from the Missions.'' Three years later, it was renamed ''Annals of the Propagation of the Faith.'' During a meeting of its Superior Council in April 1927, the Society decided to establish Fides News Service, ''to make the missions known to the People of God'' through the press. Fides was to ''provide to the Propagation of the Faith Directors of the world two classes of publicity material: (1) news copy and photos, the timeliness of which is such that they will be valuable not only to the Annals but for the non-mission press of each country; and (2) Studies of contemporary mission conditions of religious and social affairs throughout the world so far as they affect the conversions of non-Christians'' (First Statutes of Fides). Fides was launched immediately after the feast of Saint Francis Xavier in 1927, the first news bulletins being issued in English and French. The Italian edition began in 1929, the Spanish in 1930 and the German in 1932. Fides provides a mission statistics service and assists in the worldwide promotion of missionary publications. With more than 100 volumes in English and other languages, Fides is a source of accurate documentation of the work of evangelization throughout the world.

Bibliography: A. GUASCO, *Oeuvre de la Propagation de la Foi: Ses origines, . . . ses progres* (Paris 1911). *Act Apostolicae Sedis* 14 (1922) 321–330, 647–649; 15 (1923) 77–80. D. LATHOUD, *Le Secret des origines de la Propagation de la Foi*, v.1 of *Marie Pauline Jaricot*, 2 v. (Paris 1937). J. M. GOIBURU, *El problema misionero*, v.1 (Madrid 1946) 72–102. S. PAVENTI, *La chiesa missionaria* (Rome 1950) 41–51. E. J. HICKEY, *The Society for the Propagation of the Faith* (Washington 1922). JOHN XXIII, ''La Propagazione della Fede,'' *Scritti di A. G. Roncalli* (Rome 1958).

[F. J. SHEEN/EDS.]

PROPASSIONS OF CHRIST

From the times of St. Jerome and St. John Damascene theologians have customarily used the term ''propassions'' to designate the functions of the concupiscible and irascible sensitive appetites of Christ's hypostatized human nature (e.g., love, desire, hope, fear, sadness). It is likely that the prefix *pro* (in place of, for, instead of) was originally employed by the early writers to deny to Christ the passions as then imperfectly understood. Because of the prevailing influence of Greek philosophy, and of Stoicism in particular, these lower powers of man were generally thought to involve, essentially, a state of irrationality or rebellion and opposition to the higher powers (reason).

St. Thomas Aquinas, arguing from the Aristotelian philosophical view that the passions are in themselves perfections of human nature, states (*Summa theologiae,* 3a, 15.4) that Christ truly possessed all the psychological or animal passions, properly understood, in a most perfect and eminent fashion.

Respectful, as always, of past traditions, however, Thomas retained the term ''propassions'' in order to stress the fact that in Christ the passions were always perfectly subject to reason and were never a source or result of sinful excess by reason of object, principle, or effect (*ibid.*).

Modern psychological considerations of the unparalleled psychosomatic unity of Christ's sinless sensual faculties emphasize the resultant extreme sensitivity of these powers and, consequently, the intensity of Christ's suffering, especially in His Passion.

See Also: JESUS CHRIST (IN THEOLOGY) 3; IMPECCABILITY OF CHRIST.

Bibliography: E. HUGON, *The Mystery of the Incarnation,* tr A NUN OF ST. DOMINIC'S PRIORY, CARISBROOKE (London 1925)

228–232. I. SOLANO, *Sacrae theologiae summa,* ed. Fathers of the Society of Jesus, Professors of the Theological Faculties in Spain, 4 v. (Madrid 1961) 3.1:361–369. A. MICHEL, *Dictionnaire de théologie catholique,* ed. A. VACANT et al., 15 v. (Paris 1903–50) 8.1:132–32. B. M. XIBERTA Y ROQUETA, *Enchiridion de Verbo Incarnato* (Madrid 1957), Index Doctrinarum 22.

[D. R. GRABNER]

PROPERTIES, DIVINE PERSONAL

By divine personal properties Trinitarian theology understands that which is proper to and exclusive to one of the Divine PERSONS, to the exclusion of the other two. The very existence of three Persons necessarily implies the existence of differentiating qualities.

The name Father expresses that which is most intimate and necessary in the First Person, i.e., the act of generating the Son. In order to express this divine fecundity as a necessary and inseparable feature of the Father, Greek theology often refers to Him as the source, root, and principle of the other two Persons (Basil, Athanasius, Cyril of Alexandria, John Damascene; Tertullian among the Latins). These expressions convey the idea not of efficient causality, but rather of self-diffusion by communication of the same NATURE. If the act of generating a Son consubstantial to Himself belongs so intimately to the Father, then He cannot be understood except through an essential relation to the Son: the Father is paternity itself, nothing but an eternal, subsistent, generative act.

As a consequence the Son, necessarily generated by the Father, is ''the radiance of the Father's splendor and the full expression of his being'' (Heb 1.3). Just as divine paternity exclusively constitutes the Father, so also divine FILIATION constitutes the Person of the Son. The paternal act of generation is essentially productive of a perfect image of the Father, and this paternal image is an exclusive personal property of the Son. As such, the Son is the perfect replica of His Father; He manifests His Father and is consubstantial with Him. The second of these three qualities is at the root of the divine mission that constitutes the Incarnation. Divine filiation is considered as the act of an intellectual faculty (Latins) or as an operation of the entire nature, proceeding from the innermost core of the divine substance (Greeks). In any case, generation and filiation are essentially correlative terms, each constituting a different Person.

It is the same with regard to the Spirit. A constant Greek tradition sees in divine sanctity an exclusive, personal trait of the Spirit, as constitutive of a Divine Person as generation and filiation. ''In God, whatever appertains to nature is common . . . but the Person is known by the character of paternity, or filiation, or sanctifying power'' (St. Basil, *Epist.* 214.4; *Patrologia Graeca* 32:789). This conception, common in the 4th century, is further supported by Athanasius, Gregory Thaumaturgus, Cyril of Alexandria, Gregory of Nazianzus, Eulogius, and John Damascene. Sanctity as a personal property of the Spirit is, however, conceived not merely as an internal act, like generation and filiation, but with an outward bent: the Spirit is sanctity to be poured out on men. In addition to this sanctifying power, the Spirit possesses also as a personal character an ineffable intimacy with the Son originating from a special immanence in Him. Greek theology conceives the origin of the Divine Persons as it were in straight line, with the Father as divine principle of the Son, and the Son as the only immediate source of the Spirit. This was the current conception in 4th-century Cappadocia (Basil) as well as Alexandria (Athanasius, Cyril). On the contrary, for the strictly rational, almost geometrical conception of the Latins, the only differentiating personal property of the Spirit is passive SPIRATION, His being breathed forth, as though from equidistant points, by Father and Son. In this view, sanctity is not a personal property of the Spirit but rather a common treasure equally shared by all three. In current Western theology, therefore, divine personal properties are only three: generation, filiation, and passive spiration; at times, broadening the concept, two more are included: *agennētos* for the Father, and common spiration, common to Father and Son.

See Also: ACTS, NOTIONAL; CONSUBSTANTIALITY; GENERATION OF THE WORD; MISSIONS, DIVINE; PATERNITY, DIVINE; PERSON (IN THEOLOGY); RELATIONS, TRINITARIAN; TRINITY, HOLY, ARTICLES ON.

Bibliography: M. SCHMAUS, *Lexikon für Theologie und Kirche,* (Freiburg, 1957–66) 8:805–806. T. DE RÉGNON, *Études de théologie positive sur la Sainte Trinité,* 4 v. (Paris 1892–98). M. J. SCHEEBEN, *The Mysteries of Christianity,* tr. C. VOLLERT (St. Louis 1946). C. WELCH, *In This Name: The Trinity in Contemporary Theology* (Toronto 1953).

[A. M. BERMEJO]

PROPERTY (LOGIC)

Property (Gr. ἴδιον, Lat. *proprium*), one of the five PREDICABLES described in the *Isagoge* of PORPHYRY, designates an attribute or characteristic that is peculiar to a thing of a certain type. It is important in the logic of DEFINITION. In examining the differences that can be used to distinguish a given SPECIES classified within a common GENUS and thus to help in formulating the definition of the species, one discovers several kinds. (1) Common differences predicate no more than some otherness in the condition of the subject; e.g., Plato as an adult differs from himself as a boy. They are called predicable accidents; if used in formulating definitions, several must be used in a conjunction proper to the species. (2) A more proper difference is an accident that is inseparable from an individual, that belongs to him and is proper only to him (e.g., a scar, an aquiline nose). (3) The most proper differences are those that are commensurable with the specific nature; any one of these will serve to differentiate a nature. The difference that is the most proper determination by which a nature may be designated, and is also the reason for all other proper differences, is given a special name, specific difference (e.g., rational as said of man). The other proper differences that are outside the nature but follow necessarily on it, and are convertible with it, retain the more generic name of property or *proprium.* This is defined as the universal said of a species as belonging only, necessarily, and always to that species, and to every individual of that species.

Properties in this strict sense may follow either on the specific nature or on generic natures to the extent that these are definable by a difference. For example, having a nervous system is a property of the genus, animal, following on sensibility. In a broader sense property is frequently understood as designating an attribute that belongs to something always, but neither only, nor necessarily (e.g., two-footed, as said of man).

In the logic of reasoning property also designates one of the four kinds of predicates enumerated by ARISTOTLE in his *Topics* (101b 11–37; 128b 14–139a 20) as constituting one type of dialectical problem.

In strict scientific reasoning, i.e., that which employs a proper cause, properties are demonstrated of their subject through the real definition of the subject (*see* DEMONSTRATION). Predication of an attribute of its proper subject is the second mode of per se PREDICATION (*Anal. post.* 73a 35–73b 24). The aim of SCIENCE is to reduce attributes to their proper cause, so far as this is possible. The methodology of each science must determine the kind of property to be proved of the subject of the science, the causes through which they are to be proved, and in what order this is to be done.

See Also: DIALECTICS; METHODOLOGY (PHILOSOPHY); LOGIC.

Bibliography: V. MIANO, *Enciclopedia filosofica,* 4 v. (Venice–Rome 1957) 3:1168–70. P. FOULQUIÉ and R. SAINT-JEAN, *Dictionnaire de la langue philosophique* (Paris 1962) 584–585. R. EISLER, *Wörterbuch der philosophischen Begriffe,* 3 v. (4th ed. Berlin 1927–30) 1:301–303.

[W. BAUMGAERTNER]

PROPERTY, EARLY CHURCH

This article deals with Church property in the first six centuries and the doctrine on property among early Christian authors.

Church Property before Constantine. The question of Church property does not seem to have arisen in the Christian communities before the middle or end of the 2d century. Confusion with the Jews, as Suetonius attests (*Claudius* 25), apparently permitted the first Christians to benefit from the juridical statute that the Jewish community had enjoyed since Caesar (Josephus, *Ant. Jud.* 14.25).

Religious gatherings in private houses and burial in cemeteries belonging to private families, such as the catacombs of Priscilla or Domitilla in Rome, made it possible for a community to function without property. Even though it was not under continual persecution, the Church was not recognized by the government and had no legal existence. This was a precarious regimen since a proprietor could refuse to offer hospitality to religious services; and in the cemeteries, Christians and pagans were buried side by side, as the excavations under Saint Peter's in the VATICAN attest.

A deposit of funds did exist, however, in the 2d century. During the reign of Antoninus (138–61), MARCION gave 200,000 sesterces to the Church of Rome (Tert., *De praescrip.* 30) and Tertullian spoke of a collection, augmented by monthly contributions and used for charitable purposes (*Apol.* 39.5). Literary testimony, epigraphy, and archeology prove that after the end of the 2d century, cemeteries and churches were no longer the property of private individuals. In 198 Pope ZEPHYRINUS confided the administration of a cemetery to the deacon Callistus, who seems to have functioned as the agent of the community (*corpus*). In the course of the 3d century this property (belonging to a group not legally recognized) existed at least in fact.

The suspect testimony of the *Historia Augusta* (*Vita Alex. Sev.* 49.6) reports a debate before the emperor between the Christians and the wine merchants of Rome concerning the use of a *locus publicus* between 222 and 235. Of more certain value is the testimony of EUSEBIUS OF CAESAREA concerning the granting to the Christians places for religious worship by the Emperor Gallienus (*Ecclesiastical History* 7.13). The text adds that they were enabled to take possession of their cemeteries in 260 and that a decision given by Aurelia (270) in favor of the Christians of Antioch against the heretical Bishop PAUL OF SAMOSATA gave the property of the house of the Church to the bishop who was in epistolary relation with the bishops of Rome and Italy (*Ecclesiastical History*

7.30). Excavations and inscriptions in Rome, Africa, and Asia as well as papyri from the end of the 3d and beginning of the 4th century name churches and funerary monuments that imply a form of property holding. The restitutions of property to the Christians under Galerius in 305 (*Ecclesiastical History* 8.2, 9.10), by Maximian (*ibid.* 9.10.11), and finally by Constantine I and Licinius in 313 (*ibid.* 10.5.9–12; Lactantius, *De mort. pers.* 47.7–9) point to an even earlier recognized possession.

The confusion of Christians with the Jews could not have endured very long. But the use by the Christian communities of a juridical form of association proper to a lower class (*collegia tenuiorum*), as suggested by G. de Rossi and accepted by G. Monti, although not inconceivable, raises too many difficulties, as has been pointed out by L. Duchesne and others. Nor is there proof for a kind of "corporate" holding, or for the legal existence of a *corpus* (or juridically recognized body), since the thesis of a recognition by the pagan state making the community licit is hard to accept. Finally, there is no evidence for maintaining, with G. Bovini, that from the beginning of the 2d century, churches had a civilly recognized patrimonial capacity.

The development of Christianity and the support it received from at least the 3d century on, in the entourage of certain emperors, explain the tolerance of actual appropriation, but an appropriation that was necessarily precarious and without juridical title. According to whether the policy, locally or temporarily, was tolerance or persecution, the Christians could have held their landed property, disposed of it, been deprived of it, or obtained restitution for it.

In any case, it is certain that the title holder of these possessions was not the community of the universal Church. It was the local community, directed by its bishop, that used the churches and cemeteries. Eusebius makes this clear with many instances; and the restitution ordered by Constantine and Licinius confirms it: the goods are rendered *ad jus corporis eorum id est ecclesiarum* (Lactantius, *De mort. persec.* 48).

Christian Community as Proprietor. The right of the Christian communities to be proprietors of immobile property cannot be doubted after the Edict of MILAN. In 321 Constantine authorized the donation of property to the Church (*Corpus iuris civilis, Codex Iustinianus*, ed. P. Krueger, 1.2.1), and he himself proved generous. His donation of the Lateran property to the bishop of Rome is the most celebrated manifestation of his great generosity.

However, the actual juridical condition of this property is still not known with precision: was it the property of the local community considered as a moral person? Of the bishop, who in some fashion "incarnated" it? The attribution of the property to God or to a saint? Or a patrimony given for a pious cause or charitable foundation? There are as many solutions as there are texts offered in proof; but none of the solutions is without difficulty. A. Steinwenter believes in an evolution leading from the ecclesiastical corporation under Constantine to an ecclesiastical institution under Justinian. The form of such a development appears perhaps in the law of Justinian. Before that, ecclesiastical goods were doubtless considered the property of the local church under the bishop, whose development, administration, and privileges are discussed by J. Gaudemet in *L'Église dans l'empire romain* (Paris 1958) 299–315.

Patristic Doctrine on Property. If the exigencies of cult and charity required ecclesiastical property, the Christian teaching was also occupied with formulating certain principles in regard to the right of private property, its purpose, and its legitimacy. Certain decisions were gathered in canonical collections and are embodied in the Decree of Gratian (*Corpus iuris canonici*, ed. E. Friedburg, D.47, c. 8; c. 14.q.4.c.11). Taken out of context, they have given rise to contestable interpretations of patristic thought. Very often they are not principles but counsels given in particular cases and from which one cannot generalize without abusing their meaning.

Economic and Social Situation. The economic and social situation of the later empire made it legitimate for the moralists to intervene. Wars, invasions, and local revolts aggravated the misery of many, while the masters of the great landed properties already prefigured the medieval lords. But the Christian authors are rare who made much of this political crisis. LACTANTIUS denounced the economic troubles of his times (*Div. inst.* 5, 6). His ideal was that of the golden age of the pagan poets. He desired a fraternity conformable to the gospel, but had no thought of the introduction of a communism, which he considered dangerous, impossible, and unjust (*ibid.* 3, 21; Epitome 38).

SALVIAN also underlined the social disequilibrium (*De gub. Dei* 3). But he neglected the other causes, such as the invasions and the inefficacy of political institutions. If he saw in a man's fortune the occasion for numerous sins, it was the bad use of riches that he condemned, not riches themselves (*Ad eccl.* 1.7.35).

With Saint Ambrose it was the same (*De Nabuthae*). He criticized the attachment of his contemporaries to their riches (*De Off.* 2.21). Councils, such as Toledo I (c. 11) denounced the abuses of the powerful and invited the bishops to excommunicate them if they did not amend. The council appealed to the emperor to protect the poor against the rich (*Codex eccl. Afric.* c. 75). In regard to riches, patristic doctrine oscillates between the evangelical counsel of renouncement and the Roman regimen of private property. It did not solve the conflict by a prescription of absolute poverty, of perfect equality, or of holding riches in common. But it preached the disdain of riches and the necessity of almsgiving.

In patristic writings, private property was not considered the basic form that the use of earthly goods should take, for God had created these goods for the use of all. Hence one should not be an egoist in the employment of his private goods, but should use them generously in succoring the less favored. More than the proprietor of riches he has not created; man is the custodian (*custos*) or the steward (*minister*) of them. He should act as custodian and not as absolute master.

Teaching of the Eastern Fathers. In the East, Fathers such as BASIL of Caesarea, GREGORY OF NAZIANZUS, and GREGORY OF NYSSA evoked an ideal state of absolute equality and of holding goods in common. But while they condemned usury, they did not reject private property. It is in detachment from riches, disdain toward that which so often causes sin, and generosity toward the unfortunate that they found a conciliation between the egalitarian ideal and the juridical regimen of their times, which they had no intention of overthrowing. But as Saint JOHN CHRYSOSTOM made clear, man owns nothing of his own (*In Ep. 1 ad Cor. hom.* 10.2; *Patrologia Graeca*, ed. J. P. Migne, 61:84). God alone is the true proprietor of all goods.

According to S. Giet, the Greek Fathers, and in particular Basil, had distinguished between the common destination and the private ownership of goods (*Hom. in illud Lucae: Destruam* 7; *Patrologia Graeca* 31:2768).

But this doctrine, for lack of a good knowledge of Greek, was misunderstood in the West. Ambrose of Milan and Rufinus of Aquileia transformed this condemnation of exclusive use into a reprobation of private property. Thus is explained the famous interjection of Ambrose: *usurpatio jus fecit privatum,* usurpation gave rise to private right (*De off.* 1.28.133). If the Fathers evoked a primitive state before the fall in which private property was unknown (*ibid.* 1.28.132), thus confusing Paradise and the golden age of the pagans, they did not condemn the established order or the Roman right of property. In any case, a community of goods does not belong to sinful man. AUGUSTINE proposed community of goods to the priests of Hippo without being able to impose it upon them.

The essential in the patristic attitude is the determination of the limits and the purpose for property. Man has a relative proprietorship, since God is the sole and true master of goods. Man is only the custodian of property. He may use what is necessary for his well being, but he should dispense the surplus to those who are in need (Augustine, *Sermo* 61.11–12; Leo, *Serm.* 6.11.1; 18.3; 20; 49.6; 85.1, etc.).

Bibliography: B. BIONDI, *Il diritto romano cristiano,* 3 v. (Milan 1952–54) 3:297–324. G. BOVINI, *La proprietà ecclesiastica . . . in età precostantiniana* (Milan 1948). E. F. BRUCK, *Kirchenväter und soziales Erbrecht* (Berlin 1956). S. CALAFATO, *La proprietà privata in S. Ambrogio* (Turin 1958). S. GIET, ''La Doctrine de l'appropriation des biens chez quelques-uns des Pères,'' *Recherches de science religieuse* 35 (1948) 55–91. J. GAUDEMET, *L'Église dans l'Empire romain* (Paris 1958) 299–315. H. R. HAGEMANN, ''Die rechtliche Stellung der christlichen Wohltätigkeiten,'' *Revue internationale des droits de l'antiquité* 3 (1958) 265–83; *Die Stellung der piae causae nach dem justinianischen Rechte* (Basel 1953). I. SEIPEL, *Die wirtschaftsethischen Lehren der Kirchenväter* (*Theol. Studien der Görresgesellschaft* 18; Vienna 1907). G. KRÜGER, *Die Rechtsstellung der vorkonstantinischen Kirchen* (Stuttgart 1935). G. M. MONTI, ''I *Collegia tenuiorum* e la condizione guiridica della proprietà ecclesiastica nei primi tre secoli del cristianesimo,'' *Studi in onore di Salvatore Riccobono,* 4 v. (Palermo 1936) 3:71–95. J. R. PALANQUE, *Saint Ambroise et l'Empire romain* (Paris 1933). AMBROSE, *De Nabuthae,* ed. and tr. M. R. P. MCGUIRE (Catholic University of America, *Patristic Studies* 15; (Washington 1927). A. STEINWENTER, ''Aus dem kirchlichen Vermögensrechte der Papyri,'' *Zeitschrift der Savigny-Stiftung für Rechtsgeschichte, Kanonistische Abteilung* 75 (1958) 1–34. F. DE VISSCHER, ''Le Régime juridique des plus anciens cimetières chrétiens à Rome,'' *Analecta Bollandiana* 69 (1951) 39–54; *Le Droit des tombeaux romains* (Milan 1963).

[J. GAUDEMET]

PROPHECY (IN THE BIBLE)

The primary sense of prophecy in the Bible is not prediction, but rather the word of a man inspired by God to speak in His name. First and foremost, it was revelation and admonition, though the element of prediction was never lacking, and it became increasingly important as Biblical revelation progressed. However, the effort to fix more exactly the Biblical concept of prophecy runs up against a familiar problem: the Bible does not itself provide definitions. Still, the Bible does have a quasi-technical vocabulary in the area of prophecy as well as certain regular ways of utilizing sayings considered prophetic. This vocabulary and these uses are the means to a more exact idea of the Biblical concept of prophecy. *See* REVELATION, CONCEPT OF (IN THE BIBLE).

The belief that the prophet received and communicated the word (*dābār*) of Yahweh, was expressed in the formula ''thus says Yahweh'' that was used to introduce the prophetic ORACLE. This same idea is contained in the phrase ''utterance [*n*ᵉ'*ūm*] of Yahweh,'' which became more and more common as a designation of the prophetic saying in later times. The use of vision (*ḥāzôn*) to designate the prophetic word points up another aspect of OT prophecy. The older Hebrew vocabulary, then, emphasized that prophecy was revelation from God to the prophet, which he passed on to others, rather than prediction.

However, the concept of prophetic promise and fulfillment was early associated with Hebrew prophetic activity, as is seen in Nathan's promise that David's line will endure (2 Sm 7.8–16). Indeed, the regular appearance of prophets whose words are fulfilled in the history of the kings of Israel and Judah is a basic part of the theological interpretation of Israel's history as the working out of God's word, as may be seen in the Books of KINGS. Again, Deutero-Isaiah (*see* ISAIAH, BOOK OF) points up the future reference of God's word when he uses the fulfillment of Yahweh's prophecies as an argument for His supremacy over the gods of the nations (e.g., Is 41.26–29; 42.9; 43.12). Actually, the argument runs: Yahweh, not another god, foretold these things; but the one who can best foretell is the one who produces something; therefore Yahweh must have produced the things foretold, and so He alone must be the effective God, that is, the only true God. An idea such as this probably represents the high point of sophistication in the OT theological conception of prophecy.

The men of the last centuries of OT times were much concerned with the fulfillment of prophecies (e.g., Dn 11.14; Sir 36.14–17), so much so that prediction, especially the foretelling of the last things, tended to obscure the other elements in the old concept of prophecy. *See* ESCHATOLOGY (IN THE BIBLE). In this atmosphere it is not surprising that at a later period predictions were sought in every part of the OT, not merely in the strictly prophetic books. Even so, the older idea of revelation and admonition, God's word directed to the prophet's contemporaries, was not lost; e.g., in Sir 46.20, the elements of prediction and of admonition were neatly combined.

The NT sees the coming of Christ and the Church as the definitive fulfillment of prophecy, which it therefore conceives primarily as prediction. The Gospel according to St. MATTHEW develops this concept most thoroughly, but the argument from fulfillment of prophecy is basic to the NT kerygma from its beginnings (see Acts 2.14–36). In the manner of the times prophecy as used in this argument is not limited to the words of the OT prophets strictly so-called. For the NT the whole of the OT spoke of Jesus Christ. (*See* TYPE AND ANTITYPE.)

Finally, it must be noted that the NT Church was fully conscious of its own charismatic prophets, members of the community whose prophecies not only predicted

The Prophet Ezechiel.

the future (e.g., Acts 11.28) but served for the present edification of the community (e.g., 1 Cor 14.3, 31).

See Also: PROPHET; PROPHETIC BOOKS OF THE OLD TESTAMENT; PROPHETISM (IN THE BIBLE).

Bibliography: *Encyclopedic Dictionary of the Bible,* tr. and adap. by L. HARTMAN (New York 1963) from A. VAN DEN BORN, *Bijbels Woordenboek,* 1929–30. J. CHAINE, *God's Heralds,* tr. B. MCGRATH (New York 1955). H. H. ROWLEY, ed., *Studies in O.T. Prophecy* (Edinburgh 1950). O. EISSFELDT, "The Prophetical Literature," *The O.T. and Modern Study,* ed. H. H. ROWLEY (Oxford 1951) 115–161. A. FEUILLET, "Les Prophètes écrivains et la préparation de l'Évangile," *Cahiers Évangiles* 3 (1951) 27–54. T. C. VRIEZEN, "Prophecy and Eschatology," *Vetus Testamentum* 3 (1953) 199–229.

[D. J. MCCARTHY]

PROPHECY (THEOLOGY OF)

The theology of prophecy has never formed a specific treatise in theological manuals. Parts of it are scattered in fundamental, dogmatic, Biblical, and mystical theology, as well as elsewhere.

Prophecy in Tradition

For the scriptural theology of prophecy, *see* PROPHETISM (IN THE BIBLE). Here the theology of prophecy is first of all studied in the tradition of the Church (positive theology).

Beginnings until Montanism Inclusive. The New Testament shows that some received a special share in Christ's prophetic Spirit (Eph 4.7–11; 1 Cor 12.28; Acts 11.27; 13.1; etc.), while others shared this CHARISM in a more general way (Acts 2.17, 33–38; 19.6; 1 Cor 11.4–5; 14.26, 29–33). Abundant evidence indicates the continuation of the prophetic Spirit in the early Church: *Didache* 11–13; *Ascension of Isaia* 3.25–27; Justin, *Dial.* 87; Irenaeus, *Haer.* 2.32.4; 4.33.15; etc.

According to the *Didache,* prophets were more respected than bishops and deacons. They performed a similar service for the community, possibly a priestly service also (15.1–2; 10.7; 13.3). What they spoke ''in the Spirit'' was to be accepted (11.7). Some of the HIERARCHY enjoyed this charism in a special way: Ignatius of Antioch (*Philad.* 7.2; *Polyc.* 1.3; 2.2), and Polycarp of Smyrna (*M. Polyc.* 16.2).

False prophets, on the other hand, do not have ''the ways of the Lord'' about them (*Didache* 11.8). Hermas warned against the false prophets who are not Christlike (*Mand.* 11.7–10). Justin ascribed Gnostic ideas and Greek myths to them (*Dial.* 82.1; 35.3; 51.2; 8788; etc.). Though Irenaeus rejected the teaching of the false prophet Montanus, he also rejected the extreme position of the Alogi, who rejected prophecy (*Haer.* 3.11.9; cf. 2.49.3; Eusebius, *Ecclesiastical History* 5.7.5).

Asiatic Christianity with its history of prophets, MILLENARIANISM, and exaggerated Johannine teachings was a fertile soil for the Montanistic explosion of prophecy; as the ''inspired'' spokesperson for the Paraclete, Montanus, *c.* A.D. 172, inaugurated the era of the Paraclete (cf. Jn 16.12–13). Charismatic ministers ranked above the hierarchy (Jerome, *Epist.* 41.3). One sees the trend toward a purely spiritual Church in the writings of its great convert Tertullian, *c.* A.D. 207 (*De pudicitia* 21, 12). Although never officially anathematized, MONTANISM was condemned by local synods for, among other reasons, its ecstatic exaggerations (Eusebius, *Ecclesiastical History* 5.16–18). After the Montanistic experience the role of prophets in the Church diminished. Origen (d. 254) acknowledged traces of this charism in his day, but says that there were no more prophets like those of the Old Testament (*Cels.* 1.2.46; cf. *Acta* of Perpetua and Felicity; Cyprian, *Epist.* 16.4; 2.3–4).

After Montanism. Subsequent to the Montanist episode, two main streams of charismatic prophecy continue down to the present day: a mystical, sometimes ecstatic, tradition of seers and heralds, and a more rational tradition of interpreters of the Spirit in the Scriptures.

Mystical (Ecstatic) Tradition. The roots of this tradition reach back into Greek and Hebrew history. Origen was mainly responsible for introducing to Christianity the Hellenistic prophetic tradition of Plato, Posidonius (d. after 51 B.C.), and the Jew, Philo (d. 1st century A.D.). This Greek-Hebrew tradition influenced the Alexandrians and, through them, the Cappadocians, especially Gregory of Nyssa (*Vita Moysis*). The pagan Plotinus (d. A.D. 270) developed this same tradition with his Neoplatonic ideas. He so emphasized ECSTASY that the prophet became a mere mouthpiece of God. His teachings in turn influenced St. Augustine's theory of visions and prophecies (*Gen. ad litt.* 12). Pseudo-Dionysius the Areopagite (*c.* A.D. 500) also continued in the tradition of Plotinus and Nyssa, and was further influenced by the emanationism of Proclus (d. 485). Gregory the Great (d. 604) follows this same tradition in his mystical homilies that he delivered on Ezechiel.

According to this mystical tradition, the monks and martyrs retained the charismatic gifts of the early Church. The classical PROPHETS were models of the monastic ideal for their virtues, not their charismatic gifts, which were allegorized to serve as models for all monks (Nyssa's *Vita Moysis*). This trend confused inner charismatic gifts and gifts of the Holy Spirit. The monks considered the charismatic gifts to be signs, even the essence, of perfection. In Syria (*c.* A.D. 350) this trend led to Messalianism, a heresy analogous to Montanism (condemned at Ephesus, 431). It founded Christian perfection upon the confused idea of charismatic gift. The exaggerated Messalian emphasis on charism died quietly, but helped the Areopagite's anticharismatic mysticism triumph in the East throughout the Middle Ages. In the West down to the scholastics the theology of prophecy may be studied in a theology of mysticism derived from Augustine and St. Gregory and in hagiographies of saintly people to whom the prophetic charism was attributed.

Joachim of Fiore (d. 1202) announced a third dispensation of the Holy Spirit to begin in 1260, causing a Montanistlike revival among many groups, especially the Fraticelli (condemned 1317–23 by Pope John XXII). By the 16th century the Church had stamped out many forms of spiritual enthusiasm, but they found new life in the Reformation's non-Catholic sects. R. Knox distinguishes mystical and evangelical streams of this tradition that have continued down to the present day (*Enthusiasm* 581–591).

While the revival of enthusiastic prophetism in the 1200s had little influence on scholastic treatises, St. Thomas Aquinas (d. 1274) did make discriminating use of a Jewish-Arabic stream of prophetic tradition. The Arabic philosophers Avicenna (d. 1037) and Averroes (d.

1198) and the Jewish philosopher Moses Maimonides (d. 1204) wrote of their respective prophets, Mohammed and Moses, and transmitted with varying emphases a Neoplatonic tradition of a natural prophecy.

Tradition of Rational Interpretation. The tradition of the prophet as interpreter appears in Aaron's relationship to Moses as prophetic interpreter (Ex 4.16; 7.1), as well as in the prophetic interpreters of the ecstatic Pythia of Delphi (see Fascher, 11 and following). In the New Testament, Christ is *the* interpreter of previously unintelligible Old Testament prophecies (Lk 24.27, 44–45; cf. Justin, *Apol.* 1.32.2). In 1 Corinthians ch. 14, Paul stresses the prophet's role as interpreter. As speaking in tongues lessened, the interpretation of the Spirit incarnated in Scripture became the content of prophecy.

The anti-Montanist reaction focused interest on the tradition of prophetic interpreters. St. John Chrysostom (d. 407) depicts Christian prophets as conscious, moderate people in contrast to the senseless, ecstatic pagan diviners (*Hom. 29 in 1 Cor.* 1; *Patrologia Graeca* 61:241). The twofold aspect of prophecy is concisely stated by Ambrosiaster: ''Prophets may be understood in two ways: both those foretelling the future and those revealing the Scriptures'' or ''interpreting Scriptures'' [on 1 Cor. 12.28, Eph 1.11 (*Patrologia Latina* 17:249, 378); cf. (Pseudo-) Jerome, *Comm. in epist. 1 ad Cor.* 12 (*Patrologia Latina* 30:756); Eucherius, d. *c.* 450, *Instruct. liber,* 2, 1 ad Cor. (*Patrologia Latina* 50: 805); Cassiodorus, d. *c.* 583, *In psalt.,* praef., 1 (*Patrologia Latina* 70:12–14); *Glossa ordinaria,* 12th century, *Lib. psalm.,* prothemata (*Patrologia Latina* 113:842)]. The prophetic interpreter became the preacher who used the literal sense as a point of departure for exegeting the spiritual, prophetic, allegorical, and mystical sense of Scripture [*see* EXEGESIS, BIBLICAL, 5]. For other references in this tradition, see: Sedulius, *c.* 850, *Coll. in epist. 1 ad Cor.* 14, *Patrologia Latina* 103:155; R. Maurus, d. 856, *In epist. ad Rom.* 12, *In epist. ad Eph.* 4; Haimo of Halberstadt, d. 853, *In epist. 1 ad Cor.* 14, *Patrologia Latina* 117:587; Bruno the Carthusian, d. 1101, *In epist. 1 ad Cor.* 12–14, *Patrologia Latina* 153:189–197; R. Ardens, d. 1200, *Hom. 20, In epist. ad Rom.* 12.6, *Patrologia Latina* 155:1740; Abelard, d. 1142, *In epist. Pauli ad Rom.* 12, *Patrologia Latina* 178:939; St. Bonaventure, *De prophetia,* Cod. Assist, 186 fol. 11b. St. Thomas reproduces this tradition in his Scripture commentaries, but makes little use of it in the *Summa* (*In epist. ad Eph.* 3.5, lect. 1; *In epist. ad Rom.* 12.6, lect. 2; *In epist. 1 ad Cor.* 14, lect. 5; see P. Benoit, ''Révélation et inspiration'' 334).

Later Emphasis. Since the time of these scholastics the emphasis has been on the mystical (ecstatic) tradition of prophecy. The commentaries on the *Summa* of St. Thomas by the Dominicans—Cajetan, Cano, Soto, D. Báñez—and the Jesuits—Salmerón, Suárez, and De Lugo—have continued this tradition. Extraordinary prophets also manifest the continuance of this charism in the Church (e.g., Catherine of Siena, Teresa of Avila, Margaret Mary, Catherine Labouré, etc.). The 19th-century rationalists forced the Church to defend the miraculous character of supernatural prophecies of the future (see ''Prophecy and Apologetics,'' below); Modernists forced the Church to safeguard the doctrinal, transcendental character of revelation. Prophecy as interpretation received little attention, though it harmonized better with the post-World War II development of prophecy. In scattered allusions in *MYSTICI CORPORIS* and in more elaborate studies of Y. M. J. Congar, K. Rahner, C. Journet, et al., the prophetic role of Christ in the Church has received greater attention. Vatican Council II's *Dogmatic Constitution on the Church* expresses this broader understanding of the nature of prophecy [12, 35; *Acta Apostolicae Sedis* 57 (1965) 16–17, 40–41].

In the *Constitution* one is told that all the people of God share in Christ's prophetic office through their anointing by the Spirit (1 Jn 2.20, 27). This charism may be extraordinary or more simple and widely diffused, but in any case ''suited to and useful for the needs of the Church'' (12).

The hierarchy continues Christ's office by teaching in His name and with His authority. Moreover, the discernment of the genuine character and proper use of this charism belongs to them. They are not to extinguish the Spirit but to test all things and hold fast what is good.

The laity's prophetic role is to bear witness socially (Eph 6.12). Their living and spoken testimony, especially in married and family life, have a special force in the ordinary surroundings of life. For this purpose God has given them understanding of the faith (*sensus fidei*) and an attractiveness in speech (Acts 2.17–18), and so they must cooperate in the external spread and dynamic growth of the Church. To accomplish this mission the laity should acquire a more perfect grasp of revealed truth and pray for the gift of wisdom.

Prophecy and Apologetics

Prophecy is also a subject of concern to APOLOGETICS (practical theology).

Historical Background. The fulfillment of Old Testament prophecies has been a motive of credibility since the earliest days of the Church (see Acts 2.30, 34; 3.18, 22–26; 4.11; 7.52; 13.16–41; and the Evangelists, Mt 1.23; 2.6, 15; 4.15; Mk 9.11; 12.36; Lk 4.18; 22.37;

24.25–27; Jn 3.14; 5.46; 12.14–16). The early apologies to the Jews continued in this vein; in fact most of the OT prophecies used are found in the NT. See: Epistle of Barnabas; Justin's *Apology* 1, and especially his *Dialogue with Trypho*; Irenaeus's *Demonstration of the Apostolic Teaching* 42–97; and other passages in Tertullian's *Adversus judaeos* 8–9 and *Adversus Marcionem* 4–22; Origen's *C. Celsum, passim;* Cyprian's *Quod idola dii non sint* 13–14; Lactantius's *Divinae institutiones* 4.11; 5.3; Chrysostom's *Quod Christus sit Deus* 11; Augustine's *In psalm.* 66.9; *Fid. invis.* 5–9; etc. Apologists of the Middle Ages also used this argument: Amulo, Fulbert of Chartres, Peter Damien, Guibert of Nogent, Gislebert, Peter the Venerable, Abelard, Peter of Blois, etc. St. Thomas referred to this argument briefly (*C. gent.* 1.6) but concentrated on the theology of prophecy. The tradition of this argument survives to the present in the apologetics developed in the 17th century against deism and rationalism.

Faced with rationalism and liberalism in philosophical and theological thought of the 19th century, Pius IX twice defended prophecies as valid arguments for the divine origin of the faith (Denz 2779, 2907). Vatican Council I reemphasized this point: ''Miracles and prophecies . . . constitute the surest signs of divine revelation suitable to everyone's understanding'' (Denz 3009, cf. Oath against Modernism, Denz 3539).

Apologetic Proof from Old Testament Prophecies. There are presuppositions regarding the purpose and significance of Old Testament prophecies. (1) Only the general and consistent tenor of these prophecies was meant to be literally fulfilled in the great majority of cases. Only certain repeated major themes are true predictions, and these were fulfilled in a surpassing way in the NT. These general theme-fulfillments form the basis for the argument from OT prophecies. (2) NT fulfillment was not just equal to OT expectations, but surpassed them. Although the Prophets had no blueprint of the messianic era, they would have recognized in it the overfulfillment of their prophecies. (3) Ordinarily details in the OT prophecies cannot be used in a prophetic proof for a number of reasons. There is a poetic element in OT prophecy, conveying an idea by concrete details. But it is the idea and not the details that the author intends. There is a lack of temporal perspective. Though separated in time, events may be united in the prophetic perspective. There is sometimes a conditional element, even when the condition is not clearly stated. The Messiah and messianic era are described in terms of their own generation. The contemporary coloring of the prophecies is largely artificial and representative of unknown but ideal desires, personalities, etc., of the messianic era. The Prophets knew that their prophecies were only approximations, that the new covenant would be different from the old, even though their knowledge and their mentality forced them to describe the new covenant in terms of the old, which they knew.

Furthermore, the starting point for the proof should lie in the NT fulfillment and not in OT prophecy. The NT fulfillment greatly surpasses the OT prophecies. If one tries to find in OT prophecy what would come to pass in the NT, he is trying to find the greater in the less. The conclusion would contain more than the premises warrant. Hence, this method compels adjustments and modifications in the meaning of the OT prophecies to equate them to their NT fulfillment. On the other hand, beginning with the NT fulfillment, the greater, one can show that the OT prophecies relate to this NT overfulfillment.

20th-Century Theologizing

Attention may be directed to recent theologizing (speculative theology) concerning prophecy.

Prophecy in General. The current theology of prophecy is a modified descendant of St. Thomas's somewhat mystical explanation of prophecy in the Scripture Prophets. Accordingly, prophecy is a special charism of knowledge given for the instruction of mankind in whatever is necessary for salvation (*De ver.* 12.2). As a charism of knowledge it primarily affects the prophet's mind, not his will (*Summa theologiae* 2a2ae, 171.1; 174.3–4). This knowledge concerns truths normally hidden to the prophet's mind and is supernatural, if not in its essence, at least in its manner of acquisition (*Summa theologiae* 2a2ae, 171.2; 173.1; 174.3; *De ver.* 12.7).

Prophecy and Revelation. The manner in which the prophet receives his instruction involves two distinct elements. The principal element is an intellectual light illuminating the object and permitting the prophet to form a judgment about it. The secondary element consists in representations (ideas and, antecedently, the sensations and images from which the ideas are abstracted); these furnish the subject matter for the intellectual light.

The degree of revelation granted the prophet will vary according to his reception of light and representations (see *Summa theologiae* 2a2ae, 173.2; 174.2 and ad 3; 174.3; *De ver.* 12.7). (1) The highest degree of prophetic knowledge (revelation in the strict sense) occurs when the prophet receives both intellectual light and new ideas, e.g., oracles of OT Prophets, Jer 28.16–17. (2) The prophet may receive light alone (revelation in the broad sense). In this instance the ideas may come from another (e.g., Joseph received light to interpret the dreams of the Pharaoh) or may be already familiar to the prophet but now with supernatural certitude and firmness of judgment. Hence, the light of revelation and of inspiration (see below) may intermingle and represent a borderline case of prophecy. This case did not concern St. Thomas but interests modern theologians. (3) When one receives representations alone without intellectual light for judgment of them, it is not strictly a matter of revelation or prophecy, e.g., Pharaoh's dreams.

In a somewhat different approach, K. Rahner stresses three points in his theory of prophetic knowledge. (1) Prophecy involves the whole mind in all its capacities. It usually takes the form of an imaginary vision. God contacts the depths of the prophet's soul, and a sensory experience results. Vision and auditory elements intermingle in keeping with the nature of God's contact. The echo or reflex of this experience in the rest of the prophet's sensibilities is influenced by all his dispositions: elements of fantasy, attitudes of expectation due to religious training or historical situation, etc. (2) The subjective principle of the experience must be a divine reality, grace as a self-communication of God; otherwise it could be a parapsychological experience. (3) The objectification of this grace-experience in words does not give full expression to it. Evidence for the agreement between the grace-experience and its objectification may be: a miracle; inner evidence, a conviction of being spoken to by God; the transcendental character of the grace-experience making the prophetic insight self-evident. In the case of revelation in the OT and NT a supernatural saving providence of God controlling and guaranteeing this agreement is presupposed. (See discussion of private revelations below.)

Prophecy and Inspiration. Prophecy involves not merely revelation, but inspiration also. St. Thomas cites Peter Lombard's definition of prophecy (*Comm. in ps.,* praef.), an abbreviation of Cassiodorus's (*In psalt.,* praef., 1): ''Prophecy is a divine inspiration or revelation announcing the issue (*eventus*) of things with invariable truth'' (*Summa theologiae* 2a2ae, 171.6 sed c.). In this definition, revelation and inspiration are complementary ideas (*Summa theologiae* 2a2ae 171.1 ad 4). Revelation concerns the perception of divine truth through intellectual light and representations. Inspiration connotes a preparatory elevation of the mind to the supernatural level by a movement of the Holy Spirit. Commentators have tended to oversimplify St. Thomas's notion of inspiration by restricting it to a supernatural light or judgment without any representations (Zigliara, Lagrange, Vosté, Bea; see P. Benoit, ''Révélation et inspiration'' 322–324). St. Thomas, however, says inspiration may involve intellectual visions (*De ver.* 12.12 sed c.; *ibid.* 12.9 corp.).

Prophecy as Revelation and Inspiration. In distinguishing revelation and inspiration as aspects of prophecy, St. Thomas was limited by the problematic of his time. It viewed prophecy in the speculative, abstract, Greek tradition of truth. Viewed in the Semitic tradition, prophetic revelation and inspiration take on a broader meaning. Revelation in the Bible is a concrete, living manifestation of the personal God in the holiness of His being as creator and savior, truth and life. It does not require a direct ''vision'' or ''hearing'' of some spectacle or divine oracle, although this is often the case. It can take place through the varied manifestations of history in which God makes Himself visible to His people. From the psychological viewpoint of the prophet, revelation includes all the activity of speculative knowledge brought about by the supernatural light of the Holy Spirit. Its central and specific element is the supernatural judgment or knowledge attaining truth with a divine certitude, whether the truth be revelation in the strict or broad sense (*see* REVELATION, THEOLOGY OF).

Inspiration directs all the practical activities of the prophet as he is involved in communicating these revealed truths. This inspiration also enlightens his judgments: (1) Speculative-practical judgments that deal with the truths revealed to him; sometimes through inspired intellectual visions, further revelation in the broad sense results. Revelation and inspiration may thus intermingle. (2) Practical judgments that direct the concrete execution of the work in conformity with the end intended; the end of this inspiration might be to speak, to act, or to write the truths that are communicated.

Revelation and inspiration are not clearly distinct. All supernatural revelation requires a supernatural elevation of the mind, an inspiration. On the other hand, every inspiration or supernatural elevation of the mind enlightening judgment leads to some perception of revelation.

Prophecy and Private Revelations. Revelations are ''private'' not because they are addressed to a few (they may concern many), but because they do not belong to the DEPOSIT OF FAITH (closed since the death of the last Apostle, Denz 3421). They are not prophetic assertions, but commands showing the Church how to act in a concrete historical situation. In approving them, the Church does not act infallibly but acknowledges such revelations as worthy of human faith. Since they lack the providential safeguards of public revelation, the prophet's subjective involvement sometimes misrepresents the grace-experience. Even saints and blessed have communicated historical and theological errors (see K. Rahner, *Visions and Prophecies,* 64–75). Hence, much uncertainty surrounds the content of their message and must be left to the personal judgment of each inquirer.

In particular, genuine supernatural prophecies of the future must be distinguished from (1) magical, (2) parapsychological, (3) national, and (4) fabricated prophecies that do not involve revelation. Supernatural prophecies tell one nothing essentially new beyond the perspective of Scripture, but manifest God as Lord of history. Usually they announce a call to penance, prayer, trust. Their authenticity depends somewhat on the prophet's personal piety, integrity, and mental and bodily health. The only absolute proof is a miracle confirming the prophecy itself (*see* REVELATIONS, PRIVATE).

Prophecy in the Community and in the Hierarchy. As was noted above, the NT charism of prophecy is shared by all God's people, laity and hierarchy. The broader community of baptized non-Catholics and even non-Christians oriented to God also share in it to some extent. Regarding the individual prophet, his inspiration and revelation (private or public, as the case may be) have a community or ecclesial context. One cannot say how much their prophesying has been influenced by a more general revelation and inspiration in the community, but prophets enjoy their charism to a greater or lesser degree as spokesmen representing a common understanding, attitude, or need of God's people (see P. Grelot).

The role of the hierarchy is to safeguard and preserve the faith and to discern the prophetic Spirit. While the hierarchy has this gift of discernment, it must not extinguish the Spirit. It is a duty, not a condescension, for the hierarchy to heed the suggestions of God's people as long as they are not contrary to the Spirit. The Church is both charismatic and institutional (Eph 2.20); exaggeration of either aspect distorts the nature of the Church. Understanding is necessary for the prophetic Spirit to manifest itself harmoniously in both the hierarchy and the community (1 Cor 14.33).

See Also: FREEDOM, INTELLECTUAL; FREEDOM OF SPEECH (IN CHURCH TEACHING); MIRACLES (THEOLOGY OF); SYMBOL IN REVELATION.

Bibliography: Prophecy in Tradition. H. U. VON BALTHASAR, *Besondere Gnadengaben und die zwei Wege menschlichen Lebens* (Die Deutsche Thomas-Ausgabe 23; Heidelberg 1954). E. FASCHER, ΠΡΟΦΗΤΗΣ *Eine sprach- und religionsgeschichtliche Untersuchung* (Giessen 1927). R. A. KNOX, *Enthusiasm* (New York 1950; repr. 1961). J. LINDBLOM, *Prophecy in Ancient Israel* (Philadelphia 1962). N. FUGLISTER, ''Prophet,'' H. FRIES, ed., *Handbuch theologischer Grundbegriffe* (Munich 1962–63) 2:350—372. Prophecy and Apologetics. A. MICHEL, *Mystery and Prophecy,* tr. C. J. MOELL (West Baden Springs, Ind. 1954). B. VAWTER, ''Messianic Prophecies in Apologetics,'' *Catholic Theological Society of America, Proceedings* 14 (New York 1960) 97–119. R. MURPHY, ''Notes on OT Messianism and Apologetics,'' *The Catholic Biblical Quarterly* 19 (Washington 1957) 5–15. Contemporary Theologizing. P. SYNAVE and P. BENOIT, *Prophecy and Inspiration,* tr. A. DULLES and T. L. SHERIDAN (New York 1961). P. BENOIT, ''Révélation et inspiration,'' *Revue biblique* 70 (Paris 1963) 321–370. P. GRELOT, ''L'Inspiration scripturaire,'' *Recherches de science religieuse* 51 (1963) 337–382. K. RAHNER, *Visions and Prophecies,* tr. C. HENKEY and R. STRACHAN (Quaestiones Disputatae 10; New York 1963); *The Dynamic Element in the Church,* tr. W. J. O'HARA (*ibid.* 12; 1964). L. VOLKEN, *Visions, Revelations, and the Church,* tr. E. GALLAGHER (New York 1963). Y. CONGAR, *Lay People in the Church,* tr. D. ATTWATER (Westminster, Md. 1957). K. RAHNER, *Lexikon für Theologie und Kirche*[2], ed. J. HOFER and K. RAHNER, (2d new ed. Freiburg 1957–65) 8:800–805. A. JEPSEN, *Die Religion in Geschichte und Gegenwart* (3d ed. Tübingen 1957–65) 5: 627–638. A. MICHEL, *Dictionnaire de théologie catholique*, ed. A. VACANT et al. (Paris 1903–50; Tables générales 1951–) 13:708–737.

[R. X. REDMOND]

PROPHET

This article is limited to the Biblical notion of prophet. For general information and bibliography, *see* PROPHETISM (IN THE BIBLE).

The etymology of the Greek προφήτης, from which prophet derives, suggests the fundamental note in the definition of a prophet: he is one who speaks (φημί) for (πρό) another, i.e., in the present case, for God.

It is not clear that the Hebrew word for prophet, *nābî',* has exactly this significance. Most likely it is a passive participial form of a root meaning to call (cf. Akkadian, *nabû*); that is, it designates someone called by God, although it is possible that the Hebrew word is active in form and so designates a speaker (for God). In any event, the central concept is surely one of divine communication; and if etymology cannot determine the concept completely, the actual history of the Prophets of the Bible makes it clear that they were men who brought God's word to others.

The basic sources of information on what constitutes a Prophet are the accounts of the call to prophecy in the Old Testament (Is 6.1–13; Jer 1.4–19; Ez 1.1–3.21; Am 3.7–8; 7.14–16). These and other passages reveal the following essential factors in the prophetic role: the Prophet is delegated to speak for Yahweh (Is 6.8–9; Jer 1.9); the prophetic vocation is compelling even though the Prophet be reluctant or untalented (Am 3.7–8; Jer 1.7–8); God communicates His word to the Prophet (Is 6.9; Jer 1.7–9; Ez 2.8–3.3); and this communication involves visions and auditions, states analogous to those known in later mystics. The last assertion is often denied, but this is largely because of confusion concerning the meaning of mystic. Thus, the Biblical Prophet is one who has heard God's call and brings God's word to men. Primarily, then, the Prophet is an inspired speaker.

The Prophets did not write the books now called prophetic. Their words were preserved in oral tradition, and inspired writers recorded and arranged the traditional words; thus, it is the prophetic word as edited, arranged, and even added to by these writers that the Church now possesses in the inspired text. The modern interest in history has emphasized the effort to sift out the original prophetic message. This is important for reconstructing the history of Israel and its religion, but for theological interpretation it is the inspired prophetic book that counts. A study of the prophetic book in its present structure along the lines of *Redaktionsgeschichte* is often a fruitful avenue of interpretation. [*See* EXEGESIS, BIBLICAL].

The Prophets of the Old Testament are divided into the four Major Prophets (Isaiah, Jeremiah, Ezekiel, and Daniel) and the 12 MINOR PROPHETS, Hosea, Joel, Amos, Obadiah, Jonah, Micah, Nahum, Habakkuk, Zephaniah, Haggai, Zechariah, and Malachi. The terms major and minor have nothing to do with the relative importance of these men and their message; they simply refer to the respective extent of the PROPHETIC BOOKS OF THE OLD TESTAMENT. It must be remembered also that in the Old Testament the prophetic name and office were not confined to the 16 canonical Prophets of the modern Bible, the so-called writing Prophets. There are other men who appear in Israel's history, men such as ELIJAH and ELISHA, who were equally the inspired bearers of God's word, although few of their words have been preserved in writing.

The New Testament offers few details about the experiences of the prophets in the early Church; but since they had much the same function as the Old Testament Prophets, admonition and prediction, one may conclude that the New Testament concept of prophet carries on that of the Old Testament.

Prophetess. In the Old Testament a number of women are referred to by the designation prophetess (Hebrew *n*ᵉbî*'â,* feminine of *nābî*), but little is told of the nature and function of the office. Presumably they acted and were regarded as being much the same as the male prophets. The earliest to be so designated are Miriam and Deborah. Miriam, the sister of Moses, is called a prophetess on the occasion of her song of triumph after the crossing of the Red Sea (Ex 15.20). Deborah was a "judge" in Israel, one who regularly decided cases brought to her (Judges 4.4–5). However, she is doubtless called prophetess because of her inspired (charismatic) intervention to save Israel and, more especially, because of her connection with the song found in Judges chapter 5.

The name prophetess is, to be sure, an anachronism in the time of Miriam and Deborah, as the Old Testament itself witnesses (1 Sm 9.9). The name is attributed to the two women by later writers, and the reason seems to be their connection with songs considered inspired. It is not likely, however, that the attribution would have been made unless later writers knew of women who functioned

"Prophetess Being Inspired," frescos by Giovanni Battista Tiepolo. (©Elio Ciol/CORBIS)

as prophets and spoke under inspiration at a later stage of Israel's history.

Direct evidence of the presence of female prophets in Israel is found in 2 Kgs 22.14–20. When a book of the law was found on the occasion of the Temple restoration, Josiah consulted a prophetess, Huldah. (*See* DEUTERONOMY, BOOK OF.) Further, a false prophetess (and an effective false prophetess implies the acceptance of the possibility of a true one), Noadiah, opposed Nehemiah's efforts to restore Jerusalem (Neh 6.14).

Isaiah's wife is called a prophetess in Is 8.3. Some have thought this should be taken strictly, i.e., that she functioned as a prophetess, and have argued from Isaiah's connection with her that he and she belonged to a band of professional prophets. However, the attribution is sufficiently explained by her connection with Isaiah, who considered that the members of his family were caught up in his own prophetic activity (Is 8.18).

The New Testament speaks of a number of prophetesses: Anna who recognized Jesus as the Messiah (Lk 2.36–39), the daughters of PHILIP THE DEACON (Acts 21.9), and the false prophetess Jezebel (surely a symbolic name; Rv 2.20–23). The last two passages suggest that it was possible for a woman to act as a prophetess, i.e., to teach in the early Church. Presumably the Christian prophetesses had the same function as the Christian prophets.

See Also: PROPHECY (IN THE BIBLE)

[D. J. MCCARTHY]

Prophet Ezekiel. (Archive Photos)

PROPHETIC BOOKS OF THE OLD TESTAMENT

Biblical writings composed by or attributed to the Prophets of the Old Testament. In all Bibles, except Jewish ones, it is customary to distinguish between the so-called four Major Prophets and the 12 MINOR PROPHETS. The distinction, which goes back to St. Augustine (*Civ.* 18.29; *Corpus scriptorum ecclesiasticorum latinorum* 40.2.306), is merely one of relative length, not one of relative importance. Following the Septuagint (LXX), the Vulgate (Vulg) and all other Christian versions of the Old Testament consider the Book of DANIEL to be the fourth of the Major Prophets, the first three being the Books of ISAIAH, JEREMIAH, and EZEKIEL. In the LXX, Jeremiah is followed by the Book of BARUCH and LAMENTATIONS; in the Vulg and Catholic vernacular versions, by Lamentations and Baruch; in Protestant versions, by Lamentations alone, since these versions place Baruch among the so-called apocrypha. Only in the LXX are the Minor Prophets (in a somewhat different order among themselves) put before the Major Prophets.

All the books of the Hebrew Bible and of Jewish versions derived from it are divided into three main groups: the Torah (Pentateuch), the Prophets (*n^e^bî'îm*), and the Writings (*k^e^ tûbîm*). The Prophets are divided into the First Prophets (*n^e^bî'îm rī'sônîm*) including Joshua, Judges, Samuel, and Kings, which were believed to have been written by Prophets, and the Later Prophets (*n^e^bî'îm 'aḥărônîm*) including Isaiah, Jeremiah, Ezekiel, and the 12 Minor Prophets (reckoned as a single book). The Hebrew Bible puts Lamentations and Daniel among the Writings, and it does not have Baruch at all.

See Also: BIBLE.

[L. F. HARTMAN]

PROPHETISM (IN THE BIBLE)

I. Engnell and some other Scandinavian scholars have argued that much of the prophetic material, and the Old Testament in general, had a very long history of oral tradition, being fixed in writing only at a late period. As prophetic disciples and schools passed on the materials, they were reinterpreted and adapted to ever new situations. As a result, they thought, the line between the prophet's original words and later adaptations was virtually non-existent and the attempt to recover the *ipsissima verba* of the prophet became impossible. S. Mowinckel, on the other hand, had argued early for the importance of a careful investigation into the role of both oral and written tradition in shaping the prophetic tradition. Other scholars have been attempting to demonstrate from the prophetic books that, in some cases at least, the beginning of the written tradition goes back to the prophets themselves.

The formation of the prophetic books as we have them remains an elusive process. There is general agreement that, in most cases, the process began with smaller collections, which, through a gradual process of expansion and combination, resulted in our canonical books. Ever new theories continue to be put forth on the specific procedure in the case of each book. H. Barth has attempted to reconstruct a so-called *Assur-Redaktion* of Isaiah 1–39, according to which many passages that relate to the downfall of Assyria would have been added around the time of that nation's demise; he is closely followed by Clements, who speaks, rather, of a Josianic redaction; how widely this theory will be accepted remains to be seen.

Important work has been done on the redaction of Jeremiah by E. W. Nicholson. Whereas it had become commonplace to distinguish three types of material in Jeremiah, poetic oracles by the prophet himself, biographical prose (attributed to Baruch), and prose discourses (the prophet's words as preserved among the circle of his followers), Nicholson argues that the prose sections (in which he rejects the distinction implied above) are all the work of the deuteronomists, whose interest was not biographical but rather concerned the function of God's word through the prophet, human reaction to it, obedience to the law, results of disobedience, etc. The book in its edited form was intended for the exiles and vindicates their claim to be the ''true'' Israel over those who remained in the land. Nicholson does not thereby deny that the prose discourses rest on genuine words of Jeremiah or the historical truth of the events related or the traditional link with Baruch.

The redaction and organization of Deutero-Isaiah (Is 40–55) continues to be debated. T. N. D. Mettinger's analysis places emphasis on eight hymns of praise and argues for a closely knit, tightly organized structure, while Clifford divides the composition into 17 speeches aimed at persuading the exiles to return home. Clifford suggests a date after Cyrus has already issued his decree permitting the exiles to return; C. Stuhlmueller sees chs. 41–48 dating to before the fall of Babylon, chs. 49–55 to after the fall and initial return of the exiles, with the Servant Songs (42:1–4; 49:1–6; 50:4–9; 52:13–53:12) and ch. 40 composed by Deutero-Isaiah but added at a later stage of redaction, by him or a disciple. The Servant of the Lord continues to be the object of extensive study, though with no one solution finally accepted. Mettinger denies the Servant can be distinguished from Israel in the oracles of Deutero-Isaiah; for Clifford the Servant is Deutero-Isaiah and those who go back with him in the new Exodus-Conquest; Blenkinsopp thinks the first song refers to a royal figure (Cyrus or possibly Jehoiachin or Zerubbabal), the second to the exiled community (but later expanded by the prophetic group reflected in chs. 56–66), the third to (and by) Deutero-Isaiah, and the fourth to Deutero-Isaiah and his prophetic group; for Elliger the Servant is to be identified with Deutero–Isaiah himself.

Ezekiel's book has undergone many vicissitudes since C. C. Torrey suggested (1930) that it was not written by Ezekiel and was to be dated to late postexilic times. Such extreme views are no longer current. Scholars generally agree with W. Zimmerli that Ezekiel was responsible for a solid core of the book (not including chs. 38–39), which has been fleshed out with later reworkings by his disciples. Which parts are to be attributed to the latter continues to be a disputed question, but, contrary to the view of the Scandinavian scholars referred to above, bases are found for making the distinction.

See Also: PROPHECY (IN THE BIBLE); PROPHECY, (THEOLOGY OF); PROPHET; PROPHETESS; PROPHETIC BOOKS OF THE OLD TESTAMENT; PROPHETISM (IN THE BIBLE).

Bibliography: H. BARTH, *Die Jesaja-Worte in der Josiazeit* (Neukirchen 1977). R. E. CLEMENTS, *Isaiah and the Deliverance of Jerusalem* (Sheffield 1980). R. J. CLIFFORD, *Fair Spoken and Persuading: An Interpretation of Second Isaiah* (New York 1984). K. ELLIGER, *Jesaja II* (Neukirchen-Vluyn 1970–78). I. ENGNELL, ''Prophets and Prophetism in the Old Testament,'' *A Rigid Scrutiny: Critical Essays on the Old Testament*, ed. J. T. WILLIS (Nashville 1969) 123–79. B. GERHARDSSON, ''Mündliche und schriftliche Tradition der Prophetenbücher,'' *Theologische Zeitschrift* 17 (1961) 216–20. T. N. D. METTINGER, *A Farewell to the Servant Songs* (Lund 1983). E. W. NICHOLSON, *Preaching to the Exiles: A Study in the Prose Tradition in the Book of Jeremiah* (Oxford 1970). C. STUHLMUELLER, ''Deutero-Isaiah: Major Transitions in the Prophet's Theology and in Contemporary Scholarship,'' *The Catholic Biblical Quarterly* 42 (1980) 1–29. W. ZIMMERLI, *Ezekiel 1* (Philadelphia 1979); *Ezekiel 2* (Philadelphia 1983).

[J. JENSEN]

PROPORTIONALITY, PRINCIPLE OF

It is a common sense axiom that there should be a reasonable balance between human activity and its consequences. In Roman Catholic moral theology, the principle of proportionality states that the moral rectitude of an action is a function of the preponderance of human value over disvalue that results through the action.

Attention to proportionality, as pertinent to the moral evaluation of behavior, has long been part of the Catholic ethical tradition. The *principle of the* DOUBLE EFFECT, for instance, holds that an action having both good and bad effects is permissible if four conditions are fulfilled. One of those conditions is that there be a ''proportionate reason'' for tolerating the evil consequences. Similarly, the *principle of* TOTALITY justified attacks on a part of the human body if the whole body/person stood to benefit and if there was ''proportionate reason'' to tolerate the attack. The idea of proportionate reason also appeared in discussions of material cooperation in evil, the *just war theory,* and the permitting of passive scandal.

Within the Catholic theological tradition, this perspective was also evidenced in the emphasis upon the virtue of *prudence* in the living of the moral life. Thomas Aquinas, for example, viewed prudence as the central moral virtue (I–II, 61, 2), since deciding rightly among concrete options in a finite world is utterly dependent upon the skill of comparative assessment. Thus, it can be said that prudence is the virtue by which one rightly discerns the proportionate reasons for acting or not acting, and for selecting one action in preference to another.

Implied in these traditional usages is the insight that it is not humanly possible to avoid all injury/harm. Even more, it is not possible to do all possible good. For example, one cannot always safeguard professional secrets without (deliberately) deceiving others; one cannot at times defend oneself against aggressors without a violent response. Similarly, to visit a sick friend in the hospital is to take time away from family, prayer, study, etc. In a finite world all decisions are choices *among* values. Hence, the Christian's central moral duty is to do "as much good as possible and as little harm as necessary," to give attention to all the various values and disvalues that are simultaneously part of the concrete action.

Points of Controversy. Although discussions about the most accurate way to define the principle of proportionality continue, it has for many Catholic theologians achieved the status of a fundamental moral norm. And that, in turn, has led to controversy. The controversy is not about whether the principle is useful in some settings. Rather, it is about its universality and about its applications.

With regard to its universality, the question is asked if there are some actions which are never morally proper, no matter how little harm may result. The responses fall into two broad categories divided along basic approaches that various authors take to moral issues, *Teleologists* (Gr. *telos,* end or result) deny that actions can be adjudged morally proper or improper apart from reference to their actual impact on human life for, in their judgment, it is precisely the fact of overwhelmingly destructive results that is the reason for the action's immorality. Some proponents of this approach would describe it as "consequentialist," because of its emphasis on the results and/or consequences of actions. *Deontologists*, who judge the fundamental rectitude of an act in categories of duty and obligation (Gr. *deontos*) assert that some actions are always wrong, not for reasons of disproportionate harm but because of either intrinsic impropriety for human persons or specific divine prohibition. (These philosophical categories are, perhaps, used with less than complete precision in depicting the alternatives in this theological debate. According to some Catholic authors, moral philosophies defy simple categorization into teleological-deontological polarities.)

This debate is sometimes obfuscated by the accusation that the principle of proportionality amounts to an assertion that "the end justifies the means," and that its proponents are prepared to tolerate the doing of moral evil for an allegedly greater good. But defenders of the principle presume that all human acts involve both helpful and harmful, constructive and destructive aspects, and that an act is *moral* precisely because it is proportionately more positive than negative. Thus, an "end" never justifies an immoral means, since such a means counts as immoral precisely and only because it is unduly and unnecessarily destructive. Hence, all Catholic ethicists agree that the end does not justify an immoral means. The debate is about whether acts can be characterized as moral or immoral apart from attention to the proportion of good and harm involved.

The controversy also reveals itself in the application of the principle of proportionality. There is no doubt that some authors, spiritual directors, and confessors have used the principle to justify artificial contraception, remarriage after divorce, and certain forms of homosexual behavior. Thus, debates about the principle are often, in fact, disguised debates about the morality of these behaviors. But, at least in theory, the two debates are separable. That is, one could affirm a fundamentally teleological understanding of morality and could accept the principle of proportionality as an adequate norm for prudential judgment, and at the same time reject all of the behaviors mentioned above. Similarly, one could espouse a more deontological moral theory and support these behaviors.

The clarification of the principle of proportionality has occurred in the process of a thorough reassessment of Catholic moral theology, especially as it was articulated in the 18th, 19th, and early 20th centuries. That relatively recent moral tradition seemed in the eyes of a number of reputable Catholic writers in Europe and America to have become improperly legalistic, detaching moral norms from the concrete assessment of complex human behaviors. The desire of these authorities is to retrieve a teleological understanding based on the ends and consequences of human actions and the richer approaches and visions of earlier ethical writings. At the same time, their negative assessment of the moral tradition of the past two or three centuries shows itself in a willingness to question the concrete application of moral norms which were, until recently, so much a part of standard textbooks. In particular, they question the confidence with which very detailed, concrete behaviors, especially sexual behaviors, were evaluated, judged immoral, and prohibited. They further question whether the conventional answers of a just war theory and the principle of double effect in medicine are credible in the face of advances in modern science and technology.

Thus the retrieval of the traditional notion of proportionate reason and its elevation to the position of fundamental principle has occurred in the context of that more general renaissance in Catholic moral theology.

See Also: MORAL THEOLOGY; TELEOLOGICAL ETHICS

Bibliography: C. A. CURRAN and R. A. MCCORMICK, eds., *Readings in Moral Theology No. 1: Moral Norms and Catholic Tradition* (New York 1979). R. A. MCCORMICK and P. RAMSEY, eds., *Doing Evil to Achieve Good: Moral Choice in Conflict Situations* (Chicago 1978). R. A. MCCORMICK, *Notes on Moral Theology: 1965 through 1980* (Washington, D.C. 1981); *Notes on Moral Theology: 1981 Through 1984* (Lanham, MD 1984). J. J. WALTER, "Proportionate Reason and Its Three Levels of Inquiry: Structuring the Ongoing Debate,'' *Louvain Studies* 10 (Spring 1984) 30–40. L. S. CAHILL, ''Teleology, Utilitarianism, and Christian Ethics,'' *Theological Studies* 42:4 (Dec. 1981) 601–629.

[T. E. O'CONNELL]

PROPOSITION

A proposition is often said to be a verbal expression that can be true or false. This definition is imprecise for two reasons. First, a proposition is the sense of the sentence that expresses it; one proposition can be expressed by several sentences in different languages or in the same language. Secondly, TRUTH and FALSITY belong neither to sentences nor to propositions, but to judgments; only the intellectual act of JUDGMENT assenting to the proposition expressed by the sentence is in the proper sense true or false. To say that a proposition is true or that it is false is to say that anyone asserting it would be judging truly or falsely. Nevertheless, with the understanding that the usage is elliptical, sentences are here called propositions, and they are declared to be true or to be false.

Kinds of Proposition. Propositions are either assertoric or modal. The former merely declare that a given state of affairs obtains; the latter qualify such declarations as necessary, contingent, possible, or impossible. Hence there are four kinds of modals. Obviously, every assertoric proposition can be qualified by each mode, so that there are four modals for every assertoric. Assertoric propositions are of two kinds: categorical and compound. A categorical proposition is one in which an attribute (signified by the predicate) is said to characterize or not to characterize something (signified by the subject). These terms, SUBJECT and predicate, constitute the *matter* of the categorical. Its *form,* making it a proposition of a specific kind, is the copula, which affirms or denies the predicate of the subject. There are thus two species of categorical, affirmative and negative. Based upon the matter is the division into singular propositions, whose subjects are proper names or demonstrative words or phrases, and general propositions, whose subjects are common nouns or descriptive phrases. Also based upon the matter is the division into universal and particular propositions. UNIVERSALS are those in which the predicate is affirmed or denied of everything denoted by the subject; they are identified by some such modifier of the subject as ''all,'' ''every,'' ''none.'' The subjects of universals are said to be distributed. Particular propositions are those in which the affirmation or denial is extended only to some of the things the subject signifies; such restriction of PREDICATION is indicated by the use of ''some,'' ''not every,'' or the like to modify the subject. The restriction does not positively exclude from the predication anything the subject denotes; the particular proposition is noncommittal as to whether the predication could be truly made of everything the subject denotes. Subjects of particulars are said to be undistributed.

Reflection on the nature of affirmation and denial discloses that the distinction between distributed and undistributed terms applies to predicates also; for to deny a predicate of a subject is to state that nothing the predicate denotes is referred to by the subject, or that everything the predicate denotes is excluded from the subject's referents. Affirmation has no such exclusive force, but leaves unanswered the question whether the attribute the predicate signifies belongs to other things besides the subject's referents. Hence, predicates of negative propositions are distributed, while those of affirmatives are undistributed. Since both of these can be either universal or particular, there are four kinds of categorical propositions: *A.* Universal affirmative, with subject distributed, predicate undistributed (Every *S* is *P*). *I.* Particular affirmative, with subject undistributed, predicate undistributed (Some *S* is *P*). *E.* Universal negative, with subject distributed, predicate distributed (No *S* is *P*). *O.* Particular negative, with subject undistributed, predicate distributed (Not every *S* is *P*). When these propositions have the same subjects and predicates, they constitute two pairs of contradictories: *A* and *O* are mutually exclusive and also exclusive of a middle, as are *I* and *E.*

Existential Import and Equivalence. With what has been said up to this point, logicians are in general agreement; concerning another aspect of categoricals, their existential import, there is no such consensus. Concerning this aspect, there are three schools of interpretation: the first understands particulars as stating that what their subjects signify exists in some realm of discourse, and understands universals as leaving the question of existence open; the second understands affirmatives as requiring for their truth the existence of whatever their subjects signify, and understands negatives as true if what their subjects signify does not exist; the third holds all categoricals to be alike in existential import, either all existential or all nonexistential.

Conversion and Obversion. Modification of a proposition's matter or form produces a new proposition, whose relation to the original interests the logician. Conversion affects the matter; it is the interchange of subject and predicate, the copula remaining unaffected. There are two kinds of conversion: simple conversion, in which the propositions are the same in quantity; and conversion by limitation, in which the new proposition is particular, the original being universal. Obversion has to do with the proposition's form; it is the change of quality from affirmative to negative or vice versa, with the compensating substitution for the predicate of its contradictory term. The older logicians discussed another process, called equipollence, by some mistakenly identified with obversion, which it superficially resembles. It is effected by the insertion of *non* at appropriate places in Latin sentences, expressing propositions to produce other propositions equivalent to the contradictories, contraries, subalterns, and superalterns of the original (*see* OPPOSITION). The resulting equivalents are not obverses, however, for they are of like quality, both affirmative or both negative. They are not different propositions at all, but different sentences expressing one proposition; they have identical matter and form, and differ only in syntax.

Contraposition and Inversion. The product of obversion is a proposition having the same subject as the original; that of conversion is a proposition whose subject is the predicate of the original. Two other processes, contraposition and inversion, consist of alternating obversions and conversions. The contrapositive, product of the former, is a proposition whose subject is the contradictory of the original predicate. The full contrapositive is of the same quality as the original and has for its predicate the contradictory of the original subject; the partial contrapositive is of opposite quality and has the original subject as its predicate. The inverse has for its subject the contradictory of the original subject. The distinction between full and partial inverses is analogous to the distinction between full and partial contrapositives.

Implications. A proposition implies another derived from it in any of these ways, if and only if (1) any term distributed in the derived proposition is also distributed in the original, and (2) either the original is existential or the derived proposition is nonexistential. It follows that when distribution and existential import are the same for both propositions they imply each other, that is, they are equivalent. Whichever interpretation be accepted, these conditions are fulfilled in the simple conversion of *I* and But since subject and predicate differ as to distribution in *A* and *O,* neither of these implies its converse; *A* and *O* are independent of their converses. For the second school of interpretation, however, a universal implies its converse by limitation: ''Every man is just'' implies ''Some just being is a man''; and ''No man is just'' implies ''Not every just being is a man.'' The first school, of course, rejects this implication. For this school, on the other hand, every proposition implies its obverse, and *A* and *O* imply their contrapositives. Contrariwise, for the second school, only affirmatives imply their obverses. It holds, therefore, that *A* propositions imply their partial contrapositives, but that full contrapositives are independent. For instance, ''Every man is just'' implies ''No not-just being is a man,'' but neither implies nor is implied by ''Every not-just being is a not-man.''

The first and second schools hold that a proposition and its inverse are independent. Since for the second, the full contrapositive is not implied by the original, neither is the inverse, which is derived from it. The first accepts the equivalence of contrapositives, but rejects conversion by limitation, whereby one derives the inverse from the contrapositive. However, the third school holds that *A* and *E* imply their inverses. It teaches that ''Every man is just'' implies ''Some not-man is not-just'' and ''Not every not-man is just.'' The term ''just,'' however, which is undistributed in the original, is distributed in the partial inverse. For this reason the first and second schools hold that contradictories differ not only in quality and quantity, but in existential import also.

Compound Proposition. A compound proposition has for its *matter* two propositions, categorical or themselves compound; its *form* is a conjunction affirming or denying a given relation between these two. Instead of the one relation of characterization they may hold between terms, four basic relations are possible between pairs of propositions, namely: 1. Implication, the first implying the second; 2. Subimplication, the first being implied by the second; 3. Contrariety, the two excluding each other; 4. Subcontrariety, the two excluding any other that denies both. Letting *p* and *q* represent propositions, and ~*p* and ~*q,* their contradictories, one may affirm and deny these relations by means of the following compound propositions: Of the propositions affirming relations, the first two are conditional, the third is disjunctive, the fourth is alternative; all those denying relations are of the same kind, and are called conjunctive. These then are the four species of compound propositions.

Every conjunctive denies each of these relations between one or another pair of propositions, and consequently contradicts four other compound propositions. Thus ''Both *p* and *q*'' contradicts these: 1. If *p,* then ~*q* 2. If *q,* then ~*p* 3. Not both *p* and *q* 4. Either ~*p* or ~*q* Consequently, these four are equivalent. Similarly, each of the other three conjunctives composed of *p, q,* ~*p,* and ~*q* contradicts two conditionals, a disjunctive, and an alternative, which are therefore equivalent. The equivalent conditionals are said to be contrapositives, the relation among their parts being analogous to the relation among the parts of categorical contrapositives. The contradictories of converse conditionals are contraries to each other: ''If *p,* then *q*'' and ''If *q,* then *p*'' contradict respectively ''Both *p* and ~*q*'' and ''Both *q* and ~*p,*'' which are contraries. Since contradictories of contraries are subcontraries, such is the relation of these conditionals: one of the converse conditionals must be true.

Modal Proposition. Concerning the modal propositions corresponding to categoricals little need be said. To determine whether a modal implies another derived from it by obversion or conversion, one must add to the conditions mentioned above a third: that either the original proposition is in the MODE of NECESSITY or of impossibility or the derived one is in the mode of POSSIBILITY. Between modal and assertoric compounds, however, there is an important difference. The necessary conditional, like the assertoric, is equivalent to its contrapositive; unlike the assertoric conditional, it is not subcontrary to its converse. For the contradictory of the necessary conditional is a conjunctive in the possible mode, and a possible proposition does not imply a necessary one. Thus the contradictory of ''If *p,* then necessarily *q*'' is ''Possibly both *p* and not ~*q,*'' which does not imply ''If *q,* then necessarily *p.*'' A necessary conditional and its converse are therefore independent of each other.

See Also: LOGIC, SYMBOLIC; TERM (LOGIC).

Bibliography: V. MIANO, *Encilopedia filosophica* (Venice-Rome 1957) 3:1662–63. J. A. OESTERLE, *Logic: The Art of Defining and Reasoning* (2d ed. Englewood Cliffs, N.J. 1963). V. E. SMITH, *The Elements of Logic* (Milwaukee 1957). E. D. SIMMONS, *The Scientific Art of Logic* (Milwaukee 1961). O. BIRD, *Syllogistic and Its Extensions* (Englewood Cliffs, N.J. 1964).

[J. J. DOYLE]

PROPRIETARY CHURCHES

Term denoting a system of private ownership of churches and monasteries that developed in Western Europe from the 7th and 8th centuries and lasted until the 12th. The essential features were control of the temporal possessions (*ius proprietatis*) and the right to nominate the priest, abbot, and in some cases the bishop. Usually such churches were in the hands of laymen who had founded them or taken them under their protection, but it was not unusual, especially after the 10th century, for monasteries and bishops to hold proprietary churches. In this sense the Church became feudalized.

The origin of the institution is a disputed question. The major disagreement is whether proprietary churches were Germanic or Roman in origin; but the most likely explanation is that any one or a combination of causes led to proprietary churches in such countries as Germany, France, England, Italy, and Spain. It was a development that coincided with and formed part of the rise of FEUDALISM in secular institutions.

Until the GREGORIAN REFORM the system as such was accepted by the Church. Abuses, of course, were inevitable when the overlord could treat a church or monastery as a piece of property to be sold, given away, transmitted to one's heirs, and inherited. The lord also took a share of the income, which in effect led to neglect of the spiritual needs and function of the Church.

Attempts at reform were made from the 8th century onward, e.g., to control the type of person elected, and in the 9th century to strengthen episcopal authority (*see* FALSE DECRETALS).

Contrary to accepted opinion, the CLUNIAC REFORM had little direct influence on the system; nor did the popes of the early Gregorian reform (LEO IX to ALEXANDER II) attack the institution, but only its abuses. However, some laymen began to dispose of their churches and monasteries by donating them to other monasteries or by putting them under the protection of the Holy See.

GREGORY VII was the first to attack the system as such. His attack, together with the attempt to eliminate lay INVESTITURE, brought about a major struggle between the papacy and the lay powers. By the end of the 12th century, a compromise of lay and reform demands had been reached. The lay lord or monastery had become the patron. The patron would nominate the parish priest, who would receive the revenues, but the bishop had the right to approve the nominee. The transformation of the *ius proprietatis* into the *ius patronatus* was largely the work of the canonists, and it was to have significant effects on subsequent attitudes toward the LAITY IN THE MIDDLE AGES.

Bibliography: U. STUTZ, ''The Proprietary Church as an Element of Mediaeval Germanic Ecclesiastical Law,'' *Mediaeval Germany, 911–1250,* tr. G. BARRACLOUGH, 2 v. (Oxford 1938) 2:35–70. C. E. BOYD, *Tithes and Parishes in Medieval Italy* (Ithaca, N.Y. 1952). G. TELLENBACH, *Church, State, and Christian Society at the Time of the Investiture Contest,* tr. R. F. BENNETT (Oxford 1959). W. M. PLÖCHL, *Lexikon für Theologie und Kirche* (Freiburg, 1957–66) 3:733-734. R. J. COX, *A Study of the Juridic Status of Laymen in the Writing of the Medieval Canonists* (Washington 1959). T. SCHIEFFER, ''Cluny et la querelle des Investitures,'' *Revue historique* 225 (1961) 47–72. C. VAN DE KIEFT, ''*Une Église privée de l'abbaye de la Trinité de Vendôme au XI*[e] *siècle,*'' *Moyen-âge* 69 (1963) 157–168.

[J. GILCHRIST]

PROSPER OF AQUITAINE, ST.

Lay theologian and papal secretary; b. apparently Limoges, France, *c.* 390; d. probably Rome, Italy, after 455. Nothing is known of Prosper's background other than that he had an excellent classical education, was married, and read deeply in theology. He spent some time with the monks at Marseilles and proved himself a strong opponent of SEMIPELAGIANISM. With his friend Hilary he wrote to AUGUSTINE in Africa (428–429) concerning the opposition to Augustine's doctrine on grace among the monks (Aug. *Epist.* 225). Augustine wrote his *De praedestinatione sanctorum* and *De dono perseverantiae* in reply.

With Hilary, Prosper journeyed to Rome in 431 to obtain a favorable judgment of Augustine's doctrine from Pope CELESTINE I. In Rome he seems to have modified the strict Augustinian doctrine by insisting on God's universal, salvific will and to have participated in the formulation of the Roman document called the *Capitula Caelestiana* sent to the bishops of Gaul. After 440 he was associated with Pope LEO I and aided the pope with his correspondence and theological writings against the NESTORIANS, and particularly with Leo's tome to Flavian (Gennadius, *Vir. ill.* 48).

Adopting the technique used by St. Augustine in his anti-Donatist hymns for popular chanting, Prosper wrote a 1,102 hexameter poem *De ingratis* (On Those without Grace); *Poema conjugis ad uxorem* (Poem of a Husband to His Wife) in 16 anacreontic verses and 53 distichs found among the works of PAULINUS OF NOLA (*Corpus scriptorum ecclesiasticorum latinorum* 30:341–344) is probably Prosper's. The *De providentia divina* in 876 hexameters and 48 distichs is almost certainly not authentic, as it appears to have been written *c.* 417. A series of epigrams, including three against the Semipelagians and an ironic *Epitaphium Nestorianae et Pelagianae haereseos,* seem to be of his composition. Another series of *Epigrammata ex sententiis s. Augustini* represent a summa of *Sententiae ex operibus s. Augustini.* Prosper also wrote a defense of Augustine against VINCENT OF LÉRINS and two Genoan priests (*Pro Augustino responsiones*); a *Contra collatorem,* against John CASSIAN; and a *Psalmorum a C ad CL expositio* after the Council of Ephesus. Although the authorship of a *Confessio* and the *Letter to Demetrias* have been questioned, the second is most probably authentic.

His *Epitoma chronicorum* is a synthesis of the chronicles of JEROME (to A.D. 378), SULPICIUS SEVERUS, and OROSIUS (to 433), but appears to reflect his own experience from 433 to 455. It was reedited and added to by CASSIODORUS and PAUL THE DEACON.

In *De vocatione omnium gentium,* Prosper tried to modify Augustine's views on predestination. He considered the problem of the great mass of mankind who have no certain knowledge of salvation in Christ and asked how this fact can be reconciled with the scriptural statement that God wills the salvation of all. Augustine held that God predestined a part of mankind and simply refrained from selecting others. Since man has free will but needs specific graces to achieve salvation, the nonpredestined are damned. Prosper threw the mystery of damnation back to God's foreknowledge. He insisted on the gratuitousness of grace and of human freedom and on God's salvific will for all. Although he did not solve the problem, he softened the Augustinian rigidity and left room for later development. The *Letter to Demetrias* is one of several received by this Roman lady from contemporary Church leaders in reference to her vocation to an ascetic way of life.

Feast: June 25.

Bibliography: *De vocatione,* ed. and tr., P. DE LETTER, *Ancient Christian Writers*, v. 14 (1952). *Monumenta Germaniae Historica: Auctores antiquissimi* (Berlin 1826–) 9.1:341–499. C. T. HUEGELMEYER, ed. and tr., ''Carmen de ingratis,'' Catholic University of America *Patristic Studies* 95 (1962). M. K. C. KRABBE, ed. and tr., ''Epistula de Demetriadem de vera humilitate,'' *ibid.* 97 (1965). M. CAPPUYNS, *Revue Bénédictine* 39 (1927) 198–226, ''De vocatione,'' *ibid.* 41 (1929) 156–170, ''Capitula coelestiana'' *Recherches de théologie ancienne et médiévale* 1 (1929) 309–337. G. DE PLINVAL, *Recherches Augustiniennes* 1 (1958) 339–355. G. BARDY, *Dictionnaire de théologie catholique,* 15 (Paris 1903–50) 13.1:846–850. L. PELLAND, *S. Prosperi Aquitani doctrina de praedestinatione* (Montreal 1936). J. GAIDIOZ, *Revue des sciences religieuses* 23 (1949) 270–301. V. GRUMEL, *Revue des études augustiniennes* 2 (1956) 59–66. J. PLAGNIEUX, *ibid.* 391–402. J. J. YOUNG, ''Studies on the Style of *De vocatione omnium gentium,*'' Catholic University of America *Patristic Studies* 87 (1952). R. HELM, *Paulys Realenzyklopädie der klassischen Altertumswissenschaft* 23.1 (1957): 80–897. R. LORENZ, *Zeitschrift für Kirchengeschicte* 73 (1962) 217–252. B. ALTANER, *Patrology* (New York 1960) 535–537. S. MUHLBERGER, *The Fifth-Century Chroniclers: Prosper, Hydatius, and the Gallic Chronicler of 452* (Leeds 1990). A. ELBERTI, *Prospero d'Aquitania: teologo e discepolo* (Rome 1999).

[F. X. MURPHY]

PROSTITUTION

Prostitution is common lewdness for hire, the act or practice of a woman who permits a man who will pay her price to have sexual intercourse with her. It is a universal phenomenon with moral, social, cultural, psychological, medical, and other aspects. Although male prostitution is also found, that involving males exclusively is best considered as part of the general problem of HOMOSEXUALITY.

History. Social attitudes toward prostitution have changed through the ages and go on changing. It is difficult to generalize about primitive societies in which prostitution was generally obviated by an early age of marriage, the existence of polygamy or ease of divorce, and the sexual freedoms of some peoples. Instances of prostitution of slaves captured in war are reported, as are customs providing for the earning of dowries by prostitution. In a few African and American Indian tribes, parents

Women prostitutes sitting in windows, Amsterdam, Netherlands. (©Todd Haimann/CORBIS)

and husbands prostituted their women for gain. Some advanced peoples also associated prostitution with puberty rites or fertility cults, and some type of prostitution as a religious duty was common among the peoples of the eastern Mediterranean or western Asia. *See* PROSTITUTION (SACRED). Although condemned, prostitution was prevalent in ancient Palestine.

In ancient Greece expectations of chastity were confined to wives and daughters and to prohibitions against adultery. After 451 B.C., when Athenian citizenship was rigidly defined, the main profession left open to alien women was that of the hetaerae (companions). A large proportion of women of this class, including most of the temple prostitutes, were slaves, often obtained by rearing female infants exposed by fathers unwilling to rear them; freedwomen in this class were mostly freeborn aliens. The virtual lack of any sense of degradation in prostitution allowed the hetaerae to rise socially to the level of their intellectual attainments (which, because of the freedom permitted them, were often superior to those of other women). There was a profitable, organized, international traffic in prostitution.

While the Greeks had few principles of sexual morality but a well-preserved sense of public decency, the Romans held much more exalted personal and family ideals but came to exhibit a general moral depravity of which prostitution was only one form. In this development prostitution remained shameful per se, for both parties. A system of police registration and taxation was developed very early. The names of prostitutes could never be removed from the register, they were required to wear distinctive dress, and they were deprived of full civil rights. Greek influence, along with the increase of wealth and luxury, assisted in the spiritual decay of the Republic until even the upper strata of society yielded recruits to prostitution. Corrective measures attempted by some emperors were unsuccessful, as was a sixth-century attempt at a monastic refuge established by Justinian, who also removed some of the civil disabilities of prostitutes.

Christianity, while condemning the procurer, introduced a charitable attitude toward the prostitute. There developed an interest in the reformation of prostitutes and the suppression of vice. The Church established rescue missions, convents for the reception of penitents, and dowries to enable prostitutes to marry. Innocent III commended the marrying of a prostitute. Gregory IX denounced those who drew profit from prostitution, counseled that brothel-keepers should not be allowed to prevent prostitutes from attending missions, and urged bachelors to marry repentant girls or the latter to enter the cloister.

In general, however, prostitution was tolerated as a necessary evil throughout the Middle Ages. The availability of prostitutes was commonly thought to protect the integrity of families. Systems of local regulation and licensing were used to control disorders. Traffic in women became financially profitable, as always, and some cities even established public brothels for revenue. Opinion began to change at the end of the 15th century as a result of fears associated with the spread of syphilis, which devastated first southern, then northern Europe. Demands for the closing of brothels also resulted from the Reformation and Counter Reformation. Venereal disease persisted nevertheless, and by the end of the 17th century attempts at the suppression of prostitution gave way to sanitary control. This was usually a matter of police regulation. In Great Britain, brothels were made illegal about the middle of the 18th century.

Prostitution increased again during the 19th century, largely as a result of the growth of urban communities after the industrial revolution. Official regulation was instituted over a large part of Europe. The British Criminal Law Amendment Act of 1885 was an attempt to stop importation of women from the Continent. In the U.S., although in most states houses of ill repute were never legal, prostitution flourished in the ''redlight districts'' of cities. The reports of successive municipal investigations, such as the Lexow Investigation in New York during the 1890s, reflect the prevalence of these districts and the large number of houses of ill-repute within them. Police corruption was almost universal, and political control was widespread. Shortly after 1900, civic groups that sprang up in many places called for abolition of the districts. They attained their first success in Chicago, in 1912, and subsequently virtually every city abolished such districts. Meanwhile the Congress passed, in 1910, the Mann Act or White Slave Traffic Act, which made interstate transportation of women for immoral purposes a federal offense.

Bibliography: V. L. BULLOUGH, *The History of Prostitution* (New York 1964). A. HERMANN and H. HERTER, *Reallexikon für Antike und Christentum*, ed. T. KLAUSER (Stuttgart 1941 [1950]–) 3:1149–1213. H. HERTER, ''Die Soziologie der antiken Prostitution im Lichte des heidnischen und christlichen Schrifttums,'' *Jahrbuch für Antike und Christentum* (Münster 1958–) 3 (1960) 70–111. T. E. JAMES, *Prostitution and the Law* (London 1951). A. C. KINSEY, *Sexual Behavior in the Human Male* (Philadelphia 1953). J. M. MURTAGH and S. HARRIS, *Cast the First Stone* (New York 1957). C. H. ROLPH, ed., *Women of the Streets* (London 1955). W. W. SANGER, *History of Prostitution* (New York 1858). United Nations Publication ST/SOA/SD/8, *Study on Traffic in Persons and Prostitution* (New York 1959).

[J. M. MURTAGH]

PROSTITUTION (SACRED)

A rite or form of worship connected with certain fertility cults. It is first attested historically for ancient Babylonia, where it appears in a fully developed form in the Code of Hammurabi and is assumed as a traditional institution in the Epic of Gilgamesh. The practice is to be explained as an act of acknowledgment for the blessings of fertility to the great Mother Goddess or Goddess of Love and as an expression of a desire for their continuance. It is necessary to distinguish two forms of sacred prostitution. Every Babylonian woman was expected before marriage to serve at least once as a prostitute in a temple. After fulfilling this obligation, she was free to return home and was held in esteem for having offered her virginity to the goddess. The more typical prostitutes were the hierodules who engaged more or less permanently in their profession within the temple precincts and whose earnings were a source of temple revenue. However, their service was regarded as an essential part of the cult.

Imitative magic was combined with religion in this fertility cult and was evident especially in the annual sacred marriage between the king or high priest and a priestess. The priestess, however, should not be identified with the ordinary hierodules; she had a special status. This marriage was intended to symbolize in a realistic way, and to guarantee, the reawakening of the great cosmic forces of nature and their promotion of fertility in plants, animals, and men.

Sacred prostitution had a wide distribution in the area influenced by Babylonian civilization, in Canaanite religion, in Egyptian religion, in the cult of the Great Mother of Asia Minor, and in the cult of Aphrodite at Corinth. Male prostitution of this kind is also found, but to a rather limited degree. There is a survival of sacred prostitution connected with certain temples in modern India.

Bibliography: B. THUM, *Lexikon für Theologie und Kirche*, ed. J. HOFER and K. RAHNER (Freiberg 1957–65) 3:1041–42. W. VON SODEN, *Die Religion in Geschichte und Gegenwart* (Tübingen 1957–65) 5:642–643. D. G. HOGARTH and G. A. BARTON, *Encyclopedia of Religion and Ethics*, ed. J. HASTINGS (Edinburgh 1908–27) 6:672–676. W. J. WOOHDOUSE and W. CROOKE, *ibid.* 10: 404–408.

[M. R. P. MCGUIRE]

PROTERIUS, PATRIARCH OF ALEXANDRIA, ST.

Patriarchate 451–57; d. Alexandria, Egypt, March 28, 457. As the archpriest, Proterius was chosen by the nobles of Alexandria at the suggestion of the emperor MARCIAN to replace DIOSCORUS as patriarch after Dioscorus had been deposed by the Council of CHALCEDON (451). To maintain his position against popular uprisings in favor of Dioscorus stimulated by the Egyptian monks, Proterius had to depend on the imperial soldiery. He attempted to conciliate the monastic leaders TIMOTHY AELURUS and Peter Mongus, but in 456 he had them exiled from the city. Upon the death of Marcian (Jan. 24, 457) Timothy Aelurus returned to Alexandria and had himself consecrated patriarch (March 16, 457) to succeed Dioscorus, who had died in exile (Sept. 4, 454). The imperial governor was unable to prevent the followers of Timothy from invading the city and taking possession of the churches. On March 28 they besieged the church of St. Quirinus, where Proterius was celebrating the Liturgy, assassinated Proterius, dragged his body through the streets, burned it, and scattered the ashes. His name was erased from the diptychs; but he was later accepted by the bishops of Thrace as a martyr.

Feast: Feb. 28.

Bibliography: *Acta Sanctorum* Feb. 3:735–742. A. FLICHE and V. MARTIN, eds., *Histoire de l'église depuis les origines jusqu'à nos jours* (Paris 1935–) 4:279–282. J. MASPÉRO, *Histoire des patriarches d'Alexandrie* (Paris 1923) 44–45. A. GRILLMEIER and H. BACHT, *Das Konzil von Chalkedon: Geschichte und Gegenwart,* 3 v. (Würzburg 1951–54) 2:22–35, 255–257. L. DUCHESNE, *Early History of the Christian Church,* 3 v. (London 1909–24) 3:329–332, Eng. tr. from 4th Fr. ed.

[F. CHIOVARO]

PROTMANN, REGINA, BL.

Foundress of the Sisters of Saint Catherine (*Katharinenschwestern*); named sometimes spelled Prothmann; b. *c.* 1552, Braunsberg, Warmia (Ermland; now Braniewo, Poland); d. there Jan. 18, 1613.

Regina, daughter of the merchants Peter Protmann and Regina Tingels, left her family in 1571 to serve God with two other young women, who were soon joined by others. They lived as Beguines in an inherited house and tended the sick daily in their homes. In 1583, Protmann wrote the group's ascetic rule and placed the fledgling congregation under the patronage of Saint Catherine of Alexandria. On Mar. 3, 1583 their ministry received the approbation of Bishop Martin Kromer (*c.* 1512–89) and spiritual direction from the Jesuits.

Initially the Sisters of St. Catherine cared for plague victims in modern northeastern Poland. As they spread to Wormditt (1586), Heilsberg (*c.* 1586), and Rössel (*c.* 1593), their contemplative spirituality was combined with further active Apostolates, including instructing children and providing pastoral care to women. A new rule, written with the assistance of two Jesuits, was approved by the bishop and recognized by the papal nuncio (1602). Since that time the congregation has been closely associated with the Jesuits, as acknowledged in the writings of Jesuit Superior General Claudius Acquaviva.

The first *vita* (*Das Leben der gottseligen Jungfrau Regina Protmann,* 1623) of Mother Regina is presumed to have been written by her Jesuit spiritual director, Engelberg Keilert. Uncharacteristic for the period, Protmann had her spiritual daughters instructed in theology. By the time of her death, the order had 35 sisters in four convents.

Regina Protmann was declared venerable on Dec. 17, 1996. A miracle attributed to her intercession was approved on Apr. 6, 1998, leading to her beatification in Warsaw, Poland, by John Paul II on June 13, 1999.

Feast: Jan. 18.

Bibliography: E. M. WERMTER, ed., *Quellen zur Geschichte der ersten Katharinenschwestern und ihrer Gründerin Regina Protmann* (Münster 1975). G. BELLGARDT, *Die Bedeutung der Kongregation der hl. Katharina für die Erziehung der Mädchen* (Berlin 1931). A. BOENIGK, *Regina Protmann und die Kongregation der Schwestern von der hl. Katharina* (Braunsberg 1933). H. HÜMMELER, *Regina Prothmann, und die Schwestern von dr. hl. Katharina* (Siegburg 1955). J. GRUNENBERG, *Die Congregation der hl. Jungfrau und Märtyrin Katharina. Ihr Entstehen, ihr inneres Leben und Wirken, wie es durch den Wandel der Stifterin und durch die Satzungen der Ordenregel vorgezeichnet ist* (Braunsberg 1868; reprinted Berlin-Wilmersdorf 1961). C. FELDMANN, *Neuer Geist sucht neue Formen* (Freiburg 1999). M. TREU, *Die katholische Kirche ehrt eine Braunsberger Bürgertochter: Regina Protmann seliggesprochen* (Münster 1999).

[K. I. RABENSTEIN]

PROTO-EVANGELIUM

The term Proto-evangelium, meaning "the first gospel or good news," is traditionally applied to Gn 3.15 where God curses the serpent who had just enticed the first woman to break His commandment. It reads:

> I will put enmity between you and the woman, between your seed and her seed; He shall crush your head, and you shall lie in wait for his heel.

Christian tradition has seen in this passage the first announcement of the salvation to come. However, there is much disagreement among modern exegetes about its exact interpretation. Five problems are involved in the dispute: the Vulgate translation, the identity and significance of the serpent, the identity of the woman and her descendants, the meaning of the key word *šûp,* and the use of this verse in Christian tradition.

Vulgate Translation. The translation of Gn 3.15 has been a source of difficulty in the past. The pronoun ''he'' in the CCD construes the Hebrew pronoun *hû'* which refers to ''her seed'' and could be translated as ''it'' (*ipsum*), or, since it relates back to a collective noun, as ''they.'' In the LXX, because of a more specific development of messianic ideas, *hû'* was translated by the masculine pronoun αὐτός, although the antecedent Greek noun is neuter. This may be an intended reference to the Messiah who would ''grasp'' the head of the serpent. Finally, in the Vulgate as it is now, *hû'* is translated by *ipsa,* ''she,'' although the Old Latin versions have *ipse,* ''he'' (very likely the original Vulgate reading too). Whether by scribal error or intent, the *ipsa,* referring to the woman, later called Eve (Gn 3.20), has greatly influenced the Latin tradition concerning this passage. It agrees with no other version and is certainly wrong. Latin theologians, however, have constantly evoked from this mistranslation the picture of Mary Immaculate crushing the head of the serpent in her role as the new Eve.

The Serpent. The serpent (*nāḥāš*) is clearly described as an enemy of God and man, an evil personal force who entices the woman to break the single covenant law of PARADISE. He is later identified as the DEVIL or the adversary or SATAN in Wis 2.24 (see also Jn 8.4; Rv 12.9; 20.2; Jb 1.6) and in the whole of Christian tradition. The reason for using this image for God's archenemy is found in the complex serpent symbolism of the ancient Near East. The primary symbolism comes from the Canaanite fertility cults, which have left to us many representations of fertility goddesses with serpents in their hands or entwined around their bodies. Serpents were also thought to have magical qualities and were often deified by Israel's neighbors. Because of his enticement, the serpent is cursed by God and condemned to a continual battle with the descendants of the woman. Thus, the Canaanite cults of nature worship, fertility rites, and magic, which were a constant temptation to Israel, are condemned by the sacred author.

The Woman. Most independent authors reject any allusion to Mary in our text. Catholic scholars, however, are generally of the opinion that, behind the literal sense, some Mariological meaning is to be found in either a typical or fuller sense. (*See* HERMENEUTICS, BIBLICAL)

From the context it is clear that the woman is the one who has just committed the first sin. She is the first man's *'iššâ,* woman or wife (Gn 2.23). Obviously, therefore, the image of Mary has been found in our text only because of some hidden signification not patent there.

Although the LXX has taken the seed of the woman as a male individual, the Hebrew word is collective and refers to all mankind, the woman's offspring. The enmity, therefore, will be between the serpent and the woman and between their races. Both groups will be injured, but not equally.

The Key Word. In Gn 3.15b of the CCD the verbs ''crush'' and ''lie in wait'' are traditional translations from the Vulgate of the same word *šûp,* the meaning of which is obscure in the three places it occurs in the MT—here, Jb 9.17; Ps 138(139).11. It would seem preferable to use an identical verb in both clauses as does the LXX and many modern versions, such as, ''grasp,'' ''bruise,'' or ''strike.'' Nevertheless, because of the relative position of the ''attackers,'' one striking at the head, the other at the heel, we are left to infer that the woman's seed will be victorious. This inference is strengthened by the fact that the verse is found in the malediction of the serpent. If man were not victorious, would not the serpent's punishment be incomplete? And so many have seen here a promise that man will triumph over the serpent's evil power.

Christian Tradition. In the New Testament, Jesus Christ, ''born of a woman'' (Gal 4.4), is proclaimed as the definitive victor over ''the prince of the world'' by His Passion, Death, and Resurrection (Jn 12.31; 16.11; 1 Jn 3.8). St. Paul describes an antithetical relationship between Adam and Christ (Rom. 5.12–19) which later suggested a similar antithesis between Eve and Mary. Many Fathers of the Church contrasted Eve, who brought sin and death into the world, with Mary who gave birth to the victor over sin and, thus, became the mother of all those alive in Christ. These Fathers did not use Gn 3.15 to support their thesis because they saw no reference to Mary there. It was only after the sixth century, because of the erroneous Vulgate reading, that Latin writers made frequent use of the Proto-evangelium to express Mary's victory over evil and the devil.

Some theologians argue that, since Gn 3.15 has been used in a Mariological sense in the encyclicals *Ineffabilis Deus* of Pius IX and *Munificentissimus Deus* and *Fulgens corona* of Pius XII, the literal sense must apply to Mary. However, these documents refer to the traditional Latin interpretation of Gn 3.15 as a witness of the common belief that Mary conquered all sin in her Immaculate Conception. They do not intend to settle all questions concerning the literal meaning of the text.

As Biblical studies advance, the question of the Proto-evangelium will receive new clarification and will, no doubt, be extended to other texts of the third chapter of Genesis that reveal God's loving concern for His creatures even after they had sinned.

Bibliography: J. COPPENS, ''Le Protoévangile,'' *Ephemerides theologicae Lovanienses* 26 (1950) 5–36. B. RIGAUX, ''La Femme et son lignage dans Genèse III, 14–15,'' *Revue biblique* 61 (1954) 321–348. G. LAMBERT, ''Le Drame du jardin d'Eden,'' *Nouvelle revue théologique* 76 (1954) 917–948, 1044–72. *Encyclopedic Dictionary of the Bible*, tr. and adap. by L. HARTMAN (New York 1963) 1945–48. X. M. LE BACHELET, *Dictionnaire de théologie catholique*, ed. A. VACANT et al., (Paris 1903—50) 7.1: 849–861. P. F. CEUPPENS, *De Mariologia Biblica* (Rome 1951).

[D. A. PANELLA]

PROTUS AND HYACINTH, SS.

Third-century martyrs mentioned in the *Depositio martyrum* (*c.* 350) as buried in the cemetery of Bassilla on the Via Salaria. The grave of Protus and Hyacinth was identified in 1845 in a double crypt; the *loculus* was intact with the epitaph of Hyacinth still in place; but the remains of the martyrs were carbonized. The tomb had been obstructed by a 4th-century landslide and had been repaired by Pope DAMASUS I. In the late and legendary *Passio S. Eugeniae* (*Bibliotheca hagiographica latina antiquae et mediae aetatis*, 2 v. [Brussels 1898–1901; suppl. 1911] 2666) they are described as brothers, who as eunuchs served the noblewoman St. Eugenia, accompanied her to Alexandria, and were given to the virgin (St.) Bassilla, whom they converted to Christianity. During the persecution of VALERIAN (257) they were arrested after a popular uprising and taken to a temple to offer sacrifice. When their prayer reduced the statue of the god to dust, the prefect Nicetius had them executed.

Feast: September 11.

Bibliography: H. DELEHAYE, *Étude sur le légendier remain* (Brussels 1936) 171–186. A. FERRUA, ed., *Epigrammata Damasiana* (Vatican City 1942) 190–194.

[E. HOADE]

PROVENCHER, JOSEPH NORBERT

First bishop of Saint Boniface and founder of the Catholic hierarchy of the Canadian West; b. Baye-du-Febvre, Quebec, Canada, Feb. 12, 1787; d. Saint Boniface, Canada, June 7, 1853. He was the son of Jean Baptiste and Elizabeth (Proulx) Provencher. After attending the local seminary, he was ordained Dec. 21, 1811. In 1818 he went to Red River and lived temporarily at Fort Douglas of the Selkirk colony while awaiting the building of small lodgings that were to serve as a rectory and church. A year later he began the construction of a separate church, which was completed in 1825. He was named bishop, with the title of Juliopolis, and vicar apostolic of the Northwest in 1820, and was consecrated May 30, 1822, by Bp. Joseph O. Plessis of Quebec, whose auxiliary for the Northwest he was. In a land where everything was yet to be done, he had to serve as missionary and bishop and concern himself with the religious, intellectual, and even material needs of a local population made up of Canadians, métis, Indians, Scotch colonists, Meuron soldiers, and others. The school he established, where Latin was taught to two pupils, was the foundation of what later became the College of Saint Boniface. He also established a school of household arts directed by two young ladies. In 1833 he began building a stone cathedral, which was completed in 1839 and destroyed by fire Dec. 14, 1860. To help minister to his people, including the native people spread out over his vast territory—Cree, Saulteaux, Chippewayans, and others—he secured the services of Rev. G. A. Belcourt (1831), Rev. J. B. Thibault (1833), four Grey Nuns (of Charity) of Mére D'Youville (1844), and the Oblates of Mary Immaculate (1845). Under his direction missions were established slowly, and the Native American groups were visited in the North, along the Mackenzie River, in the West and Southwest, as far as the Pacific, and along the lower Co-

Joseph Norbert Provencher.

lumbia. There two bishoprics were established through his efforts, one at Vancouver, the other in the American territory then called Oregon. At his request A. A. TACHE, OMI, was appointed coadjutor in 1851. Provencher's remains lie in the crypt of the cathedral of Saint Boniface.

Bibliography: Archives de l'Archevêché de Saint-Boniface. J. N. PROVENCHER, *Lettres in Bulletin de la Société historique de St. Boniface* 3 (St. Boniface, Manitoba 1913). G. DUGAS, *Mgr. Provencher et les missions de la Rivière-Rouge* (Montreal 1889). A. G. MORICE, *History of the Catholic Church in Western Canada . . . from Lake Superior to the Pacific,* 1659–1895, 2 v. (Toronto 1910); *Dictionnaire historique des Canadiens et des Métis français de l'Ouest* (Quebec 1908). D. FRÉMONT, *Mgr. Provencher et son temps* (Winnipeg 1935).

[A. CHAMPAGNE]

PROVERBS, BOOK OF

The Hebrew title of the Book of Proverbs is *mišlê šᵉlōmōh*. The Greek renders the Hebrew title as Προιμίαι Σο(α) λομῶντος. The title in the Vulgate is Proverbia Salomonis, whence comes the English title, Proverbs of Solomon, or Proverbs. Neither the term parable nor proverb does justice to the Hebrew term *māšāl* (plural, *mišlê*), which has a more comprehensive signification. *Māšāl* denotes a relatively brief saying, universal in scope, but quite specific as to the object described and its application. Such wisdom sayings are usually cast in one of the molds that has come to be called parallelism (*see* HEBREW POETRY). Satire, hyperbole, irony, and wit are often present. As for the subject matter of such a ''proverb,'' few areas of human activity or interest seem excluded. For information concerning the nature and rise of wisdom literature in the ancient Near East and in Israel, *see* WISDOM (IN THE BIBLE).

This article treats the relation of Solomon to the book and gives an analysis of each of the nine collections of proverbs.

Solomonic Authorship. In Israel, as in her neighboring lands, the literary genre of ''proverbs'' or ''wisdom sayings'' is very old. And, in Israel, as in the other ancient Near Eastern lands, the life-setting of the proverbs was the royal court (see 1 Kings 4.29–34; 10.1–9). The titles of the collections referring to SOLOMON, King Lamuel, and Agur reflect this courtly background and indicate that the compiler is publishing the sayings as a collection of royal wisdom.

The book is called Proverbs of Solomon because it contains collections of wise sayings which were anciently attributed to Solomon. Collections II (10.1–22.16) and V (25.1–29.27) are the most ancient in the book and are ascribed to Solomon. In view of the many references made in the Bible to Solomon's wisdom, and in view of all that is known of the influence of Egyptian institutions on Israel's court life (*see* EGYPT, ANCIENT, 3), it cannot be doubted that Solomon and the learned men around him promoted the wisdom movement in Israel; but it is impossible to determine their precise contributions. The tradition that is represented in these collections goes back at least to the time of Solomon, who may have composed or collected the original nucleus. Collection I (1.1–9.18) is also attributed to Solomon in 1.1, but this collection is generally considered to be postexilic, even though its phraseology depends on earlier biblical books.

The book as a whole represents the final stage of a long tradition which was put in final form in postexilic time. It was completed, however, before the end of the Persian period, for Hellenistic influence cannot be proved with certainty anywhere in the book.

Nine Collections. A step-by-step analysis of the nine constituent parts of the Book of Proverbs will show plainly its anthological nature.

Collection I (1.1–9.18). This collection forms the introduction to the whole book. A few pivotal ideas are developed at length in prose-like fashion, not in the brief, pithy manner of the classical proverb with its parallel stichs. After the title, the author states his purpose: to teach wisdom. Then, in verse 7, he defines true knowledge in almost dogmatic fashion: ''The fear of the Lord is the beginning of knowledge.'' Some of the external forms of traditional wisdom literature are prominent, e.g., the affectionate ''Hear, my son'' (1.8); ''My son'' (1.10, 15; 2.1; 3.1); ''Hear, O children'' (4.1); and every effort is made to arouse the interest of the reader. A subtle substructure underlies this first section, alluded to in 9.1: ''Wisdom has built her house, she has set up her seven columns.'' These ''seven columns'' are to be found in the arrangement of chapters 2 to 7 into seven units of 22 verses each [see P. W. Skehan, ''The Seven Columns of Wisdom's House in Proverbs 1–9,'' and ''A Single Editor for the Whole Book of Proverbs,'' *The Catholic Biblical Quarterly* 9 (1947) 190–98; 10 (1948) 115–30.]

Collection II (10.1–22.16). These 375 Solomonic proverbs, the core of the book, are cast mostly in antithetic parallelism as far as ch. 16, and thereafter, mostly in synthetic parallelism. The tone of the couplets is entirely different from the tone of the preceding part; the environment of the royal court is sensed repeatedly; a primitive shrewdness shows through. However, its earthy humanism has been subjected to the spiritual dynamism of Yahwistic religion and given a spiritual orientation, even though this may not be directly evident in many instances. That ''the fear of the Lord is the beginning of knowledge'' (1.7) casts its aura over the whole book should not be forgotten.

Collection III (22.17–24.22). A difference in style is immediately noticed in ''the sayings of the wise.'' Instead of unrelated, simple, two-lined maxims, ideas are spelled out in strophe form. The tone, as in Collection I, is direct and personal, like that of a father admonishing his son or a teacher instructing his pupil. Of special note is the author's indubitable sympathy for Egyptian wisdom, shown by the formerly vexing line, ''Have I not written for you the 'Thirty''' (22.20), preceded in the Confraternity Version by the explicit mention of Amen-em-Ope (a solid conjectural reading for the obscure Hebrew text). Since the publication, in 1923, of the *Instruction* of Amen-em-Ope, a collection of maxims in 30 chapters or ''houses,'' as he called them (J. B. Pritchard, *Ancient Near Eastern Texts Relating to the Old Testament,* 421–24), a comparison of the judgments in this part of Proverbs with the statements of that Egyptian sage are to be found in most commentaries. The parallels, at times annoyingly close, are always intriguing.

Collection IV (24.23–34). The caption in verse 23, ''These also are the sayings of the wise,'' sets these 12 verses apart as a separate collection. The influence of Amen-em-Ope is no longer present, but the general style is the same as that of the preceding section. Notable in particular is the advanced ethical thinking of verse 29, ''Say not, 'As he did to me, so will I do to him; I will repay the man according to his deeds.'''

Collection V (25.1–29.27). This part consists of Solomonic proverbs, similar in form and content to those in the first Solomonic collection. The editor's note preceding the first proverb contains an authentic message: there is no reason to deny that scribes at the court of Hezechiah compiled an anthology of contemporary wisdom sayings. However, since wisdom was a common possession, later sages, including the final editor of Proverbs, felt free to modify the arrangement, the slant, and the contents. There is no way of reconstructing the Hezechian original apart from the application of specifics touching the theological, cultural and linguistic variations proper to the kingdom and the postexilic era.

Collection VI (30.1–14). This section is entitled ''The words of Agur, son of Yakeh, the Massaite.'' Whether the reflections of this unknown individual terminate with verse 6 or continue on to verse 14 is debated. The style, exclusive of that of verse 10, can hardly be called typically proverbial. Agur's short message is most concerned with a frequent theme in wisdom literature: the inaccessibility of wisdom for man.

Collection VII (30.15–33). The position of this collection of numerical proverbs in the Septuagint (after 24.34) as well as the mode of employing digits in it, sets it apart as an independent collection. The numerical style follows this pattern: a number is given (for instance, 3) in the first member; then in the second member the next higher number (here, 4) is given; and in the following members the same number of persons, things, or situations as the number given in the second member are enumerated. The purpose of this procedure is not to affirm the value of the number but to fix attention on the completeness of the enumeration. It would be best not to seek moral lessons in these numerical proverbs, at least not in their original form. Observations on nature and the habits of animals occasion sentiments of wonder, astonishment, incomprehensibility. The collection gives evidence of antiquity; it is cited as an exemplification of 1 Kgs 4.33, ''And he [Solomon] treated about trees from the cedar that is in Lebanon, unto the hyssop that cometh out of the wall; and he discoursed on beasts, and of fowls, and of creeping things, and of fishes.''

Collection VIII (31.1–9). The instruction given Lamuel by his mother comprises the collection; it warns against dissipation and exhorts to care for the poor. As is suggested in 31.1, this brief unit with its somewhat unusual message and numerous Aramaisms may well have had its origin in the Ismaelite tribe of Massa in northern Arabia (see Gn 25.14). The incorporation of a passage authored by a woman, especially a non-Israelite, into Israel's sacred writings is a rarity.

Collection IX (31.10–31). The concern of this part is the ideal wife. Harsh statements made about women throughout the book are counterbalanced by a concluding unit—an alphabetic poem of 22 verses, each of which begins with a successive letter of the Hebrew alphabet. Apart from 31.30b, which could possibly be a later scribal modification, the virtues attributed to the ideal wife are wholly in the natural order: she seemingly has no other purpose than laboring for husband and household. However, these passages may be a final example of how secular compositions were taken over by the wisdom editors and spiritualized by being immersed in the wisdom context, which oriented all human endeavor toward God. Verse 30b, then, would be an authentic expression of the sacred author's mind and purpose.

In the Septuagint the collections are found in the following order: 1, 2, 3, 6, 4, 7, 8, 5, 9. The secondary collections are enclosed between the two great Solomonic syntheses, while wisdom personfied as a woman begins the compilation, and wisdom exemplified in the ideal housewife ends it.

Bibliography: A. COHEN, *Proverbs: Hebrew Text and English Translation with an Introduction and Commentary* (New York 1945). V. HAMP, *Das Buch der Sprüche* (*Echter Bibel* 8; Würzburg 1949). H. DUESBERG, *Les Scribes inspirés,* 2 v. (Bruges 1938–39) v.1, *Les Livres des Proverbes.* P. F. ELLIS, *The Men and the Message of the Old Testament* (Collegeville, Minn. 1963). *The Book of Prov-*

erbs, comm. J. T. FORESTELL (*Paulist Pamphlet Bible Series* 37; New York 1960). R. E. MURPHY, *Seven Books of Wisdom* (Milwaukee 1960). J. M. MCGLINCHEY, *The Teaching of Amen-em-ope and the Book of Proverbs* (Washington 1939). M. J. DAHOOD, *Proverbs and Northwest Semitic Philology* (Rome 1963).

[W. G. HEIDT]

PROVIDENCE OF GOD (IN THE BIBLE)

In the Bible God's providence, that is, his loving care of men, is a well-known theme. Although Hebrew has no technical term to express it, *p^equddâ,* meaning care or charge, is used in Jb 10.12 of God's providence. The Greek word πρόνοια, literally "forethought," often expresses the idea of divine providence (Wis 14.3; 17.2).

In the Old Testament. For the inspired authors the concept of God's providence embraces the creation, government, and care of all things in the created order and their subjection to His will [Gn 8.21–22; Jer 5.22–24; Psalm 103(104); 148.6]. Perhaps its most beautiful expression is in Job ch. 38 to 43 and Psalm 138(139). The idea is closely related to that of God's activity in the world expressed by the Hebrew word *bārā'* (to create: Ex 34.10; Nm 16.30; Is 43.1, 15; 45.7; 48.7), considered as continuous creation through preservation and governance of all that is created. Not only does God's providence embrace all things in the lower orders of nature, but with special significance does it encompass man [Ps 103(104).29–30; Is 42.5; Jb 10.8–11]. Closely related is God's election of certain men for special roles and functions (Gn 12.1–3; 18.19; Ex 3.1–4; Nm 17.20; Am 7.15; Is 6.8; Jer 1.5–10; Ex 2.2–8).

God's providence especially is evident in the election of Israel, chosen by Him from all the peoples of the world for unique relationship in the covenant of Sinai [Ex 19.4–6; Psalm 89(90); 94(95).6; Is 43.1, 15], delivered by Him from servitude (Ex 12.31–36), guided by divinely selected leaders in the desert of Sinai (Ex 14.10–31), nourished by Him there (Ex 16.1–35), and brought at last into the land promised to its fathers (Jos 3.10). Israel is eminently the beneficiary of divine solicitude, witnessing in its own history God's providential care. Throughout the OT, God's acts on behalf of His people are constantly extolled as proofs of His providence [Ps 77(78); 104(105); 105(106); Jos ch. 24; Jgs ch. 5]. It is evident in the elevation of the Prophets to speak His word. God's care of Israel is the great argument pointing to the unique malice of its infidelity to His will [Ps 105(106); Dt 7.6–9; Ez 16.59–63].

Gradually there emerges, especially in the writings of Amos, the idea that God's providence embraces not only Israel, but all the nations of the world directed by Him to carry out His plans even against their will (Am ch. 1–2; Is 7.17–19; 10.5–14; Jer 25.9–14). All is ordered to the establishment of the kingdom of Yahweh (Is 2.2–5; 10.12; 18.7). The whole tradition of the DEUTERONOMISTS sets the history of Israel in the light of divine providence. Historical events are God's acts in reward or punishment of Israel in accordance with its observance or violation of the conditions of the covenant (Jgs 2.11–22; 3.7–12; 4.14; 10.6–9).

The problem of evil in relation to divine providence is treated in several ways in the OT. To the Semitic mind, God is the cause of all things; there is no direct recognition of the interplay of secondary causes (Gn 16.2; Is 45.7; Am 3.6). The physical evil of suffering and misfortune is seen as a means of discipline, conversion, and purification (Jb 33.15–30; Wis 3.5; 11.9–11; 12.13–27; 2 Mc 6.16; 7.18, 32–36). The Israelites await a future solution of physical evil in the Day of the Lord when the Messianic restoration will bring an end to Israel's trials (Jl ch. 3–4). The inspired writers of the later books of the OT see retribution for suffering in the resurrection from the dead in the messianic kingdom (Dn 12.2–3) and the reward in the hereafter as recompense for suffering on earth (2 Mc 7.9, 13, 23, 26; Wis 3.1–9; 5.15–16).

Moral evil, always regarded as incompatible with God's holiness, has its cause in the free will of man, which is emphatically affirmed and always presupposed in the OT (Dt 11.26–28; 30.15–20; Jer 31.8; Sir 15.11–20). God's dominion over man's will is equally affirmed and always presupposed [Jer 18.6; Prv 21.1; Ps 32(33).15; Zec 12.1]. True to Semitic mentality, no effort is made to reconcile these seemingly variant truths. God's activity is the cause of all, and yet that activity is not seen as taking away man's freedom and responsibility for his own acts. There is complete omission of reference to any secondary cause; God is said even "to harden men's heart" in punishment for sin (Ex 4.21; 7.3; 10.1; Dt 2.30; Jos 11.20; Jgs 9.23; 2 Sm 17.14; Is 29.10; 63.17). Even of actions in which the human will cooperates, the Semitic mind attributes the whole effect to God and makes no distinction between what He directly causes and what He merely permits or occasions (2 Sm 24.1). But where evil is encountered, it is always presented as serving the order of God's providence. Even in the seeming irrationality of the prosperity of the evil-doers and of the suffering of the righteous, God's providence is effective.

In the New Testament. The same perspective and thought categories as those of the OT are retained in the NT. However, God's providence in the NT is more strongly emphasized, especially in its universal and infallible aspect (Mt 5.45; Lk 6.35; Mt 6.25; 10.28; Acts

14.15–17; 17.26–28; Rom 1.19–20; 11.14–16). There is a clearer delineation of the concept in relation to the total eternal salvific plan (Rom 10.9; 1 Cor 1.21; 1 Pt 3.21). God's providence is seen as the constant manifestation and realization of His love for His creatures and His will to save them; it is stressed as the motive for complete and absolute confidence in Him (Rom 8.2–4; Gal 4.7). The meaning of suffering is set in clearer focus (Mt 10.24, 38–39; 16.24–26; Rom 5.3; 8.28; 1 Cor 1.27). All is ordered to bring man to divine adoption and ultimate glorification in Christ (Rom 8.9–22; Eph 1.3–14).

Bibliography: *Encyclopedic Dictionary of the Bible,* tr. and adap. by L. HARTMAN (New York 1963) from A. VAN DEN BORN, *Bijbels Woordenboek,* 1951–54. P. VAN IMSCHOOT, ''Le Gouvernement du monde: La Providence divine,'' *Théologie de l'Ancient Testament,* 2 v. (Tournai 1954–56) 1:107–113. A. M. DUBARLE, ''Le Gouvernement divine et l'homme,'' *Les Sages d'Israël* (Paris 1946) 177–186.

[M. R. E. MASTERMAN]

PROVIDENCE OF GOD (THEOLOGY OF)

God's providence, which pertains to His intelligence and will, is the act whereby He causes, cares for, and directs all creatures to their particular ends, in attaining which each one contributes to the final purpose of the universe—the manifestation of His external glory. (*See* GLORY OF GOD [END OF CREATION].) Other related questions arise: how is the existence of providence consistent with the presence of evil in the world and with the existence of human freedom? The definition, while precise in Catholic theology, undergoes various modifications in other cultures, depending on their understanding of God's nature and attributes and of the destiny of man.

In Greek Philosophy. For the present consideration, among the Greek philosophers Aristotle is taken as the focal point. Democritus and the atomists, Socrates, and Plato precede him; the pantheism of the Stoics and the materialism of the Epicureans follow.

The atomists denied providence, explaining the world not by intelligent purpose but by an accidental and mechanical interplay of atoms. For Socrates the principle of causality pointed to the existence of the gods; yet he was not especially concerned with monotheism. Whatever has a use must be the work of intelligence or wisdom. This is present in all things, determining them according to its good pleasure. Plato's thoughts on the subject were conditioned by contemporary mythology. He seems to have admitted a threefold providence: (1) that of the supreme god, whose main concern is for spiritual beings and then for universal categories, such as classes, species, causes; (2) that of lesser gods, who move the heavenly bodies and take care of individual things; and (3) that of the demons, who are midway between man and the gods and who look after human affairs.

Aristotle held to one god, whose life is contemplative thought—with which the exercise of providence over individual things would be incompatible. Ordinarily his care extends to species only. He is interested in particular things only insofar as they share in this common nature (cf. St. Thomas, *In 1 sent.* 39.2.2).

An interpretation of providence according to the Stoics must take into consideration their teaching on god as the soul of the universe. There are two ultimate principles, matter and force. The first is without motion and form; the second is active, inseparably joined to the former. In the universe this force is god; in man it is the soul, which is part of the deity. Epicurus, accepting the atomism of Democritus, found it unnecessary to postulate mind as a moving cause. The gods exist, but interest in human affairs would be inconsistent with their happiness. Under the influence of fear and ignorance—the basis of religion—men attribute natural happenings to providence.

In Jewish Thought. The term ''providence'' (πρόνοια) is used in Jewish literature for the first time in the Septuagint. The idea, however, is biblical. Among these people the notion of the Divinity was more exalted than that held in pagan circles. Likewise, under successive revelations their knowledge of the future life, of human responsibility, and of the problem of evil became more explicit. God is the omniscient author of the universe and cares for all creatures. Everything happens according to His plan. A distinction is not always made between His absolute and permissive will; at times there is a tendency to consider the effects of secondary causes as His direct action.

Among the Hellenistic Jews Philo showed a somewhat different development. He firmly held to divine providence; he wrote a book on the subject. Yet he followed the Platonic notion that God can have no direct contact with finite beings. His explanation of the production of the world through the Logoi, as the intermediaries of the divine action, is a mixture of Plato's teaching on preexisting ideas, of the Stoic idea of world-soul, of the biblical account of the angels, and of the Greek concept of the demons in their mythology.

The traditional Jewish teaching on providence was also affected by later considerations on man's free will. In Josephus's account (*Antiquities* 18.1.4) the Sadducees, to safeguard human freedom, denied divine influence. In general, at the time of Christ, it was held that God acted on external events, particularly those of a national or worldwide character. Two opinions were prevalent about His operation in man's inner life: He either gave virtue or persuaded man to exercise it.

Patristic Period. With the more complete revelation of man's final destiny, the notion of providence undergoes greater precision. Thus Redemption by Christ, action under grace (sanctifying and actual), predestination to eternal life, and final reprobation are within its scope. (*See* PROVIDENCE OF GOD [IN THE BIBLE].)

Augustine's teaching is representative of early ecclesiastical writers. All things are caused by divine OMNIPOTENCE. If at any time this power were withdrawn, everything would cease existing (*Gen. ad litt.* 4.12.22; *Patrologia Latina,* ed. J. P. Migne, 271 v., indexes 4 v. [Paris 1878–90] 34:304). This care extends to the whole world and to its smallest part (*Conf.* 3.11.19; *Patrologia Latina* 32: 692). No one is released from sin except by the grace of the Redeemer (*Pecc. orig.* 29.34; *Patrologia Latina* 44:402). In his actions man is free (*Serm.* 125.5; *Patrologia Latina* 38:692–693). To react against the evils in this world by denying God's existence, or providence, or justice is great impiety (*In Psalm.* 31.25; *Patrologia Latina* 36:273). These evils, if borne properly, are useful in proving one's love for the Creator, in making satisfaction for faults, in leading one to desire and strive more fully for heaven, where true happiness exists. (*Trin.* 13.16.20; *Patrologia Latina* 42:1030). Future good things have been prepared for the just that the unjust will not enjoy; and evil things for the wicked with which the virtuous will not be tortured (*Civ.* 1.8.1; *Patrologia Latina* 41.20).

In early Christianity, however, there were false views on divine providence, as, for example, those given by GNOSTICISM and MANICHAEISM. The first, introduced by Marcion in the middle of the 2d century, made a distinction between the father-god, the supreme cause of all being, and the creator and law-giver of the OT, who held a subordinate rank. In the 3d century Manes, a Persian convert, taught the concept of two eternal principles, one good, the other bad. From this latter comes all evil, physical and moral.

Boethius greatly influenced later Christian thought. He gives the classical definition: providence is the divine intelligence that is above all things and directs them (*De consol. phil.* 4 prosa 6; *Patrologia Latina* 63:814). God is responsible for the production, change, and motion of everything. Some interrelated philosophical and theological problems are also discussed: fate, chance, divine knowledge and predestination, and freedom of will.

St. Thomas Aquinas. The teaching of St. Thomas, together with the pronouncements of the magisterium, gives a very detailed picture of providence. Thomas considers this the principal part of the virtue of prudence, whose object is the proper ordering of things toward their end, or purpose (*Summa theologiae* 2a2ae, 49.6 and ad 1). Divine providence is twofold, insofar as it is conceived as directing things to a natural end or intellectual creatures to one that is SUPERNATURAL.

Existence of Providence. Several proofs can be given for the existence of this natural providence. One proceeds from God to creatures. He is the first and universal cause. Since His divine simplicity excludes any composition, His intelligence and will are identified with this causality, and thus He knows and wills all things (*Summa theologiae* 1a, 45.5; 19.4).

Another is based on an analogy between the activities of the creature and the Creator. If a person enters a well-arranged house, he can safely assume a reasonable cause behind the order. In the world, in the great majority of cases, there is a pattern whereby things turn out for the better. This regularity cannot be explained except in terms of the overall directing providence of the author of the universe, God (*Summa theologiae* 1a, 103.1).

The same argument is presented with a slight variation. All good must be attributed to God. This would include not only the mere existence of individual beings but also the order found in and between them, e.g., the regular succession of seasons or the benefits of living in a well-organized society. These things, clearly recognizable as good, are the work of divine providence (*Summa theologiae* 1a, 22.1).

Providence Described. While the analogical argument is based on similarities between the things compared, it still recognizes their differences. So divine providence is quite unlike its human counterpart. It is infinite and eternal, not limited and temporal. It exists in God's intelligence and presupposes His will, yet it is not multiple or successive, but one simple act identified with His essence (*Summa theologiae* 1a, 21.1 ad 3). Man can direct himself and others toward a goal. God, the last end of all things, is incapable of any determination to something outside Himself; His providence extends not to Himself but only to creatures (*Summa theologiae* 1a, 22.1).

God, the first cause of all things, disposes them to the end that He intends (*Summa theologiae* 1a, 22.2). Everything is eternally in Him, and in this way He immediately cares for them. This is the meaning of providence in the strict sense. The execution of His plan, however, takes place in time and is called governance (*Summa theologiae* 1a, 22.1 ad 2). For it He usually employs instruments, and thus His watchfulness is also mediate.

Such use does not imply any defect in Him. It is rather a sign of His infinite goodness, whereby others are allowed to share in His causality (*Summa theologiae* 1a, 22.3).

Creatures either possess or lack intelligence. The former are free, capable of self-determination. The others are without freedom. They tend toward an end that is either apprehended by the senses (as the actions of brute animals indicate) or completely unknown (as in the case of plants and minerals). This diversity in beings is the work of providence and contributes to the perfection of the universe (*Summa theologiae* 1a, 22.4; 1a2ae, 1.2).

In addition to existing on the natural level, man is also destined by divine providence to a supernatural last end, God as He is in Himself. Human reason alone cannot prove this; an appeal must be made to revelation. As Vatican Council I stated: Revelation must be said to be absolutely necessary, "because God out of His infinite goodness ordered man to a supernatural end, namely to share in the divine goods, which completely surpass the understanding of the human mind" (H. Denzinger, *Enchiridion symbolorum,* ed. A. Schönmetzer [32d ed. Freiburg 1963] 3005).

Such a direction of man, or predestination, falls under divine providence; yet differences are to be noted. These are to be considered only from the part of the creature affected and from the end toward which he is directed. In God there is no distinction. Providence is the more general term. It applies to all things, rational and irrational, good and evil, and to both natural and supernatural orders. Predestination considers only the intellectual being and his principal purpose, his final union with God, something above the power of unaided nature. It touches on such things as the eternal choice for glory, sanctifying grace, actual grace, and other means in this order (*De ver.* 6.1).

Difficulties. Providence involves both God's foreknowledge and His omnipotence. Relative to these attributes some difficulties, philosophical and theological, arise. There is the riddle of good and evil. If God has care of all things, how can evil, both physical and moral, be explained? There is also the question of human freedom. If from all eternity man's actions are divinely known and willed, how can he be free?

Insofar as these problems deal only with the natural order, human reason supplies an answer without leading to complete understanding. Its knowledge of the divine essence is analogical, which by its very nature is not exhaustive. Thus God wills evil not in itself but for the good toward which it is directed. For example, a man in charge of a single thing will exclude a defect from it insofar as he can. One with more extended authority may permit some imperfection in a particular thing under his charge to ensure the general welfare. Since He cares for all things, God allows deficiencies in individual instances to bring about the good of the universe (*Summa theologiae* 1a, 19.8, 22.2 ad 2).

Likewise on the purely natural level it cannot be said that God's providence destroys man's free will. God is the first and universal cause of all things. As such He moves all things according to the nature He has given them—irrational creatures without freedom, rational beings with the possibility of choice. To be free one need not be primary cause of his actions; as a secondary cause, however, he must be capable of true self-determination (*Summa theologiae* 1a, 103.7, 83.1 ad 3).

When these same difficulties are placed in the supernatural order, however, it is impossible for human reason alone to give an answer. Here entrance is had into the realm of mystery—predestination to eternal life, the supernaturalization of the soul and its actions, the freedom of the will under the influence of actual grace, final reprobation, the sufferings of the just in this life and the good fortune of the evil. Recourse must be had to the teachings of faith.

Magisterial Teaching. In various documents the Church clearly sets forth the nature of divine providence. Its universality is declared in the profession of faith required of the Waldensians desirous of returning to unity: "we believe . . . also the Father, Son, and Holy Spirit . . . to be the creator, maker, ruler, and . . . disposer of all things" (H. Denzinger, *Enchiridion symbolorum,* 790). Vatican Council I enunciates the same truth, making mention of man's freedom: "All things that He founded God by His providence protects and governs, 'reaching from end to end mightily and governing all things well' (cf. Wis 8.1). 'For all things are naked and open to His eyes' (Heb 4.13), even those things which are future by the free action of creatures" (H. Denzinger, *Enchiridion symbolorum,* 3003).

From several local councils there are indications on predestination. Thus the Council of Quiercy (May 853) substantially follows Augustine: "The good and just God according to His foreknowledge chose from the same mass of perdition those whom through grace He predestined to life, and for them he predestined eternal life: the others, however, whom in the judgment of His justice He left in the mass of perdition, He knew would perish, but He did not predestine them to perish, although He predestined eternal punishment for them, because He is just" (H. Denzinger, *Enchiridion symbolorum,* 621). The Council of Valence (Jan. 8, 855) states: "this foreknowledge of God has not imposed necessity . . . the evil perish not because they could not be good but because they did not want to be good'' (H. Denzinger, *Enchiridion symbolorum,* 627).

Divine providence allows both moral and physical evil in the world. God permits man's sin, without being its cause; the human being is responsible for his actions. The Council of Trent decreed: ''If anyone says that it is not in man's power to make his ways evil, but that God works evil as He does good, not permissively only but properly and per se . . . let him be anathema'' (H. Denzinger, *Enchiridion symbolorum,* 1556). In his encyclical *Libert as praestantissimum,* Leo XIII touches on the question of the physical evils that afflict man. ''Although this most provident God is of infinite goodness and can do all things, yet He allows evils in the world, partly that greater goods be not impeded and partly that greater evils be prevented'' (H. Denzinger, *Enchiridion symbolorum,* 3251). A correct perspective on these evils is indicated elsewhere. Against M. Baius Pope St. Pius V stated that the afflictions undergone by the just are not always a punishment for sins (H. Denzinger, *Enchiridion symbolorum,* 1972). Clement XI, rejecting the position of Pasquier Quesnel, taught that God does allow the innocent to suffer, that these troubles are not always a punishment for or a purification from sin (H. Denzinger, *Enchiridion symbolorum,* 2470).

See Also: DESTINY, SUPERNATURAL; EVIL; FREE WILL AND PROVIDENCE; GOD, ARTICLES ON; GRACE, ARTICLES ON; MERCY OF GOD; OMNISCIENCE; SCIENTIA MEDIA; WILL OF GOD

Bibliography: H. D. SIMONIN, *Dictionnaire de théologie catholique,* ed. A. VACANT et al., 15 v. (Paris 1903–50) 13.1:941–960. A. RASCOL, *ibid.* 961–984. R. GARRIGOU-LAGRANGE, *ibid.* 985–1023; *Providence,* tr. B. ROSE (St. Louis 1944). ''Vorsehung,'' *Lexikon für Theologie und Kirche,* ed. J. HOFER and K. RAHNER, 10 v. (2d, new ed. Freiburg 1957–65) v. 10. THOMAS AQUINAS, *Providence and Predestination,* tr. R. W. MULLIGAN (Chicago 1961). ST. AUGUSTINE, *Divine Providence and the Problem of Evil,* ed. and tr. R. P. RUSSELL (New York 1942). C. F. D'ARCY, *Providence and the World Order* (London 1932). M. C. D'ARCY, *The Pain of This World and the Providence of God* (New York 1952). C. S. LEWIS, *The Problem of Pain* (New York 1944). J. M. MARLING, *The Order of Nature in the Philosophy of St. Thomas Aquinas* (Washington 1934). A. G. SERTILLANGES, *Dieu gouverne* (Paris 1942). P. SIWEK, ''God and Evil,'' *Homiletic and Pastoral Review* 58 (1957–58) 879–885, 961–970. J. HARRINGTON, ''The Concept of Chance and Divine Providence,'' *American Catholic Philosophical Association. Proceedings of the Annual Meeting* 28 (1954) 176–183. H. D. ROQUEPLO, ''Est-il possible que Dieu s'occupe de nous?'' *La Vie spirituelle* 106 (1962) 319–335. W. L. YSAAC, ''The Certitude of Providence in St. Thomas,'' *Modern Schoolman* 38 (1961) 305–321.

[E. J. CARNEY]

PROVIDENTISSIMUS DEUS

Encyclical letter of Pope LEO XIII on the study of Holy Scripture, published Nov. 18, 1893. This article discusses its background, its contents, and its effects.

Background. The rapid progress of the natural and historical sciences made the 19th century more conscious of the human aspects of the Bible. Rationalist scholars began to study it as a purely human document. In the last two decades of the century a division took place among Catholic Biblical scholars: the so-called ''liberals'' tried to distinguish between the undoubted scientific achievements and the unacceptable philosophical bias in the work of liberal Protestants, whereas the conservatives, afraid of rationalism and confusing traditionally accepted opinions on scientific and historical matters with the dogmatic tradition of the Church, opposed the new views.

Thus *Providentissimus Deus* appeared at the very beginning of the Catholic effort to harmonize newly acquired scientific and historical knowledge with the traditional teaching of the Church. It was occasioned by an article written by Msgr. d'Hulst in *Le correspondant* of Jan. 25, 1893, reporting the opinions of the ''left wing'' theologians, according to whom the Bible, though inspired in its entirety, is inerrant only in matters of faith and morals.

Contents. The encyclical sought to encourage the study of the Bible and to impart to it ''a direction suitable to the needs of the present day.'' The encyclical may be summarized as follows.

The Church has always considered the Bible an inexhaustible repository of divine truth and a source of prayer and meditation. Rationalist errors, however, were destroying the true belief in the inspired word of God in the minds of many.

In view of this danger, the following directives were given for the defense of the Bible and a fuller presentation of its doctrine.

The study of Scripture in seminaries and universities was to be given the place proportionate to its great importance. Professors must be properly prepared. The courses given should enable the student to defend the Bible, to interpret it correctly, and teach him to love it and use it ''for the advantage of religion and piety.'' The text to be used was the Latin Vulgate. Where the Vulgate is not sufficiently clear, one could turn to other ancient versions and, above all, to the original texts. While ''a wide field is still left open to the private student'' who should feel free to go beyond the achievements of the past, he must never forget that the Church is the infallible interpreter of the Bible in matters of faith and morals. A unanimous interpretation given by the Fathers is likewise free from error.

Another directive dealt with difficulties raised by rationalism. Since the Bible offered many proofs of the Church's claims, its trustworthiness as a human document must be vindicated. Its defenders must be well versed in Oriental languages and the art of criticism to be able to combat the exaggerations of rationalist higher criticism.

To refute the assertion that findings of the natural sciences contradict the Bible, the encyclical pointed out that there could be no contradiction between the theologian and the scientist, as long as each remains within his own field. The sacred writers had no intention to teach about the nature of the universe; they, like their contemporaries, spoke of things as they appear to the senses. Opinions of the Fathers in this field are not binding. "The principles here laid down will apply to cognate sciences, and especially to history." This statement became the object of much discussion and was clarified by BENEDICT XV and PIUS XII.

Having indicated various ways of defending the trustworthiness and truthfulness of the Bible, the encyclical singled out one method of solving difficulties as being incompatible with the traditional doctrine: that of limiting either the inspiration or inerrancy to the passages that deal with matters of faith and morals.Whatever the Bible contains was written by men moved by the Holy Spirit who cannot be the author of error.

Effects. *Providentissimus Deus* served as a firm guide to Catholic Biblical scholarship. It endorsed a gradual liberation from undue traditionalism; it made fruitless disputes with findings of the natural sciences unnecessary; it encouraged a judicious acceptance of contemporary scientific and historical discoveries and the desire to return to the original texts. With its definition of inspiration in terms of motion, rather than revelation and suggestion, it led toward a more adequate concept of inspiration.

Bibliography: E. MANGENOT, *Dictionnaire de théologie catholique,* ed. A. VACANT et al. (Paris 1903–50) 7.2:2177–2266. LEO XIII, "Providentissimus Deus," *Acta Sanctorum Sedis* 26 (1893–94) 269–292. English tr. *Rome and the Study of Scripture* (7th ed. rev. and enl. St. Meinrad, Ind. 1962). J. LEVIE, *The Bible, Word of God in Words of Men,* tr. S. H. TREMAN (New York 1962). J. DIDIOT, *Traité de la Sainte Écriture d'après S. S. Léon XIII* (Paris 1894). M. D'HULST, "La Question biblique," *Le Correspondant* 170 (1893) 201–251. J. BRUCKER, "La 'Question biblique,'" *Études* 58 (1893) 361–387; "L'Apologie biblique, d'après l'encyclique 'Providentissimus Deus,'" *Études* 61 (1894) 545–565; 62 (1894) 619–641. M. J. LAGRANGE, "À propos de l'encyclique Providentissimus," *Revue biblique* 4 (1895) 48–64; "L'Inspiration et les exigences de la critique," *Revue biblique* 5 (1896) 496–518. A. F. HEWIT, "The Encyclical Providentissimus Deus," *American Ecclesiastical Review* 12 (1895) 318–328, 395–404, 454–465.

[A. M. AMBROZIC]

PROVISION

In the medieval Church, "provision" generally designated one of the extraordinary roads to benefices, particularly that of "papal provision," which began to develop in the century after the GREGORIAN REFORM. Originally a benefice was a concession of land for or to a church, but by the time of Gregory VII there was emerging the concept that a benefice was actually distinct from the office (parish church, canonry, etc.) that it was designed to support. Ordinarily the *COLLATIO*, or disposal, of these benefices rested with a bishop or other patron; but with the development of new forms of education in the wake of the Gregorian reform, some educated clerics found that their qualities were better appreciated at Rome than by local patrons of churches. The oldest form of papal provision, that of Pope Innocent II in 1137, was in fact nothing more than a simple request to a bishop to provide a certain cleric with a benefice. By the time of Pope Honorius IV (1154–59), however, the request was turning into a formal mandate *de providendo,* and from the time of Alexander III (1159–81) onward there was a movement toward a stabilized system of provisions. In fact the practice was so well established by 1240 that it was almost notorious. Some of the opposition directed against it was no doubt due to vested interest (*see* NEPOTISM), but many bishops, sincere in their pastoral duties, viewed the system with misgivings, judging from the GRAVAMINA presented to the Council of LYONS in 1245 by the English Church (*see* ROBERT GROSSETESTE). If, as was claimed, the practice provided a way of curbing abuses in ordinary collation, it also afforded the papacy an opportunity of consolidating its authority. Only in 1265, however, did the papacy formulate in theory what it had achieved in the course of the preceding century: in the decretal *Licet ecclesiarum* (Aug. 27, 1265; *Corpus iuris canonici* VI° 3.4.2), Pope Clement IV set out for the first time the papal right to dispose of all ecclesiastical benefices. After additional legislation by Boniface VIII, Clement V, and John XXII, the system had grown into an efficient if not profitable business by 1350, and it was to occasion stiff opposition in several countries, notably in England (Statutes of PROVISORS of 1351, 1353, 1365, 1385). However, since a papal provision granted a right only to be considered by the ordinary collator, a relatively small number of the these provisions had final efficacy, and normal rights of collation were rarely trampled upon.

Bibliography: E. VON OTTENTHAL, *Regulae cancellariae apostolicae: Die päpstlichen Kanzleiregeln von Johannes XXII bis Nicolaus V.* (Innsbruck 1888). K. LUX, *Constitutionum apostolicarum de generali beneficiorum reservatione . . . collectio et interpretatio* (Breslau 1904). U. BERLIÈRE, ed., *Suppliques de Clément VI.* (1342–1352) (*Analecta Vaticano-Belgica* 1; Brussels 1906). G. MOLLAT, *La Collation des bénéfices ecclésiastiques sous les papes d'Avignon, 1305–1378* (Paris 1921); *Dictionnaire de droit* *canonique*, ed. R. NAZ, 7 v. (Paris 1935–65) 2:406–449. G. BARRACLOUGH, *Papal Provisions* (Oxford 1935).

[L. E. BOYLE]

PROVISORS, STATUTE OF

This statute of 1351 was directed against the practice of ''papal provisions,'' i.e., the appointment of clerics to offices in the English church by the pope. Such appointments, which began to be made on a large scale in the 13th century, were always unpopular since the papal appointees were often absentee foreigners and a petition against them was presented at the Parliament of Carlisle in 1307. Subsequently the outbreak of the Hundred Years' War at a time when a line of French popes was established at Avignon increased English resentment against alien provisors and in the 1340s there were several more parliamentary petitions on the subject. The statute eventually enacted declared that ecclesiastical electors and ecclesiastical patrons in England were to exercise freely their right to elect or to present to church offices. If the Roman Curia attempted to make any provision ''in disturbance of the free elections, collations or presentations aforementioned,'' the right of collation was to fall for that occasion to the king. Any provisor who attempted to disturb the nominee of the king or of an ecclesiastical patron was to be imprisoned until he paid a fine to be fixed at the king's discretion and undertook not to defend his claim by a suit before the Roman Curia. The statute was never systematically enforced. So far as royal rights of presentation were concerned, the development of case law by mid-14th century had provided the king with ample means of enforcing his will without recourse to the statute.

Bibliography: H. GEE and W. J. HARDY, *Documents Illustrative of English Church History* (New York 1896) 112–121, statutes of 1351 and 1390. G. BARRACLOUGH, *Papal Provisions* (Oxford 1935). F. CHEYETTE, ''Kings, Courts, Cures, and Sinecures: The Statute of Provisors and the Common Law,'' *Traditio* 19 (1963) 295–349.

[B. TIERNEY]

PROVOST, JAMES H.

Priest, Canon lawyer, and university professor. b. Washington, D.C., Oct. 16, 1939; d. Takoma Park, Maryland, Aug. 27, 2000. The third of four children born to Oscar and Mary Provost, James Provost spent most of his formative years in Missoula, Montana, where he attended local schools. After graduating from Carroll College in Helena, Montana, with degrees in philosophy and mathematics, he studied theology at the Catholic University of Leuven and was ordained to the presbyterate for the service of the Diocese of Helena in Leuven in 1963. After a short period as a parish priest, he earned his doctorate in canon law (J. C. D.) at the Pontifical Lateran University in Rome with a dissertation entitled *Interecclesial Communion in the Light of the Second Vatican Council.*''

From 1967 to 1979, Provost served as chancellor and officialis of the Diocese of Helena under Bishop Raymond Hunthausen. Active in ecumenical affairs, Provost was a founding member of the Montana Association of Churches and served on the ARC-MONT, the Anglican-Roman Catholic dialogue, from its inception. For the last few years before his death, he was a member of the Anglican-Roman Catholic Conversation (ARCIC) for the United States.

Provost was a leading member of the Canon Law Society of America (CLSA) for over thirty years, serving as its vice-president from 1976 to 1977, its president from 1977 to 1978, and its executive coordinator from 1980 to 1986. In 1979, Provost joined the faculty of canon law at the Catholic University of America. He chaired the department from 1987 to 1998 and was the managing editor of *The Jurist* from 1980 until his death. Provost was also one of the editors of the church order section of the international theological journal *Concilium* and a member of the board of the *Consociatio Internationalis Studio Iuris Canonici Promovendo*. In 1991, the CLSA awarded him its highest award, the Role of Law Award, for his contribution to the reform of church law.

Provost saw the great task of canon law in the last four decades of the twentieth century to be translating the ecclesiological vision of the Second Vatican Council, whose sessions he had observed while a student in Rome, into concrete reality. As a result, he approached canon law as an instrument not to exert control over the faithful, but to facilitate the actualization of the Church's self understanding expressed in its theology. For him, the study and teaching of canon law was not a purely academic undertaking, but ministry that was deeply pastoral. For many years, he directed the Canon Law Society's Permanent Seminar, a study group that brought together scholars from various disciplines. This seminar produced several collections of essays including *The Church as Communio, The Church as Missio, Official Ministry in a New Age*, and *Protection of Rights in the Church.* To each of these collections, Provost contributed a concluding essay which synthesized the other contributions and projected a vision of the shape of the Church in the future and the challenges, practical and intellectual, to realizing that vision. Provost also made important contributions to the two commentaries on the 1983 Code of Canon Law sponsored by the Canon Law Society of America. He wrote the sections on the rights and obligations of the Christian faithful (cc. 204–231) and the supreme authority of the Church (cc. 330–367) for *The Code of Canon Law: A Text and Commentary* (1985) and the section on ecclesiastical office (cc. 145–196) for *A New Commentary on the Code of Canon Law* (2000). Provost also published numerous studies, both scholarly and popular, on such subjects as matrimonial jurisprudence, diocesan administration, rights in the Church, and the governance of the Apostolic See when the see is impeded. Through his writings, teaching, and lecturing, Provost's influence extended well beyond the United States and shaped a whole generation of canon lawyers.

[J. P. BEAL]

PROXY (CANON LAW)

The fundamental principle of canon law regarding proxy is that one can do through others what one can do oneself. There are, of course, many exceptions to this principle, arising either from the nature of the case or from the law itself. The law expressly forbids the use of proxies in diocesan synods or eparchial assemblies (*Codex iuris canonici* c. 464; CCEO c. 239), in a profession of faith demanded by the law (*Codex iuris canonici* c. 833), and in the taking of oaths where required or permitted by the law (*Codex iuris canonici* c. 1199 § 2). Non-Catholic Christians or non-Christians can act validly as proxies in ecclesiastical matters, but not lawfully without a grave reason. Proxies are either extrajudicial or judicial. An oral authorization (mandate) is, in general, sufficient for the valid appointment of extrajudicial proxies.

Proxies for the contracting parties in matrimony in the Latin Church require for validity a special mandate for the contracting of marriage with a specific person, signed by the person giving the mandate and by the pastor or ordinary of the place or a priest designated by one of these priests, or by at least two witnesses (*Codex iuris canonici* c. 1105). If the mandate is revoked or the party giving the mandate develops *amentia* before the proxy contracts, the mandate is invalidated immediately (*Codex iuris canonici* c. 1105 § 4). A minister is generally not to assist at a marriage in which one of the parties is represented by a proxy without first obtaining the permission of a local ordinary (*Codex iuris canonici* c. 1071 § 1, 7°).

Generally speaking, one who possesses legal capacity to enter or defend a suit in person is free to appoint a proxy (attorney or procurator) to represent him in the course of the trial (*Codex iuris canonici* cc. 1481 § 1, 1482, 1483; CCEO cc. 1139 § 1, 1140, 1141). However, the law or the judge may at times demand personal appearance (*Codex iuris canonici* c. 1477; CCEO c. 1135). On the other hand, the law demands that some persons (e.g., juridic persons; minors, in certain cases), in order to stand in court at all, must act through proxies (*Codex iuris canonici* cc. 1478, 1480; CCEO cc. 1136, 1138).

For the validity of judicial appointment, the principal must give his proxy a special written and signed mandate authorizing the proxy to represent him in judicial matters (*Codex iuris canonici* c. 1484; CCEO c. 1142). Some judicial acts require a further specific authorization by the principal (*Codex iuris canonici* c. 1485, CCEO c. 1143).

A proxy may be rejected by the judge for cause or removed by the principal at any time (*Codex iuris canonici* c. 1487; CCEO c. 1145).

Bibliography: J. ABBO and J. HANNAN, *The Sacred Canons* (St. Louis 1960). S. WOYWOD, *A Practical Commentary on the Code of Canon Law,* rev. and enl. C. SMITH (New York 1963). C. CONNORS, *Extra-Judicial Procurators in the Code of Canon Law* (Catholic University of America Canon Law Studies, 192; Washington 1944). J. HOGAN, *Judicial Advocates and Procurators* (Catholic University of America Canon Law Studies, 133; Washington 1941).

[J. D. KING/J. STAAB]

PRUDENCE

The Greek φρόνησις, the Latin *prudentia* (by contraction from *providens* according to Cicero, from *porro videns* according to the *Etymologies* of St. Isidore); the English word ''prudence'' has been inflected in ethical writing by the *Klugheit* of Kant and has ceased to convey the confidence, enterprise, and generosity of what perhaps is better now called ''practical wisdom.''

Aristotle. Of the five intellectual virtues set out by Aristotle, prudence is the only one to be taken into Christian moral theology, which treats understanding, science, and wisdom as gifts of the HOLY SPIRIT, and art as outside its scope. It is a steady disposition of the practical reason to right-doing and therefore directly involves morality; accordingly it appears throughout the *Nicomachean Ethics* and enters the perennial debate whether good or bad conduct can be resolved into knowledge or ignorance or whether affective factors are more decisive. To Aristotle, who combined the statement of universal truths with a strong sense of individual reality, which, he maintained, was an interest for the rational part of man, prudence was like a bridge flung out from necessary principles to contingent occasions in human living. He originated the distinction between the theoretical and the practical reason; and though he recognized the function of appetite in ἠθική, or morals, a dialectic of love the Christian theolo-

Prudence, detail from "The Allegory of Good Government," fresco by Ambrogio Lorenzetti, the Palazzo Publico, Siena, 1338–1340. (©Archivo Iconografico, S.A./CORBIS)

gians were to explore at greater depth, he remained faithful to the teaching of Socrates and always qualified it by reason; the final step, he said, and was later echoed by St. Thomas, may be called either appetitive intelligence or intelligent appetite.

This decisive knowledge held in prudence is therefore experimental. It is elicited from the opinative, or calculative, part of the soul, not from the scientific; its regard moves from the abstract and general principles of moral theory to their embodiment in particular practice; hence prudence is to be looked for in men of affairs such as Pericles, rather than in philosophers such as Thales and Anaxagoras. It consists in putting meaning into the moral virtues that otherwise could be represented merely as laudable tendencies toward fair, brave, and temperate dealing—to name only the cardinal virtues from Aristotle's repertory. An act deserves to be called virtuous because it goes to an object, not as happening to be good, but for the reason that it good; it is not only that it is according to right reason, κατά τον ὀρθόν λόγον, by behaviorist tests, or because it manifests goodwill and honest feeling, but because by prudence it is charged with right reason, μετά τοῦ ὀρθοῦ λόγου. So prudence enters into the activity of all the moral virtues; in fact there is no question of acting prudently prudent, but of acting prudently just or courageous and so forth.

The Fathers. The moral science of the patristic writers and of the Latin Stoics whose lessons they digested was less analytic and more descriptive, and it was not until after the middle of the 13th century, when Aristotle was rediscovered, that the special character of prudence was explored and mapped in the scheme of the virtues. Yet in acknowledging its importance, the patristic writers did not soften its intellectual accent. The Scriptures, of course, offer no set of psychologico-moral treatises; yet the conduct of life according to good sense runs as a current throughout the Old Testament, notably in the Sapiential books; the New Testament, notably in the parables (for instance, of the unjust steward and of the wise virgins), enjoins men to use their wits. They are to emulate the cunning of serpents, and the contrast between worldly prudence and the folly of the cross does nothing to detract from the apostolic insistence on an intelligent appreciation of how men should conduct themselves.

Accordingly, SS. Ambrose, Jerome, Augustine, and Gregory the Great helped to form the theological tradition that prudence is the first of the cardinal virtues; and its cognitional content was reinforced by the Vulgate words *discernere, disceptatio,* and *discretio,* which represented key ideas in the monastic teaching of Cassian, St. Benedict, and St. Bernard. Discretion is the salt that preserves the virtues, and Richard of Saint-Victor said that without it they go to waste.

St. Thomas Aquinas. The specific notion of prudence, though somewhat more developed by Philip the Chancellor, working on St. John Damascene, Cicero, and Macrobius, than by Peter Lombard, was not isolated from the general characteristics of inspired common sense that St. Thomas treated as the components, or integral parts, of the virtue. He did not mention some proposed by Chrysippus, εὐλογιστία, or right reckoning; ἀγχίνοια, or ready wit; νουνέχεια, or discreetness; εὐμηχανία, or being fertile with expedients. He listed *memoria,* which profits from past experience; *intelligentia,* which grasps the point at issue; *docilitas,* or teachableness; *eustochia* and *solertia,* which swiftly find the mark for themselves; *ratio,* which comes to the conclusion of a practical decision; *providentia,* or foresight; *circumspectio,* which attends to the relevant circumstances; and *cautio,* which does not mean a cautious playing for safety (an attitude later frowned on by the Church under the name of TUTIORISM) but a wary escaping from the evil that may take on the color of good in the mixture of interests involved in any practical course. These eight headings (*Summa theologiae* 2a2ae, 49), taken from Robert Grosseteste's translation of the περί παθῶν of the Pseudo-Andronicus, together with the treatment of the vices against prudence (*ibid.* 2a2ae, 53–55), provided a clearly articulated summary of the moral theology of prudence as St. Thomas found it.

The vices fall into two classes, of the too little and the too much. The first, generally called imprudence, includes ill-advisedness, carelessness in judgment, and negligence and inconstancy in execution. The second, or false prudence, covers giving in to the wiles of the flesh, the *prudentia carnis* of the Vulgate; craftiness, *astutia,* expressed in guile and deceit; and the over-solicitude about temporal things and the morrow the Gospel tells us to avoid.

The precision of St. Thomas's treatment of prudence as a special virtue is prepared for by his two psychological studies—first, on the distinction of human powers (*Summa theologiae* 1a, 77–83, in particular 79.11–13); next, on the analysis of the partial acts integrating a complete human act (*ibid.* 1a2ae, 8–17, in particular 16–17)—and by his ethical study of intellectual and moral virtue (*loc. cit.,* 55–61, in particular 57–58). He writes as an intellectualist who holds that an act of mind is constitutive, though not completive, of happiness and of the moral activity that teleologically gets reality and meaning from that end. His detailed study of virtuous activity in the *Secunda secundae* starts from the high theological virtues whose object is nothing less than God himself. The moral virtues, which come afterward, are concerned with penultimate values in man. In addressing himself to these, he begins with prudence, which strikes the note of intelligence in action.

St. Thomas's notion of prudence is built up in four stages: (1) prudence is about means to ends, (2) which are individual, (3) about which it comes to a practical decision, (4) leading to effective execution. These should not be taken to represent more than four abstract moments that, like the virtues themselves, flow into one another in the acting singleness of a human person; nevertheless it will be convenient to consider them separately.

Concerned with Means to Ends. St. Thomas drew from Aristotle and from St. Gregory the Great for his teaching on the contemplative and active lives. Christian contemplation, which surpasses the ideal of philosophy and of natural mysticism, is of God Himself, in heaven seen face to face and on earth immediately ''intended'' by faith, hope, and charity and the accompanying gifts of the Holy Spirit, above all through the love-knowledge of Wisdom. The moral virtues are on the lower plane of the active life, and the prudential knowledge that charges them is less final in its reach and bears on more particularized objects. These are called *ea quae sunt ad finem,* or realities that are Godward; this can be translated as ''means to an end'' as long as this is not taken to mean that they are mere utilities having no value in themselves and desirable only because of an extrinsic reference to an ulterior end. They are the creaturely objects of moral virtue manifesting reason and grace. In any given situation it is the office of prudence to decide where they are to be found.

Concerned with What Is Individual. Consequently, moral activity neither begins nor ends with prudence. That the theological virtues are already engaged is presupposed (*Summa theologiae* 1a2ae, 58.4, 5; 65.2), and so also the habit of SYNDERESIS (*ibid.* 1a, 79.12) and the bent of the moral virtues each to its own proper type of good (*ibid.* 2a2ae, 47.6), together with an instructed moral science. The dialectic of prudence is to bring these premises to bear on an individual course of action in an operative syllogism, so called because it partly resembles a demonstrative syllogism: not rarely St. Thomas compares the process of making up one's mind to the discourse of reasoning. Hence prudence is said to be *collativa* and *consiliativa;* it is deliberative and not contemplative; it has to make do with evidences that are more multiple, variable, and contingent than those of scientific argument; and the conclusion it comes to cannot be wholly resolved into necessary premises.

It is true that necessary principles are established in the theoretical mind by abstraction from experience; yet a man can remain in a sort of fastness if he merely thinks about things without trying to do something about them. Prudence involves the reflection by which the mind applies itself again to the experience of individual things; and though this attachment implies the appetite for things as they are in themselves and not in the mind, prudence itself is an act of reason reaching past the general meaning to the reality beyond, past *quidditas carnis* to *ipsa caro* (*Summa theologiae* 1a, 86.1; 1a2ae, 27.2 ad 2; 2a2ae, 47.3; *In 3 anim.* 8).

Arrival at Practical Decisions. The judgment of prudence is practical; it states not what is, but what is to be done. Though the generalizations of moral science can show the necessity of good intention and define the types of good activity, they cannot legislate for individual circumstances. Moreover, the judgment issues from an interaction of mind and will in the field of morals and friendship, where appetitional factors are peculiarly untranslatable into cognitional terms; the possession of virtue sets up a sympathy that requires no rational exposition or justification (*Summa theologiae* 1a, 1.6 ad 3), and on earth God can be loved more than He is known (*ibid.* 2a2ae, 27.4). On these three counts, then—namely, because it is individual, practical, and in love—the judgment of prudence goes beyond the findings of moral philosophy and theology, though not beyond the sacra doctrina of revelation (*ibid.* 1a, 1.3–7).

Effective Execution. At this third stage the judgment is an act of conscience, which itself is not a virtue (*ibid.* 1a, 79.13). A sincere and truthful conscience is not enough to ensure virtuous conduct; one may stop there or act against its dictate. Even a conscientious person may not be a prudent person. So prudence moves from the indicative to the imperative, from the mood of stating a preference, that this and not that is to be done, to the mood of commanding, do this and not that. Moreover, in this command the forces of the will are gathered so that the deed is effectively executed. In this implanting of truth into action consists the act of prudence as a specific virtue; in the preceding stages of taking counsel and making a choice St. Thomas sees the operation of the associated virtues of *eubulia, synesis,* and *gnome,* soon to be noticed.

He treats effective command, *imperium,* in reference to both the dynamic psychology of a human act (*ibid.* 1a2ae, 17.1) and the political ordinance of law (*ibid.* 1a2ae, 90.1) as an act of mind and not of will, in which some later scholastic theologians disagreed with him: for the technicalities of the discussion, which includes the meaning of *usus,* whereby what is intended is actually carried out, the student is referred to the commentators (*ibid.* 1a2ae, 16.1; 17.3). His own formula is that the reason is *dirigens,* the will is *movens,* while another power may be *exequens;* in this context he speaks of ''application'' as the act of prudence to refer to taking the abstract universal to the concrete individual and also to bringing intention into execution.

A Moral Virtue. It is by this commitment to good doing, in which good living consists, that prudence is a moral virtue, surpassing the condition of intellectual virtue, which takes a detached view of things, and of art, which governs the making of external things. And because it is *recta ratio agibilium* putting ''good-as-meant,'' *ratio boni,* into what is done, it forms the link connecting the activities of all the moral virtues. As inclinations they may pull apart (thus, for example, friendliness and sobriety), and as defined by types of activity they are distinct from prudence; nevertheless their practice on any occasion is truly virtuous only when directed by prudence. St. Thomas here crystallizes the doctrine received from the Stoics and the Fathers, according to which each virtue represents one general condition of virtue, and all virtue is composed of them all; thus prudence and justice and courage enter into the texture of temperance (*ibid.* 1a2ae, 58.4, 5; 65.1; 2a2ae, 47.6, 7). Now he is saying more, namely, that prudence as a special virtue commands the acts of all the moral, though not the theological, virtues.

The governing role of prudence extends from the conduct of a single personal life, *prudentia monastica,* to the business of the commonwealth. It is like justice, which includes the general or legal justice safeguarding and promoting the *bonum commune.* So there is a type of prudence comprehensively called ''political,'' πολιτική, possessed by all free and responsible citizens in a regime and given the special names of *regnativa* and *legis positiva,* βασιλική and νομοθετική, in the ruling and legislating authority (*ibid.* 2a2ae; 47.10; 50.1, 2); this last, it is worth noting, repeats the prudential dialectic and does not deduce decisions like conclusions from principles but produces them like works of art freely answering to the general specifications (*ibid.* 1a2ae, 95.2). Two other types may be noticed for directing infrapolitical groups: the domestic prudence, *economica,* οἰκονομική, for running a family or household, a neighborhood or tribal community, and a business company; and the *prudentia militaris* of good generalship. Pseudo-Andronicus mentions this στρατηγική; there may have been biographical reasons why St. Thomas devoted a special article to it (*ibid.* 2a2ae, 50.4) and treated soldierliness as a prudence and not just an art.

More directly needed by everybody are the companion virtues of prudence, its potential parts: *eubulia,* εὐβουλία, good counsel; *synesis,* σύνεσις, sound judgment in the ordinary run of affairs; and *gnome,* γνώμη, which decides about exceptional cases. For Aristotle these three enter into the field of prudence, but St. Thomas was more precise about treating them as distinct and special virtues; to be well-advised is not the same as being judicious in day-to-day events or when the laws do not fit the occasion; and to be judicious does not necessarily amount to an effective precept that carries out what should be done (*ibid.* 2a2ae, 51). *Gnome* is of particular interest because of its intimate relation with equity, EPIKEIA, ἐπιείκεια, the highest part of justice (*ibid.* 2a2ae, 120.2). They check pharisaism (even the noblest), are set on the spirit rather than the letter, and expand in the freedom of the Gospel as against the constraint of positive law (*ibid.* 1a2ae, 106–108).

Gnome stands as a comment, neglected in some periods of moral theology, on the attempts of the various quasi-legal moral systems to convert a doubtful conscience into a sufficient guide for conduct and in effect to provide a reassurance against sin by a reference to a code or to glosses on it. It shows that prudence does not seek legality as such, but to be reasonable in a unique situation. It may make mistakes and has a healthy fear of the consequences; yet it is not overanxious, for its truth is measured by conformity more to fair loving than to an objective fact (*ibid.* 1a2ae; 57.5 ad 3). Not looking for a guarantee of fixed evidence that its variable matter cannot provide or for the kind of security not allowed by Providence, it is marked by a robustness and an abandon to God that philosophers are unable to teach and jurists unable to prescribe. In short, there is nothing mean, tame, or timid about prudence, nor is it tangled in regulations; like all the virtues, it gives a strength and ease and, indeed, an elegance about what is best.

This best is nothing less than living in the society of the divine Persons of the Blessed Trinity. Though St. Thomas's treatise on prudence reproduces the structure of Aristotle and the mood of the Stoics, the virtue itself is seen in the setting of Christian theology against the grandeur in the background of St. Augustine's teaching of the eternal law and lit by the revelation of God's majesty and mercy and friendship. It is a virtue infused with grace; its measure exceeds that of living merely according to reason—its measure is the mind of Christ; its purpose is not to be respectable but to be a fellow citizen of the saints and a familiar of God (*ibid.* 1a2ae, 63.4). It springs from and lives only in charity, without which one may be shrewd but cannot be prudent (*ibid.* 1a2ae, 65.2, 3; 2a2ae, 47.13, 14). Furthermore it is touched by the Spirit to act with heroism in the gift of counsel (*ibid.* 2a2ae, 52.2).

Of all qualities, mercy is the most divine (*ibid.* 1a, 21.3, 4). And St. Thomas, taking his cue from St. Augustine, who with sure instinct if at some strain of literary artifice attributes a corresponding evangelical beatitude to each gift of the Holy Spirit, perceives in counsel a practical compassion (*ibid.* 2a2ae, 52.4) for which Our Lord has given His promise: Blessed are the merciful, for they shall find mercy.

Bibliography: THOMAS AQUINAS, *La Prudence* (*Summa theologiae* 2a2ae, 47–56), ed. and tr. T. H. DEMAN (2d ed. Paris 1949). H. D. NOBLE, *Dictionnaire de théologie catholique*, ed. A. VACANT et al., 15 v. (Paris 1903–50) 13.1:1023–76. A. RAULIN, "Prudence," in *The Virtues and States of Life*, ed. A. M. HENRY, tr. R. J. OLSEN and G. T. LENNON (Theology Library 4; Chicago 1957) 209–50. A. M. HENRY et al., *Prudence chrétienne* (Paris 1948). J. PIEPER, *Prudence,* tr. R. and C. WINSTON (New York 1959). C. SPICQ, "La Vertu de prudence dans l'A. T.," *Revue biblique* 42 (1933) 187–210. A. GARDEIL, *La Vraie vie chrétienne* (Paris 1935) 99–189. O. LOTTIN, "Les Débuts de traité de la prudence au moyen-âge," *Recherches de théologie ancienne et médiévale* 4 (1932) 270–93. J. R. CONNERY, "Prudence and Morality," *Theological Studies* 13 (1952) 564–82. W. A. GERHARD, "The Intellectual Virtue of Prudence," *The Thomist* 8 (1945) 413–56.

[T. GILBY]

PRUDENTIUS

Aurelius Prudentius Clemens, the greatest Christian Latin poet and the only layman regarded as a Latin Father; b. 348, probably at Calahorra, Spain; d. after 404. All knowledge of his life is based on what he says in his works. He had a normal Roman education. He "twice ruled noble cities," made a journey to Rome for personal reasons, and in his 56th year felt a sense of compunction for the way his life had been spent.

His *Cathemerinon* consists of 12 hymns, six for daily use (cockcrow, morning, etc.) and six for special occasions (for the dead, Christmas, Epiphany, etc.). The *Peristephanon* (Crowns of Martyrs) includes poems on SS. Lawrence, Eulalia, Vincent, Cyprian, and Agnes. A long poem on St. Romanus is usually printed as *Peristephanon* 10, but does not belong to that work. Most of the *Peristephanon* poems appear to be written for singing by a Christian congregation, probably at Calahorra, at the celebration of the feast (*annua*) of martyrs. The *Cathemerinon* belong to domestic cult, being designed for use in a household of the Roman type. The poems of both collections are in lyric meters, and selections from them form hymns used in both the Roman and Mozarabic rites.

Three poems in hexameters, *Apotheosis, Hamartigenie,* and *Psychomachia* are marked as books 1, 2, and 3; but the title of the combined work is not extant. The *Apotheosis* deals with the deification of man through the actions of Christ; the *Hamartigenia* concerns the origin of sin and evil; and the *Psychomachia* is an allegorical poem in which the Soul assisted by specific Virtues rescues the Body from the attack of Vices. It concludes with a description, based on the Apocalypse, of the construction of a Temple of Holy Wisdom in the soul.

A poem in two books, *Contra Symmachum,* attacks the Roman pagan religion and is related to the controversy over the removal of the altar of Victory from the Senate in Rome. Prudentius' arguments parallel those of St. AMBROSE. Most striking in this work are his vision of the Roman world as one people (*una propago*) formed out of many by common laws and institutions and his vigorous attack on gladiatorial shows.

Prudentius saw Christianity as involving not the overthrow of Rome and its institutions but rather the fulfillment of Rome's essential civilizing function, since paganism and barbarism are frequently opposed to Christianity and civilization. Just as works of sculpture are begrimed with soot and grease through the rituals of ancient religious sacrifice but can be made pure and clean by being washed and scrubbed, revealing themselves as works of art and beauty, so also could Roman institutions, by Christianization and baptism, achieve a more adequate realization of their essential purpose and function in the design of Providence.

Prudentius had a firm command of the resources of the Latin language. His writings show a fondness for Lucretius, Vergil, and Juvenal; but he was a slavish imitator of none. His sentences vary from the short and pithy to periods of 17 lines. For extended imagery he preferred examples and figures drawn from Scripture or nature to traditional simile or metaphor.

Especially notable is his ability to project personalities and actions of Sacred History or Christian legend in vivid detail. His descriptions of the denial of Peter (*Cath.* 1); the fury of Herod and his soldiers, as well as the Holy Innocents playing with their crowns of martyrdom in heaven (*Cath.* 12); Abraham rescuing Loth (*Psych.* praef.); and Lawrence on his gridiron (*Perist.* 2) have led to charges that Prudentius was prolix and gruesome and that he offended against good taste; but his technique seems appropriate to the social context for which the poems were intended.

Prudentius soon became a Christian classic. He was quoted by GREGORY OF TOURS and many others. His works formed a staple item in the monastic schools of the ninth century and were provided with commentaries and glosses. His writings, especially the *Psychomachia,* were early provided with illustrations, which in turn inspired a rich group of illustrated manuscripts of the early and high Middle Ages.

In the post-Renaissance period a lack of sympathy with Prudentius' aims and artistic ideals led to neglect of his work.

Bibliography: *Works,* ed. J. BERGMAN (*Corpus scriptorum Christianorum ecclesiasticorum latinorum* 61; 1926); ed. M. LAVARENNE, 4 v. (Budé ser.; Paris 1943–51), with Fr. tr.; ed. and tr. H. J. THOMSON, 2 v. (Loeb Classical Library; 1949–53). E. K. RAND, ''Prudentius and Christian Humanism,'' *American Philological Association: Transactions and Proceedings* 51 (1920) 71–83. R. J. DEFERRARI and J. CAMPBELL, *A Concordance of Prudentius* (Cambridge, Mass. 1932). B. M. PEEBLES, *The Poet Prudentius* (New York 1951). C. GNILKA, *Studien zur Psychomachie des Prudentius* (Wiesbaden 1963). L. PADOVESE, *La cristologia di Aurelio Clemente Prudenzio* (Rome 1980). A. KURFESS, *Paulys Realenzyklopädie der klassischen Altertumswissenschaft,* ed. G. WISSOWA et al. (Stuttgart 1893) 23.1 (1957) 1039–72.

[M. P. CUNNINGHAM]

PRUDENTIUS OF TROYES, ST.

Theologian; b. Spain; d. Troyes, 861. He came of a refugee family, was educated at the Palatine School, and served as chaplain at the court of Louis the Pious before becoming bishop of Troyes in 843 or 846. In the predestination controversy he supported GOTTSCHALK OF ORBAIS against HINCMAR OF REIMS, defending the doctrine of double predestination in his *Epistola ad Hincmarum* (*c.* 849) and again in his treatise *De predestinatione contra Joannem Scotum,* i.e., against JOHN SCOTUS ERIGENA, whose aid Hincmar had solicited. Prudentius differed with Gottschalk, however, in limiting God's salvific will to believers in Christ. Apparently he subscribed to the anti-Augustinian propositions of the Synod of Quiercy (853), but in 856 in his *Epistola Tractoria,* addressed to Wenilo of Sens, he challenged these propositions and professed a strictly Augustinian doctrine. Prudentius wrote also a continuation of the *Annales Bertiniani* for the years 835 to 861, valuable for the history of the Frankish Empire, as well as a scriptural floritegium, a *Sermo de vita et morte gloriosae Maurer,* and some poetry. A Pontifical erroneously attributed to him (Paris B. N. ms. lat. 818) is in reality an 11th-century Missal-Ritual.

Feast: April 6.

Bibliography: A critical ed. of the continuation of the *Annales Bertiniani* by G. H. PERTS, *Monumenta Germaniae Historica: Scriptores* 1:429–454; PRUDENTIUS' complete works (except for poetry) in *Patrologia Latina* ed. J. P. MIGNE (Paris 1878–90) 115:965–1458; *Monumenta Germaniae Historica: Poetae* 2:679–680; *Monumenta Germaniae Historica: Epistolae* 5.1:323–324; 5.2:631–633. J. GIRGENSOHN, *Prudentius und die bertinianischen Annalen* (Göttingen 1872). M. MANITIUS, *Geschichte der lateinischen Literatur des Mittelalters* (Munich 1911–31) 1:344–348. A. WILMART, ''Le Vrai pontifical de Prudence de Troyes,'' *Revue Bénédictine* 34 (1922) 282–293. F. STEGMÜLLER, *Repertorium biblicum medii aevi* 4:7015–17. K. VIELHABER, *Lexicon für Theologie und Kirche*, ed. J. HOFER and K. RAHNER (Freiburg 1957–65) 8:846–847.

[A. H. TEGELS]

PRÜM, ABBEY OF

Former Benedictine Abbey of the Holy Savior, Eifel, Archdiocese of Trier, founded in 721 by Bertrada of Mürlenbach. A generation later Pepin the Short brought it under Carolingian protection, granting it immunity from the local lord. Prüm, with a market and a mint (861), had economic and political importance under the Carolingians. It was a stronghold, and Charlemagne imprisoned his son Pepin there. Norman raids in 882 and 892 caused no serious setback, and by 893 Carolingian gifts brought the abbey's holdings to 1,530 estates. Its position as an imperial abbey was strengthened in 919 by the right to choose its own *Vogt* (*advocatus*). The abbey played an important role in the Empire through the early Middle Ages, and until the 18th century its abbot had a seat in the Reichstag.

The peak of its spiritual and intellectual life occurred in the 9th century under abbots Tancred, Markward, Eigil, and ANSBALD. Its cloister school was noted in the Carolingian period, and the *Annales Prumienses* are the best history of the Empire for the 10th century. The Lotharingian reform of 1003–04 began at Prüm, and in the 11th and 12th centuries active building took place there.

In the 13th century discipline was relaxed, debts accumulated, and the abbey had quarrels with its *Vogts,* who were closely allied with the counts of Luxembourg. To maintain their freedom against this combination, the abbots turned to the prince-archbishops of Trier, but in the next three centuries Prüm and its estates became an appendage of the Electorate of Trier. There was a revival of spiritual life in the 18th century under energetic priors. A new abbey church was begun in 1721. In 1794 the abbey was besieged by revolutionary troops, and in 1802 it was one of the ecclesiastical territories secularized by Napoleon I to reimburse German princes for the lands they lost to France.

Bibliography: L. H. COTTINEAU, *Répertoire topobibliographique des abbayes et prieurés,* 2 v. (Mâcon 1935–39) 2:2371. P. SCHMITZ, *Histoire de l'Ordre de Saint-Benoit,* 7 v. (Maredsous 1942–56). J. SEMMLER, *Lexikon für Theologie und Kirche,* ed. J. HOFER and K. RAHNER, 10 v. (2d, new ed. Freiburg 1957–65) 8:848–850.

[P. P. BECKMAN]

PRÜMMER, DOMINIKUS

Dominican moral theologian and canonist; b. Kalterherberg, near Aachen, Germany, Sept. 3, 1866; d. Fribourg, Switzerland, June 9, 1931. Prümmer became a Dominican in 1884, studied philosophy and theology at the University of Louvain, and was ordained in 1890.

While continuing his studies, he also wrote and taught theology at Venlo and at Düsseldorf, where he served for three years as prior. In 1906 he went to England to teach moral theology in the Dominican house of studies at Hawkesyard near Rugeley in Staffordshire. He received his doctorate in Canon Law in 1908 at the Collegio Angelico in Rome and was then assigned to teach moral theology at the University of Fribourg. There he spent the remainder of his life. Prümmer's writings included books and articles on moral theology, Canon Law, psychopathology, and history. Among his works were the treatise *Manuale theologiae moralis secundum principia S. Thomae Aquinatis* (3 v., Freiburg im Breisgau 1914); the *Vademecum theologiae moralis in usum examinandorum et confessariorum* (an epitome of the *Manuale,* Freiburg im Breisgau 1921), and the *Manuale iuris ecclesiastici* (2v. Freiburg im Breisgau 1907–09). All these works went through several editions. Prümmer was a frequent contributor to many ecclesiastical journals and edited the *Fontes vitae S. Thomae Aquinatis notis historicis et criticis illustrati* (Toulouse 191–137). Toward the end of his life, Prümmer devoted much time to the problem of the relationship between moral theology and psychopathology, but his untimely death kept him from completing his works on this subject.

Bibliography: *Analecta Sacri Ordinis Praedicatorum* 39 (1931) 247–249.

[C. LOZIER]

PSALMS, BOOK OF

The book of Psalms, or Psalter, is unique in the Bible. It is a collection of prayers, for the most part without reference to date or specific events or persons. Thus, more than any other part of the Bible, it is timeless.

The Book

Text and Versions. The primary text used in study and translation of the book of Psalms is the traditional Hebrew version, called the Masoretic Text. Other versions that are most helpful in determining the meaning of the psalms are the Septuagint, the Greek translation made around the 2d century B.C., and the three Latin translations made by Jerome in the late 4th century A.D.: the Roman Psalter, translated from the Old Latin with an eye on the Septuagint; the Gallican Psalter, translated from the Greek with an eye on Origen's *Hexapla;* and the Hebrew Psalter, translated from the Hebrew text. The Gallican Psalter is included in the Vulgate.

The best extant copies of the Masoretic Text are from the 10th to the 11th century A.D., but the discovery of several scrolls and fragments at the Dead Sea has provided versions of Hebrew psalms from the period between the 2d century B.C. and the 1st century A.D. These scrolls have helped to explain difficult words or phrases, but they have also provided new questions. For example, a scroll from Cave 11 at Qumran has many psalms from the last half of the Psalter, but they are in a different order than the one found in the Masoretic Text or the Septuagint (*see* QUMRAN COMMUNITY.)

Structure of the Book. The most notable feature regarding the structure of the book of Psalms is its division into five books of unequal length. Each of these books is marked off by a doxology at the end (see Ps 41.14; 72.18; 89.53; 106.48; 150). These doxologies are a later addition to these psalms to give the book a fivefold structure like the Pentateuch.

The book of Psalms is a collection of collections. These collections were apparently formed before the book reached its final stage. The psalms of David (Ps 3–41; 51–72) may include some psalms written by David the king. The attribution, however, is honorary, recognizing David as the patron saint of the Psalms. Other attributions categorize the psalms by groups of singers: Asaph (Ps 50; 73–83) and the Korahites (Ps 42–49; 84–85; 87–88). There is a collection entitled Songs of Ascent, probably pilgrimage psalms (Ps 120–134), a couple of collections of Hallel Psalms (Ps 113–118; 146–150; see also Ps 104–106; 111–112), and a collection of psalms celebrating the Lord's kingship (Ps 93–99).

A further characteristic indicates different collections or origins. The psalms from 1–41 frequently use the proper name of Israel's God, Yahweh. Ps 42–89 most often use the generic term ''Elohim'' for God. A comparison of Ps 14 and 53 demonstrates the difference.

Superscriptions. More than half the psalms begin with a verse or two that gives information about the collection and the performance of the psalm. Musical notes indicate the melody (e.g., ''according to Lilies,'' Ps 45; 69; 80) and the instrumentation (''strings,'' Ps 4; 6; 54; 55; 61; 67; 67; ''flute,'' Ps 5). Liturgical notes suggest the proper day for the psalm (e.g., Ps 92 on the Sabbath) or the special event (Ps 38 for the memorial sacrifice). Some superscriptions in the David collection connect a psalm to an event (e.g., ''when David fled from Saul into the cave,'' Ps 57). These notes suggest the occasion and mood for praying a psalm.

Numbering. The numbering of the psalms has been a particular problem. The problem begins with Ps 9–10, which are two psalms in the traditional Hebrew Bible but one psalm in the Greek translation, the Septuagint. Thus from Ps 10 on, each psalm has two numbers, a higher one in the Hebrew Bible and a lower one in the Greek (and Latin) Bible. This situation continues until Ps 146–147, which are two psalms in the Septuagint but one psalm in the Hebrew Bible. There is also a minor confusion around Ps 114–116. Hebrew Ps 114 and 115 are combined in the Septuagint as Ps 113; Hebrew Ps 116 is divided in the Septuagint into Ps 114 and 115. Virtually all recent translations use the Hebrew numbering.

There is also a divergence in verse numbering. The King James Bible and those that follow its tradition (New Revised Standard Version [NRSV], Revised English Bible) do not number the superscriptions, whereas the New American Bible (NAB) follows the Hebrew verse numbering (so too the Septuagint and the Vulgate). Thus Ps 51 has 21 verses in the NAB and only 19 in the NRSV.

Canonization. The earlier consensus that the book of Psalms reached its final form around the 4th century B.C. has been challenged because of discrepancies found in scrolls at the Dead Sea. The question of when the Psalter was included in the canon of Scripture is also debated. It seems to have been included in the Hebrew Scriptures at least by the 2d century A.D., and perhaps sooner (see, for example, the references to ''the law, the prophets, and the psalms;'' Lk 24.44). Christian writers as early as the 2d century also presume that the Psalms are a part of Scripture (*see* CLEMENT OF ALEXANDRIA; IRENAEUS; JUSTIN MARTYR).

Miniature from French manuscript psalter; finest psalter specimen in United States.

Interpretation

Genre. Through the 20th century, influenced by Hermann Gunkel, the primary way of interpreting the psalms was by considering their genre. The whole gamut of human emotions is covered by the various categories of psalms. The lament (e.g., Ps 22, 51) is a cry for help in suffering and a complaint to God who allows this to happen. Most laments, however, turn toward hope. Two categories develop from this turn. The psalm of thanksgiving (e.g., Ps 18, 107) captures the moment after pain. When God delivers the sufferer, the story must be told. The storytelling itself is thanksgiving. The repeated experience of God's deliverance leads to trust, which is expressed in the psalms of confidence (e.g., Ps 23, 27). Then there are moments when the focus turns to God alone. All creation—human and otherwise—is called to join the song of praise, the hymn (e.g., Ps 100, 146).

The two major genres—lament and hymn—are distinguished by form as well as content. The lament usually begins with a cry to God. A middle section may contain any of these elements: a description of suffering, a complaint, a prayer for vengeance, a promise to offer sacrifice in thanksgiving. The lament usually concludes with a prayer of thanksgiving or confidence. Most hymns begin with a call to prayer, a call for help in giving praise to God. Those called may be one's own being, faithful people, all nations, angels, or other created things such as animals, sun and stars, musical instruments. Ps 148 shows a rich variety of those called to help give praise. The call to praise in a hymn is followed by the reasons for praise. For example, God is just, compassionate. God delivers those in trouble, feeds the hungry. Ps 117 is a perfect example of a hymn with call to praise (v. 1) and reasons for praise (v. 2).

Each of these genres is found either as the prayer of an individual or as a communal prayer. Other minor categories are distinguished by content alone: historical psalms, wisdom psalms, songs of Zion, liturgies.

Shape and Shaping. Toward the end of the 20th century scholarly interest turned to the Psalter as a book. Questions were raised concerning the editorial purpose of the arrangement of the psalms and the effect of that ar-

"The Pius II Book of Psalms," illumination from a Medieval manuscript with Gregorian Chant annotations. (©David Lees/ CORBIS)

rangement. Ps 1–2, without superscriptions and set off by beatitudes at beginning and end, were recognized as the introduction to the Psalter. Ps 1 sets a wisdom tone and praises the one who ponders God's law day and night. Ps 2 is a recognition of God's action in history especially through the anointed king, the messiah. Ps 150 is the great concluding doxology. There are more lament psalms at the beginning of the Psalter and more hymns at the end.

The concluding psalms of books 2 and 3, Ps 72 and 89, are royal psalms. Ps 72, which concludes the David collection, paints a glowing picture of the king. In Ps 89 the monarchy is in trouble. Book 4 begins with a Psalm of Moses, the pre-monarchical leader, and continues with the collection acclaiming God as the king.

Other studies have been made of the positioning of the various collections and their relationship to other parts of the Old Testament. Michael D. Goulder, for example, links the Psalms of Asaph to the Pentateuch and the psalms in Book Five to Ezra-Nehemiah and the return from exile.

Translations. New translations of the Psalms continue to appear. Many are revisions of previous translations, e.g., the NRSV, and the revised psalms of the NAB. The International Commission on English in the Liturgy (ICEL) prepared a Psalter for liturgical use, using the principle of dynamic equivalence rather than that of formal correspondence. Dynamic equivalence is an attempt to capture the meaning in idiomatic English without echoing specifically the Hebrew grammar. Compare, for example, Ps 51.3 in the ICEL translation (''Have mercy, tender God, forget that I defied you'') with the NAB translation (''Have mercy on me, God, in your goodness; in your abundant compassion blot out my offense'').

Theology of the Psalms

The psalms portray God as the creator, ruling over and delighting in all that exists. They also portray God as the redeemer who works in history and delivers the people from their enemies. There is a strong sense of awe in the presence of the divine as well as a confidence that anyone in need can call upon God. God is especially solicitous for the helpless—the poor, the widow, the imprisoned, the oppressed.

In the psalms human beings are presented in all their diversity and fallibility. Sin is acknowledged but innocence is also claimed. The gamut of emotions is represented from joy to despair, anger to love. The physical body is significant in the psalms: bones ache, the throat is dry, the heart rejoices, the body rests. It is impossible to pray the psalms as disembodied spirits.

The psalms are a communal prayer. There are communal laments, communal thanksgivings, and the narration of the people's history. But even the individual psalms turn frequently to the community. For example, both Ps 130 and 131 end with a prayer for Israel.

Christians pray the psalms in the spirit of Christ. The New Testament shows Jesus praying in the words of the psalms (see Mt 27.46; Mk 15.34; Lk 23.46). Early Christian writers heard the psalms as Christ's prayer, as prayer to Christ, or as meditation on Christ.

Christian Use of the Psalms

Liturgical Use. The primary place the Catholic Christian meets the psalms is in the Liturgy of Word in the Eucharist. The responsorial psalm that follows the first reading distills the message of the readings and allows the participant to enter into them. For example, on the feast of Christ the King Year A the first reading is from the book of Ezekiel. In the reading God who chastises the selfish leaders of the people and declares: ''I myself will look after my sheep.'' The congregation claims God's care by singing Ps 23: ''The Lord is my shepherd.'' In the first reading of the Twelfth Sunday of Year

A Jeremiah complains to God about his enemies. The congregation sings Ps 69 in the voice of Jeremiah: ''Lord, in your great love, answer me.'' An excellent way to meditate on the readings from the Sunday liturgy is to begin with the responsorial psalm and to read the other readings through its lens.

The other major Christian use of the psalms is in the LITURGY OF THE HOURS, the daily prayer of the Church. At morning and midday, evening and night, Christians sanctify time through prayer. The bulk of this prayer consists of the psalms, arranged in a regular order, so that within a set period of time—anywhere from one to four weeks—the whole Psalter is prayed. A few psalms that are particularly violent are often omitted: Ps 58, 83, and 109.

Personal Prayer. Many Christians use the psalms for personal prayer. Ps 23, ''The Lord is my shepherd,'' has become a favorite for believers across denominations, as demonstrated by its use for occasions as different as a Fourth of July celebration and a funeral. Psalm books are published listing psalms to be prayed in sickness, in trouble, in thanksgiving, at times of joy, and so on. Often the Psalter is published alone with the New Testament, showing its preferred status among the Old Testament books.

Problems. Praying the psalms is not without difficulty, however. Three problems are critical: the difficulty caused by the age and cultural presuppositions of the psalms; a contemporary distaste for lament; and the violence and desire for vengeance expressed in the psalms.

The psalms were written in ancient Hebrew, a language that ceased to be a living language in the last few centuries B.C. They reflect the culture of the first millennium B.C., a primarily agrarian milieu in the Middle East. Many of the images and practices reflected in the psalms are foreign to a reader in the third millennium A.D. Nonetheless, the effort to understand is well rewarded. The human situation reflected in the psalms and the relationship of the believer to God remain remarkably similar.

Most of the psalms are laments. Contemporary culture frowns on lament or any demonstration of weakness and vulnerability. The bitter complaints, the hot anger, and the attempt to ''persuade'' God by whatever means are all distasteful to people today. Psychologists and spiritual directors, however, point out that the inability to lament is a sickness in our society and makes individuals sick as well. The lament psalms are good teachers and healthy prayers.

One characteristic of the lament in particular is difficult for believers: the prayer or wish for vengeance against enemies. One who prays the psalms regularly discovers phrases such as ''Crush their teeth in their mouths'' or ''May they dissolve like a slug in the sun.'' These prayers seem in direct contradiction to the command to love one's neighbor. It is possible simply to avoid the difficult psalm. It is also possible to consider what today's enemies are. One can pray against cancer: ''Crush its teeth.'' Or against homelessness, ''May its memory disappear from the earth.'' Or against war: ''Wipe it out from the earth.'' These psalms reflect the spirit of the quintessential Christian prayer, which concludes, ''Deliver us from evil.'' This prayer is the necessary corollary to ''Thy kingdom come.''

The psalms are central to Christian prayer. As the New Testament bears witness, they are the prayer of Jesus.

Bibliography: Commentaries and General Studies of the Psalter. B. W. ANDERSON with S. BISHOP, *Out of the Depths: The Psalms Speak to Us Today* (3d ed. rev.; Louisville, Ky. 2000). R. DAVIDSON, *The Vitality of Worship: A Commentary on the Book of Psalms* (Grand Rapids, Mich./Cambridge, Eng. 1998). W. L. HOLLADAY, *The Psalms through Three Thousand Years: Prayerbook of a Cloud of Witnesses* (Minneapolis 1993). J. L. MAYS, *Psalms* (Interpretation; Louisville, Ky. 1994). J. D. PLEINS, *The Psalms: Songs of Tragedy, Hope, and Justice* (Bible and Liberation Series; Maryknoll, N.Y. 1993). Genre and Form. H. GUNKEL, *Introduction to Psalms: The Genres of the Religious Lyric of Israel,* completed by J. BEGRICH; tr. J. D. NOGALSKI (Macon, Ga. 1998). Shape and Shaping of the Psalter. M. D. GOULDER, *The Prayers of David (Ps 51–72): Studies in the Psalter II* (Sheffield, Eng. 1990); *The Psalms of Asaph and the Pentateuch: Studies in the Psalter III* (*Journal for the Study of the Old Testament Supplement Series* 233; Sheffield, Eng. 1996); *The Psalms of the Return (Book V, Ps 107–150): Studies in the Psalter IV* (*Journal for the Study of the Old Testament Supplement Series* 258; Sheffield, Eng. 1998). J. CLINTON MCCANN, JR., *A Theological Introduction to the Book of Psalms: The Psalms as Torah* (Nashville 1993). Biblical Prayer and the Liturgical Use of the Psalms. P. D. MILLER, *They Cried to the Lord: The Form and Theology of Biblical Prayer* (Minneapolis 1994). I. NOWELL, *Sing a New Song: The Psalms in the Sunday Lectionary* (Collegeville, Minn. 1993). T. P. WAHL, *The Lord's Song in a Foreign Land: The Psalms as Prayer* (Collegeville, Minn. 1998).

[I. NOWELL]

PSALTERS, METRICAL

Metrical translations of the Psalms into the vernacular for the chief purpose of congregational singing. Although examples of metrical Psalters from earlier periods are known, the Reformed Churches of the 16th through the 18th centuries placed particular emphasis upon this type of text, the most notable exception being the Lutheran chorale, which, because it admitted the element of non-biblical poetic and religious thought, was generally rejected outside of Germany.

An attempt to survey in a limited space the history of metrical psalmody must be highly selective. Short titles will be used; and indicated dates refer not necessarily to the first edition but rather to the first complete, or most nearly complete edition of a specific title.

The earliest significant Psalter of the 16th century is the *Souterliedekens* of 1540. Printed in Antwerp, this Psalter, which was intended for use in the home and at social gatherings, contains the Psalms, the *Te Deum,* and five of the biblical CANTICLES; 33 editions are known to have been published between 1540 and 1613.

Two basic trends, one French, the other English, are to be observed in the history of metrical psalmody. The French concept was developed in the *Genevan Psalter* of 1562, translated by Clément Marot and Théodore de Bèze with music selected, edited, and in some instances apparently newly composed primarily by Louis Bourgeois. Translated into Dutch verse and keeping the same tunes, this Psalter became the *Dutch Psalter* of 1566. The English concept was developed in the Psalter of Thomas Sternhold and John Hopkins, published in its complete form by John Day in 1562 and known as *Sternhold and Hopkins* or, later, the ''Old Version.'' In its variety of stanza forms and its flexibility and subtlety of melody, the French concept was artistically superior; but the use of the familiar ballad stanza patterns and a formalized type of melody, made the English concept of greater practical value.

Toward the middle of the 16th century religious persecution in England drove various Protestant groups to the Continent. Under the influence of the *Genevan Psalter*, they reworked *Sternhold and Hopkins* and completed the *Anglo-Genevan Psalter* in 1561. A similar development produced the *Scottish Psalter* of 1564. In 1612 Henry Ainsworth completed a new Psalter for the English ''Separatists'' who had settled in Amsterdam. Known as the *Ainsworth Psalter* and brought to America by the Pilgrims in 1620, this Psalter borrowed music from both *Sternhold and Hopkins* and the *Dutch Psalter.* Mention should be made also of the *BAY PSALM BOOK*, published in America in 1640.

The second half of the 17th century witnessed a general trend toward revision. Changes in the French language threatened to make the Marot-Bèze version unintelligible; and in 1679 a ''revision,'' to all intents a new translation, was completed by Valentine Conrart. The English ''Old Version'' was gradually superseded by the ''New Version'' of 1696, completed by Nahum Tate and Nicholas Brady and known as *Tate and Brady.* The *Scottish Psalter* of 1650, surrendering artistic vitality for practical usefulness, reduced the varied metrical patterns of its earlier editions to the monotony of the English common meter.

The publication in 1719 of Isaac Watts's *The Psalms of David Imitated in the Language of the New Testament* marks a turning point in the history of metrical psalmody. Although it is ostensibly a Psalter, the freedom with which Watts paraphrases the Psalm texts is very different from the strict adherence to the Hebrew required in the earlier Psalters; the Psalter served as a model for the writers of the hymns that gradually replaced the Psalms as the basic texts for congregational singing in the majority of Protestant churches. The change from psalmody to hymnody met with considerable opposition, particularly from churches with strong Calvinistic backgrounds. Not until 1861 did the Established Church of Scotland authorize the singing of hymns.

Bibliography: M. PATRICK, *Four Centuries of Scottish Psalmody* (New York 1949). W. S. PRATT, *The Music of the French Psalter of 1562* (New York 1939). E. PARKS, *The Hymns and Hymn Tunes found in the English Metrical Psalters* (New York 1966) R. ILLING, *Est-Barley-Ravenscroft and the English Metrical Psalter* (Adelaide 1969) R. J. MILLER, *John Calvin and the Reformation of Church Music in the Sixteenth Century* (Ann Arbor 1971). R. G. APPEL, *The Music of the Bay Psalm Book* (Cambridge, MA 1975). R. LEAVER, ''English Metrical Psalmody,'' *The Hymnal Companion*, ed. R. GLOVER (New York 1990), 321–48. R. A. LEAVER, *''Goostly Psalmes and Spirituell Songes'': English and Dutch Metrical Psalms from Coverdale to Utenhove, 1535–1566* (Oxford 1991).

[A. GARRETT/EDS.]

PSEAUME, NICOLAS

French prelate active at the Council of Trent and in the Counter Reformation; b. Chaumont-sur-Aire (Meuse), Dec. 11, 1518; d. Verdun, Aug. 10, 1575. Though his family was not wealthy, Pseaume (Psaume, Psalmaeus) was sent to school first at the Norbertine Abbey of St. Paul in Verdun, then to Paris, Orleans, and Poitiers. In 1538 he returned to Verdun where he joined the Norbertines, subsequently replacing his uncle as abbot of St. Paul's (1540). A year later he was awarded a doctorate in theology from the University of Paris. In 1548 Pseaume was made bishop of Verdun. When sent to Trent in 1551 as a representative of the Norbertine Order, Pseaume spoke out strongly against the prevailing system of benefices held *in commendam* and advocated residence for bishops. While at the Council, he kept a diary of the proceeding, which was later published in Paris and Verdun. Returning to Verdun (1552), Pseaume attended to the administration of his diocese. He rebuilt St. Paul's Abbey, which had been destroyed by war, and reorganized the hospital and reformed the municipal institutions of the city. To further the cause of Catholic education in his diocese, he helped establish a Jesuit college in Verdun. Called back to Trent in 1563, Pseaume took part in the final sessions and subsequently edited the acts of the Council. He lies buried in the cathedral of Verdun.

Pseaume's publications include a number of religious treatises defending Catholicism against the reform movement: *Le Vrai et naïf portrait de l'église catholique; Advertissement à l'homme chrétien pour cognoistre et fuir les hérétiques de ce temps; Préservatif contre le changement de religion.*

Bibliography: J. J. I. VON DÖLLINGER, *Ungedruckte Berichte und Tagebücher zur Geschichte des Concils von Trient,* 1 v. in 2 (Nördlingen 1876). C. N. GABRIEL, *Étude sur Nicolas Psaulme, évêque et comte de Verdun* (Verdun 1867). C. L. HUGO, *Sacrae antiquitatis monumenta . . . ,* 2 v. (Étival-Saint-Dié 1725–31) 1:9–21. N. ROUSSEL, *Histoire ecclésiastique et civil de Verdun,* 2 v. (Bar-le-Duc 1863–64). A. ERENS *Dictionnaire de théologie catholique,* ed. A. VACANT et al. (Paris 1903–50) 3.1:1086–93. A. K. HUBER, *Lexikon für Theologie und Kirche,* ed. J. HOFER and K. RAHNER (Freiburg 1957–65) 8:863–864.

[C. HOLMES]

PSEUDO-CLEMENTINES

A collection of early Christian writings, wrongly attributed to Clement of Rome, which includes two *Epistles to Virgins,* the Pseudo-Clementine *Homilies,* and *Recognitions,* and several fragments known as the *Epitomes.* The two *Epistles to Virgins* (*Ad virgines*) are exhortations in the form of letters supposedly addressed by Pope Clement I to men and women leading celibate lives. Both writings explain the ideals toward which these persons are to strive and the dangers they must avoid. In each work the author sternly reproves those ''who under the pretext of piety live with virgins (*see* VIRGINES SUBINTRODUCTAE) and expose themselves to danger'' (*Ad virgines* 1.10). Numerous texts and examples are cited from both the Old and New Testaments to support the author's viewpoint. Only fragments of the original Greek text survive in quotations by the 7th-century Palestinian monk Antiochus of the monastery of St. Sabas, but a complete text of the letters has survived in a Syriac translation. The original author is unknown, but a Coptic translation of the first *Epistle* (1–8) attributes this letter to St. ATHANASIUS. As objections to the practice of ascetics of both sexes living under the same roof are raised for the first time in extant Christian literature toward the middle of the 3d century, scholars generally assign the *Epistles* to this date. The place of composition seems to have been Palestine.

Pseudo-Clementines, more specifically, is the name given to a long didactic novel whose central figures are the Apostle Peter and his disciple Clement of Rome, a man of noble birth diligently in search of truth. At the direction of Barnabas, Clement sets out for the East, meets Peter in Caesarea, becomes the Apostle's companion on his missionary journeys, and witnesses the encounter with SIMON MAGUS. These experiences are related in 20 *Homilies* in Greek and ten books of *Recognitions* now extant in their abbreviated Latin translation by RUFINUS OF AQUILEIA.

The *Homilies* (*Homlilae*) purport to be the missionary sermons of Peter. They clearly show influences of Judaist-Ebionite teaching, and even admit the existence of two principles, one good, the other evil. Christ, as portrayed in the *Homilies,* is a true prophet come to restore the pristine purity of the Law, but He is not the Redeemer. Paul is described as a ''hostile man'' distorting the Law, which Peter preaches in its purity. Two letters, one from Peter, the other from Clement, addressed to James the Less, Bishop of Jerusalem, serve as a preface to the *Homilies.* Peter begs James to allow only duly approved persons to read the sermons. In addition to a certain prestige attached to the church of Jerusalem some scholars see in Peter's letter a report of a missionary submitted to the mother church and its bishop.

Clement's letter addresses James as ''bishop of bishops,'' informs him of Peter's martyrdom, and states that shortly before his death the Apostle appointed Clement bishop of Rome, handing over to him the chair (*cathedra*) of preaching and teaching and the power to bind and loose. This is probably the earliest extant formal reference to the bishop of Rome as the heir of the Petrine powers. These letters were written some time in the early 3d century.

The narrative materials of the *Recognitions* (*Recognitiones*), supposedly a detailed account of the experiences of Clement and members of his family, are basically the same as those in the *Homilies.* Unusual circumstances separate father, mother, and three sons. Through Peter's intervention they are reunited, and the recognition scenes give this work its name. Its didactic content is clearly Christian in tone; Judaistic elements are minimized and the doctrine of the Trinity is clearly set forth. The Christian elements may be the interpolations of the Latin translator Rufinus.

A study of the relation between the *Homilies* and the *Recognitions* entails complicated problems of literary criticism and theological interpretation. It is now generally admitted that both works go back to a basic source mentioned by ORIGEN, entitled *Periodoi,* which incorporates materials from two earlier accounts of Peter's preaching and journeys. In their present form the *Homilies* date from 325 to 380, and the *Recognitions* from 360 to 380.

The *Epitomes* (*Epitomae*) preserve two Greek excerpts from the *Homilies,* to which are added details from Clement's supposed letter to James and a *Martyrium Clementis* by Symeon Metaphrastes. Two Arabic excerpts from the narrative portions of the *Homilies* and *Recognitions* also are extant.

Bibliography: F. DIEKAMP, ed., *Patres apostollci,* v.2 (3d ed. Tübingen 1913), *Epistles. Die Pseudoklementinen* (Die griechischen christlichen Schriftteller der ersten drei Jahrhunderte 51; Leipzig 1964), v.1 *Homilien,* ed. B. REHM; v.2 *Die Rekognitionen,* ed. B. REHM and F. PASCHKE. J. QUASTEN, *Patrology,* 3 v. (Westminster, MD 1950–) 1:58–63. B. REHM, *Reallexikon für Antike und Christentum,* ed T. KLAUSER 3:197–206. J. DANIÉLOU, *Théologie du Judéochristianisme* (Tournai 1938) 71–76. B. ALTANER, *Patrology,* tr. H. GRAEF from the 5th German ed. (New York 1960) 103–106. W. ULLMANN, *Journal of Theological Studies* NS 11 (1960) 295–317; *Studia Patristica* 4 (Texte und Untersuchungen zur Geschichte der altchristlichen Literatur 79; 1961) 330–337. F. S. JONES, ''The Pseudo-Clementines: A History of Research [2 pts],'' *Second Century, Second Century* 2, No 1 (Spring 1982), p. 1–33, 2, No 2 (Sum 1982), 63–96. G. STRECKER, *Das Judenchristentum in den Pseudoklementinen* (Berlin 1981).

[H. DRESSLER]

PSEUDO-DIONYSIUS

Dionysius the Areopagite is the name assumed by the author of four Greek treatises on liturgical and mystical theology that appeared at the beginning of the 6th century and were first referred to by the Monophysite theologians in the train of SEVERUS OF ANTIOCH. The author claims apostolic sanction for his writings by publishing them as the work of the Dionysius, who was baptized after listening to a sermon St. Paul preached in the Areopagus of Athens (Acts 17.34). These writings were quoted by the Monophysite leader in the colloquy of the orthodox and Severian bishops held in Constantinople in 532, but immediately challenged by Hypatius of Ephesus, the orthodox spokesman, as unknown to such older Fathers as Cyril and Athanasius. Translated into Syriac by SERGIUS OF REŠAINA (d. 536), they were the subject of an early 6th-century commentary by JOHN OF SCYTHOPOLIS.

These four treatises, strongly Neoplatonist in concept and terminology, deal with (1) the celestial hierarchy, (2) the ecclesiastical hierarchy, (3) the divine names, and (4) mystical theology. They were used by both the Chalcedonian and Monophysite theologians during the 6th and 7th centuries. Their influence was greatest in the Latin West, however, where in 827 they were first introduced in the translation of Abbot HILDUIN OF SAINT-DENIS made from the Greek uncial manuscript (*Codex Paris* gr. 437) sent by the Emperor Michael II as a gift to Louis the Pious. The translation of JOHN SCOTUS ERIGENA in particular supplied the scholastic theologians and medieval mystics with material for Neoplatonic speculations regarding the Trinity and the ecclesiastical hierarchy that had been only touched upon by St. Augustine.

Authorship. Only occasionally during the Middle Ages was the Dionysian authorship of these writings questioned. But Lorenzo VALLA (d. 1457) had challenged their dating in a commentary on Scripture that was first published by ERASMUS (Paris 1505) on the score that the Neoplatonist terminology as well as the liturgical and hierarchical notions could not have been produced in the 1st century. A considerable controversy followed during the 16th, 17th, and 18th centuries in which theologians attempted to defend the 1st-century authorship. But in 1895 H. Koch and J. Stiglmayr, working independently, proved that these writings could not have been composed before the 5th century, since the doctrine of evil, for one thing, was of a strictly Nonplatonic origin.

The date for the composition of the Pseudo-Dionysian writings is set by the fact that there is no mention of them before the 5th century, that their Christological teaching reflects post-Chalcedonian doctrine, such as that of the HENOTICON (482), and that the first indisputable citation of these writings is made by Severus of Antioch between 518 and 528. In 171 the Dominican Orientalist M. LE QUIEN offered arguments to prove that the true author was Peter the Fuller, the Monophysite patriarch of Antioch (d. 488), whose use of the writings of the Neoplatonist philosopher Proclus (d. 485), and whose influence in the composition of the Henoticon as well as in the introduction of the Creed in the Mass, rendered him the most likely candidate.

Of the 5th- and early 6th-century authors capable of having produced these documents, the Syrian Neoplatonist and mystic, author of the Book of Hierotheus, STEPHEN BAR-ṢŪDHAILĒ; the Monophysites Peter the Iberian, Peter the Fuller, Severus of Antioch, and Sergius of Rešaina; and the Chalcedonian John of Scythopolis have all been proposed as responsible, but despite the most elaborate study of style, theological cross-reference, and historical coincidence, modern criticism has not accepted any of these candidates as the author.

Contents. The body of Dionysian documents consists of four treatises and ten letters that further elaborate both the theological content and the pseudo-1st-century atmosphere in which they were supposedly written.

The Divine Names. This treatise deals with man's knowledge of God from His revelation of Himself in the Scriptures. These manifestations proceed from His ineffable and invisible unity. Of the three persons in the Trinity, the Son alone became incarnate, thus expressing in the universe the presence of the ineffable and inexpressible One in the world of sin and multiplicity. After a chapter on the effects of prayer, which is indispensable in theological investigation, the author gives an account of the different names that can be applied to God, beginning with the Good and proceeding to Unity and Trinity, Beauty, Love, Being, Life, Wisdom, Intelligence, Reason, etc. In all this he is reflecting the Neoplatonic thought of PROCLUS.

Mystical Theology. This treatise is a compact description of the negative dialectic that prepares and renders possible the mystical experience that by its very nature is inexpressible and indescribable, for it deals with "the divine darkness." Notable here is the lack of reference to love as the cathartic and unifying factor in the mystical approach to God. In this treatise the author contents himself with discussing the sensible and intelligible preparations that are necessary before the soul is raised to ecstasy. Letters 1 and 3 complete this treatise.

The Celestial and Ecclesiastical Hierarchy. The hierarchies of heaven and of the Church are described, in this work, on a triadic principle, proceeding from the Trinity and descending in threes through the nine angelic orders, thence to the ecclesiastical organ of bishops, priests, and deacons charged with initiating the monks, saints, and purified in a divine way of life through the process of purification, illumination, and perfection or union with the divine Being. The two aspects of the Dionysian universe, that of angelic and that of incarnate or human intelligence, complement each other, one being the image of the other. The nature and function of these intelligences are described in Scripture mainly through symbols, and Pseudo-Dionysius maintains that the triadic order pervades throughout the Old Testament and New Testament, tradition, and the history of the Church.

In the roles ascribed to bishops, priests, and deacons in the Church, the practice of the 5th century is reflected, with the bishop sanctifying by ordaining bishops and priests and consecrating monks; the priest aiding the bishop particularly in his function of illuminating the faithful through preaching the Word of God; and the deacons in charge of the purification ceremonies connected with preparation for Baptism, and the care of the poor and unfortunate.

The four treatises are completed by the letters. Letters 1 and 4 describe the divine darkness and inaccessible light of the mystical theology; letter 2 deals with the transcendence of the divine names; letters 8, 9, and 10 detail the respect to be paid to the Church's hierarchy, mercy for sinners, and fortitude in persecution; letters 3 and 5 examine Christological questions; letter 6 condemns polemics in theology; and letter 7 describes the prodigies of the noonday darkness and the earthquake that accompanied Christ's death.

Influence. The doctrinal content of the Pseudo-Dionysian corpus forms a complete theology, from the Trinity and angelic world through the Incarnation and Redemption to the last things, and provides a symbolic and mystical explanation of all that is. Its extremely spiritual doctrine gave great satisfaction to the theologians and spiritual writers of the Middle Ages and the Renaissance both in the Orient and in the West; hence the failure to question its authorship and the essentially Neoplatonic quality of its mystical excursions.

In the East, these writings were influential but not as pervasive as was once believed; rather they were incorporated into a stream of spiritual and mystical theology that was formed by the Alexandrian and Cappadocian Fathers. They were synthesized to a large extent by MAXIMUS THE CONFESSOR in the 7th century, having contributed to the Christological debates of the 6th century, and were appropriated extensively by both parties in the Palamite controversy of the 14th century, without contributing substantially to either crisis.

In the West, the legendary biography identifying Pseudo-Dionysius with both the Areopagite and the patron of Paris, which was composed by the Abbot Hilduin and attached to his Latin translation of the Dionysian writings, set the tradition that prevailed down to modern times. The Dionysian writings were cited in part by GREGORY I for his commentaries on the angels, and by Pope MARTIN I at the Lateran synod of 649. They are further mentioned by Pope AGATHO (680), BEDE, Pope PAUL I, and Pope ADRIAN I before the translation by Hilduin that was redone by John Scotus Erigena at the request of Charles II, the Bald, between 860 and 862, and then retouched by ANASTASIUS THE LIBRARIAN in 875. In the scholastic and later period John Sarrazin, ROBERT GROSSETESTE, Ambrose Traversari, and Marsilio FICINO produced Latin versions along with commentaries, and the corpus was further commented upon in whole or in part by HUGH OF SAINT-VICTOR, THOMAS GALLUS, ALBERT THE GREAT, THOMAS AQUINAS, Jean GERSON, and DENIS THE CARTHUSIAN.

Down to the first decade of the 17th century, the authority of these writings was unchallenged by Catholic and many Protestant theologians. Thereafter, though most theologians refused to consider the evidence objectively, men of the caliber of Prosper Lambertini (later BENEDICT XIV), in his treatise on the *Beatification of Saints,* expressed great caution in utilizing these works. Recent scholarly investigation has demonstrated beyond question the late date and provenience of the Dionysian writings.

Bibliography: *Patrologia Graeca,* ed. J. P. MIGNE, 161 v. (Paris 1857–66) v.3–4 (no critical edition exists). *Works,* tr. J. PAR-

KER (London 1897). H. KOCH, *Pseudo-Dionysius Areopagita in seinen Beziehungen zum Neuplatonismus und Mysterienwesen* (Mainz 1900). J. STIGLMAYR, *The Catholic Encyclopedia,* ed. C. HERBERMANN et al., 16 v. (New York 1907–14; suppl. 1922) 5:13–18. R. ROQUES, *L'Univers dionysien* (Paris 1954); *Reallexikon für Antike und christentum,* ed. T. KLAUSER (Stuttgart 1950–) 3:1075–1121. R. ROQUES et al., *Dictionnaire d'histoire et de géographie ecclésiastiques,* ed. A. BAUDRILLART et al. (Paris 1912–) 14:265–310; *Dictionnaire de spiritualité ascétique et mystique. Doctrine et histoire,* ed. M. VILLER et al. (Paris 1932–) 3:244–429. U. RIEDINGER, *Byzantinische Zeitschrift* 52 (1959) 276–296; "Der Verfasser der pseudo-dionysischen Schriften," *Zeitschrift für Kirchengeschichte* 75 (1964) 146–152. P. ROREM, *Pseudo-Dionysius: A Commentary on the Texts and an Introduction to Their Influence* (New York 1993). R. BLUM and A. GOLITZIN, *The Sacred Athlete: On the Mystical Experience and Dionysios, Its Westernworld Fountainhead* (Lanham, Md. 1991). A. LOUTH, *Denys, the Areopagite* (London and Wilton, Ct. 1989). P. ROREM, *Biblical and Liturgical Symbols within the Pseudo-Dionysian Synthesis* (Toronto 1984). G. SHAW, "Theurgy and Dionysius the Areopagite," *Journal of Early Christian Studies* 7:573–599. J. WILLIAMS, "The Apophatic Theology of Dionysius the Pseudo-Areopagite," *Downside Review* 117:157–172. S. J. BEGGIANI, "Theology at the Service of Mysticism: Method in Pseudo-Dionysius," *Theological Studies* 57, 201–223.

[F. X. MURPHY]

PSYCHICS

A term of opprobrium used by TERTULLIAN as a MONTANIST to describe Catholics whom he accused of laxness in fasting and in forgiving sins against purity (*De pudicitia* 1.10; 6.14; 10.8; 16.24; 18.2; 21.16). In Greek ψυχικοί, and in Latin *psychici,* the word is taken from St. Paul (1 Cor 2.14), where it means the "natural" man as opposed to the "spiritual" (πνευματικός) man. But Tertullian, who employed the word also in his *Adversus Marcionem* (4.22), *De monogamia* (1.1), *De jejuniis* (1.1), and *Adversus Praxean* (1.6), understood it as signifying "materialminded," a meaning similar to that previously given to it by certain Gnostic sects.

Bibliography: Tertullian, *De paenitentia,* ed. and tr. P. DE LABRIOLLE (Paris 1906) 138–143; *Adversus Praxean,* ed. and tr. E. EVANS (Society for Promoting Christian Knowledge; 1948) 187–188; *Treatises on Penance,* ed. and tr. W. P. LE SAINT (*Ancient Christian Writers* 28; 1959) 194–195.

[F. HAUSER]

PSYCHOLOGISM

A philosophy or viewpoint regarding the empirical CONSCIOUSNESS of the subject as the source of knowledge of all reality; it thus teaches that the data of consciousness have ontological value. In a general way psychologism is equatable with SUBJECTIVISM and is traceable to R. DESCARTES. Whereas Descartes limited his commitment to clear and distinct ideas, however, subsequent thinkers attributed metaphysical reality to all thoughts and sensations. This type of psychologism is opposed by those who hold for OBJECTIVITY in human knowledge.

In a stricter sense, psychologism is the theory that psychology is the basis of philosophy and of the social and normative sciences, if not of all sciences. The most forceful advocates of this view, which is a reaction to Kantian apriorism, were the German philosophers J. F. Fries (1773–1843) and F. E. Beneke (1798–1854). For them, the critical examination of reason (*Vernunft*) does not yield, as Kant maintained, a priori propositions whose synthesis is due to the activity of the mind independently of experience; it yields only the empirical facts of consciousness. According to Fries, all the basic principles and ideas of philosophy can be attained merely by psychological INTROSPECTION (*Selbstbeobachtung*), and therefore, philosophy is not founded on speculation but on pure experience. Similarly, Beneke held that the only possible groundwork of philosophy is EXPERIENCE (*Erfahrung*) and, more specifically, psychological experience. Metaphysics, he felt, should rest on psychology and not psychology on metaphysics.

Cultural science psychology (*geisteswissenschaftliche Psychologie*), promoted especially by Wilhelm DILTHEY, maintains that psychology provides the foundation for the cultural sciences. The latter aim at the understanding of the meaning, value, and purpose of events and phenomena, in contradistinction to the natural sciences, which try to explain the causal relationships between phenomena and reduce them to general laws. The task of psychology is to understand the products of the human mind. The mind of man reveals itself in what he has achieved in the world—works of art; science; justice and law; philosophical and moral systems; language; social, economic, and political institutions; and religion. The sciences concerned with these expressions of the human mind, such as philology, ethnology, aesthetics, history, economics, ethics, and philosophy of religion, are called *Geisteswissenschaften*—literally, sciences of the spirit. The term is often translated as cultural or socio-historical sciences.

Other types of psychologism may be designated as logical, ethical, and aesthetic. These maintain that the normative sciences of logic, ethics, and aesthetics are founded exclusively on the data of experience. The argument on which they are based runs somewhat as follows: psychology is altogether an empirical science; logic, ethics, and aesthetics rest on psychology; therefore, these disciplines must be empirical also. Logical psychologism, advocated by Beneke, T. Lipps (1851–1914), J. S. MILL, W. WUNDT, and C. Sigwart (1830–1904), holds that logical laws have no universality or necessity, but only tentative value. Ethical psychologism is the view of moral relativists such as F. Hutcheson (1694–1746), D. HUME, F. H. JACOBI, J. F. HERBART, Beneke, H. SPENCER, and J. DEWEY. For them the laws of morality do not hold for all times and all peoples, since they rest on moral sentiment or moral sense that differs from period to period and from individual to individual.

See Also: SCIENTISM; LOGICISM.

Bibliography: F. E. BENEKE, *Erfahrungsseelenlehre als Grundlage alles Wissens* (Berlin 1820); *Lehrbuch der Psychologie als Naturwissenschaft* (Berlin 1832; 2d ed. 1845). J. F. FRIES, *Neue oder anthropologische Kritik der Vernunft*, 3 v. (Heidelberg 1807); *Handbuch der psychischen Anthropologie*, 2 v. (Jena 1820–21). H. PFEIL, *Der Psychologismus im englischen Empirismus* (Paderborn 1934). G. DEL VECCHIO, *Materialismo e psicologismo storico* (2d ed. Rome 1953).

[J. H. VAN DER VELDT]

PSYCHOLOGY (CLASSICAL)

A term meaning the study of the soul, coined from the Greek ψυχή (soul) and λόγος (concept) by R. Goclenius (1547–1628). The branch of knowledge it designates has taken on a distinctive form since 1850, but its beginnings can be traced to the ancient Greeks. Aristotle is generally considered the ''Father of Psychology,'' both because he wrote extensive treatises on expressly psychological questions and because he grounded his studies as a natural science on a broad empirical base. Nevertheless, even before Aristotle, the Greek thinkers were speculating on psychological questions.

Development of the Concept. For the Greeks the study of living organisms was only one part of the general study of nature. ARISTOTLE distinguished between natural bodies that are not moved except by others, and natural bodies that are able to move themselves. The latter, living things including plants, brute animals, and men, form the subject of a special part of the science of nature. He undertook to classify living things, to examine their structures and functions, and to formulate definitions of the principle within them by which they were able to move themselves, which he called the soul. His treatise *De anima* (On the Soul) served as a fundamental text in psychological science for over 2,000 years.

After Aristotle, psychology developed mainly along three lines. A few Greek and Arabian philosophers wrote fresh treatises on matters that Aristotle had touched only lightly or not at all, but most contented themselves with writing commentaries on the master's works, or commentaries on other commentaries. The Greek and Arabian physicians contributed shrewd insights from their clinical observations, but introduced errors also. Finally, moral philosophers and the Christian Fathers enlarged the scope of descriptive psychology, especially in the areas of human passions, habits, attitudes, and will, in treatises whose main focus was the living of the good life and the avoidance of vice.

In the 12th and 13th centuries, when the universities began to flourish in Europe, psychology experienced a new vigor. By this time the study of plants and animals had been largely separated from the study of human life, and a new purpose animated philosophers. Their aim was to formulate a systematic science of human nature, culminating in a definition of the human soul and its relationship to the body. The medieval philosophers drew heavily on the Greek, Arabian, and Christian traditions, especially on PLATO and Aristotle, AUGUSTINE, GREGORY I (THE GREAT), JOHN DAMASCENE, GREGORY OF NYSSA, AVERROËS, and AVICENNA, but they did not hesitate to adapt the ideas they used to the demands of their own systems of thought.

Method. The psychology of St. THOMAS AQUINAS exemplifies the medieval approach to the subject. He followed Aristotle in holding that the study of living things was a special part of the science of nature, but his interests were directed almost exclusively to human psychology, He maintained that as a science it should be based on strictly empirical data, but he was willing, as were all philosophers of the day, to speculate on the basis of these data, sustaining conclusions that could not themselves be demonstrated by direct evidence. He accepted data both from observation and from INTROSPECTION.

Observation was mostly a matter of general and common experience; controlled and systematic observation was not yet part of the scientific method. The procedure was first to determine the most general principles governing an area of investigation, and then to divide the matter into parts and determine the principles of each subdivision, and so on. Thus, if the purpose of the investigation were scientific knowledge of sensation, the first step would be the definition of the nature of knowledge in general. Then the difference between intellectual and sense knowledge would be established. Next would come the distinction between internal and external sensation, and then the specific kinds of internal and external sensation, and finally the variety of modes or functions of which each specific sense is capable. In the investigation, search would be made for all the causes governing the nature of the given object at each level of generalization. The causes include the final cause or purpose, the efficient cause or agent, the formal cause or specific feature, and the material cause, or elements out of which the thing was made (*see* DEMONSTRATION). When the four causes had been determined, the investigation would have achieved its purpose.

The validity of this procedure rests on the accuracy and thoroughness of the empirical data on which it is based, and the rigor of the logical formulations and deductions. The method is successful in establishing the general principles and canons of psychology and in framing its broader conclusions, but for more detailed knowledge and for practical applications of knowledge, the facts of general experience must be augmented and refined by data from controlled observations, experiments, clinical experience, and the variety of techniques being evolved in contemporary research.

Contents. Scholastic philosophers are generally agreed on most of the major theses concerning the human soul and human nature, although they differ among themselves on points of interpretation, emphasis, and approach.

Life. They define life as self motion, that is, the capacity of an organism to move itself from potentiality to activity. From another point of view, the distinctive feature of vital operations is their IMMANENCE, that is, the characteristic of self-perfecting action that is involved in living activity. In a broad sense, for instance, nourishment perfects the organism nourished. In a stricter sense, knowledge is the perfection of the mind knowing. Both characteristics, i.e., self movement and immanence, imply that living things exist and operate on a higher scale than inorganic bodies, for living things move themselves to full perfection and maturity through their interactions with other bodies, whereas inorganic bodies lose their energies and even their existence when they interact with others.

The Soul. The principle of life in living things is called the SOUL. In essence, the soul is the factor in virtue of which living bodies have their special organization, and thus are able to function in special ways. The soul is not necessarily immaterial or spiritual; in animals and plants it is purely material. Only in man is there evidence of its transcending purely material being.

Since living things operate through parts that have special functions (organs) and yet are single units whose various operations are directed to the survival, development, and propagation of the whole, the soul, as the principle of the whole, is conceived by Thomists as something essentially simple but capable of several distinct operations, fewer in lower forms of life and most numerous in man. These capacities for distinct operations are called FACULTIES OF THE SOUL. Other scholastics acknowledge the faculties, but argue that there is more than one principle of life, or soul, in higher organisms.

Scholastics generally agree on five genera of vital faculties: vegetative faculties, powers of local movement, sensitive faculties, intellective faculties, and powers of appetition. They generally agree also in assigning three specific faculties to the vegetative order, viz, nourishment, growth, and reproduction. The study of these vegetative processes would probably have been given scant attention if the requirements of a philosophical system alone were in question. But scholastics devoted considerable thought to processes such as reproduction or birth, because some of the key mysteries in Christian revelation were couched in these terms. The Second Person of the Blessed Trinity is born of the Father, and again born of the Virgin Mary. A baptized person is reborn of water and the Holy Spirit. To interpret these mysteries, scholastics wanted precise knowledge of the natural process of birth, and thus this topic became a matter of prime interest.

Sensation. In considering the category of SENSATION, scholastics distinguish between external and internal SENSES, but differ on their number. Most are agreed on five external senses, with the sense of touch being a compound sense attaining several distinct objects, such as temperature, resistance, pain, and pleasure. After St. Thomas, internal senses were generally held to be four, viz, the CENTRAL SENSE, IMAGINATION, MEMORY, and the COGITATIVE POWER. But some 20th-century scholastics question the existence of the central sense, the cogitative power, or both.

All scholastics make a sharp distinction between the senses, which know concrete and singular objects, and the intellect, which knows objects in abstract and universal forms. They divide appetition along the same lines as knowledge, i.e., into sense appetites and the intellectual appetite or will, although there is some disagreement over details.

Knowledge. A key point in any psychological theory is the theory of knowledge, i.e., the precise explanation of the operation by which man knows objects distinct from himself (*see* KNOWLEDGE, THEORIES OF). It is a curious fact that outside the scholastic tradition no attempt is made to face the full requirements of an adequate theory of knowledge. Much is written by philosophers concerning the validity of knowledge acts and concerning the logical force of knowledge processes, and more is written by psychologists on the acquisition of knowledge and on its physiology, but the phenomenon whose validity, processes, acquisition, and physiology are under investigation is itself left undefined. According to the traditional theory of knowledge the objects of KNOWLEDGE are the forms of things, namely, all the determinants that make a thing to be what it is. The process of knowledge involves the reception of these forms into the knowing powers of the knower, but it is a reception that is somehow immaterial (*see* KNOWLEDGE, PROCESS OF). Unlike the process by which a stone is heated (receiving the form of heat from another) or wax is imprinted by a seal (receiving the shape of the seal), the FORM received in a knowledge act is undetectable in the knower and known to be present only by himself. Hence it follows that the form is present in a way unlike the way physical forms are present, and hence it is termed "immaterial," meaning not received in the knower as a simple physical effect. Then, since materiality is the reason two like forms are distinct from each other, the immaterial presence of the form in the knower leaves it somehow indistinct from the form in the thing known. Thus the OBJECTIVITY that is an experiential feature of knowledge acts is capable of reasonable explanation.

This theory of knowledge purports to be the fundamental explanation of all acts of knowledge, whether of sensation or of intellection. The difference between these two operations lies in the difference in the mode of the form received. In sensation the concrete, individual forms of an object are received, viz, its visible, palpable, audible, etc., features, as, being present, they impress themselves on the subject, or as they are later recalled. In intellection the mind attains the abstract, and hence universal, ideas drawn from the sensible experience of its objects.

The clear-cut distinction that scholastics place between sensation and intellection presents them with a problem that a purely materialistic or a purely idealistic psychology does not face. They must explain how the mind can form UNIVERSALS, and abstract ideas of concrete and singular objects. To account for this process of ABSTRACTION, an agent INTELLECT is posited, as an active power of the mind by which intelligible species are formed out of the sensible images of things, and then impressed on the knowing intellect. The intellect then knows its objects as the universal, abstract essences, or definitions, of the concrete, singular objects from whose sensible images it has drawn its knowledge.

Appetition. In scholastic psychology, the appetitive processes are, functionally subsequent to knowledge processes. They are responses to known objects, in the form of inclinations toward good objects and away from evil objects; At the sense level, APPETITE begins with the sensations of pain and pleasure, and operates to orient the organism toward pleasant objects and away from painful objects. This simple pleasure-pain appetite is called the concupiscible appetite. In cases of emergency, a second sense appetite, the irascible appetite, operates to overcome difficult objects.

The highest appetite in man is the rational appetite, called the WILL, which operates to seek out the reasonable good and avoid the reasonable evil. The will follows whatever the intellect proposes as good, and whenever the intellect proposes several goods, none of which is compelling, the will is free to elect among them (*see* FREE WILL). The will is the highest motive force in man, controlling his other powers, although not all to the same extent. It commands overt behavior "despotically," as the scholastics say, but has only "political" control over the lower appetites and knowledge faculties. In comparing the intellect and the will from the point of view of excellence, St. Thomas and Thomists argued for the superiority of the intellect; DUNS SCOTUS and his followers urged the superiority of the will; other scholastics held for an equality of excellence (*see* INTELLECTUALISM; VOLUNTARISM).

Man. The process of determining the elements of human nature, namely, body and soul, and the specific faculties with which it is equipped is the analytic part of scholastic psychology. The synthetic part is the definition of the whole human composite made up of these elements and the assessment of the structure of human nature. (*See* MAN, 2.)

In the classic definition, man is a rational animal, that is, an animal like other animals, but distinct by having the power of universal, abstract reason, and all that follows from it. One of the principal conclusions scholastics draw from this is that the soul of man is spiritual and therefore immortal, that is, that after death the vital principle of the human composite does not decay or corrupt or pass away, but persists in existence and in vital operation (*see* IMMORTALITY). The question then arises as to how the union of a spiritual principle and a physical body is to be conceived. At one extreme, the soul was conceived as something quite separate from the body and dwelling in the body like a man in a prison, or like a driver in a machine. Another opinion, deriving from the Arabian philosophers, was that the intellect was a separate entity, one for all men, in whose ideas all men, although physically distinct, somehow participated. St. Thomas fought vigorously for the concept of the unity of the human composite—perhaps in the field of psychology this was his major preoccupation—insisting that the soul and the body were incomplete principles that when joined together formed one, single entity, the soul being the determining element and the body the element determined (*see* SOUL, HUMAN, 4). Therefore, even though the soul could exist and act after death, it was in an extreme state of violence, and, naturally speaking, as miserable as it could be. After St. Thomas, scholastics did not generally hold opinions that separated soul and body as radically as those mentioned above, but some scholastics, for instance, Duns Scotus and F. SUÁREZ, held for more than one vital principle in man, the rational soul being his major soul, while other vital forms gave him lower levels of life.

While all men, in virtue of having rational souls, are essentially alike, different men can have the various powers of life in different degrees and different proportions; therefore there is a basis for asserting various diversities among men. Some of these differences are inborn—the scholastics pointed out the obvious differences of the two sexes and supported the classical theory of TEMPERAMENT according to which the different proportions of the basic humors in the human body affect men psychologically as well as physically. They maintained that individuals differ in native talent and psychological tendencies, so that some men are naturally noble and born to rule whereas others are naturally base and more fit to serve.

Given the inborn differences among men, the disparities between one man and another can be increased by acquired differences. According to St. Thomas, who developed much of his psychology of habit formation within the context of moral philosophy and theology, an acquired HABIT may be partly natural, as coming from native propensities, or purely acquired, by repeated acts. The intellect and will are the subjects of the most numerous and important habits, but the sense appetites can also be affected by habit formation. He did not consider the senses themselves and the physical functions and organs apt for habit formation except in a secondary and ancillary way.

Relation to Other Disciplines. The traditional psychology of the scholastics, which is today called philosophical psychology, or the philosophy of man or of human nature, is still considered a part of the general science of nature, or natural philosophy (*see* PHILOSOPHY OF NATURE). The principles that explain bodies in general, and the laws that govern them, are applicable to living bodies as well, and in living bodies often find their clearest exemplification.

When the scholastic psychologies were being formulated, the sphere of living organisms was set apart as one area of investigation. Today this area is studied in numerous more or less distinct branches of science, e.g., biology, psychology, zoology, botany, physiology, taxonomy, morphology, genetics, embryology, ecology, and evolution; but the basic unity of these diverse sciences is gradually regaining recognition in studies under the title of life sciences. The relation of these life sciences, and especially of modern psychology, to traditional psychology is a matter of dispute among contemporary scholastics. At the level of broad and basic principles, traditional psychology and the modern sciences often raise the same kind of questions for discussion. At the level of empirical research, experimentation, and formulation of data, the relationship is not so clear. Some hold that rational and empirical psychologies are distinct and unrelated, others hold that they are distinct and complementary, while still others hold that they are not distinct sciences but stages or grades of development within one science.

In relation to other philosophical disciplines, traditional psychology holds a key position. Discerning and defining the acts and processes of the intellect, it supplies the materials of the sciences of logic and epistemology. It is necessary for the science of metaphysics, which reaches the highest causes of things, because ''if the nature of the possible intellect were unknown to us, we could not know the order of the separated substances'' (St. Thomas Aquinas, *De anim.* 1.7). By defining human acts, analyzing the conditions of free and deliberate behavior, and elucidating the possible goals and the limits human nature can achieve, psychology provides the elements of study with which moral philosophy or ethics deals. Consequently, psychology enters into all the special parts of ethics, into politics, economics, social sciences, education, etc.

The relationship of psychology to the theological disciplines is equally vital. Much of scholastic psychology is found in the context of theological discussion, in which the concepts and conclusions of psychological investigation are brought to bear to elucidate the terms of the mysteries of revelation. The concepts of the human soul and its powers of intellect and will are basic to concepts of God and the angels and their intellects and wills. The Trinity and its processions and relations are understood in terms of analogies with the intellect and intellection and love. Man's rebirth in grace, his growth in grace, the nature of the theological and infused moral virtues, man's destiny in terms of his divine vocation, the gifts and fruits of the Holy Spirit, and the beatitudes are all understood by comparison with psychological realities. It can be asserted without hesitation that an understanding of the contents of rational psychology is an essential part of the understanding of all rational philosophy and Christian theology.

See Also: SOUL, HUMAN; MAN, 2, 3.

Bibliography: THOMAS AQUINAS, *Aristotle's De Anima and Commentary of St. Thomas Aquinas,* tr. K. FOSTER and S. HUMPHRIES (New Haven 1951); *The Soul,* tr. J. P. ROWAN (St. Louis, Mo. 1949); *In Aristotelis libros De sensu et sensato, De memoria et reminiscentia commentarium,* ed. R. M. SPIAZZI (3d ed. Turin 1949); *Summa theologiae*, tr. Eng. Dominican Fathers (New York 1947), 1a, 75–92, on the structure of human nature; 1a2ae, 1–17, on goals and the acts of the will; 1a2ae, 22–60, on passions and habits; *Truth,* tr. R. W. MULLIGAN et al., 3 v. (Chicago 1952–54), questions 10, 12, 13, 15–17, 22, 24–26; *On Aristotle's Love and Friendship,* tr. P. CONWAY (Providence, RI 1951), books 8 and 9 of the Commentary on the *Nichomachean Ethics*. ARISTOTLE, *Works,* ed. W. D.

ROSS, 12 v. (New York 1908–52), v.3 *De Anima.* R. E. BRENNAN, *Thomistic Psychology* (New York 1956). J. F. DONCEEL, *Philosophical Psychology* (2d ed. New York 1961). H. D. GARDEN, *Introduction to the Philosophy of St. Thomas Aquinas,* tr. J. A. OTTO, 4 v. (St. Louis, MO 1956). É. H. GILSON, *The Spirit of Medieval Philosophy,* tr. A. H. C DOWNES (New York 1936). J. GREDT, *Elementa philosophiae Aristotelico-Thomisticae,* ed. E. ZENZEN, 2 v. (13th ed. Freiburg 1961), v.1. E. HUGON, *Cursus philosophiae Thomisticae* (Paris 1905) v. 3–4, *Philosophia naturalis: Biologia et psychologia; metaphysics psychologica.* G. P. KLUBERTANZ, *The Philosophy of Human Nature* (New York 1953). O. LOTTIN, *Psychologie et morale aux XIIe et XIIIe siècles,* 6 v. in 8 (Louvain 1942–60), v.1 *Problèmes de psychologie.* M. MAHER, *Psychology* (9th ed. New York 1921). J. MARITAIN, *Distinguish to Unite, or The Degrees of Knowledge,* tr. G. B. PHELAN (New York 1959). T. V. MOORE, *The Driving Forces of Human Nature and Their Adjustment* (New York 1948). A. C. REGIS, *St. Tomas and the Problem of the Soul in the Thirteenth Century* (Toronto 1934). J. E. ROYCE, *Man and His Nature* (New York 1961). J. WILD, *Introduction to Realistic Philosophy* (New York 1948).

[M. STOCK]

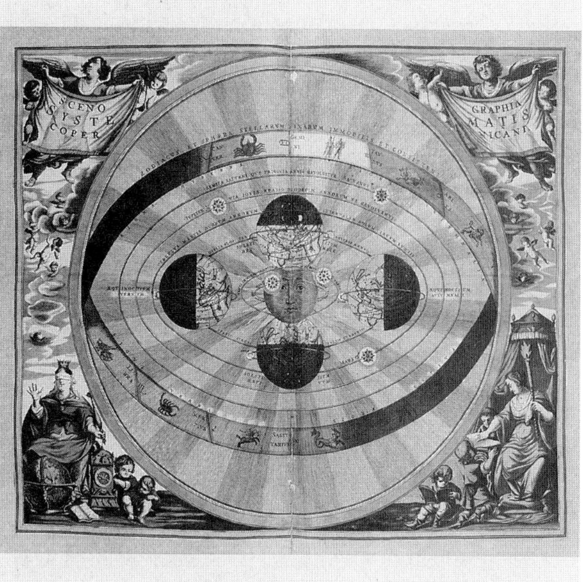

A print by Andea Cellario, entitled ''Harmonia Macrocosmica,'' showing Ptolemy's geocentric system of the world. (©Enzo & Paolo Ragazzini/CORBIS)

PTOLEMY (CLAUDIUS PTOLEMAEUS)

Astronomer, mathematician, and geographer; author of the famous *Almagest* (Syntaxis mathematica), the standard work on astronomy from the 2d century until the 16th century. Ptolemy's biographical data are uncertain, except the fact that he lived and worked in Alexandria, Egypt. According to later sources, he was born probably at the end of the 1st century and died during the reign of Marcus Aurelius, i.e., between 161 and 180. Of Ptolemy's major writings mentioned here, the *Almagest* was by far his most influential work. It consists of 13 books that contain the main tenets of geocentric cosmology, and it gives a systematic summary of the achievements of Greek astronomy up to Ptolemy's time, including certain results of his own investigations. The first two books give mainly the geometrical theorems forming the basis of his mathematical astronomy and the basic assumptions of the geocentric hypothesis, i.e., the spherical shape of the earth and its state of rest in the center of the finite universe bounded by the sphere of the fixed stars. The third book deals with the movement of the sun, and the fourth and fifth with that of the moon. In these books, as well as in the other parts of his work, Ptolemy, in order to construct a consistent model accounting for the apparent motions of the celestial bodies, makes use of the theory of epicycles and eccentric circles. An epicycle is a small circle along whose circumference the star is carried while the center of the epicycle moves along the circumference of a larger circle round the earth. The center of this circle either coincides with that of the earth or, in the case of eccentric motion, is situated at some distance from the earth. The next two books deal with the fixed stars and contain also a catalogue of more than a thousand stars with their positions and magnitudes. The last five books expound the theory of the five planets—the two inner planets Mercury and Venus, and the three outer ones Mars, Jupiter, and Saturn. Ptolemy also confirms Hipparchus's discovery of the precession of the equinoxes, giving, however, a slightly less accurate value than Hipparchus.

The *Almagest* was held in highest esteem during late antiquity and the Middle Ages until COPERNICUS's *De revolutionibus* (1543). It was translated into Arabic and commented on by several Islamic astronomers from the 9th century on; and it was also the principal astronomic source book in the Western scholastic world, as can be seen by the numerous quotations in, e.g., THOMAS AQUINAS, JOHN DE SACROBOSCO, and ROGER BACON, and by various commentaries, for example, the *Epitome* (1496) of Regiomontanus.

In another astronomical work, ''Hypotheses of the Planets,'' Ptolemy gives several improvements on the results of the *Almagest* and polemizes against attempts to return to the Aristotelian model of a single set of homocentric spheres; he reveals himself as a Platonist who believes that each planet is driven by a vital force emanating from its soul. His astrological work, *Tetrabiblos,* was one of the most famous of its kind during the Middle Ages. He is also the author of a geography, containing tables of the latitudes and longitudes of the main places of the inhabited world known at his time. His *Harmonics* is the last great systematic work of antiquity on musical harmony containing a theory of musical intervals and scales. In his *Optics* (extant only in a Latin translation), Ptolemy deduces mathematically, and verifies experimentally, several optical laws, e.g., the laws of reflection and refraction of light.

Bibliography: F. LAMMERT, *Paulys Realenzyklopädie der klassischen Altertumswissenschaft,* ed. G. WISSOWA et al. (Stuttgart) 23.2 (1959) 1788–1859. J. L. E. DREYER, *A History of Astronomy from Thales to Kepler* (2d ed. Dover pa; New York 1953).

[S. SAMBURSKY]

PUBLIC ORDER (CANON LAW)

Public order (canon law) is a legal term referring to the stability that exists in a society when its most urgent laws are obeyed and its security is assured. Nineteenth-century canon lawyers borrowed this term from civil law chiefly to indicate the measure of the traveler's subjection to local statutes.

Civil jurists developed the notion of public order with reference to the alien and the laws of the country he visits. His legal relations are generally somewhat different from those of the citizen. In continental Europe, jurists look upon nationality as the factor determining a person's rights and duties. They have developed theories of private international law to decide the individual's nationality, to define the rights enjoyed by the alien, and to resolve the conflicts that arise with respect to these rights.

The situation is different in England and in the United States. Domicile rather than nationality governs the legal status of the individual. The alien is regarded before the law as being much the same as the citizen. His distinctive rights are specified in public international law, which chiefly concerns relations between nations and is often described simply as international law.

The most frequent conflict of laws facing U.S. courts is the choice between the rule of law of the individual's domicile and the place where the court sits. Normally this involves competing laws of several states rather than of independent nations. Hence the solution of these jurisdictional questions is known in the United States as conflicts of law, and not private international law.

Occasionally a U.S. court is faced with a choice of law involving the statute of a foreign country. In the Anglo-American tradition, civil statutes are generally conceived of as territorial, affecting the person in and through the locality. They bind all who are present, aliens and nationals alike. It may happen by exception that a court will find it useful to apply to an alien the law of his own country, but this is purely a matter of comity. It is inadmissible whenever a question of public policy arises affecting the nation's vital interest.

In the 19th century, several European jurists rejected this strictly territorial concept of law. Pasquale Stanislao Mancini (1817–88) taught that laws are closely linked, not with the place but with the persons for whom they are enacted. Since the legislator acts with a view to the needs of his own people, the laws of each country are best suited to serve the interests of its citizens, wherever they may be. From this principle, Italian private international law concludes that the individual has the right to be governed by the laws of his own country. Every state is bound to guarantee this right for the alien as well as for its citizens. A notable exception to the rule arises from the need to protect the public order. Whenever the vital interest of the community is involved, the alien must submit to the local statute just as though he were a citizen.

Resolving conflicts of law is a fundamental problem for the canonist as well as for the civil jurist. The earliest commentators on Gratian's Decree regarded travelers as subject to all local laws. Later, Francisco SUÁREZ (1548–1617) took this position and developed the juridic principles that serve as its basis. He taught that the welfare of the community requires the uniform observance of its laws, not only by its subjects, but by all who happen to be present, even for a short time.

Later decretists and decretalists taught that, apart from exceptional cases, the traveler is free from the obligation to observe local statutes because he is not a resident. Tómas SÁNCHEZ (1551–1610) accepted this theory, explaining that the ruler's exceptional jurisdiction is based upon the need to protect the community from harm.

By the 19th century, canonists generally regarded the opinion of Sánchez to be the more probable, although they did not add substantially to the reasoning of its earlier defenders. Philippus de Angelis (1824–81), Franciscus Santi (1830–85), and others did, however, introduce a new phrase into canonical literature. They borrowed from civil law the term ''public order'' to define what had become the commonly accepted canonical doctrine, the legislator's exceptional jurisdiction over the traveler. Both the new term and the opinion of Sánchez received full legal force by their incorporation in the 1917 Code of Canon Law.

In defining this concept, it is helpful to bear in mind that all laws tend to promote order in the community and to foster the common good in one of two ways. Either the law seeks to provide some advantage to the individual, affecting the community only in a secondary way, and this is the private good; or it has for its object something that is not proper to any individual but is to the advantage of all. This is the social and public good.

The resident is bound to obey all the laws of his community, for at least indirectly he thereby contributes to the social well-being. The traveler is bound to observe only the law that has a public good as its object and directly affects the society as such. Moreover, he is obliged to do this only to the extent that uniform observance of the law is an indispensable condition for the welfare of the place he visits. When he does so, he helps to secure public order, which is that pattern of conduct prescribed by a law having for its object a public good that is found to be essential to the security of society.

Bibliography: G. MICHIELS, *Normae generales juris canonici. Commentarius libri I. Codex iuris canonici,* 2 v. (2d ed. Paris-Tournai-Rome 1955): 1:391–402. G. ONCLIN, *De territoriali vel personali legis indole* (Glembaci 1938) 257–260; 331–351. A. VAN HOVE, ''Leges quae ordini publico consulunt,'' *Ephemerides theologicae Lovanienses* 1 (1924) 153–167. E. ROELKER, ''The Traveller and the Local Statute,'' *Jurist* 2 (1942) 105–119. J. H. HACKETT, *The Concept of Public Order* (*Catholic University of America Canon Law Studies* 399) (Washington 1959). A. PILLET and J. NIBOYET, *Manuel de droit international privé* (Paris 1924). M. WOLFF, *Private International Law* (New York 1945).

[J. H. HACKETT]

PUBLIC PROPRIETY (IMPEDIMENT TO MARRIAGE)

Public propriety may be defined as a certain propinquity of persons or quasi-affinity arising from an invalid marriage after common life has been established or from public or notorious concubinage. In deference to public decency, such unions create an impediment that invalidates the marriage of either party with the blood relations of the other party within the first degree of the direct line.

Most authorities maintain that the impediment of public propriety in church law derived from Roman law. The impediment in Roman law had its source in betrothal—the Roman law *Sponsalia.* The canons in which Gratian presents impediments are considered by many to be apocryphal. The Council of Trent restricted the scope of the impediment (sess. 24, *de ref. matr.,* c. 3). The decree *Ne temere* made a further restriction [*Acta Sanctae Sedis* 40 (1907) 525].

Similar legislation prescribes the impediment of public propriety in both Latin and Eastern church law (*Codex iuris canonici,* c. 1093; *Codex canonum ecclesiarium orientalium,* c. 810). It is apparent from the terms of the law that public propriety springs from a twofold source: invalid marriage after the establishment of common life, and public or notorious concubinage.

To give rise to the impediment under the rubric of invalid marriage after the establishment of common life, the union must have the semblance of marriage (*species matrimonii*). As the so-called civil marriage of persons bound to the canonical form (*Codex iuris canonici,* c. 1108; *Codex canonum ecclesiarium orientalium,* c. 828) lacks this semblance of marriage, such a civil union is not, strictly speaking, an invalid marriage. However, such a civil union followed by cohabitation does give rise to the impediment (Response of the code commission, *AAS* 21 (1929) 171; *Codex canonum ecclesiarium orientalium,* c. 810 §1, 3°).

The second source of the impediment is concubinage. Only such concubinage as is either public or notorious gives rise to the impediment of public propriety. The term *public* means that the concubinage is known in the community. The term *notorious* signifies that concubinage is publicly known and lived in the community so that it cannot be concealed or excused.

This impediment is an ecclesiastical law impediment. Therefore, the local ordinary can dispense from it (*Codex iuris canonici,* c. 1078; *Codex canonum ecclesiarium orientalium,* c. 795).

See Also: MARRIAGE LEGISLATION (CANON LAW).

Bibliography: A. BRIDE, *Dictionnaire de droit canonique,* ed. R. NAZ, 7 v. (Paris 1935–65) 5:1179–1203. J. F. GALLAGHER, *The Matrimonial Impediment of Public Propriety* (*Catholic University of American Canon Law Studies* Washington 1916–) 304. W. HÖRMANN, *Quasiaffinität,* 2 v. (Innsbruck 1897–1906) 2:466–467. P. GASPARRI, *De matrimonio . . . ,* 2 v. (Rome 1932) 1:728–248. J. P. BEAL in J. P. BEAL et al., *New Commentary on the Code of Canon Law* (New York 2000) 1294–1295.

[J. F. GALLAGHER]

PUBLICANS

Publicans were collectors of various revenues and taxes in the province of the Roman Empire. Roman taxes were of two types, direct (property, poll, and income; Lat. *vectigalia*) and indirect (fees on sales and purchases, export and import customs; Lat. *portitoria*). Instead of collecting the indirect taxes through government officials and under public control, the state usually auctioned them out to rich contractors. These tax farmers divided their territory into districts and employed local agents to do the actual work of collecting revenues. These subagents were the custom house officers who examined merchandise, assessed its value more or less arbitrarily, and exacted the levy. The tax farmers were, in the strict sense, the publicans, for the Greek term used in the New Testament, τελῶναι (from τέλος and ὠνέομαι), means literally to farm taxes; yet the word came to be loosely extended to the subordinates, or the *portitores,* and these are the publicans (from the Latin *publicani*) so frequently mentioned in the Gospels.

The complicated system doubtless saved the government—central and local—a great deal of trouble and expense, but it opened the way to flagrant injustices. The unscrupulousness and rapaciousness of the publican became proverbial; he was universally hated (Cicero, *De officiis,* 1.42). The Jews had additional reasons for despising him. Most of them looked upon taxes, not as a legitimate requirement for the preservation of the social order, but as a tribute exacted by a hated conqueror, and those of their race who exacted this badge of subjection were regarded as base and despicable. They were classified with sinners (Mt 9.11, 11.19; Mk 2.15–16; Lk 15.1), heathens (Mt 18.17), and harlots (Mt 21.31–32). No publican was allowed in the Temple or synagogue; his testimony in a court of justice was not accepted. St. Matthew stresses the horror with which the publican was viewed by the people (Mt 5.46–47, 9.10–11, 11.19, 18.17), and he is the only Evangelist who indicates that Levi, the publican called to be an Apostle, was Matthew himself (cf. Mt 9.9–13 with Mk 2.14–17). (*See* MATTHEW, APOSTLE, ST.) All three Synoptics emphasize Our Lord's compassion for these outcasts of society (Mt 9.9–13, 11.19; Mk 2.15–17; Lk 7.29–34, 15.1, 18.9–14).

Bibliography: *Encyclopedic Dictionary of the Bible,* tr. and adap. by L. HARTMAN (New York 1963) from A. VAN DEN BORN, *Bijbels Woordenboek,* 1960–61. J. JEREMIAS, *Die Religion in Geschichte und Gegenwart,* 7 v. (Tübingen 1957–65) 6:1927–28. J. SCHMID, *Lexikon für Theologie und Kirche,* ed. M. BUCHBERGER, 10 v. (Freiburg 1930–38) 10:1092.

[J. M. DOUGHERTY]

PUCCI, ANTONIO MARIA, ST.

Servite pastor; b. Poggiole di Vernio (Tuscany), Italy, April 16, 1819; d. Viareggio (Tuscany), Jan. 12, 1892. His parents were peasants who tended a small herd and tilled the fields. Eustachio, as he was named at baptism, followed this simple life until his 18th year, when he joined the SERVITES in Florence and received (July 10, 1837) the name Anthony in religion. After classical and theological studies at the Hermitage of Monte Senario, near Florence, he was ordained (Sept. 24, 1843). Appointed pastor (1844) in the new parish of St. Andrew in Viareggio, he spent his next 45 years there. To his flock and to all who knew him, he became known as ''the little parish priest'' (*curatino*). His spiritual achievements were remarkable, despite a lack of natural endowments. He was not handsome; his voice was unpleasantly nasal; he was withdrawn and very sparing in words. Yet he was entirely devoted to his flock's spiritual and temporal welfare. From 1883 to 1890 he was also prior provincial of the Servites' Tuscan province. He was beatified June 22, 1952, and canonized Dec. 9, 1962.

Feast: Jan. 14 (formerly 12).

Bibliography: I. FELICI, *Il curatino santo B. Antonio M. Pucci dei Servi di Maria* (Florence 1952). P. M. PERRONI, *Il beato curatino di Viareggio: Il beato Antonio Maria Pucci dei Servi di Maria* (Rome 1953). G. PAPÀSOGLI, *Il beato curatino di Viareggio* (Rome 1962).

[J. M. RYSKA]

PUCCINI, GIACOMO

Opera composer; b. Lucca, Italy, Dec. 22, 1858; d. Brussels, Belgium, Nov. 29, 1924. His ancestors for four generations were church musicians, and he was expected to carry on the tradition. After studies at the Lucca and Milan conservatories and two posts as church organist, however, he devoted himself almost entirely to opera composition. Of his 12 operas, *Manon Lescaut* (1892), *La Bohème* (1896), *Tosca* (1900), *Madame Butterfly* (1904), *Gianni Schicchi* (1918), and the unfinished *Turandot* are most popular. They are characterized by a melodious style, superb orchestration, idiomatic vocal writing, and a telling sense of theater. ''Lax in his religious beliefs, if not actually an unbeliever'' (Carner), he did, however, produce a Mass in A-flat (1880, published 1951 as *Messa di Gloria*), nonliturgical and highly operatic throughout (the Agnus Dei was later used in *Manon Lescaut*). An early motet for the feast of St. Paulina and an unpublished *Requiem* (1905) are his only other essays in church music, although he used religious ceremonies for dramatic effect in *Tosca* and *Suor Angelica.*

Bibliography: G. PUCCINI, *Letters,* ed. G. ADAMI, tr. E. MAKIN (London 1931). A. BONACCORSI, *Puccini* (Milan 1950). G. R. MAREK, *Puccini* (New York 1951). M. CARNER, *Puccini* (London 1958). F. BONAVIA, *Grove's Dictionary of Music and Musicians,* ed. E. BLOM 9 v. (5th ed. London 1954) 6:987–991. A. W. ATLAS, ''Crossed Stars and Crossed Tonal Areas in Puccini's *Madama Butterfly,*'' *19th Century Music* 14 (1990) 186–196; ''Mimì's Death: Mourning in Puccini and Leoncavallo,'' *The Journal of Musicology* 14 (1996) 52–79. M. GIRARDI, *Giacomo Puccini: l'arte internazionale di un musicista italiano* (Venice 1995). H. M. GREENWALD, ''Verdi's Patriarch and Puccini's Matriarch: 'Through the Looking-Glass and What Puccini Found There','' *19th Century Music* 17 (1994) 220–36. J. C. PETTY, ''The Ravished Flower: A Major Poetics in *Madama Butterfly,*'' *The Opera Journal* 30/4 (1997) 2–20. M. ROSENTHAL-ENGLISH, *Giacomo Puccinis 'La fanciulla del West': Eine neue Opern-konzeption im Oeuvre des Komponisten* (Berlin 1997). D. SCHICKLING, ''Puccini's 'Work in Progress': The So-Called Versions of *Madama Butterfly,*'' *Music and Letters* 79 (1998) 527–537.

[R. M. LONGYEAR]

PUCELLE, JEAN

Head of a Parisian workshop producing illuminated religious MSS; active *c.* 1320 to *c.* 1360. Pucelle's existence is attested by only five 14th- to early 15th-century sources; three fall within his lifetime: his name appears in two books produced in his shop, and *c.* 1320 he was paid for designing a seal for a Parisian confraternity, traced through MSS from his workshop. His chief works are the Belleville Breviary (Paris, Bibl. Nat. Lat. 10483–84) and the Hours of Jeanne d'Evreux (The Cloisters, New York). These are distinctive, first, by reason of their decorative detail, typical of his products: the MSS abound with grotesque animals, or heads and figures, or scenes from everyday life (though in this they reflect the general decorative fashion of the times). More remarkable is his apparent knowledge of contemporary Italian art; reminiscences of Tuscany and Tuscan art are frequent, and his experiments in pictorial space mark him as a pioneer in French MS illumination. Most of these features were developed and imitated by later Parisian illuminators, and literal quotations from Pucelle are still found in work of the early 15th century.

See Also: MANUSCRIPT ILLUMINATION.

Bibliography: K. MORAND, *Jean Pucelle* (Oxford 1962). E. PANOFSKY, *Early Netherlandish Painting,* 2 v. (Cambridge, Mass. 1953). J. DUPONT and C. GNUDI, *Gothic Painting,* tr. S. GILBERT (New York 1954). L. BAER, U. THIEME, and F. BECKER, eds., *Allgemeines Lexikon der bildenden Künstler von der Antike bis zur Gegenwart,* 37 v. (Leipzig 1907–38) 27:442–443.

[A. MARTINDALE]

Giacomo Puccini.

PUDENS, PUDENTIANA, AND PRAXEDES, SS.

Early Christian saints and titular churches. The earliest source in which the name Pudentiana appears is an inscription of 384, *Leopardus lector de Pudentiana* (G. de Rossi, *Inscript. Christ.* 1:384). This refers to a titulus, i.e., a place of cult and not a saint, because in the fourth century it was not the custom to dedicate a church directly to a saint.

Pudentiana is an adjective, and in the present church the old inscription reads: *Dominus conservator ecclesiae Pudentianae,* meaning that the founder was a certain Pudens. Sometime in the sixth century the *titulus Pudentis* was reevaluated and Pudens was canonized. Misreading the adjective *Pudentianae* as a person created ''St.'' Pudentiana.

In the seventh century there appeared a legendary *Gesta Pudentianae et Praxedis* that states that Praxedes, after the death of her sister Pudentiana, ''who was buried on May 19 beside her father Pudens in the cemetery of Priscilla, with the consent of Pope PIUS I, dedicated the Baths of Novatus as a church, under the name of the Bl. Virgin Pudentiana, in the *vicus patricius*''—the patrician suburb. Prior to this, the same *Gesta* narrates that Pudens had constructed a church over the same house. The author of the *Gesta* thus identified the *titulus Pudentis* with the *titulus Pudentianae,* and since there was only one church on the site, he concluded that it referred to a Sancta Pudentiana, who could only be a real person, a virgin, saint, and martyr.

During the next centuries the name fluctuates between Pudens and Pudentiana, but from the ninth century on it is the church of St. Pudentiana, and in time her feast was entered in the LIBER PONTIFICALIS.

The Roman MARTYROLOGY lists SS. Pudentiana and Pudens, Senator, on May 19, with Praxedes on July 21. A son of Pudens is mentioned on June 20.

A Pudens is mentioned by St. Paul (2 Tm 4.21). Excavations beneath the church reveal the ruins of Roman houses, one of which near the Baths of Novatus could be that of Pudens. The tradition that St. Peter lived there need not be excluded. The house of Pudens was probably turned into a church by Pius I (140–155), and when re-

Madonna and Child with SS. Praxedes and Pudentiana. (©Gianni Dagli Orti/CORBIS)

built by Pope SIRICIUS (384–399), extended over the baths. Pope PASCHAL I (817–824) transferred the body of a St. Potentiana from the cemetery of Priscilla to the church of St. Pudentiana, and the same pope transferred hundreds of bodies to the nearby church of St. Praxedis.

Praxedes, according to the *Gesta,* was the sister of Pudentiana; in fact, she was foundress of the *titulus Praxedis,* which certainly existed in 489 as we know from an inscription. The ITINERARIA of the seventh century indicate her tomb in the Priscillan cemetery beside her sister Pudentiana. Her feast is first found in the Capitulary of Wissenburg (seventh–eighth century).

Feast: May 19.

Bibliography: *Acta Sanctorum* May 4:298–300. J. P. KIRSCH, *The Catholic Encyclopedia,* ed. C. G. HERBERMANN et al. (New York 1907–14) 12:344–345. H. DELEHAYE, *Les Origines du culte des martyrs* (2d ed. Brussels 1933); *Étude sur le légendier romain* (Brussels 1936) 264–266. R. U. MONTINI, *Santa Pudenziana* (Rome 1959). A. AMORE, *Antonianum* 39 (1964) 30–33, 36–37.

[E. HOADE]

PUEBLA

The Third General Conference of the Latin American Episcopate (CELAM III), took place in Puebla, Mexico, in January 1979. The meeting, originally intended to mark the tenth anniversary of CELAM II at Medellín, had to be postponed because of the deaths of Pope Paul VI and Pope John Paul I. Paul VI's apostolic exhortation *EVANGELII NUNTIANDI* provided the theological background. The presence of John Paul II, especially his remarks in three major homilies, set the tone.

Meeting Overview. The CELAM Secretariat, strongly influenced by Bishop Alphonso Lopez Trujillo, prepared a preliminary document which concentrated on the problem of secularization and the role of the Church in Latin America's transition from a rural-agrarian society to an urban-industrial society. At the outset divisions emerged among the voting bishops and non-voting participants. Many felt that the preliminary document was a betrayal of the program established at Medellín. Gradually a consensus emerged. CELAM president, Cardinal Aloisio Lorsheider of Brazil was instrumental in bringing the perspective of the meeting closer to the social analysis, methodology, and human rights concerns of Medellín. Unofficial *periti,* mainly Latin American liberation theologians, also influenced the process leading to the final document.

The bishops recognized that the social, economic, and political problems of 1968, not only remained, but had become more serious. Secularization was not the principal obstacle to spreading the gospel. Evangelization in Latin America meant that the Church had to address once again the problems of poverty, structural injustice and social sin. Once this situation was faced, the discussions took on more of a liberationist perspective. The final document, to some degree, reflects this perspective, ". . . a cry is rising to heaven, growing louder and more alarming all the time. It is the cry of a suffering people who demand justice, freedom and respect for the basic rights of human beings and peoples" (par. 87).

Final Document. The final document is divided into five parts: Pastoral Overview of the Reality That is Latin America; God's Saving Plan for Latin America; Evangelization in the Latin American Church; Communion and Participation; A Missionary Church Serving Evangelization in Latin America; Under the Dynamism of the Spirit: Pastoral Options. The conference's view of Jesus is significant for its attempt to hold a middle ground within the contemporary Latin American theological context. It lamented the attempt to distort the message of Jesus and use it for ideological purposes. "That can be done in one of two ways: either by turning him into a politician, a leader, a revolutionary, or a simple prophet on the one hand; or on the other hand, by restricting him, the Lord of history, to the merely private realm" (par 178).

Two dominant themes emerged: "Communion and Participation" and "A Preferential Option for the Poor"

On the one hand the central motif of communion and participation appeared to try to replace liberation as the dominant theological message. The preferential option for the poor, however, recalled and reinforced the message of liberation. ''We affirm the need for conversion on the part of the whole Church to a preferential option for the poor, an option aimed at their integral liberation'' (par. 1134). The text continues, ''The vast majority of our fellow humans continue to live in a situation of poverty and even wretchedness that has grown more acute'' (par 1135). ''Hence service to the poor is the privileged, though not exclusive, gauge of our following of Christ'' (par. 1145).

In spite of some repetition and contrast, the final document clearly understands evangelization as liberating from personal and social sin and as fostering communion and participation both in the Church and in society at large. CELAM III endorsed a centrist position but further committed the Church to social pastoral planning, solidarity with basic Christian communities and defense of the poor.

Bibliography: CELAM III, *La Evangelizacion en el Presente y en el Futuro de America Latina: Puebla, Documento Aprobado* (Mexico 1979); J. EAGLESON and P. SCHARPER, eds., *Puebla and Beyond: Documentation and Commentary,* translated by J. DRURY (Maryknoll 1979) (References in text to paragraph numbers are the same in Spanish and English versions). P. BERRYMAN, ''What Happened at Puebla,'' *Churches and Politics in Latin America,* ed. D. H LEVINE (Beverly Hills 1979). E. DUSSEL, *The History of the Church in Latin America: Colonialism to Liberation,* trans. A. NEELY (Grand Rapids 1981). G. GUTIERREZ, *The Power of the Poor in History* (Maryknoll 1983). P. LERNOUX, *Cry of the People* (New York 1980). G. MACEOIN, *Puebla, a Church Being Born* (New York 1980).

[J. P. HOGAN]

PUERTO, NICOLÁS DEL

Bishop of Oaxaca, Mexico; b. of indigenous parents in the mountain village of Santa Catalina Minas, near Oaxaca (date unknown); d. Oaxaca, 1681. His early studies, it seems, were made with the Jesuits in Oaxaca and were continued in the Jesuit Colegio de San Ildefonso in Mexico City where he studied philosophy and jurisprudence. He then entered the diocesan seminary. After ordination, he spent some time in Oaxaca; but he left owing to what he considered discrimination, when another was chosen for an ecclesiastical post over him. He was reported to have said that he would not return to his native city except as bishop. In 1642 he entered the Colegio Mayor de Santos in Mexico City, where he received the degree of doctor, and where he later taught and was rector and chancellor. In May 1656 he was made canon of the cathedral of Mexico and in the following year was appointed commissioner general of the Cruzada. He was also consultor of the Inquisition and vicar-general of the archdiocese. The bulls from Spain formally appointing Puerto as commissioner general of the Cruzada were late in arriving, and this created a problem. The appointee resolved the difficulty by placing a seal on one of the former bulls of Cruzada. He informed the Council of the Indies of his actions, which they approved. Having studied law, Puerto also aimed at the chair of Canon Law in the University of Mexico. In two competitive examinations he was defeated. However, convinced that he had been unjustly treated in the second examination, he appealed to the royal court, which ruled in his favor. Satisfied with the decision, he did not press for the chair, which was given to his opponent. In February of 1679 Puerto was appointed bishop of Oaxaca despite his advanced years. He had been bishop for only two years when he died, but he lived long enough to see the establishment of a seminary, which his predecessor had received permission to build, and which opened in January 1681.

Bibliography: J. A. GAY, *Historia de Oaxaca,* 2 v. (Mexico City 1881). J. M. BERISTAÍN DE SOUZA, *Biblioteca hispanoamericana septentrional,* 5 v. in 2 (3d ed. Mexico City 1947).

[C. E. RONAN]

PUERTO RICO

The smallest and most easterly of the Greater Antilles, Puerto Rico is a commonwealth of the United States. Located 885 miles southeast of Florida, the island is characterized by mountainous terrain dropping to coastal plains in the north. Sandy beaches circle much of the island, combining with the region's mild climate to create a landscape inviting to tourists. Natural resources include copper and nickel, as well as the possibility of coastal oil reserves. Puerto Rico relied for centuries on agriculture for its economic stability; sugar was raised along the coast and coffee, tobacco and starchy vegetables in the mountains. After 1949 the Industrial Development Company, a government agency, encouraged U.S. investment in the region and by 2000 Puerto Rico's exports included pharmaceuticals, electronics, rum and apparel. San Juan is one of the Caribbean's largest natural harbors.

Early History. Originally inhabited by the Arawak, Puerto Rico was discovered by Columbus on his second voyage, Nov. 16, 1493, and named San Juan de Borinquén. Juan Ponce de León, searching for gold, founded a settlement at Caparra in 1598 and the following November took possession of Puerto Rico in the name of the King of Spain, becoming its governor. Spanish missionaries entered the region shortly thereafter, working from

Capital: San Juan.
Size: 3,515 sq. miles.
Population: 3,915,798 in 2000.
Languages: Spanish, English.
Religions: 3,407,661 Catholics (87%), 274,100 Protestants (7%), 234,037 without religious affiliation.
Archdiocese: San Juan, with suffragans in Ponce, Arecibo, Mayagüez, and Caguas.

the new capital city of San Juan. On Aug. 6, 1511, Puerto Rico was made an episcopal see as a suffragan of Seville, Spain, and Father Alonso Manso became the first bishop. Jurisdiction would eventually pass from Seville to Santiago, Cuba.

Within half a century the Arawaks had become extinct due to forced labor and disease, the gold mines were exhausted. The Spanish residents petitioned to leave, but were forced to remain on the island by the Spanish government. By 1600 sugar and tobacco plantations prospered, owned by Spaniards and worked by African slaves. The 17th century witnessed the origins of the island's most famous place of pilgrimage: the church of Nuestra Señora de Monserrate in the town of Hormigueros. This shrine owed its existence to alleged apparitions visited upon the daughter of Giraldo González. While lost for two weeks, the young girl was fed by the Blessed Mother, allowing her to survive until her father found her. In about 1640 Giraldo built a chapel in the parish of San German to commemorate his daughter's visions; after his wife died he donned the robes of a priest and tended the chapel.

Still under the influence of the Spanish Church, the jurisdiction of the Diocese of San Juan was restricted to the island proper in 1791, but in 1903 it was separated from Cuba and made immediately subject to the Holy See. The Diocese of Ponce was separated from San Juan in 1924, and Edwin V. Byrne was named the first bishop. In 1960 the present hierarchy was established: the Diocese of Arecibo was established under Bishop Alfred Mendez and on April 30, San Juan was made an archdiocese with James P. Davis its first archbishop. Four years later the Diocese of Caguas was created, and Rafael Grovas was consecrated its first bishop. By 1965 the jurisdiction of San Juan had expanded to include the islands of Culebra and Vieques off the eastern coast. The diocese of Mayagüez was established in 1976.

Into the 21st Century. In 1821 Spain withdrew its protection from Puerto Rico, as the island was no longer of strategic importance. The region gained home rule under Spanish hegemony until 1898 when the United States gained the island at the close of the Spanish-American War. In 1917 the Jones Act declared all inhabitants of Puerto Rico to be statutory U.S. citizens, although they were not extended the right to vote in U.S. elections. Through the constitution of July 25, 1952 the island was declared a commonwealth. Although efforts were made to make Puerto Rico the 51st of the United States, a vote in 1993 rejected that option in favor of continued status as a self-governing commonwealth.

By 2000 there were 324 parishes with resident priests in Puerto Rico, maintained by 396 diocesan and 390 religious priests: Salesians, Dominicans, Capuchins, Vincentians, Benedictines, Jesuits, Redemptorists and Marianists. The Pontifical Catholic University of Puerto Rico, located in Ponce, was founded in 1948 and by 1965 contained a college of arts and sciences, a school of education, a school of law, and operated six extensions throughout the island. Religious women maintained over 150 primary and secondary schools, as well as a number of specialized institutions of learning, in addition to operating hospitals, orphanages and homes for the elderly. The Religious of the Sacred Heart operated a small college near San Juan. Two native communities existed, the Hermanas del Buen Pastor and the Hermanas de Fatima.

PROTESTANTISM grew steadily on the island during the 20th century, with the most active groups Methodists, Presbyterians, Episcopalians, Disciples of Christ, the United Church of Christ, the Brethren and Jehovah's Witnesses. In addition to watching its influence eroded by active evangelical sects, the Church also had to contend with liberal social attitudes imported from the United States. In 1998 Redemptorist Father Richard Welsh, C.Ss.R., who was also president of Human Life International, fought an unsuccessful battle against abortion rights clinics. A euthanasia bill introduced the same year was, however, successfully defeated through his ability to mobilize Catholic opposition. Pope JOHN PAUL II also addressed the trend toward materialism and liberalized values during a meeting with Puerto Rican bishops in 1999. Noting that the commonwealth was in a transitional period, the Pope urged Church leaders to confront ''the challenges of a society which is ever more inclined toward secularization,'' citing as evidence the rising divorce rate and instance of illegitimate births on the island.

Bibliography: A. CUESTA MENDOZA, *Historia eclesiástica de Puerto Rico* (Santo Domingo 1948–). S. BRAU, *La colonización de Puerto Rico* (San Juan 1907).

[M. MCCABE/EDS.]

PUGIN, AUGUSTUS WELBY

Architect and author; b. London, March 1, 1812; d. Ramsgate, Kent, Sept. 14, 1852. The only child of Augustus Charles Pugin, he led the Gothic revival in England, striving as a Catholic for an architecture of Christian inspiration. After being professionally trained early in life by his father (an architect, illustrator, and teacher), he accompanied a party to Normandy in 1825 to study Gothic architecture. Following his conversion to Roman Catholicism in 1834, he established his reputation with *Contrasts* (1836), wherein he attributed the artistic decline to the change of religion in the Reformation; as an architect he worked chiefly within a Catholic milieu. His theories linked the social and religious convictions of an age with the quality of its art. The principles he formulated were derived from a study of medieval art (published in *True Principles,* 1841) and won him a place in the development of modern design. With their somewhat utopian view of the Middle Ages, his studies of Gothic art and the history of the liturgy contributed to a revival of interest in liturgical art. His writings, coupled with the high quality of his buildings and decorative designs, influenced both Protestant and Catholic circles.

Among his more than 25 publications are a *Glossary of Ecclesiastical Ornament* (1844) and *A Treatise on Chancel Screens and Rood Lofts* (1851). His buildings include the cathedrals of Birmingham (St. Chad, 1839–41) and Nottingham (St. Barnabas), and the churches at Brewood (St. Mary, 1834–44), Cheadle (St. Giles, 1846), and Ramsgate (St. Augustine, 1851).

Bibliography: M. TRAPPES-LOMAX, *Pugin: A Mediaeval Victorian* (London 1932). H. SIRR, "Augustus Welby Pugin: A Sketch," *Journal of the Royal Institute of British Architects* 3d ser., 25 (1917–18) 213–226. P. B. STANTON, *ibid.* 60 (1952–53) 47–54, well illus. C. L. EASTLAKE, *A History of the Gothic Revival* (London 1872). K. M. CLARK, *The Gothic Revival, an Essay in the History of Taste* (London 1928). H. R. HITCHCOCK, *Early Victorian Architecture in Britain,* 2 v. (New Haven 1954).

[P. B. STANTON]

PULCHERIA, ST.

Byzantine empress, virgin; b. Constantinople, Jan. 19, 399; d. July 453. The daughter of the Eastern Roman Emperor ARCADIUS, she was proclaimed Augusta on July 4, 414. She was regent for her brother the Byzantine Emperor THEODOSIUS II and arranged his marriage in 421 with Athenais Eudocia, the daughter of a pagan philosopher. Pulcheria had made a vow of virginity. She was noted for her benefactions, composed secular verse and church hymns, and helped reorganize the university founded by Constantine I in Constantinople. A strong adversary of NESTORIANISM, she received a letter of gratitude from St. CYRIL OF ALEXANDRIA. Because of the hostility of Empress Eudocia and the prime minister Chrysaphius, she left the court to lead a secluded life in the palace of Hebdomon, but returned after the Robber Council of EPHESUS (449) and received frequent requests for assistance in the settlement of ecclesiastical affairs from Pope LEO I.

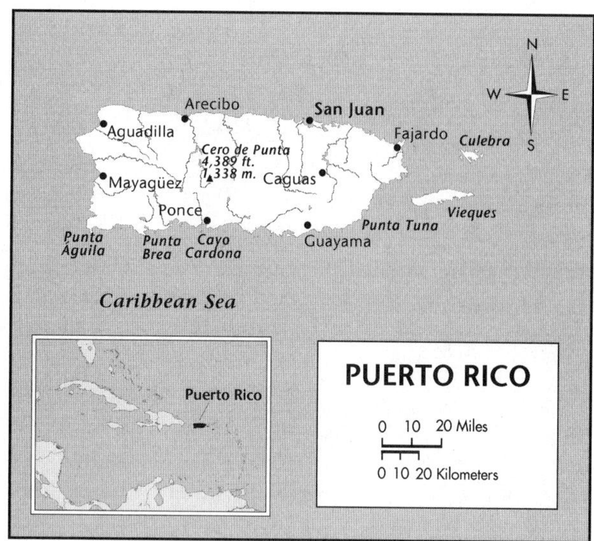

On the sudden death of Theodosius II (July 28, 450), she assumed power and married the elderly senator Marcian, who had the eunuch Chrysaphius executed. She effected the reconciliation of the Patriarch ANATOLIUS OF CONSTANTINOPLE with Rome and, despite many objections, she and Marcian convoked the Council of CHALCEDON (451) in which she took an active interest, probably being present at the sixth session.

Feast: September 10.

Bibliography: *Acta Sanctorum* Sept. 3:503–540. G. OSTROGORSKY, *History of the Byzantine State*, tr. J. HUSSEY from 2d German ed. (Oxford 1956); American ed. by P. CHARANIS (New Brunswick, N.J. 1957) 51, 55. A. B. TEETGEN, *The Life and Times of the Empress Pulcheria* (London 1907). E. SCHWARIZ, "Die Kaiserin Pulcheria auf der Synode von Chalkedon," *Festgabe für Adolf Jülicher* (Tübingen 1927) 203–212. P. GOUBERT in A. GRILLMEYER and H. BACHT, *Das Konzil von Chalkedon: Geschichte und Gegenwart* (Wurzburg 1951–54) 1:303–321.

[G. T. DENNIS]

PUNCH, JOHN

Franciscan philosopher and theologian; b. County Cork, Ireland, *c.* 1599; d. Paris, 1661. He has been frequently but erroneously called Ponce, from the Latinized surname Poncius. He entered the Franciscans at St. Anthony's College, Louvain, studied philosophy in Cologne, and then theology, first in Louvain, and from Sept. 9, 1625, at St. Isidore's College, Rome. He taught two courses of philosophy at St. Isidore's and then theology

Exterior of Ponce Cathedral at dusk, Ponce, Puerto Rico. (©Bob Krist/CORBIS)

for many years; his brother Edmund, also a Franciscan, studied under him. For a brief period, beginning July 8, 1630, he was rector of the Ludovisian College, Rome. Under its founder, Luke WADDING, St. Isidore's became the center for the 17th-century revival of Scotism. Punch collaborated with Wadding in editing the *opera omnia* of John DUNS SCOTUS.

He left Rome for France probably early in 1648. With the exception of a short stay in Lyons and a brief period as commissary of the Irish Franciscan residence, Paris, he resided at the Grand Couvent, Paris. In 1653 he found himself in the thick of a literary battle with Richard Bellings and John MacCallaghan over Nuncio Giovanni Battista RINUCCINI's censures. Having got the worst of the battle, Punch retired to his Scotist studies. In 1658 he wrote to the minister general a strongly worded defense of the Irish Franciscan exiles from Cromwellian persecution. He was the first to give a complete course of Scotist philosophy and theology, distinct from the traditional commentary on the *Sentences;* as a result he became, after Wadding, the most familiar figure of the Isidorian school of writers. A mature scholar, gifted with a subtle intelligence, he made no effort to reconcile St. Thomas Aquinas and Scotus, but accepted traditional Scotism, occasionally propounding original arguments. Even opponents, e.g., B. MASTRIUS, admitted his greatness. His major work on philosophy had five editions between 1642–43 and 1672. A course of Scotist theology was published in 1652; and in 1661, his monumental *Commentarii theologici.* Well-versed in the humanities and a facile writer, he was preeminently a metaphysician.

Bibliography: J. KAUP, in *Lexikon für Theologie und Kirche,* ed. J. HOFER and K. RAHNER, 10 v. (2d new ed. Freiburg 1957–65) 8:607. A. TEETAERT, in *Dictionnaire de théologie catholique,* ed. A. VACANT et al., 15 v. (Paris 1903–50; Tables générales 1951–) 12.2:2547–48. G. CLEARY, *Father Luke Wadding and St. Isidore's College, Rome* (Rome 1925) 43, 55–56, 83–87. B. MILLETT, *The Irish Franciscans 1651–1665* (Rome 1964). B. JENNINGS, ed., *Wadding Papers 1614–38* (Dublin 1953); "Miscellaneous Documents 1625–40," *Archivium Hibernicum* 14 (1949) 1, 3, 10, 12; "Sint-Truiden: Irish Franciscan Documents," *ibid.* 24 (1961) 184. L. WADDING, *Scriptores Ordinis Minorum* (Rome 1650; 3d ed. 1906) 149–150. J. H. SBARALEA, *Supplementum et castigatio ad scriptores trium ordinum S. Francisci a Waddingo,* 2 v. (Rome 1806; new ed. in 4 v. 1906–36) 2:118. U. SMEETS, *Lineamenta bibliographiae Scotisticae* (Rome 1942) 4, 19, 55, 109. *Father Luke Wadding: Commemorative Volume* (Dublin, London 1957). M. O'N. WALSH, "Irish Books Printed Abroad 1475–1700," *Irish Book* 2 (1963) 25–26. M. GRAJEWSKI, "John Ponce, Franciscan Scotis of the Seventeenth Century," *Franciscan Studies* 6 (1946) 54–92.

[B. MILLETT]

Catholic church in the Puerto Rican town of Isabella. (©Tony Arruza/CORBIS)

PUNIET DE PARRY, PIERRE DE

Benedictine liturgist, b. Rochefort, France, March 24, 1877; d. Abbey of Oosterhout, Holland, April 4, 1941. De Puniet, who was of a noble family of Anjou, made his profession at Solesmes on Dec. 8, 1895. Ordained on March 23, 1901, he was sent to the Abbey of Farnborough and attached to Dom Cabrol's circle. For a while he collaborated on the *Dictionnaire d'archéologie chrétienne et de liturgie.* The conference he gave at the Westminster Eucharistic Congress in 1908 on the *Dêr Balyzeh*—of such importance for the early history of the Mass—made his reputation as a liturgist. Though novice master of Oosterhout for 25 years (1917–42), he was nonetheless able to continue his scholarly writing. His chief work, *Le Sacramentaire romain de Gellone* (Rome 1938), is actually less well known than either *Le Pontifical romain: Histoire et commentaire,* 2 v. (Bruges-Paris 1930–31), of which the first volume was translated into English as *The Roman Pontifical* (New York 1932), or *Le Psautier liturgique à la lumière de la tradition chrétienne,* 2 v. (Bruges-Paris 1933–35).

Bibliography: S. G., *Ephemerides Liturgicae* 58 (1944) 316–317.

[N. HUYGHEBAERT]

PUNISHMENT

Punishment is the infliction of a penalty upon a person for a misdeed. As used here the term is to be distinguished from revenge, which is the vindictive response of an individual against one who has wronged him. As opposed to this, human punishment is here understood as the action of society against one who has transgressed its laws and so has threatened the common good.

The right to punish belongs supremely to God as to the source of all authority. In the Old Testament even natural disasters are seen as part of the punishment that God has imposed because of the infidelity of His people (e.g., Bar 2.6–10). Human lawmakers participate in God's legislative authority, and they must consequently participate in some measure in His right to punish, for without SANCTIONS their laws would have no effect. All societies bound together by laws in the proper sense of the term have therefore claimed and exercised the right of punishing transgressors of the law. The Christian sees this as a participation in God's right to punish. ''If thou dost what is evil, fear, for not without reason does it carry the sword. For it is God's minister, an avenger to execute wrath on him who does evil'' (Rom 13.4).

In most early legal codes the penalties are those of death, torture, mutilation, exile, the deprivation of civil rights or of property. In primitive societies there is commonly an effort to secure equivalence in punishment, such as the *lex talionis,* ''an eye for an eye, a tooth for a tooth'' (cf. Ex 21.28–37).

The Church claims the right to punish as following from its mandate from Christ. Ecclesiastical penalties and censures are designed to vindicate the law of God and Church and to make the offender aware of his misdeeds. Their purpose is primarily medicinal (see 1917 *Codex iuris canonici,* cc. 221–19). In a society with a single religion, the distinction between civil and religious offenses—and so of the punishments they respectively incur—can be difficult to determine. Moral sanctions extend to the total life of society. But, with the emergence of a pluralistic society, there can be only limited moral agreement among its citizens, and the relation of law to morals, and of punishment to both, is subject to radical change.

Bibliography: PIUS XII, ''Accogliete'' (message, Dec. 5, 1954) *Acta Apostolicae Sedis,* 47 (1955) 60–71, Eng. *Catholic Mind* 53 (1955) 364–373. *Dublin Review* 230 (1956) 1–88, special issue on crime and punishment by I. EVANS et al. F. A. PAKENHAM, *The Idea of Punishment* (London 1961). L. RADZINOWICZ et al., ''Punishment'' in D. S. DAVIES et al., *The Modern Approach to Criminal Law* (London 1945). 2d United Nations Congress on the Prevention of Crime and Treatment of Offenders, *Report, Prepared by the Secretariat* (New York 1961). P. DEVLIN, *The Enforcement of Morals* (New York 1965). J. CORBON in *Vocabulaire de Théologie Biblique,* ed. X. LÉON-DUFOUR (Paris 1962) 122–124. S. LYONNET, *ibid.* 345–346. C. WIÉNER, *ibid.* 919–925. E. WELTY, *A Handbook of Christian Social Ethics,* tr. G. KIRSTEIN, rev. J. FITZSIMONS (New York 1960–). W. TEMPLE, *The Ethics of Penal Action* (London 1934). A. C. EWING, *The Morality of Punishment* (London 1929).

[I. EVAN]

PURCELL, HAROLD

Missionary, editor; b. Gerardville, Pennsylvania, Jan. 3, 1881; d. Montgomery Alabama, Oct. 22, 1952. He attended Catholic schools in Philadelphia and entered the Passionist Congregation in 1897. Purcell was ordained in Union City, New Jersey, Dec. 17, 1904, and served as a home missionary for 15 years. Preaching throughout the East and Middle West, he conducted more than 300 missions and retreats. In 1921 he founded the *Sign,* a Passionist monthly magazine. Within three years he raised subscriptions to 60,000 and attracted excellent writing talent in the United States and England. The success of the *Sign* (circulation 420,000 in 1961) was due in large measure to the policies and principles Purcell established during his 13-year editorship. In 1934 he left his order to devote himself exclusively to the African American apostolate in the Mobile, Alabama diocese. Here he planned, financed, built, and directed ''The City of St. Jude,'' a $5 million complex of schools, recreation units, church, rectory, convent, hospital, and nurses' home, for the service of African Americans.

[C. J. YUHAUS]

PURCELL, HENRY

Preeminent Restoration (English) baroque composer; b. London?, 1659; d. there, Nov. 21, 1695. Purcell's father, Thomas, was associated with the private music of the royal household from the Restoration (1660) until his death in 1682. As a boy Henry sang, as did his father, in the chapel royal and attended its choir school; and in 1677 he joined his father in composing for the King's violins. He was appointed successively to the organ of Westminster Abbey (where his body rests) in 1679; to the chapel royal organ in 1682; and to the King's private music in 1689. In line with his official duties, Purcell composed for church, concert hall, and stage in an artificial, ceremonious milieu in which music—even church music—was expected only to entertain. Moreover, late Puritan ''reform'' had recently broken the last remaining links with the country's pre-Reformation liturgical traditions, so that Purcell's opportunities to create serious sacred music were limited to such forms as verse anthems, hymns, Psalm settings, sacred songs (actually solo cantatas, with texts by Cowley, Herbert, and other poets), and a few massive choral works—the *Te Deum, Magnificat, Nunc Dimittis,* and the *Jubilate* for St. Cecilia's Day (1694). On the other hand, his theater music, consisting of one complete opera, *Dido and Aeneas,* and several semioperas, enjoyed the stimulus of the flourishing Restoration stage and the unbroken masque tradition; their scores are crammed with charming songs, instrumental intermezzi, and dance interludes. Although accommodated to the taste of the times in both sacred and secular spheres, Purcell's music soars above its circumstances in an unstereotyped expression that, as the poet G. M. Hopkins put it, "uttered in notes the very make and species of man as created both in him and in all men generally." Added to this perception of the universal in the individual were his "ear-thronging" gifts of melodic and contrapuntal invention and his sensitivity to the meaning and dramatic yield of his texts. Though traditionally English in modality and tonality (the composer was called *Orpheus Britannicus* in his time), his music is probably the earliest to be considered "modern" by 20th-century norms.

Bibliography: *Works,* 31 v. (London 1878–1928, 1957–61); 22 sonatas, ed. W. G. WHITTAKER (London 1930–36). J. A. WESTRUP, *Purcell* (New York 1937); *Die Musik in Geschichte und Gegenwart*, ed. F. BLUME (Kassel-Basel 1949–) 10:1758–74. F. B. ZIMMERMAN, *Henry Purcell, 1659–95: An Analytical Catalogue of His Music* (New York 1963). J. A. FULLER-MAITLAND et al., *Grove's Dictionary of Music and Musicians*, ed. E. BLOM 9 v. (5th ed. London 1954) 6:997–1019. E. WALKER, *A History of Music in England,* ed. J. A. WESTRUP (3d ed. Oxford 1952). C. H. H. PARRY, *Music of the 17th Century,* v.3 of *Oxford History of Music,* ed. P. C. BUCK, 7 v. (2d ed. London 1929–32). G. E. P. ARKWRIGHT, "Purcell's Church Music," *Musical Antiquary* 1 (1909–10) 63–72, 234–248. M. ADAMS, *Henry Purcell: The Origins and Development of His Musical Style* (Cambridge, England 1995). M. BURDEN, "*Gallimaufry* at Covent Garden: Purcell's *The Fairy-Queen* in 1946," *Early Music* 23 (1995) 268–284. M. CAMPBELL, *Henry Purcell: Glory of the Age* (London 1993). R. R. CRAVEN, "Nahum Tate's Third *Dido and Aeneas:* The Sources of the Libretto to Purcell's Opera," *The World of Opera* 1 /2 (1979) 65–78. M. CYR, "Tempo Gradations in Purcell's Sonatas," *Performance Practice Review* 7 (1994) 182–98. C. PRICE, "*Dido and Aeneas:* Questions of Style and Evidence," *Early Music* 22 (1994) 115–25. R. SHAY, "Purcell's Revisions to the Funeral Sentences Revisited," *Early Music* 26 (1998) 457–67. I. SPINK, "Purcell's Music for *The Libertine,*" *Music and Letters* 81 (2000) 520–531.

[M. E. EVANS]

Henry Purcell, portrait by Closterman.

PURCELL, JOHN BAPTIST

Archbishop; b. Mallow, County Cork, Ireland, Feb. 26, 1800; d. St. Martin's, Brown County, Ohio, July 4, 1883. He was the third of four children of Edward and Johanna (Keefe) Purcell, who gave John an excellent classical education in the school at Mallow. At 18 he immigrated to the United States, where he obtained work as a private tutor with a prominent family on Maryland's eastern shore. In 1820 he entered Mt. St. Mary's Seminary, Emmitsburg, Md., receiving minor orders and serving on the faculty there before being sent (1824) to complete his studies at the Sulpician seminary at Paris, France. After ordination on May 20, 1826 in Notre Dame Cathedral by Abp. Hyacinthe L. de Quelen of Paris, he continued his studies at Saint-Sulpice until 1827, when he returned to the United States. At Emmitsburg he served as professor, vice president (1828), and president (1829) of Mt. St. Mary's until his appointment (1833) as bishop of Cincinnati, Ohio, to succeed its first bishop, Edward Fenwick, OP.

Bishop. Purcell was consecrated Oct. 13, 1833, by Abp. James Whitfield in the Baltimore cathedral and remained in the city to attend the sessions of the Third Provincial Council of BALTIMORE. He was installed the following November 14 in the see city of his diocese, which at the time had one church at Cincinnati, one under construction at Hamilton, and 14 others throughout the state, 9 of which had been willed by Bishop Fenwick to the Dominicans of Ohio. The new bishop lost no time in providing for the wants of the growing church in Ohio. He purchased a site for a new cathedral, and St. Peter's was completed and consecrated by Abp. Samuel Eccleston of Baltimore on Nov. 2, 1845.

After trying several locations for a diocesan seminary, Purcell laid the cornerstone (1848) of a new building on Price Hill, west of the city, and changed the name to Mt. St. Mary Seminary of the West, which was solemnly dedicated and opened with 12 seminarians in 1851. For many years it was an important center for the training of priests until its transfer (1904) to Hamilton County, Ohio. From the beginning, Purcell was an advocate of Catholic education, and under his administration parochial schools multiplied. Among the communities of religious women invited to staff them and other diocesan institutions were the Sisters of Charity, who had arrived in Cincinnati in 1829, Notre Dame sisters (1840), Precious Blood sisters (1844), Ursulines (1845), Good Shepherd sisters (1857), Sisters of Mercy and Franciscan sisters (1858), Little Sisters of the Poor (1868), the Religious of the Sacred Heart (1869), and Sisters of Christian Charity (1881). In 1840 Purcell welcomed the Jesuits and the Precious Blood fathers and, subsequently, the Lazarists (1842), the Franciscan fathers (1844), the Brothers of Mary (1849), the Passionists (1870), the Holy Cross fathers (1871), and the Holy Ghost fathers (1875).

To provide for the growing number of German immigrants in his diocese, Purcell built (1834) Holy Trinity Church, the first German-speaking parish in Cincinnati and the first west of the Alleghanies. As the German Catholic population continued to increase, numerous other such parishes were founded, directly or indirectly, from Holy Trinity. The first Catholic German periodical published in the United States was the *Wahrheitsfreund* of Cincinnati, which appeared in 1837 and continued until 1907, when the need that had brought it into existence had passed. The *Catholic Telegraph* for English-speaking Catholics had been founded in 1831 and was also used by Purcell to diffuse a correct knowledge of the Catholic faith. In 1837 the bishop's brilliant defense of Catholic teaching and practice in the debates with Alexander Campbell, a Baptist minister, not only helped to dispel much of the existing prejudice against Catholicism, but also greatly enhanced Purcell's position and reputation among his own flock and throughout the United States. When numbers of Protestant ministers began to enter the Church, Purcell urged (1853) the establishment of a fund for these highly trained men whose conversion left them without means of support.

After several visitations of his diocese, Purcell recognized the impossibility of administering the entire state properly and therefore petitioned for the erection of a new see for the northern part of the area. In 1847 the Diocese of Cleveland was erected, dividing the Diocese of Cincinnati into two parts; two years later the boundaries were adjusted by mutual agreement of the two bishops.

Archbishop. Rome recognized the rapid growth of the church in Ohio and in 1850 elevated Cincinnati to an archdiocese, making Purcell its first archbishop. He received the pallium from Pius IX the following year, during one of his many trips to Europe. When Abp. Gaetano BEDINI, who had been commissioned by Rome to investigate TRUSTEEISM in the United States, visited Cincinnati in 1853, he was the victim of a wave of KNOW-NOTHINGISM then sweeping the city. Under the leadership of Purcell, the champion of the rights of the Church in the West as Abp. John HUGHES was in the East, bloodshed was avoided and the insult to Bedini was deplored by right-minded citizens. In 1861 Cincinnati's archbishop, proclaiming himself an advocate of the Union, had the flag flown from his cathedral spire. Although this action called forth adverse criticism, Purcell continued boldly throughout the Civil War to support the North. At its close, he attended the Second Plenary Council of Baltimore (1866) and preached at one of its sessions. The conciliar decrees were sent to Rome with the usual letter to Pius IX. Later, when the text of the letter was used to support the thesis that the Second Plenary Council of Baltimore had at least implicitly affirmed papal infallibility, Purcell was one of the signers who denied the allegation.

At VATICAN COUNCIL I (1869–70), he opposed the formal declaration of papal infallibility, not only because he considered it inopportune, but also because he objected to the definition of the doctrine itself before it was clearly stated just what was meant by the pope's infallibility. Before the final vote on the question was taken, Purcell was granted permission to return home. However, once the matter had been decided, he lost no time in publicly professing his belief in the dogma as defined.

Under Purcell a number of diocesan synods were held as well as the first three provincial councils (1855, 1858, 1861). Although the question of a coadjutor came up several times, it was not until 1862 that Sylvester H. Rosecrans was appointed auxiliary to Cincinnati. His transfer to Columbus, Ohio, in 1868 again left Purcell alone until 1880, when he resigned all affairs into the hands of the new coadjutor and administrator, Bp. William H. Elder. Purcell's last days were clouded by the serious financial disaster that struck the archdiocese in 1878. The archbishop's brother, Rev. Edward Purcell, had for 40 years conducted a private banking system that had attracted many depositors, particularly after the failure of several local banks and a number of national financial panics. However, in 1878 a run on the money deposited with Purcell depleted available funds and payments were suspended. A subsequent examination disclosed the insolvent state of the banking operation and an assignment of all the resources of the bank was supplemented by the transfer of certain diocesan property. When these proved insufficient to cover all liabilities, legal action ensued (1880–1905) in state and federal courts.

The archbishop's health was affected by the strain, and in November 1879 he took up residence in the Ursuline convent in Brown County, where he died a few years later. His remains were interred in the convent cemetery. During his administration the church had made great progress; in 1833 there had been only 16 churches for about 7,000 Catholics served by 14 priests, whereas in 1883 Ohio counted 500 churches with a Catholic population of 500,000, served by 480 priests.

Bibliography: Archives, Cincinnati archdiocese. M. A. MCCANN, *Archbishop Purcell and the Archdiocese of Cincinnati* (Washington 1918). J. H. LAMOTT, *History of the Archdiocese of Cincinnati, 1821–1921* (New York 1921). M. E. HUSSEY, "The 1878 Financial Failure of Archbishop Purcell," *The Cincinnati Historical Society Bulletin* 36 (1978).

[M. P. CARTHY]

PURE ACT

Pure act is an expression used in scholastic philosophy and theology to describe the absolute or pure perfection of God, in contrast with the limited or mixed perfection of creatures. ACT here is a technical term meaning actually possessed perfection, while pure means unmixed with POTENCY, that is, with any intrinsic capacity for change or limitation. The expression is to be understood, therefore, in function of the general theory of potency and act initiated by ARISTOTLE and further developed by St. THOMAS AQUINAS and scholastic thinkers from the 13th century on (*see* POTENCY AND ACT).

This theory was originally developed by Aristotle to explain CHANGE or MOTION. Potency was conceived as a capacity for change, and not yet as a principle of LIMITATION. Hence, for Aristotle, any being that has no intrinsic potency for change but always actually possesses the full measure of perfection proper to it is a pure act. Since matter is of its nature a principle of change, a pure act must be a purely spiritual intelligence whose act or perfection consists in eternal, changeless, and blissful self-contemplation.

Although Aristotle's proof for the existence of an unmoved mover in the *Physica* (258b 10–267b 27) mentions only one such being explicitly, he seems finally to have admitted, for reasons based on the current astronomy, some 55 of these, each a prime mover for one of the heavenly spheres (*Meta.* 1073a 13–1074b 14). Perfection for him, as for pre-Christian Greek philosophy in general, seemed not to imply infinity, but rather connoted the formless, the indeterminate, and the imperfect. Thus pure act excluded change but not limitation, and there could be several different pure acts, each complete in its own act of self-contemplation.

When 13th-century Christian thinkers took over Aristotelian philosophy as an instrument of theology, they modified the Aristotelian notion of pure act and applied it to the Christian God, unique Creator of all. It then became the infinite plenitude of all possible perfection, from which all other beings received perfection in different limited degrees, each in proportion to the limiting potency or capacity of its own nature. Potency thus became a principle of limitation as well as of change, and all beings outside of God were seen to be, in some way, mixtures of act and potency. For St. Thomas, since the ultimate perfection of all things is existence itself, God is a pure subsistent act of existence, *Ipsum Esse Subsistens,* including all other perfections. At the opposite end of the scale of perfection lies pure potency or primary matter; considered in itself (though according to St. Thomas it could never exist by itself), this is pure capacity for perfection, with no act or perfection of its own (*see* MATTER AND FORM).

The few modern philosophers outside the Aristotelian-scholastic tradition who have adopted the expression use it to convey a conception of God as Absolute Spirit, thinking Himself and the world in a single pure act of thought; this group includes G. W. F. HEGEL, G. GENTILE, M. BLONDEL, and L. LAVELLE.

See Also: ASEITY (ASEITAS); GOD IN PHILOSOPHY, 3; INFINITY OF GOD.

Bibliography: THOMAS AQUINAS, *C. gent.* 1.16–18, 28, 43; THOMAS AQUINAS, *Summa theologiae,* 1a, 3–4, 7. W. N. CLARKE, "Limitation of Act by Potency: Aristotelianism or Neoplatonism," *The New Scholasticism* 26 (1952) 167–194.

[W. N. CLARKE]

PURE AND IMPURE

The OT concept of the pure and impure, a notion shared with most of the ancient religions, does not derive its origins from moral considerations. Rather, its origins are found in primitive disgust with the loathsome, a dynamic consideration of sin, and the consciousness, proper to Israel, of being a holy people, striving for holiness, separated and apart from other peoples. This article treats the pure and impure in this order: consideration that it is not a moral concept, it is related to the holy, the concept's growth and change, and its position in NT Christianity.

NOT A MORAL CONCEPT

The pure (*tāhēr*) is not to be identified with physical cleanness or moral purity; on the other hand, the impure (*tāmē'*) positively suggests something mysterious and dangerous and, consequently, to be avoided at all costs. Hence the impure is strictly forbidden or taboo. Thus a person, an animal, a certain thing or action may be impure, e.g, a woman after childbirth, a camel, a corpse. Words that convey this concept of pure or impure appear more than 500 times in the Bible. Purity seems to become a matter of national life and death, its loss causing Yahweh to turn away His face: ''According to their uncleanness and their transgressions I dealt with them'' (Ez 39.24). This attitude stems from Israel's response to the holiness of Yahweh: ''Be holy, for I, the Lord, your God, am holy'' (Lv 19.2). Cleanness or purity implies holiness; yet, in certain respects, the impure resembles the holy.

RELATED TO THE HOLY

The idea of the impure and the holy are closely related. This is well illustrated by the Semitic root *ḥrm* with its polarity of meaning, signifying both the holy and the abominable [see W. F. Albright, *From the Stone Age to Christianity* (New York 2d ed. 1948) 176]. That which is holy (*qādôš*) is untouchable (Lv 11.31–40; 15.4–12, 20–28). Therefore, after performing his sacred duties, the priest had to take off his holy garments and put on others (Ez 44.19; Ex 28.43; Lv 6.3–4; etc.). By touching sacred objects, such as the red heifer (Nm 19.1–10), one became impure; hence the priest who sprinkled the blood contracted impurity that necessitated washings before he could approach the Holy One. Although the removal of impurity is called ''sanctifying'' (Jos 3.5; 1 Sm 16.5), to be pure and to be holy are not the same. Purity seems to be a condition or prerequisite for holiness, a positive power of worthiness for approaching the ''Holy One.'' The ''holy'' God can not tolerate the impure, which shows that the foundation of the purity prescriptions in the OT are of a religious nature. [*See* HOLINESS (IN THE BIBLE)]. Since Yahweh is a jealous God and tolerates no other gods, His people become impure by worshiping other gods (Jer 2.7, 23; Hos 6.10; etc.), by consulting fortunetellers (Lv 19.31), shaving the hair above the forehead for the dead (Dt 14.1), etc.; because other gods are worshiped in foreign lands, these lands (Am 7.17; Is 52.1) and all that comes with them, including their food, (Hos 9.3; Dn 1.5–16), are impure. Consequently, Canaanite sanctuaries and their contents had to be utterly destroyed (Dt 7.5, 25) and the booty of the Madianite war had to be purified (Nm 31.20–24). Returning from Babylon, the Jews purified themselves (Est 6.20–22) and the walls of Jerusalem, which had been defiled by foreigners (Neh 12.30). As illustrated by the practice of the Jews who returned from the Babylonian Exile, the center of the laws of ritual purity in the postexilic age was the theological notion of the holiness of separation [see J. Bonsirven, *Le Judaïsme Palestinien au temps de Jesus-Christ* 2 v. (Paris 1934) 2:183–185]. In NT times the Jews are mentioned as avoiding impurity, i.e., contact with foreigners at the time of the Passover (Jn 18.28).

GROWTH AND CHANGE

The distinction between the pure and impure existed among the Israelites before the codification of the Mosaic Law. Having taken over and sanctioned the customs, the Law transformed them into religious precepts. Their observance became a sign of the holiness of the people of God (Lv 11.44) and served to preserve monotheism among the Israelites since it set them apart from the pagan nations (Dn 1.8, 12; Tb 1.10–12; etc.); moreover, because the precepts of purity were regarded as God's commandments, their observance fostered morality. In fact, this practice led to heroic deeds, such as the martyrdom of Eleazar (2 Mc 6.18–31). Nevertheless, the danger of formalism was ever present and an exaggerated zeal for ritual purity arose. The preexilic Prophets inveighed against abuses in cult practices of purification: ''This people draws near with words only and honors me with their lips alone, though their hearts are far from me, and their reverence for me has become routine observance of the precepts of men'' (Is 29.13; see also Hos 6.6; Am 4.1–5; Jer 7.21–24). The Prophets continued to emphasize that the real impurity that stained man was sin (Ez 36.17–26), a stain in man that only God could purify (Is 6.5–7). The radical purification of lips and heart and of the entire being comes with the messianic promises: ''I will sprinkle clean water upon you to cleanse you from all your impurities, and from all your idols I will cleanse you . . .'' (Ez 36.25; see also Zep 3.9; Is 35.8; 52.1).

The Psalmists also celebrate moral purity. God's goodness turns to the clean of heart [Ps 72(73).1]. Approach to the Lord is for the sinless, whose heart is clean [Ps 23 (24).4]; the Lord rewards according to one's justice [Ps 17(18).21, 25]. More than all other Psalms, the ''Miserere'' [Ps 50(51)] manifests the transition to moral purity: ''Cleanse me of sin with hyssop, that I may be purified; wash me, and I shall be whiter than snow'' (v. 9). Paralleling Ezechiel (36.25) and crowning the OT tradition, the Psalmist cries: ''A clean heart create for me, O God, and a steadfast spirit renew within me'' (v. 12). The other Wisdom teachers also stress purity of heart, hands, and prayer (Jb 11.4, 14; 16.17), while noting a radical impurity of man before God (Prv 20.9; Jb 9.30–31).

POSITION IN NT CHRISTIANITY

Side by side with the tradition accenting moral purity in postexilic Judaism, there is found also the legalistic tendency, which continued to the time of Christ, that placed increasing emphasis on the material conditions of purity, i.e., repeated ablutions (Mk 7.3–8), cup washing (Mt 23.25), avoidance of sinners (Mk 2.15–16), and the like. Jesus Himself observed certain rules of purity (Mk 1.43–44) and seemed to condemn only excesses [Mk 7.6–13; see V. Taylor, *The Gospel according to Mark*

(London1952) 342–347]. It is not likely that He explicitly and categorically abrogated the dietary laws of Judaism; otherwise, it is difficult to understand why the early Christian community had to go through such painful searchings before finally eliminating these laws (Acts 10.14; 15.28–29; Gal 2.11–17; Rom 14.14; Col 2.20–22). Yet, Jesus decisively proclaimed that moral impurity, not ritual, is the true defilement: ''Hear men, all of you, and understand. There is nothing outside a man that entering into him, can defile him; but the things that come out of a man, these are what defile a man'' (Mk 7.14–15). In this sense devils can be called ''unclean spirits'' (Mk 1.23; Lk 9.42). It is then the pure of heart (Mt 5.8) who have access to God. To see God and to come into His Presence, not only in the Temple but also into His Kingdom, moral purity is not sufficient. The active presence of the Lord is necessary; only then is man radically pure or holy: ''You are already clean because of the word I have spoken to you. Abide in me, and I in you'' (Jn 15.3; see also 13.10).

Bibliography: *Encyclopedic Dictionary of the Bible*, tr. and adap. by L. HARTMAN (New York 1963), from A. VAN DEN BORN, *Bijbels Woordenboek* 196–94. G. A. BUTTRICK, ed., *The Interpreters' Dictionary of the Bible,* 4 v. (Nashville 1962) 1:641–648. P. VAN IMSCHOOT, *Théologie de l'Ancien Testament,* 2 v. (Tournai 1954–56) 2:204–216.

[J. LACHOWSKI]

PURE NATURE, STATE OF

The term pure nature as it comes into modern theology is very much colored by the controversies over the teaching of BAIUS and C. JANSEN. As it is customarily used, it describes a possible state of man contrasted with elevated or engraced nature, and fallen or sinful nature. In the state of pure nature a man would possess all the physical and spiritual realities necessary to constitute a human being: a body and a rational soul with all their properties and capacities. In addition to this, pure nature would have a natural destiny, i.e., an end proportionate to its created capacities. This natural end would be the love of God as author of nature above all things [*see* R. Garrigou-Lagrange, *Grace* (St. Louis 1952) 33]. While no Catholic theologian would maintain that any such state ever actually existed, a very large number have insisted that only by formulating the notion of pure nature as a genuine possibility can the absolute gratuity of the SUPERNATURAL ELEVATION OF MAN be clearly understood and defended. For, once it can be ascertained what precisely belongs to nature, then the theologian is in a position to determine what GRACE is and, therefore, what must be affirmed as God's unowed gift. This approach has been used extensively against the teaching of Baius and Jansen. It is pointed out that since they deny the possibility of pure nature they make of God's gifts of grace something owed to human nature. Therefore the loss of grace through sin must necessarily corrupt the very nature of man.

In recent years, however, there has been considerable reevaluation of the notion of pure nature. Much of it began with the publication of H. de Lubac's historical study of the issue, entitled *Surnaturel* (Paris 1945). The extensive debate and discussion that followed the appearance of this book concerned itself with both issues raised by the book, although not always keeping them clearly separate. The first issue concerned the historical development of the notion itself. The correlative issue that Père de Lubac raised concerned the validity of the theological position maintaining that this notion of pure nature was necessary for the proper understanding and protection of the absolute gratuity of the supernatural [*see* P. J. Donnelly, ''The Gratuity of the Beatific Vision and the Possibility of a Natural Destiny,'' *Theological Studies* 11 (1950) 374–404]. These noteworthy issues require some elaboration.

Historical Issue. As to the historical issue, De Lubac asserted that the theological notion of pure nature found in modern theology was unknown to St. Thomas and his contemporaries. He saw it as being first formulated in the 16th century under the influence of Cajetan. In Cajetan's thought man cannot naturally aspire to what his natural powers cannot accomplish. It is possible, therefore, for an intelligent creature to exist without effective orientation to the BEATIFIC VISION. Cajetan and those who follow him hold that such a nature could be satisfied by an end or destiny proportionate to its own powers. Others would hold that even if such a nature could exist without the vision of God, nevertheless it would have a conditioned desire for it. De Lubac, however, claimed that St. Thomas never considered the idea of a spiritual being as having any end other than the vision of God.

After a lengthy debate in the many articles *Surnaturel* engendered, it would seem to be clear that St. Thomas does not explicitly treat of the possibility of a pure nature with a purely natural end. He is concerned with a pure nature (*in puris naturalibus*) in relation to the means of salvation, i.e., nature with a desire to see God but not having grace. A further question raised in the course of the debate was whether or not the internal structure of St. Thomas's theology excludes the possibility of a purely natural end. In the light of the evidence presented during the debate, it seems clear that St. Thomas's system does allow for this possibility [*see* G. de Broglie, *De fine ultimo vitae humanae* (Paris 1948)].

Theological Issue. The question of the necessity of the notion of pure nature to explain and undergird the gratuity of the order of grace is still under debate. It is clear, of course, as Pius XII affirmed in *Humani generis,* that God could have created intellectual beings not called to the beatific vision (H. Denzinger, *Enchiridion symbolorum,* ed. A. Schönmetzer [Freiburg 1963] 3891). The fact, however, of the possibility of not being called to the beatific vision is quite distinct from the possibility of pure nature, for in this latter case the use of the term nature presupposes a determined philosophical position on what precisely ''nature'' and ''natural'' are. It is this last point that has been challenged by a growing number of theologians in recent years as is illustrated by the following arguments.

In the first stage of the debate a few appeared to maintain that man's orientation to the vision of God is a necessary dynamism of a created spirit—an element of its very nature. Hence, the notion of pure nature as commonly used in theology would have neither meaning nor relevance. Something is natural only in the sense of being contrasted to the divine. It is this position that seems to be the object of the statement of Pius XII referred to above. It was a view that never gathered much support since it makes no distinction between creation and creation in Christ and so does not preserve the special gratuity of salvific grace.

Coming to the fore in the course of the debate was another opinion: that since God has in fact called man to the beatific vision, then this vocation, itself a free gift of God, enters into the total structure of man's concrete nature. In the terminology of K. Rahner, it is a SUPERNATURAL EXISTENTIAL, which of necessity brings into being a resonance and a tendency to the vision of God [*see* K. Rahner, ''Concerning the Relationship between Nature and Grace, *Theological Investigations,* v.1, tr. C. Ernst (Baltimore 1961) 295–317]. In this perspective the distinction between natural and supernatural would be reformulated. It would begin by recognizing that there is nothing in man that is not affected by the supernatural sphere. Created human nature as it exists in fact would make it impossible to set down in any detailed way a definition of the distinction between the two natures. Thus, the conception of the notion of pure nature cannot be delineated without ambiguity. For it cannot be done with either completeness or surety. Hence, while nature as distinct from the supernatural is a genuine reality and a proper order, it cannot be defined exactly. Those who follow this opinion, therefore, would tend to give much less importance to the notion of pure nature than it has had for many modern theologians and theological manuals.

See Also: DESIRE TO SEE GOD, NATURAL; DESTINY, SUPERNATURAL; MAN, 3; NATURAL ORDER; NATURE; OBEDIENTIAL POTENCY; PRETERNATURAL; SUPERNATURAL ORDER.

Bibliography: J. ALFARO, *Lo natural y lo sobrenatural desde Santo Tomás hasta Cayetano* (Madrid 1952). H. DE LUBAC, *Augustinisme et théologie moderne* (Paris 1965); *The Mystery of the Supernatural,* tr. R. SHEED (New York 1967). J. P. KENNY, ''Reflections on Human Nature and the Supernatural,'' *Theological Studies* 14 (1953) 280–287. L. RENWART, ''La Nature pure à la lumière de l'encyclique *Humani generis,*'' *Nouvelle revue théologique* 74 (1952) 337–354. H. RONDET, ''Le Problème de la nature pure et la théologie du XVIe siècle,'' *Recherche de science religieuse* 35 (1948) 481–521. D. J. M. BRADLEY, *Aquinas on the Twofold Human Good* (Washington, D.C. 1997). S. A. LONG, ''On the Possibility of a Purely Natural End for Man,'' *The Thomist* 64 (2000) 211–37.

[E. M. BURKE]

PURGATORY

According to the teaching of the Church, the state, place, or condition in the next world, which will continue until the last judgment, where the souls of those who die in the state of grace, but not yet free from all imperfection, make expiation for unforgiven venial sins or for the temporal punishment due to venial and mortal sins that have already been forgiven and, by so doing, are purified before they enter heaven.

In the Bible

Although the doctrine of purgatory is not explicitly stated in the Bible, belief in its existence is intimately related to the biblical doctrines of divine judgment [*see* JUDGMENT, DIVINE (IN THE BIBLE)], the forgiveness of sins [*see* FORGIVENESS OF SINS (IN THE BIBLE)], the mercy of God, and the temporal punishment due to sin. The essential truths known to the Israelites before the time of Christ and familiar to the writers of the New Testament were that the dead are to be judged according to their works; that their sins render it a terrible thing to be judged by God; that souls need God's mercy in order to enter heaven; and that their brethren ought to pray to God to show them mercy.

In the Old Testament. Prayer and sacrifice of expiation for the dead appear only in the last two centuries before Christ. Before this time no acts of worship directed toward the dead seem to have existed. (See R. De Vaux, *Ancient Israel, Its Life and Institutions*, tr. J. McHugh [New York 1961] 60.)

The only passage that can be cited in support of the doctrine of purgatory is 2 Mc 12.39–45. According to the text, when Judas Maccabee and his men made arrangements for the fitting burial of the soldiers of his army who had died near Adullam, it was discovered that they had worn pagan amulets, contrary to the prescriptions of the Mosaic Law. Judas concluded that God had punished the soldiers for this sinful practice; God's just judgment was praised, and prayers were offered on behalf of the victims. A collection of 12,000 drachmas was then gathered and sent to Jerusalem to have expiatory sacrifices offered for those who had fallen in battle. The inspired author of 2 Maccabees, a firm believer himself in the resurrection of the dead (2 Mc 7.9, 11, 14, 23, 29), concludes that Judas also believed in the resurrection of the dead. He, therefore, praised Judas, who acted out of consideration for the resurrection of the dead, and argued that, if he had not hoped that the slain should rise again, it would have been useless and foolish to pray for them when dead; but if he did this with a view toward the splendid reward that awaited those who died in godliness, it was a holy and pious thought. Therefore, Judas made atonement for the dead, that they might be freed from sin. *See* SIN (IN THE BIBLE).

According to the traditional interpretation of this passage, the inspired author believed that those who had otherwise led good lives were purified by prayer and sacrifice from their sins. This essentially is the Catholic doctrine on purgatory. If, however, as many modern exegetes hold, the author regarded these sacrifices as necessary for the eschatological resurrection of the dead soldiers, then these passages do not directly refer to the doctrine of purgatory. The words of Sir 7.33, ''withhold not your kindness from the dead,'' refer directly to proper mourning and burial of the dead; if, however, they are read in the light of 2 Mc 12.43–45, prayers for the deceased might also be recommended.

In Judaism. In rabbinical literature, besides the everlasting punishments of GEHENNA and the punishment of sinners, the idea was current that some people would remain only for a time in Gehenna, where they would be purified. Some rabbis interpreted the words of Zec 13.9 in this sense: ''I will bring the one third through fire, and I will refine them as silver is refined, and I will test them as gold is tested.'' The school of Shammai attributed this purification to the eschatological place of torture, where certain people, through God's mercy and goodness, would be prepared to enjoy eternal life.

In the New Testament. The New Testament shows that the disciples of Jesus were familiar with His teaching on sin and judgment (Mt 12.32, 36; 16.27; Lk 7.47;12.47–48). His words deepened their sense of God's holiness, kindled their hopes of merciful forgiveness, and inspired them to pray for the dead. He taught them the stern truths of death and judgment, and nothing suggests that only the spotlessly pure would escape hell (see Mt 8.12; Lk 12.20; 16.22; Jn 9.4; 11.9; 12.35).

Several texts can be understood as referring to purgatory at least indirectly, e.g., Mt 12.32, where mention is made of certain sins ''which will not be forgiven either in this world or in the world to come.'' Also, Paul's prayer for Onesiphorus (2 Tm 1.18), ''may the Lord grant him to find mercy from the Lord on that day,'' seems to imply the existence of purgatory. St. Paul's parable in 1 Cor 3.10–15 on various Christian preachers working to spread the kingdom of God is not concerned about purgatory, except perhaps in an accommodated sense. In the final analysis, the Catholic doctrine on purgatory is based on tradition, not Sacred Scripture.

Bibliography: *Encyclopedic Dictionary of the Bible*, tr. and adap. by L. HARTMAN (New York 1963), from A. VAN DEN BORN, *Bijbels Woordenboek* 1964–65. J. GNILKA, *Lexikon für Theologie und Kirche*[2], ed. J. HOFER and K. RAHNER, (2d new ed. Freiburg 1957–65) 4:50–51. A. MICHEL, *Dictionnaire de théologie catholique*, ed. A. VACANT et al. (Paris 1903–50; Tables générales 1951–) 13.1:1163–79. E. O'BRIEN, ''The Scriptural Proof for the Existence of Purgatory from 2 Mc. 12.43–45,'' *Sciences ecclésiastiques* 2 (1949) 80–108.

[J. F. X. CEVETELLO]

In Theology

The Catholic doctrine on purgatory may now be considered, along with indications of its basis in early tradition and in the councils. Also to be taken up is the theological speculation on the data of revelation; in the course of treating this latter, modern opinions about the nature of purgatory may be summarized.

Catholic Doctrine. Underlying the teaching on purgatory are several presuppositions. (1) The Church solemnly teaches the difference between mortal sin, which causes the eternal loss of the soul in hell (Denz 1002), and venial sin, which does not cause eternal DAMNATION and which even the just commit in daily life (Denz 1573). (2) The Church also teaches that the punishment due to sin, whether mortal or venial, is not always and necessarily forgiven along with the guilt of sin; hence this punishment is to be paid by the sinner either in this life or in the next before he can enter the kingdom of heaven (Denz 1580, 1712).

Magisterial Statements. The existence of purgatory as a state where those dying with such temporal punishment may be cleansed before being admitted to heaven and the direct vision of the divine essence is clear from the authoritative teaching of the First and Second Councils of Lyons (Denz 838, 856) and of the Council of Florence (Denz 1304), all of which expressed the common belief of both the East and the West. Finally, the Council of Trent reiterated the revealed character of the existence of purgatory against the reformers, who had denied that there was any basis for it in Sacred Scripture (Denz 1580, 1820). Since there is no solemn statement of the Church about the existence of the guilt of venial sin in purgatory, the only thing certain is that at least the punishment due to forgiven sins is exacted from the soul. In addition to the certain existence of purgatory, the Church has also authoritatively defined that the souls detained there can be helped by the prayers and other good works of the faithful on earth (Denz 856, 1304, 1743, 1753, 1820, 1867; *see* INDULGENCES). The manner in which these prayers and good works of the faithful are applied to the souls in purgatory has not been authentically determined by the Church.

Tradition. The Fathers in general are clear in their affirmation of the reality of purgation in some form. This is not to deny that some time was needed to formulate a clear and definitive idea of the purification to take place in the other world, for varying eschatological views prevented in the early centuries a uniform presentation of its nature. The witness of the Fathers to the fact of such purification after death, therefore, is beyond doubt; their explanation of the purifying process has as much validity as the reasons advanced by each one. One thing is certain: the primitive Church never accepted the belief that in each and every instance the eternal beatitude of the just began immediately after death. The widely held though false theory that heaven would begin, at least for those who were not martyrs, only at the RESURRECTION of the dead excluded this. In addition, prayers and other good works were offered for the departed souls as a matter of common practice. There can be no doubt, then, that the widespread belief of the early Church, as shown by many of the Fathers (*see* TERTULLIAN, ORIGEN, CYPRIAN, EPHRAM, AMBROSE, AUGUSTINE, CHRYSOSTOM, CAESARIUS OF ARLES, and GREGORY THE GREAT; texts in *Enchiridion patristicum*, ed. M. J. Rouët de Journel [21st ed. Freiburg im Breisgau 1960] index 587–589) and as evidenced by the liturgy, demanded the existence of a state after death in which the souls of the just would be fully purified from any remains of sin before entering heaven.

The scholastic writers accepted this teaching of the Fathers and constructed a more consistent synthesis. They taught clearly the doctrines of the existence of purgatory and the finite duration of its punishments; there was general agreement on the presence of fire as the purifying agent. On secondary points, such as the remission of venial sins, the gravity and duration of the punishments, and the location where they took place, differences were apparent. The basic teaching was then incorporated into the Councils of Lyons, Florence, and Trent, and forms the nucleus of present Catholic belief about purgatory.

The teaching of the Eastern Church today displays some differences from that of the West. The dead find themselves in an intermediate state, awaiting the day of the final judgment. The good already enjoy some foretaste of heaven, while the evil experience some of the torments of hell. Beyond this, Eastern doctrine is not too clear, although their theologians in general reject the idea that the purification takes place by fire and that a special place is set aside for it. Since neither of these points was defined in the councils, the seeming opposition between East and West in the matter of purgatory is not insurmountable. In general, the teaching of the Eastern Church reflects the primitive and somewhat undeveloped doctrine of the Fathers on the status of the departed souls.

Nature of Purgatory. Questions relating to the punishments of purgatory and allied topics are much more obscure than the question of the existence of purgatory. All theologians hold that there will be some kind of purifying punishment there (from the very etymology of the word) that will cease with the last judgment. Of its very nature, therefore, the punishment is temporary.

Duration of Purgatory. It is a false question to inquire more precisely how long purgatory will endure. First, the separated soul no longer lives in the time of this world, but in *aevum,* where duration is not measured in days and years. Second, the soul becomes very conscious of its tremendous shortcomings, of the actions it has failed to perform, or performed poorly, or not done at all, and it is wholly intent on making good for these. Thus the intensity of the suffering could well take place in an instant, or could endure for some time, without the soul being aware of it. Because of these considerations theologians have abstained from speculating on the duration of the sufferings of purgatory.

Nature of the Punishment. The temporary deprivation of the BEATIFIC VISION, for which the soul would otherwise be prepared, is surely one of the keenest punishments of purgatory. Some theologians wish to call this the pain of loss, seeing that the consciousness of being separated from the Creator, who is so near and yet so far, causes terrible suffering and longing for Him, which is heightened still more by the knowledge that the venial sins and punishment due to sin could have been expiated so easily by contrition, prayer, and other good works in this life. Others maintain that there is no pain of loss in the proper sense of the word. In regard to the pain of sense there is likewise great diversity of opinion. Many think that the total suffering of purgatory is identified with the awareness of the temporary postponement of the beatific vision, although the more common view holds that, in addition to this, there is some positive punishment, intended to repair the disorder caused by the partial aversion from God and the turning toward creatures that is the result of venial sin.

An entirely different question concerns the constitution of this pain of sense. In the Latin Church it has been generally maintained that this pain is imposed through real fire. This is not, however, essential to belief in purgatory. It is not even certain. The Greeks explicitly rejected the notion that the punishment was by means of fire, a view they were not required to change before subscribing to the statements of faith in the councils of reunion. St. Thomas explained the fire as a binding and hampering of the soul. Others hold for fire in the real sense. When the objection is raised that real fire could have no effect on the spiritual soul, these theologians are ready with an answer. The soul in purgatory, even though separated from the body, remains in some mysterious way related to the material world and open to its influence, so much so that it attains its ultimate fulfillment only at the resurrection, that is, when it is again rejoined to the body. This relationship of the soul to matter, lasting even after death, furnishes a metaphysical and salvific basis for its purification by a material agent. Even if one chooses, with the theologians of the East, to reject the idea of suffering induced by fire, one should be careful not to exclude all positive suffering from purgatory. There are still real affliction, sorrow, chagrin, shame of conscience, and other spiritual sorrows capable of inflicting true pain on the soul.

Intensity of the Punishment. This question is less discussed today than it was in medieval times. St. Bonaventure thought that the deprivation of the beatific vision was the most intense and painful suffering encountered in purgatory. Suárez was inclined to agree with him, but at the same time saw a difficulty in the case of a very holy person who entered purgatory with only the slightest punishment for which to atone. This holy soul, because it was soon to attain to a very high degree of union with God, would suffer more from the postponement of this union than another soul who was destined for a lower place in heaven. Suárez, therefore, made the following modifications: first, although the deprivation of the glory of heaven ought of its very nature to bring more suffering to the souls who are most holy, because of the mercy of God this suffering is tempered by the perfect love with which these souls accept it; second, the sorrow of the souls in purgatory also stems from the degree of glory that they have failed to attain, which makes the suffering of a less perfect soul more intense precisely because it realizes it has attained less perfection than it could have.

A veil of mystery prevents any accurate assessment of the intensity of the pain of purgatory. St. Catherine of Genoa wrote that the desire of the soul for God was an ardent fire more consuming and painful than any earthly fire. SS. Thomas and Bonaventure held that the slightest fire of purgatory was more painful than the greatest sufferings of this world. Modern authors adhere more closely to the view of Suárez, who denied the validity of such comparisons, since they deal with two entirely different orders, one of which is beyond our present experience and hence incapable of being compared with that which we know here. One should remember, at any rate, that in the midst of their sufferings these souls also experience great joy over the certainty of salvation. This point will be treated below.

It is not out of place to remark here that the terrifying descriptions of purgatory sometimes found in popular writing, sermons, and other such material are not based on the teaching of the Church. As has been shown, even the idea of fire is not universally accepted. Certain conceptions, then, stressing too much the horror and misery of purgatory, running counter to the incomparable dignity of the children of God who are detained there, and causing scandal to the faithful, should be discountenanced. They either arise from the indiscreet use of private revelations, which generally do not rise above the theological level of the recipient of such alleged apparitions, or they mirror the thought of the time. In this matter the advice of the Council of Trent is wise, insisting upon the exclusion from sermons not only of difficult and subtle questions that do not edify the people, but also of what savors of idle curiosity and superstition, and of what is scandalous and repulsive (Denz 1820). It is to the interests of both theological precision and of the dignity of this mystery to avoid all fantastic imagery in speaking of the nature of purgatory.

Purpose of the Suffering. The soul in purgatory must be freed of certain defects: (1) the guilt of venial sin; (2) inclination toward sin (inordinate desires); and (3) temporal punishment due to sin. Until quite recent times the preponderance of theological thought denied that the suffering of purgatory had as its purpose the forgiveness of the guilt of venial sin. Authors held that the guilt of venial sin was forgiven by the intense act of love of God that the soul elicited at its entrance into purgatory, an act of love that is the more intense now that the soul, freed from the trammels and drag of the body, turns toward God with the full powers of its spiritual faculties. In this state a divided, partial allegiance to God would be unthinkable. Thus the soul in purgatory is freed from the guilt of sin from the beginning and suffers only the temporal punishment due to his sins. Many authors, however, question this view.

It does not seem to take into consideration the weakness of the soul induced by lifelong habits of sin, habits acquired, it is true, through the body, but many of which affect the powers of the soul itself. The opinion also overlooks the fact that Scripture, when it refers to purification after death, speaks of the forgiveness of the guilt of venial sin in purgatory. The authority of St. Thomas is claimed by both sides of this dispute, but it is noteworthy that only after the 16th century did the view become prevalent that the guilt of sin was removed at entry into purgatory. The liturgy seems to favor the modern view also, as in the prayer for the blessing of a cemetery: ''Absolve the souls of all whose bodies are laid to rest here from every bond of sin.'' Again: ''We beseech You, O Lord, grant to the souls of your faithful whose bodies rest here the forgiveness of all their sins.'' While the probative force of these prayers may be questioned by contending that no distinction is made between the guilt of sin and punishment due to sin, they do serve as a strong confirmation for the view that the guilt of sin itself is forgiven in purgatory.

This latter opinion is also in greater conformity with the sanctity of God and the dignity of the human person. It seems more in keeping with the holiness of God that He would progressively transform and perfect the soul until it was ready for heaven than that He would continue to punish a soul otherwise worthy of the beatific vision. Of course, even if God were to punish one already freed from the guilt of sin, this would serve as an explicit revelation of the mystery of God's justice and bring once more to the consciousness of the sinner, as he stood at the threshold of heaven, the heinousness and gravity of even venial sin. But the image of God presented in Holy Scripture inclines modern authors to see the divine love, holiness, and justice combining to punish the soul still guilty of venial sins as the soul is transformed and cleansed. This would also respect the personal dignity of the created person, depriving him of the vision of God only as long as the guilt of sin remained in the soul. As soon as the last of this disappeared, the person would be ready to enter the eternal happiness of heaven.

Recent theological speculation about the nature of sin and its effects upon the whole of the human personality gives further reason for thinking that purgatory is a gradual process whereby the soul is not only punished, but also freed from the guilt of sin and especially from the evil consequences that sin has left imprinted in its very substance. The soul of the just, presuming that it is not ready for immediate admission to the sight of God, is weighed down with impurities and imperfections of varying degrees. The number and gravity of unforgiven venial sins can vary greatly, as can the punishment due to these and other forgiven sins. Even more, the ravages of CONCUPISCENCE will have made themselves felt more or less deeply in the soul. Persistent habits of sin or uncontrolled desires may have left deep spiritual scars on the faculties of the soul, scars that penetrate below the level of consciousness into the very fibers of the personality. Before the person is fully ready to enter heaven and face the unspeakable holiness and majesty of God, all of these must be removed. The whole person, in other words, must be made over, formed again in the image of God to which it was made and which sin has tried to efface by its onslaughts. Granted these deep–rooted effects of sin on the soul, one can see more clearly why modern authors do not favor the theory of the forgiveness of sins immediately upon entry to purgatory. This guilt of sin, the remains of sin in the soul, is more deeply imbedded than the person is aware. There must be quite literally a process, a purification that lays bare, so to speak, the successive layers of the personality and exposes to view the faults buried in the depths of the nature. As this purification progresses, the full personality of the individual emerges for the first time. On earth concupiscence and ingrained, subconscious habits prevented the person from acting to the fullest extent as a child of God and from displaying the wonders of its varied talents; now the person is enabled to live as its own self to the utmost for the first time and to reveal the richness of its personality. Thus purgatory is not a place of negative suffering, designed only to punish the soul, but a state of positive progress where the person is enabled to possess God by first truly possessing itself.

Manner of Suffering. Theologians distinguish the suffering endured in purgatory from that undertaken on earth in reparation for sin. The latter is called satisfaction, because the human person freely and voluntarily ''makes good'' to God the injury done by sin; such reparation is an action that is also meritorious of grace. But the soul of the departed person is no longer in the state of the wayfarer and can no longer perform satisfactory or meritorious works. Such a soul can only give satisfaction for its sins, that is, accept willingly the sufferings imposed by God for its sins. This is not to say that the sufferings of purgatory imply only passivity on the part of the souls detained there. They are rather an activity of the person under the influence of God. But there is a passive acceptance of this purification because it does not depend upon the free decision of the departed soul, but is dispensed by divine decree. This suffering, however, does not fall upon the soul as if it were a stone or a piece of wood. It is rather accepted readily and even joyfully.

State of the Souls in Purgatory. The treatment of this point can be divided into two parts: (1) the souls are confirmed in grace; (2) they are certain of salvation.

Confirmation in Grace. The theological ground for this assertion is the condemned proposition of Luther that states: ''The souls in purgatory sin without intermission so long as they crave for rest or shrink from pain'' (Denz 1489). Merit and demerit are no longer possible for the soul; the end of the earthly pilgrimage has been reached and the soul is assured that it will possess God. This assurance excludes any feelings of anguish or horror in the soul. The earliest Christian inscriptions and the liturgy constantly repeat that the departed souls "rest in the sleep of peace." Thus Luther was mistaken in attributing to them despair, anguish, and horror at the punishments they undergo. Their sufferings, as noted above, are rather undergone voluntarily and accepted as the means that will enable them to join God. This does not lessen the pain they endure, but it does render impossible any anguish or despair on their part.

Certitude of Salvation. Whether the fact of their salvation becomes known to the departed souls through the particular judgment or by any other means, it is plain that this awareness is one of the greatest joys of purgatory, preventing it from being merely a place of torture and suffering. These souls have, in substance, already achieved salvation; nothing more can imperil their final happiness, though they are not yet in possession of the beatific vision. The fact that they must still undergo a period of suffering to remove the last dross and imperfection remaining from their mortal life does not prevent an intense joy in the near anticipation of their full union with God. If they are suffering from a purifying fire, these souls are nonetheless inflamed by the Holy Spirit, who animates them as members of Christ's Mystical Body wholly given over to the Spirit. It is His strength and love that have taken complete hold of their souls and nothing can disengage them from His grasp. The suffering is there, indeed, but it is tempered by a joy and a love that literally place it beyond the power of earthly language or concepts.

Prayers for the Dead. Besides the existence of purgatory, the only other revealed dogma concerning it is that the souls in purgatory can be helped by the prayers of the faithful on earth. The basis for this assertion is the communion of saints, the community of all those who are joined in Christ, whether in heaven, purgatory, or on earth. This means that the action of any member of this community affects all others in it, although the manner in which this is accomplished is hidden in the mystery of the divine wisdom. Concretely, the souls in purgatory can be helped by works of piety, such as prayer, indulgences, alms, fasting, and sacrifices. These works are undertaken by the faithful on earth in the Spirit of Love, who also fills and animates the souls in purgatory, and they are performed for the benefit of these souls. While one cannot dictate that God apply the satisfactory value of one's personal works to the poor souls, one may certainly hope that God will hear one's petitions and help the members of the Church suffering. Because the application of these good works depends on one's petition to God, there is no infallible assurance that one's prayers help an individual soul in purgatory, or any one of them, here and now. But the mercy and love of God for the souls in purgatory, who are already so close to God, surely prompt God to speed their release from the period of purification when the faithful on earth direct their prayers to this purpose.

See Also: DEAD, PRAYERS FOR THE; FIRE OF JUDGMENT; GUILT (THEOLOGY OF); JUDGMENT, DIVINE (IN THEOLOGY); POOR SOULS; SANCTION, DIVINE; ESCHATOLOGY, ARTICLES ON.

Bibliography: For further information consult esp. the first three works. A. MICHAEL, *Dictionnaire de théologie catholique*, ed. A. VACANT et al. (Paris 1903–50; Tables générales 1951–) 13.1:1164–1326. K. RAHNER et al., *Lexikon für Theologie und Kirche*[2], ed. J. HOFER and K. RAHNER, (2d new ed. Freiburg 1957–65) 4:49–55. J. F. SAGÜÉS, *De novissimis, Sacrae theologiae summa*, ed. FATHERS OF THE SOCIETY OF JESUS. PROFESSORS OF THE THEOLOGICAL FACULTIES IN SPAIN (4th ed. Madrid 1962) 4:861–1061. M. SCHMAUS, *Von den letzten Dingen* (his *Katholische Dogmatik* 4.2; 5th ed. Munich 1959) 511–541. J. P. ARENDZEN, *Purgatory and Heaven* (New York 1960). R. GARRIGOU-LAGRANGE, *Life Everlasting,* tr. P. CUMMINS (St. Louis 1952). R. W. GLEASON, *The World to Come* (New York 1958). M. JUGIE, *Purgatory and the Means to Avoid It,* tr. M. G. CARROLL (Westminster, Md. 1949). A. WINKLHOFER, *The Coming of His Kingdom,* tr. A. V. LITTLEDALE (New York 1963). M. F. EGAN, "The Two Theories of Purgatory," *The Irish Theological Quarterly* 17 (Dublin 1922) 24–34. P. FRANSEN, "The Doctrine of Purgatory," *The Eastern Churches Quarterly* 13 (Ramsgate 1959) 99–112. V. KERNS, "The Traditional Doctrine of Purgatory," *The Irish Ecclesiastical Record* 80 (Dublin 1953) 326–342. J. LE GOFF, *The Birth of Purgatory* tr. A. GOLDHAMMER (Chicago 1984).

[R. J. BASTIAN]

PURGATORY, ST. PATRICK'S

A famous place of pilgrimage on the island of Lough Derg, County Donegal, Ireland. Although St. PATRICK preached in the neighborhood, his connection with the island remains obscure. The pilgrimage dates probably from the 12th century, when a community of Canons Regular of St. Augustine settled on Saints' Island in the lake. Jocelin of Furness, Henry of Saltrey, GIRALDUS CAMBRENSIS, and others made the little sanctuary known to the great European public. According to legend, an Irish knight named Owen (*c.* 1153) was condemned to do penance on the island and while so doing had a terrifying vision of purgatorial punishments. By 1186 the pilgrimage was efficiently organized. Each pilgrim had to be accepted beforehand by the bishop of the diocese. He then proceeded to Saints' Island, whence, after nine days, he was rowed to Station Island, where he spent a day and a night in the purgatorial cave. He then returned to Saints' Island for another nine days of prayer and penance. Pilgrims from France, Hungary, Portugal, and England left exciting accounts of their experiences and visions.

Alexander VI's order (1497) to close the cave was carried out to the letter: the cave then in use was rejected as spurious, but another was opened nearby. The pilgrimage was never interrupted, though the cave, the chapel, and all buildings were destroyed by order of the government in Dublin in 1632. By that time the Franciscans had replaced the Canons Regular as spiritual directors. A new arrangement of the exercises is mentioned by the papal nuncio to England, Chiericati, who made the pilgrimage in 1517. The cave remained in use until about 1790, when it was replaced by a chapel large enough to accommodate the ever-increasing number of pilgrims. A priest of the Diocese of Clogher, nominated prior by the bishop, succeeded the Franciscans as director. The three-day order of exercises still observed is based on a scheme drawn up in 1613. The season begins on June 1 and ends on August 15.

Bibliography: S. LESLIE, *Saint Patrick's Purgatory* (London 1932). A. CURTAYNE, *Lough Derg: St. Patrick's Purgatory* (London 1944). GEORGIUS MILES DE HUNGARIA, *Visiones Georgii,* ed. L. L. HAMMERICH (Copenhagen 1930). D. O'CONNOR, *St. Patrick's Purgatory, Lough Derg* (Dublin 1895).

[J. RYAN]

PURIFICATION

In primitive culture there is widespread belief in a mysterious supernatural energy, a sort of occult, more or less immaterial dynamic power, that attaches to persons and things and produces effects beyond the normal course of nature. In itself, this power is neutral; whether it is to be good or evil depends on how it comes into contact with man. It can be approached by especially qualified persons, but it must be avoided by others. It is taboo, that is, forbidden as being fraught with mystic danger. Being transmissible, it clings to an individual who has come into contact with it, and it can spread from him to others like an infectious disease. When a state of taboo has not been avoided or cannot be avoided, a man of primitive culture seeks an antidote or disinfectant for it by means of purification.

Methods. Since the pollution is conceived of as being material in character, the methods employed in removing it are of the same nature as those used in the cleansing and decontamination of material objects: ablution, or use of such detergents as clay, mud, charcoal, ashes, dung, eggs, wool, fleece of animals; burning; fumigation; shaving of the hair; change of clothes; use of emetics; etc. Often an abstergent is obtained from a particular source that is thought to possess especially powerful purificatory qualities, e.g., sea water or water drawn from a certain river, pool, or spring. Besides these means of purification there are many others. Noise, produced by various implements, is used to drive out the evil thing that has caused the pollution (exorcism). Persons in a state of uncleanness are required to confess their particular kind of taboo-breaking. Sometimes the accumulated pollution of a community is transferred to an animal or a human scapegoat, which is then expelled from the settlement or, less commonly, killed. Survivals of this simple primitive conception of purification were ''the emissary goat'' of Leviticus (16.7–10, 26), which, after having been declared laden with all the transgressions of Israel, was driven into the desert, and the *pharmakoí* of ancient Greece, who, by carrying away pollution, brought ''remedy'' to the city.

Ceremonies. Ceremonies of purification accompany primitive man from the cradle to the grave. The need for them is felt especially at the critical points of human life—birth, adolescence, marriage, and death—when man is thought to be more exposed than at other times to the attacks of dangerous forces. These crucial moments in human life are therefore surrounded by a series of purificatory rites. Thus a house in which a death occurs becomes defiled and, after the corpse has been carried out for burial, must be cleansed with fire or smoke or by a ritualistic sweeping. Likewise, all persons who have come into contact with the corpse must purify themselves by washing in water or a potent medicine prepared for this purpose. These proceedings may be repeated several times over a certain period.

Originally, then, purifications are intended to ward off evil forces. In the religions of the higher civilizations, this initially merely negative-apotropaic aim becomes in a further, quite natural development of the same idea transformed into a positive one. To be free from the disturbing influences of such pernicious powers also means to be in a state of purity, which seems to be necessary for persons who want to enter into communion with the divine. As a result, the old-fashioned, time-honored purificatory practices are elevated to a command of the gods who above all require purity from their worshippers.

Ritual Purity. In this way, there arises the idea of ''ritual purity.'' Anything ritually impure antagonizes the deity, especially anything connected with foreign or suppressed cults and rival demonic powers. Uncleanness, it is true, is here still conceived of as something material, as an infection that can be remedied by the external removal of the evil thing. But, by putting the notions of the pure and the holy side by side and by shaping the more elevated ideas of the divine and the demonic, of the sacred and the accursed, religion plants the seeds out of which grows the moral concept of purity. In this refining and spiritualizing process the cathartic rites, though re-

A Japanese boy offering water for purification, a Shinto shrine, Tokyo, Japan. (©G. John Renard)

taining their traditional outward forms, assume more and more a purely symbolic meaning.

Bibliography: E. N. FALLAIZE et al., *Encyclopedia of Religion and Ethics,* ed. J. HASTINGS (Edinburgh 1908–27) 10:455–505. R. HINK and R. RENDTORFF, *Die Religion in Geschichte und Gegenwart* (Tübingen 1957–65) 5:939–944, 946–948. E. STIGLMAYR and W. KORNFELD, *Lexikon für Theologie und Kirche,* ed. J. HOFER and K. RAHNER (Freiburg 1957–65) 8:1143–44, 1145–47. W. KORNFELD, *ibid.* 1150–51. L. HAMBURG, καθαρμός, *Paulys Realenzyklopädie der klassischen Altertumswissenschaft,* ed. G. WISSOWA et al. (Stuttgart 1893—) 10.2 (1919) 2513–19. G. VAN DER LEEUW, *Religion in Essence and Manifestation,* tr. J. E. TURNER (London 1938) 343–349 (par. 49). J. DÖLLER, *Die Reinheits—und Speisegesetze des Alten Testamentes in religionsgeschichtlicher Beleuchtung* (Münster 1917). E. ROHDE, *Psyche,* tr. W. B. HILLIS (New York 1925). E. FEHRLE, *Die kultische Keuschheit im Altertum* (Religiongeschichtliche Versuche und Vorarbeiten 6; Giessen 1910). T. WÄCHTER, *Reinheitsvorschriften im griechischen Kult* (*ibid.* 9.1; Giessen 1910). K. LATTE, ''Lustratio,'' in *Römische Religionsgeschichte* (Munich 1960). H. WEBSTER, *Taboo* (Stanford, Calif. 1942).

[R. ARBESMANN]

PURIFICATION (IN THE BIBLE)

In biblical usage the term ''purification'' refers to a certain rite in the external worship of God. Purification seeks to remove legal uncleanness so that the purified individual may resume normal activity in society. Special holiness arising from close contact with divine things is also something that at times requires subsequent purification.

The rites of purification are found chiefly in the section of the Priestly Code known as the Law of Purity (Lv 11–16). This postexilic codification of rituals of the period of the second Temple contains much ancient material that is used to emphasize both the separation of the Israelites from pagan peoples and the holiness of Yahweh.

Origin. The origin of these rites is lost in antiquity, since they are based on the notions of pure and impure that stem from primitive ideas of tabu (*see* PURE AND IMPURE). There are indications in the Bible that this distinction between the clean and unclean, with the consequent need of purification, was present among the patriarchs and must have been inherited from the common Semitic culture (e.g., Gn 31.35; 1 Sm 20.26). Exposure to contamination was presented by the prophets as a punishment of Yahweh for the infidelity of the people (Am 7.17; Hos 9.3–4; Ez 4.13–14). Although purification had such origins, it must likewise be recognized that the rites received a much deeper significance in the light of the covenant and of the development of religious ideas. Accordingly, a metaphorical interpretation is given to a ritual action in Ps 50(51).9.

Types. The rites of purification in the Bible are of different types and degrees. There are, first of all, simple ablutions and temporary quarantine (Lv 11.25; Dt 23.12). Then there are purifications brought about by ablution with specially prepared water (Nm 19.11–22; 31.23). The preparation of this lustral water (Nm 19.1–10) is itself related to ancient customs known to have existed in Arabia. Finally, there are purifications accomplished by letting a determined period of time pass and then offering a prescribed sacrifice (Lv 12.6–7), or by ablutions, lapse of time, and the offering of such a sacrifice (Lv 15.13–15).

The distinction between these various rites is not based on a notion of the voluntary or involuntary occurrences of contamination, as can be seen from the fact that the same rite is used for both types (cf. Lv 15.8 with Lv 11.40). Their differences may be explained as the concurrence of various traditions and a heightened sense of moral guilt leading to the use of sacrifices of expiation even for occurrences that were not voluntary (Lv 15.13–15; Lv 15.28–29).

The legal uncleanness that is to be removed by these rites may be divided into several distinct categories that have a certain aura of mystery about them. The first of these is connected with the functions of reproduction or sexual activity. Sexual intercourse itself renders the parties unclean and requires the purification of simple ablution and lapse of time (Lv 15.18), a tradition evidenced also in Ex 19.15. Nocturnal emissions or any unnatural flow is a cause of uncleanness requiring the purification of ablution and lapse of time (Lv 15.2–12; Dt 23.10). The same is true for the menstrual flow or any unnatural flow affecting women (Lv 15.19–27). Childbirth results in a legal contamination that is purified by passage of time and the offering of sacrifice (Lv 12.2–5).

Another category of legal uncleanness results from contact with dead bodies, whether of animals or human beings (Lv 11.24–25, 39–40; Nm 19.11–20). It is notable that in the tradition of Numbers, the purification is accomplished with the specially prepared lustral water mentioned above. The contamination from these dead bodies, as from all unclean objects, can be transmitted either directly or indirectly so that even objects that come in contact with such bodies must likewise be purified or broken, as in the case of articles of clothing or wooden or earthen jars (Lv 15.12).

LEPROSY or various forms of skin disease were a source of contamination, contact with which required purification. Upon being cured, the victim of such diseases could return to normal activity in society only after an involved ritual of purification (Lv 13–14).

Special holiness resulting from contact with divine things was also something that required purification. This is the signification of the sacrifices offered at the term of the NAZARITE vow (Nm 6.10–12), as also at the conclusion of the ordination of Aaron and his sons (Lv 9.1–7).

The rites of purification were used as needed, but during the last centuries of OT times some elements of these rituals were connected with a feast that was a sort of feast of national purification known as the Day of ATONEMENT (Lv 16).

The heightened sense of guilt and need for purification that existed among the Jewish people at this late period of OT history carried over into the NT, where the excessive zeal of the PHARISEES for ritual purity became the object of Jesus' condemnation (Mk 7.6; Lk 11.38). Such concern for purification was prevalent also in the QUMRAN COMMUNITY of the ESSENES, as evidenced by their writings and suggested by the architectural features of their monastery.

Bibliography: H. LESÊTRE, *Dictionnaire de la Bible*, ed. F. VIGOUROUX (Paris 1895–1912) 3.1:857–861; 5:872–874, 879–880. *Encyclopedic Dictionary of the Bible* (New York 1963) 1966–67. R. DE VAUX *Ancient Israel, Its Life and Institutions* (New York 1961) 460–466. W. EICHRODT, *Theology of the Old Testament*, tr. J. A. BAKER (London 1961) 1:133–141.

[S. M. POLAN]

PURIFICATION, SPIRITUAL

Studies on the necessity, kinds, nature, and characteristics of purification are based generally on the doctrine of St. JOHN OF THE CROSS. Theologians commonly turn to him in their discussion of these matters, since he provides the best analysis and synthesis within the Catholic tradition of the soul's purification.

Disorientation by Sin. The complex of virtues emanating from the grace with which the first man was adorned subjected perfectly the sensory or lower part of his soul to the directives of the spiritual or higher part, and the higher part to God. Once this order was lost through sin, the lower part tended toward its own satisfaction, heedless of the limits prescribed by reason, and the higher part tended to its own good also, without attention to the order God established. The reacquisition of grace did not free man from this inclination toward his own satisfaction. With great difficulty does he seek God's will only and allow himself to be guided always by the Holy Spirit.

Moreover, every personal sin, small or large, leaves embedded in the faculties, in its own measure, the very disorder produced by original sin and increases the strength of the inordinate tendencies, rooting them more deeply in their subject. The more embedded these tendencies are, the greater is the pain of their extirpation. The restoration of order consequently involves suffering.

The traditional analysis of this suffering and of the process by which order is restored is based on the essential principles of grace and the virtues, and the conditions these demand for their full evolution. Sin is a turning away from God and a conversion toward creatures; the remedy of grace in its full development involves a conversion toward God and a turning away from creatures. Grace, then, is a supernatural force destined to destroy the work of sin and restore to man an image of that first righteousness he possessed in the garden of Paradise.

Restoration through Purification. Purification makes one pure, cleanses one of all the disorder introduced by sin. By means of spiritual purification wrought through grace and the virtues, the forces of the soul, which ought to be employed in seeking God and His will as the last end in every action but which rebel against this supreme order, are redirected toward God and employed in what is for His greater glory alone.

The purifications of the two parts of the soul are also referred to as ''nights'': the ''night of the senses'' and the ''night of the spirit.'' They are effected in two ways: through the soul's active efforts (active nights) and through God's special intervention (passive nights).

In the active nights, a man, assisted by grace, strives through his own diligence to uproot all his sinful and imperfect habits. This he does by an earnest endeavor to use his sense faculties (the active night of the senses) and also his spiritual faculties (the active night of the spirit) only as God desires them to be used. Obviously, this involves much privation, and just as night entails the privation of light, so the purifications are like nights for the soul.

The passive purifications or nights are wrought mainly through a purgative contemplation that is God's gift and by which the soul is deprived passively, weaned from dependence upon spiritual sweetness, and strengthened in virtue. Purgative contemplation is an infused, obscure, mystical, or general, loving knowledge of God, which has also as its partial object the soul's own miseries and nothingness. The purgative contemplation of the night of the spirit does not differ essentially from that of the night of the senses, but comprises a more abundant knowledge. Nor are the senses fully purged until the spirit is purified, since all the imperfections and all the disorders of the sensory part are rooted in the spirit.

Purgative contemplation purifies by enlightening a man concerning his own misery and nothingness. The pain of this experience is increased by the illumination received on the infinite purity and holiness of God. Such immersion in the consciousness of his own misery will deprive the person undergoing this purgation of the joy and satisfaction formerly experienced in the operations of the faculties. This impedes the actuation of these faculties and makes every other operation outside this deep awareness, in a certain manner, impossible. Thus, even though the individual will continue, in his intense charity, to tend to and serve God with every effort, he feels frustrated in his effort and abandoned by God. The feeling of being forsaken by God, considering the person's charity, is the most painful part of the sufferings of the passive nights. Moreover, because of this deep awareness of his own misery, he will not find any comfort in spiritual books, or in the counsels given by his spiritual director, or in any other creature. The soul, deprived through this contemplation of all connatural satisfaction in its operations and impeded in these operations, will gradually lose its imperfect habits, since the satisfaction found in the operation of the faculties is what sustains the imperfect habits.

The passive purification of the senses, by which they are, in a certain fashion, reformed and accommodated to the spirit, is common; the passive purification of the spirit, by which the soul is united perfectly with God through love, is rare. The time a person must spend in the passive purifications depends on the amount of imperfection and the degree of love to which God wishes to raise him. Not all theologians agree, however, that the passive purifications occasioned by purgative contemplation are necessary in order to reach perfect union with God through charity.

Signs of Purgative Contemplation. Three signs manifest whether or not a person is receiving this purgative contemplation: (1) He finds that in spite of his efforts he is unable to meditate and make use of the imagination. (2) Deprived of satisfaction and consolation in the things of God, he derives none from creatures either. (3) He ordinarily turns solicitously and with painful care toward God, thinking that he is not serving Him but falling back.

A soul undergoes passive purification not only through this purgative contemplation but also through other sufferings. Thus, for the purification of souls God may allow war, persecution, calumny, imprisonment, injustice, abuse of authority, sickness, accident, poverty, failure, scandal, ingratitude, the loss of loved ones, conflict and misunderstanding arising from differences of opinion and temperament, and even the suffering of death. The constant daily fulfillment of the duties of one's state in life demands heroic virtue, and the burden of these duties may well serve as an instrument of purification. Severe temptations, too, will often form a part of passive purification.

These passive privations demand an active, intense life of supernatural virtue. Without this life of virtue, which withdraws man from what is not God and unites him with God alone, thus subjecting the lower part of his soul to the higher, and the higher to the divine Spirit, there is no purification.

Bibliography: A. ROYO, *The Theology of Christian Perfection,* tr. J. AUMANN (Dubuque 1962). J. DE GUIBERT, *The Theology of the Spiritual Life,* tr. P. BARRETT (New York 1953). GABRIELE DI SANTA MARIA MADDALENA, *St. John of the Cross, Doctor of Divine Love,* tr. by a Benedictine of Stanbrook Abbey (Westminster, Md. 1946). U. BARRIENTOS, *Purificación y purgatorio* (Madrid 1960). PHILIPPE DE LA TRINITÉ, *Dictionnaire de spiritualité ascétique et mystique. Doctrine et histoire,* ed. M. VILLER et al. (Paris 1932–) 4.1: 911–925.

[K. KAVANAUGH]

PURIFICATION OF MARY

The ceremony performed by the MOTHER OF GOD in the temple of Jerusalem 40 days after the birth of Christ in fulfillment of the Mosaic Law requiring the cleansing of a woman from the ritual impurity incurred at childbirth. This rite is one of several prescribed in the Old Law to render a person pure who has been legally defiled.

The rite of purification after childbirth consisted in the offering of a pigeon or turtledove as a sin offering. (The accompanying sacrifice of a yearling lamb, for which a poor woman could substitute a second pigeon or turtledove, is not part of the purification ceremony itself, but a HOLOCAUST of thanksgiving for a successful delivery.) The ceremony took place 40 days after the birth of a male child, 80 days after that of a female (Lv 12.1–8).

The sacrifice for purification was unnecessary for Mary. However, as a faithful Israelite obedient to the Law, she accomplished the prescription of the Mosaic code by offering two turtledoves. To the ceremony of purification of the mother was joined that of the dedication of the firstborn son who did not belong to the tribe of Levi. The law was fulfilled by the payment of five shekels to ''redeem'' the child—to have a LEVITE take his place in the direct service of Yahweh. There was no express regulation demanding the traditional presentation of the child to the Lord and it was therefore not necessary that this ceremony be performed by the priests. More likely it was performed by the parents, and in the case of Our Lord, also by Simeon who ''received him into his arms and blessed God'' (Lk 2.28).

This double ceremony, a mystery of the obedience of Jesus and Mary, was marked not only by the fulfillment of Simeon's desire to see the ''Christ of the Lord'' but also by his prophecy concerning the mother and child: ''Behold, this child is destined for the fall and for the rise of many in Israel, and for a sign that shall be contradicted. And thy own soul a sword shall pierce . . .'' (Lk 2.34–35). Anna, an elderly woman, joined in the praises of the Christ Child and ''spoke of him to all who were awaiting the redemption of Jerusalem'' (Lk 2.38).

The liturgical celebration of this double event originated in Jerusalem, where as early as the 4th century it was celebrated under the title of ''the fortieth day after the Epiphany.'' The feast spread to Byzantium in the 6th century as ὑπαπάντη (the ''meeting'' of Jesus and Mary with Simeon) and finally to Rome in the 7th century, where it acquired the title Purification of Mary. However, the Roman liturgy still refers in its greater part not to the Purification of Mary but to the Presentation of Jesus.

Feast: Feb. 2.

See Also: PRESENTATION OF MARY; MARY, BLESSED VIRGIN, ARTICLES ON.

Bibliography: *Encyclopedic Dictionary of the Bible*, tr. and adap. by L. HARTMAN (New York 1963) 1966–67. S. GAROFALO, *Mary in the Bible,* tr. T. J. TOBIN (Milwaukee 1961). G. M. ROSCHINI, *Mariologia,* 2 v. in 4 (2d ed. Rome 1947–48) 2.3:136–139. D. ATTWATER, comp., *Dictionary of Mary* (New York 1957) 232–233. H. J. SCHULZ, *Lexikon für Theologie und Kirche*, ed. J. HOFER and K. RAHNER, 10 v. (2d new ed. Freiburg 1957–65) 7:66.

[P. J. GAFFNEY]

PURIM, FEAST OF

The Jewish Feast of Lots, in Hebrew *pûrîm,* is celebrated on the 14th and 15th of Adar (February-March) or of Second Adar in a leap year. In 2 Maccabees 15.36, the oldest historical reference to it, it is called ''the Day of Mardochai.''

Origin. Purim is intimately associated with the OT Book of ESTHER, which is read in the synagogue on the feast. According to Esther 3.7; 9.20–32, the feast recalls the escape of the Jews of Susa, King Xerxes' Persian capital, from the destruction plotted for them by the evil min-

Students prepare Purim baskets, Ramaz Hebrew Day School, March 1, 1999, photograph by Tina Fineberg. (AP/Wide World Photos)

ister Haman, who drew lots to determine the date of their death, the 14th of Adar. The danger turned into an occasion of rejoicing when the plot was thwarted by Queen Esther and MORDECAI, and the Jews avenged themselves upon Aman and their other enemies. The Book of Esther enjoins that the feast be celebrated annually, preceded by a period of fasting and mourning; the celebration is to be marked by feasting, exchanging gifts, and giving alms to the poor.

The real origin of the feast remains obscure, however. Although the Book of Esther is designed to explain the feast and is called a ''letter on Purim'' (9.29; F. 11), the passages on the ''lots'' seem to be interpolations and the book itself is not written as a historical account. Various suggestions have been made about a pagan origin of the feast, but no specific pagan feast can be pointed to with certainty. An origin in some historical deliverance of a group of Eastern Diaspora Jews is possible. It is also possible, even likely, that the feast incorporates elements of a pagan festival, perhaps a new year's celebration, which the Jews may have adopted. The setting of the story would suggest Persia; the Babylonian loan-word used as the name of the feast and the names Mardochai and Esther, which may be related to the Babylonian deities MARDUK and Ishtar, would suggest a Mesopotamian origin. What remains most striking is the fact that Purim does not appear to have originally been a religious feast and has no original connection with the worship of Yahweh.

Historical references to the observance of Purim occur in 2 Mc 15.36; Est F. 11; Josephus, *Antiquities* 11.290–295, as well as the earlier witness of the Hebrew Book of Esther itself. A tractate of the Mishnah (*Megillah*) is devoted to Purim.

Modern Customs. The observance of Purim begins with the fast day on the 13th of Adar (the Fast of Esther). The day after the main feast day is called Purim Shushan, the 15th of Adar, recalling the date of its celebration in Susa (Esther 9.18). When Purim is celebrated in the intercalary month Second Adar in leap year, a limited observance called Purim Qatan (Little Purim) takes place on the 14th and 15th of Adar.

The principal religious ceremony is the reading of the Book of Esther, popularly called Megillah (the Scroll), on the eve and again on the morning of the 14th of Adar. The reading is introduced by three benedictions and concluded by another. When it is chanted, a traditional mode peculiar to Purim is used. The scroll is fully unrolled at the beginning, to distinguish it from Torah reading. The Talmud, which allows the Megillah to be read in any language intelligible to the audience, prescribes that all attend the reading, including women, since it was a woman, Queen Esther, who obtained the deliverance of her people. The names of Aman's ten sons (Est 9.7–10) are to be read in a single breath to indicate their simultaneous death (*Megillah* 16b). In former times it was a custom, particularly favored by the children, to drown out, by stamping and noisemakers, the name of Aman whenever it was mentioned, thus ''blotting out the remembrance of Amalek'' (Dt 25.19), the progenitor of Aman. This practice, along with other boisterous variations in the reading, created a din in the synagogue that was not out of harmony with the exuberant spirit of Purim. The Hallel [Ps 112 (113)–117 (118)], customary on religious feasts, is not sung at Purim.

Among the many other customs of the feast, the festive meal in the evening of the 14th is an important one. The joyousness of this feast may be inferred from the rabbinic exhortation to drink until one can no longer distinguish ''Cursed be Haman!'' from ''Blessed be Mordecai!'' Special cakes are often prepared for this feast, and where the tradition prevails, special songs are sung. Gifts of choice foods are sent to one's neighbors; when the Purim feast was celebrated as an open house for all, these were brought round and consumed during the long period of revelry. Purim is also a time for almsgiving, which was regarded as a strict obligation for all Jews at this feast. Collections are sometimes taken in the synagogue for this purpose.

Beginning in medieval Italy, probably under the influence of the Roman carnival, and soon spreading through Europe, masquerades and street celebrations also marked the Feast of Purim. A popular but often unruly part of this celebration was the burning in effigy of Aman. The carnival aspect has survived in the public celebration now held in modern Israel. In the Middle Ages dramatic representations of the events of Esther were held on the feast day, and in the 18th and 19th centuries, especially in Germany, there flourished a comic drama form known as *Purimspiele,* sometimes burlesquing both ancient and modern characters. More recently Purim is the occasion for playlets or satirical farces in the Jewish schools.

Bibliography: *Encyclopedic Dictionary of the Bible*, tr. and adap. by L. HARTMAN (New York 1963), from A. VAN DEN BORN, *Bijbels Woordenboek* 1967–68. R. DE VAUX, *Ancient Israel, Its Life and Institutions*, tr. J. MCHUGH (New York 1961) 514–517. J. SCHILDENBERGER, *Lexikon für Theologie und Kirche*, ed. J. HOFER and K. RAHNER, 10 v. (2d, new ed. Freiburg 1957–65); suppl., *Das Zweite Vatikanische Konzil: Dokumente und Kommentare*, ed. H. S. BRECHTER et al., pt. 1 (1966) 8:903–904. N. S. DONIACH, *Purim or the Feast of Esther* (Philadelphia 1933). J. LEWY, ''The Feast of the 14th Day of Adar,'' *Hebrew Union College Annual* 14 (1939) 127–151. V. CHRISTIAN, ''Zur Herkunft des Purim-Festes,'' *Alttestamentliche Studien: F. Nötscher,* eds. H. JUNKER and J. BOTTERWECK (Bonn 1950) 33–37. H. RINGGREN, ''Esther and Purim,'' *Svensk exegetisk årsbok* 20 (1955) 5–24. T. H. GASTER, *Purim and Hanukkah in Custom and Tradition* (New York 1950).

[G. W. MACRAE]

PURITANS

Followers of a religious movement whose definition and date of origin cannot be given with precision. The movement embodied a wide range of different sects and communities that quarreled over liturgy, dogma, political theory, and social reform both within and without the Church of England. The effective period of Puritan activity covered the span from the Elizabethan Settlement (1559) to the Restoration (1660), by which time the term ceased to be meaningful in its original sense.

Early Development. Puritanism aggravated the English religious controversy between the advocates of a simpler, fundamentalist church rooted in apostolic Christian times and a more formal, ritualistic, authoritarian church developed since that time. More specifically, Puritanism was an attitude toward religion that arose in opposition to the alleged unscriptural, Catholic forms embodied in the Act of UNIFORMITY (1559) and the THIRTY-NINE ARTICLES (1563). The Puritans generally sought to purify the Church of England of these forms, substituting Calvinistic models of ecclesiastical polity and liturgy (*see* NONCONFORMISTS). Even before the break with Rome (1534), Cambridge scholars lectured and wrote on Continental Reformation ideas, which forced many to take refuge at Geneva and elsewhere upon the accession of MARY TUDOR in 1553. They returned when ELIZABETH I assumed the throne, hoping that she would make sweeping reforms after the Genevan system, but were frustrated at the Crown's moderate Protestant posture and its unwillingness to tolerate dissent or entertain change. Thomas CARTWRIGHT assumed the earliest leadership of one faction, mostly academicians at first, who promoted PRESBYTERIANISM in place of the existing Episcopalian system of church government and who had already found common ground for opposition to Elizabeth's insistence on conformity in the Vestiarian Controversy (1566). This dispute, at first limited to Saint John's and Trinity College, Cambridge, but later involving Puritan-minded clergy in London and elsewhere, arose when Archbishop Matthew PARKER, acting on Elizabeth's order, laid down strict rules governing services and clerical dress. Coercive measures by the Anglican hierarchy followed; Puri-

Puritans going to church, painting by George H. Boughton. (©Bettmann/CORBIS)

tan scholars and clergy were suspended; and a flood of pamphlets appeared to support both sides of the question. An illustration of this opposition to religious uniformity may be seen in the publication of the Marprelate Tracts (1588–89). The invention of several Midland authors who used the pseudonym Martin Marprelate, the tracts railed against the episcopacy. They appeared despite, and perhaps because of, Archbishop John WHITGIFT's order in 1586 that all publications be censored. Several suspected authors were arrested, one of them was executed, and most of their books were burned.

Source of Faith. The Puritans disagreed over dogma, but virtually all of them stressed the Bible as the only true source of faith and conduct. Puritan divines as well as individual members of their congregations read it avidly, interpreted it as they chose, and thereupon quarreled over the form of church government it enjoined. From this Calvinistic conviction of the validity of private interpretation of the Bible grew English Protestant sectarianism.

Variant Systems of Government. By far the largest majority of Puritans went along with the episcopal system, provided the laity could share in the policymaking process and ''popish'' forms in the liturgy were expunged. This group of moderates retained general control of Puritanism until the Civil War. Other Puritans, led by Thomas Cartwright, advocated a Presbyterian ecclesiastical polity; they were originally few and largely discredited in Elizabeth's reign. With the outbreak of war in 1642 and the parliamentary alliance with the Scots that followed, the Presbyterian Puritans gained temporary ascendancy, controlling, for instance, the Westminster Assembly (1643–49), convened to reform the church. These Puritans invested ecclesiastical sovereignty in four bodies, the Kirk Session, the Presbytery, the Provincial Synod, and the General Assembly. The Separatists (known also as Brownists originally, and as Independents later on) constituted the third broad category of Puritans. As early as the 1550s groups of persons met in separate congregations (conventicles) to conduct services apart from the Established Church. Robert BROWNE, one of the early Separatist leaders, wrote several pamphlets that advocated the independence of each parish congregation from either a parental, hierarchical, or secular political control. Such Puritans professed the autonomy of each congregation under the sole supremacy of Christ and formed self-governing parishes that supposedly operated on a principle of democracy, but often became subject to the dictates of their elected ministers. From this form of

Anne Bradstreet, American poet (c. 1612–1672) wearing Puritan clothing, depicted in stained glass.

Puritanism evolved Congregationalism, some of whose adherents migrated to Holland and America to escape persecution. But others stayed to reap the rewards of Independency during Oliver CROMWELL's administration.

Doctrine and Behavior. Puritans generally shared a belief in predestination and agreed that the Bible was the sole rule of faith and morals to be interpreted individually. They maintained that one's life should in every way manifest a deep sense of devotion to Christ and to duty, and they severely criticized what they termed idolatrous forms, including vestments, statuary, the sign of the cross, the use of holy water and other sacramentals, and the position of the altar (communion table). Puritans also minimized the intermediary role of ministers and encouraged preaching. Caroline Puritans more than their Elizabethan predecessors emphasized simplicity of dress and hair styles, unostentatious ceremony, and music. They also regarded the Sabbath as a day without work, travel, or recreation that might interfere with worship (*see* SABBATARIANISM). Aside from these broad maxims of Puritan belief, they agreed upon little else.

Minor Sects. The Independents warrant particular attention if for no other reason than that they illustrate the heterogeneity of Puritanism. The Levellers, led by John Lilburne, were among the most important of the Independents. They exerted strong influence in the parliamentary army between 1647 and 1649 to effect a republican system of government that recognized the equality of all men, universal suffrage, and general religious toleration. One small faction of Social Levellers, the Diggers, directed by Gerrard Winstanley, aroused far more antagonism and put considerably more pressure on the authorities than their numbers would suggest. They preached an equalitarian, agrarian, communistic social order wherein men might put to use whatever common or wasteland lay fallow, regardless of ownership. The Diggers, like the Quakers (*see* FRIENDS, RELIGIOUS SOCIETY OF), were pacifists and offered no resistance to those who abused them on the common of Saint George's Hill (Surrey) in 1649 when they tried to dig up the ground. Others of the Independents were Millenarians, such as the politically oriented Fifth Monarchy Men and the quietistic communities of SEEKERS. The anarchistic Fifth Monarchists believed that, according to the words of the Prophet Daniel in the Old Testament, four great monarchies (Assyrians; Persians; Greeks; and Romans, who passed on their authority to the Hapsburgs) would be followed by the Second Coming of Christ, who would establish a divine kingdom on earth together with His elect. But they attempted to hurry His conquest by rebellion led by Thomas Venner in 1657 and 1661. The Seekers lived in several communities, principally in Yorkshire, Westmoreland, and Cumberland. They refused to recognize any formal church, set up congregations without any firm leadership, and practiced a pietistic faith essentially similar to that of the Quakers, with whom they had joined almost entirely by 1652. Another parallel of Puritan dissimilarity may be seen in the Family of Love and the Ranters. The former, a very small sect which originated in Flanders, was related to the Anabaptists. They symbolized pacifism and communitarianism in their traditional greeting of a kiss of peace. The Ranters, on the other hand, comprised a wide selection of unorganized Puritans who represented perhaps the most unorthodox elements of the movement. Some of them, such as Lodowick Muggleton, thought themselves sinless Messiahs; others wished to undertake another crusade to the Holy Land. Virtually all of these left wing Puritans suffered persecution and had disappeared by the Restoration, although others managed to survive until the Revolution of 1688.

Opposition from the Crown. No account of the Puritans can ignore their extraordinary role in politics during Elizabethan and early Stuart times or the constitutional changes that resulted from their activity. The Acts of Supremacy (1534, 1559) endowed the English monarch with full authority over the Church of England, and the Act of Uniformity required all Englishmen to conform to it. Since the spiritual sovereignty of the Crown was barely distinguishable from its temporal authority and since the episcopacy supported the Crown, defection from the Anglican Church was a political as well as a religious crime, the more so because of the instability of the Crown in terms of the parliamentary opposition to its prerogatives (*see* ERASTIANISM). Elizabeth and the first two Stuarts believed that religious uniformity was essential to political stability; so that Puritans and Catholics alike were treated virtually as traitors. Many of the penal laws, especially the Act of 1593 against "sectaries," were directed at the Puritans. Cartwright and Browne both went to prison several times for preaching Puritanism. Puritans hoped that James I would be more sympathetic to their views, for he had been reared a Presbyterian. For this reason a number of Puritan clergy presented the Millenary Petition (1603) soon after he crossed the Tweed from Scotland. This document, which called for moderate ecclesiastical reforms, such as the right of the clergy to choose the garb they would wear at services, the abolition of sacramentals, bowing at the name of Jesus, simplicity of worship, and release of clergymen from the necessity of accepting everything in the Book of Common Prayer so long as they subscribed to the Oath of Supremacy, James allowed to be debated at the Hampton Court Conference (1604). When Dr. Reynolds, one of the Puritan spokesmen, suggested that disputed religious questions might be referred by the bishops to presbyters, James abruptly dismissed the conference, alleging that Puritans meant to subordinate him to a Presbyterian government. The King then deprived about 300 Puritan clergy of their benefices, thereby setting them and their flocks squarely against him. From that time onward neither James nor Charles I saw eye to eye with the Puritans, who had heavy representation in the House of Commons.

Not one Parliament between 1604 and 1640 acquiesced to the royal will; not one failed to introduce legislation, petitions, or remonstrances to block many of the Crown's religious, financial, and foreign policies, or allowed the country to forget Puritan ideals. A constitutional impasse between parliamentary "rights" and royal prerogatives, frequently punctuated by lengthy periods of royal personal rule, pamphleteering, and occasional Puritan outbursts, culminated in the calling of the Long Parliament in 1640. Their series of legislative and governmental reforms caused another impasse that erupted into the Civil War and the execution of the monarch, and the creation under Cromwell of the first republic in English history.

Emigration to America. Stuart absolutism in religion, particularly during the administration of Archbishop William LAUD in the 1630s, was partly responsible for Puritan emigration to America. Laud, favoring High Church ritual and strict uniformity, relentlessly attacked the Puritans, as may easily be seen in the lives of William Prynne, Richard BAXTER, and Henry Burton. This persecution caused some Puritans to despair of ever finding a sympathetic ear in England. Those who founded Virginia in 1607 and settled in some of the Caribbean islands went largely for material gain, land, and adventure, but the Jacobean and Caroline Puritans who landed at Plymouth Rock in 1620 and Massachusetts Bay in 1628, who were joined by about 20,000 co-religionists during the 1630s, had left England to establish their own Christian commonwealths in the New World. As their towns grew, a Puritan oligarchy grew apace, and the Presbyterian system established in Massachusetts Bay Colony drove out the Antinomian Anne Hutchinson and the Seeker Roger WILLIAMS as quickly and as ruthlessly as Laud had driven the Presbyterians out. Puritanism proved to be as contentious in New England as it had been in England; the differences among Puritans were no less pronounced under Cotton Mather than they had been under Robert Browne or Thomas Cartwright.

A great academic controversy still rages among scholars of American Puritanism over the influence, for good or ill, exerted upon later generations of Americans by their Puritan forefathers. Some historians credit many American virtues to the Puritan colonials, while others speak only of Puritan oppression, intellectual stagnation, and religious intolerance. The question is not easily answered; but there is agreement that Puritanism had a lasting effect upon the moral concepts of American society.

Influence and Significance. What influences did the Puritans of England and New England have upon Anglo-Saxon civilization? Politics certainly commanded much of their attention, both theoretically and practically. Many of the 30,000 political pamphlets published in the 1640s were written by Puritans, not to mention the thousands of broadsides, tracts, and books they wrote on religious issues. Pacifists, Millenarians, republicans, social reformers, and Levellers were Puritans who created a wide literature that their countrymen read at the outset of the Civil War when newspapers were just appearing. Puritan authors contrived every conceivable political system, among them a fresh approach to democracy, which undeniably germinated under the veneer of authoritarianism that characterized the age. Puritan political agitation toppled Charles I's divine right monarchy, reformed Parliament, created a republic and, despite the interlude of the Restoration, helped to bring on the Revolution of 1688, the Bill of Rights, and limited monarchy.

Prose, poetry, and the theater felt the impact of Puritanism. John BUNYAN and John MILTON were giants of the age; William Prynne, when read seriously, could be recognized as a master of satire and a symbol of literary freedom. Conversely, Puritan prose aroused such opposition as that in Thomas Hobbes's *Leviathan.* Elizabethan drama had been far superior to early Stuart drama, which was generally poor, but the Puritan attitude toward actors and plays did much to kill it, at least temporarily, and to leave a stigma upon the stage that still lingers. Sabbatarianism was rooted in Puritanism, and ''blue laws'' flourished long after the name Puritan was forgotten. It is true that the Puritans' attitudes toward music and aesthetics have been grossly exaggerated. Moreover, the thesis about the close relationship between Calvinism and capitalism is subject to many reservations; yet there remains much about Puritan thrift, hard work, and devotion to duty that rings true. It is no coincidence that many Puritans belonged to the moneyed mercantile or professional middle class during the 17th century. Social class mobility is also associated with the Puritans. The rise of the gentry in the century from the death of Henry VIII to the outbreak of the Civil War worked its influence upon the rise of the House of Commons as a powerful force against absolutism, played a part in bringing on the Puritan Revolution and in the process narrowed the gap between the higher and lower classes of England.

Bibliography: W. HALLER, *The Rise of Puritanism* (New York 1938). A. F. S. PEARSON, *Thomas Cartwright and Elizabethan Puritanism, 1535–1603* (Cambridge, Eng. 1925). M. M. KNAPPEN, *Tudor Puritanism* (Chicago 1939). C. HILL, *Puritanism and Revolution* (London 1958). W. A. SHAW, *A History of the English Church . . . 1640–1660,* 2 v. (London 1900). H. N. BRAILSFORD, ed., *The Levellers and the English Revolution* (Stanford 1961). A. JESSOP, ''Robert Browne,'' *The Dictionary of National Biography From the Earliest Times to 1900,* 63 v. (London 1885–1900, repr. with corrections, 21 v., 1908–09, 1921–22, 1938) 3:57–61. A. SIMPSON, *Puritanism in Old and New England* (Chicago 1955). A. S. P. WOODHOUSE, *Puritanism and Liberty* (Chicago 1951). P. MILLER, *The New England Mind: The Seventeenth Century* (Cambridge, Mass. 1954). R. B. PERRY, *Puritanism and Democracy* (New York 1944). P. MILLER and T. H. JOHNSON, eds., *The Puritans,* 2 v. (New York 1938). P. A. SCHOLES, *The Puritans and Music in England and New England* (New York 1934). S. E. MORISON, *The Intellectual Life of Colonial New England* (2d ed. New York 1956). C. HILL, *Society and Puritanism in Pre-Revolutionary England* (New York 1964). J. F. NEW, *Anglican and Puritan: The Basis of Their Opposition, 1558–1640* (Stanford, Calif. 1964).

[M. J. HAVRAN]

PURPOSE OF AMENDMENT

A resolve on the part of a penitent not to sin again. It is not a mere wish, nor is it a promise, but a simple determination of will to avoid sin. In the early Church a relatively long period of actual reform was often required to precede the reconciliation of a sinner. But in the later discipline of the Church the intention to reform was, under ordinary circumstances, permitted in the Sacrament of Reconciliation to substitute for actual reform as a condition necessary for reconciliation. However, there can be no forgiveness of sin without sorrow, and sorrow is insufficient if it does not include a purpose to give up future sin; hence the purpose of amendment is an indispensable part of the true contrition necessary for the valid reception of the Sacrament. Both the Councils of Florence (*Enchiridion symbolorum,* 1323) and Trent (*Enchiridion symbolorum,* 1676) expressly associate the resolution to improve in the future with regret for past moral lapses. Although a clearly deliberate and distinct volitional proposal regarding moral reform is more helpful than a vague, undetermined, and implicit intention of amendment, the proposal to improve implicit in true contrition is sufficient in practice to ensure the validity of the Sacrament.

Theologians commonly enumerate three qualities that should mark the purpose of amendment. (1) It should be firm, i.e., the penitent's present attitude should be one of sincere determination to avoid the sin at the cost of whatever self-denial or effort may be required. (2) It should be universal. Negatively, it must exclude any present intention to sin mortally, and it should include, at least virtually, a positive intention to avoid any kind of mortal sin in the future. As regards the sins a penitent actually confesses, his purpose of amendment must therefore extend to all that are mortal. If he has no mortal sins to confess, his purpose of amendment should specifically embrace either all the venial sins he has confessed, or at least some one of them, or some sin of his past life contained in the matter of his confession. (3) It must be efficacious. This means that it must include the intention of using the means necessary to the avoidance of sin—e.g., prayer, vigilance, the shunning of the free occasions of sin. It also includes the determination to make necessary reparation for one's sins, if and when this is possible.

It must be remembered that the purpose of amendment is an act of the will, not of the mind, and it must not be confused with certainty on the part of the mind that one will succeed in implementing his proposal to reform. It is, indeed, compatible with strong doubt of mind. What is required for the purpose of amendment is not actual success, or the certain expectation of success, but a present act of will to turn away from sin. Failure to keep the resolution does not necessarily mean that a person was insincere when he made it, although frequent relapses, coupled with the neglect of obvious, necessary, and easy means may indicate that something is wanting in a penitent's purpose of amendment.

See Also: CONTRITION; PENANCE, SACRAMENT OF.

Bibliography: P. F. PALMER, *Sacraments of Healing and of Vocation* (Englewood Cliffs, N.J. 1963). C. JOURNET, *The Meaning of Grace,* tr. A. V. LITTLEDALE (New York 1960). E. H. SCHILLEBEECKX, *Christ: The Sacrament of the Encounter with God* (New York 1963). J. C. HEENAN, *Priest and Penitent: A Discussion of Confession* (London 1946).

[J. D. FEARON]

PURVEY, JOHN

Wyclifite; b. Lathbury, Buckinghamshire, England, 1353?; d. after 1407. He was ordained in 1377. Because of his close connection with John WYCLIF, he may have been an Oxford man. He was Wyclif's constant and devoted companion after the latter's withdrawal to Lutterworth in 1381. Purvey was most probably responsible for translating and revising Wyclif's original works for popular circulation among the LOLLARDS. He may have revised the translation of the Bible by Wyclif and Nicholas HEREFORD. After Wyclif's death in 1384, Purvey lived among Lollard sympathizers in Bristol, where his sermons brought a ban on preaching from the bishop of Worcester (1387). In 1388 and 1389 royal warrants authorized the confiscation of all writings of Wyclif, Hereford, Aston, and Purvey, and the arrest of their possessors. A second translation of the Bible (1396) has been ascribed to Purvey, but according to McFarlane, this "rests on slight foundation." In 1401, after some time in prison, he publicly recanted. He was presented with a living, which he resigned after two years. There is reason to believe he was alive in 1407.

Bibliography: M. DEANESLY, *The Lollard Bible* (Cambridge, Eng. 1920). K. B. MCFARLANE, *John Wycliffe and the Beginnings of English Nonconformity* (New York 1953). H. HARGREAVES, "The Latin Text of Purvey's Psalter," *Medium Aevum* 24 (1955) 73–90. A. B. EMDEN, *A Biographical Register of the University of Oxford to A.D. 1500* (Oxford 1957–59) 3:1526–27.

[J. E. HEALEY]

PUSEY, EDWARD BOUVERIE

Anglican theologian, leader of the OXFORD MOVEMENT; b. Pusey, Berkshire, England, Aug. 22, 1800; d. Ascot Priory, Sept. 16, 1882. His father, Philip Bouverie, took the name Pusey in 1789. Edward was educated at Eton and at Christ Church, Oxford. Elected a fellow of Oriel College, Oxford, in 1823, he formed close friendships there with John KEBLE and John Henry NEWMAN.

Edward Bouverie Pusey. (© Bettmann/CORBIS)

From 1825 to 1827 he attended German universities at Göttingen, Berlin, and Bonn, where he studied under Friedrich SCHLEIERMACHER, Johann August Neander, and other leaders of the higher criticism. He studied also Oriental languages before returning to England, where in 1828 he was married, ordained, and appointed regius professor of Hebrew and canon of Christ Church, offices he held until his death. In 1833 he joined Newman, Keble, and Richard Hurrell FROUDE in their effort to revive the Catholic tradition in the Church of England. Pusey's learning and prestige helped to establish the Oxford Movement as a serious force. His essay, *Scriptural Views of Holy Baptism* (1835), changed the character of the *Tracts for the Times* from pamphlets to learned studies. He also helped to found the *Library of the Fathers.* Despite his somewhat awkward preaching style, his sermons were most influential in propagating the movement's ideals.

Like Newman, Pusey was treated harshly by the Oxford authorities, who in 1843 condemned his moderately Catholic sermon on the Eucharist and suspended him from preaching for two years. Unlike Newman, Pusey refused to despair of the Church of England. Assuming leadership of the faltering movement, he sought to prevent others from following Newman into the Catholic Church by emphasizing that ANGLICANISM retained the sacraments and apostolic succession. While his treatises on the sacraments, *The Real Presence in the Fathers* (1855) and *The Real Presence* (1857), defended the High Church position, he attempted to check the spread of liberalism in the church. He tried unsuccessfully to have Benjamin Jowett, professor of Greek at Oxford, prosecuted for heresy in 1863, and he maintained the eternity of hell against the views of F. W. Farrar in 1880. Pusey believed that reunion with Rome was the most effective means of checking the spread of unbelief. His first *Eirenicon* (1865) asserted that the only obstacles to reunion were unofficial doctrines respecting the Blessed Mother, purgatory, and indulgences. His second *Eirenicon* (1869) stressed Anglican objections to the IMMACULATE CONCEPTION. Newman's discouraging reply to his appeals, however, and the definition of papal infallibility in 1870 ended his hopes.

Bibliography: *Spiritual Letters of E. B. Pusey,* ed. J. O. JOHNSTON and W. C. E. NEWBOLT (London 1898). H. P. LIDDON, *Life of Edward Bouverie Pusey,* ed. J. O. JOHNSTON and R. J. WILSON, 4 v. (London 1893–97), with list of his writings in v.4.

[T. S. BOKENKOTTER]

PUSILLANIMITY

A vice opposed to the moral virtue of magnanimity; a disposition by which the irascible appetite is inclined to desist from works of virtue because a person considers them beyond his strength when in reality they are not. This vice is also called cowardice of spirit. Such smallness of soul arises from a culpably erroneous judgment either overestimating the difficulty of the virtuous work to be done or underestimating one's strength and resources to perform the action. When pusillanimity leads to the omission of an action that a person is gravely obliged to perform, it is a mortal sin; otherwise it is a venial sin. The servant in the Parable of the Talents who buried his talent for fear of the master is the classic example of a person with the vice of pusillanimity (Mt 25.14; Lk 19.12). Pusillanimity in superiors and others having authority can easily be a serious sin because it often brings harm to the common good. It is also very serious if it causes a person to neglect spiritual works that are necessary for salvation.

Bibliography: THOMAS AQUINAS, *Summa theologiae* 2a2ae, 133. F. L. B. CUNNINGHAM, ed., *The Christian Life* (Dubuque 1959).

[R. DOHERTY]

PUSTET

A family of Catholic publishers, whose original home was the Republic of Venice. Probably in the 17th century they emigrated to south Germany, where Anton became a bookbinder in the lower Bavarian borough of Hals, near Passau. He married Anna Scheuerocher, by whom he had a son, Friedrich, on March 25, 1798. Having learned bookbinding under his father, Friedrich started a small bookstore in 1818, and in 1822 founded a separate printing establishment.

As his business prospered, Friedrich founded a publishing house in Regensburg in 1826, which developed into a worldwide enterprise. Its first catalogues show great diversity, with a leaning towards history and religious literature. Regensburg Liturgical Publications achieved wide reputation when in 1845 they issued an altar missal and shortly thereafter a breviary for use by traveling priests. In the 1850s Friedrich associated the firm with the budding reform of German church music being urged by Karl Proske and Franz Xaver Witt and the Pustet Publishing House became its most important organ. Friedrich's zeal earned for him in 1870 the title "Typographus S. R. Congregationis." Among other distinctions, his firm was entrusted by the Vatican with the *Editio Typica* of all its liturgical works. In 1860 Friedrich turned the business over to his sons, Friedrich (1831–1902), Klemens (1833–98), and Karl (1839–1910). Friedrich the elder died on March 5, 1882. The firm consistently adhered to the policies and goals set by its founder.

[R. TAPKE]

PUTZER, JOSEPH

Theologian and canonist; b. Rodenek, Austrian Tyrol, March 4, 1836; d. Ilchester, Maryland, May 15, 1904. He was professed a Redemptorist Aug. 14, 1856, studied at St. Barbara's Seminary, Mautern, and was ordained Aug. 7, 1859. For two years he was a lector at Mautern, and for 14 more he served as a missionary at Eggenburg and Innsbruck, Austria, before immigrating to America in 1876. He spent the next 11 years in the active ministry as assistant at St. Alphonsus, and St. Michael's, Baltimore, Maryland, and as superior at St. Mary's, Buffalo, New York, before going to Ilchester in 1887. There he taught theology and Canon Law for the remainder of his life, except for three years (1893–96), when he was again superior at St. Mary's, Buffalo, and assistant in St. Michael's, Baltimore. In 1893, in reediting a work previously published by Anthony Konings, CSSR, *Commentarium in Facultates Apostolicas,* Putzer so revised and enlarged it that it was a new work. Writers on both sides of the Atlantic immediately acclaimed it for its clearness, depth, and accurate scholarship. His *Instructio de Confessariis* and many articles in Catholic periodicals and newspapers also reflected his wide and exact knowledge, keen power of analysis, and unerring judgment. Bishops and priests constantly sought his opinion in difficult cases of theology and Canon Law.

Bibliography: Archives, Redemptorist Fathers of the Baltimore Province. C. MADER, *Die Congregation des allerheiligsten Erlösers in Österreich* (Vienna 1887). M. DE MEULEMEESTER, et al., *Bibliographie générale des écrivains rédemptoristes,* 3 v. (Louvain 1933–39) 2:335–336. J. F. BYRNE, *The Redemptorist Centenaries* (Philadelphia 1933). M. J. CURLEY, *The Provincial Story* (New York 1963). *American Ecclesiastical Review* 30 (1904) 614.

[M. J. CURLEY]

PYRRHONISM

Pyrrhonism is the earliest Greek skeptical movement, originating with Pyrrho of Elis (365–275 B.C.). Fragmentary evidence relating to Pyrrhonism is found in Aristocles of Messene (preserved in Eusebius's *Praeparatio Evangelica,*), Sextus Empiricus, and Diogenes Laertius in one tradition and in Cicero in another. Pyrrho himself, once a painter, seems to have accompanied Anaxarchus of Abdera on Alexander's Asian campaign. He may have assimilated Oriental ideas through association with the Magi and Gymnosophists. Democritean influence is traceable in his doctrines on knowledge and the practical life, and he may have had some contact with the CYRENAICS. He left no writings, and from ancient sources alone it is impossible to determine with certainty his philosophical positions.

Teachings. Pyrrho was essentially a moralist, not a dialectical or speculative thinker. Cicero characterized him as an austere teacher of an uncompromising ethic, one who advocated absolute indifference to the circumstances of life. He conceived philosophy as a way of life whose goal was happiness, which for him was a state of interior tranquillity (ἀταραξία). Pyrrho regarded things in themselves as wholly incomprehensible to man and consequently incapable of grounding either true or false judgment; they are wholly indifferent, neither more this way than that. Appearances alone are evident; beyond them one cannot go. Since reasons of equal weight can be advanced both for and against any opinion, the wise man withholds judgment.

Though the true Pyrrhonian did not make truth judgments, he could not be reduced to complete inactivity in the affairs of life. Pyrrho advocated the making of practical decisions not by basing them on the real values of things, for these cannot be known, but rather by following accepted usages, customs, and laws. His program for attaining inner tranquility entailed, in the speculative order, the total suppression of reason's natural desire for truth; in the moral order it demanded total conformity and the consequent abandonment of personal freedom and self-determination.

Disciples. Timon of Phlius (*c.* 325–*c.* 235 B.C.) was the apologist of early Pyrrhonism. In his prolific writings he developed the ideas of Pyrrho and also lampooned the dogmatic philosophers in verse (Σίλλοι). According to Aristocles, he summarized Pyrrho's teaching under three headings: (1) the intrinsic nature of things (they are indifferent); (2) the human situation in reference to them (man can say nothing about them); and (3) the ultimate result (man will attain tranquility). Other disciples were Philo of Athens and Nausiphanes of Teos, the Democritean philosopher who taught EPICURUS.

The movement declined after the time of Timon and enjoyed but small popularity until it was given new life through the theoretical contributions of Aenesidemus (*c.* 100–40 B.C.) at Alexandria. Sextus Empiricus (*c.* A.D. 200), the historian of Pyrrhonism, has preserved the ten tropes (τρόποι) of Aenesidemus; these are ways of achieving suspension of judgment.

See Also: SKEPTICISM; GREEK PHILOSOPHY.

Bibliography: F. C. COPLESTON, *History of Philosophy,* (Westminster, Md. 1946–) v. 1 Greece and Rome (1950). J. OWENS, *A History of Ancient Western Philosophy* (New York 1959). E. R. BEVAN, *Stoics and Sceptics* (New York 1959). L. ROBIN, *Pyrrhon et le scepticisme grec* (Paris 1944).

[L. A. BARTH]

PYRRHUS I, PATRIARCH OF CONSTANTINOPLE

Dec. 20, 638, to Sept. 29, 641, restored Jan. 8–9, 654, to June 1, 654; d. Constantinople, May 19–23, 655. A key figure in the BYZANTINE CHURCH's controversy over MONOTHELITISM, Pyrrhus was archimandrite of Chrysopolis when he succeeded his friend Patriarch SERGIUS I in the Patriarchate of CONSTANTINOPLE. Like Sergius, he espoused the Monothelitic *Ecthesis* of Emperor HERACLIUS and wrote to Pope John IV in support of Monothelitism (*Patrologia Latina* 87:1205). Because of alleged complicity in court intrigue, he was forced by Emperor CONSTANS II to leave Constantinople in 641, and he escaped to Carthage. He was replaced as patriarch by Paul II; Pope Theodore I approved the deposition of Pyrrhus, but admonished that it should have been canonical (PL 87:81). In July 645, in the presence of the exarch of North Africa, Gregory, Pyrrhus held a *disputatio* with MAXIMUS THE CONFESSOR (*Patrologia Graeca* 91:287–354), who had succeeded him at Chrysopolis and who was a resolute opponent of Monothelitism. Then, hoping for Gregory's help in his attempt to be restored to his see, Pyrrhus declared himself converted, went to Rome with Maximus, condemned the *Ecthesis,* and was received by Pope Theodore with the honors of a patriarch. However, after Gregory's death (648) Pyrrhus was induced to recant his recantation. Theodore thereupon deposed and anathematized him; this was confirmed by Pope Martin I (649) and later by Pope Agatho (680) and the sixth general council, Constantinople III. When Patriarch Paul died, Dec. 26, 653 (Pope Martin I had already been condemned), Pyrrhus was restored as patriarch for a brief period before his death.

Bibliography: J. D. MANSI, *Sacrorum Conciliorum nova et amplissima collectio* (Graz 1960) 10:859–877; 11:276, 557–572. V. GRUMEL, *Les Regestes des actes du patriarcat de Constantinople* (Kadikoi-Bucharest 1932–47) 1:118, 121. K. KRUMBACHER, *Geschichte der byzatinischen Literatur* (Munich 1897) 60–64. H. G. BECK, *Kirche und theologische Literatur im byzantinischen Reich* (Munich 1959) 109, 295, 432, 439. G. OSTROGORSKY, *History of the Byzantine State* (Oxford 1956; New Brunswick NJ 1957). O. VOLK, *Lexikon für Theologie und Kirche,* ed. J. HOFER and K. RAHNER (Freiburg 1957–65) 8:908–909.

[T. P. HALTON]

PYTHAGORAS AND THE PYTHAGOREANS

Pythagoras (fl. *c.* 530 B.C.), Greek philosopher and mathematician, was one of the most influential and creative thinkers of the pre-Socratic period. A native of the island of Samos off the western coast of Asia Minor, he is reported to have traveled extensively, but this cannot be verified. At about the age of 40 he fled from Samos to avoid the tyranny of Polycrates and migrated to Croton in southern Italy, where he lived for 20 years. It was here that he founded his famous society. His last years were spent in Metapontum, farther north from Croton, where he died on an unknown date. The Pythagorean society continued in existence for well over a century, disappearing finally in the fourth century B.C.

Pythagoras himself apparently wrote nothing, preferring to transmit his teachings orally to the members of the school. Moreover, the members of the society were supposedly sworn to secrecy on their doctrines which, if true, would militate further against the development of a written tradition. As a result, most knowledge of the Pythagoreans has come indirectly through later classical writers. Furthermore, Pythagoras was held in such high esteem by members of the school that they regularly attributed their ideas to him. Thus, although there must have been some development of the tradition, it is difficult to distinguish the teachings of the various Pythagoreans. Even Aristotle usually refers to the ''Pythagoreans'' as a common group rather than to Pythagoras himself. The later members of the school included Philolaus, Eurytus, Lysis, Xenophilos, Phanton, Echekrates, Diokles, Polymnastos, Timaeus of Locri, and Archytas of Tarentum, a friend of Plato. The authenticity of the fragments attributed to Philolaus has been questioned.

Basic Principles. The Pythagorean society was a quasi-religious community devoted to the purification of the soul and its liberation from the ''wheel of birth.'' The emphasis on communal life as a road to self-perfection, along with the doctrine of the transmigration of souls, may have derived from the earlier Orphic religious tradition. The members of the society were bound by numerous dietary and other practical proscriptions to purify the soul in accordance with their belief in METEMPSYCHOSIS. Over and above these religious and ascetic aspects, they were also actively involved in political life, which led to the eventual expulsion of the society from Croton. But above all, they placed value on the discovery and cultivation of knowledge, giving the highest place to mathematics. They held that devotion to science was the noblest form of purification.

Unlike the Homeric tradition in which the soul is merely the shadow of the man, that of the Pythagoreans held that the soul is the man and is imprisoned in the body, thus introducing the soul-body dichotomy so prominent later in Plato's thought. It is difficult to reconcile this with the doctrine, also attributed to the Pythagoreans, that the soul is the harmony or attunement of the four elements constituting the body. They also looked upon virtue as a harmonious mathematical proportion in human action.

The Pythagorean system was based on a duality of first principles: the limited, as the source of definiteness, and the unlimited, as the source of divisibility. The entire universe was a harmony of these two principles. Aristotle reports (*Meta.* 986a 23–27) that some members of the school expanded the basic duality into a table of ten opposites: (1) limited and unlimited, (2) odd and even, (3) one and plurality, (4) right and left, (5) male and female, (6) rest and moving, (7) straight and curved, (8) light and darkness, (9) good and bad, (10) square and oblong.

Mathematical Teachings. The first product of the limited and unlimited was the number one, which in turn is the principle of all the cardinal numbers. According to the testimony of Aristotle, the Pythagoreans identified number with the physical universe. This latter point is difficult to see and has been the subject of much discussion.

Number and the Universe. The theory seems to have been based on an identification, or at least an association, of arithmetical numbers, geometrical entities, and physical bodies. Aristotle suggests (*Meta.* 985b 31–986a 3) that Pythagoras's discovery that musical harmony is expressible in terms of the ratios of small whole numbers prompted him to conclude that all other phenomena in the universe are also mathematical in nature. Moreover, the Pythagoreans customarily represented numbers by placing a pebble or dot for each unit in the number. In this way the number one became a point; two, a line; three, a plane triangle; and four, a tetrahedron. Possibly because the first four numbers culminate in a solid figure, which is identifiable with an extended body, these numbers arranged in a plane triangular configuration became a sacred figure, the ''tetractys,'' and the sum of the first four numbers, that is, 10, was a sacred number. In this way the Pythagoreans could say that things are numbers: numbers were geometrized, and geometrical entities were incarnated. Though this theory may seem strange and difficult for the modern mind, it embodies a hope and an ideal of perennial recurrence, that is, the reduction of the physical universe to mathematical structure. Many of the founders of modern physical science, especially J. KEPLER and G. GALILEI, were motivated by this same ideal.

Types of Numbers. The Pythagoreans were characterized by several further mathematical teachings. Their distinction between triangular, square, and oblong numbers was based on their practice of representing a number by a corresponding group of dots. Triangular numbers (3, 6, 10, 15, etc.) were the sums of the unbroken natural number series beginning with one and arranged in a triangular pattern. The ''tetractys'' was, of course, the chief triangular number pattern. Square numbers (4, 9, 16, 25, etc.) were the sums of the odd numbers beginning with one and arranged in the form of a square. Such numbers have a rational square root. Oblong numbers (2, 6, 12, 20, etc.) were the series of even numbers beginning with two and arranged in a rectangle. Each successive addition to the latter two geometrical patterns was called a ''gnomon.''

Pythagorean Theorem. The use of the lengths 3, 4, and 5 for the purpose of constructing a right triangle dates back to the very earliest times. To Pythagoras belongs the credit of universalizing this relation into the famous theorem that still bears his name: the square on the hypotenuse of a right triangle is equal to the sum of the squares on its sides. But this discovery was a mixed blessing for the Pythagoreans. For the use of this theorem results in many cases in the uncovering of incommensurable quantities, that is, the hypotenuse and sides of the triangle are so related that no unit of measurement however small can be divided into them without a fractional remainder. This in effect was the discovery of irrational numbers, a scandal for Pythagorean cosmology. For if numbers are irrational, then so are things. Hippasos of Metapontum was reportedly drowned at sea for revealing this embarrassment. The solution to this problem of incommensurability escaped the Pythagoreans and had to wait for the theory of proportions developed by Eudoxus in the Academy. The Pythagoreans appear to have known only three of the five regular solids: the cube, tetrahedron, and dodecahedron. The discovery of the octahedron and icosahedron, along with the use of the five regular solids as cosmological principles, were later Platonic developments.

Pythagoras. (©Bettman/CORBIS)

Astronomical Views. Pythagorean astronomical theory was both ingenious and highly influential. The universe as a whole is surrounded by a ''boundless breath'' that is inhaled by the universe after the manner of a huge animal. As inhaled, this breath plays the role of empty space separating the celestial bodies. At the middle of the universe is the central fire, variously called the hearth of the world, the watchtower of Zeus, and the mother of the gods, which is never seen by us because it is always on the other side of the earth. The celestial bodies from the central fire outward are the counterearth (antichthon), earth, moon, sun, Venus, Mercury, Mars, Jupiter, Saturn, and the fixed stars. The counterearth, also never seen from our side of the earth, was posited according to Aristotle either to bring the celestial bodies up to the sacred number 10 or to explain why there are more lunar than solar eclipses. The heavenly bodies are visible as orifices in wheels of fire that revolve at a methodic pace producing the musical harmony of the heavens, which is not noticed because it is always heard. The celestial bodies periodically return to their original orientation in a time interval called the Pythagorean Great Year. Other notable elements in the theory were the doctrine of the sphericity of the earth and the distinction between the diurnal westward motion of the heavens and the slower eastward motion of planets. These astronomical views are very prominent in Plato's *Timaeus.* The early Pythagoreans clearly did not introduce the heliocentric hypothesis, an honor that must be reserved for Aristarchus of Samos (fl. 281 B.C.).

Neo-Pythagoreanism. The first century B.C. saw a Neo-Pythagorean revival that continued into the second century of the Christian Era. The emphasis in this movement was on the religious and ascetic traditions of the old school, but intellectual pursuits were not overlooked. The result was a rather eclectic combination of Pythagoreanism with Stoic, Aristotelian, and especially Platonic elements. The chief figures in Neo-Pythagoreanism were Nigidius Figulus, Plutarch of Chaeronea, Apollonius of Tyana, Nicomachus of Gerasa, Numenius of Apamea, and Philostratus of Lemnos.

See Also: GREEK PHILOSOPHY; SCIENCE (IN ANTIQUITY).

Bibliography: W. K. GUTHRIE, *A History of Greek Philosophy* (Cambridge, Eng. 1962–) v. 1. J. BURNET, *Early Greek Philosophy* (4th ed. London 1930). J. E. RAVEN, *Pythagoreans and Eleatics* (Cambridge, Eng. 1948). E. L. MINAR, *Early Pythagorean Politics in Practice and Theory* (Baltimore, Md. 1942). T. L. HEATH, *A History of Greek Mathematics,* 2 v. (Oxford 1921) 1:65–117, 141–169; *Aristarchus of Samos: The Ancient Copernicus* (Oxford 1913).

[R. J. BLACKWELL]

PYX

A container for the Blessed Sacrament. It was at first a small wooden box, usually round and with a lid. During the Middle Ages it was sometimes of metal or of ivory; when containing the Blessed Sacrament it was kept at first in people's houses, later in the sacristy, then on the altar, then suspended above the altar, sometimes inside a metal dove. When ambries, sacrament-houses, and tabernacles came into use for reserving the Blessed Sacrament, the pyx underwent a twofold development; by enlargement and the acquisition of a foot it developed into the CIBORIUM by diminution in size and the addition of a hinged lid it became the small vessel now used for carrying a few consecrated hosts to the sick. Nowadays this is the meaning usually given to the word ''pyx,'' though the name is used also for a similar vessel, a metal box that contains, inside the tabernacle, the large Host used for Benediction of the Blessed Sacrament.

Bibliography: J. BRAUN, *Das christliche Altargerät in seinem Sein und in seiner Entwicklung* (Munich 1932). C. ROHAULT DE FLEURY, *La Messe,* 8 v. (Paris 1883–89) v.5.

[C. W. HOWELL/EDS.]

Q

QATAR, THE CATHOLIC CHURCH IN

Qatar is an independent emirate occupying the peninsula of the same name which projects into the Persian Gulf southeast of BAHREIN. (For map, see the entry on the UNITED ARAB EMIRATES.) It covers an area of approximately 4400 square miles, with the capital at Doha, on the eastern coast. The land is almost entirely barren desert, with small areas of pasture; only one percent is arable. Before 1949, Qatar's main source of income was from pearl fisheries on the coast; after that date, it became an important producer of petroleum. In World War I, when its bonds with the Ottoman Empire were broken, it became an independent sheikdom under British protection; it became an independent state and a member of the United Nations on September 3, 1971.

The vast majority of Qatari people are Muslim (95 percent). The majority of Catholics are foreign workers. Qatari Catholics are under the jurisdiction of the Apostolic Vicariate of Arabia, with its seat in Abu Dhabi, in the neighboring United Arab Emirates.

[L. F. HARTMAN/EDS.]

QUADRAGESIMO ANNO

Encyclical letter of Pope PIUS XI on the reconstruction of the social order, issued May 15, 1931, ''forty years after'' Leo XIII's *RERUM NOVARUM.* Appearing in the depths of the worldwide depression which began in 1929, it attracted immediate attention as a critique of the prevailing economic system and as a program of institutional reform. A generation later, in *MATER ET MAGISTRA*, John XXIII summed up its teaching as twofold: First, the supreme criterion in economic matters ''must not be the special interests of individuals or groups, nor unregulated competition, economic despotism, national prestige or imperialism, nor any other aim of this sort. On the contrary, all forms of economic enterprise must be governed by the principles of social justice and charity.'' Second, ''man's aim must be to achieve in social justice a national and international juridical order, with its network of public and private institutions, in which all economic activity can be conducted not merely for private gain but also in the interests of the common good'' (pars. 38–40).

Quadragesimo anno begins with a review of developments following Leo's encyclical: the gradual formulation and application of a body of authoritative social teaching, the extension of social legislation, and progress in labor organization. A second section clarifies Catholic teaching on private property, the relations of capital and labor as social classes, the nature of social justice, and wages. The extension of property ownership to workers is advocated as a means toward their security and toward a fairer distribution of the fruits of industrialism. Reestablishment of an order of mutual cooperation among occupational groups analogous to the medieval guilds is presented as a demand of social justice. In this section principles of corporativism are exemplified, although Italian Fascism is explicitly rejected. The final section of the encyclical has a scathing indictment, not of the capitalist system as such, but of the trend toward concentration of economic power leading to a threefold conflict: within the economy, for the control of the state, and between states. Communism as an alternative system is condemned, and although the trend toward moderation in socialism is carefully noted, its essential doctrine is found incompatible with religion. Men are reminded that, ultimately, a solution through institutional reform will be dependent upon a prior reform of morals and of the Christian spirit.

The encyclical gave a strong impetus to Catholic social action. Attempts to give it practical effect through designs as specific as the industry council plan sometimes betrayed lack of appreciation of prerequisites for social change. But its significance for the development of Catholic thought on the economic order was made apparent by the application and development of its teaching in the pronouncements of Pius XII and John XXIII.

Bibliography: Official Latin text in *Acta apostolicae sedis* 23 (1931) 177–228. English translation in D.J. O'BRIEN and T.A. SHANNON, eds., *Catholic Social Thought: The Documentary Heritage* (Maryknoll, NY, 1992) 42–79. R. J. MILLER, *Forty Years After: Pius XI and the Social Order* (St. Paul 1947).

[R. J. MILLER]

QUADRATUS, ST.

Early second-century apologist, possibly martyr. Only a fragment of the Apology addressed by Quadratus (or Codratus) from Asia Minor to Emperor HADRIAN during a persecution (124 or 129) has been preserved by EUSEBIUS (*Hist. eccl.* 4.3.1–2). It speaks of the witness to Christ's wondrous deeds by people who had been healed or raised from the dead and were still alive. Quadratus is thought to have been a disciple of IGNATIUS OF ANTIOCH and POLYCARP OF SMYRNA (Eus., *Chron.* 2140; *Hist. eccl.* 3.37; 5.17). R. Harris has attempted to prove that the legendary Apology of St. Catherine of Alexandria quoted in the romance of BARLAAM AND JOSAPHAT was an adaptation of the Apology of Quadratus, and P. Andriessen considered the Apology to be identical with the Epistle to DIOGNETUS. However, neither of these theses has been accepted as established. Jerome (*De vir. ill.* 19; *Epist.* 70) mistakenly identified the apologist with the Bp. Quadratus of Athens who lived during the time of Marcus Aurelius. He has also been mistakenly identified with the Bp. Quadratus of Utica who was put to death in the Valerian persecution (Aug. 21, 259) and was eulogized by St. AUGUSTINE in several sermons as the patron of a church in Hippo Zarytus (Bizerte).

Feast: May 26; Sept. 27 (Byzantine Church).

Bibliography: R. HARRIS, *Expository Times* 32 (1921) 147–160; *The Bulletin of the John Rylands Library* 7 (1923) 355–383. E. KLOSTERMANN and E. SEEBERG, *Die Apologie der hl, Katharina* (Berlin 1924). É. AMANN, *Dictionnaire de théologie catholique*, ed. A. VACANT et al., (Paris 1903–50) 13.2:1428–31. P. ANDRIESSEN, *Lexikon für Theologie und Kirche*, ed. J. HOFER and K. RAHNER (Freiburg 1957–65) 6:366, s.v. Kodratos; *Recherches de théologie ancienne et médiévale* 13 (1946) 5–39, 125–149; 14 (1947) 121–156.

[F. X. MURPHY]

QUADRUPANI, CARLO GIUSEPPI

Barnabite preacher, spiritual director, and writer; b. Induno (Varese), Lombardy, 1740 (1739?); d. there, July 14, 1806. He was superior of S. Alessandro's in Milan and then provincial of the Barnabites of Lombardy. His greatest success was in preaching, for which he became famous throughout Italy. His preaching career began in the church of S. Lorenzo in Rome in 1771, and from then until the end of his life he was occupied principally with preaching in the major cities of Italy, conducting retreats for clergy and laity, hearing confessions, and giving spiritual direction. His writings went through an extraordinary number of editions and translations and were still being published in the 20th century. The *Documenti per istruzione e tranquillità della anime* (Turin 1795) was given the title *Documenti per tranquillare le anime timorose nelle loro dubbiezze* in the 30th edition (Milan 1807). He also wrote *Documenti pratici per vivere cristianamente* (published post-humously, Milan 1807), which was later published together with the first work as *Documenti di vita spirituale.*

Bibliography: O. M. PREMOLI, *Storia dei Barnabiti dal 1700 al 1825* (Rome 1925) 3:387–388. G. BOFFITO, *Biblioteca Barnabitica illustrata,* v.3 (Florence 1934) 225–234; v.4 (1937) 431.

[J. C. WILLKE]

QUALITY

A primary and universal notion that cannot be strictly defined, although it can be described and illustrated. Its Greek equivalent, ποιότης, was coined by Plato (*Theaet.* 182A) and was used by Aristotle to designate one of the CATEGORIES OF BEING. It was translated by Cicero into Latin as *qualitas.* As used in logic, quality denotes a formal property of the copula whereby the PROPOSITION is affirmative or negative. As used by Aristotle and by scholastics in metaphysics, it designates one of the ten categories and means an ACCIDENT (e.g., intelligent, white, robust) that makes an already essentially determined SUBSTANCE (e.g., man) to be of a certain kind. In modern philosophy, and generally in contemporary thought, quality refers to those characteristics of sensible reality whereby the senses are determined; for example, the color, sound, and shape of an object.

Aristotelian Division. According to Aristotle, the species of quality has the following four main divisions (*Cat.* 8b 25–11a 39). (1) Habits and dispositions. A HABIT is a firmly established condition of some nature. The man who, by repeated acts, becomes truly virtuous, acquires scientific knowledge, or develops an art conditions his nature in a certain way. Because this sort of quality is comparatively difficult to remove, it is known as habit. On the other hand, a condition of the subject that is easily changed, such as opinion, health, or disease, is called a DISPOSITION. (2) Power and incapacity. From the point of view of a nature's ability to operate, one can speak of the power or capacity to know, to will, and to resist pressure, as qualities of the being. In speaking of the powers of the soul, one frequently uses the term faculty (*see* FACULTIES

OF THE SOUL). When powers are weak, as resistance in soft things or nearsightedness in a man, they are called incapacities or impotencies. (3) Sensible qualities. These qualify the substance insofar as it is capable of affecting the senses, as colors, sounds, odors, hardness (see below). (4) Figure and shape. These are modifications of QUANTITY and tell about the kind of line or figure, as curvedness, straightness, and triangularity.

Aristotle points out that while some qualities may have contraries (as justice and injustice) and some may admit of degrees (as white and whiter), these are the exception rather than the rule.

Primary and Secondary Qualities. This division of qualities has its roots in the works of Galileo GALILEI, R. DESCARTES, and R. Boyle, and was fixed in modern terminology by John LOCKE. The division corresponds almost exactly to the traditional distinction between common and proper SENSIBLES. Common sensibles are the objects of more than one sense, as extension, shape, motion, and number. These are listed by Locke as primary qualities; but he added solidity to them. Proper sensibles are the objects of only one sense, as color and sound; and these in contemporary discourse are called secondary qualities.

The bases of differentiation for Locke and the scholastics, however, are quite different. Locke's viewpoint was the dependence of the secondary qualities on the primary, and his chief interest was in their gnoseological value. The scholastic interest was primarily psychological; its viewpoint was that of determining the formal OBJECT of each sense, or the relating of the proper sensible to the corresponding sense. Locke was influenced by current scientific theories, which stressed the mechanical explanations of the process of perception. For this point of view only the quantitative had mechanical importance. The qualitative as such was looked on as irrelevant, since it was thought to be merely the reaction of a sensitive organism to its environment.

Sensible Qualities. Sensible qualities are accidents that inhere in and determine corporeal substances and are perceived by the external senses; hence they are classified by their relation to the SENSES. Some qualities, being perceptible by one and only one sense, are referred to as the formal object of that sense: for sight, color; for hearing, sound; for taste, flavor; for smell, odor; for touch, tangibility (pressure and temperature). Other qualities are perceived by more than one sense; for example, extension can be sensed by sight, touch, and even taste. Qualities of this type include motion, rest, number, and shape. Since these are sensed by two or more senses (by means of the proper sensibles) they are called common sensibles. This classification into proper and common sensibles was traditional until the rise of modern philosophy.

Galileo and Descartes. While in some sense retaining this division, but not the terminology, Galileo and other philosophers and scientists after him claimed that the secondary qualities, being merely ''apparent'' qualities, should be reduced to and identified with their source in primary qualities. These were conceived to be the mathematical dimensions of matter in motion, which were themselves the truly real. When Descartes speaks of any reality he always means a substance (spirit as thought and body as extension) existing autonomously. Sensible qualities cannot be realities in any true sense, even as accidental determinations distinct from and inhering in the substance. For him this would mean that they were forms ''joined to substance like little souls to their bodies'' (''Letter to Mersenne,'' 1643, ed. Adam-Tannery 3:648). Although at times Descartes verbally refers to modalities or qualifications of substances, his interest is in substance as entire and present to his mind (*Prin. Philos.* 1.56; ed. Adam-Tannery 8:26).

Rationalism and Empiricism. Other rationalistic philosophers also enhance substance almost to the exclusion of qualities or accidents. B. SPINOZA could conceive only of attributes or modes of the one divine substance (*Ethics* 1. def. 4, 5) that do not determine but manifest and flow from the divine essence as corollaries follow a theorem. The monadology of G. W. LEIBNIZ presents a world made up of indivisible substances so closed off from all others that the classical meaning of accident loses all relevance. On the other hand, for the empiricists the notion of substance is an embarrassment. Locke sees it as a ''something we know not what'' to which qualities belong; G. BERKELEY denies material substance along with the extrasubjectivity of all qualities; and for D. HUME, only ideas are perceived, and substance is suggested by the association of ideas.

Modern Scientists. When the empirical scientist discusses the objectivity and nature of qualities, he enters the domain of the philosopher, whose function it is to determine the categories of being. The scientist himself is interested in the quantitative and the measureable; even in his studies on colors and sounds, it is their quantitative aspects (such as wavelengths) that occupy him. This is as it should and must be. The difficulty arises when he begins to philosophize; when he does, he often follows Locke in the reduction of quality to quantity, in the at least implicit denial of the qualitative. But modern physicists who follow Locke ''are deceived about the significance of their own discoveries. In describing perceptual experiences in terms of electrons and light-waves and so on they are explaining *how* it happens that we see things. They are not correcting our account of *what* it is we see'' [M. Cranston, *John Locke* (New York 1957) 269].

Reality and Qualities. Since the time of Galileo and Descartes, most modern philosophers (and scientists generally) have conceded the objective existence of primary qualities. Locke very clearly taught that ''ideas of primary qualities of bodies are resemblances of them, and their patterns do really exist in the bodies themselves'' (*Essay Concerning Human Understanding* 2.8.15). Except for IDEALISM and subjectivism, this position is generally maintained, although there are further differences in the explanation of how primary qualities are known.

Locke's Theory. Locke held that the mind has ''no other immediate object but its own ideas'' (*ibid.* 4.1.1.). So while quantity is truly a characteristic of reality, it is the idea of quantity that is known and that is asserted to correspond to reality. Scholastics disagree with this and hold that the real (not the idea of it) is the immediate object of both sensation and intellection.

On the question of the reality of secondary qualities there is even wider divergence. According to Locke, ''the ideas produced in us by secondary qualities have no resemblance to them at all. . . . They are, in the bodies we denominate from them, only a power to produce those sensations in us'' (*ibid.* 2.8.15). For Locke, then, these qualities are neither the immediate object known, nor are they really objective. The reasons given by Locke for the subjectivity of secondary qualities, closely paralleling those of Descartes, revolve around such considerations as the way in which a jewel changes color in slightly different light conditions, or with the change of the observer's viewpoint; the fact that the same water can feel warm to one hand, cool to the other; that pounding an almond changes its color and taste; and so on.

Berkeley's View. Berkeley insisted that any argument against the objectivity of secondary qualities told even more strongly against the primary, and he concluded that all are equally subjective. The fact of the matter seems to be that if once it is conceded that ideas are the only immediate objects of the mind, one is in the strange position of never being able to know whether or not they do conform to anything ''outside.'' In fact, in that case Berkeley might be right in looking on the outside as an unnecessary duplication, existing to no purpose. At least, if one is shut up in himself with only his ideas to contemplate, the opportunity will never be offered him to compare them with the ''originals.'' He will then be in the position of sensing various ''signals'' and having no way to discriminate between them as purely subjective or truly objective.

Scholastic Teaching. Scholastics, while disputing among themselves about the nature of sensible qualities, do agree that: (1) they are not something merely subjective, but really exist in objects; (2) there is an accidental determination in the object, a dynamic extrasubjective quality, that is not equivalent to mere local motion (as Descartes held). With these points agreed, they dispute over whether sensible qualities exist formally in things, or merely fundamentally and causally.

''Perceptionists'' (Aristotle, the early scholastics, T. PESCH, C. Boyer, et al.) hold that such qualities exist formally in things. Some of their reasons are: that this is required for the objectivity of knowledge as a conformity to what is, that otherwise there is a danger of idealism, and that the scientific objections offered are not conclusive.

''Interpretationists'' (J. BALMES, D. MERCIER, M. DE LA TAILLE, M. Maher, P. Siwek, et al.) hold for the immediate apprehension of real objective qualities by a virtual (not formal) assimilation, such as is had between a natural cause and its univocally determined effect. They claim that there is not merely a symbolic, but a true similitude. In this position they see no conflict with a realistic explanation of knowledge as truly objective, and they feel that scientific facts require it. A few of these facts will suffice here: (1) rotation of the Newtonian disk results in the seeing of white, whereas at rest the disk has the various spectral colors; (2) one and the same stimulus, e.g., electricity, causes different sensations in different organs; (3) sound varies with the distance, as experienced in the Doppler effect; this has also been verified of colors. On sound, even St. THOMAS AQUINAS says that ''sound is only potentially in the sounding body'' (*In 2 anim.* 16.441). A fuller discussion of the entire question and of other scientific facts is had in J. G. Moran's *Psychologia* 1:226 to 252.

Relation to Quantity. In scholastic philosophy both quality and QUANTITY are said to be absolutely inherent accidents; that is, they are not relative to anything outside the substance they modify. Thus shape and color, considered in themselves, merely modify the substance and bespeak no relation to another being. Other accidents, such as ACTION AND PASSION, for example, are relative.

Moreover, quantity and quality are intimately related both metaphysically and noetically. Metaphysically, quantity is the ground for the sensible qualities. By this is meant that, while all accidents properly inhere in and are sustained in being by substance, yet no sensible quality exists except as extended; thus all qualities such as color, sound, and odor require a substance that is already quantified. In the order of knowledge it is in virtue of qualities that quantity is grasped. The eye, for example, is actuated by color, and it sees extension or shape by virtue of the color. With one's back to the ocean, one can not only hear the sound of the waves, but can perceive also their magnitude. So, while sensible qualities are the primary object of the senses, these also sense the species of quantity.

Intensification of Qualities. Because physical qualities are rooted in quantity, they are indirectly quantified through the quantity of the subject in which they exist. Apart from this, however, qualities can be quantified also by reason of their intensity, which is sometimes referred to as their quantity of perfection or of power. This quantification is essentially different from that of dimensive quantity and undergoes intensification and diminution in a special way.

Dimensive quantity is increased through simple addition (and diminished through subtraction) of homogeneous parts; thus the difference of two lengths is another length. This is true also of the quantity of a quality that is based upon the quantity of the subject in which the quality inheres; in this way, the quantity of heat is increased by the simple addition or juxtaposition of hot bodies. On the other hand, the intensity of qualities, not being additive or divisible with respect to homogeneous parts, is not increased or diminished in this way. Rather it is increased or decreased by the intensification or remission of the qualitative form, i.e., by a greater or less actualization of the quality in the subject in which it is found. This is how a body becomes hotter, with a greater intensity of heat than it had previously. Such intensification is not divisible in the same sense as extensive quantity. Thus the difference between two intensities is not an intensity of the same kind; for example, the difference in heat intensity between water at 100°C and water at 80°C is not the heat intensity found in water at 20°C. This difference between the dimensive and intensive quantities of qualities becomes of special significance when one attempts the measurement of qualities.

Measurement of Qualities. Since measurement has primarily to do with size, movements, weight, and the like, it is more proximately related to quantity than it is to quality. Yet the radication of quality in quantity provides one basis for speaking of the measurable aspects of quality. Another indirect way in which qualities can be measured, and particularly their intensification, is through the effect that they produce on another body, usually called an instrument. It is in this way that the physicist measures quantitative aspects of the intensities of heat, sound, color, and so forth. The psychologist similarly measures the effects of qualities on sense receptors in terms of their response to changes either in the environment or in the individual himself.

Modern psychophysics, prescinding from the philosophical aberrations of some of its exponents, is primarily interested in studying the correlations between the physical properties of stimuli and the psychological reactions of the organism to the various stimuli, in the hope of finding laws relating these measurements. Studies along these lines have more or less determined the threshold of sensation, or the minimum stimulus needed to activate a given sense, as well as the maximum stimulus that can be sensed. E. H. Weber and T. Fechner similarly studied the perception of increased stimulation. Weber felt that his experiments led to the "conclusion that the increase in stimulation resulting in a just noticeable increase in sensory experience must be a *constant fraction* of the original stimulus" [P. Siwek, *Experimental Psychology* (New York 1959) 104]. Fechner sought to express this in a mathematical equation, with questionable results.

Occult Qualities. The hidden forces, powers, or qualities discussed by late medieval and early Renaissance writers are generally known as occult qualities. The period in which these men lived was marked by a thirst for knowledge of nature, without the aid of present-day scientific methods and instruments. Thinkers such as J. L. Vives (1492–1540), deploring the dependence on Aristotle in the study of nature, advocated independent investigations and reflections on new observations. He urged the same empirical approach even in studying the soul. Another, Peter RAMUS (1515–72), also voiced discontent with previous methods of instruction, especially with Aristotelian logic, which he held responsible for the sad state of the universities. The spirit of the times was one of reflection and criticism, of revolt against authority and tradition in the name of reason and freedom, and interest gradually centered more and more on natural science.

Not content with the plodding means of observation and experiment and lacking refined instruments, many sought shortcuts. Some felt that there were latent powers or occult forces in nature that could be discovered and used in the service of man. The way to this was through MAGIC, the use of secret arts, symbols, and mystic formulas; through ASTROLOGY, the study of planetary influences on man and his world; and through ALCHEMY, the magical transformation of metals. Agrippa von Nettesheim (1486?–1535) combined medicine with magic in the hope of learning about nature's occult qualities in herbs and minerals. Paracelsus (1493–1541) held that the physician must know not only medicine, but philosophy, astrology, and theology. He has to care for man, argued Paracelsus; and man belongs to this world through his physical body, to the sidereal world through his astral body, and to the spiritual world through his soul. So while he urged the correct use of available medicines to treat diseases, he sought to know the secret terrestrial and astral forces or occult qualities at work, and to control them by alchemy and magic. While this interest in the occult qualities of nature was extravagant and superstitious, it did foreshadow modern science in its attempt to control nature. As time went on alchemy evolved into chemistry; magic, into experiment; and astrology, into astronomy.

Qualifies and Modern Science. Because of the attitude modern scientists adopt toward sensible qualities, they generally tend to deny, or show little interest in, the qualitative as such. For example, the nonobjectivity of color, as distinct from measurable wavelengths, is almost axiomatic for scientists, and what can be said of color frequently applies to other qualities. Despite their rejection of sensible qualities, however, modern scientists are much concerned with nonsensible attributes of bodies, such as electricity, magnetism, gravity, and chemical affinity, which scholastic philosophers regard as pertaining to the qualitative order. Some of these were enumerated among the occult qualities by late medieval writers, because they cannot be directly perceived by any sense. Strictly speaking, however, they are not completely occult, because they are indirectly or reductively sensible from the effects they produce on instruments or experimental apparatus.

Granted that these are qualities, a considerable problem presents itself when one attempts to fit them into the Aristotelian category of quality. Most authors tend to locate them within the second species, as special types of active qualities. Thus gravity and IMPETUS are regarded as active powers or potencies, because of their relation to mechanical motion. Electricity and magnetism, on the other hand, are frequently listed in the third species of quality because of their close relationship to light and color, particularly when these are regarded as forms of electromagnetic radiation.

Whether mass and energy should be regarded as qualitative attributes, in a scholastic sense, is a disputed question. Since these are primarily measurements and because mass is traditionally associated with ''quantity of matter,'' there is some basis for including these under the category of quantity. Yet insofar as mass can also be regarded as a measure of gravitational or inertial tendency and since energy is commonly defined as an ability to do work, or to effect mechanical motion, there is also basis for enumerating these among the active qualities. The same appears to be true of other ''force fields'' studied in modern physics.

The difficulty in classifying these measurable attributes of bodies within traditional categories is explained by the distinctive procedures used in the physical sciences. Although the scientist investigates observable qualities of the material world, his description is usually in terms of working definitions that satisfy immediate needs. This usage, and the conceptual structures he evolves in its process, is pragmatically oriented and does not profess to offer a final explanation of the reality being described. In this way, standard scientific terminology admits of a multiplicity of philosophical interpretations when evaluated in terms of classificatory schemes that are like Aristotle's categories. The continued usage of qualitative attributes by the scientist, however, gives indication of his inability to work in quantitative terms alone and of his implicit admission that physical qualities are the means through which he comes to know the world of nature.

See Also: SENSATION; SENSE KNOWLEDGE; KNOWLEDGE; KNOWLEDGE, THEORIES OF; EPISTEMOLOGY.

Bibliography: L. M. RÉGIS, *Epistemology* (New York 1959). F. C. COPLESTON, *History of Philosophy* (Westminster, Md. 1946–); v.4, *Descartes to Leibniz*; v.5, *Hobbes to Hume*. J. OWENS, *An Elementary Christian Metaphysics* (Milwaukee 1963). J. G. MORAN, *Psychologia,* 2 v. (Mexico City 1949). F. SELVAGGI, *Cosmologia* (Rome 1959). J. GREDT, *Elementa philosophiae Aristotelico-Thomisticae,* 2 v. (11th ed. Freiburg 1956). R. J. BLACKWELL, ''The Methodological Function of the Categories in Aristotle,'' *The New Scholasticism* 31 (1957) 526–37. W. A. WALLACE, ''The Measurement and Definition of Sensible Qualities,'' *ibid.* 39 (1965) 1–25. M. J. ADLER, ed., *The Great Ideas: A Syntopicon of Great Books of the Western World*, 2 v. (Chicago 1952) 2:513–26.

[R. F. O'NEILL]

QUANTA CURA

An encyclical of PIUS IX published Dec. 8, 1864, in conjunction with the SYLLABUS OF ERRORS, which announced the Jubilee of 1865 and treated of the current errors of LIBERALISM. The opening words recall the care exercised by the papacy in nourishing the faithful with true doctrine and preserving them from error. The document deplores the attempts being made to destroy the foundations of the Catholic religion and of civil society by corrupting the minds of men, especially the young, with a false doctrine of liberty and naturalism and the teaching that civil society must be governed without reference to religion, or at least making no distinction between true and false religions. Pius IX appeals to the authority of the Fathers of the Church and to human reason in combating these errors.

Bibliography: PIUS IX, ''Quanta cura'' (encyclical, Dec. 8, 1864) *Pii IX pontificis maximi acta* 3:687–700. H. DENZINGER, *Enchiridion symbolorum,* ed. A. SCHÖNMETZER (Freiburg 1963) 2890–96. J. C. FENTON, ''Humani Generis and its Predecessors,'' *American Ecclesiastical Review* 123 (Dec. 1950) 452–458.

[W. F. HOGAN]

QUANTITY

One of the supreme CATEGORIES OF BEING, and as such incapable of strict definition. According to Aristotle, quantity answers the question ''how much?'' (Gr. ποσόν; Lat. *quantum*). It may be described as that by which a thing is said to be large or small, or to have part outside of part, or to be divisible into parts. Most philosophers in the Western tradition admit that something like quantity exists, although they are not all agreed as to precisely what it is. Those who may be identified as materialists or as mechanists, such as LUCRETIUS and Thomas HOBBES, regard quantity as a primary attribute of bodies, even though they conceive matter as bereft of all qualities. Others, such as John LOCKE and Sir Isaac Newton, list the quantitative attributes of material entities as primary or universal qualities, evidently understanding quality in the broad sense of attribute. Scholastic philosophers, following St. THOMAS AQUINAS, distinguish between physical and mathematical quantities, i.e., quantities that inhere in bodies and those that are abstracted from them. René DESCARTES, in considering extension the one primary attribute of material substance, also insisted on the reality of quantity.

Those who have denied the reality of quantity have generally done so because of an idealistic theory of knowledge or because of a dynamist theory of physical reality. Absolute idealists, denying the real existence of bodies, and therefore of quantity and extension, hold that mind or spirit is the only reality, of which bodies are only a representation. Immanuel Kant, though not denying the existence of quantity, held that it was completely unknowable in itself and made it a pure category of the mind. G. W. von LEIBNIZ also subscribed to a subjectivist view of quantity, insofar as he taught that reality is composed of simple and unextended entities, or monads, which accounted for the appearance of extension (*see* DYNAMISM; MONAD).

Many of these difficulties arise from the fact that quantity can be studied under various formalities. For example, it is considered differently by the logician, who sees it as a measure of substance and is concerned with the properties that distinguish it from the other categories; by the metaphysician, who sees it as a mode of being and considers its ontological properties; and by the mathematician, who considers quantity and the relations that follow from it as the proper subject of his science. To clarify these different formalities, this article presents an analysis of quantity as studied in logic, in metaphysics, and in mathematics, with particular reference to the Aristotelian origins and elaboration of the doctrine.

In Logic. The logician, following Aristotle, considers quantity as the first category after substance (*Cat.* 4b 20–6a 36). For him, quantity is the measure of substance in its material aspect. The logician divides quantity into the continuous and the discrete, although he is not concerned with the actual existence of either, considering only what these terms imply in their signification. Gross examples of both continuous and discrete quantity are available to the senses. A bookshelf appears to be continuous, even though the books resting on it are discrete; whether the bookshelf, upon further analysis, actually turns out to be discrete is not a logical question but one pertaining to physical science.

Parts. As a somewhat parallel division, Aristotle lists quantities whose parts have a position relative to other parts and quantities whose parts have no such relative position. The position to which he refers is the order of the parts in the whole, considering these parts in themselves, which is to be distinguished from position as a separate category, considering the parts of a whole with respect to place (*see* LOCATION [UBI]). The former position requires permanence, situation, and continuity. Permanence of parts is necessary for there to be order, since a relation of order among parts requires that they coexist. Situation further clarifies this relation: each part must be somewhere—i.e., above or below, before or after, etc.—with respect to the others. This does not mean that as parts they are in PLACE in any proper sense, since only bodies have place. The last requirement, continuity, explains how position properly distinguishes continuous quantity from discrete. By continuity is meant that all parts are joined by some common term. Thus the parts of a line are united by a point; those of the surface, by a line; and those of the body, by a surface.

Instances. As a logician Aristotle gives number and speech as instances of discrete quantity, and lines, surfaces, and bodies, together with TIME and place, as instances of continuous quantity. By speech the logician refers to sounds made by the voice and grouped into syllables that may be long or short; in pronunciation such sounds are separated, thus discrete. Among the examples of continuous quantity, the logician regards time and place as extrinsic measures of material substance, as opposed to line, surface, and body, which are intrinsic measures.

In addition to the above quantities, which the logician considers as proper, or *per se,* there are also things that are quantified by reason of something else, or *per accidens.* White, for example, is greater or smaller because of the surface in which it is found. An action is longer or shorter by reason of its duration or time. These and others like them are not considered to be quantified as such, but merely in reference to something else.

Properties. Finally, as is proper to his science, the logician gives three properties by which the quantified can be distinguished from what is not quantified. The first is that quantity has no contrary, such as is found in QUALITY. Second, quantity does not permit of more or less; e.g., one line is not more so than another, nor is one pentad more five than another. Third, quantities can be said to be equal and unequal.

In Metaphysics. The investigation by the metaphysician is quite different from the foregoing (*Meta.* 1020 a7–34). He treats quantity not as the measure of substance but as it depends upon being. Thus he studies the various modes of being that are found in the quantified. This method of dealing with the quantified leaves out certain kinds of quantity that are mentioned in the *Categories.* Thus place, as an extrinsic measure, does not indicate a different mode of being from that of surface. Also time, which is quantified by motion, is not considered in metaphysics as a per se quantity, nor is speech, which is quantified by both motion and time.

Definition. The metaphysician provides a proper definition also of the quantified, namely, that which is divisible into constituent parts each of which is naturally apt to be a unit and a particular being. Thus plurality is a quantity if it is numberable, and magnitude if it is measurable. Plurality differs from magnitude in that it is divisible into noncontinuous parts, whereas magnitude is divisible into continuous parts.

Number. Since number by definition is a plurality, the question arises how it can be one and thus a true species of quantity. The answer to this question, involving the notion of homogeneity, also presupposes that number arises from the division of the continuum. That number, as a plurality measured by the unit, arises from such division can be seen from the example of the line divided into two or more parts. The number of parts is given by the application of one of them to the multitude that results from the division. This implies that the unit or measure be homogeneous with the measured, and so a line must be measured by a line, and a surface by a surface.

In this understanding, the unity of number is possible despite its discontinuity, multiplicity, or aggregation. Yet its unity is different from that of substance, being a unity of order. The unity of number is an ordering of all the parts of the whole under one part or unit. Only a material or quantitative multitude is capable of such orderings; thus the numbering of nonmaterial things is an analogical use of the term ''numbering'' (*see* MULTITUDE). The last unit of the plurality is what gives the order, or number, to the other units; it determines that the particular multitude be three, seven, or some other number. In this way a heterogeneous whole with homogeneous parts can be expressed as a numbered plurality.

Not every order, however, gives a per se unity to that which is ordered. The unity of an army or of a city is one of order; yet the being that results is an accidental being. This is so because the ordering of these is one of relation only, and relation is not sufficient to constitute an essential unity. The unity of quantitative order, on the other hand, derives from the homogeneity of its parts and thus constitutes an essential unity.

Magnitude. Some question whether line and surface are true species of quantity because of what they call the imperfections contained in these notions. They maintain that just as point is an indivisible and is quantitative only reductively as a principle of the line, so line and surface are indivisibles and thus imperfect quantities. They argue further that these exist only in the body and have extension and measure only because of the body. Thus line and surface cannot be true species of quantity.

The answer to this objection is to be found in the description of quantity given above: that which is divisible into constituent parts each of which is naturally apt to be a unit and a particular being. Since this description is verified of both line and surface, they are proper species of quantity. If it be said that these have this divisibility by reason of body, and are thus quantified *per accidens,* it should be pointed out that the reverse is also true. Body is divisible by reason of surface and line.

Properties. Objections such as these serve to make the properties of quantity, as set forth by the metaphysician, more precise. The metaphysician sees order as the most important aspect of quantity. It is by reason of order that quantity effects a distinction of the parts of material substance. Without quantity such substance would have parts only in a confused way. The ordering of parts in a material subject, in fact, makes quantity a primary factor in the INDIVIDUATION of material substance.

The order of homogeneous parts is the basis of other properties of quantity: divisibility, extension, measurability, and impenetrability. If such parts are to be distinct, they must be separated, and this requires EXTENSION. If such extension results in an actual plurality, the quantity is discrete and the unity that of number. If the distinction produces only potential parts, the quantity is continuous and the extension that of line, surface, or body. The latter extension, in turn, is the basis of divisibility and IMPENETRABILITY.

Although these properties are real and are founded in the nature of material things, they can nevertheless be separated from their subject. For example, in the Sacrament of the Eucharist, the effects of quantity as well as of other accidents are found separated from the substances of bread and wine, which are changed into the

Body and Blood of Christ while retaining their former appearances or accidents (*see* TRANSUBSTANTIATION). Certain other miracles performed by Christ, as when He appeared through closed doors, would indicate that impenetrability also can be separated from material substance (*see* GLORIFIED BODY).

In Mathematics. The treatment of quantity by the mathematician is different from that of the logician or of the metaphysician. The science of mathematics considers its subject not only as abstracted from singulars, as does every science, but also as abstracted from sensible matter (*see* ABSTRACTION; SCIENCES, CLASSIFICATION OF). Such a consideration is possible because quantity is the first accident of substance and, by reason of its role in determining the parts of a material thing, serves as the foundation of all other accidents. Since it is thus prior to quality, quantity can be considered without the qualities that render substance sensible.

Procedure. In his proper treatment of quantity the mathematician begins by defining different species of quantity, e.g., unit, number, line, surface, and circle. With these definitions he demonstrates properties that differ from those of the logician and the metaphysician. In fact, his method of abstracting renders many properties of quantity more evident than those discerned through the more material consideration of the metaphysician. This was one of the reasons why the mathematical arts were called *disciplinales* by the scholastics; they are the easiest for the student to grasp, since they require little experience and their proofs depend on constructions that are controlled by the imagination. Yet the mathematician is not concerned with quantity exclusively. As the development of modern mathematics has shown, he can be concerned also with relations and qualities that are only remotely connected with quantity. His science, however, considers these entities in abstraction from the data of sense perception and precisely as they can be visualized in the imagination or through some form of symbolic construction.

Infinity. This explains why the mathematician, for example, can speak of lines being divisible to infinity. In the division of the mathematical line it is obvious that every division results in line segments that are further divisible. This is so because the only relevant consideration is that set by requirements of quantity itself. From the viewpoint of quantitative extension, there is no reason division should stop at any particular place. In the case of natural things, however, some point exists beyond which division cannot continue. In the division of water, for example, a point is reached when further division does not give water but some other thing; thus the division of water is terminated. The same is true for all natural substances, whose forms require a minimum of matter for their existence. This is not true of the quantities studied in mathematics, where one is not concerned with existence in the extramental sense.

See Also: CONTINUUM; EXTENSION; INDIVISIBLE; MATHEMATICS, PHILOSOPHY OF.

Bibliography: M. J. ADLER, ed., *The Great Ideas: A Syntopicon of Great Books of the Western World,* 2 v. (Chicago 1952); v. 2, 3 of *Great Books of the Western World* 2:527–545. S. CARAMELLA, *Enciclopedia filosofica,* 4 v. (Venice-Rome 1957) 3:1792–97. F. SELVAGGI, *Cosmologia* (Rome 1959). H. G. APOSTLE, *Aristotle's Philosophy of Mathematics* (Chicago 1952). V. E. SMITH, *The General Science of Nature* (Milwaukee 1958). JOHN OF ST. THOMAS, *Cursus philosophicus thomisticus,* ed. B. REISER, 3 v. (new ed. Turin 1930–37). T. DE VIO CAJETAN, *Scripta philosophica: Commentaria in praedicamenta Aristotelis,* ed. M. H. LAURENT (Rome 1939).

[R. A. KOCOUREK]

QUARACCHI

Popular name for the international College of St. Bonaventure, a Franciscan center of historical research, so called from its location at Quaracchi, a suburb of Florence, Italy. When the college moved from Quaracchi to Grottaferrata, near Rome, in 1971, it took the name with it and is now known as Frati Editori di Quaracchi, Fondazione Collegio San Bonaventura. The college was established in 1877 by Fidelis a Fanna (d. 1881) under the Franciscan Minister General Bernardino del Vago da Portogruaro for the publication of St. Bonaventure's works. After 1881 the project was completed by Ignatius Jeiler (d. 1904) in 10 volumes (1882–1902). While the work on Bonaventure was going on, the college had already begun work on other Franciscan scholastics. The results were published in the series *Bibliotheca franciscana scholastica medii aevi*, begun in 1903. At present it contains 27 volumes (Alexander of Hales, Matthew of Aquasparta, Peter Olivi etc.). A more modest series was begun the following year under the title *Bibliotheca franciscana ascetica medii aevi*, with, at present, 12 volumes. From 1940 to 1966 the college published a critical edition of the writings of Bernardine of Siena in nine volumes. A new series was begun in 1963 under the title *Spicilegium bonaventurianum*, containing to date 28 volumes. Of special importance in the series are volumes IV and V (1959–1980), with I. Brady's new edition of Peter Lombard's *Sententiae*; and volume XIII, K. Esser's *Die Opuscula des hl. Franziskus von Assisi. Neue textkritische Edition* (1976). The college also began editing historical writings in 1893 under the title *Analecta franciscana*. To date 12 volumes have appeared. A quarterly review, the *Archivum franciscanum historicum*, published its first issue in late 1907, dated to 1908, and has continued since. The college has published much else, and in particular the third edition of Luke Waddings' *Annales Minorum*, from 1933 to 1964 in 25 volumes. Recently (1999) it began a new series: *Collectio Oliviana*, devoted to writings of Peter Olivi, with three volumes to date.

Bibliography: *Archivum franciscanum historicum* 70 (1977), a special issue dedicated to Quaracchi's history. G. BUFFON, *Aspetti della vita e del governo di P. Bernardino Dal Vago da Portogruaro ofm, 1822–1895* (Porziuncola 1997), 657–730 on the founding of Quaracchi and the Bonaventure edition. F. IOZZELLI, ''Le edizioni scientifiche del Collegio S. Bonaventura di Quaracchi-Grottaferrata,'' in A. CACCIOTTI and B. FAES DE MOTTONI, eds., *Editori di Quaracchi 100 anni dopo: Bilancio e prospettive* (Rome 1997), 21–39.

[I. C. BRADY/M. F. CUSATO]

QUARESMIO, FRANCESCO

Missionary and Orientalist; b. Lodi, Italy, April 4, 1583; d. Milan, Oct. 25, 1656. Having become a Franciscan (*c.* 1598), he taught philosophy and theology for several years and held successively the offices of local superior and provincial. In 1616 he went to Palestine, where he became superior of all the Franciscan houses in the Holy Land (1618–19). During the following years he was, in turn, vice commissary apostolic of Aleppo, commissary apostolic of the East, papal commissary, and vice patriarch for the Chaldeans and Maronites of Syria and Mesopotamia. Best known of his numerous works are his *Historica . . . terrae sanctae elucidatio* (Antwerp 1634–39), an account of his travels in the Holy Land, and his *Jerosolymae afflictae . . .* (Milan 1631), in which he appealed to Philip IV of Spain to organize a campaign to reconquer the Holy Land.

Bibliography: A. TEETAERT, *Dictionnaire de théologie catholique,* ed. A. VACANT et al., 15 vol. (Paris 1903–50) 13.2:1442–44. G. FUSSENEGGER, *Lexikon für Theologie und Kirche,* ed. J. HOFER and K. RAHNER, 10 vol. (2nd ed. Freiburg 1957–65) 8:923. G. GOLUBOVICH, *The Catholic Encyclopedia,* ed. C. G. HERBERMANN et al, 16 vol. (New York 1907–14) 12:593.

[D. A. MCGUCKIN]

QUARR ABBEY

Benedictine abbey near Ryde on the Isle of Wight, off the south coast of England; the name derives from the nearby royal quarry. It was founded by Baldwin de Redvers as a daughterhouse of SAVIGNY (1132) with which it became affiliated with CÎTEAUX (1147). Its fervor and importance led to the foundation of Stanley (1151) and BUCKLAND (1278) as daughterhouses. The monk Stephen of Lexington became abbot of CLAIRVAUX (1243). Neither writings nor chartularies are available for the decline caused by coastal raids of the Hundred Years' War. Quarr was suppressed under Henry VIII (1536), and the buildings were demolished to build coastal fortifications. Monks in exile from SOLESMES rebuilt the monastery (1906–14), which became a priory (1925) and an abbey (1937) of that congregation.

Bibliography: F. BURTON, *Quarr Abbey* (Ryde 1900). P. G. STONE, *The Monks of Quarr* (Newport 1912). D. KNOWLES, *The Monastic Order in England, 943–1216* (2d ed. Cambridge, England 1962). D. KNOWLES, *The Religious Orders in England,* 3 v. (Cambridge, England 1948–60). *Quarr Abbey* (London 1960). O. L. KAPSNER, *A Benedictine Bibliography: An Author-Subject Union List,* 2 v. (2d ed. Collegeville, MN 1962); v.1, author part; v. 2, subject part. 2:251. L. H. COTTINEAU, *Répertoire topobibliographique des abbayes et prieurés,* 2 v. (Mâcon 1935–39) 2:2385.

[E. P. COLBERT]

QUARTER, WILLIAM

First bishop of Chicago, Ill.; b. Killurine, King's County, Ireland, Jan. 24, 1806; d. Chicago, April 10, 1848. He left Ireland at age 16 to enter Mt. St. Mary's College, Emmitsburg, Maryland, and was ordained for the Diocese of New York on Sept. 19, 1829. After four years as curate at St. Peter's Church, New York City, he was appointed pastor of St. Mary's, where he soon established a parochial school. When Chicago was named a diocese in 1843, Quarter was consecrated its first ordinary by Bishop John Hughes of New York on March 10, 1844. The new bishop arrived in Chicago with his brother, Rev. Walter Quarter, on May 5, 1844, and found only eight priests serving a diocese that included the entire state of Illinois. In less than a month, he opened the College of St. Mary's as a boys' school and seminary. Later the same year it was incorporated by the state legislature as the University of St. Mary of the Lake, and a university building, for which Quarter solicited funds in New York, was dedicated on July 4, 1846. At his invitation, the Sisters of Mercy opened St. Xavier's Academy for girls in September of 1846. The bishop turned over his own residence to the sisters for a convent.

Early in his administration, Quarter successfully petitioned the state legislature to enact a law constituting the Catholic bishop of Chicago and his successors a corporation sole to hold property for religious purposes. To obtain funds for expanding diocesan needs, he appealed to the Society for the Propagation of the Faith at Lyons, France, and to the LEOPOLDINEN STIFTUNG of Vienna. The two Quarter brothers also spent their personal funds to purchase property for churches and a cemetery. In addition to extensive travels throughout the diocese preaching and administering the sacraments, Quarter built 30 churches and ordained 29 priests; he kept a diary that still exists. He convened the first diocesan synod in April of 1847, and assembled what was perhaps the first theological conference in the United States in the university chapel on Nov. 12, 1847. Quarter, apparently in good health, preached on Passion Sunday, April 9, 1848, but died suddenly the following morning. His last will left all his property to the University of St. Mary of the Lake.

Bibliography: J. E. MCGIRR, *Life of the Rt. Rev. William Quarter, D.D.* (Des Plaines, Ill. 1920). G. J. GARRAGHAN, *The Catholic Church in Chicago, 1673–1871* (Chicago 1921).

[H. C. KOENIG]

QUARTODECIMANS

The term ''Quartodecimans'' refers to those Christian communities in the early Church which celebrated Easter on the 14th of Nisan (*die quarta decima*), the day of the Jewish Passover (Ex 12.6). Prevalent in Asia Minor and Syria in the second century, Quartodecimans emphasized the death of Christ, the true Paschal victim (Jn 18.28, 19.42), while Roman practice emphasized the observance of Sunday as the day of the Resurrection. Implicit in these two positions is the disputed chronology of Holy Week.

Roman efforts to induce the Quartodecimans to abandon their practice were unsuccessful. On a visit to Rome (*c.* 155), St. POLYCARP OF SMYRNA amicably discussed the question with Pope ANICETUS without, however, reaching agreement. Pope VICTOR (189–198) sought unity through a series of synods held in both East and West; all accepted the Roman practice except the Asiatic bishops. When Victor attempted coercion by excommunication, St. IRENAEUS OF LYONS intervened to restore peace (EUSEBIUS, *Ecclesiastical History* 5.23–25). During the third century Quartodecimanism waned; it persisted in some Asiatic communities down to the fifth century.

See Also: EASTER CONTROVERSY.

Bibliography: W. H. CADMAN, ''The Christian Pascha and the Day of the Crucifixion: Nisan 14 or 15,'' *Studia Patristica* 5 (1962) 8–16. C. W. DUGMORE, ''A Note on the Quartodecimans,'' *Studia Patristica* 4 (1961) 411–421. M. RICHARD, ''La lettre de saint Irénée au pape Victor,'' *Zeitschrift für die Neutestamentliche Wissenschaft und die Kunde der Älteren Kirche* 56 no 3–4 (1966) 260–282. C. C. RICHARDSON, ''New Solution to the Quartodeciman Riddle,'' *Journal of Theological Studies* ns 24 (1973) 74–84. L. SABOURIN, ''Easter in the Early Church,'' *Religious Studies Bulletin* 2 No. 1 (1982) 23–32. S.G. HALL, ''The origins of Easter,'' *Studia Patristica* 15:1 (1984) 554–567.

[J. FORD/EDS.]

Quarr Abbey, photograph by Gillian Darley. (©Edifice/CORBIS)

QUAS PRIMAS

A papal encyclical promulgated Dec. 11, 1925, by Pius XI to institute the Feast of Christ the King. In setting up the feast, Pius XI wrote that observance of Christ's royal rights, particularly those over human society, would prove the most effective answer to the challenge of secularism and communism.

Bibliography: PIUS XI, ''Quas primas,'' (Encyclical, Dec. 11, 1925) *Acta Apostolicae Sedis* 17 (1925) 593–610. *The Encyclicals of Pius XI,* tr. J. H. RYAN (St. Louis 1927).

[M. D. MEILACH/EDS.]

QUASTEN, JOHANNES

Patristic scholar, university professor; b. Homberg, across the Rhine from Duisburg, May 3, 1900; d. March 10, 1987. After a traditional classical education at the *Gymnasium* of nearby Moers, he entered the University of Münster in 1921. Following his ordination as a priest in February 1926, he pursued higher studies, especially in the area of ancient Christian literature and archaeology. Franz Joseph DÖLGER, whose school became known by the name *Antike und Christentum,* particularly inspired him. Studying the relationship between the ancient world and that of the nascent Christian Church, Quasten came to have a special love for early Christian worship. His work culminated in his doctoral thesis of 1927, *Musik und Gesang in den Kulten der heidnischen Antike und christlichen Frühzeit.* A revision of this work was published in 1930 (Eng. 1983).

Quasten was an early student of the newly founded Pontifical Institute of Christian Archaeology in Rome and participated in excavations in Sicily, Yugoslavia, and North Africa. After the preparation of his second doctoral thesis (required for university teaching in the German system) on the Good Shepherd in early Christian art, he began his teaching career as a *privatdozent* in Münster in 1931. Under the Nazi regime after January 1933, his academic activities were made increasingly difficult, and he was forbidden to teach in the fall of 1937. He returned to Rome briefly before accepting an invitation to join the theological faculty of the Catholic University of America in Washington, D.C., in the fall of 1938. His career of teaching and research continued well beyond formal retirement in 1970, and he offered graduate seminars in patristics until 1977, when he returned to Germany, taking up residence near Freiburg.

Works. Over the years, Quasten published many studies in the area of patristics, especially in the area of liturgy. While at work in Germany, he edited a series of fascicles in the series *Florilegium patristicum,* which contained Latin and Greek selections of the most significant texts bearing on the early Eucharist (*Monumenta eucharistica et liturgica vetustissima* 1935–37). After World War II, he contributed numerous articles to the second edition of the *Lexicon für Theologie und Kirche* and *The New Catholic Encyclopedia.*

His activities in the United States included the direction of numerous dissertations by his students, and his general influence helped inspire young American scholars in the field of patristics. In the mid-1940s, he collaborated with Joseph PLUMPE to publish a collection of patristic texts in English translation, *Ancient Christian Writers* (1946–). Another series he inaugurated, *Studies in Christian Antiquity* (1941–), offered to the wider public important studies by his students.

Quasten's best-known publication is his three volume *Patrology,* a standard reference work which details the lives, writings, and theological teachings of the post-Biblical authors of the early Church. Originally published in English, the volumes have been translated into French, Spanish, and Italian, each with updated bibliographies. Though unable to complete the *Patrology* himself, Quasten wrote a brief introduction to volume IV, the Italian edition, published in 1978, in which eight scholars from the *Augustinianum* in Rome completed the project. This additional volume covers the golden age of the Latin Fathers.

Among the many honors conferred on Quasten was the Cardinal Spellman award in theology (1960). Upon his retirement from the Catholic University of America in 1970, Quasten was presented with two volumes of essays and studies by colleagues and former students from around the world, titled *Kyriakon.* A complete bibliography of his writings, along with a biographical sketch, can be found at the end of the second volume.

Quasten's predilection for liturgical history made a significant contribution to the liturgical movement which preceded the Second Vatican Council. His work led him to be named a member of the council's preparatory commission for the liturgy. Next to his *Patrology,* his principal influence has been the inspiration of deeper interest in the field of patristics among American scholars.

Bibliography: P. GRANFIELD and J. A. JUNGMAN, eds., *Kyriakon: Festschrift Johannes Quasten,* 2 v. (Münster 1970). P. GRANFIELD, "Johannes Quasten, a Biographical Essay," 921–923; "A Bibliography of the Writings of Johannes Quasten," 924–938. Interview, *Theologians at Work* (New York 1967) 22–34.

[R. B. ENO]

QUEBEC ACT OF 1774

By the Peace of Paris of Feb. 10, 1763, which ended the French and Indian War, France ceded Canada and Cape Breton Island to England. Moreover, the Mississippi River was recognized as the boundary between Louisiana and British territory. Thus the area bounded by the Ohio and Mississippi Rivers and the Great Lakes, over which the war originated, was added to Britain's continental domain.

Background. Since the Proclamation of 1763 closed this area to expansion from the seaboard colonies, few Englishmen were found there. Various Native American tribes inhabited the district, and there were several French settlements in southern Illinois, at Vincennes, Detroit, and lesser ones elsewhere. With the withdrawal of French officials, civil government ceased abruptly, and only a limited jurisdiction was exercised by British commanders at the various military posts. Before long, serious problems developed.

Relying on their charters, several colonies, notably Virginia, claimed portions of this territory. But they did not exercise effective control over trade with the natives, check the trespassing of squatters, restrain the aggression of land companies, or prevent the inroads of land-hungry colonists, who, in general, defrauded the Native Americans in trade and land purchases. Actually, there was no civil government, no legal acts, no order. This situation could not be tolerated. Civil government and the control and legalizing of trade and land transfers were imperative. Aware of the growing hostility of the Native Americans over the conduct of white transgressors and intent on introducing law and order, the British government resolved to place the area under imperial government in default of colonial neglect or ineptitude. A decade of study and discussion brought forth the Quebec Act.

Provisions and reaction. Alexander Wedderburn, the solicitor general, drafted the bill, which became law on June 22, 1774. It stipulated that the Province of Quebec was to include the area circumscribed by the Allegheny, Ohio, and Mississippi Rivers and the Great Lakes. As a concession to the French settlers and to win their loyalty to the British king, French civil law and customs were to continue, but the British criminal code replaced that of France. Government was vested in a governor and a council nominated by the Crown with complete legislative power. Finally, the act allowed the inhabitants liberty to profess the ''religion of the Church of Rome . . . subject to the King's Supremacy,'' but for the oath of royal supremacy in religion, a simple oath of allegiance was substituted. Furthermore, the clergy ''may hold, receive and enjoy their accustomed dues and rights with respect to such persons only as shall profess the said religion.''

Apart from the disregard of colonial claims to portions of this country on the basis of their charters, the fact that the Quebec Act was contemporaneous with the Coercive Acts precipitated additional widespread opposition in the old seaboard colonies. The sacredness of colonial charters and their unilateral abrogation by Great Britain was stressed; the sacred right of the new British subjects to the enjoyment of British civil law with trial by jury as well as British criminal law was given emphasis; the absence of representative government was condemned.

But the granting and safeguarding of religious freedom and the right to practice the Catholic religion without interference in this territory evoked the loudest and most bitter denunciation. On this aspect of the act, rather than on disregard of colonial charters or virtual exclusion of British traders and prospective colonists, opposition was concentrated. The act was held to equate ''establishment'' of the Catholic religion and to be a violation of the royal coronation oath.

While opposition to this section of the act was general, New England, and in particular Boston and Newport, led the forefront of the crusade against popery. Writers and speakers professed to see in the act a threat to the Protestant religion and a subtle device eventually to impose popery on themselves. Some zealots joined in the campaign out of conviction, while others had less worthy motives; they simply seized the opportunity to participate in the traditional propaganda against popery and the Catholic religion. This flood of sustained criticism from clergy and men prominent in civil life became at least a contributory cause, and, for some individuals, a primary cause, for the break with England.

Effects. Unquestionably, the Quebec Act was influential in reconciling the French in Canada to their new rulers and new regime and in fostering the loyalty of priests and seigneurs during the American Revolution. When the two groups came to know of the volume of abuse of their religion in the press of the older British colonies and the pulpits of Protestant churches, and of the double-dealing of the Continental Congress in its several addresses, association or cooperation with the American patriots was precluded. It has been maintained that even today the French in Canada regard the Quebec Act as their Magna Carta of liberty. And a distinguished historian has recently lauded this remarkable act of parliament as ''one of the greatest pieces of statesmanship in the history of the empire'' [A. L. Burt, *The British Commonwealth* (Boston 1956) 39.]

Bibliography: R. COUPLAND, *The Quebec Act: A Study in Statesmanship* (Oxford 1925). C. H. METZGER, *The Quebec Act* (U.S. Catholic Historical Society 16; New York 1936). A. L. BURT, *The Old Province of Quebec* (Minneapolis, Minn. 1933). J. SOSIN, *Whitehall and the Wilderness* (Lincoln, Neb. 1961) ch. 10.

[C. H. METZGER]

QUEDLINBURG, CONVENT OF

Former Benedictine (936) and Lutheran convent (1539–40) in Saxony, Diocese of Halberstadt (patrons, SS. Servatius and Dionysius). It was founded as an imperial Benedictine convent for daughters of noble families by Matilda, widow of Emperor Henry I. Its first nuns came from Wendhausen. It was richly endowed with lands, privileges, and immunities; the abbess bore the title of imperial princess. It nurtured the Ottonian revival; probably WIDUKIND OF CORVEY and later Bp. Thietmar of Merseburg studied there. By the 14th century, the convent was weakened financially and the town of Quedlinburg, asserting its independence of the abbess, was supposed by the bishop of Halberstadt, who was infringing on the convent's ecclesiastical immunity. But under Hedwig, 1477, its lordship over the town and its independence of the bishop were regained. It became a Lutheran

Hyacinthe Louis de Quelen.

convent under Anna II, and remained so until secularization, 1803. Subordinate convents were St. Mary (Münzenberg), St. Andrew at Walbeck, and Brehna; monasteries were St. Wigbert and Michaelstein.

Bibliography: *Monumenta Germaniae Scriptores* (Berlin 1826–) 3:18–90. K. JANICKE, *Urkundenbuch der Stadt Quedlinburg,* v.2:1–2 of *Geschichtsquellen der Provinz Sachsen,* 48 v. (Halle 1870–1923). H. LORENZ and S. KLEEMANN, *Quedlinburgische Geschichte* 2 v. (Quedlinburg 1922). A. BRINKMANN, *Beschreibende Darstellung der älteren Bau- und Kunstdenkmüer des Kreises Stadt Quedlinburg,* 2 pts. (Berlin 1922–23). H. LECLERCQ, *Dictionnaire d'archéologie chrétienneet de liturgie,* ed. F. CABROL, H. LECLERCQ and H. I. MARROU, 15 v. (Paris 1907–53) 14.2:2017–19 R. JOPPEN, *Lexikon für Theologie und Kirche,* ed. J. HOFER and K. RAHNER, 10 v. (2d, new ed. Freiburg 1957–65) 8:931.

[D. ANDREINI]

QUELEN, HYACINTHE LOUIS DE

Archbishop of Paris; b. Paris, Oct. 8, 1778; d. Paris, Dec. 31, 1839. The scion of a noble family from Brittany, he entered the Seminary of Saint-Sulpice in 1801. After ordination at Saint-Brieuc (1807), he returned to Paris and was assigned to the Grande Aumônerie, whose titular was Cardinal Joseph Fesch. Appointed vicar-general of the Grande Aumônerie (December 1814), he carried on negotiations for a new concordat with the Holy See. In 1817 he was named auxiliary bishop of Paris, and in 1819, coadjutor with the right of succession. When Cardinal Talleyrand-Périgord died (Oct. 20, 1821), Quelen became archbishop of Paris. He reorganized the seminaries, initiated the practice of ecclesiastical retreats, and ordered the preaching of missions in parishes. He was elected a member of the French Academy (1824). The Revolution of July 1830 was hostile to him because of his relations with the fallen Bourbon dynasty. He was forced into hiding for several months, during which time his episcopal residence was partially demolished. The riot of Saint-Germain-l'Auxerrois (February 1831) was partly directed against him. It culminated with an almost complete rupture between him and the government of Louis Philippe. From temporary residence in various convents, Quelen continued to administer his diocese. In 1832 he demonstrated his courage by visiting persons suffering from cholera. He later founded an orphanage. In 1834 he organized religious conferences at Notre Dame Cathedral, and in 1835 he placed LACORDAIRE in charge of them. He encouraged devotion to the miraculous medal and to Our Lady of Victories. He published several works on the administration of the Sacraments and several funeral orations.

Bibliography: P. I. B. D'EXAUVILLEZ, *Vie de Mgr. de Quélen, archevêque de Paris,* 2 v. (Paris 1840). M. R. A. HENRION, *Vie et travaux apostoliques de Mgr. Hyacinthe Louis de Quélen* (Paris 1840). R. LIMOUZIN-LAMOTHE, *Monseigneur de Quelen . . .* 2 v. (Paris 1955–57). *L'Épiscopat français depuis le concordat jusqu'à la séparation 1802–1905* (Paris 1907) 453–456.

[R. LIMOUZIN-LAMOTHE]

QUEM TERRA, PONTUS, SIDERA

Office hymn that was historically prescribed for Matins on feasts of the Blessed Virgin Mary that have no proper hymn. The authorship of FORTUNATUS (*c.* 530–600) is disputed, but scholars agree that the hymn, written in iambic dimeter and showing an artistic use of rhyme, is the work of a skillful poet. The eight original stanzas of this hymn offer variations on the paradox of the Creator and Ruler of the universe housed in the womb of a simple virgin, and on the notion of Mary acting as the new Eve and as the gateway to heaven.

Bibliography: *Analecta hymnica* 50:86–87, text. J. CONNELLY, ed. and tr., *Hymns of the Roman Liturgy* (Westminster, Md. 1957), translation and commentary. S. GASELEE, comp., *The Oxford Book of Medieval Latin Verse* (Oxford 1928; reprint with corrections 1937). F. J. E. RABY, *A History of Christian-Latin Poetry from the Beginnings to the Close of the Middle Ages* (Oxford 1953).

[M. A. MALONE]

QUENSTEDT, JOHANN ANDREAS

Lutheran theologian and dogmatician; b. Quedlinburg, Aug. 13, 1617; d. Wittenberg, May 22, 1688. He was educated at the University of Helmstädt (1637–43), where he came under the influence of Georg Calixtus, whose heterodox ideas he later refuted. From 1644 to the time of his death, Quenstedt held various academic positions at the University of Wittenberg. He published the results of his years of teaching in *Theologia didactico-polemica sive systema theologicum* (Wittenberg 1685; Leipzig 1715). This represents a type of reaction to the reconstruction of dogma that had been begun by Veit Ludwig von Seckendorf (1626–92) and that was symptomatic of the intellectual revolution taking place throughout Europe. On every subject discussed there is first the presentation of theses, followed by their exposition and proof, and then the discussion of various difficulties and questions that are suggested. Because of this style the work became so thoroughly a systematized treatise on Lutheran theology that Quenstedt has been frequently called "the bookkeeper of Lutheran orthodoxy." His definitions and theses are, however, constructed almost entirely on an earlier work, entitled *Theologia positiva acroamatica,* by J. F. Koenig (1619–64).

Bibliography: J. C. ERDMANN, *Lebensbeschreibungen und litterarische Nachrichten von den wittenbergschen Theologen* (Wittenberg 1804). F. A. G. THOLUCK, *Der Geist der lutherischen Theologen Wittenbergs* (Hamburg 1852). F. LAU, *Die Religion in Geschichte und Gegenwart,* 7 v. (3rd ed. Tübingen 1957–65) 5:735.

[C. J. BERSCHNEIDER]

QUENTIN, HENRI

Biblical scholar; b. St. Thierry in the Diocese of Reims, France, Oct. 7, 1872; d. Rome, Feb. 4, 1935. He studied in the diocesan seminary in Reims and entered the Benedictine Abbey of MAREDSOUS, Belgium, in 1894, taking his vows there in 1895. In 1897 he went to the Abbey of SOLESMES, France, where he was ordained in 1902. His studies on conciliar history and hagiography brought him, in 1907, an appointment to the Commission for Revision of the Vulgate and he was sent to Rome.

There, Quentin collected a series of photographic copies of all important Vulgate manuscripts, including what is probably the oldest text, *viz,* that in the *Codex Amiatinus.* His *Mémoire sur l'établissement du text de la Vulgate* (Collectanea biblica 6; Rome 1922) was basic for the structural organization of the edition. The method of textual criticism used by Quentin, especially his theories on the relative interdependence of the manuscripts and their subsequent value for the history of the transmission of the text, remained a very controversial issue. In the Vulgate Commission presided over by F. GASQUET, Quentin was editor-in-chief of the Pentateuch (1926–36). In 1923 Quentin became a member of the Pontifical Roman Academy of Archaeology (*see* PONTIFICAL ACADEMIES), and in 1930 Pope PIUS XI appointed him to the historical section of the Congregation of Rites. Quentin had a substantial part in the creation of the new Sacred Heart liturgy, established by the encyclical *Miserentissimus Redemptor* in 1928 (*See* SACRED HEART, DEVOTION TO). In 1933 he was made first abbot of the Abbey of S. Girolamo in Rome.

Bibliography: Works. H. QUENTIN, *Jean-Dominique Mansi et les grandes collections conciliaires* (Paris 1900); *Les Martyrologes historiques du moyen âge* (Paris 1908); *Essais de critique textuelle* (Paris 1926). B. MOMBRITIUS, *Sanctuarium, seu vitae sanctorum,* 2 v. (new ed. Paris 1910). **Literature.** C. MOHLBERG, "Dom Enrico Quentin," *Rendiconti della Pontificia Accademia Romana de Archeologia* 11 (1935): 13–39, bibliog. 34–39. A. MANSER, *Lexikon für Theologie und Kirche,* 10 v. (Freiburg 1957–65) 8:934.

[H. RUMPLER]

QUESNEL, PASQUIER (PASCHASE)

French oratorian, theologian, and spiritual writer, noted for his part in the history of JANSENISM; b. Paris, July 14, 1634; d. Amsterdam, Dec. 2, 1719. A pupil of the Jesuits at Clermont College and later a student at the Sorbonne (Bachelor in Theology in 1657), Quesnel entered the Oratory in 1657, was ordained in 1659, and was first assigned to Oratorian novitiate, rue Saint-Honoré, as master of ceremonies and librarian. Strongly imbued with BÉRULLE's spirituality, he was from that time on devoted to Augustinianism, but he had little regard for Jansen's thought, which he considered too archaic and systematic. He also had no difficulty in signing on four occasions, between 1661 and 1665, the formulary condemning the book *AUGUSTINUS.*

From 1666 to 1669 he was second director of the Seminary Saint-Magloire. In this environment strongly influenced by Jansenism, he became closely allied with Antoine ARNAULD, who was hiding there. He then began his career as a writer and a polemicist. Having returned to the house on the rue Saint-Honoré, he resumed his teaching and proved to be more and more Augustinian and Gallican, at the same time endeavoring to remain faithful to Thomism in essential points. In 1675 he won the attention of the learned world by a scholarly edition of the works of St. Leo the Great, but the Gallican bias of the notes and essays that accompanied the text caused it to be placed on the Index. In 1678 the archbishop of Paris, F. de Harlay, demanded his withdrawal. He was sent to Orléans, but in 1684 he refused to subscribe to the anti-Jansenist decrees issued by the assembly of the Oratory. He preferred exile and in February 1685 rejoined Antoine Arnauld in his retreat in Brussels. He was his faithful companion until the latter's death in 1694.

Faithful to his moderate Augustinianism and his Thomism, Quesnel tried at first not to arouse the doctrinal controversies then dormant. The three volumes of his *Tradition de l'église romaine sur la prédestination des saints et sur la grâce efficace*, published from 1687 to 1690, presented grace in an entirely Bérullian perspective as a prolongation of the Incarnation. He also continued to devote himself to the composition of spiritual works; the most famous of these productions continues to be the *Prières chrétiennes* (1687), reprinted several times. It is imbued with a totally Bérullian spirituality.

Quesnel used these years of relative peace to transform Jansenism into a veritable organized party. Energetic, positive, methodical, and tenacious, he always possessed the qualities of a leader, which Arnauld lacked. Within a few years, he established a vast secret network of communication and information that operated in almost all the large cities of Europe. The awakening of the disputes provoked around 1700 by the intransigent Jansenists attracted attention to his *Nouveau Testament avec des réflexions morales* (1695), in which he expressed not only his Augustinianism bordering on Jansenism, but also his Richerism, i.e., his attachment to the extreme Gallicanism formerly professed, around 1615, by Edmond RICHER. On May 30, 1703, he was arrested in Brussels by order of the king of Spain, Louis XIV's grandson, and put in the jail of the archbishopric of Malines, whence he escaped on the following September 13. He settled in Amsterdam and reconstructed his network, which had been dispersed when his papers had been seized. He took an increasingly active part in the conflicts aroused by the *Cas de conscience* affair and by the bull *Vineam Domini* (1705). In 1710 Quesnel began with Fénelon, an adversary of Jansenism, a bitter dispute that indirectly provoked the condemnation by the bull *UNIGENITUS* (Sept. 8, 1713) of 101 propositions taken from the *Réflexions morales*.

In the years that followed, in a multitude of works of every kind, Quesnel did not cease to protest the complete orthodoxy of his thought. After having hoped for an opportunity to return to France at the beginning of the Regency, he preferred to give up the idea, but his authority over the Jansenist party continued to be very great. At the beginning of 1718 he formally adhered to the appeal of the four bishops to the general council. He died in the same sentiments, after a short illness, leaving behind him a very considerable work, for which the bibliography remains to be compiled.

Bibliography: J. CARREYRE, *Dictionnaire de théologie catholique*, ed. A. VACANT et al. (Paris 1903–50) 13.2:1460–1535. J. A. G. TANS, *Lexikon für Theologie und Kirche*, ed. J. HOFER and K. RAHNER (Freiburg 1957–65) 8:935–936; *Pasquier Quesnel et les Pays-Bas* (Paris-Groningen 1960), *Dictionnaire de spiritualité ascétique et mystique,* Doctrine et histoire, ed. M. VILLER et al (Paris 1932–) XII–2, col. 2732–2746. L. CEYSSENS and J. A. G. TANS, *''Pasquier Quesnel,'' Autour de l'Unigenitus* (Leuven 1987). J. A. G. TANS and H. SCHMITZ DU MOULIN, *La correspondance de P. Quesnel. Invantaire* (Leuven 1989); *Index analytique*, 2 v. (Leuven 1993), bibliography.

[L. J. COGNET/J. M. GRES-GAYER]

QUESNELLIANA COLLECTIO

Shortly after 1670, Pasquier Quesnel, the Oratorian priest and Jansenist, was preparing a complete edition of the works of Pope Leo the Great. In the course of his work he came upon an old, unedited canonical collection that he believed to be the oldest existing code that had been used by the Roman Church. Quesnel published this collection in his compilation of Leo's works, and it thereafter became known as the *Collectio Quesnelliana.* A printed edition of this work may be found in Migne, *Patrologia Latina* 56, 358–747.

There have been several studies of this collection since the time of Quesnel. It is presently believed to have been compiled between 494 and, at the latest, 523. There is still considerable discussion as to its exact place of origin. There are some who believe that it originated in Gaul and very likely at Arles. This contention is principally based on the fact that all 15 of the existing manuscripts of this collection originated in France, and Arles is known to have been an important center for Canon Law at that time. However, the more general belief is that this collection originated in Italy, most likely at Rome. The principal reason for this contention is that it is a collection with a universal outlook in contrast to the local collections that emanated from places such as Arles. Moreover there are positive indications that the papal archives were directly consulted in its compilation. There are no positive indications as to the identification of the author of this collection. There is a theory of W. M. Peitz that attributes this collection to Dennis the Little, but this theory has not found general acceptance.

The *Collectio Quesnelliana* consists of excerpts from various oriental councils—Chalcedon, Nicaea, Ancyra, Neocaesarea (apparently at the same time trying to avoid including anything that might be a source of friction between the Oriental and Roman churches); excerpts from African councils; certain writings in regard to the Acacian schism, Pelagianism, Eutychianism; decretals of Popes Innocent I, Zosimus, Siricius, Leo I; and finally a large number of letters of Leo I. There is no strict logical or chronological order in the arrangement of these materials. The author apparently wished to replace former collections, which contained only one type of these materials, e.g., the Greek councils, with a collection containing a compilation of the various materials available. This was the time of the Gelasian Renaissance, when there was a serious attempt to codify and centralize ecclesiastical discipline.

The *Collectio Quesnelliana* is important for the history of the sources of Canon Law. In itself it represents an important step in canonical compilation, and it provides valuable information concerning the life of the Church at the time. Furthermore, it was the principal collection used in Gaul until the mid 8th century. Finally, some of its contents passed into later collections that played an important role in the history of medieval Canon Law, such as the *HADRIANA COLLECTIO*, the *HISPANA COLLECTIO*, and the *Capitularies* of BENEDICT THE LEVITE.

Bibliography: L. LEFEBVRE, *Dictionnaire de droit canonique*, ed. R. NAZ, 7 v. (Paris 1935–65) 7:434–440. A. VAN HOVE, *Commentarium Lovaniense in Codicem iuris canonici I* v. 1–5 (Mechlin 1928–) 1:151. H. WURM, *Studien und Texte zur Dekretalensammlung des Dionysius Exiguus* (Bonn 1939). C. SILVA-TAROUCA, ''Nuovi studi sulle antiche lettere dei Papi,'' *Gregorianum* 12 (1931) 3–56, 349–425, 547–598, A. M. STICKLER, *Historia iuris canonici latini* v. 1 *Historia fontium* (Turin 1950) 41.

[J. M. BUCKLEY]

QUÉTIF, JACQUES

Dominican scholar and literary historian; b. Paris, Aug. 6, 1618; d. there, March 2, 1698. He was professed in the Dominican order in 1635 and ordained in 1642. After spending a few years in the ministry, he returned in 1652 to the priory of the Annunciation, rue Saint-Honoré, Paris, and there spent the rest of his life as librarian.

Quétif's major achievement was the launching of the monumental history of Dominican writers. He traveled widely in France, Italy, Germany, and the Netherlands and corresponded with leading contemporary scholars in his search for materials. At his death he had completed 800 articles and had gathered material on about 2,000 other lives. The work was continued and amplified by Jacques ÉCHARD, who published it between 1719 and 1721 under the title *Scriptores ordinis praedicatorum.*

Quétif also edited the *Vie de Savonarole par Pico de la Mirandole, révélations, épîtres et autres écrits de Savonarole; the Formalis explicatio summae theologiae divi Thomae* of Jerome de Medicis; and the canons of the Council of TRENT. He composed a biography of Bartholomew of the Martyrs and one of JOHN OF ST. THOMAS for an edition of his works.

Bibliography: J. QUÉTIF and J. ÉCHARD, *Scriptores Ordinis Praedicatorum* (New York 1959) 2.2:746–747. R. CREYTENS, ''L'Oeuvre bibliographique d'Échard: Ses sources et leur valour,'' *Archivum Fratrum Praedicatorum* 14 (1944) 43–71. M. GASNIER, *Les Dominicains de St. Honoré* (Paris 1950).

[J. F. HINNEBUSCH]

QUEVEDO, JUAN DE

Franciscan bishop in Panama; b. place and date unknown; d. Spain, Dec. 24, 1519. In response to the concern of King Ferdinand of Spain, Leo X in a bull dated Sept. 24, 1513, named Quevedo bishop of Darien, Panama, the first bishopric on Tierra Firme. This diocese was the fourth in the New World, preceded in 1511 by those of Santo Domingo and Concepción de la Vega on Hispaniola, and San Juan in Puerto Rico. Quevedo arrived in Darien with Gov. Pedrarias Davila in July 1514. He was accompanied by various other religious destined for the missions.

The episcopal see was established in Santa María la Antigua. His apostolic work was made difficult by the dissension between the two most famous caudillos of the conquest in Darien: Pedrarias and the Adelantado Vasco Núñez de Balboa, discoverer of the Pacific Ocean. The bishop was a consistent critic of the conduct of Pedrarias because of his cruelty to the natives. After Balboa was beheaded in 1519 on orders of Pedrarias, Quevedo returned to Spain where he engaged in a controversy with Bartolomé de LAS CASAS before the Emperor on the methods of the conquest in America.

[E. J. CASTILLERO]

QUICUMQUE CHRISTUM QUAERITIS

Office hymn that was historically prescribed for VESPERS and MATINS on the feast of the TRANSFIGURATION. The text of this hymn is taken from the 12th poem of the *Cathemerinon,* ''Hymnus Epiphaniae,'' by PRUDENTIUS (348–*c.*405). It is written in iambic dimeter and urges those who seek Christ to raise their eyes on high and to hear and believe Him who is God, the King of the Nations and of the Jews.

Bibliography: *Corpus scriptorum ecclesiasticorum latinorum* 61, *Liber Cathemerinon* text. J. CONNELLY, ed. and tr., *Hymns of the the Roman Liturgy* (Westminster, Md. 1957), tr. and commentary. H. LECLERCQ, *Dictionnaire d'archéologie chrétienne et de liturgie*, ed. F. CABROL, H. LECLERCQ, and H. I. MARROU (Paris

1907–53) 6.2:2901–28. F. J. E. RABY, *A History of Christian-Latin Poetry from the Beginnings to the Close of the Middle Ages* (Oxford 1953) 44–49. J. JULIAN, ed., *A Dictionary of Hymnology* (New York 1957), s.v. *Quicumque.*

[M. A. MALONE]

QUIDDITY

English transliteration of the Latin *quidditas,* meaning ''whatness''; in scholastic usage it designates a thing's ESSENCE taken precisely in its capacity to inform the intellect of the answer to the question ''what is it?''

Related Terms. At most a virtual minor DISTINCTION obtains between essence and quiddity: essence is the thing as capacity for existence, whereas quiddity is the thing as capacity to instruct the intellect. The quiddity of a thing, if definable, is analytically expressed in its real DEFINITION by its genus and specific difference. As such it is similar to, but more exact than, NATURE in BOETHIUS's first sense: ''anything that can be grasped (by the intellect) in any way whatever'' (*De persona et duabus naturis* 1; *Patrologia Latina,* 64:1341BC). Nature, in the more etymological and Aristotelian sense, is closer to essence than to quiddity inasmuch as nature signifies a thing's principle of operation—effective only through existence.

Such are the comparisons between these terms suggested by St. THOMAS AQUINAS (*De ente* 1, 3). To these he adds FORM and Aristotle's phrase ''the what was to be'' (τὸ τί ἦν εἶναι, *quod quid erat esse*). He defines the form that is convertible with essence and quiddity as ''the complete essential determination'' of a thing. This is the ''form of the whole'' (*forma totius,* εἶδος) according to the Avicennian interpretation of book seven of the *Metaphysics*—an interpretation rejected by Averroës but accepted by St. Thomas (*In 7 meta.* 9. 1467–69). Form in this sense includes the matter as universalizable as well as the ''form of the part'' (*forma partis,* μορφή), the substantial form as distinct from matter (*see* MATTER AND FORM). Form thus expresses the completeness of an essence's specification in itself with respect both to existence and to intellect, and in the latter respect is synonymous with quiddity. Some modern scholars concur independently in the Averroist interpretation that Aristotle excludes matter altogether from the notion of form or species and its equivalent, ''the what was to be.'' But St. Thomas insists that Aristotle holds its inclusion necessary in the case of natural substances, since it must be included universally in their definition (*In 7 meta.* 9.1468; *In I anim.* 1.24–29).

Aristotelian Meaning. The term *quidditas,* coined in the 12th century in translations of Avicenna into Latin and possibly also in paraphrasing the *Topics,* stems ultimately from Aristotle's own phrase ''the what was to be.'' From its grammar and from the probable places of its earliest appearance (*Topica* 101b 22, 132a 1), it originated in a context of DIALECTICS and PREDICATION and was designed as a verbal sort of variable representing the *full* answer to any Socratic question as to what a thing is, for example, man, virtue, the Sophist, etc. The particular reference of the phrase can be specified in any context by adding a dative, for example, ''the what was it *for a man* to be,'' or ''the being characteristic of man.'' This full answer, Aristotle says, is expressed in the definition of the thing in question.

As such the phrase must be distinguished from another Aristotelian one, ''the what is it'' (τὸ τί ἐστι, *quod quid est*), of wider range, since it not only may refer to the complete formula or definition but may also be satisfied by any one of its parts taken separately—genus, matter, difference, or form. Grammatically, the past tense, ''was'' (ἦν, *erat*), has a habitual or transtemporal sense, indicating the specifying, or formal, identity of the essence with respect to any individual of that essence at any time (*Meta.* 1031a 15–32a 11, esp. 32a 5; Aquinas, *In 7 meta.* 5) or, in the case of the separate substances, beyond time. Accordingly, in virtue of the ''what'' element the phrase has formally a noetic reference, whereas in virtue of the verbal elements ''was'' and ''to be'' it has a basic ontological connotation. Because of it's ontological reference, the phrase ''the what was to be'' is superior to the term quiddity. Among the Christian Aristotelians, who departed from Aristotle on the eternity of the world, this transtemporal character of essences is taken to refer to their self-identity as essences—including their openness to identity with their individuals, when the latter exist—or also to refer to their eternal presence as ideas to the divine mind.

Because it can refer also, by the habitual tense (ἦν, ''was''), to separate substances, including God, of which St. Thomas says one knows what they are not rather than what they are (*De anim.* 16), the Greek phrase and the Latin term coined from it do not necessarily suggest that the truly adequate answer to the implied question of ''what'' must be rational, analytical and complex, after the fashion of a definition. It may be purely intellectual and intuitive. ''It is not of the notion of quiddity that it be composite, for then a simple nature would never be found—which is false at least in the case of God—nor is it of its notion that it be simple, since certain composites are found, such as human nature'' (*In 2 sent.* 3.1.1). Quiddity can thus apply to God and the separate substances, which are undefinable by reason of their simplicity and not in virtue of any defect of unity.

Substituting the term quiddity for the more cumbersome "the what was to be," one finds that in *Meta.* 1029b 14, speaking terminologically, Aristotle defines "the quiddity of each thing" as "that which it is said to be in virtue of itself" (καθ' αὑτό). Excluding things that are only one by accident, such as "white man" or "musical man" and hence indefinable by defect of unity, he says analogically that "quiddity will belong . . . primarily and in the simple sense to substance, and in a secondary way to the other categories also—not quiddity in the simple sense, but the quiddity of a quality or of a quantity" (1030a 29–32). Finally he seems even to allow a definition, in an improper sense, of "white man" as an accidental whole, "but not in the sense in which there is a definition either of white or of substance" (b 13); however, he does not allow the notion of quiddity this improper range.

Modern Relevance. The insistence of G. W. F. HEGEL on the impossibility of philosophically discussing anything in a purely ontological way apart from its relation to mind should be reappraised in view of the convertibility of quiddity and essence and of truth and being (*see* TRANSCENDENTALS). At the same time, a realistic philosophy must maintain the absolute primacy of being and essence and also their inseparable transcendental relevance, as truth and quiddity, to intelligence on all levels, and first of all to the divine mind. In this connection, the so-called "presuppositionless method" of PHENOMENOLOGY, as proposed by E. HUSSERL, that would suspend judgment on the question of existence and real being, itself makes a supposition inasmuch as it presumes that essence can speak to mind without revealing itself as, first and radically, capacity for existence. Expressed in the above outlined language, this method appears to be an attempt to treat essence as quiddity rather than as essence. The work of the medieval disciples of St. Thomas and of John DUNS SCOTUS on these questions should be brought into dialectical confrontation with the analogous work of modern epistemologists and phenomenologists. Particularly worthy of mention are the *Quaestiones disputatae de esse intelligibili* of WILLIAM OF ALNWICK (see *History of Christian Philosophy,* 468, 768–769).

Bibliography: H. BONITZ, *Index Aristotelicus* (Berlin 1870; photo reproduction 1955) 764a 20–765a 6. M. KAPPES, *Aristoteles-Lexikon* (Paderborn 1894) 24–25. J. OWENS, *The Doctrine of Being in the Aristotelian Metaphysics* (2d ed. Toronto 1963) 180–188. E. BUCHANAN, *Aristotle's Theory of Being* (Cambridge, Mass. 1962) ch. 4, 5. ARISTOTLE, *Metaphysics,* rev. Gr. text with introd. essay and commentary, W. D. ROSS, 2 v. (Oxford 1953) 1:xciv–cxi. R. J. DEFERRARI, *A Latin-English Dictionary of St. Thomas Aquinas* (Boston 1960) 883–884. R. J. DEFERRARI and M. I. BARRY, *A Complete Index of the Summa Theologica of St. Thomas Aquinas* (Washington 1956) 292. L. SCHÜTZ, *Thomas-Lexikon* (Paderborn 1895; photo offprint Stuttgart 1958) 675. E. GILSON, *History of Christian Philosophy. Patrologia Latina,* ed. J. P. MIGNE, 217 v., indexes 4 v. (Paris 1878–90).

[J. J. GLANVILLE]

QUIERCY (QUIERZY), COUNCILS OF

Several notable assemblies held at the Frankish royal residence of Quiercy (Kiersy, Carisiacum, or Quiercy-sur-Oise), near Noyon, France. (1) When Pope STEPHEN II went to PEPIN III IN 754, the king met at Quiercy (or at nearby Braine) with his magnates and concluded an alliance with the pope against the LOMBARDS. Moreover, according to the LIBER PONTIFICALIS, it was on this occasion that the promise or so-called donation of Pepin (*see* STATES OF THE CHURCH) was made: lands in central Italy then held by the Lombards were to be restored to the papacy when conquered by the Franks. In 774 CHARLEMAGNE confirmed this grant, which is a landmark in the growth of the temporal power of the papacy. Although some have doubted that such a grant was ever made, most modern controversy has focused on the interpretation of its terms (*see* DONATION OF CONSTANTINE). (2) In 838 a council of Frankish bishops was held at Quiercy in conjunction with an imperial diet. Supporters of AGOBARD, exiled archbishop of Lyons, led by FLORUS, sought to discredit the administrator of the diocese, AMALARIUS OF METZ, by obtaining the council's condemnation of certain errors in his writings. (3) After German bishops had condemned GOTTSCHALK OF ORBAIS's doctrine of predestination at Mainz 848, he was sent to HINCMAR OF REIMS to be disciplined. At Quiercy 849, in the presence of Charles II the Bald, the prelates of Reims province, assisted by the archbishops of Sens, Tours, and Lyons, sentenced him to a life of silence and prison after deposing him from the priesthood and having him whipped. (4) Against the teaching of Gottschalk, Hincmar himself advanced four propositions—that God's predestination is only single, that man's free will is restored through grace, that God wishes all men to be saved, and that Christ suffered for all men—all of which a council of his province approved at Quiercy in 853. His propositions were in their turn attacked at VALENCE IN 855 and at LANGRES and Savonnières in 859. Councils were also held at Quiercy in 857 and 858.

Bibliography: C. J. VON HEFELE, *Histoire des conciles d'après les documents originaux* (Paris 1907–38) 3.2:923–924 (754); 4.1:101–103 (838), 150–155; 4.2:1308–10 (849); 4.1:197–199; 4.2:1324 (853); 4.1:212; 4.2:1333–34 (857); 4.1:214; 4.2:1335 (858). A. WERMINGHOFF, ed., *Monumenta Germaniae Historica: Concilia* 2.2:768–782, 835–853 (838). B. GEBHARDT, *Handbuch der deutschen Geschichte* (Stuttgart 1954–60) 1:128–131, with bibliog.

[R. KAY]

QUIET, PRAYER OF

The prayer of quiet, a form of contemplation, is an intimate awareness of the presence of God that captivates the will and often fills the body and soul with ineffable sweetness and delight. Being a gift of God, it cannot be acquired through personal effort; at the most, one can dispose oneself for it by fidelity to the practice of mental prayer and by cultivation of purity of life. Writing of it in her autobiography (ch. 14) St. Teresa of Avila says: "This state is a recollecting of the faculties within the soul . . .; the will alone is occupied in such a way that, without knowing how, it becomes captive; the other two faculties [i.e, intellect and memory] help the will so that it may become more and more capable of enjoying so great a blessing, though sometimes it comes about that, even when the will is in union, they hinder it exceedingly." In the prayer of quiet, therefore, the principal activity of the individual is affective; thus it differs from the prayer of recollection, which usually precedes it and centers its activity in the intellect.

The recollection of the will, characteristic of the prayer of quiet, does not necessarily hinder the activity of the other rational powers of man, so that his response to the demands of the active life is not impeded.

The main effects of this form of contemplation are growth in virtue, particularly in detachment; profound joy and peace; and a sense of the nearness of God, although the last is not always clearly perceived. A possible effect can be the gift of tears.

Very similar to the prayer of quiet is the phenomenon caused by exhaustion of the rational faculties through inordinate concentration upon spiritual matters, especially in prayer. It can be diagnosed by the swiftness with which it passes and the aridity it leaves in the soul.

See Also: CONTEMPLATION.

Bibliography: TERESA OF AVILA, *Complete Works,* ed. SILVERIO DE SANTA TERESA, and E. A. PEERS, 3 v. (New York 1946) v.2, *Interior Castle,* "4th Mansions." R. GARRIGOU-LAGRANGE, *The Three Ages of Interior Life,* tr. T. DOYLE, 2 v. (St. Louis 1947–48). A. F. POULAIN, *The Graces of Interior Prayer,* tr. L. L. YORKE SMITH (St. Louis 1950).

[S. V. RAMGE]

QUIETISM

The name given to a spiritual doctrine that, as proposed by Miguel de MOLINOS, was condemned as heretical, suspect, etc., by the decree of the Holy Office of August 28 and the constitution *Caelestis Pastor* of Innocent XI of Nov. 20, 1687 (H. Denzinger, *Enchiridion symbolorum*, ed. A. Schönmetzer [Freiburg 1963] 2201–69). Quietism is best described as an exaggeration of orthodox spirituality. It is, at base, a recurrence of the ultrasupernaturalism that has plagued and stimulated the Church from its earliest years. It is thus akin to and different from every other form of ILLUMINISM and enthusiasm that has existed in the Church in the past.

History. The Messalians of Asia Minor in the fifth and sixth centuries claimed to practice continual prayer and encouraged a spirit of complete indifference. In the 13th century, the monks of Mt. Athos were called "hesychasts," or quietists, but they seem to have been imbued with a more Oriental kind of self-oblivion. In the West, the Brethren of the Free Spirit were said to claim an entire passivity along with an antinomian outlook on morality. The Beghards were condemned in 1312 for holding that meditation on the Sacred Humanity was a descent from contemplation. The Devotio Moderna of medieval Germany, which would rather be able to feel compunction than define it, did much to separate theology from mysticism. As a result, the area of man's highest aspirations was left open to sentimentalists who felt called to contemplation by experiences not transcending their own emotional upheavals, and quietists who neglected everything to drift in their spiritual daydreams became self-proclaimed experts in matters spiritual.

The antecedents, then, of 17th-century quietism in Italy are manifold, but it would be impossible to trace a causal nexus positively influencing Molinos and his adherents. It is true that the aberrations of the ALUMBRADOS of southern Spain were condemned only in 1623; and although many of their confessed tenets are similar to those of Molinos, the movement was vigorously repudiated by him. It was rather the contemporary scene that provided the fertile ground for quietism. The 17th century in European spirituality was devoted to schools and to controversy. The Jansenist crisis was just abating when a new struggle developed between the adherents of the Ignatian method of meditation and those who saw in it the denial of the contemplation espoused by the great Spanish and French mystics of the preceding century. The protagonists exaggerated the approved spiritual doctrines, literalized the symbols and figures of the canonized authors, and in general made man's approach to God in prayer a matter of partisanship.

Foremost in the ranks of those defending the primacy of contemplation were Francis Malaval, the gentle recluse of Marseilles, Pier Matteo Petrucci, later to become a curial cardinal, and the enigmatic figure of Miguel de Molinos; all were to see their writings placed on the Index. Since none of these authors ever claimed to set forth a new conception of the spiritual life, it is only by reference to the orthodox doctrine of approved writers that one can recognize their version as a caricature of Catholic mysticism.

Quietist Teachings. Whereas solid doctrine holds that there is a state of contemplative passivity in which God acts in man by His operating grace and which one reaches normally only after exercising himself in the ascetical life for a long time, the quietists held, paradoxically, that the way of passive contemplation is acquired at will be the very cessation of every operation. Using the language of SS. Teresa and John of the Cross, the quietist opened the door to illuminism, since he looked upon his own intellectual activity as a refusal to adore God in spirit and in truth, for it is God who alone must work in the soul. So avid were they in removing the mental images on which meditation feeds that, for them, even the consideration of the sacred humanity itself was a distraction to be rejected. In the words of Malaval: ''Thy Humanity itself, my Saviour, . . . not being regarded as it should have been, deceived the Jews, tempted the apostles and every day keeps people of real devotion away from perfection.'' This contemplative gaze, then, became the sole measure of true mysticism and was for the quietist a single act unbroken even by sleep.

Granting their error concerning the fundamentals of contemplation, it is therefore not surprising to discover the bizarre nature of their practical moral conclusions. This way of obscure faith offers no consolations, for these are a betrayal; cares nought for the yearnings for perfect happiness, for they would be an expression of self-will and not God's; and despises any reflection on self, for that is a base infidelity to grace. As a result, the movement leaves no opportunities for the acts of virtues; prayers of petition, examinations of conscience, even confession itself become impossible for the soul perfected in the way of darkness and aridity, for these elements necessarily involve conscious activity on the soul's part.

And so the ultimate moral aberration is reached. Molinos implicitly advocated, and in his recantation admitted teaching publicly, that an exterior action objectively sinful could be consistent with the state of contemplation. The history of his arrest, conviction, and punishment can find its explanation only in the conclusion that he practiced, to some degree, what he preached. With this, 17th-century quietism in Italy came to an end. Its doctrine of love, disinterested even to the point of despair, provided the spark for the famous semiquietist debate that rocked the Church in France in the last decade of the 17th century.

See Also: GUYON, JEANNE MARIE DE LA MOTTE; FÉNELON, FRANÇOIS DE SALIGNAC DE LA MOTHE; CONTEMPLATION; HESYCHASM.

Bibliography: P. POURRAT, *Dictionnaire de théologie catholique*, ed. A. VACANT et al., (Paris 1903–50) 13.2:1537–81. P. DUDON, *Le Quiétiste espagnol: Michel Molinos* (Paris 1921). R. A. KNOX, *Enthusiasm* (New York 1950) 231–318. R. GARRIGOU-LAGRANGE, *The Three Ages of Interior Life*, tr. T. DOYLE, 2 v. (St. Louis 1947–48) 2:289–292.

[T. K. CONNOLLY]

QUIMPERLÉ, ABBEY OF

Former Benedictine monastery in the Diocese of Quimper and the department of Finistere, France (Abbey of the Holy Cross; *Kemperlegiense*). A monastery may have been founded on this site as early as 550 by St. Gunthiern with the aid of Grallon, the legendary king of Brittany. In any case, in 1029, Alain, Count of Cornuailles, installed, at the junction of the Ellé and the Isole, a group of Benedictines whose first abbot was St. Gurloès (d. 1057). St. Vigonien was superior of the monastery from 1059 to 1066. His successor, Benedict (d. 1115), son of Count Alain, enriched the abbey with numerous endowments and in 1083 had the church consecrated. The 13th century saw the monks embroiled in protracted conflict with the bishops of Quimper. Then came a period of decadence, until in the 16th century, the monastery had as abbot the infamous Odet de Coligny, Cardinal of Châtillon (d. 1571), who was divested of his benefices on becoming a Calvinist. At the end of the century only three monks remained at the abbey, assisted by three secular priests. In 1665 the MAURISTS took possession of the abbey and held it until the revolution. The abbey church of the Holy Cross, dating from the 11th century, had a curious rood screen from the Renaissance period framing the main door; it collapsed in 1862, but has been restored according to the original plan. Circular in form, the church imitates the Basilica of the Holy Sepulchre in Jerusalem and is one of the rare specimens of this style in Brittany. The rotunda is flanked on four sides by semidomes: that on the east is the apse, that on the west is the nave, while the other two form the transept. The 11th-century romanesque crypt under the circular choir contains many tombs, notably that of St. Gurloès. In addition to the church, the cloisters and the 18th-century monastery still survive; the cloisters now serve as the town hall.

Bibliography: L. H. COTTINEAU, *Répertoire topobibliographique des abbayes et prieurés,* 2 v. (Mâcon 1935–39) 2:2390–91. J. MABILLON, *Annales Ordinis S. Benedicti,* 6 v. (Lucca 1739–45) v.1, 4–6. *Gallia Christiana,* v.1–13 (Paris 1715–85), v.14–16 (Paris 1856–65) 14:900–905. *Histoire Littéraire de la France*, ed. Académie des Inscriptions et Belles-Lettres (Paris 1814–1941) 21:745. A. DE BLOIS, *Notice historique sur la ville de Quimperlé . . . suivie d'une histoire particulière de l'abbaye de Sainte-Croix . . .* (Quimperlé 1881). P. LE DUC, *Histoire de l'abbaye de Sainte-Croix de Quimperlé* (Quimperlé 1881). L.

MAÎRE and P. DE BERTHOU, *Cartulaire de l'abbaye de Sainte-Croix de Quimperlé* (Paris 1896; 2d ed. Rennes 1904).

[J. DAOUST]

QUINCTIAN OF CLERMONT, ST.

Bishop; d. 525 or 526. Quinctian (Quintian) was probably a native of Africa who, during the Arian persecutions there, fled to Gaul. In 506 he appeared as the bishop of Rodez at the synod of Agde; he also participated in the synod of Orléans (511). The Arian Visigoths in Auvergne suspected him of collaboration with their enemy, CLOVIS, and Quinctian was forced to flee from Rodez (*c.* 512). He sought refuge with Bishop Euphrasius at Clermont, where he became bishop in 515. His biographer, GREGORY OF TOURS, extols his goodness and inexhaustible energy, his concern for the needy, and his fearlessness.

Feast: Nov. 13.

Bibliography: GREGORY OF TOURS, *Historia Francorum* 2:36; 3:2, 12, 13; 4:5, 35; *Monumenta Germaniae Historica: Scriptores rerum Merovingicarum* 1.1:84, 98, 108–109, 138, 167. *Vitae patrum* 4; 6:3, *Monumenta Germaniae Historica: Scriptores rerum Merovingicarum* 1.2. *Monumenta Germaniae Historica: Concilia* 1:9. J. MANSI, *Sacrorum Conciliorum nova et amplissima collectio* (Graz 1960) 8:337. L. DUCHESNE, *Fastes épiscopaux de l'ancienne Gaule* (Paris 1907–15) 2:35–36, 40. J. L. BAUDOT and L. CHAUSSIN, *Vies des saints et des bienheureux selon l'ordre du calendrier avec l'historique des fêtes* (Paris 1935–36) 11:399–401.

[G. M. COOK]

QUINISEXT SYNOD

A synod convoked in 691 by Justinian II to furnish disciplinary measures for the 5th and 6th (hence Quinisext) Ecumenical Councils of CONSTANTINOPLE II (553) and III (680–681), which had dealt only with doctrine. It was known also as the Synod in Trullo from the hall in the imperial palace in Constantinople where it was held. It was attended by 165 Oriental bishops with no duly appointed Western legates. Of its 102 canons, several were directed against Armenian, Latin, and specifically Roman legislation (3, 12, 13, 16, 29, 30, 55): clerical celibacy was repudiated (3 and 13); canon 28 of Chalcedon, rejected by Pope LEO I as inimical to the patriarchates by giving Constantinople second place after Rome, was reasserted (36); excommunication was prescribed for fasting on Saturdays in Lent (55); and the use of blood and suffocated animals was forbidden (67; Acts 15:29). The majority of canons, however, had a beneficial purpose, reaffirming the true faith and the authority of apostolic ordinances, patristic traditions, and previous canonical legislation and condemning abuses mainly among clerics (3–39), monks, nuns (40–49), and laity (50–102), particularly in regard to superstitions and matrimonial impediments (53–54).

To the signatures of the Oriental prelates, Justinian requested that that of the pope be added. When SERGIUS I (687–701) refused, the emperor sent Count (the protospatharius) Zachary to Rome, but he was maltreated by the papal attendants. Pope JOHN VII (705–707) refused to explain Roman objections. Pope CONSTANTINE I (708–715) journeyed to Constantinople to reach a compromise, and ADRIAN I (772–795) quoted the synod and canon 82 in a letter to Patriarch TARASIUS OF CONSTANTINOPLE. ANASTASIUS the librarian attests that JOHN VIII (872–882) approved the canons "except those which were opposed to the good faith, correct morals, and customs of the Roman Church." Many of the canons are cited by medieval canonists and by Pope SIXTUS V (1585–90).

Bibliography: K. BIHLMEYER, *Lexikon für Theologie und Kirche*, ed. M. BUCHBERGER (Freiburg 1930–38) 10:312–313. J. D. MANSI, *Sacrorum Conciliorum nova et amplissima collectio* (Graz 1960) 11:921–1006. C. J. VON HEFELE, *Histoire des conciles d'après les documents originaux* (Paris 1907–38) 3:560–581. P. JOANNOU, *Discipline générale antique (IIe -IXe s.)* (Rome 1962) 1.1:98:241, a rev. and crit. ed. of fasc. 9, Fonti CICO.

[F. X. MURPHY]

QUIÑONES, FRANCISCO DE

Also called Francisco de los Angeles; Spanish cardinal and reformer, originator of the expedition of the "Twelve Apostles" to Mexico; b. 1480; d. Veroli, Oct. 27, 1540. Quiñones became a Franciscan before 1507, taking the name of Francisco de los Angeles. He was minister general of the order (1523–28), was named cardinal (Dec. 7, 1527), and was bishop of Coria (1531–33). Quiñones was a representative of the Catholic reformation prior to the Council of Trent. As a superior, he stimulated studies, the training of Franciscan youth, and the use of retreat houses as centers of intense spiritual life. His missionary vocation bore fruit in 1523 when he sent the mission of the Twelve Apostles to New Spain. In the obedience and instructions, which have been called the Magna Carta of Mexican civilization, he stressed the qualities of the missionary and referred to the standards of missionary methods.

In 1526 he conceived the project of going to Mexico, with faculties as nuncio and viceroy, to promote evangelization. He did not attain his objective, however, because Clement VII sent him on secret missions to the Emperor between 1526 and 1528. By his representations, he won the freedom of the Pope and prepared the Treaty of Barcelona of 1529. As a cardinal, he defended the interests of Spain and the reform of the Church. In Rome he surrounded himself with humanists and scholars.

Asked by Clement VII to prepare a new BREVIARY, he distributed the Psalms over the days of the week, reduced the Matins to one nocturn consisting of three Psalms and three lessons, and eliminated all elements of a choral character, such as antiphons, responsories, versicles, and hymns. Between 1535 and 1558, 100 editions of that Breviary were issued, amounting to about 100,000 copies. It influenced the BOOK OF COMMON PRAYER and was the precursor of 20th-century reforms. The Breviary was vigorously attacked by theologians and suppressed by the Council of Trent.

In 1536 Cardinal Quiñones commissioned Sansovino to make his sepulchral monument in his titular church, the church of the Holy Cross in Jerusalem. He also built a palace in Veroli.

Bibliography: F. QUIÑONES DE LEÓN Y DE FRANCISCO MARTIN [Marquis d'Alcedo], *Le Cardinal Quiñones et la Sainte-Ligue* (Bayonne 1910). J. M. LENHART, ''Quiñones' Breviary, a Best Seller,'' *Franciscan Studies* NS 6 (1946) 468. J. MESEGUER FERNÁNDEZ, ''Contenido misionológico de la Obediencia e Instrucción de Fray Francisco do los Angeles a los Doce Apóstoles de México,'' *Americas* 11 (1954–55) 473–500.

[J. MESEGUER FERNÁNDEZ]

QUINQUE COMPILATIONES ANTIQUAE

Between the *Decretum Gratiani* (*c.* 1140–41) and the Gregorian *Decretales* of 1234, canonical skill was devoted to two main tasks: the systematization of the latest Canon Law, expressed most commonly in decretal letters (*see* DECRETALS, COLLECTIONS OF) and literary commentary on the *Decretum* (*see* DECRETISTS). The five most important decretal collections from that period are the *Quinque Compilationes Antiquae*, named in sequence of composition as *prima, tertia, secunda, quarta*, and *quinta*.

It is established that *Compilatio prima* itself marked the culmination of a tradition of codification dating from the mid-1170s, and many manuscripts survive revealing the process by which the technical skill of this work was achieved. It is equally clear that other important collections were made contemporaneously with the five: by Gilbert, Alan, and RAINERIUS OF POMPOSA, BERNARD OF COMPOSTELLA THE ELDER, and so forth. Here it is significant that HOSTIENSIS in his *Aurea Summa* listed eight collections of the period, including these five, when discussing Gregory IX's plan to abrogate the antique compilations, and to reduce what was useful and necessary into a single volume. Nevertheless, the *Quinque Compilationes* acquired a preeminent reputation, were used as a basis of canonical study at Bologna and provided a standard of reference for commentators on decretals before the promulgation of the Gregorian collection. All five were the subject of important glosses, while the *tertia* and *quinta* were promulgated in papal bulls. *Compilatio prima* (1187–91), or *Breviarium extravagantium*, of Bernard of Pavia, was composed mainly of post-Gratian decretals and included the canons of the Lateran Council of 1179; it was arranged in five books entitled *iudex, iudicium, clerus, connubium*, and *crimen*, dealing respectively with ecclesiastical jurisdiction, canonical civil procedure, the state and rights of the clergy, marriage and related questions, and criminal procedure and penalties. This scheme was later adopted by the other four and taken over in the *Decretales. Compilatio tertia*, composed by Peter of Benevento for Innocent III, comprised decretals from the first 12 years of Innocent's pontificate; it was promulgated in the bull *Devotioni vestrae*, Dec. 28, 1210, and sent to Bologna, and its use enjoined *''tam in iudiciis quam in scholis.''* It is thus the first official collection in canonical history. *Compilatio secunda* was composed by JOHN OF WALES (1210–15); though third in sequence, it is named *secunda*, or *decretales mediae seu intermediae*, since it includes decretals issued between those of *Compilationes prima* and *tertia*, as well as earlier items omitted in the *prima*. It drew on the works of Gilbert and Alan. The authorship of *Compilatio quarta* is uncertain, but may perhaps be attributed to JOANNES TEUTONICUS or to Alan; it contains decretals of the later years of Innocent III and the canons of the Lateran Council of 1215. Though not certainly promulgated, it was promptly used in courts and schools. *Compilatio quinta* was made at the request of Honorius III from decretals of his own pontificate (from 1216), and promulgated in the bull *Novae causarum*, May 2, 1226; its authorship is uncertain also, but may possibly be attributed to TANCRED.

The principal permanent significance of these collections lies in their formative influence on the *Decretales* of Gregory IX, whose author, RAYMOND OF PEÑAFORT, accepted Bernard of Pavia's plan and incorporated 1,771 of the 1,971 chapters of the five collections.

Bibliography: *Quinque compilationes antiquae nec non Collectio canonum lipsiensis*, ed. E. FRIEDBERG (Graz 1956). J. F. VON SCHULTE, *Die Geschichte der Quellen und der Literatur des kanonischen Rechts* (Graz 1956) 1:76–90. S. KUTTNER, *Repertorium der Kanonistik* (Rome 1937) 322–385. A. VAN HOVE, *Commentarium Lovaniense in Codicem iuris canonici 1* (1945) 1:355–361. A. VILLIEN, *Dictionnaire de théologie catholique* et al. (Paris 1903–50) 4.1:206–212. R. NAZ, *Dictionnaire de droit canonique* (Paris 1935–65) 3:1239–41.

[C. DUGGAN]

Vasco de Quiroga.

QUIROGA, VASCO DE

Bishop, social reformer; b. Madrigal de las Altas Torres, Castilia la Vieja, Spain, in the 1470s; d. Pátzcuaro, Mexico, March 14, 1565. Little is known of his early years except that he remained a layman and obtained a licentiate in Canon Law. He entered the royal service and in 1525–26 served as a judge in the North African city of Oran. After his return to the court, his friends Juan Bernal Díaz de Luco and Cardinal Juan de Tavera recommended him to the king for a position of importance.

In 1530 he was named *oidor* of New Spain, a member of the five-man governing body, or *audiencia,* which was being sent there to maintain royal authority. After arriving in Mexico City in January 1530, he began to exert all his efforts to bring a rule of justice and charity to the native people. He tried to understand their laws and to apply Spanish law accordingly. He was particularly active in judging cases of Indian slavery, with favor toward the slaves. In 1532, out of commiseration for the plight of the native people, he established near Mexico City a hospital-town, called Santa Fe, to care for the sick and needy and to instruct the natives in the Catholic faith. It was patterned after the plan of society presented in Thomas More's *Utopia.* In 1533–34 he was sent to the province of Michoacán to visit the area and correct abuses. There he established another hospital of Santa Fe on the model of his previous foundation. The two institutions retained a prime place in his interest throughout his life and he watched over them with fatherly protectiveness.

In 1536 Michoacán was made a diocese, and Quiroga was chosen its first bishop. Probably in December 1538 he was ordained through the whole series of orders and consecrated bishop. One of his first acts as bishop was to move his see from Tzintzuntzan, former capital of the Tarascan kingdom of Michoacán, to Pátzcuaro, which seemed a more suitable location. There he established the Colegio de San Nicolás, intended primarily to train priests who would have a command of the native languages. It was the first such establishment in New Spain. He also began work on his cathedral, planned as a structure with five naves, T-shaped with the fourth and fifth naves radiating from the right angles of the T. This work, on which much money and labor was expended against the opposition of many of the Spaniards, was never completed.

In 1542 Quiroga sailed for Europe to attend the Council of Trent, but was forced to return to Mexico after a near shipwreck. In 1547 he again left Mexico and succeeded in reaching Spain. During his stay he was able to give advice on many problems facing the Spanish crown and the Church in the New World. He also obtained favorable decisions in a number of lawsuits that he had appealed to the Council of the Indies.

Having returned to New Spain in 1554, he took part in the First Provincial Council of Mexican bishops in 1555, which treated matters of great interest to him: the construction of hospitals in every town and the limitation of the privileges of the friars. His last years saw a continuation, perhaps to an increased degree, of the manifold litigations that had absorbed much of his energy throughout his career: boundary disputes with his fellow bishops, suits involving his hospitals of Santa Fe, suits with Indians and Spaniards over the construction of his cathedral and the population of his see city, and suits with the friars, especially the Augustinians, arising from his efforts to limit their privileges and freedom of action in his diocese. His will gave its principal attention to his two hospital-towns and his college, both of which continued their valuable contribution to the diocese of Michoacán for many years.

The ancient monastery at Qumran. The "Dead Sea Scrolls" were discovered here in a nearby cave in 1947. (©Richard T. Nowitz/ CORBIS)

Bibliography: *Don Vasco de Quiroga: Documentos,* ed. R. AGUAYO SPENCER (Mexico City 1939). F. B. WARREN, *Vasco de Quiroga and His Pueblo-Hopitals of Santa Fe* (Washington 1963).

[F. B. WARREN]

QUMRAN COMMUNITY

Ascetic sect of Jews who lived in the Judean Desert near the Wadi Qumran, along the northwest shore of the Dead Sea roughly between 150 B.C. and A.D. 68.

Sources. The Qumran community is known principally from the excavation of Khirbet Qumran, 'Ain Feshkha, and 11 nearby caves, as well as from the sectarian Qumran Scrolls, especially the various *pesharim*, 4QTestimonia, the Community Rule (1QS and its copies 4QS, 5QS), 1QSa,. 1QSb, 1QH, 1QM, 4QMMT, and possibly 11QTemple. Data found in the *Damascus Document* (CD and its copies 4QD, 5QD) must be used with caution; although copies of it were produced at Qumran and found in the caves, it apparently governed the communal life of "camps" in the land of "Damascus" (a code word for related Jews dwelling elsewhere). Inhabitants of such camps apparently followed a mode of life that differed somewhat from that of the Judean Desert.

Origins. The beginnings of the community are obscure, and two explanations are used: (1) The first explanation relates the community to the *Ḥăsîdîm* (Pious Ones: 1 Mc 2.42; *see* HASIDAEANS) of the Maccabean revolt (167–165 B.C.). When the Maccabees developed political tendencies and the high priesthood was assumed by Jonathan (152 B.C.), this community broke off from the Jerusalem priesthood and withdrew to the Judean desert (*See* MACCABEES, HISTORY OF THE; HIGH PRIEST). It referred to itself as *bĕnê Sādôq*, "the sons of Zadok," revealing its connection with the old line of ousted but legitimate Zadokite priestly families. According to its strict interpretation of Levitical rules, it considered the Jerusalem priests to be unclean, for they had been hellenized, had abandoned the old solar calendar for a new one in celebrating the feasts, and were notorious for their worldly pursuit of wealth.

(2) The second explanation relates the community to the ''returnees of Israel'' (CD 4.2; 6.5), that is, descendants of Jews deported to Babylon in the sixth-century Babylonian Captivity who had remained there until they heard of the success of the Maccabean revolt and then returned to Judah, only to find the form of Jewish life there far from strict enough, and so they broke with the Jerusalem priesthood (as above). In either explanation the conduct of those priests was an abomination to the strict priestly elements of the Qumran community, who refused to share in Temple sacrifice offered by such men. After 20 years of an amorphous existence (''groping,'' CD 1.12), the community was shaped by an energetic priest who came to be regarded as its founder and given the title of the ''Righteous Teacher''; his identity is unknown. He and his community were persecuted by a ''Wicked Priest'' (1QpHab 8.8–12.10), who may have been the high priest Jonathan (or a succession of high priests). Later, when Alexander Jannaeus (103–76 B.C.) persecuted the Pharisees, some of them seem to have joined the Qumran community. (*See* HASMONAEANS.)

Identification. Attempts have been made to identify the Qumran community with the PHARISEES (C. Rabin), SADDUCEES (L. H. Schiffman), EBIONITES (O. Cullmann), Jewish Christians (B. Thiering, R. H. Eisenman), or even the medieval Karaites, but none of these attempts are convincing. The best theory, proposed originally by E. L. Sukenik, A. Dupont-Sommer, and the majority of scholars, identifies it with the ESSENES. The main reason for identification is the notice in Pliny the Elder (*Natural History* 5.15.73) that locates the Essenes on the western shore of the Dead Sea south of Jericho and above 'En-Gedi and Masada. The only spot with Roman-period remains in this area that could be meant is Khirbet Qumran, the site of the community center. Even though some details of the community's mode of life known from the Scrolls do not always agree with the data of ancient writers who tell about the Essenes (Philo, Josephus, Pliny the Elder, Hippolytus), the bulk of them does coincide and suggests that the Qumran community was Essene.

Beliefs and Mode of Life. The Jews of Qumran were called simply *yahad*, ''community'' (1QS 1.1,12,16), or *harabbîm*, ''the Many'' (1QS 6.1,8,11), or even ''the Way'' (1QS 9.17–18, 21). Members who joined the community were said to ''enter the covenant'' (1QS 1.18, 20). Chosen by divine predilection, they were the remnant of Israel (CD 1.4), the new Temple (1QS 8.5), the new plantation (1QS 11.8), the new people of God (1QM 1.5; 3.13), with whom He made a ''new covenant'' (CD 6.9; 20.12; cf. Jer 31.31). Their retreat to the desert was motivated by Is 40.3, ''to prepare the way of the Lord'' (1QS 8.14–15). There they lived an ascetic life, nourished by common work, prayer, study and interpretation of the Torah and the Prophets, strict observance of levitical purity regulations, and a conviction that it was already the ''end of days'' (1QpHab 2.5; 9.6). For the day of God's visitation was imminent; soon He would descend with His angels to do battle on the side of the ''sons of light'' (i.e., the community) and wipe out all sons of darkness and sinful opposition to them (1QM 1.5–12). Living in the end time, they believed that many savings of the Old Testament Prophets were being verified in the events of their sect. Their Righteous Teacher had received special revelations from God making known to him ''all the secrets of the words of His servants the Prophets'' (1QpHab 7.5). These formed the community's esoteric interpretation of the Old Testament. They awaited the advent of a Prophet (like Moses, Dt 18.18), and of two Anointed Ones (a priestly MESSIAH of Aaron and a royal Messiah of Israel: 1QS 9.11). A striking DUALISM colored their otherwise orthodox monotheism. God ''created human beings to rule the world, and appointed for them two spirits by which they were to walk until the time of His visitation: the spirits of truth and of perversity'' (1QS 3.17–19). This ethical dualism is expressed sometimes in terms of light and darkness, the Prince of Light and the Angel of Darkness, or a conflict between God and Belial.

Community life was marked by communal ownership of property. Though one entered the community voluntarily and became a full member only after two-thirds years of probation (1QS 6.13–18), one was expected to turn all property and earnings over to the community's overseer. Communal ownership was partly motivated by a contempt for worldly riches; these were to be left to the men of perdition, whereas the members formed the ''community of the poor'' (4Qp Ps 37 2.10).

The *Community Rule (1QS)* envisages a communal life without women; this agrees with the ancient notices about celibate Essenes in Pliny (*Nat. Hist.* 5.15.73) and Josephus (*Bell. Jud.* 2.8.2 No. 120). The *Rule of the Congregation* (1QSa 1.4–8), however, mentions women and children and gives instruction about the proper age for sexual intercourse. The *Damascus Document (CD)* also speaks of ''taking wives according to the Law and begetting children'' (7.6; 19.3). Since a few female skeletons were found in an annex to the main Qumran cemetery, the community apparently at some stage had both celibate and married members (see Josephus, *Bell. Jud.* 2.8.13 No. 160–161).

Besides priests and Levites, there were also laymen in the community, divided into groups of 1,000s, 100s, 50s, and 10s (1QS 2.21–22; cf. Ex 18.21, 25). A nucleus group was composed of 12 laymen and 3 priests, experts in the Law (1QS 8.1). The main affairs of the community were settled democratically in the "assembly of the Many," but the executive administration of various affairs was in the hands of "a [lay] man appointed at the head of the Many" (1QS 6.14) and an "overseer of the [work of the] Many" (1QS 6.11, 20). The former was a sort of superior, the latter a sort of bursar; they were responsible for the admission of candidates, administration of property, and so on.

Two rites formed the main cultic exercises of daily life: purificatory washings and a common religious meal. The purificatory washings were apparently immersion baths, like those prescribed by the Old Testament for priestly cleanliness; they symbolized a sorrow for sins (1QS 3.4–5, 9; 5.13–14). Such purification was required before one partook of the common meal. The religious meal was presided over by a priest who was to bless the bread and the wine before anyone touched them. He took precedence even over the Messiah of Israel who was thought to be present (1QSa 2.11–20; 1QS 6.20–21).

In addition to these rites, there were also prayers at set hours, in the evening and at sunrise, and a liturgy of the Sabbath used by the community. The community's Psalter, containing the canonical Psalms in a different order and their own *Thanksgiving Psalms (1QH)* (*hôdāyôt*), reveal the piety of the sect. The ancient solar calendar of 364 days regulated the community's celebration of feasts, and on the Feast of Weeks each year the Covenant was renewed (*Jubilees* 6.17) and new members were admitted.

Bibliography: P. R. DAVIES, "Hasidim in the Maccabean Period," *Journal of Jewish Studies* 28 (1977) 127–44. N. GOLB, *Who Wrote the Dead Sea Scrolls?* (New York–London 1995). M. GOODMAN, "A Note on the Qumran Sectarians, the Essenes and Josephus," *Journal of Jewish Studies* 46 (1995) 161–166. L. H. SCHIFFMAN, *Reclaiming the Dead Sea Scrolls* (Philadelphia 1994). H. STEGEMANN, *The Library of Qumran: On the Essenes, John the Baptist and Jesus* (Grand Rapids, Mich. 1998). E. ULRICH and J. VANDERKAM, *The Community of the Renewed Covenant* (Christianity and Judaism in Antiquity 10; Notre Dame, Ind. 1994). M. A. KNIBB, *The Qumran Community* (Cambridge 1987). H. RINGGREN, *The Faith of Qumran* (Philadelphia 1963). For additional bibliog. *see* DEAD SEA SCROLLS.

[J. A. FITZMYER]

The Appian Way, where it is believed Peter met with Jesus. (©Bettmann/CORBIS)

QUO VADIS

Quo Vadis or *Domine, quo vadis?*, meaning Lord, where are you going?, a text from the Apocryphal *Acts of Peter* composed *c.* A. D. 190, probably in Syria or Palestine. An anecdote based on the text became a legend in patristic times and is referred to by ORIGEN (*Comm. in Joan.* 20.12; *Patrologia Graeca* 14:600) and AMBROSE OF MILAN (*Sermo Contra Auxentium* 13).

Peter is represented in flight from Rome during the persecutions of Nero; he meets Jesus on the Appian Way: "And when he saw him, he said, 'Lord, whither goest thou?' And the Lord said unto him, 'I go into Rome to be crucified.' And Peter said to him, 'Lord, art thou being crucified again?' He said to him, 'Yes, Peter, I am being crucified again.' Peter came to himself, and having beheld the Lord ascending up into Heaven, he returned to Rome, rejoicing and glorifying the Lord, because he said, 'I am being crucified,' which was about to befall Peter" (James, *The Apocryphal New Testament* 333).

The *Acts of Peter* record the condemnation of Peter by the prefect Agrippa, his request to be crucified head downward, and a long sermon that he delivered on the symbolic meaning of the cross. This discourse betrays Gnostic influence, as do certain other passages of the *Acts of Peter*. About two-thirds of the text have been recovered; small Greek and Coptic fragments and the main body in a Latin manuscript were found at Vercelli (*Actus Vercellenses*). Ambrose used the anecdote without reference to its Apocryphal character to show that, as Peter stood firmly with the Church, Ambrose would stand with the Church of Milan against the Arians.

Bibliography: M. R. JAMES, *The Apocryphal New Testament* (Oxford 1953). C. H. TURNER, "The Latin Acts of St. Peter," *Journal of Theological Studies* 32 (1930–31) 119–133. H. DANNENBAUER, *"Nochmals die römische Petruslegende," Historische Zeitschrift* 159 (1938) 81–88. J. QUASTEN, *Patrology*, (Westminster, Md. 1950–) 1:133–135. F. L. CROSS, *The Oxford Dictionary of the Christian Church* (London 1957) 1050, 1134.

[M. C. MCCARTHY]

QUODVULTDEUS, BISHOP OF CARTHAGE, ST.

Episcopate: 432 or 433 to 454. He acceded to the see in 432 or 433. Shortly after the Vandals seized Carthage in 439, their king Geiseric despoiled Quodvultdeus and placed him and a host of his fellow clergymen "naked on dangerous ships," according to Victor of Vita. Quodvultdeus arrived safely in Naples, where he spent the remainder of his life in exile. He died sometime before October 454, when Deogratias was ordained his successor. Soon after his death Quodvultdeus was honored as a saint and confessor in both Naples and Carthage.

Sometime during the years 445 to 450 Quodvultdeus composed his most substantial work, the *Liber promissionum et praedictorum Dei,* which until recently was falsely attributed to Prosper of Aquitaine. The tome is meticulously ordered into 153 chapters, based on the number of fish in the miraculous catch (Jn 21:11). Augustine's threefold schema of salvation history inspires the first three parts, each of 40 chapters: "Before the Law," "Under the Law," and "Under Grace." In the first two parts, Quodvultdeus demonstrates how various events, people and institutions of the Old Testament are types or figures of Christ and the Church. The third part consists largely of verbal Old Testament prophecies that he shows to be fulfilled in New Testament times. Next comes a section of 20 chapters titled "The Middle of Time" (*dimidium temporis*, Dn 7:25, Rv 12:14), which focuses on the three and one-half years during which Antichrist will reign before Christ's triumphant return. Following a pre-Constantinian Christian tradition, Quodvultdeus believes that the fall of the Roman Empire will precipitate the end of the world. Hence he interprets the upheaval of Roman order effected by the Vandals in Africa as a sign that the end is imminent and the apocalyptic period of tribulation is soon to come. The *Liber* ends with a section of 13 brief chapters entitled "The Glory and Reign of the Saints."

Early in the twentieth century several scholars argued that Quodvultdeus also authored a number of pseudo-Augustine sermons. R. Braun included 13 of these in his critical edition of Quodvultdeus' works. Although it is perhaps impossible to definitively prove that Quodvultdeus authored these sermons, many scholars accept the attributions, notwithstanding the objections of M. Simonetti. Certainly all the sermons come from the milieu of mid-fifth century Africa. In arguing against Judaism, paganism and heresies—especially the Arian heresy of the barbarian invaders—they solidly expound Catholic Christology. Nine of the sermons were delivered as baptismal catechesis; these contain expositions of the Creed as well as valuable information about the African baptismal liturgy. If Quodvultdeus is indeed their author, he must have delivered them in Carthage before being exiled.

Bishop Quodvultdeus is most likely the same person as the Deacon Quodvultdeus who wrote two letters to Augustine and received two responses (Augustine's *Epist.* 221 to 224) in 428 to 429. In his letters Quodvultdeus implored the Bishop of Hippo to write a treatise against heresies for use in the Church of Carthage. At first hesitating, Augustine finally conceded and composed *De haeresibus*, dedicating it to Deacon Quodvultdeus.

Bibliography: *Clavis Patrum Latinorum* E. DEKKERS, ed. (1995) 401–17b. R. BRAUN, *Corpus Christianorum Series Latina* (1976) v. 60. R. BRAUN, *Sources Chrétiennes* (1964) v. 101–02. T. FINN, *Quodvultdeus of Carthage: Three Homilies on the Creed* (Mahwah 2002). R. KALKMAN, "Two Sermons *De tempore barbarico* Attributed to St. Quodvultdeus, Bishop of Carthage—A Study of Text and Attribution with Translation and Commentary" (Ph.D. disseration Catholic University of America 1963). R. BRAUN *Dictionnaire de spiritualité* (Paris 1986) v. 13.2, 2881–89. T. FINN, *Studia Patristica* 31 (1997) 42–58. R. GONZÁLEZ-SALINERO, *Revue des Études Juives* 155 (1996) 447–59. H. INGLEBERT, *Revue des Études Augustiniennes* 37 (1991) 307–20. L. MÜLLER, *The* De haeresibus *of Saint Augustine: a Translation with an Introduction and Commentary* (Washington, D.C. 1956). R. DE SIMONE, *Augustinianum* 25 (1985) 265–82. M. SIMONETTI, *Rendiconti parte generale e atti ufficiali* 84 (1944–57) 407–24. W. STROBL, *Vigiliae Christianae* 52 (1998) 193–203. D. VAN SLYKE, "Quodvultdeus of Carthage: Political Change and Apocalyptic Theology in the Fifth Century Roman Empire" (Ph.D. dissertation Saint Louis University 2000).

[D. VAN SLYKE]

QUR'ĀN

The holy book of ISLAM, containing what are considered by the Muslims the revelations made by God to the Prophet MUḤAMMAD over the approximately 20 years of his apostolate. The English term is derived from the Arabic word *qur'ān* (from the root *qr'*, to recite aloud, read), which would seem to have been borrowed from Syriac *qiryānā,* having the specifically religious sense of a recitation or reading of Scripture. The term is used in the work itself alongside a number of other terms [e.g., *waḥy,*

The Qur'ān (Archive Photos)

tanzīl, revelation; *dhikr, dhikra, tadhkira,* calling to mind; *furqān,* that which separates good from evil (but in Syriac, "salvation"), etc.] to designate the revelation of God's word, both in the interior experience of Muḥammad and as the expressed form and content of this experience as it was spoken by him and heard by the believers. It is termed "an Arabic *Qur'ān*" (12.2; 20.112; 39.29; 41.2; 43.2), being a revelation "in the Arabic language" (46.11) as opposed to non-Arabic revelations made to other prophets, viz, those of the Jews and Christians (cf. 16.105 and 41.44).

Arrangement. The Qur'ān, in its present form, is divided into 114 units or chapters called sūras (Arabic pl. *suwar*), which, varying in length from two lines to almost 700, are arranged in an order of decreasing length. The opening sūra (*Fātiḥat al-kitāb*), which is unique in being nothing more than a short prayer, stands outside this order as do the last two, which are imprecations against enchantment and evil spirits. In the earliest texts, following a practice no doubt already begun in the lifetime of the Prophet, the sūras were separated only by the *basmala,* i.e., the formula "In the Name of God, the Compassionate, the Merciful," standing at the head of each sūra. The formula, however, certainly did not form a part of the earliest revelations but was added consistently throughout only later; and its absence at the beginning of sūra 9 would indicate that sūras 8 and 9 were originally taken to be a single unit. The earliest manuscripts contain simply a blank space between sūras, into which commonly used titles, taken generally from some distinctive element in the sūra, were later added, e.g., 2 is known as *The Cow* (cf., 2.63); 57, *Iron* (cf. 57.25); 50, *Qâf* (from the initial at the beginning); 87, *The Most High* (87.1). In contrast to the *basmala* the titles are in no way considered part of the text; they have fluctuated, and particular sūras may have more than one, e.g., 68 = *al-Qalam* or *Nūn,* 17 = *'asrà* or *banī Isrâ'īl,* while 9 has been known by many names, the most common of which are *al-Tawba* and *al-Barā'a.*

The individual sūras are divided into verses called *'āyāt,* "signs" or "tokens" (sing. *'āya*), a term used in the revelation itself (e.g., 10.1; 12.1; 13.1, "These are the 'āyāt . . ."). These verses do not necessarily coincide with sentence units, but rather form rhetorical pauses marked by a rhyming assonance called *fāṣila,* in contradistinction to the strict rhyme of poetry, which is called *qāfiya.* There is considerable variability in the strictness of the rhyme and the number of successive verses over which a single assonance may be maintained; also the length of the verses themselves varies from a single word to many lines. In the latest-written portions of the book, particularly in the legal sections, the lines are quite long with no discernible cadence and a very weak rhyme (most commonly-ūn,-īn,-īm); in contrast, some of the earlier sūras manifest a kind of *saj'* or cadenced, rhymed prose somewhat similar to that used in the oracular sayings and incantations of the ancient Arabian diviners (*kāhin*, pl. *kahana*), something which induced the pagan hearers of Muḥammad to call his utterances "the speech of a *kāhin*" (cf. 69.42 and 52.29).

Manner of Compilation. The present order of the sūras in no way reflects the chronological sequence of their composition or of the promulgation of their parts, but on the contrary roughly reverses it, the longest ones being for the most part from the Medinan period and the shortest from the earliest. Again, with a few exceptions, chiefly among the shortest, almost none of the sūras in their present form represent integral, primitive units of the revelation. Some sūras show a simple juxtaposition of two or more originally independent pieces of varying length, while frequently single verses have been introduced to qualify or expand the original text. In some cases incomplete fragments would seem simply to have been inserted into an original unit with little regard for its contextual or grammatical integration; but one must always be circumspect in making any such judgment in view of the "disjointed" appearance of much of Arabic literature on the one hand, and of prophetic literature in general. Though in some instances the parts of a particular sūra are from quite different periods of Muḥammad's career, the majority are made up of elements generally more or less contemporary. Often the combination of originally independent elements is by simple juxtaposition; and though the process of combination could hardly have been as haphazard as some scholars have assumed, it is difficult, if not impossible, to determine what principles and method underlay the process. Whatever these may have been, the grouping must have taken place very early, and been almost, if not entirely, completed during the lifetime of the Prophet, since there is no tradition whatsoever indicating any order of verses within the sūras other than that of the present received text. Certain kinds of systematic arrangement of material would seem to have been consciously avoided; legal ordinances and admonitions, for example, rather than being grouped into a kind of unified code, are to be found in a number of separate sūras, and in each case are combined with homiletic and dogmatic elements, as if to maintain them always within the matrix of the religious and spiritual context that ultimately grounds their meaning. This is most notable in sūra 2, which forms a kind of constitution of the Muslim community at Medina; or in sūra 24, where precepts regarding adultery are juxtaposed with a magnificent passage on God as the light of the world (see also sūras 33, 58, and 65). In other cases there is to be found an intentional arrangement of homiletic material with "historical" narrative and descriptions of the last day.

Historical Setting. Although the Qur'ān, especially in the Meccan sūras, contains few unambiguous references to the historical events in the life of Muḥammad, the ISLAMIC TRADITIONS (ḤADĪTH), Arabic *ḥadīt,* furnish us with abundant if not always reliable information concerning the circumstances surrounding the revelation of particular verses and groups of verses. The most important sources are the Commentary of al-Ṭabarī and the works on the "occasions of the revelation" (*'asbāb al-nuzūl*). Combining this information with a study of the style and content of various sections of the Qur'ān itself, it is possible to establish a general chronology of the sūras, i.e., to assign them to roughly designated periods of the Prophet's career. To a great extent the parts belonging to the Medinan period are distinguishable by their style and content, the whole historical context of the revelation having altered with the HIJRA. Here, too, our information concerning the history of the Muslim community becomes much more clear, and the relative chronology of many of the Medinan sūras can be established with some confidence. On the contrary, our information on the detail of the Prophet's career at Mecca is anything but clear; for the sūras of this period, the most accurate classification that can be discerned is that given by T. Nöldeke, following the pioneer work of G. Weil and grouping them into three rough periods, early, middle, and late. Exact dates simply cannot be established.

Before the Hijra. According to the tradition the first revelation consisted in v. 1–5 of sūra 96 or v. 1–7 of 74, while the last revealed was sūra 9 and precisely, according to some sources, 9.120 (the whole sūra contains 130 v.). The earliest sūras manifest an abrupt and highly elliptical style, set forth in short, heavily cadenced, rhymed verses, the effect being one of terrible intensity and a remarkable rhetorical power. They contain calls to ritual purity before God, increasingly detailed arguments for God's creative omnipotence, and vivid portrayals of the day of judgment; later one finds increasing threats against the pagans coupled with historical examples of the experience of past prophets and God's punishment of the people who refused to heed their call. In the following period we find the same themes reiterated with an increasing emphasis on the absolute unicity of God (*al-tawḥīd*) and the necessity for good works (*al-ṣāliḥāt*), but the intensity of the style and the weight and variability of the rhyme is rather decreased as the descriptions of heaven and hell and of the last day, as well as the accounts of the prophets of the past, become more elaborated. Further, one begins to find here sūras built in a loose tripartite form that is continued into the following period. Such sūras open and close with a kind of homiletic exhortation or dogmatic exposition; in between, they offer some historical examples of God's judgment, in this world and the next, of those who refuse His commands and the words of His emissaries. Some few sūras may well originally have had this form, others have been so constructed out of smaller independent units. In the third period the same themes continue, set forth ever more explicitly. The theological content becomes denser as it is more expressly elaborated.

Medinan Period. In this period many former themes are continued, such as the attacks against idolatry and polytheism, warnings of the Last Judgment, the proclamation of God's unity and omnipotence. Yet there is a considerable shift in their overall appearance and structure; a number of new elements, reflecting the completely new circumstances of the Prophet and his followers, are introduced. Here one begins to find rather long sections containing legal precepts and regulations concerning diverse aspects of the social and moral life of the community. Then too, numerous passages reflect the conflicts with the non-Muslim inhabitants of Medina, the conflicts with the Jews, and the battles with and the final victory over the Quraysh and the Meccan opposition. The sūras of this period, which vary greatly in length, often seem to have little internal structure; the style varies from the lengthy, prosaic verses of the legal and narrative passages to echoes of the preceding period in passages of dogmatic and homiletic content.

Transmission of the Qur'ān. Though primary reliance had always to be upon memory, because the early Arabic orthography was grossly inadequate, there can be little doubt that various portions of the Qur'ān were reduced to writing quite early.

To the Death of Muḥammad. Tradition has it that some revelations were written down immediately on whatever materials were available, palm leaves, sherds, scraps of leather, shoulder blades of large animals, and the like. We are told according to one tradition that the sister of the future caliph 'Umar, on the eve of his conversion, in about the year 616, possessed a copy of sūra 20 (albeit we cannot know how much of the present sūra such a copy may have contained). Later, after the establishment of the Muslim community in Medina, Muḥammad seems to have dictated various portions of the book to his secretaries, the most important of whom were Zayd ibn Thābit and 'Ubay ibn Ka'b. Though the particular story may well be of doubtful authenticity, we hear also of his supervising Zayd ibn Thābit in the ordering and revision of certain portions of the work. Concerning the state of the text at the time of Muḥammad's death, we can be certain only that a universally accepted order of the verses within the sūras was definitively established. In the case of some of the shorter and earlier sūras this may have come about through their liturgical recitation by the prophet; but in the case of the longer ones, 2 through 5 for example, it is difficult to conceive how a definitive order could have been set and have gained recognition other than by their having somehow received written form under the direction of the Prophet. Exactly how the arranging was done remains, however, altogether uncertain, and any attempted solution must be conjectural. At the death of the Prophet there existed no official, authoritative recension of the entire corpus of the revelation. There did exist a number of private collections of leaves (*ṣuḥuf*) containing more or less extensive portions of the book, as well as several collections that were complete. In all these, as in the present recension, the order of the sūras, however many the individual collection may have contained, was already one of decreasing length.

Received Text of the Qur'ān. According to tradition, following the death of a number of Qur'ān readers in the battle of 'Aqrabā, Zayd ibn Thābit at the behest of 'Umar (or according to another, less reliable tradition, of Abū Bakr) set about to make a complete written compilation of the revelation. This he accomplished working from such fragmentary materials as were available to him in writing and from recitation by those who had memorized other parts of the book. The exact circumstances surrounding the original draft of Zayd ibn Thābit are quite obscure, but it is certain that it did not constitute an official text, for at the death of 'Umar the leaves passed into the possession of his daughter Ḥafṣa. We know also of other complete collections alongside that of Zayd; some of them enjoyed considerable prestige, most importantly those of 'Abdallāh ibn Mas'ūd, 'Ubay ibn Ka'b, Abū Mūsā al-'Ash'arī, and Miqdād ibn 'Amr, whose readings were long followed at Kūfa, Damascus, Baṣra, and Homs, respectively. Other complete recensions are attributed to 'Alī ibn Abī Ṭālib and Ibn 'Abbās. Finally during the reign of 'Uthmān, the need for a universally authoritative text that would forestall the growing disputes regarding various readings of the Book became more urgent and accordingly, in about A.H. 30–35, the Caliph established a commission to produce an official text. This commission, composed of Zayd ibn Thābit, 'Abdallāh ibn al-Zubayr, Sa'īd ibn al-'Aṣ, and 'Abdarraḥmān ibn al- Ḥārith, then procured Zayd's original compilation from Ḥafṣa bint 'Umar and used it as the basis for their work. Upon the completion of the work, according to tradition, a number of copies were made, of which one was kept at Medina, while the others were sent to Damascus, Baṣra, and Kūfa along with the Caliph's orders to destroy all other copies. Whatever may be the truth of this account, the official recension almost immediately gained wide acceptance, despite the determined opposition of 'Abdallāh ibn Mas'ūd, who regarded Zayd ibn Thābit as a kind of upstart.

Variant Recensions. Though no copies of the early recensions have been preserved, some were yet in circulation as late as the 10th Christian century; their readings are widely cited in the commentaries, and they are described in a number of sources. Besides a number of variations in individual verses, the recensions of 'Ubay and Ibn Mas'ūd differ from the received text in the order of the sūras. The general principle of decreasing length is followed in all, but would seem most strict in that of Ibn Mas'ūd, whereas in that of Zayd ibn Thābit, the received text, there would seem to have been some attempt to maintain the integrity of certain groups that may have formed individual blocks of sūras in the partial collections from which he worked. This would be particularly true if we assume that the sūras beginning *ḤM* (40–46), *'LR* (10–15), *'LM* (2–3, 29–32), *ṬH* and *ṬS(M)* (20.26–28) belonged originally to individual collections designated by the initials; no. 32, for example, is notably shorter than 33. Again, the recension of Ibn Mas'ūd lacked the initial sūra (*al-Fātiḥa*) as well as the last two and combined, probably, 8 and 9 into a single unit, giving a total of 110 sūras. That of 'Ubay, on the other hand, contained, following sūra 103 of the present recension, two short sūras, no longer considered canonical, entitled respectively *Sūrat al-Ḫal'* and *Sūrat al-Ḥafd* (text in Nöldeke 2, 34–35), and may have combined into a single unit sūras 105–106 or sūras 93–94.

Teaching of the Qur'ān. The Prophet is not held to be the author of the Qur'ān, but only an emissary and witness who gives warning and announces good news (7.59–60; 48.8; 73.5; *et passim*); the words of the Qur'ān are fully distinct from Muḥammad's own words (75.16–18; 53.3–5; 69.44–46; 16.15–17; 87.6; 73.5), for the revelation forces itself upon his consciousness from without, coming unexpectedly upon him (17.88–89; 42.52).

Modes of Divine Revelation. The divine message is revealed to Muḥammad by an angel (2.91) or the Spirit of God (44.2) on "The Night of Power" (97), which traditionally is said to have been in the last 10 days of RAMAḌĀN (cf. 2.181). It is a "mighty Scripture" (41.41), completely overpowering (59.21), which was sent down by God as something preexisting (11.1; 20.99; 27.6; 3.5) in a celestial archetype (50.4; 56.77; 80.11–13), "the well-kept Tablet" (85.21) that is the core of the Scripture (43.3) and embodies God's eternal knowledge and judgment of all things (cf. 10.62; 27.77; 34.3), the total content of which is too great to be contained in any material document (18.108). Ultimately God's universal dominion is manifested in all things, and even the simplest processes of nature are signs or tokens (*'āyāt*) of His unity and creative power (*passim*). "In whatever direction you turn, there is the face of God . . ." (2.115), "who created each thing and fixed its measure" (25.2; 5.120) and "who is closer to man than his own jugular vein" (50.15). He manifests His signs within the immediacy of consciousness and in the horizons of the created world (41.53; 51.20–21), showing Himself in the simple alternation of night and day (36.37; etc.), and in the growth of man from conception to senility and death (8.5–7; 16.72; 40.69; etc.). In all things there is an allusion (*'ibra*) to God's Being (32.21; 16.68) for "those who can see" (24.44), "who will reflect and understand" (45.4, 12; 16.11–13; etc.), and will "perhaps show gratitude and be guided aright" (16.13–15; etc.). His signs are effective for those who have opened themselves to Him in faith (45.2–3; 79.26; 10.6; etc.), but this opening (*'išrāḥ*) and receptivity to God's grace is ultimately worked by God (cf. 6.125–127; 39.23; 94.1–3; 76.29–30; 74.53–55; etc.). Even when Abraham is said, in a famous passage (6.75–80), to have concluded from the observation of natural phenomena that God is One and Almighty, the text notes that "Thus we showed Abraham the kingdom of the heavens and the earth, that he might become one of those who have the certitude [of faith]."

Historical Revelation and the Qur'ān. As a gratuitous act of mercy (*raḥma, ni'ma*) toward the human race (21.84; 45.19; 11.30, 66; 28.46; 29.50; 38.42) God sends His emissaries (*rusul*) and prophets (*'anbiyā', nabiyyīn*) to humanity with the Scripture, wherein His signs are set forth explicitly and unequivocally (11.1; 10.38; 41.1; but cf. also 3.5) as a guidance (hudā), admonition, and healing (10.58; 17.74)—a calling to mind (*dhikr,* 20.99; 74.34; etc.) of His omnipotence, a warning of impending judgment and doom (6.19; 37.69; etc.) and promise of beatitude (39.19; etc.), a call to worship God alone (57.25; 29.2; 6.102; etc.) and to live according to the norms of justice and morality demanded and decreed by Him. The signs (*'āyāt*) of the Scripture are the signs par excellence, for it is through them that all other signs are brought to man's attention and made intelligible. Recited by God's emissaries (45.24; etc.), they are self-expressing in that they address themselves immediately to the understanding of the hearer in the clear form of articulate language. As opposed to the worldly and self-centered human inclinations (*al-'ahwā'*), which tend to lead them away from God (10.37; 28.50; 47.15; etc.), the revelation is given from God Himself and is taught by Him (53.3–5; 7.60; 47.16; etc.). In the acceptance of the revelation as the teaching of God lies the only true knowledge (*'ilm,* cf. 30.56; 34.6; 29.48; etc.) as opposed to merely human opinion (*ẓann,* cf. 53.39; 49.12; 10.37, 67; 4.156–158; etc.); it is the Divine Truth (*ḥaqq,* 13.1; 10.94; etc.), which destroys the vanity of untruth (17.83; 8.6–8; etc.), being the manifestation of God who is the ultimate truth (10.33; 22.6, 61; etc.); it is the light that God gives to whom He will (42.52) wherein and whereby men should be guided (6.91; 57.9; etc.) to God, the source, who is "the light of the heavens and the earth" (24.35); wherefore the true believers, when they hear these signs fall prostrate and glorify God (7.108; 32.15; etc.). In the Qur'ān, God Himself reveals Himself, the unknowable and transcendent (*al-ġayb*), in His attributes and names (*'asmā'uhu al-ḥusnā*) and thereby, since He is the maker of all creation and the ground of all being, He makes manifest to the believer the true nature (*ḥaqq*) of created existence. This notion of the Qur'ān as the supreme self-manifestation of God to His creatures is extremely important to the dogma of the miraculous inimitability (*al-'i'jāz*) of the Qur'ān and for the development, among the orthodox theologians, of the thesis that it is uncreated (*see* KALĀM) as well as for an understanding of the place of the book in Muslim piety.

Man's Response to Revelation. According to the Qur'ān, man's response to God's words ought to be immediate, for God has created him and given him all his powers of perception and understanding (32.8; 16.80; 67.23; 76.2), and at the very foundation of his being lies an innate testimony that God is his Lord (7.171). Through the Prophet He calls men to submit themselves completely to Himself, worshiping Him alone and living according to His law. Men, however, are all too frequently distracted by their engagement in the pursuit of the goods of the world (10.7; 77.16–17; 30.6; 6.69; 45.34; etc.), being seduced by their competition in "the ornaments of this life" (57.38; 64.15; 58.18; etc.). They are by nature anxious and grasping (70.19–21; cf. also 41.49–51; 11.12–13; 30.33–35; 42.50; etc.) and do not look beyond their material existence (45.22–23). The Qur'ān recognizes the importance of a number of sociological factors that blind men to God's message—group solidarity, tradition, etc. (7.27, 68; 9.23; 43.21–30; etc.)—and the obstinate pride in social position that characterizes those who refuse God's signs (7.73–75; 40.24; 74.16–23; 71.6; 63.5; 46.19; 16.25), in contrast to the attitude of the God-fearing (16.71; 21.19; etc.), who are willing to abandon these things (59.22).

Sanctions and Determinism. The insensibility to God's signs and the preaching of His word (*al-kalām;* cf. 2.70; 9.6; 7.141) appears as a kind of spiritual blindness (7.187; 8.22; 2.9; 9.126), realized in a conscious obstinacy and refusal to perceive (see 71.6); and men's perseverance in this refusal to accept God's guidance is ultimately ratified and made permanent by God who so seals their hearts (10.75; 63.3) that, regardless of what the Prophet may say or do, they will never believe (36.9; 7.192; 6.25; 17.45–49; 10.43–44; 18.55; 39.43; 30.51; 43.39). It is as if there were an impediment in their hearing (41.4, 44; 31.6) and a veil between them and the Prophet (17.47). God grants His mercy and guidance to whom He will (24.45; 76.30; 81.27–29; 6.125;39.23–24) and none can mislead him whom God guides aright (39.38). If He wished, all men would believe (6.107; 32.13), for all creatures are under God's immediate providence (11.59). He refuses, however, to guide the unjust and the sinful and those who refuse Him (9.37, 110; 28.50; 46.9; 16.109; 39.5; 40.29; etc.). In many passages the Qur'ān is deterministic: "There is no guide for those whom God leads astray, but He lets them go, to wander lost in their excess" (7.176–177; cf. also 2.14; 16.110; 6.39; 16.39; 14.4; 13.33; 18.16; 38.24; etc.). On the other hand, the Qur'ān insists at the same time that God does not wrong men, but, rather, that they wrong themselves (16.35, 119; 10.45; 18.47; etc.); He does not punish them until they themselves have done evil (8.55; etc.), each person receiving ultimately in heaven or hell the rewards of what he has done (*passim*), for this life is a test of their goodness and justice (67.1; 18.6; 16.94; 21.36; 6.165; etc.). God demands of no one more than that of which he is capable (2.233; 6.153; 7.40), for He is "merciful and forgiving" (*passim*). In the final analysis the Qur'ān does not try to solve the mystery of God's justice; what may be its final statement on the subject is put into the mouth of Jesus: "You know what is in my soul, but I do not know what is in Yours. You, indeed, have complete knowledge of the hidden . . . . If You punish them,—they are Your servants; and if you forgive them,—You are the Almighty, the All-wise . . .; to God belongs the dominion of the heavens and the earth and what is in them; over all things He is Mighty" (5.116–118).

Muḥammad, the Prophets, and Jesus. The Qur'ān contains many accounts, often extremely elliptical, of those whom God sent with His message in the past. With few exceptions [viz, Idrīs, Ṣâliḥ, Šu'ayb, Dhû 1-Kifl] all those mentioned are Biblical, though the accounts given show a greater affinity frequently to haggadic and other noncanonical sources than to the Bible itself. According to the Qur'ān, the revelation given to Muḥammad continues a long tradition (3.2; etc.) and has the same content as the "Leaves of Abraham and Moses" (87.19); as he is a Prophet to the Gentiles (*nabī 'ummī*), God has laid upon him the same injunction as upon "Abraham, Moses, and Jesus" (42.11), though he is, nevertheless, the "seal of the prophets" (33.40), Abraham is the highest example of the purest Islamic faith (37.81–82; 16.124;

22.77; etc.) and a model for all believers (60.4); he was the founder of the faith, the chosen friend of God (4.124), ''neither Jew nor Christian'' but Muslim and *ḥanīf* (3.60; 2.134; 16.121; etc.), who founded the sanctuary at Mecca (22.27; 2.118–120; etc.). Moses also, whose encounter with Pharaoh is frequently recalled, was given the Scripture (*al-Kitâb,* 2.53, etc.), i.e., the Torah (*al-Tawrāt*), which is considered a single revelation, one book; he belonged to the same faith (42.13). Later John the Baptist (Yaḥyā ibn Zakarīyā'), whose miraculous birth is recounted in sūras 3 (v. 38–40) and 19 (v. 1–3), preached the unity of God (6.83) to the Israelites. To Jesus, the Messiah (*al-Masīḥ, 'Īsâ ibn Maryam*) was revealed the Gospel (*al-'Injīl*), likewise considered as a single book of revelation (3.43). Jesus, like Adam, was created directly by God's command (3.52) and is called the ''word of God'' (3.45), i.e., His creative word ''which was cast into Mary'' (4.169; see also 3.59; 66.12), who was purified and chosen above all women (3.37). He is called ''The Spirit of God'' (4.169) and ''a sign for the human race and an act of mercy from'' God (19.21). Though giving Him a place of preeminence and proximity to God in this world and the next (3.40), the Qur'ān nevertheless denies categorically that He is God (5.19, 76–77) or the Son of God (9.30; 19.35–36); both notions Muḥammad considered idolatrous. In this way the Trinity, which is taken to be made up of God, Jesus, and Mary (4.169–170), is denounced as a tritheism; rather Jesus is simply a servant of God (*'abd*), an emissary (*rasūl*), and prophet (*nabī;* 5.116–118; 19.31), with whom God has made the same pact as with His other prophets, Muḥammad, Noah, Abraham, and Moses (33.7).

Bibliography: The two principal English translations are: M. W. PICKTHALL, tr., *The Meaning of the Glorious Koran* (London 1930). A. J. ARBERRY, tr. and ed., *The Koran Interpreted,* 2 v. (New York 1955). **Principal studies include:** K. CRAGG, *The Event of the Qu'ran; Islam in its Scripture* (London 1971). A. T. WELCH, ed., *Studies in Qur'an and Tafsir* (Chico, CA 1979). F. RAHMAN, *Major Themes of the Qur'an* (Minneapolis 1980). A. RIPPIN, ed., *Approaches to the History of the Interpretation of the Qur'an* (Oxford/New York 1988). H. GÄTJE, ed. *The Qur'an and Its Exegesis: Selected Texts with Classical and Modern Muslim Interpretations* (Rockport, Maine 1996). M. A. A. HALEEM, *Understanding the Qur'an: Themes and Style* (London/New York 1999). A. RIPPIN, *The Qur'an: Formative Interpretation* (Brookfield, VT 1999). M. A. COOK, *The Koran, A Very Short Introduction* (Oxford/New York 2000). A. WESSELS, *Understanding the Qur'an* (London 2000). J. D. MCAULIFFE and B. WALFISH, *With Reverence for the Word: Medieval Scriptural Exegesis in Judaism, Christianity, and Islam* (New York 2002).

[R. M. FRANK/EDS.]

R

RA (RE)

Sun–god of ancient Egypt and chief god of the pantheon of Heliopolis. The term *r'* (pronounced *rā'* or *rē'*) was the Egyptian word for the sun. A large part of the Egyptian religion was connected with the worship of the sun, which was the primary source of existence. Ra, the sun, in the widest and most general sense, was considered the creator of everything. Since the Egyptian state was god–given and established when the world was created, the monarchy was as old as the world, for the creator himself had assumed kingly office on the day of creation. Ra was called the first king of Egypt, and the pharaoh was his descendant and successor. As Ra put order (*ma'at*) in the place of chaos, so the pharaoh's achievements were described in exactly the same way. From the beginning the king had been the god Horus or Har–akhti (symbolized by a hawk), the son of ISIS and Osiris. During the Fifth Dynasty the king became the son of Ra at Heliopolis (On). A millennium later, the previously obscure creator god AMON of Thebes (No–Amon) was identified with Ra. Pharaoh Amenhotep IV (*c.* 1364–1347 B.C.) broke with Amonism, changed his own name to AKHNATON (AKH–EN–ATON), moved the capital from Thebes to Tell el–Amarna, and instituted the pure worship of Aton, the sun disc, in an attempt to suppress all other worship. However, throughout Egyptian history there was a tendency toward syncretism, so that the supreme god Ra could be identified with Atum (the god of "all" of the Heliopolis pantheon) and worshiped under the name of Ra–Atum or identified with other gods, so that he had such names as Amon–Ra, Ra–Har–akhti, and Khnum–Ra. This might have led (but did not) to true monotheism.

See Also: EGYPT, ANCIENT, 1.

Bibliography: K. H. SETHE, *Amun und die acht Urgötter von Hermopolis* (Berlin 1929). J. A. WILSON, *The Burden of Egypt: An Interpretation of Ancient Egyptian Culture* (Chicago 1951; pa. *The Culture of Ancient Egypt* 1956). H. FRANKFORT, *Ancient Egyptian Religion* (New York 1961). For additional bibliography *see* EGYPT, ANCIENT, 1.

[H. MUELLER]

RABANUS MAURUS, BL.

Rabanus (Hrabanus, Rhabanus) Magnentius Maurus, Benedictine theologian, *Praeceptor Germaniae,* abbot of Fulda, archbishop of Mainz; b. Mainz, of a noble family (hence Magnentius?), 776 (784?); d. Winkel (Vinicellum) on the Rhine, Feb. 4, 856. Rabanus received his early education at Fulda, where he was ordained deacon in 801. In 802 he was sent to Tours to study under ALCUIN, from whom he received the sobriquet "Maurus" (a reference to St. Maur, disciple of St. Benedict) in recognition of his scholastic abilities. Recalled to Fulda in 803, he was made director of the monastic school there, which became, under his guidance, one of the most outstanding in Germany, numbering among its pupils such famous personages as WALAFRID STRABO and Otfrid of Weissenburg. Rabanus was ordained on Dec. 12, 814. From 822 to 842, as abbot of Fulda, he furthered the spiritual, intellectual, and temporal welfare of the monastery, erected buildings and churches, collected MSS and art treasures, and continued his own scholarly, literary, and exegetical endeavors. In the political struggle between Louis the Pious and his sons, Rabanus supported Louis and, on Louis' death, gave his allegiance to LOTHAIR I. When the latter was defeated by Louis the German in 840, Rabanus fled his monastery. He returned in 841 but retired in 842 to nearby Petersberg, where he devoted himself to prayer and literary work until he was called in 847 to become archbishop of Mainz. As archbishop he was zealous in instructing clergy and laity, in combating social disorders, and in defending sound doctrine. He held three provincial synods: in 847, to deal with matters of ecclesiastical discipline; in 848, to condemn the monk GOTTSCHALK OF ORBAIS and his doctrine of PREDESTINATION to evil as well as to good; in 852 (851?), to deal with the rights and disciplines of the Church.

Temple of Ramses II, 1257 B.C., Abu Simbel, Nubia. (©Roger Wood/CORBIS)

Rabanus was a voluminous writer. He produced a study on grammar (De arte grammatica), a collection of homilies for the Church year (not all certainly his), two penitentials, a martyrology, and some Latin poetry (the *VENI CREATOR SPIRITUS* is probably not his), which reveals him as a skilled versifier but a mediocre poet. In addition, he compiled a pedagogical treatise (*De institutione clericorum*) in three books, composed not later than 819 and relying heavily on Augustine, Gregory the Great, and Isidore; an encyclopedic dictionary (usually entitled *De universo,* though more properly called *De rerum naturis*), consisting of 22 books based on the *Etymologies* of ISIDORE OF SEVILLE; and extensive commentaries on the Bible (among others, on the Heptateuch, Ruth, Proverbs, Jeremias, Ezechiel, Wisdom, Maccabees, Matthew, and the Pauline Epistles). Though a learned and scholarly man (he was probably unequaled in his lifetime for scriptural and patristic learning), Rabanus was by no means an original thinker. His writings, compiled, like those of Alcuin, with the help of pupils, consist in large part of extracts from other sources and are important more for their role in the CAROLINGIAN RENAISSANCE and in the establishment of learning in Germany than for any intrinsic merit of their own. There is no complete critical edition of his works. Rabanus was buried in the monastery of St. Albans at Mainz, but his relics were later translated to Halle by Abp. ALBRECHT OF BRANDENBURG. He is honored as a saint (or *beatus*) in Mainz, Fulda, Limburg, and Breslau.

Feast: Feb. 4.

Bibliography: Editions. *Patrologia Latina,* ed. J. P. MIGNE, 217 v., indexes 4 v. (Paris 1878–90), v.107–112, reproduces *Hrabani Mauri opera,* ed. J. DE PAMELE (d. 1587) 6 v.in 3 (Cologne 1626–27). Rabanus' extensive and important correspondence is in *Monumenta Germaniae Historica Epistolae* (Berlin 1826–), 5.2:37–533. *De institutione clericorum,* ed. A. KNOEPFLER (Munich 1900). The poems are in *Monumenta Germaniae Historica Poetae* (Berlin 1826–), 2:154–258; *Analecta hymnica* (Leipzig 1886–1922), 50:180–209. The *Life* by his disciple Rudolfus [*Patrologia Latina,* ed. J. P. MIGNE, 217 v., indexes 4 v. (Paris 1878–90), v.107] is unreliable. Literature. W. KOSCH, *Deutsches Literatur-Lexikon,* ed. B. BERGER in 1 v. (Bern 1963) 189, selected bibliog. to 1960. A. HAUCK, *Kirchengeschichte Deutschelands,* 5 v. (9th ed. Berlin–Leipzig 1958), 2:638–659, *passim.* P. LEHMANN, ''Zu Hrabans geistiger Bedeutung,'' in *Sankt Bonifatius: Gedenkgabe zum zwölfhundertsten Todestag* (Fulda 1954) 473–487. H. PELTIER, *Dictionnaire de théologie catholique,* ed. A. VACANT et al., 15 v. (Paris 1903–50; Tables générales 1951–) 13.2:1601–20, good bibliog. M. MANITIUS, *Geschichte der lateinischen Literatur des Mittelalters,* 3 v. (Munich 1911–31) 1:288–302. M. BERNARDS, *Lexikon für Theologie und Kirche,* ed. J. HOFER and K. RAHNER, 10 v. (2d, new ed. Frieburg 1957–65) 5:499–500.

[M. F. MCCARTHY]

RABBI

Title of a Jewish religious teacher. The word is derived from the Hebrew *rabbî* (literally, ''my master''), which in New Testament times was used only as a term of address. In time the force of the possessive adjective fell away and the word came to be used as title in the third person (cf. monsignor, literally ''my elder'').

In the New Testament. Although the term rabbi does not occur in the Old Testament, by the first Christian century it must have become common, for the Gospels frequently show the disciples of Jesus (Mt 26.25, 49; Mk 9.5; 11.21; 14.45; Jn 1.49; 4.31; 9.2; 11.8) and other people (Jn 3.2; 6.25) addressing Him as ''Rabbi'' (ῥαββί). In Jn 1.38 the term is explained as equivalent to διδάσκαλε (teacher), and this word is often used in the Gospels as a substitute for it in addressing Jesus (Mt 8.19; 12.38; etc.; Mk 4.38; 9.17, 38; etc.; Lk 7.40; 9.38; etc.; Jn8.4). In Luke, where the word rabbi does not occur, Jesus is often addressed by another Greek equivalent ἐπιστάτα (master: L.k 5.5; 8.24, 45; etc.). A heightened form of Semitic *rab* (chief, master) is Aramaic *rabbān,* Hebrew *rabbôn,* and the latter with the suffix -*î* (my) is *rabbônî;* Jesus is thus addressed in Mk 10.51; Jn 20.16 (usually written ῥαββουνεί in the Greek MSS). Except in addressing Jesus, the term rabbi is used in the Gospels only once in addressing John the Baptist (Jn 3.26) and twice in Our Lord's condemnation of the Scribes and Pharisees, who loved to be addressed by this title (Mt 23.7–8).

In Judaism. In current English, the word rabbi designates the spiritual leader of a Jewish community, Orthodox, Conservative, or Reform. The office of rabbi reached its present development through stages that are not always easy to pinpoint in history. In Talmudic times (roughly from 200 B.C. to A.D. 500) there were two categories of rabbi, the rabbi teachers and the rabbi judges (*dayyānîm*). The former qualified for their teaching function by their learning and ability to interpret. They did not receive a salary for their teaching activity, but supported themselves by the pursuit of some trade or profession. The rabbi judge was empowered by the Palestinian authorities on the basis of his understanding of the law and his personal integrity. He was paid a fee for the time he consumed in adjudicating a case. At times the function of teaching and judging merged in the person of one rabbi.

In the 12th century there emerged a type of rabbi comparable in position and function to the modern rabbi. To permit the rabbi to devote more time to rabbinical activity it became common to pay him for his services to the community and thereby free him from the need of working to sustain himself. In the wake of salaried rabbis it came to be customary to stipulate in writing the specific services that a given congregation anticipated from its rabbi. Among other things, a rabbi was expected to set up and preside over a community court, organize and supervise a lower school and an academy, and to participate in circumcision, BAR MITZVAH, marriage, and other ceremonies. On occasion rabbis have been charged with the performance of civil functions; for example, the collection of taxes for the government. This usage eventually grew into the office of chief rabbi maintained at various times in certain countries of Europe, e.g., Spain, Portugal, and England. The chief rabbi was in effect a government appointee authorized to oversee the taxation of Jews and to represent their interests in the particular country.

In the past the training of a rabbi consisted almost exclusively in Jewish studies. However, from the 19th century on, chiefly under the influence of Leopold Zunz (1794–1886) and Abraham Geiger (1810–74) in Germany, considerably more stress has been put upon the secular sciences. This new emphasis on the profane disciplines was intensified in some instances by civil government; for certain European states, among them France and Austria, began to require a general education of rabbinical aspirants. The main rabbinical seminaries in the United States are the Yeshiva University, New York City (Orthodox), the Hebrew Theological Seminary, New York City (Conservative), and the Hebrew Union College, Cincinnati (Reform).

Bibliography: *Encyclopedic Dictionary of the Bible*, tr. and adap. by L. HARTMAN (New York 1963) 1974–75. H. ERHARTER, *Lexikon für Theologie und Kirche*, ed. J. HOFER and K. RAHNER (Freiberg 1957–65) 8:957. E. L. DIETRICH, *Die Religion in Geschichte und Gegenwart* (Tübingen 1957–65) 5:759. M. M. BERMAN, *The Role of the Rabbi* (New York 1941). A. J. FELDMAN, *The Rabbi and His Early Ministry* (New York 1941).

Manuscript illustration depicting Rabanus Maurus being presented to St. Martin by Abbot Albinus, from "De Laude Sanctae Crusic," 9th century.

[J. C. TURRO]

RABBINICAL BIBLES

Printed editions of the Hebrew Scriptures with the Masoretic Text and the Targum in parallel columns surrounded by various rabbinic commentaries, such as those of RASHI, Abraham IBN EZRA, NAḤMANIDES, and David Kimchi, in the margins. Termed *miqrā'ôt gᵉ dōlôt* (large editions of the Scriptures) in Hebrew, they include also the apparatus of the Masora giving variant readings and other reference data. The several editions of rabbinical Bibles may differ from each other in the numbers and types of commentaries included.

The first rabbinical Bible, published by Daniel BOMBERG in Venice in 1516–17, was edited by Felix PRATENSIS, a Jewish convert to Christianity. This edition is the first to give the *qᵉrê* and *kᵉtîb* variants and to establish the division of Samuel, Kings, and Chronicles into two books each, as well as to separate Ezra and Nehemiah. Pratensis was meticulous in his attempt to fix the Biblical text insofar as the MSS at his disposal permitted, even citing the minutest variations in vocalic and accentual notation as well as the peculiar sizes and positions of certain letters.

Bomberg's second edition, 1524–25, was edited by Jacob ben Ḥayyim. It differs from the first in that Ben

Polish Rabbi, ca. 1865-1875. (©Scheufler Collection/CORBIS)

Ḥayyim sought to produce the authoritative form of the scriptural text by collating and comparing material from many manuscripts. For this purpose, he included the Masora *magna, parva,* and *finalis.* He also indicated the open and closed sections by the initial letters of the Hebrew equivalents for these terms.

His version of the Masoretic text became the standard for all subsequent editions of the Hebrew Bible, critical and otherwise, well into the 20th century. Modern studies, however, have demonstrated that Ben Ḥayyim was eclectic in his selection of variant readings and his sources were neither old nor necessarily accurate.

After Bomberg's third edition, 1546–48, edited by Cornelius Alkind, there were three subsequent publications of his rabbinical Bible: Treves, Germany (no date); Venice, 1617–19; and Basel, 1618–19. The last, by Johannes Buxtorf, the Elder, possesses a hybrid scriptural text derived from both the text of Ben Ḥayyim and that of the Complutensian Polyglot, 1513–17 (*see* POLYGLOT BIBLES).

The seventh rabbinical Bible, called *Qehillôt Mōšeh,* was published in Amsterdam by Moses ben Simeon Frankfurter in 1724–27 in four volumes. The Warsaw Rabbinical Bible issued by Abraham Baer Lebensohn in 1860–68 is in 12 volumes and contains 32 commentaries.

Bibliography: R. GOTTHEIL, *The Jewish Encyclopedia*, ed. J. SINGER (New York 1901–06) 3:158–161. P. E. KAHLE, *The Cairo Geniza* (2d ed. New York 1960) 120–124, 129–131.

[R. KRINSKY]

RABBULA

Rabbula was a fifth–century Syrian bishop of Edessa and theologian; b. Qennešrīn, near Aleppo, *c.* 350; d. Edessa, 435 or 436. Son of a pagan father and Christian mother, Rabbula was well educated and knew Greek. He entered the civil service and rose to prefect, but *c.* 400 was converted and became a monk. In 411 he was elected bishop of Edessa and devoted himself to the reform of the Church, particularly of the clergy and monks. He strongly opposed Jewish, pagan, and Gnostic influences in Syria. At the Council of EPHESUS (431) he took the part of CYRIL OF ALEXANDRIA, and in the difficulties that followed he excommunicated Andrew of Samosata and broke with Alexander of Hierapolis, charging them with Nestorian leanings (before Easter 432). At Cyril's request he translated the Alexandrian's *De recta fide* into Syriac; wrote two series of rules for priests and monks; preached against Nestorius and on the agape for the deceased. He is credited with having written some of the hymns in the Syriac (Jacobite) liturgy, but their authenticity is doubtful. The vita written apparently *c.* 450 by an Edessan ecclesiastic is only partially trustworthy. His authorship of the Syriac version of the Bible, the PESHITTA, is seriously questioned. He had difficulty with his clergy, and particularly Ibas of Edessa during the last years of his life, and seems to have been in ill health for a long time. Only fragments of his correspondence have been preserved.

Bibliography: J. OVERBECK, ed., *S. Ephraemi Syri, Rabulae Episcopi Edesseni . . . Opera* (Oxford 1865) 159–209, *Vitae,* 222–248, homilies and letters; liturgy. A. VÖÖBUS, *Investigations into the Text of the New Testament Used by Rabbula* (Pinneberg 1947); Early versions of the New Testament (Stockholm 1954); *History of Asceticism the Syrian Orient,* v.2 (*Corpus scriptorum Christianorum orientalium* (197; Paris–Louvain) 1960) 154–158; *L'Orient syrien* 7 (1962) 297–306, letter to Gemillinos; *Lexikon für Theologie und Kirche* 2, ed. J. HOFER and K. RAHNER (Freiburg 1957–65) 8:958–959; ed. and tr., *Syriac and Arabic Documents* (Stockholm 1960). P. E. PUSEY, *Sancti patris nostri Cyrilli . . . de recta fide* (Oxford 1877) 1–33. P. PEETERS, *Recherches de science religieuse* 18 (1928) 170–204. I. ZIADÉ, *Dictionnaire de théologie catholique,* ed. A. VACANT et al., 15 v. (Paris 1903–50; Tables générales 1951–) 13.2:1620–26.

[P. ROCHE]

RABELAIS, FRANÇOIS

French satirist; b. near Chinon, *c.* 1483; d. Paris, April 1553. He entered religion as a Franciscan novice probably in 1511; by 1521 he was already a priest at the Fontenay-le-Comte monastery of the Observantine Friars Minor. After difficulties with superiors over the study of Greek, he received an indult from Clement VII to join the Benedictine monastery-cathedral at Maillezais, whose abbot, Bishop Geoffroi d'Estissac, encouraged his studies. Without permission, he matriculated at the Medical Faculty, Montpellier (Sept. 17, 1530) in the garb of a secular priest. His graduation six weeks later was not as unusual as it now seems, but is proof of serious medical studies. In Rome, as personal physician to Cardinal Jean du Bellay, he obtained (1536) absolution from his irregularities and, by an agreed subterfuge, entered the Cardinal's Benedictine monastery at Saint-Maure-les-Fossés, just as it was about to be secularized. He was then named a supplementary prebendary canon. Toward the end of his life (1551) he was nominated to the cure of souls at Saint-Martin-de-Meudon, but never resided. He resigned the living on Jan. 9, 1553. He was the father of a son who died in infancy, and of two other children, legitimated by Paul III. His principal works were: *Pantagruel* (1532), *Gargantua* (1534), *Tiers livre de Pantagruel* (1546), and *Quart livre de Pantagruel* (partial version 1548, revised and completed 1552). The *Cinquiesme livre de Pantagruel* (1564), partially published 1562 as *l'Isle sonnante,* could not as it stands have been by Rabelais. Some scholars accept various parts as his, but their authenticity is not yet proved. His minor works include almanacs and prognostications (mainly evangelical and satirical in intention) and editions of works by Galen, Hippocrates, Manardi, etc. Several of his letters are extant.

Patrons and Persecution. At various times Bp. Geoffroi d'Estissac, Cardinal Jean du Bellay and his brother Guillaume, Margaret of Navarre, and Cardinal Odet de Châtilion protected Rabelais. He corresponded with Erasmus and Budé and had many learned friends, including the humanist lawyer Tiraqueau. Despite this support, all his novels were condemned on publication by the Sorbonne, the Parlement de Paris, or both, with the possible exception of *Gargantua* (condemned certainly in 1543). Francis I enjoyed his works, considered them free from heresy, and gave a fulsome privilege to the *Tiers livre.* Some months after the *Affaire des placards* (October 1534), when posters attacking the ''idolatry'' of the Mass led to severe repercussions, Rabelais abruptly abandoned his post of doctor to the Hôtel-Dieu at Lyons and for a time ''disappeared.'' Later hostile theological reaction to the *Tiers livre* caused him to flee to the imperial town of Metz. After the condemnation of the *Quart livre,* it was rumored that he was imprisoned; this is possible, but unlikely. He was buried with honor in St. Paul's, Paris.

François Rabelais. (Archive Photos)

Rabelais's Ideology. Few scholars now discern hidden atheism in his work, and his ''obscenity,'' though still shocking, is seen to serve a genuine artistic purpose. *Pantagruel* and, to some extent, *Gargantua* (both published anonymously) were presented as popular tales of giants, but their serious intent was soon recognized. In them Rabelais satirized the monastic ideal and the superstitious veneration of saints, as well as old-fashioned education and university theology. His liberal evangelism owes much to Erasmus and Lefèvre d'Étaples, and something to Luther, though Rabelais was no Lutheran. He strongly advocated the study of classical languages and thought, including law and medicine, and showed a pronounced preference for Plato over Aristotle. He opposed aggressive wars and the spread of the Gospel by force. His praise of fertile marriage was partly antimonastic in intention, but deeply Christian, indeed scholastic, in exposition. Perhaps under Lutheran influence, he tends at times to equate *fides* with *fiducia* (''faith'' with ''trust''), though in some ways his ideas retain a Franciscan mark.

Both Lutheran and Franciscan influences on his thought, however, have probably been overstressed. In the *Tiers livre* he exploits the renewed literary interest in matrimony, feminism, and antifeminism as a means of mocking ιλαυτία (self love), and he does it in the name of Christian Platonism and Stoicism, though with cynical and skeptical undertones. His evangelical propaganda is less overtly aggressive, except in his mockery of the doctrine of contrition and his condemnation of clandestine marriage. He follows the Reformers in denying the validity of ecclesiastical marriage law in the name of equity, natural law, and imperial law, with some reference to the Old Testament. He jests at Galen's opinions on the womb and the nature of semen, and advocates a Platonic-Christian morality that acknowledges the urgency of the sex-instinct in woman, but denies its necessary dominance in man. In the *Quart livre,* with the support of Cardinal de Châtillon, Rabelais took advantage of the crisis between the Holy See and the French Court (1551) to mock the Council of Trent as the *''concile national de Chésil''* (Hebrew *Kessil,* fool).

Under cover of GALLICANISM, he championed extreme evangelical opinions and followed the Reformers in calling the papal party worshippers of a *Deus in terris,* but without suggesting, as they did, that the pope desired the excesses of such worship. He satirized the DECRETALS as Antichrist's parody of the Scriptures, rejecting, as based on their ''usurped authority'' alone, all monastic orders, papal claims to rights over princes and universities, as well as the doctrines of the Keys, purgatory, and supererogation. He mocked his comic bishop for asserting that we must love our neighbors as ourselves provided they are not heretics. Rabelais was strongly anti-Calvinist, rejecting, in the name of SYNERGISM, both the enslaved will of Lutheranism and Calvinistic predestination. His theology, like that of many Christian humanists, was syncretistic with Pan as its symbol in the *Quart livre.* The dying Pan of Plutarch was, for Rabelais, no devil but Christ Himself, the Good Shepherd (Πάν), the Christian's All (Πᾶν). Despite his outspoken satire, the question of his orthodoxy, within the wide tolerance of his day in France, remains to be settled.

Bibliography: *Oeuvres,* ed. A. LEFRANC et al., 5 v. (Paris 1913–31); v.6 (Geneva 1955–), v.6 contains opening chs. of *Le Quart livre;* for complete text and recent scholarship, with listed eds. of individual works, see *Le Quart livre,* ed. R. MARCHEL (Geneva 1947). J. PLATTARD, *La Vie et l'oeuvre de Rabelais* (Paris 1939). L. P. FEBVRE, *Le Problème de l'incroyance au XVI*[e] *siècle: La Religion de Rabelais* (rev. ed. Paris 1947). M. A. SCREECH, *Rabelaisian Marriage* (London 1958); *L'Évangélisme de Rabelais* (Geneva 1959). A. J. KRAILSHEIMER, *Rabelais and the Franciscans* (Oxford 1963).

[M. A. SCREECH]

RACCOLTA

An Italian word meaning collection or gathering. It is frequently used in canonical language to signify a collection of documents regarding a particular subject, such as religious, pastors, schools, or the like. It was used in this sense in the title of the 1898 official collection of the now extinct Congregation of Indulgences and Sacred Relics, as it had been in the earliest modern private prototype of such a work, the *Raccolta di orazione e pie opere per le quali sono state concesse dai Sommi Pontefici le SS Indulgenze,* composed by Telesforo Galli, a consultor of the Congregation of Indulgences in 1807. Two new editions published by Aloysius Prinzivalli, substitute secretary of the congregation, were specially approved by a decree of Dec. 15, 1854, and it was this collection that was translated into English by Ambrose St. John of the Birmingham Oratory, with approval by Cardinal Wiseman Oct. 23, 1856, in virtue of a faculty conceded to him by Pius IX on Feb. 3, 1856. The translation was entitled *The Raccolta.*

Soon thereafter, however, the congregation itself published an authentic collection, (June 3, 1877). This was in Italian and had the same long title as the original work of Galli, as also did the official authentic collections of 1886 and 1898. The Jesuits at Woodstock made a translation of the first official collection of 1877 with permission of the congregation contained in a letter of Cardinal Oreglia, prefect of the Congregation, guaranteeing the fidelity of the translation. It also used the title *Raccolta.*

Later official Italian collections (in Latin) were called *Collectio Precum Piorumque Operum* and were translated in later editions of the Oratory *Raccolta,* still retaining the Italian name. A revised collection called *Preces et Pia Opera Indulgentiis Ditata* was promulgated by the Apostolic Penitentiary by order of Pius XI on Dec. 31, 1937. It was translated into English by Joseph P. Christopher and Charles E. Spence and published by Benziger Brothers in 1943. This, too, retained the Italian name ''raccolta'' as did the edition of 1957, which contained the translations of the ''Enchiridion Indulgentiarum'' first promulgated by the Sacred Penitentiary on Jan. 30, 1950, by command of Pius XII, but reformed and promulgated anew on March 3, 1952.

[M. T. SMITH/EDS.]

RACINE, JEAN BAPTISTE

French dramatist whose works represent the peak of dramatic art in 17th-century France; b. La Ferté-Milon, baptized Dec. 22, 1639; d. Paris, April 21, 1699. Born of bourgeois parents, Racine was orphaned at the age of three, and raised principally by grandparents. In 1649, through family connections with PORT-ROYAL he entered that important Jansenist school, where he received an excellent education, particularly in the classics. With the exception of two years spent at the college of the city of Beauvais, Racine remained under the guidance of the men at Port-Royal until 1658. He was thus witness to the turbulent period (1656–58) when the Jansenist-Jesuit quarrel was highlighted by the appearance of PASCAL's *Les Lettres Provinciales*.

Racine left Port-Royal for Paris in 1658. There, in his desire to succeed, he dedicated to the queen an ode entitled, ''La Nymphe de la Seine'' (1660), which attracted the attention of Colbert, Prime Minister of Louis XIV. However, Racine's two attempts at play writing (*L'Amasie* and *Les Amours d'Ovide*) were rejected, and on the possibility of obtaining an ecclesiastical benefice he went to Uzès in Languedoc. Despite the important diocesan post held there by his uncle Antonin Sconin, Racine's efforts were fruitless and he returned to Paris and the stage.

The Young Dramatist. In 1664 Molière's troupe presented the first of Racine's tragedies ever to be performed, *La Thébaïde,* which was followed in 1665 by *Alexandre le Grand.* Both plays were in the French classical tradition as practiced by Corneille and Quinault, but neither exhibited more than traces of the genius he was to show in *Andromaque* and for which he became famous. However, in his drive to satisfy his profound ambitions, Racine made an enemy of Molière by asking a rival theater, the Hôtel de Bourgogne, to present *Alexandre* in direct competition with Molière's production. It was also during this period that Racine quarreled openly with his former masters at Port-Royal because of their general condemnation of theatrical spectacles.

Andromaque (1667) marked Racine's departure from the tradition of heroic tragedy; for in this play he introduced a new concept of the tragic motive of passion, different from the ennobling sentiment of Corneille and the older generation. *Andromaque* revealed a violent, destructive love that consumed all in its desire to possess the beloved; it was this intimate rapport between passion and hatred that marked the innovation.

In 1668 Racine turned briefly to the writing of comedy and produced a satire on the legal profession, *Les Plaideurs,* that owed much to the *Wasps* of Aristophanes. But he returned to his particular domain in 1669 with *Britannicus,* in which he displayed his mastery of Corneille's favorite type of drama—tragedy with a Roman background. Yet within the typically Cornelian framework, the same explosive passions are at work that were discovered in *Andromaque.* A struggle for power forms the basis for an intensely cruel plot in which innocent intermediaries are caught and sacrificed to the needs of the two predatory creatures who seek complete domination—the ruthless Agrippine and her sadistic son Néron.

Jean Baptiste Racine.

Despite the relative lack of success of *Britannicus,* Racine remained with Roman history for one more play, *Bérénice* (1670). This time his efforts were crowned with a double triumph; *Bérénice* was an unqualified success at the box office and Racine saw his own adaptation of the Titus and Bérénice story preferred to Corneille's (*Tite et Bérénice*), which was first presented only eight days after the première of Racine's version. Despite much bitter criticism, largely based on antagonism toward Racine and personal affection for Corneille, Racine emerged victorious in the public eye.

After the Sophoclean simplicity of *Bérénice,* with its three characters and bloodless, though definitely tragic, conclusion, Racine once again looked to the active, mobile kind of plot, characterized by passion and death. The result was *Bajazet* (1672). He also endeavored to profit from the surge of interest in things exotic by having the action of the play performed entirely within the confines of a royal Turkish harem. Racine's personal satisfaction with the public and royal reception of his play may be measured by the fact that in the preface to the printed edition of *Bajazet* he did not deign to defend at length his creation against the inevitable criticism of rivals. It was a self-assured Racine who composed that relatively short preliminary discourse, free from the acid polemics that characterized earlier Racinian prefaces.

The Master Dramatist. Racine was at the pinnacle of his fame during the years from 1670 to 1677, and two events in 1673 are indicative: his reception to the Académie Française on January 12 and the popularity of *Mithridate* (Louis XIV's favorite Racinian tragedy), which was performed shortly thereafter. However, in Mithridate himself Racine has attempted to create a hero of Cornelian proportions, and a certain uneasiness about depicting a figure foreign to his own conception of the "fallen" hero—the man endowed with great strength who nevertheless is crushed—may serve to explain the drama's lack of intensity in comparison with preceding Racinian endeavors.

Iphigénie (1674) was the occasion of Racine's return to Greek subjects, particularly as dramatized by Euripides. Racine also wished to profit from the popularity of French opera and the consequent vogue of mythological subjects by producing a work in which not only the strong flavor of Greek fatality but also the very musicality of the verses recalled Greek tragedy with its lyrical moments of choral declamation.

With the death of Molière (1673) and the decline of Corneille, Racine was the undisputed master of the Parisian stage. Nevertheless, two and a half years elapsed before his next production, *Phèdre,* which stands at the summit of Racinian tragedy. In *Phèdre,* which owed much of its material to many predecessors, ancient and modern alike, Racine fashioned a drama about an uncontrollable passion that led not only to an event of catastrophic import (the death of Hippolytus), but also to the tragic torment. *Phèdre* is the culmination of a Racinian tendency to infuse an awful lucidity into the heroine (or hero), so that she is fully aware of her moral degradation. Moreover, by employing a mythological background Racine greatly enlarged the scope of his tragedy. This factor, plus Phèdre's acute self-consciousness, give substance to her cry that she has blackened the universe by an incestuous desire, and that the ritual of her death (on stage) is therefore tantamount to a cosmic rite of purification.

The years from 1677 to 1689, known as his *retraite,* formed a dramatic pause in the creative life of Racine. Among the most likely reasons for this period of silence are his reconciliation with the Jansenists and principally his appointment, at the same time as Boileau, as historiographer of the King. Racine's advancement in royal circles apparently inspired in him little inclination to continue his association with actors and with his "trade," as dramaturgy was considered in his day. Moreover, it was precisely in 1677 that he began his life as husband, and later, as devoted father of five girls and two boys, in a household where religion and moral principles were closely observed.

At the request of Mme. de Maintenon, Racine composed, in 1689, a play destined for the edification of the students at Saint-Cyr, a school for young girls. This was *Esther,* a three-act religious tragedy with chorus. *Athalie* (1691) was also written for the girls under Madame de Maintenon's care; and the title character is one of Racine's most powerful creations. Because of the imposing stature of Athalie, her struggle against God's will assumes titanic proportions. Thus, even when inevitably defeated, she still evokes admiration by the very magnitude of her effort.

Racine was never again strongly tempted to undertake the composition of another dramatic work, but he did continue to write, as the four beautiful *Cantiques Spirituels* (1694) and his *Abrégé de l'Histoire de Port-Royal* (not published until 1742–67) attest. It was only, however, in the last two years that remained to him (1698–99) that he irrevocably deserted the mundane existence of the courtier for the scrupulously principled life compatible with the Jansenist point of view. He died in Paris and was buried, according to his wish, in the cemetery of Port-Royal-des-Champs.

The conception of the human condition discovered in Racine's plays is a tragic one: man, deceived into believing that his acts can be efficacious, is frustrated and finally crushed by his collision with a ruthless destiny. Some have referred to this view as Jansenist, because of Racine's background; but this would not seem to be necessarily the case, since, for example, approximately the same tragic conception may be found in the works of Seneca. What is certain, however, is that life as tragedy never has found a more eloquent nor profound expression than in Racinian drama.

Racine's Genius. The most striking elements of any Racinian play are his characters; they are finely nuanced, passionate models of intensity whose very suffering excites sympathy and pathos (*le pathétique*) while their stature summons admiration. Creations such as Oreste, Hermione, Néron, Athalie, and above all Phèdre are truly unforgettable.

Racinian tragedy is well constructed to incite the many and violent emotional reactions of its characters, because it is composed with crisis at its center. Everything underlines and forces the tension of the crisis to the point of explosion: the location of the action in one defined area, the limitation of the time span to one day, and the strict subordination of details to the central conflict. Unlike Shakespearean theater, Racinian drama uses little scenic effect and employs relatively few physical actions to aid the plot's development; it remains for language to sustain the play, and Racinian verse is celebrated both for its poetical beauty and its functional use in the drama.

Indeed, the whole trend of French classical literature seemed to have paved the way for Racine so that on his arrival he found all the elements in readiness: lucidity, simplicity, concision, intellectuality, and universality. In fact, Racine may be considered as principally responsible for the death of classical French tragedy because of the perfection of his work: his art was inimitable and served only to frustrate the creative efforts of post-Racinian classical dramatists, such as Voltaire. Racinian tragedy thus remains the most exalted form of French art in a century consciously striving for artistic perfection.

Bibliography: J. B. RACINE, *Oeuvres Complètes,* ed. P. MESNARD, 10 v. (2d ed. Paris 1885–88); *Oeuvres Complètes,* ed. R. PICARD, 2 v. (Paris 1950–52). A. ADAM, *Histoire de la littérature française au 17e siècle,* 5 v. (Paris 1958–61) v.4. R. PICARD, *La Carrière de Jean Racine* (new rev. ed. Paris 1961). P. MOREAU, *Racine: L'Homme et l'oeuvre* (Paris 1943). J. GIRAUDOUX, *Racine* (Paris 1950). T. MAULNIER, *Racine* (Paris 1958). P. BÉNICHOU, *Morales du Grand Siècle* (Paris 1948). J. POMMIER, *Aspects de Racine suivi de l'histoire littéraire d'un couple tragique* (Paris 1954). E. VINAVER, *Racine and Poetic Tragedy,* tr. P. MANSELL JONES (New York 1959). J. C. LAPP, *Aspects of Racinian Tragedy* (Toronto 1955). J. D. HUBERT, *Essai d'exégèse Racinienne* (Paris 1956).

[R. W. TOBIN]

RACLOT, MATHILDE

Missionary and educator of the Ladies of St. Maur; b. Surauville (Vosges), 1814; d. Tokyo, 1911. At 18 years of age she entered the Institute of the Teachers of Charity of the Holy Child Jesus, founded by N. Barré and called the Ladies of St. Maur. She distinguished herself as an educator at Bagnoles and also at Bergiers. In 1852 she left for Malay at the head of a group of her sisters. They debarked at Penang and diligently devoted themselves to the urgent work there, founding orphanages, nurseries, and schools for the poor. Then she went to Japan, where she had been called by the vicar apostolic in 1872. She founded a house in Tokyo in 1875, and in Shidsuoka in 1903.

[J. VERBILLION]

RADBOD OF UTRECHT, ST.

Monk, bishop; b. near Namur, Belgium, *c.* 850; d. Ootmarsum, Netherlands, Nov. 29, 917. Son of a leading Frankish family, he was educated in Cologne and at the court of Emperor Charles the Bald. In either 899 or 900, Radbod became bishop of Utrecht, but he was driven out the next year by the NORMANS. Retreating only a few miles, to Deventer, he carried on not only the work of the diocese but also the Utrecht tradition of learning, as he wrote poems (*Monumenta Germaniae Historica: Poetae* 4:160–173), homilies (*Patrologia Latina* 132), and history, and a work on St. Martin (*Monumenta Germaniae Historica: Scriptores* 15:1239–44). From 1905 to 1923 the present Catholic University of Nijmegen bore St. Radbod's name.

Feast: Nov. 29.

Bibliography: *Analecta Bollandiana* 6 (1887) 5–15. M. MANITIUS, *Geschichte der lateinischen Literatur des Mittelalters* 1:603–604. A. BUTLER, *The Lives of the Saints,* rev. ed. H. THURSTON and D. ATTWATER 4:446. P. H. WINKELMAN, *Lexikon für Theologie und Kirche*[2], ed. J. HOFER and K. RAHNER (2nd new ed. Freiburg 1957–65) 8:963.

[R. BALCH]

RADEGUNDA, ST.

Queen of the Franks; d. Aug. 13, 587. Radegunda, born a Thuringian princess, fell as booty to the Frankish King Chlothar I (531) who had her educated and eventually married her. The murder of Radegunda's brother occasioned her leaving Chlothar to enter religion (*c.* 555). Chlothar helped her build a convent at Poitiers where she gathered many highborn converts (200 in 587), assembled a large collection of relics (notably one of the True CROSS, which gave the convent its name), introduced the rule of CAESARIUS OF ARLES (*c.* 570), and, having installed an abbess, strove to live as a simple nun. She maintained excellent relations with her stepsons, though not with the local bishop, and befriended the poet FORTUNATUS. Popular canonization directly followed her death, and pilgrims still seek her tomb in Poitiers.

Feast: August 13.

Bibliography: Sources. GREGORY OF TOURS, *Historiarum libri,* 3.4, 7; 6.29, 34; 7.36; 9.2, 39–42, *Monumenta Germaniae Historica* Section: Scriptoes rerum Merovingivarum 1.1; Berlin 1951) 99–100, 103–105, 295–297, 304–305, 358, 415, 460–474; *De gloria confessorum* 104, *ibid.* 1 (1885) 814–816. V. FORTUNATUS and BAUDONIVIA, *De vita sanctae Radegundis libri duo, ibid.* 2 (1888) 358–395. V. FORTUNATUS, *Carmina, Monumenta Germaniae Historica.* Auctores antiquissimi 4; Berlin 1881); *La vie de sainte Radegonde par Fortunat,* ed. R. FAVREAU (Paris 1995). Literature. O. M. DALTON, ed. and tr., *The History of the Franks . . . ,* 2 v. (Oxford 1927) 1:67–69. A. M. ZIMMERMANN, *Kalendarium Benedictinum: Die Heiligen und Seligen des Benediktinerorderns und seiner Zweige* (Metten 1933–38) 2:571–572. R. AIGRAIN, *Sainte Radegonde* (new ed. Poitiers 1952). B. PISCHEL, *Radegunde: zur europäischen Volkskunde* (Frankfurt 1997). D. KLEINMANN, *Radegunde: eine europäische Heilige* (Graz 1998).

[W. GOFFART]

RADICAL THEOLOGY

Radical theology was the name applied in the 1960s to a widely publicized current in American Protestant

"Life of Saint Radegunda: Radegunda at Mass." (©Archivo Iconografico, S.A./CORBIS)

theology which was fundamentally skeptical about modern man's ability to speak meaningfully about God. The theologians most prominently identified with the movement were William Hamilton, Paul Van Buren, and Thomas J. J. Altizer. Several other theologians were closely associated with the movement in the popular mind although their works were less radical in character. The British theologian, John A. T. Robinson, and the American theologian, Harvey Cox, shared a good deal of the radical theologians' skepticism and, like the radical theologians, Robinson and Cox advocated a religion of secular involvement rather than a religion of otherworldly salvation. Gabriel Vahanian, although not one of the radical theologians, shared their preoccupation with the challenge of contemporary secularism to Christian faith.

The theological divergencies among the radical theologians were too great for them to form a school. Nevertheless, their works are marked by a number of common convictions. Faith in the transcendent God of traditional Christian theology is no longer possible for the contemporary man. The theologian can no longer work in the church. His concerns are no longer the classical churchly concerns: liturgy, prayer, otherworldly salvation. He must move out into the world, since, like other contemporary men, his fundamental preoccupation is the struggle to maintain human values in the context of modern secular society. He can no longer speak of a God who has become meaningless to contemporary man but he must still speak of Christ. The Christ of the radical theologian, however, is the purely human Christ who is the man for others. Christ's function in contemporary society is to serve as a supremely inspiring human example, Christ is "a place to be" in the struggle for human values.

The shift away from theological activism at the end of the civil–rights struggle brought a decline of interest in radical theology. As a movement it did not survive the sixties, but the issues which it brought to prominence in America, e.g., the knowability of God, contemporary

Christology, eschatology, and social activity, continue to occupy the attention of contemporary theologians.

See Also: DEATH OF GOD THEOLOGY.

Bibliography: T. J. J. ALTIZER, *The Gospel of Christian Atheism* (Philadelphia 1966); ed., *Toward a New Christianity: Readings in the Death of God Theology* (New York 1967). T. J. J. ALTIZER and W. HAMILTON, *Radical Theology and the Death of God* (Indianapolis 1966). H. COX, *The Secular City* (New York 1965). W. HAMILTON, *The New Essence of Christianity* (New York 1961); ''The Death of God Theology,'' *Christian Scholar* 48: 27–48; ''The Shape of Radical Theology,'' *Christian Century* 82:1219–22. J. A. T. ROBINSON, *Honest to God* (Philadelphia 1963); *Exploration into God* (Palo Alto, Calif. 1967). G. VAHANIAN, *The Death of God* (New York 1961); *No Other God* (New York 1966); ed., *The God is Dead Debate* (New York 1967). P. VAN BUREN, *The Secular Meaning of the Gospel* (New York 1963); *Theological Explorations* (New York 1968). L. GILKEY, *Naming the Whirlwind: The Renewal of God Language* (Indianapolis 1969) 107–145. V. MEHTA, *The New Theologians* (New York 1966). T. W. OGLETREE, *The Death of God Controversy* (Nashville 1966).

[G. MCCOOL]

RAFFEINER, JOHN STEPHEN

Pioneer missionary; b. Mals, Austrian Tyrol, Dec. 26, 1785; d. Brooklyn, N.Y., July 16, 1861. His studies for the priesthood, at the Tyrolean Benedictine abbey in Fiecht and later in Rome, were interrupted in 1809 by the Napoleonic wars. He then turned to medicine, obtained his degree in 1813, and conducted a highly successful practice as physician and surgeon in Italy, Austria, and Switzerland. After resuming his theological studies, he was ordained at Brixen in the Tyrol on May 1, 1825. He served as assistant and pastor in his native diocese of Brixen until, in response to an appeal of Bishop Edward Fenwick of Cincinnati, Ohio, through the Leopoldine Association, he volunteered for missionary work in the United States.

Upon his arrival in 1833, he was persuaded by Bishop John Dubois to remain in New York City to minister to the fast-growing colonies of German Catholics there. With personal funds earned in his previous medical career, he rented a carpenter shop as a temporary chapel and later leased a former Baptist church, where he formally organized the first New York City congregation of German Catholics. In 1834 he bought land from John Jacob Astor for St. Nicholas's Church, New York City, which was dedicated in 1836. He visited German congregations at Macopin and elsewhere in New Jersey; at Albany, Utica, Salina, Syracuse, Rochester, Buffalo, and other missions in New York State; and, at the request of Bishop Benedict Fenwick, at Boston, where he founded Holy Trinity Church, dedicated in 1844. In all these visitations he had notable success in settling national difficulties and disputes between congregations and pastors arising from the prevalent system of incorporating church property under boards of lay trustees.

Among the 30 churches he was instrumental in establishing, including the above, were St. John's, New York City (1840), and Holy Trinity, Williamsburg, Brooklyn (1841). In 1843 Bishop John Hughes of New York appointed him vicar-general for the German Catholics of the diocese, an office in which he continued until his death. In addition, he remained pastor of Holy Trinity and acted as vicar-general of Bishop John Loughlin from the time Brooklyn was separated from New York as a new diocese (1853).

Bibliography: M. A. CORRIGAN, ''Register of the Clergy Laboring in the Archdiocese of New York from Early Missionary Times to 1885,'' *Historical Records and Studies of the U.S. Catholic Historical Society of New York* 7 (June 1914): 201. T. F. MEEHAN, ''Very Rev. Johann Stephan Raffeiner, V. G.,'' *ibid.* 9 (June 1916): 161–175. ''Documents: The Schwenninger Memorial,'' *American Benedictine Review* 10 (1959): 107–135; *ibid.* 11 (1960): 154–178.

[J. A. REYNOLDS]

RAFOLS, MARÍA, BL.

Virgin, foundress of the Institute of the Sisters of Charity of St Anne; b. Nov. 5, 1781, Villafranca del Penedés, Spain; d. Aug. 30, 1853, Saragossa, Spain.

Although María was born into a working-class family, her innate intelligence won her a place at a boarding school in Barcelona. Upon graduating she joined 12 other young women in an apostolate of charity under the direction of Father Juan Bonal, administrator of Our Lady of Grace Hospital in Saragossa, which cared for the sick, the disabled, and the mentally ill. Although Bonal appointed María superior in 1804 (age 23), the group made no formal profession until 1825 when Rafols gained formal recognition of the community.

During the devastation of the Napoleonic wars in Spain (1808–13), Rafols rendered heroic service to the sick, wounded, and the children. Imprisoned during the Carlist War, she was released and returned to her foundling home, where she died at age 71. A miracle attributed to the intercession of the woman John Paul II called a ''Heroine of Charity'' was approved by the Vatican, July 6, 1993. That same pope beatified her, Oct. 16, 1994.

Feast: Nov. 5.

Bibliography: G. GROOT, De omstreden heiligheid van madre Maria Rafols, *NRC– Handelsblad*, Aug. 19, 1987. G. L. BOUE, Moeder Maria Rafols, *Catolica* (Apr. 28, 2001) v. 6.

[K. I. RABENSTEIN]

RAFQA DE HIMLAYA, ST.

Maronite nun; also called Rebecca ar-Rayyes, ''The Little Flower of Lebanon,'' and the ''Purple Rose''; b. Himlaya (near Bikfaya, Mten), Lebanon, June 29, 1832; d. Grabta, March 23?, 1914. Born on the feast of St. Peter, her parents named her Boutrosiya (''Petronilla''). Following her mother's death in 1838, Petra's father, Mourad Saber Shabaq al-Rayes, remarried (1841). Petra lived and worked as a domestic in Syria, 1843–47.

When it was time to decide her future, her stepmother wanted her to marry her brother (Petra's step-brother), and an aunt, to marry her son (Petra's cousin). While the women quarreled, Petra became a Maryamat postulant at the convent of Our Lady of Rescue at Bikfaya. Upon Petra's acceptance as a novice, Feb. 9, 1855, she was given the name Anissa (''Agnes'').

She was sent to a convent in Ghazir where, while working in the kitchen, she learned to read and write in her spare time. Later she studied at Bait-Shahib, Shuwayr, Hammana, and elsewhere. She was teaching at Dair al-Qamar during the massacre of Christians (1860). When the monastery was attacked, she saved a Christian boy being pursued by armed soldiers by throwing her cloak over him to hide him.

In 1871 her order was united with another to form the Order of the Sacred Hearts of Jesus and Mary. Each sister was offered the choice of staying or leaving. After prayer Sister Anissa decided to become a nun in the ascetic Baladiya Order of the Maronites at Saint Simon Convent at El–Qarn, where she was known as Boutrosiya from Himlaya. At the time she made her perpetual vows, Aug. 25, 1873, she chose the name Rafqa (''Rebecca''), after her saintly mother.

Sister Rafqa was transferred in 1897 to the convent, Mar Youssef ad–Daher (Saint Joseph of Grabta). Under obedience to her new superior Mother Doumit, Rafqa related the story of her life. She told how in 1885 after praying to share in Christ's suffering, she began to suffer loss of sight and a crippling bone disease. By 1907 Sister Rafqa was totally blind, paralyzed, and in constant pain, but in spite of her cross she remained full of joy until her death seven years later. Rafqa was buried at Saint Joseph of Grabata where she died.

Sister Rafqa was beatified in Rome, Nov. 17, 1985, by Pope John Paul II. Following the acceptance of the required miracle on July 1, 2000, Rafqa was canonized as the first female saint of Lebanon on June 10, 2001.

Feast: Nov. 17 (Maronites); March 23.

Bibliography: F. M. ZAYEK, *Rafka, the Blind Mystic of Lebanon* (Still River, Mass. 1980).

[R. ABOU MOUSSA]

RAHNER, HUGO

Historian and theologian; b. Pfullendorf, Germany, May 3, 1900; d. Munich, Dec. 21, 1968. He entered the Jesuit novitiate of the North German Jesuit Province in 1919, three years before his younger brother Karl, who was later to become a more widely known theologian. Hugo Rahner studied at the University of Innsbruck, Austria, and received doctorates in philosophy and theology.

From 1935 he taught at Innsbruck, specializing in early Church history and patrology but writing on a wide variety of topics. In *Theology of Proclamation* (1939; Eng. tr. 1968) he contended that the priest's most important task was ''the reconstruction of our traditional knowledge, the fashioning out of our dogmatic theology what can be of immediate use in performing the great work to which we are called—preaching'' (pp. 12–13). In *Man at Play* (1949; Eng. tr. 1965) he analyzed the significance of play from a religious standpoint. The theme of Mary as a symbol of the Church was developed in his book *Our Lady and the Church* (1951; Eng. tr. 1961). He set forth a Christian humanism in *Greek Myths and Christian Mystery* (1957; Eng. tr. 1963), endorsing the action of the early Church in preserving the culture of Greece and Rome. He also sought to show that the piety of the ancient world had been incorporated and sanctified by the Church. The founder of his order was the subject of several of his literary efforts. He wrote *The Spirituality of St. Ignatius Loyola* (1949; Eng. tr. 1953) and *Ignatius the Theologian* (1964; Eng. tr. 1968), edited *Letters to Women by Ignatius Loyola* (1965; Eng. tr. 1960), and with the photographer Leonard von Matt produced *St. Ignatius of Loyola: A Pictorial Biography* (1956). With his brother Karl he wrote *Prayers for Meditation (1962).*

Bibliography: J. HOLDT, *Hugo Rahner: Sein geschichts–und symboltheologisches Denken* (Paderborn 1997). K. H. NEUFELD, *Die Bruder Rahner: Eine Biographie* (Freiburg im Breisgau 1994). A. P. KUSTERMANN and K. H. NEUFELD, *''Gemeinsame Arbeit in bruderlicher Liebe'': Hugo und Karl Rahner; Dokumente und Wurdigung ihrer Weggemeinschaft* (Stuttgart 1993).

[T. EARLY]

RAHNER, KARL

German theologian; b. Freiburg im Breisgau, Germany, March 5, 1904; d. Innsbruck, Austria, March 30, 1984. One of seven children of Karl Rahner, gymnasium professor, and Luise Trescher. After concluding his secondary education he entered the Society of Jesus' novitiate at Feldkirch in Vorarlberg, Austria, on April 20, 1922, three years after his brother Hugo. During his philosophical studies from 1924 to 1927, first at Feldkirch, then at Pullach near Munich, he was influenced especially by Joseph MARÉCHAL's Thomistic response to the thought of Immanuel Kant. After teaching Latin at the Feldkirch Novitiate, where Alfred Delp was one of his students, Rahner studied theology at Valkenburg in the Netherlands (1929–33). There his earlier reading of Christian spirituality was deepened through study of the Apostolic Fathers, the patristic period, and medieval thinkers such as BONAVENTURE. He was ordained a priest on July 26, 1932, and pursued his Jesuit tertianship at Saint Andrea in Carinthia, Austria (1933–34).

Early Foundations. Intended by his Jesuit superiors to be a professor of the history of philosophy, Rahner was sent to the University of Freiburg im Breisgau to prepare a doctorate. He attended Martin Heidegger's seminars with other Catholic students such as Max Müller, Gustav Siewerth, Bernard Welte, and Johannes B. Lotz. When his doctoral director, Martin Honecker, rejected his interpretation of Saint Thomas' epistemology, Rahner returned to Innsbruck. In the course of the academic year 1936–37, he was able to satisfy the doctoral and post-doctoral requirements for teaching in the University's faculty of theology and began to lecture the following year. After the Nazis abolished the theology faculty (July 1938) and the Jesuit college (October 1939), Rahner moved to Vienna to work under Karl Rudolph at the Pastoral Institute. For five years he served as a consultant there, also offering courses and occasional lectures. In the final year of World War II he became a pastor at Mariakirchen in Lower Bavaria.

For three years after the war he taught dogmatic theology at Berchmanskolleg in Pullach and then, in August 1948, returned to Innsbruck's faculty of theology, which had just been reopened. Named an *Ordinarius* the following summer, he remained at Innsbruck through the winter semester of 1964, teaching a cycle of courses on the doctrines of creation and original sin; grace and justification; faith, hope and charity; and the Sacraments of Penance, Anointing of the Sick, and Orders. In the early 1950s his doctoral students included Adolf Darlap, Walter Kern, Herbert Vorgrimler, and Johann Baptist Metz.

In these foundational years of Rahner's theological career his interests ranged from the primary philosophical studies elaborated in his doctoral dissertation and his Salzburg lectures on the philosophy of religion, through classic early publications on prayer and the Christian life, to highly technical re-examinations of questions long considered settled by the neo-scholastic theology that dominated most of Catholic thought at the time, and certainly its major official pronouncements. His Freiburg thesis *Geist in Welt* (1939) sought a contemporary retrieval of the Thomistic insight into sense experience as the enduring ground for human knowledge. Heidegger's question of Being also helped to guide his understanding of religion in its historical dependence on the transcendent self-disclosure of a personal God (*Hörer des Wortes* 1941). His first years in Innsbruck saw the publication of the meditations collected in *Encounters with Silence* (1938) and his Lenten sermons in postwar Munich appeared in an eloquent book *On Prayer* (1949).

Karl Rahner. (©Bettmann/CORBIS)

But it was his probing analyses of human existence in a world permeated by divine grace that gave Rahner's early writings their explosive force. Emphasizing the dynamics of knowledge and freedom yet guided most deeply by the mystery of God's own gift of self, he reconceived the terms of the relationship between nature and grace, took the conciliar definitions as a starting point rather than an end for christological reflection, and renewed ecclesiology by examining the Church in its origin, its sacramental actualization, and its pastoral practice. When his early theological essays were gathered in the first three volumes of the *Schriften zur Theologie* in 1954, 1955, and 1956 (English translation, *Theological Investigations*), it was clear that a wholly original dialectical mind had appeared on the Catholic scene. During this period his prodigious editorial labors began as well, and he was responsible for four editions of Denzinger's *Enchiridion Symbolorum* (1952–57) and seven editions of *Der Glaube der Kirche in den Urkunden der Lehrverkündigung* (1948–65).

Programmatic Years. A second, programmatic phase coincided roughly with Rahner's work as coeditor for the second edition of *Lexikon für Theologie und Kirche* (1957–65) and his contributions to the preparation and course of the Second Vatican Council. Continuing to teach at Innsbruck, he also lectured extensively, undertook new editorial responsibilities, and for a year (1962–63) was subject to a preliminary censorship regulation from Rome. When the University of Munich in 1963 invited him to become Romano Guardini's successor in the Chair of Christian World View and Philosophy of Religion, he received permission from his Order to accept the call and began teaching in Munich in the summer semester of 1964. In that year also, a monumental two-volume Festschrift, *Gott in Welt,* appeared in honor of his sixtieth birthday.

In view of urgent contemporary questions, Rahner had previously sought to re-appropriate Catholic tradition through a dialectical discussion with scholastic theology and the dogmatic tradition. He probed the implication of these studies and began to write more programmatically on the correlation between theology and anthropology within the historical process. In a world that is always and everywhere invited to union with God (the "supernatural existential,") he argued, responsible theology must conduct a continuing transcendental reflection on the structural conditions of possibility for salvation. In *Schriften IV* (1960) he published seminal essays on mystery, the Incarnation, the theology of symbol, and the hermeneutics of eschatological assertions. An analogy of transcendence unifies these essays materially, envisaging history as a response to the Holy Mystery that draws the world toward eternity through self-communication in Word and Spirit. In the essays of *Schriften V* (1962), the analogy was significantly broadened by his discussion of evolutionary science, world religions, and utopian views of the future. *Schriften VI* (1966) continued his effort to express the Church's new self-understanding in a secularized, pluralistic world.

In these same years Rahner published major essays in pastoral theology (*Sendung und Gnade* 1959; English translation, *Mission and Grace* 1963) and gathered a new collection of essays in spirituality (*Schriften VII* 1967). In 1962 he helped to draft a plan for the *Handbuch der Pastoraltheologie,* which subsequently appeared in five volumes (1964–72) with Rahner as one of its editors. With Heinrich Schlier he conceived the series of *Questiones Disputatae* (1958 ff.) in which appeared some of his own most original contributions on the inspiration of Scripture, the theology of death, the prophetic mission of the Church, the relation between episcopacy and papal primacy, and the renewal of the diaconate. Rahner was a founding member of the editorial committee that planned *Concilium,* chaired its section on pastoral theology, and with Edward Schillebeeckx edited its first issue in 1965. With Adolf Darlap he planned *Sacramentum Mundi* and then supervised its German edition (4 v. 1967–69).

Late Development. When it appeared that Rahner would be unable to direct doctoral students in theology at Munich and also that there were hopes for collaborating on serious reform of theological education elsewhere, he accepted the University of Münster's invitation to become Ordinary Professor of Dogmatics and the History of Dogma and moved to the Westphalian capital in the summer semester of 1967. His years at Münster were fruitful ones during which he continued to reflect on Roman Catholicism's efforts to appropriate Vatican II and developed his response to critics who found his own theological anthropology reductionistic (Hans Urs von Balthasar) or politically impractical (Johann Baptist Metz). Reflecting on the historical concreteness of Christianity and its social responsibility, three further volumes of the *Schriften* (1967, 1970, 1972) offer important insights on theology's place in the human search for meaning; careful situational analysis as a requirement for religious authenticity; the need for a contemporary introduction (mystagogy) to the experience of God; a new understanding of Jesus as humanity's way to God (Christology from below); and reform of the Church as a declericalized, more democratic and socially critical community of service to the world.

Retiring to Munich in 1971, Rahner first lived at the Jesuit writers' residence near Nymphenburg. His major project there was the preparation of his *Grundkurs* or "Introduction to the Idea of Christianity" (1976; English translation, *Foundations of Christian Faith* 1978). Though not an adequate synthesis of his thought, the book does present his typical approach to central topics of Christian doctrine. In the years immediately before it, he published several briefer works on Church reform (1972) and on an ecumenical understanding of Church office (1974), as well as *Schriften XI* (1973), which gathers his early studies on the practice and theology of penance, and *Schriften XII* (1975), which centers on the doctrine of the Holy Spirit. Having participated in the first planning of *Mysterium Salutis* (5 v. 1965–76), he continued to contribute major articles to that new, historically conceived dogmatic theology.

Final Dialectic. After moving to the Berchmanskolleg in Munich and living there for several years, Rahner returned again to Innsbruck and made it his final residence (1981–84). Between 1976 and 1984 he lectured and wrote vigorously, publishing four more volumes of the *Schriften* (v. XII–XVI: 1978, 1980, 1983, 1984); a new edition of his *Dictionary of Theology* (1976); moving essays on prayer (1977), love of neighbor and love of Jesus (1981, 1982); and a dialogical apology for contemporary faith, co-authored with Karl-Heinz Weger (1979). He was also represented by several anthologies, one of which, *The Practice of Faith* (1982), also serves well as a general introduction to his thought. He continued his editorial involvements and, fortunately, allowed himself a new candor in his autobiographical reflections.

Although his final years are remarkably consistent with his previous career, significant developments nevertheless do occur in his consolidation of a thoroughly historical Christology; in his proposal for a ''universal pneumatology'' that might precede Christology in the future; in his arguments for a truly world church and his pleas for ecumenical seriousness; in a series of moral essays on the virtues required of late twentieth-century Christians. Throughout the writings of this last phase, Rahner noted the deepening relativism and skepticism in European culture and attempted to address it. ''The old schoolmaster,'' as he styled himself, also became disturbingly frank about the climate of the Catholic Church, which he had served all his life and would serve to the end.

Systematic theologian though he was, Rahner's thought may be better characterized as a lifelong meditation on the correlation between human experience and God's self-communication. Because of his insistence that theology analyze the conditions of possibility for divine salvific action, he is most often described as a transcendental theologian. Even from the beginning, however, his method required historical research and reflection, since the dynamics of grace always unfold in an unfinished, temporal world where servitude and suffering are all too obvious. In fact, it may be even more exact to see Rahner as a Catholic dialectical theologian. His career presents a personal response to the religious issues of his day and an enduring effort to conceive human history as destined for an eternal communion with God that can only be achieved through the course of time. Thus, a concrete dialectic of transcendence in history characterized his life as well as his thought and influence.

Bibliography: The Theology Department at the University of Innsbruck in Austria maintains the collection of Rahner's manuscripts and papers at the Karl Rahner Archive. For a complete, chronological listing of Rahner's publications *see:* R. BLEISTEIN, ed., *Bibliographie Karl Rahner 1969–1974* (Freiburg 1974). R. BLEISTEIN and E. KLINGER, eds., *Bibliographie Karl Rahner 1924–1969* (Freiburg 1969). A. E. CARR, ''Karl Rahner,'' in D. G. PEERMAN and M. E. MARTY, eds., *A Handbook of Christian Theologians* (Nashville 1984): 519–542. W. V. DYCH, *Karl Rahner* (Collegeville, Minn. 1992). H. D. EGAN, *Karl Rahner: The Mystic of Everyday Life* (New York 1998). P. IMHOF and E. MEUSER, ''Bibliographie Karl Rahner 1979–1984,'' in E. KLINGER and K. WITTSTADT, eds., *Glaube im Prozess* (Freiburg 1984): 854–871. P. IMHOF and H. TREZIAK, ''Bibliographie Karl Rahner 1974–1979,'' in H. VORGRIMLER, ed., *Wagnis Theologie* (Freiburg 1979): 579–597. L. J. O'DONOVAN, ed., *A World of Grace: An Introduction to the Themes and Foundations of Karl Rahner's Theology* (New York 1980). C. D. PEDLEY, ''An English Biographical Aid to Karl Rahner,'' *Heythrop Journal* 15 (1984): 319–365. H. VORGRIMLER, *Understanding Karl Rahner: An Introduction to His Life and Thought* (New York 1986).

[L. J. O'DONOVAN]

RAIMONDI, LUIGI

Cardinal, eighth apostolic delegate to the United States; b. Oct. 25, 1912 in Lussito d'Acqui, a small town in the Piedmont region of northern Italy; d. June 24, 1975 in Rome. At a young age he entered the seminary of the Diocese of Acqui where he received his classical, philosophical and theological training in preparation for the priesthood. He was ordained a priest in Acqui, June 6, 1936.

Immediately after ordination, Fr. Raimondi was sent to Rome by his bishop in order to pursue graduate studies leading to doctorates in canon law and theology. He obtained both at the Pontifical Gregorian University in 1938. While pursuing these studies, he also prepared for a career in the diplomatic service of the Holy See as a student of the Pontifical Ecclesiastical Academy (then the Pontificia Accademia dei Nobili Ecclesiastici). In August of 1938, he received his first diplomatic assignment as secretary of the apostolic nunciature in Guatemala.

In 1942, Monsignor Raimondi became the auditor of the Apostolic Delegation in Washington. He served in this capacity throughout World War II until he was named chargé d'affaires of the Holy See's mission in New Delhi, India. While in Washington, Monsignor Raimondi worked for the then apostolic delegate, Archbishop Amleto Cicognani, and had an opportunity to travel extensively throughout the United States. On Dec. 15, 1953, Monsignor Raimondi was appointed titular archbishop of Tarsus and apostolic nuncio to Haiti. In 1957, he was transferred to Mexico to become apostolic delegate to the church in that country. Ten years later, on June 30, 1967, Pope Paul VI named Archbishop Raimondi the eighth Italian prelate to become apostolic delegate to the American Catholic Church.

During a term of almost six years Archbishop Raimondi ordained 22 new bishops, installed others as residential bishops, and oversaw the establishment of 12 new dioceses and three new archdioceses. His pastoral duties took him to virtually every part of the country and even as far as the Trust Territory of the Pacific and Alaska. Archbishop Raimondi represented Pope Paul VI at the funerals of Senator Robert F. Kennedy in 1968 and former President Dwight D. Eisenhower in 1969. The years of Archbishop Raimondi's tenure were highlighted by the tensions confronting the Church as it groped through the immediate post-conciliar era. As apostolic delegate, Archbishop Raimondi found himself dealing with these situations within the American Catholic Church from his position of papal authority, which he understood to be a function of love and pastoral solicitude.

When Paul VI created 30 new cardinals on March 5, 1973, the apostolic delegate in the United States was among them. Shortly thereafter, Cardinal Raimondi was appointed by the Holy Father to be prefect of the Sacred Congregation for Saints' Causes. In the brief time that Cardinal Raimondi served in this office, he took a very special interest in furthering the canonization process of both Mother Elizabeth Ann Seton, who was to become America's first native saint (1975), and Bishop John Nepomucene Neumann, the fourth bishop of Philadelphia, canonized in 1977. On June 24, 1975, Cardinal Raimondi was suddenly and fatally stricken with a heart attack while at the Vatican.

[J. M. WHALEN]

RAINALD OF BAR, BL.

Abbot; d. Provence, France, 1150. Rainald (Raynald) came from the family of the counts of Bar-sur-Seine and joined the CISTERCIANS at CLAIRVAUX. With the nomination of BERNARD OF CLAIRVAUX he was made abbot of CÎTEAUX *c.* 1133 or 1134, and during his administration, in 1147, the abbeys of OBAZINE and SAVIGNY, with their affiliates, were incorporated into the order. Rainald also participated in the reconciliation of Bernard with ABELARD. The only work presently attributed to him is a part of the *Instituta generalis capituli,* a collection of statutes published, not as was previously thought in 1134, but *c.* 1150 or even perhaps as late as 1151 by Rainald's successor, Goswin (d. 1155). The abbot died in Provence in the course of a regular visitation, but he was buried at Cîteaux. He was honored as early as 1491 in the Cistercian martyrology.

Feast: Dec. 16.

Bibliography: Sources. *Epistola ad Innocentium II, Patrologia Latina,* ed. J. P. MIGNE, 217 v. (Paris 1878–90) 189:671. PETER THE VENERABLE, *Epistola* 4.4, *ibid.* 305. BERNARD, *Epistola* 270.3, *Patrologia Latina,* ed. J. P. MIGNE, 217 v. (Paris 1878–90) 182:475. *Vita Iª s. Bernardi* 4.3, *Patrologia Latina,* ed. J. P. MIGNE, 217 v. (Paris 1878–90) 185:332. CONRAD OF EBERBACH, *Exordium magnum cisterciense* 1.34, ed. B. GRIESSER (Rome 1961) 94–95. Literature. A. M. ZIMMERMANN, *Kalendarium Benedictinum: Die Heiligen und Seligen des Benediktinerorderns und seiner Zweige,* 4 v. (Metten 1933–38) 3:439–441. M. A. DIMIER, *Saint Bernard, pêcheur de Dieu* (Paris 1953) 191–192. J. B. VAN DAMME, "Genèse des *Instituta generalis capituli,*" *Cîteaux* 12 (1961) 28–60. K. SPAHR, *Lexikon für Theologie und Kirche,* ed. J. HOFER and K. RAHNER, 10 v. (2d, new ed. Freiburg 1957–65) 8:978–979.

[M. STANDAERT]

RAINALD OF DASSEL

Imperial chancellor (1156–59) and archbishop of Cologne (1159–67); b. *c.* 1118; d. Aug. 14, 1167. He was a younger son of Saxon Count Rainald I, and was educated at Hildesheim and Paris. Subsequently he held posts at Goslar, Hildesheim, and Münster. He showed himself to be an ardent supporter of Emperor FREDERICK I Barbarossa, was a member of the embassy sent to EUGENE III at Rome in 1153, and became chancellor in 1156. Even after his elevation in 1159 he remained a militant statesman. The basic principle of his actions was to strengthen the empire at the expense of the papacy. He was probably responsible for the outburst at the Diet of Besançon in October of 1157, and the schism between ALEXANDER III (1159–81) and the antipopes he supported first Victor IV (1059–64) and then Paschal III (1164–68). The latter action was a mistake and against the wishes and best interests of the empire. He failed to win foreign support for his policies, was excommunicated in 1163, and died on a campaign in Italy. The extent of his influence on Frederick Barbarossa has probably been overestimated.

Bibliography: G. RILL, *Lexikon für Theologie und Kirche,* 10 v. (Freiburg 1957–65) 8:979. B. GEBHARDT, *Handbuch der deutschen Geschichte* (Stuttgart 1954–60). M. MACCARRONE, *Papato e Impero, dalla elezione di Federico I alia morte di Adriano IV, 1152–1159* (Rome 1959). R. M. HERKENRATH, "Reinald von Dassel als Verfasser und Schreiber von Kaiserurkunden," *Mitteilungen des Instituts für österreichische Geschichtsforschung* 72 (1964): 34–62.

[J. GILCHRIST]

RAINALD OF RAVENNA, BL.

Archbishop; b. Milan, Italy, *c.* 1250; d. Ravenna, Italy, Aug. 18, 1321. A member of the Concorregi family, he began his career as a papal chaplain, and from 1296 to 1303 he was bishop of Vicenza. During the year 1299 he acted as papal legate entrusted with the task of making peace between England and France, and on March 4, 1302, he became director of spiritual affairs in the Romagna. Rainald was made archbishop of RAVENNA on Nov. 19, 1303, and on Aug. 12, 1308, he was appointed a papal commissioner for the investigation of the TEMPLARS in northern Italy. Later the Templar question and the problem of Church reform occupied his attention at several provincial synods in the years 1310, 1311, 1314, and 1317, as well as at the Council of VIENNE. He was beatified by Pius IX on Jan. 15, 1852.

Feast: Aug. 18.

Bibliography: F. UGHELLI, *Italia sacra . . . ,* ed. N. COLETI, 10 v. (2d ed. Venice 1717–22) 2:382–388. C. EUBEL et al., *Hierarchia Catholica medii (et recentioris) aevi* (2d ed. Münster 1913) 1:415. *Acta Sanctorum* Aug. 3 (1863) 688–696. S. MURATORI, *Bollettino d'arte,* 2 (1908) 324–337. D. G. MOLTENI, *Biographia di S. R. Concorrezzo* (Monza 1911). J. D. MANSI, *Sacrorum Conciliorum nova et amplissima collection* (repr. Graz 1960–) 25:293–296, 449–476, 535–550, 599–628. C. J. VON HEFELE, *Histoire des conciles d'après les documents originaux,* tr. and continued by H. LECLERCQ, 10 v. in 19 (Paris 1907–38) 6.1:549–551, 629–630, 637–640; 6.2:733–736, 784–787. H. SCHMIDINGER, *Lexikon für Theologie und Kirche,* ed. J. HOFER and K. RAHNER, 10 v. (2d, new ed. Freiburg 1957–65) 8:979. H. FINKE, *Papsttum und Untergang des Templerordens,* 2 v. (Münster 1907) 1:321–. E. MÜLLER, *Das Konzil von Vienne* (Münster 1934) 89. A. TORRE, *Studi romagnoli,* 10 (1959) 112.

[R. E. GEIGER]

RAINCY, NOTRE-DAME DU

Notre-Dame du Raincy is a Catholic church in the Diocese of Versailles, France, important in the evolution of modern church architecture; designed by Auguste PERRET and built in 1923. This small (63 by 185 feet) church almost single-handedly broke the reactionary grip that eclecticism had held (and to a certain degree still holds) on church building. It is pivotal in 20th-century religious architecture because of its method of construction. For a period of some 150 years prior to Raincy, most of the world's churches were built in revival styles, e.g., neoclassic, neo-Gothic, neo-Romanesque, etc. The church at Raincy, however, engaged contemporary architectural abilities with an intelligence that provided guidelines for the future. Perret, who designed Notre-Dame du Raincy, was one of the great pioneers of reinforced concrete, and he determined to use this ''industrial'' material throughout the church. Slender columns of reinforced concrete (*béton armé*) uphold a slightly vaulted concrete nave, while the four walls are composed of precast panels of geometrically pierced concrete whose many interstices are filled with brightly colored glass designed by Maurice DENIS. The simple ''one room'' of the church is thus surrounded by panels of colored glass and is suffused with light. The revolution initiated with the nave construction has been of inestimable importance in the development of subsequent religious architecture.

See Also: CHURCH ARCHITECTURE, HISTORY OF.

Bibliography: P. COLLINS, ''The Doctrine of Auguste Perret,'' *The Architectural Review* 114 (1953) 91–98. A. HENZE and T. FILTHAUT, *Contemporary Church Art,* ed. M. LAVANOUX, tr. C. HASTINGS (New York 1956) 20–27. J. PICHARD, *Modern Church Architecture,* tr. E. CALLMANN (New York 1962) 34–38. A. CHRIST-JANER and M. M. FOLEY, *Modern Church Architecture* (New York 1962) 6–13.

[G. E. KIDDER SMITH]

RAINERIUS OF POMPOSA

Benedictine monk and deacon in the Abbey of Pomposa (Diocese of Comacchio) at the beginning of the 13th century; the first to compile a collection of decretals of Pope Innocent III. Nothing is known of his life. A confrere of his by the name of John was a member of the papal household (*capellanus papae*); to him Rainerius dedicated the collection. The work was compiled in 1201 from the registers of the papal chancery and consists of 41 titles containing 123 decretal letters, most of them dating from the first three years (only 12 of the fourth year) of Innocent's pontificate. The work, known and used by a few canonists in the school of Bologna, was soon replaced by more comprehensive collections and seems to have been forgotten by 1220. The only extant manuscript comes from the Abbey of St. Thierry, near Reims (now Reims MS 692); it was discovered and edited by E. Baluze in 1682. It was likewise in northern France, at Rouen, that an unknown canonist in the early years of the 13th century made an abstract of Rainerius's collection (now Paris MS lat. 3922A).

Bibliography: *Patrologia Latina,* ed. J. P. MIGNE, 271 v., indexes 4 v. (Paris 1878–90) 216:1173–1272. S. KUTTNER, *Repertorium der kanonistik* (Rome 1937) 71; *Studi e Testi* (Rome 1900–) 310. S. KUTTNER, *Dictionnaire de droit canonique,* ed. R. NAZ, 7 v. (Paris 1935–65) 7:583–584. G. FORCHIELLI, ''Rainerio diacono e monaco pomposiano,'' *Pomposia monasterium in Italia princeps: IX centenario del Campanile* (Comacchio 1963).

[S. KUTTNER]

RALE, SEBASTIAN

Missionary, lexicographer; b. Pontarlier, France, Jan. 4, 1657; d. Norridgewock, Maine, Aug. 23, 1724. Rale (Rasle) entered the Jesuit novitiate at Dole, France, on Sept. 24, 1675, and taught and studied at Carpentras, Nîmes, and Lyons. In 1689, he was assigned to the Canadian mission and worked for a time in the Christian

Nave of Notre-Dame Cathedral, Raincy, France. (©Archivo Iconografico, S.A./CORBIS)

Abenaki village near Quebec, mastering the language, compiling a catechism, and beginning his Abenaki dictionary. After two years with the Illinois tribe, he was assigned in 1694 to the Abenakis at Norridgewock, Maine, on the Kennebec River. Rale spent the next 30 years with these tribes, but his labors on their behalf have been overshadowed by his involvement in the Anglo-French conflict for the control of Maine. His sympathies were with the French, and, after 1713, Massachusetts authorities were determined to remove him and to scatter or subject the Abenakis. After the failure of conferences and treaties with the tribes, for which Rale was blamed, a surprise attack on Norridgewock was made on Aug. 23, 1724. English soldiers, contrary to orders, killed Rale and returned his scalp to Boston.

The missionary's strongbox, the chapel bell, and other items are in the Maine Historical Society, Portland. His dictionary, seized in the raid of January 1722, was edited by John Pickering in 1833; the manuscript copy is in the Harvard University library. A monument, dedicated in 1833 by Bp. Benedict Fenwick of Boston, Mass., in the presence of descendants of the tribe, marks the site of Rale's heroic labors and death.

Bibliography: J. F. SPRAGUE, *Sebastien Ralé: A Maine Tragedy of the Eighteenth Century* (Boston 1906). M. D. MULVEY, *French Catholic Missionaries in the Present United States 1604–1791* (Washington 1936). H. C. SCHUYLER, ''The Apostle of the Abnakis: Father Sebastian Rale, S.J., 1657–1724,'' *Catholic Historical Review* 1 (1915–16) 164–174, contains critical list of sources. *Jesuit Relations and Allied Documents,* ed. R. G. THWAITES, 73 v. (Cleveland 1896–1901; New York 1959–) 66 (1900) 346 and 71 (1901) 157, for biog. data; 67 (1900), for correspondence; 73 (1901) 270, for other references. J. P. BAXTER, *Pioneers of New France in New England* (Albany 1894), prejudiced but contains documents not found elsewhere.

[W. L. LUCEY]

Exterior of Church of the Holy Child, Shrine of the Infant of Prague, Jacksonville, Diocese of Raleigh (Raleighiensis), North Carolina, dedicated in 1963.

RALEIGH, DIOCESE OF

Established by Pius XI on Dec. 12, 1924, the Diocese of Raleigh (*Dioecesis Raleighiensis*) originally comprised the territory of the entire State of North Carolina, except for the eight counties assigned to the *abbatia nullius diocesis* of Belmont Abbey, that had been erected in 1910. In 1944 the jurisdiction of the abbot of Belmont was reduced to one county (Gaston), and in 1960, it was limited to the 827 acres of the monastery grounds. It was entirely suppressed in 1977, six years after the Diocese of Charlotte, which consists of the forty-six western counties of North Carolina, had been erected. Since the creation of a second diocese in the state (in 1971), the Diocese of Raleigh includes the fifty-four counties of the eastern part of the state. In 2001, a total Catholic population of 167,537 was reported, out of a total population of 3,697,588. It was served by 63 active diocesan and 53 religious priests, 23 permanent deacons, and 77 women religious.

The vicar general of the Archdiocese of Baltimore, William J. Hafey, became the first bishop of Raleigh upon his episcopal consecration, June 25, 1925. In 1937 he was transferred to the see of Scranton, PA, where in he died in 1954. Previously, the state of North Carolina had been included in the jurisdiction of the Diocese of Charleston, South Carolina (est. 1820), and it was constituted a vicariate apostolic in 1868. The first vicar apostolic was Bishop James Gibbons (1868–1877), who was followed in turn by Bishops John J. Keane (1878–1881) and Henry P. Northrup (1882–1887). During much of this period North Carolina lacked a resident bishop, as these vicars apostolic often served simultaneously as diocesan ordinaries elsewhere. An attempt was made to solve this pastoral difficulty by naming the abbot of Belmont Abbey, Leo M. Haid, O.S.B., as vicar apostolic in 1887. Haid served as both abbot and vicar apostolic until his death in 1924, after which the diocese was erected.

Hafey endeavored to establish a stronger institutional presence for the Church in North Carolina. He succeeded in establishing thirty new parishes (from 61 to 91), and increasing the number of "stations," where Mass was at least occasionally celebrated, from 60 to 154. He recruited several religious congregations of men and women to establish themselves in the new diocese, a few of which focused at least some of their efforts on the evangelization of the African-American population. Immigration into the state was not strong in those early years, and the number of Catholics only rose from about 6,000 to about 10,000. But the number of women religious working in the diocese, mostly in the education and health care apostolates, increased from from 84 to 199.

Eugene J. McGuiness, the second bishop of Raleigh in (1937–1944), continued many of the pastoral initiatives of Hafey, during a period of modest wartime population growth, until his transfer to the Diocese of Oklahoma City. On April 17, 1944, seven counties that had been assigned to the *abbatia nullius diocese* of Belmont Abbey (in 1910) were transferred to the jurisdiction of the Raleigh diocese, leaving only Gaston County in care of the abbot-ordinary of Belmont. (Gaston County, save the monastery property itself, was transferred to the diocese in 1960, and the *abbatia nullius* was suppressed in 1977.) Vincent S. Waters of the Diocese of Richmond, was installed as the third bishop of Raleigh in 1945.

During Waters' thirty years in office, he pursued a vigorous policy of evangelization among his fellow Southerners, and was noted for his socially progressive stances, especially with regard to "the race question." He issued a pastoral letter in 1953 (June 12) ordering the integration of all parishes, schools, and diocesan institutions and organizations, though the vision was not completely fulfilled for many years. After attending the sessions of Vatican Council II, Waters attempted a broad program of education and a cautious implementation of the conciliar and the post-conciliar decrees, which was met with impatience and frustration by a number of the diocesan priests and religious. He died in Raleigh in 1974, in the midst of the celebrations for the diocese's golden jubilee.

The Diocese of Raleigh, which had been a suffragan see of Baltimore was transferred to the Province of Atlanta when that diocese was made an archdiocese in 1962. The Diocese of Charlotte was created with Waters' full cooperation and support in 1971. He also established a diocesan newspaper, the *North Carolina Catholic* (1946), the North Carolina Laymen's Association, and a creative program for the pastoral training of newly ordained diocesan priests (1945). During Waters' episcopacy, James J. Navagh, Charles B. McLaughlin, and George E. Lynch served as auxiliary bishops in Raleigh, and Joseph Lennox Federal, Joseph L. Howze, and Michael J. Begley, all priests of the diocese, became ordinaries elsewhere. Howze was the first self-acknowledged black ordinary (Biloxi) appointed in the United States.

F. Joseph Gossman, an auxiliary bishop of Baltimore, was appointed the fourth bishop of Raleigh in 1975. In the last quarter of the twentieth century the Catholic population of the diocese rose more rapidly than ever before, as industry relocated workers from the north, immigrants moved into the state from Mexico and Central America, and military facilities expanded, drawing both active-duty and retired military personnel to the region. Retirees from around the country also established themselves in the coastal areas in record numbers. Collegiality, lay ministry, and ecumenical relationships were areas of special concern for Gossman and his administration during these years.

[J. F. GARNEAU]

RALLIEMENT

Term referring to the policy of adhering to the directives given by Pope LEO XIII to French Catholics in 1892. For historical reasons dating from the FRENCH REVOLUTION, the Third Republic (1870–1914) began with most of its supporters hostile to the Church and most Catholics eager for the return of the monarchy. ANTICLERICALISM and LAICISM characterized the outlook of Gambetta and other republicans who gained control in 1879, and legislated the expulsion of religious congregations, restrictions on Catholic education, and other laws inimical to the Church. From the beginning of his pontificate Leo XIII (1878–1903) pursued a prudent, cautious policy toward the Third Republic, illustrated notably by his encyclical *Nobilissima Gallorum gens* (Feb. 8, 1884), which asked French Catholics to defend the Church without opening themselves to accusations of hostility to established government. After the Boulanger crisis (1888–89) the pope judged that the moment had come to prescribe that Catholic political activity seek to improve the regime, not to destroy it. This policy of rallying to the Republic was launched by Cardinal LAVIGERIE, who, at papal request, pronounced a toast in Algiers (Nov. 12, 1890) in which he praised adherence unreservedly to the existing form of government. These words struck French Catholics as scandalous. The other French cardinals spoke out in favor of neutrality rather than of *ralliement*. Leo XIII waited until Feb. 16, 1892, before publishing the encyclical *Au milieu des sollicitudes,* whose contents can be resumed by a comment of the pope himself in a letter to the cardinals (May 3): "Accept the Republic . . . submit to it as representing power come from God."

These instructions provoked in elite Catholic circles a long crisis of conscience. Reactions were diverse and complex. As a rule only the young generation, especially among the clergy, comprehended Leo XIII, who was acting in virtue of his indirect power in temporal matters. Many laymen openly resisted the pontiff, arguing that this matter pertained to the temporal sphere entirely outside the pope's domain. Albert de Mun, Jacques Piou, Étienne Lamy, and Domenico FERRATA, nuncio

(1891–96), were the leading *ralliés.* Leo XIII would have preferred to see Catholics allied with moderate republicans to form a large conservative party; but in the 1893 elections the *ralliés* won only 35 seats. However, the *ralliement* triumphed for some years by agreeing with an appeasement policy of the moderate republicans, called "the new spirit." Then the Dreyfus affair, which saw the great majority of Catholics ranged against Dreyfus, reopened religious conflicts, especially from 1902 to 1906, and led to an expulsion of religious congregations, the rupture of diplomatic relations with the Holy See, and the separation of Church and State. Cardinal MERRY DEL VAL, secretary of state to Pius X, countermanded Leo XIII's instructions (1909). For the time being the *ralliement* had collapsed.

Slowly the Republic took root, and monarchical restoration appeared more and more chimerical despite the success in certain quarters of the ACTION FRANÇAISE movement. After World War I, moreover, the former combatants no longer wished to renew religious struggles. Relations with the Holy See were renewed. A measure of agreement was reached in the application of the law separating Church and State. In 1924 a return of anticlericalism hung fire. BENEDICT XV had renewed Leo XIII's policy, and PIUS XI continued to do so. He overcame the resistance of the assembly of French cardinals and archbishops, condemned Action Française (1926), and renewed Leo XIII's directives through the secretary of state Cardinal GASPARRI. This is called the second *ralliement.* It succeeded because the arguments that had blocked the first no longer held. (*See* FRANCE.)

Bibliography: A. DEBIDOUR, *L'église catholique et l'état sous la troisiàme république,* 2 v. (Paris 1906–09), laicist viewpoint. J. TOURNIER, *Le Cardinal Lavigerie et son action politique* (Paris 1913). J. PIOU, *Le ralliement et son histoire* (Paris 1928). W. GURIAN, *Die politischen und sozialen Ideen des Französlischen Katholizismus, 1789–1914* (München-Gladbach 1929). Lecanuet ÉglFrance v.2, 3. J. BRUGERETTE, *La Prêtre français et la societé contemporaine,* 3 v. (Paris 1933–38) v.2–3. Dansette v.2. P. CASTEL, *Le P. Picard et le P. Bailly dans les luttes de presse* (Rome 1962). A. SEDGWICK, *The Ralliement in French Politics* 1890–1898 (Cambridge, Mass. 1965).

[A. DANSETTE]

RALPH HIGDEN

English Benedictine chronicler; b. in the west country *c.* 1280; d. March 12, 1363–64. He became a monk of St. Werburg (Chester) in 1299 and supposedly traveled much in England. His principal claim to fame is the *Polychronicon,* a universal history, some versions of which end in 1327 and others in 1342. Ralph (Ranulph) gives some 40 authorities for his work, which is chiefly a compilation. It is divided into seven books (after the seven days of creation): the first is concerned with geography and the rest with history. The *Polychronicon,* of which more than 100 MSS survive, was enormously popular and was considered a standard work for more than 200 years. It is of interest as a compendium of medieval ideas on geography, science, and history; not even the small contemporary portion is of much value as a historical source. It was first translated into English (with additions) by John TREVISA in 1387; the translation (with a further continuation) was printed by Caxton in 1482.

Bibliography: R. HIGDEN, *Polychronicon,* ed. C. BABINGTON and J. R. LUMBY, 9 v. (*Rerum Britannicarum medii aevi scriptores* 41; 1865–86). C. L. KINGSFORD, *The Dictionary of National Biography from the Earliest Times to 1900,* 63 v. (London 1885–1900; repr. with corrections, 21 v., 1908–09, 1921–22, 1938; suppl. 1901–) 9:816–817 for Higden's other works. J. GAIRDNER, *England* (Early Chroniclers of Europe; New York 1879). J. DE GHELLINCK, *L'Essor de la littérature latine au XIIe siècle,* 2 v. (Brussels-Paris 1946) 2:264. W. A. PANTIN, *The English Church in the Fourteenth Century* (Cambridge, Eng. 1955).

[F. D. BLACKLEY]

RALPH OF DICETO

Angevin historian, theologian, outstanding 12th-century dean of St. Paul's; b. *c.* 1120 to 1130; d. Nov. 22, 1202. Most probably Ralph was of French origin and connected with the Belmeis family. He spent two periods of study at Paris, one in his youth and another after he was made archdeacon of London in 1152. In 1180 he became dean of SAINT PAUL'S CATHEDRAL, where he initiated a complete overhaul of the administration of the chapter's churches and manors, a reform of the statutes, and a vigorous building program.

Between 1180 and 1202 he composed his historical works, of which the most important are the *Abbreviationes chronicorum* (to 1147) and the *Ymagines historiarum* (from the knighting of Henry of Anjou in 1149 to 1201). Up to 1162 he relied principally on the history of ROBERT OF TORIGNY; thereafter his work becomes an important original source. In spite of his Angevin leanings, he gave a very fair and balanced account of the BECKET controversy, and from *c.* 1180 the *Ymagines* is a contemporary chronicle with its value enhanced by Ralph's shrewd political insight and careful choice of documents. He also composed a number of scriptural commentaries.

Bibliography: *Opera Historica,* ed. W. STUBBS, 2 v. (*Rerum Britannicarum medii aevi scriptores* 68; 1876). *The Domesday of St. Paul's,* ed. W. H. HALE (Camden Society; London 1858). M. GIBBS, *Early Charters of the Cathedral Church of St. Paul, London* (Camden 3d Ser. 58; London 1939). F. BARLOW, *The Letters of Arnulf of Lisieux* (Camden 3d Ser. 61; London 1939) xvii, 35–36. C.

N. L. BROOKE, "The Composition of the Chapter of St. Paul's, 1086–1163," *Cambridge Historical Journal* 10 (1951) 111–132.

[M. M. CHIBNALL]

RALPH STRODE

English scholastic philosopher and logician; dates of birth and death unknown. He was a contemporary at Oxford of John WYCLIF, with whom he once disputed. From Wyclif's reply (Strode's work is lost), *Responsiones ad Rodolphum Strodum,* Strode appears to have argued against predestination and to have supported the endowments of the Church. His famed *Logica* has not survived, but his *Consequentiae* (on syllogisms) and his *Obligationes* (on scholastic dialectic) were used in Italy and eventually printed at Padua and Venice. His conjectured authorship of the elegiac poem the *PEARL* is now generally rejected; his identification with a London common sergeant, who lived at Aldersgate and died in 1387, is unlikely, despite A. B. Emden's support. Emden thinks Strode was a fellow of Merton in 1359 and 1360, but the evidence appears inconclusive. Chaucer dedicated his *Troylus and Cryseyde* jointly to the poet GOWER and "the philosophical Strode."

Bibliography: I. GOLLANCZ, *The Dictionary of National Biography from the Earliest Times to 1900,* 63 v. (London, 1885–1990) 19:57–59. C. F. BROWN, "The Author of *The Pearl,* Considered in the Light of His Theological Opinions," *Publications of the Modern Language Association* N.S. 12 (1904): 115–153. H. B. WORKMAN, *John Wyclif,* 2 v. (Oxford 1926) 2:125–129, 412–414. A. B. EMDEN, *A Biographical Register of the University of Oxford to* A.D. *1500,* 3 v. (Oxford 1957–59) 3:1807–1808.

[F. D. BLACKLEY]

RAMAḌĀN

The ninth month of the Islamic calendar. It would seem that in the ancient Arabian calendar this month fell in the summer; with the introduction by Islam of a purely lunar calendar, however, it may fall at any season of the year. It was in this month, traditionally on one of the last ten days, that the QUR'ĀN was revealed to MUḤAMMAD (cf. Qur'ān 2.181). Beginning from the year A.H. 2 (*see* HIJRA), with the suppression of the '*āšūrā*' fast (on the 10th of al-Muḥarram, the first month of the year), Muslims have been obliged to fast during Ramaḍān (cf. Qur'ān 2.181–183). The fast (*ṣawm,* probably borrowed in this sense from Jewish Aramaic) is obligatory to all adults who are physically capable of it; but it is relaxed for the aged and infirm, pregnant and nursing women, and travelers; the last are expected later to make up the days that they have omitted. The fast is binding only during the daylight hours, during which the person who is fasting must abstain from all food and drink and from sexual intercourse; menstruation and post-partum bleeding are also considered to break the fast. The nights of Ramaḍān are often spent in various forms of social activity. The feast of the breaking of the fast (*'īd al-fiṭr*) is celebrated with the sighting of the new moon of the next month, Shawwāl.

[R. M. FRANK]

RAMBERT OF BOLOGNA

Dominican Thomist theologian and bishop; b. Bologna, *c.* 1250; d. Castello or Venice, Nov. 8 or 9, 1308. A son of the influential Primadizzi family, he entered the order at an early age. While still a young man he was sent to Saint–Jacques, Paris, for theological training; he was in Paris during the second regency of St. THOMAS AQUINAS (1269–72). By 1288 he was a bachelor in theology. Returning to Bologna before receiving the degree of master, he occupied various positions of importance. As definitor of the province of Lombardy in 1291, he attended the general chapter of Palencia that deposed the Master General, Munio of Zamorra. In 1300 and 1301 he was considered a likely candidate for the office of master general. Meanwhile, between 1290 and 1295 be returned to Paris to obtain the university's license to incept in theology; he taught as regent master between 1295 and 1299. By April 1299 he returned to Bologna and was appointed consultor to the Holy Office. On Feb. 20, 1303, he was appointed bishop of Castello, near Venice, an office he filled until his death. He is buried in the Dominican church of SS. Giovanni e Paolo in Venice.

In reply to the *Correctorium fratris Thomae* of WILLIAM DE LA MARE, Rambert wrote an *Apologeticum veritatis contra corruptorium* (ed. J.P. Müller, Vatican 1943). *see* CORRECTORIA. This reply was written in Paris before his departure in 1299. It is incomplete, ending abruptly in the middle of a sentence in article 16 instead of at the end of 118 articles. Although it follows the structure of other *correctoria* and depends noticeably on the *Correctorium "Circa"* of JOHN (QUIDORT) OF PARIS, it is highly original in that Rambert answers parallel criticisms of RICHARD OF MIDDLETON, HENRY OF GHENT, and GILES OF ROME. He refers also to SIGER OF BRABANT. Apart from this, a lost commentary on the *Sentences,* and one sermon for Easter, April 22, 1302, other works formerly ascribed to him are now known to be spurious: the *Speculum exemplare* was written by Petroboni Bentivegne of Bologna; the *Determinatio de paupertate Christi et apostolorum* was written by a Dominican known as Robert of Bologna; *De potestate regia et papali* is of unknown authorship. Only the compilation of *Quodlibeta* 1–9 of Henry of Ghent remains doubtful.

Despite the dearth of his writings, Rambert is a significant witness in the development of early THOMISM. His *Apologeticum* alone reflects the loyalty and fidelity of Italian Dominicans to Thomas Aquinas even before his canonization.

Bibliography: É. H. GILSON, *History of Christian Philosophy in the Middle Ages* 414–416. P. GLORIEUX, *Répertoire des maîtres en théologie de Paris au XIIIe siècle* 1:170–171. J. QUÉTIF and J. ÉCHARD, *Scriptores Ordinis Praedicatorum* 1.2:504. M. GRABMAN, "La scuola tomistica italiana nel XIII e principio del XIV secolo," *Rivista di filosofia neoscolastica* 15 (Milan 1923) 127–131. F. CORVINO, *Enciclopedia filosofica* 3:1845–46.

[P. GLORIEUX]

RAMEAU, JEAN PHILIPPE

Distinguished composer and theorist; b. Dijon, France, Sept. 25, 1683; d. Paris, Sept. 12, 1764. In a long, busy career Rameau was eminent in three musical areas that were much more disparate then than now. In his earlier years he was considered primarily a theorist, and his *Traité d'harmonie* of 1722 is one of the landmarks of the science. In it he proposed theories of the invertibility of triads, the "fundamental bass" (function of chord roots irrespective of inversions), and the cycle of fifths —theories definitive in virtually all texts on tonal harmony since then. He composed many harpsichord works, both solo pieces (three books: 1706, 1724, 1731) and pieces *en concert* (with other instruments, 1741). He was also an organist and produced a handful of motets in connection with his church positions. In 1733, already age 50, Rameau began a new career in opera. He produced more than two dozen works, among them *Les Indes galantens* (1735), *Castor et Pollux* (1737), and a comedy, *Les Paladins* (1760). His imaginative instrumentation and characterization caused considerable discussion; his work was always controversial. His contemporaries considered him a philosopher, and he continued didactic writing throughout his life.

Jean Philippe Rameau.

Bibliography: *Oeuvres complètes,* ed. C. SAINT-SAËNS, 18 v. (Paris 1895–1913), now somewhat outdated; the keyboard works have recently been reedited by E. JACOBI; "Traité de l'harmonie," O. STRUNK, ed., *Source Readings in Music History* (New York 1950) 564–574, excerpt. P. M. MASSON, *L'Opéra de Rameau* (Paris 1930). P. BERTHIER, *Réflexions sur l'art et la vie de Jean-Philippe Rameau* (Paris 1957). C. M. GIRDLESTONE, *Jean-Philippe Rameau* (London 1957). M. M. KEANE, *The Theoretical Writings of Jean-Philippe Rameau* (Washington 1961). *Baker's Biographical Dictionary of Musicians*, ed. N. SLONIMSKY (5th, rev. ed. New York 1958) 1303–05. D. J. GROUT, *A Short History of Opera*, 2 v. (2d, rev. and enl. ed. New York 1965). J.-M. BARDEZ, "Jean-Philippe Rameau: *Pièces de Clavecin en Concert,*" *Analyse Musicale* 25 (1991) 77–97. T. CHRISTENSEN, *Rameau and Musical Thought in the Enlightenment* (Cambridge, England 1993). C. DILL, *Monstrous Opera: Rameau and the Tragic Tradition* (Princeton 1998). B. HYER, "*Sighing Branches:* Prosopopoeia in Rameau's *Pigmalion,*" *Music Analysis* 13 (1994) 7–50. H. KREBS, "Schenker's Changing View of Rameau: A Comparison of Remarks in *Harmony, Counterpoint,* and *Rameau or Beethoven?,*" *Theoria: Historical Aspects of Music Theory* 3 (1998) 59–72. W. LANDOWSKA, "French Music Of the Past: Jean Philippe Rameau." in *Landowska On Music*, ed. and trans. D. RESTOUT (New York 1964) 267–273. P. F. RICE, "Mid-Eighteenth Century Changes in French Opera: The Two Versions of Rameau's *Zoroastre.*" *Recherches sur la Musique française classicque* 21 (1983) 128–144. P. SABY, "Le travail de la forme dans les chœurs dramatiques de Jean-Philippe Rameau," *Analyse Musicale* 20 (1990) 9–15. H. SCHNEIDER, "Rameau et sa famille: Nouveaux documents," *Recherches sur la Musique française classicque* 23 (1985) 94–130.

[E. BORROFF]

RAMOS ARIZPE, MIGUEL

Mexican priest and politician; b. Coahuila, Feb. 15, 1775; d. Mexico City, April 28, 1843. He studied at Monterrey and Guadalajara and was ordained in 1803 in the cathedral of Mexico City. In 1808 he received the doctorate in canon law in Guadalajara and in 1810 entered the Colegio de Abogados of Mexico City. During these years he held a number of posts in the bishopric of Linares. From 1811 to 1814 Ramos Arizpe was the representative of Coahuila to the Spanish Cortes. In Cádiz he became a Mason and was widely known for his extreme liberalism. He was accused of conspiracy and arrested on orders of Ferdinand VII, but the successful liberal revolution of 1820 gave him his freedom, after which he was named canon of the Puebla cathedral. In December of 1821 he arrived at Tampico and then went to Saltillo, where he devoted himself to masonic propaganda and engaged in a conspiracy against Iturbide. When Iturbide was overthrown and the republic established, Ramos Arizpe became a deputy for Coahuila and a leader of the federalist group. The Constitution of 1824 was, in part, his work. He founded the Masonic Society, Águila Negra, and collaborated with POINSETT in founding York Rite lodges. He served as minister of justice and ecclesiastical affairs (1826–28), as ambassador to Chile (1830), as a member of the junta that proposed the Plan of Tacubaya in 1841, and as a deputy in congress (1842). Beginning in 1831, he was dean of the cathedral of Puebla. He wrote a number of reports as minister of justice, and *Memoria sobre las Provincias Internas de Oriente* (Cádiz 1812; Guadalajara 1831; Eng. tr. Philadelphia 1814).

Bibliography: V. ALESSIO ROBLES, ''Noticia Biográfica,'' in M. RAMOS ARIZPE, *Memoria sobre el estado de las provincias internas de oriente* (Mexico City 1932) 7–54. ,

[E. DEL HOYO]

RAMPOLLA DEL TINDARO, MARIANO

Cardinal, secretary of state; b. Polizzi, Sicily, Aug. 17, 1843; d. Rome, Dec. 16, 1913. Of noble birth, he had to brave paternal hostility to pursue his priestly studies in Rome, receiving ordination in 1866. Following legal studies he became *doctor in utroque jure* (1870). He then served the secretariate of state in the Congregation for Extraordinary Ecclesiastical Affairs until 1875 when he went to Spain as counselor in the nunciature, becoming chargé d'affaires in 1876. Grave political disturbances were troubling Spain, with Catholics divided between the Carlists and Alfonsists. The representative of the Holy See had to try to pacify these opposing parties.

Msgr. Rampolla was called to Rome (1877) by Pius IX to become secretary for affairs of the Oriental rite in the Congregation for the PROPAGATION OF THE FAITH. Aided by his grasp of Oriental languages, he sought to end the Armenian schism; he reached a solution in 1879. He served as secretary of the Congregation for Extraordinary Ecclesiastical Affairs from Nov. 16, 1880, until his appointment, Oct. 25, 1882, as nuncio to Madrid. On Dec. 8, 1882, he was consecrated titular archbishop of Heraclea. Msgr. Della Chiesa, the future BENEDICT XV, acted as his secretary. The new nuncio urged Spanish Catholics to distinguish the cause of religion from that of political parties. In dioceses he favored lay associations promoting a rigorously Catholic program. He also contributed to the erection of an episcopal see in Madrid, which until 1885 had been dependent on the Diocese of Toledo. It was to Rampolla that Cardinal JACOBINI, Secretary of State, addressed the important letter (April 13, 1885) on the powers of nuncios. The nuncio's good offices permitted the Holy See to act as mediator between Spain and Germany in the dispute over the Caroline Islands, which was settled in December 1885.

Named cardinal (March 14, 1887), Rampolla succeeded Jacobini as secretary of state, June 1, 1887, and held the post until Leo XIII's death, July 20, 1903. It would be extremely difficult to differentiate the respective roles of Pope and secretary in the conduct of pontifical diplomacy during these 16 years. Their views were identical, according to witnesses. It is significant that LEO XIII, after some months of hesitation, chose Rampolla rather than Luigi Galimberti, who favored a *modus vivendi* with Italy and good relations with the Central Powers. As matters turned out, hope for a settlement of the ROMAN QUESTION gradually subsided. Italy's association with Germany and Austria-Hungary in the Triple Alliance led Rome to seek an entente with France and Russia. Cardinal Rampolla sympathized with France; interested himself in the southern Slavs who were subject to Austria-Hungary; sought cordial relations with Russia; wished to see the Church endorse democratic aspirations; and favored decidedly the Christian social movement in Austria. These explain Austria's hostility to the secretary of state, manifested most notoriously at the conclave in 1903 when Cardinal Puzyna stifled all chance of Rampolla's election, after he had received 29 votes, by exercising his government's veto power.

Pius X appointed Rampolla secretary of the Holy Office, and also as a member and then president of the PONTIFICAL BIBLICAL COMMISSION. His manner of life was retired, austere, and free of personal ambition.

Bibliography: C. CRISPOLTI and G. AURELI, eds., *La politica di Leone XIII da Luigi Galimberti a Mariano Rampolla* (Rome 1912). P. SINOPOLI DI GIUNTA, *Il cardinale Mariano Rampolla del Tindaro* (Rome 1923). B. CERRETTI, *Il cardinale Mariano Rampolla del Tindaro* (Rome 1929). E. SODERINI, *Il pontificato di Leone XIII*, 3 v. (Milan 1932–33). F. ENGEL-JANOSI, *Österreich und der Vatikan, 1846–1918,* 2 v. (Graz 1958–60).

[J. M. MAYEUR]

RAMSEY, ABBEY OF

Former Benedictine monastery in the county of Huntingdon (town of Ramsey) and the Diocese of Lincoln. It was founded *c.* 969 by Aylwin, Duke of East Anglia, at the prompting of OSWALD OF YORK. Richly endowed by the founder and his kinsfolk, the abbey became known as "Ramsey the rich." Twelve monks came from Westbury to occupy buildings erected by Ednoth. The abbey church was built in 974 and dedicated to Our Lady, St. Benedict, and All Holy Virgins. At Oswald's request, the abbot of Fleury sent ABBO OF FLEURY (*c.* 986) as a teacher for this new Benedictine community. Abbo wrote his *Questiones grammaticales* for the instruction of the monks and a *Passio sancti Edmundi* at their request. One of his pupils composed a life of Oswald, while Byrhtferth, another pupil, wrote commentaries on Bede's mathematical works. Further gifts to support the community of 80 monks came from Aethelric, Bishop of Dorchester, early in the 11th century, whereas an attempt by the Mercian thegn, Aelthere, to replace the monks with seculars failed. In 1143 Geoffrey de Mandeville drove out the monks and used the buildings as a fortress during the Barons' War. After Geoffrey's death Abbot Walter had to restore the abbey. Shrines of the fenland saints, Felix of Dunwich, Ethelred, and Ethelbriht, were added in 1192. Community life was fully restored and high enough standards maintained to stand severe scrutiny by Bp. ROBERT GROSSETESTE in 1239. However, the rich fenland estates of the abbey aroused the jealousy of neighbors, and the monks were involved in expensive lawsuits, which led to their being in debt by 1267. Though discipline seems to have fallen off for a time, the abbey recovered *c.* 1400, and visitations in the 15th century showed little amiss. Abbot Tichmersh began further building work, while the magnificent library was put to good use by Lawrence Holbeach in composing his Hebrew lexicon. But zeal for the religious life again fell off; and when the crisis came with HENRY VIII in November 1539, the abbey surrendered without a struggle. The monastic community was pensioned. All the buildings, except the gateway, have been destroyed.

Bibliography: W. H. HART and P. A. LYONS, eds., *Cartularium monasterii de Rameseia*, 3 v. (*Rerum Brittanicarum medii aevi scriptores* 79; 1884–93). W. D. MACRAY, ed., *Chronicon abbatiae Rameseiensis* (*Rerum Brittanicarum medii aevi scriptores* 83; 1886). *The Victoria History of the County of Huntingdon*, ed. W. PAGE et al. (London 1926–) 1:377–385. D. KNOWLES, *The Monastic Order in England, 943–1216* (2ed. Cambridge, England 1962); D. KNOWLES, *The Religious Orders in England,* 3 v. (Cambridge, England 1948–60). D. KNOWLES and R. N. HADCOCK, *Medieval Religious Houses: England and Wales* (New York 1953). J. A. RAFTIS, *The Estates of Ramsey Abbey* (Toronto 1957).

[F. R. JOHNSTON]

Mariano Rampolla del Tindaro.

RAMUS, PETER

Pierre de la Ramée, educational reformer and logician, author of many widely used works on philosophy and letters; b. Cuts (Oise), France, 1515; d. Paris, Aug. 26, 1572. Despite straitened family circumstances, Ramus went to study at Paris. The common story that for his inaugural performance as master of arts in 1536 or 1537 he defended a spectacularly anti-Aristotelian thesis is now suspect, but in 1543 his two works, *Dialecticae partitiones* (The Structure of Dialectic) and *Aristotelicae animadversiones* (Remarks on Aristotle), did violently attack Aristotle and the university curriculum as confused and disorganized. Condemned by Francis I, Ramus was reinstated by Henry II, who in 1551 appointed him professor of eloquence and philosophy in the body of professors later known as the Collège de France. He embraced the Protestant reform around 1562, retiring to Fontainebleau in 1562–63 and to Rhenish Germany and Switzerland from 1568 to 1570. C. Waddington's often-repeated story that Ramus's murder in the St. Bartholomew's Day Massacre was engineered by the physician Jacques Charpentier is without solid foundation.

Ramus's much edited works, which sparked volumes of controversy, run to 60-odd titles, supplemented by some 13 additional published works of Omer Talon

(Audomarus Talaeus, *c.* 1510–62), his literary collaborator. Besides the pivotal dialectic or logic and its complementary rhetoric, these works include also classical editions and commentaries; lectures on physics, metaphysics, and mathematics; textbooks on grammar, arithmetic, algebra, and geometry; miscellaneous orations and open letters; and the posthumously published *Commentariorum de religione Christianae libri quatuor* (1576), Ramus's only theological work, basically Zwinglian in orientation.

Ramus's most important work was the *Dialectica* or *Logica* (1555, 1556, etc.), a work related to the dialectic of R. Agricola, Ciceronian and humanistic in professed aim, but ultrascholastic in manner and in much of its content. Dialectic or logic, the art of discourse (*ars disserendi*), made up of *inventio* and *dispositio*, was to rule all thought, from mathematics to poetry, to the exclusion of any logics of the probable (such as dialectic and rhetoric had often been made out to be). Ramist rhetoric consisted merely of tropes and figures. Ramus helped set the stage for R. DESCARTES by developing concern about ''method,'' which in 1546 Ramus, almost simultaneously with MELANCHTHON and Johann Sturm, had transplanted into logic from the rhetorical manuals where it earlier appeared. ''Method,'' included under *dispositio*, meant proceeding from the general to the particular. (''Cryptic method,'' proceeding from the particular to the general, met special emergencies.) Ramists specialized in dichotomized charts to ''analyze'' both thought and reality ''methodically'': a subject was divided into two, the subdivisions again dichotomized, and so on. Ramist method provided the academic tradition of the West a major teachable organization for discursive thought other than that of the classical oration, which from antiquity had been the dominant overall form of discursive organization formally taught, though others were used (the common dialectical organization was not discursive but dependent on attack and rejoinder). Ramist method thus laid the groundwork for the modern encyclopedia article.

Into the late 17th century Ramism had countless proponents, especially in Germany, the British Isles and their American colonies, France, Switzerland, the Low Countries, and Scandinavia. Ramus's theology as such attracted little notice, beyond the condemnation of his proposal for lay church government at the Protestant synod of Nîmes in 1572. But Ramist systematizing appealed to the nonsacramental, methodical Calvinist mind, in both religious and secular matters. Countless writers, including Francis BACON, attacked Ramism as oversimplified, but its heavy reliance, overt or covert, on spatial models in its account of mental activities and extramental actuality, which has discernible antecedents in medieval SCHOLASTICISM, was typical of much of the thought even of its opponents.

See Also: DIALECTICS; DIALECTICS IN THE MIDDLE AGES.

Bibliography: W. J. ONG, *Ramus, Method, and the Decay of Dialogue* (Cambridge, Mass. 1958), exhaustive bibliog; *Ramus and Talon Inventory* (Cambridge, Mass. 1958). R. HOOYKAAS, *Humanisme, science et réforme: Pierre de La Ramée 1515–1572* (Leiden 1959). W. RISSE, *Die Logik der Neuzeit* (Stuttgart 1963) v.1.

[W. J. ONG]

RANCÉ, ARMAND JEAN LE BOUTHILLIER DE

Cistercian abbot and reformer of La Trappe, ascetic author and controversialist; b. Paris, Jan. 9, 1626; d. La Trappe, Oct. 27, 1700. He was born of an influential family of government officials and was destined early to an ecclesiastical career. He received the tonsure in 1635 and soon became a canon of Paris and the beneficiary of two priories and three abbeys, among them the Cistercian LA TRAPPE in Normandy. He pursued his studies with brilliance, particularly in patristic theology. Rancé was ordained on Jan. 22, 1651, received the licentiate of theology in the next year, ranking first in his class, and was graduated as doctor of theology from the Sorbonne in 1654. At the Assembly of the Clergy from 1655 to 1657, he defended Cardinal de Retz against Mazarin and signed the anti-Jansenist formulary, although he retained a close relationship with the French Oratory and the circle of Port-Royal. Neither better nor worse than many other worldly prelates of his era, he divided his time between occasional preaching and the fashionable diversions of Paris society.

The turning point of his life came in 1657, when the death of the celebrated beauty of the court, the duchess of Montbazon, terminated their close friendship. He left Paris and spent much time at his country home in reading, reflection, and meditation. Resolving to become a monk, he sold his estates, retaining only La Trappe, and in 1663 began his novitiate at the reformed Cistercian monastery of Perseigne. He made his monastic profession on June 6, 1664, with the intention of assuming the government of La Trappe as regular abbot. A few months after his profession, however, he was delegated by the CISTERCIANS of the Strict Observance, together with Dominic George, abbot of Val-Richer, to plead before Pope Alexander VII for the autonomy for this reformed branch of the order. He remained in Rome until 1666, but the mission was a failure; the Strict Observance remained subject to the abbot of Cîteaux. Rancé submitted to the papal decision with great reluctance. In 1673 he made a direct appeal to Louis XIV for a reversal of the decree, only to fail again. He retired from public life and devoted his energies to the reform of La Trappe, although he maintained a voluminous correspondence and published a number of books and pamphlets in justification of his peculiar monastic ideas.

His chief work was *De la sainteté et des devoirs de la vie monastique* (2 v., Paris 1683). Ignoring the indulgent character of the Rule of St. Benedict, he insisted that monasticism was basically penitential. Monks should consider themselves criminals doomed to a life of severity. The abbot must create humiliations for his monks and encourage the practice of austerity even at the cost of ruined health. The monks must feel no satisfaction in their works and exercises, must banish intellectual pursuits, and occupy their time in hard manual labor. Rancé's concept of monasticism became the object of vigorous reaction. His most notable opponent was the Maurist MABILLON who defended monastic studies. Under Rancé's administration La Trappe became a populous and much admired community, and he himself was venerated as a saint by many of his contemporaries. His health broken by austerities and exertions, Rancé abdicated as abbot in 1695 and died among his devoted monks after five years of intense suffering. Rancé's heroic asceticism was deeply impressive, though his obvious exaggerations and combative temper leave him always a figure of controversy. His immediate influence was slight, but after the Napoleonic Wars, when the Strict Observance was successfully revived by the monks of La Trappe, he became the guiding genius of the fast-growing TRAPPIST congregation and dominated its spirituality during the 19th century.

Bibliography: L. DUBOIS, *Histoire de l'abbé de Rancé et de sa réforme*, 2 v. (Paris 1866), considered the standard biography, this is a version of the panegyrical 18th-century MS of A. F. GERVAISE. J. MARSOLLIER, *La Vie de Dom Arman-Jean Le Bouthillier de Rancé* (Paris 1703). F. R. DE CHATEAUBRIAND, *Vie de Rancé* (Paris 1844). H. BREMOND, *The Thundering Abbot*, tr. F. J. SHEED (London 1930). A. CHEREL, *Rancé* (Paris 1930) and E. JEU, *M. de La Trappe* (Paris 1931), are short and popular. For list of works and full bibliography *see* J. CARREYRE, *Dictionnaire de théologie catholique,* ed. A. VACANT et al., 15 v. (Paris 1903–50; Tables générales 1951–), 13.2:1652–56.

[L. J. LEKAI]

RANDOMNESS

Randomness is a term with two principal meanings, one mathematical and the other physical. In the mathematics of probability and statistics, the term can refer to either the notion of ''random variable'' or the more imprecise concept signified by ''random sampling,'' ''at random,'' or ''random distribution.'' A random variable, best defined as ''a function defined on a given sample space'' (Feller, 204), is less important than the imprecise ''at random'' notion it helps to clarify. The latter, in the purely theoretical formulation of probability, is roughly equivalent to the equal likelihood presumed in the basic postulates of probability (*ibid.* 29). As such, it is a purely theoretical model for the explanation of experimental results that are often neither perfectly random nor truly equally likely.

In the physical world randomness is closely associated with CHANCE and with the data of such theories as quantum and statistical mechanics, which presuppose random motion of particles for the very formulation of their laws. Randomness thus seems to be a given, or datum, in at least some of the most important areas of science; J. von Neumann has attempted to demonstrate the radical character of this randomness. Nevertheless, it is a peculiarity of statistical theory that the most unexpected experimental results—equally probable or not—can be (approximately) reduced to some sort of statistical regularity. For example, consider the relations between Maxwell–Boltzmann, Bose–Einstein, and Fermi–Dirac statistics in theoretical physics (*ibid.* 38–40). This suggests that there is some sort of ORDER underlying even the most ''random'' of physical events, whether or not science ever in fact discovers it.

Bibliography: W. FELLER, *An Introduction to Probability Theory and Its Applications*, v.1 (New York 1957).

[P. R. DURBIN]

RANFAING, ELIZABETH OF, VEN.

Foundress; b. Remiremont (Lorraine), Oct. 30, 1592; d. Nancy, Jan. 14, 1649. Elizabeth (Marie Elisabeth de la Croix de Jesus) had been coerced into marriage with Dubois, an aged nobleman, who treated her brutally. She was a widow, at 24. With her three daughters she opened a refuge for fallen women in Nancy in 1631. The success of this venture, one of many such houses, convinced ecclesiastics of the permanent need for this apostolate. In 1634 the Holy See approved of her congregation under the title of Our Lady of Refuge. It spread rapidly throughout France, particularly in the late 19th century. Several independent houses of refuge became members of the congregation, which had St. Ignatius as patron and the Rule of St. Augustine as a guide. The constitution provided for three types of members: those of unblemished lives, vowed specifically to serve the penitents; penitents of altered lives, equal with the first sisters but ineligible for office; and penitents proper, following the same rule but without vows. To guarantee this apostolate to the pen-

Leopold von Ranke. (Archive Photos)

itents, the rule specified that the third group always constitute at least two-thirds of the community.

Bibliography: H. M. BOUDON, *Le Triomphe de la croix en la personne de la vénérable mère Marie-Élizabeth de la Croix de Jésus* (Liège 1686). L. GIAMBENE, *Enciclopedia Italiana di scienzi, littere ed arti,* 36 v. (Rome 1929–39; suppl. 1938–) 29:317. M. HEIMBUCHER, *Die Orden und Kongregationen der katholischen Kirche,* 2 v. (3d ed. Paderborn 1932–34) 1:650. P. HÉLYOT, *Histoire des ordres monastiques,* 8 v. (Paris 1714–19) 4:344–361. G. ALLEMANG, *Lexikon für Theologie und Kirche,* ed. J. HOFER and K. RAHNER, 10 v. (2d, new ed. Freiburg 1957–65) 3:818.

[C. LYNCH]

RANKE, LEOPOLD VON

Historian; b. Wiehe (Thuringia), Germany, Dec. 21, 1795; d. Berlin, May 23, 1886. He descended from a long line of Lutheran pastors and studied theology and classical philology at the University of Leipzig (1814–18), where his reading of Thucydides and Barthold Niebuhr turned his main interest to history. After a long period of doubt, Ranke had moved by 1818 toward a synthesis of Lutheran mysticism, Neoplatonism, humanism as propounded by Goethe and Herder, and the pantheism of Fichte. While teaching at a secondary school (gymnasium) at Frankfort on the Oder (1818–25), he completed the first part of his *Geschichten der romanischen und germanischen Völker* (1824). This won him a professorship at the University of Berlin (1825–71). His accomplishments included the discovery of the invaluable records of the Venetian ambassadors; lectures on the history of Italian poetry (1833), which inspired a new school of historiography; and joint editorship of the *Historisch-Politische Zeitschrift,* founded in 1833 to combat revolutionary extremism. He was named official Prussian historiographer (1841), served as president of the Munich Historical Commission beginning in 1858, and gained the Prussian prefix of nobility ''von'' (1865).

Ranke was the most influential and widely read historian of his century, noted for pioneer work in the systematic exploitation of archival sources and in the creation of the modern scientific approach to history. The ''Columbus of modern history,'' as Lord Acton termed him, took as the apt motto of his extremely industrious life, *Labor ipse voluptas.* His prodigious scholarly output spanned modern European history and continued for six decades until the eve of his death, which found him, half blind, at work on the sixth volume of a world history, begun in his 82d year. Although many sections of his works are outdated, many of his profound observations in them remain valid. His aim was to write history ''as it actually happened,'' avoiding political partisanship, nationalistic narrowness, moral judgments, and religious enthusiasm. His universalistic and unitary view of European history was admirable, although not devoid of his conservative Prussian political commitment. To him the driving forces of modern history have been the European states. He was a leading exponent of HISTORICISM and rejected the notion of progress. History to him was a hieroglyph of God, and Christian hope and belief in Divine Providence were dominant in his outlook. Each era, he believed, is directed to God and is fulfilled in itself, not in later generations. He tended, however, to center history too much on great personages and to concentrate on diplomatic questions to the neglect of social and juridical ones.

Chief among Ranke's books were his three volumes on Prussian history (1847–48), five volumes on French history (1852–61), and seven volumes on English history (1859–68). His five-volume history of Germany in the Reformation period (1839–47) revealed a Lutheran sympathy evident elsewhere in his treatment of religious topics. Ranke first won fame with his three-volume history of the popes during the sixteenth and seventeenth centuries (1834–39), which he extended to include Vatican Council I (1869–70) in the 6th edition (1874) and later ones. It was based on extensive archival research, although it did not include the Vatican Archives, which were not then opened to scholars. Although it overemphasized papal political and diplomatic activity, it was a masterpiece of historiography and raised this subject from its hitherto polemical level. Protestants criticized it as too favorable to Catholics; Rome placed it on the Index (Sept. 16, 1841).

Bibliography: *Sämtliche Werke,* 54 v. (Leipzig 1867–90); ed. P. JOACHIMSEN et al. (Munich 1952–); *Das Briefwerk,* ed. W. P. FUCHS (Hamburg 1949); *Neue Briefe,* ed. B. HOEFT and H. HERZFELD (Hamburg 1949). H. F. HELMOLT, *L. von Rankes Leben und Wirken* (Leipzig 1921). G. P. GOOCH, *History and Historians in the Nineteenth Century* (2d ed. London 1952). F. SCHNABEL, *Deutsche Geschichte im 19. Jahrhundert,* 4 v. (Freiburg 1927–37) 3:86–101. T. H. VON LAUE, *Leopold Ranke, the Formative Years* (Princeton 1950). H. VON SRBIK, *Geist und Geschichte vom Deutschen Humanismus bis zur Gegenwart,* 2 v. (Munich 1950–51) 1:239–292. H. HEUSER, *L. von Rankes protestantisches Geschichtsbild* (Zurich 1950). C. HINRICHS, *Ranke und Die Geschichtstheologie der Goethezeit* (Göttingen 1954). F. BAETHGEN, ''Zur geistigen Entwicklungsgeschichte Rankes in seiner Frühzeit,'' *Deutschland und Europa,* ed. W. CONZE (Düsseldorf 1951) 337–353. F. MEINECKE, *Die Entstehung des Historismus,* ed. C. HINRICHS (3d ed. Munich 1959). H. LUTZ, ''Ranke und das Papsttum'' *Rivista di storia della Chiesa iri Italia* 16 (1962): 439–450. K. KUPISCH, *Die Religion in Geschichte und Gegenwart,* 7 v. (3d ed. Tübingen 1957–65) 5:778–779. S. SKALWEIT, *Lexikon für Theologie und Kirche,* 10 v. (Freiburg 1957–65) 8:990–991.

[S. J. TONSOR]

RANSOM

The analogy of the payment of a price is employed in the New Testament to explain the death of Christ: ''The Son of Man has not come to be served but to serve, and to give his life as a ransom [Gr. λύτρον] for many'' (Mk 10.45). This saying of Christ is an allusion to the fourth Servant Song (Isaiah ch. 53; *see* SUFFERING SERVANT, SONGS OF THE). The word λύτρον means a payment for the release of a prisoner or a criminal (cf. Septuagint, Nm 35.31). A cognate notion is that of a bondsman, a role that Yahweh plays with respect to Israel (Ex 6.6; Hos 13.14), St. Paul uses this metaphor to remind the people that they do not belong to themselves but to God (1 Cor 6. 19–20; Acts 20.28). St. Peter writes: ''You know that you were redeemed . . . not with perishable things, with silver or gold, but with the precious blood of Christ . . .'' (1 Pt 1.18).

The condition from which mankind is ransomed is spoken of as captivity to the law of sin (Rom 7.23), as slavery to the Law (Rom 7.1–6), as subjection to the power of darkness (Col 1.13) and to death (Col 2.13). These ideas have a resonance in St. John (Jn 12.31; 1 Jn 3.8) and in Hebrews (2.14–15).

Man's ransom or Redemption has a positive aspect. ''Jesus Christ . . . gave himself for us that he might redeem us from iniquity and cleanse for himself an acceptable people, pursuing good works'' (Ti 2.14). This text alludes to the deliverance from Egypt and the covenant of Sinai. God freed His people from slavery that He might take them for his own and make them a holy people (Dt 7.6–11; cf. Jer 31.32–33). Similarly, by Christ's death man is acquired or purchased by Christ and becomes His own (1 Cor 7.22–24), but free. He is consecrated to God and made holy. His ransom from bondage terminates in union with God.

The concept of the saving work of Christ as a liberation achieved through ransom led some of the Fathers to picture the devil as the one to whom the ransom was paid. Satan had acquired legal rights over man and the blood of Christ had to be paid him as ransom. Although this theory was ridiculed by some, for example, by Adamantius as early as A. D. 300 (*Dialogue* 1.27; *Patrologia Graeca* 11:1756; Van de Sande Bakhuyzen, *Die griechischen christlichen Schriftsteller der ersten drei Jahrhunderte* 55), it was espoused by Origen, Gregory of Nyssa, Ambrose and others and was popular through a good part of the Middle Ages.

Bibliography: S. LYONNET, ''De notione redemptionis,'' *Verbum Donini* 36 (1958) 129–146; ''De notione emptionis seu acquisitionis,'' *ibid.* 257–269; *De peccato et redemptione*, 4 v. (Rome 1957—). A. VÖGTLE, *Lexikon für Theologie und Kirche*, ed. J. HOFER and K. RAHNER (Freiburg 1957–65) 6:1150–51.

[J. M. CARMODY]

RAPHAEL, ARCHANGEL

The angel who is one of the chief figures in the story of Tobit. The Book of TOBIT (Tobias) is the only book in the Bible that mentions him. In Hebrew his name *rᵉpā'ēl* (cf. 1 Chr 26.7) means ''God has healed.''

The stature of Raphael attained in pre-Christian Jewish and Christian belief as an instrument of divine intervention. Raphael appears as God's envoy, sent to answer Tobit's and Sarah's separate prayers by healing Tobit's blindness and by providing a husband for Sarah [Tb 3:16–17 (3.26 in Vulgate)]. Tobias, Tobit's son, is guided to Rages, Media, by Raphael, now disguised as a fellow Israelite. He leads Tobias to a happy marriage with Sarah (thus answering her prayer), collects Tobias' inheritance as a wedding gift, and finally brings the happy couple back to Tobit, whose blindness he then cures. Before returning to the heavenly court, he reveals himself to be ''one of the seven Angels who are ever ready to enter into the presence of the Lord's glory'' (12.12, 15).

The Bible mentions by name only three angels, Raphael, MICHAEL, and GABRIEL. Apocryphal works supply other names but usually in legendary fashion.

"The Archangel Leaving the Family of Tobias," painting by Rembrandt, 1637. (©Francis G. Mayer/CORBIS)

A cultus of Raphael appeared rather late and then only infrequently. A Venetian church was dedicated to him in the 7th century. Isolated references appeared honoring him on various dates, but only in the 17th century did Masses in his honor become more numerous. In 1921 Benedict XV instituted a universal feast for him, to be celebrated on October 24. The post-Vatican II reform of the Roman liturgical calendar created a combined Feast of the Archangels Michael, Gabriel and Raphael on September 29. In the Eastern Christian Tradition, the Feast of the Archangels is celebrated on November 8.

Images of Raphael before the 16th century are rare, but since then he has been widely depicted as the patron of travelers.

Bibliography: D. KECK, *Angels and Angelology in the Middle Ages* (New York 1998).

[T. L. FALLON/EDS.]

RAPID CITY, DIOCESE OF

Established first at Lead, South Dakota in 1902, the seat of the diocese was transferred to Rapid City (*Rapidopolitana*) in 1930. It is a suffragan of the metropolitan See of St. Paul-Minneapolis. The diocese includes about 43,000 square miles, all of the state west of the Missouri River. The leading Sioux reservations are located in this diocese. The first bishop was John Stariha (1902–1909), who resigned because of ill health and was succeeded by Joseph Busch (1910–1915). John Lawler (1916–1948) became bishop, followed by William T. McCarty (1948–1969), Harold J. Dimmerling (1969–1987), and Charles J. Chaput OFM Cap. (1987–1998), who was appointed archbishop of Denver ten years later. Blase J. Cupich was installed as bishop in September, 1998.

Of the more that 222,000 people in the area, about 32,000 are Catholic. Some 10,000 of these are on the Indian Reservations: Pine Ridge, Rosebud, Crow Creek, Lower Brule and the southern section of Standing Rock. A diocesan Native Concerns Office addresses the needs of the Native Americans on and off the reservations. When Martin Marty, Vicar Apostolic of Dakota Territory in the late 19th century, could find no more Benedictine priest-monks for the reservations, he recruited German Jesuit priests to staff them. They were assisted by Sisters of St. Francis, Daughters of the Heart of Mary, Benedictine nuns, Presentations and Sisters of Charity. The Oblate Sisters of the Blessed Sacrament, was organized at Marty Mission near Wagner by the Benedictine monk-missionary, Father Sylvester Eisenman, in cooperation with Mother (now Saint) Katharine DREXEL and the Pennsylvania Congregation of Blessed Sacrament Sisters who staffed the school that continues to serve the people at Marty as well as staffing Kateri Convent in Rapid City from which the Sisters tend home-bound Native Americans in the area. At Howes, the Mahpiya na Maka Center, staffed by Jesuits, is a spiritual haven for the Sioux. In Eagle Butte, on the Crow Creek Reservation, the Sacred Heart Fathers supervise the Sacred Heart Center which assists almost 1,000 Native Americans. The Chamberlain Indian School is also under the supervision of the Sacred Heart Fathers.

In 2001 the diocese claimed almost 36,000 Catholics in 97 parishes, served by 31 priests, and 27 Permanent Deacons, seven Brothers of religious orders, ten Sisters and 27 lay ministers. About 15 young men are preparing for the priesthood in out-of-state seminaries. Several congregations of Sisters have a presence in the diocese: Dominicans, Notre Dames, Franciscans, Sisters of Charity, Presentations, Sisters of the Divine Savior, and Brothers of St. Francis Xavier. The diocese has a Benedictine monastery originally from Melchtal, Switzerland. In 1888 the nuns arrived in Sturgis where their first monastery was a former wayside tavern. In 1962 the monastics relocated to Rapid City. There are 36 nuns who share their acreage with retreatants, guests, and groups utilizing their community center.

The diocese has Catholic high schools and grade schools educating over 6,000 students. Between 700 and 800 infants are baptized annually, over 90 adults, and 120 are received into full communion in the church each year. Over 500 Catholics are annually confirmed. Interfaith marriages dominate, 116 over 83 Catholic ceremonies in 2001.

Social services of all kinds, educational institutions, as well as religious and spiritual opportunities exist in the diocese for the Catholic population, non-Indian as well as Native American.

Bibliography: C. DURATCHEK, *The Beginnings of Catholicism in South Dakota* (Washington D.C. 1943); *Crusading Along Sioux Trails* (St. Meinrad, Ind. 1947). R. KAROLEVETZ, *With Faith, Hope and Tenacity* (Sioux Falls 1989); *Bishop Martin Marty: Black Robe Lean Chief* (Yankton 1980). A. KESSLER, ''First Catholic Bishop of Dakota,'' in *South Dakota Leaders,* eds. H. HOOVER et al. (Vermillion 1989).

[A. KESSLER]

RAPIN, RENÉ

Jesuit theologian, literary critic, and historian of the Jansenist movement; b. Tours, France, Nov. 3, 1621; d. Paris, Oct. 27, 1687. Rapin entered the Society of Jesus in 1639, and taught rhetoric for nine years at Tours and

Paris before commencing his career as an author. He wrote many theological and ascetical works, such as *L'Esprit du christianisme* (Paris 1672), *La Perfection du christianisme* (Paris 1673), and *La Foi des derniers siècles* (Paris 1679). His chief importance, however, lies in the prominent part he played against the Jansenists. His lively *Histoire du Jansénisme* (ed. E. Domenech, Paris 1861) and its sequel, *Mémoires sur l'Église . . .* (ed. L. Aubineau, 3 v. Paris 1865), despite strong bias, greatly illumine their subject.

As a Latin versifier and literary critic, Rapin enjoyed an even greater reputation among his contemporaries. They acclaimed his *Hortorum libri IV* (Paris 1665) worthy of the Age of Augustus. This work encouraged the vogue for ''Nature'' gardens, themselves part of the wider cult of ''Nature'' that permeated philosophy, literature, and the arts until at least the French Revolution. His influence is also recognizable in the writings of Jean de La Bruyère. Despite Rapin's conservatism, apparent for example in his *Réflexions sur la poetique d'Aristote . . .* (Paris 1676), in which he champions the ''ancients'' against the ''moderns'' in that famous quarrel, his literary criticism reflects originality.

Bibliography: J. ORCIBAL, *Les Origines du jansénisme,* 5 v. (Louvain 1947–62) v. 3. E. B. O. BORGERHOFF, *The Freedom of French Classicism* (Princeton 1950). F. COUREL, *Lexikon für Theologie und Kirche*, ed. J. HOFER and K. RAHNER (Freiberg 1957–65) 8:992–993. P. GALTIER, *Dictionnaire de théologie catholique*, ed. A. VACANT et al. (Paris 1903–50) 13.2:1663. C. SOMMERVOGEL et al., *Bibliothéque de la Compagnie de Jésus* (Brussels-Paris 1890–1932) 6:1443–58.

[J. Q. C. MACKRELL]

RAPP, JOHANN GEORG

Founder of the Harmony Society; b. Iplingen, Württemburg, Germany, Nov. 1, 1757; d. Economy, Pa., Aug. 7, 1847. He was the son of a prosperous farmer. Although he had little formal education, Rapp was deeply influenced by the writings of J. Böhme, P. J. Spener, E. Swedenborg, and other German mystical theologians, and he gathered some followers into a spiritual family. In 1803 he went to the United States to select a site for a community; his disciples joined him in 1805 to form the Harmony Society at Harmony, Butler County, Pennsylvania. All goods were held in common and after 1807 celibacy was enforced. The community migrated to New Harmony, Posey County, Indiana, in 1814 and in 1825 moved to Economy, near Pittsburgh, Pennsylvania. Rapp continued as the group's spiritual leader and virtual dictator until his death. His eclectic theology was expounded in his *Thoughts on the Destiny of Man* (1824).

Bibliography: C. KNOEDLER, *The Harmony Society* (New York 1954). J. S. DUSS, *George Rapp and His Associates* (Indianapolis 1914); *The Harmonists* (State College, Pa. 1943).

[R. K. MACMASTER]

RAPTURE

The term ''rapture,'' which is derived from the Greek *harpazō* and the Latin *raptus*, has the general meaning of something being quickly snatched away or taken by force. Traditionally it was used to describe a particularly elevated kind of mystical experience. More recently it has been used in certain fundamentalist circles with reference to the ''end time.'' In both cases, biblical texts that include forms of *harpazō*; form a basis for the use of the term in Christian life and literature; the present understanding is also profoundly affected by a long history of extra-biblical developments.

Paul's statement that he was ''caught up into Paradise and heard ineffable things, which no one may utter'' (2 Cor 12:4) is the most prominent biblical description of mystical rapture. In the later tradition of Christian mysticism, general characteristics of rapture (as distinct from other deep experiences of union with God) include: it comes upon one suddenly, without warning; one has the awareness of being irresistibly acted upon by God; one is completely entranced interiorly, losing some or all of the ability to use one's physical or mental faculties; and blissful supernatural knowledge is infused.

The term ''rapture'' is applied with different nuances by various mystics, and some use other terms for what appears to be the same phenomenon. Teresa of Avila, for example, names ''suspensions,'' ''transports, ''flights of the spirit,'' and ''impulses,'' while the Rhineland and Flemish mystics such as Hadewijch of Antwerp and Jan Ruusbroec speak of a ''storm of love.'' All of these seem to manifest the general features named above. The extreme character of these experiences sometimes leaves the body exhausted, in pain, or out of joint, but if aa rapture is genuine its long-term effects will be beneficial. Authentic raptures usually occur at an advanced point in the mystical life, when the mystic is undergoing the final purification before entering the culminating ''spiritual marriage.'' Spiritual teachers agree that these experiences are not to be sought after, especially because of the great danger of ''false raptures'' induced by causes such as mental illness, emotional or physical stress, overwrought imagination, or malevolent spirits.

Today, certain groups of fundamentalist Christians believe that at Jesus' second coming he will literally ''snatch away'' all those who have been faithful to him.

He will then wreak destruction upon the remaining sinners, after which he will return to earth with those he has saved and reign for a thousand years before the final annihilation of the earth. The basis of this belief is a literal interpretation of 1 Thes 4:17, which says that believers who are still alive at Christ's coming "will be caught up together with [those who have died] in the clouds to meet the Lord in the air." This form of fundamentalism, which is called "dispensationalist millennialism," was founded by J. N. DARBY (1800–1882) and disseminated through the very popular *Scofield Reference Bible* (1909).

Many scholars criticize this dispensationalist doctrine of the "rapture" on both biblical and theological grounds. First, the imagery of the Thessalonians text needs to be interpreted in view of its background in Jewish apocalyptic literature, in which it is not uncommon for visionaries to be "snatched up" to heaven. This genre of writing is not intended to provide literal descriptions of past or future events, but rather to offer a mythic framework of hope to communities in crisis. The larger context of 1 Thes 4:17 indicates that Paul's main purpose is to reassure grieving Christians that a day is coming when the dead and the living will be equal and together again as one community with the Lord. The dispensationalist doctrine of the rapture, on the other hand, stresses separation, vengeance, and destruction rather than reconciliation, hope, and constructive activity. An adequate understanding of "rapture" must be approached by careful study of the full range of biblical and post-biblical insights into how God acts powerfully and salvifically within human lives and communities.

Bibliography: Z. HAYES, "Fundamentalist Eschatology: Piety and Politics," *New Theology Review* 1 (1988) 21–35. R. JEWETT, *Jesus against the Rapture* (Philadephia 1979). A. T. LINCOLN, "Paul the Visionary: The Setting and Significance of the Rapture to Paradise in II Corinthians XII.1–10," *New Testament Studies* 25 (1979) 204–20. E. J. RICHARD, *First and Second Thessalonians* Sacra Pagina Series 11 (Collegeville, Minn. 1995) 224–48. TERESA OF AVILA, "Spiritual Testimony 59," in *The Collected Works of St. Teresa of Avila,* v. 1, tr. K. KAVANAUGH and O. RODRIGUEZ (Washington, D.C. 1987).

[M. FROHLICH]

RASH JUDGMENT

An act of mind that, on the basis of insufficient evidence, attributes something morally discreditable to another or denies something morally creditable. As judgment, it is an act that affirms or denies with certainty and without the hesitation that is characteristic of suspicion. In suspicion one is inclined to accept something discreditable as true, but judgment accepts it with firm conviction. Rash judgment differs much more from doubt in a similar context. In doubt judgment is suspended and one hesitates between taking either a favorable or an unfavorable view. As rash, the judgment here in question is essentially imprudent precisely because it lacks a reasonable foundation. This is true even when the judgment happens accidentally to be in accord with fact, for the rashness or temerity of the act does not depend on its disagreement with fact but on the inconclusive nature of the evidence on which it is based.

Rash judgment that goes so far as to judge not merely exterior actions but internal culpability is offensive to God because it usurps His exclusive right to judge the hearts of men (1 Cor 4.5; Rom 14.4). In addition, it does a moral INJURY to the person judged, who has a right, if not to the positive good esteem of others, at least not to be held in disesteem without sufficient reason. This right is a matter of value to him and he should not be despoiled of it unless by his conduct he has forfeited claim to it. Moreover, rash judgment is a form of injustice apt to diffuse itself and result in further injuries. The internal judgment of the mind naturally seeks external expression, which it finds either by communication to others in the form of calumny or in the denial of the marks of respect to which the injured party is entitled.

Rash judgment is contrary to charity, which, according to St. Paul, thinks no evil (1 Cor 13.5). This opposition is apparent in the nature of the act. When the mind goes beyond evidence in its judgments it is the will that supplies for the deficiency of the premises. One believes because he wants to believe. Thus the wish that is father to the kind of thought involved in rash judgment is essentially malevolent and rejoices over wickedness in contradiction to the impulse of charity (1 Cor 13.6). However, the more immediate and specific malice of rash judgment lies in its opposition to justice.

Rash judgment is held by theologians to be a serious sin whenever the conditions necessary for subjective responsibility are fully realized and the judgment is concerned with something more than slight moral shortcomings. The severity with which rash judgment is condemned in the Scriptures is evidence of the gravity of the sin according to its kind (Mt 7.1–5; Lk 6.37). However, in any particular case rash judgment is not held to be mortally sinful unless the following conditions are verified: (1) The judgment must be fully deliberate and must consist of something more than vagrant and abrupt speculation. This condition implies also the necessity of advertence to the sinfulness of the judgment as well as to the fact of its being unsupported by reasonable evidence. (2) The rashness must be notable, that is, there must be a marked insufficiency of evidence. Thus it does not appear that it would be mortally sinful to take as certain something that could reasonably be considered highly probable. (3) The discreditable thing attributed to the person rashly judged must be of a serious nature, either in itself or by reason of the circumstances of the one misjudged, as when a person in a position of dignity and responsibility is rashly judged to be a habitual liar.

It is disputed among theologians whether the same malice attaches to unfounded suspicion and doubt as to rash judgment. Some argue that it does, since the Scriptures appear to make no distinction between these different acts of mind, and ill will among men is more often founded on doubt, suspicion and opinion than upon certain judgment. Others deny this and hold that suspicion and doubt do a lesser injury because, although they diminish one's good esteem for others, they do not extinguish it.

Because one is obliged to avoid rash judgment, suspicion and doubt, it does not follow that it is immoral to take prudent precautions against the possibility that another may be sinfully inclined.

Bibliography: THOMAS AQUINAS, *Summa theologiae* 2a2ae 60.3–4. ALPHONSUS LIGOURI, *Theologia moralis,* ed. L. GAUDÉ, 4 v. (new ed. Rome 1905–12; repr. 1953) 3:962–965. J. A. MCHUGH and C. J. CALLAN, *Moral Theology,* 2 v. (New York 1930 2:55–62. H. NOLDIN, *Summa theologiae moralis,* rev. A. SCHMITT and G. HEINZEL, 3 v. (Innsbruck 1961–62) 2:576–578. D. M. PRÜMMER, *Manuale theologiae moralis,* ed. E. M. MÜNCH, 3 v. (12th ed. Freiburg-Barcelona 1955) 2:179–181. A. HOUVENIN, *Dictionnaire de théologie catholique,* ed., A. VACANT et al., 15 v. (Paris 1903–50) .2:1828–32.

[P. K. MEAGHER]

RASHI (RABBI SHELOMOH BEN YISHAQ)

One of the most famous of medieval commentators on the Bible and the Talmud; b. Troyes, France, 1041; d. there, July 13, 1105. His popular name, Rashi, is formed on the initials of his title and name, R(abbi) Sh(elomoh ben) Y(ishaq), Hebrew for Rabbi Solomon, son of Isaac.

Life. Little is known with certainty of Rashi's life. After his boyhood at Troyes in northwestern France, he studied at Worms under Rabbi Jacob ben Yaqar and at Mainz under Rabbi Isaac ben Judah. At the age of 25 he returned to Troyes, where he remained for the rest of his life. The stories about his extensive travels in Egypt, Persia, Spain, Germany, and Italy to increase his knowledge are legends with no foundation in fact. At Troyes he established a school of Jewish studies, where numerous students attended his lectures. He supported himself, however, not by tuition from his students, but by the income from his vineyard. His last years were saddened by anti-Jewish riots in the Rhineland on the occasion of the First Crusade.

Writings. Besides several minor works, Rashi wrote commentaries on almost all the books of the Hebrew Bible and on most of the tractates of the Talmud. As a biblical exegete he is best known for his commentary on the Pentateuch. Printed at Reggio in 1475, it is the first book printed in Hebrew to bear a date. In its Bologna edition of 1482, the commentary was printed with the Hebrew text of the Pentateuch, the latter in the center of the page, the former in the margin. This way of printing rabbinical commentaries was later followed in the so-called RABBINICAL BIBLES, and the semicursive form of medieval script in which these commentaries are printed in these Bibles is commonly called ''Rashi script.'' Also worthy of note among the Hebrew incunabula are his commentaries on the Song of Songs, Ecclesiastes, Ruth, Esther, Daniel, Ezra and Nehemiah (the last two probably not authentic), which were first printed at Naples in 1487. Both his commentaries on the Bible and those on the Talmud were in turn often commented on by Jewish scholars. The *editio princeps* of all his commentaries on the Bible was published in Venice in 1525. During the sixteenth and seventeenth centuries several Latin translations of his biblical commentaries were published.

Appraisal. With the exception of MAIMONIDES, Rashi probably exercised a greater influence on Jewish life and thought than any other rabbi of the Middle Ages. His principal contribution was made by his commentary on the Talmud, in which he combined sound judgment and practical sense with an extensive knowledge of rabbinical traditions. While not all his interpretations of Jewish laws were accepted by his contemporaries or by later generations, his opinions on these matters were always respected and in most cases followed.

His biblical commentaries, however, owed their popularity, more to their conciseness and general clarity than to their scientific value. For intrinsic value, the commentaries on the Sacred Scriptures by his grandson Rabbi Samuel ben Meir, popularly known as Rashbam, are superior. Yet Rashi has always been regarded by the Jews as the classical interpreter of the Bible, from whom the ordinary pious as well as students can receive spiritual nourishment. In fact, for centuries his commentaries on the biblical books constituted the manual from which young Jewish students learned to read the Holy Scriptures and obtained their first knowledge of rabbinical literature. ''Every educated Jew knows that one must begin with Rashi to enter the world of the Bible'' (A. Neher).

In his exegesis Rashi combines an interpretation of the literal sense with personal views and haggadic traditions (*see* HAGGADAH). At times he does not hesitate to insert fables or allegories into his commentaries. While he thus allows considerable space to such MIDRASH, he tries in general to give a rational exegesis and often repeats the statement of the Talmud: ''A text must not be twisted from its natural sense.'' His commentaries on the Bible were read and studied also by certain Christian scholars of the late Middle Ages and Renaissance, particularly by Nicholas of Lyra, who in turn had considerable influence on Martin Luther's translation and interpretation of the Bible.

The writings of Rashi have proved a boon in another field of study. Although on the whole he wrote in medieval Hebrew, for the sake of clarity he often inserted words or phrases taken from his native French but written in Hebrew script. More than 3,000 of such *lă'āzîm* (Hebrew for ''foreign words'') constituting a vocabulary of about 2,000 words occur in his works. Since he is consistent in his method of transcribing foreign words in Hebrew characters, these Old French words he uses are a valuable source for the recovery of the language that was spoken in the eleventh century in the province of Champagne in northern France.

Bibliography: M. LIBER, *The Jewish Encyclopedia,* ed. J. SINGER, 13 v. (New York 1901–01) 10:324–328. RASHI, *Commentary on the Pentateuch,* tr. M. ROSENBAUM and A. M. SILBERMANN, 5 v. in 2 (London 1946). American Academy for Jewish Research, *Rashi Anniversary Volume* (New York 1941). S. M. BLUMENFIELD, *Master of Troyes* (New York 1946). E. I. J. ROSENTHAL, ''Rashi and the English Bible,'' *The Bulletin of the John Rylands Library* 24 (1940): 138–167. S. FEDERBUSCH, ed., *Rashi, His Teachings and Personality* (New York 1958). H. HAILPERIN, *Rashi and the Christian Scholars* (Pittsburgh 1963). A. DARMESTETER and D. S. BLONDHEIM, *Les Gloses françaises dans les commentaires talmudiques de Raschi,* 2 v. (Paris 1929, Baltimore 1937).

[A. BRUNOT]

RASKOLNIKS

Raskol'niki, or schismatics, was the term applied to numerous members of the clergy and people of Russia who rebelled against the ritualistic reforms introduced in mid-17th century by the Patriarch NIKON. Nikon was supported by Czar Alexis in an effort to bring the ceremonial of the official church into closer conformity with the Greek usages of Constantinople and the Ukraine. The Ukrainian Rada voted allegiance to Great Russia in the year following the Nikonian reform (1654).

The famous Russian dissenters called themselves Old Ritualists or Old Believers. Their protest of 1653 was a nationalistic reaction against the introduction of foreign elements into Russian religion; it was indicative of the traditional confusion and identification of external rite (*obriad*) with the underlying dogmatic truth or faith (*vera*) symbolized by the outward sign. Thus thousands of Russians were to die as zealous martyrs for the sake of form.

Background. The precise nature of the process involved is not clear, but with the passage of years since the 10th-century conversion of St. Vladimir and his Russia to the Catholicism of Byzantium with its Greek usages, a peculiarly Russian manner of external worship developed, differing in certain details from the Greek way of Constantinople. Differences may have arisen originally with the hasty translation of Greek service books in the attempt to give Russians the Faith in something like the vernacular. The existence of such ''errors'' in formula had been apparent previously to such churchmen as Maksim the Greek and to the Council of the Stoglav in the days of Ivan IV; but all attempts at modifying the Muscovite practices in favor of the Greek failed. Thus, in their processions during the divine liturgy, priests of the Muscovite patriarchate, unlike those of Constantinople, ''marched with the sun.'' They differed from the Greeks in their spelling of the Savior's name, and intoned the Alleluia twice. The faithful made the sign of the cross with two fingers in honor of the two natures in Christ; the Greeks prescribed the use of three fingers to commemorate the Triune God. The churches of Muscovy were adorned by an eight-pointed cross.

Origin. In 1653, during a period of general unrest and riot following Czar Alexis' legal codification (*Ulozhenie* of 1649), which made serfdom the law of the land, the Patriarch Nikon issued a pastoral letter decreeing that henceforth Greek usages alone would be permitted in the state Orthodox Church. Many of the minor clergy and their people looked upon the reform as an innovation that violated Moscow's stand on the union reached at the Council of FLORENCE. To them it represented a corruption of the Greek faith, and was contrary to the tradition of Moscow as the Third Rome. The reform seemed also to undermine the position of Moscow as an independent patriarchate. The Nikonian reforms were confirmed three times by the Church Sobor (synod) in Moscow. Opponents of the liturgical changes were anathematized as schismatics (*Raskol'niki*) in 1666. Bishop Paul of Kolomna was degraded; Neronov, Loggin, Danilo, the Archpriest AVVAKUM, and others were exiled, tortured, and martyred for their recalcitrance.

History. The Russian government continued its oppressive measures against the dissenters until 1900. In the 17th century alone, more than 20,000 Old Ritualists voluntarily surrendered, or burned or buried themselves alive as fanatic martyrs for the sake of form. From the standpoint of political ideology Russia's *Raskol'niki* have constituted a nationalistic conservative group traditionally hostile to officialdom, government, and the established Church. The opposition of these right-wing revolutionaries to the czar at the time of the break was based not on the czar's assumption of ecclesiastical power at the downfall of Nikon (1666), but rather on the ruler's acquiescence in the abolition of old Russian ceremonials, his betrayal of a Russian national tradition.

Among these revolutionary Old Believer schismatics numerous offshoots and strange religious aberrations developed, and a number of Russian sects evolved: Popovtsy, Bezpopovtsy, Khlysty, Skoptsy, Molokane, Dukhobortsy, etc. In 1917, between 20 and 25 million Old Believers of one variety or another existed in Russia.

Bibliography: P. PASCAL, *Avvakum et les débuts du raskol* (new ed. The Hague-Paris 1964). S. BOLSHAKOFF, *Russian Nonconformity* (Philadelphia 1950). V. PLEYER, *Das russische Altgläubigentum* (Munich 1961). P. HAUPTMANN, *Altrussische Glaube* (Göttingen 1963); *Lexikon für Theologie und Kirche*, ed. J. HOFER and K. RAHNER, 10 v. (2d new ed. Freiburg 1957–65) 8:993–995. J. LEDIT, *Dictionnaire de théologie catholique*, ed. A. VACANT et al., 15 v. (Paris 1903–50; Tables générales 1951) 14.1:292–304.

[F. L. FADNER]

RASOAMANARIVO, VICTORIA, BL.

Lay woman; b. 1848, Tamanarive, Madagascar (now Malagasy Republic); d. there Aug. 21, 1894. Born into a leading family headed by her maternal grandfather who was prime minister, Victoria was educated by the Jesuits and St. Joseph Sisters. Victoria was baptized on March 1, 1863, and the following year (March 13, 1864) married her first cousin, a debauched alcoholic who abused her. Despite her unhappy marriage, Victoria refused divorce in the hope of influencing her husband to conversion. She baptized him herself on his deathbed following an accident (*c.* 1888).

Victoria is revered as the mother of the Malagasy Church for her role in preserving and spreading Catholicism in the absence of priests and missionaries, who had been banished following the overthrow of King Radama II (1883) and the first Franco-Malagasy war. She encouraged young lay Catholics through the Catholic Union, kept Catholic schools open, supported liturgical practice in the absence of pastors, defended imprisoned Catholics, and cared for the poor and lepers. When missionaries returned in 1886, they found the Church still vibrant.

Victoria was declared venerable in 1983 and beatified at Antanarivo, Madagascar by John Paul II, April 30, 1989. Patron of abused spouses.

Feast: Aug. 21.

Bibliography: K. L. WOODWARD, *Making Saints: How the Catholic Church Determines Who Becomes a Saint, Who Doesn't, and Why* (New York 1990): 210. *Acta Apostolica Sedis* (1989): 536–39.

[K. I. RABENSTEIN]

RASPUTIN, GRIGORIĬ EFIMOVICH

Russian religious figure; b. Pokrovskoe, Tobolsk Province, Siberia, *c.* 1871; d. Petrograd, Dec. 16, 1916. He came of a peasant family surnamed Novykh, received little formal education, and married in 1895. In 1904 he left his wife and three children to lead a wandering life. His pilgrimages to holy places took him to Mt. Athos and Jerusalem. As suited his passionate, superstitious character, he joined the *Khlysty* (People of God), a pantheistic, blasphemous sect that mingled emotional religion with debauchery. At this time he changed his name to Rasputin (licentious) and advocated the commission of sin in order to gain forgiveness. His excesses and violent acts of repentance impressed the peasants, who regarded him as a holy man with remarkable supernatural powers. Rasputin's reputation as a thaumaturge led to his introduction to the royal family (1907), on whom he made a lasting impression by seeming to cure the czarevich Alexis of hemophilia. Czar Nicholas II and his wife Empress Alexandra were convinced that Rasputin was sent by God, and accepted his advice on matters of state. Soon Rasputin dictated the choice of cabinet ministers and Orthodox bishops. His reputation increased among the populace after an unsuccessful attempt on his life in 1914, engineered by Heliodor, a well-known monk. Rasputin's ignorance of political affairs made him a pawn for reactionaries, who courted his friendship and imparted to him the ideas that he passed on to the Czar. Rasputin was shot to death in an assassination plot led by Grand Duke Dimitry Pavlovich, Prince Yussopov, and other nobles. At Empress Alexandra's orders Rasputin was buried with solemnity near the royal family's chapel in the imperial palace at Tsarkoe Selo (now Pushkin); but after the 1917 revolution a mob dug up the cadaver and burned it.

Bibliography: S. M. TRUFANOV, *The Mad Monk of Russia,* tr. from Russian (New York 1918). E. RADZIWILL, *Rasputin and the Russian Revolution* (New York 1918). R. T. M. SCOTT, *The Mad Monk* (New York 1931). R. FÜLÖP-MILLER, *Rasputin, the Holy Devil,* tr. F. S. FLINT and D. F. TAIT (New York 1928). H. LIEPMANN, *Rasputin and the Fall of Imperial Russia,* tr. E. FITZGERALD (New York 1959).

[G. A. MALONEY]

RASSLER, CHRISTOPH

Jesuit moral theologian; b. Constance, Aug. 12, 1654; d. Rome, July 16, 1723. He entered the Society of

Jesus in 1669, and from 1685 to 1714 he taught theology at Ingolstadt and Dillingen. He was rector of the college at Dillingen for two years, and in 1716 he was called to Rome to serve as revisor general of the society and prefect of studies at the German college. Rassler was deeply engaged in the theological disputes of his day that revolved around the theory of probabilism and was one of the leading German Jesuits who sought to hold a moderate position against the extremes of rigorism and laxism. After producing a number of works dealing with the subject of probabilism, he summarized his thought well in his *Norma recti* (Ingolstadt 1713). This work presents a point of view that would later be called EQUIPROBABILISM. By the time that equiprobabilism gained stature in theological circles, the work of Rassler had been forgotten. He apparently, however, influenced the thinking of Eusebius AMORT, to whom St. Alphonsus Liguori acknowledged his indebtedness, and thereby indirectly contributed to the formation of the theory of equiprobabilism.

Bibliography: C. SOMMERVOGEL et al., *Bibliothèque de la Compagnie de Jésus,* 11 v. (Brussels-Paris 1890–1932; v. 12, suppl. 1960) 6:1461–64. H. HURTER, *Nomenclator literarius theologiae catholicae,* 5 v. in 6 (3d ed. Innsbruck 1903–13); v. 1 (4th ed. 1926) 4:1298–99. R. BROUILLARD, *Dictionnaire de théologie catholique,* ed. A. VACANT et al., 15 v. (Paris 1903–50; Tables générales 1951–) 13.2:1675–77.

[J. C. WILLKE]

Grigoriĭ Efimovich Rasputin. (Archive Photos)

RASTELL, JOHN AND WILLIAM

John, printer and brother-in-law of St. Thomas MORE; b. Coventry, 1475; d. London, 1536. John Rastell entered the Middle Temple before 1500, married Elizabeth More before 1504, and was settled in London by 1510, where he added printing to his legal work. Among the earliest books he printed were More's *Pico* and Linacre's *Latin Grammar.* He served in the French war of 1512 and took part in an abortive voyage to the New World in 1517. He helped in the embellishment of the Field of Cloth of Gold and, in later years, of several London pageants. He compiled a number of law books and wrote several interludes. Under the influence of John Frith, he accepted Lutheran notions and campaigned against tithes. In spite of his friendship with Thomas CROMWELL, he was sent to prison where he died.

William, nephew of St. Thomas More; b. London?, 1508; d. Louvain, 1565. William Rastell was probably educated with the More children. He assisted his father, John, in his print shop until 1529 when he set up his own printing press and produced his uncle's controversial writings. After More's death he studied law at Lincoln's Inn and was called to the bar in 1539. He married Winifred, daughter of John and Margaret Clement, in 1544. Forced into exile under the Protestant policy of Edward VI in 1549, they settled at Louvain. After Winifred's death in 1553, William returned to England, published his uncle's *English Works* in 1557, and became a judge of the Queen's Bench in 1558. Under ELIZABETH I, he again went into exile where he published his uncle's Latin works at Louvain in 1565. He wrote a life of St. Thomas More, but only fragments referring to St. John FISHER are extant.

Bibliography: A. W. REED, *Early Tudor Drama* (London 1926). *The Dictionary of National Biography from the Earliest Times to 1900* (London 1885–1900) 16:746. J. GILLOW, *A Literary and Biographical History or Bibliographical Dictionary of the English Catholics from 1534 to the Present Time* (London–New York 1885–1902) 5:387–392.

[E. E. REYNOLDS]

RATHERIUS OF VERONA

Benedictine of LOBBES, bishop of Verona (931–968) and Liège (953–956), theologian; b. near Liège, *c.* 890; d. Namur, Belgium, April 25, 974. Ratherius was restless, ambitious, tactless, well read in the classics and the Fathers, and an accuser and defender of himself; yet he was ever the monk, intransigently set upon immediate reform of his clergy, easily finding protectors among the great, and making enemies among his subordinates. He accompanied his deposed abbot and rejected bishop, Hilduin, to Hugh of Provence, King of Italy (920), and succeeded Hilduin as bishop of Verona (931). Objecting to the king's meddling in ecclesiastical matters, he was imprisoned near Pavia (934–936) where he composed his most important work, *Praeloquia*, a guide to right living, and was subsequently exiled to Como (936–939).

Upon his release, he stopped in Provence (939–944) on his way back to Lobbes. Recalled to Verona by Hugh (946), he again had to flee to Provence (948). He campaigned with Emperor OTTO I's son Ludolph and with Otto (948–951), was summoned from Lobbes by Otto to teach in the palace school (952), and was made bishop of Liège by Otto's brother, Abp. BRUNO OF COLOGNE (953). When forced to flee after an uprising, he took refuge with Abp. William of Mainz and acted as abbot of AULNE-SUR-SAMBRE (956), where he composed *Conclusio deliberativa, Phrenesis,* and *Excerptum ex dialogo confessionali.*

Recalled to Verona by Otto (962), he finally yielded his see (968) after further struggles with his clergy and returned to Lobbes. He intrigued unsuccessfully against Abbot FOLCWIN of Lobbes and was forced to return to Aulne. He died on a visit to the Count of Namur. Besides the works mentioned and a number of pamphlets composed at Verona (962–968) and at Aulne, he left 34 letters and several sermons.

Bibliography: Works. *Patrologia Latina,* ed. J. P. MIGNE (Paris 1878–90) 136:9–768, on which cf. É. AMANN, *Dictionnaire de théologie catholique*, ed. A. VACANT et al., (Paris 1903–50) 13.2:1679–88. F. WEIGLE, *Die Briefe des Bischofs Rather von Verona* (*Monumentua Germaniae Historica Die Briefe der deutschen Kaiserzeit* 1; Weimar 1949); "Die Briefe Rathers von V.," *Deutsches Archiv für Erforschung des Mittelalters* 1 (1937) 147–194; "R. von V. im Kampf um das Kirchengut 961–968," *Quellen und Forschungen aus italienischen Archiven und Biblilttheken* 28 (1937) 1–35; "Zur Geschichte des Bischofs R. von V.," *Deutsches Archiv für Erforschung des Mittelalters* 5 (1942) 347–386. A. VOGEL, *R. von V. und das 10. Jahrhundert,* 2 v. in 1 (Jena 1854). B. SCHWARK, *Bischof R. von Verona als Theologe* (Königsberg 1916). M. MANITIUS, *Geschichte der lateinischen Literatur des Mittelalters* (Munich 1911–31) 2:34–52. A. ADAM, *Arbeit und Besitz nach R. von V.* (Freiburg 1927). G. MONTICELLI, *Raterio, vescovo di Verona, 890–974* (Milan 1938). G. MISCH, *Geschichte der Autobiographie,* v.2.2 (3d ed. Frankfurt a.M. 1955) 519–650. H. M. KLINKENBERG, "Versuche und Untersuchungen zur Autobiographie bei R. von V.," *Archiv für Kulturgeschichte* 38 (1956) 265–314. C. LEONARDI, "Raterio e Marziano Capella," *Italia medioevale e umanistica* 2 (1959) 73–102. G. BILLANOVICH, "Dal Livio di Raterio (Laur. 63, 19) al Livio del Petrarca (B.M. Harl. 2493)," *ibid.,* 103–178.

[J. N. GARVIN]

RATIO STUDIORUM

The abbreviated term for the Jesuit curricular and methods guide, which appeared in 1599 under the title *Ratio atque Institutio Studiorum Societatis Iesu.*

Organization. This document is a collection of 30 sets of practical regulations for administrators, teachers, and students of Jesuit establishments. When fully developed, these institutions offered instruction in three faculties or curricular areas, and the Ratio's rules referred to one or all of these. In the faculty of letters or classical language studies, the program was divided into five main sections: three grammar classes, whose readings and exercises the Ratio gave in detaïl; humanities, which emphasized poetry; and rhetoric. The arts faculty provided a three-year course in philosophy together with some science and mathematics. Studies in the theology faculty covered four years and were normally pursued only by candidates for the priesthood. Not every Jesuit college possessed each of these faculties but all had at least the faculty of letters, which constituted a secondary or middle school between the abecadarian exercises of elementary education and professional specialization in such university faculties as theology, medicine, and law. The prestige of 16th- and 17th-century Jesuit educators was chiefly associated with these middle schools, and the Ratio deals principally with their work or that of the arts curriculum.

Origin. An account of the Ratio may conveniently consider its origins and its contents. IGNATIUS OF LOYOLA (1491–1556), founder of the Society of Jesus (*see* JESUITS), began the process that culminated in the Ratio of 1599. The Fourth Part of the *Constitutions,* which Ignatius wrote for the Society, dealt with the Jesuits' own training and with their schools. Its 13th chapter called for eventual construction of a "separate treatise" detailing particulars of schedules, curricula, and pupil exercises. During the quarter-century following Ignatius's death, numerous discussions of these matters emerged from Jesuit schools. These have been collected in *Monumenta Paedagogica,* a volume appearing in Madrid in 1901, as part of the continuing series *Monumenta Historica Societatis Jesu.* It was Claudio Aquaviva, however, elected fifth general of the Society in 1581, who brought the Ignatian directive to fulfillment. He appointed a six-man delegation that in 1586 produced a trial version of the Ratio. This consisted mainly of essays on the conduct of classes, repetitions, and disputations; on teacher formation and the various curricula, vacations, time-orders, prizes, and degrees. After review by Aquaviva and his advisers together with committees in each province of the order, this draft was revised in 1591. The material remained substantially unchanged but was organized into rules and omitted theoretical discussions. After further experimentation, a final, more polished version was formally promulgated by Aquaviva in 1599.

The 1586 and 1591 drafts are very rare, but the 1586 and 1599 texts were published by G. M. Pachtler, SJ, in the series *Monumenta Germaniae Paedagogica* as part of a four-volume critical edition of early Jesuit educational documents: *Ratio Studiorum et institutiones scholasticae Societatis Iesu.* The Ratio guided Jesuit schools until the order's suppression in 1773. After the restoration in 1814, a revision was planned and an experimental emendation, which placed more emphasis on science and vernacular literature, appeared in 1832 but was never definitively promulgated.

Contents. The contents of the Ratio are similar to those of other Renaissance school plans, for it drew from the best contemporary practice and theory. In Ignatius's own day the Jesuit schools had adopted the sequence of studies and the procedures used at the University of Paris, many of them inspired by Quintilian (*see* PARIS, UNIVERSITY OF). The schools of the BRETHREN OF THE COMMON LIFE were also an influence. The success of the early Jesuit institutions was due not to curricular novelty but largely to four characteristics owed to Ignatius himself. Their teachers were carefully prepared and inspired with an apostolic dedication. The schools charged no tuition fees. In light of available knowledge of methodology and psychology, the course of studies and the pupils' activities were carefully organized to promote learning in graduated steps. But this concern for order did not eliminate innovation and reconstruction, since Ignatius had directed in the *Constitutions* that all provisions of the anticipated Ratio were to be adapted to places, times, and persons. This made it possible for the spirit of the Ratio to remain influential even when its concrete details became obsolete.

At first sight the letter of the Ratio may appear to obscure its spirit since few theoretical principles are enunciated. The curricular and methodological details, however, imply some theory. The aim is both moral and intellectual formation, with primacy of honor going to the former and most attention to the latter. The letters and arts curricula center on a Renaissance Christianization of the Greco-Roman tradition of literary and philosophical culture directed toward writing Latin like Cicero and thinking like Aristotle. In theology St. Thomas is the precribed author. The chief methodological emphasis is on student activity, and the Ratio prescribes an abundance and variety of written and oral exercises. One of its few general statements is: Variety is good because satiety is bad. Hence there are provisions for academic contests, the *concertatio,* pitting individuals or groups against one another; for academies in which gifted students do advanced work; and for dramas, fêtes, games, and vacations. To facilitate teaching, the Ratio recommends dividing large classes into *decuriae,* groups of ten, each with a captain who has some monitorial duties. The teacher's work includes hearing recitations, correcting exercises, and explaining in a "prelection" (lecture) the problems posed by an assignment. He is advised to motivate pupils not by chastisement but by the attraction of honor and the rewards of scholastic success. This Renaissance accent on glory, however, is counterbalanced by the assertion on the first page of the Ratio that the whole of schooling should be designed to bring students to the knowledge and love of God.

Bibliography: E. A. FITZPATRICK, ed., *St. Ignatius and the Ratio Studiorum* (New York 1933). F. DE DAINVILLE, *La Naissance de l'humanisme moderne* (Paris 1940). A. P. FARRELL, *The Jesuit Code of Liberal Education* (Milwaukee 1938). *Monumenta paedagogica Societatis Jesu,* ed. C. O. GOMEZ RODELES et al. (Madrid 1901). G. M. PACHTLER, ed., *Ratio Studiorum et institutiones scholasticae Societatis Jesu per Germaniam lim vigentes collectae. . . ,* 4 v. (Monumenta Germaniae paedagogica 2, 5, 9, 16; Berlin 1887–94). B. DUHR, *Die Studienordnung der Gesellschaft Jesu* (Bibliothek der katholischen Pädagogik 9; Freiburg i.Br. 1896).

[J. W. DONOHUE]

RATIONALISM

A theory or system that exaggerates reason's independence from the senses in philosophy or from supernatural revelation in religion. Although it appears in many forms, in nearly all a doctrinaire insistence on the sovereignty of reason displaces a native trust in the reasonableness of human thought, and an arbitrary insistence is placed on the former as uniquely representative of free scientific inquiry. This article treats first of philosophical rationalism, giving its historical outline and characteristics, and then of religious rationalism, both negatively as denying the supernatural and affirmatively as an aid to understanding revealed truth.

Philosophical Rationalism

Philosophical rationalism is commonly associated with certain philosophers of the 17th and 18th centuries in Continental Europe, notably R. DESCARTES, B. SPINOZA, and G. W. LEIBNIZ. Generally it holds that reason rather than sense experience is the source of knowledge and the ultimate test of truth. Its opposite is EMPIRICISM or POSITIVISM, which maintain that ideas and propositions not directly verifiable by sensory observation are meaningless. Usually rationalistic knowledge is thought to originate in reason itself, being a system of universal and necessary truths based on principles or starting points not discovered in experience.

As an attitude of mind resulting from philosophical positions, rationalism tends to single out and magnify abstract human reason while minimizing other human powers, such as sense, imagination, and free will. Logical ideals of order, procedure, and method predominate over empirical data and experimental technique. As a philosophical position, rationalism usually involves the following theories relating to being and knowledge, methodology, and sufficient reason.

Being and Knowledge. Most rationalist systems rest on Plato's theory of a dual universe, wherein eternal, necessary truths somehow exist apart from the world of human experience but remain accessible to human reason. This concept of a "duoverse" was further developed by Descartes, who considered material substances or extended bodies in mechanical motion as independent units, distinct and separate from spiritual substance or thinking mind. Even in man, the meeting place of the two realms of body and spirit, this separation held.

Hence, for neither Plato nor Descartes could the material world of sense experience be a source of genuine knowledge. Adopting a theory of innate ideas, Plato's epistemological rationalism held that human reason had "seen" in a previous existence the necessary and eternal truths. By recollection of these ideas, the mind obtains real knowledge even though it is surrounded by a shadow world of change that is basically unintelligible. Plato's Socratic dictum, "Virtue is knowledge," also founded a type of ethical rationalism.

Descartes's theory was more complex and did not involve the Platonic notion of recollection. He thought of the human mind as born with the materials of knowledge, e.g., certain fundamental concepts such as "God," "being," "soul," "material substance," "cause," "number," "time," "space," and "motion," as well as general propositions such as "I think, therefore I am"; "Every event has a cause"; and "God is perfect and cannot deceive me." These, as well as the basic truths of ethical obligation, are discovered in the mind itself and not in extramental reality, even though experience may help clarify and make explicit what the mind contains (*see* INNATISM). Derided by empiricists as empty a priori forms, these, for the rationalist, were the starting points of deductive movements of the mind toward further truths, including the results of applying universal concepts to empirical data. Descartes, for instance, could build on them an argument for the existence of a material world otherwise not known with certainty to exist. For him, the truths of faith were not among the certitudes of reason, but depended rather on the will—a position designed to safeguard the supernatural but later to lead to religious rationalism and the denial of revealed truth.

Some types of rationalism admit that ideas are supplied to reason either from sense experience or in self-reflection. Reason, however, still functions to discover real knowledge by seeing relations and necessary connections or by deducing further consequences from the resulting intelligibility. Some rationalists think of reason as an instrument for bridging the gap between itself and reality. For them, knowledge is attained by applying to experience concepts or meanings discovered in reason. Characteristic of all such rationalism is the tendency to view ideas or concepts rather than things themselves as the objects of thought. For thinkers such as I. KANT and G. W. F. HEGEL, the gap between the meanings of reason and the things of experience stimulated a critical rationalism that ultimately reduced all of reality to reason and absolute mind.

Besides attempting to deduce from fundamental laws of logic the basic propositions of a universal system of knowledge, Leibniz developed a rationalist theory that depended explicitly on the existence and functioning of an infinite intelligence.

Methodology. Mathematics, with its clear and distinct ideas and rigorous demonstration, was the ideal knowledge and method for most rationalists. Seventeenth-century scientists such as J. KEPLER, G. GALILEI, and, later, I. Newton devised physical theories that were heavily mathematical in character. As their new and powerful method for describing the physical universe was perfected, philosophers tried to introduce the rigor of mathematics into every department of knowledge. H. GROTIUS is a good example of this, with his secularization of law. As rationalists, these thinkers tended to narrow their conception of genuine knowledge to that obtained by the methods of physical science, restricted though these may have been.

Spinoza and Leibniz exemplify attempts to solve a crucial problem that immediately came into focus, namely, how to use such methods to construct a rationalistic system that could embrace mind and God as well as matter. Boundless confidence in the power of reason for a time overcame the natural repugnances these systems encountered from common sense. In the end there was no escaping the fact that such methods had nothing to say about the meaning of man, of human values, and of freedom, none of which exhibit mechanical or mathematical characteristics.

But some popularizers of the new learning unreasonably concluded that what these methods could not treat did not exist, and they somehow won for themselves the title of rationalists, combining a valid rejection of prejudice, ignorance, credulity, and superstition with an irrational rejection of revelation and religious authority.

Others refused to straitjacket the mind in the mathematical-physical method, and kept philosophy open to genuine knowledge of man, God, and freedom. This tension continued into the 18th-century Age of the Enlightenment, with its practical applications of rationalism to questions of authority in religion, theories of government in politics, and further developments of method in science. In the common confusion between philosophical rationalism and the new scientific methods, older philosophers and overzealous Churchmen, conscious of the philosophical errors in rationalism, condemned the new science as erroneous philosophy and acted at times to interfere with free scientific inquiry.

Sufficient Reason. One of Leibniz's followers, C. WOLFF, sought to advance philosophical knowledge by transferring the new ideals of method and some of its nonphilosophical procedures into metaphysics, philosophy of man, and ethics. He accepted Leibniz's distinction between ''truth of fact'' and ''truth of reason,'' and made extensive use of the principle of SUFFICIENT REASON to transform all contingent elements to rational elements, thus attempting to bridge the chasm between experience and reason. This resulted in a rationalistic system wherein each form of empirical knowledge, such as physics or psychology, was supplemented by a corresponding rational form that functioned to raise the former to the level of genuine knowledge by deducing it from the principles of general ontology and cosmology.

Wolff's voluminous work was condensed into handy manuals by his followers, who embodied his basic rationalistic view of a duoverse and the deductive ideal of a system of knowledge. These were widely used in Protestant seminaries and universities and became well known to scholastics. Philosophy textbooks modeled on Wolff's were produced by German Jesuits between 1750 and the suppression of the Society of Jesus (1773), and the work was continued by Franciscans and others who imitated Wolff's scholasticism. Catholic manual writers were to come under the influence of such German rationalism as late as the 20th century. In the absence of adequate historical studies of scholasticism at the time, this type of rationalism was considered to be genuinely scholastic and led many to accept its demolition by Kant as a final destruction of scholastic philosophy [see J. E. Gurr, *The Principle of Sufficient Reason in Some Scholastic Systems, 1750–1900* (Milwaukee 1959)]. Many theology manuals followed a similar method, beginning with definitions of theological realities and then seeking a greater insight by relating concepts or by analyzing definitions to discover their full logical implications.

Kant, who was nurtured on this kind of philosophical rationalism, set out to destroy it; at the same time he wished to safeguard ultimate truths about man and God with a new critical, as opposed to a dogmatic, rationalism. His attempts to remove such truths from the sphere of reason, however—since they neglected the native, spontaneous reasoning powers of the human mind—actually dissolved the rational basis of faith and morals and led eventually to advanced forms of religious rationalism.

Religious Rationalism

Religious rationalism has both a philosophical and a social dimension. As derived from philosophical rationalism, it is a negative and limited view of reason as supremely competent in matters of faith and morals. Thus it holds that an adequate theory of man, of his relations with God, and of his destiny can be had from human intelligence alone; it thereby excludes revelation and the evidence of any authoritative witness. As resulting from the positive use of reason to penetrate, understand, and defend truths known by faith, religious rationalism is a form of theological activity.

Negative Aspect. Early Greek thinkers who rejected explanations of the world of experience in terms of the gods and goddesses of mythology to substitute the principles and causes of philosophy were rationalists without being antireligious. Rationalist elements—in the sense of questioning existing institutions and ways of doing or thinking, or of criticizing abuses, real or imagined—are present in the oldest Biblical documents.

But modern religious rationalism—from the Averroists of the late Middle Ages, through the humanists of the Reformation and the *philosophes* of the Enlightenment, to 20th-century evolutionists—mutilates by its negations the power of reason to range beyond finite personality and the natural world. The present narrow form of this doctrine is SCIENTISM, which teaches that the natural sciences study all of reality and that their methods are the only valid way to knowledge.

As involving practical conflicts between Church authorities and those who confuse scientific method with metaphysics, rationalism is itself an ideology finding expression in a sustained war on prevailing creeds and institutions, whether these be Catholic, Protestant, or Jewish. English deists such as J. LOCKE, whose influence still is felt in freemasonry, and French ENCYCLOPEDISTS such as P. BAYLE and VOLTAIRE personify this ideology. These men were committed to eliminating from Christianity, in the name of sovereign reason, whatever was above human comprehension. Biblical accounts of creation, God's dealings with the Jews, miracles, the Incarnation, the Resurrection, prayer, providence, and a divine teaching authority in the Church were all refused credence. In Germany and France the ENLIGHTENMENT (Ger. *Aufklärung,* or clearing up) aimed at banishing all mystery and the supernatural, specializing in the application of restricted standards of reason to art, literature, and political and social activity. On Nov. 10, 1793, this practical doctrinaire rationalism culminated in the French National Convention's selecting a Madame Maillard to represent the goddess of reason and enthroning her in the Cathedral of Notre Dame in Paris—designated for a time as the Temple of Reason.

By the end of the 1800s, antireligious rationalism manifested itself in various forms of naturalism, positivism, scientism, secularism, and MATERIALISM. In a less sophisticated form it still survives as a kind of folklore tradition that (1) reason in an age of science has demolished all forms of spiritual and supernatural reality and knowledge; (2) only rationalism inspires hatred of hypocrisy and teaches moral and intellectual honesty, inspiring courage in the fight for social justice; and (3) only those who deny Christianity, and embrace ATHEISM are true rationalists.

Positive Aspect. Religious or theological rationalism may also refer to the fact that the Jewish, Muslim, and Christian religions, although based on divine revelation, expect reason to perform its natural work of inquiry, consideration, and formulation. This results in a theological expression of revealed truth, an organized effort to understand what one believes, sometimes referred to as rationalistic theology. From the early Apologists of the 3d century, through NICHOLAS ORESME to L. E. M. BAUTAIN, the Catholic Church has condemned thinkers who unduly minimize reason; similarly, theological systems holding that revelation has been given man as a substitute for all other knowledge have been rejected. The distinction between reason and faith has been steadily maintained, however, and when these are seen in proper relation, the individual believer is free to use understanding and reason in many ways. St. Paul's reference to inexcusable ignorance of the existence of God (Rom 1.20) itself initiated an untiring effort to blend religious faith with rational speculation. Catholic theology, as a consequence, presupposes the truths of natural reason as *preambula fidei.*

Medieval Thought. For St. Augustine, the perfect kind of rational knowledge was the philosophy of Plato and Plotinus. St. ANSELM OF CANTERBURY regarded logical knowledge as true rational knowledge, but his *Credo ut intelligam* implied that, with faith as a necessary condition, a deeper understanding of religious truth could be achieved by the application of reason. His ontological argument for the existence of God was rationalistic, however, in the sense that it proceeded independently of natural experience, although within the context of faith and the truths guaranteed by authority.

Pope Pius IX, in the 19th century, defended the SCHOLASTICISM of the high Middle Ages against the suspicion of rationalism raised by A. BONNETTY, maintaining that "the method which St. Thomas and St. Bonaventure and other scholastics after them used does not lead to rationalism . . ." (H. Denzinger, *Enchiridion symbolorum*, ed. A. Schönmetzer, 2814). Yet the use of Aristotelian dialectic in medieval scholasticism did give birth to a system of purely rational truth out of which modern philosophy was to be born.

Unlike the Jewish philosopher Moses MAIMONIDES, the Muslim Averroës stressed that philosophy should be kept apart from theology. He justified a complete separation on the rationalistic principle that what was necessarily and genuinely true in philosophy could contradict the teaching of Christian revelation, in his case, the Qur'ān (*see* DOUBLE TRUTH, THEORY OF). Christian theologians such as SIGER OF BRABANT promoted a Latin AVERROISM that the condemnations of 1270 and 1277, by Étienne TEMPIER, Bishop of Paris, could not completely eradicate. This influence continued through the Averroistic Aristotelians at Padua to the libertines of the 17th and 18th centuries.

Reformation. Among Protestants, P. MELANCHTHON developed a Christian rationalism designed to meet the age-old need of understanding what was known by faith. In Italy, SOCINIANISM exemplified a Protestant rationalist position in theology that was destructive of the revealed doctrine of the Trinity. Similarly, in 18th-century Germany, Protestant theologians accepted a distinction proposed by J. S. Semler between religion (understood more as an ethics) and theology, together with a similar separation of religion from theological opinion and religious usage fostered by J. G. HERDER. Such distinctions, made originally to safeguard religion from attacks on theology and Biblical history, led eventually to a disavowal of the true supernatural nature of revelation as the word of God. It left reason and its resources supreme and, by the end of the 19th century, led to the very antireligious naturalism that Protestant theological rationalists had sought to prevent.

Meanwhile, F. D. E. SCHLEIERMACHER maintained that religion consists in neither knowledge nor action, but rather in the consciousness of absolute dependence on God. Thus he replaced the Church by a purely individual commitment and opened the way to a philosophy of power that was fatal to both rationalism and Christianity. These developments provided scriptural exegetes with new critical principles whose application led to extremes of naturalism in such works as the *Leben Jesu* of D. F. STRAUSS.

Modern Thought. Nineteenth-century Catholic theologians such as G. HERMES and A. GÜNTHER attempted unsuccessfully to relate Catholicism to the pure rationalism of post-Kantian philosophy. But with God, reason, and faith united in the Hegelian system, they could not avoid reducing faith to a work of unaided reason, thereby denying the gratuity of revealed truth. The Danish Lutheran, S. A. KIERKEGAARD, on the other hand, gave attractive expression in his writings to an acceptable position; this regards faith as a personal commitment that neither results from a rationalistic (or historical) mode of argumentation nor is a rational exercise associated with the unfolding of Absolute Mind.

The failure of some contemporary Catholic writers to represent adequately the Catholic view of the relationships between faith and reason and between theology and philosophy has caused reactions against rationalist philosophy to be interpreted as attacks on THOMISM or on other scholastic syntheses. Some of the literature of EXISTENTIALISM augments this confusion, for its horror of the systematized and the objectivized is basically an aversion from the excesses of rationalism.

Critique. Both philosophical and religious rationalism must be criticized for neglect of evidence. Philosophical rationalism fails to take into account prephilosophical and prescientific knowledge, tending to consider specialized attitudes or techniques as the only rational method. Religious rationalism too often simply makes an act of faith in the all-embracing character of a currently successful method of knowing; it refuses even to consider the data of revelation, and thus cuts itself off completely from the highest source of human knowledge.

See Also: REASONING; KANTIANISM; DEISM; THEISM.

Bibliography: F. C. COPLESTON, *History of Philosophy* (Westminster, Md. 1946–); v.4, Descartes to Leibniz; v.5, Hobbes to Hume (1959); v.6, Wolff to Kant (1960). C. CONSTANTIN, *Dictionnaire de théologie catholique*, ed. A. VACANT et al., 15 v. (Paris 1903–50) 13.2:1688–1778. C. MAZZANTINI, *Enciclopedia filosofica*, 4 v. (Venice-Rome 1957) 3:1870–83. O. MUCK, *Lexikon für Theologie und Kirche*, ed. J. HOFER and K. RAHNER, 10 v. (2d, new ed. Freiburg 1957–65) 8:1005–06. K. OEHLER and H. HOHLIVEIN, *Die Religion in Geschichte und Gegenwart*, 7 v. (3d ed. Tübingen 1957–65) 5:790–800. R. EISLER, *Wörterbuch der philosophischen Begriffe*, 3 v. (4th ed. Berlin 1927–30) 2:579–84. A. W. BENN, *The History of English Rationalism in the Nineteenth Century*, 2 v. (New York 1962). J. B. BURY, *A History of Freedom of Thought* (2d ed. New York 1952). É. H. GILSON, *Reason and Revelation in the Middle Ages* (New York 1961). G. BOAS, *French Philosophies of the Romantic Period* (New York 1964). J. D. COLLINS, *God in Modern Philosophy* (Chicago 1959) 55–89. R. DERATHÉ, *Le Rationalisme de Jean-Jacques Rousseau* (Paris 1948). J. M. F. LAPORTE, *Le Rationalisme de Descartes* (Paris 1945). P. HAZARD, *The European Mind (1680–1715)*, tr. J. L. MAY (New York 1963). J. S. SPINK, *French Free-thought from Gassendi to Voltaire* (London 1960). L. I. BREVOLD, *The Brave New World of the Enlightenment* (Ann Arbor 1961). A. BREMOND, *Religions of Unbelief* (Milwaukee 1939). M. C. D'ARCY, *Belief and Reason* (London 1944).

[J. E. GURR]

RATISBONNE, MARIE THÉODORE AND MARIE ALPHONSE

Brothers, co-founders of the CONGREGATION OF NOTRE DAME DE SION and the FATHERS OF SION. Théodore: b. Strasbourg, France, Dec. 28, 1802; d. Paris, Jan. 10, 1884. He was the second eldest son of the most important Jewish family in Alsace and was educated at the Royal College at Strasbourg. He labored to alleviate the social and economic conditions of the Jews in the Strasbourg ghetto. His study of the Bible and Church history led to his conversion (1827). Because of his family's bitter opposition, he was baptized secretly, assuming the name Marie at this time. After ordination (1830) he taught in the minor seminary of the Diocese of Strasbourg until 1840, when he went to Paris and worked in the Archconfraternity of Our Lady of Victories. To promote understanding between Christians and Jews and to bring about the conversion of the Jews, he and his brother Marie Alphonse founded the Congregation of Notre Dame de Sion for women (1843) and the Fathers of Sion (1852). Among his numerous writings the best known are his two-volume *Histoire de St. Bernard et de son siècle* (1840; 11th ed. 1903); *Manuel de la mère chrétienne* (1859; 11th ed. 1864); *Nouvelle manuel des mères chrétiennes* (1870; 22d ed. 1926); and *La question juive* (1868).

Alphonse: b. Strasbourg, France, May 1, 1814; d. Ain Karim, Palestine, May 6, 1884. The ninth child of the family, he became a lawyer and banker. Like his brother Théodore he was eager to aid his fellow Jews. So bitterly anti-Christian was he that he could not forgive Théodore for becoming a Catholic in 1827. But on his way to the East, he visited Rome, where he was suddenly converted after a vision of the Blessed Virgin Mary in the church of St. Andrea della Fratte (Jan. 20, 1842). At the time of his Baptism (Jan. 31), he took the name Marie. A few months later he joined the Jesuits. After his ordination (1848) he received permission to leave the Society of Jesus and collaborate with his brother in working for the conversion of the Jews. He collaborated with Théodore in founding their two congregations. In 1855 he went to Palestine, where he spent the remainder of his life laboring to convert Jews and Muslims. He established for the Sisters of Sion the Ecce Homo monastery (1856) and later opened two orphanages.

Bibliography: M. J. EGAN, *Christ's Conquest: The Coming of Grace to Theodore Ratisbonne* (Dublin 1945); *Our Lady's Jew, Father M. A. Ratisbonne* (Dublin 1953).

[M. R. NÔTRE]

RATRAMNUS OF CORBIE

Theologian; d. after 868. Ratramnus entered the Benedictine abbey of Corbie in Somme, France, about 825, and there became a priest and teacher. Little is known of his life. His writings reveal an independent mind, wide learning, and dialectical skill.

Ratramnus' best known work is on the Eucharist, *De corpore et sanguine Domini* (*c.* 850), requested by Charles the Bald, king of the West Franks. It was intended to rectify the tract by Ratramnus's former teacher and abbot, Paschasius Radbertus, whose doctrine Ratramnus found excessively realistic and not consonant with a more symbolic interpretation then in favor. Ratramnus stressed the figurative aspects of the Sacrament and the mysterious mode of Christ's Eucharistic presence, but denied the identity of His sacramental and historical body, as insisted upon by Paschasius. Neither a full treatment nor a devotional piece, the *De corpore*'s unconventional language and subtlety help to explain the conflicting judgments passed upon it. It was condemned as a supposed work of JOHN SCOTUS ERIGENA at the Council of Vercelli (1050). Cited with favor by St. John Fisher in 1527, it was later used by some of the Protestant theologians as a precedent for their doctrine and was widely translated. Partly because of Protestant patronage, it was listed in the first Index of Prohibited Books in 1559 and retained until the 1900 edition. Catholic opinion remains divided, but recent studies have upheld its orthodoxy.

In his *De praedestinatione* (850), again at the instance of King Charles, Ratramnus opposed Archbishop Hincmar of Reims. Ratramnus set the mystery of predestination in the context of God's governance of the world (bk. 1), and defended the disputed ''double predestination'' of St. Augustine, i.e., the predestination of the gratuitously elect to salvation and of the culpably reprobate to their just punishment (bk. 2), although, Ratramnus points out, God is neither the author of their evil-doing nor is their perdition His will (*Patrologia Latina* 121:42).

His last and best dogmatic work, *Contra Graecorum opposita,* was one result of Nicholas I's letter in 867 urging the Frankish hierarchy to a united defense against the anti-Latin charges of the Byzantine court and the Patriarch Photius, then in conflict with the Roman See. Ratramnus pleaded for unity of faith as the one essential, and for a legitimate diversity of customs; he defended the double procession of the Holy Spirit from Father ''and Son'' (*Filioque*) with impressive erudition (bks. 1–3), and defended Latin usages and the Roman primacy with some originality (bk. 4).

His *De nativitate Christi,* holding that the Blessed Virgin Mary's parturition was entirely natural, was opposed by Paschasius who defended the miraculous birth. Ratramnus wrote two tracts on the nature of the soul. In one he opposed the teaching of Marius Scotus on the universal soul.

Bibliography: *Opera Omnia, Patrologia Latina.* ed. J. P. MIGNE (Paris 1878–90) 121:11–346, 1153–56; *De Corpore et sanguine Domine,* ed. J. N. BAKHUIZEN VAN DEN BRINK (Amsterdam 1954); Eng. tr. in C. P. FARRAR and A. P. EVANS, *Bibliography of English Translations from Medieval Sources* (New York 1946) 3267–72; *Letters,* ed. E. L. DÜMMLER, *Monumenta Germaniae Historica Epistolae* (Berlin 1826–) ser. 18, 6:149–158; *Liber de anima ad Odonem Bellovacensem,* ed. C. LAMBOT (Namur 1952). J. FAHEY, *The Eucharistic Teaching of Ratramn of Corbie* (Mundelein, Ill. 1951). I. BACKES, *Lexikon für Theologie und Kirche*, ed. M. BUCHBERGER (Freiburg 1930–38) 8:642–643. J. GEISELMANN, *Die Eucharistielehre der Vorscholastik* (Paderborn 1926). H. PELTIER, *Dictionnaire de théologie catholique*, ed. A. VACANT et al. (Paris 1903–50) 13.2: 1780–87.

[J. J. RYAN]

RAUSCH, JAMES

Bishop, Church official; b. Albany, Minn., Sept. 4, 1928; d. Phoenix, Ariz., May 18, 1981. He was the son of a storekeeper in a small rural community and was educated at Crosier Seminary, Onamia, Minn., and St. John's Seminary, Collegeville. Following his ordination as a priest of the Diocese of St. Cloud, Minn., on June 2, 1956, he fulfilled several parochial assignments while serving as instructor at Cathedral High School. He pursued graduate studies in education at the College of St. Thomas, St. Paul, Minn., and received his doctoral degree in pastoral sociology from the Gregorian University, Rome, in 1969.

In 1967 Rausch was named an associate of the Justice and Peace Commission of the United States Catholic Conference (USCC). At the beginning of 1970, he became its assistant general secretary and was unanimously elected general secretary of both the USCC and NCCB December 1972. He was ordained a bishop by John Cardinal Krol in St. John's Abbey Church, Collegeville, as an auxiliary of the bishop of St. Cloud while continuing to serve as general secretary of the USCC and NCCB.

Rausch brought his direct and incisive leadership ability to his new post. He spoke extensively on the role of the Church in the areas of civil and human rights, political involvement of the Church in moral concerns, and the decisive role of the Catholic laity in both political and ecclesiastical life. He was a leading figure in the ''Call to Action'' convention of the Catholic laity that met in Detroit in 1979. He was recognized as one of the promising young bishops of the U.S. advocating the major social concerns of the times. In this cause he met opposition from the conservative wing of the Catholic Church of that period, both lay and clerical.

Installed as the second bishop of Phoenix, Ariz. on March 22, 1977, Rausch brought his pastoral zeal to bear on the issues of poverty, discrimination, civil and human rights. He was a vigorous advocate of the underprivileged, resulting in an unfortunate alienation of some of the more conservative and affluent members of his flock.

He died of a sudden heart attack at a shopping center in Phoenix. During his brief tenure as bishop of Phoenix he ordained eighteen priests, established seven new parishes, and supervised the building of six homes for the aged. He performed a prophetic role in providing for the future of the diocese which, unfortunately, was not recognized by many of his clergy and people. In the exercise of his episcopal office he proved to be a man ahead of his time.

[V. A. YZERMANS]

RAUSCHENBUSCH, WALTER

Chief exponent of the SOCIAL GOSPEL in American Protestantism; b. Rochester, N.Y., Oct. 4, 1861; d. Rochester, July 25, 1918. After graduating in 1886 from Rochester Theological Seminary, he served for 11 years as pastor of the Second German Baptist Church on the edge of New York City's notorious Hell's Kitchen. From this ministry and from his reading of Henry George, Tolstoi, Marx, Bellamy, and the Webbs came *Christianity and the Social Crisis* (1907), a book that challenged the individualism and pietism of 19th-century American Protestantism. In subsequent works, *Christianizing the Social Order* (1912), *The Social Principles of Jesus* (1916), and *A Theology of the Social Gospel* (1917), he preached the theme of the ''Kingdom of God,'' which emphasized social transformation and economic betterment as the purpose for which the church exists. In addition to his writing, Rauschenbusch also served as professor of New Testament (1897–1902) and of church history (1902–18) at Rochester Theological Seminary. He was active in civic affairs until World War I, which left him crushed in spirit. His theology was largely superseded by neo-orthodoxy after the war.

Bibliography: *A Rauschenbusch Reader: The Kingdom of God and the Social Gospel,* comp. B. Y. LANDIS (New York 1957). H. F. WARD, *Dictionary of American Biography,* ed. A. JOHNSON and D. MALONE, 20 v. (New York 1928–36; index 1937; 1st suppl. 1944; 2d suppl. 1958) 15:392–393. D. R. SHARPE, *Walter Rauschenbusch* (New York 1942). R. NIEBUHR, ''W. R. in Perspective,'' *Religion in Life* (Autumn 1958).

[E. DUFF]

RAUSCHER, JOSEPH OTHMAR VON

Cardinal, archbishop of Vienna; b. Vienna, Oct. 6, 1797; d. Vienna, Nov. 24, 1875. After studying philosophy, theology, and law at Vienna, he was ordained in 1823. In 1825 he became professor of theology in Salzburg, and in 1832, titular abbot and director of the Oriental Academy in Vienna and adviser for religious affairs to the government. In this capacity he negotiated, at the direction of Emperor Francis II, the conditions under which the Jesuits were permitted to work in Austria. In 1844 he taught philosophy to the later Emperor Francis Joseph I and his brothers. In 1849 he became prince bishop of Seckau and played an important role in the negotiations between the Austrian episcopate and the government concerning the abolition of JOSEPHINISM. He spent two years as the emperor's representative negotiating with the papal nuncio Michele Viale-Prelà the concordat signed on Aug. 18, 1855. Rauscher became prince bishop of Vienna (1853) and cardinal (1855). Later he successfully defended the concordat against the attacks of liberalism in the press and *Reichstag,* even though his methods were not always approved by other bishops. At VATICAN COUNCIL I he disapproved the definition of papal infallibility as inopportune, and he also opposed the doctrine itself. When his efforts to prevent the definition failed, he left Rome before the final voting, but by Aug. 8, 1870, he published the decree in his archdiocese.

Bibliography: C. WOLFSGRUBER, *Joseph Othmar Cardinal Rauscher* (Freiburg 1888); *The Catholic Encyclopedia,* C. G. HERBERMANN, ed., 16 v. (New York 1907–14) 12:660–662. E. C. BUTLER, *The Vatican Council,* 2 v. (New York 1930). É AMANN, *Dictionnaire de théologie catholique,* 15 v. (Paris 1903–50) 13.2:1787–1789. F. ENGEL-JANOSI, *Österreich und der Vatikan, 1846–1918,* 2 v. (Graz 1958–60) v. 1.

[F. MAASS]

RAUTENSTRAUCH, FRANZ STEPHAN

A key figure of Josephinism; b. Blottendorf, Bömisch-Leipa, July 26, 1734; d. Erlau, Hungary, Sept. 30, 1785. He joined the Benedictines in 1750 and was chosen abbot of his monastery at Břevnov (Braunau, 1773); he was appointed director of the theological faculty in Prague (1774) and later served in the same capacity in Vienna, where he was simultaneously imperial-royal councilor and president of the commission for ecclesiastical affairs. Modern attempts to extenuate his aims and activity in state and Church overlook two facts. In 1769 Empress Maria Theresa, urged by her advisers, forced the archbishop of Prague, who had condemned Rautenstrauch's *Prolegomena in jus ecclesiasticum* (1769), to decorate the Benedictine monk with a gold medal bestowed upon him by the empress for this very same book. In 1776 the monarch decreed that in the future in all public and private ecclesiastical schools of studies only such theological matters might be taught as were contained in Rautenstrauch's *Synopsis juris ecclesiastici publici et privati* (1769). Important religious truths of the Catholic deposit of faith, such as papal infallibility and supremacy as well as the Immaculate Conception of Mary, were not contained in this book and thus might not be taught any longer.

Bibliography: B. MENZEL, *Beiträge zum Wirken des Abtes Rautenstrauch* (Diss. Prague 1932). J. MÜHLSTEIGER, *Die Wiener Tätigkeit des Abtes Rautenstrauch* (Diss. Innsbruck 1960). J. MÜLLER, *Lexikon für Theologie und Kirche,* ed. J. HOFER and K. RAHNER, 10 v. (2d, new ed. Freiburg 1957–65) 8:1018–1019. K. G. STECK, *Die Religion in Geschichte und Gegenwart,* 7 v. (3d ed. Tübingen 1957–65) 5:805.

[F. MAASS]

RAVALLI, ANTONIO

Missionary; b. Ferrara, Italy, May 16, 1812; d. Stevensville, Mont., Oct. 2, 1884. He entered the Society of Jesus in the province of Emilia in Italy on Nov. 12, 1827. Prior to ordination he devoted several years to teaching in Turin, Piedmont, and other parts of Italy. Desiring to work in the Native American missions of the Oregon Country, he prepared himself by studying medicine and acquiring mechanical trades. He accompanied Pierre DE SMET, SJ, from Belgium to the Oregon Country, 1843–44. After spending a winter among the Kalispel people on the Upper Columbia River, he was transferred to St. Mary's Mission among the Flathead people in western Montana. He remained there until the mission was temporarily abandoned in 1850 because of hostile Blackfeet. Following assignments with other tribes and at Santa Clara College, California (1860–63), he returned to St. Mary's Mission after it was reestablished in 1866. There he combined priestly endeavors with his ministry of medicine. He lived among the Native Americans for almost 40 years and was held in an esteem that rivaled De Smet's. When he died at St. Mary's, the natives, as he had requested, buried him in their cemetery there. A monument marks his grave, and he is commemorated in Montana by having a station of the Northern Pacific Railroad, located about 40 miles north of Missoula, named after him.

Bibliography: L. B. PALLADINO, *Indian and White in the Northwest: A History of Catholicity in Montana* (2d ed. rev. Philadelphia 1922).

[J. B. MCGLOIN]

RAVASCHIERI, BALTHASAR, BL.

Franciscan; b. Chiavari, 1419; d. Binasco, Oct. 17, 1492. Ravaschieri was born into a noble family whose ancestors were the counts of Lavagna. His father, Count Cattaneo, died in 1421 shortly after Balthasar's birth. His aunts Ginevra and Tobia, both Franciscan tertiaries, were responsible for instilling in him a sense of piety and morality. He entered a friary of Franciscan Observants, located near his home. He was a model religious, a good theologian, and a zealous confessor. In addition he practiced extraordinary mortifications. He was appointed superior and later vicar provincial. But he spent the best years of his life at Santa Maria del Campo Seminary in Binasco. As early as 1456 he had made a visitation of the Third Order there; he returned there at the conclusion of his duties as provincial because he was attracted to a life of prayer and to the apostolate. At this time he is said to have made some conversions and performed some miracles.

At the general congregation in Pavia in 1478 he came to know BERNARDINE OF FELTRE. Ravaschieri was inflicted with a crippling case of gout, which he accepted as a means to draw him closer to God. In spite of this affliction he preached and heard confessions whenever he could. One winter day someone left the crippled Ravaschieri in the garden during a storm, but the snow fell around him leaving him dry. His cult began immediately after his death, and he is still venerated today. In 1805 his relics were transferred to Pavia and in 1812 to Basilica. His cult was confirmed Jan. 7, 1930, for the Franciscans and for the Dioceses of Pavia and Genoa.

Feast: Oct. 25.

Bibliography: B. DA CARASCO, *Il Beato Baldassare Ravaschieri dei Frati Minori* (2d ed. Chiavari 1930). J. L. BAUDOT and L. CHAUSSIN, *Vies des saints et des bienheueux selon l'ordre du calendrier avec l'historique des fêtes,* 12 v. (Paris 1935–56) 10:562–563. J. GOYENS, *Dictionnaire d'histoire et de géographie ecclésiastiques,* ed. A. BAUDRILLART (Paris 1912–) 6:428.

[J. CAMBELL]

RAVENNA

A city in Emilia-Romagna, northeast Italy, seven miles from the Adriatic Sea, with which it is connected

Baptistery of the cathedral, Ravenna. (©Gérard Degeorge/CORBIS)

by a canal. The Archdiocese of Ravenna has been a metropolitan since the sixth century, and in 1947 Cervia (known in 501) was perpetually united to it. In 2001 it had 208,270 Catholics in a population of 215,570; there were 89 parishes, six churches, 97 secular and 26 religious priests, five permanent deacons, 35 members of men's religious institutes, 237 members of women's religious institutes, 21 educational institutes, and 12 charitable institutes.

HISTORY

Ravenna is one of the main historical and artistic centers in Emilia. Once surrounded by lagoons and extensive pine forests (praised by Dante and Byron), it was Umbrian in origin and developed under Caesar Augustus, who built the important naval base of Classe nearby. Ravenna was capital of the Italian province of Flaminia and Picenum in the fourth century, before Honorius II made it the capital of the Empire in the West (402). It flourished in the fourth and fifth centuries and was the residence of the empress Galla Placidia (424–450) and Valentinian III (450–455) who saw the clear advantages of its geographical position. The Gothic Odovacer lived there after 476, and the Ostrogoth THEODORIC I established himself there (493–526). Taken by BELISARIUS in 540, it served as the capital of Italy, and was the seat of a Byzantine exarchate until 751. From the ninth to the eleventh centuries the archbishops, supported by German emperors, became great feudal lords and pursued intensive religious and political activity throughout their domain. Ravenna, which had a flourishing school of law before that in Bologna, began to decline with the rise of its commune. Rudolph I of Hapsburg bestowed it on the popes (1276), and it continued in the States of the Church, undisputedly from 1509 to 1859, except for periods under Venice (1441–1509, 1527–29, and 1797–1815). In 1859 it became part of the Kingdom of Italy.

Lateral view of the colonnaded nave of the Church of S. Apollinare Nuovo, c. 504, Ravenna. (Alinari-Art Reference/Art Resource, NY)

Church History. From *c.*150 to *c.* 400 the episcopal see, suffragan to Milan, was in Classe, a port with merchants and voyagers from the East. When it moved to Ravenna, the clergy in Classe retained much of their autonomy for some time. Under St. PETER CHRYSOLOGUS in 430 Ravenna became metropolitan over Forlì, Faenza, Imola, Bologna, and Modena, all previously under the jurisdiction of Milan. In the thirteenth century all Emilia from Piacenza to Rimini was under the archbishop's jurisdiction. In 1582, however, Bologna and several dioceses in east Emilia were detached, and other jurisdictions have been detached since.

The episcopal list of 137 names is complete and includes 22 saints and one blessed. The oldest list, the *Liber pontificalis ecclesiae Ravennatis,* compiled by the priest Agnellus under Archbishop George (835–846), was probably derived from older diptychs. The first bishop, Apollonaris (*c.* 200), is venerated as a martyr. Later accounts made him a disciple of St. Peter, who supposedly sent him to Ravenna. His 11 successors, also buried in Classe, were called Columbine because their election was said to have depended on the intervention of the Holy Spirit; St. Severus attended the Council of (348). Ursus (d.429) moved the see to Ravenna and consecrated the five-nave Basilica of the Anastasis, later called Ursiana. Peter Chrysologus (d. 450), Neon (d. 458), and Ecclesius (d. 534) built splendid Christian monuments. Maximian (546–556), a native of Nola who was consecrated in Patras, Greece, by Pope Vigilius, governed in times difficult for orthodoxy; he was appointed by Justinian to promote the latter's own ecclesiastical policies. An energetic scholar-prelate, he organized his church, reformed the liturgy, and built monuments. The see supported Justinian in the Three Chapters Controversy against Milan and Aquileia, and the archbishop Agnellus (557–578) was rewarded with the property of the Arian Church; the Arian basilica, S. Apollinare Nuovo, was given over to Agnellus and Arianism, which had flourished under Theoderic the Great, came to an end in Ravenna. Agnellus also began the organization of rural parishes, which was completed around 1200.

Belisarius was replaced by Narses, who restored Italy to Byzantium from the Goths (554–567); but the Lombard invasion of 568 caused Justinian I by 584 to replace the civil Praetorian Prefect for Italy with a military exarch, who in the seventh century assumed control also of civil administration. The Exarchates of Carthage and of Ravenna thus straddled the middle Mediterranean. Ravenna, the center of Byzantine power and administration, where army and navy bases and the treasury were located, separated the Lombard duchies of Benevento and Spoleto from the rest of Lombard Italy. Ravenna continued after the sixth century as a center for trade, luxury goods and Latin literary activity, especially liturgy, geography, medicine and hagiography. The Greek monastic presence, however, dwindled, and no Greek works from this period survive.

The Greek Exarchs, with patrician rank, who headed a corps of Greek officials and a Greek colony, confirmed papal elections as representatives of the emperor. However, during the seventh and eighth centuries there were a number of small revolts as Ravenna tried to secure its position between Byzantium, Rome, and the Lombards. In 709 the Emperor Justinian II sent a force to punish the disloyalty of the leading citizens, and in the 720s, with renewed Lombard attacks, increased taxation and the beginning of the iconoclast movement in Byzantium, Ravenna participated in the general Italian revolt of 727. After being captured by the Lombards in 732 and liberated for Byzantium by the Venetians, it fell again to the Lombard king Aistulf in 751 and was subsequently handed over to the popes (754). At the same time its commercial role declined with the silting up of the harbor and the rise of Venice only 75 miles (121 km) to the north. The capture of Ravenna was a key turning point, since it left the way open for complete Lombard domination of Italy.

However, Ravenna remained important as a powerful ecclesiastical center and for centuries Ravenna's archbishops struggled against Rome in defense of their autonomy. Beginning with Maximian (546–556), the claim reached a peak under Maurus (648–671) when Emperor Constans II in 666 recognized his independence of Rome. Reparatus (671–677) reiterated the claim, but the privilege was revoked by the Emperor Constantine IV. The struggle continued intermittently for some time. A schism occurred when Archbishop Guilbert became Antipope CLEMENT III (1080), but from the twelfth century Ravenna was constantly faithful to Rome. Against Milan, its archbishops gained the privilege to sit at the right of the pope in the absence of the emperor (1047). Three

Christian statue, Ravenna. (©Gérard Degeorge/CORBIS)

prelates of Ravenna became popes: John XII (Pope John X, 914–928), Gerbert of Aurillac (Sylvester II, 999–1003), and Cosmato Meliorato (Innocent VII, 1404–06). Anselm of Havelberg was Archbishop of Ravenna (1155–58). Ravenna had many councils in the tenth and eleventh centuries, some attended by popes, and in the thirteenth century, especially under Philip Fontana (1253, 1259, 1261, 1270).

From the fourteenth century the prelates turned more to religious activity. Bl. Rainald defended the Templars in synods (1307, 1311). Guilio Feltrio della Rovere (d. 1578) founded the seminary (1567). Cristoforo Boncampagni (d. 1603), Pietro Aldobrandini (d. 1621), and Liugi Capponi (d. 1645) applied the Tridentine reform in pastoral visits and diocesan and provincial synods. Antonio Codronchi (1785–1826) and C. Falconieri (1826–59), friend of Pius IX, had difficult times, the one under Napoleonic rule and the other during the Risorgimento. When Ravenna joined the kingdom of Italy in 1859, a dechristianization marked by violent intolerance was loosed; but a Christian renaissance began with Abp. Pasquale Morganti (1904–21), author of ascetic works.

Ravenna's archives are rich: 13,000 parchments in the episcopal archives and 8,000 in the state archives. The public library Classense continues that of the Camal-

St. Apollinare, detail of 6th century Italo-Byzantine mosaic, in the Basilica of Sant' Apollinare, Classe, Ravenna. (©G. E. Kidder Smith/CORBIS)

dolese. Since 1911 the review *Ravenna Felix* has published historical and archaeological studies. The earliest Christian relic is a funeral stela of *c.* 200 found at Classe, where excavations are still continuing. Dante died in Ravenna (1321), as did the humanist Cardinal Bessarion (1472). The canal to the sea was begun by Cardinal Alberoni (1736).

Monasteries. Many monasteries near famous basilicas fostered religious and cultural life. Eastern monks settled near S. Andrea (fifth century), S. Lorenzo di Cesana, and S. Apollinare in Classe (founded by Bishop John in the sixth century). Benedictines near S. Giorgio (founded by Bishop John V in 750), S. Giovanni Evangelista (ninth century), and S. Vitale (tenth century). King St. Stephen I of Hungary founded the nearby monastery of S. Pietro in Vincoli (1040) as a hospice for Hungarians travelling to and from Rome. In the eleventh century St. Peter degli Oresti founded outside the city S. Maria in Porto, from which Canons exercised a great influence even beyond the province; the monastery was destroyed in World Way II. Near the monastery of Classe the hermit revival began under St. Romuald (d. 1027), founder of the Camaldolese. Romuald's fame was celebrated by St. Peter Damian (d.1072), also of Ravenna. Fransiscans came to the city in 1261, Dominicans a few years later. Pre-Tridentine reform was fostered by Bl. Margherita da Russi, Bl. Gentile Giusti, and Ven. Gerolamo Malucelli. Most monasteries became inactive after suppression by the French *c.* 1800.

Bibliography: T. S. BROWN, *Gentlemen and Officers: Imperial Administration and Aristocratic Power in Byzantine Italy A.D. 554–800* (London 1984); ''The Aristocracy of Ravenna from Justinian to Charlemange,'' *Corsi di Cultura sull'arte ravennate e bizantina* 33 (1986) 135–149. F. W. DEICHMANN, *Ravenna,* 6 v. (Wiesbaden 1958–1989). A. GUILLOU, ''Ravenna e Giustiniano,'' *Corsi di Cultura sull'arte ravennate e bizantina* 30 (1983) 333–343. J. HERRIN, *The Rise of Christendom* (Oxford 1987). R. A. MARKUS, ''Ravenna and Rome, 554–604,'' *Byzantion* 51 (1981) 556–578. A. MERCATI et al., eds., *Rationes decimarum Italiae nei secoli XIII e XIV. Aemilia: I, Ravenna* (Vatican City 1932). G. MESINI, *Ravenna* (Bologna 1954). J. MOORHEAD, *Theodoric in Italy* (Oxford 1992). A. RANDI, *Storia di Ravenna* (Ravenna 1952). A. RANDI, *Pagine di storia ravennati* (Ravenna 1957). O. G. VON SIMSON, *Sacred Fortress: Byzantine Art and Statecraft in Ravenna* (Chicago 1948, repr. 1976). C. WICKHAM, *Early Medieval Italy: Central Power and Local Society, 400–1000* (London 1981). A. VASINA, ''Cento anni di studi sulla Romagna 1861–1961,'' *Bibliografia storica nazionale*, ed. G. LATERZA (Faenza 1963).

[G. D. GORDINI/F. NICKS]

EXARCHATE

The Exarchate of Ravenna comprised Byzantine Italy after its government was reorganized. This reorganization, like that which occurred simultaneously in North Africa, laid the foundation of the theme system established under the Heraclian Dynasty (610–710).

The Exarchate of Ravenna (or of Italy) was created as a defense against the Lombards who invaded Italy under Alboin. In five years most of north Italy fell, including the greater part of inland Venetai, Liguria, and Tuscany. Anarchy followed the murder of Alboin, and the Lombards broke up into 35 groups led by dukes. Dukes Farwad and Zotto established Lombard duchies beyond the Apennines in Spoleto and Benevento. Fear of a Lombard conquest of all Italy moved Byzantium quickly to reform the government of Italy. Thus, the exarchate emerged. Government offices were rebuilt and a separate palace of the exarch was added to Theodoric's. Emperor MAURICE (582–602) was probably responsible for the reform, since it is first reported in 585; an Exarch Smaragdus is mentioned in a letter of Pelagius II in that year.

Italy was administered by an exarch residing in Ravenna who served as a governor-general and vice-regent of the emperor in Constantinople. He possessed civil and military powers, the right to make war and peace, to act as a supreme judge, and to nominate military officials and perhaps even civil prefects and vicars. At times he confirmed papal elections. The most important member of his staff was the *consiliarius,* a judge-advocate. The provinces were governed by *magistri militum* responsible to the exarch; below them were the tribunes who commanded towns and fortresses. Such decentralization of imperial power was unusual in this period but it must have been seen as a measure to reduce problems in governing the reconquered territories and in coping with continued military threats.

The extent of the exarchate varied: *c.* 600 it included Istria, Maritime Venetia, Aemilia, the Pentapolis (Ariminum, Pisaurum, Fanum, Senigallia, Ancona), and the three duchies of Rome, Naples, and Perugia, Calabria, Bruttium and Maritime Liguria; by 700, however, the exarchate had lost Maritime Liguria and Calabria. Several exarchs fell victim to the period of instability of the seventh and eighth centuries; John I (616), John Rizokopas (710) and Paul (926) were murdered, and usurpers included Eleutherios (619) and Olympios (c.651/2). The of Leo III (717–741), and general dissatisfaction with Byzantium's fiscal polices led to the revolt of Ravenna in 727. The Lombards exploited the disunity by an offensive that ended in the seizure of Ravenna (751).

The fall of Ravenna ended the exarchate and ended Byzantine control of north Italy. The greater part of the area was handed over by PEPIN III to Pope STEPHEN II (III) (756) and incorporated into the States of the Church.

Bibliography: O. BERTOLINI, *Roma di fronte a Bisanzio e ai Longobardi* (Bologna 1941). T. S. BROWN, ''The Interplay between Rome and Byzantine Traditions and Local Sentiment in the Exarchate of Ravenna,'' *Settimane di Studio del Centro Italiano di Studi sull'-alto medioevo* (1988) 127–60. C. DIEHL, *Etudes sur l'administration byzantine dans l'exarchat de Ravenne, 568–751* (Paris 1888). A. GUILLOU, *Régionalisme et indépendance dans l'Empire byzantin: l'exemple de l'Exarchate et de la Pentapole d'Italie* (Rome 1969). L. M. HARTMANN, *Untersuchungen zur Geschichte der byzatinischen verwaltung in Italien, 540–750* (Leipzig 1889).

[N. TOBIAS/F. NICKS]

ART

Ravenna was the center of Byzantine influence in Italy until the eighth century (*see* BYZANTINE ART). Sieges, invasions, and war damage, not to mention the restoration of nineteenth-century enthusiasts, have obliterated much of Ravenna's artistic past; but what remains, particularly of the fifth through eighth centuries, is quite valuable. In no other place in Europe, save perhaps Venice, has the Byzantine style blended with the Western to so great a degree. Although usually classified as Byzantine much of the architecture, colonnades, and mosaics are not so much Byzantine as they are representative of early Christian art with strong Eastern inspiration and resemblances (*see* ART, EARLY CHRISTIAN). The basilicas and other structures at Ravenna are of special architectural interest, because contrary to what one often finds in Italy, the exteriors have been but slightly tampered with. The rugged brick work as well as the typically round campaniles can be studied to advantage in many buildings.

Early Period, 402 to 455. The time from the transferal of the imperial residence to Ravenna under Emperor Honorius in 402 to the death of VALENTINIAN III in 455 was the first great era of postclassical building activity in Ravenna. Numerous palaces and ecclesiastical buildings were erected; the two outstanding monuments that survive are the Orthodox Baptistery and the Mausoleum of Galla Placidia.

St. Ursus, archbishop of Ravenna under Honorius, constructed the cathedral, which in addition to the main nave had four aisles, but this structure was destroyed (1734–44); only the crypt, the round campanile, and a few inscribed stones remain. The present cathedral museum contains several early Christian sarcophagi, a silver cross of the eleventh century, and the famous wood and ivory throne of Archbishop Maximian (546–556). S. Giovanni Evangelista was erected by Galla Placidia, half sister of Honorius and mother of Valentinian III, in fulfillment of a vow made on her voyage from Constantinople. The present structure has been entirely rebuilt, though the columns are ancient. The Gothic portal is excellent, and the church contains a mosaic pavement (1213) with representations of the ill-famed Fourth Crusade and some frescoes by Giotto painted during a visit to Dante (1317–20).

The so-called Mausoleum of Galla Placidia (440–450) was probably first a chapel dedicated by the Empress to St. Lawrence or SS. Nazarius and Celsus. The plan is that of a Greek cross, its four arms having vaulted ceilings with a dome on pendentives over the central intersection. The exterior conceals the dome with a short square tower. Though the whole chapel appears as a plain brick mass from the outside, the small interior is a gem of color. Covered with mosaics on ceiling and dome and provided with a marble wainscot, the interior is illuminated by small alabaster windows which admit a soft light.

The four windows under the dome are flanked by pairs of Apostles in blue tunics with white mantles. The image of St. Peter is especially notable since it makes use of the key as his symbol perhaps for the first time in iconography. The dome mosaic is of rich blue with golden rosettes and the victorious cross in the middle. The symbols of the four EVANGELISTS adorn the spandrels between the four supporting arches. The total effect is one of richness and regality.

Two important mosaics are to be found in the lunettes of the entrance and back walls. In the first, Christ surrounded by sheep and holding the cross of victory in His hand is seated on a boulder in a meadow with a rocky background interspersed with bushes. But here ends any similarity with the usual Good Shepherd of early Christian portrayal. The beardless Christ here is clothed in a royal purple mantle with a golden dalmatic ornamented with blue clavi, and His head is surrounded with the glory of a golden nimbus. The youthful Christ, as a victorious warrior, gathers His faithful sheep into the fold. The lunette on the back wall depicting St. Lawrence the martyr approaching his gridiron is a lively designed and richly colored composition.

The Orthodox Baptistery (S. Giovanni in Fonte) was built by St. Ursus and decorated by Bishop Neon. It is a tall octagonal structure domed on the inside and encrusted with blue ground mosaics, multicolored marble, and stucco reliefs. The focus of attention is the top of the dome in the portrayal of the Baptism of Christ by St. John. The Apostles stride in an impressive circular zone around the central motif, bearing their crowns of martyrdom. Between each Apostle formalized gold foliage sets off the reiterated figures. The outer zone depicts the interiors of contemporary churches with the Book of the Gospels enthroned on the altar or the jeweled vacant Throne of Judgment awaiting the Second Coming of the Savior. The general color scheme is lively; light and delicate tones are offset by the frequent dark backgrounds of the lower mosaic.

Second Period, 493 to 526. The second great period of Ravenna art was that associated with Theodoric the Ostrogoth (493–526). To this era belong the great Basilica of S. Apollinare Nuovo, part of the octagonal church of S. Vitale, the Mausoleum of Theodoric, the Arian Baptistery, the rebuilt Archbishop's Chapel, and Theodoric's Palace. The last survives only in the famous mosaic portrayal of it in the Church of S. Apollinare Nuovo. The small Archbishop's Chapel is the only remaining portion of the archiepiscopal palace. Rebuilt during Theodoric's reign, the chapel is a simple, square-vaulted building with a small apse at one end and a narrow alcove off the other. The bust portraits in mosaic under the chapel's arches are extremely well done in the classical style and were probably copied from painted portraits of the Greco-Roman or COPTIC school. The Arian Baptistery is a small structure, built by Theodoric on the model of the Orthodox Baptistery. The central theme of the dome mosaic is the Baptism of Christ in the Jordan. Despite the destruction of the lower ring mosaic of the dome, a magnificent series of the 12 Apostles approaching a throne on which is placed a cross remains beneath the Baptism. The Mausoleum of Theodoric is a circular building covered by a low dome of monolithic stone about 33 feet in diameter. It is thought that the dome was intended to suggest a crown and might have been brightly colored and gilded.

S. Apollinare Nuovo, the most important basilica in Ravenna, was built by Theodoric to be the largest Arian church and was originally dedicated to St. Martin. In the ninth century it was rededicated to St. Apollinaris on the occasion of the translation of his relics there. The interior of the hall-like basilica has 24 marble columns with almost uniform capitals. The great mosaics of the life of Christ adorning the walls of the nave represent the best work of the period. In addition to 26 Gospel scenes set high above the windows and large figures of Prophets and Apostles between the windows, are the characteristic processions of virgins and martyrs depicted in mosaic from the church entrance to the apse. Moving from the town of Classe through green meadows and palm trees the cortege of crown-bearing virgins leads to the Virgin Mother enthroned with the Child and being offered gifts by the Magi. Across from the Virgin on the opposite wall the majestic and bearded Lord with four angels awaits on His throne the procession of male saints emanating from the imperial palace of Theodoric and led by St. Martin. It is thought that the original mosaics probably contained portraits of Theodoric, his wife, and retinue, but that after the reconquest by Justinian they were reworked to eliminate any reminder of the Arian king.

Final Period, after 527. The last great artistic period of Ravenna occurred with the reconquest of Italy from the Goths by Justinian, who completed the octagonal church of S. Vitale and was responsible for the building of S. Apollinare in Classe (dedicated in 549), the great basilica which today is all that remains of the ancient port of Classis. S. Apollinare is dominated by its high cylindrical campanile and has a fine narthex. On the interior beneath the great apsidal cross is the heroic mosaic of the martyr St. Apollinaris who was originally buried here.

S. Vitale, begun by Abp. St. Ecclesius (524–534), was completed and dedicated by Archbishop Maximian during the reign of Justinian (547). The centrally planned building is composed of two octagons, one enclosing the other. The dome is over the inner octagon, and between the two a second-story open gallery probably seated the women of the congregation. The sanctuary is situated on one side in a room added to the octagon and terminating the apse. Opposite it the entry hall or narthex is flanked by two cylindrical towers. The brick exterior is bare, with the result that the gorgeous decoration of the interior overawes the viewer.

The Byzantine-inspired plan of this church attracted Charlemagne, who so admired the structure that he built the palace church at AACHEN in the same style. Mosaic work and marble were taken from S. Vitale and other Ravenna buildings to build the church in Aachen. Despite the eighteenth-century redecoration of the central area, a considerable amount of the original decor remains.

The choir-apse area is the most remarkable feature. Here the walls seem to disappear as the mosaicist creates his colorful vision of space. In the apse the beardless, triumphant Christ in Majesty sits upon the sphere of the universe attended by angels who usher into His presence St. Vitalis, the patron of the church, and St. Ecclesius, who presents a model of the building itself. The vault and ceiling are profusely decorated with brilliant floral and animal forms. Moses, Jeremiah, Isaiah, Melchizedek, Abraham, Abel, and the Apostles are among the many figures represented in the choir. The two rectangular panels facing each other on the side walls are the finest surviving works of the period. On the left side stands Justinian surrounded by soldiers, courtiers, and Archbishop Maximian with attendant deacons. The emperor presents an enormous golden vessel, his dedication gift to the church. On the right Empress Theodora, accompanied by courtiers and ladies in waiting, similarly presents a gift. The embroidered Magi on the hem of Theodora's gown continue the theme of donation. Vested in sumptuous robes of brilliant colors, bedecked with jewels and embroidery, the figures present a magnificent scene of an Oriental court. They are true portraits, but beyond that the realism ends. They are weightless, flattened out, and float in mid-air. The abstract rhythmic pattern of shapes and colors is typical of this period of transition from the early Christian to the new Byzantine spirit. The artist now conceives new canons of proportion; uninterested in distance, he expresses in a solemn and hieratic way a vision of the world outside time and space.

Bibliography: I. ANDREESCU-TREADGOLD and W. TREADGOLD, ''Procopius and the Imperial Panels of S. Vitale,'' *Art Bulletin* 79/4 (1997) 708–723. F. W. DEICHMANN, *Frühchristliche Bauten und Mosaiken von Ravenna* (Weisbaden, 1958); *Rom, Ravenna, Konstantinopel, Naher Osten: gesammelte Studien zur spätantiken Architektur, Kunst und Geschichte* (Wiesbaden 1982). C. IHM, *Die Programme der christliche Apsismalerei* (2d ed. Wiesbaden 1992). M. JOHNSON, ''Towards a History of Theodorics' Building Program,'' *Dumbarton Oaks Papers* 42 (1988) 73–96. E. KITZINGER, *Byzantine Art in the Making: Main Lines of Stylistic Development in the Mediterranean Art, Third–Seventh Centuries* (Cambridge, MA 1977). S. KOSTOF, *The Orthodox Baptistery of Ravenna* (New Haven 1965). H. MAGUIRE, *Earth and Ocean: The Terrestrial World in Early Byzantine Art* (University Park, PA 1987). C. R. MOREY, *Early Christian Art* (Princeton 1953). O. VON SIMSON, *Sacred Fortress: Byzantine Art and Statecraft in Ravenna* (Chicago 1948, repr. 1976). W. F. VOLBACH, *Early Christian Mosaics from the Fourth to the Seventh Centuries, Rome, Naples, Milan, Ravenna* (New York 1946).

[A. JACOPIN/L. JONES]

RAVIGNAN, GUSTAVE FRANÇOIS XAVIER DE

Jesuit, popular pulpit orator and preacher of conferences and retreats; b. Bayonne, Dec. 1, 1795; d. Paris, Feb. 26, 1858. After an early and distinguished career in law, during which he rose to the rank of deputy attorney general at the Royal Court, Ravignan caused a sensation by retiring to the Sulpician seminary at Issy in May 1822. In November of that same year he entered the novitiate of the Society of Jesus at Montrouge. He was ordained July 25, 1828.

Ravignan taught dogmatic theology at St. Acheul near Amiens for two years, moving with his students during the revolution of 1830 to Brieg in Switzerland, where he continued to teach until 1835. During this time his missions and retreats began to win for him a fame that was augmented by his stirring Lenten sermons in the cathedral at Amiens and at St. Thomas d'Aquin in Paris. In 1836, the Archbishop of Paris, Monsignor de Quelen, called him to succeed Lacordaire in the pulpit of Notre Dame. Ravignan's preaching was characterized more by the magnetism and conviction of his own personality than by the eloquence or imagination of the words themselves.

Gustave François Xavier de Ravignan.

Most of his sermons and conferences were published only posthumously from notes made by listeners, although he was prevailed upon before his death to edit 39 of the conferences given at Notre Dame from 1836 to 1847. These form the bulk of *Conferences du R.P. Ravignan* (Paris 1860), upon which his oratorical fame is largely based. In 1841 Ravignan began the custom of concluding the Lenten conferences with a retreat during Holy Week. This proved such a success that it was necessary for him to preach several retreats concurrently.

During the quarrels over the Falloux Law and the use of pagan classic literature in secondary schools, Ravignan sided with the party of Dupanloup, Montalembert, and Berryer. He refused, however, to take any active public or political role, such as the post of deputy, which was offered to him in 1848. Dupanloup wanted to associate him with the direction of *L'Ami de la Religion,* but the general of the Society of Jesus would not allow it. Only to defend his own order against its attackers did Ravignan take to the public forum. His book, *De l'existence et de l'institut des jésuites* (1844), made its mark, although it had little effect upon the policies of the government of Louis Philippe. His two volumes on Clement XIII and Clement XIV (1854) served at least to bring to light the shameful circumstances that had given rise to the suppression of the Jesuits in the 18th century.

Bibliography: A. DE PONLEVOY, *The Life of Father de Ravignan* (New York 1869). P. DUDON, *Dictionnaire de théologie catholique*, ed. A. VACANT et al., 15 v. (Paris 1903–50; Tables Générales 1951–) 13.2:1793–1802. C. SOMMERVOGEL et al., *Bibliothèque de la Compagnie de Jésus*, 11 v. (Brussels-Paris 1890–1932; v.12, suppl. 1960) 6:1499–1509.

[J. H. CAMPANA]

RAVOUX, AUGUSTIN

Missionary; b. Langeac, Auvergne, France, Jan. 11, 1815; d. St. Paul, Minn., Jan. 17, 1906. After three years in the minor seminary at Le Puy, France, he entered the major seminary there, receiving the subdiaconate on May 20, 1837. He then transferred to the diocese of Dubuque, Iowa, and completed his studies at Mount St. Mary's, Emmitsburg, Maryland, and at Dubuque. He was ordained on Jan. 5, 1840, and he subsequently ministered to frontiersmen at Prairie du Chien, Wisconsin, for a year and a half. In 1841 he began his missionary labors among the Sioux in the Minnesota River valley. As the first priest to serve the area in almost 100 years, he mastered three native dialects and published in 1843 a catechism and hymnal titled *Wakantanka Ti Ki Chanku, or The Path to the House of God.* The indigenous peoples had great respect for him; all but five of the 38 Native Americans condemned to be hanged for leading an uprising in 1862 chose him to prepare them for death. He was the only priest in Minnesota from 1844 to 1851, when the first bishop of St. Paul, Joseph Cretin, arrived. In those years Catholics in the St. Paul area required most of his time, but he visited Sioux villages occasionally, and twice he ministered to isolated Catholics as far west as the Missouri River in South Dakota. In 1850 the diocese of St. Paul was created, chiefly through his efforts, and the land that he had acquired became the basis of its material prosperity. He was vicar-general of the diocese from 1857 to 1859. He declined, in 1868, the appointment as first vicar apostolic of the vicariate of Montana. He was made a domestic prelate on March 1, 1887. He lived in retirement at the cathedral rectory in St. Paul, where he wrote *Reminiscences, Memoirs, and Lectures* (1890; French ed. 1892), *Labors of Mgr. A. Ravoux at Mendota, St. Paul, and Other Localities* (1897), *Catholic Life in St. Paul* (1899), and *Tempus tacendi et tempus loquendi* (1901).

Bibliography: J. M. REARDON, *The Catholic Church in the Diocese of St. Paul* (St. Paul, MN 1952).

[P. H. AHERN]

RAYMOND MARTINI

Dominican theologian, Orientalist; b. Subirats, Catalonia, *c.* 1220; d. Barcelona, 1285. He taught in the

School of Arabic Studies, Tunis, and the School of Hebrew Studies, Barcelona, founded by his order to Christianize North African Muslims and Spanish Jews. He was adviser to King Louis IX of France on his crusade against Tunis and acted as censor of books for Aragon under James I. His works include *Explanatio symboli apostolorum, c.* 1256 [ed. J. March, *Anuari del Institud d'estudis catalans* (Barcelona 1908)]; *Pugio fidei,* completed 1278 (Paris 1642, 1651; Leipzig 1687), based on Islamic and Jewish works and the *Summa contra Gentiles* of St. Thomas Aquinas; and *Capistrum Judaeorum,* written 1267, in MS. His authorship of other works ascribed to him is doubtful.

Bibliography: J. QUÉTIF and J. ÉCHARD, *Scriptores Ordinis Praedicatorum* (New York 1959) 1.1:396–398. A. BERTHIER, "Un maître orientaliste du XIII(e) siècle," *Archivum fratrum praedicatorum* 6 (1936) 267–311.

[P. F. MULHERN]

RAYMOND NONNATUS, ST.

Ransomer of Christian captives; b. Portello, Spain, *c.* 1204; d. Cardona, Catalonia, probably Aug. 31, 1240. His surname derives from his reputed birth by Caesarean section following his mother's death. In the absence of reliable contemporary sources, it is impossible to establish the events in his career. He is generally credited with noteworthy activity in ransoming Christian captives in Moorish North Africa and in Spain, and his zeal served as a model for the work of the MERCEDARIAN order. The claim that Raymond was created cardinal by GREGORY IX is historically uncertain. His intercession is invoked by mothers in childbirth and by the innocent charged with crime. In 1657 ALEXANDER VII permitted Raymond's name to be entered in the Roman MARTYROLOGY.

Feast: Aug. 31.

Bibliography: *Acta Sanctorum* Aug. 6:729–776. G. VÁZQUEZ NÚÑEZ, *Manual de la historia de la orden de N. S. de la Merced,* v.1 (Toledo 1931). B. DE GAIFFIER, *Analecta Bollandiana* 58 (1940) 88. A. BUTLER, *The Lives of the Saints*, rev. ed. H. THURSTON and D. ATTWATER, 4v. (New York 1956) 3:449–450.

[O. J. BLUM]

"St. Raymond Nonnatus Preaching," painting by Venetian artist Carlo Saraceni.

RAYMOND OF CAPUA, BL.

Dominican master general, reformer, hagiographer; b. Capua, Italy, *c.* 1330; d. Nuremberg, Germany, Oct. 5, 1399. Born of the royal Delle Vigne family, Raymond studied at Bologna, and was especially gifted in Scripture and patrology. He became a Dominican *c.* 1347, and served as lector from 1358 to 1362 in various Dominican priories. In 1363 he was assigned as spiritual director to the monastery of Montepulciano. In 1367 he was elected prior of Santa Maria sopra Minerva, Rome. Later, when regent of studies at Siena, Raymond met CATHERINE OF SIENA and was appointed her spiritual director in 1374. Together, the two helped victims of the plague, tried to begin a new crusade, and attempted to reconcile Florence and the Tuscan League with the pope. Raymond collaborated with Catherine in effecting the return of GREGORY XI to Rome, ending the AVIGNON PAPACY.

When the WESTERN SCHISM began in 1378, URBAN VI sent Raymond, once again prior of the Minerva, as papal legate to France to seek the adherence of King Charles V to Urban. The mission failed when Raymond was refused admittance to France. He was elected master general of the DOMINICANS in 1380, and a decade later inaugurated the Dominican reform movement, which sought to restore primitive observance. Raymond is the author of official and personal letters, of biographies of Catherine [Eng. tr. G. Laub (London 1960)] and AGNES

OF MONTEPULCIANO, and of a treatise on the Magnificat. He died while on a visitation to Germany. He is buried at St. Dominic's, Naples. Leo XIII confirmed his cult on May 15, 1899.

Feast: Oct. 5.

Bibliography: RAYMOND OF CAPUA, *Opuscula et litterae,* ed. H. M. CORMIER (2d ed. Rome 1899). G. GIERATHS, *Lexikon für Theologie und Kirche*, ed. J. HOFER and K. RAHNER (Freiberg 1957–65) 8:974. A. W. VAN REE, "R. de Capoue: Éléments biographiques," *Archivum Fratrum Praedicatorum* 33 (1963) 159–241.

[A. DABASH]

RAYMOND OF FITERO, BL.

Abbot of the Cistercian monastery of Fitero in Navarre; d. probably before 1161. He is considered the founder of the military Order of CALATRAVA. In January 1158, King Sancho III of Castile, accepting Raymond's offer to defend Calatrava against the Moors, granted the fortress to him. Raymond transferred most of his monks to Calatrava and welcomed warriors who offered their help. Many of them also assumed the monastic habit. In this way the Order of Calatrava came into being, though it did not receive papal approbation until 1164. Raymond was buried at Ciruelos, "where, as it is said, God worked miracles through him," but his remains repose today in the cathedral of Toledo. He was never formally canonized, but his cult was confirmed in 1719.

Feast: March 15.

Bibliography: J. F. O'CALLAGHAN, "The Affiliation of the Order of Calatrava with the Order of Cîteaux," *Analecta Sacri Ordinis Cisterciensis* 15 (1959) 178–191. F. GUTTON, "Le Culte de Saint Raymond, Abbé," *Cîteaux* 14 (1963) 25–32.

[J. F. O'CALLAGHAN]

RAYMOND OF PEÑAFORT, ST.

Canonist; b. Vilefranca de Penades, near Barcelona, 1175–80; d. Barcelona, Jan. 6, 1275; canonized by Pope CLEMENT VIII in 1601. Raymond completed the trivium and quadrivium at the cathedral school in Barcelona, where he then taught rhetoric and logic. After eight years of legal studies at Bologna, he became master of law in 1218. Three years later he returned to Barcelona, where he received the Dominican habit in the convent of St. Catherine of Alexandria.

In 1229 Raymond was associated with the work of the papal legate in Spain, John of Abbeville. The following year GREGORY IX summoned Raymond to the papal court as his confessor and, shortly thereafter, named him chaplain and penitentiary. The pope also entrusted to him the task of collecting the papal decretal letters into one volume. This work, which came to be called the *Decretales Gregorii IX,* was officially promulgated by the bull *Rex Pacificus* in 1234. Raymond refused the proffered archbishopric of Tarragona and asked permission to return to Spain. He reached Barcelona in 1236, having relinquished all his offices but that of penitentiary, which he held until 1237–38.

At the general chapter of 1238 he was elected the third master general of the Dominicans. Raymond did not change the customs that had been adopted under St. Dominic, but he did give the constitutions of the Order of Preachers a juridical arrangement.

His task completed, he resigned as general in 1240 and returned to Spain, where he turned his attention to the extirpation of heresy and the apostolate to the Jews and Moors. As a member of the papal household he had been instrumental in establishing the Inquisition in Aragón in 1232. His work at the papal chancery had brought to his attention reports from missionaries to the Moors. He used his influence to inaugurate a school of Arabic studies and to induce St. Thomas Aquinas to compose his *Summa contra gentiles,* a presentation of the truths of faith adapted to a pagan mentality. Raymond's lifetime of almost a century ended on the Epiphany 1275. His body was first placed in the chapel of his convent of St. Catherine in Barcelona. In 1878 the chapel of SS. John and Paul in the cathedral of Barcelona became his final resting place.

Raymond's writings exercised a vast influence. His *Decretales Gregorii IX* and his revision of the Dominican Constitutions remained part of the law of the Church and of his order until the present Code of Canon Law was promulgated.

His first canonical treatise, the so-called *Summa juris canonici* (Barcelona 1945), was interrupted when Raymond left Bologna in 1221 and was never completed. In the only extant manuscript the first two of seven projected parts are found.

His principal literary work was the *Summa de casibus poenitentiae,* written (1222–29) at Barcelona. The work, which originally was in three books, was reissued by the author in 1235 with the addition of a fourth book, which was really a revision of Tancred's popular *Summa de matrimonio.* While earlier penitentials had contained little more than lists of sins and corresponding penances, confessors could find in Raymond's work a practical and systematic treatment of doctrinal and canonical matters of interest to them. In Book One, Raymond treated sins committed against God (in 16 titles); in Book Two, sins commited against one's neighbor (in 8 titles); and in Book Three, such questions as irregularities, impediments, dispensations, and sentences (in 34 titles). Hundreds of extant manuscripts and several published editions (Rome 1603,1619; Avignon 1715; Verona 1744) testify to the *Summa's* popularity and to Raymond's fame as an authority on the internal forum.

His minor works include a digest of his *Summa* for the use of Dominican confessors; the *Dubitabilia cure responsionibus,* containing cases of conscience; and the *Diversae consultationes,* containing replies to missionary superiors in Tunis. Of interest to the student of medieval canon law are his glosses on the *Decretum,* and perhaps also on the *Compilatio IV,* as well as his commentary on the *Arbores consanguinitatis et affinitatis.*

Feast: Jan. 7 (formerly 23).

Bibliography: T. M. SCHWERTNER, *St. Raymond of Pennafort,* ed. C. M. ANTONY (Milwaukee 1935). F. VALLS TABERNER, *San Ramón de Penyafort* (Barcelona 1936; Barcelona 1979). F. BALME, et al., eds., *Monumenta ordinis praedicatorum historica,* v.4 of *Raymundiana* (Rome 1898–1901). J. RUIS SERRA, *Diplomatario San Raimundo de Penyafort* (Barcelona 1954). A. COLLELL, ''Raymundiana,'' *Analecta Sacra Tarraconensia* 30 (Barcelona 1957) 63–95. P. RIBES MONTANÉ, *Relaciones entre la potestad eclesiástica y el poder secular, según san Ramón de Penyafort : estudio histórico-jurídico* (Rome 1979). J. J. PIQUER JOVER, *La vida i els miracles de Sant Ramon de Penyafort segons un gravador flamenc* (Barcelona 1980), iconography. V. FORCADA COMINS, *San Ramón de Peñafort* (Valencia 1994). A. TEETAERT, *Dictionnaire de théologie catholique,* ed. A. VACANT et al., (Paris 1903–50; Tables générales 1951–) 13.2: 1806–23. R. NAZ, *Dictionnaire de droit canonique* (Paris 1935–65) 7:461–464. S. KUTTNER, *Repertorium der Kanonistik* (Rome 1937) 443–445. S. KUTTNER, ''The Barcelona Edition of St. Raymond's First Treatise on Canon Law,'' *Seminar* 8 (1950) 52–67; ''Zur Entstehungsgeschichte der Summa de casibus poenitentiae des hl. Raymund von Penyafort,'' *Zeitschrift der Savigny-Stiftung für Rechtsgeschichte, Kanonistische Abteilung* 39 (Weimar 1953) 419–434.

[P. STENGER]

RAYMOND OF RODA-BARBASTRO, ST.

Bishop; d. Huesca, Spain, June 21, 1126. The most reliable source for his career is the vita written by a contemporary canon, Elias of Roda. Raymond was prior of the monastery of St. Saturninus in Toulouse before he was made bishop of Roda and Barbastro in northern Aragon. He soon acquired fame as a zealous bishop of outstanding personal virtue, but he could not escape the political and ecclesiastical conflicts of the time. Stephen, bishop of Huesca, with the help of Alfonso I, the warrior king of Aragon, drove Raymond out of Barbastro and annexed the area of this see to his own diocese. Despite Raymond's appeal to Rome and the strong letters addressed to Alfonso and to Stephen by Pope Paschal II, Barbastro was not restored to Raymond. He accepted the situation and, at the request of Alfonso, accompanied him in the campaign culminating in the battle of Cutanda, and in Alfonso's famous expedition as far as Malaga. In returning from this second campaign, Raymond fell ill and died at Huesca. His body was subsequently transferred to Roda. Alfonso made amends for his earlier injustice and restored Barbastro to the jurisdiction of Roda.

Feast: June 21.

Bibliography: *Acta Sanctorum* June 5:110–115. *Bibliotheca hagiographica latina antiquae et mediae aetatis,* 2 v. (Brussels 1898–1901; suppl. 1911) 2:7074–78. H. FLÓREZ et al. *España sagrada,* 54 v. (Madrid 1747–1957) 46:149–157, 247–263. A. UBIETO ARTETA, ''Disputas entre los obispados de Huesca y Lerida en el siglo XII,'' *Estudios de edad media de la corona de Aragón* 2 (Saragossa 1946) 187–240. J. VINCKE, *Lexikon für Theologie und Kirche,* ed. J. HOFER and K. RAHNER, 10 v. (2d, new ed. Freiburg 1957–65) 8:977–978.

[M. R. P. MCGUIRE]

RAYMOND OF SABUNDE

Philosopher; b. Barcelona; d. Toulouse, 1436. Having degrees in arts, medicine, and theology, he taught theology at the University of Toulouse, and in time was ordained a priest. His only work is the *Theologia naturalis,* or *Liber creaturarum,* written between 1434 and 1436 and widely circulated throughout Europe. According to its author, the aim of this work is to study the nature of man as well as the things prerequisite to this study, i.e., natures subject to man. God has placed at man's disposal two books, created nature and the Bible, the latter being given to him when, blinded by sin, he could not read the former. Since both books come from God, they cannot obliterate, falsify, or contradict each other. As a result, philosophy is the study of nature, especially human nature. Man, then, should be the first object of knowledge, and God should be the end to which all human thoughts and actions are ordered. Because Sabunde's claim that he encountered in the study of nature all the truths contained in Sacred Scripture was taken to be equivalent to saying that revelation is unnecessary, the Council of Trent put the prologue of his work on the Index.

Bibliography: C. C. L. KLEIBER, *De Raimundo quem vocant de Sabunde vita et scriptis* (Berlin 1856). F. HOLBERG, *De theologia naturali R. de Sabunde* (Halle 1860). T. and J. CARRERAS Y ARTAU, *Historia de la filosofía española: Filosofía cristiana de los siglos XIII al XV,* 2 v. (Madrid 1939–43) 2:101–174, with extensive bibliog.

[D. CABANELAS]

RAYMOND OF TOULOUSE

Name of several members of the ruling family of the County of Toulouse.

Raymond IV, founder of the Latin County of Tripoli in the Holy Land; b. *c.* 1043; d. Tripoli, Feb. 28, 1105. Raymond became Marquis of Provence in 1066 and Count of Toulouse in 1093, upon the death of his elder brother, Count William IV. In 1095, shortly after the Council of Clermont, Raymond took the cross and set out for the Holy Land in October of 1096. After the capture of Antioch (1098), Raymond attempted to gain control of the city on behalf of Byzantine Emperor ALEXIUS I COMNENUS, but he was thwarted by Bohemond I. When the crusaders took Jerusalem (1099), Raymond also attempted unsuccessfully to establish himself there. He then allied himself with the Byzantines and subsequently joined forces with the Crusade of 1101. He escaped the general massacre of that unsuccessful expedition and then returned to Syria, where he took Tortosa and commenced a further campaign against Tripoli. Although Raymond died before the capture of Tripoli (1109), he is usually regarded as the founder of the Latin County of Tripoli (*see* CRUSADES; CRUSADERS' STATES).

Raymond VI, defender of Provence against the Albigensian Crusade; b. Oct. 27, 1156; d. August 1222. Raymond inherited the County of Toulouse from his father, Count Raymond V (1134–94), and in the early years of his reign secured a settlement of the war begun by his father with RICHARD I, King of England. In 1207 INNOCENT III excommunicated Raymond for protecting and fostering the ALBIGENSES or CATHARI. After the assassination of papal legate PETER OF CASTELNAU by one of Raymond's officers in 1208, a crusade was launched against the Albigenses and against Raymond, as their protector. Following the disastrous battle of Muret on Sept. 12, 1213, Raymond went into exile. He endeavored to clear his name at the Fourth LATERAN COUNCIL (1215) but he was condemned instead to the loss of his lands, which were turned over to SIMON DE MONTFORT L'AMAURY. Raymond then returned to Provence, where he was able to recover a part of his former domains before his death. Although he was married five times, Raymond left only two legitimate children: a daughter, Constance, and a son, Raymond VII, who succeeded him.

Raymond VII, the last Count of Toulouse; b. Beaucaire, July 1197; d. Milhau, Sept. 27, 1249. He continued to fight against the Albigensian Crusade and the Montfort family. After Simon de Montfort's heir, Amaury, transferred his claims in Provence to the French king (1226), Raymond had to face the perils of a renewed campaign. Eventually he made peace with his enemies under the harsh terms of the Treaty of Meaux (1229), which stripped him of most of his possessions. The marriage of his only daughter, Jeanne, to Alfonse de Poitiers, brother of King LOUIS IX of France, assured that at Raymond's death his remaining lands would pass under the control of the French monarchy.

Bibliography: C. DE VIC and J. VAISSETE, *Histoire générale de Languedoc,* 15 v. (rev. ed. Toulouse 1872–93) v. 3, 4, 6. A. P. MOLINE DE SAINT-YON, *Histoire des comtes de Toulouse,* 4. v. (Paris 1859–61) v. 2–4. J. H. and L. L. HILL, *Raymond IV de Saint Gilles* (Toulouse 1959). P. BELPERRON, *La Croisade contre les Albigeols* (Paris 1942).

[J. A. BRUNDAGE]

RAYMOND OF TOULOUSE, ST.

Patron of Toulouse, France; d. Toulouse, July 3, 1118. Raymond was born a free man of Toulouse and was dedicated by his parents to the service of St. Saturninus. He abandoned the religious life and married. His wife died within a few years, however, and Raymond thereupon devoted himself completely to charitable works. Prominent among these was the building and endowment of a hospital or college for 13 poor clerics, next to the Church of St. Saturninus, which he also rebuilt. Raymond later became a regular canon of this church. His cult was established in 1652, after an epidemic in Toulouse was believed to have been ended through his intercession. His life was apparently written by a regular canon in the 13th century.

Feast: July 8.

Bibliography: *Acta Sanctorum* July 1:589–603. J. L. BAUDOT and L. CHAUSSIN, *Vies des saints et des bienheureux selon l'ordre du calendrier avec l'historique des fêtes* (Paris 1935–56) 7:70–72. A. BUTLER, *The Lives of the Saints* (New York 1956) 3:43.

[J. A. BRUNDAGE]

RAYNAUD, THÉOPHILE

Jesuit theologian and author; b. Sospello, near Nice (now Sospel, Alpes-Maritimes), Nov. 15, 1583; d. Lyons, Oct. 31, 1663. Raynaud entered the Society of Jesus in 1602 and was ordained in 1613. He taught humanities in Avignon and philosophy and theology in Lyons. An erudite and versatile scholar, he produced 92 separate works covering almost the entire field of theology. He was regarded as the most learned theologian of his time by many, and Cardinal Richelieu sought his assistance when the Spanish Jesuit, Hurtado de Mendoza, attacked the cardinal's political alliance with the Huguenots. In 1645 he was called to Rome to refute Pierre de Marca's *De concordia sacerdotii et imperii.* Raynaud entered with vigor into the theological disputes of his time, occasionally showing a lack of taste, judgment, and discretion. His style was classical, although often verbose and obscure. His theological works are rarely consulted today, but his writings on the Congregation of the Index remain significant for Church historians.

Raynaud's collected works, which he revised shortly before his death, were published in 19 volumes (Lyons 1665). A 20th volume, entitled *Apopompaeus* (i.e., the Scapegoat), and containing a number of writings that Raynaud had purposely excluded from his collection, was published, supposedly in Cracow, but actually in Lyons, in 1669 by an anonymous editor; this volume was condemned by the Congregation of the Index. The following list of subjects taken from the *Opera* suggests the nature and scope of his writings: *Theologia Patrum, Christus Deus Homo, De attributis Christi, Moralis disciplina, De virtutibus et vitiis, Theologia naturalis, Opuscula Eucharistica, Marialia, Ascetica,* and *Polemica.*

Bibliography: C. SOMMERVOGEL et al., *Bibliothèque de la Compagnie de Jésus.* (Brussels-Paris 1890–1932) 6:1517–50. R. BROUILLARD, *Dictionnaire de théologie catholique*, ed. A. VACANT et al. (Paris 1903–50) 13.2:1823–29.

[J. G. BISCHOFF]

REA, ALONSO DE LA

Franciscan chronicler; b. Querétaro, Mexico, 1606?; d. place unknown, 1660? He is called also Fray Alonso de Larrea; some bibliographers erroneously call him Roa. He was the natural son of the Spaniards Tomás Angulo and Francisca de la Rea. He took the habit in November 1624, in the convent of Valladolid (today Morelia). He became a lector in philosophy and theology, a definitor of the order, chronicler (1637), and first Creole provincial of the Franciscans of Michoacán (1649). He wrote *Crónica de la Orden de N. Seráfico P. S. Francisco, Provincia de San Pedro y San Pablo de Mechoacán en la Nueva España,* published by the widow of Bernardo Calderón (Mexico 1643, 1822). Rea was a truthful and precise historian with a clear and concise style. He described the artistry of the Tarascans (natives of the province) in their featherwork mosaics, paintings of indigenous lacquer, religious sculptures of sugarcane pulp, especially their famous "Christs of Michoacán," as well as their ability as metal workers. An eyewitness to the plague that devastated the region, he described the charity of the Franciscan missionaries in curing and burying the native Mexicans and reported that towns of 20,000, such as Tzintzuntzan, dropped to 200 and that in the whole province five out of every six Tarascans died.

Bibliography: J. M. BERISTAIN DE SOUZA, *Biblioteca hispano americana setentrional,* 5 v. in 2 (3d ed. Mexico City 1947).

[E. GÓMEZ TAGLE]

READING, ABBEY OF

A reformed Benedictine house, County Berkshire, England. It was founded by King Henry I in 1121, and originally colonized by monks from CLUNY and the Priory of LEWES. Reading, liberally endowed with lands and privileges, was one of the ten richest and most important abbeys in medieval England. Throughout the 12th century it had strong links with the Cluniac Order but never became a member of it; by the later 13th century Reading was virtually an ordinary Benedictine house. The first abbot, HUGH OF AMIENS, was appointed in 1123 and made archbishop of Rouen in 1130. The abbey church, which housed the tomb of Henry I, was dedicated in 1164 by Thomas BECKET. Abbot William I (1164–73) became archbishop of Bordeaux and Abbot Hugh II (1186–99) was elected abbot of Cluny. By grant of Clement III in 1191, the abbot was mitered. Reading's most important relics were the hand of St. James the Great, given by Henry I, and the head of St. Philip, given by King John in 1205. The abbey was the scene of John of Gaunt's marriage to Blanche of Lancaster in 1359, and of the announcement of King Edward IV's marriage in 1464. Parliament assembled there in 1453. Dependent houses were Leominster Priory (County Hereford) and, until the late 13th century, May Priory, Scotland. Reading was dissolved in 1539, after the execution of the last abbot, Hugh Cook Faringdon, who denied the royal supremacy. Some ruins remain today.

Bibliography: J. B. HURRY, *Reading Abbey* (London 1901). J. C. COX, "The Abbey of Reading," *The Victoria History of Berkshire,* ed. P. H. DITCHFIELD and W. PAGE, 4 v. (London 1906–24) v.2. D. KNOWLES and R. N. HADCOCK, *Medieval Religious Houses: England and Wales* (New York 1953) 74. D. KNOWLES, *The Monastic Order in England, 943–1216* (2d ed. Cambridge, England 1962). L. H. COTTINEAU, *Répertoire topobibliographique des abbayes et prieurés,* 2 v. (Mâcon 1935–39) 2:2417.

[B. R. KEMP]

READING, SPIRITUAL

Spiritual reading is the reading of those things that help one make progress in the spiritual life, done precisely with the aim of nourishing and strengthening this life. It differs from vocal prayer, meditative reading, and study, inasmuch as it presupposes in the reader a disposition that is more receptive than active. However, insofar as it gives him new matter for consideration, it serves, at least as a moral cause, to bring about a certain actualization of the reader's internal faculties in the direction of contemplation.

Aim. God has given man a share in His own life and has thereby raised him to the supernatural order. Thus, the preservation and constant growth of this divine life, with a view to possessing it eternally in heaven through the direct vision of God, the Supreme Good, is the essential problem of the spiritual life. The aim of spiritual reading, therefore, is to have man know as many aspects of this life as possible and thereby to facilitate the accomplishment of his supernatural destiny. The need and importance of devoting part of his time to spiritual reading, then, arises from human indigence, since man is in constant need of instruction and new impulses if he is to make progress in the life of virtue and apostolic activity. This need grows along with growth in profane culture, since there must be not only an ever more adequate knowledge of the problems and concerns of the spirit, but also a strengthened ability to rebut error and to protect oneself against spiritual loss through absorption in secular interests.

Matter. Books for spiritual reading embrace the Bible primarily, which contains God's own words; then the writings of the Fathers, and Doctors of the Church, who have developed the Biblical expression of God's teaching; and, in general, every work that serves to explain Catholic teaching about human perfection or to manifest its realization in the lives of the saints.

The Bible. The Bible is the principal book for spiritual reading since it contains the principles and rules of Christian perfection, especially as these are exemplified in the life of our Lord. The four accounts of the Gospel, then, comprise the most important part of the Bible for the purpose of spiritual reading, since they contain not only the narration of what our Lord did and taught, but also the manner wherein He fulfilled the prophecies. Moreover, these accounts represent His life, not only with respect to His personal perfection, but also with respect to His perfection as the king and savior of the human race. Yet to appreciate God's whole plan of salvation, one should strive to read the whole Bible, from the first page to the last.

The Fathers. The Fathers of the Church developed their teaching by exploring the content of the Bible. While their writings are in general a rich source for spiritual reading, the organization of excerpted material in St. Thomas Aquinas's *Catena Aurea* (*The Golden Chain*) is of special value. There the reader can find the Fathers' own explanation of the social context of Christ's words and actions and can see the relation between this social context and his own, as well as the symbolic meaning of many of Christ's words.

The Doctors of the Church. While many of the Fathers are also Doctors of the Church, there are many Doctors who are not Fathers. They are important for spiritual reading, not only because of their analyses of Christ's teaching, but also because of the discipline in logic contained in their writings. Very few persons have the habit of logic so perfectly as to avoid all the pitfalls of sentimentalism even during the time devoted to spiritual reading. By serving to discipline the mind, then, the Doctors of the Church serve also to discipline the emotions, and this discipline helps to remove the obstacles to thorough penetration of the doctrine presented.

History. Historical accounts, too, can be suitable for spiritual reading. This is true especially of the history of the Church, wherein one can read the history of salvation and the spread of Christ's mystical body throughout the world. Inasmuch as the saints reflect Christ's own perfection and His constant work of sanctifying souls, the accounts of their lives, too, are good sources for spiritual reading. In this regard, however, one must make a careful selection. Extremely poetic and rhetorical reports of the lives of the saints militate against, rather than serve, the purpose of spiritual reading, since they not only misrepresent the true holiness of the particular saint, but also distort the mind of the reader by focusing attention on what is not genuinely holy in this person's life or by emphasizing what can have a sensational appeal.

Dispositions. The personal advantage of spiritual reading presupposes certain dispositions in the reader. First among these are the theological virtues: faith, hope, and charity. Faith is needed so that the reader is ready to accept God's word without questioning its truthfulness. Hope is necessary as a foundation for perseverance in the practice of spiritual reading, as well as for a habitual readiness to rely upon God's help for the penetration of what is read. Charity is needed so that the reading may be motivated by love for God, and that joy and peace may predominate in the course of the reading; a person engaged in spiritual reading must be preoccupied with what is good rather than with what is evil, and must have considerable freedom from both internal and external agitation. Among the moral virtues, piety has a special importance, since the reader must be habitually disposed to accept God as the principal teacher; the Apostles, Fathers, and Doctors as secondary teachers under God; and other authors as teachers who share in a lesser degree the excellence of the foregoing authors. Studiousness causes a person to apply what he reads to himself and inclines him to penetrate what he reads, rather than to read many books without really delving into their meaning. Humility, of course, is a most basic disposition, since it causes the reader to recognize his true spiritual condition and thereby prevents him from adopting an unrealistic view of what he reads, for instance that involved in fantastic comparisons of himself with certain saints, as though he had the same degree of perfection.

Benefits. The two principal advantages of spiritual reading are habitual encouragement to strive for perfection in one's thoughts, words, and actions; and a disposition for frequent meditation based upon what has been read. From meditation, the soul can be raised to contemplation, the most perfect act of man's mind, inasmuch as it involves union with God. Spiritual reading, then, becomes a source of contemplative prayer, wherein charity is inflamed and wherein the soul here contemplates, in the darkness of faith, the Supreme Good, whom it will contemplate forever in the light of glory.

Bibliography: R. GARRIGOU-LAGRANGE, *The Three Ages of the Interior Life,* tr. M. T. DOYLE, 2 v. (St. Louis 1947) 1:247–55. A. ROYO, *The Theology of Christian Perfection,* tr. J. AUMANN (Dubuque 1962). J. EUDES, *La Vie et le royaume de Jésus dans les âmes chrétiennes* (Oeuvres Choisies de Saint John Eudes 1; Paris 1931). E. BERTAUD, ''Dialogues Spirituels,'' *Dictionnaire de spiritualité ascétique et mystique. Doctrine et histoire,* ed. M. VILLER et al. (Paris 1932–) 3:834–850; ''Entretiens spirituels,'' *ibid.,* 4.1:763–774. E. BERTAUD and A. RAYEZ, ''Echelle spirituelle,'' *Dictionnaire de spiritualité ascétique et mystique. Doctrine et histoire,* ed. M. VILLER et al. (Paris 1932–) 4.1:62–86. T. CAMELOT, ''Lecture et oraison,'' *La Vie spirituelle* (Paris 1919–); title varies, 78 (1948) 640–659. J. DE GHELLINCK, *Lectures spirituelles dans les écrits des Pères* (Paris 1935). A. LEFÈVRE et al., ''Écriture sainte et vie spirituelle,'' *Dictionnaire de spiritualité ascétique et mystique. Doctrine et histoire,* ed. M. VILLER et al. (Paris 1932–) 4.1:128–278.

[E. BERTAUD]

REALINO, BERNARDINE, ST.

Jesuit humanist, patron of Lecce; b. Carpi (near Modena), Italy, Dec. 1, 1530; d. Lecce, Apulia, Italy, July 2, 1616. Realino studied at nearby Modena and at the University of Bologna, where he was made a doctor in *utroque jure* in 1556. Because of an argument during which he had wounded an adversary, Bernardino was forced to make his career elsewhere, and he went in 1556 to Milan. The governor, Cardinal Cristofero MADRUZZO, appointed him to the first of several minor mayoralties and fiscal posts. In May 1564 the Marquis of Pescara brought Realino to Naples to supervise some of his holdings. He was admitted into the Society of Jesus by Alphonso Salmerón and made his novitiate at the Jesuit college in Naples. In 1567 he was ordained and shortly afterward was appointed master of novices by (St.) Francis BORGIA, general of the Jesuits. In 1574 Realino was assigned to Lecce. Here he remained for 42 years, founding a college and building a noble baroque church. Direction of souls soon became his chief occupation, and his winning charity and compassionate skill in the confessional earned him a reputation for sanctity. A sodality for priests, which he inaugurated, seems to have been the first of its kind under Jesuit auspices. Numerous miraculous cures and prophecies were attributed to him, and several visions of the Blessed Virgin and of Jesus crucified. The Bollandists refer to him as *notae sanctitatis thaumaturgus.* On his deathbed, at the petition of the mayor and council of Lecce, he agreed to be the city's protector in heaven. He was beatified by Leo XIII and canonized June 22, 1947, by Pius XII. In his youth Bernardino was a prolific writer, mainly on the classics, and wrote verses even in the last years of his life. At 21 he had published a commentary on a poem of Catullus, *In nuptias Pelei et Thetidis catullianas commentarius* (Bologna 1551). Although on becoming a Jesuit he destroyed all the copies he could find, at least 22 survive in the great libraries of the world.

Feast: July 2 (Jesuits).

Bibliography: B. DE REALINO, *Lettere spirituali inedita . . .,* ed. G. BOERO (Naples 1854). G. GERMIER, *San Bernardino Realino* (Florence 1943). F. SWEENEY, *Bernardine Realino: Renaissance Man* (New York 1951); *Every Man My Brother* (Boston 1976). J. N. TYLENDA, *Jesuit Saints & Martyrs* (Chicago 1998) 195–97. A. BUTLER, *The Lives of the Saints,* rev. ed. H. THURSTON and D. ATTWATER, 4 v. (New York 1956) 3:13–14. *Acta Apostolicae Sedis* 39 (Rome 1947) 249–253, 391–398. C. SOMMERVOGEL et al., *Bibliothèque de la Compagnie de Jésus,* 11 v. (Brussels-Paris 1890–1932; v. 12 suppl. 1960) 6:1554–56.

[F. SWEENEY]

REALISM

Realism, in the language of modern and contemporary philosophy, is a general theory concerning the relationship between the mind of man and what is commonly called REALITY. Because of this, a doctrine affirming or denying realism pertains to the branch of philosophy known as EPISTEMOLOGY, which treats of the subject of KNOWLEDGE. Although philosophers are not in agreement as to whether epistemology is a philosophical discipline distinct from METAPHYSICS, the nature of the subject under discussion permits one to abstract from this question. In any event, the epistemologist must ultimately square his conclusions about knowledge with his metaphysics of being.

Realism vs. Idealism. In its broadest terms, realism asserts that the ultimate factor or principle in being is not the mind of man, but rather what exists in reality beyond the mind or ''outside'' the mind. The word ''outside'' is not here taken in a spatial sense, as though the mind were located within the human brain and reality were situated outside it. Although this may be true in a qualified sense, spatial localization has little to do with the meaning the Western philosophical tradition has given to extramental reality. Nor must realism be taken to imply that the contents understood by the mind are real and the mind itself is not. Realism, in its many forms, does not deny the reality of mind in order to assert the reality of what is not mind. On the contrary, realism maintains that the term of the act of knowing is not to be identified with that very act. Knowledge is always about something that is not itself knowledge. Hence realism attributes an independent existence to the term of knowledge. In a word, realism maintains that there is a world and that the function of the mind consists primarily in coming to terms with that world in order to understand it as it is in itself.

In its most general notion, realism is opposed to IDEALISM. Idealism, prescinding from differences existing between idealist philosophers, maintains that the ultimate principle from which philosophy takes its point of departure is mind, whether mind is differentiated into individual intelligences or is itself an undifferentiated principle. Idealism therefore asserts that reality issues forth from intelligence or from spirit, and is ultimately nothing more than a dimension of that same spirit. The idealist begins with the ''I'' thinking reality, whereas the realist affirms that thinking or knowing depends upon the reality known or thought.

Absolute Realism vs. Nominalism. Historically, such differences did not arise as a result of the modern idealist-realist controversy but as a result of a controversy that centered around the status of UNIVERSALS. The dispute originated in Greek philosophy, and its underlying presupposition is the evident truth that man possesses universal concepts or networks of meaning that are applicable indifferently to many subjects of judgment. What, precisely, is the status of ''man'' as predicated of John and of Paul? The answer of PLATO gave birth to what the philosophical tradition of the West calls absolute realism (*Soph.* 242–264B; *Parm.*). Reasoning from the data at hand, Plato concluded that both John and Paul participate in a common meaning designated by the word ''man.'' But since no individual man exhausts the meaning of man, this intelligibility or form cannot be identified with either John or Paul. Plato's problem hinged upon his having to discover the status of a predicate that is participated among many subjects. He concluded that meanings or forms (ideas) have an absolute status quite apart from the things that participate in them. He thus postulated two orders of reality: an order of absolutely real being that corresponds to the judgment of identity, ''*A* is *A*''; and an order of second-rate reality that imperfectly shares in the being of the forms and that corresponds to the judgment of participation, ''*A* is *B*.'' In the latter judgment the predicate is not identified completely with the subject. What is most important for an understanding of Plato's absolute realism in his contention that the universal CONCEPT in all its universality is being, and that the role of the mind is reduced to ascertaining this being.

Plato's doctrine entered into early medieval philosophy through the writings of BOETHIUS and through the *Isagoge* of PORPHYRY; here it was opposed by NOMINALISM, which asserted a position in flat contradiction to that of Plato. Nominalism in its earlier phase is associated with ABELARD, and in its later stages with WILLIAM OF OCKHAM. Whereas Plato had attended to the evident reality of meanings in things, nominalists looked to the evident reality of singularly existing things. Outside the mind there simply are no universal realities. The universal, by definition, is a community of meaning predicable of many singulars. But a community of meaning can never be found in actual existence. Man never encounters the universal. Arguing thus, and urged on by their insistence that only the singular is real, nominalists concluded by denying any reality whatsoever to the universal. The universal was reduced to the spoken or written or imagined word, which itself is singular. Thus all meaning disappeared from the universe. The more sophisticated nominalism of the 20th century, associated with LOGICAL POSITIVISM, states that universals are convenient tools with which man organizes the continuum of sensation. But all nominalists, both medieval and modern, agree that universal meaning has no extramental or metaphysical status whatsoever.

Conceptualism and Scotism. CONCEPTUALISM is a position between that of absolute realism and nominalism. While granting that the mind does in fact possess universal ideas, conceptualism maintains that there is no basis outside the mind for this universality. The universal serves as an instrument for grouping singular objects. Conceptualism thus bears an affinity to both nominalism and to logical positivism.

A late medieval attempt to close the gap between Platonic absolute realism and the nominalistic insistence upon the ultimate reality of the singular was that of John DUNS SCOTUS. While agreeing with Plato that the form or idea has an extramental or metaphysical status, Scotus took account of the irreducibility of the singular to the universal. The form of man, let us say, must receive the additional form of ''thisness'' (*haecceitas*) or of individuality that seals reality and binds existent meaning to this concrete singular reality. The difficulty in Scotus's position would seem to reside in the impossibility of conceiving a form that is a form and at the same time individual.

Aristotle's Moderate Realism. The realism of Aristotle, as distinguished from that of Plato, is usually called moderate realism. The Aristotelian critique of Platonic realism can be divided methodologically into two moments, one experimental and the other metaphysical (*Cat.* 2–10; *Meta.* 1017–18; *Part. animal.* 642b–644b). In the order of experience man does not discover universals as he discovers things. Slavery is not experienced, but rather slaves. It follows that Plato's theory of PARTICIPATION is useless in man's search for the universal.

Induction and Abstraction. For Aristotle, the universal emerges in the mind as the result of an accumulation of EXPERIENCE that serves to form an INDUCTION. When the experience in question is sufficient, the universal is produced by an intellectual power or faculty known in the scholastic tradition as the agent INTELLECT. The universal, being the product of an act of mind, is made by the mind; therefore its metaphysical status as a universal is owed strictly to the intellect. But the mind is able to form the universal, and thus predicate it of the singular, because within reality itself there is a basis or foundation for the universal. This foundation is the energizing principle that organizes each thing, giving it consistency and direction or finality. Aristotle called this principle the FORM. Form in extramental reality is always individualized by MATTER, which functions as a passive limitation upon form. Granted that forms are repeated throughout nature, the basis for the universal is reality itself, and reality as form or as ACT.

Ultimately what separates Aristotelian from Platonic realism is Aristotle's insistence that human knowledge is basically abstractive, and that ABSTRACTION depends upon a series of confrontations or experiences with reality through the medium of the senses. For Plato knowledge is basically intuitive, and hence proceeds from the general to the particular, at least ideally.

Objections to Plato. Aristotle's metaphysical objection to Platonic realism rests upon Aristotle's conviction that nature is essentially active or dynamic (*Meta.* 1013a–1017a). Even if there were Platonic ideas, these could not explain a changing universe. What does not initiate activity does not itself have being. The Aristotelian form not only structures a thing; it is its internal energy or actuality. Since Plato's ideas do not do anything, they are incapable of serving as a basis for such explanation. The Platonic form is, however, a model or an exemplary cause; as such, it does have meaning in a world of art where the carpenter, for example, fashions a chair from the preexistent idea of chair that he entertained (*see* EXEMPLARY CAUSALITY). In the world of art and technology, the idea precedes the reality; in this order Plato's theory of participation applies with perfect justice. But the world of nature would seem to correspond more closely to the Aristotelian position.

Inherent Difficulties. Aristotle's realism nonetheless contains a number of difficulties that were pointed out by both nominalists and realists during the famous medieval controversy. The chief difficulty in Aristotelian moderate realism is one of explaining how the selfsame form can exist in two orders of reality, in extramental being as actuality and in the mind as universality. The difficulty is rooted in Aristotle's theory of BEING. For Aristotle, being is ultimately reducible to SUBSTANCE, itself a composition of an active principle (form) and a passive principle (matter). Being must serve to answer the question ''what is a thing''; and this ''what'' (QUIDDITY) or ESSENCE is ultimately the form as related to matter. But if being is substance, and especially substance as form, there is no difference between the being of a man and that man himself (*Meta.* 1003b 28). How then is it possible that man ''be'' (i.e., exist) in the mind, if being is defined as identical with substance?

Aquinas's Moderate Realism. The metaphysics of St. THOMAS AQUINAS is probably the most ambitious attempt within Western philosophy to preserve the doctrine of moderate realism by surmounting difficulties of this type. While conserving in its fullness Aristotle's notion of substance as composed of matter and form, as well as the Aristotelian theory of abstraction, St. Thomas Aquinas made important emendations in the Aristotelian doctrine relating to being. His principal contribution in this area was the clear and explicit distinction he introduced between essence and existence (*see* ESSENCE AND EXISTENCE).

Since essence (and therefore form) is not identically its own existence, nothing prohibits the selfsame form from existing in different individuals. The form remains identically the same within any given species, while it is existentially diverse because of its different acts of existing. Thus the form that exists singularly in the order of being can come to exist within the human intelligence as universal. The latter special mode of existence is known within Thomism as intentional existence [see Y. R. Simon, *Introduction à l'ontologie du connaître* (Paris 1934)].

Within a Thomistic context, INTENTIONALITY must not be thought of simply as an act of being. Intentional existence does not make a thing exist; rather it makes a thing be known. The knower is thus literally the thing known; yet the union between them is not physical. Neither knower nor thing known loses its proper identity in the world of being. The act of knowledge is thus conceived to be a relational act; the term of the relation is the reality grasped in knowledge.

Critical Realism. The moderate realism of Aristotle and the medievals was challenged first by the nominalism of Ockham and others, and then in the Renaissance by René DESCARTES. The position of Descartes may be identified as a critical realism, an attempt to justify realism on grounds that belong strictly to the intelligence. Strongly influenced by the success of mathematics in reducing the complex to the simple, Descartes professed a systematic and universal doubt about everything he had hitherto accepted as true, and then proposed to remove that doubt through the application of mathematical methods. Fixing upon the irreducible certitude of the ''I'' or ego, the existence of which cannot be doubted, Descartes wished to proceed from the ego to the world, rather than from the world to the ego. This marked a radical departure from the Thomistic and Aristotelian contention that man's knowledge of self, as revealed in his CONSCIOUSNESS, is a consequence of the knowledge he already possesses of the world.

Descartes established his realism by direct appeal to divinity; for him, the idea of God, whose existence is guaranteed by an identification of His perfection with the concept of existence or being, combines with the fact of experience to prove the existence of the world. All men reason spontaneously to the being of the world from the sensations they possess. The only adequate cause of these sensations is the things represented by them. God's veracity guarantees the validity of the reasoning process, because God would not permit the whole human race to be deceived.

Critical Idealism. The critical realism of the late 19th and early 20th centuries was an attempt to improve the Cartesian thesis by transcending its weakness. Nevertheless, Descartes's realistic intentions were soon absorbed into the idealism of the classical German philosophers of the 18th and 19th centuries. Immanuel Kant affirmed the extramental reality of the world, but he denied that there was any necessary relationship between such reality and the laws of the mind. He admitted that the human intelligence is forced to think in terms of the law of causality, which declares an inexorable link between propositions and ideas. But, for him, CAUSALITY itself is not found in reality; rather, the real is made up of discrete elements that are not related by causal necessity. Nature contains no laws within itself. Law, being universal and necessary, comes from reason and is thus prior to experience. Kant, of course, did speak of a ''thing-in-itself'' beyond experience. But this escapes the order of judgment, which is restricted, according to him, to the phenomena of experience; the mind ought therefore not to affirm or deny the existence of the ''thing-in-itself.'' Kant's critical idealism, itself containing a minimum of realism, was thereupon expanded into the absolute idealism of J. G. FICHTE and G. W. F. Hegel, which denied the ''thing-in-itself'' as superfluous.

The realist objections to the Kantian position can be stated under two headings. (1) Kant's sharp opposition between the PHENOMENA, or the events of experience that are always singular, and the NOUMENA, or laws of the mind that are always universal, is itself an opposition between two mental concepts. The universal is not opposed to the singular, except logically; rather the universal is discovered by the mind in the singular. Realism thus denies the basis upon which Kant built his system by denying an existential opposition between singularity and the universality. Universality is grounded in form or actuality; this is always individuated in matter, before the mind abstracts its formal intelligibility and sees it as a complexity of meaning common to many things. (2) The Kantian insistence that human knowledge is restricted to phenomena introduces a distinction between ''things-in-themselves'' and ''things-in-man's-sensibility'' that is purely assumed and in no sense evident.

Nonscholastic Realism. Contemporary nonscholastic realism has taken many forms, most of which reflect the influence of Kant and his insistence that law belongs to the mind and not to things. Thus H. BERGSON and W. JAMES reduce the mind to a tool that is capable of working out human problems but is incapable of coming to grips with reality itself. Reality must be grasped, according to Bergson, by an INTUITION that bypasses the logical structure of the intelligence. A similar philosophy has been developed by George SANTAYANA. Asserting the reality of the idea as of an essence given whole and entire to the human intelligence, Santayana asserts that the reality of the existent is accepted on a purely animal faith. It follows that the less existence an idea or an essence has, or the less it is involved in the world, the more real it becomes. Santayana's explanation through animal faith, while differing in many respects from the PHENOMENOLOGY of F. BRENTANO, E. HUSSERL, and M. SCHELER, has in common with this doctrine a realism of essence that prescinds from a realism of EXISTENCE. From a scholastic point of view the realist philosophies proffered by G. E. Moore, B. RUSSELL, A. N. WHITEHEAD, S. ALEXANDER, and N. HARTMANN also force an excessive separation between essence and that of existence.

Modern EXISTENTIALISM has attempted to surmount the traditional opposition between realism and idealism by its insistence upon the truth that man always encounters himself within a world. This situation of ''being-in-a-world'' belongs to the very constitution of man, who, for M. HEIDEGGER, is a project or a ''being-towards-and-in-a-world.'' It is impossible to conceive of man and of the world in isolation; man and world essentially involve one another.

The criticism leveled against realism by these thinkers is prompted by the basic realist contention that the world is not man. Existentialists deny the supposed opposition, and thus claim to have transcended the dispute between idealism and realism. The strength of the existentialist position would seem to reside in its insistence that man is meaningless apart from the world, a thesis that seems, however, to strengthen rather than weaken the realist position. The ambiguity in the existentialist transcendence of both realism and idealism is located in the concept of world. If this means a related, meaningful whole, actually intelligible or known, then the existentialist notion of world corresponds roughly to the realist. But if world is taken to exclude actual intelligibility, then the existentialist position can be reduced to an idealism, and thus it in no sense transcends the dispute between realism and idealism.

See Also: KNOWLEDGE, THEORIES OF; AESTHETICS.

Bibliography: F. D. WILHELMSEN, *Man's Knowledge of Reality* (Englewood Cliffs, N.J. 1956). F. VAN STEENBERGHEN, *Epistemology,* tr. M. J. FLYNN (New York 1949). J. MARITAIN, *Distinguish to Unite: The Degrees of Knowledge,* tr. G. B. PHELAN (New York 1959). B. J. F. LONERGAN, *Insight: A Study of Human Understanding* (New York 1957). L. M. RÉGIS, *St. Thomas and Epistemology* (Milwaukee 1946). E. H. GILSON, *Le Réalisme méthodique* (Paris 1936); *Réalisme thomiste et critique de la connaissance* (Paris 1939). I. M. BOCHEŃSKI, *Contemporary European Philosophy,* tr. D. NICHOLL and K. ASCHENBRENNER (Berkeley 1956). F. H. PARKER, ''Realistic Epistemology,'' *The Return to Reason,* ed. J. D. WILD (Chicago 1953). M. M. GORCE, *Dictionnaire de théologie catholique*, ed. A. VACANT et al., 15 v. (Paris 1903–50) 13.2:1833–1910. A. COLOMBO and V. MATHIEU, *Enciclopedia filosofica*, 4 v. (Venice-Rome 1957) 3:1889–1901. R. EISLER, *Wörterbuch der philosophischen Begriffe*, 3 v. (4th ed. Berlin 1927–30) 2:622–25.

[F. D. WILHELMSEN]

REALITY

Reality denotes the realm of things existing outside of, and independently of, the mind. Derived from the Latin *res,* ''thing,'' the word is often applied to the world of the SENSES. By contrast, the world of reality is distinguishable from the realm of IMAGINATION or that of intellectual ABSTRACTION. The absolute intelligibility and even the existence of a world of reality have been challenged, most notably in modern philosophy (*see* KNOWLEDGE, THEORIES OF).

Two questions might be asked concerning reality: ''Are things as they appear?'' and ''Do they even exist at all?'' Light from a white object, passing through a green pane of glass, might convey to an observer behind the glass the impression that the object itself was green. René DESCARTES, in his *Discourse on Method,* suggested the possibility that the senses themselves transform the impressions they give of objects in a similar manner. In his *Critique of Pure Reason,* Immanuel KANT answered that one knows reality only as previously transformed by his own senses and intellect. What one knows, therefore, is not things themselves but certain subjectively transformed appearances, PHENOMENA. Hence the philosophy of PHENOMENALISM. A further step would then be to ask if anything at all corresponds outside the mind to the appearance within the mind. A negative answer yields the philosophy of SOLIPSISM, which affirms that internal appearances are all that exist, that oneself is the sole existing reality.

Since the knower has no way of verifying the existence and nature of reality except by the use of his senses and INTELLECT, whose objective validity phenomenalism and solipsism call into question, the legitimacy of the foregoing questions must be examined. To question whether other things exist besides oneself, one must imply his own EXISTENCE, which he knows in the same way as he knows the existences called into question. To acknowledge one's own existence, therefore, is equivalent to acknowledging the existence of other things. Similarly, when one asks if things are as he conceives them to be, the question presupposes an awareness of the identity of the senses as distinct from the object of perception. It further presupposes that, with due caution and attention, the mind can forestall any misinterpretation of sense data. To one who has a cold, for example, food may seem tasteless; yet he realizes that it is not the food that has lost its savor, but rather his senses that are not normal. So one may invent questions leading to solipsism and phenomenalism, but the mind does not actually raise them. In fact those who profess such doubts do not adhere to them in practical life.

Although the term ''reality'' as denoting the totality of things existing independently of mind is usually identified with reality as perceived by the senses, one cannot arbitrarily restrict the scope of existing things to the sensible world alone. If immaterial things such as SOUL, ANGELS, and GOD, exist, they too are real and actually constitute, by their plenitude of being, a superior realm of reality.

See Also: DISTINCTION, KINDS OF; KNOWLEDGE; REALISM.

Bibliography: ARISTOTLE, *Meta.* 1003a.20–1012b.30. THOMAS AQUINAS, *In 4 meta.* 1–17; *De ver.* 1.1. V. MATHIEU, *Enciclopedia filosofica,* 4 v. (Venice–Rome 1957) 3:1903–13.

[P. CONWAY]

REASON, CULT OF GODDESS OF

A civic, naturalistic religion of the FRENCH REVOLUTION, dedicated to the worship of Reason and Liberty and intended as a substitute for Christianity. The Paris Commune, under the leadership of Pierre Chaumette, inaugurated the cult with a ceremony in the cathedral of Notre Dame (Nov. 10, 1793), three days after Jean GOBEL, the constitutional bishop of the capital, had been induced to abdicate his priesthood. In the cathedral a shrine was erected in honor of Reason and Liberty. In front of the choir a sacred mountain was constructed, surmounted by a small Greek temple in honor of Philosophy. Surrounding it were busts representing leading figures in the ENLIGHTENMENT (probably Montesquieu, Rousseau, Voltaire, and Benjamin Franklin). A young opera singer, whose name remains uncertain, posed as Liberty and was dubbed ''Goddess of Reason.'' A flame, symbolic of truth, burned on an altar, while white-clad young girls, wearing tricolored sashes representative of allegiance to the Republic, carried torches up and down the sacred mountain. Meanwhile the congregation sang André Chenier's hymn: ''Come, Holy Liberty, dwell in this temple; become the Goddess of the French people.''

As the cult spread to other parts of France, modifications were introduced. Some temples of Reason recognized the Supreme Being; others venerated Brutus or Jean Marat. The revolutionary extremists, who were trying to dechristianize the country, claimed that Christianity was too otherworldly to oppose tyranny and was nearing extinction. They hoped to speed the process with the new cult. One of their chief vehicles of propaganda was *Moniteur du culte de la raison,* edited by Pierre Chantreau. Jacobins eagerly adopted the cult, even in the provinces. By order of the commune (Nov. 24, 1793), all churches in Paris were transformed into temples of Reason. The Cult of Reason vanished quickly, after its chief exponents, Chaumette and Jacques Hébert, were guillotined (March 24, 1794); it was supplanted by the Cult of the SUPREME BEING (May 1794).

Bibliography: F. AULARD, *Le Culte de la raison et le culte de l'Etre Suprême, 1793–94* (Paris 1892). A. SICARD, *À la recherche d'une religion civile* (Paris 1895). A. MATHIEZ, *Les Origines des cultes révolutionnaires, 1789–1792* (Paris 1904); *Contributions à l'histoire religieuse de la révolution française* (Paris 1907). A. LATREILLE, *L'Église catholique et la révolution française,* 2 v. (Paris 1946–50).

[M. LAWLOR]

REASON, USE OF

Reason is an individual's possession of a capacity to employ his thinking and volitional powers here and now in the direction and control of his behavior in such a way that his actions can be accounted truly human and morally imputable. It thus differs from the age of reason, or the time in life when a person becomes more or less stably capable of moral judgment.

No doubt consciousness of any kind in a human being involves some operation on the part of his intellect and will, as well (in his earthly mode of existence) as of his sensory powers. But only when these several principles of activity are sufficiently sound in their separate and combined functions to enable a man to formulate a reasonable judgment concerning an end to be pursued (appraised from the point of view of ultimate human values), or the means suitable to its attainment, can he be said to enjoy the ''use'' of reason, i.e., the capacity to employ it freely in the pursuit of objectives specifically human in their value. If the function of his powers is impeded or impaired in such a way that he is incapable of judgment of this kind, although reason and its associated powers may be operative, a man does not possess the free use of them to human purposes and his actions cannot, therefore be classified either as perfectly human or as perfectly moral.

The use of reason may be lacking or impaired by a variety of defects. The most radical of these is an insufficiency in the development of the power of abstract thinking, or a present incapacity to exercise it, that makes a man unable to distinguish absolute from relative values and to see beyond the particular goods that appeal to his immediate desire. If this capacity is wanting, one is incapable of any truly human or moral activity whatever. Other defects may diminish one's use of reason without destroying it entirely. These may occur in consequence of malfunction of sensory perception (as in hallucinations), or of ignorance or inadvertence on the part of the mind itself, or of turbulent emotional disorder. For the influence of these defects on the use of reason and hence on moral responsibility, *see* IGNORANCE; HUMAN ACT; VOLUNTARITY.

[P. K. MEAGHER]

REASONING

The process by which the human INTELLECT passes from what it already knows to what it does not yet know, without having recourse to new information. Since KNOWLEDGE is expressed in propositions, reasoning may be characterized also as the process by which the mind passes from two or several propositions, called the premises or the antecedent, to another proposition, called the conclusion or the consequent. It may be noted that passing directly from one PROPOSITION to another, e.g., by conversion, is not considered reasoning because the conclusion has the same content as the premise, differing from it only in form; thus no new knowledge results. Only by bringing together two or more knowledge-contents does the mind grasp a new knowledge-content.

(The direct passage from one proposition to another is sometimes called immediate inference, although the term "inference" is here used in an improper sense.)

Matter and Form. In reasoning there are two aspects to consider, namely, matter and form. The matter is the content with which the reasoning is concerned, i.e., the objects and properties mentioned in the propositions involved in the reasoning. The form is the manner in which the elements of the reasoning are linked together; it is what characterizes the reasoning when abstraction is made from its content. Corresponding to the distinction between form and matter is that between the validity and the truth of a reasoning process; a consideration of validity and truth may thus assist the understanding of form and matter as they are applied to the reasoning process.

Validity of Reasoning. Reasoning is valid, or correct, when the consequent follows necessarily (with a logical necessity) from the antecedent, i.e., when the antecedent cannot be true without the consequent's being true also. It is then said that the consequent is inferred from the antecedent or that there is an inference (in the strict sense) from the antecedent to the consequent. Valid reasoning thus expresses an inference.

The validity of reasoning depends only on its form. In other words, the validity is independent of the objects and properties about which the reasoning is concerned, and therefore, of the truth or falsity of the propositions involved in it. If, in valid reasoning, each mention of an object or of a property is replaced by the mention of another object or another property, the resulting reasoning also is valid.

Reasoning can be valid even if its conclusion is false, as when one of the premises is false. Again, invalid, or incorrect, reasoning can come to a true conclusion; when this occurs, however, it is by accident and not in virtue of the deductive link the reasoning establishes between true premises and the conclusion drawn. When any given reasoning is incorrect, it is always possible to replace it by another with the same form and with true premises that leads to a false conclusion.

The necessary condition of the validity of a given reasoning process is the following: "in all reasoning having the same form, if the premises are true the conclusion is also true" (Dopp, 15).

Truth of Reasoning. The reasoning process that establishes the TRUTH of a proposition is called DEMONSTRATION. A proposition is demonstrated to be true only if it expresses the conclusion of a valid reasoning process all of whose premises have been previously recognized as true, i.e., as being evident in themselves or as having in turn been demonstrated. According to Aristotelian doctrine, a distinction must be made between demonstration in the strict sense, which concerns what is necessarily true, and demonstration in the improper sense, which concerns what is only probable. The first leads to SCIENCE (*scientia*) as such, which is knowledge of the necessary, whereas the second pertains to DIALECTICS, which is concerned with probable knowledge.

The study of reasoning can be undertaken from the viewpoint of validity only, which considers form alone, or from the viewpoint of demonstration, which considers form and matter conjointly. The first viewpoint is that of formal logic, the second, that of material logic (*see* LOGIC).

Evolution of Concept. Various conceptions of reasoning have evolved with the history of logic. According to the scholastic conception, which to a great extent was inherited from Aristotle, logic is the study of acts of the mind that relate to the acquisition of truth. In this view, conditions affecting the validity of reasoning and those affecting its truth are based upon the characteristics of the intellectual acts that are involved in the reasoning process and in demonstration. Since those acts can be attained only through philosophical REFLECTION, logic, in this conception, has a philosophical base.

According to the modern conception, which is at the root of contemporary mathematical logic, formal logic must be considered as a science in the same sense as mathematics and must be developed in abstraction from all philosophical preconceptions. The study of reasoning is there attempted in terms of facts and without reference to acts of the mind; it considers only the properties of the objects of thought. This viewpoint finds its most radical expression in formalism. (*See* LOGIC, SYMBOLIC.)

Scholastic Analysis. It is common scholastic teaching that reason or intellect has three fundamental operations: simple APPREHENSION, JUDGMENT, and reasoning. In each, a distinction is made between the operation as such, which is an act of the intellect, and the product of the intellect that results from this operation. This product is to be distinguished from its oral or material expression. The term "reasoning" may denote the operation of the mind in apprehending a group of propositions (the antecedent) as inferring another proposition (the consequent) and concluding from the antecedent to the consequent. It may denote also the product of this operation, called ARGUMENTATION, which is the logical whole formed by the antecedent and the consequent: "a group of propositions in orderly sequence one of which (the consequent) is posited as inferred by the others (the antecedent)" (Maritain, 154). The term "argumentation" may denote the product of reasoning either as a mental object or as the oral or material expression of this object.

The consequence (*consequentia*) is the logical link that the reasoning establishes between the antecedent and the consequent; it is the manifestation of an inference. Reasoning, as an act, is really a motion of the mind, a *discursus* wherein the mind, perceiving two propositions as true and as standing in some type of mutual relationship, perceives in this very connection the truth of a third proposition, which it itself forms and to which it gives its assent. Thus the mind, put in motion by the antecedent, finds its rest in the consequent. The antecedent may therefore be regarded as a cause of the consequent. The essential law that governs this process is the following: in a correct reasoning, it is impossible that the antecedent be true and the consequent false.

Deduction and Induction. There are two types of reasoning: DEDUCTION and INDUCTION. In deduction, the mind moves only on the plane of the intelligible; it makes manifest "the truth of the proposition in so far as it is contained in the *universal truth* from which it is derived" (Maritain, 161). The best known and most celebrated form of deductive reasoning is the assertoric SYLLOGISM. This is *"an argumentation in which, from an antecedent that unites two terms to a third, a consequent is inferred uniting these two terms to each other"* (*ibid.* 169). Aristotelian and scholastic logicians have considered also other forms of deductive reasoning, in particular those of modal logic and of propositional logic.

In induction, the mind moves from the sensible plane to the intelligible plane. Induction is *"an argumentation in which the mind infers an universal truth from sufficiently enumerated singular cases"* (*ibid.* 259).

Analysis and Synthesis. Induction and deduction may be further characterized in terms of analysis and synthesis. ANALYSIS, or DIVISION, is an operation that resolves a complex whole into its parts; it thus passes from the complex to the simple. SYNTHESIS is the reverse of this; it passes from the simple to the complex, from the parts to the whole. Induction may be regarded as a type of analysis: it goes from facts to laws, i.e., to the universal principles upon which the facts depend; these may be regarded as wholes of which the facts are parts. It proceeds by a *resolutio materialis,* resolving the conclusion into the elements from which the mind has drawn it as from its matter. Deduction, on the other hand, may be regarded as a type of synthesis: it goes from principles to their consequences. It proceeds by a *resolutio formalis,* resolving the conclusion to the intelligible truths on which it depends and finally to FIRST PRINCIPLES that are self-evident. (It should be noted that not every analysis or synthesis involves reasoning; thus division of a concept is an analysis and judgment is a synthesis.)

Practical Reasoning. Demonstration in the strict sense, founded ultimately on the first principles of intellectual understanding, generates speculative, or theoretical, science. Apart from such science there is also practical science, which has human action and the regulation of this action as its object. Reasoning has a role to play in the practical order because, although human action as such proceeds from the will, the intellect presents the will with its object. And it is the intellect that deliberates, prior to the will's election, so as to make possible a judgment concerning means that can lead to the end proposed by the will (*see* HUMAN ACT).

Human action is concerned with the particular and the contingent. But there are first principles in the practical order, as in the speculative, and a corresponding habit that enables man to come to knowledge of such principles, namely, SYNDERESIS. Right reason (*recta ratio*), starting with the principles furnished by synderesis and using the rules of reasoning (exactly as in the speculative order), establishes conclusions that constitute the rules of morality. CONSCIENCE applies these rules to particular situations, to what must be done by the individual here and now. The judgment of conscience is located between moral science, which is knowledge of the principles and rules of action, and the last practical judgment, which decides the course of action to be taken. The judgment of conscience is directed by PRUDENCE, a habit that enables man to judge rightly the data of a practical problem and choose means adequate to the end in view. It makes use also of the COGITATIVE POWER, an internal sense that enables man to perceive the goodness or harmfulness of an object and thus to make comparisons in the realm of practical knowledge.

Modern Analysis. In recent thought, a clear-cut distinction is made between the philosophical and the formal study of reasoning. Philosophical logic, much like scholastic logic, investigates norms of correct reasoning and the conditions required for the acquisition of truth. But logicians from the 19th century onward, applying mathematical methods to the study of the logical problems, have succeeded in creating a discipline that may be considered as a branch of mathematics, namely, mathematical, or symbolic, logic. H. B. Curry compares the relationship between this logic and philosophical logic to the relationship that exists between geometry considered as a pure mathematical science and geometry considered as a physical theory of real space.

Formal Methods. Mathematical logic investigates certain categories of formal systems considered in themselves and abstracting from particular philosophical positions or problems (*see* AXIOMATIC SYSTEM). Such formal methods have shown themselves particularly useful in studying the foundations of mathematics; metatheoretical studies of this type likewise make use of the methods of mathematical logic. Using such methods, for example, important work has been done in the elucidation and resolution of paradoxes (*see* ANTINOMY). Scholastic logic had already contributed considerably to this subject, but modern logic has undertaken the study with more rigorous and strictly formalized methods.

Study of Content. The procedures of mathematical logic can be used also to study the content of reasoning. Since its beginnings, mathematical logic has been preoccupied chiefly with problems of deduction, and a great variety of deductive systems have been elaborated; these offer a much wider field for deductive reasoning than that provided by traditional logic.

Research on inductive reasoning, although less developed, is pursued in the same manner. Here the notion of probability plays a central role; thus investigations of induction are closely related to studies of the foundations of probability. An allied topic of research is the problem of decision. R. Carnap's work is particularly significant for having elaborated a program of inductive logic in the spirit of mathematical logic.

Finally, modern studies of scientific methodology have successfully employed the methods of formalism to study problems pertaining to the acquisition of truth. Studies of induction are partially concerned with such problems. Important studies have examined also the process of VERIFICATION, the notion of explanation in modern science, the structure of scientific theories, the role of models, and special problems raised by the particular sciences.

See Also: METHODOLOGY (PHILOSOPHY).

Bibliography: M. J. ADLER, ed., *The Great Ideas: A Syntopicon of Great Books of the Western World,* 2 v. (Chicago 1952); v. 2, 3 of *Great Books of the Western World* 2:546–568. J. MARITAIN, *Formal Logic,* tr. I. CHOQUETTE (New York 1946). I. M. BOCHEŃSKI, *Formale Logik* (Freiburg 1956), Eng. *A History of Formal Logic,* ed. and tr. I. THOMAS (Notre Dame, Ind. 1961). J. DOPP, *Notions de logique formelle* (Louvain 1965). H. B. CURRY, *The Foundations of Mathematical Logic* (New York 1963). R. CARNAP, "The Aim of Inductive Logic," in *Logic, Methodology and Philosophy of Science: Proceedings of the 1960 International Congress,* ed. E. NAGEL et al. (Stanford 1962) 303–318.

[J. A. LADRIÈRE]

REASONING, THEOLOGICAL

The New Testament gives witness to the confidence of the first Christians in the ability of human reason to receive God's self-revelation and to foster its transmission through understanding, articulation, and proclamation. The announcement in the Gospel of John that "the Word became flesh" (1.14) affirms directly the mystery of the Incarnation, but indirectly it also indicates the dignity and efficaciousness of human reason (*logos*), derived from and reflective of the divine Logos. The Apostle Paul does not hesitate to remind his readers that "invisible realities, God's eternal power and divinity, have become visible, recognized through the things he has made" and so people "certainly had knowledge of God" (Rom 1.20–21). In his letters he uses logic to refute his opponents (e.g., Gal ch. 2), as well as analogies drawn from history (e.g., Rom ch. 4) and experience (e.g., 1 Cor ch. 12).

The confidence of the Church in the ability of human reason in matters divine is well summarized in Vatican I's Dogmatic Constitution *Dei Filius* (1870). The Council teaches that "God, the source and end of all things, can be known with certainty from the things that were created, through the natural light of human reason" (DS 3004; J. Neuner and J. Dupuis, ed., *The Christian Faith* [New York 2001], no. 113). But the Council also affirms that "revelation is to be judged absolutely necessary . . . because God in His infinite goodness has ordained us to a supernatural end (DS 3005; *The Christian Faith,* no. 114). There are, therefore, truths revealed by God not accessible to human reason (e.g., God as Triune, the mystery of the Church, etc.), which human beings accept through the gift of faith. Even in regard to these truths, however, there is a role for human reason, as Vatican I declared: "Nevertheless, if reason illumined by faith inquires in an earnest, pious and sober manner, it attains by God's grace a certain understanding of the mysteries, which is most fruitful, both from the analogy with the objects of its natural knowledge and from the connections of these mysteries with one another and with man's ultimate end" (DS 3016; *The Christian Faith,* no. 132).

Christians have always discovered fruitful insight into the mysteries of revelation by using analogies drawn from natural knowledge. Some have been quite simple, e.g., comparing the unity of Christians gathered in communion with Christ at the Eucharist to the grains in a loaf of bread. Some have been quite complex, e.g. St. AUGUSTINE's psychological analogy of the human experience of memory, understanding, and will for insight into the mystery of the Trinity.

Throughout the centuries theologians have striven to connect the mysteries of revelation with one another in order to achieve greater understanding through such a synthesis. Since Vatican II, a particularly effective connection has been that of seeing ecclesial communion in the light of Trinitarian communion. In the Middle Ages, the most successful and enduring synthesis was the *Summa theologiae* of St. THOMAS AQUINAS. In the twentieth century, the most influential systematic work has been the *Church Dogmatics* of the Protestant theologian Karl

Barth, who maintained that the best apologetic was good dogmatics.

The effort to connect the mysteries of revelation with the ultimate destiny of human beings has manifested itself in the twentieth century with the concern to show the coherence of revelation with the structures of human knowing and loving in the quest for transcendence. This has led to the reshaping of fundamental theology from a more anthropological perspective and reflects the modern ''turn to the subject.'' Investigation into human knowing and loving have been intrinsic to the work of such theologians as Bernard LONERGAN, S.J., and Karl RAHNER, S.J.

Efforts to achieve greater understanding of the mysteries of revelation have to rely on the intellectual resources of a particular culture, especially philosophy. In Western Christianity the philosophy of St. Thomas Aquinas, derived from Aristotle but also modified by him to be more consonant with the Christian tradition, was for a long time the dominant force. As Pope JOHN PAUL II noted in his encyclical *FIDES ET RATIO* of 1998, ''The most influential Catholic theologians of the present century, to whose thinking and research the Second Vatican Council was much indebted, were the products of [the] revival of Thomistic philosophy'' (no. 57). Many theologians of the twentieth century, however, have also been influenced by other philosophical systems, e.g., existentialism, process philosophy, and phenomenology. Pope John Paul II himself insists that ''the Church has no philosophy of her own nor does she canonize any one particular philosophy in preference to others'' (*Fides et Ratio*, no. 49).

Theological reasoning, however, also has a critical function because of ''the historical condition that affects the expression of revelation,'' as this is described in the Declaration *Mysterium ecclesiae* from the Congregation for the Doctrine of the Faith in 1973 (A. Flannery, ed., *Vatican Council II: More Post Conciliar Documents* [Northport, N.Y. 1982], pp. 433–34). The Declaration notes that dogmatic formulas are conditioned by ''the expressive power of the language used at a certain point in time and in particular circumstances,'' by incomplete (though not false) formulation at first but fuller expression later ''in a broader context of faith or human knowledge,'' by concentration on ''solving certain questions or removing certain errors,'' and by traces of ''the changeable conceptions of a given epoch.'' The Declaration goes on to define the work of theologians as ''seeking to define exactly the intention of teaching proper to the various formulas, and in carrying out this work they are of considerable assistance to the living Magisterium of the Church, to which they remain subordinated.''

Vatican II led to the use of other resources for theological reasoning besides philosophy. In discussing the participation of the People of God in Christ's prophetic office, the Council states that in adhering to the Christian faith the People ''penetrates it more deeply through right judgement, and applies it more fully in daily life'' (*Lumen gentium*, no. 12). This has led to greater theological reflection on the practice of faith by the members of the Church. Praxis has become a source of insight into the implications of the Gospel and the Christian tradition for teaching and action. Thus, for example, liberation theology, insofar as it is theological reflection on the plight of the poor and their Gospel-based actions to improve their condition, underlies the Church's recognition that ''there is a special presence of Christ in the poor, and this requires the Church to make a preferential option for them'' (Pope John Paul II, *Novo Millenio ineunte*, no. 49).

Theologians have also turned to the sciences—empirical and social—either engaging them as conversation partners with the Christian tradition or using them to gain deeper insight into the unfolding of the tradition. Pope John Paul II notes that ''reference to the sciences is often helpful, allowing as it does a more thorough knowledge of the subject under study, but it should not mean the rejection of a typically philosophical and critical thinking that is concerned with the universal'' (*Fides et ratio*, no. 69).

Vatican II also encouraged young Churches to ''borrow from the customs, traditions, wisdom, teaching, arts, and sciences of their people everything which could be used to praise the glory of the Creator, manifest the grace of the Savior, or contribute to the right ordering of Christian life'' (*Ad gentes divinitus*, no. 22). The Council encouraged theological investigation in each of the great socio-cultural regions so that ''the facts and words revealed by God, contained in Sacred Scripture, and explained by the Fathers and Magisterium of the Church, [could be] submitted to a new examination in the light of the tradition of the universal Church'' (ibid.). Pope John Paul II notes that the Church of the future ''will judge herself enriched by all that comes from today's engagement with Eastern cultures and will find in this inheritance fresh cues for fruitful dialogue with the cultures which will emerge as humanity moves into the future'' (*Fides et ratio*, no. 72).

In sum, the Church maintains a positive regard toward the role of reason in the relationship of human beings to God. Reason can come to know the existence of God by its own natural light, and it can achieve a deeper understanding of God's self-revelation through the use of philosophical systems, the sciences, praxis, and dialogue with other cultures.

[J. STRYNKOWSKI]

REBIRTH (IN THE BIBLE)

The concept of a rebirth is one of the ways by which the NT seeks to explain the riches of Redemption that have been communicated to the Christian; before taking up the NT teaching, however, this article will refer to some passages from the OT intertestamental literature that throw light on the subject.

Old Testament and Intertestamental Literature. The idea of a new birth or rebirth is well represented in the philosophical and religious literature of the Greco-Roman world, but it is absent from Jewish writings prior to Philo. In the OT, Israel—and later its king and people—could be described as ''sons of God'' (Dt 1.31; 8.5; Hos 11.1; 2 Sm 7.14; Is 30.1, 9; etc.), but this relationship was not thought of in terms of a birth or rebirth. Such ideas had polytheistic and idolatrous associations and were therefore avoided (Jer 2.27). Even those expressions that might suggest a divine generation of Israel or its king [Ex 4.22; Dt 32.18; Ps 2.7; 109(110).3 (Septuagint)] are subject to a moral or ''adoptionist'' interpretation. To express the idea of a new beginning, which is implied in the term rebirth, the OT speaks of a New Creation (Is 65.17–18; 66.22–23), which was ultimately given a futurist eschatological setting and associated with the inbreaking of the eternal age to come (Ethiopic Henoch 72.1; 91.16–17; Jubilees 1.29; 2 Bar 32.6; 4 Ezr 7.75). This doctrine is reflected also in the Qumran documents (*Serek hayyahad (Rule of the Community, Manual of Discipline)* 4.25; *Hôdâyôt (Thanksgiving Hymns from Qumran Cave 1)* 13.11–12), and it is made a present reality for those candidates entering the eschatological community (*Hôdâyôt (Thanksgiving Hymns from Qumran Cave 1)* 11.10–13); but these events are never described as a rebirth. This concept was foreign to Jewish thought.

New Testament. The concept of a new birth or rebirth is found in a limited number of passages in the NT. In the Johannine literature it is described as a being born of God (Jn 1.13; 1 Jn 2.29; 3.9; 4.7; 5.1, 4, 18) or being born anew or from above (Jn 3.3, 7), terms that stress the source of this new birth. In the other texts the terminology is more elastic, with the noun rebirth (παλιγγενεσία; Mt 19.28; Ti 3.5) or the verbs to regenerate (ἀναγεννάω; 1 Pt 1.3, 23) or to bring forth (ἀποκυέω; Jas 1.18) being employed to describe the total process. With the exception of Mt 19.28, which reflects Stoic terminology and refers primarily to the Jewish idea of the renewal of the cosmos in the age to come, all these passages describe a personal rebirth, the reception of a new, spiritual principle of life during the present physical existence. The rebirth concept is not found in the Synoptics, the closest contact being their insistence on the need for a conversion and beginning in life, becoming like a little child, in order to enter the kingdom (Mt 18.3; Mk 10.15). Nor does this notion occur in St. Paul, who remains within the Jewish framework of a general renewal. For him man has become a new creature (2 Cor 5.17; Gal 6.15); the Old Covenant has yielded to the New (2 Cor 3.6); the old man has been put off, the new put on (Col 3.9–10; Eph 4.24; cf. 2 Cor 4.16); all men are created a new man in Christ (Eph 2.10, 15).

In those passages in which this notion of a personal rebirth occurs, it has an eschatological content. The individual's new birth is brought about by God the Father (Jas 1.17–18; 1 Pt 1.3) through the Resurrection (1 Pt 1.3) or glorification of Christ (Jn 3.13–15; Ti 3.6), in the hope of salvation and eternal life (Ti 3.7) in the kingdom of God (Jn 3.3, 5). These are eschatological goods that, according to the ''realized'' aspect of Christian eschatology, are already present in Christ and His work. [See ESCHATOLOGY (IN THE BIBLE)]. Rebirth is therefore more than a conversion and new beginning; it is the attainment of a new life and salvation by the Christian. It is based on faith; it makes Christians the first fruits of God's creatures (Jas 1.18; cf. Ex 4.22) and the children of God (Jn 1.12–13). It is at present reality communicated to the Christian by the word of God (1 Pt 1.23) and the Spirit (Jn 3.5, 8), the principles of this new birth. The word is the revelation of God found in the gospel. It is planted as a seed in the human heart (Mk 4.1–20), where it remains and confers eternal life (Jn 6.63, 68). This develops the OT themes of the word of God as the law of God (Dt 29.28) put in the hearts of men (Dt 30.11–14; Jer 31.31–34) as a guide for their lives. It is the Wisdom of God (Wis 9.1–2) that itself is the law of God (Sir 15.1–10; 24.23–34); it is a source of life (Wis 7.12) and immortality (Wis 6.17–18; 8.13) to those who possess it. The Spirit is the life-giving power of God that is poured out upon the Christian community (Acts 1.8; 2.1–11). This suggests the OT themes of the Spirit as the principle of physical life (Gn 6.17; Jb 34.14–15) and eschatological life (Ez 11.19; 36.26; Is 32.15; Jl 3.1–2), as well as a means of understanding, interpreting, and expressing the Word in both the OT and the NT. It is at Baptism that the new life of the resurrected Christ is given (Rom 6.3–11) and that the Spirit is communicated to man (Mt 28.19; Acts 2.38), and so it is Baptism that is the moment of rebirth (Jn 3.5; Ti 3.5), the moment when the interacting Word and Spirit of God produce their effect.

Although the terminology used in these passages shows the influence of Greek thought, the ideas expressed are Christian. They develop themes found in the OT and are not merely borrowed from the Greco-Oriental MYSTERY RELIGIONS. This terminology was employed to explain to Gentile converts the true significance of the baptismal event.

See Also: BAPTISM (IN THE BIBLE).

Bibliography: J. DEY, Παλιγγενεσία (Münster 1937). R. REITZENSTEIN, *Die Vorgeschichte der christlichen Taufe* (Leipzig 1929) 103–126. E. SJÖBERG, "Wiedergeburt und Neuschöpfung im palästinischen Judentum," *Studia Theologica* 4 (1950) 44–85; "Neuschöpfung in den Toten-Meer-Rollen," *ibid.* 9 (1955) 131–136.

[S. PARSONS]

REBUSCHINI, ENRICO, BL.

Mystic, priest of the Order of Clerics Regular, Servants of the Sick (CAMILLIANS); b. Apr. 28, 1860, Gravedona on Lake Como, Piedmont, Italy; d. May 10, 1938, Cremona, Lombardy, Italy. Although Enrico was born into a wealthy family, he was always sensitive to the needs of the poor. When his father opposed his priestly vocation, Enrico submitted. He enrolled at the University of Pavia, but found its anticlerical atmosphere intolerable. Remaining docile to his father's wishes, Enrico entered military service, studied accounting, then joined his brother-in-law's silk factory for two years. No longer able to dismiss his vocation, he attended the Pontifical Gregorian University at Rome until he fell gravely ill. Upon his recovery, he engaged in rigorous asceticism in order to give himself totally to God. He entered the Camillians, Servants of the Sick, at Verona (1887) and was ordained (1889) by the future Pope Saint PIUS X. He was the hospital chaplain at Verona (1891–99), then assigned to that position in Cremona. He administered the new clinic at Cremona (1903–37), and, for the last 11 years of his life, he was superior of the community. Pope John Paul II, who beatified Rebuschini on May 4, 1997, noted his "extraordinary love for the Eucharist and constant devotion to the sick and suffering" (beatification homily).

Bibliography: L. MIGLIOLI, *Il messaggio d'amore di padre Enrico Rebuschini* (Milan 1969). *Acta Apostolicae Sedis* (1997): 599. *L'Osservatore Romano,* English edition, no. 29 (1995): 5.

[K. I. RABENSTEIN]

RECAPITULATION IN CHRIST

In profane usage recapitulation (Greek, ἀνακεφαλαίωσις; Latin, *recirculatio*) had the meaning, among other things, of a summary, a restatement of the main point, a repetition. St. Paul used the term of Christ in Eph 1.10: "This his good pleasure he [the Father] purposed in him [Christ] to be dispensed in the fullness of the times: to re–establish all things in Christ, both those in the heavens and those on the earth." The cognate term head (Greek, κεφολή; Latin, *caput*) occurs in the proximate context of Eph 1.22: "And all things he made subject under his feet, and him he gave as head over all the Church, which indeed is his body, the completion [πλήρωμα] of him who fills all with all."

In Pauline theology recapitulation refers both to the headship of Christ over His body, the Church, and to the unity of all things, the whole cosmos, under Christ: the latter meaning being probably intended in reply to a Gnostic myth of a primitive first man, lord of creation (where κεφαλή was ἀρχή, power, as in Col 2.10).

St. Irenaeus. To St. Irenaeus (d. 202), more than to any other ancient author, belongs the credit for first developing in Christian theology the scriptural teaching of the recapitulation of all things in Christ. He enriched his Christology with various uses of recapitulation.

Historical Recapitulation. Historical recapitulation is the record of the interventions of the Incarnate Word for mankind. This is the salvation history outlook, where the coming of the Word is the last and supreme act of God, condensing all previous interventions. Christ gains salvation for all men (ἐν συντόμῳ). Irenaeus regarded all Biblical events from creation onward as "mysteries," and this mystery–content in human history is centered and depends for its meaning on Christ. The primordial mysteries are repeated and fulfilled in Him. The fullness of the divinely decisive times is achieved in Christ. The three covenants with Adam, Noah, and Abraham are included and surpassed by the Word made man. Mankind was in its infancy in Adam; hence Christ came as an infant to gather the whole course of human history and raise it up to the vision of God. The faith that comes through Christ is a renewal of the faith of Abraham, Old Testament champion of faith.

Redemptive Recapitulation. The mystery of redemptive recapitulation for Irenaeus is not simply the repairing of a plan that had gone wrong in the fall of man. Even before the world began, all men and indeed all creation were preordained, predestined for the Incarnation of the Logos. In taking up again the substance of the first creation, Christ recreates, renews His creation. He came unto His own. As man He is not only head of the Church but also king of material creation and keystone of the universe. In place of the "earthly man," Christ the "heavenly man" (1 Cor 15.47) has come to lead humanity back home and with mankind all the cosmos.

Primacy of Christ. The incarnate Word by His human existence reestablished His primacy over all visible beings, especially over men. He joined together again heaven and earth, invisible creation and men. The recapitulation of invisible creation (the angels) has been accomplished already, but the work of the Word, the extending of the primacy of Christ to all men, is an ongoing process of transformation. The recapitulation of man fallen in Adam is realized through renewal in grace and the final full restoration in the resurrection of the flesh (the concept of ''recirculation'' in Irenaeus). Only they achieve this goal who are one with Christ, the first–born from the dead (Col 1.18), i.e., only those who have followed Him in obedience.

Recapitulation in Irenaeus was part of a unified theological outlook that included likewise continuity (restoration) and transformation (perfection). Irenaeus is often regarded as an early example of the physical theory of redemption, which roots the mystery of redemption in the Incarnation, and his theology of recapitulation (new Adam, new head of humanity, etc.) is offered as evidence. In fact, the death of Christ in obedience is also a core part of Irenaeus's theory of recapitulation, as it is of his redemptive outlook.

Other Early Authors. Recapitulation is explained by other authors also: Hippolytus, Methodius, Athanasius, Hilary, Ambrose, and Augustine. Indeed the theme of recapitulation runs through almost all patristic attempts to explain the redemptive work of Christ; all men were present in the first Adam, all are present too, or can be, in the second Adam. Hippolytus teaches that the Word was born from the Virgin in order to restore and recapitulate in Himself the original Adam. Methodius takes up Irenaeus's recapitulation in attenuated form, to the neglect of the atoning death. Hilary combines the language of recapitulation with a strong stress on the voluntary sacrifice of Christ. St. Ambrose joins recapitulation to substitution: because He shares human nature, Christ can substitute for sinful men, undergo punishment in their place. Greek authors of the 5th century bring out realist theories of redemption in a recapitulation setting, e.g., Theodore of Mopsuestia.

Later Theology. In postpatristic thought the East remained aware of the relationship of the Logos to the cosmos. In the West the accent shifted from the work of Christ to His Person. A Christocentric recapitulation was not a significant concept in scholastic theology, in spite of such exceptions as St. Bernard, Richard of Saint–Victor, Eckhart, and Nicholas of Cusa. The deep piety toward Christ of post–Reformation saints and thinkers (Ignatius of Loyola, Teresa of Avila, John of the Cross, Pascal) had little effect on contemporary theology. Reformed theology did not concern itself with the recapitulation of all things in Christ as God's plan. In K. Barth, Protestant theology of the 20th century has been given a Christocentric emphasis. In recent Catholic thought, through investigation of the Scriptures and the Fathers, there has been an intense revival of interest in recapitulation.

The writings of Teilhard de Chardin are another factor in the reawakened interest in the recapitulation of the cosmos in Christ. It was the peculiar genius of de Chardin, ''pilgrim of the future on my way back from a journey made entirely in the past'' (as he wrote from China in 1923, where he was exploring traces of primitive man), to capture again the Christocentric concept of recapitulation and to restate it in keeping with the evolutionary dimensions of the universe in contemporary thought.

Bibliography: R. HAUBST, *Lexikon für Theologie und Kirche*[2], ed. J. HOFER and K. RAHNER, 10 v. (2d, new ed. Freiburg 1957–65); suppl., *Das Zweite Vatikanische Konzil: Dokumente und Kommentare,* ed. H. S. BRECHTER et al., pt. 1 (1966) 1:466–467. H. KÜNG, *ibid.* 2:1169–74. H. SCHLIER, ''Kephale, Anakephalaioomai,'' G. KITTEL, *theologisches Wörterbuch zum Neuen Testament* (Stuttgart 1935–) 3:681–682; *Der Brief an die Epheser* (3d ed. Düsseldorf 1962). J. I. HOCHBAN, ''St. Irenaeus on the Atonement,'' *Theological Studies* 7 (1946) 525–557. J. QUASTEN, *Patrology,* 3 v. (Westminster, Md. 1950–) v.1. L. S. THORNTON, ''St. Irenaeus and Contemporary Theoloy,'' *Studia patristica* 2 (1957) 317–347. D. UNGER, ''Christ's Role in the Universe according to St. Irenaeus,'' *Franciscan Studies* 26 (1945) 3–20, 114–137. P. TEILHARD DE CHARDIN, *The Divine Milieu* (New York 1960); *The Phenomemon of Man,* tr. B. WALL (New York 1959). C. F. MOONEY, ''The Body of Christ in the Writings of Teilhard de Chardin,'' *Theological Studies* 25 (1964) 576–610; ''Teilhard de Chardin and the Christological Problem,'' *Harvard Theological Review* 58 (1965) 91–126.

[E. R. CARROLL]

RÈCHE, JULES-NICOLAS, BL.

Known in religion as Brother Arnould (Arnold), religious of the Brothers of Christian Schools; b. Sept. 2, 1838, Landroff, Lorraine, France; d. Oct. 23, 1890, Rheims, France. Nicolas was the eldest of the eight surviving children of a cobbler, Claude Rèche, and his wife, Anne Clausset. He attended the village school for a few years until he was able to work in his father's shop and run errands to help support his family. When he was old enough to leave home, he worked as a coachman for a wealthy family in Raville–Fouligny, then as a teamster for the construction of Notre Dame Church at Charleville, where he became acquainted with the Brothers of the Christian Schools while attending evening classes. He entered the novitiate on Dec. 23, 1862, receiving the name Brother Arnould, and was solemnly professed in 1871. He taught at the boarding school in Rheims for 14 years, while continuing his own studies in theology, mathematics, science, and agriculture. Brother Arnould was awarded the Bronze Cross for the care he gave the sick and wounded of both sides during the Franco–Prussian War (1870). He was appointed novice master (1877) at Thillois, France, because of his exemplary conduct. He continued in this role when the novitiate was moved (1885) to Courlancy near Rheims. Arnould died soon after his appointment as director general of the formation center. His grave in the cemetery at Rheims became a pilgrimage site. Pope John Paul II beatified Brother Arnould on Nov. 1, 1987.

Feast: Oct. 23 (LaSallian Brothers).

Bibliography: C. LAPIERRE, *Si le grain de blé: frère Arnould* (Paris 1986). *L'Osservatore Romano,* English edition, no. 47 (1987): 7–8.

[K. I. RABENSTEIN]

RECLUSE

Recluse, or an anchorite, or hermit, designates a religious–minded person who embraces the eremitical life in one of its most extreme forms, to retire as far as possible from human society. The earliest–known Christian recluses were the Fathers of the Egyptian desert who inhabited natural cells or abandoned tombs, or sometimes even open deserted areas, to achieve seclusion. Recluses of the Middle Ages often had themselves walled in cells; these were sometimes attached to churches and shrines. Their motive was to do penance and make reparation for sin but, above all, to achieve the greatest possible union with God through uninterrupted prayer.

Inclusion was perpetual, as in the case of St. Paul of THEBAÏD, or for certain long periods of time, as in the case of St. ANTHONY OF EGYPT. Since the life involved severe penances and grave spiritual difficulties, the Church began to regulate this type of asceticism by legislation in the seventh century and required at least previous training in a monastery. Recluses were to be found throughout the Christian world in early Christian and medieval times, but rarely since then. GREGORY OF TOURS describes recluses in Merovingian Gaul; and AELRED OF RIEVAULX wrote a rule for an anchoress in 12th–century England, as did also the anonymous author of the ANCRENE RIWLE (probably of the 13th century).

Bibliography: H. ROSWEYDE, ed., *Vitae Patrum* (Antwerp 1628) 157:626. J. CASSIAN, *Conlationes,* ed. M. PETSCHENIG in *Corpus scriptorum ecclesiasticorum latinorum* (Vienna 1866–) 13; 1886. ATHANASIUS, *The Life of Saint Anthony,* ed. and tr. R. T. MEYER in *Ancient Christian Writers,* ed. J. QUASTEN et al. (Westminster, Md.–London 1946–) 10; 1950. GREGORY OF TOURS, *De gloria confessorum; Patrologia Latina,* ed. J. P. MIGNE, 217 v., indexes 4 v. (Paris 1878–90) 71:828–912. AELRED, *De Vita eremitica; Patrologia Latina,* ed. J. P. MIGNE, 217 v., indexes 4 v. (Paris 1878–90) 32:1451–74. J. MORTON, ed. and tr., *The Ancren Riwle* (London 1853); *The Nun's Rule: Being the Ancren Riwle Modernized* (London 1905). J. BESSE, *Dictionnaire de théologie catholique,* ed. A. VACANT et al., 15 v. (Paris 1903–50; Tables générales 1951–) 1.1:1134–41. C. LIALINE, *Dictionnaire de spiritualité ascéiqtque et mystique. Doctrine et histoire,* ed. M. VILLER et al. (Paris 1932–) 4:936–953.

[M. C. MCCARTHY]

RECOLLECTION

A type of attention whereby the individual excludes voluntary distractions, internal and external, to concentrate all his powers on introspection. Although there are various types of natural recollection, in the spiritual life recollection signifies a concentration of one's powers on God or something related to God. It may be a transitory concentration or a habitual practice whereby the individual directs his faculties to God in order to live in the presence of God. Recollection refers also to one of the required dispositions for prayer or to certain species of prayer.

As a spiritual practice, to live in the presence of God or recollected in God consists in recalling as often as possible that God is present in all places and especially in souls in the state of grace; the former is a presence of immensity, and the latter is the indwelling of the Trinity. Two principal methods of rising this practice are to visualize God as seeing all things at every moment and of directing all things by His providence (this is greatly aided by the use of visual symbols such as crucifixes and paintings) and, second, to live with an awareness of God's presence in the soul, either by the presence of immensity or the indwelling through sanctifying grace. This recollection turns the soul inward, not to seek self, but to seek the God who dwells in the self. Such habitual recollection is a great aid in the practice of prayer, in motivating all one's actions supernaturally, and in overcoming temptations to sin.

As a required disposition for prayer, whether vocal or mental, recollection refers to the attention given to the words of the prayer, the meaning of the words, or the one to whom prayer is addressed (St. Thomas Aquinas, *Summa theologiae* 2a2ae, 83.13). Vocal prayer requires attention to the words spoken; meditation requires attention to the meaning of the words; all prayer requires attention to God, who is the one addressed in prayer. In the higher degrees of prayer there is little attention to words and meanings, but an absorbing recollection in God. Obstacles to recollection in prayer may proceed from a variety of causes: temperament, vivid imagination, weak powers of concentration, uncontrolled passions, sensate nature, physical or mental illness, bad habits, environmental factors, or even diabolical intervention. Moreover, the human mind is not capable of maintaining unwavering concentration over a long period of time.

The prayer of recollection is a special type of prayer classified by St. Teresa of Avila as acquired recollection and called by Bossuet the prayer of simplicity. Other authors refer to it as the prayer of simple gaze, of the presence of God, or the simple vision of faith. It is also called acquired contemplation, to signify that it is the highest degree of ascetical or active prayer and the bridge to mystical or passive prayer. Unlike meditation, which is discursive and intellectual, or affective prayer, which utilizes the will predominantly, acquired recollection is a simple loving gaze upon God or some mystery related to God, and all the powers are recollected in this unified activity.

The prayer of infused recollection, known also as infused contemplation, is the first degree of truly mystical prayer, which operates under the gifts of the Holy Spirit. It is a supernatural prayer that cannot be cultivated by one's own efforts, even with the help of ordinary grace, but is due to the intervention of God, who gathers the soul and all its faculties and concentrates them on Himself. It is accompanied by a sense of God's presence, a vivid illumination of the intellect, and a suspension of the lower powers. All the ascending degrees of mystical prayer are characterized by recollection and passivity. The prayer of infused recollection especially affects the intellect; the prayer of quiet engages the will; the prayer of union captivates all the internal faculties. In the prayer of simple union the external senses are still free; in the prayer of ecstatic union the external senses are recollected in God and withdrawn from their natural objects. The awareness of God's presence becomes so intense that the soul is led at last to the prayer of the transforming union or mystical marriage, which is the immediate disposition for the beatific vision.

Bibliography: A. ROYO, *The Theology of Christian Perfection,* ed. and tr. J. AUMANN (Dubuque 1962) 505–570. TERESA OF ÁVILA, *The Way of Perfection,* ch. 28–31; *Interior Castle,* 4th Mansions, 7th Mansions. J. G. ARINTERO, *Stages in Prayer,* tr. K. POND (St. Louis 1957). A. F. POULAIN, *The Graces of Interior Prayer,* tr. L. L. YORKE SMITH, ed. J. V. BAINVEL (St. Louis 1950). G. LERCARO, *Methods of Mental Prayer,* tr. T. F. LINDSAY (Westminster, Md. 1957).

[J. AUMANN]

RECONCILIATION, MINISTRY OF

The ministry of reconciliation is a phrase that summarizes the economy of salvation. God's design is a ''coming from'' and a ''return'' to him. The ''let the world be'' of creation is at the same time the ''let God be all in all'' of the eschaton. Salvation history is the story of God committing himself more and more deeply to his creation that it might achieve perfect reconciliation with him. At the center of this plan is the Incarnation. Jesus Christ is the completely comprehensive reality that embraces all of creation. All things achieve their purpose, their right ordering, by being ordered to the Incarnate Word who has become not simply part of creation, but its center (Eph 1.9–10). The ''already'' of the reconciliation accomplished by Christ must be balanced off by the ''not yet'' of his second coming. In the time between, the ministry of reconciliation continues and the Church exists as the Sacrament and agent of this redemptive work.

Objectives. The objective of this ministry is more than the juxtaposition of created realities in peaceful coexistence. Rather it is a radical and definitive reordering that can be accomplished only in Christ, the ontological principle of unity. Creatures are reconciled with one another because they are reconciled with God. Paul is clear on this point when writing to the quarrelsome Corinthians. In seeking their reconciliation with one another and with him, he asked that they participate more deeply in the profound reconciliation achieved by Christ (2 Cor 5.16–21).

Vatican Council II speaks of reconciliation in a variety of contexts (unity among Christians, peace among nations, sacrament of reconciliation) but the primary referent is always the fundamental reconciliation achieved by Christ. While it is fully achieved only in relationship to God, this cannot excuse Christians from dealing directly with one another in seeking unity. The commandments to love God and love neighbor are in fact one (Mt 22.34–40). The ministry of reconciliation, then, involves not only an individual's relationship to God, not only bringing others to him, but also the personal relationship with others.

Exercise of Reconciliation. God has taken the decisive initiative in exercising the ministry of reconciliation, and human efforts must always be seen as a participation in this. This means not only passive openness but a positive initiative toward reconciliation. In saying that we should leave our gift at the altar and first become reconciled, the Lord is talking about reconciliation with a person who has something *against* us (Mt 5.23–24). Christians are called upon to take the initiative in reaching out as salt, light, leaven, ministers of Christ's reconciliation to the world.

Full reconciliation will be achieved only in the Kingdom, but the call is to achieve partial realizations during this time between the Lord's first and second coming. Results may be incomplete and transitory, but they serve as anticipations of the Kingdom. The incomplete and imperfect nature of reconciliation during this present journeying raises a major difficulty. Reconciliation very often seems illogical, premature, prophetic. The logical inclination would be to wait until perfect at-one-ment is achieved, when all things will fit together as they should. Christ, however, called upon his followers to engage in this ministry now, to be forgiving, to build peace and unity even in this imperfect state (contrast the attitude of the brother of the prodigal son). The first Eucharistic Prayer for Masses of Reconciliation carries the reminder that now is the time of reconciliation.

Ministry of the Community. Christian communities, as communities, exercise a ministry of reconciliation partly by being a sign and foreshadowing of the unity of the Kingdom. That is why the current disunity among Christians presents such a monumental problem. Called to be a sign of reconciliation, Christianity has made the world spectator to its own divisions for nearly the last millennium. Given the central place of the ministry of reconciliation, the unity of Christians has to count as one of the highest priorities. Ecumenical developments hold promise. Yet, while interdenominational unity appears to be increasing, intradenominational unity is becoming a serious concern. Disunity is not to be confused with healthy diversity and plurality which actually serve to enhance unity; Christian communities are experiencing fragmentation and polarization at various levels.

These problems have to be taken as seriously as Paul took them at Corinth. The Christian community exercises its ministry of reconciliation most forcefully when its unity has no apparent reason other than Christ, when people worship together celebrating bonds of oneness that go deeper than the differences that normally keep people at odds—differing political views, race, culture, prejudice.

The Ordained Ministry. The ministry of reconciliation exercised by public ministers in the Church brings with it additional considerations. The public minister is called upon to forego certain rights as an individual Christian in order to serve the wider community. The attitude of the Apostle Paul must prevail—the attempt to be all things to all people. This is not to be taken in the sense of having all the answers or holding all the resources, but precisely in the sense of serving the cause of unity. ''I became like a Jew to the Jews. . . . To those bound by the law I became like one who is bound. . . . To those not subject to the law I became like one not subject to it. . . . To the weak I became a weak person . . .'' (1 Cor 9.20–22).

In its Decree on the Ministry and Life of Priests Vatican Council II says that, in the interest of building the Christian community, priests are never to put themselves at the service of any ideology or human faction (*Presbyterorum ordinis* 6). The 1971 Synod of Bishops, in its document on the Ministerial Priesthood makes a similar point in reference to political involvement: ''But since political options are by nature contingent and never in an entirely adequate and perennial way interpret the Gospel, the priest, who is the witness of things to come, must keep a certain distance from any political office or involvement'' (Synod MinPr p. 21).

This ''certain distance'' from causes that can interfere with the ministry of reconciliation presents various problems. On the one hand, true peace requires justice and development (Paul VI PopProgr 87) and the Church cannot remain silent or removed from all issues. On the other hand the Church cannot claim competence in all secular affairs and specific solutions should not be confused with the Gospel message (*Gaudium et spes* 54, cf. Synod JustWorld pp. 42–43). In this matter one has but to recall how the Church, at the time of the Reformation, was closely allied with national and political interests, and the effects that this had.

The Church must be conscious of her distinctive role as a reconciler, i.e. ministering a gift that goes much deeper than practical solutions. It is often when the Church is least of the world that it can do most for the world. This must always be motivated not by the self-interest of the Church, but rather in the interests of placing itself more fully at the service of the world in the ministry of reconciliation.

Bibliography: J.-F. COLLANGE, ''Appel à la réconciliation,'' *Énigmes de la deuxième Epître aux Corinthiens* (Cambridge 1972) 18:226–80. Y. M.-J. CONGAR, *Sainte Église* (Paris 1964). R. COSTE, ''Le prêtre et la politique,'' *Nouvelle revue théologique* 94 (1972) 912–32. Pro Mundi Vita. *New Forms of Ministries in Christian Communities* Bulletin 50, (Brussels 1974). PAUL VI, *On Reconciliation.* Apostolic Exhortation, *Paterna cum benevolentia*, Dec. 8, 1974 (USCC Publ. Office, Washington, D.C. n.d.).

[K. UNTENER]

RECTOR POTENS, VERAX DEUS

The office hymn that was traditionally prescribed for Sext in the Roman BREVIARY. Its authorship is usually ascribed to St. AMBROSE. It resembles his acknowledged hymns in that it is strictly quantitative, in iambic dimeter, and yet has a well-marked rhythm based on accent. It is found in many of the Ambrosian MSS; it is acknowledged as genuine by Biraghi and is included by Dreves in his list of 18 authentic hymns of Ambrose. However, Walpole defends it as not unworthy of Ambrose in thought and expression, arguing that its brevity (two stanzas instead of the eight usual in the hymns of Ambrose) is evidence against its genuineness. The fact that it is not included in the lists of CAESARIUS OF ARLES and of AURELIAN OF RÉOMÉ or in the MSS of the early hymnaries also militates against Ambrose's authorship. This hymn seems to be by the same author as the *Nunc sancte nobis Spiritus* (Terce) and the *RERUM DEUS TENAX VIGOR* (None). Of these three, Raby states that if Ambrose did not compose them, they are the work of a poet of equal genius. Szövérffy, however, feels that Simonetti's *dictum* that no evidence exists for Ambrosian authorship is not sufficiently supported. *Rector potens,* sung about noon, invokes God as the mover of day in its course and the source of the changes in nature. Referring to the noonday heat, it asks God to quench the fires of strife and the heat of our passions and to grant us bodily health and peace of heart.

Bibliography: G. M. DREVES, *Aurelius, Ambrosius, "Der Vater des Kirchengesanges"* (St. Louis 1893). J. JULIAN, ed., *A Dictionary of Hymnology* (New York 1957) 953. J. MEARNS, *Early Latin Hymnaries* (Cambridge, Eng. 1913) 72. M. BRITT, ed., *The Hymns of the Breviary and Missal* (new ed. New York 1948). A. S. WALPOLE, ed., *Early Latin Hymns* (Cambridge, Eng. 1922) 21–26, 110–111. M. SIMONETTI, "Studi sull'innologia popolare cristiana dei primi secoli," *Atti d. Accad. nazionale dei Lincei: Memorie* 4 (1952) 341–484. F. J. E. RABY, *A History of Christian-Latin Poetry from the Beginnings to the Close of the Middle Ages* (Oxford 1953) 32–44. J. CONNELLY, *Hymns of the Roman Liturgy* (Westminster MD 1957) 32–33. J. SZÖVÉRFFY, *Die Annalen der lateinischen Hymnendichtung* (Berlin 1964–65) 1:51, 214.

[A. J. KINNIREY]

RECTORS

The appointment, functions and removal of rectors are determined by the law for each of the several types of rector.

Rectors of Churches. Rectors of churches are priests who have charge of churches that are neither parochial nor capitular nor annexed to the house of a religious community or society of apostolic life (*Codex iuris canonici* c., 556; *Codex Canonum Ecclesiarium Orientatium* c., 304). In the case where one has the right according to law to present or elect the rector, the diocesan bishop's approval must be secured. This approval is necessary even if the church belongs to an exempt religious institute. If the Church is connected with a seminary or college under the care of clerics, the superior of the seminary or college is the rector of the church, unless the diocesan bishop makes other provisions (CIC c., 557 §3; CCEO c., 305 §3).

Functions reserved to pastors (CIC c., 530; CCEO c., 290 §2) may not be performed by the rector of a church (CIC c., 558; CCEO c., 306 §1). However, he may celebrate divine services solemnly in his church in accordance with the terms of the legal foundations and without prejudice to parochial rights (CIC c., 559; CCEO c., 306 §2). He possesses the right to give permission to say Mass there, to administer the Sacraments and to perform other sacred functions according to law. The rector is responsible, under the authority of the local ordinary, for the administration of the property of the church, as well as for its maintenance (CIC c., 562; CCEO c., 309). In certain circumstances, the local ordinary may regulate the hours of divine services in the church and he may also require the rector to celebrate certain functions in his church and to make the church available for use by certain persons or groups (CIC c., 560; CCEO c., 307).

The rector may be removed for a just cause. If the rector is a religious, the provision of CIC c., 682 §2 or CCEO c., 1391 §2 is to be applied (CIC c., 563; CCEO c., 310).

Rectors of Seminaries. The rector of a seminary is the immediate representative of the diocesan bishop in the internal government and supervision of the diocesan seminary. The rector is appointed by the diocesan bishop and he may be removed by him.

By virtue of the exemption of the seminary from parochial jurisdiction (CIC c., 262; CCEO c., 336 §2), the rector possesses all the rights of a pastor over those who dwell therein, with the exception of certain restrictions concerning Matrimony and Penance. Only a local ordinary, the pastor of the local parish or his delegate can validly assist at marriages there, and the rector may hear the confessions of his students only when they seek him out for that purpose and freely request it in particular cases (CIC c., 985; CCEO c., 734 §3). He can dispense from the laws of fast and abstinence and from feasts of obligation (CIC c., 1245). The rector also enjoys the right to attend the diocesan synods (CIC c., 463 §1, 6°; CCEO c., 238 §1, 4°).

Rectors of Universities. To qualify as a Catholic university, the institution must be approved by competent ecclesiastical authority (CIC c., 808; CCEO c., 642 §1). Ecclesiastical universities are established through erection by the Holy See or with its approval (CIC c., 816 §1; CCEO c., 649). In the Latin Church, rectors of Catholic and ecclesiastical universities are called to particular councils and have a consultative vote in them (CIC c., 443 §3, 3°).

Bibliography: J. ABBO and J. HANNAN, *The Sacred Canons,* 2 v. (2d ed. St. Louis 1960) 1:358, 479–486; 2:891, 1368. J. B. COX, *The Administration of Seminaries* (*Catholic University of America Canon Law Studies,* 67; Washington 1931). J. J. MARKHAM, *The Sacred Congregation of Seminaries and Universities of Studies* (*Cath-*

olic University of America Canon Law Studies, 384; Washington 1957). *Codex iuris canonici* (Rome 1918; repr. Graz 1955).

[R. J. MURPHY]

RECUSANT

A term coming to mean, in the course of Elizabeth I's reign, a person who refused (Lat. *recusare*) to attend the services of the Established Church, as commanded by the 1559 Uniformity Act, reinforced by later statutes. The penalty for absence, originally twelvepence for each offense, was increased in 1581 to 20 pounds per lunar month, while later acts empowered the monarch to seize a recusant's goods and two-thirds of his lands in lieu of the fine. Recusants might be prosecuted in both civil and ecclesiastical courts and, if convicted, became liable not only to financial penalties but to expulsion from London, restriction to their own dwelling-places, and excommunication (possibly involving loss of civil rights and refusal of burial). Names of convicted recusants, fined by the county sheriffs, occur first in the Pipe Rolls and then, from 1592 to 1691, in a separate series of Recusant Rolls. Acts of 1593 (35 Eliz. I, cap. 1, 2) distinguish popish from Protestant recusants, but the Rolls rarely indicate religious allegiance and include numerous Protestants, especially in Charles II's reign. The Rolls record fines and forfeitures owed by convicted recusants, not sums paid. Of those convicted, only a very small minority were fully penalized, and many recusants escaped conviction altogether (e.g., because in the initial reports their periods of absence from church were altered to less than four weeks). In 1689 (1 Wm. and Mary, sess. 1, cap.8, 15) those refusing the oaths of allegiance and supremacy and the Test declaration of 1678 (for wording, *see* ROYAL DECLARATION) were deemed guilty of ''constructive recusancy'' and from 1693 onward such persons might be punished by a double land tax, which in practice was exacted only spasmodically, while (by 12 Anne, st. 2, cap. 14) the concept of constructive recusancy was widened to embrace ''every Papist or Person making Profession of the Popish Religion.'' The offense of recusancy was abolished by the Catholic Relief Act of 1791.

Bibliography: M. D. R. LEYS, *Catholics in England, 1559–1829: A Social History* (London 1961). E. I. WATKIN, *Roman Catholicism in England . . .* (New York 1957). A. O. MEYER, *England and the Catholic Church under Queen Elizabeth,* tr. J. R. MCKEE (London 1916). W. R. TRIMBLE, *The Catholic Laity in Elizabethan England, 1558–1603* (Cambridge, Mass. 1964). M. J. HAVRAN, *The Catholics in Caroline England* (Stanford, Calif. 1962). The increasing study of recusancy at the local level is exemplified in H. AVELING, *Post-Reformation Catholicism in East Yorkshire* (York 1960), and J. A. WILLIAMS, *Bath and Rome: the Living Link* (Bath 1963). H. BOWLER, ''Introd.,'' in *Publications of the Catholic Record Society*, v.57 (1965). J. A. WILLIAMS, ''Recusant Rolls,'' *History* (1965), in ser. ''Short Guides to Records.'' See also *Recusant History* (1951—), a journal devoted exclusively to English Recusant history.

[J. A. WILLIAMS]

RECUSANT LITERATURE

Though technically the term ''recusant'' applied to all who, contrary to the Act of Uniformity of 1559, refused to attend Anglican services (*see* RECUSANTS), recusant literature is a convenient term covering religious works by English Catholics in penal times. This literature stems from the late medieval and early Tudor religious writers, but increasingly reflects contemporary trends, particularly in Italian and Spanish devotional works, thus acting as a medium for their transmission to the main body of English literature. The highest point in quality and quantity of recusant literature was the late Elizabethan period, when such writings shared in the general richness and variety characteristic of the age and responded with a frequency and force to match the intensity of persecution and controversy. Then came a gradual decline common to all religious writing, the nadir being reached in the 18th century; and it did not receive a fresh impetus until after the Emancipation Act of 1829, the indirect effect of the OXFORD MOVEMENT, and the general Catholic revival. This falling off was mainly the result of Catholics' becoming an underprivileged minority with a weakening cultural tradition and few educational opportunities; and while those who were exiles could obtain a thorough academic training, they tended to lose touch with English thought and idiom. Thus, some of the best writers were converts (permanent or otherwise), such as William Alabaster (1567–1640), Richard Crashaw, and John Dryden, and it was on converts that the literary movement of the ''second spring'' was mainly dependent.

Publishing Difficulties. In assessing the achievements of recusant writers, it should be remembered that until well into the 17th century a large number of their works were composed in Latin, or if expressly aimed at Continental readers, in one of the European languages. Further, the imperfections sometimes found in their compositions may be attributable not to lack of ability but to necessary haste or the adverse conditions under which most recusant books were printed. Analysis is further complicated because many works are anonymous (mainly for reasons of security) or of composite authorship.

Despite the difficulties in publishing recusant works in the early period owing to lack of funds and the rigorous legislation of the English government, more than 250 books in English alone were printed during the reign of

Elizabeth I, some on secret presses at home, but most of them abroad, especially in France and the Low Countries, generally by foreign printers, though sometimes under English supervision. They were then dispatched to the main centers of English Catholic life on the Continent and smuggled into England. Distribution was fairly successful, important polemic and devotional works being eagerly sought after by Protestants as well.

The leading English Catholics, especially Cardinal William ALLEN, Thomas STAPLETON, and Gregory MARTIN, were acutely aware of the value of the written word as a weapon of Catholic action and were themselves among the chief and most successful writers. The Jesuits, however, explored the different fields with the greatest concentration and effect, the foremost being Robert PERSONS, Robert SOUTHWELL, Henry GARNET, and Edmund CAMPION.

Prose Writings. Recusant prose grew and withered with its counterparts in other fields of English. Basically, it derived many of its characteristics from Thomas MORE: its fullness of vocabulary, its relatively plain style, some of its graphic description, its cogency and occasional sleight of hand in argument; but it lacked More's deep sense of humor, and at best rose only to a blatant irony in polemic. For all its virtues, it cannot be claimed as the only true mainstream of English prose between More and Dryden (J. S. Philimore's theory, *Dublin Review*, 1913, which held currency until very recently), nor can More be accorded the sole paternity of modern English [as R. W. Chambers implied in *The Place of St. Thomas More in English Literature and History* (London 1937) and in *On the Continuity of English Prose* (London 1932)].

Early Apologetic Prose. The early phase of recusant prose, mainly apologetic in scope, is characterized by the Louvain group of theologians, chief among them being Thomas Harding, John RASTELL, Thomas Stapleton, and Nicholas SANDER, all of whom participated in the ''Great Controversy,'' a 64-book saga occasioned by Bishop John JEWEL's ''Challenge Sermon'' of 1559. They all show great intellectual power and scholarship in a style that is formal, lucid, and relatively simple, with a tendency to balanced sentences and syllogisms, especially in the work of Harding, the most distinguished of the group, whom the poet Gabriel Harvey praised as a ''thunder and lightning orator in divinity.'' By the 1580s prose style became infinitely more varied, animated, and vigorous, losing much of its academic rigor in its calculated appeal to the general reader. In the best writers, especially Persons and Southwell, there was a successful blend of native and classical elements in language, syntax, and allusion, but subject matter was never buried by excessive euphuism. The new vigorousness of style resulted partly from a more conversational if not colloquial diction, but it was reinforced also by a vehemence of fury in the face of political and religious oppression. At best, as in Southwell's *Humble Supplication* (1595), this style has an overpowering cogency, but it can degenerate into a torrent of invective in which no adjective is too base for inclusion, as sometimes happened in the controversies between the secular clergy and the Jesuits, especially in the pamphlets of Antony Copley (*see* ARCHPRIEST CONTROVERSY; BLACKWELL, GEORGE).

Marked contrasts in this period are to be found not only between, for example, the almost frigidly formal style of Garnet and the vigorous, though rhythmically harsh writing of Campion, but also within a single writer, who might follow a quietly eloquent preface to the ''Catholic reader'' with an intemperate tirade against the object of his particular aversion. Perhaps the most marked contrasts are to be found in the works of Cardinal Allen, if one compares the graceful and controlled *True, Sincere and Modest Defence* (1584) with the violent *Admonition to the Nobility and People of England* (1588). Persons towers above the rest as the most prolific and versatile writer, equally at home in polemic and devotional writing, and, though he lacks geniality, he has many other gifts: clarity, flexibility, conversational ease, and a timelessness justly praised by Swift [*Tatler,* No. 230 (1710)].

The Rheims New Testament and Devotional Writing. The great achievement of the early period was the Rheims translation of the New Testament (1582) effected mainly by Gregory Martin, and followed by the complete Bible in 1609. Despite its numerous unnatural Latinisms, which resulted from following the Vulgate too literally, it has a fine feeling for phrases and cadences, and was used as a source for nearly 3,000 readings in the Authorized Version (1611).

Whereas until the New Testament was published writers were fully engaged in burning controversies on the origins of the Church in England, the political position of Catholics, the persecution of missionary priests and similar issues, devotional works now made their appearance and soon dominated and renewed the life of recusant prose, while controversial works began to lose their directness and relevance and became clumsy and desiccated in style; there were a few notable exceptions, such as the graceful and penetrating works of Edmund Lechmere (d. *c.* 1640). The two main types of devotional literature were: first, translations of new and traditional prayers and meditations, including the popular *Manual* compiled by George Flinton (1583), the *Jesus Psalter* (1575), and the *Primer* or *Office of the Blessed Virgin* published by Richard VERSTEGAN in 1599 and often reprinted until the 18th century; and second, treatises on how to live a good Christian life, among them numerous translations of the *IMITATION OF CHRIST*, and the writings of Spanish mystics, such as LOUIS OF GRANADA, Diego de Estella, and Gaspar Loarte. Such works were to have a marked influence on English literature, especially because the Protestants, having little similar literature, were heavily dependent on them. The most influential of the English devotional treatises was Persons's *Christian Directory* (originally published as *The First Booke of Christian Exercise,* 1582). Based on the Ignatian prayer of self-surrender, it derived much of its material from Loarte and Louis of Granada, but is less baroque and shows affinities with the medieval tradition of ROLLE and HILTON. Skillfully integrated, with a perfect balance of intellectual and emotional appeal, the work proved so popular that it was pirated by the Protestant divine, Edmund Bunny, while writers as diverse as Robert Greene and Richard Baxter bore testimony to its influence.

Southwell also exerted influence, for through his baroque *Marie Magdalen's Funeral Teares* (which ran to at least 20 editions) and his penitential poems, he introduced from the Continent the post-Tridentine literature of tears and linked the English elegiac temperament to a religious theme. Thomas Nashe and Thomas Lodge are among those who immediately reflect his influence. Other leading devotional writers are the versatile Sir Tobie Matthew (1577–1655), author of two fine original works and nine masterly translations, including that of the *Confessions* of Saint Augustine, and the two mystics, Benet Canfield, who, in the tradition of Hilton, used a very fundamental and abstract approach, and his disciple, David Augustine BAKER, whose voluminous works combine boundless aspiration for union with God with a sober, practical sense.

Effective prose writers from the late 17th century onward are scarce, the most distinguished being Richard CHALLONER. His devotional works (e.g., *Garden of the Soul*), with their deep, unostentatious spirituality, long set the pattern for English devotional reading; his other achievements include a competent revision of the Douay-Rheims Bible and the remarkably acute and accurate *Memoirs of English Missionary Priests* (1741–42). Able controversialists include John Gother, highly praised by Dryden and Butler; Robert Manning, a learned, fair-minded, and fluent writer; and Joseph and Simon Berington, the former having a particularly vigorous and sustained style. There were also two notable historians: the lively but prejudiced Charles Dodd and the scrupulously fair and objective John LINGARD.

Poetry. Much recusant poetry is mediocre and anonymous, scattered in commonplace books. It is devotional in character, and when it deals in apologetics, it normally fails (as in Miles Hoggard's works); the notable exception is Dryden's controlled and artistic *Hind and the Panther* (1687). The chief theme of the early period was the traditional *de contemptu mundi,* though usually with a greater emphasis on the joys of heaven than in the medieval period (''Jerusalem, my happy home'' being a classic example). Combined with this was the theme of penitence, generally based on the subject of Mary Magdalen or Saint Peter as a starting point for meditations (as in Southwell and Richard Verstegan). While Marian devotion is strongly represented (e.g., in Henry WALPOLE, John Brerely, and Crashaw), Christ dominates, especially in the early 17th century, when particular emphasis was placed upon His Passion—a highly relevant theme in time of fierce persecution. There were also a large number of poems on individual saints, normally grouped in a collection of sonnets (e.g., in William Alabaster, Henry Constable, and Tobie Matthew).

Recusant verse began in a plain native tradition, with a simple, forceful diction but also a rhythmical clumsiness that makes the lyrics seem heavy compared with those of the 15th century. It is at its best in the poems of Thomas More and Thomas Vaux, and in the ballads on stirring subjects such as the PILGRIMAGE OF GRACE and, later, the martyrdom of Campion. The clumsiness, the jog-trot iambic regularity, and the excessive alliteration did not materially, alter until Southwell, Constable, and Alabaster instilled a more classical smoothness, and introduced Petrarchan and baroque elements, especially the conceits. Despite a seeming artificiality, Southwell used language in a highly emotive way particularly fitted to his method of meditation. Typical of his style is *The Burning Babe,* a poem much admired by Ben Jonson, but the most influential of his meditative poems is the frequently imitated *St. Peter's Complaint* (1595). Though they employed secular elements, Southwell and his contemporaries strongly believed that poetry should be used only for religious subjects, a feeling echoed by Alabaster and Constable, who signified their change of heart in spiritual sonnets, Alabaster's being founded on scriptural tradition, Constable's based on Tansillo, Tasso, and Jacque de Billy.

Southwell's influence pervaded much of 17th-century religious verse, particularly that of Crashaw, who was, however, even more exuberant in his use of language. Though a poet in his own right, Crashaw was highly derivative; for example, he borrowed from FRANCIS DE SALES, especially from the *Treatise on the Love of God,* echoing it not only in general spirit but also in the use of metaphor and in the technique of associating the spiritual with everyday life. Apart from the emblematic work of Henry Hawkins, *Parthenia Sacra*, there was little else of distinction in the 17th century, and the 18th century was in general as barren of good religious verse as of love poetry. The main literary form became the hymn (among the best settings being the translations of Dryden), and it was not until Gerard Manley HOPKINS that a truly great Catholic religious poet again emerged.

Drama and Novel. Recusant literature has practically no drama, for even in the 17th century, when there was a distinguished group of Catholic dramatists, only a handful of plays reflected pronounced Catholic sympathies: Philip Massinger's *Virgin Martyr* (1622) and *The Renagado,* which has a Jesuit as a leading character and deals with Penance and baptismal regeneration; and James Shirley's *Grateful Servant,* which glorifies the Benedictine Order, and his *St. Patrick for Ireland.* The novel made a tentative Catholic start with Eliza Inchbald's *A Simple Story* (1791) and Henry Digby Beste's *Four Years in France* (1826), but it is largely out of the Oxford Movement controversies that the Catholic novel and the new Catholic literature in general developed. This development was stimulated mainly by the work of John Henry NEWMAN.

Bibliography: A. F. ALLISON and D. M. ROGERS, *A Catalogue of Catholic Books in English . . . 1558–1640,* 2 v. (London 1956). J. B. COLLINS, *Christian Mysticism in the Elizabethan Age* (Baltimore 1940). J. GILLOW, *A Literary and Biographical History or Bibliographical Dictionary of the English Catholics from 1534 to the Present Time*, 5 v. (London-New York 1885–1902; repr. New York 1961). L. I. GUINEY and G. BLISS, eds., *Recusant Poets* (New York 1939). M. HAGEDORN, *Reformation und spanische Andachtsliteratur* (Leipzig 1934). E. HUTTON, *Catholicism and English Literature* (London 1942). P. JANELLE, *Robert Southwell, the Writer* (New York 1935). L. L. MARTZ, *The Poetry of Meditation* (New Haven 1954; repr. pa. 1962). H. E. ROLLINS, ed., *Old English Ballads: 1553–1625* (Cambridge, Eng. 1920). O. SHIPLEY, ed., *Carmina Mariana,* 1st series (London 1893), 2d series (London 1902). A. C. SOUTHERN, *Elizabethan Recusant Prose, 1559–1582* (London 1950). A. WARREN, *Richard Crashaw* (repr. pa. Ann Arbor 1957). P. CARAMAN, ed., *The Other Face* (New York 1960).

[A. G. PETTI]

RED MASS

The solemn votive Mass in honor of the Holy Spirit, celebrated annually at the opening of the judicial year. Judges and lawyers attend in a body, joined by public officials and law faculty members. Although this Mass is used at the opening of legislative assemblies and school terms, indications suggest it was first associated with the law profession, and the appellation Red Mass customarily refers to the Mass initiating the legal year.

This venerable custom originated in Europe in the 13th century. From the time of Edward I the Mass was offered at Westminster Abbey at the opening of Michaelmas term. It received its name from the fact that the celebrant was vested in red and the Lord High Justices were robed in a brilliant scarlet. They were joined by the university professors, the doctors among them displaying red in their academic gowns.

Celebrating Red Mass in Westminster Cathedral. (©Bettmann/ CORBIS)

In France the inauguration of the judicial year was celebrated annually at the famous Sainte–Chapelle. Although the chapel was desecrated during the French Revolution, it was restored by Louis Philippe and dedicated exclusively to the use of the *Messe Rouge.* In 1906 the *Parlement* secularized the Chapelle and the celebration of Red Mass was transferred to Saint-Germain-l'Auxerrois.

The Red Mass has also been traditionally identified with the opening of the Sacred Roman Rota, the supreme judicial body of the Catholic Church.

The inauguration of the Red Mass in the United States occurred in New York City on Oct. 6, 1928. This Mass was celebrated at old St. Andrew's Church on Duane Street with Cardinal Patrick Hayes presiding. Other localities followed, e.g., Boston, Chicago, New Orleans, San Francisco, and Washington, DC. In the U.S. not only Catholic but also Protestant and Jewish members of the judiciary and the legal profession attend the Mass.

The Red Mass is offered to invoke divine guidance and strength during the coming term of court. It is celebrated in honor of the Holy Spirit as the source of wisdom, understanding, counsel, and fortitude, gifts which must shine forth preeminently in the dispensing of justice

Red Sea and Coral Island in Egypt, photograph by Klaus D. Francke. (©Klaus D. Francke/Peter Arnold, Inc.)

in the courtroom as well as in the individual lawyer's office.

Bibliography: E. R. TIEDEBOHL, ''The Red Mass: A Legal and Judicial Tradition,'' *University of Detroit Law Journal* 18 (1954) 59–62; ''The Votive Mass of the Holy Spirit,'' *Catholic Lawyer* 1 (1955) 215–216, 253; ''Background of the Red Mass,'' *Ave Maria* NS 72 (Oct. 21, 1950) 519–523. H. C. WATTS, ''The Red Mass for Judges and Lawyers,'' *America* 67 (Oct. 3, 1942) 712–713.

[L. J. HIEGEL/EDS.]

RED SEA

In Greek and Roman times, the Red Sea was located at the northwestern reaches of the Indian Ocean including the Persian and Arabian gulfs. The origin of the term (Heb. *yam sûp,* ''Sea of Rushes''; in the Septuagint, ἡ ἐρυθρὰ θάλασσα, ''the Red Sea'') is obscure. A plausible suggestion maintains that it was derived from the reddish corals that line the sea's bottom and are visible from its shores.

In the Old Testament the term Sea of Rushes refers to either of the two narrow arms of the Arabian Gulf that embrace the eastern and western shores of the Sinai peninsula, whose modern names are the Gulfs of Aqaba and Suez. In 1 Kgs 9.26 it denotes the Gulf of Aqaba, whence Solomon's ships embarked; probably it has this denotation also in Jgs 11.16. In Ex 10.19, where the locusts are carried into this sea by the west wind, it seems to mean some swampy part of the Suez isthmus, a meaning also likely in Ex 13.18; 15.4, 22. The earliest tradition probably referred to a lake or bay full of reeds, but the later Greek translators understood the Sea of Rushes to be a branch of the Red Sea that was familiar to them.

Exodus does not refer to the Gulf of Suez itself, whose water was as deep then as it is now. What the Israelites crossed was very likely a shallow body of water, a marshy, southern bay of Lake Menzaleh or the northern tip of Lake Timsah. The earliest account of the crossing of the sea, found in the YAHWIST tradition, says that Yahweh caused the sea to recede by a strong east wind—the extremely hot desert wind, the sirocco—which blew all night and dried up the marsh. The chariot wheels of the Egyptians became clogged in the mud, and pursuit of the Israelites, who were afoot, became impossible. By morning, when the wind abated, the waters flowed back to their normal depth. Seeing this marvel, the Egyptians fled, finally convinced that Yahweh was fighting for Israel (Ex 14.21b, 24–25, 27b).

Today the term Red Sea usually signifies the main part of the gulf of the Indian Ocean that separates Africa from Arabia, extending from the Straits of Aden to the Sinai Peninsula and now joined to the Mediterranean by the Suez Canal.

Bibliography: *Encyclopedic Dictionary of the Bible,* tr. and adap. by L. HARTMAN (New York 1963) from A. VAN DEN BORN, *Bijbels Woordenboek,* 2004–05. A. LUCAS, *The Route of the Exodus of the Israelites from Egypt* (New York 1938).

[M. J. HUNT]

REDEMPTION (IN THE BIBLE)

The English word ''redemption'' comes from the Latin *redemptio* (derived from the verb *redemere*, to buy back) and signifies literally the process of buying back, liberating by payment of a price or ransom. This article is concerned mainly with the Redemption of humankind wrought by God in Jesus Christ, as set forth in the NT; however, because the ''buying back'' or ''ransoming'' involved in the literal meaning of the word can be only an image, it is necessary to investigate the whole background of the concept in the OT in order to arrive at an understanding of the reality that lies behind the image.

The process of redeeming or ransoming was, in the first place, a human act that came to be applied, later, to the dealings of God with humans. This article, therefore, investigates first the biblical concept of redemption as a human act, then redemption attributed to God in the OT, and finally the redemptive work of God in Jesus Christ in the NT. In the first and second sections, the emphasis rests on the development of Hebrew thought that lies behind the NT terms and ideas, for that is where they took their origin; but attention is given also to the Greek words by which Hebrew terms were translated in the Septuagint (LXX), because the usage in the LXX determined to some extent the content of the terms as they were understood by the NT writers.

Human Redemption

The OT concepts of ransom and redemption rest partly on legal, social, and religious customs that are not found in modern cultures. Therefore, only by an investigation of these customs is it possible to arrive at an understanding of what redemption means when transferred to other spheres. With a human as the acting subject, there is reference to redemption or ransom of people from death and slavery, of animals from death, and of property from the possession of another. The Hebrew roots most frequently used are *pdh, g'l,* and *kpr*. Because of their significance for this study and because they have different shades of meaning, each of these roots is discussed separately.

The root pdh. The verb *pādâ* is a legal term in which the accent lies upon an actual substitution for the person or animal delivered; the substitution may be either money or another animal. The object to be redeemed is always a living being, and in almost all cases it would be put to death (at least in theory) if it were not redeemed; the only exceptions to this would seem to be in Jb 6.23; Lv 19.20; and Ex 21.8. An important use of this verb is in the legislation concerning the first-born.

Every first-born male, whether of man or of beast, belonged to Yahweh. In theory, all were to be given to Yahweh by sacrifice; this did, in fact, happen in the case of ritually clean animals, but human first-born and the first-born of ritually unclean animals were to be redeemed (Ex 13.13; 34.20; Nm 18.15–16). In redeeming a first-born son, originally an animal was substituted; later a fixed sum of money was to be paid (Nm 18.16). The firstborn of unclean animals, since they were not acceptable for sacrifice, were either redeemed by the substitution of a sacrificial animal or simply slain (Ex 13.13; 34.20; Nm 18.15).

A person or animal could also become liable to death by sacrifice through being vowed to the Lord. The Mosaic Law did not permit the redemption of persons or clean animals so dedicated, but unclean animals could be redeemed by paying one-fifth more than their value (Lv 27.26–29). A somewhat similar case is described in 1 Sm 14.24–45: Saul laid a curse upon anyone who should eat on the day of a particular battle; and when he learned that his son Jonathan (ignorant of the curse Saul had pronounced) had, in fact, eaten, he bound himself by an oath to put him to death. The people, however, intervened and ''ransomed'' [*pādâ*] Jonathan, possibly by substituting an animal (or, less probably, another person) in his place.

Also of interest is a Ps text that says that no person can redeem himself. The context indicates that it would be a question of saving one's life by paying a ransom to God—something not even the richest would be able to do [Ps 48(49).7–10].

Of the derivatives of *pādâ* the ones of special interest are *p^e^dûyīm, pidyôm,* and *pidyōn,* substantives that signify money paid in ransom; here, too, the one ransomed is regularly delivered, in theory at least, from death. In Nm 18.16 *p^e^dûyīm* designates the money paid to redeem a first-born. It is used in the same sense in Nm 3.46–51, where it is said that Yahweh will take for His service the whole tribe of Levi instead of demanding the Israelite first-born; since, however, the number of the first-born exceeds the number of Levites, a price must be paid to ransom the additional ones. The term *pidyōn* is used in Ex 21.30, where legislation is given concerning the punishment meted out to the negligent owner of an ox that habitually gores people; normally such an owner would be put to death; ''If, however, a fine [*kōper*] is imposed upon him, he must pay in ransom [*pidyōn*] for his life whatever amount is imposed on him.'' In Ps 48(49).9 the term is used of the price necessary (too high for anyone to pay) to redeem one's life.

The verb *pādâ* and the substantives discussed, when they refer to human activity, are usually translated in the LXX by λυτρόω or λύτρον. The substantive λύτρον is derived from the verb λύω, to loose, and designates that which must be paid in order to deliver a prisoner, i.e., ransom; it is normally used in the plural. From λύτρον is derived, in turn, the verb λυτρόω, to hold for ransom, to release upon payment of ransom. In both the LXX and the NT, it is regularly employed in the middle voice; in this voice, the basic meaning is to obtain release by the payment of ransom, though it will be seen that other meanings are derived from the basic one. The substantive λύτρωσις is also found, sometimes designating the act of ransoming, sometimes the price paid.

The root g'l. The verb *gā'al* is a term of family law and suggests the vindication for oneself of some person, property, or right to which one has a previous claim through kinship or prior possession. An important instance of such ''redemption'' is found in the legislation of Lv 25.47–49: an Israelite who has had to sell himself into slavery because of poverty may be redeemed by a brother, uncle, or clansman; he may also redeem himself. The family aspect is seen also in the case of property that must be sold because the owner has become impoverished; the man's closest relative has the right (and apparently the obligation) of buying it either from him or from the one to whom he had sold it (Lv 25.24–25; Jer 32.6–9). The object of this law was to keep property within the family. The verb is used also for the buying back of property or goods that have become the possession of God, such as tithes (Lv 27.31), unclean animals (27.13), houses (27.15), and fields (27.19) that have been vowed to God. Although this last usage is similar to that of *pādâ* (and the two verbs are used in a like sense in Lv 27.27), it is clear that the idea of substitution and ransom is absent from *gā'al.*

Worthy of special note is *gō'ēl,* the participle of *gā'al.* It is often translated ''redeemer,'' though more exactly speaking the term indicates the person upon whom devolved all the duties, which were very diverse, of the next of kin. These duties would be all of those suggested by the verb *gā'al*: the redemption of relatives from slavery, of property from foreign possession, etc., as discussed above, as well as the marrying of the childless widow of a near relative in order to fulfill the obligations of the law of LEVITATE MARRIAGES, and the exacting of BLOOD VENGEANCE on the murderer of a near relative. According to the levitate legislation (Dt 25.5–10), only the brother of the dead man had the obligation of marrying the widow and so assuring progeny to continue the name and lineage of the dead man, but the practice reflected in the Book of Ruth indicates that at least in some periods it was extended to more distant relatives. When a murder had been committed, the *gō'ēl* fulfilled his duty as next of kin by exacting vengeance on the murderer (Nm 35.16–19; Dt 19.11–13); some see in this a redemption of innocent blood by the spilling of the blood of the guilty.

The LXX usually translated *gā'al,* when used of human activity, by some form of λυτρόω, though sometimes by ἀγχιστεύω, to be next of kin. The human *gō'ēl* is almost always represented by the participle of ἀγχιστεύω.

The root kpr. The basic meaning of the verb *kāpar* is to cover; in the intensive conjugation (*piel*) it can mean to cover over sin, atone, make expiation (*see* EXPIATION (IN THE BIBLE)). Of special interest for this study, however, is the substantive *kōper*, ransom (it may also mean bribe). In a number of texts, it is translated by λύτρον (sometimes in the plural) in the LXX, and in each of these cases it signifies a price paid for a life that has become forfeit. In a text already discussed, *kōper* signifies that which the negligent owner of an ox that has killed someone must pay as ransom for his own life (Ex 21.30); in Ex 30.11–16 the money each one pays is considered a ''forfeit for his life'' to guard against the dangers believed to be involved in taking a CENSUS (see 2 Sm 24.1–17). On the other hand, no such price may be accepted to save a murderer from paying for his crime with his life (Nm 35.31–32), and in Prv 6.35 it is said that an enraged husband will accept no amount in place of the vengeance (viz, of death) that is to be visited upon the defiler of his wife; see also Prv 13.8. When λύτρον (λύτρα) is used to translate *kōper* in these texts, it is in a sense akin to its proper meaning of ransom; yet here the price paid is not to deliver one person from another who holds him captive, but from a death he would otherwise have to undergo.

God as Redeemer in the Old Testament

The object of God's redemptive activity is usually the people as a whole, rather than individuals. God is said to ''ransom'' His people and to be their *gō'ēl.* His work of redemption is closely connected with the messianic deliverance the Israelites expected from Him.

Deliverance from captivity. The beginning of God's redemptive work is seen in the deliverance of His people from the slavery of Egypt; this is often described as a ransoming; e.g., ''For remember that you too were once slaves in the land of Egypt, and the Lord, your God, ransomed [*pādâ*] you'' (Dt 15.15); ''I will rescue (*gā'al*) you by my outstretched arm and with mighty acts of judgment'' (Ex 6.6). Redemption or ransom, as practiced among men, involves the deliverance of someone from the power of another (or from an unfavorable fate) by the payment of a price or by a substitution. When the same terminology is used with God as the acting subject, redemption or ransom is obviously an image: God does deliver, but never by paying a price. ''The Lord's are the earth and its fullness'' [Ps 23(24).1]; He should not, would not, pay a price, for no one could ever have such power over any creature of His that His own rights would have to be purchased. Those for whom God was concerned were held captive by the power of a hostile people; God intervened to deliver them, and this was called, not unnaturally, redemption. The texts do not speak of a price being paid (for one apparent exception, see below), but rather stress that God has intervened in might and power, ''by my outstretched arm and with mighty acts of judgment'' (Ex 6.6); to bring out from slavery and to ransom from Egypt mean the same (Dt 13.6). Once the accounts of the Exodus from Egypt had established the equivalence between redemption and deliverance, the same imagery and terminology were applied to other acts of deliverance, especially to the restoration after the Exile (Is 29.22; 35.10; 43.1; 44.22; Jer 31.11; etc.). Both *pādâ*; and *gā'al* occur without appreciable difference in meaning; e.g., ''The Lord shall ransom [*pādâ*] Jacob, he shall redeem [*gā'al*] him from the hand of his conqueror'' [Jer 31.11; see also Ps 68(69).19]; they are also used in parallel with other verbs that signify deliverance and salvation: ''I will free [*hiîl*] you from the hand of the wicked, and rescue [*pādâ*] you from the grasp of the violent'' (Jer 15.21); ''He saved [*hôšîă'*] them from hostile hands and freed [*gā'al*] them from the hands of the enemy'' [Ps 105–106.10].

It is clear from these examples that the idea of payment of ransom is absent. Sometimes the idea of ransom is explicitly rejected, as in Is 52.3: ''you were sold for nothing, and without money you shall be redeemed [*gā'al*]''; the meaning is that the people, taken captive because of their sins, were set free by the power of God when their guilt had been expiated. In one text, it is said that ransom is paid for the exiles who are about to be released from Babylonia: ''I give Egypt as your ransom, Ethiopia and Saba in return for you. . . . I give men and peoples in exchange for your life'' (Is 43.3–4). But this is clearly an example of poetic imagery. Lands and peoples would, indeed, pass under the control of Cyrus in the series of conquests that would result in the freeing of the Jewish captives; these victories are given him so that he might, according to God's plan, release God's people. Yet the riches of conquest are more properly hire than ransom, for the one who received them was not the one who held captive, and he that did received nothing. Elsewhere it is said more accurately, ''He [Cyrus] Shall . . . let my exiles go free without price or ransom'' (Is 45.13).

The LXX translation reflects the fact that *pādâ* and *gā'al* have a somewhat altered sense when they refer to God's activity; although λυτρόω is still used in the majority of the cases, ῥύομαι, to deliver, and σῴζω, to save, and other verbs that have no direct connection with ransom are used as well.

God as gō'ēl. A number of OT passages designate Yahweh as *gō'ēl* (Redeemer), usually of Israel, though sometimes of pious individuals. The discussion above of this term and the root from which it is derived indicates that it conveys the idea of close family relationship and the rights and obligations that spring from it. When applied to God, the term would suggest the certainty of Israel's redemption, since it rested in the hands of one who is not only almighty but also had the obligation of the next of kin to redeem those who were otherwise helpless. This usage is found most frequently in Deutero-Isaiah (*see* ISAIAH, BOOK OF) as the great exilic Prophet consoled the exiles with the assurance of the release soon to come (Is 41.14; 43.14; 44.24; 48.17; 49.7, 26; etc.). Sometimes the term is used along with other expressions that signify God's power and nearness, such as SAVIOR (49.26), husband, and maker (54.5). Some passages stress the punishment that is to come upon the Babylonians, Israel's captors, and in these is seen the duty of blood venegeance that is incumbent upon the *gō'ēl*. The same idea is present in Jer 50.34; see also Prv 23.11.

A passage of special interest is Jb 19.25: ''But as for me, I know that my Vindicator [*gō'ēl*] lives, and that he will at last stand forth upon the dust.'' The expectation expressed here is not that Job will be delivered from sin; his trial is, in fact, that he seems to stand convicted of sin, whereas he knows himself to be innocent. God will vindicate him in showing him to be innocent of all charges, even though this should happen after Job's death; the idea of the next of kin who vindicates innocent blood is present also. Thus, in spite of Job's many complaints, he here expresses his conviction that God is near and concerned about him.

Redemption and messianism. There is a very close connection between the OT teaching on redemption and Israel's messianic hope, and the two concepts evolved hand in hand. MESSIANISM, in its broadest aspects, included the conviction that God had chosen Israel in a special way in order to bestow upon it the blessings of salvation and redemption, in which the nations also would share.

What was understood by ''salvation and redemption'' underwent considerable evolution in the course of OT revelation. The historical beginning of messianic hope for Israel as a people may be dated to the time of the Exodus, for here God demonstrated His special choice of them and that He had a plan for their welfare that would be worked out in history; the patriarchal traditions that Israel had treasured during the centuries since Abraham—the promises of numerous progeny, possession of land, etc. —took on new meaning in the light of the Exodus. It was at this time as well that He revealed Himself as a God of deliverance, a savior who redeems His people. In the beginning, then, redemption was more or less equivalent to the release of the people from Egypt. In later times, in the face of enemy threats or actual captivity, they continued to expect deliverance from their God. When the great Prophets of the 8th and 7th centuries predicted exile and captivity because of the sins of the people, they foretold also deliverance (redemption) and restoration because of the saving plan of God; during the Exile itself Prophets arose (especially Ezekiel and Deutero-Isaiah) who promised restoration. But when the Prophets thus predicted deliverance and restoration, they did not think merely of a freeing from captivity, a return to the land, and a reestablishment of political institutions; such a return to the status quo ante would have had little meaning for them. The restoration to which the Prophets looked forward embraced the final establishment of God's messianic kingdom, including a fundamental conversion from sin, the establishment of perfect justice, obedience to God, peace among all people, and abundant prosperity. Such expectation is seen in Jeremiah's promise of a new covenant (Jer 31.31–34) and Ezekiel's promise of a new heart, purification with clean water, and the gift of God's spirit (Ez 36.24–32), as well as in the utopia he pictures in ch. 40–48. Much of this passed into the content of the OT terms for redemption.

The connection between messianic redemption and the role of the personal Messiah of the line of David who was expected is not easy to define. Neither Jeremiah nor Ezekiel contains many authentic references to a personal MESSIAH, nor does a Messiah seem to play a significant part in bringing to pass the expected redemption promised in their oracles. When Jeremiah says that ''he shall reign and govern wisely, he shall do what is just and right in the land. In his days Judah shall be saved, Israel shall dwell in security'' (Jer 23.5–6), he suggests a connection between the restoration and the ideal king without actually attributing it to his activity. Even the more enthusiastic oracles of Isaiah (e.g., 9.1–6; 11.1–9), while closely associating the messianic king with the ideal days to come, do not say that he is the cause of salvation; in general, it is attributed directly to God's activity (Is 9.6). The least that can be said, however, is that the king, by virtue of his role in their society and of their conception of the function of the royal office, would be the mediator of the blessings God intended to bestow upon them and would have a direct role in the establishment and maintenance of justice. He was not, however, presented as a savior.

Redemption from sin. There is only one OT passage that speaks explicitly of redemption from sin. In Ps 129(130).8 it is said that God ''will redeem [*pādâ*] Israel from all their iniquities.'' This isolated passage, however, probably refers to deliverance from captivity or other distress (and so conforms to the meaning of redemption found elsewhere) considered to have been occasioned by sin, rather than from the guilt of sin (*see* GUILT (IN THE BIBLE)). This conclusion is strengthened by the parallel expression in Ps 24(25).22: ''Redeem [*pādâ*] Israel, O God, from all its distress!'' A similar explanation is probably in order for a couple of passages in which redemption is found parallel with forgiveness of sins: ''I have brushed away your offenses like a cloud, your sins like a mist; return to me, for I have redeemed [*gā'al*] you'' (Is 44.22); ''He pardons all your iniquities, he heals all your ills. He redeems [*gā'al*] your life from destruction'' [Ps 102(103).3–4].

This is not to say, however, that there was no belief in a reconciliation after the estrangement brought about by sin nor in a remission of guilt. The pattern of punishment for sin and messianic restoration described above supposes that sin would be expiated by the punishment of the Exile (Is 40.2), after which the blessings of the messianic era would be conferred by God. That remission of sin and freedom from sin is part of the expected redemption is clear from many texts; see Jer 31.34; 50.20; Ez 36.24–33; Dn 9.24.

Even apart from the remission of sin that would precede and accompany the messianic redemption, the OT authors knew the need for remission of sin and entertained a lively hope that it could be obtained. A high point in OT spirituality is reached in Ps 50(51), a fervent and hopeful prayer for forgiveness by one who is convinced that God will not spurn a contrite and humble heart (v. 19). Another high point is reached in the last of the Servant of the Lord Oracles (Is 52.13–53.12), in which sinful mankind stands aghast and comes a step nearer to obtaining a ''contrite and humble heart'' in recognizing that the innocent victim suffered because the sins of all had been placed upon him (53.4, 6, 10–12). Not only does the Servant expiate the sins of others in some mysterious way, but his suffering has also a more positive aspect: ''But he was pierced for our offenses, crushed for our sins; upon him was the chastisement that makes us whole, by his stripes we were healed'' (53.5). The Servant is not identified with the Messiah in this text, nor is there anything to connect him with the Davidic kingship; nevertheless, because his mission is to give ''his life as an offering for sin . . . , and the will of the Lord shall be accomplished through him'', his work deserves to be characterized as messianic and redemptive in the highest sense of the words.

Redemption in Christ

The message of the NT is summed up in large part by the assertion that the long-awaited redemption has arrived, that Israel's messianic hope has been fulfilled in the person and mission of Jesus Christ, who has become mediator of salvation for all people. Because redemption was accomplished through Him, He obtains a far more central and essential role than was accorded the Messiah in the OT or in later Jewish tradition.

New Testament meaning of redemption. No simple explanation of the NT concept of redemption is possible because it is exceedingly rich and complex. However, it can be briefly described as the deliverance, through the death and Resurrection of Christ (Rom 4.25), from the state of estrangement from God (Ti 2.14) that prevailed from the earliest days of human existence (Gn 3.1–11.9), ratified by each person by his own sins (Rom 3.23); this redemption includes all of creation, for it ''was made subject to vanity'' because of human sin (Rom 8.20); the final stage, to be realized only at the Parousia and the general resurrection, will bring with it the end of all the ills that afflict humankind, but many of the messianic benefits are already enjoyed by the redeemed. In many respects redemption can be identified with SALVATION (σωτνρία).

Some of the elements of this description were already contained in the OT concept of redemption, though not so explicitly expressed. In the OT, however, deliverance of the Jewish nation from political domination was an important element; and popular Jewish expectation, as seen in some of the intertestamental writings, often tended to emphasize this aspect in a narrow, restrictive manner. The NT sometimes speaks of redemption in quite general terms that have more or less the same content as the OT expectation. This is true of the use of the term in the opening of the Benedictus (Lk 1.68; cf. 1.71: ''Salvation from our enemies, and from the hand of all who hate us''). Probably nothing other than this is to be seen in the disappointed expectation of the disciples on the road to Emmaus: ''But we were hoping that it was he who should redeem Israel'' (Lk 24.21). Obviously these men did not at that time regard Jesus' death as redemptive, nor were they awaiting His Resurrection; the fact that He had been put to death seemed to them evidence that He was not the awaited Redeemer. Their mistaken notions were corrected by Jesus Himself (Lk 24. 25–27), and the concept of deliverance from sin, death, and God's anger precisely through Jesus' death and Resurrection is the normal content of NT redemptive terminology.

The NT uses many of the Greek terms found in the LXX, but usually with the specifically Christian content just described. There is but a single passage in which λύτρον occurs (Mk 10.45; Mt 20.28), but it is a very significant one. The verb λυτρόω (in the middle voice) occurs a few times, as does its substantive λύτρωσις much more frequent, but without apparent difference in meaning, is the compound ἀπολύτρωσις. The last two terms usually mean the state of redemption, though they sometimes refer to the act by which redemption is accomplished. Other important terms are mentioned in the course of this article.

Redemptive death of Jesus. Although the total redemptive work of Jesus includes His Incarnation, life, Passion, death, and Resurrection, it cannot be denied that the NT emphasizes His death as the cause par excellence of redemption. The question of how the death of Jesus is redemptive does not find a single, clear, explanation in the NT. Various approaches are used—ransom, sacrifice, expiation, etc.—but none of them can exhaust the mystery. Moreover, these approaches are presented in thought categories largely foreign to the modern Western mind. Nevertheless, it is necessary to investigate the mystery in terms such as these, for they are the only kind the NT presents (*see* BIBLICAL THEOLOGY).

Jesus' Conception of His Mission. The NT recognizes Jesus as the Messiah and the bearer of salvation. He Himself generally avoided the title, which was largely associated with the political notions of His contemporaries concerning the type of redemption the Messiah would bring. His ministry was marked by a series of miracles that signified the overthrow of the kingdom of Satan in order to make way for the KINGDOM OF GOD. Near the beginning of His ministry He made clear the moral dispositions required of those who would enter this kingdom, but He fled from an enthusiastic following that wanted to make Him king (Jn 6.15). While avoiding the title of Messiah, Jesus constantly referred to Himself as Son of Man. This title, found in Dn 7.13 and applied to a transcendant, heavenly being in later Jewish writings, notably 1 Enoch and 4 Esdras, did not have the narrow political overtones attached to Messiah in popular Jewish expectation. But even to the title Son of Man Jesus gave a new content by identifying His mission with that of the Servant of the Lord of Deutero-Isaiah. Although Jesus did not explicitly call Himself the Servant of the Lord, sayings recorded in the Gospels explain His mission in terms that were drawn from the description of that OT figure. For example, the pattern of rejection, humiliation, death, and resurrection found in the Passion predictions (Mk 8.31; 9.29–30; 10.32–34; and parallels) follows that of the fourth Servant oracle. In the logia preserved in Mk 9.11 and 14.21 it is affirmed that Scripture foretold the necessity of the suffering of the Son of Man; yet no text of Scripture contains such a prediction (nor do even the non-biblical texts speak of the Son of Man suffering), and it is clear that the sayings apply to Jesus as Son of Man the things said of the Servant of the Lord. In one text He explicitly applied to Himself the words written of the Servant (Lk 22.37). The Evangelists and other NT writers, too, liberally applied to Him the Servant texts and terminology; see, e.g., Mt 8.17; 12.18; Jn 12.38; Acts 4.27, 30; 8.32–35; Rom 15.21; 1 Pt 2.22–25. Another passage that is of special importance for understanding Jesus' conception of His mission, Mk 10.45, requires a fuller investigation.

A Ransom for Many. The logion found in almost identical form in Mk 10.45 and Mt 20.28 is particularly important because in it Jesus characterized His understanding of His whole mission. In order to counter the tendency toward ambitious self-seeking on the part of His disciples, Jesus insisted on the need for humility and readiness to serve others, concluding with the words: ''for the Son of Man also has not come to be served but to serve, and to give his life as a ransom for many.'' There is little need to question the authenticity of this saying; the objections made in the past, that this verse is an expansion made under the influence of Pauline teaching or that St. Luke's version of the ''service logion'' (Lk 22.24–27) is more primitive, have been amply refuted.

The background against which this saying is to be interpreted is, in all probability, Jesus' conception of His mission as Servant of the Lord. This position has been denied by some (e.g., C. K. Barrett), but the arguments in its favor are very strong. It must be admitted that the language of the passage does not approach very closely to the LXX version of the fourth Servant oracle, but the thought expressed is very similar: in each case it is a question of one whose mission can be summed up as service and whose life is given in place of ''many'' (Is 53.11). Further, if the immediate context in Mark is taken into account, it may be said that the pattern of abasement, death, and exaltation appears in each text, for in Mk 10.43–44 Jesus explains to His disciples that the way to true greatness lies in humiliation and service, and then He goes on (in v. 45) to apply this to Himself: ''for the Son of Man also.'' When one adds to this the conviction that Jesus interpreted His own mission in the light of the Servant figure, it becomes clear that this also is the background against which must be understood the saying in which Jesus solemnly summarizes the meaning of His life's work.

How, then, should the ''ransom'' be understood? Some have suggested that the λύτρον recalls the *'āšām* of Is 53.10: the Servant is said to give his life as an ''offering for sin''; but this is probably incorrect, for *'āšām* is never translated by λύτρον. More probably λύτρον represents the idea contained in the occurrences of *kōper* discussed above: a price given in place of (the proper meaning of ἀντί) a life that is forfeit. The meaning, then, is that Jesus dies in order to deliver ''many'' (a term that does not necessarily imply any restriction) from a situation in which their own lives were forfeit. The ''situation'' in question is man's state as sinner and the consequences deriving from it (ultimately death). This corresponds closely to the mission of the Servant. However, the image of a price or ransom cannot be pressed too far; man is held in bondage to sin (and thus liable to death) through the activity of Satan, but it cannot be thought that the price (the life of Jesus) is delivered to Satan; he has no rights over God's creatures. Jesus does die in obedience to the will of the Father and to offer Him a sacrifice on behalf of all, and in this sense His life might be said to be paid to God. Yet this must not be understood in a crudely substitutionary sense, as though an irate God accepted the death of the innocent Jesus in place of that of sinners and thus was appeased. It was the loving Father who initiated His merciful plan of salvation by sending His Son. Moreover, the life of Jesus was given to release sinners from the state of bondage, a state in which they are not kept by God, and to enable them to serve God properly.

Jesus' Death as a Sacrifice. If Jesus interpreted His sufferings and death in the light of the Servant passages, it would appear that He viewed His death as a sacrifice; the same implication is found in the words of institution of the chalice at the Last Supper: ''This is my blood of the new covenant, which is being shed for many'' (Mk 14.24)—words that allude both to the blood of the Sinai covenant sacrifice (Ex 24.8) and to the Servant oracles. It is not possible to enter here into a full discussion of Israel's concept of sacrifice, but it is helpful to recall certain features that are pertinent to the present investigation. Sacrifice had various functions, some more prominent in certain types of sacrifice than in others. The emphasis was not upon the destruction of the victim, but upon the offering of life made to God. The ends of the offering were worship, reconciliation, and fellowship with God. Sacrifice, when offered in the proper spirit, implied a giving of self; the imposition of the hands of the offerer upon the head of the victim signified his identity with it and so signified total surrender and the desire to be accepted by God as the victim would be. Sacrifice was understood to effect reconciliation by removing the obstacles to union with God caused by sin; this was the function of guilt offerings and sin offerings, which were understood to be effective through the mysterious power of blood (*see* BLOOD, RELIGIOUS SIGNIFICANCE OF), the shedding of which signified the release of life. It is to be noted that the life thus presented to God was not a substitute for the life of the guilty. The expiation involved consisted in the wiping out of sin so as to restore the relationship of community between the sinner and God, not in placating the anger of God. Sacrifice also effected communion or fellowship with God in two ways: the blood of the victim, with which the offerer was in some way identified, was presented to God by being splashed on the altar; and (in some types of sacrifices) the offerer shared in the victim, now transferred to the sphere of the divine through acceptance by God, by a sacred meal.

These are elevated concepts, but the disadvantages of the OT practice are apparent. The victim itself had no intrinsic value as an offering to God, nor could a dumb animal partake in any way in the free offering that is the essence of sacrifice. The total value, then, derived from the dispositions of the offerer. These, however, were often lacking; the sacrifice could be viewed in a somewhat mechanical way, as effecting something automatically—as the condemnations of the Prophets eloquently indicate.

The sacrificial death of Jesus, however, was not vitiated by these imperfections. The mission He had received from His Father of establishing the kingdom of God and instructing men in its true nature roused against Him the hostility of Satan and wicked men and issued ultimately in His death. That His death would be an outcome of His fidelity to His mission Jesus clearly foresaw; this is explicit in the Passion predictions, implicit in His identification of Himself with the Servant of the Lord. Nevertheless, He adhered to the path that He knew would lead to His death in obedience to the will of His Father, and in so doing became a conscious, willing victim (Jn 10.11, 15–18); the Passion of Christ was not simply a circumstance but a necessity (Lk 12.50; 24.26). Sinless and innocent Himself, Jesus willingly underwent death in obedience to the will of the Father in the full knowledge that in so doing He was accomplishing the redemption of all; by His obedient death as Servant, He offered a sacrifice in which all can share, which all can make their own. Because Jesus freely offered Himself, He was not only victim, but also priest. (The function of the priest in the OT was not to slay the victim but to offer it to God; the slaughter was often carried out by a layman.) This truth became the basis for a theme developed at length in the Epistle to the Hebrews and found in other places in the NT.

It may be asked why God required the sacrifice of Jesus as the price of redemption for all and did not simply forgive sin freely; it might be thought that this would involve a higher conception of God and one that is already found in the OT. In answer it may be said that the OT, even though it sometimes seems to speak of sin being freely pardoned, did recognize and teach the necessity for reparation for sin; this is witnessed by the practice of guilt offerings and sin offerings, the Day of ATONEMENT, the belief that punishment for sin must precede the messianic restoration, the teaching on the mission of the Servant of the Lord, and in many other ways. A proper estimate of sin recognizes it as something that not only offends God but, in a real way, induces a disorder into one's very being, because it perverts one's ordering of oneself to God, in which one's total good as creature consists. The fallen condition, from which springs our need for redemption, is the result of the sin of disobedience (rebellion); this goes back to the origin of the human race (Gn ch. 1–11), in which each individual is inserted and grounded (*see* ORIGINAL SIN). Only by a definitive rejection of all that is evil, by a new act of perfect obedience in which God would be chosen in preference to self, could a new beginning be made. Yet, paradoxically, this is precisely what human nature, wounded as it now was by sin, was not able to effect; humankind, in the greatest need, found itself in a state of helplessness. It is at this point that God in His merciful design takes the initiative to rescue man, by means of the Incarnation, from a state in which he cannot rescue himself. Jesus, sinless and in no way partaker of man's moral weakness, offers in the name of all His obedience unto death. In so doing, He both undergoes the penalty of death for sin in the name of sinners and repairs the disorder caused by disobedience.

From this it is clear that there is a substitutionary element in the sacrifice of Jesus; this is implied also in the connection of His death as ransom with the OT kōper (see above). The substitutionary element is seen partly in the fact that He has done for man what man could not do for himself. Yet a fuller understanding of Jesus' death as redemptive must go far beyond this; Jesus does not die simply in place of sinful mankind, but must in some way be identified with those for whom He died. This identification proceeds in two directions: Jesus dies in the name of sinners, and sinners, in turn, make Jesus' sacrifice their own. It is not without significance that the only Servant passage that Jesus explicitly applied to Himself (Is 53.12) implied His association with sinful mankind: "For I say to you that this which is written must yet be fulfilled in me, 'And he was reckoned among the wicked'" (Lk 22.37; for the forceful expressions of St. Paul, see Rom 8.3; 2 Cor 5.21; Gal 3.13). Objectively the sacrifice of

Jesus, offered in the name of sinners, accomplishes total reparation and redemption; but it does not operate in an automatic way in reconciling the individual sinner to God. Each person must make the sacrifice his own, expressive of his own dispositions of contrition for sin and willingness to make reparation; as in the case of any sacrifice, it avails only for the individual who makes it a vehicle of his own oblation of self. Ultimately this means that the offerer wills to render personally the perfect obedience of Jesus to God, obedience even unto death (Phil 2.5–8; 2 Cor 5.14–15).

That Jesus intended men to appropriate His sacrifice as their own is clear from His institution of the Eucharist. In this rite, the broken loaf and of wine are effective signs of His body slain and His blood ''shed for many'' (Mk 14.22–24), and the invitation to eat of them is an invitation for each person to make his own the sacrifice of Jesus. The covenant aspect that is present (''This is my blood of the new covenant . . .''; cf. Ex 24.8; Jer 31.31–34) implies that Jesus' death makes possible fellowship between God and those who share in it.

Teaching of New Testament Writers. There is no possibility of presenting here a complete synthesis of the diverse and complex approaches used by the NT writers in explaining the redemptive nature of the death of Christ; a description of some of the more basic lines of thought is all that is attempted.

St. Mark's Gospel indicates that the immediate effect of Jesus' death is reconciliation with God. Whereas in St. Matthew's Gospel the rending of the veil of the Temple is one of a series of marvels that follows the death of Jesus (Mt 27.51–53), in Mark's account it stands alone (Mk 15.38) and is sandwiched into the narrative for the sake of what it signifies—the way of access to God is now open. A comparable teaching on access to God through the veil by virtue of the death of Christ is found in Hebrews (Heb 10.19–22). Paradoxically, it is at the moment of Jesus' death in rejection and apparent abandonment that Mark places the recognition of His divinity (Mk 15.39). When N. Ferré; says that ''Calvary shows the depth of God's redemptive love for man and thus alone is the full revelation of God'' [*The Christian Faith* (New York 1942) 161], he makes explicit something that is implicit in Mark's account. St. John and St. Paul also see God's redemptive act in Christ as the supreme manifestation of His love (Jn 3.16; Rom 5.8; 8.32).

The image of redemption accomplished through the payment of a price is reflected in many NT passages. Of special interest is 1 Tm 2.6, for it is clearly a paraphrase of the ransom passage in Mk 10.45: ''who [Jesus Christ] gave himself a ransom [ἀντίλυτρον] for all.'' By substituting ''all'' for ''many,'' the passage excludes any suggestion of a limitation of redemption to some segment of humankind. See also Ti 2.14; 1 Pt 1.18–19. Even when λύτρον and its derivatives are not used, the idea is sometimes expressed in other terms, such as ἀγοράζω, to purchase (1 Cor 6.20; 2 Pt 2.1; Rv 5.9; 14.3); ἐξαγοράζω, to buy back, redeem (Gal 3.13; 4.5); and ἐλευθερέω, to deliver, free, e.g., from sin, death, or slavery (Rom 6.18, 8.2, 21; Gal 5.1). The same concept is present as well in references to the price (sometimes specified as the precious blood of Christ—Acts 20.28; Eph 1.7; 1 Pt 1.18–19; Rv 5.9) by which man is redeemed (1 Cor 6.20). The passages in which these expressions occur allude at least implicitly to the sacrificial nature of the death of Christ; the reference to sacrifice is found also in Rom 3.25: ''whom [Jesus] God has set forth as a propitiation [ἱλαστήριον] by His blood ''(*see* EXPIATION (IN THE BIBLE)). See also, e.g., 1 Cor 5.7; Eph 5.2. In 1 Thes 1.10 Paul says that believers have been delivered (ῥύομαι) from God's wrath. In biblical terminology the wrath of God stands for vindictive punishment to be visited upon sinners through divine judgment on the last day, whereas the justice of God stands for the benign plan of God to save man from sin. In Rom 5.9 salvation (σῴζω) from God's wrath is attributed to the blood of Christ. (For other aspects of Paul's distinctive teaching on Redemption, *see* PAUL, APOSTLE, ST.).

The image of redemption as a buying or a purchase contains another important element, namely, the acquisition of the redeemed for God as His own people—already an important part of OT thought. Thus St. Paul can speak of ''the Church of God which he [Christ] has purchased with his own blood'' (Acts 20.28) or say that Jesus ''gave himself for us that he might redeem us from all iniquity and cleanse for himself an acceptable people'' (Ti 2.14). St. Peter can call the Christians ''a purchased people'' (1 Pt 2.9). In 1 Cor 7.22–24 St. Paul tells his readers, slaves and free, that having been bought at a price, they have been set free (i.e., of the powers that formerly held them) in order to become slaves of Christ. In a similar sense, Jesus had said that when He had been ''lifted up'' He would draw all to Himself (Jn 12.32) and had compared Himself to a grain of wheat that falls into the ground and dies in order to bring forth much fruit (Jn 12.24–25).

The means by which we can appropriate for ourselves the sacrifice of Christ are set forth in various ways. St. Paul speaks of faith, incorporation into the body of Christ, sacramental participation in the redemptive mystery (through Baptism in Rom 6.3, through the Eucharist in 1 Cor 11.26), etc. Of special import is Paul's presentation of Christ as Second Adam (Rom 5.12–19; 1 Cor 15.44–49). Just as Adam, the total embodiment of humanity at the beginning, encompassed all of humankind in his fall, so Christ incorporates all of humankind in

Himself in His act of perfect obedience on the Cross: ''For just as by the disobedience of the one man the many were constituted sinners, so also by the obedience of the one the many will be justified'' (Rom 5.19). The same is said more briefly in 2 Cor 5.14: ''[S]ince one died for all, therefore all have died.'' The conclusion to be drawn from this is that the redeemed are dead to sin and thus able to be the recipients of a new life (Rom 6.2–3; 2 Cor 5.15; Col 3.1–4).

Redemption and the Resurrection. Although Jesus taught the redemptive value of His death, He did not clearly indicate, at least in the authentic sayings that have been preserved, the redemptive significance of His Resurrection. Even the fourth Servant oracle, which was the background of Jesus' interpretation of His mission, seems to view the Servant's resurrection almost solely as a vindication of his innocence and the means of making known to others that it was not for his sins but for the sins of ''the many'' that he died; the emphasis is placed on his death: ''through his suffering, my servant shall justify many, and their guilt he shall bear'' (Is 53.11).

Yet the NT writers have correctly seen the importance of the RESURRECTION OF CHRIST for a proper understanding of the Redemption. The NT does not emphasize the redemption of souls—a concept that rests upon a Platonic and quite un-biblical view of the human situation (*see* MAN, 1)—but of the redemption of the person. A correct view extends Redemption to include our bodily nature, society, and all of creation; any redemption that did not include this would be incomplete.

In rising from the dead, Christ did not simply return to the mortal life He had known before, but He was glorified and exalted to the right hand of the Father (Mk 16.19; Acts 2.32–33). Further, the new life He now possessed was something all the redeemed were also to share in. In order to grasp the full meaning of this, it is necessary to understand the force of the concepts of death and life in Scripture. In biblical thought ''death'' often signifies far more than simply the loss of bodily life. Death entered the world as the result of sin (Gn 3.17–19; Rom 5.12), and the ultimate stage of it is eternal damnation (Jas 1.15; Rom 5.21; 6.21; Rv 20.14); this would be the inescapable fate of fallen man if God had not intervened. As it is, Christ has overcome death through His Resurrection. The raising of Christ from the dead is usually attributed to the Father, just as the initiative in the Redemption is regularly presented as coming from Him; because of Christ's divine nature and because of His perfect victory over evil in His own life, however, it can be said also that the realm of death had no power to hold Him (Acts 2.24). In His dying and Resurrection, death and the powers of death have been destroyed (2 Tm 1.10; Heb 2.14).

The positive aspect of this victory is the bestowal of life on all those united to Christ; indeed, this gift of life can be considered to be the completion of His redemptive mission: ''I have come that they might have life, and have it more abundantly'' (Jn 10.10). Life, too, is a pregnant concept in Scripture; just as ''death'' can describe man's unredeemed state and all its consequences, so ''life'' can comprise the totality of the gift of God, including Redemption and supernatural blessedness. This life is conferred on the believer in virtue of the Resurrection of Christ; St. Paul can say that ''even when we were dead by reason of our sins, [God] brought us to life together with Christ'' (Eph 2.5). Solidarity with Adam brought death; solidarity with Christ brings life: ''For since by a man came death, by a man also comes resurrection from the dead. For as in Adam all die, so in Christ all will be made to live'' (1 Cor 15.21–22). The Resurrection of Christ and that of the redeemed are so closely linked as cause and effect that to deny the resurrection of the dead is, implicitly, to deny the Resurrection of Christ (1 Cor 15.12–21). Sometimes this link is explained in terms of sacramental action. St. Paul speaks especially of Baptism in this regard: ''For you were buried together with him in Baptism, and in him also rose again through faith in the working of God who raised him from the dead'' (Col 2.12); ''For we were buried with him by means of Baptism into death, in order that, just as Christ has arisen from the dead through the glory of the Father, so we also may walk in newness of life. For if we have been united with him in the likeness of his death, we shall be so in the likeness of his resurrection also'' (Rom 6.4–5). St. John sees this effected through the Eucharist: ''He who eats my flesh and drinks my blood has everlasting life and I will raise him up on the last day'' (Jn 6.55).

The Christian's share in the Resurrection of Christ includes both the life of grace now (walking ''in newness of life''—Rom 6.4) and the resurrection of the body on the last day. The life of grace is granted through the believer's intimate union with Christ (Eph 2.4–7) and the gift of the Spirit (Rom 8.1–11), which Christ is able to bestow in virtue of His Resurrection and exaltation (Acts 2.33; Jn 7.39, 20.22;). The possession of the SPIRIT OF GOD renders the receivers SONS OF GOD and joint heirs with Christ (Rom 8.14–17).

Bestowal of the Spirit not only restores integrity to the individual, but also brings to an end the divisions within the human community caused by sin and existing since the earliest generations (Gn 11.1–9). The creation of one community for all, long expected by the Prophets as an effect of the messianic redemption (Is 2.2–4; 19.18–25), is realized at least germinally at Pentecost (Acts 2.5–11) and continued in the process of the building up of the body of Christ, the Church, in which all divisions are brought to an end (Gal 3.28; Col 3.11; Eph 2.13–22).

Because man is the crown of creation and because all other creatures were made for him and placed under his dominion (Gn 1.26–28; 2.18–19), all creation shared in man's fall and became subject to the vanity of his sin (Rom 8.20); the earth was cursed because of him (Gn 3.17–18). The Prophets, therefore, looked forward to a redemption in which the disorders introduced by the Fall would be undone and in which all creation would share (Is 11.6–9; Hos 2.20; Am 9.13)—a cosmic redemption calling for the creation of a new heaven and a new earth (Is 65.17–25). This cosmic aspect is seen also in the NT teaching on redemption, even though its completion will be realized only on the last day. St. Paul expects that ''creation itself also will be delivered from its slavery to corruption into the freedom of the glory of the sons of God'' (Rom 8.21). Something of the same idea is contained in 1 Cor ch. 15, where St. Paul speaks of the day when death and every evil force will be destroyed and all other things will be subject to God in their proper order to the end ''that God may be all in all'' (1 Cor 15.24–28; see also Eph 1.10). In a sense, this is already accomplished in the Incarnation (Col 1.15–17).

Redemption and eschatology. In many prophetic texts, especially (or perhaps exclusively) in those after the Exile, the fulfillment of the expected messianic redemption is seen to coincide with the end of human history, of the present world, and of the present age, and to introduce a new world in a new age (see, e.g., the ''new heavens and new earth'' oracle in Is 65.17–25 referred to above). With the exaltation of Christ and the sending of the Spirit, the Apostles recognized that in Christ the decisive act of salvation history (Heilsgeschichte) had been accomplished and the new age had been ushered in; this is a central element of the NT proclamation. Nevertheless, the NT continues to look forward to the Parousia (Second Coming) of Christ as the final act of the redemptive work that, until that moment, must remain, in a sense, incomplete. Until sin, death, and every hostile force is brought to an end, the kingdom of God cannot be considered to be perfectly established; until the redeemed share in the glory of the Resurrection of Christ through the glorification of their own bodies, Redemption will not be complete (see Lk 21.28; Rom 8.23; Eph 1.14; 4.30). This state of affairs leads to a tension between present and future that is inherent in the NT message. Some modern authors would resolve this tension by seeing all the goods of the messianic age already present, with no further extraordinary intervention of God on earth to be expected. Such ''realized eschatology'' (term of C. H. Dodd), however, is hardly consistent with all the data of the NT. But the theory does contain important elements of truth. Many of the benefits of Redemption are already possessed in this life: deliverance from God's wrath, reconciliation with God, the gift of the Spirit, adoption as sons of God, and the messianic community (the Church) that is potentially the sphere of salvation and unity of all men (see Rom 3.24; 1 Cor 1.30; Eph 1.7; Col 1.14). Even the gifts that are not yet fully possessed are to a degree already proleptically present for the Christian in virtue of union with the glorified and exalted Christ. The various writers of the NT stress now one, now the other of these two poles, so that only a somewhat mitigated form of ''realized eschatology,'' sometimes termed ''inaugurated eschatology,'' truly represents their thought. (*see* ESCHATOLOGY (IN THE BIBLE)).

Christians have been given the means of bettering the world; they can and must work for justice, equality of opportunity, peace, the extinction of every evil, and the acquisition of every good. But the perfect establishment of the kingdom of God, according to the mind of the NT, will be accomplished not by the gradual success of human endeavors, but only by the return of the Son of Man.

See Also: HOPE OF SALVATION (IN THE BIBLE); JUSTIFICATION.

Bibliography: *Encyclopedic Dictionary of the Bible,* tr. and adap. by L. HARTMAN (New York 1963) 1994–2003. J. GEWIESS, *Lexikon für Theologie und Kirche,* ed. J. HOFER and K. RAHNER (Freiburg 1957–65) 3:1016–20. P. VIELHAUER, *Die Religion in Geschichte und Gegenwart* (Tübingen 1957–65) 2:579–584. H. J. KRAUS and P. VIELHAUER, *ibid.* 2:586–590. H. SCHLIER, *Theologisches Wörterbuch zum Neuen Testamentm,* ed. G. KITTEL (Stuttgart 1935—) 2:484–500. O. PROCKSCH and F. BÜCHSEL, *ibid.* 4:329–359. M. M. BOURKE, *Passion, Death, and Resurrection of Christ* (Glen Rock, N.J. 1963). D. M. STANLEY, *Christ's Resurrection in Pauline Soteriology* (*Analecta biblica* 13, Rome 1961). F. X. DURRWELL, *The Resurrection,* tr. R. SHEED (New York 1960). L. CERFAUX, *Christ in the Theology of St. Paul,* tr. G. WEBB and A. WALKER (New York 1959) 69–192. V. TAYLOR, *The Atonement in New Testament Teaching* (3d ed. London 1958); *Jesus and His Sacrifice* (New York 1955). C. NOVEL, *Essai sur le Développement de l'idée biblique de Rédemption* (Lyons 1954). J. DUPONT, *La Réconciliation dans la théologie de St. Paul* (Paris 1953). A. KIRCHGÄSSNER, *Erlösung und Sünde im N.T.* (Freiburg 1950). J. BONSIRVEN, *L'Évangile de s. Paul* (Paris 1948) 144–174. J. J. STAMM, *Erlösen und Vergeben im A. T.* (Bern 1940). R. G. BANDAS, *The Master Idea of St. Paul's Epistles on the Redemption* (St. Paul, Minn. 1926). J. WACH, *Der Erlösungsgedanke und seine Deutung* (Leipzig 1922). S. LYONNET, ''The Redemption of the Universe'' in H. RAHNER et al., *The Church: Readings in Theology* (New York 1963) 136–158; *Introduction à la Bible,* eds. A. ROBERT and A. FEUILLET (Tournai 1959) 2:840–889; ''De notione redemptionis,'' *Verbum Domini* 36 (1958) 129–146. C. K. BARRETT, ''The Background of Mark 10:45,'' *N. T. Essays: Studies in Memory of T. W. Manson,* ed. A. J. B. HIGGINS (Manchester, Eng. 1959) 1–18. A. R. JOHNSON, ''The Primary Meaning of the Root g'l,'' *Vetus Testestamentum* suppl. 1 (1953) 67–77. R. CROUZEL, ''Le Dogme de la Rédemption dans l'Apocalypse,'' *Bulletin de Littérature Ecclésiastique* 58 (1957) 65–92. B. VAWTER, ''Resurrection and Redemption,'' *Catholic Bib-*

lical Quarterly 15 (1953) 11–23. J. JEREMIAS, ''Das Lösegeld für viele (Mk. 10, 45),'' *Judaica* 3 (1948) 249–264. J. RIVIÈRE, ''Expiation et Rédemption dans l'A.T.,'' *Bulletin de Littérature Ecclésiastique* 47 (1946) 3–22. J. B. COLON, ''La Conception du salut d'après les évangiles synoptiques,'' *Recherches de science religieuse* 10 (1930) 370–415; 11 (1931) 27–72, 193–223. B. WARFIELD, ''The N.T. Terminology of Redemption,'' *Princeton Theological Review* 15 (1917) 201–249. J. UNTERMAN and G. S. SHOGREN, ''Redemption,'' *Anchor Bible Dictionary* (New York 1992) 5:650–657.

[J. JENSEN]

REDEMPTION (THEOLOGY OF)

The term ''Redemption'' in Christian theology refers to the mystery of God's deliverance of mankind from the evil of sin and His restoration of man to the state of grace by an act of divine power and merciful love. This redemptive act spans the whole of man's history from the time of his first sin and fall from grace. ''God . . . wishes all men to be saved and to come to the knowledge of truth'' (1 Tm 2.4).

INTRODUCTION

The salvific act of God as it encounters men has progressive realizations and various manifestations. God works His saving will in history in an ever-expanding power of action and clarity of revelation. In the Old Testament, the first realization and revelation of God's redemptive act, a Redemption is promised in Gn 3.15 (*see* PROTO-EVANGELIUM) and has the beginnings of its realization in the call of Abraham, the election of Moses, the Exodus from Egypt, the covenant of Sinai, the life of the people of God in the Promised Land, the exile and the return of the people, and their waiting in hope for the Messiah of God to come and give ''help to Israel . . . as he spoke to . . . Abraham and to his posterity forever'' (Lk 1.54–55).

Salvation history traces a pattern of God's redemptive activity and will provide many of the theological categories within which Christian theology will reflect upon the decisive and definitive Redemption that God works in behalf of mankind in and through Christ. Although a complete theology of Redemption must include all that can be known of God's act of deliverance and restoration, Christian theology has concentrated on the revelation of the New Testament, which marks the ''fullness of time'' in SALVATION HISTORY when ''God sent his Son, born of a woman . . . that he might redeem . . . that we might receive the adoption of sons'' (Gal 4.4).

For the NT writers, Redemption may refer to the purpose of Christ's work in its total accomplishment (e.g., Rom 8.23; Eph 4.30; Rv 5.9) or in its partial accomplishment here on earth (e.g., Eph 1.7; Col 1.14). The term also designates the plan of Christ's work (e.g., Rom 3.24; Ti 2.14). Finally, Redemption and its cognate forms can refer to the very accomplishing of the work of Christ in terms of what is done and how the work is effective.

This article considers Redemption chiefly as a process in which the redeeming activity of God is mediated in and through the life and death and Resurrection of the Incarnate Word. The investigations are polarized to the side of Redemption as it is something objective. This is to say that the Redemption is considered as the decisive and definite act of God in Christ on behalf of mankind so that, as regards the divine activity in this order of things, Redemption is accomplished ''for once and for all.'' In the consideration of Redemption as objective, the focus is on God's efficient activity rather than on man's reception of and response to the redemptive act of God. The objective of this article is to present a doctrinal survey that indicates the main lines of theological reflection upon this mystery. This article is not an effort to construct an integral theology of the Redemption according to any one soteriological theory. The Redemption is a mystery properly so called. In certain epochs and according to certain schools of theology, different aspects of the mystery have been put in relief while others have been passed over almost unnoticed. No single theory of the Redemption has ever been total or complete. The investigation proceeds, in general, through scriptural themes and dogmatic formulations by the Church, the doctrinal context of the Redemption, and finally, theories of the Redemption considered within the doctrinal context.

SCRIPTURAL THEMES AND DOGMATIC FORMULATIONS

These themes and formulations serve as points of departure for the reflections of the Church and the articles of faith toward which are addressed the theological questions for an intelligence of the mystery.

Scriptural themes. There are seven themes that can be derived from the NT as theological points of departure for the inquiring Christian who asks the question: how and by what means is man delivered from the evil of sin and restored to grace with God? Although not all these themes are equally central in the mystery, each of them, nonetheless, provides a clue for insight into the various aspects of the mystery.

First, Redemption is revealed as achieved by the very fact that the Word of God assumes human nature and becomes the mediator between God and man. The theme is derived from the Fourth Gospel. The sources are also Pauline (e.g., 1 Tm 2.5; Heb 8.6; 9.15). Compare the re-establishment of all things in Christ (Eph 1.10; Col 1.15–20) and the Christ-Adam parallel (Rom 5.12–19; 1 Cor 15.21–22, 45–49).

12th-century apse mosaic of combined Redemption motifs, Church of S. Clemente, Rome.

Second, Redemption is accomplished through Christ's giving His life as a price of purchase, or RANSOM, as it were (Mk 10.45; 1 Cor 6.20; 7.23; 1 Tm 2.6; Ti 2.14; 1 Pt 1.18–19; Rv 5.9).

Third, Redemption is effected through the sufferings and death of Christ undergone because of SIN and in behalf of sinners (Jn 1.29; Rom 4.25; 5.6–21; 1 Cor 15.3; 2 Cor 5.15; Gal 2.20; Eph 5.2; Col 2.13–14).

Fourth, Redemption is performed through the sacrifice of Christ offered on the cross (from the account of the institution of the Eucharist in the Synoptic Gospels; the Epistle to the Hebrews; Rom 3.25; 1 Cor 5.7; Eph 5.2;1 Jn 4.10). (*See* SACRIFICE OF THE CROSS.)

Fifth, Redemption is acquired through Christ's victory over the devil (Jn 14.30; Col 1.13; 2.15; 1 Jn 3.8), sin and death (Rom 5.21; 6.6–23; 8.3; 1 Cor 15.20–58).

Sixth, Redemption is attained through the obedience of Christ (Jn 10.18; 14.31; Phil 2.5–11).

Seventh, Redemption is carried out by the RESURRECTION OF CHRIST (Rom 1.4; 4.25; 1 Cor 15; 2 Cor 5.15) and His INTERCESSION in heaven with the Father (Rom 8.34; Heb 7.25).

These themes are scattered throughout the NT. The texts cited are simply some examples in the Scriptures whence these themes can be derived. They converge on the central truth of Christian revelation—man's deliverance from sin and his restoration to union with God by means of Christ's coming, His life, and especially His death and Resurrection. The NT authors scarcely go beyond the statement of the mystery. They illustrate various aspects of the mystery with comparisons to similar things in the world of man.

The Redemption wrought by God in Christ is something absolutely and entirely unique. Faith in the redemption accomplished by Christ was a living experience far richer than their attempted formulations of the experience. The writers formulated their experience not to set out ideas in a system, but rather to set out ideas in various contexts and on different occasions in order to foster the faith and sustain this living experience in the infant Church.

God invites man to participate in the mystery and intends that man read out of his living experience of the mystery some understanding of the reasons why. This is precisely what happened in the Church when these scriptural themes became the points of departure for the subsequent theological reflections made within the living experience of the Redemption [*See* REDEMPTION (IN THE BIBLE)].

Dogmatic formulations. Definitions of the Church are usually formulated in response to questions raised in controversy or in answer to a heresy.

Before the Council of Trent. There are no salient pronouncements on the subject of the Redemption by the authoritative teaching Church before the Council of Trent. No serious controversies arose in the Church over the redemptive work of Christ before the Council of Trent. It is true that the logic of the early Christological heresies and Pelagianism could have had repercussions in the doctrine of the Redemption, but unorthodoxy did not press its principles into applications in this field of the faith. The Church was satisfied to aim its anathemas at the principles themselves.

The creeds can be considered the earliest formulations of the faith on the Redemption. Employed for catechetical and baptismal purposes, the creeds are statements of the fundamental articles of the faith with a minimum of doctrinal development. In the earliest creeds, the belief in Christ as SAVIOR is professed. There is a recital of the great events of His life: Christ is born, is crucified, is buried, and rising on the third day sits at the right hand of the Father. Forgiveness of sins and life eternal are confessed, at least in an implied manner, as the fruits of the life and death and Resurrection of the Savior (cf. H. Denzinger, *Enchiridion symbolorum* 1–6).

As such, creeds develop further; one may note that a reason is assigned for the coming of the Savior. Thus in the NICENE CREED: "For us men and for our salvation He came down and was enfleshed, made man, suffered, and rose on the third day, [and] ascended into heaven" (*ibid.* 125). The Creed of Constantinople (381) goes one doctrinal step further by inserting: ". . . crucified also for us under Pontius Pilate" (*ibid.* 150).

Until the time of the Council of Trent, the faith of the Church relative to the Redemption appears in certain doctrinal pronouncements, but it does so incidentally, with other subjects. The doctrine is usually expressed in the terminology of the Scriptures or of the creeds and without any real doctrinal advance (cf. *ibid.* 539, 700, 801, 852). It is in the 14th century that the concept of MERIT as applied to Christ's sufferings and death begins to appear in the ecclesiastical documents (cf. H. Denzinger, *Enchiridion symbolorum* 1027, 1347).

Council of Trent and After. Significant doctrinal advances were made within the formulations issued by the Council of Trent. In defining the hereditary character of ORIGINAL SIN, the council employed the notion of merit to explain the forgiveness of sins (*ibid.* 1513). The concept of satisfaction is also adjoined to the notion of merit to explain the manner in which man is redeemed by

Christ (*ibid.* 1529). This notion of satisfaction for sins offered to God in the sufferings of Christ is mentioned again in the council's treatment of the Sacrament of Penance (*ibid.* 1689–90; cf. 1713). (*See* SATISFACTION OF CHRIST).

The meaning of merit and satisfaction as applied to the Redemption will be taken up later. Only the employment of these concepts is noted here. J. Rivière remarks: ''In these passages there is no question of a doctrinal definition. This was not called for. Nevertheless, by the very fact of being included in the solemn decree of justification the two categories of merit and satisfaction which were already current in the schools as describing the work of Christ acquired a kind of official character'' (*Dictionnaire de théologie catholique* 13.2:1919).

The sacrificial character of the Redemption was affirmed by the council in its defense of the Holy Mass against the objections of the reformers (H. Denzinger, *Enchiridion symbolorum* 1739–42).

While the council was still in session, Pope Paul IV in 1555 condemned the proposition of the Socinians: ''Jesus Christ did not submit to the most cruel death of the cross to redeem us from sins and from eternal death and to reunite us with the Father unto eternal life'' (*ibid.* 1880).

This formula affirms the objective character of the Redemption against those who would see in the Passion of Christ only the value of an example—an opinion to be proposed again by certain 19th-century liberal Protestant theologians.

Modern Times. Vatican Council I included in its program a general schema on Christian doctrine in which the doctrine of the Redemption was to have had a prominent place. The schema included a canon that would have declared heretical the affirmation that Christ could not and did not truly and properly satisfy for sins; that vicarious satisfaction of one mediator for all men is repugnant to divine justice. These canons do not have the authority of a pronouncement of the Church, but they manifest the thinking of the Church current at that period.

Summary. In great part these formulations from the magisterium are paraphrases of the themes derived from the text of Scripture. The teaching Church puts particular insistence on the role of the sufferings and death of Christ in the work of Redemption, but not more emphasis than the NT itself does (see 1 Cor 1.23–25; 2.2).

In the mind of the Church, the death of Christ has the value of a supreme lesson for and example to mankind. But more than that. Christ's sacrificial death is objectively and sovereignly efficacious in the work of delivering man from the evil of sin and of re-establishing the union between God and man.

There is a doctrinal advance in Trent's explanation of that efficacy by way of the theological categories of merit and satisfaction. The council did not canonize any particular theory of merit or of satisfaction in relation to the work of the Redemption. Neither did it sanction any theory of sacrifice. The council and the subsequent official teaching of the Church do, however, direct that authentic Catholic theology will explain the manner of the Redemption within some valid conception of merit and satisfaction. That is, the work of Christ somehow earns or acquires the deliverance from sin and the reunion of man with God; Christ in His sacrificial death in some real way compensates for the evil of sin and thereby becomes for man ''God-given wisdom, and justice, and sanctification, and redemption'' (1 Cor 1.30).

In employing these categories of merit and satisfaction, the Church has interpreted the data of revelation and sanctioned some principal currents of doctrine in tradition.

THE FATHERS ON REDEMPTION

The thought of the Fathers of the Church on the mystery of the Redemption is unsystematic. It is difficult (if not impossible) to summarize their doctrine briefly, accurately, and without distortion. Their thought is not always clear-cut or precise.

Problems in patristic thought and method. The Fathers' doctrine on the Redemption contains fixed elements derived from the Scripture, the creeds, and the liturgy. In the early Church, especially among the Greeks, the decisive moment of the Redemption in the life of the Incarnate Word is never pinpointed. In the West, the sufferings and death of Christ very soon became the events that specially focus the act of Redemption, whereas in the theology of the East, one finds a moving viewpoint according to which it is sometimes the very fact of the Incarnation in which Redemption is accomplished, sometimes the total life of Christ. Yet even in the East there is a marked emphasis on the death of Christ.

In the Scriptures, the Redemption is something God does in and through Christ for the SALVATION of sinful men. But Redemption is also something that Christ, as man, offers to God on man's behalf. The Redemption is a work that takes place in God and in man with an effectivity, apparently, in opposite directions. The Greek Fathers tend to emphasize the first conception; the Latin Fathers, the second. Though both conceptions might be affirmed side by side, an emphasis on one tends to become an underestimation of the other.

Furthermore, a writer's general approach to the Christian religion will exercise a determining influence on his doctrine of the Redemption. If Christianity is conceived of primarily as a code of conduct, Redemption through the teaching, example, and inspiration of Christ will become a key concept. If Christianity is considered a cult rather than a code, Redemption will take place through some religious event or experience in which the faithful are to participate.

In the West, cult is considered generally after the manner of an exchange. Christ offers His humanity in loving obedience to the Father in the event of His sacrificial death to obtain from the Father for sinful mankind forgiveness of sins and eternal life. The faithful participate objectively in this exchange because Christ performs the work in the name of all mankind.

In the East, cult is a mystical transplantation rather than a sacrificial exchange. Man does not so much achieve something as experience something in cultic action. The Word of God is made flesh, and by living in human history He releases into the world of men a new dynamism that is able to effect a moral reorientation and a mystical transfiguration. As a power of moral reorientation, the Christian dynamism is able to rescue man from the power of evil. As a power of transfiguration, it is able to cure him of his involvement in sin, his weakness and death, and all the other deprivations consequent to the Fall. The faithful participate objectively in this power because it has been made available to the experience of all in the life of the Church. Such divergent conceptions will set a theology of Redemption on different courses.

Summary. Historians of doctrine both Catholic and non-Catholic trace different patterns of thought and divergent lines of progress in the development of the doctrine in tradition. Each author can adduce long lists of impressive names and pages of patristic dicta to support his conclusions.

The monumental work of J. Rivière was an effort to defend a fundamental unity of doctrine in tradition against the works of A. Ritschl, L. A. Sabatier, and A. von Harnack. For the theology of Ritschl, see E. Bertrand, *Une Nouvelle conception de la rédemption* (Paris 1891); for Sabatier, *The Doctrine of the Atonement and Its Historical Evolution,* tr. V. Leuliette (London 1904); for Von Harnack, *History of Dogma,* tr. N. Buchanan et al., 7 v. (New York 1961) 3:310–315; 5:55–60.

These authors underlined the discordance between Scripture and tradition, between the Greek and Latin Fathers, and between primitive Christianity and the Middle Ages. The disunity is certainly not so serious and sharp as Rivière's adversaries contend. But neither is there such an obvious unity as Rivière seemed to propose amid the multiplicity of divergent ideas found in the writings of the Fathers [see G. Oggioni in *Problemi e orientamenti di teologia dommatica* (Milan 1957) 2:312–314, 318].

Rivière ably defended a unity in the tradition of the East and of the West, of the ancient and the modern in exposing a line of doctrinal development that leads to a theory of vicarious moral satisfaction. But he did this at the expense of failing to integrate into a theology of the Redemption other important scriptural themes and significant developments in tradition. In a section entitled ''Definitive Organization in the Catholic Church,'' Rivière wrote, ''Upon the basis of the Anselmian system, with some superficial modifications, the Catholic dogma of the Redemption rapidly took the form which it has today'' (*Dictionnaire de théologie catholique* 13.2:1947). Today most Catholic theologians find that judgment deficient and one-sided. There has been an extensive renewal of biblical studies in the Church and a return of theology to a critical study of the sources of the faith. This renewal and return are exerting a full and fruitful influence in the theology of the Redemption. It is being seen with an ever-greater clarity that a theology of the Redemption that pays exclusive attention to the death of Christ and explains its redemptive value chiefly in terms of a moral satisfaction offered God for the sins of men is an unbalanced and impoverished theology. Besides, it is a theology not altogether faithful to the rich data in Scripture and tradition.

DOCTRINAL CONTEXT

The doctrine of the Redemption is presently in the process of an awakened and rapidly unfolding development. The development is the result of an effort to integrate the modern scholarship in Scripture and the more recent critical studies in the history of doctrine. The development is also in terms of an extension of the field of inquiry as new questions, new methodology, and new contexts are introduced into the investigations. In view of this recent theological unfolding, it is not out of place to examine the doctrinal context of the Redemption.

By ''context'' is meant the galaxy of subjects, issues, and multirelated divine and human facts that are to be related and integrated into a comprehensive theology of the Redemption. By ''doctrinal'' it is implied that what is said of these matters is verifiable in the commonly accepted doctrines of reputable theologians, biblical exegetes, and other scholars.

There are other reasons to examine this doctrinal context. First, the context provides a framework in which to organize the reflections of the more important Fathers of the Church. Second, the context affords a frame of reference in which to situate the systems of the theologians as well as those areas of present doctrinal development.

The Redemption is the mystery of God's redeeming act in and through Christ whereby mankind is delivered from the evil of sin and reunited in grace with God. This general definition implies three fundamental and distinct subjects related in the mystery: first, the redeeming activity of God in and through Christ; second, the evil of sin; third, the reunion in grace. These subjects in their theological implications are the three dimensions, as it were, of the doctrinal context of objective Redemption.

Divine Redeeming Act. The Redemption must be considered as an act accomplished both by God and by Christ. There are two phases, as it were, in the salvific act of God's merciful love.

Redeeming Act of God through Christ. The origin of the Redemption is the absolutely free love and MERCY OF GOD, who wills to incarnate His Son and send Him into the world and into human history to deliver mankind from the evil of sin and to reunite man with Himself. This statement indicates that the initiative in the redeeming act is with God. The motive is God's free love and mercy offering for man's Redemption, nothing less than the gift of Himself. The means by which the redeeming act is accomplished is the Word made flesh in His human life. The purpose is to deliver man from the evil of sin in order to unite man with God. God's act is a deliverance *from* something and *into* something. It is a deliverance-acquisition. God enables Christ as man to undertake and accomplish the work of deliverance and reunion by inspiring Christ with that love and obedience whereby the Word Incarnate freely performs in His life and in His humanity that work of liberation and ATONEMENT.

This affirmation declares that the divine redeeming activity is essentially performed by means of the human acts of the Word Incarnate motivated by love and obedience. As human acts performed in His humanity, these acts operate in the physical order. As inspired by love and obedience, these acts are operative in the moral order. Consequently, there are two parallel effectivities able to be considered in Christ's acts: a physical effectivity and a moral effectivity. As physical, Christ's acts are related to the effects that the very acts themselves produce as a result of their own operative efficiency. As moral, Christ's acts obtain a moral right that God acts to produce some effect. God raises Christ from the dead in order that the crucified and risen Lord might be able to communicate to mankind His grace of deliverance and reunion. This proposition proposes that the act of God resurrecting Christ is an essential part of the activity of God redeeming, so that the sufferings and death of Christ are not to be considered as redemptive independently of the Resurrection. It implies besides that it is by means of the Death-Resurrection event, two aspects of one mystery, that Christ, ''who was delivered up for our sins, and rose again for our justification'' (Rom 4.25), becomes for mankind ''God-given wisdom, and justice, and sanctification, and redemption'' (1 Cor 1.30).

Redeeming Act of Christ. Although the divine redeeming activity has its first and eternal origin in the love of the Blessed Trinity for sinful man (Eph 2.4), in a second moment and in ''the fullness of time God sent his Son . . . that he might redeem . . . that we might receive the adoption of sons'' (Gal 4.4–5). Christ is the mediator of God's redeeming activity, becoming Himself for mankind the cause of their deliverance from sin and the cause of their reunion with God in grace.

The Incarnate Word exercises this function of mediating the redemptive act of God in four ways: first, in the fact of His becoming man; second, in the mediation of His life as messiah-king, as prophet-teacher, and as high priest; third, in the mediation of His death as victor, as redeemer, as priest-victim; fourth, in the mediation of His Resurrection as savior and as intercessor.

In the very fact of the Word of God's becoming man there is an assumption by the Word not only of a human nature but also of a redemptive history. The INCARNATION is an actual and decisive event, an intervention in the current of human history. It is an event capable in itself of interrupting the processes of human history and of setting history on the course of a new direction.

The redeeming activity of God is mediated by Christ as messiah-king. Christ establishes the KINGDOM OF GOD and the new covenant by making disciples and winning their faith, love, and loyalty. In making disciples and in giving them the new law, Christ establishes the lines of that community in which deliverance from the evil of sin and reunion with God might take place and, when realized in the members, might be lived in freedom.

As prophet-teacher, Christ instructs mankind in the way of God's salvific will, in the way of response to God. Christ points out the way of life and the way of death; what is true and what is a lie. Christ becomes for mankind the way, the truth, and the life in order that men might know how they are to be delivered from evil and from what evil they are to be liberated; how to be reunited with God and what the realities and terms of that union are.

As high priest, Christ establishes the new priesthood and the new cult so that by means of the acts of cult, mankind might be enabled and inspired to hate the evil of sin and love the goodness of God.

The redeeming activity is mediated by Christ in His death as victor, as redeemer, and as priest-victim. This area of the doctrinal context bears the burden of the traditional theology of the Redemption. At this point should be set out, along general lines, the doctrine that, as variously interpreted by the theologians, is used to support their doctrinal theories.

Christ is considered as victor in His death from two points of view. In the first place, Christ is seen as victorious over the powers of evil itself. For although the death of Christ was plotted by Jews, pronounced by Pilate, and executed by Roman legionnaires, behind these men were the forces of evil itself. Our Lord Himself speaks not simply of His human assassins but of the ''prince of this world'' (Jn 14.30) and the ''power of darkness'' (Lk 22.53). Under this attack of His enemies and even in the agony of His sufferings, Christ is victorious in His supreme resolution lovingly and obediently to do as the Father commanded (Jn 14.31). Christ dies but to rise on the third day.

Second, Christ is victor in His death because by the power of His obedient charity He is able to vanquish the objections and the revulsions of His human nature in the terrors of the CRUCIFIXION. It is in the real and historical circumstances of His death that Christ finds the opportunity for the full expression of His loving obedience (cf. Jn 15.13). It is in the actual circumstances of His sufferings that Christ's human nature becomes fully actuated by the mighty power of His grace. As redeemer, Christ, in accepting His death out of love and obedience, accomplishes in behalf of mankind that work by means of which man is delivered from his complicity in and his liability to and his oppression by sin and death. As priest-victim, Christ offers Himself in the bloody sacrifice of the cross, thereby reconciling sinful mankind to God.

How Christ as victor, redeemer, and priest-victim mediates the deliverance of man from sin and reunites him with God will be taken up shortly. How the victory affects man, how the work of deliverance is accomplished, and how the sacrifice is a reconciliation—all these questions are answered variously in the theological systems.

The redeeming activity is mediated, finally, by Christ as savior and intercessor. It is the grace of the crucified and risen Savior, the grace formed in Him by the death-Resurrection event, which is to be communicated to the faithful. This grace when shared will make those ''in Christ'' die to the flesh and be transformed to live to Christ in the grace of His Resurrection and in the grace of the Spirit. Moreover, Redemption is mediated by the risen Christ insofar as it is the risen Christ in the grace of His Resurrection who is the efficient cause of man's justification (cf. Rom 4.25; 6.1–11; 8.23; St. Thomas, *Summa theologiae* 3a, 56.1–2).

Summary. The redemptive act is performed by God in and through Christ. The act of redeeming has its origin in God, who loves man and wills to be merciful to him. This act of God is mediated by means of the activity of the Incarnation. The redeeming activity of the Word made flesh is manifold and mediated by His very assumption of human nature, by the redemptive roles He exercised in His life, death and Resurrection and Ascension to the Father. It is this totality that accomplishes once and for all the work that is able to deliver man from the evil of sin and to reunite him in grace with God.

Evil of sin. The second dimension of the doctrinal context is the subject the evil of sin. A theology of Redemption must explain how the salvific activity of God mediated through Christ is directed to the deliverance of man from sin in all the actual or possible aspects of evil in sin (*see* SIN).

As introduction, it is to be remarked that sin is taken here in a biblical conception that names as sin anything defecting from what God wills to be realized in man. This conception of sin is altogether objective. It prescinds from the subject's attitude toward, or even knowledge of, the fact of this defect. It is assumed, however, that such an objective defect from God's will enters the world of man by a deliberate abuse of intellect and will. Sin is introduced by man's knowing and willing refusal to acknowledge God and by his failure to choose the good that God wills for him. It is this conscious and deliberate refusal and failure that introduces the evil of sin into man's history, into his society, into his person, and consequently into his activity toward his destiny. The evil of sin, therefore, has four main aspects: evil in relation to man's destiny; evil in relation to his person; evil in relation to his society; evil in relation to his history.

In Relation to Man's Destiny. The evil of sin is related to man's destiny as a condition of fallen nature. This condition is caused by man's alienating himself from God in the act of his free choice. This act of free choice is an act of alienation when man, in his freedom, refuses to love and obey God. This act of alienation causes a state of alienation that implies, first, a loss of the supernatural gifts of GRACE; second, a withdrawal of his life from God as his final destiny; third, a choice of what he determines for himself to be his destiny.

From a moral point of view, man's act of alienating himself from God can be understood as an act dishonoring God, or as an act violating God's just will, or as an act injuring God's supreme majesty, or as an act offending God's infinite goodness. The state of man's alienation may be considered as a debt, since man is in default of payment to God of what is His due, or as a fault, inasmuch as man's refusal of love and obedience is a rupture of the right order between God and man.

It should be noticed that when the evil of sin is described either as the human act and state of alienation or as dishonor, offense, debt, and fault the identical reality is being described. These are two viewpoints on the same thing. God's honor is verified in man's free love and obedience. Man pays his debt to God in retaining his gifts of grace. Man will never default if he seeks God above all things. The act of alienation and its consequent state describe a physical condition of man theologically considered. Dishonor, offense, debt, and fault describe those same realities in a transposition of understanding into the moral order.

In Relation to Man's Person. The evil of sin in relation to man's person is, in the first place, damaging. The immediate result of man's alienation from God is his loss of the gifts of grace. Implied in his act of refusal to love God is a withdrawal of his life from God as his final destiny. In this act of withdrawal there is contained a choice of self. This act of choice in which a man determines for himself what will be good for him introduces within his person a condition of disintegration and disability so that his very nature as man is in a damaged condition.

There is a disintegration, an ''infirmity,'' in what man is, because, having rejected what God wills for him, man is without that principle that must integrate both the various powers of activity within himself and his activity in relation to his fellow men. God's will determines man's nature to be what it is (cf. *Summa theologiae* 1a, 19.4). It is man's correspondence with that divine will that alone is the principle of social and personal integration. Without this principle, men are left to the devices of their own wills and to the autonomous desires of their own persons. Man is led in life by what St. Paul would call the spirit of the flesh (cf. Rom 7.13–25; 8.5–13). Governed solely by his own will, man is in bondage to sin. He comes to fear himself and his fellow men (cf. Rom 8.15; 7.13–25). The refusal to obey God's will is a refusal of freedom. ''Everyone who commits sin is a slave of sin'' (Jn 8.34; cf. Rom 6.15–23). The damaged condition of man becomes a disability, a ''weakness,'' besides. Once a man has lost the gifts of grace, he is unable to accomplish what God wills him to achieve. As alienated from God's will, man has cut himself off from the sources of ''life'' that God grants to those united with Him. Man is left only with the resources of his nature now disintegrated. In Pauline terms, he is reduced to the existence of the ''flesh'' and his life becomes ''death'' (cf. Rom 7.13–25; 8.2).

Living without grace and in alienation from God, man has a disabled life. It is unproductive from God's point of view, a succession of nothing to be terminated by physical death without the hope of eternal life. Physical death ratifies and makes final what has been taking place continually: a dying in man's person from the disintegration and the disability. The result of this damage is the fact that a man is without the powers to produce what the very nature of man requires for its own well-being: ordered, purposeful activity that is good for the whole man and for the common good of society. Sin disintegrates and disables man and through him sin disorders society.

In Relation to Society. A society established by men inspired by the ''lust of the flesh, and the lust of the eyes, and the pride of life'' (1 Jn 2.16) becomes a fallen society. Like the sinful men who compose it, society incorporates within itself the alienation from God and damaged condition of men. Society is alienated from God as it seeks its own self-assigned destiny. Society becomes disintegrated as groups within society are at counterpurposes. The social body becomes disabled in its efforts, by reason of its lack of unity in the quest for the common good. In Johannine terms, this society is the ''world'' that is ''not from the Father'' (1 Jn 2.16), that hates Christ (cf. Jn 15.18), that does not know the Word of God (cf. Jn 1.10).

It is such a society, perverted by its sinful members, that in its turn becomes a force of evil to pervert its members. In the dynamism of social influence, man is induced into sinful ways of living as his social milieu endorses his sin and provides him opportunity for the expression of his sinful person. Furthermore, fallen society enforces its mores on its members as it rewards those who adopt its standards and goals. The world loves what is its own (cf. Jn 15.19). ''They are of the world; therefore of the world they speak and the world listens to them'' (1 Jn 4.5).

Besides inducing its sinful members further into their personal sin, society also seduces its members into sin by engendering its ways of sin, conforming them to this world (Rom 12.2) so that they walk ''according to the fashion of this world'' (Eph 2.2). This seduction is imperceptible. It happens unconsciously, and without a man's being aware of it he defects from the good God wills for him. Seduced, he becomes like a sheep gone astray (1 Pt 2.25). This seduction also happens previous to the time when a man is competent to exercise his personal freedom. Personal sin mediates sin to society. Social sin and personal sin, as it has a social aspect, mediate sin into history.

In Relation to History. The evil of sin in relation to history is a kind of deviation. This deviation takes place in two historical frames of reference: first, in the history of the race as a whole and, second, in the history of the individual. By history is meant this plain fact: the condition of man and his activity at one point of time in his existence affects his condition and his activity at succeeding points along the line of time.

There is an interlocking of the *before* and the *after* in man's historic existence. This interlocking is a process in which the *before* affects the *after* in terms of continuity, causality, immanence, and transcendence. There is in the process the effect of continuity, for the *after* is always, at least in something, contained in the same order of things as the *before*. What is before is the matrix of what comes after. There is the effect of causality because there is a correlation between the existence of the *before* and the existence of the *after*. What is before is the condition of possibility for what comes after. There is the effect of immanence insofar as there is some presence of the *before* in the *after*. What is before is a determinant of what comes after. Finally, there is the effect of transcendence inasmuch as the *after* is able, in something, to go beyond the *before* by means of the unique contribution of the *present*, the *now*.

First, in the actual history of the race, the sin of Adam at the beginning of history causes Adam's condition to be that of fallen man, alienated, damaged in his disintegration and disability. This condition is the beginning of a process in which the *before* affects the *after* and in which the *after* is able to transcend the *before*.

The first man passes on to those after him a condition like his own. Men are born alienated from God, damaged in view of God's will that man be elevated to grace. Man becomes disintegrated as soon as the choice of self, proceeding from his person deprived of grace and of nature's integrity, becomes actual. This process is repeated as generation follows generation. The process is also transposed to the social order as the social lines of a sinful society at any given point of time are affected by the social dimensions of a previous society in terms of continuity, causality, immanence. The process compounds itself through the effect of transcendence as both men and society make their unique contributions to the alienation and damage of sin. The result is a perpetuation of evil, a process of continual, ever-widening deviation from the will of God.

Second, when the evil of sin is considered in relation to the history of the individual, certain considerations must be introduced. In the context of concrete existence, the human individual may be considered a ''person'' insofar as he freely disposes of himself by personal decision and possesses his own reality in the act of making a free decision about himself. In this same method of considering man, the individual is also a ''nature,'' that is, all in him that is given and is prior to this personal and free disposal of himself.

Nature is the object-given, the passivity, the reception, the spontaneous in man. Nature is the condition of his possibility. Person is the subject-positing, the activity-determining, the man in his freedom to determine himself as a whole in relation to what is good.

The terms ''person'' and ''nature'' with this meaning must be distinguished from these same terms as they have been traditionally used in scholastic theology. The use of the terms here is in the context of the modern metaphysics of existence. Some such terms are necessary because there is a need to distinguish between that in man which is given, which is structured and dynamic within him but without his freely disposing himself as such, and that in man which is such as it is by reason of his free disposition of himself. This is the distinction that common sense sees partially in the division between ''what I am'' and ''what I want to be and try to be.''

In the personal history of man and in the context of this dualism, nature is prior to person. Nature is acted upon and has its specific activity before a person acts to posit that which the subject freely wishes to be. This dynamism of nature is the necessary presupposition of the conscious, free decision of the person. And although the free decision of person should comprehend and transform the prior and spontaneous act of nature, the act of nature and the determinations already set up in nature come to affect the act of person.

It happens that before person in man is sufficiently awakened and before he is able to dispose of himself as a whole toward what is good simply, and before the inner core of the subject-person is able to posit what he will be and modify what he actually is, nature has already been determined in a deviation toward sin. Nature has already been determined as born alienated from God, damaged in view of God's will concerning the ELEVATION OF MAN to grace. Nature is potentially disintegrated and disabled because, lacking a positive conversion to God, the man is potentially converted to self.

The potential conversion to self becomes actual from three agencies. (1) The spontaneous dynamisms of ''nature'' tend to the particular good, not to good simply but to what is good in the here and now for the subject. Such tendencies induce the subject into acts of choice toward particular goods. And such a choice becomes equivalent to a choice of self, given the lack of a ''personal'' conversion to good simply. These acts lay down habituations and sets of determinations that are dynamic elements within the subject when the person is first called upon to make the free decision of person. Consequently, antecedent to the subject's determination of himself by personal decision, dynamic orientations are already there within the subject's nature toward specific self-related values. In the dynamism of these determinations, freedom of personal choice is jeopardized because the determinations of nature tend to specify the act of person in terms of a continuity with nature, a causality from nature and in an immanence of nature. Person penetrates nature with difficulty. Nature must be reformed and person fortified in its own dynamism before free decision succeeds completely in making its way without being deviated by nature. (2) Personal choice is further deviated by the influence on the subject by other sinful persons. (3) Personal determination is deviated by the influence exerted by sinful society. Until a person is able to take up a stand, command and comprehend its freedom, the human subject is related to others and to his society in a relationship of profound dependency. In this dependency nature is open and a person is susceptible to whatever modifications the external personal and social environment introduces. In the concrete circumstances of his human history, a man's personal freedom is jeopardized so that he is not able to overcome what he is by nature through the free decision of person.

Summary and Conclusions. It is in man and in man's world where sin is situated as something real and concrete. Sin in its reality is fundamentally something (or, to put it more accurately, something *missing*) in man. But given the facticity of sin in man, one can go on and consider the evil of sin in other categories of intelligibility.

From a moral point of view, the evil of sin is transposed in understanding and is seen as a rupture of the interpersonal relations between God and man. One goes on to speak of how God regards sinful man and how man dares to regard God. One speaks of the rights of the person offended, of the obligation and the manner of making a suitable satisfaction for the offense. The categories of explanation of sin and deliverance from it are contained within the field of amicable, interpersonal relationship.

From a juridical point of view, the evil of sin is transposed into the order of law. Sin is seen as a violation of law incurring the penalties that justice decrees as corrective or vindictive punishments. One speaks of the expiation of crimes, of penalties undergone to avoid the retributive punishments determined by law. The categories of explanation of sin and of man's deliverance from sin are retained within the context of jurisprudence.

These transpositions in the understanding of sin are an enrichment of the conceptions of the fact of sin. The mystery of sin is related to familiar analogies in human affairs. But these conceptions tend to become an impoverishment and, possibly, a distortion of the fact. Sin is a rupture of the relations between God and man. Sin is a violation of law. Nevertheless, the reach and applications of these conceptions fall short of comprehending the totality of aspects in the reality of man's sin. It is never theologically safe to discuss the WILL OF GOD and His law without looking at the reality and seeing it steadily. God's law is God's will. God's actual will is the cause of the reality of things such as they are.

It is necessary to understand sin not only in the moral and juridical orders but primarily in the physical order of man's actual condition. In this physical order, sin is something done to man. Sin is also something happening to man. If the Redemption is to be the deliverance from this evil, then Redemption must be both something done (completed) and something happening (continued) to deliver him from all the aspects of reality in sin.

Reunion in grace. Like the subject of sin, the reunion in grace has several aspects insofar as the realities of this reunion are transposed into various frames of understanding. The reunion in grace may be considered in relation to the physical order, the moral order, the juridical order.

In the Physical Order. The reunion in grace has the aspect of identity with the deliverance from sin when this reunion is considered in the physical order. As God has determined things, there is no deliverance from sin without a reunion in grace (cf. *Summa theologiae* 1a2ae, 113.2). If sin be an alienation, mankind is delivered from this evil by the gift that will convert him to God and sustain that conversion. If sin be a damage, man is delivered by the gift that restores the integrity and the ability of his nature. If sin be a social perversion, society is delivered by the gift that reforms the lines of perverted society. If sin be a historical deviation, history is delivered by the gift that reorients the processes of human history.

In this frame of reference, theology must explain how the redeeming activity of Christ is related to the grace of conversion for mankind, the grace of personal restoration, the grace of social reform, and the grace of historical reorientation.

In the Moral Order. Sin is conceived, in the moral order, as an offense against God. Offense is given when several wills regard the same object and there is contrariety of choice and conflict of act between those wills. One person wills and acts contrary to the will and act of another person. This other person is offended if he has equal or superior rights over the subject. God wills that man love and obey Him. In sinning, man refuses this love and obedience. God is offended by this will and act of man for God has absolute rights over man. Man has the obligation to reverence his Creator.

To be reunited to God, man must willingly and with love do that which God loves more than He hates the offense. In this moral frame of reference, theology explains how the work of Christ is something God can love more than He hates the sin of mankind, so that by reason of this compensating work of Christ, satisfaction is made for the offense and grace is given man by God.

Another consideration in the moral order understands sin as a fault or a debt. As a fault, sin is a defection destroying the right order that must obtain between God and man. From this aspect, theology shows how the work of Christ accomplishes a mutual reconciliation through the act of propitiation. As a debt, sin is the refusal of man to offer what he owes to his Creator. From a basis in this understanding, theology proposes how the work of Christ offers a payment or ransom so that man, redeemed from his debt and solvent through Christ's work, may avail himself freely of God's grace for a life of love and obedience.

In the Juridical Order. Sin is understood in the juridical order as a violation of the just law of God that demands that the sinner be punished according to his crimes. From this conception, theology will describe how the work of Christ is an EXPIATION for the penalty due to sins so that, God's justice being satisfied, He may freely and lovingly give the grace of pardon to man.

It will be noticed that when the understanding of sin is transposed into the moral and juridical orders, the redeeming activity appears as a work that Christ as man offers to God on behalf of man. The effectivity of Christ's work has a term in (or at least a direction toward) God. Man comes to God in the Redemption achieved by Christ. However, when sin is seen in the physical order, the redeeming activity is a work done by God in Christ and offered to man. Both the term and the direction of the effectivity are immediately related to man. God comes to man in the Redemption performed by Christ.

These two conceptions of the Redemption point up a significant fact. In the moral order, it is man who must reunite himself to God, for God never ceases to love man. In the physical order, it is God who must reunite Himself to man, because, once man loses this supernatural union with God, there is nothing man can do to regain this union.

THEOLOGICAL REFLECTION ON INCARNATION ITSELF

In this section and the corresponding one that follows, the more important theories will be situated within the doctrinal context. The first dimension of the context, namely, the divine redeeming activity in and through Christ, will provide the points of departure in this discussion.

Considered first will be the theories based on the Incarnation itself as redemptive. According to such theories, the Incarnation is like a new act of creation; or better, a new moment in the creational act of God when God purposes to create all things anew in Christ. This doctrine is a theme in the writings of St. John and St. Paul. In it the very coming of Christ and His life as a totality are understood as redemptive.

Mystical explanation. St. Irenaeus founds his redemptive theory of RECAPITULATION in Christ on this scriptural basis. His insight was to conceive an identity of pattern and a parallelism of action between the course of man's history, beginning with creation and Adam's sin, and Christ's salvific life. Irenaeus traces a pattern of identity and a parallelism of contrasts in these two courses of history with a remarkable ingenuity. For Irenaeus, Christ recapitulates humanity. Christ is a compendium of human history by summarizing in His life the course of human history as willed by God and by reiterating in His life the human processes, being victorious where man fell in defeat. The conception most notable in Irenaeus is the understanding that Christ comes and shares all the experiences of humanity, sin only excepted. Living our life in the circumstances of our history, Christ conquers the forces of evil at work in the world and thereby reverses the processes of human history. Instead of man's history leading him to sin and death, by the work of Christ, those men who are united with Him are brought to divinization and immortality.

Realistic explanation. Modern theology returns to this idea left in tradition by St. Irenaeus and echoed by Tertullian and St. Methodius. In becoming man, Christ entered the world formed by the history of apartness from God. This alienation causes ''sin and death'' (in the Pauline eschatological sense of definitive separation from God). Although Christ could not be touched by the moral guilt of sin, He took upon Himself the historic conditions of our sinful existence. He came ''in the likeness of sinful flesh'' (Rom 8.3) and ''did not consider being equal to God a thing to be clung to, but emptied himself, taking the nature of a slave and being made like unto men'' (Phil 2.7). He became ''one tried as we are in all things except sin'' (Heb 4.15) and even ''learned obedience from the things that he suffered'' (Heb 5.8).

In His Incarnation, Christ as man chose a self-emptying, a condition in which the fullness of His grace was not able to have its full effects. It was the very life history of the Incarnation in the actual unfolding of His life that provided, under God's providence, those opportunities permitting the full expression of His grace and those conditions allowing the Spirit of God to penetrate fully and to possess entirely His created nature. In this abasement, Christ accepted a historic solidarity with the sinful human race (*see* KENOSIS).

F. X. Durrwell writes that ''the redemption of human nature is a drama unfolding first of all in Christ. It takes place in him as a sanctifying transformation from the state of sinful flesh to the holiness of divine life which is its direct opposite'' (*The Resurrection* 58). This act of God transforming the humanity of Christ in the circumstances of His lifetime from the state of sinful flesh to full participation in the divine life is the redemptive act mediated by Christ to sinful man for the reorientation of his history. The redeeming act of God is not a single, static act. It is a continual irruption into history: into Christ's history first, and then through Him into the history of mankind. The Redemption begins from the first moment of the Incarnation and spans the lifetime of Christ, so that the life of Christ as a unit has the aspect of efficiency in relation to the deliverance from the evil of sin and to the return in grace in their historical dimensions.

Moralistic explanation. Another theological viewpoint that conceives the Incarnation in its totality as the cause of man's Redemption is the so-called moralistic, or exemplarist, theory. This theory considers the life of Christ as the supreme example of how man is to encounter the circumstances of his life and how God is prepared to act to deliver man from sin and to unite man to Himself. In this conception, Redemption is accomplished primarily by God's grace and only secondarily through the revelation, example, and inspiration in the life of Christ. The life of Christ is a work performed by God in humanity to be seen and considered by man and thereby to become the occasion for faith in God's redemptive act. Christ's life is a living lesson of faith and a lesson for living the free gift of faith offered men by God.

The theory stated in such general terms has a scriptural basis and is represented in the writings of the Fathers, particularly: Ignatius, Clement of Alexandria, the apologists in general, Origen, and Augustine. The theory is valid because the example and teaching of Christ are redemptive insofar as there is presented objectively for all mankind the revelation of God's redemptive will and that source of inspiration to motivate men to respond to God's saving grace.

No Catholic theologian will question the fidelity of this theory to Scripture and tradition until it is pressed to the conclusion that the life of Christ has the value only of an example, that the efficacy of His life is exclusively that of revelation and inspiration. Abelard seems to have held this conclusion, and later the Socinians. More recently, it has become the preferred theory of many liberal Protestant theologians, who follow the current of 19th-century rationalism or the existentialist interpretations of Christianity fostered by R. Bultmann [see J. Rivière, *The Doctrine of the Atonement* 1:18–33; L. Malevez, SJ, *The Christian Message and Myth,* tr. O. Wyon (Westminster, Md. 1958) 67–117].

Christ messiah-king and high priest. Although no redemptive theory has been elaborated on the specific doctrine of Christ messiah-king and high priest, modern theology would insist upon integrating into the theology of the Redemption Christ's life activity of making disciples and establishing the foundations of that community of life and cult wherein the deliverance from the evil of sin might take place and the reunion, once begun, might be fostered and sustained. It is Christianity as the community formed by Christ that becomes redemptive of society's perversion. The Christian community by means of the dynamism of social influence counters and corrects the seducing influence of the ''world.'' This is an area of present doctrinal development.

THEOLOGICAL REFLECTION ON VICTOR, REDEEMER, VICTIM

The redeeming activity of God is mediated by Christ in His death as victor, as redeemer, and as victim. This doctrinal statement embraces five of the seven scriptural themes on Redemption. It is, besides, a doctrinal summary of the greater part of the official teaching of the Church. As well, it is a compendium of the central body of doctrine presented by the Fathers and the theologians and is a foundation for several theories of the Redemption. Only the barest outline of these systems is offered here.

Christ as victor. Christ's victory over the devil, ''sin and death,'' is a theme from Scripture, and from the earliest times there was a tradition of developing a theory of the Redemption around this favorite theme or idea. The theme began to be developed as early as St. Ignatius, and it was carried in the current of tradition both in the East and in the West until the time of St. Thomas Aquinas.

Devil's Rights. The theory of the devil's rights, as it has been called, has almost as many variations as there are writers handling it. But fundamental to the doctrine is the representation (this is a product of image-thinking) of a contest between Christ and the devil, who holds man in the bondage of ''sin and death.'' In the theory, sin and death are personifications of the dynamic forces of evil within man's life and the allies of the devil. Christ conquers sin because the devil cannot tempt Christ from His resolution to obey even in the terrors of the Crucifixion. Christ conquers death in His rising from the dead in divine power. As a result of Christ's victory, the devil is a vanquished foe of man. God delivers all those united to Christ the Victor from the power of the evil one.

When the theory of the devil's rights is understood in sympathy with image-thinking, the theory appears to be an effort to explain how the work of Christ delivers man from that evil of sin that is nonpersonal and beyond the evil present only in the disordered and deliberate will of the individual. Such a nonpersonal and transcendent evil is the evil of sin in its social and historical aspects.

Person vs. Nature. A new development in theology would see the victory of Christ in another way. In the actual assumption of the human nature by the Word, Christ's human nature is in the condition of ''sinful flesh.'' This condition allows that, although Christ is personally sinless and although His humanity is endowed with a fullness of grace, He will suffer unto death in His humanity in performing the will of God. This suffering is significant. The very fact that Christ is able to suffer is evidence of the fact that nature in Christ is able to have its own determinations, its own ''will'' as St. Thomas calls it (cf. *Summa theologiae* 3a, 18.3–4). St. Thomas also quotes St. John Damascene to the effect that ''the divinity of Christ permitted His humanity to do and to be done to in whatever manner is proper to human nature'' (*ibid.* 3a, 46.8).

Therefore in the terrors of the Crucifixion (and even in the less difficult situations of Christ's life) nature in Christ is able to protest. Pain and sorrow are the signs of nature's objections, of the protest that nature does not want that which both external causes and personal decision force upon it. The Crucifixion was the external condition that nature in Christ violently refused, as is apparent in the agony in the garden (Lk 22.39–45). But the mighty act of free decision of Person in Christ, fortified by divine love and obedience, conquers the act of nature in Christ's obedient choice of His death. This act of free decision in Christ has as its first effect a disposition of nature itself. Nature is penetrated by Person, and Person succeeds in having its way. ''By sending his Son in the likeness of sinful flesh [that is, with a nature able to object and protest to what is concretely to be performed to fulfill God's will] he has condemned [conquered] sin in the flesh'' (Rom 8.3).

Christ as Redeemer. In the present context, redeeming means specifically the act of delivering from sin. There are three general theories explaining the deliverance of mankind from sin by the death of Christ the Redeemer.

Substitutional Penal Expiation. The evil of sin may be conceived primarily in the juridical order, as a violation of the divine law that decrees rewards for virtue and punishment for vice. Analogies from jurisprudence are employed to illustrate this theory. Redemption is accomplished according to this system by the objective fulfillment of divine laws eternally enacted. Divine law decrees that for sins committed there must be punishment equal to the crime. If the sinner does not repent, the punishment is inflicted upon him. Should he repent, he must voluntarily accept punishment to make up for his evil act. As voluntarily accepted, the punishment becomes satisfaction rather than vindictive punishment.

In the case of man's sin, adequate satisfaction is impossible. Deprived of grace, man is forever unable to love God as he ought. Besides, as the crime of a creature against his Creator, man's sin takes on an infinite magnitude. Since God cannot forgive sins according to His justice until an equitable satisfaction is made, man is hopelessly in his sin and under the threat of punishment. Yet because God loves man, even when he is a sinner (Rom 5.9), God decrees in mercy to send His Son, who in His sufferings and death offers the satisfaction that divine justice demands. Christ, as divine and sinless, offers an infinite satisfaction. Christ, as man, takes our place and suffers the punishment divine justice imposes for the sins of mankind.

Such an explanation can be sustained by plausible interpretations of Scripture. It has been proposed in the writings of many Fathers, theologians, and especially orators. The theory was accepted in great part by the reformers, who recast it somewhat in view of their principle of imputed justice. For the leaders of the Reformation, the sins of all mankind are gathered and burdened on Christ. Christ suffers the condemnation and the punishment once and for all so that man might be free of it. Freed from the judgment on sin, men are imputed just by reason of the death of Christ, which cancels the sentence of condemnation and punishment (*see* IMPUTATION OF JUSTICE AND MERIT).

At its best, this system of penal substitution proposes to the faithful the doctrine of the inexorability of punishment for sin and the necessity of satisfaction. It presents the cross of Christ as the great manifestation of the evil of sin. But when it affirms that Christ assumed the punishment so that man would not have to suffer it, or that Christ offered satisfaction so that men need not make it, the theory is theologically unsound. When it affirms that God delivered Christ to His cross to manifest to the world not only the evil of sin but also how severely sin is punished, this is nothing less than terrorism.

If sin is inexorably punished (and it is), this is because the sinner himself passes a sentence of suffering upon himself and his world in his very sin, which damages himself and contributes to the perversion of his society and to the deviation of history. God need do nothing but let the laws of man work themselves out. If satisfaction is necessary, it is because even after repentance a man must positively do something to compensate for the evil done in his nature by the act of sin, to his society, and to human history. If the cross of Christ is a manifestation of the evil of sin, this is because it was evil men who hated the Person who would save them from themselves.

But the theory has an insight. It can be said that Christ takes away the punishment due to sin and makes satisfaction in man's place because, by reason of Christ's work, man will not have to suffer the kind of punishment from sin that would have been man's fate if Christ had not come to bring grace and truth to the world. It can be said that Christ makes satisfaction for sin in man's place because, by reason of the grace of Christ for man's person, his society, and his history, man is not required to compensate for the evil perpetrated by his sin in the manner that would have been necessary (indeed, impossible) had not Christ come ''to serve and give his life as a ransom for many'' (Mk 10.45).

Vicarious Moral Satisfaction. In this system, the evil of sin is considered in the moral order as an offense of God, destroying the interpersonal relationship between God and man. The theory intends to explain why God loves sinful man and forgives his sins while he is yet a sinner and offers the grace of restoration.

God sends His Son into human nature and inspires in Him an indomitable charity for and obedience to God and a boundless love for mankind. United to mankind by the bonds of flesh and blood and charity, Christ is willed by God to become the head of humanity, so that what Christ does is done for Himself and also in behalf of His members, who are as one mystical person with Him (*Summa theologiae* 3a, 48.2 ad 1). Christ, in our name and on our behalf, offers God His love and obedience in His sufferings and death. It is this offering that God can love more than He hates the offense of mankind.

Christ, as head of humanity, is given grace not only for Himself but also for His members, and His works are referred to Himself and to others as the works of another man are referred simply to himself (*ibid.* 3a, 48.2). Consequently, since God gives as a reward for a man's actions that for which He gave him the power to act (*ibid.* 1a2ae, 114.1), and since God gives grace to Christ for the attainment of salvation, Christ merits glorification for Himself and salvation for all men (*ibid.* 3a, 48.1; 49.6).

Such is St. Thomas's doctrine simply stated and without the many doctrinal implications to be drawn out by the application of other principles in his thought. This theory avoids all the improprieties of the theory of substitutional juridical satisfaction. The doctrine centers on the love and obedience of Christ as the cause of man's deliverance from sin and his reunion in grace. The efficiency of Christ's loving obedience in the delivering of man from sin is by way of moral compensation or satisfaction. The efficiency of Christ's obedient love in reconciling man with God is by way of merit. Satisfaction and merit are considered as operative in the moral order. Christ performs the redemptive work not in our place but rather in our behalf, as united to us in a moral solidarity.

Representative Physical Satisfaction. The third theory would transpose the understanding of Redemption from the moral order to the physical order. This transposition is encouraged by St. Thomas's doctrine of ''capital grace.'' This doctrine affirms that it is the very grace resident in Christ in its physical entity that becomes the source and cause of grace for all men (*ibid.* 3a, 8; *De ver,* 29.4, 5: *Comp. theol.* 214). Or to put the same fact in another way, it is the Sacred Humanity in its physical entity as ''graced'' that is the conjoined instrument of God in the production of grace in all mankind (*Summa theologiae* 3a, 13.2; 19.1; 62.5).

With this doctrine as the premise, this theory affirms that it is the actual event of the Crucifixion that forms the grace in Christ so as to be the source of grace delivering men from the evil of sin. In other words, it is the historic event of Christ's sufferings and death in which the Sacred Humanity becomes in a fullness the instrument of God for the production of that grace which will deliver man from sin.

The act of person in free decision has as its first effect a disposition of the subject himself. Christ's personal act of loving obedience sustained in His sufferings overmasters the act of nature that as nature refuses the cross. The effect of this act within Christ Himself is a victory of transformation of the nature of Christ Himself, so that nature joins with Person in the cry of victory: ''Father, into thy hands I commend my spirit'' (Lk 23.46). ''It is consummated!'' (Jn 19.30). This transformation in Christ is real and pertains to what Christ actually is as man. It is in this transformation that the grace of Christ becomes disposed so as to be the grace for all mankind delivering them from sin. What happened to Christ was physical.

What happened in Christ is also satisfactory in the sense that the redemptive power of Christ and His grace more than offset the power of evil in mankind. ''Where the offense has abounded, grace has abounded yet more'' (Rom 5.20). God can love what Christ does in loving obedience more than He hates the evil of man's sins because Christ's loving obedience when communicated to mankind actually effects more good in the world than sin causes evil.

What happened in Christ is, furthermore, meritorious, for the transformation in the Sacred Humanity is that very effect which God gave Christ the power to accomplish. Merit is not only a right to a reward for an act performed; merit is also the accomplishment and the possession of the actual effects of one's acts.

Finally, Christ in this transformation is representative rather than vicarious or substitutional. The transformation itself is representative in the order of signs, for what happened in Christ manifests what must happen in man in order that he be delivered from sin, namely, a death to the flesh when person, fortified by grace, resists to death the sinful ways of nature. Christ Himself is representative in the order of physical reality, for Christ, in solidarity with human history, is the event that reorients history's deviation; in solidarity with human society, He is that social Person who is able to reshape the form of social living; in solidarity with men, He is that Person who is able to convert man's person and restore his nature.

Christ as priest-victim. Sacred revelation presents the death of Christ in the context of sacrifice. Christ mediates the redemptive activity of God as priest-victim. Scripture reveals simply the fact that the death of Christ is a sacrifice of reconciliation of man to God. The Sacred Text does not reveal precisely how the death of Christ is to be understood as sacrificial. Neither has the Church designated any precise sacrificial theory in which the faithful are to understand this sacrifice.

When theologians attempt to explain the death of Christ in the context of sacrifice, there are two doctrinal controls that guide their explanations. First, the sacrifice of Christ must be explained in some continuity with the ritual of sacrifice in the Old Law, the figure of things to come. Second, the sacrifice of the cross must be explained in a coherence with the doctrine of Christ's death as redemptive in delivering from sin.

Sacrifice of Expiation. If the theory of the redemptive death is cast in the juridical order, the death of Christ will be understood as a sacrifice of expiation. Theologians who hold this theory see Christ's death in an analogy with the expiatory sacrifices of the Old Law in which (so these writers consider) an animal was symbolically loaded with the sins of the people and then ritually slain. The animal is substituted for sinful man, and man, seeing the death of the animal, may understand what his sins deserve and how severe are God's punishments. By means of this sacrifice, God's anger is appeased and His wrath averted.

The theory has had many adherents among both Catholics and Protestants, especially among the reformers themselves. But biblical research has questioned, indeed attacked, this understanding of the death of Christ in terms of such an expiatory sacrifice. It is affirmed in this theory that the sins of mankind are imputed to Christ. God permits, even wills, that Christ be slain both to appease His anger and to manifest to the world the evil of sin and the fact that God will not forgive without satisfaction being made either by the innocent or by the guilty. It does not matter. This is nothing short of amorality, even immorality. In such an understanding of the Redemption, God does not keep His own command to man to forgive without demanding satisfaction (Mt 5.38–48).

Sacrifice of Propitiation. If the redeeming death is understood in the moral order, then the sacrifice of the cross is conceived of as a sacrifice of propitiation or reconciliation. In the OT sacrifices, so this doctrine explains it, there was: a victim (something suitably representing man), an offering (to represent man's gift of himself to God), the act of immolation (some sacred action done to the victim to express man's irrevocable dedication of himself to God), an official priest to offer the sacrifice in the name of the community that participates in the victim offered.

St. Thomas fits these essential sacrificial lines over the offering of Christ on the cross. Christ is a suitable victim representing man, as having His humanity to offer and being the head of humanity. There is an offering in Christ's willingly going to His death. There is an act of immolation in His fatal Crucifixion. Christ Himself is the priest offering what is most acceptable to God. The faithful are able to participate in the victim through Christ's gift of the Eucharist (*Summa theologiae* 3a, 48.3).

Recent Thought. A more recent trend in Catholic thought finds something more involved in Christ's sacrifice. After investigating the idea of sacrifice in the OT, many theologians are recasting the conception of the immolative act, and in this recasting the significance of sacrifice is somewhat modified. Sacrifice is a ritualistic expression of man's dedication to God. It is, besides, an effort to attain an actual union with the divinity. Man offers himself in sacrifice, and God is understood as actually accepting man by giving him a participation in the divinity in and through the sacrifice itself.

In the moral order the purpose of sacrifice is conceived of as man's effort to please God. In the physical order the purpose of sacrifice is to effect in man what is pleasing to God, to produce in man what is in itself the reconciliation with God.

Transposing the understanding of sacrifice into the physical order, the act of immolation has as its purpose the ending of the form of existence the victim had had hitherto in order that the *oblata* might become sacred to God. The act of immolation signified a transfer of the profane and human thing to divine ownership. The rite was a sort of consecration, an invitation for God to make it His own and transform it into something divine. The offerers expected God to accept the gift, sanctify it, and impregnate it with His divinity so that all those who partook of it might share in the divine holiness and be in communion with God.

The rite of immolation has two moments. First, there is the act of transfer, when the gift is taken out of the realm of the profane and placed in the realm of the divine. Second, there is the act of transformation, when the gift is sanctified in God's very acceptance of it.

Applying this doctrine to the sacrifice of the cross, the act of transfer is verified in the following manner. Christ's consent to undergo His sufferings is the offering of the victim of sacrifice. The historical event of His Crucifixion presented Christ with that final and full opportunity for the free act of Person to transform nature by bringing nature into full submission to and perfect acceptance of the will of Person. This transformation of nature is the transfer of the Sacred Humanity from the condition of ''likeness of sinful flesh.'' In the death of Christ, the first moment of the immolative act is accomplished.

It is the Resurrection in which the second moment is fulfilled, when God raises Christ from the dead and His humanity is transformed by the fullness of participation in the divine life and the complete possession of the Spirit. ''In the light of [this] sacrificial theory, the glorification of Christ appears as a necessary phase of his oblation. It is the completion without which his sacrifice is essentially mutilated and is therefore no sacrifice—just as there can be no movement which does not arrive anywhere, and no gift where there is no one to accept it. His glorification not only completes his sacrifice in itself, but also makes it beneficial; in the divinized victim, God communicates himself to the offerer and to all who eat at the altar'' (Durrwell, *The Resurrection* 76).

Redemption mediated by the risen Christ. One last point of the doctrinal context needs be discussed: the mediation of the Redemption through the Resurrection of Christ. St. Thomas considered the Resurrection, as well as the sufferings and death of Christ, as being an integral part of Christ's redemptive work (*Summa theologiae* 3a, 56). But St. Thomas's contemporaries and his successors made little of this doctrine as long as the theology of Redemption was dominated by the concepts of merit and satisfaction as understood in the juridical and moral orders.

The contribution of modern biblical research to the theology of the Redemption is the growing understanding of the data demonstrating that in the mind of St. Paul the Resurrection is inseparable from the Passion in the work of salvation. Christ ''was delivered up for our sins, and rose again for our justification'' (Rom 4.25). Following out the line of thought in which the Redemption is conceived of as something happening in the physical order, the Resurrection is the event in human history that reorients its course of deviation. The risen Christ becomes the redemptive source of social reform and the cause of personal conversion and restoration.

The event of the Resurrection reorients the course of human history, for it is an intervention by God through an event that interrupts the course of continuity, causality, and immanence set up in history by sin. In resurrecting Christ, God establishes Him as a new principle of continuity. By the power of the risen Christ, God sends His Spirit into men to enable them to do the same work in history that Christ Himself performed in His lifetime. A new order of things begins. In the Resurrection, Christ has the power to communicate His nature to men, the nature transformed by grace in His Resurrection. A new form of man's existence begins. Through the Resurrection, Christ is enabled to communicate His Person to men in the mystery of Christ (cf. Col 1.24; Eph 3.17; Rom 16.25–27). A new immanence of God in Christ begins in man's history.

The risen Christ is the source of social reform as being the head of the Church. Christ engenders in it His Spirit, His life, and His Person, enabling it to deliver men from the evil of sin and reunite them to God through its preaching of Him, through its administration of His sacrifice and Sacraments, and through its life for and service of mankind.

The risen Christ is the source of personal restoration and conversion to God, because the grace formed in the Crucifixion and communicated to Christ's members is a grace enabling them to die to the flesh. As a grace filled with the Spirit in the Resurrection, it is a grace enabling men to live unto God in the fullness of the Spirit. ''Jesus Christ our Lord was established Son of God in power according to the spirit of holiness by resurrection from the dead, through whom we have received grace and apostleship to bring about the obedience to faith among all the nations'' (Rom 1.4–6).

Conclusion. The deliverance of man from the evil of sin and the reunion of man with God are realized in the mystery of the encounter of God's loving act, which in saving man will involve him in his being delivered up for his sins and rising again for justification (cf. Rom 4.25). Redemption for sinful mankind is the reproduction within man's person, within his society, and within his history of the pattern of person and nature and life-purpose that God established in Christ the Savior.

See Also: SOTERIOLOGY; MAN, 3; PASSION OF CHRIST, I (IN THE BIBLE); PASSION OF CHRIST, II (DEVOTION TO), PERSON (IN THEOLOGY).

Bibliography: J. RIVIÈRE, *Dictionnaire de théologie catholique,* ed. A. VACANT et al. (Paris 1903–50) 13.2:1912–2004; *The Doctrine of the Atonement,* tr. L. CAPPADELTA (St. Louis 1909); *Le Dogme de la rédemption dans la théologie contemporaine* (Albi 1948). J. GEWIESS et al., *Lexikon für Theologie und Kirche,* ed. J. HOFER and K. RAHNER (Freiburg 1957–65) 3:1016–30. A. D'ALÈS,

Dictionnaire apologétique de la foi catholique, ed. A. L'ALÈS (Paris 1911–22) 4:542–582. F. BAMMEL et al., *Die Religion in Geschichte und Gegenwart* (Tübingen 1957–65) 2:576–600. C. ANDRESEN, *Reallexikon für Antike und Christentum* ed. T. KLAUSER [Stuttgart 1941 (1950)—] 6:54–219. J. GNILKA and W. DETTLOFF, *Handbuch theologischer Grundbegriffe,* ed. H. FRIES (Munich 1962–63) 1:303–319, A. MÉDEBIELLE, *Dictionnaire de la Bible,* suppl., ed. L. PIROT (Paris 1928—) 3: 1–262. A. RICHARDSON, *The Interpreters' Dictionary of the Bible,* ed. G. A. BUTTRICK (Nashville, Tenn.) 168–181. G. AULEN, *Christus victor,* tr. A. G. HEBERT (New York 1931). J. BONSIRVEN, *The Theology of the New Testament,* tr. S. F. L. TYE (Westminster, Md. 1963). F. X. DURRWELL, *The Resurrection: A Biblical Study,* tr. R. SHEED (New York 1960); *In the Redeeming Christ,* tr. R. SHEED (New York 1963). R. S. FRANKS, *The Work of Christ* (New York 1962). T. H. HUGHES, *The Atonement* (London 1949). B. J. F. LONERGAN, *De Verbo Incarnato* (3d ed. Rome 1964). S. LYONNET, *De peccato et redemptione,* v.1–2 (Rome 1957–61); ''Conception paulinienne de la rédemption,'' *Lumière et vie* 7 (1958) 35–66; ''La Valeur sotériologique de la résurrection du Christ selon saint Paul,'' *Gregorianum* 39 (1958) 295–318; ''De notione redemptionis,'' *Verbum Domini* 36 (1958) 129–146. L. MORALDI, *Espiazione sacrificale e riti espiatori . . .* (Analecta biblica 5; Rome 1956). PHILIPPE DE LA TRINITÉ, *What Is Redemption?,* tr. A. ARMSTRONG (New York 1961). L. RICHARD, *Le Mystère de la rédemption* (Tournai 1959). L. SABOURIN, *Rédemption sacrificielle* (Bruges 1961). V. TAYLOR, *The Atonement in New Testament Teaching* (3d ed. London 1958); *Jesus and His Sacrifice* (New York 1955). H. E. W. TURNER, *The Patristic Doctrine of Redemption* (London 1952). A. VONIER, *The Incarnation and Redemption,* v. 1 of *Collected Works,* 3 v. (Westminster, Md. 1952–53). P. DE LETTER, ''Theology of Satisfaction,'' *Thomist* 21 (1958) 1–28. P. GRECH, ''Protestant Theories Explaining the Redemption,'' *Theology Digest* 5 (1957) 183–188.

[E. L. PETERMAN/EDS.]

REDEMPTOR HOMINIS

Pope JOHN PAUL II's sixth encyclical letter, issued on March 4, 1979. *Redemptor hominis* (RH) can be viewed, especially in the light of subsequent documents and events, as a programmatic statement revealing many of the themes that have come to define the pontificate. Foremost among these is the anticipation of the year 2000. Already in the first paragraph the Pope announces that the millennial year ''will be the year of a great Jubilee.'' It becomes clear that John Paul envisions his papal ministry as the continued unfolding and reception of the Second Vatican Council in anticipation of the Jubilee Year 2000. The Church prepares to enter the 21st century precisely by deepening its understanding and implementation of the directions taken at Vatican II.

The encyclical comprises four sections: ''Inheritance'' (1–6), ''The Mystery of the Redemption'' (7–12), ''Redeemed Man and His Situation in the Modern World'' (13–17), and ''The Church's Mission and Man's Destiny'' (18–22). Although a number of the documents of Vatican II are cited, clearly it is *Gaudium et spes* that provides the encyclical with a specific point of reference.

John Paul brings his vision of Christian personalism to bear in analyzing the conditions within which men and women live in the late 20th century. Of particular importance is a statement of *Gaudium et spes* 22: ''The truth is that only in the mystery of the Incarnate Word does the mystery of man take on light'' (cited in no. 8). This is coupled with the statement of *Gaudium et spes* 24 that ''man can fully discover his true self only in a sincere giving of himself.'' The dignity of each person guides the Christian approach to the world, to economics and politics, and to an understanding of the Church itself. So John Paul emphasizes ''the primacy of the person over things'' (no. 16) and the welfare of the ''person in the community'' as ''the essential criterion for all programs, systems, and regimes'' (no. 17).

There is also a striking application of personalism to ecclesiology in RH 21. The Church is portrayed as the ''community of disciples'' in which ''each member has his own special gift,'' which is ''a personal vocation and a form of participation in the Church's saving work.'' Each member of the ''deeply personal'' society that is the Church receives a ''singular, unique, and unrepeatable grace'' for the Church's communion and mission. Every human being is ''the way'' for the Church (no. 14) precisely because Christ, above all in the Incarnation and Redemption, is the way of self-discovery for each unique, ''unrepeatable'' human being (no. 13).

Another prominent theme of the pontificate is heralded in RH 6—the call to Christian unity. The Church does not have the right to risk being unfaithful to Christ's prayer ''that they may all be one.'' These words, *ut unum sint,* become the title of a groundbreaking encyclical on ecumenism published in 1995. Here again, it is a matter of extending the initiatives of the Second Vatican Council in the attempt to overcome divisions with Christians in both the East and the West.

With the publication of the subsequent encyclicals DIVES IN MISERCORDIA (1980) and DOMINUM ET VIVIFICANTEM (1986) it becomes evident that RH is also the first of the ''Trinitarian encyclicals'' of John Paul. The three documents focus successively on the Son, the Father, and the Spirit. A Trinitarian dimension, spelled out in the apostolic letter TERTIO MILLENNIO ADVENIENTE (1994) likewise accrues to preparations for the Jubilee Year. John Paul draws in particular upon those scenes from the Gospels that take place in the ''Upper Room'' in order to develop this perspective. His ''theology of the Upper Room'' begins to take shape in RH and comes to fuller expression in the later documents.

Other significant themes of the pontificate also find their place in RH. For example, the importance of the saints (no. 19) and Mary (no. 22) is underscored. Elements of Catholic social teaching are also referenced. In sum, RH stands as a key that unlocks the vast treasure of documents and events comprising the pontificate of John Paul II.

Bibliography: For the text of *Redemptor hominis,* see: *Acta Apostolicae Sedis,* no. 71 (1979): 266–324 (Latin); *Origins* 8, no. 40 (March 22, 1979): 625, 627–644 (English); *The Pope Speaks* 24 (1979): 97–147 (English). For commentaries and summaries of *Redemptor hominis,* see: A. DULLES, *The Splendor of Faith: The Theological Vision of Pope John Paul II* (New York 1999). R. T. GAWRONSKI, ''Redemptor Hominis,'' in *The Thought of Pope John Paul II: A Collection of Essays and Studies,* J. M. MCDERMOTT, ed. 221–230 (Rome 1993).

[M. PELZEL]

REDEMPTORIS MATER

Pope JOHN PAUL II's sixth encyclical letter, issued on the feast of the Annunciation (March 25) in 1987, presaging the Marian year (Pentecost 1987 to Assumption 1988). In the introduction (nos. 1–6), Pope John Paul emphasizes the fact that the mystery of Christ is indissolubly united with that of Mary as the God-Bearer (THEOTOKOS), solemnly defined at the Council of Ephesus in 431. This dogma is essentially and primarily a christological doctrine in which Mary is portrayed as the ''spotless'' and perfect archetype of the Church from the moment of her Immaculate Conception. On the threshold of the new millennium or 2,000th birthday of the Son of God incarnate, the Holy Father reflects on the salvation history of the Bible in the light of a meditation on Mary's unique role in our redemption as a ''New Eve'' or companion of Christ.

The first of the three sections, ''Mary in the Mystery of Christ,'' constitutes a biblical reflection upon what Vatican II aptly described as Mary's ''pilgrimage of faith'' (*LUMEN GENTIUM* 58). The pope points out that this ''pilgrimage'' represents a constant focus for the Church and, in a sense, for all humanity. He pursues the same christocentric and ecclesiotypical Mariology as taught in chapter 8 of *Lumen gentium.* Just as Christ cannot be contemplated apart from the redemptive activity from which his MYSTICAL BODY originated, so Mary must be considered closely connected with the Incarnation and the Redemption if she is to be viewed as the archetype of the Church uniquely redeemed by her Immaculate Conception and the consummation of the whole Body of Christ in her glorious Assumption. The pope begins by citing the Pauline writings on the divine plan of salvation; the unique relationship between Mary and her Son in this story of grace thus becomes the focus of his meditation on the texts from the Synoptics, John, and Acts that concern Mary.

In the second section, ''The Mother of God at the Center of the Pilgrim Church,'' the pope speaks of Mary's indissoluble link to the mystery of the Church born on the first Pentecost, called by Christ to give apostolic witness to all nations (Matt. 28:19–20). He devotes special attention to the ecumenical issues concerning Mary, especially with respect to the East, longing for the time when both the East and the West will be the one Church again breathing with ''both lungs'' (no. 34). He sees this as also helping the dialogues between the Catholic Church and the churches and ecclesial communities of the West. This will lead to the one Church of Christ singing her Magnificat, which continuously ''re-echoes'' in her heart as she recites the Canticle of Mary at Vespers each day.

In the third section, ''Maternal Mediation,'' the pope is careful to affirm Mary's salutary influence upon each one of us by her maternal mediation and intercession. He develops what Vatican II calls her spiritual motherhood, ''a motherhood in the order of grace'' (*Lumen gentium* 62). As in the case of the intercessory role of all the saints in heaven, it is entirely dependent upon and subordinate to the unique mediation of Christ. Mary's maternal mediation finds its origin in her ''fullness of grace,'' embodied in her total selfgiving to God at the Annunciation. Perfected through her Assumption into glory, it extends as far as the redemptive work of her Son. Furthermore, since motherhood is always a personal relation, the maternal mediation of Mary is a way for every Christian to enter into a more intimate and immediate encounter with Christ. The special meaning of the Marian Year, beginning on Pentecost and ending on the feast of the Assumption, is that the Church should reflect on what the mystery of Mary reveals about the Church's mission and hope.

Mary's mediation is the effective maternal presence sharing in the many complex problems of our lives. She is invoked to transform the Church through her role of relating us more closely to the incarnate and saving Christ.

Bibliography: For the text of *Redemptoris Mater,* see: *Acta Apostoliae Sedis* 79 (1987): 361–433 (Latin); *Origins* 16, no. 43 (April 9, 1987) 745–766 (English); *The Pope Speaks* 32 (1987): 159–197 (English). For commentaries and summaries of *Redemptoris Mater,* see: *Mary: God's Yes to Man—John Paul's Encyclical ''Redemptoris Mater,''* introduction by J. RATZINGER, commentary by H. VON BALTHASAR (San Francisco 1988). F. M. JELLY, O. P., ''Ecumenical Aspects of *Redemptoris Mater,*'' *Marian Studies* 39 (1988): 115–129.

[F. JELLY]

REDEMPTORIS MISSIO

Pope JOHN PAUL II's eighth encyclical *Redemptoris missio* (RM), issued on Dec. 7, 1990, celebrates the 25th

Miguel Angel Isla Lucio (left), Spanish missionary seen in this undated photo with children in a mission, Zaire, was found dead along with two other missionaries on Nov. 8, 1996. (AP/Wide World Photos)

anniversary of *Ad Gentes* (Vatican II's decree on missionary activity) and the 15th anniversary of *EVANGELII NUNTIANDI* (Paul VI's apostolic exhortation on evangelization). RM has the significant subtitle: ''On the Permanent Validity of the Church's Missionary Mandate'' the pope sounds a clarion and urgent call to all Church sectors to renew their enthusiasm and commitment to evangelize the world. Composed of eight chapters plus an introduction (nos. 1–3) and conclusion (no. 92), RM has a ''doctrinal'' section (nos. 4–30) and a ''pastoral'' section (nos. 31–91), respectively treating the ''why'' and ''how'' of contemporary mission.

The pope begins by stating his conviction about ''the urgency of missionary activity'' (no. 1). The pope asserts: ''Missionary activity specifically directed 'to the nations' (*ad gentes*) appears to be waning . . . a fact which must arouse concern among all who believe in Christ'' (no. 2). Missionary evangelization remains urgent because ''it is the primary service which the Church can render to every individual and to all humanity in the modern world'' (no. 2).

RM's doctrinal section of three chapters affirms the foundations of mission theology from Vatican II; it also clarifies specific ''doubts and ambiguities regarding missionary activity *ad gentes*'' (no. 2). Chapter 1, ''Jesus Christ, the Only Savior,'' treats core elements of dogmatic theology in relation to mission (e.g., revelation, faith, christology, and soteriology). Chapter 2, ''The Kingdom of God,'' is biblically based and describes the intimate relationship of Kingdom to Christ and the Church. Chapter 3, ''The Holy Spirit, the Principal Agent of Mission,'' examines the role of the Holy Spirit in the Church's life and its mission. In his strong reaffirmation of these basics of Church teaching, the pontiff continually links mission and faith: ''Mission is an issue of faith'' (no. 11); ''It is only in faith that the Church's mission can be understood and only in faith that it finds its basis'' (no. 4; see also nos. 2, 36, 49).

A holistic vision of evangelization underlies all of RM, particularly its second section on concrete approaches to mission. This vision is in continuity with *Evangelii nutiandi* (nos. 17–24) and emphasizes what contemporary missiological terminology calls ''integral evangelization.'' ''Jesus came to bring integral salvation'' (no. 11); ''evangelical witness . . . is directed toward integral human development'' (no. 42); ''action on behalf of integral development and liberation . . . is most urgently needed'' (no. 58).

By viewing mission with its various complementary and mutually enriching elements, evangelizers are able to appreciate fully that ''Mission is a single but complex reality, and it develops in a variety of ways'' (no. 41). ''This mission is one and undivided, having one origin and one final purpose; but within it, there are different tasks and kinds of activity'' (no. 31). Indeed, integral evangelization is an interpretive key to linking harmoniously the numerous themes and subjects treated in RM.

Several topics are insightfully discussed in RM as they directly relate to mission: Christian family (nos. 42, 80); personal conversion (nos. 47, 59, 60, 81); missionary institutes (nos. 66, 67, 72); youth (nos. 82, 86, 89); local church (nos. 26, 39, 48–52, 62–64, 83–85); interreligious dialogue (nos. 55–57); mission vocations (nos. 32, 65, 66, 79, 84); women (nos. 70, 71); inculturation (nos. 25, 52–54, 76); basic ecclesial communities (no. 51); proclamation (nos. 44–46); mission spirituality (nos. 87–91). This enumeration is much more than a random listing of topics; underlying it is a broad, practical, integral vision for effective evangelization.

The encyclical has several strengths: RM presents solid traditional and biblical theology along with the thought of Vatican II and *Evangelii nuntiandi* and offers several trult original insights, e.g., the threefold situation of mission (nos. 32–34); mission in various ''new worlds'' (no. 37); paschal mystery and mission (nos. 6, 10, 28); and pneumatology and mission (nos. 21–30).

RM opens many avenues of theology, spirituality, mission vision, and concrete responses to contemporary problems, as the Church faces the challenge of ''bringing the Gospel, by witness and word, to all people and nations'' (no. 92). The missionary Church accomplishes its evangelizing task as it ''proceeds along *the path* already trodden by the Virgin Mary'' (no. 92).

Bibliography: For the text of *Redemptoris missio,* see: *Acta Apostolicae Sedis* 83 (1991): 249–339 (Latin); *Origins* 20, no. 34 (Jan. 31, 1991): 541, 543–568 (English); *The Pope Speaks* 36 (1991): 138–183 (English). For commentaries on *Redemptoris missio,* see: W. BURROWS, ed., *Redemption and Dialogue: Reading Redemptoris Missio and Dialogue and Proclamation* (Maryknoll, NY 1993). J. KROEGER, *Living Mission: Challenges in Evangelization Today* (Maryknoll, NY 1994). There are also commentaries to be found in *Omnis Terra.* They are written by DEGRIJSE (Feb. / Mar. 1993); KROEGER (Dec. 1991 / Jan. 1995); LAVERDIERE (Sep.–Oct. 1991); ODORICO (Feb. 1994 / Jul.–Aug. 1994); WOLANIN (Dec. 1994); ZAGO (Feb. 1991 / Nov. 1991 / Nov. 1992).

[J. KROEGER]

REDEMPTORISTINES

Popular name for the Order of the Most Holy Redeemer, *Ordo Sanctissimi Redemptoris* (OSSR; Official Catholic Directory #2010), a contemplative order of nuns founded in 1731 in Scala (Naples), Italy, by Ven. Celeste Crostarosa (1696–1755) through the instrumentality of St. ALPHONSUS LIGUORI. Sister Celeste was a member of the community of VISITATION NUNS in Scala and claimed to have received private revelations concerning the foundation of a new religious order devoted exclusively to the perfect imitation of Christ. When St. Alphonsus was convinced that these revelations were authentic, he composed a rule based on them and introduced it into the Visitation community at Scala. This rule received papal approval in 1750.

The Redemptoristines seek to carry on the work of redemption in, with, and through Christ. As a strictly contemplative and cloistered order the Redemptoristines take solemn vows, recite the Liturgy of the Hours in choir, and observe papal enclosure. The habit consists of a red tunic, blue scapular, and blue choir mantle. Attached to the scapular is a picture of the Sacred Heart, and suspended from the cincture is a 15-decade rosary. The veil is black over white.

Each community is autonomous, but in some countries the monasteries have joined into federations for mutual assistance in remunerative work and novitiate training. These federations limit in no way the independence of each community. Each monastery strives to be self-supporting. The type of work varies with the locale. In many houses the nuns manufacture church vestments and banners, altar linens, and habits for the Redemptorists. Painting, writing, mimeograph work, bookbinding and making altar breads are among the other remunerative works.

All Redemptoristines were in Italy until 1831, when a monastery was founded in Vienna and a new era of expansion began. With the opening of the first house in Africa (1963) every continent possessed at least one convent. In the United States there was a community in Esopus, N.Y., founded in 1957, and another in Liguori, Mo., started in 1960.

Bibliography: OSSR, Official Catholic Directory, #2010. J. B. FAVRE, *A Great Mystic of the 18th Century, The Venerable Maria Celeste Crostarosa,* tr. a Redemptoristine of Chudleigh (London 1935). J. M. SCOTT, *Life of the Venerable Maria Celeste Crostarosa* (Chudleigh 1949).

[M. M. WILKINSON/EDS.]

REDEMPTORISTS

(CSSR, Official Catholic Directory #1070); the Congregation of the Most Holy Redeemer (Congregatio Sanctissimi Redemptoris) was founded by Saint Alphonsus Liguori (1696–1787) under the direction of Bp. Tommaso Falcoia (1663–1743) of Castellammare di Stabia, Italy. Moved by the spiritual neglect of country people in the Kingdom of Naples, Liguori founded the Redemptorists ''to follow the example of Jesus Christ, the Redeemer, by preaching the word of God to the poor.'' The congregation does this ''by responding with missionary thrust to the pressing pastoral needs of the most abandoned, especially the poor, by devoting itself entirely to evangelization.'' Canonically, it defines itself as ''a clerical missionary religious institute of pontifical rite, enjoying the privilege of exemption, and having members belonging to various rites'' (CSSR Rule, Constitution 1).

As a community of priests, permanent deacons, and lay brothers ministering in 724 foundations in 73 countries, its total membership in 2001 consisted of 5,556 professed religious: bishops (43); priests (4,160); and deacons, brothers, and students (1,353). Worldwide the congregation is organized into 40 provinces, 26 vice provinces, 11 regions, and 10 mission outposts. The members bind themselves to the work of evangelization by the vows of poverty, chastity, and obedience, together with a vow and oath of perseverence in the congregation. An essential law for Redemptorists is to ''live in community and to carry out their apostolic work through community'' (Constitution 21). To enable them to fulfill their vocation in the Church of preaching the gospel to the most abandoned, Redemptorists, like their founder, cultivate a markedly Christocentric spirituality orientated to ''crib, cross, and sacrament.'' Devotion to Mary under the title of Our Lady of Perpetual Help is integral to the spiritual life of a Redemptorist. The motto of the congregation is ''With Him there is Plenteous Redemption'' (Ps 130:7).

History. Liguori established the first community of the Redemptorists in the small town of Scala, near Naples, in 1732. Neapolitan regalism made the beginning extremely difficult. Only after a foothold was gained in the Papal States and the rule and constitutions were approved by Benedict XIV in 1749, was the future growth and success of the congregation assured. A severe crisis was occasioned in 1780 by the *Regolamento.* This was a rule drawn up by several Redemptorists who were commissioned to seek royal approval for the congregation. In order to placate the Neapolitan regalists, the original rule, approved by Benedict XIV, was so watered down that the nature of the institute was changed in the new document. Alphonsus, already in his 80s and suffering from severe physical handicaps, signed the *Regolamento,* unaware of the betrayal by his confreres. In an act of reprisal directed at the Neapolitan government, Pius VI withdrew his approval of the Neapolitan Redemptorists. Only those in the Papal States were looked upon with favor by him. Alphonsus thus came under a cloud, since he resided in the Neapolitan area. Only after his death was his good name cleared and his innocence in the matter of the *Regolamento* established. By 1793 all the Redemptorists were united again.

Sister Maria Celeste Crostarosa.

Development in Italy. The period following the founder's death (1787) must be seen from two points of view: the one concerns the Redemptorists in Italy, the other centers around the Redemptorists in the vicariate north of the Alps. From the days of Alphonsus down to 1855, the world headquarters of the congregation was in Nocera dei Pagani, in southern Italy, where the superiors general resided. For a period of 70 years the congregation grew at a fair pace in the Kingdom of Naples and in the Papal States. In spite of the Napoleonic invasions and the economic hardship that followed, the number of members grew steadily during the regimes of the superiors general Andrea Villani (1787–92) and Pier Paolo Blasucci (1793–1817). Nineteen foundations were established throughout Italy. Progress in Italy was slower during the administrations of Nicola Mansione (1817–23), Celestino Maria Cocle (1824–31), Giovanni Camillo Ripoli (1832–50), and Vincenzo Trapanese (1850–53). By the middle of the 19th century an effort was being made to have the headquarters moved to Rome in order to free the Redemptorists from the regalistic restrictions of Naples, but the king of Naples refused to countenance this administrative move. As a result, Pius IX in 1853 reluctantly divided the institute again, allowing Neapolitans to have their own superior general and ordering the other Redemptorists to elect a superior general with a residence in Rome. The actual opening of the new Roman headquarters took place in 1855. This dual administration lasted until 1869, when all Redemptorists throughout the world were united under the sole jurisdiction of the superior general in Rome.

Development outside Italy. Meanwhile, a great impetus had been given to the congregation north of the Alps by (St.) Clement HOFBAUER, who after taking his vows as a Redemptorist in the Papal States, moved to Vienna, Austria, in 1785 to establish a branch in northern Europe. Balked in Vienna, Clement moved northward to Warsaw, Poland, in 1787. For 20 years he had extraordinary success there, and as vicar-general of the Redemptorists north of Italy, won many recruits for the congregation until the legions of Napoleon uprooted and destroyed his work. Aware of the danger to his foundation in Warsaw, Clement strove to establish the congregation on German soil, sending his lieutenant, Joseph Passerat (1772–1858), with a group of clerics and their teachers to Jestetten, southern Germany, in 1803. The wanderings of these Redemptorists for 15 years from Warsaw to Bavaria and then to Switzerland form a saga of patience and perseverance. They finally found a home in Valsainte, Switzerland.

When Clement himself was exiled from Warsaw in 1808, he went to Vienna, where he sought once again to establish his congregation. Emperor Francis I of Austria finally consented to a Redemptorist foundation in that city, but Clement, who died shortly afterward, never saw it in operation. At the time of his death in 1820, he had only two precarious foundations to show for his 35 years of labor, one in Switzerland and the other in Romania. There were also some Redemptorists still in Poland. Nevertheless, Clement had gathered together a group of missionaries who, operating out of Switzerland and Vienna, were to spread the congregation into northern Europe and North America.

For 28 years (1820–48) Joseph Passerat was the vicar-general in northern Europe. Thanks to his energy and to the spirit of the men Clement had trained, the Redemptorists advanced successfully across border after border. They went into France in 1820, Portugal in 1826, Belgium in 1831, Bulgaria in 1835, Holland in 1836, Germany in 1841, and England in 1843. During this same period they also came to the United States (1832). The forward movement north of the Alps was temporarily checked by the Revolution of 1848. After two years a new vicar-general was chosen in the person of Rudolf Smetana, who held this post until 1855. During his term of office the Redemptorists were established in Luxemburg in 1851 and in Ireland in 1853.

Uniting of the Two Branches. By mid-century the vicariate had outstripped, in the number of its personnel and of its new foundations, the Italian division of the congregation. Two moves were made that sought to improve the administration of the whole organization. The first was the decree of Rome in 1841 dividing the whole congregation into 6 provinces, 3 in northern Europe and 3 in Italy and Sicily. The second was the effort to bring the headquarters of the entire institute to Rome. Because of the civil conditions of Italy, this effort resulted for a time (1855–69) in the creation of a dual administration. Nevertheless, the establishing of the Roman headquarters and the election of a rector major (superior general) in 1855 favored the growth of the congregation. From that time on it prospered under the successive superiors general: Nicolas Mauron, a Swiss (1855–93); Matthias Raus, a Luxemburger (1894–1909); Patrick Murray, Irish (1909–47); Leonardus Buijs, a Hollander (1947–53); William Gaudreau, American (1954–67); Tarcisio Amaral, Brazilian (1967–73); Josef Pfab, German (1973–85); Juan Lasso de la Vega, Spaniard (1985–97); and Joseph Tobin, American (1997–).

Mauron and Raus increased the foundations in Europe (Czech Republic) and North America and introduced the Redemptorists into South America (1859), Australia (1882), and Africa (1899). During the administration of Murray the number of foundations in these places was increased, and the Redemptorists began to establish themselves in Asia (the Philippines, 1906) so that the congregation became truly worldwide. These advances were made despite many serious setbacks. Like other religious orders, the Redemptorists suffered from suppression and confiscation in Alsace in 1830, Lisbon in 1833, Switzerland in 1847, Austria in 1848, Italy in 1860, Spain in 1868, Germany during the Kulturkampf, France in 1902, Mexico in 1926, and Spain in 1936. During World War II every foundation in one province of Germany was lost, and the whole Redemptorist community of Warsaw was wiped out. Under communist regimes, especially in the Ukraine, Czechoslovakia, and Vietnam, Redemptorists suffered severe persecution, and several shed their blood for the faith.

Government and Apostolate. The Redemptorists are ruled by a superior general known as the rector major.

He is elected for a term of six years by the sole legislative body of the congregation, the capitulars assembled in a general chapter. The chapter elects also a group of regional consultors as the cabinet of advisers to the general. Their term of office terminates with the convocation of the following general chapter. General chapters are held every six years or on the occasion of the death or resignation of the superior general. Two other officials complete the administration, the procurator general and the general econome (bursar). These also are elected by the capitulars. The procurator general is the liaison with the Holy See on official business. The general chapter is composed of the Roman officials, the provincial of each province, and delegates elected by the fathers in their respective provinces and vice provinces. The provincials, provincial vicars, rectors, and local superiors are selected according to the electoral law enacted in each unit, after approbation by the general government.

The main service rendered the Church by Redemptorists is the preaching of missions, retreats, and novenas, the administration of parishes, and foreign missions. It took the Redemptorists almost 40 years to inaugurate their missions in northern Europe, but once established, they became known among the foremost preachers in various countries. Well known for their eloquence were Michael Neubert (1805–82) in Baden and Alsace; Bernard Hafkenscheid (1807–65) in Holland; John Furniss (1809–65) in England; Victor DECHAMPS, later Cardinal of Malines in Belgium; Johannes Zobel (1815–93) in Germany; Achille Desurmont (1828–98) in France; and Joseph Wissel (1830–1912), who preached missions for over 50 years in the United States. The eminence of Liguori in moral theology, emphasized by the Holy See in declaring him patron of that study, has naturally interested his followers in that important branch of ecclesiastical learning. Among those who have won recognition by their publications in the field are: Anthony Konings (1821–84), Joseph Aertnys (1828–1915), Cornelius Damen (1881–1953), Willem VAN ROSSUM, Clément Marc, Francis Connell (1888–1967), Bernard Häring (1912–98), Marciano Vidal (1937–), and Brian Johnson (1959–). In 1957 the Redemptorists founded the Academia Alfonsiana, a special institute of moral theology in Rome, which was incorporated into the Pontifical Lateran University in 1960. In 2000 the student body, which annually averages 300, represented 60 countries. To date, 539 doctorates have been granted.

Another special apostolate of the congregation is its work among Ukrainian Catholics. Begun by the Belgian fathers laboring in Galicia, in Poland, this apostolate later spread to Canada and the United States. The Redemptorist fathers and brothers of the Byzantine rite in North America form the Yorkton province. These Byzantine rite houses number seven, with their headquarters in Winnipeg, Canada. In the United States they are established in Newark, New Jersey. In the course of their history the Redemptorists have served the Church in many other ways. Alphonsus fought JANSENISM and strenuously upheld the rights of the Holy See against FEBRONIANISM. Hofbauer worked to save the Church's prerogatives during the Congress of Vienna. Passerat and Friedrich von Held (1799–1881) strove to stem the title of irreligious liberalism in northern Europe. Redemptorist missionaries promoted the Confraternity of the Holy Family and fostered devotion to the Blessed Virgin under the title of OUR LADY OF PERPETUAL HELP. Dechamps was a leader at Vatican Council I in promoting the declaration of papal infallibility. In all, 131 Redemptorists have been chosen as bishops; five have been nominated cardinals. Four have been canonized: Saints Alphonsus Liguori, Gerard Majella, Clement Hofbauer, and John Neumann. Declared blessed: Peter Donders (Netherlands/Surinam), Kaspar Stanggassinger (Germany), Gennaro Sarnelli (Italy), Francis Xavier Seelos (USA); in 2001 Pope John Paul II beatified five Redemptorist martyrs, four from the Ukraine and one from Slovakia; 16 causes are at various stages of progress.

Development in the U.S. The growth of the Redemptorists in the United States began slowly. For the first seven years they failed to obtain a stable footing, but following the foundation in Pittsburgh in 1839, they grew, rapidly. Answering the appeal of the bishops of the country, they undertook the care of German immigrants. Not all the early Redemptorists came from a Germanic background, however. Many were of French, Dutch, Belgian, and Slavic origin; four of the first six superiors in the United States were non-Germans. By 1850, when the first American province was erected, there were nine foundations stretching from New York City to New Orleans, Louisiana. Their work was not restricted to the Germans, however, since they also established American, French, and Bohemian parishes. A permanent mission band, devoted exclusively to giving missions in English, was organized in 1851 under the direction of Hafkenscheid.

Through the years Redemptorists conducted missions, retreats, and other preaching events in English, German, French, Italian, Bohemian, Polish, Spanish, and Portuguese. Today such preaching is conducted mostly in English and Spanish; a number of missionaries minister to the special needs of the hearing challenged. The preaching apostolate is also continued in a number of retreat houses in the states of Arizona, California, Florida, Kansas, Louisiana, New Jersey, New York, Virginia, and Wisconsin. Redemptorists continue their tradition of ministering in large parochial centers, where special stress is placed upon frequent preaching, impressive services, and spiritual and social societies and organizations. This work for the immigrant was instrumental in giving badly needed support to incoming European immigrants, insecure and confused in their new home. Faithful to their charism of seeking out the marginalized and spiritually abandoned, especially the materially poor, Redemptorists today are frequently found in the inner city, working for African Americans, those from a Latin background, and new arrivals.

The Redemptorists' parochial centers have always given much attention to the parochial schools. Since this phase of their activity at first centered on the German immigrant, they were forced to provide Catholic schools using the German language in order to preserve the faith of the immigrant. These in time became schools of both German and English, and then entirely English. A similar effort to attend to the spiritual and corporal works of mercy resulted in the provision of Catholic homes and asylums for orphaned children. In Baltimore, Maryland; Philadelphia and Pittsburgh, Pennsylvania; New York, Rochester, and Buffalo, New York; and New Orleans, Louisiana, the Redemptorists undertook this task with notable success. American Redemptorists have continued the apostolate of the pen initiated by St. Alphonsus. Liguorian Publications is one of the largest publishing houses of Catholic literature in the United States and the *Liguorian,* a periodical aimed at the average American Catholic, is one of the leaders in circulation.

Two Redemptorists served as chaplains in the Civil War. During World War II, the American Redemptorists had 188 chaplains serving the armed forces, and in 1943 the provincial of the Baltimore province, William McCarty, was consecrated bishop to assist the military vicar, Cardinal Francis Spellman. Redemptorists from the United States established their first houses in Canada at St. Patrick's, Quebec, in 1872 and at Ste-Anne-de-Beaupré in 1878. Redemptorist fathers and brothers in the United States are divided into two provinces, Baltimore and Denver, and two vice-provinces, Richmond and New Orleans. There are three provinces in Canada: the English-speaking Edmonton-Toronto province, the French-speaking Ste-Anne-de-Beaupré, and the Ukrainian province of Yorkton.

The foreign mission field has been staffed with many missionaries from these provinces. In the 1900s Redemptorist fathers and brothers from the United States and Canada went overseas on missions to: Puerto Rico 1902; Virgin Islands 1917; Vietnam, Laos, and Cambodia 1925; Mato Grosso, Brazil 1929; Asunción, Paraguay 1934; Amazon region 1943; Dominican Republic 1946; Thailand 1948; Japan 1948; Uruguay 1968; Haiti 1980; Nigeria and St. Lucia 1987. Since 1950 the congregation worldwide has made foundations in: Lebanon 1952; Angola and Guatemala 1954; Nicaragua 1955; Indonesia and Siberia 1956; Malaysia and Zimbabwe 1960; Iraq 1962; Panama 1964; Madagascar 1967; Kenya and Byelorussia 1990; Korea 1991; China (Hong Kong); Russia, Kazakhstan, and the Ivory Coast 1993; Ghana 1994; Congo 1995; and Cuba 2001.

Bibliography: G. BASS *Working for Plentiful Redemption: History of the Redemptorist Vice Province of New Orleans, 1952–1995* (New Orleans 1995). J. F. BYRNE, *The Redemptorist Centenaries* (Philadelphia 1932). F. CHIOVARO, ed. *The Origins (1732–1793),* v. 1 of *The History of the Congregation of the Most Holy Redeemer,* tr. and ed. R. FENILI (Liguori, Mo. 1996). M. J. CURLEY, *The Provincial Story: A History of the Baltimore Province of the Congregation of the Most Holy Redeemer* (New York 1963). E. DAY, "The Beginnings of the Redemptorists in the United States: 1832–1840," Diss. CU (Louvain 1948). M. DE MEULEMEESTER, *Bibliographie générale des écrivains rédemptorists,* 3 v. (Louvain 1933–39). J. P. DOLAN, *Catholic Revivalism: The American Experience 1830–1900* (Notre Dame, Ind. 1978). F. DONLAN, *Southeastern Redemptorist Heritage, 1926–1986* (privately printed 1986). J. GAUCI, *Redemptorist Apostolates in the Caribbean of the Nineteenth Century* (Puerto Rico 1989). P. GEIERMANN, *Annals of the St. Louis Province of the Congregation of the Most Holy Redeemer,* 3 v. (St. Louis 1923). G. LAUENSTEIN, *Fully Devoted: the Hispanic Apostolate in the St. Louis Province of Redemptorists* (Denver 1996). P. LAVERDURE, *Redemption and Renewal: The Redemptorists of English Canada, 1834–1994* (Toronto 1996). N. MUCKERMAN, *Redemptorists on the Amazon: The First 50 Years* (privately printed 1992). T. SKINNER, *The Redemptorists in the West* (St. Louis 1933). *Spicilegium Historicum CSSR* (Rome 1953–). J. WISSEL, *The Redemptorist on the American Mission,* 3 v. (New York 1978). J. WUEST, *Annales Congregationis SS. Redemptoris, Provinciae Americanae,* 5 v. in 11 parts (Ilchester, Md. 1888–1924).

[M. J. CURLEY/C. HOEGERL]

REDON, ABBEY OF

A former Benedictine monastery in the Diocese of Vannes, department of Ille et Vilane, France. It was founded in 823 or 832 by St. Convoyon (d. 868), who became first abbot, on land ceded by a Breton lord, Ratuili. Destroyed by the Normans in 869, it was restored in the 10th century under Abbot Catwallon, who extended its property holdings. Involved in Breton political strife, it was pillaged anew by Duke John of Brittany. In the 13th century, it was refurbished, and in the 14th century it became the center of a small city walled by Abbot Jean de Tréal and was considered by Bretons a sanctuary of national independence. At the request of Duke Francis I (d. 1450) MARTIN V made Redon an episcopal see, a status it retained only briefly. It became the object of favors of LOUIS XI, who visited it *c.* 1461. Reforms were attempted under a succession of commendatory abbots (*see* COMMENDATION) such as Cardinal Salviati, Bp. Arthur d'Epinay, who rebuilt extensively and introduced monks of the Congregation of Brittany in 1620, and Cardinal RICHELIEU, who established MAURISTS at Redon in 1628 and continued repairs. Three Choiseul-Praslin abbots governed the monastery in the 17th century, and two cardinals de la Tour d'Auvergne, from 1681 to 1722. The church, which has a notable romanesque tower and 13th-century choir and ambulatory chapels, now serves as a parish church. The abbey was suppressed in 1790, and the cloisters today are used as a school under the direction of the EUDISTS.

Bibliography: G. HEER, *Lexikon für Theologie und Kirche,* ed. J. HOFER and K. RAHNER, 10 v. (2d, new ed. Freiburg 1957–65) 8:1066. L. H. COTTINEAU, *Répertoire topobibliographique des abbayes et prieurés,* 2 v. (Mâcon 1935–39) 2:2422–23. H. LECLERCQ, *Dictionnaire d'archéologie chrétienne et de liturgie,* ed. F. CABROL, H. LECLERCQ and H. I. MARROU, 15 v. (Paris 1907–53) 14.2:2176–78. A. M. DE COURSON DE LA VILLENEUVE, ed., *Cartulaire de l'abbaye de Redon en Bretagne* (Paris 1863).

[G. E. GINGRAS]

REDUCTIONS OF PARAGUAY

Jesuit mission establishments that existed in Rio de la Plata from the beginning of the 17th century until the expulsion of the society from America in 1768. They were organized internally according to the Spanish mission system. [*See* ALDEIAMENTO SYSTEM IN BRAZIL; MISSION IN COLONIAL AMERICA, I (SPANISH MISSIONS), 1.] The reductions, however, took on added importance because of their location on the borders of Spanish and Portuguese colonial claims. They were established among the Guarani, an extensive linguistic group who had developed a culture that included some agriculture, raising of domesticated animals, pottery, weaving, and the use of efficient tools and weapons.

History. At the end of 1609 Hernando Arias (1564–1645), Governor of Asunción, and Bishop Lizárraga requested Jesuit missions for Paraguay. The first Jesuit provincial of the area, Diego de Torres, sent three pairs of missionaries out to start the chain of missions. The first, founded in the southern part of Paraguay, was San Ignacio Guazú. Ultimately more than 50 reductions were founded in the modern areas of southern Brazil, Paraguay, Uruguay, and northeastern Argentina.

From 1612 to 1656 the Paulistas of Brazil harassed the settlements with their slave raids. In 1627 and again in 1631, particularly severe attacks destroyed those nearest São Paulo, and the Jesuits were obliged to move the reductions further west. In the Treaty of Limits of 1750, settling the border dispute between Portuguese Brazil and the neighboring Spanish colonies, Spain ceded to Portugal an area in which seven reductions were located. The reductions were to be moved into Spanish territory, but the native peoples in them rebelled and had to be subjugated by force of arms. On the expulsion of the Jesuits, Spain divided the government of each reduction between a civil administrator and the priest. This began the decline of the missions.

Organization. The reductions were native villages from which European settlers were excluded. The population of each ranged from about 1,000 to 8,000, the average being between 3,000 and 4,000. In the peak period, 1730 to 1740, there were more than 100,000 native peoples in about 30 missions.

The settlements were usually located on or near a river in a fertile area and were grouped around a plaza. On one side were the church, the priests' house, a home for widows and orphans, the cemetery, storehouses, and offices. The other three sides were made up of native homes, long buildings housing many families in separate apartments. Frequently the church, and sometimes the house for the priests, was built of stone or hardwood depending on the materials available in the area. In each reduction were the pastor and at least one other priest, caciques, and the *cabildo.* Members of the *cabildo* were elected each year by the outgoing group, except for the chief magistrate who was appointed by the governor on the pastor's recommendation. Save for this slight connection, the reductions remained politically apart from the colonial administration. On occasion the governor of Paraguay visited them, as did visitors sent out by the *audiencia* of Charcas. Economically, as well, the reductions remained aloof. The Jesuits organized the settlements on a combination of private and collective property. Agriculture was largely a communal project, but each Indian family had its own gardens and sometimes a cow or horse. Domestic industries were encouraged, and their products, as well as agricultural surpluses, were sold by the Jesuits to the outside world to procure any items needed in the mission economy. The natives were taught Christian doctrine, reading, writing, and singing. Their native abilities in painting and sculpture were encouraged and used in decorating the churches. All work and play was tied in with communal religious prayers, songs, and processions.

Consequences. After the expulsion of the Jesuits and the transfer of the control of the reductions to civil and secular authority, the settlements gradually declined in prosperity and population. The natives did not immediately revert to a more primitive life as some critics of the system have charged. Many of them were absorbed into colonial society. The whole concept and operation of the Jesuit reductions has been a subject of controversy: in the

18th century, because of the political overtones; in the 20th century, because of the sociological implications. Cunninghame Graham notes that even the most bitter opponents of the system agree that in the reductions the Jesuits ''instilled into the Indians that the land on which they lived, with missions, churches, herds, flocks, and the rest, was their own property. Of equal importance, the Jesuits told them they were free, and that they had the King of Spain's own edict in confirmation of their freedom, so that they never could be slaves.''

Bibliography: A. ARMANI, *Ciudad de Dios y ciudad del sol* (Mexico City 1996). P. CARAMAN, *The Lost Paradise* (New York 1975). R. B. C. GRAHAM, *A Vanished Arcadia* (London 1901). M. DURÁN, ''The Reductions,'' in Enrique Dussel (ed.), *The Church in Latin America, 1492–1992* (Maryknoll, N.Y. 1992) 351–362. G. FURLONG, *Misiones y sus pueblos guaraníes* (Buenos Aires 1962). E. J. A. MAEDER, *Misiones del Paraguay: Conflictos y disolución de la sociedad guaraní (1768–1850)* (Madrid, Mapfre 1992). B. MELIÀ and M. A. LIANE, *Guaraníes y jesuitas en tiempo de las misiones: una bibliografía didáctica* (Asunción, Paraguay 1995). M. MÖRNER, *The Political and Economic Activities of the Jesuits in La Plata Region*, trans. by A. READ (Stockholm 1955). S. PALACIOS and E. ZOFFOLI, *Gloria y tragedia de las misiones guaraníes* (Bilbao 1991). F. J. REITER, *They Built Utopia: The Jesuit Missions in Paraguay, 1610–1768* (Potomac, Md. 1995). T. WHIGHAM, ''Paraguay's *Pueblos de Indios*: Echoes of a Missionary Past,'' in E. LANGER and R. H. JACKSON (eds.), *The New Latin American Mission History* (Lincoln, Nebraska 1995) 157–188.

[H. STORNI/J.L. KLAIBER]